THE NEW

PALGRAVE

DICTIONARY OF

ECONOMICS AND THE LAW

THE NEW PALGRAVE DICTIONARY OF ECONOMICS AND THE LAW

EDITED BY

PETER NEWMAN

2

E–O

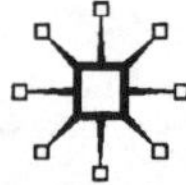

The New Palgrave Dictionary of Economics and the Law
Edited by Peter Newman, in three volumes

First published in hardcover 1998

First published in paperback 2002 by
PALGRAVE MACMILLAN
Houndmills, Basingstoke, Hampshire RG21 6XS and
175 Fifth Avenue, New York, N. Y. 10010
Companies and representatives throughout the world

PALGRAVE MACMILLAN is the global academic imprint of the Palgrave Macmillan division of St. Martin's Press, LLC and of Palgrave Macmillan Ltd. Macmillan® is a registered trademark in the United States, United Kingdom and other countries. Palgrave is a registered trademark in the European Union and other countries.

ISBN 0–333–67667–X hardback (*outside North America*)
ISBN 1–56159–215–3 hardback (*in North America*)
ISBN 0–333–99756–5 paperback (*worldwide*)

This book is printed on paper suitable for recycling and made from fully managed and sustained forest sources.

A catalogue record for this book is available from the British Library.

The Library of Congress has cataloged the hardcover edition as follows:
The new Palgrave dictionary of economics and the law / edited by Peter Newman.
3 v, : ill. : 27cm.
Includes bibliographical references and index.
Contents: 1. A-D – 2. E-O – 3. P-Z.
ISBN 1–56159–215–3 (U.S. : set) – ISBN 0–333–67667–X (U.K. : set)
1. Law–Economic aspects–Dictionaries. 2. Law and economics–Dictionaries. 3. Law–Economic aspects–United States.–Dictionaries. I. Title: Palgrave dictionary of economics and the law. II. Title: Dictionary of economics and the law. III. Newman, Peter K., 1928–

K487.E3 N49 1998
330'.03–dc21 2001316174

10 9 8 7 6 5 4 3 2 1
11 10 09 08 07 06 05 04 03 02

CONTENTS

LIST OF ENTRIES A–Z

One-line cross-references are shown in *italics*.

VOLUME 1

VOLUME 2

VOLUME 3

SUBJECT CLASSIFICATION

The Classification lists the 399 essays in the Dictionary under 75 subheadings, which are themselves gathered together in seven sections. A given essay is very likely to occur more than once in the classification (the listings below contain 781 items in all), in one or more sections.

1. SOCIETY

(a) civil society and others
  (i) civil society
  (ii) disorder

(b) conventions and norms
  (i) conventions
  (ii) network externalities
  (iii) norms and rules

(c) institutions

(d) game theory
  (i) theory
  (ii) applications

2. ECONOMY

(a) political economy
  (i) constitutional economics
  (ii) welfare economics

(b) property rights (*see also 5b, 5g(i)* and *6c(iv)*)
  (i) general
  (ii) applications

(c) privatization

(d) fiscal structure
  (i) general
  (ii) taxation

(e) transaction and agency costs

(f) individual behaviour, risk and uncertainty

(g) international economics

3. POLITY

(a) political philosophy

(b) justice

(c) law and the state

(d) public choice

(e) administration and bureaucracy

(f) European polity
  (i) European Union
  (ii) Central and Eastern Europe

4. LAW IN GENERAL

(a) jurisprudence and legal history
  (i) jurisprudence
  (ii) history of legal and economic doctrine
  (iii) history of law

(b) legal systems
  (i) common law
  (ii) civil law
  (iii) private law
  (iv) comparative law

(c) law-and-economics
  (i) general
  (ii) efficiency in the law

5. COMMON LAW SYSTEMS

(a) legal organization and procedure
- (i) legal rules and standards
- (ii) judiciary
- (iii) legal profession
- (iv) trial and settlement
- (v) settlement of disputes outside the courts

(b) property (*see also 2b, 5g(i)* and *6c(iv)*)
- (i) possession
- (ii) real property
- (iii) intellectual property
- (iv) privacy and free speech

(c) contracts
- (i) general
- (ii) contract enforcement
- (iii) contracts by type of activity

(d) torts
- (i) general
- (ii) liability and negligence
- (iii) cost rules
- (iv) damages
- (v) torts by type of activity

(e) criminal law

(f) family law

(g) ownership
- (i) general (*see also 2b, 5b* and *6c(iv)*)
- (ii) corporate law
- (iii) corporate governance
- (iv) bankruptcy
- (v) non-corporate firms

6. REGULATION

(a) general theory

(b) organization of regulation

(c) economic regulation
- (i) general
- (ii) competition law and antitrust
- (iii) financial regulation
- (iv) land and housing (*see also 2b, 5b* and *5g(i)*)
- (v) employment and wages
- (vi) economic activities by type

(d) social regulation
- (i) general
- (ii) information and media
- (iii) health and safety
- (iv) environment
- (v) discrimination

7. BIOGRAPHIES

(a) economists

(b) philosophers

(c) lawyers

(d) other social scientists

1. SOCIETY

(a) civil society and others

(i) civil society

- civil society
- Ferguson, Adam
- Hobbes and contractarianism
- Scottish Enlightenment and the law
- social justice
- spontaneous order
- state of nature and civil society
- Tocqueville, Alexis de

(ii) disorder

- corruption
- corruption in transition economies
- gangs and the state of nature
- legal reform in Eastern Europe
- organized crime
- stability of anarchic societies

(b) conventions and norms

(i) conventions

- common knowledge
- conventions
- conventions and transaction costs
- conventions at the foundation of law
- focal points
- Hayek, Friedrich von
- Hume, David
- informational cascades and social conventions
- invisible hand explanations
- legal formalities
- Menger, Carl
- spontaneous order

(ii) network externalities

- cheap talk and coordination
- informational cascades and social conventions
- network effects and externalities
- network externality and convention
- path dependence

(iii) norms and rules

- customary law
- efficient norms
- emergence of legal rules
- preference shaping by the law
- rule-guided behaviour

(c) institutions

- American institutional economics and the legal system
- anthropological law-and-economics
- Coase, Ronald
- Commons, John R.
- disestablishment, economics of
- Ely, Richard T.
- legal pluralism
- neoinstitutional economics
- trust
- Weber, Max

(d) game theory

(i) theory

- cheap talk and coordination
- commitment
- common knowledge
- coordination games
- evolutionary game theory
- focal points
- game theory and states of the world
- non-cooperative games
- paradoxes of game theory
- prisoners' dilemma

(ii) applications

- bounded rationality
- comparative negligence
- contract formation and interpretation
- conventions
- conventions and transaction costs
- conventions at the foundation of law
- customary law
- disclosure and unravelling
- division of powers in the European constitution
- economic theory of liability rules
- efficient norms
- emergence of legal rules
- freedom of expression
- games of secession
- game theory and the law
- Hobbes and contractarianism
- international sanctions
- joint and several liability
- most-favoured-customer clauses
- network externality and convention
- opportunity costs and legal institutions
- prisoners' dilemma and the theory of the state
- reliance
- social norms and the law
- stability of anarchic societies
- tax compliance
- trust

2. ECONOMY

(a) political economy

(i) constitutional economics

- Austrian School of Economics and the evolution of institutions
- Buchanan, James M.
- constitutional economics
- division of powers in the European constitution
- evolution of the economic constitution of the European Union
- fiscal federalism
- Freiburg school of law and economics
- Hayek, Friedrich von
- Menger, Carl
- subsidiarity and the European Union
- Wicksell and public choice

(ii) welfare economics

- contingent valuation
- Kaldor–Hicks compensation
- Pareto optimality
- value maximization
- wealth maximization

(b) property rights *(see also 5b, 5g(i) and 6c(iv))*

(i) general

- Coase, Ronald
- Coase theorem
- common property
- corruption
- evolution of property rights
- first possession
- holdouts
- inalienability
- investment incentives and property rights
- local common property rights
- Locke, John
- markets and incommensurability
- opportunity costs and legal institutions
- possession
- property rights
- property rights in civil law
- restitution for benefit or liability for harm
- self-governance of common-pool resources
- standing
- State power
- takings

(ii) applications

- auctions of rights to public property
- common carriers
- corruption in transition economies
- property rights in aboriginal societies
- property rights in prisoners of war
- property rights in the electromagnetic spectrum
- riparian rights
- transfer of property rights in Eastern Europe
- unitization
- wildlife law

(c) privatization

- disestablishment, economics of
- privatization
- privatization in Central and Eastern Europe
- rate-of-return regulation versus price regulation for public utilities
- regulatory rule-making: privatized utilities in the UK
- transfer of property rights in Eastern Europe

(d) fiscal structure

(i) general

- Buchanan, James M.
- fiscal federalism
- legal obligation, non-compliance and soft budget constraint
- Wicksell and public choice

(ii) taxation

- countervailing duties
- inheritance taxation
- retroactive taxation
- taxation of international transactions
- tax compliance

(e) transaction and agency costs

- agency cost and administrative law
- agency costs and corporate governance
- Coase, Ronald
- Coase theorem
- conventions and transaction costs
- countertrade and transaction costs
- lawyers as transaction cost engineers
- neoinstitutional economics
- opportunistic behaviour in contracts
- trespass and nuisance

(f) individual behaviour, risk and uncertainty

- attitudes towards risk
- bounded rationality
- cognition and contract
- commitment
- contingent valuation
- game theory and states of the world
- rule-guided behaviour
- valuing life and risks to life

(g) international economics

- antidumping
- countertrade and transaction costs
- countervailing duties
- immigration policy
- international sanctions
- most-favoured-nation obligations in international trade
- taxation of international transactions

3. POLITY

(a) political philosophy

Bentham, Jeremy
Buchanan, James M.
conventions
Hayek, Friedrich von
Hobbes and contractarianism
Hume, David
Locke, John
modern contractarianism
modern utilitarianism
prisoners' dilemma and the theory of the state
state of nature and civil society
Tocqueville, Alexis de
trust

(b) justice

criminal justice
distributive justice
eminent domain and just compensation
equity
Hume, David
justice
just price
legal aid
modern utilitarianism
rule of law
social justice

(c) law and the state

constitutional economics
division of powers in the European constitution
eminent domain and just compensation
games of secession
gangs and the state of nature
judicial review
legislative intent
political control of the bureaucracy
rule of law
secession
social norms and the law
State power
statutory interpretation and rational choice theories

(d) public choice

Buchanan, James M.
corruption
judicial independence
public choice and the law
rent from regulation
rent seeking
State power
Statute of Frauds
transition in Eastern Europe
Tullock, Gordon
Wicksell and public choice

(e) administration and bureaucracy

agency cost and administrative law
agency discretion and accountability in regulation
bureaucracy
bureaucracy in Eastern Europe and the former Soviet Union
comparative administrative law
corruption
corruption in transition economies
judicial independence
judicial review
legislative intent
political control of the bureaucracy
statutory interpretation and rational choice theories

(f) European polity

(i) European Union

centralized and decentralized regulation in the European Union
competition law in the European Union and the United States
division of powers in the European constitution
European competition policy
evolution of the economic constitution of the European Union
harmonization of law in the European Union
ownership and control in Europe
regulation of capital markets in the European Union
subsidiarity and the European Union

(ii) Central and Eastern Europe

bureaucracy in Eastern Europe and the former Soviet Union
corruption in transition economies
economic legality and transition in Russia and Eastern Europe
legal obligation, non-compliance and soft budget constraint
legal reform in Eastern Europe
privatization in Central and Eastern Europe
transfer of property rights in Eastern Europe
transition in Eastern Europe

4. LAW IN GENERAL

(a) jurisprudence and legal history

(i) jurisprudence
- American legal realism
- Austin, John
- Bentham, Jeremy
- conventions at the foundation of law
- emergence of legal rules
- Fuller, Lon L.
- Hart, H.L.A.
- Holmes, Oliver Wendell
- Kelsen, Hans
- legal positivism
- rule of law
- rule of recognition

(ii) history of legal and economic doctrine
- Adam Smith and the law
- American institutional economics and the legal system
- Austrian School of Economics and the evolution of institutions
- Calabresi, Guido
- Chicago school of law and economics
- Coase, Ronald
- Coase theorem
- evolution of property rights
- just price
- Maine, Henry
- possession
- riparian rights
- Savigny, Friedrich von
- Scottish Enlightenment and the law
- Statute of Frauds
- Western legal tradition

(iii) history of law
- Blackstone, William
- emergence of legal rules
- English common law
- equity
- evolution of commercial law
- informal contract enforcement: lessons from medieval trade
- Law Merchant
- Roman law

(b) legal systems

(i) common law
- English common law
- equity
- fiduciary duties
- precedent
- standing
- stare decisis
- Statute of Frauds
- trespass and nuisance

(ii) civil law
- conspiracy
- efficient statute law
- harmonization of law in the European Union
- just price
- property rights in civil law
- Roman law
- Western legal tradition

(iii) private law
- evolution of commercial law
- informal contract enforcement: lessons from medieval trade
- Law Merchant
- private commercial law
- private law-making and the Uniform Commercial Code
- social norms and the law

(iv) comparative law
- choice of law
- civil procedure in the USA and civil law countries
- common law, statute law and economic efficiency
- comparative administrative law
- comparative common law: the consequences of differing incentives to litigate
- comparative corporate governance
- comparative law and economics
- conflict of laws
- customary law
- dispute resolution in Japan and the United States
- legal formants
- legal pluralism
- plea bargaining: a comparative approach
- property rights in civil law
- Western legal tradition

5. COMMON LAW SYSTEMS

(a) legal organization and procedure *(cont.)*

(iv) trial and settlement

accuracy in adjudication
allocation of litigation costs: American and English rules
civil procedure in the USA and civil law countries
class actions
comparative common law: the consequences of differing incentives to litigate
discovery
juries
nuisance suits
plea bargaining: a comparative approach
precedent
private information and legal bargaining
rules of evidence and statistical reasoning in court
selection of cases for trial
sequential and bifurcated trials
settlement of litigation
stare decisis
suits with negative expected value

(v) settlement of disputes outside the courts

alternative dispute resolution
anthropological law-and-economics
arbitration
arbitration in the shadow of the law
dispute resolution in Japan and the United States
evolution of commercial law
informal contract enforcement: lessons from medieval trade
international sanctions
Law Merchant
legal pluralism
private commercial law
self-governance of common-pool resources
self-regulation of private organized markets

(b) property *(see also 2b, 5g(i) and 6c(iv))*

(i) possession

evolution of property rights
first possession
legal formalities
possession

(ii) real property

adverse possession
coming to the nuisance
holdouts
land title systems
land-use doctrines
riparian rights
takings
trespass and nuisance

(iii) intellectual property

computer law
copyright
droit de suite
incentives to innovate
intellectual property
ownership of market information
patents
performance rights
trademarks
trade secret

(iv) privacy and free speech

freedom of expression
privacy

(c) contracts

(i) general

asset specificity and vertical integration
cognition and contract
contract formation and interpretation
contracts
contracts and relationships
default rules for incomplete contracts
fraudulent conveyance
gratuitous promises
hold-up problem
incomplete contracts
Karl Llewellyn and the early law and economics of contract
opportunistic behaviour in contracts
quasi contracts
relational contract
secured credit contracts
standard form contracts
Statute of Frauds
symbiotic arrangements

(ii) contract enforcement

breach remedies
contract renegotiation and option contracts
contracts
impossibility doctrine in contract law
informal contract enforcement: lessons from medieval trade
Law Merchant
options pricing and contract remedies
penalty doctrine in contract law
private commercial law
reliance
specific performance
unconscionability
unjust enrichment

(iii) contracts by type of activity

breach remedies
cropshare contracts
employment contract law
franchise contracts
instalment credit contracts
insurance law
marriage as contract
sex discrimination and the equal good of pensions

(d) torts

(i) general

accuracy in adjudication
class actions
crime as a distinct category of behaviour
customary practices and the law of torts
remote risks and the tort system
types of tort

(ii) liability and negligence

auditing standards and legal liability
causation and tort liability
civil liability under RICO: unintended consequences of legislation
comparative negligence
contributory and comparative negligence: empirical comparisons
due care
economic theory of liability rules
Good Samaritan rule
insurance, deterrence and liability
joint and several liability
last clear chance
Learned Hand rule
legal standards of care
liability rights as contingent claims
products liability
rescue
restitution for benefit or liability for harm
third-party liability
unlimited shareholder liability
vicarious liability

(iii) cost rules

accuracy in adjudication
allocation of litigation costs: American and English rules
comparative common law: the consequences of differing incentives to litigate
conditional fees in Britain
contingent fees

(iv) damages

accuracy in adjudication
judgment-proofness
punitive damages
total offset rule in damage awards
valuing life and risks to life

(v) torts by type of activity

automobile accidents, insurance and tort liability
medical malpractice
occupational disease and the tort system: the case of asbestos
products liability

(e) criminal law

accuracy in adjudication
Becker, Gary S.
capital punishment
civil liability under RICO: unintended consequences of legislation
computer law
conspiracy
corporate crime and its control
corruption
corruption in transition economies
crime as a distinct category of behaviour
criminal attempts
criminal conviction and future income
criminal justice
criminal sanctions for product safety
default rules for incomplete contracts
drug prohibition
economic approach to crime and punishment
fraud-on-the-market
fraudulent conveyance
gangs and the state of nature
gun control
insider trading
insurance law
juries
organized crime
plea bargaining: a comparative approach
precommitment and prohibition
preference shaping by the law
privacy
public enforcement of law
punitive damages
rule of law
rules of evidence and statistical reasoning in court
third-party liability
vicarious liability

(f) family law

Adam Smith and the law
adoption
alimony
Becker, Gary S.
child custody
divorce
inheritance law
marriage as contract
no-fault divorce
Roman law

(g) ownership

(i) general (see also 2b, 5b and 6c(iv))

employee ownership of firms
inheritance law
ownership of the firm
possession
privatization
residual rights of control

(ii) corporate law

civil liability under RICO: unintended consequences of legislation
competition for state corporate law
corporate crime and its control
corporate law
fiduciary duties
limited and extended liability regimes
professional corporations and limited liability
unlimited shareholder liability
vicarious liability

(iii) corporate governance

agency costs and corporate governance
auctions and takeovers
boards of directors
comparative corporate governance
competition for state corporate law
corporate governance
independent directors
law-and-economics in action
leveraged buyouts
market for corporate control
ownership and control in Europe
ownership of the firm
shareholder activism and corporate governance in the United States
symbiotic arrangements
tender offers

(iv) bankruptcy

bankruptcy and its reform
Chapter 11
corporate bankruptcy
corporate reorganizations
fraudulent conveyance
leveraged buyouts
personal bankruptcy
personal bankruptcy in the United States
secured credit contracts

(v) non-corporate firms

joint ventures
law firms
partnership

6. REGULATION

(a) general theory

auctions of rights to public property
bargaining with regulators
informal contracts and regulatory constraints
privatization
public franchising
rate-of-return regulation versus price regulation for public utilities
regulation and deregulation
regulatory competition
regulatory impact analysis: a cross-country comparison
regulatory rule-making: privatized utilities in the UK
rent from regulation
rent seeking
risk assessment
risk regulation
State power
takings

(b) organization of regulation

agency discretion and accountability in regulation
auctions of rights to public property
bureaucracy
centralized and decentralized regulation in the European Union
licensing and certification systems
regulatory agencies and the courts
regulatory rule-making: privatized utilities in the UK

(c) economic regulation

(i) general

common carriers
comparative regulation
consumer protection
disclosure and unravelling
mandatory disclosure
regulation and deregulation
regulatory capture
self-regulation of private organized markets
Simons, Henry C.
Stigler, George J.

(ii) competition law and antitrust

agreement under the Sherman Act
antitrust policy
asset restructuring and union bargaining
asset specificity and vertical integration
auctions and takeovers
cartels and tacit collusion
cheap talk and coordination
competition law in the European Union and the United States
Director, Aaron
European competition policy
evolution of the economic constitution of the European Union
exclusionary agreements
horizontal mergers
most-favoured-customer clauses
ownership and control in Europe
patents
path dependence
per se rules
predatory pricing
regulation of financial holding companies
regulation of the professions
resale price maintenance
rule of reason in antitrust
Stigler, George J.
tender offers
tying
unitization
vertical mergers and monopoly leverage

(c) economic regulation *(cont.)*

(iii) financial regulation

auditing standards and legal liability
civil liability under RICO: unintended consequences of legislation
derivative securities regulation
disclosure and unravelling
fraud-on-the-market
insider trading
instalment credit contracts
mandatory disclosure
ownership of market information
regulation of automated trading systems
regulation of capital markets in the European Union
regulation of financial holding companies
securities regulation
self-regulation of private organized markets
third-party liability

(iv) land and housing (see also 2b, 5b and 5g(i))

compensation for regulatory takings
Ely, Richard T.
eminent domain and just compensation
Kaldor–Hicks compensation
land development controls
land title systems
land-use doctrines
rent control
restitution for benefit or liability for harm
takings
unitization

(v) employment and wages

alternative dispute resolution
arbitration
asset restructuring and union bargaining
discrimination in employment
employee ownership of firms
employment contract law
insurance for workplace injuries
minimum wage regulation

(vi) economic activities by type

airline deregulation
common carriers
pharmaceutical regulation
property rights in the electromagnetic spectrum
rate-of-return regulation versus price regulation for public utilities
regulating the hours of shopping
regulation of telecommunications
regulatory rule-making: privatized utilities in the UK

(d) social regulation

(i) general

contingent valuation
disestablishment, economics of
remote risks and the tort system
risk assessment
risk regulation
trespass and nuisance
valuing life and risks to life

(ii) information and media

computer law
freedom of expression
information regulation
property rights in the electromagnetic spectrum

(iii) health and safety

addiction
alcohol control
automobile accidents, insurance and tort liability
criminal sanctions for product safety
drug prohibition
gun control
insurance for workplace injuries
medical malpractice
occupational disease and the tort system: the case of asbestos
occupational health and safety regulation
pharmaceutical regulation
precommitment and prohibition
products liability
regulation of hazardous wastes
regulation of toxic substances
valuing life and risks to life

(iv) environment

economic incentives for environmental regulation
endangered species
harmonization of law in the European Union
regulation of hazardous wastes
regulation of toxic substances
regulatory impact analysis: a cross-country comparison
riparian rights
takings
tradeable pollution permits
wildlife law

(v) discrimination

discrimination in employment
immigration policy
law-and-economics from a feminist perspective
sex discrimination and the equal good of pensions
sexual harassment

7. BIOGRAPHIES

E

easements. *See* LAND-USE DOCTRINES.

economic approach to crime and punishment. Crime, particularly violent non-financial crime, appears to be among the least rational of all human activities. The mind of the murderer or the rapist seems so distant to many of us that standard economics might seem to offer little help in understanding criminal behaviour. After all, crime does not have well-defined formal markets or well-defined prices or even well-defined products. Nevertheless, the economics literature on crime and punishment, which began with Smith (1776, see Book V, Chapter 1, Part II) and was brought into its modern form by Becker (1968), has been among the most successful and convincing expansions of the domain of neoclassical economics. This remarkable extension of economic reasoning to criminal behaviour is both a high water mark of what economics has done and a clear signal of what economics can do in explaining even the seemingly least rational of human actions.

This essay presents a brief tour of the economic approach to criminal behaviour. I will present the basic apparatus of Becker (1968), which is the underlying structure of all the economics of crime. I focus on the supply of crimes, and the inputs into both the level of the supply curve and its elasticity. The essay ends with a discussion of what should determine and what does determine the level and structure of punishment and deterrence.

THE LEVEL OF CRIME. Becker's model of crime and punishment ultimately comes from looking at the optimization problem of the prospective criminal. People who choose to commit crimes receive benefits (denoted B_i for person i) if their crimes succeed (which they will with probability S_i). Criminals pay costs for their crimes which must be paid whether or not they are caught (these will be denoted C_i) and they must also pay additional costs of K_i if they are caught, which they will be with probability P_i. With this notation a risk-neutral criminal will commit a crime if:

$$S_iB_i > C_i + P_iK_i. \qquad (1)$$

This simple inequality forms the core of Becker's analysis. Individuals are more likely to commit crimes when the probability of success is higher, when the benefits from a successful crime are higher, when the costs are lower and when the probability of apprehension is lower. Perhaps the most important element of this approach is that criminals are not viewed as diseased or malfunctioning, but rather as rational individuals for whom the benefits of crime are greater than the costs of crime.

Inequality (1) implies that increasing either the probability of arrest or the severity of punishment should deter criminals. Much of the empirical literature on crime and punishment has focused on finding out whether harsher punishments and better enforcement actually deter crime (e.g. Ehrlich 1975, Witte 1980 and (with international data) Wolpin 1978, Archer and Gartner 1984 and Wong 1995). The evidence at this point for the importance of the deterrence hypothesis seems quite strong and supports the model, but there is still much disagreement about the magnitude of these deterrence effects (see Ehrlich 1996).

One implication of the theory is that we should expect high levels of recidivism. Before people enter prison, the costs to them of crime were lower than the benefits they expected from crime. When convicted criminals leave prison, usually the costs of crime to them have only mildly changed. Prisoners get older in jail and age seems to increase the costs of crime substantially (Wilson and Herrnstein 1985); also, the state often increases punishment for repeat offenders. But as long as these cost changes are fairly small, which they will be for relatively minor crimes with short prison terms, we should not expect a prison term to generate significant changes in a criminal's decision to commit crimes. Thus the observed high levels of recidivism (see Needels 1994) are evidence for the theory.

There is also evidence that released prisoners may move up to deadlier crimes (see DiIulio 1996a), and this evidence may also be understood with the basic model. Prisons can increase the benefits of crime, since they may act as schools to form more effective criminals. Moreover, once a person has been imprisoned the stigma associated with a second prison term may diminish, so the costs of crime may fall.

THE SUPPLY OF CRIMES. In calculating the supply of crimes it is useful to distinguish between the extensive and the intensive margins, i.e. individuals choose both whether to commit any crimes at all and how many crimes to commit once they have committed a first crime. Criminals commit many crimes and there is a great variety in the number of crimes across criminals (see Chaikin 1978 and Piehl and DiIulio 1994). I will not deal with the intensive margin in this essay, but rather assume that each criminal commits just one crime (or, equivalently, any *fixed* number of crimes). The basic economics of the intensive margin closely resembles the economics of the extensive margin, and empirical work distinguishing between these two margins is sadly almost nonexistent.

The probability of success, S_i, the benefits per crime, B_i, and the costs of crime, C_i, are functions of the percentage of people in society who are criminals (denoted N). I will index individuals so that $S_iB_i - C_i$ is increasing in 'i' (for a given level of N). From here on I assume that the probability of arrest P_i and the cost of imprisonment K_i are independent of i, so that everyone faces the same criminal justice system, and, more problematically independent of N (I will return to that later). I will also make three simplifying assumptions (which are necessary for the algebra, but not for the intuition of the results): (1) if $S_iB - C_i$ is increasing in i for one level of N, it is increasing in i for all levels of N; (2) $S_1(0)B_1(0) - C_1(0)$ is arbitrarily large (so that there is at least one criminal); and (3) $S_1(1)B_1(1) - C_1(1)$ is zero or negative (so that there is at least one law-abiding citizen). The supply of crimes will be determined by the marginal criminal who is denoted i^* and is defined from the following perturbation of inequality (1):

$$\begin{aligned} &S_{i^*}(N)B_{i^*}(N) - C_{i^*}(N) \\ &= S_{i^*}(1-i^*)B_{i^*}(1-i^*) - C_{i^*}(1-i^*) \\ &= PK \end{aligned} \qquad (1')$$

All persons with i's greater than i^* will become criminals; all persons with i's below i^* will not. The proportion of criminals will be $1 - i^*$. Figure 1 shows the equilibrium graphically; the upward sloping line is the crime supply curve. The two horizontal lines represent P times K, the punishment-related costs of criminal activity. The number of criminals is shown graphically by the distance above the i^* intersection of the crime supply curve and the punishment line.

As Figure 1 shows, if the supply function is well behaved and upward sloping then an increase in P times K, i.e. an upward shift in the (horizontal) punishment line, will reduce the number of crimes. The steeper the crime supply curve (the line $SB - C$) the smaller the decrease in the quantity of crime caused by an increase in PK. In general, the extent to which changes in P or K reduce the amount of crime depends on the elasticity of the crime supply function.

One set of forces that determines this elasticity is the heterogeneity of talents for crime, opportunities for crime and costs of the crime (i.e. the heterogeneity of S, B and C). When these traits are distributed very heterogeneously then $S_iB_i - C_i$ (for a given level of crime) will be rising sharply with i and demand will be more inelastic. Small increases in P or K will induce only a small fall in the level of crime because as i^* rises the marginal criminal rapidly becomes much more effective and has much lower costs of crime. This suggests that marginal increases in law enforcement will be more effective in more homogeneous societies.

The second feature that determines the elasticity of the supply of crimes is the extent to which increases in the number of criminals change the $S(N)$, $B(N)$ and $C(N)$ functions. To examine this easily, temporarily assume that there is no heterogeneity across criminals, so the equilibrium condition will be determined by $S(1-i^*)B(1-i^*) - C(1-i^*) = PK$. The overall elasticity of crimes with respect to punishment is given by the following equality:

$$1/\varepsilon^{N}_{PK} = (SB(\varepsilon^{S}_{N} + \varepsilon^{B}_{N}) - C\varepsilon^{C}_{N})/SB - C \qquad (2)$$

where I follow the notational convention of letting $\varepsilon^{X}_{Y} = (Y/X)\partial X/\partial Y$.

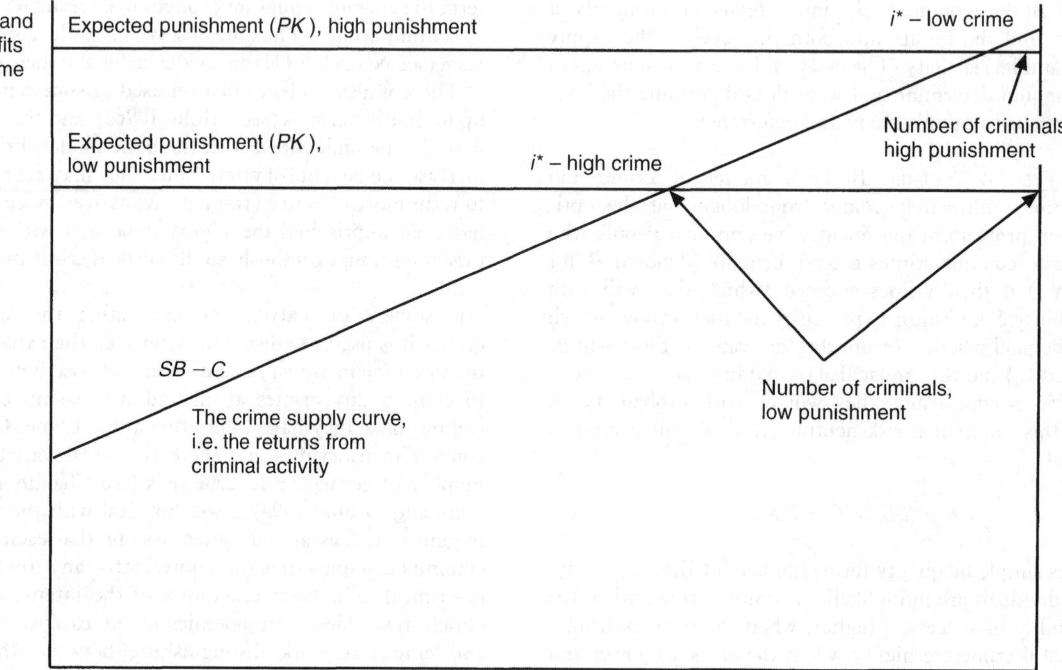

Figure 1 The supply of crime

It seems plausible that the $S(.)$ and $B(.)$ functions are decreasing with respect to the number of criminals, so ε^S_N and ε^B_N will be negative. As the number of criminals rises, since the most lucrative and the most unprotected crimes will already have been committed the marginal criminal will be forced into crimes that are both less lucrative and less accessible. As these elasticity terms become more sharply negative, the overall elasticity of the supply of crimes gets smaller. Of course, forces can drive against these effects. If criminals learn from each other then $S(.)$ may be rising in the number of criminals, in which case the elasticity will be larger.

The cost function may also be falling in the number of criminals (i.e. ε^C_N is negative). For example, the cost of crime may consist mainly of the reputational stigma of leading a criminal lifestyle, which is presumably less important when the entire community is made up of criminals. If the cost function reflects foregone legal earnings and if high levels of crime reduce the returns from legal activity, then ε^C_N will be negative (as in Murphy, Shleifer and Vishny 1993). As ε^C_N becomes more negative, the supply of crimes becomes more elastic. Eventually, if ε^C_N is sufficiently negative ε^N_{PK} will be positive, which means that the crime supply curve slopes down.

If the supply function is downward sloping around an equilibrium, then that equilibrium will not be stable. The intuitive explanation of this instability is that if the crime supply curve is downward sloping then a marginal increase in the number of criminals (a fall in i^*) will increase the benefits of crime for the marginal criminal (so benefits will be greater than PK), the new marginal individual will also become a criminal and the number of criminals will increase further. As a small increase in the number of criminals spurs a larger increase in the number of criminals, the equilibrium is unstable. This instability usually implies multiple steady states, which means that there can be both high- and low-crime equilibria in any environment.

An alternative model of multiple equilibria is Sah (1991), who argues that higher levels of crime will reduce the probability of arrest for a given level of law enforcement (which would mean that P is a function of $1 - i^*$). In this model there can be a high-crime, low-probability-of-arrest equilibrium and a low-crime, high-probability-of-arrest equilibrium. Multiple-equilibria models are particularly appealing to policy pundits because they suggest that it is possible to catapult a society from a high-crime equilibrium to a low-crime equilibrium with no changes in the level of punishment.

THE OPPORTUNITY COST OF TIME. The forces that make up the costs of crime (C) may include elements such as social stigma, the pangs of one's conscience and the opportunity cost of time. Stealing small-value items makes little sense when an individual is making much more money legally. The opportunity cost of time affects crime in two ways. First, the time spent committing crimes is time taken away from legal pursuits. Second, since the criminal system often penalizes by means of time spent in jail, the well-paid will lose more income as they spend time incarcerated.

There is empirical evidence at the micro level that suggests a weak connection between foregone earnings and criminal behaviour (Witte 1980, but see Myers (1983) for a rebuttal). More aggregate studies using time series evidence for the UK (Wong 1995) and cross-city data in the US (Glaeser and Sacerdote 1996) also find a connection between crime and proxies for the opportunity cost of time (schooling, unemployment rates, poverty). A policy implication of this analysis is that raising the returns from legal activity for the poor could lower crime rates. Also, by giving individuals in jails better skills and better earnings in the legitimate sector, released prisoners may be induced to follow legitimate careers.

EMPIRICAL PUZZLES AND ALTERNATIVE EXPLANATIONS OF CRIME. There are a variety of significant empirical puzzles about crime rates, which are difficult to explain with only the opportunity cost of time and the level of punishment. These puzzles push us towards a broader theory of criminal behaviour. For example, the young are much more prone to crime than the old, men are much more prone than women, and most explosively, there seems to be a connection between race and crime as well (see Wilson and Herrnstein (1985) for a discussion of all these facts). There is also a striking variance of crime rates across countries, cities and neighbourhoods that cannot be explained with standard variables.

Some of the connection between youth and crime may occur because of lower opportunity cost of time for the young and because full legal penalties are not always enforced against individuals under the age of 18. However, the age effect remains large for people over the age of 18 (who are subject to full adult penalties) and seems to be much stronger than any effect that would be implied by lower earnings for the young. One explanation of the age–crime connection is that younger people are evolutionarily coded to be more aggressive (see Daly and Wilson 1988). Another possible explanation is that younger people are less patient and crime may be more appealing to people who live for the present; crime seems to offer immediate rewards, and the costs of crime, especially lengthy prison sentences, are paid for only over time (see Banfield (1974) for a discussion).

One finding of the criminological literature that supports the role of patience is that crime is much more responsive to increased probabilities of arrest than to increased durations of sentences (see Grogger 1991). Short time horizons suggest that criminals would be frightened by a higher probability of facing arrest now, but would care much less about how long they will spend in prison if they are caught. My own work on this topic (Glaeser and Sacerdote 1996) finds a connection between crime and various proxies for impatience (not having a savings account, smoking, having sex without contraception, the age at which one first smoked, drank or had sex) even controlling for a wide battery of individual economic and social characteristics. Impatience may help explain criminal behaviour and may be connected to the connection between youth and criminal activity.

The connection between criminal behaviour and gender is even harder to explain. Since men usually earn more than women and are not thought to be treated more leniently by the courts, neither lower opportunity cost of time or lighter penalties can explain this gender difference. An evolutionarily-based connection between gender and aggression could explain this fact (again see Daly and Wilson 1988). It is also possible that the social influences on men are more oriented towards crime or that men live more for the present.

The racial difference in the propensity towards crime is also something of an anomaly. Empirical work in this area is also difficult because of possibly discriminatory behaviour on the part of police officers, who may arrest blacks more readily than whites. However, even controlling for this fact and relying only on victimization surveys, there is a substantial tendency of blacks to commit more crimes, particularly against black victims (see DiIulio 1996b). It is certainly true that blacks have lower earnings, but the earnings gap is generally not large enough to explain the racial gap in crime. An alternative explanation is that blacks are subject to much more arbitrary justice; the basic theory predicts that as penalties become more arbitrary, the marginal cost of committing a crime get much lower.

Finally, it is possible that being black is not itself important, but blacks in the US are generally brought up in a different social environment from whites and it is this social environment that matters. One piece of evidence for this hypothesis is that a raw correlation between the crime rate in a city and the percent black in that city is strongly positive. However, once one controls for the number of single-parent families in that city the connection between race and crime disappears (see Glaeser and Sacerdote 1996).

A final set of empirical puzzles relate to spatial differences in crime rates. The US has a much higher crime rate than most of Western Europe; the murder rate is ten times higher in the US than in Japan. Within the US, some cities and neighbourhoods are remarkably law-abiding while other very similar areas are remarkably violent and criminal. Some of these differences can be explained with observable differences, such as differences in inequality. For example, high American inequality suggests that there are rich people to rob from and poor people who have a low opportunity cost of crime, and this is seen as one explanation of high US crime rates. Usually, though, observables can only explain a small part of the spatial variance in crime rates.

Glaeser, Sacerdote and Scheinkman (1996) argue that this high variance of crime rates is a prediction of models where social influences determine the level of crime. (A high variance of crime rates is also predicted by models with multiple equilibria.) With social interactions, one person's choice about crime influences many of his neighbours and therefore small events can trigger large differences in average crime rates. Since small shocks are ubiquitous, we should expect large differences in crime rates over space. Our work also provides a natural index of social interaction and we find high levels of social interaction for minor crimes (larceny, robbery) and almost no social influence in murder or rape.

Direct evidence confirms the importance of social influence on criminal behaviour. Case and Katz (1991) found that people whose friends are criminals are more likely to be criminals themselves. Freeman (1986) found that church attendance is closely and negatively linked to criminal behaviour among young black males; a natural explanation of this result is the set of social influences associated with church going. In criminology, models of social influence have substantial empirical support and are identified with the differential association school of Sutherland (1939).

The role of social influence can work through learning about criminal opportunities and techniques, or because peers are unlikely to stigmatize a criminal if they are themselves criminals, or through the development of ethical standards or a 'conscience'. Social influence may also work by encouraging a taste for revenge (revenge seems to be important in many crimes). A taste for vengeance can be explained as an evolutionarily dominant personality feature, because even if vengeance is costly and inefficient in the short run, in equilibrium, vengeance may be useful since few people will try to cheat or steal from individuals who are known to be particularly vengeful (see Romer 1995). A taste for vengeance will be more useful in hostile environments so we would expect to see more vengeful behaviour if a child was raised in a dangerous neighbourhood or a violent country.

THE LEVEL OF PUNISHMENT. The previous section has taken the two punishment variables P and K as exogenously determined variables, or as potential policy instruments. Becker's original paper (1968) viewed these things as choice variables to be chosen optimally by the policy maker, i.e. he proposed a normative approach to punishment that responded to his positive approach to criminal behaviour. Indeed, the line between a positive and a normative theory blurs once governments are assumed to be maximizing social welfare. With this assumption normative predictions also become positive predictions about what we should expect to find governments actually doing.

An important normative implication about punishment is that it is not necessarily optimal to eliminate all crimes. If the criminal is willing to pay more than the social cost of the crime to commit the crime, then a crime should take place. To get the optimal quantity of crimes, the government should set the expected punishment (P times K) equal to the social cost of the crime (see Stigler 1970).

However, higher probabilities of arrest and higher levels of punishment both have social costs. Prisons and police are both expensive. Becker (1968) argued that we could make penalties much cheaper by using fines, rather than prison sentences. Once penalties are sufficiently cheap, the state could save by making apprehension probabilities sufficiently small and by making punishment sufficiently draconian. The question why governments in the real world seem not to impose more severe penalties in order to save on policing costs has emerged as an empirical puzzle.

One possible answer to this puzzle is that we have omitted the costs of risk aversion and the large costs that may come from mistakenly punishing innocent people with large penalties. Even if apprehension is perfect (in the sense that the innocent are never falsely accused), Polinsky and Shavell (1979) have shown that risk aversion on the part of criminals makes it optimal to limit penalties.

A second explanation of why punishment does not look

like the predictions of Becker (1968) or Stigler (1970) is given by Friedman (1995). Friedman argues that constitutional rules (both in the US and elsewhere) are designed to limit the trouble caused by governmental institutions which maximize their own, occasionally perverse, objective functions while working within the constitutional rules. Limits on penalties are then needed to limit the ability of police officers to use criminal penalties to extract bribes from the innocent. As an aside, it is worth stressing that the mere presence of corruption and bribes does not invalidate the basic Beckerian approach. If criminals bribe policemen not to prosecute them to avoid the courts, then criminals are still paying a punishment for their crimes and as long as the police are effective enough in extracting bribes crime will be limited by this punishment (see Becker and Stigler 1974).

The problem with bribery occurs when police and the courts use the criminal justice system to control the innocent. Unlimited penalties for minor offences give police and the courts power with which to extract bribes, or punish their enemies. Even if the courts are honest, as long as the prosecutors have some chance of convicting an innocent man, when punishments get high enough everyone will be willing to bribe a policeman to avoid taking their chances in court. Historical documents such as the Magna Carta and the US Constitution suggest that limits on criminal penalties were set to check the overreaching power of the government.

A third explanation for why we see limited penalties is: given the current US institutional arrangements, it is often possible for juries or judges to undo legislative rules which were designed to enforce minimum penalties. McCoy (1984) argues that the California courts undid the State of California's attempts to impose more severe sentencing rules; Kessler and Piehl (1996) argue that the courts overresponded to new rules. If the state is working under the constraints imposed by the judicial system, then our penalties may be the highest that the system allows. Of course, this theory must explain why the judicial system was designed the way it was, and why juries seem unwilling to impose heavy penalties mandated by legislative rules; we currently understand little about what either judges or juries maximize (despite recent work in this area by Richard Posner).

A second puzzle in punishment is why jail time is used so much more often than fines, given that fines would seem to be much less socially costly. Fines may not be used because they are 'unfair' (because the rich find them easier to pay) or ineffective (perhaps because the poor are unable to pay them). A particular advantage of jail time is that while criminals are in jail they cannot commit crimes against the general population; Levitt (1996) finds that the primary effect of increased prison time on crime works through incapacitation, not deterrence. A final problem with fines is that if the state punishes prisoners by extracting fines for itself, the state has an incentive to overextract penalties to fill its own coffers.

Much less work has been done on the decisions undertaken by the victim (as opposed to the criminals or the police), which is a little surprising since the decisions victims make about self-protection (especially choice of locale) have much more impact on their being victimized than the decisions local police make about deterrence. We also have very good information on victims (from the National Crime Victimization Survey). For example, we know that victims tend to resemble criminals in many ways. Victims tend to be unmarried, live in apartment buildings, rent rather than own, be young, be male, be members of racial minorities and be poor (again see Glaeser and Sacerdote (1996) for some basic facts). Some interesting early work on this topic is Ehrlich and Becker (1972) which models the choice of self-protection (limiting the possibility of an attack) or self-insurance (limiting the size of an attack when it comes), and Landes and Posner (1975) who present a useful model of private legal enforcement.

The economic theory of crime and punishment is not just a success in its ability to explain crime, but it has also led to substantial improvements in related areas. Unsurprisingly, the basic Beckerian approach serves as the basis for the economics of riots and corruption (Murphy, Shleifer and Vishny 1993), but it has also provided a large set of insights that have been borrowed by incentive theory (as in Lazear 1979, Shavell 1979 or Shapiro and Stiglitz 1984) and many other branches of economics.

EDWARD L. GLAESER

See also BECKER, GARY S.; CAPITAL PUNISHMENT; CRIME AS A DISTINCT CATEGORY OF BEHAVIOUR; CRIMINAL ATTEMPTS; CRIMINAL CONVICTION AND FUTURE INCOME; CRIMINAL JUSTICE; GANGS AND THE STATE OF NATURE; LAW-AND-ECONOMICS FROM THE PERSPECTIVE OF LAW; ORGANIZED CRIME; PLEA BARGAINING: A COMPARATIVE APPROACH; PREFERENCE SHAPING BY LAW; PUBLIC ENFORCEMENT OF LAW; STIGLER, GEORGE J.

Subject classification: 5e.

BIBLIOGRAPHY

Archer, D. and Gartner, R. 1984. *Violence and Crime in Cross-National Perspective*. New Haven: Yale University Press.

Banfield, E.C. 1974. *The Unheavenly City Revisited*. Boston: Little, Brown.

Becker, G.S. 1968. Crime and punishment: an economic approach. *Journal of Political Economy* 76: 169–217.

Becker, G.S. and Stigler, G.J. 1974. Law enforcement, malfeasance, and compensation of enforcers. *Journal of Legal Studies* 3: 1–18.

Case, A. and Katz, L. 1991. The company you keep: the effect of family and neighbourhood on disadvantaged youth. NBER Working Paper No. 3705.

Chaikin, J. 1978. RAND prison inmate survey. RAND Working Paper WN-10107-DOJ.

Daly, M. and Wilson, M. 1988. *Homicide*. New York: A. de Gruyter.

DiIulio, J. 1996a. Help wanted: economists, crime and public policy. *Journal of Economic Perspectives* 10(1): 3–24.

DiIulio, J. 1996b. My black crime problem, and ours. *City Journal* 6(2): 14–28.

Ehrlich, I. 1975. The deterrent effect of capital punishment: a question of life and death. *American Economic Review* 65: 397–417.

Ehrlich, I. 1996. Crime, punishment and the market for offenses. *Journal of Economic Perspectives* 10: 1, 43–67.

Ehrlich, I. and Becker, G.S. 1972. Market insurance, self-insurance and self-protection. *Journal of Political Economy* 80(4): 623–48.

Freeman, R. 1986. Who escapes?: the relation between churchgoing and other background factors to socioeconomic performances of black male youths from inner-city tracts. In *The Black Youth Employment Crisis*, ed. R.B. Freeman and H.J. Holzer, Chicago: University of Chicago Press.

Friedman, D. 1995. The efficiency of inefficient punishment. Santa Clara Law School, mimeograph.

Glaeser, E.L. and Sacerdote, B. 1996. Why is there more crime in cities? NBER Working Paper No. 5430.

Glaeser, E.L., Sacerdote, B. and Scheinkman, J.A. 1996. Crime and social interactions. *Quarterly Journal of Economics* 111(2): 507–48.

Grogger, J. 1991. Certainty vs. severity of punishment. *Economic Inquiry* 29: 297–309.

Kessler, D. and Piehl, A. 1996. How important is discretion under determinate sentencing? Stanford University, mimeograph.

Landes, W. and Posner, R. 1975. The private enforcement of law. *Journal of Legal Studies* 4: 1–46.

Lazear, E. 1979. Why is there mandatory retirement? *Journal of Political Economy* 87: 1261–84.

Levitt, S. 1996. How do increased arrest rates reduce crime: deterrence, incapacitation or measurement error? *Economic Inquiry*, forthcoming.

McCoy, C. 1984. Determinate sentencing, plea bargaining bans and hydraulic discretion in California. *Justice System Journal* 9: 256–75.

Murphy, K.M., Shleifer, A. and Vishny, R.W. 1993. Why is rent seeking so costly to growth? *American Economic Review* 83(2): 409–14.

Myers, S. 1983. Estimating the economic model of crime: employment versus punishment effects. *Quarterly Journal of Economics* 98: 157–66.

Needels, K. 1994. Go directly to jail and do not collect?: a long-term study of recidivism and employment patterns among prison releasees. PhD Dissertation, Princeton University.

Piehl, A. and DiIulio, J. 1994. 'Does prison pay?' revisited. *Brookings Review* 13: 21–5.

Polinsky, M. and Shavell, S. 1979. The optimal tradeoff between the probability and the magnitude of fines. *American Economic Review* 69(5): 880–91.

Romer, P. 1995. Preferences, promises and the politics of entitlement. In *Individual and Social Responsibilities*, ed. V. Fuchs, Chicago: University of Chicago Press.

Sah, R.K. 1991. Social osmosis and patterns of crime. *Journal of Political Economy* 99: 1272–95.

Shapiro, C. and Stiglitz, J. 1984. Equilibrium unemployment as a worker discipline device. *American Economic Review* 74: 433–44.

Shavell, S. 1979. Risk sharing and incentives in the principal and agent relationship. *Bell Journal of Economics* 10: 55–73.

Smith, A. 1776. *An Inquiry into the Nature and Causes of the Wealth of Nations*. Modern Library Edition, New York: Random House, 1947.

Stigler, G. 1970. The optimum enforcement of laws. *Journal of Political Economy* 78(3): 526–36.

Sutherland, E.H. 1939. *Principles of Criminology*. 3rd edn, Philadelphia: Lippincott.

Wilson, J.Q. and R. Herrnstein. 1985. *Crime and Human Nature*. New York: Simon and Schuster.

Witte, A. 1980. Estimating the economic model of crime with individual data. *Quarterly Journal of Economics* 94: 57–84.

Wolpin, K. 1978. Capital punishment and homicide in England: a summary of results. *American Economic Review* 68: 2, 422–7.

Wong, Y. 1995. An economic analysis of the crime rate in England and Wales. *Economica* 62: 235–46.

economic constitution. *See* EVOLUTION OF THE ECONOMIC CONSTITUTION OF THE EUROPEAN UNION; FREIBURG SCHOOL OF LAW AND ECONOMICS.

economic incentives for environmental regulation. Nearly all environmental policies consist of two components, either explicitly or implicitly: the identification of an overall goal (such as a degree of air quality) and some means to achieve that goal. This essay considers the second component, the means – the 'instruments' – of environmental policy, and focuses, in particular, on the use of economic-incentive or market-based policy instruments.

1. ECONOMIC CRITERIA FOR POLICY INSTRUMENT CHOICE. A variety of criteria – both economic and others – can be brought to bear on the choice of policy instruments to achieve some environmental goal or standard. Among these criteria, three stand out: static cost effectiveness; dynamic cost effectiveness; and distributional equity. Static cost effectiveness refers to the minimization of the short-term aggregate costs of achieving a particular level of pollution control. Similarly, dynamic cost effectiveness refers to the minimization of the present discounted value of the future stream of aggregate costs. Distributional equity refers to the 'fairness' of the distribution of the benefits and costs of the environmental policy, both cross-sectionally (among geographic regions, income groups, etc.) and intertemporally.

We begin by considering a cost-minimizing pollution control programme for a uniformly mixed flow pollutant. For such an environmental problem, we can focus on aggregate emissions per unit of time, where aggregate emissions are simply the sum of emissions from a set of individual firms or sources, where emissions from each source are the difference between unconstrained emissions and emission reductions. A cost-effective emission-control programme is one that controls aggregate emissions from all sources at minimum total cost. It is well known that if the control cost functions are convex in their relevant ranges, then the necessary and sufficient conditions for cost minimization are that the marginal cost of control be the same among all sources that carry out positive levels of control (Baumol and Oates 1988). Thus, in a cost-effective allocation of the pollution-control burden among sources, any and all sources that exercise a non-zero level of control must experience the same marginal abatement cost.

To achieve this cost-effective allocation of the pollution-control burden, the government could conceivably establish a non-uniform (source-specific) standard to ensure that all firms would control emissions at the same marginal cost of control, but this would require detailed information about the costs faced by each source, information that could be obtained by the authority only at very great cost, if at all. One way out of this impasse is through the use of economic-incentive or market-based policy instruments.

2. WHAT ARE ECONOMIC-INCENTIVE POLICY INSTRUMENTS? Economic-incentive instruments are regulations that encourage behaviour through price signals rather than through explicit instructions on pollution control levels or methods (Hahn and Stavins 1991). These policy instruments, such as tradeable permits and pollution charges, have been described as 'harnessing market forces' because, if they are properly implemented, they encourage firms to

undertake pollution control efforts that are in their financial self-interest and that will collectively meet policy goals (Stavins 1988, 1991).

Conventional approaches to regulating the environment are frequently referred to as 'command-and-control' regulations since they allow little flexibility in the means of achieving goals. Early environmental policies in the United States and other industrialized nations relied almost exclusively on these approaches (Portney 1990).

In general, command-and-control regulations force firms to shoulder identical shares of the pollution-control burden, regardless of the relative costs. Command-and-control regulations do this by setting uniform standards for firms, the most prevalent of which are technology-based and performance-based standards. Technology-based standards specify the method, and sometimes the actual equipment, that firms must use to comply with a particular regulation. For example, all electric utilities might be required to employ a specific type of 'scrubber' to remove particulates. A performance standard sets a uniform control target for firms, while allowing some latitude in how this target is met. For example, a regulation might limit the number of allowable units of a pollutant released in a given time period, but might not dictate the means by which this is achieved.

Holding all firms to the same target can be expensive and, in some circumstances, counterproductive. While standards can effectively limit emissions of pollutants, they typically exact relatively high societal costs in the process, by forcing firms to resort to unduly expensive means of controlling pollution. A survey of eight empirical studies of air pollution control found that the ratio of actual, aggregate costs of the conventional, command-and-control approach to the aggregate costs of least-cost benchmarks ranged from 1.07 for sulphate emissions in Los Angeles to 22.0 for hydrocarbon emissions at all domestic DuPont plants (Tietenberg 1985). Because the costs of controlling emissions may vary greatly between firms, and even within the same firm, the appropriate technology in one situation may be inappropriate in another.

Furthermore, command-and-control regulations tend to freeze the development of technologies that might otherwise result in greater levels of control. Little or no financial incentive exists for businesses to exceed their control targets, and both technology-based and performance-based standards discourage experimentation with new technologies. A firm adopting a new technology may be 'rewarded' by being held to a higher standard of performance, and not given the opportunity to benefit financially from its investment, except to the extent its competitors have even more difficulty reaching the new standard.

Characteristics of economic-incentive policy instruments. Economic-incentive instruments have captured the attention of environmental policy-makers in recent years because of the potential advantages they offer over traditional command-and-control approaches. In theory, properly designed and implemented economic-incentive instruments allow any desired level of pollution cleanup to be realized at the lowest possible overall cost to society, because they provide incentives for the greatest reductions in pollution by those firms that can achieve these reductions most cheaply. Rather than equalizing pollution levels among firms, economic-incentive instruments equalize the incremental amount that firms spend to reduce pollution (their marginal abatement costs).

As suggested above, command-and-control approaches could theoretically achieve this cost-effective solution. However, this would require that different standards be set for each pollution source, and, consequently, that policy makers obtain detailed information about the compliance costs each firm faces. Such information is simply not available to government. By contrast, economic-incentive instruments provide for a cost-effective allocation of the pollution control burden among sources without this information. Additionally, in contrast to command-and-control regulations, economic-incentive instruments have the potential to provide powerful incentives for firms to adopt cheaper and better pollution-control technologies (Magat 1978; McHugh 1985; Downing and White 1986; Malueg 1989; Milliman and Prince 1989; Jaffe and Stavins 1995).

Types of economic-incentive instruments. Economic-incentive instruments can be divided into five categories: pollution charges, tradeable permits, deposit-refund systems, reductions in market barriers, and government subsidy elimination (US Environmental Protection Agency 1991; Organization for Economic Cooperation and Development 1994; US Congress 1995).

Pollution charge systems assess a fee or tax on the amount of pollution a firm generates. For example, a pollution charge might take the form of a charge per unit of sulphur dioxide (SO_2) emissions. The choice of whether to tax pollution quantities, activities preceding discharge, inputs to those activities, or actual damages will depend upon tradeoffs between costs of abatement, mitigation, damages, and programme administration, including monitoring and enforcement. With a charge system in place, it becomes worthwhile for each firm to reduce pollutant emissions to the point at which its marginal cost of control is equal to the pollution-tax rate. Since all sources equate their marginal abatement costs with the same tax rate, marginal abatement costs will be identical across all sources. Hence, the imposition of a pollution tax leads to the cost-effective allocation of the pollution-control burden among sources. By internalizing the previously external pollution costs, firms control pollution to differing degrees, with high-cost controllers controlling less, and low-cost controllers controlling more.

A.C. Pigou (1920) is generally credited with developing the idea of a corrective tax to discourage activities which generate externalities, such as environmental pollution. But, the difficulty with charges is figuring out where to set the tax. If environmental damages are quantified in economic terms, then the charge should be set equal to social damages at the efficient level of control, that is, at the level of control where marginal benefits (avoided marginal damages) are equivalent to marginal abatement costs. It is rare, however, that reliable economic valuations of damages are available. Instead, policy makers may seek to identify the tax rate that will lead to the politically-determined level of aggregate abatement. But it is difficult for government to know beforehand how firms will respond to a given level of taxation. Despite the availability in a few cases of relevant elasticity estimates, in general it is difficult for government to ascertain with precision what level of cleanup will result from any given charge.

Tradeable permits can achieve the same cost-minimizing allocation of the pollution control burden as a charge system, while avoiding the problem of uncertain responses by firms. Coase's (1960) classic treatment of externality problems – originally intended as a critique of the Pigovian corrective tax approach – appears to have stimulated the subsequent literature on quantity-based economic incentive approaches, i.e. tradeable permit systems (Dales 1968; Montgomery 1972; Hahn and Noll 1982). Under such a system, an allowable overall level of pollution is established and then allotted among firms in the form of permits. Firms that keep their emissions below the allotted level may sell or lease their surplus permits to other firms or use them to offset excess emissions in other parts of their facilities.

In this case, each firm that carries out a non-zero degree of abatement will find it in its own interest to control up to the point at which its marginal abatement cost is equal to the market-determined permit price. Since all sources are equating their marginal abatement costs with the same permit price, marginal abatement costs are identical across sources. Hence, the environmental constraint is satisfied and the cost-effective allocation of the pollution-control burden is achieved.

A special case of a pollution tax is a *deposit refund system*, under which consumers pay a surcharge when purchasing potentially polluting products. Upon return of the product to an approved centre for recycling or proper disposal, the deposit is refunded. A number of American states, Canadian provinces, and European nations have successfully implemented this system through 'bottle bills', to control litter from beverage containers and to reduce the flow of solid waste to landfills (Bohm 1981; Menell 1990). This concept has also been applied to lead-acid batteries.

Reducing market barriers can also help to curb pollution. In some cases, substantial gains can be made in environmental protection simply by removing existing government-mandated barriers to market activity. For example, measures that facilitate the voluntary exchange of water rights promote more efficient allocation and use of scarce water supplies (Willey and Graff 1988).

Elimination of government subsidies can be a powerful economic incentive for environmental protection. Subsidies are the mirror image of various taxes and, in theory, can provide economic incentives to address environmental problems. In practice, however, many subsidies promote inefficient and environmentally unsound economic development. A prime example is the below-cost sale of timber by the US Forest Service, which does not allow for the recovery of the cost of making timber available for harvesting by private firms.

In the simplest models, as indicated above, pollution taxes and tradeable permits are symmetric, but that symmetry begins to break down in actual implementations. First, permits fix the level of pollution control while charges fix the costs of pollution control. Second, in the presence of technological change and without additional government intervention, permits freeze the level of pollution control while charges increase it. Third, with permit systems as adopted, resource transfers are private-to-private, while they are private-to-public with ordinary pollution charges. Fourth, while both charges and permits increase costs on industry and consumers, charge systems make the costs more explicit to both groups. Fifth, permits adjust automatically for inflation, while some types of charges do not. Sixth, permit systems may be more susceptible to strategic behaviour, because of the barriers to entry that implemented forms of these systems frequently provide. Seventh, significant transaction costs can drive up the total costs of compliance, having a negative effect under either system, but particularly with tradeable permits. Eighth and finally, in the presence of uncertainty, either permits or charges can be more efficient, depending upon the relative slopes of the marginal benefit and marginal cost functions (Weitzman 1974) and any correlation between them (Stavins 1996).

The degree of abatement achieved by a pollution tax and the tax's effect on the economy will depend – in part – on what is done with the tax revenue. There is widespread agreement that revenue recycling (that is, using revenues to lower other taxes) can significantly lower the costs of a pollution tax (Jorgenson and Wilcoxen 1994; Goulder 1995). Some researchers have suggested, further, that all of the abatement costs associated with a pollution tax can be eliminated through revenue recycling in the form of cuts in taxes on labour (Repetto et al. 1992). There is now common recognition, however, that this stronger claim is not valid (Bovenberg and de Mooij 1994; Bovenberg and Goulder 1996). Indeed, some pollution taxes can exacerbate distortions associated with remaining taxes on investment or labour. The revenue raised by an auction of tradeable permits can also be used to finance a reduction in some distortionary tax (Goulder et al. 1996; Fullerton and Metcalf 1996).

3. APPLICATIONS OF ECONOMIC-INCENTIVE INSTRUMENTS. There have been six major applications of economic-incentive instruments in the United States: the US Environmental Protection Agency's (EPA) Emissions Trading Program, the leaded gasoline phasedown, water quality permit trading, the chlorofluorocarbon (CFC) phaseout, the SO_2 allowance system for acid rain control, and the RECLAIM programme in the Los Angeles metropolitan region.

The Emissions Trading Program. Beginning in 1974, EPA experimented with emissions trading as part of the Clean Air Act's programme for improving local air quality. Firms that reduced emissions below the level required by law received credits usable against higher emissions elsewhere. Firms could employ the concepts of 'netting' or 'bubbles' to trade emissions reductions among sources within the firm, so long as total combined emissions did not exceed an aggregate limit (Tietenberg 1985; Hahn 1989). The 'offset' programme, which began in 1976, went further in allowing firms to trade emission credits. Firms wishing to establish new sources in areas that are not in compliance with ambient standards can offset their new emissions by reducing existing emissions. This can be accomplished through internal sources or through agreements with other firms. Finally, under the 'banking' programme, firms may retain earned emission credits for future use. Banking allows for either future internal expansion or the sale of credits to other firms.

EPA codified these programmes in its Emissions Trading Program in 1986 (US Environmental Protection Agency 1986), but the programmes have not been widely used. States are not required to use the programme, and uncertainties about its future course seem to have made firms reluctant to participate (Liroff 1986). Nevertheless, numerous firms have traded emissions credits, and a market for transfers has long since developed (Main 1988). Even this limited degree of participation in EPA's trading programmes may have saved between $5 billion and $12 billion since the programme's inception (Hahn and Hester 1989b).

The leaded gasoline phasedown. The purpose of the lead trading programme, developed in the 1980s, was to allow gasoline refiners greater flexibility in meeting emission standards at a time when the lead-content of gasoline was reduced to ten percent of its previous level. In 1982, the EPA authorized inter-refinery trading of lead credits (US Environmental Protection Agency 1982). If refiners produced gasoline with a lower lead content than was required, they earned lead credits. In 1985, EPA initiated a programme allowing refineries to bank lead credits, and subsequently firms made extensive use of this. EPA terminated it at the end of 1987, when the lead phasedown itself was complete.

The lead programme was successful in meeting its environmental target, and the high level of trading activity achieved suggests that it was relatively cost-effective. In each year it operated, more than sixty percent of the lead added to gasoline was associated with traded lead credits, and over half of all refineries participated in trading with other firms (Hahn and Hester 1989a). EPA estimated savings from the lead trading programme of approximately twenty percent over alternative programmes that did not provide for lead banking, a cost savings of about $250 million per year (US Environmental Protection Agency 1985). The programme experienced some relatively minor implementation difficulties related to the importation of leaded fuel, but it is not clear that a comparable command-and-control approach would have done better in terms of environmental quality (US General Accounting Office 1986).

Water quality permit trading. Non-point sources of water pollution, particularly agricultural and urban runoff, constitute the major remaining American water quality problem (Peskin 1986). An experimental programme to protect the Dillon Reservoir in Colorado demonstrates how tradeable permits could be used, in theory, to reduce nonpoint-source water pollution. The reservoir is the major source of water for the city of Denver. Nitrogen and phosphorus loading threatened to turn the reservoir eutrophic, despite the fact that point sources from surrounding communities were controlled to best-available technology standards (US Environmental Protection Agency 1984). Rapid population growth in Denver, and the resulting increase in urban surface water runoff, further aggravated the problem.

In response, state policy makers developed a point-non-point-source control programme to reduce phosphorus flows, mainly from non-point urban and agricultural sources (Hahn 1989), which was implemented in 1984. It allowed publicly owned sewage treatment works to finance the control of non-point sources in lieu of upgrading their own treated effluents to drinking water standards. EPA estimated that the plan could save over $1 million per year (Hahn and Hester 1989a), due to large differences in the marginal costs of control between non-point sources and sewage treatment facilities. However, no trading ever occurred under the programme, apparently because high regional precipitation essentially eliminated its need.

The CFC phaseout. A market in tradeable permits was used in the United States to help comply with the Montreal Protocol, an international agreement aimed at slowing the rate of stratospheric ozone depletion. The Montreal Protocol called for a 50 percent reduction in the production of CFCs from 1986 levels by 1998. In addition, the Protocol froze halon production and consumption at 1986 levels beginning in 1992. The market places limitations on both the production and consumption of CFCs by issuing allowances that limit these activities. The Montreal Protocol recognizes the fact that different types of CFCs are likely to have different effects on ozone depletion. Therefore, each CFC is assigned a different weight on the basis of its depletion potential. If a firm wishes to produce a given amount of CFC, it must have an allowance to do so, calculated on this basis (Hahn and McGartland 1989).

Through mid-1991 there were 34 participants in the market and 80 trades. However, the overall efficiency of the market is difficult to determine, because no studies were conducted to estimate cost savings. The timetable for the phaseout of CFCs was subsequently accelerated, and a tax on CFCs was introduced. Indeed, the tax may have become the binding (effective) instrument. Nevertheless, relatively low transaction costs associated with trading in the CFC market suggest that the system was relatively cost-effective.

The SO_2 allowance system for acid rain control. A centrepiece of the Clean Air Act Amendments of 1990 is a tradeable permit system that regulates sulphur dioxide emissions, the primary precursor of acid rain (US Clean Air Act 1990). Title IV of the Act reduces sulphur dioxide and nitrous oxide emissions by 10 million tons and 2 million tons, respectively, from 1980 levels (Ferrall 1991). The first phase of sulphur dioxide emissions reductions was achieved by 1995, with a second phase of reduction to be accomplished by the year 2000.

In Phase I, individual emissions limits were assigned to 111 electrical utilities. After 1 January, 1995, these utilities could emit sulphur dioxide in excess of limitations only if they qualified for extensions or substitutions, or if they obtained allowances for their total emissions. During Phase I, the EPA allocated each affected utility, on an annual basis, a specified number of allowances related to its capacity, plus bonus allowances available under a variety of special provisions (Joskow and Schmalensee 1995). Cost-effectiveness was promoted by permitting allowance holders to transfer their permits among one another.

Under Phase II of the programme, beginning 1 January 2000, almost all electric power generating units will be brought within the system. Certain units are excepted to compensate for potential restrictions on growth and to reward units that are already unusually clean. If trading permits represent the carrot of the system, its stick is a penalty of $2,999 per ton of emissions that exceed any year's allowances (and a requirement that such excesses be offset the following year).

A robust market of bilateral SO_2 permit trading has emerged, resulting in cost savings in the area of $1 billion annually, compared with the anticipated costs under a command-and-control regime. Nevertheless, the programme has fallen short of predictions, with fewer permits traded and at lower prices than originally anticipated (Burtraw 1995). This may have more to do with faulty predictions than problematic performance, however. Despite earlier concerns that state regulatory authorities would hamper trading in order to protect their domestic coal industries, preliminary evidence suggests that this has not been a major problem (Bailey 1996). Similarly, in contrast to early assertions that the structure of EPA's permit auction market would cause problems (Cason 1995), the evidence now indicates that this has had little or no effect on the vastly more important bilateral trading market (Joskow et al. 1996).

The RECLAIM programme. The South Coast Air Quality Management District (SCAQMD), which is responsible for controlling emissions in a four-county area of Southern California, launched a tradeable permit programme in January 1994 to reduce nitrogen oxides (NO_x) and sulphur dioxide emissions in the Los Angeles area (Johnson and Pekelney 1996). As of June 1996, 353 participants in this Regional Clean Air Incentives Market (RECLAIM) programme have traded more than 100,000 tons of NO_x and SO_2 emissions, at a value of over $10 million (Brotzman 1996). The RECLAIM programme, which operates through the issuance of permits that authorize decreasing levels of pollution over time, governs stationary sources only, but the authority is considering expanding the programme to allow trading between stationary and mobile sources (Fulton 1996).

4. ASSESSING THE APPLICATIONS: LIMITED USE OF INSTRUMENTS. Notwithstanding the varying levels of success in the implementation of specific programmes, economic-incentive instruments have yet to transform the landscape of environmental policy in fundamental ways. Indeed, economic-incentive instruments still exist only at the fringes of regulation, and have not become a central component of private firms' environmental decision making. It is beyond the scope of this essay to provide a thorough treatment of the positive political economy of instrument choice in environmental policy (Keohane et al. 1997), but it is possible to identify several important factors that have limited the use of economic-incentive policies.

The role of interest groups. Traditional regulatory programmes require regulators with a technical or legal-based skill-set, but economic-incentive instruments require market-trained thinkers, including MBAs, economists, and others. It is understandable that, under these circumstances, members of the government bureaucracy should rationally resist the dissipation of their human capital (Hahn and Stavins 1991). Although some environmental advocacy groups have welcomed the selective use of economic-incentive instruments (Krupp 1986), others are concerned that increased flexibility in environmental regulation will result in the reduction of the overall level of environmental protection. In parts of the environmental community, the sentiment remains that environmental quality is an inalienable right, and that economic-incentive programmes condone the 'right to pollute'. In addition, some of these environmental professionals, like their government counterparts, may be resisting the dissipation of *their* human capital.

Ambivalence towards better regulation. Many firms applaud economic-incentive instruments in the abstract because of their promise of flexibility and cost savings, but few have actively supported specific incentive-based policies. Much of the hesitation stems from a reluctance to promote any regulation, no matter how flexible or cost effective. Private firms perceive – perhaps seasoned by experience – that political forces beyond their control might unfavourably distort the design and implementation of these instruments.

First, there is a concern that any cost savings will be used to increase the overall degree of environmental clean up. Second, the actual design of instruments may distort their flexibility and penalize some firms. Third, the regulated sector may fear that the rules will change over time. Environmental investments can often be very large (e.g., tens of millions of dollars). For businesses to optimize these investments, regulations not only have to be flexible, but predictable. In the case of acid rain, for example, changes have been proposed by EPA in the permit bidding process, and the American Lung Association has sued EPA in an attempt to force them to tighten SO_2 standards (Lobsenz 1996). Finally, firms are concerned that 'buying the right to pollute' under emission trading programmes could lead to negative publicity. Even though the trade of permits is legal, and helps improve the environment at lower overall cost to society, some citizens may perceive this behaviour as unethical.

Consumer experience. The slow penetration of economic-incentive instruments into environmental policies is also a function of these instruments not being well understood by the public. Economic-incentive instruments – especially charges – may suffer from making environmental costs transparent. While encouraging individuals to link environmental costs consciously to environmental benefits may be a good thing, it can undermine the enthusiasm with which economic-incentive instruments are embraced. These instruments have been an easy target for opponents who paint a picture for consumers that firms are simply paying to pollute. While the fallacy of such arguments is clear, particularly in the context of command-and-control instruments that actually *give away* the right to pollute, the imagery has been compelling.

5. ASSESSING THE APPLICATIONS: A MIXED RECORD ON PERFORMANCE. In section 4, I examined some of the reasons why economic-incentive instruments have not been widely used in the environmental policy arena. In this section, I consider the reasons why, when they have been used, economic-incentive instruments have not always performed as well as predicted.

Inaccurate predictions. One of the major reasons why economic-incentive instruments have fallen short in delivering the cost savings predicted is that the predictions themselves have often been unrealistic – they were premised on perfect performance under *ideal* conditions. That is, these predictions have implicitly assumed that the cost-minimizing allocation of the pollution-control burden among sources would be achieved, and that marginal abatement costs would be perfectly equated across all sources. In a frequently cited table, Tietenberg calculated the ratio of the cost of an actual command-and-control programme to a least-cost benchmark (Tietenberg 1985). Others have mistakenly used this ratio as an indicator of the potential gains of adopting specific economic-incentive instruments. The more appropriate comparison would be between actual command-and-control programmes and either actual or reasonably constrained theoretical economic-incentive programmes (Hahn and Stavins 1992).

In addition, predictions made during policy debates have typically ignored a number of factors that can adversely affect performance: transaction costs involved in implementing economic-incentive programmes (Stavins 1995); uncertainty as to the property rights bestowed under programmes; concentration in the permit market (Hahn 1984; Misolek and Elder 1989) or product market (Malueg 1990); the preexisting regulatory environment (Bohi and Burtraw 1992); and the inability of firms' internal decision-making capabilities to fully utilize programme opportunities (Walley and Whitehead 1994).

The SO_2 allowance trading programme is a high-profile example where overly optimistic predictions were made. The programme was originally predicted to cut the cost of achieving SO_2 reductions by up to $3 billion annually (ICF, Inc. 1986). It is now predicted to result in savings of about $1 billion annually (Hahn and May 1994). The price and quantity of permit trading has been lower than originally predicted, partly because the marginal cost of abatement has been lower than expected for reasons related to changes in input markets, primarily the fall in the price of low-sulphur coal, due to railroad deregulation (Ellerman and Montero 1996) and innovations in fuel blending that have enabled more fuel switching (Burtraw 1995). Furthermore, permit prices may have been lower than marginal abatement costs because of: utilities' reluctance to consider new options; constraints imposed on utilities by contractual precommitments (Coggins and Smith 1993); the preexisting regulatory environment, including locally binding regulations and rate-of-return regulations; regulatory uncertainty; permit property rights questions (Bohi and Burtraw 1992); and transaction costs.

Design problems. Many of the factors cited suggest the need for changes in the design of future economic incentive instruments. While some programme design elements reflect miscalculations of market reactions, others were known to be problematic at the time the programmes were enacted, but nevertheless were incorporated into them to ensure adoption by the political process. One striking example is the adoption of the '20 percent rule' under EPA's Emission Trading Program. This rule, adopted at the insistence of the environmental advocacy community, stipulated that each time a permit is traded, the amount of pollution authorized thereunder is reduced by 20 percent. Since permits that are not traded retain their full value, this regulation discourages trading and thereby increases abatement costs.

Limitations in firms' internal structures. A third set of explanations for the mixed performance of implemented economic-incentive instruments reflects limitations in private firms' internal structures and skill sets (Hockenstein, Stavins and Whitehead 1997). Economic-incentive instruments require a very different set of decisions than do traditional command-and-control approaches, and most firms are simply not equipped internally to make the decisions necessary to take full advantage of these instruments. Since economic-incentive instruments have been used on a limited basis only, and firms are not certain that these instruments will be a lasting component on the regulatory landscape, most firms have not reorganized their environmental, health and safety (EH&S) departments in a manner necessary to exploit fully potential cost savings. Rather, most firms continue to have organizations that are experienced in minimizing the costs of complying with command-and-control regulations, not in making the *strategic* decisions required by economic-incentive instruments (Walley and Whitehead 1994).

In general, EH&S staff members are poorly equipped to handle emerging environmental issues in a business context. As lawyers and engineers, not MBAs, they are experienced in interpreting detailed regulatory rules and in designing technological solutions to comply with them; they are unprepared to implement the cost-saving decisions that economic-incentive regulations allow. EH&S departments need to be staffed with market-trained thinkers who can analyse the strategic implications of the new options which firms face.

Businesses are further impaired by the fact that EH&S functions are not sufficiently integrated with those of the business units. Links have rarely developed between environmental decision-makers and business unit decision-makers. In many cases, environmental costs are not fully measured and are not considered by the business units from which they derive. This has limited firms' abilities to make even the few strategic decisions allowed under command-and-control approaches. When firms face the much broader set of strategic issues raised by market-instruments, the lack of integration of environmental with business units becomes an even more pressing problem. Absent this integration, the full potential of economic-incentive instruments – cost-effectiveness and improved incentives for technological change – will not be realized.

6. CONCLUSIONS. Some eighty years ago, Pigou proposed the use of a corrective tax to internalize environmental or other externalities; and fifty years later, the portfolio of potential economic-incentive instruments was expanded to include a quantity-based mechanism, tradeable permits. Thus, economic-incentive approaches to environmental protection are by no means a new policy idea. Over the past two decades they have held varying degrees of prominence in environmental policy. But these instruments remain on the periphery of environmental policy, and when they have been implemented, they have frequently not performed as predicted. Does this suggest that economists and legal scholars should abandon their advocacy of these instruments? The historical record, reviewed in this essay, suggests that the answer is 'no'.

Economic-incentive instruments have delivered attractive results where implemented and promise additional future benefits. To date, their effectiveness has been undermined by unrealistic expectations, lack of political will, flaws in design, and constraints imposed by the internal structure of firms. These are all remediable. Thus, rather than abandoning the use of market-based instruments, policy-makers should direct their efforts to making future applications work better than those that came before.

ROBERT N. STAVINS

See also CONTINGENT VALUATION; ENDANGERED SPECIES; REGULATION AND DEREGULATION; REGULATION OF HAZARDOUS WASTES; REGULATION OF TOXIC SUBSTANCES; REGULATORY IMPACT ANALYSIS: A CROSS-COUNTRY COMPARISON; REMOTE RISKS AND THE TORT SYSTEM; RISK ASSESSMENT; RISK REGULATION; TRADEABLE POLLUTION PERMITS; VALUING LIFE AND RISKS TO LIFE.

Subject classification: 6d(iv).

BIBLIOGRAPHY

Bailey, E.M. 1996. *Allowance trading activity and state regulatory rulings: evidence from the U.S. Acid Rain Program.* MIT-CEEPR 96–002 WP, Center for Energy and Environmental Policy Research, Massachusetts Institute of Technology.

Baumol, W.J. and Oates, W.E. 1988. *The Theory of Environmental Policy*. 2nd edn, New York: Cambridge University Press.

Bohi, D.R. and Burtraw, D. 1992. Utility investment behavior and the emission trading market. *Resources and Energy* 14: 129–53.

Bohm, P. 1981. *Deposit-Refund Systems: Theory and Applications to Environmental, Conservation, and Consumer Policy*. Baltimore: Johns Hopkins University Press for Resources for the Future.

Bovenberg, A.L. and de Mooij, R. 1994. Environmental levies and distortionary taxation. *American Economic Review* 84: 1085–9.

Bovenberg, A.L. and Goulder, L.H. 1996. Optimal environmental taxation in the presence of other taxes: general-equilibrium analyses. *American Economic Review* 86: 985–1000.

Brotzman, T. 1996. Opening the floor to emissions trading. *Chemical Marketing Reporter* 27 May, p. SR8.

Burtraw, D. 1995. Cost savings sans allowance trades? Evaluating the SO_2 Emission Trading Program to date. Discussion Paper 95–30. Resources for the Future.

Cason, T.N. 1995. An experimental investigation of the seller incentives in EPA's emission trading auction. *American Economic Review* 85: 905–22.

Coase, R.H. 1960. The problem of social cost. *Journal of Law and Economics* 3: 1–44.

Coggins, J.S. and Smith, V.H. 1993. Some welfare effects of emission allowance trading in a twice-regulated industry. *Journal of Environmental Economics and Management* 25: 275–97.

Dales, J. 1968. *Pollution, Property, and Prices*. Toronto: University of Toronto Press.

Downing, P.B. and White, L.J. 1986. Innovation in pollution control. *Journal of Environmental Economics and Management* 13: 18–27.

Ellerman, A.D. and Montero, J.P. 1996. Why are allowance prices so low? An analysis of the SO_2 Emissions Trading Program. Center for Energy and Environmental Policy Research, Massachusetts Institute of Technology.

Ferrall, B.L. 1991. The Clean Air Act Amendments of 1990 and the use of market forces to control sulphur dioxide emissions. *Harvard Journal on Legislation* 28: 235–52.

Fullerton, D. and Metcalf, G. 1996. Environmental controls, scarcity rents, and pre-existing distortions. Paper presented at the National Bureau of Economic Research workshop, 'Public Policy and the Environment', Cambridge, MA.

Fulton, W. 1996. The Big Green Bazaar. *Governing Magazine*. June, p. 38.

Goulder, L. 1995. Effects of carbon taxes in an economy with prior tax distortions: an intertemporal general equilibrium analysis. *Journal of Environmental Economics and Management* 29: 271–97.

Goulder, L., Parry, I. and Burtraw, D. 1996. The Choice Between Revenue-Raising and Other Instruments for Environmental Protection in a Second-Best Setting. Paper presented at the National Bureau of Economic Research workshop, 'Public Policy and the Environment', Cambridge, MA.

Hahn, R.W. 1984. Market power and transferable property rights. *Quarterly Journal of Economics* 99: 753–65.

Hahn, R.W. 1989. Economic prescriptions for environmental problems: how the patient followed the doctor's orders. *Journal of Economic Perspectives* 3: 95–114.

Hahn, R.W. and Hester, G.L. 1989a. Marketable permits: lessons for theory and practice. *Ecology Law Quarterly* 16: 361–406.

Hahn, R.W. and Hester, G.L. 1989b. Where did all the markets go? An analysis of EPA's Emissions Trading Program. *Yale Journal on Regulation* 6: 109–53.

Hahn, R.W. and May, C. 1994. The behavior of the allowance market: theory and evidence. *Electricity Journal* 8: 28–37.

Hahn, R.W. and McGartland, A.M. 1989. Political economy of instrumental choice: an examination of the U.S. role in implementing the Montreal Protocol. *Northwestern University Law Review* 83: 592–611.

Hahn, R.W. and Noll, R. 1982. Designing a market for tradeable permits. In *Reform of Environmental Regulation*, ed. W.A. Magat, Cambridge, MA: Ballinger Publishing Co.

Hahn, R.W. and Stavins, R.N. 1991. Incentive-based environmental regulation: a new era from an old idea? *Ecology Law Quarterly* 18: 1–42.

Hahn, R.W. and Stavins, R.N. 1992. Economic incentives for environmental protection: integrating theory and practice. *American Economic Review, Papers and Proceedings* 82: 464–72.

Hockenstein, J.A., Stavins, R.N. and Whitehead, B.W. 1997. *Environment*, forthcoming.

ICF, Inc. 1986. *Analysis of Six and Eight Million Ton 30-Year/NSPS and 30-Year/1.2 Pound Sulphur Dioxide Emission Reduction Cases.* Washington, DC.

Jaffe, A.B. and Stavins, R.N. 1995. Dynamic incentives of environmental regulations: the effects of alternative policy instruments on technology diffusion. *Journal of Environmental Economics and Management* 29: S–43–S–63.

Johnson, S.L. and Pekelney, D.M. 1996. Economic assessment of the regional clean air incentives market: a new emissions trading program for Los Angeles. *Land Economics* 72: 277–97.

Jorgenson, D. and Wilcoxen, P. 1994. The economic effects of a carbon tax. Paper presented to the IPCC Workshop on Policy Instruments and their Implications, Tsukuba, Japan, January 17–20.

Joskow, P.L. and Schmalensee, R. 1995. The Political Economy of Market-based Environmental Policy: The 1990 U.S. Acid Rain Program. Draft manuscript, MIT.

Joskow, P.L., Schmalensee, R. and Bailey, E.M. 1996. Auction Design and the Market for Sulphur Dioxide Emissions. Paper presented at the National Bureau of Economic Research workshop 'Public Policy and the Environment', Cambridge, MA.

Keohane, N.O., Revesz, R.L. and Stavins, R.N. 1997. The Positive Political Economy of Instrument Choice in Environmental Policy. Paper presented at the Allied Social Science Associations meeting, New Orleans, Louisiana, 4–6 January.

Krupp, F. 1986. New environmentalism factors in economic needs. *Wall Street Journal*, 20 November, p. 34.

Liroff, R.A. 1986. *Reforming Air Pollution Regulations: The Toil and Trouble of EPA's Bubble.* Washington, DC: Conservation Foundation.

Lobsenz, G. 1996. Lung association sues EPA over SO2 standard. *The Energy Daily*, 22 July, p. 3.

Magat, W.A. 1978. Pollution control and technological advance: a model of the firm. *Journal of Environmental Economics and Management* 5: 1–25.

Main, J. 1988. Here comes the big new cleanup. *Fortune* (November): 102–118.

Malueg, D.A. 1989. Emission credit trading and the incentive to adopt new pollution abatement technology. *Journal of Environmental Economics and Management* 16: 52–7.

Malueg, D.A. 1990. Welfare consequences of emission credit trading programs. *Journal of Environmental Economics and Management* 18: 66–77.

McHugh, R. 1985. The potential for private cost-increasing technological innovation under a tax-based, economic incentive pollution control policy. *Land Economics* 61: 58–64.

Menell, P. 1990. Beyond the throwaway society: an incentive approach to regulating municipal solid waste. *Ecology Law Quarterly* 17: 655–739.

Milliman, S.R. and Prince, R. 1989. Firm incentives to promote technological change in pollution control. *Journal of Environmental Economics and Management* 17: 247–65.

Misolek, W.S. and Elder, H.W. 1989. Exclusionary manipulation of markets for pollution rights. *Journal of Environmental Economics and Management* 16: 156–66.

Montgomery, W.D. 1972. Markets in licenses and efficient pollution control programs. *Journal of Economic Theory* 5: 395–418.

Organization for Economic Cooperation and Development. 1994. *Managing the Environment: The Role of Economic Instruments.* Paris: OECD.

Peskin, S. 1986. Nonpoint pollution and national responsibility. *Resources* (Spring): 10–11.

Pigou, A.C. 1920. *The Economics of Welfare.* New York: AMS Press, 1978.

Portney, P.R. (ed.) 1990. *Public Policies for Environmental Protection.* Washington, DC: Resources for the Future.

Repetto, R., Dower, R., Jenkins, R. and Geoghegan, J. 1992. *Green Fees: How a Tax Shift Can Work for the Environment and the Economy.* Washington, DC: World Resources Institute.

Stavins, R.N. (ed.) 1988. *Project 88: Harnessing Market Forces to Protect Our Environment.* Sponsored by Senator Timothy E. Wirth, Colorado, and Senator John Heinz, Pennsylvania; Washington, DC.

Stavins, R.N. (ed.) 1991. *Project 88 – Round II, Incentives for Action: Designing Market-Based Environmental Strategies.* Sponsored by Senator Timothy E. Wirth, Colorado, and Senator John Heinz, Pennsylvania; Washington, DC.

Stavins, R.N. 1995. Transaction costs and tradeable permits. *Journal of Environmental Economics and Management* 29: 133–47.

Stavins, R.N. 1996. Correlated uncertainty and policy instrument choice. *Journal of Environmental Economics and Management* 30: 218–32.

Tietenberg, T. 1985. *Emissions Trading: An Exercise in Reforming Pollution Policy.* Washington, DC: Resources for the Future.

US Environmental Protection Agency. 1982. *Regulation of Fuel and Fuel Additives* 49, 322–4 (final rule).

US Environmental Protection Agency. 1984. Case studies on the trading of effluent loads, Dillon Reservoir. Final Report.

US Environmental Protection Agency. 1985. *Costs and Benefits of Reducing Lead in Gasoline, Final Regulatory Impact Analysis.* Washington, DC: Office of Policy Analysis.

US Environmental Protection Agency. 1986. *Emissions Trading Policy Statement*, 51 Fed. Reg. 43,814 (final policy statement).

US Environmental Protection Agency. 1991. *Economic Incentives: Options for Environmental Protection.* Office of Policy, Planning, and Evaluation. Washington, DC: US Government Printing Office.

US Clean Air Act. 1990. Amendments, Public Law No. 101–549, 104 Statute 2399.

US Congress, Office of Technology Assessment. 1995. *Environmental Policy Tools: A User's Guide.* OTA-ENV-634. Washington, DC: US Government Printing Office.

US General Accounting Office. 1986. *Vehicle Emissions: EPA Program to Assist Leaded-Gasoline Producers Needs Prompt Improvement.* GAO/RCED-86-182. Washington, DC: US General Accounting Office.

Walley, N. and Whitehead, B. 1994. It's not easy being green. *Harvard Business Review* 72(3): 46–52.

Weitzman, M.L. 1974. Prices vs. quantities. *Review of Economic Studies* 41: 477–91.

Willey, W.R.Z. and Graff, T.H. 1988. Federal water policy in the United States – an agenda for economic and environmental reform. *Columbia Journal of Environmental Law*: 349–51.

economic legality and transition in Russia and Eastern Europe. 'Economic legality' can be defined as (1) a mutually consistent set of laws that govern economic activity; and (2) a belief by the population in the stability and enforcement of those laws. This definition is closely related to the concept of rule by law as opposed to the discretion of individuals. The establishment of economic legality requires credible commitment for supporting trust in contractual agreements, including economic policies. The presence of economic legality in any given country or organization is a matter of degree, and depends critically on the beliefs of the population. Economic legality refers not to the formal existence of stable and enforced economic laws, but to expectations of the public as to their existence.

Research in economics and political economy has emphasized the importance of many aspects of economic legality for economic development. Greif, Milgrom and

Weingast (1994) present a theory of merchant guilds as institutions capable of building economic legality through the multilateral enforcement of rules. North and Weingast (1989), North (1990) and Weingast (1995) have emphasized the central role of credible commitment to the enforcement of rules in the emergence of rapid economic growth in several countries, particularly in eighteenth-century England. More recently, La Porta et al. (1996) found strong evidence for the importance of 'trust' for explaining the performance of large organizations.

In recent years, problems in economic legality have become quite visible during the process of economic transition in Eastern Europe and the former Soviet Union. The Soviet-type economic system, which had formerly prevailed in these countries, operated with a very low degree of economic legality. The two primary principles that explained the functioning of the system were the discretionary authority of superiors over subordinates in the hierarchy, and reputation effects from personal, often informal, bilateral long-run ties (Litwack 1991). Economic transition has had a very disruptive effect on the nature and value of former ties and dependencies, and has made imperative the development of economic legality to support well-functioning markets.

The creation of this environment presents one of the foremost challenges of economic transition. The above-cited studies in economic history indicate that the development of economic legality in the Western world occurred over a number of centuries, often involving the formalization of rules that previously had been enforced implicitly, and associated with the development of autonomous organizations. A strategy for economic transition aims at accelerating the development of economic legality through a second-mover advantage. Indeed, most of the constitutions and basic economic laws adopted in these countries are based on existing models in Western countries. The experience of a number of Asian countries since World War II suggests that such a second-mover advantage can indeed be important.

Some aspects of the experience in Asia are also indicative of difficulties that can accompany attempts to import Western laws and practices in the absence of a similar tradition of economic legality. For example, after World War II, the United States moved to set up a framework for economic law in Japan that was strikingly similar to its own. But the economic system that emerged, and its corresponding institutions of economic legality, are distinctively different. This system involves the operation of financial-industrial groups (*keiretsu*) around a particular 'main bank', in which repeated relationships, cemented through debt contracts and cross-shareholding, play a critical role in defending economic legality and mutual trust within their respective organizations (Aoki 1988). In some sense, the Japanese system is a hybrid that has combined both the importation of legal institutions from the West and the activities of indigenous institutions that play a similar role to those autonomous organizations around which economic legality first emerged in the Western world.

During the period of transition, the development of economic legality has exhibited substantial heterogeneity across Eastern Europe, reflecting quite different histories, traditions, and geographies. The Central European countries, by and large, participated directly in the process by which economic legality was created in the Western world. A number of these countries were able to fall back on laws and traditions that prevailed before World War II. Also, privatization programmes in some of these countries have transferred substantial assets to foreign investors, who have brought with them developed business practices and a strong lobby for promoting polices consistent with economic legality.

With the exception of Estonia, Latvia and Lithuania, which had traditions dating from before World War II, the process of development of economic legality in the countries of the former Soviet Union has proceeded on a rather different basis. As in Central Europe, most of these countries rapidly moved to adopt constitutions and basic economic laws that borrow heavily from the experience of the West. But the specific institutional environment of these countries had made the creation of economic legality through such means more complicated. After five years of economic transition in the Russian Federation, for example, a plethora of constantly changing laws, decrees, regulations, and instructions, emanating from numerous government bodies and often mutually-inconsistent with one other, continues to compromise the goal of establishing rule of law in the country. In this context, parallel to explicit attempts to promote economic legality through the adoption and implementation of laws, the organizational evolution of the economy has favoured the development of implicit means for contract enforcement and the promotion of trust, as reflected in the recent rise to prominence of large financial-industrial groups (OECD 1997).

One area that has been particularly problematic for the creation of legality in the Russian Federation is that of taxation. State banks that held the accounts of all economic organizations under the former planned economic system provided an automatic mechanism for the collection of (implicit) taxes. Furthermore, rules affecting the distribution of income were regularly revised to siphon off the 'excess profits' of more successful organizations. At the outset of transition in 1991, a new comprehensive law was intended to provide the foundation for a completely new system of taxation, including a well-defined division of authority and revenue between various different levels of government. Six years later, while some limited progress has been made on the basis of this document, the development of legality in this area has nevertheless proceeded very slowly. Fiscal relations between various levels of government, as well as between the state and economic organizations, continue to be determined largely through special bilateral agreements. In addition, these agreements, like other laws and regulations concerning taxation, are themselves highly unstable. The Russian government has yet to be successful in combating the expectations of the population, which were formed during the Soviet period, that economic success will lead to discretionary adjustments in tax rates to siphon off additional profits. State tax revenue has declined continually during the transition period amidst widespread tax avoidance and regular emergency campaigns of the state to crack down on evasion and collect tax arrears. These campaigns have often been carried out in explicit violation of basic economic laws, including provisions in the Civil Code that protect workers and secured creditors in cases of insolvency (OECD 1997). The expenditure side of the budget mirrors the problems on the revenue side. The allocation of state expenditures has deviated sharply from legal budgetary obligations, often depriving state employees and pensioners of earned wages and benefits.

This environment has fostered a growing trend toward the formation and growth of financial-industrial groups. The most important such groups exist around several large Moscow banks and natural monopolies. While a primary motivation for the formation of these groups has been the fostering of trust and commitment within the organization, particularly for the enforcement of debt contracts, the development of special relations with government organs is also an important goal. In fact, a political lobby exists in Russia that proposes an entire development strategy revolving around bilateral agreements between financial-industrial groups and the government in taxation, customs duties, licensing, and other areas. This lobby was sufficiently powerful to push through the government a Law on Financial Industrial Groups in 1995 that authorizes the granting of various special government favours to registered groups. As of late 1997, the government had granted very few such explicit favours. Nevertheless, a number of registered, as well as unregistered, financial-industrial groups appear to have profited significantly from informal favours from various government organs, including special tax conditions, authorized participation in state financial programmes, and privileged access to privatization auctions. Such special relations with state organs are still widely understood as a prerequisite for success in the Russian business community.

Simultaneous with these developments, many government bodies and policy-makers in the Russian federation continue to pursue another model of economic development, based upon rule of law, a 'level playing field', and a high degree of competition, including that from foreign investors who possess the physical and human capital to accelerate the restructuring process. The emerging economic system in the Russian Federation already includes a complicated mix of developing institutions for the promotion of economic legality. Current policy choices may have a critical effect on determining the nature of the Russian economic system in the medium and long term.

JOHN M. LITWACK

See also BUREAUCRACY IN EASTERN EUROPE AND THE FORMER SOVIET UNION; CORRUPTION IN TRANSITION ECONOMIES; LEGAL OBLIGATION, NON-COMPLIANCE AND SOFT BUDGET CONSTRAINT; LEGAL REFORM IN EASTERN EUROPE; TRANSFER OF PROPERTY RIGHTS IN EASTERN EUROPE; TRANSITION IN EASTERN EUROPE.

Subject classification: 3f(ii).

BIBLIOGRAPHY

Aoki, M. 1988. *Information, Incentives, and Bargaining in the Japanese Economy*. Cambridge: Cambridge University Press.

Greif, A., Milgrom, P. and Weingast, B. 1994. Coordination, commitment, and enforcement: the case of the merchant guild. *Journal of Political Economy* 102: 745–76.

La Porta, R., Lopez-de-Silanes, F., Shleifer, A. and Vishny, R. 1996. Trust in large organizations. NBER Working Paper No. 5864.

Litwack, J. 1991. Legality and market reform in Soviet-type economies. *Journal of Economic Perspectives* 5(4): 77–89

North, D. 1990. *Institutions, Institutional Change, and Economic Performance*. Cambridge: Cambridge University Press.

North, D. and Weingast, B. 1989. Constitutions and credible commitments: the evolution of the institutions of public choice in 17th century England. *Journal of Economic History* 49(4): 803–32.

OECD. 1997. *OECD Economic Surveys: The Russian Federation 1997*. Paris: OECD.

Weingast, B. 1995. The economic role of political institutions. Institute for Policy Reform Working Paper, 46.

economic theory of liability rules. The economic theory of liability rules is a body of analysis of the economic consequences of tort liability rules. Since tortious harm can be avoided to some degree by taking precautions, the economic theory of liability is grounded in the economics of precautions. Tort law governs relations between strangers who hurt one another. The strangers are not dealing with one another in organized markets nor have they contracted with one another. It is not an analysis of organized markets. Instead, it is an analysis of economic behaviour in the face of accidents that might or might not happen, where costly precautions may or may not be put to use, and where, if an accident happens, a potential injurer may have to pay damages, or a potential victim may not be able to collect damages.

SCOPE: ECONOMICS APPLIED TO TORT LAW RATHER THAN CONTRACT LAW

Legal rules of liability for torts have an impact on economic behaviour. Whether the impact is socially beneficial or perverse, whether the rules have a large or a small impact, these are the subject of the economic theory of liability.

A tort is any wrongful act, other than a breach of contract, for which a civil lawsuit may be brought by a private person. Our discussion will be limited to cases where the parties are strangers to each other, in the sense that they have not had or taken the opportunity to enter into agreements or contracts with each other about the consequences of potential harm caused by one to the other.

Liability rules describe the circumstances under which a court will grant damages for injuries to oneself or one's resources. Liability rules are distinct from property rights, which allow one to exclude all others from the use of that resource. I may not be able to prevent you from hitting my car, but through the application of liability rules, I can get a court to force you to pay damages to me for hitting my car.

The economic behaviour at issue is the extent to which parties take costly precautions which can protect others or themselves from harm.

The economic theory of contracts and contract enforcement involves very different considerations and is beyond the scope of this essay. Still, it should be pointed out that where parties have a contract with each other, but the contract does not cover a contingency that in fact occurs, then the parties might be considered as strangers, and often tort law concepts can provide structure and background to any analysis, whether legal or economic.

THE ECONOMICS OF PRECAUTIONS

The production of precautions. The economics of precautions is, in part, an exercise in the standard economic theory of production. Here, the good produced is a level of accident avoidance which is best expressed as a probability of the accident being avoided (one minus the probability of the accident). In the standard case, production of a level of accident avoidance requires amounts of two inputs or precautions. Later we shall let one of the precautions be under the control of the injurer and one under the control of the victim. The standard neoclassical production theory is usually developed under the assumptions of positive and declining marginal products for each input and the inputs are available at fixed prices. One can determine efficient combinations of the two inputs to produce any particular level of accident avoidance. In the simplest case, when both precautions and the cost of the accident are simply denominated in dollars, and the cost of the accident is fixed, one can easily identify the least cost combination of precautions and accident probability. See Figure 1 for a standard representation of production where the product is accident avoidance, increasing upward to the right. Standard isoquants show different combinations of precautions that jointly produce equal levels of accident avoidance, and the straight lines represent equal cost combinations of precautions. The optimal combination, the combination that would be chosen if both precautions and the cost of the accident were under common control, will be where the isoquant and isocost lines are tangent. Of the many tangencies, that will be chosen where the marginal cost of increased production is the same as the marginal benefit of accident avoidance.

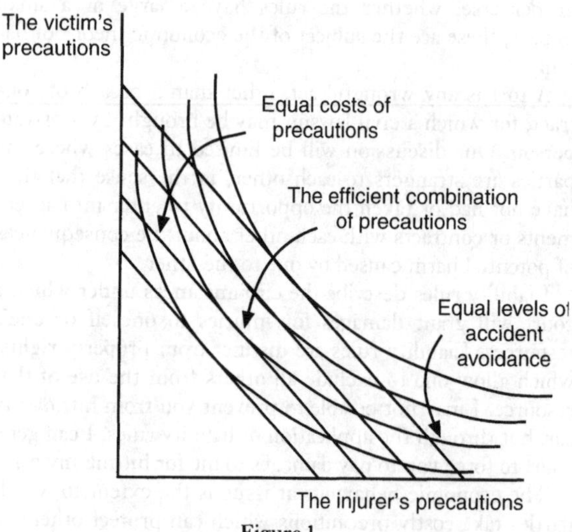

Figure 1

As the economist would have it, at the best combination of precautions the marginal cost of each precaution is equal to the value of its marginal product of accident probability reduction. At less than the optimal level of either precaution, the marginal benefits of increased precaution are greater than the marginal cost of the precaution. Whenever less than appropriate levels of precautions are being taken, it can be said that there are further precautions that can be taken, should be taken, but are not being taken.

In general, of course, the least cost level of accidents, or probability of accidents, is not zero, and requires some positive level of both precautions. Of course, there are simpler cases, where one of the precautions is unnecessary, or the least cost solution is to use enough precautions to avoid the accident altogether. These corner solutions are easily dealt with, but we shall ignore them here.

CENTRALIZED CONTROL OVER PRECAUTIONS

The classic tort case during the nineteenth century was a fire in ricks of flax stacked near the railroad tracks awaiting shipment to market, and the fire was caused by sparks flying from a passing train. In these cases there are two available precautions: arrest more of the sparks before they leave the engine by adding an expensive spark arrester, or move the flax to a less convenient location farther from the tracks. If, as was occasionally the case, the train and the land were both owned by the same party, say the Union Pacific, then there would be no lawsuit after a fire.

Where both precautions are in the control of the same person or firm – the Union Pacific – and the accident costs are borne by them, then the Union Pacific has every incentive to choose the optimal level of each precaution and hence the optimal level of accident avoidance. If something other than the best combination of precautions were taken, the Union Pacific would reduce its costs by changing the level of precautions toward the best level. If the marginal benefits of the precaution were greater than their marginal costs, the owner would increase the precaution, whether by moving the flax farther from the tracks or by using a more effective spark arrester.

This centralized solution is the standard for testing the efficiency of legal rules. The legal rules play out in the same technology under the same costs, but the harm and one of the critical precautions are under separate control by people who are strangers unless they meet in court after an accident.

Coase in his classic 'The Problem of Social Cost' (1960) took Pigou to task for what Coase considered a misunderstanding of these and other railroad accidents. (See Grady (1984) for application of the economic theory of liability to railroad fire cases.)

DECENTRALIZATION TO TWO PARTIES WITH LIABILITY RULES

With this background in hand, we can now turn to the analysis of liability. In the context of a tort case, the precautions are controlled by two strangers rather than one person or company. The strangers have typically not communicated at all prior to the accident, let alone negotiated about joint precautions. They now come together in court, and their case is decided according to the rules of liability to be applied. It is the tradition of the economic analysis of liability rules to ignore many of the important complexities and costs incurred in the courts to focus on the rules themselves. So courts are typically assumed to act without mistake and without cost. It is a further simplification to assume that damages, if awarded by the court, are the same as the full cost of the accident to the victim. See Calfee and Craswell (1984) for the effects of uncertainty in the courts on the incentives to take precautions.

This analysis is carried out under the assumption that the lack of precaution by the injurer caused the accident that harmed the victim. Causation itself is a complex area that has received significant attention by economists as well as legal scholars.

LIABILITY RULES

It is useful to separate liability rules into two groups, rules based on negligence by one party or the other, and two simpler rules, strict liability for the injurer and no liability for the injurer. We treat the simple rules first, then describe negligence and finally treat the negligence-based rules.

The simple rules. There are two very simple liability rules that require no judgment on the part of the court, except to decide if the rule applies. They are no liability and strict liability. No liability simply means that a victim cannot collect damages from an injurer.

Under strict liability, the injured plaintiff need only present the case to the court in order to collect damages from the injurer. This rule is the symmetric opposite of no liability.

Equilibrium under the simple rules. Equilibrium under these simple rules is equally simple. Under a rule of no liability, the injurer has no incentives to take precautions to avoid the accident, and the victim will take the most cost effective precautions under her control, operating under the assumption that the injurer will take no precautions. Of course, this is not the same solution as if there were a single owner. Typically, the injurer will take too few precautions, and the victim will take too many, and the result will be too many accidents. The rule is inefficient.

Under a strict liability rule, where the injurer will fully reimburse the victim for the full cost of the accident, the victim has no incentive to take any precautions and the injurer will take the most cost-effective precautions under the assumption that the victim will take none. Again, as compared to the centralized decision, the rule will be inefficient. The injurer will take too many precautions and the victim will take too few. Again, injuries will be higher, as well.

Negligence, the standard of care, and efficient precautions. Negligence is a central concept in the common law and in the economic theory of liability. Following an accident or tort, a party is negligent if the fact-finder determines that he or she did not meet the appropriate standard of care, or as it is sometimes said, did not use due care. Or equivalently, a party is negligent if there is a precaution that the party could have taken, should have taken, and did not take.

The central result of the economic theory of liability is that, under circumstances that economists consider usual, if the standard of care of the negligence rule is the same as the amount of care that would be taken under centralized control, then a negligence rule will lead to efficient choice of precautions by both injurer and victim. For an early statement of this result see Brown (1973), and for a more complete statement of the mathematics see Kornhauser and Revesz (1989).

The negligence-based rules. It is possible to distinguish a number of negligence-based rules (see Brown 1973 for example). This discussion is limited to the most important: the negligence rule and the negligence rule with a contributory negligence defence.

Negligence rule. Under the negligence rule the victim cannot collect from the injurer unless the injurer is found negligent.

Negligence rule with a contributory negligence defence. Under the negligence rule with a contributory negligence defence, the injurer is liable if he is negligent *and* the victim is not.

One of the earliest cases in American tort law that laid out the rule of negligence with a contributory negligence defence was the 1850 Massachusetts case of *Brown v. Kendall*, where the defendant or injurer took up a stick to separate fighting dogs belonging to the plaintiff – the victim – and the defendant. In the course of beating the dogs the defendant accidentally hit the plaintiff in the eye, injuring him severely. Chief Justice Shaw laid down the rule:

> if both plaintiff and defendant at the time of the blow were using ordinary care, or if at that time the defendant was using ordinary care, and the plaintiff was not, or if at that time, both the defendant and the plaintiff were not using ordinary care, then the plaintiff could not recover [60 Mass. (6 Cush.) 292 (1850)].

Other rules. The analytical structure that is applied to the simple rules and the negligence-based rules can be applied to any well-defined liability rule. The huge literature in the economic theory of tort liability is, to a large degree, the application of this structure to an amazing variety of issues.

Equilibrium under negligence-based rules. It is the essence of a precaution that the level of precaution is chosen prior to the accident, typically prior even to knowing that the accident would happen or knowing who the other party would be. Because of the jointness of production between the precautions of the two parties, the efficacy of the precaution I take depends on the amount of precautions you take, whoever you may be. That decision is certainly one made under uncertainty and is usefully thought of as a strategy in a two-person non-cooperative game. Then, the outcome of the game can be considered with the tools of game theory. The economic theory of liability is traditionally a study of the properties of the non-cooperative equilibria of these games. An equilibrium for a game is a pair of choices of precautions by the two parties such that, given the choice by the other party, neither party has an incentive to change his or her own choice.

To construct an equilibrium, we first construct response functions for each party like those in Cournot's analysis of duopoly. A response function shows the least cost response of one party to a particular level of precaution taken by the other. Where those response functions intersect is the equilibrium to the game. The cost of a response takes into account both the cost of the precaution taken and the cost of the liability for the accident. To make the discussion symmetric, we shall say that the victim is liable for the accident if he or she cannot collect in court from the injurer, and we shall abstract from differences between the judgment and the cost of the accident by assuming them to be the same.

To prepare the way, consider the simpler response functions assuming that each party would bear the full costs of the accident. Figure 2 shows these functions. The injurer's response function shows his cost-minimizing response to any given level of precaution by the victim, assuming that he will bear the full cost of the accident. In turn, the victim's response function shows her cost-minimizing response to any given level of precaution by the injurer, assuming that she will bear the full cost of the accident. The full-cost response functions are equivalent to the first order conditions of minimization of the total cost of the accident and its precautions. As a result they intersect at the joint level of precautions which minimizes the total cost, the combination that would have been chosen if there were centralized joint control over both precautions. Thus it is the case that if both the injurer and the victim were forced to bear the full cost of the accident, their incentives would lead them to choose the most efficient combination of precautions. But, of course, such double jeopardy does not conform to the legal rules in any real jurisdiction.

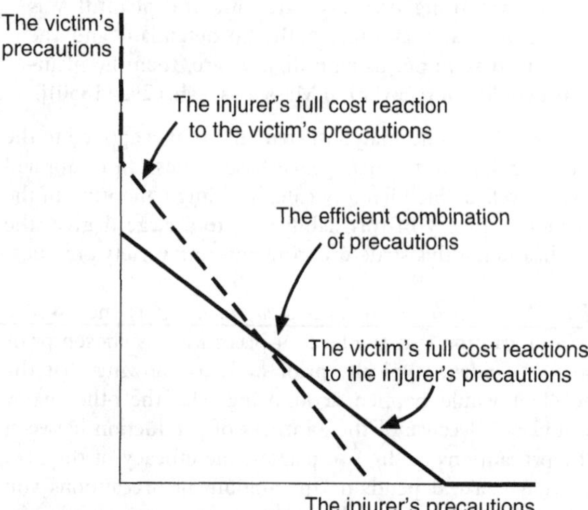

Figure 2

From these full cost reaction functions, we can construct reaction functions for the various rules.

Under a negligence rule with a contributory negligence defence, the victim will pay the full cost of the accident, unless the defendant injurer is negligent and the victim is not, in which case the victim will collect the full cost of the accident from the injurer. That is, if the injurer uses less care than the standard of care would call for and the victim meets the standard of care, the victim will not pay for the accident, and will have no incentive to take any precautions beyond meeting the standard of care. If the injurer meets the standard of care, the victim will bear the full cost of the accident and has the full incentive to take precautions, depending on the level of precautions of the injurer. But once the injurer has met the standard of care he has no further incentive to take more care because he bears no further responsibility for the cost of the accident. See Figure 3 for the response functions of victim and injurer under a negligence rule with a contributory negligence defence. The shaded area denotes the combination of precautions where an injurer will be found liable for the cost of the accident. The response functions show the minimum cost response of one party to the other party's precautions. The injurer responds to the victim's choice of precautions, measured vertically, and the victim responds to the injurer's choice of precautions, measured horizontally. Notice that the response functions are consistent (they cross) at the efficient combination of precautions, the same levels of precautions that would be chosen under centralized control. This is an equilibrium which is efficient.

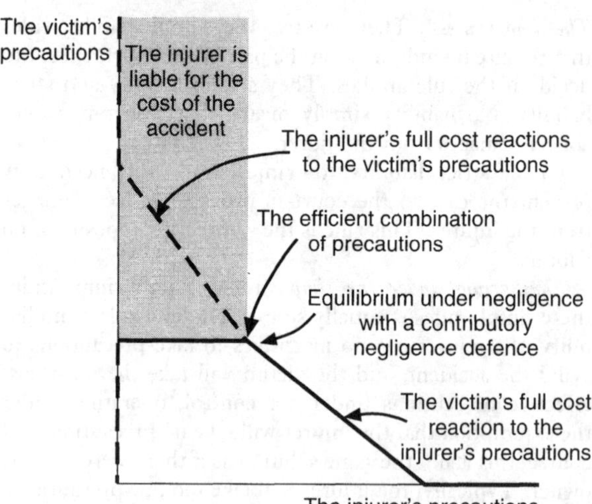

Figure 3

For the negligence rule without a contributory negligence defence, the same methods can be used to show that the efficient combination of precautions is again the unique equilibrium under this rule (see Brown 1973).

Indeed, the equilibrium will be efficient as long as the rule requires that the injurer pays when the injurer is negligent and the victim is not, and that the victim pay when the victim is negligent and the injurer is not. Efficiency is not affected by shifts in liability either when both parties have met the standard of care or when neither has met the standard of care.

Efficiency. The standard of efficiency is the standard provided by centralized control: what precautions would be taken if all precautions were taken by, and all harm was borne by, a single person.

CHANGING THE AMOUNT OF THE ACTIVITY

In some situations the parties to potential accidents control not only the level of precautions that they take, but also the amount of the potentially dangerous activity, as well. One can choose how carefully to drive and how much to drive.

Just as decisions about care should take into account the risks imposed on others, so should decisions about the amount of the risky activity to be undertaken. It would be best if liability rules provided incentives for the proper level of activity, as well as the proper level of care. Unfortunately, as Shavell (1980) has shown, there is no liability rule that simultaneously provides appropriate incentives for both injurer and victim to take the appropriate level of care and choose the appropriate amount of activity. This negative result may go too far; if a court can consider negligence in terms of both care and amount of activity, the original analysis can apply.

UNCERTAINTY ABOUT THE OUTCOME OF THE COURT

There are many sources of uncertainty in cases coming before courts. Parties can be uncertain about the level of care actually taken, because of momentary lapses in care or attention. Courts can improperly identify the level of care actually taken because of evidentiary difficulties. Courts can also incorrectly identify the standard of care because they do not correctly consider all the costs and benefits of precautions. These uncertainties have been widely studied in the literature (see especially Diamond 1974; Green 1976; Shavell 1983; Calfee and Craswell 1984) Many of these results show that uncertainty will lead parties to take more than the appropriate level of care.

OTHER COMMENTS

The analysis of liability rules has been carried out at a high level of abstraction. This is a frequent source of frustration or irritation for lawyers steeped in the common law. Liability rules apply to a bewildering variety of situations. Tort cases are nothing if they are not concrete, and are won by careful analysis of particular facts. That high level of abstraction is probably appropriate given the extraordinary variety of cases in which the rules are applied. It is the general rules that are the subject of analysis, not the particular cases. It is general rules that can inform people's choices of levels of care before accidents do – or usually do not – occur.

These common law notions are very robust under changes in technology, unlike many statutory or regulatory rules. Negligence is a meaningful concept where due care is meaningful. The rule has been applied to separating fighting dogs, but it can be just as sensibly applied to accidents that take place electronically or on the World Wide Web, or in the control room of a nuclear reactor.

It is an interesting aspect of negligence rules that the courts do not more and more carefully set out what appropriate precautions might be. Indeed that is typically the role of the jury, not the judge. We do not find courts setting out particular standards, which are then refined by later litigation. Instead, the jury determines if a party met the standard of due care or not, and reports that judgment, without identifying what the standard might be.

A theory of negligence is helpful in thinking about decisions among liability rules. It is only part of any analysis of the choice between liability rules and other forms of control, such as regulation or taxation of potentially dangerous behaviour. One must also have a theory of regulation or taxation in order to avoid the obvious pitfalls of comparing a carefully analysed system found flawed with a stylized and apparently perfect alternative. Then decisions might be made on the basis of the extent of the analysis, rather than on the merits of the alternatives.

JOHN PRATHER BROWN

See also COMPARATIVE NEGLIGENCE; DUE CARE; JOINT AND SEVERAL LIABILITY; LEGAL STANDARDS OF CARE.

Subject classification: 1d(ii); 5d(ii).

CASES

Brown v. Kendall, 60 Mass. (6 Cush.) 292 (1850).

BIBLIOGRAPHY

Brown, J.P. 1973. Toward an economic theory of liability. *Journal of Legal Studies* 2: 323–49.

Calfee, J. and Craswell, R. 1984. Some effects of uncertainty on compliance with legal standards. *Virginia Law Review* 70: 965–1003.

Coase, R. 1960. The problem of social cost. *Journal of Law and Economics* 3: 1–44.

Cooter, R. and Ulen, T. 1988. *Law and Economics*. Reading, MA: Addison Wesley Publishing; 2nd edn, 1996.

Diamond, P. 1974. Single activity accidents. *Journal of Legal Studies* 3: 107–64.

Grady, M. 1984. Proximate cause and the law of negligence. *Iowa Law Review* 69: 363–449.

Green, J. 1976. On the optimal structure of liability laws. *Bell Journal of Economics* 7: 553–74.

Kornhauser, L. and Revesz, R. 1989. Sharing damages among multiple tortfeasors. *Yale Law Journal* 98: 831–90.

Landes, W. and Posner, R. 1987. *The Economic Structure of Tort Law*. Cambridge, MA: Harvard University Press.

Shavell, S. 1980. Strict liability versus negligence. *Journal of Legal Studies* 9: 1–25.

Shavell, S. 1983. Torts in which the victim and injurer act sequentially. *Journal of Law and Economics* 26: 589–612.

Shavell, S. 1987. *Economic Analysis of Accident Law*. Cambridge, MA: Harvard University Press.

efficient norms. A great deal of behaviour is maintained by social norms and non-legal sanctions, rather than by legal rules and sanctions. Such norm-governed behaviour raises many important legal issues. Should courts determine negligence by using a cost–benefit standard like the Hand test or by evaluating the conduct against social norms? Should courts fill gaps in contracts by trying to divine the intentions of the parties or by assuming conformity to business norms? One cannot answer these questions without understanding how norms function and whether they provide efficient standards of behaviour.

Turning from private law to public law, the significance of social norms is even clearer. On one view, welfare causes illegitimacy by reducing the opportunity cost of bearing children out of wedlock. But on another view, welfare causes illegitimacy by weakening social norms that have traditionally supported the family. On one view, people file for bankruptcy because generous exemption laws allow them to do better than they would if they paid their debts.

But on another view, people file for bankruptcy because generous exemption laws have over the years eroded the stigma that once attached to those who have failed to pay their debts. On one view, people commit crimes because the expected gain from the criminal conduct exceeds the expected cost of punishment. But on another view, people commit crimes because a criminal reputation enhances status among members of the relevant community. When economic models fail to predict observed behaviour, economists, all but admitting defeat, sometimes suggest that exogenous social norms account for the discrepancy. (The classic example is that of wage-stickiness.) But this suggestion begs the question: why do such social norms exist?

So deeply do social norms penetrate everyday life that one can understand important legal phenomena only if one understands social norms. Yet writers in law and economics have generally neglected social norms. The reason for this neglect is that their best-understood and most frequently used models assume a world consisting of individuals, on the one hand, and a government with a monopoly of force, on the other. The government influences citizens' behaviour by creating rules and enforcing them with sanctions. These models cannot be used to analyse social norms because social norms are enforced spontaneously by individuals acting together in intermediate groups, like families and labour unions, or by an individual's conscience, or even by strangers exploiting gains from coordination. More complicated models are needed.

I. NORMS. Start by contrasting 'legal order' and 'spontaneous order' (see Hayek 1973). Legal order arises when the state enacts laws and punishes those who violate them. Spontaneous order arises when people engage in stable patterns of behaviour because few people or no one gains by deviating, even in the absence of effective legal deterrents. The term 'norm' is used by writers to refer both to the regularities in behaviour that emerge in spontaneous orders (sometimes called in this context 'statistical norms') and to regularities in behaviour that have some moral content ('moral norms'). For example, it might be the norm among a particular group that people wear their hair parted from left to right, but this norm does not necessarily have moral content in the sense that if one person wears his hair parted from right to left, others will disapprove. The price of a commodity can be considered a statistical norm because most sellers of that commodity charge that price. But it does not follow that people will disapprove of a seller who charges either a lower or higher price. Sometimes, people do disapprove of sellers who charge higher prices, for example, when the price of kerosene rises after a hurricane strikes an area. Thus, the distinction between statistical and moral norms frequently blurs: mere regularities in behaviour are often regarded as morally valuable.

To explain why regularities in behaviour may acquire moral content, some writers rely on psychological theories of internalization (compare Sugden 1986 and Cooter 1994). A second approach treats the norm that requires enforcement of a statistical norm as itself a statistical norm. For example, the relevant norm to be explained is not the norm that one should charge the old price for kerosene despite a hurricane-induced shortage, but the norm that most people will punish the person who charges the high price for kerosene. However, people appear to obey norms both in order to avoid being sanctioned by others ('shame') and in order to avoid being sanctioned by their conscience ('guilt'). The problem with the second approach is that it cannot explain guilt. But the problem with the first approach is that its assumptions about guilt are not sufficiently rigorous to enable predictions about which norms are internalized and which are not. Whether a theory of social norms should incorporate a psychological theory of internalization (thus losing rigour) or can safely ignore this phenomenon (thus losing realism) remains to be seen.

Another ambiguity in the word 'norm' results from its use both for rules self-consciously issued by institutions and for rules that evolve without the guidance of any agency. People may respect a picket line because their union tells them to, or they may respect a picket line spontaneously – at the behest of no particular institution or even of any particular person. 'Social norm' seems to be a more apt label for the second phenomenon than the first; indeed, the union's order is obeyed only because social norms give the union authority.

But if social norms are not produced by an agency, how do they evolve? To answer this question, it is helpful to think of the common law process. When a court decides a dispute, it may allow itself to be guided by prior decisions but it also makes an irreducibly particular judgment about the dispute before it. When a court looks for guidance in prior decisions, it will usually generalize those decisions as a rule, but this rule is always provisional on how future courts decide cases based on similar facts. It is thus misleading, if not altogether false, to say that a court 'applies' a rule. Similarly, norms can be understood as generalizations about prior behaviour. In trying to decide what to do, a person may generalize from the behaviour of others in similar situations, and allow himself to be guided by that generalization, but again his decision always has an irreducibly specific aspect to it. This is why norms can be simultaneously described in highly general terms ('do not kill another human being') and in highly specific terms that seem to contradict the general statement ('do not kill another human being unless acting in (justified) defence, or in a (just) war', a statement that can be fully fleshed out only by considering an indefinitely large number of hypothetical situations).

A final issue arises from the concern that norms may have different functions or structures in different contexts. Some norms govern relations between strangers (for example, tipping a taxi driver); others govern relations between repeat players (for example, norms of professional courtesy). Some norms are stable over long periods of time (for example, shaking hands to seal a contract); other norms are not (for example, miniskirts). Indeed, some patterns of behaviour change so rapidly that the term 'social norm' does not fit at all. Behaviour during a bank panic is predictable but few people would say that the depositors act in conformity with a social norm. The distinctions between these behaviours are so slippery, however, that it is best to analyse them together.

That different norms describe different contexts nevertheless suggests that any attempt to develop a general theory of norms is likely to be frustrated. The better approach, and the one followed in the literature, is to use different models for different situations. A few examples follow; no effort is made to be complete. (Interested readers can find many citations to the economics literature in Koford and Miller 1991, and to the law and economics literature in the *University of Pennsylvania Law Review* 1996.)

One approach treats norms as a description of the pattern of behaviour that emerges in iterated prisoner's dilemmas. The folk theorems show that when parties care sufficiently about the future they may reach an equilibrium in which both parties cooperate and produce a collective good. To solve the problem of multiplicity of equilibria, some authors incorporate in their models emotions or involuntary physiological responses that make cheating difficult (see, e.g., Hirshleifer 1987, Frank 1988). Further research on bounded rationality may suggest other solutions to this problem (see Conlisk 1996).

A second approach treats norms as a description of the pattern of behaviour that emerges in signalling games. Bernheim (1994), for example, argues that if people care sufficiently about how others judge their motivations, they will signal that they have the right motivations by conforming to the pattern of behaviour in which people with those motivations generally engage (see also Posner 1998). Conformity can also be generated if everyone has partial information with respect to the value of a particular behaviour, and knows that everyone else has partial information: 'herd behaviour' results when each individual rationally takes a stream of consistent prior choices as evidence of the value of that behaviour, and imitates it (see Bikhchandani, Hirshleifer and Welch 1992).

A third approach assumes that people have other-regarding preferences. Becker's rotten kid theorem shows a family producing collective goods because the head is an altruist and the other members recognize that they maximize the value of transfers from the head to themselves by cooperating in the production of collective goods (see Becker [1981] 1991). If people care about others outside their family, this approach can be generalized (see Becker 1996). McAdams (1997) argues that social norms derive from competitions for status.

One problem with these three approaches is that they assume that norms govern the interaction of people who know each other, and not that of strangers. But it is clear that norms that govern the interaction of strangers are quite important; indeed, many repeat games could not begin without such norms because the players are strangers prior to the first move.

To deal with these problems, another approach is needed. The fourth approach to explaining social norms uses evolutionary game theory. Suppose that when people come toward each other on single-lane roads, they must choose whether to pass on the right or on the left. In this coordination game, both agents do equally well when they choose the symmetrical moves and equally poorly when they choose the wrong combination of moves. If everyone decides in advance to choose one move or the other, or to choose a mix, over time more and more people will choose the symmetrical moves. At some point, enough people choose those moves that a single strategy will be adopted by all, and the norm of using that strategy will be impervious to the occasional mutation (Sugden 1986). Note that individuals are assumed to be boundedly rational. They choose from a limited set of strategies and have neither perfect memory nor perfect foresight, and deviate from their strategies either by mistake or in order to experiment (Young 1996).

Another example of the evolutionary approach relies on the hawk–dove game, in which each player does best if he plays the aggressive move ('hawk') and the other player plays the passive move ('dove'), second best if both he and the other play the passive move, and worst if both players play the aggressive move. This game can result in various equilibria in which each player mixes strategies, but a more interesting result is an equilibrium that reflects a focal point around which the parties coordinate their moves. One such focal point is possession. Suppose that the two moves refer to the aggressiveness with which one tries to seize resources. A norm according to which the possessor of the resources plays 'hawk', while non-possessors play 'dove' might be the source of modern property rights (see Hirshleifer 1982; Sugden 1986). See Picker (1997) for a computer model of the spread of norms according to evolutionary principles.

A fifth approach is institutional. Institutions evolve through spontaneous processes, and put power in the hands of one person or a small group of people, and these people use their power to create and enforce new rules. One must explain, of course, how institutions evolve, and such an explanation must incorporate the theories reflected in the other four approaches. But a focus on institutions allows one to understand how the cooperative energies harnessed in an organization may enable that group to coerce people outside that group, in the process requiring them to conform to some of the group's own norms.

The five approaches share the assumption that the state does not produce order, but that order emerges 'spontaneously', given minimal assumptions about cooperative institutions and tastes. The suitability of each approach depends on what kind of spontaneous order is the subject of interest. Notice that each of the approaches explains the emergence of statistical norms, not moral norms. The norms simply describe the strategies that are chosen in equilibrium. Self-interested union members, for example, choose the strategy 'don't cross the picket line' in equilibrium because they do not want to lose the chance to obtain future gains through union participation, not because they believe that crossing the picket line is morally wrong. That is to say, whether or not they believe that crossing the picket line is wrong, this belief is not necessary for the equilibrium to be sustained.

II. EFFICIENT NORMS. There is confusion in the law and economics literature over what it would mean for a norm to be efficient and why this matters, and even whether a single conception of efficiency would be appropriate for different models of social interaction. Some authors seem to argue that the relevant question is whether a norm is Pareto optimal (or welfare-maximizing). A moment's reflection, however, should convince the reader that probably no social norm meets this standard, as one can always imagine a slight variation in a norm that would make one person better off without making anyone else worse off, or that increases social welfare. The better approach is to take a set of norms as given, and ask whether a particular legal intervention would produce a Pareto improvement or an increase in a social welfare function. But since several authors take the first approach, we discuss it in this part, and defer discussion of the second approach to Part III.

Ellickson (1991) argues that if one looks around in the world, one finds many examples of welfare-maximizing norms prevailing in closely knit groups. At first sight, Ellickson's empirical work, as well as related work by legal writers (e.g., Bernstein 1996), and economists (e.g., Greif 1993), and a vast common pool literature (e.g., Ostrom 1990), appears to support his argument. But the empirical work must be interpreted carefully. The work does show, and strikingly so, that social norms are powerful, and support complex forms of cooperation in the absence of legal intervention. But the studies do not show that social norms are necessarily or even likely efficient. First, they do not, for obvious reasons, reveal all of the possible cooperative gains that would be obtained through state intervention but are not obtained because the appropriate social norms have failed to evolve. Second, the studies are consistent with the possibility that the same norms that support an enterprise restrict production. Pending further study, our presumptions about the efficiency of norms must rest on theoretical arguments.

Let us then discuss some of the theoretical approaches mentioned in Part I. Ellickson argues that the repeat-game analysis gives hope that norms are efficient, and he is right. But the folk theorem by itself does not guarantee an efficient outcome. In equilibrium the parties may play strategies that do not enable them to capture all of the cooperative surplus. Various equilibrium refinements suggest conditions in which parties behave more or less efficiently, but research on equilibrium refinements is inconclusive. There is thus as yet little reason for believing that norms that emerge from repeated games are efficient in the sense of enabling players to capture all the gains from cooperation.

Other approaches have similar problems. The equilibria that emerge in signalling games are not, as is well known, predictably Pareto-optimal. When people conform to a pattern of behaviour in the hope of achieving popularity, they incur signalling costs and they deny themselves the satisfaction of nonreputational preferences; moreover, in equilibrium people may not even succeed in distinguishing themselves from those with outlier preferences (or if they do, those with outlier preferences are injured). Efforts to signal type may also externalize costs on others (see, e.g., McAdams 1995). Herd behaviour magnifies harm caused by chance and error. The 'rotten kid theorem' applies only under special conditions: among other problems, altruists find it difficult to cooperate because their altruism undermines the credibility of their threat to punish in case of deviation (see Bernheim and Stark 1988).

The equilibria that emerge in evolutionary games also bear no necessary relationship with efficiency. In Britain, the pass-on-the-left norm may have initially been superior to no norm, and of equal value to a pass-on-the-right norm; but once international automobile markets opened, Britain was put at a competitive disadvantage (see Cooter 1994). The property norms that arise from the hawk–dove game do not allow for leases, mortgages, security interests in chattels, bailments, equity investments, and other valuable transactions that require the separation of ownership and possession. These transactions usually require recording systems, but recording systems cannot 'evolve' the way norms do. Evolution builds on and entrenches past practices, whereas efficiency often demands the self-conscious modification of old understandings (Posner 1996a).

Private institutions might be thought to issue efficient rules, on analogy to the behaviour of firms in the market. However, information problems and strategic behaviour undermine their efficiency unless they face competition from other groups; but competition from other groups weakens their ability to punish defectors (see Posner 1996c). Unions have often been successful in coordinating behaviour, but they also have successfully lobbied for legal protections which restrict competition. Religious groups also coordinate behaviour well, but these groups sometimes produce severe externalities, which themselves are a direct result of the characteristics, such as the passionate commitment to a totalizing world view, that make religious groups so powerful and valuable as norm-producers (see Posner 1996b).

III. LAW AND NORMS. Should the state, or its courts, enforce social norms as law? Consider a contract for the sale of goods that neglects to allocate the risk of delay caused by labour strife at the manufacturer's plant. There are three possible approaches to enforcing the contract: (1) give the buyer damages if the hypothetical *ex ante* value-maximizing contract would assign the risk to the seller; (2) give the buyer damages if the custom in the industry is for the seller to bear the risk; and (3) give the buyer damages just because on a literal reading of the contract the promise is not conditional on good labour relations at the manufacturer's plant. The first approach is standard in the academic literature. The second approach has a long history in the law, is reflected in the Uniform Commercial Code, and has recently been advocated by Cooter (1994). The third approach can be called 'formalistic'.

Which approach is optimal? If we doubt the competence of courts to reconstruct the value-maximizing contract, we must reject the first approach. But if we doubt the courts' ability to reconstruct the value-maximizing contract, can we have confidence in their ability to discover business norms? Suppose we think courts can, we must consider the likelihood that business norms are efficient. This question can be answered only by choosing among the various models of norm-production. Do business norms fit the model of repeat interactions or the signalling model; or are they usually issued by centralized institutions such as trade associations? One's choice of model, which may vary from industry to industry, will influence one's conclusions about efficiency. Norms that reflect herd behaviour are likely to be inferior to those that describe strategies in repeat games; and the efficiency of either kind of norm is likely to differ from the efficiency of norms that arise in evolutionary games. Moreover, it is unclear whether business norms that are efficient in a regime of nonlegal enforcement would also be efficient in a regime of legal enforcement. Because courts lack the information and many of the sanctions that members of the business community have, business norms that presuppose nonlegal enforcement may become inefficient when enforced by courts. The formalistic approach may therefore appear desirable, because it forces the parties to reveal in the contract the norms they would want enforced. But if transaction costs are high, and courts are fairly competent, this approach will be inferior to the others.

Another issue concerns the extent to which the state can and should change norms. Suppose that the erosion of norms against illegitimacy and norms against filing for bankruptcy is socially harmful. One response is to attack the problems directly by increasing the cost of having illegitimate children (e.g., by reducing welfare benefits to unwed mothers) and by increasing the cost of filing for bankruptcy (e.g., by reducing the generosity of exemptions). But if norms are sufficiently powerful, direct legal responses of this kind will have little effect. The other response is to change the norm. But whether and how the state can change a norm depends on how one models norm production in a particular sector of society.

If, for example, these norms are sustained in repeat games, the state must use stronger sanctions than it uses when people do not act out of a desire to maintain a cooperative relationship. The optimal criminal sanction must be higher when a person commits a crime both to obtain the criminal gains and to avoid being ostracized by his friends, than when a person commits a crime solely to obtain the criminal gains. If norms are sustained in coordination or signalling games, a similar analysis applies; but it is also the case that the state may be able to bump agents into a socially more desirable equilibrium by using education or publicity to change focal points. Effective advertising campaigns convince people that smoking or drinking are not high-status activities (see Lessig 1995; Sunstein 1996); to signal one's social desirability, then, one may substitute to less harmful behaviour, such as athletic prowess. If norms are highly influenced by intermediate groups, such as religious organizations, the state may be able to modify the norms by subsidizing some groups and taxing others (see Posner 1996c).

The state sometimes unintentionally weakens social norms in its pursuit of unrelated goals. It is often argued, for example, that erosion of norms against illegitimacy arise as an unintended consequence of the welfare system, and that the cooperative ties that prevail in minority groups are weakened by well-meaning efforts by the government to promote assimilation. The discontinuity of norm-governed behaviour (see especially Bernheim 1994) creates hazards for the state: a gradual increasing of a sanction may have no effect on equilibrium behaviour until a threshold is reached, at which point a radically different equilibrium obtains. Norms are thus both robust and delicate. Their robustness creates a false sense that some social policies do not have harmful side-effects; their delicacy comes into view when years of accumulating pressure on a norm finally causes its collapse. Although economists have long understood that individuals frustrate interventionist policies by 'bargaining around' them, they have not understood the extent to which more complicated norm-driven patterns of behaviour frustrate such policies. Norms are an ocean on which the state precariously floats, a rickety boat.

ERIC A. POSNER

See also BOUNDED RATIONALITY; CONVENTIONS; CUSTOMARY PRACTICES AND THE LAW OF TORTS; EVOLUTIONARY GAME THEORY; INFORMAL CONTRACT ENFORCEMENT: LESSONS FROM MEDIEVAL TRADE; INFORMATIONAL CASCADES AND SOCIAL CONVENTIONS; PREFERENCE SHAPING BY THE LAW; PRISONERS' DILEMMA; PRIVATE COMMERCIAL LAW; SELF-GOVERNANCE OF COMMON-POOL RESOURCES; SOCIAL NORMS AND THE LAW; SPONTANEOUS ORDER; TRUST.

Subject classification: 1b(iii); 1d(ii); 4c(ii).

BIBLIOGRAPHY

Becker, G.S. 1981. *A Treatise on the Family*. Cambridge, MA: Harvard University Press; enlarged edn, 1991.

Becker, G.S. 1996. *Accounting for Tastes*. Cambridge, MA: Harvard University Press.

Bernheim, B.D. 1994. A theory of conformity. *Journal of Political Economy* 102: 841–77.

Bernheim, B.D. and Stark, O. 1988. Altruism within the family reconsidered: do nice guys finish last? *American Economic Review* 78: 1034–45.

Bernstein, L. 1996. Merchant law in a merchant court: rethinking the Code's search for immanent business norms. *University of Pennsylvania Law Review* 144: 1765–1822.

Bikhchandani, S., Hirshleifer, D. and Welch, I. 1992. A theory of fads, fashion, custom, and cultural change as information cascades. *Journal of Political Economy* 100: 992–1026.

Conlisk, J. 1996. Why bounded rationality? *Journal of Economic Literature* 34: 669–700.

Cooter, R. 1994. Structural adjudication and the new law merchant: a model of decentralized law. *International Review of Law and Economics* 14: 215–31.

Ellickson, R.C. 1991. *Order Without Law: How Neighbors Settle Disputes*. Cambridge, MA: Harvard University Press.

Frank, R.H. 1985. *Choosing the Right Pond*. Oxford: Oxford University Press.

Frank, R.H. 1988. *Passions Within Reason*. New York: Norton.

Greif, A. 1993. Contract enforceability and economic institutions in early trade: the Maghribi traders coalition. *American Economic Review* 83: 525–48.

Hayek, F.H. 1973. *Law, Legislation, and Liberty*: Volume 1: *Rules and Order*. Chicago: University of Chicago Press.

Hirshleifer, J. 1987. On the emotions as guarantors of threats and promises. In *The Latest on the Best: Essays on Evolution and Optimality*, ed. J. Dupré, Cambridge, MA: MIT Press.

Hirshleifer, J. 1982. Evolutionary models in economics and the law: cooperation versus conflict strategies. *Research in Law and Economics* 4: 1–60.

Koford, K.J. and Miller, J.B. (eds.). 1991. *Social Norms and Economic Institutions*. Ann Arbor: University of Michigan Press.

Lessig, L. 1995. The regulation of social meanings. *University of Chicago Law Review* 62: 943–1045.

McAdams, R.H. 1995. Cooperation and conflict: The economics of group status competition and race discrimination. *Harvard Law Review* 108: 1003–84.

McAdams, R.H. 1997. Law, economics, and the origin of norms. *Michigan Law Review* 96 (forthcoming).

Ostrom, E. 1990. *Governing the Commons: The Evolution of Institutions for Collective Action*. Cambridge: Cambridge University Press.
Picker, R.C. 1997. Simple games in a complex world: a generative approach to the adoption of norms. *University of Chicago Law Review* 64 (forthcoming).
Posner, E.A. 1996a. Law, economics, and inefficient norms. *University of Pennsylvania Law Review* 144: 1697–1744.
Posner, E.A. 1996b. The legal regulation of religious groups. *Legal Theory* 2: 33–62.
Posner, E.A. 1996c. The regulation of groups: The influence of legal and nonlegal sanctions on collective action. *University of Chicago Law Review* 63: 133–97.
Posner, E.A. 1998. Signals, symbols, and social norms in politics and the law. *Journal of Legal Studies* 27 (forthcoming).
Sugden, R. 1986. *The Economics of Rights, Co-operation, and Welfare*. Oxford: Basil Blackwell.
Sunstein, C.R. 1996. Social norms and social roles. *Columbia Law Review* 96: 903–68.
University of Pennsylvania Law Review. 1996. Symposium: Law, economics, and norms. 144: 1643–2339.
Young, H.P. 1996. The economics of convention. *Journal of Economic Perspectives* 10: 105–22.

efficient statute law. Due to its development from different sources such as common law and equity as brought across the ocean from England, the Code Civil in Louisiana, widely divergent state law, and federal statute law, regulations and jurisdiction, American civil law has traditionally been hard to comprehend and therefore also hard to teach. On the basis of the teachings at the University of Chicago School, notably by Aaron Director, Richard Posner (Posner 1977) built a legal doctrine and textbook presentation of American law, especially American civil law, on the hypothesis that it can be described and taught as if it had been designed with economic efficiency in mind. This hypothesis seems to fly in the face of both legal history and the received body of public choice theory, including the economic theory of rent seeking. It is therefore necessary to show under what conditions we can expect the law to develop so as to facilitate market exchange, by reducing transactions costs and thereby allowing for a deep division of labour in the economy. This essay offers a simple model-based discussion of why not only the common law but also statute law can be expected to develop towards efficiency, and spells out the conditions of this development. It is argued that statute law moves towards efficiency not only through legislation but also through jurisdiction.

I. THE DEBATE ON THE EFFICIENCY OF THE COMMON LAW. A steady flow of papers over recent decades in the economic analysis of law suggests that the common law evolves toward efficiency (Posner 1977; Priest 1977, Rubin 1977, 1982; Goodman 1978; Landes and Posner 1979; Cooter and Kornhauser 1980; Terrebonne 1981; Hirshleifer 1982); but with reservations – the implication being that statute law does not. There are others who disagree: for example, Posner himself is now 'distinctly skeptical about the claim' (personal communication). The notion has nevertheless become so deeply rooted in the folklore of the law and economics subdiscipline that it has rendered meaningful discussions about efficient legislation by code or statute very difficult. Despite the different formulations, the suggestion turns on the proposition that inefficient law creates large transactions costs: hence, parties gain from having inefficient legal arrangements removed. It follows that inefficient legal rules will be litigated again and again, until they approach efficiency. Michelman (1980) showed that this tendency should hold for judicial behaviour under either type of law, common or enacted. We should therefore observe a tendency toward efficiency in judicial rule making, independent of the particular legal culture in which a judge opines.

Whereas Michelman's amendment to the Posnerian argument considerably weakens the case for the superiority and singular efficiency of the common law, it refocuses attention on the body of law to which judicial decision making gives rise. That judicial decision making tends toward 'efficient' (defined as wealth maximizing) legal rules (Posner 1981 and, from a critical viewpoint, Samuels 1981) is quite consistent with another contention, dating back to Bentham (1789, 1838–43), that the common law, as a system of rules, lacks coherence and rationality and hence is less efficient than a code (one might add 'can conceivably be'). The successive judicial decisions groping towards efficiency may reach a local optimum, an optimum that can be inferior, as Pareto emphasized, to an inefficient solution reached otherwise.

Further doubt is cast on the notion that the common law converges towards efficiency, since the supposition that inefficient rules will be re-litigated rests on the assumption that the judiciary is a monopolistic provider of legal decisions. Inefficient legal arrangements need not be re-litigated. Parties will engage in litigation only if each of them expects the benefits from litigation to exceed the costs. When inefficient verdicts are expected, parties will be reluctant to litigate and prefer rather to settle out of court. The tendency toward efficiency is not a dependable one. As Priest and Klein (1984) have shown, litigation depends largely on how close the parties estimate the dispute to remain to the court's established decision standard. 'Close' cases are most likely to be re-litigated, as are those in which one party has a relatively larger stake than the other. It follows that both efficient and inefficient decision rules can be perpetuated (This begs a related question: Where will those parties turn that have been frustrated by inefficient court rulings? Answers to this question of substitute re-litigation will, of course, hinge on the availability of alternative sources of adjudication.) Disregarding for the moment private avenues of adjudication, it appears that whether the law is efficient will depend more on the performance of legislatures than the prevailing literature suggests.

In the following section I propose three variations of a simple model to show under what conditions we can expect the legislature to enact efficient law.

II. THREE SIMPLE MODELS. In keeping with Michelman's (1980) distinction, we assume that there are two types of law in any society: law that every incremental enactment or judicial opinion builds on (Michelman calls it 'background law'), and law that was a 'deal' to redistribute income away from one group and toward another. In this transfer, the legislator is seen as a broker who acts for a fee (McCormick and Tollison 1981). 'Deal law' may then be efficient in maximizing the wealth of the society in the long run, but it need not be. Conventionally, 'background law' should tend toward efficiency, although my preceding remarks leave this supposition in doubt. 'Background law' may be either common law or codified case law, consisting of pure codifications or a combination of these elements. Hence, we can assume, in each jurisdiction, a certain amount of competition between the legislature and the judiciary in providing 'background law'. While Michelman's distinction between 'background law' and 'deal law' is a straightforward one, identifying a particular piece of legislation as being either 'background law' or 'deal law' may be less so. It is perfectly possible that an act of parliament contains both. As Posner has pointed out, the distinction may require some deeper analysis in each individual case. He notes that 'courts cannot readily identify purely redistributive legislation, in part because such redistributive legislation may be defensible on efficiency grounds by reference to problems of social peace, free rider problems and so forth' (see Posner 1987, at note 12).

Fortunately for the purpose of this essay, this distinction need not be operationalized (Aretz 1993). For a study of a particular legislative process, the distinction would have to be established by developing a model that is able to capture the impact of the legislation on the performance of the affected natural or legal persons.

A. Political entrepreneurs. Assume a legislature made up of representatives who broker their legislative services for a fee. They are individual wealth maximizers, an assumption which is standard in the American context although one may wonder whether it contains a reasonable description of political processes in Europe, where political parties tend to play a much greater role than in the United States. Still, important interest groups are expediently and reliably served by their parties or caucuses, and particular politicians specialize in particular interest groups.

The demand for legislative income transfers is fairly straightforward. It requires a group so small that the benefit bestowed upon it is clearly perceptible for each member, sufficiently well organized as to prevent dissipation of the benefit, and able to provide the necessary brokerage fee in terms of either votes or pecuniary (and lawful) benefits. The suppliers of wealth transfers must, in turn, be difficult to organize and inelastic in their response to legislation. A threat of facing a one dollar loss as a consequence of legislation will not result in a one dollar increase in expenditure to fight it; the expected individual costs of mounting a political defence exceed the expected individual gains from not being coerced into a wealth transfer. The opportunity costs of resisting the wealth transfer must exceed the *per capita* amounts transferred.

The more durable the enactment and the larger the transfer it provides, the more the receiving interest group is willing to pay. Yet, for the providing group, the more durable the enactment and the larger the transfer, the higher will be the benefit from resisting the transfer, whereas opportunity costs remain unaffected. Hence, wealth transfers are subject to a scale restriction that is determined by the (transactions) costs of resisting them. We should therefore observe multiple small transfers involving different groups of suppliers.

The main cost element facing groups that are either seeking or resisting wealth transfers are start-up costs; hence, once they are borne, they no longer affect marginal costs. Established interest groups, then, enjoy an advantage in both seeking and resisting wealth transfers. This advantage amounts to a strong incentive for an established clientele of transfer recipients. A transfer may be large and durable, yet only affect each supplier to a small extent. Still, the larger the group of suppliers and the larger or more durable the transfer (or both), the higher the benefits will be from resisting. Votes and wealth can be assumed to be convertible. Since brokers compete for wealth or votes, political entrepreneurs may seek out groups of suppliers and, in return for their votes, oppose transfer programmes on their behalf. The larger the group of suppliers involved, or the larger or more durable the transfer sought, the higher the probability that a competing broker will organize resistance to a proposed wealth transfer. It follows that 'deal law' should be of relatively shorter durability than 'background law'. Likewise, 'deal law' should strongly benefit established groups and only mildly harm small, scattered groups; that is, 'deal law' should not impose considerable welfare losses on the general public. There are clearly tendencies in society that contain the social loss from rent seeking (Tullock 1980).

Assuming convertibility between wealth and votes, legislative brokers can either seek to serve established interest groups or appeal to large groups of general interest voters. They will probably do both; they have an incentive to produce legislation that benefits many while harming few. Generous transfers are largely precluded since a transfer that is perceptibly to benefit many must impose a heavy burden on a few. Such a transfer will not be supplied because the benefits from resisting it will generally exceed the opportunity costs of forgoing the resistance. It follows that legislative brokers have an incentive to produce legislation that is capable of producing wealth for the general public; the more durable this wealth-producing legislation, the larger the benefit from it and, presumably, the larger the expected return in votes. Legislators face incentives to produce durable wealth-enhancing legislation side by side with incentives to broker transfers of relatively limited duration. This holds true under the assumption that legislators have sufficient information. While obviously legislators are not omniscient, they can rely on their clients to possess and process the relevant information. Wealth-reducing legislation will be brought to the attention of the legislators by those whose wealth is being affected as well as by the press.

We conclude that brokers in the legislature face incentives to produce both efficient 'background law' as well as (mildly) inefficient 'deal law'. 'Mildly' inefficient is a deliberately loose term, since the argument is cast in terms of tendencies, not precisely quantifiable magnitudes. I mean to suggest that the (negative) welfare costs of deal law in this scenario will be relatively minor as compared to the (positive) welfare effects of background law.

B. The open jurisdiction. The second model differs from the first in two respects. It assumes that the jurisdiction is open in the sense that citizens and corporations can either resist or escape unwanted legislation. They may escape into other jurisdictions or into an extralegal domain within the jurisdiction, such as an underground or shadow economy. The first alternative is relatively straightforward, the equivalent to the small open economy in international trade theory. The smaller the jurisdiction and the more flexible the agents it comprises, the more elastic we can expect the evasive response to be. Even if the jurisdiction is 'big' and closed, however, the room for avoidance may be substantial. Regulations can be avoided by taking up other lines of business. Conflicts can routinely be settled out of court or conflict prone transactions can be avoided altogether. Alternative forms of dispute resolution can be resorted to or initiated. Finally, producers can withdraw from market transactions and shift exchanges of goods and services into an organization designed to reduce transactions costs (Williamson 1981).

None of these developments is included in what has been labelled the shadow economy, which itself is reputed to be a sizeable extralegal sector in advanced Western economies (Simon and Witte 1982; Tanzi 1982). The shadow economy, then, can be assumed to provide scope for escape in addition to the avoidance strategies already listed above (Frey and Weck 1983; Frey and Ramser 1986).

This modification of our model has two implications: the larger the potential for evasive action, the smaller the citizens' incentive will be to resist 'deal' law that aims at extracting transfers, and the smaller the extracted transfer, particularly in the long run. While this leaves the demand for transfers unaffected, increasing the scope for avoidance dries up the supply and raises the legislators' cost of providing transfers, or 'deal laws'. Secondly, the larger the scope for escape, the stronger the competitive pressure will be on legislators to produce efficient legal arrangements. And the stronger those competitive pressures are, the more likely it is that the economy will experience an expansion of its production possibility frontier.

The efficiency effect of 'deal law' when supply dries up is essentially secondary, that is, that efficiency loss occurs in terms of productive activities foregone in an economy. These are the opportunity costs of 'deal law'. Obviously, they depend on the extent to which opportunities for wealth production are foreclosed by 'deal law'. This effect implies that the general welfare loss of 'deal law' increases with the scope for evasive action.

Where resistance to 'deal law' weakens and transfers decline, a large number of 'deal laws' will be enacted. This observation reinforces the aforementioned tendency for 'deal laws' to be numerous but of relatively limited direct impact on attained wealth. By the same reasoning, however, 'deal laws' contract the production possibility frontier of the economy as a whole and hence affect citizens' attainable wealth positions.

We can conclude that in an 'open' jurisdiction, legislators face even stronger incentives to produce efficient 'background law', whereas incentives to produce 'deal law' become weaker relative to the first model.

C. Introducing Leviathan. The third model expands on the second in featuring an open jurisdiction, a Leviathan legislature (Buchanan and Brennan 1980) that seeks to maximize revenues from taxation, and a judiciary that adjudicates litigation by professional standards of jurisprudence and remains unaffected by the revenue maximization behaviour of the legislature. Hence, an independent judiciary is assumed. Model C is designed to capture the long-run implications of legislators' activities on the efficiency of the whole body of law.

In Leviathan models legislators are again assumed to maximize the sum of political profits from taxation, on the one hand, and regulation (i.e. 'deal law') on the other. Taxation and regulation are not only interchangeable as political means. While policies based on either invariably burden the citizenry, the size and fertility of the tax base is itself affected by the extent of regulation (Posner 1986), a trade-off long noted in economics (see Backhaus and Wagner 1987). Thus, the regulatory domain shrinks as the burden of taxation increases, and conversely reducing the burden of taxation opens up the regulatory domain. From this simple argument it follows that the production of 'deal law' impairs the fertility of the tax base. Hence, 'deal laws' generate negative externalities for the legislature as a whole by reducing the tax pie.

In the Leviathan literature (Buchanan and Brennan 1980; Buchanan and Lee 1982) it is customary to assume that Leviathan acts myopically. The long-run tax rate is assumed to exceed that rate which would yield the maximum stream of tax revenues; likewise the long-run regulatory intensity exceeds that intensity which would maximize the production of 'deal law' in the long run. Frey and Ramser (1986) have shown, however, that the short-run optimization of tax rates as well as regulatory intensities (considered simultaneously) can yield overregulation in tandem with undertaxation. It then appears that Leviathan's myopia is at odds with the beast's appetite. Short-run optimization does not yield a maximum political profit.

By way of clarification, suppose there is a unicameral legislature (according to McCormick and Tollison 1981 a unicameral legislative is more conducive to interest group, i.e. 'deal law', legislation than a bicameral legislature, especially if the two houses are of uneven size) and delegates may be re-elected. Then we can classify the delegates into cohorts according to the length of their tenure in the legislature. Whereas seniority can safely be assumed to carry additional power, there will always be a cohort that contains more members than a given one chosen at random. The larger cohort will be composed of younger delegates than the smaller one. This rule applies to all but the youngest cohort, which will be the largest. Hence, votes tend to be concentrated with younger delegates. The longer the tenure of a delegate, the shorter, *ceteris paribus*, is his expected future tenure, and thus the shorter his time horizon can be in taking political decisions.

Empirically, we also observe that elected officials' re-election probabilities are a positive function of the length of their past tenure. The empirical base is McCormick and Tollison's (1981). In a majority voting system based on districts, districts will compete for the most viable candidates in order to garner a majority, notably in a multi-party system. An under-researched case is the Imperial German democracy. The leading politician of the (Catholic or ultra montane) Centre party, Count Ballestrem, had his estate in Upper Silesia and was elected there for the district of Oppeln to the Imperial Diet in 1872. He was a leading adversary of Bismarck in the confrontation with the Pope, was first vice president of the Diet (1890–93) and representative of Meppen at the very Western border of the Empire (1891–4) for the Royal Prussian Diet. The point is that districts will compete for candidates, and the competition will land the most viable candidates in the safest candidacies.

The relatively lower re-election chance of younger representatives affects the length of their time horizon only insofar as political gains and losses of 'deal law' can be more heavily discounted in the immediate future where re-election is uncertain. Long-run effects, however, will be important for younger elected officials who can expect to be held responsible for 'deal' legislation they supported. Hence, elder delegates should be observed to be more prone to 'deal law' than younger delegates. Conversely, the 'newcomers' are more likely to take a long-run view, since they stand a greater chance not only of being confronted with the adverse consequences of sizing down the tax base or regulatory domain but of profiting individually from a large future tax base and unimpaired regulatory domains. Their opportunity cost of exposing deals is lower than that of longer serving legislators; it may even be nil. Since powerful interest groups will turn primarily to senior legislators who can deliver better deals, exposing those deals may be the best strategy in trying to depose long serving incumbents. Thus, gains from exposing 'deal law' and introducing 'background law' are likely to be highest for junior candidates, even if their expected tenure in office may remain relatively low due to lower (re-)election chances. In turn, delegates who take a long-term view outnumber their elder colleagues; more particularly, they have an incentive to produce 'background law' that broadens the tax base and increases its fertility by expanding the production possibility frontier of the economy. All this suggests that 'deal laws' will often be opposed by younger politicians who try to build political coalitions of transfer victims, thus seeking votes in the present while preserving their political power base for the future. This tendency should be observable in particular where politicians can claim revenue sources or regulatory domains, i.e., when political property rights are allowed to develop.

CONCLUSION. Will democratic legislatures largely engage in producing 'deal law' at the expense of providing the economy with 'background law'? Under the strict assumptions that legislatures consist of political brokers who act in a Leviathan environment, the conclusion is a resounding no. Brokers in the legislatures face incentives to produce efficient 'background law' as well as (mildly) inefficient 'deal law'.

Although these incentives hold in a closed jurisdiction, in an open jurisdiction legislators face even stronger incentives to produce efficient 'background law', whereas incentives to produce 'deal law' become weaker relative to the first model. Finally, taking a long-run view, one notes that 'deal laws' will often be opposed by younger politicians who try to build political coalitions of transfer victims, thus seeking votes in the present and preserving their political power base for the future. This tendency should be observable in particular where politicians can claim revenue sources or regulatory domains, i.e., when political property rights are allowed to develop.

JÜRGEN G. BACKHAUS

See also COMMON LAW, STATUTE LAW AND ECONOMIC EFFICIENCY; EFFICIENT NORMS; POSNER, RICHARD A.; RENT FROM REGULATION; RENT SEEKING; VALUE MAXIMIZATION; WEALTH MAXIMIZATION.

Subject classification: 4b(ii); 4c(ii).

BIBLIOGRAPHY

Aretz, E. 1993. Efficient law. PhD Dissertation, University of Maastricht.

Backhaus, J.G. and Wagner, R.E. 1987. The Cameralists: a public choice perspective. *Public Choice* 53: 3–20.

Bentham, J. 1789. *An Introduction to the Principles of Morals and Legislation*. London: T. Payne & Son. Reissued, ed. J.H. Burns, H.L.A. Hart and F. Rosen, Oxford: Clarendon Press, 1996.

Bentham, J. 1838–43. *The Works of Jeremy Bentham*. 11 vols, ed. J. Bowring, Edinburgh: William Tait.

Bentham, J. 1970. *Of Laws in General*. Ed. H.L.A. Hart, London: Oxford University Press.

Buchanan, J.M. and Brennan, G. 1980. *The Power to Tax. Analytical Foundations of a Fiscal Constitution*. Cambridge: Cambridge University Press.

Buchanan, J.M. and Lee, D.R. 1982. Politics, time, and the Laffer curve. *Journal of Political Economy* 90: 816–19.

Cooter, R. and Kornhauser, L. 1980. Can litigation improve the law without the help of judges? *Journal of Legal Studies* 9: 139–63.

Frey, B.S. and Ramser, H.J. 1986. Where are the limits of regulation? *Journal of Institutional and Theoretical Economics* (*Zeitschrift für die gesamte Staatswissenschaft*) 142: 571–80.

Frey, B.S. and Weck, H. 1983. What produces a hidden economy? an international cross section analysis. *Southern Economic Journal* 49: 822–32.

Goodman, J.C. 1978. An economic theory of the evolution of the common law. *Journal of Legal Studies* 7: 393–406.

Hirshleifer, J. 1982. Evolutionary models in economics and the law: cooperation versus conflict strategies. *Research in Law and Economics* 4: 1–60.

Landes, W.M. and Posner, R.A. 1979. Adjudication as a private good. *Journal of Legal Studies* 8: 235–84.

McCormick, R.E. and Tollison, R.D. 1981. *Politicians, Legislation, and the Economy. An Inquiry into the Interest Group Theory of Government*. Boston/The Hague: Martinus Nijhoff.

Michelman, F.I. 1980. Constitutions, statutes, and the theory of efficient adjudication. *Journal of Legal Studies* 9: 431–61.

Posner, R.A. 1977. *Economic Analysis of Law*. 2nd edn, Boston: Little, Brown; 3rd edn, 1986.

Posner, R.A. 1981. *The Economics of Justice*. Cambridge, MA: Harvard University Press.

Posner, R.A. 1987. The constitution as an economic document. *George Washington Law Review* 56(1).

Priest, G.L. 1977. The common law process and the selection of efficient rules. *Journal of Legal Studies* 6: 65–82.

Priest, G. and Klein, B. 1984. The selection of disputes for litigation. *Journal of Legal Studies* 13: 1–55.

Rubin, P.H. 1977. Why is the common law efficient? *Journal of Legal Studies* 6: 51–63.
Rubin, P.H. 1982. Common law and statute law. *Journal of Legal Studies* 11: 205–23.
Samuels, W. 1981. Maximization of wealth as justice. *Texas Law Review* 60: 147–72.
Simon, C. P. and Witte, A. D. 1982. *Beating the System: The Underground Economy*. Boston: Auburn House.
Tanzi, V. (ed.). 1982. *The Underground Economy in the United States and Abroad*. Lexington, MA: Lexington Books.
Terrebonne, R.P. 1981. A strictly evolutionary model of common law. *Journal of Legal Studies* 10: 397–407.
Tullock, G. 1980. Efficient rent seeking. In *Toward a Theory of the Rent Seeking Society*, ed. J.M. Buchanan, R. Tollison and G. Tullock, College Station: Texas A&M University Press, 3–15.
Williamson, O.E. 1981. The modern corporation: origins, evolution, attributes. *Journal of Economic Literature* 19: 1537–68.

electromagnetic spectrum. *See* PROPERTY RIGHTS IN THE ELECTROMAGNETIC SPECTRUM.

Ely, Richard Theodore (1854–1943). Richard Theodore Ely, 'that excellent German professor in an American skin' (Schumpeter 1954: 874), was born to a devout Presbyterian family in Ripley, New York on 13 April 1854. Awarded a fellowship to study philosophy in Germany following his graduation from Columbia College in 1876, he turned instead to political economy, earning a PhD at Heidelberg under Karl Knies in 1878. In 1881, Ely became the first lecturer in his field at Johns Hopkins, where he combined the historical inductivism of his German teachers with his own commitment to Christian Socialism to produce a normatively charged, interdisciplinary economics that strongly challenged the deductive methods and laissez-faire prescriptions of English classicism. Ely left his intellectual mark on a distinguished group of students at Hopkins, among them Frederick Jackson Turner, John R. Commons, E.A. Ross, Albion Small, Newton D. Baker and Woodrow Wilson, before leaving in 1892 to direct the new School of Economics, Political Science and History at the University of Wisconsin. There, after a notorious trial before the university's regents in 1894 at which he was exonerated of charges that he had advocated socialism and encouraged strikes, he maintained his faith in social legislation but gradually became more conservative as the nation adopted the progressive politics of his youth, a shift reflected in Theodore Roosevelt's remark that Ely 'first introduced me to radicalism in economics and then made me sane in my radicalism' (Taylor 1994: 135). Ely left Wisconsin in 1925, first for Northwestern University and then for New York, where he led a small research institute and completed an autobiography (1938) before his death, in his ninetieth year, on 4 October 1943.

Ely is best remembered not for his economics, but for his central role in the creation of the American Economic Association in 1885 and as the mentor of a host of scholars and men of affairs more accomplished than he; it is hard to dispute the conventional view that 'his original contribution to economic theory is negligible' (Coats 1987: 129). But Ely's economics was always more prescriptive than analytic. Though his positions on matters of distribution and institutional organization changed over time, the positive theory that motivated the questions he asked and the normative principle that governed the answers he gave remained constant throughout his life. The theory was that of his German teachers, that institutions circumscribe economic life and determine distribution, that law and custom, always in flux, determine institutions, and thus, as the founding principles of the AEA put it, that the 'progressive development of economic conditions . . . must be met by a corresponding development of legislative policy' (Ely 1938: 140). The normative principle, expressed first as a commitment to the ideal of brotherhood (Ely 1889: 67–8), was a consistent subordination of individual interest to the welfare of society that Ely called 'utilitarianism in the highest sense' (Ely 1914: 504). The unity of economics and law this implied was manifest in Ely's own writing and has animated work at their interface to this day, a development that would not have surprised Ely, who was comfortable with legal sources and saw the two disciplines as 'different approaches to the same territory' (Ely 1938: 188). During Ely's own lifetime, Commons (1924) sharpened and extended Ely's vague positive analysis of the effects of legal institutions on economic outcomes, a perspective revived years later in the seminal works of the 'new law and economics' (Coase 1960; Calabresi and Melamed 1972). And despite his own chagrin late in life at some of its practical manifestations, Ely's view that all policy, and thus all law, should promote social welfare ultimately found expression in both the progressive labour and antitrust economics of the New Deal and postwar eras and the conservative, wealth-maximizing social ethic of Richard Posner (1981: 48–115).

All these themes are apparent in *Property and Contract in Their Relations to the Distribution of Wealth* (1914), a treatise twenty years in the making that Ely (1938: 270) called 'my most important work'. For Ely, who subsumed contractual rights in the larger category of property, the relation implied by the title was fundamental. Distribution is determined neither by the character or behaviour of men, nor by any natural endowment of personal rights society is bound to respect, but by the way society, acting in its own interest through the state, chooses to define the rights that individuals may exercise over things. Property thus has a social as well as an individual side, and as societies mature, the social side grows in importance, as changing conditions increasingly require that prerogatives once enjoyed by individuals be transferred by positive law to the public. American law presents two ancient mechanisms to accomplish this transfer, eminent domain, which requires compensation of these individuals, and the police power, which does not. Though neither Ely nor any of his successors have ever managed to elucidate the distinction between them authoritatively, the extended discussion of these powers in *Property and Contract* anticipates many of the questions that have vexed courts and commentators alike in the years since 1914.

Ely saw the continuous delineation and refinement of the state's police power as the means by which courts maintained the shifting balance between the social and individual sides of property. In deciding the validity of legislation that adversely affected private interests against a claim that a compensable taking of property had occurred, courts fixed the 'metes and bounds' of private property and gave it 'a content at each particular period in our development which fits it to serve the general welfare' (1914: 206–7). There could thus be no question of compensation where such a statute was upheld; because the court's decision *defined* the property right at stake, it was held from the moment of its creation by the state, so the individual had not been deprived of anything he had owned before. But Ely maintained that once a right *had* been vested in an individual by a court or legislature, the state could only effect the transfer by eminent domain and compensate the owner for its full value. In 1914, this was not the law; compensation for value in land lost through regulation was required only when title actually passed to the state. But in 1922, speaking in *Pennsylvania Coal Co. v. Mahon* through Justice Holmes, who had sympathetically read *Property and Contract* in manuscript, the Supreme Court adopted Ely's broader view and held that if state action deprived the owner of a vested right in land of its entire economic value, compensation was required even though title remained in the owner. As courts redraw the shifting line between the two powers in this way, Ely believed, they make 'the idea of property a flexible one, adapted to the actual situation', and protect the public against both the tyranny of a robber-state and the 'excessive development of vested rights' (1914: 209–10).

A central point of this analysis is that the actual determination of this line is the province of the courts. But Ely did not hesitate to offer his own views, and in the course of his long treatise, perhaps in reflection of his drift to the right over the period of its composition, he seemed to contradict himself. Always solicitous of society's needs, he believed that both the police and eminent domain powers ought to be exercised freely, though, like Michelman (1967) decades later, his utilitarianism was sensitive both to the administrative costs of achieving compensation and the demoralization that might attend a failure to compensate that disappointed the expectations of investors (1914: 209, 497–505). Early in the work, he criticized the Supreme Court's controversial 1905 decision in *Lochner v. New York* that a statute regulating working hours must yield to the right of free contract, arguing generally that judges' lack of training in the social sciences inclined them to give too little scope to the police power (1914: 212–26). But later (1914: 755–91), and in his autobiography (1938: 269–74), he supported a broad expansion of compensable vested rights to protect not just the owners of traditional property against the state but the interests of workers in their trades against the advance of technology; if, he argued, such reallocations truly are beneficial to society, the payment of compensation entails no loss and serves as a middle ground between pursuit of social change regardless of its costs and resistance to any change at all. Though Ely derided the ideas of natural rights and social contract, this later position resembles the explicit Lockeanism of Epstein (1985), itself a reaction to Michelman's utilitarian approach to the compensation problem.

Contemporary reviews of *Property and Contract* were mixed. Learned Hand found it 'always moderate, never pungent, seldom novel', while Roscoe Pound could see 'nothing else on the subject worth talking about' (Rader 1966: 197, 199), evaluations not necessarily in contradiction. But if Ely's contribution to economic theory as such is in fact negligible, this work alone demonstrates his ability to range across disciplines and penetrate to the heart of difficult problems of political economy, and to identify questions that his successors would have to address.

RICHARD ADELSTEIN

See also AMERICAN INSTITUTIONAL ECONOMICS AND THE LEGAL SYSTEM; AMERICAN LEGAL REALISM; COMMONS, JOHN R.; TAKINGS.

Subject classification: 1c, 6c(iv); 7a.

SELECTED WORKS

1889. *An Introduction to Political Economy*. New York: Chautauqua Press.

1914. *Property and Contract in Their Relations to the Distribution of Wealth*. 2 vols, New York: Macmillan; reprinted 1971, Port Washington: Kennikat Press.

1938. *Ground Under Our Feet: An Autobiography*. New York: Macmillan.

CASES

Lochner v. New York, 198 US 45 (1905).

Pennsylvania Coal Co. v. Mahon, 260 US 393 (1922).

BIBLIOGRAPHY

Calabresi, G. and Melamed, A.D. 1972. Property rules, liability rules and inalienability: one view of the cathedral. *Harvard Law Review* 85: 1089–1128.

Coase, R.H. 1960. The problem of social cost. *Journal of Law and Economics* 3: 1–44.

Coats, A.W. 1987. Ely, Richard Theodore. In *The New Palgrave: A Dictionary of Economics*, ed. J. Eatwell, M. Milgate and P. Newman (London: Macmillan), Vol. 2: 129–30.

Commons, J.R. 1924. *Legal Foundations of Capitalism*. New York: Macmillan.

Epstein, R.A. 1985. *Takings: Private Property and the Power of Eminent Domain*. Cambridge, MA: Harvard University Press.

Michelman, F.I. 1967. Property, utility, and fairness: comments on the ethical foundations of 'just compensation' law. *Harvard Law Review* 80: 1165–1258.

Posner, R.A. 1981. *The Economics of Justice*. Cambridge, MA: Harvard University Press.

Rader, B.G. 1966. *The Academic Mind and Reform: The Influence of Richard T. Ely in American Life*. Lexington: University of Kentucky Press.

Schumpeter, J.A. 1954. *History of Economic Analysis*, ed. E.B. Schumpeter, New York: Oxford University Press.

Taylor, H.C. 1944. Richard T. Ely. *Economic Journal* 54: 132–8.

emergence of legal rules. The emergence of legal rules refers to the process whereby new law comes into being or existing law is modified. The terms require some clarification. 'Emergence' is broader than 'creation'. It encompasses not merely official acts of declaring legal rules in legislation or judicial decisions, but also processes whereby legal rules appear in the course of human interaction, without a specific design or explicit state mandate to that effect. The term emergence suggests that law need not originate with 'an omnipotent authority standing high above society, and issuing *downwards* its behests. [It allows for law to be] spontaneous, growing *upwards*, independently of any dominant will' (Allen [1927] 1964: 1).

Legal rules or norms are the constitutive elements of the law. They are to be distinguished both from prescriptions of morality and from social conventions and other rule systems. The distinction between law and morality opposes natural law theories and legal positivism. The distinction between law and other rule systems opposes legal pluralism to legal centralism. All these theories come in many shades and varieties.

Natural law theories hold that besides products of human lawgiving, the law consists of elements stemming from the natural order of things, human nature or divine revelation. They concern the morality or justice of the law and fundamental legal principles. These principles are judged to be the necessary foundation of positive law as well as an essential source of inspiration for lawgivers in law reform; they may be invoked to criticize unjust legislation as not being law and hence as having no claim to be obeyed. Proponents of natural law theories of the seventeenth and eighteenth centuries, such as Grotius, Pufendorf and Wolff, held that the principles of natural law could be discovered by human reason. They derived from them rather specific prescriptions in family law, the law of property, the law of successions and the law of torts.

Legal positivism, in the works of Bentham and Austin, was a reaction against this form of natural law thinking, judged too unreliable a source, too much open to contradictory interpretations and too easy an escape from obligations imposed by positive law. The common element of legal positivism, including its modern proponents Kelsen and Hart, appears to be the thesis that all law is created by authorized human lawgivers and that no law exists outside this source. The validity of laws is to be judged not by their content, but by the authority underpinning their creation.

An early example of natural law being invoked against positive law is Antigone's reply to Creon in Sophocles' play bearing her name. Asked why she had buried her brother in spite of Creon's decree forbidding it, she declares that the king's decrees are powerless to set aside the obligations resulting from the higher and timeless laws of divine origin. In contemporary discourse, the natural law idea finds expression in the doctrine of fundamental rights common to all human beings. Whilst positivists may acknowledge these ideas as expressions of what the law ought to be, they believe them to become part of positive law only by being recognized, even articulated in legislation, judicial decisions or other instruments of positive law. In the 1982 Postscript to his classic treatise, Hart, qualifying himself as a 'soft positivist', admits that the rule of recognition may designate moral principles or substantive values amongst the criteria for valid law (Hart [1961] 1982: 250).

Principles to which the defenders of natural law would appeal are generally unwritten; positive law is generally written. Yet the opposition between positivism and natural law does not turn on the question of whether law is written. Even in a positivist conception, there is room for unwritten rules. In the Canadian constitutional tradition, for instance, the written constitution is complemented by 'constitutional convention' and other unwritten rules, which are considered binding and recognized by the courts (*Re Resolution to Amend the Constitution*, 774–5). Unwritten rules may play a role in other fields of law as well, as in commercial practices and usage. Conversely, natural law theories acknowledge the important role played by written law, but contest that it is the exclusive source of law.

The practice of writing down the laws of a community was invented in antiquity (Gilissen 1979: 53). Until then, the law was indistinct from social custom. Within closed communities unwritten custom may be sufficient reference to solve disputes (Stein 1984: 4). As communities grow, and trade with outsiders develops, custom is no longer a clear and sure enough base to prevent disputes and to resolve those that could not be prevented (Gagarin 1986: 135). It was the hope of preventing conflict that led the Greek city states to have their laws written down. The task proved beyond the talents of the local authorities and had to be entrusted to specialized craftsmen such as Draco and Solon.

Drafting the laws did not consist merely in recording customary rules. Citizens were only dimly aware of the rules by which they lived (much like the grammatical rules followed in speech). The task lawgivers faced was to formulate rules at once in broad agreement with existing custom and acceptable to community members for future cases. Laws thus codified were solemnly proclaimed for all to know and as a result had an imperative claim on citizens to be obeyed. They were meant to be fixed for all times. Written laws in fact clarified and simplified customary rules and provided certainty about what the law was. They thereby contributed to social peace and to equality of citizens before the law.

These benefits were sought and found again in Western Europe during the thirteenth to sixteenth centuries, when groups of subjects asked their Emperor, King or other supreme ruler for assistance in writing down and then formally proclaiming their local or regional customs. The rulers may have found it in their interest to provide such help as a means of checking the power of the local nobles and of strengthening their own. It should be noted that the decrees they issued on their own behalf were initially restricted to issues of public order, money and taxation (van den Bergh 1982: 10, 28–9). They steered clear of the ordinary relationships amongst citizens, which were thought to be the proper subject matter of custom.

The process of writing down the laws or customs of a society reveals the role which law plays in society: that of articulating non-violent solutions to potential conflicts as well as the procedures and institutions by which the solutions are to be brought about. Writing down the laws has the effect of divorcing the written law from its living source, which is custom and the record of resolved conflicts. The law becomes a body of abstract and formally proclaimed rules; knowledge of the law becomes a separate profession. Written law has a certain solemnity and rigidity about it, which may make it difficult to keep pace with evolving custom (Stein 1984: 69).

Law as an instrument of social peace makes it a concern for those in charge of maintaining peace in society, the rulers. While initially they may be content merely to lend their authority to written law as a record of custom and to courts as agencies for dispute resolution, in due course they will find it to their advantage to take charge of the lawmaking as a sovereign prerogative. They may attempt to use it as an instrument of power – that is, to decree rules of their choosing, overriding customary rules, codified or not. This practice gives credence to the idea that rulers and, in modern times, legislatures can create new law, indeed that they are the primary source of it.

On such a view, custom is at best a secondary source of law. In the last century, the Historical School in Germany, under the inspiration of F.C. von Savigny, held that such a view was misguided and that custom was ultimately the only valid source of law. These views, though widely discussed, have had little influence. In particular, they have not stopped the codification of the civil law in Germany (BGB of 1900).

These considerations bring us to the opposition between legal pluralism and legal centralism. Legal centralism and legal positivism are joined in viewing the law of a given society as a single unified system. The question of whether a given norm is a valid legal rule is answered by identifying the authority behind it and determining whether it is duly authorized by higher authority to issue such a norm. This view implies a hierarchical conception of power.

Legal positivism provides the comfort of a clear criterion for determining whether a norm is a legal rule or a mere social convention, which is not part of it, such as taking one's hat off to a lady (Hart [1961] 1982: 44). On a positivist view, custom enters the law only in as much as it is admitted through legislation or judicial decision. Yet even such a distinct positivist as Kelsen expressly allows for the possibility of a constitution, itself unwritten, establishing custom as a law-creating fact and ordinary citizens as its enforcers (Kelsen [1934] 1970: 224).

Within civil society, numerous distinct communities live by rules of their own making: churches, charitable organizations, schools and academies, clubs, business communities, to name a few (Rocher 1996: 131). One might speak of the customary law of semi-autonomous communities. In a formal sense, this form of rule-making is authorized, or at least condoned, by state authority. But this must not be taken to imply the clearly misguided view that state authority could effectively re-order those rules at will. Throughout history, rulers have had to learn at their expense the limitations of their power to change the ways of their subjects and the undesired side effects, from civil disobedience to rebellion, produced by attempts to overstep those limits. In our day, Ellickson's study (1991) shows that the farmers of Shasta county, California, in their reciprocal dealings ignored the official property and tort law in favour of rules evolved amongst themselves. Formally valid law need not be effective.

These considerations set the scene for a pluralistic view, according to which the law of a society consists of numerous distinct legal orders, each with its own enforcement machinery and metarules about rule-making and conflict resolution (Fuller 1969; Ellickson 1991; Cooter 1996; Rocher 1996). Some orders are better articulated than others; the state legal order is generally the best articulated of them all. There exists a loose hierarchical relationship amongst the orders, with the state legal order being generally, but not invariably, the dominant one. Rules may be carried from one order into another, a phenomenon for which Carbonnier ([1977] 1979) proposed the term 'internormativity', which has gained currency amongst sociologists of law. On a pluralistic view, it is not easy to determine whether a particular rule is valid law. Validity of rules is a matter of degree, turning on the extent to which rules are considered binding and effectively observed within the relevant community. Carbonnier ([1969] 1992: 17–18) warns against the temptation to see law everywhere ('*panjuridisme*') and explicitly leaves open the possibility of matters where one would expect law, but there is none ('*non-droit*').

Where custom conflicts with written positive law, there is the problem of deciding which is to prevail. Historically, local custom (including the liberties and powers conferred by city charters) has been invoked to oppose uniform written law imposed by rulers as a means of centralization (van den Bergh 1982: 5, 51). Conversely, codification was demanded to do away with the imprecision and arbitrariness of powers based on customary law (van den Bergh 1982: 5, 52). In modern societies, to a positivist, written law prevails where custom conflicts with it. A pluralist is likely first to observe that they are part of different legal orders and may reach the opposite conclusion. The practices of the legal community tend towards the former view.

And yet at the margin, one encounters cases which sit uncomfortably with a strictly positivist view. Article 293 of the Dutch Criminal Code explicitly criminalizes assistance (even by a doctor) to a person wishing to end his or her life. A practice has developed whereby the public prosecutor's office will not prosecute doctors in cases of mercy killing (euthanasia), provided the patient's desire is unequivocal and the doctor has obtained the assent of two colleagues for the intervention and filed a detailed form on the case with the local prosecutor's office. Each case of mercy killing is widely discussed in the country and the practice has gradually been extended to different types of case (comatose, severely handicapped, etc.). The Supreme Court has expressly accepted the practice, all the while maintaining the general validity of Article 293 of the Criminal Code. The government does not intend to introduce in Parliament legislation that would modify the Criminal Code to decriminalize mercy killings, presumably because the matter is still controversial amongst the population.

What is the law in this case? One could scarcely discount the Code provision, which still stands as a rampart against insufficiently careful mercy killing. And yet its explicit text does not fully describe the law. What appears to be happening is this. Mercy killing is a sufficiently grave matter to call for explicit rules. Yet the machinery which generates written rules cannot operate in the absence of an underlying substantial agreement on what the rule should be. The opinions about mercy killing (and about abortion) vary widely amongst citizens. It is a matter of such moment that under the rule of law, a majority ought not to impose its preferred rule on the minority. The ambivalence one observes in Holland seems to reflect a strategy of discovery through 'tâtonnement' (groping): maintain the formal prohibition, but allow the dissonant rule to work in limited fashion and in restricted contexts; develop experience with its advantages and disadvantages; attempt to broaden agreement on a new rule based on accumulated experience, clearing the way for legislation (or for maintaining the status quo and disallowing the dissonant practice).

This discovery procedure is at odds with a strict positivist–centralist point of view. Such a view offers no easy answer to the question of how a society finds the contents of new rules to be adopted in controversial matters.

What can the economic analysis of law contribute to the understanding of these issues? A preliminary question to be clarified concerns the reason for using rules. If people are rational optimizers, as traditional economic theory would picture them, why do they follow rules in their private decisions and in their interactions with others, even where in a given instance this does not lead to the optimal result? The answer is that rules economize on the information required for reaching a decision. In most situations humans face, there are serious practical limitations on the information which can be brought to bear on the decision, as Herbert Simon's work has demonstrated. First, there is uncertainty – questions about which no information other than one's guesses is available; then, there are matters on which information can be had, but at too high a cost, considering what is at stake, leading the decision-maker to remain 'rationally ignorant'; finally, time and talent available to deliberate are finite. These considerations make it rational to reach decisions by relying on rules. Rules simplify decision problems by focusing the attention of the decision-maker on a few key aspects of the problem which alone are to be taken into consideration in deciding.

Rules are constructed on the basis of recurrent situations, in which they lead to satisfactory, though not necessarily optimal results. They reflect an implicit trade-off between the quality of a decision (as reflected in the benefits or the regret it causes) and its (information) cost. Rules are transmitted by teaching or imitation. Humans thus develop a repertoire of rules for a variety of circumstances. Rules make their behaviour to a certain extent predictable. Heiner (1983, 1986, 1990) has proposed a formalization of rule-guided behaviour. He explains amongst other things why the more complex the problem, the likelier the decision-maker is to resort to rules in order to resolve it (and the more stereotypical his response will be).

If legal rules articulate non-violent solutions to potential conflicts as well as models for cooperation, they are, as Ullmann-Margalit (1977) was the first to demonstrate, a proper subject for game theory, which studies human interaction. A first distinction flowing from game theory is between coordination games and cooperation games. In the former, participants arrive at the best solution by adopting the same or complementary strategies. By contrast, cooperative games have a strategic component to them in that cooperation is profitable, but each participant may be tempted to profit more by exploiting the others.

Coordination games are exemplified in driving on the same side of the road, speaking the same language, conforming to compatibility standards for electrical or telephone plugs or for television signals and computer software. Non-conforming (deviant) behaviour entails its own sanction, which makes these norms largely self-enforcing. Coordination norms often present network externalities: the more numerous are those who follow the norm, the stronger will be the interest of the uncommitted to adopt it as well. Interactions of this kind often have several, more or less equivalent equilibria. This suggests dynamics whereby an initial impetus favouring a particular solution – chosen by some for features considered salient within the community or for fortuitous reasons (Schelling 1960, 1978) – will in due course propagate that solution to the norm for the group as a whole. The law has a limited role to play here: articulating, for greater certainty, the solution on which the norm-generating process is converging.

Conflict may arise where different communities within a larger society have evolved incompatible coordination norms, which clash as economies of scale and other forces push towards a single norm for the entire society. More than a coordination problem is at stake here. Whilst all members of the larger society stand to gain from adopting a common norm, the community whose norm is generalized gets a free gift, whereas all others face conversion or adaptation costs. The tensions around a common language amongst different linguistic groups exemplify the problem.

These tensions point to the second class of games, the games of cooperation, which are more significant for law. These games have in common that, whilst all participants gain from adopting cooperative strategies, each faces the temptation of trying to exploit the others (non-cooperative strategy) from which higher gains result for him or her, but losses for the others. If all participants give in to the temptation, cooperation breaks down – a Pareto inferior outcome. Prisoner's dilemma, the chicken or hawk–dove game, the assurance game and their variants are examples.

Cooperation games do not converge on an equilibrium in the self-enforcing manner of coordination games. The puzzle in these games is to explain how cooperation might arise without being imposed from above. The recent literature on game theory has been able to show that the problem of cooperation is solvable under certain conditions (Axelrod 1984; Sugden 1986; Taylor 1987). The most important amongst these conditions are enduring relationships amongst the participants to the game and the ability of participants to distinguish correctly between cooperative and non-cooperative strategies adopted by the other participants. Enduring relationships may be found in ties based on kinship, friendship, ethnicity or religion (Cooter 1996: 151).

People locked into relationships which can be described as prisoner's dilemmas or hawk–dove games about scarce resources and their exchange are likely to reach equilibria reflecting core principles of contract (respecting one's word; reciprocity) and of property law. But equilibrium strategies do not of themselves constitute rules. They become rules when players 'internalize' them, consider them binding and observe them whenever applicable, and expect others to do the same. People may sanction others who do not follow the rules (Sugden 1986: 147 f.; Cooter 1996).

These principles are brought to light in the course of people's interactions and it is not surprising that they should have been discovered everywhere. This sheds new light on the idea of law as a spontaneous order, which Hayek has given new currency in recent years. It gives us a handle on natural law ideas: they might reflect constraints inherent in all human interaction, but developed only when people actually engage in such interaction, much as Piaget and Kohlberg have maintained for children learning moral principles. Fuller (1971) said as much for law.

The concrete rules in which the principles are crystallized, and the range of situations to which they apply, depend on what scarce resources have become the object of interaction. As technology advances, new objects are drawn into interactions which lead people to discover the rules by which they should handle them. The question of what should be the contents of legal rules for new situations might now be answered by directing one's attention to situations where participants are locked in interactions which are bound to make them discover the proper rules. The adequacy of the rule, on such a view, depends on the incentives bearing upon those articulating it to get it right, and on the information available to them. A wealth of literature explores this theme for the 'new' (and older) merchant law and for communities formed 'around a technology such as computer software, a body of knowledge such as accounting, or a particular product such as credit cards' (Cooter 1996: 147; see also Benson 1989, 1992; Ellickson 1989; Milgrom et al. 1990; Bernstein 1996; Mackaay 1996).

In many situations, individuals have a common interest in the pursuit of some endeavour. Game theory shows that securing this collective aim by bundling individual efforts is not always a simple matter. Some participants may attempt to 'free ride' on the efforts of others (externalities are a variant of this); some may 'hold out' in the hope of securing a larger share of the spoils for their participation; yet others may overexploit a common resource. If collective efforts are steered through an organization, the directors may have an incentive to pursue their private interest in opposition to that of the group. All these problems are part of the paradox of collective action (Olson 1989), which can be elucidated as a cooperative game with numerous players. One must fear that some worthwhile collective endeavours (public goods) will not be undertaken because of these dangers and this is used as an argument for having them provided by the state.

In the course of history, numerous institutions have been developed to overcome collective action problems in particular contexts. State coercion is one of them, but by no means the only one. Indeed the state itself might be seen in its origins as an instrument for collective action, be it defence of the group or the creation of public works such as irrigation systems. Solutions to collective action problems are reflected in legal rules. It may therefore often be fruitful to analyse new legal rules as responses to collective action problems or to problems with institutions already in place for that purpose. Studies on the law of corporations are one source of largely private rules dealing with collective action problems (Easterbrook and Fischel 1991; Romano 1993).

Once the state has come into being, it tends to expand and crowd out other modes of organization. A plethora of legal rules has been developed for the purpose of dispersing coercive power and structuring the supervision of its exercise (Benson 1994; Mackaay 1997). The exercise of power, including legislative power relevant here, is the object of the public choice literature. This literature is generally pessimistic about the likelihood that in representative democracies state action faithfully reflects the preferences of the citizenry. A recent contribution questions this conclusion by drawing attention to the competition amongst centres of power, in formally federal states as well as in unitary ones (Breton 1996).

The state acts through representatives, whose actions it must control. This poses an agency problem. One must expect much administrative law to reflect constraints inherent in this form of representation (Bishop 1990). In allocating their services to the population otherwise than through the price system, state agencies face the problem of priorities. This requires legal rules. Game theory may provide suggestions of the forms these rules may take (Brams and Taylor 1996).

The economic analysis of law has been taxed with confining itself to a positivist-centralist conception of the law (Ellickson 1987: 81). This criticism appears to be rash. Indeed, law and economics has much to contribute to a pluralistic view of the emergence of legal rules.

EJAN MACKAAY

See also CONVENTIONS; CONVENTIONS AT THE FOUNDATION OF LAW; CUSTOMARY LAW; EVOLUTION OF COMMERCIAL LAW; LEGAL POSITIVISM; PRISONERS' DILEMMA; PRIVATE COMMERCIAL LAW; RULE-GUIDED BEHAVIOUR; RULE OF RECOGNITION; SOCIAL NORMS AND THE LAW.

Subject classification: 1b(iii); 1d(ii); 4a(i); 4a(iii).

CASE

Re Resolution to Amend the Constitution, [1981] 1 SCR 753–912 (Supreme Court of Canada).

BIBLIOGRAPHY

Allen, C.K. [1927] 1964. *Law in the Making*. 7th edn, Oxford: Clarendon Press.

Axelrod, R. 1984. *The Evolution of Cooperation*. New York: Basic Books.

Axelrod, R. and Dion, D. 1988. The further evolution of cooperation. *Science* 242: 1385–90.

Benson, B. 1989. The spontaneous evolution of commercial law. *Southern Economic Journal* 55: 644–61.

Benson, B. 1992. Customary law as a social contract: international commercial law. *Constitutional Political Economy* 3: 1–27.

Benson, B. 1994. Emerging from the Hobbesian jungle: might takes and makes rights. *Constitutional Political Economy* 5: 129–58.

van den Bergh, G.C.J.J. 1982. *Wet en Gewoonte – Historische grondslagen van een dogmatisch geding* [Statute and custom – historical foundations of a doctrinal dispute]. Deventer: Kluwer.

Bernstein, L. 1996. Merchant Law in a Merchant Court: rethinking the Code's search for immanent business norms. *University of Pennsylvania Law Review* 144: 1765–1821.

Bishop, W. 1990. A theory of administrative law. *Journal of Legal Studies* 19: 489–530.

Brams, S.J. and Taylor, A.D. 1996. *Fair Division: from cake-cutting to dispute resolution*. Cambridge: Cambridge University Press.

Breton, A. 1996. *Competitive Governments: an economic theory of politics and public finance*. Cambridge: Cambridge University Press.

van Caenegem, R.C. 1992. *An Historical Introduction to Private Law*. Cambridge: Cambridge University Press.

Carbonnier, J. [1969] 1992. *Flexible droit – textes pour une sociologie du droit sans rigueur*. Paris: Librairie générale de droit et de jurisprudence.

Carbonnier, J. [1977] 1979. Les phénomènes d'internormativité. In *Essais sur les lois*, ed. J. Carbonnier, Paris: Répertoire du notariat Defrénois.

Cooter, R.D. 1994. Structural adjudication and the new Law Merchant: a model of decentralized law. *International Review of Law and Economics* 14: 215–31.

Cooter, R.D. 1996. The theory of market modernization of law. *International Review of Law and Economics* 16: 141–72.

Easterbrook, F.H. and Fischel, D.R. 1991. *The Economic Structure of Corporate Law*. Cambridge, MA: Harvard University Press.

Ellickson, R.C. 1987. A critique of economic and sociological theories of social control. *Journal of Legal Studies* 16: 67–99.

Ellickson, R.C. 1989. A hypothesis of wealth-maximizing norms: evidence from the whaling industry. *Journal of Law, Economics, and Organization* 5: 83–97.

Ellickson, R.C. 1991. *Order without Law – How Neighbors Settle Disputes*. Boston: Harvard University Press.

Fuller, L.L. 1969. *The Morality of Law*. 2nd edn, New Haven: Yale University Press.

Fuller, L.L. 1971. Human interaction and the law. In *The Rule of Law*, ed. R.P. Wolff, New York: Simon & Schuster.

Gagarin, M. 1986. *Early Greek Law*. Berkeley: University of California Press.

Gilissen, J. 1979. *Introduction historique au droit – Esquisse d'une histoire universelle du droit – Les sources du droit depuis le XIIIe siècle – Éléments d'histoire du droit privé*. Bruxelles: Bruylant.

Hart, H.L.A. [1961] 1982. *The Concept of Law*. 2nd edn, Oxford: Clarendon Press.

Heiner, R.A. 1983. The origin of predictable behavior. *American Economic Review* 73: 560–95.

Heiner, R.A. 1986. Imperfect decisions and the law: on the evolution of legal precedent and rules. *Journal of Legal Studies* 15: 227–62.

Heiner, R.A. 1990. Rule-governed behavior in evolution and human society. *Constitutional Political Economy* 1: 19–46.

Kelsen, H. [1934] 1970. *Pure Theory of Law*. Berkeley: University of California Press.

Mackaay, E. 1996. The economics of emergent property rights on the internet. In *The Future of Copyright in a Digital Environment*, ed. P.B. Hugenholtz, The Hague: Kluwer Law International.

Mackaay, E. 1997. The emergence of constitutional rights. *Constitutional Political Economy* 8: 15–36.

Milgrom, P.R., North, D.C. and Weingast, B.R. 1990. The role of institutions in the revival of trade: Law Merchant, private judges, and the Champagne fairs. *Economics and Politics* 2: 1–23.

Olson, M.L. 1989. Collective action. In *The New Palgrave: A Dictionary of Economics*, ed. J. Eatwell, M. Milgate and P. Newman, London: Macmillan; New York: Stockton Press; reprinted in *The Invisible Hand*, ed. J. Eatwell, M. Milgate and P. Newman, London: Macmillan, New York: W.W. Norton, 61–9.

Parisi, F. 1995. Toward a theory of spontaneous law. *Constitutional Political Economy* 6: 211–31.

Rocher, G. 1996. Pour une sociologie des ordres juridiques. In *Études de sociologie du droit et de l'éthique*, ed. G. Rocher, Montréal: Éditions Thémis.

Romano, R. (ed.) 1993. *Foundations of Corporate Law*. New York: Oxford University Press.

Schelling, T.C. 1960. *The Strategy of Conflict*. Cambridge MA: Harvard University Press.

Schelling, T.C. 1978. *Micromotives and Macrobehavior*. New York: Norton.

Stein, P. 1984. *Legal Institutions: The Development of Dispute Settlement*. London: Butterworth.

Sugden, R. 1986. *The Economics of Rights, Co-operation and Welfare*. Oxford: Basil Blackwell.

Sugden, R. 1989. Spontaneous order. *Journal of Economic Perspectives* 3: 85–97.

Taylor, M. 1987. *The Possibility of Co-operation*. Cambridge: Cambridge University Press.

Ullmann-Margalit, E. 1977. *The Emergence of Norms*. Oxford: Clarendon Press.

eminent domain and just compensation. Eminent domain is the power of government to take property regardless of whether compensation is paid. When a government agency informs property owners that it is going to take their property by eminent domain, they have no legal power to resist except, in the United States, under the 'public use' doctrine. The best owners can do in most nations of the world is to make a claim for just compensation, an amount determined by a process established by statutes, constitutions and judicial interpretations. In most countries, 'just compensation' is considered to be the market value of the property at the time the government takes it.

Eminent domain and just compensation so often raise strong normative stances about property rights that it can be difficult to see how economic analysis might be applied. It may be useful instead to approach eminent domain as a simple budgetary issue. This approach will be used to address a positive question about a normative practice: Why do nearly all nations of the earth compensate owners of land when their property is taken? (Garner 1975).

Suppose that a government proposes to build a dam across a river that will flood (and thus render unusable for private purposes) land that is owned by some of its citizens. The government has the power to tax, and the bulk of the taxes are on personal income. If the government seizes the land for the dam without compensation, it will not have to raise taxes. If it does pay compensation, taxes will have to rise, and the usual problems of additional deadweight loss will afflict the economy.

Seen in this light, the issue raised by eminent domain is to decide who should be taxed – the landowners (whose property is rendered unusable by the dam) or the taxpayers. If just compensation is paid to the landowners, then the 'property' (mostly labour income) of general taxpayers is taken. If just compensation is not paid, the landowners bear the financial burden. Just compensation is, in this formulation, no more than a tax problem, and optimal taxation theory could be – but generally has not been – brought to bear on the issue. (Optimal taxation theory attempts to formulate taxes in such a way as to minimize the deadweight losses of the taxes. One of its tenets is that taxes should be levied on factors whose supply is relatively inelastic.)

I have formulated this problem as a question of whether the government should compensate landowners rather than owners of other types of property. It is easy to see why most governments pay for most physical capital and the services of government workers (other than soldiers, to be discussed presently). If the government did not pay its workers, their services would not be forthcoming, or they would be forthcoming only with the greatest of effort. Seizure of capital without compensation would likewise discourage its formation by private saving and investment, and encourage its emigration to lands whose politics were more favourable to property owners (Stoebuck 1972: 563; Been 1991).

The deadweight loss of collecting the 'tax' by uncompensated expropriation of labour and capital would usually exceed (one presumes) the deadweight loss of a general income tax. Because substantial deadweight loss is an evolutionary drawback, government purchase of the services of labour and capital would become the norm. But for the same reason, it seems likely that owners of land would seldom be compensated in such societies. Land is typically fixed in supply. Economists have known for almost two centuries (and kings for much longer) that resources that cannot run away are more efficiently taxed than those that can.

It follows from the foregoing that there must be some reason other than the usual efficiency considerations (about deadweight loss) that nearly all nations pay just compensation to landowners. It is unlikely that the habit of just compensation comes from a high regard for property itself. On the one hand, most of the formerly socialist countries paid at least some compensation for taking land (Garner 1975: 11). On the other hand, even the country whose historical regard for private ownership of land is arguably greatest, the United States, typically pays no more than the market value of the land it acquires, and at various times in its history has paid even less than that (Ely 1992). American states and the federal government do not compensate owners for personal, above-market valuations for their property, and many states fail to compensate for indirect losses, such as business goodwill. And all American governments resist demands for compensation by landowners whose property has been devalued by a change in regulations.

Another possible reason for the nearly universal practice of just compensation for land is to promote government efficiency. If land has no price-tag attached to it, this story goes, government agencies will regard it as a free input and overuse it relative to factors of production. Special interest groups might shift private activities to the public sector in order to get their favoured projects at a lower cost (Levmore 1991). As a result of such 'fiscal illusion', too many public dams, roads and other projects will be built. There are some solid economic studies as well as a host of anecdotes that suggest that government's willingness to acquire land is sensitive to whether it has to pay the full price (Cordes and Weisbrod 1979).

But even this appealing (at least to economists) rationale for just compensation does not explain why just compensation should be a *uniform* practice, one required by constitutions (and constitution-like common law practices), not just by legislation. The opportunity cost of many parcels of land that the government seeks to acquire (as in rural areas) is often lower than the transaction costs of acquiring the land. Allowing a government agency some discretion as to whether to pay would seem to be more efficient than a uniform just-compensation rule. Moreover, if governments are interested in efficient operations, they could command their agencies to incorporate market-based appraisals of the land they take into their calculations. Appraisal is in fact the typical method by which eminent domain trials are resolved, so there is nothing novel about this method.

The reader may be impatient with the author's obvious oversight in the previous analysis. The 'tax' on landowners in most eminent domain situations is in one important dimension completely unlike the general income tax to which it is compared. The uncompensated burden on landowners entails enormous horizontal inequities. Only a few landowners are selected to pay the tax (by government's failure to compensate them), and the tax often takes all of their asset, not just a small part of it. It is the nearly universal anxiety about such inequities, I submit, that has made some form of 'just compensation' the qualifier of eminent domain for all property, not just that which is elastic in supply.

Economists have given a puckish response to the horizontal equity argument. They ask why landowners should not be expected to insure against uncompensated takings (Blume and Rubinfeld 1984; Kaplow 1986). 'Just compensation' could be provided by policies from the Allstate Insurance Company as well as by all states. Perhaps just compensation should be granted by the government when landowners are in a poor position to purchase insurance or self-insure, but otherwise, goes this argument, why rely on the state for compensation?

The answer must be that the prospect of uncompensated takings presents an anxiety that is different from that which arises from other insurable events. Government takings of land are seldom randomly determined. The person whose land is taken without compensation thus perceives that his well-being is being deliberately subsumed to that of other members of the polity (Farber 1992). This is more profoundly alienating than either random losses of the same magnitude or systematically generated losses of the same magnitude from government-imposed burdens that are widely shared (Michelman 1967: 1217 & 1169 n.5; Fischel and Shapiro 1988). This proposition will be explored with an example that is seldom considered in the eminent domain context.

The military draft is a taking of young people's 'property' – their right to choose an occupation and domicile – with considerably less than what would pass in most other situations as 'just compensation' (Fischel 1996). Nor is this taking of the quotidian variety. Foregoing several years' private income (less the income of a private) very likely exceeds the value of property sacrificed by most owners subject to traditional eminent domain.

Military drafts are most readily accepted when they take almost everyone in the class deemed most suitable for military service. By most accounts, the military draft of American men during World War II did not generate much opposition. Nearly three-quarters of men of draft age were in fact inducted at some time during that conflict, so that few could argue that they were being singled out (Lee and McKenzie 1992). Opposition that eventually ended the draft came during the Vietnam War era, in which a much smaller fraction of eligible young men were required to fight. (Similar arguments might be advanced for the remaining example of conscription, jury service.)

Of course, it mattered that the net benefits of fighting World War II were widely regarded as being high, while the Vietnam War's benefits seemed both remote and problematical. But nonetheless, the acceptance of a large burden by draftees and their sympathizers during the earlier war suggests that it is not just the amount of the loss caused by eminent domain (in the traditional property context) that warrants just compensation. The perceived unfairness of deliberately concentrating public costs on a few landowners, even if it were insurable, must account for the nearly universal practice of compensation for land under eminent domain.

THE ECONOMIC FRAMEWORK OF DEMORALIZATION V. SETTLEMENT COSTS

The previous section attempted to account for why just compensation is both a uniform rule within countries and why almost all countries offer some form of just compensation when they take property. This section will place the previously-identified reasons for compensation in a more formal model, which was first developed by Frank Michelman (1967) and was elaborated by Fischel and Shapiro (1988) and Fischel (1995). The following section will employ this vocabulary to examine some prominent issues of eminent domain and just compensation.

Michelman's framework envisages the government contemplating projects such as a dam. He makes the supposition that the dam generates benefits in excess of costs. That is, he does not assume (at least not explicitly) that the purpose of just compensation is to guide the government away from undertaking inefficient projects. Once the dam passes the Kaldor–Hicks test, so that there are positive net benefits from the dam, the question is whether compensation should be paid to those adversely affected. That is, should the government apply something closer to the Pareto-superior test, in which there are no losers, or should it allow losses to fall where they may? (The invocation of Pareto's test is not exact because under eminent domain, losers are required to accept compensation rather than, as in the Pareto-superior rule, asked to give their consent.)

For a utilitarian government of the type that economists envisage, the question of whether to pay depends on the relative costs of paying versus not paying. Michelman dubs all of the costs to society of making compensation 'settlement costs'. For people familiar with law and economics terminology, these are the transaction costs of making compensation. To focus on the particular transaction costs of just compensation, I will divide settlement costs into three categories:

(a) *Procedural costs.* If the government pays, it endures the transaction costs that are endemic to eminent domain. Assessments of property values and the services of experts must be obtained. In the event that there are disputes about the amount that cannot be resolved by a referee process (Green 1988), a jury trial may ensue. Most government agencies that regularly acquire land are acutely aware of these costs (Stoebuck 1969).

(b) *Deadweight loss of taxes.* To the procedural costs must be added any additional deadweight losses from taxation (or deficit finance) that arise when government revenue must be raised to finance both the just compensation payments and the costs of the procedural mechanism endured by the government.

(c) *Moral hazard.* The prospect of compensation can induce landowners to game the system and otherwise behave in inefficient ways (Blume, Rubinfeld and Shapiro 1984). Moral hazard is the consequence of anticipating payments that are independent of one's behaviour. It is the same problem that economists analyse under the rubrics of tort and contract and which complicate the lives of insurance executives (Cooter 1985). The prospect of a damages remedy for tort and breach of contract discourages potential victims from taking precautions to avoid the harm.

Settlement costs are avoided if compensation is not paid. But nonpayment induces other unhappy results, which Michelman aggregates into a term called 'demoralization costs'. These may be divided into two categories: (a) suboptimal avoidance costs and (b) unfairness costs.

(a) *Avoidance.* Most obvious to economists are the avoidance costs of not compensating owners. Some were noted at the beginning of this essay as the deadweight losses of the 'tax' on landowners of not compensating. It is the drop in productive activity occasioned when owners of property realized that the fruits of their labour or investment could be snatched away. Not all drops in productive activity are suboptimal, however. Closing a polluting factory may cost some productive activity, but closure may be a desirable outcome if the pollution is sufficiently harmful and abatement costs are prohibitive. The prospect that the government will 'take' the factory by closing it down will deter some owners from opening factories. Thus the productive losses to be counted in demoralization costs are only the net losses in the value of 'goods' minus 'bads'.

Even if private owners could purchase insurance for uncompensated takings of productive activity, the additional costs of insurance (for a hazard that would not arise if the potential taker were a private citizen) would deter much private investment. Of course, people do insure against theft, but this is different from attempting to insure against legalized theft by the government. It is also true that domestic firms can insure against uncompensated expropriation by foreign governments. But that is different from having to insure against opportunistic actions by one's own government. Foreign governments are, for domestic firms, an exogenous factor. They can be regarded in many ways as external forces over which owners have no control and so can be insured against as random hazards.

(b) *Unfairness.* The other component of demoralization costs is the unfairness that owners feel even if the taking results in no inefficient avoidance activity, as might be the case in the government's taking of unimproved private land. As was noted in the previous section, the horizontal inequities of selective takings probably account for the near universality of compensation for land. Taking without compensation from the many (as in a nearly universal military draft) is less demoralizing. Thus a critical component of the 'unfairness' test is disproportionate, concentrated burden relative to other property owners who might reasonably be put in the same classification.

Michelman suggested that the unfairness aspects of demoralization costs are also likely to be higher under the following circumstances (1967: 1217–18):

(i) When losers suspect that government's supposedly favourable benefit–cost calculation works only if they are not compensated. This condition implicitly restores the precondition of a favourable benefit–cost calculation (the Kaldor–Hicks test) to Michelman's framework. The implication is that citizens in a democracy are more favourably disposed toward particular government projects (as distinct from general and purposive income redistribution) if they at least meet Kaldor–Hicks efficiency standards. The failure to meet the test raises demoralization costs and is thus injurious, if not fatal, to the government's decision not to compensate.

(ii) When the losers are members of a domestic group that is systematically disfranchised from participation in the government, so that they have little chance of recouping their losses through logrolling or other legitimate political activity now and in the future. Political disfranchisement of groups that democratic principles would ordinarily admit to the polity is in itself questionable, but further damage is done to members of such groups if they are not compensated for takings. I have suggested that the US Supreme Court's solicitousness for the property of American Indians (whose reservation-dwelling members do not vote in US elections) may be accounted for by this (*Hodel v. Irving*; Fischel 1995: 165).

(iii) When the costs of making compensation seem low, so that failure to compensate is not easily justified on the basis of settlement costs. The assumption here is that property owners are sympathetic to the argument that additional taxes and other settlement costs would be excessive if compensation were made. This again implies that citizens regard wasteful economic activity – here entailed by making compensation rather than by undertaking inefficient projects – as something to be avoided.

(iv) When the benefits of the project do not accrue to those not compensated, so that burdens are not offset by, as Justice Holmes called it, 'an average reciprocity of benefit' (*Pennsylvania Coal v. Mahon* 1922: 415). This condition looks at the distribution of benefits as well as the distribution of costs. In the earlier coal mining case to which Holmes was referring (and distinguishing the regulation at issue in *Pennsylvania Coal*), mine owners unarguably benefited as a group from a regulation that prevented mining in one area from causing flooding in adjacent mines. Examining only the substantial costs of the regulation to each owner would have overlooked the closely tied and substantial benefits to mine owners that flowed from the same regulation. Indeed, compensation for such regulation by general taxpayers might have unfairly enriched claimants and, in an elastic view of just compensation, been an unfair taking of taxpayers' assets (Epstein 1985: 295).

The economic calculation that results from Michelman's utilitarian framework is simply to minimize the sum of demoralization and settlements costs of the project, assuming its benefits exceed its costs. If demoralization from disappointed owners is too high, then endure the settlement costs; if settlement costs of offering compensation are too high, then endure the demoralization costs. More generally, the government should (policed by its constitution, courts, or its sense of rationality and fairness) maximize net benefits from all projects, where the three costs to be subtracted from gross benefits are ordinary opportunity costs, settlement costs, and demoralization costs.

The usefulness of this framework, particularly the vocabulary of settlement and demoralization costs, will be explored in the following section. I will attempt to explain the existence of some otherwise peculiar practices in the field of eminent domain and just compensation. All of these are offered in the context of American cases, rules, and history.

ISSUES THAT MAY BE ILLUMINATED BY THE MICHELMAN FRAMEWORK

Physical invasion v. regulation. The government is said always to be obliged to pay compensation when it causes a permanent physical invasion to occur. Building a public road on even a small corner of one's estate is held compensable, as is flooding from a dam or requiring an owner to tolerate hikers to cross one's land. The length of the doctrine's reach was suggested by a case that arose in New York City. The state required owners of apartment buildings to accommodate, without compensation, bread-box-sized, rooftop facilities for cable-TV companies. The US Supreme Court held that this was a compensable taking, notwithstanding the trivial nature of the physical invasion (*Loretto v. Teleprompter*).

Such a rule seems to assume that, for physical invasions, demoralization costs always exceed settlement costs. This seems peculiar for two reasons. One is that it is not true. It is widely accepted that governments can destroy private buildings without compensation in order to contain the spread of an urban conflagration (*Bowditch v. Boston*) or to prevent property from falling into enemy hands (*Respublica v. Sparhawk; US v. Caltex*). Destruction of property in such cases was surely more serious than affixing a cable-TV box on the roof.

The other and more important source of peculiarity is that the physical invasion rule is usually offered as a means of distinguishing the rule for regulations. Devaluation of property by burdensome regulations is seldom compensated in the United States and virtually never in the rest of the world (Ogus 1990). But this is an empty distinction, too. The government can often substitute regulation for acquisition, for example, by zoning for open space rather than buying land for a park. The government can also demand, as a condition for exceptions to its regulation, that the owner 'voluntarily' donate land to the government (*Nollan v. California Coastal Commission*; Epstein 1993).

A defence of the physical invasion test for compensation is that in most instances of physical invasion, settlement costs are low, at least compared to the settlement costs for regulatory takings of similar magnitude. One component of settlement costs is establishing exactly what the private owner has given up. By focusing on rights that can be measured in acres or hectares, the physical invasion standard reduces the settlement costs of eminent domain trials. Moreover, visible invasions by the government cause a special sense of personal demoralization that is perhaps lacking when only the police power of government is invoked, as in regulations. These reasons may explain why physical invasions, even trivial ones, are almost always compensable.

Few commentators, however, have put up convincing defences for the idea that physical invasion should be the *only* compensable event. The casebook characterization of property as a bundle of sticks, in which physical possession is only one of the sticks, makes it difficult for lawyers of even modest sophistication to maintain that government should pay when only one of those sticks – the right to be free of physical occupation by another – is foregone (Fischel 1995).

Alternatives to eminent domain. Governments are not compelled to invoke eminent domain. Most acquisitions of personal property (that is, property other than buildings and land) by the government do not differ from those in the private sector. The government goes out and purchases the resources it wants. High settlement costs (in this case, chiefly trial costs) by themselves encourage government agencies to use voluntary exchange in most situations where there are competitive markets.

The situation is different, however, when particular parcels of real estate are to be acquired. Because government agencies must develop site plans in the sunlight of public scrutiny, they cannot assemble contiguous parcels or purchase a key lot through the use of straw buyers, as modern developers often do. This leads to the potential for holdouts and protracted negotiations over economic rents, rather obvious settlement costs.

One much-cited study has demonstrated some of the high settlement costs (without using the term) of eminent domain (Munch 1976). Acquisition of Chicago real estate parcels for urban renewal projects generally compensated owners by about one-third more than market value. Much of the excess arose because owners of high-valued property tended to get proportionately larger settlements, apparently because they hired better lawyers.

Munch concluded that her results 'leave unproved' the superiority of eminent domain to market acquisition. She did not, however, address how actual governments dealing in the market might be able to overcome holdout problems. Many holdouts do not want to sell for any price, as may be shown by the amusing configuration of some large private properties whose developers lacked the power of eminent domain (Alpern and Durst 1984).

Evidence that eminent domain has few practical alternatives may be inferred from the academic debate about the merits of property rules, which allow owners to dictate the terms of trade (including refusal to trade at all), and liability rules, which allow owners only to collect financial compensation – usually determined as the market value of the asset (Calabresi and Melamed 1972; Krier and Schwab 1995). Eminent domain is the premier example of a liability rule. Private owners may refuse to sell to other private parties, but they must yield to the government if it offers compensation.

With only a few exceptions, law and economics scholars have concluded that liability rules are preferable for resolving multiparty private disputes (Kaplow and Shavell 1996). This suggests that eminent domain does not have many close substitutes for resolving multiparty strategic bargaining. It must also be noted again that the government can forgo the use of eminent domain and deal with property owners through the usual market mechanisms. That eminent domain continues to be used by practical-minded, budget-conscious government agencies that have a wide range of private options open to them is prima facie evidence that forced sales are a necessary power of government.

Public use. The takings clause of the US Constitution is the tail-end of the Fifth Amendment, which concludes, 'nor shall private property be taken for public use without just compensation'. Although it may not be immediately clear that 'public use' truly limits the government, many state constitutions make it clear that a limitation is intended. For example, New York's Constitution added to its requirement of just compensation for takings the following:

> The use of property for the drainage of swamp or agricultural lands is declared to be a public use, and general laws may be passed permitting the owners or occupants of swamp or agricultural lands to construct and maintain for the drainage thereof, necessary drains, ditches and dikes upon the lands of others . . .

I infer that the adoption of this amendment was occasioned by court interpretations that such laws were not for public use, and one may also suppose that private uses not enumerated as such remained outside the scope of eminent domain.

The public use limitation may be seen as an attempt to add a constraint on government action because 'just compensation' does not cover all the interests affected. The economic framework proposed in the first section regards eminent domain as a contest between two potential sets of taxpayers. If compensation is paid, the general public bears the cost; if compensation is not paid, property owners bear the tax.

But suppose that both sets of potential taxpayers were concerned, at some constitutional moment, that government officials would pose the dilemma too often. Officials may be detached from the political process and thus be inclined to advance public projects that, on balance, do not provide net benefits for either taxpayers at large or property owners. The same inefficient decisions might result from excessive influence by interest-groups in government decisions. In anticipation of such possibilities, constitution-framers might want to impose some limits on eminent domain that are not imposed on the political process as a whole. In this light, the public use provisions may be intended as a special barrier against rent seeking by government officials and special interest groups.

One problem with the public use limitation is drawing the lines. Economists make a distinction between public goods and private goods, the former having the characteristic of being available for all if they are provided for one and being consumable by additional citizens without subtracting from the enjoyment of any other. Richard Epstein (1985: 166) has proposed that the public use qualification in eminent domain should be interpreted as allowing forced acquisition only if it involves the provision of a public good.

The trouble with Epstein's economic translation of public use is not that it contradicts the apparent intent of constitution makers. The trouble is the same that any professor of economics has in explaining the difference between a private good and a public good to bright undergraduates. National defence falls neatly into the category of public goods, while hamburgers do not. But what about the vast number of other activities that are only partially non-rival in consumption, such as rural highways, or for which exclusion is possible but costly, such as outdoor public art? Perhaps as a result of such line-drawing problems, few American courts invoke the public use doctrine any longer (*Hawaii Housing Authority v. Midkiff*).

Despite this washing of hands by the judges, however, explicit condemnation of property and transferring it to other private parties is relatively uncommon. One reason is suggested by Thomas Merrill (1986). Eminent domain itself has substantial transaction costs aside from the deadweight loss of taxation. In situations lacking a holdout problem, it is cheaper for most legislatures and agencies to buy property on the open market. Thus the procedural demands of eminent domain can in most cases be relied upon to deter the government from forcing sales when the private market is a viable alternative.

I suggest another reason why the public use doctrine has declined and is less troublesome to courts than it once was. The economic role of government – both state and federal – is much larger than it was before the Great Depression. The US court system is also far more deferential to transparently special-interest legislation (*US v. Carolene Products*; *Williamson v. Lee Optical*). As a result of their enormous increase in economic control, politicians no longer find eminent domain as attractive as it once was. If the government wishes to confer an advantage on individuals in order to garner political support, it nowadays has a host of ways to do so. Tax breaks, pork-barrel projects, and exceptions to regulations are generally much less costly (to the government) than instituting eminent domain proceedings, for which tax money must be paid.

Outright taking from one private party to give to another private party also has the disadvantage to the government of being open, and thus subject to a level of public scrutiny that can be embarrassing to both the government and the beneficiary. In one of the most notorious cases, the city of Detroit was permitted by the Michigan courts to use its power of eminent domain to acquire land for a private automobile plant (*Poletown v. Detroit* 1981). In doing so, it dispossessed residents of a well-established ethnic neighbourhood, albeit with compensation. Both Detroit and General Motors have been roundly criticized for this action from both ends of the political spectrum (Paul 1987; Schultz 1992). Given such political costs plus the more ordinary settlement costs of eminent domain, it seems likely that courts will have few occasions to call upon the public use requirement.

Moral hazard. Although there are few practical alternatives to using eminent domain to deal with holdout problems in real estate, settlement costs remain. Moral hazard, as mentioned earlier, is one aspect of these costs. There have been instances of landowners subdividing or otherwise enhancing their property solely to increase eminent domain awards. Less dramatic instances of moral hazard arise because landowners simply ignore the probability that their land will be taken, given that just compensation will be paid in any event.

In an efficient world, landowners who anticipate that the government will build a road across their property next year should not erect buildings there. Knowledge that the government will pay will induce owners to discount such contingencies and result in a waste of capital if the government must remove it from the site. Although some scholars have questioned how large the moral hazard problem is in relation to the costs of not compensating (Burrows 1991; Usher 1995), it has been the principal basis for academic questioning of the fundamental merits of paying just compensation and the inspiration for some imaginative alternatives (Blume and Rubinfeld 1984; Hermalin 1995; Miceli and Segerson 1996).

The moral hazard problem has typically been analysed as an aspect of settlement costs. That is, if the government is committed to compensate (and thus endure settlement costs and avoid demoralization costs), property owners may behave in morally hazardous ways. More recently, however, economists have begun to analyse moral hazard as an aspect of demoralization costs (Dana 1995; Riddiough 1997).

Instead of arising when the government does pay, this moral hazard on the part of landowners arises when property owners respond to the realization that they will not be compensated. Apartment owners who anticipate the adoption of stringent rent controls have been known to tear buildings down so that they would not be compelled to subsidize renters. Owners of buildings likely to be designated as historic treasures (without offsetting benefits or compensation) have demolished them before the rules take effect (Fischel 1985: 174). Such inefficient destruction of capital might have been forestalled if regulations were compensable. Moral hazard does not always cut against compensation.

The benefit-offset principle. The benefit-offset principle holds that owners whose property is partially taken may have their compensation reduced by the amount that the remaining property increases in value. If a roadway is cut through the centre one-third of Ms Adam's property, the government may be able to reduce the amount it owes her for the taking by the increase (if any) of the remaining two-thirds of her property. This practice is symmetrical with the idea of 'severance damages'. If Ms Adam's remaining property is reduced in value by having the roadway split it in two (for example, by making both remaining parcels substandard in size), the government owes her for the value of the land it takes plus the reduction in value of her remaining land. In both cases, the property owner is left in the same financial condition that she was before the government acted.

The use of benefit offsets became controversial by the middle of the nineteenth century (Scheiber 1973). Railroad builders, lent the power of eminent domain by states eager for better transportation, would take part of a rural landowner's property for the right of way. Courts would deduct from the amount owed as 'just compensation' the increase in value of the remaining land. Because early rail lines usually greatly increased the value of all territory that they served, the landowner's remaining property was often much more valuable than the entire tract had been before the railroad arrived. This practice often resulted in nominal compensation awards of $1.

Many commentators have regarded the benefit offset as a subsidy to railroads, with the implication that it resulted in excessive railroad development (Horwitz 1977). But this is not necessarily so. Public projects that especially benefit a particular geographic area are often best financed by increments in land value that result from those projects (Pines and Weiss 1976). To the extent that railroad developers could not internalize all the benefits of the existence of a railroad through passenger and freight charges, obtaining additional revenue by, in effect, taxing affected landowners is not immediately offensive to economic principles.

The problem with the benefit offset was not that it was a subsidy, but that it was not enough of a subsidy. Nearby landowners whose property was not taken by the railroad generally benefited from its existence as much as those whose property was actually taken. To tax those who actually surrendered some property but collect nothing from those who did not seemed unfair. It was for this reason that many state constitutions were amended to eliminate the benefit-offset practice (Cooley 1890: 702). For example, the revised Ohio Constitution of 1850 declared that 'where private property shall be taken for public use, a compensation therefore shall first be made in money . . . without deduction for benefits to any property of the owner.'

Within Michelman's demoralization/settlement cost framework, the benefit offset illustrates how a practice that reduced one component of settlement cost (the deadweight loss of general taxation or other means of financing railroads) happened to increase demoralization costs (the unfairness of being singled out to bear a disproportionate share of the cost). The popular revolt against the benefit offset occurred in a political society that was dominated by landowners who were eager for railroads (Freyer 1981). This may be taken as another illustration of the power of the disproportionate-burden component of demoralization cost.

Exactions. Landowners who seek permission to develop are often faced with demands by municipal authorities to pay 'exactions' (Altshuler and Gómez-Ibáñez 1993). Exactions are in lieu of having the developers themselves put in roads, sewers, and other additional public infrastructure that is deemed by authorities to be warranted by the project. Exactions are usually assessed on a case-by-case basis, but some municipalities have regularized them by establishing a schedule of 'impact fees' to be applied to categories of development.

The problem with exactions is that the government may use them as an occasion to extract some of the landowner's value from the project for the benefit of citizens at large. As in other areas of eminent domain, the most pressing issue is disproportionate burden. Suppose permission to build would increase the land's value by $100,000. Expenditures by the builder of $30,000 would leave the community in no worse position – in terms of congestion of public facilities and neighbourhood effects – than it was without the development. The community might nonetheless attempt to extract some of the $70,000 increment by means of exactions.

The obvious reason that such practices are controversial is that they take private property without compensation. If there were no external constraint on the practice, municipalities may be tempted, especially when the landowner is a stranger to their polity, to extract all incremental land values for the benefit of local residents. While general, community-wide land-value taxation may be equitable and efficient (Oates and Schwab 1997), exactions represent selective taxes whose disproportionate burden increases demoralization costs (Sterk 1988).

The US Supreme Court has attempted to limit the scope of exactions, and its formulations of doctrine in this area are far more concrete than in other areas of regulatory takings. It has, supposedly following the practice of a majority of states, demanded that exactions be no more than a payment (in cash on in kind) which is 'roughly proportionate' to that needed to alleviate the otherwise external costs of the project (*Dolan v. Tigard*). If a commercial building causes additional traffic, the owner may be charged the portion of the cost of a new road that is attributable to her project. She may not be charged for benefits to the public at large.

Whether this supposed restatement of state rules by the US Court will result in more equitable exaction policies at the local level remains to be seen. The hazard of court limitations on the terms of trade between governments and landowners is that it could foreclose some mutually desirable exchanges. Exactions can verge into takings, but prohibiting them altogether would eliminate an important transactions medium by which much development gets done (Gyourko 1991; Fischel 1995: 341).

Adequacy of market compensation. Market value has almost always been the standard for 'just compensation'. One line of criticism holds that governments often fail to tender what would normally be paid when two private parties exchange property, notwithstanding the previously mentioned evidence of overpayment found by Munch (1976). The government sometimes denies compensation for off-site damages and intangible losses. It also often refuses compensation for neighbourhood blight flowing from abandonment by tenants in the face of condemnation (Kanner 1973). Many (not all) of these failures have been remedied by legislation, but intellectual arguments about the shortfalls of compensation persist. They have focused on the inadequacies of market values, even if fully paid, to make owners whole.

The most obvious fault is that financial compensation does not cover non-financial attachments to property. These can take the form of personal and neighbourhood attachments. Indeed, there is a logical case that perfectly appraised market compensation is inadequate in almost all cases. If the owner had wanted to sell the property, it would already have been on the market. Only if there were a coincidence of timing between owner's desire to sell and the government's desire to purchase would market value fully compensate.

It is sometimes suggested that the undercompensation inherent in market value should be offset by a premium. Epstein (1985: 4) argues that the purpose of compensation should be to maintain each owner's share of the total wealth. Suppose there are two owners in the polity. Initially, A owns $100 of the wealth and B owns $200 of the wealth. The government proposes a wealth-enhancing project that will add $99 to total wealth. Epstein submits that compensation should be arranged so that after all is said and done, A should own $133 and B should own $266, which preserves the initial 1:2 ratio of A's wealth to B's.

Epstein's criterion is more stringent than that of Pareto superiority, which would be satisfied in the previous example if either A or B got all of the $99 increment in wealth, or any combination that left neither party worse off than before. Epstein does not rigorously insist on this share-preserving idea in his subsequent discussions of takings and eminent domain, but it is interesting to note that the criticism of the benefit-offset principle discussed above is akin to his criterion. Courts that reduced compensation for a partial taking by the amount of the gain in value on the remainder of the property were meeting the Pareto superiority test. That state constitution makers and other lawgivers eventually ended much of this practice suggests that Epstein's 'super-Pareto-superior' rule has some popular appeal.

The more frequent arguments for compensation above market value stem from notions akin to consumers' surplus. The government should offer extra compensation when personal values are at issue, as in residential acquisition or for properties for which there are poor substitutes (Knetsch 1983; Radin 1984). Some scholars, anticipating that such a scheme would raise the settlement costs of acquiring land as residents overstated their personal attachments, have suggested simply offering a fixed premium for eminent domain (Ellickson 1973: 736). The premium would reflect some estimate of the average consumers' (and producers'?) surplus from having to surrender their property.

Once again, however, it is impossible to escape the offsetting costs. While the premium would quell some demoralization costs, it would raise settlement costs, especially the moral hazard problem. If the premium were large enough, landowners might lobby government planners to steer the project in their direction, which could lead to even more inefficiency. It is surely for these reasons that experiments with compensation for more than market value, such as that of New Hampshire, are anecdotal (*Head v. Amoskeag* 1885: 14).

CONCLUSION: RULES VERSUS DISCRETION

This essay has reviewed eminent domain and just compensation law and theory from the perspective of an economic analysis first developed by Frank Michelman, whose utilitarian framework is akin to the optimal taxation approach. Michelman's criteria, which balance the benefits of government projects against three distinct types of costs, are of the same calculus that drives economic analysis. Economists may nonetheless be uncomfortable with the approach because it casts the question of compensation in terms of balancing one cost (demoralization) against another (settlement), whose elements are often difficult to determine in advance.

Susan Rose-Ackerman perhaps best summarized economists' impatience with a process that even its defenders refer to as 'ad hoc balancing'. She titled her comment on a later paper by Michelman (1988): 'Against ad hocery: a comment on Michelman'. She argued therein that 'even a very imperfect, but clearly articulated, formal takings doctrine is likely to be superior to open-ended balancing' (Rose-Ackerman 1988: 1697). She went on to sketch some principles that might characterize such firm rules, but her main point was that it is better to have firm rules than to be constantly balancing things. Commitment to even imperfect rules allows property owners to plan and to assist the government in keeping its promises (Kydland and Prescott 1977).

The analysis in the present essay should not be construed as an argument against Rose-Ackerman's programme. What I have tried to show is that Michelman's framework can give a useful positive account of why certain rules have developed and, sometimes, faded away. It is also a framework for normatively evaluating suggested reforms in these practices. As an operational system, however, there is no doubt that rules have many utilitarian advantages over discretion. The nearly talismanic rule of compensation for physical invasions may seem questionable when explored on a case-by-case basis, but few would deny that it has great value as a formal rule.

Yet I do not want to give away too much to formal rules. This relevance relates to the other reason why economists are often uncomfortable with Michelman's framework. Its demoralization costs include, in addition to the usual losses of future production from excessive precaution, a special feeling of outrage by disappointed claimants who regard themselves as unfairly treated. It is not just risk aversion, which could, of course, be covered by insurance. It is that special feeling that makes us feel differently about accidentally losing a valued possession and having it stolen. It is perhaps related to the reason that almost all societies distinguish between negligent homicide and murder. Having one's well-being deliberately subsumed to that of others involves a greater anxiety than randomly generated harms.

It is for reasons such as these that judges, whether operating under a formal constitution or not, have to be able to invoke a balancing rule even where formal rules are relatively simple and clear. I have sat on a local zoning board for ten years. Zoning boards are the 'quasi-judicial' administrative bodies that grant minor exceptions to land use regulations. They are the lowest courts in the land, bound by a detailed document. Yet hardly a month passes without the need to consider extenuating circumstances and unclear rules and, yes, unfair implications of clear rules. Even at the lowest and seemingly least complicated level of dispute resolution, 'balancing – or, better, the judicial practice of situated judgment or practical reason – is not law's antithesis but a part of law's essence' (Michelman 1988: 1629).

WILLIAM A. FISCHEL

See also COMPENSATION FOR REGULATORY TAKINGS; HOLDOUTS; INALIENABILITY; KALDOR–HICKS COMPENSATION; LAND DEVELOPMENT CONTROLS; LAND-USE DOCTRINES; MARKETS AND INCOMMENSURABILITY; PROPERTY RIGHTS IN PRISONERS OF WAR; RENT CONTROL; TAKINGS; TRESPASS AND NUISANCE.

Subject classification: 3b; 3c; 6c(iv).

CASES

Bowditch v. Boston, 101 US 16 (1879).
Dolan v. Tigard, 512 US 687 (1994).
Hawaii Housing Authority v. Midkiff, 467 US 229 (1984).
Head v. Amoskeag Manufacturing Co., 113 US 9 (1885).
Hodel v. Irving, 481 US 704 (1987).
Loretto v. Teleprompter Manhattan CATV Corp., 458 US 419 (1982).
Nollan v. California Coastal Commission, 483 US 825 (1987).
Pennsylvania Coal Co. v. Mahon, 260 US 393 (1922).
Poletown Neighborhood Council v. Detroit, 304 NW2d 455 (Mich. 1981).
Respublica v. Sparhawk, 1 US 357 (Pa 1788).
US v. Caltex (Philippines), Inc., 344 US 149 (1952).
US v. Carolene Products Co., 304 US 144 (1938).
Williamson v. Lee Optical of Oklahoma, Inc., 348 US 483 (1955).

BIBLIOGRAPHY

Alpern, A. and Durst, S. 1984. *Holdouts!* New York: McGraw-Hill.

Altshuler, A.A. and Gómez-Ibáñez, J.A. 1993. *Regulation for Revenue: The Political Economy of Land Use Exactions*. Cambridge, MA: Lincoln Institute of Land Policy.

Been, V. 1991. 'Exit' as a constraint on land use exactions: rethinking the unconstitutional conditions doctrine. *Columbia Law Review* 91: 473–545.

Blume, L.E. and Rubinfeld, D.L. 1984. Compensation for takings. *California Law Review* 72: 569–628.

Blume, L.E., Rubinfeld, D.L. and Shapiro, P. 1984. The taking of land: when should compensation be paid? *Quarterly Journal of Economics* 99: 71–92.

Burrows, P. 1991. Compensation for compulsory acquisition. *Land Economics* 67: 49–63.

Calabresi, G. and Melamed, A.D. 1972. Property rules, liability rules, and inalienability: one view of the cathedral. *Harvard Law Review* 85: 1089–1128.

Cooley, T.M. 1890. *A Treatise on the Constitutional Limitations Which Rest Upon the Legislative Power of the States of the American Union* 6th edn, Boston: Little, Brown.

Cooter, R. 1985. Unity in tort, contract and property: the model of precaution. *California Law Review* 73: 1–51.

Cordes, J.J. and Weisbrod, B.A. 1979. Government behavior in response to compensation requirements. *Journal of Public Economics* 11: 47–58.

Dana, D.A. 1995. Natural preservation and the race to develop. *University of Pennsylvania Law Review* 143: 655–708.

Ellickson, R.C. 1973. Alternatives to zoning: covenants, nuisance rules, and fines as land use controls. *University of Chicago Law Review* 40: 681–782.

Ely, J.W., Jr. 1992. *The Guardian of Every Other Right: A Constitutional History of Property Rights*. New York: Oxford University Press.

Epstein, R.A. 1985. *Takings: Private Property and the Power of Eminent Domain*. Cambridge MA: Harvard University Press.

Epstein, R.A. 1993. *Bargaining with the State*. Princeton: Princeton University Press.

Farber, D.A. 1992. Economic analysis and just compensation. *International Review of Law and Economics* 12: 125–38.

Fischel, W.A. 1985. *The Economics of Zoning Laws*. Baltimore: Johns Hopkins University Press.

Fischel, W.A. 1995. *Regulatory Takings: Law, Economics, and Politics*. Cambridge, MA: Harvard University Press.

Fischel, W.A. 1996. The political economy of just compensation: lessons from the military draft for the takings issue. *Harvard Journal of Law and Public Policy* 20: 23–63.

Fischel, W.A. and Shapiro, P. 1988. Takings, insurance, and Michelman: comments on economic interpretations of 'just compensation' law. *Journal of Legal Studies* 17: 269–93.

Freyer, T. 1981. Reassessing the impact of eminent domain in early American economic development. *Wisconsin Law Review* 1981: 1263–86.

Garner, J.F. (ed.). 1975. *Compensation for Compulsory Purchase: A Comparative Study*. London: United Kingdom National Committee of Comparative Law.

Green, G.H. 1988. Mediating eminent domain awards: a state-by-state review of refereeing practices. *Appraisal Journal* 56: 381–90.

Gyourko, J. 1991. Impact fees, exclusionary zoning, and the density of new development. *Journal of Urban Economics* 30: 242–56.

Hermalin, B.E. 1995. An economic analysis of takings. *Journal of Law, Economics, and Organization* 11: 64–86.

Horwitz, M.J. 1977. *The Transformation of American Law, 1780–1860*. Cambridge, MA: Harvard University Press.

Kanner, G. 1973. Condemnation blight: just how just is just compensation? *Notre Dame Lawyer* 48: 765–810.

Kaplow, L. 1986. An economic analysis of legal transitions. *Harvard Law Review* 99: 509–617.

Kaplow, L. and Shavell, S. 1996. Property rules versus liability rules: an economic analysis. *Harvard Law Review* 109: 715–90.

Knetsch, J.L. 1983. *Property Rights and Compensation: Compulsory Acquisition and Other Losses*. Toronto: Butterworths.

Krier, J.E. and Schwab, S.J. 1995. Property rules and liability rules: the cathedral in another light. *NYU Law Review* 70: 440–83.

Kydland, F.E. and Prescott, E.C. 1977. Rules rather than discretion: the inconsistency of optimal plans. *Journal of Political Economy* 85: 473–91.

Lee, D.R. and McKenzie, R.B. 1992. Reexamination of the relative efficiency of the draft and the all-volunteer army. *Southern Economic Journal* 58: 644–54.

Levmore, S. 1991. Takings, torts, and special interests. *Virginia Law Review* 77: 1333–68.

Merrill, T.W. 1986. The economics of public use. *Cornell Law Review* 72: 61–116.

Michelman, F.I. 1967. Property, utility, and fairness: comments on the ethical foundations of 'just compensation' law. *Harvard Law Review* 80: 1165–1258.

Michelman, F.I. 1988. Takings, 1987. *Columbia Law Review* 88: 1600–1629.

Miceli, T.J. and Segerson, K. 1996. *Compensation for Regulatory Takings: An Economic Analysis with Applications*. Greenwich, CT: JAI Press.

Munch, P. 1976. An economic analysis of eminent domain. *Journal of Political Economy* 84: 473–97.

Oates, W.E. and Schwab, R.M. 1997. The impact of urban land taxation: the Pittsburgh experience. *National Tax Journal* 50: 1–22.

Ogus, A. 1990. Property rights and freedom of economic activity. In *Constitutionalism and Rights: The Influence of the United States Constitution Abroad*, ed. L. Henkin and A. Rosenthal, New York: Columbia University Press.

Paul, E.F. 1987. *Property Rights and Eminent Domain*. New Brunswick: Transaction Books

Pines, D. and Weiss, Y. 1976. Land improvement projects and land values. *Journal of Urban Economics* 3: 1–13.

Radin, M.J. 1984. Property and personhood. *Stanford Law Review* 34: 957–1015.

Riddiough, T.J. 1997. The economic consequences of regulatory taking risk on land value and development activity. *Journal of Urban Economics* 41: 56–77.

Rose-Ackerman, S. 1988. Against ad hocery: a comment on Michelman. *Columbia Law Review* 88: 1697–1711.

Scheiber, H.N. 1973. Property law, expropriation, and resource allocation by government: the United States 1789–1910. *Journal of Economic History* 33: 232–51.

Schultz, D.A. 1992. *Property, Power and American Democracy*. New Brunswick: Transaction Publishers.

Sterk, S.E. 1988. Nollan, Henry George, and exactions. *Columbia Law Review* 88: 1731–51.

Stoebuck, W.B. 1969. The property right of access versus the power of eminent domain. *Texas Law Review* 47: 733–65.

Stoebuck, W.B. 1972. A general theory of eminent domain. *Washington Law Review* 47: 553–608.

Usher, D. 1995. Victimization, rent-seeking and just compensation. *Public Choice* 83: 1–20.

employee ownership of firms. Once considered largely either a theoretical curiosity or an ideological aspiration, employee ownership of enterprise has attracted considerable interest in recent years as a practical matter of organization. In the West, this interest derives in considerable part from the decline of unionism and the resulting search for other means of assuring efficiency and equity in labour contracting, while in the East, interest in worker ownership has been stimulated by the rapid collapse of state socialism and the subsequent search for market-oriented ownership structures that stop short of a direct leap into full finance capitalism.

1. VARIETIES OF EMPLOYEE PARTICIPATION. Ownership of a firm involves two rights: (1) the right to control the firm (which, in a large firm, may take the somewhat attenuated form of a right to vote in electing the firm's directors and on major corporate transactions); and (2) the right to receive the firm's residual earnings. In any given firm, employees may participate in either or both of these rights to a greater or lesser degree. The term 'employee ownership' has been used to refer to a variety of different arrangements of this character. For purposes of economic analysis, it is helpful to differentiate somewhat among these arrangements.

Direct employee ownership. To begin with, there are firms in which rights to votes and earnings are apportioned among employees directly according to the amount of work they contribute to the firm. The most straightforward way to organize such a firm is as a cooperative corporation or as a partnership, although a stock corporation can be employed as well, with shareholdings manipulated to maintain proportionality to the amount of work contributed rather than the amount of capital.

In principle it is possible to form a firm with only partial employee ownership of this sort – the remaining ownership rights being given, say, to investors of capital. But such a structure is unusual among large firms – that is, those with substantial numbers of employee owners – for important reasons explored below. For this reason, and to avoid ambiguity, the term 'direct employee ownership' will be used here to refer only to firms that are fully employee owned – that is, in which ownership of the firm is entirely in the hands of some or all of its employees.

Direct employee ownership is rare in the industrial sectors of most economies. In the United States, the most conspicuous exception is plywood manufacturing, where a number of relatively small worker-cooperatives have together maintained substantial market share over many decades.

In contrast, direct employee ownership is quite common in the service sector. In particular, firms of this character have long been the dominant mode of organization in professional services, such as law, accounting and management consulting. To be sure, ownership of these firms is typically not shared among all of the firm's employees, but rather is confined to professionals, and even then is awarded only to those who have survived a period of apprenticeship. Within any given firm, however, those professionals may number in the hundreds, and even in the thousands. Moreover, it is not just in professional service firms that ownership is confined to a subset of the firm's employees, but rather in nearly all firms that exhibit direct employee ownership – a significant fact to which we shall return.

Outside the professions, there are several other service sectors in which direct employee ownership is relatively common. One of these is transportation – including bus services, taxicab services and trucking – where firms are often owned collectively by their drivers.

Employee stock ownership. An alternative method for giving earnings and control to workers is to structure the firm as a conventional investor-owned business corporation, in which votes and earnings are allocated according to amounts invested, and then sell some or all of the stock to the firm's employees.

A reductive form of this approach, in which senior executives of corporations are compensated with stock or stock options, has long been routine in the United States. In more recent years, management buyouts, in which senior executives acquire a controlling share in their firms, have also become common. Though the distinction is a bit artificial, we shall not be concerned here with managerial ownership of this sort. Rather – whether discussing employee stock ownership or direct employee ownership – the term 'employee ownership' will be used here to refer only to situations in which ownership is shared by a substantial fraction of a firm's workforce.

Over the past twenty-five years, employee ownership through stock purchase has become common in US industry, principally in the form of deferred compensation plans such as ESOPs (employee stock ownership plans), in which stock is deposited in a trust fund that holds the stock for the benefit of the firm's employees, frequently as the reserve fund for the employee's pensions. In most firms with such plans, employee stock ownership extends to only a minority share of the firm's stock. It is estimated, however, that there are roughly 1,000 firms in the United States in which a majority of the outstanding shares are held in ESOPs.

While the fraction of a firm's stock held in such plans is a reasonably accurate reflection of the extent to which employees participate in the firm's earnings, the degree of effective control that employees achieve is generally much smaller. One reason for this is that ESOPs that hold a substantial fraction of an employer's stock are typically found in closely held firms in which – as is permitted by the relevant pension and tax law – the stock held by the ESOP is voted by the trustee of the ESOP rather than by the employees, and the firm's managers appoint the ESOP trustee. Perhaps for this reason, nonmanagerial employee representatives are only rarely found on boards of directors in firms with ESOPs.

Earnings rights only. Employees sometimes have sole claim on a firm's net earnings but no control. For example, the most successful recent experiments with large-scale employee-owned industrial enterprise in Britain, the ICOM cooperatives, were structured with beneficial employee ownership of this sort, the firms being managed on behalf of their workers by autonomous trustees who are not elected by the workers.

A partial share in earnings with no control can be found in investor-owned firms with profit-sharing plans. This is also effectively the situation in many firms with ESOPs, as we have noted.

Control rights only. The reverse pattern, in which employees are given a share in control while having no claim on the firm's residual earnings, can also be found. The most conspicuous example is the worker codetermination that is imposed on all large German firms by law, in which employee representatives are given half the seats on a firm's (upper-tier) board of directors. A more modest version of this approach has been adopted in the Scandinavian countries, where employees have a right to between one and three seats on a firm's board.

II. BENEFITS OF EMPLOYEE OWNERSHIP. Employee ownership, like any form of ownership, has both benefits and costs, and these must be balanced against each other to determine when that form of ownership is efficient (see OWNERSHIP OF THE FIRM). We begin with the potential benefits.

Employee incentives. Employees are often difficult to monitor, with the result that there is a degree of moral hazard in contracting for all but the simplest forms of labour. It is often suggested that employee ownership – and perhaps merely participation in earnings without control – can mitigate this problem by giving employees a greater stake in the fruits of their labour. Of course, where employees are numerous, individual employees bear only a trivial fraction of the costs of their own shirking even with full employee ownership. But incentives for workers to monitor each other are also augmented by employee ownership. Moreover, ownership – especially of publicly traded stock, with its clear price signals – might yield productivity gains simply by making the firm's overall performance more salient to the workers. The effects of employee ownership on productivity are therefore difficult to predict *a priori*. The empirical evidence to date, though substantial, is inconclusive, suggesting but not confirming that there may be modest productivity gains from partial or full worker ownership (see Blasi and Kruse 1991).

The incentive argument has also led to the claim that employee ownership should be expected in those industries in which employees are hardest to monitor (e.g., Alchian and Demsetz 1972). While there may be some support for this claim if one considers only *beneficial* employee ownership, in which employees participate in earnings but not control, so far as direct employee ownership is concerned the observed pattern is just the reverse. Employee ownership is most commonly found among the types of workers – such as lawyers and truck drivers – whose individual productivity can be, and often is, monitored remarkably closely. Conversely, direct employee ownership is extremely rare in settings where individual productivity is extremely hard to measure, as where employees work in large teams or have extensive supervisory or managerial tasks.

Firm-specific investments. Employees must sometimes make substantial investments whose value can be maintained only if they continue to work for their current employer. These firm-specific investments may be job-related, such as the acquisition of skills or knowledge specialized to the employer, or they may be personal, such as the establishment of strong roots in the local community. Investments of this character create the potential for exploitation by the employer, who may be able to capture their value through lower wages or inferior working conditions. And workers, foreseeing this, may take costly measures to avoid such vulnerability – for example, by refusing to make investments that would otherwise be valuable to them or their employer.

Employee ownership – or at least direct employee ownership, in which the employees actually control the firm – holds the promise of mitigating these contracting problems by removing much of the firm's incentive to exploit its employees' firm-specific investments, and has sometimes been advocated on these grounds (see Blair 1995). As it is, however, direct employee ownership seems seldom to serve this purpose, since it is typically found in industries where employees have unusually generic skills and are highly mobile – as, again, in the case of lawyers and truck drivers.

Strategic bargaining. In industries where employees are unionized, there is a potential for strategic bargaining behaviour between employees and the firm that can result in costly strikes or lockouts and in inefficient wage bargains. Employee participation in earnings can reduce the incentive for such behaviour by aligning the financial interests of workers and the firm more closely, and employee participation in control can mitigate both the informational asymmetries that give rise to strategic behaviour and the willingness of the parties to exploit them.

This consideration is surely important in transactional uses of employee ownership, discussed below. It may also be an advantage of employee participation in earnings, and of employee seats on the board of directors such as those provided for in Scandinavian and German law. It does not, however, seem much of a stimulus for direct employee ownership, which is generally found in firms and industries where unions do not play an important role.

Monitoring managers. As compared to the anonymous and fragmented investors who share ownership of many publicly traded firms, employees have the potential advantage of being reasonably effective monitors of a firm's managers. Employees have substantial knowledge of the firm and its personnel simply by virtue of their jobs; they have a large personal stake in the efficiency with which the firm is managed; and they can be organized relatively easily for collective action. Consequently, one might expect employee ownership to economize on the agency costs of delegated management.

As a rule, however, the only firms in which employees exercise a meaningful degree of control are relatively small firms in which the agency costs of delegated management would be modest even under investor ownership. In large firms, as we have noted, employees often participate significantly in earnings, but rarely are given any meaningful role in governance. Or at least this is true outside of those jurisdictions, such as Germany, where worker participation in governance is mandated by law.

III. COSTS OF EMPLOYEE OWNERSHIP. From the preceding we see that, while employee ownership holds the promise of both (1) reducing the costs of labour contracting – by increasing incentives for worker productivity, protecting employees' firm-specific investments, and reducing the costs of strategic bargaining – and (2) reducing the agency costs of delegated management, in practice employee ownership, and particularly employee control, is found most commonly in situations in which these costs are relatively modest. Consequently, if survival in the marketplace is an indication of efficiency, there must be some countervailing costs of employee ownership that are more important than these potential benefits.

Raising capital. When employees own a firm, they have two alternatives for raising capital: borrow it, or provide it themselves. The costs of both methods are likely to be higher than are the costs to an investor-owned firm of raising capital from its investor-owners. The costs of borrowing are likely to be high because the lenders will be concerned that the worker-owners might behave opportunistically, appropriating some or all of the borrowed funds through excessive wages or investments that sacrifice profit for employment. The costs of raising capital from the employees themselves, in turn, are likely to be high because of the substantial illiquidity and risk that this imposes on the employees.

These capital costs presumably help explain why direct employee ownership is far more common in the service sector than in the industrial sector. Yet there is substantial evidence that capital costs are not the most serious obstacle to employee ownership. Some service industries with substantial direct employee ownership, such as investment banking, are capital intensive. The largest and most successful employee-owned industrial firm in the world, the group of affiliated worker cooperatives in Mondragon, Spain, has not had difficulty raising capital and has in fact become a net lender; and employees in many US industries have been willing to invest heavily in their own firms through ESOPs even without obtaining thereby a meaningful role in firm governance.

Risk-bearing. In any firm in which employees have full ownership, and also in firms in which employees participate only in earnings and not control, the employees must bear some or all of the residual risk associated with the enterprise. Because of their inability to diversify their sources of income by working for a number of firms simultaneously, employees are generally in a worse position to bear this risk than are investors of capital, and thus poor risk-bearing is another cost of employee ownership. This cost is particularly high, of course, in capital-intensive firms, where employees must either lever their net earnings through borrowing or else sacrifice investment diversification by investing their own savings in the firm.

Yet risk-bearing, even more than the related problem of capital supply, does not in itself seem to be a major obstacle to employee ownership. For example, the only US industry with substantial direct employee ownership, plywood manufacturing, is both moderately capital intensive and highly volatile. Likewise, poor risk-bearing has not prevented employees from investing heavily in their own employers through ESOPs. Moreover, at least in the United States, employees commonly bear a substantial share of the risk even in investor-owned firms, which have traditionally placed a high premium on paying a constant shareholder dividend while at the same time hiring and firing workers with some liberality.

Collective decision-making. We noted above that, in important respects, employees are often in a better position to oversee a firm's managers than are investors. But investors have – or can be structured to have – one important advantage in governing a firm that employees generally lack: substantial unanimity of interest.

Employees' interests can diverge concerning many aspects of a firm's operations. Most obviously, employees are likely to differ among themselves concerning the relative wages they are to be paid. Likewise, employees may differ concerning working conditions, the kind and amount of work each is assigned, and – when things go poorly – which jobs are to be eliminated and who is to be laid off. Older workers, who are generally more risk-averse and who will generally have more capital invested in the firm, may also differ with younger workers over both the desirable level of risk for new investments and the appropriate division of the firm's earnings between labour and capital. These and other differences of interest among a firm's employees are likely to grow, moreover, as the division of labour and diversity of tasks within a firm increase.

Conflicting interests among a firm's employees can make employee governance costly in two ways. First, they can increase the costs of the decision-making process by increasing the time and effort needed to achieve a workable consensus. Second, they can increase the likelihood that substantive decisions made by the firm will be inefficient, reflecting disproportionately the interests of a controlling group or constituting an awkward compromise between different interests.

The resulting costs – the costs of collective decision-making – appear to play a crucial role in determining when and where employees participate in firm governance, suggesting strongly that these costs commonly dominate the other costs and benefits of employee ownership surveyed here.

To begin with, direct employee ownership is typically found only where there is substantial homogeneity of interest among the employees involved. The employees who participate in ownership commonly do similar work within the firm and have similar kinds and levels of skill, and rarely exercise much hierarchical authority over each other. This is conspicuous in professional service firms: the partners in a law firm, for example, are all lawyers of similar skill and productivity who work more or less independently of each other; rarely does one partner exercise much supervisory authority over another. Similarly, the semi-skilled worker-owners in the US plywood cooperatives are unspecialized, and commonly rotate among the jobs in the firm; the firm's manager, who is the only employee who has different skills and performs a conspicuously different role, is commonly not a member of the cooperative but rather is hired on a salaried basis. The drivers who own the transportation cooperatives are yet another obvious example.

Furthermore, firms with full employee ownership typically adopt strategies – sometimes at conspicuous cost – to reduce potential conflicts of interest among the employee-owners. For example, many US law firms, including some of the most prominent and prosperous, use lock-step compensation schemes in which a partner's earnings are determined solely by the number of years he has been with the firm – a scheme that gives up all financial incentives for productivity for the sole purpose, it would seem, of avoiding costly conflicts among the partners over division of earnings. The plywood cooperatives also generally allocate earnings equally and, as noted, rotate jobs rather than encourage specialization.

Finally, firms with substantial employee participation in earnings typically involve little employee participation in control if there is significant heterogeneity of interest among the firm's employees – as, for example, where there is substantial division of labour. Thus, as we have noted, the large British industrial cooperatives have been run on behalf of their employees by autonomous trustees whom the employees do not elect. Likewise, the many US firms that have adopted ESOPs rarely provide for meaningful employee participation in control. Of course, in the latter situations, in which outside investors typically retain a substantial ownership stake, employee participation in governance would be attended not only by the complications arising from diversity of interest among the employees, but more seriously by divisions between the employees and the investors, and this is presumably another important reason such participation is rare. (A conspicuous recent exception to the general pattern is United Air Lines where, following a recent partial employee buyout, a meaningful sharing of control between employees and investors has been attempted – though, as noted below, this is a transaction-driven structure that may prove only a temporary expedient.)

If capital liquidity or risk-bearing were more important obstacles to employee ownership than the costs of collective decision-making, one would expect to see the reverse pattern: substantial employee participation in control, but little participation in earnings or in the provision of financial capital. The only place one finds the latter pattern, however, is in codetermined firms in Germany. The fact that codetermination is imposed in Germany by law, that nothing like it has been adopted by firms in jurisdictions where it is not mandated, and that it is so much at variance with the general pattern of employee participation observed elsewhere, all suggest that codetermination is relatively inefficient as a form of corporate governance. This conclusion is consistent, moreover, with other features of German corporate management, such as the weakness of the supervisory boards of directors on which employee representatives sit, and the fact that many important decisions concerning matters of employment are not made by that board, but rather are made at a lower level by the works councils or at a higher level through industry-wide collective bargaining.

IV. EMPLOYEE OWNERSHIP AS A TRANSACTIONAL EXPEDIENT. Employee ownership has played a special role in restructuring firms that require substantial concessions from their employees to remain viable. In the early 1990s, for example, several of the leading firms in the US airline industry gave large blocks of stock to their employees in return for wage and work-rule concessions that the airlines needed from their unionized workers to compete successfully following deregulation (see Gordon 1995). The most noteworthy of these transactions was undertaken by United Air Lines, in which two unions – one representing the airline's 7,000 pilots and the other representing most of the rest of the firm's employees – obtained for the employees 55% of the firm's stock, held primarily in ESOPs.

Giving employees stock in return for their concessions in these transactions has several important advantages. Management's willingness to offer stock is credible evidence that givebacks are truly necessary for the firm's health. Further, stock ownership guarantees the employees that, if the firm succeeds as a result of the concessions, they will receive a well-defined proportion of the resulting gains. And, if continued participation in ownership proves unattractive once the crisis has passed, the employees remain free to sell their ownership stake and reinvest their funds elsewhere.

Similar considerations arguably underlay the Russian government's decision to give employees a substantial ownership stake in former state enterprises when they were privatized: this was a uniquely simple and credible way of assuring employees that they would share in the benefits of privatization, and not simply bear its costs.

All of this suggests, of course, that these arrangements may only be temporary, and that the extent of worker ownership in these firms will decrease over time.

V. IS SURVIVORSHIP A GOOD TEST? The discussion here has proceeded on the assumption that survival is a reasonable test of the efficiency of employee ownership. In general, that assumption seems sound. There are, to be sure, subsidies and regulations that affect the pattern of ownership that we observe. Nearly all of these favour employee ownership. In the United States, for example, these advantages include exemption from corporate taxation for firms with direct employee ownership; special tax privileges for ESOPs; and a prohibition on investor-owned law firms. If these and other forms of legal favouritism were removed, there would almost surely be less employee ownership, but it would probably appear in roughly the same types of firms, and take roughly the same forms, as it does now. And with some exceptions, such as German codetermination and employee stock ownership in privatized Russian firms, much the same seems true of other countries as well – a conclusion reinforced by the fact that the observed pattern of employee ownership is similar in its basic features across all developed economies.

Consequently, it seems reasonable to infer that this pattern is roughly efficient. True employee ownership, in which employees participate meaningfully both in earnings and control, is quite effective in a broad range of circumstances so long as control of the firm can be placed in the hands of a class of employees who have highly homogeneous interests. But where, as is common, this condition cannot be met, other forms of ownership have the advantage.

HENRY HANSMANN

See also ASSET RESTRUCTURING AND UNION BARGAINING; COMPARATIVE CORPORATE GOVERNANCE; LAW FIRMS; OWNERSHIP OF THE FIRM; PARTNERSHIP; PROFESSIONAL CORPORATIONS AND LIMITED LIABILITY; REGULATION OF THE PROFESSIONS; RESIDUAL RIGHTS OF CONTROL.

Subject classification: 5g(i); 6c(v).

BIBLIOGRAPHY

Alchian, A. and Demsetz, H. 1972. Production, information costs, and economic organization. *American Economic Review* 62: 777–95.

Blair, M. 1995. *Ownership and Control*. Washington, DC: The Brookings Institution.

Blasi, J and Kruse, D. 1991. *The New Owners: The Mass Emergence of Employee Ownership in Public Companies and What It Means to American Business*. New York: HarperBusiness.

Blasi, J. and Shleifer, A. 1996. Corporate governance in Russia: an initial look. In *Corporate Governance in Central Europe and Russia, Vol 1: Banks, Funds, and Foreign Investors*, ed. R. Frydman, C. Gray and A. Rapaczynski, Budapest: Central European University Press.

Bonin, J., Jones, D. and Putterman, L. 1993. Theoretical and empirical studies of producer cooperatives: will ever the twain meet? *Journal of Economic Literature* 31: 1290– 1320.

Gordon, J. 1995. Employee stock ownership as a transitional device: the case of the airline industry. In *The Handbook of Airline Economics*, ed. D. Jenkins, New York: McGraw Hill.

Hansmann, H. 1990. When does worker ownership work? ESOPs, law firms, codetermination, and economic democracy. *Yale Law Journal* 99: 1749–1816.

Hansmann, H. 1996. *The Ownership of Enterprise*. Cambridge, MA: Harvard University Press.

employment contract law

employment contract law. Traditionally, scholars of the employment relationship have focused on legal developments in the unionized sector of the economy – a field that American lawyers commonly call 'labor law'. In recent decades, however, US union membership as a percentage of total employment has plummeted. The relative importance of 'labor law' as a field has declined, and both courts and legislatures have developed countless new legal rules affecting the nonunion workplace. As a result, a distinct field of 'employment law' has arisen that focuses on individual employment rights rather than on the problems associated with collective bargaining. Employment contract law is an important element of this new field.

For nearly a century, a virtually irrefutable presumption that employers could terminate employment contracts 'at will' made American contract law an unpromising source of legal rights for non-union employees. More recently, however, state courts have relied upon employee handbooks, oral assurances, and other circumstances to extend contractual protection against discharge. This flurry of cases and an increasingly lively academic debate among employment law scholars have fuelled a renewed interest in the law governing nonunion employment contracts.

NON-UNION EMPLOYMENT CONTRACT PRACTICES. In theory, formal written contracts might govern a wide range of employment terms including wages, hours, working conditions, promotion, discipline, and termination. Indeed, federal statutes such as the Fair Labor Standards Act and the Employee Retirement Income Security Act contain complex regulatory provisions concerning critical matters such as wages, hours, and benefits. Union collective bargaining agreements similarly specify in great detail the terms and conditions of employment and provide arbitral procedures for resolving grievances. In stark contrast, only a small proportion of non-union employees negotiates and executes a formal written contract (see Verkerke 1995).

Despite the absence of formal contracts, employers nevertheless use a variety of written documents to structure the employment relationship. Indeed, the majority of companies issue an employee handbook or personnel policy manual that establishes expectations for employee performance. Many firms also include contractually significant terms in employment applications or offer letters. Increasingly, courts have begun to give such statements binding effect. However, these decidedly incomplete expressions of contractual intent leave many important issues unspecified. And incumbent employees are far less likely than those who have been discharged to assert their legal rights in a judicial forum (see Donohue and Siegelman 1991). As a result, contract law exerts remarkably little constraint during the term of employment. Thus, for example, nonunion employers typically have a unilateral right to modify wages, benefits, and working conditions. Instead, employment contract law focuses almost exclusively on two issues: the duration of the contract and the rules governing its termination.

The duration of an employment contract may be for a definite term (e.g., five years) or the parties may agree to an employment relationship that will continue for an indefinite period. Definite term contracts predominate in some industries and occupations. School teachers, for example, commonly work under one-year term contracts, and business executives often have individual contracts extending for a three- to five-year term. However, the overwhelming majority of employees have no contractual agreement concerning the duration of their employment. Indefinite term employment is thus by far the most common arrangement (see Verkerke 1995). In keeping with this empirical predominance, employment contract law has focused principally on providing rules governing the termination of these indefinite term contracts.

THE AT-WILL PRESUMPTION AND ITS EROSION. Beginning in the late nineteenth century, US courts began to presume that a hiring for an indefinite period was terminable 'for good cause, for no cause or even for cause morally wrong' (see *Payne v. Western & Atlantic R.R.*). Commonly called the 'employment-at-will' rule, this approach to employment contracts gives employers wide latitude to terminate indefinite term employment relationships and freedom from judicial scrutiny of their discharge decisions.

Although the rule itself is clear enough, its historical origins are clouded in controversy. Critics contend that Horace Gay Wood, a prolific treatise writer of the period, pronounced the at-will rule widely accepted at a time when more careful analysts would have described the law as unsettled (see, e.g., Feinman 1976, 1991). They also claim that courts subsequently embraced Wood's at-will rule in order to promote industrial development and to protect the economic power of business owners. However, other commentators have defended Wood's reading of the contemporary case law (Freed and Polsby 1990) and questioned the connection between industrial development and the adoption of the at-will rule (Morriss 1994). Whatever one's position in this historical debate, there can be no doubt that by the early 1900s the at-will presumption had become firmly established throughout the United States.

In recent years, however, judges, legislators and legal scholars have actively debated whether this presumption should be maintained, modified or eliminated altogether. During its heyday, the at-will rule virtually barred employees from attempting to prove that an employer had promised some measure of job security. In most jurisdictions, however, employees may now argue that written disciplinary policies, oral statements, and various other assurances of job security provide contractual protection against discharge for other than just cause (see Postic 1994). These doctrinal innovations have left the at-will rule significantly eroded.

The most widely accepted doctrinal erosion of the at-will rule enforces the terms of an employee handbook or a policy manual as an implied contract. In *Toussaint v. Blue Cross & Blue Shield*, for example, the employer's handbook stated that it was the 'policy' of the company to discharge employees 'for just cause only'. The Michigan Supreme Court held that this statement was enforceable as a contractual promise limiting the employer's power to terminate the contract. Many other jurisdictions have similarly indicated that written assurances of job security contained in employment manuals or other documents can be enforced despite the indefinite term of the resulting employment contract (see Postic 1994). Indeed, only Florida and Missouri have unequivocally rejected the argument that an employee handbook can form an indefinite term just cause contract.

In all of the jurisdictions that enforce handbook provisions, a closely related doctrine enforces written disclaimers and confirmations of at-will status. Thus, employers who wish to avoid extending just cause protection can quite easily restore the at-will presumption. They may include language explaining that handbook disciplinary standards and procedures are not intended to form an employment contract and that those policies may be varied at the discretion of the employer. For more reliable protection, they can confirm expressly that employees may be 'terminated at any time with or without cause'. The available empirical evidence shows that such a confirmation of at-will status is the most commonly used written term governing discharge (see Verkerke 1995).

Although less widely accepted than the enforceability of employee handbook provisions, most courts will also consider claims involving oral assurances of job security. Courts have thus enforced informal oral commitments not to discharge an employee without good cause. By far the most formidable barrier to such claims is the Statute of Frauds. The Statute bars enforcement of contracts that cannot be performed within one year unless the parties memorialize their agreement in a signed writing. In a number of jurisdictions, this rule bars any attempt to prove an oral agreement to form an indefinite term just cause contract (see Postic 1994). In the majority of states, however, courts consider such claims, relying on the fact that the employee may quit or die before the end of a year or that the employee has rendered part performance under the asserted contract (see, e.g., *Burton v. Atomic Workers Federal Credit Union*). But even those courts that entertain contract claims based on oral statements appear to demand proof of more specific assurances of job security than if the same statements were in writing.

Although no other doctrinal erosions are as widely accepted as employee handbook and oral assurance claims, several other theories have found occasional success. For example, individuals sometimes move their families long distances, give up secure employment, or incur other substantial costs to accept a new position. Some courts protect the 'reasonable reliance' of such recent movers for a 'reasonable time' against their new employer's arbitrary decision to rescind an offer of employment or to discharge them (see, e.g., *Grouse v. Group Health Plan, Inc.*). However, many other courts have rejected similar claims (see, e.g., *Romack v. Public Service Co.*). Similarly, long-term career employees form a strong bond with one company and rely heavily on their prospects for continued employment. Thus, in some jurisdictions, an employee's longevity of service may be relevant to finding an implied just cause contract (see, e.g., *Pugh v. See's Candies, Inc.*). But in most it is not (see Verkerke 1995). Finally, a few courts scrutinize all employment terminations under a general good faith standard (see, e.g., *Crenshaw v. Bozeman Deaconess Hospital*). However, the overwhelming majority of jurisdictions have rejected this theory (see Postic 1994).

As this abbreviated account no doubt suggests, existing employment contract law has a somewhat chaotic character. Nevertheless, it is possible to identify two significant unifying tendencies. First, the central feature of existing law is dramatic jurisdictional variation. States divide roughly into liberal, conservative, and centrist jurisdictions. In liberal jurisdictions, courts recognize a broad array of exceptions to employment-at-will and tend generally to construe alleged assurances of job security in favour of employees. Conservative jurisdictions exhibit opposite tendencies, strictly limiting doctrinal erosions of the at-will rule and finding virtually all employer statements unenforceable. Between these two extremes, a large number of states pursue a more or less centrist approach to employment contract law, typically recognizing some but not all of the new doctrinal theories.

Focusing principally on the centrists, one can identify a second important unifying tendency. Courts in these jurisdictions ordinarily decide cases according to whether employment documents or alleged oral assurances are sufficiently definite and specific to contract around the at-will default. Courts ruling against discharged employees almost always explain that the alleged assurances were too vague or generalized to be construed as a promise. In contrast, the same courts, in upholding other employees' claims, emphasize that a reasonable person would understand the employer's definite and specific language as a legally enforceable commitment. Thus, a traditional focus on the objective meaning of alleged contractual assurances animates most decisions in this area.

As we have seen, the strict at-will rule has been eroded past the point of recognition. An overwhelming majority of courts now entertain claims that would have had absolutely no chance of success during the heyday of the at-will presumption. Nevertheless, courts in virtually every American jurisdiction continue to presume that an indefinite term employment contract is terminable at will by either party. Indeed, despite confident predictions of the doctrine's imminent demise, courts have steadfastly refused to jettison the at-will presumption. Thus, even the most vociferous critics of employment-at-will must acknowledge its pervasive and durable role in the judicial consideration of employment contracts.

THE JUST CAUSE DEBATE. There remains then a significant normative question: Is employment-at-will with all of its erosions a desirable legal default rule? A growing scholarly literature debates whether lawmakers should instead adopt a just cause standard for the termination of nonunion employment contracts. Early arguments for just cause rested primarily on intuitive moral notions of fairness and on general complaints about inequality of bargaining power (see, e.g., Peck 1979). Although these arguments had, and continue to have, a certain rhetorical force, their proponents never offered a rigorous account of what 'bargaining power' meant and how 'fairness' should determine case outcomes. So long as such critical terms remain ill specified, these arguments provide a profoundly ambiguous foundation for legal policy.

These same commentators often compared the at-will regime unfavourably to the just cause protection commonly contained in union collective bargaining agreements. Many critics have also noted that employment laws in most other industrialized countries mandate far more generous protections against discharge (see, e.g., Beermann and Singer 1989). To a great extent, however, such comparative arguments beg the fundamental policy question of whether a judicially enforceable just cause standard is superior to the at-will alternative. They also tend to ignore fundamental differences between union and nonunion employment and between foreign and domestic economic performance (see Estreicher 1985, Freed and Polsby 1989, Verkerke 1995).

More recently though, both advocates of a just cause standard and defenders of employment-at-will have displayed an increasing technical sophistication in their arguments. Indeed, it is fair to say that economic theory now structures the academic debate. The economics literature on internal labour markets, theories based on the economics of information, and a nascent empirical literature are the most influential strains in current employment contract scholarship.

Internal labour markets. Economists have theorized that within an internal labour market firms pay career employees supra-competitive efficiency wages. More precisely, some models of this relationship call for late-career employees to receive wages greater than their marginal product in exchange for having produced a marginal product greater than their wage during midcareer. This deferred compensation bonds workers to the firm, thus allowing the firm to invest in providing firm-specific training that increases productivity. The threat of losing the late-career bonus also powerfully deters employees from shirking.

Drawing on an extensive literature describing the implicit bargain that firms offer to these career employees, Stewart Schwab argues that courts should provide 'life-cycle just cause' protection (Schwab 1993). He contends that workers are most vulnerable to opportunistic discharge at the beginning and end of their careers. Thus, courts should offer protection to early career workers who have incurred some substantial cost in accepting a new job. An at-will relationship is appropriate during the midcareer period. However, late-career workers have fulfilled their part of an implicit life-cycle bargain and deserve protection against opportunistic discharge.

By selectively examining leading cases in several different jurisdictions, one can construct a pattern of decisions consistent with the life-cycle just cause approach (Schwab 1993). However, the theory ultimately fails as a positive description of existing law (Verkerke 1995). In fact, longevity of service plays at most a subsidiary role in contemporary employment contract law. Courts rely instead on traditional legal analysis of employment documents and other assurances. As we have seen, the presence or absence of contractual protection against discharge depends most often on the definiteness and specificity of the alleged assurances of job security.

The normative case for life-cycle just cause is also questionable (see Verkerke 1995). Private employers might well conclude that having an informal understanding about career employment enhances productivity. However, Schwab's approach would transform an implicit self-enforcing agreement into a judicially enforceable contract. Critical elements of the resulting 'contract' are far too uncertain for judicial enforcement. For example, the life-cycle rule conditions important employment rights on the transition from one stage of the career to the next. It seems extraordinarily unlikely that courts can obtain adequate information to determine, even roughly, when a career employee's productivity dips below his or her current wage. Moreover, it would be extremely difficult to define what just cause should mean under a life-cycle contract. Schwab would protect late-career workers against being fired for 'slowing down' or 'failing to pull their weight' or 'being paid more than they are worth'. However, each of these vague statements could also describe a late-career employee who has breached his or her side of the implicit contract by shirking under the cover of the life-cycle just cause standard for discharge. Finally, the recent statutory prohibition on mandatory retirement and the utter lack of empirical evidence identifying occupations or industries in which firm-specific human capital is important make it doubtful that courts would be able to determine to which employment relationships a life-cycle just cause rule should apply.

In fact far from supporting legal intervention, the existence of an internal labour market with its own set of norms governing discharge substantially undermines the case for legally enforceable just cause protection. Edward Rock and Michael Wachter argue that the difficulty of administering a just cause standard explains a seeming paradox of nonunion employment relationships (see Rock and Wachter 1996). Employers carefully preserve their legal right to discharge employees at will. Simultaneously, however, they structure their internal disciplinary procedures to ensure that employment terminations occur only for good cause. Firms can ill afford to develop a reputation for treating employees unfairly, and they must particularly guard against the devastating effects that arbitrary discipline would have on internal morale and productivity. In short, Rock and Wachter contend that a self-enforcing just cause norm protects nonunion workers. The existence of this norm dramatically reduces the marginal benefit that employees might obtain from legally enforceable just cause protection and undermines the case for adopting such a just cause rule.

One can fairly object that Rock and Wachter base their argument on stylized facts rather than on a rigorous empirical investigation of the role of norms in the internal labour market. However, no one can deny that norms are a tremendously powerful force in structuring workplace relations. Rock and Wachter have identified a critically important disciplinary norm that warrants further investigation.

The many problems associated with a legally enforceable just cause standard have led other scholars to consider alternative means for protecting long-term career employees. One possible approach, proposed by Samuel Issacharoff, would be to create a mandatory severance pay obligation (Issacharoff 1996). Terminated workers would receive severance pay calculated as some multiple of their years of service. Issacharoff would also establish an administrative procedure for resolving any disputes that arise. Severance payments would be excused, as under the unemployment compensation system, whenever an employer can prove that a worker was discharged for wilful misconduct.

This more stringent 'wilful misconduct' standard for avoiding severance payments silences objections based on the difficulty of defining life-cycle just cause. Similarly, the challenging problem of determining when late-career protection begins gives way to an automatic formula for computing the amount due to a terminated employee. However, concerns about the proper scope for the rule and the prohibition on mandatory retirement remain. Moreover, legally mandated severance payments diminish the sanction available to deter shirking under long-term employment contracts. Career employees could conceivably take advantage of the rule by engaging in misbehaviour or work slowdowns short of wilful misconduct. Employers would then be faced with a difficult choice between tolerating lower productivity or discharging the worker and paying a substantial severance payment. To the extent that the right to severance payments becomes vested and invariant to an employee's level of effort, deferred compensation loses its ability to motivate employees.

The political feasibility of such a severance system is also an interesting question. In more liberal jurisdictions, employers might willingly exchange their uncertain liability under the common law for a more predictable monetary severance payment. A calculation of precisely this sort led Montana employers to support a statutory good cause standard to replace the unpredictable and expansive tort doctrine of good faith and fair dealing that the state's courts had begun to develop. However, in most centrist jurisdictions, it seems likely that employers would resist efforts to impose a mandatory severance pay regime.

The economics of information. Informational problems of two types – cognitive and strategic – have also produced important arguments for just cause protection. Many commentators have argued that workers misperceive the value of just cause protection (see, e.g. Issacharoff 1996). The theory of cognitive dissonance suggests that newly hired workers will ignore the unpleasant possibility that they may someday be unjustly discharged. Similarly, prospect theory teaches us that workers may underestimate the expected losses from relatively remote, low probability events such as discharge.

Although these are plausible cognitive biases, equally plausible errors might well lead workers to make the opposite mistake. It is unpleasant to be guilty of the sort of misconduct that would justify a disciplinary discharge. Thus, the theory of cognitive dissonance suggests that workers will be overly optimistic about their job performance. Somewhat surprisingly, this optimism leads them to *overvalue* just cause protection. More formally, let $p(D)$ equal the true probability of discharge and $p(C|D)$ equal the probability that there exists just cause for a given discharge. Assuming for the sake of simplicity that judicial processes are costless and perfectly accurate, the value of just cause protection will be a positive function $V(\cdot)$ of the quantity $p(D)\cdot(1 - p(C|D))$. Underestimating $p(D)$ therefore reduces an employee's estimate of the expected value of just cause protection, $E(V)$. But underestimating $p(C|D)$ has the opposite effect and creates an upward bias in the estimate of $E(V)$. Thus, the relationship between the employee's estimate of $E(V)$ and its true value depends on the relative magnitude of the two errors. There is no *a priori* basis for concluding that one or the other misperception will dominate.

If, however, the employee sets $p(D)$ to zero, then he or she will completely discount the value of just cause protection and no amount of bias in the estimate of $p(J|D)$ can counteract the misperception. This possibility provides a potential justification for legal intervention, but no mere default rule can hope to overcome the inefficient consequences of these worker misperceptions. Lawmakers must instead adopt a mandatory rule. Otherwise, misguided workers would readily agree to waive just cause protection that they find valueless. However, such a policy prescription requires an extremely strong sense of paternalistic certainty about employees' 'true' preferences. Establishing the existence of significant cognitive problems is only the first step in justifying intervention. Proponents of such a mandatory just cause rule must also bear the burden of demonstrating that a majority of workers in fact value just cause protection at more than its cost. The existing evidence for this underlying preference is equivocal at best.

A second type of informational problem may arise when employers are less well informed than job applicants are about the applicants' productivity. Employers generally cannot know, and an applicant may often know, whether he or she is highly productive and motivated or instead less productive and more prone to shirk. This asymmetric information about productivity can produce two strategic barriers to workers' efforts to contract for just cause protection: signalling and adverse selection. Whether an employer has just cause for discharge is imperfectly verifiable. As a result, a legally enforceable just cause requirement provides a form of 'insurance' against discharge, including discharges for unverifiable shirking. This 'insurance' is most valuable to those comparatively unproductive workers who expect to be discharged. In a signalling model, job applicants thus choose not to bargain for job security because they fear that employers will interpret their requests as a signal of low productivity. Similarly, adverse selection could occur if those firms offering just cause contracts find that this protection against discharge tends to attract less motivated and competent workers.

Several commentators have argued that these strategic informational problems explain why nonunion workers fail to contract for just cause protection (see Levine 1991, Kamiat 1996). However, it is quite unlikely that either signalling or adverse selection explains the predominance of at-will contracts. First, the signalling problem is formally symmetric. According to the theory, employers should be equally concerned that their refusal to provide legally enforceable just cause protection will signal that they are unusually prone to discharge employees for arbitrary and unfair reasons. Proponents of the signalling model have thus far failed to resolve this inherent ambiguity. The model produces determinate predictions only if employers can safely ignore the possibility that their own behaviour signals their type.

Second, the signalling model presumes that, in the absence of strategic informational problems, workers would engage in individual negotiations concerning job security. It is difficult to evaluate such a counterfactual proposition. However, the available evidence concerning other important aspects of the nonunion employment contract makes such individual negotiations seem quite improbable. Job applicants seldom bargain in any meaningful sense about most terms and conditions of employment. It seems unlikely that signalling problems explain why workers so seldom obtain individualized treatment in their employment contract. Indeed, if the need to standardize employment terms across the workforce is compelling for matters as diverse as wage scales, benefits, vacation policies, and parking arrangements, then one should expect similar uniformity for terms governing discharge. Indeed, as critics of the at-will regime have long complained, nonunion employment contracts consist mostly of take-it-or-leave-it terms. The fear of signalling that one is a shirker could theoretically deter an applicant from inquiring about just cause protection. However, the structure of employment contracts in the nonunion sector suggests strongly that even in the absence of these fears, such individual bargaining would rarely ever take place. With no serious prospect of individual negotiation, there is simply no opportunity for signalling.

Strategic informational problems still might explain the absence of just cause terms if employers' fear of adverse selection prevented them from offering contractual job security. However, several inconvenient empirical facts make such theoretical speculation implausible. First, union collective bargaining agreements typically provide just cause protection, but union employers manage to maintain a reasonable level of productivity. Even more troubling for the adverse selection argument is empirical evidence indicating that a significant number of nonunion employers offer just cause protection (Verkerke 1995). In a sample of 220 employers, roughly 15% indicated that they intended to provide legally enforceable just cause protection to their employees. The existence of these voluntary just cause contracts contradicts the fundamental premise of the adverse selection argument. Contrary to the theory, perfectly ordinary employers seem quite willing and able to select productive workers without fear that just cause protection will attract a disproportionate share of shirkers.

Finally, it is worth noting that any legal effort to overcome strategic informational problems would almost certainly require a mandatory just cause rule. For example, if we assume that applicants but not employers must worry about signalling, then a default rule of just cause protection is unlikely to affect contractual behaviour. Employers could quite easily frustrate the purpose of adopting such a rule by imposing a routine requirement that all newly hired employees execute an express confirmation of at-will status. Any employee who refused to sign such an agreement would send precisely the same signal of low productivity that the model indicates a request for just cause protection now entails. Thus, as in the case of legal measures designed to remedy cognitive errors, the proponent of legal reform should be required to show more than the existence of a barrier to free contracting. Advocates of a mandatory rule must also demonstrate that workers value just cause protection at more than its cost.

Empirical investigation of employment contracts. Despite its growing technical sophistication, the theoretical debate over just cause reforms has proven difficult to resolve. Many fundamental disagreements between critics and defenders of the at-will rule are ultimately disputes about empirical assumptions – about how the world actually works. As we have seen in discussing the adverse selection model, evidence on actual contract practices sometimes allows us to test the predictions of theoretical arguments for legally enforceable just cause protection. A new empirical literature, now in its infancy, seeks to provide data relevant to these questions.

In earlier work, I conducted a preliminary survey of nonunion employment contract practices (Verkerke 1995). In a sample of 220 employers from five different states, express at-will contracts predominated. However, a significant fraction of employers (15%) chose to provide legally enforceable just cause protection. Approximately one-third of all employers had no written terms governing discharge. Using data on the characteristics of employers who contracted expressly, I used a multinomial logit model to predict what type of contract those employers who had not contracted expressly would choose. The results of this statistical exercise supported the prevailing at-will default rule. No statistically identifiable subgroup of employers or employees has revealed a market preference for just cause protection. Finally, the article examined a number of theoretical arguments for legal reform. In each case, I analysed whether the observed pattern of contracting behaviour was consistent or inconsistent with the assumptions underlying those arguments. Although it is important to emphasize the relatively small sample size and the somewhat tentative nature of these conclusions, I found no support for the empirical implications of these theoretical arguments for just cause protection.

Work such as mine, defending the at-will rule, generally assumes that workers are reasonably well informed about their lack of legal protection under an employment-at-will contract. I was able to offer only indirect evidence that workers such as attorneys, who presumably know the prevailing legal rules governing termination, seem to form at-will contracts at the same rate as those whom we would expect to be less knowledgeable. In order to examine this assumption more directly, Pauline Kim recently tested terminated workers applying for Missouri unemployment insurance benefits about their knowledge of employment law principles relevant to job security (Kim 1997). Kim found that her subjects substantially overestimated the extent of their legal protection against discharge.

These results present an important challenge to theories that depend on contrary informational assumptions. If employees are so poorly informed about the legal rules governing employment terminations, then it is much harder to argue that they will accurately determine the value of contractual just cause protection. Future empirical work should seek to confirm these findings using a population of recently employed rather than recently terminated employees. It is possible that employment termination itself influences workers' attitudes and beliefs about their legal rights. A follow-up study might also attempt to refine the method for distinguishing generally accepted workplace norms and workers' moral beliefs from their expectations about legal rules and litigation outcomes. Even Kim's careful cautionary instructions may have been insufficient to overcome respondents' overwhelming tendency to view employment terminations as an ethical rather than as legal matter.

If further investigation confirms that employees systematically overestimate their legal protections against discharge, we will have to determine whether these findings justify legal reform. The informal just cause norm that Rock and Wachter have identified suggests that employees enjoy considerable, though legally unenforceable, protection against unjust discharge. In light of this norm, the expected returns from litigation might simply be too low to make it worthwhile for employees to learn the intricacies of employment contract law. Thus, as we have seen before, identifying a potential market failure falls far short of establishing the case for reform. Nevertheless, Kim's results rightly focus attention on the extent of employees' legal knowledge. Future work will need to consider more carefully how contract rules influence what employees know about their legal rights.

CONCLUSION. Scholars of employment contract law have thus far focused almost exclusively on whether just cause or at-will is a better legal rule for the termination of indefinite term contracts. Their attention has produced a fascinating theoretical debate that draws on sophisticated internal labour market models and on the economics of information. More recently, a valuable empirical literature has begun to address the same question. Like the field of employment law of which it is a part, however, the study of employment contracts is at an early stage of its development. One interested in discovering where the truth lies can only hope that the future brings us more and better empirical work. Nevertheless, the case has yet to be made convincingly for displacing the traditional default rule of employment at will.

J. HOULT VERKERKE

See also ARBITRATION; ASSET RESTRUCTURING AND UNION BARGAINING; DISCRIMINATION IN EMPLOYMENT; MINIMUM WAGE REGULATION; STATUTE OF FRAUDS.

Subject classification: 5c(iii); 6c(v).

CASES

Burton v. Atomic Workers Federal Credit Union, 803 P2d 518 (Idaho 1990).

Crenshaw v. Bozeman Deaconess Hospital, 693 P2d 487 (Mont. 1984).

Grouse v. Group Health Plan, Inc., 306 NW2d 114 (Minn. 1981).

Payne v. Western & Atlantic R.R., 81 Tenn. 507, 519 (Tenn. 1884).

Pugh v. See's Candies, Inc., 171 Cal. Rptr 917 (Cal. 1981).

Romack v. Public Service Co. of Indiana, 499 NE2d 768 (Ind. 1986).

Toussaint v. Blue Cross & Blue Shield of Michigan, 292 NW2d 880 (Mich. 1980).

BIBLIOGRAPHY

Beermann, J.M. and Singer, J.W. 1989. Baseline questions in legal reasoning: the example of property in jobs. *Georgia Law Review* 23: 911–95.

Donohue, J.J. and Siegelman, P. 1991. The changing nature of employment discrimination litigation. *Stanford Law Review* 43: 983–1033.

Estreicher, S. 1985. Unjust dismissal laws: some cautionary notes. *American Journal of Comparative Law* 33: 310–23.

Feinman, J.M. 1976. The development of the employment at will rule. *American Journal of Legal History* 20: 118–35.

Feinman, J.M. 1991. The development of the employment-at-will rule revisited. *Arizona State Law Journal* 23: 733–40.

Freed, M.G. and Polsby, D.D. 1989. Just cause for termination rules and economic efficiency. *Emory Law Journal* 38: 1097–1144.

Freed, M.G. and Polsby, D.D. 1990. The doubtful provenance of 'Wood's Rule' revisited. *Arizona State Law Journal* 22: 551–58.

Issacharoff, S. 1996. Contracting for employment: the limited return of the common law. *Texas Law Review* 74: 1783–1812.

Kamiat, W. 1996. Labor and lemons: efficient norms in the internal labor market and the possible failures of individual contracting. *Pennsylvania Law Review* 144: 1953–70.

Kim, P.T. 1997. Bargaining with imperfect information: a study of worker perceptions in an at-will world. *Cornell Law Review* 83 (forthcoming).

Levine, D.I. 1991. Just-cause employment policies in the presence of worker adverse selection. *Journal of Labor Economics* 9: 294–305.

Morriss, A.P. 1994. Exploding myths: an empirical and economic reassessment of the rise of employment at-will. *Missouri Law Review* 50: 679–773.

Peck, C.J. 1979. Unjust discharges from employment: a necessary change in the law. *Ohio State Law Journal* 40: 1–49.

Postic, L.J. 1994. *Wrongful Termination: A State-by-State Survey*. Washington, DC: Bureau of National Affairs.

Rock, E.B. and Wachter, M.L. 1996. The enforceability of norms and the employment relationship. *Pennsylvania Law Review* 144: 1913–52.

Schwab, S.J. 1993. Life-cycle justice: accommodating just cause and employment at will. *Michigan Law Review* 92: 8–62.

Verkerke, J.H. 1995. An empirical perspective on indefinite term employment contracts: resolving the just cause debate. *Wisconsin Law Review* 1995: 837–918.

encryption. *See* COMPUTER LAW.

endangered species. The worldwide rate of species extinction has increased dramatically in recent decades. Estimates of both the total number of extant species and the current extinction rate vary dramatically, yet even conservative estimates peg current species loss to be three or four orders of magnitude greater than the historical average. Some scientists estimate that at the current rate of extinction, only half of the world's current species will survive to the end of the 21st century. Although problematically high everywhere, extinction rates peak in developing tropical regions, where expanding human populations are encroaching on species-rich habitat.

Concerns over extinction rates have spawned new laws and treaties. Internationally, the Convention on International Trade in Endangered Species of Wild Fauna and Flora (CITES) regulates international trade in endangered species, while the Convention on Biological Diversity encourages governments to protect areas of high biological diversity. An increasing number of countries have also adopted local protection laws – the United States Endangered Species Act (ESA) being the most notable. Stemming the tide of extinction, however, has not proven easy, partly because of the diverse causes.

OPEN ACCESS REGIMES AND OVEREXPLOITATION. Open access to fish and wildlife constitutes one reason for species loss. Although the common law gives landowners 'constructive' possession of species while on their property, non-domesticated animals become *ferae naturae* and capturable by anyone as soon as they wander. As Gordon (1954) and Clark (1973) demonstrated, open access leads to overexploitation because no one recognizes the full benefit of conservation and everyone tries to bag their prize before someone else does. Open access regimes can lead not only to overexploitation, but to the extinction of a species where the consumptive value of the species is greater than the harvesting costs even at low population levels, and the species' population growth rate is inadequate to offset the harvesting losses. Under these conditions, no sustainable equilibrium population level may exist.

For several reasons, governments have not responded by eliminating the commons in favour of private property in animals. Unless rights are awarded over an entire local population, defining and policing rights in migrant species is technologically expensive if not impossible. Moreover, private property rights would both subvert the wildness of wildlife and violate the societal norm – dating at least to the Institutes of Justinian – that access to wildlife should be common and universal.

Governments have thus taken regulatory approaches to the risk of overexploitation and extinction. Fish and game commissions have directly regulated the taking of local species through quotas and licensing since the late nineteenth century. Since the Convention for the Regulation of Whaling (1931), a series of international treaties have similarly regulated the taking of whale species. Although initially these regulatory regimes merely capped harvesting levels to ensure 'maximum sustainable yields', more recently they have imposed complete moratoria where species have been at risk of extinction. New laws such as the ESA also prohibit the capture or killing of endangered species. While direct regulation has worked reasonably well where there have been effective enforcement points (such as in the commercial catching and sale of whales) or strong local support for regulation and high expected penalties (such as under the ESA), many developing countries lack the incentive and resources to effectively police numerical restrictions or moratoria.

Alternative regulatory approaches have focused on decreasing the profitability of taking species. Many jurisdictions, for example, have attempted to increase harvesting costs by restricting the equipment or methods used to take particular species. Although often easier to enforce than direct take limits because violations are harder to disguise, process restrictions encourage inefficiently high levels of harvesting investment, seldom help species on the brink of extinction, and again leave implementation and enforcement in the hands of often reluctant countries. CITES, by contrast, tries to reduce the value of taking an endangered species by restricting international trade in the species. If species are 'threatened with extinction' and 'are or may be affected by trade', CITES prohibits international trade except where 'scientific authorities' of the exporting and importing countries have advised that the trade will not be 'detrimental to the survival' of that species (art. III). The ESA similarly forbids anyone from importing an endangered or threatened species into the United States except in limited situations (§ 9).

COMPETITION FOR HABITAT. Overexploitation is the principal threat to survival primarily for ocean species. On land, loss of habitat to farming, mining, and land development is typically far more important. The benefits of commercial or domestic land use normally far exceed the direct benefit to a private owner of habitat preservation. Efforts to reduce overexploitation by regulating the taking of, or reducing demand for, a species will not address the habitat problem and can be counterproductive. By reducing the commercial value of a species, such efforts reduce the economic incentive to conserve the habitat in order to commercially exploit the species.

Property rights in habitat unfortunately do not internalize all the economic benefits of habitat preservation. Owners of land and water at best enjoy nonexclusive rights to most fish and wildlife dependent on their property for habitat and thus generally lack significant economic motivation to forego use of the property. Although landowners enjoy exclusive access to plants and other non-nomadic species on their property, landowners do not enjoy rights to all significant commercial uses of the species. The genetic information encoded in a species can carry substantial pharmaceutical, industrial, or agricultural value; the rosy periwinkle of Madagascar, for example, yielded cures for both lymphocytic leukaemia and Hodgkin's disease. Yet patent rights to genetic resources currently go to the companies converting the resources into commercial products, not to the countries or owners of land harbouring the contributing species.

Many commentators have argued that sharing the commercial value of genetic resources with the originating countries or landowners would reduce habitat destruction. The Convention on Biological Diversity thus encourages 'fair and equitable' sharing of the benefits from commercial utilization of genetic resources (articles 15(7) & 19(2)). Early economic estimates that placed high genetic value on habitat preservation strongly supported this approach. Simpson, Sedjo and Reid (1996), however, have concluded that internalization of genetic value is unlikely to influence many landowners' decisions. Early studies ignored the fact that, where several species contain a useful genetic compound, value is not additive across the species; only the first discovery of the compound adds significant value. Correcting for this error, Simpson, Sedjo and Reid calculate that pharmaceutical companies are unlikely to pay more than about $20 per hectare (2.47 acres) to protect the species-rich habitat of western Ecuador, $2.50 in the uplands of western Amazonia, and $1 in prime habitat regions of Asia and Africa.

THE DISPARITY BETWEEN COMMERCIAL AND NON-COMMERCIAL VALUE. Proposals to reduce extinction rates by restructuring property rights inevitably confront the problem that the commercial value of most endangered species is small. The major exceptions – those species with high harvesting value – face the greatest risk of overexploitation. Although some wild species might lend themselves to commercial ranching or farming, low growth rates often preclude economic viability. Only one in 25,000 species, at best, is projected to produce commercially valuable genetic discoveries – yielding an expected value per species of less than $10,000. A few species produce nonconsumptive tourism value: whales, for example, support a $200 million whale-watching industry in California alone. Yet the vast majority of endangered species are insufficiently charismatic to add tourism value (more clams than mammals are endangered in the United States).

Endangered species, by contrast, enjoy sizeable noncommercial value. Biodiversity increases the overall productivity of ecosystems (e.g., by promoting plant growth or nutrient retention) and helps ecosystems both recover from environmental shocks such as droughts and storms and adjust to long-term environmental change (Gowdy 1997). However, the value of individual species is too complex, indeterminate, and diffuse to be effectively valued in the market. Efforts to identify and place rough estimates on the *overall* value of biodiversity are in an infant stage (Daily 1997). The consequences of a *single* species' loss are even less understood and typically linked to the fate of other species. Ecosystem value, moreover, is a public good which the market is not well structured to provide.

Contingent valuation studies also suggest that endangered species enjoy sizeable existence and bequest value. Most individuals report that they are willing to pay significant amounts to preserve species with little or no commercial value. Annual willingness-to-pay amounts have ranged from $5–$10 per household for some lesser known fish such as the striped shiner to $95 per household for the northern spotted owl (Loomis and White 1996). Like ecological value, existence and bequest values are public goods. The existence, now or in the future, of a species is both nonrivalrous and nonexclusionary.

THE ENDANGERED SPECIES ACT. Species' public-good attributes have inevitably led to direct governmental regulation and protection of habitat. The United States ESA, prototypical of laws in a number of other jurisdictions, guards species that the government identifies and lists as endangered or 'threatened' (defined as species 'likely to become an endangered species within the foreseeable future').

Although section 9 of the ESA protects against over-exploitation by proscribing direct harm to, or trade in, listed species, the bulk of the act addresses habitat. Section 5 authorizes the federal government to acquire habitat. Section 7 prohibits federal agencies from taking any action, including the authorization or funding of private actions, that might 'jeopardize the continued existence' of a listed species or 'result in the destruction or adverse modification' of the species' critical habitat. Regulations promulgated under section 9 forbid 'significant habitat modification or degradation', by anyone, that 'actually kills or injures [protected] wildlife by significantly impairing essential behavioral patterns, including breeding, feeding, or sheltering' (50 CFR §17.3). A landowner can develop his property in violation of the latter proscription only by developing a 'habitat conservation plan' that minimizes the development's impact on listed species and helps ensure the species' continued survival and recovery. Section 4 tries to coordinate the government's preservation efforts by requiring the government to develop a recovery plan for each listed species.

The ESA has proven controversial in many respects. First, the ESA began with an 'emergency room' approach to saving species. The ESA ignored species until they were on the brink of extinction and then, with the species' habitat nearly eliminated, was forced to undertake Herculean efforts to preserve the species. Given the inefficacy of this approach, the ESA has moved in the mid-1990s toward a regional habitat approach in which efforts are made throughout a region to evaluate the needs of all species of potential concern, often including non-listed species, and to develop region-wide habitat conservation plans capable of protecting those species.

Second, the ESA treats all listed species as if they are of infinite value. In deciding whether to list a species, the government must rely only on biological, not on economic, information. Once listed, species are entitled to the basic protections of the ESA no matter what the private or public cost (*TVA v. Hill*, 184). In the only significant exception, section 7 exempts federal agency actions from the normal restrictions if a cabinet-level Endangered Species Committee finds, inter alia, that the benefits of the action 'clearly outweigh the benefits of alternative courses of action consistent with conserving the species or its critical habitat' and the action is in the 'public interest'. The Endangered Species Committee has granted an exemption from the ESA in only one instance (involving timber sales that jeopardized the Northern Spotted Owl), and that exemption was vacated after the courts questioned its procedural validity on procedural grounds (*Portland Audubon Society v. Oregon Lands Coalition*).

To many members of the public, the refusal to factor economics into the protection of an endangered species is a matter of moral principle: a species' value, in their view, is incommensurate with the costs of preserving the species. Yet the government behaves as if there is a trade-off. Economics, banned from explicit consideration, still affects implementation of the Act. Economic concerns, typically voiced through political opposition, have delayed or prevented species from being listed, weakened conservation plans, and influenced which species will receive the limited governmental funding that the United States has been willing to invest in recovery efforts (Thompson 1997). Even if a more open and rigorous balancing of costs and benefits would be valuable, however, we lack adequate biological and economic information to place an absolute or comparative value on specific species.

Third, the ESA's regulation of private habitat has often been counterproductive and raised constitutional concerns over the taking of private property. Almost 80 percent of all listed species in 1993 had some or all of their habitat on private land. Although section 5 of the ESA authorizes the United States to purchase needed habitat, the government has instead relied primarily on its section 9 power to regulate the development or modification of habitat – not surprisingly, since purchases require public appropriations, while regulation is uncompensated and thus can be accomplished 'off budget' (Epstein 1997).

Threat of uncompensated governmental regulation, unfortunately, has encouraged landowners to take evasive actions undermining the ESA's goals. Section 9 regulates only *existing* habitat of *listed* species. Property owners can avoid regulation by destroying habitat before a species is listed or preventing a species from taking up residence on his property. Because of weak enforcement, many property owners can also uproot listed species before the government discovers the species' presence on their land. Although there is no estimate of how much evasion occurs, it is prevalent enough to have its own acronym: 'shoot, shovel, and shut up', or the Three-S Syndrome. The evasive efforts lead to unnecessary or temporally premature land use and endanger the very species that the ESA tries to protect (Thompson 1997).

The perverse economic effect of uncompensated regulation does not necessarily mean that purchase or condemnation of needed habitat would be economically superior. Attacks on uncompensated regulation often forget that taxes used to fund habitat acquisition can distort taxpayer behaviour and lead to often sizable deadweight losses – economic inefficiencies parallel to those generated by regulation. Whether to regulate or acquire habitat thus reduces to a question of comparative inefficiency. Assuming that inefficiency loss increases at an accelerating rate as the burden on property owners or taxpayers increase (a standard assumption in economic tax literature), the ideal policy is likely to be regulation with partial compensation (Thompson 1997).

Although few legal challenges have yet arisen, courts to date have been unreceptive to complaints of private property holders. In *Babbitt v. Sweet Home*, the United States rejected the statutory argument that Congress had not intended to regulate habitat modification under section 9 (which does not explicitly refer to habitat preservation), but expected the government to purchase any needed habitat under section 5. And two lower courts have rejected claims that state regulation of habitat requires compensation pursuant to the Fifth and Fourteenth Amendments to the United States Constitution (*Florida Game & Fresh Water Fish Commission v. Flotilla, Inc.*; *Southview Associates, Ltd v. Bongartz*). Courts have thus left reform to legislative and administrative bodies which, because they have a broader arsenal of potential curative measures, are better equipped to address regulatory deficiencies.

MARKET APPROACHES TO HABITAT PRESERVATION. Both supporters and critics of the ESA agree that reform is needed. The ESA has improved the long-term prognosis for many species under its protection. The health of listed species is positively correlated with its time listed: each year of protection makes it 1.5 percent more likely that a species is stable or improving rather than declining. Nearly half of all listed species, nonetheless, remain in decline, and 15 species have become extinct while under the ESA's protection. The success of the ESA, moreover, has been significantly lower where listed species have faced economic conflicts (Rachlinksi 1997).

Proposed reforms suggest at least four principles for effective habitat protection. First, as already discussed, planning for the needs of multiple species on a regional basis is both more effective and efficient than attempting to identify and save individual species that have reached the brink of extinction. Second, governments can use guarantees against future regulation to stimulate current cooperation by property owners. Under the ESA 'safe harbor' programme, for example, the United States has begun to encourage property owners to create new habitat for endangered species by promising not to invoke its regulatory authority under the ESA if the owner later wishes to destroy or alter that habitat. The United States has also successfully sought to entice landowners to agree to restrictive habitat conservation plans through a 'no surprises' policy under which no new land restrictions will be imposed in the future if the plan later proves inadequate to protect all species (Thompson 1997).

Third, the creation of 'transferable development rights' (TDRs) can reduce the overall economic cost of habitat protection and fine tune the economic incentives facing landowners. Proposed regional habitat conservation plans have incorporated several variants of TDRs. Under the simplest TDR system, property owners who voluntarily choose to preserve habitat in sensitive areas receive tradable rights that can be used to exceed density standards elsewhere. By letting the market determine which habitat to preserve, a simple TDR system encourages property owners to voluntarily assemble a specified preserve at the lowest economic cost (Thompson 1997). Olson, Murphy and Thornton (1993) have promoted a more complex trading system, dubbed the Habitat Transaction Method (HTM), in which property owners willing to preserve habitat would receive credits based on the overall value of the habitat to local species. Anyone wishing to develop habitat would need to acquire credits in amounts again varying with the biological value of the habitat and reflecting the total amount and quality of the habitat the government wishes to preserve.

Fourth, market incentives can more effectively protect habitat than direct regulation. Proposals have included not only TDRs, but tax incentives, environmental assurance bonds, and debt-for-nature swaps (Clark and Downes 1995). Isolated examples exist of the actual adoption of incentives. Minnesota, for example, exempts undisturbed wetlands and prairie from property taxation. The United States has offered to excuse some debts in exchange for habitat preservation. The budgetary costs of most incentives, however, have deterred governments from actively using them.

GOVERNMENTAL SUBSIDIZATION OF HABITAT DESTRUCTION. Many governments magnify the market biases against species preservation by subsidizing or otherwise encouraging activities that destroy species or their existing habitat. In the United States, for example, the principal threats to species on federal lands are timber and mining operations, livestock grazing, and recreation – all of which are permitted by the federal government at prices below market value and, in the case of timber and mineral extraction, at below federal costs. Water and forests are underpriced throughout the world. Most countries allow water to be diverted for free and also subsidize the cost of treating and delivering the water. Governments directly subsidize the harvesting of ocean fisheries; for this reason, the cost of ocean fishing far outstrips the value of the catch (Stone 1995). Like fiscal incentives, however, eliminating subsidies has proven a difficult political sell.

CONCLUSION. Direct governmental regulation, where used, has effectively protected most species from overexploitation, but has been far less efficacious in preventing habitat destruction. Because habitat regulation imposes often significant costs on landowners without countervailing economic gains, landowners seek to escape regulation either through political and legal opposition (which weakens regulatory implementation) or by destroying habitat before regulation takes effect (thereby harming the very species regulation is designed to protect). A combination of habitat acquisition, new economic incentives, and the elimination of counterproductive governmental subsidies would far better preserve necessary habitat. Unfortunately, habitat acquisition and incentives would require substantial increases in governmental funding which politicians, despite contingent valuation studies showing high public valuation of species protection, have been unwilling to support given the free regulatory alternative in place. Elimination of subsidies faces concentrated political opposition. As evidence grows of the limits of the current regulatory regimes, however, pressure will mount for effective, market-oriented reform.

B.H. THOMPSON

See also COMMON PROPERTY; CONTINGENT VALUATION; ECONOMIC INCENTIVES FOR ENVIRONMENTAL REGULATION; INALIENABILITY; MARKETS AND INCOMMENSURABILITY; PROPERTY RIGHTS; TAKINGS; WILDLIFE LAW.

Subject classification: 6d(iv).

STATUTES

Convention for the Regulation of Whaling, 155 LNTS 349 (1931).

Convention on Biological Diversity, 31 ILM 818 (1992).

Convention on International Trade in Endangered Species of Wild Fauna and Flora, 993 UNTS 243, 27 UST 1087, TIAS No. 8249, 12 ILM 1085 (1973).

Endangered Species Act of 1973, 16 USC §§1531–1544.

CASES

Babbitt v. Sweet Home Chapter of Communities for a Great Oregon, 515 US 687 (1995).

Florida Game & Fresh Water Fish Commission v. Flotilla, Inc., 636 S2d 761 (Fla Dist. Ct App 1994).

Portland Audubon Society v. Oregon Lands Coalition, 984 F2d 1534 (9th Cir. 1993).

Southview Assoc., Ltd v. Bongartz, 980 F2d 84 (2d Cir. 1992).

TVA v. Hill, 437 US 153 (1978).

BIBLIOGRAPHY

Clark, C. 1973. Profit maximization and the extinction of animal species. *Journal of Political Economy* 81: 950–61.

Clark, D. and Downes, D. 1995. *What Price Biodiversity? Economic Incentives and Biodiversity Conservation in the United States*. Washington, DC: Center for International Environmental Law.

Daily, G.C. (ed.) 1997. *Nature's Services: Societal Dependence on Natural Ecosystems*. Washington, DC: Island Press.

Epstein, R. 1997. *Babbitt v. Sweet Home Chapter of Oregon*: the law and economics of habitat preservation. *Supreme Court Economic Review* 5: 1–57.

Gordon, H.S. 1954. The economic theory of a common property resource: the fishery. *Journal of Political Economy* 62: 124–42.

Gowdy, J.M. 1997. The value of biodiversity. *Land Economics* 73: 25–41.

Loomis, J.B. and White, D.S. 1996. Economic benefits of rare and endangered species: summary and meta-analysis. *Ecological Economics* 18: 197–206.

Olson, T.G., Murphy, D.D. and Thornton, R.D. 1993. The habitat transaction method: a proposal for creating tradable credits in endangered species habitat. In *Building Economic Incentives into the Endangered Species Act*, ed. H. Fischer and W.E. Hudson, Washington, DC: Defenders of Wildlife.

Rachlinksi, J.J. 1997. Noah by the numbers: an empirical evaluation of the Endangered Species Act. *Cornell Law Review* 82: 326–87.

Simpson, R.D., Sedjo, R.A. and Reid, J.W. 1996. Valuing biodiversity for use in pharmaceutical research. *Journal of Political Economy* 104: 163–85.

Stone, C.D. 1995. What to do about biodiversity: property rights, public goods, and the earth's biological riches. *Southern California Law Review* 68: 577–619.

Swanson, T.M. 1994. The economics of extinction revisited and revised: a generalised framework for the analysis of the problems of endangered species and biodiversity loss. *Oxford Economic Papers* 46: 800–21.

Thompson, B.H. 1997. The Endangered Species Act: a case study in takings and incentives. *Stanford Law Review* 49: 305–80.

English common law. Western Europe has produced two major systems of legal thought, or legal traditions. One, much the oldest in its origins, is the Roman or civil law tradition. Ultimately this goes back to the foundation of Rome, traditionally dated to 753 BC. Roman lawyers, particularly in the late republican period and early Empire, developed a highly sophisticated body of private law. The lawyers who created it were called jurists; they were private legal scholars, who acquired status and honour through their achievement in expounding a body of civil law to regulate the social relationships of Roman citizens. Jurists were neither judges, nor practitioners before law courts.

The other tradition is that of the English common law. It is much younger, but nevertheless at least eight hundred years old. Until very modern times it was evolved as an aspect of the practical work of lawyers directly engaged in court work, either as counsel, or as judges. Only in fairly recent times has it come to be influenced to any significant degree by non-practitioners, working in university law schools.

A legal tradition is not the same thing as a legal system. Apart from international law – either general international law or regimes established under treaties of one kind or another – legal systems, in the sense of bodies of working law and institutions, are today associated with individual nation states – for example New Zealand, the US, Ghana or whatever. But systems of legal thought, legal traditions, are an aspect of general culture, and are usually not home-grown emanations of individual nation states. Most nation states have imported either their legal culture, or some significant part of it, from elsewhere. This is true, for example, of the three nation states mentioned. All three states operate legal systems which are quite distinct from one another, and do so while at the same time preserving in part their own indigenous legal cultures and the law derived from them. Thus in the US, Native American law is still in operation in reservations, and in Ghana a number of different bodies of African customary law regulate, for example, property in land, and some aspects of family law. Ghanaian contract law is, however, an import from England.

Individual legal systems in some ways resemble languages, and legal traditions are in some ways like the family groups into which we divide languages, such as Romance languages. But the analogy is not precise. For whereas an Italian speaker may not be able to understand Spanish, the law of states which share the same legal tradition is always mutually intelligible. Thus an English lawyer who moves to New Zealand will have not the least difficulty in understanding the New Zealand legal system, in handling New Zealand legal materials, or in conducting a legal argument before the New Zealand courts.

The Roman or civil law tradition, as it exists today, was developed from the twelfth century onwards in university law schools around the exegesis of a set of legal texts. The earliest such school was that established at Bologna in north Italy; in the course of time other schools were established, for example in Paris. The ancient texts which formed the basis for the Civil Law tradition, the *Corpus Iuris Civilis*, comprised a comprehensive restatement of the law of the Roman Empire, which had been compiled in Byzantium in the sixth century under instructions from the Emperor Justinian. The law and legal system of the ancient Roman world, which generated these texts, evolved out of a system of formalized dispute resolution established in Rome centuries before the Christian era. The rediscovery of Justinian's restatement in the twelfth century enabled Roman law to enjoy a curious second life, in which a version of Roman legal thinking, developed in academia, as learned law, the law of professional legal scholars, came to dominate the legal world of almost the whole of Western Europe.

This second life of Roman law began about the same time as the common law tradition began to crystallize. In the course of time, indigenous customary law in Europe was either supplanted, or re-expressed in Romanist form. Graduates of the university law schools infiltrated the administrative and judicial world, and brought to it the system of legal thinking in which they had been schooled. So it was that the Roman tradition achieved its dominance. The process whereby this came about is called the reception of Roman law. In relatively recent times the Roman law tradition came to be expressed in the form of comprehensive legal codes, the most celebrated being the Code Napoleon. But for most of its history the Roman law tradition, though text based, was not expressed in such codes.

Civilian legal culture has been exported from Europe to many other parts of the world – to South America for example; in geographical coverage it is a more successful tradition than that of the English common law.

Only one indigenous customary system of law generated a rival system of legal thought, and that was the legal system of England. The most remarkable fact about this system of thought is that it exists at all. The English common law tradition had its origin in customary processes of adjudication. Unlike the medieval civil law tradition, it did not evolve out of the exposition of a basic text or set of texts. Nor was it the product of the English universities of Oxford and Cambridge. Indeed the English universities were not involved with the teaching and exposition of English law until the nineteenth century, although in the eighteenth century William Blackstone delivered some extra-curricular lectures on the subject in Oxford. Oxford and Cambridge, like other European universities, taught Roman law and the canon law of the Western Christian Church.

THE ORIGINS OF THE COMMON LAW. The common law began life as comprising the customary practices followed by royal officials in the court, or entourage, of the king, when the court was engaged in the resolution of disputes and conflicts, that is in the provision of justice.

It is natural to wish to place a date on the origin of the common law. Of course an indigenous system of law does not have any precise moment of birth, but there is fairly general agreement among historians that the formative era of the common law system, the period during which it came to achieve a distinctive character, was the twelfth century, and in particular the reign of Henry II (1154–89). A few historians might dispute this, and part of the reason for their disagreements may be merely definitional. It is certainly the case that bodies of settled customary law long predate the Norman Conquest. Indeed, we have texts of royal laws as early as the reign of Ethelbert of Kent (*c*560–616). His laws, complied in about 602, constitute the earliest surviving text in the English language. In pre-Conquest England, dispute resolution involving the monarch was governed by settled customary practices, and certain characteristic features of the medieval common law system can definitely be traced back to Saxon times. One example is the use of writs to communicate Royal instructions. Other characteristic features, for example the use of juries to determine guilt and innocence, belong to a much later period, in this instance to the thirteenth century, though there are traces of the ancestor of the jury in Saxon law.

But it was in the reign of Henry II that critical steps were taken which led to the ultimate creation of a distinctive national legal system. In his time the royal entourage, in addition to cooks and carvers and other necessary persons, included a number of clerks – that is, literate churchmen – who specialized in the management of adjudication and were engaged in establishing efficient institutional arrangements which extended the scope of the early common law throughout the realm. They had evolved a powerful system, and we fortunately possess a contemporary description of how it worked, for one of Henry II's clerks – it is not certainly known who he was – wrote an account of the practices followed in his time, the *Treatise on the Laws and Customs of England*. This has come to carry the name of Ranulf de Glanvill (*d* 1190), who was a more senior royal official of the time, holding the office of Justiciar from 1180 onwards. The treatise was, so its author explains, intended as an *aide mémoire*. What it described and systematized was an oral tradition as to the proper practice followed in managing adjudication in the Royal court. This tradition was not based upon an authoritative text, nor was it the product of a single legislative decision. It was rooted in practice. Glanvill gives a systematic account of the procedures followed, and sets out the texts of some of the formal written documents, the writs, then employed in the commencement and conduct of litigation. The fact that such a book could be written so early – for nothing like it appeared elsewhere in Europe – makes it clear that by this time there existed a settled body of customary practice, the embryonic common law, which clustered around the formal processes associated with the writs. From that date the common law has had a continuous history up to the present time.

The state of the sources makes it inherently difficult to say how much earlier we can trace back important elements of the system Glanvill describes. The Norman conquest had produced a strong central monarchy: the conquest of one people by another can encourage the development of state institutions as a mechanism for retaining power. The Normans certainly brought with them a tradition of efficient bureaucratic administration, and made use of the ecclesiastical technology of the written text. It may be that the attribution of the birth of the common law to the reign of Henry II puts the date rather too late, but it is certainly not too early.

The first notable characteristic of the embryonic common law is that it is royal law, backed by royal power, and administered by royal officials. Early medieval monarchs had two principal functions – the making of war, and the administration of justice. This second function was in part a consequence of the first – a military leader must take steps to ensure unity and cohesion amongst his followers. Not all disputes were or could be the business of the royal court, only those which because of their seriousness, or because important people were involved, or because, through some other factor, they specially concerned the monarch, were its concern. The traditional practices followed in the resolution of these disputes, and thought to be obligatory, became the common law.

Until quite late in the medieval period the monarch might in person sit in court and participate in adjudication; the last king who attempted to do this was James I, by whose reign this had become an anachronism. But as early as Henry II's reign personal involvement of the monarch in court work was becoming unusual, and a small number of royal clerks were regularly doing the work for the king.

From the fact that the law which is being administered is royal law derives a second characteristic of the common law tradition, the central role of the judge. For the royal clerks of Henry II's time are the ancestors of the modern judges of the common law system. They derive their power and status from the fact that they are acting as deputies to the monarch, exercising royal power over litigants on the monarch's behalf. They are not arbitrators, umpires or mediators; they are judges, and in the common law system judges remain the central actors, the high priests of the law, the oracles of the law. Since their power derives from the hierarchical structure of society the law which they administer – mainly a system of formal procedures – is imposed law, not law which emanates from the traditional customs of local communities.

The reign of Henry II also saw the birth of a specialist professional legal culture, a body of esoteric knowledge, and this is yet another characteristic of the common law. The starting point is the existence of clerks, such as the author of Glanvill, whose regular business it is to manage the conduct of litigation. The clerks who managed litigation in the royal court were bureaucrats, whose basic skill was the ability to read and write; this ability, in an illiterate society, no doubt contributed to the process of professionalizing the customary law of dispute resolution. Once written documents were involved only the literate could run the system. The clerks not only made use of written documents, typically issued in the name of the monarch, to initiate litigation and procedures associated with litigation; soon they took to keeping a written record of the proceedings. Their knowledge of the correct forms and procedures, which the author of Glanvill wrote down, conferred upon them the power of the specialist. Thus royal law was already in course of becoming a distinct body of esoteric knowledge. Given that it was developed by the literate, one might expect that authoritative written texts would come to comprise the common law. But in spite of the use of writing in legal procedure, and the existence of legislative texts of one kind or another, the law which the clerks administered retained the character of an orally transmitted tradition. To this day it is a basic feature of the common law system that its supposed rules and principles are never to be found in an authoritative text. Its rules, indeed, have no canonical text.

We can also see in Glanvill's account the establishment of the procedural system known as the forms of action, which characterized the common law until the mid-nineteenth century, and provided it with its basic structure. Disputes are categorized by the bureaucrats, and must then proceed to decision through highly formalized procedures. Each step in the process is initiated by the issue of a formal written instruction, called a writ, which is a warrant authorizing the royal judges to deal with the case. The original writs (that is, the writs which initiate litigation) are issued by the royal Chancery, the division of the royal court which issues documents in the name of the monarch. To start an action, such a writ must be purchased by the litigant. The forms of writs appropriate to different sorts of complaint become stereotyped, and the procedures associated with particular forms of writ also become settled. What already exists in embryo is what is known as the forms of action; the common law becomes the learning associated with the writs and the procedures they initiate. If you sue to recover a debt you have to use a particular writ form, the writ of debt, and the case will be determined by a particular procedure, in this case by oath swearing, if no document under seal can be produced to prove the debt. If you sue to assert hereditary right in land you use a quite different writ form, and elaborate procedures exist, designed, for example, to compel the defendant's presence in court. Eventually the case may come to decision, but the procedure is quite unlike that used in debt claims – there can be trial by battle, or trial by a form of jury trial. So in Glanvill's treatise the early common law is portrayed as largely consisting in the forms of writs and the procedural rules and practices associated with them.

Yet another important characteristic of the early common law is that its typical mechanism for determining cases, jury trial, already makes its first appearance. Early law everywhere makes use of procedures involving supernatural agencies to whom is entrusted the power of ultimate decision, and the early law of England was no exception. But in Henry II's time there is evidence of the introduction in royal law of the use of what seems to us to be a more rational process of decision, a form of jury trial, a mechanism of great importance in the development of common law. The context is that of land disputes, and the newer procedure functions to supersede the Norman practice of determining land disputes by an appeal to God through battle. The jury will become one of the most characteristic mechanisms of the common law.

COMMON LAW AS THE LAW OF THE LAND. Originally this early body of royal law had a fairly limited scope; only certain matters were thought to be the special concern of the monarch, and thus be appropriate for royal adjudication. Hence, in civil matters, the need for a royal writ authorizing the royal judges to handle the case at all. The early common law was concerned with the graver crimes, known as the pleas of the Crown. The persons most obviously concerned with crimes are the victims or their kin, and arrangements whereby they could invoke the blood feud, or some substitute for it, have a history going back to early Anglo-Saxon times. But by now the monarch is thought to be concerned too, on the theory that grave crimes, wherever committed, and whoever was the direct victim, disturbed the monarch's own tranquillity, the royal 'peace'. Hence a national criminal law already existed, in which, as we would say today, crimes are viewed as offences against the state and not simply against their immediate victims. In this period, landownership was the principal source of wealth and power, and royal law was in the process of taking control over all land disputes between freeholders, though the process was not yet complete. So the early common law was concerned both with the disputes which arose between the monarch's more important feudal tenants, most commonly disputes over property rights in land, and it was encroaching more generally on feudal courts. By Glanvill's time all litigation concerning freehold land had to be commenced by royal writ, and was coming to be supervised by royal law.

Royal law was, however, still only one among many bodies of customary law. Indeed, the author of Glanvill explains that it would have been quite impossible in his time for anyone to give an account of all the bodies of law in force in England, since nobody could possibly know what they all were. The world in which the common law originated was thus a world in which there were multifarious courts, all making use of local custom to resolve disputes. Under the feudal structure of society, lords held courts for their tenants; the monarch was himself the lord paramount, and in this capacity acted as other lords did. Some of the feudal courts, the courts of manors, survived until very recent times. Then there was the Church; many matters concerning lay persons were thought to lie within its jurisdiction, for example issues arising out of marriage or connected with testamentary succession. The Church also asserted jurisdiction over persons in holy orders. The Church possessed its own elaborate hierarchy of courts (as indeed it still does), as well as its own law, the canon law. Then there were courts of counties and courts of hundreds; there were courts of towns and cities, and courts of fairs and markets. By custom certain trades ran their own courts – for example the courts of the miners of Cornwall, the stannary courts. So the royal courts and the royal law existed in a world of multifarious local and personal laws.

This provides in part the explanation for the use of the term 'common' to characterise the royal law. Just as a common prostitute is available to everyone, so the royal law, where it applied, was 'common' in much the same sense, and where grave crime was in issue would be applied to everyone in the realm. Hence it formed a national body of law, unlike, for example, the Church's canon law, which applied throughout Christendom and was thus international in character, and unlike, for example, the customary law of a manor, with its essentially local character. There was but one monarch, and one realm, and therefore one single body of royal common law. This national character was strengthened by the fact that the monarch's law could be set in operation and enforced through a nationwide system of royal officials, for example through the sheriffs in each of the counties. The common law came to be viewed as the law of the land, and is still viewed in this way, although the reality of the matter is, even today, that it forms only one of the various bodies of law in force.

ADMINISTERING THE COMMON LAW. Courts administering the common law, as we know them, are emanations of the royal court, the royal entourage, institutions which eventually break away from their parent structure, and acquire their own staff, their own records, and their own traditional practices. The royal entourage moved with the monarch, who travelled about the kingdom in part as a mechanism for maintaining his power. In the thirteenth century the institutions through which the common law was administered began to become more elaborate, and courts distinct from the royal entourage came to be established. There evolved two distinct 'Courts of Common Law', originally possessing separate functions, jurisdiction and personnel. One was originally called the Bench or the Common Bench, and came to be called the Court of Common Pleas. Its essential feature was that it was a stationary court, sitting in Westminster Hall in London. The idea of having such a stationary court probably originated in Henry II's time. It was staffed by its own justices, and dealt with civil suits between subject and subject. Around this court developed a London-based legal profession. The second court was the Court of King's Bench, and notionally at least it determined cases in the very presence of the monarch. Consequently it originally travelled with him; its function was to deal with matters in which the monarch had some special interest. This included criminal cases.

Within the royal court the handling of finance early became the business of a distinct department, the Exchequer; an ancillary adjudicative body, the Court of Exchequer, whose judges were called Barons of the Exchequer, handled matters to do with the revenue.

By the close of the medieval period all three courts had acquired more or less the same civil jurisdiction, and had come to sit in the same building in London, Westminster Hall. The three courts became the Courts of Common Law, and continued as such until the court system was reorganized in the late nineteenth century. It was in Westminster Hall that the common law was elaborated.

This did not mean, however, that the common law system operated solely in London. There had also evolved, as early as Henry II's time and perhaps before, arrangements distinct from the moving King's Bench, whereby royal officials, judges, travelled about the country to make the common law available everywhere, and not simply where the monarch and his court happened to be. The form this system took changed over time. Thus most criminal trials took place locally before the travelling judges, as did jury trials in civil cases. The judges who operated this system were authorized by commissions, and rode around the country to conduct what were called the assizes; lawyers travelled the assize circuits with the justices of assize. Versions of this system survive to the present time. The system of travelling justices used lawyers, mainly judges, from the London courts to run the system; this tended to preserve uniformity in the nationwide common law. Those who administered the system formed a small group of professionals, working much of the year in London during the law terms when legal court business went on, and carrying the law with them as travelling justices in other parts of the year.

These arrangements can be viewed as mechanisms which extended the common law system territorially; within the realm the common law became ubiquitous.

THE DOMESTIC EXPANSION OF THE COMMON LAW. Over the centuries other forms of expansion took place. Thus in the twelfth century the range of disputes within the customary jurisdiction of the common law was fairly limited. Thus disputes over private contracts were not regularly handled by royal judges. In so far as contracts were enforced by the law it was not by the common law; contract business was handled in the local courts of towns and markets and ports. Over time this changed. By the close of the medieval period the common law had established an extensive jurisdiction over contracts entered into by formal instruments under seal; these in effect bound the contracting party to pay a penalty unless the contract was performed, and provided an extremely flexible and effective mechanism for making any kind of agreement obligatory. The common law by then was also beginning to acquire a general jurisdiction over 'parole' contracts, that is, contracts made by word of mouth. Out of this body of law evolved the contemporary general law of contract. Again, what are now called tort actions – actions claiming damages for wrongs – began to be regularly tried before royal justices in the thirteenth century. Such actions were mainly instituted by a writ form known as the writ of trespass, and stereotyped forms were evolved to cover trespass to the person, to goods and to land. Early trespass actions were regarded as in part criminal in nature, and for this reason lay within royal jurisdiction. Later, the range of tort actions was much extended by allowing suits to be commenced by what were called writs of trespass on the case, which could be altered in form to reflect the special circumstances of the case – hence their name. But the expansion was a slow process. Thus it was not until the sixteenth that actions for defamation of character were entertained, and although some forms of negligent injury were remediable at common law as early as the fourteenth century – for example, medical negligence – it was not until the nineteenth century that a general principle of liability for negligence evolved.

Some of this expansion of the common law simply involved the transfer of litigation from other courts to the courts of common law. Thus before the sixteenth century, defamation suits were handled by the ecclesiastical courts. Earlier, a similar process had transferred land disputes from seigniorial courts to the royal judges. Since little evidence survives about many of the courts which lost business in this process, for they kept no written records, the effects of the transfer cannot be fully investigated. The pressure which brought about this expansion of the common law at the expense of other jurisdictions must have come primarily from litigants, who must have preferred royal justice if it could be had. The process may have been assisted by the fact that the royal judges and court officials were paid out of fees, and thus had an economic motive for expanding their jurisdiction. But not all developments can be explained in this way.

In the thirteenth and early fourteenth centuries the mechanism whereby the common law expanded was primarily the development of new 'original' writs, that is writs initiating litigation. Such writs were issued by the clerks of the royal Chancery, who were thus in a position to control the scope of the common law. They kept precedent books of writ forms, known as Registers of Writs, and the expansion of the common law took place by the expansion of the Register. From the late fourteenth century (though this is controversial) it appears that the control passed to the common law judges, operating through the extension of the scope of existing writ forms. The writ form of trespass on the case was itself flexible, and could therefore readily be employed in this way. Whatever the precise chronology, what is certain is that by the late medieval period the courts themselves controlled the scope of the common law. The movement seems to have been always towards expansion. Where other jurisdictions were recognized the common law judges asserted, and to some degree acquired, a power to restrain what they viewed as inferior courts from exceeding what they thought to be the proper limits of their jurisdiction. Other courts, and other bodies of law, were conceived to exist by leave and licence of the common law.

Some of the expansion of the common law involved the creation of entirely new legal rights and responsibilities, a process typical of contemporary common law. Thus in relatively modern times it has become possible for employees to sue their employers over injuries suffered in the course of employment through the employer's negligence – the first known suit took place in 1836. Here the expansion of the common law did not involve a transfer of jurisdiction, for before 1836 there was no other court which provided a remedy in such a case. In modern times the law of tort has been an obvious example of this form of expansion, driven in part by economic considerations, and in part perhaps by changing social attitudes to responsibility for accidents.

THE OVERSEAS EXPANSION OF THE COMMON LAW. As English power increased, the common law system came to be applied to new areas – the earliest examples are Wales and Ireland. In the colonial and imperial period the common law, often in a modified form, came to be imposed upon or imported into large parts of the globe – for example to New Zealand, Australia, most of Canada and the US, to Ghana, Nigeria, Kenya, Hong Kong and India, to mention but a few. This expansion of the common law has taken place even in countries whose original settlers were anxious to escape from what they regarded as evil features of the legal system of their home country. This was the case with some of the early American colonists. But in the end the English common law was received in the US; this happened in the late eighteenth and early nineteenth centuries.

Legal theories were evolved to regulate this expansion. Thus in settled territories, where there existed no developed system of indigenous law, the settlers automatically took with them so much of the common law as was thought appropriate to their condition. In ceded or conquered territories, where there was developed local law, for example in India, the local law remained in force unless altered by Crown action or legislation. In the course of time, as systems of local government came to be established, the application of the common law was usually regulated by legislation. The spread of common-law ways of thought was also assisted by the fact that many lawyers who worked in overseas territories were trained in England. The end product of this expansion of the common law has generally been that the common law system exists side by side with indigenous legal cultures; this is today the position in virtually every country to which the common law has been exported. Examples are India, Nigeria and the US. The relationship between imported and indigenous law is both extremely complex and sometimes very uneasy. In modern times there have been powerful movements to protect the rights of indigenous peoples who, in earlier times, were not regarded as having any law or legal rights at all, as was the situation, for example, in Australia. Claims for the protection of land rights enjoyed under indigenous customary law, but in the past often denied by the imported common law system, have become a particularly controversial matter.

The expansion of the common law has also converted the legal system of England into an international legal tradition. Although versions of the common law were in existence outside the United Kingdom before then, it is only in the nineteenth century that courts and lawyers outside its country of origin made any significant contributions to the common law tradition. The position changed with the evolution of a powerful legal profession and an elaborate system of legal education in the US in the nineteenth century. Today many other national legal systems, where the common law tradition has been received, are in like case. They have ceased to be simply recipients of the common law tradition, and have become major actors in its modification and development.

THE PROFESSIONALIZATION OF THE COMMON LAW. The evolution of a sophisticated legal tradition goes hand in hand with the evolution of a legal profession. Already in Henry II's time the management of legal business had passed into the hands of expert bureaucrats – the clerks in the royal Chancery who issued the formal documents required, and the clerks who acted as royal deputies in the management of disputes. These early legal experts were officials in Church orders. The bureaucratic regulation and elaboration of the formalities involved in civil litigation generated complexity, and this in its turn a need for expert representatives who would present claims in court. There was also a need for experts to take formal steps in litigation, acting as agents for litigants. Once professionals manage dispute resolution, the assistance of other professionals becomes necessary for those who wish to participate in the process. The need for assistance before the judges created court lawyers, the ancestors of the modern barrister, and the need for legal agents to conduct business outside the court generated professional attorneys.

Early common law legal procedure involved litigants telling their stories to the court in highly formalized language, or formally denying such stories. The early court lawyers were thus called story tellers, 'counters', from the French *conter*. Very little is known of the early history of the counters, but by around the end of the thirteenth century the profession which had grown up around the common law courts appears to have established arrangements for teaching law; some form of law school already existed. By the time we reach the fourteenth century the judges are being appointed from those who practise before the common law courts; the bench is being recruited from the bar.

In the course of the fourteenth and fifteenth centuries there evolved what amounted to a London-based legal university, established in the Inns of Court and the lesser Inns of Chancery. This provided an intellectual centre for the common law culture, where law was taught and studied, and where those who hoped to rise in the legal system received their education. This university was established in a legal quarter of London around Holborn, Chancery Lane and Fleet Street. There the lawyers established fraternity houses, *hospicia*, four of which survive as the Inns of Court – the Inner Temple, the Middle Temple, Gray's Inn and Lincoln's Inn. There they lived, worked and taught. By the mid-fifteenth century, and probably long before, an ambitious young student would start his legal studies in one of the ten or so Inns of Chancery, institutions which were originally the homes of the clerks who worked in the royal Chancery. There he would study the learning of the writ system; after a few years he would move to one of the four Inns of Court, and by participating in moot case arguments, and in lecturing, might eventually rise to a senior position in his Inn. Then, if fortunate, he would be summoned to become a Serjeant at Law, the equivalent of a doctorate in the Universities, and thus become one of the handful of court lawyers who monopolized business in the Court of Common Pleas, where all the major civil litigation was conducted. Eventually perhaps he might become one of the judges of the common law courts, who were recruited from amongst the Serjeants at Law.

The establishment of a distinct common law legal profession, possessing its own educational institutions and practices, separated the common law system from the Church. The legal university of London formed the only wholly secular higher educational system in Europe. The common law, as we have seen, was not taught or studied in the universities of Oxford or Cambridge, where only Civil and Canon law were on the curriculum. Its possession of its own intellectual centre made possible the survival of common law as the second legal tradition produced by Western Europe. There could have been a reception of Roman law in England but there never was, though some branches of the common law have been considerably influenced by Roman law.

With the emergence of the common-law legal profession went the development of a professional literature. This principally comprised texts related to the formal documents involved in litigation – for example, Registers providing texts of standard writ forms – and texts related to the practices followed by the courts – for example, reports of arguments presented in tricky cases to the judges, the ancestors of the modern law report. Virtually all early legal literature is of a severely practical nature.

LAW, FACT AND LEGAL PROCEDURE. The early common law was largely concerned with procedural matters. Thus Glanvill's account of a land case is concerned with such questions as how the claim is initiated, and what is to be done if the defendant fails to turn up in court, for instance if he claims to be ill. He describes the next procedural step – a writ is to be issued so that four knights ride to the defendant's residence and check whether he really is ill or not. Eventually, if the appropriate procedures are followed, the dispute is taken to the point of decision, and in early English law decision regularly involves supernatural intervention. Thus the standard Norman mechanism for determining land disputes was to submit the dispute to battle. Litigants could employ champions to fight on their behalf, and the battle was elaborately regulated. In the end God would ensure that the right prevailed. Other forms of decision involved oath taking, and in criminal law various forms of ordeal – for example, carrying a red hot iron a certain number of paces. After an interval the hand that carried the iron was inspected; its condition determined guilt or innocence. No doubt some of these apparently supernatural mechanisms were manipulated – the local priest supervised the ordeal and may well have adjusted matters in the light of his own knowledge.

In this world there was little place for what we now call substantive law, that is to say law which sets out rights, obligations, defences, principles of land ownership and so forth. Similarly there is no function for abstract criminal law, defining what counts as murder, or rape, or whatever. If criminal guilt or innocence is decided by God through the ordeal, there is no need for the legal experts to concern themselves with the analysis of criminal guilt, or the presumption of innocence, much less with a law of evidence. God does not require the assistance of experts, though a priest may be needed to call upon his assistance. But already in the twelfth century the royal common law had begun to provide alternative methods of trial; a defendant in a land dispute could choose trial by a jury of twelve knights instead of defending his title by battle. There also developed newer forms of action in which jury trial was the only system of trial permitted. In Henry II's times this was the rule when a land suit was brought before the Royal Justices by a new procedure called the Assize of Novel Disseisin – a suit alleging recent dispossession from the claimant's land. In the thirteenth century the tort actions – actions of trespass – which the common law came to entertain, always entailed trial by jury. As newer forms of action were introduced they made use of the more modern procedure, and the older forms, which involved more archaic procedures, tended to pass out of use.

In the criminal law, jury trial came in after 1215, when the Western Church withdrew its support for the use of ordeals. Without the intervention of a priest the secular common lawyers could not involve the Deity in the proceedings. Yet criminals had somehow to be tried, and a system of accusation of crime by a local jury had long existed. So jury trial came into the criminal law because nobody could think of anything else. But since God, who alone could be certain of the truth, was not directly involved, the accused had to consent to this second-rate form of trial. As jury trial became the norm those who did not consent were, it came to be settled, to be tortured by pressing them with heavy weights until they either did consent, or died untried and unconvicted. Although other forms of trial survived until very recent times, jury trial became the typical method of trial both in civil and criminal law.

JURY TRIAL AND SUBSTANTIVE LAW. A jury was a body of relatively important local males, required to come to court, swear an oath to speak the truth, and determine the dispute. Various pressures were put on them to ensure that they performed their duty – for example they were starved until they gave their verdict. Early juries were 'self informing', that is, they were supposed to speak the truth of their own knowledge, and they were not judges of evidence presented to them in court, which they were later to become. The jurymen were summoned from the place where the subject matter of the dispute arose; ideally at least they knew what had happened before they came to court. They simply reported what they already knew by giving a general verdict, in a criminal case 'Guilty' or 'Not Guilty'. They did not have to explain themselves, and the jury functioned in much the same way as earlier supernatural modes of trial.

The rise of the jury had profound effects upon the common law system. Once lay persons, rather than God, became involved in a legal system managed by expert professionals, the latter were tempted to suppose that they might know better than the inexpert jurymen, at least in some situations, especially those of great complexity, how the case should be decided. What was needed, according to this mode of thought, was some mechanism which distinguished between matters which it was appropriate for the lay jury to decide – questions of fact – and matters which might be thought more appropriate for expert decision – questions of law. The latter might, for example, involve the legal consequences of the facts.

The earliest mechanism which was developed in the civil law to separate issues for the jury from issues for the judge was special pleading. Special pleading separated off a range of issues which were for expert decision only, and created an area of substantive law which served to limit the discretion of juries. The system of pleading was hugely elaborated in the fourteenth and fifteenth centuries and relied upon a process of allegation and counter-allegation, whereby the litigants, through their lawyers, came to an agreement as to what precisely the dispute was really about. The counters now became pleaders, experts in this process. The 'issue' identified by pleading would either be one of fact, to be determined by the jury, or an issue of law, which was to be settled by the court.

Suppose, for example, that Robert is suing Hugo by action of trespass, alleging that Hugo beat him, and caused him severe injuries for which he claims compensation in damages. And suppose that what in reality had happened was that Robert was Hugo's servant, and Hugo beat him for insolence and poor work. If Hugo simply pleads a general plea, a general denial – not guilty of the said trespass – the case will go to a jury to decide one way or the other. If, for example, the jury, which is inscrutable, finds for the defendant, we shall have a decision, but this will generate no legal rule as to the powers of masters over servants, even though the jurymen thought that the chastisement in the case was permissible. Under the more elaborate system of special pleading Hugo can tender a plea which confesses that he did beat Robert, but allege that Robert was his servant and was being lawfully chastised. Robert may now deny these facts, and the parties have now agreed to differ on a narrow question which the jury will decide. Or Robert may admit the facts and raise the abstract question of law – is a master entitled to chastise his servant? If the parties agree to differ on this then the matter will be decided by the judges, and their decision can generate a rule of substantive law. In effect the system of pleading has created a distinction between matters of law, matters to be settled by expert professional legal opinion, and questions of fact, to be settled by lay common sense.

Various other procedural mechanisms were evolved to

express and create the distinction between questions of law and questions of fact, but special pleading was how it all began, and special pleading was a reaction to the rise of the jury. For there to be an intellectualized legal tradition there must be some mechanism which identifies issues of law in this way.

For the common lawyer, substantive law consists of the way in which such questions as that about the beating of Hugo are answered by the judges in conformity with expert tradition. Substantive common law, setting out the rights and responsibilities of individuals, and their duties and obligations, and creating structures of responsibility, and excuses and justifications, is simply the product of this take over by the lawyers of the power to decide matters which would otherwise be left to lay common sense. The distinction between matters of fact for the jury, and matters of law for the court, does not exist in the nature of things. A jury could perfectly well settle the power of a master over his servant on a case-by-case basis.

Under the common law system the decision as to where the line should be drawn rests with the court; the law determines what is law. The tendency over the centuries has been for law to expand at the expense of fact. As the system continues the area conceived to be that of law continually increases and the law in consequence becomes increasingly complex and abstruse.

JURY TRIAL AND THE CHARACTER OF THE SYSTEM. Until very recent times the legal profession which created the common law was extraordinarily small. There were around twelve judges of the three common law courts – the 'twelve men in scarlet' – and the number of court lawyers who practised before them in civil cases was small; until well into the eighteenth century lawyers were little involved in criminal cases. As the common law expanded to encompass the more important civil litigation, and the more serious criminal cases, the use of juries was one of the mechanisms which made it unnecessary to develop a large professional judiciary. The small scale of the profession, together with the fact it was based in the capital, did much to create cohesion in the transmission of the oral tradition of the common law.

The jury also brought into the administration of justice a popular element, and, although this was not originally the position, it came to be established that a jury was immune from any form of punishment if it reached what the professionals regarded as a perverse verdict. The character of the jury changed too when the practice of presenting evidence to the jury in court evolved in the late medieval and early modern period. As a supposedly impartial judge of the facts, the ideal jury was now one which came to court wholly ignorant of the facts of the cases. In the seventeenth and eighteenth centuries the immunity of the jury came to be viewed as a means to protect liberty, particularly political liberty, against governmental power. A jury could throw out a state prosecution, for example, even in the teeth of the evidence, and in defiance of the views of the trial judge. In a sense the jury brought a democratic element into the administration of justice since jurymen, though admittedly subject to a property qualification, were drawn from varied ranks in society.

Yet the institution of the jury had its dark side. The lack of ultimate control over jury verdicts by professional lawyers meant that juries could be regarded as an institution which was a threat to the ideal of the rule of law. For under the rule of law disputes should be decided in accordance with the law, and juries might freely ignore the law.

THE MYSTERIOUS SCIENCE OF THE LAW. In the fourteenth and fifteenth centuries the common law developed into a highly complex and technical body of law. The criminal law which was administered locally, either by the travelling judges riding the assize circuits, or by the lay justices of the peace in quarter sessions, was relatively under-elaborated. Legal elaboration is intimately connected with where the money is to be had, and there was little to be had in the criminal courts. The civil law, in particular the law of property in land, was intensely complex, being endlessly refined at the hands of the ablest lawyers of the time. It was the law of the affluent, not the law of the poor. Its centre was the Court of Common Pleas, where the great property disputes were litigated, and the intellectual leaders of the profession, the Serjeants at Law, argued with each other and with the judges, whilst aspiring students sat in court to hear the great masters perform. The common law was by no means rigid or incapable of development, but it was naturally rooted in tradition, and in consequence, perhaps, slow to adapt to new pressures. It was also increasingly esoteric.

Its character as a mystery is most simply illustrated by the languages it employed. The court clerks kept their records of the pleadings in the case, and of the formal stages in litigation, in Latin, the written language of the Church from which the clerks who invented the system had once come. The written language of the common law was, however, not Latin, but Norman French, once the spoken language of the royal court. Until the mid-seventeenth century this remained the situation – law reports, for example, were written in this language. What language was actually spoken in the common law courts in the late fifteenth century is not at all clear – probably the pleadings, delivered orally at least in some cases, were spoken in French and enrolled in Latin, and French may well have been still used for legal argument in the central courts, particularly in the Court of Common Pleas. The populace spoke English, and this would be the only language understood by most jurymen. The complexities of the common law, together with its arcane rituals, must have tended to reinforce a certain inflexibility in the system.

LAW, CONSCIENCE AND EQUITY. During the fifteenth century there developed what is perhaps the most curious feature of the common law system – a distinct court, the Court of Chancery, whose function was conceived to be that of correcting defects in the administration of the common law. Since the common law courts – Common Pleas, King's Bench, and Exchequer, administered the common law, the commodity with which the Court of Chancery dealt could not be characterized as law at all. Instead it came to be called 'equity', an entirely distinct commodity.

Briefly how this came about is that in the medieval world those who thought they were not receiving justice from the law and legal system could petition the King or his Council, setting out their complaint, and asking for a remedy. Such petitions could, for example, be remitted to Parliament for attention, which might respond with legislation. In the fifteenth century the practice developed of referring petitions complaining of defects in the common law to the Chancellor for attention. The Chancellor was the King's principal minister and head of the royal secretariat which, amongst other things, issued the writs used to initiate actions at common law. By about 1450 a large volume of such petitions was being handled in this way, and the Chancellor was making orders, known as decrees, as to what should be done about them; such decrees might provide a remedy when the common law failed to provide one. Out of the Chancery evolved a distinct court, the Court of Chancery. Precisely what the basis for its authority was is not entirely clear, but in the medieval world there were no precise rules as to what the King or his chief minister might do. Probably the Chancellor's powers were thought to arise by way of delegation from the monarch.

Thus the common law did not recognize or enforce what we would today call trusts. Suppose that a landowner was going abroad on some hazardous enterprise; he might formally transfer his lands to two friends, on the understanding that if he did not return they were to hold the lands not for their own benefit, but for the benefit of his infant son, and hand them over when the child became adult and able to manage his own affairs. If this trust was not performed (suppose the friends prove treacherous and use the lands for their own benefit) the common law did not recognize the informal arrangement as giving rise to any enforceable rights. It therefore provided no mechanism to compel the performance of the trust. At common law the friends owned the lands, and that was that; owners could use what they owned as they liked.

If a complaint was made to him by petition, for example by the son, the Chancellor would compel the performance of the trust, if need be by threatening imprisonment if his order was not observed. As complaints of this and other kinds came to be common, there evolved a court with a distinctive procedure to investigate complaints and settle what action to take. The Chancery did not make use of juries; officials investigated the matter, making use of questions, interrogatories, and written statement under oath, affidavits, to get at the truth. By the end of the fifteenth century this court, in addition to enforcing trusts, was also regularly intervening in numerous other types of case. For example it enforced forms of informal contract, ordered specific performance of land contracts where the common law only provided damages, and intervened in cases where fraud or mistake affected formal transactions, when the common law refused to do this.

The medieval Chancellors were senior ecclesiastics who usually had legal qualifications in either Civil law, or Canon law, or both. They must have had some intellectual basis for what could be seen as an illegitimate interference with the course of the law. Although the evidence is not at all satisfactory, during the fifteenth century the predominant idea seems to have been that the Chancellor was not administrating law of any kind, but rather 'conscience'. In the thought of the time, conscience was the faculty which human beings possessed which enabled them to avoid sin and, ultimately, hellfire; in complex matters, however, expert advice might be needed as to what a rightly directed conscience would dictate. Legal rights could be abused in the sense that they could be used in ways which were not in accordance with good conscience, and the Chancellor, in ordering a trust to be performed, or whatever, was in no way seeking to undermine the law. He was merely insisting that law and legal rights should not be used in sinful ways. This was indeed in the long-term interests of the defendant. There was no contradiction involved. According to this theory the Court of Chancery was a court of conscience, not a court of law.

This may explain a feature of Chancery procedure – the Chancellor was said to act *in personam*, against the person. Thus the investigation of the case was designed to discover the state of the defendant's individual conscience, and orders issued by the Chancellor took the form of orders to the individual to act properly, for example to perform the trust, or, in the case of contracts, to perform the contract.

In the sixteenth century a rather different rationale became more prominent, though it too is found in fifteenth century sources, though less prominently. This was that the Court of Chancery was dealing in equity. The theory derives from Aristotle's *Ethics*. The argument was that law operates in the pursuit of justice, and does so through general rules. But as a mechanism for achieving justice general rules are inevitably imperfect. The reason is that it is quite impossible to formulate a general rule which will lead to a just result in all the possible circumstances which can arise. Human beings are incapable of anticipating the infinite combinations of circumstances which lie in the future, and therefore cannot make provision for them in a perfect general rule. Hence what is needed, if justice is to be achieved, is for there to be a power to depart from general rules as a corrective to their inescapable imperfection. This power to depart from rules, when justice requires this, is equity, and cannot itself be governed by general rules. For any attempt to regulate the exercise of the power simply recreates the initial problem.

In the seventeenth century a statement of the theory of the Court of Chancery made in a leading case (*The Earl of Oxford's Case*) combines the older idea of the court of conscience with the more modern idea of a court of equity:

> The office of the Chancellor is to correct mens' consciences for frauds, breaches of trusts, wrongs and oppression of whatever nature they be, *and to soften and modify the extremity of the law.*

The passage I have italicized embodies the conception of equity; the opening of the passage embodies the earlier notion.

Relations between the Chancellor and the common law could however be viewed as involving conflict; it turned upon how they were described, and how convincing the rationalizing theories were thought to be. Thus in the case of a trust the issuing by the Chancellor of an injunction against the legal owners of the property could be viewed as a direct interference with the common law right of property. In the seventeenth century it came to be settled, after considerable controversy, that if there was conflict, equity should prevail. This rule eventually became statutory in England. In the course of the time the original discretionary character of equity, though required by the Aristotelian theory, came to be replaced by a respect for stability and precedent, so that equity turned into a form of law, often as rigid as the common law it was supposed to correct. Throughout the common law world the institutionalized distinction between law and equity, that is to say their enforcement in distinct courts, has gone. But it is part of the common law tradition as it exists today to think of the rules and principles evolved in the old Court of Chancery as conceptually separate from those evolved in the common law courts. Thus where a contract is broken the *legal* remedy is damages, whereas the *equitable* remedy is a decree of specific performance, and the latter, unlike the common law remedy, is conceived to be discretionary, though this discretion has come, with the systematisation of equity, to be governed in its turn by reasonably settled rules. Perhaps the greatest institutional creation of the Court of Chancery is the trust, which continues to flourish as a mechanism for separating legal title and powers of management over property from the right to the beneficial enjoyment of its products.

GENERAL CHARACTERISTICS OF THE COMMON LAW: CASUISTRY. No two writers are likely to achieve complete agreement on the central characteristics of the developed common law tradition, or the relative emphasis to be placed upon them. Some important characteristics which I have already mentioned tend to be taken for granted by those familiar with the system, so that their importance is not noticed.

Thus the common law, notwithstanding the Christian world in which it originated, is a secular system, quite unlike, for example, Islamic law. This feature is an aspect of the division between Church and State which developed in England after the Conquest, and was expressed, for example, in the establishment of a distinct system of Courts Christian. It was expressed in the evolution of a secular, literate legal profession, transmitting the body of legal knowledge through its own secular legal university in London, but cause and effect here are difficult to separate.

Again those within the system today see nothing remarkable in the prominent and indeed dominating position of the judge in the tradition; throughout the common law world the judges of the senior courts are the heroes and sometimes the villains of the common law. Their status, and the conventions governing their behaviour, differ strikingly from those of the judges of the civil law tradition; the explanation is of course historical. Their elevated status originally derived from their being deputies for the monarch; the manner whereby they perform their duties – for example in delivering individual idiosyncratic opinions – derives from the fact that they are recruited from the bar, and carry onto the bench the habits of behaviour formed there. Thus it is that the form of the common law judicial opinion is that of an argument.

But if these two features would not normally excite attention few would disagree on the casuistic nature, in the literal sense of the term, of the common law tradition. To a lawyer from the civil law tradition the foundation for law is typically a text, whereas to a common lawyer it is a case. In the common law world there has, from the very beginning, been legislation, embodied, at least ideally, in a canonical text. But even today, when a very large proportion of the law is embodied in legislative texts, common lawyers are less interested in what the legislation says than in what the courts have made of it in actual cases. The centrality of the case goes back to the early history of the common law. Reports of argument in cases form a major part of early legal literature, the early reports being called *Yearbooks* because of their chronological arrangement. They begin back in the late thirteenth century, and reports of cases continue to be the typical from of professional legal literature at the present time, now made available through computerized systems.

The centrality of the case is continually emphasised in modern common law legal education; much of it takes the form of the detailed analysis of reported cases. In the United States a whole system of legal education, the case system of instruction, originated in Harvard in the late nineteenth century around the idea that students could best achieve an understanding of law by the study of a limited number of particularly notable leading cases. Versions of this system, now somewhat confused as to their rationale, dominate American legal education at the present time. The centrality of the study of cases for a common lawyer goes right back to the medieval period; so it was that when Chaucer in the Prologue to the *Canterbury Tales* wanted to present a picture of a common lawyer, the Serjeant at Law, he equipped him with a set of law reports.

The casuistic character of the common law means that it has evolved over the course of time in the practical setting of litigation, where real problems are presented to a court in concrete terms. The common law does not express a view as to the criminal responsibility of the insane, or liability for the escape of fire, until confronted with an insane murderer, or a real escaping fire. Its development has not been the product of speculative thought, but a reaction to immediate problems. To some this has been a chief merit of the common law way of making law. By proceeding from case to case, as they are presented for decision, the common law is built up slowly and cautiously. At the same time the consequence is that the common law tends to be extraordinarily rich in detail, and one of the more entertaining features of a common law education is reading of the more extraordinary events recorded in the law reports, out of which has emerged the common law. A classic example in modern English tort law is the case *Behrens v. Bertram Mills Circus*, where the largest elephant in England trampled on the smallest dwarf in England who worked in the circus with the elephant, which, though not normally in any way dangerous, had been upset by meeting with a Pomeranian dog unlawfully introduced onto the premises by an unknown third party. Out of such incidents emerges the common law, here the law on the circus's liability to compensate the dwarf and his distressed wife although no negligence could be shown.

HOW CASES ARE DECIDED. Given the fact that the common law has been developed in this case-by-case way, it might be thought that it would possess a clear basic theory as to how cases are decided, and how they should be decided. In fact no very clear answer can be given to either of these two questions. A possible answer might be to say that cases, except when the system is subject to some sort of error or mistake, are and ought to be decided in conformity with the common law. But this does not get us much further. Not only is it often notoriously controversial what the law is, so far as it relates to a particular case, but there are acute philosophical difficulties in providing a satisfactory theoretical account of what the common law is anyway. Jeremy Bentham, for example, argued that if one understood a system of law to comprise a system of general rules, the common law simply did not exist at all; it was indeed a myth employed to conceal the exercise of arbitrary power by the judges.

Although the language in which it has been expressed has differed over the centuries, the traditional lawyers' theory of the common law conceives of it as comprising a body of general principles which in some rather mysterious sense underlie the practice of dispute resolution by the Courts, or are consistent with it. An example of such a basic principle would be the principle that a person ought not to profit from their own wrongdoing. This sort of theory is first explicitly stated in about 1470 by Sir John Fortescue, a former Chief Justice, in his *De Laudibus Legum Angliae* (*In Praise of the Laws of England*). The deep principles – called also 'maxims' or 'universals' or 'grounds' – were, according to an Aristotelian scheme, thought to possess special qualities. They were ultimate in that they could not be supported by further arguments; hence it was idle to argue with anyone who denied them. For example if you cannot see that a person should not profit from their own wrong, nothing can be done by way of offering you some proof, or trying to derive this principle from some higher principle. Secondly, they were self evident, as, it can be argued, this principle is, if you reflect upon it. How could you have a legal system at all which was based on the principle that people should profit from their own wrongdoing? Thirdly, they had always been accepted, timeless features of a timeless system. Fourthly, although any intelligent person could have an understanding of them, their working out and application in complex human affairs required the special skills of the lawyer, achieved only after long years of study and experience.

Such a conception of the common law arose, at least in part, as a response to the apparently disorderly appearance of a system of law which develops on a case-to-case basis. In much the same way we think that underneath the disorderly process of human communication there exists a system of linguistic rules and conventions, without which the process of communication would not be possible. Those who engage in communication may not of course be able to say what these rules and conventions are in any detail; only scholars can do this, and they may well disagree to some extent as to what they are. Similarly, only skilled lawyers have any deep understanding of the fundamental principles of the common law, without which the process of judicial decision would be simply arbitrary. And they, like professional linguists, may disagree about precisely what these principles are, and how they are best formulated.

Versions of this kind of vision of the common law remain very influential today and, particularly in the nineteenth century, became associated with the notion that the law constituted a body of knowledge, a science, which could, like any other body of knowledge, be set out in the form of an elaborate working out of the implications of a limited number of fundamental principles. The discovery and enunciation of these principles formed the work of the legal scientist, whose function it was to expound and systematize the law. The typical product of legal science was the legal treatise, which purports to set out and explain the principles which underlay the practice of the courts, as recorded in the law reports. Formulations of the common law, according to the theory of legal science, both describe the practice of the courts and prescribe what it should be, since the normal or accepted practice is the proper practice. But such formulations are inherently corrigible, since further reflection or study may improve upon them; furthermore, since courts may err there can well be a lack of correspondence between the law and the practice in particular cases.

A somewhat different approach to the theory of the common law is to explain it in terms of what are called 'sources of law'. If the casuistic process of decision is thought to be a rational process, as opposed to an arbitrary one, this seems to presuppose some canon of what counts as a good reason for a legal decision. One sort of reason much relied upon in the practice of the courts is precedent – conformity to the precedents counts as a good reason. This can be rationalized further by saying that it makes the law predictable, or on the ground that it treats people equally, or because unless there is some consistency of decision it is hard to see that the law can be thought to involve general rules at all. Elaborate theories of precedent as a source of law, and of other supposed sources of law – for example the opinion of text writers – have been developed.

The literature on the supposed theory of precedent is elaborate but not very satisfactory. To simplify this somewhat, one long popular view is that each case is supposed to have been decided by reference to a legal rule or principle, called the *ratio decidendi*; if this can, as it were, be extracted from the case, it provides authority for decisions in similar cases in the future. Theoretical writers have attempted to construct rules as to how the *ratio* is to be determined. The *rationes decidendi* of senior courts, for example appellate courts, may bind future courts lower down in the hierarchy, or may simply provide persuasive but not binding guidance. Unfortunately all such theories assume that the processes of judicial decision are simpler and more cohesive than is in reality the case. They depend upon the idea that there is some fixed, and established, and clear set of conventions as to what constitutes a good legal argument, whereas this is not so. The conventions as to what counts as a good argument, and what does not, and the conventions as to what arguments are more powerful than others, are relatively loose. In the law, as in other branches of practical reasoning, there are no conclusive arguments, and no closed list of possible arguments. Hence theories which attempt to give precision to the conception of the common law by supposing that there exist tests as to what constitutes a rule of the common law, and how they are determined, which are reflected in the conventions of legal argument, run into severe difficulties.

Another way of looking at the matter is to conceive of the common law method as involving analogy; cases should be decided in the same way as earlier cases which are analogous to them. Thus the perception of similarities and differences between cases is the typical method of the common lawyer.

THEORIES OF THE COMMON LAW. To a historian, purportedly merely interested in giving a description of the system, the common law is essentially a body of practices observed and ideas received amongst a caste of lawyers. These practices and ideas are used by them in providing guidance as to rational determination of disputes decided by them, and in the various activities which are parasitic upon dispute resolution – for example in deciding whether to settle a dispute out of court, or initiate litigation. These ideas and practices exist only in the sense that they are in fact used within the group of experts, and accepted as identifying appropriate and inappropriate forms of behaviour. They are transmitted by example and precept as the membership of the group changes, typically by educational mechanisms. They are traditional in the sense that they are passed down through time as a received body of knowledge and learning. All these notions are imprecise. Cohesion in a traditional system of law of this character will depend on a variety of factors, and may exist to a greater or lesser degree. In the early common law the small scale of the profession, and the system under which lawyers lived and ate together, no doubt contributed to produce a high level of agreement as to what was and what was not appropriate.

Theories as to the nature of the common law developed by legal thinkers are not simply concerned to describe or explain what happens. They are directed more towards the legitimation of the system. In particular they may be seen as attempts to make sense of the belief that the process of legal decision in the common law system is compatible with the ideal of the rule of law, and rational. The most extreme form in which this claim can be put forward is one in which it is supposed that there always exists, at least in theory, a uniquely correct answer to every legal problem There is a long tradition, however, of an iconoclastic nature which, to a greater or lesser degree, denies that the common law is capable of controlling the outcome of cases. This is well illustrated by an exchange between two common law judges which took place as long ago as 1345 in the Court of Common Pleas, where counsel had raised the question of how cases ought to be decided; he argued that the judges should decide as others had done in the past, for otherwise nobody would know what the law was. An iconoclastic judge, one Hillary, replied to him that 'Law is the will of the Justices'. His view was vehemently denied by another judge, Stonore. 'Certainly not. Law is reason' (*Anon.*). The exchange encapsulates three contrasting conceptions of the common law – arbitrary will, conformity to tradition and common-sense rationality. Their interrelation will always generate controversy.

EVOLUTION AND CHANGE IN THE COMMON LAW. Common lawyers of the medieval and early modern period conceived of the common law as a timeless system, which had existed in more or less the same form since the time of the Roman occupation of Britain. They were not conscious of legal evolution and change. Today we are conscious of the fact that a legal tradition has a history, and has been formed in response to social and political pressures which are external to the tradition itself, though it is by no means easy to identify how these pressures have operated. To some degree legal systems are autonomous, and regulate the conditions of their own development. That is to say some legal developments do not seem to be explicable in terms of external social, economic or moral factors.

In a customary or traditional body of law such as the common law, conceptions and ideas and principles may have their origins in the fairly remote past. The law, indeed, can in some respects resemble an archaeological site. Thus the modern common law of property in land employs a terminology and set of basic conceptions which were mainly developed in the medieval period. Land was then the principal source of wealth and power, and in consequence the law of land ownership came to be elaborated at an early period. And many of the more general elements of the common law tradition can be traced back to its early history. This is true, for example, of its casuistical nature, its secular character, its essentially unsystematic nature. Many of its institutional peculiarities are also of early origin. This is true of its use of the jury and of the central place it accords to the office of judge. The form of the common law judicial opinion – argumentative, rhetorical, disorderly in structure – is another example. The judges are recruited from the bar, and carry onto the bench the habits they have acquired as advocates. Indeed the modern judicial opinion originated in the form of arguments presented by judges in court before any decision was reached.

But much of the substantive common law and its associated concepts, now spread throughout the common law world, is a product of the English legal system of the eighteenth and nineteenth centuries. This is true, for example, of the general law of contract. Although common law courts had been enforcing contracts, mainly those evidenced by documents under seal, since the twelfth century, and had also in the early modern period created a law for contracts entered into informally, either by word of mouth or by signed documents, even by the beginning of the nineteenth century there had been no great elaboration of substantive law. Issues such as the assessment of damages for breach of contract, now an elaborate branch of the law, were apparently largely left to jury discretion, so that there was virtually no law on the subject at all. But in the nineteenth century the courts developed complex law as to how and when contracts became binding, how damages for breach of contract should be assessed, when a change of circumstances would absolve parties to contracts from the obligation to perform or pay damages, and on many other matters. Much of this law seems to have been imported into the common law system from the world of Roman law, which had earlier addressed these questions and provided solutions to them. The vehicle for this process was the legal treatise – writers of such treatises borrowed ideas from continental writers when the common law cases provided no guidance.

What thereby happened to contract law was that jury discretion was restricted by the expansion of substantive law. One possible explanation of this phenomenon is that it represented an increased commitment to the ideal of the rule of law – dispute resolution should be governed by settled rules rather than by unregulated jury discretion.

The same phenomenon is met in other branches of law, for example in the law of torts. Thus the nineteenth century saw both the development of a general principle of tortious liability for negligence, and an elaboration of the law defining what was meant by negligence, and when it was actionable, and what defences might be put forward to a negligence suit. Again in criminal law the principles of criminal liability were elaborated; for example the relevance of insanity to criminal responsibility came to be spelled out by the judiciary. This was not because insane criminals were a new invention; it was just that there was very little law on what should be done about them. The whole process went hand in hand with the evolution of more effective mechanisms for controlling juries, and ensuring that, so far as possible, they followed the law. Thus judicial instructions to juries became much more elaborate than they had been in earlier times. In England, though not in the US, the nineteenth century also saw the beginning of a process whereby the jury began to pass out of use completely in civil litigation.

THE COMMON LAW AS AN INTELLECTUAL SYSTEM. The common law of the medieval and early modern period had evolved into a highly technical body of esoteric learning. It could only be learned by direct involvement in practice; in so far as it would be derived from texts, many of them were still written in an artificial legal language, the lawyers' version of Norman French. Court records were kept in Latin until well into the eighteenth century. The procedures of the courts were in some respects little short of bizarre, and archaic institutions, such as trial by battle, survived in a vestigial way even into the nineteenth century. The Court of Chancery, because of administrative defects, became a byword for delay and, in the form in which it operated in the early nineteenth century, was parodied by Charles Dickens in *Bleak House* in his account of the interminable case of *Jarndyce v. Jarndyce*, which had been going on so long that nobody could recall what it was about. No doubt in spite of all its defects the system in its way worked; criminals were tried, civil suits were determined. But in comparison with the systems of law developed in the universities of continental Europe the common law appeared to be an intellectually impoverished system, and this was reflected in the character of its literature. Thus at the start of the eighteenth century there existed no coherent exposition of the law of civil injuries, of tort law, and not a single published account of the law of contract. There were multifarious reports of cases, going back to the fourteenth century, and a variety of works which attempted, with greater or lesser success, to systematize the case law and make it accessible. There were form books of one kind or another, and numerous procedural texts and more or less practical guides. But even the law of property in land had not been set out in a coherent form; lawyers had to learn about it from an elaborate gloss written by Sir Edward Coke in the seventeenth century on a tiny fifteenth century account, written by a judge of that period, Thomas Littleton. The system lacked a literature which portrayed either the common law generally, or particular branches of it, as a rational and coherent body of thought. Furthermore the nature of the legal texts which were available made the law inaccessible; there are numerous accounts of the horror which reading law books inspired even in those who were determined to enter the profession.

All this changed with the publication, between 1765 and 1769, of William Blackstone's *Commentaries on the Laws of England*. Blackstone (1723–1780) wanted to become the Professor of Roman Law in Oxford, but failed to secure the appointment. Instead he became the holder of the first Chair of English Law established in an English university, and before he obtained this position he delivered a series of extra-curricular lectures which were in due course worked up into a four-volume comprehensive account of the entire common law system. The *Commentaries* comprise the first, and indeed the last, elegant literary exposition, in a highly readable form, of the common law system as a whole, in which was included an account of the British constitution. Blackstone's *Commentaries* were hugely successful and presented the common law, albeit in some relatively minor respects defective, as an intellectually respectable system embodying both the accumulated wisdom of the ages and a commitment to the protection of the rights and freedoms enjoyed by the English, who enjoyed a degree of liberty denied to those who lived under more repressive systems of law. He also presented the history of the common law in a curious manner, whereby over the course of the centuries it has purged itself of harmful characteristics introduced by the Normans, to the detriment of the ancient Saxon laws.

Blackstone was by no means the first common lawyer who idealized the system; Fortescue had done so in the fifteenth century in the work already mentioned. But he gave the most notable expression to what is perhaps a somewhat romanticized vision of the common law. This idealization came to be influential; thus British colonialism was in part rationalized and justified as bringing the benefits of the common law to those who had the good fortune to be ruled by the British. And today this Blackstonian tradition, albeit modified, is by no means wholly extinct, though the forms it now takes are various, and have changed since Blackstone's time. Thus the common law method, whereby the law is built up by degrees in the light of experience, is thought by some to be preferable to the generation of law through legislation, given the fact that legislatures can be captured by sectional interests. Again, those who are generally suspicious of governmental activity, as tending to distort the natural working of the market, view the operation of the common law not so much as a form of governmental activity, but rather as simply providing a minimalist and politically neutral level of social regulation, which makes it possible for individuals to work out their own plans and desires without any more interference or direction from the state than is necessary if other individuals are to be allowed to do the same. Another view which has achieved some currency sees the common law as a system which can be best understood as driven by some inner mechanism towards the pursuit of economic efficiency. Thus the system whereby it is built up – decision following decision in litigated cases – may provide a means whereby inefficient rules are weeded out over the course of time, and more efficient rules, which will tend not to be challenged in litigation, will come to the fore. Those of a Marxist persuasion see the common law differently, for example as a mechanism to legitimate an unjust society. General views of this nature are unfortunately very difficult to relate to empirical evidence; for all that, they may provide important insights into the character of the common law tradition.

A.W. Brian Simpson

See also BLACKSTONE, WILLIAM; EQUITY; INHERITANCE LAW; JURIES; LAND-USE DOCTRINES; LAW MERCHANT; POSSESSION; PRECEDENT; ROMAN LAW; STARE DECISIS; STATUTE OF FRAUDS; WESTERN LEGAL TRADITION.

Subject classification: 4a(iii); 4b(i).

CASES

Anon. (1345) YB 19 Edw. III (Rolls Series) 337, plea 3.
Behrens v. Bertram Mills Circus Ltd [1957] 2 QB 1, 1 All ER 583.
The Earl of Oxford's Case (1615) 1 Ch. Rep. 1.

BIBLIOGRAPHY

Baker, J.H., *An Introduction to English Legal History* (3rd edn London: Butterworths, 1990) provides an up-to-date and very lucid general survey, and has extensive lists of further reading.
Milsom, S.F.C., *Historical Foundations of the Common Law* (2nd edn London: Butterworths, 1981) though less useful as an introductory survey, is notable for its analytical power.
Cornish, W.R. and Clark, G. de N., *Law and Society in England 1750–1950* (London: Sweet and Maxwell, 1989) deals more broadly with the modern history, and also provides full lists of further reading.
Pollock, F. and Maitland, F.W., *The History of English Law Before the Time of Edward I* (2nd edn by S.F.C. Milsom, Cambridge: Cambridge University Press, 1968) retains its position as a classic account of the early period.
Horwitz, M.J., *The Transformation of American Law 1780–1860* (Cambridge, MA: Harvard University Press, 1977) and *The Transformation of American Law 1870–1960* (New York: Oxford University Press, 1992) offer a contextual history of the development of the common law in the USA.
Atiyah, P.S., *The Rise and Fall of Freedom of Contract* (Oxford: Clarendon Press, 1979) is far and away the most ambitious attempt to relate a body of legal doctrine to its social, moral, political and economic context. No study of comparable quality exists for any other branch of private law.
Simpson, A.W.B., *A History of the Common Law of Contract. The Rise of the Action of Assumpsit* (Oxford: Clarendon Press, 1975) provides a purely doctrinal history of contract law up to 1677.

There exist no substantial monographs on other branches of private law, such as tort law or property law. The same author's *A History of the Land Law*, 2nd edn (Oxford: Clarendon Press, 1986) offers, however, a concise introduction to the history of the law of property in land.

The claim that common law development is to some degree driven by the pursuit of economic efficiency is explored in the following articles:

Posner, R.A. 1972. A theory of negligence. *Journal of Legal Studies* 1: 29–96.
Priest, G.L. 1977. The common law process and the selection of efficient rules. *Journal of Legal Studies* 6: 65–82.
Goodman, J.C. 1978. An economic theory of the evolution of the common law. *Journal of Legal Studies* 7: 393–406.
Rubin, P.H. 1977. Why is the common law efficient? *Journal of Legal Studies* 6: 51–63.

There is no major work applying Marxist theory to the history of the common law, but the potential is well illustrated by a collection of essays by D. Hay, P. Linebaugh and E.P. Thompson, *Albion's Fatal Tree* (London: Allen Lane, 1975).

The casuistic nature of the common law is explored in A.W.B. Simpson, *Leading Cases in the Common Law* (Oxford: Clarendon Press, 1995).

English rule. *See* ALLOCATION OF LITIGATION COSTS: AMERICAN AND ENGLISH RULES.

environmental regulation. *See* ECONOMIC INCENTIVES FOR ENVIRONMENTAL REGULATION.

equitable remedies. *See* EQUITY; SPECIFIC PERFORMANCE.

equity. According to Maitland's famous definition, equity in the sense that lawyers use the term is 'that body of rules administered by our English courts of justice which, were it not for the operation of the Judicature Acts, would be administered only by those courts which would be known as Courts of Equity' (Maitland 1932: 1). In other words, 'equity' refers to the doctrines and remedies that originated in the English Court of Chancery, in contrast to the 'common law' which is the body of rules developed by the King's courts.

The definition is a poor one, as Maitland himself conceded. It draws attention to the institutional origins of equity, but it tells the inquirer nothing directly about equity's philosophical underpinnings or the complexity of its relationship with the common law. The truth is that neither the nature of equity nor the significance of Maitland's definition can be appreciated properly without reference to historical considerations. A brief account follows.

Equity began to develop in the Chancellor's office during the Middle Ages as an antidote to the inflexibility of the common law. A plaintiff could only sue at common law if the wrong complained of came within the scope of a recognized form of action, and the common law courts over time became increasingly reluctant to innovate. Subjects who had no claim at common law began to petition the Chancellor for relief. Petitions were also brought in cases where the claimant was too poor to sue or defend a case at common law, and where justice was likely to be denied at common law due, for example, to the power and influence of the defendant.

The Chancellor's concern was to grant relief in hard cases. Initially, this was done on an *ad hoc* basis, without reference to precedent. The earlier Chancellors were nearly always ecclesiastics, and in resolving disputes they relied on their sense of the rights and wrongs of the case informed by their schooling in canon law. In short, decisions were made on grounds of conscience. The Chancellor's office gradually metamorphosed into a court, but its decision-making continued to rely heavily on appeals to conscience. This led inevitably to charges of arbitrariness by equity's opponents, for example Seldon's well-known barb:

> Equity is a roguish thing. For law we have a measure . . . [but] equity is according to the conscience of him that is Chancellor, and as that is longer or narrower, so is equity. Tis all one as if they should make the standard for the measure a Chancellor's foot (quoted in Holdsworth 1956 i: 467–8).

Canon law was the main source of intellectual inspiration for the early Chancellors. A little later, alternative support was found in the writings of Aristotle. In the *Nicomachean Ethics*, Aristotle distinguished between the rule of law, which was universal in its application, and equity, which was concerned with doing justice in the individual case. The rule of law, applied strictly, may work hardship in particular cases and Aristotle says that the function of equity is to avoid such outcomes (Aristotle, Bk V. Ch. 10). The virtue of the rule of law lies in its certainty and predictability, whereas equity's strength is its flexibility. There is an obvious and unavoidable tension between universal justice or certainty and individual justice or flexibility, which all mature legal systems must come to terms with. Most legal systems have some facility for dispensing individual justice in the face of the rule of law. The unique feature of the English system was that, by historical accident, the two kinds of justice came to be administered in separate courts (Meagher, Gummow and Lehane 1992: 6).

In equity's formative stages, therefore, the relationship between common law and equity could at least loosely be characterized by reference to the dichotomy between universal justice and individual justice. Seldon's statement, quoted above, reflects the tension. However, the relationship changed between the later part of the sixteenth century and the early part of the nineteenth. During this period, equity lost its *ad hoc* character and became increasingly systematized. The Chancellors were no longer bishops, but lawyers; equity cases were reported; and, with the advent of equity reports, a system of precedent emerged. Equity developed settled doctrines, and in terms of judicial technique it became virtually indistinguishable from the common law. Chancellors proclaimed the importance of predictability, and downgraded conscience. Lord Eldon, the most prominent Chancellor of the period, in a belated response to Seldon's attack on equity, remarked:

> Nothing would give me greater pain in quitting this place than the recollection that I had done anything to justify the reproach that the equity of this Court varies like the Chancellor's foot (quoted in Holdsworth 1956 i: 468–9).

Hanbury and Martin (1993: 4) summarize the modern position as follows:

> Principles of justice and conscience are the basis of equity jurisdiction, but it must not be thought that the contrast between law and equity is one between a system of strict rules and one of broad discretion. Equity has no monopoly over the pursuit of justice . . . Just as the common law has escaped from its early formalism, so over the years equity has established strict rules for the application of its principles. Indeed, at one stage the rules became so fixed that a 'rigor aequitatis' developed; equity itself displayed the very defect it was designed to remedy . . . Today, some aspects of equity are strict and technical, while others leave considerable discretion to the court.

In other words, common law and equity have substantially converged. The two systems have become 'not rivals, but partners in the work of administering justice' (Holdsworth 1956 v: 668). This explains the poverty of Maitland's definition, quoted above. The point of the definition is that the only meaningful distinction left between the two systems is the historical one.

THE JURISDICTION OF EQUITY. The early Chancellors intervened in disputes to mitigate the harshness of the common law. One form of intervention was to issue an injunction preventing the defendant from enforcing an unconscionable judgment obtained at common law (for example, a judgment obtained by fraud, or abuse of power or influence). The effect of the injunction was to make the judgment inoperative, and equity's inter-meddling was bitterly resented by the common law judges. The issue came to a head in the *Earl of Oxford's Case* (1615), which resulted in a dispute between the Chief Justice (Sir Edward Coke) and the Chancellor (Lord Ellesmere) over the Court of Chancery's jurisdiction to grant injunctions. The King intervened and ruled in favour of the Chancellor. This ruling established the modern position, namely that in the event of a conflict between common law and equity, the rules of equity take precedence.

Another form of intervention by Chancery was to develop new causes of action to cater for wrongs that were not recognized by the common law courts, and innovative remedies to deal with cases where, for one reason or another, the common law remedy of damages was inadequate. Meagher, Gummow and Lehane (1992: 5) list some of these innovations as follows:

> (i) the recognition, protection and development of uses and trusts . . .; (ii) the enforcement of contracts on principles unknown to the common law – for example, sometimes recognising contracts not under seal, long before the simple contract was accorded recognition at law; (iii) interference with the rigidity of the law in cases where the presence of fraud, forgery or duress would render the enforcement of strict legal rights unconscionable; (iv) the giving of remedies unavailable at law, for example, injunction or specific performance; (v) the development in the equitable action of account of a much more flexible and beneficial instrument than its common law counterpart; and (vi) the giving of common law remedies

where they theoretically existed at law, but in practice were not available – owing, for example, to local rebellion, bias and 'the violence' (as it was put in many petitions) of the defendant.

The *Earl of Oxford's Case* established equity's superiority over the common law, but only in a limited sense. Equity did not claim to be superior to the common law courts in the sense that it could tell the courts themselves what to do. However, it was superior in the sense that it could prevent a party from going to the common law courts, whereas the common law courts could not prevent a party from going to equity (Maitland 1932: 9–10). On the other hand, there was an important sense in which equity was inferior to the common law:

> Equity was not a self-sufficient system, at every point it presupposed the existence of common law. Common law was a self-sufficient system. I mean this: that if the legislature had passed a short act saying 'Equity is hereby abolished,' we might still have got on fairly well; in some respects our law would have been barbarous, unjust, absurd, but still the great elementary rights, the right to immunity from violence, the right to one's good name, the rights of ownership and of possession would have been decently protected and contract would have been enforced. On the other hand had the legislature said, 'common law is hereby abolished' this decree if obeyed would have meant anarchy. At every point equity presupposed the existence of common law. Take the case of the trust. It's of no use for Equity to say that A is a trustee of Blackacre for B unless there be some court that can say that A is the owner of Blackacre. Equity without common law would have been a castle in the air, an impossibility (ibid.: 19).

Equity could intervene to correct deficiencies in the common law, but it had no jurisdiction over areas where the common law was adequate. So, for example:

(1) Equity has no jurisdiction to determine property entitlements recognized by common law, but it can direct a legal owner to hold property for the benefit of another (this is the basis of the trust);
(2) The equitable remedies of injunction and specific performance can be awarded to prevent wrongs recognized at common law (trespass, for example, and breach of contract), but only in cases where the plaintiff cannot be compensated adequately in damages; and
(3) Equity's intervention to deter cheating was necessary because the common law took a narrow view of what amounted to fraud (compare, for example, *Derry v. Peek* and *Nocton v. Lord Ashburton*).

For the reasons that have just been discussed, the subject matter of modern equity's jurisdiction is limited. Hanbury and Martin (1993: 40) list the following subject areas by reference to the matters that have been assigned to the Chancery Division in England by the Supreme Court Act 1981:

> The sale, exchange or partition of land, or the raising of charges on land;
> The redemption or foreclosure of mortgages;
> The execution of trusts;
> The administration of the estates of deceased persons;
> Bankruptcy;
> The dissolution of partnerships or the taking of partnership or other account;
> The rectification, setting aside or cancellation of deeds or other instruments in writing;
> Probate business, other than non-contentious or common form business;
> Patents, trade marks, registered designs or copyright;
> The appointment of a guardian of a minor's estate;
> All causes and matters involving the exercise of the High Court's jurisdiction under the enactments relating to companies.

This list, though not exhaustive, is sufficient to convey the flavour of what equity is about, both in England and in other jurisdictions that have inherited the English system.

THE JUDICATURE ACTS. The separation of the common law and equity courts was inconvenient for litigants. The Court of Chancery had almost exclusive equity jurisdiction, and the common law courts did not recognize equitable entitlements. At the same time, Chancery had no power to rule on disputed common law rights. This meant, for example, that in order to raise an equitable defence to a common law action, the defendant had to obtain an injunction from the Court of Chancery to stay the proceedings in the common law court and then start a new action in Chancery to obtain a ruling on the defence (Hanbury and Martin 1993: 4).

These difficulties were addressed by a number of statutory reforms culminating in the Judicature Acts of 1873 and 1875. The Judicature Acts abolished the old separate courts and replaced them with a single court constituted in divisions, including a Queen's Bench Division and a Chancery Division. Each division exercises both legal and equitable jurisdiction. Any issue can be adjudicated in any division, and any part of law or equity can be raised in any division. Cases are allocated to the divisions according to their subject-matter, but only for the sake of administrative convenience. Each division is a court of complete jurisdiction (Hanbury and Martin 1993: 15–16). The Judicature Act reforms were a practical necessity for the reasons mentioned earlier, but they also represented the logical next step in the convergence of common law and equity that had already been taking place. Nearly all jurisdictions which have inherited the English legal system adopted comparable reforms, though the Australian State of New South Wales did not do so until 1972.

The orthodox view is that the Judicature Act reforms were purely procedural. They achieved a fusion of common law and equity in the sense that both bodies of doctrine can now be administered together by a single court, but they did not abolish the distinction between common law and equity or in any way change the shape of pre-existing doctrines and remedies. In Ashburner's words, 'The two streams of jurisdiction, though they run in the same channel, run side by side, and do not mingle their waters' (Ashburner 1933: 18). 'Legal rights remain legal rights, and equitable rights remain equitable rights, though administered in the same court' (Hanbury and Martin 1993: 21). Today, this distinction is maintained with varying degrees of fervour from one jurisdiction to another. In the United States, the distinction has virtually disappeared. There is, of course, still a law of trusts and principles governing fiduciary obligations and so on, but judicial doctrines tend not to be classified any more according to whether they are legal or equitable in origin. By contrast, in Australia, the distinction is still quite vigorously maintained perhaps, in part, due to the lateness of the Judicature Act reforms in New South Wales, the most populous state. Equity is taught as a separate subject in all Australian law schools, and there is a proliferation of textbooks devoted to equity doctrines and remedies. The attitudes in other common law countries, including England itself, New Zealand and Canada, probably fall somewhere between these two extremes.

EQUITABLE REMEDIES. The main common law remedy is damages. Equity has developed a wide range of alternative forms of relief. The most important are the injunction, which is an order requiring the defendant to perform an act or restraining the performance of an act, and specific performance, which is an order requiring the defendant to perform a contract. Common law damages are available as of right, but equitable remedies are discretionary. For example, an injunction may be refused on the ground of the plaintiff's own unconscientious behaviour, whether or not it amounts to an actionable wrong against the defendant. Furthermore, an injunction to restrain a common law wrong (such as a trespass) and specific performance can only be awarded in cases where damages are an inadequate remedy.

Other equitable remedies include: the account of profits, which requires the defendant to surrender gains made in consequence of a wrong done to the plaintiff; rescission, which involves the setting aside of contracts and restoring the parties to their pre-contractual position; and compensation (payment for loss caused by the defendant's wrongdoing). Equitable compensation is similar to common law damages, except that it is limited to cases involving equitable causes of action, for example breach of fiduciary duty or breach of confidence. By contrast, damages are awarded in respect of common law wrongs (such as breach of contract, defamation, negligence or trespass).

Equity may also order constructive trust relief. A constructive trust is an order declaring that the defendant holds the disputed property on trust for the plaintiff. The consequence is to give the plaintiff equitable (or beneficial) ownership of the asset, and this entitles the plaintiff to claim the asset *in specie* from the defendant. So, for example, if company directors divert to themselves a business opportunity they were under a duty to secure for the company, the court may declare a constructive trust over the profits in the company's favour (*Cook v. Deeks*). Again, if an employee accepts a bribe or secret commission, the court may impose a constructive trust on the payment in the employee's hands or, if the employee has invested the payment, on the investment (*Attorney-General for Hong Kong v. Reid*). The constructive trust is also commonly used in some jurisdictions as a means of achieving a fair settlement of property disputes following the breakdown of *de facto* relationships (*Baumgartner v. Baumgartner*; *Pettkus v. Becker*). (Property disputes between married couples are governed by legislation, and in some jurisdictions now this is true also of disputes between *de facto* partners.) The constructive trust is a remedy imposed by the court, in contrast to the express trust which depends on the intention of the party creating the trust (express trusts are discussed further in the next section). The constructive trust is a kind of judicially created proprietary entitlement in the plaintiff's favour. The granting of the remedy is controversial in cases where the defendant is, or may be, insolvent because it gives the plaintiff a prior claim to the disputed asset in the defendant's bankruptcy over other creditors (contrast *Lister v. Stubbs* and *Attorney-General for Hong Kong v. Reid*, and see Paciocco 1989 and Sherwin 1989).

THE TRUST. Maitland described the development of the trust idea as one of the greatest achievements of English law (Maitland 1936: 129). At the heart of the trust is the separation of legal title to property from equitable or beneficial ownership. The trustee is legal owner of the trust property, but this is only a nominal title. Effective ownership, in the sense of entitlement to the benefits deriving from the trust property, is vested in the beneficiary.

The modern trust owes its origins to the medieval use. For various reasons, a landowner (A) might want to transfer the land to another person (B) subject to an undertaking that B will hold the land for the use and benefit of a third party (C). What was A's or C's remedy if B breached the undertaking and misappropriated the benefits? At common law, A might have a claim for damages against B for breach of covenant, but no right to compel B to observe the undertaking while C, not being a party to the covenant between A and B, would have no common law rights at all.

The Chancellor intervened on the basis that it would be unconscionable for B to ignore the undertaking. The Chancellor had no power to deny B's legal title to the land, because issues relating to title were matters exclusively for the common law courts. However, what he could do was make an order directed to B in person, compelling B to keep the legal title only, and to give all the benefit of the land to C. Moreover, if B transferred the land to D and D had notice of B's undertaking, the Chancellor would enforce the undertaking against D. Over time, by a process of ellipsis, C's right to compel B (or D) in equity to observe the terms of the undertaking came to be treated as proprietary in character: B (or D) was the legal owner of the land, but C was the owner in equity. Thus was born the notion of the equitable proprietary entitlement distinct from, but co-existing with, legal title to the subject property.

One significant advantage of the use was that it allowed landowners to avoid feudal dues. It was an early form of tax avoidance. The Statute of Uses 1535 was enacted to suppress the use, but it proved to be only a temporary impediment. The legislation was not comprehensive and, besides, it lost its purpose as the feudal system declined. The courts eventually began giving effect to forms of transaction that were aimed at avoiding the operation of the statute (the so-called 'use upon a use'), and these developments led to the emergence of the trust in its modern form.

The modern trust performs a wide range of economically valuable functions. These all derive from the principal characteristic of the trust, namely the separation of legal title from beneficial ownership. For example:

(1) The trust can be used to split entitlements among two or more beneficiaries successively (to C1 then C2). This feature of the trust makes it useful as an instrument of family settlement. The vesting of legal title in the trustee (B) ensures continuity of ownership during any periods when there is no beneficiary with a present entitlement. Furthermore, B's involvement means that there is someone available to preserve the trust assets and ensure that the entitlements are distributed among the beneficiaries in accordance with A's wishes. (In some countries, tax considerations affecting the family settlement have led to the adoption of alternative methods of disposition.)

(2) Entitlements can also be split contingently by means of the trust, so that the benefit is put in suspense pending fulfilment of a condition (for example, to C1 upon her marriage). The founder of a trust may want to postpone the decision concerning allocation of benefits so that future events can be taken into account. For example, the founder may want to benefit persons not yet born or allocate benefits among beneficiaries depending on their relative future needs or deserts. These objectives can be met by giving the trustees power to make the appointment in future. In the meantime, as in the previous example, entitlements are held in suspense. This is the basis of the so-called 'discretionary trust'. In some countries, the discretionary trust is a favoured method of disposition for tax reasons.

(3) The trust can also be used to split entitlements concurrently (to C1 and C2 in proportions designated by the founder of the trust or, in the case of a discretionary trust, to be determined by the trustees). This feature of the trust is relied on in the context of family arrangements. However, it is also useful in contexts where, whether for legal or practical reasons, the group of persons intended to benefit is too large to have them made co-owners holding legal title. Instead, legal title can be transferred to a small number of trustees who hold the assets on trust for the group. Voluntary associations are sometimes constituted in this way, though less commonly nowadays since the enactment in many jurisdictions of legislation to facilitate the incorporation of associations. Other applications include collective investment activity (debenture trusts, unit trusts, private pension or superannuation funds, and the like) and charitable fund-raising.

(4) The trust enables management and control of assets to be separated from beneficial entitlement. This may be important in cases where the entitlement is in investments. An investment portfolio needs active management, and good management depends on expertise. The intended beneficiaries may be too numerous or lack the time and experience to assume a management role. The appointment of a suitably qualified trustee to control and manage the fund on the beneficiaries' behalf is a common solution to the problem (Moffat 1994: 5–10).

The purposes of the trust vary somewhat from one country to another, depending on statutory restrictions and tax considerations. Moffat identifies the common purposes of the modern trust in England as follows:

> concealing ownership, facilitating land conveyancing and other types of dealing in property, holding and controlling property for the sake of large groups of people (particularly in the fields of collective investment and charitable and other non-profit-orientated activity), providing for the founder's family in various ways over long periods of time (before and after his or her death), protecting property from creditors and from the extravagance of individual members of the family, and cutting down tax liabilities, particularly on the transfer of private capital (Moffat 1994: 10).

Modern trust law has evolved to meet this range of applications. So, for example, Chancery developed investment guidelines for portfolio management by trustees, and also rules relating to the delegation by trustees to brokers and other agents of their management responsibilities (these rules have since been partly codified and supplemented by legislation); trustees are subject to equitable duties of care and skill (to prevent shirking) and good faith (to prevent misappropriation of trust assets and other forms of cheating); and a wide range of remedies has been made available to the beneficiary against the defaulting trustee (among other things, trustees can be ordered to give accounts of their financial administration of the trust, pay compensation for loss or damage they have caused to the trust estate, and make restitution of profits they have wrongfully made for themselves by virtue of their position as trustees (Moffat 1994: 33–5)).

THE PREVENTION OF FRAUD. Equity has a wide jurisdiction to intervene in cases involving fraud. The development of the trust, recounted above, is associated with this jurisdiction but it is only one of many applications.

The concern of the common law courts was primarily with *representations* that were fraudulent. Furthermore, fraud came to be defined narrowly, the courts insisting on proof of an intention to cheat (*Derry v. Peek*). Accordingly, a deliberate lie would be actionable at common law if it caused the plaintiff loss (for example, if the lie caused the plaintiff to enter into an unprofitable contract). However, other more subtle forms of cheating went unpunished while, in the case of deliberate lies, the law did nothing to facilitate the plaintiff's problems of proving the defendant's mental state.

By contrast, the concept of fraud in equity has always been a fluid one. In the words of Lord Hardwicke:

> As to relief against frauds, no invariable rules can be established. Fraud is infinite, and were a Court of Equity once to lay down rules, how far they would go and no farther, in extending their relief against it, or to define strictly the species or evidence of it, the jurisdiction would be cramped, and perpetually eluded by new schemes, which the fertility of man's invention would contrive (quoted in Sheridan 1957: 2).

Equity's robust approach to the definition of fraud is closely linked with the idea of conscience and reflects the ecclesiastical origins of equity's jurisdiction. In the equitable sense, fraud consists of conduct that the court considers to be against conscience, whether or not it involves an express representation and even if there is no provable intention to cheat.

On the other hand, equity's jurisdiction in relation to fraud is not at large. The varieties of fraud may be infinite, but courts of equity no longer dispense *ad hoc* justice. A successful claim depends on the plaintiff being able to show that the defendant's conduct falls within some established category of wrongdoing recognized by the court. The following are some examples.

(a) *Innocent misrepresentation.* Equity will set aside a contract that was induced by misrepresentation regardless of whether the representor had an intention to mislead. In the leading English case *Redgrave v. Hurd*, Sir George Jessel M.R. suggested the following alternative ways of stating the rationale (at 12–13):

> A man is not allowed to get a benefit from a statement which he now admits to be false. He is not allowed to say, for the purpose of civil jurisdiction, that when he made it he did not know it to be false; he ought to have found that out before he made it.

and

> Even assuming that moral fraud must be shewn in order to set aside a contract, you have it where a man, having obtained a beneficial contract by a statement which he now knows to be false, insists upon keeping that contract. To do so is a moral delinquency: no man ought to seek to take advantage of his own false statements.

An economic explanation would be to say that the rule acts as an incentive for the representor to be careful in two senses. First, it induces the taking of cost-justified precautions to ensure the accuracy of the statement. Secondly, it encourages representors to be circumspect, in cases where they cannot be sure of their information, by making disclaimers. A disclaimer is a signal to the representee either that there are no economical means of discovering the truth or, alternatively, that it is cheaper for the representee to investigate (Bishop 1980).

(b) *Undue influence.* The use of undue influence to pressure a party to enter into a contract or make a gift is another example of fraud in equity. The typical case is where the plaintiff is in a dependent relationship with the defendant such as parent and child, guardian and ward or solicitor and client. In such cases, equity will set aside the transaction once the existence of the relationship has been established, unless the defendant can prove that there was no undue influence in fact exercised (for example, by pointing to the fact that the plaintiff was independently advised). In other words, undue influence is presumed so that the plaintiff is not required to prove it. Meagher, Gummow and Lehane say (1992: 344–5):

> Much of the value of the jurisdiction to the weaker party arises from the presumption against transactions in the course of a relationship of influence. Further, the cases usually concern plaintiffs who entered happily, if not euphorically, into the transaction.

Why should a transaction be set aside if the plaintiff entered 'happily, if not euphorically,' into it? The answer is that the plaintiff's 'happiness' is exogenous. As much as the transaction itself, it is a product of the defendant's influence. Free of influence, the plaintiff is likely to have chosen differently. All victims of fraud are presumably happy until the fraud is unmasked. Victims of duress make choices unhappily, but fraud and duress are different in this respect, though they both affect the quality of the victim's consent. Equity's intervention in undue influence cases acts as a deterrent against exploitation by the defendant of the plaintiff's position of dependency. The justification for reversing the onus of proof has to do with the evidentiary difficulties the plaintiff would be likely to encounter if undue influence had to be proved affirmatively. Typically, the relations between the parties will be 'so close as to make it difficult to disentangle the inducements which led to the transaction' (*Johnson v. Buttress*, 134–5).

(c) *Conflicts of interest.* The equitable rules governing fiduciary obligations were developed initially in the context of the trust. Trustees are subject to equitable duties of care and loyalty. The duty of loyalty precludes trustees from using their office as a means of personal gain, and it requires them to avoid actual or potential conflicts of interest. Similar rules apply to company directors in relation to their company, solicitors in relation to their clients, partners in relation to each other, and so on.

A wide range of conduct is affected. So, for example: a trustee is prohibited from misappropriating or self-dealing in assets; company directors may not divert corporate business opportunities to themselves; solicitors are prevented from acting for both parties to litigation; employees may not accept bribes or secret commissions. The usual remedy for breach of the duty of loyalty is disgorgement of profits, regardless of harm caused to the beneficiary. Moreover, a reverse onus rule applies. Once the plaintiff has established certain basic facts, the onus shifts to the defendant fiduciary of justifying the conduct that has been complained of. So, for example, company directors who divert a business opportunity to themselves are deemed to have breached the duty of loyalty. They must account to the company for the gains unless they can prove that the transaction took place with the shareholders' fully informed consent.

From an economic perspective, these rules represent the courts' response to the impossibility of writing fully specified agreements covering long-term contractual relations. The rules reflect the kinds of provision the parties themselves are likely to have included in the contract if transactions costs had not been prohibitive. A trustee who insisted, in negotiations, on the right to misappropriate trust assets would stand very little chance of appointment; the inclusion of such a right in the contract would undermine the whole purpose of establishing a trust in the first place. The same reasoning applies to company directors in respect of business opportunities and other corporate assets. Clients, as a general rule, contract on the assumption that they will receive undivided loyalty from their solicitor; litigants employ lawyers to improve their chances of success in litigation, not to prejudice them. Employers would be likely to insist, if they directed their minds to the matter at the outset, on employees accounting for any bribes received. Bribes drive a wedge between the employer's interests and the employee's interest, and a rule requiring the employee to hand over the payment restores the employer's control. The parties would also be likely to contract for some kind of evidentiary concession in relation to the duty of loyalty, as a way of countering A's high monitoring costs. In the absence of such a rule, A would have difficulty establishing whether, for example, loss of an asset was due to B's misconduct or legitimate business misfortune – or, correspondingly, whether a gain was attributable to good management on B's part or just good luck. There would be no point in stipulating for a detailed set of obligations on B's part if A's inability to discriminate in this way meant that breaches routinely went undetected; in that event A would be just as vulnerable to B's wrongdoing as if there had been no stipulations at all.

In summary, fiduciary obligations are a gap-filling device. They are no more or less than contractual implied terms. The consequence is to leave the parties free to write relatively short, open-ended contracts. The courts then fill in the details in the manner just described. Parties who do not want the standard fiduciary package remain free to bargain around it. This will necessarily involve writing a longer contract, but it is cheaper to allow parties to contract out of a standard package in the minority of cases than to require parties in the majority of cases to contract in. The philosophy underlying the implied warranties in sales law is exactly the same (Easterbrook and Fischel 1993).

(d) *Relief against forfeiture.* Consider the following case:

> A agrees to purchase land from B and pay the price by instalments. The contract provides that the instalments must be paid punctually, otherwise B may rescind the contract and recover the land. A goes into immediate occupation and, to B's knowledge, builds a house on the land. Partly as a consequence of A's improvements, the land increases substantially in value. A is two days late in paying an instalment. B refuses to accept the payment and invokes the rescission clause.

This scenario is based loosely on the facts of the Australian case *Legione v. Hateley*. At common law, the position is likely to be governed by the terms of the contract, strictly interpreted. However, in equity the court may be prepared to grant A relief against forfeiture of the property by prohibiting the exercise of B's strict legal rights under the contract and ordering specific performance of the contract in favour of A. The likelihood of such an outcome will be increased if it is proved that B contributed to A's breach (for example, by leading A to believe that late payment would be acceptable). The use by B of surprise tactics as a means of securing a windfall gain from rescinding the contract is another example of fraud in equity.

This kind of intervention is similar in policy terms to the rules governing fiduciary obligations, discussed above. It is an attempt to fill in the gaps of an incompletely specified contract. In the example given, the contract appears to have been drafted without the parties giving thought to the possibility that A – with B's consent – might build on the land and, perhaps more significantly, without express reference to the parties' rights in the event that B contributes to A's breach. If the parties had thought about the matter at the outset, they would be likely to have agreed that there would be no right of rescission in these circumstances. The consequence otherwise would be to leave A exposed to a substantial risk of manipulation by B, and A is unlikely to have wanted an agreement on those terms. In short, to enforce the contract according to its letter would be contrary to the parties' likely *ex ante* preferences and would result in a misallocation of resources.

(e) *Estoppel* The leading English case *Central London Property Trust v. High Trees House Ltd* concerned a lease agreement for a London block of flats that was signed just before the outbreak of World War II. The lessor and lessee were related companies and the lessee intended to sublet the flats and pay the rent out of the profits. The war made it difficult to find occupants for the flats, due to the absence of people in London, and the parties agreed informally to reduce the rent. The lessor company later went into receivership, and at the end of the war the receiver claimed arrears of rent from the lessee. At common law the lessee would have had no defence because of the rule that a lease under seal could only be varied by deed. However, Denning J. held that the lessee had a good defence in equity. The lessor had made a promise intended to be binding and to be acted on by the lessee. The lessee had acted on the promise by maintaining its involvement in what would otherwise have been an unprofitable venture, and the lessor was estopped from going back on its word.

In the Australian case *Waltons Stores Ltd v. Maher*. Brennan J. reformulated the equitable estoppel doctrine as follows (at 428–9):

> In my opinion, to establish an equitable estoppel, it is necessary for a plaintiff to prove that (1) the plaintiff assumed or expected that a particular legal relationship exists between the plaintiff and the defendant or that a particular legal relationship will exist between them and, in the latter case, that the defendant is not free to withdraw from the expected legal relationship; (2) the defendant has induced the plaintiff to adopt that assumption or expectation; (3) the plaintiff acts or abstains from acting in reliance on the assumption or

> expectation; (4) the defendant knew or intended him to do so; (5) the plaintiff's action or inaction will occasion detriment if the assumption or expectation is not fulfilled; and (6) the defendant has failed to act to avoid that detriment whether by fulfilling the assumption or expectation or otherwise.

The lessee in the *High Trees* case gave no consideration in exchange for the lessor's promise (at common law, an agreement to accept a lesser sum in discharge of a larger debt is not good consideration). Nevertheless, the lessor was still held to be bound. Equitable estoppel thus poses a threat to the established common law doctrine of consideration. The economic justification for the consideration doctrine is that consideration is an outward manifestation of the parties' intention to be bound by their statements. The courts' insistence on consideration avoids the costs that would otherwise be incurred if evidence had to be led in every case of the parties' actual intentions. The reduction of a promise to the form of a deed under seal serves the same function, and this explains the courts' willingness to waive the consideration requirement for deeds. To the extent that the *High Trees* case made inroads into this position, the decision was a costly one.

On the other hand, there are offsetting benefits. Given the particular facts of the case, it is a fair inference that both parties' *ex ante* preference would have been that the lessor's promise should be binding. The lessee would have wanted to receive a commitment from the lessor to reduce the risk of its continued involvement in the project and, correspondingly, the lessor would have wanted to make a commitment to prevent the lessee's withdrawal. Why, then, did the parties not execute a deed of variation, to put the matter beyond doubt? The answer is almost certainly that it did not occur to them at the time that formalities were necessary. In other words, it cannot be inferred from their failure to execute a deed that they did not intend to be bound. The decision enforcing the lessor's promise was therefore efficient in the sense that it gave effect to the parties' likely *ex ante* preferences, and also in the related sense that it provided a deterrent against promisors in future inducing wasted reliance expenditure by promisees. These benefits need to be offset against the costs of an equitable estoppel rule flowing from increased uncertainty in the litigation of contract disputes. However, the equitable estoppel rule is quite closely circumscribed as Brennan J's statement, quoted above, makes clear, so that in the majority of contract disputes the doctrine of consideration will still apply (Craswell 1996; Katz 1996).

CONCLUSION. Maitland's view was that there is no longer any meaningful distinction between common law and equity, except the historical one. By contrast, some modern equity writers claim that equity is a superior system of justice. Equity, it is said, is concerned with imposing higher moral standards on the community, whereas the common law encourages self-interested behaviour and is ruggedly individualist in its outlook. For example, Parkinson says (1996: 52):

> The principles of equity . . . ensure that a much greater standard of altruism is required in business and other relations than was the case a hundred years ago. Equity is resurgent.

This assessment is consistent with views expressed by other commentators (for example Finn 1987 and Finn 1989) and judges in a number of countries (for example McLachlin 1993).

However, while it is true that equity judgments are often heavily laced with appeals to conscience, it is important not to be beguiled by the rhetoric. In the end, it is not the language judges use that count so much as the results they actually reach. The truth is that, notwithstanding the rhetoric of conscience, large areas of equity doctrine can be accounted for in economic terms and hence are referable to considerations of parties' self-interest rather than to altruism (see the previous section).

To deny that equity is motivated by altruistic concerns is not to suggest that other-regarding behaviour should be discouraged or that greed is good. The point is simply that the courts' capacity for enforcing standards of morality is limited. It is critically important to be aware of these limitations, otherwise the lawmaker is likely to end up doing more harm than good (Duggan 1996).

ANTHONY J. DUGGAN

See also ENGLISH COMMON LAW; FIDUCIARY DUTIES; INCOMPLETE CONTRACTS; INHERITANCE LAW; JUSTICE; JUST PRICE; SOCIAL JUSTICE; TRESPASS AND NUISANCE; UNCONSCIONABILITY.

Subject classification: 3b; 4a(iii); 4b(i); 5a(ii).

STATUTES

Statute of Uses 1535 (27 Hen. VIII, c. 10).
Supreme Court Act 1981 (Eng).
Supreme Court of Judicature Act 1873 (36 & 37 Vict., c. 66).
Supreme Court of Judicature Act 1875 (38 & 39 Vict., c. 77).

CASES

Attorney-General for Hong Kong v. Reid [1994] 1 AC 324.
Baumgartner v. Baumgartner (1987) 164 CLR 137.
Central London Property Trust v. High Trees House Ltd [1947] KB 130.
Cook v. Deeks [1916] 1 AC 554.
Derry v. Peek (1889) 14 App Cas 337.
Earl of Oxford's Case (1615) 1 Ch R 1; 21 ER 485.
Johnson v. Buttress (1936) 56 CLR 113.
Legione v. Hateley (1983) 152 CLR 406.
Lister & Co. v. Stubbs (1890) 45 ChD 1.
Nocton v. Lord Ashburton [1914] AC 932.
Pettkus v. Becker (1980) 117 DLR (3d) 257.
Redgrave v. Hurd (1881) 20 ChD 1.
Waltons Stores (Interstate) Ltd v. Maher (1988) 164 CLR 387.

BIBLIOGRAPHY

Aristotle. *Nicomachean Ethics*. Trans. H. Rackham. Cambridge, MA: Harvard University Press, 1968.
Ashburner, W. 1933. *Principles of Equity*. 2nd edn, London: Butterworths.
Bishop, W. 1980. Negligent misrepresentation through economists' eyes. *Law Quarterly Review* 96: 360–79.
Craswell, R. 1996. Offer, acceptance and efficient reliance. *Stanford Law Review* 48: 481–553.

Duggan, A.J. 1996. Is equity efficient? Paper presented at European Law and Economics Association Conference August 1996 and Canadian Law and Economics Association Conference September 1996.

Easterbrook, F.H. and Fischel, D.R. 1993. Contract and fiduciary duty. *Journal of Law and Economics* 36: 425–46.

Finn, P.D. 1987. Equity and contract. In *Essays on Contract*, ed. P.R. Finn, Sydney: Law Book Company.

Finn, P.D. 1989. The fiduciary principle. In *Equity, Fiduciaries and Trusts*, ed. T.G. Youdan, Toronto: Carswell.

Hanbury, H.G. and Martin, J.E. 1993. *Modern Equity*. 14th edn, London: Sweet & Maxwell.

Holdsworth, W.S. 1956. *A History of English Law*. 7th edn. 17 vols, London: Methuen & Co; Sweet and Maxwell (1st edn 1903).

Katz, A. 1996. When should an offer stick? *Yale Law Journal* 105: 1249–1309.

Maitland, F.W. 1932. *Equity*. Ed. A.H. Chaytor and W.J. Whittaker, Cambridge: Cambridge University Press.

Maitland, F.W. 1936. *Selected Essays*. Freeport, NY: Books for Libraries Press, Inc.

McLachlin, B.M. 1993. The place of equity and equitable doctrines in the contemporary common law world: a Canadian perspective. In *Equity, Fiduciaries and Trusts 1993*, ed. D.W.M. Waters, Toronto: Carswell.

Meagher, R.P., Gummow, W.M.C. and Lehane, J.R.F. 1992. *Equity Doctrines and Remedies*. 3rd edn, Sydney: Butterworths.

Moffat, G. 1994. *Trusts Law Text and Materials*. 2nd edn, London, Dublin and Edinburgh: Butterworths.

Paciocco, D.M. 1989. The remedial constructive trust: a principled basis for priority over creditors. *Canadian Bar Review* 68: 315–51.

Parkinson, P. 1996. The conscience of equity. In *The Principles of Equity*, ed. P. Parkinson, Sydney: LBC Information Services.

Pettit, P.H. 1993. *Equity and the Law of Trusts*. 7th edn, London, Dublin and Edinburgh: Butterworths.

Sheridan, L. 1957. *Fraud in Equity: A Study in English and Irish Law*. London: Pitman.

Sherwin, E.L. 1989. Constructive trusts in bankruptcy. *University of Illinois Law Review* [1989]: 297–365.

ESOPS. *See* EMPLOYEE OWNERSHIP OF FIRMS.

estoppel. *See* CLASS ACTIONS; COLLATERAL ESTOPPEL; CONTRACT FORMATION AND INTERPRETATION; EQUITY.

European competition policy. Competition policy is one of the pillars of the economic constitution of the European Union. The Treaty of Rome (1957), subsequently incorporated, unamended, in the Maastricht Treaty on European Union (1992), gives the European Commission extensive executive powers to deal with anti-competitive practices by private enterprises, as well as certain behaviour of Member State governments or state owned enterprises that distort competition and inhibit integration of markets across Europe. According to Article 3(f) of the Treaty of Rome, competition policy has the central remit to ensure '*that competition in the common market is not distorted*'. Articles 85–94 then specify the founding principles under which European competition policy operates. Articles 85 and 86 address private enterprises with respect to restrictive agreements and abuses of a dominant position, whereas Articles 90 and 92–94 address government protection of state monopolies and financial support to specific companies that may distort competition. These Treaty Articles are complemented by a number of Regulations that form the basis of actions of the Commission in the area of competition policy. Of particular importance are Regulation 17/62, which governs the implementation of Articles 85 and 86, and the Merger Regulation 4064/89, which gives the Commission powers to vet mergers with a Community dimension.

The Commission has used these wide powers to great effect. It is generally acknowledged that today the EU has one of the most developed antitrust policies in the world, which exerts a great influence over the behaviour of business. The role of European competition policy goes, however, much beyond that traditionally assigned to competition policy regimes in other countries. European competition policy is unique in that it subsumes competition policy under the much broader goal of integration of the national economies. The creation of a single market where national borders do not matter is the ultimate goal. The Single Market Programme, launched in 1985, aims to complete the internal market by reducing non-tariff barriers between Member States and opening up national markets for other European competitors. The measures taken within this programme range from directives that seek to open up public procurement markets, to measures that facilitate the harmonization of technical standards. Competition policy is integral to this process because it seeks to ensure that trade barriers are not replaced by new constraints. In particular, companies are not allowed to thwart the emerging internal market through restrictive agreements or mergers that would allow them to maintain and exploit market partitioning. More generally, competition policy, in the words of the commissioner, Karel Van Miert, must '*ensure that the single market with its efficiency gains becomes a reality and not only a theoretical possibility*' (Van Miert 1996: 2). European competition policy seeks to guarantee sound markets across the EU just as the planned European Monetary Union seeks to guarantee sound money across the EU. It is arguable that European competition policy has, over the last forty years, been influential in promoting European integration through actions taken by the Commission, and backed by the European Court of Justice, to support the free movement of goods and services throughout the Community.

INSTITUTIONS AND PROCEDURES. In its execution of competition policy the Commission acts through the Directorate General for Competition – or DG IV as it is commonly known. There is an important distinction between the political arm, the Commission, and the administration headed by a Director General who, by tradition, has so far always been German. The Commissioner in charge of competition policy resides in the same building as his fellow Commissioners, rather than with his officials in DG IV, underlining the political nature of Commission decisions in the application of competition policy and his distinct role vis-à-vis the administration for which he is responsible.

DG IV is structured into seven main Directorates, listed in Table 1.

Table 1
Composition of DG IV

Directorate:	*Description:*
A	General competition policy and co-ordination
B	Merger Task Force
C	Information, communication and multimedia
D	Services
E	Basic industries
F	Capital and consumer goods industries
G	State aids

Directorate A does not become directly involved in individual cases. Directorate B applies the Merger Regulation. Directorates C to F apply Articles 85/86 and, when applicable, Article 90 to specific sectors.

DG IV is unusual among the institutions of the European Union in several respects. Other directorates actively promote policy in fields such as external affairs, harmonization of national legislation in the Member States (e.g. product liability, toy safety, environmental regulation) or are responsible for spending large funds for support of particular industries or regions (in 1995, 6.76 billion ECU was spent on the Social Fund and almost 40 billion ECU was spent on support and structural measures for the agricultural sector). In contrast, DG IV is relatively small with only just over 400 staff. While small in terms of numbers of staff and budget, DG IV's actions directly affect individual businesses in a significant way. With a warrant from a local judge, its staff can enter business premises to search for documentary evidence of anti-competitive conduct and can force businesses to provide commercially sensitive information. Moreover, negative decisions reached after an investigation by DG IV into restrictive practices and abuse of monopoly power are enforced in national courts and can result in heavy fines, reaching a maximum of 10% of a company's turnover.

The Commission's case load is substantial. Since the 1960s, when the Commission became active in this area, a significant number of cartels have been heavily fined and thousands of contracts have been vetted. Fines have become larger and more common since the early 1980s. Table 2 shows the number of new cases registered, mainly under Articles 85/86, in each year since 1988. The cases are split by type: notifications, complaints and *ex officio* cases (cases opened at the Commission's own initiative):

Table 2
New cases registered by DG IV during the year

	1988	1989	1990	1991	1992	1993	1994	1995
Notifications	376	206	201	282	246	266	236	368
Complaints	83	93	97	83	110	111	140	145
Ex officio	44	67	75	23	43	27	16	46
Total	503	366	373	388	399	404	392	559

Source: XXV Report on Competition Policy 1995.

In recent years there has been an active policy to reduce the list of pending cases. This has resulted in the number of open cases falling from 3,451 at the end of 1988 to 1,178 at the end of 1995. There remains, however, a substantial criticism by business that DG IV is under-resourced and therefore operates too slowly, thus creating delays and uncertainty. Exempt from this criticism is the Merger Task Force which operates along strict deadlines. There is one month for an initial phase (after which mergers that do not indicate any competition problems are cleared) and another four months for making a decision if an in-depth investigation is thought necessary. Since the Merger Regulation took effect in 1990, only seven mergers have been blocked by the Commission while a significant number of others were cleared only after the Commission extracted substantial concessions. Up to the end of 1996 over 500 notifications were received by the Commission. Most concentrations – the legal term for notifiable mergers and joint ventures – were cleared within one month and fewer than 35 in-depth investigations were opened.

In its dealings on monopoly rights and state aids the Commission has faced some major political battles when investigating support provided by national governments to enterprises that are considered to have an adverse impact on competition. The fact that the ultimate decisions on state aid (and competition policy matters) have to be taken by the Commission as a whole, sometimes leaves room for pork-barrel politics where political considerations, often supported by affected Member States and the respective industry directorates within the Commission, may override the purely competitive aspects of an individual case. Among the more controversial cases in the 1990s have been those dealing with the massive support to airlines which were feeling the impact of liberalization, and which previously benefited from substantial protection as government-owned flag carriers.

SUBSIDIARITY. Competition policy in the EU is executed not only through the European Commission, but also through the competition authorities of Member States and through national courts. In fact, national competition legislation predates that of the European Union in some of the major European countries which have established their own policies and legislative framework. The UK, for example, has had competition legislation since 1948 and conducts competition and consumer protection policy through the Office of Fair Trading (set up in 1973) and the Monopolies and Mergers Commission (set up in 1948). The German Federal Cartel Office was established in 1958 but unfair trade laws have been in force since 1909 (the Gesetz gegen den unlauteren Wettbewerb). In contrast, several European countries have only introduced formal EU-style antitrust legislation in the last ten years (Belgium, Greece, Italy, Portugal, Spain, Finland and Sweden). In the case of Italy, EC competition legislation has been adopted as a whole, including a binding commitment to respect case law of the Commission and the European courts. Even countries outside the European Union (such as Hungary, the Czech Republic, Poland and Romania) have adopted a broadly similar national competition policy regime, making European competition policy a rare example of an export of a legal framework.

What rules govern the application of European as distinct from national competition laws? What are the rules that provide powers to the Commission, rather than national authorities? What is the role of national courts to enforce Community law? These complex constitutional questions of subsidiarity and decentralization have spawned a great debate over the division of labour between the Commission and Member State governments on the one hand and the respective roles of national and Community law on the other. The extension of the powers of the Commission, and introduction of majority voting in the Council in the run-up to the Maastricht Treaty on European Union (1992), was accompanied by strong moves to reduce the scope of action taken at Community level. As a result, the principle of subsidiarity is now formulated in Article 3B(2) of the Treaty of Maastricht:

> In areas which do not fall within its exclusive competence, the Community shall take action, in accordance with the principle of subsidiarity, only if and in so far as the objectives of the proposed action cannot be sufficiently achieved by the Member States and can therefore, by reason of the scale or effects of the proposed action, be better achieved by the Community.

The principle of decentralization, among others, has been addressed through a Notice, published in February 1993 by the Commission, on cooperation between the Commission and national courts in the application of Articles 85 and 86, and has now been extended by a similar notice on the application of state aid rules. The Commission argues that since authorities are often closer to the companies and markets in question, they may be better able to perform the role of 'competition watchdog'.

The Treaty rules that govern cartels and abuse of monopoly create supremacy of European competition law in cases where trade between Member States is affected. However, while the policies on restrictive practices and monopolies are determined at the supra-national level, they can – with the exception of Art 85(3) – be enforced through private actions in national courts. This now happens frequently with often devastating effects, either through injunctions or companies arguing that clauses are void and unenforceable as contrary to EC rules. In important key areas of competition policy, however, the Commission has sole jurisdiction, for example in mergers, where the Merger Regulation of 1989 gives it an exclusive role (the one-stop shop) to vet mergers between very large companies which operate in more than one Member State of the European Union. Mergers that do not meet the turnover thresholds of the Merger Regulation or where the activities mainly affect a distinct market in a single Member State (the so-called 'German clause') are still the prerogative of national laws. While these jurisdictional rules give Member States an increased role, there is another clause, the so-called 'Dutch clause', which allows Member States without merger regulations to refer a case to Brussels (which has so far happened only on occasion – four times up to 1997).

ANTI-COMPETITIVE AGREEMENTS. Article 85 prohibits a large range of anti-competitive agreements and practices among firms. The policy aim is to prevent coordinated market behaviour. Article 85(1) casts a wide net by declaring void all agreements or concerted practices which have as their object or effect the prevention, restriction or distortion of competition in the common market. The list of practices in Article 85(1) covers cartels, price fixing and market sharing agreements as well as exclusionary practices that disadvantage third parties. These agreements can be of a horizontal nature (between competitors) or vertical restrictions between parties at different levels of the market. Article 85(3) allows for exemptions from this wide ranging prohibition and narrows down the impact of Article 85(1) in cases where agreements or concerted practices provide significant benefits in terms of improved production, distribution or innovation. The control of restrictive practices in European competition policy is, therefore, at the same time wide and narrow. In principle, any agreement between market participants which have more than a minimal share of the market is caught by Article 85(1). The scope for exemption is, however, very wide and the Commission spends much time vetting contracts for their compatibility with the common market, often without coming to any decision.

European competition policy towards restrictive practices has been particularly successful in hunting down cartels, but not always successful in having its decisions upheld by the courts. Large fines for producers of woodpulp accused of operating a cartel were quashed by the European Court of Justice in 1996 after a nine-year court battle. Equally, a decision against several producers of soda ash was reversed in 1995 after the European Court of First Instance found the Commission failed to give information to allow a fair hearing.

Anti-trust enforcement is generally difficult. This applies to the execution of European competition policy as well as to anti-trust regimes elsewhere. Evidence of price fixing or market sharing is hard to obtain, even though the Commission has extensive powers to collect documentary evidence. DG IV is well known for its dawn raids where its staff, supported by officials from Member States, turn up early in the morning and request access to all files that relate to a particular type of business or transaction. However, collusive pricing is often difficult to distinguish from the outcome of competition in markets with few competitors. *Woodpulp* is just one case where defendants argued successfully in the European Court of Justice that the observed pricing in the market was the outcome of oligopolistic competition rather than collusion among producers.

Nevertheless, the Commission has effectively challenged a number of large EU-wide cartels with quite formal structures that maintained coordination among firms in different Member States. Cartonboard, cement and steel products are just some of the more recent examples where cartels have been fined hundreds of millions ECU for agreeing pricing initiatives, production quotas and generally exchanging commercial information. Some examples are given in Table 3.

One response has been to introduce incentives for cartel members to inform the Commission of anti-competitive practices by cartels. The so-called 'whistle-blower' notice of 1996 offers reduced fines to those firms who come forward.

Table 3
Examples of fines imposed under Articles 85 and 86

Date	Case	Fines	
		ECU m.	£m.
December 1990	ICI and Solvay fined for soda ash cartel	47	37
July 1991	Tetrapak fined for abuse of dominant position in liquid packaging (article 86)	75	59
February 1994	16 companies in steel beams cartel fined	104	81
July 1994	19 carton board producers fined for 'pernicious' cartel	132	104
December 1994	33 cement producers and associations fined for prolonged cartel	248	193

Source: Wilks and McGowan, 'Competition policy in the European Union', in *Comparative Competition Policy*, eds Doern & Wilks (1996).

OTHER COOPERATIVE AGREEMENTS BETWEEN FIRMS. Apart from collusion on prices and production, there are other forms of agreements between firms which restrict competition yet may have efficiency-enhancing effects. Such agreements, even if their efficiency effects are obvious, nevertheless have to be notified to the Commission, which can then grant an exemption under Article 85(3). In particular, there are two types of cooperation which have the potential to be exempted on efficiency grounds: horizontal agreements on joint research and development activities; and vertical agreements related to the production and/or distribution of goods.

The Commission is generally fairly lenient towards agreements that deal with R&D joint ventures or with licensing agreements. The policy approach has been to look favourably at such forms of cooperation when it allows firms to remain competitive with the rest of the world, or when it furthers the integration of the common market. As a result, European competition law contains some quite wide-ranging block exemptions for R&D and technology licensing agreements as well as a number of individual exemption decisions (ten a year) to the general prohibition under Article 85(1). Many agreements receive a non-binding comfort letter from the Commission which suggests that action is unlikely. This positive attitude has been supported by the expectation that the single market would lead to more cross-border cooperation by firms in an integrating market and that this would contribute to integration. The fact that the number of cooperation agreements between European firms related to R&D has not significantly increased does not, however, justify this more lenient approach. What in fact has been observed is an increase in marketing agreements between European firms and the rest of the world.

A perennial source of debate is the Commission's treatment of vertical restraints, typically in agreements between manufacturers and distributors or distributors and retailers. At the moment, DG IV vets many agreements each year for the degree of exclusivity that they provide for a downstream firm. In the 1997 Green Paper on vertical restraints, the Commission reveals that following the coming into force of Regulation 17/62 it had dealt with nearly 30,000 agreements. The Commission has recognized that some modification is needed to the system of notifications for vertical agreements that are never likely to cause any damage to consumers and simply occupy valuable resources within DG IV. Economists have argued for some time now that unless either upstream or downstream markets are concentrated or subject to certain types of regulation, vertical restraints are likely to be pro-competitive or at least neutral in their effects on competition. Yet DG IV's traditional form-based assessment of vertical restraints cannot deal with a policy that is primarily effects-based. The Commission finds itself caught in a situation of legal precedence that is increasingly at odds with the economics of distribution, and more generally with vertical relationships that depend on cooperation. To deal with these tensions the Commission has enacted a number of block exemptions for certain types of agreements and certain industries and this has lessened the problem without silencing all critics. It is fair to say that this debate over the acceptability of vertical restrictions in agreements between suppliers and distributors or retailers will continue well into the next millennium.

Yet there may be a defence of the Commission's practice. The overriding goal of integration as set out in the Treaty of Rome is clearly at odds with agreements which operate along national borders, and which can, in some circumstances, give rise to serious obstacles to competition and integration. The national organization of distribution may be justified and supported by national purchasing habits that are based on objective factors such as climate, geography, cultural preferences or language. These national purchasing habits, however, make it particularly easy for firms to reinforce national market segmentation through agreements or types of behaviour which limit intra-brand competition and may also reduce the intensity of inter-brand competition or deter entry.

For example, both the car and beer industries exhibit strong patterns of national purchasing habits and are characterized by an organization of distribution in the form of agreements that contain restrictions on sale of competing goods, resale restrictions and clauses granting exclusivity. The block exemptions for the beer and car industries were renewed by the Commission in the mid-1990s, after extensive debate and also lobbying by the respective industries. Without here judging the merits of these individual cases, it is fair to say that many of these agreements do tend to reinforce national market segmentation. The Commission, supported by the European Courts in its interpretation of the Treaty of Rome, naturally focuses on the scope for market segmentation, and has insisted on measures that prevent dealers having sole or 'absolute' territorial protection. The Commission insists on the option for consumers to buy parallel imports and benefit from some degree of cross-country arbitrage.

MARKET DOMINANCE. Article 86 of the Treaty of Rome deals with the abuse of a dominant position through anti-competitive practices which have the effect of damaging competitors or restricting competition at the expense of customers. Monopoly behaviour will be investigated following a complaint by an actual or potential competitor about being forced out of the market, or by customers facing unfair or unequal trading conditions. Article 86 challenges only the abuse of a dominant position and not the mere existence or acquisition of market power. The types of abuse that are outlawed are set out in Article 86 in a non-exhaustive manner and include price discrimination, access restrictions and foreclosure, tying, exclusionary pricing, as well as excessive pricing.

Article 86 is aimed primarily at the conduct of a single dominant company. The extension of such provisions to so-called joint dominance is fairly recent and controversial. The controversy has arisen because it was believed by some that the abuse of a dominant position by one or more undertakings referred to in Article 86 only related to undertakings within the same economic unit or corporate group. Hence cases of collective dominance in oligopolistic markets were excluded. In *Italian Flat Glass* (1990), however, the Commission dealt with the case of two or more economically and legally independent firms and considered them to hold a collective dominant position under Article 86.

A dominant position has been defined by the European Court of Justice in a number of cases as the power of a firm to behave to an appreciable extent independently of its competitors, customers, and ultimately of consumers. To establish that a dominant position exists, the Commission first has to define the relevant market. It then takes account of market shares and of other indicators of dominance, such as high barriers to entry into the relevant market, that reinforce or support any market power in the short to medium term. For example, in the case of *United Brands* (1978), the Commission found, and the Court confirmed their view, that dominance was supported by a very strong brand name, vertically integrated operations in shipping and banana plantations, access to the international capital market and economies of scale. Both the excessive reliance on market share as an indicator of dominance, and the listing of every activity or genuine competitive advantage based on superior efficiency of the dominant undertaking, has been criticized by economists. Proving an abuse of a dominant position is exceedingly difficult. Several of the practices listed in Article 86 have an efficiency justification as well as potentially being a manifestation of monopoly power. Furthermore, it is sometimes difficult to distinguish between the legitimate competitive process of rivalry which leads to the exit of inefficient firms and the abusive behaviour of dominant firms.

A comparison of European competition policy towards monopolies with similar national policies shows that excessive pricing as a form of exploitation of monopoly power does not figure prominently in the application of EU competition law. There have been very few cases of excessive or predatory pricing. The *United Brands* case, which went to the European Court of Justice, is a case in point. Here the Court ruled against the Commission for failing to demonstrate the existence of prices above costs but accepted other forms of abuse such as refusal to supply a banana ripener and charging differential prices between Member States. In fact, there are quite a few cases of discriminatory pricing where an entry-deterring pricing strategy was effectively challenged by the Commission. There are also numerous cases of tying, refusal to supply and foreclosure, particularly with respect to competitors or entrants from other Member States. For example, in *Commercial Solvents v. Commission*, the ECJ upheld the Commission's decision that Commercial Solvents had abused its dominant position by refusing to supply nitrophone to an existing customer (Zoja) which would, as a result, be forced to leave the market. More generally, the cases examined by the Commission under Article 86 show that its overriding concern is to protect existing competitors in the interest of integration rather than challenging market power in the single market.

In addition to Article 86, Article 90 is directed at monopoly situations which have at their source monopoly (exclusive or special) rights granted by or protected by national governments. It obliges national governments not to enact or maintain in force any measure contrary to the Treaty. State monopolies and government regulation are often a major source of monopoly in many industries (particularly infrastructure industries such as gas, electricity, telecommunications and transport). With the general trend towards deregulation and privatization in the 1990s, there is increasing scope for DG IV to deal with government-backed monopolies, and the role of DG IV in securing a pro-competitive outcome in these industries is becoming even more important. Disputes over access to airport and seaport facilities are one area where the interface of competition policy and the regulation of markets with a tendency towards monopoly situations has become more prevalent, opening new areas of activities for DG IV. This has led to the development of an 'essential facilities doctrine' through a number of leading cases supported by Commission notices.

MERGERS. European merger policy is fairly recent. The Merger Regulation 4064/89 gives the Commission substantial powers to vet mergers and concentrative joint ventures, but it was enacted only after more than a decade of political controversy. As a political compromise, designed to pacify opponents of ever increasing powers for the Commission, the Merger Regulation only covers deals involving large companies with an aggregate world-wide turnover of more than 5 billion ECU. Further, the relevant jurisdictional test is also based on geographic turnover in the EU (more than 250 million ECU for each party). The nationality of the head office of the parties does not matter: the Merger Regulation can therefore apply to transactions involving no European company. In practice, this has meant that most major mergers of US companies have needed clearance by both the Commission and the US authorities. This fact, plus some other widely publicized parallel antitrust investigations on both sides of the Atlantic, have led to increased efforts at international cooperation on competition policy.

The guiding principle in the Commission's analysis of mergers is that a concentration which '*creates or strengthens a dominant position as a result of which effective competition would be significantly impeded in the Common Market or in a substantial part of it, shall be declared incompatible with the Common Market*' (Article 2 of the Merger Regulation). In some cases, the Commission has also intervened to prevent the strengthening or emergence of non-competitive oligopolies (most notably *Nestlé/Perrier* 1992). The key role of merger policy is thus in the first instance to identify and control market power. Conversely, mergers which do not create dominance should be approved without delay.

It is of course also possible that mergers promote efficiency gains in the form of cost savings for the merging parties. These may go some way to offsetting the allocative efficiency losses from the increase in market power, and indeed it is conceivable that the overall welfare effect of a merger may be positive even if it leads to an increase in concentration. However, like other national merger authorities in Europe (for example Germany), the Commission's approach is heavily focused on changes in market structure and does not easily accept efficiency defences. The interpretation of the Merger Regulation by the Merger Task Force places far more emphasis on market structure, and its centrepiece is therefore the analysis of dominance.

STATE AID. The Commission takes decisions with respect to aid granted by national or local government bodies in Member States under Articles 92–94 of the Treaty. State aid may have a distorting effect on competition and can change market structure in an undesirable way. If, for example, a government supports a relatively inefficient firm through extensive subsidies, then exit of a more efficient rival in another Member State may be one of the consequences. In this way state aid adversely affects productive efficiency. When several firms in an industry are simultaneously affected by major changes in their markets, then a race between firms may ensue whereby firms seek support from their respective governments. In particular, when such an industry has a high concentration of employment in one geographic area, or when national champions are affected, then state aid races can easily occur.

Although a framework for control of state aid at the European level has been in place since the foundation of the EC, its importance has increased with the completion of the single market. The air travel sector offers an example of an industry where liberalization and deregulation provoked substantial restructuring of a sector that had hitherto benefited from significant protection. The invariable response of some Member States has been to grant huge subsidies to help domestic flag carriers adjust to the new and more competitive environment. It is arguable that economically justifiable reasons for state aid were not present in these cases. Most state aid cases in the airline sector have been controversial and have been dealt with by the Commission in a highly political environment. Even the Commission has had to admit that national governments may be looking for measures to protect the economic interests of their own airlines. The irony is that when the Commission gives way to the political pressures from Member States and accepts state aid, it inevitably undermines the objectives of the process set in motion by the Commission's liberalization measures.

THOMAS A. HOEHN

See also ANTITRUST POLICY; CENTRALIZED AND DECENTRALIZED REGULATION IN THE EUROPEAN UNION; COMPETITION LAW IN THE EUROPEAN UNION AND THE UNITED STATES; EVOLUTION OF THE ECONOMIC CONSTITUTION OF THE EUROPEAN UNION; OWNERSHIP AND CONTROL IN EUROPE; SUBSIDIARITY AND THE EUROPEAN UNION; VERTICAL MERGERS AND MONOPOLY LEVERAGE.

Subject classification: 3f(i); 6c(ii).

STATUTES

Green Paper on Vertical Restraints in EU Competition Policy, adopted by the European Commission 22 January 1997.
Merger Regulation 4064/89, 1989 OJ L 395/1.
Commission Notice 93/C 39/05, 1993 OJ C 39/6.
Council Regulation 17/62, 1962 OJ 13 204/62.
Treaty of Rome (1957).
Treaty on European Union (1992).

CASES

Commercial Solvents v. EC Commission [1974] 1 CMLR 309.
Re Italian Flat Glass [1990] 4 CMLR 535.
Re Nestlé/Perrier 1992 OJ L 356/1.
Re Soda Ash 1995 OJ C 208/21.
Re United Brands [1978] 1 CMLR 429.
Wood Pulp, Case C-73/95 P, judgment of 24 October 1996.

BIBLIOGRAPHY

Brittan, L. 1992. *European Competition Policy: keeping the playing field level.* London: Brassey, for Centre for European Policy Studies.

Commission of the European Communities. *Annual Reports of the Commission on Competition Policy.* Luxembourg: Office for Official Publications of the European Communities.

Doern, G.B. and Wilks, S. (eds.) 1996. *Comparative Competition Policy: National Institutions in a Global Market.* Oxford: Clarendon Press.

London Economics, Instituto de Análisis Económico/Fundán de Economá Analíatica, Barcelona, Fachhochschule für Wirtschaft, Berlin. *Single Market Review 96: Competition Issues.* Report for the European Commission. Luxembourg: Office for Official Publications of the European Communities, 1997.

Neven, D., Nuttall, R. and Seabright, P. 1993. *Merger in Daylight.* London: Centre for Economic Policy Research.

Posner, R.A. 1976. *Antitrust Law: An Economic Perspective.* Chicago: University of Chicago Press.

Van den Bergh, R. 1996. Economic criteria for applying the subsidiarity principle to the European Community: the case of competition policy. *International Review of Law and Economics* 16:3, 363–83.

Van Miert, K. 1996. The proposal for a European competition agency. *Competition Policy Newsletter* 2:2, 1–4.

Whish, R. and Sufrin, B. 1993. *Competition Law.* 3rd edn, London: Butterworths.

Wilks, S. and McGowan, L. 1996. Competition policy in the European Union: creating a federal agency? Ch. 8 in Doern and Wilks (1996).

event studies. *See* COMPETITION FOR STATE CORPORATE LAW.

evolutionary game theory. Evolutionary game theory provides an answer to questions like: Where do conventions and social norms come from? What determines which convention will dominate within a community? By a convention, I mean a pattern of behaviour within a community that is 'self-enforcing'. Examples include giving way to the right at intersections and the use of equal division in bargaining interactions (Elster 1989, Sugden 1989 and Young 1996 have many examples). In many of these examples, the interaction between members of the community can be thought of as being the result of random meetings. I will refer to members of the community as agents.

When two agents meet, they play a coordination game, that is, a game in which each agent prefers to choose the action chosen by the other agent (irrespective of which action it is). A coordination game, then, has multiple symmetric Nash equilibria. Moreover, these equilibria are strict: each agent has a strict incentive to follow their part of the equilibrium. For example in the coordination game in Figure 1, if everyone in society is playing A, then all agents will continue to play A. On the other hand, if all members of society are playing B, then all agents will continue to play B.

		column player	
		A	B
row player	A	1, 1	0, 0
	B	0, 0	1, 1

Figure 1 Both (A, A) and (B, B) are symmetric strict equilibria

These questions about conventions are instances of two important questions at the heart of non-cooperative game theory: Why do agents play Nash equilibrium? And, given that agents play Nash equilibrium, which equilibrium do they play? Suppose an agent is asked to play the coordination game of Figure 1 against an unfamiliar opponent, and each agent knows absolutely nothing about the opponent. Suppose, moreover, that the agents are not permitted to communicate and must make their choices independently in different rooms. Then it is highly implausible that both the agent and his opponent will successfully coordinate their behaviour. Thus, the assumption that agents play Nash equilibrium is an assumption that agents can successfully coordinate on some equilibrium. The important aspect of this assumption is that it requires an agent to know the behaviour of the opponent. If each agent knows the behaviour of the other, and both are optimizing, then the behaviour is necessarily a Nash equilibrium. The difficulty is to explain where this knowledge comes from.

Evolutionary game theory, like the learning literature (see, for example, Fudenberg and Levine 1993), starts from the presumption that agents do not know the behaviour of their opponents. In an evolutionary model, there is a population of agents interacting over time, with their behaviour adjusting over time in response to the payoffs that various choices have historically produced. Since agents observe the results of the choices of others, evolutionary models describe situations of social learning. An important feature is that the agents are assumed to be boundedly rational. In making their choices, agents believe the world is stationary and, as a corollary, they do not believe that they can influence the future path of population play. Moreover, agents are myopic, so that in each period they are attempting to maximize payoffs in that period (and not the expected value of the stream of payoffs). Agents do not properly understand the payoff implications of different choices; they may not even understand all the available choices.

As an illustration, consider a pair of agents drawn randomly from a population to play the game in Figure 1. Suppose, moreover, that in each period, agents observe (perhaps imperfectly) what has happened in the last period. Suppose also that agents are naively attempting to optimize as described above. Then, if more than half the agents chose A in the last period, the number choosing A this period will probably increase. This suggests that over time eventually all agents will play A. If, on the other hand, over half played B last period, then eventually everyone will play B. Thus the explanation in this setting of why people play Nash is that the history of actual play provides sufficient information for the agents to coordinate their behaviour. Moreover, the inertia in group behaviour explains which equilibrium will be played this period: it is the same equilibrium as last period. There is another feature of this example that is noteworthy: the equilibria are stable. If everyone in the population is playing A, say, then even if one or two agents were to change their choice of action (as an experiment, for example), eventually population play would return to everyone playing A.

Evolutionary models do not directly model learning of boundedly rational agents. Rather, they take as given the idea that behaviour which appears to be successful will increase its representation in the population, while behaviour that appears to be unsuccessful will not. This style of modelling does not lend itself to small numbers of agents. If there is only a small population, is it plausible to believe that the agents are not aware of this? And if agents are aware, then imitation is not a good strategy. Evolutionary dynamics that are motivated by learning have the property that, in large populations, if they converge then they converge to a Nash equilibrium. This is a reasonable criterion for the model to be a good model of social learning: if behaviour converges so that the population environment is stationary and there is a behaviour (strategy) that yields a higher payoff, then some agent will eventually figure this out.

There is a good chance that evolutionary models (together with explicit models of learning) will eventually provide a satisfactory foundation for equilibrium analysis in non-cooperative game theory. This is to be contrasted with the similar earlier attempt to provide a dynamic adjustment foundation for Walrasian equilibrium, which is widely viewed as having been a failure (see Hahn 1982 for a survey). While there are certainly examples where evolutionary or learning dynamics fail to converge, we should not conclude that a learning approach is deficient if in some examples agents cannot learn how to coordinate on an equilibrium; examples in which learning (convergence) under some process does not occur often serve to delineate the class of games for which dynamics converge. The encouraging results in evolutionary game theory arise because, unlike the earlier work on Walrasian equilibrium, global convergence is not the goal. It is not necessary that every Nash equilibrium be capable of being learned. Theories of learning will discriminate between different Nash equilibria (for example, some Nash equilibria are not evolutionarily stable), thus indicating, under varying assumptions on learning, which equilibria can be learned, and which cannot.

Surveys of evolutionary game theory can be found in van Damme (1987, ch. 9), Kandori (1997), Mailath (1992), and Weibull (1995). Results discussed below that lack specific citation can be found in one or other of these sources.

EVOLUTIONARY STABLE STRATEGIES AND REPLICATOR DYNAMICS. The starting-point of evolutionary game theory is the seminal work of Maynard Smith and his co-authors. Of particular importance was the notion of an evolutionary stable strategy (ESS), introduced by Maynard Smith and Price (1973). Excellent references on biological dynamics and evolution are Maynard Smith (1982) and Hofbauer and Sigmund (1988). In biology, the game is interpreted as a contest between animals over some resource (such as food or shelter). If an animal is successful in the contest, then the animal will have more offspring. The payoff in the game is thus interpreted as 'fitness', with fitter strategies having higher reproductive rates (reproduction is asexual). Animals are programmed (perhaps genetically) to play particular strategies. While economic agents wish to choose a strategy to maximize stage payoffs, learning is assumed to result in strategies with relatively higher payoffs being played by relatively more agents. Thus, the dynamics of population behaviour are similar. The idea underlying evolutionary stable strategies is that a stable pattern of behaviour in a population should be stable to perturbations. The biological origin of the perturbations is typically an invasion by 'mutants'. In the learning context, new behaviour could be the result of experimentation. Thus, if a population pattern of behaviour is to eliminate invading mutations (different behaviour), it must have a higher fitness than the mutant in the population that results from the invasion.

The standard game used to illustrate evolutionary stable strategies is Figure 2. The story is that the contest involves two animals fighting for a resource, and that there are two strategies, 'hawk' and 'dove'. Hawk and dove refer to different behaviours of the same animal, not different birds. A hawk fights until serious injury; a dove displays threateningly, but gives up at the first sign of real aggression. The resource is beneficial for survival, thus increasing the likelihood of the animal having offspring, while an injury reduces the likelihood of the animal having offspring. If a hawk fights a dove, the hawk receives the resource with no injury while the dove leaves, uninjured, with nothing. If two doves fight, the outcome is decided randomly with no injury. If two hawks fight, the outcome is decided randomly with the loser being seriously injured. The resource has value or fitness V, no resource has fitness 0, and an injury imposes a cost of C.

Denote by S the collection of available behaviours (*pure strategies*). The payoff to the agent choosing i when his opponent chooses j is $\pi(i, j)$. We follow most of the

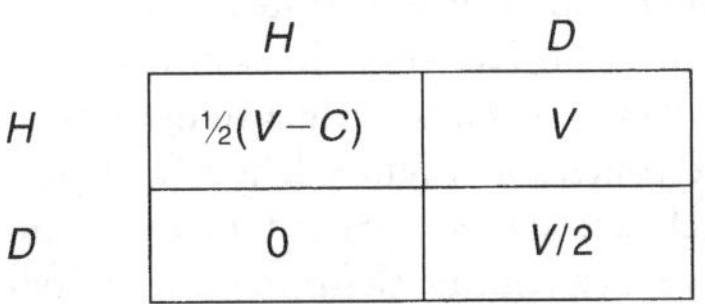

	H	D
H	½(V−C)	V
D	0	V/2

Figure 2 The Hawk–Dove Game

literature in assuming that there is only a finite number of available strategies. A *mixed strategy* is a probability distribution over pure strategies.

While any pure strategy can be viewed as the mixed strategy that places probability one on that pure strategy, it will be useful to follow the convention that the term 'mixed strategy' always refers to a mixed strategy that places strictly positive probability on at least two strategies. Mixed strategies have two leading interpretations as a description of behaviour in a population: either the population is *monomorphic*, with every member of the population playing the same mixed strategy, or the population is *polymorphic*, with each agent playing a pure strategy, and the fraction of the population playing any particular pure strategy equals the probability assigned to that pure strategy by the mixed strategy. The average payoff to strategy i against the strategy q is $\pi(i, q) = \Sigma_{j\in S}\pi(i, j)q_j$. The average payoff to the possibly mixed strategy p against q is $\pi(p, q) = \Sigma_{i\in S}\Sigma_{j\in S}\,\pi(i, j)p_iq_j$.

Definition 1. A (potentially mixed) strategy p is an Evolutionary Stable Strategy (ESS) if for all $q \neq p$, there exists $\varepsilon' > 0$ such that for $\varepsilon \in (0, \varepsilon')$,

$$\pi(p, \varepsilon p + (1-\varepsilon)q) > \pi(q, \varepsilon p + (1-\varepsilon)q).$$

Thus, p is an evolutionary stable strategy if it has a higher payoff against the perturbed population that results from a small invasion of agents playing q than do the agents playing q. In other words, the perturbation does not destabilize the population play of p. By taking ε to zero, we obtain the characterization:

Proposition 1. *The strategy p is an* ESS *if and only if*

1. $\pi(p, p) \geq \pi(q, p)$; and
2. if $\pi(p, p) = \pi(q, p)$ and $p \neq q$, then $\pi(p, q) > \pi(q, q)$.

While every strict (symmetric) equilibrium strategy is an ESS (if p is a strict symmetric equilibrium, then $\pi(p, p) > \pi(q, p)$ for all $q \neq p$), there are other ESS. For example, in Figure 2 there is a unique ESS, given by the mixed strategy that assigns probability $V/(V+C)$ to H and $C/(V+C)$ to L.

The concept of ESS is most easily interpreted if it is assumed that agents can learn (imitate) mixed strategies, or in the biological context, that animals can inherit mixed strategies. The *replicator dynamic* is an explicit dynamic that focuses on inheritance of pure strategies only (although it can be extended to the inheritance of mixed strategies). Suppose individuals choose only pure strategies. The mixed strategy p^t is now interpreted as the proportion of the population choosing strategy i in period t.

This interpretation of mixed strategies is important in

its own right. Interpreting mixed strategies as a randomization by the agent is problematic. It is difficult to believe that agents play games by consulting a roulette wheel when needed. For the contest in Figure 2, it is less plausible to believe that each animal at each interaction randomizes between the two behaviours than to have a population divided into two groups, the Hawks and the Doves, with a fraction $V/(V+C)$ of Hawks in the stable population. Due to the random matching between members of the population, the probability that an animal meets a Hawk is then $V/(V+C)$.

In the replicator dynamic, the fraction playing strategy i is determined by how well i fares, relative to the population average fitness ($\pi(p^t, p^t) = \Sigma_{ij}\ \pi(i, j)p^t{}_i\ p^t{}_j$). It can be derived by assuming that $\pi(i, j)$ is the number of offspring to i when playing j, that the population is large (so that the number of offspring to a strategy is the fitness of the strategy against the population), and that the entire population dies each period and is replaced by offspring. The general discrete time formulation of the *replicator dynamic* is, assuming $\pi(i, j) > 0$ for all $i, j \in S$,

$$p_i^{t+1} = p_i^t + p_i^t \times \frac{(\pi(i, p^t) - \pi(p^t, p^t))}{\pi(p^t, p^t)} \tag{1}$$

The continuous time version is:

$$\frac{dp_i^t}{dt} = p_i^t \times (\pi(i, p^t) - \pi(p^t, p^t)). \tag{2}$$

Two properties of the replicator dynamic are worth noting: the fraction playing any strategy that receives an above average payoff will increase, not just the strategy that maximizes current payoff; and if a strategy is not currently being played, then it will never be played, even if it would yield a higher payoff. Thus, any state in which the same pure strategy is played by every agent is a rest point of the replicator dynamic; so being a rest point is *not* a sufficient condition for a Nash equilibrium. While being an ESS is a sufficient condition for asymptotic stability under the continuous time replicator dynamic, it is not necessary. The reason that a strategy can be asymptotically stable and yet fail to be an ESS is that the definition of an ESS effectively assumes that mixed, as well as pure, strategies can be inherited (learned), while the replicator dynamic (as formulated above) does not.

Our discussion so far has assumed that agents cannot condition their behaviour on their role, row or column. This assumption, called *no role identification*, is a strong assumption that is often violated. Any asymmetry between the agents can serve to allocate roles. For example, in the Hawk–Dove game, the larger animal, or the current owner of the resource, may be the row player. In that example with role identification, the only stable outcomes are the two asymmetric Nash equilibria (in which one role plays Hawk and the other Dove). Moreover, in many contests, the game itself is not symmetric. The notion of an ESS and replicator dynamics can be applied to such games by simply specifying a separate population for each role. However, every ESS in such a game is a strict equilibrium (Selten 1980). This is an important negative result. Most games (in particular, non-trivial extensive form games) do not have strict equilibria and so ESSs do not exist for most asymmetric games. Nonetheless, these non-strict equilibria (particularly in non-trivial extensive form games) do have important stability properties.

DETERMINISTIC DYNAMICS. Replicator dynamics are somewhat restrictive, and there has been some interest in extending the analysis to more general dynamics. *Monotone dynamics* (also called payoff monotone dynamics) require that on average agents switch from worse to better (not necessarily the best) pure strategies. These dynamics preserve most of the essential features of the replicator dynamics.

Since, by definition, a Nash equilibrium is a strategy profile with the property that every agent is playing a best reply to the behaviour of the other agents, every Nash equilibrium is a rest point of any monotone dynamic. On the other hand, since the dynamics may not introduce behaviour that is not already present in the population, not all rest points are Nash equilibria. If a rest point is asymptotically stable, then the learning dynamics, starting from a point close to the rest point but with all strategies being played by a positive fraction of the population, converge to the rest point. But if the rest point is not a Nash equilibrium, some agents are not optimizing and the dynamics will take the system away from that rest point.

If an equilibrium is strict, it is asymptotically stable. Moreover, asymptotic stability in asymmetric games implies almost strict Nash equilibria, and if the profile is pure, it is strict. For the special case of replicator dynamics, a Nash equilibrium is asymptotically stable if and only if it is strict.

These negative results are due in large part to an inappropriately phrased question: what are the stability properties of a single strategy profile? It is now clear that in complicated interactions, some drift should be expected. In particular, in the play of an extensive form game, play at information sets that are not reached is undisciplined. Recall that a strategy is a plan that specifies an action at every possible contingency. If a contingency does not arise, then an agent may not learn that his intended play is suboptimal. Moreover, different agents may have different plays planned for an unreached contingency, and since the contingency is unreached, any tendency for an agent's intended play to 'drift' over time is unchecked by negative payoff implications. (This is an implication of the property that in an extensive form there are typically many strategy profiles, differing only in choices at unreached information sets, that yield the same outcome.) A single strategy profile describes the aggregate pattern of behaviour within the population. A set of strategy profiles is a *collection* of such descriptions. Loosely, we can think of a set of strategy profiles as being 'evolutionarily stable' if behaviour within the population, once near any profile in the set, converges to some profile within it and never leaves the set. The important feature is that behaviour within the population need not settle down to a steady state; rather, it can 'drift' between the different patterns within the 'evolutionarily stable' set.

With this viewpoint, the situation improves somewhat. In particular, sets of strategy profiles that are asymptotically stable under plausible deterministic dynamics have strong strategic stability (in the sense of Kohlberg and Mertens 1986) properties (Swinkels 1993). A similar result under different conditions was subsequently proved by Ritzberger and Weibull (1995), who also characterize the sets of profiles that can be asymptotically stable under certain conditions. It is still not clear, however, how small these sets of asymptotically stable strategy profiles are. The results can only be viewed as positive if the asymptotically stable sets are small relative to the strategy space.

STOCHASTIC DYNAMICS. The replicator dynamic and its generalizations are deterministic. They assume that while the original invasion may have been the result of a random event, the probability of another such event is sufficiently low that it can be ignored until the dynamics have converged. As illustrated earlier, this assumption yields long-run results that are history dependent, i.e. long-run behaviour that depends upon its starting-point. In particular, all strict equilibria are asymptotically stable: even if a small fraction of the population changes its behaviour, the optimality of the existing behaviour is unchanged. However, even at an intuitive level, there is a sense in which some strict equilibria are more likely than others. For example, if in the game described by Figure 1, the payoff to (A, A) is changed to (5, 5), then (A, A) seems more likely than (B, B). There are several ways this can be phrased. Certainly, (A, A) seems more 'focal'. Alternatively, consider the basins of attraction of the two equilibria under deterministic dynamics (they will all agree in this case, since the game is so simple). The set of initial fractions of the population from which the dynamics converge to (A, A) (i.e. its basin of attraction) is five times the size of that of (B, B), and so if we imagine that the initial condition is chosen randomly, then the A pattern of behaviour is five times as likely to arise. There is a more recent perspective that makes the last idea more precise by eliminating the need to specify an initial condition.

Recall that the motivation for the concepts of ESS and (asymptotic) stability was a desire for robustness to a single episode of perturbation. By looking at asymptotic stability, the focus is on the 'long-run'. Foster and Young (1990) have argued that the notions of an ESS and attractor of the replicator dynamic do not adequately capture long-run stability when there are continual small stochastic shocks. If explicit attention is paid to the possibility that, while unlikely, the perturbations are continual, then the perspective can be viewed as being 'ultra-long-run' (see Binmore, Samuelson and Vaughan 1995).

There is a difficulty that must be confronted when explicitly modelling randomness that does not arise in deterministic dynamics. If the mutations (experimentation) occur at the individual level, with an infinite population there will be no aggregate impact and the resulting evolution of the system is deterministic with no 'invasion events'. There are two ways to approach this. One is to consider aggregate shocks (this is the approach of Foster and Young 1990). The other is to consider a finite population and analyse the impact of individual experimentation (this is the approach of Kandori, Mailath and Rob 1993).

The finite population models analyse finite state Markov processes. The state space is the set of all possible distributions of play in the population (which is finite since the population is finite), denoted Z. A Markov process, with transition probability matrix B describing learning, is first specified on the state space (this dynamic is sometimes called a selection or Darwinian dynamic). This process is a stochastic version (since agents may switch to a better action with a probability less than one) of the dynamics described in the previous section. Typically, Nash equilibria (or, more accurately, states in which all agents choose the same Nash equilibrium action) are absorbing states of B. Perpetual randomness is then incorporated by assuming that, in each period, each agent independently switches his action with some small probability, ε, to an arbitrary action. This corresponds to another Markov process with transition matrix $Q(\varepsilon)$. The Markov process studied has transition matrix $Q(\varepsilon)B$. Thus, in each period, there are two phases: the learning phase and the experimentation phase. Note that after the experimentation phase (in contrast to the learning phase), with positive probability, fewer agents may be choosing a best reply to last period's state.

Under $Q(\varepsilon)B$, every state is reached with positive probability from any other state (including those states that are absorbing under B). Thus, the Markov chain is irreducible and aperiodic. Such a Markov chain has a unique stationary distribution, denoted $\mu(\varepsilon)$. The goal is to characterize the limit of $\mu(\varepsilon)$ as ε becomes small. This, if it exists, is called the *stochastically stable distribution* (Foster and Young 1990) or the *limit distribution*.

Consider the case of 2×2 symmetric games with two strict symmetric Nash equilibria. Any monotone dynamic divides the state space into the same two basins of attraction of the equilibria. The *risk-dominant equilibrium* is the equilibrium with the larger basin of attraction. The risk-dominant equilibrium is 'less risky' and may be Pareto dominated by the other equilibrium (for example in Figure 3, (A, A) Pareto dominates (B, B), while (B, B) is the risk-dominant equilibrium). Kandori, Mailath and Rob (1993) show that the limit distribution puts probability one on the risk-dominant equilibrium. The non-risk dominant equilibrium is upset because the probability of a sufficiently large number of simultaneous mutations that leave society in the basin of attraction of the risk-dominant equilibrium is of a higher order than that of a sufficiently large number of simultaneous mutations that cause society to leave the basin of attraction.

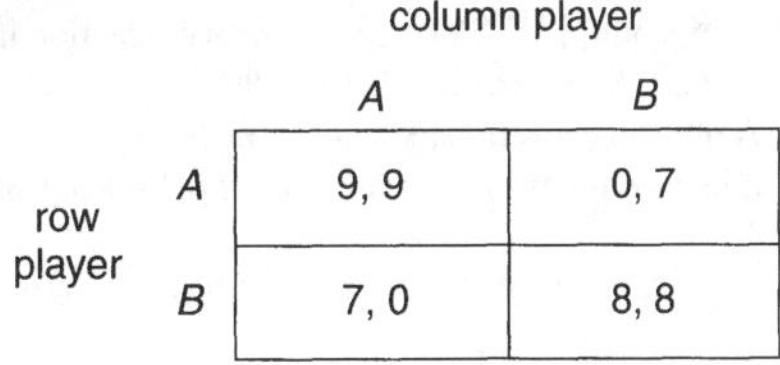

		column player	
		A	B
row player	A	9, 9	0, 7
	B	7, 0	8, 8

Figure 3 (A, A) Pareto dominates (B, B), while (B, B) is the risk-dominant equilibrium

In contrast to deterministic dynamics, there is a unique outcome (or distribution over outcome). History does not matter. This is the result of taking two limits: first, time is taken to infinity (which justifies looking at the stationary distribution), and *then* the probability of mutation is taken to zero (looking at small rates).

Models based on stochastic dynamics, with both uniform random matching (that is, where any agent is equally likely to meet any other agent) and local interactions (that is, each agent only interacts with a subset of the population), have contributed substantially to our understanding of equilibrium analysis. See Mailath (1993) for details.

GEORGE J. MAILATH

See also CONVENTIONS; CONVENTIONS AND TRANSACTION COSTS; CONVENTIONS AT THE FOUNDATION OF LAW; EFFICIENT NORMS; FOCAL POINTS; NETWORK EXTERNALITY AND CONVENTION; NON-COOPERATIVE GAMES; SOCIAL NORMS AND THE LAW; SPONTANEOUS ORDER.

Subject classification: 1d(i).

BIBLIOGRAPHY

Binmore, K.G., Samuelson, L. and Vaughan, R. 1995. Musical chairs: modeling noisy evolution. *Games and Economic Behavior* 11: 1–35.

Elster, J. 1989. Social norms and economic theory. *Journal of Economic Perspectives* 3: 99–117.

Foster, D. and Young, H.P. 1990. Stochastic evolutionary game dynamics. *Theoretical Population Biology* 38: 219–32.

Fudenberg, D. and Levine, D. 1993. Steady state learning and Nash equilibrium. *Econometrica* 61: 547–73.

Hahn, F. 1982. Stability. In *Handbook of Mathematical Economics, Volume II*, ed. K. Arrow and M. Intriligator, New York: North Holland: 745–93.

Hofbauer, J. and Sigmund, K. 1988. *The Theory of Evolution and Dynamical Systems*. Cambridge: Cambridge University Press.

Kandori, M. 1997. Evolutionary game theory in economics. In *Advances in Economics and Econometrics: Theory and Applications. Seventh World Congress of the Econometrics Society*, ed. D.M. Kreps and K.F. Wallis (Cambridge: Cambridge University Press): 243–77.

Kandori, M., Mailath, G.J. and Rob, R. 1993. Learning, mutation, and long run equilibria in games. *Econometrica* 61: 29–56.

Kohlberg, E. and Mertens, J.-F. 1986. On the strategic stability of equilibria. *Econometrica* 54: 1003–37.

Mailath, G.J. 1992. Symposium on Evolutionary Game Theory: Introduction. *Journal of Economic Theory* 57, 259–77.

Mailath, G.J. 1993. Perpetual randomness in evolutionary economics. *Economics Letters* 42: 291–9.

Maynard Smith, J. 1982. *Evolution and the Theory of Games*. Cambridge: Cambridge University Press.

Maynard Smith, J. and Price, G.R. 1973. The logic of animal conflict. *Nature* 246: 15–18.

Ritzberger, K. and Weibull, J.W. 1995. Evolutionary selection in normal-form games. *Econometrica* 63: 1371–99.

Selten, R. 1980. A note on evolutionary stable strategies in asymmetric animal conflicts. *Journal of Theoretical Biology* 84: 93–101.

Sugden, R. 1989. Spontaneous order. *Journal of Economic Perspectives* 3: 85–97.

Swinkels, J.M. 1993. Adjustment dynamics and rational play in games. *Games and Economic Behavior* 5: 455–84.

Van Damme, E. 1987. *Stability and Perfection of Nash Equilibria*. Berlin: Springer-Verlag.

Weibull, J.W. 1995. *Evolutionary Game Theory*. Cambridge, MA: MIT Press.

Young, H.P. 1996. The economics of convention. *Journal of Economic Perspectives* 10(2): 105–22.

evolution of commercial law. Pospisil (1978: 63) emphasizes that understanding legal dynamics requires recognition that some laws are 'customary', and others are 'authoritarian'. Pospisil's observation applies to commercial law. Authoritarian legislation is easily recognized, of course, but the significant contribution of custom to the evolution of commercial law is less obvious. Therefore, while some impacts of authority on commercial law will be discussed (*see also* ARBITRATION IN THE SHADOW OF THE LAW and LAW MERCHANT in this regard), the focus here is on custom.

A key distinguishing characteristic of customary law is that rules of obligation are initiated by individuals' decisions to behave in particular ways under particular circumstances and then spread through observation and imitation by other individuals (Mises [1957] 1985: 192). Adopting such behaviour creates expectations and accompanying obligations (Hayek 1973: 96–7). But an obligation that achieves the status of a 'customary law' must be widely recognized and accepted by the individuals in the affected group, so such a rule is widely viewed among members of the affected community as desirable, and even indispensable (Pospisil 1978: 63–4). In contrast, a rule imposed by a legal authority (an individual or institution with a concentration of coercive power to induce compliance) need not be viewed as desirable by even the majority of the group, as the authority can enforce the rule for the benefit of himself or a powerful minority (Pospisil 1978: 64).

The claim that custom plays an important role in the evolution of law is not accepted by all legal scholars, of course. The opinion frequently traced to Sir Henry Maine ([1864] 1873: 74) but shared by many (e.g. Hart 1961; Landes and Posner 1979; Brunet 1987), is that custom is static, or at least very slow to change. The fact is, however, that flexibility and change often characterize customary law systems (Pospisil 1971, 1978; Benson 1988), and in commercial law, it is the flexibility of customary processes that allow practical and rapid legal adaptations to the changing requirements of commerce (Mitchell 1904; Berman 1983; Trakman 1983; Benson 1989). In fact, during some periods of history custom has dominated the evolution of commercial law to the virtual exclusion of authority (Mitchell 1904; Bewes 1923; Berman 1983; Trakman 1983; Benson 1989), and while at other times authority has substantially altered commercial law (Trakman 1983), custom remains a primary source of evolving law for substantial segments of today's business community (Lew 1978; Berman and Dasser 1990; Benson 1992, 1995, 1997).

There are actually several ways that a change in customary rules can be initiated. As suggested above, an individual may simply begin behaving in a particular way under certain circumstances, others observe the behaviour, come to expect it, perhaps adopting similar behaviour under similar circumstances, and an implicit obligation develops. At times, such observation and imitation has been very important in the transmission of commercial customs among expanding networks of traders (Mitchell 1904: 7–9; Bewes 1923: 138; Trakman 1983: 11; Greif 1989) but there are other more important mechanisms for the evolution of customary commercial law. Two such mechanisms are dispute resolution, explored in Section I, and contracting, examined in Section II (*see* LAW

MERCHANT for historical examples). Section III concludes with a discussion of some implications of the interaction between custom and authority for the evolution of commercial law, focusing on potential authoritarian impacts on dispute resolution and contracting.

I. DISPUTE RESOLUTION AND CUSTOMARY COMMERCIAL LAW. The potential role of public courts as a means of extending customary law has been widely recognized. Indeed, as Hogue ([1906] 1985: 6) points out, one proposed definition of common law is 'a body of law based on custom alone'. Hogue (ibid.: 188–215) correctly rejects this definition, of course, pointing out that while custom was the 'principle source' of common law before Parliament was firmly established as a law-making institution, medieval common law judges who assumed the authority to determine what was 'good custom' refused to accept some custom, and they also recognized various royal 'enactments' as a source of law that could alter or negate custom. Today such a definition is even less appropriate, given the facts that common law judges also must consider disputes in light of statute law and that judges themselves appear to be 'legislating' significant departures from common law precedent, at least in some areas of law (Benson 1996). Indeed, modern common law judges rarely explicitly recognize custom as a source of law (see for example Ebke 1987: 613). Nonetheless, such a definition is revealing of the potential role that dispute resolution might play in evolving customary law, and of the very important impact that custom has had on the evolution of state-backed law during at least some historical periods.

Perhaps more important than the fact that judges can and do at times recognize custom as a source of law, however, is the fact that most business disputes in medieval England were not resolved by judges (Berman 1983; Trakman 1983; Benson 1989), and the same is true today (Berman and Dasser 1990; Bernstein 1992; Benson 1992, 1995, 1997). Negotiation is probably the primary means of dispute resolution among businessmen, but if direct negotiation fails, they generally turn to providers of Alternative Dispute Resolution (hereafter, ADR) such as mediators and arbitrators, rather than to courts (reasons for choosing ADR and for accepting ADR rulings are explored in ARBITRATION UNDER THE SHADOW OF THE LAW), and ADR providers generally base their decisions on business custom (Lew 1978: 584–5; Berman and Dasser 1990; Benson 1997). Furthermore, new customary rules can be initiated as individuals resolve their disputes (Wooldridge 1970: 104; Lew 1978: 584–9; Fuller 1981: 90, 110–11; Benson 1988), whether through direct negotiation (as discussed below) or ADR, and this appears to be a particularly important source of change in customary commercial law (Benson 1989, 1997). For instance, suppose a dispute arises between two businessmen because some technological or institutional change occurs, making a previously unwanted and therefore non-owned resource valuable, or because a contingency arises that was not anticipated in a contract. The parties turn to an ADR provider, and the resulting dispute resolution creates behavioural rules specific to the situation and parties involved (Hayek 1973: 99; Fuller 1981: 128), but it can also provide new or extend existing customary law if it is seen as an appropriate and beneficial guide to future behaviour (Fuller 1981; Benson 1988, 1989, 1997). This may occur because the ADR provider explains and justifies the decision in the context of existing custom, as they often do (Lew 1978; Benson 1997), but even if the reasons for a decision are not explicitly stated, affected and potentially affected parties will perceive or guess some reason, generally in the context of their understanding of existing rules, and adjust their conduct accordingly (Fuller 1981: 90).

In contrast to this claim that private dispute resolution can be an important source of new rules of behaviour, Landes and Posner (1979: 238–9, 245) argue that ADR providers seeking to maximize profits actually have incentives not to clarify rules because doing so will reduce the number of disputes to be resolved, and they conclude that ADR in the commercial area is 'not a source of rules or precedents'. Similarly, Brunet (1987: 19) contends that precedent law produced by public judges is a 'public good' which is not going to be produced at efficient levels through ADR. He emphasizes that ADR results are 'internal' to the parties involved and that the secrecy that characterizes ADR means that others will not be able to learn about the outcome of any particular dispute anyway (Brunet 1987: 14–15). Such arguments fail to recognize that when external benefits (e.g. producing new customary law) are significant, strong incentives exist to develop institutions (property rights, contracts, organizations) that can internalize them (Demsetz 1967; Benson 1997). This can be an important source of incentives underlying the formation of trade associations and other commercial groups, for instance (Benson 1995, 1997), and within such an organization, institutional arrangements easily can create incentives to minimize disputes by making clear rulings (as Landes and Posner (1979) recognize). Thus, Fuller (1981: 110–11) contends that incentives can be exactly the opposite of those suggested by Landes and Posner (1979) and Brunet (1987): when an ADR provider must be concerned with the acceptability of his decisions to more than just the parties involved there are strong incentives to get the facts and relevant law (custom) right and to justify the ruling in the context of those facts and customs.

Consider Bernstein's (1992) examination of the systematic rejection of state-created law by the diamond industry in favour of its own internal rules (including ADR institutions and privately produced sanctions; *see* ARBITRATION IN THE SHADOW OF THE LAW regarding such sanctions), wherein she explains that the diamond merchants' Boards of Arbitrators resolve disputes on the basis of industry 'trade custom and usage'. But she also finds that within some trading clubs in the diamond industry the outcome of arbitration is 'officially kept secret' as long as the ruling is complied with (Bernstein 1992: 124), perhaps supporting the view that custom is static. Such 'official' secrecy does not mean that new rules are not created or spread, however, or even that too few customary rules exist, for at least four reasons (Benson 1997): (1) parties to the dispute will consider the outcome in future dealings and contracts under similar circumstances even with different trading partners; (2) there is a tremendous 'unofficial' flow of information through word of mouth (gossip) within and between diamond trading clubs (Bernstein 1992: 121) so that arbitration results do 'become known through gossip'

(Bernstein 1992: 126); (3) there are important mechanisms for initiating new customary rules in addition to dispute resolution, as suggested below; and (4) ADR mechanisms are very flexible so if external benefits become attractive, a group can change its dispute resolution procedures to capture them. In regard to this last point, for instance, Bernstein (1992: 150) notes that diamond dealers have begun to recognize that these secrecy practices create uncertainty, and many trading clubs have begun to change their institutions. Within some trading clubs, arbitrators now publish written announcements of the principles used to decide novel cases even though they keep the parties and identifying facts secret. Thus, Bernstein (1992: 117) concludes, in contrast to those who see customary law dominated by private dispute resolution (and sanctions) to be relatively inefficient, that 'The private regime must be Pareto superior to the established legal regime in order to survive.'

The fact is that there are many alternative ADR mechanisms (Benson 1997), so a variety of incentive structures can be created for ADR suppliers depending on the potential value of creating new rules. Therefore, for instance, international commercial arbitrators base their rulings on international commercial custom rather than on any national system of law, and they attempt to demonstrate the correctness of rulings by explaining how it is consistent with several existing customary rules (Lew 1978: 584–5). That is, international commercial law might well be characterized as a 'body of law based on custom', even though common law cannot be so defined, since disputes are generally resolved by looking to past rulings, practices, traditions and usage when it is necessary to extend the law and cover new issues. The same applies within at least some domestic commercial groups (Benson 1995, 1997). Indeed, the law-making consequences of commercial arbitration led Wooldridge (1970: 104) to suggest that its substantial growth in the United States is a 'silent displacement of not only the judiciary but even the legislature'. But even when a particular ADR process does not appear to clarify existing or produce new customary rules, it may just be that dispute resolution is a relatively unimportant source of legal change for the relevant group. After all, as suggested above, there are a number of ways for new customary rules to be introduced beyond dispute resolution. A very important source of new rules in commercial custom is bilateral negotiation and contracting.

II. CONTRACTING AS A SOURCE OF CHANGE IN COMMERCIAL LAW. Contract negotiation and drafting does much more than simply set prices: they 'also establish the rules that will govern the transaction' (Rubin 1995: 115). If conditions change, for example, and two individuals decide that, for their purposes, behaviour that was attractive in the past has ceased to be useful, they can voluntarily devise a new contract stipulating any behaviour that they wish. That is, old custom can be quickly replaced by a new rule of obligation toward certain other individuals without prior consent of or simultaneous recognition by everyone in the group (or of some legal authority). Others enter into contacts with the two parties and are informed of the contractual innovation (or observe the results of a new contractual stipulation), so if it provides a more desirable behaviour rule than older custom, it can be rapidly emulated. Many contracts spread as 'standard forms' throughout the relevant business community, for instance, serving as 'powerful norms' with obvious 'legal character' (Rubin 1995: 115). Indeed, since a major portion of commercial law really is contract law, some observers see customary commercial law almost exclusively as rules created through and about contracting (e.g. Draetta et al. 1992). Furthermore, many of commercial law's innovations have been initiated through contracts (see for example Mitchell 1904: 12; Berman 1983: 349–55; Draetta et al. 1992). An expanding use of explicit contracting is actually a natural event in the evolution of customary law. As cooperative legal arrangements evolve and are improved upon, they tend to become more explicit, and therefore, more contractual. In addition, a carefully constructed and enforceable contract can substitute for localized sources of trust, allowing a group to expand.

In this context, as Fuller (1981: 224–5) explains,

> the term *contract law* . . . refers primarily, not to the law *of* or *about* contracts, but to the 'law' a contract itself brings into existence. . . . If we permit ourselves to think of contract law as the 'law' that the parties themselves bring into existence by their agreement, the transition from customary law to contract law becomes a very easy one indeed.

While customary law and contract law are typically sharply differentiated, Fuller (1981: 176) argues that this is inappropriate. He explains, for instance, that if contingencies arise which were not explicitly anticipated in a contract, they will generally be resolved by asking what 'standard practice' is with respect to similar issues. Are the parties subject to customary law, or did they tacitly agree to incorporated standard practice into the terms of the contract? Actually, contract and customary law often are simply different terms for the source of a particular behavioural obligation. A contract may be implied entirely from the conduct of the parties, for instance, because they conducted themselves in such a way that a tacit exchange of promises occurred.

It should be noted that the roles of dispute resolution and contracting in the evolution of commercial law, while treated separately here, are actually tightly intertwined. For instance, the displacement of trust relationships by contracts means that disputes requiring third party assistance may become more prevalent. Through contracts parties can specify that arbitration or some other ADR will be employed rather than more adversarial adjudication processes. Furthermore, ADR procedures often play a direct role in contracting: 'That there is a close connection between *mediation* and the ordering principle of contract certainly requires no demonstration' (Fuller 1981: 179), for instance. In fact, one of the most common uses of a mediator is to act as a go-between to facilitate contract negotiation.

The role of contracting also reinforces the idea that many modern 'laws' that appear to emanate through authoritarian channels are customary in the sense that they are effective only to the degree that they are voluntarily adopted. After all, under certain circumstances 'the *right to contract around the rule* indirectly yields unanimity: all those parties who do not wish to be bound by a particular rule ... generally have the opportunity to adopt any other rule that is mutually satisfactory' (De Alessi and Staaf 1991: 112). This can be true even if the rule that the parties wish to nullify has been produced by a third party dispute resolution process, whether that third party is a private ADR provider or a public court. Indeed, De Alessi and Staaf (1991) emphasize that the historic ability to contract around the rules implied by common law decisions has been an important safeguard against judicial legislation and/or judicial error that could lead to the creation of inefficient common law rules. But contractual nullification can even apply to authoritarian legislation if the authority is not able to enforce its rules (see for example Umbeck's (1981) and de Soto's (1989) examinations of privately established property rights to supposedly 'publicly' owned lands). Indeed, displacement of custom by authority requires limits on the use of both ADR and contracting.

III. CONCLUSIONS: CUSTOM VERSUS AUTHORITY IN COMMERCIAL LAW. A rule that favours a particular minority cannot be imposed if individuals who do not benefit from the rule can either: (1) turn to a customary legal system like the medieval Law Merchant (Benson 1989) or modern trade associations (Benson 1995), where a different rule is applied; or (2) find another claimant to authority who applies a different rule (Berman 1983; Benson 1994). Thus a legal authority often attempts to eliminate or absorb alternative legal arrangements. For instance, many widely held customary rules are selectively codified and/or enforced, perhaps in order to imply that the relevant source of these laws is also authority and/or in an effort to give authoritarian legislation the same 'dignity and respect' (Hayek 1973: 126) that applies to widely accepted customary law. Even an apparently authoritarian legal system, therefore, generally involves a mix of custom and deliberately designed and imposed rules.

Codification of customary commercial law has a long history (see Mitchell 1904: 11; Berman 1983: 341; Benson 1989) that continues to this day. For instance, Chen (1992: 93) argues that the modern Law Merchant (i.e., customary commercial law) provides an important basis for American commercial law, but attributes this to the Uniform Commercial Code (UCC) which 'captures the essence of the law merchant ... enabling the law of trade to change alongside actual practice'. He contends that the UCC's section regarding usage is 'superior' to the common law courts' treatment of custom prior to passage of the UCC, so the relative degree of court acceptance of evolving business practice and usage reflects statutory mandates. Still others reject any claim that custom is important to American commercial law because common law courts rely upon it explicitly only infrequently (Ebke 1987: 613). But the test of how important evolving custom is as a source of commercial law may not be in how often courts refer to practices, usage, or custom, or even whether generally accepted commercial standards are easily discernable by the judiciary. Rather, the test is whether customary law governs commercial behaviour. In fact, within the jurisdiction of a legal authority, parallel 'systems of law' can arise if the costs of complying with the authority exceed the costs of establishing an alternative. Thus, 'informal' sectors within the geographic jurisdiction of a legal authority often establish and enforce rules, and resolve disputes (e.g. de Soto 1989; Ellickson 1991).

Customary commercial law enforced within groups such as trade associations using private sanctions (Bernstein 1992; Benson 1992, 1995) and ADR can be an example of such a parallel legal system. For instance, common law courts were established in the British colonies of North America, and they obviously remained in place after the revolution. However, they did not apply commercial law in what the American merchant community considered to be a just and expeditious fashion: 'Not only did courts, according to one New York merchant, dispense "expensive endless law"; they were slow to develop legal doctrine that facilitated commercial development' (Auerbach 1983: 32). Therefore, businesses relied on negotiation and contracting to make rules, and commercial organizations such as the New York Chamber of Commerce developed arbitration arrangements very quickly in each of the American colonies (Jones 1956; Auerbach 1983; Benson 1995, 1997) to provide third-party dispute resolution under evolving customary law for the merchant community. Negotiation and ADR continued as the primary means of resolving business disputes after the revolution (Jones 1956; Benson 1995) despite considerable hostility by common law judges who did not feel compelled either to enforce contracts or to uphold ADR decisions.

Even as American common law courts became relatively less hostile, showing an increasing willingness to enforce contracts and to apply business practice and usage to resolve commercial disputes, new sources of ADR continued to emerge. Widespread and growing use of arbitration by business groups is particularly evident for the last four decades of the nineteenth century, for example (Jones 1956: 214–15; Wooldridge 1970; Auerbach 1983; Macneil 1992; Benson 1995). Uncertainty regarding the credibility of public courts' implicit commitment to support business contracts was apparently increasing during this period because judges also must look to statutes, and authoritarian legislation regarding commerce was beginning to expand: 'The growth of the regulatory state unsettled advocates of commercial autonomy, who turned to arbitration as a shield against government intrusion' (Auerbach 1983: 101). By the end of World War I, the courts clearly were a secondary recourse in many areas of commercial activity and completely irrelevant in others (Wooldridge 1970: 101). Under such circumstances, contracts and ADR options clearly can serve as mechanisms for nullifying some authoritarian legislation (Wooldridge 1970: 101).

The availability of contracting and ADR does not imply that custom rules to the exclusion of authority, of course. Indeed, through authoritarian actions, including judicial legislation, the relative costs of using ADR, and the potential scope of custom and contract can both be limited. For instance, when a group of motion picture producers agreed to place arbitration clauses in all contracts with motion picture exhibitors, *and* to boycott any exhibitor who refused arbitration or refused to accept an arbitration ruling (see ARBITRATION IN THE SHADOW OF THE LAW for discussion of the boycott sanction in backing arbitration), the boycott agreement was held to be illegal in 1930 (*Paramount Lasky Corporation v. United States*) despite the fact that there was no evidence that the purpose of the agreement was anything other than to make arbitration effective (e.g., it was not an attempt to police a cartel). What may appear to be a liberalization of this ruling was rendered in 1963 (*Silver v. New York Stock Exchange*). Enforcement of stock exchange rules by boycott was not held to be in violation of the antitrust laws, given that adequate procedural safeguards existed in the exchange's procedures. However, prior to this case, it was generally believed that the self-governing institutions of the regulated exchanges were exempt from antitrust scrutiny (Landes and Posner 1979: 257). Clearly, governments can claim the authority to control private institutions of governance, and under many circumstances they have wielded that authority (Trakman 1983; *see also* ARBITRATION IN THE SHADOW OF THE LAW and LAW MERCHANT).

Another significant threat to custom as a source of commercial law is limitations on the scope of contracting. For instance, product liability used to be a contract issue in the United States. Manufacturers owed a duty of care only to those who contracted directly with them, and damages could be specified by contract, particularly if harms were likely or if courts made inefficiently large or small damage awards. However, beginning with *MacPherson v. Buick Motor Co.* in 1916, this duty has gradually expanded. By 1960, manufactures' duty had clearly been extended well beyond contractual linkages to include anyone likely to use or be exposed to a product. Then, in 1960 (*Henningsen v. Bloomfield Motors, Inc.*), a manufacturer was declared to be liable under an 'implied warranty principle' for the first time in a product case, despite the lack of any convincing evidence of negligence by the manufacturer, or of any defect, and no expressed contractual warranty covering the claimed failure of the product. This implied warranty principle contributed to the movement away from the negligence standard of tort liability toward strict liability. Thus, the potential for contracting around inefficient statutes and court-made rulings regarding product liability has been significantly limited. Since 1960, product liability tort litigation has exploded, tort rules have changed dramatically, and entire domestic industries are threatened with extinction (Benson 1996). And this is only one example of the 'tortification of contract' (Olsen 1992).

Clearly, custom is not the only source of the evolving law of commerce. Legislation, including judge-made law, can have a significant influence on this process (see for example Trakman 1983 and Benson 1995). As Rubin (1995: 124) emphasizes, however, influence is not the same as control and, furthermore, influence can flow in both directions. New rules for business behaviour continue to develop through evolving practices and contractual negotiations, and some of them continue to be implicitly and even explicitly recognized by judges. Furthermore, even when they are not (perhaps because they conflict with authoritarian statutes), businessmen need not treat judicial decisions (or statutes) as permanent determinants of behavioural rules. They may be able to write contracts that specify different types of behaviour and opt for ADR. The tortification of contract does limit the potential for contracting around some undesirable rules, of course, but even then, institutional innovations may reestablish contractual options (e.g. many Health Maintenance Organizations have arbitration clauses in their contracts with patients, in an effort to move medical malpractice issues out of tort and into contract). Other options also arise. For instance, since custom still dominates in international commercial law (Lew 1978; Berman and Dasser 1990; Benson 1992), and to greater or lesser degrees in other countries' commercial law, investments can be relocated to avoid authoritarian influences. The increasing mobility of capital constrains legal authorities more and more all of the time. Thus, while many contend that law is what judges say it is, this is only true to the extent that judicial remedies are, or are expected to be sought; when they are not sought, other consideration can and often will control the parties' conduct (Rubin 1995: 118), so much of evolving commercial law within the United States remains, if not independent, at least insulated from authoritarian regulations (Rubin 1995: 124; Benson 1995).

BRUCE L. BENSON

See also ALTERNATIVE DISPUTE RESOLUTION; ARBITRATION IN THE SHADOW OF THE LAW; CONTRACT FORMATION AND INTERPRETATION; CUSTOMARY LAW; CUSTOMARY PRACTICES AND THE LAW OF TORTS; EMERGENCE OF LEGAL RULES; INFORMAL CONTRACT ENFORCEMENT: LESSONS FROM MEDIEVAL TRADE; LAW MERCHANT; MAINE, HENRY; PRIVATE COMMERCIAL LAW; PRIVATE LAW-MAKING AND THE UNIFORM COMMERCIAL CODE.

Subject classification: 4a(iii); 4b(iii); 5a(v).

CASES

Henningsen v. Bloomfield Motors, Inc., 32 NJ 358, 161 A2d 69 (1960).

MacPherson v. Buick Motor Co., 217 NY 382, 111 NE 1050 (1916).

Paramount Famous Lasky Corporation v. United States, 282 US 30 (1930).

Silver v. New York Stock Exchange, 373 US 341 (1963).

BIBLIOGRAPHY

Auerbach, J.S. 1983. *Justice Without Law?* New York: Oxford University Press.

Benson, B.L. 1988. Legal evolution in primitive societies. *Journal of Institutional and Theoretical Economics* 144: 772–88.

Benson, B.L. 1989. The spontaneous evolution of commerical law. *Southern Economic Journal* 55: 644–61.

Benson, B.L. 1992. Customary law as a social contract: international commerical law. *Constitutional Political Economy* 2: 1–27.

Benson, B.L. 1994. Emerging from the Hobbesian jungle: might takes and makes rights. *Constitutional Political Economy* 5: 129–58.

Benson, B.L. 1995. An exploration of the impact of modern arbitration statutes on the development of arbitration in the United States. *Journal of Law, Economics, & Organization* 11: 479–501.

Benson, B.L. 1996. Uncertainty, the race for property rights, and rent dissipation due to judicial changes in product liability tort law. *Cultural Dynamics* 19: 19–51.

Benson, B.L. 1997. Arbitration. In *The Encyclopedia of Law and Economics*, ed. B. Bouckaert and G. De Geest, Aldershot: Edward Elgar (forthcoming).

Berman, H.J. 1983. *Law and Revolution: The Formation of Western Legal Tradition.* Cambridge, MA: Harvard University Press.

Berman, H.J. and Dasser, F.J. 1990. The 'new' Law Merchant and the 'old': sources, content, and legitimacy. In *Lex Mercatoria and Arbitration: A Discussion of the New Law Merchant*, ed. Thomas E. Carbonneau, Dobbs Ferry, NY: Transnational Juris Publications.

Bernstein, L. 1992. Opting out of the legal system: extralegal contractual relations in the diamond industry. *Journal of Legal Studies* 21: 115–58.
Bewes, W.A. 1923. *The Romance of the Law Merchant: Being an Introduction to the Study of International and Commerical Law With Some Account of the Commerce and Fairs of the Middle Ages.* London: Sweet & Maxwell.
Brunet, E. 1987. Questioning the quality of alternative dispute resolution. *Tulane Law Review* 62: 1–56.
Chen, J.C. 1992. Code, custom, and contract: the Uniform Commercial Code as Law Merchant. *Texas International Law Journal* 27: 91–135.
De Alessi, L. and Staaf, R.J. 1991. The common law process: efficiency or order? *Constitutional Political Economy* 2: 107–26.
Demsetz, H. 1967. Toward a theory of property rights. *American Economic Review*, Papers & Proceedings 57: 347–59.
de Soto, H. 1989. *The Other Path: The Invisible Revolution in the Third World.* New York: Harper & Row.
Draetta, U., Lake, R.B. and Nanda, V.P. 1992. *Breach and Adaptation of International Contracts: An Introduction to Lex Mercatoria* Salem, NH: Butterworth Legal Publishers.
Ebke, W.F. 1987. Review of *The Law Merchant: the evolution of commercial law*, by Leon E. Trakman. *The International Lawyer* 21: 606–16.
Ellickson, R.C. 1991. *Order Without Law: How Neighbors Settle Disputes.* Cambridge, MA: Harvard University Press.
Fuller, L. 1981. *The Principles of Social Order.* Durham, NC: Duke University Press.
Greif, A. 1989. Reputation and coalitions in medieval trade. *Journal of Economic History* 49: 857–82.
Hart, H.L.A. 1961. *The Concept of Law.* Oxford: Clarendon Press.
Hayek, F.A. 1973. *Law, Legislation, and Liberty*, Vol. I. Chicago: University of Chicago Press.
Hogue, A.R. [1906] 1985. *Origins of the Common Law.* Indianapolis, IN: Liberty Press.
Jones, W.C. 1956. Three centuries of commerical arbitration in New York: a brief survey. *Washington University Law Quarterly* 1956: 193–221.
Landes, W.M. and Posner, R.A. 1979. Adjudication as a private good. *Journal of Legal Studies* 8: 235–84.
Lew, J.D.M. 1978. *Applicable Law in International Commerical Arbitration: A Study in Commerical Arbitration Awards.* Dobbs Ferry, NY: Oceana Publications.
Macneil, I.R. 1992. *American Arbitration Law.* New York: Oxford University Press.
Maine, Sir H.S. [1864] 1873. *Ancient Law.* 3rd American edn from 5th English edn, New York: Henry Holt & Co.
Mises, L. von [1957] 1985. *Theory and History: An Interpretation of Social and Economic Evolution.* Auburn, AL: Ludwig von Mises Institute.
Mitchell, W. 1904. *An Essay on the Early History of the Law Merchant.* Cambridge: Cambridge University Press.
Olsen, W. 1992. Tortification of contract law: displacing consent and agreement. *Cornell Law Review* 77: 1043–8.
Pospisil, L. 1971. *Anthropology of Law: A Comparative Theory.* New York: Harper & Row.
Pospisil, L. 1978. *The Ethnology of Law.* Menlo Park, CA: Cummings Publishing.
Rubin, E.L. 1995. The nonjudicial life of contract: beyond the shadow of the law. *Northwestern University Law Review* 90: 107–31.
Trakman, L.E. 1983. *The Law Merchant: The Evolution of Commercial Law.* Littleton, CO: Fred B. Rotham & Co.
Umbeck, J. 1981. *A Theory of Property Rights with Applications to the California Gold Rush.* Ames, IA: Iowa State University Press.
Wooldridge, W.C. 1970. *Uncle Sam, The Monopoly Man.* New Rochelle, NY: Arlington House.

evolution of property rights. The evolution of property rights is a subject with a distinctly mixed intellectual history. Illustrious commentators of the past have suggested that humanity might have been far less strife-ridden if property – particularly individual property – had never evolved at all. Plato forbade individual property to the Republic's 'guardians', on the ground that property would lead to distracting discord among them; Rousseau (1755) argued more generally that the seeds of war and domination were sown when human beings acquired the concept of mine and thine. In the same vein, a frequent feature of utopian communities has been the effort to do away with private property, which presumably gives vent to selfishness and aggression (see Hardy 1979; Barry 1992). And of course Marx (1867–83) depicted the origins and evolution of property as a story of economic rapine.

On the other hand, the western intellectual tradition also incorporates an exactly opposite opinion of property. From John Locke onward, a variety of considerable intellects have argued that property offers an escape from an aggressive, warlike and chaotic state of nature, and indeed that an evolving property rights regime might lead humankind toward a new kind of earthly Paradise (see Merchant 1995, 1997).

The modern law and economics movement, though of course thoroughly secular, is on the whole more likely to see the evolution of property rights in the latter light rather than the former. Indeed, law and economics writers explicitly state why property rights might deliver us to what is effectively a secular Eden of peace and plenty. In an earlier and more theologically inclined era, the proposition might have been expressed as follows: property yokes the sinful propensities of human beings to the Biblical command to labour.

PROPERTY LEADS TO PARADISE? In the original Eden, fruits and berries and other natural bounties presumably fell without requiring human effort; but the very injunction to labour suggests that nature outside the Garden has become a place not of bounty but of scarcity. Unfortunately, sinful human beings (or as we are more modernly called, self-interested rational actors) have little interest in labour; we would rather loaf and grab things from others than work. Thus, as one may easily extrapolate from Hobbes (1651), the problem of nature in a state of scarcity is that people behave badly. We fight over whatever fruits and berries are still around. We trample down the bushes and knock over the trees in our anxiety to take while the taking is good, and in so doing, we exacerbate the scarcity and reinforce Hobbes's famous line that life in a state of nature is 'nasty, brutish, and short'.

But in the argument that began most explicitly with Locke (1690) and that has continued through the modern law and economics movement, property has been presented as the chief institution that can save us from that sorry state, because property mobilizes self-interested humans to labour as nothing else does. Property encourages human beings to expend our efforts on the things we own – in Lockean terms, mix our labour with them – safe in the understanding that we ourselves will reap the rewards of our labours, and aware as well that we will suffer the pain that results from sloth and poor management. That is, property 'internalizes the externalities' of labour, concentrating its fruits on the labourer himself. As Richard Posner (1992: 32) has more recently remarked, 'All this has been well known for hundreds of years.'

But there is more: by defining rights and identifying the owners of various resources and laboured-upon things, property makes it possible for people to trade the things on which they have laboured for other things that they want, rather than grabbing everything in sight and fighting with others. Indeed, trade adds even more to the enticement to labour, since, as Adam Smith (1776) so famously noted, trade allows us to specialize; specialization in turn makes our labour all the more productive and valuable. Thus on this now quite standard view, retold in a variety of contexts, property rights help to mollify aggression, mobilize self-interest toward useful labour, and restore a new Eden of plenty and prosperity.

There is a problem with this thesis, however. The problem is that it has an analytic gap. Underlying the thesis is a rational actor model of self-regarding behaviour; that is, human beings can be induced to invest labour and effort, but only if property rights allow them to reap the ensuing fruits. But that same self-regarding rationality presents a problem when it comes to the origins and development of property. Consider person A, Ann: Let us suppose that she does mix labour with some resource in the state of nature; that is, she invests in the resource. Say, she prunes the berry bushes. From the perspective of person B, Bart, the best of all scenarios would be to hang around and wait for Ann to complete her investment, and then for him, Bart, to harvest the now more plentiful berries. Putting it briefly, Ann cannot have property all by herself. She needs Bart's cooperation in the form of his forbearance, but unfortunately Bart would rather cheat and take the things Ann has created. Moreover, self-regarding Ann feels the same way about Bart; she would rather take the fruits of his labours than do the work herself.

Thus purely self-regarding rational actors Ann and Bart are in a Prisoner's Dilemma (PD). Collectively, they are better off if they cooperate and create a little mutual property regime where each respects the other's rights, but their individual self-regarding motivations lead them to cheat and shirk instead – and hence no property regime arises (see Rose 1994). Eighteenth-century thinkers transformed self-regard from 'sin' into the more moderate sounding 'self-interest' (see Hirschman 1977), but self-interested rational actors are just the same old sinners when it comes to solving the problem of inventing property.

Locke famously solved this problem by kicking it upstairs: Ann and Bart create a state to police their property for them. But the state does not solve the analytic problem. As James Krier (1992) points out, the people who have to form the state are just a lot of Anns and Barts, and none of them wants to do the committee work to get the state organized; nor do they later want the task of monitoring the government itself, which is itself also made up of more Anns and Barts.

How then do rational actor theories get property to evolve? The answer is simple: the theorists fill in the analytic gap by telling a story. Locke did so in the late seventeenth century, and although the parts are somewhat scattered through the Second Treatise, they form an identifiable narrative: at first, people's initial property signifies no more than that they simply appropriate foodstuffs at the time they eat them; next, they begin to keep durables like nuts and even money, and of course they enclose land; and at the conclusion they establish a system of governance to safeguard their property. Blackstone (1765–9) told an almost identical story three-quarters of a century later, pointing out the relationship between growing scarcity and increasingly sophisticated forms of property and finally governance; and in our own time, the economist Harold Demsetz (1967) told it once again, using the example of the Northern Canadian Indians' development of property rights regimes in beaver habitat in response to the European demand for furs. And others have told variations on this narrative as well, using a variety of examples (see North and Thomas 1973; compare North 1990; Krier 1992).

All these narratives have the same general structure: first, resources are plentiful, more or less free for the taking. Next, resources become more scarce – either as a result of gradual development or more rapid perturbation – whereupon humans begin to create more complex forms of property in these scarce resources. Finally (once adequate measures are taken for protecting property), human beings get rich, because well-defined property rights help them to mediate conflicts and encourage investment and trade. Historical or pseudo-historical tales like these make the invention and evolution of property seem plausible – even as they gloss over the analytic PD gap. As narrative theorists point out, that is what stories are for. These stories are in some ways hortatory, as if to say, 'see, we simply *did* it; and we can do it again if we try' (see Rose 1994).

Unfortunately, as is well known in the modern law and economics literature, there is another version of the story. In this version, humans do not invent property when faced by the problem of scarcity. Instead, they wind up fighting and wasting resources – that is, they fail to solve the PD problem, and instead sink into a Hobbesian state of nature. Among modern economists, Scott Gordon (1954) told a well-known version of that story using the example of open-access fisheries, whose tendency is toward resource depletion, management failure and poverty for fishermen. But the modern story is perhaps best known for the name it received from the biologist Garrett Hardin (1968), that is, 'the Tragedy of the Commons', a tragedy that is itself just another version of the Prisoner's Dilemma. The Tragedy directly challenges the more optimistic just-so property story. It argues very forcefully that in the face of scarcity, sinful (or self-interested) rational actors are quite unlikely to invent property after all.

Given these two quite similar stories with such divergent outcomes, the evolution of property rights seems a much more contingent matter. Property does not just happen, as the optimistic just-so story suggests; instead, property from the start requires inventiveness, effort, favourable circumstances, and perhaps some measure of good luck – even some measure of what used to be called godliness, in the form of human willingness to cooperate.

At a minimum, given the possibility of the pessimistic outcome, the evolution of property must be recognized as a social institution, and studied as such.

PROPERTY AS A SOCIAL EVOLUTION. Some of the modern law and economics literature on property has begun to modify self-interested rational actor approaches and has taken a considerably more institutional approach. This literature often analyses property regimes as norm systems, and inquires about the circumstances that favour and disfavour the invention and elaboration of property norms appropriate to the subject matters to which they apply. One obvious factor smoothing the way to efficient norms in general, and to property regimes in particular, is small group size. Another smoothing factor for the construction of property norms is pre-existing cohesiveness on a variety of other fronts, such as religion, kinship, or mixed social and commercial relations. These factors can support the group effort – and the individual self-restraint – necessary to negotiate and abide by social norms. Thus Edna Ullman-Margalit (1977) predicts that small groups can overcome the PD problems embedded in the creation of norms; thus Avner Greif (1994) traces historical merchant groups' commercial norms back to other shared cultural norms, while Lisa Bernstein (1992) does the same for modern merchants; thus Robert Ellickson (1991) predicts the proliferation of efficient norms – including property norms – among 'close-knit' groups sharing a variety of social and economic relations.

Once invented, however, property regimes may require further refinement and reinvention, since first-cut property rights may well leave behind externalities or common-pool problems that at first seem trivial, but that later require readjustment in the face of new or unexpected scarcities. Gary Libecap (1989) has described this readjustment process as 'contracting for property rights', and has identified a number of factors that either assist or impede readjustment. Among the expediting factors are the magnitude and the obviousness of common-pool losses stemming from misaligned definitions of property; but among the impediments – increasing the costs of 're-contracting' – are again numbers and heterogeneity of stakeholders in the older regime, as well as difficulties in spreading more or less evenly the gains from property redefinitions.

Even when property rights are successfully 'negotiated', another contingency may arise collaterally, as it were: a sharp definition of property rights in one aspect of a resource may exacerbate common-pool problems with some other aspect. Nineteenth-century whalers, for example, invented a variety of informal property rights to divide each captured cetacean among the various participants in its capture and rendering. These 'local' property regimes, however, may have hastened the demise of larger global whale stocks simply by turning the whalers into more efficient hunters (see Ellickson 1991).

Yet another set of contingencies arises because sharply defined property rights may display a quite unattractive appearance *ex post*, especially when a more informed person appears to use hard-edged entitlements to the disadvantage of a less knowledgeable or less capable person. Under these circumstances, courts often fold muddying exceptions into what had seemed to be well-defined *ex ante* systems of rights, much to the consternation of some members of the law-and-economics community (see Easterbrook 1984). Mortgage law, for example, is full of extensions, forgivenesses, and 'reliefs from forfeiture' that respond to hard-luck stories, but that also cloud the parties' entitlements and entangle precise planning (see Rose 1994). Concerns over constitutional issues or human rights can similarly blur property definitions, for example when solicitude for free speech 'trumps' an owner's claim to exclusive control of her property (see for example *PruneYard Shopping Center v. Robins*).

All these matters suggest that property regimes evolve not in some necessary and natural lockstep, but rather in a considerably chancier way. But for some of the most interesting examples of what might be called the contingent evolutions of property, we may turn to the general area denoted as 'environmental law'.

ENVIRONMENTAL EVOLUTIONS. One important achievement of the law and economics approach to property has been the lesson that contractual and property regimes are not costless (see Coase 1960; Demsetz 1964). That fact in itself suggests one way to understand the evolution of property regimes: property as a management technique is most likely to emerge earliest where property rights can be defined relatively inexpensively. Institutional and social factors play an obvious role in the expense of property rights; as discussed above, different features of groups – size, cohesiveness etc. – lead to greater or lesser expenses in 'contracting' for property rights. Holding institutional factors constant, however, another major factor lies in the characteristics of the resource itself.

Land is clearly a resource that responds to investment, and it is also relatively easy to turn into property. Under many if not most conditions, land can be divided into individual parcels; moreover, land stands still, so that each claimant can mark it and stake out claims recognizable to others. The claimant can fence land to keep out trespassers, and can observe and chastise those trespassers who do enter without invitation. Small wonder, then, that land is so ubiquitous a subject of property rights (see Ellickson 1993).

But land lies adjacent to other resources, notably air, water and wildlife stocks; these environmental resources are considerably more difficult to divide into individual properties. Indeed, it is this common and indivisible nature that makes us think of such resources as 'environmental': they do not seem to belong to anyone in particular.

A quite typical pattern connects individual property usage to environmental resources: owners of land often 'piggy-back' uses of these common resources onto their uses of land. When farming, they may allow waste matter to be carried off in adjacent streams; they may hunt and fish the wildlife that roams through the area, and they may allow odours and dust to permeate the air. As Dean Lueck (1989) points out, spillover effects may be obviated if individual landholdings are large enough or if contracting is feasible, but quite often, individual landowners' uses of such common-pool resources create externalities to the neighbouring landowners. Even these externalities are unimportant when individual uses are thinly spread over wide spaces. Indeed, it is typical of environmental problems that they really are *not* problems at the outset. They only become so as increasing numbers of landowners piggyback more intense uses of the unpropertized common resources, and as the marginal cost of each additional use increases. At some point these common pool costs rise high enough that it is worth a common effort to try to limit them (see Rose 1996).

Here too, the law and economics literature suggests that the cheapest common management techniques may be used first (see Anderson and Hill 1975). Thus a typical first public response to pollution problems is simply to forbid new or expanded uses, or even more typically, to close off the use to outsiders (see Cheung 1970; Rose 1991). A Massachusetts community, for example, attempted to limit the malodorous effects of a city dump by forbidding all but residents from using it (see *Town of Warren v. Hazardous Waste Facility Site Safety Council*); in a famous US constitutional case, for another example, New Orleans adopted land use controls that confined slaughter-houses to a particular area in the city (see *Slaughter-House Cases*). Similarly, the lobster-fishing communities on certain Maine islands preserve the plentiful lobster stocks nearby by cutting the traps of any outsiders who venture in to fish for them (see Acheson 1988). In the same pattern, British aristocrats of earlier centuries maintained the wild game they liked to hunt by limiting the take to themselves alone (see Lueck 1995). Riparian law preserves riverflows for adjacent watermills by prohibiting the interbasin transfer of water (see Rose 1994). And so on and so on.

All these 'keep-out' methods effectively convert the environmental resource from an open-access state – free for the taking by anyone – into a limited common property, that is, held in common only among a particular group of 'insiders'. One difficulty with the keep-out approach is that outsiders and latecomers may continue to crash at the gate, so that the success of this conservation regime depends to some degree on the ability of the insiders to monitor and police those gate-crashers. A second difficulty is that the insiders themselves may overuse the resource, and hence may require some internal policing.

In the face of greater pressure on some valuable resource, either from the outside or from the inside or both, a community may adopt a somewhat more expensive method to preserve common-pool resources – that is, constraints on the *manner* in which the resource is used, often (but not always) overlaid on top of keep-out regimes. Such constraints are more difficult to monitor than the simple prohibition on outsider entry; as Ellickson (1993) points out, it is easier to limit entry at the gate than to monitor the behaviour of persons who are entitled to be inside. Nevertheless, manner-of-use constraints are embodied in legal regimes like riparian rights and nuisance law, where the relevant groups of resource users are expected to use the resource no more than 'reasonably'. The hallmarks of such regimes are moderation and equality: a 'reasonable' use typically means one that accords with the general practice of the community, and that is compatible with a like use by others (see *Embrey v. Owen*).

Manner-of-use constraints have been updated and considerably complicated in some modern environmental controls, especially in uniform performance standards aimed at controlling pollution. Under such regulatory regimes, a factory can 'use' the air to deposit pollution, but only after filtering the pollutants through the 'best available technology'. These modern technological requirements, however, reveal some of the weaknesses of manner-of-use constraints: they work best among homogeneous resources users, but much less well among heterogeneous ones (witness the proliferation of uniform 'new source performance standards' under the United States Clean Air Act). Moreover, entitlements structured on equal use stifle transfers from lower-value to higher-value users (see Ackerman and Stewart 1988).

Under still greater resource pressure, communities may turn to a new version of individual, alienable property rights. Modern fishery management, for example, is increasingly moving toward individual transferable quotas (ITQs), while air pollution control moves toward tradeable emission rights. These hybrid types of regulatorily-created property have the advantage of constraining overall usage while allowing Pareto-superior transfers (see Dales 1968; Tietenberg 1985; Ackerman and Stewart 1988; Stewart 1990). But it only makes sense to use such hybrid, market-based regulatory rights if their advantages overcome their chief disadvantage: hybrid regulatory rights may be even more difficult to monitor than manner-of-use regulations. Thus it is likely to be easier to tell if a manufacturer has installed a sulphur-reducing scrubber in a factory exhaust pipe than to determine whether the factory's sulphurous fumes exceed the limits of the owner's tradeable emission permit; it is easier to tell if a fishing boat carries only a certain type of tackle than to discern whether the fisherman has surreptitiously exceeded his allotted quota of the catch. But given increasing concern about depletion of the underlying resources, it might be worth the cost to shift to market-based regulatory regimes, with their explicit attention to allowable resource use (see Krier and Montgomery 1973).

In environmental matters, then, there is still another version of the optimistic property story – that is, environmental management regimes become increasingly sophisticated as resources come under increasing pressure. As with the old Lockean story, resources initially open to all tend to evolve into property, even if that property is only a hybrid regulatory creation. But three matters are worth noticing about the environmental variant on this classic tale.

First, the environmental story suggests that the evolution of property is not unidirectional. Despite the evolution towards more sharply defined property rights, in the environmental story the new hybrid market-based rights are no more than very limited consumptive entitlements on the surface of resources that are in large part conserved as common pool goods. Tradeable emission rights do not completely consume the air; far from it, the bulk of the air remains open for non-consumptive common usage (for example, for views). Individual fishing quotas do not completely consume the fish stock; indeed, the whole point is to retain an unconsumed stock that can regenerate itself, while the quotas are simply one way to allocate a moderate consumption at the fringe of that stock. Thus the environmental evolutionary story suggests a procession of resource management not toward complete individual property, but rather to something quite different: in the case of public goods, the progress of resource management is toward a community property or public property, in which individual rights merely allocate entitlements of a consumable fringe.

Second, the environmental evolutionary story is no more logically compulsory than the more general optimistic property story. The successful evolution of environmental management regimes – from open access through keep-out and manner-of-use regimes to hybrid property rights – is quite as much a just-so story as the Lockean story. Management regimes for environmental resources are no more likely than individual property to evolve successfully. Perhaps it would be *nice* if public goods generated increasingly sophisticated management regimes when increases in demand warranted such shifts; but the niceness of the thought does not make it happen. If anything, because public goods management involves mixed techniques – stock preservation at the centre combined with consumption management at the fringe – and because this mixed management necessarily involves a whole community of decision-makers, the likelihood of success is even lower.

The third point follows from the second: the evolution of environmental management regimes is a highly contingent matter, one that requires a great variety of adjustments and compromises. Here too, as in the evolution of property rights generally, the alteration of management regimes entails Libecap's (1989) 'contracting for property rights'. In particular, stakeholders in an earlier management regime can undermine efforts to move to more effective management. For example, landowners are frequently stakeholders in an earlier regime that allows them to 'piggyback' environmental resources such as air or water onto their landed property; they may come to regard an earlier open access regime as a matter of permanent right, and indeed may make capital expenditures based on those expectations. Meanwhile, later purchasers typically demand the same rights on grounds of equality (see Rose 1996).

Much of the highly contested American law of 'takings' can be seen as an effort to mollify such stakeholder claims, while at the same time permitting some breathing room to communities to alter management regimes in order to deal with increased pressure on common or environmental resources. Similarly, new environmental legislation may incorporate a variety of mollifying and compromising features, most notably the 'grandfathering' of pre-existing practices. Needless to say, what seem at first to be temporary and minor expedients can become tremendous sticking points at some future time; 'grandfathered' legislative exemptions can become enormously valuable rights in themselves, enjoying the status of semi-monopolies.

For these reasons as well as others, changes in environmental regulation often have a distinctly lumpy character. Nevertheless, we have enjoyed some modest measure of success on the environmental front, and the movement of environmental law towards even a very lumpy set of property-like regimes should yield at least a muted optimism about the human capacity to use property to manage scarce resources. Optimism is warranted because we have in fact been able to address some environmental problems through property; but that optimism must be muted because the evolution toward both private and public 'environmental property' has such frequent lurches and sways.

Given those sways and lurches, it would be difficult to think, upon reflection, that property really will lead to a new Eden, even a secular one. But it would be even more difficult to believe, with some philosophers, that property is chiefly an inducement to human avarice and discord. On the contrary, the various evolutions of property rights, uneven and contingent though they are, suggest that this is a vitally important institution for socializing self-interested human beings, and for allowing us to break through our self interest and work toward mutually desirable ends in a modestly cooperative fashion (see Hirschman 1982). Indeed, theologians of an earlier age might have posited that human beings can only create and nurture property regimes because property itself perfectly comports with the human condition: the institution most prominently reflects our fallen and sinful nature – but also our very slight glimmer of divinity.

CAROL M. ROSE

See also BLACKSTONE, WILLIAM; COMMON PROPERTY; ECONOMIC INCENTIVES FOR ENVIRONMENTAL REGULATION; ENDANGERED SPECIES; FIRST POSSESSION; LOCAL COMMON PROPERTY RIGHTS; LOCKE, JOHN; PROPERTY RIGHTS; TRADEABLE POLLUTION PERMITS; WILDLIFE LAW.

Subject classification: 2b(i); 4a(ii); 5b(i).

CASES

Embrey v. Owen (1851) 6 Ex. 353, 154 Eng. Rep. 1047.

Prune Yard Shopping Center v Robins, 447 US 74 (1980).

Slaughter-House Cases, 83 US 36 (1872).

Town of Warren v. Hazardous Waste Facility Site Safety Council, 466 NE2d 102 (Mass. 1984).

BIBLIOGRAPHY

Acheson, J.M. 1988. *The Lobster Gangs of Maine*. Hanover, NH: University Press of New England.

Ackerman, B.A. and Stewart, R.B. 1988. Reforming environmental law: the democratic case for market incentives. *Columbia Journal of Environmental Law* 13: 171–99.

Anderson, T.L. and Hill, P.J. 1975. The evolution of property rights: a study of the American West. *Journal of Law and Economics* 18: 163–79.

Barry, B.J.L. 1992. *America's Utopian Experiments: Communal Havens from Long-Wave Crises*. Hanover, NH: University Press of New England.

Bentham, J. 1802. Principles of the Civil Code. In *The Theory of Legislation*, London: Kegan Paul, Trench, Trubner & Co.; New York: Harcourt, Brace & Co., 1931.

Bernstein, L. 1992. Opting out of the legal system: extralegal contractual relations in the diamond industry. *Journal of Legal Studies* 21: 115–57.

Blackstone, W. 1765–9. *Commentaries on the Laws of England*. 4 vols, Oxford: Clarendon Press.

Cheung, S.N.S. 1970. The structure of a contract and the theory of a non-exclusive resource. *Journal of Law and Economics* 13: 49–70.

Coase, R.H. 1960. The problem of social cost. *Journal of Law & Economics* 3: 1–44.
Dales, J.H. 1968. *Pollution, Property and Prices*. Toronto: University of Toronto Press.
Demsetz, H. 1964. The exchange and enforcement of property rights. *Journal of Law and Economics* 7: 11–26.
Demsetz, H. 1967. Toward a theory of property rights 1967. *American Economic Review (Papers & Proceedings)* 57: 347–59.
Easterbrook, F.H. 1984. The Supreme Court Review 1983 Term – Forward: the Court and the economic system. *Harvard Law Review* 98: 4–60.
Ellickson, R.C. 1991. *Order Without Law: How Neighbors Settle Disputes*. Cambridge, MA; London: Harvard University Press.
Ellickson, R.C. 1993. Property in land. *Yale Law Journal* 102: 1315–400.
Gordon, H.S. 1954. The economic theory of a common-property resource: the fishery. *Journal of Political Economy* 62: 124–42.
Greif, A. 1994. Cultural beliefs and the organization of society: a historical and theoretical reflection on collectivist and individualist societies. *Journal of Political Economy* 102: 912–50.
Hardin, G. 1968. The tragedy of the commons. *Science* 162: 1243–8.
Hardy, D. 1979. *Alternative Communities in Nineteenth Century England*. London, New York: Longman
Hirschman, A.O. 1977. *The Passions and the Interests*. Princeton: Princeton University Press.
Hirschman, A.O. 1982. Rival interpretations of market society: civilizing, destructive, or feeble? *Journal of Economic Literature* 20: 1463–84.
Hobbes, T. 1651. *Leviathan*. Ed. C.B. MacPherson, Harmondsworth, Middlesex; Baltimore: Penguin Books, 1968.
Krier, J.E. 1992. The tragedy of the commons, Part II. *Harvard Journal of Law and Public Policy* 15: 325–47.
Krier, J.E. and Montgomery, W.D. 1973. Resource allocation, information cost and the form of government intervention. *Natural Resources Journal* 13: 89–105.
Libecap, G. 1989. *Contracting for Property Rights*. Cambridge: Cambridge University Press.
Locke, J. 1690. *Two Treatises of Government*. Ed. P. Laslett, Cambridge: Cambridge University Press, 1960.
Lueck, D. 1989. The economic nature of wildlife law. *Journal of Legal Studies* 18: 291–324.
Lueck, D. 1995. Property rights and the economic logic of wildlife institutions. *Natural Resources Journal* 35: 625–70.
Marx, K. 1867–83. *Capital*. Ed. F. Engels, New York, London, Toronto: Encyclopedia Britannica, 1955.
Merchant, C. 1995. Reinventing Eden: Western culture as a recovery narrative. In *Uncommon Ground: Toward Reinventing Nature*, ed. W. Cronon, New York; London: W.W. Norton.
Merchant, C. 1997. Paradise and property: Locke's narrative and the transformation of nature. Paper delivered at the American Society for Environmental History, Baltimore, MD.
North, D.C. 1990. *Institutions, Institutional Change and Economic Performance*. Cambridge: Cambridge University Press.
North, D.C. and Thomas, R.P. 1973. *The Rise of the Western World. A New Economic History*. Cambridge: Cambridge University Press.
Ostrom, E. 1990. *Governing the Commons: The Evolution of Institutions for Collective Action*. Cambridge: Cambridge University Press.
Plato. *The Republic*. Trans. F.M. Cornford, New York, Oxford: Oxford University Press, 1945.
Posner, R.A. 1973. *Economic Analysis of Law*. Boston: Little, Brown & Co.; 4th edn, 1992.
Rose, C.M. 1991. Rethinking environmental controls: management strategies for common resources. *Duke Law Journal* 1991: 1–38.
Rose, C.M. 1994. *Property and Persuasion*. Boulder, CO: Westview Press.
Rose, C.M. 1996. A dozen propositions on private property, public rights, and the new takings legislation. *Washington and Lee Law Review* 53: 265–98.
Rousseau, J.-J. 1755. *Discourse on The Origin of Inequality*. Ed. P. Coleman, Oxford: Oxford University Press, 1994.
Smith, A. 1776. *An Inquiry Into the Nature and Causes of the Wealth of Nations*. Ed. E. Cannan, New York: Modern Library, 1937.
Stewart, R. 1990. Privprop, Regprop and beyond. *Harvard Journal of Law and Public Policy* 13: 91–8.
Tietenberg, T.H. 1985. *Emissions Trading: An Exercise in Reforming Pollution Policy*. Washington, DC: Resources for the Future.
Ullman-Margalit, E. 1977. *The Emergence of Norms*. Oxford: Clarendon Press.

evolution of the economic constitution of the European Union. The present economic constitution of the European Union is the result of a development that began only a few years after World War II. Before analysing this evolution in detail, we must set out our frame of reference, i.e. the concept of an *economic constitution*. This has its origins in a particular tradition of law and economics, the Freiburg School, which can be regarded as a precursor of modern institutional economics (Streit 1992) and emphasizes the role of legal rules within the process of economic interaction.

The term 'economic constitution' can be used in a descriptive way. In this sense, it refers to all legal rules which constrain the conduct of economic agents, i.e. to rules which are particularly relevant to the economy as a societal subsystem. The term can also be used in a functional way. In this sense, it refers to those legal rules which can be identified as constitutive for or conducive to a specific type of economic system, for example a market system.

The two meanings of economic constitution can be linked analytically. Properties which are related to the second meaning can serve as a frame of reference when assessing an observable economic constitution (the first meaning) as to its functional quality. As a result, it should be possible to state whether and to what extent observable legal rules correspond to the functional requirements of a market system. Further, economic analysis has provided empirically relevant results which allow statements on at least some of the likely economic consequences in those cases where properties of observable rules deviate from those required from a functional point of view. Methodologically, it is important to note that statements which can be derived in this way are positive statements and not normative ones.

The functional interpretation of 'economic constitution' implies that we can identify abstract qualities of rules which are conducive to the functioning of a market economy as a self-organizing system. These qualities can be summed up by the criterion of universalizability (Streit 1992: 682 ff.), i.e. that the rules are: abstract in the sense of being 'applicable to an unknown and indeterminable number of persons and instances' (Hayek 1973: 50); they are open in the sense of describing merely those actions which are not allowed and thus leave it to the individuals also to discover and take unprecedented actions; they are certain in the sense that individuals can trust in their continuance and are able to identify in practice those actions which are not allowed (Leoni [1961] 1991: 76ff).

The corresponding rules serve the purpose of securing

the voluntary exchange of property rights by autonomous agents. Translated into the language of law, they are an important part of private or civil law. This is why a society whose members are predominantly subjected to this kind of law and consequently also enjoy autonomy as to government interference would be a 'private law society' (Böhm [1966] 1989).

The structure of the economic constitution in this sense is similar to the structural elements of the constitution of political systems which are designed to secure a government under the law (Mestmäcker 1974). On the one hand, autonomy is granted to those who are entitled to set rules and to govern. But since, on the other hand, autonomy tends to provide opportunities to exercise power, infringing on the freedom of the citizens, a sophisticated system of checks and balances is required to prevent an arbitrary use of such political power. Similarly, the constitutional structure of a market system consists of secured opportunities to act in an autonomous, self-responsible way. But equally, institutional provisions are required to prevent an arbitrary use of the concomitant economic power infringing on the freedom of others to compete.

Modern economic constitutions – in the descriptive sense – are usually quite far away from the model of a 'private law society'. They are, instead, dominated by political efforts to assign particular economic results to specific groups. Consequently, legal rules no longer correspond to the criterion of universalizability. They are transformed into 'materialized law' (Weber [1921] 1985: 397) by introducing 'ethical imperatives or (. . .) political maxims' (ibid; our translation) which allow the pursuit of specific objectives. The ensuing legislation not only undermines the rules of private law. It tends to turn the political systems into a welfare state. The systemic consequences of this development for the functioning of a market economy have been thoroughly analysed. Mancur Olson's label 'institutional sclerosis' (Olson 1982) stands for the decline of the systems' self-organizing and self-regulating capacity as the consequence of relentless rent-seeking activities.

Two approaches to economic integration. When applying the concept of economic constitution to economic integration in general and to the European Union (EU) in particular, two approaches to integration can be identified which influenced the evolution of the economic constitution of the EU right from the beginning (Mussler and Streit 1996): *integration by competition* and *integration by intervention*. They reflect two opposing views of the market system or, more precisely, of the possibilities of shaping economic development according to political objectives. Correspondingly, they require different legal rules and imply different conceptualizations of integration.

Integration by competition starts from the following reasoning: Competition as a 'discovery procedure' (Hayek [1968] 1978: 179) and as a controlling device is not only effective within the borders of a national state, but can also be used as a means of integration. This kind of integration is, first, related to the economic domain *per se*, i.e. to the economic benefits resulting from the opening up of national markets allowing border-crossing competition and an international division of labour. Secondly, integration by competition can also allow for institutional competition, i.e. competition among political suppliers of different institutional (legal) systems to attract mobile resources. As a consequence, private agents have the opportunity to make use of possibilities to choose (i) between goods and services within a common market and (ii) between various locations and thus various legal systems in the different member states.

This approach to integration can also be labelled 'integration from below' because it leaves it to the citizens themselves to discover and exploit the opportunities provided by a legal framework which allows both economic and institutional competition. This means that the integration process does not need to be centrally planned. Rather, integration is channelled by the individual objectives and choices of the economic actors, which are the crucial 'medium' of integration, and supported by rules conducive to both types of competition.

The second approach, integration by intervention, is characterized by attempts to direct the integration process politically 'from above' with the aim of serving politically defined common objectives. It consists of those common policies which discriminate between different economic activities in pursuing specific targets. In the European Union, this approach is characteristic of the common sectoral policies or the common policies in the area of R&D. They are regarded as effective instruments to serve common purposes such as 'European competitiveness' or 'the common European interest'. This implies attempts to set concrete objectives for parts of the economic system. The approach necessarily suggests a centralization of intervention power on the European level and a far-reaching harmonization of legal rules.

In this case, integration is not related to the actions of economic agents but to sovereign actions of politicians and bureaucrats. The degree of integration depends on the concrete results achieved by the interventions of the central authority.

Regarding legislation and the function of legal rules, the two approaches differ correspondingly. Integration by competition means that the economic and political actors accept (a) that universal or abstract rules are effective in coping with the endemic lack of knowledge of all economic actors (Hayek 1945), and (b) that competition of legal systems within the Community (Union) can help to improve the institutional framework in an unpredictable way. Contrarily, integration by intervention implies an interpretation of law as a 'conditional planning programme' (Mestmäcker 1993; our translation). Legislation of this kind is based on an understanding of the economic system which wrongly presumes relatively simple and stable patterns of causation. It suffers from a pretence of knowledge.

A 'European Economic Constitution'. The competitive approach to integration needs further elaboration because we can derive from it the requirements for a 'European economic constitution' in the functional sense. It contains the simple idea that the functional properties of market systems should be secured by law in the context of border-crossing transactions as well. Market systems can be characterized by the following functional properties: (i) private subjects act on their own authority by pursuing individual purposes (*private autonomy*); (ii) the patterns of economic activities emerging from the use of private autonomy are the evolutionary outcome of *self-coordination* through exchange and of *self-control* through competition.

In an international context, these properties only become effective on a large scale if the economic actors pursuing individual purposes are not constrained by national governments. This implies that national economies are open systems, i.e. that they allow the free movement of goods and services, but also of persons and capital, beyond national borders: the core of integration by competition is a common market. Regarding Europe, this kind of market integration requires a set of legal rules which we might call the European economic constitution. It implies that certain national powers be transferred to a European authority for the purpose of enforcing those rules. The rules have to meet the following requirements (Mussler and Wohlgemuth 1995: 24–6):

(1) With regard to the citizens of the European Union, economic liberties such as freedom of trading goods and services, of settlement and of domicile have to be granted. These liberties must be universally applicable to all citizens of the European Union. To this effect they must be superior to national law and hence enforceable by court decision in case of conflict. The individual freedom of action granted to the EU citizens by the aforementioned liberties has to be secured by prohibition of private restraints on trade.

(2) With regard to the Member States, it is necessary that their discretionary power, i.e. their sovereignty, be limited in a specific sense. All those activities of Member States' authorities which impede border-crossing transactions in a discriminatory way, and thus restrict the individual liberties and property rights of the citizens, are prohibited.

(3) With regard to the European level of 'government' and jurisdiction, the powers of European authorities must be strictly limited to the protection of economic liberties and of competition throughout the whole of the Union. It is particularly important that the economic liberties granted to citizens by limiting interventions into the market process by the Member States are also secured against potential interventions by the Union authorities themselves. This means that not only interventions by the Member States but also those by the European Commission and the European Council have to be prohibited. Furthermore, it is important that the removal of trade barriers within the Union not be accompanied by erection of (new) trade barriers towards countries outside the Union. This would be discrimination against those who do not want to confine the use of their economic liberties to transactions within the integration area. In other words, the competitive approach to integration is ultimately directed towards an open world economy.

If the aforementioned economic liberties are granted to citizens, it becomes possible to deal also with impediments to trade resulting from the territoriality of law. This leads to the second dimension of integration by competition, namely institutional competition, or the competition of legal systems. For these economic liberties imply also that citizens are able to choose among the different legal systems of the nation states, i.e. by their choices they can initiate institutional competition.

Institutional competition. Institutional competition is a process in which elements of economic and political competition interact in a rather complex way (Wohlgemuth 1995). Like its two constituent forms of competition, this process of interaction is channelled by rules, which define the possibilities that private agents have to choose among the various territorial legal systems. The actual range of opportunities to choose is defined by the degree of openness of the systems considered. Furthermore, that openness depends on rules which effectively prevent governments from interfering with border-crossing activities of citizens when the disciplinary effects of institutional competition make themselves felt. Originally, the discussion of institutional competition centred around international factor movements. To allocate mobile factors in a specific country necessarily implies that their further use is subjected to the corresponding territorial private and public law or to specific legislation on resources owned by foreign nationals.

Differences in territorial law can be among those factors which influence decisions on locating mobile resources. Adam Smith ([1776] 1982: 848–9) discussed the potential influence of differences of profits after tax on international capital flows. Extending that reasoning beyond fiscal dimensions, it can be argued that transnational allocation of mobile factors always implies institutional arbitrage. Political actors as suppliers of institutional arrangements may either observe such factor movements and interpret them to be the result of a choice of systems by private agents, or their attention will be drawn to it through 'voice' by those – particularly owners of immobile factors – who are negatively affected by this kind of 'exit' (Hirschman 1970). Institutional competition would become effective in the country considered if political actors were induced to revise their institutional supply in order to improve the attraction of their constituency for mobile factors.

Apart from different analytical problems of institutional competition which require further research, two basic conjectures about institutional competition can be suggested. (i) Institutional competition is a procedure allowing private competitors to test the expediency of available institutional arrangements. At the same time it induces political competitors to develop more attractive institutional innovations (institutional competition as a discovery procedure). (ii) Institutional competition is initiated as a consequence of actual and political substitution of institutional arrangements by private competitors. This, in turn, has a controlling effect on political competitors as suppliers of old and new institutional arrangements (institutional competition as a controlling device).

THE ECONOMIC CONSTITUTION OF THE EEC TREATY

Steps towards a European Union. The evolution of the economic constitution of the European Union can be traced by studying the various treaties preceding the

Union and the related jurisdiction. The first step was the Treaty of 1951 establishing the European Coal and Steel Community (ECSC Treaty), which secured common political control of the 'key industries' of the time, considered to be of strategic importance in view of the experience of the two world wars. The central idea of this treaty has been characteristic of European integration ever since: political objectives should be obtained primarily by means of economic integration. This is clearly expressed in the preamble of the Treaty, where the signatories declare their firm intention 'to substitute for age-old rivalries the merging of their essential interests; to create by establishing an economic community, the basis for a broader and deeper community among peoples long divided by bloody conflicts'.

While attempts in the 1950s to build a European Political Community or a European Defence Community failed, economic integration appeared to be more conducive to the political objectives of integration than political integration itself. Political integration would have required that the Member States give up a considerable part of their national sovereignty. This requirement was not apparent in the case of economic integration, and that may have been the reason why at their conference at Messina in 1955 the Foreign Secretaries of the ECSC Member States charged a commission under the chairmanship of the Belgian Foreign Secretary Paul-Henri Spaak to examine further steps towards economic integration. The resulting Spaak Report of 1956 suggested the establishment of a common market. This report was the basis for the Treaty establishing the European Economic Community (EEC) which was concluded by the Member States at Rome in 1957 and came into force in 1958.

Whereas the ECSC Treaty reflects a concept of sectoral and therefore partial integration, the EEC Treaty aims at a common market. It was constituted by the legal rules for a customs union, granting basic economic liberties and establishing common rules on competition. Further, the Community was vested with authority in the fields of agriculture, transport and commercial policy with non-Member countries.

The EEC Treaty became and still remains the legal basis for European integration. It has been fundamentally amended twice, by the Single European Act (SEA) of 1986 and by the Treaty on European Union (TEU; 'Maastricht Treaty') of 1992. The SEA contained rules on the 'Completion of the Internal Market' and the extension of Community powers in different fields of economic policy. The TEU changed the name of the EEC Treaty to EC Treaty and involved a further extension of Community powers. Furthermore, it established rules for a monetary union and a timetable for its introduction. The provisions introduced at the same time on cooperation in the fields of foreign policy, security policy, and justice and home affairs, remain mere declarations of intent.

The evolution of the economic constitution of the EU was determined not only by the treaties and their amendments. The jurisdiction of the European Court of Justice (ECJ) was equally important because it created the specific constitutional quality of the EEC Treaty. Further, this constitutional development was influenced by the production of secondary law which partly served as a precedent for the amendments to the Treaty.

The EEC Treaty: provisions for integration by competition. There is sufficient evidence to argue that the Treaty provides a framework for a common market as a self-organizing system (Streit and Mussler 1994: 330–31).

(1) In order to allow unimpeded self-coordination of economic actors through market transactions, it is a part of the activities of the Community to eliminate tariff as well as non-tariff barriers to the import and export of goods between Member States (Art. 3a) and to abolish 'obstacles to freedom of movement for persons, services and capital' (Art. 3c).

(2) In order to allow self-control of economic actors through competition and to contain economic power, the Community establishes 'a system ensuring that competition in the common market is not distorted' (Art. 3f).

(3) So far as external markets are concerned, the Community not only establishes 'a common customs tariff' and 'a common commercial policy' (Art. 3b) but is also committed 'to contribute, in the common interest, to the harmonious development of world trade, the progressive abolition of restrictions on international trade and the lowering of customs barriers' (Art. 110).

As a whole, these activities describe sovereign tasks of the Community with the aim of improving the institutional framework for autonomous economic decisions of private actors. They imply a clear demarcation of the private and the public sphere whereby it is the duty of the Court of Justice to 'ensure that in the interpretation and application of this Treaty the law is observed' (Art. 164).

The requirements for rules of an economic constitution conducive to integration by competition (see above) are met by the Treaty:

(1) The most essential part of the Treaty are the basic economic liberties (free movement of goods: Arts. 9ff, esp. Arts. 30ff.; free movement of persons, services and capital: Arts. 48ff.). Because of their specific legal character, they are not mere declarations but must be interpreted as basic individual rights of EU citizens. They are complemented by common rules on competition (Arts. 85ff.).

(2) Simultaneously, the basic liberties imply safeguards against restrictions of competition which result from the activities of the Member States: forming a common market represents an obligation to remove existing restrictions of trade (Art. 3c) and hence of competition between Member States. In addition, those distortions of competition which may result from aids granted by Member States (Arts. 92ff.), from regulations or administrative action (Arts. 101ff.) and from measures related to 'public undertakings and undertakings to which Member States grant special or exclusive rights' (Art. 90) are considered incompatible with the Treaty.

(3) The legitimization of Community action is functionally constrained to the establishment of a common market.

From the perspective of an economic constitution, the specific legal quality of the basic liberties must be explained in more detail. It has been developed by the ECJ and represents a particular solution to the problem of territoriality of law. Border-crossing transactions can only be legally safeguarded if the corresponding liberties of economic actors are protected against interventions of the otherwise sovereign Member States. In case of violation it must be possible to gain a legal title enforcing those rights. According to the interpretation of the ECJ, the EEC Treaty differs fundamentally from other integration programmes based on public international law. The Court stated in 1991 that the Treaty is 'the constitutional charter of a community based on the rule of law' (ECJ 1991). According to this, the ECJ specified the content of the basic liberties in the following respects: first, the obligations of the Member States to eliminate any restraints of trade among themselves were transformed into individual rights of EEC citizens; and second, because of a far-reaching interpretation of these obligations, the restrictions imposed upon the economic liberties of citizens were most effectively removed.

The basic liberties as constitutionalized individual rights. The specific constitutional quality of the EEC Treaty is the result of its enforcement mechanism. Public international law can normally be enforced only by the nation states themselves. In the case of the EEC Treaty the situation is quite different. All Member States are subject to the obligatory jurisdiction of a common court of justice. In a sense, the mechanism of law enforcement in the Community is novel. It takes advantage of the fact that national governments are bound by the jurisdiction of their (national) courts: according to Art. 177 (EEC Treaty), the national courts are obliged to submit to the ECJ any case which raises questions as to the interpretation of the Treaty and which is pending before a court or tribunal of a Member State. To put it more concretely, the national courts must apply European law. This means that for the citizens of the Union their liberties can be enforced by the ECJ or by national courts even against the powers of the Member States. The corresponding doctrines of 'direct effect' and of 'supremacy' of European law developed by the court in its 'Van Gend & Loos' and 'Costa' rulings of 1963 and 1964 brought about a 'constitutionalization' (Mestmäcker 1994, 622–4) of the basic liberties: the obligation of the Member States according to public international law was transformed into individual rights of citizens of the Community, which can be claimed in court. According to this interpretation, the basic liberties define economic spheres of action which cannot be infringed upon by the Member States. These spheres can be used by the citizens in the common market according to their economic requirements within the framework of private law (Behrens 1992: 147).

The basic liberties as the pacemaker of European integration. Due to the jurisdiction of the ECJ, the basic liberties became a far-reaching instrument of economic integration. At the beginning, the integrative effects of the liberties were quite limited because of their interpretation in accordance with Art. 7 (EEC Treaty), which prohibits any discrimination on grounds of nationality. This implied, for example, that product safety regulations of a Member State were equally effective for domestic products and for products originating from other Member States. However, this interpretation still impeded trade between Member States considerably since, for example, the import of goods from countries with low-level regulation into countries with high-level regulation was made very difficult. From the perspective of a common market there were two solutions to this problem. The first is set out in Art. 100 (EEC Treaty) which asks the Council to 'issue directives for the approximation of such provisions laid down by law, regulation or administrative action in Member States as directly affect the establishment or functioning of the common market'. But since the realization of such approximation turned out to be nearly impossible, the court also tried the second alternative: the restriction of regulatory power of the Member States in such a way that the impeding effects on trade caused by non-discriminatory regulations are eliminated. The court took this direction by interpreting Art. 30 (EEC Treaty) by which 'quantitative restrictions on imports and all measures having equivalent effect' between Member States are prohibited. This prohibition was made more precise by the court in the famous *Dassonville* ruling of 1974: 'All trading rules enacted by Member States which are capable of hindering, directly or indirectly, actually or potentially, intra-Community trade are to be considered as measures having an effect equivalent to quantitive restrictions' (ECJ 1974: 873).

Thus the free movement of goods implies a general prohibition of any restraint of trade among Member States. Apart from some qualifications in detail, the court upheld this judgment in further rulings and extended it to the free movement of services, persons and capital (Behrens 1992). This evolution towards far-reaching economic liberties strengthened the economic constitution of the Community as a constitution for market integration, i.e. integration by competition in the economic domain. It can also be interpreted as a move from the *country of destination* principle to the *country of origin* principle. From this point of view, it can be argued that the ECJ established at the same time important rules for institutional competition.

The *country of destination* principle corresponds to the non-discrimination principle in the sense mentioned above: goods, services and persons are subject to the legal system of their destination in the context of border-crossing transactions. The *country of origin* principle, however, requires the country of destination to recognize the regulations of the country of origin as equivalent to its own regulations. With regard to the common market, this mutual recognition makes sure that every good can circulate in the whole of the integration area if it corresponds to the regulations of its country of origin. Mutual recognition is a precondition for institutional competition because the economic actors are enabled to choose among different regulations and can thus initiate competition among (the political suppliers of) such regulations. The suppliers of goods and services choose a regulation regime adequate to their purposes by locating their business accordingly, whereas the demanders get the opportunity to choose among different goods and services produced under various regulation regimes.

The ECJ 'discovered' the *country of origin* principle more or less by chance: the decisive statement can be found in the Court's famous *Cassis-de-Dijon* ruling of 1979:

> There is therefore no valid reason why, provided that they have been lawfully produced and marketed in one of the Member States, alcoholic beverages should not be introduced into any other Member State; the sale of such products may not be subject to a legal prohibition on the marketing of beverages with an alcohol content lower than the limit set by the national rules (ECJ 1979: 664).

The rules on competition. These rules (Arts. 85ff., EEC Treaty) are the counterpart to the basic liberties. They are equally addressed to the Member States and to the economic actors, particularly to the companies located in the Member States. As far as they concern the Member States themselves, they complement the basic liberties: the latter imply a prohibition of negative discrimination against foreigners by the domestic government, whereas the rules on competition (especially the prohibition of subsidies) are designed to prevent any positive discrimination in favour of domestic companies by domestic governments. As far as they apply to private economic actors, they prohibit as incompatible with the common market any kind of activity which has as its object or effect 'the prevention, restriction or distortion of competition within the common market . . .' (Art. 85). These rules refer particularly to cartels and comparable agreements (Art. 85) and to the abuse of a dominant position within the common market (Art. 86).

Considering a third direction in which the liberties require protection, there exists no clear impediment to the Community itself becoming a source of restrictions imposed upon the economic freedom of its citizens. At first glance there should be no doubt that the constitutionally secured basic liberties and the principle of undistorted competition have also to be considered as safeguards against Community interference (Petersmann 1993b: 408). But the Treaty itself does not make sufficiently clear that the principles of open markets and the rules of competition, which are addressed to the Member States, apply equally to the Community. In view of the more recent political moves in the process of European integration, it is necessary to recall a fundamental constitutional problem of the nation state again, this time with regard to the Community: 'The new . . . challenge consists of the obligation of the Community authorities to Community law' (Mestmäcker 1992; our translation).

Functional legitimation of Community action. The activities of the Community authorities are restricted by the Treaty. They are, according to Art. 3, 'provided in this Treaty'. This implies that the Community authorities need a legal basis resulting from the Treaty for any of their activities. These authorizations are, on the whole, related to the requirements of the common market. The authorizations reflect the 'principle of functionally limited enumerated powers' (Mestmäcker 1994: 631), i.e. the Community is legitimized to act only as far as is necessary to enforce the rules of a market system: 'It is the task of the community to guarantee and implement a policy of open markets and undistorted competition, while the Member States retain legislative and executive powers that are compatible with open markets' (Mestmäcker 1994: 633). It can hardly be denied, however, that the authorizations of the Community mentioned above are formulated somewhat vaguely. This holds particularly true for Art. 235 (EEC Treaty) which enables the Community to take measures 'to attain . . . one of the objectives of the Community' if the Treaty 'has not provided the necessary powers'. But since even this article clearly refers to the common market, the Community has no 'Kompetenz-Kompetenz', i.e. the Community is not permitted to grant powers to itself.

Non-market elements of the EEC Treaty. The elements of the EEC Treaty analysed above characterize it as an economic constitution for a market system. This interpretation, however, does not fail to recognize that (1) the restraining effects of the Treaty on the Member States with regard to their propensity to intervene could not have been foreseen by the representatives of the Member States when signing the Treaty; and that (2) we can also find considerable parts of the Treaty which are dominated by integration by intervention. The most prominent examples are the rules on agriculture (Arts. 38ff., EEC Treaty) and on transport (Arts. 74ff., EEC Treaty). They have the same functional deficiencies as their precursor, the ECSC. The ECSC Treaty favours integration by intervention almost throughout. Even Art. 65 referring to 'normal competition' pays only lukewarm tribute to market principles in view of the plethora of provisions which allow direct interventions or imply private restraints to trade in order to become effective.

Considering the economic experience with sectoral policies, the Commission had to admit after four decades what some economists expected right from the beginning:

> The experience of the 1970s and 1980s has shown that sectoral policies of an interventionist type . . . have failed to make industry competitive by delaying the requirement to implement necessary adjustments, led to grave misallocation of resources and exacerbated problems of budgetary imbalances. Especially grave problems of adjustment have been tackled at Community level in the past, for instance for steel, textile and shipbuilding (Commission 1990: 19).

The experience with the CAP has probably been worse. This policy turned out to be a 'subsidized folly' (Petersmann 1993a: 30), burdening the European taxpayer and consumer with extremely high costs. It absorbs most of the Community's budget, partly by also covering the costs of denaturalizing, destroying, recycling and dumping the surpluses. And instead of winning approval, it provokes violent protests even among its beneficiaries. In addition, the CAP is a permanent source of conflict in international trade policy because it requires to be flanked by variable tariffs and by quotas. Like the policy for steel, textile and shipbuilding, its built-in protectionism is particularly detrimental to the trade and development of less-developed countries and to some of the countries in transition in Eastern Europe. As a result, the Community's aid to less-developed countries and its preference policy – which in itself is quite problematic – is largely a compensatory effort with limited beneficial effect.

Considering this experience, the ECSC and the CAP

live by objectives and not by achievements. Art. 3 (ECSC Treaty) contains an impressive number of specific targets concerning supply to the common market, price formation, production and productivity, working conditions and international trade. Many of these targets are stated in an interventionist way: by defining, for example, lowest prices on a cost-plus basis, by requiring a harmonization of working conditions, by aiming at equitable limits in export pricing and by seeking an orderly expansion of production in view of foreign competition. The corresponding catalogue of targets concerning agricultural policy (Art. 39, EEC Treaty) reads in a quite similar way.

In both cases, the treaties contain a corresponding set of organizations and interventions that are intended to secure the desired results or cope with possible problems. The failure of both sectoral policies is basically caused by a totally inadequate view of the functioning of markets. They are supposed to be instruments to obtain desired results by manipulating their operating conditions and dodging undesired results, but again and again, the impossibility of acquiring all the relevant knowledge to control development, even within one section of the open market system, has proved to be decisive.

The sectoral policies turned out to be not only an economic failure. They did not contribute to the objective of political integration either. In the history of the European Union they became the object of redistribution struggles between the Member States and were the most striking examples of 'eurosclerosis' (Giersch 1985). The attempts to achieve the objective of political unity 'from above' failed. The alternative, the growing together of European citizens 'from below', by relying on the use of individual liberties, was more successful with regard to political objectives as well.

In the domain of common commercial policy, the Treaty itself is as ambiguous as political practice in that field. On the one hand, the Community is obliged 'to contribute to the harmonious development of world trade, the progressive abolition of restrictions on international trade and the lowering of customs barriers' (Art. 110, EEC Treaty). In this respect, the Treaty pays tribute to the idea that the competitive approach to integration should not be limited to free movement within the Union. But on the other hand, the Treaty provides several exemptions from this self-commitment, especially in Art. 115. Further, EU citizens cannot claim a direct application of Art. 110 in court. On various occasions the ECJ has rejected claims of importing companies in EU Member States which referred to restrictions of trade erected by the Community.

FROM ROME TO MAASTRICHT

Driving forces: centralization and constitutional displacement. Looking back at the history of European integration between 'Rome' and 'Maastricht', we propose to distinguish two driving forces which manifested themselves in the administrative practice of the Commission and the Council and in consecutive changes of the relevant treaties. The first is centralization. This can be convincingly explained by modern political economy (e.g. Vaubel 1992). The principle of enumerated powers was undermined more and more by efforts of the Community, based on proposals of the Commission, to take measures which were considered necessary according to Art. 235 (EEC Treaty) (Weiler 1991: 2434ff.). The European Court is not on the record for having opposed the extensive use of this provision. In addition, it is quite plausible that the Community can be and is used by the Member States as a kind of wild card to serve special and sometimes public interests via Brussels in view of domestic opposition.

The second force emerged from a kind of constitutional displacement of the original Member States. In the course of the integration process, they gained new experience in a twofold sense. First, they had to accept the restrictions of their discretionary powers in different political fields due to the interpretation of the treaty by the ECJ. It is plausible to argue that they would not have agreed to the treaty had they foreseen these restraining effects. One might interpret this constellation as a constitutional 'veil of ignorance' in a Rawlsian sense (Mestmäcker 1993). Second, the enlargement of the Community had a constitutional displacement effect in the sense that the *'acquis communautaire'* was partly questioned by the new members. Some of them obtained exemptions, others simply ignored parts of their obligations, following examples set by the original Member States. The unforeseen consequences of the Treaty and the experience of the enlargements have probably provided strong incentives to the Member States to reconsider the constitutional situation with regard to the constraining effects of the Treaty. This has to be taken into account when considering the two steps of constitutional recontracting: the Single European Act (SEA) and the Treaty on European Union (EU).

Recontracting the Treaty: the SEA. Considering the dichotomy between integration by competition and integration by intervention, the SEA established further ambiguities. On the one hand, the completion of the internal market that 'shall comprise an area . . . in which the free movement of goods, persons, services and capital is ensured' (Art. 13, SEA) clearly seemed to be a project inspired by the competitive approach to integration even if it did not represent anything novel with regard to the content of the previous Treaty. However, the SEA gave a new stimulus in that direction. It was based on the Commission's White Paper on Completing the Internal Market (Commission 1985) and gained political momentum with the Cecchini Report of 1988 (Cecchini 1988).

On the other hand, the SEA introduced several interventionist policies at the Community level. First, after several attempts of the Commission to establish a European industrial policy, the SEA provided for such a policy in a special form: the promotion of research and technological development (R&TD; Art. 24 SEA). It gave a firm legal basis to a policy which had become effective already in 1984 when the so called ESPRIT programme ('European Programme for Research in Information Technology') was initiated. At that time, twelve big European firms did not need much encouragement by Commissioner Davignon to pool their lobbying activities into forming a 'European Information Circle' and assist the Commission in convincing a partly reluctant Council of

Ministers that industry was in need of a 'European technology community'. Half of the European Community's financial support providing for some 240 projects during the first phase of the programme (1984–88) was given to the 'Big 12', the same twelve who also developed the basic concept for ESPRIT. The legal backing of this policy by the SEA initiated a bewildering variety of R&TD programmes of the Community and 'an amazing alphabet soup of trendy acronyms' (Curzon Price 1991: 136). It opened a new field of purpose-oriented sectoral policies favouring anew vested interests at the expense of the European citizens.

Another part of the SEA – on social and economic cohesion (Art. 23, SEA) – widened the legal basis for a policy direction which had already been initiated by the EEC Treaty (Arts. 117ff.) and by the establishment of the European Fund on Regional Development in 1975. As a consequence, the EC authorities have an amazing variety of different 'funds' at their disposal. They allow attempts at reducing or removing interregional differences in economic development that reflect market assessments of different locations. Apart from the dysfunctional, purpose-oriented character of such funds, they reveal another constitutional problem. Their use implies political discretion, thus initiating a redistribution struggle within the Community. The criterion of 'social and economic cohesion' can hardly be assessed by the courts. As a 'weasel word', it allows the EC authorities to start programmes and use funds in the name of almost every conceivable 'social' purpose. It encourages interest groups, as well as those national governments not able to finance projects of regional development out of national funds, to demand new financial privileges by referring to the objective of economic and social cohesion. And these demands are welcome to the Commission because they correspond to its attempts to increase the degree of centralization in regional policy.

The new legal rules aiming at the completion of the internal market were based on the aforementioned White Paper of the Commission which contained the 'new approach' to integration (Pelkmans 1987). It stressed explicitly the role of mutual recognition of national regulations as a means of integration and seemed therefore to serve as the basis for regulatory competition (Streit and Mussler 1995: 83–90). At the same time, the White Paper suggested the harmonization of a considerable number of national regulations. This ambiguity is reflected in the articles inserted into the EEC Treaty by the SEA. Art. 100b seems to establish the principle of mutual recognition. But as far as we can see the Community authorities made no use of this article. On the other hand, Art. 100a mandates the Community to 'adopt the measures for the approximation of the provision laid down by laws, regulations or administrative actions in Member States which have as their object the establishment and functioning of the internal market'. This provision is not only a clearer embodiment of harmonization in the Treaty than Art. 100. Furthermore, it is a general authorization to discretionary Community measures because it is up to the Community to define which rules had as their objects the establishment and functioning of the internal market (Petersmann 1993b: 412).

THE CONSTITUTIONAL CHANGE: MAASTRICHT

Ambiguities as a characteristic feature. When evaluating the changes of the economic constitution of the EU brought about by the TEU ('Maastricht Treaty'), we have, first of all, to refer to the changes in the text of the Treaty. In doing so, we do not ignore that further evolution of the economic constitution will depend considerably upon post-constitutional practice, especially upon the jurisdiction of the court. This is important to note because the EC Treaty leaves much more room to interpretations and is less justiciable than before. But nevertheless, there is good reason to argue that the economic constitution is now mainly characterized by interventionist traits despite declarations to the opposite which can also be found in the text of the Treaty.

According to Art. 3a(1) (EC Treaty), the economic policy adopted by the Community and the Member States will be 'conducted in accordance with the principle of an open market economy with free competition'. Equally, self-coordination of private agents through market transactions and self-control through undistorted competition as well as a further opening-up of the EU towards countries outside are confirmed by Arts. 3c, 3g and 110(1), respectively. However, it is very difficult – if not impossible – to see how this basic decision can be upheld in view of the new competences attributed to the Community according to Art. 3. Considering this provision, the new activities are of equal rank when compared with those conducive to 'an open market economy with free competition'. The additional activities necessarily discriminate, for example, between sectors, enterprises, special activities (e.g. types of applied research) and occupations. This means, however, that distortions of competition are becoming unavoidable in practice. And given the material content of the provisions, it is hardly possible to challenge them in court, except for the observance of rules of competence and procedure.

Besides its ambiguity, the TEU establishes direct and indirect links between the various fields of interventionist activities. This can best be demonstrated by analysing industrial policy introduced into the new EC Treaty (Art. 130). Because of these linkages, the articles on industrial policy provide a kind of superstructure to the interventionist policies introduced already by the SEA. In addition, these policy mandates themselves have been widened by the TEU. In Table 1, we try to illustrate these two arguments. The table shows (1) the linkages between industrial policy as a 'constitutional cornerstone' and the other policies, and (2) the expansion of interventionist Community policies according to the SEA and the Maastricht Treaty.

The provisions on R&TD were supplemented by the clause that the Community shall promote 'all the research activities deemed necessary by virtue of the Chapters of this Treaty' (Art. 130f.(1)). This represents a more or less general authorization for the Community to promote any kind of research activities interpreted as 'necessary'. The same extension of discretionary Community activities can be observed in the field of economic and social cohesion. First, a new fund – the 'cohesion fund' – was added to the already existing funds. Second, a corresponding general authorization for equivalent Community action which was

Table 1
*European industrial policy; basic provisions according to the Treaty on Political Union**

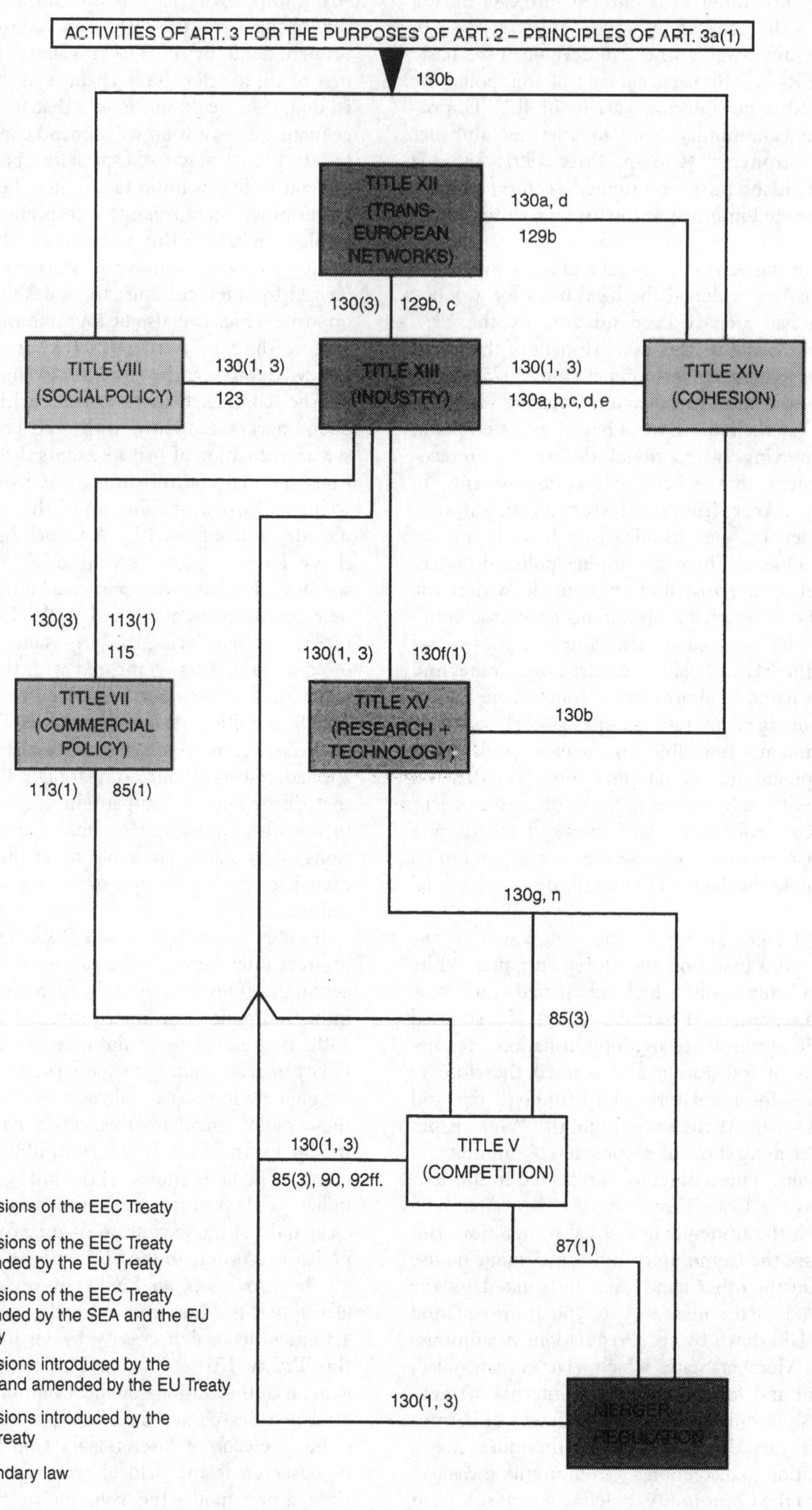

not provided by the SEA can be found now in Art. 130b: 'If specific actions prove necessary outside the Funds and without prejudice to the measures decided upon within the framework of the other Community policies, such actions may be adopted by the Council.' Apart from this, the Treaty establishes further new fields of Community action, such as education, vocational training and youth (Art. 126f.), culture (Art. 128), public health (Art. 129), consumer protection (Art. 129a), and trans-European networks (Art. 129b and c).

Together with the encompassing authorization to industrial policy, these regulations offer a considerable number of opportunities for the EC authorities to follow discretionary policies. This changes the constitutional situation profoundly. Before, the Member States were constrained in their discretionary policies in view of the principle of undistorted competition. Now, the EC authorities themselves are encouraged to take actions which are likely to be incompatible with this principle, but seemingly compatible with a new objective of the Community: 'to ensure that the conditions necessary for the competitiveness of the Community industry exist' (Art. 130(1)). This may even lead to a situation where the Community would have to tolerate an activity by a Member State – for example, the granting of aid in pursuing an industrial policy – which previously could be prevented according to Art. 92.

A constitutional cornerstone: industrial policy. Considering more closely the mandate of Art. 130 (EC Treaty), the new constitutional quality which was obtained by this extension of the SEA is a key to a whole network of possible interventions (see Table 1). Single policies like the promotion of R&TD, the use of regional and structural funds or social policy no longer stand for themselves. They are now part of an encompassing mandate oriented towards 'competitiveness of the Community's industry'. In other words, industrial policy has become a kind of constitutional cornerstone.

However, it should be pointed out that Art. 130 is yet another example of the ambiguities of the EC Treaty. A 'faith healing' interpretation (Möschel 1992: 418) would begin with Art. 3a(1) and 'the principle of an open market economy with free competition'. Then, it could refer to the Titles on industry and on trans-European networks where 'a system of open and competitive markets' (Arts. 129b(2), 130(1)) is stated. Furthermore, Art. 130(3) does seem to set clear limits to an industrial policy: 'This title shall not provide a basis for the introduction by the Community of any measure which could lead to a distortion of competition.' However, almost all the activities which are envisaged by the network of provisions necessarily imply selective measures.

The key question is simple. If no interventionist approach to industrial policy was intended, why did the signatories not content themselves with Arts. 2 and 3 of the EEC Treaty? These articles allow what may be called a framework approach to industrial policy (Streit 1993: 388ff.). It consists essentially of providing an infrastructure which is likely to promote the development of all economic activities in a non-discriminatory way. This would include an institutional infrastructure (i.e. rules conducive to a market system) as well as a material infrastructure ranging, for example, from the supply of a diversified education system to the promotion of basic research by non-profit organizations.

The network of provisions allowing an interventionist industrial policy. The interventionist or planning approach to industrial policy has been popularized with the motto 'picking the winners and helping the losers'. The basic objective of this approach is to speed up structural change and economic development by promoting so-called sunrise industries on the one hand and to 'buy time' for the adjustment of so-called sunset industries on the other. Given these objectives, the approach must necessarily be discriminatory, interfere with the freedom to compete and presuppose a correspondingly detailed knowledge about the effectiveness of the instruments used as well as of future developments. If we take the provisions of the Treaty on industrial policy and those related to other policies together, it is possible to argue that the Treaty allows for a broadly based policy of protecting the losers and trying to pick the winners.

Regarding protecting the losers, the links between Titles XIII (Industry), XIV (Economic and Social Cohesion) and VIII (Social Policy, Vocational Training and Youth) come into focus. According to Art. 130(1), Community action shall be aimed at 'speeding up the adjustment of industry to structural changes'. And this should be done 'through the policies and activities it pursues under other provisions of this Treaty' (Art. 130(3)). In Art. 130c (Title XIV), we find that the Regional Development Fund should be used to help 'in the conversion of declining industrial regions' given the overall objective to strengthen the Community's 'economic and social cohesion' (Art. 130a). A possible link between Title XIII and Title VIII can be established when taking into account Art. 123. One of the objectives pursued with the Social Fund is 'to improve employment opportunities for workers' by facilitating 'their adaptation to industrial changes and to changes in production systems'. Taken together, the above provisions not only allow discrimination between regions, but also between industrial activities and types of employment by providing adjustment assistance to those considered to be adversely affected by structural changes. No strings are attached to this kind of aid by requiring that it should be provided only for a limited period and at a declining rate, something most economists would ask for in order to avoid adverse incentives.

A policy to speed up adjustment by 'picking the winners' could rely primarily on the links between Titles XIII and XV, explicitly established by Arts. 130(3) and 130f(1). In terms of policy content, 'fostering better exploitation of the industrial potential of policies of innovation, research and technological development' (Art. 130(1)) would mean for the Community not only to 'encourage undertakings, including small and medium-sized undertakings, research centres and universities in their research and technological development and demonstration programmes' (Art. 130f(2)). It could even 'set up joint undertakings or any other structure necessary for the efficient execution of Community research, technological development and demonstration programmes' (Art. 130n). These and other activities in accordance with Art. 130g would be subjected to planning in terms of a 'multi-annual framework programme' (Art. 130i). The few quotations should suffice to demonstrate the mandate for a diversified and highly selective approach in the Community's R&TD policy.

It is not difficult to imagine that the discretionary promotion of specific economic activities – for example, 'key industries' in order to facilitate structural change – will require a complementary protectionist policy. In this respect, modern versions of the infant-industry argument suggesting a 'strategic trade policy' are very convenient despite the fact that they assume more knowledge than there is to know (Streit 1993: 403ff.). There is every reason to assume that the EU will continue the protectionist policy which has become conspicuously apparent on various occasions (Petersmann 1993a).

From an economic perspective, the concept of competition revealed by the text of the Treaty and by the practice of the Commission is completely different from the view compatible with the functional properties of market systems. For the Community authorities, competition is an instrument to achieve certain objectives. These objectives require that competition has to be conditioned by means of industrial policy: '. . . the main issue is which conditions need to be present in order to strengthen the optimal allocation of resources by market forces, towards accelerating structural adjustment and towards improving industrial competitiveness and the industrial and particularly technological long-term framework' (Commission 1990, 1). On corresponding policy objectives, the Commission is very explicit: 'Those policies which favour firms' initiative and guide them in the direction of a long-term perspective founded on the Community's interests are to be preferred' (ibid., 11). Hence, what matters most are the Community's interests and not private objectives. This is hardly reconcilable with a market process which leaves it to private agents and to competition to identify viable industrial and technological developments.

Towards a rent-seeking community. Given the aforementioned position of the Commission, it is important to examine how the Community's interests are determined, i.e. what the decision process on this question within the Union looks like. The answer is that in all domains where Community interventions are legitimate, we can observe the same procedure already established by the ECSC Treaty and within the CAP: a cartelization of specific interests cooperating with national governments (ultimately the Council) and a Commission which is principally interested in gaining more influence.

A key proposition in this context is probably the 'active partnership between all the interested parties (firms, social partners, scientific bodies, local, regional, national and Community authorities)'. It is considered by the Commission as an adequate procedure to define the 'Community's interest' in the context of industrial policy. In other words, the Community's interest should be identified in a corporatist way, or, formulated less benevolently, by a 'conspiracy of ambitious politicians and incompetent industrialists' (Starbatty 1993: 21; our translation). This is quite in accordance with the role attributed by the Treaty to the Economic and Social Committee and to the Committee of the Regions. And it certainly would further encourage lobbying activities outside these organizations.

The opportunities for interregional redistribution increased markedly after 'Maastricht'. The Committee of the Regions (Art. 189a) is directly involved in decisions concerning trans-European networks (Art. 129d), and particularly in matters of social and economic cohesion (Arts. 130b, d, e). Furthermore, the Committee will be informed in all those cases in which the Economic and Social Committee has been consulted (Art. 198c(3)). And it can issue an opinion on its own initiative which will be forwarded to the Council and to the Commission (Art. 198c). Taking into account the network of provisions related to industrial policy and the involvement of the Economic and Social Committee, the new employment opportunities for industrial lobbies and regional as well as local politicians and their staff should be splendid. By itself, this may already be quite annoying to the taxpayer who has to foot the bill. What matters more for the Community are the long-term consequences that may result from a legal arrangement favouring a corporatist structure of interlocking political and private interests and thus an interpenetration of state and society. It is likely to produce collective irresponsibility.

The corporatist tendency will probably become further enhanced by the so-called 'social union' constituted by the Agreement on Social Policy (which has not been signed by the United Kingdom). It assigns to the associations of organized 'management and labour' a much more important role than before: They have to be consulted by the Commission before submitting proposals in the field of social policy (Art. 3) and are authorized to enter into 'contractual relations, including agreements' (Art. 4). The first steps undertaken to get such an agreement aim at a harmonization of labour and social policies at a high level. A corresponding European agreement on working conditions would be quite helpful to those Member States where labour markets are already regulated densely and at a high level. But since this would affect the competitiveness of the other Member States unfavourably, their consent will have its price, for example, in terms of additional transfers through the cohesion fund, the regional fund etc. This example should suffice to demonstrate again that integration 'from above' will be a source of further demands for redistribution between Member States.

The same holds true for the monetary union envisaged by the Treaty. It can be considered as a regime of definitively fixed exchange-rates. After conversion to the common currency, transfers must compensate for changes of real exchange-rates between Member States as a reaction not only to emerging differences in competitiveness in relation to other Member States but also to countries outside the Union. In short, transfers are a kind of substitute for exchange-rate flexibility. Besides the considerable enlargement of Community power, the Maastricht Treaty seemingly provides a constraint to centralization: the principle of subsidiarity. According to Art. 3b (EC Treaty), the Community shall take action 'only if and in so far as the objectives of the proposed action cannot be sufficiently achieved by the Member States'. However, the doubts about the effectiveness of this principle (e.g. Cass 1992) seem to be justified because of its lacking justiciability. The doubts have been clearly expressed by the former president of the ECJ, Lord Mackenzie-Stuart: 'To decide whether a given action is more appropriate at Community level, necessary at the Community level, effective at Community level is essentially a political topic. It is not the sort of question a Court should be asked to decide' (Mackenzie-Stuart 1991: 42).

New challenges to the economic constitution of the EU. Considered as a whole, the Maastricht Treaty favours integration by intervention almost throughout. Whereas this approach to integration represents the exception in the Treaty of Rome, it seems to be the rule of European integration now. It serves as the legal basis for an integration strategy which replaces self-coordination through markets by political discretion and self-control through competition by corporatist structures quite similar to those of the Member States. There are many indications that the traditional strategy of the Community was overstretched: without sufficient consensus on the structure and extent of political union, additional measures of economic integration in the interventionist style were employed. This shows that the Maastricht Treaty implies a backward-looking view on European integration which is not appropriate to the new economic and political situation in Europe. The economic constitution of the EU is thus challenged from within as well as from outside.

The redistribution struggle within the Union will intensify when taking into account the fiscal problems which all Member States are facing. All newly established activities of the Community require additional financial resources. And immediately after Maastricht, the Commission asked for additional funds including the right to incur public debts (which was turned down by the Council). The increased number of discretionary activities represents a standing invitation to rent-seeking at the level of the Union. These problems are of course well known in every nation state. However, there is an important difference with regard to the Union as a still undefined political entity. Since the redistribution struggles take place at a level removed from the citizens, it should not be expected that there will be much loyalty from those who will have to foot the bill. It is thus plausible to argue that the Union will be exposed to disintegrative forces much more than before: a Community under the law would survive more easily than a rent-seeking Community.

Secondly, the Union has put itself under severe strain with the project of a monetary union. Political will, self-imposed requirements of stability and economic realities are extremely difficult to reconcile. Without exploiting the vagueness of the criteria for access to this union and without renouncing intentions to back up the common currency by imposing more fiscal discipline on the Member states, 'from above', the EU will be split into a few members and many non-members. And it can easily be imagined that such a split will be a source of conflict.

Thirdly, the present decision-making structure would simply become inoperable when trying to enlarge the Union towards the east and the south of the continent (Streit and Voigt 1997). Regarding the economic constitution, the inclusion of the countries of Central and Eastern Europe into the different funds of agricultural, structural, and regional policy would be prohibitively expensive, and would simultaneously impede structural change in those countries. Furthermore, an adaptation of the regulations in those countries to the harmonized level in the EU would be simply impossible. An opening of the EU in accordance with integration by competition would cause fewer problems. It would consist mainly of the application of the basic liberties and rules on competition to those countries. This opening of the European markets would also favour the political integration of Central and Eastern Europe (Stehn 1996).

This kind of opening of the EU indicates, at the same time, what the future integration of the European continent as a whole could look like. Given the tremendous problems and the corresponding reluctance of the present Member States to move ahead with a political union that is yet to be clearly defined, it may be worthwhile to reflect on the success story of the Union. That success was much more related to integration by competition than to integration by intervention. It was the latter strategy which led to a problem of legitimation of Community action. Its solution requires political integration, which has not yet received sufficient acclaim by the governments and the people of the Member States and is now to be promoted by the project of a monetary union. Hence, European integration at large may well be better served by relying on '*doux commerce*' (Hirschman 1977: 60) than on moves towards political union.

MANFRED E. STREIT AND WERNER MUSSLER

See also CENTRALIZED AND DECENTRALIZED REGULATION IN THE EUROPEAN UNION; COMPETITION LAW IN THE EUROPEAN UNION AND THE UNITED STATES; CONSTITUTIONAL ECONOMICS; DIVISION OF POWERS IN THE EUROPEAN CONSTITUTION; EUROPEAN COMPETITION POLICY; FISCAL FEDERALISM; FREIBURG SCHOOL OF LAW AND ECONOMICS; HAYEK, FRIEDRICH VON; OWNERSHIP AND CONTROL IN EUROPE; REGULATORY COMPETITION; RENT SEEKING; SUBSIDIARITY AND THE EUROPEAN UNION.

Subject classification: 2a(i); 3f(i); 6c(ii).

CASES

Case 26/62 (*van Gend & Loos v. Nederlandse administratie der belastingen*), ECR 1963, 1 (ECJ 1963).

Case 6/64 (*Flaminio Costa v. ENEL*), ECR 1964, 585 (ECJ 1964).

Case 8/74 (*Procureur du Roi v. Benoît et Gustave Dassonville*), ECR 1974, 837 (ECJ 1974).

Case 120/78 (*Rewe Zentral AG v. Bundesmonopolverwaltung für Branntwein* [*'Cassis de Dijon'*]), ECR 1979, 649 (ECJ 1979).

Opinion relating to the creation of the European Economic Area 1/91, OJEC 1992 C 110/1 (ECJ 1991).

BIBLIOGRAPHY

Behrens, P. 1992. Die Konvergenz der wirtschaftlichen Freiheiten im europäischen Gemeinschaftsrecht. *Europarecht* 27: 145–62.

Behrens, P. 1994. Die Wirtschaftsverfassung der Europäischen Gemeinschaft. In *Verfassungen für ein ziviles Europa*, ed. G. Brüggemeier (Baden-Baden: Nomos): 73–90.

Böhm, F. 1966. The rule of law in a market economy. In *Germany's Social Market Economy: Origins and Evolution*, ed. A. Peacock and H. Willgerodt, London: Macmillan, 1989: 46–67.

Cass, D.Z. 1992. The word that saves Maastricht? The principle of subsidiarity and the division of powers within the European Community. *Common Market Law Review* 29: 1107–36.

Cecchini, P. et al. 1988. *The European Challenge 1992*. Aldershot: Gower

Commission of the European Communities. 1985. *Completing the Internal Market*. White Paper, Brussels.

Commission of the European Communities. 1990. *Industrial Policy in an Open and Competitive Environment*. Communication of the Commission to the Council and to the European Parliament, 16 November, Brussels. [COM (90) 556 final.]

Curzon Price, V. 1991. The threat of 'fortress Europe' from the development of social and industrial policies at the European level. *Aussenwirtschaft* 46: 119–38.

Giersch, H. 1985. *Eurosclerosis*. Kieler Diskussionsbeiträge 112, Institut für Weltwirtschaft, Kiel.

Hayek, F.A. 1945. The use of knowledge in society. *American Economic Review* 35, 519–30.

Hayek, F.A. 1968. Competition as a discovery procedure. In F.A. Hayek, *New Studies in Philosophy, Politics, Economics and the History of Ideas* (London: Routledge, 1978): 179–90.

Hayek, F.A. 1973. *Law, Legislation and Liberty, Vol. 1: Rules and Order*. Chicago: University of Chicago Press.

Hirschman, A.O. 1970. *Exit, Voice, and Loyalty*. Cambridge, MA: Harvard University Press.

Hirschman, A.O. 1977. *The Passions and the Interests*. Princeton: Princeton University Press.

Leoni, B. 1961. *Freedom and the Law*. 3rd edn, Indianapolis: Liberty Fund, 1991.

Mackenzie-Stuart, Lord. 1991. Assessment of the views expressed and introduction into a panel discussion. In *Subsidiarity: The Challenge of Change – Proceedings of the Jacques Delors Colloquium*. European Institute of Public Affairs, Maastricht: 37–41.

Mestmäcker, E.-J. 1974. Power, law, and economic constitution. *Law and the State* 10: 117–32.

Mestmäcker, E.-J. 1992. Widersprüchlich, verwirrend und gefährlich. *Frankfurter Allgemeine Zeitung* (236), 10 October: 15.

Mestmäcker, E.-J. 1993. Der Kampf um die Rolle des Rechts. *Frankfurter Allgemeine Zeitung* (294), 18 December: 13.

Mestmäcker, E.-J. 1994. On the legitimacy of European law. *Rabels Zeitschrift für Ausländisches und Internationales Privatrecht* 58: 615–35.

Möschel, W. 1992. EG-Industriepolitik nach Maastricht. *Ordo* 43: 415–21.

Mussler, W. and Streit, M.E. 1996. Integrationspolitische Strategien in der EU. In *Europäische Integration*, ed. R. Ohr (Stuttgart: Kohlhammer): 265–290.

Mussler, W. and Wohlgemuth, M. 1995. Institutionen im Wettbewerb–Ordnungstheoretische Anmerkungen zum Systemwettbewerb in Europa. In *Europas Arbeitsmärkte im Integrationsprozeß*, ed. P. Oberender and M.E. Streit (Baden-Baden: Nomos): 9–45.

Olson, M. 1982. *The Rise and Decline of Nations*. New Haven: Yale University Press.

Pelkmans, J. 1987. The new approach to technical harmonization and standardization. *Journal of Common Market Studies* 2: 249–69.

Petersmann, E.-U. 1993a. Constitutional principles governing the EEC's commercial policy. In *The European Community's Commercial Policy after 1992: The Legal Dimension*, ed. M. Maresceau (Boston: Kluwer): 21–61.

Petersmann, E.-U. 1993b. Grundprobleme der Wirtschaftsverfassung der EG. *Aussenwirtschaft* 48: 389–424.

Smith, A. 1776. *An Inquiry into the Nature and Causes of the Wealth of Nations*. Indianapolis: Liberty Press, 1982.

Starbatty, J. 1993. Europäische Industriepolitik und die Folgen – Zur Immanenz industriepolitischer Dynamik. Diskussionsbetrag 28, Wirtschaftswissenschaftliches Seminar, Tübingen.

Stehn, J. 1996. Vertiefung und Osterweiterung der Europäischen Union: Ein Widerspruch? In *Europa reformen – Ökonomen und Juristen zur zukünftigen Verfaßtheit Europas*, ed. M. E. Streit and S. Voigt (Baden-Baden: Nomos): 68–81.

Streit, M.E. 1992. Economic order, private law and public policy: the Freiburg School of law and economics in perspective. *Journal of Institutional and Theoretical Economics* 148: 675–704.

Streit, M.E. 1993. European industrial policy: an economic and constitutional challenge. *Staatswissenschaften und Staatspraxis* 4: 388–416.

Streit, M.E. 1995. Dimensionen des Wettbewerbs – Systemwandel aus ordnungsökonomischer Sicht. *Zeitschrift für Wirtschaftspolitik* 44: 113–34.

Streit, M.E. 1996. Competition among systems, harmonisation and European integration. Discussion Paper 01/96, Max Planck Institute for Research into Economic Systems, Jena.

Streit, M.E. and Mussler, W. 1994. The economic constitution of the European Community: from Rome to Maastricht. *Constitutional Political Economy* 5: 319–53.

Streit, M.E. and Mussler, W. 1995. Wettbewerb der Systeme und das Binnenmarktprogramm der Europäischen Union. In *Europa zwischen Ordnungswettbewerb und Harmonisierung*, ed. L. Gerken (Berlin: Springer): 75–107.

Streit, M.E. and Voigt, S. 1997. Toward ever closer union – or ever larger? In *Constitutional Law and Economics of the European Union*, ed. D. Schmidtchen and R. Cooter (Cheltenham: Edward Elgar): 223–47.

Vaubel, R. 1992. The political economy of centralization and the European Community. *Journal des Économistes et des Études Humaines* 3: 11–48.

Weber, M. 1921. *Wirtschaft und Gesellschaft – Grundriß der verstehenden Soziologie*. Tübingen: Mohr (Siebeck); 5th edn, 1985. 4th edn. translated *Economy and Society* ed. G. Roth and C. Wittich (Berkeley, CA: University of California Press), 1978.

Weiler, J.H. 1991. The transformation of Europe. *Yale Law Journal* 100: 2403–83

Wohlgemuth, M. 1995. Economic and political competition in neoclassical and evolutionary perspective. *Constitutional Political Economy* 6: 71–96.

exclusionary agreements. An exclusionary agreement says: 'You agree not to buy from anyone but me.' American antitrust law calls that agreement 'exclusive dealing'. Like many things in life, exclusive dealing has been hard to understand. Comparing its law and economics reveals shortcomings in both. The law of exclusive dealing is aged and unsupported, and embodies hostility toward exclusive dealing that is unwarranted by legislative intent or by economic analysis. This economic analysis in turn is helpful but incomplete. There are two new strands. One is the important transactions cost literature, which undercuts current law by suggesting the many ways that exclusionary agreements can benefit consumers. This literature has been empirically confirmed but has yet to offer definitive accounts of the governing cases – the type of evidence most persuasive to the judges who craft American antitrust policy and who must grapple with precedent. A different literature about predatory vertical foreclosure postulates conditions under which exclusionary agreements may harm consumers. These theories are largely empirically unverified, and commonly require – as current law does not – that the excluding firm have market power or special access to unusual market conditions. This body of theory does not, and does not purport to, offer support for reigning Supreme Court law about exclusive dealing.

This essay focuses on US law: specifically, on exclusive dealing rather than boycotting (where *competitors* agree with each other to refuse to deal with some party). I concentrate on §3 of the Clayton Act but note that the Sherman and FTC Acts provide similar causes of action. I assume that antitrust law aims to promote efficiency or consumer welfare (see Wiley 1986: 748–51, but see Bok 1961: 306 and fn106).

I. THE LAW OF EXCLUSIVE DEALING. The Clayton Act outlaws exclusive dealing where the effect 'may be to substantially *lessen competition* or *tend to create a monopoly* . . .'. In passing this Act, Congress delegated an enigma to federal judges by failing to specify when exclusive dealing indeed would 'lessen competition' or would 'tend to create a monopoly'. The judges who have interpreted these words have possessed no necessary training in economics but have done their best to do as Congress asked. Their interpretations have created law that today is simple to summarize, uncertain to apply, and hard to justify.

A. Simple to summarize. The Supreme Court's most recent law on exclusive dealing is literally a footnote. The *Jefferson Parish* majority recited that an exclusive dealing contract '*could* be unlawful if it foreclosed so much of the market from penetration by [the excluding firm's] competitors as to unreasonably restrain competition in the affected market . . .' (1984: 31 fn. 51 [my emphasis]). As authority for this simple-sounding rule, the Court cited its 1949 *Standard Stations* and 1961 *Tampa Electric* decisions: two earlier decisions that had reached opposite results. *Standard Stations* outlawed Standard Oil's exclusive dealing where (depending on the statistic selected) the foreclosure covered either 16% or 6.7% of a regional gasoline market. The 16% statistic derived from the number of retail gas stations with which Standard had exclusive contracts; the 6.7% statistic derived from the number of gallons these stations sold (295). Twelve years later, *Tampa Electric* upheld exclusive dealing that foreclosed only 0.77% of a regional coal market (333). The *Tampa Electric* Court recited the 16% outlet statistic and omitted the more logical 6.7% gallonage statistic when recounting the *Standard Stations* precedent (328–9). This background suggests a naive interpretation of *Jefferson Parish's* footnote: exclusive dealing is legal when the foreclosure is 0.77% or less but illegal when the foreclosure is 16% or more.

B. Uncertain to apply. This interpretation is naive because it takes the Supreme Court decisions at face value when the matter is not so simple. These decisions indeed are perfectly consistent in some ways. For instance, the *Tampa Electric* Court began by redefining the relevant market so as to cause the foreclosure statistic in the case to fall from 18% to 0.77% (330–33). That *Tampa Electric* bothered at all with market definition – a neglected issue in the lower court opinions – suggested that the *Tampa Electric* Court thought an 18% foreclosure share would be illegal and that *Standard Stations* still was valid law. Some later analysts plausibly have reached contrary conclusions, however, claiming for instance that *Tampa Electric* (333–5) 'flatly overruled *Standard Stations*, without so acknowledging' (Ross 1993: 313, compare Bok 1961: 282, Joskow 1991: 62).

Interpreting these decisions is thus difficult (see Sullivan 1977: 472–484, compare Steuer 1986). Uncertainty arises even from *Jefferson Parish's* unexplained usage that exclusive dealing 'could' (rather than 'would') be unlawful under the stated condition. To illustrate the uncertainty about this rule in a different and pertinent way, consider two extreme positions on just one issue: the relevance of efficiency justifications for exclusive dealing.

(1) One extreme: efficiency is irrelevant. One extreme is the *Standard Stations* approach: efficiency justifications are irrelevant. *Standard Stations* affirmed a lower court result that had 'excluded as immaterial' the evidence about the benefits of exclusive dealing (306–7, 298, 299). The *Standard Stations* Court gave two bad reasons why efficiency evidence was thus to count for nothing. First, this inquiry would be 'ill-suited for ascertainment by courts' (310). The dissent aptly retorted that this inquiry might be 'tedious' and 'not too enlightening, but without it a judicial decree is but a guess in the dark' (322, see also *Continental TV* 54–56, *Broadcast Music* 19–23). Second, the Court incorrectly reasoned that the practice of exclusive dealing, if beneficial, would continue without the need for exclusive dealing contracts (313–14, see Schwartz 1949: 15). Reliable *promises*, however, are often essential prerequisites to efficient conduct because businesses may require a guarantee of cooperation from others before proceeding. *Standard Stations'* decision to exclude efficiency evidence was thus unwarranted. The Court, however, has never expressly renounced this approach. If anything, the literal language in *Tampa Electric* and *Jefferson Parish* seems only to approve of *Standard Stations*.

(2) The opposite extreme: only efficiency counts. The opposite extreme is Judge Easterbrook's view in *Paddock Publications* (1996), a case about a small newspaper's suit against the exclusive distributor arrangements between news services and larger newspapers. Judge Easterbrook upheld the arrangements by recounting their efficiency justification (43, compare *Interface Group*, 11–12, and *Barry Wright*, 236–8). Judge Easterbrook said that to assess '"foreclosure" of sales to competitors without proof of injury to consumers' – the method of *Standard Stations* – 'reflects a bygone day in antitrust analysis' (46). He labelled one such Supreme Court precedent 'a derelict' and referred to a different one as 'another antique antitrust opinion that is unlikely to be reaffirmed if the Supreme Court revisits the subject'. Judge Easterbrook distinguished the exclusive distributorships at issue (which limited *seller* options) from exclusive dealing arrangements (which limited *buyer* options, as in *Standard Stations*), but he also made apparent his view that the *Standard Stations* approach would be unlikely to command support from a modern Supreme Court. In Judge Easterbrook's estimation, then, the approach of *Standard Stations* is no longer reigning law.

It is thus unclear how to apply the *Jefferson Parish* rule. Rather than debate the ineffable, this brief essay accepts the naive interpretation. So stated, the *Jefferson Parish* rule is hard to justify.

C. Hard to justify. The exclusive dealing rule from *Jefferson Parish* is hard to justify because it expresses hostility to exclusive dealing in at least two ways. First, the rule reduces the question of illegality to the question whether exclusive dealing forecloses a market. This law seems to outlaw all exclusive dealing that covers a 'substantial' share, say 16%, of a market, even though a practice may be common for good as well as bad reasons. Second, this rule does not require that the firm doing the exclusive dealing have market power. This premise – that exclusive dealing must be bad whenever common, even when used by a firm without market power – is powerfully hostile.

Statutory language does not support this hostility. The Clayton Act forbids exclusive dealing only when its effect 'may be to substantially lessen competition or tend to create a monopoly . . .'. When is that? Literally, these words seem to require judges to evaluate in each case whether exclusive dealing may 'lessen competition' or 'tend to create a monopoly' (Bok 1961: 272). These words do not support blanket condemnation of all pervasive exclusive dealing, irrespective of competitive effect. Nor can one maintain that the Clayton Act must simply state a harsher test than the Sherman Act rule, because §3 of the Clayton Act changed the previous Sherman Act rule by clarifying that antitrust laws do indeed apply to exclusive dealing (Lockhart and Sachs 1952: 938).

Neither does legislative history support this hostility. The Supreme Court has been of two minds about whether this history is relevant at all. (Compare *Standard Fashion*, 362, with *Jefferson Parish*, 10 and fn. 15 [tying].) In analysing this legislative history, moreover, the original *Standard Stations* opinion committed a serious factual error that the Court purported to correct with a reworded but still misleading analysis. (Lockhart and Sachs 1952: 933–40). Lockhart and Sachs also show that this legislative history does not support categorical hostility to exclusive dealing in any event. (Compare Bok 1961: 308 and fn108, Schwartz 1949: 21 fn40 ['[t]he debates resist rational summary'].)

Like legislative language and history, economic analysis also does not support a general hostility towards exclusive dealing.

II. THE ECONOMICS OF EXCLUSIVE DEALING. Economic analysis of exclusive dealing is enlightening but has yet to reach a consensus. One relevant vein is the transactions cost literature, a booming field that suggests a wide range of efficient explanations for exclusive dealing. Joskow (1988a, 1991), Perry (1989) and Shelanski and Klein (1995) survey this field's sturdy empirical foundations, but the field has yet to offer definitive accounts of the ruling legal precedents. In a second vein, theorizing about vertical foreclosure is recent but without much empirical support. Both procompetitive and anticompetitive theories for exclusionary agreements thus exist, but so far only the procompetitive explanations can claim a robust and demonstrated basis in reality. Economic analysis therefore does not support a generalized hostility to exclusive dealing.

A. Procompetitive explanations for exclusive dealing. Exclusive dealing is a form of vertical integration by contract (Kessler and Stern 1959). Our understanding of vertical integration has expanded in the last decades, thanks to transactions cost scholarship. This intellectual development has arisen since the 1961 *Tampa Electric* decision and shows how vertical integration can surmount opportunism that otherwise impedes desirable business conduct (Williamson 1975, 1985, 1996; Goldberg 1976; Klein, Crawford and Alchian 1978; Marvel 1982; Joskow 1985, 1988a: 63, 1991). Empirical testing has 'overwhelmingly confirm[ed]' many of this literature's predictions (Shelanski and Klein 1995: 352). Thus exclusion can serve consumers in a host of ways, as the three leading Supreme Court cases may illustrate.

(1) *Jefferson Parish*: efficient management of a professional department? The case of *Jefferson Parish* demonstrates that exclusive dealing can facilitate efficient management of a hospital department. The relationship in *Jefferson Parish* was between a hospital and the anaesthesiology firm of Roux & Associates. Roux provided all of the anesthesiology services for the hospital. Anaesthesiologist Hyde applied for hospital privileges, which the hospital refused to grant because Dr Hyde was not employed by Roux. The Supreme Court majority rejected Hyde's attack on the hospital's exclusive arrangement with Roux. Justice O'Connor's concurrence (joined by three other justices) found that this exclusive dealing 'ensure[d] stable markets and encourag[ed] long term, mutually advantageous business relationships' (43–4, 45).

Lynk and Morrisey (1987) explain this conclusion in more detail. If a hospital does not hire anaesthesiologists as employees, it can either enter an exclusive dealing relationship with a professional anaesthesiology corporation or it can maintain an open-staff policy with a range of independent anaesthesiologists among whom admitting doctors choose (400). Exclusive dealing has been the norm, both at New Orleans hospitals and in health care generally (*Jefferson Parish* 44; Lynk 1994: 394). Lynk and Morrisey speculate about why this is so by telling a standard transactions costs story: desirable cooperation between the anaesthesiologists and the hospital (or among the anesthesiologists) can produce durable benefits, but the opportunistic threat that one party might later appropriate these benefits can jeopardize this cooperation. An open-staff policy could hamper an upgrade of the department, for instance, if the prospect that hospital management would later admit new staff doctors discouraged existing doctors from investing correctly in new equipment or procedures. Or the anaesthesiologists might benefit if a colleague devoted time to studying and teaching them new techniques. An open-staff policy that paid anaesthesiologists per surgery would discourage this action, while an anaesthesiology firm could assign and compensate this helpful work (Lynk and Morrisey 1987: 404–5). If these suggestions are correct, then exclusive dealing was an efficient way to combat opportunism and promote helpful cooperation.

Empirical verification would inspire greater confidence in this plausible but unconfirmed analysis of *Jefferson Parish*. Case studies of this sort hold special promise for antitrust law reform. By being vague, Congress has in effect deputized federal judges to be the reluctant authors of American competition policy. It might seem like an odd way to run a country, because judges are trained in the case method and not in economic theories. But judges do enjoy a good reputation for brains and the right motivation. The *stare decisis* rule rivets their attention on the governing cases. Detailed and reliable empirical evaluations of cases like *Jefferson Parish* would pack special persuasive punch with this audience.

(2) *Tampa Electric: minimizing production costs by assuring long-run coordination?* The *Tampa Electric* case may illustrate a different way in which exclusive dealing can promote productive cooperation. The Supreme Court rightly rejected a monopoly explanation for the exclusive dealing between coal buyer Tampa Electric Company (TECO) and coal seller Nashville Coal Company (NCC). The contract locked up the parties for a very long time – twenty years – but covered only 0.77% of a coal market. The Court did not give a positive explanation for the exclusiveness of this contract, and again we have no definitive economic analysis of this case. It appears, however, that TECO's exclusive dealing allowed it to shift efficiently from costly oil fuel to cheap coal (See Liebeler 1981: 188–96; Joskow 1985, 1987, 1988b, 1990; and Goldberg and Erickson 1987).

Before 1955, TECO burned only oil to generate electricity for Tampa, Florida (*Tampa Electric* 1960: 776, 768). In 1955, TECO switched to coal for its new plants – something no other utility in peninsular Florida had tried before (*Tampa Electric* 1961: 322) Coal plants cost more than oil plants to build (323), but TECO bet that cheap fuel would make coal plants cheaper in the long run. TECO thus contracted to buy all the coal it needed for twenty years from NCC, which was one of the 700 coal producers that could have supplied TECO (*Tampa Electric* 1958: 461).

This long-run commitment apparently reduced TECO's and NCC's costs in several ways. Again we speculate; the lower courts ruled out such investigations as 'irrelevant' (*Tampa Electric* 1961: 324–5; 1960: 773; 1958: 463). TECO and NCC perhaps reduced their search and contracting costs and shifted risk from TECO to NCC subject to an escalation clause (323, see Joskow 1988b). Of greater potential significance, both sides invested large sums in reliance on this contract (see 323). Some of this investment may have been specific to this particular contract. Coal varies by BTU, sulphur, moisture, and chemical content, and TECO may have designed its particular coal plants to burn a specific type of coal. TECO thus may have required assurance of guaranteed coal price and availability before locking itself into this large investment. Otherwise, fear of hold-ups by NCC might have persuaded TECO to build a more versatile but less efficient plant (see Joskow 1987: 171). Likewise, on NCC's side, this contract required it to barge enormous amounts of coal from one particular field to a distant area where little coal had previously been shipped (*Tampa Electric* 1960: 769, 781). NCC may have had to construct or to improve canals to the Florida area, for instance – canals that NCC would not be able to use if TECO opportunistically shifted coal suppliers in an effort to hold up NCC for a lower coal price. NCC's fear of this hold-up problem could have deterred or reduced this desirable investment (Goldberg 1976; Klein, Crawford and Alchian 1978, compare Mullin and Mullin 1997: 83). By conquering these opportunistic threats, exclusive dealing apparently facilitated investments that produced cheaper electricity for TECO's customers. Empirical verification of this speculation again would be helpful. As Harold Demsetz asks, for instance, was TECO's contract price lower than the price(s) it would have paid on the open market?

(3) *Standard Stations: combating dealer free-riding?* The *Standard Stations* case illustrates a different way in which exclusive dealing may have combated business opportunism. At issue were exclusive supply contracts that obligated thousands of independent gas stations to buy all of their gasoline (and sometimes other products as well) from Standard Oil. The Court described these stations as 'independent', but the common description today probably would be 'franchisees'.

These exclusive dealing contracts were not monopoly devices. Their duration was brief – often only six to twelve months – and commonly they were terminable on 30 days notice after six months (*Standard Oil*: 296). These fleeting obligations could give Standard no durable power to lock its independent gas stations away from competing gasoline refiners (Posner 1976: 201; Marvel 1982: 7). With a stable market share of only about 23% (by gallonage) and with more than 75 competitors, moreover, Standard had no monopoly (Director and Levi 1956: 293, compare Kessler and Stern 1959: 32 and fn139). Standard did not use exclusive dealing to sell its full 23% market share; its exclusive contracts with independents covered only 6.7% (by gallonage) or 16% (by number of outlets) of the retail gasoline market. Standard sold the balance of its market share through its wholly owned stations or to industrial users (*Standard Oil*, 295–6). Standard's major competitors all used similar exclusive dealing contracts with their independent retailers, suggesting that Standard's exclusive dealing served some purpose other than the desire of a market leader to raise entry barriers (*Standard Oil*, 295, 309; Marvel 1982: 6; see Liebeler 1981: 191). Moreover, as Victor Goldberg comments, the government's goal of split-pump stations did not and apparently still do not exist in substantial numbers in the United States – suggesting that the exclusive dealing arrangement in this competitive retail market remains robust for some presumably efficient reason.

If not monopoly, what was the specific goal of Standard's exclusive dealing? Again we have no definitive empirical investigation. One suggestion is that these contracts helped national oil companies safeguard investments in brand-promoting efforts (such as advertising) from free-riding by gas station operators. Without exclusive dealing, Standard might be vulnerable to opportunistic conduct by independent gas stations. Standard's national advertising would generate customers for all independent stations that displayed 'Standard' signs. Once these customers drove into the independent station, opportunistic independents could divert the buyer to similar but unadvertised gasoline brands. Consumers would then lose if the national companies' fear of dealer free-riding reduced the national companies' willingness to invest in trustworthy national trademarks beneficial to consumers (Marvel 1982: 6–8;

Hovenkamp 1994: 387). Judge Posner embraced this logic in his *Roland Machinery* opinion (1984: 395), but only in an abstract way and without reference to the *Standard Stations* facts.

Benjamin Klein suggests to me that Standard's exclusive dealing may have helped oil companies prevent dealers from fraudulently selling cheaper off-brand gasoline under the oil company's trademark. In a different opinion, Judge Posner reports that such conduct 'has long been a problem in the retail gasoline business' (*General Electric Co. v. Speicher*, 534).

These inventive speculations possibly make sense out of the *Standard Stations* facts. They also suggest that the Court moved the ball in the wrong direction for consumers when it outlawed Standard's contracts. The Court's damage to efficient consumer service may have been only modest, however, for oil companies have used alternative arrangements to accomplish their same basic exclusivity goal (e.g., Kessler and Stern 1959: 38–9). But we really do not know for sure. Saul Levmore for instance notes that the free-rider explanation depends on the questionable ability of gas station operators to divert customers to another brand, while the fraud account neglects the range of other fraudulent possibilities (midnight deliveries from other suppliers; pumping regular instead of premium gasoline, etc.) that remain open to unscrupulous dealers (see also P'ng and Reitman 1995). Reassuring to judges who may one day reconsider this precedent would be reliable scholarly proof about the true function of exclusive dealing in this historic case.

These three examples of efficient exclusive dealing illustrate but do not exhaust the extensive range of efficiencies that exclusive dealing can facilitate (see Lockhart and Sachs 1952: 920–22, 926–7; Liebeler 1981; Areeda and Kaplow 1988; Ornstein 1989; Hovenkamp 1994: 386–8). The general point is simple. As Judge (now Justice) Breyer stated, exclusive dealing 'often' serves legitimate business purposes (*Interface Group*: 11).

B. Anticompetitive explanations for exclusive dealing. A monopoly problem would arise if a firm used exclusive dealing to foreclose rivals' access to all possible product outlets (Director and Levi 1956: 293). Circa *Standard Stations*, analysts thought this anticompetitive danger to be obvious and likely. Lockhart and Sachs (1952: 922), for instance, wrote confidently that exclusive dealing 'can be used to handicap competing suppliers and secure or preserve as large a share of the market as possible'. Since then, however, Chicagoans Director and Levi (1956), Bork (1954, 1965), Bowman (1956), and others have assailed unwarranted monopoly fears about vertical integration. Despite vulnerability to some theoretical (Kaplow 1985: 525) and empirical (Grimm, Winston, and Evans 1992) criticisms, this analysis has established that the foreclosure tactic poses no simple and obvious competitive hazard.

The standard example about 'giant can maker Alpha' illustrates the force of this Chicago analysis. Alpha could foreclose the market and achieve a monopoly *if* all food canners would agree to buy exclusively from Alpha (Areeda 1974: 775; compare *American Can*, 875, 881–4). Yet food canners ordinarily will reject such a programme, unless Alpha offers lower prices or better products – or bribes. To the fear that a firm would bribe its customers into exclusive dealing and thereby gain a monopoly, the basic reply is that it would not be profitable for this firm to do so (Posner 1976: 199–200, 202–5; Bork 1978: 137–44, 304–5; Hovenkamp 1994: 341–6, 384). The excluder's potential monopoly gain cannot exceed the consumer surplus lost as a consequence. So long as the excluder will have to pay bribes of this magnitude, it will not be able profitably to use exclusive dealing to foreclose the market inefficiently or to achieve a monopoly. The literature later stated this argument formally (Rasmusen, Ramseyer and Wiley 1991: 1139–40; Rasmusen 1991: 372–5). The debunking of simple foreclosure fears convinced leading Chicagoans that inefficient exclusive dealing was unlikely (Posner 1976: 205) or utterly nonexistent (Bork 1978: 309).

Analysts from across the spectrum have come to agree that the standard vertical foreclosure argument is 'woefully inadequate' (Ordover, Salop and Saloner 1990: 133), and have responded by investigating whether new theories could support a rational fear of exclusive dealing. These 'post-Chicago' models postulate some unusual conditions under which inefficient vertical foreclosure may be possible. Thus there is no consensus among modern theorists that vertical integration must always be innocuous or beneficial to consumers. But these new vertical foreclosure theories all rely on special conditions to obtain their results. And unlike the transactions cost economics, these theories have not been proven empirically. In particular, there has been no factual showing that a firm without market power can use exclusive dealing to gain a monopoly. This new literature about vertical foreclosure thus does not support current law's hostility to exclusive dealing.

This brief essay does not do justice to this lively literature, but does seek to convey its extent. One branch of recent foreclosure theory suggests that dominant firms under special conditions might use vertical integration to foreclose markets or to raise their rivals' costs. Krattenmaker and Salop (1986a, 1986b), Hovenkamp (1994: 285–90), and Rey and Tirole (1996) survey this theory, which remains controversial (Lopatka and Godek 1992; Reiffen and Vita 1995) and empirically unsupported (Mullin and Mullin 1997, but see Grimm, Winston and Evans 1992). Even if accepted as proposed, moreover, these theories condemn vertical integration only in special cases. A second line of theory follows the Aghion and Bolton model (1987) and debates whether a monopolist's customers would accept inefficient exclusive dealing contracts enforced by liquidated damages penalties. Again, however, the model applies only in highly specialized situations, and the limited empirical work on actual practices does not yield much support for the theories (Snyder and Kauper 1991: 567–72).

A third approach explores the possibility that a dominant firm with a minimum efficient scale could impose exclusionary contracts on customers through a divide-and-conquer strategy (Rasmusen, Ramseyer and Wiley 1991; Rasmusen 1991; Segal and Whinston 1998). Innes and Sexton (1994) correctly point out that a corollary to this approach is that buyers can defeat this strategy when they can form coalitions among themselves and can contract with potential entrants. They offer a number of useful empirical applications, including the richly documented case of *Sewell Plastics v. Coca-Cola* (1989). Sewell may indeed have been a modern 'giant can maker Alpha'. Sewell once was the largest manufacturer of plastic soft drink bottles in the US, but its own disgruntled customers organized a new bottle-making firm to compete with it. The district court reported that the economic consequences were 'dramatic': within four years, bottle prices dropped by 50%, production increased and became more efficient, and consumers benefited (1199, 1208–20). Competition, not monopoly, triumphed.

In sum, this large and recent literature on vertical foreclosure does not support a generalized legal hostility to exclusive dealing. It implies disapproval of vertical integration only in special situations that allow firms to raise prices. Leading theorists in this school commonly agree that foreclosure effects are 'complex and not fully understood', and speculate that their work may support only such traditional antitrust policy tests as to whether a relevant market is highly concentrated (Bolton and Whinston 1991: 225). Moreover, all of this new foreclosure theory lacks firm empirical foundations. As Joskow (1991: 58 fn4) aptly comments, 'the assumptions embedded in these models do not fit real markets very well' (cf. Fisher 1989; Joskow 1991: 80; Peltzman 1991: 206–7). Vertical foreclosure models to date aim to show problems that could conceivably exist. They do not try to show, and do not show, that inefficient exclusion is a serious problem or that it has ever actually occurred – even once.

III. CONCLUSION. American law embodies unwarranted hostility to exclusive dealing. The US Supreme Court would make this law mesh with current economic wisdom first by recognizing that exclusive dealing has a large and proven potential for consumer benefit, and second by asking plaintiffs to explain in particular cases how the exclusive dealing in fact may 'lessen competition' or 'tend to create a monopoly'. Economists could assist the Supreme Court by establishing the precise function of exclusive dealing on the facts of the leading precedents, and by assessing the theoretical robustness and empirical significance of the recent economic literature on vertical foreclosure.

JOHN SHEPARD WILEY JR

See also ANTITRUST POLICY; ASSET SPECIFICITY AND VERTICAL INTEGRATION; COMPETITION LAW IN THE EUROPEAN UNION AND THE UNITED STATES; VERTICAL MERGERS AND MONOPOLY LEVERAGE.

Subject classification: 6c(ii).

STATUTES

Clayton Act §3, 15 USC §14.
FTC Act §5, 15 USC §45.
Sherman Antitrust Act, 15 USC §§ 1–2.

CASES

Barry Wright Corp. v. ITT Grinnell Corp., 724 F2d 227 (1st Cir. 1983).
Broadcast Music, Inc. v. Columbia Broadcasting System, Inc., 441 US 1 (1979).
Continental TV v. GTE Sylvania, 433 US 36 (1977).
General Electric Co. v. Speicher, 877 F2d 531 (7th Cir. 1989).
Hyde v. Jefferson Parish Hospital District No. 2, 513 F Supp. 532 (La 1981).
Interface Group, Inc. v. Massachusetts Port Authority, 816 F2d 9 (1st Cir. 1987).
Jefferson Parish Hospital District No. 2 v. Hyde, 466 US 2 (1984).
Paddock Publications, Inc. v. Chicago Tribune Co., 103 F3d 42 (7th Cir. 1996), cert. denied, 65 USLW 3728 (1997).
Roland Machinery Co. v. Dresser Industries, Inc., 749 F2d 380 (7th Cir. 1984).
Sewell Plastics, Inc. v. Coca-Cola Co., 720 F Supp. 1196 (NC 1989), aff'd, 912 F2d 463 (4th Cir. 1990).
Standard Fashion Co. v. Magrane-Houston Co., 258 US 346 (1922).
Standard Oil Co. v. United States (Standard Stations), 337 US 293 (1949).
Tampa Electric Co. v. Nashville Coal Co., 168 F Supp. 456 Tenn. 1958), aff'd, 276 F2d 766 (6th Cir 1960), rev'd and remanded, 365 US 320 (1961).
United States v. American Can Co., 230 F 859 (Md 1916), cert. denied, 256 US 706 (1920).

BIBLIOGRAPHY

Aghion, P. and Bolton, P. 1987. Contracts as a barrier to entry. *American Economic Review* 77: 388–401.
Areeda, P. 1974. *Antitrust Analysis: Problems, Text, Cases*. Boston: Little, Brown & Co.; 4th edn with L. Kaplow, 1988.
Bok, D.C. 1961. The *Tampa Electric* case and the problem of exclusive arrangements under the Clayton Act. *Supreme Court Review* 1961: 267–332.
Bolton, P. and Whinston, M.D. 1991. The 'foreclosure' effects of vertical mergers. *Journal of Institutional and Theoretical Economics* 147: 207–26.
Bork, R. 1954. Vertical integration and the Sherman Act: the legal history of an economic misconception. *University of Chicago Law Review* 22: 157–201.
Bork, R. 1965. Contrasts in antitrust theory: I. *Columbia Law Review* 65: 401–16.
Bork, R. 1978. *The Antitrust Paradox*. New York: Free Press; 2nd edn, 1993.
Bowman, W.S. 1956. Review of Carl Kaysen's '*United States v. United Shoe Machinery Corporation*, an economic analysis'. *Yale Law Journal* 66: 303–14.
Carlton, D.W. and Perloff, J.M. 1990. *Modern Industrial Organization*. Glenview, IL: Scott, Foresman & Co.
Director, A. and Levi, E.H. 1956. Law and the future: trade regulation. *Northwestern University Law Review* 51: 281–96.
Fisher, F.M. 1989. Games economists play: a noncooperative view. *RAND Journal of Economics* 20: 113–24.
Goldberg, V.P. 1976. Regulation and administered contracts. *Bell Journal of Economics* 7: 426–48.
Goldberg, V.P. and Erickson, J.R. 1987. Quantity and price adjustment in long-term contracts: a case study of petroleum coke. *Journal of Law and Economics* 30: 369–98.
Grimm, C.M., Winston, C. and Evans, C.A. 1992. Foreclosure of railroad markets: a test of Chicago leverage theory. *Journal of Law and Economics* 35: 295–310.
Hovenkamp, H. 1994. *Federal Antitrust Policy: The Law of Competition and Its Practice*. St. Paul, MN: West Publishing Co.
Innes, R. and Sexton, R.J. 1994. Strategic buyers and exclusionary contracts. *American Economic Review* 84: 566–84.
Joskow, P.L. 1985. Vertical integration and long-term contracts: the case of coal-burning electrical generating plants. *Journal of Law, Economics, and Organization* 1: 33–80.

Joskow, P.L. 1987. Contract duration and relationship-specific investments: empirical evidence from coal markets. *American Economic Review* 77: 168–85.

Joskow, P.L. 1988a. Asset specificity and the structure of vertical relationships: empirical evidence. *Journal of Law, Economics and Organization* 4: 95–117.

Joskow, P.L. 1988b. Price adjustment in long-term contracts: the case of coal. *Journal of Law and Economics* 31: 47–83.

Joskow, P.L. 1990. The performance of long-term contracts: further evidence from coal markets. *RAND Journal of Economics* 21: 251–74.

Joskow, P.L. 1991. The role of transaction cost economics in antitrust and public utility regulatory policies. *Journal of Law, Economics and Organization* 7: 53–83.

Kaplow, L. 1985. Extension of monopoly power through leverage. *Columbia Law Review* 85: 515–56.

Kessler, F. and Stern, R. 1959. Competition, contract, and vertical integration. *Yale Law Journal* 69: 1–129.

Klein, B., Crawford, R. and Alchian, A. 1978. Vertical integration, appropriable rents, and the competitive contracting process. *Journal of Law and Economics* 21: 297–326.

Krattenmaker, T.G. and Salop, S.C. 1986a. Competition and cooperation in the market for exclusionary rights. *American Economic Review* 76: 109–13 (*Papers and Proceedings*).

Krattenmaker, T.G. and Salop, S.C. 1986b. Anticompetitive exclusion: raising rivals' costs to achieve power over price. *Yale Law Journal* 96: 209–93.

Liebeler, W.J. 1981. Antitrust law and the new federal trade commission. *Southwestern University Law Review* 12: 166–229.

Lockhart, W.B. and Sachs, H.R. 1952. The relevance of economic factors in determining whether exclusive dealing arrangements violate section 3 of the Clayton Act. *Harvard Law Review* 65: 913–54.

Lopatka, J.E. and Godek, P.E. 1992. Another look at *Alcoa*: raising rivals' costs does not improve the view. *Journal of Law and Economics* 35: 311–29.

Lynk, W.J. 1994. Tying and exclusive dealing: *Jefferson Parish Hospital v. Hyde*. In Kwoka and White, *The Antitrust Revolution*; 2d edn 1994, New York: HarperCollins CollegePublishers.

Lynk, W.J. and Morrisey, M. 1987. The economic basis of *Hyde*: are market power and hospital exclusive contracts related? *Journal of Law and Economics* 30: 399–421.

Marvel, H.P. 1982. Exclusive dealing. *Journal of Law and Economics* 25: 1–25.

Mullin, J.C. and Mullin, W.P. 1997. United States Steel's acquisition of the Great Northern Ore properties: vertical foreclosure or efficient contractual governance? *Journal of Law, Economics, and Organization* 13: 74–100.

Ordover, J., Salop, S. and Saloner, G. 1990. Equilibrium vertical foreclosure. *American Economic Review* 80: 127–42.

Ornstein, S.I. 1989. Exclusive dealing and antitrust. *Antitrust Bulletin* 34: 65–98.

Peltzman, S. 1991. The *Handbook of Industrial Orgainization*: a review article. *Journal of Political Economy* 99: 201–17.

Perry, M.K. 1989. Vertical integration: determinants and effects. In *Handbook of Industrial Organization*, ed. R. Schmalensee and R.D. Willig, 2 vols (Amsterdam: North-Holland): 183–255.

P'ng, I.L.P. and Reitman, D. 1995. Why are some products branded and others not? *Journal of Law and Economics* 38: 207–24.

Posner, R.A. 1976. *Antitrust Law, An Economic Perspective*. Chicago: University of Chicago Press.

Rasmusen, E.B. 1991. Recent developments in the economics of exclusionary contracts. In *Canadian Competition Law and Policy at the Contenary*, ed. R.S. Khemani and W.T. Stanbury (Halifax, N.S.: Institute for Research on Public Policy): 371–88.

Rasmusen, E.B., Ramseyer, J.M. and Wiley, J.S. 1991. Naked exclusion. *American Economic Review* 81: 1137–45.

Reiffen, D. and Vita, M. 1995. Is there new thinking on vertical mergers? Comment. *Antitrust Law Journal* 63: 917–40.

Rey, P. and Tirole, J. 1996. A primer on foreclosure. Unpublished manuscript.

Ross, S.F. 1993. *Principles of Antitrust Law*. New York: Foundation Press.

Schwartz, L.B. 1949. Potential impairment of competition – the impact of *Standard Oil Co. of California v. United States* on the standard of legality under the Clayton Act. *University of Pennsylvania Law Review* 98: 10–40.

Segal, I.R. and Whinston, M.D. 1998. Naked exclusion and buyer coordination. *American Economic Review* (forthcoming).

Shelanski, H. and Klein, P.G. 1995. Empirical resarch in transaction cost economics: a review and assessment. *Journal of Law, Economics and Organization* 11: 335–61.

Snyder, E.A. and Kauper, T.E. 1991. Misuses of the antitrust laws: the competitor plaintiff. *Michigan Law Review* 90: 551–98.

Sullivan, L.A. 1977. *Handbook of the Law of Antitrust*. St. Paul, MN: West Publishing Co.

Williamson, O.E. 1975. *Markets and Hierarchies: Analysis and Antitrust Implications*. New York: Free Press.

Williamson, O.E. 1985. *The Economic Institutions of Capitalism*. New York: Free Press.

Williamson, O.E. 1996. *The Mechanisms of Governance*. New York: Oxford University Press.

Wiley, J.S. 1986. A capture theory of antitrust federalism. *Harvard Law Review* 99: 713–89.

expectation damages. *See* BREACH REMEDIES; CONTRACTS; RELIANCE.

experimental law and economics. There has been little research devoted exclusively to experimental law and economics. However, much of the work in general experimental economics is directly applicable to law and economics. Hence, this essay addresses the general methodology of experimental economics, reviews some of its results of interest to scholars in law and economics, and outlines in detail some major research programmes and their results, hoping thereby to challenge scholars in law and economics to think of ways to incorporate laboratory experiments into their research. For surveys on experimental economics in general, see Berg et al. (1995a), Davis and Holt (1993), Hey (1991), and Kagel and Roth (1995). For surveys of experimental law and economics, see Hoffman (1997) and Hoffman and Spitzer (1985b), from which this essay draws heavily.

A laboratory experiment in economics can be described as a carefully controlled, synthetic economic environment in which subjects participate in one or more economically relevant decisions for real monetary payoffs. Each experiment begins with a set of instructions to the participants. The instructions describe the economic environment, the rules governing exchange of messages among participants, and the schedule of monetary payoffs for specific individual or group decisions. The basic assumption underlying the use of monetary payoffs is that subjects prefer more money to less and that the experimenter can use this incentive to 'induce' a set of preferences for outcomes in an experiment using those monetary payoffs.

A typical experimental economics research agenda

involves conducting a series of controlled experiments in which the experiment is replicated several times under one set of conditions; then, changing one or more of these conditions and conducting a second series of controlled experiments; then finally, comparing the individual or group decisions under the first set of conditions with the individual or group decisions under the second set of conditions. The change from one set of experiments to the next might be in the economic environment itself, in the way subjects exchange messages with one another, or in the relationship between the monetary payoffs to individuals and the group's messages.

Economists use laboratory experiments to inform their research in several different ways. From the beginning of the development of the subfield of experimental economics, economists have used laboratory experiments to test fundamental theoretical models. In fact, many economists believe that laboratory experiments provide the cleanest tests of fundamental theories in economics. This is because most economic theories specify little or no institutional detail, and so can be modelled quite easily in the laboratory. By inducing in subjects preferences that conform precisely to a model's specification, and by excluding all the 'noise' of the natural world, the experimenter can produce an environment in which a theory has, on its own terms, the best chance of predicting behaviour. Part of the process of testing an economic theory is to test for the comparative statics effects of changing different parameters of the model and determining whether subjects in the experiment then change their behaviour as the model predicts. If the theory fails under these circumstances, there is little reason to believe its predictions will fare better in the less hospitable conditions of the natural world.

Experiments can also be used to distinguish among theoretical models, especially when they make substantially different predictions about economic outcomes. In particular, a series of experiments may allow an economist to reject one theory in favour of an alternative theory that predicts the experimental data better.

A second way that economists use laboratory experiments is to explore the domain of a theoretical model, particularly when a model is used to predict behaviour in the natural world. First, the experimenter tests the applicability of the model under the stark assumptions of the fundamental statement of the model. If the results conform to the model's predictions, the experimenter then creates laboratory environments that more closely parallel the natural environments being studied and observes whether the model continues to predict correctly in these new environments.

This is the way laboratory experiments can be valuable in law and economics. One of the interests of scholars in law and economics is the impact of different laws and legal systems on economic decisions. Often, they use economic theory to inform their analyses. Laboratory experiments that first test the predictions of the fundamental model and then explore the domain of the model in the legal environments being considered can help scholars in law and economics develop better economic analyses.

DOUBLE AUCTION AND POSTED OFFER MARKETS. To illustrate how laboratory experiments can be used first to test economic theory and then to inform scholars in law and economics, we describe the classic market experiment first designed by Smith (1962). He was interested in whether the competitive equilibrium predictions of the simple model of supply and demand are correct. The problem with this model for the kind of policy analysis used by scholars in law and economics is that the competitive equilibrium is a static economic concept such that all trades are assumed to take place at the equilibrium price. No trading institution is actually specified in developing the basic model.

Moreover, the institution generally described by theorists for reaching such a static equilibrium is the *tâtonnement* process, in which an auctioneer adjusts relative prices among goods until all markets clear. At that point the auctioneer allows all trades to take place. With the possible exception of the London gold market, no naturally occurring markets use such a market clearing process.

Almost all naturally occurring markets allow sequential trading at prices which may differ from one trade to the next. No one checks to see if an equilibrium has been reached before the next trade takes place. Some markets, such as stock and commodity markets, allow considerable information exchange among participants as the market proceeds. Others, such as used car and housing markets, involve individuals bargaining with one another to determine a price which might or might not be revealed to other potential participants in such a market. In retail food and clothing markets, sellers 'post' prices and buyers passively decide whether to buy or not buy at the posted prices. The simple model of supply and demand assumes all these different market institutions will lead to the same equilibrium price and quantity traded.

Smith decided to test that proposition. He began his experimental study by modelling a stock or commodity market in the laboratory. His experiments were usually conducted in a classroom. Approximately half the subjects were told that they were buyers and half that they were sellers. Each buyer was given a private schedule of prices that declined as the number of units purchased increased. Buyers were told they could buy units of a fictitious commodity from sellers for prices less than or equal to the reservation values on their schedules. Profits, which were theirs to keep, could be earned as the difference between the reservation value of a unit and the purchase price. Each seller was given a private schedule of prices that rose as the number of units each seller sold increased. Sellers were told they could sell units of a fictitious commodity to buyers for prices greater than or equal to the costs on their schedules. Profits, which were theirs to keep, could be earned as the difference between the selling price of a unit and its cost.

The stock market structure of the trading rules has come to be known as the double auction or double oral auction. Most such experimental markets are now run on computer networks, but we will describe the original, oral version. Buyers can make verbal bids to purchase one unit each at specified prices. Sellers can make verbal offers to sell one unit each at specified prices. The lowest offer and the highest bid form the standing bid-ask spread in the market. To enter the market, a buyer must bid higher than the standing bid and a seller must offer to sell for less than the standing offer price. Bids and offers outside the standing bid–ask spread are arranged in ascending and descending order, as in a specialist's book. At any time, any buyer can accept the standing offer and any seller can accept the standing bid. Once a bid or offer is accepted, there is a binding contract between the buyer and the seller for one unit of the fictitious commodity at the accepted bid or ask price. The buyer and the seller involved in the transaction enter the market price and their respective profits on their transaction sheets. At that point, the next best bid or offer becomes the standing bid or offer and the solicitation of new bids and offers continues.

The market is organized into trading 'days' that typically last a few minutes. At the end of each trading day, the buyers and sellers get a new (or the same) set of reservation values and costs, and the market runs for another trading day. A typical experiment runs for 5–10 trading days.

Smith found that the double auction experimental market converged to the predicted equilibrium price and quantity in only a few trading days (2–4) with the same reservation values and costs. Nearly 100% of the possible profits were paid out to buyers and sellers in the market. This result has been replicated in thousands of experimental settings, in many countries around the world, both in the described classroom setting and over a computer network, for more than 40 years. It has become the classic illustration of how competitive markets work.

This result tells us that the New York Stock Exchange, the Chicago Board of Trade, and the many other stock and commodity markets around the world are likely to lead traders to equilibrium prices and quantities. But, it does not necessarily tell us about market results in most retail trade markets that rely on either one-on-one negotiation or posted prices.

The next institution that Smith studied (with Charles Plott) was the posted offer market (Plott and Smith 1978). Using the same reservation values and costs as in the double auction market, each seller in a posted offer market posts a price which must hold for a trading day. In their eagerness, buyers queue to accept the most profitable offers. Buyers cannot make counterbids. When the buyers have purchased all the units they are willing to buy, the market trading day closes. The market is then repeated with the same or different reservation values and costs.

This simple institutional change turns out to have a powerful effect on market outcomes. If sellers can produce to order, rather than for inventory in advance of the market, prices in a posted offer market start out significantly higher than the equilibrium price and converge down to the equilibrium only very slowly. Moreover, convergence to a new equilibrium after a change in supply or demand is significantly more rapid in the double auction market than in the posted offer market.

This institutional difference even carries over to a market in which there is only one seller and several buyers, the classic monopoly (Smith 1981). If a monopolist can post prices each trading period, the monopolist will search for, and likely find, the profit-maximizing price, and then post that price each trading period, earning monopoly profits. However, if a monopolist must face a set of buyers who bid low, the buyers may be able to force the monopolist to accept lower bids or not sell enough units. Similarly, a small number of sellers who post prices can charge higher prices and earn higher profits than the same number of sellers who face buyers in a double auction market (Isaac and Plott 1981).

This set of results has had a powerful impact on regulatory policy, for they suggest that the market institution is at least as important as the number of sellers in a market in determining whether or not sellers can exercise monopoly power. This insight has forced regulators to re-evaluate policies regarding changing market institutions.

For example, in the mid-1970s, the railroad industry petitioned the Interstate Commerce Commission (ICC) to force the barge industry along the Mississippi river to post their prices 15 days in advance of any price changes. The railroads claimed they could not compete effectively with the barge industry, since they did not know what the barge industry's prices were. The barge industry was run as a telephone negotiation market at that time. Grain sellers, wishing barge transport down the Mississippi river, would call barge owners and negotiate prices.

The results on posted offer versus double auction markets were just becoming available at that time. Economists at the ICC saw that forcing the barge industry to post prices might result in higher prices in the barge market. So, they commissioned Plott to conduct a study of the potential effect of the proposed institutional change (Hong and Plott 1982). He designed a set of experiments that have become a model of parallelism in research in experimental law and economics.

The experiments were run on several successive evenings at the California Institute of Technology. Each subject was given a private office with a telephone. The parameters of the market were designed to parallel the existing Mississippi river barge industry. There were large and small buyers and sellers, with the relative numbers and relative costs and reservation values parallel to, but scaled down from, the naturally occurring barge market. There were two kinds of trading days: one corresponding to a peak demand period and the other corresponding to an off-peak period. During the peak demand period, all sellers could make some profits; but, during the off-peak demand period, some sellers had costs that were too high to remain profitable.

For the first two evenings, the market institution was a two sided telephone market. Buyers and sellers could call one another and negotiate prices, with both sides free to make bids or offers. Experimenters monitored calls to make sure subjects did not reveal their private reservation value and cost information to one another. The difference between this market and the double auction market was that the bids and offers were private to each telephone pair. Thus, less information was communicated to the entire market. For the third and fourth evenings, sellers posted prices at the beginning of each trading period and buyers called to place orders.

The results were exactly as expected, given the previous results on posted offer versus double auction markets. The two-sided telephone market showed more variation in prices than a comparable double auction market, but the prices were dispersed around the equilibrium price. Moreover, by the end of the first evening the prices had converged close to the equilibrium price. However, as soon as the posted offer was instituted, prices rose significantly above the equilibrium price and stayed above for the rest of the experiment. This result convinced the ICC to disallow the railroad's complaint and made clear the importance of laboratory experiments in evaluating proposed changes in trading institutions.

THE ALLOCATION OF PUBLIC GOODS: VOLUNTARY CONTRIBUTION, COASEAN BARGAINING, AND SYNTHETIC ALLOCATION MECHANISMS. Another area of importance to the law to which results from laboratory experiment have provided important insights is in the allocation of public goods and the payment for externalities. Much of the law deals with the allocation of public goods and with the payment for externalities: national defence, national parks and monuments, highways, the welfare system, and clean air and water to name a few. Until recently, public policy in most countries has been based on a perceived need to have the government provide for public goods and to regulate pollution. This perceived need arises from the theoretical statement of the free-rider problem: individuals, acting in their own self interest, will underprovide public goods and positive externalities and overprovide negative externalities, relative to those quantities necessary for the maximization of social welfare. In the limit, with pure public goods such as national defence, and no appropriability, no public goods will be provided.

(i) Voluntary contribution. This proposition suggests that voluntary contribution drives will not be effective in providing public goods. Yet, we see local and national voluntary contribution drives for United Way, the American Cancer Society, and a host of other organizations that provide public goods. In light of that observation, economists and sociologists have examined voluntary contributions in a large number of experimental studies.

The classic experiment in voluntary contribution was first designed by the sociologists Marwell and Ames (1979, 1980, 1981), and later clarified by the economists Isaac and Walker (Isaac, Walker and Thomas 1984; Isaac and Walker 1988a). In the classic experiment, as revised by Isaac and Walker, each subject in a group of known size is given a set of tokens that can be redeemed from the experimenter for cash. The tokens can be invested in a private account, that returns \$.01 per token, or in a group account, that returns less than \$.01 per token plus an amount that is an increasing function of the total contributions of all the individuals in the group. The experiment is designed so that the incentive of the individual acting alone is to contribute 0 tokens to the group account; however, each individual earns the most if 100% of the tokens of *all* the participants are contributed to the group account. Thus, the social incentive is directly opposite to the private incentive. This provides a stark experimental test of the free-rider hypothesis.

The results of a series of experiments by Isaac and Walker and a number of different coauthors (Isaac, Walker and Thomas 1984; Isaac, McCue and Plott 1985; Isaac and Walker 1988a, 1988b; Isaac, Schmidtz and Walker 1989; Isaac, Walker and Williams 1994) neither confirm the free-rider hypothesis nor suggest that voluntary contribution alone will provide an optimal allocation of public goods. Isaac, Walker and Thomas (1984) and Isaac and Walker (1988a) considered group sizes of four and ten subjects, individual returns to the group account of \$.003 or \$.0075, and differences in the amount of experience subjects have had with the task. Each experiment was run for ten contribution periods. They found that subjects in all treatments contributed more than 0 tokens to the group account in almost every contribution period. Averaging over replications of the same treatment, contributions ranged from 40% to 60% of tokens in period 1, which fell to 20% to 40% of tokens in period 10. Subjects tended to contribute less with repetition or experience, and with a lower individual return from contributions to the group account. Holding individual payoffs constant, group size did not have a significant effect. Thus, subjects converged to neither the socially optimal nor the individually rational outcome. The free-rider problem existed, in that a suboptimal quantity of the public good was provided. On the other hand, some amount of the public good was provided, leaving some room for voluntary contribution.

These results have led to a significant change in the focus of experimental research on voluntary contribution mechanisms. Having determined that the free-rider problem is partially but not completely verified, experimental economists have turned to studies of factors that contribute to more or less free riding. From a legal perspective, this research has led to a renewed emphasis on the possibility of the private provision of public goods.

The results of this new line of research show quite clearly why some strategies for generating voluntary contributions for public goods are successful. The most powerful treatment turns out to be communication (Isaac and Walker 1988b). If experimental subjects can talk for a few minutes before each decision period, contributions to the group account rise to 100% of the total tokens, and stay there. This suggests that groups of people who can regularly communicate with one another can successfully provide public goods for themselves.

Another powerful treatment turns out to be establishing a target level of contributions, which is less than 100% of the tokens. If that target level is achieved, the public good is provided. If the target level is not achieved, the public good is not provided and the tokens are automatically invested in the private account. The target level is referred to in the literature as a provision point (Isaac, Schmidtz and Walker 1989). Under a provision point treatment, subjects get only the individual return to contributions to the group account up to a certain number of total tokens contributed. After that point, there are substantial group returns. The provision point provides a focal point for contributions to the group account, and raises contributions relative to treatments with no provision point. This suggests that groups with specific monetary goals that they can communicate effectively to potential contributors are more likely to be successful in providing public goods voluntarily.

Sequential provision of public goods provides evidence of the role of commitment in mechanism design. Robert Dorsey (1992) compares the level and path of contributions in a real-time voluntary contribution environment. In this environment, subjects make initial contributions to the group account, followed by a 180 second period, during which subjects can update their contributions to the group account in real time. In one treatment, in which subjects can either increase or decrease their contributions to the group account, contributions average 11.53%. However, in a second treatment, in which subjects can only increase their contributions to the group account, total contributions average 20.24%. Sequential provision with commitment allows subjects to engage in reciprocity as they increase contributions. This principle of reciprocity in contributions applies in local funding drives, such as the United Way, and in international negotiations, such as in the several rounds of GATT negotiations (The General Agreement on Tariffs and Trade), that recently concluded with a significant reduction in world-wide tariffs.

(ii) Coasean bargaining. While most economists and legal scholars have focused their attention on the free-rider problem and governmental solutions to the allocation of public goods and externalities, some economists and legal scholars have focused their attention on the seminal work of Ronald Coase (1960). Coase suggested that individuals will realize the benefits from collective action and form private organizations to provide public goods and solve problems created by externalities. His theoretical work was written before the above experimental research on voluntary provision was conducted, but there is striking similarity between the statement of the Coase theorem and the conditions found to foster voluntary contribution.

In its simplest form, the Coase theorem states that parties to a bargain who can do harm to one another will bargain to a unique allocation of that harm, regardless of the liability rule determining which party has the right to make production or consumption decisions unilaterally. This theorem can be shown to hold in a simple environment in which there are two parties to a bargain who have common knowledge, no transactions costs, no wealth effects, a clearly defined interior Pareto-optimal allocation of the externality, and contracts between parties are signed and strictly enforced. This result has formed the basis for an alternative view that the role of government should be limited and that decisions about the allocation of public goods and externalities should be decentralized.

Hoffman and Spitzer (1982) initiated an experimental agenda to test the prediction of the Coase theorem in the simple environment outlined above and to examine the extent to which its predictions were valuable in a more realistic legal environment. Their initial experiment proceeded as follows. Two subjects who did not know one another sat in a room across a table; a monitor was present. The subjects were presented with a payoff table that associated a payment to each participant with each of a series of numerical outcomes. One subject would be paid nothing for the lowest numerical outcome and $12.00 for the highest outcome. The other subject would be paid $12.00 for the lowest numerical outcome and nothing for the highest numerical outcome. One outcome yielded $14.00 for the two subjects jointly. By a flip of a coin, one subject was chosen the 'controller'. The controller had the right to make the decision without consulting the other person. This right was clearly explained in the instructions. The other subject could persuade the controller, possibly by monetary transfer, to choose some other number. Any bargain involving monetary transfer was to be signed by both parties and enforced by the monitor. The predicted outcome was for the two subjects to agree to choose the number that gave a joint payoff of $14.00 and for the controller to earn at least $12.00 through a transfer from the other participant to the controller.

Hoffman and Spitzer (1985a) followed this initial experiment with an experiment in which the controller had to earn the right to be the controller, and that right was reinforced by a public statement that the controller had earned the right, and by a series of experiments involving three, four, five, ten, and twenty subjects (Hoffman and Spitzer 1986). They found that almost every pair or group of subjects bargained to the joint-profit maximizing outcome, thus strongly supporting the primary prediction of the Coase theorem. They also found that subjects were more likely to bargain to the predicted distribution of profits if the controller (or controllers, in the larger experiments) had earned the right and had that right publicly reinforced.

These results provide support for a more decentralized view of the role of government in the allocation of public goods and externalities. When differential property rights have social legitimacy and the government can enforce private contracts, small to medium sized groups of people can privately determine the optimal allocation of public goods and externalities and tax themselves. Combined with the results on voluntary contributions, summarized above, laboratory experimental results have changed economists' evaluations of the role of government in the allocation of public goods and externalities.

(iii) Synthetic allocation mechanisms. Theoretical and experimental results on the design of mechanisms for the allocation of public goods have lent further credibility to the decentralized perspective on the role of government in the allocation of public goods. William Vickrey (1961) outlined a new auction mechanism, the second-price auction. He showed that participants in such an auction have a dominant strategy to bid their true values. The reasoning is simple, yet profound. In a second-price auction the highest bidder wins the auction but only pays the second-highest bid price. Since the winner does not have to pay his or her bid price, the best strategy is to reveal true value.

In the 1970s a number of theorists used Vickrey's insight about private values auctions to develop decentralized incentive-compatible mechanisms for the allocation of public goods, mechanisms that induced participants to reveal their true marginal values for public goods instead of engaging in free riding (see, for example, Clarke 1971; Groves 1976; Groves and Ledyard 1977). Vernon Smith (1979a, 1979b, 1980) and others (for example, Ferejohn, Forsythe and Noll 1979; Harstad and Marrese 1981; Binger, Hoffman and Williams 1987; Banks, Plott and Porter 1988; Bagnoli and McKee 1991) have analysed the behavioural properties of public goods allocation mechanisms in laboratory implementations. The results have led to the design of new mechanisms that are less purely incentive compatible from a theoretical perspective, but that are more likely to lead to the optimal allocation of public goods in actual implementations.

For example, the Smith Auction Mechanism, designed by Vernon Smith (Smith 1979a, 1979b, 1980) after he found that purer mechanisms consistently failed to lead subjects to reveal their true values, combines insights from both the theoretical literature on incentive compatible mechanisms and the experimental literature on voluntary contribution mechanisms. In the Smith Auction Mechanism each subject submits a message to a dispatch centre, indicating how many units of the public good the subject wants the group to provide and how much he or she is willing to contribute to that provision. The dispatch centre then calculates the average quantity proposed by the members of the group, the sum of the individual contributions, and whether or not the contributions cover the cost of provision. The centre reports back to each participant that average quantity and a proposed cost share calculated as the total cost of that provision minus a prorated sum of the other participants' contributions. A subject can either ratify that proposal by sending that message back to the dispatch centre, or change his or her proposal. Smith investigated several stopping rules, including unanimity voting on the final allocation and repetition of the last proposal by all participants. He found that subjects participating in such a mechanism generally selected the Pareto-optimal allocation of the public good and volunteered to contribute a sufficient amount to provide it. While this research is still in its early stages, it promises to move us further along the road to a more decentralized approach to the allocation of public goods.

THE ROLE OF EXPERIMENTAL ECONOMICS IN THE DEREGULATION OF COMPLEX MARKETS. The experimental results summarized above demonstrate the importance of laboratory experimental results in informing regulatory law and policy in markets for simple commodities: one good sold by one seller to one buyer. Recently, however, there has been a worldwide move to deregulate more complex commodities: electric power, natural gas and water in arid lands. In each of these commodities, producers supply the product to a joint distribution system (a power grid, a gas pipeline, or a set of canals, respectively). Once a producer's product is in the joint distribution system, it cannot be distinguished from any other producer's product; it is a public good. Buyers withdraw units of the product from the distribution system at their ends, but the units they withdraw cannot be tied back to any one producer. Moreover, in the case of electric power and water in arid lands, some of the product gets lost in transmission. The complexity of these markets requires some coordination among buyers, sellers, and owners of distribution systems to properly allocate sales and purchases, set prices, and account for transmission losses. Prior to a recent, world-wide move to deregulate such markets most governments believed their intervention was required to maintain 'fair' allocations and prices in such markets.

As governments have moved to deregulate markets for these complex commodities, research on synthetic mechanisms has focused on the design of 'smart' computer-assisted markets for the allocation of such commodities. These new markets draw upon insights gained from research on the design and implementation of mechanisms for allocating public goods. For example, the computer-assisted market for natural gas (see McCabe, Rassenti and Smith 1991) is designed as follows. Communities wishing to buy gas submit location-specific bids to buy quantities of gas, delivered to their locations, at specified prices. Well-head producers submit location-specific offers to sell quantities of gas at their locations at specified prices. Owners of pipelines submit offers of capacity to transmit gas, over specified pipeline legs, at specified prices. A computer program incorporates all this information to determine prices at each node and for transmission, so as to maximize the gains from exchange in the system, according to the revealed demand, supply, and transmission functions. Buyers and sellers who can trade profitably at these nodal prices, according to their revealed schedules, constitute the active dispatch program.

They use a two-sided extension of the Vickrey auction as a market mechanism: a uniform-price, double-auction mechanism. In this market, buyers submit limit orders to buy specified quantities of gas at specified prices. Sellers and owners of pipelines submit limit orders to sell or transmit specified quantities of gas at specified prices. The computer algorithm combines the buyer and seller bids and offers with transmission offers to suggest prices at each node that maximize the revealed gains from exchange. Buyers, sellers, and pipeline owners can revise their limit prices for a prescribed length of time until the market closes. Dispatch continuously updates market-clearing prices on the basis of new information. When the market closes, all buyers who bid greater than or equal to the market price (including transmission costs) purchase units, and all sellers who offer to sell for prices less than or equal to the market price (minus the transmission costs) sell units. Excess demand or supply at the market price can be rationed in a variety of ways, including random selection and first into the market.

Smith and his colleagues have studied the uniform-price double-auction market extensively, both as a simple market and embedded in a smart, computer-assisted market for electric power or natural gas. They find that buyers and sellers generally under-reveal the value of inframarginal units in such markets. That is, buyers submit bids less than their true induced values and sellers submit offers higher than their costs. However, like the double-auction market discussed above, the uniform-price double-auction market mechanism forces buyers and sellers of marginal units to truthfully reveal the value of those marginal units or be forced out of the market. In general, within a few trading periods these markets converge to prices and quantities that maximize the true gains from exchange.

This success in designing and testing laboratory prototypes of smart, computer-assisted markets has led to considerable interest in implementing such markets for the sale of real commodities. For example, the Arizona Stock Exchange, which operates daily after the close of the New

York Stock Exchange, is the first fully computerized stock exchange to use a uniform-price double-auction market mechanism. Large investors, such as TIAA/CREF, use the market because they can trade at prices well below the commissions charged by the New York Stock Exchange. There is also considerable interest in smart markets for electric power, natural gas, and water, both by governments considering privatization and by companies and government agencies already operating in deregulated markets.

PRIVATIZATION, PROPERTY RIGHTS AND LEGITIMACY. The increasing importance of decentralization and privatization in public policy raises important questions about the legitimacy of property rights and the role of social norms in legitimizing political decisions. Cooter (1996) refers to the rule of state law and the rule-of-law state. In a rule-of-law state, social norms determine what is just and citizens obey the law because they respect those norms. Decentralization and privatization require a well-functioning rule-of-law state. But, economic theory has little to say about the role of social norms in the functioning of a market economy.

Previous research by Hoffman and Spitzer (1985a), as well as recent research by Berg, Dickhaut and McCabe (1995b), Hoffman, McCabe, Shachat and Smith (1994), Hoffman, McCabe and Smith (1996, forthcoming), and McCabe, Rassenti and Smith (1996) demonstrate the importance of norms of equality, equity, and reciprocity in determining economic outcomes. They find, in particular, that property rights that lead to differential economic outcomes (some people richer than others) may need to be legitimized by means consistent with social norms in order for economic agents to approximate Nash equilibrium outcomes. In addition, the norm of reciprocity mediates economic behaviour, leading to more cooperation than non-cooperative Nash equilibrium theory would predict. As literature in law and economics responds to the world-wide decentralization, privatization, and deregulation movement, we need to pay attention to the interplay between local social norms and private markets. Just as experimental economists found that trading institutions affect market outcomes, we may find that differences in local social norms affect the way that different economies develop under decentralization and privatization.

CONCLUSION. Laboratory experimental research holds great promise for the future of law and economics. Previous research in experimental economics has shown that market institutions significantly affect competitive market outcomes; that voluntary contribution mechanisms, Coasian bargaining, and incentive-compatible mechanisms can be used for the decentralized provision of public goods; and that complex commodities such as natural gas and electric power can be efficiently allocated through computer-assisted 'smart' markets. Moreover, recent research suggests strongly that local social norms will mediate the impact of decentralization and privatization. As governments world-wide move to privatized, decentralized economic systems, these results have increasing importance in analyses in law and economics.

ELIZABETH HOFFMAN, KEVIN MCCABE AND VERNON L. SMITH

See also AUCTIONS OF RIGHTS TO PUBLIC PROPERTY; COASE THEOREM; EFFICIENT NORMS; SELF-GOVERNANCE OF COMMON-POOL RESOURCES; SOCIAL NORMS AND THE LAW.

Subject classification: 4c(i)

BIBLIOGRAPHY

Bagnoli, M. and McKee, M. 1991. Voluntary contribution games: efficient private provision of public goods. *Economic Inquiry* 29: 351–66.

Banks, J.S., Plott, C.R. and Porter, D.P. 1988. An experimental analysis of unanimity in public goods provision mechanisms. *Review of Economic Studies* 55: 301–22.

Berg, J., Dickhaut, J. and McCabe, K. 1995a. The individual versus the aggregate. In *Judgment and Decision-Making in Accounting and Auditing*, ed. R. Ashton and A. Ashton (New York: Cambridge University Press): 102–34.

Berg, J., Dickhaut, J. and McCabe, K. 1995b. Trust, reciprocity, and social history. *Games and Economic Behavior* 10: 122–42.

Binger, B.R., Hoffman, E. and Williams, A.W. 1987. Experiments on a tâtonnement mechanism for allocating public goods. Public Choice Society Annual Meetings.

Clarke, E.H. 1971. Multipart pricing of public goods. *Public Choice* 11: 17–34.

Coase, R.H. 1960. The problem of social cost. *Journal of Law and Economics* 3: 1–44.

Cooter, R.D. 1997. The rule of state law and the rule-of-law state: economic analysis of the legal foundations of development. In *Annual Bank Conference on Development Economics 1996*, ed. M. Bruno and B. Pleskovic, Washington, DC: The World Bank.

Davis, D.D. and Holt, C.A. 1993. *Experimental Economics*. Princeton: Princeton University Press.

Dorsey, R. 1992. The voluntary contributions mechanism with real time revisions. *Public Choice* 73: 261–82.

Ferejohn, J.A., Forsythe, R. and Noll, R. 1979. An experimental analysis of decision making procedures for discrete public goods: a case study in institutional design. In *Research in Experimental Economics*, vol. 1, ed. V.L. Smith (Greenwich, CT: JAI Press): 1–58.

Groves, T. 1976. Information, incentives, and the internalization of production externalities. In *Theory and Measurement of Economic Externalities*, ed. S.A.Y. Lin, New York: Academic Press.

Groves, T. and Ledyard, J. 1977. Optimal allocation of public goods: a solution to the 'free rider' problem. *Econometrica* 45: 783–809.

Harstad, R.M. and Marrese, M. 1981. Implementation of mechanisms by processes: public good allocation experiments. *Journal of Economic Behavior and Organization* 2: 129–51.

Hey, J.D. 1991. *Experiments in Economics*. Oxford: Basil Blackwell.

Hoffman, E. 1997. Public choice experiments. In *Perspectives on Public Choice: A Handbook*, ed. D. Mueller (Cambridge: Cambridge University Press): 415–28.

Hoffman, E., McCabe, K., Shachat, K. and Smith, V.L. 1994. Preferences, property rights, and anonymity in bargaining games. *Games and Economic Behavior* 7: 346–80.

Hoffman, E., McCabe, K. and Smith, V.L. 1996. Social distance and other-regarding behavior in dictator games. *American Economic Review* 86(3): 653–60.

Hoffman, E., McCabe, K. and Smith, V.L. 1996. Behavioral foundations of reciprocity: experimental economics and evolutionary psychology. *Economic Inquiry* (forthcoming).

Hoffman, E. and Spitzer, M.L. 1982. The Coase theorem: some experimental tests. *Journal of Law and Economics* 25: 73–98.

Hoffman, E. and Spitzer, M.L. 1985a. Entitlements, rights, and fairness: an experimental examination of subjects' concepts of distributive justice. *Journal of Legal Studies* 14(2): 259–97.

Hoffman, E. and Spitzer, M.L. 1985b. Experimental law and economics: an introduction. *Columbia Law Review* 85(5): 991–1036.

Hoffman, E. and Spitzer, M.L. 1986. Experimental tests of the Coase theorem with large bargaining groups. *Journal of Legal Studies* 15: 149–71.

Hong, T. and Plott, C.R. 1982. Rate filing policies for inland water transportation: an experimental approach. *Bell Journal of Economics* 13: 1–19.

Isaac, R.M., McCue, K.F. and Plott, C.R. 1985. Public goods provision in an experimental environment. *Journal of Public Economics* 26: 51–74.

Isaac, R.M. and Plott, C.R. 1981. The opportunity for conspiracy in restraint of trade. *Journal of Economic Behavior and Organization* 2: 448–59.

Isaac, R.M., Schmidtz, D. and Walker, J.M. 1989. The assurance problem in a laboratory market. *Public Choice* 62: 217–36.

Isaac, R.M. and Walker, J.M. 1988a. Group size effects in public goods provision: the voluntary contribution mechanism. *Quarterly Journal of Economics* 103: 179–99.

Isaac, R.M. and Walker, J.M. 1988b. Communication and free-riding behavior: the voluntary contributions mechanism. *Economic Inquiry* 26: 585–608.

Isaac, R.M., Walker, J.M. and Thomas, S.H. 1984. Divergent evidence on free riding: an experimental examination of possible explanations. *Public Choice* 43: 113–49.

Isaac, R.M., Walker, J.M. and Williams, A.W. 1994. Group size and the voluntary provision of public goods: experimental evidence utilizing large groups. *Journal of Public Economics* 54: 1–36.

Kagel, J.H. and Roth, A.E. 1995. *Handbook of Experimental Economics*. Princeton, NJ: Princeton University Press.

Marwell, G. and Ames, R.E. 1979. Experiments on the provision of public goods I: resources, interest, group size, and the free rider problem. *American Journal of Sociology* 84: 115–1360.

Marwell, G. and Ames, R.E. 1980. Experiments on the provision of public goods II: provision points, stakes, experience and the free rider problem. *American Journal of Sociology* 85: 926–37.

Marwell, G. and Ames, R.E. 1981. Economists free ride, does anyone else? *Journal of Public Economics* 15: 295–310.

McCabe, K.A., Rassenti, S.J. and Smith, V.L. 1991. Smart computer-assisted markets. *Science* 254: 534–8.

McCabe, K.A., Rassenti, S.J. and Smith, V.L. 1996. Game theory and reciprocity in some extensive form experimental games. *Proceedings of the National Academy of Science* 93: 13421–8.

Plott, C.R. and Smith, V.L. 1978. An experimental examination of two exchange institutions. *Review of Economic Studies* 45: 133–53.

Smith, V.L. 1962. An experimental study of competitive market behavior. *Journal of Political Economy* 70: 111–37.

Smith, V.L. 1979a. Incentive compatible experimental processes for the provision of public goods. In *Research in Experimental Economics* (Greenwich, CT: JAI Press) 1: 59–168.

Smith, V.L. 1979b. An experimental comparison of three public good decision mechanisms. *Scandinavian Journal of Economics* 81: 198–215.

Smith, V.L. 1980. Experiments with a decentralized mechanism for public good decisions. *American Economic Review* 70: 584–99.

Smith, V.L. 1981. An empirical study of decentralized institutions of monopoly restraint. In *Essays in Contemporary Fields of Economics in Honor of E.T. Weiler (1914–1979)*, ed. J. Quirk and G. Horwich (West Lafayette, IN: Purdue University Press): 83–106.

Vickrey, W. 1961. Counterspeculation, auctions, and competitive sealed tenders. *Journal of Finance* 16: 8–37.

externalities. *See* COASE THEOREM; LAW-AND-ECONOMICS FROM THE PERSPECTIVE OF CRITICAL LEGAL STUDIES.

F

fair trade. *See* RESALE PRICE MAINTENANCE.

fair use. *See* COPYRIGHT.

Ferguson, Adam (1723–1816). It is possible that Ferguson would have been somewhat puzzled by his inclusion in this Dictionary. He did not consider either 'œconomy' or the law to be the true mainstays of civil society. As the Scottish Enlightenment moved towards legalistic theories of political economy, Ferguson launched a spirited critique of the ideas associated with his friends David Hume and Adam Smith. Yet he was deeply interested in some of the new ideas, and – by an ironic twist in the history of ideas – became closely associated with one of the Scottish insights best remembered by economists. The idea of unintended consequences in human affairs was given one of its clearest expressions in Ferguson's *Essay on the History of Civil Society* (1767):

> Like the winds, that come we know not whence, and blow whithersoever they list, the forms of society are derived from an obscure and distant origin; they arise, long before the date of philosophy, from the instincts, not from the speculations, of men. The croud [sic] of mankind, are directed in their establishments and measures, by their circumstances in which they are placed; and seldom are turned from their way, to follow the plan of any single projector.
>
> Every step and every movement of the multitude, even in what are termed enlightened ages, are made with equal blindness to the future; and nations stumble upon establishments, which are indeed the result of human action, but not the execution of any human design (Ferguson [1767] 1995: 119).

These lines are so quotable that one may easily forget that what Ferguson called the 'vicissitudes of human affairs' were only one part of his understanding of the progress of civil society, pointedly balanced off by a strong theory of individual agency and moral action. Friedrich Hayek, who was particularly fond of this passage and cited it repeatedly (e.g., Hayek 1967: 96; [1973] 1982: 1,150; 1978: 264), saw Ferguson as a faithful disciple of Mandeville and a like-minded colleague of Hume and Smith. Ferguson, in Hayek's reading, coined a felicitous phrase which summed up Mandeville's idea of cumulative spontaneous order from *The Fable of the Bees* (1714). 'The Results of Human Action but not of Human Design' even became the title of a chapter in Hayek's *Studies in Philosophy, Politics and Economics* (1967).

A careful reading of the rest of Ferguson's most important book should reveal, however, that Hayek got him wrong. Ferguson's own rhetoric had done him a disservice, and his famous passage on the unintended nature of human establishments casts a very misleading light on his ethics, politics and historiography. *An Essay on the History of Civil Society* is seen all too often as a book about the 'unintended outcomes of social life' (cf. Brown 1984: 92; Ullman-Margalit 1978: 284). Ferguson himself is accordingly taken for a somewhat coarse, but effective, contributor to the political-economist discourse of spontaneous order.

In order to trace the depth of Ferguson's distance from Hume and Smith – a distance which amounted to a fork in the road of the Scottish Enlightenment toward an analysis of modernity – we may look at his equally salutary words on the division of labour. This passage, which seems to stem directly from his treatment of unintended consequences in general, earned the respect of Karl Marx, who used it to hail Ferguson as Smith's teacher (Marx [1867] 1954: 123n, 354, 362n). Unaware that Smith's lectures on jurisprudence included an analysis of the division of labour preceding the publication of Ferguson's *Essay*, Marx especially applauded Ferguson's discussion 'Of the Separation of Arts and Professions', then widely considered to be the earlier and seminal formulation of the idea, which reads:

> [A] people can make no great progress in cultivating the arts of life, until they have separated, and committed to different persons, the several tasks, which require a peculiar skill and attention. . . . The artist finds, that the more he can confine his attention to a particular part of any work, his productions are the more perfect, and grow under his hands in the greater quantities. Every undertaker in manufacture finds, that the more he can subdivide the tasks of his workmen, and the more hands he can employ on separate articles, the more are his expences diminished, and his profits increased.
>
> [. . .] By the separation of arts and professions, the sources of wealth are laid open; every species of material is wrought up to the greatest perfection, and every commodity is produced in the greatest abundance (Ferguson [1767] 1995: 172–3; cf. 1996a).

The division of labour is thus yet another spontaneous process of change which brings about the unintended result of technological and material advance. Ferguson, however, did not write this to support Smith's ideas of progress but to subvert them. He believed, thereby earning a further round of applause from Marx, that specialization was destructive. Mechanical arts 'succeed best under a total suppression of sentiment and reason . . . where the workshop may, without any great effort of imagination, be considered as an engine, the parts of which are men'. The same metaphor applies, with graver results, to 'the higher departments of policy and war', where the over-specialized soldiers and statesmen are 'equally blind with the trader to any general combination' (Ferguson [1767] 1995: 173).

Blindness, then, is bad. It is particularly bad for citizen-soldiers and for any person active in the public sphere. These men, not in the capacity of traders or manufacturers, were Ferguson's subject matter and intended reading public. With them lay the responsibility of checking the blind forces of history and the unintended motions of the multitude, and making sense of the given circumstances in their pursuit of a vigorous, robust polity. The 'blind forces' shape the physical contours of human existence, like Montesquieu's climate and geography; but there is also a moral sphere, inspired by Machiavelli's republican theory of political *virtù*, where human agents are at work, constantly alert and pointedly unprofessional. These men are neither legislators nor economic planners: Ferguson emphatically parted from the myth of Solon and Lycurgus, and rejected all utopias and pencil-drawn governments (cf. Forbes 1966). But they are individuals all right, citizens in the classical republican sense, ready to fight enemies and to debate issues, and ever responsible for the public spirit which must animate any 'establishment' which the nation had stumbled upon. No piece of legislation can carry any meaning without this living basis of public spirit, and even the Habeas Corpus Act 'requires a fabric no less than the whole political constitution of Great Britain, a spirit no less than the refractory and turbulent zeal of this fortunate people, to secure its effects' (Ferguson [1767] 1995: 160). This was the part of Ferguson ignored by Hayek, and a crucial part it is.

From this premise stemmed Ferguson's rebuke against the economists and their language. Republicanism is moral, but it is by no means economical:

> We are not only obliged to admit numbers, who, in strict œconomy, may be reckoned superfluous, on the civil, the military, and the political list; but because we are men, and prefer the occupation, improvement, and felicity of our nature, to its mere existence, we must even wish, that as many members as possible, of every community, may be admitted to a share of its defence and its government (Ferguson [1767] 1995: 225).

Ferguson thus pleaded with authors conversant in 'speculations on commerce and wealth', like his friend Smith, 'not to consider these articles as making the sum of national felicity, or the principal object of any state' (Ferguson [1767] 1995: 140). Modern commercial society is in constant danger of losing its civic vitality precisely because of its unintended tendency towards specialized skills and Mandevillian dissipation:

> while it seems to promise improvement of skill, and is actually the cause why the productions of every art become more perfect as commerce advances; yet in its termination, and ultimate effects, serves, in some measure, to break the bands of society, to substitute form in place of ingenuity, and to withdraw individuals from the common scene of occupation, on which the sentiments of the heart, and the mind, are most happily employed (Ferguson [1767] 1995: 206–7).

Ferguson was thus not in the business of supporting Mandeville and spreading the principle of 'private vices, public virtue', but of undermining it. No vice can produce virtue, and Mandeville was a clear target for a moralist's attack (Ferguson 1996b: 213). The parallel between beehives and human communities has limits, like all other animal metaphors for human behaviour. Ferguson was anxious to draw those limits and show that a moral sphere of active choice exists beyond the natural similarities between 'the establishment of men' and 'the artifices of the beaver, the ant, and the bee' (Ferguson [1767] 1995: 173; [1792] 1975: 1, 54–5). Man's moral edge is not constituted by his sociability alone, but by his use of language, his 'talent for communication and intercourse' and his 'wonderful talent for the use and interpretation of signs' (Ferguson [1792] 1975: 1, 46–7).

It is here that Ferguson's genuine, and largely overlooked, contribution to economic discourse can finally be found. His deep interest in voluntary social interaction and in man's endless inventiveness focused his attention on play, the human action which reflects our social, active and communicative nature with unique clarity. Ferguson must have been one of the earliest modern thinkers to pay attention to the rational aspect of games men (though not women) play. He was fascinated by the role of intelligent play as a matrix for human 'business' in general, involving variety and choice, competition and conflict, risk-taking and social bonding. In a broad sense, he may have been the first game theorist. 'We are soon tired', he wrote,

> of diversions that do not approach to the nature of business, that is, that do not engage some passion, or give an exercise proportioned to our talents, and our faculties. The chace [sic] and the gaming-table have each their dangers and difficulties, to excite and employ the mind. All games of contention animate our emulation, and give a species of party-zeal. The mathematician is only to be amused with intricate problems, the lawyer and the casuist with cases that try their subtilty [sic], and occupy their judgement.
>
> . . . [W]hy may not the man whose object is money, be understood to lead a life of amusement and pleasure . . . even as much as the virtuoso, the scholar, the man of taste . . . ? ([1767] 1995: 52).

It is no coincidence that the thinker who was soon to create a subtle modern theory of play, Friedrich Schiller, and members of the early generation of German sociologists and economists in our century, were avid readers of Ferguson's works.

F. Oz-Salzberger

See also ADAM SMITH AND THE LAW; CIVIL SOCIETY; HAYEK, FRIEDRICH VON; HUME, DAVID; INVISIBLE HAND EXPLANATIONS; LAW-AND-ECONOMICS FROM THE PERSPECTIVE OF ECONOMICS; SCOTTISH ENLIGHTENMENT AND THE LAW; SPONTANEOUS ORDER; STATE OF NATURE AND CIVIL SOCIETY.

Subject classification: 1a(i); 7d.

SELECTED WORKS
1767. *An Essay on the History of Civil Society*. Edited with an introduction by F. Oz-Salzberger, Cambridge: Cambridge University Press, 1995.
1792. *Principles of Moral and Political Science: Being Chiefly a Retrospect of Lectures Delivered in the College of Edinburgh*. Repr. with an introduction by J. Hecht, 2 vols, Hildesheim and New York: Georg Olms Verlag, 1975.
1996a. Of the separation of departments, profesions [sic] and tasks resulting from the progress of arts in society. In A. Ferguson, *Collection of Essays*, edited with an introduction by Y. Amoh, Kyoto: Rinsen Books.
1996b. Of the principle of moral estimation: David Hume, Robert Clerk, Adam Smith. Ibid.

BIBLIOGRAPHY
Brown, R. 1984. *The Nature of Social Laws, Machiavelli to Mill*. Cambridge: Cambridge University Press.
Forbes, D. 1966. Introduction. A. Ferguson, *An Essay on the History of Civil Society*, Edinburgh: Edinburgh University Press.
Hayek, F. 1960. *The Constitution of Liberty*. London: Routledge & Kegan Paul.
Hayek, F. 1967. *Studies in Philosophy, Politics and Economics*. London: Routledge & Kegan Paul.
Hayek, F. 1978. *New Studies in Philosophy, Politics, Economics and the History of Ideas*. London and Henley: Routledge & Kegan Paul.
Hayek, F. 1982. *Law, Legislation and Liberty*. Vol. 1 (1973), reprinted in the corrected three-volume edition, London, Melbourne and Henley: Routledge & Kegan Paul.
Hamowy, R. 1968. Adam Ferguson, Adam Smith and the division of labour. *Economica* 35: 249–59.
Hamowy, R. 1987. *The Scottish Enlightenment and the Theory of Spontaneous Order*. Carbondale: Southern Illinois University Press.
Kettler, D. 1965. *The Social and Political Thought of Adam Ferguson*. Columbus: Ohio State University Press.
Marx, K. 1867. *Capital*. Moscow: Foreign Languages Publishing House, 1954.
Oncken, A. 1909. Adam Smith und Adam Ferguson. *Zeitschrift für Socialwissenschaft* 12: 129–37, 206–16.
Ullman-Margalit, E. 1978. Invisible-hand explanations. *Synthese* 39: 263–91.

fiduciary duties. Fiduciary duties fall into two broad categories: the duty of loyalty and the duty of care. These duties vary with different types of relationships between fiduciaries and their counter-parties ('entrustors'). History helps explain the variety of fiduciary relationships and the flexibility of fiduciary law. Fiduciary law has evolved in categories, each of which addressed a class of relationship, as it appeared at a different time in history. Thus, with the rise of trusts in the middle ages, ecclesiastical courts and later courts of equity developed trust law (see Scott and Fratcher [1939] 1987). As partnerships evolved in the thirteenth century, equity courts developed partnership law (see Bromberg and Ribstein [1988] 1996). Agency law responded to the emergence of this relationship in the 1800s, and statutory corporate law imposed fiduciary duties on directors and officers as corporations were recognized in the seventeenth century (see Fletcher [1917] 1990). Recently, courts have imposed fiduciary duties on union officers, physicians and clergymen.

Fiduciary relationships appear in many legal contexts: contracts, wills, trusts and elections (e.g., of corporate directors). However, fiduciary duties and remedies draw on a common source – equity. Thus, in addition to damages – a remedy in common law – fiduciaries must account for ill-gotten profits even if their entrustors suffered no injury – a remedy in equity. The similarities and differences among fiduciary relationships explain why law regulates fiduciaries in the first place, and why the regulation varies with different classes of fiduciaries. Therefore, before discussing fiduciary duties we discuss the features by which fiduciary relationships can be recognized.

FEATURES OF FIDUCIARY RELATIONSHIPS. (1) *Fiduciary relationships are service relationships, in which fiduciaries provide to entrustors services that public policy encourages.* Bailees, escrow agents, agents, brokers, corporate directors and officers, partners, co-venturers, lawyers and trustees all render service to entrustors. Some fiduciaries, such as partners, may be both fiduciaries and entrustors of each other.

(2) *To perform their services effectively, fiduciaries must be entrusted with power over the entrustors or their property ('power').* The extent of entrusted power varies with the parties' desires and terms of their arrangements. For example, entrustors who seek investment advice, but intend to make the investment decisions themselves, vest less power in their investment advisers than entrustors who wish to leave these decisions to their advisers. Arrangements in which entrustors are precluded from controlling their fiduciaries in the performance of their services, categorized in law as 'trust', vest far more power in the fiduciaries than arrangements, categorized in law as 'agency', in which entrustors control their fiduciaries in the performance of their services. The extent of vested power depends also on the freedom of entrustors to remove their fiduciaries and retrieve the entrusted property. For example, trustees have more power than agents because under the trust model beneficiaries may not remove their trustees, while under the agency model principals may remove their agents. When removal powers of entrustors are limited to election dates, as in the case of shareholders and their directors, directors have more power than agents but less than trustees. The magnitude of the powers entrusted to fiduciaries is also related to the cost of specifying the fiduciaries' future actions. Thus the services of escrowees and bailees, which do not require broad discretion, can be spelled out easily in advance, while the services of investment managers and trustees, which require broader discretion, can be described only in general terms because the details depend on future unknown circumstances.

(3) *The sole purpose of entrustment is to enable fiduciaries to serve their entrustors.* Entrustment enables fiduciaries to use entrusted power for other purposes – for their own use or the use of third parties. Entrustors' losses from abuse of entrusted powers can be higher than their benefits from the fiduciaries' services. Therefore, an entrustor will not hand over $100 to a fiduciary if the probable loss of the $100 from the fiduciary's embezzlement, (e.g., a 50% chance) exceeds the expected gain from the relationship (e.g., $5).

(4) *Entrustors' costs of monitoring fiduciaries' use of entrusted power are likely to exceed entrustors' benefits from the relationship.* For example, if the advisers' interests conflict with those of the entrustors, the value of their advice, even their expert advice, is doubtful. Monitoring such conflicts of interest is costly. Similarly, the very utility of the relationship for clients would be undermined if the clients must watch over their discretionary investment managers to prevent abuse of power.

(5) *Entrustors' costs of monitoring the quality of fiduciary services are likely to be very high, because most fiduciary services involve expertise that entrustors do not possess.* These monitoring costs may exceed the benefits to entrustors from the relationship. For example, if clients must check the quality of their investment advisers' recommendations, the advice is worth little. Similarly, clients cannot evaluate legal services except by hiring other lawyers or undertaking a costly study of law. In addition, the quality of some services cannot be determined by their results: a defendant may lose his case even if his lawyer has performed brilliantly. The quality of some services cannot be easily established at the time of performance: it may take years to discover that a will is faulty.

(6) *The fiduciaries' costs of reducing the entrustors' monitoring costs may exceed the benefits to fiduciaries from the relationship.* Fiduciaries can reduce entrustors' monitoring costs by 'bonding', insurance and third-party guarantees, provided their costs do not exceed their benefits from the relationship. Because of these limits, their efforts may not be enough to fully cover the entrustors' risks of loss.

(7) *Alternative external controls that reduce entrustors' risks, such as market controls, either do not exist or are too weak.* Courts recognize new fiduciary relations when, in their opinion, the historical protections of entrustors have eroded. For example, physicians recently joined the family of fiduciaries as they became involved in conflict of interest situations – when physicians own pharmacies that supply their patients' medicines, or when the interests of the physicians' employers conflict with the patients' optimal medical treatment (see Rodwin 1993). Similarly, recognizing that church controls over clergymen have weakened, courts have recently categorized members of the clergy as fiduciaries (see Cruz 1991). The Supreme Court of Canada declared accountants giving investment advice to be fiduciaries. The Court found that an accountant breached his fiduciary duties when he recommended to a client tax-sheltered investments without disclosing his personal interest in these investments (see *Hodgkinson v. Simms*).

The reverse is also true. When outside controls over fiduciaries tighten, courts are likely to relax their supervision over these fiduciaries. For example, in the United States, courts impose limited fiduciary duties on securities brokers, depending on the circumstances of the relationship. Courts may believe that the controls exerted by the markets, the Securities and Exchange Commission, and the National Association of Securities Dealers provide alternative protection to investors, and perhaps judges have concluded that the judicial system has been overutilized as claims against brokers have increased dramatically. In short, the weakening of entrustors' protection may trigger recognition of new fiduciary relationships and stricter duties on existing fiduciaries, while the strengthening of alternative protection may reduce or even eliminate fiduciary duties (see Frankel 1983 and 1993).

Notwithstanding the language in some court decisions, undue influence, confidence and trust, personal dependence, and actual reliance by one person on another do not create fiduciary relationships. As the discussion on points 4–7 demonstrates, economic analysis of 'agency costs' has become an integral part of the theory and design of fiduciary law. Although the disciplines of law and economics differ in vocabulary and focus (see Clark 1985), economic theories on principals' costs of monitoring and disciplining their agents, and the mechanisms for reducing these costs, have greatly influenced legal thinking on fiduciary law (see Jensen and Meckling 1976; Fama 1980; Arrow 1985). Some scholars define fiduciary relationships as contracts involving high costs of specifying the parties' terms and of monitoring the fiduciaries' performance (see Macey 1991). In their opinion, these costs (and not property and power entrustment) are the only justifications for recognizing fiduciary relationships (see Easterbrook and Fischel 1993). We revisit this issue in the last section of this essay.

THE PURPOSE AND EFFECT OF FIDUCIARY DUTIES. Fiduciary duties are imposed when public policy encourages specialization in particular services, such as money management or lawyering, and when the entrustors' costs of specifying and monitoring the fiduciaries' functions threaten to undermine the utility of the relationship to entrustors. The ultimate effect of the law is to provide entrustors with incentives to enter into fiduciary relationships, by reducing entrustors' risks and costs of preventing abuse of entrusted power, and of ensuring quality fiduciary services. Judicial enforcement of fiduciary duties shifts entrustors' costs to taxpayers. The law imposes on fiduciaries duties that limit their freedoms but increases their marketability by endowing them with a reputation for honesty backed by regulation.

JUDICIAL DENIAL OF FIDUCIARY STATUS. Courts are likely to deny a fiduciary status to relationships that do not involve property, perhaps because the historical purpose of regulating fiduciaries was to protect property owners. Further, courts may refuse to extend fiduciary law when its application would present doctrinal problems (see Singer 1988; Frankel 1993) or because these parties can fend for themselves by specific contract terms. For example, US courts refused to impose fiduciary duties on corporate directors towards corporate bondholders and employees; these are deemed to be creditors of the corporation, not entrustors (see McDaniel 1986). Similarly, courts did not impose fiduciary duties on banks towards their depositors (see *Morse v. Crocker Natl Bank*) and on insurance companies towards their policyholders (see *Rochester Radiology Assocs, PC v. Aetna Life Ins. Co.*) and held both institutions to be debtors. As trustees, banks and insurance companies would have had to segregate deposits or reserves, undermining the very utility of banking and insurance, which requires pooling. In contrast, legislatures freely apply fiduciary duties piecemeal, as the regulation of banking and insurance demonstrates. Legislation imposes duties of loyalty and care on these institutional debtors, which, doctrinally, is a contradiction in terms.

JUDICIAL CREATION OF FIDUCIARY DUTIES. Courts apply fiduciary law in three steps. They (1) define the functions that particular fiduciaries are expected to serve; (2) determine the powers vested in the fiduciaries to perform these functions, which vary, depending on the parties' agreements and actions, and circumstances of the relationships; and in light of these functions and powers (3) design the regulatory regime for the particular cases before them. As the Supreme Court of the United States declared more than fifty years ago: '[T]o say that a man is a fiduciary only begins analysis; it gives direction to further inquiry. To whom is he a fiduciary? What obligations does he owe as a fiduciary? In what respect has he failed to discharge these obligations? And what are the consequences of his deviation from duty?' (*SEC v. Chenery Corp.*, 85–6). Courts also determine the degree of skill that fiduciaries must possess in performing their functions. Unless the fiduciaries profess to possess certain skills, or the parties specify them, the courts derive the degree of required skill from the type of expected services, the circumstances surrounding the relationships (e.g., the responsibility involved in providing the services) and the fees paid for them. Having determined the functions and powers of a fiduciary in a particular relationship, courts regulate the fiduciary in the exercise of these powers mainly to reduce entrustors' risk from misappropriation of entrusted power, and secondarily, from inappropriate performance.

DOCTRINE OF FIDUCIARY DUTIES. Fiduciary law vests in entrustors the *legal right to rely on the honesty of their fiduciaries* by imposing on fiduciaries a corresponding duty of loyalty and other specific duties to deter dishonesty. In enforcing these duties, which constitute the bulk of fiduciary law, courts follow principles similar to those underlying the crime of embezzlement (see LaFave and Scott [1972] 1986) and the tort of conversion (see Prosser and Keeton [1941] 1984; *Moore v. Regents of the University of California*). The duty of loyalty addresses the risk of abuse of entrusted power to which entrustors are exposed. Further, fiduciary law vests in entrustors the *legal right to receive quality fiduciary services, commensurate with reasonable expectations of entrustors*, by imposing on fiduciaries a corresponding duty of care in the performance of their services. Breach of this duty is similar to the tort of negligence, and addresses the entrustors' risk of low-quality fiduciary services.

DUTY OF LOYALTY. Some court decisions may suggest that the duty of loyalty requires fiduciaries to be altruistic: to commit fully to the interests of entrustors, and put these interests before their own. The substance of these decisions suggests a narrower interpretation. Fiduciaries need not sacrifice their property and interests to benefit entrustors. The duty of loyalty is limited to the entrusted power that fiduciaries receive for the purpose of performing their services. The duty requires fiduciaries to be honest: refrain from converting entrusted power to unauthorized uses. The enforcement of the duty of loyalty is implemented by preventive duties that dampen temptation, especially when fiduciaries deal with entrusted property over long periods. Here are a number of examples:

(1) *Fiduciaries should segregate and earmark entrusted assets.* This duty protects entrustors from claims of creditors of fiduciaries in financial difficulties. Segregation constitutes notice to potential creditors that assets, which fiduciaries seem to own, belong to others. Earmarking prevents fiduciaries from allocating losing investments to entrustors and successful investments to themselves, after the fact. Because people are creatures of habit, segregation and earmarking also reduce the likelihood that fiduciaries would view other people's assets as their own. Segregation and earmarking remind fiduciaries every time they look at, or think about, entrusted property, that they do not own it even if they control it.

(2) *Fiduciaries may not create situations in which their interests conflict with those of the entrustors*, for example, buying entrusted property while acting on behalf of entrustors. The prohibition is based on a rebuttable presumption, borne out by experience, that conflict of interest transactions would benefit fiduciaries at the expense of entrustors, and is designed to avoid temptations to use entrusted powers for the fiduciaries' own benefit. However, because such transactions could benefit both parties, the law does not disallow them altogether. Such transactions are permitted with the consent of the entrustors, or third parties on their behalf, or – under corporate law – third parties and the courts, or – under the Investment Company Act of 1940 – the Securities and Exchange Commission. Such consents are aimed to assure that the terms of the transactions will mirror those reached at arm's length negotiations.

The prohibition on conflict of interests transactions does not preclude fiduciaries from having interests that conflict with those of their entrustors, for example in seeking compensation. Sometimes the line between permissible and impermissible conflicts of interest is blurred. For example, while employees may use for their own benefit knowledge, information and some of the personal contacts they acquired during their employment, they may not, in contemplation of terminating the employment, take with them proprietary information, nor entice clients away from their employer before leaving. Similarly, controlling shareholders may sell their shares at a premium over market price because of cost savings and other advantages that controlling blocks of shares present. The better view, however, is that they hold their power over the minority shareholders' interests as fiduciaries, and may not sell the control over the minority's shares, especially if the shares have no liquid market.

Similarly, although a trustee may not usually have conflict of interest with his beneficiaries, a court may refuse to remove such a trustee if he is a son, appointed by his deceased father as trustee for the benefit of himself and his mother, in order to continue operating the family business. In this case the father is presumed to have known the son's integrity far better than the court, his familial relationship would protect the mother, even if she perceives otherwise, and, presumably, the son will operate the family business better than any outsider.

(3) *Fiduciaries may not compete with their entrustors.* Competition would tempt fiduciaries to use their entrusted powers for their own benefit. Because competition is unlikely

to benefit entrustors, entrustors' consent will be closely examined to ensure that it is informed and independent.

(4) *Fiduciaries must provide their entrustors with information and accounting*. Information and accounting as to the use of entrusted power helps reduce both temptation and the entrustors' costs of monitoring.

THE DUTY OF CARE. Like the duty of loyalty, the duty of care is triggered when the entrustors' high costs of monitoring the quality of fiduciaries' services might deter entrustors from entering the relationship. As compared to the duty of loyalty, the duty of care is generally considered the lesser fiduciary duty. Arguably, it is imposed when there is a suspicion of conflict of interest but no proof. The duty of care requires fiduciaries to perform their services with care and skill that can be reasonably expected of them in the particular situation. If fiduciaries possess or purport to possess certain skills, they must use them to benefit entrustors. Reflecting the tort of negligence, 'care' denotes caution, and is especially relevant for trustees, required to preserve trust capital. The duty is broader, however, and relates to the fiduciaries' decision-making process. It requires them to (1) gather pertinent information; (2) focus – pay attention – and deliberate before making a decision; and (3) use their skills in the process.

The standard of care that fiduciaries must exercise is often measured by the care that they would exercise in their own affairs. In corporate law the standard follows the profession: care exercised by holders of similar positions. The distinctions between private fiduciaries that service a small number of entrustors (whether individuals or entities) and those that service many entrustors is not well developed. Yet, this distinction plays a role in shaping fiduciary duties because the strictness of these duties generally depends on entrusted powers, monitoring and controls that entrustors can exercise in each situation.

THE DESIGN OF FIDUCIARY DUTIES. The objectives of fiduciary law and the circumstances which give rise to problems inherent in fiduciary relationships explain why fiduciary duties are not uniform. Fiduciary duties vary with the costs of specifying and monitoring entrustors' services, the degree of potential risk of losses from the relationship to entrustors, and the extent to which there are no alternative mechanisms to protect entrustors from such risks.

Thus, because escrow agents and bailees can perform their services with little discretion over property entrusted to them, and their duties can be easily specified, their duties of loyalty and care are relatively slight. In contrast, trustees need substantial discretionary powers and title to trust property in order to perform their functions, and their functions cannot be itemized with specificity, especially when they are long term. Further, beneficiaries usually do not choose their trustees and are locked into the relationships; unless the power of removal is reserved to them, they cannot remove the trustees except by court order, after a showing of wrongful behaviour. Beneficiaries are unable to influence the trustees' decisions and unable to exit the relationships. Therefore, trustees are subject to strict fiduciary duties and active judicial supervision.

As compared to trustees, directors are not regulated as strictly. They do not have as much power over shareholders' property, and no title to the corporation's property. Shareholders can exit the relationship by selling their shares, although they may sustain significant losses if the market for these shares is illiquid. Shareholders have alternative mechanisms to control directors, such as voting the directors out of office (although these powers are weak for small shareholders). Therefore, as compared to trustees, directors are subject to a lower standard of fiduciary duties, and less judicial supervision. If shareholders are locked into the corporation, for example because their shares have no market, courts may impose stricter fiduciary duties of loyalty on the directors and controlling shareholders (see *Donahue v. Rodd Electrotype Co.*). Agents and advisers to individual or small groups of clients are subject to lower duties than directors because, as principals, clients can control and direct their advisers and can terminate the relationships, usually with little cost.

Thus, the strictness of the duty of loyalty and the preventive duties imposed on fiduciaries are a function of the entrusted power in the fiduciaries' hands and the self-protection attached to the particular kind of fiduciary relationship. Similarly, the duty of care is imposed only to the extent that entrustors' costs of monitoring the quality of services and terminating the relationships are relatively high. As compared to trustees, corporate directors are subject to a lower duty of care not only because shareholders elect the directors and can terminate the relationship by selling their shares or electing other directors, but more importantly, because, unlike trust situations, shareholders expect directors to act as entrepreneurs and take business risks. Arguably, the cost of a higher duty of care would deter directors from serving on boards. Hence, in America, the 'business judgment rule' protects corporate directors from liability for breaching the duty of care. The rule constitutes a conclusive presumption that the directors' decisions are right, and courts will not examine them on the merits if the directors had no conflicts of interest with the corporations and their shareholders, and if their decisions were made in an informed and deliberate manner. In contrast, trustees must comply with a higher standard of caution, subject to the directives in the trust instruments, the state of the estates and the needs of beneficiaries.

The same principles apply when fiduciaries serve entrustors with diverse interests, e.g., life beneficiaries and remaindermen of a trust, or the holders of corporate common and preferred stock. The courts will defer to the fiduciaries' judgments unless the fiduciaries' decisions are tainted by conflicts of interest with their entrustors, or the fiduciaries have shown a clear bias towards one entrustor over another, or made their decision in violation of the procedural requirements of the duty of care.

FIDUCIARY DUTIES AS DEFAULT RULES. Whether entrustors may waive, or bargain around, fiduciary duties owed to them is a complex issue. Arguably, the very idea of fiduciary rules as default rules conflicts with the fiduciary duty of loyalty and reliability. When bargaining with their fiduciaries, entrustors must fend for themselves, and their right to rely on their fiduciaries, indeed the very relationship, must be eliminated during the bargaining. Fiduciary law allows such termination of the relationship with respect to specified transactions with the entrustors' consent. Therefore, the parties must follow a certain procedure designed to ensure an effective transition from the fiduciary mode – in which entrustors are entitled to rely on their fiduciaries – to a contract mode – in which entrustors cannot rely on these fiduciaries. (1) Fiduciaries must put entrustors on notice that, regarding the specified transaction, entrustors are on their own; (2) entrustors must have legal capacity to enter into bargains with their fiduciaries as independent parties; (3) to enable entrustors to make informed decisions, fiduciaries must provide them with information regarding the transaction, especially if the information was acquired in connection with the performance of their services to entrustors. This procedure is, as indeed it should be, mandatory. If this procedure is not followed, it is likely that the entrustor's waiver will not be legally binding. Courts may refuse to recognize waivers of fiduciary duties when they (1) doubt the quality of entrustors' consent (especially when given by public entrustors, such as shareholders); (2) find that the parties' own agreements limit their ability to contract around fiduciary duties; (3) have paternalistic concerns that the particular entrustors cannot fend for themselves; (4) assert their power to classify relationships and determine their legal consequences, and preclude parties from doing so by agreement; (5) recognize the importance of providing society with a legal model of a trust relationship.

FIDUCIARY AND CONTRACT RELATIONSHIPS. Some scholars view fiduciary relationships solely as contracts that involve unusually high costs of specification of the parties' terms and monitoring of parties' performance. In their opinion, courts should fill in the gaps in these contracts to reflect the parties' intent, as, without admitting it, courts actually do (see Macey 1991; Easterbrook and Fischel 1993). These scholars then make a quantum leap from an economic concept of contracts (consensual relationships) to a legal concept of contracts, subsume fiduciary law into contract law (see Easterbrook and Fischel 1993; but see Romano 1993) and eradicate its property law underpinning (see Langbein 1995). While economics-based explanations of fiduciary relationships are extremely helpful to the understanding of the law, legal reclassification of loosely consensual arrangements as exclusively contractual is unwarranted.

Eliminating fiduciary law as a separate category and its reclassification as contract has far-reaching consequences in the context of the Anglo-American legal system. First, reclassification obliterates the historic building block of fiduciary law, that is, trust law. It is a unique invention of English judges, splitting property rights into legal title – held by the trustee, and beneficial interests – held by beneficiaries. In the market place the trustee can deal with trust property as if he were its owner; towards his beneficiaries, he must abide by the terms that he agreed to follow. This duality allows the parties to limit the trustee's use of entrusted property, and avoid chaotic property law by maintaining traditional standard forms of ownership.

Second, denying the property aspects of fiduciary law dilutes the rights of beneficial owners against their trustees and eliminates the remedy of accounting for breach of fiduciary duties. Conversion of trust assets would constitute a breach of contract (resulting in payment of damages). This result weakens beneficial property rights considerably. Third, judicial discretion in designing the parties' duties under contract law is far more limited than under fiduciary law. American judges exercise self-restraint in interpreting and creating contract-based duties, especially preventive duties. Fiduciary duties would be derived from the express or implied terms of contracts, shifting to entrustors the burden of showing contract-based duties. Fourth, the contract regime would require courts to enforce entrustors' waivers of fiduciary duties without added protections. Fifth, many current fiduciary relationships might not constitute contracts; unless they find a new home, they remain without legal enforcement altogether.

The contract regime does govern fiduciary relationships in civil law systems (e.g., the German and French legal systems). However, contract in civil law and contract in Anglo-American law differ. Civil law does not recognize the concept of beneficial ownership, but has widened the reach of contract law to include many types of fiduciary relationships. Civil law judges exercise broad discretion in interpreting the duties of contract parties, including their duty of 'fair dealing', and have developed under this heading duties akin to fiduciary duties (see Schlesinger, Baade, Damaska and Herzog [1950] 1988).

Fiduciary relationships are consensual, but they are not necessarily contractual. For example, if, upon my request, my friend accepts $50 in order to buy me flowers, he is my agent and fiduciary. He cannot buy flowers for $40 and pocket the difference without my informed consent. He is not entitled to compensation for his services unless I agreed to pay him, or unless he could claim under the equitable doctrine of *quantum meruit*. Further, even without compensation, my friend would violate his fiduciary duties to me by using my money for other purposes or by losing the money negligently.

Although some contract situations (such as franchises, construction agreements, and so-called 'relational contracts', long-term agreements) pose problems similar to those of fiduciary relationships, and may overlap with them at the fringe, the basic prototypes of these relationships differ. The distinctions do not preclude coexisting fiduciary and contract relationships, such as directors contracting with their corporations, except that if the two conflict, fiduciary law would trump contract.

Arguably, fiduciary duties and remedies may deter fiduciaries, such as corporate directors, from serving. Even so, courts can relax the duties and reduce the severity of the remedies; legislatures may do so and cap awards of damages. The problem does not call for the drastic solution of eliminating fiduciary law altogether. Such a solution may deter entrustors from entering the relationship, and that may be socially more harmful.

Thus far, American courts have refused to sweep fiduciary duties under the contract rug. Some decisions have tended to limit the reach of fiduciary duties, and others expanded the reach of fiduciary law by converting aspects of contract into property. The United States Supreme Court ordered a Central Intelligence Agency employee, who violated his contract with the Government by publishing a book about the Agency without pre-clearance, to account to the Government for his profits from the publication. The court characterized the information in the book as the Government's property and ordered accounting, even though the information was public, and the Government failed to prove injury (see *Snepp v. United States*). Hence, it is highly unlikely that fiduciary law will soon disappear into the contract category.

TAMAR FRANKEL

See also AGENCY COSTS AND CORPORATE GOVERNANCE; BOARDS OF DIRECTORS; CORPORATE CRIME AND ITS CONTROL; CORPORATE LAW; EQUITY; FRAUD-ON-THE-MARKET; INHERITANCE LAW; PARTNERSHIP; SECURITIES REGULATION.

Subject classification: 4b(i); 5a(i); 5g(ii).

CASES

Donahue v. Rodd Electrotype Co. of New England, Inc., 328 NE2d 505 (Mass. 1975).
Hodgkinson v. Simms (1994) 117 DLR (4th) 161 (SCC).
Moore v. Regents of the University of California, 793 P2d 479 (Cal. 1990).
Morse v. Crocker Natl Bank, 190 Cal. Rptr 839 (Cal. 1983).
Rochester Radiology Associates, PC v. Aetna Life Insurance Co., 616 FSupp 985 (NY 1985).
SEC v. Chenery Corp., 318 US 80 (1943).
Snepp v. United States, 444 US 507 (1980).

BIBLIOGRAPHY

Arrow, K.J. 1985. The economics of agency. In *Principals and Agents*, ed. J.W. Pratt and R.J. Zeckhauser, Boston: Harvard Business School Press.

Bromberg, A.R. and L.E. Ribstein. 1988. *Bromberg and Ribstein on Partnership*. Boston: Little, Brown & Co.; revised ch. 1, 1996.

Clark, R.C. 1985. Agency costs versus fiduciary duties. In *Principals and Agents*, ed. J.W. Pratt and R.J. Zeckhauser, Boston: Harvard Business School Press.

Cruz, E. 1991. When the shepherd preys on the flock: clergy, sexual exploitation and the search for solutions. *Florida State University Law Review* 19: 499–523.

Easterbrook, F.H. and Fischel, D.H. 1993. Contract and fiduciary duty. *Journal of Law and Economics* 36: 425–46.

Fama, E.F. 1980. Agency problems and the theory of the firm. *Journal of Political Economy* 88: 288–307.

Fletcher, W.M. 1917. *Fletcher Cyclopedia of the Law of Private Corporations*. Ed. C.R.P. Keating and G. O'Gradney, Deerfield, IL: Callaghan & Co.; permanent edn revised, 1990.

Frankel, T. 1993. Fiduciary law: the judicial process and the duty of care. In *The 1993 Isaac Pitblado Lectures, Fiduciary Duties/Conflicts of Interest*, Manitoba: The Law Society of Manitoba.

Frankel, T. 1983. Fiduciary law. *University of California Law Review* 71: 795–836.

Jensen, M.C. and Meckling, W.H. 1976. Theory of the firm: managerial behavior, agency costs and ownership structure. *Journal of Financial Economics* 3: 305–60.

LaFave, W.R. and Scott, A.W. Jr. 1972. *Handbook on Criminal Law*. St. Paul, MN: West Publishing Co.; 2nd edn, 1986.

Langbein, J.H. 1995. The contractarian basis of the law of trusts. *Yale Law Journal* 105: 625–75.

Macey, J.R. 1991. An economic analysis of the various rationales for making shareholders the exclusive beneficiaries of corporate fiduciary duty. *Stetson Law Review* 21: 23–44.

McDaniel, M.W. 1986. Bondholders and corporate governance. *Business Lawyer* 41: 413–56.

Prosser, W.L. and W.P. Keeton. 1941. *Prosser and Keeton on the Law of Torts*. St. Paul, MN: West Publishing Company; 5th edn, 1984.

Rodwin, M.A. 1993. *Medicine, Money and Morals*. New York: Oxford University Press.

Romano, R. 1993. Comment on Easterbrook and Fischel, 'Contract and fiduciary duty'. *Journal of Law and Economics* 36: 447–51.

Schlesinger, R.B., Baade, H.W., Damaska, M.R. and Herzog, P.E. 1950. *Comparative Law*. Mineola, NY: The Foundation Press; 5th edn, 1988.

Scott, A.W. and Fratcher, W.F. 1939. *The Law of Trusts*. Boston: Little, Brown & Co.; 4th edn, 1987.

Singer, J.W. 1988. The reliance interest in property. *Stanford Law Review* 40: 614–751.

financial holding companies. *See* REGULATION OF FINANCIAL HOLDING COMPANIES.

fine print. *See* STANDARD FORM CONTRACTS.

first, role of. *See* COMING TO THE NUISANCE.

first possession. First possession has been the dominant method of establishing property rights (Epstein 1979; Berger 1985; Rose 1985). This rule grants an ownership claim to the party that gains control before other potential claimants. First possession is both more prolific and more viable than suggested by the exotic treasure trove and wild animal cases that typically come to mind. In fact, first possession has been applied widely in both common and statute law in such varied settings as abandoned property, adverse possession, bona fide purchaser, fisheries and wildlife, groundwater, intellectual property, land, non-bankruptcy debt collection, nuisance law, oil and gas, pollution permits, the radio spectrum, satellite orbits, seabed minerals, spoils of war including prisoners and slaves, treasure trove, and water rights. First possession is also a powerful norm (Ellickson 1991) tightly woven into the fabric of Anglo-American society, where it is better known as 'finders keepers' or 'first come, first served', in cases ranging from street parking and cafe seating to setting up fishing huts on frozen lakes. First possession has also been a fundamental component of civil law, traditional African and Islamic legal systems, as well as informal and customary rule-making around the world (Lawson 1975; Dukeminier and Krier 1993). Indeed, the application of first possession rules touches on important issues in law and economics such as the role of transaction costs in shaping legal institutions, the link between private contracting and government action, and the relative efficiency of common law, norms, and statutes. Perhaps just as important, rules of first possession are intimately related to the 'justice of acquisition', a major topic in philosophical and political discussions of distributive justice (Nozick 1974).

I. A BRIEF INTELLECTUAL HISTORY

Despite its persistent use, most scholars have had little good to say about first possession rules. Legal scholars and political philosophers have considered it to be unjust (Cohen 1927; Becker 1977) and economists have considered it to be inefficient. More recently, however, first possession rules have been argued to be both efficient and just (Epstein 1979 and 1986; Rose 1985; Lueck 1995).

A. POLITICAL AND LEGAL THEORIES. In John Locke's (1690) labour theory of property, each man has a natural right to himself and can gain ownership of natural resources such as land or game by 'mixing' his labour with the resource. Thus, a man acquires ownership to a plot of virgin land by tilling and cultivating it. By this process, people can establish private property rights to the earth's abundance that was given by God 'to all mankind in common'. Many scholars have noted the limits of Locke's theory (e.g., Nozick 1974; Epstein 1979; Rose 1985), particularly for his vague specification of labour and the extent of the resulting property claim, for what has become known as the Lockean proviso that a labour-based property claim must have 'enough and as good left in common for others' (Locke 1690: II §27), and for the ambiguity surrounding his use of the term 'things held in common'. Despite these faults, Locke's theory of property remains a powerful defence of individual rights, more or less consistent with real-world application of the rule of first possession. Nozick (1974) attempts to salvage Locke's theory by modifying his proviso, implicitly arguing that first possession is a just method of acquiring holdings.

Two of the greatest common law jurists – William Blackstone (1766) in England and Oliver Wendell Holmes (1881) in America – defended the rule without hesitation. Yet neither took pains to develop a theory of first possession. Blackstone, for instance, noted (Book II, Chapter 1,2):

> There is nothing which so generally strikes the imagination, and engages the affections of mankind, as the right of property; or that sole and despotic dominion which one man claims and exercises over the external things of the world, in total exclusion of the right of any other individual in the universe. And yet there are very few, that will give themselves the trouble to consider the original and foundation of this right.

Indeed Gaius, the first-century Roman commentator, stated the rationale simply: 'What presently belongs to no one becomes by *natural reason* [my emphasis] the property of the first taker' (Mommsen et al. 1985, Book 41, §1).

Among contemporary legal–political theorists, Epstein (1979, 1986) offers the strongest defence of first possession as a legitimate method of establishing property rights. Epstein argues that first possession is valuable because it promotes decentralized ownership and thus is consistent with a minimal state (a Lockean view), and that a time-based rule like being first is a clear, simple way to mark things which reduces transaction costs. Epstein, notably impressed with the historical dominance of first possession rules and sceptical of those who dismiss them, is the first to attempt a positive theory that explains their dominance. Similarly, Rose (1985) notes the persistence and virtues of first possession but stresses the variation and subtleties in the way in which possession is determined, arguing that first possession tends to create clear property claims that reward 'useful labor'. The work of both Epstein and Rose has an advantage over that of other scholars for two reasons. First, they examine the actual practice of first possession in both law and custom. Second, they heavily rely on the economic theory of property rights. Berger's (1985) study has a similar economic theme.

B. MODERN ECONOMICS. Economic analysis of first possession began when Barzel (1968) examined the question of the optimal timing of innovation. He showed that the potential gains could be completely dissipated in a race to develop the innovation; because no one potential innovator could claim ownership of the idea, the race would cause the innovation to be introduced 'too early', thus reducing the present value of the innovation to zero. In essence, Barzel rediscovered the analysis of open access along a time dimension (Knight 1924; Gordon 1954). Wright (1983), in fact, shows that the race equilibrium is exactly analogous to Gordon's average-product rule for exploiting an open access resource. Barzel's study quickly spawned a highly theoretical literature on innovation and patent races whose notable contributors include Loury (1979), Dasgupta and Stiglitz (1980), and Mortensen (1982). This voluminous literature, which developed as game theory was making inroads into industrial organization, is summarized by Reinganum (1989).

The literature on innovation developed rapidly and remained narrowly focused on theoretical optima; yet there was little applied work on the larger issue of first possession. Economists tended to examine first possession rules on a case-by-case basis, ignoring the connection between seemingly distinct bodies of law. For instance, in studies of homesteading (Anderson and Hill 1990), oil and gas (Libecap and Wiggins 1984) and water (Williams 1983), first possession was criticized as an inefficient rule. Unlike political philosophers and legal scholars, the criticism from economists has emphasized that first possession has the potential to dissipate wealth, either from a wasteful race to claim an asset or as a rule of capture which leads to over-exploitation. Haddock (1986) generalized Barzel's argument and gave it wide application in the law. In concluding that first possession rules are generally wasteful, Haddock directly counters Epstein (1979, 1986) and Rose (1985). At the same time, in studies of the broadcast spectrum (Hazlett 1990), homesteading (Allen 1991), and patents and mining (Kitch 1977), economists argued that first possession can be an efficient method of establishing ownership. Taken together, the literature shows considerable disagreement among law and economics scholars on the merits of first possession rules (Merrill 1986). In recent work on property rights to monopoly gains, however, Barzel (1994) argues that dissipation from racing is likely to be mitigated because of heterogeneity among potential claimants. More recently, Lueck (1995) provides a generalization by linking models of racing with models of resource over-exploitation, and focusing on how subtle changes in legal rules can greatly reduce the potential dissipation inherent in first possession.

II. EFFICIENCY AND DISSIPATION UNDER FIRST POSSESSION

In his classic *The Common Law*, Oliver Wendell Holmes (1881: Lecture VI, 216) wrote: 'To gain possession, then, a man must stand in a certain physical relation to the object and to the rest of the world, and must have a certain intent. These relations and this intent are the facts of which we are in search.' As Holmes implied, first possession rules can operate on different margins. For instance, the rule can grant ownership of a barrel of oil to the first person that brings the oil to the surface, under the so-called rule of capture, or it can grant ownership of the entire underground reservoir to the first person that locates the reservoir. The behaviour of the possessor and the use of the oil will obviously differ in the two cases. In the former case, first possession applies to the *flow* of output from the *stock* of underground oil, while in the latter case the rule applies to the stock itself, a distinction recognized long ago by Blackstone (1766: Book II, ch. 1). Beginning with an unowned asset, the rule of first possession sets in motion a well-specified pattern of behaviour (Lueck 1995). If applied to a stock, private property rights are established directly through possession. On the other hand, if only a flow (or a portion of the stock) can be possessed, the rule of capture ensues. Even within these broad categories the precise meaning of possession can be important, as in the famous case of *Pierson v. Post* where the court was divided over whether possession of a wild fox was determined by 'hot pursuit' or physical capture.

First possession rules often vary as to the duration of the granted ownership right. For example, possession could grant ownership of a pasture in perpetuity or it could simply grant ownership of the grass currently being grazed by one's livestock. Perpetual ownership means ownership of the stock, while a shorter term of ownership means ownership of some flows. Rights to stocks implies ownership to the future stream of flows, so the formal economic model is intertemporal, while rights to flows means ownership is a one-time event, so the formal economic model examines just one period.

Consider an asset, such as a plot of land, an oil reservoir, or a new idea, that yields an instantaneous (net) flow of benefits $R(x(t))$, where $x(t)$ is the amount of a variable input supplied by private owners at time t. Let r be the interest rate and assume the flow value, $R(t)$, grows over time at the continuous rate $g < r$, so that the value of the asset grows over time, and that each period's return is independent of past returns. This formulation recognizes the usual case that during 'early' periods assets are not sufficiently valuable to cover the costs of establishing ownership. The first-best full-information value of the asset is

$$V^{FB} = \int_0^{\infty} R(x^*(t))e^{-(r-g)t}dt, \qquad (1)$$

where $x^*(t)$ is the optimal input level in period t. In general, V^{FB} is not attainable because of the costs of both establishing and enforcing rights that efficiently allocate use of the resource. Several possible first possession regimes are examined below and summarized in Table 1. Each regime is characterized by specific values for the time of possession (t), the number of users (n), the level of the variable input (x), the periodic rent (R), the cost of establishing ownership (C), and the net present value of the resource (V).

A. FIRST POSSESSION AND THE RACE TO ESTABLISH OWNERSHIP OF AN ASSET. Ownership under first possession goes to the first person to obtain possession of the entire stock. Assume that the method of possession does not damage other resources and that continued possession costs are zero. The first claimant thus obtains exclusive rights, into the indefinite future, to the flow of rents, $\int_0^{\infty} R(t)dt$, generated by the assets. Since establishing a bona fide claim will be costly and because $g < r$, rights may not be worth enforcing. Property rights to the asset will emerge, after an initial period without ownership, as the value of the asset increases (Demsetz 1967). As in Barzel (1968), maximizing resource value is a problem of optimally timing the establishment of rights under first possession.

The single claimant. Assume there are one-time costs, C, of establishing enforceable rights or demonstrating possession which give the claimant exclusive right to the stream of production for all time. If there is a single potential claimant, the flow from the asset is available after rights to the stock are established. The decision to claim the stock is the result of private maximization. The optimal time to establish ownership (t^s) is when the marginal return from waiting (the present value of the asset's rental flow) equals the marginal cost of waiting (the present value of the opportunity cost of establishing rights), so $V^S < V^{FB}$. This is because the net value of the asset must now account for the costs of establishing ownership and the fact that these costs delay ownership and production to t^s from $t = 0$ (see Table 1). If there is a competitive race among homogeneous claimants, rights are established 'too early' at t^R, where $t^R < t^S$ (Barzel 1968; Mortensen 1982). More important, the race equilibrium implies that the rental stream is fully dissipated; that is, $V^R = 0$.

Efficient claiming: heterogeneity and the race for lower costs. Heterogeneity among potential claimants can reduce, even eliminate, the dissipation of wealth (Barzel 1994; Lueck 1995). Assume there are just two competitors (i and j) for ownership of the asset with possession costs $C_i < C_j$. Also assume that neither party knows each other's costs. In a race, person i gains ownership just before the closest competitor makes a claim, at time $t^i = t^R - e$, and earns rent equal to the present discounted value of his cost advantage, V^{R_i}. The key implication is that as the heterogeneity of claimants ($C_j - C_i$) increases the level of dissipation will decrease. The analysis remains the same with rental value differentials such as $R_i \neq R_j$ or different expectations about the rate of growth of the flow value, $g_i \neq g_j$. In the extreme case, where just one person has costs less than the net present value of the asset's flows, the first-best outcome is achieved. Since only one person enters the race, there is no dissipation.

Table 1
Asset values for various first possession outcomes

ownership regime	present value of asset	t	n	x	R	C
First-best						
	$V^{FB} = \int_0^\infty R^*(t)e^{-(r-g)t}dt$	0	1	x^*	R^*	0
Single Claimant						
one-time claiming costs	$V^s = \int_{t^s}^\infty R^*(t)e^{-(r-g)t}\,dt - Ce^{-rt^S}$	$t^s > 0$	1	x^*	R^*	C
Race						
(a) Homogeneous claimants	$V^R = \int_{t^R}^\infty R^*(t)e^{-(r-g)t}dt - Ce^{-rt^R} = 0$	$t^R < t^s$	1	x^*	R^*	C
(b) Heterogeneous claimants *incomplete information*	$V^R_i = \int_{t^i}^\infty R[C_j - C_i]e^{-rt}dt$	$t^i < t^R$	1	x^*	R^*	$C_i < C_j$
(c) Heterogeneous claimants *complete information*	$V^R_i = V^S$	t^s	1	x^*	R^*	C_i
Open Access	$\lim_{n^{OA}\to\infty} V^{RC} = \int_0^\infty \sum_{i=1}^{n^{OA}} [R^{RC}_i(t,n^{OA})]e^{-(r-g)t}dt = 0$	0	n^{OA}	x^{OA}	0	0
Common Property *group size = n^C*	$V^C = \int_0^\infty \sum_{i=1}^{n^C} = [R^{RC}_i(t,n^C) - p(n^C)]e^{-(r-g)t}dt$	0	$n^C < n^{OA}$	x^C	R^{RC}	0
State Auction	$V^A = \int_{t^A}^\infty R^*(t)e^{-(r-g)t}\,dt - [C^A + C^E]e^{-rt^A}$	t^A	1	x^*	R^*	$C^A + C^E$

Source: Lueck (1995). t = time of resource use and possession
n = number of resources users
$p(n)$ = policing costs for common property
x = level of variable input use
R = periodic rent from resource

Altering the assumption about information can alter the racing equilibrium. Fudenberg et al. (1983) and Harris and Vickers (1985) show that if competitors have complete information about each other's talents a race will not ensue because only the low-cost individual will have a positive expected payoff of entering the race; that is, V^S is achieved if $C_i < C_j$, $i \neq j = 1, \ldots n$.

Even though claimant heterogeneity can limit, even eliminate, racing dissipation, there arises the possibility that a claimant can gain a cost advantage by expending resources, thereby altering the margins of dissipation (McFetridge and Smith 1980). For example, if competing claimants can acquire the technology to achieve the minimum costs (C_i), then homogeneity and the full dissipation equilibrium is re-established. This extreme result, however, relies on the questionable assumption that homogeneity can be attained easily by investing in the low cost claimant's technology. The more likely reality is that claimant costs depend not only on endogenous investment decisions but also on exogenous forces that generate and preserve heterogeneity. Consider two possibilities. First, if the distribution of talent across individuals is not equal, some people will have innate advantages that will be difficult or impossible to overcome with investment. Second, if there is random variability in opportunities, then some individuals will be in the position of being the low cost claimant; again, investment is unlikely to destroy the random advantage.

Because first possession is a rule that restricts competition to a time dimension, there is another reason why investment cannot routinely eliminate heterogeneity. Cost advantages, no matter how they were gained initially, are expected to diminish over time because potential investors ultimately will gain information that allows them to mimic the behaviour of the low cost person (Kitch 1977; Suen 1989). As long as costs depend on exogenous factors, dissipation will be incomplete. In the worst-case race equilibrium, the first claimant will own just the value of his exogenous advantage; in the best-case, extreme heterogeneity or the full information game theory equilibrium, the first claimant will own the full potential value, V^S, of the asset.

B. FIRST POSSESSION AND THE RULE OF CAPTURE FOR ASSET FLOWS. When the costs of enforcing a claim to the asset are prohibitive, ownership can be established only by capturing or 'reducing to possession' a flow from the asset. The rule of capture – simply a derivation of the rule of first possession – will occur when enforcing possession of the flow is cheaper than enforcing possession of the stock. Wildlife and crude oil are the classic examples: ownership is established only when a hunter bags a pheasant or when a barrel of oil is brought to the surface. The stock itself, be it the population of pheasant or the oil reservoir, remains unowned. As a result, the new 'race' is to claim the present flow, $R(t)$, by capturing the product (e.g., the dead pheasant) first.

Epstein (1986) notes that as a rule of capture, first possession can lead to classic open access dissipation. Under the rule of capture no one owns the asset's entire stream of flows, $\int_0^\infty R(t)dt$. As a result, the formal economic analysis of dissipation is now one-period, rather than inter-temporal as in the race. Assume *n* people have unrestricted access to the stock and that each maximizes his own rent subject to the rule of capture, which means that each person captures the flow in proportion to his share of total capture effort. Assuming homogeneous claimants, rent dissipation will increase with the number of users and in the limiting case of a large number of claimants, no one earns rent ($R_i^{RC} = 0$), so the aggregate per-period rent and the present value of the asset is also zero, or $V^{RC} = 0$ (Cheung 1970).

Common property: contractual–legal limits on the rule of capture. Restricting access to the stock creates a new ownership regime – common property – which is an intermediate case between open access and private ownership. Common property may arise out of explicit private contracting (e.g., unitized oil reservoirs, groundwater districts) or out of custom (e.g., common pastures and forests); it may have legal (e.g., riparian water rights) or regulatory (e.g., hunting and fishing rules) origins that have implicit contractual origins (Ostrom 1990). Contracting to form common property effectively creates a group that has exclusive rights to the resource (Eggertsson 1992; Lueck 1994). Acting together individuals can realize economies of enforcing exclusive rights to the asset.

A simple, customary common property rule is one allowing equal access to each group member (Blackstone 1766; Ostrom 1990). Equal sharing avoids the explicit costs of measuring and enforcing individual effort, but it does create a rule of capture *within the exclusive group*. Because individual effort is not explicitly part of the contract, each member chooses his own effort (X_i) as he captures his share of the resource's product in competition with other members. In a common property pasture, for example, this internal rule of capture might emerge as competition among members for that part of the pasture with the best grazing, whether for better grass or fewer predators. The size of the group is chosen in order to maximize group wealth subject to the constraints of each member's rule of capture effort level (X^{RC}) and the costs of excluding outsiders. Optimal group size is thus a trade-off between the increased resource use associated with a larger group and the increased exclusion costs associated with a smaller group (Eggertsson 1992; Lueck 1994). Common property falls short of the potential optimum (V^S), yet, given the prohibitive costs of establishing private rights to the asset, it provides an important alternative that limits open access dissipation and generates positive rents.

Homogeneous groups and common property. Dissipation from internal capture can be limited by maintaining a homogeneous membership (Lueck 1994, 1995). With equal sharing rules, a homogeneous membership actually maximizes the present value of a common property resource. Once a group chooses an equal sharing rule there is an incentive to maintain homogeneity. With heterogeneous members and equal shares, highly productive individuals will supply too little effort and the less productive will supply too much, so dissipation will increase. In effect, equal-sharing rules increase group wealth when homogeneity among group members is enforced. This provides an economic rationale for preserving homogeneity by screening potential members, by indoctrination, or by restricting the transfer of memberships.

C. EFFICIENT RESTRICTIONS ON TRANSFERRING RIGHTS. The distinction between stocks and flows also has implications for the efficient transfer of rights. When property rights are well defined, voluntary transfer is always wealth enhancing. If not, transfers can cause wealth-reducing externalities. (Epstein 1985; Rose-Ackerman 1985). Well-defined rights mean that exclusive rights are defined to the stock and, accordingly, its stream of flows over time. This implies that the law should allow rights transfers when first possession establishes clear ownership of resource stocks.

When first possession triggers the rule of capture, however, the rights to the stock remain ill defined. Legal and contractual restrictions on access can limit dissipation. If individuals having access rights under the rule of capture are allowed to trade their rights, however, dissipation can be even greater than when trade is restricted (Epstein 1985). For example, if a member of a common fishery sells his membership to an outsider with a superior fishing technique, the new member will 'over-fish', damaging the common resource and reducing its value to the other members who were not party to the exchange.

D. AUCTIONS AND ADMINISTRATIVE ALTERNATIVES. Law and economics scholars studying first possession have overwhelmingly recommended auctions as the efficient method of establishing rights without closely examining the costs of auctions (e.g., Coase 1959; Barzel 1968; Williams 1983; Haddock 1986; Posner 1992). Assuming the same costs of establishing the rights (C), the winner of the 'ideal' auction pays V^S and begins production at t^S, thus maximizing the value of the asset. Yet, in practice, auctions will entail real and often large costs (Epstein 1979; McMillan 1994). Under first possession, private claimants must bear the cost, Ce^{-rt}, of enforcing a claim to the resource. Similarly, before the auction can take place, the state must establish rights to the asset at a cost, C^Se^{-rt}, and also incur costs, C^Ae^{-rt}, of administering the auction. In addition, the state must survey and police the resource. The state also must determine what size parcels of the asset to sell, the method of auction to use, and so on (McMillan 1994). In addition, if the state cannot protect property rights adequately after the auction, potential buyers will bid less than V^*. Epstein (1979) also notes that interest groups will attempt to alter the auction rules to suit their own advantage leading to further dissipation of rent. Indeed, he notes that administrative alternatives simply were not available (i.e., too costly) during much of the development of the common law. As a result, only if the state's costs $(C^S + C^A)e^{-rt}$ are less than Ce^{-rt} will V^* result from an auction. The choice between auctions (or other administrative policies) and first possession is ultimately a trade-off between costly auctions and potential dissipation from races. In some cases – future patentable innovations, sunken treasure, and the unused electromagnetic spectrum – the resource cannot be auctioned because it has yet to be identified. Haddock (1986), despite his general criticism of first possession, favours first possession rules in these cases too.

III. THE DESIGN OF THE LAW: IMPLICATIONS AND EVIDENCE. Once the two potential paths of dissipation (racing and over-exploitation) are recognized, an analysis of the law of first possession reveals an economic logic (Lueck 1995). When first possession has the potential for a race, the law tends to mitigate dissipation by assigning possession when claimant heterogeneity is greatest. On the other hand, when first possession breeds a rule of capture, the law tends to limit access and restrict the transfer of access rights to limit open access exploitation. A strictly legal definition of 'first possession' applies to a relatively small set of circumstances such as unclaimed land and deep-sea treasure. The economic approach, on the other hand, recognizes many applications of first possession. Judicial opinions and statutes may use such terms as 'first in time, first in right', 'priority in time', or the 'rule of capture'. The definitions provided by legal scholars vary too. For instance, Dukeminier and Krier (1993: 3) call first possession 'acquisition of property by discovery, capture, creation'. Regardless of the precise legal terminology, all of the subjects examined below are governed by rules in which legitimate ownership is created by establishing possession before anyone else. Table 2 summarizes the first possession rule in each of the cases discussed below.

A. FIRST POSSESSION: ESTABLISHING OWNERSHIP OF AN ASSET. In those cases where first possession rules establish ownership in a resource stock, a number of common principles are evident. First, possession is defined so that valid claims are made at low cost and before dissipating races begin, thus exploiting claimant heterogeneity. Second, once rights are established the transfer of rights to the resource is allowed routinely. Third, the use of auctions or other administrative allocation mechanisms are high cost alternatives.

Unowned and unclaimed chattels. In *Armory v. Delamirie*, the classic English case, a chimney sweep is awarded title to a jewel found on the job. Essentially, the 'finder can acquire title against all the world' by demonstrating the intent to acquire the property and demonstrating possession or a high degree of control (Schoenbaum 1987). The law of finds, which has both common law and statutory authority, includes lost property (involuntary parting), abandoned property (voluntary parting), salvaged property (property retrieved from the ocean), and treasure trove. Under property law, the finder tends to get either all or none of the find, but salvage rules under maritime law allow for a division of the spoils (sunken ships and their cargo) between the finder and the former owner. The salvor, however, does have priority rights over all other claimants besides the original owner. In a recent sunken treasure case, *Columbus-America Discovery Group, Inc. v. Atlantic Mutual Ins. Co.*, the court allowed the establishment of rights through the use of remote video cameras which produced live images – coining the term 'telepossession' – and did not require physical possession. The court held that the first finder could legitimately use cameras to show its capability of retrieving the treasure. Granting ownership prior to the bulk of the production process prevented costly duplication in exploration.

Land. Throughout history land has been reduced to ownership via first possession, often called 'initial occupation'. First possession of land has determined initial ownership under the English Common Law (*terra nullius*), traditional Subsaharan African law, and Islamic law (Blackstone 1766; Lawson 1975). Within the United States, the establishment of private rights to extensive government holdings relied on both first possession rules and land sales. In *Johnson v. M'Intosh*, Chief Justice John Marshall traced the original title of the entire United States to first possession ('discovery' of *terra nullius*) by the white man. Rose (1985) argues that first possession, not discovery, better describes the case, since arguably in many cases tribes never possessed clear title.

Table 2
Examples of first possession rules

Resource	Possession rule	Stock-flow and duration of right
Chattels (abandoned, lost, unclaimed)	recover or show intent to recover	stock – permanent
Commons (pasture, forest, turf)	graze, gather wood or turf	share of stock – internal capture rule
Groundwater – absolute ownership	bring water to surface	flow – current pumping
Groundwater – correlative rights	bring water to surface	share of stock – internal capture rule
Intellectual property	first to invent, write	stock – varies (17–100 years)
Land	occupation, cultivation	stock – permanent
Minerals (hard rock)	locate mineral deposit	stock – permanent
Ocean fisheries	land fish	flow – current catch
Petroleum	bring oil to surface	flow – current production
Radio spectrum	broadcast a signal	stock – permanent
Water – appropriation doctrine	develop a diversion plan	stock – permanent
Water – riparian doctrine	pump or divert	flow – current use
Wild game	kill or capture	flow – current kill

After the American Revolution the states ceded their unsettled western lands to the federal government for the purposes of disposal to the citizenry. Although early disposal policies emphasized sales, first possession became the dominant policy. Squatting was common from the beginning of the Republic. The Preemption Act of 1830, as well as other preemption laws, legitimized the claims of squatters. The Homestead Act of 1862 went further, establishing a formal system of land claims based on first possession. The growth of squatting and its formal recognition by the preemption acts indicate that the cost of enforcing rights to land by non-users was increasing as the frontier rapidly expanded beyond established settlements (Kanazawa 1996). Similarly, the move to homesteading and the abandonment of land sales indicated the high cost of policing land in a distant frontier by non-resident owners (Allen 1991). Under preemption and squatting there were rules that limited the size of claims and defined the terms under which legitimate possession could be obtained. Squatters formed local associations known as 'claim clubs' that established rules for governing claim sizes and for settling disputes between competing claimants (Kanazawa 1996); federal homesteading policies limited the acreage that could be claimed and typically required some active form of use (e.g., cultivation, timber harvest) before the claim matured into legal title.

Hard rock mining. In both England and the United States, the common law doctrine of *ad coelum* grants landowners the exclusive rights to subsurface minerals (Barringer and Adams 1900; Lindley 1903). The mineral rights are severable and transferable just like other attributes of real property. Extensive public land holdings in the United States, however, required a modification of the common law approach. As usual, exceptions to this rule could be found. In England, the Crown retained rights to all gold and silver or 'royal' mines and in some areas – notably the tin regions in Cornwall and Devon – a custom developed whereby those first discovering a vein of ore gained legal title to that vein wherever it led them. In the United States similar customs developed on unsettled public lands, most notably in the gold fields of California during the middle of the nineteenth century. Lindley (1903) documents how these customs were introduced into America by both Cornish miners who had initially settled in the Midwest and by Mexican miners who moved to California after the discovery of gold there. A complex body of custom and law quickly emerged to govern the size of claims and settle disputes over conflicting claims to a body of ore (Umbeck 1977).

The General Mining Law of 1872 (still in force, though amended) codified these customary rights, allowing people to establish bona fide claims to tracts of public land for the extraction of minerals. To get a patent to mineral land, the miner must find a valuable deposit, locate the claim, do assessment work, and finally apply for a patent. While prospecting, and before discovery, the miner's claim is legally protected under the customary doctrine of *pedis possessio* (Leshy 1987). Mining law gives full transferable title to the mineral bearing land to the first person who discovers a deposit. Claimants need not show that the deposit is commercially important, but only that surface mineralization is present. Granting patentable title early on in the process effectively limits excessive investment.

Intellectual property. The protection of intellectual property – copyrights, patents, and trademarks – has it roots in the common law and the US Constitution (Blackstone 1766; Chisum and Jacobs 1992). Because intellectual property is perhaps the most conspicuous kind of undiscovered (i.e., unowned) property, the auction alternative makes little sense. Accordingly, Dukeminier and Krier (1993) call this first possession rule 'acquisition by creation'. The rules for establishing possession of intellectual property assets address the potential for wasteful races by granting ownership 'early', when claimant heterogeneity is still large. The limited duration of the right (17 years for patents and 100 years for copyrights) also can mitigate dissipation even when a race occurs. Haddock (1986) notes that the public good character of ideas might reduce the incentive to race. Exclusive and transferable patent rights are acquired under a 'first to invent' policy (Chisum and Jacobs 1992). Patentable ideas do not require commercial success, but only evidence that the invention will work regardless of its likely value. Like patents, copyrights are also exclusive and transferable; they are established automatically when a work is created. Although historically copyright protection has required notice and registration, these formalities have recently been removed. As a result, current copyright protection is simple to obtain. Because a work must be original to receive copyright protection, first possession is the rule for rights acquisition. Trademark law, just like patents and copyrights, grants exclusive and transferable rights to marks that distinguish a merchant's product from those of others. Similarly, trademarks are acquired by adoption and use. The mark must be original and distinct from the marks of others and, in case of conflicts, 'first to use' determines priority. Grady and Alexander (1992) point out that dissipation might occur at both the initial idea stage and later when improvements are developed. More important, they examine numerous cases and show convincingly that court decisions regarding patentable subject matter and the scope of patents implicitly consider various margins for dissipation.

The radio spectrum. Although the regulation and use of the radio spectrum has generated significant attention from economists ever since the seminal studies by Coase (1959) and Herzel (1951), little attention has been given to the early days of radio broadcasting during which rights to spectrum use were assigned using a first possession rule. During the 1920s, the initial assignment of broadcast rights in the spectrum were granted on a 'priority-in-use' rule by the Commerce Department, which had licensing authority under the 1912 Radio Act (Hazlett 1990). These rights were exclusive, transferable, and traded in an active market. When, in 1926, the Commerce Department officially abandoned the first possession rule, the spectrum devolved from private property to open access, resulting in a period of 'chaos' fraught with 'wave jumping' and frequency 'pirates' and other symptoms of over-exploitation. Tremendous dissipation – manifest as chaos – created incentives to re-establish spectrum ownership and the state courts were quickly awash with interference cases. In *Tribune Co. v. Oak Leaves Broadcasting System*, the court assigned property rights to radio broadcasting on the priority-in-use basis used by the Commerce Department a few years earlier. Other courts appeared likely to follow the example in *Oak Leaves*, but by February 1927 the Radio Act was law; the federal government had claimed ownership of the spectrum. The radio spectrum is a neat illustration of first possession rules establishing ownership in a previously undiscovered resource. Auctions during the 1920s would have been unworkable during the initial era of radio use. Beginning in 1994, however, the FCC auctioned off spectrum previously used by the military for use in personal communications services ('PCS') such as pocket telephones, portable fax machines, and wireless computer networks (McMillan 1994). Notably, the auction does not establish property rights but merely reallocates existing rights.

Water: prior appropriation. In nineteen western states, case law and statutes have now codified a system of customary law that originally developed among miners in the 1800s (Trelease and Gould 1986; Scott and Coustalin 1995). During this period, those claiming the vast unsettled public lands of the West for mineral exploitation required the diversion and use of water at locations distant from adjacent ('riparian') land. The common law doctrine available at the time excluded the use of water by those who did not own riparian land. As a result, miners developed a new customary system of water rights called prior appropriation, which separated rights to water from rights to land. Many state court decisions supported these customs. *Coffin v. Left Hand Ditch Co.*, in particular, is often cited as a leading case because the Colorado Supreme Court formally established the prior appropriation doctrine and explicitly rejected the older common law doctrine of riparian rights. The doctrine of prior appropriation severs water rights from the land by granting permanent ownership of a portion of surface water body on a priority-in-use basis.

Possession under prior appropriation requires the *diversion* of water with the *intent* of beneficial use, typically for such out-of-stream uses as irrigation or mining. Establishing bona fide appropriation does not require the completion of water projects or specific use. Moreover, in modern administrative systems, state water authorities often date appropriation from the time of permit application, so no actual diversion is initially required. By allowing claims to be made 'early' in the process of water use, the costs of possession remain low and the potential for races is reduced. In fact, diversion need not always be physical to establish beneficial use. Uses such as livestock watering, natural irrigation, and recently, in-stream uses have been recognized as legitimate appropriations (Tarlock et al 1993).

B. FIRST POSSESSION: THE RULE OF CAPTURE FOR ASSET FLOWS. In certain cases, establishing possession of an entire stock is especially costly and leads to the rule of capture, as in the case of so-called 'fugitive' resources (Rose 1986) such as oil and wildlife. In these cases a number of common principles can be found. First, the rule of capture may not produce severe dissipation when there are but a few users or when there are 'plenteous' goods (Rose 1986). Open access may persist optimally as in the case of nineteenth-century whaling. Second, when dissipation becomes severe, access to the resource tends to be limited through legal, contractual, or regulatory methods. Third, transfer of rights to capturable flows tends to be restricted, unlike the previous legal domains where rights tend to be freely transferable.

The commons. In feudal England, both custom and common law doctrine often defined rights – which inhered to groups – to certain attributes of what was otherwise private land. The commons of pasture (grass), estover (wood), diggings (coals and stones), turbary (sod), and piscary (fish), for example, allowed township citizens access to these characteristics of the land (Blackstone 1766; Rose 1986), while the cultivated crops remained private. Under the law of 'commons' the rule of capture was limited by establishing common property rights. English villagers had equal access to the common resources and transfers of these rights were not allowed. Although equal sharing can appear to be a rule of capture, the exclusion of outsiders generates rents for members of the group. The routine prohibition of selling one's membership presumably enhances homogeneity among users by effectively restricting each member's rights to use only for household consumption.

Similar common property arrangements have been found throughout the world, including in the United States (Lawson 1975; McCay and Acheson 1987; Ostrom 1990). During the Colonial Period there was extensive use of commons for grazing, wood gathering, and even fruit collection. In the northern states common pastures seem to have been replaced by private holdings in the late 1800s, but in the South grazing commons (under open range or 'fence-out' laws) persisted until the late 1970s. In 1922, Justice Holmes (*McKee v. Gratz*) noted the widespread American tradition of allowing local citizens common hunting access on undeveloped private lands. Today this type of common property is rare in the formal law, although the lobster territories in Maine are an informal case.

Wild game. The rule of capture has been the fundamental property doctrine for wildlife since the beginning of the English common law (Lueck 1989). In one of the most famous American property law cases, *Pierson v. Post*, the court considered the possession, and hence, ownership of a wild fox, and ruled that the first possessor gains ownership of the wild fox. Further, the court ruled that possession required physical capture and not simply 'hot pursuit'. The manifestly high cost of establishing possession of live animal populations meant that they were not subject to ownership until *individual animals* were killed (the usual case) or otherwise physically captured. The potential for open access dissipation, in turn, created incentives for the modification of legal institutions.

By the nineteenth century the common law had effectively established ownership rights in wild game to English landowners, essentially creating private ownership of live stocks. Meanwhile, in the United States, where private ownership of live stocks of game was prohibitively expensive because of both small, scattered private landholdings and wide-ranging species, states were granted extensive regulatory control over access and use of wildlife. In the United States, there are severe restrictions and outright prohibitions on wildlife product markets; in Great Britain, however, legal game markets thrive.

Ocean fisheries. Not surprisingly, the legal history of ocean fisheries is comparable to the history of wild game (Edwards 1994). Like wild game, the dominant rule was the rule of capture. Even here the rule could vary, as Holmes (1881) and later Ellickson (1989) noted in nineteenth-century Atlantic whaling. The rule of capture typically required that a whaler's harpoon be fixed to the mammal before a legitimate ownership interest was established, the 'fast-fish, loose-fish' rule. In the case of the aggressive sperm whale, however, the 'iron holds the whale' rule granted ownership to a whaler whose harpoon first was affixed to the whale so long as the whaler remained in fresh pursuit. Holmes and Ellickson clearly recognize how the precise way in which possession is defined will influence the outcome and how the law tends to define possession so that waste (e.g., fruitless whaling effort) will be minimized.

As expected, the potential for rent dissipation under a rule of capture was often great enough to lead to the formation of rights to live fish stocks. Because of the economies of group enforcement, common property rights to fisheries have been widespread in North America and around the world (McEvoy 1986; Durrenberger and Palsson 1987; McCay and Acheson 1987). In the United States, antitrust suits brought against fishermen's associations in the middle of this century have prevented groups from further limiting access to fishery stocks. In other cases, new technologies (e.g., large capacity fishing vessels) led to the erosion of informal common property fisheries. Also, until the Fishery Conservation and Management Act of 1976 (FCMA) gave the United States the authority to limit foreign fishing within 200 miles of the coast, there was no mechanism to establish a formal system of rights to ocean stocks. Historically, the eight Regional Fishery Management Councils established by FCMA have simply regulated total catch or fishing effort; because these rules do not limit access to the stocks, dissipation is still severe in many fisheries.

In the past decade, however, the regional councils have altered their policies by establishing individual transferable quotas (ITQs) systems in several fisheries (e.g., Atlantic wreckfish, Pacific halibut, sablefish). An ITQ system limits total annual catch and allocates a permanent, transferable share of the catch through quotas. By establishing limits to periodic claims on flows, ITQs indirectly establish rights to the fish stocks. ITQ policies have also been implemented in Australia, Canada, Iceland, and New Zealand, and may well be the preferred policy for future fisheries management. Once an ITQ system is chosen to govern a specific fishery, the initial allocation of 'quota' must be determined. As a rule, existing fishermen have been given quota rights based on historical catch records. In essence, this or any other 'grandfather' rule is a first possession rule. This is especially true for the Atlantic wreckfish and the orange roughy in New Zealand. Both of these fish stocks were discovered during the 1980s and the overwhelming share of ITQs was formally allocated to those fishermen who first discovered and exploited those stocks.

Oil and gas. As with hard rock minerals, the doctrine of *ad coelum* gives landowners the rights to drill for oil and gas, yet oil and gas law has more in common with wildlife law than the law of hard rock minerals. The fluidity of oil and gas beneath the surface of numerous landowners makes it prohibitively costly for surface owners to establish rights to 'their' stocks as against those of neighbouring drillers, leading to the rule of capture (Hardwicke 1935; Kramer and Martin 1989). The principle, if not the term 'rule of capture', emerged first in the 1889 case of *Westmoreland Natural Gas Company v. DeWitt* in which the Supreme Court of Pennsylvania clearly stated that ownership of land is not sufficient to have ownership of the gas lying below it. In *Westmoreland* the court also made the analogy between wild animals and oil and gas. Under this rule of capture rights to the stock of oil or gas remain ill-defined, but rights to the flows are clear once they have been brought to the surface.

As with wildlife, there have been legal-contractual modifications to the rule of capture that have arisen to mitigate waste (Craft 1995; Lueck and Schenewerk 1996). Because oil, like wildlife and water, is attached to land, contracting among landowners offers a solution to the rule of capture. Private 'unitization' contracts have sometimes emerged to coordinate the actions of those with surface access to oil and gas. In many cases, however, the cost of forming units is prohibitive (Libecap and Wiggins 1984). Statutory 'conservation' regulation has emerged in two prominent ways to mitigate rule of capture waste by limiting access to the stocks of oil and gas underlying numerous surface holdings. First, most oil and gas producing states have well-spacing requirements that limit the density of wells and prevent adjacent surface owners from drilling along their property lines to deplete their neighbours' reserves. Second, nearly all states compel the formation of units if a super-majority of the surface owners agree (Kramer and Martin 1989). The regulations governing the Outer Continental Shelf (OCS) lands are in direct contrast to regulations for on-shore production on private land. OCS resources, owned by the US government and administered by the Minerals Management Service (MMS), are available for private exploitation through a system of leasing in which large tracts are leased in competitive auctions. In this case, oil 'land' is essentially owned by a single entity (MMS) so that rule of capture problems are usually avoided, except in cases where adjacent lessees have access to the same reservoir.

Water: riparian doctrine. The traditional legal doctrine governing water in the United States is the riparian doctrine. The riparian system, in contrast to the appropriation doctrine, limits the rule of capture by creating common property rights in the water stock among riparian landowners. In *Tyler v. Wilkinson*, Justice Story settled a dispute by stating that among riparians a stream was owned 'in perfect equality of right'. Riparian rights are governed by the common law and in their modern form grant 'correlative' and 'reasonable use' rights to water for landowners whose property borders a body of water. Riparian water rights are tied to the riparian land, require that water be used only on that land, and may not be sold apart from the land. The law implicitly defines the group (riparians) that equally shares access to the water resource (Epstein 1985; Rose 1990). The common property analysis shows, however, that an element of the rule of capture is still present. This means that dissipation increases with the number of riparians. Statutory restrictions on new uses have emerged in many riparian jurisdictions, presumably to further limit excessive water exploitation among a large group of users. And, like many common property regimes, riparian law prohibits transfers of water rights.

Groundwater law has similarities with the law of oil and gas as well as riparian water law. In ruling on a conflict between two parties drilling in the same aquifer, an English court developed the 'absolute ownership' rule on groundwater (*Acton v. Blundell*). By this doctrine the landowner has 'absolute' rights to pump underground water without liability to any other groundwater users. Despite the name, this is identical to the rule of capture doctrine in oil and gas law. The plaintiff in *Acton v. Blundell* had been pumping water for twenty years longer than the defendant and claimed, by first possession, perpetual ownership of the quantity of water he had, historically, been using. On the other hand, the defendant claimed, again by first possession, ownership of any water he could bring to the surface from his well. The debate in this case exactly mimics the stock–flow distinction made earlier in this essay. American law adopted this English rule but, as expected, the absolute ownership doctrine has led to overexploitation problems in areas where the number of users has become large relative to groundwater supplies. In some cases, private landowners have effectively unitized aquifers by forming groundwater districts (Ostrom 1990). In many other jurisdictions, however, the development of 'reasonable use' and 'correlative rights' doctrines limited the rule of capture by making groundwater users liable for at least some of the effects on neighbouring wells. Both of these rules are like riparian rights to surface water because they create an equal-sharing rule for those landowners whose holdings overlie the groundwater basin. As with surface water, western states have tended to go one step further by establishing a prior appropriation doctrine which, following the argument by the plaintiff in *Acton v. Blundell*, grants a perpetual right to withdraw a specific quantity of groundwater.

IV. COMPLICATIONS AND EXTENSIONS. The evidence supports an economic logic inherent in first possession rules, yet many issues remain unexamined. I briefly discuss four such issues: abandonment and continued possession efforts; defining possession to assets with many valuable characteristics; applications to new resources; and first possession in the private sector.

What must be done to maintain a legitimate claim? Though the law tends not to require a claimant to continually exert the effort required for an initial claim, he cannot remain an owner without incurring some continued possession costs (Holmes 1881). An owner must actively and continuously enforce his ownership claim, regardless whether he obtained ownership by first possession or by subsequent method such as purchase, inheritance, or bankruptcy. The law has two responses to a party lax in exerting effort at continued possession. If an owner intentionally ignores the property it can become abandoned and subject to being reclaimed under first possession. In certain cases (e.g., minerals, trademarks, water), specific rules, often lumped together as use-it-or-lose-it, have developed to determine precisely when the right has been abandoned. If an owner is simply inattentive enough to allow another party to establish continued use of the property, the adverse users can ultimately gain ownership under the doctrine of adverse possession (Dukeminier and Krier 1993). Each of these crucial issues – first possession, continued possession, and abandonment – is made clear in *Haslem v. Lockwood*, an 1871 case from Connecticut involving a dispute over manure piles. In *Haslem* the plaintiff was a farmer who gathered into 'heaps' manure from the ditch along a public highway, leaving them overnight while he returned to his farm to get a cart for transport of the heaps. Before he returned the defendant had begun to load the heaps and take them away. The court, in deciding for the plaintiff, ruled that the manure was abandoned property in the public ditch, that the plaintiff established ownership via first possession by piling the dung into heaps, and finally, that the plaintiff having established ownership did not have to exert the same effort to maintain possession and was therefore justified in returning home to fetch his carts. Implicit in this case and elsewhere is the fact that collective institutions (e.g., courts, custom, police) actively enforce property rights once they are established, thus minimizing the resources devoted to continued possession. The general trend of not requiring the same effort for continuing possession as for establishing possession is plausibly a recognition of economies of enforcement by collective institutions and a protection of specific investments by the original claimant.

Most, if not all, assets have numerous valuable attributes. An important case is land, valuable not only for surface uses but also possibly for game, minerals, oil, and water. A first possession rule that leads to an optimal system of ownership for one attribute can leave rights unspecified to another attribute. Establishing rights to land for farming, for instance, might create a system of rights inconsistent with the optimal use of wildlife or groundwater. The process of establishing possession might cause damage to adjacent environmental assets, as when the diversion of water under prior appropriation damages instream resources (Leshy 1987; Sprankling 1996). Indeed, the application of first possession to environmental goods (e.g., scenic view) is not well developed in the law. Private contracting to consolidate land holdings is a possible solution to the ownership problem for the attached resource, but this is an imperfect solution when contracting costs are positive (Libecap and Wiggins 1984). For example, detailed property rights to small, urban parcels of land can lead to severe open access dissipation for subsurface oil and gas production.

Possession rules can also swing dramatically from a rule of capture to a perpetual right to a stock. Water law illustrates the issue clearly. Under absolute ownership a landowner can claim groundwater under the rule of capture by pumping water to the surface; under prior appropriation, however, a successful first claimant earns a permanent withdrawal right to a measured quantity extracted each year. Indeed, such a switch in regimes begs the question of what is the actual stock that is valuable to potential users. Is the bison herd the valuable stock, or is a single bison (which can yield meat and hides) a valuable stock in its own right? Ultimately the answer depends on the uses of the resource as well as on the relative costs (e.g., claiming possession, enforcing common property).

While their treatment in legal texts suggests otherwise, first possession rules are still relevant and likely to be important in the future. Berger (1985) notes many cases not examined here where first possession is the primary rule. For example, while the common law has tended to move away from the 'coming to the nuisance' doctrine, nearly all states have enacted 'right to farm' statutes which effectively codify this first possession principle, namely that no one can make a legitimate nuisance claim for activities in place prior to a location decision by the affected party (Berger 1985). The recent trend in environmental regulation toward using transferable emissions permits requires initial allocations of the permits. As with fisheries ITQs, current polluters are usually grandfathered in to the permit system based on historical emissions as in the case of the sulphur dioxide trading programme under the Clean Air Act amendments of 1990. Some economists have considered this a 'free distribution' (Stavins 1995) or 'give away', but it is more appropriately viewed as an allocation based on first possession. In these cases, first possession may protect the specific investments made by the original users of the assets and avoid the administrative and rent-seeking costs of auctions. Though it might seem reasonable to think that the era of discovering new resources has long passed, space (McDougal et al. 1963) and the deep sea may have surprises to offer. In space, geosynchronous satellite orbits have been claimed by first possessors, but the deep sea has been treated differently. Epstein (1979) noted that the Law of the Sea conference rejected first possession rules for allocating claims to deep sea minerals.

The use of customary first possession rules in businesses, families, and other social settings is universal. In business, first possession is used to establish rights to customer service and to claim merchandise for later purchase (e.g., earnest money, 'holds'). Most of this customary first possession is arguably used for claims on assets whose demand changes frequently and whose prices are costly to change. In families, first possession is used to allocate household goods such as books, chairs, and tools. Within families, first possession is arguably an internal rule of capture associated with common property ownership of family resources and is simply a cheap method of allocating temporary uses of an asset. First possession is also well known in labour contracts where it manifests itself as 'seniority' privileges for layoffs, overtime and other perquisites (Berger 1985). In all of these cases there is either an unowned resource or an unspecified attribute of the resource.

V. CONCLUSIONS. Property rights are an important social invention because they create incentives for people to maintain and invest in resources which leads to specialization and trade. Yet, property rights themselves are economic goods that must be created. Overwhelmingly, first possession has been the chosen method by which rights are established both in custom and in law. Compared to the real alternatives, first possession rules are neither systematically inefficient nor are they routinely unjust. Systematic inefficiency is contradicted by a close inspection of the law which reveals an implicit recognition of potential dissipation and systematic efforts to reduce or avoid it. Routine injustice is contradicted by a system that protects the investments of individuals from the arbitrary claims of others. People tenaciously stick to the rule of first possession because it works to establish the property rights necessary for the creation of wealth.

DEAN LUECK

See also AUCTIONS OF RIGHTS TO PUBLIC PROPERTY; COMMON PROPERTY; JUSTICE; LOCKE, JOHN; POSSESSION; PROPERTY RIGHTS IN THE ELECTROMAGNETIC SPECTRUM; RIPARIAN RIGHTS; SELF-GOVERNANCE OF COMMON-POOL RESOURCES; UNITIZATION; WILDLIFE LAW.

Subject classification: 2b(i); 5b(i).

STATUTES

Fishery Conservation and Management Act of 1976 (codified at 18 USCA §§1972, 1973).
Homestead Act of 1862 (codified at 43 USCA §§161 et seq. repealed in 1976).
Mining Law of 1872 (codified at 30 USCA §§22–39).
Preemption Act of 1830 (codified at 43 USCA §§174, 251, 890 et seq.).
Radio Act of 1927 (codified at USCA 47 §1515 et seq.).

CASES

Acton v. Blundell (1843) 12 M&W 324.
Armory v. Delamirie (1722) 1 Str. 505.
Coffin v. Left Hand Ditch Co., 6 Colo 443 (Colo 1882).
Columbus-America Discovery Group, Inc. v. Atlantic Mutual Ins. Co., 974 F2d 450 (4th Cir. 1992).
Haslem v. Lockwood, 37 Conn. 500 (1871).
Johnson v. M'Intosh, 21 US 543 (1823).
McKee v. Gratz, 260 US 127 (1922).
O'Reilly v. Morse, 56 US 62 (1853).
Pierson v. Post, 3 NY Rep. 175 (NY 1805).
Tribune Co. v. Oak Leaves Broadcasting System, (Cir. Ct. Cook County, Illinois, 1926) reprinted in 68 Cong. Rec. 216 (10 December 1926).
Tyler v. Wilkinson, 24 F Cases 472 (RI 1827).
Westmoreland Natural Gas Company v. DeWitt, 18 A 724 (Pa 1889).

BIBLIOGRAPHY

Allen, D.W. 1991. Homesteading and property rights: or, 'how the West was really won'. *Journal of Law and Economics* 34: 1–23.

Anderson, T.L. and Hill, P.J. 1975. The evolution of property rights: a study of the American west. *Journal of Law and Economics* 18: 163–79.

Anderson, T.L. and Hill, P.J. 1990. The race for property rights. *Journal of Law and Economics* 33: 177–98.

Barringer, D.M. and Adams, J.S. 1900. *The Law of Mines and Mining in the United States*. V. 2 St. Paul: Keefe-Davidson.

Barzel, Y. 1968. The optimal timing of innovations. *Review of Economics and Statistics* 50: 348–55.

Barzel, Y. 1994. The capture of wealth by monopolists and the protection of property rights. *International Review of Law and Economics* 14: 393–409.

Becker, L.C. 1977. *Property Rights: Philosophical Foundations*. London: Routledge & Kegan Paul.

Berger, L. 1985. An analysis of the doctrine that 'first in time is first in right.' *Nebraska Law Review* 64: 349–88.

Blackstone, W. 1766. *Commentaries on the Laws of England, Book II*. Chicago: University of Chicago Press, 1979.

Cheung, S.N.S. 1970. The structure of a contract and the theory of a nonexclusive resource. *Journal of Law and Economics* 13: 49–70.

Chisum D.S. and Jacobs, M.A. 1992. *Understanding Intellectual Property Law*. New York: Matthew Bender.

Cohen, M.R. 1927. Property and sovereignty. *Cornell Law Quarterly* 13: 8–30.

Coase, R.H. 1959. The Federal Communications Commission. *Journal of Law and Economics* 2: 1–40.

Craft, R.L. 1995. Of reservoir hogs and pelt fiction: defending the *ferae naturae* analogy between petroleum and wildlife. *Emory Law Journal* 44: 697–733.

Dasgupta, P. and Stiglitz, J. 1980. Uncertainty, industrial structure, and the speed of R&D. *Bell Journal of Economics* 11: 1–28.

Demsetz, H. 1967. Toward a theory of property rights. *American Economic Review* Papers and Proceedings 57: 347–59.

Dukeminier, J. and Krier, J.E. 1993. *Property*. 3rd edn, Boston: Little, Brown.

Durrenberger, E.P. and Palsson, G. 1987. Ownership at sea: fishing territories and access to sea resources. *American Ethnologist* 14: 508–22.

Edwards, S.F. 1994. Ownership of renewable ocean resources. *Marine Resource Economics* 9: 253–73.

Eggertsson, T. 1992. Analyzing institutional successes and failures: a millennium of common mountain pastures in Iceland. *International Review of Law and Economics* 12: 423–37.

Ellickson, R.C. 1989. A hypothesis of wealth-maximizing norms: evidence from the whaling industry. *Journal of Law, Economics, and Organization* 5: 83–97.

Ellickson, R.C. 1991. *Order Without Law*. Cambridge, MA: Harvard University Press.

Ellickson, R.C. 1993. Property in land. *Yale Law Journal* 102: 1315–1400.

Epstein, R.A. 1979. Possession as the root of title. *Georgia Law Review* 13: 1221–43.

Epstein, R.A. 1985. Why restrain alienation? *Columbia Law Review* 85: 970–90.

Epstein, R.A. 1986. Past and future: the temporal dimension of the law of property. *Washington University Law Quarterly* 64: 667–722.

Fudenberg, D., Gilbert, R., Stiglitz, J. and Tirole, J. 1983. Preemption, leapfrogging, and competition in patent races. *European Economic Review* 22: 3–31.

Gordon, H.S. 1954. The economic theory of a common-property resource: the fishery. *Journal of Political Economy* 62: 124–42.

Grady, M.F. and Alexander. J.I. 1992. Patent law and rent dissipation. *Virginia Law Review* 78: 305–50.

Haddock, D.D. 1986. First possession versus optimal timing: limiting the dissipation of economic value. *Washington University Law Quarterly* 64: 775–92.

Hardwicke, R.E. 1935. The rule of capture and its implications as applied to oil and gas. *Texas Law Review* 13: 391–422.

Harris, C. and Vickers, J. 1985. Perfect equilibrium in a model of a race. *Review of Economic Studies* 52: 193–209.

Hazlett, T.W. 1990. The rationality of U.S. regulation of the broadcast spectrum. *Journal of Law and Economics* 33: 133–75.

Herzel, L. 1951. 'Public interest' and the market in color television regulation. *University of Chicago Law Review* 18: 802–16.

Holmes, O.W. 1881. *The Common Law*. Boston: Little, Brown; 40th printing, 1946.

Johnson R.N., Gisser, M. and Werner, M. 1981. The definition of a surface water right and transferability. *Journal of Law and Economics* 24: 273–88.

Kanazawa, M.T. 1996. Possession is nine points of the law: the political economy of early public land disposal. *Explorations in Economic History* 33: 227–49.

Kitch, E. 1977. The nature and function of the patent system. *Journal of Law and Economics* 20: 265–90.

Kitch, E. 1980. Patents, prospects, and economic surplus: a reply. *Journal of Law and Economics*. 23: 205–7.

Knight, F. 1924. Some fallacies in the interpretation of social cost. *Quarterly Journal of Economics* 38: 582–606.

Kramer, B. and Martin, P.H. 1989. *The Law of Pooling and Unitization*. 3rd edn, New York: Matthew Bender.

Lawson, F.H. (ed.) 1975. *International Encyclopedia of Comparative Law*, Volume VI. Paris: J.C.B. Mohr.

Leshy, J.D. 1987. *The Mining Law*. Washington, D.C.: Resources for the Future.

Libecap, G.D. and Wiggins, S.N. 1984 Contractual responses to the common pool: prorationing of crude oil. *American Economic Review* 74: 87–98.

Lindley, C.H. 1903. *A Treatise on the American Law Relating to Mines and Mineral Lands*. 2nd edn, San Francisco: Bancroft-Whitney Company.

Locke, J. 1690. *Two Treatises of Government*. Ed. P. Laslett; 2nd edn, Cambridge: Cambridge University Press, 1963.

Loury, G.C. 1979. Market structure and innovation. *Quarterly Journal of Economics* 93: 395–410.

Lueck, D. 1989. The economic nature of widlife law. *Journal of Legal Studies* 18: 291–324.

Lueck, D. 1994. Common property as an egalitarian share contract. *Journal of Economic Behavior and Organization* 25: 93–108.

Lueck, D. 1995. the rule of first possession and the design of the law. *Journal of Law and Economics* 38: 393–436.

Lueck, D. and Schenewerk, P. 1996. An economic analysis of unitized and non-unitized production. *Proceedings of the 1996 Society of Petroleum Engineers Annual Technical Conference* (1996): 67–76.

McCay, B.J. and Acheson, J.M. 1987. *The Question of the Commons*. Tucson: University of Arizona Press.

McDougal, M.S., Lasswell, H.D., Vlasic, I.A. and Smith, J.C. 1963. The enjoyment and acquisition of resources in outer space. *University of Pennsylvania Law Review* 111: 521–636.

McEvoy, A.F. 1986. *The Fisherman's Problem*. Cambridge: Cambridge University Press.

McFetridge, D.G. and Smith, D.A. 1980. Patents, prospects, and economic surplus: a comment. *Journal of Law and Economics* 23: 197–203.

McMillan, J. 1994. Selling spectrum rights. *Journal of Economic Perspectives* 8: 145–62.

Merrill, T.W. (ed.). 1986. Roundtable discussion: symposium on time, property rights, and the common law. *Washington University Law Quarterly* 64: 793–865.

Mommsen, T., Krueger, P. and Watson, A. (eds). 1985. *The Digest of Justinian*. Philadelphia: University of Pennsylvania Press.

Mortensen, D.T. 1982. Property rights and efficiency in mating, racing, and related games. *American Economic Review* 72: 968–79.

Nozick, R. 1974. *Anarchy, State, and Utopia*. New York: Basic Books.

Ostrom, E. 1990. *Governing the Commons*. New York and Cambridge: Cambridge University Press.

Posner, R. 1992. *Economic Analysis of Law*. 4th edn, Boston: Little, Brown; 1st edn 1972.

Reinganum, J.F. 1989. The timing of innovation: research, development, and diffusion. In *Handbook of Industrial Organization*, ed. R. Schmalensee and R.D. Willig, Amsterdam: North-Holland.

Rose, C.M. 1985. Possession as the origin of property. *University of Chicago Law Review* 52: 73–88.

Rose, C.M. 1986. The comedy of the commons: custom, commerce, and inherently public property. *University of Chicago Law Review* 53: 711–81.

Rose, C.M. 1990. Energy and efficiency in the realignment of common-law water rights. *Journal of Legal Studies* 19: 261–96.

Rose-Ackerman, S. 1985. Inalienability and the theory of property rights. *Columbia Law Review* 85: 931–69.

Schoenbaum, T.J. 1987. *Admiralty and Maritime Law*. St. Paul, MI: West Publishing.

Scott, A. and Coustalin, G. 1995. The evolution of water rights. *Natural Resources Journal* 35: 821–979.

Sprankling, J.G. 1996. The anti-wilderness bias in American property law. *University of Chicago Law Review* 63: 516–90.

Stavins, R.N. 1995. Transaction costs and tradeable permits. *Journal of Environmental Economics and Management* 29: 133–48.

Suen, W. 1989. Rationing and rent dissipation in the presence of heterogeneous individuals. *Journal of Political Economy* 97: 1384–94.

Tarlock, A.D., Corbridge, J.N. and Getches, D.H. 1993. *Water Resource Management*. 4th edn, Westbury, NY: Foundation Press.

Trelease, F.J. and Gould, G.A. 1986. *Cases and Materials on Water Law*. 4th edn, St. Paul: West Publishing.

Umbeck, J. 1977. A theory of contract choice and the California gold rush. *Journal of Law and Economics* 20: 421–37.

Williams, S.F. 1983. The requirement of beneficial use as a cause of waste in water resource development. *Natural Resources Journal* 23: 7–22.

Wright, B.W. 1983. The economics of invention incentives: patents, prizes, and research contracts. *American Economic Review* 73: 691–707.

fiscal federalism. Fiscal federalism is the branch of economics devoted to the analysis of issues that arise in the context of a federal system of government, although aspects of the analysis developed within fiscal federalism are applicable more generally to systems of government that involve decentralized government policy-making within a formally unitary state, or in the context of relations between nations. The debates on local government taxation within unitary states such as the UK, or on tax harmonization in Europe, stand as examples of this broader applicability. The development of fiscal federalism may be characterized as starting from narrow concerns with specific fiscal problems of federal states, and expanding to consider wider economic and political aspects of federal organization. This expansion is still incomplete, but fiscal federalism is able to make a contribution to the debate on federalism and the structure of government from a distinctively economic perspective.

The central questions confronting fiscal federalism include: Why adopt a federal structure at all? In a federal society, how should government be organized and which public activities should be pursued by each branch of government? What are the consequences of free mobility of people or assets between jurisdictions? What is the role of inter-governmental transfer payments, and what form should they take? What kind of tax system is most appropriate in a federal structure? In addressing these and other questions, fiscal federalism draws on a wide range of economic ideas. Beginning from roots in the traditional analysis of public finance, fiscal federalism has incorporated aspects of the theory of externalities and public goods, the theory of clubs, the theory of optimal taxation, public choice theory, economic geography and international economics.

An overview of fiscal federalism might start by drawing a rough distinction between a concern for efficiency in the supply of public services, and a concern for equity in the treatment of regions or states as well as individuals within nations. (Oates 1972, Breton and Scott 1978, and the articles collected in Grewel et al. 1980 provide a good introduction to the issues.) We shall begin by sketching some of the basic ideas associated first with the supply of public goods in a federal setting, and then with redistribution in a federation and the use of intergovernmental grants. With these ideas in hand, we shall then return to some of the central questions listed above. While this plan reflects the public finance orientation of fiscal federalism, we hope to be able to indicate something of the development of the broader political dimension of fiscal federalism as we proceed.

PUBLIC GOODS, DECENTRALIZATION AND MOBILITY. The analysis of public goods provides the basis for a discussion both of the decentralization of government policy and of the potential role of mobility in improving the efficiency of government policy delivery. The non-rival and non-excludable characteristics of public goods raise distinct issues which pull in opposite directions. Non-excludability means that individuals cannot be excluded from consumption, even if they refuse to contribute to the cost of the public good. This creates the classic 'free-rider' problem in the case of attempts to provide public goods through market processes. A standard response to the free-rider problem involves the use of a compulsory tax to raise the relevant revenue. But an analogue of the free-rider problem is reintroduced in the case of the provision of tax-financed public goods by local governments. If the benefits of the public goods spill over onto the citizens of neighbouring jurisdictions, those neighbours will effectively enjoy a free ride. As in the case of market provision, this free-rider problem will lead to under-provision of the public good. This same problem arises in the case of national governments if benefits are not confined to national boundaries – as in the case of attempts to control greenhouse gas emissions to moderate global warming.

Essentially, what is required in cases of this type is a more inclusive jurisdiction that covers the geographical range of the public good in question. This points to the fact that government jurisdictions can be too small to overcome the free-rider problem. If the non-excludability property of public goods was all that was at issue, it might seem that a single world government might be the optimal means for providing public goods. An argument for decentralization can, however, be constructed on the basis of the non-rivalness characteristic of public goods.

Non-rivalness implies that the quantity of any public

good supplied cannot generally be set so as to match each relevant individual's preferences. In the textbook case of private goods, an efficient allocation can be achieved by charging all individual consumers a price equal to the marginal cost of production and allowing each individual to choose a quantity to consume at that price. However, in the case of a public good, all individuals within a jurisdiction must consume the same quantity of the good, so the best that can be achieved is to supply the quantity that equates the social marginal valuation to the marginal cost of production. Essentially, the problem here is that the uniformity of consumption imposes a constraint on the satisfaction of individual preferences.

The decentralization of government policy can offer at least a partial response to this problem. By allowing the level of supply of a public good to vary as between states, additional degrees of freedom are introduced so that each state can provide a level of supply which corresponds more closely to the particular preferences of its citizens. The extent to which efficiency gains are available in any particular case will depend on considerations such as the extent of variations in preferences across states and any economies of scale in the supply of the public good. Nevertheless, the general point that a more flexible, decentralized pattern of public good supply will allow a closer correspondence between individual preferences and policy seems clear enough.

The simple decentralization thesis that lies at the heart of much of fiscal federalism balances these two lines of argument to argue for an optimal degree of decentralization. This thesis is linked to what is often called the 'layer-cake' model of federalism. On this view, each public good has an optimal 'range' – that is, an optimal size of jurisdiction. For street lighting, this range is narrow, so that street lighting should be decentralized to a local level of government; for defence, this range is wide, so that defence policy should be located at the national level. Decision-making with respect to each public good should then be decentralized to the appropriate layer of government, with the pattern of layers dictated largely by the technical nature of the goods to be provided and the costs of operating each layer of administration.

Notice first that this approach to federalism focuses on the expenditure side of government activity. As we shall see below, attempts to decentralize taxation can lead to difficulties and, in particular, to the problem that states may not be able to raise the revenue required to finance the efficient level of public good supply. The separation of the expenditure-assignment problem from the tax-assignment problem is common in fiscal federalism, and is one reason for the importance of the issues of inter-governmental grants and revenue-sharing schemes, to which we will return below.

Notice also that this view of federalism implicitly assumes that each government will supply public goods in efficient quantities subject only to the limits of feasibility. However, the decentralization thesis does not in itself identify a mechanism that justifies this assumption. In particular, it does not overcome a further basic problem of public goods – the problem of the revelation of preferences. It is here that Tiebout's famous discussion (1956) of the potential efficiency effects of mobility becomes important. The basic point here is that, *ceteris paribus*, individuals will face an incentive to migrate to the state in which the pattern of public good supply most closely matches their own preferences: citizens will vote – or at least reveal their preferences – with their feet. In an idealized setting involving the absence of any barriers to mobility, individuals will sort themselves into homogeneous groups so that each group receives their common ideal package of public goods, and full efficiency results. Clearly, the introduction of mobility costs of one sort or another will place limits on the efficiency gains to be achieved by the Tiebout mechanism.

An alternative view of the possibility of decentralizing the supply of a public good derives from the theory of clubs (Buchanan 1965). Here, the basic idea is to allow private profit-seeking clubs with no geographic base to compete for members. Each member will pay a membership fee or user charge in return for access to consumption of the club good. Clearly, for this idea to be applicable, clubs must have the ability to exclude non-members from consumption. In this type of model, it can be shown that a set of competitive clubs can implement the fully efficient allocation of a local public good. In this simple case, then, the provision of a local public good could be decentralized within the private sector.

The basic idea of private profit-seeking clubs can be extended to incorporate more realistic geographic considerations. Clubs can have locations. Members must then move to those locations in order to join, and mobility can be costly. In this somewhat richer model, membership fees or user charges will no longer be sufficient to implement efficient allocations. Even here, efficiency may be restored if the clubs own the land and so collect land rents as well as user charges. If we depart from the private sector nature of the clubs, this might translate into states with powers to raise land taxes and user charges but no other revenues.

More serious problems arise when we consider the need to provide more than one local public good. Clearly, if the clubs/states associated with good 1 own the land (or the right to tax land rents), the clubs associated with good 2 cannot – unless the same clubs provide all local public goods. But all-purpose clubs cannot ensure efficiency unless the geographic regions associated with the optimal supply of all local public goods are identical. In general, all-purpose clubs or states may only achieve efficiency if there exist particular transfers or subsidies from a central government that effectively internalize the externalities arising between clubs. This shifts the focus of attention firmly back to the public sector.

Indeed, the approach based on the Tiebout model and the clubs approach might be argued to converge in the interesting case of many geographically local public goods with non-identical ranges and imperfect mobility. The user charges and land rents of the clubs model effectively perform the same role as the lump-sum taxes in the Tiebout model.

The Tiebout model and the clubs model each provide a partial specification of a federal mechanism for the supply of local public goods, but neither is by any means complete

(Hamlin 1991). In short, both models lack any specification of the political aspects of federalism.

The political dimension of federalism introduces several further ideas into the analysis. The first is the idea of political competition between states. Competition can take many forms, but a key idea is that states may compete for mobile resources – whether those resources are people or capital. Competition may also operate in many domains, but it is in the domain of tax policy that competition has been particularly stressed within fiscal federalism. The basic point here emphasizes potential inefficiencies in the taxation policies adopted by competitive states in a world of mobile resources. The Tiebout model ensures efficiency by specifying the use of lump-sum taxes within each state. Once this extreme assumption is relaxed, a variety of potential tax inefficiencies may arise as a result of attempts by states to export taxes or pursue a range of 'beggar-thy-neighbour' policies. In particular, if many resources are mobile, competition between states may drive tax rates down below the point required to finance efficient levels of expenditure.

One possible reaction to such competitive tax inefficiencies at the state level is to look for policies at the national level that might restore efficiency. And, indeed, combinations of regulations on the types of taxes that may be levied by states and grants-in-aid can often be argued to allow a decentralized structure to achieve efficiency. This is exemplified in the clubs model, sketched above, where taxes are restricted to land taxes and user charges, and supplemented by central subsidies. However, there remains the question of whether such policies will actually be selected at the national level, even when they are available. Here again, we require an analysis of the political decision-making process. One possibility is that the central or federal government may be made up of representatives from the various states – each pursuing their own state's interests rather than any conception of the national interest. In this setting, policy outcomes at the central level will depend on the detailed structure of bargaining and log-rolling at the level of national government, but there can be no presumption that policies that restore overall efficiency to the system will emerge.

The idea of competition between states provides direct links from the analysis of tax competition to many other areas of debate in economics – most obviously on questions such as trade policy and the competitive pressures on exchange rates, and on monetary policy and the competitive determination of interest rates. In these areas, too, analysis reveals inefficiencies resulting from unregulated competition between states and points to remedies that require a more inclusive political jurisdiction. The debate on the European exchange rate mechanism and monetary union provides a clear example.

A second explicitly political aspect of fiscal federalism derives from the public choice school that characterizes federalism as a constitutional restriction on governmental power, rather than as a means of providing an essentially benign government with more powerful and flexible policy instruments. The basic idea here is that federalism divides and separates the powers that might otherwise be concentrated in a single centralized government authority. It is then argued that this restructuring of power acts in the interests of citizens by restraining the monopoly power associated with government. This essentially political advantage of federalism is largely independent of the decentralization thesis, but is still related to the idea of mobility. It is where individuals have the 'exit option' provided by mobility that the monopoly power of government is most likely to be significantly reduced.

Notice that this public choice perspective on the value of federalism may pull in the opposite direction to more standard lines of economic argument. For example, consider the case of tax competition between two state governments attempting to tax a potentially mobile resource. If the resource is freely mobile, neither government may be able to sustain any non-zero tax rate. From the perspective of standard welfare economics, this may be seen as a cost of federalism. Essentially the taxable capacity of the economy as a whole is reduced and the pattern of taxes may be distorted away from the optimum. But from the perspective of public choice theory or constitutional economics, this disadvantage of federalism may be offset by the effect of federalism in limiting the use of the government's monopoly power to tax.

These two perspectives differ most obviously in their underlying views of the motivation of government agencies. Conventional economics tends to view governments (whether state or federal) as motivated to maximize the welfare of their citizens. Public choice tends to view governments as being structures of procedural and other rules that are operated by individuals acting in their own interests.

The introduction of popular voting as an important aspect of decision making both within states and at the national level provides a further crucial step towards a more fully rounded analysis of democratic federalism. The key issues here include the extent to which voters take account of the long-run incentives for migration in determining their voting behaviour. However, since it is clear that voting is driven by distributional concerns as much as by efficiency concerns, we should turn to providing a sketch of some of the more important ideas on redistribution in federations before picking up the theme of the interaction between voting and economic policy in federations.

Before doing so, however, it is worth noting a quite different perspective on the politics of federalism, which arises from the recognition that federalism institutionalizes a plurality of sovereignties, with each state claiming a degree of independence. This plurality effectively offers federalism as a solution to the problems arising from strong loyalties within groups, and antagonisms between groups, within a larger polity. On this reading, federation accommodates the existence of different basic political identities, rather than differences in demands for public goods.

This perspective on federalism goes with a view of politics in which political process is seen less as a means of satisfying citizens' demands, and more as an expressive means by which citizens attest to their social identities. Where differences in ethnic, cultural, racial, tribal or other loyalties have a geographic dimension, decentralization can permit those separate identities to gain political expression, with less strain on the stability of the more inclusive polity. Where such loyalties do not initially have a geographical dimension, federalism may allow spatial restructuring to occur via Tiebout-like processes. In political history, local loyalties of this kind have probably been a more common ground for pressures calling for the adoption of federal structures than has any concern to harness the efficiency advantages of decentralization with respect to public goods (Gutmann 1992; Smith 1995).

REDISTRIBUTION IN A FEDERATION. The idea of redistribution in a federation has a number of dimensions. One might be concerned with redistribution between individuals – perhaps from the rich to the poor – and interested in the question of the implications of a federal structure for such redistribution. Alternatively, one might be concerned with redistribution between states – perhaps from the rich to the poor – and interested in the question of the optimal design of such transfer policies.

A convenient starting-point for the discussion of redistribution in federations involves identifying the limits imposed by a federal structure combined with mobility on the extent of redistributive policy. In the case of redistribution between individuals, a variation on the tax competition argument mentioned above implies that any attempt by any one state to redistribute from rich to poor might be expected to result in the in-migration of relatively poor individuals and the out-migration of relatively rich individuals. In the Tiebout-like limit in which mobility is costless and taxes are lump-sum, no redistribution by states may be possible. While costly mobility and inefficient taxation reintroduce the possibility of redistribution at the level of the state, many would argue that the incentive to migrate effectively limits the redistributive powers of state governments (Epple and Romer 1991).

As in the case of tax competition, this result may be interpreted in either of two ways. In conventional economics, the tendency is to conclude that interpersonal redistribution must be seen as the responsibility of national governments, or other units of government with relatively limited migration possibilities. An obvious corollary would be that the removal of international barriers to mobility (as, for example, in the case of Europe) would tend to reduce even national governments' ability to pursue redistributive policies. The alternative interpretation, associated with the public choice view, would see the move to federal structures as imposing a constraint on what might otherwise be seen as excessive redistributive activity.

Just as the possibility of mobility between states limits the possibility of redistribution within states, so the possibility of exit by states limits the possibility of redistribution between states. In other words, if states have a right to secede this will place a limit on the ability of a federal government to redistribute between states, since no state would tolerate being made worse off than it would be as an independent entity. Of course, these limits on the power of federal governments may not be very restrictive in practice, but mobility/secession is not the only issue in the analysis of redistributive policy in federations.

The political aspects of federal decision making imply that the extent of redistribution may depend upon the way in which policies are structured as much as their content – even in the absence of mobility or threats of secession. This is particularly true with respect to the necessarily complicated structure of voting within a federation. For example, consider two alternative policy proposals in a federation made up of just two states, and assume that there is no mobility between states. Policy A operates by first transferring resources from the richer state to the poorer state and then setting each state government the task of transferring resources between richer and poorer individuals within its own jurisdiction. At each stage, decisions are taken by majority voting within the relevant jurisdictions. Policy B, by contrast, operates in one stage with a direct vote at the national level on the extent of redistribution between richer and poorer individuals regardless of their location – even though this will normally imply some net redistribution between the states.

At first sight, it might seem that these two policies should yield identical outcomes provided that voters are fully informed. In each case, one might think, voters should focus on the ultimate consequences in terms of the impact on individuals (including themselves) and vote so as to achieve their desired level of redistribution. But the differing voting procedures built into these two policies undermine this line of argument. Under policy A, the natural coalitions of voters in the national vote are simply the states: members of the richer state (whether richer or poorer as individuals) will have a shared interest in reducing the transfer to the poorer state, and *vice versa*. Under policy B, the natural coalitions are richer and poorer individuals regardless of their state of residence: richer individuals have a shared interest in reducing the extent of redistribution, and *vice versa*. The political outcomes under each policy will therefore depend upon the details of the distributions of richer and poorer individuals across the richer and poorer states, and the relative sizes of the two states and the two classes of individuals. Roughly, if the richer state is the larger, we would expect little or no inter-state redistribution under policy A even if, under policy B, considerable inter-state transfers might be majority approved. Equally, if the ratio of richer and poorer individuals varies sharply as between states, the extent of intra-state redistribution might vary sharply in the two states under policy A, whereas it is constant (by definition) across states under policy B.

One might go on to enquire which further constitutional arrangements would tend to promote policy A over policy B, or *vice versa*. One possibility is that decisions between options of this type must be made at the national level; another might require a majority of states to agree; still another might require unanimity amongst the states. Each of these constitutional arrangements would carry differing implications for the formation of voting coalitions in the vote between A and B; and again, these implications will also depend on the detailed distribution of individuals across states and classes (Persson and Tabellini 1996b).

This simple example serves to indicate the potentially complex interactions between federal political arrangements – including voting arrangements – and the choice of economic policy. It also serves to illustrate the more general importance of even relatively detailed constitutional arrangements. Federalism – interpreted as the simple idea of some decentralization of decision making – is only one aspect of a constitution, and without more detailed specification of the remaining aspects it is not normally possible to make firm predictions regarding the impact of federalism on the design and operation of economic policy.

GRANTS AND REVENUE SHARING. As we have seen, both redistributive and efficiency considerations may give rise to a policy of inter-governmental grants or revenue-sharing arrangements whereby tax revenues are raised disproportionately at the national level and then shared with state governments. The analysis of inter-governmental grants has formed another major theme within fiscal federalism. The traditional approach to this topic has been to investigate the differential effects on the behaviour of the recipient of differing types of grant. For this purpose, grants have been divided into the broad categories of general grants, which are not conditional on the money being used to support any particular activity or expenditure; and specific grants, which are. Specific grants may be further subdivided into lump-sum grants, matching grants with cash limits and open-ended matching grants. A still more detailed taxonomy is possible.

The traditional discussion is typically presented in terms of indifference-curve analysis, with the preferences of the grant recipient interacting with a budget constraint that is shifted in one way or another by the particular type of grant in question. In a positive reading of these models, the recipient might be thought of as a state planner, or as a representative individual, median voter, or some other decisive individual in the political process of the state. In this way, the more political aspects of federalism are pushed into the background. Alternatively, the exercise can be construed in normative terms with the preferences representing a state social-welfare function. In this case, of course, the question under investigation is how *should* the recipient state respond to this or that grant, rather than how *will* it respond?

The broad conclusion of this line of analysis is that open-ended matching grants have the strongest stimulating effect on the behaviour of the recipient, and therefore should be used wherever the underlying purpose of the grant is efficiency related. Essentially, the detailed terms of the matching grant may be constructed so as to internalize relevant externalities. On the other hand, where the underlying purpose of the grant is redistributive in nature, grants should be lump-sum general grants, so as to interfere as little as possible with state-level decision making.

There is some doubt as to the fit between these models of grants and reality. One particular area of dispute is the so-called 'flypaper effect'. Consider a state receiving a lump-sum general grant, and compare the effects of the receipt of this grant with those of a simple increase in the aggregate private income of the state. The simplest theory suggests that these two events should have the same impact (since they are represented by identical shifts in the state's budget constraint) and, in particular, that the division of the increase in state income as between public and private sectors should be the same in each case. This is not borne out in practice. Increases in general grant income are spent disproportionately in the public sector when compared with increases in private income. This is the flypaper effect: money sticks where it hits.

The flypaper effect may be explained in a number of ways. One possibility is to abandon the idea of a state planner, or of a decisive median voter, in favour of a state government run by bureaucrats with agenda-setting powers used in pursuit of their own interests. Another is to recognize that, from the point of view of the recipient state, the social cost of public funds may be lower in the case of a grant than in the case of an increase in private income, since no inefficient local tax is involved. However, it is also possible to argue that the apparent flypaper effect can be understood as a product of the fact that even general grants are politically endogenous to the federal system of voting (unlike, for example, international grants that might be more appropriately seen as exogenous to the recipient country). As we suggested above, state taxation may be relatively inefficient as a means of raising revenue. Equally, a national tax combined with a set of grants to states may be approved by a national majority (depending crucially on the distribution of voters both across states and across other relevant dimensions) if it offers a more efficient way of providing local public services. In this case it will be the relative efficiency of central taxation that drives the logic of the flypaper effect, and the nature of the federal voting system that realizes that logic (Brennan and Pincus 1996).

CENTRAL QUESTIONS. Federalism is a simple term that stands in place of a complex set of interrelated principles and ideas, some of which are institutional, some political and some economic. The economic analysis of federalism offers one perspective on the structure and implications of this set of ideas. It provides both a framework within which the various ideas can be explored, and a method of analysing and evaluating the implications of federalism.

One noteworthy aspect of the debates on both efficiency and redistribution in federations is that, although they began as relatively narrow exercises in traditional economics, they have developed to incorporate many of the more political aspects of federalism. Whether it is through the incorporation of formal models of voting, or through the more constitutional perspective of public choice theory, it is surely the case that fiscal federalism is increasingly interested in the detailed political institutions of federalism and their normative implications, including their impact on the design and operation of economic policy.

We began this essay by identifying five central questions confronting fiscal federalism. Why adopt a federal structure? In a federal society, how should government be organized and which public activities should be pursued by each branch of government? What are the consequences of free mobility of people or assets between jurisdictions? What is the role of inter-governmental transfer payments, and what form should they take? What kind of tax system is most appropriate in a federal state? Fiscal federalism provides no simple or fully satisfactory answers to these questions. However, fiscal federalism has made some contribution towards a deeper understanding of the issues at stake and the interconnections between the questions. We conclude by attempting to pull together some of the strands of argument sketched above to provide partial and tentative answers to some of these questions. We will focus on taxation, the structure of government and the allocation of responsibilities, and the ultimate question of the balance of arguments for and against federalism itself.

Taxation policy in a federation is an area that seems relatively tractable so long as one abstracts from the details of political process. The analysis of tax exportation and other forms of tax competition between states seems to point clearly towards a tax system that provides state governments with access to only a restricted range of tax instruments or imposes federal regulation on allowable state tax rates. Federal taxes and a system of grants can then be designed to complete the picture. The most obvious example of the former strategy would restrict states to the use of resident-based taxes – a simple rule that would outlaw the most obvious forms of tax competition, although it does not solve all of the problems. The latter strategy can be seen at work in the type of tax-harmonization proposals being introduced in Europe, which allow member states to choose particular tax rates within a specified range. Such schemes may be seen as attempts to limit the scale of tax competition while protecting revenues and limiting the extent to which members' domestic tax systems are distorted.

Similar arguments operate in the area of redistribution. Left to their own devices we might expect states to impose relatively regressive tax systems, since higher-income households tend to be more mobile. This suggests that restrictions that impose proportionality or a degree of progressivity may be beneficial. One way in which this may be institutionalized is to restrict state governments to adding a surcharge to an existing federal income tax scheme.

These and other similar conclusions seem to flow quite easily from the economic analysis. However, these conclusions derive from an essentially normative model designed to address the question of how federal governments should respond to problems at the state level. This model does not fully account for the political structure of federalism. Once both federal and state policy making are endogenized via a structure of voting which gives individuals voting rights at both the state and federal level, it is by no means clear that we can rely upon federal policy to take the normatively required actions with respect to state taxation powers, or the pattern of inter-governmental grants. Indeed, there are often good reasons to suggest that the opposite is the more likely outcome, with the operation of politics at the federal level acting to amplify the inefficiencies created by the operation of politics at the state level (Inman and Rubinfeld 1996).

The wider question then concerns the relationship between alternative constitutional structures and the likely outcomes of those political structures in terms of both federal and state tax policies. This question is only just beginning to receive attention in fiscal federalism.

A similar pattern holds true when we shift attention to the design of government structures and the allocation of responsibilities between agencies. The simple 'layer cake' model of federalism based on the decentralization thesis seems to offer the prospect of efficiency in simple, largely apolitical, models. But once the models are extended to include a range of local public goods and a political structure of decision making, the appeal of the layer-cake view is sharply reduced.

One way of thinking about this issue is as a debate between a vision of federalism as a network of single-purpose authorities, each providing a single local public good over some defined area, and an alternative vision of consolidated state governments, each defined with respect to a particular geographic area and charged with supplying a full range of services. The single-purpose authorities have the advantages of fitting their geographic areas to the characteristics of the specific good supplied, and of being politically accountable on a single issue via what would essentially be a hypothecated tax or user charge. The corresponding disadvantages include the fact that single-purpose authorities would have no exclusive access to any tax base – since any individual (or any piece of land) would be situated within many authorities – so that tax externalities would be encouraged. Consolidated states face the opposite menu of advantages and disadvantages. Compromise between these two extreme visions of federalism is the only real possibility, but the balancing of the arguments is problematic and will again depend upon the political structure put in place alongside any institutional structure. Are the single-purpose authorities to be elected, or are they to be appointed, or perhaps companies will bid for franchises to be offered by the federal government? As always, the devil is in the detail (Hochman et al. 1995; Persson and Tabellini 1996a).

And so we come to the big questions. Why adopt federalism at all? What are the advantages and disadvantages of federalism and why might federalism be appropriate in some contexts and not in others? All of the foregoing arguments (and many more) bear on these questions.

Alexis de Tocqueville famously argued that federalism is an attempt to combine the advantages of small and great nations, but that the major and unavoidable disadvantage of federal countries was the result of the complicated nature of the means that they must employ. It is clear that there are potentially both economic and wider political advantages from adopting a federal structure: economic advantages in the provision of local services and political advantages in the separation and division of powers, the rendering of democracy as an accountable and responsive system, and the structuring of sovereignty to accommodate genuine local loyalties. But it is equally clear that there are potentially both economic and wider political disadvantages from adopting a federal structure: economic disadvantages in terms of the potential loss of efficiency in taxation and wasteful competition between states; and political disadvantages, including the risk of encouraging regional factionalism. If federalism can combine the advantages of small and great nations, so too can it combine their disadvantages. Fiscal federalism has made considerable progress from its beginnings in the analysis of very specific questions concerning fiscal policy, but it still has some way to go before it can claim to offer a fully rounded account of federalism from an economic perspective.

GEOFFREY BRENNAN AND ALAN HAMLIN

See also CENTRALIZED AND DECENTRALIZED REGULATION IN THE EUROPEAN UNION; COMPETITION FOR STATE CORPORATE LAW; CONSTITUTIONAL ECONOMICS; DISTRIBUTIVE JUSTICE; DIVISION OF POWERS IN THE EUROPEAN CONSTITUTION; REGULATORY COMPETITION; SUBSIDIARITY AND THE EUROPEAN UNION.

Subject classification: 2a(i); 2d(i).

BIBLIOGRAPHY

Brennan, G. and Pincus, J.J. 1996. A minimalist model of federal grants and flypaper effects. *Journal of Public Economics* 61: 229–46.

Breton, A. and Scott, A. 1978. *The Economic Constitution of Federal States*. Toronto: University of Toronto Press.

Buchanan, J.M. 1965. An economic theory of clubs. *Economica* N.S. 32: 1–14.

Epple, D. and Romer, T. 1991. Mobility and redistribution. *Journal of Political Economy* 99: 828–58.

Grewel, B., Brennan, G. and Matthews, R. (eds). 1980. *The Economics of Federalism*. Canberra: Australian National University Press.

Inman, R.P. and Rubinfeld, D.L. 1996. Designing tax policy in federalist economies: an overview. *Journal of Public Economics* 60: 307–34.

Gutmann, A. (ed.). 1992. *Multiculturalism and 'The Politics of Recognition.'*: an essay by Charles Taylor, with commentary by Amy Gutmann, editor. Princeton: Princeton University Press.

Hamlin, A.P. 1991. Decentralization, competition and the efficiency of federalism. *Economic Record* 67: 193–204.

Hochman, O., Pines, D. and Thisse, J.-F. 1995. On the optimal structure of local governments. *American Economic Review* 85: 1224–40.

Oates, W.E. 1972. *Fiscal Federalism*. New York: Harcourt Brace Jovanovich.

Persson, T. and Tabellini, G. 1996a. Federal fiscal constitutions: risk sharing and moral hazard. *Econometrica* 64: 623–46.

Persson, T. and Tabellini, G. 1996b. Federal fiscal constitutions: risk sharing and redistribution. *Journal of Political Economy* 104: 979–1009.

Smith, G. 1995. *Federalism: The Multicultural Challenge*. London: Longman.

Tiebout, C.M. 1956. A pure theory of local expenditures. *Journal of Political Economy* 64: 416–24.

fishing expedition. *See* CIVIL PROCEDURE IN THE USA AND CIVIL LAW COUNTRIES; DISCOVERY.

focal points. In a 1957 article Thomas Schelling introduced the concept of a focal point. The article, reproduced as chapter 3 of the modern classic, *The Strategy of Conflict* (1960), laid the foundations for much of the later work on the subject. His point of departure was the state of game theory at that time, which centred on the minimax solution to zero sum games. In zero sum games there is no scope for mutual collaboration. The main point of his book was to argue that the theory developed for zero sum games is not an appropriate starting-point for analysing nonzero-sum games: being unpredictable is the main guide for rational behaviour in zero sum games, whereas the reverse may very well be true in other types of games, in particular in games with common interests.

Schelling tried out nine examples of coordination games on what he termed 'an unscientific sample of respondents' (1960: 55); two of these examples will be discussed in some detail below. It turned out that in all nine examples, players were often very well able to coordinate their actions. He observed that, not only do people in everyday life use symbolic details (the labels of strategies) in order to coordinate their activities, but also that game theory loses some of its relevance if it does not take this empirical evidence into account. He also argued that, from a normative point of view, a theory of rational play should take the symbolic details into account. In his own words:

> a normative theory must produce strategies that are at least as good as what people can do without them. More, it must not deny or expunge details of the game that can demonstrably benefit two or more players and that the players, consequently, should not expunge or ignore in their mutual interest (Schelling 1960: 98).

Schelling's theoretical remarks about focal points have two distinct elements: imagination and logic. A clear example in which logic seems to be the dominant factor explaining individuals' choices is a coordination game in which individuals are asked to write down a positive integer. If they coordinate on the same integer they get a positive reward; if not, nothing. Schelling reports that in this game two-fifths of all people chose the number 1, whereas if they were asked just to write down an integer (without the necessity of coordinating with somebody else) they wrote down a large variety of numbers. Schelling explains:

> And there seems to be good logic in this: there is no unique 'favored number'; the variety of candidates like 3, 7 and so forth is embarrassingly large, and there is no good way of picking the 'most favorite' or most conspicuous. If one then asks what number, among all positive numbers, is most clearly unique, or *what rule of selection would lead to unambiguous results*, one may be struck with the fact that the universe of all positive numbers has a 'first' or 'smallest' number (1960: 94).

In other examples, it seems that logic plays a less important role. When people are asked to coordinate on 'heads' or 'tails', the majority chooses 'heads' even though there does not seem to be an argument that makes 'heads' logically superior to 'tails'. In examples like this 'prominence' or 'conspicuousness' seems to play a key role. In other examples, prominence is a consequence of precedence: the reason for choosing a certain alternative now is that it has been chosen successfully in the past. In most cases, both imagination and logic have to be used, however: 'Logic helps . . . but usually not until imagination has selected some clue to work on from among the concrete details of the situation' (Schelling 1960: 58).

Subsequent work on focal points has taken various routes. I first discuss some of the experimental work that has been done, and then in Sections 2 and 3 go into some of the aspects of incorporating focal points into a theory of rational play in games. Section 4 discusses boundedly rational behaviour and the evolution of focal points, and Section 5 concludes with some general observations on the relevance of focal points outside situations of pure coordination, and on the applicability of the different theories on focal points discussed in the preceding sections.

1. SOME EXPERIMENTS. Schelling (1960) reported the results of many informal experiments which he had performed to show that people actually do use focal points. Apart from the nine coordination games mentioned above, he also carried out eight informal experiments on tacit bargaining. In a series of articles Mehta, Starmer and Sugden (1992, 1994a, 1994b) were, however, the first to do *controlled* experiments on whether agents employ focal points in deciding what to choose in pure coordination games. Other experiments on coordination games, such as Van Huyck et al. (1990), concentrate on coordination games with Pareto-ranked equilibria and do not study the impact of the labels of strategies on the choices that are made. The experiments of Mehta et al. were not really meant to test any formal theory and can, therefore, be discussed before actual theories about focal points. They consisted of two parts. Part I was an attempt to replicate Schelling-type results, asking questions such as 'name a car manufacturer', 'name a mountain', 'name a year' and so on; Part II consisted of ten so-called assignment games.

The authors' main hypothesis is based on Schelling's work: before deciding what to choose, players first inquire into the rules of selection that could be used as a base for one's decision, and players then choose from this set a rule that, if followed by both players, is most likely to result in coordination. They call this form of salience 'Schelling salience'. Apart from Schelling salience, the authors distinguish primary and secondary salience. According to primary salience, players just choose what first comes to their mind. According to secondary salience, players expect their opponents to play the option that is primarily salient for them and maximize expected payoffs given this belief. If players have a common culture, all forms of salience may explain that players are able to coordinate their actions. Mehta et al. (1994a) test which of these forms of salience is best able to explain the experimental results. On the other hand, Mehta et al. (1994b) inquire into the actual rules of selection that people use. The latter are important in order to develop an explanatory theory of focal points because, as the authors rightly observe, 'when one explains coordination in terms of 'salience', there is a danger that one is providing nothing more than an *ex post* rationalization' (Mehta et al. 1994b: 167). On the other hand, were we to possess some rules of selection that people actually use, we would be able to predict the decisions they will make. Accordingly, for the ten assignment games three hypotheses were proposed and tested.

Mehta et al. (1994a, 1994b) define a *coordination index* which measures the probability that two individuals chosen at random from the population of participants give the same answer. If players were simply to randomize in a coordination game with n actions each, the coordination index would equal $1/n$. In the three examples from Part I mentioned above, the coordination indexes were 0.80, 0.79 and 0.51, respectively. This indicates that, indeed, people are well able to coordinate their answers. Moreover, when players do not play a coordination game, but instead are just asked to give an answer, they do much worse. This indicates that in pure coordination games players are guided by Schelling (or secondary) salience, but not by primary salience.

It turns out that the three proposed hypotheses did fairly well in explaining most of the responses given by the participants. In all the games (apart from one) in which the hypotheses made predictions about which outcomes were to be expected, the predicted outcomes were also those most frequently observed in the sample. However, taking the coordination index as a measure of how successful participants are in coordinating their answers, it turned out that the players were almost as successful in the two games in which the hypotheses did *not* make a prediction about which outcome to expect as in the eight games in which they did. Apparently, also in the games for which the hypotheses are silent about what to expect, the participants are able to find rules of selection that help them to coordinate their answers.

Of course, in none of the games of the experiment did all the participants coordinate on the same answer, i.e., the coordination index never equalled 1. This implies that a theory which explains that players of coordination games have a higher chance of coordinating their actions than they would have if they simply randomized over all possible choices, should also explain that there are quite a few cases in which players do not manage to coordinate.

2. ON THE DIFFICULTIES OF INCORPORATING FOCAL POINTS INTO A THEORY OF RATIONAL PLAY IN GAMES. Even though Schelling (1960) argued that rational players should take the symbolic details of strategies into account, he did not attempt to incorporate his analysis of focal points into a more formal theory of games. The first attempt to do so was by Gauthier (1975). The example he used is a coordination game in which meeting at one of two railway stations in London, Marylebone and St Pancras, is at stake. Suppose the matrix below specifies the payoffs for the two players.

Table 1

	Marylebone	St Pancras
Marylebone	5, 5	0, 0
St Pancras	0, 0	5, 5

As one of the persons is travelling from Leicester and as trains run from Leicester to St Pancras but not to Marylebone, Gauthier argued that going to St Pancras is the salient option. Given this evidence, he goes about analysing the game in the following way. First, he argues that the way the players describe the game to themselves is different from the one provided above. According to Gauthier, the players consider two options, namely 'seeking salience' and 'ignoring salience'. In the latter option the players randomize between going to either one of the two stations. The transformed game with expected payoffs in the cells of the matrix is as follows.

Table 2

	Seeking	Ignoring
Seeking	2.5, 5	2.5, 2.5
Ignoring	2.5, 2.5	2.5, 2.5

Given this transformed game, Gauthier argues that the only rational choice for both players is to seek salience and go to St Pancras. In order to arrive at this conclusion he introduces a *Principle of Coordination* according to which rational players should play their part of a unique Pareto-efficient equilibrium, if there is one. Note that applying the criterion of risk-dominance to this transformed game yields the same conclusion.

Looking at Gauthier's analysis more closely, it is clear that the two key elements are: (i) a transformation of the game and (ii) the Principle of Coordination. In the next section it will turn out that both elements are also present in later attempts to incorporate an analysis of focal points into a theory of games. Here, I would like to concentrate for a moment on the *particular* way Gauthier has transformed the original game. As Gilbert (1989) has argued quite convincingly, Gauthier does not seem to have a good reason to restrict the options of the transformed game to two. More specifically, if we stick to Gauthier's interpretation of 'ignoring salience' as choosing each of the two options with probability 1/2, there seems to be at least one other alternative, namely 'seeking the non-salient', i.e., if a player thinks about the possibility of 'seeking salience', then it seems natural to assume that the possibility 'seeking the non-salient' also comes to his mind. Allowing for this third option, however, destroys Gauthier's analysis. To see this note that the new transformed payoff matrix is as below and that there are (again) two Pareto-efficient equilibria. Accordingly, the Principle of Coordination cannot operate successfully in this case.

Table 3

	Seeking	Ignoring	Seeking NonS
Seeking	2.5, 5	2.5, 2.5	2.0, 0
Ignoring	2.5, 2.5	2.5, 2.5	2.5, 2.5
Seeking NonS	2.0, 0	2.5, 2.5	2.5, 5

As pointed out by Goyal and Janssen (1996), a similar problem occurs in the analysis of Crawford and Haller (1990), which tried to explain how rational players can use past play to coordinate their actions in the future. Their analysis was based on precedence: once players have successfully coordinated their actions in one period (suppose, in the example above, coordination on St Pancras railway station), they will do so ever after, because they can repeat the action combination that yielded a coordinated outcome. However, in 2×2 games players could also guarantee a coordinated outcome by both switching to the action that was not chosen in the first period in which a coordinated outcome was reached (in the example above, the players could also try to coordinate on Marylebone in the period after they coordinated on St Pancras). Hence, after a coordinated outcome has been reached there are two equally efficient ways (namely, meeting at St Pancras *and* meeting at Marylebone) to guarantee a coordinated outcome in the next period; and there is no way that rational players can individually distinguish between them. Accordingly, something much stronger than Gauthier's principle of coordination is needed to choose between the two equilibria. A similar argument can be made with respect to Kramarz (1996). It deserves mention, however, that Crawford and Haller's analysis is not vulnerable to the same criticism in 3×3 coordination games, because an asymmetry between the one action combination that resulted in coordination and the other two is created once players have coordinated the first time.

Thus, one of the difficulties of incorporating focal points in a theory of rational play in games is to create an asymmetry between the option that is considered to be salient and those that are not. In 2×2 games, Gauthier's analysis fails because if one action is salient (by some criterion), the other is in some sense also salient, because it is the only action that is not salient according to the first criterion. Hence, there is no asymmetry between the two actions. The same applies to several of the games analysed in Crawford and Haller (1990), as there is no asymmetry between continuing playing the action that yielded a coordinated outcome and switching to the other action.

3. RATIONALIZING FOCAL POINTS. Recently, Bacharach (1993), Janssen (1995) and Sugden (1995) have made some progress in circumventing the problems outlined above. The present discussion focuses mainly on Bacharach's contribution. The main ideas of his analysis are best understood by means of an example. Suppose two players are asked to choose one out of ten wooden blocks. Of the blocks, two are yellow and eight are red and those who look at the blocks carefully will see that one of the red blocks has a wavy grain, whereas the grain of each of the other nine blocks is straight. If the two players each choose the same block, Bacharach is ready to give each a prize of £100. If they choose different blocks they get nothing. What would constitute a rational choice in this case?

Bacharach first introduces the notion of *availability*, which is the likelihood that a particular way of conceiving the coordination problem comes to the mind of a player. In the above example, there are two clues available: colour and grain patterns. The availability of colour is the likelihood that a player sees that the blocks have a colour and that he considers basing his choice on the colour of the object. Similarly, the availability of grain is the likelihood that a player sees that the blocks have a grain and that he considers basing his choice on the grain of the object. For simplicity, we will assume that the colours are very distinct so that the availability of colour is 1. The availability of grain is denoted by v, where it is assumed that $v < 1$. Accordingly, it may be that (i) each player conceives of both ways to partition the blocks; (ii) only one player thinks about both ways while the other thinks only about colours; and (iii) each player thinks only about colours. It is assumed that availability v also measures the conditional probability that the grain structure comes to the mind of the opponent, given that it has come to the mind of a particular player.

The next step in the argument is to transform the game. In particular, Bacharach argues that given the different ways that come to the mind of a player, she only has a limited number of options. For example, if both grain structure and colour come to mind, she can (i) ignore all characteristics and randomize with probability 1/10 over all objects, (ii) choose a yellow block, (iii) choose a red block, (iv) choose the block with the wavy grain or (v) choose a block with a straight grain. As she does not have any reason to distinguish, for example, the two yellow objects from one another, she cannot decide to choose a *particular* yellow object. Therefore, the Principle of Insufficient Reason tells us that the player's choice should be such that it gives both yellow blocks the same probability. The same holds true, *mutatis mutandis*, for the red objects and the blocks with the straight grain. The transformation of the game described above is different from Gauthier's transformation, because in Bacharach's analysis all potentially possible ways to describe the game have been incorporated; in particular, the notion of salience has *not* been used in transforming the game.

Finally, Bacharach uses a Principle of Coordination that is similar to Gauthier's. It says basically that players choose one of the Pareto-dominant equilibria of the transformed game. Applying the Principle in the example discussed here gives the following result: if $v > \frac{1}{2}$, players who observe both ways to partition the objects choose the block with the wavy grain, and if $v < \frac{1}{2}$, they choose each of the yellow objects with probability $\frac{1}{2}$. Players who do not observe the grain of the blocks choose each of the yellow objects with probability $\frac{1}{2}$.

Bacharach's analysis formalizes the two elements of Schelling's theoretical remarks on focal points: conspicuousness and logic (unicity). The notion of availability formalizes how conspicuous an aspect of the objects is. The Principle of Insufficient Reason and the Principle of Coordination together formalize the logical (or uniqueness) aspect of focal points: if the availability of all characteristics is the same, then rational players should randomly choose blocks that are rarest, because this gives the highest chance of coordination. In the example above, there is a tradeoff between rarity and availability. Hence, the result: if (and only if) the availability is large enough, the rarity aspect dominates.

Janssen (1995) generalizes and modifies Bacharach's analysis. He allows for objects to have an arbitrary number of attributes and he shows that in all generic cases, players receive a higher payoff following the procedure outlined above than they would receive if they neglect the information contained in the labels of the strategies and randomize over all objects. He obtains his result by using a more strict version of the Principle of Coordination, which says that rational players will choose their part of the *unique* Pareto-efficient equilibrium if there is one.

Sugden (1995) stays closer to the conventional game theoretic framework. His basic game is essentially the game in normal form. Players play this basic game, however, under a certain private description. This description is assigned to players by a random labelling procedure. Sugden shows that depending on whether the labelling procedure is perfectly correlated, uncorrelated or somewhere in between, the principle of coordination (what he terms the principle of collective rationality) may or may not assure coordination.

The approaches taken by Bacharach (1993) and Janssen (1995) have the following general structure in common. Each player observes a certain number of attributes of the strategies. How many attributes one player observes is beyond conscious control. The attributes she observes are potential clues for solving the coordination problem. The analysis shows how people choose one out of the set of potential clues and choose an action according to the clue that is used. The analysis may also be used to show why coordination may fail as it does in some circumstances (as we all know from daily experience and from the evidence reported in Section 1 and in Schelling 1960). One reason for this offered by the analysis above is that if some attributes come to the mind of one player and she thinks it likely that they will also come to the mind of the other player, she may decide on a particular action. However, the particular attribute which lies at the basis of her decision may not have come to the mind of the other player at all. To illustrate with the example used above: a player who observes both attributes of the wooden blocks chooses the block with the wavy grain if $v > \frac{1}{2}$. The other player may, however, fail to notice the grain of the blocks altogether. Hence, a coordination failure occurs. A second reason may lie in the fact that even if the same attributes come to the mind of different players, they may have assigned different probabilities to the event that an attribute also comes to the mind of the other player, i.e., the availabilities may be subjective and differ across players.

What the analysis achieves is that it establishes a way players may reason about what to choose in coordination games. If after the game is played you are asked by the other player why did you choose that particular option, then you have an answer: Given your assessment of the probabilities that the other player did in fact observe what you did, you maximized the chance of coordination. Of course, this analysis does not rationalize the assessment of availabilities. In this sense, the analyses discussed here still assume the existence of some kind of (primary) salience, because successful coordination is only guaranteed if the probabilities which players assign to the other player observing what you did are sufficiently similar.

Another point that deserves attention is the falsifiability of the theory. If availability cannot be measured independently of the choice which individual players make, then from the above it follows that almost any choices can be rationalized. Indeed, in their experimental paper testing the theory outlined above, Bacharach and Bernasconi (1997) try to measure the value of subjective availabilities in a certain experiment, on the basis of earlier experiments with the same subjects and from the subjects' written reports. It turns out that the joint hypotheses that the theory is correct *and* that availabilities can be measured in the proposed way do quite well in explaining the experimental results.

A final question is the extent to which the Principle of Coordination is reasonable in the present context. Two versions of the Principle have to be distinguished. The version Bacharach (1993) employs, which is also implicitly used by Crawford and Haller (1990), should be criticized on the grounds that it assumes too much coordination capacity on the part of the individual players: how can players, each of them deciding individually, guarantee themselves an equilibrium payoff if the equilibria are payoff symmetric? The second version employed by Gauthier

(1975), Janssen (1995) and Sugden (1995) does not suffer from this criticism. Their solution concept is only applicable, however, if there is a unique Pareto-efficient equilibrium. Of course, one may argue that the second version of the Principle of Coordination is also an equilibrium selection device and that it goes beyond the standard notion of individual rationality usually employed in game theory. I think this potential criticism is too conservative in the present context. I have two arguments. First, other arguments that have been used for equilibrium selection purposes such as risk dominance (Harsanyi and Selten 1988) and its generalization, $\frac{1}{2}$-dominance (Morris, Rob and Shin 1995), yield the same results if applicable in many pure coordination games. Second, and more substantively, arguments have been made in favour of the principle of coordination. Sugden (1991), among others, argues that in pure coordination games rational players should consider themselves as being members of a team. Being a member of a team, they should think about a rule of behaviour that if followed by both is best for both players, i.e. it is Pareto-efficient. If such a rule exists and is unique, each player *reasoning individually* will discover the rule and is sure that the other player will discover the same rule. Hence, individual rational players have a reason to use the Principle of Coordination. (For completeness, note that the Principle of Coordination does not prescribe that rational players should choose to cooperate in one-shot Prisoner's Dilemma games, because in such games there are three Pareto-efficient allocations.) Along different lines, Colman (1997) also argues in favour of the Principle of Coordination.

4. EVOLUTION AND FOCAL POINTS BASED ON PRECEDENCE. Schelling (1960) already argued that precedence is one of the ways in which focal points come about. Above, it was argued that the notion of precedence is inherently difficult to incorporate into a theory of games that is based on common knowledge of rational behaviour. The reason is that rationality is essentially forward looking: a strategy is rational at a certain moment in time if it maximizes the player's expected payoff *from that moment onwards*. On the other hand, precedent is, by definition, something based on the past. The reason why precedent may work to establish a focal point is that it helps players to coordinate their expectations on one out of many conceivable choices. However, if rationality is common knowledge, players' expectations about other players' future behaviour are based on their supposed rationality. Any equilibrium configuration, and not just the one that has been played before, is consistent with common knowledge of rationality. Hence, when common knowledge is assumed structural characteristics of the game are what matters and not historical accident.

A framework in which the way that precedence helps to shape focal points can be better understood as one in which the behaviour of individuals is boundedly (instead of fully) rational. Such an evolutionary game theoretic framework has recently been developed by Kandori, Mailath and Rob (1993) and Young (1993), among others. The basic model has players randomly drawn from a population playing a certain game. Players do not know with whom they are playing the game, but they have some (partial) observations on how the game has been played in the recent past. Players assume that past play is a good indicator of what their opponent will play in the game they play. Hence, expectations about opponent's play are not based on the supposition that they are rational. It is here that the assumption of boundedly rational behaviour is used most intensively. Given these adaptive expectations, players (gradually) adjust their behaviour towards the strategies that perform best. A final element that is important in the basic model is that at any moment in time people may behave in some unexplainable way. This is modelled by allowing any action to be chosen in any period with some (very small) probability.

The above-mentioned articles show that if the random deviations have sufficiently low probability and if interaction is uniform, i.e., all players meet each other with the same probability, then most of the time most of the population will play according to one of the equilibria. The reason is twofold. First, because of the chance element, eventually one particular way of solving the coordination problem will always be used more frequently than the other(s). Second, once a particular way of solving the coordination problem gains an edge, it is likely that more people hear about it and that they expect more people to use it. Hence, it becomes best to join the majority. For any positive probability of random deviations, there is a chance, however, that there is a sequence of random events by which one convention replaces another. When this probability is small, a convention is stable for a long time, but will be replaced eventually.

Young (1996) has shown how evolutionary game theory can be used to analyse the origin of two different types of conventions: (i) the historical development that eventually led every country in continental Europe to drive on the right side of the road, and (ii) the widely used norm in distributive bargaining to split the surplus in two equal parts.

5. CONCLUDING REMARKS. Schelling (1960) argued that focal points are important not only in pure coordination games, but also that they seem to play a key role in many other economically relevant areas such as tacit and explicit bargaining. This is confirmed by Young (1996). At first sight, one may expect focal points to be irrelevant in bargaining situations as there is an element of pure conflict: the larger share of the surplus one party gets, the less does the other. On closer inspection, however, the importance of focal points may be revealed. Especially when the stakes are high, it is important for both parties to reach an agreement, no matter what its exact content is, if the alternative outcome may be that no agreement is reached at all. Hence, as Schelling observed (1960: 70), 'most bargaining situations ultimately involve some range of possible outcomes within which each party would rather make a concession than fail to reach agreement at all . . . and very often the other party knows it'. Focal points are important in social life, because they help stabilize mutual expectations in case many conceivable choices exist.

There are basically two alternative stories to tell about how focal points come about. One story is based on the way players make rational use of the observed labels (attributes) of strategies and their beliefs about the labels their opponent observes. The second story is based on precedence governing the (adaptive) expectation about future play of the opponent. The stories have different domains of applications and are, therefore, not inconsistent with one another. The rationality story based on the unicity of certain attributes of strategies is best used in case people have to coordinate in situations they have not encountered before. The precedence story applies to recurrent situations in which a focal point gradually emerges out of the historical process which is partly governed by chance.

MAARTEN C.W. JANSSEN

See also COMMITMENT; CONVENTIONS AT THE FOUNDATION OF LAW; COORDINATION GAMES; EVOLUTIONARY GAME THEORY; SOCIAL NORMS AND THE LAW.

Subject classification: 1(b); 1d(i).

BIBLIOGRAPHY

Bacharach, M. 1993. Variable universe games. In *Frontiers of Game Theory*, ed. K. Binmore, A. Kirman and P. Tani, Cambridge, MA: MIT Press.

Bacharach, M. and Bernasconi, M. 1997. The variable frame theory of focal points: an experimental study. *Games and Economic Behavior* 19: 1–45.

Colman, A. 1997. Salience and focusing in pure coordination games. *Journal of Economic Methodology* 4: 61–82.

Crawford, V. and Haller, H. 1990. Learning how to cooperate: optimal play in repeated coordination games. *Econometrica* 58: 571–95.

Gauthier, D. 1975. Coordination. *Dialogue* 14: 195–221.

Gilbert, M. 1989. Rationality and salience. *Philosophical Studies* 57: 61–77.

Goyal, S. and Janssen, M. 1996. Can we rationally learn to coordinate? *Theory and Decision* 40: 29–49.

Harsanyi, J. and Selten, R. 1988. *A General Theory of Equilibrium Selection in Games*. Cambridge, MA: MIT Press.

Janssen, M.C.W. 1995. Rationalizing focal points. Tinbergen Institute Discussion Paper 95–35, Rotterdam, The Netherlands.

Kandori, M., Mailath, G. and Rob, R. 1993. Learning, mutation and long run equilibria in games. *Econometrica* 61: 29–56.

Kramarz, F. 1996. Dynamic focal points in n-person coordination games. *Theory and Decision* 40: 277–313.

Lewis, D. 1969. *Convention: A Philosophical Study*. Cambridge, MA: Harvard University Press.

Mehta, J., Starmer, C. and Sugden, R. 1992. An experimented investigation of focal points in coordination and bargaining. In *Decision Making Under Risk and Uncertainty: New Models and Empirical Findings*, ed. J. Geweke, Dordrecht: Kluwer.

Mehta, J., Starmer, C. and Sugden, R. 1994a. The nature of salience: an experimental investigation of pure coordination games. *American Economic Review* 84: 658–73.

Mehta, J., Starmer, C. and Sugden, R. 1994b. Focal points in pure coordination games: an experimental investigation. *Theory and Decision* 36: 163–85.

Morris, S., Rob, R. and Shin, H. 1995. P-dominance and belief potential. *Econometrica* 63: 145–57.

Schelling, T.C. 1960. *The Strategy of Conflict*. Cambridge, MA: Harvard University Press.

Sugden, R. 1991. Rational choice: a survey of contributions from economics and philosophy. *Economic Journal* 101: 751–85.

Sugden, R. 1995. A theory of focal points. *Economic Journal* 105: 533–50.

Van Huyck, J., Battalio, C. and Bell, R. 1990. Tacit coordination games, strategic uncertainty and coordination failure. *American Economic Review* 80: 234–48.

Young, H.P. 1993. The evolution of conventions. *Econometrica* 61: 57–84.

Young, H.P. 1996. The economics of convention. *Journal of Economic Perspectives* 10: 105–22.

folk theorems. *See* GAME THEORY AND THE LAW.

foreseeability in contracts. *See* CONTRACTS.

form contracts. *See* STANDARD FORM CONTRACTS.

forum shopping. *See* CONFLICT OF LAWS.

forward contracts. *See* DERIVATIVE SECURITIES REGULATION.

franchise contracts. Franchising is an organizational form lying between markets and hierarchies, and can follow either a business-format or a simpler dealership model. Business-format franchising, in which the franchisor supplies a brand name and also a model business for the franchisee to copy, is the growing sector of franchising and covers businesses like vehicle rental and fast-food restaurants. Many of the differences between business-format franchising and dealerships (e.g., cars or petroleum) are disappearing over time as manufacturers provide a wide range of support for their dealers. Theoretical and empirical work on franchising has developed from agency theory and from ideas about asset specificity and opportunism associated with transactions-cost analysis. Franchising is in fact a very good area in which to study many of the questions raised in the economics of contracts.

A common view amongst businessmen, also held by some academics, is that firms franchise to raise capital for expansion. This argument makes no sense unless we assume that the franchisor is more risk averse than the franchisee (Rubin 1978), which is implausible. Even if franchisors could not use normal capital markets, they could sell shares in a portfolio of all outlets. The shares would diversify risk for the buyers but impose no costs on the franchisor. Franchisees would pay less for undiversified investments if they are risk averse, which implies smaller returns for franchisors. Any capital-market advantages from franchising must come from shifting risk to the franchisee, which only makes sense if the franchisor is the more risk averse.

The foregoing dismissal of the capital-raising explanation of franchising does, however, depend upon an assumption of zero transaction costs. Franchising can in fact be a capital issue under less restrictive assumptions (Norton 1995) and this should be remembered when experiencing discomfort at undermining the widely held view in business that capital structure drives franchising. However, the best reason for generally denying the relevance of capital structure is that empirical work by economists supports other organizational costs as the driving force behind franchising. As an example, increases in the capital cost of opening stores typically reduce the proportion of franchised outlets in a chain, which is contrary to the capital-raising story. Furthermore, interviews with franchisors show them often to emphasize the incentive aspects of franchising rather than capital issues: the capital-raising argument is not universally held within the business world.

The best explanations of the features of franchising embody solutions to serious monitoring problems. In retail networks where the satellite business is remote from the head office, monitoring is difficult and it pays to develop an incentive system that encourages the avoidance of shirking. A profit-sharing agreement gives the franchisee sufficient residual profits to make shirking too costly. The franchise chain will show more total profit if shirking is controlled. Franchisors will not pay any more profit to franchisees than is necessary to remove the incentive to shirk. In a competitive market, prospective franchisees should be willing to pay lump-sum franchise fees equal to the difference between franchise profits and the managerial earnings available in similar occupations.

We do not usually observe franchise contracts of this kind. Instead, franchisees pay a lump-sum initial fee plus a continuing royalty payment related to sales, in return for residual profits. The most plausible explanation is that the franchisee requires protection against poor post-contract performance by the franchisor. The franchisor's duties cover such things as providing managerial support and the monitoring of standards of operation throughout the franchise system. Monitoring of the system is necessary to control a classic externality problem: if one franchisee allows quality to deteriorate, he benefits by the full amount of the savings from reduced quality but incurs only part of the costs as other franchisees will suffer some of the loss of business. This type of externality is best regarded as horizontal free riding (Mathewson and Winter 1985).

The importance of monitoring by the franchisor suggests several predictions. Increasing the geographical density of outlets should make operating company stores more attractive. Also, franchisors should buy back their outlets as their chains become more mature, the density of outlets increases and distance-related monitoring costs become lower per outlet. Buy-backs are in fact observed in mature chains and much econometric work supports the importance of geographical density in explaining franchising. Another important observation is that increases in the value of the franchisor's inputs increase the royalty payment relative to the franchisee's lump-sum fee, which supports the view that franchise contracts are partly constructed to control the franchisor's opportunism.

Horizontal externalities, although apparently of practical importance, are not actually necessary to explain franchise contracts. Monitoring difficulties arise for the franchisor even when there is only one territory. However, vertical externality (the franchisee chiselling on the franchisor's standards) is an ever-present problem. The franchisor could impose a large penalty if the franchisee were caught cheating, making the franchisee's income the same across different demand conditions and giving a pure risk-sharing contract with no profit-sharing. This could be done regardless of the degree of risk aversion on the part of the franchisee, which is therefore also not a central issue in explaining franchise contracts. However, the required penalty may be unfeasible owing to wealth constraints affecting the franchisee, and this suggests a need for some form of profit sharing.

Given a constraint on the wealth of franchisees that prevents them from sinking large investments into franchises, franchisors must rely on rewards rather than the penalty of termination to maintain franchisees' standards. Incentive compatibility between the franchisor and franchisee can be achieved by careful tailoring of the contract. For example, the franchise contract must ensure that the profit accruing to the franchisee from correctly declaring good demand states and applying the correct effort level exceeds the profit from wrongly declaring a poor state and adjusting effort downward. If the franchisee is to participate in the contract at all there must be sufficient profit for the franchisee to pay a royalty fee. Agency theorists have used insights like these to construct models giving precise predictions of franchise fees, franchise effort in different demand states, the level of brand-name investment by the franchisor (including advertising) and the frequency of monitoring.

If franchisees did not face wealth constraints, they could post bonds to guarantee good performance. Bond posting, however, is problematic, as the franchisor might behave opportunistically. The expected value of any posted bond would have to be less than the profits accruing to the franchisor from the proper delivery of services; otherwise, there would be an incentive for the franchisor to abscond with the lump sum, possibly by contriving some reason for contract termination. Thus the royalty fee, or its equivalent, is always likely to be the engine for rent extraction by the franchisor. 'Dual distribution' is an important franchising phenomenon, in which the franchisor simultaneously operates some stores and franchises others. Dual distribution may be a method through which a franchisor signals the profitability of the franchise chain by making his own returns dependent on the revenues of the company stores (Gallini and Lutz 1992). The value of this may be greatest for a new franchisor with no track record.

Suppose that a new franchisor knows that conditions are favourable so that stores should be unusually profitable. The problem is to convey this information in a credible manner to prospective franchisees. A high-profit franchisor chooses the proportion of company stores, the lump-sum and the royalty to establish a 'separating equilibrium' defining a contract that a low-profit franchisor could never offer and stay in business. A contract can be designed so that low-profit franchisors will always make more profit from truthfully declaring quality and franchising all stores, compared with emulating the dual-distribution strategy of the high-profit franchisor.

A number of predictions may be made on the basis of signalling theory, but they are not supported by empirical work. To take one as an example, the high profitability of some franchises would be recognized over time and there would be no need for franchisors to operate company stores as a signal. We should see mature franchise chains concentrating on franchising, rather than the operation of company stores. However, there is often a buy-back phenomenon as the chain matures, which is quite the opposite of the prediction.

Dual distribution could be a device through which the franchisor gathers and uses local information. This theory is Austrian in character and emphasizes the key role played by information in the competitive process. There are examples where the franchised and company stores operate in close proximity to each other. For example, in Sacramento, California, 34 Taco Bell restaurants covered a 30-mile radius, of which seven were company owned (Minkler 1992). In such cases, franchisors may be drawing on the local knowledge of franchisees concerning local tastes and market conditions. The franchisor might be unable to direct the satellite business, even if monitoring costs were zero, because of ignorance. Franchising allows the use of the trade mark to be exchanged for the franchisee's local entrepreneurship, which is defined as noticing and acting upon opportunities. The franchisee's local entrepreneurship reduces the cost of search for new business.

So far, I have concentrated on property-rights and organizational explanations of the franchise contract. Within the mainstream industrial-organization literature there are papers which show that a firm with monopoly power supplying an intermediate product into a competitive industry has an incentive to exercise vertical control if downstream input substitution is possible. It is worth spending a little time explaining why these monopoly-power stories are not relevant to the understanding of franchising.

Vertical restrictions principally comprise refusal to supply, tied-in sales, and exclusive-dealing contracts. The arguments of several economists that there are efficiency reasons for all of these practices are reflected in the specialist economic analysis of franchising, and in the benign view taken by European competition law towards franchising. For example, against simple claims that a monopolist could foreclose a downstream market by refusing to supply unless buyers were tied into a restrictive contract, it may be argued that it is profitable to allow access to inputs at monopoly prices to more efficient downstream firms. Although, to be fair, some recent analysis has revealed conditions under which refusal to supply (Bolton and Whinston 1993) is a credible policy committing a firm to compete aggressively in the downstream market and deterring entry.

Analyses of franchising based on monopoly-power explanations of vertical restrictions are typically less general than theories based on the economics of organization. As a very simple example of lack of generality, note that monopoly-power theories of vertical restrictions usually deal with product franchises (whereas most business-format franchises are based on services) and would seem to have relevance only for brand-and-trade-name franchising. The relevance of the market-power approach is also questioned by a lack of supporting empirical evidence: for example, the proportion of franchised outlets *decreases* as franchisor input sales increases (Lafontaine 1992). A further problem is the tendency to regard individual controls like resale price maintenance (RPM) and franchise fees as perfect substitutes for one another. In general, franchising firms select particular contractual devices with great regularity and cannot possibly be indifferent between them and devices that are rarely or never used.

Efficiency-based explanations of vertical restrictions are descended from Telser's (1960) analysis of RPM. A retailer could provide service levels such as advice and product demonstrations only to find that consumers made use of these and then bought the product at a low price from a no-frills retailer. There is a free-rider problem among retailers implying that no retailer would provide services. If service levels matter in promoting sales for the manufacturing and retailing industries combined, and are not separable, a means like RPM must be found to defeat free riding. Exclusive dealing, which is a common feature of franchising, may be explained in a similar fashion (Marvel 1982). When a manufacturer with a valuable brand supplies an outlet, it endorses the retailer's business and centralized advertising may promote the retailer's sales more generally. Exclusive dealing prevents retailers from diverting business to other brands and wasting advertising.

Franchisors may use tied-in sales either to control the quality of the final service, or to measure the sales of franchisees (Klein and Saft 1985). Where the franchisee cannot substitute away from the input, a mark-up on a tie-in is equivalent to a fixed-percentage sales royalty if price is predictable. Tie-ins may also develop where the franchisor wishes to ensure that franchisees use inputs of specific quality. Rather than monitoring the required technical properties of more generic inputs, the franchisor has the much simpler problem of ascertaining whether anything else was used.

Moving back to organizational questions, transactions-cost analysis shows that franchise contractual provisions that are often regarded as unfair in the law have important implications for efficiency (Klein 1995). Fully contingent, costlessly enforceable, explicit contracts are not usually feasible. Uncertainty implies a large number of possible contingencies and some aspects of contractual performance are difficult to measure. Individuals have an incentive to renege on agreements and hold-up any contracting partner who has made specific investments, by taking advantage of unspecified or unenforceable aspects of contracts. Full vertical integration between trading partners will not always be observed: for instance, integration of human capital is outlawed by the prohibition of slavery.

One method of safeguarding performance is for a potential cheater to post a bond (a 'hostage'), possibly in an implicit form if the cheater is required to make an investment in a highly specific form with a very low salvageable value. In both cases, the same purpose is served. Franchise contracts typically require franchisees to pay lump-sum fees to franchisors and to make highly specific investments in equipment. The franchisor usually takes the right to terminate the contract at will if the franchisee is not maintaining quality standards. For any hostage to be effective it must set the franchisee's expected gain from cheating equal to zero. This implies that hostages will be worth much more than the actual gain when monitoring costs are positive. Cheating by the franchisor is controlled by possible increases in operating costs. A franchisor known to appropriate hostages opportunistically would lose franchisees and find it hard to recruit new ones, forcing him to use more costly organizational forms. As long as the franchisee's bond is greater than the franchisee's expected gain from cheating and is less than the cost penalty imposed on the franchisor on moving to some other organizational form, a hostage can support their relationship. The hostage is a low-cost substitute for costly monitoring and enforcement devices.

Of particular interest is an argument put forward by Benjamin Klein (1980) that the franchisor's right to terminate the contract at will (or perhaps just for good cause: although Klein claims in his later paper (1995) that US courts have allowed termination at will) supports a number of hostages. Given the franchisor's prerogative over termination, the common requirement that franchisees lease their properties from the franchisor can be explained. The franchisee could be forced to move premises and sacrifice valuable leasehold improvements, which would revert to the franchisor as lessor. This gives the franchisor a hostage with which to control franchisee behaviour and enables monitoring to be reduced with an associated cost saving. In recent years, Klein has moved to the view that the rents attached to the non-salvageable investment should be the focus in valuing the franchisee's potential loss, at least in cases where there are no binding legal constraints on the franchisor's behaviour.

It is important to recognize the rich variety of devices used to support contracts. The use of restrictive covenants in franchise agreements can also be explained in terms of hostages. Covenants usually prevent a franchisee from competing in a market area for some period after leaving the franchise system, implying that the non-availability of an alternative rent stream is used to constrain the franchisee's behaviour: i.e., he cannot cheat and leave for better pastures. A new franchisee's future level of skill is not known, but if he becomes highly adept at his business he might be tempted to set up on his own. A covenant prevents the franchisee from simply removing the franchisor's investment in his training. Also, termination by the franchisor can cause the loss of the hostage.

It is possible to lay down some principles to aid hostage selection. Implicit hostages are less vulnerable to opportunistic appropriation by trading partners compared with pecuniary hostages. A hostage can be selected to be unattractive to its holder. An ideal hostage is like an 'ugly princess': the medieval king with two equally cherished daughters would be wiser posting the ugly one as a hostage, as she is less likely to be appropriated by the captor (Williamson 1985).

A number of common observations can be made in examining franchise chains (Dnes 1993). Franchising increases the specificity of investment for the satellite business, compared with independent operation: for example, leasehold improvements are trade-marked and hard to adapt to other uses. Also, lump-sum fees are typically small in relation to sunk investment for the franchisee and appear to be linked to the franchisor's costs of establishing the franchisee (training and launch advertising). The implicit aspects of contracts are important and show adjustments that favour the interests of both franchisees and franchisors.

Another real-world consideration is that the feasibility of placing disciplinary hostages with franchisors is qualified by the explicit and implicit details of franchise contracts, which often set out conditions under which the franchisor must buy-back assets in the event of termination. Statute law in some countries, like the US, also makes it difficult to call in a hostage for disciplinary reasons. Principles of common law, such as the prohibition against penal damages for breach of contract, may also make disciplinary hostages illegal in an Anglo-American setting.

It is not surprising that franchisees are careful to avoid hostage penalties in their contracts: investments in such things as leasehold improvements are not ugly princesses but are of potential direct value to the franchisor. There are several questions about the real-world feasibility of disciplinary hostages, regardless of whether these are measured as rent streams or as the book value of sunk investments. Sunk investment by the franchisee may well have mainly a screening function, serving to demonstrate confidence in his own competence.

The last decade has witnessed much progress in the scientific understanding of franchising. Several theories have been constructed to explain franchising, most of which emphasize savings of monitoring costs in an agency framework. The dominant concern has been with the contractual devices used to suppress opportunism on the part of both franchisors and franchisees. In many key respects, in result although not in principle (as the lawyers say) the transaction-cost analysis and agency analysis of franchising often appear to be two different languages describing the same franchising phenomena and very similar economic mechanisms.

ANTONY DNES

See also ASSET SPECIFICITY AND VERTICAL INTEGRATION; CONTRACTS AND RELATIONSHIPS; EXCLUSIONARY AGREEMENTS; HOLD-UP PROBLEM; OPPORTUNISTIC BEHAVIOUR IN CONTRACTS; PUBLIC FRANCHISING; RELATIONAL CONTRACT; RESALE PRICE MAINTENANCE; SYMBIOTIC ARRANGEMENTS; TYING.

Subject classification: 5c(iii).

BIBLIOGRAPHY

Blair, R.D. and Kaserman, D.L. 1982. Optimal franchising. *Southern Economic Journal* 48: 494–505.

Bolton, P. and Whinston, M. 1993. Incomplete contracts, vertical integration and supply constraints. *Review of Economic Studies* 60: 121–48.

Brickley, J.A. and Dark, F.H. 1987. The choice of organizational form: the case of franchising. *Journal of Financial Economics* 18: 401–20.

Dnes, A.W. 1991. The economics of franchising and its regulation. In *Franchising and the Law: Theoretical and Comparative Approaches in Europe and the United States*, ed. Ch. Joerges (Baden-Baden: Nomos): 133–42.

Dnes, A.W. 1993. A case-study analysis of franchise contracts. *Journal of Legal Studies* 22: 367–93.

Dnes, A.W. 1996. The economic analysis of franchise contracts – survey article. *Journal of Institutional and Theoretical Economics* 152, 297–324.

Gallini, N.T. and Lutz, N.A. 1992. Dual distribution and royalty fees in franchising. *Journal of Law, Economics and Organization* 8: 471–501.

Klein, B. 1980. Transaction cost determinants of unfair contractual arrangements. *American Economic Review* 70: 356–62.

Klein, B. 1995. The economics of franchise contracts. *Journal of Corporate Finance: Contracting, Governance and Organization* 2: 9–38.

Klein, B. and Saft, L.F. 1985. The law and economics of franchise tying contracts. *Journal of Law and Economics* 28: 345–61.

Lafontaine, F. 1992. Agency theory and franchising: some empirical results. *RAND Journal of Economics* 23: 263–83.

Lafontaine, F. 1993. Contractual arrangements as signaling devices: evidence from franchising. *Journal of Law, Economics and Organization* 9: 256–89.

Martin, R.E. 1988. Franchising and risk management. *American Economic Review* 78: 954–68.

Marvel, H. 1982. Exclusive dealing. *Journal of Law and Economics* 25: 1–25.

Mathewson, G.F. and Winter, R. 1985. The economics of franchise contracts. *Journal of Law and Economics* 28: 503–26.

Minkler, A. 1992. Why firms franchise: a search cost theory. *Journal of Institutional and Theoretical Economics* 148: 240–59.

Norton, S.W. 1988. An empirical look at franchising as an organizational form. *Journal of Business* 61: 197–218.

Norton, S.W. 1995. Is franchising a capital-structure issue? *Journal of Corporate Finance: Contracting, Governance and Organization* 2: 75–102.

Rubin, P.H. 1978. The theory of the firm and the structure of franchise contract. *Journal of Law and Economics* 21: 223–33.

Sass, T.R. and M. Gisser. 1989. Agency cost, firm size, and exclusive dealing. *Journal of Law and Economics* 32: 381–99.

Schanze, E. 1991. Symbiotic contracts: exploring long-term agency structures. In *Franchising and the Law: Theoretical and Comparative Approaches in Europe and the United States*, ed. Ch. Joerges, Baden-Baden: Nomos: 67–103.

Telser, L. 1960. Why should manufacturers want fair trade? *Journal of Law and Economics* 3: 86–105.

Thompson, R.S. 1994. The franchise life cycle: a contractual solution to the Penrose effect? *Journal of Economic Behavior and Organization* 24: 207–18.

Williamson, O.E. 1985. *The Economic Institutions of Capitalism.* New York: Free Press.

fraud-on-the-market. 'Fraud-on-the-market' describes a legal theory which identifies misrepresentations and the withholding of information as fraudulent behaviour adversely affecting both purchasers and the securities market in general. This theory is

> based on the hypothesis that, in an open and developed securities market, the price of a company's stock is determined by the available material information regarding the company and its business. . . . Misleading statements will therefore defraud purchasers of stock even if the purchasers do not directly rely on the misstatements (*Basic v. Levinson*, 241–2).

It is intended to benefit investors who are presumed harmed by misleading or misdirecting statements by officers or directors of a corporation. The courts established the fraud-on-the-market theory to allow plaintiffs to recover when the material information made available to them is either incomplete or incorrect.

The primary flaw in the courts' application of this theory lies in its failure to recognize the competing interests of fiduciary duties and property rights in information. Not all misrepresentations or material omissions are harmful to purchasers. In fact, corporate officers or directors may often have a duty to withhold or misrepresent information in the interest of the shareholder, and those actions will often prove beneficial to shareholders. The fraud-on-the-market theory is unlikely to benefit investors until courts make the theory compatible with the efficient allocation of property rights in information within the corporation. This reconciliation could easily be accomplished by combining the fraud-on-the-market theory with the theory of fiduciary duties of disclosure. Such a modification of fraud-on-the-market theory would allow officers and directors to maintain their obligations to shareholders while protecting the market from harmful behaviour.

The United States Supreme Court first embraced the fraud-on-the-market theory in *Basic, Inc. v. Levinson* (*Basic v. Levinson*, 224). The Court validated a new method by which a plaintiff may show reliance on material misstatements or omissions by the defendant in a lawsuit brought under Rule 10b–5, which is the SEC's general rule prohibiting insider trading and misleading or deceptive trading practices. Under the fraud-on-the-market theory, a plaintiff may show that he was entitled to rely on the 'integrity' of the market price for the securities he bought or sold. According to the Court, the market price for a security has integrity if the trading market for the security is efficient in the sense used by financial economists, who describe the market for a security as efficient if it adjusts rapidly to reflect new information. Plaintiffs buying or selling stocks that trade in efficient markets need no longer meet the traditional requirement that they actually read or heard the material containing the relevant misstatement or omission.

In *Basic*, the Court held that plaintiffs must prove that a security trades in a semi-strong efficient market in order to recover under the fraud-on-the-market theory. This requirement as applied by the Court is both underinclusive and overinclusive from an economic perspective. It is overinclusive because stock prices of some firms may be highly efficient with regard to some information, but inefficient with regard to other information. For example, a widely traded stock may respond promptly to information about a stock split, but slowly to information about a change in projected quarterly earnings. The Court's application of the efficiency test is underinclusive, because even stock that exhibits low levels of information efficiency with respect to most information may respond in a highly efficient manner to some types of information, such as news about a pending hostile takeover. Thus, in a securities fraud case brought under the fraud-on-the-market theory, courts should not consider the question of whether a security is traded in an efficient market in isolation from the particular disclosure issue being litigated. Furthermore, three different variables will have important effects on market efficiency: the type of firm-specific information being released, the market in which the security is traded, and the type of security being traded. Only one of these variables – the market in which the security is being traded – was considered relevant by the Court in *Basic*.

The disclosure responsibilities of officers and directors suggested by the Court in *Basic* are inconsistent with the principle that nonpublic corporate information is simply another form of corporate asset that should be used for the benefit of the firm that owns it. Thus, the fraud-on-the-market theory must be reconciled with a theory of property rights in information in order to produce a coherent theory of 10b–5 liability that will promote the efficient allocation of nonpublic corporate information.

A primary function of assigning and protecting property rights is to ensure that property owners bear all the costs and enjoy all the benefits generated by the assets they own. Requiring that the owner bear all the costs associated with owning an asset helps to ensure that third parties do not bear these costs. Allowing the owner to enjoy the benefits associated with owning the asset (including the benefit derived from being able to sell the asset for a profit) ensures that property owners have the appropriate incentives to create and deploy assets in the most productive ways. This analysis is as true for intangible property, such as nonpublic information, as for tangible property such as land.

The Supreme Court's opinion in *Chiarella v. United States* is illustrative of a theory of insider trading liability that is entirely consistent with a theory of property rights in information (*Chiarella v. United States*, 222). The defendant, Vincent Chiarella, obtained material, nonpublic information in the course of his work as a financial printer. He discovered the identities of firms that were about to be the target of tender offers or merger proposals by deciphering the encoded names in disclosure documents delivered to his printing firm by the companies making the tender offers or merger proposals.

The firms making the tender offers and merger proposals clearly owned the information in question. They created the information, and their research investment was going to lead to the increases in wealth associated with these corporate combinations. Prior to the public announcement of an acquisition, secrecy was of the utmost importance to the acquiror – premature disclosure would cause the price of the target firm's stock to increase, thereby making the acquisition more costly and less likely to occur.

These acquirors attempted to preserve their property interests in this material, nonpublic corporate information by contractually obligating the printing company to maintain the confidentiality of the information it obtained in the course of its work. The printing company consequently enforced this obligation on its employees.

The Court's selected method for enforcing property rights in information was a declaration that material, nonpublic information could be protected by a 'fiduciary duty' owed to the owners by those in contractual privity with them. The Court linked the property rights in inside information to a preexisting contractual obligation that engenders a fiduciary duty. Thus, if Chiarella owed any legal obligation, it was to the acquiring companies whose information he had stolen. Subsequent cases have made it clear that liability for violating Rule 10b–5 will henceforth be based on a business property theory, implemented in turn by a preexisting fiduciary duty test.

The Supreme Court's opinion in *Dirks v. SEC* reinforced the economic underpinnings and the property rights perspective of its *Chiarella* analysis (*Dirks v. SEC*, 646). Dirks, an investment analyst, obtained nonpublic information about an ongoing fraud of epic proportions at Equity Funding, an insurance holding company. Dirks obtained this information from a former officer at Equity Funding and disclosed it to his clients, in some cases with the expectation of future trading commissions.

The Court based its decision on 'a theory that recognizes the value to society of protecting property rights in inside information'. In *Dirks*, the Court emphasized that the 'initial inquiry' in an insider trading case should be 'whether there has been a breach of duty by the insider'.

In *Basic, Inc. v. Levinson*, the Court failed to follow the implications of the sound economic reasoning it developed in *Dirks* and *Chiarella*. In particular, the Court failed to distinguish adequately those situations in which the defendants in a Rule 10b–5 suit owe a fiduciary duty to the plaintiffs from the smaller set of situations in which the defendants breach that duty. The point is illustrated with reference to the fact pattern presented in *Basic* itself.

The plaintiffs in *Basic* were one-time shareholders in Basic, a large manufacturing company whose shares traded on the New York Stock Exchange. Beginning in September 1976, Basic's officers and directors were involved in negotiations concerning a possible merger with Combustion Engineering, a manufacturing company in a related field. Although Basic made three public statements during 1977 and 1978 denying that it was engaged in merger negotiations, Basic's board of directors announced publicly on 20 December 1978 its approval of Combustion Engineering's tender offer for all of its outstanding shares.

Shareholders who sold Basic shares between the time of the first public statement denying merger negotiations and the public announcement of the tender offer brought suit claiming that Basic and certain of its officers and directors had violated Rule 10b–5. The plaintiffs alleged that they had been harmed because they sold Basic shares at prices 'artificially depressed' by Basic's false and misleading statements about the pendency of serious merger negotiations with Combustion Engineering.

Chiarella and *Dirks* emphasized that traders owe no generalized duty to the marketplace. By contrast, in *Basic*, the Court defended its adoption of a fraud-on-the-market approach on the ground that the theory will protect the securities markets generally.

Basic's management clearly would have breached their fiduciary duties to their shareholders had they purchased Basic stock for their own accounts while in possession of inside information about the pending merger with Combustion Engineering. But Basic's officers and directors did not purchase any stock. Their only wrongdoing was issuing a misleading press release. Under these facts, the real issue in *Basic* should have been whether the officers and directors breached a fiduciary duty to Basic's shareholders by falsely denying that Basic was engaged in merger negotiations. The Court, however, did not even consider whether management had breached this fiduciary duty.

Fiduciary duties function economically to regulate the complex structure of the corporate enterprise. Within the modern publicly held corporation, investors delegate authority to directors, who in turn delegate authority to other agents operating at many levels within the enterprise. This delegation is efficient because it allows directors and officers to specialize in management and investors to specialize in risk bearing. The fiduciary principle is a relatively low-cost approach, substituting deterrence for costly and ineffective direct supervision of agents' behaviour.

From an economic perspective, fiduciary principles, including the fiduciary principle proscribing insider trading, are simply contractual devices. The principle that officers and directors owe a fiduciary duty to shareholders serves as a 'standard-form penalty clause' in contracts to which investors are interested parties. This economic perspective is important because it generates a mechanism by which courts can decide cases. In particular, when scrutinizing managerial behaviour, courts should treat an allegation of a breach of fiduciary duty as they would treat any alleged breach of contract. This analytic method is often described as the 'hypothetical bargain' approach. Under this approach to fiduciary duty, courts would evaluate whether the managers' actions were consistent with the terms of a hypothetical fully specified, contingent contract that informed, value-maximizing investors would have agreed to *ex ante*. The Court's analysis in *Basic* is flawed because of its failure to employ this 'hypothetical bargain' perspective. It did not consider even briefly whether its decision enhanced or diminished investor welfare.

News that merger negotiations were in progress would signal to other investors that Basic was an attractive merger prospect, allowing them to 'free ride' on Combustion's investment in information about Basic. The simple identity of valuable takeover targets is information that lends itself to free riding. The free-rider problem adversely affects investor wealth maximization to the extent it discourages acquirors who would otherwise pay shareholders a takeover premium for the shares they own. No firm wants to be the first bidder unless it has some advantage, such as speed, over subsequent bidders to compensate for the fact that only it had to incur monitoring costs. And, of course, if there is no first bidder there will be no later bidders and no tender premium. For this reason, among others, it is well settled that premature disclosure of merger discussions may thwart the merger and its value. All shareholders, including the plaintiffs, would have been made worse off if premature disclosure of the merger negotiations caused Combustion Engineering to withdraw its offer.

Nondisclosure of merger negotiations may thus encourage mergers and increase shareholder wealth. It seems clear that Basic's misleading press releases should enjoy the protection of the business judgment rule. The Court, therefore, should reconcile its decision in *Basic* with its earlier decisions in *Chiarella* and *Dirks*, which emphasize the relationship between culpability under Rule 10b–5 and the breach of a preexisting fiduciary duty to investors.

Nonetheless, a tension exists between the goal of wealth maximization, which at times can only be achieved through strategic misrepresentation or nondisclosure, and the goal of creating an efficient market. Nondisclosure or misleading disclosures will inhibit an accurate reflection of all information known about the firm. But market efficiency has never been an end unto itself. Efficient markets are beneficial because they allow investors to purchase and sell stock in reliance on market prices. The reliance saves investors' resources because it replaces costly research into firm values. Efficient markets also increase allocative efficiency by ensuring that capital flows to its highest valuing users.

While a strongly pro-disclosure regime would increase market efficiency, shareholder wealth would suffer because fewer mergers would be consummated. This diminution in mergers would reduce the possibility that shareholders will receive a premium for their shares, thereby reducing shareholder and societal wealth. It seems clear that, given a choice between wealth maximization and market efficiency, investors would gladly exchange efficiency for the opportunity for increased wealth.

The second attribute of market efficiency identified above was the improvement of allocative efficiency. If securities are efficiently priced, prices will accurately reflect all known information about firms' future prospects. Investments will then flow to those firms and projects having the greatest chance of succeeding. The Supreme Court's opinion in *Basic* heavily favours disclosure as a means of protecting the allocative efficiency of the market. Strategic misrepresentation is not even considered as a possible option for firms faced with a disclosure dilemma. In fact, the Court goes so far as to suggest that mere nondisclosure may be as bad as outright manipulation.

Although efficient markets are clearly important to capital allocation decisions, the policy advocated here does little to harm the capital allocation process. Firms may not engage in nondisclosure or strategic misrepresentations merely at their whim. They must have a compelling reason, such as the need to protect the confidentiality of ongoing merger negotiations or a new corporate discovery or invention. Furthermore, the nondisclosure or misrepresentation may last only so long as necessary to protect shareholder interests.

Moreover, there is little danger of harm to the capital allocation process because the costs of misrepresentations or nondisclosures, in terms of increased capital costs, are generally borne by the firm making the nondisclosures or misrepresentations. For example, to the extent they were believed, the defendants' misrepresentations in Basic caused the price of Basic shares to trade at artificially low levels, thus raising the costs to Basic of attracting new capital.

The costs of some value-maximizing nondisclosures and misrepresentations will not be internalized by the firms making them. These sorts of nondisclosures or misrepresentations should not be permitted. For example, suppose that a firm is not a takeover target, but the directors and officers of the firm are aware of the substantial premiums available to target shareholders and would like to attract an outside bidder. These directors and officers also are aware that bidders are more likely to surface if it becomes known that the firm already is 'in play' – that is, it is currently the subject of a merger proposal. These circumstances might tempt management to fabricate rumours that the firm is involved in merger discussions in order to attract outside bidders.

Although these misrepresentations might increase shareholder wealth, they should not be permitted, because they reduce allocative efficiency in ways that are not internalized by the relevant firms and create negative externalities. Potential bidders will waste resources sifting through the false information being disseminated by would-be takeover targets. Investors would also be disadvantaged by the distortions created by these sorts of misrepresentations. Thus, nondisclosures and misrepresentations should only be permitted where the costs of such behaviours are internalized by the firms making such nondisclosures and misrepresentations. These typically will be strategic misrepresentations that cause shares to trade at artificially low rather than artificially high prices. Misrepresentations that cause a firm's share prices to shift from an efficient level to an inefficient level will cause negative externalities and should be discouraged. On the other hand, misrepresentations or nondisclosures that allow the price of a firm's share to continue to trade at an inefficient level in order to preserve the confidentiality of corporate information should not be discouraged.

In modern, sophisticated financial markets, officers and directors of public corporations must occasionally employ subterfuges such as nondisclosure and misrepresentation in order to protect the value of their firms' investments. It should also be clear, however, that misrepresentations should only be permissible where necessary to protect existing investments or legitimate corporate opportunities. Otherwise, such misrepresentations create the negative externalities and allocative inefficiencies described above. This theory does not condone or justify strategic misrepresentations, except in those limited situations where such misrepresentations are necessary in order to facilitate transactions that are themselves socially beneficial.

Valuable corporate information should not be disclosed if, in the business judgment of the officers and directors involved, such disclosure would jeopardize the aggregate value of the firm's shares. If, for example, management legitimately believes that disclosure of preliminary merger negotiations would threaten the success of such negotiations, then it should not be compelled to make such a disclosure, regardless of the materiality of those negotiations, until the merger is complete. Similarly, management should be allowed to deny rumours which it knows to be correct and even to make affirmative misstatements if doing so is necessary to protect aggregate share value. These strategic misrepresentations should not be punished where management commits them in adherence to its fiduciary duty to shareholders. As the information processors within the capital markets have become more sophisticated, the old fashioned 'no comment' statements that management used to make in order to protect confidential information no longer suffice to protect shareholder wealth. In light of current decoding techniques among market professionals, management must be free to take bolder steps. An exception to this policy of permitting certain corporate misrepresentations would be applied to cases in which the firm making the false statements does not internalize the costs to the capital market associated with such misstatements. This exception will eliminate any distortions to the capital allocation process caused by the general rule favouring strategic misrepresentations.

Thus, plaintiffs should be allowed to recover under the fraud-on-the-market theory under only two circumstances. The first is in cases where the officers and directors making the material omission or misrepresentation breached a fiduciary duty in doing so. The second is where the firm about which the misrepresentations were made is not seeking to protect a preexisting property right in information, so that it does not internalize the costs associated with the misrepresentation.

The fraud-on-the-market theory need not be rejected by the courts. Instead, the judiciary's application of finance theory should be refined to make it conform to principles of economic theory. The fraud-on-the-market theory can be both good finance and good economics.

J.R. MACEY

See also CIVIL LIABILITY UNDER RICO: UNINTENDED CONSEQUENCES OF LEGISLATION; CORPORATE CRIME AND ITS CONTROL; CORPORATE LAW; FIDUCIARY DUTIES; INSIDER TRADING; LAW-AND-ECONOMICS IN ACTION; OWNERSHIP OF MARKET INFORMATION; PROPERTY RIGHTS; SECURITIES REGULATION; TENDER OFFERS; UNJUST ENRICHMENT.

Subject classification: 5e; 6c(iii).

CASES

Basic, Inc. v. Levinson, 485 US 224 (1988).
Chiarella v. United States, 445 US 222 (1980).
Dirks v. SEC, 463 US 646 (1983).

BIBLIOGRAPHY

Macey, J.R. and Miller, G.P. 1990. Good finance, bad economics: an analysis of the fraud on the market theory. *Stanford Law Review* 42: 1059–92.

Macey, J.R. and Miller, G.P. 1991. The fraud-on-the-market theory revisited. *Virginia Law Review* 77: 1001–8.

Macey, J.R., Miller, G.P., Mitchell, M.L. and Netter, J.N. 1991. The fraud-on-the-market theory. *Virginia Law Review* 77: 1017–67.

fraudulent conveyance. Creditors ordinarily must bargain for specific terms in their debt contracts to gain rights against their debtor. Creditors commonly protect themselves by monitoring their debtors, taking security, and making their debt short-term or callable on short notice. Moreover, creditors can protect themselves by insisting on a variety of loan covenants, such as one that forbade dividends, incurring of additional debt, and purchase of new capital equipment (see Smith and Warner 1979). In the absences of such terms, they must rely on a handful of general legal doctrines to protect their rights. Among these, perhaps the most important is fraudulent conveyance law (see Clark 1977). Fraudulent conveyance statutes give creditors the right to prevent their debtors from engaging in transactions that are so contrary to the interests of creditors that creditors would nearly always insist on them as a matter of contractual right. Fraudulent conveyance law is, in other words, an 'off-the-rack' term the law supplies to debt contracts just as implied warranties are implicitly part of a sales contract (see Baird and Jackson 1985).

PRINCIPLES OF FRAUDULENT CONVEYANCE LAW. Fraudulent conveyance law first took statutory form in 1571 (see Glenn 1931). Transfers made and obligations incurred with the intent to delay, hinder or defraud creditors are fraudulent and void as against creditors. Although written in general terms, the basic transaction at which the statute was first aimed is quite simple. A debtor, hounded by creditors, transfers everything to a friend for a trivial sum. This debtor hopes to shield assets from creditors. When the creditors come to enforce their claims, the debtor will assert that there are no assets on which they can levy. By invoking fraudulent conveyance law, the creditors can pierce through form and go to substance. The transfer is a sham, and the creditors can ignore the transfer and levy on the goods in the friend's hands as if the transfer had never taken place.

A person in search of a loan could never bargain for the right to make transfers or incur obligations for the purpose of delaying, hindering and defrauding the person who was making the loan. For this reason, the core of fraudulent conveyance law remains uncontroversial. Creditors are better off if they can always take action when their debtor tries to defraud them and do not have to bargain for such a right explicitly. Given that creditors are going to be much less willing to make loans when they lack this ability, the core of fraudulent conveyance law benefits debtors as well.

Fraudulent conveyance law, however, has grown beyond its original scope. It applies to transactions that are not 'fraudulent' in the traditional sense at all. The first step came in 1601. The court in *Twyne's Case* found that a transaction was a fraudulent conveyance not because one could prove that the debtor acted with actual fraudulent intent, but rather because there were 'badges of fraud' associated with the transaction, conditions so likely to exist only in the presence of actual fraud, that one could conclusively presume fraud from these conditions. If a debtor sells assets for a pittance to a relative, we can assume that mischief is afoot.

As the doctrine developed, however, these 'badges of fraud' ceased to be merely proxies for fraud and in addition covered transactions that, although perhaps not fraudulent, were also ones to which creditors would object. The essence of fraudulent conveyance law can be put simply: insolvent debtors cannot make transfers without receiving 'fair consideration' or 'reasonably equivalent value'. If the insolvent debtor is a corporation, any such transfer must not leave it with an unreasonably small amount of capital. Similarly, an insolvent debtor who incurs an obligation and receives too little or nothing in return makes a fraudulent conveyance.

The easiest case to imagine is a gift. An insolvent debtor gives a birthday present to a parent. A ban on such transfers makes good sense. First, large gifts to parents while in dire financial straits may in fact be motivated as much by a desire to keep assets from creditors as from filial devotion. So many of the transactions in which an insolvent debtor gives away something and receives nothing or too little in return are fraudulent that one is better off voiding all of them, rather than engaging in elaborate case-by-case inquiries into fraud. Second, gifts while a debtor is insolvent are gifts of someone else's money. When your assets are large and your debts small, your hands are free. If you are insolvent, however, they are not. When your assets exceed your liabilities, the assets are not really yours, but rather your creditors'. The justification for the law is not that such transactions are inevitably or even typically associated with bad intent, but rather that we can be confident that creditors and debtors before the fact would agree to ban them if they negotiated over the question explicitly. Fraudulent conveyance law simply supplies terms that would be part of the fully dickered bargain between debtor and creditor (see Baird and Jackson 1985).

Corporations typically do not make gifts. Nevertheless, there are a wide variety of corporate transactions that, from the perspective of a creditor, involve a transfer for which the corporation receives nothing or very little in return. Consider, for example, an ordinary dividend. Assets flow out of the corporation's coffers away from reach of creditors and nothing comes in return. Similarly, the repurchase of stock brings the creditors nothing of value. To be sure, the corporation acquires stock, but stock has no value in the hands of a corporation that issued it. We can take the simple case of a corporation with a single shareholder. There is no difference between declaring a dividend of $1 million and repurchasing $1 million in stock from the shareholder. In both cases, the shareholder owns the entire corporation after the transaction as before. The only difference is that the shareholder is $1 million richer and the creditors look to a correspondingly smaller amount of assets in corporate solution to satisfy their claims.

MECHANICS OF FRAUDULENT CONVEYANCE LAW. Fraudulent conveyance statutes take several different forms. In the United States, most states have adopted a fraudulent conveyance statute promulgated by the National Conference of Commissioners on Uniform State Laws (either the Uniform Fraudulent Conveyance Act or the more recent Uniform Fraudulent Transfer Act). The federal bankruptcy statute has its own fraudulent conveyance provision. These use slightly different definitions and statutes of limitations. Rights under one may be available to some creditors that are not available to those creditors under a different enactment. In a bankruptcy case, creditors (or, more likely, the bankruptcy trustee) can use both the federal and state enactments. The same basic principles, however, animate all of them.

As noted, outside cases of outright fraud, fraudulent conveyance law applies principally to transactions in which the debtor fails to receive 'fair consideration' or 'reasonably equivalent value'. The way in which these terms are defined is one of the most important ways in which the limits of fraudulent conveyance laws are established. Trading one asset for another of roughly similar value is an exchange in which there is 'fair consideration' or 'reasonably equivalent value'. Hence, such a transaction is not a fraudulent conveyance, even if the debtor is insolvent. Creditors are stuck with the business decisions its debtor makes as long as the debtor remains in control. Moreover, creditors are powerless to reach assets once they have been placed in the hands of a good-faith purchaser for value.

Even when an insolvent debtor pays off a creditor, the creditor is conclusively presumed to give 'fair consideration' and 'reasonably equivalent value'. Such transfers on account of an antecedent debt may affect how assets are distributed among the different creditors, but they do not affect the pool of assets available to the creditors. Creditors as a group are not worse off when one is paid and others are not. A creditor can challenge a payment to another creditor under the fraudulent conveyance laws only if the payment was done with actual fraudulent intent. Such a payment may be a voidable preference, but it is not a fraudulent conveyance. (The law of preferences itself grows out of the law of fraudulent conveyances, and until the end of the eighteenth century they were not distinct from each other.)

The effect of these provisions is to take many transactions outside the scope of the fraudulent conveyance laws. It makes no sense to have a general doctrine that prohibits debtors from engaging in transactions that leave some creditors worse off. Creditors are always worse off when the debtor takes assets whose value is certain (such as cash) and exchanges assets whose value is uncertain. A new machine may or may not make production more efficient. Creditors must choose debtors whom they believe able to make competent decisions about how to run their businesses. To the extent that they want to be able to stop the debtor from taking some kinds of actions, they must bargain for the right. The 'fair consideration' and 'reasonably equivalent value' provisions prevent creditors from using fraudulent conveyance law to second-guess their debtor's business decisions. Creditors who want to stop what they think is misbehaviour must bargain for the right to declare a default and then exercise the right (see Smith and Warner 1979).

The 'insolvency' test further narrows the scope of the fraudulent conveyance laws. Applying the insolvency test requires us to ask a simple question: would a solvent buyer be willing to pay a positive price to take on all the debtor's assets and all the debtor's liabilities (see *Covey v. Commercial National Bank*)? A debtor has guaranteed a $10 million debt of its parent corporation and otherwise has no other obligations. The debtor's assets are worth $1 million. If you were solvent, whether you would pay to acquire the assets and liabilities of this debtor would turn on whether the chance that you will be called upon to honour the guarantee was greater or less than one in ten. No one who was solvent would agree to take an asset worth $1 million if it came with a fifty–fifty chance of having to pay $10 million. On the other hand, a risk-neutral buyer would willingly pay a positive price to acquire an asset worth $1 million if the chance that it would have to pay $10 million were, let us say, only one in twenty. Hence, the debtor is insolvent in the first instance and solvent in the second.

The insolvency test is based on a sound and straightforward idea: when a firm's debts are greater than its assets, the shareholders are the residual claimants. They enjoy each additional dollar the firm brings in and they lose each additional dollar the firm loses. Because they are the residual owners, they internalize the benefit of making the right decisions and the cost of the wrong ones. When a firm is insolvent, the shareholders enjoy some of the upside if the firm's fortunes improve enough, but they bear none of the downside risk. By adding an insolvency requirement, we can ensure that creditors are able to upset only those transactions where the shareholders do not internalize all the costs of their decisions. If creditors do not trust the shareholders to make decisions when their incentives are correctly aligned, they must bargain for it explicitly.

The insolvency requirement, however, is underinclusive. A firm can be solvent and the shareholders can still have the incentive to engage in transactions that run contrary to the creditor's interest. Assume that a firm owes its creditors $10 and has a little more than $20 in assets. One asset is $10 in cash and the other is a lottery ticket that has a one-in-ten chance of paying $101. If it declared a dividend of $10, the firm would still be solvent. (It would have debt of $10 and a lottery ticket worth a little more than $10.) Nevertheless, the dividend would change dramatically the creditor's chances of being repaid. They drop from being certain to being only one-in-ten. The creditor is paid only if the lottery ticket turns out a winner.

A more serious problem may arise if courts are not able to determine whether a firm is insolvent at any point in time. Consider the case in which a firm's sole asset is an oil-drilling venture. Its only creditor is owed $100. At the time the firm declares a dividend, the firm is drilling ten wells. There is a 90% chance that at least one of them will hit oil. For this reason, the firm is worth $500. There is, however, a 10% chance that none of the wells will produce. In this event, the firm will be worthless. A year passes and all the wells prove to be dry holes. Can the creditor attack the dividend on the ground that the firm was insolvent at the time of the dividend?

In one sense, the firm was insolvent. None of the sites had any oil beneath it. Yet this conclusion seems wrong. The determination of insolvency should be tied to what was known at the time the dividend was made. If the 'insolvency' standard permits second-guessing after the fact, fraudulent conveyance law may interfere with ordinary commercial transactions. Much fraudulent conveyance litigation takes place only after things have gone badly. To work effectively, fraudulent conveyance laws depend upon judges who can put themselves in the position of the parties at the time of the initial transaction.

There is one respect in which existing fraudulent conveyance laws seem conspicuously defective. They may not distinguish sufficiently present and future creditors. Consider, for example, a firm that issues a huge dividend to its shareholders and the dividend leaves the firm insolvent. Anyone who was a creditor at the time of the dividend should, of course, have a fraudulent conveyance action against the shareholders. But what about the creditors who came on the scene after the dividend? Unless they lent because they were misled by the past financial health of the firm, they are no different than creditors who lend to a firm that has become insolvent through a market reverse. Ordinarily, those who lend to a thinly capitalized firm's creditors have no right to reach that firm's shareholders in the event it fails. Such a right (called a right to pierce the corporate veil) typically exists only when there has been abuse of the corporate form. If creditors want shareholders to become liable for the firm's obligations, they must insist upon a guarantee, as indeed many do.

THE STEP-TRANSACTION DOCTRINE. Perhaps the hardest single part of modern fraudulent conveyance doctrine concerns not whether a fraudulent conveyance exists, but rather the person against whom the fraudulent conveyance remedy should apply (see *Lippi v. City Bank*). Consider, however, the following case. The same debtor goes to a jewellery store, gives the store $100, and asks it to give a gold ring to a parent. In this case, we have a transfer of $100 from the debtor to the jewellery store and a transfer of the ring from the store to the parent. If a creditor tries to recover the ring from the parent, can the latter argue that the creditor has no right to the ring because its debtor (the child) never owned it? In other words, can the parent argue that the fraudulent conveyance is the child's transfer of $100 to the jeweller, not the transfer of the ring from the jeweller to the parent?

Most of us would reject this argument. In form, there might have been a transfer between the insolvent debtor and the jeweller and then the jeweller and the parent, but the substance is the same as if an insolvent debtor bought the ring and then gave it to the parent. Hence, a fraudulent conveyance action should lie against the parent, but not the jeweller. Applying fraudulent conveyance law in the corporate context also requires recharacterizing the form of the transaction to get at its economic substance. The 'substance' of such a transaction, however, is harder to intuit. The business of stepping together discrete transactions often cannot be done without some underlying conception of the policies that fraudulent conveyance law is intended to promote. A simple case involving a leveraged buyout makes this point.

Firm owes $2 million to a group of general creditors and it has assets of about $3 million. It has ten shareholders. Entrepreneur buys the shares of one shareholder for $100,000. Firm borrows $900,000 from Lender and Lender will take a security interest in all of Firm's assets. Firm then buys back the shares of the old shareholders. Entrepreneur now owns Firm. Firm still has assets of about $3 million, but $2.9 million in debt. Because Lender took a security interest, Lender is entitled to be paid in full before the general creditors receive anything. The general creditors' equity cushion has shrunk dramatically or perhaps disappeared altogether. Let us assume that a court would find that the stock repurchase was a fraudulent conveyance because the repurchase gave Firm nothing of value and left it either insolvent or 'with unreasonably small capital'. A fraudulent conveyance exists, but against whom? Entrepreneur? Lender? The old shareholders?

If there is an actual recovery against Entrepreneur or the shareholders, there should be no additional recovery against Lender. But Lender is a more inviting target in the first instance. The shareholders are likely to be diverse or they may have had little to do with the leveraged buyout, while Lender may have overseen it at every turn. Entrepreneur is likely to be judgment proof. Moreover, the general creditors do not need to recover any assets from Lender. They need only keep Lender from sharing in Firm's assets.

A court may well refuse to allow a fraudulent conveyance attack against Lender. The court could conclude that Lender, unlike the shareholders, did not get something for nothing. Lender gave up cold, hard cash in return for its security interest. Moreover, Firm was, from one point of view, far from being insolvent at the end of its transaction with Lender. At the end of *that* transaction, Firm had $2.9 million in debt and almost $4 million in assets. Before and after the transaction with Lender, there was a million-dollar equity cushion for the other creditors. The trustee cannot hold Lender responsible for Firm's decision to use the proceeds of the loan to buy back shares of its stock. Under this view, there are two separate transactions: (1) the deal between Lender and Firm, and (2) the deal between Firm and its shareholders. One can argue that these two transactions should not be collapsed into one. If they are kept separate, the second transaction is a fraudulent conveyance for all the reasons we have already discussed, but the first is not. It is simply a business deal done at arm's length between strangers. The general creditors may have to watch out for such transactions, but the general rule for creditors is that each must watch out for its own interest and cannot rely on someone else to do it for them.

A court, however, may not be willing to separate the loan to Firm from the buyout. The loan from Lender to Firm made the transaction between Firm and the shareholders possible. Collapsing the two transactions may not be unreasonable if we care about substance rather than form. In order to make the case that there was only one transaction (and thereby reach Lender), one begins by observing that the funds from Lender went into Firm and then out to the old shareholders in the blink of an eye. Lender was in a good position to police against fraudulent conveyances, and we want to encourage it to do that policing. Lender should not be able to pretend that it was giving value to Firm. It was just as if Lender made a loan to shareholders and Firm promised to pay Lender back. To bring a fraudulent conveyance attack against Lender, however, one ultimately has to conclude that, as a matter of sound policy, Lender should be held accountable for what Firm does with the money it lends, at least to some extent. Embracing such a policy, at least when Lender was closely involved with the structuring of the leveraged buyout, may be consistent with the norms that have long been a part of fraudulent conveyance law. Creditors who do not operate at arm's length with the debtor are not in the same position as those who do.

The step-transaction is a part of fraudulent conveyance law, but there are few cases that discuss it explicitly. The issue does not even arise until the court finds that a transaction was a fraudulent conveyance. In a case in which only the lender is being sued, a court may conclude that a transaction was not a fraudulent conveyance at all, rather than hold that it was, but that the lender who financed it is not liable. In those cases that have faced the question, some courts have analysed the problem in terms of a party's knowledge or 'good faith'.

Some courts have allowed fraudulent conveyance actions against those who financed leveraged buyouts on the grounds that these lenders had not acted in good faith (see

United States v. Tabor Court Realty Corp.). This approach, however, is misguided. It strains the traditional meaning of good faith without confronting the underlying issue: the conditions under which we can justify 'stepping' the loan to the firm and the payout to the shareholders together. In these cases, the honesty of the lender or any other person against whom the action is brought is not an issue. We are asking whether, under all the circumstances, the transaction, as a matter of substance and not merely form, was one in which the party gave fair consideration or reasonably equivalent value to its debtor. Answering the question requires asking how much the transaction was at arm's length and how much one party should be asked to monitor its debtor on behalf of its other creditors.

Reducing everything to the Procrustean inquiry of whether the party exercised good faith is unlikely to illuminate things. The alternative standard that some have proposed – asking whether the party had knowledge of the overall transaction – is affirmatively suspect, as such a rule rewards ignorance and stupidity, something that the law, as a general matter, should not do.

INTERCORPORATE GUARANTIES AND OTHER TRANSACTIONS. The net of fraudulent conveyance law spreads wide. Pious debtors who tithe out of religious conviction may expose their churches to fraudulent conveyance attacks for the entire period in which they are insolvent. The law here remains unclear (see *Christians v. Crystal Evangelical Free Church*). Fraudulent conveyance attacks are possible even when a 'transfer' takes place as a result of inaction on the part of the debtor. Consider a firm that is hopelessly insolvent. Its location is perfect. The franchise is very popular. Its managers, however, are inept, and they give up. The landlord terminates the lease and rents the premises to another tenant at a higher rent. The franchisor terminates the franchise agreement and finds someone else to sell its products in that territory. The loss of these rights through the debtor's inaction may be a 'transfer' under fraudulent conveyance law.

Fraudulent conveyance law is implicated in virtually any transaction that affects the capital structure of an enterprise. Consider, for example, the fraudulent conveyance issues that arise when an enterprise consists of a group of related corporations (see *Rubin v. Manufacturers Hanover Trust*). Parent borrows $100,000 from Bank on January 1 and Subsidiary, a wholly owned subsidiary with a lot of assets, guarantees the obligation and secures it with all of its assets. On November 1, Parent and Subsidiary both file for bankruptcy. Can Bank's security interest in Subsidiary's assets be set aside on the grounds that it is a fraudulent conveyance?

Does Subsidiary get 'reasonably equivalent value' or 'fair consideration'? What were the benefits of the loan that inured *to Subsidiary*? If the proceeds of the loan went to Parent, the benefits to Subsidiary seem trivial relative to the harm the guarantee brings to Subsidiary (and its creditors). In many cases, however, a loan will be made to a corporate group and the bank will ask for guarantees for the entire loan from all the subsidiaries. In such a case, the obligation that Subsidiary is assuming may be commensurate with the benefits it will receive from the loan. Consider, for example, the case that would have arisen in the event that Parent had guaranteed a loan made to a solvent and wholly owned subsidiary. In principle, the value of its equity interest in Subsidiary increases by a dollar for each dollar that Subsidiary receives from a lender.

CONCLUSION. Fraudulent conveyance law is a general rule that prevents debtor misbehaviour. Sometimes we encounter a transaction that leaves everyone but a few insiders worse off, yet we cannot readily point to a specific violation of substantive law. In these cases, the first question we should ask is whether a fraudulent conveyance has taken place. Because it looks to substance, rather than to form, fraudulent conveyance law reaches transactions that have been structured to evade the letter of particular statutes and loan covenants.

For as long as there have been debtors, some have sought ways to prevent their creditors from recovering what they are owed. Any successful legal system is likely to have developed a general principle that gives creditors a way to protect themselves from at least the most egregious conduct. Fraudulent conveyance law is the way in which Anglo–American law embodies this principle.

DOUGLAS G. BAIRD

See also CORPORATE BANKRUPTCY; LEVERAGED BUYOUTS; SECURED CREDIT CONTRACTS.

Subject classification: 5c(i); 5e; 5g(iv).

CASES

Christians v. Crystal Evangelical Free Church, 82 F3d 1407 (8th Cir. 1996).

Covey v. Commercial National Bank of Peoria, 960 F2d 657 (7th Cir. 1992).

Lippi v. City Bank, 955 F2d 599 (9th Cir. 1992).

Rubin v. Manufacturers Hanover Trust Co., 661 F2d 979 (2d Cir. 1981).

Twyne's Case (1601) 3 Co. Rep. 80b, 76 Eng. Rep. 809.

United States v. Tabor Court Realty Corp., 803 F2d 1288 (3d Cir. 1986), cert. denied, 483 US 1005 (1987).

BIBLIOGRAPHY

Baird, D.G. 1991. Fraudulent conveyances, agency costs, and leveraged buyouts. *Journal of Legal Studies* 20: 1–24.

Baird, D.G. and Jackson, T.H. 1985. Fraudulent conveyance law and its proper domain. *Vanderbilt Law Review* 38: 829–55.

Brudney, V. and Clark, R.C. 1981. A new look at corporate opportunities. *Harvard Law Review* 94: 998–1062.

Clark, R.C. 1977. The duties of the corporate debtor to its creditors. *Harvard Law Review* 90: 505–62.

Glenn, G. 1931. *Fraudulent Conveyances and Preferences*. New York: Baker, Voorhis & Co.; revised edn, 1940.

Smith, C.W. and Warner, J.B. 1979. On financial contracting: an analysis of bond covenants. *Journal of Financial Economics* 7: 117–61.

freedom of expression. The economics of freedom of expression has both positive and normative aspects. Positive analyses show how economics can help explain the structure of laws, adopted by either legislatures or courts that control freedom of expression. Normative analyses reveal the structure of optimal laws and legal institutions that govern freedom of expression.

POSITIVE ANALYSIS. Positive analysis assumes that judges, legislators and private individuals are rationally self-interested. These actors play a game that is defined by the institutional structures, such as Article 1, Section 7 of the United States Constitution. Each actor tries to achieve an outcome of the game that is best according to his or her self-interest. The equilibrium of this game is law. This approach, which goes by the name of 'positive political theory', has been applied to many areas of the law, including topics in freedom of expression. Legislators are presumed to desire (among other things) reelection, and hence reflect the ideological and material interests of their constituents. But federal judges in the United States serve for life. Each is free to pursue his own vision of the public interest. Characterizing the judges' objectives is difficult, but is needed to make the analysis work.

Ideally, positive political theory aspires to explain the core questions in freedom of expression, including: Why are US broadcast media licensed and controlled but print media are unlicensed and subject to much less onerous content controls? Why has the US Supreme Court protected speech markets but not economic markets? Why has the US Supreme Court fashioned the First Amendment doctrines that it has chosen? Positive political theory currently does a pretty good job on the first two questions, but has a long way to go on the third.

Broadcasting. According to the standard positive political theory view, the US broadcast media are licensed and content-controlled as part of a mutually beneficial arrangement between broadcasters, Congresspersons, and bureaucrats (Hazlett 1990; Spitzer 1996). Broadcasters want protection from competition and free spectrum, leading to supracompetitive profits. By licensing broadcasters and limiting the number of licences, Congress has provided broadcasters with protection from competition. By charging no cash payment for the licences, Congress provides spectrum for 'free' in exchange for the expectation that broadcasters will self-censor. Congress expects that extremist political groups, such as neo-Nazis or Communists, will be denied coverage as anything other than lunatic fringe groups. In addition, this implicit 'contract' mandates that incumbents receive greater coverage than electoral challengers, and that any serious challenge to the Democrat and Republican duopoly, such as Ross Perot's party, receive sceptical broadcast coverage. Broadcasters are to avoid angering the voters by broadcasting foul language or explicit sexual material. To accomplish all this self-censorship, Congress attaches to licences a duty to broadcast *in the public interest.* Because broadcasting in the public interest is understood to entail all this self-censorship, voters have one less reason to be angry, new entry by a political force is unlikely, and incumbents tend to be reelected. The Federal Communications Commission, a bureaucracy that issues broadcast licences and regulates broadcaster behaviour, is a creature of Congressional statutes. In turn, the FCC has promulgated and enforced regulations that enforce the public interest deal between broadcasters and Congresspersons.

Why are print publications left unlicensed and uncontrolled while broadcasters are licensed and controlled? Congress would seem to want the same deal with newspapers and magazines. The US Supreme Court will not allow newspapers to be licensed and controlled in the same way. Broadcasting, on the other hand, was regarded as different because it required radio spectrum. Regulating interference on the radio spectrum between different broadcasters was regarded as more like an issue of economic regulation. Hence, the government could license broadcasters in the public interest and issue regulations. Of course, this leads to the question why economic regulation is not subject to the same scrutiny as direct speech regulation.

Speech markets and economic markets. Sullivan (1995), in an excellent synthetic survey, points out that, since the New Deal, US constitutional law protects markets in speech but fails to protect economic markets. This means, in essence, that when Congress passes a law that restricts speech, the courts demand a very good reason, directly supported by evidence linking the regulation to the rationale, before the regulation can stand. In contrast, any regulation regarded as economic need only be justified by a rational basis, and the connection between the rational basis and the regulation can be exceedingly weak. Shapiro (1978) provides the most convincing explanation for the distinction, arguing that New Deal Supreme Court Justices, the majority of whom were liberal Democrats, created and nurtured the distinction so as to enable Congress to serve New Deal constituents. New Deal voters wanted to redistribute property to themselves, and so New Deal Congresspersons desired reduced constitutional protections for economic markets. Voters wanted to be secure in their civil rights, and where their economic interests, such as welfare rights, were threatened by propertied interests, the Court would sometimes redefine the issue as a protected civil right, such as the 'right to travel' (*Shapiro v. Thompson*). The biggest problems with Shapiro's explanation are that the Court started eroding protections for economic markets before the New Deal (Epstein 1992) and the Court has not fundamentally altered the hierarchy between speech markets and economic markets even though the New Deal has been gone for decades.

To explain the persistent difference between speech markets and economic markets, one should focus on the political beliefs and incentives of today's judges. Modern judges protect speech as a strategy to affect current and future political outcomes. Rational judges should decide to protect speech if that protection allows private parties to behave in ways that produce outcomes that the judges prefer. Thus, for example, judges should protect, as freedom of speech, unlimited spending of personal money by candidates if judges like the outcomes of elections with unlimited spending. Although some law professors have been groping toward such a positive political theory (Balkin 1990; Schauer 1993), most of the work remains to be done.

Because federal judges have life tenure and secure income, they are insulated substantially from political pressure. One could try to create other theories, relying on different judicial objective functions, to try to explain the difference between the treatment of speech rights and economic rights. For example, consider the following argument, based on Coase (1974: 389–90). One could assume that judges identify themselves as intellectuals, and that intellectuals are driven by self-esteem to value their work – the production and communication of ideas – over that of people in other markets. Self-interested writers and publishers resist regulation, partly because they like to be free, and partly for economic reasons. Controversy – including many false ideas – is needed to pump up demand for communications, and freedom of speech promotes this condition. Judges, identifying with the writers and publishers (as fellow intellectuals), implement their interests by protecting speech. Other market endeavours, however, are regarded by judges as merely economic, and left to the tender mercies of Congress.

Coase's explanation resembles that of political economists who explain the tendency of Congressional committees to protect particular industries. Congressional committees identify with particular industries because of the Congressmen's need to be reelected. In Coase's explanation the judge's psychology takes the place of the Congressman's electoral connection. By assuming that judges 'identify' with a particular economic interest, one can predict protective doctrine for that interest. One could focus on other economic interest groups and use the same form of argument (McChesney 1988) to predict other protective doctrines.

Specific doctrines. An economic analysis of specific doctrines in freedom of expression has the same general form as the analysis of the big issues above. Justices are presumed to be self-interested government actors, deciding issues within a sequential game in which Congress, the President and the States also have moves. The Justices vote and the Court chooses doctrines strategically, anticipating the reactions of the other branches so as to effectuate the Justices' most preferred available outcomes. The difference is that the object of analysis is a much more specific rule within the area of freedom of expression.

For example, the Court scrutinizes rules that apply only to certain content – termed 'content-based' – much more closely than regulations that apply equally to all messages – termed 'content-neutral'. Because content-based speech regulations will often be struck down in circumstances where content-neutral regulations will be allowed to stand, the Court's decisions must be understood to require that many speech regulations be content-neutral. Spiller and Spitzer (1992: 17) suggest that when the Court requires Congress to use only content-neutral speech regulations, Congress is restricted to a content-neutral subset of the policy space. The Court restricts Congress, or not, depending on the Court's preferences over the resulting policy equilibria. For example, assume the Court must decide whether Congress may restrict the content of projects supported by National Endowment for the Arts money (e.g. no obscene or antireligious art). Given the Court's ruling, Congress will choose a funding level for the NEA – presumably more money with funding restrictions, less without. The Court will choose to allow content-based funding restrictions, or not, depending on the Justices' preferences for a smaller budget with unrestricted NEA grants compared to a larger budget with restricted grants.

Other doctrines, such as the distinction between commercial and noncommercial speech, special categories for fighting words and hate speech, and the overbreadth doctrine, can be analysed in a similar fashion. Most of the existing work in this area tends to assume that judges and courts, but not legislatures, are social welfare maximizers. This converts the positive economic analysis into a search by courts for optimal doctrine, in essence a normative enterprise.

NORMATIVE ANALYSIS. Normative analysis of regulation of freedom of expression must avoid several traps that are peculiar to this field of law. To see this, consider the following general framework for analysing speech regulation, corresponding to Posner (1986). Any regulation that targets speech will make two types of errors. First, the regulation will fail to deter some targeted speech. Second, it will catch and suppress some nontargeted speech. Hence, the level of both targeted speech, TS, and nontargeted speech, NS, will be a function of the level of regulation, ρ. There will be both social benefits and social costs associated with TS and NS, which we denote SB(TS(ρ)), SC(TS(ρ)) and SB(NS(ρ)), SC(NS(ρ)). A court reviewing the constitutionality of a speech regulation calculates the net costs and benefits of the regulation by asking if this regulation is better than having no regulation at all, rather than asking if this regulation is globally optimal. Thus, the total change in costs and benefits due to the change in targeted speech from instituting a regulation is SB(TS(ρ)) − SB(TS(0)) − SC(TS(ρ)) + SC(TS(0)). We have a similar expression for nontargeted speech: SB(NS(ρ)) − SB(NS(0)) − SC(NS(ρ)) + SC(NS(0)). The costs and benefits must be discounted to present value and for probability of occurring, and then summed to give the net benefit from regulation. Because the social costs and benefits of TS or NS may arrive at different times we have the following total expression for net benefit:

$$\begin{aligned}&SB(TS(\rho))P_1(1+r)^{-n1} - SB(TS(0))P_2(1+r)^{-n2}\\&- SC(TS(\rho))P_3(1+r)^{-n3} + SC(TS(0))P_4(1+r)^{-n4}\\&+ SB(NS(\rho))P_5(1+r)^{-n5} - SB(NS(0))P_6(1+r)^{-n6}\\&- SC(NS(\rho))P_7(1+r)^{-n7} + SC(NS(0))P_8(1+r)^{-n8},\end{aligned}$$

where P_i is a probability of that term happening, *ni* is the time at which that term will happen, if it occurs, and r is the discount rate, which is intended to incorporate the idea that future benefits (costs) are less valuable (costly).

In Posner (1986), which is the leading article on efficient design of First Amendment free speech doctrine, Richard Posner uses a simplified version of this general approach. Posner's discussion implicitly assumes:

$P_1 = P_2 = P_5 = P_6 = 1$ (Both targeted and nontargeted speech have social benefits)

$n1 = n2 = n5 = n6 = 0$ (Social benefits arrive immediately)

$P_7 = P_8 = 0$ (There are no social costs to non-targeted speech)

$P_3 = 0$ (There are no social costs to targeted speech once the regulation has been implemented. This is assumed in his formula, but not in all discussions)

Using this framework, Posner gives special attention to the nature of externalities in speech. Because some speech – scientific, aesthetic, political or moral – produces large externalities that speakers cannot recapture, it is underproduced. Analogising speech regulations to taxes and analogising special constitutional protections for speech to subsidies, Posner concludes that striking down regulations and giving special protections represent economically efficient doctrines. Political speech, in particular, represents the clearest example of the press producing externalities – by examining and often rejecting claims of organized, rent-seeking interest groups. Commercial advertising, in contrast, allows the speaker to recapture external benefits, and hence is hardier and needs less protection.

This form of analysis, though perhaps useful as a starting point, can be misleading. First, there is no market price for many of these costs and benefits and no obvious method of hedonic estimation. Consequently, the application seems likely to reflect any particular judge's or author's idiosyncrasies (Hammer 1988; Hasian, Jr. and Panetta 1994). For example, Posner excludes consumers' utility from reading and viewing in his analysis, preferring to see the only purpose of communication as the transfer of information or persuasion. Second, and closely related, the types of costs and benefits associated with regulation are likely to appear *discontinuously* in consumers' utility functions. Thus, just 'knowing' that one lives in a society that allows free speech may please a libertarian, and similarly knowing that society allows pornography may displease a conservative. Such costs and benefits resist appraisal. Third, Posner's framework treats regulations as taxes. Although regulations and taxes both burden speech, they alter the incentives of speakers and listeners in different ways. A careful economic analysis should incorporate the different effects of regulations. Fourth, speech that produces external benefits that cannot be recaptured does not automatically merit special protection from regulation. The existence of such benefits means that the market equilibrium prior to regulation will produce, when compared to an equilibrium in which the external benefits *can* be recaptured, a less-than-optimal quantity of the speech. But this tells us little when comparing two other equilibria, in one of which speech is regulated but in both of which the speech is plagued by the inability to recapture external benefits. If the external benefits combine with regulation to produce a particularly sharp drop in the social benefits from targeted speech, then the regulation may be inadvisable. In general, one must pay special attention to the economics of the particular medium being regulated (see Owen 1975) and compare the relevant states of the world.

None of this is to say that normative analysis is impossible, but it must be done with a real sense of its limitations and uncertainties. The central point about speech often producing positive externalities that are impossible to capture seems right, at least for certain types of speech (Hammer 1988; Farber 1991). Communications covering political, scientific, economic, or other social matters convey information that can often be replicated at low cost and distributed to others. Thus, those that produce this sort of communication will be undercompensated and consequently produce too little of it. Regulations may reduce the volume of communication even further, thereby further reducing the amount of positive externalities. This might be sufficient to raise a presumption of invalidity for political speech regulations.

Commercial speech may sometimes produce external benefits (Cass 1988; Estreicher 1990) but whether it does so to the same extent as political, scientific, and economic expression is highly debatable. In addition, those producing political, scientific and economic speech will often be getting pleasure from the act of expression (Neuborne 1989: 15–18), whereas commercial speakers garner no such pleasure. Thus one could plausibly argue that the presumption of invalidity for regulation of commercial speech should be lower than a similar presumption for noncommercial speech. In addition, one could use these arguments to suggest that, contrary to the heartfelt criticism of numerous commentators (Director 1964; Coase 1974: 389–90; Epstein 1992), the market for expression deserves special solicitude (Michelman 1992).

There are some unexplored literatures in economics that may yet illuminate topics in freedom of speech. The topics covered below explicate the 'marketplace of ideas' – the idea that somehow the free interchange of communication produces truth. In the game theoretic literature upon which we will draw, truth is defined socially, as a consensus among citizens.

First, consider the interaction between the truth-seeking function of the marketplace of ideas and the economics literature on 'agreeing to disagree'. Robert Aumann (1976) showed that if two Bayesians start with common priors about some event, observe different information relevant to that event, and then share their posterior beliefs about the likelihood of the event as common knowledge, then their final posterior beliefs are identical. This means that if (Bayesian) people start by agreeing, and honestly share their beliefs, they must finish by agreeing. The crucial concept, common knowledge, requires not only that *A* knows that *B* knows the item of knowledge and that *B* knows that *A* knows it, but that *A* knows that *B* knows that *A* knows that . . . for any length of 'knows that' statement. Thus, for example, if *A* and *B* together observe an event, it becomes common knowledge.

An example, based on theorems in Geanakoplos and Polemarchakis (1982), may make this result clearer. Suppose that two baseball scouts, *A* and *B*, who work for the same team and who trust each other are trying to evaluate a minor league baseball player's ability to hit major league pitching. The scouts, who know only that the typical minor league baseball player can get a hit 20% of the time against major league pitching, will watch the player try to hit 100 pitches by a major league pitcher. They agree to divide the work, with each scout separately watching part of the batting practice. After the practice the scouts, *A* and *B*, get together to share their opinions of the player's hitting ability. *A* says '17%' and *B* says '35%'. Based on these statements *A* can deduce that *B* must have seen the player hit a bunch, while *B* can deduce that *A* saw a dismal performance. Based on the deductions, as well as their own observations, *A* and *B* will revise their opinions and announce new estimates. *A* says '25%' and *B* says '28%'. Now *A* and *B* can revise their opinions again, based on the information embedded in the new statements. After a finite number of announcements their opinions will converge, and the scouts will agree.

There are several important aspects of such a consensus-producing process. First, agreement occurs without sharing the observed information – note that each scout only observed part of the batting practice and did not even tell the other scout directly how many hits the player made. Second, only the posterior opinions based on the information need be shared – the scouts shared their revised opinions of the players' hitting ability. Third, the agreement will usually be the same regardless of whether the people share the information in the observations or just their posterior opinions. Fourth, as Geanakoplos and Polemarchakis (1982) show, for any number of rounds, an example can be constructed where we observe no change in the announced opinion of the scouts until the final round, when they agree completely. Thus, if there were an appropriate set of scouts' beliefs and scout-observed hits in batting practice, we could observe ten rounds where scout A says '*x*%' and B says '*y*%', but on the eleventh round they both suddenly announce the same opinion.

These results have been extended in a number of directions (Milgrom and Stokey 1982; Nielsen et al. 1990). If there is a public statistic that is an additively separable, monotonic function of individual beliefs, then opinions will converge (McKelvey and Page 1986). Publicly identifying individuals with the highest (or lowest) values also produces consensus (Hanson 1997).

There are some obvious differences between the economic literature and the traditional marketplace of ideas. First, the economics literature is about agreement. The marketplace of ideas is usually thought to be a search for truth. One could define truth socially, so that complete agreement produces truth. Or one could view the First Amendment as protecting a search for agreement rather than for truth. Second, the economics literature seems geared to disputes about factual matters, such as scientific events, batting averages, or crop yield. It is not clear what happens when one shifts to disagreements about values. Third, the economics literature thus far presumes common priors, or other fairly stringent conditions on priors (Geanakoplos and Sebenius 1983). It seems likely that if priors differ, so can posteriors. However, if priors are common knowledge, the logic of the proofs in this literature would suggest that commonly known posterior beliefs could produce stable disagreements. (Kalai and Lehrer 1994) Last, the existing literature is about sufficient (rather than necessary) conditions needed to produce agreements. The First Amendment protects particular institutions. If the economics literature is to be relevant we must be able to say that the failure to protect particular institutions will destroy the ability to reach consensus, or will delay agreement, or will make agreement more expensive. The current literature is no more than suggestive in these regards.

Nevertheless, there may be some direct applications of the existing economics literature to legal topics. The Geanakoplos and Polemarchakis (1982) result about lack of apparent convergence could suggest implications for the doctrine of 'fighting words'. The Court has held that words that are likely to lead to fights and which are not designed to persuade or communicate are not protected by the First Amendment (*Chaplinsky v. New Hampshire*, 571–2):

> There are certain well-defined and narrowly limited classes of speech, the prevention and punishment of which have never been thought to raise any Constitutional problem. These include the lewd and obscene, the profane, the libelous, and the insulting or 'fighting' words – those which by their very utterance inflict injury or tend to incite an immediate breach of the peace . . . [S]uch utterances are no essential part of any exposition of ideas, and are of such slight social value as a step to truth that any benefit that may be derived from them is clearly outweighed by the social interest in order and morality.

Consider the sequence of shouted words 'I'm right!' 'No, I'm right!' 'No, I'm right!'. The Geanakoplos and Polemarchakis result suggests that the sequence of shouts could eventually lead to consensus rather than a fight. Or, it could lead to a fight. This might imply that courts should be chary of including the apparent nature of rhetoric, including the ability of speech to persuade immediately, as part of the calculus of whether speech should be protected. More particularly, this result suggests that courts should refrain from extending the 'fighting words' category of unprotected speech to heated disagreements that are seemingly making little headway toward consensus.

The Hanson result, that identifying those with extreme views can lead to agreement, may have implications for another doctrine. In *McIntyre v. Ohio Elections Commission* the Supreme Court held that a state may not require those who produce and distribute political literature to put their names on the literature. It is possible that this decision could interfere with the operation of the marketplace of ideas. If the political tracts were about factual issues (e.g. the rate of inflation) and it is clear from the materials which estimate is the highest, knowing the identities would help produce agreement. Similarly, the SEC's refusal to require an investment newsletter to inform its readers that articles were prepared by the subject of the article could be critiqued (Neuborne 1989: 39–40, claiming *no* value in disclosure). Of course, the Court's *McIntyre* decision might also have some good properties, making it harder for the government to retaliate against critics, among other things. The value of economics here is to highlight a possible, nonobvious cost.

The 'agreeing to agree' literature utilized above described the theory and implications from situations where there are no incentives to misrepresent one's opinions. The following discussion concerns games with communication that have incentives for the players to lie.

Consider the following 2-person game, whose payoffs are given in Table 1.

Table 1

	x_2	y_2
x_1	5, 1	0, 0
y_1	4, 4	1, 5

Each player must choose x_i *or* y_i (for i=1, 2). There are several possible equilibria. Both (x_1, x_2) and (y_1, y_2) are Nash equilibria in pure strategies, and there is an equilibrium where both players choose randomized strategies and which gives expected payoffs of (2.5, 2.5).

With communication between the players, however, they can do even better. With a fair coin, the players can agree to choose (x_1, x_2) if the coin comes up heads and (y_1, y_2) if it comes up tails. If the parties can agree on a mediator, they can agree to a self-enforcing plan that will pay each (3 1/3, 3 1/3). The mediator will roll a fair 6-sided die and privately advise player 1 to play x_1 if the mediator sees 1 or 2, but to play y_1 if the mediator sees another number. The mediator privately will advise player 2 to play x_2 if the mediator sees 1, 2, 3, or 4, and y_2 otherwise. As long as neither player can learn of the recommendation to the other, following the mediator's suggestion is a Nash equilibrium. If the players can learn of the mediator's recommendation the equilibrium is destroyed.

There are more complex, n-person versions of such games involving uncertainty of players' *types*, where the payoffs in the game depend on the players' types (Myerson 1994). The players send signals about what types they claim to be, and based upon the signals received from other players, and based on each player's prior probability distribution over various player types, each player chooses an action. Such games can become quite complicated. As in the example with which we started this section, the players can often improve their expected outcome by agreeing to use a mediator, where communication between each player and the mediator is private and unobservable.

The literature on correlated equilibria can illuminate legal issues involving the ability to keep communication private to enable mediation devices. One place where this might be an issue is in United States administrative law, where the Government in the Sunshine Act and the Freedom of Information Act make it difficult for government agencies to receive confidential communications. Assume for the moment that several interest groups, each with private information, routinely appear before an administrative agency. Each interest group will get some payoff, contingent on the true state of the world (which is the cross product of all their private knowledge), and contingent on each interest group's choice of how to behave. These behaviours could be anything from deciding to develop new technology, to lobbying Congress for protective legislation, to contesting statutes in court. If the administrative agency were willing to act as mediator, and if the interest groups could confide *privately* to the administrative agency, then the agency could suggest correlated strategies to the interest groups, suggestions that would not fully reveal each interest group's information and strategies to the others, but which would preserve some coordination between the groups. Such correlated strategies could often produce higher expected payoffs for the interest groups than could actions with only public pronouncements. The Government in the Sunshine Act and the Freedom of Information Act could interfere with private communication, and thereby disrupt the mechanism for achieving a correlated equilibrium.

Is this a good or a bad thing? From a social standpoint it might well be desirable to disrupt these correlated equilibria. Helping interest groups achieve their own desired ends may well work against the public interest.

This branch of the game theoretic literature likely has other applications to rules requiring openness in communication. In this case, note that a robust marketplace of ideas can preclude certain equilibria from forming. Depending on the nature of the excluded equilibria, this may provide an argument in favour of or against enhanced freedom of expression.

MATTHEW L. SPITZER

See also COMMON KNOWLEDGE; INFORMATION REGULATION; JUDICIAL INDEPENDENCE; LEGISLATIVE INTENT; PRIVACY; PUBLIC CHOICE AND THE LAW.

Subject classification: 1d(ii); 5b(iv); 6d(ii).

STATUTES

Freedom of Information Act, 5 USC 552 (1996).

Government in the Sunshine Act, 5 USC 552b (1996).

CASES

Chaplinsky v. New Hampshire, 315 US 568 (1942).

McIntyre v. Ohio Elections Commission, 514 US 334 (1995).

Shapiro v. Thompson, 394 US 618 (1969).

BIBLIOGRAPHY

Aumann, R.J. 1976. Agreeing to disagree. *Annals of Statistics* 4: 1236–9.

Balkin, J.M. 1990. Some realism about pluralism: legal realist approaches to the first amendment. *Duke Law Journal* 1990: 375–430.

Cass, R.A. 1988. Commercial speech, constitutionalism, collective choice. *University of Cincinnati Law Review* 56: 1317–82.

Coase, R.H. 1974. The market for goods and the market for ideas. *American Economic Review, Papers and Proceedings* 64: 384–91.

Director, A. 1964. The parity of the economic market place. *Journal of Law and Economics* 7: 1–10.

Epstein, R.A. 1992. Property, speech, and the politics of distrust. *University of Chicago Law Review* 59: 41–89.

Estreicher, A.G. 1990. Securities regulation and the First Amendment. *Georgia Law Review* 24: 223–326.

Farber, D.A. 1991. Free speech without romance: public choice and the first amendment. *Harvard Law Review* 105: 554–83.

Geanakoplos, J.D. and Polemarchakis, H.M. 1982. We can't disagree forever. *Journal of Economic Theory* 28: 192–200.

Geanakoplos, J. and Sebenius, J. 1983. Don't bet on it: contingent agreements with asymmetric information. *Journal of the American Statistical Association* 78: 424–6.

Hammer, P.J. 1988. Free speech and the 'acid bath': an evaluation and critique of Judge Richard Posner's economic interpretation of the first amendment. *Michigan Law Review* 87: 499–536.

Hanson, R. 1997. Consensus by identifying extremists. *Theory and Decision* (forthcoming).
Hasian, M. Jr., and Panetta, E. 1994. Richard Posner's redefinition of the 'marketplace of ideas': a law and economics interpretation of the first amendment. *Free Speech Yearbook* 32: 33–49.
Hazlett, T.W. 1990. The rationality of U.S. regulation of the broadcast spectrum. *Journal of Law and Economics* 33: 133–76.
Kalai, E. and Lehrer, E. 1994. Weak and strong merging of opinions. *Journal of Mathematical Economics* 23: 73–86.
McChesney, F.S. 1988. A positive regulatory theory of the First Amendment. *Connecticut Law Review* 20: 355–82.
McKelvey, R. and Page, T. 1986. Common knowledge, consensus, and aggregate information. *Econometrica* 54: 109–27.
Michelman, F.I. 1992. Liberties, fair values, and constitutional method. *University of Chicago Law Review* 59: 91–114.
Milgrom, P. and Stokey, N. 1982. Information, trade and common knowledge. *Journal of Economic Theory* 26: 17–27.
Myerson, R.B. 1994. Communication, correlated equilibria and incentive compatibility. *Handbook of Game Theory* 2: 827–47.
Neuborne, B. 1989. Lecture: the first amendment and government regulation of capital markets. *Brooklyn Law Review* 55: 5–63.
Nielsen, L.T., Brandenburger, A., Geanakoplos, J., McKelvey, R. and Page, T. 1990. Common knowledge of an aggregate of expectations. *Econometrica* 58: 1235–9.
Owen, B.M. 1975. *Economics and Freedom of Expression: Media Structure and the First Amendment*. Cambridge, MA: Ballinger Publishing Co.
Posner, R.A. 1986. Free speech in an economic perspective. *Suffolk University Law Review* 20: 1–54.
Schauer, F. 1993. The political incidence of the free speech principle. *University of Colorado Law Review* 64: 935–57.
Shapiro, M. 1978. The Constitution and economic rights. In *Essays on the Constitution of the United States*, ed. M. Harmon, Port Washington, NY/London: Kennikat Press.
Spiller, P. and Spitzer, M.L. 1992. Judicial choice of legal doctrines. *Journal of Law, Economics, and Organization* 8: 8–46.
Spitzer, M.L. 1996. Dean Krattenmaker's road not taken: the political economy of broadcasting in the telecommunications act of 1996. *Connecticut Law Review* 29: 353–72.
Sullivan, K.M. 1995. Free speech and unfree markets. *U.C.L.A. Law Review* 42: 949–65.

free riders. *See* HOLDOUTS; PRISONERS' DILEMMA AND THE THEORY OF THE STATE.

Freiburg school of law and economics. The school was founded in the 1930s at the University of Freiburg in Germany by economist Walter Eucken (1891–1950) and jurist Franz Böhm (1895–1977). They were joined by jurist Hans Grossmann-Doerth (1894–1944), who was killed in World War II. Besides holding joint seminars on law and economics themes, the three collaborated in research, as reflected in their founding, in 1937, of the series of publications entitled *Ordnung der Wirtschaft* (The Order of the Economy).

Also known under the name of *Ordo-liberalism*, the ideas of the Freiburg School constituted a major part of the theoretical foundations on which the social market economy in post-World War II Germany was based. The school is often subsumed under the rubric of German neo-liberalism, which also includes such authors as Alfred Müller-Armack, Wilhelm Röpke and Alexander Rüstow. Yet though the two groups of authors shared important common ground, there are significant differences between them. In particular, the somewhat interventionist, outcome-oriented flavour of the concept of the *social market economy* was much more representative of the thoughts of Müller-Armack, who invented the term, and of Röpke and Rüstow, than of the procedural and rule-oriented *Ordo-liberalism* of the Freiburg School.

Outside the German-speaking academic world, and in particular in Anglo-American academia, the ideas of the Freiburg School have received relatively little attention as most of its scholarship has been published only in German and little has been translated into English. At the suggestion of F.A. Hayek, T.W. Hutchison prepared an early English translation of Eucken's *Grundlagen der Nationalökonomie*, originally published in 1940, which appeared in 1950 as *The Foundations of Economics*. Yet, as the translator notes in his preface to the 1992 reprint, the original translation aroused very little interest in Britain and the United States. More recently, the school's research programme has attracted attention, due to the growing recognition that it has much in common with certain modern approaches in economics, particularly constitutional political economy and other sub-fields within the new institutional economics (Tumlir 1989: 126; Sally 1996: 250f).

Walter Eucken was born in 1891, son of the philosopher and Nobel Laureate (in literature) Rudolf Eucken. He took his doctorate in economics at the University of Bonn in 1914 and, after military service from 1914 to 1918 in World War I, he completed his Habilitation in 1921 at the University of Berlin, where he taught as Privatdozent until 1925, the year he was appointed Professor of Economics at the University of Tübingen. In 1927 Eucken accepted a chair at the University of Freiburg, where he remained until his death in 1950. Eucken was the only non-emigrant German who took part in the 1947 conference at Mont Pelerin in Switzerland, initiated by F.A. Hayek, which resulted in the founding of the Mont Pelerin Society. Hayek also arranged for Eucken's views on central planning to be published in *Economica* (1948) and, together with Lionel Robbins, invited Eucken to give a course of lectures at the LSE in 1950. During this visit, Eucken died in London. His lectures were posthumously published under the title *This Unsuccessful Age*.

Franz Böhm was born in 1895. After military service in World War I, he earned law degrees at the University of Freiburg in 1922 and 1924. From 1925 to 1931 he worked at the Cartel Department of the Ministry of Economics (Reichswirtschaftsministerium) in Berlin. In 1931 he returned to Freiburg where he took his doctorate (1932) and his Habilitation (1933), with Eucken and Grossmann-Doerth on his committee. He taught at Freiburg as Privatdozent until 1936 when he was appointed professor of law at the University of Jena, a position from which he was dismissed in 1938 because of his critical comments on the National Socialist regime's treatment of Jews. Shortly after the war Böhm was appointed Professor of Law at the University of Freiburg, and in 1946 at the University of Frankfurt, but the centre of his activities shifted to politics. He served from 1948 on as advisor to West Germany's Department of Economics, was a member of the Bundestag (for the CDU) from 1953 to 1965, and was one of the principal drafters of West Germany's anti-cartel legislation (the final result of which he considered, however, as too much 'watered down' by concessions to special interests). Böhm died in 1977.

The 'second generation' of the Freiburg School includes Friedrich A. Lutz, an assistant of Eucken, Paul Hensel, Hans Otto Lenel and Ernst-Joachim Mestmäcker, a disciple of Franz Böhm. The yearbook *ORDO*, founded by Eucken and Böhm in 1948, continues to be one of the principal outlets for publications in the tradition of the Freiburg research programme.

Freiburg University's 'Fakultät für Rechts- und Staatswissenschaften', including law as well as economics, provided a congenial framework for the combination of legal and economic perspectives characteristic of the Freiburg School and the Ordo-liberal tradition. As Böhm said in retrospect, the founders of the school were united in their common concern for the question of the constitutional foundations of a free economy and society. In the first volume of their jointly edited publication series *Ordnung der Wirtschaft* (Böhm 1937), the three editors included a programmatic introduction, entitled 'Our Task' (Böhm, Eucken and Grossmann-Doerth 1989), in which they emphasized their opposition to the, then, still influential heritage of Gustav von Schmoller's Historical School, and to the unprincipled relativism that, in their view, this heritage had brought about in German jurisprudence and political economy. By contrast, they stated as their guiding principle that the 'treatment of all practical politico-legal and politico-economic questions must be keyed to the idea of the economic constitution' (ibid.: 23), a task for which, they said, the collaboration of law and economics 'is clearly essential' (25).

Eucken developed his own work as an explicit alternative to Schmoller's programme and its continuing influence on economic thought and economic policy in Germany. Under Schmoller's leadership, he maintained, German economists had given up theoretical analysis and had lost the ability to look at specific issues of economic policy within the context of the broader issue of the economic constitution as a whole (Eucken 1938: 79). With his *Staatliche Strukturwandlungen und die Krise des Kapitalismus*, published in 1932, and his two major works, the *Grundlagen der Nationalökonomie* (1940) and the *Grundsätze der Wirtschaftspolitik* (1952), he wanted to provide an alternative to the Historical School's atheoretical approach to economic analysis as well as to its unprincipled discretionary approach to economic policy (Eucken 1940: 503). His aim was to develop a systematically integrated approach to the theoretical study and the political shaping of a constitutional social-economic-political order, or – to use the German terminology – a systematic approach to *Ordnungstheorie* and *Ordnungspolitik*.

As the term *Ordnung* (order) is *the* central concept in the research programme of the Freiburg School, it is important to note that, in the context of that programme, it is related to the concept of the *economic constitution*, in the sense of the *rules of the game*, upon which economies or economic systems are based (Eucken 1992: 314). Eucken and Böhm, and their followers, used *Ordnung* as an analytical concept that is meant to emphasize the systematic relation between the rules of the game, the economic constitution, and the order or patterns of economic activities that result under different kinds of rules or economic constitutions. It is definitely not meant to imply any of the conservative or authoritarian connotations that the word 'Ordnung' – or the English term *order* – may have had, or does have, in other uses.

By *economic order* (*Wirtschaftsordnung*) is meant the typical structure and systematic patterns of economic activities, or the regularities of the economic process, that characterize particular economies, in the sense in which one may speak of, for instance, the Athenian economic order in the age of Pericles, or the economic order of the Flemish towns around 1270 (Eucken 1992: 308). As Eucken insists (1992: 80), all economic activities take place within some economic order and can be adequately understood only in the context of that order. The question guiding research must be: 'What are the rules of the game?' (Eucken 1992: 81). The main message is that economic orders must be understood in terms of their underlying *economic constitution*, which means primarily the formal legal–institutional framework but which is also meant to include informal conventions and traditions that govern economic activities in the respective communities (Eucken 1990: 377). According to Eucken (1990: 21), the large variety of specific economic orders that have existed in the past and which exist in the present can be understood as varied compositions of two basic principles – the decentralized *coordination* of economic activities within a framework of general rules of the game on the one hand, and, on the other, the principle of *subordination* within a centralized administrative system (Eucken 1992: 118). One of the major themes of the Ordoliberal school was the contrast between a centrally planned economy, like the German war economy or the socialist economies, and the exchange or market economy (*Verkehrswirtschaft*). They developed a critique of central planning (*Zentralverwaltungswirtschaft*) with arguments very similar to those advanced by von Mises and Hayek (Eucken 1990: 361ff.).

Factual economic orders may, of course, be more or less efficient or desirable (Eucken 1992: 313f.), and the founders of the Freiburg School emphasized that the principal means by which economic policy can seek to improve on them is by improving the rules of the game, i.e. by implementing appropriate economic constitutions (ibid.: 378). What motivated their work was an interest in applying theoretical insights from law and economics to the practical problem 'of understanding and fashioning the legal instruments for an economic constitution' (Böhm, Eucken and Grossmann-Doerth 1989: 24), a concern that they saw as part of the broader project of inquiring into the constitutional foundations of a functioning and humane socio-economic-political order. To describe such an order Eucken adopted the Latin word *Ordo*, a term with apparent natural law connotations, which can, however, be separated from such connotations and be interpreted in the straightforward sense of an order that is desirable for the human beings who live in it (Vanberg 1997). Eucken and Böhm emphasized that their interest was not in developing a research programme as a purely academic enterprise, but in seeking for answers to the practical question of how a desirable economic order may be created and maintained, a question that they approached as a problem of *constitutional choice*, i.e. as a question of how a desirable economic order can be generated by creating an appropriate economic constitution (Eucken 1992: 314f.). The joint efforts of law and economics were to them an indispensable prerequisite for what they called *Wirtschaftsverfassungspolitik* (constitutional economic policy), a policy that seeks to improve the resulting economic order in an *indirect* manner, by reforming the rules of the game, by contrast to an economic policy that seeks to improve outcomes directly by way of specific interventions in the economic process (Eucken 1990: 336). The general aim that, in their view, such constitutional economic policy had to pursue was to create conditions under which economic actors in seeking to further their own interest also promote the common interest (Eucken 1938: 80; 1990: 360). In other words, they considered it the task of *Wirtschaftsverfassungspolitik* to *create* conditions under which the 'invisible hand' that Adam Smith had described can be expected to do its work.

Against historicist notions of an unalterable course of societal evolution, whether in their Marxian or other versions, Eucken and Böhm emphasized that the socio-economic orders in which people find themselves are to a significant extent subject to collective, political choice (Böhm 1960: 164). They acknowledged that all actual societies and economies are to a considerable degree the product of evolutionary forces and not the creation of a master plan (Eucken 1992: 82), and that, in particular, the market order had not been invented or implemented by deliberate design but had gradually evolved over millennia. They insisted, nevertheless, that economic orders are subject to human design and can be improved upon by deliberate reform. As Eucken (1992: 314) said about the problem of achieving a functioning and humane economic order:

> The problem will not solve itself simply by our letting economic systems grow up spontaneously. The history of the last century has shown this plainly enough. The economic system has to be consciously shaped. The detailed problems of economic policy, trade policy, credit, monopoly, or tax policy, or of company or bankruptcy law, are part of the great problem of how the whole economy, national and international, and its rules, are to be shaped.

It is in this sense that the Freiburg Ordoliberals spoke of an *economic constitution* as the inclusive decision of a community about how its economic life is to be ordered. And they took care to point out that an effective constitutional economic policy has to pay attention to the complex ways in which the various elements of the legal-institutional framework may interact (Eucken 1942: 42f.). As the founders of the school put it, it is essential to understand that such areas of law as 'bankruptcy law, . . . the law of obligations, real estate law, family law, labour law, administrative law, and all other parts of the law' (Böhm, Eucken and Grossmann-Doerth 1989: 24) together constitute the economic constitution, and that between them systematic interdependencies may exist that *Ordnungspolitik* has to pay attention to.

In the sense noted, the research programme of the Freiburg School can be said to comprise a *theoretical paradigm* as well as a *policy paradigm*. The theoretical paradigm is based on the premise that an adequate analysis and explanation of economic phenomena has to account for the nature of the constitutional framework, or the rules of the game, under which they occur. The policy paradigm is based on the premise that economic policy should seek to improve the framework of rules, the economic constitution, such that a well-functioning and desirable economic order results, rather than seeking to bring about desired outcomes directly by specific interventions into the resulting economic order. *Ordnungstheorie* is the name for the explanatory part of the Freiburg research programme, the paradigm of systematically studying the working properties of alternative institutional-constitutional arrangements, and the complex interdependencies between various components (company law, patent law, tax laws, labour law, etc.) of a nation's economic constitution. *Ordnungspolitik* is the name for its policy paradigm, for an integrated approach to the various components of the legal-institutional framework in which a market economy is embedded. In terms of Hayek's (1969) useful distinction between the *order of rules* and the *order of actions* that results under the rules, the explanatory paradigm of the Freiburg School can be said to focus on the question of how differences and changes in the order of rules result in differences or changes in the emerging order of actions, while the policy paradigm can be said to focus on the question of how the resulting economic order or order of actions can be improved by suitable reforms in the economic constitution or the order of rules.

While the founders of the Freiburg School placed themselves firmly in the tradition of classical liberalism, they emphasized, in contrast to some varieties of liberalism, that a free market order is not simply what one would find if and where government is absent, that it is not a natural event but a political-cultural product, based on a constitutional order that requires careful 'cultivation' for its maintenance and proper functioning. In this regard they found it necessary to distance themselves from a *laissez-faire* liberalism that failed to appreciate the essential positive role that government has to play in creating and maintaining an appropriate framework of rules and institutions that allows market competition to work effectively. They took care to distinguish between the spontaneous working of markets, provided an appropriate legal-institutional framework is in place, and the issue of how the framework itself comes about. In other words, they clearly distinguished between the *sub-constitutional* issue of how market competition works within given rules, and the *constitutional* issue of how the rules that make market-competition work are themselves established and enforced.

That the founders of the Freiburg School accused some of their nineteenth-century liberal predecessors of an unjustified 'confidence in the spontaneous emergence of the natural order' (Eucken 1989: 38) does not mean that they did not fully share the classical liberals' confidence in the self-regulating properties of market processes. It only means that they saw no justification for extending such confidence to what they called the *Ordnungsrahmen*, i.e. the legal-institutional framework. An appropriate *Ordnungsrahmen* for market competition, they argued, cannot be assumed to be self-generating, to evolve naturally and spontaneously.

The essence of the *free market economy* or a *free economic constitution* (Böhm 1937: 67) the Freiburg Ordoliberals saw to be in its nature as an order of *free competition*, in which all economic players meet as legal equals and in which voluntary exchange and voluntary contract are the only means by which economic activities are coordinated (ibid.: 105). They knew of course that the principles of equality and voluntariness are nowhere perfectly realized, and they pointed out that any criticism of the 'market economy' must distinguish between the issue of how well or imperfectly particular institutional realizations actually work, and the issue of what kind of legal-institutional framework might make for a well-functioning market order. They regarded these principles as normative standards against which existing economic orders and potential reforms could be judged, and as a reference criterion that can provide guidance to efforts in constitutional reform (Böhm 1937: 124f.). They saw a major historical step towards the realization of an economic order that meets these criteria in the liberal movements of the late eighteenth and early nineteenth centuries (Eucken 1982: 124) that marked the transition from the feudal society to what Böhm (1989: 46ff.) called the *Privatrechtsgesellschaft* (private law society) or *Zivilrechtsgesellschaft* (civil law society). The driving force of these movements was the idea of transforming the feudal 'multi-tier society into a private law society consisting of equally free people with equal rights' (Böhm 1989: 54), 'the idea that in society everyone should have the same rights and status, namely the status of a person under private law' (46). Its foremost goal was to eliminate inequalities in the law, the most objectionable of which were seen in 'the feudal sovereign rights . . . and the trade and industrial privileges' (56).

The market economy is, as Böhm (1989: 54) noted, the twin of the private law society, 'that the functioning of the free market system presupposes the existence of the private law society':

> The exchange agreement and its fulfilment is the characteristic mode of co-operation between independent traders with equal rights. In this respect, therefore, the private law system is very decisively involved in controlling free market processes.

In other words, the emergence of the market economy can be seen as a byproduct of the transition from the feudal order to the order of civil law, a transition that meant the abolition of feudal privileges and a multitude of restrictions on economic activities, creating an economic arena in which individuals are free to trade and to compete as legal equals. Böhm and Eucken insisted, though, that creating and maintaining a well-functioning competitive market order requires more than replacing feudal privileges and restrictions by free trade and freedom of contract. It requires, they claimed, an economic constitution that in its entirety is tuned to upholding competition in the face of anti-competitive interests; and a policy that aims at creating and maintaining such an economic constitution they considered to be something quite different from *laissez-faire*.

The Ordoliberals' critique of *laissez-faire* was probably motivated more by their concern to fend off stereotypic misrepresentations of the classical liberal doctrine than by their wish to provide a balanced account of nineteenth-century liberal doctrine. It should therefore be assigned lesser weight than the positive part of their message, i.e. their argument that an appropriate economic constitution is a prerequisite of a well-functioning market economy. They conceded that the policy of *laissez-faire* did not aim at a 'staatsfreie Wirtschaft' (Eucken 1990: 26), an economy without the state, but realized the importance of property rights, contract law, corporation law, patent law, etc. They pointed out, however, that it failed to recognize that the monitoring of the economic order at large is a political task but instead assumed that a suitable economic order would evolve spontaneously within the framework of the law (Eucken 1982: 116). By contrast, the founders of the Freiburg School took care to point out that there is not simply '*the* free market' that emerges wherever and whenever property rights are enforced, and where free trade and freedom of contract are realized. They emphasized that markets can work quite differently and that it depends on the nature of the entire framework of rules of the game whether market competition exhibits desirable working properties. Their principal message was that the free market economy is more than a free play of economic forces; rather, it is a constitutional regime with particular rules of the game and its proper functioning depends on the nature and the effective enforcement of those rules. They considered it to be of utmost importance to recognize that opting for a market economy is a matter of *positive constitutional choice*, that it implies the adoption of a particular economic constitution that must be upheld against adverse interests if market competition is to work to the common benefit of all the players involved.

The whole logic of the Freiburg research programme rests on the distinction between the *constitutional level* at which political choices regarding a society's economic constitution are made, and the *sub-constitutional level* at which private choices *within* the constitutionally determined rules of the game are made. As the Ordoliberals put it: 'The economic constitution must be understood as a general political decision as to how the economic life of the nation is to be structured' (Böhm, Eucken and Grossmann-Doerth 1989: 24). The free market order is seen as 'a political and constitutional-legal order' (Böhm 1937: 18), as an order that is adopted by explicit constitutional choice, not an order that would be self-creating and self-maintaining in the absence of a political-constitutional will to sustain it. As a constitutional order it is subject to political-constitutional choice, even though the very nature of the market as a constitutional regime is that it provides for an arena in which private voluntary transactions can be carried out protected from government interference. Eucken and Böhm were quite clear about the fact that 'the power to establish generally binding norms is essentially a political power' (Böhm 1989: 55), and that the decision in favour of the market as an arena of private, voluntary co-ordination is, in itself, a political choice. In this sense, they recognized that there is logical priority of the political-constitutional choice *of* a market order over the sub-constitutional choices made *within* that order.

Central to the Freiburg approach is the notion that the choice of the rules of the game is one that is made on behalf of the entire constituency of a jurisdiction, and that individual 'players' or members of a jurisdiction cannot be allowed to abrogate or renegotiate the rules at the sub-constitutional level by way of private contracting (Böhm 1960: 39ff.). As Eucken (1982: 120) argued: 'Keeping markets open helps to promote a country's economy. Hence, private pressure groups cannot be given the right to eradicate this. That right forms part of the regulative policy (*Ordnungspolitik*) and it must not be left to private persons.' This is the issue that the Ordoliberals had in mind when they insisted that the *freedom of contract*, which is of obvious importance for a competitive market economy, cannot be allowed to serve as an instrument 'to eliminate competition and to establish monopolistic positions' (Eucken 1982: 123) and must not be permitted to be 'used for the purpose of entering into contracts which restrict or eliminate the freedom of contract' (ibid.: 125). They insisted, in other words, that it is incompatible with the notion of playing according to rules if the players retain the right to change the rules unilaterally by separate agreements among sub-coalitions, and that it is, in particular, incompatible with the constitutional decision for a competitive economy to allow economic agents to excuse themselves, through private contracting, from the constraints that the rules of the game of competition are meant to impose on them (Böhm 1960: 27ff.; 1980: 233ff.). This is Böhm's principal argument why cartel agreements are in principle incompatible with a competitive economic constitution, and why he considered the decision of the highest German court, in 1897, to grant the protection of the law to cartel agreements a fundamental judicial mistake (Böhm 1937: 150ff.; Eucken 1989: 55). And this is why they did not see any reason to believe that the *selbstgeschaffene Recht der Wirtschaft*, the 'self-produced law of the business community' (Grossmann-Doerth 1933; Eucken 1989: 56), can be trusted generally to serve the common interest, rather than serving producer interests at the expense of consumer interests. As Eucken (1989: 32) noted: 'It must be asked whether the rules and regulations made by economic power groups to control activity among themselves in fact are tending to take the place of statute law. How far has such 'self-made' law transformed the legal order? The question is of great importance in the modern industrialised world.'

Böhm was concerned with *The Problem of Private Power* (the title of a 1928 publication of his) and the threat that it poses to the viability of a competitive order, a concern that he shared with Eucken. Expressly agreeing with the classical economists of the Scottish School, he emphasized in *Wettbewerb und Monopolkampf* (1933) that consumer interests are 'the sole directly justifiable economic interests' (Böhm 1982: 107) and that the essential function of competition is 'to place the entrepreneur's pursuit of profit in the direct service of the consumer' (109). Referring to Adam Smith's view that the impulse of human selfishness loses its 'anti-social aspects under the impact of competition' (112), Böhm described competition as 'the moral backbone of a free profit-based economy' (110), invoking the basic theme that runs through his entire work, the notion that, as he phrased it in later writings (Böhm 1960: 22), 'competition is by no means only an incentive-mechanism but, first of all, an instrument for the deprivation of power (*Entmachtungsinstrument*),' that 'competition is the most magnificent and most ingenious instrument of deprivation of power in history' ('Der Wettbewerb ist das grossartigste und genialste Entmachtungsinstrument der Geschichte').

The Freiburg Ordoliberals made it clear that the desirable working properties that the classical liberals attributed to market competition cannot be expected from any unqualified competitive process *per se*, but only from what they called *Leistungswettbewerb*, 'achievement-' or 'performance-competition', i.e. competition in terms of better service to consumers (Eucken 1990: 43), as opposed to *Behinderungswettbewerb*, 'prevention-competition', i.e. competition by means that are directed at preventing competition from other producers, rather than improving one's own performance (Böhm 1937: 123ff.; Eucken 1990: 329, 358f.). Creating and maintaining an appropriate framework of 'rules of the game of *Leistungswettbewerb*' (Eucken 1942: 38) is, in their view, a genuine and indispensable political task, a task for *Wirtschaftsverfassungspolitik* or *Ordnungspolitik* (Eucken 1990: 266f.). This task they likened to the activities of a gardener who does not construct things, like an engineer, but provides for conditions that are conducive to the natural growth of what is considered desirable, while holding back the growth of what is not desired. As Böhm (1980: 200) put it, to maintain a well-functioning market economy requires continuous nursing and gardening, comparable to creating and maintaining a highly cultivated park ('die dauernde Pflege und Verbesserung einer ganzen Reihe von politischen, rechtlichen, sozialen und zivilisatorischen Vorbedingungen, das Vorhandensein einer ziemlich hochgezüchteten sozialen Parklandschaft').

Ordnungspolitik in the Freiburg sense is first and foremost *competition policy*, a policy that aims at securing a competitive process with desirable working properties, one that works to the benefit of consumer interests. Yet, while Eucken and Böhm were fairly clear about the general aim that they wanted competition policy to pursue, namely to realize *consumer sovereignty* to the largest possible extent, some ambiguity arose in their more specific recommendations for how such policy should proceed. They introduced, in addition to the criterion of *Leistungswettbewerb* (performance competition), another criterion that should guide competition policy, namely 'complete competition' (*vollständige Konkurrenz*), a criterion that does not appear to be quite compatible with the first, nor which seems compatible with the procedural logic of the Freiburg paradigm. The concept of *Leistungswettbewerb* clearly points in the direction of a rule-oriented competition policy that would seek to specify rules of the game that define which kinds of competitive strategies should, and which should not, be permitted because they can be predicted to work (or not to work) to the benefit of the consumer. To be sure, there may be considerable scope for disagreement on where the dividing line between permissible and prohibited strategies should be drawn, and the

Leistungswettbewerb-criterion is not immune to being misused in support of anti-competitive interests. Yet, it clearly constitutes a *procedural* criterion that is in line with the logic of *Ordnungspolitik* or constitutional policy, and that can be rationally discussed in terms of the appropriateness of its particular applications. By contrast, the criterion of 'complete competition' (*vollständige Konkurrenz*), is *outcome-oriented*, in the sense that it looks at the resulting market structure, identifying as desirable a situation where on both sides of the market there are numerous economic players without any market power (Böhm 1937: 105f.; 1960: 62f.; Eucken 1992: 270).

The problem with the concept of perfect competition is, of course, that it is in contrast to the procedural thrust of *Ordnungspolitik* and that it may lead to policy recommendations that conflict with the concept of *Leistungswettbewerb* (Eucken 1990: 375f.). Since the latter's focus is on the nature of the procedures by which outcomes are generated rather than on the outcomes as such, it would have to allow for market structures that deviate from complete competition as long as they are the result of *Leistungswettbewerb*, while the former criterion would recommend against such structures even if they are solely the result of *Leistungswettbewerb*. That the views which Eucken and Böhm voiced on competition policy are in need of clarification has often been noted, and these views have been further developed within the Freiburg School, just as the theoretical outlook regarding competition has changed considerably over the past fifty years in the rest of the economics profession. These issues, important as they are, should be considered, however, of secondary importance relative to the general notion that the Ordoliberals sought to advance, namely that an appropriate competitive order, one that exhibits desirable working properties, is not a self-generating and self-maintaining gift of nature but something that needs to be actively pursued and cultivated. There is clearly scope for argument on what may be the most suitable kind of *Ordnungspolitik* to serve that purpose, and one may well disagree with some of what the founders of the Freiburg School had to say on this issue, while still agreeing with their principal argument that *market competition* is not just any kind of competition but one that requires appropriate rules of the game.

To what extent 'private economic power' poses, indeed, a threat to a properly working competitive market order (Eucken 1990: 359) is an issue that many of today's economists, even among those working in the Freiburg tradition, would judge somewhat differently, sharing fewer of the concerns that moved Eucken and Böhm, and seeing the roots of anticompetitive contrivances more in the political than in the private arena. If, as Böhm (1960: 32) argues, the essence of economic power lies in the ability of inferior suppliers to prevent customers from gaining access to more attractive alternatives, the question arises of how such power may be obtained within a properly enforced order of private law, and in the absence of legal privileges. In fact, Eucken and Böhm were not blind to the fact that many of the problems which they discussed under the rubric of 'private economic power' are indirect consequences of misguided government interventions or of defects in the existing legal-institutional framework. As Eucken noted (1989: 33):

> The formation of monopolies can be encouraged by the state itself through, for example, its patent policy, trade policy, tax policy *et cetera*. This has happened often in recent times. The state first encourages the formation of private economic power and then becomes partially dependent on it.

However one may judge the contemporary relevance of what the founders of the Freiburg School thought about the need to defend a competitive economic constitution against threats from private power, what is clearly still most relevant, and much in line with modern political economy, is what they had to say about a problem that they described as *refeudalization* and which in contemporary economics is discussed as the problem of *rent-seeking* (Streit 1992: 690f.). As noted above, the Ordoliberals saw the essential feature of the competitive market order in the fact that it is a privilege-free, non-discriminating constitutional order within which economic actors meet as legal equals. The transition from the privilege-based feudal order to the civil-law society that had marked, in their view, the major historical step towards the realization of such an order, had been motivated by the liberal principle that 'the state should on no account be allowed to confer privileges' (Böhm 1980: 141; 1989: 57). Accordingly, they regarded the granting of special privileges to particular groups as a violation of the very principles on which a competitive market order is built, as a violation of the fundamental constitutional commitment that is entailed in opting for the market order and the privilege-free civil law society (ibid.: 164). Privilege-seeking and privilege-granting is, as they emphasized, in essence a movement back to the kind of discriminatory order of privileges that had been characteristic of the feudal society. It is a 'refeudalization of society' (ibid.: 258), a process about which Eucken (1990: 329) said that it reminds the observer of descriptions of the medieval feudal system. In no lesser clarity than modern public choice discussions on the problem of rent-seeking, the Freiburg Ordoliberals described the fatal political dynamics that result where governments and legislators are empowered to grant privileges and where, in consequence, special interest groups work the political process in order to obtain such privileges. As Böhm phrased it (1980: 166; 1989: 66), the government

> is constantly faced with a considerable temptation to meet the contradictory demand of many pressure groups. . . . The fact that this tendency is, as it were, in the nature of things makes it a weakness of the system which must be taken seriously.

What the Ordoliberals made clear with their constitutional approach to market competition was that the competitive order must be considered a public good, and that – as in all public good cases – it is important to distinguish clearly between a person's interest in enjoying the benefits of a public good and her interest in contributing to its production. Applied to the competitive order as a public good, it is important to distinguish between, on the one side, the issue of whether it is desirable for a person to live within a competitive market environment and, on the other, the issue of whether it is in that person's interest to comply with the rules that constitute a competitive market order. That legislator and government act in accordance with their 'constitutionally determined mandate . . . to create, preserve and manage that regulative framework' which guarantees the functioning of the free market

> is desired not only for itself, it is also in the interest of all citizens of the state that the government adheres strictly to this mandate (Böhm 1989: 63f.).

Despite this common interest, however, 'it is possible for any participant and for any group of participants to obtain benefits by violating the rules, . . . at the expense of other participants or groups of participants' (64), be it by direct rule-violations such as the forming of cartels or by lobbying for special privileges. The latter strategy is, as Böhm pointed out, particularly attractive because:

> in this case, the individual does not expose himself to the odium of cheating but demands are made of the legislator or the government to elevate cheating to a legislator or governmental programme . . . Protective duties, tax privileges, direct subsidies, price supports, initial support for establishing monopoly or 'orderly markets' can be demanded. . . . It is the state itself which is to be enjoined to override the rules of the prevailing order in favour of one group and at the expense of other groups or citizens.

Even if they did not use the term 'public good', nor the concepts of game theory, the Ordoliberals most clearly recognized that the 'game of competition' represents a prisoners' dilemma, in the sense that while all players are better off living under a competitive regime, compared to potential alternative regimes, everybody has an interest in being exempted from the constraints that competition imposes. Yet, if all successfully seek protection from competition for themselves, they will end up in a thoroughly protectionist regime that is desirable for nobody, and which no one would choose over the competitive alternative if the choice were between the two. It is in order to escape from that dilemma that all can benefit from committing to a competitive economic constitution, if that commitment is made credible by the presence of a government that effectively enforces the rules of the game of competition. And it is a violation of such commitment, a violation of the rules of the game, if players seek to escape the discipline of competition through private contrivances or by the means of politics (Böhm 1937: 126). This is the logic behind the Ordoliberals' diagnosis that the competitive market order is not self-generating and self-maintaining but needs the assistance of *Ordnungspolitik*. In today's language one might say that to them a major and principal task of Ordnungspolitik is to allow the economic players to escape from prisoners' dilemmata.

In assigning to the state the task of acting as 'guardian of the competitive order', as *Hüter der Wettbewerbsordnung* (Eucken 1990: 327), the Freiburg Ordoliberals found themselves facing a fundamental dilemma. The logic of their argument implied that the solution to the problem of guarding the competitive order had to come from an agency, the government, that they recognized, at the same time, to be a major source of the defects that it was supposed to cure. Certainly, they did not suppose that, under the existing political structure, government could be expected to do what is in the common interest, and they explicitly criticized the illusionary belief that government can be trusted to act as a benign and omniscient agent of the common good (Eucken 1932: 323). Yet, they also insisted that the existing political order should not be taken as unalterable fate, but should be regarded as something that can be and must be reformed (Eucken 1990: 338), in the awareness that the real problem is, in the political realm no less than in the economy, to establish a framework that induces ordinary, self-interested people to do, in pursuit of their own interest, what is in the common interest (Eucken 1940: 490f.). In other words, they recognized, much in line with modern Constitutional Economics, that the solution to the problem of rent-seeking must ultimately be found in the political constitution (Eucken 1990: 327). They saw that before the state can be trusted to be a reliable guardian of the competitive economic constitution, the constitutional order of 'the state', or the rules of the game of politics, are in need of reform. And they were aware, of course, of the fact that such reform can, again, only be achieved through the political process, and that therefore there can be no guarantees that a solution to the twofold constitutional problem will be achieved. But to them this was not an acceptable excuse for not making an effort to address this problem.

That the dilemma exists is not the fault of the Freiburg research programme; it lies in the nature of things. And it speaks to the intellectual honesty of the founders of this programme that they did not pretend to be able to offer an easy answer. A phrase that they used, and that has often been misunderstood, is the argument that a 'strong state' is needed to fend off interest group pressures. This was clearly not meant as an argument in favour of an authoritarian state with large discretionary power. On the contrary, the Freiburg Ordoliberals expressly noted that it is the modern growth of the state's apparatus and activities that have made it 'a plaything in the hands of interest groups' (Böhm 1980: 258; Eucken 1990: 326). The formula 'strong state' was meant by them as a shorthand for a state that is constrained by a political constitution that prevents government from becoming the target of special interest rent-seeking (Böhm 1989: 61). What such a constitution was to entail, i.e. how constitutional safeguards might be installed that effectively prevent the dynamics of privilege-seeking and privilege-granting, they did not discuss in detail. But they would have certainly subscribed to the general recommendation that the authority and the power must be taken away from governments and legislators to discriminate among citizens by granting privileges (Eucken 1990: 337).

Eucken, in particular, emphasized the importance of extending the logic of *Ordnungspolitik* from the realm of the economic constitution to that of the political constitution. He explicitly stated that, just as Ordnungspolitik is needed in order to establish and to maintain an appropriate economic constitution, Ordnungspolitik is also needed at the level of politics in order to establish and to maintain an appropriate political constitution (Eucken 1990: 331f.). His early death prevented Eucken from working out his thoughts on the notion of Ordnungspolitik for the political realm. But the paradigm that he and Böhm launched clearly invites such an extension of its logic from the market arena to the political arena, and it remains a task to be pursued by those who carry on the Freiburg tradition.

VIKTOR J. VANBERG

See also CONSTITUTIONAL ECONOMICS; EVOLUTION OF THE ECONOMIC CONSTITUTION OF THE EUROPEAN UNION; HAYEK, FRIEDRICH VON; MENGER, CARL; PRISONERS' DILEMMA AND THE THEORY OF THE STATE; RENT SEEKING.

Subject classification: 2a(i).

BIBLIOGRAPHY

Böhm, F. 1933. *Wettbewerb und Monopolkampf – Eine Untersuchung zur Frage des wirtschaftlichen Kampfrechts und zur Frage der rechtlichen Struktur der geltenden Wirtschaftsordnung*. Berlin: Carl Heymann; reprinted 1964. (Excerpts in English translation published as Böhm 1982.)

Böhm, F. 1937. *Die Ordnung der Wirtschaft als geschichtliche Aufgabe und rechtsschöpferische Leistung*. Stuttgart and Berlin: W. Kohlhammer. (Vol. 1 of *Ordnung der Wirtschaft*, ed. by F. Böhm, W. Eucken and H. Grossmann-Doerth.)

Böhm, F. 1950. Die Idee des Ordo im Denken Walter Euckens. *ORDO* 3: xv–lxiv.

Böhm, F. 1960. *Reden und Schriften*. Karlsruhe: C.F. Müller.

Böhm, F. 1980. *Freiheit und Ordnung in der Marktwirtschaft*. Baden-Baden: Nomos.

Böhm, F. 1982. The non-state ('natural') laws inherent in a competitive economy. In W. Stützel et al. (eds.), 107–113. (Excerpts in English translation from Böhm 1933.)

Böhm, F. 1989. The rule of law in a market economy. In Peacock and Willgerodt (eds) 1989a: 46–67. (English translation of 'Privatrechtsgesellschaft und Marktwirtschaft' in Böhm 1980, 105–168.)

Böhm, F., Eucken, W. and Grossmann-Doerth, H. 1989. The Ordo Manifesto of 1936. In Peacock and Willgerodt (eds) 1989a: 15–26. (Originally published in German as 'Unsere Aufgabe' in Böhm (1937): vii–xxi).

Eucken, W. 1932. Staatliche Strukturwandlungen und die Krise des Kapitalismus. *Weltwirtschaftliches Archiv* 36: 297–323.

Eucken, W. 1938. Die überwindung des Historismus. *Schmollers Jahrbuch* 62: 63–86.

Eucken, W. 1940. Wissenschaft im Stile Schmollers. *Weltwirtschaftliches Archiv* 52: 468–506.

Eucken, W. 1942. Wettbewerb als Grundprinzip der Wirtschaftsverfassung. In G. Schmölders (ed.), *Der Wettbewerb als Mittel volkswirtschaftlicher Leistungssteigerung und Leistung-sauslese*, Berlin: Duncker & Humblot (Schriften der Akademie für Deutsches Recht, Gruppe Wirtschaftswissenschaft, Vol. 6.)

Eucken, W. 1948. On the theory of the centrally administered economy. An analysis of the German experiment. *Economica, N.S.* 15: 79–100 (Part I), 173–93 (Part II).

Eucken, W. 1951. *This Unsuccessful Age*. Edinburgh: William Hodge.

Eucken, W. 1982. A policy for establishing a system of free enterprise. In Stützel et al., 115–131 (Excerpts in English translation from Eucken 1990.)

Eucken, W. 1989. What kind of economic and social system? In Peacock and Willgerodt (eds) 1989a: 28–45.

Eucken, W. 1990 (orig. 1952). *Grundsätze der Wirtschaftspolitik*. 6th edn, Tübingen: J.C.B Mohr (Paul Siebeck). (Excerpts in English translation published as Eucken 1982.)

Eucken, W. 1992. *The Foundations of Economics – History and Theory in the Analysis of Economic Reality*. Berlin, New York: Springer. (Reprint of the first English edition published in 1950 by William Hodge, London; English translation of *Die Grundlagen der Nationalökonomie*, first published in 1940, 9th edition published in 1989 by Springer, Berlin.)

Grossekettler, H.G. 1989. On designing an economic order: the contributions of the Freiburg School. In *Perspectives on the History of Economic Thought*, ed. D.A. Walker, Vol. II (Aldershot: Edward Elgar): 38–84.

Grossmann-Doerth, H. 1933. *Selbstgeschaffenes Recht der Wirtschaft und staatliches Recht*. Freiburg: Wagner (Freiburger Universitätsreden, 10).

Hayek, F.A. 1969: Rechtsordnung und Handelnsordnung. In *Freiburger Studien*, Tübingen: J.C.B. Mohr (Paul Siebeck): 161–98.

Johnson, D. 1989. Exiles and half-exiles: Wilhelm Röpke, Alexander Rüstow and Walter Eucken. In Peacock and Willgerodt (eds) 1989b: 40–68.

Kasper, W. and Streit, M. 1993. *Lessons from the Freiburg School. The Institutional Foundations of Freedom and Prosperity*. The Center for Independent Studies, Australia.

Lenel, H.O. 1989. Evolution of the social market economy. In Peacock and Willgerodt (eds) 1989b: 16–39.

Peacock, A. and Willgerodt, H. (eds) 1989a. *Germany's Social Market Economy: Origins and Evolution*. London: Macmillan.

Peacock, A. and Willgerodt, H. (eds) 1989b. *German Neo-Liberals and the Social Market Economy*. London: Macmillan.

Peacock, A. and Willgerodt, H. 1989. Overall view of the German Liberal Movement. In Peacock and Willgerodt (eds) 1989b: 1–15.

Sally, R. 1996. Ordoliberalism and the social market: classical political economy from Germany. *New Political Economy* 1: 233–257.

Schmidtchen, D. 1984. German 'Ordnungspolitik' as institutional choice. *Zeitschrift für die gesamte Staatswissenschaft* 140: 54–70.

Streit, M. 1992. Economic order, private law and public policy – the Freiburg School of law and economics in perspective. *Journal of Institutional and Theoretical Economics* 148: 675–704.

Streit, M. 1994. The Freiburg school of law and economics. In *The Elgar Companion to Austrian Economics*, ed. P.J. Boettke (Aldershot: Edgar Elgar): 508–15.

Stützel, W. et al. 1982. *Standard Texts on the Social Market Economy*. Stuttgart and New York: Gustav Fischer.

Tumlir, J. 1989. Franz Böhm and the development of economic-constitutional analysis. In Peacock and Willgerodt (eds) 1989b: 125–41.

Vanberg, V. 1997: Die normativen Grundlagen von Ordnungspolitik. In *Ordo*, forthcoming.

Willgerodt, H. and Peacock, A. 1989. German Liberalism and Economic Revival. In Peacock and Willgerodt (eds) 1989a: 1–14.

frivolous suits. *See* NUISANCE SUITS; SUITS WITH NEGATIVE EXPECTED VALUE.

Fuller, Lon Luvois (1902–1978). Described as 'unquestionably the leading secular natural lawyer of the twentieth century in the English-speaking world' (Summers 1984), Lon L. Fuller has had a major influence on contemporary jurisprudence. Formerly a professor of law at the universities of Oregon and Illinois, and at Duke University, Fuller taught at Harvard Law School from 1939 until 1972, becoming Carter Professor of General Jurisprudence (the chair formerly held by Roscoe Pound) in 1948. From 1942 to 1945, Fuller worked part-time for a Boston firm, and the experience of legal practice affected his subsequent work on legal process and his views about legal education. His casebook on Contract drew on his experience both in practice and as an arbitrator, as did his work on the 'science of social ordering', or 'eunomics' as he termed it – the study of the different legal techniques corresponding to various forms of social order. Author of an influential report by the Harvard Law School Curriculum Committee, which he chaired, he argued that the law school was too preoccupied with appellate decisions, neglecting the skills of successful legal planning, such as drafting and negotiation. His work in legal theory made an important contribution to a wider body of American scholarship, which included the influential (though unpublished) materials by Henry Hart and Albert Sacks on the legal process on which Fuller's mark was clear (see Duxbury 1995).

Believing that there were only a limited number of processes of social decision-making and that each made a distinctive contribution to the problem of social order, Fuller attempted to identify the main characteristics of each. He considered adjudication, customary law, contract, legislation, arbitration and mediation, objecting to the view held by theorists such as John Stuart Mill and Isaiah Berlin, that questions of process were always subservient to independently formulated objectives: social ends were neither fully comprehensible nor attainable without attention to available means. Public procedures and institutions embodied intrinsic moral values which placed limits on the objectives which they could properly be invoked to secure. Fuller argued, for example, that the moral force and legitimacy of common law adjudication might be undermined if it were extended to areas which lay outside its proper scope. If courts were required to perform tasks unsuited to adjudication, the result would not only be ineffective administration but the risk of damage to the standing of the judicial process itself, weakening respect for law. In particular, adjudication was an inappropriate vehicle for the resolution of 'polycentric' problems, involving the consideration of a variety of interdependent factors where no single issue can be determined in isolation from all the others. In his important essay, 'The Forms and Limits of Adjudication', published posthumously, Fuller argued that the essential feature of adjudication was its according an affected party a particular form of participation – that of presenting proofs and reasoned arguments for a decision in his favour. The moral force of a judgment was greatest where the judge confined his decision to an existing controversy between the parties, and decided the matter solely on the basis of the evidence and arguments which they have presented.

Lon Fuller was, above all, a perceptive and forceful critic of both legal positivism and legal realism. Each movement, he considered, suffered from a disastrous attempt to divorce the study of law from its ethical purpose. A purely descriptive or 'scientific' theory of law must choose between the realm of pure fact and that of pure assumption. Realism chose the former and made itself useless for any practical purpose: its attempt to study judicial behaviour as an independent phenomenon deprived it of any significance for the conduct of human affairs. By contrast, Hans Kelsen's attempt to give coherence to the legal system by deriving the validity of all its rules from a 'basic norm', a mere fiction or hypothesis, only distorted the complex reality it purported to explain. Hobbes's theory of the sovereign as the source of positive law had been grounded, unlike those of his modern successors, in *normative* principles which viewed the maintenance of peace and order as the fundamental purpose of legal rules and institutions.

Fuller repudiated the positivist's rigorous distinction between law and morality, emphasizing the crucial part played by reason and morality in determining the content of law in any particular case; and he rebuked positivist thinkers for allowing their passion for analytical definitions of law to deflect their attention from more pressing matters of substance. In seeking to contest the distinction between fact and value, which positivists had inherited from David Hume, Fuller also sought to undermine the moral subjectivism, or ethical non-cognitivism, which underlay the instrumentalist outlook of contemporary thinkers. His own extensive work on legal processes, distinguishing between different ways of resolving disputes, was inspired by a strong commitment to the rule of law and a belief in the importance of the lawyer's distinctive contribution to good government. Law consisted of both reason and fiat – of 'order discovered and order imposed' (1946) – and neither element could be ignored in its analysis.

Although legislation explicitly introduced reform, Fuller stressed the impossibility of drawing any clear distinction between the application of existing law and its evolution and development in the context of the common law. A positivist might wish to draw a clear line between law and morality, but a judge deciding a case at common law could not escape responsibility for the law's improvement – for bringing the law, within the narrow constraints of the particular case, closer to the requirements of justice. Fuller's celebration of judge-made law reflected his belief in the power of reason to guide the organization of human relations. He observed that positive law always existed within a much broader field of general understanding and shared assumptions – a spontaneous ordering of human relations, dependent for its effectiveness not on state decrees but on the power of ideas. The judicial process was much better suited to development of autonomous order than statute law: the common law reflected, and contributed to, people's beliefs about the rightness of certain forms of conduct, thereby ensuring their willing compliance.

Fuller's critique of positivism was sharpened in the course of his famous debate with H.L.A. Hart, the Oxford legal philosopher, in the late 1950s and 1960s. Hart, following John Austin and Jeremy Bentham, urged the desirability of keeping the question of a law's validity distinct from questions about its morality or title to obedience: intellectual clarity was assisted by such a division, which would also serve to emphasize the importance of independent moral scrutiny. Fuller, by contrast, objected that the positivist's distinction between validity and moral acceptability weakened the ideal of fidelity to law. If the law's content could always be ascertained without the exercise of moral judgment, it was difficult to explain the view, widely held by legal theorists, that the citizen has a moral obligation to obey the law. The ideal of fidelity to law was intimately related to the integrity of those legal processes through which social order was attained.

In Fuller's view, law was a purposive enterprise which required the collaboration of official and citizen: it was wrongly identified with the commands of a sovereign power, whatever their moral content. The existence of a legal system depended on its conformity to a set of procedural norms which Fuller described as constituting an 'inner morality of law'. Generality of law was achieved by the existence of rules; promulgation of the rules enabled them to be generally known and applied; prospectivity ensured that the rules could be followed, retroactive statutes being generally an abuse of legislative power, at least in the criminal law; rules must be clear because obscure and incoherent laws could provide no guidance; they must not contradict each other, or command the impossible; there must be reasonable constancy in the rules because frequent changes undermined the citizen's ability to obey; and the actions of officials, including judges, must be congruent with the rules declared.

The rule of law, as Fuller explains it, therefore imposes *reciprocal* obligations on government and governed: significant departure from these standards of formal legality constitutes a breach of faith. The existence of a legal order was essentially a matter of degree because a failure to guarantee the inner morality of law could be more or less serious. In the most serious case, of which Nazi Germany was Fuller's principal example, it would be doubtful whether a legal system, capable of generating obligations of obedience, existed at all. In a number of cases after 1945, German courts had tried and punished local war criminals, spies, and informers, who had assisted the Nazi regime. The defendants appealed to laws of the regime in force at the relevant time to justify their actions, even though some had procured the imprisonment or execution of personal enemies by reporting trivial offences to the authorities. Hart advocated the enactment of retroactive legislation, frankly acknowledging breach of the precept *nulla poena sine lege*, as a lesser evil than leaving such informers unpunished. By contrast, Fuller doubted the legality of the rules to which the defendants appealed. He questioned whether the abuse of legal procedure under the Nazi regime had not made untenable an informer's claim to have acted in accordance with existing law: many statutes had purported to authorize whatever suited the regime in particular cases, and their precise terms were in any case often disregarded by the German courts.

Fuller's critics objected to his identification of formal legality with morality, pointing out that oppressive or iniquitous laws could be drafted with precision and uniformly applied to those within their purview. Hart observed that a group of slaves might be denied even the minimum protection from violence or theft under laws which otherwise satisfied Fuller's canons of legality. In Hart's view, Fuller had mistaken purpose for morality: law might be inherently purposive but that proved only that the principles of legality were efficient means to substantive ends, whatever the merits of those ends (see Hart 1965). It has even been suggested that both Hart and Fuller exaggerated the significance of the terms in which legal and moral conflicts are debated, the substantive questions being essentially independent of their semantic, or analytic, presentation (see Posner 1990: 228–39).

There was much more truth to Fuller's claims than his critics were willing to allow. Respect for formal legality is necessary to protect the citizen's dignity, acknowledging his rationality and autonomy, his ability to take account of legal rules in planning his future conduct. The rule of law, in the sense of Fuller's precepts of legal morality, expresses a relationship of reciprocity between government and governed which has independent moral value, a point which Fuller underlined by the distinction he drew, in response to his critics, between law and 'managerial direction'. Moreover, Fuller was right to insist that a social institution can be understood only in the light of its purpose or point. The inherent connection Fuller sought between law and justice can be explained in this way. As MacCormick (1992) has argued, law is intelligible only by reference to the ends or values it should serve – justice and the common good. The law must at least *purport* to serve the common good, even if we think it fails to do so, or we would be unable to recognize its demands as claims to our obedience, asserting the existence of legal *obligations*.

The principal themes of Fuller's work reflect a wider movement of American jurisprudence focusing on the nature of legal process. Other writers also stressed the value of purposive interpretation in regard to statutes; and the important role of legal principles in the resolution of 'hard' cases, in which existing rules appeared to provide no solution, had been affirmed by such writers as John Chipman Gray, Benjamin Cardozo and, more recently, Roscoe Pound. Although Fuller appears to have developed his ideas largely in opposition to other schools of thought, whose defects he exposed with vigour and insight, his genius lay in forging significant connections between themes which were already current in contemporary debate. While embracing the widespread rejection of legal formalism, which had formerly minimized the creative role of judges in extracting the law from settled rules and concepts, he nevertheless repudiated the moral scepticism and behaviouralism of the 'realist' writers of the 1930s, such as Karl Llewellyn and Jerome Frank. Instead, he highlighted the role of reason as the basis of an approach to law which emphasized principle, purpose and morality.

In his rejection of the positivist's distinction between fact and value in the description of law, and in his emphasis on reason and morality as crucial to legal interpretation, Fuller laid the foundations for the later work of Ronald Dworkin. Dworkin's famous distinction between principle and policy, the former the concern of common law adjudication and the latter that of government or legislature, echoed Fuller's characterization of judicial activity as founded on reason. The purposive interpretation of legal rules, on which Fuller insisted, entailed the articulation of those principles or values which underlay society's general legal arrangements. Principled consistency was a necessary concomitant of the fundamental idea that like cases should be decided alike. Accordingly, the rights and duties enforced by the courts were always determined by reflection on principles of political morality already implicit in existing law: 'a right is a demand founded on a principle' (1978). Although Fuller did not quite anticipate Dworkin's attempt to identify substantive *criteria* of political morality, his work should nonetheless be understood as a contribution to liberal political theory (see Covell 1992). The role of reason was allied to the values of individual freedom and constitutional democracy: it was only in a liberal democracy that ideas could flourish in accordance with their merit, as opposed to their sponsorship by those in power. And the precepts which composed the 'inner morality of law' ultimately derived their importance from their contribution to legitimate constitutional government.

T.R.S. ALLAN

See also AMERICAN LEGAL REALISM; CONVENTIONS AT THE FOUNDATION OF LAW; HART, H.L.A.; RELIANCE; RULE OF LAW.

Subject classification: 4a(i); 7c.

SELECTED WORKS

1934. American legal realism. *University of Pennsylvania Law Review* 82: 429–62.
1936 (with William R. Perdue, Jr.). The reliance interest in contract damages. *Yale Law Journal* 46: 52–96, 373–420.
1940. *The Law in Quest of Itself.* Evanston, IL: Northwestern University Press.
1946. Reason and fiat in case law. *Harvard Law Review* 59: 376–95.
1947 (with Robert Braucher). *Basic Contract Law.* St Paul: West Publishing Co.; 2nd edn, 1964 (with Melvin Aron Eisenberg); 3rd edn, 1972; 4th edn, 1981.
1949. *The Problems of Jurisprudence.* Mineola, MN: Foundation Press.
1949. The case of the Speluncean explorers. *Harvard Law Review* 62: 616–45.
1954. American legal philosophy at mid-century. *Journal of Legal Education* 6: 457–85.
1955. Freedom – a suggested analysis. *Harvard Law Review* 68: 1302–25.
1956. Human purpose and natural law. *Journal of Philosophy* 53: 697–705.
1958. Positivism and fidelity to law – a reply to Professor Hart. *Harvard Law Review* 71: 630–72.
1964. *The Morality of Law.* New Haven: Yale University Press; revised edn, 1969.
1967. *Legal Fictions.* Stanford: Stanford University Press.
1968. *Anatomy of the Law.* Chicago: Britannica Perspectives; Harmondsworth: Penguin Books Ltd; New York: Praeger.
1978. The forms and limits of adjudication. *Harvard Law Review* 92: 353–409.
1981. *The Principles of Social Order* (posthumous). Durham: Duke University Press.

BIBLIOGRAPHY

Covell, C. 1992. *The Defence of Natural Law: A Study of the Ideas of Law and Justice in the Writings of Lon L. Fuller, Michael Oakeshott, F.A. Hayek, Ronald Dworkin, and John Finnis.* New York: St Martin's Press.
Duxbury, N. 1995. *Patterns of American Jurisprudence.* Oxford: Clarendon Press.
Hart, H.L.A. 1965. Lon L. Fuller: the morality of law. *Harvard Law Review* 78: 1281–96; reprinted in Hart, *Essays in Jurisprudence and Philosophy*. Oxford: Clarendon Press, 1983.
MacCormick, N. 1992. Natural law and the separation of law and morals. In *Natural Law Theory: Contemporary Essays*, ed. R.P. George. Oxford: Clarendon Press.
Posner, R.A. 1990. *The Problems of Jurisprudence.* Cambridge, MA: Harvard University Press.
Summers, R.S. 1984. *Lon L. Fuller.* London: Edward Arnold; Stanford, CA: Stanford University Press.

futures contracts. *See* DERIVATIVE SECURITIES REGULATION.

G

games of secession. All the issues surrounding secession have attracted new interest in the wake of Yugoslavia's bloody breakup, the collapse of the Soviet Union, and the separation of the Czech Republic and Slovakia – events that have accompanied new secessionist strains in fragile federations like Canada, Belgium and India, as well as pressures for decentralization in Malaysia, Nigeria, France, Spain and the United Kingdom. Not surprisingly, the tool of game theory has been applied to such situations by scholars in economics and political science. These efforts have shown some promise. They have provided new understanding of the calculations involved in secession, and they have illuminated the dynamics of particular cases. But they have also demonstrated some of the limitations of game theory in politics, several of which might be overcome by future work.

Amidst the efflorescence of the literature on secession, it is useful here to cut away those clusters of work that are not central to games of secession. One is normative studies, primarily in political philosophy and law, that concern the legitimacy of secession (see Buchheit 1978; Buchanan 1991; Heraclides 1992; McGee 1992). While arguments about justice are powerfully deployed by all secessionist movements and their adversaries, and while norms of fairness help order citizens' preferences about constitutional arrangements, these are not the stuff of secession games. Neither are strictly legal arguments about the international and domestic law governing secession (see Sunstein 1991 and Cassese 1995). Not only is the relevant international law ill defined (in part because of the rareness of the event and the particular circumstances of each case), but a successful secession depends ultimately on the capacity of the new state to exercise authority over its territory and to be recognized by other sovereign entities. These are fundamentally political questions rooted in domestic solidarity on the one hand and nations' foreign policy on the other. A third strand of work that is relevant but not central focuses on the ultimate causes of secessionist movements, whether located in a globalizing world often claimed to be conducive to decentralization or fragmentation – because of the greater economic security offered by international regimes (see Schroeder 1992; Cable 1995), or in the socio-economics of ethnic solidarity and nationalist mobilization (see Rogowski 1985; Frye 1992; Meadwell 1993; Breton and Breton 1995; Keating 1996). But conditions and causes do not capture the strategic dynamics of secessions. Yet another literature treats constitutional design, some of which concerns revolution and secession (see Ordeshook 1992; Elster 1993; Chen and Ordeshook 1994), yet this does not explain how movements came to the point of successful separation from an existing state. Finally, there are accounts of how secession happens. Beyond the many extant case studies, some of these works present empirical generalizations about the process based on historical experience (see Bookman 1993; Young 1994c); others analyse more abstractly the pattern of alternatives open over the course of secessions to both secessionist movements and their opponents (see Wood 1971; Hechter 1992). The former usefully show how secessions are historic events in which choices are possible, critical, and often irreversible, but they do not capture the effects of actors' preferences with the clarity achieved by game theory. The latter emphasize that secessions (with the partial exception of decolonizing empires) are contested, politically or militarily or both. But they do not involve close analysis of the strategic interactions that determine particular choices.

Standard economics is more relevant. Leaders and citizens will always make calculations of the relative costs and benefits of alternative constitutional arrangements. Out of the public-finance and fiscal-federalism traditions, a literature has been built on the original analysis by Buchanan and Faith (1987) of the possibility of 'internal exit' through secession. Much of this work explores the implications of economies of scale in public-goods provision, the efficiency of redistribution and mutual insurance across different units, and the relationship of political integration with economic integration and efficiency (see Casella and Feinstein 1992; Bolton, Roland and Spolaore 1996). A second branch stems from a paper by Friedman (1977). In this 'macro' tradition, the size and shape of nations is endogenous, a function of the economic value of territory, the cost of tax collection, economies of scale and scope, the external economic environment, and military and other technologies (see Dudley 1991; Wittman 1991; Alesina and Spolaore 1995).

These economic treatments are suggestive and useful, but they are not adequate to deal with secession. Those in the public finance tradition have generally assumed perfect information about the relative costs of different constitutional arrangements. But this is not the case when secession is contemplated, precisely because future economic performance will depend on political arrangements. For example, the long-term prospects of Slovakia or Quebec are in part a function of the trading and other relationships that can be established with the Czech Republic and the rest of Canada, and until the secession takes place these are unknown. More seriously, these analyses neglect the costs of transition to different constitutional arrangements. Generally, economists distinguish the long-term costs (and benefits) of secession (which include elements like the fiscal burden, access to foreign markets, national solidarity, and new economic policies) from the short-term effects of the secession. These latter 'transition costs' include the transactions costs of negotiating the secession and implementing new administrative arrangements, and costs caused by uncertainty. The latter include the *premia* to be paid creditors and investors – because of uncertainty about the currency, the ability of the new state(s) to carry debt, and the treaty and policy environments that will prevail – but they are potentially much broader: the uncertainties during a secession affect individuals' decisions about migration and savings and firms' decisions about sources of inputs, markets, and investment (see Economic Council 1991: 77–93). Some transition costs are fixed, or inevitable, but most are variable. They depend on the politics of the secession. If negotiations break down or violence accompanies a contested secession, then the transition costs can be immense, as Yugoslavia shows, and even without war, heavy transition costs can have enduring structural effects that cripple a state's long-term performance (see Young 1995a: 94–100). All of this implies that the uncertainty about the economic effects of secession will be critical in determining citizens' willingness to support secessionist movements, and that leaders on both sides will deploy arguments about these costs, strategically, to advance their cause. It also implies that the costs of secession will depend on the interaction between the sides, including the deployment of threats and the capacity to make credible commitments. The public-finance treatments miss these elements of secession.

The 'macro' tradition suffers from a different problem – the same functionalism that often infuses analyses in the 'new institutional' school, where it seems that if efficient outcomes require a different set of institutions, then they will emerge. In analyses of secessions (and conquests), the same logic is found.

> Consider two nations, each claiming the same piece of territory. Each may try to gain its ends by force, threats, or offers of payment or exchange. It seems reasonable to suppose that the outcome will be efficient, that the territory will end in the control of the nation willing to pay the higher price (Friedman 1977: 59).

Similarly, 'two nations would join together (separate) if the economies of scale and scope and the synergy produced by their union created greater (smaller) benefits than costs' (Wittman 1991: 129). The problem here, empirically, is that there are often long lags between the existence of the facilitating conditions and the occurrence of the event, so while such analyses may clarify the advantages and disadvantages of particular constitutional arrangements, and they may explain *ex post* why it was rational for secessions or other changes to take place, they do not capture the stakes as perceived by actors *ex ante*, and these, presumably, are what lead to particular secessionist moves and countermoves. (Indeed, 'rational' depictions of the costs and benefits of secession are a big part of secessionist debates.) Nor do they generally capture the strategic interaction that characterizes secessions, or the uncertainty about costs and benefits that is itself a product of those political (and military) interactions.

This brings us, finally, to specific treatments of secession using game theory. Unfortunately, these are very few and, as yet, they are elementary. But, unlike the literatures just described, they should focus on the strategies involved in secession, clarify actors' preferences, stress the interaction between secessionists and their opponents, incorporate the high degree of uncertainty about the future that is intrinsic to secessions, and explain particular choices over the course of the process.

The first such treatment was produced by Louis Imbeau (1991). This was stimulated by the long constitutional negotiations between Quebec and Canada, which had produced in 1987 an agreement on the terms for Quebec's acceptance of the 1982 Canadian constitution (see also Imbeau 1990). But this agreement – the Meech Lake Accord – failed to be ratified, so Imbeau aimed to predict how the situation might evolve, and especially whether Quebec would secede. The setup was standard. First, the interaction was modelled as a game between two actors, Quebec and the rest of Canada. Second, Imbeau described the possible outcomes: C, a compromise (rather like the Meech Lake Accord, perhaps); FQ, one favouring Quebec, perhaps with much decentralization of powers or an asymmetrical arrangement amounting to 'special status' within the federation; FC, one favouring Canada, with minimal change from the status quo; and Impasse, or no agreement. Third, each player had two possible strategies, conventionally called 'cooperation' and 'defection'. The basic game then took the form depicted in Figure 1.

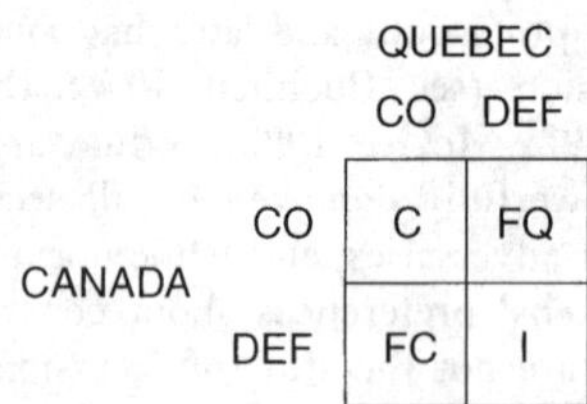

Figure 1 Constitutional Negotiations between Quebec and Canada

Next, Imbeau described each actor's possible preference functions over these outcomes. All the preferences are transitive orderings. For example, a 'centralist federalist' might order the outcomes as FC > C > FQ > I, while a 'hardcore sovereigntist' might prefer I > FQ > C > FC, on the expectation that an Impasse would result in secession. With 24 possible preference orderings for each player, there are 576 possible games, but these reduce to 78 that are strictly distinct (see Rapoport and Guyer 1966). Within this framework, Imbeau was able to analyse a range of possible outcomes, including those where Compromise was a natural outcome, and those where it could result from one side having the power to threaten the other. Focusing on the most plausible preference orderings, he concluded that Quebec had been prepared to Compromise by accepting the Meech Lake Accord, but Canada had been ready to risk Impasse by rejecting it; hence, Quebec now had to show that it was willing to accept Impasse – and political sovereignty – in order to attain a stable constitutional Compromise.

This analysis revealed several features of simple game theory as it applies to secessions. First, the preference orderings over the possible outcomes are crucial in determining the shape of the game. However, each player can misperceive the other's preferences (and, in reality, preferences may change over the course of events). Second, the starting point of the game is important, because the available moves depend on this. As well, players may exercise threats, both 'compellent' (threatening not to change position no matter what the opponent does) and 'deterrent' (threatening retaliation should the opponent change position). Finally, the credibility of an opponent in communicating both his preferences and his determination crucially affects the other's choices.

This last point was stressed by Brams (1994: 159–63) in an analysis of the attempted secession of the Confederacy. There were four possible outcomes: Compromise (with, perhaps, slavery permitted in the South but restricted elsewhere), Union Submits (with slavery permitted in the United States, or else an uncontested secession by the Confederacy), Confederacy Submits (with slavery abolished), and Civil War. Brams suggests that the Union's ranking of these alternatives (where 4 is the most valued and 1 the least) was 3, 1, 4, 2, while the Confederacy, weaker in military power, ranked them 3, 4, 2, 1. In this game, while the Union would have preferred Compromise, it would definitely not cooperate in the extension of slavery throughout the United States; hence, if the Confederacy defected, it would fight. But the Confederacy, by choosing in fact to defect, might have been aiming to force the Union to accept a Compromise; alternatively, argues Brams, the Confederate leaders may have believed that an early, massive show of force might have induced the Union to allow an uncontested secession. This was a miscalculation, because Lincoln was 'determined to make it palpably clear that the North could better withstand the breakdown state' [of civil war] (Brams 1994: 162). The Confederacy did not have threat power, and underestimated the Union's preference for war over submission.

Young (1994b) pushed Imbeau's analysis into the realm of actual secession rather than merely Impasse. This treatment took account of the economic calculations about long-term costs and transition costs discussed above, because in the debate about Quebec secession these had figured prominently. In particular, the sovereigntists in Quebec had argued that Canada would cooperate in a secession, since a difficult transition would impose costs on both parties. In order to minimize costs, it would be in the predecessor state's interest to facilitate an orderly transfer of responsibilities, conduct efficient negotiations about substantive matters so as to reduce uncertainty, and aim towards a high level of long-term economic integration. But Canadian spokesmen refused to admit there would be any economic cooperation between Canada and a sovereign Quebec, and some predicted that the secession would be acrimonious and the transition very costly (perhaps, even, involving partition of the seceding province). These threats were obviously intended to deter Quebecers from voting Yes in a referendum on sovereignty, but for many voters they were not credible. As the sovereigntists argued, it made perfect sense for the federalists, who wanted to avoid the costs secession would impose on themselves, to emphasize the difficulties of the transition and the costly absence of long-term economic integration. However, these threats were a bluff. Were Quebecers to ignore them, and to choose sovereignty, then a Canada seeking to minimize its losses would change its strategy, opting for cooperation, for the tranquil management of the transition, for joint assurances that would diminish uncertainty – especially among foreign investors – and for an economic association that would avoid the costs to itself of fragmenting the common economic space.

Simple game theory illuminated this situation, and it can easily be generalized to most cases of potential secession because they typically follow protracted constitutional negotiations, have a range of possible outcomes, and feature the deployment of threats about a highly uncertain future. Assume that a constitutional crisis involves two players, Unity and Autonomy, the latter of which may secede. Assume also that the crisis can have four possible results:

C: a compromise on a new set of mutually satisfactory constitutional arrangements;

SA: sovereignty-association; that is, Autonomy achieves sovereignty but maintains a high level of economic integration with Unity;

SQ: the status quo, which favours Unity; and

RR: a rupture of relations after Autonomy declares sovereignty, possibly involving military conflict but certainly entailing high economic costs both in the transition and the longer term.

In the first game, assume that the Autonomists' preference function is SA > C > SQ > RR. For their part, the Unitans prefer SQ > C > SA > RR. These are quite realistic preferences in many potential secessions, and they produce the well known game of Chicken, depicted in Figure 2. As ever, each player can cooperate or defect. (The figures in brackets refer to the values attached to each outcome by the players, with Autonomy's values on the right.)

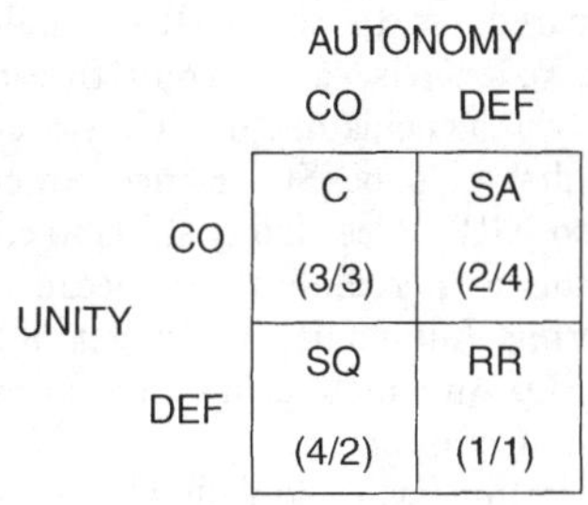

Figure 2 Secession as Chicken

In this game, neither player has a dominant strategy. In choosing to defect and achieve the outcome most favourable to it, each risks that the other will do the same, producing the disastrous outcome RR. So one's best strategy choice depends on the choice of the other, and also on the capacity to make threats. If Unity can threaten noncooperation through declaring itself prepared to live with the RR outcome, and can do so with credibility, then it can force Autonomy to accept SQ because Autonomy prefers this to RR. Similarly, Unity may have to accept SA if Autonomy refuses to compromise and appears ready to stick at RR at all costs. So the threat of moving to RR is crucial to attain one's preferred objectives. Note, though, that if each player knows the other's preferences, the same threat can produce a stable outcome at C. For example, Unity can adopt a cooperative attitude, knowing that it could react to a defection towards SA by Autonomy through moving towards RR. Autonomy can make the symmetrical calculation. With foresight, the players can achieve Compromise.

If preferences are different, of course, the players are not engaged in the game of Chicken. Perhaps the Autonomists really do find the Status Quo intolerable, so they prefer RR to it, and have the preference function SA > C > RR > SQ. Assume as well that opinion in Unity has also hardened, so its preferences are SQ > C > RR > SA. Figure 3 shows the resulting game of Prisoners' Dilemma.

		AUTONOMY	
		CO	DEF
UNITY	CO	C (3/3)	SA (1/4)
	DEF	SQ (4/1)	RR (2/2)

Figure 3 Secession as Prisoners' Dilemma

In this game there are two stable results, RR and C. If each actor pursues its first preference by adopting a non-cooperative attitude, RR is the result, and this is a stable outcome because neither side then has an incentive to shift towards cooperation. In order to attain the Compromise result, each player must renounce, in a credible manner, the pursuit of its best alternative. However, each also has to demonstrate its preparedness to accept RR should the other defect; that is, to exercise a deterrent threat. For example, if Autonomy is conciliatory but Unity remains intransigent, the result would be SQ. Hence Autonomy would threaten to choose RR unless Unity shifts to cooperate – and note that this is a credible threat because with this preference ordering Autonomy would get a better result at RR than at SQ. Anticipating this train of events, the two players can find Compromise.

One further consideration has to do with whether secession involves 'one-shot' or 'repeated' games. This is germane to arguments like those advanced by the Quebec sovereigntists to the effect that post-secession cooperation is inevitable. In either Chicken or Prisoners' Dilemma, a credible threat is essential to achieve Compromise, and also to avoid being left with the sucker's payoff, and the sovereigntists were arguing that Canadian threats were not credible. But, as is well known, the surest way to have a current threat be credible is to have made similar ones in the past, and to have executed them. If games are to be repeated, therefore, a rational player may accept the short-term losses caused by carrying out a threat in order to establish credibility in a future game where the stakes are greater. Moreover, it seems that the best way to ensure cooperation over the long term is to adopt the meta-strategy (governing many games) of being cooperative, but threatening non-cooperation should the other player defect, and carrying out that threat if necessary: this is playing 'Tit-for-Tat' (see Axelrod 1984). Now cases of secession always involve repeat play. Despite the frequent use of the analogy, a secession is not a 'divorce', because no one is 'leaving': immutable geography makes it inevitable that games between the two actors will continue, whatever the constitutional framework. But from this observation one cannot draw the conclusion that cooperation also is inevitable. Indeed, retaliatory non-cooperation could be seen as the strategy most likely to produce mutually beneficial compromise in the long run. In the Quebec case, therefore, while there is little credibility to federalist threats of 'permanent retaliation' (a meta-strategy that punishes defection with eternal non-cooperation in all future games), it remains true that non-cooperation by Canada could be entirely rational, within the meta-strategy of Tit-for-Tat. If Canada and Quebec are indeed playing Prisoners' Dilemma or Chicken, repeated or not, then simple game theory shows that Quebecers (like Canadians) must be prepared to endure a situation where relations rupture entirely, in order to achieve their objectives.

While these simple games can clarify the dynamics of particular choices on the road to secession, they have some obvious weaknesses. One is that they involve only ordinal rankings of preferences. It may be, for example, that one player finds very little difference between a Compromise and the Status Quo, but ranks the latter very much more highly than a Rupture of Relations. While this would not change the essential strategy of moves, it would affect the determination with which they are made and sustained. Another problem is whether the 'rules' of the game limit the number of moves that can be made (see Zagare 1984). In a Chicken secession game, for example, is Sovereignty-Association or a Rupture of Relations a stable equilibrium when the first can be eroded over time and the second lead to a collapse by one player or the other? Secessions raise this problem acutely because some of the potential outcomes may have irreversible political or economic consequences – such as formal sovereignty or the creation of a new currency – just as in the Cuban Missile Crisis when the players could not have cycled through the (1, 1) result in Chicken because this outcome represented nuclear war (see Brams 1994: 130–38). Similarly, it may not be obvious where in the game the players actually are, whether it is a one-shot or a repeated game. Did Canada, for instance, defect by defeating the Meech Lake Accord (when it was actually accepted by the great majority of the provinces)? Did the government of the Czech Republic defect by pressing through with market reforms that disproportionately disrupted the Slovak economy? The answers to such questions are not evident, but are a matter of how the events are framed by political leaders. Yet they shape the strategy to be taken in the next move.

More seriously, these treatments of secession are modelled as two-player games. This misrepresents reality in two important ways. First, the political leaders who are directly involved in negotiations have to balance their strategy vis-à-vis their opponents with the currents of domestic public opinion within which they operate. The two sides are not pure unitary actors. A decision to break off negotiations (to defect), for example, will fail if it is not supported by the citizenry. It is possible to avoid this problem in theory by simply taking the preference function of, say, Autonomy, as the politically weighted vector-sum of all societal preferences. But this misses many of the constraints on political leaders, and, equally important, it neglects the degrees of freedom open to them when playing what are really two-level games (see Putnam 1988). Leaders can claim in negotiations that certain outcomes cannot be carried 'back home', and they can also manipulate domestic public opinion because only they were present at the negotiating table. Further, leaders can affect opinion in the other unit, by design or otherwise, a dynamic that was most apparent in the polarization between the Czechs and Slovaks that preceded the dissolution of Czechoslovakia (see Young 1994a). In modern secessions, public opinion is crucial, not only in establishing preference orderings, but in fostering the political solidarity that underpins decisive and determined action, and existing game-theoretic models are too simple to capture the interplay of public opinion and leaders' preferences.

The second defect of the unitary-actor assumption concerns secessions from federations. In such states, the two 'sides' are not clearly delineated. Instead, the potential secessor is a sub-unit within the federation, represented in its central institutions, so its interlocutor may actually not be a distinct player but rather the very locus of negotiations. In Canada, for example, the Quebec sovereigntists generally address themselves to the federal government, but this agent does not directly represent the other provinces; instead it includes representatives from both the rest of the country and also Quebec, and it is within the federal cabinet that bargaining positions are determined. These complexities have not been modelled, except in the case of individual politicians (see Simard 1991). But they imply that simple game theory is most applicable when federal governments are devoid of representation from potentially seceding sub-units or, more generally, when federations are dyadic. As was shown in the Czechoslovakian case, where power simply ebbed from the centre as the governments of the two opposing republics squared off, dyadic federations are notoriously unstable (see Duchacek 1988).

In light of the strengths and limitations of work on secession games, what are the promising avenues of future research? There are several possibilities. One straightforward extension would be to examine the interplay between preference orderings that may fit particular cases or iterations better than the standard Chicken and Prisoners' dilemma games. The work of both Imbeau and Brams shows the richness of the alternatives that can be explored. Another avenue is to expand the number of strategies available, moving beyond 2×2 games. This would require depicting the results in game trees, and would complicate matters considerably, but it would allow for strategies of longer range and greater intricacy than can be accommodated by the standard setup, which might be more realistic (see Monahan 1995). On the other hand, there is much to be said for the simplicity of 2×2 games, which can be arrayed sequentially. A third possibility is to model secessions as two-level games – promising but difficult (see Weaver 1996). As well, there is scope for applying much more sophisticated game theory to secessions, though the limiting assumptions necessary for solutions are likely to restrict conclusions to a portion of the secession process, as in recent work by Wittman (1996) on credible commitments and by Austin (1995) on the excludability of members of a seceding coalition.

Two other avenues of work seem particularly promising. One concerns polarization, which is intrinsic to secessions, because they involve growing estrangement between two communities and, often though not always, greater solidarity within each. The mechanisms through which polarization occurs are quite unclear, but it is evident that secessionist leaders attempt to foment it, and that their opponents, having reached some saddle-point, may shift to hard-line strategies that accelerate the process. In other words, polarization can underlie changes in preference ordering. Theoretical work explicitly focusing on polarization is in its infancy, and has concentrated mainly on class (see Esteban and Ray 1994). But there is certainly scope for applying to secession new game-theoretic and other models derived from the study of labour relations and class conflict (see Alesina and Drazen 1991). The other intriguing area for future research concerns political discourse. Secessions are led by politicians who deploy arguments, and these cluster around a limited number of dimensions. Arguments and dimensions are selected strategically, as the brilliant analysis by Riker (1986) demonstrated – especially with respect to Lincoln's position on slavery. In both the Czech–Slovak case and the 1995 Quebec referendum on sovereignty, it was evident that the interplay of competing discourses was both sequential and strategic: leaders clearly had preferences about what dimensions to emphasize and what positions to take on them (because of the effects they would have on public opinion, the commitments they embodied, and the openings they left for opponents). There was also advantage to be had, at times, through being ambiguous (see Young 1995b). While it is not obvious how competing discourses could be formally modelled in game-theoretic terms, accomplishing this would represent a major contribution of modern economics to the study of secessions, and also to the study of legal argument more generally.

Of course, this is a very speculative approach to secession, but one thing about this whole topic is quite certain: around the world, games of secession will continue. It is worth trying to clarify and comprehend them.

Robert Young

See also CENTRALIZED AND DECENTRALIZED REGULATION IN THE EUROPEAN UNION; DIVISION OF POWERS IN THE EUROPEAN CONSTITUTION; FISCAL FEDERALISM; PRISONERS' DILEMMA; PRISONERS' DILEMMA AND THE THEORY OF THE STATE; SECESSION; STABILITY OF ANARCHIC SOCIETIES; SUBSIDIARITY AND THE EUROPEAN UNION.

Subject classification: 1d(ii); 3c.

BIBLIOGRAPHY

Alesina, A. and Drazen, A. 1991. Why are stabilizations delayed? *American Economic Review* 81: 1170–88.

Alesina, A. and Spolaore, E. 1995. On the number and size of nations. NBER Working Paper Series 5050, National Bureau of Economic Research, Cambridge, MA.

Austin, D.A. 1995. Coordinated action in local public goods models: the case of secession without exclusion. *Journal of Public Economics* 58: 235–56.

Axelrod, R. 1984. *The Evolution of Cooperation*. New York: Basic Books.

Bolton, P., Roland, G. and Spolaore, E. 1996. Economic theories of the break-up and integration of nations. *European Economic Review* 40: 697–705.

Bookman, M. 1993. *The Economics of Secession*. New York: St. Martin's Press.

Brams, S. 1994. *Theory of Moves*. Cambridge: Cambridge University Press.

Breton, A. and Breton, M. 1995. Nationalism revisited. In *Nationalism and Rationality*, ed. A. Breton, G. Galeotti, P. Salmon and R. Wintrobe, Cambridge: Cambridge University Press.

Buchanan, A.E. 1991. *Secession: the Morality of Political Divorce from Fort Sumter to Lithuania and Quebec*. Boulder: Westview Press.

Buchanan, J. and Faith, R. 1987. Secession and the limits of taxation: toward a theory of internal exit. *American Economic Review* 77: 1023–31.

Buchheit, L. 1978. *Secession: the Legitimacy of Self-Determination*. New Haven: Yale University Press.

Cable, V. 1995. The diminished nation-state: a study in the loss of economic power. *Daedalus* 124: 23–53.

Casella, A. and Feinstein, J. 1992. Public goods in trade: on the formation of markets and political jurisdictions. Working Papers in Economics E-92-12, The Hoover Institution, Stanford University, Stanford, CA.

Cassese, A. 1995. *Self-determination of Peoples*. Cambridge: Cambridge University Press.

Chen, Y. and Ordeshook, P. 1994. Constitutional secession clauses. *Constitutional Political Economy* 5: 45–60.

Duchacek, I. 1988. Dyadic federations and confederations. *Publius* 18: 5–31.

Dudley, L. 1991. Constitutions as the outcome of imperfect spatial competition. In *The Competitive State*, ed. A. Breton, G. Galeotti, P. Salmon and R. Wintrobe, Dordrecht: Kluwer Academic Publishers.

Economic Council of Canada. 1991. *A Joint Venture: the Economics of Constitutional Options*. Ottawa: Minister of Supply and Services Canada.

Elster, J. 1993. Constitutional bootstrapping in Philadelphia and Paris. *Cardozo Law Review* 14: 549–75.

Esteban, J.-M. and Ray, D. 1994. On the measurement of polarization. *Econometrica* 62: 819–51.

Friedman, D. 1977. A theory of the size and shape of nations. *Journal of Political Economy* 85: 59–77.

Frye, T. 1992. Ethnicity, sovereignty and transitions from non-democratic rule. *Journal of International Affairs* 45: 599–623.

Hechter, M. 1992. The dynamics of secession. *Acta Sociologica* 35: 267–83.

Heraclides, A. 1992. Secession, self-determination and nonintervention: in quest of a normative synthesis. *Journal of International Affairs* 45: 399–420.

Imbeau, L. 1990. Voting games and constitutional decision: the 1981 constitutional negotiation in Canada. *Journal of Commonwealth Studies* 28: 90–105.

Imbeau, L. 1991. Le compromis est-il encore possible? La négotiation constitutionnelle de l'après-Meech à la lumière de la théorie des jeux [Is compromise still possible: the constitutional negotiations after Meech in light of game theory]. In *Le Québec et la Restructuration du Canada 1980–92 [Quebec and the Reconfiguration of Canada 1980–92]*, ed. L. Balthazar, G. Laforest, and V. Lemieux, Sillery (Québec): Les éditions du Septentrion.

Keating, M. 1996. *Nations Against the State*. London: Macmillan; New York: St. Martins Press.

McGee, R. 1992. The theory of secession and emerging democracies: a constitutional solution. *Stanford Journal of International Law* 28: 451–76.

Meadwell, H. 1993. The politics of nationalism in Quebec. *World Politics* 45: 203–41.

Monahan, P. 1995. *Cooler heads shall prevail: assessing the costs and consequences of Quebec separation*. C.D. Howe Institute Commentary 65, C.D. Howe Institute, Toronto, Ontario.

Ordeshook, P. 1992. Constitutional stability. *Constitutional Political Economy* 3: 137–75.

Putnam, R. 1988. Diplomacy and domestic politics: the logic of two-level games. *International Organization* 42: 427–60.

Rapoport, A. and Guyer, M. 1966. A taxonomy of 2×2 games. *General Systems* 11: 203–14.

Riker, W. 1986. *The Art of Political Manipulation*. New Haven: Yale University Press.

Rogowski, R. 1985. Causes and varieties of nationalism: a rationalist account. In *New Nationalisms of the Developed West*, ed. E. Tiryakian and R. Rogowski, Boston: G. Allen & Unwin.

Schroeder, G. 1992. On the economic viability of new nation-states. *Journal of International Affairs* 45: 549–74.

Simard, P. 1991. Compétition électorale et partage des pouvoirs dans un état fédéral [Electoral competition and the division of powers in a federal state]. *Canadian Public Policy* 15: 409–16.

Sunstein, C. 1991. Constitutionalism and secession. *University of Chicago Law Review* 58: 633–70.

Weaver, K. 1996. Canadian constitutional negotiations as an evolving two-level game. Paper presented to the Canadian Political Science Association Annual Meeting, St. Catharines, Ontario.

Wittman, D. 1991. Nations and states: mergers and acquisitions; dissolutions and divorce. *American Economic Review Papers and Proceedings* 81: 126–29.

Wittman, D. 1996. Mergers and devolutions of states: the role of credible commitments and hysteresis. Paper presented to the 7th Villa Colombella Seminar, Rome.

Wood, J. 1971. Secession: a comparative analytical framework. *Canadian Journal of Political Science* 14: 107–34.

Young, R. 1994a. *The Breakup of Czechoslovakia*. Kingston, Ontario: Institute of Intergovernmental Relations, Queen's University.

Young, R. 1994b. The political economy of secession: the case of Quebec. *Constitutional Political Economy* 5: 221–45.

Young, R. 1994c. How do peaceful secessions happen? *Canadian Journal of Political Science* 27: 773–92.

Young, R. 1995a. *The Secession of Quebec and the Future of Canada*. Montreal: McGill-Queen's University Press.

Young, R. 1995b. 'Maybe yes, maybe no': the rest of Canada and a Quebec 'oui'. In *Canada: the State of the Federation 1995*, ed. D. Brown and J. Rose, Kingston, Ontario: Institute of Intergovernmental Relations, Queen's University.

Zagare, F. 1984. Limited-move equilibria in 2×2 games. *Theory and Decision* 16: 1–19.

game theory and states of the world. In a game, each player (henceforth, GP) chooses which strategy to play, and the outcome of a strategy for GP depends on the other players' behaviour. What criteria should guide GP's choice? Since all other players are involved in a decision problem similar to the one faced by GP, this is a non-trivial question even assuming – as is common in economics – full rationality on the part of the agents.

Indeed, the very definition of rationality becomes problematic when it comes to games: the rationality of GP's choice depends on the behaviour of the other players, whose rationality in turn depends on GP's choice. This kind of interdependence is absent in the case of individual decision-making in non-strategic contexts.

However, the cornerstone of game theory is the so-called 'Bayesian approach', which uses an axiomatic theory of rational *individual* behaviour under uncertainty in order to model rational choices in a game. In other words, the Bayesian approach manages to subject the behaviour of an agent in a game to the same kind of analysis used for non-strategic decision-making.

In a problem of individual decision-making under uncertainty (henceforth, decision problem), the outcome for the decision-maker (henceforth, DM) depends on two sets of variables. The first set includes the variables under DM's control, which, following Savage (1954), are called *acts*. These variables are the object of DM's decision. The second set includes the variables whose realisation is outside DM's control. These are the object of DM's uncertainty and are called, in Savage's terminology, *states of the world* (*sw*).

In a game, the strategy combination chosen by the players other than GP is outside his control, and may be uncertain from his viewpoint. There is thus an analogy between games and decision problems. According to this analogy, in a game the *sw* for GP are the strategy combinations played by the other players, and the acts are represented by the strategies. The question is whether such an analogy is complete to the extent that the principles of rationality and the modelling techniques devised for decision problems can be transferred to games. Only in this case will the Bayesian approach to game theory be justified.

PERSONAL PROBABILITY. An act can be seen as a map from the set of available *sw* to the set of available consequences (the latter set is treated as primitive in a decision problem). By means of the act-*sw* framework, Savage (1954) was able to define a notion of subjective probability as an expression of *rational* or *consistent* preference. Specifically, a *binary preference relation* of DM on the entire set of conceivable acts is postulated as a primitive. Then, some consistency requirements ('axioms') are imposed on this preference ordering, which imply the existence of a *likelihood ordering* on the (power) set of the *sw*. For the purposes of our discussion, it is necessary to be precise on this point. Assume for simplicity that consequences are amounts of money and that both acts and *sw* are finite in number. In this way, DM's problem can be easily visualized as a matrix of numbers, whose rows represent the available acts and each column of which represents the amounts of money gained in a given *sw* for all the different acts. At the purely mathematical level, the procedure used by Savage consists of:

(a) defining a binary relation L on the power set of columns on the basis of the primitive binary relation P on the set of rows;

(b) demonstrating that, if P possesses certain properties, then the defined binary relation L is an ordering (a complete transitive relation), which in addition possesses the same properties of a (qualitative) probability ordering.

However, the assertion that the relation L expresses anything about DM's beliefs (i.e., his likelihood ordering on *sw*) is entirely a matter of *interpretation*. The mathematics simply shows how to translate the properties of one relation on the rows of a given matrix into the properties of another relation on its columns. Especially when the Savage framework is used in contexts for which it was not originally devised (such as games), the interpretation of the derived ordering L is in need of careful scrutiny even when the formal structure of the problem is the same.

Some further axioms, which ensure that the structure of the set of *sw* is sufficiently rich, yield the result that the likelihood ordering can be represented by a probability function. Such a probability function is a manifestation of DM's *personal* (or subjective) preferences over acts. In this sense it has no objective basis: hence the term *personal (or subjective) probability*. Finally, it is possible to use the personal probabilities thus constructed to imply the existence of a *utility function* which represents DM's preferences over consequences (interpreted as constant acts); and DM's preferences over acts can be represented by an *expected* utility function, that attaches with each act the sum of the utilities of the consequences obtained in the various *sw*, weighted by the personal probabilities attached to them.

Savage's was not the first definition of subjective probability (e.g. Ramsey 1926; De Finetti 1937), nor the last (e.g. Anscombe and Aumann 1963), nor demonstrably the best. It is, however, one in which economists and game theorists have shown a particular interest, and our discussion of personal probabilities in games will focus on his approach. Similar arguments could be used in relation to other approaches.

GAMES. The similarity between decision problems and games has been noted before. Many game theorists have moved from this similarity to the assertion that Savage's results, or equivalent ones such as those of Anscombe and Aumann, can be applied to games (Harsanyi 1977 and Myerson 1991 are outstanding and influential examples). The major implication of this conceptual leap is that GP's behaviour can be modelled as if he attached a personal probability to the event that any given strategy combination will be played by the other players. Given personal probabilities and utilities, GP will choose one of the strategies that maximize his expected utility. The task of the game theorist in this Bayesian approach becomes essentially one of restricting the set of personal probabilities that can be held by a player in a game. This is made possible by specifying more precisely what each player knows about the rationality of the other players. For example, if a player knows that the other players abide by the Savage axioms, he should not attach positive probability to strategy combinations which involve other players playing dominated strategies (this follows from the mathematical fact that a dominated strategy – one which yields a payoff inferior to some other strategy no matter how the other players behave – cannot maximize expected utility for any personal probability distribution). With more stringent assumptions about the players' knowledge of each other's rationality, it is possible to narrow down even further the beliefs of each player about the others' choices of strategy, and consequently to narrow down even further his own choice of strategy (notable efforts in this direction are Bernheim 1984, Pearce 1984, and Aumann 1987).

The possibility of applying personal probability theory to games is, with few exceptions, asserted informally and acritically – no matter how formal the analysis that follows such applications. There are, however, a number of differences between the decision problems and games, which make the specification of the exact procedure to be used to define personal probabilities in games non-trivial. It is noteworthy that in the early and unsurpassed analysis of game theory by Luce and Raiffa (1957) the application of subjective decision theory axioms to games was viewed with some scepticism. Essentially, the difficulties stem from the fact that the notion of *sw* does not immediately match that of a strategy combination played by the opponents in a game. An *sw* in a decision problem is thought of as 'passive' with respect to DM's choice problem, in a sense which is clearly not true of the strategy chosen by a rational opponent of GP. Before listing some of the difficulties involved, a relatively innocuous difference is noted first. In the standard description of a game (von Neumann and Morgenstern 1947), payoffs are already expressed as utilities, whereas in a decision problem outcomes are described as physical consequences. This problem can easily be overcome by appropriately redefining what a game is. Alternatively, if one sticks to the traditional definition of a game in terms of utilities, interpretations of personal probability different from that of Savage will have to be adopted (e.g., Nau and McCardle 1990 use De Finetti's 1937 definition).

The following issues have been discussed more amply in Mariotti (1995, 1996, 1997).

Choice vs. preference. DM is assumed to have a *preference* ordering over acts. However, the language of game theory is really one of *choice* between, rather than preference over, strategies. Presumably, it can be said that a strategy is preferred to one that it dominates; or even that an equilibrium strategy is preferred to a non-equilibrium one. But it is not at all clear what it can mean to have a preference between two dominated or two non-equilibrium strategies. Savage himself was very concerned to give DM's preference an interpretation in terms of choice. This is not too difficult in the context he studied, as long as one is willing to consider hypothetical choice situations between pairs of acts: then, the assertion that DM prefers act A to act B can be interpreted as the assertion that DM would choose A from the set {A,B}. Now, if one tries to apply the same interpretation to preference over strategies in a game, things become more complicated. What exactly does it mean to confine the choice of a player in a game to two strategies? The game itself is crucially changed when this restriction on the strategy set of a player is made. In particular, the other players' behaviour cannot be expected to be the same, in general, in the original game and in the restricted game. On the other hand, if the choice from {A,B} were offered 'outside' the game, it would not be clear why such a choice should have any relevance at all for the game itself.

Virtual acts. DM's preference ordering over acts is postulated to hold *on all conceivable acts*, that is, not only on those which are feasible in the specific decision problem, but also on all those 'virtual acts' which it is possible to construct using the available consequences and *sw*. For example, if there are two *sw*, two consequences c and d, and only the two acts (c, d) and (c, c) (in obvious notation) are available, it will also be necessary to consider DM's preference for the acts (d, c) and (d, d). Once again, the meaning of this construction is far from being transparent when applied to games. While the realization of a *sw* cannot be expected to be influenced by alterations in DM's choice set, the same is certainly not true for the strategy played by an opponent in a game, when GP's strategy set is enriched with 'virtual strategies' not present in the original game. A specific additional problem which arises in the context of games is: what payoffs for the other players should be associated with GP's 'virtual strategies'?

Games as consequence. It is a characteristic of the Savage framework that essentially no restriction is imposed on what a 'consequence' may be (Savage's own examples include omelettes and picnics). In particular, there is no difficulty associated with the notion that a consequence may be itself a decision problem. Similarly, in the theory of choice under risk, with objective probabilities, compound lotteries may be considered. It may thus seem that, once games are treated as (collections of) decision problems, one should be able to conceive of a game as a consequence. In fact, an assertion such as 'GP prefers to be player 1 in game G rather than player 2 in game G′' should make sense in the Bayesian approach. It is, however, not difficult to construct examples where this leads to paradoxes (Mariotti 1995). The point is that there is no obvious connection between preferences held *outside* a game and preferences held *within* a game, where they can influence the other players' choices.

PERSONAL PROBABILITIES FOR GAMES. Two possible resolutions to the difficulties just discussed have been proposed. They are both attempts to overcome the basic problem that *sw* in games are not 'passive' as needed in the Savage framework. The idea they share is to devise – given a game – an enlarged decision problem where it is possible to 'test' GP's preferences over strategies (or consequences) without the other players being affected.

Battigalli's construction. Battigalli (1996) has proposed the following construction (the version of Battigalli's idea given by Hammond (1997) is followed here). Suppose we want to define player i's personal probabilities in a game G. Then, modify game G by introducing a fictitious player, i^*, whose preferences are identical to i's preferences. This 'clone' i^* moves before all the other players choose in game G, and the other players do not know the choices made by i^*. In addition, i^*'s choices have no effect whatsoever on the payoffs of the players in G, including i. The payoff for i^* depends not only on his move, but on the strategies chosen by the players different from i in G. Denoting the enlarged game G′, it is assumed that the behaviour of all players in G is the same as their behaviour in G′. It can then be said that, from the point of view of player i^*, the strategies chosen by the players in G are like *sw* in an individual decision problem, since their realization does not depend on whatever feasible set is given to i^*. It is then possible to apply Savage's axioms to i^*'s decision problem and derive his personal probabilities. Moreover, since i^*'s preferences are exactly the same as i's preferences, such personal probabilities can be interpreted as effectively expressing i's beliefs.

Hammond's construction. The following alternative construction has been proposed by Peter Hammond (it appears in an early draft of Hammond 1997; the version expounded here is a modification of that version to take into account the fact that Hammond's original proposal uses the framework of Anscombe and Aumann 1963, rather than that of Savage). Once again the given game G for which i's subjective probabilities must be derived is enlarged, as follows. Suppose that there exists in the world another pair of states (in addition to the various strategy combinations), say S and T, which are both considered possible. Then consider the following hypothetical situation. If S is realized, then the original game G is played. If T is realized, however, a different game G' is played where player i chooses between his strategies, with their corresponding payoffs, and the other players have no choice and get a fixed payoff. Note that in this hypothetical situation *either* the original game G is played, *or* the game which tests i's subjective beliefs is played. To see that the beliefs that are being tested are really the 'right' ones, suppose that all players make their choices before it is known whether S or T is realized: so they choose among *conditional* extended strategies, or, in other words, they choose strategies in an extended game, denoted G^E. A form of subjective independence axiom (or sure-thing principle) implies that the behaviour of all players different from i must be the same when G is being played for sure and when there is a chance that G' will be played (in which case they get the assigned fixed consequence). And, therefore, i must believe that whatever likelihood a certain strategy combination has in G, it must have the same likelihood in G^E conditional on S being realized and so G being played. So his conditional choice in G' should say something about his subjective beliefs about any strategy combination being played in G.

CONCLUDING REMARKS. As has been emphasized before, the question whether a subject's preference over behavioural variables reveals something about his personal probabilities attached to events is a matter of interpretation; after all, as De Finetti (1970: x) summarized his thesis: 'probability does not exist'. The connection between preference and the definition of probability is quite obvious and natural in Savage's original framework. In the previous section two possibilities for adapting that framework to the case of strategic uncertainty – and in particular for interpreting the strategy combinations played by one's opponents in a game as *sw* – have been illustrated. Independently of whether one accepts either of those proposals, it is evident how in both cases the connection between preference and beliefs becomes more tenuous than in the single-person case. Battigalli's proposal depends on introducing fictitious 'clones' of the decision-maker in a game. In this construction, the personal probability of player i in a game is identified with the personal probability that his clone would have in an enlarged game: note that it cannot be i himself whose beliefs are being directly studied, for in that case the game would be effectively changed, i's payoffs being different. The interpretational difficulty associated with this construction is that postulating the existence of 'clones' is dangerously close to simply assuming away the problem itself. In addition, the construction seems to make it particularly difficult to achieve an operational definition of personal probability for games, that is, one that could in principle be elicited in a laboratory. On the other hand, Hammond's framework is free from such difficulties, although it relies heavily on an independence axiom. Once again, this creates a wedge with the single-person case, where independence axioms are only needed to give probability an additive structure, rather than for the definition itself.

Be that as it may, one cannot conclude this discussion without observing that many Bayesian game theorists would be happy simply to *postulate* personal probabilities for game players, without worrying about their axiomatic foundations ('players just *have* probabilities', one sometimes hears asserted). This more 'pragmatic' approach demands that Bayesian game theory should be judged on its own merits. But once transformed into a mere working hypothesis, it appears difficult to justify the pre-eminence that the Bayesian approach has been accorded in the past, and the opinion that solution concepts and models which are not justified by 'Bayesian rationality' are somehow less fundamental or complete. In this respect, Binmore (1992) illustrates some difficulties with the Bayesian approach; and Greenberg (1990) is an example of a unified game-theoretical framework where Bayesian rationality is not presupposed (nor denied).

MARCO MARIOTTI

See also ATTITUDES TOWARDS RISK; BOUNDED RATIONALITY; GAME THEORY AND THE LAW; NON-COOPERATIVE GAMES.

Subject classification: 1d(i); 2f.

BIBLIOGRAPHY

Anscombe, F.J. and Aumann, R.J. 1963. A definition of subjective probability. *Annals of Mathematical Statistics* 34: 199–205.

Aumann, R.J. 1987. Correlated equilibrium as an expression of Bayesian rationality. *Econometrica* 55: 1–18.

Battigalli, P. 1996. Comment on Mariotti. In *Rationality in Economics*, ed. K. Arrow, E. Colombatto, M. Pearlman and C. Schmidt (London: Macmillan): 149–54.

Bernheim, D. 1984. Rationalizable strategic behaviour. *Econometrica* 52: 1007–28.

Binmore, K. 1992. Foundations of game theory. In *Advances in Economic Theory. Sixth World Congress, Vol. 1*, ed. J.J. Laffont, Econometric Society Monographs, Cambridge: Cambridge University Press.

De Finetti, B. 1937. La prévision: ses lois logiques, ses sources subjectives. *Annales de L'Institut Henri Poincaré* 7: 1–68. Translated in Kyburg and Smokler (1980).

De Finetti, B. 1970. *Teoria delle probabilità. Sintesi introduttiva con appendice critica*. Turin: Einaudi, 2 vols. Trans. as *Theory of Probability*, 2 vols, New York: Wiley, 1974–5.

Greenberg, J. 1990. *The Theory of Social Situations: An Alternative Game-Theoretic Approach*. Cambridge: Cambridge University Press.

Hammond, P.J. 1997. Utility theory for non-cooperative games. Ch. 15 of *Handbook of Utility Theory*, ed. S. Barberà, P.J. Hammond and C. Seidl, Amsterdam: Kluwer Academic Publishers (in preparation).

Harsanyi, J.C. 1977. *Rational Behaviour and Bargaining Equilibrium in Games and Social Situations*. Cambridge: Cambridge University Press.

Kyburg, H.E. and Smokler, H.E. (eds). 1980. *Studies in Subjective Probability*, 2nd edn., Huntington, NY: Krieger.

Luce, D. and Raiffa, H. 1957. *Games and Decisions*. New York: John Wiley & Sons.

Mariotti, M. 1995. Is Bayesian rationality compatible with strategic rationality? *Economic Journal* 105: 1099–1109.

Mariotti, M. 1996. The decision theoretic foundations of game theory. In *Rationality in Economics*, ed. K. Arrow, E. Colombatto, M. Pearlman and C. Schmidt (London: Macmillan): 133–48.

Mariotti, M. 1997. Decisions in games: why there may be a special exemption from Bayesian rationality. *Journal of Economic Methodology* 4: 43–60.

Myerson, R.B. 1991. *Game Theory: Analysis of Conflict*. Cambridge, MA: Harvard University Press.

Nau, R.F. and McCardle, K.F. 1990. Coherent behaviour in noncooperative games. *Journal of Economic Theory* 50: 424–44.

Pearce, D. 1984. Rationalizable strategic behaviour and the problem of perfection. *Econometrica* 52: 1029–50.

Ramsey, F.P. 1926. Truth and probability. In F.P. Ramsey, *The Foundations of Mathematics and Other Logical Essays*, New York: Harcourt, Brace and Co. 1931; reprinted in Kyburg and Smokler (1980).

Savage, L.J. 1954. *The Foundations of Statistics*. New York: John Wiley & Sons.

von Neumann, J. and Morgenstern, O. 1947. *Theory of Games and Economic Behaviour*, 2nd edn., Princeton: Princeton University Press.

game theory and the law. Game theory possesses a distinctive vocabulary that may at times accentuate the differences between it and traditional law-and-economics. If we take a few steps backwards, however, we are likely to see that the differences are ones of emphasis. Game theory is useful not because it is different from traditional law-and-economics, but because it provides additional tools to anyone interested in understanding the structure of legal rules and the way they affect the way people behave (see Ayres 1990). The easiest way to see this is to begin with the most familiar example in law-and-economics.

Coase (1960) analyses the question of how liability should be allocated when the owner of a railroad must decide how much to invest in spark arrestors and farmers must decide how close to the tracks to plant their crops. This problem can be captured as a conventional normal form game. The two players are the farmer and the railroad. The farmer's strategy choices are how close to the tracks to plant his crops; the railroad's strategy choices are whether and how much to invest in spark arrestors. The payoff to the farmer is the revenue from selling corn. This amount depends on the number of bushels of corn harvested. The size of the harvest turns on how much is planted and how much of that is burned by sparks from the railroad. The payoff to the railroad is the revenue it collects, less its costs, including the costs of spark arrestors and any liability it owes farmers whose crops burn. Transaction costs are high, and the farmer and the railroad cannot negotiate with each other.

As set out here, the game is one in which the strategies available to each player form a continuum. Hence, it cannot be set out in the two-by-two bimatrix that is ubiquitous in the law reviews, but otherwise it is a most conventional example of a normal form game. It does focus our attention on some important issues.

Game theory would tell us that after we set out the game involving the farmer and the railroad, we need to ask whether we can predict the strategy choices that the players would make. Predictions about how people play games are 'solution concepts'. Traditional economics is powerful precisely because it rests on the simplest possible axioms about how people behave. So too with game theory. Few would take issue, for example, with the solution concept known as dominance: a dominant strategy in a game for a player is a strategy that is a best choice for that player for every possible choice by the other player. One strategy 'strictly dominates' another strategy when it always leads to a better outcome no matter what the other player does. This idea expressed as a solution concept takes the following form: A player will choose a strictly dominant strategy wherever possible and will not choose any strategy that is strictly dominated by another. Few would take issue with the idea that individuals are likely to choose a strategy when they always can do better in their own eyes choosing that strategy than by choosing any other.

Game theory and the law, however, rests primarily on a different, and perhaps less compelling, solution concept called the Nash equilibrium (see Nash 1950b; Kreps 1990a: 28–36). From the perspective of the traditional law-and-economics scholar, there is no novelty in using the Nash equilibrium solution concept. Brown (1973) and Shavell (1987) rely on it explicitly and Landes and Posner (1987) implicitly. The difference lies in making the solution concept the centre of focus.

The Nash equilibrium solution concept is that the combination of strategies that players are likely to choose is one in which no player could do better by choosing a different strategy given the one the other chooses. The strategy of each player must be a 'best response' to the strategy of the other. A little reflection shows both the power of the concept and how it is a formal way of capturing how many of us have long thought about the law.

A strategy combination that is not a Nash equilibrium is unlikely to be the solution to the game. We can see this by assuming for a moment the opposite, that a particular strategy combination that is not Nash *is* the solution to the game. If it is the solution to a game, both players should be able to identify it as such beforehand. If the strategy is not Nash, however, it follows that one of the players is choosing a strategy that is not a best response given what the other player is doing. This does not make sense. Put yourself in the position of the player whose strategy is not a best response. Why should you choose the strategy that is asserted to be part of the solution to the game? Given what the other player is supposed to do in this purported solution, you can do better. You are not acting rationally if you pick a strategy that does not maximize your own payoff.

The Nash equilibrium solution concept gives us a familiar answer to the question of the outcome in the game in which the railroad is strictly liable for all damage to the farmer's crops. Is it likely both that the railroad will invest the optimal amount in spark arrestors and that the farmer will choose the optimal distance from the tracks to plant the crops? The answer is no. Because the railroad is liable for all damage from fire, the farmer has no incentive to plant the crops away from the track. The farmer will deviate from any proposed equilibrium in which the farmer is planting crops at the optimal place. This lesson here is, of course, a familiar one. Imposing legal burdens on one party is likely to affect the behaviour of those with whom that other party interacts. It takes two to tango.

To be useful, game theory needs to do more than replicate the familiar lessons of law-and-economics. Game theory, however, has two distinct contributions to make even in these simple cases. First, it aids our intuition. Whenever we hear someone suggest that a legal reform is a good idea because it will bring about a particular result, the easiest way to test the claim is to focus on the outcome that is claimed for the legal rule and ask whether this outcome is in fact a Nash equilibrium. Is the advocate of reform in fact positing a Nash outcome in which all affected parties are making a best response given the way that everyone else is supposed to be behaving?

Too often advocates of law reform assume that people do not make adjustments in the face of legal change. The Nash equilibrium concept is a formal way to sharpen our intuitions and prevent us from making this sort of mistake. We have to imagine the world once the legal reform is put in place and ask if we are in fact positing a world in which everyone still has the incentive to behave the way we predict.

The Nash equilibrium concept is useful for a second and quite different reason. By reducing interactions to simple components, it becomes easy to compare different legal rules and understand how they work. The different tort regimes under Anglo-American law, such as regimes of negligence, strict liability with contributory negligence, and comparative negligence provide a good example. Tort law tries to affect behaviour by requiring an injurer to compensate victims under specified circumstances. Posner (1973) shows that the standard common law rule of negligence coupled with contributory negligence creates an environment in which both the injurer and the prospective victim have the incentive to act efficiently. Throughout the 1970s, many articles, beginning with Brown (1973), showed that other rules, such as comparative negligence, also proved efficient. Once all these different rules are reduced to simple normal form games it quickly becomes apparent that the efficiency of all these rules is no coincidence. Each regime is best seen as variations on a single principle, rather than as discrete rules (see Baird, Gertner and Picker 1994: 24–5). All of these liability rules share three features:

(1) The legal regimes are ones of compensatory damages. Parties always bear their own cost of care. The legal rules never require an injurer to pay more than is necessary to compensate the victim for the injury.
(2) An injurer who exercises at least due care pays no damages whenever the victim does not exercise at least due care, and a victim is made whole whenever the victim exercises at least due care and the injurer does not.
(3) When both the injurer and the victim exercise at least due care, the costs of the accident are borne by one or the other or divided between them in some way.

These features are themselves sufficient to ensure that both the injurer and the victim take due care. As long as a rule has these features (as all the different tort regimes we see around us do), parties will have the right set of incentives in the plain environment in which these rules were first analysed. The common law is 'efficient' in the limited sense that it gives the parties the correct incentives under a number of strong assumptions, but so do many other legal regimes. Choosing among these different rules requires us to ask about their distributional consequences and all the other things that are assumed away in this environment, such as whether a rule is likely to lead to more litigation or whether a court is more likely to make errors in enforcing it.

'Refinements' of the Nash equilibrium concept are tools developed to solve games, of which there are all too many, that have more than one Nash equilibrium. Multiple Nash equilibria, for example, can arise even in the simple case in which one party threatens to retaliate if the other player takes a particular action. In these cases, multiple equilibria exist because the Nash equilibrium concept does not take into account whether it is in a player's self-interest to carry out a threat when called upon to do so.

A lender will tell a debtor that it will sue if the loan is not repaid, but the lender will not necessarily carry out the threat. If litigation is expensive (and reputational effects are for some reason irrelevant), the lender might find the cost of bringing suit would be greater than the amount of the loan that remained unpaid. As long as the debtor knows that the lender will not have the incentive to follow through on the threat, the threat will not be taken seriously. We should therefore reject a proposed solution in which the debtor repays the loan. Nevertheless, it is a Nash equilibrium for the lender to make the loan and sue in the event of default and for the debtor to pay rather than default. Given that the lender will sue, paying off the loan is a best response; given that the debtor will repay, being willing to sue is a best response. Each player is acting optimally given what the other does. (Being willing to sue brings the same payoff as suing when the debtor never defaults.) We need some way to distinguish this Nash equilibrium from the equilibrium that seems the much more likely outcome: the equilibrium in which the lender does not make the loan in the first place because it knows that the debtor will not repay the loan and it will not bring a suit against the debtor after default.

For interactions such as this one, a refinement of the Nash equilibrium solution concept (known as 'subgame perfection') not only allows us to predict a single likely course of play, but it does so in a way that makes intuitive sense. It excludes strategy combinations that, even though they are Nash, make implausible assumptions about the actions that the players would take, but do not in fact take under the proposed equilibrium. The concept of subgame perfection, in other words, takes account of actions that are off the equilibrium path.

There are many other refinements of the Nash equilibrium (see, e.g., Cho and Kreps 1987). Some have proved quite useful in identifying which Nash equilibrium is the likely outcome of an interaction. Like subgame perfection and the way it identifies credible threats, these refinements provide a formal way to identify one equilibrium when many are possible, but only one captures how individuals are likely to interact. A number of refinements, however, do the job of identifying a single equilibrium from many candidates, but not in a way that is convincing. These refinements are both complex and bereft of a logic or intuition that gives us confidence that they tell us much about how individuals are likely to behave.

THE LIMITS OF GAME THEORY. As the preceeding discussion of refinements suggests, we must understand the limits as well as the strengths of using simple normal form games to understand strategic behaviour. Paradigmatic games can provide useful benchmarks. It may seem unduly limiting to begin with a game in which there are only two players and two strategies, but such simple games can capture the dynamics of many interactions. When we can use these games, we can make the forces that are at work readily apparent.

Nevertheless, one should use these paradigms with caution. First, one always wants to examine the strategic elements in a given situation and take care to avoid being drawn too quickly to a well-known paradigm such as the prisoner's dilemma. It is better to capture the problem in normal form and then look for the appropriate paradigm, rather than shoehorn the problem into one at the outset. The prisoner's dilemma, for example, captures the basic feature of collective action and common pool problems, but a model with more elements will reveal details that the prisoner's dilemma does not (see Gibbons 1992: 27–9). If one is interested in the dynamics of a particular collective action problem, the prisoner's dilemma may not be useful.

One must also guard against looking at interactions between players in isolation. A problem that may look like a prisoner's dilemma or some other simple two-by-two game may be part of a much larger game. One cannot assume that, once embedded in a larger game, the play of the smaller game will be the same (see Baird, Gertner and Picker 1994: 188–218). Moreover, many interactions between individuals are inherently dynamic. They interact over time and make decisions in response to what the other does. Two-by-two games that model simultaneous decision-making are not useful vehicles for analysing such problems.

FOLK THEOREMS AND REPEATED GAMES. There are many environments in which players interact with each other over time. We can model some of these as simple games that are repeated indefinitely. Game theorists have long known that patterns of cooperation can emerge when games are repeated that do not emerge when the game is played only once. Players who find themselves in a repeated prisoner's dilemma may end up in an equilibrium in which neither defects. For example, it might be an equilibrium for players to adopt a strategy in which they cooperate initially, but defect after any round in which the other defected. This strategy of tit-for-tat on the part of both players may be one that is an equilibrium (see Axelrod 1984). Given that each will punish the other in the event of a defect, neither ever defects, even though each would defect if the game were played only once. These models are useful because, among other things, they show how oligopolists can engage in what appears to be collusive behaviour without actually ever having talked with each other.

There is a danger, however, in assuming too much about cooperation in repeated games. To say that cooperation *can* emerge in repeated games is not to say that it *will* emerge or even that it is likely to emerge. This is the lesson of various 'folk theorems'. These are theorems in game theory that have been so much part of the received wisdom that they are not associated with any individual. They show how in repeated games an infinite number of equilibria are possible, and few of them involve cooperation (see Fudenberg and Tirole 1991). The idea of cooperation emerging naturally and the robustness of the strategy of tit-for-tat have long been exaggerated in the legal literature. The following example provides an illustration.

A town council has decided to take decisive action to solve a recurring problem. Every spring and fall, wild deer cross the various highways near the town. Motorists cannot always see them in time. The deer, the motorists and their cars suffer mightily in the event of a collision. If the owners of the land adjacent to the highways maintained their fences better and were careful to keep the gates closed, the number of these accidents would go down dramatically. Law enforcement officers, however, have no way to tell whether the fences are being well maintained and the gates are kept closed. Even after the fact, they cannot tell, at reasonable cost, whether the landowners took reasonable steps. Hence, the town council has decided to fine the landowner on each side of the road $25 in the event of an accident between a deer and a motorist. The idea is that the fine will induce each landowner to take care without requiring officials to assess blame. Does this scheme make sense?

To begin to think about this problem, let us examine the case in which there are two landowners, each on the opposite side of the road. Under the law, each pays $25 in the event of an accident. The landowners cannot enter into an enforceable agreement in which each promises to maintain their fences and keep their gates shut. Each landowner may move away to a different town with some probability before each spring or fall. Neither knows whether the other takes care before deciding whether to take care. Each learns whether the other took care after the fact with very high probability, but has no way to prove it in court. (In other words, whether a landowner takes care is observable, but non-verifiable, information.)

It costs each landowner $100 to maintain a fence properly each season and keep his gates shut. If both take care (at a cost of $100 each), there will be one accident in the spring (requiring each to pay a $25 fine) and another in the fall (requiring each to pay another $25 fine). If one takes care and the other does not, there will be three accidents each spring (requiring each to pay $75 in fines) and three more in the fall (requiring each to pay another $75 in fines). If neither maintains, there will be six accidents each spring (requiring each to pay $150 in fines) and another six in the fall (requiring each to pay another $150 in fines). There is no civil action against either landowner or other cost apart from the costs of maintaining the fence and the $25 fine. This game is set out in Figure 1.

	Maintain	Not Maintain
Maintain	−125, −125	-175, −<u>75</u>
Not Maintain	−<u>75</u>, −175	−<u>150</u>, −<u>150</u>

Figure 1

In this game, the consequences of setting the fine too low are manifest. In the one-shot game, not maintaining strictly dominates maintaining. The game has the same structure as a prisoner's dilemma. Tit-for-tat, however, is not a strategy that produces an equilibrium in which the players cooperate. (I would rather cycle between paying $75 in one period and $175 in the next than paying $125 in each period, as long as the discount rate is positive.)

In this world, the legal regime has at least two obvious problems when seen through a game-theoretic lens. First, if the parties are likely to sell their property and move away to another town, there may be no equilibrium in which both parties maintain the fence. Second, the solution to the game is not obvious as a matter of theory. Even though it may be an equilibrium in which both parties maintain, there are many other equilibria as well, and in many of these the parties do not behave optimally.

Folk theorems provide a powerful counter to those who assert that, as a matter of theory, cooperation naturally emerges over time. It is worth noting, however, that some empirical data suggest that, in such interactions between neighbours in small communities, a variety of pressures push parties towards acting cooperatively independent of the legal regimes that are in place (see Ellickson 1991).

INFORMATION, GAME THEORY AND LEGAL RULES. The problem the town council faced in the case just discussed arose because information about a central issue (how well landowners in fact maintained their fences) was not available to a court. The problem is a pervasive one. Most legal rules make assumptions both about what individuals know and what information courts are able to gather. A law may mandate a fine for a motorist who fails to drive carefully. Such a law, however, is unlikely to do much good unless the motorist knows what it means to drive carefully and unless after the fact a court has some way to determine whether in a particular case the motorist drove carefully.

Information itself plays a crucial role in the way individuals interact. Many of the basic ideas are well known and have long assumed a central place in law-and-economics. Most familiar, perhaps, are the related ideas of moral hazard and adverse selection. These often arise simultaneously. Both problems, for example, explain why no insurance company will sell a policy to cover a person's gambling losses in Las Vegas. There is an adverse selection problem because those who want such a policy and are willing to pay its premium are those most likely to have large losses. There is also a moral hazard problem. Once you have a policy that insures your gambling losses, you will gamble more recklessly than you would otherwise.

The concepts of moral hazard and adverse selection arise when information is not verifiable. Important problems also arise in situations in which information is verifiable, cases in which information can be readily checked once it is revealed. (The combination to a safe is the simplest example of verifiable information. The combination, once revealed, either opens the safe or it does not.) The most important principle game theory brings to problems of verifiable information is known as the unravelling result (see Grossman 1981).

Someone with favourable information has an incentive to disclose it. Hence, an uninformed party can infer that someone who fails to disclose has unfavourable information. The unravelling result identifies a limit on what legal rules can do. Consider whether we can in fact protect the rights of criminal defendants not to testify against themselves. Given the logic of unravelling – that someone with information will disclose it, rather than be subject to the inference that arises from the failure to disclose when one can do so – the privilege against self-incrimination becomes meaningless unless steps are taken to prevent the adverse inference from being drawn. A jury instruction may make the problem worse because it may alert the jurors to their ability to draw inferences from a defendant's failure to testify.

The unravelling result also calls into question two standard legal approaches to revelation of information – inquiry limits and disclosure duties (see Baird, Gertner and Picker 1994: 90–95). Inquiry limits attempt to prevent decision-makers from obtaining information thought to be an inappropriate basis for decision. For example, the Americans with Disabilities Act bars an employer from asking whether an applicant has a disability and also bars pre-offer medical tests. There are also limits on the kinds of inquiries that can be made of an applicant to rent or purchase a dwelling. Other regulations forbid inquiry into the marital status of an applicant for employment at or admission to a school receiving federal funding. Many US states bar pre-employment inquiries into religious or political affiliations for prospective public school teachers or for all prospective state employees. A firm may be barred from asking prospective employees whether they have filed workers' compensation claims. Inquiry limits are especially common under rules of evidence. The general protection for privileged matters – usually matters between attorney and client, physician and patient, or spouses, for example – is a form of inquiry limit, as are rules forbidding questions regarding a victim's prior sexual history in rape trials.

Inquiry limits, however, may be ineffective unless there is some mechanism that prevents voluntary disclosure of the information. Barring an employer from asking whether an applicant has a disability might not affect whether the employer learns of the disability. When applicants who are not disabled also know the legal rule, they can disclose this information when it is verifiable. As soon as the healthiest applicants disclose the results of their medical tests, the slightly less healthy ones may follow suit. The inability of the employer to require a medical test before making an offer may be irrelevant if applicants know that their employer wants the information, but cannot ask about it. They can simply volunteer it. Information problems can turn our usual intuitions upside down. We usually think that parties must know the legal rule for it to be effective. In this context, a legal rule barring inquiry might work best if the applicants did not know it.

LEGAL RULES AND POOLING AND SEPARATING EQUILIBRIA. Legal rules matter most in situations where markets are undeveloped. In exactly these situations, information may not be available to the court or even to all of the parties. Inferences can be drawn from the actions that informed parties take, but whenever one party possesses private, nonverifiable information, there is a potential for inefficient outcomes, even when parties can negotiate with each other easily. The private gain to one party from hiding information may induce that party to behave in a way that, though privately beneficial, is not socially optimal.

A game-theoretic focus on these problems is again one that centres on the idea of an equilibrium. Let us assume that there are two kinds of sellers in the marketplace. One makes expensive radios that are unlikely to break; the other builds radios that are more likely to break, but cost significantly less. Both kinds of radios break down, however, and there is no way for either buyers or courts to tell whether any given radio was well made or not. There are also two kinds of buyers. One is willing to pay a premium for reliability, and the other is not. The buyers who value reliability buy the better radios and pay more for them. The other buyers pay less, but also get the kind of radio best suited to their needs.

Of central importance is the type of equilibrium that emerges. A 'pooling' equilibrium is one in which players of different types adopt the same strategies and thereby prevent an uninformed player from drawing any inferences about an informed player's type from that player's actions. By contrast, a 'separating' equilibrium is one in which players of different types adopt different strategies and thereby allow the uninformed player to draw inferences about an informed player's type from that player's actions. A separating equilibrium might emerge if sellers can elect to sell their goods with a warranty (see Grossman 1981). Selling a radio with a warranty costs the seller of reliable radios less because over the long haul there will be fewer claims under the warranty. The ability to adopt a warranty may allow separation, and the separating equilibrium may leave us better off than the pooling equilibrium in which all radios are sold at the same price.

Unfortunately, there are no fixed rules about what equilibrium brings about an outcome that leaves the players in the aggregate better off. Warranties are costly. Those who buy a radio with a warranty have less of an incentive to use it carefully. If we lived in a world in which there were only one kind of seller and buyer, we might find that this moral hazard problem would keep any sellers from offering a warranty. In a world in which there are different types of buyers and sellers, the private benefit of distinguishing among different kinds of buyers might exceed the cost of the warranty. The cost of granting a warranty to the high-quality seller might exceed the costs of distinguishing itself from low-quality sellers (and therefore charging a higher price). The seller must make a tradeoff.

In making this assessment, the seller is focusing on private costs of selling with a warranty and the private costs of living in a world in which there is a pooling equilibrium in which all sellers are indistinguishable and all radios are sold for the same price. The private calculus of the individual seller, however, does not weigh the bad incentives that come with the signal against the benefits that come with buyers sorting themselves by type. Hence, one cannot be sure that the market will reach an efficient outcome.

Our inability to know whether a warranty is desirable in this context, however, does not prevent this example from providing us with guidance about the kind of legal rules that we want. This case identifies a potential flaw in a legal rule that requires goods to be sold with a warranty. Mandating a warranty creates a moral hazard problem for all buyers, not just some. At the same time the rule extinguishes the signalling value of the warranty and therefore eliminates any benefit that arises from buyers being matched with the right radio. It provides all the costs of a signal while destroying all the benefits. Mandatory warranties might be justified in some contexts, but these costs need to be taken into account.

The ability of different types of players to sort themselves out may turn as much on the market as on the legal rules. The existence of many different options may make it less likely that those with unfavourable information will mimic the others. Similarly, the more ability parties have to negotiate with each other, the more they may be able to devise mechanisms that transform non-verifiable information into verifiable information.

When problems of private, non-verifiable information exist, however, we cannot be confident about the efficiency of the outcomes we see in the market. There may be little that legal rules can do to improve things, but understanding legal rules in this context requires developing a set of intuitions about how people draw inferences from actions. One of the best ways of doing this is to connect predictions about the effects of legal rules to the kind of equilibrium that we think will emerge once the legal rule is in place.

BARGAINING AND THE LAW. There are many rich areas of game theory and the law that remain largely unexplored. Perhaps the most prominent concerns the bargains that people reach with each other and the way laws affect these bargains and the ways courts must take the dynamics of bargaining into account. This is also the area in which non-cooperative game theory, the branch of game theory used almost exclusively in analysing the law, can give way to cooperative game theory (see Nash 1950a; Osborne and Rubinstein 1990: 9–27).

Formal models can help us understand both how parties reach agreement and, if they do, how they divide the gains from trade between themselves (see Gul, Sonnenschein and Wilson 1986). An owner values possessing a book at $10. A buyer will spend as much as $15 to acquire the same book. The different values a buyer and a seller place on the book make a mutually beneficial trade possible, and legal rules should ensure that parties who want to make this trade are able to do so. After all, such a trade can leave both parties better off. Legal rules, however, do more than simply facilitate trade. They also may affect the way the parties divide the potential gains from any trade (in this case the $5 difference between $10 and $15). Two labour laws might be equally efficient, but one might create a bargaining environment that leaves the workers with higher wages than the other.

In any particular case, much will turn on the specific facts and the reputations and other characteristics of the parties. One party, for example, may be willing to forego any benefit from reaching a deal in order to establish a reputation as a tough negotiator. The two individuals may live in a culture in which there are strong norms about how such divisions are to be made. The fear of ostracism may drive them towards a particular division. When our focus is on how the law affects bargaining we want to understand the bargaining environment and how a change in the legal rules is going to change it. Much of the recent scholarship in game theory has returned to cooperative game theory, and its explicit focus is on the question of the bargains that rational players are likely to reach with each other.

A recent case illustrates how an understanding of strategic behaviour is essential to understanding and applying the law. *In re Hoskins* is a dispute of a most conventional sort. An individual files a Chapter 13 bankruptcy petition, and applicable law allows the debtor to keep his car, provided that the creditor who has a security interest in the car is paid an amount equal to the 'value' of the car. Everyone agrees that bankruptcy law should look outside bankruptcy to determine the car's 'value'. Everyone also agrees that, if no bankruptcy petition had been filed and the creditor were to repossess the car and sell it, the creditor would realize $3,000. Everyone also agrees that if no bankruptcy petition were filed and the debtor were to go out and purchase a similar car, he would pay $5,000.

The Court in this case began by noting that neither valuation reflected the result that would likely exist outside bankruptcy. Outside bankruptcy, we would encounter a bilateral monopoly: the creditor had the right to seize the car and realize $3,000, but the car was worth $5,000 to the debtor. Outside bankruptcy, the creditor and the debtor would recognize the potential gains from bargaining. Hence, the Court found, the outcome in bankruptcy should take into account the dynamics of bargaining outside.

We have long recognized that people bargain in the shadow of the law (see Mnookin and Kornhauser 1979). Legal rules form a background against which people negotiate. What is less commonly recognized is that the opposite is also true. To have legal rules that function effectively, they must also take into account the way in which people bargain. This region of the law, like so many others, remains unsurveyed and, again like so many others, game theory may provide some of the tools we need.

DOUGLAS G. BAIRD

See also DISCLOSURE AND UNRAVELLING; GAME THEORY AND STATES OF THE WORLD; NON-COOPERATIVE GAMES; PRISONERS' DILEMMA; PRIVATE INFORMATION AND LEGAL BARGAINING; SOCIAL NORMS AND THE LAW.

Subject classification: 1d(ii); 4c(i).

CASES

In re Hoskins, 102 F3d 311 (7th Cir. 1996), disapproved by *Associates Commercial Corp. v. Rash*, 117 S.Ct. 1879 (1997).

BIBLIOGRAPHY

Axelrod, R. 1984. *The Evolution of Cooperation*. New York: Basic Books.

Ayres, I. 1990. Playing games with the law. *Stanford Law Review* 42: 1291–1317.

Baird, D. and Picker, R. 1991. A simple noncooperative bargaining model of corporate reorganizations. *Journal of Legal Studies* 20: 311–49.

Baird, D.G., Gertner, R.H. and Picker, R.C. 1994. *Game Theory and the Law*. Cambridge, MA: Harvard University Press.

Brown, J.P. 1973. Toward an economic theory of liability. *Journal of Legal Studies* 2: 323–49.

Cho, I.-K. and Kreps, D. 1987. Signaling games and stable equilibria. *Quarterly Journal of Economics* 102: 179–221.

Coase, R.H. 1960. The problem of social cost. *Journal of Law and Economics* 3: 1–44.

Ellickson, R. 1991. *Order Without Law: How Neighbors Settle Disputes*. Cambridge, MA: Harvard University Press.

Fudenberg, D. and Tirole, J. 1991. *Game Theory*. Cambridge, MA: MIT Press.

Gibbons, R. 1992. *Game Theory for Applied Economists*. Princeton: Princeton University Press.

Grossman, S. 1981. The informational role of warranties and private disclosure about product quality. *Journal of Law and Economics* 24: 461–83.

Gul, F., Sonnenschein, H. and Wilson, R. 1986. Foundations of dynamic monopoly and the Coase conjecture. *Journal of Economic Theory* 39: 155–90.

Hardin, G. 1968. The tragedy of the commons. *Science* 162: 1243–8.

Hardin, R. 1982. *Collective Action*. Baltimore: Johns Hopkins University Press.

Kreps, D. 1990a. *Game Theory and Economic Modeling*. Oxford: Clarendon Press.

Kreps, D. 1990b. *A Course in Microeconomic Theory*. Princeton: Princeton University Press.

Landes, W. 1971. An economic analysis of the courts. *Journal of Law and Economics* 14: 61–107.

Landes, W. and Posner, R. 1987. *The Economic Structure of Tort Law*. Cambridge, MA: Harvard University Press.

Mnookin, R. and Kornhauser, L. 1979. Bargaining in the shadow of the law: the case of divorce. *Yale Law Journal* 88: 950–97.

Nash, J. 1950a. The bargaining problem. *Econometrica* 18: 155–62.

Nash, J. 1950b. Equilibrium points in n-person games. *Proceedings of the National Academy of Sciences (U.S.A.)* 36: 48–9.

Osborne, M. and Rubinstein, A. 1990. *Bargaining and Markets*. San Diego: Academic Press.

Posner, R. 1973. *Economic Analysis of Law*. Boston: Little, Brown; 4th edn, 1992.

Priest, G. and Klein, B. 1984. The selection of disputes for litigation. *Journal of Legal Studies* 13: 1–55.

Shavell, S. 1987. *Economic Analysis of Accident Law*. Cambridge, MA: Harvard University Press.

gangs and the state of nature. Gangs are organizations whose defining characteristic is the provision of protection services. For protection to be necessary, and therefore for a demand for protection services to exist, there must be a power vacuum, 'anarchy' or the philosopher's 'state of nature'. Gangs are also involved in other more traditional economic activities, both legal and illegal, such as garbage collection, the restaurant business, gambling, prostitution and drug dealing. Such activities, although they can often absorb much of a gang's energy, are nevertheless secondary to the gang's primary role; without protection and the means of its enforcement, those other activities would quickly dwindle, taken over by other gangs or, in the case of legal business activities and in the absence of coercion, by ordinary business firms.

As organizations, gangs have a hierarchical structure that typically goes beyond that of a commonly recognized leader. They are also distinct from ephemeral teams of bandits or robbers who join together for the accomplishment of a specific task, after which the team disbands. By contrast, gangs have temporal continuity and, in addition, some territorial continuity, an area within which the gang possesses a near-monopoly in the use of force.

Because the gang engages in the production or distribution of some services or goods, it could be viewed as a firm and thus be subject to the same type of economic analysis as regular business firms. The market for the goods and services that gangs provide could, in principle, be similarly analysed. Protection, however, is not any ordinary service. It is supposed to make the ownership of other goods and services safe from theft and make their contractual exchange enforceable. But how does one make the provision of protection enforceable when what is provided is itself the means of enforcement? Therein lies the puzzle and peculiarity of protection that makes gangs less akin to firms and more similar to the traditional provider of protection, the state.

In what follows I will discuss gangs first in their emergence from the state of nature, then in their organizational characteristics, and finally in their market structure. The account draws on recent contributions to the economic analysis of organized crime (as can be found, for example, in Fiorentini and Peltzman 1995). The concept of the gang employed here includes both youth gangs and organized crime groups like the Mafia. Much of the discussion applies also to the emergence, organization and market structure of those pre-modern states that have had minimal division of labour in their governance and the absence of a codified legal system.

GENESIS. Gangs emerge out of conditions that resemble the state of nature. Individuals and groups have to fend for themselves in such settings and defend against bandits, robbers and, when disputes arise, against one another. These conditions can have different sources: geographic and social distance from the centres of power, the turmoil of transitional historical periods, and state policies prohibiting the production and distribution of certain commodities. Geographically remote areas (such as the mountainous regions of Albania, Montenegro, the Caucasus or Corsica, to name a few) have often been effectively outside the control of states and rule within them has alternated between anarchy and fragmented tribal lordships, the latter having similar characteristics to gangs.

Transitional periods following wars, famines or revolutions are also often times of anarchy, since the traditional enforcement mechanisms weaken or completely disappear while equivalent new ones are slow to take their place. Today, broad swathes of the former Soviet Union fall into this category, in addition to numerous other locations across the globe, from Colombia to Somalia to Afghanistan. These are times when gangs step in to fill the vacuum, either temporarily for a few years or for much longer, when they become permanent players in the economic and political landscape. As an example of the latter type, the Mafia in Sicily grew significantly during the transitional three decades of the last century that followed the unification of Italy (Gambetta 1993, ch. 4), and in spite of the ups and downs in its fortunes over the intervening years it is still there today.

Distrust of centralized authorities and the police by the local population reduces the effectiveness of the state in maintaining order in that area. This distrust can have economic or social origins, as in the case of American inner cities, now and in the past, where some recent immigrants and minorities have often felt alienated from the larger society or excluded from its economic benefits. In the absence of other communal institutions that would substitute for the internal security provided by the state, youth gangs emerge as alternative providers of security (which is another, more respectable name for protection). Such has been the origin of Irish, African-American, and Hispanic youth gangs in Boston, New York and Los Angeles.

The gangs of Prohibition-era Chicago, however, had a different origin: prohibition itself. When the state prohibits the production and distribution of certain commodities, with drugs and alcohol being the prime examples, private parties can no longer use the legal system to write and enforce contracts that pertain to the production and exchange of these commodities. Therefore, with prohibition there is effective anarchy in the industry that surrounds the production and distribution of the affected commodities, including their inputs and financing. In this case, gangs usually both provide the protection that is then naturally demanded and engage in the lucrative production and distribution of the prohibited commodity. The profits are abnormally high not just because of the risk of apprehension by the police but also, and probably more so, because of the high-stakes risks involved in the life-and-death contests among rival groups.

Members of gangs and mafias, irrespective of their origin and location, need to have the ability to use force when called upon to do so. The successful mafioso, although he may rarely resort to violence in the ordinary conduct of his affairs, needs to have applied physical force at least once and in such a way that both potential customers and rivals have taken notice. An integral part of initiation in most youth gangs is a fight against an existing gang member, and valour and performance in battles against other gangs is an important factor of a member's position within the pecking order of the gang's social system, although not necessarily for the position within the formal hierarchy.

In contemplating whether to enter the business of organized crime, a prospective mafioso or gang member has to weigh the expected benefits of such a career, with violence as its centrepiece, against those of a more conventional life in the legal sector of the economy. (Of course, sometimes both career paths are pursued; in that case our discussion applies to the path that is emphasized, in terms of time spent or income earned.) Since the ability to use force is a skill different from those usually required in the legal sector of the economy, there will be a strong tendency for gang members to be selected from those individuals who are relatively better able to use force, those who are better in predation. Or, to use the more conventional terminology of economics, gang members tend to become those who have a comparative advantage in predation (as opposed to production, which for simplicity we consider as the main alternative in the legal sector of the economy).

Although no society can completely avoid expending resources both on predation itself and in defensive measures against it, anarchic conditions encourage a disproportionate share of resources to be devoted to such activities. And because predation does not contribute directly to production, indeed takes away resources and manpower from production, we can expect areas with near-anarchy and significant gang activity to be poorer. Perhaps of greater importance for the poverty of such areas, it is not the proportion *per se* of manpower and resources that is devoted to predation and protection at any given time, but rather the chronic insecurity and unpredictability of economic activity, which moulds the incentives for investment in physical, human and social capital in ways that are detrimental to material growth.

Ordinary businesses, for instance, having to pay for protection, face higher costs of operation, invest less and bias the investments they make against anything that can be easily destroyed. Youths, seeing that a gang career pays and has higher prestige in the neighbourhood, tend to invest in the skills that will confer on them a comparative advantage in predation; which implies that they will value, and so go to, school less, and be less able to succeed in the legal economic sector later on. That does not of course imply that gang members are intrinsically less able in general and less resourceful. On the contrary, as argued by Jankowski (1991, ch. 4), gang members in American inner cities are recruited from among the most stable, entrepreneurial and responsible youths of the neighbourhood; that is, precisely those individuals who under different conditions would be conventionally successful and would provide community leadership. Poor areas with gang activity also encourage emigration to richer and more secure neighbourhoods, thus reducing their population. With a smaller population, agents can no longer take full advantage of the agglomeration economies present in cities, thus further increasing costs, emigration and the slide towards impoverishment.

ORGANIZATION. Private and public organizations typically have a hierarchical structure, and gangs are not exempt from this rule. In industrialized societies, however, firms, government agencies and voluntary organizations are viewed by economists as cooperative and consensual in their make-up, which can also promote the general good of society at large. Membership in such organizations is based on written contracts as well as on informal rules and social norms.

Although gangs can be seen from their members' perspective as cooperative organizations, it would be difficult to view them as promoters of the general good. That is one difference between gangs on the one hand, and firms and other such legal organizations on the other. Another originates precisely from the extra-legal status of the gang: it cannot be party to contracts and its members cannot write enforceable contracts with the gang or with one another, at least in matters that lie within the boundaries of what is considered illegal. They can of course have their own types of contracting and informal constraints in their behaviour since, after all, the gang as a provider of protection services is the ultimate authority in its area. As such, it can enforce some (unwritten) contracts even more effectively than the state; penalties can be much more severe within gangs than they are in a modern polity. Physical punishment, even death, is a form of penalty used much more often by gangs. But the severity of penalties is not enough to balance the multiple uncertainties surrounding the fulfillment of contracts and the arbitrariness that often exists in enforcing contracts in the gang's territory and within the gang's organization.

In the long run, what provides much of the glue that binds members of organizations together is not explicit contracts but informal constraints, behavioural norms and ideological constructs. So it is with gangs. A gang's success – as measured by its size, territory, and longevity – very much depends on how well it articulates a 'mission' to its members and develops a workable culture and ideology. A central element of the ideology of American youth gangs, as described by Jankowski (1991, ch. 3), is that American society systematically discriminates against their kind. Another element in this ideology is that illegality and predatory behaviour are in fact operative and even encouraged in the larger society; 'everybody does it'. The gang, then, is viewed as an organization that contributes to the advancement of its members and – because in their overwhelming majority gangs are organized along ethnic lines – of their ethnic group, just as other organizations do in the larger society. The poverty of their community and the hostility of media and the authorities reinforce beliefs and legitimize their actions in their own eyes.

The mafioso of rural Sicily, who used to engage in intermediary and judicial functions in addition to providing protection, had the self-image of performing public service, and local society in general appears to have largely agreed on that. Even the occasional outburst of grisly violence was perceived by the mafioso, if not by the community, as a necessary sacrifice to the altar of public order. Such traits must have persisted in some of the organized crime syndicates of urban North America, but with time the lack of legitimacy in the larger society should have worn away the veneer of such a self-image and replaced it by a straightforward self-seeking business ethic.

The fact that the Mafia is referred to as 'family' by its own members as well as others points to another significant element of the ideology of gangs which attempts to liken the organization to this most durable human institution. American youth gangs also actively promote a 'brotherhood' ideology, but not because their members do not have stable biological families (as some media reports, falsely, might make us believe). It is because while gang members are ambitious, entrepreneurial and defiantly individualistic, as well as being good with guns and knives, it is an excellent survival strategy to maintain a semblance of cooperation within the organization by telling and abiding by, though not necessarily believing in, a strong binding myth. What better such myth is there than everyone being biologically of the same stock? The presence of this myth across many different localities and types of gangs suggests that it has good long-run stability properties.

Some gangs, like Chicano gangs in Los Angeles and Irish gangs in Boston, have a rather loose and flat organizational structure and leadership that is informally recognized rather than formally elected or appointed (Jankowski 1991: ch. 3). Others, like some New York youth gangs, have developed a more elaborate division of labour with several different levels of formal hierarchy. And over the past twenty years it has become more evident that the Sicilian Mafia has more hierarchy and communication across geographically distant locations than originally thought (compare the discussions and evidence in Hess 1973 and Gambetta 1993).

Whereas the degree of comparative advantage in predation is an important prerequisite for gang membership, it is not clear whether and how a member's comparative advantage in predation determines success and advancement within the gang. To be sure, a minimum of demonstrable physical prowess is required for someone to achieve a leadership position, but beyond that level sophisticated political and administrative skills become most important. The planning and execution of tasks, coalition-building, the capacity to build political support over time and the ability to motivate the troops are examples of the skills that are helpful in becoming a successful leader in any organization, including gangs. Since these skills are very different from those that are required of a good fighter, it appears that leaders would be selected among those with a comparative advantage in politics and administration, provided they have a minimum level of competence – which can still be high relative to others – in the use of force. This, however, is a hypothesis that has yet to be confirmed.

MARKET STRUCTURE. Measures of protection against theft and arbitrary seizure of property can be, and in fact always are, taken by agents individually. Normally, however, these measures are supplemented, and often taken over, by communities and the state through laws, the police and the judicial system. Since the provision of protection has public good characteristics there is a strong tendency for its monopolistic provision within a certain territory. As was known by the kings and lords of the past, and as the kleptocratic dictators of today quickly learn, the monopolistic provision of protection is extremely profitable; the king, the lord or the dictator can bring order against banditry and robbery but, with the coercive apparatus at his disposal and no other checks on his rule, he can appropriate much of the surplus that order generates. Nevertheless monopoly can never be absolute, for there will always be pretenders, suitors and alternative nation-saviours contesting these monopoly profits through force. Much of warfare in human history and many political as well as military battles in today's Third World can usefully, though cynically, be viewed as struggles over monopoly protection rents. Qualitatively, this condition is not different from the way the market for protection is organized in the areas controlled by gangs. The differences in scale and organizational capabilities from predatory states can have a substantially different impact on the economic welfare of the affected areas, but nonetheless the basic similarities between gangs and predatory states are hard to escape.

The structure of the market for protection resembles that of monopolistic competition. Each gang controls a certain area within which it has the local monopoly of protection. The absence of alternative providers means that the gang can set a price that is close to the alternative each individual customer would have faced under the state of nature. Moreover, the gang, unlike lawful firms, can force everyone within their area to pay up. On the cost side, the gang has to expend the resources of its members to police its area and defend it against other gangs that continually attempt to encroach on its territory, or to attack the territory of other gangs. For a given number of gangs, the size of the area controlled by each gang, and its profits, depend on the technologies of protection and conflict, where the latter determines the resources the gang must expend to maintain rule within a given territory. These profits can be divided among gangs members or spent in the creation and maintenance of club houses and the provision of entertainment and other services to gang members.

In the long run, with free entry, these profits should be reduced to those available elsewhere in the economy. Thus, excess profits in the long run should be competed away and the initial reaction of someone versed in economics might be that this is a good thing, an efficient state of affairs. Quite to the contrary, however, since in terms of production and economic welfare such a market structure could well be as bad as the state of nature. First, individual producers in a gang's territory do not have to be better off than they were under the state of nature; what was extracted by bandits and robbers under the state of nature could now be extracted by the gang as tribute and tax, ostensibly in exchange for the protection services provided. The gang might even be capable of extracting more than the bandits. And whatever costly self-protection measures were to be undertaken against bandits would now be replaced by tribute-avoidance measures, also costly, against the gang. Second, it is unclear whether the total number of producers would be increased under the presence of gangs compared with the state of nature. That would happen only if there were appropriate incentives to produce and keep what is produced and, as we have just seen, an individual producer might not have the incentives to produce more under the gang. Thus it is conceivable that economic welfare under the gang might be no better than under the state of nature – those who were bandits under the state of nature just become organized into gangs.

In fact, the condition with competing gangs can also be described as a state of nature, as anarchy, albeit at a level in which a subset of the original actors have coalesced into gangs. For the overcoming of conflict within a group and the emergence of cooperation can lead to conflict that previously could not exist with other groups (Hirshleifer 1995). Clans can unite and fight one another until they themselves unite to form a tribe, which can then engage in conflict with other tribes, which can also later on collectively form a state. The main difference of gangs from predatory states (and examples of that include most empires and kingdoms of the past and many Third-World states of today) is size. Size means that many internal disputes are not settled wholly through guns, but somewhat more efficiently through politics, no matter that politics are likely to be coercive, and also implies that much of the uncertainty and unpredictability of shifting gang rule can be avoided. In the limiting case of Leviathan – a monopolistic predatory state without challengers and neighbours to worry about – production and trade could in principle flourish, but Leviathan could drive all his subjects down to their reservation levels of welfare, i.e. those achievable under the state of nature, and keep his enormous rents to build magnificent pyramids in the sand.

Studying gangs and the state of nature can help understand the primitive inner layers of the state when one takes away its historically more recent functions, in the absence of the rule of law, constitutions, self-governance or representative democracy. Recent events throughout the world remind us that those inner layers are far from dormant and that we know very little of how and why they thrust themselves into view.

BIBLIOGRAPHIC NOTE. Gambetta (1993) has forcefully and clearly argued for protection as the defining characteristic of the Mafia. Hess (1973) and Jankowski (1991) are two other excellent monographs on gangs, the first on the Mafia and the second on American youth gangs. Schelling (1967, 1971) has provided an early economic analysis of organised crime, emphasizing aspects of its industrial organisation. Anderson (1995) and Dick (1995) have used the transaction-cost method to examine the industry. Shavell (1992) and Konrad and Skaperdas (1995, 1996) have identified the different negative economic affects of gangs; the section above on market structure is based on the last paper. Polo (1995) has also examined aspects of the market structure of gangs and their internal organization using a principal–agent approach. Skaperdas and Syropoulos (1995) develop the analogy between gangs and primitive states. Konrad and Skaperdas (1997) examine the credibility problem in gangs: how they can back up words with deeds. Grossman (1995) takes the view that competition between the State and a mafia can be welfare-enhancing; this result appears to depend on the treatment of the good provided by the State as an ordinary public good. Grossman and Noh (1994), Marcouiller and Young (1995) and McGuire and Olson (1996) have examined the policies of a monopolistic predatory state, which also provides a public good that enhances private production.

STERGIOS SKAPERDAS

See also DRUG PROHIBITION; ECONOMIC APPROACH TO CRIME AND PUNISHMENT; GUN CONTROL; ORGANIZED CRIME; RULE OF LAW; STABILITY OF ANARCHIC SOCIETIES; STATE OF NATURE AND CIVIL SOCIETY; TRUST.

Subject classification: 1a(ii); 3c; 5e.

BIBLIOGRAPHY

Anderson, A. 1995. Organised crime, mafia and governments. In Fiorentini and Peltzman, *op. cit.*

Dick, A.R. 1995. When does organized crime pay? A transaction cost analysis. *International Review of Law and Economics* 15: 25–45.

Fiorentini, G. and Peltzman, S. (eds). 1995. *The Economics of Organised Crime*. Cambridge: Cambridge University Press.

Gambetta, D. 1993. *The Sicilian Mafia: the Business of Private Protection*. Cambridge, MA: Harvard University Press.

Grossman, H. 1995. Rival kleptocrats: the Mafia versus the State. In Fiorentini and Peltzman, *op. cit.*

Grossman, H. and Noh, S.J. 1994. Proprietary public finance and economic welfare. *Journal of Public Economics* 53: 187–204.

Hess, H. 1973. *Mafia and Mafiosi: The Structure of Power*. Lexington, MA: Lexington Books, D.C. Heath & Co.

Hirshleifer, J. 1995. Anarchy and its breakdown. *Journal of Political Economy* 103: 26–52.

Jankowski, M.S. 1991. *Islands in the Street: Gangs and American Urban Society*. Berkeley: University of California Press.

Konrad, K. and Skaperdas, S. 1995. Extortion. Working Paper, University of California, Irvine.

Konrad, K. and Skaperdas, S. 1996. The Market for Protection and the Origin of the State. Working Paper, University of California, Irvine.

Konrad, K. and Skaperdas, S. 1997. Credible threats in extortion. *Journal of Economic Behavior and Organization* 33: 23–39.

Marcouiller, D. and Young, L. 1995. The black hole of graft: the predatory state and the informal economy. *American Economic Review* 85: 630–46.

McGuire, M.C. and Olson, M. 1996. The economics of autocracy and majority rule: the invisible hand and the use of force. *Journal of Economic Literature* 34: 72–96.

Polo, M. 1995. Internal cohesion and competition among criminal organisations. In Fiorentini and Peltzman, *op. cit.*

Schelling, T.C. 1967. Economics and the criminal enterprise. *Public Interest* 7: 61–78; reprinted in Schelling 1984, ch. 7.

Schelling, T.C. 1971. What is the business of organized crime? *Journal of Public Law* 20: 71–84; reprinted in Schelling 1984, ch. 8.

Schelling, T.C. 1984 *Choice and Consequence*. Cambridge, MA: Harvard University Press.

Shavell, S. 1992. An economic analysis of threats and their illegality: blackmail, extortion, and robbery. Harvard Law School, Discussion Paper no. 118, Cambridge, MA.

Skaperdas, S. and Syropoulos, C. 1995. Gangs as primitive states. In Fiorentini and Peltzman, *op. cit.*

gaps in contracts. *See* DEFAULT RULES FOR INCOMPLETE CONTRACTS; INCOMPLETE CONTRACTS.

gatekeepers. *See* THIRD-PARTY LIABILITY.

generic drugs. *See* PHARMACEUTICAL REGULATION.

Good Samaritan rule.

> A New England farmer comes into the country store and after a few minutes says: 'Alonzo Smith hung himself in his barn.' Someone then asks: 'Did you cut him down?' And the farmer answers: 'No, not until he stops twitching.'

Should the farmer have an affirmative duty to rescue the person hanging? A person is lying unconscious across a railroad track. Should a passerby be compensated for saving the unconscious person's life or be found liable for not saving? In general, Anglo-American courts require no affirmative duties of bystanders, and rarely is there a legal obligation to compensate the rescuer for the minor costs incurred in rescuing. In contrast, the Continental rule imposes Good Samaritan duties on mere bystanders when the cost of rescue is trivial and entitles the successful rescuer to a reward. Which system is better?

The answer is not found by arguing that the unhelpful bystander did not 'cause' the death of the unconscious person or by claiming that the bystander was guilty merely of a sin of omission rather than of commission. Economic reasoning shows such distinctions to be meaningless since it is clearly cost effective for a bystander to rescue the unconscious person and without such a rescue the unconscious person will die.

THE ECONOMIC LOGIC UNDERLYING THE CONTINENTAL RULE. The Continental rule is more consistent with economic logic. If a person can be rescued at low cost, it is clearly economically efficient to do so. The Continental rule encourages these low cost rescues in two ways. First, the rescuer is compensated for the small costs of rescue; second, if the potential rescuer's costs are somewhat higher than the average so that the reward does not fully cover all of his costs, then the threat of a more severe fine (or being liable for damage to the potential rescuee) will motivate the person to rescue. The rule also provides the appropriate incentives for those who might need rescue. By charging for the average cost of the rescue, the rescuee takes the appropriate level of care. A higher price for rescue would result in the potential rescuee being overly cautious and needing too few rescues. On the other hand, if the price paid to rescuers is lower than the costs that they incur in rescue, then either there will be too many people needing rescue and being rescued (if the low price does not affect the supply of potential rescuers) or there will be too few rescuers and as a consequence too few people putting themselves at risk (if the low price reduces the supply of potential rescuers below the optimal; for example, ships undertaking circuitous routes to avoid areas where there are boat people in need of rescue).

In a nutshell, in order for there to be the correct economic incentives, both liability by the rescuee for being rescued and liability by the rescuer for non-rescue must be in place. The Continental rule employs both. The Anglo-American rule employs neither.

THE ANGLO-AMERICAN RULE. If the Continental rule is so sensible, why have the Anglo-American courts ruled otherwise? There have been a number of attempts to find an economic explanation, but, despite the cleverness of the ideas, none of the suggested answers is fully convincing. For example, Landes and Posner (1978) argue that people either are truly altruistic or desire to have a reputation for being altruistic and that a law which made people liable for non-rescue would interfere with this motivation – people could not claim that their behaviour was altruistically motivated if the law punished them for not behaving in an 'altruistic' way. There are several problems with such an explanation. It is not clear why a law backing up desirable behaviour diminishes it. Much desirable behaviour is reinforced by legal sanctions and many religions use the threat of eternal damnation if the person does not act righteously. In the example at hand, the altruistic person could always give back the money for rescuing. And it is hard to conceive of the case where punishing for non-rescue would deter an altruistic person from rescuing.

Landes and Posner's counter-argument is that people are altruistic when it is a choice of someone losing a life and their being slightly inconvenienced; once there is an imposed payment, the choice is between collecting or not collecting, and not collecting means that the Samaritan is giving up something to benefit someone else by an equal amount. Therefore the altruistic motive will no longer be operative and the rescuer will want to collect on the reward. If most people are altruists when it comes to saving lives, then the effect of requiring an award will be a needless costly transaction. But there are also problems with this counter-argument. If people do not have to pay for their rescue, people will take too many risks (as Landes and Posner demonstrate elsewhere in their article). Furthermore, once we allow altruism as a motivation for the rescuer's behaviour, we may have to reconsider the motivation of the rescued person as well. For example, would something akin to altruism motivate the rescued person to reward the rescuer? Finally, do we want to argue that a system of rewards and punishments is not needed in English speaking countries because they are more altruistic?

Rubin (1986) suggests that the cost of tracking down non-rescuers could be so large (it may be hard to discover who was in the area or whether they witnessed the event) that the benefits of such a rule would be undermined. There are problems with such an argument. The person will be tracked down only if the cost of tracking is less than the liability which is the cost of non-rescue. Since by hypothesis the cost of rescue was slight, even in the presence of search costs it is efficient to make the non-rescuer liable. Rubin also brings up the issue of multiple tortfeasors: if there were ten people watching someone drown, there is the question of how to allocate liability. But the problem of multiple tortfeasors can be handled by making them jointly and severally liable or by creating a more complicated scheme if the tortfeasors vary in their ability to rescue.

Rather than trying to justify the Anglo-American rule, it may be more insightful to see the many exceptions. There are numerous special cases in Anglo-American law that require restitution for rescue or liability for non-rescue. A physician who treats an unconscious person can collect her regular fee. A number of statutes require a driver who is involved in an accident to offer assistance to the accident victims regardless of fault. In most American jurisdictions, the captain (or ship owner) is liable if he fails to take reasonable measures to rescue passengers or crew who fall or jump overboard even if the need for rescue is not the captain's fault. Passengers (crew) pay for these rescue services via higher ticket prices (lower wages). More important, 'individuals in charge of a vessel shall render assistance to any individual found at sea in danger of being lost, so far as the . . . individual in charge can do so without serious danger to the . . . individual's vessel or individuals on board' (46 USC §2304; also see Canada Shipping Act, RSC 1985, and the UK Maritime Conventions Act, 1911). Failure to do so may lead to a fine and/or imprisonment. As a final example, if it is not dangerous to do so, a driver must swerve out of the way of a person lying unconscious on the street; that is, if the costs are relatively minor, the driver must rescue the person in distress by swerving or be liable for the resultant injuries.

EXTENSIONS. The cost of rescue is not always trivial and because of that people are sometimes prevented from undertaking certain risky actions in the first place. Eagle Sarmount wanted to fly his hang glider (powered with a snowmobile engine) from New York to Paris. But when he got to Canada, the Royal Canadian Mounted Police would not let him fly over the Atlantic even though he claimed that it was his life to lose (*Santa Cruz Sentinel*, 23 July 1980). The Canadians realized that if his plane did go down in the Atlantic, they would be responsible for saving him. They knew that Eagle did not have the wherewithal to pay for his rescue, and they knew that Eagle knew this also. Rather than allowing him to impose such a cost on others, they prevented him from flying any further.

There are other solutions besides regulation. In some mountain climbing areas, climbers must post bond for their rescue. Poor swimmers can risk drowning in public swimming pools because the price of admission includes a life guard. On the open seas, ships are liable to their rescuers; if they were not, professional rescuers and salvage ships would not be available (see Landes and Posner (1978) for a discussion of professional salvage). There is no need for liability for non-rescue since the profit from rescue is sufficient to encourage rescue attempts when it is efficient to do so.

CONCLUDING REMARKS. We have investigated high transaction cost situations where the cost of rescue is trivial but the cost of non-rescue is great. A two-part rule, liability by the rescuee for being rescued and liability by the potential rescuer for non-rescue, creates the proper incentives for all actors. The rule thus emulates many market situations where a person purchases a service, but the service provider is liable if the service is negligently provided. This two-part rule also puts brakes on the use of affirmative obligation. For example, Epstein (1973: 199) argues that a natural extension of the Good Samaritan rule would require the rich to give charity to the poor. But a two-part liability rule does not involve redistribution – those that are saved must pay for their rescue.

DONALD WITTMAN

See also LAST CLEAR CHANCE; RESCUE.

Subject classification: 5d(ii).

STATUTES

Canada Shipping Act, RSC 1985, c. S-9, s. 451(1).
UK Maritime Conventions Act, 1911, 1 & 2 Geo. 5, c. 57, s. 6.
46 USC § 2304.

BIBLIOGRAPHY

Epstein, R. 1973. A theory of strict liability. *Journal of Legal Studies* 2: 151–204.

Landes, W. and Posner, R.A. 1978. Salvors, finders, Good Samaritans and other rescuers: an economic study of law and altruism. *Journal of Legal Studies* 7: 83–128.

Levmore, S. 1986. Waiting for rescue: an essay on the evolution and incentive structure of the law of affirmative obligation. *Virginia Law Review* 72: 879–941.

McInnes, M. 1992. The economic analysis of rescue laws. *Manitoba Law Journal* 21: 237–63.

Ratcliffe, J.M. (ed.). 1966. *The Good Samaritan and the Law*. Garden City, NY: Doubleday Company/Anchor Books.

Rubin, P. 1986. Costs and benefits of a duty to rescue. *International Review of Law and Economics* 6: 273–6.

Weinrib, E.J. 1980. The case for a duty to rescue. *Yale Law Journal* 90: 247–93.

Wittman, D.A. 1984. Liability for harm or restitution for benefit. *Journal of Legal Studies* 13: 57–80.

gratuitous promises. It is standard doctrine in Anglo-American contract law that a promise is not enforceable without 'consideration': normally, a *quid pro quo* for which the promise was exchanged. It follows that the gratuitous or benevolent promise will be denied legal effect, no matter how clearly the promisor may have wished to bind himself. By contrast, any promise made as part of a bargain carries with it a presumptive guarantee, furnished at state expense, in the form of legal enforceability. Assuming that the promisor is free not only to make or withhold a promise, but also to make it on such terms and conditions as he chooses, the possibility of assuming a legally enforceable obligation can only be beneficial to both parties; since to the extent the bonded (i.e. enforceable) promise is more valuable to the promisee, it must be correspondingly more valuable to the promisor as well, whether this added value is realized through an ordinary exchange or an interdependent utility function.

The problem traditionally associated with gratuitous promises, taking the doctrine of consideration at face value, is thus to explain why the common law denies to the gratuitous transaction a value-enhancing facility that it extends automatically to the most mundane exchange. The traditional problem rests on a misconception, however, because the majority of the gratuitous promises that come before the courts are actually enforced under one rubric or another. We might more accurately say that, whereas a promise made in a bargain context carries a presumption of enforceability, the proponent of a gratuitous promise must persuade the court that the promise merits enforcement – judged by such *a priori* criteria as the promisor's intent or the promisee's reliance.

The different doctrinal standing of gift and bargain promises is often explained by an argument that enforcement of gift promises would yield lesser benefits, at greater cost, than the enforcement of bargains. Gratuitous transfers are said to be 'economically sterile transactions' (von Mehren 1982: I-29), where they are not positively harmful: 'frequently made in highly emotional states brought on by surges of gratitude, impulses of display, or other intense but transient feelings' (Eisenberg 1979: 5), such promises may be better left unenforced simply because they are unwise. Alternatively, a 'general rule of nonenforceability' might be appropriate because gratuitous promises are *de minimis*. Such a rule would be the consequence of 'an empirical hunch' on the part of common-law judges 'that gratuitous promises tend both to involve small stakes and to be made in family settings where there are economically superior alternatives to legal enforcement' (Posner 1977: 417).

Enforcement of gratuitous promises is thought to involve higher costs. Because gratuitous promises, by definition, lack the formal safeguards that Fuller (1941) found implicit in the doctrine of consideration, it is more difficult to ascertain either their existence or their terms with the requisite certainty; enforceability would thus carry an unacceptable risk of enforcing promises that were never made or not intended as such (see Fuller 1941: 815; Eisenberg 1979: 4–5). Posner (1977: 419) expresses the concern that 'the standard unilateral promise' may be only 'a figment of the promisee's imagination'.

These attempts to justify legal orthodoxy are unsatisfactory for a number of reasons. One is the *post hoc*, essentially conjectural nature of much of the argument. If it were true, for instance, that gratuitous promises were economically sterile, difficult to prove, or typically made without adequate deliberation, such observations would indeed tend to explain a general rule of non-enforceability; but since these propositions have no particular plausibility as empirical statements (see Kull 1992: 51–5), the explanations appear to be derived from the rule rather than the other way around. Posner's 'empirical hunch' that most gratuitous promises involve small stakes and are more efficiently enforced by non-legal sanctions looks like an accurate observation, but the same might be said of most bargains. Indeed, the relevant set of gratuitous promises strongly resembles the bargain promises with which the law is concerned, since it consists necessarily of promises actually made, substantial enough to justify the cost of litigation, as to which non-legal means of enforcement have proved ineffective.

Arguments that contrast the intrinsic merits of gifts and bargains encounter a historical objection as well. The common law made no distinction whatever between gift and bargain promises, as long as the test of enforceability was that a promise be contained in a sealed writing. Nor, despite the alleged shortcomings of gift promises, did the subsequent ascendancy of consideration doctrine put any significant obstacle in the way of one who sought to make such a promise with legal effect, as long as the formality of the seal remained easily and commonly accessible. The seal was abandoned because it lost its efficacy as ritual, not because of a judgment that gift promises did not merit enforcement (see *Aller v. Aller*); so that the disfavoured legal position of the gratuitous promisor has been, as a practical matter, merely an unintended consequence of the decline of the seal.

Any attempt to explain why our legal system treats gratuitous promises as presumptively unworthy of enforcement is therefore starting from a false premise. A more realistic question is a more modest one: why, following the virtual disappearance of the seal, has the law not recognized a mechanism by which one might make a legally effective promise of a gift?

Efforts to remedy this deficiency have taken two essentially opposing tacks. One recurring suggestion has been to create a new validating formality that would take the place of the seal, the most interesting example being Samuel Williston's Uniform Written Obligations Act. Originally proposed in 1925, the act makes a written promise enforceable without consideration if it contains 'an additional express statement, in any form of language, that the signer intends to be legally bound'. The model act is law only in Pennsylvania, where its principal effect has been to add another clause to the stereotyped recitals in business contracts prepared by lawyers. The utter failure of Williston's idea suggests, among other things, the futility of trying to impose socially meaningful formality by legislative enactment – the more so if the attempt is to replace arcane ritual with a conclusory statement in plain language.

The opposite approach to the problem of gratuitous promises is not to resurrect formalities but to rationalize the doctrine of consideration. If we assume with Lord Wright (1936: 1225) that the *a priori* test of enforceability should be 'whether there is a serious and deliberate intention to enter into obligations enforceable at law' – a test implicitly conceded by writers who justify consideration by asserting that gratuitous promisors lack such intentions – then consideration is at best an imperfect proxy for the existence of the underlying criteria. Assuming that the context of a bargain makes a relatively reliable, easily ascertainable index of seriousness and deliberation, the presence of consideration makes an efficient test for validating a promise. But to treat its absence as invalidating involves a *non sequitur*, since the absence of consideration can be no indication of the absence of the criteria when a promise is intended to be gratuitous.

Lord Wright (1936) and the other members of the Law Revision Committee (1937) urged that consideration doctrine be reformed to make the existence of a bargain a sufficient condition of enforceability but not a necessary one: evidence 'that the parties intend to create a relationship binding in law' might be supplied 'equally well either by consideration regarded as evidence of that intention or by some other evidence of that intention' (1937: ¶28). Proposals of this kind, repeated many times since, have had negligible effect on the written law of contracts. There could be, indeed, no sufficient impetus to reform of the doctrine unless the received rules were felt to obstruct desirable results in a significant number of instances. But such is evidently not the case.

The doctrine of consideration has been permitted to ossify because the meritorious promises to which it ostensibly denies enforceability are in fact being enforced. Enforcement can be justified by finding consideration, nominal or 'invented' if need be (see Treitel [1962] 1991: 67–8); or by finding that the promise is of a type enforceable without consideration (see *Restatement* §§82–94); or by finding that the promise has induced action in reliance on the part of the promisee. Indeed, it is the ready applicability of reliance analysis to most issues of enforceability that explains, more than anything else, the persistence of antiquated consideration doctrine, since a judge is unlikely to pursue the matter beyond the first serviceable explanation that comes to hand. Because the dominant reason for promising is precisely to facilitate reliance of a beneficial kind (see Goetz and Scott 1980: 1267), a promise that has *not* been relied on in some respect must tend to be the exception.

There continue to be, assuredly, numerous cases in which judges explain that a particular promise is unenforceable for want of consideration. What is difficult to find, by contrast, is a case in which the want of consideration appears to be the real objection. In an extensive survey of modern US decisions, Wessman (1996) reports that the doctrine of consideration serves almost invariably as an 'overlapping' reason for refusing enforcement to alleged promises open to objection on other grounds: because they are of doubtful genuineness, or indefinite, or coerced, or one-sided. The same use of consideration as pretext is apparent in the decisions refusing to enforce gift promises (see Kull 1992: 44–5). The test case would of course be one in which a promise that is fully established by the evidence, and unobjectionable on any grounds either of formation or fairness, is nevertheless refused enforcement because it lacks consideration; and such a case, in the US at least, would today be a rarity and an anachronism. Developments elsewhere may lag significantly, making the foregoing generalizations about consideration doctrine appear unduly casual. But the tendency in Commonwealth jurisdictions is evidently in the same direction (see Atiyah 1986: ch. 8).

The divergence between law and doctrine is tolerated, in part, because cases that test the central proposition of consideration doctrine are few and far between. Gratuitous promises are, properly speaking, non-existent in a business context, where consideration must be easy to find as long as we assume that people are not in business for their health (see *Pillans v. Van Mierop*). This observation remains heretical, of course, since most of the real difficulties associated with the doctrine of consideration have stemmed from the courts' readiness to suppose that business engagements might indeed be undertaken gratuitously. But the tendency of modern contract law has been systematically to eliminate each of the points, involving such matters as firm offers or modifications, at which a supposed lack of consideration once prevented the enforcement of real bargains.

'Gratuitous promises', therefore, comprise only promises of gifts; and within this narrow category, the number of promises that present squarely the issue of enforceability is further reduced by a series of important limits. The promise must have been intended by the promisor to create a legally enforceable obligation (see *Balfour v. Balfour*; *Jones v. Padavatton*); where a gift promise is made in a family setting there may be legitimate and substantial doubt that such an obligation was intended. The promised gift must be of a size substantial enough to justify litigation. Equally important, the disappointed promisee must be prepared to sue the promisor in the event of non-performance. Understandable scruples about suing one's benefactor explain, in part, the predominance of executors and administrators as defendants in these cases.

The number of gratuitous promises actually sued upon is therefore exceedingly small; and of this number, the majority are concededly *enforceable* under recognized exceptions to the requirements of consideration. Marriage settlements (*Shadwell v. Shadwell*) and, in the US, charitable subscriptions (see *Restatement* §90 (2)), are routinely enforced; as is any other promise that has induced substantial reliance on the part of the promisee. This leaves us, as a real-life test of the abstract proposition about enforceability, little more than the classic scenario in which a benevolent uncle promises a gift to his nephew. Because nephews do not sue their uncles to recover promised gifts, the typical case is actually one in which the nephew sues the uncle's estate. Here, too, the gratuitous promise is generally enforced, even when it falls within no recognized exception to the consideration requirement (*Devecmon v. Shaw*; *Hamer v. Sidway*; *Ricketts v. Scothorn*; *Webb v. McGowin*). Where gratuitous promises are asserted against executors, an ostensible problem of consideration becomes – as Fellows (1988) points out – a question of donative transfers and testamentary substitutes: whether the law should acknowledge a disposition of the decedent's estate that fails to comply with the Wills Act. What is noteworthy in these cases is the courts' evident reluctance to allow purported rules of consideration to obstruct the realization of the parties' presumed intentions.

Examining the outcomes of cases rather than judicial statements, the truth of the matter seems to be that judges examine gratuitous promises against substantive criteria of enforceability, including, of course, the relative certainty that the promise alleged was actually made and the quality of the promisee's reliance. If meritorious gift promises are denied enforcement it is because a key element of the equation, the intent to create legal relations, is ordinarily so difficult to assess. Nearly everyone agrees, after all, that a 'serious and deliberate intention to enter into obligations enforceable at law' (in Lord Wright's words) is one that ought to be respected, whether one's 'general theory of promise-keeping' derives from notions of autonomy or utility or both (see Trebilcock 1993: ch. 8). But outside the context of bargain, where it is understood that enforceable promises constitute the medium of exchange, the difficulty is to identify the requisite intention. Trebilcock justifiably complains that 'an autonomy-based theory of promise-keeping provides absolutely no assistance in determining, at least outside the context of sealed promises, which gratuitous promises can reasonably be interpreted as intended to be legally binding and which cannot' (1993: 184). The law meets this difficulty, it would seem, by enforcing only those gratuitous promises in which the promisor's intent to be bound is essentially uncontested.

One result of this solicitude toward the gratuitous promisor is to make it impossible for uncle to bind himself by an irrevocable promise of a gift, but the absence of this particular legal facility is presumably the consequence of a lack of demand. Very few promisors would choose to make themselves liable to suit on an unperformed promise of a gift, whether the reason for non-performance was change of circumstances or change of heart. Although the promise might be made subject to stated conditions, the essentially subjective nature of the contingencies that might cause the promisor to seek to be released from his obligation, and the consequent inability of the courts to verify their occurrence (Shavell 1991: 407), render the conditional obligation scarcely more attractive to the promisor. In the donative context, moreover, a promise will ordinarily carry a sufficient degree of reliability without the additional security – costly to the donor, and hence to the donee as well – afforded by legal enforceability. The ordinary, revocable donative promise is warranted against revocation by non-legal sanctions that are likely to be highly effective; Shavell's formal analysis (1991: 419–21) supports the intuition that the mere statement of intention to give a gift will usually induce the desired degree of reliance on the part of the prospective donee. Where a revocable promise does not adequately secure the promisee's expectations, the donor's normal recourse is to make a present gift or settle a trust.

What both promisor and promisee ordinarily require, by contrast, is a mechanism by which the unperformed and unrepudiated gift promise may be enforced against the deceased promisor's estate; and this, as we have seen, the law effectively supplies. *Hamer v. Sidway* (or *Ricketts v. Scothorn*, or *Webb v. McGowin*) reveals a promisor who never repudiated and apparently never regretted his promise, who took appropriate steps to perform during his lifetime, and who died without completing performance. The meaningful question about intent in such a case is not whether the promisor intended to expose himself to suit during his lifetime, but whether he intended that the promise be recognized as an obligation of his estate, to the extent that he left it unperformed.

The practical need is thus for a hybrid sort of gift promise, one that is revocable during the life of the donor but enforceable *post mortem*: a promise, in short, that acts like a will. Promises having these characteristics are impossible as a matter of contract law but easy to find in the cases. True, the absence of either consideration or seal to serve as validating formality makes the proof of such a promise more costly, by opening it to judicial scrutiny of the *a priori* desirability of enforcement; but here it may be that gift promises, rather than bargains, reflect the emerging standard of enforceability.

Contemporary legal thought is both hostile to legal formality and sceptical of the individualistic ideals that underlie classical contract doctrine. The more characteristic modern assertion is not that we should develop substitutes for the seal, but rather that we should anticipate 'a more candid set of principles to determine which promises should be enforceable in terms of the fairness of each type' (Fried 1981: 39), employing 'an expanded, paradigmatic concept of unconscionability' to condition enforceability directly on 'the quality of the bargain' (Eisenberg 1982: 754). On this converse side of the consideration question – summed up in the notion that adequacy of consideration is not a requirement of enforceability – law and doctrine diverge as well; courts have shown themselves ready to pass on the quality of the bargain without waiting for a candid set of principles. Considered in light of the most pronounced changes in contract law over the last century, the more telling question is not why we have failed to re-establish formal means of validating gift promises, but how long bargains will continue to be accorded presumptive legal validity.

ANDREW KULL

See also CONTRACTS; INHERITANCE LAW; LEGAL FORMALITIES; RELIANCE.

Subject classification: 5c(i).

STATUTE

Uniform Written Obligations Act (1925).

CASES

Aller v. Aller, 40 NJL 446 (1878).
Balfour v. Balfour [1919] 2 KB 571.
Devecmon v. Shaw, 14 A 464 (Md 1888).
Hamer v. Sidway, 27 NE 256 (NY 1891).
Jones v. Padavatton [1969] 2 All ER 616.
Pillans v. Van Mierop (1765) 3 Burr. 1663.
Ricketts v. Scothorn, 77 NW 365 (Neb. 1898).
Shadwell v. Shadwell (1860) 9 CBNS 159.
Webb v. McGowin, 168 S 196 (Ala 1935).

BIBLIOGRAPHY

Atiyah, P.S. 1986. *Essays on Contract*. Oxford: Clarendon Press; reprinted 1990.

Eisenberg, M.A. 1979. Donative promises. *University of Chicago Law Review* 47: 1–33.

Eisenberg, M.A. 1982. The bargain principle and its limits. *Harvard Law Review* 95: 741–801.

Fellows, M.L. 1988. Donative promises redux. In *Property Law and Legal Education: Essays in honor of John E. Cribbet*, ed. P. Hay and M.H. Hoeflich, Urbana, IL: University of Illinois Press.

Fried, C. 1981. *Contract as Promise*. Cambridge, MA: Harvard University Press.

Fuller, L.L. 1941. Consideration and form. *Columbia Law Review* 41: 799–824.

Goetz, C.J. and Scott, R.E. 1980. Enforcing promises: an examination of the basis of contract. *Yale Law Journal* 89: 1261–322.

Kull, A. 1992. Reconsidering gratuitous promises. *Journal of Legal Studies* 21: 39–65.

Law Revision Committee. 1937. *Sixth Interim Report (Statute of Frauds and the Doctrine of Consideration)*. Cmd. 5449. London: His Majesty's Stationery Office.

von Mehren, A. 1982. A general view of contract. In *International Encyclopedia of Comparative Law* (fasc VII–1), Tübingen: J.C.B. Mohr (Paul Siebeck).

Posner, R.A. 1977. Gratuitous promises in economics and law. *Journal of Legal Studies* 6: 411–26.

Restatement (Second) of Contracts. 1981. St Paul, MN: American Law Institute.

Shavell, S. 1991. An economic analysis of altruism and deferred gifts. *Journal of Legal Studies* 20: 401–21.

Trebilcock, M.J. 1993. *The Limits of Freedom of Contract*. Cambridge, MA: Harvard University Press.

Treitel, G.H. 1962. *The Law of Contract*. London: Sweet & Maxwell; 8th edn, 1991.

Wessman, M.B. 1996. Retraining the gatekeeper: further reflections on the doctrine of consideration. *Loyola of Los Angeles Law Review* 29: 713–845.

Wright [Lord]. 1936. Ought the doctrine of consideration to be abolished from the common law? *Harvard Law Review* 49: 1225–53.

gun control. Firearms are more closely regulated than most other consumer products because of the hazard of accident and suicide that they pose to their owners, and, more important, the threat that they pose to others should they be put to criminal use. But the regulations on private ownership of firearms are controversial because of the beneficial uses of guns, which go beyond sport to include protection against crime. Indeed, many believe that the widespread ownership of firearms tends to deter criminals and even tyrants. Economic analysis cannot resolve this controversy, but provides a useful framework for analysing the likely effects of regulation on firearms commerce, and for structuring the public-interest debate. The economic perspective, by incorporating the full array of positive and negative consequences, differs substantially from either the public health approach, which focuses on the prevention of firearm injury but affords little interest in the benefits of guns, and the criminological perspective, which is chiefly concerned with the dissuasion or punishment of potential or actual gun offenders.

GUN USE AND MISUSE. Crime, particularly unjustified homicide, is the major concern associated with gun misuse, though accidents and suicides involving guns also warrant attention. In recent years in the United States there have been more than 30,000 firearm deaths annually; firearm suicides are slightly more frequent than firearm homicides, while gun accidents (which have been declining rather steadily in recent decades) account for less than 5% of the total. Males are much more likely than females to be the victim of a gun homicide or suicide. Older white males predominate among firearm suicides, while younger black males are the most likely homicide victims. Non-fatal firearm injuries are also quite significant; for every firearm fatality, there are three or more non-fatal shootings (Zawitz 1996). Fear of becoming a victim (intended or accidental) of a firearm attack must be reckoned another social cost associated with gun misuse.

Benefits associated with firearms arise from personal protection (or the perception of protection), hunting, target shooting, collecting, etc., as well as the use of firearms in certain professions, such as public and private security, animal slaughtering, vermin control and race starting. In some circles, conspicuous gun ownership or use may contribute to respect and social standing. Private gun ownership also provides a general deterrent against some types of crime.

REGULATING FIREARMS. An ideal gun control would reduce gun misuse, without any reduction (or possibly an expansion) in the beneficial uses of guns, and the control would be inexpensive to implement and enforce. Real-world regulations, however, present tradeoffs: rules that have the potential to reduce gun misuse may raise barriers to beneficial gun use, too, and could involve a complex or intrusive administration.

The economic approach to gun controls might initially suggest a direct regulatory strategy involving Pigovian taxes, in which the external costs and benefits from firearm use are internalized via appropriate taxes and subsidies. In practice, however, this 'punish the bad guys' strategy has serious shortcomings; most particularly, many gun users are effectively judgment-proof, either because they are not identified after an unjustified shooting or because they are unable to pay a compensatory fine (Cook and Leitzel 1996). For this reason, governments supplement *ex post* penalties for gun misuse with *ex ante* gun controls. Similar combinations of regulations are applied in many other regulatory domains involving health and safety. Examples of *ex ante* controls in other social spheres include driver licensing, workplace safety rules, food inspection, and some forms of environmental protection.

In the case of guns, controls can be placed on various pre-use aspects of firearm behaviour, such as production, sale, possession, or carrying. Typical *ex ante* controls take the form of bans on the possession of specific types of weapons, bars on ownership by groups of individuals (felons and children, say), and 'place and manner' ordinances that restrict firearm carrying or use in high-risk areas, such as public parks or congested urban areas. Such an array of regulatory discriminations among weapons, owners, and uses can be viewed as providing a rough form of an *ex ante* Pigovian tax, where higher controls are placed on those people, firearms, and intended applications that present higher expected external costs. Subsidies to the arming and firearm training of public police officers, whose firearm use is geared toward creating public benefits, is another aspect of this standard regulatory approach.

In analysing the impact of a gun regulation, an initial issue concerns whether the control will actually reduce the costs of gun crime. A common argument is that there will always be plenty of guns available informally (via black markets, say) to meet the demands of criminals, irrespective of the regulatory regime. Implicit in this logic is the notion either that criminals have a perfectly inelastic demand for firearms, or that regulations cannot raise the effective price of guns to criminals. The evidence, however, is that some regulations can be effective in reducing the quantity demanded of firearms. The introduction of a mandatory one-year prison sentence in Massachusetts in 1975 for any person convicted of carrying a gun without a licence apparently reduced, in the short run, the percentage of robberies and assaults that involved guns (Pierce and Bowers 1981). In locations that are policed intensively, such as inside prisons or aboard commercial aircraft, gun availability is minuscule. Some controls can effectively, though not perfectly, limit firearm availability, even to relatively determined individuals. Nor should it be assumed that high-risk gun users are particularly determined in acquiring guns. Teenage criminals often go long periods without guns, and most robberies in the US do not involve firearms, despite the advantages of guns in enforcing compliance during a robbery attempt (Cook 1991; Cook, Molliconi and Cole 1995). In one study of juvenile offenders in Atlanta, more than half of those who had owned a gun acquired their first gun passively, in an unplanned fashion (Ash et al. 1996).

If *ex ante* controls dissuade criminals or other potential firearm misusers from acquiring or using guns, there remains the issue of what these individuals choose to do as an alternative. It is possible that they will still carry out their activity, substituting other weapons that are equally deadly, or, in the extreme case, weapons that entail even higher social costs. Broadly speaking, however, violent encounters that do not involve a firearm tend to be significantly less deadly than those in which a gun is involved. Zimring's (1968) analysis of Chicago-area violent assaults, for instance, found that a gun attack was five times more likely than a knife attack to result in a fatality.

Concerns with weapon substitution might be most germane with respect to controls that apply to only one type of gun, and thereby could induce a substitution to a more deadly firearm. Effective handgun controls, for example, could result in a shift by criminals towards the use of shotguns, which can be more deadly at close range (Kleck 1984). Concealability of a weapon, however, tends to be very important for the type of crimes committed in public areas, muting any potential substitution to long guns. The general structure of firearm controls (including *ex post* penalties), which typically attempts to control high social-cost firearms most closely, also tends to restrict the potential for the creation of perverse incentives for criminals to substitute more dangerous weapons in the face of controls targeted at a subset of firearms.

A control that is effective in reducing the availability of guns to high-risk users, and that does not induce undesirable weapon substitution, must still be examined for its impact on low-risk users. Opponents of gun controls frequently point out that controls might disproportionally affect law-abiding citizens. If low-risk users are differentially disarmed, and if this disarmament is a sufficient spur to criminal activity, then crime, particularly burglary, could increase following 'effective' gun control. Of course, many controls, such as background checks on buyers or licensing and oversight of dealers, hold little potential to restrict the access of law-abiding citizens to guns. Nor is it clear that possession of a firearm for defensive purposes offers a particularly good option for many individuals, when traded-off against the increased risk of gun suicide, accident and even homicide, that seems to accompany firearm ownership (Kellermann et al. 1992, 1993). In any case, all else equal, a gun control will be more desirable to the extent that it is better targeted, in the sense of protecting the desirable uses for guns while limiting the socially costly uses.

THE US AND THE UK. The relative costs and benefits of gun availability will differ among countries, or among regions of a single country, and so the optimal firearm regulatory regime will also vary. Consider, for example, a ban on handguns. In the US, handguns are quite prevalent, with approximately one-quarter of households owning at least one handgun, and a total stock of perhaps 70 million. In the UK, by contrast, only 200,000 handguns were legally in private hands in 1996, predominantly held by sports people engaged in target shooting. An effective ban on handguns in the United States, then, would impose costs on a wide cross-section of individuals, many of whom own handguns for personal protection. In the UK, however, a ban (or a partial ban on handguns above .22 calibre, as was adopted in early 1997) imposes direct costs on a relatively small and identifiable group, who can be compensated for the ban. Further, the black market for guns, which is supplied in substantial measure by diversions (theft or otherwise) from the legal stock, is much smaller and perhaps easier to contain via policing than in the relatively gun-saturated US.

All else equal, it appears that a high prevalence of guns is accompanied by higher social costs from violent activity, relative to low firearm prevalence. This is not to say that more guns implies more violence, a counterexample being the combination of high-gun prevalence and low violence in some rural areas of the US; rather, the violence that does take place will tend to be more deadly. 'The serious assault rate in the United States is about 30% greater than in England. The homicide rate is 530% greater' (Zimring 1995: 8, footnote omitted). Further, the much greater firearm availability in the US appears to be responsible for much of the difference in levels of deadly violence. About 70 per cent of US murders in 1995 involved a firearm, as opposed to only 10 per cent in the UK. More generally, there is a substantial positive correlation internationally between gun prevalence and homicide (Killias 1993), though there is no simple and invariant causal relationship linking an increase in guns with an increase in homicide or other crime.

GUN PREVALENCE AND POLICY. Consideration of the US and the UK suggests that even with similar levels of violence, there might exist fairly distinct low-gun prevalence and high-gun prevalence 'equilibria'. The optimal regulatory policies in a low-gun equilibrium can be expected to differ markedly from those appropriate in areas where gun ownership is widespread. Employing epidemiological terminology, the appropriate intervention in situations that have not gone through an epidemic of gun violence will focus on prevention, while in situations in which the 'disease' is already widespread, mitigation of the costs of the infection takes on increased prominence.

One difficulty with trying to maintain a low-gun prevalence society is that such a situation, in the absence of regulation, may be inherently unstable. An exogenous increase in gun ownership or violence by certain groups (drug dealers, perhaps) can set off an arms race, by increasing the incentives for others to acquire more and better guns (Philipson and Posner 1996). Strict firearm controls, then, to the extent that they can support the reasonable belief that others are not armed with firearms, might be required to prevent transition to the high gun prevalence situation. Alternatively, in situations that are already marked by high levels of gun prevalence and violence, an attempt to increase the severity of gun controls will be less able to convince individuals that others have been effectively disarmed, if for no other reason than the informal market is likely to be larger and more difficult to suppress. The imposition of stricter controls in high prevalence areas, then, could paradoxically be less beneficial than in relatively low-gun crime situations. While perhaps more difficult to implement successfully, however, strict controls in high prevalence areas are not doomed to failure, as the success of airport metal detectors and some police stop-and-search campaigns indicate.

The experiences in the US and the UK seem to reflect the difference between regulating high- and low-gun prevalence situations. In recent decades, the UK has employed much stricter controls than the US, and has a much smaller stock of firearms (approximately two million legally-owned weapons in 1995, including shotguns). The number of legally owned weapons in the UK has fallen considerably in recent decades, whereas the US stock, now on the order of 200 million guns, has risen significantly in the past forty years. Indeed, annual additions to the US stock, some 4.5 million guns per year, easily exceed the entire supply in Britain. Following the shooting deaths of sixteen children and their teacher in Dunblane, Scotland, in March 1996, the UK moved to ban all handguns above .22 calibre, and to restrict the remaining handguns to storage at approved target ranges. With only 60,000 legal handgun owners (who were partially compensated for their newly banned weapons), and a small amount of crime conducted with illegally owned guns, this new restriction received strong support across the political spectrum. As handguns have not been legitimate weapons for personal protection in Britain, there was almost no concern that the new laws would lead to more violence against law-abiding citizens. (It should be noted that the distinction between criminals and law-abiding citizens is not absolute and eternal; both the Dunblane massacre, and a 1987 attack in the English town of Hungerford that took seventeen lives including the gunman's, were carried out by legal gun owners.)

In the United States, on the other hand, the relatively high gun-crime setting increases the perceived need by some law-abiding citizens for firearms for personal protection. One response in recent years has been a trend towards liberalized state laws governing the conditions under which citizens can legally carry concealed firearms. The impact of these liberalizations on crime, and more generally, the effectiveness and prevalence of firearm use for defensive purposes, are very contentious issues in current US firearms research (Guns and Violence Symposium 1995; Lott and Mustard 1997; Black and Nagin 1998). Such issues are well beyond the range of firearm public policy debates in the UK, just as the British policy of banning handguns above .22 calibre seems significantly more restrictive than any US federal legislation is likely to be for the foreseeable future. Again, these divergent policies can be traced to the different approaches required to maintain existing low-gun violence, versus controlling the costs of violence with high-gun prevalence. A handgun ban (and even the limited firearm carrying by police officers) in the UK can be useful in preventing an arms race, whereas such a ban in the US would be widely viewed as a disarmament pact between law-abiding citizens and criminals, where the citizens may well doubt whether the criminals would either have the intention or face the compulsion to abide by the terms of the 'treaty'.

BLACK MARKETS. Of course, criminals in the UK need not feel compelled to abide by a handgun ban, but the general unavailability of weapons is such that few of them are likely to acquire handguns in the face of a ban (just as few did so prior to the ban). An important determinant of the effectiveness of gun controls that attempt to lessen firearm availability to high-risk individuals, then, is the readiness with which firearms can be acquired outside the regulated arena by such individuals. What determines the size of the black market for guns? Because most of the informal supply originates in the domestic formal sector (home-produced firearms and smuggled imports being exceptions), the size of the formal sector is one factor. In particular, theft of firearms is quite common. In the US, where there is no safe-storage requirement for legal gun ownership, some half a million firearms are stolen annually.

Other leakages outside the formal sector also fuel black-market firearms supplies. In the United States, while transfers from dealers to gun consumers are regulated, further transfers between individuals are, in practice, almost entirely unregulated, though it is illegal knowingly to transfer a gun to a felon or a handgun to a youth. (This is in stark contrast to Britain, where transfers among individuals are subject to the same legal requirements as transfers from dealers.) As a result, the informal market offers fairly ready access of firearms to criminals. Thus, gun control measures are unlikely to greatly restrict the availability of guns to high-risk users unless this gaping regulatory loophole is closed, perhaps by requiring all transfers of firearms to be routed through dealers and their record-keeping requirements. Other gateways to the informal market can be reduced in scope as well. For example, the state of Virginia enacted a 'one gun a month' rule limiting individuals to at most a single handgun purchase per month, a law which appears to have had a fairly major impact on the extent to which Virginia serves as a source of black-market supply to more tightly regulated areas such as New York City (Weil and Knox 1996). Policing the black market directly, and back-tracing guns used in crimes, are other areas where increased efforts in the US could put pressure on the extent of informal gun markets.

In both the US and the UK, detailed information about the nature of the black market is extremely scarce, despite its importance as a factor in the outcome of gun control measures. Experience with bans on other commodities, such as drugs or alcohol, is sometimes culled for strategies to disrupt the black market for guns (Koper and Reuter 1996), or, alternatively, offered as evidence of the futility of attempted restrictions on supply. Because firearms are durable goods, repeat black market purchases do not feature as prominently as they do for drugs. Much of the black market trade is presumably itinerant, as when a thief steals a gun and sells it to an acquaintance. This suggests that disruption efforts should be aimed at preventing the initial flow (e.g., the theft) into the informal market, and at relatively well-organized sources of black market supply, such as registered dealers who also engage in off-the-books trade.

THE SECOND AMENDMENT. The United States is unique in that the Second Amendment to the Constitution relates to firearms. It reads: 'A well regulated Militia, being necessary to the security of a free State, the right of the people to keep and bear Arms, shall not be infringed.' The meaning of this amendment is the subject of continuing debate, most notably concerning whether the right to arms is an individual or a collective right (Kates 1984). As with other constitutional protections, however, the right to keep and bear arms is not absolute, and no federal gun control measure has ever been found unconstitutional by the Supreme Court on Second Amendment grounds. Nevertheless, opponents of US gun controls frequently invoke the Second Amendment, and it could be interpreted in future court decisions to rule out some restrictive legislation. Further, the concern that is often claimed to underlie the amendment, that an unarmed population would have no protection against governmental tyranny, would be just as relevant irrespective of constitutional interpretation. It is hard to know how to account for this concern in the cost–benefit calculus with respect to a given gun control, however, or how a given control might contribute to the Constitutional intentions of ensuring domestic tranquility and promoting the general welfare.

POTENTIAL SOURCES OF CHANGE. The technology of offensive and defensive weapons has changed dramatically over the centuries, and there is no reason to expect that this evolution will not continue. In recent years, for instance, there has been a marked shift by criminals in the US towards the use of semiautomatic pistols and away from revolvers. As firearm technology evolves, the appropriate regulatory apparatus will also change. Technology already exists whereby firearms could be discharged only by a given individual, who would be identified by fingerprints or a special ring worn on the finger. If this were to become a standard feature of guns (whether by mandate or otherwise), accidents would likely be reduced, as would the usefulness of stolen guns. Improvements in non-fatal alternatives to firearms, such as stun guns or pepper sprays, might provide the same ease of use and similar ability to control a potentially violent encounter as would a gun, and at much lower social cost. The regulatory environment could then shift to promote substitution to such relatively benign alternatives, both by criminals and defensive users. Another potential source of change involves detection technology, which could improve and become less intrusive, thereby making it easier to assure individuals of a firearm-free environment in a wider range of circumstances than is currently available at reasonable cost. Alternatively, firearms themselves could become less detectable, and render much of current detection technology useless. Improved data collection and processing to better identify individuals who are ineligible for firearm ownership could have a substantial impact on the nature of an optimal regulatory regime, as would a large change in the availability and effectiveness of *ex post* sanctions.

Whatever the nature of future changes, it is likely that *ex ante* firearm controls will continue to be seen as desirable in many settings. Nor are the basic principles likely to change: restrictions will be more severe on those firearms, users, and intended applications that present the highest social costs relative to their benefits. Within a family or a small group of people, efforts are made to keep children and other high-risk individuals away from dangerous commodities. Within the larger community, public measures aimed at firearms can usefully serve a similar end.

PHILIP J. COOK AND JAMES A. LEITZEL

See also DRUG PROHIBITION; GANGS AND THE STATE OF NATURE; JUDGMENT-PROOFNESS; OCCUPATIONAL HEALTH AND SAFETY REGULATION; PUBLIC ENFORCEMENT OF LAW.

Subject classification: 5e; 6d(iii).

BIBLIOGRAPHY

Ash, P. et al. 1996. Gun acquisition and use by juvenile offenders. *Journal of the American Medical Association* 275: 1754–8.

Black, D.A. and Nagin, D.S. 1998. Do 'right-to-carry' laws deter violent crime? *Journal of Legal Studies* 27 (forthcoming).

Cook, P.J. and Leitzel, J.A. 1996. 'Perversity, futility, jeopardy': an economic analysis of the attack on gun control. *Law and Contemporary Problems* 59: 91–118.

Cook, P.J., Molliconi, S. and Cole, T.B. 1995. Regulating gun markets. *Journal of Criminal Law and Criminology* 86: 59–92.

Guns and Violence Symposium. 1995. *Journal of Criminal Law and Criminology* 86(1).

Kates, D.B., Jr. 1984. Handgun prohibition and the original meaning of the Second Amendment. *Michigan Law Review* 82: 204–73.

Kellermann, A.L. et al. 1992. Suicide in the home in relation to gun ownership. *New England Journal of Medicine* 327: 467–72.

Kellermann, A.L. et al. 1993. Gun ownership as a risk factor for homicide in the home. *New England Journal of Medicine* 329: 1084–91.

Killias, M. 1993. Gun ownership, suicide, and homicide: an international perspective. In *Understanding Crime and Experiences of Crime and Crime Control*, ed. A. del Frate, U. Zvekic and J.J.M. van Dijk., UNICRI Publication No. 49, Rome: UNICRI.

Kleck, G. 1984. Handgun-only gun control: a policy disaster in the making. In *Firearms and Violence: Issues of Public Policy*, ed. D.B. Kates, San Francisco: Pacific Institute for Public Policy Research; Cambridge, MA: Ballinger Publishing Co.

Koper, C.S. and Reuter, P. 1996. Suppressing illegal gun markets: lessons from drug enforcement. *Law and Contemporary Problems* 59: 119–46.

Lott, J.R., Jr. and Mustard, D.B. 1997. Crime, deterrence, and right-to-carry concealed handguns. *Journal of Legal Studies* 26: 1–68.

Philipson, T.J. and Posner, R.A. 1996. The economic epidemiology of crime. *Journal of Law and Economics* 39: 405–33.

Pierce, G. and Bowers, W. 1981. The Bartley–Fox gun law's short-term impact on crime in Boston. *Annals of the American Academy of Political and Social Science* 455: 120–37.

Weil, D.S. and Knox, R.C. 1996. Effects of limiting handgun purchases on interstate transfer of firearms. *Journal of the American Medical Association* 275: 1759–61.

Zawitz, M.W. 1996. Firearm injury from crime: firearms, crime, and criminal justice: selected findings. US Department of Justice, Office of Justice Programs, Bureau of Justice Statistics, NCJ-160093, Washington, DC.

Zimring, F.E. 1968. Is gun control likely to reduce violent killings? *University of Chicago Law Review* 35: 21–37.

Zimring, F.E. 1995. Reflections on firearms and the criminal law. *Journal of Criminal Law and Criminology* 86: 1–9.

H

Hadley v. Baxendale. *See* BREACH REMEDIES; CONTRACTS; RELATIONAL CONTRACT.

Hand formula. *See* LEARNED HAND RULE.

harmonization of law in the European Union. Harmonization of the law, in Europe and elsewhere, can be a theory-driven process in which law and economics research can play an important role. With the example of a recent German case, the waterpenny case, and an established piece of legislation, the Civil Code, it may be shown that economic reasoning can enter into the process of jurisdiction, as well as legislation. Broader lessons can be drawn from these studies.

I. THE GERMAN WATERPENNY CASE: A PARADIGM FOR THE EMERGING COMMON LAW OF EUROPE. Sometimes, arcane cases come before the high courts and require a specific ruling. The German waterpenny case (*Bundes Verfassungs Gerichts Entscheidung*, Gen. 413/88 and 1300/93) is such an instance. At stake was not just the issue of who would ultimately have to bear the costs of using artificial fertilizer that may contaminate groundwater. Rather, in settling this issue the court faced a decision space of uncertainty and had to settle a basic issue on which an entire system of rulings settling liability claims would have to rely in the future. The decision space was one of uncertainty and not risk (see Knight 1921) because neither the set of conceivable outcomes nor the attributable probabilities could be known beforehand. Even the legal system in which the ruling would ultimately serve as a precedent was no longer known since the German constitutional court, like other highest courts within the European Union, now operates in the context of harmonization attempts that link the different legal systems of Member States – as well as of those aspiring to become members – to one another. There is substantial pressure toward a convergence of these legal systems, when by architecture and built-in procedures they operate according to different rhythms. Ultimately, common features and traits will become apparent, and these will be principles that may not have guided any single decision of courts or other rule makers but may be able to further understanding of the decisions and rules as if these had been guided by them.

Europe is an area with many different jurisdictions. The attempts at harmonization of law have focused on legislated law rather than on the free movement of legal professionals, still less on understanding how law is being made in the different constituent parts of the European Union. In this context, it has been suggested (see Kötz 1992) that the American example be followed and economic analysis employed as a unifying framework. In particular, law and economics as a subdiscipline of economics may provide such a unifying ingredient. The more European lawyers, attorneys, barristers, prosecutors and judges as well as the rule-drafting civil servants think in terms of law and economics concepts, the easier it will be for them to settle their differences, sharp as those may be in particular cases.

II. ANTECEDENTS: THE ORIGINS OF THE GERMAN CIVIL CODE. The issue of legal harmonization is not new in Europe. Outstanding examples are the great codifications, such as the *Code Civil de Napoléon* and the German Civil Code. The German Civil Code can actually even be considered an explicit attempt at efficient legislation. The Civil Code was, in its ultimate form, passed with the explicit input of the leading economists of their time in Germany, and based on explicit economic reasoning. How this came about is worth recounting briefly.

In 1848, when the first German democratic parliament convened in the Church of St Paul in Frankfurt, there were no less than 56 different legal systems governing bills of exchange. This exceeded by far the number of Member States of the German Federation at that time. It was obvious that such splintering of the legal system stood in the way of the rapidly developing market economy, and the Frankfurt parliament attempted to initiate a common German Civil Code as well as a Commercial Code. However, the parliament had a short life, and dissolved before it had even seriously started the task. There were new initiatives in 1866 and 1869 in the northern German Federation, the precursor of the Reich, but only after the unification of the German states as a confederation of principalities in 1871 could the task be resumed, and this happened with initiatives in 1873 in both the imperial parliament and the imperial council (the representation of the confederated princes). In 1874 the pre-commission of five members was established, and in the same year a commission of eleven was established under the chairmanship of Pape. This commission issued a report in 1887, and the Act of Introduction with various drafts of bylaws was issued in 1887 and 1889 to provide for a broad discussion. However, Gustav (von) Schmoller, the editor of the leading economics journal in Germany at the time, the *Jahrbücher für Gesetzgebung, Verwaltung und Volkwirtschaft im deutschen Reich* (Annals of Legislation, Administration and Political Economy in Germany), together with his colleagues in the German Economics Association (*Verein für Socialpolitik*), agreed that the draft was impractical because it did not build on established economic practices and their respective legal counterparts, rather providing a deductively reasoned set of norms based on the Roman law tradition, and hence not corresponding to the economic practices of a developed industrialized market economy. Entire issues of the journal were devoted to critiques of the draft act, the articles by Otto (von) Gierke having the strongest influence. This unsolicited advice led in 1890 to the establishment of a second commission which provided a completely revised draft Code in 1895 and this was duly passed, after stormy discussions in the imperial parliament, on 1 July 1896 with 222 votes in favour and 48 against, on 4 July in the imperial council, and ratified by the Emperor on 18 October. The Code took effect on 1 January 1900. With numerous smaller revisions, it has remained unchanged since. This episode illustrates that efficient legislation is possible, although it also demonstrates that had the economics profession not intervened, legislation would probably have been imposed that would have burdened the German economy with high and persisting transactions costs. The Code would not have become the export article it proved to become, to the present date.

III. REPRISE: THE WATERPENNY CASE CONTINUED. Instead of harmonizing law by codification, the German waterpenny case, which not only vindicates the Coase theorem as a conceivable tenet of legislation, but also deals with a problem recurring in every one of the Member States of the European Union, provides a good example for showing how the theory-driven process of harmonization of European law could take place without infringing on the sovereignty of any one Member State. Hence, European legal harmonization may not only result in but may even require efficiency in statute law.

When the waterpenny decision was published, there was an outburst of popular discontent with the constitutional court (see, e.g., *Frankfurter Allgemeine Zeitung*, 1996). Rarely has the constitutional court been so harshly criticized in the popular press (with only one recent instance rivalling the waterpenny commotion, when the court ruled on the separation of church and state). The farmers were said to be dumping their 'poison' on the fields, and now they were being bribed to impose less harm on the natural resource of water. Under the cloak of the market economy, this political instrument appeared, in violation of the 'polluter pays principle', 'a late ['*spät*'] victory of Lothar Späth, but defeat of reason'. (Lothar Späth had been the Prime Minister of the state of Baden Württemberg where the waterpenny was initiated at the behest of economists from the University of Constance. The Prime Minister had later resigned over a travel funding dispute and started a new career as a promoter of industrial development in the new federal state of Thuringia.) In the face of such steamy rhetoric, it is probably worth considering the case itself. It had been brought by water authorities in Baden Württemberg and Hesse against the states of Baden Württemberg and Hesse (separately), claiming violation of the Federal constitution in Baden Württemberg. For extracting groundwater, water authorities had been charged between one and ten pfennings per cubic meter, in Hesse between ten and fifty pfennigs, eventually one Mark per cubic meter.

The total revenue from these levies amounted to between 145 and 165 million German Marks per year in Baden Württemberg and between 25 million German Marks and eventually 160 million German Marks in Hesse. The water authorities claimed violation of articles 2.1 Basic Law (general guarantee of freedom and personal integrity), 3.1 (equality), 12.1 (freedom of choice of profession and line of business), 14.1 (guarantee of private property), as well as procedural violations. Violation of article 12 had been claimed only by the paper industry, which had joined the suit.

A definitional issue blurs a clear cut analysis of the case. Under German law, there is a difference between *fees* charged for specific services rendered by a public institution, *special charges* levied for specific purposes, *taxes* and *prices*. Roughly speaking, fees (*Gebühren*) require specific services rendered and in general have to mirror in value the benefit provided or the costs of the provision. The revenues from charges (*Abgaben*) have to be committed to the specific purpose for which they are levied, i.e. they have to be earmarked. Taxes (*Steuern*) are levied for the general fund with no specific offsetting benefit granted, while prices (*Preise*) are subject to the forces of supply and demand. Under this terminology, the states could not levy a tax for lack of competence, the water charges could not qualify as fees or prices, nor could they qualify as special charges (*Sonderabgaben*) because the beneficiaries were not identical to the stated purpose. Most of the argument revolves around these definitional issues, through which the court cut by stating that the traditional notions and definitions were irrelevant and only the function of the policy instrument had to be considered in the light of their guarantees and protections provided by the fiscal constitution (Statement (*Leitsatzt*) 1). Secondly, the court decided that water as a natural resource was a common property, and using it created a specific advantage which could be taxed away (*Abschöpfen*) either in part or in whole.

On several occasions, the court explicitly cites 'economists' and 'economics' and even uses economic jargon, such as 'externalities', 'market failure' and functional instruments to 'internalize' external costs. It cites incentive effects of the waterpenny and legislative discretion between different functional instruments. Finally, the court emphasizes the care that the legislatures have taken in preparing the legislation in Baden Württemberg and Hesse, relying on experts in environmental economics and environmental law and the overwhelming consensus of these experts in drafting their respective legislation. This is not the first time economics has taken a prominent position in German law. Harmonization of law can also be effected through legislation, and here again economics can play an important function, as the previously discussed legislation of the Civil Code suggests [sect. II].

From an economic point of view, the implications of the waterpenny legislation in Baden Württemberg and Hesse are clear enough. The ecological problem of reducing water pollution through fertilizer use can clearly and effectively be addressed by subsidizing the farmers and taxing the water authorities, a standard economic solution. However, the polluter pays principle is being invoked from an equity point of view. Although the waterpenny levied on the water authorities and generating the subsidy to the farmers is not more burdensome to the consumers of water than the zero alternative which involves high costs of water cleaning, the polluter pays principle is charged with political overtones that defy standard public finance analysis and belong to those political premises that the economic analyst has to take for granted. From the point of view of legal harmonization, the relevant theoretical aspects involve the position of the Coase theorem in jurisdiction, a specific economic theory of institutions developed by the court under the name of a theory of functions, and the doctrine of legislative due care.

IV. EXTERNALITIES AND MARKET FAILURE. With this decision, the constitutional court in Karlsruhe has juxtaposed the economic principles of neoclassical public finance with the received doctrine that served to classify public revenues. By buying into modern public finance, which is a dogmatic system by itself, the court has substituted for an old dogmatic system – the old classificatory doctrine of public revenues that had strong public law underpinnings – the modern theory of public finance as it has emerged consequent to the development of the theory of market failure (see Bator 1958). From the point of view of constitutional legal doctrine, this juxtaposition did not require any particular change in methods. One economic system can serve as well as another, so long as there is a linkage that can translate the economic notions into legal ones. That linkage is provided by the theory of functions which the court has been using for some two decades now in the most diverse subareas of constitutional litigation.

V. THE THEORY OF FUNCTIONS. For many years now, the court has developed the theory of functions (of legal institutions or legal arrangements) that serves as a port of entry for almost any kind of a scientific argument into its jurisdiction, much as the Brandeis brief does in the United States (see Senn 1998). The court has had ample opportunity to test this theory, since the German constitution has been broadly conceived and can be interpreted and tested as serving to protect many specific institutions. For instance, such institutions as capital markets, labour markets, collective bargaining and its equilibrating forces, private property, vested rights of university scholars in their traditional forms of research, corporate forms such as joint stock companies, limited liability companies, limited liability companies on shares, etc., to name only a few, are all protected under the constitution in their basic viability. The doctrine of viability which serves as the standard test that the court uses in order to judge the constitutionality of particular acts of parliament requires that the basic function of the institution in question not be impaired. A rule passes muster before the constitution if the institution in question, such as a corporation under the codetermination act, to name just one example, is still viable after application and implementation of the act under review. In order to determine whether an institution is viable under changed conditions, one has to determine first what constitutes its viability, i.e. in the notions of the court, what is its function. If, for instance, the function of the corporation is held to be that capital owners have a chance to invest and earn a return on their capital that reflects both the scarcity of capital and their business acumen, and to give workers a chance to be employed in a particular community, then these three functions must be possible to be discharged even after any rule has been imposed and without major impediments in the sense that such impediments cannot be overcome by the kind of management that can be expected to run such a corporation. Likewise, and to move the discussion closer to the case at hand, a specific public revenue source may be said to have the function to fulfil the revenue needs of a specific public institution that is dedicated to a specific need (*Anstalt*), and then the doctrine has to serve the purpose of protecting both the institution in terms of its revenue needs and the captive customers of the institution from overcharging. This is the reason for the dogmatic theory of revenue sources that the court cut through for the case at hand. It argued, instead, that a Pigovian tax (the court did not use that term) is not a revenue seeking instrument of taxation but rather an incentive oriented instrument to seek a particular response on the part of the taxpayer, and hence it falls outside the received doctrine. Then the purpose must be to show that the function of affecting those incentives in the desired manner can well be accomplished by the instrument used and in the way the instrument is being used. Hence, if the desired purpose is to reduce reliance on the natural resource of water by reducing water consumption, and if it can be shown that a water charge imposed on the water authorities and passed along to the customers serves that purpose, then this specific fiscal instrument can be considered functional and it therefore passes the constitutional test.

Yet a popular sentiment insists that the waterpenny flies in the face of the 'polluter pays principle' and therefore violates the most basic principle of civil law. Of this, the court had to find an answer in terms of its theory of functions, which it did. Nothing in the theory of Pigovian taxes implies that the charges levied on those whose behaviour imposes externalities on others have to benefit those very inducers of externalities, nor need they be used for otherwise containing harm resulting from the externalities. Under Pigovian doctrine the revenues from the charges, if they occur, can be used for any purpose. The point of the Pigovian levy is to correct for an externality. Pigou cuts through the link made by Wicksell (1896) always to consider public outlays and public revenues together as one and only one decision. So the court argues correctly that it is within the discretion of the government to levy the charge, and it is likewise within the discretion of the government to use the resulting revenue according to its policies. Furthermore, the court argues that if a programme can be designed that uses the revenues so as to further the policies envisaged, nothing in the test of functionality prevents a government from pursuing that course.

It is here that the Coase theorem enters. The 'polluter pays principle' does not make a distinction between allocation and distribution in an economy. The agent who 'causes' an externality is responsible in the sense of being liable, that is he is responsible for correcting the allocation of resources as well as the resulting redistribution of income or wealth. The Coase theorem, instead, makes the standard distinction in economics that separates issues of the allocation of resources from issues of income or wealth. In order to achieve this result for the waterpenny, that is, in order to reject the argument that the consumers who ultimately bear the burden of the waterpenny – private households, industrial corporations, etc. – should also somehow benefit from the charge intended to reduce water consumption, the court has to disconnect the allocation part: creating incentives for prudent water use; from the distribution aspect: who benefits from the revenues of the waterpenny? Since the Coase theorem is the vehicle for this argument, the court invokes the consensus among economists (the assumption by the court was correct: Ronald H. Coase had received the Nobel Prize in economics about when the litigation started) and through its theory of functions applies the Coase theorem to the waterpenny case.

By using the theory of functionality as a vehicle to introduce the evidence from social sciences into jurisprudence and notably the jurisdiction of the constitutional court, the court runs the risk of using theoretical results that have not been sufficiently corroborated. The results from social science research are, of course, always subject to the caveat that (1) conditions may change and (2) the evidence may simply have been misleading and what appeared to have been a thorough result, for instance, may rather be the result of spurious correlations.

While some courts in the United States have strongly relied on even recent social science research results in ordering strong measures (the bussing decisions on the basis of James Coleman's research being one particularly conspicuous example), the German constitutional court has been more circumspect in designing a test with a specific consequence. It is here that the notion of legislative due care (*Sorgfaltspflicht des Gesetzgebers*) comes in.

VI. LEGISLATIVE DUE CARE. Repeatedly, the German constitutional court has offered this reasoning in upholding controversial legislation. The instance was probably pioneered when the University Constitution Act was challenged, and it was perfected when the Codetermination Act of 1976 was under review. In such instances, when a specific arrangement due to a rule, an act or the composite result of different rules, acts, rulings etc. results in a specific, clearly circumscribed outcome, and parties claim to be violated in their basic rights, the functional test as described above for the institution in question is applied. For instance, it could and has been argued that the waterpenny makes it impossible for the Hessian paper industry to compete fairly in international paper markets, against foreign competition to supply the big printing locations in Frankfurt. Against this has to be weighed the concern for water conservation which can, so the functional argument for the waterpenny goes, be accomplished by on the one hand discouraging water use by end consumers and on the other hand discouraging water pollution by farmers through fertilizers and (possibly) pesticides. Yet, what if farmers cannot be discouraged from polluting groundwater, and end consumers cannot be discouraged from using ever increasing amounts of water, with water authorities being rendered unable to make ends meet and fulfil their functions? In that case, the court has consistently argued, the factual evidence on which the decision rested, that has been introduced through the functionality theory, is erroneous; and consequently, the decision may be (but also may not be) erroneous as well since *ex falso quodlibet*! In that case, and if the institution in question can clearly not perform the function attributed to it by the legislation and the court, it is the duty of the legislature to correct the act of parliament. (If parliament does not re-enact, the court will correct the law by substituting it through its ruling.) The German parliament had repeatedly (but not often) to work under this regimen.

This requirement to correct an erroneous act of parliament is to my knowledge, as far as constitutional courts go, an invention of the judges in Karlsruhe. It is an interesting fruit of the eternal German *Werturteilstreit*, the struggle over the meaning of different scholarly methods, and it is the ultimate corrective on the doors swung wide open to introduce social science evidence into jurisdiction. The requirement to correct erroneous legislation opens the door as wide as possible to introduce empirical social science evidence. Yet, it provides its own regulator in imposing a duty of correction on the parliament. Who would want to repeal his own legislation because of factual errors about its consequences? Given the requirement of erroneously based acts of parliament to be subject to review, and given the traditional emphasis on certainty in the law that characterizes every Western legal system, the court designed a doctrine of due legislative care in order to safeguard against sudden reversals of jurisdiction and legislation. In addition to considering the constitutionality of a particular arrangement such as an act of parliament, a directive, European legislation involving German persons (legal or personal), lower court rulings or administrative rulings, the constitutional court has designed a two pronged procedure to allow social science evidence into the law.

On the one hand, through the theory of functions, almost any type of respectable social science result can enter right into the decisions of the court. This is even the case for feminist jurisprudence so long as it is scholarly. The current president of the court promotes this course. On the other hand, the court has always insisted, and consistently does so, that legislatures, when introducing social science evidence into their considerations as they should, should also take due care in not glossing over the evidence and being circumspect in gathering enough of it. Hence, particularly when far-reaching decisions have to be taken and much evidence mounted by either side before the parliament and its committees, the court raises the standard of legislative care in requiring extensive hearings prior to the legislation. That is, if any parliament, either one of the sixteen constituent federal states or the federal parliament itself, wishes to pass an act of legislation that can be expected to be challenged in front of the constitutional court, that parliament now has to engage in an extensive procedure of fact finding and hearings prior to legislating, just in order to make sure that the act under controversy will survive before the constitutional court, of course always under the proviso that the evidence does not overwhelmingly change.

Hence, by on the one hand lowering the threshold for

admissible evidence and on the other opening the doors for social science research results, the court at the same time has increased the threshold of evidence on the legislatures by forcing them to consider and divulge that same social science evidence beforehand. This may be the wider implication of the functionality theory for German jurisdictions. It amounts to a strong emphasis on background law and a severe discouragement of deal law.

By upholding the waterpenny legislation of the states of Baden Württemberg and Hesse, the court, from the point of view of legal harmonization, did three things: it first introduced the Coase theorem explicitly into jurisdiction and thereby opened the door for other aspects of economic analysis to follow; secondly, it reaffirmed its theory of functions implying that legislation can be criticized from a transactions cost and property rights point of view if it can be shown that it renders economically relevant institutions operationally inefficient; and thirdly, the theory of legislative due care reaffirms a type of liability for legislatures that do not adhere to this quality standard with legal consequences of remedial requirements.

VII. EUROPEAN IMPLICATIONS. From a European point of view, the musings of the German constitutional court over the implications of the provisions of the German Basic Law of 1949 may appear to be rather immaterial. What is the law in Kehl may not necessarily be the law across the River Rhine in Strasbourg. Yet, the specific approach taken by the court in interpreting this Basic Law, the main provisions of which can, by the way, also be found in various European treaties, by far exceeds the boundaries of the German territories. First of all, legal doctrine is also a scholarly discipline that is internationally interconnected. The so-called German *Rechtskreis* also includes Greece and most of the Central European countries in transition. So, *nolens volens*, German legal doctrine enters the doctrine of other European states as well. These states are members of the Council of Europe, and in that capacity they also influence the process of European legal harmonization. Others are members of the European Union and in that capacity they enter their concepts into the process of European harmonization in law.

A more important because less obvious element needs to be emphasized. The law in any country deals with the behaviour of people, and the social sciences have only in the last one hundred years taken a meteoric rise, while law as a scholarly discipline is several thousand years old. This scholarly confrontation has been met in different ways by different legal systems, but the American system with the Brandeis brief and the German system with the theory of functionality have been particularly open to social science research. Social science itself is international, and social scientists are competing internationally, subjecting their research to international scrutiny as it appears. Hence, social science research is becoming ever more powerful as an element of the set of data anyone, and therefore also a judge, needs to consider. The legal doctrine that gains a lead will be one that finds a way to systematically integrate social science research into jurisdiction without compromising the core of the body of the law. With its pioneering decisions, of which the waterpenny case is only one, the German constitutional court has shown how this integration can be accomplished without doing damage to the core of the law. In doing this, the court, of course, does not export German jurisprudence in the sense of the specific relevant stipulations of German legislation, including the Basic Law, into other countries undergoing the same process of harmonization; what it exports is the specific method that is at variance with, for instance, the French method of jurisprudence that is based more strongly on Latin doctrine and emphasizes specific notions and their interpretation. The dispute over the classification of taxes is a very good point of illustration, as in that area Germany used largely to follow French administrative legal doctrine.

In opening this door to social science, and also providing for the requisite safeguards that any high court needs to maintain when admitting uncontrollable streams of evidence, the court necessarily opted for those social sciences that have the strongest evidence to marshal. At the present moment, economics is among these sciences, and law and economics is the discipline through which the results of economic science can be filtered into legal doctrine. Economic science, like any social science, is, of course, international and as such not bound by specific jurisdictions. In this sense, active law and economics research that filters into the decisions of high courts is itself a motor of the harmonization of law to the extent that courts are willing to follow the example of the German constitutional court, as has been demonstrated in the waterpenny case.

JÜRGEN G. BACKHAUS

See also COASE, RONALD; COASE THEOREM; ECONOMIC INCENTIVES FOR ENVIRONMENTAL REGULATION; EFFICIENT STATUTE LAW; WICKSELL AND PUBLIC CHOICE.

Subject classification: 3f(i); 4b(ii); 6d(iv).

BIBLIOGRAPHY

Bator, F. 1958. The anatomy of market failure. *Quarterly Journal of Economics* 72: 351–79.

Frankfurter Allgemeine Zeitung. 1996. 17 February, Nr. 41, p. 2.

Knight, F. 1921. *Risk, Uncertainty and Profit*. Boston: Houghton Mifflin; Chicago: University of Chicago Press, 1971.

Kötz, H. 1992. A common private law for Europe. In *The Common Law of Europe*, ed. Bruno de Witte and Caroline Forder (Deventer: Kluwer): 31–42.

Senn, P. 1998. Science as a source of the law. In *The Elgar Companion to Law and Economics*, ed. J. Backhaus, Aldershot, UK: Edward Elgar.

Wicksell, K. 1896. *Finanztheoretische Untersuchungen*. Jena: Gustav Fischer.

Hart, Herbert Lionel Adolphus (1907–1993). Hart was Professor of Jurisprudence at Oxford University from 1952 until 1968, and continued actively contributing to the philosophy of law until his death in 1993. Although his initial university education was in philosophy (at New College, Oxford, under H.W.B. Joseph), Hart only turned to philosophy as a career in middle life. On graduating, he qualified as a lawyer and practised at the English Bar throughout the 1930s. During the war of 1939–45 he was employed in defence intelligence, in a department related to that where Stuart Hampshire and Gilbert Ryle were working. After the war, responding to an invitation pressed upon him more than once, he returned to Oxford as Fellow in Philosophy at New College and became involved in the new linguistic philosophy then revolutionizing the philosophy faculty. An interest in 'performative utterances' (Hart suggested calling them 'operative utterances') showed the relevance of his legal work (mainly in trusts and tax) to the new philosophy. When in 1952 the Chair of Jurisprudence unexpectedly fell vacant on the resignation of A.L. Goodhart, Hart was eventually chosen, and to his own surprise was able to bring together his prior interests in law and his current philosophical concerns. The combination was to prove a happy one.

Hart was undoubtedly one of the most important and influential legal philosophers of the twentieth century; he put forward what is generally considered one of the most powerful statements of a positivistic theory of law and is often treated as the standard version of legal positivism, both by its supporters and its opponents. His approach to the problems of law and legal theory falls within the school of analytical philosophy, to which he made significant contributions, especially in the development of the 'linguistic-analytical' approach in post-1945 Oxford.

In his main work, *The Concept of Law* (the title was chosen to echo Gilbert Ryle's *The Concept of Mind*), he offered an account of law as conceptually distinct from morality. Hart followed the tradition initiated by Jeremy Bentham and John Austin, but did not endorse their idea of the law being the sovereign's command. Instead, he developed a theory of legal systems as comprising social rules, some of which have coercive sanctions. The important flaws Hart saw in Bentham's and Austin's theories of law did not prevent him from undertaking a critical but sympathetic study of their work. His *Essays on Bentham* is generally considered an authoritative account of both the problems and the insights of Bentham's legal thought.

Hart argued that Bentham and Austin tried to reduce the law to a set of brute facts such as habits, threats and the like. In their place, he distinguished two different perspectives from which a given group's social rules might be viewed: the *external* and the *internal* point of view. The internal point of view is that of the members of the group, who accept and use these rules as patterns guiding their conduct. From this standpoint, the rules are seen not as threats or statements about the likelihood of future events, but as *rules*, that is, as normative statements capable of bringing about duties and obligations. The external point of view is that of the observer, someone who does not share this understanding (the standard example in legal literature being that of the anthropologist who observes the customs of a primitive society without participating in them). Only from the former's point of view is it possible to make sense, according to Hart, of the normative language we all use when speaking about the law. The use of statements such as 'I have the obligation to . . .', 'I have the right (or duty) to . . .' are distorted when translated to the (external) language of simple observation.

Hart also opposed the idea (held by Hans Kelsen among others) that all legal material can be formulated in the form of 'if–then' punitive norms, that is, of norms that impose sanctions for their transgression. Instead, he argued that 'the key to the science of jurisprudence' was to be found in the union of two different categories of rules which, according to him, are present in any developed legal system. Rules of the first kind (*primary rules*) are those that lay down duties to perform or to abstain from performing a given act, while rules of the second kind (*secondary rules*) are rules that are related in a systematic way to primary rules. Regarding the nature of this relation, secondary rules can in turn be divided into three different types: first, *rules of adjudication*, which empower individuals to make authoritative determinations of the question whether, on a particular occasion, a primary rule has been broken; they determine, for example, whether some rules are to be applied by courts or by other state agencies and which procedures shall be followed when applying such laws. Rules of adjudication include rules that empower officials to exact sanctions from those who are judged to have committed breaches of primary rules. Secondly, *rules of change*, which regulate the ways in which other rules are to be created, modified or derogated. Rules of this kind specify who has authority to change the primary rules and how this authority is to be exercised. These include both wide-ranging public powers, such as those vested in a national legislature, and also private powers to change one's legal position, for example through contract or transfer of property. Lastly, he argued that in every legal system there must be one *rule of recognition*, which specifies the criteria all the other rules have to fulfil in order to be part of such a legal system.

Hart's contention was that a legal system comes into existence when two conditions are fulfilled: on the one hand, the (bulk of the) population complies with the (bulk of the) primary rules (for whatever reasons); on the other hand, the functionaries (judges, administrators, and the like) regard the rules as *rules*, i.e. they share the *internal point of view*. Hart was eager to deny that this latter requirement demanded from the functionaries a *moral* upholding of the rules: his position was that they have to *accept* them, for whatever reasons (moral reasons being just one among many possible types of reason). In such a way, Hart was able to build up a theory of law which can be explained and understood with reference not to moral standards, but to social practices alone. His theory of law soon gained widespread acceptance, to such an extent that today it is difficult to find a book on legal theory where his views are not extensively discussed, even if not wholly accepted.

But Hart's work covered a wider range of issues than those treated in *The Concept of Law*. His first major work, *Causation in the Law* (written with Tony Honoré, 1958), contains a thorough discussion of the problems posed by the notion of causation, with its vital role in many branches of the law, yet seemingly with roots both in common sense and in the scientific explanation of natural phenomena. One of the most remarkable features of this work is the way in which it combines the utilization of the methodological tools of analytical philosophy with the peculiarities of legal analysis. *Law, Liberty and Morality* (1963), on the other hand, was a powerful restatement of the moral limits of law, and made Hart one of the most important liberal thinkers of the second half of this century. In this book, he made what is now a commonplace distinction between critical and positive morality. Hart's argument was that the law's proper function is that of preventing people from harming others, not to prevent infractions of a moral code nor, except in extreme cases, to prevent people from behaviour which harms only themselves.

Finally, in *Punishment and Responsibility* (1968), Hart tackled some of the perplexities surrounding the justification of punishment. He held that there is no reason why the principles that justify the socio-legal institution of punishment should be the same as those that justify the distribution of punishment in particular cases. Thus he found a way out of the traditional difficulties faced by both the retributionist and utilitarian justifications of punishment, establishing a middle way between a utilitarian justification of the practice of punishing people, with general deterrence as its main aim, and a retributive principle for the particular distribution of punishment, with the allocation and measure of the justified punishment according with the offender's deserts.

In Hart's works it is possible to discern the influence of philosophers like Ludwig Wittgenstein and J.L. Austin (indeed, a quotation from Austin is given as a justification of the methodological approach followed in *The Concept of Law*). The way he applied to legal analysis the most important insights of analytic philosophy is one strong reason for his continuing influence.

The approach of 'the Oxford school' of linguistic analysis to philosophical problems has lost momentum, and is today somewhat unfashionable. Given the considerable influence that school had on Hart's work on legal theory, have Hart's contributions suffered from the fall, if not from grace at least from fashion, of that philosophical approach? It seems safe to argue that Hart's work in causation, criminal responsibility and punishment, as well as his work on Bentham, have not been greatly affected by that change of philosophical outlook.

Regarding *The Concept of Law*, however, the answer does not seem so straightforward. It could be argued that the growing criticism that work has encountered in the last decade or so is precisely related to the differences between the kind of philosophical reflection favoured by that school and the concerns of legal theorists writing today. To single out one example of this shift of interests, one of the main topics in modern jurisprudence is a theoretical explanation of *legal interpretation* (both of the legal practice as a whole and of particular laws). Hart's position, based on the open-textured nature of natural languages (i.e. the fact that the application of a word to a particular in the world can be dubious and controversial: is a pamphlet a book?) does not seem to offer a complete explanation of the need for interpretation. In recent years, however, there has been a growing interest in the application of the late writings of Wittgenstein to the problems of legal theory. Some theorists working in this context have offered new arguments to further and support Hart's positions in ways that, though not necessarily those he would have chosen, are sympathetic with the main tenets of his theory of law (for good examples, see Marmor 1989; Bix 1993).

While it is hard to find a work on legal theory that does not discuss Hart's ideas, it is equally hard to find one where his ideas are completely endorsed. Hart's last reply to his critics (mainly to Ronald Dworkin) is to be found in the Postscript to the posthumous edition of *The Concept of Law* (1994). Hart's work has set the agenda for analytical jurisprudence in the last thirty years, and it remains today very much a focus of debate.

Fernando Atria and Neil MacCormick

See also AUSTIN, JOHN; BENTHAM, JEREMY; CONVENTIONS AT THE FOUNDATION OF LAW; FULLER, LON L.; KELSEN, HANS; LEGAL POSITIVISM; RULE OF LAW; RULE OF RECOGNITION.

Subject classification: 4a(i); 7c.

SELECTED WORKS

1958. *Causation in the Law* (with Tony Honoré). Oxford: Clarendon Press. 2nd edn, 1985.

1961. *The Concept of Law*. 2nd edn, ed. J. Raz and P. Bulloch. Oxford: Clarendon Press, 1994.

1963. *Law, Liberty and Morality*. Oxford: Clarendon Press.

1968. *Punishment and Responsibility*. Oxford: Clarendon Press.

1982. *Essays on Bentham*. Oxford: Clarendon Press.

1983. *Essays on Jurisprudence and Philosophy*. Oxford: Clarendon Press.

BIBLIOGRAPHY

Bayles, M. 1992. *Hart's Legal Philosophy: An Examination*. Dordrecht: Kluwer.

Bix, B. 1993. *Law, Language and Legal Determinacy*. Oxford: Clarendon Press.

Dworkin, R. 1977. *Taking Rights Seriously*. Cambridge, MA: Harvard University Press

Fuller, L. 1969. *The Morality of Law*. New Haven: Yale University Press, revised edn.

Gavison, R. 1987. *Issues in Contemporary Legal Philosophy. The Influence of H.L.A. Hart*. Oxford: Clarendon Press.

MacCormick, N. 1981. *H.L.A. Hart*. London: Edward Arnold.

Marmor, A. 1989. *Interpretation and Legal Theory*. Oxford: Clarendon Press.

Martin, M. 1987. *The Legal Philosophy of H.L.A. Hart: A Critical Appraisal*. Philadelphia: Temple University Press.

Raz, J. and Hacker, P.M.S. 1977. *Law, Morality and Society. Essays in Honour of H.L.A. Hart*. Oxford: Clarendon Press.

Hayek, Friedrich August von (1899–1992). Hayek was born in Vienna, into an academic family. His father was a botanist at the University of Vienna, and two brothers also became academics (1994: 1, 37–40). He came from that background in educated Viennese society which has had a profound influence upon intellectual developments throughout the twentieth century and he enjoyed cordial relations with others from that background who had moved to wider spheres of influence (1994: 57–8), notably Karl Popper. After education at the University of Vienna and service in the First World War, Hayek entered the Austrian Civil Service. He quickly encountered the remarkable figure of Ludwig von Mises, and Mises was undoubtedly the most important intellectual influence on Hayek. In 1931 Hayek, as a result of an initiative by Lionel Robbins, left Vienna and was appointed to a Chair at the

London School of Economics. He remained there until 1950 when he moved to Chicago. He left Chicago in 1962, and moved to the University of Freiburg, where he held a Chair until 1969. In 1974 he was awarded the Nobel Prize in Economics jointly with an economist of whose work he had been very critical, Gunnar Myrdal. He died in Freiburg on 23 March 1992.

The interrelationship between economics and law is the background to his critique of 'scientism' and constructionism published in the early 1940s (Hayek 1941, 1942–1944). (According to Hayek, in his preface to the republication of these articles (1952: 5), they formed 'part of a single comprehensive plan'.) It is a central theme of Hayek's work from 1944, when he published *The Road to Serfdom.* He devoted two major works to the subject: *The Constitution of Liberty* (1960) and his great three-volume work, *Law, Legislation and Liberty* (1973–79). Although he had established a significant reputation as an economist in the 1930s – indeed as Keynes's most important opponent (O'Brien 1994b) – his economics training was narrow and he qualified at Vienna in Law and Economics (though the latter degree was *doctor rerum politicarum*). His transmutation into a philosopher – and, in particular, into a philosopher of law – was thus relatively straightforward. It was aided by an extraordinary erudition, manifested in familiarity with a wide range of sources in a number of languages (O'Brien 1994a: 344–5).

In understanding Hayek, these are important factors. So also is one which has been relatively neglected, but which explains many of the implicit assumptions of his work, especially in *The Road to Serfdom*. This was his anglophilia. He became naturalized in 1938 (as 'von Hayek' because the British authorities naturally insisted on seeing his birth certificate even though the title 'von' had been abolished when Austria became a Republic in 1918 (1994: 107)) and Hayek acknowledged this anglophilia explicitly (1944: 100, 159–60; 1994: 98–101). It may also help to explain his remarkable tolerance, something which was commented on with surprise bordering on admiration by Popper and which led Schumpeter to accuse him of politeness to a fault (Schumpeter 1946; Hayek 1973–9: I, 70, 161; O'Brien 1994a: 370; 1994b: 348).

Hayek's fundamental moral standard was freedom. It was necessary that this be acknowledged as an overriding principle (1973–9: I, 61). It was freedom which permitted the development of both social and economic organization and of the individuals within a society, and protected those individuals from the threat of arbitrary action – even horrible action, as in an example given by Hayek (1944: 63n) – by a government unconstrained by general rules.

It was the English common lawyers whom Hayek believed to have been responsible, in the seventeenth century, for both articulating and developing this fundamental concept of freedom. They did so in the face of executive power and of its apologists, especially Thomas Hobbes. (see for example 1960: 181; 1973–9: I, 9–11, 33, 91, 95, II, 45, 58; 1978a: 158). This led Hayek to categorize writers as either heroes who recognized the evolutionary nature of society and the freedoms which this brought or 'constructivist' villains who sought to impose artificial arrangements on society (1973–9: I, 52, 74). The first category included the seventeenth-century common lawyers, notably Coke and Hale, as well as John Locke (1960: 58; 1967: 107, 162; 1968: 23, 25; 1973: 10–11; 1973–9: I, 22–4, 85), and the great names more familiar to economists – Adam Smith, Adam Ferguson and Edmund Burke (1949: 4, 7; 1960: 172–4; 1967: 77, 98–9; 1973–9: I, 22–4; 1978a: 124–5, 264). Hayek was particularly impressed not only with Smith's criticisms of the 'Man of System' (1973–9: I, 35, 155) but with Ferguson's emphasis on social and economic phenomena which were the result of human action but not of human design (1973–9: I, 20–1; 1978a: 264). However his real heroes in this connection were Mandeville and Hume. It was Mandeville who had developed the way in which the *unintended* consequences of individual actions under partial information interacted so as to produce social benefit (1968: 9; 1973–9: I, 22–4, 29–31; 1978a: 11, 73, 249–66; 1988: 71). It was Hume who had exposed the limits of human reason and the fallacies of 'constructivism' as embodied in the work of Bacon and Hobbes, and whose critique was applicable to the constructivist villains who followed, from Saint-Simon and Comte to Marx and, indeed, Galbraith (1960: 63; 1968: 15, 21; 1973–9: I, 4, 6, 22–4, 29–31, 52, 67, 92, 113, II, 1, 16, 17, 34, 62, III, 105). It was Hume, in particular, who was responsible for establishing the idea of the evolution of social and economic institutions, an idea which preceded the work of Charles Darwin who had himself been influenced by it (1960: 59; 1973–9: I, 23, III, 154). It was unfortunate that the 'Social Darwinists' who came after him neglected this heritage and concentrated their attention on social evolution relating to individuals rather than to institutions.

Hayek himself was an agnostic (1994: 41). Yet in contrast to both Lionel Robbins and Jacob Viner, who were strongly opposed to religious beliefs (O'Brien 1988: 7), Hayek showed some sympathy towards, and appreciation of, not merely individual Catholics (Lord Acton was one of the individuals whom Hayek admired most; 1960: 177; 1973–9: I, 8, 107) or even the Catholic church as a whole (Hayek stressed the opposition which the Nazis had encountered from the Catholic church as then constituted in Germany; 1967: 143) but writers writing within the Thomistic tradition, notably Molina. Hayek emphasized that for Molina the Just Price was simply the price in a competitive market (1967: 170; 1973–9: I, 20–1; 1978a: 255); he noted that Molina appreciated the concept of orderliness which was not produced directly by human will (1967: 98), and pointed out that the 'Calvinist ethic' owed at least as much to strands in Catholic thinking and behaviour (1973–9: II, 145, III, 203).

Not surprisingly, Hayek also emphasized the evolutionary elements to be found in Menger's *Untersuchungen* (1883) even though he recognized that Menger himself had received the British evolutionary tradition through German sources (1967: 99–103; 1973–9: I, 22, 47; 1978a: 265). Hayek also showed appreciation of the work of Bastiat (1973–9: I, 57).

Many of these threads came together in Hayek's admiration for the English legal system. It was only England which had succeeded in building up the concept of liberty under the law with the Common Law as a barrier to executive power (1973–9: I, 84). It was this, rather than any separation of powers, which had produced British liberty. The British tradition of liberalism was grounded on this, and on the writings of the common lawyers and of John Locke. It contrasted with Continental liberalism which was deeply infected with constructivism (1949: 28–9, 110; 1960: 55–7, 407; 1967: 160; 1978a: 119–20). In his appreciation of the English Common Law, Hayek manifested a romanticism which made him vulnerable to criticism. Yet Hayek had a substantial point; even now, a public functionary defying a court order would run a serious risk of contempt of court, whereas in France he would simply open negotiations with the judge (Lebrecht 1996: 229). This remains true even though, as Hayek recognized, Britain has witnessed a remarkable development of that administrative law which had previously been thought to be a Continental vice (1973–9: III, 29); and, especially under the auspices of EU directives, the bureaucracy in Britain has assumed quasi-legislative powers far beyond those which alarmed Hayek when they were employed, in particular, during the era of the post-war Labour government (1973–9: III, 115, 144–5; Booker and North 1994).

THE NATURE OF LAW. Hayek distinguished between law and legislation. Law was much older than legislation and became gradually articulated in words after being long established (1967: 102; 1973–9: I, 72, 76–8, 95, III, 33–4). The idea that society preceded law was a fallacy common to the constructivists and the legal positivists. The idea of a social contract was factually false (1967: 102; 1973–9: I, 11). The rules by which man lives 'have by a process of selection been evolved in the society in which he lives' (1973–9: I, 11) and groups which evolved good rules would themselves prosper (1967: 67–81; 1973–9: I, 99, III, 166). The so-called 'Calvinist ethic' was an example of this (1973–9: II, 145). Hayek was able to find support for his view in the literature of ethology and cultural anthropology (1973–9: I, 74–6). Some of the rules might well remain non-legal (1973–9: II, 31, 34). But it was fundamentally necessary for people to follow rules of some sort because everybody operated under limited information, and rules evolved in such a way as to enable society to cope with this problem (1978a: 3–22, 59, 67–8, 71; 1988: 21). People did not need to understand the rules – indeed they usually did not – but the rules had evolved in such a way as to function precisely when people were in a state of ignorance (1960: 29; 1967: 79–80, 115; 1973–9: I, 11–15, 30, II, 8, III, 155). Without such rules, human action would have resulted in chaos. The actual rules for behaviour were 'genuine social growths' (1967: 243). But they were of fundamental importance: they were nothing less than the key to group survival (1973–9: I, 81). These rules resulted in strong moral beliefs (1967: 229–36). Indeed 'a free society will work well only where free action is guided by strong moral beliefs' (1967: 230).

On this basis the articulation of the accepted rules of conduct as a legal system then proceeded. The example which, above all, Hayek had in mind was the English Common Law; but the early development of Roman Law also involved codification of accepted norms (1973–9: I, 81–90). Of course in the development of all this there was a continuous process 'in which every step produces hitherto unforeseen consequences' (1973–9: I, 65) and the judiciary had to seek to produce an internally consistent system of rules in the course of dealing with particular problems (1973–9: II, 25–9, 40). The role of the judiciary in all this was thus central; it had to select the good rules, ensure internal consistency, and apply the body of law to particular cases (1973–9: I, 94–8, 118–20). This did not however mean the maintenance of the status quo; indeed legal evolution could sometimes lead to laws which favoured particular groups and this 'ought clearly to be corrected' (1973–9: II, 131). The development of law had, too, to take account of the factual setting (1973–9: I, 105–6).

The rules which provided the framework in which society operated represented one kind of rule (1973–9: I, 48–52). There were, however, two kinds. There were the general rules, of the kind discussed so far, which Hayek called *Nomos*; and there were rules which had a definite purpose, which Hayek called *Thesis*. The two categories of rule related to two different kinds of order; the first, Hayek called *Cosmos*, meaning a spontaneous order, and the second he called *Taxis*, meaning an organized system (1967: 163; 1968; 1973–6: I, 35–54, 124–44, II, 15). The vast majority of legislation related to the rules of organization (1973–9: I, 127–40).

As Hayek noted at a number of points, these categories corresponded to ones used by Oakeshott, though with different terminology (Nomocracy for Cosmos and Teleocracy for Taxis; 1967: 163; 1973–9: II, 15). But, perhaps more fundamentally, the ideas also corresponded to a central element in classical economics, articulated in our own time by Lionel Robbins (1952) and by Warren Samuels (1966). This is the idea that all economic activity, and, in particular, the pursuit of self interest, has to be limited by a framework of law, religion and custom.

The rules called Nomos governed just conduct. It was the essence of rules of just conduct that *all* power should be limited.

> The thesis of this book [*Law, Legislation and Liberty*] is that a condition of liberty in which all are allowed to use their knowledge for their purposes, restrained only by rules of just conduct of universal application, is likely to produce for them the best conditions for achieving their aims; and that such a system is likely to be achieved and maintained only if all authority, including that of the majority of the people, is limited in the exercise of coercive power by general principles to which the community has committed itself (1973–9: I, 55).

Government must thus come under the law (1973–9: I, 130–1, III, 128; 1978a: 65–6).

The framework produced in this way resulted in expectations which could form the basis of action, and the reconciliation of different aims (which included the disappointment of some expectations through negative feedback to equilibrium) through the market (1973–9: I, 97, II, 12, 124; 1978a: 184). When people pursued their own ends subject to such rules, a spontaneous order resulted (1973–9: I, 38–46).

Following Hume, Hayek emphasized that the most fundamental rules related to property – stability of possession, and transference by consent. Equally important was the performance of promises. The market required the prevention of violence and fraud, the protection of property, the enforcement of contracts, and the recognition of the equal rights of all individuals to produce and sell in quantities and at prices they chose (1944: 78; 1949: 110–11; 1960: 140, 229; 1973–9: I, 107–8, II, 40).

It was legitimate for the State to use coercion to enforce such general rules; but it was only such rules, which were end-independent (1960: 148–61, 208; 1973–9: II, 3, 20–1, 31, 123), that justified the coercive powers of the State (1960: 205; 1967: 165; 1973: 11; 1973–9: I, 141, III, 5, 109, 139). End-independence was of the essence of such rules; they were designed to fit a range of situations and to limit conduct within those situations. Like J.S. Mill, Hayek did not believe that the coercive powers of the State should be employed to enforce moral standards which did not relate to the necessity of protecting the private domain of individuals (1973–9: II, 57).

As Lionel Robbins also emphasized in *The Economic Problem in Peace and War* (1947), Hayek insisted that a market economy did not involve a single social purpose or indeed an agreed set of social purposes. Rather, the role of a market economy was to enable individuals to pursue their own ends, as a result of which resources would be used in a more efficient way than if common ends were imposed (1967: 163; 1973–9: II, 1–2, 23). Individuals could do this by observing the rules of just conduct which were essentially prohibitions (1973–9: II, 35–38), protecting the domain of fellow men (1967: 166). Laws had to lay down the boundaries of freedom of action – Hayek quoted Robert Frost's view that 'good fences make good neighbours' (1967: 167; 1973–9: I, 107). The rules of just conduct were not natural law 'in the sense that they are part of an external and eternal order of things' but they were rules, adherence to which efficient social function required (1973–9: II, 59–60). They were essentially concerned with commutative justice (1967: 258; 1973–9: II, 87). The freedom which individuals enjoyed under them was productive of what Hayek called 'The Great Society' which 'arose through the discovery that men can live together in peace and mutually benefiting each other without agreeing on the particular aims which they severally pursue' (1973–9: II, 109; see also 1960: 35; 1967: 163–4). Hayek referred to the resulting economic order as 'Catallaxy' (1967: 164; 1968; 1973–9: II, 107–32). 'A catallaxy is thus the special kind of spontaneous order produced by the market through people acting within the rules of the law of property, tort and contract' (1973–9: II, 109). (The study of such a system was thus 'catallactics'; 1973–9: III, 69.) The resulting order did not amount to making 'economic ends' prevail for the simple reason that, as Robbins (1932) had pointed out, there was no such category of ends (1973–9: II, 113, III, 168). Rather, it enabled individuals freely to pursue whatever ends they chose and to engage in the decisive step of exchange (1973–9: II, 109). Constrained by rules in this pursuit, they produced a complex order far more sophisticated than anything that the human mind could design (1973–9: I, 110–14). Because they used their own knowledge they optimized the use of resources as a result of which society was able to afford more benefits for more people than under any other system (1973–9: II, 106, 118).

The market processes generated knowledge, without any such aim on the part of participants (1973–9: II, 111, 115). Prices transmitted unknown wants to potential producers (1973–9: II, 116; 1978a: 182).

> The manufacturer does not produce shoes because he knows that Jones needs them. He produces because he knows that dozens of traders will buy certain numbers at various prices because they . . . know that thousands of Joneses, whom the manufacturer does not know, want to buy them (1973–9: II, 116).

The information contained in prices resulted from competition (1973–9: II, 117). Competition is thus a discovery process (1973–9: II, 71, III, 67–70, 75; 1978a: 179–80). Hayek's insight was vividly illustrated by experience with 1960s British attempts at governmental 'picking winners' which indicated that the market is far better fitted to perform this function than the State. Indeed economists were fundamentally misled by assuming that producers had certain knowledge – 'No theory can do justice to it [competition] which starts from the assumption that the facts to be discovered are already known' (1973–9: III, 68). Typically, of course, and indeed increasingly, economists have assumed perfect competition, with its ludicrous assumptions about perfect knowledge. Hayek was emphatic that the kind of competition which he was talking about was certainly not perfect competition (1949: 92–106; 1967: 174; 1973–9: III, 65). Indeed, the fixation of economists with perfect competition led them to misunderstand completely the magnitude of the achievement of a competitive system. Competition made it possible for resources to be used in the way which best reflected the wants of society, taking account of the alternative uses of those resources (1973–9: III, 74–6; 1978a: 185). No central direction could accomplish such cost minimization and consumer satisfaction. Where government did not interfere with it, the competitive system worked extremely well. The truth of this was demonstrated by the difficulty of finding unexploited profit opportunities. The market served minorities as well as majorities (1973–9: III, 49) and reconciled the desires of different consumers through price adjustment (1973–9: II, 112). It did not bestow power in the way that political action did; Hayek tellingly contrasted the power of men over men bestowed by socialism with the position of the mail-order company Sears Roebuck, which could not be said to have power in that way (1973–9: III, 80–81).

Because the market gave voice to both minorities and majorities, it was superior to a system which only served the majority (1960: 110–11). But an increasing public sector share served only that majority (1973–9: III, 53). Hayek was understandably critical of writers like Galbraith and Downs who seriously maintained that the public sector was too small (1967: 317; 1973–9: III, 53). The converse was the case, because of the way in which democratic government operated, satisfying different groups at public expense in order to produce a political majority. Hayek was equally dismissive of the idea that the balance of power between such groups could produce anything other than a suboptimal outcome (1973–9: III, 92).

GOVERNMENT. Hayek recognized a substantial legitimate role for government (1949: 22–3, 110–15; 1960: 231; 1967: 165–6; 1973–9: I, 46–8, III, 41–64). This included such matters as 'building regulations, pure food laws, the certification of certain professions, the restrictions on the sale of certain dangerous goods . . ., as well as some safety and health regulations for the processes of production' (1973–9: III, 62) and even compulsory purchase if general rules applied and were subject to court control. Hayek was not advocating a minimal state: government should provide a wide range of public goods. He discussed issues such as market failure, the standard characteristics of genuine public goods, and the issue of externalities. Government should also ensure that all were entitled to a minimum basic income (1944: 89–90; 1949: 112; 1960: 285–305; 1967: 175; 1968; 1973: 17; 1973–9: II, 87, 136, III, 55, 142). Unemployment relief was necessary (1960: 300).

The finance of government activities through taxation should not, however, involve progression (1949: 118; 1960: 307; 1967: 175; 1973–9: III, 127). Indeed Hayek's exposition reflected (and acknowledged) the writings of J.R. McCulloch, who said that once the principal of proportionality was abandoned we were at sea without a rudder or a compass – a phrase which, indeed, Hayek quotes (1960: 308). However this did not rule out *individual* taxes, such as income tax, being progressive; it was the overall tax burden which Hayek looked at. Not only did progression involve legislatures voting for higher taxes when the legislators themselves would not have to pay them, as McCulloch had envisaged ([1845] 1975: 147), but it even encouraged government to pursue inflationary policies in order to benefit from fiscal drag (1960: 315).

Much of Hayek's approach here is not fully worked out. Although he appears to be taking a benefit approach to taxation (1960: 315–6; 1973–9: III, 52, 127), he does not make this explicit. Moreover, although he was concerned about the progressive increase in the size of government expenditure beyond that which voters would have preferred, he does not explore the issue of public debt, a prime tool for government in this context.

Although, armed with its revenue, government might finance a range of services, it did not necessarily follow that it had to provide them as well (1973–9: III, 46). In particular Hayek favoured Friedman's scheme for education vouchers. He emphasized, like John Stuart Mill, that where government provided it should not have a monopoly (1967: 175; 1973–9: III, 147). Like Marshall, he objected to the government monopoly of the postal service (1973–9: III, 57), and he objected strongly to the idea of a government monopoly of education (1960: 376–94; 1973–9: III, 60–1).

In approaching government regulation of private sector activities, Hayek was guided by the principle that such regulation should be according to rules and not a matter of discretion. Price controls, quite apart from their interference with markets, were to be rejected since they were necessarily discretionary (1960: 227–8); by contrast, factory legislation was perfectly acceptable (1944: 28, 60; 1960: 224–5). Housing and town planning posed serious problems even though there was certainly a case for public involvement, if only because of the problem of externalities (1960: 340–57; 1967: 321–38). Agricultural policy was generally counter-productive (1960: 358–75).

GOVERNMENT AND INDUSTRY. Hayek made a number of suggestions for changes in the legal framework within which companies operated. In particular, he objected to companies assuming to themselves a role as social benefit providers, using for this purpose funds which belonged to shareholders (1967: 300–312; 1973–9: III, 82), and he proposed amending the law so that each individual shareholder could vote on the proportion of earnings per share which the company might retain (1967: 307). To prevent abuse of power through interlocking share holdings, however, he proposed that companies with such share holdings should be barred from voting (1967: 309–10).

He adopted a somewhat sceptical attitude towards competition policy (1960: 136; 1967: 176–7; 1973–9: III, 66–7, 71–3, 78, 82–3, 86–7). This is important because when the opposition to that policy became fully articulated in Chicago in the 1970s, Hayek's position was influential, and indeed acknowledged to be such; the most important of such writers, Harold Demsetz, has acknowledged Hayek's contribution (Demsetz 1989: 219, 223). Hayek believed that in so far as there was a monopoly problem, this stemmed very largely from government encouragement and re-enforcement of monopolies (1967: 176; 1973–9: III, 78). With the growth of large diversified firms the concept of industry, and thus of industrial concentration, had become virtually meaningless, and, like P.W.S. Andrews, Hayek believed that firms were under perpetual threat of competitive attack from other firms already established but active in different parts of the market system (1973–9: III, 78–9; Andrews 1964).

Hayek was insistent, in line with his general position, that competition policy, in so far as it was operated at all, must not be discretionary (1960: 265). He would thus have been dismayed by developments in Britain, in which the legal system established in the 1950s has been very largely superseded by administrative discretion (O'Brien 1982).

Competition policy was, in any case, seriously handicapped by the fact that costs were not in any sense given, but could be assumed to be minimized if there was entry into the industry. Size itself was of no significance – except where distorted by government, the choice of size was the result of the market process (1973–9: III, 78).

Interference based upon supposed knowledge of prices and costs was completely misguided. The idea of given cost curves was 'one of the chief sources of error in this field' (1973–9: III, 69). Indeed cost curves depended on the extent and nature of the competition (1973–9: III, 69) – a valid observation, but one destructive of whole areas of microeconomics. How people would behave under competition was unknown even to them, let alone anyone else. No outsider could know whether normal profits were being earned and firms could not be expected to take risks and then, if successful, be forced to equate price with marginal cost. It was part of the nature of competition that its pressure brought about a search for improvement which led to a divergence between price and marginal cost in the form of a temporary monopoly (1973–9: III, 71).

However, Hayek had positive proposals for competition policy. The main harm which he believed to be done by monopoly occurred when a monopolist was in a position to exclude entrants into the industry (1973–9: III, 72–3). Accordingly, Hayek proposed to utilize the availability of private knowledge through prohibiting this exercise of market power via a civil claim using a multiple damages approach. Actions would be conducted on a contingency basis (1960: 136; 1973–9: III, 85–7). (There was no recognition of the problem of moral hazard which has manifested itself in this area.) To avoid the use of a discretionary approach towards cartels, it was best to prohibit them, but to do so simply by making them unlawful (1967: 176–7; 1973–9: III, 86), an approach which essentially relied upon the pressure to break ranks within such organizations.

MACROECONOMIC POLICY. One area in which Hayek's views showed a sharp change in late life concerned government's monopoly of the monetary base. For a long while Hayek took the position that government should be prepared to seek stability in macroeconomic policy (1944: 90; 1960: 223, 324–39) – and indeed, at least after the controversies of the 1930s, he was prepared to concede in principle that public investment should be scheduled in a counter-cyclical manner (1944: 90–1; 1973–9: III, 59). In *The Constitution of Liberty* (1960) he rejected the idea of removing money supply from the ambit of government even though he recognized the propensity of government to inflate. To control this propensity, he suggested a commodity-based standard (since return to the Gold Standard was not practicable) (1949: 209–219; 1960: 335). But in *Law, Legislation and Liberty* Hayek put forward proposals for 'denationalisation' of the money supply (1973–9: III, 57–8, 148; 1976a, 1976b; 1978a: 224–8). Because government had 'shamelessly abused' (1973–9: III, 58) the money supply in order to obtain command over resources, its control should be removed from the purview of government. Indeed, he claimed that the market system would 'never again work satisfactorily' (1973–9: III, 148) until control was removed. In the 1990s this almost apocalyptic tone seems unwarranted; but viewed against the macroeconomic chaos of the 1970s, with broad money in the UK increasing by more than 60 percent in two years, his tone is understandable.

The proposal was, however, remarkably short on detail – although Hayek made the point that Gresham's Law only operated with fixed ratios of exchange between competing money supplies so that his proposal was not vulnerable on that score (1967: 318–20; 1976: 41). (In other contexts, however, he actually favoured fixed exchange rates as a monetary discipline; 1978: 201–2, 214.) Indeed, his proposal was, as one critic complained, remarkably vague (Fischer 1986: 433). But when the details were worked out by others it became clear that Hayek's proposal related essentially to the supply of bank notes (Dowd 1988). The argument for freedom of issue turned out to depend upon the ancient fallacy known in the mid-nineteenth century as the doctrine of 'Reflux' under which banks could not over-issue, as excess notes would be returned to them by their customers. Since the argument depended crucially upon the absolute price level being fixed in some other way it could not be applied in a twentieth century context, even had it been applicable – which is doubtful – under the gold standard. In fact most of the issues had been comprehensively dealt with by Henry Thornton in his critique of the Real Bills Doctrine in 1802, in a work subsequently re-issued in a fine scholarly edition by Hayek himself (Thornton 1802). But in any case, in a late twentieth-century context, the proposals were massively irrelevant; competition already exists in the supply of bank deposits, which is overwhelmingly the means of payment, and government, as by far the largest borrower, cannot help but influence this supply.

There are, however, two points which may be made in Hayek's defence. Firstly, his proposal may have helped to strengthen the case of those who have argued for independence of central banks from government, and recent research has indeed demonstrated a negative association between the degree of independence and the propensity of government to debase the currency. Secondly, Hayek's proposal may well have lain behind the 1980s British case for currency competition rather than European monetary union, and in view of the subsequent debacle of British membership of the Exchange Rate Mechanism in Europe there was much to be said for this.

The propensity of government to inflate the money supply was greatly strengthened by the privileged position of trade unions in Britain during much of Hayek's lifetime. Hayek regarded the Trade Disputes Act of 1906 as exemplifying a measure passed in the name of democratic control which was actually not desired by the vast majority of the population but which reflected the reality of assembling a political majority (1960: 267–84; 1973–9: III, 31–2). It bestowed upon trade unions a private power of coercion which should not have been available to them (1949: 117; 1967: 281–93), and enabled them to interfere with the operation of the market, thus lowering national income (1967: 255). But most seriously it led government persistently to inflate the money supply to offset the unemployment-creating effects of trade union activity (1967: 270–9; 1980). Ultimately inflation became the standard tool with which to counter unemployment (1978a: 191–231). Unfortunately, money illusion was eroded, and thus it became progressively necessary to increase the rate of inflation (1967: 282, 295–9). Hayek's exposition of this is based around the Austrian trade cycle theory, though without reference either explicitly to that theory or to the concept of the period of production. Without the privileged position enjoyed by trade unions, Hayek believed that an important motive for debasing the money supply would have been removed.

THE MYTH OF SOCIAL JUSTICE. The privileged position enjoyed by the trade unions was defended – not least by the trade unions themselves – on the grounds of social justice. Hayek denounced the concept as simply meaningless (1973: 13; 1980: 44). In the face of his relentless critique – the title of the second volume of *Law, Legislation and Liberty* is *The Mirage of Social Justice* – it is indeed difficult to maintain the position that the phrase has any meaning. Hayek was scathing about it. Pursuit of this mirage was not merely pointless; it did positive harm (1973–9: II, 133) and, since it damaged the market system, it actually prolonged poverty (1973–9: II, 139). But it had become a new religion – one attractive to the purveyors of the older religions who were losing faith in them (1973–9: I, xvi, II, 66–7, 80) – and a cloak for dishonesty.

> The phrase 'social justice' is not . . . an innocent expression of good will towards the less fortunate, but . . . a dishonest insinuation that one ought to agree to a demand of some special interest which can give no real reason for it . . . the term is intellectually disreputable, the mark of demagogy or cheap journalism (1973–9: II, 97).

The word 'social' had simply become a replacement for 'moral' in the secular society even though it functioned as a cloak for envy (1967: 239, 245).

The idea of imposing measures in the name of social justice was meaningless since, as David Hume had shown, there was no possibility of an agreed welfare standard (1973–9: II, 1, 62, 80–4). As Hayek pointed out, 'the word "social" *presupposes* the existence of known and common aims behind the activities of a community, *but does not define them*' (1967: 242). The phrase 'value to society' was meaningless except in so far as such value was reflected in market valuation (1967: 172). But the market did not reflect, or require, agreed aims for society as a whole.

The more closely Hayek examined the concept 'social justice' the flimsier it seemed. At what point did one draw a frontier? Were we concerned with social justice for foreigners as well? (1973–9: II, 88–91). The essentially empty nature of the concept was brought out most clearly by pointing out that it was a slogan of totalitarian governments (1973–9: II, 66, 78–80, 136).

Nonetheless, the pursuit of 'social justice' had led to a mass of legislation (1973: 12; 1973–9: I, 141–3), resulting in the abandonment of the principle that coercion was only justified in relation to rules of just conduct. Social justice involved the use of coercion in a discriminatory rather than a uniform manner, and was linked to the development of the 'rights' culture (1973–9: II, 101–106), commentary on which led Hayek to the sarcastic remark (concerning the United Nations Declaration) that 'The conception of a "universal right" which assures to the peasant, to the Eskimo, and presumably to the Abominable Snowman, "periodic holidays with pay" [article 24] shows the absurdity of the whole thing' (1973–9: II, 105).

However, the supposed claims of 'social justice' had led to legislation to favour particular groups in society. In truth 'social justice' ultimately represented a struggle between groups (1973–9: II, 137, III, 9–11, 138). While selfish actions of individuals, constrained by law in the form of the rules of justice, produced benefit for all, the selfish actions of groups produced harm (1973–9: II, 138, III, 89). Ultimately, indeed, egalitarianism could end cultural evolution (1973–9: III, 172–3).

DISTRIBUTION. Hayek's basic position on the question of distribution was that as long as the competitive system was fair – just – and applied the same rules to all, there were bound to be unequal outcomes (1960: 87) and that it was the operation of competition, not the outcome, with which we should be concerned (1972–3: II, 38, 73). The market outcome might be regarded as unjust, but it emerged from a just system (1973–9: II, 64, 73–4). We had a choice between maintaining the market system and destroying it by altering the outcomes through redistribution. Market clearing factor rewards had nothing to do with individual merit, but acted simply as resource allocation signals (1967: 233; 1973–9: II, 72). There was, if we accepted the benefits of the market system, an unavoidable discrepancy between moral merit and reward. Hayek pointed out in *The Road to Serfdom* that income differences in the Soviet Union were as great as in the United States (1944: 77).

The rules of justice determined the chances of economic actors, not the outcomes. But the chances for any randomly selected person were maximized in a free society (1973–9: II, 114, 126, 132; 1978a: 184). *'The Good Society is one in which the chances of anyone selected at random are likely to be as great as possible'* (1973–9: II, 132). The matter of the relationship between Hayek's work and that of Rawls will be addressed below, but it is worth noting that this proposition is in Hayek's 1968 paper reprinted in *New Studies* (1978a: 184).

Hayek can hardly have been unaware of the qualifications to such a position, dating from the previous century, notably the Mill–Cairnes concept of non-competing groups. But he clearly took the view that the way to deal with this was through the removal of barriers to labour mobility (including education) rather than through redistribution. In any case, the plea for social justice in relation to some occupations simply amounted to a demand for the protection of entrenched interests (1973–9: II, 93–6, 140).

Redistribution, as a form of socialist activity, was irreconcilable with the rule of law according to Hayek, because instead of everybody standing equally before the law it involved subordinates receiving and superiors allocating funds. The resulting interference was cumulative: the demand for equality was probably often based on a belief that existing inequalities were the result of somebody's decision rather than of market processes, and, once outcomes were altered through administrative decision, that belief had a firm foundation (1973–9: II, 80–87). It thus led to demands for further intervention. The result was necessarily *ad hoc* (1960: 302). Indeed, socialism itself was based on 'the atrocious idea that political power ought to determine the material position of the different individuals and groups' (1973–9: II, 99; see also II, 136, III, 13) and this led him to interpret incomes policies – more often, in truth, the last resort of governments that had seriously mishandled macroeconomic management – entirely in such socialist terms, an interpretation which seems to have been influenced by his familiarity with the work of Barbara Wooton (1973–9: III, 13, 95). But such interference in a 'catallaxy' could never be just because it replaced the spontaneous order, produced by the rules of justice, with disorder (1973–9: II, 128).

DEMOCRACY. Hayek, only too well aware of the nature of tyranny, regarded democracy as the only defence against oppression. He was thus alarmed by the evidence of disillusionment with democracy (1973–9: III, 1–19, 98). The essential reason for this lay in the fact that democratic assemblies had assumed powers which were completely unlimited by general laws (1973–9: II, 61, III, 15, 33, 99, 128); they had then become the forum for the operation of pressure groups, and for the imposition of legislation to satisfy those pressure groups in order to be able to command a majority of the votes (1973–9: III, 99). This assumption of power was buttressed by the writings of legal positivists on sovereignty which regarded such sovereignty, once vested in a democratic legislature, as unbounded (1973–9: II, 61). But the domination of government by coalitions of organized interests was 'the inescapable result of a system in which government has unlimited powers to take whatever measures are required to satisfy the wishes of those on whose support it relies' (1973–9: III, 15) and such coalitions could be assembled in the name of social justice dispensing 'gratuities at the expense of somebody else *who cannot be readily identified*' (1973–9: III, 103).

Because of the difficulties which democracy was encountering, and because of the abuse of the term democracy (both in such strange concepts as 'people's democracy' and in its use in demands by interest groups to gain control of a particular institution), Hayek preferred the term 'Demarchy' (1968, 1973–9: III, 38–40). He put forward proposals for an ideal constitution (1973–9: III, 35–8) with a three-tiered system of representative bodies, separating consideration of issues of government from rules of just conduct and the framework of the constitution. The separation of powers (1973–9: III, 105–127) would make clear a distinction between rules of just conduct and the institutions of government and establish the basic principle of such a constitution – that coercion was only for rules of just conduct. Historically the need to limit the powers of the executive had been recognized, and it was the doctrine of the Old Whigs. But sight of this had been lost with the increase in the franchise, so that even in Britain the executive was unconstrained and there were substantial areas of administrative law (1973: 15–22; 1973–9: III, 20; 1978b: 66).

CONSTRUCTIVISM. Hayek's whole thesis, as outlined so far, was developed in opposition to what he called constructivism – the belief that society could be designed by the efforts of the human mind (1973–9: I, 10, 14–15, 24–6, 73, II, 59, III, 155, 173). This supposedly positivist approach employed spurious aggregates such as 'society' and rested upon two related fallacies: that an unplanned system must necessarily be chaotic rather than coherent, and a belief that it could be replaced (1942–4: III, 29–30; 1978a: 3–22). Although Hayek recognized the origins of this in the writings of Saint-Simon and his followers, especially Comte (1941: III, 307–12; 1942–4: II, 50–63), Bentham and his followers attracted his particular ire (e.g. 1973–9: I, 22, 128–9, II, 17–23, 44–8), thus ensuring in turn the hostility of Lionel Robbins towards Hayek's position. Hayek believed that until Bentham, and James Mill, the idea of the separation of powers and of government under the law, with government occupying a limited role, had been accepted. The fundamental fallacy of the pain/pleasure calculus was the assumption that *all* effects could be known. What Hayek called 'rule' utilitarianism, which he associated with Paley (1973–9: II, 19–20), he regarded as less harmful although it too assumed that all the effects of rules could be known. In clear contrast, Hayek's position was that rules were needed precisely because of ignorance. The Benthamites aspired to build a society; but societies grew and were not built:

> From the insight that the benefits of civilization rest on the use of more knowledge than can be used in any deliberately concerted effort, it follows that it is not in our power to build a desirable society by simply putting together the particular elements that by themselves appear desirable (1973–9: I, 56).

The efforts of the constructivists had been much encouraged by bad economic history, which continuously misrepresented the nineteenth century experience and concealed the enormous rise in real wages and general well-being that had occurred (1967: 207–8; 1973–9: I, 67–8, II, 131). In the edited volume *Capitalism and the Historians* (1954), Hayek attempted to assemble a counter-statement, but the process is a never-ending one, as even a cursory survey of more recent economic history literature makes clear. Nonetheless, as he was able to point out, there was one inescapable piece of evidence – the huge rise in population had occurred simply because capitalism had made it possible for far more people to survive than had been possible ever before in history (1960: 118–19). Economic historical work of the distorted kind had also led to bogus historical laws which had been employed by Comte and Marx (1973–9: I, 23–4). Indeed, the origins of totalitarianism could be found in the 'scientism' Hayek associated with Comte – the misguided attempt to apply methods of natural science to the vastly more complex social world (1941; 1942–4: I, 280; 1973–9: I, 15–17, 64).

But the urge to plan society was flattering to the vanity of the would-be planners (1973–9: I, 8–9, III, 130; 1988) and there was also, Hayek insisted, a persistent problem of reverting to pre-market, tribal values in which individual welfare was the concern of group arrangements (1973–9: II, 133–52, III, 165). This problem came about essentially because many people in modern society worked in large organizations and had no feel for the operation of the market. The academics were particularly to the fore; it should 'not surprise us that academic philosophers in their sheltered lives as members of organizations should have lost all understanding of the forces which hold the Great Society together and, imagining themselves to be Platonic philosopher-kings, should propose a re-organization of society on totalitarian lines' (1973–9: II, 105). Socialism was thus a reactionary doctrine – a revival of tribal instincts (1973–9: III, 169). Ultimately, constructivism led not to the triumph of reason but to the 'enthronement of the will' (1973–9: I, 32) in an environment without rules.

The intellectual basis for this error was provided in part by legal positivists, who lacked any understanding of the true nature of law and of a spontaneous market order (1967: 101; 1973–9: I, 66–7, 114, II, 47–56). In his comments on the legal positivists, Hayek was no respecter of persons: Glanville Williams is equated with Humpty

Dumpty (1973–9: II, 48). Hayek was particularly incensed, and on strong ground in his specialist knowledge, by the fact that the legal positivists had been defenceless before the Nazis (1973–9: II, 55–6), since they had validated State action as law, and German legal theories for decades before Hitler had helped to prepare the way for totalitarianism (1960: 234–9, 1967: 169).

The appearance of a regime like that of the Nazis might be an extreme case; but there was – or should be – a fundamental distinction between law and the activities of discretionary, interventionist government (1949: 18; 1978: 134). Unless government were limited by law, recognition of principles was not enough; in a contest between principles and expediency, between long-term uncertain effects and short-term immediate benefits, expediency would always triumph (1973–9: I, 55–93). But interference with the catallaxy always had unintended consequences which led to further interference (1967: 264–5; 1973–9: III, 18). There was thus cumulative interference (1973–9: I, 58–61, 63).

SOCIALISM AND PLANNING. Hayek, like his mentor Mises, was a sustained and ultimately successful critic of the concept of the planned economy, despite the myth, propagated even by those who were not Marxist, that Lange and Taylor had in some sense been able to meet the objections raised by Mises and Hayek. In the present context, however, it is the introduction of planning into a basically market oriented system which is more interesting. Hayek as early as 1944 pointed to the myth that economic planning was somehow 'inevitable' (1944: 32–41). In fact 'in social evolution nothing is inevitable but thinking makes it so' (1944: 35). The whole idea was based upon a fundamental failure to understand the complexity of economic life (1973–9: III, 164). Once extended beyond the national frontier, its ludicrous nature became apparent (1944: 164–6), as Robbins had pointed out in the 1930s (Robbins 1937). However, the vanity of economists, in particular, caused the ideas involved in planning to resurface at regular intervals, even in the United States. Hayek was able to point to the failure of 'indicative planning' in France which had so attracted western intelligentsia and was highly critical of the proposal, involving Leontief, to employ input–output tables as a planning tool; he pointed out, with some justification, that these represented no more than economic history (because they have no prices; 1978: 232–46).

Planning would indeed increase uncertainty and produce tensions between conflicting ends that could only be solved by political means (1944: 42–53, 66–75). Individual freedom was in any case incompatible with the imposition from above of social ends (1944: 150–62). It was also incompatible with the replacement of known laws by the discretion necessarily employed under planning (1944: 54–65).

Of course not all planning involved totalitarianism – and Hayek did not argue this in *The Road to Serfdom* (1944: 100–123). (He did however provide cogent reasons, based on the German experience, for believing that moral standards were impossible under totalitarianism and he entitled chapter 10 of *The Road to Serfdom* 'Why the Worst Get on Top'.) But socialism, even in a dilute form, damaged individual moral responsibility – indeed he held that it 'must lead to the extinction of all moral responsibility of the individual' (1973–9: III, 129). Indeed he seems to have foreseen, in *The Constitution of Liberty*, the present crisis in welfare provision, with the State assuming responsibility for so many decisions of the individual, that is now afflicting Western societies (1960: 290–92).

But though there was a clear distinction between socialist interventions in a market system and totalitarianism, Hayek did not believe that a so-called 'middle way' represented a viable long-term position (1973–9: III, 150). This was because of the activities of groups; group concessions bred further ones until socialism was significantly advanced. Socialism did not, however, simply represent different values; it was not that the socialist simply attached greater weight to equality (1988: 66–88). By failing to understand the achievements of the market system, socialism was

> based on an intellectual error which makes its adherents blind to its consequences. This must be plainly said because the emphasis on the alleged difference of the ultimate values has become the common excuse of the socialists for shirking the real intellectual issue (1973–9: II, 136).

Hayek lived throughout most of the century during which socialism, including Marxism, appeared to be an important intellectual force. Hayek did not share this view. Marxism he regarded as 'merely one among many characteristic 19th-century products' of the 'theory of history' variety, (1942–4: II, 59) and it was not even a particularly refined example – Marx even lacked an understanding of the price system (1973–9: III, 170). His contempt for Marx was coupled with that for Freud, whose activities, he believed, had undermined the necessary human adherence to rules (1973–9: III, 174). As the end of the century approached, though writing before the collapse of the Berlin Wall, Hayek saw these twin currents drying up.

> If our civilization survives, which it will do only if it renounces those errors, I believe men will look back on our age as an age of superstition, chiefly connected with the names of Karl Marx and Sigmund Freud. I believe people will discover that the most widely held ideas which dominated the 20th century, those of a planned economy with a just distribution, a freeing ourselves from repressions and conventional morals, of permissive education as a way to freedom, and the replacement of the market by a rational arrangement of a body with coercive powers, were all based on superstitions in the strict sense of the word (1973–9: III, 175–6).

PRECONCEPTIONS AND INFLUENCE. Although Hayek's work has attracted a great deal of critical comment, even the best of it (e.g. Barry 1979) does not bring out fully the twin foundations on which the vision sketched in this account rests. We have seen how Hayek envisaged law as a body of rules coming into existence spontaneously, and gradually being articulated so as to produce a society in which diffused information could be coordinated through a price system. In this system, economic maximization by the individual was constrained by the legal system buttressed by religion and custom. Such a view is entirely consistent with the tradition stemming from Adam Smith. However, in the case of Hayek there are two particular historical episodes, with the associated literature, which drove forward his statement of this vision, and which – and this is extremely important to emphasize – provided him with implicit assumptions which critics, especially in the United States, have not immediately sensed. The first of these eras was the period 1933–1944 in Germany, when an apparently civilized and highly developed country fell suddenly into the grip of an extreme totalitarian regime, the nature of which was hardly grasped by many people in Britain. The second was the period of the post-war Labour government in Britain, spanning the years 1944–1951.

As someone with a first-hand knowledge not merely of Germany but of German socialist and anti-capitalist literature, and of German legal writings, Hayek was almost uniquely qualified to appreciate the true roots of National Socialism. It was an appreciation of the intellectual roots of Nazism which led to comments such as the following, which infuriated his critics:

> It is indeed the concept of 'social justice' which has been the Trojan Horse through which totalitarianism has entered (1973–9: II, 136).

Viewed against the intellectual background of Nazism and a century of German socialist writings, the background of *The Road to Serfdom*, this is perfectly understandable; but it infuriated English critics both because of their lack of real appreciation of the nature and origins of Nazism and because they believed that Hayek's attitude was formed solely by the experience of Britain in the years 1944–51. Nor had they any appreciation of the true horrors of a totalitarian regime. As Hayek dryly remarked, it was those with some direct experience of a totalitarian regime who had 'a clearer conception of the conditions and value of a free society' (1967: 150).

At the time he wrote *The Road to Serfdom*, Hayek clearly discerned amongst the intellectual classes strongly fashionable currents which mirrored those to be found in Germany twenty-five years before (1944: 135–49). He cited in particular the Marxist work of E.H. Carr, which poured scorn on liberalism and put forward a collectivist view that was indistinguishable from that of the Nazis, including writings on 'The Moral Foundations of War' [sic.] (1944: 138–41). At the same time scientists, naive as ever about social matters, agitated for planning (1944: 141–4), large firms looked to government to strengthen their market position (1944: 144–7) (as had indeed happened during the War; Swann, O'Brien et al. 1974: 46) and organized labour fell under the influence of people like Harold Laski who explicitly advocated the continuation of wartime controls after the end of the war (1944: 149). Hayek warned against this at the very beginning of *The Road to Serfdom* (1944: 2).

But the actual experience of Britain in the years 1945–51, while it did not fulfil Hayek's worst nightmares, did provide for him a sort of mental conditioning which was at the back of his mind henceforth. *The Road to Serfdom* was published as it indeed became evident that wartime controls would be continued in the postwar period, and Hayek lived through the era of the postwar Labour government. This, because of the particular make-up of the commentating community, has had a much better press than it deserved, and only isolated exceptions – such as Jewkes (1948) – give any flavour of what it was like to live through that era, above all the winter of 1947. Indeed an apparently unimportant piece by Hayek on Town and Country Planning (1967: 321–38), which is hardly referred to at all in the secondary literature (though see Barry 1979: 121), is actually of key importance. For here we have all the concerns which lay behind much of his more elliptical writings: discretionary legislation, enabling acts, retrospective powers, confiscation of property (the Crichel Down affair eventually came to the public light, although not until after this era) and wide public disquiet. Lewis (later Lord) Silkin, the minister responsible for town and country planning, told the inhabitants of Stevenage, a very small town north of London, which was at that time hardly more than a built-up section of the A1 road (there were only 4,810 on the electoral roll – *Times* 20 May 1946, 2a), that they were going to have a new town. The residents demanded an enquiry; Mr Silkin made it clear that they were going to have a new town anyway. He referred arrogantly to the 'backward people of Stevenage' (*Times* 12 July 1946, 6e). Protestors changed the railway station signs to 'Silkingrad' (*Times* 21 December 1946, 2f). Viewed against the experience of that era by someone who lived through it, many of the paradoxes which American critics apparently see in Hayek's work are easily explained. One knows what he is getting at. But the existence of these implicit assumptions reduces the generality – hence the criticisms. Had this era not come to an end, many critics would have had much less difficulty in understanding what Hayek was driving at. As it was, even in postwar Germany under Allied control, the price controls were lifted – leading corporatist economists, as Hayek was later able to note sardonically, to tell anybody who would listen that the removal of these controls would wreck the German economy (1992: 194; cf. Galbraith 1948), a somewhat unfortunate prophecy at the start of a decade in which the German economy grew in real terms at the rate of nine percent per annum, an achievement unparalleled in the history of the developed world (Yeager 1976: 485).

It was the experience of this period in Britain which led to Hayek's later observation that there occurred an accelerated ending of the rule of law under the postwar Labour government (1967: 224–7). But it was much more than this development which made an indelible impression on Hayek's outlook. As the study by Jewkes shows, the era was characterized by absurdly detailed regulations, massive incompetence, shoddy goods of the kind later familiar in Eastern Europe, and a rampant black market (Jewkes 1948: 179–85, 212–13, 217–22, 224–5). Yet in the minds of many on the Left this era was – indeed continues to be – viewed with a roseate glow; a prominent Labour politician in the 1970s repeated the absurd claim made during this era (Jewkes 1948: 205) that diet had improved during wartime food shortages, causing one to wonder what it was that politicians (as distinct from, say, nurses; Dickens 1978: 91, 98) were eating.

Hayek himself was well aware that the reception of *The Road to Serfdom*, by both critics and admirers, failed to take account of the English background. As he observed in an interview in the posthumously published autobiographical volume *Hayek on Hayek* (1994), *The Road to Serfdom* 'was written so definitely in an English frame of reference – and it was, of course, received in a completely different manner' (1994: 102). Hayek felt that, to some extent, British socialists had understood the background, even if they disagreed; but in the United States he 'was exposed to incredible abuse, something I never experienced in Britain at the time. It went so far as to completely discredit me professionally' (1994: 102–3). (The most extreme example of this, cited by Hayek himself (1967: 218) was Herman Finer; e.g. Finer 1945.)

Later commentators, including those from the United States, have been able to see Hayek's message in much better perspective (Gissurarson et al. 1984). This is only just. Many, including many sympathetic to Hayek's general position, have the impression that *The Road to Serfdom* is some kind of hysterical pamphlet, an impression which is a tribute to the success of the enemies of liberalism in implanting this idea. In truth, the work is the best compact statement of Hayek's views, one which is much easier to digest than the later more diffuse ones. It is true that Hayek's views developed further, and that, in particular, his seminal analysis of the central importance of uncertainty was still to be reflected fully in his treatment of markets, an achievement culminating in *Law, Legislation and Liberty* (1973–9). But *The Road to Serfdom* is an important and scholarly book. At the time of its publication, a number of reviewers appreciated this. Thus even Pigou, who might well have been unsympathetic, wrote that 'This is a scholarly and sincere book' (1944: 217). Jewkes explicitly linked his study of Britain under planning with Hayek's book (1948: ix).

Yet Hayek was aware that there was much hostility, even though not always publicly expressed, amongst his fellow economists, many of whom regarded planning as rather *chic*:

> I discredited myself with most of my fellow economists by writing *The Road to Serfdom*, which is disliked so much. So not only did my theoretical influence decline, most of the departments came to dislike me, so much that I can feel it to the present day. Economists very largely tend to treat me as an outsider, somebody who has discredited himself by writing a book like *The Road to Serfdom*, which has now become political science altogether (1994: 143).

Reviewing events after twelve years, Hayek wrote that the book was 'a warning to the socialist intelligentsia of England' (in 1967: 216–17); unfortunately it took until 1989 for many of them, unscathed by events in 1956 and 1968, to heed this warning.

Hayek's isolation – for that is what it became (O'Brien 1994b: 364–6) – was made easier by the fact that, like Lionel Robbins (O'Brien 1988: 22, 71), he showed occasionally a tendency to alarm verging on panic (e.g. 1973–9: I, xx). There was at times almost an apocalyptic element in his work. As late as 1979 he was claiming that the only way to stop the ratio of government expenditure to GDP rising to 100% was a complete reform of financial legislation (1973–9: III, 127) and that the role of trade unions in forcing government to inflate the money supply to accommodate wage inflation 'must before long destroy the whole market order, probably through the price controls which accelerating inflation will force governments to impose' (1973–9: III, 144). Similarly in 1976 he prophesied that '*Attempts to "correct" the order of the market lead to its destruction*' (1973–9: II, 142). But remarks like this have to be seen in context. Viewed against the history of the 1970s, the three-day week, and the experiences under the Heath government, this did not seem as far fetched when published as it does now.

Hayek's scathing remarks about intellectuals also failed to endear him to the academic community (1944: 121; 1967: 178–94, 201–5, 216–7; 1973–9: III, 130). He wrote about the Treason of the Intellectuals, castigated by Benda (1973–9: III, 136), and the support of intellectuals for the construction of society and the reductions of individuals' liberty in the name of 'positive liberty' and social justice, leading to the subsidization of 'socialist experiments' in low income countries (1973–9: III, 133). 'Only fools believe that they know all, but there are many' (1973–9: III, 130). In an essay on 'The Intellectuals and Socialism' Hayek pointed out that socialism had never been a working-class movement and poured scorn on intellectuals as 'people who understand nothing in particular especially well, and whose judgement on matters they themselves understand shows little sign of special wisdom' (1967: 178–94, at 182). The socialist interpretation of economic history was a prime example of what he was complaining about (1967: 201–15). As a university teacher in England, Hayek was acutely sensitive as World War II neared its end to a contempt for individual liberty amongst a significant section of the intellectual classes and indeed to the anti-free enterprise teaching in universities (1944: 97, 114–23). These people were, in his view, playing with fire; though he continued to insist that many of them meant well, he was acutely aware that Nazism was indeed National Socialism (1944: 3–4) and that anti-capitalism and anti-semitism in Germany were from the same source (1944: 104). The roots of National Socialism went back 150 years and the movement gained intellectual dominance in the 1920s, producing a union of the anti-capitalist forces of the right and left, assisted by the destruction of the middle classes (by the 1923 inflation; 1944: 124–34). Hayek was intensely aware of the way in which German socialist, and more general anti-free market, writings had prepared the way for the Nazis, who, of course, had a substantial, democratically elected, parliamentary representation in 1933. But even today the origins of Nazism, and the mechanisms by which Hitler assumed power, are not well appreciated in western societies, partly because so many western intellectuals have been so anxious to differentiate the Nazis from the communist regimes in Eastern Europe, and to depict communism as the opposite of Nazism instead of being, as Hayek (and indeed the journalist Malcolm Muggeridge, who had observed matters at first hand) insisted, national variants of the same thing (Muggeridge 1972: I, 268; see also Ingrams 1995: 50–76; Wolfe 1995: 98–124). (In this the intellectuals were only following the same line as the East German radio which, virtually until the day the Berlin Wall fell, seemed at times obsessed with detecting Nazis in other countries, 44 years after the end of the Nazi regime.)

CONCLUSION. Partly through the activities of the Institute of Economic Affairs, in the foundation of which Hayek's advice had been influential (O'Brien 1994b: 357), his own views seem to have enjoyed a resurgence of interest – with a nice irony, as the limitations of Keynesian policies became clear for all to see in the 1970s. His view that the mixed economy did not represent a stable long-run solution has received support (Littlechild 1978), and even his scheme for privatization of the money supply has been articulated and developed by Kevin Dowd (1988). His more general political programme has been articulated by a number of able writers, notably Barry (1979, 1988) and Butler (1983), and his impact on the latter-day Chicago School has also been acknowledged (Demsetz 1988, 1989). This represents something of an advance from a situation in which even natural allies, such as Viner and Robbins, were critical of him. Viner (1961) did not believe that Hayek's positive proposals for government intervention were consistent with the rule of law as set out by Hayek, and this view was shared by Robbins (1961). Robbins also objected to Hayek's treatment of the Benthamites as 'constructivist' and he made the telling point that Hayek's view of the evolved body of Common Law was exceptionally romantic – a view which, as Robbins was able to point out, certainly contrasted with that of Acton whom Hayek so much admired. On this there is no doubt that Hayek was vulnerable; the evolved legal system, as criticized by Bentham and satirized by Charles Dickens, was characterized not only by significant anomalies but by a form of evolution which gave the maximum scope for producer (i.e. lawyer) power.

But subsequent developments have shown the way in which Hayek's insights could be developed. Thus the Virginia School has developed the concept of the maximizing bureaucrat, one which is wholly consistent with Hayek's criticism of the 'Pigovian' vision of a benign omniscient government; and Olson has produced work on the group conflict which so worried Hayek in the context of democracy, work which Hayek endorsed and indeed drew upon (1973–9: III, 97, 143).

There remain however two major areas where the position bequeathed by Hayek is unclear and in which there are unresolved ambiguities. The first of these concerns the framework of evolved rules; the second relates to social justice.

With regard to evolved rules, Hayek insists that these pre-date legislation and that they emerge in such a way as to enable societies which adopt good rules to flourish. But any society is likely to contain different groups with different moral precepts, and essentially Hayek's position amounts to acceptance of majority values with some possible assimilation of minority insights. After all, different religious groupings have very different views on commutative justice (Wilson 1996). It is even possible that tensions in this area may have made some contribution to the anti-semitism in Germany which, generalized to anti-capitalism, was viewed by Hayek as an important intellectual source of National Socialism.

The problem of social justice has two aspects. The first, is the difficult question of the relationship between Hayek's position and that of Rawls. Some critics believed Hayek to be indebted to Rawls for the idea that under a just system the chances of the least advantaged would be maximized. In fact, however, the idea pre-dates Rawls's 1972 book, being found in a 1966 paper by Hayek:

> An optimal policy in a catallaxy may aim, and ought to aim, at increasing the chances of any member of society taken at random of having a high income, or, what amounts to the same thing, the chance that, whatever his share in total income may be, the real equivalent of this share will be as large as we know how to make it (1967: 173).

This explains why Hayek did not believe there were fundamental differences between himself and Rawls (1973–9: I, xvii, II, 100, 114, 188–9). It is hardly necessary to emphasize that there are elements in Rawls's work which were not acceptable to Hayek (DiQuattro 1986; Barry 1979: 143–7). Rather, the point is that some of Rawls's recommendations, notably his apparent enthusiasm for governmental redistribution, do not seem to follow from his basic starting-point.

Yet the question of social justice, and the matter of redistribution, raise a final difficulty. For it is not clear why Hayek himself *necessarily* had to rule out redistribution, *so long as* this was according to known and clear rules. Thus, for instance, a negative income tax system, as endorsed by Milton Friedman, would indeed have avoided precisely that kind of *discretionary* intervention which Hayek regarded as unacceptable and subversive of law, while permitting a degree of redistribution which the majority of the population – and indeed a majority of not merely Hayek's fellow intellectuals but even Hayek's fellow economists – would find preferable to a system in which an unfortunate outcome in the 'game of catallaxy' (to use Hayek's own phrase) would (subject only to the minimum income qualification) have to be borne without amelioration.

D.P. O'BRIEN

See also AUSTRIAN SCHOOL OF ECONOMICS AND THE EVOLUTION OF INSTITUTIONS; CONVENTIONS; HUME, DAVID; MENGER, CARL; RULE OF LAW; SOCIAL JUSTICE; SOCIAL NORMS AND THE LAW; SPONTANEOUS ORDER.

Subject classification: 1b(i); 2a(i); 3a; 7a.

SELECTED WORKS

1941. The counter revolution of science. Part I, *Economica* NS 8, Feb.: 9–36; Part II, May: 119–50; Part III, Aug.: 281–320.

1942–4. Scientism and the study of society. Part I, *Economica* NS 9, Aug. 1942: 267–91; Part II, *Economica* NS 10, Feb. 1943: 34–63; Part III, *Economica* NS 11, Feb. 1944: 27–39.

1944. *The Road to Serfdom*. London: Routledge.

1949. *Individualism and Economic Order*. London: Routledge.

1952. *The Counter-Revolution of Science*. Glencoe, IL: Free Press. Reprinted London: Collier-Macmillan.

1954. (ed.) *Capitalism and the Historians*. London: Routledge.

1960. *The Constitution of Liberty*. London: Routledge.

1967. *Studies in Philosophy, Politics and Economics*. London: Routledge.
1968. *The Confusion of Language in Political Thought*. Occasional Paper No. 20. London: Institute of Economic Affairs.
1973. *Economic Freedom and Representative Government*. Occasional Paper No. 39. London: Institute of Economic Affairs.
1973–9. *Law, Legislation and Liberty*. Vol. I, *Rules and Order*, 1973; Vol. II, *The Mirage of Social Justice*, 1976; Vol. III, *The Political Order of a Free People*, 1979. London: Routledge.
1976a. *Denationalisation of Money*. Hobart Paper 70; 3rd edn, London: Institute of Economic Affairs, 1990.
1976b. *Choice in Currency*. Occasional Paper No. 48, London: Institute of Economic Affairs.
1978a. *New Studies in Philosophy, Politics, Economics and the History of Ideas*. London: Routledge.
1978b. Will the democratic ideal prevail? In *Confrontation: Will the Open Society Survive to 1989?*, ed. A. Seldon, London: Institute of Economic Affairs.
1980. *Unemployment and the Unions*. Hobart Paper No. 87; 2nd edn, London: Institute of Economic Affairs, 1984.
1988. *The Fatal Conceit: The Errors of Socialism*. London: Routledge.
1992. *The Fortunes of Liberalism*. Ed. P. Klein, London: Routledge.
1994. *Hayek on Hayek*. Ed. S. Kresge and L. Wenar, Chicago: University of Chicago Press.

BIBLIOGRAPHY
Andrews, P.W.S. 1964. *On Competition in Economic Theory*. London: Macmillan.
Barry, N. 1979. *Hayek's Social and Economic Philosophy*. London: Macmillan.
Barry, N. 1988. *The Invisible Hand in Economics and Politics*. Hobart Paper No. 111, London: Institute of Economic Affairs.
Booker, C. and North, R. 1994. *The Mad Officials*. London: Constable.
Butler, E. 1983. *Hayek. His Contribution to the Political and Economic Thought of our Time*. London: Temple Smith.
Demsetz, H. 1988. *Ownership, Control, and the Firm*. Oxford: Blackwell.
Demsetz, H. 1989. *Efficiency, Competition, and Policy*. Oxford: Blackwell.
Dickens, M. 1978. *An Open Book*. London: Heinemann.
DiQuattro, A. 1986. Rawls versus Hayek. *Political Theory* 14: 307–10.
Dowd, K. 1988. *Private Money*. Hobart Paper No. 112, London: Institute of Economic Affairs.
Finer, H. 1945. *Road to Reaction*. Boston: Little Brown.
Fischer, S. 1986. Friedman versus Hayek on private money. *Journal of Monetary Economics* 17: 433–9.
Galbraith, J.K. 1948. The German economy. In *Foreign Economic Policy for the United States*, ed. S.E. Harris, Cambridge, MA: Harvard University Press.
Gissurarson, H. et al. 1984. *Hayek's 'Serfdom' Revisited*. Hobart Paperback No. 18, London: Institute of Economic Affairs.
Ingrams, R. 1995. *Muggeridge*. London: Harper Collins.
Jewkes, J. 1948. *Ordeal by Planning*. London: Macmillan.
Lebrecht, N. 1996. *When the Music Stops*. London: Simon & Schuster.
Littlechild, S.C. 1978. *The Fallacy of the Mixed Economy*. Hobart Paper No. 80, London: Institute of Economic Affairs.
McCulloch, J.R. 1845. *A Treatise on the Principles and Practical Influence of Taxation and the Funding System*. Ed. D.P. O'Brien. Edinburgh: Scottish Academic Press, 1975.
Menger, C. 1883. *Untersuchungen über die Methode der Socialwissenschaften und der Politischen Oekonomie insbesondere*. Trans. F.J. Nock, ed. L. Schneider as *Problems of Economics and Sociology*, Urbana: University of Illinois Press, 1963.
Muggeridge, M. 1972. *Chronicles of Wasted Time*. 2 vols, London: Collins.
O'Brien, D.P. 1982. Competition policy in Britain: the silent revolution. *Antitrust Bulletin* 27: 217–39. Reprinted in D.P. O'Brien, *Methodology, Money and the Firm*, Aldershot: Edward Elgar, 1994.
O'Brien, D.P. 1988. *Lionel Robbins*. London: Macmillan.
O'Brien, D.P. 1994a. Hayek as an intellectual historian. In *Hayek, Co-ordination and Evolution*, ed. J. Birner and R. van Zijp, London: Routledge.
O'Brien, D.P. 1994b. Friedrich August von Hayek 1899–1992. *Proceedings of the British Academy* 84: 347–66.
Pigou, A.C. 1944. Review of F.A.v. Hayek, *The Road to Serfdom*. *Economic Journal* 54: 217–19.
Rawls, J. 1972. *A Theory of Justice*. Oxford: Oxford University Press.
Robbins, L.C. 1932. *An Essay on the Nature and Significance of Economic Science*. London: Macmillan.
Robbins, L.C. 1937. *Economic Planning and International Order*. London: Macmillan.
Robbins, L.C. 1947. *The Economic Problem in Peace and War*. London: Macmillan.
Robbins, L.C. 1952. *The Theory of Economic Policy in English Classical Political Economy*. London: Macmillan.
Robbins, L.C. 1961. Hayek on liberty. *Economica* N.S. 28: 66–81.
Samuels, W. 1966. *The Classical Theory of Economic Policy*. Cleveland: World Publishing.
Schumpeter, J.A. 1946. Review of Hayek, *The Road to Serfdom*. *Journal of Political Economy* 54: 269–70.
Swann, D., O'Brien, D.P., Maunder, W.P. and Howe, W.S. 1974. *Competition in British Industry*. London: Allen & Unwin.
Thornton, H. 1802. *An Enquiry into the Nature and Effects of the Paper Credit of Great Britain*. Ed. with an intro. by F.A.v. Hayek, London: Allen & Unwin, 1939.
Viner, J. 1961. Hayek on freedom and coercion. *Southern Economic Journal*, 27: 230–6.
Wilson, R.J.A. 1996. *Economics, Ethics and Religion: Jewish, Christian and Muslim Economic Thought*. London: Macmillan.
Wolfe, G. 1995. *Malcolm Muggeridge*. London: Hodder & Stoughton.
Yeager, L.B. 1976. *International Monetary Relations*. New York: Harper & Row.

hazardous wastes. *See* REGULATION OF HAZARDOUS WASTES.

hazard warnings. *See* INFORMATION REGULATION; PRODUCTS LIABILITY.

hedonic damages. *See* VALUING LIFE AND RISKS TO LIFE.

Hicks–Kaldor compensation. *See* KALDOR–HICKS COMPENSATION.

Hobbes and contractarianism. Hobbes's social contract theory is, first and foremost, a theory of political legitimacy. It purports to justify the institution and maintenance of an absolute political sovereign. Contemporary Hobbesian contractarians have deployed Hobbes's basic framework to explore not only its potential for justifying the state, but also for deriving morality from individual rationality. In both endeavours, contemporary Hobbesian contractarianism makes extensive use of the tools of rational choice and game theory. In this essay, I provide a brief overview of the philosophical stakes in Hobbesian contractarianism and explain how it emerged as the dominant alternative to Rawlsian contractarianism. But my principal aim will be to explain how Hobbesian contractarianism deploys game theory to analyse the structure and solutions to various collective action problems that arise within the contractarian framework. Apart from its obvious philosophical importance, Hobbesian contractarianism offers lawyers and economists insight into the application of game theoretic models.

I. HISTORICAL AND PHILOSOPHICAL BACKGROUND

In *Leviathan*, Thomas Hobbes presented a theory designed to justify the creation and maintenance of an absolute political authority. Despite its unprecedented rigour, most of Hobbes's contemporaries ignored, dismissed or ridiculed his theory for its unpalatable rejection of any conditions on the moral legitimacy of a political sovereign. For Hobbes, this position was compelled by two conclusions to which his analysis had led: that morality required no more nor less than individual rationality, and that life without a political sovereign was so intolerable that everyone would fare better under any political sovereign, even an arbitrary and tyrannical one. As Hobbes famously wrote, life in the state of nature – Hobbes's term for the state of anarchy – would be 'solitary, poore, nasty, brutish, and short' (Hobbes [1651] 1968: 186). John Locke and Jean-Jacques Rousseau followed Hobbes with their own, more moderate, contractarian justifications for the state. Locke in particular premised his contractarian theory on the rejection of Hobbes's argument for an absolute political sovereign. In rejecting Hobbes's claim that life under even a tyrannical sovereign could not be as bad as life in the state of nature, Locke wrote,

> As if when Men quitting the State of Nature entered into Society, they agreed that all of them but one, should be under the restrain of Laws, but that he should still retain all the Liberty of the State of Nature, increased with Power, and made licentious by Impunity. This is to think that Men are foolish that they take care to avoid what Mischiefs may be done them by *Pole-cats* or *Foxes*, but are content, nay think it Safety, to be devoured by Lions (Locke [1690] 1980: 50).

For all its detail and insight, Hobbes's theory was brushed aside as radically implausible. Contractarian theory was dominated instead by discussion of Locke's tacit consent theory and Rousseau's concept of the General Will. Locke's critics, however, doubted that citizens could be said to give even tacit consent, given the practical limits on rejecting their government. Rousseau's critics rejected the concept of the General Will as a metaphysically tendentious and hopelessly vague abstraction. By the end of the nineteenth century, contractarian thought gave way to comprehensive utilitarianism, which offered a unified moral and political theory. But by the mid-twentieth century, utilitarianism appeared to have succumbed to two fundamental criticisms: it seemed to be subject to a *reductio ad absurdum* – namely, that in principle it might treat as morally justified acts everyone would consider morally outrageous, and it required cardinal, interpersonal comparisons of utility, which most people rejected as impossible. By the mid-twentieth century, with contractarianism and utilitarianism both apparently discredited, political philosophy itself fell into disrepute.

In the 1950s, John Rawls began exploring the limits of utilitarianism and by 1971 published *A Theory of Justice*. Rawls began by restating the fundamental Kantian objection to utilitarianism that by trading off one person's disutility for another's utility it failed to take the distinction between persons seriously. To build a plausible alternative political theory, Rawls turned to Kant's contractarianism, rather than Hobbes's. Given that utilitarianism failed for its lack of respect for the individual, Kant's theory was attractive because it began with a commitment to treating individuals as ends in themselves. But despite its Kantian inspiration, Rawls's theory constituted a distinct and significant innovation in political theory. Rawls melded the insights of moral ideal observer theories with the methodology of the traditional contractarians. Instead of modelling a state of nature, and tracing justification to self-interest, tacit consent, or a General Will, Rawls imagined an 'original position' in which the idealized actors under morally idealized circumstances would decide on principles of justice that define the conditions for the legitimate exercise of political authority. The normative significance of the principles decided on in the original position derived from the ideal moral properties of decisions made in the original position. Rawls designed the original position to reflect the basic and relatively uncontroversial moral intuition that justice can be viewed as fairness. The famous Rawlsian 'veil of ignorance', for example, is designed to ensure that the decisions in the original position are not tainted by factors 'irrelevant from a moral point of view', such as one's current social or economic status, race, or gender.

Rawls's contractarian theory revitalized political theory itself, as well as contractarian methodology. The latter was due, in part, to Rawls's introduction of the formal tools of rational choice and game theory to moral and political philosophy. Rawls used a contractarian framework to reduce the question of what justice requires to the question of what rational choice requires in the original position. His theory was extraordinarily well-received, not only within political and moral philosophy, but within the humanities and social sciences generally. But a number of criticisms soon emerged, chief among them the view that despite its normatively minimal pretensions, Rawls's theory built into its analysis of the original position a number of question-begging assumptions. For example, some argued that it invoked a normatively loaded theory of primary goods – the maximand for rational utility maximizers deciding on principles behind the veil in the original position. Others argued that it presupposed a controversial and unacceptable conception of the person. Rawls then further developed his views in a series of articles spanning from the mid-1970s through the 1980s, culminating in his 1993 publication of *Political Liberalism*. By the mid-1980s, it was clear that Rawlsian contractarianism either presupposed controversial normative, metaphysical and epistemological premises, or, as Rawls insisted, presupposed a controversial conception of political philosophy that had no epistemological or metaphysical presuppositions at all.

Contemporary Hobbesian contractarianism emerged in the mid-1980s as the principal contractarian alternative to Rawlsian contractarianism. One of its chief attractions was its relative simplicity, clarity, and normative minimalism. Whatever else its faults, Hobbes's theory certainly did not begin with robust or question-begging normative assumptions. Instead, Hobbes begins with the view that morality consists in the rational pursuit of individual self-interest. Nor did Hobbes's theory require the view that moral and political philosophy could be independent, as Rawls came to maintain. Hobbes purports to derive the justification for the state from his theory of morality, which reduces morality to individual rationality. From this normatively minimal premise, Hobbes claims to derive the ultimate justification for political authority – the justification of an unfettered political sovereign. Rawls's theory had already rejuvenated interest in contractarian theory, and demonstrated the power of combining rational choice theory within normative political theory. Contemporary Hobbesians shared Rawls's conviction that rational choice theory could provide a powerful tool for moral and political theory, and that contractarian theory offered an attractive framework for employing rational choice theory. But they rejected Rawls's view that the rational choice modelled should be embedded within a normatively idealized choice situation. Instead, they mined Hobbes's original theory for its insights into the use of rational choice theory within the state of nature: a realistic rather than idealistic hypothetical model of human interaction. Hobbesian contractarianism promised to avoid the complex and potentially question-begging normative assumptions critics found in Rawls's theory, while at the same time maintaining the commitment to transforming the abstract philosophical inquiries of moral and political philosophy into the relatively precise problems answered by the formal logic of game and decision theory.

II. THE STRUCTURE OF CONTRACTARIAN THEORIES

All contractarian theories have three stages: a stage-one definition of a hypothetical scenario, a stage-two analysis of decisions, choices, or interactions in that scenario, and a stage-three argument for the normative significance of the outcomes in stage two. For political contractarians, who hope to provide a justification for political authority, there are two distinct kinds of stage-three arguments. The first is based on Hobbes's theory. Hobbes holds a meta-ethical view that reduces morality to individual rationality. Thus, the justification of the state for Hobbes requires a demonstration of its individual rationality. To provide this demonstration, Hobbes uses the hypothetical scenario of the state of nature. His strategy is to demonstrate that every individual would be worse off living in the state of nature than living under any effective political authority. Demonstrating the individual rationality of creating and maintaining a political authority, for Hobbes, is simply a matter of comparing one's prospects under political authority to one's prospects without political authority. Hobbes's definition of the state of nature is therefore intended to provide an accurate model of what life would be like for us without political authority. Thus, we might say that Hobbes follows a 'realistic' strategy for defining the state of nature.

The second stage-three strategy for political contractarians is based on Rawls's theory. Rawls's strategy was to think of the principles of justice as the outcome of a normatively ideal or purified decision procedure. Since his insight was to conceive of justice as fairness, he hoped to determine the content of the principles of justice by deriving it from a rational choice made under ideally fair conditions. He therefore designed the original position to embed the fundamental ideals of fairness. Thus, we might say that Rawls follows an 'idealistic' strategy for defining the original position.

The details of any contractarian theory, therefore, turn on the contractarian's stage-three argument for the normative significance of her hypothetical scenario. Hobbes's state of nature is designed to be realistic because he uses it as a basis for comparing the individual rationality of political authority to anarchy. Rawls's original position is designed to be idealistic because he uses it as a device for demonstrating the content of the principles of justice that follow from a commitment to viewing justice as fairness.

For the most part, Hobbesian contractarians share Hobbes's commitment to the realistic strategy for defining the state of nature. As we have seen, the classic Hobbesian contractarian argument eschews potentially question-begging ideals as first premises and seeks instead to ground legitimacy in simple individual rationality. Although some Hobbesian contractarians blend realistic and idealistic strategies, I will focus on the traditional approach. To demonstrate the individual rationality of political authority, the traditional Hobbesian contractarian undertakes two separate analytical demonstrations. The first is that life in the (realistic but hypothetical) state of nature would consist in what Hobbes called a war of all against all. This demonstration in turn is broken down into proofs that individuals would persistently compete physically against one another and would be unable to engage in long-term cooperation. In contrast, Hobbesians argue, an effective political authority will monopolize the use of force, thus preventing citizens from using force on one another, and can enforce contracts, thus preventing defection from cooperative agreements. The second demonstration is that an empowered sovereign would emerge from the interaction of minimally rational individuals in the state of nature. One way the sovereign might emerge is by 'institution'. The institution of a sovereign can be broken down into two stages. In the first, Hobbesians attempt to show that individuals in the state of nature would be able to select a sovereign. In the second, they attempt to show that the individual selected could be empowered as a sovereign. But Hobbes himself also argues that a sovereign might emerge from the state of nature not by institution but by 'acquisition'. Hobbes imagines that various warring, if temporary, factions in the state of nature might interact over time in such a way that one dominant faction with one leader emerges over time. Whether by institution or acquisition,

Hobbesians claim that the emergence of a sovereign in the state of nature demonstrates the individual rationality of political authority: political authority would result from the rational choice or rational interactions of individuals living in anarchy. Thus, they argue, individuals living under political authority now should find it individually rational to maintain their political authority. Finally, traditional Hobbesians conclude that this demonstration of the individual rationality of political authority also constitutes a demonstration of its moral legitimacy.

Thus, the contemporary political Hobbesian contractarian employs game theory to demonstrate the impossibility or unlikelihood of rational cooperation in the state of nature and to demonstrate that a sovereign would emerge from the state of nature, either by institution (by virtue of a concerted effort to select and empower a sovereign) or by acquisition (through the dynamics of group competition in the state of nature).

III. GAME THEORY AND HOBBESIAN CONTRACTARIANISM

The first application of game theory in Hobbesian contractarianism is in the demonstration that life in the state of nature will consist in a war of all against all. The line of analysis closest to Hobbes's original view identifies two distinct accounts of this conflict, each of which relies on Hobbes's account of human psychology. The clearest, most developed, and most sophisticated game-theoretic explication of Hobbes's original theory is provided in Jean Hampton's *Hobbes and the Social Contract Tradition* (1986). When presenting the traditional Hobbesian view, I will for the most part follow Hampton's characterizations and reconstructions of his position.

A. MODELS OF CONFLICT IN THE STATE OF NATURE. Hobbes begins with the assumption that human beings are psychological egoists: they necessarily seek to satisfy their desires. He also holds that human beings are predominantly rational psychological egoists: they are typically fully informed of relevant facts, reason free of distorting influences, and are free of diseases that produce abnormal desires. Finally, Hobbes stipulates that resources are moderately scarce in the state of nature. Based on these assumptions, Hobbes provides the 'rationality account' of conflict in the state of nature. This account is based on the view that interaction in Hobbes's state of nature has the structure of a single-play Prisoner's Dilemma (PD). Thus, the dominant strategy in cooperative games will be defection and no cooperation will be possible in the competition for scarce resources. One objection to the rationality account argues that interaction in the state of nature will have the structure of an iterated, rather than single-play, PD. When two individuals interact in a PD repeatedly over time, it is no longer the case that defection from a cooperative agreement is the dominant strategy. Although a short-term calculation would recommend defection, a long-term calculation must take into account the possibility of achieving long-term benefits over time through cooperation. By keeping an agreement in the first play of an iterated PD, one party can signal to the other that he or she is prepared to cooperate over the long run if the other will cooperate as well. As a result, indefinitely iterated PDs have some cooperative equilibria. There is also considerable evidence that minimally rational individuals will sometimes use a 'tit-for-tat' strategy in an iterated PD to punish defection and reward cooperation, resulting in a cooperative equilibrium over time (Axelrod 1984).

The second account of conflict in the state of nature is based on another of Hobbes's psychological assumptions. Hobbes claims that human beings have 'passions' that motivate them to act contrary to reason. In particular, they have a passion for 'glory' that will drive them to ignore the benefits of cooperation and irrationally risk even their self-preservation. One problem with this account is that it appears to be at odds with Hobbes's assumption that human beings are predominantly rational. But both the rationality and passions account of conflict are subject to the objection that they undermine Hobbes's later argument for the claim that a sovereign can be instituted in the state of nature by virtue of the rational actions of the individuals in the state of nature.

A third account of conflict, Jean Hampton's own account, holds that individuals in the state of nature are 'shortsighted'. This is not the view that individuals simply desire present benefits more than future benefits. Rather, it is the view that individuals engage in mistaken reasoning that leads to the creation of false beliefs. Thus, some individuals in the state of nature might simply 'not understand that the long-term advantages of cooperation would be much greater [than non-cooperation]' (Hampton 1986: 82). These individuals might fail to appreciate the rationality of cooperating even in an iterated PD. Still others might fail to appreciate that their interaction has the structure of an iterated PD rather than a single-play PD. If even a significant minority of individuals in the state of nature is shortsighted, then even non-shortsighted individuals will fear interacting with them and rationally refuse to cooperate. In addition, some individuals may be overcome by the passion for glory and forgo cooperation because they overestimate their own superiority. As a result, cooperation may well be irrational even though interaction has the structure of an iterated PD.

A fourth account of conflict in the state of nature is provided by Gregory Kavka in *Hobbesian Moral and Political Theory* (1986). Kavka begins by defining the state of nature as subject to mild scarcity of resources and populated fairly densely by ideally rational, predominantly self-interested, forwardlooking individuals. He then distinguishes between two different kinds of individuals in the state of nature. The first, called 'dominators', 'desire conquest, dominion, and power over others for its own sake'. The other, called 'moderates', 'desire power over others, if at all, only as a means to protect and secure themselves and their possessions' (Kavka 1986: 97). According to this analysis, it is possible that the only rational strategy for both dominators and moderates to follow in the state of nature, given that there will be both types in the state of nature, is 'anticipation'. That strategy requires 'striking first or gathering power over others so that one will be in a stronger relative position when battle erupts' (ibid.). If nearly everyone in the state of nature anticipates, not only will individuals lack personal security, but they will be unable to cooperate.

Anticipation imposes actual loses as well as opportunity costs in the state of nature. But anticipation may not be the only rational strategy. Another possibility, 'lying low', recommends that individuals not actively attack others and instead keep to themselves in the hope of being left alone. Lying low may be rational, especially for moderates who take no intrinsic pleasure in dominating others, if sufficiently few others anticipate. Once the percentage of individuals who anticipate exceeds a threshold, it will likely be rational for all individuals to anticipate. But if that percentage of individuals is below a threshold, it would be rational for moderates not to anticipate. If moderates refuse to anticipate, they would find it rational to cooperate. This analysis concludes that the state of nature will probably, but not certainly, consist in a war of all against all. Thus, it holds that defection from cooperative agreements is not dominant for all individuals in the state of nature, but is instead, at least for moderates, 'quasi-dominant': '[A] move by one party in an n-person game is quasi-dominant if and only if that move yields a higher payoff for that player than any other move for every likely, plausible, or reasonably expectable combination of moves by other players' (Kavka 1986: 113). Thus, interaction in the state of nature for moderates has, according to this analysis, the structure of a 'quasi-PD'.

B. MODELS OF SOVEREIGN SELECTION IN THE STATE OF NATURE. The second application of game theory in Hobbesian contractarianism is to solve the sovereign-selection problem. Hampton models this problem as a coordination game. A pure coordination game is one in which each player cares only that he choose the same alternative as everyone else, and is indifferent to which alternative that turns out to be. Rowing a boat is an example (Hume's). The solutions to pure coordination problems are stable equilibria because neither player has any incentive to deviate from the coordination solution.

There are two methods for solving a pure coordination game. The first Hampton calls a selective incentive strategy. This strategy is to change the structure of the game to make only one equilibrium (e.g., both row forward) the most attractive for both players (e.g., by paying a dollar to everyone who rows forward). The second method for solving a pure coordination game is by using a 'salience strategy'. By making one strategy more salient than all the others, every player might expect that every other player will employ that strategy. As David Lewis explains,

> [Players] might all tend to pick the salient as a last resort, when they have no stronger ground for choice. Or they might expect each other to have that tendency, and act accordingly; or they might expect each other to expect each other to have that tendency and act accordingly, and act accordingly; and so on. Or – more likely – there might be a mixture of these. Their first- and higher-order expectations of a tendency to pick the salient as a last resort would be a system of concordant expectations capable of producing coordination at the salient equilibrium (Lewis 1969: 35–6).

An alternative might be made salient as a result of a pre-existing convention or practice, an explicit or implicit agreement, or some peculiar or distinctive property it has uniquely (among the alternatives) and that therefore makes it obvious.

Mixed coordination games, like pure coordination games, are ones in which each player prefers that all players coordinate their action to achieve a mutually desired result. But unlike pure coordination games, the coordination equilibria of mixed coordinations games distribute the gains of coordination unequally among the possible alternatives. Thus, players are not indifferent among the alternative solutions. The classic example is the so-called 'Battle-of-the-Sexes', in which a husband and wife prefer going out together to going out alone, but the husband prefers to see a prize fight and the wife prefers a ballet. The wife prefers both at the ballet, the husband prefers both at the prize fight, and both prefer being together at their less favourite event than being apart at their favourite event. Like pure coordination games, mixed coordination games can be solved by incentive strategies that make one alternative preferable to both players (e.g., pay the husband enough money for attending the ballet so he prefers it over attending the prize fight). Salience strategies, however, are not likely to work in mixed coordination games, particularly if they are iterated, or allow for decision changes following the initial decision. For example, if husband and wife both show up at the ballet, say because husband and wife know that the only event whose location is known to both is the ballet, the husband can simply inform his wife, at the ballet, of the prize fight location and leave for the fight. Mixed coordination equilibria are, for this reason, unstable: each party has an on-going incentive to upset an already achieved coordination solution.

Hampton models the sovereign selection problem as a mixed coordination problem because everyone in the state of nature prefers political authority to anarchy, but everyone prefers to be the sovereign. She argues that a salience strategy will solve this coordination problem. Through the use of successive elections, Hampton claims, one individual can be selected and made salient as the 'sovereign-elect'. She argues that individuals will not seek to upset the results of an election by 'holding out' to be selected themselves and instead will 'give in'. Although individuals may bluff holding out, bluffing may well lead to deadlock. She claims that giving in is a rational solution to the deadlock that bluffing will create. Hampton also argues that individuals in the state of nature face a *de facto* deadline for creating a sovereign because of the danger of living in the state of nature. As the effective deadline approaches, Hampton claims that the probability for agreement decreases. Thus, when facing a deadline for agreement on selecting a sovereign, Hampton claims that individuals with large stakes in achieving coordination should give in rather than risk undermining a sovereign election which constitutes the first step of creating a political authority from which they have the most to gain. Thus, Hampton maintains, those with lower stakes will hold out and those with larger stakes will give in, conditional on others doing so as well.

C. MODELS OF SOVEREIGN EMPOWERMENT IN THE STATE OF NATURE. The third application of game theory in Hobbesian contractarianism is to model and solve the sovereign-empowerment problem. As I have noted, Hobbes contemplates two methods by which a sovereign could emerge from the state of nature: by institution or by acquisition. In either case, the central problem is to explain how even a selected sovereign could come to wield the power necessary to achieve effective rule. To achieve this power, the sovereign must have what Hampton calls an effective 'punishment cadre': a group of individuals who will obey and enforce the sovereign's commands.

1. *Sovereign empowerment by institution.* Hampton offers two accounts of the creation of an effective cadre in the institutional scenario for the emergence of political authority in the state of nature. The first turns on a distinction between different game-theoretic models for the provision of different types of collective good problems. The second relies on the rationality of cooperation in an iterated prisoner's dilemma.

A punishment cadre constitutes a collective good. A collective good provides benefits from which it is either impossible or impractical to exclude those who did not contribute to its production or do not contribute to its maintenance. Russell Hardin (1982) has shown that the provision of some collective goods has the structure of a single-play PD. Thus, given that non-cooperation is the dominant strategy in a single-play PD, such a collective good could not be produced in the state of nature. But Hampton argues that the particular collective good of an effective punishment cadre cannot be modelled as a single-play PD. Instead, she claims it has the structure of a particular kind of mixed coordination game in which free riding is irrational. This is a game in which individuals attempt to create a collective good that is a 'step-good' rather than an 'incremental good'. An incremental good is one that comes into existence gradually, as a matter of degree. There is no one point before which it does not exist and after which it does exist. Like the concept of a 'heap', one grain of sand more or less will not make the difference between there being or not being a heap. The collective good of national defence is one example – one airplane or soldier more or less will not affect the existence of an effective national defence. Although it is possible to specify levels of funding that are either necessary or sufficient for the provision of an incremental good, there is no precise level of funding that is both necessary and sufficient for the provision of an incremental good. A step good, however, does come into existence at a discrete, identifiable point in time. Pure step goods come into existence immediately after a certain threshold is met, and then cannot be increased in magnitude by further contributions. An example is a bridge, which constitutes no good at all before it fully spans a gap, but fully constitutes a good once it does so. It makes no sense to say that an individual contribution to an uncompleted bridge increases the magnitude of a collective good. Until the bridge is complete, no benefits can be derived from it as a functioning bridge.

Hampton argues that incremental collective goods have the structure of a single-play PD, but step goods have the structure of a mixed coordination game in which free riding will be irrational. Hampton reconceives the problem of creating an effective punishment cadre as that of creating a *minimally effective* punishment cadre. She then argues that one person's contribution to a punishment cadre – joining it – can make the difference between it being effective or not. Hampton argues that the sovereign can create her own punishment cadre by accurately selecting exactly the number of individuals she would need for a minimally effective punishment cadre. Each individual will realize that his contribution will make the difference between the existence or non-existence of the cadre. Given that everyone is better-off with an empowered sovereign than in the state of nature, the selected cadre members will join even if they prefer not to be in the cadre at all. Just as the husband prefers the ballet with his wife to the prize fight without her, Hampton claims the selected cadre members prefer being cadre members for an effective sovereign to being out of the cadre but in the state of nature as a result.

Hampton also claims that cooperating in the formation of a punishment cadre is rational because the cadre formation game has the structure of an iterated-PD. Thus, if the cadre is successfully formed, the sovereign-elect can promise to reward cadre members and punish those who refused to join. The iterated nature of a prospective cadre member's interaction with the sovereign and her potential future cadre, according to Hampton, makes joining a punishment cadre rational. One problem with this approach is its apparent conflict with Hampton's assumption that there are sufficiently many shortsighted individuals in the state of nature to cause a war of all against all, despite the fact that interaction in the state of nature has the structure of an iterated-PD.

2. *Sovereign empowerment by acquisition.* The acquisition scenario of the emergence of a sovereign in the state of nature takes as its first premise the realistic inequalities of individuals in the state of nature. Hobbes argues that some individuals will be better warriors than others, and thus better able to attack and to defend themselves in the state of nature. Hampton reconstructs Hobbes's argument as holding that 'weak warriors' will enter into 'confederacy agreements' with 'strong warriors'. Eventually, many confederacies will exist, but ultimately one might emerge as dominant and its head will be the effective sovereign that transforms the state of nature into a polity. Of course, this scenario requires the possibility of rational cooperation in a confederacy agreement in the state of nature, even though Hobbesians argue that cooperation is generally not rational in the state of nature. Hampton argues that confederacy agreements will not have the structure of a single-play PD, but will instead have the structure of what she calls a 'contingent-move agency game'. In this game, cooperation is individually rational for both parties even though the game does not iterate. In the agency game, one party performs before the other performs, but the party performing second has no incentive to defect. Her example of an agency game is the following Ruler–People game (Figure 1).

In the Ruler–People game, the people will empower the ruler so long as the ruler governs in their best interests. In this game, the ruler must move first. Provided the ruler

Ruler	People	Ruler	People
Govern according to terms of empowerment	Keep in power	2	1
	Depose	4	3
Ignore terms of empowerment	Depose	3	2
	Keep in power	1	4

Figure 1 Ruler-People agreement as an agency game

rules in the best interests of the people, the people have no incentive to defect from the cooperative agreement. Hampton's claim is that so long as the strong warrior 'moves first', and continues to protect the weak warrior, the weak warrior will have no incentive to defect.

D. GAME THEORY AND MORAL CONTRACTARIANISM. In *Morals by Agreement* (1986), David Gauthier argues that morality can be modelled as the outcome of a purely rational bargain among the inhabitants of Hobbes's state of nature. Gauthier's project can be divided into three stages. In the first stage, he must demonstrate that individuals in the state of nature would find it rational to bargain at all. Because individuals would find it rational to bargain only if compliance with the outcome of the bargain will be rational, Gauthier must demonstrate that rational individuals would comply with the outcome of bargains reached in the state of nature. For this demonstration, Gauthier relies on his theory of 'constrained maximization', according to which cooperation can be individually rational even in the single-play PD. In the second stage, Gauthier must show that the bargaining problem which individuals would face in the state of nature would admit of a solution, rather than stall in hopeless deadlock. To solve this problem, Gauthier argues that rational individuals in the state of nature would follow his bargaining strategy of 'minimax relative concession'. In the third stage, Gauthier must show that the principles generated as the outcome of rational bargaining in the state of nature can plausibly be described as moral principles. Gauthier argues that to qualify as moral principles, the principles must be fair. To demonstrate that the principles agreed to in the state of nature would be fair, Gauthier defends a theory of fair initial entitlements, a theory of the fairness of rational bargaining, and a theory of the unique rationality of complying only with fair bargains (or what he calls 'narrow compliance'). Below, I provide a selective overview of Gauthier's positions in each of these stages of his moral contractarian argument.

A. Constrained maximization. As we have seen, Hobbes begins by arguing that morality can be reduced to individual rationality. Hobbes's view therefore rejects the traditional claim that morality necessarily has the potential to conflict with the demands of individual rationality. Thus, on the traditional account of morality, keeping an agreement is *ceteris paribus* morally praiseworthy, especially when doing so conflicts with the demands of individual rationality. But on Hobbes's view, keeping an agreement to cooperate in a single-play PD would be immoral precisely because doing so conflicts with the demands of individual rationality. Gauthier also argues that morality can be reduced to individual rationality. And like Hobbes, Gauthier denies that morality necessarily has the potential to conflict with the demands of individual rationality. But instead of eliminating the potential conflict between morality and individual rationality by abandoning the traditional conception of morality, Gauthier abandons the traditional Hobbesian conception of individual rationality as direct utility maximization. On his view, individual rationality, properly understood, requires individuals sometimes to forgo directly utility-maximizing strategies, like the strategy of defection in the single-play PD. Thus, Gauthier argues that it can be individually rational to keep an agreement to cooperate even in a single-play PD. Gauthier therefore not only subscribes to the traditional conception of morality which ordinarily requires the keeping of agreements, but argues that this moral obligation can be explained by demonstrating that it is entailed by the dictates of individual rationality, even in the single-play PD.

Gauthier argues that individuals in the state of nature are likely to have many interactions that have the structure of a single-play PD over the course of their lifetime. In order to exploit the potential gains from these interactions, individuals would maximize their overall utility by resisting the direct utility-maximizing strategy of defection and instead following the indirectly utility-maximizing strategy of cooperation, so long as they could be reasonably certain that they are interacting with others similarly disposed to cooperate in single-play PDs. He claims that individuals can develop a psychological disposition to ignore direct utility-maximization strategies in the single-play PD so long as they are interacting with others similarly disposed. He argues that when two people so disposed interact in the single-play PD, it is individually rational for them to cooperate. Thus, Gauthier describes his theory of individual rationality as sometimes requiring direct utility-maximization (e.g., when individuals are dealing with others not disposed to cooperate with them in a single-play PD) and sometimes requiring what he terms 'constrained maximization' (e.g., when individuals are dealing with others who are disposed to cooperate with similarly disposed individuals in the single-play PD). The plausibility of Gauthier's thesis turns first on whether individuals can in fact develop the requisite psychological disposition to cooperate in single-play PDs with others similarly disposed, and second, on whether individuals can determine with reasonable certainty that they are in fact interacting with someone who has the same disposition. Gauthier claims that individuals' psychological dispositions for cooperation will be neither 'opaque' nor 'transparent' to others, but instead will be 'translucent.' Finally, the individual rationality of constrained maximization also requires that there be sufficiently many others disposed to cooperate in the single-play PD to make it worth the risk of mistakenly cooperating in a single-play PD with a non-cooperator. The odds of interacting with another cooperator and the ability of the cooperators to differentiate between cooperators and non-cooperators together will determine whether constrained maximization will maximize utility over time for those who predispose themselves to cooperate with others similarly disposed to cooperate in the single-play PD.

B. Minimax relative concession. Gauthier's project requires him not only to demonstrate the individual rationality of constrained maximization, but also that rational individuals would be able to agree on a distribution of the surplus created by their cooperation. Toward that end, Gauthier argues for his own brand of rational bargain theory, which he calls 'minimax relative concession'. That theory holds that 'in any co-operative interaction, the rational joint strategy is determined by a bargain among the co-operators in which each advances his maximal claim and then offers a concession no greater in relative magnitude than the minimax concession.' The minimax concession is 'the maximum concession (or one of the maximum concessions) with least relative magnitude required to bring about an outcome represented by a feasible concession point' (Gauthier 1986: 142). A feasible concession point is one that constitutes a distribution of any cooperative surplus over which the parties are bargaining (a 'point in the outcome-space').

C. Narrow compliance. Finally, Gauthier's theory requires not only that individuals will comply with cooperative agreements, but also that they will comply only if those agreements are fair. Gauthier labels individuals who will comply with any cooperative agreements as 'broad compliers', and those who will comply only with fair agreements as 'narrow compliers'. He then provides a series of arguments for the claim that narrow compliance is uniquely rational.

IV. CONCLUSION

This essay provides a summary overview of a number of the applications of game and decision theory to the philosophical problems addressed by contemporary Hobbesian contractarianism. Virtually all of the positions described are subject to extensive criticism and elaboration, as is the philosophical foundation for the entire Hobbesian contractarian project itself. An extensive discussion of the normative significance of Hobbesian contractarianism, as well as a detailed presentation and critique of the game and decision theoretic models discussed here, can be found in *The Limits of Hobbesian Contractarianism* (Kraus 1993). The philosophical promise of contractarianism lies in its ability to transform abstract and normatively complex questions into relatively tractable analytic exercises in formal modelling. The chief attraction of Hobbesian contractarianism is its promise to do this without making extensive normative presuppositions, such as those arguably required in Rawlsian contractarianism. Whether or not Hobbesian contractarianism ultimately satisfies its philosophical ambitions, it has already succeeded in providing a philosophical backdrop for state-of-the-art applied game and decision theory.

JODY S. KRAUS

See also BUCHANAN, JAMES M.; CONVENTIONS; CONVENTIONS AT THE FOUNDATION OF LAW; FOCAL POINTS; LOCKE, JOHN; MODERN CONTRACTARIANISM; MODERN UTILITARIANISM; PRISONERS' DILEMMA; PRISONERS' DILEMMA AND THE THEORY OF THE STATE; STATE OF NATURE AND CIVIL SOCIETY.

Subject classification: 1a(i); 1d(ii); 3a.

BIBLIOGRAPHY

Axelrod, R. 1984. *The Evolution of Cooperation*. New York: Basic Books, Inc.

Gauthier, D. 1986. *Morals by Agreement*. New York: Oxford University Press.

Hampton, J. 1986. *Hobbes and the Social Contract Tradition*. New York: Cambridge University Press.

Hardin, R. 1982. *Collective Action*. Baltimore: Johns Hopkins University Press.

Hobbes, T. 1651. *Leviathan*. Ed. C.B. Macpherson, Harmondsworth: Penguin Books, 1968.

Kavka, G.S. 1986. *Hobbesian Moral and Political Theory*. Princeton: Princeton University Press.

Kraus, J.S. 1993. *The Limits of Hobbesian Contractarianism*. New York: Cambridge University Press.

Lewis, D. 1969. *Convention: A Philosophical Study*. Cambridge, MA: Harvard University Press.

Locke, J. 1690. *Second Treatise of Government*. Ed. C.B. Macpherson, Indianapolis: Hackett Publishing Company, 1980.

Rawls, J. 1971. *A Theory of Justice*. Cambridge, MA: Harvard University Press.

Rawls, J. 1993. *Political Liberalism*. New York: Columbia University Press.

holdouts. The meaning of holdouts can best be illuminated by contrasting them with freeriders. Both are well-worn terms in the lexicon of law and economics. Unfortunately, the two expressions are often applied rather too loosely and interchangeably. Though they are members of the same family and have some resemblance, they are not identical twins. Each refers to an effort by the owner of a property right to appropriate quasi-rents from an entrepreneur who launches a wealth-increasing project that touches on that property right. That said, holding-out and freeriding differ in their technical and legal antecedents, their likely consequences and their behavioural imperatives. But, these causes, consequences and strategies are not the underlying phenomena. The ordinary language meaning of the two words captures the fundamental difference between the two concepts: the freerider wants to go along for the ride, while the holdout wants to hold his interlocutor over a barrel and cut a deal. Why, then, are the two phenomena so often confused? It is because the attractiveness of becoming a holdout itself creates a meta-freerider problem; multiple market actors encountering the possibility of becoming holdouts will each routinely behave as a sort of freerider.

The best way to reveal the essential nature of holdouts and freeriders is through a concrete illustration. Let us suppose that Edith Entrepreneur has gradually acquired three-quarters of a block in a rundown residential section of town. She intends to acquire the neighbouring 8¼ blocks, build a department store on the centre block and rehabilitate all the housing on the other eight blocks. Henry Holdout owns and operates a sanitarium on the remaining quarter block of the proposed department store. Its value in its current use is $400,000. Eight hundred identical Fred Riders each owns one of the eight hundred houses on the surrounding eight blocks. Each house has both a market value and subjective value to its current owner of $80,000.

Henry and Fred will now be further stylized so that they represent archetypes of holdouts and freeriders respectively. Towards that end, assume the following: (1) Edith's interest in Henry's property rests on scale economies in department-store construction and operation; in other words, a department store covering one full block is more than 33% more productive than one covering ¾ of a block; (2) because of negative externalities of department stores on sanitariums and any other plausible use of Henry's property, if Edith did erect a ¾-block department store it would reduce the value of Henry's property; (3) Edith's department store will confer $50,000 of positive external benefits on each Fred's property; and (4) if Edith builds a department store without acquiring the Freds' properties, each Fred will find it in his interest to renovate his property in exactly the same fashion that she would if it were hers.

In determining that the benefits of her proposed project exceed its costs, Edith has included in her calculations the standard transaction costs of negotiating contracts of sale with Henry and the eight hundred similarly situated Freds, assuming that they are unaware of her plan and of its effect on the value of their property, i.e. the substantial scale economies and external diseconomies for Henry, and the positive externalities for Fred. Simply put, Henry and the Freds (wrongly) believe that Edith could purchase property of equal value to her at a well-established market price only slightly above the value that each of them places on his separate property in its current use. No such property is in fact available. Henry and the Freds therefore have no incentive to engage in strategic bargaining. As holding-out and freeriding are conscious acts that require a knowledgeable actor, neither Henry nor Fred will be an obstacle to Edith's plans. Under these assumptions the cost of negotiating the deal will be a modest $1,000 per contract, or a total of $801,000.

But, if Henry and Fred learn of Edith's plans, their incentives and strategies change radically. In a colloquial sense Henry will become a holdout and Fred a freerider. Henry will try to extract a portion of the gain from Edith's project by refusing to sell his property to her unless she offers him a price that incorporates that gain, and the Freds will each try to sit back silently and enjoy all the gains that accrue to their property from Edith's project.

What if we relax the assumption that Edith can keep her plans secret, but impose a new assumption that transaction costs do not increase as a result of the information leak? The resulting changes, though substantial, are purely distributive rather than allocative. Since both the social value of the project and its total transaction cost remain unchanged the project will still go forward. But the gains will no longer flow exclusively to Edith. Henry and the various Freds will be in a position to extract some portion of the gain from Edith. How the pie is divided is not our present concern. It suffices to note that it will be a function of the reservation prices and bargaining prowess of the various parties.

If Henry and the Freds have no knowledge of Edith's plans, and perhaps even if they do, Edith must negotiate contracts with them. But what will they agree to exchange? At first blush the answer seems obvious: the property that each owns in exchange for money. But this answer rests on certain unspoken assumptions that hold for Henry but not for the Freds.

Consider a world bereft of *all* transaction costs. In such a world the character of the problems that Henry and Fred pose for Edith are largely indistinguishable from one another and purely distributional. If they have no knowledge of her plans they pose no problem, and if they have knowledge their revised bargaining behaviour will not reduce social wealth, but only redistribute it. Both Henry and Fred will gain a portion of the profit attributable to Edith's project.

In this zero transaction cost world, moreover, Edith need acquire none of her neighbours' properties. Other forms of contract and exchange are equally satisfactory and plausible. Contracts for the sale of the properties may be replaced by contracts for sidepayments to Edith from the various Freds (of a sum less than the $50,000 external benefit to each parcel) to induce her to go ahead with the project, and a contract for coordination of the use of Henry's property with Edith's. Henry could retain ownership of his property and agree to develop his quarter of the department store in perfect coordination with Edith. The bricks, girders and glass would all join perfectly at the property line, and in the operation of the store, product lines and personnel would be perfectly coordinated, as costless electronic scanners ensure that no patrons exit through Edith's portion of the department store with articles taken from Henry's and vice versa. All that distinguishes Henry from Fred is the plausible monetary range over which each can extract rents from Edith.

Neither the world of zero transaction costs nor even the world of transaction costs unaffected by the possibility of strategic bargaining is the one in which we live. In our world economic space is contoured by the omnipresence of the various species of the genus transaction costs. Transaction costs are a useful summary term, but it is crucial to understanding how they function to remember that they are an amalgam of subsidiary costs: negotiation costs, coordination costs, monitoring costs, etc. They are, in short, all the distinct categories of costs that might result when two or more people conduct business with one another and those people, as all people, have separate wills, knowledge and interests. Further, the character and magnitude of those costs affects and is affected by strategic opportunities. It is those considerations that ultimately distinguish Henry's relationship to Edith from Fred's.

Now, as we consider the unreality of our assumption of zero transaction costs, we must reflect in more detail on the differing ways in which transaction costs manifest themselves with respect to Henry *vis-à-vis* the Freds. The prospect of Henry and Edith trying to coordinate activities perfectly in their separately owned portions of a department store would perhaps make a suitable plot for a *Monty Python* farce, but not for a real-life business transaction; coordination and monitoring costs would dwarf any scale economies of the enterprise. As a result the only economically reasonable outcome is for Edith to acquire ownership of Henry's property. While the coordination costs between Edith and the Freds are zero, those between Edith and Henry are close to infinite. What of the negotiation costs?

Since Henry knows that scale economies in department stores make his property worth more to Edith than the $400,000 it is worth to him, the transaction costs of negotiating a transfer of the property will undoubtedly increase. A seller will expend more effort bargaining if he believes that the value of his property to the buyer differs from his own reservation price by $2 million than if he believes that the gap is only $2,000. But that increased transaction cost is unlikely to have any *ex-post* allocative effects. In the end Henry will sell his property to Edith. Why?

Henry is a pure holdout. He knows that if Edith builds the department store around his sanitarium he will be a freerider in only a darkly ironic sense. The externalities that a department store would provide to his property are negative, not positive. While a breakdown of negotiations between the parties as a result of poor information or strategy is not inconceivable, it is anomalous. Because it is in the interest of both parties to conclude a contract and they know it, it is also in their interest to limit the costs of reaching that contract. Neither party can fool the other by pretending that he or she does not want to successfully conclude negotiations as quickly and cheaply as possible. Even if the negotiating costs when Henry knows of Edith's plans are several times greater than when he does not, those costs will still be well below the increased gain of the transaction, and so it is highly likely that the two sides will reach agreement (Coase 1988: 161–3). Once more, only in a *Monty Python* farce would the parties expend so much in negotiating that they exhausted all or even most of the gain from the transaction.

Not so with Fred, or more accurately, the set of eight hundred Freds. Each Fred faces a very different set of transaction costs, both in character and magnitude. Imagine a situation in which Edith acquires 20% of the Freds' property and all of Henry's without tipping her hand. Assume that, at that point, the remaining Freds learn of her plans, and rightly conclude that her level of ownership makes it in her interest to proceed with the project. Recall our earlier assumption that if Edith goes forward with the department store each Fred will find it in his interest to renovate his property in precisely the same way Edith would were it hers. Under these assumptions no further contracting with the Freds, and no transaction costs, would be either necessary or sensible. Edith cannot credibly threaten to shoot herself in the foot by not going forward with the project. Accordingly, she cannot acquire the Freds' property at prices less than the enhanced value that results from her project. Although all the Freds become pure unadulterated freeriders, they present no allocative freerider problem. Edith will go forward with the project, and the remaining Freds will happily capture all the external gains to their property.

Let us change the scenario slightly. Assume once again that Edith has acquired 20% of the Freds' property and all of Henry's when her plans become known to all concerned. Only now Edith must capture some portion of the benefits that her project will provide for the remaining six hundred and forty properties in order to make her project viable. She needs to contract with some fraction of the remaining Freds. Let us assume that if she is able to capture $24 million of the $32 million increase in the value to the remaining Freds' property that will result from the project she will go forward.

Unlike in the case of Henry, for the Freds there is no unique set of contracts that answer the questions *whom* she must contract with, *how many* contracts she must make, and *what* those contracts must provide for. The same allocative end can be reached, in the sense that the department store will be built and the surrounding property will be renovated, by a wide variety of different contracts. It does not matter one whit whether she receives an outright subsidy to build the department store or a bargain sale of the surrounding property. In fact, the simpler and less costly solution of a side-payment from the various Freds to Edith, which would have been inconceivable if her plans remained secret, now becomes not only feasible but preferable. All that needs to be negotiated is how much each Fred will pay Edith to go ahead. And there is the rub.

There is no incentive for any of the Freds to accept even a *pro rata* share of the gain. Instead each Fred will want to play hardball in the hope that the others make the necessary sacrifices. More than that, each will find it in his interest to signal to Edith that the transaction costs of negotiating with him will be very high, and that she should go elsewhere for his share of her $24 million. Unlike the negotiations between Henry and Edith, in which Henry knew, and Edith knew that Henry knew, that it was not in his interest that she go ahead with the project without acquiring his property, in Fred's case it is clearly in his interest that Edith go ahead with the project without him. The express and implied haggling over price that this will induce will have a pernicious allocative effect; many projects will simply be abandoned as the freerider problem cannot be overcome.

The examples of Henry Holdout and Fred Rider are stylized, archetypical end-points on a set of continua. Henry exemplifies the case of negative externalities under uncoordinated separate ownership of the respective properties; the impossibility of coordinating the use of the properties; and only two parties. Fred sits at the opposite poles: positive externalities; perfect and costless coordination without consultation; and a very large number of parties. Of course, in the real world the two separate statuses, freerider and holdout, get muddled. Economic life offers up numerous situations that lie at intermediate points along the lines separating Henry and Fred, thereby partaking of the difficulties endemic to both sorts of problems.

The greatest source of the confusion over the difference between holdouts and freeriders arises from the common circumstance of multiple potential holdouts. Imagine that Henry's sanitarium is replaced with the offices of twenty-five independent psychotherapists, each of whom knows that Edith must acquire all of their properties in order to go forward with her project. Multiplying Henry by twenty-five does not change his status as a potential holdout, but now we recognize that something else is at play. These multiple Henry's have in some sense become freeriders, but not in the sense that they would be perfectly happy if the project went ahead without them, for they would then suffer substantial negative externalities. They have become freeriders not on Edith's department store, but on each others' contracts with Edith. In other words, unlike the Freds, each Henry wants to contract with Edith, but each also wants to be the last one to do so, when he will then be in a position to exact a much higher price from Edith. Because the prospect of multiple potential holdouts is so common, and routinely gives rise to a meta-freerider problem, the two are often confused.

The fundamental difference between holdouts and freeriders and the allocative and distributive effects associated with each rests on the differing character and magnitude of transaction costs required to do business successfully with each. And the source of those differences in transaction costs are immediately related to: (1) the direction of the externality if there is no coordination; (2) the cost of coordination; and (3) the number of parties. Moreover, each of these immediate causes is itself rooted in both the technical characteristics of the project and the background legal rules. But though these technical and legal roots are the source of the character and magnitude of transaction costs, it is the nature of the transaction costs and not their source that is the defining characteristic of holdouts and freeriders.

Because holding-out and freeriding derive from different economic phenomena, they also require different skills. Holdouts are, in the end, bilateral monopolists engaged in negotiations on how to divide up the pie. They must therefore act with a degree of skill not required of a freerider. The freerider may simply sit and wait. Even if a project will be abandoned because of collective freeriding, each individual freerider is usually helpless to change his fate. The holdout, on the other hand, holds his fate in his hands. He must search for just the right moment to act. The successful holdout requires accurate information and a high degree of negotiating, bargaining and bluffing skills. To the extent that he lacks that information and those skills he may either sell too soon and too cheap or, out of fear of selling too soon, hold out too long and lose everything.

Intelligent entrepreneurs do not harbour the illusion that they will generally be able to acquire all the property they need to assemble without the sellers catching on. They recognize that before the day is done they are likely to be faced by freeriders, holdouts, or those hoping to become holdouts by freeriding on other potential holdouts contracting with the entrepreneur. In order to avoid these costs entrepreneurs will undertake heroic efforts to maintain secrecy. And when the cat is out of the bag they will employ imaginative contractual tools to overcome the problems. But even though these tactics are costly they may nonetheless fail. The costs from holdouts and freeriders not only manifest themselves as quasi-rents in the period of direct negotiation, they also influence behaviour when they are only an opportunity cost for the entrepreneur not yet committed to the venture. He will abandon otherwise profitable projects if he anticipates that the costs of freeriders and holdouts will be too great.

When secrecy breaks down and holdouts and freeriders present themselves in full bloom they each require a different tactical response from the entrepreneur. The holdout presents him with a difficult, but hardly a unique, business problem. The holdout and the entrepreneur are simply bilateral monopolists locked in tough negotiations. Each has something the other wants, and each will do his best to gain the lion's share from the negotiations. Freeriders, on the other hand, present special and peculiar problems. The entrepreneur will often be forced to try some more creative negotiating tactic, such as mutually contingent contracts: Edith might offer each of the Freds $90,000 for their property contingent on *all* of them agreeing. Such a ploy does not guarantee success. But without some device to move each potential freerider from the back row to the margin, none of the Freds will want to enter negotiations, and transaction costs will bury the project.

Holdouts and freeriders are both a potential threat and an unpleasant reality in a multitude of economic circumstances. The market for control of corporations is but one of those circumstances. It is, however, a particularly illuminating illustration because the property rights that inhere in share ownership have a much less fixed character than other property rights. Corporate shares are a modern invention. They lack a long cultural heritage that prescribes a particular set of property rights. In addition, corporate shares are a more *narrowly* economic form of property, than, for example, real property. Therefore, in fashioning and limiting the rights that attach to them, the public, the legislatures and the judiciary are more comfortable in giving due weight to the desire to reduce transaction costs in order to increase wealth. So, let us examine how the definition of the property rights that attach to share ownership will affect the prospects of freerider and holdout problems in the market for corporate control.

Assume that the value of some publicly held corporation could be substantially increased by a change in management. For an entrepreneur to bring about such a change he must acquire a sufficient stockholding to control a majority of the board of directors. What stockholding should be legally sufficient? And how does the entrepreneur acquire it? The first is an issue of legal policy and the second one of business strategy. Both questions require that one address potential holdout and freerider problems.

The possibility of freeriding and holding out in a takeover battle and the incentives to engage in each are entirely a function of the legal rules for acquiring and exercising control of a corporation. Consider a legal rule that permitted boards of directors to be totally self-perpetuating unless all the outstanding shares were owned by a single entity that wished to remove the board. Such a rule would leave no room for an ordinary freerider problem, no current shareholder could hope to be a minority shareholder in the corporation after the change in management. Its shortcoming, however, is that it would generate a holdout and meta-freerider problem with a vengeance. A potential raider would be faced with multiple potential holdouts. And both the raider and the current shareholders would know from the beginning that at the end of the process of acquiring shares some knowledgeable shareholder will block the raider's path to control of the corporation. That shareholder will demand a large portion of the gain expected to result from a change in control of the corporation. The anticipation of this will encourage each shareholder to withhold his shares in the hope of becoming the final holdout, that is, to freeride on the sale of the others' shares to the raider. The potential raider, faced with the prospect of overcoming the reluctance to sell of this multitude of potential holdouts, then to confront the last holdout in bilateral negotiations, will be drained of all enthusiasm for the venture. Moreover, no increase in the value of the firm expected to result from a takeover will correct the problem; the greater the expected gain from a takeover, the greater the potential gain to a holdout.

If the legally required stockholding necessary to change the board is reduced to a mere majority the holdout and meta-freerider problem will be eliminated. In that very process, however, a prosaic, but nonetheless disabling, freerider problem will be created. Current shareholders who believe that a change in management will substantially increase the value of their shares will prefer to hold on to them rather than sell for less than the expected enhanced value.

The raider could try to acquire a majority holding quietly without alerting the shareholders. This is generally more difficult in the case of corporate shares than in the case of real property. Rationally ignorant shareholders believe that the market price of their shares reflects their fundamental value. And so they will not sell even in response to an immodest rise in the price. They must be jarred into action by the publicity of a tender offer (Cohen 1990). Regardless of the reason, if the raider must tip his hand a seemingly insoluble freerider problem will arise. It is simultaneously in the interest of each shareholder that the raider succeeds in acquiring a majority and that the shareholder retains his shares and thereby partakes in the gains generated by a change in control of the corporation.

Solving this problem has required granting legal rights to entrepreneurs in the market for corporate control not generally available to other private actors. The law permits the raider, in effect, to condemn privately the shares of erstwhile freeriders. After he acquires control, the raider can force the remaining shareholders to surrender their shares in exchange for their pre-raid value. And so the freerider problem is solved by making corporate raids 'front-end loaded'; the raider offers the shareholders more for their shares now then they will be able to receive after he acquires control. The market for corporate control illustrates how the possibility of freeriding and holding out are ultimately a function of the rights that attach to property and the transaction costs associated with exercising those rights.

To summarize and conclude, while I have employed concrete examples to illustrate the nature of, and distinctions between, holdouts and freeriders, those examples are not meant in any way to cabin the application of the definitions offered. Those definitions are generic and can be applied fruitfully to all putative instances of the respective phenomena. The holdout is a current owner who recognizes that: because of positive externalities in the planned, well-coordinated use of the entrepreneur's and the holdout's property, his parcel has risen in value *to the entrepreneur*; the holdout cannot perfectly or even approximately coordinate the use of his property with that of the entrepreneur if they are separately owned; and, if the holdout retains ownership of his property, there will be no (or a much smaller) positive externality from the entrepreneur's planned use of his property. The holdout can then only gain by selling to the entrepreneur. The freerider, by contrast, will receive positive external benefits from the entrepreneur's project regardless of whether he contracts with the entrepreneur or not. He has a strong incentive to stand on the sidelines and thereby reap what others have sown. A variation on the freerider phenomenon, that for lack of literary imagination I infelicitously call a meta-freerider problem, arises when there are many *potential* holdouts. Each potential holdout then has an incentive to freeride, *not on the entrepreneur's project*, but on the capitulation of the other potential holdouts, in the hope that he will become the ultimate holdout.

Holdouts, freeriders, and meta-freeriders are different theoretical problems. In their operational manifestations such problems do not simply hang in the air. Each has causes, both technical and institutional, and consequences of significant economic import. Those potential consequences in turn generate responses both personal and institutional which have been touched on in this short essay.

LLOYD COHEN

See also AGENCY COSTS AND CORPORATE GOVERNANCE; COASE THEOREM; MARKET FOR CORPORATE CONTROL.

Subject classification: 2b(i); 4c(i); 5b(ii).

BIBLIOGRAPHY

Coase, R.H. 1988. *The Firm, The Market, and the Law*. Chicago: University of Chicago Press.

Cohen, L.R. 1990. Why tender offers? The efficient market hypothesis, the supply of stock, and signaling. *Journal of Legal Studies* 19(1): 113–43.

Cohen, L.R. 1991. Holdouts and free riders. *Journal of Legal Studies* 20(2): 351–62.

hold-up problem. The essential elements of 'the hold-up problem' can be illustrated with the following example. A builder constructs a house on land he does not own, but only leases short term. Perhaps the builder believes he has an understanding with the landowner on the future purchase price of the land. However, after the initial land lease expires, the landowner violates the intent of the contractual understanding by threatening to raise the land rent unless the builder agrees to buy the land at an exorbitant price. This simple example illuminates the three factors necessary for the occurrence of a hold-up.

First of all, the builder's investment must be specific to the particular piece of land. If the house were built on wheels and it were costless to move it to another piece of land, a hold-up could not take place. The landowner could not threaten to increase the sale price of the land after the builder made its investment because the builder's entire investment would be costlessly transferable. More generally, if some element of the builder's investment were specific to the particular piece of land and hence non-salvageable, this element would be the maximum amount by which the landowner could increase the price of the land.

Secondly, the contract governing the relationship between the landowner and house builder must be incomplete. In this case the land lease did not cover future years. If the land lease had fixed the rent for all future years, the landowner could not engage in this particular hold-up.

Thirdly, the landowner must find it profitable to engage in a hold-up. Although the presence of an incomplete contract and of specific investments creates an opportunity for the landowner to hold up the builder, the landowner may decide not to take advantage of this opportunity if doing so entails additional costs. For example, the landowner may be planning to transact with the builder in the future. As a result, engaging in a hold-up would jeopardize the landowner's future relationship with the builder and thereby lead to lost expected future profits. A hold-up occurs only when a transactor, taking these future effects into account, decides it is wealth-maximizing to take advantage of contractual incompleteness to expropriate the rents on the specific investments made by its transacting partner. Each of these three factors, specific investments, incomplete contracts and the conditions of wealth maximization, are discussed in turn below.

SPECIFIC INVESTMENTS. The first factor, the presence of specific investments, is all-pervasive in the economy. The very nature of exchange implies continuing relationships and the necessity for individuals to make investments in assets or in information that are specific to their particular transacting partners. As a result, it is generally costly for transactors to switch partners. Therefore, the potential for a hold-up is almost always present in continuing relationships. However, the fact that transactors are to some extent 'locked in' to one another after they make their specific investments does not imply the presence of market or monopoly power. The market may well be competitive at the relevant point in time when transactors are making their investment decisions: for example, there may be a large number of essentially equivalent pieces of land on which a house can be built. Moreover, contrary to the exercise of market power, the ability to take advantage of specific investments to engage in a hold-up requires imperfect contracts and, as we shall see, unanticipated events.

Perhaps the most extensively discussed example in the economic literature of a hold-up due to the presence of specific investments is the Fisher Body–General Motors case (originally presented in Klein et al. 1978). The case deals with the supply of automobile bodies by Fisher to General Motors in 1919. In order to produce automobile bodies for General Motors, Fisher Body had to make an investment in stamping machines and dies that was highly specific to General Motors. Fisher Body's investment could not be used to make bodies for any other automobile manufacturer. As a result, a significant potential was created for General Motors to hold up Fisher. In particular, after Fisher Body made its specific investment, General Motors could have threatened to reduce its demand for Fisher-produced bodies, or even to terminate its relationship with Fisher completely, unless Fisher reduced its prices.

In most cases involving specific investments, transactors attempt to control the hold-up problem by designing their contracts before any such investments are made. In this case the contract adopted by General Motors and Fisher Body included a ten-year exclusive dealing clause which required General Motors to buy all its closed metal automobile bodies from Fisher for a period of ten years. This prevented General Motors from appropriating the rents from the Fisher investment by threatening to switch suppliers of its bodies.

Obviously, such a contract also had to set the price at which Fisher would supply the bodies to General Motors, or Fisher would charge General Motors a monopoly price during the contract term. The transactors agreed upon a formula where the price was set equal to Fisher's 'variable cost' plus 17.6 percent. The use of an upcharge over variable costs, rather than a formula based on Fisher's total cost, was probably employed because Fisher was selling automobile bodies to many different companies and it was difficult to isolate and measure precisely the capital and overhead costs associated with General Motors shipments.

INCOMPLETE CONTRACTS. The contract adopted by Fisher Body and General Motors was, like all contracts, not complete. What is unusual about this case, however, is that Fisher took advantage of the contractual incompleteness to hold up General Motors. Fisher was able to hold up General Motors because, after the parties signed their contract, the demand for closed automobiles increased dramatically. Fisher took advantage of the contractual incompleteness in the face of the large demand increase for automobile bodies to adopt an inefficient, highly labour-intensive production process. From Fisher's point of view there was no economic reason to make capital investments when, according to the contract, they could instead hire a worker and put a 17.6 percent upcharge on the worker's wage. In addition, Fisher used the contract to locate its body-producing plants far away from the General Motors assembly plant. There was no economic reason for Fisher to locate their plant close to the General Motors assembly plant when, according to the contract, they could profit by locating their plant far away from the General Motors plant and put a 17.6 percent upcharge on their transportation costs. The result was automobile bodies that were highly profitable for Fisher to produce, but very costly for General Motors to purchase.

This type of hold-up, where a transacting party uses the court to enforce a long-term imperfect contract in a manner that is contrary to the intent of all the contracting parties, may appear different from the hold-up that occurred in the house construction example, where the landowner took advantage of the absence of a long-term contract to hold up the builder after the short-term land lease expired. The court was unable to protect the builder in the house construction case, whereas in the Fisher–General Motors case the court is actually effectuating the hold-up by strictly enforcing the written contract terms. But although this distinction may be important for contract law, the hold-ups involved in both cases are analytically similar.

Both hold-ups are caused by a transactor using the court to take advantage of an imperfection in the contract governing an economic relationship. In the Fisher Body–General Motors case, court enforcement of the imperfect cost-plus contract permitted Fisher to charge General Motors arbitrarily high prices. Similarly, in the house construction case, court enforcement of the imperfection in the contract, namely that the contract only covered a short period, permitted the landowner to charge the builder an arbitrarily high price after the short-term land lease expired. (We are assuming for simplicity in this discussion that the court only enforces written terms and does not enforce unwritten terms. Contract law is, of course, more complicated, with courts often interpreting both written and unwritten (but understood) terms. One should merely think of 'written terms' throughout the discussion here as referring to the terms that, in fact, are enforced by the court under the principles of contract law.)

The only difference in the two hold-up cases is that it is the long-term contract in the Fisher–General Motors case, not its investments in order to supply General Motors, which creates the specificity that permits Fisher Body to hold up General Motors. In fact, in this case the particular contract adopted by the parties to prevent General Motors from holding up Fisher actually created the potential for a much greater hold-up by Fisher Body of General Motors. Once the long-term exclusive dealing contract was signed, essentially all of General Motors' assets became specific to Fisher Body.

The Fisher Body–General Motors case illustrates a major cost associated with contractual specification. Because contracts are inherently imperfect, writing something down to be enforced by the court creates rigidity. Written contracts are inherently imperfect because some elements of performance cannot be measured in such a way that breach can be demonstrated unambiguously to a court. Consider, for example, the energy an employee puts towards a task, or the taste of a hamburger. Transactors cannot expect to cover such performance in their written contracts.

In addition, contracts are imperfect because it is too costly for transactors to attempt to cover every possible contingency over the life of a contract. The costs of attempting to cover every possible contingency are not the 'ink costs' of writing down many contract terms, but the substantial negotiation costs involved in specifying a contractual response to every possible contingency. These costs include the costs to transactors of discovering all the possible things that can happen in the future, figuring out the optimal response for all these hypothetical (largely irrelevant) states, and then bargaining over mutually acceptable contingent contractual arrangements for all these possibilities. Much of this activity involves largely redistributive rent dissipation, with transactors merely attempting to obtain an informational advantage over their transacting partners, hoping to place themselves in a position where they will be more likely to collect on (and less likely to pay for) hold-ups, with little or no allocative benefit. Therefore, rather than attempting to determine all of the many events that might occur during the life of a contractual relationship and writing a prespecified response to each, transactors increase the gains from exchange by using imperfect, incomplete contracts.

Because contract terms are inherently imperfect, writing something down in a contract may present transactors with an opportunity to engage in a hold-up. A hold-up can be effectuated by a transactor deciding to use the court to enforce the imperfect contract term rigidly, even if the literal contract term is contrary to the intent of the contracting parties. This is what occurred in the Fisher–General Motors case.

This does not mean that writing down contract terms is not beneficial to transactors. Writing terms has the obvious benefit that the court can be used to enforce performance. However, because court enforcement of contract terms may also be the mechanism by which a transactor engages in a hold-up, one must recognize that contractual specification not only has benefits but also costs. In fact, it is the very benefit associated with contract specification, that the court can be used to enforce literal performance, that creates the harm of contractual rigidity. For some easily measurable elements of performance there may be no trade-off in terms of added rigidity associated with writing down contract terms. However, when transactors must use a less than perfect proxy for performance in a contract, there is a trade-off. Including the proxy in the contract may help in enforcing the understanding but it may also do harm by making the contractual arrangement more rigid.

As the Fisher–General Motors case vividly illustrates, once an agreement is formalized in a written contract it may not be breached cheaply if unanticipated changes occur in the market. The only limit on the cost to General Motors of not performing to the literal terms of the imperfect contract when market conditions deviate substantially from *ex ante* expectations is essentially their declaration of bankruptcy. If, on the other hand, a contractual understanding is not formalized in a written contract, the understanding is much more flexible, with transactors able to opt out of the agreement more cheaply if subsequent market conditions deviate substantially from expectations. As a result, at some point adding additional contract terms implies a net expected cost so that transactors often decide to avoid the rigidity associated with written terms by intentionally leaving many elements of intended performance unspecified in their contract.

THE CONDITIONS OF WEALTH MAXIMIZATION. Although specific investments and incomplete contracts are pervasive in the marketplace, this does not imply that transactors will always take advantage of contractual incompleteness to engage in a hold-up. This leads us to the third necessary factor for a transactor to engage in a hold-up, the presence of conditions under which a hold-up is wealth maximizing. In particular, the transactor must expect the short-run gains from engaging in the hold-up to outweigh any long-run costs imposed by the transactor being held up. These long-run costs involve the future losses to a transactor engaging in a hold-up by termination of the relationship. The magnitude of this sanction will depend upon the amount of specific capital possessed by the transactor engaging in the hold-up since that is what will be lost upon termination.

In general, transactors enforce their contractual relationships not solely with the threat of court imposed sanctions, but also with the use of these privately imposed sanctions. The magnitude of the privately imposed sanction can be referred to as private enforcement capital. A transactor deciding whether to engage in a hold-up will trade off the short-run gains from engaging in a hold-up with these privately imposed sanctions that it will bear from engaging in a hold-up. If the private sanctions are greater than the hold-up gains, transactors will not engage in a hold-up. It is because of the existence of this private enforcement mechanism that transactors generally feel comfortable leaving their contracts incomplete.

The quantity of private enforcement capital possessed by transactors defines what can be called the self-enforcing range of the contractual relationship, which measures the extent to which market conditions can change without precipitating a hold-up by either party. Changes in market conditions may alter the magnitude of the hold-up potential. Yet as long as the relationship remains within the self-enforcing range, where each transactor's hold-up potential gain is less than the private sanction that can be imposed for violating the intent of the contractual understanding, a hold-up will not take place. Only when changes in market conditions move transactors outside the self-enforcing range, so that the one-time gain from breach exceeds the private sanction, will a hold-up occur (see Klein 1996).

This is what occurred in the General Motors–Fisher Body case. Fisher and General Motors found themselves outside the self-enforcing range because of a very large increase in demand by General Motors for Fisher-produced bodies. This increase in demand increased the Fisher hold-up potential so much that it became larger than the private sanction that could be imposed on Fisher by General Motors. As a result, Fisher found it profitable to violate the intent of the contractual understanding by taking advantage of the imperfect terms of the agreement.

The change in market conditions that permitted Fisher to take advantage of General Motors in this way must have been unanticipated. If the parties had known that a big increase in demand was likely, they would certainly have used a different contract that explicitly handled the contingency. However, when the contract was entered into in 1919 the dominant production process for automobiles consisted of individually constructed, largely wooden open bodies; the closed metal bodies supplied by Fisher were essentially a novelty. After 1919, demand for closed metal bodies grew dramatically, and by 1924 they accounted for about two-thirds of General Motors' automobile sales. This unanticipated shift in demand increased the extent by which the contract forced General Motors to rely on Fisher and made it profitable for Fisher to take advantage of the contract to hold up General Motors. The large increase in demand increased Fisher's hold-up potential of General Motors so that it became greater than the private sanction that could be imposed on Fisher by the loss of future sales to General Motors after the contract expired. If this large change in demand had not occurred, the Fisher–General Motors contract would have been self-enforcing and the malincentives associated with the cost-plus contract terms would not have mattered. Fisher would have known that they could not take advantage of the literal terms of the contract without being punished by General Motors and this punishment would have been greater than any hold-up gain.

Transactors believe, given the particular contract terms they choose and the private enforcement capital they possess, that their relationship will remain within the self-enforcing range, where market conditions can change and the parties will perform as intended. However, transactors also know at the time they enter their contractual relationships and make their specific investments that their private enforcement capital is limited, that their written contract is imperfect and incomplete and, therefore, that there is some probability of a hold-up occurring. In particular, transactors know that there is some probability that market conditions may change sufficiently (and the value of the rents accruing to one of the parties increase sufficiently) so that one party may find it in its interest to engage in a hold-up.

This probabilistic hold-up framework implies a fundamental complementarity between court enforcement and private enforcement. Court enforcement and private enforcement are not alternative enforcement mechanisms, where transactors are assumed to rely upon one or the other enforcement mechanism, but never both. Instead, because of the costs associated with writing contract terms to be enforced by the court, transactors can be expected to rely as much as possible on private enforcement. However, given the fact that private enforcement capital is limited, transactors can be expected to use written contract terms and the assistance of the court as a supplement to private enforcement. Where private enforcement capital possessed by transactors is large relative to the hold-up potential, this court assistance will be small. Contracts will be 'thinner', with transactors writing out only the essential elements of the agreement, or perhaps even proceeding on the basis of a verbal understanding and a handshake. Alternatively, where private enforcement capital is small, written contracts will be 'thicker', with transactors attempting to specify more elements of performance and provide for more contingencies.

The role of contract terms within this framework is very different from the standard economic view of contract terms. Rather than thinking of contract terms as creating optimal incentives on some court-enforceable proxy for performance, contract terms are designed to maximize the probability that transactors remain within the self-enforcing range. In general, the goal of contractual specification is to economize on the amount of private enforcement capital necessary to make a contractual relationship self-enforcing by 'getting close' to desired performance in a wide variety of circumstances (without creating undue rigidity) and to let the threat of private enforcement move performance the remainder of the way to the desired level.

This may explain the exclusive territory or the *de facto* resale price maintenance terms used in franchise or distribution contracts. Such terms serve to shift the private enforcement capital of the franchisor or manufacturer to the franchisee or distributor, so that the latter has something to lose if it does not perform as desired. The contract terms can be thought of as shifting the location of the self-enforcing range so that private enforcement capital coincides more accurately with the transactors' hold-up potentials under likely future conditions. By more closely relating actual private enforcement capital to likely requirements, transactors widen the *ex post* market conditions that are likely to fall within the range where performance remains assured.

This probabilistic view of hold-ups should be contrasted with Williamson's view of 'opportunism' which he identifies with lying, stealing, cheating, and more subtle forms of deceit such as incomplete or distorted disclosure of information (Williamson 1985: 47). The hold-up may have occurred in our illustrative house construction example because the landowner deceived the builder with a low up-front land rental price and vague promises about the future. However, relying on one transactor taking advantage of the naivety or ignorance of another transactor is a highly unsatisfactory way to explain the incidence of hold-ups. Explanations of hold-up behaviour based upon transactor deception are often clearly inconsistent with the facts. For example, the Fisher–General Motors case involved a transaction between two large, sophisticated business firms with no evidence of any pre-contract deception on either transactor's part.

It is much too unlikely an explanation to rely on General Motors' naivety or on Fisher's deception to explain why General Motors accepted such an imperfect, incomplete contract which placed it in a position where it could be held up by Fisher. General Motors and Fisher Body were clearly aware of the hold-up problems inherent in their relationship, and both Fisher and General Motors had to have been aware that the contract they adopted to solve their hold-up problem was 'defective' in the sense that it was incomplete and, as a result, contained obvious malincentives. Yet General Motors and Fisher adopted this incomplete and imperfect contract because they believed it would have been more costly to write a more complete (and rigid) contract and, given the magnitude of the transactors' private enforced capital, they expected the incomplete contract to work in most circumstances they would be likely to encounter in the future. That is, General Motors and Fisher knowingly entered into their incomplete contract because they believed that this contract, while imperfect, was optimally designed to minimize the probability of a hold-up occurring.

Unfortunately, conditions developed that permitted Fisher to use the incomplete contract profitably to hold up General Motors. If General Motors and Fisher had known ahead of time what was to happen – in particular, the very large increase in demand for closed auto bodies – no doubt they would have written their contract to take account of the problems that developed. In that sense the Fisher hold-up of General Motors was an unexpected surprise. However, in an uncertain world where complete contractual specification is impossible, transactors knowingly use incomplete contracts, recognizing that they leave themselves open to the possibility of hold-ups. Transactors recognize that a hold-up could occur if particular conditions develop, but these particular conditions are considered unlikely to develop. Because it is costly to negotiate contract terms and because contract terms create the danger of rigid enforcement, these unlikely conditions are not taken account of in the contract. Rather than thinking of hold-ups occurring because transactors are ignorant or deceived, transactors (such as General Motors and Fisher Body) should be thought of as designing an optimal contract where they assume the risks of a hold-up, recognizing that it is too costly for them to try to specify in advance perfect contract terms for all contingencies.

BENJAMIN KLEIN

See also ASSET SPECIFICITY AND VERTICAL INTEGRATION; CONTRACT FORMATION AND INTERPRETATION; CONTRACTS; CORPORATE GOVERNANCE; FRANCHISE CONTRACTS; INCOMPLETE CONTRACTS; LAW FIRMS; OPPORTUNISTIC BEHAVIOUR IN CONTRACTS.

Subject classification: 5c(i).

BIBLIOGRAPHY

Goldberg, V.P. 1976. Toward an expanded economic theory of contract. *Journal of Economic Issues* 10(1): 45–61.

Klein, B. 1996. Why hold-ups occur: the self-enforcing range of contractual relationships. *Economic Inquiry* 34(3): 444–63.

Klein, B., Crawford, R.G. and Alchian, A.M. 1978. Vertical integration, appropriable rents and the competitive contracting process. *Journal of Law and Economics* 21(2): 297–326.

Klein, B. and Murphy, K.M. 1988. Vertical restraints as contract enforcement mechanisms. *Journal of Law and Economics* 31(2): 265–97.

Williamson, O.E. 1985. *The Economic Institutions of Capitalism*. New York: Free Press.

Holmes, Oliver Wendell, Jr. (1841–1935). Oliver Wendell Holmes, Jr. (he dropped the 'Jr.' when his father, Oliver Wendell Holmes, died) is the outstanding figure in the history of American law. His relation to the law and economics movement is significant but complex and even ambivalent – and easily overstated. In his best-known essay, 'The Path of the Law', he deplored 'the present divorce between the schools of political economy and law', said that 'every lawyer ought to seek an understanding of economics', and famously declared that 'for the rational study of the law the black-letter man may be the man of the present, but the man of the future is the man of statistics and the master of economics' (Holmes 1897: 170, 174). These passages convey, however, an exaggerated impression of Holmes's founding relation to the economic analysis of law.

Holmes was born in 1841, the son of a distinguished medical scientist and belles-lettrist and, on his mother's side, the descendant of men who had played important roles in the early history of Massachusetts. Raised in Boston, a childhood friend of William and Henry James and Henry Adams and acquainted through his father with Emerson, Holmes was educated at Harvard, served three years as an officer in the Union Army in the Civil War (surviving three serious wounds), and graduated from the Harvard Law School in 1866. He practised law for fifteen years in Boston, while doing extensive scholarly writing on the side and participating in Boston intellectual circles that included Charles Sanders Peirce, William James and other founders of pragmatism. He was appointed to a professorship at the Harvard Law School in 1881, but within a year of his appointment he resigned it to become a Justice of the Supreme Judicial Court of Massachusetts. The series of lectures published in 1881 as *The Common Law* had established Holmes as a preeminent legal scholar, and he continued to write notable articles, including 'The Path of the Law', during his two decades of service on the Massachusetts court, of which he eventually became the Chief Justice. He was appointed to the US Supreme Court in 1903, retired in 1932, and died three years later, shortly before his ninety-fourth birthday. Despite the advanced age (62) at which he was appointed to the Court, very few Justices have exceeded the length of his tenure.

Holmes is most famous within the legal profession for his jurisprudential ideas, including his debunking of the role of logic in law ('The life of the law has not been logic: it has been experience' (Holmes 1881: 1)), his 'bad man' theory of law, his positivism, his concept of judicial self-restraint, and his 'objective' theory of criminal liability, and for a series of opinions, mostly dissenting, in the US Supreme Court involving free speech, federalism, and federal habeas corpus (see Posner 1992). None of these aspects of Holmes's work and thought is central to the economic analysis of law; and even his heralding of the economic approach in the passages quoted above from 'The Path of the Law' was not much noticed until the law and economics movement was well established. The founders of the movement, such as Ronald Coase, were either unaware or only barely aware of Holmes's remarks about economics.

Nevertheless, at least in hindsight, it is possible to view Holmes as a significant precursor of the modern economic analysis of law – though not because of any specifically economic insights, and not as significant as, say, Bentham. Holmes was not trained in economics and appears not to have read extensively in it, and although he had strong economic intuitions they lacked subtlety and accuracy. His dominant economic intuition was that issues of income distribution were unimportant because wealthy people could not consume their wealth, and that allocative issues (such as those presented by monopoly and cartelization) were unimportant because there was always competition from distant if not from close substitutes. Holmes was right of course that a wealthy person does not literally consume his money but instead uses it to buy goods and services, and that since the production and supply of those goods and services require labour, the wealthy person's money ends up in the pockets of the people who are providing the goods and services he consumes. But this recirculation of wealth is neither inconsistent with gross disparities in the standard of living nor proves that efforts at the redistribution of income or wealth are doomed to utter futility because 'the crowd' has it all already, as Holmes liked to say (see, e.g., Holmes 1904: 128; Holmes 1913: 146). Holmes's second point, about the importance of competition from distant substitutes (see, e.g., *Dr. Miles Medical Co. v. John D. Park & Sons Co.*, 412), amounts to little more than that no prices are infinite, because people's resources are limited and no one can monopolize the production of *all* goods and services and thereby wipe out the competition of distant substitutes. Holmes also failed to distinguish between a partnership, which eliminates competition between the partners, and a merger that enables monopoly because the merging firms were the principal competitors in the market (see *Northern Securities Co. v. United States*, 410).

Holmes's economic intuitions sketched above incited in him a stubborn and rather unreasoned opposition to the antitrust laws, though he was right in his dissent in the resale price maintenance case (*Dr. Miles*) to note the implausibility of supposing that control of a single brand of a product, in that case 'Dr. Miles' patent medicines, could confer monopoly power. However, even though in hindsight his scepticism about the antitrust laws was not wholly lacking in merit, the grounds that he offered for that scepticism will not commend themselves to economists.

Antitrust was not the only area of the law in which Holmes expressed economic views, and in others he can be seen as laying some of the foundations of the modern economic analysis of law. He was prescient in emphasizing in his books and articles (particularly Holmes 1881 and Holmes 1897) that the threat of sanctions for the violation of a legal duty could affect behaviour even if the person threatened felt no moral obligation to comply with legal duties. Hence damages for the breach of a contract could be viewed simply as the price of breach, so that a contractual promiser could be expected to break the contract if the cost of complying with it exceeded the damages – and this was fine. Holmes thus anticipated the concept of 'efficient breach', a concept fundamental to the economic analysis of contract law.

Holmes recognized, moreover, that an important function of contracts is simply to allocate the risk of unavoidable breakdowns in the performance of a contract. Hence, as he pointed out, there is no paradox in promising to do something that may turn out to be impossible, since all such a promise really means is that the promisor will insure the promisee against the consequences should the contingency that prevents performance occur (Holmes 1881: lect. 8). Extending this insight to tort law, Holmes argued that a universal rule of strict liability, by making injurers liable for their unavoidable as well as their avoidable accidents, would in effect convert tort law into a scheme for social insurance (Holmes 1881: lect. 3). Holmes's famous metaphor of the market of ideas (*Abrams v. United States*, 630) foreshadowed the economic analysis of freedom of speech. And he grounded the doctrine of adverse possession in an intuitive version of the principle of diminishing marginal utility (Holmes 1897: 176).

Holmes's greatest oversight with regard to the economics of the common law was his failure to recognize the deterrent function of tort law. He was emphatic about the deterrent function of criminal law, and this explains his belief that criminal liability should be objective, that is, should be based on the dangerousness of the criminal's conduct rather than on his state of mind (Holmes 1881: lect. 2). Holmes could not assign a social *function* to tort law, however. He seems to have regarded it purely as a system of allocatively irrelevant wealth transfers from injurers to victims, and so was left to argue rather lamely that the only basis for shifting a loss from victim to injurer through the tort system was that the injurer had been blameworthy. He did not realize that the threat of liability might be used to deter behaviour that is negligent in the sense of creating a risk of injury disproportionate to the cost of avoiding it, and that this might be a more efficient system of accident control than using the criminal law. He may have been influenced by scepticism as to whether most accidents are deterrable, for in 'The Path of the Law' he suggests that industrial accidents may be an unavoidable by-product of industrial activity and, if so, should perhaps be governed by a system of no-fault accident insurance rather than by tort law (Holmes 1897: 167–168).

Holmes's greatest significance for modern economic analysis of law lies neither in the manifestos in 'The Path of the Law' nor in the specific applications of economics to law that he essayed from time to time in his academic and judicial writings. It lies rather in his functionalism and, what is closely related, his hostility to legal formalism and to natural law. Holmes considered law to be at bottom a policy science, in which the choice between legal rules is determined by 'weighing considerations of social advantage', and in which 'we learn that for everything we have to give up something else, and we are taught to set the advantage we gain against the other advantage we lose and to know what we are doing when we elect' (Holmes 1897: 168, 174). This 'balancing' approach to legal issues became the reigning method of deciding difficult legal issues in most fields of law in the 1950s and 1960s, and it was easily recast as cost–benefit analysis by economic analysts of law in the following decades. Holmes's moral scepticism, which played such a large role in his thinking about law, cleared the ground for cost–benefit analysis by disparaging with great rhetorical power the possibility that law could be guided by loftier moral themes.

RICHARD A. POSNER

See also AMERICAN LEGAL REALISM.

Subject classification: 4a(i); 4c(i); 7c.

CASES

Abrams v. United States, 250 US 616 (1919).

Dr. Miles Medical Co. v. John D. Park & Sons Co., 220 US 373 (1911).

Northern Securities Co. v. United States, 193 US 197 (1904).

SELECTED WORKS

1881. *The Common Law*. Boston: Little, Brown & Co.

1897. The path of the law. In Holmes (1992); 160–177.

1904. Economic elements. In Holmes (1992); 128–30.

1913. Law and the court. In Holmes (1992): 145–8.

1953. *Holmes-Laski Letters: The Correspondence of Mr. Justice Holmes and Harold J. Laski, 1916–1935*. Edited by Mark DeWolfe Howe, Cambridge, MA: Harvard University Press.

1992. *The Essential Holmes: Selections from the Letters, Speeches, Judicial Opinions, and Other Writings of Oliver Wendell Holmes, Jr.* Edited by Richard A. Posner, Chicago and London: University of Chicago Press.

1995. *The Collected Works of Justice Holmes: Complete Public Writings and Selected Judicial Opinions of Oliver Wendell Holmes*, Edited by Sheldon M. Novick (3 vols), Chicago and London: University of Chicago Press.

BIBLIOGRAPHY

Novick, S.M. 1989. *Honorable Justice: The Life of Oliver Wendell Holmes*. Boston, MA: Little, Brown & Co.

Posner, R.A. 1992. Introduction. In *The Essential Holmes: Selections from the Letters, Speeches, Judicial Opinions, and Other Writings of Oliver Wendell Holmes, Jr.*, ed. R.A. Posner (Chicago and London: University of Chicago Press): ix–xxxi.

White, G.E. 1993. *Justice Oliver Wendell Holmes: Law and the Inner Life*. Oxford: Oxford University Press.

horizontal mergers. Horizontal mergers are mergers between direct competitors, i.e. two firms which provide the same good or service. The term 'merger' is used here in its most general sense and we do not distinguish among various corporate forms such transactions can take; nor do we distinguish between 'friendly' mergers and unfriendly ones, often referred to as 'takeovers'. Like any other kind of merger (e.g. vertical or conglomerate), there can be a wide variety of motives for any given horizontal merger, including greater efficiency, tax savings, or simply a desire for larger size on the part of corporate management, and a correspondingly wide range of economic effects (see, generally, Varian 1988, and Paulter and O'Quinn 1993: 742–7). However, because any horizontal merger reduces the number of independent competitors providing a good or service, horizontal mergers raise special concerns and have typically been subject to greater regulatory scrutiny than other types of mergers. That such scrutiny is appropriate is not particularly controversial; the much tougher problem is deciding which specific mergers should be permitted and which should not. Economic theory and empirical research have contributed much to the resolution of this legal problem; but there is still an element of art rather than science to the exercise.

AN OVERVIEW OF THE PROBLEM. In the extreme case where there were only two competitors before the merger, the merger results in a monopoly, and the potential economic losses from monopoly are well understood. But horizontal mergers are a concern even when they do not result in a monopoly because economic theory and empirical research have established that, in the most general sense, the vigour of competition can be affected by the number of competitors, and therefore that a merger which reduces the number of effective competitors, say from three to two, can have adverse economic consequences even though the resulting market structure falls short of monopoly if firms, either individually or collectively, are able to exercise 'market power', i.e. the ability profitably to charge prices above the competitive level. This is not to suggest that such adverse consequences are certain, but simply to point out that there are special questions raised by horizontal mergers, and not merely mergers which result in monopoly.

One solution to the possible adverse consequences which can flow from a horizontal merger is to prohibit all such mergers, allowing only those vertical mergers (mergers between a purchaser of good or service and a seller of that same good or service) which do not themselves raise competitive problems and all purely conglomerate mergers (mergers in which there is no competitively relevant relationship between the parties). But such a policy would be overkill, since it is also possible that horizontal mergers can increase efficiency. In part this is because a horizontal merger, like any other kind of merger, can be a way of displacing inefficient management, and the threat of such a merger can provide an effective incentive for existing management to strive for efficiency. Indeed, one would expect that the 'market for corporate control' would work significantly less well if all horizontal mergers were prohibited, since it is eminently plausible that someone in the same line of business would be particularly capable of spotting an underperforming firm and correcting the problem after a merger. In addition, horizontal mergers can be a source of other kinds of efficiencies not obtainable from vertical or conglomerate mergers, which we can label, generally, 'economies of scale', meaning that unit costs for any given firm fall, at least up to some point, with increased output of a given product.

Since a blanket prohibition of horizontal mergers would almost certainly be unwise (and no modern economy has adopted such a policy), regulators are confronted with the task of deciding precisely which horizontal mergers are in the public interest (i.e., the benefits outweigh the costs) and which are not. In this branch of law, the role of economics in assisting the decision maker is potentially significant. There are generally, however, three practical constraints on the use of economic analysis in formulating merger policy.

First, the answer about whether a given merger is in the public interest has usually to be given before the effects of the merger are known, since the policy decision is normally whether the merger should be allowed to take place at all. Hence the role of economics is not that of measuring the net effect of a merger that has already occurred, but that of predicting which mergers are likely to turn out to have benefits which exceed the costs (Schmalensee 1987: 42–3).

Second, in part because the analysis is performed before the merger has occurred, it is particularly difficult to predict with any confidence the degree to which the merger will produce efficiency gains, either those specific to the merger or those which flow from the general enhancement of the market for corporate control (Pitofsky 1992: 210). Rather than attempting a specific benefit–cost tradeoff in every case, the more common approach is to require that the anti-competitive consequences surpass a given threshold before a merger will be challenged. The implicit assumption is that for the rest, benefits likely exceed costs. Only where the potential anti-competitive consequences are anticipated to be significant is there any need to attempt a specific forecast of efficiencies likely to be achieved and to attempt to balance the anti-competitive potential against the forecast efficiencies.

Third, mergers are very expensive to organize and timing is often crucial. The business community has a very strong interest in being able to anticipate the conclusion a regulator is likely to reach about a particular merger so that mergers which will ultimately be prohibited can be avoided in the first instance and energies can be channelled into selecting candidates for mergers which will not be challenged. The result is a desire that merger policy be expressed in the form of 'guidelines' which set out in advance the steps the regulatory agency will take in analysing a given merger and the criteria it will apply. Hence in many modern economies, including the US, the European Union, Canada, Australia and New Zealand, there are now formal 'Merger Guidelines' (e.g. US Department of Justice and Federal Trade Commission 1992) and a major contribution of economics and economists in those jurisdictions has been in the precise formulation of those guidelines. The job, then, is in two parts: understanding what economic theory and empirical research have to say about the economic consequences of mergers, and using that information to formulate guidelines that can be applied to any particular merger.

THE POSSIBLE ANTI-COMPETITIVE CONSEQUENCES OF A MERGER. A number of different models have been used to analyse the possible anticompetitive effects.

(a) *Monopoly*. In the extreme case, where prior to the merger there were only two competitors, the merger results in a single seller; i.e., a monopoly. (A merger of two buyers can result in a situation where there is only a single buyer, i.e. monopsony, with effects parallel to those discussed herein.) The economic consequences of monopoly are well known: higher prices and reduced output. The result is both a transfer from consumers to the monopolist (the consumer pays higher prices and the monopolist earns higher profits) and a reduction in allocative efficiency since, on the margin, the added value to consumers of the lost output exceeds the relevant costs of producing that output. The exercise of market power may take other forms, such as reduced quality, and the analysis generalizes readily to those other effects. Another possibility is that the merged firm loses the incentive to remain technically efficient, i.e., to keep unit costs of production to a minimum.

A necessary condition for the adverse effects of monopoly to occur is the presence of some barriers to entry; otherwise, the higher prices will simply induce new firms to enter. In addition, in rare cases, monopoly power on the selling side could be offset by monopsony power on the buying side, possibly negating the anti-competitive consequences of the merger. But otherwise, the major potential difficulty in analysing a merger to monopoly is that of defining the proper market, since whether the resulting firm is in fact a monopolist in the economic sense depends upon whether there are adequate substitutes for the 'monopolized' product. Thus, after a merger, there may be only a single producer of cellophane, but that producer will not have any significant monopoly power if consumers can and will switch readily to other wrapping materials if the price of cellophane is increased above the competitive level. The same general principle applies if there is only one producer in a given country, but consumers in that country can and will turn readily to imports from producers in other countries.

The modern test for market definition (US Department of Justice 1992) is matched perfectly to the problem as it arises in the analysis of mergers. According to that test, one assumes that there is only a single seller of a given product in a given geographic area and asks whether this 'hypothetical monopolist' could profitably raise prices above competitive levels for any sustained period of time. The word 'profitably' is key, since any firm or group of firms can raise prices, but those without genuine market power will lose so much business that it will not be profitable. Therefore, the approach assumes a given price increase, large enough to be regarded as non-trivial, and asks whether, in response to that increase, large numbers of consumers would turn to alternative products (substitutes) or to the identical product sold by firms located in other geographic areas (imports). If so many consumers would switch that an attempted price increase would not be profitable, technically the conclusion is that the product or geographic market has been drawn too narrowly and must be expanded to include the source of competitive pressure. If, on the other hand, a 'hypothetical monopolist' could profitably raise price – i.e., most consumers would not switch – then a 'relevant market' has been identified and the approach then proceeds to an analysis of competition within the market. This is not to suggest that market definition is easy in practice: there are many technical and data availability problems which can arise in any given situation. But the basic conceptual framework for market definition, at least for fairly homogeneous products, is widely supported by economists and has been adopted by regulatory authorities as a way of analysing mergers in many of the modern industrial economies which have formulated explicit procedures (Crampton 1993; Hay and Walker 1993; Werden 1993).

(b) *Unilateral effects falling short of monopoly.* In markets characterized by product differentiation, it is recognized (Shapiro 1996) that there can be monopoly-like effects from a merger even where several competitors remain. In a market consisting of a large number of firms, each producing one variant of a non-homogeneous product, each producer faces a downward-sloping demand curve so that small (unilateral) increases in price will not cause the total loss of customers (as would be the case in a market for homogeneous goods), and prices, in general, will exceed marginal costs. If the two merging firms happen to produce products that, in the eyes of at least some consumers, are the closest possible substitutes for one another, then, when the price of one product rises, some consumers will switch to the other, and vice versa. In this case, after the merger, the firm will recognize that at least some of the sales that would otherwise have been lost as a result of a price increase will be captured by the other product that is now sold by the same firm. In such a case, the revenues will not really be lost and the result is that the equilibrium price for each of the two products will be higher. (The same analysis can be applied to homogeneous products that are sold at different geographic locations in a world where consumers have preferences as to where they shop. If the two nearest competitors merge, the equilibrium price charged by each will be higher. Hence, a merger results in a price increase which can have ripple effects on the prices of other 'nearby' producers, without any collusion or other form of coordination among the firms. Observe that the model assumes limits on the abilities of firms to 'relocate', i.e. to change the characteristics of the product or location so as to occupy the product or geographic niche where prices have been increased.

In analysing mergers involving differentiated products where the relevant concern is unilateral price increases, the market definition process is of no real help. Indeed, different mergers involving the same market shares in the same overall 'market' can have quite different effects. Instead, if data permit, the preferred approach is to try to estimate directly the price increase likely to result from a given merger. In the most basic formulation of the 'unilateral effects' model, the two key pieces of information required are the pre-merger price-cost margin and the 'diversion ratio' – the percentage share of all sales that company A, if it raised price, would lose to company B, the prospective merger partner, although in practice the analysis is often considerably more complicated (Froeb and Werden 1994; Overstreet, Keyte and Gale 1996).

(c) *Oligopoly models.* The vast majority of horizontal mergers do not result in a monopoly but simply a smaller number of competitors and increased concentration. In addition to the possibility of unilateral effects discussed above, there are a number of other possible anticompetitive consequences of a merger which creates or enhances a situation of oligopoly, i.e. a relatively small number of major sellers that recognize their mutual interdependence (see generally Jacquemin and Slade 1989).

(1) *Explicit collusion.* As a result of the reduction in the number of independent firms, the remaining firms may find it easier to engage in collusion with respect to price or other terms of sale. The literature on cartels indicates that a great many factors influence the likelihood of successful collusion (Hay and Kelley 1974), but two (related) significant factors are the number of firms and the degree of concentration. The greater the number of firms that participate in a cartel, *ceteris paribus*, the more difficult it will be to coordinate the actions of the group (e.g. agree on the profit-maximizing cartel price) and the more difficult it will be to detect and deter cheating by individual members

of the cartel (Stigler 1964). While a cartel could attempt to reduce these internal coordination and discipline problems by limiting the number of firms that are included, the cartel cannot afford to exclude significant market participants or they will undermine the cartel from the outside. A merger of two significant market participants reduces by one the number of significant firms whose actions have to be coordinated and increases the ability of the cartel to detect cheating among its members, and thus makes the likelihood of successful collusion greater.

(2) *Tacit collusion.* If, as a result of increased concentration, the market will become more 'oligopolistic' in nature, this can facilitate so-called 'tacit collusion', a situation where firms, recognizing their interdependence, behave as if they had met and agreed to collude but without actually engaging in any kind of explicit communication (Shapiro 1989). In the extreme case of 'pure' tacit collusion, the result is a price approaching or equal to that a cartel would set, but since there is no explicit communication or any other explicit facilitating practice (Hay 1982), there is probably nothing to attack as inappropriate behaviour from a legal perspective (Turner 1962). As in the case of explicit collusion, there are many other factors that are relevant to whether tacit collusion is likely to be successful in achieving supracompetitive prices, but it is widely believed that, *ceteris paribus*, higher concentration increases the likelihood of supracompetitive prices being achieved through tacit collusion. Since tacit collusion, at least in its simplest form, may not be actionable under the laws dealing with cartels, merger policy which seeks to prevent such high concentration is a crucial policy instrument (Hay and Werden 1993). An alternative is price regulation of highly concentrated markets, but the trend in almost all modern economies has been away from reliance on price regulation and towards trying to use merger policy and laws against cartels to ensure that markets are structurally and behaviourally competitive.

(3) *Non-cooperative equilibria.* A different way of looking at the effects of a horizontal merger, developed more than 150 years ago but emphasized by modern game theorists, involves non-collusive models of oligopolistic interaction, in which firms make certain assumptions about their rivals' behaviour but otherwise seek to maximize individual profits. The Cournot model (and its progeny), which in the most basic variant has each firm assuming that its rivals' output will not change as a result of its own decision, is the most widely known. As Hay and Werden (1993: 174) point out, despite the apparent naivety of the most basic model, the Cournot framework has withstood a century of criticism, and modern game theoretic models support its basic intuition that there is a predictable relationship between concentration and the equilibrium price of a non-cooperative game, which can support a merger policy based in part on concentration.

A CONCENTRATION-BASED MERGER POLICY. Where the concern is about one or more of these 'oligopoly' effects, the typical merger policy begins by defining the market (see the discussion above) and measuring the degree of concentration and how much it will be increased by the merger. There are various measures of concentration that can be used. The traditional measure is the 'four-firm concentration ratio', the sum of the market shares of the leading four firms. More recently this has been replaced, at least in the US, by the Herfindahl– Hirschman Index (HHI), which is calculated by summing the squares of the individual market shares of all the firms in the market. While this measure may seem exotic, under certain Cournot-type assumptions there is a recognized mathematical relationship between the HHI and the equilibrium price (Jacquemin and Slade 1989: 430–32).

The most controversial step in formulating a concentration-based merger policy comes in defining a threshold, below which the possible benefits of a merger are presumed to outweigh the costs, so that mergers below the threshold will normally be permitted. Mergers above the threshold are typically subject to further analysis to determine whether other factors make it more likely than not that the potential adverse effects of concentration will be realized and will offset any potential efficiency gains.

The main problem with trying to create concentration-based thresholds is that, while the qualitative link between concentration and the likelihood of supracompetitive prices is not especially controversial (at least most would agree that high concentration is a facilitating factor even if it is not determinative), even those who feel most strongly about the existence of *some* relationship would acknowledge that the quantitative relationship is not known with any degree of precision. Is there a particular threshold of concentration below which the likelihood of successful collusion is so low it can be ignored? Starting at any given level of concentration, what is the precise impact of a particular increase in concentration on the likelihood of successful collusion? These and similar questions are matters on which economists can make educated guesses but probably no more than that (Hay and Werden 1993: 173).

Moreover, it is highly unlikely that the same threshold is appropriate for every market in a given economy, yet having a different numerical rule for every market frustrates the legitimate needs of the business community for well-established and predictable rules of merger enforcement. In addition, as we look across different economies, it is certain that the same rule is not ideal for all. In relatively small economies, firms may need to achieve substantial market shares in order to come close to minimum efficient scale. In such economies, it may be appropriate to tolerate higher thresholds. Fortunately, this can be (and is) done without causing confusion or inconsistency within any jurisdiction – the US, Australia and New Zealand, for example, each use a concentration-based formula in their published guidelines, but the market share thresholds used in the various countries are different, reflecting the size and scale concerns that are a function of the size of the economy.

When a given merger exceeds the concentration threshold, it is necessary to evaluate the merger more closely to see if other factors indicate that anti-competitive effects are likely. The principal factors to consider are those aspects of the market (other than concentration) which affect whether an oligopolistic industry will be able to achieve a consensus on price and be able to prevent cheating. Many factors are relevant but among the most important are the fungibility of the product (the more fungible the product, the easier to reach a consensus in price) and the degree to which actual prices charged by one seller are promptly known by other sellers (the more transparent each seller's prices, the easier to detect cheating). In addition, if entry barriers are very low, even high concentration should not produce any significant anti-competitive effect. Finally, where the structural conditions suggest a high likelihood of an anti-competitive effect, there must be an examination of the specific efficiencies claimed for the merger since unusually large efficiencies may overturn the inference about the effects of the merger that can be drawn from the structural conditions. This can be either because unusually large efficiencies may themselves reduce the likelihood of a cooperative equilibrium or because the efficiencies are so large that the merger should be allowed despite the anti-competitive potential (see, generally, FTC 1996, chapter 2).

GEORGE A. HAY

See also AGREEMENT UNDER THE SHERMAN ACT; ANTITRUST POLICY; CARTELS AND TACIT COLLUSION; COMPETITION LAW IN THE EUROPEAN UNION AND THE UNITED STATES; EUROPEAN COMPETITION POLICY; MARKET FOR CORPORATE CONTROL; VERTICAL MERGERS AND MONOPOLY LEVERAGE.

Subject classification: 6c(ii).

BIBLIOGRAPHY

Crampton, P. 1993. The DOJ/FTC Horizontal Merger Guidelines: a Canadian perspective. *Antitrust Bulletin* 38: 665–714.

Federal Trade Commission Staff Report. 1996. Enhancing the analysis of efficiencies in merger evaluation. *Anticipating the 21st Century: Competition Policy in the New High-Tech, Global Marketplace.*

Froeb, L. and Werden, G. 1994. The effects of mergers in differentiated products industries: Logit demand and merger policy. *Journal of Law, Economics, and Organization* 10: 407–26.

Hay, G. 1982. Oligopoly, shared monopoly, and antitrust law. *Cornell Law Review* 67: 439–81.

Hay, G. and Kelley, D. 1974. An empirical survey of price fixing conspiracies. *Journal of Law and Economics* 17: 13–38.

Hay, G. and Walker, J. 1993. Merger policy and the TPC's Draft Merger Guidelines. *Competition & Consumer Law Journal* 1: 1–32.

Hay, G. and Werden, G. 1993. Horizontal mergers: law, policy, and economics. *American Economics Review* Papers & Proceedings 83: 173–77.

Jacquemin, A. and Slade, M. 1989. Cartels, collusion, and horizontal merger. In *Handbook of Industrial Organization*, Vol. I, ed. R. Schmalensee and R. Willig, Amsterdam: North-Holland.

Paulter, P. and O'Quinn, R. 1993. Recent empirical evidence on mergers and acquisitions. *Antitrust Bulletin* 38: 741–97.

Pitofsky, R. 1992. Proposals for revised United States merger enforcement in a global economy. *Georgetown Law Journal* 81: 195–250.

Schmalensee, R. 1987. Horizontal merger policy: problems and changes. *Journal of Economic Perspectives* 1(2): 41–54.

Shapiro, C. 1989. Theories of oligopoly behavior. In *Handbook of Industrial Organization*, Vol. I, ed. R. Schmalensee and R. Willig, Amsterdam: North-Holland.

Shapiro, C. 1996. Mergers with differentiated products. *Antitrust* 10 (Spring): 23–6.

Stigler, G. 1964. A theory of oligopoly. *Journal of Political Economy* 72: 44–61.

Turner, D. 1962. The definition of agreement under the Sherman Act: conscious parallelism and refusals to deal. *Harvard Law Review* 75: 655–706.

Overstreet, T., Keyte, J. and Gale, J. 1996. Understanding econometric analysis of the price effects of mergers involving differentiated products. *Antitrust* 10 (Summer): 30–34.

US Department of Justice and FTC. 1992. *Joint Horizontal Merger Guidelines.* Washington, DC: Government Printing Office.

Varian, H.L. (ed.). 1988. Symposium on takeovers. *Journal of Economic Perspectives* 2(1): 3–82.

Werden, G. 1993. Market delineation under the merger guidelines: a tenth anniversary perspective. *Antitrust Bulletin* 38: 517–56.

hostile takeovers. *See* TENDER OFFERS.

Hume, David (1711–1776). This essay focuses on the character and salience of Hume's contributions to economics and the law, and the relationship between them. Hume's economic and legal theories, like his political and social ideas, were not developed independently of one another in separate treatises devoted to specific subjects. The scope of Hume's interests was vast and the extent of his influence on the modern, and more or less discrete, disciplines of economics, political theory, moral philosophy, comparative law, history, psychology, sociology and aesthetics amply demonstrates that his intellectual reach did not exceed his grasp.

While the range of Hume's intellectual concerns exemplifies an age in which the disciplinary boundaries of the social sciences had yet to be drawn, much of the twentieth-century interest in Hume has in fact been shaped by the concerns of analytical philosophy. This tendency directed scholarly attention almost exclusively towards one relatively narrow aspect of Hume's thinking contained in the first part of the *Treatise of Human Nature*, and it generated a received wisdom that restricted Hume's lasting contributions to questions concerning cause and effect and/or our knowledge of the external world. On this reading, Hume's writings on historical, moral, political, legal and economic subjects – upon which his eighteenth-century reputation was established and which largely sustained it for a nineteenth-century audience – were passed over as being either unsystematic and fragmentary, or of less serious import. Harold Laski's assessment of Hume's political thought as containing no more than 'a series of pregnant hints' (1920: 155) is, for example, representative of this view. In economics, this received opinion is represented by the still prevailing idea that while Hume might have made interesting (and important) contributions to particular aspects of economic theory (the quantity theory of money, the balance of payments, the theory of interest and public finance), his economics lacked the coherence of either Adam Smith or the physiocrats. Unfortunately, these opinions seem unnecessarily to limit the relevance of Hume's contributions to contemporary economics and the law. Accordingly, we shall spend no time at all on the well-known aspects of Hume's contributions to economic theory; for these the reader may consult the original *New*

Palgrave: A Dictionary of Economics. We shall concentrate, instead, upon how Hume developed an approach to the analysis of a class of coordination problems which he applied directly to understanding both the basis of the private contractual order, private property rights and their enforcement, and the origins and nature of justice, legitimate government and the rule of law.

1. SKETCH OF HUME'S LIFE AND INFLUENCE. The details of Hume's life that are of most interest here are those pertaining to his role in bringing the Continental Enlightenment to Scotland and in transmitting the Scottish Enlightenment to the Continent and beyond. For more extensive biographical coverage, the reader may consult Burton (1846), Greig (1931) and Mossner (1954).

Born in Edinburgh on 26 April 1711, Hume was the youngest of three children. He entered the University of Edinburgh in 1723, but left without taking a degree. After the early death of their father, the Hume children were brought up by their mother. Of his early intellectual interests Hume singled out 'a passion for literature' and commented: 'My studious disposition, my sobriety, and my industry, gave my family a notion that the law was a proper profession for me; but I found an unsurmountable aversion to every thing but the pursuits of philosophy and general learning' (*Essays*, xxxiii). In 1734, following a short and abortive attempt to enter into a commercial career at Bristol, he set out to France, visiting Paris, Rheims and settling at La Flèche. During his three years there he wrote his *Treatise of Human Nature* which appeared in 1739/40 but, as Hume put it, that great work 'fell dead-born from the press' (*Essays*, xxxiv, italics omitted). In an unsuccessful attempt to publicize its main arguments he published an anonymous *Abstract* of the *Treatise* in 1740. The publication of the two *Enquiries (Human Understanding* in 1748 and the *Principles of Morals* in 1751), representing Hume's attempt to recast the arguments of the *Treatise* in a more digestible form, was scarcely more successful. His *Essays*, however, the first volume of which appeared in 1741, garnered a more favourable reception – one that Hume recorded made him 'entirely forget my former disappointment' (*Essays*, xxxiv). In 1752 his *Political Discourses* appeared; 'the only work of mine that was successful on the first publication' (*Essays*, xxxvi). With the *Discourses*, Hume's contemporary reputation was finally secured.

Hume's reputation in France was both wide and deep – being especially high among thinkers such as Montesquieu, Rousseau, Turgot, Morellet, d'Holbach and d'Alembert. Nor was it only through his own works that Scottish thought was presented to French intellectual circles of the day. Despite his own distinctive contributions to economic theory (that were taken up directly by the physiocrats), Hume was a tireless advocate of Adam Smith's *Theory of Moral Sentiments* to an eager French audience. A measure of Hume's own fame in France may be gathered by his self-deprecating remarks about the laudatory reception he received on his visit to Paris in 1763 (*Essays*, xxxix). In Scotland, of course, his contributions were more often than not the critical starting point for many of the most lasting contributions of Adam Smith, William Robertson, Thomas Reid, James Millar and Adam Ferguson.

Hume died in Edinburgh on 25 August 1776, just five months after the publication of Smith's *Wealth of Nations*. Adam Smith wrote: 'Upon the whole, I have always considered him, both in his lifetime and since his death, as approaching as nearly to the idea of a perfectly wise and virtuous man, as perhaps the nature of human frailty will permit' (*Essays*, xlix).

Together with Adam Smith, David Hume is the most wholly modern thinker of the Scottish Enlightenment. However, it is precisely the comparatively neglected aspects of Hume's thought that speak most clearly to theoretical issues of contemporary concern – namely, his economic and political thought. Yet, contrary to Hume's own stated view, treatment of his economic and political thought (when they are treated at all) is often compartmentalized – each is taken to be both logically and conceptually independent of the other. Since our concern is with the lasting resonance of Hume's arguments in the contemporary discourse of economics and the law – and since we are interested in presenting the conceptual core around which Hume's economic and legal thought was developed – we shall examine Hume's contributions to two intellectual projects which occupy central positions in modern economic, legal and political philosophy: (1) private contract and the problem of coordination, and (2) social collectivities and the problem of social order.

Understanding Hume in this broader light has gained significant support relatively recently. Hayek's claim that Hume gave us 'probably the only comprehensive statement of the legal and political philosophy which later became known as liberalism' (Hayek 1967: 109), David Lewis's reconsideration of Hume in his pathbreaking philosophical investigation into convention (Lewis 1969), John Rawls's affirmation of Hume's account of the preconditions for justice (moderate scarcity and mutual disinterest) in the course of unfolding his own theory (Rawls 1971), and Duncan Forbes's reconnection of Hume to the natural jurisprudence tradition (Forbes 1975), independently but collectively marked the beginning of a renewed interest in Hume's larger economic, political and legal concerns.

If one turns to the third book of the *Treatise*, as well as to Hume's more mature writings in the *Enquiries*, the *History* and several of his *Essays*, one finds him addressing a set of much larger considerations concerning the origins of government, the origin and nature of justice and the constitution of human nature which makes justice possible. Far from being philosophically peripheral, these considerations of self-interest, coordination, justice, law and property, remain matters of central concern throughout his work. They are intimately connected to Hume's efforts to examine the principles of human nature, to illuminate those elements of human understanding and passions which he claims all men share, and to delineate the narrow bounds of human reason and thus challenge the traditional understanding of natural law.

2. SELF INTEREST AND 'A SENSE OF COMMON INTEREST'. According to the model of market mechanism central to modern economics and the law, exchange proceeds as self interested individuals, constrained by their initial endowments in a well-defined regime of property rights, seek to maximize their individual utilities by reallocating

those endowments through trading voluntarily among themselves in mutually advantageous ways. In the absence of market imperfections, liberty of trade will bring about a social optimum – in the sense that the outcome of an exchange process (populated by many traders) will yield an allocation of resources that cannot be improved upon for any subset of individuals without making some other subset of individuals worse-off in terms of their own utility. This last proposition is often said (rightly or wrongly) to capture in a more formal and precise way the old idea of Adam Smith that it is not from the benevolence of others that we should expect our dinner, but from their regard to their own self interest.

Hume's analysis of voluntary exchange proceeds along parallel but different lines. Self interest is manifestly also at work in exchange: 'The chief spring or actuating principle of the human mind is pleasure or pain' (*Treatise*, III.III.i, 574). However, self interest here is not to be understood as that narrow utilitarian pursuit of pleasure *without regard to others*, but rather what Hume terms a 'sense of interest [that] has become common to all our fellows' (*Treatise*, III.II.ii, 490). He then provides a simple illustration of exactly what it is he has in mind: '[t]wo men, who pull on the oars of a boat, do it by an agreement or convention, tho' they have never given promises to each other' (*Treatise*, III.II.ii, 490). This view of self interest remained unchanged through the revisions of the *Enquiries*, where the same point is made in the following terms:

> [T]wo men pull the oars of a boat by common convention, for common interest, without any promise or contract: thus gold and silver are made the measures of exchange; thus speech, and words, and language, are fixed by human convention and agreement (*Enquiry 2*, Appendix III, 306).

The common interest Hume speaks of here is that shared interest of each individual in the *orderly* conduct of their private affairs. Failure to act on common interests of this kind renders an individual materially *worse off* in the sense that it leads to the impossibility of any coordinated interaction at all. As Hume puts it: 'if men pursu'd the publick interest naturally [. . .] they wou'd never have dream'd of restraining each other by [. . .] rules; and if they pursu'd their own interest, without any precaution, they wou'd run head-long into every kind of injustice and violence' (*Treatise*, III.II.ii, 496–7). To put it another way, free-riding by individuals, on this line of argument, is not a problem: it is in every individual's *private* interest, according to Hume, that their own actions, and those of others, conform to certain conventions which render the *successful* coordination of those individual actions possible:

> [I]t is evident, that every man loves himself better than any other person, he is naturally impelled to extend his acquisitions as much as possible; and nothing can restrain him in this propensity, but reflection and experience, by which he learns the pernicious effects of that licence, and the total dissolution of society which must ensue from it (*Essays*, 480).

Self interest is thus foundational to Hume's account of individual behaviour, but this self interest must be properly understood as involving an interest in the orderly functioning of affairs; a private interest in the public good which arises from the immediate experience of the necessities of coordinated social interaction itself:

> The general societies of men are absolutely requisite for the subsistence of the species; and the public conveniency, which regulates morals, is inviolably established in the nature of man, and of the world, in which he lives. [. . .] Common interest and utility beget infallibly a standard of right and wrong among the parties concerned (*Enquiry 2*, IV, 210).

The difference between this construal of the idea of self interest and that made familiar by Benthamite utilitarianism is marked and of no small importance. On the latter argument, constraints on the unhindered operation of private interests had to be imposed *exogenously*, so to speak. Indeed, in the hands of Bentham and James Mill the whole of the utilitarian theory of government, for example, proceeded from just such a presupposition. For Hume, on the other hand, those same constraints were *endogenous* components of private interests themselves.

The similarity between this argument and Adam Smith's deployment of the idea of 'sympathy' in his *Theory of Moral Sentiments* is, of course, quite apparent here (as are its common origins in Francis Hutcheson's earlier observations on the same subject). However, the precise way in which 'sympathy' operates in the arguments of Smith and Hume respectively differs in important details. For Smith, 'sympathy' modifies narrow self interest thanks to a *social-psychological* mechanism whereby individuals are able to see themselves, and their own actions, as others do. Most importantly for Smith's argument, individuals are thereby able to judge their own actions as if they were an 'impartial spectator' to them. For Hume, on the other hand, individual actions conform to conventions which directly modify self interest narrowly conceived because they permit the coordination of the actions of many. Thus, the 'whole scheme [. . .] of law and justice is advantageous to society; and t'was with a view to this advantage, that men, by their voluntary conventions, establish'd it. After it is once establish'd by conventions, it is naturally attended with a strong sentiment of morals; which can proceed from nothing but our sympathy with the interests of society' (*Treatise*, III.III.i, 579–80).

> [B]y convention be meant a sense of common interest; which sense each man feels in his own breast [. . .] and which carries him, in concurrence with others, into a general plan or system of actions, which tends to public utility (*Enquiry 2*, Appendix III, 306).

The mechanism through which 'sympathy' operates for Hume does not, therefore, seem to require the mediation of the kind of social-psychological processes so characteristic of Smith's *Moral Sentiments*. It is not by deferring to the moral judgements of an impartial spectator that individuals regulate private passions through self command, but by their direct observance of conventions which are in the individual interest of all:

> It is only a general sense of common interest; which sense all the members of the society express to one another, and which induces them to regulate their conduct by certain rules. I observe, that it will be for my interest to leave another in the possession of his goods, *provided* he will act in the same manner with regard to me. He is sensible of a like interest in the regulation of his conduct. When this common sense of interest is mutually express'd, and is known to both, it produces a suitable resolution and behaviour (*Treatise*, III.II.ii, 490).

Of course, it is worth remembering that although differing in detail, these two accounts of self interest yield essentially the same characterization of the kind of behaviour by individuals in economic affairs which is most conducive to the economic advancement of society. In this arena Hume, like Smith, endorses prudence and frugality: '[A]ll prospect of success in life, or even of tolerable subsistence, must fail, where a reasonable frugality is wanting' (*Enquiry 2*, VI.i, 237).

3. CONVENTION, COMPETITION AND THE CONTRACTUAL ORDER. If we return to the model of exchange on competitive markets familiar in contemporary economic theory, it is possible to appreciate that a rather different view of this process (and its outcomes) emerges from Hume's distinctive consideration of the operation of self interest and convention. In the competitive model of market exchange, the coordination problem is solved by non-cooperative behaviour by individual agents. On Hume's account the coordination problem is solved by cooperative behaviour.

The private contractual regime emerges as a stable order precisely because it has its basis in a sense of common interest. Of course, as society grows, as its industry and commerce expand, the situation becomes more complex and convention is backed by legal sanctions. But for Hume, conventions not only precede the *making* of promises to fulfil voluntary agreements (contracts) but they also ensure the *performance* of such promises. As Hume observes: 'convention is not of the nature of a promise: [f]or even promises themselves [. . .] arise from human conventions' (*Treatise*, III.II.ii, 490, italics omitted). Contract law, understood as the legal enforcement of property rights, appears at a later stage; as a necessary, but secondary pillar reinforcing already established conventions in a complex market economy. In the final analysis, for Hume it is convention rather than competition (or the threat of it) that renders market exchange at once possible and orderly:

> [A] promise wou'd not be intelligible, before human conventions had establish'd it; and [. . .] even if it were intelligible, it wou'd not be attended with any moral obligation (*Treatise*, III.II.v, 516; italics omitted).

It is the sense of common interest each agent shares in conforming to established property rights which provides an individual motive for contractual solidarity, rather than the secondary threat of recourse to the law of property. For Hume,

> every member of society is sensible of this interest: Every one expresses this sense to his fellows, along with the resolution he has taken of squaring his actions by it, on the condition that others will do the same [. . .] every single act is perform'd in expectation that others are to perform the like (*Treatise*, III.II.ii, 480).

Indeed, Hume argued that this motive would be at work even as economies become larger and comprehend a more complex and diverse set of contractual agreements:

> The mutual dependence of men is so great, in all societies, that scarce any human action is entirely complete in itself, or is performed without some reference to the actions of others, which are requisite to make it answer fully the intention of the agent [. . .]. In proportion as men extend their dealings, and render their intercourse with others more complicated, they always comprehend [. . .] a greater variety of voluntary actions, which they expect [. . .] to cooperate with their own (*Enquiry 1*, VIII.i, 89).

Hume provides a very concrete example of the pivotal role of this sense of common interest to the orderly functioning of market economies when he turns to the analysis of monetary arrangements. Here Hume defers to convention, rather than an argument about the formal sanctions associated with legal tender, to explain why objects which act as means of exchange (money) are acceptable in the discharge of debt. Thus, he argued, 'gold and silver become the common measures of exchange, and are esteem'd sufficient payment for what is of a hundred times their value' (*Treatise*, III.II.ii, 490). Of course, in large and complex economic systems, where present and future contracts are customarily denominated in money terms, formal regulations regarding what is and is not legal tender eventually emerge. But for Hume money still remains a matter of convention, and these laws and regulations are to be viewed as emanating from already existing conventions about the acceptable objects which constitute that system's media of exchange.

At this point it should be noted that for Hume the *same* model which underpins the stability of the private contractual order also reveals the secret of the real foundation of the social and political order. As he puts it: '[t]he case is precisely the same with the political or civil duty of *allegiance*, as with the natural duties of justice and fidelity' (*Essays*, 480):

> All men are sensible of the necessity of justice to maintain peace and order; and all men are sensible of the necessity of peace and order for the maintenance of society. Yet, notwithstanding this strong and obvious necessity, such is the frailty or perverseness of our nature! it is impossible to keep men, faithfully and unerringly, in the paths of justice [. . .] frequently [an individual] is seduced from his great and important, but distant interests, by the allurement of present, though often very frivolous temptations (*Essays*, 38).

Returning to the analysis of the market mechanism, while for Hume threats to the stability of the private contractual order of the market are eliminated primarily by the general observance of conventions about property rights and monetary arrangements, this is not to say either that Hume saw the breakdown of these conventions as the only source of instability to that order, or that he imagined legal rules to be irrelevant to their enforcement. For example, Hume is perfectly well aware in the passage just cited that difficulties may arise where individuals weigh their *present* interests too heavily in relation to their more *distant* ones, and that this must be palliated by instituting 'some persons, under the appellation of magistrates, whose peculiar office it is, to point out the decrees of equity, to punish transgressors, to correct fraud and violence, and to oblige men, however reluctant, to consult their own real and permanent interests' (*Essays*, 38). In short, if the private contractual order *originates* from the sense of common interest in following conventions, it is reinforced by formal rules whose origins are the same.

4. SOCIETY, PROPERTY AND THE ORIGINAL CONTRACT. In his account of the origin of social order, Hume seeks to clarify the problem that justice was invented to solve – not threats to life and limb, but the insecurity of possession of transferable goods – and puts forward an argument with all the hallmarks of that which he deployed in his discussion of the market mechanism and the private contractual order. Indeed, Hume's insights into the manner in which coordination of private activities is secured in exchange relations between self-interested individuals is applied without significant modification to the larger project of understanding political order and the legal framework which underwrites it.

Neither a Lockean 'golden age' nor a Hobbesian 'war of all against all' characterize Hume's vision of the early and rude state of society. In fact, Hume's version of society's beginnings is so primitive as barely to be a society at all – and it is precisely in this sense that he writes about it having universally and empirically taken place in the *Treatise* (III.II.ii, 485). Hume's moral history of the rise of society is drawn in deliberate and rather pointed contrast to the biblical story of Genesis. In the biblical fable, society is the result of punishment. Men live by the collective sweat of their brow by necessity, following a fall from a physical condition of plenty and a moral condition of mastery and virtue. On Hume's account, however, men begin weak, inferior and in exceptional need. What rescues individuals from the vicissitudes of fortune and accident is cooperation, so that individuals manage to bootstrap themselves into society which gives them 'mutual succour' as well as 'force, ability, and security' against 'fortune and accidents' (*Treatise*, III.II.ii, 485, italics omitted; see also *Enquiry 2*, Appendix III, 307).

This early form of societal cooperation gives way to formal government as the populousness and complexity of society demands uniformity. In this sense, government is a further form of cooperation – not based on promising or contract, but (as in the case of the private contractual order) on convention:

> It has been asserted by some, that justice arises from Human Conventions, and proceeds from the voluntary choice, consent, or combination of mankind. If by convention be here meant a promise (which is the most usual sense of the word), nothing can be more absurd than this position [. . .]. But if by convention be meant a sense of common interest [. . .] it must be owned, that, in this sense, justice arises from human conventions (*Enquiry 2*, Appendix III, 306, italics omitted).

According to Hume, a convention is a kind of mutual agreement that arises from the perception that there may a common interest in either performing or not performing some particular action. Justice is just such a convention, or cooperative virtue, with its origins in the family. Furthermore, stable possession protected by justice is what we call property: 'the origin of justice explains that of property. The same artifice gives rise to both' (*Treatise*, III.II.ii, 490). Property, then, is a social derivation, where society is initially nothing more than a collection of men (families) competing for scarce resources to meet their needs according to the rules of justice. Importantly, the artificial constructions of justice and property antedate the creation of government in Hume's theory.

Hume objected to the theory of an original social contract on a number of historical and philosophical grounds. On historical grounds, he argued that no evidence suggested that government originated in this way. Instead, according to Hume, '[a]lmost all the governments, which exist at present, or of which there remains any record in story, have been founded originally, either on usurpation or conquest, or both, without any pretence of a fair consent' (*Essays*, 471). On philosophical grounds, he held that the doctrine of original contract contained a logical flaw in suggesting that men might promise or contract their way into society when the concept of promising already presupposed a set of societal rules in order to give the concepts of promise or contract meaning. On both historical and philosophical grounds, then, Hume resisted the arguments for the justification of political authority or the legitimacy of particular forms of rule based on arguments from contract:

> The state of society without government is one of the most natural states of men, and may subsist with the conjunction of many families, and long after the first generation. Nothing but an encrease of riches and possessions cou'd oblige men to quit it; and so barbarous and uninstructed are all societies on their first formation, that many years must elapse before these cou'd encrease to such a degree, as to disturb men in the enjoyment of peace and concord (*Treatise*, III.II.viii, 541).

Hume holds that the political obligation (or, what amounts to the same thing, submission to authority) which individuals choose to recognize is based on the interest which all men have in the security and protection of property afforded by government. A promise then takes place: '[w]hen men have once perceiv'd the necessity of government to maintain peace, and execute justice, they wou'd naturally assemble together, wou'd chuse magistrates, determine their power, and promise them obedience. As a promise is suppos'd to be a bond or security already in use, and attended with a moral obligation, 'tis to be consider'd as the original sanction of government and as the source of the first obligation to obedience' (*Treatise*, III.II.viii, 541, italics omitted).

Government is thus a late invention for Hume – after justice, after property, after promising – which seems to arise as indispensable in the maintenance of the rules of justice in handling the unintended consequences of the economic progress of society (e.g. greater avidity; greater scarcity). Government is in some sense a psychological crutch forcing us to make what is in our long term interests also in our short term interest, so that our 'violent propension to prefer contiguous to remote' (*Treatise*, III.II.vii, 537) will not lead us to sacrifice our greater to our lesser good.

> Here then is the origin of civil government and allegiance. Men are not able radically to cure, either in themselves or others, that narrowness of soul, which makes them prefer the present to the remote. They cannot change their natures. All they can do is to change their situation, and render the observance of justice the immediate interest of some particular persons, and its violation their more remote (*Treatise*, III.II.vii, 537).

Hume differs from other putatively liberal thinkers by disengaging property from the nature of man and denying any notion of either natural rights or claim rights (right to what is due) in his theory. Hume's theory of property stood most opposed to the theory of the natural origin of property through occupation found in the labour theory of property of Locke. Locke's conjoined labour theory of property argued that a man might claim by natural right any objects appropriated through his own labour. In order to demonstrate the artificial rather than natural origins of property, Hume had to refute Locke's argument for a natural right to property.

> Some philosophers account for the right of occupation, by saying, that every one has a property in his own labour; and when he joins that labour to any thing, it gives him the property of the whole: But [. . .] we cannot be said to join our labour to any thing but in a figurative sense. Properly speaking, we only make an alteration on it by our labour. This forms a relation betwixt us and the object; and thence arises the property according to the preceding principles (*Treatise*, III.II.iii, 505–506n).

Property was thus for Hume 'a species of cause and effect' in which the cause must be conceived of separately from the effect, with only 'constant conjunction' uniting the two ideas. Locke's labour theory of property was thus a confusion in the theory of cause and effect. On Hume's account, what property a man has is strictly a matter of convention – what the rules of justice allocate to him and protect in use. 'A man's property is some object related to him. This relation is not natural, but moral, and founded on justice' (*Treatise*, III.II.ii, 491). The original distribution of possessions is assumed by Hume to have been established by violence and submitted to by necessity. Hume becomes, by turns, socially radical and jurisprudentially conservative; but becomes so on the basis of a singularly consistent and profound argument.

5. NATURAL LAW AND NATURAL JURISPRUDENCE. Without a doubt it is law that does the heavy lifting in Hume's thought by superimposing and sustaining habits of order when other regulative devices elude us. 'From law arises security: From security curiosity: And from curiosity knowledge' (*Essays*, 118). Hume's contribution to a distinctively modern theory of law is that he rendered it possible to discuss it without appealing either to natural rights or to their metaphysical and religious foundations in a natural law, as had been discussed by earlier writers such as Locke.

It is well known that Locke had remained confident that there were natural laws of justice and property which, though not innate in men's knowledge, remained available to them through the use of reason with the same clarity as the laws of mathematics. Natural laws in this sense rested on one side of an age old divide between the normative and empirical realms. Locke's claim that the content and character of natural law strictures transcended empirical experience enabled his theory to generate potentially revolutionary criticism of existing law and government. Hume's effort was to deprive rationalist natural law theory of what he believed was an ill-founded and politically destabilizing message, and he did so by challenging the psychological and moral efficacy of reason in the sphere of conduct.

While Hume argued that reason might well be thought of as the faculty of understanding, pure reason remained incapable of making normative demands on the world of experience: '[r]eason is wholly inactive, and can never be the source of so active a principle as conscience, or a sense of morals' (*Treatise*, III.I.i, 458). Knowledge is one thing; to be moved by it to action is another. 'Morality, therefore, is more properly felt than judg'd of' (*Treatise*, III.I.ii, 470). In this way, Hume pointed to the confusion in attributing to reason a motivating power which belonged to the faculty of imagination (the principle of association of ideas) and the passions.

This reversal of the priority of reason over passion in Hume's sceptical critique overturned one tradition of natural law thinking which reached back to classical antiquity, without, however, abandoning altogether the tradition of natural jurisprudence. There might be, as Hume argued, no direct connection between justice and any natural inclination – no general love of humanity, no 'simple original instinct' (*Enquiry 2*, II.II, 201) for property. Yet the very constitution of human nature with its limited generosity and intellectual imperfections, combined with the external setting of unalterable scarcity common to the species, underpins the construction of three fundamental rules of justice: stability of possession, transfer by consent and performance of promises (*Treatise*, III.II.vi, 526). These rules, by which Hume claims

> property, right, and obligation are determin'd, have in them no marks of a natural origin, but many of artifice and contrivance. They are too numerous to have proceeded from nature: They are changeable by human

laws: And have all of them a direct and evident tendency to public good, and the support of society. This last circumstance is remarkable [. . .] because, tho' the cause of the establishment of these laws had been a *regard* for the public good, as much as the public good is their natural tendency, they wou'd still have been artificial, as being purposely contriv'd and directed to a certain end (*Treatise*, III.II.vi, 528–9).

In this important sense, justice was for Hume, an 'artificial' rather than a natural virtue. Of course, Hume claimed, the artificial construction of justice would have little sticking power if these rules did not draw on natural, non-rational passions and tendencies in human nature. These Hume draws out through his method of introspection and observation.

> [T]he laws of justice arise from natural principles in a manner still more oblique and artificial. 'Tis self-love which is their real origin; and as the self-love of one person is naturally contrary to that of another, these several interested passions are oblig'd to adjust themselves after such a manner as to concur in some system of conduct and behaviour. This system, therefore, comprehending the interest of each individual, is of course advantageous to the public; tho' it be not intended for that purpose by the inventors (*Treatise*, III.II.vi, 529).

Two points concerning Hume's conception of justice arise here. First, justice is a rather narrow virtue concerned with the regulation of the 'interested passions', that is, with restraining the 'love of gain'. In this sense, justice is not the core of all morality for Hume, rather it is 'purposely continued and directed to a certain end', namely, solving the problem of the insecurity of possession of transferable goods (*Treatise*, III.II.vi, 489). The limits of property and justice are coincident (coterminous?) and both considerations precede the foundation of government. Second, in arguing that the 'artificial' virtue of justice has ultimate 'causes' as 'natural' as any natural virtue, it appears that Hume may have undercut the importance of the natural/artificial distinction. However, the point for Hume would not seem to be that justice has no natural antecedents, but rather that justice is a complex set of social practices (numerous and changeable) rather than a simple set of natural motives.

The more important distinction Hume is making is rather that between those rules of justice which are intentionally created to serve an end or purpose and those natural tendencies which lack (as do all things in nature) human intentions. That Hume would make such a distinction is hardly surprising. After all, as has already been noted, what particularly interested Hume in the *Treatise* was the basis of natural jurisprudence in the workings of the imagination. As already mentioned, through the experience of social life, Hume believed men come to share accepted rules of behaviour – acceptable because they worked to bring about the stability of possession and the orderly transference of goods which all men need and seek. In the third book of the *Treatise* these basic social rules of justice – we are allowed even to call them 'natural laws' – are seen as emerging spontaneously to meet the growing needs of society.

Hume's construal of justice in the *Treatise* as an unintended consequence of individual actions permitted him to retain many of the benefits of natural law and legal positivism without their attendant pitfalls of either an excessive rationalism or complete constructivism, both of which Hume abhorred (*Treatise*, III.II.iii, 500). However, this move could not be accomplished without weakening the distinction between natural (unintended) and artificial (intended) action and effectively creating a third category of human action – those unintended (natural) outcomes of intended (artificial) actions.

That Hume necessarily understood he was revising this distinction and placing justice in yet a third category is debated – Hayek claims he did (1973: 20), Haakonssen claims he did not (1981: 24). However, what does seem clear is that in the revised considerations of justice in the *Enquiry* Hume puts forward several arguments to support a far more intentionalist claim that 'public utility is the sole origin of justice, and that reflections on the beneficial consequences of this virtue are the sole foundation of its merit' (*Enquiry 2*, III.i, 183, italics omitted).

6. 'PUBLIC UTILITY' AND JUSTICE. In the *Enquiry* Hume drops much of the evolutionary language concerning the origins and development of society and justice characteristic of the *Treatise*, and relegates the idea of the artificiality of justice to a footnote (*Enquiry 2*, Appendix III, 307n). In the *Enquiry*, greater emphasis is placed instead on the concept he refers to as 'public utility':

> Thus, the rules of equity or justice depend entirely on the particular state and condition in which men are placed, and owe their origin and existence to that utility, which results to the public from their strict and regular observance (*Enquiry 2*, V.ii, 188, capitalization omitted).

The laws of justice are useful – that is, have utility – in the sense that they serve as means to a *public* or common end. Our sympathy with this usefulness or utility (derived from experience) is both what gives these laws their moral character and what accounts for their origin. Thus, the public interest is not why men pay their debts but it is why we approve of them morally when they do, so that what Hume claims is inadequate as a motive for action may still be the source of its moral character in the opinion of others:

> Usefulness is only a tendency to a certain end; and it is a contradiction in terms, that any thing pleases as means to an end, where the end itself no-wise affects us. If usefulness, therefore, be a source of moral sentiment, and if this usefulness be not always considered with a reference to self; it follows, that every thing, which contributes to the happiness of society recommends itself directly to our approbation and good-will (*Enquiry 2*, V.ii, 219).

While Hume here makes reference to the general happiness of society, created through the means of justice, he says very little about happiness as the content of the 'certain end' of either justice or the utility that determines our moral approbation of it. When he speaks of the public interest as useful to our private interests the content of those private interests also seems irrelevant. Hume, in fact, rarely discusses the content of the 'ends' of individual justice seekers other than to say that they must be mutually compatible.

Despite the change in language, however, nothing essential has changed from the underlying model set out in the *Treatise*. 'Public utility' is nothing other than that 'sense of common interest' in coordination and social order, embodied in individual adherence to established conventions, which accounts for the origin of justice and which gives to it its moral character. The greater good, as Hume put it, emerges spontaneously from the self-interested actions of individuals, but in a way more subtle than that which later utilitarian theory would comprehend. It is, therefore, this model that properly can be seen as constituting the lasting element of Hume's investigations into economics, politics and the law – it provides, as we have seen, the unifying theme around which the whole of his account of the economy and the law is constructed.

MURRAY MILGATE AND SHANNON C. STIMSON

See also CONVENTIONS; HAYEK, FRIEDRICH VON; JUSTICE; LOCKE, JOHN; MODERN UTILITARIANISM; SCOTTISH ENLIGHTENMENT AND THE LAW; SPONTANEOUS ORDER.

Subject classification: 1b(i); 3a; 3b; 7b.

SELECTED WORKS

Note: Titles are listed here according to the date of their original publication. The details of the relevant edition used in this essay (when not the original) follows each entry.

1739–40. *A Treatise of Human Nature*. Edited by L.A. Selby-Bigge. 2nd edn with text revised and variant readings by P.H. Nidditch, Oxford: Clarendon Press, 1978.

1740. *An Abstract of a Treatise of Human Nature*. Edited by John Maynard Keynes and Piero Sraffa, Cambridge: Cambridge University Press, 1938.

1741–2. *Essays, Moral and Political*. Reprinted in *Essays* (1777b).

1748. *Three Essays* ['Of natural character', 'Of the original contract' and 'Of passive obedience']. Reprinted in *Essays* (1777b).

1748. *Enquiry Concerning Human Understanding*. Edited by L.A. Selby-Bigge; 3rd edn revised by P.H. Nidditch, Oxford: Clarendon Press, 1975. Referred to herein as *Enquiry 1*.

1751. *Enquiry Concerning the Principles of Morals*. Edited by L.A. Selby-Bigge; 3rd edn revised by P.H. Nidditch, Oxford: Clarendon Press, 1975. Referred to herein as *Enquiry 2*.

1752. *Political Discourses*. Nine of the twelve essays in this volume are collected by Eugene Rotwein in Hume's *Writings on Economics* (1955) and all are reprinted in *Essays* (1777b).

1754–62. *History of Great Britain from the Invasion of Julius Caesar to the Revolution of 1688*. Six volumes.

1757. *Four Dissertations* ['The natural history of religion', 'Of the passions', 'Of tragedy' and 'Of the standard of taste'].

1776. *My Own Life*. As reprinted in *Essays* (1777b).

1777a. *Two Essays* ['Of suicide' and 'Of the immortality of the soul']. Reprinted in *Essays* (1777b).

1777b. *Essays, Moral, Political and Literary*. Edited by Eugene F. Miller. Indianapolis: Liberty Press (revised edition). 1987.

1779. *Dialogues Concerning Natural Religion*. Edited by John Valdimir Price. Oxford: Clarendon Press, 1976. This edition also contains 'The natural history of religion'.

Hume's correspondence

Greig, J.Y.T. (ed.). 1932. *The Letters of David Hume*. 2 vols, Oxford: Clarendon Press.

Klibansky, R. and Mossner, E.C. (eds). 1954. *New Letters of David Hume*. Oxford: Clarendon Press.

Mossner, E.C. and Ross, I.S. (eds). 1977. *The Correspondence of Adam Smith*. Oxford: Oxford University Press. Being volume six of the Glasgow Edition of Adam Smith's *Works and Correspondence*. [Contains Smith's side of the Hume–Smith correspondence.]

Rotwein, E. (ed.). 1955. Relevant extracts from Hume's correspondence. In his edition of *David Hume: Writings on Economics* (details given below). [Contains correspondence from A.R.J. Turgot, Lord Kames and James Oswald.]

BIBLIOGRAPHY

Burton, J.H. 1846. *Life and Correspondence of David Hume*. 2 vols, Edinburgh: William Tait.

Forbes, D. 1975. *Hume's Philosophical Politics*. Cambridge: Cambridge University Press.

Greig, J.Y.T. 1931. *David Hume*. London: Jonathan Cape.

Haakonssen, K. 1981. *The Science of a Legislator: Natural Jurisprudence in David Hume and Adam Smith*. Cambridge: Cambridge University Press.

Hayek, F.A. 1967. *Studies in Philosophy, Politics and Economics*. Chicago: University of Chicago Press.

Hayek, F.A. 1973. *Law, Legislation and Liberty*. Volume 1. Chicago: University of Chicago Press.

Laski, H.J. 1920. *Political Thought in England from Locke to Bentham*. London: Hume University Library; New York: Henry Holt Company.

Lewis, D. 1969. *Convention: A Philosophical Study*. Cambridge, MA: Harvard University Press.

Mossner, E.C. 1980. *The Life of David Hume*. 2nd edn, Oxford: Clarendon Press (1st edn 1954).

Rawls, J. 1971. *A Theory of Justice*. Cambridge, MA: Belknap Press of Harvard University Press.

Rotwein, E. (ed.). 1955. *David Hume: Writings on Economics*. London: Nelson; reprinted, Madison: University of Wisconsin Press, 1970.

Rotwein, E. 1987. Hume, David. In *The New Palgrave: A Dictionary of Economics*, ed. J. Eatwell, M. Milgate and P. Newman (London: Macmillan), Vol. 2: 692–5.

I

immigration policy. As of the late 1980s, approximately 100 million people were resident outside their nations of current citizenship. Roughly 35 million were in sub-Sahara Africa alone and approximately 13–15 million each in the prosperous regions of Western Europe and North America. Another 15 million or so were in the Middle East or Asia (Russell and Teitelbaum 1992; 1, 9). The United Nations estimates that over 60 million people, or 1.2 percent of the world's population, now reside in a country where they were not born (United Nations 1989: 61). Although most immigrants choose a traditional destination (over one-half go to the United States, Canada or Australia), many other countries are also receiving relatively large immigrant flows, including Germany, Switzerland, France and the United Kingdom. Of the total number of immigrants, as of 1993, about 18 million were refugees, most of whom were located in Africa and Asia, up from 8 million in 1980 and 2.5 million in 1970 (*The Economist*, 23 December 1989: 17; *The Economist*, 13 November 1993: 45). The following table describes immigrants as a percentage of the population for most OECD countries in 1981 and 1991.

Table 1
Immigrants as a Percentage of the Total Population

	1981	*1991*
Australia	20.6	22.7
Austria	3.9	6.6
Belgium	9.0	9.2
Canada	16.1	15.6
Denmark	2.0	3.3
Finland	0.3	0.7
France	6.8	6.3
West Germany	7.5	8.2
Italy	0.6	1.5
Luxembourg	26.1	28.4
Netherlands	3.8	4.8
Norway	2.1	3.5
Spain	0.5	0.9
Sweden	5.0	5.7
Switzerland	14.3	17.1
United Kingdom	2.8	3.1
United States	6.2	7.9

Source: OECD (1994)

This table obscures locational concentrations of immigrants within countries: for example, 21.7 percent of the population of California is foreign-born (Friedberg and Hunt 1995: 27); almost one-quarter of the populations of Ontario and British Columbia in 1991 were immigrants, including 38 percent of the population of Toronto and 30 percent of the population of Vancouver (Badets and Chui 1994: 7, 10).

A number of features of contemporary immigration trends have precipitated major political controversies in host countries around the world, including the US, Canada, Australia, New Zealand and Western Europe. These features include the sheer scale of immigration; the changing composition of source countries; and the dramatic increase in the number of refugees, all of which have focused attention in receiving countries on the impact of immigrants on native participants in domestic labour markets; the impact on social programme expenditures; and the impact on social and cultural homogeneity and cohesiveness.

I. IMMIGRATION POLICY IN HISTORICAL PERSPECTIVE. In the US, the first great migration wave occurred between 1881 and 1924, when almost 26 million people entered the country. Reacting to the increase in immigration and to the widespread perception that the new immigrants differed from the old, Congress closed the floodgates in the 1920s by enacting the National Origins Quota System that allocated entry visas according to the ethnic composition of the US population in the 1920s. During the 1930s, only 0.5 million immigrants entered the US. Since then, the number of legal immigrants has increased at about the rate of 1 million per decade and by 1993, nearly 800,000 people were being admitted annually (Borjas 1994: 1668). The number of illegal immigrants has also steadily increased and is now estimated at between 200,000–300,000 per year. The illegal immigrant population was estimated at around 3.4 million in 1992 (equal to 1.3 percent of the US population). About 40 percent of the illegal immigrants have come to the US from Mexico (Friedberg and Hunt 1995: 27). Amendments in 1965 to the Immigration and Nationality Act repealed the national origins restrictions and made family ties to US residents the key factor that determines whether immigrants are admitted into the country. Partly as a result of these changes, the composition of source countries of immigrants to the US has changed dramatically in recent decades. In the 1950s over half of all immigrants to the US came from Europe. Currently fewer than one in five immigrants is European. Almost 40 percent of recent immigrants are from Asia (especially Southeast Asia) and a roughly equal number originate in Mexico, the Caribbean and Latin America (Friedberg and Hunt 1995: 26).

Canadian immigration policy in much of the past century has been similar to that of the US: a major influx of immigrants between 1890 and the late 1920s, minimal immigration through the depression and World War II years, and a steady increase in immigration levels thereafter, with current levels running at about 200,000 per year. For much of this period, Canada explicitly excluded most immigrants from non-European source countries. Beginning in 1963 and formalized through the adoption of a point system in 1967, Canada abandoned selection criteria based on country of origin and admitted immigrants on the basis of family ties and in the case of independent immigrants assessments of various factors, including education and occupational skills considered likely to influence the ability of immigrants to resettle successfully in Canada. Initially the point system applied to about fifty percent of immigrants. Since the 1980s the family sponsorship class has come to dominate independent entrants assessed under the point system (Green 1995). Ninety percent of immigrants who arrived in Canada before 1961 were born in Europe. This proportion fell to 69 percent for those who arrived between 1961 and 1970; 36 percent for those who immigrated between 1971 and 1980; and one-quarter for those who arrived between 1981 and 1991. At the same time the proportion of immigrants born in Asia and other non-European countries has increased. People born in Asia and the Middle East made up almost one-half of immigrants who came to Canada between 1981 and 1991, but only three percent of those who came before 1961 (Badets and Chui 1994: 13).

European immigration since World War II falls into four phases (Zimmerman 1995). The period of war adjustment and decolonization covers the period between 1945 until the early 1960s. The number of people displaced by the war was estimated at about twenty million. For instance, twelve million Germans had to leave Eastern Europe by 1950 with about eight million going to West Germany. Great Britain, France, Belgium and the Netherlands were affected by return migration from European colonists and the inflow from workers from former overseas territories. The second period – 1955 to 1973 – reflected considerable labour migration. Labour shortages in some countries induced openness and sometimes active recruitment policies. Germany and some other Western European countries established guest worker systems. Net immigration to the north from the Mediterranean countries was about five million. The third period – from 1974 to 1988 – was one of restrained immigration throughout Western Europe reflecting recessionary conditions after the first oil price shock. Labour recruitment ceased, although it proved difficult to induce return migration by foreign workers. Family and political migration dominated migration patterns during this period. The last period from 1988 to the present day reflects the dissolution of Communist and Socialist regimes in Eastern and Central Europe, which dramatically increased the flow of east–west immigrants, predominantly to Germany. The migration potential from Eastern Europe is estimated in the range of 5–50 million, mostly over a period of 10–15 years. One estimate suggests a potential immigration flow of three percent of the current population size in Eastern Europe for the next fifteen years, which implies a migration inflow of about three million ethnic Germans and ten million others (Layard et al. 1992). Additional immigration pressures are likely to be caused by south–north migration, particularly from Turkey, Egypt, and other countries in Northern Africa (Zimmerman 1995: 48).

II. THE WELFARE IMPLICATIONS OF IMMIGRATION. The welfare implications of immigration pose many complex issues. One threshold issue is the perspective to be adopted in evaluating these implications, particularly whether the perspective should focus only on the impact of immigration on domestic welfare in a receiving country; or whether a more global perspective should be adopted including the impact of immigration on the welfare of immigrants themselves; and the impact of immigration on the welfare of residents of sending countries who remain behind. Another threshold question is whether a narrowly economic conception of welfare should be adopted or whether the welfare calculus should include non-economic factors such as humanitarian, social, cultural, and distributional concerns.

From the perspective of immigrants themselves, it seems obvious that in most cases immigration is likely to enhance their welfare, either economically or psychically (in cases where they are escaping political, religious, or ethnic persecution in their home countries), otherwise they are unlikely to incur the economic and emotional costs of uprooting themselves and moving to a foreign country. From a global economic perspective, it seems equally clear, applying standard international trade theory paradigms, that global welfare is enhanced by relatively unrestricted migration. For example, Hamilton and Whalley provide estimates from 1977 that the gains from removing all restrictions on international immigration could exceed world-wide GNP in that year. More qualified estimates would still yield gains constituting a significant proportion of world GNP and exceeding gains from removing all trade restrictions (Hamilton and Whalley 1984). The premise behind these estimates is that open immigration encourages human resources to move to their most productive uses, whatever the localized impact in countries of emigration or immigration. The most important qualification to this proposition is fiscally induced migration driven by a desire to access non-contributory entitlement systems such as social welfare and public health care systems in other countries. Obviously, migration undertaken for these reasons may not entail a redeployment or relocation of human resources to more productive uses (Sykes 1995).

The effects of emigration on the welfare of citizens in sending countries is far from clear. Arguably, owners of capital receive a reduced return (and consumers may pay higher prices) if wage rates among workers who remain increase (although these workers are to that extent better off). Negative externalities from population density may be reduced, but some advantages from population density and size (e.g. ease of communication and transportation) may also be reduced. While the brain drain from source countries has often elicited concern, this requires the assumption that highly skilled professionals, business people, or workers are not capturing in their returns the full value of their marginal product, but are creating positive externalities that will be lost when they leave (e.g. imparting skills or knowledge to younger individuals). To the extent that their education has been financed by their home governments, their departure may entail a loss of this investment, but on the other hand taxes paid by parents, may, on average, reflect these costs. To the extent that emigrants are younger and more productive than the home population on average, the sending country loses their taxes with which to finance social programmes for older citizens and children (Simon 1989: ch. 14; Bhagwati 1991: chs 18–20). Largely mitigating or even offsetting many of these costs to sending countries are substantial remittances sent home by immigrants – estimated at about US $66 billion world-wide in 1989 (Russell and Teitelbaum 1992: 18–32).

Most of the theoretical and empirical research undertaken to date on the welfare implications of immigration has focused on the impact of immigration on the welfare of the native population in receiving countries. This research had focused principally on economic impacts. An assessment that included non-economic impacts of immigration would need to to take account of, on the one hand, humanitarian considerations that may favour generous family reunification and refugee policies, and on the other hand, concerns over erosion of cultural and social homogeneity and cohesiveness (Schlesinger 1992; Brimelow 1995). The principal findings of research that has focused on the economic impacts of immigration on the welfare of native populations in receiving countries is briefly reviewed below.

Economic research in the early 1980s reached highly optimistic findings regarding the impact of immigration on native economic welfare. For example, Chiswick in an analysis of the 1970 US census found that at the time of arrival, immigrants earn about 17 percent less than the natives. However, immigrant earnings overtake native earnings within 15 years after arrival. After 30 years in the US the typical immigrant earned about 11 percent more than the comparable native workers (Chiswick 1978). Simon's influential book, *The Economic Consequences of Immigration* (1989), substantially extended these findings, and not only concluded that immigrants out-perform comparable native workers in the long run but that immigrants have little or no effect on wage and employment levels of the native population, including unskilled native workers, and that they contribute substantially more in taxes than the costs they impose on social programmes (and indeed that their net fiscal contribution on average was greater than the native population). The 'catch-up' and overtaking effect was largely attributed to initial challenges in overcoming language and skill deficits and the greater drive and ambition of immigrants who had decided to incur the wrenching costs of leaving their home countries and resettling in a foreign country (a self-selection effect).

While Borjas in 1990 reached many similar findings, he also found that recent immigrants were under-performing previous generations of immigrants and in some cases the native population (Borjas 1990). In subsequent writings, he has elaborated on this theme (Borjas 1994, 1995). For example, in 1970, the typical immigrant who had just arrived in the US had 11.1 years of schooling, as compared to 11.5 years for the typical native worker. By 1990, the typical immigrant who had just arrived in the US had 11.9 years of schooling, as compared to 13.2 years for natives. The most recent arrivals enumerated in the 1970 census earned 16.6 percent less than natives. By 1990, the wage disadvantage between the most recent immigrant wave and natives had grown to 31.7 percent. In 1970 immigrants were less likely than natives to receive public assistance. By 1990, the welfare participation rate of immigration households had risen to 9.1 percent, or 1.7 percentage points higher than the participation rate for native households (Borjas 1995: 3–4). According to Borjas, the changing national origin mix of immigrants explains over 90 percent of the decline in educational attainment and relative wages across successive waves of immigrants between 1960 and 1980 (Borjas 1994: 1685).

In evaluating the impact of immigrants on native participants in US labour markets, Borjas estimates the impact of immigrant workers on native worker wage levels and compares this loss to gains by employers and indirectly consumers from lower input costs. He estimates that currently native workers lose about 1.9 percent of GDP, or $133 billion in a $7 trillion economy, while native employers and consumers gain about 2 percent of GDP, or $140 billion, yielding an immigration surplus of $7 billion. This implies a sizeable redistribution of wealth from native workers to the users of immigrant labour, and implies in turn that debates in receiving countries over immigration policy are likely to focus more on these distributional impacts than on the relatively small efficiency gains entailed (Borjas 1995). As Borjas puts it, analogizing to theories of the effects of international trade liberalization, 'no pain, no gain', so that studies that find no or minimal impacts of immigrants on labour markets in receiving countries imply that immigrants capture all the returns from immigration and the native population in receiving countries none. Borjas argues that greater selectivity in immigration that focuses on screening out unskilled immigrants and admitting mostly skilled immigrants would raise the immigration surplus substantially, reflecting the fact that factor prices for skilled labour appear to be more elastic than for unskilled labour and that complementarities between skilled labour and capital in production are greater than complementarities between skilled and unskilled labour or between unskilled labour and capital, particularly in an advanced economy like that of the US. With respect to the fiscal impacts of immigration in the US (sometimes discussed in terms of the dependency ratio), estimates vary dramatically, with some estimates reporting net annual fiscal benefits from immigration of $27 billion and other estimates reporting fiscal losses of over $40 billion. These estimates are highly speculative, because beyond estimating the impact of immigrants on social welfare programmes, it is difficult to estimate the marginal impact on the vast array of other public services that they utilize (Borjas 1994: 1704–8). Again, skilled immigrants are less likely to be unemployed than unskilled immigrants and hence less likely to become dependent on social welfare programmes.

Despite these recent research findings on the deteriorating performance of recent waves of immigrants to the US, the consensus position among researchers remains that the impact of immigration on the labour market outcomes of natives is small, both in terms of employment and wage levels (Friedberg and Hunt 1995). Evidence from other receiving countries supports this view. Canadian researchers have concluded that immigrants have a minimal impact on employment or wage levels of native workers (Economic Council of Canada 1991; Akbari and De Voretz 1992) and that immigrant households, including recent immigrants, pay more in taxes than they receive in benefits and that their contribution exceeds the average Canadian-born household lifetime contribution (Akbari 1995), although the net fiscal contributions of immigrants, while still positive, have been declining significantly in the case of more recent immigrants.

As to whether the performance of more recent immigrants to Canada has deteriorated more generally relative to earlier immigrants and relative to the native-born population of Canada, an extensive analysis by the Economic Council of Canada (1991) reaches cautious conclusions. The proportion of persons with only elementary education has slightly increased amongst recent immigrants, but the latter also include a higher proportion of university-educated persons than the native population. Knowledge of the English language has also declined with recent waves of immigrants. The Council found no evidence that immigrants from the new source countries have consistently lower labour force participation rates than those from traditional source countries, although there has been a decline in the general participation rate for immigrants arriving in the 1980s. While unemployment rates are generally lower for immigrants than natives (8.2% compared to 10.8%), for immigrants arriving between 1978 and 1983 the rate has been slightly higher: 11.2% compared to 10.8% for natives, and for immigrants arriving in the period 1983 to 1986, the unemployment rate was 16%. However, the Council was unable to find any significant changes in the characteristics of the most recent immigrants relative to those who had arrived between 1978 and 1982, and was therefore not prepared to attribute changes in labour force participation rates to changing immigrant characteristics. With respect to participation in welfare programmes, 12.5% of immigrants who came during the period 1981 to 1986 received welfare compared to 1.7% of immigrants who came between 1976 and 1980 and 13.8% of the native-born population. Contrary to Borjas's findings in the US, refugees do not seem to perform markedly less well than other immigrants or the native born population.

A recent study by Statistics Canada (Badets and Chui 1994) analysing data from the 1991 Census largely confirms the Economic Council's findings. In 1991, the overall dependency ratio for immigrants was 29.8 while that for the Canadian-born was 52.9; thus immigrants have a higher proportion of people of working age than do the Canadian-born. Immigrants were also more likely to have higher levels of education than the Canadian-born – about 16% of immigrants aged 15 and over had university degrees compared to 11% of the Canadian-born, although a higher proportion of immigrants (19%) than the Canadian-born (13%) had less than Grade 9 education. Of immigrants who came between 1981 and 1991, 17% had a university degree, compared with 9% of immigrants who arrived before 1961. For those aged 25 and over, the difference is even more pronounced: 21% of recent immigrants had a university education, compared with 9% of immigrants who came before 1961. In 1991, the overall labour force participation rate of immigrants was 65.2%, slightly higher than in 1984 (64.7%) and only slightly lower than the Canadian-born (68.7%). However, 71% of immigrants who came to Canada between 1981 and 1991 reported a mother tongue other than English or French, compared with 59% of those who came before 1961.

With respect to the European experience, research on the impact of immigration on native participants in labour markets in receiving countries seems broadly consistent with the US and Canadian evidence, finding minimal impact on wage and employment levels, despite higher unemployment levels in Europe and less flexible labour markets (often reflecting the role of centralized unions) (Zimmerman 1995).

It should be noted with respect to most of the foregoing studies of the impacts of immigration on native workers in labour markets in receiving countries that they assume constant returns to scale. It might be argued that countries with a larger and more rapidly growing population will be able to sustain some industries and some social infrastructure which would not be viable at smaller population sizes. Apart from scale effects *per se*, dynamic effects, such as broader diffusion of technological and other ideas, and greater possibilities for learning-by-doing, may generate significant positive effects on average native incomes from a larger population (Simon 1989: ch. 8; Economic Council of Canada 1991: 25). These arguments are not especially convincing, particularly in a country the size of the US, or even in the case of smaller countries, given a liberal international economic environment where scale effects, especially in capital rather than labour intensive industries, can often be captured by trading into foreign markets and do not require a large local employment or consumer base (Borjas 1995: 12).

III. IMPLICATIONS FOR IMMIGRATION POLICY. Commentators concerned with the deteriorating performance of recent immigrants to receiving countries and the diminishing domestic returns to immigration associated therewith typically argue that immigration policy should focus more on screening for skilled immigrants (Borjas 1994, 1995; De Voretz 1995: 23–9). This proposed policy reorientation raises a number of difficult issues. With respect to refugee claimants, most receiving countries are signatories to the UN Convention on Refugees, which entails commitments to admit refugees who satisfy the UN Convention definition. While there appears to be high variability from one country to the other in how this commitment is interpreted and applied, it nevertheless implies a limited latitude to alter radically refugee intake policies, at least with respect to inland refugee claimants, although a good deal more latitude with respect to admission or sponsorship of offshore refugees. With respect to the family sponsorship category, proposals to limit entry in this category entail either narrowing the class of eligible relatives to immediate family members; treating this category as the residual category within over-all immigration quotas after independent immigrants have been screened for skills; or requiring family sponsors to assume financial responsibility for sponsored relatives by, for example, purchasing surety bonds against the risk of sponsored relatives becoming dependent on social welfare programmes (the value of such a bond has been estimated at $20,000 in Canada; De Voretz 1995: 8). None of these measures is likely to prove uncontentious in receiving countries. With respect to independent immigrants who are screened for skills, two problems arise. The first is that receiving countries do not unilaterally determine the skill set of immigrants seeking entry. This is in significant part determined by conditions in sending countries. Both 'push' and 'pull' factors are relevant. Sending countries that are generally impoverished are likely to send mostly unskilled immigrants. Sending countries with high degrees of inequality of wealth are again likely to send mostly unskilled immigrants, with skilled residents for the most part facing few inducements to emigrate. Only skilled workers from countries that 'tax' directly or indirectly the earnings and opportunities of high performing skilled workers, where receiving countries permit higher dispersions in returns to human capital, are likely to find it attractive to emigrate. This may be a relatively small applicant pool. If receiving countries were to confine themselves exclusively or almost exclusively to this pool, this may entail substantial curtailment of total current levels of immigration.

A second problem relates to how skilled workers are selected by receiving countries. Even assuming a substantial skilled applicant pool, presumably not all skills are in equal demand in receiving countries. The challenge then becomes of screening amongst various classes of skilled prospective immigrants. The Canadian experience with the point system that was implemented in 1967 suggests that attempts at fine-tuning screening criteria by occupation or class of skill imply an accuracy in manpower forecasting that is mostly unwarranted, and they have been of limited efficacy (Green and Green 1995; De Silva 1997). Screening on some very basic variables such as age, health, language skills, and level of education may be as far as screening criteria can usefully go.

In response to the limitations and deficiencies of bureaucratically administered entry policies, many economists see virtues in an auction system for quotas, assuming entry is to be limited (Trebilock 1995). It is argued that the immigrants who purchase these quotas will be those who value the opportunity to emigrate most highly, principally because they are confident that the employment or business opportunities available to them in the country of immigration will warrant the investment in the quota, reflecting the higher value that residents place on their potential contributions. One can also view an auction system as a means of extracting monopsony rents from immigrants analogous to the optimal tariff in trade theory (Sykes 1995). However, there seem compelling reasons in principle why an auctioned quota system cannot be assigned a central role in allocating entry positions to immigrants. Assuming that there are good humanitarian and compassionate reasons for preserving a significant role for family reunification policies, there would seem to be no role here for an auctioned quota system. Equally, it is obviously untenable to screen refugees on this basis. With respect to independent immigrants, an auction system seems both inefficient and unfair: inefficient because given the well-known difficulties of borrowing money against future employment income or human capital (which is the rationale for, for example, most student assistance programmes), many efficient relocation decisions may not be made; and unfair simply because it penalizes those with few present resources, whatever the future contributions they may make to the country of immigration. Business or investor-class immigrants may be more amenable to an auctioned quota system. At present, Canada admits a small number of immigrants in this category (about two to three percent of the annual immigration flow) by requiring as a condition of entry the investment of several hundred thousand dollars in approved Canadian projects, which resembles an auctioned quota system (Kunin and Jones 1995).

The category of temporary workers warrants brief comment. Here there is a compelling argument that foreign students in receiving countries on student visas, on successful completion of their studies, should be entitled to apply for permanent residence status, fairly much of right (Simon 1989: 315–18). This would clearly seem to be in the domestic interest of the receiving country. Whether it is welfare enhancing from the global perspective entails the somewhat indeterminate debates about the effect of the brain drain on developing countries. But given that this is also entailed in a number of the other long-established immigrant categories, it is not quite clear why this is a particular objection to providing successful students with the opportunity to become permanent residents. To the extent that they receive financial assistance with their studies from their countries of origin, presumably these countries can demand bonds or security from the student or his or her family to ensure reimbursement of this assistance. With respect to other temporary workers, there are serious difficulties in designing and administering programmes providing for legal, unskilled, temporary immigrants. While it is true that temporary workers often contribute positively to the dependency ratio, partly because of their age, and partly because they are often not entitled to non-contributory forms of public assistance, the European experience suggests that it is very difficult to send these people home if they have been temporary workers for a number of years and they and their families have established roots in the community. Simon (1989: 302) suggests various financial bonding arrangements to ensure departure on the expiration of temporary work visas, and Sykes (1995) sees such a programme as a strong substitute for illegal or undocumented immigration. However, many temporary workers may simply go 'underground' upon the expiration of their visas and become illegal or undocumented aliens. With a transient population such as is often involved with unskilled guest worker programmes, it is not clear how easy it would be to design and enforce the bonding arrangements that Simon proposes. In any event, both efficiency and humanitarian considerations seem to dictate that if a guest worker has worked productively in the country of immigration for any significant period of time, he or she should be entitled to apply for permanent resident status, treating his or her work experience as a substitute for other forms of education, training, or financial assets.

One last aspect of immigration policy requires comment. In making initial eligibility determinations (health, criminality, national security risk), inland refugee determinations, family sponsorship entitlements, and deportation decisions, designing legal processes that, on the one hand, accord immigrants some basic measure of due process, and, on the other hand, avoid miring the administration of immigration policy in costly and protracted legal processes, has proved a daunting challenge for many countries, with the appropriate balance between the two sets of considerations often the subject of ongoing and unresolved debates.

MICHAEL J. TREBILCOCK

See also COMPARATIVE ADMINISTRATIVE LAW.

Subject classification: 2g; 6d(v).

BIBLIOGRAPHY

Akbari, A. and DeVoretz, D. 1992. The substitutability of foreign-born labour in Canadian production: circa 1980. *Canadian Journal of Economics* 25: 604–14.

Akbari, A. 1995. The impact of immigrants on Canada's treasury circa 1990. In De Voretz (ed.) 1995.

Badets, J. and Chui, T. 1994. *Canada's Changing Immigrant Population*. Ottawa: Statistics Canada.

Bhagwati, J. 1991. *Political Economy and International Economics*. Cambridge, MA: MIT Press.

Borjas, G.J. 1990. *Friends or Strangers: The Impact of Immigrants on the US Economy*. New York: Basic Books.

Borjas, G.J. 1994. The economics of immigration. *Journal of Economic Literature* 32: 1667–1717.

Borjas, G.J. 1995. The economic benefits from immigration. *Journal of Economic Perspectives* 9(2): 3–22.

Brimelow, P. 1995. *Alien Nation*. New York: Random House.

Chiswick, B.R. 1978. The effect of Americanization on the earnings of foreign-born men. *Journal of Political Economy* 86: 897–921.

DeSilva, A. 1997. Earnings of immigrant classes in the early 1980's in Canada. *Canadian Public Policy* 23: 179–202.

De Voretz, Don J. (ed.) 1995. *Diminishing Returns: The Economics of Canada's Recent Immigration Policy*. Toronto: C.D. Howe Institute.

Economic Council of Canada. 1991. *Economic and Social Impacts of Immigration*. Ottawa: The Council.

Friedberg, R.M. and Hunt, J. 1995. The impact of immigrants on host country wages, employment and growth. *Journal of Economic Perspectives* 9(2): 23–44.

Green, A.G. 1995. A comparison of Canadian and US immigration policy in the twentieth century. In De Voretz (ed.) 1995.

Green, A.G. and Green, D.A. 1995. Canadian immigration policy: the effectiveness of the point system and other instruments. *Canadian Journal of Economics* 28: 1006–1041.

Hamilton, B. and Whalley, J. 1984. Efficiency and distributional implications of global restrictions on labour mobility: calculations and policy implications. *Journal of Development Economics* 14: 61.

Kunin, R. and Jones, C.L. 1995. Business immigration in Canada. In De Voretz (ed.) 1995.

Layard, R. et al. 1992. *East–West Migration: The Alternatives*. Cambridge, MA: MIT Press.

OECD. 1994. *Trends in International Migration*. Paris: OECD.

Russell, S. and Teitelbaum, M. 1992. *International Migration and International Trade*. Washington, DC: World Bank Discussion Paper No. 160.

Schlesinger, A. 1992. *The Disuniting of America*. New York: W.W. Norton.

Schwartz, W.F. (ed.) 1995. *Justice in Immigration*. Cambridge: Cambridge University Press.

Simon, J.L. 1989. *The Economic Consequences of Immigration*. Oxford: Basil Blackwell.

Sykes, A.O. 1995. The welfare economics of immigration law. In Schwartz (ed.) 1995.

Trebilcock, M.J. 1995. The case for a liberal immigration policy. In Schwartz (ed.) 1995.

United Nations. 1989. Dept. of International Economic and Social Affairs. *World Population at the Turn of the Century*. New York: United Nations.

Zimmerman, K. 1995. Tackling the European migration problem. *Journal of Economic Perspectives* 9(2): 45–62.

impossibility doctrine in contract law. Several bodies of doctrine in the law of contracts provide for the discharge of contractual obligations under certain unusual contingencies as long as nothing in the contract evidences a contrary intention of the parties. One of these doctrines is the 'impossibility' doctrine, which excuses the obligations of a promisor with no requirement that damages be paid, if performance becomes 'impossible'. Related doctrines under the Uniform Commercial Code excuse performance when it has become 'commercially impracticable', or when goods identified to the contract are destroyed through no fault of the promisor. These doctrines are akin to '*force majeure*' clauses found in many contracts, although impossibility and impracticability cases do not rest on any express provisions of the contract (other than the absence of express intent to negate them), and they encompass contingencies that typical *force majeure* clauses do not.

Claims of impossibility or impracticability have arisen in a variety of settings. The leading early case on impossibility, *Taylor v. Caldwell*, held that the owner of a concert hall had no liability to the promoters of a concert for lost profits when the hall burned down and the owner was unable to provide the promised concert facility. A number of cases have held that an obligation to deliver crops grown on a particular tract of land is discharged in the event of crop failure. In addition to these cases involving 'destruction of the means of performance', impossibility has been found to exist when the cost of performance has risen dramatically and unexpectedly. Thus, for example, *Mineral Park Land Co. v. Howard* held that a promise by a construction company to take its requirements of gravel from the plaintiff's land was discharged when much of the gravel was unexpectedly below the water table, raising the cost of excavating it by ten to twelve fold – a 'difference in cost so great [as to make] performance impracticable'. Cases refusing to apply this extension of the doctrine include several in which shipping companies claimed commercial impracticability due to an unexpected closure of the Suez Canal, and a well-publicized case in which Westinghouse Electric Corporation asserted that a dramatic rise in the spot price of uranium due to the activities of a uranium cartel made it impracticable for Westinghouse to perform its fixed-price contracts to supply nuclear reactor fuel to various utilities (see Joskow 1977).

Impossibility and impracticability decisions have been the focus of considerable economic commentary, much of it from the economic perspective. The earlier writers tended to view the doctrine fairly favourably, although later writers have been more critical.

I. THE RISK-SHARING/DIVERSIFICATION JUSTIFICATION. Posner and Rosenfield (1977) suggest that the impossibility doctrine efficiently allocates the risks of certain unfortunate contingencies to the promisee under circumstances where the promisee is best able to bear them, either because the promisee is less risk-averse or because it is better suited than the promisor to lay the risk off in insurance markets. Likewise, they argue, when the promisor can take measures to avoid or insure against the risk in question more easily, the doctrine does not and should not apply (see also Joskow 1977 and Bruce 1982).

As one illustration of their discussion, Posner and Rosenfield defend the results in the crop-failure cases by suggesting that a contract to deliver crops grown on a particular tract of land is usually a contract between a risk-averse farmer and a wholesale buyer. The buyer, they suggest, can lay off the risk of non-performance by diversifying its purchases geographically. The seller/farmer, by contrast, has no comparable strategy for reducing risk. The impossibility doctrine discharges the liability of the farmer for any excess of the spot price over the contract price on the agreed date of delivery, and avoids heaping this additional loss on the risk-averse farmer who has already suffered a substantial loss due to the destruction of his crops and loss of his investment in them.

Sykes (1990) and others have been critical of the proposition that impossibility decisions generally can be justified on these grounds. In particular, nothing in the doctrine is expressly sensitive to the factors that might indicate whether the promisor was a comparatively poor risk bearer in a given case. Rather, the focus is on matters such as the 'unforeseen' nature of the contingency that interferes with performance or the magnitude of the increase in cost of performance (see especially Triantis 1992). As a result, large agribusiness interests have been the beneficiary of the crop-failure doctrine, and non-profit corporations have been the beneficiary of the doctrine in *Taylor v. Caldwell* at the expense of individual performing artists. Similarly, large cost increases may be experienced by all sorts of promisors, not just those that are relatively risk averse – there is little reason to think that the landowner in *Mineral Park*, for example, was less risk averse than the construction company that was excused from performing. A review of other cases further suggests that many of the promisors who have successfully invoked the impossibility doctrine have been large, publicly held companies, whose shareholders can typically diversify away the kinds of risks that trigger impossibility.

Moreover, the division of risk between promisor and promisee that results from the impracticability doctrine can be quite peculiar. Consider, for example, the *Mineral Park* case involving an increase in the cost of excavating gravel on the promisee's land. The case suggests that the promisor's liability is discharged only if costs rise because of some unusual contingency and only if they rise above some critical threshold. Thus, the promisor bears the risk of potentially sizable cost increases (or at least remains liable for damages in the event of breach) up to, say, a several-fold increase in cost, but the risk of losing the benefits of the bargain abruptly shifts to the promisee when the cost increase becomes sufficiently large and unusual (there, ten- to twelve-fold). Such an arrangement surely fails to approximate even remotely the first-best state-contingent contract between a risk averse promisor and the promisee (see Sykes 1990). Put differently, a rule discharging the promisor in these circumstances, and in other types of cases to which the impossibility doctrine applies, is certainly not a first-best damages rule (see Perloff 1981, Polinsky 1983 and White 1988).

As to the question whether the allocation of risk that results from the impossibility doctrine may nevertheless be better in a second-best sense than the allocation that results from requiring the promisor to perform or pay ordinary contract damages (expectation damages) all the time, the formal analysis is typically inconclusive. To continue with *Mineral Park* as an illustration, assume that the allocation of risk between a risk-averse promisor and a (risk-neutral or risk-averse) promisee is the only efficiency issue. Suppose further that the cost increase required to trigger the impossibility doctrine is high enough to ensure that the promisor is never discharged when performance remains jointly efficient. Then, the impossibility doctrine does not really prevent the promisor from having to incur unusually high costs, because the promisor would find it optimal to breach and pay expectation damages rather than to incur those costs. Instead, the doctrine simply defines some states of the world – a subset of those in which breach is efficient anyway – and excuses the obligation of the promisor to pay expectation damages in those states. The value of the contract to the promisee is thereby reduced somewhat, *ceteris paribus*, and the promisee will pay a somewhat lower price for the promisor's good or service as a consequence (as long as the promisee is well informed, discussed further below). In turn, the expectation damages payable in states where breach occurs are somewhat higher: expectation damages are equal to the difference between the value of performance to the promisee, and the price that the promisee must pay for performance – this difference has risen because of the impossibility doctrine because the price paid by the promisee has fallen. As a consequence, it is not possible to show in general that an impossibility rule dominates a rule under which the promisor is always obligated to pay expectation damages in the event of breach, *even when the promisee is risk neutral and thus a clearly better risk bearer*. The impossibility doctrine reduces downside risk for the promisor in some states and increases it in others, and without more assumptions about the precise utility function of the promisor (beyond mere risk aversion) it is impossible to be sure that the parties can benefit from the introduction of an impossibility rule.

If we relax the assumption that discharge is never permitted when performance is jointly efficient, another potential problem arises – the danger that the impossibility doctrine will lead to inefficient breach or to the renegotiation costs necessary to avoid it. Likewise, if the promisee is also somewhat risk averse, the utility of shifting any risk to the promisee is plainly reduced. Similar types of issues arise with respect to the risk allocation that results from the impossibility doctrine in other types of cases (Sykes 1990).

Not only is the risk-sharing issue by itself a potentially complicated one depending on the case, but the shifting of risk to the promisee that results from the impossibility doctrine may have unfortunate incentive effects. The benefits of the bargain to the promisee are external to the promisor and will not be considered by the promisor in taking precautions against adverse contingencies (unless those precautions are contractible at reasonable cost). Thus, perhaps the owner of a music hall, as in *Taylor*, may as a result of the impossibility doctrine take inadequate precautions against fire and other events that would put the hall out of service. Sellers who are subject to potentially dramatic cost increases may also have precautions available to them, such as buying inputs under forward contracts (see Joskow 1977). The incentive for promisors to expend resources gathering information that may bear on the need for such precautions is also diminished by the impossibility doctrine.

Related to these moral hazard concerns, information asymmetries may reduce or eliminate any gains from shifting risk to a less risk-averse promisee, as Posner and Rosenfield (1977) acknowledge. Promisors may often have better information about the likelihood of events that may make their performance 'impossible'. Unless the discharge of the promisor under the impossibility doctrine is made conditional on disclosure of this superior information at the time of contracting, various problems may arise. Promisees may enter contracts with negative expected value, for example, or may fail to take certain precautions themselves that are valuable. Yet, the cases often seem to pay little attention to these issues (see Bruce 1982 and Sykes 1990).

The vagueness of the impossibility doctrine in many cases also casts doubt on its utility as an *ex ante* risk-sharing device. Although the crop-failure rule is fairly clear and simple, the rule of cases like *Mineral Park* is not. Contracting parties know that a court may relieve a promisor of the obligation to perform under extreme cost conditions, but precisely what those conditions are often cannot be forecast with any confidence. Thus, the risk allocation that results is in fact unknown to the parties *ex ante* except in a very rough way (Sykes 1990; Triantis 1992).

In the cases where the impossibility precedents do afford a rule that is fairly clear and precise – such as the crop-failure cases – the transaction costs of including a clause in the contract to serve the same function seem small. For example, it would not be difficult for contracts between farmers and their customers to include a single sentence stating that the farmer's liabilities are discharged in the event of a crop failure. The Posner and Rosenfield justification for the doctrine in such cases thus reduces to the notion that it saves the parties a relatively trivial transaction cost of reducing things to writing (why not a standard form?), while the skeptics might suggest that the absence of an express provision covering such a simple and seemingly important contingency perhaps warrants an adverse inference about its efficiency.

Finally, because the impossibility and impracticability doctrines apply only in the event of contingencies that are unusual, some of them may not be within the contemplation of the parties *ex ante*. If so, the doctrine has no *ex ante* effects. A focus on its *ex post* implications for the welfare of the parties, including its impact on litigation costs, may then be more proper (see Joskow 1977 and Trimarchi 1991).

In sum, although it is assuredly *possible* in the abstract that the impossibility doctrine might efficiently shift risk to promisees who are less risk-averse or better able to insure and diversify, this justification for the doctrine seems quite speculative. The division of risks that impossibility decisions create in practice can be quite peculiar and unpredictable, and a matter of substantial litigation expenditure after the fact in some instances. Various moral-hazard and information concerns may reduce or eliminate any attendant risk-sharing benefits. Further, the doctrine on its face focuses on the 'impossibility' or 'impracticability' of performance and on the question whether the contingency that makes performance impracticable is sufficiently extreme or unforeseen, while paying little attention to observable factors that might bear on the relative risk-bearing capacities of the parties.

II. OTHER POSSIBLE JUSTIFICATIONS. Even when the promisee is no less risk-averse or better able to diversify or insure the risk, the impossibility doctrine may have some valuable consequences. These include a reduction in the promisee's incentive to over-rely on the contract, an improvement in the promisee's incentive to mitigate damages, and an avoidance of certain costs associated with the potential bankruptcy of the promisor.

1. *Reliance.* Promisees 'rely' on contracts by making various expenditures to enhance the value of performance to them, such as by preparing workers and real property for the arrival of new capital equipment. It is well known from the work of Shavell (1980) and others that when these reliance expenditures by the promisee are not constrained by the contract, ordinary expectation damages will lead to excessive reliance. The reason is that the promisor becomes an insurer of the benefits of the bargain to the promisee under expectation damages, yet in states of the world where the promisor opts to breach and pay expectation damages, performance is no longer jointly efficient (assuming damages are fully compensatory). Thus, as to the states of the world in which breach occurs, reliance expenditures yield a transfer from the promisor that is privately valuable to the promisee but is of no social value, and reliance tends to be excessive as a result. The problem is even worse under reliance damages.

If the jointly optimal level of reliance were cheaply observable by a court, the court could induce it directly, as by conditioning any recovery of damages by the promisee on an absence of excessive reliance. But where optimal reliance is unobservable, a court might move the level of reliance towards the joint optimum by reducing somewhat the set of states in which the promisor acts as the insurer of the benefits of the bargain to the promisee. The impossibility doctrine does just that and, as long as it does not overshoot or introduce other inefficiencies (such as the moral-hazard concerns noted above), the doctrine might produce joint gains because of its effects on reliance (Sykes 1990).

This is an uncomfortable justification for the doctrine, however, for at least two reasons. First, if the courts are unable to ascertain the efficient level of reliance by hypothesis, they will have great difficulty weighing any benefits of reducing excessive reliance against possible adverse consequences of the impossibility doctrine *ex ante* and *ex post* (litigation costs). Second, this rationale for discharging the promisor some of the time applies whenever excessive reliance is a significant problem, yet the impossibility doctrine applies only in the event of unusual contingencies that affect the promisor's costs or ability to perform – the materialization of such contingencies on the promisor's side of the bargain would seem rather a poor marker for circumstances in which excessive reliance on the promisee's side is a serious concern. Any benefits of the impossibility doctrine in reducing excessive reliance, therefore, seem totally fortuitous.

2. *Mitigation of damages.* Goldberg (1988; see also Bruce 1982) advances yet another rationale for the impossibility doctrine. If the promisor acts as insurer of the promisee's benefits of the bargain under the expectation damages rule, the promisee will have no incentive to mitigate damages in the event of a breach by the promisor. Contract law attempts to correct this problem by introducing a mitigation of damages requirement, foreclosing recovery of damages that the promisee could have avoided through reasonable mitigation efforts. But if the mitigation of damages requirement is difficult to enforce because proper mitigation efforts are hard to observe by a court, the expectation damages rule may lead to inadequate mitigation of damages after breach.

By discharging the promisor's obligations under certain contingencies, the impossibility doctrine forces promisees to internalize the benefits of efficient mitigation of damages in the event of those contingencies, and may thus produce better efforts at mitigation. Goldberg suggests that this fact weighs in favour of discharging the promisor in states of the world where, *ex ante*, the expected costs of discharge to the promisee are small. Thus, for example, if the promisor is unable to perform because of a fire in his factory, and if the item that will not be delivered as a result is produced in many other locations, the promisee can likely find a substitute source of supply without much difficulty, at a price that is not expected to be much higher than the contract price *ex ante*. If the promisor's obligation is discharged under these circumstances, therefore, the expected cost to the promisee is small and the promisee will have an incentive to mitigate quickly and efficiently. Of course, a valuable incentive to mitigate might also be created by discharge even where the expected cost to the promisee *ex ante* is high, and the promisee could be compensated by a reduction in the contract price, but a broader rule of discharge could well introduce other problems.

The difficulty with this justification for the impossibility doctrine parallels the difficulty with the reliance justification. If courts cannot tell when mitigation is appropriate, they will have a difficult time determining when the benefits of improved incentives to mitigate damages outweigh their possible costs in the form of moral hazards, risk-bearing inefficiencies and litigation costs. For example, even if the expected cost of discharging the promisor under the contingency in question is small *ex ante* to the promisee, that may be of little comfort to a risk-averse promisee who receives a bad draw from the urn. Further, as a positive matter, one observes impossibility decisions that discharge the promisor under circumstances where it is difficult to imagine the promisee engaging in any useful mitigation behaviour (*Mineral Park*, for example). And more generally, the contingencies that make performance impossible or impracticable on the promisor's side do not seem closely correlated with the circumstances in which mitigation is especially important on the promisee's side and difficult to police. Some of Goldberg's own examples are suggestive on this last point – where a close substitute for the promised good is widely available from other sources of supply, it is not difficult for courts to verify that the promisee mitigated properly by purchasing a substitute promptly rather than sitting around accumulating damages.

3. *Bankruptcy costs.* The bankruptcy of a firm can trigger sizable transaction costs. These costs are presumably worth incurring in most cases so that poor management can be replaced and resources redeployed to more valuable uses. But where bankruptcy would result not from a poor management decision or a change in the competitive position of the enterprise, but instead from a freakish event that could not have been anticipated or avoided and that does not signal the need for redeployment of resources, society might gain at times from avoiding the associated bankruptcy costs. Such reasoning might suggest a justification for discharging certain obligations of firms that would otherwise force them into bankruptcy.

If the impossibility doctrine were limited to contingencies that met these conditions, and did not at the same time create other difficulties such as by shifting risk to poorer risk-bearers or by inducing unproductive leverage as a strategic response, a concern for the costs of bankruptcy proceedings might afford some justification for it. But once again, the correspondence between the cases and this putative justification for the doctrine seems thin at best.

At this point, the reader may wonder whether, even if no one justification for impossibility and impracticability decisions seems terribly satisfactory, perhaps the various justifications collectively provide adequate rationale. To that query the response is at best 'may be'. My own assessment is that many of the cases in practice have no plausible fit with any of the possible justifications for discharging the promisor's obligations (Sykes 1990). Even if I am correct, however, that observation does not prove that the doctrine is on balance harmful, and assuredly does not establish that an improved doctrine would not be worth retaining.

ALAN O. SYKES

See also ATTITUDES TOWARDS RISK; CONTRACTS; RELIANCE; SPECIFIC PERFORMANCE.

Subject classification: 5c(ii).

CASES

Mineral Park Land Co. v. Howard, 156 P 458 (Cal. 1916).
Taylor v. Caldwell (1863) 3 B & S 826.

BIBLIOGRAPHY

Bruce, C. 1982. An economic analysis of the impossibility doctrine. *Journal of Legal Studies* 11: 311–32.
Goldberg, V. 1988. Impossibility and related excuses. *Journal of Institutional and Theoretical Economics* 144: 100.
Joskow, P. 1977. Commercial impossibility, the uranium market and the *Westinghouse* case. *Journal of Legal Studies* 6: 119–76.
Perloff, J. 1981. The effects of breaches of forward contracts due to unanticipated price changes. *Journal of Legal Studies* 10: 221–35.
Polinsky, A.M. 1983. Risk sharing through breach of contract remedies. *Journal of Legal Studies* 12: 427–44.
Posner, R. and Rosenfield, A. 1977. Impossibility and related doctrines in contract law: an economic analysis. *Journal of Legal Studies* 6: 83–118.
Shavell S. 1980. Damage measures for breach of contract. *Bell Journal of Economics* 11: 466–90.
Sykes, A. 1990. The doctrine of commercial impracticability in a second-best world. *Journal of Legal Studies* 19: 43–94.
Triantis, G. 1992. Contractual allocations of unknown risks: a critique of the doctrine of commercial impracticability. *University of Toronto Law Journal* 42: 450–83.
Trimarchi, P. 1991. Commercial impracticability in contract law: an economic analysis. *International Review of Law and Economics* 11: 63–82.
White, M. 1988. Contract breach and contract discharge due to impossibility. *Journal of Legal Studies* 17: 353–76.

impracticability in contract law. *See* IMPOSSIBILITY DOCTRINE IN CONTRACT LAW.

inalienability. In 1972, Guido Calabresi and Douglas Melamed justified alternative entitlement rules in economic efficiency terms. They distinguished between property rules and liability rules. Under a property rule, property could not be alienated without the owner's consent. Under a liability rule, consent was not required, but compensation must be paid at a level set by the state. Calabresi and Melamed recognized a third category, inalienability, but did not analyse it thoroughly, and they failed to see that inalienability rules could have an economic grounding.

Over ten years later, in 1985, I tried to remedy the lacuna in Calabresi and Melamed's original approach by developing a taxonomy of inalienability and asking when economic analysis could justify restrictions on entitlements (Rose-Ackerman 1985). I distinguished between restriction on (1) who may hold the entitlement; (2) what actions the entitlement holder is required to perform or forbidden from doing and (3) what kinds of transfers are permitted. My focus was on the way market failures – such as externalities, monopoly power, information imperfections, and coordination and agency problems – could justify various types of restrictions. I did, however, also distinguish between justifications based on the inefficiency of markets and those that further distributive justice or enhance the legitimacy of government. In commenting on my paper, Richard Epstein argued that I had strayed too far in rationalizing restrictions and contended that all valid restraints on alienation could be justified as efforts to control external effects and to deal with common pool problems (Epstein 1985). Margaret Jane Radin, in contrast, found my analysis normatively flat (Radin 1987).

At about the same time Carol Rose (1986) argued that one ought to distinguish between public property managed by the state, such as bridges and airports, and 'inherently public property' open to all without state management. My analysis focused on cases where private ownership was unquestioned, but where the scope of ownership might be restricted by state imposed restraints on alienability. Rose's work, in contrast, makes problematic the background condition of private ownership. She isolates situations where it is not desirable for the state to establish either private property regimes or public management regimes. She discusses resources that are very plentiful and almost unbounded such as the oceans and the air, but her primary interest is in the kinds of market failures discussed in my article. She shows how factors which produce arguments for restrictions on private rights under my analysis, produce arguments for unrestricted public access under her view. Thus our work can be seen as complementary efforts to demonstrate that, even in a basically free market system, unrestricted private property rights are not universally efficient.

The inalienability framework has spawned a diverse literature. There are applications to takings law and property, to health care and the provision of body parts, to cultural artifacts such as the Parthenon Marbles, to intellectual property, to reproductive freedom and surrogate motherhood, to environmental issues, to bankruptcy, and to voting in corporations and political jurisdictions. I incorporate the most interesting of these applications into the discussion below, which follows the framework of my earlier paper. I begin with efficiency and fairness rationales, go on to discuss citizenship, and conclude with an assessment of Margaret Jane Radin's focus on personal identity.

EFFICIENCY AND FAIRNESS. The efficiency rationales for inalienability rules are second-best responses to market failures that arise because of externalities, imperfect information, or difficulties of coordination. The straightforward responses of internalizing the externality through fees or taxes, of subsidizing the provision of information, and of facilitating joint action may be costly. In such cases, restricting market trades becomes a realistic possibility. Inalienability rules establish prohibited or required actions that make market incentives less, rather than more, important.

Externalities provide the most commonly recognized rationales for inalienability (Epstein 1985). When transaction costs are high, market incentives and tort law may be ineffective tools. If there is a strong statistical relationship between some characteristic of product users and an external cost, the most effective policy may be an outright ban on use of the product by this type of person. Thus blind people and children are forbidden from driving automobiles even if some of them might, in fact, be quite safe drivers. Other types of externalities can be controlled by regulating use of a product. Speed limits and traffic signals control driving over and above tort rules which penalize negligent behaviour.

Markets also frequently work poorly because information is imperfect and asymmetrical. Then inalienability rules may be an effective response in two situations. First, buyers and sellers may have asymmetric information. Sellers can claim that a product is high quality, and buyers have no way to judge quality on their own before purchase (Akerlof 1970). In extreme cases, it may be most efficient to outlaw sales and encourage uncompensated gifts (Arrow 1972). The number of cases in which such conditions hold is likely to be small. On the one hand, appeals to altruism must be feasible, and on the other hand, alternative strategies – such as the provision of information or the imposition of tort liability – must be costly and ineffective. Some have argued, for example, that human blood should be acquired only through donations in the absence of fully effective tests for contaminants such as hepatitis or AIDS and that human organ donations would fall if sales were also permitted. Richard Titmuss (1971), for example, stressed the problem of the transmission of hepatitis through contaminated blood. This raises the possibility that an entirely donative system of supply might be more efficient than a world which permits both gifts and sales. We do not have good data, but such results are, at least, possible (Thorne 1994).

It does seem likely that market substitutes reduce giving in areas where people are urged to sacrifice for the public good. Why should you sacrifice if others are being paid to do the same thing? Thus if blood and body parts are purchased from some, donations can be expected to fall (Thorne 1994). The same may be true when mandatory retirement ages are outlawed, as has recently happened in the United States. If some employees demand large severance payments in return for retiring, even those who believe that retirement at a fixed time is the right thing to do may demand a similar payoff. One's feelings of moral obligation may be undermined by the payment of compensation. Instead of feeling under an obligation to take an action or accept a burden without payment, one may feel entitled to compensation (Rose-Ackerman 1985: 945–8; 1997). According to Margaret Jane Radin (1987: 1913; 1996: 96–101), a 'domino effect' may operate. Permitting the commodification of a service, such as sexual relations, may reduce the value of free gifts of the same service.

The quality control argument for outlawing sales does not provide a general argument against sales of body parts. For many organs useful in transplants there is no quality control argument against market sales (Jones 1994: 577–9). A recent article provides a political economy argument for the continued lack of a market in cadaveric organs. The authors point out that the number of hospitals in the United States doing heart transplants increased over 600 percent between 1983 and 1988, evidence that the transplant business is profitable. They argue that physician and hospital support for the altruistic supply system is due in part to the enhanced profitability created by the policy (Blair and Kaserman 1991: 419). The medical doctor who commented on their paper, however, claims that permitting sales would have little impact on the supply of organs. The main problem is the failure of hospitals and doctors to request donations (Guttmann 1991).

Second, two products may look alike but one can be legally possessed while the other cannot. For example, laws protecting rare birds prohibit the taking of specimens after a set day but permit possession of those killed in the past. Suppliers might then fraudulently claim that their illegal products are in the legal category. Buyers are not harmed by this misrepresentation, but some other policy – for example, the preservation of an endangered species – is undermined. A modified alienability rule – that is, a rule permitting gifts but not sales – may resolve both of these problems. Such a practice was followed by the United States Secretary of the Interior. A law prohibited the killing of eagles after a certain date. The Secretary issued a regulation prohibiting the sale of anything containing eagle products even if the eagles had been killed before that date. Since there is no reliable way to date eagle feathers, an outright ban is administratively simpler than the alternatives. The effect of the regulation is to convert Indian artifacts made of 'old' eagle feathers from goods protected by a property rule to ones protected by a modified inalienability rule. The owners challenged the rule as an unconstitutional 'taking' of property and sought compensation. They lost in the case of *Andrus v. Allard*. Although the Supreme Court never discussed the issue, it is important to recognize that payment of compensation would have undermined the purpose of outlawing sales unless the government set up a system to pay compensation before the ban on hunting took effect. Even then, the government would have had to watch for people seeking to shoot eagles before the deadline (Rose-Ackerman 1985: 944–5).

Finally, difficulties of coordination may lead to inefficiencies. The coordination problem is most clear in the case of a pure public good consumed in common by a large group. Outlawing sales but permitting gifts can help achieve conservation goals while retaining considerable freedom for private action. Examples of babies and the conservation of wild animals and indigenous cultures fall into this category. Permitting the sale of babies might make population control goals harder to achieve. A number of states outlaw the sale of wild fish and game to limit their commercial potential. Some Alaskan native groups in the United States are permitted to hunt endangered and threatened species integral to their traditional way of life but are not permitted to sell them (Rose-Ackerman 1985: 942–3).

Closely analogous to this case is the 'prisoners' dilemma' where all would benefit from coordination, but where independent action is inefficient. Consider the problem of developing a new geographic region. Everyone would be better off if other people settle first, but no one has an incentive to be the first settler. To alleviate this problem, policy makers may provide land cheaply and attach coercive conditions, such as the United States Homestead Acts' requirement that owners actually live on and develop their land in order to perfect their title. An underlying prisoners' dilemma may also justify restrictive conditions in urban housing programmes designed to improve neighbourhood quality (Rose-Ackerman 1985: 957–9). Similarly, when close-knit settlements have beneficial spillovers, restrictions on alienation are a way to maintain these benefits (Ellickson 1993: 1378–80). Similar motivations appear to be behind restrictions on resale and subleasing in private real estate contracts where the value of property in a shopping centre or condominium complex is partly a function of who else lives there.

Agency/principal problems may produce similar questions. An inalienability rule can supplement other contractual controls in such cases. Thus the law protects creditors by preventing a person close to bankruptcy from giving away assets. Similarly, mineral leases that require royalty payments equal to a percentage of profits may include diligence requirements (Rose-Ackerman 1985: 950, 959).

Incentives for predation and violence may result from permitting certain kinds of market trades. Claiming that truly contractual slavery is rare, William K. Jones (1994: 551–6) argues that 'the most potent argument against slavery and other forms of involuntary servitude' is that they 'are rooted in violence and ultimately beget more violence'. Violence produces deadweight losses: 'a seemingly endless stream of deaths, woundings, diseases, displaced persons, and devastated economies'. Similarly, part of the opposition to permitting a market in body parts comes from those worried that criminals will injure or murder people to obtain their valuable organs.

The imposition of restrictions on alienability will generally have distributive as well as efficiency consequences. Sometimes the distributive effects are the primary justification. If policy makers wish to benefit a particular sort of people but cannot identify them *ex ante*, they may impose restrictions that are less onerous for the worthy group than for others. For example, the coercive conditions imposed on the use of land under the Homesteading Acts can be justified as a way to assure that most of the land went mainly to those formerly landless people willing to live on and farm the property (Rose-Ackerman 1985: 960–61). In other cases, the distributive impact is an unwelcome side effect. Therefore, policy makers might decide to compensate the losers. Fundamental conflicts arise when a group does not deserve to bear the costs of the restraints but where compensation would undermine the purpose of the restraint. For example, compensating blood donors for the fact that they cannot sell their blood would convert the process into something similar to a market trade and would undermine the use of a modified inalienability rule to assure high-quality blood supplies. Similar problems would arise if women were compensated for not practicing prostitution or surrogate motherhood.

The law places many more impediments on the alienability of human capital than it does on physical capital. Employment law is reluctant to enforce covenants not to compete, prohibits certain kinds of personal service contracts, and safeguards the employee's income against the employer's claims. Bankruptcy and family law also treat human capital more favourably than physical and financial capital. Stewart Sterk (1993) argues that the existing justifications for this differential treatment are weak and that the distributional consequences are perverse. He recommends that United States law be rethought with the goal of treating human capital more like other forms of capital in the modern world where human capital is of increasing importance.

CITIZENSHIP. The analysis of inalienability helps to illuminate a theme that has preoccupied students of capitalist democracy: How insulated should the state be from market pressures? When constitutional rights can be purchased by the state from willing citizens, there is a risk that the government will accumulate an unacceptable amount of power. This worry is exacerbated by the fact that government funds are raised from taxation so that its willingness to pay may bear little relation to the economic value of the right. If rights are meant to protect individuals from majority will, the majority's interest in obtaining someone's right does not provide a persuasive justification for permitting its purchase by the state (Kreimer 1984: 1391).

To further develop this theme in the context of inalienability, I demonstrate how alternative conceptions of citizenship have different implications for voting, military service, and jury selection (Rose-Ackerman 1985: 961–8).

Consider, first, alienable and inalienable rights. Under the weakest conception of citizen responsibility, citizenship services are obtained under a regime of alienable property rights. Votes can be sold, given away, or left unused. The state sets basic voting qualifications, and those who obtain voting rights can sell or give them to other qualified people. Both soldiers and jurors are obtained in the labour market by offering compensation to qualified people willing to participate.

The argument for permitting people to assign their votes to others turns on the poor information available to most voters and their lack of an incentive to become informed. In the corporate world shareholders can give their votes to management or other proxies, a practice that is justified by the better information available to managers and large shareholders. Thomas André (1990) argues that sales of corporate voting rights in tender offers should be permitted as a way of reducing the influence of incumbent managers. He claims that his analysis is consistent with the concern of other scholars that sale of votes separate from a sale of the underlying ownership interest will result in excessive agency costs (Easterbrook and Fischel 1983: 411). Agency costs are unimportant, he argues, because his proposal is limited to tender offers where the goal is to obtain the entire equity interest.

In the political realm, agency costs would be severe since politicians could pay off sellers with public money (Epstein 1985: 987–8). Furthermore, outright sales could concentrate political power in the hands of the wealthy (Karlan 1994). As Seth Kreimer (1984: 1390) argues, free rider and prisoners' dilemma issues arise in the voting context:

> If an economically and socially disadvantaged group is to improve its collective lot, political action is necessary . . . The government deals primarily in public or quasi-public goods – sewers, antidiscrimination legislation, and the like. It is advantageous for any given member of the least well-off group, if votes are alienable, to sell her vote rather than use it to attempt to obtain a public good for her group. If others sell their votes, she is no worse off for having sold her vote, and

if other members of her group retain their votes and vote for the public good, she will obtain the good in any event. On the other hand, if she retains her vote and her compatriots do not, she will have gained nothing, and she knows that her compatriots, faced with the same choices, will probably 'rationally' choose to sell.

Laws that prohibit the sale of individual votes are, according to Pamela Karlan (1994: 1467), 'best justified as protecting the integrity of the political system rather than the autonomy of individual voters'. Vote buying transforms a 'relational agreement and ongoing conversation' between voter and politician into a discrete contract (ibid.: 1469–70). Karlan then raises the important question of why most democracies distinguish between the illegal purchase of individual votes and legal campaign promises of economic benefit to voters. To her, the difference depends upon three factors. The pledge is made openly; the benefits extend to a significant group of taxpayers and citizens; and there is no direct *quid pro quo*. The outcome depends not on an individual vote, but on the candidate obtaining majority support (ibid.: 1468). Sometimes, however, campaign promises have the quality of vote purchases. In Singapore more than 85% of the population lives in public housing and a single party has controlled the government for many years. In a recent election observers reported that the dominant party threatened that housing located in districts that did not support its candidates would not be allocated adequate renovation funds ('Ring in the old: voters extend the PAP's lease on power yet again', *Far Eastern Economic Review*, 16 January 1997: 16–17).

On the supply side the government is a market participant. An all-volunteer military has the advantage of forcing taxpayers to finance the opportunity cost of personnel. Some commentators object to this shift of responsibility on citizenship grounds, claiming that choosing soldiers who prefer military service to other options is undesirable in a democracy. A country may be overly likely to engage in militaristic adventures if its soldiers are people who prefer fighting more than does the rest of the population.

Analysts have seldom viewed jury duty as a job like any other that should be made available to qualified applicants. Yet it is difficult to see why a sharp distinction should be made between jurors and soldiers. Paying market rates for jurors would impose the cost of the system on the general public and those attracted to jury service would include those with an interest in participating. The objections, however, parallel those made for the military draft. Jury duty is viewed as a duty of citizenship and the process itself might be undermined if the system were staffed by volunteers. Those serving on juries would not be a cross section of the population – an outcome that would raise constitutional objections in the United States. Using the market would imply that military service and jury duty are rights, not duties.

Suppose then that we view voting, military service, and jury duty as duties that may or may not be alienable. An inalienable duty is imposed by the state with no possibility of transfer to others. The coercive nature of duties can be softened by making them alienable by gift or sale.

In some countries voting is not only inalienable, but also required. The state sets a price for not voting by fining those who stay at home on election day. Such coercion can overcome the familiar free rider problem inherent in democratic choice – no one has an instrumental reason to vote since the chance of affecting the outcome is vanishingly small. Karlan proposes that the state pay those who show up at the polls, converting a penalty into a benefit with the same incentive effect. However, if many voters are poorly informed or indifferent to the outcome, including them in the electorate may not preserve democratic values. Karlan dismisses this argument on the grounds that those who know they will vote under her incentive scheme may become better informed. To counter arguments that outright monetary payments are inappropriate, she suggests that people might be given vouchers to assign to nonprofit charities (Karlan 1994: 1472–4).

The arguments for forced jury duty and military service are somewhat different. If both are viewed as citizenship duties, a draft based on a lottery with no buy out possibilities seems to impose the duty most fairly. Multiple lotteries could be constructed if the goal is not just to impose the duty equally but to produce juries that represent a cross section of the population. The cost of such systems is the inefficiency in the use of the country's labour resources (Fischel 1996).

Suppose, however, that these duties are made alienable. Those called to the military or jury service may purchase substitutes or try to induce their friends or relatives to serve in their place. Such a system has little to recommend it. It reduces both the fairness and the efficiency of the system. To see this, consider the situation during the United States Civil War. In both the North and the South draftees could either buy their way out or buy a substitute. The system amounted to a volunteer army financed by wealthy draftees instead of taxpayers as a whole. The governments in planning military strategy had no incentive to take into account the opportunity cost of soldiers' time and the risks they faced. Therefore, they lacked incentives to economize on manpower. It was also viewed as unfair in both the North and the South and broke down. In the North state and local governments appropriated funds to enable every one to buy his way out (Rose-Ackerman 1985: 967–8).

If, then, we rule out alienable duties, we are left with a choice between market-based systems of rights or inalienable duties. Each has something to recommend it and a mixed strategy may be desirable. For example, a volunteer army could be used in peacetime with a draft based on a lottery introduced during war. Jurors in cases involving substantial time and expertise might be recruited and paid the market wage. When a cross-section of the population is required by law, jury service could be an inalienable duty with pay levels set equal to the average wage so that the state pays the opportunity cost of jury service.

PERSONAL AND NATIONAL IDENTITY. Many commentators view the economic approach to inalienability as overly reductionist and normatively impoverished. The most interesting attempt at a broader perspective is by Margaret Jane Radin in a 1987 article that has been incorporated into her book, *Contested Commodities* (1996). To her, cost-benefit analysis is like a flat map of the world. It is 'easy to use at the point of projection, but difficult and misleading at the edges' (Radin 1996: 85).

The aspect of Radin's argument most relevant to the field of law and economics is her claim that treating something as an alienable commodity can affect its value. In particular, aspects of one's personhood that are intimately tied up with one's ability to flourish as a person may be devalued and undermined by being available for sale (Radin 1987, 1996: 87–101). She recognizes, however, that some things are the same whether or not they are bought and sold, and others are different. She claims (1996: 95) that:

> At present we – at least the mainstream group of 'us' – tend to think that nuts and bolts are pretty much the 'same' whether commodified or not, whereas love, friendship, and sexuality are very 'different'; we also tend to think that trying to keep society free of commodified love, friendship, and sexuality morally matters more than does trying to keep it free of commodified nuts and bolts.

She is also concerned that even if one does not oneself participate in market trades, the mere existence of a legal market can be detrimental to one's sense of self (ibid.: 97).

These concerns make Radin sceptical of proposals to legalize prostitution, establish an adoption market for babies, permit surrogate motherhood, or allow the sale of body parts (ibid.: 131–53). Thus Radin is raising the important question of whether the existence of the market enhances or undermines value. She recognizes, however, the 'double bind' at the heart of proposals to outlaw prostitution or surrogate motherhood. Commodification may lead to exploitation, but prohibition of these activities will simply make women poorer in the absence of alternative equally well-paid employment or large-scale redistributive programmes (1987: 1916–17; 1996: 131–53). Radin proposes compromise solutions. Prostitution should be 'incompletely commodified'. To her, this means decriminalization, regulation to ban brokerage (pimping) and recruitment, maintaining the unenforceability of prostitution contracts and a ban on advertising (1996: 134–6). Paid surrogacy and adoptions cause her more difficulties because of the existence of a third person, the baby, not a party to either market or altruistic arrangements (ibid.: 137). After canvassing the pros and cons, she concludes that market inalienability – outlawing sales, but permitting gifts – is the best regime 'for now' (ibid.: 148). On this issue, I must admit to sharing Jones's (1994: 579) view that surrogacy benefits both the infertile couple and the surrogate mother and produces a child with excellent prospects for healthy social development. There is, however, a need for regulation because of the especially serious problem of opportunistic behaviour by both the birth mother and the father once the baby is born.

Radin is in some respects the mirror image of Thorstein Veblen who, in the early years of the twentieth century, claimed that some goods became more valuable to people the higher their price since price was taken as a measure of a good's social value. He argued that consumers make obvious costliness a measure of a good's serviceability so that merit is identified with cost, and he quotes the maxim 'A cheap coat makes a cheap man' (Veblen [1899] 1925: 156, 158). Wealth, he argued, is held sacred 'primarily for the sake of the good repute to be got through its conspicuous consumption' (ibid.: 118). Thus Veblen, focusing on the demand side, claims that society attributes moral value to people who spend money on conspicuous consumption. Radin, in contrast, argues that the sale of certain goods and services lowers the moral value not just of the seller, but of potential sellers, even those with a moral aversion to such sales. These are both empirical claims for which little solid evidence exists. Radin argues that her view is normatively correct; Veblen is critical of those who equate price with merit.

Both authors raise the question of whether the pervasiveness of the market undermines the desirable features of interpersonal links based on trust and respect. According to Viviana Zelizer's work on the social meaning of money (1994: 71–118), however, this result does not follow. Markets in some goods and services can easily coexist with altruistic transfers. People give food, clothing and shelter to the poor undeterred by the existence of a market in these commodities. Others support cultural institutions in music and art despite an active for-profit entertainment sector. College graduates give to their alma mater even though most students also pay tuition. Furthermore, even within the zone of compensation interpersonal relationships frequently reflect underlying social relationships. This is especially likely to occur in the workplace where people interact daily over long periods of time. Alternatively, relationships based on trust and friendship may be undermined by some kinds of payments within those relationships. In contrast to the jeremiads of some writers, Zelizer stresses the peaceful coexistence of different forms of exchange in modern societies.

Even if the 'guilt by association' argument does not always hold with respect to market trades, some kinds of sales, or even gifts, may so undermine the identity of the original owners that they should be outlawed. An interesting attempt to extend this claim beyond individuals to communities is provided in a student note in the *Cornell Law Review* (Moustakas 1989). The author argues that cultural artifacts that bear a strong link to a nation's identity should be strictly inalienable. In other words, neither sales nor gifts should be permitted. To the author, the Parthenon Marbles taken to England by Lord Elgin are in this category for the Greek people. The Greeks themselves should not be permitted to give away or sell artifacts so essential to 'Greek groupness' and 'communal flourishing'. Strict inalienability, as opposed to modified inalienability, is justified because the artifacts are unique, actual possession is necessary, and intergenerational justice limits the rights of the current generation. Not all artifacts should be inalienable, however, especially those that are available in multiple variants. At some point, limits on transferability become fetishistic.

CONCLUSION. In the years since the concept of inalienability was introduced into property law by Calabresi and Melamed, a rich literature has developed around this topic.

Inalienability has proved a fruitful way to organize and think through the arguments for restraining property rights. Restrictions on transferability, ownership, and use of property can be justified under a range of different assumptions based on imperfect information and transaction costs. Inalienability is frequently useful, not as an ideal policy, but as a second-best response to the messiness and complexity of the world. It is generally possible to conceive of an alternative policy that would be superior if transaction costs were lower. The major exceptions, where some form of inalienability is the preferred response, involve the ideal of citizenship and cases where market sales undermine other values such as Radin's conception of personhood or Moustakas's concept of national identity.

SUSAN ROSE-ACKERMAN

See also ADOPTION; COMMON PROPERTY; EMINENT DOMAIN AND JUST COMPENSATION; ENDANGERED SPECIES; JURIES; MARKETS AND INCOMMENSURABILITY; PROPERTY RIGHTS IN PRISONERS OF WAR; STANDING.

Subject classification: 2b(i); 4c(i).

CASES

Andrus v. Allard, 444 US 51 (1979).

BIBLIOGRAPHY

Akerlof, G.A. 1970. The market for 'lemons': quality, uncertainty and the market mechanism. *Quarterly Journal of Economics* 84: 488–500.

André, T. 1990. A preliminary inquiry into the utility of vote buying in the market for corporate control. *Southern California Law Review* 63: 535–636.

Arrow, K. 1972. Gifts and exchanges. *Philosophy and Public Affairs* 1: 343–62.

Blair, R.D. and Kaserman, D. 1991. The economics and ethics of alternative cadaveric organ procurement policies. *Yale Journal on Regulation* 8: 403–52.

Calabresi, G. and Melamed, D. 1972. Property rights, liability rules, and inalienability: one view of the cathedral. *Harvard Law Review* 85: 1089–1128.

Easterbrook, F. and Fischel, D. 1983. Voting in corporate law. *Journal of Law and Economics* 26: 395–427.

Ellickson, R. 1993. Property in land. *Yale Law Journal* 102: 1315–1400.

Epstein, R. 1985. Why restrain alienation? *Columbia Law Review* 85: 970–90.

Fischel, W.A. 1996. The political economy of just compensation: lessons from the military draft for the takings issue. *Harvard Journal of Law and Public Policy* 20: 23–63.

Guttmann, R.D. 1991. The meaning of 'The economics and ethics of alternative cadaveric organ procurement policies'. *Yale Journal on Regulation* 8: 453–62.

Jones, W.K. 1994. A theory of social norms. *University of Illinois Law Review* 1994: 545–96.

Karlan, P.S. 1994. Not by money but by virtue won? Vote trafficking and the voting rights system. *Virginia Law Review* 80: 1455–75.

Kreimer, S.F. 1984. Allocative sanctions: the problem of negative rights in a positive state. *University of Pennsylvania Law Review* 132: 1293–1397.

Moustakas, J. 1989. Group rights in cultural property: justifying strict inalienability. *Cornell Law Review* 74: 1179–1227.

Radin, M.J. 1987. Market-inalienability. *Harvard Law Review* 100: 1849–1937.

Radin, M.J. 1996. *Contested Commodities*. Cambridge, MA: Harvard University Press.

Rose, C. 1986. The comedy of the commons: custom, commerce, and inherently public property. *University of Chicago Law Review* 53: 711–81.

Rose-Ackerman, S. 1985. Inalienability and the theory of property rights. *Columbia Law Review* 85: 931–69.

Rose-Ackerman, S. 1997. Bribes and gifts. In *Economics and Values*, ed. A. Ben-Nur and L. Putterman, Cambridge: Cambridge University Press, 1997.

Sterk, S.E. 1993. Restraints on alienation of human capital. *Virginia Law Review* 79: 383–460.

Thorne, E.D. 1994. The Economics of Market-Inalienable Human Organs. PhD dissertation, Department of Economics, Yale University, New Haven.

Titmuss, R. 1971. *The Gift Relationship*. London: Allen & Unwin.

Veblen, T. [1899] 1925. *The Theory of the Leisure Class: An Economic Theory of Institutions*. London: George Allen & Unwin.

Zelizer, V.A. 1994. *The Social Meaning of Money*. New York: Basic Books.

incentives to innovate. Protection of intellectual property creates incentives to invent. In the case of patents, it also creates incentives to disclose new technologies to the benefit of competitors. Much of the economics literature is directed at understanding how this incentive system works. The purpose of this essay is to expose the disheartening message contained in that literature as a whole: patents are a very crude incentive mechanism with many pernicious side effects. On the positive side, I discuss some of the remedies that have been suggested, mostly staying within the structure of legal doctrine and practice, but also straying beyond it. I organize the discussion around defects of the patent system.

PATENTS DO NOT REFLECT COSTS. Perhaps the most limiting aspect of the patent system and other forms of intellectual property protection is that there is no formal mechanism by which the extent of protection can reflect R&D costs. Since the patent life is independent of R&D costs, the tradeoff identified by Nordhaus (1969) is fundamental: Long patents are undesirable because they prolong monopoly distortions beyond the minimum required to reimburse costs, and short patents are undesirable because some inventors are dissuaded from investing. The optimal patent life balances these two social costs.

While it seems obvious that the patent system would be improved if patent values were individually chosen to cover R&D costs, I argue that, because patents are awarded after costs are sunk, this is infeasible.

Suppose that the patent office tried to tailor patent values to R&D costs. It would face the following problems: (i) Since most R&D firms are pursuing several patents, they must allocate overhead costs among innovations, which makes it easy to misrepresent R&D costs. (ii) At best the patent authority can observe what the firm actually spent on R&D, but not what the most efficient firm would have spent, or what the inventor would have spent if it had invested efficiently. It is the latter that should be reimbursed. (iii) If the firm is only reimbursed for costs when R&D is successful, then it will make negative profit in expectation if success is not assured. Hence it will not invest.

To some extent these problems could be avoided by contracting *ex ante*. If the patent authority auctioned a contract for doing the research, the most efficient firm would win the bid, and they would win at a price that reflects its true assessment of how overhead costs should be allocated, as well as compensating in expectation for the prospect of failure. An *ex ante* auction goes a long distance toward solving all three *ex post* problems, and since the payment could be lump-sum rather than in the form of a patent, the auction could also avoid granting a monopoly. However, such a solution departs radically from current practice, by which patents are granted *ex post*. (A discussion of other alternatives to the patent system can be found in Wright 1983.) And the auction is not available with only one firm, which can easily misrepresent its cost to the patent authority. With only one firm and costs that are unobservable to the patent authority *ex ante*, the patent cannot be tailored to the cost.

PATENTS CANNOT BE TAILORED TO THE MARKET. Even if patent value could be tailored to costs, there would be the additional problem of how to structure it. Two obvious patent instruments are the patent life and the breadth of claims that are allowed. Klemperer (1990) and Gilbert and Shapiro (1990) have pointed out that to provide a given patent value, the patent can either be long with narrow claims or short with broad claims. They investigate which combination minimizes the deadweight loss from market power. Instead of repeating their arguments, which respectively pertain to rather special circumstances, I would like to emphasize an aspect that they obscure, namely, that the most efficient type of patent depends on the nature of oligopolistic competition and demand. Such market details are not considered in granting patents. Instead, patents are awarded purely on technical considerations such as whether the innovation is novel and nonobvious, and the claims are limited to what the patent examiner thinks the inventor invented.

Another market condition that should inform the granting of patent rights is network externalities, possibly created by the establishment of standards, for example, a computer operating system that permits the development and use of compatible software. If the underlying standard is not protected, then the inventor who facilitates the network will not be reimbursed. On the other hand, networks can create such strong market power that property rights are unnecessary to support innovation. Indeed, property rights can give unduly large rewards to an innovator who by happenstance created a network without much investment in R&D. The resolution of these tensions has not been worked out (Farrell 1995).

AGGREGATE INFORMATION IS NOT USED EFFICIENTLY. A typical defence of patents is that firms have better information about the costs and benefits of research than the patent authorities have. According to the general principle that decisions should be located with the parties who have the best information, R&D decisions should be decentralized, and this justifies the patent system.

In my view, this line of reasoning is misguided. It is surely true that firms should contribute their private information to the decision process, but the extreme form of decentralized decision-making inherent in the patent system is not a very good way to accomplish this.

The problem of aggregating private information takes several guises, which I will address in a simple unified model. Suppose that two firms have different, privately known, costs (say c_L or c_H) of investing in, say, a vaccine. In addition they have different signals, L or H, about the benefits of such an investment. The signal might represent the probability of success or the extent of the market. Two problems are represented in this model: There is the problem of an efficient *decision* (should investment occur at all?) and the problem of efficient *delegation* (which firm should invest?). The efficient decision depends on whether the lowest cost is c_L, and on whether, for example, the signals of value are (L, L), (L, H) or (H, H). Efficient delegation is obviously to the least-cost firm.

Since a patent race cannot aggregate the information, it cannot ensure that research effort is efficiently delegated or that the efficient decision is taken. To first see the delegation problem, suppose that the benefits of the innovation are known, and that the costs are such that at most one firm will invest. If both invested, then each would receive the patent with probability one-half, which I will suppose is not profitable enough to justify investment. Suppose, however, that if only one firm invests, investment is worthwhile whether the costs are c_L or c_H. Then it is an equilibrium for either firm to invest, and that is inefficient if a high-cost firm invests when a low-cost firm is present. Gandal and Scotchmer (1993) show in a more general model how the delegation problem can be solved by research joint ventures, but possibly with an offsetting inefficiency of reducing aggregate investment or the speed of innovation.

Now suppose that only the benefits are unobservable, but the costs are either commonly known or the same for all firms. Each firm cares about a common underlying value of the innovation, and each firm's signal adds information about that value. Hence each firm can make a better decision if it can infer something about the other firm's signal by observing its investment behaviour. This is a problem addressed by Minehart and Scotchmer (1997), who show that the following problem can occur.

Suppose that investment is efficient for a firm with signal L, provided it believes with probability at least one-half that the other firm has signal H. Investment is inefficient if the signals are known to be (L, L). Suppose that the signals turn out to be (L, L), but each firm knows only its own signal. Then there can be an equilibrium in which each firm invests because it puts probabilities one-half on the other firm having signal L or H. Neither firm learns anything about the other firm's signal in equilibrium. But there can be another equilibrium where neither firm invests, thus revealing to each firm that the other firm has signal L. The example illustrates that although firms might learn from each other's investment behaviour, there can also be a self-reinforcing equilibrium in which they jointly take an inefficient action. Not all of their private information will be revealed in a decentralized equilibrium where they observe each other's actions.

Finally, suppose that neither firm can observe the other

firm's costs or information on value. Suppose that the cost and signal of value for one firm is (c_L, L) and of another is (c_H, H). The low-cost firm might not invest because it is pessimistic about the payoff to such an investment, and the high-cost firm might not invest because its costs are too high. These decisions could be inefficient: a social planner in possession of all the information might direct the low-cost firm to invest on the basis of information about benefits possessed by the high-cost firm. A decentralized system of patent incentives cannot achieve this outcome because the information is not aggregated. This problem is addressed by Cremer and Scotchmer (1997), who characterize an incentive mechanism by which a social planner could get the firms to reveal their aggregate information.

DUPLICATION OF R&D INVESTMENTS. Even when firms have the same information, patent incentives may lead to inefficiencies through patent races. The literature has produced two views of patent races: that they inefficiently duplicate costs, and that they efficiently encourage higher aggregate investment. Of course 'duplication' is a form of 'higher aggregate investment', so these two views obviously presume different models of R&D. Inefficient duplication arises where R&D costs have a large fixed component; e.g., the natural interpretation of the model above is that the R&D cost for achieving the innovation is fixed, and if two firms invest, the cost is needlessly duplicated. The incentive for two firms to enter instead of one could be remedied by restricting the patent value (patent life), but that solution is stymied by the inability of patents to reflect costs (see above).

On the other hand, participation of many firms might be efficient if there are no fixed costs of R&D, and if there is no cumulative learning within each firm. These are the two premises of a large patent race literature based on the Poisson R&D process (see Reinganum 1989), in which patent races may actually improve efficiency because they accelerate innovation. The patent race literature based on the Poisson model focuses on the fact that R&D investment is a flow over time. Since the patent value is less than the social value, the marginal benefit of increasing the aggregate rate of investment is greater to a social planner than to a single private firm. As a consequence a single private firm would invest too slowly and delay the invention.

Patent races increase the rate of investment, and in conjunction with a well chosen patent life, may therefore overcome the tendency toward underinvestment. Under mild conditions with the Poisson technology, efficiency demands the participation of many firms: dividing a fixed rate of investment among several firms stochastically decreases the waiting time. For this reason, and also because the total rate of investment will be higher in a patent race, patent races stochastically reduce the time until the invention, and this may be a social improvement.

However, the optimal patent value does not simply reflect *ex post* verifiable R&D costs. Consider the obvious possibilities: Suppose that the patent life were chosen to reimburse the aggregate expected R&D costs of the firms in the race, when they invest at the efficient rate. Then if all firms invested at the efficient rate, they would have equal probabilities of winning the patent, and would make zero profit in expectation. However, this will not be an equilibrium. A firm can make positive expected profit by reducing its rate of investment. Suppose instead that the winning firm is given a patent that reimburses its actual accumulated R&D costs. Then only one firm will race, since otherwise the firms would make negative expected profit, and the advantages of a patent race are then undermined. Even if investment by only one firm were efficient, the policy of reimbursing actual accumulated costs would suffer the problem of not reimbursing for the *ex ante* possibility of complete failure.

CUMULATIVE INNOVATION, THE PROBLEM OF DIVIDING PROFIT. When more than one firm is involved in developing a technology, a new problem arises: how to divide their joint profit such that both cover their individual costs (Scotchmer 1991; Green and Scotchmer 1995). In particular, suppose that there are two stages of research: basic and applied, or first-generation and second-generation. Second-generation products are of at least three types: accessories (new products that can be sold to the consumer separately from the initial products, but are complements, e.g., computer software for some previously invented hardware), improvements (innovations that cannot be sold separately but must be integrated into them; e.g., an automatic switch that shuts off an iron), and applications (new uses not described in the initial patent claims, such as laser surgery using laser technology).

I first assume for expositional purposes that although the first technology facilitates the second, the two products serve different markets, so that the profit of selling one does not depend on whether the other is also sold. For example, the first product could be the genetic code for disease resistance introduced to a food crop, and the second product could be the same genetic code applied to a fibre crop.

Suppose that the market value of the initial invention is x per period, and that a firm other than the first patent-holder will have an idea (s, c_2) for a second-generation product, say an application, where s is the per-period market value of the application and c_2 is its cost. Let $\pi(s, T)$ be the market value of the application if it receives a patent of length T. Similarly, let $\pi(x, T)$ be the market value of the first innovation. One may assume that the social values of the innovations, say $W(x, T)$ and $W(s, T)$, are respectively larger than $\pi(s, T)$ and $\pi(x, T)$, since a monopolist seldom collects the entire social value as profit and since social value continues beyond the patent's expiration. $\pi(s, T)$ increases with T, since T increases the patent life, but $W(s, T)$ decreases with T, since T increases the deadweight loss from monopoly distortions.

Since the second-generation product is facilitated by the first product, the social value of the first product includes the expected value of the second product. The value of the second product is a random variable that has value 0 or ($W(s, T) - c_2$) according to whether the innovation occurs. Since at best there will be investment in the second-generation product if $\pi(s, T) - c_2 \geq 0$, the best that can be hoped for is that such investment occurs whenever this holds. In fact, there are two goals: (1) to ensure investment in the second product whenever $\pi(s, T) - c_2 > 0$, and (2) to transfer the entire surplus $\pi(s, T) - c_2$ to the first innovator. The first innovator will in general have too little incentive for the first innovation, especially if, for example, $x = 0$. In that case the entire value of the first innovation resides in the second-generation products it facilitates, and the first innovator is in jeopardy of not covering his costs c_1.

I now ask how well these goals are met under current laws and practice. Unless the second product infringes the first patent, there is no vehicle to transfer profit to the first innovator. Patent infringement forces licensing, which is a vehicle to transfer profit. Indeed, Kitch (1977) argues for broad protection of basic research precisely on the grounds that through licensing, broad patents give the initial patentholder an incentive to support investment in later products.

The licensing negotiation will divide the surplus that is available by achieving a bargain. Costs are sunk when the negotiation occurs, so the bargaining surplus is $\pi(s, T)$. Suppose the innovators anticipate that the bargaining surplus $\pi(s, T)$ will be divided in nonnegative shares k, $1 - k$, for example, one-half each. When the second innovator decides to invest, he anticipates the *ex post* negotiation, and his anticipated profit is $(1 - k)\pi(s, T) - c_2$. Hence it might be unprofitable to invest, even if $\pi(s, T) - c_2 > 0$. One solution is to increase the patent life T, but this reduces social welfare in the event that the innovation occurs, another expression of the Nordhaus (1969) tradeoff.

Another solution is to permit *ex ante* licensing agreements. Suppose $(1 - k)\ \pi(s, T) - c_2 < 0 < \pi(s, T) - c_2$. If the licensing agreement can be negotiated before c_2 is sunk, the bargaining surplus is $\pi(s, T) - c_2$, and investment will occur whenever this is positive. However, there is still no reason to believe that the first innovator will receive all the surplus. If again they have bargaining power represented in bargaining shares k, $1 - k$, the first innovator will receive only a fraction $k(\pi(s, T) - c_2)$.

The main policy conclusion that emerges from these arguments is that if research is decentralized among several innovators, such as with basic and applied innovations achieved by sequential innovators, patent lives will have to be longer than if the whole research line is concentrated in one firm. The patent life can be shorter if firms are allowed to form *ex ante* licensing agreements so that basic research and second-generation products are effectively 'owned' by the same firm. However, such agreements might run afoul of antitrust doctrine when the two generations are substitutes (see Green and Scotchmer 1995).

The cumulative problem takes on a new complexion in the opposite extreme case where successive products serve the same market and are successive improvements on each other (quality ladders). Suppose there is an endless stream of innovations instead of two generations, e.g., the 286 computer chip, the 386 chip, the 486 chip, etc. Each innovator might have to license prior patents, but might also be a licensor to future innovators, and each firm's profit is governed by the expected time until the next non-infringing innovation. O'Donoghue, Scotchmer and Thisse 1998) call the time between non-infringing innovations the *effective patent life*. The effective patent life is governed at least as much by *patent breadth* and the *patentability (or novelty) requirement* as by the statutory patent life (see Scotchmer and Green 1990; O'Donoghue 1996; O'Donoghue, Scotchmer and Thisse 1998). There arises a similar tradeoff to the one Nordhaus identified: If the effective patent life is increased, then innovation might increase, but at the expense of more monopoly power. In the case of cumulative innovation, monopoly power arises from consolidation of property rights along the quality ladder. With a longer effective patent life, there will be a larger quality gap between competing, or successive, non-infringing innovations.

CONCLUSIONS. The effectiveness of patent law is undermined by at least three features of patents that are common to all patent systems: (i) they are granted *ex post* after all research costs have been sunk, (ii) they cannot depend on the costs of R&D, and (iii) they depend only on technical considerations, but not on market considerations. This system should be contrasted with government procurement, such as for weapons, where the government contracts with firms before the innovation has occurred (Laffont and Tirole 1986, 1987).

Some of the problems that arise can be remedied by allowing the firms themselves to coordinate their actions in research joint ventures. See Katz and Ordover (1990) for a general discussion. Firms in a joint venture have incentive to delegate to the least-cost firm (Gandal and Scotchmer 1993), and also have incentive to share their information on the benefits of research, to the extent that it does not undermine their respective competitive positions. However, a side effect is that the joint venture will typically reduce R&D investments. The reduction may be inefficient if it retards innovation, but is efficient to the extent that it avoids duplication of costs. According to their 1995 Guidelines, the US Department of Justice is sceptical of mergers between R&D firms that are in the same 'innovation market', mainly on the theory that competition in R&D spurs investment.

SUZANNE SCOTCHMER

See also COMPUTER LAW; INTELLECTUAL PROPERTY; JOINT VENTURES; NETWORK EFFECTS AND EXTERNALITIES; PATENTS; TRADE SECRET.

Subject classification: 5b(iii).

BIBLIOGRAPHY

Arrow, K. 1962. Economic welfare and the allocation of resources for invention. In *The Rate and Direction of Inventive Activity*, ed. R.R. Nelson, Princeton: Princeton University Press.

Cremer, J. and Scotchmer, S. 1997. Optimal R&D procurement: why patents? Mimeograph, University of California, Berkeley.

Dasgupta, P. and Maskin, E. 1987. The simple economics of research portfolios. *Economic Journal* 97: 581–95.

Farrell, J. 1995. Arguments for weaker intellectual property protection in network industries. *StandardView* 3: 46–9.

Gandal, N. and Scotchmer, S. 1993. Coordinating research through research joint ventures. *Journal of Public Economics* 51: 173–93.

Gilbert, R. and Shapiro, C. 1990. Optimal patent length and breadth. *RAND Journal of Economics* 21: 106–12.

Green, J. and Scotchmer, S. 1995. On the division of profit in sequential innovation. *RAND Journal of Economics* 26: 20–33.

Katz, M.L. and Ordover, J. 1990. R&D cooperation and competition. In Martin Neil Baily and Clifford Winston (eds.), *Brookings Papers on Economic Activity: Special Issue* 137–91.

Kitch, E.W. 1977. The nature and function of the patent system. *Journal of Law and Economics* 20: 265–90.

Klemperer, P. 1990. How broad should the scope of patent-protection be? *RAND Journal of Economics* 21: 113–30.

Laffont, J.-J. and Tirole, J. 1986. Using cost observation to regulate firms. *Journal of Political Economy* 94: 614–41.

Laffont, J.-J. and Tirole, J. 1987. Auctioning incentive contracts. *Journal of Political Economy* 95: 921–37.

Merges, R.P. and Nelson, R.R. 1990. On the complex economics of patent scope. *Columbia Law Review* 90: 839–916.

Minehart, D. and Scotchmer, S. 1997. Ex post regret and the decentralized sharing of information. GSPP Working Paper 230, University of California, February.

Nordhaus, W. 1969. *Invention. Growth and Welfare*. Cambridge, MA: MIT Press.

O'Donoghue, T. 1996. A patentability requirement for sequential innovation. Math Center Discussion Paper 1185, Northwestern University.

O'Donoghue, T., Scotchmer, S. and Thisse, J. 1998. Patent breadth, patent life, and the pace of technological improvement. *Journal of Economics and Management Strategy* 7: 1–32.

Reinganum, J. 1989. The timing of innovation: research, development and diffusion. Ch. 14 in *Handbook of Industrial Organization*, Vol 1, ed. R. Schmalensee and R. Willig, New York: North-Holland.

Scotchmer, S. 1991. Standing on the shoulders of giants: cumulative research and the patent law. *Journal of Economic Perspectives* 5: 29–41.

Scotchmer, S. 1996. Protecting early innovators: should second-generation products be patentable? *RAND Journal of Economics* 27: 322–31.

Scotchmer, S. and Green, J. 1990. Novelty and disclosure in patent law. *RAND Journal of Economics* 21: 131–46.

US Department of Justice. *1994 Merger Guidelines*. Washington, DC: Government Printing Office.

US Department of Justice and Federal Trade Commission. 1995. *Antitrust Guidelines for the Licensing of Intellectual Property*. Washington, DC: US Government Printing Office.

Wright, B. 1983. The economics of invention incentives: patents, prizes and research contracts. *American Economic Review* 73: 691–707.

incomplete contracts. The recent literature about incomplete contracts seeks to explain contracting behaviour. This law and economics essay inquires into the normative implications of the new learning. Restricting a discussion of incomplete contracts to the points of contact between these contracts and the legal system, however, risks not confining the subject very much. A complete contract prescribes payoff-relevant actions for every possible state of the world and the payoffs for these actions. A party who signs a complete contract thus could have only one reason to breach: the other party has made a sunk cost investment and so could be exploited in a renegotiation. Making the contract legally enforceable reduces this incentive to breach. Breach also would be deterred when a contract only prescribes payoff relevant actions for every future state (though not payoffs) but the court will specifically enforce the actions. As a consequence, in advanced legal systems complete contracts are rarely breached. The state's task, broadly speaking, is to regulate incomplete contracts. Every legal field dealing with private transactions, from contract law itself to corporations, corporate finance, commercial law, property, some aspects of tort, and bankruptcy, thus must cope with the incomplete contracts problem. Is there anything general to say about such a vast subject?

This essay reaches two conclusions. First, a long-standing research paradigm in law and economics, to supply default rules that decision makers can use to complete contracts, should be rethought. Creating helpful defaults is either impossible or appears not worth the creation cost in a large number of cases. Second, specifically enforcing a contract's verifiable terms is often a more useful approach to incompleteness than attempting to complete the contract with a default rule. An implication of this conclusion is that courts should continue to pursue the traditional approach of enforcing contracts 'as written'. The early stage of economic research into incompleteness suggests that these two conclusions should be taken with a grain of salt. A more solidly grounded view would hold that a sound private law approach to the regulation of incomplete contracts is yet to be developed.

This essay begins by defining contractual incompleteness and then summarizes the economic reasons for it. It next shows that when contracts are incomplete because of high transaction costs, the state could seldom complete them efficiently. Then the recent Nash implementation literature is reviewed. It is shown that when transaction costs are zero but there is hidden action and hidden information, the state cannot write efficient defaults but private parties sometimes can write optimal contracts (in theory), if courts specifically enforce those contracts. The essay concludes with a summary of normative implications.

1. CONTRACTUAL INCOMPLETENESS. In the lawyer's view, a contract is incomplete when it has a true gap: for example, the contract is silent respecting the parties' payoffs if one of them breaches. Economists have not settled on a definition of incompleteness but agree on a paradigm case: a contract is incomplete when it is insufficiently state contingent. This definition is used here. To see how to apply it, consider a typical sales contract: the seller is to supply ten widgets at \$50 per widget to a dealer buyer, delivery on 1 July, two months hence. Let demand in the buyer's market on 1 July take on two values – high or low. If demand is high, the price at which the buyer expects to resell is \$60; if low, the expected reselling price is \$45. The probability of high demand is 0.9, so the contract is profitable: the buyer expects to make \$8.50 (0.9×10 plus $0.1 \times -5 = 8.50$). Nevertheless, the contract is incomplete. There are two possible future states of the world, but the transaction price is not made to depend on the realized state: rather, the price is fixed. The buyer thus has an incentive to breach if the low demand state materializes. A fully state contingent contract would specify a price for the high demand state and a price for the low demand state. Alternatively, the contract could excuse performance in the low demand state. The simple contract in this example did neither.

Incomplete contracts sometimes will not condition on payoff-relevant information – here the nature and probabilities of future states of the world – even when both parties know it. The parties throw this information away. A contract also may be incomplete when there is information that only one party knows. In this case, of 'hidden information', one party does not know the other party's type. For example, consider a contract to trade a product that can malfunction. The odds of malfunction increase with intensity of use, and the seller has a comparative advantage at making repairs. There are two buyer types, high intensity users and low intensity users, but the seller does not know which is which. In the usual case, the contract will warrant against defects in materials and workmanship for a limited period. This contract also is incomplete on the definition used here. A fully contingent contract would give a more extensive warranty to the intense user, or charge that user a higher price for the same coverage, or exclude warranty coverage for that user. The contract in this second example is incomplete because the seller offers the same warranty coverage to everyone.

The contracts in these two examples, however, are sufficiently complete for a court to apply standard contract remedies; the contracts are 'obligationally complete' (see Ayres and Gertner 1992). In the first example, a court could award market damages if the buyer breached in the low demand state – the difference between the contract and market prices. Courts commonly can learn the contract quantity and price and the market price at breach time. In the second example, a court could grant specific enforcement of the warranty or damages for its breach if the seller refused to service the high-demand customer. That a contract is incomplete does not imply that the court cannot grant a remedy. The remedy, however, may not be optimal. In the first example, if performance in the low demand state would be inefficient, a remedy that would induce performance also would be inefficient. When the decision maker sees an incomplete contract, can it do better than enforce or excuse?

This question cannot be answered without knowing, at least in a rough way, why parties fail to complete their own contracts. Transaction costs are commonly invoked to explain incompleteness. Three such costs are most frequently mentioned.

(a) The costs of specifying an action in a particular state of the world would exceed the gains from specification (see Hart and Moore 1988). This explanation obviously holds at some level. For example, if the state space is infinite and it is costly to describe discrete elements of it, then parties cannot write a complete contract that will make every feasible action contingent on a possible future state: parties cannot incur infinite costs. The contracting cost story is itself 'incomplete', however, because it cannot explain why contracting parties throw away so much information. Parties apparently can write more complete contracts than the simple sales contracts described above.

(b) Future states cannot be fully foreseen. When an unforeseen state materializes, the contract will not have specified an action or payoff for that state. This story is problematic for reasons similar to those just given. While some future states are literally unforeseeable, contracts like the contract in the initial sales example do not condition on future states that seem easy to foresee, such as the likely state of demand in the next period.

(c) People are boundedly rational. This may cause them not to foresee certain future states, be unable to calculate highly complex action correspondences, or be unable to process complex information. Bounded rationality probably does explain some incompleteness (see Williamson 1985). How much is difficult to say because there is no worked-out theory of bounded rationality from which predictions about actual behaviour can be derived.

The difficulties with transaction cost explanations of contractual incompleteness have led to a research programme that attempts to make incompleteness endogenous. Models in this tradition assume that the transaction costs described do not exist. Then a contract is 'endogenously incomplete' when it is insufficiently state contingent in consequence of asymmetric information, either between the parties themselves or between parties and decision makers. Return to the two simple examples used above. In the first, assume that the seller cannot observe demand in the buyer's market. This assumption is plausible if the seller sells to numerous buyers who have different end uses. If the contract set a price for the high demand state and a price for the low demand state, there would be moral hazard: every buyer would have an incentive to claim *ex post* that demand was low in order to get the low price. Alternatively, if a contract excused the buyer when demand was low, some buyers experiencing high demand might falsely claim that demand was low, if such buyers thought that the seller would prefer to renegotiate the price down rather than lose the sale. A seller thus may prefer to write a simple contract that ignores information about the likelihood and character of payoff-relevant future states when the seller cannot observe the realized state. Similarly, in the warranty example, if the seller offered a contract that charged a high price to a high-intensity user and a low price to a low-intensity user for the same coverage, but the seller could not observe a buyer's type *ex ante*, all buyers would claim to be low-intensity users to get the low price. Sellers thus usually offer warranties that do not condition on the buyer's type.

In these examples, contracts are incomplete because information is asymmetric, thereby making moral hazard or adverse selection possible. Recent explanations add that contracts can be incomplete when one party has private information about payoff-relevant variables, and when offering a contract would communicate some of that information to the other party, to the disadvantage of the contract proposer (see, e.g., Allen and Gale 1992). To get a better idea of what is meant, consider a sales contract where the seller's costs are partly a function of an exogenous shock. The buyer cannot observe these costs but can observe a signal that correlates with them – for example, some accounting measure of cost. The seller, however, can manipulate the signal. If the seller is risk averse and the supplier is risk neutral, there is an opportunity for beneficial risk sharing, in which the transaction price is conditioned on the signal (a signal of high cost would generate a high price). Then assume that there are two seller types, a bad type who can distort the signal cheaply and a good type who faces high distortion costs. A complete contract would condition the trading price on the cost signal while an incomplete contract would throw away the information in the signal (which can be valuable when the correlation between signal and state would remain non-trivial after seller manipulation). In the latter case, there would be pooling on an incomplete contract: both seller types would offer a simple sales contract that does not condition on a cost signal.

Pooling is the probable equilibrium contract. The bad seller type would like to condition the price on the signal because it can distort the signal more easily than the good type can. For this reason, though, the buyer may infer that the proposal of a contract conditional on the signal is made by the bad type, and thus penalize a seller who proposes a contingent contract in the price term. As a result, the bad type may prefer to be thought good by proposing a non-contingent contract; and since the proposal of a contingent contract is taken by the buyer as a signal that the seller is bad, the good seller type also would propose a non-contingent – that is, incomplete – contract. In this story, again parties throw away relevant information (evidence of what the actual state of the world is) because the incomplete contract is privately optimal. There are a number of similar stories.

Contracts also may be incomplete even when parties can observe all relevant information, if parties cannot verify some of that information to third party decision makers such as courts. In many cases, information is easier for a party to observe than to establish in a litigation. In the first sales example above, then, suppose that the seller can roughly infer the state of demand in the buyer's market from market 'clues', but cannot verify demand to a court: hiring economic experts and lawyers to prove the true *ex post* state would not be worth the gain. Then the parties may write an incomplete contract, for if the contract excused the buyer in the low demand state, a buyer may prefer falsely to claim low demand and take its chances in court or in a renegotiation rather than pay the high demand state price. In this last case, contracts may be said to be incomplete not because of transaction costs but because of enforcement costs – the costs of verifying pay-off-relevant information to a decision maker.

2. TRANSACTION COSTS AND DEFAULT RULES. A contract may be incomplete because transaction costs are high or it may be incomplete because of asymmetric information. Part 2 begins with the former reason. It will review arguments that the state could seldom complete contracts at less cost than parties could. Part 3 discusses the state's role when contracts are incomplete in consequence of the parties' strategic choices (these are endogenously incomplete contracts).

If transaction costs prevent parties from completing contracts with efficient terms, the state should supply such term – enact 'problem solving defaults' – when the state has lower contracting costs than parties do. In a large economy, there will be considerable diversity in party preferences over terms. This suggests that the comparative cost condition is hard to satisfy (see Schwartz 1994). To pursue this possibility, define a market 'type' as the set of parties that prefers a particular solution to a contracting problem – choosing an optimal payment term, say. N types are in the relevant political unit, so a particular type can be denoted $n_i \in N$. There are t sets of parties of each type ($1 \leq t < \infty$). A solution to a contracting problem is indexed by x. To say of two parties that they belong to n_i implies that they prefer solution x_i to any other solution. Each party dyad of type n_i must incur a cost c_{pi} to create a solution to its contracting problem, and this cost is assumed to be identical for every dyad in the contracting type.

There are two relevant cases. In the first, the cost of creating a solution is less than the parties' gain so private parties would solve their problem – complete their contract – if the state did not. Let it be costless for parties to use a rule that the state creates. The cost to the state of creating a problem solving default rule for a particular type is c_{si}, where $c_{si} > c_{pi}$, and the state is as expert as private parties. Respecting the cost assumption, the state creates rules through legislation, administrative rule making or a series of litigations. These processes are expensive, so it is likely to be more costly for the state to solve a problem than it would be for a party dyad to create a solution of their own. On this view, creating a public default rule can be efficient only because the state must incur a one time creation cost, after which all parties of the relevant market type can costlessly use the public default.

To express this insight formally, the state should create a problem solving default rule for a market type n_i when $c_{si} < \sum_1^{t_i} c_{pi}$: the one time state creation cost is less than the sum of the total costs private parties would otherwise have incurred to solve the problem for themselves. This condition becomes harder to satisfy as t falls. Therefore, when party preferences over contractual solutions are diverse (N contains many sets of market types but the number of parties in each set is small), and state rule creation is costly, the state can seldom optimally solve contracting problems that parties would otherwise have solved for themselves.

In the second relevant case, the cost to a particular type of creating a solution to a contractual problem would exceed the gain, so parties of this type would write incomplete contracts. The benefit to each set of parties of type n_i from having a solution is b_{xi}, so it is now assumed that $c_{pi} > b_{xi}$. The efficiency condition for the state to create a default rule for parties of type n_i is thus $c_{si} < \sum_1^{t_i} b_{xi}$ – the state should solve the problem when the state's cost would be less than the total private party gain. Once again, this condition becomes harder to satisfy as the number of parties of a particular type falls. In addition, a court, legislature or administrative agency could not easily learn the benefit (b_{xi}) that parties within a particular market type would obtain from a solution to a contracting problem that these parties may face. A state legislature, for example, would find it hard to know how much surplus parties in the home construction industry would derive from a well drafted liquidated damage clause or an optimal payment schedule. Without such knowledge, the legislature could not decide intelligently whether to create default liquidated damage clauses or payment schedules for the home building industry.

The state may thus be unable to give parties much help when contracts are incomplete because of high transaction costs. Completing incomplete contracts by supplying the parties with problem solving default rules is a sensible enterprise when (i) a large number of parties face the same contracting problem; (ii) typical parties of that type would not find it cost justified to solve the problem on their own; (iii) the cost to the state of finding and supplying a solution is less than the benefit parties would derive from the solution; (iv) the state can know when condition (iii) is satisfied; and (v) the state is as good as, or not very much worse than, private parties at solving contracting problems. Standard views of judicial competence and the diverse preferences over contract content that probably exist in large economies suggest that these conditions are hard to satisfy. When they cannot be satisfied, legislative or administrative drafters should not attempt to create problem solving default rules.

When a court decides a case, it must apply a 'rule of law', and that rule will be the operative default until changed. Thus, if a default rule is a rule that will govern unless parties change it, defaults will always exist. When the five conditions set out here are not satisfied, however, judicial problem solving defaults would not be worth writing. This raises the question what other normative bases there should be for default rules when contracts are incomplete because of high transaction costs.

An answer to this question is beyond this essay's scope, but consideration should be given to the view that courts in these cases should not attempt to develop defaults but rather should direct the *ex post* efficient result. A court could do this only if it were informed about the relevant economic variables, but courts usually are informed by parties. If particular parties were symmetrically informed *ex post*, however, bargaining theory teaches that they would renegotiate to the efficient result, so the dispute would be settled. A court therefore would be called on to act only when asymmetric information has caused bargaining breakdown, and the court then could not direct an efficient outcome unless it could obtain information that at least one of the parties lacked. As will appear below, it is hard to see how this condition can be satisfied.

The analysis can be summarized thus: transaction cost explanations for contractual incompleteness are unsatisfactory positively because there is apparently more incompleteness than these explanations permit, and because this aspect of transaction cost theory is poorly worked out. Consequently, it is hard to know when incompleteness in a contract is due to one or another type of transaction cost or to strategic behaviour. Even if one can be sure that incompleteness is due to high transaction costs, the question whether the state can play a constructive role is open. The conditions under which a state agency can create efficient default rules seem quite limited, and it is difficult to see how a court could direct the *ex post* efficient outcome in a particular case.

3. ENDOGENOUS INCOMPLETENESS. A contract will be endogenously incomplete when parties are asymmetrically informed respecting relevant economic variables at the contracting stage, the renegotiation stage, or both. A contract will also be endogenously incomplete if asymmetric information between the parties is resolved *ex post* but relevant variables remain unverifiable. The state could not write efficient problem solving defaults in any of these cases. A default would have to condition on information that is unavailable to the parties – when uncertainty is never resolved – or condition on information that is unavailable to the court – when relevant variables are unverifiable. Private parties do not condition contracts on unobservable or unverifiable information, and so would reject defaults that did. Defaults that parties will not use cannot be efficient.

A second possible state role is to direct the *ex post* efficient result. Respecting this possibility, an incomplete contract may be interpreted as choosing a mechanism to achieve efficiency. If the parties anticipate that uncertainty will later be resolved, they can be said to choose renegotiation as their mechanism. Renegotiation under symmetric information will yield the efficient outcome. If the parties expect that uncertainty will not be resolved, they would choose the court as the mechanism to achieve *ex post* efficiency if the court will have information at the adjudication stage that the parties will lack at the renegotiation stage, and the court could use this information to achieve the right result. The condition 'informed and capable courts; uninformed parties', however, is unlikely to be satisfied in practice. As said above, courts learn from parties, not independently. When a contract is endogenously incomplete, a court thus should not attempt to direct the *ex post* efficient outcome either because doing this is unnecessary – renegotiation works – or because the court will lack the data (and perhaps the ability) to do the job.

Recent work in implementation theory suggests another judicial role, to enforce specifically on the basis of the verifiable variables. This can be a constructive role for a court when asymmetric information is resolved for the parties – they become symmetrically informed *ex post* – but the court remains uninformed. As said above, when the parties are informed, they can bargain to the *ex post* efficient outcome. The issue in this literature thus becomes whether parties can use *ex post* efficient renegotiation to induce optimal investment when parties must act before uncertainty is resolved (Moore 1992; Tirole 1994). For example, can parties write a contract that will induce optimal reliance when reliance is itself noncontractible – the court cannot learn the level of reliance actually undertaken – and the court also cannot learn the value that parties place on performance?

The answer is yes in theory, if courts will grant specific performance. To understand this answer, Part 3 first sketches the general Nash implementation model and then gives a concrete illustration. Assume that transaction costs are zero so the parties can describe all possible states of the world and actions in a contract, but the parties do not know which state of the world will prevail. The contractual surplus is a function of a stochastic state variable θ and sunk cost investments a_i that either or both parties can make to increase the value of performance. After the state of the world is realized, the parties take another action z (to trade or not). The parties' contracting task is to ensure that the investment actions are optimally chosen and that trade is *ex post* efficient. The timing is given by Figure 1.

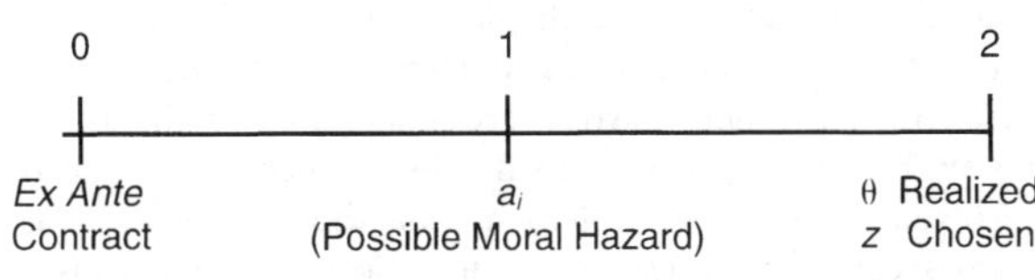

Figure 1

The state of the world θ and the vector of relation specific investment actions $a = (a_1, a_2)$ determine the parties' *ex post* 'types': $\eta = (\eta_1, \eta_2)$, where $\eta_i = \gamma(a, \theta)$. A buyer's type is the buyer's realized valuation v; a seller's type is the seller's realized cost c. A party's gross surplus depends on its type and on the second stage decision z: letting $Y_i(\eta_1, z)$ denote gross surplus and r_i denote party i's income, a party gets net surplus from the deal of $r_i + Y_i(\eta_i, z)$. The disutility of taking the stage one action is $b_i(a_i)$ so party i's preferences are given by

$$v_i(r_i, a, \theta, z) = u_i(r_i + Y_i(\eta_i, z)) - b(a_i).$$

At stage two, the parties send messages $m_i \in M_i$ to each other – a message may be an offer to trade at a stated price – and take actions – to trade or not.

Respecting the model's information structure, the parties can observe their realized types η_i and can verify *ex post* messages and actions (such as whether a party traded) to courts. The parties may be able to observe the investment actions a_i and the *ex post* state of the world θ. The court, however, does not know the investment actions, realized state or the party types.

In this model, the contract defines the message space for each party (M_1 and M_2) and specifies the actions $z(m_1, m_2)$ and transfers $t_i(m_1, m_2)$ that are contingent on the messages sent. The court is assumed to enforce the contract by directing parties to perform the actions that are contingent on the messages and by ordering parties to make the message contingent transfers. Trade will be optimal at stage two because information is symmetric then. How this contracting set-up, in connection with a court's willingness to grant specific performance, induces optimal investment is best shown by example.

Consider the problem of inducing a seller and buyer to make optimal relation specific investments (see Hermalin and Katz 1993 and Noldeke and Schmidt 1995). There are four relevant variables: the seller's investment a_s, which can reduce production cost; the buyer's investment a_b, which can increase the value of performance; the seller's realized cost c (the seller's type); and the buyer's realized value v (the buyer's type). Both the seller's realized cost and the buyer's realized value are partly a function of a stochastic state variable θ (so as above the parties' types are a function of their investment actions and the state of the world). Contracting costs are zero so that all actions and states can be described in the contract, but the parties cannot verify the investment actions, the state of the world or their realized types to a court. The court, however, can observe the written contract and the parties' *ex post* messages and actions. The parties are symmetrically informed at the time of contracting and later can observe the seller's cost and the buyer's valuation. The object is to induce trade only when the buyer's benefit exceeds the seller's cost ($v > c$), and to induce optimal investment.

The parties can reach first best with a contract that sets a transfer schedule T that is a function of the transaction price and quantity to be traded. After the values c and v are realized, the seller announces a price – sends a message – and the buyer chooses a quantity q. The buyer pays pq plus the negative transfer T, where

$$T = -\int_0^p (p - c)g(c; a_s^*)\mathrm{d}c + r.$$

Costs are distributed on $g(\cdot)$, a_s^* is the seller's optimal investment and r divides the rents.

The seller sets the price and so will make a take it or leave it offer at the highest possible price ($p = v$ because the seller can observe the buyer's valuation). Since the seller will not trade unless $c < v$, trade will be efficient. The transaction price pq is reduced by the expected trade surplus (the term in the integral with p equalling v). The buyer thus has an incentive to invest optimally: the price is reduced by the expected surplus $v - c$, so the buyer wants to invest in order to maximize v. Note that T is a function of the seller's optimal action a_s^*, not the action the seller actually takes. The seller's pay off is $\pi_s = pq - T - c$. The separation between the seller's pay off and its action, and the seller's ability to obtain the entire realized surplus, thus induces the seller to invest in order to minimize c.

In this story, breach would entail the seller not naming a price, the buyer not specifying a quantity, the seller refusing to deliver, or the buyer refusing to pay. Parties concerned about breach could create an additional set of monetary transfers that would ensure performance. For example, the seller must pay a specified penalty if she fails to name a price. The mechanism in the contract thus will ensure first best if the court grants specific performance – orders the seller to deliver, orders the seller to pay the penalty for not naming a price, and so forth. Specific performance is feasible because the parties can verify their messages and *ex post* actions to the court.

Models of the type described have been extended to cases in which a party cannot observe many of the relevant variables *ex post* (see Aghion, Dewatripont and Rey 1994, and Edlin and Reichelstein 1996). If the contract can allocate all *ex post* bargaining power to one party, as in Aghion et al., or if the parties can renegotiate to vary the amount to be traded, the results are the same: when transaction costs are zero, the parties can achieve first best with mechanisms that entail parties taking actions and making transfers that are contingent on the messages they send *ex post*, *provided that* courts specifically enforce the contract's verifiable terms (provided, that is, that the contracts are obligationally complete and courts enforce the obligations).

These results should be viewed with caution for two reasons. First, the implementation literature has identified few actual contracts that appear to embody the theoretical mechanisms. Second, there is only one trading opportunity in the models described here: the buyer always purchases if $v > c$. In some cases, there may be several *ex post* trading opportunities: the seller's performance has a stochastic element and some realizations will turn out to be better for the buyer than others. As the number of later trading opportunities increases, the parties' ability to achieve first-best shrinks (see Segal 1996). This is partly because it is too complex to describe the full message game in a contract when message spaces must be created for numerous trading opportunities (another way to put this is that the zero transaction cost assumption becomes unrealistic when the number of trading opportunities becomes large). Nevertheless, specific performance is a better grounded theoretical response to endogenously incomplete contracts than state attempts to complete these contracts with efficient terms or judicial attempts to direct the efficient *ex post* outcome.

4. CONCLUSION. An analysis of the causes of, and the parties' best responses to, contractual incompleteness suggests a narrow role for the state. The traditional law and economics view holds that incompleteness is a consequence of high transaction costs, and that the state should respond to incompleteness by supplying the public good of default rules. These rules are meant to solve contracting problems that it is not cost justified for parties to solve on their own. Analysts also suggest that courts should sometimes direct *ex post* efficient outcomes – for example, to excuse when performance would be inefficient.

Transaction cost explanations account for less incompleteness than is observed. Even when these explanations hold, state supplied defaults are seldom cost justified. This is due to high costs of state rule creation, party heterogeneity (too many contractual solutions are needed), the inability of the state to know what the benefits of good defaults are, and the state's relative lack of expertise in creating efficient contract terms. In addition, parties can bargain to *ex post* efficient outcomes when the relevant economic variables are observable, so a court could usefully direct such an outcome only when it knows things that parties do not know. It is unclear how courts can get such information.

Recent theory shows that contractual incompleteness is often endogenous. Even when transaction costs are zero, parties will not write complete contracts either because they cannot observe relevant economic variables, because they cannot verify those variables to courts, or because they prefer not to disclose relevant information about themselves (their 'types'). The state cannot write better contracts for parties than parties could write for themselves were transaction costs zero. As an application of this insight, if parties will not condition contracts on unverifiable information, they will contract out of default rules that condition on unverifiable information. Thus the state cannot complete endogenously incomplete contracts with defaults that solve parties' contracting problems.

When parties are concerned only with trade and not investment, and anticipate that uncertainty will be resolved *ex post*, they may write incomplete contracts that in effect choose renegotiation as the mechanism to achieve *ex post* efficiency. The contract's verifiable terms – for example, the price and quantity – become the disagreement points in these renegotiations. Because sophisticated parties choose verifiable terms with renegotiation in mind, a refusal by courts to enforce the verifiable terms would change the renegotiation game and thus defeat the parties' chosen mechanism. When parties are concerned with investment and trade, and considerable uncertainty will be resolved *ex post*, the implementation literature shows that parties can sometimes achieve first best with mechanisms that create a message space, and then constrain the contractual actions and transfers to be a function of the messages the parties send. If courts refuse to enforce these contracts specifically, again they will defeat the parties' mechanism.

This analysis suggests that courts should enforce the verifiable terms in endogenously incomplete contracts. Given the difficulty of identifying whether incompleteness is a consequence of high transaction costs or asymmetric information, and the few cases in which the state can intervene optimally when transaction costs are the culprit, it would perhaps be best for courts specifically to enforce a contract's verifiable terms in general. Other decision makers such as legislatures should then create defaults that would condition on verifiable information (contract/ market damages in contract law, for example), but only when the cost savings from these defaults seem clear.

There is evidence that courts sometimes act as this essay suggests they should (see Schwartz 1992). For example, long-term contracts seldom condition transaction prices on the seller's current period costs or the buyer's current demand. Such information is often unobservable and commonly is unverifiable. These contracts, however, tend to be obligationally complete (they specify a mechanism for setting a price and state quantities). If a party breaches, courts do not attempt to complete the contracts with better pricing terms nor do courts attempt to direct the efficient *ex post* outcome. Rather, the common legal remedy for breach in these cases is specific performance. And courts in general prefer granting damages based on the contract's verifiable terms or enforcing specifically when the incompleteness appears endogenous. The stated law, however, permits more extensive judicial interventions, and legal scholars commonly urge them.

This essay shows that many questions remain open. On a normative level, is there a fairness value that courts could implement when the traditional judicial roles of writing contract completing defaults or directing efficient *ex post* outcomes are inappropriate? When parties are asymmetrically informed *ex post*, the specific performance remedy may not yield first best. What else is a court to do? On a positive level, can the theory of bounded rationality be made sufficiently precise to ground predictions? To what extent does the implementation literature describe actual contracting behaviour? An analysis of the current state of the art thus suggests a limited role for the state and a more extensive one for the scholars.

ALAN SCHWARTZ

See also BOUNDED RATIONALITY; CONTRACTS; CORPORATE GOVERNANCE; DEFAULT RULES FOR INCOMPLETE CONTRACTS; RESIDUAL RIGHTS OF CONTROL; SPECIFIC PERFORMANCE.

Subject classification: 5c(i).

BIBLIOGRAPHY

Aghion, P., Dewatripont, M. and Rey, P. 1994. Renegotiation design with unverifiable information. *Econometrica* 62: 257–82.

Allen, F. and Gale, D. 1992. Measurement distortion and missing contingencies in optimal contracts. *Economic Theory* 2: 1–21

Ayres, I. and Gertner, R. 1992. Strategic contractual inefficiency and the optimal choice of legal rules. *Yale Law Journal* 101: 729–73.

Edlin, A.S. 1996. Cadillac contracts and up-front payments: efficient investment under expectation damages. *Journal of Law, Economics and Organization* 12: 98–118.

Edlin, A.S. and Reichelstein, S. 1996. Holdups, standard breach remedies, and optimal investment. *American Economic Review* 86: 478–501.

Hart, O. and Moore, J. 1988. Incomplete contracts and renegotiation. *Econometrica* 56: 755–85.

Hermalin, B.A. and Katz, M.L. 1993. Judicial modification of contracts between sophisticated parties: a more complete view of incomplete contracts and their breach. *Journal of Law, Economics, and Organization* 9: 230–55.

Moore, J. 1992. Implementation in environments with complete information In *Advances in Economic Theory*, ed. J.J. Laffont, Sixth World Congress, Cambridge: Cambridge University Press.

Noldeke, G. and Schmidt, K.M. 1995. Option contracts and renegotiation: a solution to the hold-up problem. *RAND Journal of Economics* 26: 163–79.

Schwartz, A. 1992. Relational contracts in the courts: an analysis of incomplete contracts and judicial strategies. *Journal of Legal Studies* 21: 271–318.

Schwartz, A. 1994. The default rule paradigm and the limits of contract law. *Southern California Interdisciplinary Law Journal* 3: 389–419.

Segal, I. 1996. Complexity and renegotiation: a foundation for incomplete contracts. Department of Economics, University of California at Berkeley.

Tirole, J. 1994. Incomplete contracts: where do we stand? Institut d'Economie Industrielle, Toulouse and Ceras, Paris.

Williamson, O.E. 1985. *The Economic Institutions of Capitalism*. New York: The Free Press.

indemnity principle. *See* INSURANCE LAW.

independent directors. Over the last twenty-five years the boards of directors of large US public companies have come increasingly to contain a majority of independent directors. In the literature on corporate governance, directors are categorized as *inside directors* (persons who are currently officers of the company), *affiliated outside* directors (former company officers, relatives of company officers, and persons who have or are likely to have business relationships with the company, such as investment bankers and lawyers – all these sometimes called *grey* directors) and *independent directors* (outside directors without such affiliations). Bhagat and Black (1997) find that more than two-thirds of the 957 largest US public corporations in 1991 had boards with a majority of independent directors. They also find that the median firm in this sample of 957 firms in 1991 had an eleven member board, which includes seven independent directors, one affiliated outsider, and three insiders (typically including the chief executive officer and chief financial officer). The median of three inside directors in 1991 might be as low as two today, due to changes in this period in the composition of a typical board.

An increasing number of boards have 'supermajority' independent boards, with only one or two inside directors. SpencerStuart (1996) in their survey of 100 of the largest US public corporations report that *half* of the surveyed firms had only one or two inside directors.

Many commentators applaud this trend. For example, a recent report by the National Association of Corporate Directors (1996) notes with apparent approval the increasing number of firms whose only inside director is the CEO, and recommends that boards have a 'substantial majority' of independent directors. Greater board independence remains high on the agenda of activist institutional investors.

It has often been argued that independent board members are more effective monitors of senior corporate managers. Hence, companies with more independent board members are more likely to be managed in the interest of shareholders. We consider here the evidence on whether the trend toward greater board independence rests on a sound empirical footing regarding the impact of board independence on firm performance. An increasing number of studies document differences in the *behaviour* of majority-independent and non-majority-independent boards. But studies of overall firm performance have found no convincing empirical evidence that firms with majority-independent boards achieve better performance than other firms.

There is an even greater lack of empirical support for the recent trend toward supermajority-independent boards. The differences between majority-independent boards and supermajority-independent boards, either for discrete board tasks or for overall performance, have not been carefully studied. But the limited evidence that we have suggests caution: there is some evidence that having a reasonable number of inside directors could improve corporate performance.

The weak empirical support for majority- or supermajority-independent boards is mirrored by mixed anecdotal evidence. Independent directors often turn out to be lapdogs rather than watchdogs. The majority-independent board of General Motors did nothing for a decade, while GM floundered. The majority-independent board of American Express fired former CEO James Robinson only when faced with open shareholder revolt, despite a decade of business problems with a few scandals along the way. Many other companies – including IBM, Kodak, Chrysler, Sears, Westinghouse and Borden – performed abysmally for years despite majority-independent boards. And the compensation of chief executives has exploded over the same period during which independent directors became dominant on the boards of large firms (Crystal 1991).

We first review the evidence on how board composition affects the board's action on discrete tasks, such as firing the CEO or approving a takeover bid. Next, we survey the evidence on whether board composition affects overall firm performance. Finally, we note some implications of these research findings.

BOARD COMPOSITION AND DISCRETE BOARD TASKS. A central board task is replacing the CEO when necessary. Warner et al. (1988) find that only very poor performance, for an extended period of time, leads to measurably shorter tenure in office. There is also evidence that the firm's performance improves modestly, on average, after a CEO is replaced (Denis and Denis 1995). Scott and Kleidon (1994) find that firms with majority-outside boards who replace CEOs have worse pre-replacement stock price performance than firms without such boards.

These studies suggest that independent directors behave differently from inside directors with respect to the task of firing the old CEO. But it isn't clear whether these differences in behaviour lead to better or worse decisions, on average. Moreover, there are severe limits on what those studies, which focus on only *one* directorial task, can tell us about how board composition affects overall firm performance. Even if independent directors perform better with regard to the task of firing the old CEO, that need not produce superior economic performance on average.

For every CEO who leaves another must be hired, not only when the old CEO is fired but in the more common case when the former CEO retires or leaves voluntarily. Suppose that majority independent boards (1) are better at firing underperforming CEOs, but (2) know less about the company's business and are therefore worse at choosing new CEOs. Negative effect (2) would occur at *all* companies with majority independent boards and could easily swamp positive effect (1), which would occur only at poorly performing companies. Borokhovich et al. (1996) report that firms with a high proportion of outside directors are more likely to choose an outsider as a new CEO, but we know little about whether these choices are better or worse than the insiders chosen by other boards.

More generally, even if majority-independent boards are better at monitoring tasks, such as firing the new CEO or approving a takeover bid, they may be worse at advising CEOs, because independent directors usually know less about the firm and its industry. This relative ignorance is strengthened by the Clayton Act, which bars director interlocks between competing firms. Whatever its antitrust justification, this ban tends to reduce the quality of independent directors.

Byrd and Hickman (1992) report that tender offer *bidders* with majority-independent boards earn roughly zero returns on average, while bidders without such boards suffer statistically significant losses. Bidders with majority-independent boards also offer lower takeover premia. Apparently, independent directors are less willing to overpay to acquire another company. However, the economic significance of this tendency is small. Only a minority of firms are active acquirers, and the improvement in returns to these firms is modest. Moreover, the general concern expressed above remains: even if firms with majority-independent boards are less likely to overpay for other firms, these firms' boards may perform less well at other tasks.

Cotter et al. (1997) found that tender offer *targets* with majority-independent boards realized roughly 20% higher stock price returns between 1989 and 1992 than targets without majority-independent boards. Their study, however, suffers from possible selection bias. The higher returns to targets with majority-independent boards come at the expense of lower bidder returns. In a rational expectations equilibrium, acquirers will realize this and will make fewer takeover bids for firms with majority-independent boards. Shareholders of *potential* target firms may not benefit from majority-independent boards, even if shareholders of *actual* targets realize higher returns if they have majority-independent boards.

There is some evidence in the Cotter et al. study to support this conjecture about selection bias. The target firms in their sample had, on average, only 36% independent directors – far lower than the 60% or so independent directors found in other contemporaneous studies (Yermack 1996; Bhagat and Black 1997). This could reflect the smaller size of takeover targets, compared to the large firms that other researchers on boards of directors have studied. But it could also reflect bidders avoiding targets with a high proportion of independent directors.

Brickley et al. (1994) report that when firms adopt poison pill defences, the stock market reaction is significantly positive if the firm has a majority-independent board, and significantly negative if it does not. This suggests that investors believe that majority-independent boards are more likely to use this weapon to receive a higher takeover price than to block a control transaction altogether. But the higher premia from those auctions could be offset by a lower incidence of takeover bids. Moreover, Bhagat and Jefferis (1991) find that as the fraction of votes controlled by outside directors increases, the company is less likely to propose anti-takeover amendments, including poison pills.

The proportion of independent directors correlates with the likelihood that a firm will adopt a golden parachute plan to protect its senior executives if the company is acquired (Cotter et al. 1997). These plans reduce the likelihood that a firm will resist a takeover bid (Machlin et al. 1993), so they may be value-enhancing if the payout is a small fraction of company value. This is usually but not always the case (Lambert and Larcker 1985).

Kosnik (1987) reports that firms with a high proportion of outside directors are less likely to pay greenmail. But the effect is subtle: it was significant only for a subset of firms whose CEOs owned little stock, relative to their cash compensation. Bhagat and Jefferis (1994) find that CEOs and officers and directors, as a group, control fewer votes in companies that pay greenmail than a group of control firms selected on the basis of size and industry.

Holthausen and Larcker (1993) report that CEO compensation correlates with the proportion of outside directors on a company's board, and that the predicted component of CEO compensation is negatively correlated with future performance. Apparently, outside directors are not very good at compensating the CEO (including developing appropriate incentive compensation) – perhaps because many outside directors are themselves current or former CEOs. The outside directors' largesse filters down – pay for other executives is also higher at firms with a high percentage of outside directors.

Rosenstein and Wyatt (1990) find that stock prices increase, on average, when companies appoint additional outside directors. This increase, while statistically significant, is economically small and could be due to signalling effects. Appointing an additional independent director could signal that a company plans to address its business problems, even if board composition doesn't affect the company's ability to address these problems.

Numerous studies examine the correlation between share ownership and company performance (for a survey, see Black 1992). Taking the studies as a whole, inside stock ownership correlates with improved performance up to some level of ownership (perhaps as low as five percent), but there is mixed evidence about the correlation between inside ownership and performance at higher ownership levels, and some evidence that CEO stock ownership serves more as a reward for past performance than as an incentive for future performance.

The possible correlation between inside ownership and the firm's performance implies that studies of whether board composition affects performance must control for inside stock ownership. Firms with high inside ownership tend to have fewer independent directors, partly because large owners want their own representatives on the board, which leaves fewer seats for others. Large outside blockholders also often insist on representation on a company's board of directors. If companies with large outside blockholders perform better, then a study that doesn't control for the presence of outside blockholders might mistakenly ascribe this correlation to the presence of independent directors; Bhagat and Jefferis (1998) provide a more general treatment of the endogeneity problems that affect conclusions in most of the literature on corporate governance and control.

Yermack (1996) reports a strong negative correlation between board size and Tobin's *q*, and a similar negative correlation between board size and several accounting measures of profitability. He hypothesizes that many corporate boards are simply too large. However, Bhagat and Black (1997) report that Yermack's results are not robust to the choice of performance measure.

Hermalin and Weisbach (1988) report that the proportion of independent directors on the boards of large firms increases slightly when a company has performed poorly. In contrast, Klein (1996) finds no tendency for firms in the bottom quintile for 1991 stock price returns to add more independent directors between 1992 and 1993 than firms in the top quintile. Chaganti et al. (1985) find no significant tendency for failed firms to increase their proportion of outside directors in the five years before failure. Taking these studies together, firms appear to adjust their board composition slowly, if at all, in response to poor performance.

BOARD COMPOSITION AND FIRM PERFORMANCE. The studies discussed above evaluate whether majority-independent boards behave differently from other boards on discrete tasks. They do not address the underlying question of whether firms with majority-independent boards perform better (worse) than firms without such boards.

The direct evidence that board composition affects corporate profitability is weak. Baysinger and Butler (1985), and Hermalin and Weisbach (1991) all report no significant contemporaneous (same year) correlation between board composition and various measures of corporate performance.

Several studies suggest that firms with more independent directors perform *worse*. Yermack (1996) reports a significant *negative* correlation between proportion of independent directors and contemporaneous Tobin's *q*; Agrawal and Knoeber (1996) report a similar negative correlation between proportion of *outside* directors and Tobin's *q*. However, as detailed below, Bhagat and Black (1997) find that these results are not robust to alternative measures of performance.

Klein (1996) studies whether the existence and staffing of board committees affects the firm's performance. She finds little evidence that 'monitoring' committees – audit, compensation, and nominating committees, usually dominated by independent directors – affect performance, regardless of how they are staffed. In contrast, inside director representation on a board's investment committee correlates with improved firm performance. However, companies with supermajority-independent boards may have too few inside directors to perform this role.

Bhagat and Black (1997) undertook the first large sample study (957 large public US corporations), with long time-horizon (1983–95), of whether the proportion of independent or inside directors affects firm performance. They found no consistent evidence that the proportion of independent directors affects future firm performance, across a wide variety of stock price and accounting measures of performance. A high proportion of independent directors correlates with slower growth and, less strongly, with lower stock price returns in the recent past (before the date when we measure board composition). However, this correlation disappears for future performance (after the date when we measure board composition). They find evidence that proportion of inside directors correlates with higher past (but not future) stock price returns, and with greater profitability for some accounting measures of performance (both retrospectively and prospectively).

IMPLICATIONS. The neutral evidence in Bhagat and Black (1997) on the value of independent directors on large firm boards can be interpreted in a number of ways. First, it could reflect the limited power of the tests. Stock price and accounting data are noisy, especially over long time horizons. Second, perhaps today's 'independent' directors aren't independent enough. Perhaps, as Gilson and Kraakman (1991) argue, 'corporate boards need directors who are not merely independent [of management], but who are *accountable* [to shareholders] as well'. But if so, institutional investors may need to put their own representatives on boards of directors, a step that few are interested in and which is hard for them to take under current US legal rules (Roe 1994).

Perhaps too, some directors who are classified as independent are not truly independent of management, because they are beholden to the company or its current CEO in ways too subtle to be captured in customary definitions of 'independence'. For example, some nominally independent directors may serve as paid advisors or consultants to the company, or may be employed by a university or foundation that receives financial support from the company. Unfortunately, the data needed to capture these relationships are not available. Perhaps, too, some directors have personal relationships with the CEO that affect their independence in subtle ways. This possibility is consistent with evidence that directors who were appointed during the current CEO's tenure are more generous in determining the CEO's compensation (Holthausen and Larcker 1993; Yermack 1996).

A third possibility is that optimal board structure is not the same for all firms but dependent on firm-specific characteristics. For example, slowly growing firms may need a high proportion of independent directors to control managers' incentives to reinvest the firm's cash flow rather than pay dividends, even when the firm lacks profitable reinvestment opportunities. Optimal board composition could also vary with a firm's principal industry. This endogeneity/cash flow conflict story is consistent with the correlation that Agrawal and Knoeber (1996) and Yermack (1996) find between a high proportion of independent directors and lower Tobin's q (which is a measure of growth prospects), and evidence in Bhagat and Black (1997) that a high proportion of independent directors correlates with slower *past* growth across a number of accounting variables, although not slower future growth. This could reflect the possibility that companies who face slow growth increase the proportion of independent directors on their boards. This endogeneity story, however, suggests that the current push by commentators and institutional investors for greater board independence at *all* firms may be misguided.

Another plausible endogeneity hypothesis is that alternate mechanisms for controlling agency costs in large firms (including independent directors, leverage, CEO stock ownership, and large outside blockholders) act either as substitutes or complements. These interaction effects are a potentially fruitful avenue for further research.

A fourth explanation, suggested by Baysinger and Butler (1985), is that an optimal board contains a mix of inside, independent, and perhaps also affiliated outside directors, who bring different skills and knowledge to the board. Including insiders on the board may also make it easier for other directors to evaluate them as potential future CEOs (Vancil 1987). This 'mixed board' explanation is consistent with the hints in our data about the value of having at least some inside directors on the board, and with Klein's (1996) finding that inside director representation on investment committees of the board correlates with improved firm performance. If so, then many large companies may have too few inside directors to perform this role. However, the test by Bhagat and Black (1997) of the hypothesis that it is valuable for a board to have a threshold percentage of inside directors produced inconclusive results.

Fifth, perhaps some types of independent directors are valuable, while others are not. Maybe CEOs of companies in other industries (who are, by number, the majority of independent directors) are often too busy with their own business, know too little about a different business, and are overly generous in compensating another CEO. Maybe 'visibility' directors – well-known persons with limited business experience, often holding multiple directorships and adding gender or racial diversity to a board – are not effective on average. But this explanation, too, suggests that the current push for greater board independence may be fruitless or even counterproductive, unless independent directors have particular attributes, which are currently unknown.

Then, too, the obvious explanation – that board independence isn't very important, on average and over time, compared to other factors that influence corporate performance – could be the right one. That hypothesis is consistent with recent studies that find, more generally, mixed evidence on wealth gains from corporate governance activism by institutional investors targeted at specific companies (Smith 1996; Wahal 1996), and with evidence that social connections are important in determining who is chosen to fill board seats, while home-firm performance is not (Davis 1993).

SANJAI BHAGAT AND BERNARD BLACK

See also AGENCY COSTS AND CORPORATE GOVERNANCE; BOARDS OF DIRECTORS; COMPARATIVE CORPORATE GOVERNANCE; LAW-AND-ECONOMICS IN ACTION; MARKET FOR CORPORATE CONTROL; SHAREHOLDER ACTIVISM AND CORPORATE GOVERNANCE IN THE UNITED STATES; TENDER OFFERS.

Subject classification: 5g(iii).

BIBLIOGRAPHY

Agrawal, A. and Knoeber, C.R. 1996. Firm performance and mechanisms to control agency problems between managers and shareholders. *Journal of Financial and Quantitative Analysis* 31: 377–97.

Baysinger, B. and Butler, H. 1985. Corporate governance and the board of directors: performance effects of changes in board composition. *Journal of Law, Economics and Organization* 1: 101–24.

Bhagat, S. and Black, B. 1997. Do independent directors matter? Columbia University Law School working paper.

Bhagat, S. and Jefferis, R.H., Jr. 1991. Voting power in the proxy process: the case of antitakeover charter amendments. *Journal of Financial Economics* 30: 193–225.

Bhagat, S. and Jefferis, R.H., Jr. 1994. The causes and consequences of takeover defense: evidence from Greenmail. *Journal of Corporate Finance* 1: 201–31.

Bhagat, S. and Jefferis, R.H., Jr. 1998. *The Impact of Corporate Ownership, Performance, and Governance on Takeovers and Managerial Turnover.* Cambridge, MA: MIT Press (forthcoming).

Black, B. 1992. The value of institutional investor monitoring: the empirical evidence. *UCLA Law Review* 39: 895–939.

Borokhovich, K.A., Parrino, R. and Trapani, T. 1996. Outside directors and CEO selection. *Journal of Financial and Quantitative Analysis* 31: 337–55.

Brickley, J.A., Coles, J.L. and Terry, R.L. 1994. Outside directors and the adoption of poison pills. *Journal of Financial Economics* 35: 371–90.

Byrd, J.W. and Hickman, K.A. 1992. Do outside directors monitor managers?: evidence from tender offer bids. *Journal of Financial Economics* 32: 195–22.

Chaganti, R.S., Mahajan, V. and Sharma, S. 1985. Corporate board size, composition and corporate failures in retailing industry. *Journal of Management Studies* 22: 400–17.

Cotter, J.F., Shivdasani, A. and Zenner, M. 1997. Do independent directors enhance target shareholder wealth during tender offers? *Journal of Financial Economics*, forthcoming.

Crystal, G. 1991. *In Search of Excess: The Over-compensation of American Executives.* New York: W.W. Norton.

Davis, G.F. 1993. Who gets ahead in the market for corporate directors: the political economy of multiple board memberships. *Academy of Management Best Papers Proceedings* 202–6.

Denis, D.J. and Denis, D.K. 1995. Performance changes following top management dismissals. *Journal of Finance* 50: 1029–57.

Gilson, R.J. and Kraakman, R. 1991. Reinventing the outside director: an agenda for institutional investors. *Stanford Law Review* 43: 863–906.

Hermalin, B.E. and Weisbach, M.S. 1988. The determinants of board composition. *RAND Journal of Economics* 19: 589–606.

Hermalin, B.E. and Weisbach, M.S. 1991. The effect of board composition and direct incentives on firm performance. *Financial Management* 20(4), 101–12.

Holthausen, R.W. and Larcker, D.F. 1993. Boards of directors, ownership structure and CEO compensation. Working paper, Wharton School, University of Pennsylvania.

Kaplan, S.N. and Reishus, D. 1990. Outside directorships and corporate performance. *Journal of Financial Economics* 27: 389–410.

Klein, A. 1996. Firm performance and board committee structures. NYU working paper.

Kosnik, R.D. 1987. Greenmail: a study of board performance in corporate governance. *Administrative Science Quarterly* 32: 163–85.

Lambert, R. and Larcker, D. 1985. Golden parachutes, executive decision-making, and shareholder wealth. *Journal of Accounting and Economics* 7: 179–203.

Machlin, J., Choe, H. and Miles, J. 1993. The effects of golden parachutes on takeover activity. *Journal of Law and Economics* 36: 861–76.

National Association of Corporate Directors. 1996. *Report of the NACD Blue Ribbon Commission on Director Professionalism*. Washington, DC: NACD.

Roe, M.J. 1994. *Strong Managers, Weak Owners: The Political Roots of American Corporate Finance*. Princeton: Princeton University Press.

Rosenstein, S. and Wyatt, J.G. 1990. Outside directors, board independence, and shareholder wealth. *Journal of Financial Economics* 26: 175–91.

Scott, K.E. and Kleidon, A.W. 1994. CEO performance, board types and board performance: a first cut. In *Institutional Investors and Corporate Governance*, ed. T. Baums, R. Buxbaum and K. Hopt (New York: W. de Gruyter): 181–99.

Shivdasani, A. 1993. Board composition, ownership structure and hostile takeovers. *Journal of Accounting and Economics* 16: 167–98.

Smith, M.P. 1996. Shareholder activism by institutional investors: evidence from CalPERS. *Journal of Finance* 51: 227–52.

SpencerStuart. 1996. *1996 Board Index: Board Trends and Practices at Major American Corporations*. New York: SpencerStuart.

Vancil, R.F. 1987. *Passing the Baton: Managing the Process of CEO Selection*: Boston: Harvard Business School Press.

Wahal, S. 1996. Pension fund activism and firm performance. *Journal of Financial and Quantitative Analysis* 31: 1–23.

Warner, J.B., Watts, R.L. and Wruck, K.H. 1988. Stock prices and top management changes. *Journal of Financial Economics* 20: 461–92.

Yermack, D. 1996. Higher market valuation of companies with a small board of directors. *Journal of Financial Economics* 40: 185–212.

independent judiciary. *See* JUDICIAL INDEPENDENCE.

informal contract enforcement: lessons from medieval trade. Exchange fosters economic efficiency by enabling the reallocation of endowment and products, increasing specialization and motivating innovations. For efficiency enhancing exchange to take place, the parties to the exchange have to be able to commit *ex ante* not to breach a contract *ex post*. They must commit to respect the property rights generated by their contractual arrangement. Hence, contract enforcement institutions which enable such commitment determine the discrepancy between the set of optimal exchange relations and that of feasible exchange relations. Formal contract enforcement institutions, that is, the legal system and the private order institutions that evolve in the shadow of the law, often enable such commitment (Williamson 1985). Yet the ability of formal institutions to support exchange is limited, due to asymmetric information and the boundaries of the state's jurisdictional power. Thus the discrepancy between the sets of optimal and feasible exchange relations in an economy is also determined by the nature of the available informal contract enforcement institutions, namely, institutions that enable commitment in the absence of a legal system with authority over (all) those parties to the exchange who can gain from breaching the contract.

The importance of informal contract enforcement institutions (henceforth ICEIs) is well reflected by the large extent to which exchange in pre-modern, modern, developed and undeveloped economies takes place outside the domain of the legal system (for a survey, see Greif 1997a). Macaulay (1963), for example, found that among businessmen in Wisconsin 'many, if not most, exchanges reflect no [contractual] planning or only a minimal amount of it' (p. 60). A survey of 224 randomly selected Kenyan manufacturing firms found that 58 percent of them borrowed from informal sources without legal contracts or collateral (Fafchamps et al. 1993). In Russia, despite the lack of an appropriate legal system prior to (and after) its market reform, informal exchange has been extensive (Greif and Kandel 1995).

What are the origin, nature, and implications of a society's ICEIs? This essay advances the following perspective. ICEIs emerge spontaneously as a response to efficiency-enhancing opportunities. Yet they are a product of the larger economic, cultural, social and political processes of which they are an integral part. Cultural, social and political factors affect ICEIs by coordinating actions and expectations, determining the availability of information, influencing the ability to initiate collective action, determining the ability to use coercive power in the pursuit of economic ends and influencing the existing set of formal contract enforcement institutions. At the same time, existing ICEIs can reinforce the social structures and cultural features which led to their emergence, and influence processes of formal and informal institutional innovations and change. In short, although ICEIs reflect and affect economic needs and outcomes their particularities and implications reflect their interrelations with the broader organization of society (Greif 1994). They shape the cultural and social aspects of the relevant society as well as its formal institutions. Thus, they are not necessarily 'optimal' in the sense that they can support the exchange relations required to bring an economy to the (constrained) Pareto frontier, given the economy's enforcement technology, endowments, preferences, and production technology. Furthermore, ICEIs exhibit path dependence (David 1988) in being incapable of evolving significantly away from the forms and functions shaped by their historical origins. Consequently, they may have a lasting economic impact.

This essay substantiates these points by briefly presenting and elaborating on several private order institutions which facilitated exchange during the late medieval commercial revolution – the developmental epoch stretching from the eleventh to the fourteenth centuries, which witnessed the re-emergence of Mediterranean and European long-distance trade after an extended period of decline. This place and period lend themselves to an examination of the role of ICEIs in facilitating exchange, since the emergence of long-distance commerce depended on the mitigation of contractual problems despite the absence of appropriate legal enforcement provided by the state. Furthermore, the nature, origin and implications of ICEIs during this period have recently been the subject of several studies which have advanced a new methodology for their investigation. It combines explicit game-theoretical models and detailed, micro-level historical analysis (Greif 1997d).

Common to all these studies is a reliance on the game-theoretical formulation of the idea that when contractual relations are expected to be repeated, a reputation mechanism can provide the basis for informal contract enforcement among self-interested individuals. Conditioning future exchange on past conduct creates a linkage between past conduct and the future utility stream. If the long term cost of losing future gains from exchange is higher than the short run gains from a breach, one acquires a reputation for honesty: he can credibly commit *ex ante* not to breach a contract *ex post*.

To identify the ICEI which governs a particular exchange it is thus necessary to examine theoretically and empirically how the linkage between past conduct and the future utility stream is created. It requires identifying the exact nature of the sanctions which would be imposed following a breach of contract, how the appropriate information is obtained and disseminated, who applies the sanctions, how the sanctioners learn or decide what sanctions to apply, why they do not shirk from their duty, and why the offenders do not flee to avoid sanctions. Once this identification takes place, the examination of the ICEIs can be further advanced to study their origin and implications and interrelations with various economic, social and political features.

The essay proceeds as follows. The first section briefly presents several ICEIs. The second section examines the interrelations between them and the cultural, social and political aspects of the relevant societies. The third section examines the efficiency and path dependence of these institutions. Due to space limitations, these sections neither present the methodology utilized to link the game-theoretical and historical analyses nor delineate the relevant evidence. The methodological approach is discussed in Greif (1997c), while the relevant historical evidence is provided in the works cited below.

I. INFORMAL CONTRACT ENFORCEMENT INSTITUTIONS

(1) *Institutions which governed the relations between rulers and alien merchants.* As discussed in Greif, Milgrom and Weingast (1994), since the political units during the late medieval period were relatively small, spatial specialization in production required trade across political boundaries. But a difficulty arose: having a local monopoly over coercive power, any medieval ruler faced the temptation to abuse alien merchants who frequented his realm and their property. Without an institution which enabled the ruler to commit *ex ante* to secure their rights, alien merchants were not likely to frequent that ruler's territory, thereby depriving its population, the ruler and the merchants of the benefits of trade.

Since trade relationships were expected to repeat, one may conjecture that an ICEI based on a bilateral reputation mechanism (in which a merchant whose rights were abused ceased trading), or based on an uncoordinated multilateral reputation mechanism (in which a subgroup larger than the one that was abused ceased trading), could surmount this commitment problem. The Folk theorem of repeated game theory suggests that since these mechanisms created an *ex ante* linkage between past conduct and the future income stream, a ruler who valued future income highly could credibly commit himself *ex ante* not to abuse merchants' rights *ex post*.

Yet, although each of the mechanisms above can support some level of trade, neither can support the *efficient level of trade*. The bilateral reputation mechanism fails because, at the efficient level of trade, the value of future trade of the '*marginal*' traders to the ruler is zero, and hence the ruler is tempted to abuse their rights. In a world fraught with information asymmetries, slow communication and plausibly different interpretations of facts, the multilateral reputation mechanism is prone to fail for similar reasons.

Theoretically, to overcome the ruler's commitment problem at the efficient level of trade an organization that *coordinates* traders' responses is required. When coordination is achieved, the threat by *all* the merchants to cease trading if *any* merchant were to be abused enables the ruler to commit – given that the merchants' threat of retaliation is credible. Unfortunately, however, the threat is not credible: it entails a complete boycott during which trade would shrink below the level at which, for example, a bilateral reputation mechanism is effective. Hence some traders would renegotiate with the ruler to resume trading. This impedes the coordinating organization's ability to surmount the commitment problem by reducing the penalty threatened to be imposed on the ruler. Thus to support the efficient level of trade, a multilateral reputation mechanism must be supplemented by an organization with the ability to coordinate responses *and* to ensure traders' *compliance* with boycott decisions. The traders must have some mechanism which makes the threat of collective action credible.

Historical evidence indicates that during the Commercial Revolution an institution with these attributes – the *merchant guild* – emerged and supported trade expansion and market integration. Merchant guilds exhibited a range of administrative forms – from a subdivision of city administration, such as that of the Italian city-states, to an intercity organization, such as the German Hansa. Yet their functions were the same: to ensure the coordination and internal enforcement required to make the threat of collective action credible. (Note that the argument does not relate to craft guilds.)

The German Hansa is perhaps one of the best examples of a guild's contribution to fostering trade expansion. For historical reasons, membership in the basic organizational unit that coordinated the activities of German merchants abroad – the *Kontor* – was not conditional on residency in one particular town. Any German merchant who arrived in a non-German city could join the local *Kontor*. Hence, a *Kontor* could coordinate the responses of the German merchants in disputes with the town, but it lacked the ability to enforce sanctions against its members.

In 1252, a *Kontor* of German merchants obtained extensive trading privileges from the city of Bruges (Flanders), which was the main trading centre of Northern Europe at that time. Despite promises to the contrary, the property rights of alien merchants in Bruges were continually abused. An embargo imposed by all alien merchants on Bruges from 1280 to 1282 secured the property rights of the Italian and Spanish traders, but failed to secure the German traders' rights. The relatively large and well-organized political units of the Italian and Spanish merchants furnished them with a state-provided mechanism to supplement the self-enforcing relations between them and Bruges by making their threat of future trade embargoes credible. In contrast, because the *Kontor* encompassed only the German merchants actually present in Bruges – rather than all the potential German traders who might want to trade during a boycott – its threat of sanctions against Bruges was not credible.

Another embargo by the German merchants, from 1307 to 1309, was required to force Bruges to respect their property rights. Its successful conclusion enabled the commerce between Flanders and Germany to flourish and expand for the next fifty years. What had changed between 1280 and 1307 was the ability of the German towns to coordinate their responses and enforce their embargo decisions on each other. A milestone occurred in 1284 when merchants from the city of Bremen refused to cooperate in an embargo against Norway, and the other German towns excluded Bremen's merchants from all German *Kontore*. The German towns had achieved the coordination needed to exclude one of their members from the economic rent generated by their common activities. The ability to exclude, in turn, was used to make their decisions self-enforcing.

The importance of the German towns' ability to impose their decision on their own traders to strengthen the operation of a multilateral reputation mechanism is seen clearly when their relations with Bruges were strained. The war between England and France around the middle of the fourteenth century increased the cost to Bruges of securing the German traders' property and lives. Increasing the level of protection required the Hansa to enhance its ability to impose a trade embargo on Bruges and to demonstrate this ability. In 1356 the German Hansa held its first *Diet* (assembly of representatives from all the Hansa's towns), and its authority over the *Kontor* of Bruges was declared. The enhanced ability of political units to exercise their coercive power over their merchants fostered the operation of the institution that governed the relations between these merchants and Bruges. In the Hanseatic embargo against Bruges in 1358, it was announced that any disobedience, whether by a town or an individual, was to be punished by perpetual exclusion from the Hansa. Bruges attempted to defeat the embargo by offering trade privileges to individual cities, including both non-Hanseatic ones like Kampen and a Hanseatic one, Cologne, but only the non-Hanseatic cities accepted Bruges's terms. The embargo proved to be a success and, in 1360, Bruges came to terms with the Hansa.

(2) *Institutions which governed the relations between merchants and overseas agents.* During the Commercial Revolution market expansion and integration were facilitated by the employment of *overseas agents* who enabled merchants to reduce the cost of long-distance trade by saving the time and risk of travelling, diversifying sales, and so forth. The contribution of agency relations to reducing the cost of trade, and hence to fostering market integration, has been recognized in the context of many pre-modern trading systems. For agency relations to promote efficiency, however, overseas agents had to have control over a merchant's capital abroad, enabling them to act opportunistically and expropriate that capital. Hence in the absence of institutions limiting opportunism, merchants would not hire agents.

But such institutions did come into existence: the institution which governed agency relations among the Maghribi traders, who operated in the Muslim Mediterranean during the eleventh century, is a striking case-in-point (Greif 1989, 1993). Agency relations among the Maghribis were governed by an economic institution that can be referred to as a *coalition* – a nonanonymous institution based on a multilateral reputation mechanism. The Maghribis employed each other as agents, and all of them retaliated against any agent who had cheated a coalition member. Their social and commercial network provided the information required to detect and announce cheating, and the multilateral punishment was self-enforcing since what kept an agent honest in his dealings with a specific merchant was the fear of losing the rent stream available to him from his future dealings with *all* the Maghribis. Hence if it was expected that a specific agent would not be hired in the future, he did not stand to lose the value of future relations with the Maghribis if he was caught cheating. Therefore, to keep such an agent honest, a Maghribi merchant had to provide him with a rent much higher than the one which would have kept an alternative agent honest. The merchant had to pay this unusually high rent in order to make the future value of their relations high enough to induce the agents to be honest in the absence of collective punishment. Since that implied a reduction in the merchant's own profit, each merchant was induced to hire only agents who were expected to be hired by others, making collective punishment self-enforcing.

Collective punishment enhanced efficiency and profitability relative to bilateral punishment, since it enabled the employment of agents even when the relations between a specific merchant and agent pair were not expected to recur. The resulting additional gains from cooperation, the value of the information flows and the expectations concerning future hiring ensured the 'closedness' of the coalition. That is, Maghribis were motivated to hire and to be hired only by other Maghribis, and non-Maghribis were discouraged from hiring Maghribis.

Besides traders from the Muslim world, Italian traders were very active in Mediterranean trade, particularly during and after the twelfth century. These traders also benefited from institutions which governed agency relations, but, in contrast to the coalition, agency relations among Genoese traders were governed by a Patron system based on a bilateral reputation mechanism facilitated by state enforcement (Greif 1994). In other words, among the Genoese an agent was induced to be honest, fearing that his relations with a particular merchant (who could have represented a family or even a clan) would be terminated if he were not. Furthermore, the legal system contributed to inducing honesty by providing contract registration facilities in many trade centres, specifying a minimum rate of return in case accounts were not furnished and holding an agent's property and family hostage until the agent's return.

(3) *Institutions which governed relations among merchants with limited information.* Market formation and integration during the Commercial Revolution required the appropriate governance for exchange relations characterized by separation in time or space between the *quid* and the *quo*. Credit markets, insurance markets and markets for future delivery could not be sustained otherwise. Yet, the separation between the *quid* and the *quo* made opportunistic behaviour possible. While local courts could enforce property rights generated in spot exchange or among members of the same community, they were unable, by themselves, to provide the contract enforcement required for exchange characterized by separation between the *quid* and the *quo* among merchants from *different* localities.

Yet the historical records indicate that exchange relations characterized by separation between the *quid* and the *quo* were frequently established among individuals from different localities during the Commercial Revolution. Such inter-community exchange relations contributed greatly to trade expansion during the Commercial Revolution. The 'take-off [of the Commercial Revolution] was fueled not by a massive input of cash, but by a closer collaboration of people using [commercial] credit' (Lopez 1976: 72). What institutions governed these contractual arrangements?

Milgrom, North and Weingast (1990) have maintained that contract enforceability over time at the Champagne Fairs was achieved by a Law Merchant System, in which the court was used to supplement a multilateral reputation mechanism. In particular, they present the following theoretical analysis. Suppose that each pair of traders is matched only once and each trader knows only his own experience. Since the fairs' court lacked the ability to enforce judgment once a trader had left the fairs, assume that the court is capable only of verifying past actions and keeping records of traders who cheated in the past. Acquiring information and appealing to the court is costly for each merchant. Despite these costs, symmetric sequential equilibrium exists in which cheating does not occur and merchants are induced to provide the court with the information required to support cooperation. It is the court's ability to activate a multilateral reputation mechanism by controlling information that provides the appropriate incentives. Hence a local court can ensure contract enforcement through time even if it cannot use coercive power against cheaters.

The historical records indicate that another ICEI was operating which supported exchange among traders from various localities, despite the absence of a legal system with jurisdiction over these localities (Greif 1997c). This institution took advantage of intra-community (formal and informal) contract enforcement institutions and the large extent to which community affiliation during the medieval period was common knowledge. By placing the future trade of all the members of his community as a bond, an alien was able to commit, for example, to repay a debt despite the lender's inability to locate and sue him.

Specifically, the lender's local court (as well as other courts) held all members of a community responsible for the default of any member. They were held responsible in the sense that following a default by one community member, the lender's court implemented a strategy which called for confiscating the goods of any member of the defaulter's community present in its jurisdiction. The goods were confiscated until the loss was recovered or the defaulters' community advanced compensation for the default. A community was thereby provided with the incentive to employ its intra-community contract enforcement institution to *ex post* punish one who defaulted in inter-community exchange. Since this was known *ex ante*, a lender could commit to *ex post* repay his debt. Hence, the Community Responsibility System enabled inter-community impersonal exchange relations characterized by separation over time and space.

Once this situation is modelled as a repeated, imperfect monitoring game the analysis reveals the rationale for various patterns of behaviour reflected in the historical records. Modelling the situation as one of imperfect monitoring seems appropriate since the historical records indicate that at times the courts of different communities disagreed about whether a breach of contract had indeed occurred. Among other insights, the model indicates that in the equilibrium which sustains exchange, a finite period of retaliation would follow disagreement among courts. During a period of retaliation inter-community trade ceased, and each community's court confiscated the goods of the members of the other community. While such retaliation periods are costly, the model indicates that they were unavoidable: had the communities been expected not to retaliate, they would have provided disincentives to the courts to reveal their private information about cheating even when there was no genuine disagreement. This, however, would have motivated borrowers to breach their contractual obligations. Hence, the model provides a rationale for behaviour that was considered 'barbaric' by an earlier generation of historians.

This section briefly presented several ICEIs which governed various exchange relations during the Commercial Revolution. By providing the contract enforcement required to enable commitment, institutions such as the Merchant Guild, the Coalition and the Community Responsibility System enabled exchange and the emergence, operation and integration of markets.

II. INFORMAL CONTRACT ENFORCEMENT AND THE ORGANIZATION OF SOCIETY. The above ICEIs were a response to efficiency enhancing opportunities but their origins and natures reflect more than economic factors; each of them was embedded in a broader cultural, social and political context. They were part of the organization of society: the inter-related web of complementary economic, legal, political, social and moral features which is the essence of a society's nature. It is within this broader context that one has to comprehend the origin, nature, change and implications of ICEIs. To further substantiate this assertion, this section briefly elaborates on some of the inter-relations between cultural traits, social features, political factors and the above ICEIs.

(1) *Cultural factors.* The origin, nature and implications of the distinct institutions which governed agency relations among the Maghribi and Genoese traders illustrate the relations between cultural factors and ICEIs (Greif 1994). A main distinction between the Coalition and the Patron System relates to expectations off-the-path-of-play, namely, in situations which do not transpire. Only among the Maghribis were there the expectations for a collective punishment to be inflicted on an agent who cheated. While a game theoretical analysis of agency relations indicates that each set of expectations is self-enforcing, cultural factors (as well as the social factors discussed below) determine which expectations prevailed in each group.

Cultural factors among the Maghribis made expectations for a collective punishment a focal point. The Maghribis were *mustarbin*, that is, non-Muslims, who adopted the values of the Muslim society. Among these values was the view that they were members of the same *umma*. This term, although translated as 'nation', is derived from the word *umm* meaning 'mother,' reflecting the basic value of mutual responsibility among the members of that society. Further, *umma* members shared the fundamental duty not only to practise good, but also to ensure that others did not practise sin. In addition, the Maghribis were part of the Jewish community, within which it was a prominent idea that 'all Israel is responsible for every member'. In contrast, Genoa's cultural environment did not make collective punishment a focal point. The Genoese traders were part of the feudal world in which bilateral patronage relations prevailed. Furthermore, Christianity during that period placed the individual rather than his social group at the center of its theology, advancing the creation of a new society based on the individual.

While these cultural aspects of the two societies made distinct expectation focal points, their concrete embodiment in particular ICEIs transformed these expectations into cultural beliefs: ideas and thoughts common to several individuals which govern interaction – between these people, and between them, their gods and other groups – and which differ from knowledge in that they are not empirically discovered or analytically proven. In other words, the expectations which crystallized with respect to a particular game became part of the 'view of the world' of members of these societies, and thus provided the basis for extrapolating behaviour in situations that had not been encountered before. As such, they affected outcomes following exogenous change in the rules of the game and provided incentives for particular trajectories of organizational change. Hence, they directed the evolution of the organization of society by influencing institutional change, organizational innovations, social structure and the formation of values and identities (Greif 1994).

With respect to organizational change, for example, the 'collectivist' cultural beliefs associated with the operation of the coalition and the 'individualistic' cultural beliefs had profound and lasting implications. Theoretically, the individualistic cultural beliefs of the Genoese, but not the Maghribis' collectivist cultural beliefs, provided an incentive to establish a 'firm' through which the wealth of several merchants was aggregated. Such a firm did not prevail among either the Genoese or the Maghribis when they began operating as traders. Yet, it was the Genoese, but not the Maghribis, who adopted the family firm during the thirteenth century (Greif 1996, 1997a). Individualist cultural beliefs, but not collectivist cultural beliefs, also provided incentives to use a bill of lading. Indeed, the first historical evidence for its use in Europe is from late medieval Genoa. In sharp contrast, the Maghribis, although familiar with the bill of lading, did not utilize it. Hence, distinct ICEIs led to and reinforced distinct cultural features, which, in turn, directed these two groups along separate paths of organizational development. The importance of distinct cultural beliefs to the evolution of a society's organization is further exemplified below through the examination of their implications on other formal organizations and social structures.

(2) *Social features.* By directing available information and specifying social identities, a society's social features affect the set of feasible ICEIs. At the same time, ICEIs and their implications affect the evolving nature of these social features. In some cases they re-enforce them while in others they undermine them. Social structures and ICEIs thus shape, and are shaped, by each other.

The emergence of the Maghribi traders coalition reflects a particular social structure. The Maghribis were the descendants of Jewish traders who, during the tenth century, had left the increasingly politically insecure surroundings of Baghdad and emigrated to North Africa. By coordinating expectations and providing a social network to transmit information, immigration made the initiation of collective punishment possible while, as discussed above, cultural factors made it a focal point. In contrast, the social environment within which agency relations were initially established among the Genoese forestalled, rather than encouraged, the formation of a coalition. Toward the end of the twelfth century, the number of Genoese active in trade rose dramatically, while Genoa experienced a demographic expansion despite a high mortality rate. This demographic and social setting did not support the stable social networks required for the development of a coalition based on collective punishment.

While the initial social setting within which agency relations were organized among the Maghribis and Genoese affected their ICEIs, these distinct ICEIs influenced the nature and evolution of the associated social structures. For example, the details of collective punishment among the Maghribis were such that they implied that one's investment in trade enhanced his ability to commit to being honest while serving as an agent. Merchants, therefore, were motivated to hire other merchants who also invested in trade as agents, thereby determining the social characterization of the Maghribis. One does not observe the existence of two separate 'classes' among them – an agents' class and a merchants' class. Socially, the Maghribi traders group was a homogeneous group of middle class traders and each of them operated as a merchant and as an agent at the same time. This was not the case among the Genoese traders, however. The lack of collective punishment implied that one's investment in trade diminished his ability to commit to being honest while serving as an agent. This determined the social characterization of Genoese traders among whom one can recognize two distinct subgroups, that of the merchants and that of the agents. In the long run, these social characterizations affected economic mobility and wealth distribution (Greif 1994).

The interrelations between the initial social characterizations of the Maghribis and the Genoese and the distinct cultural beliefs associated with their ICEIs also influenced other social features of these groups. Specifically, following various military and political changes in the Mediterranean, both groups had the opportunity to expand their trade to areas previously inaccessible to them. Commercially, both groups responded similarly and expanded their trade from Spain to Constantinople. Socially, however, their responses differed: the Genoese responded in an 'integrated' manner while the Maghribis responded in a 'segregated' manner. The Maghribis expanded their trade by employing other Maghribis, who emigrated from North Africa as agents, rather than employing Jewish or non-Jewish local merchants. For generations the descendants of Maghribis continued to cooperate with the descendants of other Maghribis. The Genoese also responded to the new opportunities by emigrating abroad, and agency relations among them prevailed. Yet, although the historical sources are biased toward reflecting agency relations among Genoese, they nevertheless clearly indicate the establishment of agency relations between Genoese and non-Genoese.

The rationale behind the different responses of the Maghribis and the Genoese to the same exogenous change in the rules of the game is clear once one considers the relations between cultural beliefs and equilibrium selection. Agency relations among the Maghribis were governed by the expectations for collective punishment within the coalition. Yet, since agency relations were not established with a non-coalition prior to the point in time in which such relations became feasible, there was uncertainty about whether collective punishment would be relevant in agency relations with non-coalition members. After all, the existing cultural beliefs implied that merchants would continue to hire only agents who were coalition members. Hence, it led to the 'closedness' of the coalition: since agency relations within the coalition were more profitable even when less efficient, the Maghribis were motivated to hire and to be hired only by other Maghribis. For similar reasons non-Maghribis were discouraged from hiring Maghribis. Such closedness did not prevail among the Genoese, however. Without expectations for collective punishment, the same uncertainty about it in agency relations with non-Genoese did not influence the profitability of hiring an agent. Hence, Genoese merchants were motivated to hire non-Genoese agents whenever such agency relations were efficient (Greif 1994, 1996).

This symbiosis between social structures and the nature of the associated economic institution is well reflected in the later history of Maghribi traders. The Maghribi traders retained their separate identity within the Jewish communities as long as they were active in long-distance trade. During the second half of the twelfth century, however, they were forced by the Muslim rulers of Egypt to abandon that trade. At that point, as far as we know, they integrated completely within the Jewish communities and vanished from the stage of history. In other words, as long as the Maghribis traded, the nature of the economic institution that governed agency relations contributed to maintaining their social entity.

The Community Responsibility System (henceforth CRS) reflects the fact that the operation of an ICEI may depend crucially on the extent to which social affiliations are common knowledge. Under the late medieval CRS, unless a lender knew the community affiliation of a borrower, lending could not have taken place since no punishment could have been imposed on the borrower in a case of default. In other words, a particular feature of the late medieval society – merchants' affiliations with particular communities and the large extent to which these affiliations were common knowledge – enabled the operation of an ICEI. At the same time, the CRS reflects that ICEIs may undermine the social feature of the society on which it is based. The same processes that the CRS fostered – processes through which trade expanded and merchants' communities grew in size, number, and economic and social heterogeneity – reduced the economic efficiency and the intra-community political viability of the CRS over time. This occurred since the economic impact of the CRS segmented communities and made it relatively easy to falsify, and difficult to verify, one's community affiliation (Greif 1997c).

(3) *Political factors and formal organization.* ICEIs are also inter-related with political factors and formal organizations. Formal organizations influence the feasible set of ICEIs, political factors influence the ability to alter them, and the nature of available ICEIs affects the demand for formal contract enforcement institutions.

Examination of the timing of the emergence of merchant guilds in various localities in Europe indicates that it was determined by political and social factors. For example, the major Italian city states grew large because of political and social events around the Mediterranean. Italian trade expanded since each city functioned as a merchant guild, and its size implied that its traders were not 'marginal'. Although the potential gains from trade in the Baltic Sea were substantial as well, that region's settlement process resulted in small towns which could not assure the safety of their traders abroad. Only after a long process of institutional evolution were these towns incorporated into an intercity merchant guild, the German Hansa, which enabled Baltic trade to prosper. If all these small cities had been part of a unified political regime, this long period of institutional evolution would not have been required. (Greif 1992). The history of the German Hansa presented above also illustrates the complementary nature of the relations between formal and informal means for contract enforcement. The relations between the German towns, members of the Hansa and non-member political units were informal. The relations between any individual German merchant and the Hansa, however, were based on a formal institution – the legal authority of the town in which he dwelled.

The history of the CRS illustrates the extent to which political factors and formal organization influence the ability to alter ICEIs. In the second half of the thirteenth century attempts were made in England, France, and Italy to abolish the CRS. Yet, the extent to which communities could have replaced this ICEI with an alternative formal institution based on a legal system depended on their political environment. The kings of England and France were able to provide traders with a legal procedure enabling relatively fast and cheap contract enforcement based on individual legal responsibility. This, however, was not the case in politically fragmented Italy. Due to a lack of central authority, the repeated attempts of the Italian city-states to abolish the CRS failed. In the absence of a third party – a king – able to provide a legal system whose decisions did not reflect the community's self-interest, the Italian city-states could not adopt the institutions implemented in France and England (Greif 1997c).

While the above discussion indicates that political factors affected the ability to abolish ICEIs, it is also true that ICEIs affected society's formal institutions. Consider, for example, the Maghribis and the Genoese. Among the Maghribis, agency relations were governed by an institution based on self-enforcing, collective, economic punishment, and supported by the closedness of the coalition and an ingroup social communication network. In such a 'collectivist society' the enforcement required to support collective actions and facilitate exchange could be achieved without 'formal' – legal or political – organizations which specialized in communication and enforcement. In contrast, among the Genoese agency relations were governed by an institution based on bilateral punishment which reduced the benefit of informal communication. Such an 'individualistic' society had a relatively low level of informal economic enforcement over its members. Hence to support collective actions and facilitate exchange, it needed to develop formal – legal and political – enforcement organizations (Greif 1994).

Indeed, the Genoese developed formal organizations to support collective actions and exchange, whereas the Maghribis abandoned them. During the twelfth century the Genoese quit entering contracts with a handshake and developed an extensive legal system for registering and enforcing contracts. This system supplemented the operation of the patron system, as agents were legally required to provide merchants with verifiable accounts regarding their expenses and revenues. An agent who failed to submit such an account was legally obliged to provide a minimum return on the merchants' investment. Furthermore, the customary contract law which governed the relations between Genoese traders was codified as permanent courts were established. In contrast, despite the existence of a well-developed Jewish communal court system, the Maghribis entered contracts informally, used an informal code of conduct to govern exchange and attempted to resolve disputes informally.

The emergence of the family firm and the adoption of the bill of lading, discussed above, also reflect the impact of distinct ICEIs on organizational development. The development is further reflected, for example, in the formation of merchant guilds in these two societies. Among the Maghribis compliance with embargo decisions was assured through informal means. After the Muslim ruler of Sicily abused the rights of some Maghribi traders, they responded by imposing, *circa* 1050, an embargo on Sicily. This embargo was organized informally, although the Maghribis could have utilized the Jewish court system or the formal Jewish communal organization. In contrast, among the Genoese the city of Genoa itself functioned as a formal enforcement organization to ensure compliance with collective actions. After the city authorities declared that a certain area was a *devetum*, that is, prohibited for trade, any merchant who was found in that location was subject to legal prosecution.

III. INSTITUTIONAL EFFICIENCY, CHANGE AND PATH DEPENDENCE. ICEIs enhanced efficiency during the Commercial Revolution. This does not necessarily imply, however, that they were optimal in the sense of enabling exhaustion of all the gains from trade that were feasible given that period's production, information and contract enforcement technology. As a matter of fact, the above discussion of the processes that moulded these non-market institutions suggests that they were not optimal.

For example, an analysis of the Law Merchant suggests that the centrality of the Fairs of Champagne in European trade reflects economies of scale in the operation of a multilateral reputation mechanism. If that is the case, the geographical distribution of much of the European trade of the period reflects the historical process that led to the emergence of that institution at that specific time and place. As theoretical studies of path dependence indicate, this process need not be optimal.

The institutions that governed agency relations do not seem to have been optimal either. The Maghribis' coalition and the patron system were different institutions linked to specific historical, political, and social processes of which they were integral parts. These processes, rather than merely economic efficiency, determined the nature of these institutions and the timing of their emergence and disappearance. Indeed, the evolution of these institutions and the details of their operations suggests that neither of them could have supported the set of optimal exchange relations. Among the Maghribis, the extent of agency relations was limited by the coalition's size, which had been determined by immigration and cultural beliefs. The historical evidence indeed indicates that the Maghribis did not establish efficient relations with non-Maghribis, preferring more profitable but less efficient agency relations among themselves. This deficiency could have been remedied by an appropriate coordinating organization but none emerged (Greif 1993).

Was the institutional infrastructure provided by the above ICEIs converging to an optimal one? Was it inducing organizational or technological innovations which were growth enhancing? The historical and theoretical analyses indicate that it was not. Rather, this institutional infrastructure was path dependent in the sense that its capacity to change was constrained by its own history. Examination of the sources, manifestations, and implications of this path dependence reinforces further the conclusion regarding the non-optimality of the period's institutional structures.

The emergence of merchant guilds in the Latin world entailed the consolidation of political and legal entities which shaped and constrained later institutional and commercial development. In particular, the emerging German Hansa was a new political entity aimed at preserving the property rights of German merchants. Although its establishment enabled Northern European trade to flourish, once organized, its concern was not efficiency but profitability. In its constant effort to preserve trade rights and supremacy, the Hansa crushed the advances of other traders' groups without considering their comparative efficiencies. In 1368, for example, the King of Sweden provided the German Hansa with control over the autumn fairs of Skania (the southern province of Sweden). Before then English merchants were selling West European cloth at these fairs and using the proceeds to purchase herring and salt. The English merchants were able to compete successfully with Hanseatic merchants, who were also importing West European cloth to that area. In February 1370, a Hanseatic diet ruled that English, Welsh and Scottish merchants would no longer be allowed to engage in such trade. The complaints of the English king, Edward III, were to no avail. Distributional considerations took precedence over efficiency (Greif 1992).

The sources of path dependence in institutions which governed agency relations are much more complex. Cultural beliefs, as have been discussed above, directed institutional path dependence by providing distinct incentives for organizational innovations. The relative efficiency of these separate organizations, in turn, depended on the economic environment. Yet, since cultural beliefs are uncoordinated expectations, a society lacking the appropriate cultural beliefs would be unable to take advantage of the superior organizations. Similarly, the dependence of the Maghribi traders' coalition on uncoordinated collective punishment by merchants located at different trade centres implied another source for path dependence. For the threat of collective punishment to be credible, 'cheating' must have been defined in a manner that ensured collective response. If some merchants considered specific actions to constitute 'cheating' but others held a different opinion, the effectiveness of the collective threat would have been undermined. To mitigate this problem, the Maghribis employed a set of cultural rules of behaviour which specified how an agent should act to be considered honest in circumstances not mentioned in the merchant's instructions. These rules were shared by all the Maghribi traders and served as a default contract between agents and merchants. This set of rules promoted efficiency by providing a coordination device necessary for the functioning of the coalition, economizing on negotiating cost and enabling flexibility in establishing agency relations. Yet, in the absence of any mechanism able to coordinate changes, this set of rules among the Maghribis was a source of rigidity and path dependence. It imposed rigidity on the system because its process of adjustment was impeded by agents' concerns regarding what others would be thinking about their actions rather than what the outcome of their actions would be (Greif 1993).

The above short discussion illustrates that ICEIs during the Commercial Revolution exhibited path-dependence and were not necessarily converging to optimal institutions. They gave rise to political units which employed their coercive power to affect distribution at efficiency cost, and even the self-enforcing institutions were based on expectations that, in the absence of coordinating mechanisms, impeded efficient adaptations. Furthermore, various institutions and their associated cultural beliefs provided a separate impetus to the introduction of different organizations, leading to institutional path dependence (Greif 1994, 1997a). Hence, different societies, even when encountering similar organizational problems, can be 'locked in' to different trajectories of institutional development, each of which will have distinct economic implications in various possible situations.

IV. CONCLUSIONS. Adam Smith's intellectual heritage includes the view that much of the institutional framework provided by the state and aimed at directing the economy can be replaced by the 'invisible hand' generated by the uncoordinated interactions among self-interested individuals. Menger (1963) has further advanced this view to claim that such interactions provided the basis for all social institutions, including contract enforcement institutions. Some have taken this view to mean that informal contract institutions emerge spontaneously to advance exchange. They provide an efficient, welfare maximizing enforcement that Pareto dominates the enforcement provided by the state (e.g. Benson 1989; Ellickson 1991; Cotter 1997).

The study of informal contract enforcement institutions during the late medieval period challenges this view. It provides support to other studies of ICEIs which concluded that efficient institutions would not necessarily be forthcoming (De Soto 1989; Putnam 1993). Its contribution to this line of argument is not limited to additional case studies. By combining explicit game theoretical analysis and detailed historical examination, it is able to present a comparative study of institutions over time and space which reveals their underlying rationale and their complementary nature with other aspects of society.

Understanding the functioning of economies and processes of economic growth and stagnation in various societies requires an examination of their nexus of contract enforcement institutions. In particular, it requires comprehending the interrelations between cultural factors, endogenous social features, formal organizations, political factors and ICEIs. It demands an understanding of how a society's ICEIs interrelated with the other features of that society's organization, thereby influencing its economic performance and institutional changes.

AVNER GREIF

See also ANTHROPOLOGICAL LAW-AND-ECONOMICS; COMMITMENT; EMERGENCE OF LEGAL RULES; EVOLUTION OF COMMERCIAL LAW; LAW MERCHANT; PATH DEPENDENCE; PRIVATE COMMERCIAL LAW.

Subject classification: 4a(iii); 4b(iii); 5a(v); 5c(ii).

BIBLIOGRAPHY

Benson, B.L. 1989. The spontaneous evolution of commercial law. *Southern Economic Journal* 55: 644–61.

Cotter, R.D. 1997. The rule of state law and the rule-of-law state: economic analysis of the legal foundations of development. In *Annual World Bank Conference on Development Economics 1996*, ed. M. Bruno and B. Pleskovic, Washington, DC: The World Bank.

David, P.A. 1988. Path-dependence: putting the past into the future of economics. Technical report number 533, IMSSS, Stanford University Economics Dept., Stanford, CA.

De Soto, H. 1989. *The Other Path*. New York: Harper & Row.

Ellickson, R. 1991. *Order Without Law*. Cambridge, MA: Harvard University Press.

Fafchamps, M., Biggs, T., Conning, J. and Srivastava, P. 1993. Enterprise finance in Kenya. World Bank, Africa Region, Regional Program on Enterprise Development. Washington DC: The World Bank.

Greif, A. 1989. Reputation and coalitions in medieval trade: evidence on the Maghribi traders. *Journal of Economic History* 49: 857–82.

Greif, A. 1992. Institutions and international trade: lessons from the commercial revolution. *American Economic Review, Papers and Proceedings* 82: 128–33.

Greif, A. 1993. Contract enforceability and economic institutions in early trade: the Maghribi traders' coalition. *American Economic Review* 83: 525–48.

Greif, A. 1994. Cultural beliefs and the organization of society: a historical and theoretical reflection on collectivist and individualist societies. *Journal of Political Economy* 102: 912–50.

Greif, A. 1996. On the study of organizations and evolving organizational forms through history: reflection from the late medieval family firm. *Industrial and Corporate Change* 5: 473–502.

Greif, A. 1997a. On the inter-relations and economic implications of economic, social, political, and normative factors: reflections from two late medieval societies. In *Frontiers of the New Institutional Economics*, ed. J.N. Drobak and J. Nye, New York: The Academic Press.

Greif, A. 1997b. Contracting, enforcement, and efficiency: economics beyond the law. In *Annual World Bank Conference on Development Economics, 1996*, ed. M. Bruno and B. Pleskovic, Washington, DC: The World Bank.

Greif, A. 1997c. On the historical development and social foundations of institutions that facilitate impersonal exchange: from the community responsibility system to individual legal responsibility in pre-modern Europe. Working paper # 97–016, Department of Economics, Stanford University, Stanford, CA.

Greif, A. 1997d. Microtheory and recent developments in the study of economic institutions through economic history. In *Advances in Economic Theory, Vol. II*, ed. D.M. Kreps and K.F. Wallis, Cambridge: Cambridge University Press.

Greif, A., Milgrom, P.R. and Weingast, B.R. 1994. Coordination, commitment and enforcement: the case of the merchant guild. *Journal of Political Economy* 102: 745–76.

Greif, A. and Kandel, E. 1995. Contract enforcement institutions: Historical perspective and current status in Russia. In *Economic Transition in Eastern Europe and Russia: Realities of Reform*, ed. E.P. Lazear, Stanford, CA: Hoover Institution Press.

Lopez, R.S. 1976. *The Commercial Revolution of the Middle Ages, 950–1350*. Cambridge: Cambridge University Press.

Macaulay, S. 1963. Noncontractual relations in business: a preliminary study. *American Sociological Review* 28: 55–70.

Menger, C. 1963. *Problems of Economics and Sociology*. Transl. F.J. Nook, ed. L. Schneider, Urbana: University of Illinois Press.

Milgrom, P.R., North, D.C. and Weingast, B.R. 1990. The role of institutions in the revival of trade: the Law Merchant, private judges, and the Champagne Fairs. *Economics & Politics* 2: 1–23.

Putnam, R.D. 1993. *Making Democracy Work*. Princeton: Princeton University Press.

Williamson, O.E. 1985. *The Economic Institutions of Capitalism*. New York: The Free Press.

informal contracts and regulatory constraints. Contracts provide parties with a means of projecting their exchanges into the future. Nothing in their language or form guarantees performance. Enforcement, instead, comes from the governance structure supporting the agreement. Regulation, like markets, courts, internal organization and private orderings, is a form of contractual governance. All governance structures place limits on the scope and range of permissible contracting. Where the costs of those limits outweigh the benefits provided by them, the parties are apt to search for alternative means of protecting their contractual arrangements. Typically, the discussion of alternatives to regulatory schemes focuses on legislative action, litigation, and capture of the administrative structure. However, regulatory constraints can be circumvented or altered through the use of informal, legally unenforceable arrangements as well. My purpose here is to document this assertion with reference to the contracting between rail-freight carriers and their shippers (see generally Palay 1984, 1985).

RAIL-FREIGHT TRANSACTIONS. Conceptually, the contracting between rail-freight carriers and their shippers is straightforward. The agreements that evolve are similar in nature to any intermediate product market buyer–seller relation. Supplier (carrier) provides an input (transportation) for purchaser's (shipper's) production function. In short, buyer procures through contract the technology necessary to move inputs or outputs from point A to point B. However in the US, at least through the late 1970s, the comprehensive regulatory scheme of the Interestate Commerce Act (ICA) placed severe limitations on the range and scope of permissible contracting between the rail carriers and their shippers. These constraints were all the more problematic because many rail-freight transactions required sizeable investments in idiosyncratic physical and human capital.

By idiosyncratic capital I refer to those investments in physical and human assets that have little alternative use outside the transaction for which they were initially procured. Where parties make investments of this type, any competitive conditions observed prior to contract initiation are generally lost once contract performance commences. Competition disappears because the specialized requirements of the transaction limit the availability of substitute sources of purchase or supply. For example, at the time of this study (Palay 1981, 1984, 1985) shipper A was a major shipper of automobiles. Its finished vehicles were produced at only a few locations. To reach final markets, A had to ship large numbers of automobiles over long distances. Rail carrier X acted as a conveyor belt to move A's finished automobiles to the next step in the production and marketing process.

To transport A's finished vehicles from assembly point to destination, carrier X employed open trilevel autoracks fastened atop rented flatcars. The autorack rail car was developed specifically to handle the size, weight, and design characteristics of finished automobiles. Essentially multilevel parking ramps fastened atop oversized flatcars, the $40,000 to $70,000 autoracks could carry fifteen to eighteen finished automobiles and, importantly, were specific to the shipper's finished vehicles. The configuration of the decks and tie-downs made it costly to transfer the cars either between manufacturers or across automobile models. The carrier's only use for the autoracks was on the shipper's routes. Once built, their worth in their next best use was roughly equivalent to their scrap metal value. In addition, trilevel autoracks were generally higher than standard eastern bridge and tunnel clearances. To alleviate the obvious difficulties, the carrier had to raise its clearances. The railroad also had to undertake other investments, such as the construction of off-loading ramps, solely for the benefit of the finished automobile movements.

THE PROBLEM. Parties to transactions heavily dependent upon investment in idiosyncratic capital must somehow devise contractual relations that safeguard those investments. However, at the time of this study the Interstate Commerce Act created a regulatory environment in which such formal contracting was severely constrained.

The Act required the parties to move all traffic pursuant to a formal rate tariff. To do otherwise was expressly prohibited (49 USC 10761–2, 1978). Through the tariff the railroad offered to carry a particular commodity or class of commodities from origin to destination at a designated price. However, the official tariff did not commit the shipper to actually use the rail service. The formal agreement covered price but not the commitment of volume. Only the tendering of the commodity to the railroad imposed a legal obligation on the shipper. Thus the carrier's obligations were long term, while the shipper's obligations resembled those associated with spot market transactions.

The formal contracts resulting from this arrangement were inherently incomplete and inadequate to the task of facilitating the complex transactions at issue. First, the contract form required by the ICA made it difficult for the parties to secure expectations. Because an enforceable contract existed only if cargo was actually tendered the formal agreements were short term and provided no expectation about future exchange. Legally each successive exchange required a separate and wholly distinct contract. With little prospect for future interaction, the parties would lack the incentive to develop the long-term continuing relationships needed to support transactions involving idiosyncratic investments (Palay 1985).

Second, the ICA place limitations on the commitment of volume to carriers (Locklin 1972: Palay 1985). At the time of this study, except where cost savings were immediately evident or where competition from other modes dictated, a shipper could not commit a percentage of its output or some volume per time period to a particular carrier. Similarly, the Commission did not allow railroads to offer favourable prices for any such commitments. The restrictions on volume commitments made carrier investment in idiosyncratic capital problematic. If A did not ship the vehicles promised, X's investment in trilevel autoracks would be at risk. Nevertheless, the ICA precluded them from reaching a formal accord on annual volume or similar types of commitments.

A third problem with the agreements prescribed by the ICA was the common understanding that the Act prevented shippers and carriers from formally contracting over service standards and on-time performance incentives. For instance, in order to maintain a large and consistent outbound flow of finished vehicles automobile shipper A requires a consistent supply of rail cars and dependable schedules. Nevertheless, the ICA made it illegal to provide incentives for meeting turnaround time or on-time performance standards.

Finally, the zone-of-reasonableness constraints on rates placed obvious restrictions on prices. This was of particular concern to parties unable to arrange effective contracting safeguards.

Each of these problems contributed to making the tariff an inadequate contracting format for rail-freight transactions, especially those that entailed relatively idiosyncratic investments in physical and human capital. Carriers did not want to make transaction-specific investments without shippers' assurance that they would actually use the service. Shippers could not make those commitments using the contracting format provided by the ICA. Similarly, shippers would not be enthusiastic about committing a large volume to a particular carrier without knowing that the railroad had the equipment and expertise to move it and to move it on time.

THE SOLUTION. To overcome the contracting problems created by the regulatory scheme, the parties, in essence, restructured the regulatory constraint by supplementing their formal contracts with informal, legally unenforceable agreements. These provided some price flexibility and, more importantly, helped to arrange, implement and monitor contractual safeguards.

The informal agreements were 'handshake' understandings between the shipper's transportation division and the railroad's marketing or sales department. For the most part, documentation was limited to a letter of understanding or memorandum to the files. Typically, the informal agreements were oral, though subsequent written confirmation of essential terms was not unusual. They were often as short as a brief paragraph dealing with some combination of three subjects: (1) the commitment of volume; (2) the promise of equipment; and (3) the guarantee of specified service standards. The informal contracts were collateral to the formal official tariff and effectively restructured the regulatory relation governing many of the carriers and shippers. In a strict sense, some of the informal promises were really just spot market contracts made merely to complete formal tariffs rather than mechanisms for restructuring the regulatory scheme. However, none of the spot market contracting involved transactions in which idiosyncratic capital was at issue. Where investments were made in idiosyncratic assets, informal contracting worked to make the governance structure more compatible with the necessities of rail-freight transactions.

First, informal contracting was used to extract price concessions. Usually negotiated in the context of fixing formal tariff rates, price concessions might represent either a revaluation of the transaction or a restructuring of contracting safeguards. Where the price concession implemented a revaluation strategy one party typically offered to support a tariff change in exchange for an informal guarantee of some sort. For instance, a railroad might lower its price per unit of volume in exchange for a shipper's informal but 'firm' commitment to move a minimum annual volume. Similarly, a shipper might provide a necessary investment incentive by offering to pay the railroad a price premium in return for the carrier's informal pledge to procure and assign a specified amount of specialized rail equipment.

Price concessions might also represent a restructuring of the contracting safeguards used by the parties to support the transaction. Williamson (1983) has suggested that parties to transactions requiring idiosyncratic investments can protect their investment in either of two ways. On the one hand, one party can offer the other protection by paying a premium above the marginal cost of the service. The resulting price deviates from efficient pricing principles but includes an insurance premium of sorts. On the other hand, the parties can attempt to devise nonprice safeguards – hostages, incentive schemes and private orderings – to protect their investments. Thus where one observes a shipper agreeing to make a credible commitment of volume in exchange for a guarantee of equipment and a downward adjustment of price, one might interpret this as a readjustment of the contract price to reflect the fact that new contractual safeguards made a preexisting premium no longer necessary. The contract between auto parts shipper B and carrier Z reflected this type of understanding. Like shipper A discussed above, B is a major producer of automobiles and automobile parts. Parts consist of everything from batteries, spark plugs and light bulbs to engines, sheet metal stampings, axles and frames. B's production process was such that it generally procured the necessary parts from locations throughout the United States and shipped them to various assembly plants. The carrier acted as an interstate conveyor belt for the shipper's assembly line. This required both large transportation capacity and consistent service. To meet the shipper's transportation needs, both parties had to make specialized investments in rail cars, parts racks, plant layout, and coordination and communications networks.

Carrier Z for its part was concerned about price, though of course price was irrelevant if shipper B did not actually ship the promised components. Just prior to the interview, the carrier had realized that if it were to lower its rate on a particular movement of auto parts it might be able to capture volume then travelling by truck. The railroad believed that the lower price was justified by the increased volume, which would reduce unit costs and better utilize fixed capital. What is more, the additional volume would justify and protect the investment in specialized service and equipment. Carrier Z was reluctant, however, to publish the lower rate without receiving a credible commitment of volume from shipper B. Z was concerned that once it published the lower rate, railroad T – interested in the potential large volume, but presently not involved in the movement – might follow suit. Shipper B might then choose to divide the traffic between the two carriers, leaving Z in a worse financial position than it would have been in before it decided to compete for the truck traffic. Carrier Z lowered the price on the move only after shipper B's vice president for transportation personally assured the railroad that the new traffic was forthcoming. After many years of dealing with the vice president, Z felt confident in his promise (Palay 1981: 117; Palay 1984: 277–8).

Second, informal contracting that did not involve price concessions was used to restructure the contractual relation into one with more secure expectations about future exchanges. Because a carrier's obligations were relatively long term, while a shipper's were merely of a spot market type, the railroads perceived themselves as particularly susceptible to opportunistic behaviour. Informal agreements on such issues as the commitment of volume alleviated some of the problem by restructuring the contract to one where both parties' obligation would be of the same scope and duration. This helped to establish an ongoing relation and permitted the parties to take advantage of adaptive sequential decision making (Williamson 1976).

Finally, informal agreements were used to implement hostage exchanges. In the rail-freight context both shipper and carrier made investments in idiosyncratic assets that could be 'destroyed' if either party failed to perform its part of the agreement. Vulnerable assets acted as hostages and played important roles in securing investments in idiosyncratic capital (Williamson 1983). The carrier's hostages were easy to identify. They included specialized rail cars and transaction-specific investments in track and clearances. The shipper's hostages might be a little less obvious to the casual observer. In some instances shippers located or designed plants to effectively preclude the use of alternative modes of transportation. In addition, some shippers made investments in their own idiosyncratic rail equipment. Chemical shippers, for example, owned most of their own rail cars. Automobile manufacturers also made nontrivial investments in the highly specialized assets such as the shipping racks needed to load and secure parts inside boxcars. The racks acted as a hostage because they were only good for moving automobile parts in boxcars and were vehicle make- and model-specific. A change in the design of an automobile component or a decision to ship by truck could render a rack worthless.

GOVERNING INFORMAL CONTRACTS. Contracts themselves do not guarantee performance. They simply specify or codify the proposed actions of the parties. Negotiation, monitoring, adaptation and enforcement of the agreement comes from the governance structure supporting the contract. Governance structures take different forms depending upon the characteristics of the underlying transaction (Williamson 1976; Palay 1984, 1985). Markets, judicial or quasi-judicial enforcement, internal organization, and private orderings are all useful forms of governance under the right circumstances. What makes rail-freight contracting interesting is that we typically think of judicial and quasi-judicial governance as providing the bulk of contractual governance – an assumption that is not altogether warranted (Macaulay 1963; Macneil 1974; Palay 1984). However, as discussed above, recourse to the courts or administrative bodies was not available to the contracting parties studied here. Instead, they relied upon markets, private orderings, and vertical integration (Palay 1984).

In general, the type of governance supporting rail-freight transactions changed as investment characteristics varied (Palay 1984). The concern uppermost in the minds of the parties was how they were to obtain the performance promised when the contract in question was not enforceable in a court of law. The issue was not so much on how parties would force their contracting opposites to provide specific performance, but on how they would ensure that they received the services they needed, regardless of the source of those services. In general the data supported the hypothesis that where investment is standardized, the enforcement mechanism tends to be market oriented. However, as the investment becomes more idiosyncratic, the means of ensuring enforcement tends, as predicted, to be transactions specific (Palay 1984).

By market oriented I am referring to an emphasis on fulfilling the terms of the agreement by recourse to substitute sources, rather than on enforcing the existing agreement. For example, carrier R moved sanitary tissue paper for shipper K. To do so, the railroad invested heavily in both physical and human capital, little of which was particularly specialized. The rolling stock tended to be free-running general service rail cars that were easily transferable among shippers, carriers, and uses. Either the fifty-foot/seventy-ton or the sixty foot/one-hundred-ton boxcar was used. The railroad indicated that its primary protection from shipper's ability to take advantage of him at the renegotiation or recontracting phase was market related. If shipper failed to live up to the agreement carrier could transfer its cars to some other user. When it came right down to it, R's willingness to bind its future to K was premised on its knowledge that it did not have to trust shipper to fulfil its end of the bargain. If K failed to deliver on its promise, R would suffer only momentary losses and could stop delivering equipment. Similarly, it was clear that carrier appreciated the constraints imposed on it because shipper had alternative means of transporting its sanitary paper to final customers. As the carrier stated, 'Competiton from truck is what keeps us from raising our prices too high. Our costs, and competition from other railroads, keeps us from setting them too low.'

Where investments were only moderately idiosyncratic – i.e., where it is difficult, but not impossible to find alternative uses for capital assets used in the transaction – enforcement tended to be of a mixed type. In most of the cases studied the parties talked of both the existence of alternatives and the reputation for fair dealing of the parties with whom they dealt (Palay 1984).

For instance, carrier T moved large quantities of aluminum sheet and plate to fabricating facilities owned by shipper D and located at various destinations throughout the United States. The transaction involved moderately idiosyncratic investment. Semi-finished aluminum is transferred in covered coil cars or specially designed and outfitted boxcars. These cars can be shifted between shippers of semifinished metals, but their value is significantly reduced outside the movement of coils and sheet. The contract between T and D entailed trading volume commitments for specified service standards and a guarantee of railcars. When asked to describe what it was that held the informal contractual relations together, T equivocated. In one breath it clearly mentioned and talked about trust and realized mutuality of interest.

> 'We've been dealing with [shipper D] from the beginning. When they located and designed their plant they knew we'd be one of their primary carriers. I believe what they tell us. They know how we operate; that we're an honest bunch of people. Neither one of us plays games. I like dealing with them.' Nevertheless, in the next breath carrier T was careful to point out its potential market alternatives: 'We work very hard to maintain our image of integrity and fair play. We're very business-like. But I guarantee you that [shipper D] knows that if he pushes me once too often he'll find himself sitting around with a lot of aluminum sheet and no cars. Alternatively, we could stop investing money in new equipment for him' (Palay 1984: 275).

Where investments were highly idiosyncratic, enforcement was premised either on a realized mutuality of interest (private orderings) or internal organization. Before investors make expenditures on idiosyncratic capital, their expectations must be reasonably secure. To facilitate the process both shippers and carriers felt it crucial to maintain reputations for honesty, integrity, and trustworthiness. Opportunistic conduct could destroy any established reputation effects. Concern over appearing honest, therefore, seems to have forced the parties to be so. In order to maintain reputations, shippers and carriers simply did not take advantage of the *ex post* small-numbers bargaining conditions. Instead, trust relations developed.

For instance, with respect to the movement of finished automobiles described above, both parties were asked to describe what, if anything, kept the other party from backing out of its commitments. Each party emphasized that 'we need them as much as they need us,' and the 'business-like' behaviour of the other. The parties had developed a relationship that, as carrier admitted, other divisions viewed with a mix of envy, that advantageous accommodations could be reached so readily, and suspicion, that an affinity with one's customer might lead to overly generous concessions. Shipper, too, noted the duality of responses from others within its company and was careful to describe the situation as being 'strictly a good faith' relation, 'honest and business-like, but not social'.

Both shipper and carrier were apparently reluctant to exploit short-term advantages if it would lead to harm in the long-run relation. For example, amortization agreements were used to offset the risk that slumping auto sales, an auto industry strike, or a major design change might render the existing auto racks useless. Neither party, though, believed that the rack-car amortization agreements were legally enforceable. The understandings were primarily used to reduce ambiguity, to reinforce shipper's 'moral commitment' to share the risk of idiosyncratic investment, and to reduce the unease of some of carrier's operations (as opposed to marketing) people. Despite the legal unenforceability of amortization agreements, shipper had several times paid off the unamortized portion of cars when it was shipper's actions that rendered the rolling stock useless. Both parties pointed to the example of the 'Epsilon' railcar, produced exclusively to move shipper's Epsilon model automobile. When shipper drastically altered the design of the automobile the rail cars were rendered useless. The automobile manufacturer subsequently reimbursed carrier slightly more than $1 million for the unamortized portion of the investment, though it believed it had no legally enforceable obligation to do so.

The development of the relationships that underlie private orderings takes both real resources and time. However, once the relations are successfully developed, both parties have the ability to make credible requests, reject inadequate offers, and make long-term commitments.

Alternatively, some of the parties who made highly idiosyncratic investments safeguarded contracts by combining the realized mutuality of interest described above with vertical integration. A good example of this type of enforcement involves shipper E, a major producer of chemical products. Of those chemicals that were moved by rail, most travelled in tank cars or in covered hoppers. The former were among the most specialized cars in general use. They were usually constructed to be substance-specific. Glass or rubber linings, specialized pressure valves, and damage control equipment are but a few examples of the unique equipment employed. Quality control and safety concerns prevented the transfer of cars across products or manufacturers. Utilization patterns simply made it too costly to attempt to modify a car to handle a new product after each trip, and cleaning involved expensive facilities and technologies. In addition, shipper used carrier in a pipeline capacity. Thus specialized coordination and handling were required to maintain a constant flow.

To guarantee safety and quality control, shipper employed a governance structure premised on vertical integration. It owned in excess of ten thousand rail cars. To enforce the other aspects of any agreement realized mutuality of interest was employed. The chemical industry is, in the words of one market manager, a 'handshake industry, where your word is your bond'. Shipper E, for instance, wanted to move a million tons of a substance from origin to destination. Carrier X offered to transport the substance at a price of 69 cents per hundredweight. Carrier Y, however, offered to publish a rate of 63 cents per hundredweight. E readily accepted X's offer because (1) it felt it to be more realistic, but, more important, (2) it knew that when X's representative promised a particular rate that price would be in force for a significant period. Even after Y changed its filed rate to 75 cents per hundredweight, carrier X did not raise its price. As carrier X's chemical manager stated: 'It's far more important that they believe I'm reliable than that we jack the price up on them. Maybe I could have gotten more out of them, but now I have them on the hook. Besides, they believe me when I come calling.' E could have accepted Y's initial offer and then switched to X if the former raised its price. However, it was unable to accept the performance losses associated with any switch over. In addition, shipper was concerned that switching to railroad Y would create the impression that it was willing to deal 'fast and loose' with the railroads.

CONCLUSION. I have argued that informal contracting was an important method of effectively altering the regulatory scheme of the Interstate Commerce Act. Informal contracting has several virtues to commend it as a means of avoiding regulatory constraints. First, it can be transaction- or firm-specific. There is no need to develop 'industry-wide' policies. To 'fine tune' a regulation the parties need do nothing more than fix the particular problem that concerns them. There is, for instance, no need to reach a compromise with potential coalition partners in the legislature as would be necessary in effectuating comprehensive reform. In addition, informal contracting is more timely than other strategies. Regulation, litigation, or lobbying involves substantial lags. Informal contracting provides the parties a means of making adjustments in relatively short order. Finally, informal contracting has the added virtue of preserving the fundamental structure of an existing regulatory cartel, and any accompanying monopoly profits, while effectively permitting the parties to cheat on their cartel partners. The parties can avoid the constraints of the cartel with respect to some transactions but remain in it with regard to others.

THOMAS PALAY

See also ASSET SPECIFICITY AND VERTICAL INTEGRATION; CONTRACTS AND RELATIONSHIPS; CORPORATE GOVERNANCE; LAWYERS AS TRANSACTION COST ENGINEERS; OPPORTUNISTIC BEHAVIOUR IN CONTRACTS; REGULATION AND DEREGULATION; RELATIONAL CONTRACT.

Subject classification: 6a.

STATUTES

Interstate Commerce Act 49 USC A7; §10101 et seq. *as amended by* Public Law No. 95–473 (October 17, 1978).

BIBLIOGRAPHY

Goldberg, V. 1976. Regulation and administered contracts. *Bell Journal of Economics* 7: 426–48.

Klein, B., Crawford, R. and Alchian, A. 1978. Vertical integration, appropriable rents, and the competitive contracting process. *Journal of Law and Economics* 21: 297–326.

Locklin, D.P. 1972. *Economics of Transportation*. Homewood, IL: Richard D. Irwin.

Macaulay, S. 1963. Non-contractual relations in business. *American Sociological Review* 28: 55–70.

Macneil, I. 1974. The many futures of contracts. *Southern California Law Review* 43: 691–816.
Palay, T. 1981. The governance of rail-freight contracts: a comparative institutional approach. PhD Dissertation, University of Pennsylvania.
Palay, T. 1984. Comparative institutional economics: The governance of rail freight contracting. *Journal of Legal Studies* 13: 265–87.
Palay, T. 1985. Avoiding regulatory constraints: contracting safeguards and the role of informal agreements, *Journal of Law, Economics, and Organization* 1: 155–75.
Williamson, O.E. 1975. *Markets and Hierarchies: Analysis and Antitrust Implications*. New York: Free Press.
Williamson, O.E. 1976. Franchise bidding for natural monopolies – in general and with respect to CATV. *Bell Journal of Economics* 7: 73–104.
Williamson, O.E. 1979. Transaction-cost economics: the governance of contractual relations. *Journal of Law and Economics* 22: 233–61.
Williamson, O.E. 1983. Credible commitments: using hostages to support exchange. *American Economic Review* 73: 519–40.

informational cascades and social conventions. A striking regularity of human society is localized conformity. At one school teenagers experiment with drugs and sex while at another they 'just say no'. Time variation is striking as well, as with swings across decades among college-aged youths between pacifism and enthusiastic enlistment for war. Social popularity and acceptance of different religious practices, crime, vices and musical styles have fluctuated rapidly.

Localization in time or place may seem to cast doubt upon the rationality of decision-makers, since variations in behaviours and social conventions often are not associated with obvious variations in costs and benefits. In such cases, how can both old and new behaviours be optimal for those that engage in them? For example, if a Teenage Mutant Ninja Turtle children's toy is preferred by most children one year, what makes Beanie babies preferable another year?

The main theme of this essay is that learning by observing the actions of others can explain the conformity, idiosyncrasy, and fragility of many types of social behaviour. When people within a group observe one another's behaviour, they very often end up making the same choices. Thus, localized conformity. The decisions of an informed individual are a valuable resource to those who decide later. Self-interested individuals will not try to act in a way that makes their actions as informative as possible to followers. Thus, if early-movers err, followers are likely to imitate the mistake, leading to idiosyncrasy. If later on a few people start behaving differently for whatever reason, then the old convention may be swept away by rational imitation of the new behaviour; hence fragility. Such imitation can explain either transient fads or permanent choices among alternative products, sexual and marital options, scientific theories, and religious beliefs.

Social conventions are practices, procedures or rules for acceptable behaviour in a group. Often there is strong reason to have a convention, while its specific form is relatively arbitrary (as with driving on the right- versus left-hand side of the road). In other cases, the alternatives are not equally good for those involved, as with a convention that members of an organization are not permitted (or are permitted) to speak first in the presence of higher-ranking members.

There are several possible mechanisms for maintaining conventions, most of which imply rigid behaviour in the face of changing circumstances. For example, the threat of sanctions upon deviants (e.g., Akerlof 1976, 1980; Coleman 1987; Kuran 1989, 1991; and Hirshleifer and Rasmusen 1989), can lock a dysfunctional social convention in place. Only seldom can a small shock affect the behaviour of many individuals.

Payoff interactions can cause one individual's action to increase directly the benefit to another of doing the same thing (see Schelling 1978; Farrell and Saloner 1985; Arthur 1989; Katz and Shapiro 1994; for a sceptical viewpoint, see Liebowitz and Margolis 1994). Thus, conventions such as driving on the right-hand side of the road are self-enforcing. Relatedly, individuals may have a direct conformity preference to do the same things that others are doing, or may have a preference to follow accepted norms of behaviour (Elster 1989; Lindbeck 1995). The stable action may not be the best one (Jones 1984). As Becker (1991) shows, a seller may price close to the edge of demand instability.

With parallel reasoning, everyone independently figures out the best alternative. With direct communication, those who figure out the best choice pass their information on to others. Neither theory explains why poor conventions (or more general, poor choices) may be fixed upon.

The tendency of individuals to imitate means that conventions can be maintained voluntarily, even when suboptimal. Errors begun by a few individuals can be transmitted through society, often leading to a mistaken outcome that is at least temporarily stable. Such imitation can be based upon rational weighing of pros and cons. Individuals arriving in sequence to buy film tickets, for example, can gain useful information about the quality of the show by observing queues of earlier arrivers. An individual may imitate the choices of predecessors even if his own limited information is opposing. Welch (1992) and Bikhchandani, Hirshleifer and Welch (1992) call such ignoring of own-information an *informational cascade* (see also Banerjee 1992).

Often, conventions will be maintained by a combination of forces, including sanctions, conformity preference, and rational imitation. During stable times, sanctions may be highly effective. However, during times of possible change, people will be hungry for information about whether the current social convention will remain in place. As a result, actions by a few individuals may again become extremely influential, leading to idiosyncratic outcomes.

The self-reinforcing effects of imitation give sellers of consumer products a strong incentive to induce early-movers to buy, as when new restaurants and performers hire people to attend and display enthusiasm conspicuously. The common phenomenon of low introductory prices for new products is thus a natural response by sellers to the possibility of buyer cascades.

Bikhchandani, Hirshleifer and Welch (1992) (henceforth BHW) show that informational cascades often develop spontaneously on the basis of very little information. People converge upon one action quite rapidly, and their decisions are *idiosyncratic* and *fragile*. In the BHW model, a sequence of individuals make successive choices (e.g., between two films) based on both private information received by each individual and on the observed decisions of earlier movers. With many individuals, with virtual certainty a point is reached where an individual rationally ignores his private information and bases his decision solely upon what he sees predecessors do. The accumulated evidence from predecessors outweighs his private information. The decision of this individual n is uninformative to later choosers. Thus, individual $n + 1$ is no better informed than individual n, so she also joins the cascade. This reasoning extends to all later individuals. (Of course, this conclusion does not *always* follow: later movers may have different costs and benefits from adopting, or different accuracy of their private information signals.) For example, consider the stigma placed upon gaps in a personal resumé. A rational employer can reasonably infer that other employers have probably detected something negative about the applicant. After enough rejection, even a good worker may become virtually unemployable.

In the cascades model, actions fluctuate randomly until the system lands at a *precariously stable* resting point, like a car teetering on the edge of a precipice. As decisions are made, evidence (in the form of past decisions) gradually accumulates in favour of one action or another. An action is fixed upon when the weight of the decision history grows just strong enough to overcome one individual's opposing information. At that point, if the next individual is similar, he also is barely willing to ignore his own information signal, i.e., he is in a cascade. Since all further identical individuals do the same thing, a very small preponderance of evidence causes a landslide in favour of one alternative. Thus, a very small shock such as new public information can alter the behaviour of many. So the restaurant, clothing style or political election campaign that is 'in' this week may be 'out' the next for no apparent reason.

Precarious stability is unlikely to last forever. An initially mistaken cascade can be corrected quite quickly as new information arrives. Of course, if the cascade is for a non-repeated activity (such as seeing a given movie or buying shares of a given initial public offering) or an infrequent activity (such as buying a car), this corrective force is less powerful.

The possibility of cascades does not mean that all social conventions are precarious. Those enforced by strong payoff dependence (driving on the right hand side of the road) or powerful sanctions (expressing support for a dictatorial superior) can be very stable. Others can be stable by virtue of their arbitrariness. The convention of shaking hands as a greeting is unlikely to suddenly shift to an alternative such as clasping arms since it is clear that neither has any strong inherent superiority. However, a social convention that cohabitation will occur only after marriage may change partly as a result of conspicuous violations by individuals.

Conventions enforced by social stigma have multiple levels. At the basic level is the prescribed or proscribed action (e.g., do not cohabit before marriage), but a higher punishment level (reject those who cohabit before marriage) and further levels (e.g., reject those who fail to reject those who cohabit before marriage) are also needed. Information effects can be important at each meta-level. If the parents of a cohabiting couple fail to impose sanctions, other parents may conclude that this is the best response. If a cascade of not imposing sanctions starts, the convention will collapse.

1. THE BASIC MODEL. Consider a setting where each individual observes only the *actions* of predecessors, not their information signals. ('Actions speak louder than words.') Each individual in a sequence observes the decisions (smoking or not) of all predecessors. Everyone has the same costs and benefits from adopting the behaviour. If smoking is healthful its net value is +$1, and if harmful, –$1, with equal probability. Each individual then privately observes a private signal: H (favourable to smoking) versus L (unfavourable), which is informative, but inconclusive.

If adoption is the optimal action (adoption value +$1), each individual has a 3/4 chance of observing H, and a 1/4 chance of observing L. These probabilities are reversed if rejection is optimal (adoption value –$1). Given the optimal action, signals are independent, so Berenice may see L even if Ahmet sees H.

Each individual decides after observing his own information signal and the actions of predecessors. (If indifferent, he flips a fair coin.) In Figure 1, Ahmet, the first individual, adopts if he observes signal H and rejects if he sees L. So Berenice can infer that Ahmet adopted if and only if his signal was H. If Ahmet adopted, Berenice should also adopt if her signal was H. If Berenice's signal is L, it is offset by Ahmet's H signal, so she tosses a coin to decide. Similarly, if Ahmet rejected, Berenice rejects if she sees L, and tosses a coin if she sees H.

For Charles, if (1) both Ahmet and Berenice adopted, Charles adopts too, because he knows that Ahmet observed H, and that Berenice probably did too (though she may have seen L and flipped a coin). So Charles adopts even if he sees an L signal; he is in a *UP cascade*. Similarly, if (2) both predecessors rejected, Charles is in a *DOWN cascade*. If (3), Ahmet adopted and Berenice rejected (or vice versa), Charles knows that Ahmet observed H and Berenice observed L (or vice versa). Since these signals cancel, Charles follows his own signal.

In the cascades case wherein both predecessors adopted, since Charles adopts regardless of his signal, his action provides no information to successors about the desirability of smoking. So even if both Charles and Desi have L signals, Desi continues the UP cascade. This reasoning extends to Eric, Fiona, ... Linda, ... Zorro ... and so on. Since opposing information remains hidden, an early preponderance toward either adoption or rejection, however mistaken, is self-reinforcing.

The overall outcome is therefore idiosyncratic and history-dependent, even though individuals' information would, if combined, yield very accurate decisions. The discreteness of actions reduces their informativeness and, owing to cascades, increases the likelihood of error. There is indeed evidence that individuals' choices influence observers, as when farmers observed neighbours' adoption of hybrid corn (Ryan and Gross 1943). Going beyond the numerical example, cascades can form even if individuals observe only a few 'neighbours', or observe only a summary statistic of past actions.

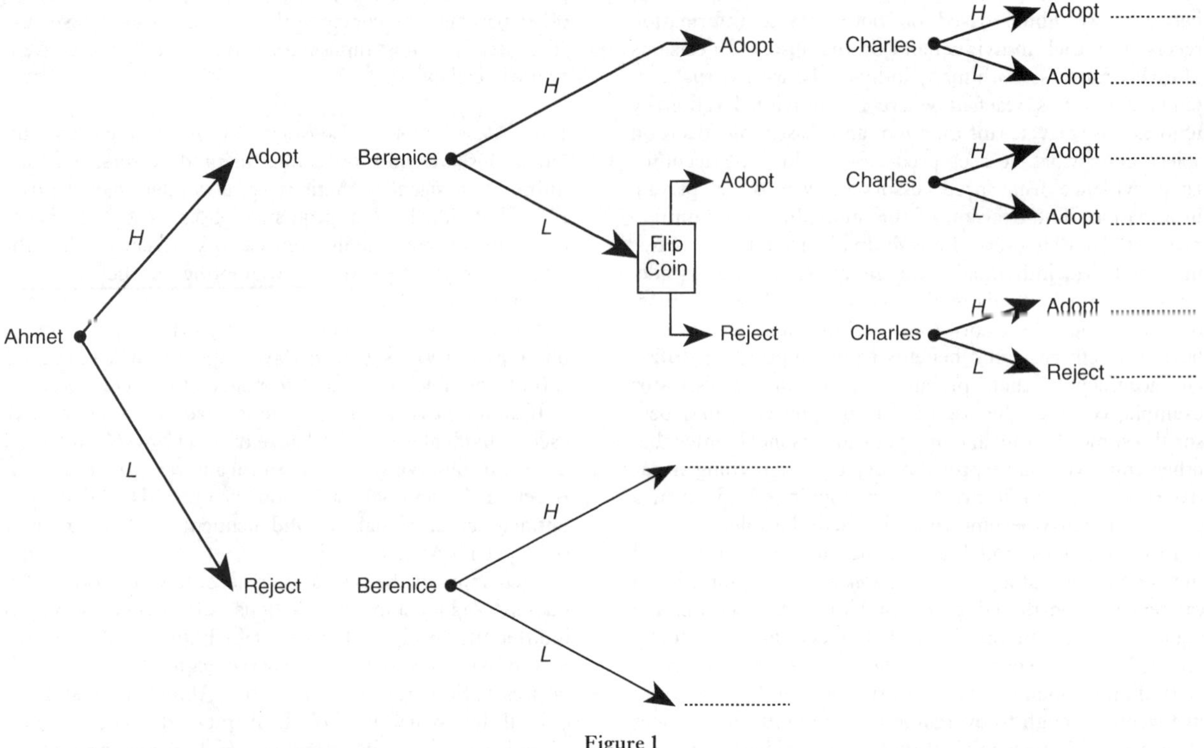

Figure 1

The fallibility of cascades makes them fragile. If some individuals have more precise signals than others, or if public news is revealed at a later date, or if the relative desirability of adopting versus rejecting changes, then cascades are easily reversed. Thus, cascades help explain fads in which the actions of large groups of individuals suddenly change in response to a very small stimulus.

In this setting, cascades must arise eventually (see BHW 1992; Banerjee 1992). Intuitively, information keeps accumulating until a fairly mild preponderance of evidence favours one or the other action. Once this happens, a cascade starts, so the public information pool is not very conclusive. Typically, cascades begin surprisingly soon. For example, even if signals are almost pure noise, the probability of a cascade forming after ten individuals is greater than 99%!

The probability of a DOWN cascade after two individuals *given that in fact adopting is superior* can be remarkably high. With a signal accuracy of 60%, so that when adopting is preferable 60% of the time an H signal is observed, about 1/3 of the time the wrong cascade results. Owing to cascades, long-term outcomes depend heavily on chance circumstances and early choices.

1.1 *Fashion leaders.* When information precisions differ, the idiosyncrasy of cascades can become more extreme. In the binary signal example, the action of a single initial expert may cause millions to follow. If everyone knows that Ahmet, a doctor, has slightly better information about whether or not to eat oat bran, and if Ahmet acts first, a cascade starts *immediately*. Berenice should imitate her better-informed predecessor, making her action uninformative. If Charles is like Berenice he also imitates, and the cascade continues indefinitely. Ahmet sways a long train of followers even though his information is far less accurate than the *combined* information of a thousand individuals like Berenice.

When individuals decide *when* to move, BHW conjecture that higher-precision individuals will tend to act first, since they have less to gain from observing others (see Zhang 1997). Thus cascades should form extremely rapidly (after one individual), which may be disastrous.

In contrast, if Ahmet has slightly *lower* information precision than those who follow him, his action does *not* start a cascade; Berenice should follow her own signal. This hurts Berenice slightly, but now her action is informative to all who follow. Charles and all successors therefore benefit substantially. Thus, modest early differences in precision can make a big difference later. If a higher-precision individual shows up late, he can shatter a cascade, because he is more inclined to use his own information signal. His action then conveys valuable information to those who follow him.

This suggests that decision-makers should be ordered inversely to their precisions. Perhaps this is why, according to the Talmud, the ancient Hebrew judges of the Sanhedrin voted in inverse order of seniority, a practice also followed in US Navy courts-martial. More generally, judges sitting in lower-level courts making initial judgments are normally less experienced (less precise?) than those in higher appellate courts.

There is indeed evidence that ill-informed decision-makers imitate accurate ones (see the applications below). Experiments have found that a human subject's failure in a task raises the probability that in further trials he will imitate a role-model (Thelen et al. 1979). Children instinctively imitate their parents and teachers. Newborns as early as 42 minutes old imitate the facial expressions of adults. Indeed, Meltzoff (1988) suggests that imitation is such a fundamental propensity of the human infant that we should be called '*homo imitans*'. Imitation of high prestige individuals may be based on a belief that the prestigious are good decision-makers. As Bandura (1977) says, 'in situations in which people are uncertain about the wisdom of modeled courses of action, they must rely on such cues as general appearances, speech, style, age, symbols of socio-economic success, and signs of expertise as indicators of past successes.'

2. FRAGILITY OF CASCADES: THE PUBLIC RELEASE OF INFORMATION. The conformity brought about by cascades remains brittle even after many individuals adopt. Thus, the arrival of a little information, or the mere possibility of a value change (even if the change does not actually occur), can shatter an informational cascade.

The release of public information *prior to the start of a cascade* can make some individuals worse off (in an *ex ante* sense). Public information release has two effects on an individual: (i) it provides information directly, and (ii) it changes the decisions of predecessors, and hence the information conveyed thereby. A film review that provides very noisy information is only slightly useful to Berenice. However, an adverse review may lead Ahmet to reject when he would otherwise have marginally accepted. This can make rejection by Ahmet less informative to Berenice. This indirect disadvantage to Berenice of public information release can sometimes outweigh the direct benefit.

Thus, it is not obvious that health authorities should quickly disseminate noisy information. Sketchy disclosures of possible advantages of oat bran, fish-oil, or Prozac can trigger harmful fads. Of course, clear-cut information (e.g., smoking causes cancer) is likely to benefit all users.

Once a cascade starts, individuals' decisions convey no further information. An informative public disclosure at this point cannot reduce the information conveyed by individuals' decisions. So identical individuals welcome public information. Such a public disclosure may therefore be beneficial. How much public information is required to shatter an established cascade? Even a public signal less informative than the private signal of a single individual can do the trick. Thus, a film reviewer whose information is not better than others' can still sway thousands.

In the illustrative model given earlier, suppose that adoptions and rejections are evenly split until Eric and Fiona both adopt. Successors recognize two possibilities: (1) both received favourable (H) signals, or (2) Eric observed H and Fiona observed L, leading her to flip a coin. Consider a film review almost as informative as a typical viewer's signal. Gerard can reason that even if Eric and Fiona *both* observed H, a negative film review almost cancels out one H. So if Gerard observes L, he is almost indifferent. Since Fiona may actually have observed L, Gerard should reject, breaking the cascade.

3. EXAMPLES. Cascades occur when individuals with inconclusive private information make discrete decisions sequentially. This section discusses how well the cascades model's assumptions and implications fit some actual applications. Some criteria pertaining to model assumptions are: (i) Do individuals observe the actions of others?; (ii) Do individuals learn from direct discussion with others?; and (iii) Are informational effects more important than other effects?

Point (ii) is not crucial, since 'actions speak louder than words'. Regarding (iii), non-informational factors (sanctions against deviants, payoff interdependence, desire to conform) are often present. Thus, we cannot conclude from uniformity of behaviour that cascades are present. However, sometimes payoff interactions are negative, which *opposes* uniformity. An early entrant in a new line of business is a potential competitor to followers. If such entrance attracts followers, this suggests that information effects are overcoming negative payoff interaction. When payoff interactions, sanctions, or conformity preference do support uniformity, learning by observing the actions of others and informational cascades may still describe the process which determines which alternative is fixed upon.

A second group of criteria pertains to implications of the theory: (i) Is behaviour localized and idiosyncratic (often mistaken)? (ii) Is behaviour fragile? and (iii) Do individuals follow predecessors in opposition to their own private information? These implications help distinguish informational cascades from non-informational theories that are generally inconsistent with implications (i) – (iii).

3.1 *Peer influence and stigma.* Why does crime vary widely over time and location, even after holding constant socio-economic factors such as poverty? According to Kahan (1997), a crucial source of variation is that individuals learn about what sort of behaviour is profitable and acceptable by observing the actions of others. Thus, either high- or low-crime equilibria are possible under a given set of external conditions. Consistent with the cascades approach, he suggests that policies which affect the ability of individuals to observe criminal behaviour of others (such as curfews, anti-loitering, and 'zero tolerance' policies) can dramatically affect overall crime rates.

According to Keegan (1987), based on his personal conduct on the battlefield Alexander the Great was '... the supreme hero'. For example, 'at Multan, he attempted to take the city virtually single-handed. It was thus that he suffered his nearly fatal wound.' The example of Alexander's astonishing courage inspired others to fight harder. Pakenham (1979: 133) describes the willingness of English officers to risk their lives in order to rally the troops in the Boer War. More generally, in battle, waves of optimism or pessimism often make the difference between victory and defeat. A deserter not only denies *aid* to comrades (payoff interaction), but may cause an *inference* that he viewed victory to be unlikely. Thus, heroic leadership may have an informational basis. As in the fashion leader model, the actions of officers who know more about the prospects for victory should strongly influence the morale and behaviour of the troops.

Conformity to peers in general is often assumed

automatically to be due to coercion rather than informational effects. (Contrast the popularity of the pejorative phrase 'peer pressure', with the more neutral term 'peer influence'.) The cascades theory emphasizes the voluntary nature of conformity, especially among the inexperienced and uninformed. Genuine coercion can arise from the threat of stigma, a shared negative treatment of someone who violates group norms. But stigma may sometimes have informational roots: a frequent job- or marriage partner-switcher may have been rejected by others.

3.2 *Politics.* The political scientist Bartels (1988) has discussed 'cue-taking' in presidential nomination campaigns, in which one person's assessment of a candidate is influenced by the choices of others: '. . . "25,000 solid New Hampshirites (probably) can't be too far wrong."' Several studies have found that respondents who are aware of favourable poll results rate a candidate more favourably. Bartels points out (consistent with the cascades theory) that 'There need not be any actual process of persuasion . . . the fact of the endorsement itself motivates me to change my substantive opinion of . . . [the candidate].' While non-informational theories can explain why poll results influence *voting*, they do not explain why poll results influence *approval ratings*. According to the cascades theory, approval ratings of a candidate should increase after early victories. Bartels found such an 'internalized effect' in the early stages of the 1984 Hart–Mondale contest for the Democratic nomination.

A common criticism of the primary system is that voters in early primaries carry disproportionate weight, as with the Iowa voters who gave an obscure candidate named Jimmy Carter a conspicuous early success in the 1976 US presidential campaign. As a result, many Southern states have coordinated their primaries on the same date ('Super-Tuesday'). Many regard early reporting of election results as undesirable because results may influence later voters. Several European countries prohibit publication of poll results close to the dates of elections.

Public protests, demonstrations and political riots can also convey information to observers. In Lohmann (1992), such actions occur repeatedly over time, and turnout fluctuates until a cascade forms. Since people have different gains from a political regime change, and choose when to protest, protests convey information gradually over time. An unexpectedly high turnout, even if the numbers are small, communicates stronger opposition to the regime, stimulating further turnout. Based on evidence from sequences of polls of demonstrators in five cycles of protest in Leipzig and the public at large, Lohmann (1994) argues that a dynamic informational cascades model provides the most satisfactory explanation for the process by which communism fell in then-East Germany.

3.3 *Zoology.* Even for animals, vicarious learning beats hard experience. Animals frequently copy the behaviour of others in territory choice, mating and foraging. Territorial animals cluster more than can be accounted for by the clustering of high-quality sites; territories are often not clumped at the best available sites (Stamps 1988). According to the cascades theory, the location of clusters will be fairly idiosyncratically determined by the choices of a few early settlers. Indeed, some zoologists argue that males take the presence of nearby males' territories as an indicator of high resource quality.

In several species, females copy other females in choosing a mate. Pomiankowski (1990) discusses evidence of imitation by females in fallow deer and sage grouse. Gibson et al. (1992) found that sage grouse females make more uniform mate choices when they arrive at the male mating display area together, so that they can observe which males other females choose. The unanimity of mate choice is not explained by any characteristics of males or sites detectable to human researchers. This arbitrariness is consistent with informational cascades.

Remarkably, Dugatkin (1992: 1388) shows that

> . . . females [of the Trinidadian guppy *Poecilia reticulata*] copy the choice of mates made by other females by viewing such interactions, remembering the identity of the chosen male, and subsequently choosing that male in future sexual endeavors.

Dugatkin and Godin (1993: 291) find that '. . . younger females copy the mate choice of older females, but older females do not appear to be influenced by the mate choice of younger individuals.' This is consistent with the 'fashion leader' model at the end of Section 1. Older females, being more experienced at choosing males, are presumably able to interpret environmental cues more accurately than younger females. Dugatkin and Godin (1992) established that:

> . . . copying can even override a female's original preference of mates . . . That is, a female's preference for a particular male . . . can be reversed if she has the opportunity to see a (model) female choose the male she herself did not choose previously.

This experiment identifies a key aspect of informational cascades, that an individual's private information can be overridden by the observation of others' actions.

3.4 *Medical practice and scientific theory.* Most doctors are not at the cutting edge of research; their inevitable reliance upon what colleagues have done or are doing leads to numerous surgical fads and treatment-caused illnesses ('iatroepidemics') (Taylor 1979; Robin 1984). The cascades theory predicts fads, idiosyncrasy, and imitation in medical treatments. The practice of bleeding to remove bad blood, popular until the nineteenth century, is a familiar example. Many dubious practices seem to have been adopted initially based on weak information. Examples include the popularization in the 1970s of elective hysterectomy (the routine surgical removal of the uterus of women past child-bearing age), and routine tonsillectomy (the surgical removal of tonsils). An English panel (quoted in Taylor 1979) asserted that tonsillectomy was being '. . . performed as a routine prophylactic ritual for no particular reason and with no particular result'. Also notable are the extreme differences in tonsillectomy frequencies in different countries and regions.

Burnum discusses 'bandwagon diseases' diagnosed by physicians who behave

. . . like lemmings, episodically and with a blind infectious enthusiasm pushing certain diseases and treatments primarily because everyone else is doing the same (1987: 1221).

Since even one adoption can start a cascade, patients seeking a second opinion should consider withholding the first doctor's diagnosis.

Academia is notorious for fads and fashions. The volume and complexity of material a scholar must process makes it impossible to examine criticially the evidence underlying all major theories relevant for a line of research. Since knowledge is interrelated, scholars are compelled to specialize and then accept useful theories and techniques from other areas because *others have done so*.

In the fashion leader model, the decision by the first (well-informed) individual persuaded everyone after to imitate. In academics, nascent theories do seem to enjoy greater success when the initiator is famous and from a major university. The cascades theory implies that academic eminence is itself idiosyncratic. Since it is costly to assess the achievements of another researcher, we accord respect to those who have been acclaimed. As Ghiselin says: 'The mere fact of eminence provides a cheap substitute for inquiring as to the basis upon which that eminence rests' (1989: 160–61). Similarly, an academic job applicant who receives a few prestigious interviews or early job offers may become a 'star', attracting offers widely as a result. Similar imitation is common in tenure decisions and the appointments to chaired professorships. The idiosyncrasy of academic eminence makes the choices of academic fashion leaders noisier, which can cause errors in the initial acceptance or rejection of new ideas.

3.5 *Finance.* Foresi and Mei (1991, 1992) provide evidence consistent with imitation in corporate investment decisions. An important discrete investment is the purchase of another firm. Firms that are 'put into play' by a takeover bid often receive immediate competing offers. Yet competing for an in-play target is more expensive than buying a target not sought by a competitor. This suggests that potential bidders learn from the first bid that the target is an attractive candidate for takeover. More broadly, takeover markets have been subject to seemingly idiosyncratic booms and crashes, such as the wave of conglomerate mergers in the 1960s and 1970s, in which firms diversified across different industries, and the subsequent refocusing of firms through restructuring and bust-up takeovers in the 1980s.

Several models of individual investment are based on imitation of predecessors. Welch (1992) focuses on informational cascades among purchasers of equity being issued publicly for the first time; see also Noah (1997). When a distressed firm seeks to renegotiate its debt, the refusal of one creditor may make others more sceptical. Similarly, if some bank depositors withdraw their funds from a troubled bank, others may follow, leading to a bank run. In both examples, there is a payoff as well as an informational interaction: early withdrawals hurt loyal depositors. However, at the very start of the bank run, when only a few depositors have withdrawn, the *information* conveyed by actions may be the dominating influence upon other depositors. An analysis of informational cascades in the start of bank runs is provided by Corb (1993). Chen (1993) examines contagious cascades of runs between banks.

Stock market price fluctuations have often been described with such phrases as 'manias', 'panics', 'fads', 'animal spirits', 'investor sentiment' and 'bubbles'. In the basic cascades model the cost of 'adopting' (buying a stock) is constant. In practice, a wave of purchases will drive up price. Lee (1993) has shown that market booms and crashes can occur in a cascades model that endogenizes price. Gervais (1995) shows that cascades can occur that limit the information investors learn through price about other investors.

4. FADS. Customs and standards sometimes shift abruptly without obvious reason. Since in the basic cascades model individuals make irrevocable decisions in strict sequence, *fads* are defined here as shifts in behaviour between early and later individuals based on little news. However, the cascades concept extends to settings in which individuals choose a time to switch from one behaviour to another (Lohmann 1992; Chamley and Gale 1994; Caplin and Leahy 1994; Grenadier 1997).

The kind of shock to the system considered here is a small probability that the underlying value of adopting versus rejecting can change after the 100th individual (say). If it used to be better to adopt, and now it is better to reject, then people may notice this fact and act accordingly. More interestingly, the cascade can switch not just because the right action has changed, but because people think it may have changed. Since individuals are not confident that the initial cascade was correct, they shift at the slightest provocation. For example, even if adopting was optimal and the original cascade was correct, individual 101 may happen to observe an L signal and wrongly switch to rejecting because he thinks that now rejection has become superior. Thus, the likelihood of an action change (from a cascade of rejection to one of acceptance, or *vice versa*) can be far greater than the probability that the correct choice has changed. BHW (1992) provide a numerical example in which, after the 100th individual, there is a 5% chance of a switch in best action (from Adopt to Reject, or vice versa). This leads to a probability of over 9.35% that the cascade is at some point reversed, which is 87% higher.

I have focused on one source of fads, value changes. Other types of noise or shocks can have similar effects. For example, individuals who can't perfectly observe or recall what predecessors did (as in Banerjee and Fudenberg 1995; Cao and Hirshleifer 1995a), or think their costs and benefits differ, may be inclined to switch. Again, this can lead to abrupt shifts in the behaviour of many.

5. THE DECISION TO ACQUIRE INFORMATION. It is cheaper to rely on the decisions of others than to investigate yourself. Suppose that identical individuals decide in sequence whether to pay to investigate or to decline, and then whether to adopt or reject. Then, whenever an individual declines to investigate, all followers do likewise. For example, if Desi declines, then Eric knows no more than Desi, and his decision problem is identical. This reasoning extends to all successors.

A late individual is virtually sure to be in a cascade, in which case he would not use any purchased information. Thus, individuals who are late in the queue virtually never acquire information. Rogers and Shoemaker (1971) conclude from twelve empirical studies on diffusion of innovations that 'early adopters seek more information about innovations than later adopters'.

Even when individuals observe the *signals* of predecessors (not just actions), cascades can form and bring about idiosyncratic behaviour and fragility (see Smith and Sorenson 1995; Cao and Hirshleifer 1995b). As soon as public information favours one action over another enough to dominate one individual's signal, later individuals will imitate without investigating. The ability to observe predecessors can even reduce decision quality, if followers stop investigating and observe predecessors with noise (Cao and Hirshleifer 1995a). This is consistent with evidence of Gibson et al. (1992) that decision quality in sage grouse apparently declined when there were opportunities to observe others.

6. CONCLUSION. The theory of informational cascades helps explain how conventions arise, are maintained, and are broken. Since cascades start readily, based on very weak information, the conformist outcome is often mistaken. While this cascade of conventional behaviour can become quite long, it is not strong. A small shock, such as a public information disclosure, a value change, or even the possibility of such a change, can lead to an abrupt shift. In some theories of change, actions are unstable only if the system coincidentally is balanced near a knife-edge. Under informational cascades the system *systematically* moves to a precarious position; everyone is doing the same thing but just barely prefers to do so.

The basic cascades model implies occasional, irregular bouts of sudden change when people reestimate the costs and benefits of decision alternatives. In some theories of fads or fashion, change occurs regularly because individual preferences over alternatives directly depend on what others are doing. For example, whether a short skirt is acceptable this season depends on what others do. In practice, several forces may operate simultaneously. But even if people want to conform, for example, they face the informational issue of determining what decision others are expecting to be the norm (e.g., short or long skirts). Cascades theory suggests that in such situations the actions of the first few individuals will still be extremely influential, and can help explain the process by which society switches from one steady state to another.

I will mention two possible further extensions of the cascades approach to social conventions and change. First, in designing organizations or societies, it may be desirable to separate groups and later combine them, so that the information of several cascades can be aggregated. Khanna and Slezak (1994) study information flows in organizations. If subordinates have useful but noisy information, then an upward flow of project recommendations may preserve their information much more effectively than a decision process that moves downward through the hierarchy.

Second, if costs of adoption vary across individuals, then cascades of adoption can be broken. Hirshleifer and Welch (1995; in progress) show that cascades are just a special case of a more general phenomenon which we call inertia. When an individual such as a corporate manager can observe previous decisions (of his predecessor) but not previous signals, the new manager is often biased in favour of continuing and even *escalating* the old policies.

DAVID HIRSHLEIFER

See also CONVENTIONS; EFFICIENT NORMS; NETWORK EFFECTS AND EXTERNALITIES; NETWORK EXTERNALITY AND CONVENTION; PATH DEPENDENCE; SOCIAL NORMS AND THE LAW.

Subject classification: 1b(i); 1b(ii).

BIBLIOGRAPHY

Akerlof, G.A. 1976. The economics of caste and of the rat race and other woeful tales. *Quarterly Journal of Economics* 90(4): 599–617.

Akerlof, G.A. 1980. A theory of social custom, of which unemployment may be one consequence. *Quarterly Journal of Economics* 94: 749–75.

Arthur, W.B. 1989. Competing technologies, increasing returns, and lock-in by historical events. *Economic Journal* 99: 116–31.

Bandura, A. 1977. *Social Learning Theory*. Englewood Cliffs, NJ: Prentice Hall.

Banerjee, A. 1992. A simple model of herd behaviour. *Quarterly Journal of Economics* 107: 797–817.

Banerjee, A. and Fudenberg, D. 1995. Word of mouth learning. Mimeo, MIT, September.

Bartels, L.M. 1988. *Presidential Primaries and the Dynamics of Public Choice*. Princeton: Princeton University Press.

Becker, G.S. 1991. A note on restaurant pricing and other examples of social influences on price. *Journal of Political Economy* 99: 1109–16.

Bikhchandani, S. Hirshleifer, D. and Welch, I. 1992. A theory of fads, fashion, custom and cultural change as informational cascades. *Journal of Political Economy* 100(5): 992–1026.

Burnum, J.F. 1987. Medical practice à la mode: how medical fashion determines medical care. *New England Journal of Medicine* 317(19): 1220–22.

Cao, H. and Hirshleifer, D. 1995a. Limited observability, reporting biases, and informational cascades. Mimeo, University of Michigan, August.

Cao, H. and Hirshleifer, D. 1995b. Costly investigation and informational cascades. Mimeo, University of Michigan, April.

Caplin, A and Leahy, J. 1994. Business as usual, market crashes, and wisdom after the fact. *American Economic Review* 84: 548–65.

Chamley, C. and Gale, D. 1994. Information revelation and strategic delay in a model of investment. *Econometrica* 62: 1065–85.

Chen, Y. 1993. Payoff externality, information externality, and banking panics. UCLA Anderson Graduate School of Management, October.

Coleman, J. 1987. Norms as social capital. In *Economic Imperialism: The Economic Approach Applied Outside the Field of Economics*, ed. G. Radnitzky and P. Bernholz, New York: Paragon House.

Corb, H.M. 1993. The nature of bank runs. Graduate School of Business, Stanford University.

Dugatkin, L.A. 1992. Sexual selection and imitation: females copy the mate choice of others. *American Naturalist* 139: 1384–9.

Dugatkin, L.A. and Godin, J.-G.J. 1992. Reversal of female mate choice by copying in the guppy *Poecilia reticulata. Proceedings of the Royal Society of London*, Series B, 249:179–84.

Dugatkin, L.A. and Godin, J.-G. J. 1993. Female copying in the guppy *Poecilia reticulata*: age-dependent effects. *Behavioural Ecology* 4: 289–92.

Elster, J. 1989. Social norms and economic theory. *Journal of Economic Perspectives* 3(4): 99–117.

Farrell, J. and Saloner, G. 1985. Standardization, compatibility, and innovation. *RAND Journal of Economics* 16(1): 70–83.

Foresi, S. and Mei, J. 1991. Do firms 'keep up with the Joneses?': evidence on cross-sectional variations in investment. NYU Salomon Center Working Paper S-91–41, June.

Foresi, S. and Mei, J. 1992. Interaction in investment among Japanese rival firms. Mimeo, NYU, August.

Galef, B.G., Jr. 1976. Social transmission of acquired behaviour: a discussion of tradition and social learning in vertebrates. *Advances in the Study of Behaviour* 6: 77–100.

Gervais, S. 1995. Market microstructure with uncertain information precision: a multiperiod analysis. Mimeo, University of California at Berkeley, November.

Ghiselin, M. 1989. *Intellectual Compromise: The Bottom Line*. New York: Paragon House.

Gibson, R.M., Bradbury, J.W. and Vehrencamp, S.L. 1992. Mate choice in Lekking sage grouse revisited: the roles of vocal display, female site fidelity, and copying. *Behavioural Ecology* 2: 165–80.

Grenadier, S.R. 1997. Information revelation through option exercise. Mimeo, Stanford University Graduate School of Business.

Hirshleifer, D. and Rasmusen, E. 1989. Cooperation in a repeated prisoners' dilemma with ostracism. *Journal of Economic Behaviour and Organization* 12: 87–106.

Hirshleifer, D. and Welch, I. 1995. Institutional memory, inertia, and impulsiveness. University of Michigan Business School, Mitsui Life Working Paper No. 95–27.

Hirshleifer, D. and Welch. I. Institutional memory, escalation, and investment decisions. (In progress).

Jones, S.R.G. 1984. *The Economics of Conformism*. Oxford: Basil Blackwell.

Kahan, M. 1997. Social influence, social meaning, and deterrence. *Virginia Law Review* 83(3): 349–95.

Katz, M.L. and Shapiro, C. 1994. Systems competition and network effects. *Journal of Economic Perspectives* 8(2): 93–115.

Keegan, J. 1987. *The Mask of Command*. (New York: Elisabeth Sifton Books–Viking): 13–91.

Khanna, N. and Slezak, S. 1994. The effect of organizational form on information aggregation and project choice: the problem of informational cascades. University of Michigan Business School, September.

Kuran, T. 1989. Sparks and prairie fires: a theory of unanticipated political revolution. *Public Choice* 61: 41–74.

Kuran, T. 1991. Now out of never: the element of surprise in the East European revolution of 1989. *World Politics* 44: 7–48.

Lee, I.H. 1993. Market crashes and informational cascades. UCLA Economics Department.

Liebowitz, S.J. and Margolis, S.E. 1994. Network externality: an uncommon tragedy. *Journal of Economic Perspectives* 8(2): 133–50.

Lindbeck, A. 1995. Welfare state disincentives with endogenous habits and norms. *Scandinavian Journal of Economics* 97(4): 477–94.

Lohmann, S. 1992. Rationality, revolution and revolt: the dynamics of informational cascades. Graduate School of Business Research Paper No. 1213, Stanford University, October.

Lohmann, S. 1994. The dynamics of informational cascades: the Monday Demonstrations in Leipzig, East Germany, 1989–91. *World Politics* 47: 42–101.

Meltzoff, A.N. 1988. The human infant as *homo imitans*. In *Social Learning: Psychological and Biological Perspectives*, ed. T.R. Zentall and J.B.G. Galef (Hillsdale, NJ: Lawrence Erlbaum Associates): 319–41.

Noah, R.B. 1997. Reputation effects, sequential cascades and speculative investment. Mimeo, University of Michigan.

Pakenham, T. 1979. *The Boer War*. New York: Random House.

Pomiankowski, A. 1990. How to find the top male. *Nature* 347 (October): 616–17.

Robin, E.D. 1984. *Matters of Life and Death: Risks vs. Benefits of Medical Care*. New York: Freeman & Co.

Rogers, E.M. and Shoemaker, F.F. 1971. *Communication of Innovations: A Cross-Cultural Approach*. 2nd edn, New York: Free Press.

Rogers, E.M. 1983. *Diffusion of Innovation*. 3rd edn, New York: Free Press; London: Collier Macmillan.

Ryan, B. and Gross, N.C. 1943. The diffusion of hybrid seed corn in two Iowa communities. *Rural Sociology* 8: 15–24.

Schelling, T.C. 1978. *Micromotives and Macrobehavior*. New York: Norton.

Smith, L. and Sorenson, P. 1995. Pathological outcomes of observational learning. Mimeo, MIT, November.

Stamps, J.A. 1988. Conspecific attraction and aggregation in territorial species. *American Naturalist* 131 (March): 329–47.

Taylor, R. 1979. *Medicine Out of Control*. Melbourne: Sun Books.

Thelen, M.H., Dollinger, S.J. and Kirkland, K.D. 1979. Imitation and response uncertainty. *Journal of Genetic Psychology* 135: 139–52.

Welch, I. 1992. Sequential sales, learning and cascades. *Journal of Finance* 47: 695–732.

Zhang, J. 1997. Strategic delay and the onset of investment cascades. *RAND Journal of Economics* 28: 188–205.

information regulation. The economic theory of regulation provides justification for a variety of forms of regulation to address well-known and well-accepted forms of market failure. Examples of these market failures include monopoly power (controlled through, for example, rate regulation), externalities (addressed by, for example, emission taxes and standards), and public goods (accounted for through, for example, establishing property rights linked to permits). While students of price theory recognize that for markets to function efficiently consumers must have adequate information about the prices and the quality of the goods and services they purchase, it has only been in the last thirty years that economists have focused on regulatory remedies for these information-based market failures. The first part of this essay outlines the theory behind informational market failures and the possible remedies implied by this theory. The second part relates information-processing theories of consumer behaviour to information-based market failures. This analysis identifies an additional source of market imperfections related to information beyond those due to the unavailability of perfect information. In so doing, it points towards additional means by which government intervention in the form of regulation or information provision could, in principle, improve the efficiency with which markets operate. The final section applies these economic and information-processing theories of market failure to the use and design of product labels, an important example of information regulation.

ECONOMIC THEORIES OF INFORMATION REGULATION. Consumers acquire information about the goods and services they consider for purchase from a variety of different sources. If the products are readily available and the relevant quality characteristics are evident upon direct observation of the product, then observation serves to provide the requisite information. For characteristics which may not be so observable, sellers often provide information with the product on labels and in inserts (e.g., booklets and videos). Once the product or service is purchased, the relevant product characteristics usually become evident through experience.

Beyond information provided from direct observation and experience and from labels, information is also available from third parties. Some are independent sources such as general audience newspapers and magazines targeted solely at providing product information (e.g., *Consumer Reports*), while others are supported directly or indirectly by the product manufacturers, for example trade associations and the products' retailers and middlemen. Several indirect sources provide information about product quality through signals such as prices, advertising, and seller reputation, and through contract terms such as warranties and service guarantees.

When the information available to consumers from all of these sources is insufficient to provide complete information about a good or service, then competitive markets yield inefficient allocations and there is at least a potential role for government regulation to 'correct' for these informational market failures. Of course, government intervention can also fail to correct the market failures because accurate information is either costly or impossible to acquire and communicate, and often because government agencies lack the incentives either to acquire accurate and complete information or to act upon that information appropriately. Thus, the relevant policy question is whether government agencies can and will design information remedies that effectively address the information-based market failures at a cost less than the efficiency benefits that they provide.

Akerlof's famous 'lemons' market paper (1970) provides an early example of how the non-observability of product characteristics produces an inefficient market outcome in which sellers of high-quality products are willing to sell at prices below the amount that buyers are willing to pay, yet, without a credible way to convey, or guarantee, the high quality level of their products, no mutually beneficial exchanges take place. Consider the stylized example of a used car market with only 'good' and 'bad' cars, and in which buyers cannot observe the quality of cars offered for sale, yet sellers know the quality of their cars. Because buyers cannot distinguish between good and bad cars, all cars must sell at the same price. In addition, that price must be below the value of a good car for if the price equalled the value of a good car then buyers, knowing they would, on average, receive a car worth less than the price, would refrain from any purchases. With price below the value of a good car, no good cars will be placed on the market.

While provocative, the Akerlof model omits some important characteristics of market behaviour which reveal the product quality information possessed by sellers. Under some conditions prices convey information about product quality, although there is not always an equilibrium, and in some models there may be dispersion across consumers in the equilibrium prices (Salop and Stiglitz 1977). Beyond price, a variety of market signals provide information to consumers about product quality (Spence 1973, 1974). Much has been written about advertising as a market signal, but signals can take many other forms, such as sales effort, product labels, and quality certification. Signals work as a method of revealing information about product quality as long as they are costly to firms to produce and, in addition, the marginal cost of increasing the level of the signal is inversely related to the quality of the products sold. Under some circumstances these market signals lead to a fully separating equilibrium and product quality is fully revealed, while there are other cases in which a separating equilibrium does not exist.

The reputation of the sellers for the quality of their products can also serve as an effective signal of quality to buyers. Generally, reputation by itself is not sufficient to induce firms to supply the optimal level of product quality (Shapiro 1982), but this is possible, especially with the use of warranties.

Market signalling through advertising, reputation building, and other costly activities may not be necessary for a fully revealing equilibrium to occur if product quality is fully observable *ex post*, or if the losses suffered from low quality products are observable *ex post* (Viscusi 1978; Grossman 1981). First, consider a market in which consumers cannot observe the quality of products sold to them in advance of purchase, but after purchase the quality of the products becomes easily known to them. No seller would lie by claiming that its product quality was of higher quality than the truth for it could be prosecuted for fraudulent claims. While a seller could understate the quality of its product, it would have no incentive to do so for this would only lower its profits. In this market all sellers, with the exception of the one with the lowest quality product, will fully and voluntarily disclose the true quality of their products. Now consider the second case in which the losses suffered, but not the product quality itself, are easily observable. Sellers will offer warranties that fully insure consumers against losses, thus creating the incentive for producers to raise their product quality levels to those that would occur under complete information.

These research results demonstrate that making disclosure rules and enforced warranties mandatory is unnecessary, and can even be counterproductive, as long as the costs to the firms of disclosing the quality information are low and the costs to consumers of gathering and processing the information and enforcing warranty claims are also minimal. Stated another way, the implied role of government concerning information about product characteristics is only as a facilitator to allow natural market forces to provide the incentives to reveal the quality of products. Beales et al. (1981) categorize these information remedies into three classes: (1) removing information restraints; (2) correcting misleading information; and (3) encouraging the supply of additional information.

The best-known example of the first remedy of removing information restraints is the action of several state governments and the US Federal Trade Commission to prohibit restrictions on advertising by professionals such as optometrists (Benham 1972), dentists, accountants and lawyers. A second example is the remedy of prohibiting the practice in some industries of imposing restrictions on their members' ability to use comparative advertising, which reduces the amount of information available to consumers and raises the cost of information acquisition. As a final example of an information remedy, cancelling generic trademarks, such as aspirin and cellophane, enhances the ability of firms to compete with the holder of the original trademarked product.

The logic behind the second information remedy of correcting misleading information flows from the observation that for information to be useful to consumers it must be both truthful and believed to be truthful. Hence the need for legal restrictions on fraudulent claims in product advertising and on product packaging.

The third category of information remedy, increasing consumer information, can be accomplished in several ways. Standardization of the definition of terms and the establishment of scoring systems for measuring important product characteristics help consumers understand the quality of products and carry out comparison shopping. If the conditions that lead firms to disclose information voluntarily do not exist, then mandating disclosure of product quality information can assist consumers in making better purchase decisions and thus will improve market efficiency. Often this mandated disclosure is linked to a standardized metric for the information (e.g., the monthly energy cost of operating a refrigerator). Finally, because of the public goods characteristic of some product information, it is sometimes useful for the government to produce the information and supply it as cheaply and as easily as possible to potential users of that information. The US Environmental Protection Agency's automobile gasoline mileage ratings are a good example of this type of policy.

CONSUMER INFORMATION-PROCESSING THEORIES. The starting point for the economics literature on information-based market failures is the lack of complete information possessed by consumers about product characteristics and prices in markets. Implicit in these analyses is the assumption that once information is made available to consumers, they will be able to use that information to make informed decisions. The recent scholarship from psychology and marketing on how consumers acquire, process, and use information to make decisions questions this implicit assumption and offers a rich set of models for how consumers do use information in decision making. These models also provide guidance to public policy makers on how to design information remedies in order that consumers act upon the information provided to them under the remedies (chapter 2 in Viscusi and Magat 1987).

The theory starts from the recognition that people have limits on their abilities to process information, and that processing information is costly in terms of time and mental effort. Thus, they adopt heuristics that allow them to cope with tasks of acquiring and processing information in order to make decisions. Sometimes so much information is available about a product choice that consumers choose to ignore some of it, or focus on only a subset, for example that provided by experts. Other times so little information is available that consumers have to choose how much and where to search for that information. Even given fairly complete information about a product or choice, consumers have difficulty processing that information in ways that lead to rational decisions. Sometimes this information processing problem occurs because the information is technically complex (e.g., about a hazardous waste siting decision), while other times the information is understandable but only to consumers with training in statistics, economics, or some other discipline that provides frameworks for combining the information into a form useful for decision making. Consumers faced with complex problems of acquiring, processing and using information for decision making often adopt simplifying strategies such as focusing on only one characteristic of a product at a time (e.g., whether an automobile has airbags), or starting the decision process by anchoring on one possible choice (such as the status quo, or the current product being used) and comparing all other choices to that anchor. This behaviour implies that the decisions people reach about purchasing and using products depend upon both the information used in the decision and the rules for combining that information and reaching decisions.

These theories of consumer information processing provide useful frameworks for understanding how to design successful information remedies. These frameworks indicate how much information to provide for different decisions depending on the state of prior knowledge and the education of the consumers. They suggest how to present the information in terms of location (e.g., television advertisements and package inserts), the use of symbols (e.g., for hazard warnings), summary measures of the effectiveness of the product (e.g., energy efficiency ratings for appliances), and who should convey the information (e.g., company officials, government agencies, or impartial experts). Finally, these frameworks provide guidance on the maximal effectiveness that policy-makers can expect to achieve from information remedies such as product labels. Thus, they suggest when to rely upon informational remedies that address the market failures due to lack of information and when to either use other more direct and restrictive forms of regulation, such as product bans and product quality standards that override market decisions, or accept that the most efficient social policy is to allow markets to operate with imperfect information and without any government intervention.

THE DESIGN OF PRODUCT LABELS. Product labels provide an important and instructive example of an information remedy that is used to address the lack of adequate information for many products, particularly information about product risks. Research has shown that for a label to be effective, consumers must not only read, comprehend, and believe it, but also store the information in memory and accurately retrieve the information when it is time to act. This extensive list of cognitive processes suggests that the effectiveness of a product label can be compromised if any of the steps is missed. In practice, the effectiveness of product labels is mixed.

(a) Examples of the efficacy of product labels. Warning labels on cigarettes are one of the earliest and best known examples of product labelling. In 1965, the US Congress required that cigarette packages and advertising contain the phrase 'smoking may be hazardous to your health', strengthened in 1969 to 'smoking is dangerous to your health', and further expanded in 1984 to require a series of

four rotating warnings covering the risks of cancer, pregnancy, carbon monoxide and other risks (Viscusi 1994). The evidence on awareness of these labels indicates that virtually all adults have heard the basic cigarette warning message, and there was a decline in per capita cigarette consumption in the US after the 1965 and 1984 warnings were imposed. However, due to the variety of other events affecting cigarette consumption around the time the labelling requirements were imposed, econometric studies have been unable to sort out the separate impacts of the labels from events such as the 1964 publication of a highly publicized report on smoking by the Department of Health, Education, and Welfare and the 1971 ban on advertising cigarettes on television and radio.

Congress used the cigarette warning programme as a model for the alcohol warnings which were required to be placed on all alcoholic beverages in November 1989, with the warnings alerting consumers to the risks of automobile accidents, birth defects, and other health problems. The consensus of the literature is that the warnings have not been identified with any significant changes in risk-taking behaviour and that public perceptions of the risk from alcohol consumption have not changed much (Hilton 1993). One notable exception is that light drinkers decreased their drinking during pregnancy but heavy drinkers did not (Hankin et al. 1993).

The US Food and Drug Administration (FDA) has required nutrition labels since 1975 on all food products for which a nutrition claim was being made. The 1990 Nutrition Labeling and Education Act expanded the earlier requirement to cover health as well as nutrition claims, to standardize serving sizes, and specifically to cover fat, saturated fat, dietary fibre and cholesterol, with new labels required in 1994. While the impacts of the 1990 Act are too recent to assess, there is good evidence from a natural experiment in 1985 when a FDA ban on claims linking diet to disease risks was lifted. Following the lifting of this ban, the consumption of fat, saturated fat, and cholesterol in foods went down (Ippolito and Mathios 1994). On the specific link between fiber consumption and cancer, Ippolito and Mathios (1990, 1991) found that lifting the ban led to an awareness of this fibre–cancer link, the development of more nutritious cereals, and an increase in the consumption of cereals containing high fibre content.

(b) Design and efficacy issues. Determining the impact of a particular product label used in practice is difficult because other factors such as media attention and government reports often tend to affect product sales and use in the same time period as the labels are introduced. However, experimental studies have been successfully used to control the information received by consumers and to measure the impacts of various information policies (Viscusi and Magat 1987; Smith and Johnson 1988; Magat and Viscusi 1992). These studies are also useful for assessing the impacts of various elements of the design of information policies.

It is now well established that providing too much information on a product label can be counterproductive in the sense that label clutter reduces total recall of the information on it. A related problem is associated with excessive use of warnings. Consumers stop paying attention to the warnings, or they fail to distinguish between the severity of risks associated with products subject to warnings.

A variety of attributes of the structure and format of labels affects their ability to convey information. Label effectiveness is improved by techniques such as using standard language, employing well-established warning symbols, relying upon graphical representations of statistical information, and organizing the information in a hierarchical format which mirrors the way the information is to be used (Hadden 1986; Magat and Viscusi 1992).

These examples of the use of product labelling illustrate many of the issues involved in using information as a regulatory tool. Consumers often lack complete information for decision making, but they have cognitive limits on how much they can learn from information programmes administered by both product sellers and the government. While there are a variety of approaches for improving the effectiveness of information programmes, the limits to their effectiveness mean that public policy makers must choose among less than perfectly effective information-based policies, imperfect forms of direct regulation, such as product bans and standards that override market decision making, and unregulated but inefficient markets.

WESLEY A. MAGAT

See also BOUNDED RATIONALITY; COGNITION AND CONTRACT; CONSUMER PROTECTION; DISCLOSURE AND UNRAVELLING; MANDATORY DISCLOSURE; PRODUCTS LIABILITY; REGULATION OF THE PROFESSIONS; RISK ASSESSMENT; STANDARD FORM CONTRACTS; TRADEMARKS.

Subject classification: 6d(ii).

BIBLIOGRAPHY

Akerlof, G.A. 1970. The market for 'lemons': quality uncertainty and the market mechanism. *Quarterly Journal of Economics* 84: 488–500.

Beales, H., Craswell, R. and Salop, S.C. 1981. The efficient regulation of consumer information. *Journal of Law and Economics* 24: 491–539.

Benham, L. 1972. The effect of advertising on the price of eyeglasses. *Journal of Law and Economics* 15: 337–52.

Grossman, S.J. 1981. The informational role of warranties and private disclosure about product quality. *Journal of Law and Economics* 24: 461–83.

Hadden, S.G. 1986. *Read the Label: Reducing Risk by Providing Information*. Boulder, CO: Westview.

Hankin, J.R. et al. 1993. The impact of the alcohol warning label on drinking during pregnancy. *Journal of Public Policy and Marketing* 12(1): 10–18.

Hilton, M.E. 1993. An overview of recent findings on alcoholic beverage warning labels. *Journal of Public Policy and Marketing* 12(1): 1–9.

Ippolito, P.M. and Mathios, A.D. 1990. Information, advertising and health choices: A study of the cereal market. *RAND Journal of Economics* 21: 459–80.

Ippolito, P.M. and Mathios, A.D. 1991. Health claims in food marketing: Evidence on knowledge and behaviour in the cereal market. *Journal of Public Policy and Marketing* 10: 15–32.

Ippolito, P.M. and Mathios, A.D. 1994. Information, policy, and the sources of fat and cholesterol in the U.S. diet. *Journal of Public Policy and Marketing* 13(2): 200–217.

Magat, W.A. and Viscusi, W.K. 1992. *Informational Approaches to Regulation*. Cambridge, MA: MIT Press.

Salop, S.C. and Stiglitz, J.E. 1977. Bargains and ripoffs: A model of monopolistically competitive price dispersion. *Review of Economic Studies* 44: 493–510.
Shapiro, C. 1982. Consumer information, product quality and seller reputation. *Bell Journal of Economics* 13: 20–35.
Smith, V.K. and Johnson, F.R. 1988. How do risk perceptions respond to information? The case of radon. *Review of Economics and Statistics* 70: 1–8.
Spence, A.M. 1973. Job market signaling. *Quarterly Journal of Economics* 87: 355–74.
Spence, A.M. 1974. Competitive and optimal responses to signals. *Journal of Economic Theory* 7: 296–332.
Spulber, D. 1989. *Regulation and Markets*. Cambridge, MA: MIT Press.
Viscusi, W.K. 1978. A note on 'lemons' markets with quality certification. *Bell Journal of Economics* 9(1): 277–79.
Viscusi, W.K. 1994. Efficacy of labeling of foods and pharmaceuticals. *Annual Review of Public Health* 15: 324–43.
Viscusi, W.K. and Magat, W.A. 1987. *Learning About Risk: Consumer and Worker Responses to Hazard Information*. Cambridge, MA: Harvard University Press.

inheritance law. This essay discusses common law, equity and statutory rules governing gratuitous transfers of assets in the United States and Great Britain. These transfers often occur at the death of the donor or in the anticipation of death, but can also occur much earlier in life. The recipient of these gratuitous transfers is usually a member of the family, a friend or a charity. One of the recurring questions of inheritance law is how to increase the chances of reaching the result the transferor wanted. Another issue is how far to allow the transferor's intent to control future ownership of property, in other words, to what extent to allow property to be governed by 'the dead hand of the past'. The theme of rules adopted to constrain donors followed by creativity in circumventing the constraints repeats often. Sometimes in tension with the goal of following the decedent's intent are the objectives of reducing the individual costs of transfer and minimizing the societal costs of maintaining the dispute resolution system. As in many areas, legal rules reflect a balancing of these various concerns. In its discussion of intestate succession, wills, and trusts, this essay highlights those interwoven policy threads in the fabric of inheritance law.

Compared to the valuable insights law-and-economics has produced in areas such as torts, crimes, contracts and some areas of property, it has said little about inheritance law. (There are exceptions, of course, such as the obvious, but important, point that the prudence of trust management should be judged by looking at the entire portfolio of investments rather than by determining whether each investment is too speculative.) A number of reasons suggest themselves for this relative paucity. It may be that many rules of inheritance are quite technical, making them difficult for the economist to approach, and that the economic issues embedded in inheritance are quite subtle and sophisticated, making them hard for the legally trained to see. Perhaps many subtleties of the deep economic structure will be exposed only when the topic is tackled by someone with advanced training in both economics and estates.

On the other hand, the reason for the dearth might be just the opposite. It could be that inheritance rules have very few incentive effects, leaving those who would focus on the behavioural consequences of inheritance law with little to say. There are substantial administrative concerns and massive distributional consequences, but those may be so manifest that no one sees their exposition as being worthwhile. The various policy threads are perhaps too obvious to make an enlightening lesson. Or modern law-and-economists may feel that the subject has received adequate treatment by economists during the last couple of centuries (see Goody 1987; Pechman 1987).

Another possible reason, connected to the foregoing, for the absence of weighty law-and-economic insights relating to inheritance is that the rules in this area have balanced competing values well, leaving little room for an economic critique. That reason, however, hardly suffices if inheritance law, especially primogeniture and the land tenure system, led to inefficiency in production from land. Moreover, the role of inheritance law in perpetuating huge disparities in wealth is worth examining even if that outcome was and is consistent with the desires of the various dominant interests. Finally, inheritance law today differs from that of yesterday, so either the law has changed as the goals of the rule-makers have changed through the ages, or some of the rules did not serve well in the past or do not serve well now. In any case, there should be an interesting law-and-economics tale to tell. The goal here is to suggest a few points of that story.

INHERITANCE AT COMMON LAW. At the start it should be noted that though we now assume that rights in things may be transferred freely to others, the common law has not always supported inheritance of land. In the early years of the English feudal system, shortly after the conquest by William, Duke of Normandy, land did not automatically pass from parent to child. Instead, a tenant's rights in land terminated at his death and his overlord was given the opportunity to grant the lands to a new tenant, as the tenurial relationship could be established only if the lord accepted the tenant's homage. The lord would usually accept the child of the old tenant as his new tenant, but could require the child to buy back the lands (see Simpson [1961] 1986).

It is easy to see how this arrangement could lead to suboptimal investment in land. Tenants hesitate to make long-lasting investments because a portion of such expenditures inures to the benefit of the overlord if the tenant dies and the tenant's expenditures increase the amount the lord can demand from the tenant's child for the child to continue his father's possession. Overlords invest too little because their tenants might live longer than expected. A mutually negotiated sharing of the rewards of the investment while the tenant is in possession would lead to inadequate effort by the tenant or require difficult monitoring of the tenant's diligence in farming and harvesting. As an alternative, a lord and tenant might share the costs of improvement, but that too is problematic. Cautious overlords refrain from offering to share the costs of current improvements with tenants because of the adverse-selection problem: such offers will be accepted only by tenants who will stay too long for the landlord to get an adequate return (see Basu 1989).

Thus, the limitation of tenurial estates to the life of the tenant created situations fraught with temporal externalities. Perhaps in part to internalize these externalities, the law soon recognized a method for a tenant to acquire rights that would survive his death. By the twelfth century, a tenant would require his overlord to give assurance that the tenant's heir could take after him (see Moynihan [1962] 1988). In this early method of inheritance planning, Earl could provide for Blackacre to pass to his son Robert by insisting that Earl's grantor make his grant of Blackacre 'to Earl and his heirs'. The words 'and his heirs' became terms of art and were necessary to the creation of the *fee simple* estate, the only alienable estate of potentially infinite duration.

The use of the word 'heirs' in this context should not be misconstrued. Under the method of descent predominating at early common law, called 'primogeniture', land passed according to a set of rules much like those governing the succession of the English Crown. In priority, issue preceded other relatives, males preceded females, elder males preceded younger males but females all took equally as 'coparceners', and inheritance through male ancestors preceded inheritance through female ancestors. The usual result was that land passed from the decedent to his eldest son. Assuming that Earl had two surviving sons, Robert and his younger brother Donald, only Robert would take. The 's' on the end of 'heirs' was not meant to include Donald as a taker. Instead, that 's' meant that after Robert's death Earl's next heir, Robert's eldest son, or daughters if he had no son, would take Blackacre.

Though primogeniture predominated for devolution of land, other rules existed. Some jurisdictions in Wales, Ireland and Kent followed the custom of gavelkind, under which land passed in equal parts to all males of the same (and closest) degree. Borough English was another local custom deviating from primogeniture in that younger sons were preferred to older. One explanation of this custom is that eldest sons were more likely to leave and younger sons were more likely to stay and take care of the family. Another explanation, declared fanciful by some authorities, relates the disfavour of older sons in Borough English to the *jus primae noctis*, the right of the lord to enjoy the first night with a tenant's new bride (see Megarry and Wade [1957] 1984).

Personalty did not pass to the sole heir, but instead passed to the next of kin. The next of kin were determined according to the following rules of priority: surviving spouse first, widower taking all, widow taking one-half if there were no surviving issue, but only one-third if issue survived; issue taking *per stirpes*, by the stocks or lines; father; mother and siblings taking equally with children of a deceased sibling taking their parent's share; and then next of kin of the same degree, taking *per capita*.

Personalty includes interests in everything other than land. It even includes some interests in land, such as leaseholds, which were considered not to be realty because the holder lacked seisin. Of course, some things are so connected to the enjoyment of land that to pass them to someone other than the landowner would be inefficient. The title deed to land would generate the most utility in the hands of the landowner, being quite helpful to his proof of ownership. The Crown jewels might best be held by the king. Efficiency would also support passing the fish in a fishpond to the owner of the pond rather than other relatives, who would have to collect their inheritance, transport it, and find an appropriate place for live storage. At a minimum, appropriate initial allocation saves the costs of transactions needed to get the asset into the hands of the landowner. Early law avoided these potential inefficiencies by the doctrine of heirlooms. Heirlooms were chattels that passed by the laws of realty to the heir rather than the next of kin. The law of heirlooms can, on rare occasion even today, have some effect if a will gives realty to one person and personalty to another.

Primogeniture has some obvious advantages for devolution of land. Given time for market transactions to occur, land should be divided or collected into efficiently sized parcels. Inheritance by multiple recipients either will divide the land into smaller than optimal parcels or will result in multiple ownership, which creates 'commons' problems. Owners will hesitate to improve land when their investment will be shared by all, and will harvest too much when the depletion will be borne in part by others. By primogeniture, the common law preserved optimally sized parcels. On the other hand, the early rules also recognized, in their application of primogeniture only to realty, that cash and other personalty need not be collected in packages of certain size to be useful. Though it may be allocatively efficient when applied to land, primogeniture may be distributionally objectionable. In addition to giving nothing to some children in a family and all to another, this one-winner approach can result in highly concentrated economic wealth and political power.

For political, and perhaps economic, reasons, primogeniture was rejected early in America. Initial acquisitions of land were not always limited to parcels optimal for farming by a single owner and little time had passed for market transactions to divide land ownership. Therefore, descent of the family farm to the eldest son would not necessarily preserve an efficiently sized parcel. Moreover, since there was no peerage, there was no need for, and indeed there was an aversion to, primogeniture as a means for determining who would govern.

The fee simple estate was not the only common-law estate designed to achieve succession by descendants. Just as the words 'and his heirs' created one early form of succession, the words 'and the heirs of his body' were used to create another form of succession. By these words, a transferor intended to create an estate that would pass from one descendant of the grantee to another, down through the generations. Unlike the grantor of a fee simple, however, a grantor transferring 'to Lawrence and the heirs of his body' did not intend to allow free alienation by Lawrence or his successors in possession. Lawrence could transfer the right to possession during his life, but at his death the land was intended to pass to his lineal descendant. If, at some point in time, there were no surviving descendants of Lawrence, the land was to pass back to the original grantor rather than passing to a collateral heir (a descendant of an ancestor) of Lawrence. Hence a father transferring to his son 'and the heirs of his body' attempted to give a series of possessions to his son, then in turn to his grandson, then his great grandson, and so forth. By use of 'and the heirs of his body', grantors attempted to control ownership of land long into the future, keeping the land in the family.

While the fee simple had beneficial economic effects, the intended effects of a grant to the grantee 'and the heirs of his body' were not so benign. Although the tenant could still sell some interest, he could not sell an everlasting interest in the land. While his land might often descend to the person to whom he might want it to pass, it would not always do so. Nor, when he was young, could a tenant count on having any issue survive him. Therefore, an estate that was only partially alienable, as desired by the grantor, created some of the same temporal externality problems that had existed before lands were inheritable. Responding perhaps to such potential inefficiencies, judges refused to follow the intent of the grantor and instead interpreted the 'and the heirs of his body' language as creating an estate, called the fee simple conditional, that could be transferred, in fee simple, to a new owner once a child was born to the tenant. Thus the courts preserved the alienability of lands and increased the efficiency of land use. The necessary consequence was, of course, that the tenant could disinherit persons the original grantor had intended to benefit.

In 1285 this judicial enabling of disinheritance was countered by legislation, the Statute De Donis Conditionalibus, which forced courts to follow the grantor's intent. After passage of De Donis, the 'heirs of the body' language created the *fee tail* estate, an estate which did not allow the tenant to transfer control out of the family. This estate proved popular with the nobility as it tied their heirs to the land and protected the familial lands from forfeiture. As time passed, the number of parcels held in fee tail increased, certainly limiting land alienability and likely impairing land development. Nevertheless, being popular with the nobility, the fee tail was not repealed by the legislature.

As might be expected, owners bridled at the control of the dead hand of the past and attempted in various ways to free their lands from its grip. By the time *Taltarum's Case* was decided a couple hundred years after De Donis, these attempts were receiving a sympathetic judicial ear. Reacting partly to the efficiency problems created by the fee tail, the courts allowed convoluted legal manoeuvres to turn the relatively inalienable fee tail into an alienable fee simple. Holders of fee tail estates gained freedom from the past while holders of fees simple lost some control of the future. The theme of attempts to control future ownership followed by attempts to loosen lands from the grip of the past continued through the ensuing centuries as the courts gradually allowed bolder and simpler means of 'disentailing' the fee tail estate.

The fee tail was abolished entirely in most American jurisdictions two centuries ago, with at least one statute reciting an entail's discouragement of improvements (see Orth 1992), and where it remains it is easily disentailed. It lives on in England. Indeed, the latest step in the dance has been another legislative endorsement of the fee tail concept in the form of an expansion allowing personalty to be entailed (Law of Property Act 1925, Section 1). However, in England only equitable interests, whether realty or personalty, can be entailed (see Megarry and Wade [1957] 1984). Because the legal estate is held in fee simple, the land or other asset remains fully alienable by the trustee. Thus English law now affords donors substantial freedom in passing assets as they please without raising problems of inefficient allocation caused by inalienability.

The rules of primogeniture made no provision for surviving spouses. Instead, spousal inheritance was handled under the common-law doctrines of *dower* and *curtesy*. Upon the birth of their live issue, a husband acquired an 'estate by the curtesy initiate' in his wife's estates in land inheritable by such issue. This tenancy 'by the curtesy of England' lasted until the husband died. If his wife died before him, his estate became an 'estate by the curtesy consummate'. In such case, the effect was to give him an inheritance in her lands, or one half of her lands for some tenures, for the remainder of his life. Because the feudal death taxes sometimes took the form of the overlord getting the benefit of the land for a year after the death of the tenant and because a husband's curtesy took priority over such taxes, the survival by the husband could have the effect of denying the overlord the compensation he expected at the succession by the new generation. The curtesy of England survived transatlantic passage to the United States, but protects few widowers today on either side of the Atlantic.

Dower performed a parallel function for widows, giving them life estates in any legal interests in land that could have been inherited by their children, whether or not they had any. However, it differed from curtesy in important ways. While dower applied only to one-third of the husband's lands, in England before 1833 and in the United States until much later it applied to any lands he held during their marriage, even lands which he had sold before his death. This rule caused substantial litigation and uncertainty because it was sometimes unclear whether a previous owner of land was ever married and, if so, whether he sold his land while he was married. If the sale occurred during coverture and without his wife's consent, then she retained a dower interest as long as she remained alive. While this clogged up transactions in land, one benefit was that the husband could not easily sell family assets without the knowledge of his wife.

Another difference between the rules of dower and curtesy is that the former, unlike the latter, required a certain form of good behaviour. If a wife left her husband for a paramour and was not reconciled to her husband, no matter what bad behaviour on his part triggered her leaving, her dower interest was terminated. This rule clearly created an incentive for wifely fidelity, regardless of opportunistic behaviour by her husband.

The tenancy in common, *tenancy by entireties* and *joint tenancy* are, like coparcenary mentioned above, all forms of concurrent ownership in which one asset is owned by more than one person at a time. The tenancy by entireties and joint tenancy are special in that they can be employed to pass assets at death without a will. Tenants holding an asset in one of these tenancies have a 'right of survivorship' which means that the death of one tenant terminates his or her interest in the asset, leaving ownership in the survivor or survivors. The tenancy by entireties can exist only between a husband and wife; the joint tenancy can exist between any individuals. If, at the time he purchases Blackacre from Burt, Robert wishes his wife Bernadine to take Blackacre when he dies, he tells Burt to make the conveyance to both of them as tenants by entireties. When one spouse dies, the surviving spouse becomes the sole owner of Blackacre. The joint tenancy can be used the same way.

One major difference between the two tenancies is that joint tenants can unilaterally sever the tenancy, changing it into a tenancy in common and destroying the right of survivorship, while tenants by entireties cannot sever unilaterally. Furthermore, since the Partition Act (1539) joint tenants have been able to get a partition, dividing the asset and destroying the common ownership. The joint tenancy hence has the advantage of allowing a tenant to terminate the relationship, other than by homicide, if she is bothered by problems of the commons. In the distant past, the problems of multiple ownership had little opportunity to arise in tenancies by entireties because the husband controlled his wife's assets and even today the marital relationship between the owners reduces those problems. In some jurisdictions the tenancy by entireties, not being severable or partitionable by one party acting alone, carries the advantage of protecting the asset from the creditors of one owner.

Perhaps for the reasons supporting primogeniture, the common law preferred tenancies with a right of survivorship to tenancies in common, which did not carry a right of survivorship. The death of a tenant in common could leave the land in more hands after her death than held it before her death. The death of a joint tenant or tenant by entireties, by contrast, would leave ownership in fewer hands, all of whose ownership stemmed from the same original grant, reducing commons problems and making it easier for the land to pass in commerce to its highest use. 'The law loves not fractions of estates, nor to divide and multiply tenures' (*Fisher v. Wigg*, 392, *per* Holt, CJ). To reduce problems in conveyancing in England, this common-law preference for joint tenancies has been codified (Law of Property Act 1925, s. 34(2)) in a rule that prohibits a legal estate from being held by tenancy in common (see Megarry and Wade [1957] 1984). Equity, by contrast, did not favour the right of survivorship. 'Survivorship is looked upon as odious in equity' (*R. v. Williams*, 343, *per cur*). The unfairness of the one-winner approach might have been enough alone to put joint tenancy in disfavour in courts of equity, but it is also worth noting that courts of equity need not concern themselves with inalienability. The legal title holder could still control the asset without concern for the number of equitable interests being served.

MODERN STATUTORY INHERITANCE. Dower, curtesy and primogeniture have for the most part been displaced by modern statutes describing who takes property on an owner's death intestate (without a will). These statutes apply to chattels as well as land and, indeed, bear more resemblance to the old rules governing personalty than the rules for realty. There are four stages of priority under most statutes: the spouse, sometimes taking all of the estate if it is small or there are no surviving issue or parents; the surviving children or other issue; ancestors and collaterals if no descendants survive; and the state, if none of the above can be found.

There are interesting issues of policy embedded in the rules of intestate succession. One standard goal is to distribute the decedent's assets as he would have wished. Our guess as to what decedents would have wanted is not, however, the same for all decedents. Moreover, there is reason to believe that the variation in desire is not entirely random. Some empirical research suggests that the richer the person, the greater the desire that children or other relatives share with the surviving spouse (Sussman et al. 1970; Contemporary Studies Project 1978). In addition, from a Darwinian presumption that people wish to aid in the survival of their genes combined with a presumption that there is a diminishing marginal survival utility to money, we would predict that rich persons would like to spread their assets to a wider set of relatives than would poor persons (Stake 1990).

If the goal of the rules of intestate succession is to anticipate the preferences of decedents but donative preferences differ, upon whose preferences ought the rules be based? That depends on why the law should follow a decedent's intent. If we wish to minimize the need for the drafting of wills, the law should mimic the wishes of those who can be spared the drafting of a will by the appropriate intestate rules. That group would be those who have substantial assets. However, we should exclude the very rich as they are likely to engage in estate planning regardless of the default rules. For them, the transactions costs of planning represent only a tiny fraction of the assets being controlled.

By contrast, if we wish to maximize the frequency of achieving the intent of the decedent, then we ought to let those having the resources to hire a lawyer do just that. The rules of intestate succession should mimic the intent of those who cannot or will not write a will, poorer persons, but not those so poor they leave nothing behind. The rules need not be aimed, however, at the average preference of this group. In creating a set of default rules intended to achieve the intent of the decedent, we need to consider whether deviations from the default are equally easy in both directions. With regard to the share given to spouses, if signalling problems make it very costly for a person writing a will to give her spouse less than would the law of intestate succession, but easy to give more, the laws of descent should be biased slightly against the surviving spouse so as to allow more people to achieve their intent. Consideration ought also to be given to the degree to which the laws of intestate succession might have shaped current dispositive preferences and might shape future preferences.

In the past, statutes leaned toward the desires of the wealthy, giving a lot less of the intestate estate to the surviving spouse than a person of poor or moderate means would desire. Both the Intestates' Estates Act 1952, Section 1, in England and the 1990 Uniform Probate Code in the US (National Conference of Commissioners on Uniform State Laws 1993) adopt a compromise which to some degree finesses the issue by granting a fixed amount to the spouse in addition to a fraction of the estate exceeding that amount.

Perhaps a similar approach could be applied with regard to issue. Under both the common law rules determining the next of kin and the modern statutory replacements, a grandchild takes only if her parent is dead. This division into fewer shares makes sense if there is little wealth to go around. It is probably inappropriate, however, for large estates. The first assets could be divided among the children. Then, after each child inherits a given amount, the remaining assets could be divided equally, or by degree of consanguinity, among all living descendants. Collateral relatives could be included as a third stage. One arguable disadvantage of such a scheme, which makes a gift to issue of living descendants, is that it creates an incentive to procreate. If Robert's children can inherit from Earl while Robert is alive, Robert can increase the share for his branch of the family by having more children. Current law avoids creating such incentives.

The same issue of encouraging fertility lurks in the choice between distribution *per stirpes* and distribution *per capita*. When assets pass *per stirpes*, as under some statutes, the assets are divided by the number of lines of descent at each generation. Suppose Earl dies, survived only by seven grandchildren, four by his son Robert and three by son Donald. Taking *per stirpes*, Robert's four children each take one-fourth of his half and Donald's three children each take one-third of his half. Under a *per capita* distribution, assuming again that Robert and Donald predeceased Earl, all seven grandchildren would take equal sevenths. Seeing this possibility before he dies, Donald can increase his family's portion of Earl's estate from three-sevenths to one half by having another child.

Do people wish to create an incentive, however tiny, for their children or other relatives to have more children? If so, and if we wish to mimic their intent, then the law should choose *per capita* distribution. On the other hand, if we wish not to create any incentive to procreate, the law ought to distribute assets *per stirpes*. English law takes the latter approach. The law in the US varies widely, from *per stirpes* to various forms of *per capita*.

Perhaps it is appropriate to balance this speculation about incentives for creating life with a word about incentives for ending life. Unlike primogeniture, modern statutes distribute assets to a group of persons rather than one heir. One of the advantages, besides fairness, of today's statutes over primogeniture is that they create less incentive for rent seeking. As the movie *Kind Hearts and Coronets* pointed out, the common law system of succession created a large prize for the eldest surviving person most closely related to the decedent. Under that system, one might stand to inherit a sizeable estate (even the Crown, as in the case of Richard III and the Princes in the Tower) if the intervening heirs apparent were somehow to shuffle off their mortal coils. By spreading the inheritance across the family, the more even-handed modern statutes create less opportunity for others to gain at the death of an heir apparent, thereby perhaps reducing the frequency of mysterious disappearances.

As noted above, however, rules of intestacy that distribute assets broadly have the potential to divide ownership into inefficiently small packages of rights. This potential has been realized on Native American reservations. Ownership of some reservation lands has become so fractionated that no owner has a sufficient interest in managing the lands to make them productive. The same modern laws of succession that have fractionated Native American lands apply, of course, to nonreservation lands. Such lands have not, however, become so afflicted with multiple ownership. The different results may stem from the difference in cultures. By the time modern rules of intestate succession were adopted, the British and their descendants in America had experienced hundreds of years of individual ownership, enough to create a cultural expectation. The British cultural preference for individual ownership adequately counteracted the tendency of the law, after primogeniture ended, to subdivide ownership. Private transfers kept most lands from being held by too many hands. The Native Americans had a different cultural heritage, one of tribal ownership, or no ownership at all. Indeed, individual ownership was forced upon Indians by the US government. Native American culture, being less oriented toward individual ownership, did not counter the unproductive tendencies of the modern rules of succession. Once the problem was recognized, it was too large to deal with effectively. It was not worth the effort of any single Native American to transfer her interests to a single successor because other owners would probably not do so and the land would continue to be unmanageable and unproductive.

WILLS. The word 'inherit' has a narrow technical meaning, referring only to taking by the laws of descent and distribution just discussed. The word is used in this essay in a broader sense, to include taking by will or even, un-idiomatically, taking from an *inter vivos* trust. The rules of descent discussed above apply only when people die without a will or having a will that fails to dispose of some of their assets. Those rules have, since at least 1540, been default rules, applying only if the decedent fails to specify otherwise. We now turn to the issue of how a decedent can avoid those default rules. One way to avoid the laws of descent and distribution is to make a will, a testament.

There are a number of requirements for making a valid will. The testator must have the general capacity to execute a will. This requirement includes subrequirements of legal age and mental capacity, which means a sound mind. Why does the law refuse to honour the products of an unsound mind? Perhaps the best rationale is that the law's refusal to give effect to the testamentary rantings of a lunatic assures us that the plans we make so carefully today will not be upset if we go mad in the future. It is comforting to know that the law will not follow our wishes after we lose control. Moreover, the psychological downside of the capacity requirement is small because few of us think we are crazy now. We are not upset by the thought that the law will not follow the instructions of the insane because that is someone else.

The capacity requirement has other costs, however. One is rent seeking in the form of legal battles over the decedent's estate. Another cost is the damage done to the feelings of those close to the decedent. It upsets us to hear arguments that father was incompetent and hurts even more if the court declares its agreement. Third, because capacity is not easily determined, this fuzzy requirement leaves a lot of discretion in the finder of fact, be that judge or jury. The indeterminacy of the 'capacity' requirement allows judges to impose their prejudices.

The law will not admit a will to probate if the testator was subjected to fraud, which involves some form of misrepresentation, or undue influence, which is the loss of free agency through psychological domination. In addition to these vague and difficult-to-apply standards, there are more determinate rules aimed at preventing products of coercion from being admitted to probate. The point of these formalities is to achieve justice, assuming justice is doing what the testator wanted done. There are, however, other approaches to that goal that would not involve formalities. The law could say that it is the job of courts to follow the will of the decedent in every case. If the courts did a good job at it, that straightforward approach might maximize justice. The law has not taken that tack, presumably because it would cost too much to hold the necessary hearings to determine intent and could leave too much discretion in the hands of judges.

The law imposes specific formalities upon those wishing to make a valid will. These formalities include requirements that the testator sign and acknowledge the will, sometimes in the presence of witnesses, and that witnesses attest to the will. Even when it was absolutely clear that a document was intended by the decedent to be his will, courts have denied probate because the testator or his lawyer failed to observe some formality, such as the requirement that the witnesses be in the presence of each other at the time the will was acknowledged (see *In re Eagles*).

Commentators have disparaged this high level of formality as unwarranted and have proposed various reforms giving courts the discretion to dispense with the formalities. To this end, South Australia granted courts a 'dispensing power' (South Australia Wills Act Amendment Act 1975, Section 9), and the neighbouring state of Queensland joined a few years later (Queensland Succession Act 1981, Section 9(a)). Langbein, an early proponent of relaxing the formalities, studied 41 cases involving the dispensing power and concluded that Americans should 'shudder that we still inflict upon our citizens the injustice of the traditional law, and we should join in this movement to rid private law of relics so embarrassing' (Langbein 1987: 54). Dukeminier predicted that malpractice liability for lawyers would lead to reform (Dukeminier 1979) and Section 2–503 of the Uniform Probate Code (UPC) now follows the Australian lead.

An obvious question arises as to whether this relaxation of formalities improves the law. One gain is the increased frequency of passing assets to the truly intended recipient where the will was defectively executed. But rarely did courts refuse to adopt an obvious Pareto improvement and, therefore, we should not expect that gain to be cost free. Litigation is one potential cost. By replacing, in some cases, relatively determinate formal inquiries, such as whether two witnesses signed, with an indeterminate standard that looks to the subjective intent of a dead person, the reform probably increases the frequency of litigation. The cost of each litigated case might also increase since a greater bulk of evidence can be proffered on the question of intent than on the question of whether there are two signatures.

It is even possible that justice will not increase. First, if testators respond to the reformed law by worrying less about formalities, being sloppier in expression, and consulting lawyers less often, they may express their intent less clearly and courts will get it wrong more frequently. The traditional formalities encourage testators to engage in careful planning and generate clear evidence of their intent. Second, although reducing the formalities will reduce erroneous exclusions from probate, it might increase erroneous admissions to probate. Even assuming the number of fraud or undue influence attempts remains stable, wills generated by fraud or undue influence will be admitted to probate more often because the reformed law offers an additional avenue of admission. As a potential example, take *In re Williams*, which held admissible a will that the wife had not signed. It is possible that she had not signed because the will reflected her husband's desires rather than hers. Moreover, the amount of rent seeking via attempts to exercise undue influence or fraud will likely increase because the signing and witnessing requirements will no longer discourage dishonesty. Strike suits will be more common because threats of alternative wills will be more credible. Furthermore, the degree of injustice under the reform and the traditional law are not the same. It is more unjust to pass assets to an unintended recipient that has committed a wrong to get those assets, as is possible under the reform, than to pass assets to an innocent family member, as happens under the old rule.

Perhaps most important, as the number of cases of fraud and overreaching increase and the public learns of such cases, people will lose confidence that their well-considered dispositions will be followed. This result is not ineluctable, but it is possible and the costs of this uncertainty, should it occur, are very hard to gauge. The rigidity of the traditional law causes occasional injustice, but it also provides comfort.

This last cost of UPC 2–503, and perhaps some of the others, could be minimized by allowing a testator to decide for herself whether UPC 2–503 applies to her estate. Free individual choice is not always best. There are good reasons, such as judicial economy, that a state might insist on the traditional formalities. It is harder to see, however, why the state should insist that all persons' estates be subjected to the costs and uncertainties of 2–503. The whole point of 2–503 is to follow the intent of the decedent more often. If the decedent prefers the protections of the formalities, why should the state deny them? Testators should be able, in a valid will, to elect that their subsequent wills be admissible only if they comply with the traditional requirements. Ulysses ordered his crew to lash him to the mast to protect him from his own future behaviour. The law, like Ulysses' crew, ought to help people protect themselves from the siren songs of today.

In addition to the basic requirements aimed at achieving the decedent's intent, there are many other rules of inheritance law that help courts to achieve the likely intent of the testator. There is, for example, a rule that murderers do not inherit, by will or intestate succession, from their victims. In the context of intestate succession, this rule can be justified as nullifying incentives for homicide. For decedents with wills, however, that justification fits less well because wills are often kept secret before death and the potential killer will less often know he stands to inherit. This one-should-not-profit-from-his-wrong rule, which applies to both testate and intestate decedents, can be justified as a term that most decedents would want in their wills if they thought about it. The law saves transactions costs by writing it into wills automatically.

Many rules relating to wills help effectuate the intent of the testator, but some are designed to do just the opposite – to prevent certain testamentary goals from being achieved. In the past, some persons were disabled from making a will at law. Wives could not make wills passing legal interests in land. Still today, minors cannot dispose of their assets by will unless, in some jurisdictions, they are in the armed services. Nor can incompetent persons make a will. Perhaps the best justification of this latter rule is that it assures testators that the plans they make while sane will not be undone by subsequent acts of insanity. That rationale does not explain, however, why a person could not opt out of that limitation by his own will, or why persons who have always been insane cannot make wills.

Although the rules of succession in common-law jurisdictions allow decedents to disinherit their children, they prohibit decedents from disinheriting their spouses. These modern statutory protections, creating the 'forced share', either replace or supplement the common-law rules of dower and curtesy discussed above. Although the limitations vary widely, the surviving spouse is usually given the option of waiving the will and taking a share similar to what he or she would have received had the decedent died intestate. Despite the fact that these rules limit individual freedom of disposition, Posner ([1972] 1992) has explained them as implied contractual terms. Because contracts to make a bequest are enforceable, spouses could, and probably would, agree not to disinherit each other. The law spares them those unsavoury negotiations and legal fees.

Decedents occasionally attempt to control the behaviour of their friends or relatives after they die. Some wills include gifts predicated on the recipient marrying a person of a specified religion. Such limitations will be upheld in the US if they are reasonable, which requires that the limitation not reduce the likelihood of marriage too much. The outcome depends on effect of the limitation rather than the motive or purpose of the testator. By contrast, the validity of nonreligious limitations on marriage such as a gift to 'my niece for so long as she is not married' sometimes depends, curiously enough, on the motive behind the restraint rather than on the incentives it places before the niece. If the decedent's purpose, divined by the court, was to discourage marriage, the restraint is void. If the dominant motive behind the gift was to provide support until marriage, the restraint is good even though its incentive effect is to discourage marriage. It is questionable whether the dead hand should be granted such influence over the living.

Courts have recently begun facing issues relating to whether decedents can leave money to persons willing to have their children. Suppose T's will leaves $10,000,000 and his frozen gametes in trust, the income to be paid to the first woman who bears and cares for his child. Should T's gametes be considered to be his property and, if so, should we honour his wish to have a posthumous child? Should we allow testamentary gifts of money and gametes to an unlimited number of unspecified persons who are willing to have the children? Until these difficult issues can be worked through, perhaps the law ought to refrain from granting rights to control gametes by will, because it is far more difficult to retract rights later than to give additional rights.

On the other end of the spectrum, suppose that a testator instructs her executor to bury her in her pink Cadillac automobile and destroy her personal papers. There is authority for ignoring instructions to destroy valuable assets. But clearly the testator, before death, had the legal authority to burn her personal diaries. Why then should the law stop her executor, her posthumous alter ego, from carrying out her wishes? Part of the answer may lie in the difference in our confidence about the testator's strength of preference. If she burns her assets before death, we can deduce from the fact that the market did not outbid her that she took more pleasure in their destruction than others would take from their preservation. When she tells her executor to burn the papers after death, we are less sure that her preference was stronger than others' because, unlike when she is alive, she never has to bear the loss. Another part of the answer might be that net societal utility does not include the utility of dead persons. On that ground we ought not to care about her wishes after she is dead, except to the extent that a rule against honouring her intent would upset the living. If the law overrides intent in 'burn-my-papers' cases, we can infer that the living are not too troubled by that law since they can burn the papers themselves if they care deeply that the papers not survive. Although that rationale applies equally to the simple destruction of a Cadillac, it will not work as a justification for ignoring instructions to bury the decedent in the Cadillac for that is something the testator could not comfortably accomplish while alive.

TRUSTS. Except in a few localities, the English courts of law did not honour attempted testamentary transfers of interests in real property prior to 1540. The Court of Chancery, possibly seeing an opportunity to increase its jurisdiction, supplied what the courts of law would not, a method of land testation. To qualify, the owner had to create a 'use', an interest recognized in equity but not in courts of law. O would transfer Blackacre 'to T and his heirs, to the use of O and his heirs'. After such a transfer T held legal title for the benefit of O. O could then leave written instructions telling T to transfer Blackacre to B upon T's death. Because uses were also used to reduce feudal death taxes, and had become quite popular, they were eventually abolished by the Statute of Uses in 1535. The unintended casualty of the Statute of Uses was testamentary transfers of land. That was soon remedied by the Statute of Wills which in 1540 allowed for the first time legal estates in land to be passed by will.

Recognizing the potential usefulness of separating control of assets from the benefit, and despite the express language of the Statute of Uses, English courts held that the Statute did not execute uses if the legal title holder had some active duty to perform. Thus the courts authorized what we now call the trust. Although courts of law and equity have merged, a trust still today refers to essentially the same division of ownership attributes with respect to the trust property, or '*res*'.

The key characteristic of a trust is the separation of management from benefit. The trustee (often an institution) has the power to manage the trust property. The trustee is bound by a fiduciary duty to manage the *res* prudently, to administer it according to the terms of the trust, and to apply it for the sole benefit of the beneficiaries. The trust is 'mandatory' if trust terms instruct the trustee as to how to apply the income; it is 'discretionary' if the trustee has latitude in choosing when or how much to distribute to the beneficiaries. The enviable job of the beneficiary, the '*cestui que trust*' or '*cestui*,' is to relax and enjoy the benefits. While the trustee has important obligations, its identity is usually not considered critical to the trust and it is often said that 'a trust will not fail for want of a trustee'. It is essential, however, that a private, noncharitable trust have beneficiaries because the trustee must act for the benefit of someone or something other than itself. Trusts allow settlors (creators of trusts) to achieve their distributional goals without gumming up the allocation of resources. The trustee holds legal title and can sell the trust property, allowing it to pass to a higher and better use, while the beneficiaries of the trust, often a group and often including minors or incompetents, remain those specified by the original donor.

In some ways, American courts follow the intention of the settlor more closely than English courts. In England, the beneficiaries, if all are identified, competent, and in agreement, may terminate the trust and distribute its assets. Under the Claflin doctrine accepted in the US, beneficiaries of a trust cannot terminate the trust if doing so would defeat a material purpose of the settlor. However, to prevent the dead hand from controlling assets too long, the beneficiaries may terminate the trust after the period of the Rule against Perpetuities has run.

The spendthrift trust again sounds the refrain of owners attempting to control ownership of assets into the future. It also shows American courts giving greater deference to settlors' intentions. Like the Claflin doctrine, this particular dynastic device started in the US in the late 1800s. The settlor of a spendthrift trust aims to assure lifelong financial security for the beneficiary by providing an income stream that cannot be reached by the beneficiary's creditors. Thus spendthrift trusts allow owners to impose restraints on alienation, although only on the equitable interest and not on the legal title to the asset. Although nearly all of the states now recognize spendthrift trusts, considerable opposition remains. Critics are bothered by the possibility that spendthrift beneficiaries can live in luxury while their creditors starve. Critics also note that, since a person cannot create a spendthrift trust for herself, income from inherited wealth has more protection than income earned from labour. A person who knows he has a genetic predisposition to some form of dementia is not allowed to settle a trust on his assets to protect himself from his future indiscretions. Spendthrift trusts are not allowed in England, but settlors there can create a protective trust which changes from a mandatory to a discretionary trust if the *cestui* attempts to alienate her interest.

Settlors use charitable trusts to set up perpetual foundations dedicated to achieving charitable purposes. Unlike ordinary private trusts, charitable trusts need not have a specified beneficiary. Posner ([1973] 1992) makes the point that governing boards of charitable foundations lack adequate incentives to manage assets efficiently. The beneficiaries cannot complain about managerial sloth because there are no beneficiaries. And in the provision of charitable services, charitable foundations often do not compete for customers with other suppliers. Thus charitable foundations are accountable only to themselves and operate without the beneficial checks of the competitive market.

When the purpose of a charitable trust becomes impossible to achieve, courts will often '*cy pres*', modifying the trust to come as close as possible to the settlor's original intent. The court has wide discretion in modifying the ends of the trust and there can be a number of parties with an interest in the outcome. As a result, the *cy pres* doctrine can lead to considerable rent seeking. It is worth wondering whether it might be better to terminate impossible trusts rather than trying to modify them. This would create an incentive for settlors to be more careful in specifying the goals of the trust and the conditions of termination, and might save substantial litigation. The *cy pres* doctrine raises, once again, the issue of whether courts should work as hard as they do to follow the intent of now deceased persons who were insufficiently careful in setting out their intentions.

Charitable and spendthrift trusts are but two of the infinite possible variations on the trust theme. In addition to being useful for accomplishing goals that cannot be achieved via a will, trusts can be used today to accomplish virtually anything that can be accomplished by will. A settlor can place his assets in a revocable trust while he is alive and specify in the trust document who is to receive the assets when he dies. The assets then pass to those trust beneficiaries at his death, without ever entering his probate estate. Because the settlor need not comply with the formalities required for a will and because the revocable *inter vivos* trust avoids probate, such trusts have become quite popular. The revocable *inter vivos* trust plays an important role in the nonprobate revolution.

Other devices that can be used as substitutes for a will, transferring property at the moment of death, are the pension fund, the pay-on-death account, and life insurance. For many years, many of these will substitutes were rejected by courts when the governing instrument was not executed in compliance with the wills formalities, but they are now well accepted. All of these devices share the advantages of the revocable trust; the assets do not pass through the court-operated probate system and the decedent thereby spares his beneficiaries the delays and costs of judicial supervision. Because of these advantages, nonprobate transfers are pushing the probate system into the background. According to Langbein, '[t]he law of wills and rules of descent no longer govern succession to most of the property of most decedents' (1984: 1109).

The development of these will substitutes makes a point somewhat related to the Coase theorem. The proposition they seem to support is that private parties will attempt to set up by contract their own private, alternative, legal regimes when the transaction costs of the public law regime are unjustifiably high. When the costs of private contracting are low enough, contracts can be used to reduce the transaction costs imposed by entirely distinct public legal regimes. The enforceability of contractual relationships has freed individuals from many restrictions of the law of wills.

THE RULE AGAINST PERPETUITIES. We saw earlier that common law courts frowned on attempts to use the fee tail to control future land ownership. Should owners of land, using the flexible power of wills and trusts, be able to control who will possess the land, or what they do with it, in the distant future? Traditional law again answers in the negative. Although charitable trusts can last indefinitely, many other interests created by wills or trusts, or presumably other will substitutes, are subject to the Rule against Perpetuities. The Rule says that an interest is void if it might vest in interest too late; and too late is more than 21 years after the last death of persons alive when the interest was created. An interest vests when its taker can be identified and all conditions precedent to taking have been satisfied. The purpose of the Rule, it might be said, is to prevent people from even attempting to control ownership beyond the generation they know well, their children. As put by Lord Hobhouse:

> A clear, obvious, natural line is drawn for us between those persons and events which the Settlor knows and sees, and those which he cannot know or see. Within the former province we may trust his natural affections and his capacity of judgment to make better dispositions than any external Law is likely to make for him. Within the latter, natural affection does not extend, and the wisest judgment is constantly baffled by the course of events. I submit, then, that the proper limit of Perpetuity is that of lives in being at the time when the settlement takes effect (Hobhouse 1880: 188).

However, the assumption that a settlor is ignorant does not lead inexorably to the conclusion that the law's reallocation of rights is superior. Certainly any restraint on testation that might upset settlors ought to be justified with a showing, not just that the settlor knows not what he does, but that the law knows better. To make that showing, to describe the operation of the Rule and to see some of the benefits of its operation, it is helpful to look at specific examples.

A benefit of the rule in some cases is that it frees land from restrictions on use.

Example 1, where O, B, and C are all alive: O conveys Blackacre 'to B, but if the premises shall be used for the consumption of liquors then to C's widow'. C's widow's interest is void and B takes a fee simple absolute. The Rule improves resource allocation by directly eliminating the restriction on use. B need not refrain from drinking on Blackacre, and Blackacre becomes more enjoyable as it is put to better use by its possessors.

Example 2: T dies, leaving a will that devises Blackacre to his sister, who is 80 years old, for her life, then 'to my sister's daughters for life, then to my sister's granddaughters then living'. W is T's heir. Suppose that P wishes to buy Blackacre because he would enjoy residing there much more than would the sister's family. Without the Rule against Perpetuities, P would have some difficulty because some of the owners, the granddaughters, might not even be born yet. Following *Jee v. Audley*, however, a court would hold that the interest in the granddaughters violates the Rule and is void. The application of the Rule in such cases has been attacked as absurd, but the result is a clear improvement in resource allocation. As a result of the Rule, Blackacre's owners are the sister, her daughters, and W; and P can purchase a reasonably secure title. The Rule has eliminated a practical restriction on alienation, allowing the land to pass to a more appreciative owner. (New cases like these first two examples cannot arise in England because English law has since 1926 allowed such future interests to be created only in trust.)

Example 3: Assume the same facts as in Example 2, except that the sister is only 30 years old and has no granddaughters yet. As before, by the Rule, W becomes an interest holder instead of the granddaughters. W will probably never take possession, but that does not prevent W from enjoying her ownership. Unlike the unborn granddaughters who cannot possibly enjoy their ownership, she derives utility from her ownership (and may enjoy passing it along in her will) even though she will never take possession. The contingent interests invalidated by the Rule are like lottery tickets to lotteries that might not be held for scores of years. By taking those lottery tickets and reallocating them to a person who is alive today, the Rule places them in the hands of someone who can enjoy ownership. Thus the Rule accelerates the enjoyment of interests. Unlike the two points above, this benefit of the Rule obtains even when the interests in question are held in trust.

Example 4: T bequeaths $100,000 in trust, 'the income to be paid monthly to my nephew Ben and his descendants, but if a Libertarian wins a national office then to my nephew Sam and his descendants'. If this bequest were enforced as written, it would create uncertainty that diminishes the utility of the *res* of the trust. The Rule resolves the uncertainty by invalidating the interest in Sam, leaving Ben's family as the sole owners.

Although it could be argued that dividing rights is sometimes beneficial, such as when ownership is divided between a landlord and tenant or between a gambler and a bookmaker, the kinds of divided rights that violate the Rule rarely increase the net value of the divided asset. Some evidence that such divided rights decrease utility is that the market almost never creates ownership that could remain uncertain for a century or more. With the exception of poorly drafted option contracts, for which an exception might be appropriate, interests that violate the Rule against Perpetuities are almost always created by gift.

Of course, by his making of the gift, the donor tells us that the sum of the utility he takes from subdividing the ownership and the utilities of the donees is greater than the market offers for those assets. So executing the instrument does not reduce net utility at the time of execution. Later, however, when the donor dies, his utility drops to zero and the total utility derived from the asset is less with ownership divided in an uncertain manner than it would be with expectations made certain. The effect of the Rule, then, is to increase utility after the donor's death and decrease utility before his death.

One beauty of the Rule against Perpetuities is that its complexity, which has been elided here, minimizes the donor's utility losses before death. Certainly some donors will be frustrated by their inability to accomplish their dynastic designs and, knowing that, some potential donors may even consume more and accumulate less. That effect, however, should be small because, in actual operation, the Rule frustrates very few donors. According to Leach, '[p]ractically anything a testator is likely to want can be done within the limits of the Rule against Perpetuities' (1938: 669). Moreover, it is not in a lawyer's interest to say to the client that he is sorry that he cannot accomplish the client's ends. The lawyer has strong incentives to find a way. If the lawyer succeeds, the Rule causes the client no discontentment. If the lawyer mistakenly drafts a provision that violates the Rule, the client can usually correct the mistake if he discovers it before dying. If the client does not discover the mistake, his utility is not diminished by the Rule. Thus the Rule rarely decreases the utility that living persons derive from their assets. Many critics have called for reform of the Rule, and many statutory reforms have been adopted, always with the effect of reducing the frequency of the Rule's application. But the statutory reforms seem to reflect little recognition that the case law process created what could never be achieved through the legislative process, a wonderfully efficient Rule for freeing assets from the dead hand of the past.

CONCLUSION. It seems likely that testators will continue to invent ways to extend their influence into the future, and likely that the law will continue to find that some of those attempts have unacceptable consequences for successors. Despite adherence to some basic limitations, however, it appears that the law increasingly struggles to follow the dispositive intent of the decedent. We should expect societies, as they grow wealthier and more successful at providing basic needs, to grow more willing to use discretionary funds to pay for justice. We should be not too alarmed when that good absorbs an increasing portion of our consumption expenditures. Yet it is still appropriate to question whether the current trend has taken us beyond the current optimum. It may be that the law should not require courts to work so hard to achieve decedents' goals, especially where the decedent himself has expended little effort in expressing those goals.

J.E. STAKE

See also COMMITMENT; ENGLISH COMMON LAW; EQUITY; FIDUCIARY DUTIES; LEGAL FORMALITIES; PRECOMMITMENT AND PROHIBITION.

Subject classification: 5f; 5g(i).

STATUTES

De Donis Conditionalibus (1285), in the Statute of Westminster II, 13 Edw I c.1.

Statute of Uses 1535, 27 Hen VIII c.10.

Partition Act 1539, 31 Hen VIII c.1.

Statute of Wills 1540, 32 Hen VIII c.1.

Law of Property Act 1925, 15 & 16 Geo V c.20.

South Australia Wills Act Amendment Act (No. 2) 1975, amending Wills Act 1936, 8 South Australia Stat. 665.

Queensland Succession Act 1981, 1981 Queensland Stat. No. 69.

CASES

Fisher v. Wigg (1700) 1 Salk. 391.

In re Eagles (1990) 2 QdR 501.

In re Williams (1984) 36 SASR 423.

Jee v. Audley (1787) 1 Cox Rep. 324, 29 Eng. Rep. 1186.

R. v. Williams (1735) Bunb. 342.

Taltarum's Case (1472) YB 12 Edw IV 19.

BIBLIOGRAPHY

Basu, K. 1989. Technological stagnation, tenurial laws, and adverse selection. *American Economic Review* 79: 251–55.

Bogert, G.G. and Bogert, G.T. 1921. *Handbook of the Law of Trusts*. St. Paul: West Publishing Company; 5th edn, 1973.

Contemporary Studies Project. 1978. A comparison of Iowans' dispositive preferences with selected provisions of the Iowa and Uniform Probate Codes. *Iowa Law Review* 63: 1041–1152.

Dukeminier, J. 1979. Cleansing the stables of property: a river found at last. *Iowa Law Review* 65: 151–75.

Goody, J. 1987. Inheritance. In *The New Palgrave: A Dictionary of Economics*, ed. J. Eatwell, M. Milgate and P. Newman (London: Macmillan Press), Vol. 2: 851–5.

Hobhouse, A. 1880. *The Dead Hand: Addresses on the Subject of Endowments and Settlements of Property*. London: Chatto & Windus.

Katz, S.N. 1976. Thomas Jefferson and the right to property in revolutionary America. *Journal of Law and Economics* 19: 467–88.

Kurtz, S.F. and Hovenkamp, H. 1987. *Cases and Materials on American Property Law*. St. Paul: West Publishing Company; 2nd edn, 1993.

Langbein, J.H. 1984. The nonprobate revolution and the future of the law of succession. *Harvard Law Review* 97: 1108–1141.

Langbein, J.H. 1987. Excusing harmless errors in the execution of wills: a report on Australia's tranquil revolution in probate law. *Columbia Law Review* 87: 1–54.

Langbein, J.H. 1988. The twentieth-century revolution in family wealth transmission. *Michigan Law Review* 86: 722–51.

Leach, W.B. 1938. Perpetuities in a nutshell. *Harvard Law Review* 51: 638–71.

Megarry, R. and Wade, H.W.R. 1957. *The Law of Real Property*. London: Stevens & Sons; 5th edn, 1984. (A detailed treatment of English property law.)

Moynihan, C.J. 1962. *Introduction to the Law of Real Property*. St. Paul: West Publishing Co.; 2nd edn, 1988.

National Conference of Commissioners on Uniform State Laws. 1993. *The Uniform Probate Code*. St. Paul: West Publishing Company; 1995 edn.

Orth, J.V. 1992. After the revolution: 'reform' of the law of inheritance. *Law and History Review* 1992: 33–44.

Orth, J.V. 1997. Tenancy by the entirety: the strange career of the common-law marital estate. *Brigham Young University Law Review* 1997: 35–49.

Pechman, J. 1987. Inheritance taxes. In *The New Palgrave: A Dictionary of Economics*, ed. J. Eatwell, M. Milgate and P. Newman (London: Macmillan Press), Vol. 2: 855–7.

Posner, R.A. 1973. *Economic Analysis of Law*. Boston: Little, Brown & Co.; 4th edn, 1992.

Simpson, A.W.B. 1961. *An Introduction to the History of the Land*

Law. London: Oxford University Press. 2nd edn, retitled *A History of the Land Law*, Oxford: Clarendon Press, 1986. (A concise and authoritative summary of the development of many English inheritance rules.)

Stake, J.E. 1990. Darwin, donations, and the illusion of dead hand control. *Tulane Law Review* 64: 705–81.

Sussman, M.B., Cates, J.N. and Smith, D.T. 1970. *The Family and Inheritance*. New York: Russell Sage Foundation.

Waggoner, L.W., Alexander, G.S. and Fellows, M.L. 1991. *Family Property Law*. Westbury: The Foundation Press, Inc.; 2nd edn, 1997.

inheritance taxation. Many nations impose a final settling of fiscal accounts on the occasion of a person's death. In the United States and the United Kingdom, this settlement is accomplished by assessing a tax against the decedent's estate, before its distribution to heirs. In many of the continental European nations, this settlement is assessed against the inheritances that are transmitted to heirs. In this essay, these alternative forms for taxing the transfer of assets from one person to another are referred to generically as 'inheritance taxation'.

It seems quite clear that governments could increase considerably the vigour with which they seek to tax inheritance, as through raising rates and lowering the value of exemptions, deductions and exclusions. This does not mean that it would be wise for them to do so. The scholarly literature on the wisdom of inheritance taxation contains two branches, which may be called the fiscal and the social. The fiscal branch asks whether inheritance taxation is a good means for financing government, and the scholarship in this branch seeks to assess inheritance taxation against the canons of taxation that tax philosophers have articulated over the years. The social branch of inquiry is not concerned so much with the revenues that are raised as with the impact of inheritance and its taxation upon society. The claims advanced within this branch of inquiry range from the argument that inheritance is socially cancerous, with the taxation of inheritances being a means for removing the cancer, to claims that inheritance is socially beneficial, in which case inheritance taxation is socially harmful.

FISCAL JUSTIFICATIONS FOR INHERITANCE TAXATION. Is there any plausible justification for a tax on inheritance as a means of financing the general activities of government? While the writings of the tax philosophers contain plenty of disputation, they also reflect a fairly broad, though not universal, consensus regarding the general superiority of broad-based, nondiscriminatory forms of taxation over narrow-based, discriminatory forms. From a purely personal point of view, the best tax is surely one that someone else pays. The political generalization of this point of view, however, is a tax system whereby those who are politically successful secure tax privileges at the expense of those who are not. A principle of broad-based taxation can help to resist this political expression of personal interest, by subjecting potential political outcomes to a requirement that people whose tax bases are the same pay the same tax regardless of their political status.

Actual tax practice, however, is never so simple as a statement of principle might seem to suggest. A broad-based tax on income would seem to require that all people with the same income pay the same tax. People would not bear different tax liabilities depending simply on differences in the sources or uses of their incomes. Yet what constitutes income for tax purposes is something that is defined politically. It is easy for the products of political favouritism and domination to be characterized by the victors as national goals or needs. Further, the debates over such things as the degree of progressivity, or of exemptions and exclusions from tax liability, show that there is plenty of scope for apparent tax discrimination to be reconciled with support for a principle of nondiscrimination. However uneasy one may judge the case for progressive taxation to be (Blum and Kalven 1953), there nonetheless would be little dissent from the proposition that equally situated people should contribute equally to those revenues that are used to finance the general activities of governments. Indeed, this principle of uniformity or nondiscrimination in taxation is but one particular application of the principle of equality before the law.

Where does inheritance taxation fit into a principled support for a broad-based tax on income or consumption? What justification is there for some shift toward inheritance taxation? One straightforward line of argument follows from the Haig–Simons approach to the definition of income (see Simons 1938). Under this definition, annual income is the sum of consumption and any change in net worth. This approach would clearly treat the receipt of an inheritance as income to the recipient. Symmetry might seem to require that the value of an inheritance received by a donee should be treated as a negative income item to the donor, because the net worth of a donor falls by the amount of transfer. Most of the scholarly commentary, however, rejects this outcome, and treats the Haig–Simons approach as requiring that inheritances be added to the income of donees without being subtracted from the income of donors. Under this approach, there would exist no separate taxation of estates or inheritances, however, as wealth transfers through inheritance would be incorporated into the income tax.

What has been generally overlooked in the widespread usage made by fiscal scholars of the Haig–Simons approach is that its concepts and categories have been selected not for their economic coherence but for their fit with American political practice. It has been standard American tax practice to treat capital appreciation as an item of income, even if it is taxed at a different rate than other items of income. In contrast, capital appreciation is not treated as income in many nations throughout the world. In this alternative treatment, those nations have chosen, even if unwittingly, an economically coherent approach to the definition of income.

The Haig–Simons approach confounds two disjunct economic categories, capital and income. Moreover, this confounding was noted by Irving Fisher (1912), long before any writing by Haig or Simons. Income is the value of a flow of services generated by a set of assets over some interval of time; capital is the present valuation of the anticipated future income to be generated by those same assets. Capital and income are simply two different approaches to evaluating the same object. Through capitalization, any evaluation of income is concomitantly an evaluation of capital.

From this reciprocal nature of the relationship between capital and income, it follows that capital appreciation cannot be defined as income in any economically coherent manner. Capital appreciation is not one among many separable components of income, but rather is simply the capitalized reflection of the increased income yielded by an asset. An apple orchard that yields a net income of £100,000 may carry a value of £1 million, reflecting a ten-percent rate of capitalization. Now suppose the net income rises to £150,000, perhaps through some combination of an increased demand for apples and lower cost of production. The market value of the orchard will rise to £1.5 million. Income during the year is £150,000. It is not £650,000. The £500,000 of capital appreciation is not income, but is simply the capitalized reflection of the £50,000 increase in income.

To tax capital appreciation as income is a form of double taxation, as the increased yield of income and the increased value of the assets are simply two different manifestations of the same thing. The Fisherian conceptual framework, with its simple and symmetrical connection between capital values and income flows, does not, however, always fit easily with actual convention and practice. We can speak of human capital, but no direct capitalization takes place. There is a well-known line of argument that an income tax favours physical over human capital because maintenance and depreciation are not incorporated into measures of the net income from human capital. This type of argument has, in turn, been used to advocate an added tax on physical capital to achieve parity in tax treatment between physical and human capital. From this point of departure, some have suggested that a periodic tax upon death could substitute for an annual tax on net worth. This leads to a fiscally based justification for inheritance taxation.

Such arguments about a bias against human capital would have merit if the formation of human capital were financed through the same market processes as is the formation of physical capital. The formation of human capital, however, is subsidized heavily through state-financed education. This subsidization works to offset what might otherwise be a bias against human capital, perhaps even reversing any bias that might exist. With education being an object of heavy subsidization, it would seem difficult to press with any vigour a claim for a net worth tax, whether levied annually or only upon death, as a means of promoting neutrality between human and physical capital. There is simply no sound foundation for inheritance taxation in the standard normative lines of argument regarding methods for financing government.

INHERITANCE TAXATION, TAX SHIFTING AND FISCAL POLITICS. Tax policy is enacted by politicians and not by tax philosophers. It would seem relatively easy to explain the use of inheritance taxation through recourse to some simple notions of political arithmetic. Suppose revenues from an inheritance tax replace what would otherwise have been revenues from a broad-based tax on income. Any shift from an income to an inheritance tax will typically modify the distribution of tax liability within the population. Under normal presumptions about the distributions of inheritance and income, a greater reliance on inheritance taxation will reduce taxes for a majority of people. The simple political arithmetic of majority voting would seem to explain some use of inheritance taxation as a means of shifting tax burdens.

Indeed, what would seem to call for explanation is the limited use of inheritance taxation in spite of such political arithmetic. Inheritance taxation hits relatively few taxpayers directly, though it may hit a greater number indirectly. Some scholars have argued that inheritance taxation, by reducing the net return to capital, reduces the accumulation of capital in a nation, which in turn lowers wages and incomes. In this manner, the burden of an inheritance tax is spread onto those on whom no tax liability would have been directly assessed (see, for example, Wagner 1993).

Moreover, the actual politics of taxation is not so simple as such simple numerical exercises would suggest. The simple arithmetic of majority voting must be amended to allow for differential effectiveness and influence among people. Those who belong to relatively effective interest groups take on added weight compared with those who do not. Even if wealthy people might not constitute an interest group in the absence of inheritance taxation, the adoption of an inheritance tax would transform them into one. There is plenty of theoretical reason and empirical support for the claim that wealth increases the effectiveness of an interest group. This consideration suggests that inheritance taxes would be employed to a lesser extent than the simple arithmetic of majority voting would lead one to expect. Still, the claim that the presence of inheritance taxes in a government's fiscal arsenal can be explained as a form of tax shifting to minority groups remains valid, only those minority groups are able to reduce the extent of such tax shifting through their effectiveness in mustering political opposition to inheritance taxation.

While it is simple to offer an explanation for the use of inheritance taxation based upon the arithmetic of majority rule, this does not imply that the use of inheritance taxation must necessarily be a result of its ability to shift tax burdens. It is possible to imagine a situation where inheritance taxation is generally agreeable, and not a simple matter of a majority imposing itself upon a minority. Features of such an argument are set forth in Buchanan (1967). Suppose people were to choose their tax systems prior to their possession of any knowledge concerning their own economic position. Further suppose that the alternative to inheritance taxation is a flat-rate tax on income. Is it conceivable that there would be general support for some replacement of the income tax with an inheritance tax? Under the postulated circumstances, people who end up as potential testators or heirs will be in a position somewhat analogous to lottery winners. Arguments grounded in a diminishing marginal utility of income could be used to adduce that some shifting of the tax burden away from incomes onto estates or inheritances would represent a kind of fiscally mediated purchase of insurance.

In this setting, it would be possible to justify inheritance taxation on purely fiscal grounds. The problem with this line of justification, of course, is that it envisions a process of fiscal choice that is analogous to the choice of rules in advance of actually playing the game. In actuality, taxes are chosen and revised while the game is in play and people pretty much know their economic interests. This returns us to the simple arithmetic of majority rule, but it does not deny that some purely fiscal rationale that has plausible normative foundations can be constructed, even if those normative foundations may weigh but lightly in the full range of considerations concerning inheritance taxation.

INHERITANCE TAXATION AND THE CORRECTION OF SOCIETAL DEFORMITY. The bulk of the literature on inheritance taxation focuses not on its merits as a means of generating revenues for governments, but on its qualities in correcting alleged societal deformities that some think would otherwise characterize a market economy. A regime of free inheritance is presumed to be socially cancerous, in that it promotes the transmission and magnification of material inequality across generations. The wealthy are wealthy not because of what they have accomplished but because their parents were wealthy. The poor are poor not so much through any failure to accomplish as through a foreclosure of the possibilities of accomplishment in society, due to the transmission of material position through inheritance. Through its perpetuation of inequality across generations, inheritance imparts elements of a caste system into society. These claims are often buttressed by analogies drawn from the operation of compound interest, which, when compounded at a common rate, leaves unchanged the rank orderings of the fortunes of people and their descendants through time.

Against this background, inheritance taxation is portrayed as a means for promoting some measure of equality of opportunity, by reducing the heritability of economic position. In a commonly used analogy, the receipt of an inheritance is likened to the receipt of a head start in a footrace. To be sure, inheritance has more dimensions than material wealth. Families can differ in the educational opportunities they provide for their children, in the experiences and the nurturing they furnish, and in the contacts and connections they make available, to say nothing of the importance of genetics. Furthermore, efforts to restrict material forms of inheritance, as through inheritance taxation, will induce some substitution into these other forms. Still, a programme of inheritance taxation is portrayed as a means of helping to promote equality of opportunity among people, which in turn is construed as a situation where everyone starts the race from the same position, as against some people receiving head starts based on the advantages provided by their parents.

The allure of this popular analogy would seem to lie in its simplicity. It surely seems unfair to let some racers start ahead of others, and if economic life is thought of as a race, it might seem axiomatic to claim that the bequeathal of estates should be disallowed, at least to individuals. This simple analogy, however, is at least as erroneous as it is alluring, as it is both economically incoherent and situationally inapt. Equal starting positions in a race may indicate some modicum of fairness and equality of opportunity to the participants, but this is only because those participants have arrived at that starting line through a lengthy social process of open competition, where many one-time competitors dropped out along the way because they were not fast enough. Those who dropped out were those who were naturally not so fast as those who remained. When some people happen to be quicker than others by virtue of birth, those who were born naturally slow would not face an equal opportunity of winning the race should they be made to start at the same place as those who were naturally fast. Fairness would seem to require a set of handicaps where those who were naturally quicker would start further back. How much further back? So long as those who were handicapped by starting in the rear still finished in the front, it would seem as though the handicap was not sufficient to provide equal opportunity. When the footrace analogy is applied in a context where people differ in their talents, equality of opportunity becomes indistinguishable from equality of results.

Moreover, the footrace analogy is incoherent when it is applied to economic life. In a footrace there is one winner and many losers. Placing a handicap on a projected winner increases the odds that someone else will win. Increased odds of success for some racers comes at the expense of reduced odds of success for other racers. This zero sum character, where one person's gain is someone else's loss, surely characterizes footraces. But it most surely does not describe economic life. An Isaac Singer may become wealthy through developing a sewing machine, but at the same time millions of other people are able to become better clothed, as well as to become healthier because they can now afford new clothes, whereas before they had to wear used clothes, which often were sources of disease. The footrace analogy construes economic life as fundamentally a matter of wealth redistribution, whereas in fact it is wealth creation (and dissipation) that is centrally important to the quality of economic well-being.

There can be no doubt that a person's family situation exerts an influence in many ways over their prospects and opportunities in life. At the same time, that family situation is far from being absolutely controlling. There is a great deal of fluidity in the transmission of economic positions across generations. While children whose parents were of above-average wealth tend to have above-average wealth themselves, they also fare less well than their parents on average. Similarly, children whose parents were of below-average wealth also tend on average to be of below-average wealth, but yet also wealthier than their parents. Some process of regression toward the mean seems clearly to characterize relative economic positions across generations, as well as within the same set of people followed over a number of years.

This is not to deny the existence of serial correlation in economic position. Indeed, a world without such correlation would be unrecognizable, as, among other things, it would require the operation of different principles of biology and genetics than those to which we are subject. It would also mean that parents were totally ineffectual in raising their children. What the evidence does deny, however, is the applicability of any kind of reasoning based on analogies with compound interest applied to different initial starting points. Competitive market economies are far removed from caste societies. Material inheritance is not a dominant influence over one's economic position. Lawrence Lindsay (1992) reports that less than half of the top one percent of American wealth holders received any inheritances at all, and in the aggregate for those people inheritances were less than 10 percent of their reported wealth.

Arguments about equality of opportunity are often joined by arguments about the moral superiority of earned over unearned wealth. By making it possible for people to live on the unearned incomes that have been bequeathed to them, and which substitute for what would otherwise have to be efforts to earn their own way, inheritance promotes slothfulness and indulgence. It is noteworthy in this respect that the widely cited Rignano programme for inheritance taxation would apply only a 50 percent rate to the first generation of inheritance, while confiscating the inheritance that remains for the second generation. The Rignano programme represents one effort to institutionalize the belief that inheritance is a normatively inferior form of wealth, with the degree of inferiority rising with the passing of time.

There is no doubt that a large fortune can support a lot of slothfulness and indulgence. But it is also the case that such a fortune will be a fortune that is on its way to dissipation. Inherited wealth cannot perpetuate itself without effort. Someone may inherit a company that manufactures breakfast cereals. Regardless of the company's value at the time of inheritance, if it simply rests on past accomplishments and fails to develop new products or to adapt, for example, to changing consumer concerns and beliefs about such things as nutrition, it will lose out to competitors. In a competitive market economy, all asset positions are open to continual challenge, whereby wealth, once earned, must be re-earned continually or else it will be lost. Wealth earned by age fifty will not perpetuate itself automatically until age eighty, regardless whether that wealth was created by the holder or received through inheritance.

PROPERTY, THE FAMILY AND HUMAN FLOURISHING. It is possible to support inheritance taxation even if it is recognized that claims about the socially cancerous nature of inheritance rest on weak foundations. If inheritance were socially neutral, so would be its taxation. The taxation of inheritance might affect the distribution of wealth within society, but there would be no effect upon the character of society in any relevant dimension. In contrast to this Coase-like proposition, however, there is much reason and evidence to support the claim that inheritance is socially beneficial, which in turn would render the taxation of inheritance a source of harm.

The taxation of inheritance strikes at two of the primary institutions of civil society: property and the family. Inheritance taxation is a limitation on rights of property beyond those contained in broad-based taxes during life. Inheritance taxation imposes an additional tax on the mere transfer of an asset from one person to another, and thus transforms private property into common, with the rate of transformation varying directly with the rate of tax. A 50 percent rate of tax, for instance, shifts one-half of private property into the state-governed commons upon death.

The ability of inheritance taxation to convert private property into common resonates well with the famous controversy between Plato and Aristotle over the raising of children. Plato, in *The Republic*, advocated that children be raised in common, as a way of abolishing the advantages that result when particular children are raised in particular families. Plato sought to promote a form of equal opportunity, whereby no children would derive particular advantages because they were raised in family situations that were better in one way or another. Plato argued that the movement of child rearing from particular families to the state-governed commons would result in all parents coming to feel and act paternally toward all children. In commenting on this Platonic scheme, Aristotle noted in his *Politics* that this would lead to all parents acting with equal and universal indifference toward all children. As Aristotle put it quite succinctly: 'It is better to be own cousin to a man than to be his son after the Platonic fashion' (p. 44). For children to be raised with parental interest and not indifference, it is necessary to call upon the natural partiality of parents for their own children.

The family and private property are two of the primary institutional foundations of a flourishing society. Inheritance taxation strikes at both by restricting their range of operation. Inheritance taxation seeks to impose penalties upon families that are successful in accumulating wealth, in the name of promoting fairness for everyone else. Without doubt, many people start life with what amount to negative legacies. But what is the appropriate response to the presence of such negative legacies? Inheritance taxation, and its attack on property and the family, seeks to scale down the positive legacies that are bequeathed, much as Plato sought to scale back what he regarded as positive parental legacies.

An alternative approach would look to the elimination of negative legacies as an important element in a positive programme for a flourishing society. Rather than seeking to penalize those who were successful in creating positive legacies, it would seek to cultivate conditions that were less conductive to the persistence of negative legacies. Such a programme for a flourishing society would seek to reform those institutions that restrict opportunity, rather than to curtail those institutions, like private property and freedom of inheritance, that foster it. The precise characteristics of such an approach are outside the scope of this essay, however, and point in part to territory that is now under examination in the widespread rethinking of the welfare state that is well underway.

The attenuation of property rights that inheritance taxation creates is typically mitigated when transfers are earmarked for certain kinds of philanthropic activities and organizations. Indeed, it is often claimed that this tax exemption, in conjunction with high tax rates on transfers to individuals, serves to promote bequests to such organizations. If this claim were accurate, it would point to the apparent paradox that those mediating institutions that are an important part of the framework of a flourishing society become supported more strongly as property and family are weakened through inheritance taxation.

That paradox, however, is fictive, though it is easy to see how the claim might have gained currency. An increase in the tax rate does lower the price of leaving charitable bequests, when those bequests are exempt from tax. Under the estate tax approach used in the United States, it costs a donor £1.25 million to leave £1 million to personal heirs when the tax rate is 20 percent. It costs but £1 million to leave the same amount to philanthropic organizations. With an estate tax rate of 50 percent, it would cost £2 million to leave £1 million to personal heirs. As the rate of tax rises, the relative cost of charitable bequests falls. With a 20 percent rate of tax, a charitable bequest is 80 percent as costly as a personal bequest. With a 50 percent rate of tax, the charitable bequest is only 50 percent as costly as a personal bequest.

The effect of inheritance taxation on charitable bequests cannot be gauged on the basis of such imputed price comparisons alone. The combination of high rates of tax and charitable exemptions may well lead to an increase in the share of net bequests that go to philanthropic organizations while decreasing the total volume of philanthropic bequests. As estates become larger, charitable bequests rise relative to personal bequests. The limiting form of this observation is a case where people have a target level for their personal bequests, and leave the remainder to philanthropic organizations. As the rate of inheritance tax rises, the amount that a testator spends to leave the desired amount of personal bequest will rise, which in turn will leave less for philanthropic bequests.

To postulate a target level of personal bequests is to postulate a zero elasticity of demand for such bequests. Under ordinary assumptions about elasticity, increases in the rate of inheritance tax will reduce the volume of personal bequests left, though the amount of wealth devoted to leaving those bequests will have increased, provided only that the demand for personal bequests remains inelastic. As a result, philanthropic bequests will be lower at higher rates of tax, and would be lower still if those bequests were not exempt from tax.

This point about the negative effect of inheritance taxation upon philanthropic support can also be approached through a comparison of extremes: free inheritance on the one hand and taxation at 100 percent on the other. Under the 100 percent rate of tax, personal bequests are impossible. Estates will be accumulated only to the extent that testators choose to leave charitable bequests. Otherwise, people will convert their wealth into annuities, increasing the applicability of the life cycle model of saving in the process. Inheritance taxation would seem to impinge strongly on the support for philanthropic organizations, though legal rules governing the creation and operation of such organization are also important components of the robustness of such organizations.

WEALTH, INHERITANCE, AND THE FORMS OF DEMOCRACY. The social concerns that comprise the larger portion of the literature on inheritance taxation would seem to have only modest merit in an open-market economy. Such a form of economic organization has as its counterpart a system of liberal democracy. This is an approach to democratic governance whereby the state is subject to the same principles of property and contract as are other participants in society. Liberal democracy is accompanied by a system of open competition, governed only by the general principles of property and contract. Under liberal democracy, any wealth position is subject to challenge. There is no conductor who monopolizes the determination of whether someone can challenge for first violin.

The liberally democratic approach to economic and political organization has been under strenuous challenge throughout most of the twentieth century, with the democratic challenge coming from a system of social democracy. Under social democracy, the state is not limited by prior principles of property and contract, because the state serves as the arena within which property rights are granted, removed, or abridged, as well as the arena within which the substance of contract is rewritten through legislation and regulation. Competitive pressures are as intense in a system of social democracy as they are in one of liberal democracy. Those pressures, however, manifest themselves differently, often with significant economic consequence.

Social democracy operates in many areas to replace open competition with a system of closed or moderated competition, where the principles of property and contract have been relegated to the background through legislation and regulation. Social democracy forecloses paths of competition and creates sheltered positions where wealth positions may be more secure, and with that security purchased through political insurance, in one form or another. The state becomes a partisan of well-organized and well-financed interests, which injects a bias in favour of those who are established over those who are not. The competition for first violin is no longer open to all, but is open only to those who are invited. In this way the natural process of regression toward the mean may be slowed through political control and the complementarity that is created between private wealth and public power. Hence, inherited wealth may be socially beneficial in a system of liberal democracy, where the state acts as something of a referee or night watchman, and yet take on cancerous characteristics in a system of social democracy.

RICHARD E. WAGNER

See also DISTRIBUTIVE JUSTICE; INHERITANCE LAW; SIMONS, HENRY C.; SOCIAL JUSTICE.

Subject classification: 2d(ii).

BIBLIOGRAPHY

Aristotle. *The Politics of Aristotle*. Ed. and trans. E. Barker, Oxford: Clarendon Press, 1946.

Blum, W.J. and Kalven, H. 1953. *The Uneasy Case for Progressive Taxation*. Chicago: University of Chicago Press.

Brittain, J.A. 1978. *Inheritance and the Inequality of Material Wealth*. Washington, DC: Brookings Institution.

Buchanan, J.M. 1967. *Public Finance in Democratic Process*. Chapel Hill: University of North Carolina Press.

Fisher, I. 1912. *The Nature of Capital and Income*. New York: Macmillan.

Hall, A.P. 1997. *The Concept of Income Revisited: An Investigation into the Double Taxation of Saving*. Washington, DC: Tax Foundation.

Lindsay, L.B. 1992. Why the 1980s were not the 1920s. *Forbes 400* (October 19): 78ff.

Meade, J.E. 1974. *The Inheritance of Inequalities: Some Biological Demographic, Social and Economic Factors*. Third Keynes lecture in economics, 5 Dec 1973; London: Oxford University Press, 1974.

Plato. *The Republic*. Ed. and trans. B. Jowett, London: Macmillan, 1892.

Rignano, E. 1924. *The Social Significance of the Inheritance Tax*. Trans. W. Shultz, New York: Knopf.

Simons, H.C. 1938. *Personal Income Taxation*. Chicago: University of Chicago Press.

Tait, A.A. 1967. *The Taxation of Personal Wealth*. Urbana: University of Illinois Press.

Tullock, G. 1971. Inheritance justified. *Journal of Law and Economics* 14: 465–74.

Wagner, R.E. 1977. *Inheritance and the State*. Washington, DC: American Enterprise Institute.

Wagner, R.E. 1993. Federal transfer taxation: a study in social cost. Washington, DC: Institute for the Study of Taxation.

Wedgewood, J. 1929. *The Economics of Inheritance*. London: George Routledge & Sons.

insider trading. Insider trading, in the sense of one party to a transaction knowing something about the subject matter that the other party does not, is presumably as old as the history of exchange. To economists, exchange under conditions of asymmetric information is a situation with which parties and markets have long contended. When does the extent, or the source, of the asymmetry create a problem with which the parties themselves cannot adequately deal? In general, the law has historically prohibited (that is, afforded a remedy for) the knowledge of significant misstatements by one party on which the other party has reasonably relied, but beyond that they are left to their own information and judgment as to whether to enter into the transaction.

That is no longer the case with regard to transactions in securities, unlike most other property. Instead, a complicated jurisprudence has grown up for securities transactions, going beyond misrepresentation to non-disclosure and beyond the actual transaction parties to other persons. That process began, fairly slowly, in the United States in the 1930s and has now increasingly spread to securities markets in Europe and elsewhere.

The central legal issues have been to define what constitutes insider trading and what precisely is the problem with it. After economists became interested in the subject, their central concerns have been to measure the magnitude of insider trading and to assess its effects (usually theoretically rather than empirically) on the internal efficiency of the firm and on the performance of capital markets.

In the US, the Securities Exchange Act of 1934 contained two provisions relevant to insider trading: §16 and §10(b). Section 16 required insiders (defined as officers, directors and 10% stockholders) to file public reports of changes in their stock holdings with the Securities and Exchange Commission (SEC), not to make short sales, and to pay to the company any 'profit' resulting from matching sales and purchases within six months of each other. Although the stated statutory purpose of this 'short-swing' trade liability was that of 'preventing the unfair use of information which may have been obtained', there was no requirement that the trades have actually been based on any inside information.

Interestingly, the liability was enforced not by the SEC but by private suits; either the company or any shareholder could bring an action to recover the profit for the company. The action was usually brought by an attorney, who followed the trading reports and bought a qualifying share of stock, in order to be awarded attorney's fees if successful. This enforcement mechanism was quite effective, and largely wiped out short-swing trading by insiders; litigation was devoted to the boundaries, such as when mergers were to be treated as sales or what securities were economic equivalents. What was not eliminated was actual profiting from the use of inside information. A purchase or sale founded on inside information created no liability, provided there was no transaction the other way within six months. Ultimately, the section became primarily a trap for the unlucky or unwary.

Section 10(b) of the 1934 Act was just a delegation of authority to the SEC, to adopt rules prohibiting 'any manipulative or deceptive device or contrivance' in connection with the purchase or sale of securities. Not until 1942 did the SEC adopt the now-famous rule 10b–5, making it unlawful for any person, in connection with the purchase or sale of a security, to engage in any fraud or to 'make any untrue statement of a material fact or to omit to state a material fact necessary in order to make the statements made, in the light of the circumstances under which they were made, not misleading'.

The Securities Act of 1933 in §17 (a) already applied that same standard to the sale of securities; rule 10b–5 merely extended it to purchases. In both cases, the standard was enforced by the SEC, in broker/dealer regulation or in injunction or criminal proceedings; those sections did not purport to create any private rights of action. But in 1947 a federal district court applied the rule to a private lawsuit by stockholders in a closely held company against directors who purchased shares without disclosing that they were negotiating a sale of the business.

Other federal courts gradually agreed that rule 10b–5 created private causes of action, in exchange transactions as well as direct dealings, and the door was opened for judges to define the elements of the lawsuit as they saw fit, without guidance or limitation from a Congress which had never thought about the issue. The *Texas Gulf Sulphur* decision by the 2d Circuit Court of Appeals in 1968 triggered an explosion in rule 10b–5 lawsuits by the SEC and private parties, and in the scope of situations to which it was applied (Grundfest 1994); there are now more than 8,000 federal court decisions citing the rule.

Acting as an unguided and uncoordinated legislature, the federal courts had to address and determine all the requirements of a cause of action. The possibilities presented by the language of the rule were numerous, as lawyers soon discovered, and over time at least four distinguishable categories of cases were developed:

(1) Actions based on misrepresentations by defendants who bought or sold securities. This category was mostly a federal version of the common law action for deceit that existed under state law anyway.

(2) Actions against a defendant who purchased or sold without disclosure of important information.

(3) Actions against non-traders, such as a company or its

officers who had put out an inaccurate financial statement or been dilatory in releasing a press statement on some significant matter, thereby affecting the trading market.

(4) Actions against corporate management for violations of their fiduciary duty to stockholders under state law, converted into a federal action on a theory of failure to disclose the violation.

The only category which will be explored further here is the second, in the context of transactions over an exchange, which probably best comports with the common understanding of insider trading. But unfortunately for clarity of discussion and analysis, these are all treated as 'rule 10b–5 actions' in judicial decisions, and statements made in one context are often applied without distinction to quite different situations. Rational jurisprudence is not thereby advanced.

As the courts proceeded to shape the cause of action, they had to specify its necessary elements, without assistance from any legislative history, and both the SEC and Congress have consistently resisted providing a definition of insider trading. There is no mention in the rule of insiders or inside information; it refers to 'any person' and 'material facts'. Would it apply to transactions in the secondary trading market between persons unconnected to the company?

Must the plaintiff be a person who transacted with the defendant, and what would such a requirement mean in the case of anonymous transactions through a securities exchange? What is the extent of the defendant's liability, and how is it to be measured? How are we to determine which facts are material? The rule uses the language of misrepresentations and half-truths; must they be intentional? Could 'pure' non-disclosure constitute a violation? Does the source of the non-disclosed information matter?

Presumably it would help in answering such questions to have a clear idea of the purpose of the rule, and of the costs and benefits of different positions. As formulated in the *Texas Gulf Sulphur* decision, the rule requires that 'anyone in possession of material inside information must either disclose it to the investing public, or . . . must abstain from trading in or recommending the securities concerned while such inside information remains undisclosed.' Over time, judges came up with allusions, usually brief, to various rationales for what they were deciding, which can be sorted into at least three lines (Scott 1980).

First, there is a concern with fairness in the stock market, sometimes rephrased as a concern with public confidence in the market. The SEC saw 'inherent unfairness' where one party has information not available to others, and the *TGS* court referred to a 'justifiable expectation of the securities marketplace that all investors trading on impersonal exchanges have relatively equal access to material information'. This 'fair game' approach has a number of implications. The source of the informational advantage or status of the one possessing it seem irrelevant. It is not evident why the concern should not extend beyond information to any other advantage that one trader may possess, in terms of capital or acumen or experience, over the other. The injury is to the other player, who should be made whole by a rescission of the unfair trade.

Second, some courts felt the purpose of the rule was to enhance the flow of information to the stock market, to contribute to the accurate pricing of securities and the efficient allocation of capital resources. If non-disclosure is the essence of the wrong, then the injury is to all who traded in the opposite direction during the period before ultimate disclosure, and damages are to be measured by the stock price adjustment. Of course, the *TGS* rule of 'disclose or abstain' really means 'abstain', since disclosure first would remove the gain from trading. A no-trading rule for insiders might have a minor effect on promoting corporate disclosure, though it is arguable, while removing from the market price discovery process the signalling effect of such trades. But it seems an indirect and ineffective way to mandate disclosure of new information by the firm, if that is the objective of the 'informed market' position.

Third, some courts have seen the rule as affording protection to valuable business property from 'misappropriation' by employees and others. In the *TGS* case itself, the insiders were buying company stock on the basis of a major mineral strike, which the company was keeping confidential while it acquired the surrounding land; the resulting activities would tend to fuel rumours and drive up the price of both the stock and the land, the latter to the company's detriment. If the rule is to protect the value of investment in the production of useful information, then the injured party would be the owner of the stolen information (not traders) and the measure of damages would be the reduction in that investment's value (not stock price changes). But why should it matter whether the thief is an 'insider' to the company, or whether the information originated within the company? and is it a function of the federal securities laws to protect corporate property rights?

A sequence of decisions has answered some of these questions, though not in a particularly coherent way. To begin with, and to simplify a bit, the defendant must be an insider, a term that is nowhere defined but has been held to include actual company employees, directors and agents; 'temporary' insiders (such as lawyers, printers, accountants or consultants who are performing a confidential assignment for the company); and 'tippees' who receive the information from one who they know has breached a fiduciary duty in telling them. The Supreme Court in *Chiarella* (1980) and *Dirks* (1983) rejected the expansive 'fair game' approach that the mere possession of non-public information would violate a parity of information standard; there had to be a breach of some fiduciary duty.

Usually the information will also be 'inside' – that is, nonpublic information derived from within the company whose shares are being traded. But under the misappropriation theory, what if the information is external – an acquirer is about to make a tender offer for the company, or it is about to be awarded a major contract – and someone in a fiduciary relationship to the external source trades on the advance knowledge? This has been disputed terrain. Most courts found misappropriation of information to be a basis for criminal prosecution or civil enforcement against the outsider, but not for private lawsuits under rule 10b–5 and the Supreme Court endorsed the misappropriation theory, at least for criminal prosecutions, in *O'Hagan* (1997). (However, the SEC in 1980 issued a separate rule 14e–3 to protect tender offerors, which may also create a private right of action, and Congress followed with an express private action for contemporaneous traders in 1988.)

As the language of the rule states, the non-public information traded on must be 'material'. No one doubts that people running a company know a lot more about its affairs than outsiders; if they trade, when have they violated the rule? The Supreme Court's standard is that 'an omitted fact is material if there is a substantial likelihood that a reasonable shareholder would consider it important in deciding' (whether to buy or sell). So a jury decides *ex post* whether some information strikes it as sufficiently important; *ex ante*, the insider gets little help from the verbal formula. *TGS* involved what was characterized as one of the richest ore strikes of the century, but of course subsequent cases moved away from situations so clear cut. Section 10(b) also has a fraudulent intent or 'scienter' requirement; in the omission context, that means only that the insider must know the information has not been publicly disseminated.

If the insider does trade impermissibly, who is entitled to damages, and in what amount? The Supreme Court has held that the plaintiff must be a purchaser or seller of the securities, though not necessarily with the defendant; that ruled out an almost infinite class of those who claimed they decided *not* to purchase or sell due to material misrepresentations or omissions. But then what is the required 'connection' to the defendant? The answer is that the plaintiff must be merely one of those who traded in the opposite direction to the defendant, during some period still uncertain – possibly just while the defendant was trading, but probably all the way to the time of disclosure.

Since such plaintiffs are numerous, the doctrine gave rise to class actions covering a trading volume greatly in excess of the defendant's own transactions. If the measure of damages was the plaintiffs' aggregate losses, the sum could be enormous – in the *TGS* case, exceeding the entire net worth of the company as well as of the individual defendants (Ruder 1968). And in precisely what way did the defendant's action cause losses to the plaintiffs? They were making independent decisions to buy or sell, and the defendant's impact on the market price, if any, would be to have caused it to move in a direction favourable to them (Manne 1966).

The court decisions appear to have settled on a 'disgorgement' approach to damages; the insider's gain (or loss avoided) is divided pro rata among the public traders. Congress adopted that measure of damages in the 1988 legislation, but that was limited to 'contemporaneous' public traders and did not affect rule 10b–5. Of course, a disgorgement rule is open to criticism on the grounds of inadequate deterrence; what does the insider have to lose by trying, except for legal costs (and sometimes a prospect of criminal prosecution)? The stakes were increased in 1984, when Congress authorized the SEC to sue for up to three times the amount of profit gained or loss avoided, as a penalty paid to the government.

This tour of US insider trading law, condensed though it is, should make it clear that the concept and the rules are not simple. In the postwar years, other countries have made their own entries into the field, whether from conviction or from pressure by the SEC as it pursued transactions hidden in foreign accounts. Criminal sanctions were adopted in Japan in 1948, in France in 1970 and in the United Kingdom in 1980; prosecutions ranged from non-existent to occasional. German companies and exchanges adopted voluntary guidelines in 1970, to be incorporated into managerial employment contracts which allow the company to seek restitution after a finding by a stock exchange review panel; it is not clear that a finding of violation of the guidelines has ever occurred. Italy had no rules on insider trading. A country-by-country review of the legal status of insider trading can be found in Gaillard (1992).

In Europe the picture changed toward greater consistency with the adoption by the Council of the European Communities of the Insider Dealing Directive in 1989, to which Member States are obliged to conform their laws. The Directive is clearly influenced by US law, but departs from it in a number of ways. The inside information covered is defined as not only non-public but (instead of 'material') as 'of a precise nature' and 'likely to have a significant effect' on the securities price; the source may be either internal or external. Insiders may be primary (directors, employees, contractors, shareholders) or secondary (knowing tippees). Both categories are prohibited from 'taking advantage' of their inside information by trading; primary insiders are prohibited from tipping.

The Directive does not have the force of law; it has to be implemented by the Member States, which retain discretion over enforcement and the selection of penalties 'sufficient to promote compliance'. Most countries appear to be relying on administrative or criminal sanctions; notably absent (except for Ireland) are provisions expressly creating a private right of action, which in the United States proved a potent additional enforcement mechanism.

Economists have made a number of significant contributions to understanding some of the insider trading issues, although their impact on legal developments is less apparent. Empirically, they have sought to demonstrate the existence and magnitude of the insiders' advantage, in several ways. One was to examine the mass of reports filed every month by §16 insiders – that is, directors, officers and 10% shareholders. Both early studies by Scholes (1972), Jaffe (1974) and Finnerty (1976), and more recent ones such as by Seyhun (1986) and Lin and Howe (1990), have consistently found such insiders earning positive abnormal (that is, adjusted for market price movements; see Brown and Warner 1985) returns; the range is roughly 2% to 8%, depending on time period and methodology. Whether there is anything illegal about such excess returns depends, of course, on whether they derived from 'material' information or from something lesser.

If insiders reap excess returns, at whose expense are they obtained? The argument that the price impact of the insider's actions can only be to move the price against him suggests that the opposing trader can only be benefitted by having the insider in the market. But that views the opposing trader as a member of the uniformed public and a price-taker, making occasional and unsolicited portfolio trades for rebalancing or liquidity or savings/consumption purposes. Professional traders holding inventories, such as dealers or market makers, know that they will at times be trading against, and losing to, informed insiders; they identify them when they can and adjust the price, but otherwise have to treat the adverse selection as a cost of business and cover it in the bid-ask spread charged all customers. Seyhun (1986) provides supporting evidence. (The implication is that the private plaintiffs in insider trading cases are mostly reaping windfalls.)

Is there any justification for the insiders' excess returns? One argument is that the stock market is a market for information, that obtaining information generally has a cost, that insiders are led to impart information (even when it is not favourable) to the market by their trading, and that a market which quickly and accurately adjusts prices is the best protection for the public investor. That takes us back to the 'informed market' theory, and the question of whether (or under what circumstances) insider trading or its prohibition is the best way to achieve it.

A number of empirical studies have found information content in insider trades (Meulbroek 1992). But if greater price efficiency is coupled with higher transaction costs and lower market liquidity, the overall welfare verdict becomes theoretically indeterminate (Leland 1992).

Another argument in justification, of which Manne (1966) is the primary proponent, is that insider trading profits are an effective form of incentive compensation for entrepreneurial effort and innovation. Were it otherwise, we would have observed firms making their own efforts to restrict insider trading (Carlton and Fischel 1983). Other commentators have been more inclined to see them as an example of principal/agent costs, in the tradition of Jensen and Meckling (1976).

The agency cost view has developed a substantial literature of its own, mainly theoretical, devoted to the effects of insider trading opportunities on management behaviour (Bebchuk and Fershtman 1994). The models address such issues as risk aversion, the level of management compensation and effort, the selection of investment projects for the firm, and the timing of corporate disclosure. Not surprisingly, different assumptions lead to different outcomes, and little of the literature is empirical.

From a shareholder's point of view, the existence of insider trading is a known risk of investing; to the extent it is not diversifiable, it would have to be compensated for by the expected return. For shareholders in general, then, the game remains fair. The real concern is a social one, with respect to firm and market efficiency, the cost of capital and returns on investment – as compared to a more perfect world in which all insider trading (by some definition) is costlessly eliminated.

What effect has the regulation of insider trading had on the actual amount of insider trading? Has it been worth the resources devoted to it? In Europe, there is little evidence that the adoption of insider trading regulations had a significant impact on European securities markets (Estrada and Pena 1995). Of course, enforcement efforts have also been minimal. In the United States, however, the SEC has made insider trading regulation a major enforcement priority, and judicial proceedings are plentiful; the laws and sanctions have been progressively made more severe. Nonetheless, empirical studies have found an increase in both the volume and profitability of insider trading since 1975 (Seyhun 1992). Where there apparently has been an impact is on trading prior to major announcements of corporate takeovers and earnings (Arshadi and Eyssell 1991). The exchanges and SEC have a computerized stock watch programme that looks at unusual trading, particularly just before corporate releases that cause a significant movement in the price, and that not infrequently turns up trading on inside information. But trading which does not meet this description seems to have a low probability of detection. To sweep more broadly, Fried (1997) has proposed that §16 insiders be required to give electronic notice shortly in advance of entering an order, so that the market might be alerted to its possible information content.

Thus far, the lawyers and the economists have not come together on any consensus on what is the problem with insider trading and where there is a need for some form of mandatory regulation. Some facts are evident: insiders will always have an asymmetric information advantage, and will always be able to benefit from it in deciding when *not* to trade – that is, in postponing purchases until after the release of bad news and sales until after the release of good news. Given that, the question of when additional regulation increases social welfare is surprisingly complicated.

KENNETH E. SCOTT

See also CIVIL LIABILITY UNDER RICO: UNINTENDED CONSEQUENCES OF LEGISLATION; CLASS ACTIONS; CORPORATE CRIME AND ITS CONTROL; CRIMINAL CONVICTION AND FUTURE INCOME; FRAUD-ON-THE-MARKET; LAW-AND-ECONOMICS IN ACTION; MANNE, HENRY G.; OWNERSHIP OF MARKET INFORMATION; SECURITIES REGULATION; UNJUST ENRICHMENT.

Subject classification: 5e; 6c(iii).

STATUTES

Council Directive of 13 November 1989 coordinating regulations on insider dealing (89/592/EEC) OJ 1989 No. L 334 at 30.
Rule 10b–5, 17 CFR § 240.10b–5.
Securities Act of 1933, 15 USC § 77.
Securities Exchange Act of 1934, 15 USC § 78.

CASES

Chiarella v. United States, 445 US 222 (1980).
Dirks v. SEC, 463 US 646 (1983).
SEC v. Texas Gulf Sulphur Co., 401 F2d 833 (2d Cir. 1968), cert. denied, 394 US 976 (1969).
United States v. O'Hagan, 117 S Ct 2199 (1977).

BIBLIOGRAPHY

Arshadi, N. and Eyssell, T. 1991. Regulatory deterrence and registered insider trading: the case of tender offers. *Financial Management* 20: 30–39.

Bebchuk, L. and Fershtman, C. 1994. Insider trading and the managerial choice among risky projects. *Journal of Financial and Quantitative Analysis* 29: 1–14.

Brown, S.J. and Warner, J.B. 1985. Using daily stock returns: the case of event studies. *Journal of Financial Economics* 14: 1–31.

Carlton, D. and Fischel, D. 1983. The regulation of insider trading. *Stanford Law Review* 35: 857–95.

Estrada, J. and Pena, J.I. 1995. Empirical Evidence on the Impact of European Insider Trading Regulations. Working Paper 95–46, Departamento de Economia de la Empresa, Universidad Carlos III de Madrid.

Finnerty, J.E. 1976. Insiders and market efficiency. *Journal of Finance* 31: 1141–48.
Fried, J. 1997. Towards reducing the profitability of corporate insider trading through pre-trading disclosure. *Southern California Law Review* 70 (forthcoming).
Gaillard, E. (ed.) 1992. *Insider Trading: the Laws of Europe, the United States and Japan*. Boston: Kluwer Law and Taxation Publishers.
Grundfest, J. 1994. Disimplying private rights of action under the federal securities laws: the Commission's authority. *Harvard Law Review* 107: 961–1024.
Jaffe, J. 1974. Special information and insider trading. *Journal of Business* 47: 410–28.
Jensen, M.C. and Meckling, W.H. 1976. Theory of the firm: managerial behavior, agency costs, and ownership structure. *Journal of Financial Economics* 3: 305–60.
Leland, H.E. 1992. Insider trading: should it be prohibited? *Journal of Political Economy* 100: 859–87.
Lin, J. and Howe, J. 1990. Insider trading in the OTC market. *Journal of Finance* 45: 1273–84.
Manne, H. 1966. *Insider Trading and the Stock Market*. New York: Free Press.
Meulbroek, L.K. 1992. An empirical analysis of illegal insider trading. *Journal of Finance* 47: 1661–99.
Ruder, D. 1968. Texas Gulf Sulphur – the second round. *Northwestern University Law Review* 63: 423–50.
Scholes, M.S. 1972. The market for securities: substitution versus price pressure and the effects of information on share price. *Journal of Business* 45: 179–211.
Scott, K. 1980. Insider trading: Rule 10b–5, disclosure and corporate privacy. *Journal of Legal Studies* 9: 801–18.
Seyhun, H.N. 1986. Insiders' profits, costs of trading, and market efficiency. *Journal of Financial Economics* 16: 189–212.
Seyhun, H.N. 1992. The effectiveness of the insider-trading sanctions. *Journal of Law and Economics* 35: 149–82.

instalment credit contracts. An instalment credit contract is an agreement by which credit is extended on terms that it is to be repayable by instalments. The modern history of instalment selling began early in the nineteenth century with the sale of furniture and household effects. It then spread to sewing machines as the result of an initiative by the Singer Sewing Machine Company, and to pianos (see Seligman 1927:17–22). Several factors have contributed to the huge growth of instalment credit: the development of mass production techniques for motor cars, machinery and household goods; the evolution of specialist finance houses; the post-war expansion in the range of available consumer goods, accompanied by fierce competition for their custom among stores and financiers; and the introduction of credit cards and other revolving credit facilities which kept customers in a continuing relationship with card issuers and suppliers.

The never-ending pressure on suppliers and financiers to produce new credit products has resulted in a bewildering variety of instalment credit forms. These have evolved differently in different countries (see Farnsworth 1972:3–20). The law governing them also varies greatly from one legal family to another and within a given legal family. However, in the field of consumer instalment credit, legislation has been found necessary in most jurisdictions to deal with abuses in selling and lending practices, with a high degree of similarity both in the forms of abuse and in the remedial measures taken to prevent or correct it. These remedial measures vary according to the characterization of the instalment credit agreement, and a striking feature is the extent of commonality in the systems of classification adopted, whether in legislation or by the courts.

Instalment credit may be retail or wholesale. The former involves the extension of credit to the end-user of goods, the latter the provision of financial support for dealers to enable them to acquire their stock (inventory). Wholesale credit in the form of a floor (or stocking) plan may be provided by loan secured on the dealer's inventory and accounts or by means of a bailment, by which the finance house purchases the required inventory from the supplier and supplies it to the dealer on conditional sale or hire-purchase.

CHARACTERIZATION OF INSTALMENT CREDIT CONTRACTS. In all legal systems the characterization of transactions is of fundamental importance. The classifications of particular relevance to instalment credit law are: loan (lender) credit versus sale (vendor) credit; fixed-sum credit versus revolving (or running-account) credit; and debtor-creditor-supplier (or connected) credit versus debtor-creditor (or unconnected) credit.

(1) *Loan credit and sale credit.* Of the three classifications mentioned above, the first is the most fundamental. In the loan form money is advanced to the borrower, or to a third party at his request, which is repayable by instalments, usually with interest. Under an instalment sale, or one of its variants, the credit is extended by way of deferment of the price for the supply of land, goods, services or other things, the price and any credit or finance charge being repayable by instalments. Forms of price-deferment contract include credit sale, in which ownership passes to the buyer from the outset, conditional sale, in which title is retained by the seller until completion of payment, and hire-purchase, in which the goods are hired with an option, but not an obligation, to buy them at the end of the hire period. Pure rental agreements do not involve the extension of credit, but finance leases, in which the rent is fixed so as to amortize the capital cost and desired return on capital over the useful life of the leased equipment, are equated with sales on credit in accounting convention and are vulnerable to treatment as sales and secured loans in North American legal systems, though not usually elsewhere.

The laws of most countries outside North America, whether common law or civil law systems, distinguish sharply between sale credit and purchase-money loan credit, even though the economic effect of the two transactions is the same. For example, in England usury legislation never applied to the credit charge payable on instalment sales, this being considered merely a 'time-price differential' between the price for immediate payment and the price if credit were taken. That was established in 1827 in *Beete v. Bidgood*, involving the sale of a half share of a plantation, including a number of slaves, in Demerara (now Guyana) under conditional sale agreements. The plaintiff's contention that the credit charge (inaccurately referred to in the agreement as interest) fell outside the usury legislation was triumphantly vindicated (no one appeared to be concerned about the fate of the slaves). Again, except in the United States and Canada the retention of title under a conditional sale agreement is not categorized as a form of chattel mortgage, for the buyer is not giving rights in security over his own goods but is merely agreeing that he would not become the owner until payment. This form of agreement therefore avoids both the legislation governing the form and registration of chattel mortgages and the rules of equity by which a mortgagee who sells the mortgaged property on default has to account to the mortgagor for the surplus. A form of agreement that evolved in England is hire-purchase, an agreement for hire under which the hirer has an option, but no obligation, to buy. Hire-purchase is thus a hybrid which combines elements of lease and sale but is distinct from both and falls outside legislation governing sales. It is not generally recognized as a distinct legal category in civil law countries or in North America, being there treated either as a lease or as a sale and, in the United States and Canada, as a security equivalent to a purchase-money chattel mortgage.

The loan credit/sale credit dichotomy is a specific manifestation of a wider issue with which legal systems have had to grapple, namely that of form versus substance, the theme of an influential work by Atiyah and Summers (1987). This is also the issue which has traditionally divided legal theory from accounting convention. Until the middle of the twentieth century most courts tended to apply formal reasoning to legal questions and to characterize transactions by reference to the legal form in which they were cast rather than according to their economic substance or to social or policy considerations. There was thus considerable consternation when in 1963 the Nebraska Supreme Court ruled in *Elder v. Doerr* that a finance charge on an instalment sale was usurious interest and that the retail instalment sales legislation which had appeared to validate it was unconstitutional, thereby rendering unenforceable outstanding retail instalment sales liabilities estimated at $400 million and bringing about an almost total cessation of this type of business in Nebraska until the problem was eventually resolved by new legislation. More recently, the rent-to-own agreement (the American equivalent of the English hire-purchase agreement) has provoked attack on the ground that its payment structure makes it in substance an instalment sale and as such a type of agreement regulated by instalment sales legislation. In revolving credit transactions the courts veered uneasily between categorisation of the transaction as a loan and as a sale.

Characterization is of still greater importance in commercial transactions. In *American President Lines Ltd v. Lykes Steamship Co., Inc.* the United States Bankruptcy District for the Middle District of Florida held, in relation to a sale and lease-back of a number of ships, that the leases which appeared on traditional criteria to possess all the features of a true lease, were properly to be characterized as secured loans, on the basis of 'economic realities', with the result that the 'lessee' was to be regarded as the owner and the interest of the 'lessor' was restricted to a security interest.

The strength of the formal rather than the functional approach to classification is that it aids predictability, an objective to which great importance is attached in world financial centres such as London and New York. The weakness of such an approach is that it fragments the legal treatment of instalment credit and creates artificial distinctions between the rules governing one credit form and those governing another which is intended to fulfil the same economic purpose. Article 9 of the American Uniform Commercial Code was the first model law to recognize the economic identity of title retention under sales contracts and the purchase-money chattel mortgage, and to treat both forms of credit as secured transactions governed by the same rules. Article 9 has been adopted throughout the United States and in the personal property security legislation of many Canadian provinces. Other countries have yet to follow this path, which was recommended for the United Kingdom in the 1971 Crowther Report on Consumer Credit but was rejected by the government. However, the Consumer Credit Act 1974 did make a root and branch reform of consumer credit, abolishing the traditional distinction between sale credit and loan credit and replacing this with an integrated approach to consumer credit in which new classifications were introduced based on the structure of party relationships and the way in which the credit is provided.

Accounting convention has long favoured substance over form. So goods supplied on conditional sale are treated in the buyer's balance sheet as its assets from the beginning. The same is true of finance leases, where the lessee may never acquire ownership but is considered to be the economic owner, the equipment being shown in its balance sheet as an asset and the future rental capitalized as a liability. This substantive approach works well enough where the enterprise is solvent; its drawback is that it does not show the security link between the liability and the asset and thus (in the absence of relevant notes to the accounts) gives the false impression that assets held on conditional sale or finance lease will be available for the general body of creditors of the buyer or lessee in the event of its liquidation.

(2) *Fixed-sum credit and revolving credit.* The types of transaction described above are all examples of fixed-sum credit, in which the amount of the credit is determined in advance and is reduced and eventually extinguished by payment. Fixed-sum credit is to be contrasted with revolving credit, a facility in which the debtor is given a line of credit on which to draw as and when required, each drawing reducing the remaining credit and each repayment topping it up again. Revolving credit may be loan-based, as in the case of a bank overdraft, or sale-based, the debtor being allowed to acquire goods or services up to the credit limit, making agreed monthly payments. The great advantage of revolving credit from the viewpoint of the creditor is that it creates a continuing business relationship between creditor and debtor, whereas in fixed-sum credit this ends with the completion of payments. For his part the debtor can draw on the credit when he chooses and incurs interest charges only on his drawings. It is this feature which makes it necessary to give revolving credit distinctive treatment in consumer credit legislation. Since it is not known in

advance when the credit will be taken and when it will be repaid, rules requiring disclosure of the amount of credit, mode of repayment and the annual percentage rate of charge cannot be applied in the same way as to fixed-sum agreements.

(3) *Debtor-creditor-supplier credit and debtor-creditor credit.* The third distinction drawn in legal systems is between debtor-creditor-supplier credit, in which the credit is extended by the supplier or by a creditor pursuant to arrangements with the supplier, and debtor-creditor credit, which is any other form of credit. This distinction is of particular importance in relation to three-party credit in which a financier lends money to a customer for the purchase of goods or services from a supplier, the loan being repayable by instalments. In traditional legal theory the loan transaction is independent of the sale transaction, even where there are standing arrangements between lender and supplier for the making of loans to customers introduced by the supplier. But modern consumer credit law tends to treat such arrangements as linking the contracts, thereby recognizing that economically they constitute an integrated package. This has a number of consequences. In German law a sale for cash financed by an instalment loan pursuant to an arrangement between lender and seller is treated by the courts as falling within the scope of the 1894 *Abzahlungsgesetz* (Instalment Sales Act), the first special instalment sale statute to be enacted in Europe and one which influenced a number of other European countries (von Marschall in Goode 1978: 234; Reich and Micklitz 1980: 137). The European Court of Justice, which tends to adopt a strongly policy-oriented and expansionist approach in its decisions, has taken the same line in *Société Bertrand v. Paul Oil KG*, 1446) when construing a reference to 'contracts for the sale of goods on instalment credit terms' in section 4 of the 1968 Brussels Convention on Jurisdiction and the Enforcement of Judgments. The United Kingdom Consumer Credit Act 1974 makes the creditor under a debtor-creditor-supplier agreement is made jointly and severally liable with the supplier for the latter's misrepresentations and breaches of contract.

STRUCTURE OF RELATIONSHIPS. The typical instalment credit transaction involves either two or three parties, though more complex structures are common, particularly in commercial leasing and conditional sale in which a head lessor or seller is brought in as a funder to acquire the equipment and supply it to the intermediate lessor or seller for the purposes of sub-lease. In the two-party arrangement credit is extended by a seller or lender without the involvement of any party other than the buyer or borrower. The evolution of the specialist finance house enabled the burden of providing credit to be removed from the retail seller, thereby greatly expanding the instalment credit market.

The English form of fixed-sum large-unit credit (e.g. for motor vehicles) typically involves direct collection, that is, the sale of the goods by the supplier to a finance house, which then sells it on instalment terms or lets it on hire-purchase to the supplier's custom. The effect is to bring the finance house into a direct contractual relationship with the customer, so that the customer's claim for defects in the goods lies against the finance house rather than the physical supplier. By contrast in the North American model (and for small-unit business in England) the credit is indirect, the supplier entering into the instalment credit agreement with the customer and then discounting it to the finance house, while continuing to collect payments on its behalf. Usually no notification of the assignment is given to the customer, who may therefore never be aware that the finance house is involved. The finance house as assignee incurs no positive liability under the agreement, though it can be met with all defences that the customer would have against the supplier.

Three-party fixed-sum credit can also arise in the context of a debtor-creditor-supplier loan for the acquisition of land, goods or services. The common law treated the loan transaction as quite separate from the sale, so that the lender was not responsible for the defaults of the supplier and could enforce the loan agreement regardless of any breach of the sale contract. But modern legislation often treats the two transactions as interdependent, regarding the relationship between creditor and supplier as being to some extent in the nature of a joint venture. This may be significant for several reasons. For example, the debtor's exercise of a statutory right to cancel the loan agreement may result in the sale agreement being automatically cancelled also by force of law; and the lender may be exposed to liability or to rights of set-off in respect of breaches of contract by the seller.

Sale-based revolving credit, like fixed-sum credit, was initially extended by the suppliers themselves, and expanded hugely when credit institutions offered facilities to take over the credit burden, by purchasing the revolving account portfolios or by issuing credit cards against which suppliers would provide goods or services, collecting payment from the card issuer, which would recover its outlay by instalments from the cardholder.

RIGHTS OF THE PARTIES. Standard-term instalment credit agreements tend to be weighted heavily on the side of the credit provider. In relation to commercial transactions most legal systems allow the wide parties a wide, though not unlimited, freedom of contract. Such contracts typically contain provisions exempting the creditor from liability for defects in any goods or services supplied on credit and confer on him a range of remedies in the event of the debtor's default, including, in the case of an instalment loan, acceleration of liability and enforcement of any security and, in the case of an instalment sale under reservation of title, termination of the agreement, repossession of the goods and damages for the loss of the future instalments. The common law is sympathetic to contractually agreed self-help remedies, such as the possession and sale of security or repossession of goods supplied under retention of title; the civil law tends to be more hostile to self-help, requiring recourse to the court for the exercise of the more important remedies.

TERMS CONTROL AS AN ECONOMIC MEASURE. Restrictions on instalment credit terms may be imposed not as consumer protection measures but in the wider interests of the national economy. In particular, regulations may prescribe minimum downpayments, maximum payment periods and rate ceilings at times when the economy is in danger of over-heating and it is thought prudent to curb the growth of consumer instalment credit. Apart from limited short-term effects such measures are of doubtful utility, and attempts to evade them have been widespread (see Farnsworth 1972: 27–8). In the United Kingdom, at a time when there were such controls over instalment sales, hire-purchase and hire agreements, the Crowther Committee was set up with the objective, among others, of finding ways of extending the controls to cover lending, a technically difficult matter. However, the committee's report, far from recommending the extension of terms controls, expressed the view that they were inequitable and ineffective and should find no place among the weapons of economic policy (Crowther 1971: 360). The controls were subsequently revoked. Similar, if somewhat less trenchant, views had been expressed in the earlier study by McCracken, Mao and Fricke (1965).

SELLER'S RIGHTS AGAINST THIRD PARTIES. The buyer or hirer under a conditional sale or hire-purchase agreement may wrongfully sell it to a third party before completing the payments due under the agreement. Whether the seller's rights prevail in this situation varies from legal system and also depends on the circumstances even within a given system. The common law starts from the principle that rights of ownership are to be protected, the civil law takes as its starting point the protection of the innocent purchaser. All legal systems have seen some degree of convergence between the two approaches. In many countries sellers have sought to extend their retention of title so that it covers not only the price of the goods but other sums due from the buyer and carries through to products resulting from the commingling of the seller's goods with other goods and to proceeds of authorized resales by the conditional buyer. The effectiveness of such contractual provisions varies greatly from one legal system to another, and in certain jurisdictions they are considered to constitute a disguised form of security and to be subject to rules governing registration of security interests.

SECURITIZATION. Instalment sale and instalment loan contracts are saleable assets and are frequently discounted to financial institutions, thus providing the supplier with increased liquidity. The growth and increased sophistication of the financial markets, coupled with the desire of banks to off-load their non-cash financial assets in order to increase their return on capital and reduce their capital adequacy commitments, led to the perception that installment receivables could not only be discounted but could be repackaged so as to become assets tradable on the capital and money markets. This conversion process is known as securitization. Receivables of a given type – e.g. mortgage instalments, personal loans, credit card receivables – are pooled by the owner (the originator) and sold to a special-purpose vehicle (SPV), which finances the purchase by the issue of bonds or loan notes on the credit of the issuer, backed by any credit enhancement, e.g. a demand guarantee or standby credit. The SPV then charges the portfolio to a trustee for the investors. Alternatively the originator transfers the receivables to a trustee for the investors, who are issued with certificates recording their equitable ownership of an undivided share of the trust fund.

CONSUMER PROTECTION. Most countries have enacted legislation to protect the consumer entering into credit transactions (see Farnsworth 1972). Among the most comprehensive models are the United Kingdom Consumer Credit Act 1974, the American Uniform Consumer Credit Code (also known as the U3C) and the Australian Consumer Credit Code. All of these, though lengthy and detailed, are buttressed by subordinate legislation. Within the European Union the legal treatment of consumer credit has been harmonized by a 1986 Directive designed to set minimum standards of protection for the consumer, while leaving member states free to adopt more stringent provisions. The need for protection is seen to arise not merely from the debtor's status as a consumer but also from the fact that the facility of paying on easy terms can all too easily lull the consumer into unaffordable commitments. The scope of the legislation raises a number of policy questions: who is to be considered a consumer? how is a consumer credit transaction to be distinguished from a commercial credit transaction? what types of transaction should be excluded from the scope of the legislation? In European Community Directives a consumer is usually defined as a natural person who is acting for purposes outside his trade, business or profession. The United Kingdom legislation does not follow this approach – partly, at least, because of the perceived problem of treating credit for the acquisition of multi-purpose goods such as cars – but instead focuses on the legal character of the debtor. An unincorporated debtor is protected by the Act, even if it is a business partnership, a corporate debtor is not. As in many countries, the legislation is confined to transactions within a given ceiling of credit.

Various forms of protection are available, and often the legislation uses them in combination. The relevant statute may itself lay down rules conferring rights on the debtor and circumscribing the rights and remedies of the creditor; the court may be given powers and discretion over the orders it makes; and an administrative body may be given certain regulatory functions, e.g. to license creditors or credit-brokers or to approve standard forms of contract. The form and content of consumer credit agreements may also be regulated. Issues that have attracted particular attention from legislators are the following:

(1) *Rate disclosure.* It is generally considered that the credit consumer should know the true cost of the credit in percentage terms, so that he can shop around for the cheapest bargain. The available evidence suggests, however, that consumers are relatively insensitive to credit rates, particularly where the credit transaction is financing a purchase and is being concluded at the point of sale. It seems likely, therefore, that if rate disclosure has any effect at all it is because credit institutions feel the need to advertise rates lower than those of their competitors. The bottom end of the consumer credit market is characterized

by high rates and an inability on the part of the consumer to engage in any effective bargaining. Rules for expressing the rate can be complex. They need to ensure that credit charges are not concealed in the cash price. The formulae adopted depend on the extent to which the compounding effects of different payment periods are to be taken into account. In the case of revolving credit the actual rate cannot be stated in advance, for it depends on the way the credit is drawn and repaid. Moreover, the elements that go into the credit charge and distinguish it from the credit itself can be difficult to work out and are peculiarly dependent on local conditions and practices. The mass of litigation generated in the United States by Regulation Z of the Truth in Lending Regulations graphically illustrates the problems involved in rate disclosure. The European Community Directive on consumer credit prescribes on a transitional basis a standard formula for computation of the effective annual percentage rate; this is to be replaced by a new Directive specifically devoted to rate computation. The policy underlying this requirement is unclear, given the lack of evidence of significant cross-border shopping for credit within the European Union.

(2) *Rate control.* The control of interest rates in loan agreements is of long standing, going back at least as far as the ancient Laws of Manu, which allowed the remarkably generous rate of two percent a month. The medieval Church declared that usury was a damnable sin, and at one time treated any loan at interest as usurious, on the ground that the sale of time belongs only to God. But faced with the compelling need of merchants to do business, and of governments to borrow, the Church showed itself every whit as ingenious as the secular lawyers in circumventing the strictness of doctrine, so that eventually it became recognized that the lender was entitled to charge for his risk and expenses, and interest was unobjectionable so long as it was moderate. The credit charge in consumer instalments contracts is in most countries subject to control either by the legislature or by the courts. Even where the legislature does not itself fix a ceiling rate, the courts may disallow a rate which they consider excessive or extortionate. The policy dilemma is whether to set an absolute standard or one which involves unconscionable behaviour on the part of the creditor, as by taking advantage of the borrower's financial predicament or inexperience. The difficulty with an absolute standard is that it is likely to be either so low that it does not reflect the credit risk or so high that the maximum becomes the norm. Moreover, it may exclude the high-risk borrower from access to credit altogether except from the illegal loan shark (Caplovitz 1978: 137–8). On the other hand, to allow *any* rate of charge so long as it is commensurate with the risk borne by the creditor may result in rates so staggeringly high as to suggest that such transactions should be prohibited altogether (Crowther 1971: 275).

(3) *Cooling-off period.* To counter the abuses that can occur when instalment credit agreements are negotiated on the consumer's doorstep or in their home, legislation in many countries allows the consumer a limited period within which to cancel the transaction and recover any payments made. Within the European Union this right of cancellation is guaranteed by the Directive on contracts negotiated away from business premises.

(4) *Restrictions on creditors' remedies.* These may take a variety of forms: prohibiting certain types of remedy; limiting the debtor's monetary liability or the effectiveness of penalty clauses and liquidated damages provisions; prescribing a statutory rebate of charges for early settlement; requiring the creditor to obtain an order of the court instead of resorting to self-help; and empowering the court to reschedule accrued and future indebtedness.

(5) *Imposing liability on connected creditor.* In the case of a three-party debtor-creditor-supplier agreement the legislation may make the creditor jointly liable for the defaults of the supplier, either without limit or up to the amount of the credit advanced, on the basis that supplier and creditor are in effect engaged in a joint venture to their mutual advantage and that the creditor is in a better position than the debtor to select the suppliers with whom the creditor will deal and to control their business conduct (Crowther 1971: 242–3, 250).

(6) *Efficacy of consumer protection measures.* The usual procedure for law reform in the field of instalment credit, as in other fields of regulation, is to identify the mischief, enact legislation to remedy it and then assume that the problem has been solved. There is a tendency in some countries, particularly the major common law jurisdictions, to over-regulate, in an attempt to deal with every conceivable situation and stop up every imaginable loophole. Primary legislation, lengthy enough in itself, is reinforced by regulations of daunting detail and complexity which embody a mass of technical minutiae. Though this is intended to provide certainty, all too often its effect is to create doubt and to confine legitimate transactions within a strait-jacket of prolix rules which only the specialist can understand and which are applied in a mechanical way without regard to the legislative policies and purposes. Thus while protection of the consumer in instalment credit transactions may seem good on paper, its effects in practice may in certain respects be adverse and will usually be limited, because of ignorance of the law, fear of resorting to lawyers and the courts and the existence of more compelling pressures of life.

Consumer credit legislation is often associated with the protection of the low-income consumer. This is an illusion. The consumer who is homeless and unemployed has more pressing problems than those addressed by consumer credit law and is anyway ill-equipped to take advantage of measures designed for his protection. Consumer credit law operates only on a minority of cases in a minority of debt situations (see Goode 1978: 98, 100). The indigent need to pay less for their goods and services but invariably they pay more (Caplovitz 1963, 1978). Perhaps the greatest effect of instalment credit legislation is its influence on contract terms and on business attitudes as to what constitutes acceptable credit behaviour.

ROY GOODE

See also CONSUMER PROTECTION; PERSONAL BANKRUPTCY; PERSONAL BANKRUPTCY IN THE UNITED STATES; STANDARD FORM CONTRACTS; UNCONSCIONABILITY.

Subject classification: 5c(iii); 6c(iii).

STATUTES

Convention on Jurisdiction and the Enforcement of Judgments in Civil and Commercial Matters signed at Brussels, 27 September 1968.

Council Directive on Contracts Negotiated away from Business Premises, 85/557/EEC, 1985 OJ L 372/31.

Council Directive on Consumer Credit 87/102/EEC, 1987 OJ L 42/48, as amended by Council Directive 90/88/EEC, 1990 OJ L 61/14.

Abzahlungsgesetz (Instalment Sales Act) 1894 (Germany).

Consumer Credit Act 1974 (United Kingdom).

Laws of Manu. Translated by W. Doniger and B.K. Smith, London: Penguin Books, 1991.

Truth in Lending Regulations (Regulation Z), being Part 226 of Title 12 of the US Code of Federal Regulations.

Uniform Commercial Code (American).

CASES

American President Lines Ltd v. Lykes Steamship Co., Inc., 196 Bank. R. 574 (1996).

Beete v. Bidgood (1827) 7 B & C 453.

Elder v. Doerr, 122 NW2d 528 (Neb. 1963).

Société Bertrand v. Paul Ott KG, Case 150/77, [1978] ECR 1431.

BIBLIOGRAPHY

Atiyah, P.S. and Summers, R.S. 1987. *Form and Substance in Anglo-American Law.* Oxford: Clarendon Press.

Caplovitz, D. 1963. *The Poor Pay More.* New York: Free Press.

Caplovitz, D. 1978. The social benefits and costs of consumer credit. In *Consumer Credit*, ed. R.M. Goode, Leyden/Boston: A.W. Sijthoff.

Consumer Credit: Report of the Committee (Chairman: Lord Crowther). 1971. London: Her Majesty's Stationery Office (Cmnd. 4596, 2 vols).

Curran, B. 1965. *Trends in Consumer Credit Legislation.* Chicago: University of Chicago Press.

Farnsworth, E.A. 1972. VIII International Encyclopaedia of Comparative Law, Chapter 4: *Installment Sales.* Tübingen: J.C.B. Mohr (Paul Siebeck).

Federal Reserve Board. 1957. *Consumer Instalment Credit.* Washington DC: Board of Governors of the Federal Reserve System (6 vols).

Goode, R.M. 1974. A credit law for Europe? *International and Comparative Law Quarterly* 23: 227–91.

Goode, R.M. (ed.). 1978. *Consumer Credit.* Leyden/Boston: A.W. Sijthoff.

Goode, R.M. and Ziegel, J.S. 1965. *Hire-Purchase and Conditional Sale: A Comparative Survey of Commonwealth and American Law.* London: British Institute of International and Comparative Law Special Publication no. 8.

Johnson, R.W. 1967. Regulation of finance charges on consumer instalment credit. *Michigan Law Review* 66: 81–114.

Jordan, R.L. and Warren, W.D. 1966. Disclosure of finance charges: a rationale. *Michigan Law Review* 64: 1285–1322.

McCracken, P., Mao, J. and Fricke, C. 1965. *Consumer Instalment Credit and Public Policy.* University of Michigan Bureau of Business Research.

Peden, J. 1974. *Stock-in-Trade Financing.* Sydney: Butterworths.

Reich, N. and Micklitz, H.-W. 1980. *Consumer Legislation in the EC Countries: A Comparative Analysis.* New York: Van Nostrand Reinhold Co.

Runcie, N. 1969. *The Economics of Instalment Credit.* London: University of London Press.

Seligman, E.R.A. 1927. *The Economics of Instalment Selling: A Study in Consumers' Credit with Special Reference to the Automobile.* New York: Harper (2 vols).

Ziegel, J.S. 1962. Retail instalment sales legislation: a historical and comparative survey. *University of Toronto Law Journal* 14: 143–75.

institutional shareholders. *See* SHAREHOLDER ACTIVISM AND CORPORATE GOVERNANCE IN THE UNITED STATES.

insurance, deterrence and liability. The tort liability a party can expect to encounter is due to several factors. One is the set of risky activities the party chooses to engage in – in conjunction with the relevant rules of tort liability. (A general rule renders a party liable for harms negligently caused, but several particular strict-liability rules impose liability for harms caused, regardless of negligence.) Second is the factor of chance, which determines whether a risky activity materializes in injury, and whether the resulting injury is minor or severe.

A party concerned about the operation of chance has an interest in purchasing a liability insurance policy. Economists who emphasize the diminishing marginal utility of income tend to assume that most parties are indeed risk averse. Given this assumption, a broad demand for liability insurance is easy to understand. On the other hand, insurance companies, by writing many liability policies, can in most circumstances succeed in pooling the risks surrounding individual insureds in a way that largely cancels out these risks. Since the Law of Large Numbers enables these companies to largely eliminate risk, they are willing to supply liability insurance.

Overall, then, there is a natural economic logic in favour of liability insurance. This logic, however, does not always dominate. For one thing, insurance policies have an inevitable overhead or 'load' (including the insurance company's own profits), which is commonly at least ten percent of the insurance premium. In deciding whether to purchase a liability insurance policy, the potential insured needs to compare this load to the benefits of risk reduction which the policy can provide. The larger the insured's own enterprise, the more the insured can pool risks internally, and hence the less substantial are the advantages it receives from liability insurance. It is not surprising, then, that large corporations and other major entities such as public agencies are increasingly tending to 'self-insure' – that is, to dispense with liability insurance and merely set aside reserves to cover what may be the eventual cost of liability.

Secondly, the Law of Large Numbers on which insurers rely assumes that the liability risks posed by individual insureds are independent and uncorrelated. Concede, for example, that many motorists sometimes absent-mindedly take their eyes off the road; even so, only a small proportion of this absent-mindedness may result in accidents, and the number of absent-minded accidents may well be actuarially predictable. Hence the practice of liability insurance can make sense. Yet some of the time, the liability risks associated with various insureds seem correlated. Assume, for example, that courts have under consideration some new legal rule that would expand the extent of liability in a general way (by recognizing, for example, 'loss of enjoyment' as a separate heading of damages). If, during the policy year, the courts decide in favour of this new rule, the increased liability exposure will apply to each and every policy the insurer might have written at the beginning of the year. Since the insurer can foresee that the aggregation of risks will not enable it to reduce overall risk levels, the insurer will be less willing to offer liability policies.

Further, the basic logic favouring liability insurance presupposes insurance policies that are voluntarily entered into. In many fields, however, legislatures have rendered obligatory the purchase of liability insurance. For example, legislatures often mandate that employers – subject to liability for injuries to workers – protect themselves with liability insurance. Also, many jurisdictions require all motorists to purchase liability insurance. Furthermore, in many American states automobile insurers, under assigned-risk plans, are required to offer insurance to high-risk motorists at rates that are well below market levels. When insurance does not result from the voluntary choices of insureds and insurers, the basic logic favouring liability insurance can no longer be affirmed.

The market for liability insurance can also be disturbed by moral hazard – the reduction of the insured's efforts to avoid those instances of harm which he knows are covered by his liability policy. Indeed, in light of moral hazard, liability insurance calls into question what many see as the primary purpose of tort liability. Tort liability is commonly understood as designed to deter parties from taking unreasonable risks. This basic deterrence objective can be frustrated by liability insurance: a party, having purchased an insurance policy, might find inadequate reason to adopt costly precautions and to restrain himself from participating in risky activities.

To be sure, many insurance policies are partial rather than complete. The liability policy purchased by a manufacturer, for example, will typically include some significant per-occurrence deductible and likewise a policy maximum or 'cap' – expressed in either per-occurrence or per-annum terms. That the manufacturer is exposed to liability below the deductible and above the cap reduces the moral hazard effects of liability insurance. Other manufacturers self-insure for the basic range of expected liability, but then purchase a 'catastrophic' policy to cover them in the unlikely event of a liability disaster. That these manufacturers are subject to full liability except in unusual circumstances obviously limits the moral hazard problem. However, when insurance is mandatory, the reasons relied on by the state in imposing this mandate often lead the state to insist on insurance in an unlimited form. For example, the liability insurance policy that British motorists are required to purchase is a 'first dollar' policy which begins to run from the very beginning of liability and then covers liability for an unlimited amount.

The extent of the moral hazard problem of liability insurance also depends on the ability of the insurance company to 'monitor' or 'observe' the behaviour of the insured. Monitoring permits the insured to adjust the terms (including the price) of the policy in a way that takes into account the actual risktaking in which the insured engages. The extent of monitoring by insurance companies obviously depends on the ratio of costs to benefits. On the cost side, how much of a burden is it for insurers to review the behaviour of their insureds? On the benefit side, how substantial are the advantages the insurer receives by taking account of the information derived from reviews in developing more refined schemes of premium classifications? Monitoring is often studied in the context of principal–agent, and on-the-scene employers often face relatively low costs in continually observing the behaviour of their employees. For a physically remote insurance company, any such process of continuing observation is obviously an impossibility.

There are, however, various methods available to the insurer. It can, for example, inspect the facilities of a commercial landowner before issuing a landowner's liability policy, and in doing so identify physical hazards that might pose some risk of injury. While it would not usually be cost-effective for the insurer to inspect the premises of individual homeowners before issuing a homeowner's liability policy, the insurer can condition its issuance of a policy on the insured providing accurate information in the insurance application. Under California law, dog-owners are strictly liable for all dog bites; and many California insurers refuse to write policies for homeowners whose application forms show that they own dangerous breeds of dogs such as pit bulls, Rottweilers and Doberman pinschers.

The insurance company can also take into account the insured's past record in committing or avoiding tortious conduct. When, for example, a motorist's negligence produces an accident or when the motorist is ticketed for a moving violation, the insurance company can regard this specific instance of bad driving as indicative of the motorist's more general tendency towards bad driving. The insurance company, engaging in 'merit rating' or 'experience rating', can then raise the premium it charges the motorist for future policies. While experience rating is relied on in many fields of liability insurance, much depends on the predictive value of the insured's past 'experience'. Experience rating is routine in setting the insurance premiums for large enterprises such as manufacturers, whose experience is rich enough to have predictive value. Malpractice claims against doctors, however, remain relatively uncommon; moreover, the information provided by an individual claim is often stale, since claims are frequently filed a year or more after the alleged malpractice incident. Given these factors, malpractice insurers believe that individual malpractice claims lack predictive value; accordingly, at least until recently these insurers have declined to practise experience rating. In short, the feasibility of experience rating is a function of several variables. Still, to the extent it is feasible, insurers by adjusting policy premiums can segregate potential insureds so as to limit problems of adverse selection; and insureds' own interest in avoiding premium increases gives them an incentive to avoid tortious conduct in a way that reduces the problem of moral hazard.

On balance, the costs of observation are rarely so prohibitive as to prevent insurers from taking *any* action to respond to the risky conduct of insureds; yet these costs are almost always high enough to prevent *complete* monitoring. Therefore, the terms and price of insurance will respond – but only to a moderate extent – to the level of the insured's tortious conduct. Insofar as the prospect of liability would otherwise discourage the actor from engaging in tortious conduct, almost every liability insurance policy creates some intermediate prospect of moral hazard. (The reader can probably affirm this point by introspection. Consider how much more scrupulous you would be in complying with highway speed limits if for some reason you were to find yourself without auto liability insurance on your car.)

From this recognition, several points follow. One is that the insurer, appreciating the prospect of moral hazard, will be inclined to include a moral hazard surcharge in the price of the insurance policies it offers. At some point, as the price of insurance goes up, parties who would otherwise purchase insurance may determine that it is cheaper to dispense with insurance and engage in a more genuine effort in reducing the tortious risks their conduct generates. Given this possibility, there is error in the common assumption that the legal system is malfunctioning when liability insurance seems unaffordable. Instead, the explanation might be that legal rules are properly targeting for liability risky conduct that parties can feasibly prevent, and that it is cheaper for parties to do without insurance and avoid that conduct than to purchase insurance and be lured by moral hazard into engaging in the conduct.

Indeed, at some point the prospect of moral hazard becomes so obvious that insurance becomes altogether unavailable. Thus insurance companies refuse to offer coverage for intentional torts. Moreover, parties are generally unable to acquire coverage for their liability for breach of contract; insurance companies perceive that contractual breaches are largely (even though not entirely) within the control of the party committing the breach. Indeed, since the standard economic account of negligence is that negligence consists of a party's deliberate choice to engage in conduct whose expected harm exceeds its expected benefit, it can easily be argued that the moral hazard surcharge an insurer will include in a liability policy will make it cheaper for a potential insured to forgo insurance and simply avoid negligent conduct (Shavell 1987: 211–12). Yet in fact there is a huge voluntary market for negligence liability insurance. This market suggests that the economist's account of negligent conduct is unduly stylized, and that a significant fraction of this conduct is as a practical matter unpreventable by the parties who engage in it (Grady 1988).

One factor that somewhat minimizes the moral hazard problem concerns the ability of liability insurers, in writing policies and processing claims for many actors, to acquire expert knowledge about a range of accidents and accident causes. Given the sophistication that insurers can develop, they can be in a position to develop safety strategies and offer these strategies to insureds by way of recommendations. Of course, these recommendations might be expensive to implement; and insureds, subject only to a limited measure of experience rating, might not always be willing to bear those expenses. In fact, the significance of insurer safety recommendations varies sharply from one context to another. Companies insuring employers for liability for workers' injuries frequently offer a wide range of quite significant safety services and recommendations. Yet insurers make no real effort to offer safety services to motorists or physicians.

In any event, even if insurers' safety services are taken into account, a significant prospect of insurance-induced moral hazard remains. Given this prospect, one can indeed wonder whether the rules of the legal system that validate liability insurance policies are efficient. To be sure, so long as insurance markets are voluntary, the purchase of insurance signifies that both the insured and the insurer are advantaged. But a third party who would have avoided injury had the insurance policy not been written now suffers injury because of the way in which moral hazard reduces the insured's safety efforts. Admittedly, this victim receives tort compensation for his injury. On the assumption that tort damages fully compensate the victim for his losses, economists have argued that the efficiency of liability insurance can be affirmed: the insurance policy, while benefiting the insurer and insured, avoids disadvantaging the victim (Shavell 1987).

In reality, however, tort damages often do not fully compensate. For one thing, to secure the full recovery the law allows, many victims need to hire a lawyer, and the lawyer's fee – in the United States, one-third of the victim's recovery – results in net compensation for the victim that does not completely compensate her for her losses. Furthermore, when the accident produces a fatality, the victim is obviously not compensated by the tort system after the accident in any way that is meaningfully restorative. Moreover, serious accidents can often result in ongoing pain and suffering. A tort award, designed with deterrence in mind, will be geared to the *ex ante* value of the pain-and-suffering risk imposed on potential victims. Yet once the accident happens, the experience of ongoing pain and suffering can reduce the utility of money to the victim. Accordingly, even the victim who receives what tort law regards as adequate compensation for his pain and suffering may end up with less utility than he would have obtained had the injury been avoided in the first place (Friedman 1982). Overall, since many victims are rendered worse off when the moral hazard effects of liability insurance convert the deterrence of risky conduct into a package of injury-plus-compensation, it may be difficult to determine whether the legal rules approving of those policies are consistent with the efficiency norm.

The above discussion of moral hazard invites reconsideration of the mandate for liability insurance imposed on motorists. Most motorists have reachable assets that are less than the size of a verdict that might be entered against them if their negligence produces a serious injury; indeed, many motorists are quite poor. Without insurance, the liability payments these low-asset motorists would actually end up making would often be dramatically less than the liability which the tort system seeks to impose. The prospect of liability might therefore be quite inadequate in deterring these motorists from engaging in negligent driving. Similarly, the premium for liability insurance policies might seem unattractively high to such motorists, since once a policy is written the insurer is not able to take advantage of the *de facto* immunity from liability originally enjoyed by the uninsured motorist. Accordingly, the motorist might be inclined to do without insurance, and also make an inadequate effort to avoid negligent driving.

At this point, the legislature's decision to mandate insurance can be given a generous evaluation. Admittedly, once the motorist is insured, moral hazard can dull incentives to avoid negligence. But at least in deciding whether to drive in the first place, the motorist will need to compare the benefits he receives from driving with the average costs of motorist liability – as reflected in the premium for the insurance policy the motorist is required to purchase. In making this comparison, some will decide not to drive at all. In the context, then, of low-wealth persons, compulsory insurance enables tort liability rules to achieve at least one of their goals – giving parties incentives to make appropriate choices about engaging in risky activities.

Discussed above have been the moral hazard problems associated with liability insurance. Similar problems can perhaps be created by first-party insurance policies purchased by potential victims. From an economic perspective, the combination of tort liability rules and affirmative defences are designed to provide incentives for appropriate behaviour by both potential injurers and potential victims. It has recently been argued that victims are commonly protected by first-party insurance policies (such as health and life insurance) that lack any features of experience rating; therefore, the argument goes, the package of liability rules and defences fails in its effort to modify the behaviour of potential victims appropriately (Hanson and Logue 1990).

This argument is intriguing and original in the way it extends the moral hazard concern from liability insurance to first-party insurance. Nevertheless, the argument is badly overstated. Health insurance in the United States is certainly widespread, yet it often includes deductibles or cost-sharing features that leave with the insured some fraction of the cost of health-care services. Moreover, in the United States 'disability' insurance – covering the loss of wages or self-employed income – is very uneven; problems of adverse selection and various kinds of moral hazard have evidently depressed the disability insurance market. Furthermore, first-party insurance for pain and suffering is quite uncommon and, according to American juries, pain and suffering accounts for about half of the overall harm of accidental injuries. Even given that first-party insurance is often lacking in experience-rating features, the victim will typically be covered by this insurance for significantly less than half of her potential accident losses. Also, under the American version of the collateral source rule, the victim who is reimbursed by first-party insurance can receive a second round of compensation from a defendant whose tortious conduct has been a cause of the victim's injury. So long as the victim's conduct is understood in narrow economic terms, the victim's interest in pursuing the asset of a tort recovery will give the victim a strong incentive to modify his conduct so as to comply with tort law's rules and defences and hence render himself eligible for tort compensation.

Attention has until now been given to the effect of liability (and first-party) insurance on the efficacy of tort liability in achieving its objective of appropriately controlling the conduct of injurers and victims. But there is quite another way in which the function of insurance can be deemed relevant to tort liability rules. Even once tort liability rules achieve whatever deterrence is within their power, many accidents remain unprevented. One effect of tort liability is to provide victims with 'insurance' against the harms produced by unprevented accidents. This insurance for accidental injuries can be achieved by imposing liability on large entities capable of absorbing and spreading losses. Insurance can also be provided to victims by imposing liability on individual defendants such as motorists, homeowners and physicians, with the expectation that these individuals will protect themselves by purchasing liability insurance policies.

Observers have long claimed that juries, desiring to compensate badly injured plaintiffs, often resolve factual doubts in favour of liability, appreciating that the defendant is a large enterprise or an insured individual. If this claim is correct, then juries are in essence relying on an insurance rationale in expanding the scope of actual liability. Furthermore, since the early 1960s, American judges have dramatically extended the coverage of liability rules, and many scholars allege that the primary factor driving this expansion has been the desire by judges to expand the insurance available through the tort system (Priest 1987). This allegation is plausible: one can certainly find rhetoric in some judicial opinions commending the insurance effects of tort liability. Yet this rhetoric is often part of larger passages that otherwise stress deterrence, and the rhetoric is simply absent in most other opinions (Stapleton 1995). Partly for this reason, other scholars, while conceding that the insurance rationale has played some role in the expansion of liability, have contended that this role has generally been secondary (Schwartz 1992).

Putting to one side the 'positive' debate about the motives of judges in expanding liability, at the normative level there is a considerable consensus that the tort system operates ineffectively as a technique for insuring potential accident victims. For one thing, as noted above, first-party insurance commonly includes features such as deductibles, cost sharing, ceilings on recovery, and fixed limitations on services provided (such as the length of hospitalization); these features help assure that accident victims covered by first-party insurance do not go overboard in consuming insurance benefits. Such constraints are typically lacking in tort awards, which afford 100 percent compensation for all health-care costs and income losses that juries deem reasonable. Secondly, the insurance rationale for tort liability overlooks the fact that most Americans already have substantial insurance for health-care costs and at least limited insurance for disability. Moreover, as noted above, under the collateral source rule the victim, having secured first-party insurance benefits, can then receive a full round of additional benefits from the tort system. From an insurance perspective, this doubling up makes no sense; and subrogation – as a possible solution to the problem of double recoveries – proves not feasible in most instances. Furthermore, tort awards include substantial compensation for pain and suffering; and most economists agree that efficient insurance policies would not seek to provide coverage for non-monetary losses of this sort (Priest 1987).

Finally, the tort system is strongly committed to doctrines such as defendant fault and victim contributory fault which are both expensive and time-consuming to litigate. Accordingly, the tort system incurs high administrative costs; and it frequently delivers compensation only after substantial delays. These features do not seem inconsistent with a deterrence rationale for the tort system; but they do suggest it is unwise to expect that system to serve as an efficient source of insurance for accident victims.

GARY T. SCHWARTZ

See also AUTOMOBILE ACCIDENTS, INSURANCE AND TORT LIABILITY; INSURANCE FOR WORKPLACE INJURIES; INSURANCE LAW; JURIES; MEDICAL MALPRACTICE; PRODUCTS LIABILITY; VALUING LIFE AND RISKS TO LIFE.

Subject classification: 5d(ii).

BIBLIOGRAPHY

Abraham, K.S. 1986. *Distributing Risk*. New Haven: Yale University Press.

Friedman, D. 1982. What is 'fair compensation' for death or injury? *International Review of Law and Economics* 2: 81–93.

Grady, M.F. 1988. Why are people negligent? Technology, nondurable precautions, and the medical malpractice explosion. *Northwestern Law Review* 82: 293–334.

Hanson, J. and Logue, K.D. 1990. The first-party insurance externality: an economic justification for enterprise liability. *Cornell Law Review* 76:129–96.

Priest, G.P. 1987. The current insurance crisis and modern tort law. *Yale Law Journal* 96: 1521–90.

Schwartz, G.T. 1990. The ethics and the economics of tort liability insurance. *Cornell Law Review* 75: 313–65.

Schwartz, G.T. 1992. The beginning and the possible end of modern American tort law. *Georgia Law Review* 16: 601–702.

Shavell, S. 1987. *Economic Analysis of Accident Law*. Cambridge, MA: Harvard University Press.

Stapleton, J. 1995. Tort, insurance and ideology. *Modern Law Review* 58: 820–45.

insurance for workplace injuries. This essay focuses on the legal structure and economic effects of workplace injury insurance. In particular, it describes the workers' compensation insurance programmes as they have evolved and now exist in the United States. In many ways, the US workers' compensation programmes are typical of other social insurance programmes both within the US and in other developed economies. In other important ways, they are not.

1. HISTORICAL DEVELOPMENT. Prior to the introduction of workers' compensation insurance in its current form, workplace injury law in the United States was governed by a common-law negligence standard. In order to recover damanges from an injury in the workplace, a worker had to establish that the owner had not exercised due care in providing a safe workplace. As described in Kantor and Fishback (1996), even a negligent employer could escape liability for a workplace accident if he could prove that the employee was aware of the risks inherent in the job and had assumed them, or that a co-worker had caused the accident, or that the worker's own negligence had contributed to the accident. Delays of up to five years were typical in the resolution of claims, and workers and their families often received no compensation whatsoever from the employer.

The adoption of modern workers' compensation programmes around the turn of the century sought to redress these two problems (settlement lags and low, uncertain payments) by replacing the existing systems with one that promised speedy payment for known amounts sufficient to support the worker and his family over the period of recovery. Thus the two major features of new workers' compensation programmes were a switch from the negligence standard to one of strict liability on the part of the employer, and the adoption of well-defined benefit schedules for injuries of various severity classifications. Some liability remained with the worker, as recovery amounts were capped, and the right to sue the employer for damages was given up.

The new systems were designed to provide rapid resolution of claims through the strict liability rule, and to limit the potential losses to employers by setting limits on payment amounts and eliminating the worker's right to sue. As Kantor and Fishback illustrate in their historical study, payments to injured workers increased considerably subsequent to these changes, with benefits to fatally injured workers typically doubling over their previous levels. However, a significant gap still existed between the benefits available and the losses of lifetime earnings suffered by fatally injured workers.

2. STRUCTURE. Workers' compensation benefits are determined at the state level in the US. Important structural features that vary across states include the nature of the administrative process used to regulate the systems, the extent of coverage, benefit levels and their durations, the mix of public and private funds provided by insurers, and the duration of mandatory waiting periods for the resolution of claims.

Benefit structure. The prototypical workers' compensation programme in the US is governed by a strict liability standard. Injuries are classified into one of four severity classes: temporary total, permanent partial, and permanent total disability, and fatalities. A key feature of these systems is that determination of the nature and extent of the injury is often unclear and, despite the litigation-free aspects of the system available through the strict liability standard, a great deal of litigation results from disputes over the proper classification of injury severity.

Benefit levels for lost earnings are governed primarily by the state average weekly wage. Payment schedules are nonlinear, as each state sets a maximum and minimum benefit amount that limits the range of payments available to the worker. Benefit maxima are typically set at two-thirds of the state average weekly wage. However, benefits are tax exempt, so that the after-tax replacement rate can be quite high, on the order of 80 to 90 percent of preinjury earnings. Between the minimum and maximum benefit amounts, most states set payments at two-thirds of the worker's actual pre-tax weekly wage.

The second type of benefit available to workers compensates them for medical expenses incurred as a result of their injury. These benefits are not subject to the same limitations as are payments for lost earnings.

Benefit durations vary both within state as a function of the injury severity, and across states as a matter of legislative or administrative discretion.

3. ECONOMIC EFFECTS. There are at least five important economic effects associated with workers' compensation. These include (i) the incentives created for workers to file claims; (ii) incentives for taking care on the part of workers and employers; (iii) incentives to return to work on the part of employees; (iv) wage effects; and (v) precautionary motives for saving. Since workers' compensation is similar in many respects to other forms of insurance, the lessons learned from research on each of these phenomena is applicable to a wide range of social insurance schemes.

The economic forces underlying these responses are well understood. Butler and Worrall (1991) have termed the first two of these 'claims reporting' and 'risk bearing' moral hazard. In the first case, as benefit levels increase, the attractiveness of a claim becomes greater and workers become more likely to file. Likewise, as benefit levels increase, the cost of a successful claim to a firm rises, and firms will exert more effort disputing the legitimacy and severity of the claim. Duration of time away from work will rise as the net loss of earnings (wages less benefits) decreases, so that workers will stay out of work longer, and firms will attempt to hasten the return to work.

The extent of risk-taking and risk-prevention efforts should also vary with benefit levels. Although pain and suffering is possibly the largest component of the costs of an injury to the worker, there is also variation in the financial and medical losses on the margin that may affect worker risk-taking behaviour somewhat.

An important feature of existing state programmes is the degree to which firms are rated according to their safety record. Large firms and firms that have a history of accidents are typically rated perfectly (i.e., in accordance with their own claim history), with others lumped into risk pools, so that the safety incentive effects to these latter firms are dampened.

A major problem facing researchers in this area has been the inability to separate out these two effects. Since the outcome of the reporting and care-taking processes is the same (i.e., a reported injury) and since data on firms' and workers' efforts to take care are limited at best, researchers can only observe the joint outcome of a four-way process: efforts by firms to reduce claims, and those by workers to file a claim, given that an injury has occurred (the claims reporting effect), and efforts by workers to take care and by firms to provide a safe workplace prior to the occurrence of an injury.

Given this observability problem, researchers on the incentive effects of workers' compensation were able to reach conclusions only about the net effect of these four processes. Until recently, the received view was that the worker claims reporting effect was dominant in general, and that evidence of precautionary behaviour on the part of firms, in particular, was practically nonexistent.

A key development in this area resulted from the observation that, for important classes of injuries, the claims reporting effect would be *a priori* negligible, so that the effects of benefits on these types of injuries could be used to identify the risk-bearing and risk-prevention effects. In particular, Moore and Viscusi (1989) focused on the effects of increases in benefit maxima on occupational fatality rates. Clearly, many dimensions of claims reporting moral hazard are limited here: there is no dispute about the severity of the injury, and the locus and timing of the injury are clear (in particular, reporting cannot be postponed as discussed in Smith 1990). In the data analysed, Moore and Viscusi find a systematic negative relationship between the generosity of benefits and fatality rates, i.e., more generous benefit levels led to fewer occupational fatalities. Furthermore, the extent of the tradeoff varies with firm size, lending support to the prediction that the degree of experience rating, which varies positively with firm size, moderates the safety incentive effects.

A heretofore unappreciated distinction in the previous literature is also noted in Moore and Viscusi's work. Some previous studies (Chelius 1982 and Fishback 1987, in particular) had found a negative relationship between benefit levels and injury rates for more severe injuries. The importance of distinguishing between the effects of benefit levels on more or less severe injuries appears to have been neglected at the time, but in retrospect evidence of strong safety incentives had been around for years, primarily due to these research efforts. Since the publication of the Moore and Viscusi result, their results have been replicated with more disaggregated data by Ruser (1991) and others.

Wage effects are important for various reasons. First, compensation for accidents on the job can take two forms: *ex ante* compensation in the form of compensating differentials for potential job risks, and *ex post* compensation for injuries that have actually occurred. The importance of the former has been established by a number of studies (see Viscusi 1993 for a survey). The compensating differentials, if sufficiently high, can provide strong incentives for safety provision. Moore and Viscusi (1989), for example, compare the incentives provided by the marketplace to the potential fines firms face under Occupational Safety and Health regulation, and find the difference considerable.

As regards the effect of *ex post* compensation such as workers' compensation, we would expect workers' compensation benefits to replace wages, particularly in more risky contexts. These benefits represent a form of compensation that becomes more valuable in expected terms, the riskier the job. Second, an important related question concerns the incidence of benefit costs. These will depend on the ability of firms and workers to find alternatives at least as attractive elsewhere. To the extent that costs of the system are passed on to workers, employer claims of financial duress are mitigated. Finally, as in the 'value of life' literature associated with compensating differentials for job hazards, observed wage-risk and wage-benefit tradeoffs can be used to isolate the valuation of nonpecuniary, or health-related, losses of job accidents from those associated with anticipated financial losses. In particular, in the absence of any earnings replacement for on-the-job injuries, compensating differentials for job risks would reflect both the financial and health related losses inherent in a risky job. If financial losses are limited by injury insurance, however, the compensating differentials for these losses will not be reflected in higher wages, so that observed compensating differentials for job risks at full earnings replacement can be interpreted as reflecting the health losses only (Viscusi and Moore 1987).

Liability rules. Three important questions in workers' compensation are of more general importance in other risky contexts. First, what was the effect of moving from a negligence standard to one of strict liability? Second, will a movement towards '24 hour' insurance, where individuals are protected by state insurance regardless of where or when an accident occurs, as is practised in many European countries and is being contemplated in many states, eliminate the safety incentives provided by workers' compensation? Third, has the movement to strict liability reduced litigation costs?

For the first question the evidence is quite clear. Chelius (1982) and Fishback (1987) both find a significant downward effect on mortality rates of the movement to strict liability in the early part of the century. This suggests, among other things, that transaction costs are important in limiting workplace safety negotiations between workers and firms. If this were not the case, the location of liability would, of course, be irrelevant, and the optimal level of safety would have been provided regardless of the liability regime.

As regards the effects of 24-hour coverage, it is clear that if firms do not pay for job safety insurance, some of the costs of job accidents will be eliminated. However, in the absence of insurance, labour market equilibrium should lead to a wage adjustment to compensate workers for the expected losses associated with an accident. This wage adjustment will include expected financial losses, pain and suffering, and medical expenses. It will also provide a substitute incentive for safety on the part of employers. Workers who do not have a reasonable amount of job mobility would suffer, as their wages would not adjust to reflect the reduced benefit. On the other hand, these workers were most likely paying for most of the cost of workers' compensation anyway, via the wage-benefit offset.

As for the effect of strict liability on litigation costs, it is clear that the system is far from litigation-free. Workers still sue over the severity classification, and whether the injury was job related. In many instances, as shown by Viscusi (1989), workers will sue the manufacturers of products involved in their accidents in a product liability action, thus avoiding the cap on payments. It is also clear that litigation costs are inordinately high relative to losses for less severe injuries. That much of the litigation is related to these less severe injuries should not be surprising. As Smith (1990) noted, many sprains and strains, for example, are reported on Monday mornings, suggesting that workers who injure themselves over the weekend might postpone reporting the injury until coming to work in order to collect. These claims will often be disputed, resulting in costly litigation. Obviously, more severe injuries cannot be postponed, and there will be less doubt as to their cause and, consequently, less litigation. As load factors increase, it may become prudent to adopt a system of deductibles to eliminate claims for less severe injuries, in order to remain solvent enough to compensate workers for extreme losses.

Recent trends do not bode well for the system. Mental health and stress-related claims and claims for occupational disease have skyrocketed in recent years. In both cases, the contribution of the job to the severity of the impairment is much less clear than in the case of occupational injury. Also, workers may use the workers' compensation system to recover the more extensive benefits available, rather than collect for job loss due to unemployment, plant closings, and the like. For example, a claim for cumulative trauma such as hearing loss or breathing impairment could result in a lifetime of benefits under workers' compensation following a job loss, whereas benefits under the state unemployment system would run out after a few months.

MICHAEL J. MOORE

See also DUE CARE; INSURANCE, DETERRENCE AND LIABILITY; INSURANCE LAW; MEDICAL MALPRACTICE; OCCUPATIONAL DISEASE AND THE TORT SYSTEM: THE CASE OF ASBESTOS; OCCUPATIONAL HEALTH AND SAFETY REGULATION; PRODUCTS LIABILITY; VALUING LIFE AND RISKS TO LIFE.

Subject classification: 6c(v); 6d(iii).

BIBLIOGRAPHY

Butler, R. and Worrall, J. 1991. Claims reporting and risk bearing moral hazard in workers' compensation. *Journal of Risk and Insurance* 58: 191–204.

Chelius, J. 1982. The influence of workers' compensation on safety incentives. *Industrial and Labor Relations Review* 35: 235–42.

Fishback, P. 1987. Liability rules and accident prevention in the workplace: empirical evidence from the early twentieth century. *Journal of Legal Studies* 16: 305–28.

Kantor, S. and Fishback, P. 1996. Precautionary saving, insurance, and the origins of workers' compensation. *Journal of Political Economy* 104(2): 419–42.

Moore, M. and Viscusi, W. 1989. Promoting safety through workers' compensation: the efficacy and net wage costs of injury insurance. *RAND Journal of Economics* 20: 499–515.

Ruser, J. 1991. Workers' compensation and occupational injuries and illnesses. *Journal of Labor Economics* 9(4): 325–50.

Smith, R. 1990. Mostly on Monday: is workers' compensation covering off-the-job injuries? In *Benefits, Costs, and Cycles in Workers' Compensation Insurance*, ed. P.S. Borba and D. Appel, Norwood, MA: Kluwer Academic Publishers.

Viscusi, W.K. 1989. The interaction between product liability and workers' compensation as ex post remedies for workplace injuries. *Journal of Law, Economics, and Organization* 5(1): 185–210.

Viscusi, W.K. 1993. The value of risks to life and health. *Journal of Economic Literature* 31: 1912–46.

Viscusi, W.K. and Moore, M. 1987. Workers' compensation: wage effects, benefit inadequacies, and the value of health losses. *Review of Economics and Statistics* 69: 249–61.

insurance law. Insurance law is a body of law governing insurance contracts. In the common law world, the law of insurance is founded on common law principles dating back to the eighteenth century. Most of the basic principles survive in Anglo-American jurisdictions, but many of these principles are now embodied in statutes. The hypothesis presented here is that the insurance principles embodied in the common law can be explained by economic concepts such as moral hazard and adverse selection or by a desire of courts to prevent harm to third parties.

One of the striking features of insurance law is the degree to which the law seems to impose judicial control over private contracts. For example, the ability of an insurer to avoid payment of benefits because the insured lacks an 'insurable interest' would appear to interfere unnecessarily with a private contract. This essay, which is drawn largely from Rea (1993), presents several of the principal insurance law doctrines and examines the economic basis for these principles.

A basic assumption of economics is that those engaged in exchange will make every effort to draw up efficient contracts, taking into account only interests of the parties to the contract. That is, the individual features of the contract will be such that no change can be made that can make one party better off without making the other worse off. If a court decision leads to inefficiency, there will be pressure *from both parties*, including the party favoured by the decision, to change the outcome and the rule. Furthermore, the market will attempt to negate the impact of the inefficient decision.

Despite such market responses, there are at least two economic justifications for contract law. First, the law provides standard terms for contracts, reducing the cost of negotiation; and second, the law may alter market outcomes which are not Pareto efficient. The first justification clearly underlies much of insurance law because of the complexity of the contracts. However, in the absence of government intervention one would expect the market to provide more complete contracts, without an enormous increase in transactions costs. The second possibility offers a more compelling argument for government action because it suggests that private parties may not negotiate efficient contracts. There are two types of inefficiencies. In the first, asymmetric information can lead to contracts which are inferior for all parties in a market. For example, some contract clauses that one party might want to include would be seen as a signal of high cost to the other party. By making some clauses mandatory the law might make everyone in the market better off. The second type of inefficiency arises when two parties enter into a contract that makes a third party worse off. Judicial intervention can prevent such inefficient contracts.

INSURABLE INTEREST. A fundamental requirement for the enforcement of an insurance contract is that the insured have an 'insurable interest'. That is, the insured must have an expectation of a loss that is covered by the insurance. If there is a lack of insurable interest, the insurer can refuse to pay for any losses that occur.

The conventional explanations of the insurable interest doctrine focus on two major arguments. First, without insurable interest the insurance contract is a wager and therefore 'against public policy'. Second, the insured without insurable interest will have an incentive to create the loss. These are referred to as the anti-wagering and moral hazard arguments, respectively.

The moral hazard argument has been criticized because the ability to affect the risk in subtle ways is greatest for those who are closely involved with the object of the insurance. Someone insuring another's ship is unlikely to be able to affect the probability that the ship founders. On the other hand, there are other situations in which someone without a direct ownership interest might be able to affect the risk. For example, an employee might be in a very good position to increase the probability that an employer's property is destroyed but would not have a legally enforceable insurable interest. The insurable interest doctrine seems to be designed to avoid a costly investigation of the amount of care by focusing on the insured's interest.

The anti-wagering explanation can be criticized as inconsistent with the legalization of many other forms of gambling. Historically, the controls on gambling were somewhat selective and did not apply to wagers. The 1664 anti-gambling act applied only to betting on specific games and sports. Disputes regarding wagers were considered in the courts before and after a 1774 act that required insurable interest for insurance contracts. In *Good v. Elliott* the 1774 act was held to apply to insurance policies, not wagers. That is, a wagering contract did not require an insurable interest. As an explanation for the insurable interest doctrine, anti-wagering policy is not historically valid.

A more plausible explanation for the insurable interest doctrine is the externality that is created when one party insures another's property. Insurance without insurable interest creates an incentive to take less care with respect to that property or deliberately to inflict loss. This incentive differs from the usual moral hazard. Most insurance reduces the insured's incentive to take care because it is not efficient for insurers to monitor perfectly the care taken by the insured. When there is insurable interest, the added expected loss caused by the moral hazard is borne by the two parties to the insurance contract. When a third party owns the property, that party bears the increased risk of loss without compensation. Therefore, an insurance contract without insurable interest is not Pareto efficient. The contract makes the insured better off and the owner of the property worse off. This essay argues that the insurable interest doctrine exists to prevent such inefficient contracts. The externality argument and the moral hazard argument both arise because of increased risk, but the externality argument is based on concern for third parties, not increased risk by itself.

The case of *Da Costa v. Jones* illustrates that Lord Mansfield, the most influential figure in forming insurance law, was more concerned with externalities than wagering. The two parties had wagered on whether or not Chevalier d'Éon, who appeared as a man, was in fact a woman. During the trial witnesses offered personal information on d'Éon, convincing the jury that he was a woman. Lord Mansfield stated that

> Indifferent wagers upon indifferent matters, without interest to either of the parties, are certainly allowed

by the law of this country, ... [but] ... suppose a wager that affects the interest or the feelings of a third person ... Would it be endured? Most unquestionably it would not.

The judgment was reversed because the case was 'manifestly a gross injury to a third person'.

Lord Mansfield took a liberal view of the extent of interest required (*Le Cras v. Hughes*), but in a subsequent case, *Lucena v. Craufurd*, there were two competing theories of insurable interest, one requiring a legally enforceable right and the other a factual expectancy of loss. Keeton and Widess present two US cases which are based on these two approaches. In *National Filtering Oil Co. v. Citizens Insurance Co.* the insured had a fire insurance policy on Ellis & Co.'s works because a fire would reduce royalties paid by Ellis to National Filtering. The court found that National Filtering had an insurable interest. In contrast, a turnpike company (*New Holland*) was found to lack an insurable interest in a county-owned bridge, despite the loss of profits that would occur if the bridge were destroyed. (See *Farmers Mutual Insurance Co. v. New Holland Turnpike Co.*) The lack of a legally enforceable right in the later case was crucial.

On first impression, it seems obvious that a turnpike company would suffer a loss if a bridge were destroyed and that it would be reasonable to insure such a loss. Yet, if the turnpike company reduces the level of care because of the insurance, the county will suffer a loss. In *National Filtering* a contract explicitly allocated to National Filtering the risk of loss of royalties by fire. One could argue that Ellis knew about the insurance and might have been compensated in the contract for any increased risk. In other words, these two cases could be distinguished by the presence of a contractual relationship in *National Filtering* which was absent in *New Holland.* A finding of lack of insurable interest in *New Holland* does not eliminate the possibility of insuring such a loss, it induces the parties in such a situation to explicitly contract for insurance.

Canada has recently returned to the factual expectancy test. In *Constitution Insurance Co. of Canada v. Kosmopoulos* a sole owner of a corporation was found to have an insurable interest in the company's assets. The Supreme Court explicitly accepted the factual expectancy test and overruled previous precedents. Clearly, there are no externalities in this situation.

Insurance law explicitly deals with the externality in the case of life insurance. In Ontario the Insurance Act states that a contract for life insurance is not void for lack of insurable interest if the insured agrees. This law would not be consistent with the wagering or moral hazard theories of insurable interest. An employer may have an insurable interest in an employee and a creditor may have an insurable interest in a debtor. An employer may take less care with respect to employees who are insured, but there is no externality because the employer and employee have a contractual relationship. The employee can be compensated for any added risk through higher wages.

Tort law is also consistent with the externality argument. In the United States courts in several cases have found that an insurance company owed a duty of care to the subject of life insurance. Failure to take reasonable care in determining whether the customer had an insurable interest would make the company liable for damages suffered by the injured person (in the case of an unsuccessful murder attempt) or the survivors (in the case of a murder).

A number of features of insurance law are examined below in order to determine if the externality justification for the insurable interest requirement is consistent with the law.

ASSIGNMENT. The wagering and moral hazard justification for the insurable interest doctrine would prevent the owner of an insurance policy on his life from selling the policy. After the sale, the new owner would have an incentive to murder the subject of the insurance and would be wagering on his death. Yet, courts ultimately accepted the assignment of life insurance policies. The externality argument can explain this exception to the insurable interest doctrine. When the owner of a policy gives up his rights, he does so for some consideration and with knowledge of the incentives created.

The individual assigning a policy to someone he trusts must recognize that the assignee may, in turn, assign the policy to a third party. As in the employment case, there is no externality because the person whose life is insured can be compensated in the original transaction for any added risk.

LIABILITY INSURANCE. It is accepted that an individual has an insurable interest in his liability for someone else's damages, subject to such insurance being against public policy (see below). The ability to insure against a liability for someone else's loss poses an interesting test of the externality theory. Given a potential liability, the insured clearly has an expected loss and cannot be considered to be wagering. The moral hazard argument and the externality argument both assume that the victim bears additional risk if the insured takes less care and the insurance company cannot monitor care. However, Shavell (1982) has pointed out that the cost of the moral hazard is not borne by the victim as long as there is full compensation. If there is full compensation, the acceptance of liability insurance in the common law is consistent with the wagering argument (there is no gamble) and the externality argument (there is no externality), but not the moral hazard argument (care is reduced).

If victims receive less than full compensation from tort awards, the liability insurance imposes an externality on the victim. However, the impact is mitigated if the insurance raises the probability that the victim will receive compensation for accidents from an injurer with limited wealth. We will return to a discussion of liability insurance below in the context of the public policy rule against insuring criminal acts. At this stage it is sufficient to conclude that the eventual acceptance of liability insurance is consistent with the externality argument if the value of the added compensation paid to victims is sufficiently large. Liability insurance does not create wagering but is inconsistent with the moral hazard argument.

WHY ONLY THE INSURER RAISES THE INSURABLE INTEREST ISSUE. One puzzling aspect of the insurable interest is that the insurer can raise the issue and profit *ex post* from a lack of insurable interest. If the doctrine is designed to prevent externalities, why can't the party with the insurable interest raise the issue and receive the benefits? Why should the insurer, who has received a premium, profit from the defence when a claim would otherwise be payable? An alternative approach was used in Texas. Prior to 1953 Texas had a rule that the beneficiaries of an estate could receive the insurance benefits if the designated beneficiary was found to lack an insurable interest. The rule was changed because it limited assignment of life insurance policies.

An explanation for the insurer's role in policing insurable interest is that third parties may not know about insurance contracts written on their property. In the absence of an insurable interest requirement, neither the insurer nor the insured would have an incentive to reveal this information *ex ante* or *ex post*. By allowing the insurer to raise the issue *ex post*, there is a private incentive to prevent any externalities. *Ex post* monitoring may be less costly than *ex ante* monitoring because the monitoring does not have to be done frequently.

IMPERFECT INFORMATION AND INSURABLE INTEREST. A final possible explanation for a mandatory insurable interest provision is that the market might induce contracting parties to avoid the provision. If the insurer and the potential insured are both uncertain about the probability of a loss occurring, the process of contracting between the parties may signal each party's information. Those lacking insurable interest are likely to believe that insurance is underpriced. The consequences of errors by insurers in estimating costs will be magnified by the existence of groups who attempt to profit from insurers' mistakes. Insurers might attempt to separate those with a need for insurance from the speculators in order to reduce the 'winner's curse'. However, an insurer who insisted on an insurable interest provision might signal an inability to monitor care, attracting higher risk customers, or might signal an inability to assess risk, attracting customers who believe that they have better information. The insurable interest provision might not survive in the market, despite its advantages for insurers and those with an insurable interest. These groups could be made better off by a mandatory insurable interest provision. As an explanation for the development of the doctrine, the externality argument is more convincing than one based on imperfect information, but it appears that the early legislation was designed to separate speculators from those requiring insurance.

INDEMNITY. A fundamental feature of insurance law is the indemnity principle. This principle states that the insured cannot receive more compensation than the value of what was lost. The indemnity principle allows an insurer to reduce the compensation, if necessary, but unlike the insurable interest doctrine, does not void the contract. The indemnity principle applies to all insurance except life and accident and sickness insurance.

The indemnity principle appears to be a reasonable term in an insurance contract. An insured offered fair insurance will want to insure for the amount of the loss, not more. Excess coverage would increase the insured's risk compared to full coverage. If the principle is so obvious, what is the economic explanation for the development of the legal doctrine? Wouldn't the term be included in insurance contracts in the absence of the principle?

One traditional explanation for the indemnity principle is that the courts do not want to enforce wagering contracts, but this explanation has been dismissed in the discussion of insurable interest. A second explanation is moral hazard. If insurance coverage exceeds the value of the loss, there is a positive incentive to induce the loss. The explanation, as usually stated, is not convincing in that there is no externality. Any inducement to cause the loss will be reflected in the premium, inducing contracting parties to reduce the coverage. Most contracts with moral hazard will include less than complete coverage as a compromise between the cost of added coverage and the value of risk reduction.

More recent developments in economic theory indicate that moral hazard can create externalities. If an insurance contract is subject to moral hazard and the insurers cannot monitor the quantity of insurance purchased, an insurer who sells additional insurance to a customer with existing insurance coverage will raise the probability of the loss occurring and reduce the profits of the first insurer. Some degree of co-ordination is necessary if this externality is to be avoided. The indemnity principle might be seen as a crude way of accomplishing this co-ordination, but it is not complete because the externality also exists if total coverage does not exceed the loss. In any event, there is nothing to prevent an insurer from including a clause that limits subsequent purchases of insurance. If the purchase of multiple policies is not observable *ex post*, neither private contracting nor the indemnity principle will be of assistance.

Adverse selection also produces an externality. High risk customers raise the price for low risk customers when they buy the same policy. Furthermore, those who know that they face a high risk will wish to buy more than complete coverage if the premium is sufficiently attractive. As above, the indemnity principle deals with this problem in a crude way, but private contracting might produce the same result.

Imperfect information on both sides of the market could eliminate some provisions from the marketplace, as discussed in the context of insurable interest. Under some assumptions about the pattern of information this could justify the use of mandatory contract provisions such as the principle of indemnity.

The introduction of the indemnity principle through private contracts, rather than the courts, may be difficult, particularly if insurers have conflicting provisions. For example, two insurers may include clauses that make the coverage excess to other coverage. The indemnity principle allows the courts to be flexible in their response to these situations.

An analysis of the indemnity principle must explain the existence of insurance contracts which are not classified as contracts of indemnity. Non-indemnity contracts are most likely to arise when the pecuniary value of the loss is not easy to measure. Since *Dalby v. India & London Life-Assurance Co.*, life insurance contracts are not contracts of indemnity. On the other hand, why is a 'valued policy', which fixes the amount to be paid *ex ante*, considered to be an indemnity contract? The answer must be that valued contracts arise when it is easier to monitor the value of the loss *ex ante* than *ex post*. For example, jewellery will generally be insured with a valued policy. *Ex ante* the insurer will require that the stated value be reasonable and may require *ex ante* appraisal. Non-indemnity insurance contracts, such as life insurance, involve losses which are difficult to measure both *ex ante* and *ex post*.

Insurance for replacement value would seem to violate the indemnity principle. When someone loses a durable good, it is likely that the replacement cost is greater than the market value of a used good. One reason for this is that the 'lemons' problem makes the quality in the used market lower than the quality of used goods not offered for sale. Someone who is given the cash value of a used good will not usually be fully compensated for the loss. Provided the moral hazard is not too great, insurers will offer replacement coverage. In most cases they will not provide cash compensation unless a replacement purchase is made. This helps to control moral hazard but has the disadvantage that some insureds would rather have cash compensation.

Unlike the doctrine of insurable interest, parties can contract out of the indemnity principle by specifying that a contract is not indemnity insurance (see *Glynn v. Scottish Union & National Insurance Co.*). This flexibility casts doubt on externalities or anti-wagering as explanations for the indemnity principle. One can conclude that the indemnity principle is a default rule that would have been chosen in any case by most parties to insurance contracts. It does not appear to prevent any externalities that could not be prevented with private contracting, but it facilitates co-ordination of conflicting insurance policies and guides the courts when new problems arise.

SUBROGATION. Subrogation is a doctrine which permits the insurer to compensate the insured but to pursue whatever rights the insured has against a third party. The subrogation doctrine follows from the indemnity principle. Subrogation is in the interest of the insured because it permits him or her to avoid the uncertainty of a lawsuit and to insure only for what is lost. Premiums will be lower to the extent that the insurer collects from a third party. At the same time it preserves incentives for the third party to take care by permitting the lawsuit to proceed despite compensation by the insurer.

Subrogation, like indemnity, is a flexible doctrine that permits the parties to tailor the amount of coverage to the actual loss. The insurer can forgo subrogation rights in a contract, but otherwise they form an implicit part of the contract. Subrogation applies to legal obligations of third parties, not voluntary payments. Third parties would not make voluntary payments to victims if they knew that insurers would reduce benefits by an equal amount. It would not be in the joint interest of insurers and insureds to provide for subrogation in this situation because the provision would simply reduce joint profits.

'UTMOST GOOD FAITH'. Parties to an insurance contract must reveal all relevant facts to the other party. Failure to do so is grounds for nullifying an insurance contract.

Why are parties to an insurance contract held to a higher standard than other contracting parties? An unusual feature of insurance contracts is that the characteristics of the *buyer* affect the costs of the seller. That is, a high-risk customer will cost more than a low-risk customer. The importance of the buyer's risk characteristics to the insurer gave rise to the idea that contracts of insurance required 'utmost good faith' in order to induce the buyer to reveal his or her risk characteristics.

There are several types of costs that arise if information on the nature of the risk is not revealed. If the insured is able to conceal information from the insurer, adverse selection may result. One possible result of adverse selection is that low risk customers signal their low risk status by buying less insurance. The resulting equilibrium may be Pareto inferior to an outcome in which minimum insurance rules are enforced. Gravelle (1991) concludes that incentives to reveal information can make both honest and dishonest insureds better off. Furthermore, more correct pricing of risky activities will benefit third-party victims. Finally, revelation of information will reduce expenditures by insureds to conceal information and expenditures by insurers to detect that information.

There are some costs associated with rules that require revelation of information. It is possible that the benefits from gathering additional information may, in fact, be smaller than the costs (see Rea 1991). If insurers can occasionally eliminate their obligation to pay benefits, the insured will be forced to incur costs to make sure that additional information is revealed, and some residual fraction of the time insurance will not be payable. As a result the insurance is incomplete and the advantage of insurance is reduced. The added transactions costs and the reduction in coverage may reduce the demand for insurance.

Insurance law has adapted to the costs of hidden information by setting up a mechanism for inducing revelation of information. Insurance law requires both parties to the contract to disclose all information which might influence the other to enter into the contract or to settle a claim. The 'utmost good faith' (*uberrimae fidei*) doctrine in Canadian and English insurance law arises most frequently when an insurer refuses to pay an insurance claim on the grounds that the insured withheld information prior to the formation of the contract. The information must be such that it would have influenced the premium that would have been charged or the insurer's decision to accept a risk. There are two striking features in these cases. First, the information does not have to have any causal relationship with the event that arose, and second, the remedy is rescission (nullification of the contract), not damages. These two features give the doctrine a punitive element not often found in contract law. That is, the remedy seems designed to deter insureds from withholding information, not to compensate the insurer.

In ordinary contracts rescission results in the loss of lost expectation profits for both parties, provided some adverse event has not occurred. Rescission of an insurance contract after an insured contingency has arisen strongly favours the insurer. If the contingency does not occur, the insurer keeps the premium. If it occurs, the insurer can return the premium. The insurer is obviously better off if the insured withholds information.

One could imagine an alternative remedy in which the benefit paid is reduced to account for the higher risk. Accident and Sickness insurers in Ontario are permitted by statute to vary either the premiums or the benefits in order to reflect a misstatement of the age of the insured. This remedy would not adequately deter insureds from withholding information if some fraction of those doing so would go undetected. Deterrence seems to be the explanation for the more conventional rescission remedy.

The merits of the 'utmost good faith' doctrine for inducing revelation of information become less obvious when there is a possibility of mistake by the insured. In *Henwood v. Prudential Insurance Co. of America* the insured had seen a physician for treatment of normal teenage emotional problems. A year later she responded negatively to a question in an insurance application whether she had ever been treated for a 'nervous or mental disorder'. The expert witnesses were divided whether her previous medical condition fell in this category. Nevertheless, the court held that the insurance contract was void because there was material non-disclosure of information. The fact that she died in an automobile accident, completely unrelated to the previous medical problems, was not even an issue.

The *Henwood* case illustrates several features of the insured's obligation to disclose. First, the lack of a relationship between the fact not disclosed and the specific event that is insured adds another punitive element to the law. Any non-disclosure can be used by the insurer to void the contract. Despite the apparent harshness of this rule, there are practical reasons for its use. Insurers frequently use easily-measured variables that are correlated with unmeasured variables that are causally related to risk. For example, those who have been treated by psychiatrists may face greater risk, regardless of how severe the problem. There are also rating variables that are related to exposure, such as miles driven per year or geographical area of operation in the case of automobile insurance. It would not be possible to say that a particular accident had been *caused* by misrepresentation of variables such as these.

The second problem illustrated by *Henwood* is the burden it places on the insured to know what information is material. General questions such as this may leave substantial room for alternative interpretations. The application process is not usually conducive to the provision of detailed information. The insured is not familiar with the types of questions and the insurance agent assisting the applicant will be anxious to sell the insurance quickly.

An economic argument can be made that the applicant should not be penalized if it is not reasonable to believe that the information is material. If the applicants do not appreciate that some information affects the probability of loss, there cannot be adverse selection. Similarly, information that the insured acquires after purchasing insurance cannot be the source of adverse selection. The insurer simply faces a more heterogeneous risk pool. The common law of insurance does not require that the insured disclose subsequent information.

INTENTIONAL ACTS. In early cases insurance contracts were not enforced, as a matter of public policy, if the loss resulted from a criminal act by the insured (see *Amicable Society v. Bolland*). The courts believed that to enforce such contracts would increase the amount of crime. Subsequently, as motor vehicle accidents resulting from illegal acts became common, the rule has been modified by statute to restrict the public policy rule to intentional acts. It is also an implied term of insurance contracts that the insurance does not cover intentional acts, regardless of the legality of the acts. In *Co-Operative Fire & Casualty Co. v. Saindon* the insured, Saindon, raised a running lawn mower up to the face of his neighbour during an argument. The mower cut off the neighbour's fingers. Saindon then continued to mow the lawn as he said he 'only had a little strip to finish'. The neighbour was awarded damages and Saindon attempted to recover under a Comprehensive Personal Liability section of his insurance policy. The insurer declined to pay on the grounds that it was contrary to public policy to compensate the insured for an intentional criminal act. The Supreme Court of Canada accepted the insurer's argument.

The *Saindon* case illustrates the conflict between several economic and social objectives. On the one hand, the law should encourage potential injurers to take an efficient amount of care. On the other hand courts will desire to compensate victims of crime. As discussed above in the context of insurable interest, Shavell's model suggests that there is no externality when insurance induces the insured to take less care because the tort compensation is assumed to compensate fully the third party for his or her injuries. As a practical matter, full compensation is not awarded by the courts (most obviously in the case of wrongful death), and the defendant may not have adequate funds. The dissent in *Saindon* and the subsequent criticism of the case were undoubtedly motivated by a concern that the victim would not be able to recover the entire award from the impecunious injurer. Denial of insurance coverage will effectively deny full compensation for the victim.

What is the role for a public policy rule against enforcement of contracts for insurance against liability for intentional acts? Insurers will not sell insurance for intentional acts because of moral hazard. Consequently, a public policy rule should not be needed as a protection for third parties. On the other hand, potential injurers, faced with the possibility of momentary carelessness or capricious courts, will want insurance against liability for unintentional negligence. Somewhere between these two extremes is the 'calculated risk' in which the injurer hopes to profit by taking too little care and the 'reckless disregard for the lives or safety of other persons'. Insurers may be willing to sell insurance for liability created by these acts, but in doing so, they *may* create a higher risk for potential victims. The word 'may' is crucial because the judgment-proof injurer will not have any incentive to take care *with or without* insurance. Furthermore, the victim who is completely judgment-proof will have no reason to buy any liability insurance! More realistically, most potential injurers are likely to incur some cost as a result of a civil suit and will desire insurance. Since the insureds will have limited wealth, the insurance provides compensation to the victim for the accident. Given that this compensation is not complete, the insurance may make the victims worse off if the losses caused by the greater frequency of accidents (which are under-compensated) dominate the additional compensation which is received from injurers with limited wealth. It is possible that the additional compensation dominates the value of the added risk. A side benefit is that the insurance premium may place more of the costs of risky activities on potential injurers, perhaps reducing the extent of these activities. Without insurance, partially judgment-proof injurers would face unreasonably low costs for these activities.

One possible solution method of dealing with insurance for criminal acts is to require that the insurer pay the victim but permit the insurer to recover from the injurer. This approach was used in New Jersey in *Ambassador Insurance Co. v. Montes.* The flaw with this remedy is that there is no incentive for the insurer and the insured to enter into contracts that benefit third parties. Following such a decision one would expect that insurance contracts would be refined so as to explicitly exclude coverage for the sorts of acts that would be covered by this decision. A further problem with this approach is that the insurer has a duty to defend the insured in the liability claim and will have a conflict of interest if it intends to ask for indemnification from the insured.

Intentional acts may also impose losses on the insured, members of the household, and others with a contractual relationship to the insured such as mortgagees. In *Scott v. Wawanesa Mutual Insurance Co.* the insured's fifteen-year-old son deliberately set fire to the family home. The policy excluded 'loss or damage caused by a criminal or wilful act or omission of the Insured . . .'. Elsewhere, the term 'Insured' was defined to include members of the same household. The majority of the court rejected an argument that the son had no insurable interest in the home (which would have excluded the son from being an 'insured') and held that the exclusion prevented recovery. Similar issues arose in other cases when a woman deliberately set fire to a house co-owned with her husband and a mortgagee attempted to collect insurance proceeds after an owner scuttled the ship.

A dissenting judge in the *Scott* case concluded that a reasonable person would not expect to recover for his or her own acts but would expect to recover if a spouse burned down the house. An economic perspective does not necessarily support this conclusion. The insurance contract will involve a compromise between risk reduction and lower premiums. In the absence of moral hazard the insured will want full insurance without exclusions. If there is significant moral hazard for some types of risks, it will be in the interest of the insured to exclude those risks. In the situation illustrated by *Scott* the insured is in a much better position than the insurer to monitor the actions of members of the household. If deliberate destruction can be prevented by the insured at relatively low cost, it is efficient to exclude this type of risk from the coverage.

Consider the situation in which a house is insured for the benefit of a mortgagee and an owner. There is a risk that the owner or members of his family might deliberately damage the structure. How should this risk be allocated? Neither the insurer nor the mortgagee will be able to monitor the deliberate acts of the insured or his family. The insured could monitor his or her own actions and the actions of members of the family. It seems possible that the most efficient outcome is for the insurance to exclude coverage for the insured's share of the loss resulting from a family member's acts and to provide coverage for the mortgagee. Whether or not the mortgagee would be covered would depend on the relative risk aversion of the mortgagee and the comparative advantage of the insurer and the mortgagee in determining which families are likely to impose a risk of deliberate destruction. Many lenders will implicitly provide income insurance for borrowers, but it is not clear where the comparative advantage lies as between mortgagee and insurer. The insurance company, having paid the mortgagee, would have subrogation rights against the insured to the rights of the mortgagee. If there is no coverage, the mortgagee can attempt to recover from the insured's other assets. Either way, all of the loss will fall on the insured if there is deliberate destruction.

What is the role of the law in dealing with this type of intentional act? The *Saindon* and *Scott* cases differ in that the former more directly involves third parties who will not be protected in a contract. The losses in *Scott* are internalized and one might expect the insurance contract to reflect all of the costs. In such cases the contract itself should be given more weight than in situations affecting third parties. However, there are potential externalities when the intentional acts involve arson or the scuttling of a ship. In the case of the ship, innocent crew members will be placed at risk and others may feel obligated to rescue the survivors. This suggests that the insured should not recover for his or her own acts and he or she should have an additional obligation to monitor family members. On the other hand, it is possible that exclusion clauses arise because of adverse selection, not because of moral hazard. The market may produce too many such exclusion clauses as insureds without delinquent children attempt to signal their low-risk characteristics. In such a situation it is possible that a ban on such exclusion clauses would make both low-risk and high-risk customers better off.

A hybrid of *Saindon* and *Scott* arises when a child, who is insured under the policy, commits a deliberate act which injures a third party and the parents are found to be vicariously liable for negligently failing to monitor the child. United States courts have tended to permit recovery under the parents' liability insurance policy. Apparently, the concern for the third party and the absence of parental intent tip the balance toward enforcement. If the parents had committed the deliberate act the liability insurance coverage would not be enforceable.

In summary, intentional acts create a dilemma for courts. Enforcement of insurance contracts provides compensation to third party victims but may increase the number of injuries. Forcing the insurance company to compensate the victim and to attempt recovery from the insured will lead to greater exclusions and increased risk for innocent insureds. The economic approach suggests a difference between situations in which there are no externalities (child intentionally floods basement) and those in which third parties actually or potentially suffer losses. In the former situation greater weight should be placed on the ability of the insured to monitor family members. The emergence of more widespread first-party insurance coverage should reduce the importance of compensating victims and increase the importance of deterring intentional harms.

SAMUEL A. REA, JR.

See also AUTOMOBILE ACCIDENTS, INSURANCE AND TORT LIABILITY; INSURANCE, DETERRENCE AND LIABILITY; INSURANCE FOR WORKPLACE INJURIES; JUDGMENT-PROOFNESS; MEDICAL MALPRACTICE; PRODUCTS LIABILITY; SEX DISCRIMINATION AND THE EQUAL GOOD OF PENSIONS; VALUING LIFE AND RISKS TO LIFE.

Subject classification: 5c(iii).

CASES

Ambassador Insurance Co. v. Montes, 388 A2d 603 (NJ 1978).
Amicable Society v. Bolland (1830) 4 Bligh NS 194.
Constitution Insurance Co. of Canada v. Kosmopoulos [1987] 1 SCR 2.
Co-Operative Fire & Casualty Co. v. Saindon (1975) 56 DLR (3d).
Da Costa v. Jones (1778) 2 Cowp. 729, 98 Eng. Rep. 1331.
Le Cras v. Hughes (1782) 3 Dougl. 81, 99 Eng. Rep. 549, at 552.
Dalby v. India & London Life-Assurance Co. (1854) 15 CB 365, 139 Eng. Rep. 465.
Farmers Mutual Insurance Co. v. New Holland Turnpike Co., 15 A 563 (Pa 1888).
Glynn v. Scottish Union & National Insurance Co. (1963) 40 DLR (2d) 929.
Good v. Elliott (1790) 3 B & P 195, 100 Eng. Rep. 808.
Henwood v. Prudential Insurance Co. of America (1967) 64 DLR (2d) 715.
Lucena v. Craufurd (1806) 2 Bos. & Pul. (NR) 269, 127 Eng. Rep. 630.
National Filtering Oil Co. v. Citizens Insurance Co., 13 NE 337 (NY 1887).
Scott v Wawanesa Mutual Insurance Co. [1989] 1 SCR 1445.

BIBLIOGRAPHY

Abraham, K. 1986. *Distributing Risk.* New Haven: Yale University Press.
Gravelle, H. 1991. Insurance law and adverse selection. *International Review of Law and Economics* 11: 23–45.
Keeton, R.A. and Widiss, A.I. 1988. *Insurance Law: A Guide to Fundamental Principles, Legal Doctrines, and Commercial Practices.* St. Paul, MN: West Publishing Co.
Rea, S.A. 1991. Insurance classifications and social welfare. In *Contributions to Insurance Economics,* ed. G. Dionne (Boston: Kluwer Academic Publishers): 377–96.
Rea, S.A. 1993. The economics of insurance law. *International Review of Law and Economics* 13: 145–62.
Schwartz, G.T. 1990. The ethics and the economics of tort liability insurance. *Cornell Law Review* 75: 313–65.
Shavell, S. 1982. On liability and insurance. *Bell Journal of Economics.* 13: 120–32.

intellectual property. The fundamental question in the economics of intellectual property is the degree of protection to be afforded creators of intellectual property against the copying of their works by other producers. (Another branch of the economics of intellectual property involves the analysis of unauthorized use by final consumers rather than by producers. See, for example, Besen and Kirby (1989) for an analysis of the effect of 'private' copying of copyrighted works.) This question itself subsumes several others: Is any protection appropriate? How much protection should there be? Should the extent of protection be measured by its duration or its breadth? In determining the appropriate amount of protection, how should the interests of other producers be taken into account? Does the amount of protection depend on the nature of the intellectual property and, if so, in what way?

IS ANY INTELLECTUAL PROPERTY PROTECTION APPROPRIATE? As a preliminary matter, it is useful to address the question of whether any form of intellectual property protection is needed. Indeed, a branch of economic analysis that has been sceptical about the need for intellectual property protection goes back at least to papers by Plant (1934a, 1934b) in the 1930s. More recently, Breyer (1970) makes a similar argument against the copyright system and, even more recently, Samuelson (1984) has argued against copyright protection for computer programs.

These papers argue vigorously that the patent and copyright systems are unnecessary, both because much innovative activity occurs independently of the resulting financial rewards and because there are means other than legal protection by which creators can benefit from their efforts before others can copy them. These papers argue further that the systems are inefficient because they apply to all innovations although protection of only a limited number is justified.

Although this line of argument remains outside the mainstream, some indirect justification for more limited patent protection can be found in a survey of 'high-level R&D managers' conducted by Levin et al. (1987). Respondents were asked to rate each of the following for its effectiveness in 'protecting the competitive advantages of new or improved processes and products': patents, secrecy, lead time, moving quickly down the learning curve, and sales or service efforts. The findings were that:

> for new processes . . . patents were generally rated the least effective of the mechanisms of appropriation . . . [and although] patents for products were typically considered more effective than those for processes . . . generally, lead time, learning curves, and sale or service efforts were regarded as substantially more effective than patents in protecting products.

Levin et al. conclude 'that improving the protection of intellectual property is not necessarily socially beneficial . . . Stronger appropriability will not yield more innovation in all contexts and, where it does, innovation may come at excessive cost' (1987: 816).

HOW MUCH PROTECTION SHOULD THERE BE? Assuming that some intellectual property protection is necessary, how much should there be? During the period of protection, the competition faced by the innovator is limited and he is thus able to earn supranormal returns that permit him to cover the costs and risks of undertaking the search for the innovation. The extent to which the innovator is sheltered from competition depends on both the scope of protection and the availability of imperfect substitutes for the innovation.

Consider a single isolated innovation that, but for intellectual property protection, would not be created at all. Assume, further, that there are no issues of breadth, so that only the length of the period of protection is at issue. Also assume that only one level of innovative activity is possible, i.e. that the innovation cannot be accelerated or improved by expending additional resources (which is, of course, at variance with the basic assumption in the 'patent race' literature). Assume, finally, that other innovative activity is unaffected by the extent of protection that is given.

In this simple case, the appropriate period of protection is that which permits the innovator to cover the risk-adjusted cost of innovative activity, but no longer. If a shorter period of protection were provided, the innovation would not be made. If protection were for a longer period, the competitive supply of those innovations that would have occurred with less protection would be unnecessarily delayed, with the resulting loss in social welfare.

Suppose now that the 'optimal' period of protection differs among innovations but that, perhaps for reasons of administrative simplicity, it is necessary to apply the same period of protection to a large number of different innovations. As the (common) period of protection is lengthened, additional innovations are encouraged but the diffusion of innovations that would have occurred even with a shorter period of protection is inefficiently delayed. The choice of the optimal period of protection thus involves balancing the benefits from encouraging additional innovative activity against the social costs of deferring the competitive supply of the innovation. (The same type of tradeoff arises where the intensity at which a particular innovative activity is undertaken can be varied. Nordhaus (1969) and Scherer (1972) develop formal models of this tradeoff for the case of 'run-of-the-mill' process innovations.) A 'one-size-fits-all' regime results in too much protection for some innovations – those that would have occurred even if the period of protection had been shorter – and too little for others – those that would have eventuated if the period of protection had been longer.

It is important to note here that, although all patented inventions have the same term, patents are granted for much shorter terms than are copyrights. In the United States, for example, copyrights extend for the author's life plus fifty years while patents provide for only seventeen years. (For a discussion of these and other aspects of the copyright, patent, trade secret and trademark regimes, see Besen and Raskind 1991.) In addition, the patents for some products are effectively longer than others because of differences in the way in which they are administered. For example, in the United States, the patent protection period may be extended by as long as five years for pharmaceuticals and medical devices to allow for the Federal review and approval process, while design patents are protected for only fourteen years. In addition, separate legal regimes with different periods of protection are sometimes created for particular products, as in the case of the ten-year term for the protection of 'mask works' embodied in semiconductor chips in the United States.

WHAT FORM SHOULD PROTECTION TAKE? LENGTH VS. BREADTH. For many years, economists who studied the patent system focused almost exclusively on the length of the period of protection. More recently, however, attention has been directed at the breadth of protection, which can be defined loosely as the range of innovations over which a patent holder is given exclusive domain. Broad protection, as defined by Klemperer (1990), means that a patent holder has exclusive rights to develop and market 'adjacent' innovations while narrow protection limits the holder to the specific innovation for which protection has been granted. Alternatively, as Gilbert and Shapiro (1990) observe, increased breadth can take the form of greater latitude in the practices permitted to the patent holder in exploiting the patent grant, for example by allowing the use of exclusive territories or tying arrangements in the sale of the patented item.

The broader is protection, the greater the flow of profits emanating from the innovation during the period in which the protection is in force. Because a given flow of profits can result from a very large number of combinations of patent length and breadth, allowing numerous ways in which the cost of innovation can be covered, the question arises as to what is the appropriate combination.

Two contrasting results have arisen in the literature. (Although this literature has focused on patent length and breadth, it also has relevance to the nature of copyright protection.) Gilbert and Shapiro (1990) find that under certain assumptions, very narrow, infinitely lived patents are optimal. Under different assumptions, Klemperer (1990) finds that broad, short-lived patents may be preferred.

The basic assumption that produces the Gilbert–Shapiro result in their 'reduced-form' model is that the social cost of expanding the breadth of protection increases at an increasing rate while the social cost of lengthening the patent life increases at a constant rate. They also show that the same result obtains where greater breadth is interpreted as the ability of the patent holder to set a higher price for a homogeneous product.

Klemperer analyses a model in which all consumers prefer the same product type but may differ in the extent to which they are willing to substitute alternatives to their preferred type. As the breadth of protection is increased, the range of products that can be offered by competitors to the patent holder is reduced. This permits the patent holder to raise his price, which both reduces the consumption of the patented product and induces some consumers to purchase less preferred products from competitors. The social cost of very broad patents primarily takes the form of reduced consumption, while that of very narrow patents results primarily from consumers switching to less preferred alternatives. Which effect dominates depends on the nature of consumer demand.

If all consumers are similar in their willingness to substitute away from the patented product (i.e. they have similar 'transport costs' if they choose less preferred alternatives), the patent holder must set a price that induces few shifts to alternatives. In this case, narrow, long-lived patents are optimal because they induce the patent holder to set a low price. By contrast, if all consumers have similar reservation prices for the patented product, broad but short-lived patents are optimal. This is because, at the (common) reservation price, the social costs resulting from reduced consumption will be small.

It is interesting to note here that patents generally provide relatively broad and short-lived protection while copyrights are narrow and long-lived. Two identical works can both be copyrighted if they are the result of independent creation. Copyright protection covers 'expression' but not the underlying 'ideas'. (Section 102 (b) of the United States Copyright Act of 1976 states that 'In no case does copyright protection . . . extend to any idea, procedure, process, system, method of operation, concept, principle, or discovery . . .'.) Moreover, under the case law, copyright protection may not extend even to expression if only a limited number of ways exist to express an idea, in which case the idea is said to have 'merged' with the expression. In addition, facts cannot be copyrighted, although compilations of facts may be. (However, in *Feist Publications, Inc. v. Rural Telephone Service Co.*, 499 US 340 (1991) the United States Supreme Court ruled that a telephone directory could not be copyrighted because it did not display 'the minimal creative spark required by the Copyright Act . . .'.) At the same time, however, Section 103 of the Copyright Act extends protection to any 'derivative work' such as 'a translation, musical arrangement, dramatization, fictionalization, motion picture version, sound recording, art reproduction, abridgment, condensation, or any other form in which a work may be recast, transformed, or adapted', which tends to broaden the scope of protection.

More recently, especially in the case of computer software, attempts have been made to broaden the protection afforded by copyrights. This, in turn, has led to proposals (e.g., Chisum 1986; Menell 1987) to require creators of computer software to obtain patents, for which the standards required to obtain protection are more stringent, if they wish broader protection.

Unlike the copyright regime, where independent protection is a defence, patent protection is available only to a single innovator under either the 'first to invent' or 'first to file' rule. Indeed, under the 'doctrine of equivalents', patent infringement may be found if there is substantial, functional identity between the patented and the alleged infringing items.

HOW DOES THE SCOPE OF PROTECTION AFFECT THE COST OF INNOVATION? The discussion to this point has focused on the relationship between a single innovator and the users of the innovator's product where the welfare trade-offs involve comparing the *rewards* to innovation and either the social costs of delaying the competitive provision of the product or limitations on the competitive supply of substitutes for it. Recently, however, there has been renewed interest in the effect of the scope of protection on the *cost* of innovation. Put simply, although tighter intellectual property protection increases the *returns* to holders of patents or copyrights, and thus presumably spurs innovative activity, it may also increase the *costs* of innovative activity to other inventors, because much innovative activity is cumulative, with one creator building on the efforts of others. If later innovators cannot freely build on the work of others, or must pay to do so, they may be less likely to engage in inventive activity themselves.

If intellectual property protection is tight, it is more likely that the creator of an 'early' innovation will be able to control future developments, either through licensing 'later' innovators, or by undertaking the follow-on innovation himself. If, on the other hand, later innovators can build freely on the work of their predecessors, the costs of the former are reduced because they do not have to obtain licences to use the work of others. (Where intellectual property protection is weak, innovators may be induced to use trade secrecy rather than patents or copyrights because they must disclose their innovations in order to obtain legal protection.)

Landes and Posner (1989: 337) note that:

> the cost of expression to authors of copyrighted works increases as copyright protection increases. The less material an author . . . can borrow from other copyright holders without infringing their copyrights, the greater will be the cost of creating his work.

They conclude (1989: 344) that 'the more the cost of expression rises as [the level of copyright protection] increases . . . the lower will be the optimal degree of copyright protection'.

Where Landes and Posner suggest that the scope of protection for intellectual property should be narrow in order to lower the costs of later innovators, Kitch (1977) contends that United States patent law, as interpreted by the courts, does, and should, provide broad protection. Kitch contends that the 'reward theory', which is the basis of much analysis of the patent system, is incomplete because it ignores the 'prospect' function of that system. In this view, a principal benefit of the patent system is that it promotes efficient *exploitation* of an invention by granting a patent holder the exclusive rights to innovations that grow out of his work.

Kitch argues (1977: 276–7), for example, that:

> the patent owner has an incentive to make investments that maximize the value of the patent without fear that the fruits of the investment produce unpatentable information appropriable by competitors . . . Only in the case of a patented product is a firm able to make the expenditures necessary to bring the advantages of the product to the attention of the customer without fear of competitive appropriation if the product proves successful . . . a patent system lowers the cost for the owner of technological information of contracting with other firms possessing complementary information and resources.

In Kitch's view, there are significant benefits from restricting the access of later innovators to earlier works because doing so avoids the social costs of the inefficient exploitation of those works. Implicitly, these benefits are judged to be greater than the higher costs that the later innovators must incur.

Scotchmer (1991) also analyses how the relationship between earlier and later innovators is affected by the scope of patent protection. She assumes that innovators can benefit from access to earlier innovations because, for example, they reduce research and development costs, and that in some cases the later innovation may be impossible without either an agreement with, or a licence from, the early innovator. She also assumes that the later innovator may be better situated to produce follow-on innovations. In these circumstances, early innovators may need to be able to share in the surplus obtained by later innovators in order to cover their own costs, but if they capture too much of the surplus they may discourage efforts to discover the follow-ons.

Scotchmer shows that if patent protection is broad and the first innovator has all the bargaining power, there can be efficient later innovation, essentially for the reasons given by Kitch. That is, early innovators will contract to provide later ones with access to their works at licence fees that permit the later innovators to cover their costs. And, for some early innovators, licence fees permit them to cover their research and developments costs.

What Scotchmer also shows, however, is that if the patent system divides the bargaining power between earlier and later innovators, both types of innovation may be carried out inefficiently. The reason is that a division of revenues that is sufficient to cover the costs of early innovation may leave too little for later innovators, while an arrangement that is sufficient to compensate later innovators may yield revenues that are inadequate to cover the costs of early innovators.

SHOULD INTELLECTUAL PROPERTY PROTECTION BE WEAKER IN NETWORK INDUSTRIES? Determining the appropriate scope of intellectual property protection in so-called 'network industries' poses special problems. In network industries a single way of doing something may become the standard to the total exclusion of what may be as good or even superior alternatives. Thus, for example, all users of computer applications software may come to expect that the keystrokes required to perform certain repetitive tasks are the same regardless of the vendor from whom they purchase their products, or all purchasers of portable telephones may expect to be able to access the public network regardless of vendor, or all purchasers of compact discs may expect to be able to play them on any player. Because, other things equal, consumers prefer to be on large networks, it may become difficult for small networks to survive once one network achieves a critical size. This phenomenon is known as 'tipping' (see Besen and Farrell 1994 for a discussion of business strategies in network industries. For a formal treatment of 'tipping' see Arthur 1989).

Because 'tipping' is a common phenomenon in network industries, strong intellectual property protection may convey a great deal of market power to the owner of a standard. For this reason, a number of authors have argued that intellectual property protection should be more limited in those industries.

Farrell (1995) argues for weaker protection primarily on the basis of three factors. First, higher prices in network industries harm not only those who choose to buy less of the product as a result, but also those who would have benefited from their larger purchases, i.e. some 'network externalities' are lost. Second, because network industries tend to 'tip', the owner of a standard may be less constrained by competition than are intellectual property owners in other industries. Finally, Farrell observes that a given standard might represent only a modest technical advance, and could even be inferior to technologies that it defeated.

The argument for weaker intellectual property protection has been made especially strongly in the case of computer software, where network effects can be extremely important. For example, Menell (1987) has called for limiting intellectual property protection for computer operating systems both by protecting only important innovations (essentially by requiring that innovations meet the higher patentability requirements of novelty and non-obviousness instead of the weaker copyright requirement of originality), and by limiting the term of protection. In his words, legal protection for operating system software 'should be hard to come by and relatively short in duration' (p. 1364). In addition, Menell would require the owner of an operating system to license it to others on reasonable terms in order to limit the ability of the owner of a standard to disadvantage its rivals.

The law in this area is still evolving but there have been numerous attempts to provide broad protection under the copyright law to certain standardized features of computer software or other products. Some of these initiatives have met with success, although some courts have attempted to draw a line between standards, which receive little or no intellectual property protection, and non-standardized features for which considerable protection is provided. (See, e.g., *Lotus Development Corp. v. Paperback Software Intern'l*, and *E.F. Johnson Co. v. Uniden Corp.*)

CONCLUSION. Determining the appropriate scope of protection for intellectual property is a difficult undertaking. The law employs two broad regimes. Copyrights are easy to obtain, extend for a long period of time, and generally provide only limited protection against the development of close substitutes because they protect expression alone and not underlying ideas. Patents are difficult to obtain and are granted for relatively short periods, but provide considerable protection against potential infringers, even those who employ substantially different technologies.

Historically, the copyright system has been employed to protect literary and artistic works, for which the market structure is monopolistic competition, while patents have covered tangible products and industrial processes, where there are likely to be fewer close substitutes. The fairly recent development of computer software has challenged this traditional separation because the product combines features of both literary and industrial products, and because the existence of network effects may argue for more limited protection.

STANLEY M. BESEN

See also COMPUTER LAW; COPYRIGHT; INCENTIVES TO INNOVATE; NETWORK EFFECTS AND EXTERNALITIES; NETWORK EXTERNALITY AND CONVENTION; PATENTS; TRADE SECRET.

Subject classification: 5b(iii).

STATUTE

The Copyright Act of 1976, Public Law 94–553, 90 Stat. 2541, as amended.

CASES

E.F. Johnson Co. v. Uniden Corp. of America, 623 F Supp 1485 (Minn. 1985).

Feist Publications, Inc. v. Rural Telephone Service Co., Inc., 499 US 340 (1991).

Lotus Development Corp. v. Paperback Software International, 740 F Supp 37 (Mass. 1990).

BIBLIOGRAPHY

Arthur, W.B. 1989. Competing technologies, increasing returns, and lock-in by historical events. *Economic Journal* 99: 116–31.

Besen, S.M. and Farrell, J. 1994. Choosing how to compete: strategies and tactics in standardization. *Journal of Economic Perspectives* 8: 117–31.

Besen, S.M. and Kirby, S.N. 1989. Private copying, appropriability, and optimal copying royalties. *Journal of Law and Economics* 32: 255–80.

Besen, S.M. and Raskind, L.J. 1991. An introduction to the law and economics of intellectual property. *Journal of Economic Perspectives* 5: 3–27.

Breyer, S. 1970. The uneasy case for copyright: a study of copyright in books, photocopies, and computer programs. *Harvard Law Review* 84: 281–351.

Chisum, D.S. 1986. The patentability of algorithms. *University of Pittsburgh Law Review* 47: 959–1022.

Farrell, J. 1995. Arguments for weaker intellectual property protection in network industries. *StandardView* 3: 46–9.

Gilbert, R. and Shapiro, C. 1990. Optimal patent length and breadth. *RAND Journal of Economics* 21: 106–12.

Kitch, E.W. 1977. The nature and function of the patent system. *Journal of Law and Economics* 20: 265–90.

Klemperer, P. 1990. How broad should the scope of patent protection be? *RAND Journal of Economics* 21: 113–30.

Landes, W.M. and Posner, R.A. 1989. An economic analysis of copyright law. *Journal of Legal Studies* 18: 325–63.

Levin, R.C., Klevorick, A.K. Nelson, R.R. and Winter, S.G. 1987. Appropriating the returns from industrial research and development. *Brookings Papers on Economic Activity* 3: 783–820.

Menell, P.S. 1987. Tailoring legal protection for computer software. *Stanford Law Review* 39: 1329–72.

Nordhaus, W.D. 1969. *Invention, Growth and Welfare: A Theoretical Treatment of Technological Change*. Cambridge, MA: MIT Press.

Plant, A. 1934a. The economic theory concerning patents for inventions. *Economica* NS 1: 30–51, reprinted in Plant, A. 1974. *Selected Economic Essays and Addresses*. (London: Routledge & Kegan Paul, Chapter 3: 35–56.

Plant, A. 1934b. The economic aspects of copyright in books. *Economica* NS 1: 167–95. Reprinted in A. Plant, *Selected Economic Essays and Addresses* (London: Routledge & Kegan Paul, 1974): 57–86.

Samuelson, P. 1984. CONTU revisited: the case against copyright protection for computer programs in machine-readable form. *Duke Law Journal* 1984: 663–769.

Scherer, F.M. 1972. Nordhaus' theory of optimal patent life: a geometric reinterpretation. *American Economic Review* 62: 422–7.

Scotchmer, S. 1991. Standing on the shoulders of giants: cumulative research and the patent law. *Journal of Economic Perspectives* 5: 29–41.

international sanctions. A prerogative of government is its right to take coercive measures, such as confiscation and incarceration, to discourage undesirable behaviour. Normally the legitimacy of such measures ends at the borders of a government's jurisdiction, but governments often seek influence beyond these borders.

International sanctions are one means by which a national government, often called the *sender*, tries to affect what happens in another country, the *target*. Sanctions involve the threat or use of a measure intended to harm the target.

Sanctions fall short of the direct extraterritorial exercise of coercion, what Schelling (1960) calls 'brute force', such as a military attack. Instead, sanctions involve measures enforced domestically but aimed at a target. Various actions taken by the allied powers against Iraq after its 1991 occupation of Kuwait illustrate the distinction: the boycott of Iraqi oil was a sanction imposed (unsuccessfully) to persuade Saddam Hussein to abandon Kuwait; the attack that ultimately removed his soldiers constituted brute force.

International sanctions have generated two controversies. One is the narrower, more positive question of whether they are effective in achieving their sender's objectives. Some spectacular failures (trade restrictions against Italy after Mussolini's occupation of Abyssinia, the nearly forty years of commercial isolation that the United States has tried to impose on Cuba, the case of Iraq) have led observers to conclude that sanctions do little to influence their targets (see, e.g., Bartlett 1985). In these cases, however, senders sought major reversals of the target's policies. We review five studies that assess quantitatively the use of sanctions in recent history, usually with more modest objectives. A common conclusion is that sanctions often do work, especially when their objectives are limited. But because these successes are more minor, they command less attention.

A broader, more normative controversy is whether international sanctions make a useful contribution to world welfare. Some observers have been especially critical of the increased role sanctions have played in US law (see Bhagwati and Patrick 1990, various contributions). Concerns are that unilateral sanctions threaten national sovereignty, undermine multilateral agreements, and put small countries at an unfair disadvantage (see Chayes and Chayes 1995). Others, however, argue that unilateral sanctions help enforce international agreements and fill in gaps in these arrangements. As for bias against small countries, trade measures might actually damage a large country more since it has more trade to divert, while a large country might more often find itself a target since its behaviour has more effect on others (see Sykes 1992).

I. BASIC FEATURES. Sanctions have three basic features: (i) the parties involved (the sender and target), (ii) their objective (the aspect of the target's behaviour that the sender seeks to influence), and (iii) their measures (what the sender does or threatens to do to the target for not complying with its wishes).

The parties. Targets are usually individual states, although there are examples in which sanctions have targeted groups within states. Senders have been individual countries or groups of countries acting in concert. Sanctions may be initiated by the sender's government or by private individuals.

Objectives. Countries have used sanctions to pursue a wide range of objectives. While motives are often mixed, a few broad categories can be distinguished.

Sanctions have been a response to the target's military actions, such as its invasion or occupation of territory (e.g., Iraq in Kuwait or the Soviet Union in Afghanistan).

A target's treatment of the sender's nationals has also led to sanctions. An example here is the US response to the kidnapping of its diplomats in Iran.

Sanctions have been aimed at economic policies that the sender perceives as damaging. Senders have used sanctions to seek greater access to foreign markets for their exports, enhanced overseas protection of their physical and intellectual property, and repayment of external claims.

Environmental protection has been another objective of sanctions. Early examples are their use in disputes over international fisheries, where the issues were primarily commercial (see Elagab 1988). More recent applications have concerned protecting endangered species and the atmosphere.

Finally, senders have used sanctions to pursue ethical and human rights concerns. Examples here are the sanctions imposed against South Africa during apartheid, and the Jackson–Vanik amendment conditioning US trade with communist countries in Eastern Europe on emigration rights of their citizens (see Martin 1992). Here the sender seeks to influence the target state's policies towards its own nationals rather than its policies toward other states (see Stremlau 1996).

An important legal issue is whether the objective is to enforce a treaty or international law. In many cases sanctions have been used for this purpose, but US law includes provisions for sanctions against behaviour that does not break international law or a treaty obligation (see Sykes 1992).

Whatever the sender's objective, two key aspects are: (i) the cost to the target of complying with the sender's demand and (ii) the benefit to the sender of achieving its objective.

Measures. Most commonly, sanctions threaten measures such as embargoes, boycotts, and limitations on financial interaction that restrict some form of commerce with the target. Senders have seized or blocked assets owned by the target or its nationals under the sender's jurisdiction. Senders have also punished a target by restricting its participation in international organizations, by stopping aid, by banning its athletes from international sporting events, and by boycotting sporting events that the target is sponsoring (see Carter 1988).

Most measures appear to be what Malloy (1990) terms 'directive', and are meant to encourage the target to alter its behaviour to avoid or to end the measure. Some measures appear to be 'defensive', however, intended to weaken a target state militarily or to render it more vulnerable to overthrow. The US embargoes on exports of helium to Nazi Germany and of high-technology goods to Communist countries, along with the current sanctions against Iraq, seem to fall more into this category. Yet a third motive for imposing sanctions might be 'communicative', simply to express disapproval of a target or its actions. Finally, sanctions might serve to signal the sender's willingness to use tougher measures such as brute force down the road (see Stremlau 1996). Depending on what the sender has in mind, different analytic methods and criteria for success apply. Where these distinctions matter, the focus here is on 'directive' sanctions, since they appear most common and raise the most interesting analytic issues.

Just as objectives differ as to whether a breach of international law or a treaty obligation is at issue, measures differ according to whether they would constitute, if taken without provocation, a breach on the sender's part. A reprisal that, in isolation, would break international law is nevertheless legal if: (i) the sender establishes that the target itself broke international law, (ii) the reprisal follows an unsuccessful attempt to obtain reparation, and (iii) the harm imposed by the reprisal is not disproportional to the damage initially inflicted by the target (see Elagab 1988).

Two basic features of a measure are the damage it does to the target and the cost to the sender of imposing it. Both theory and evidence indicate that the effectiveness of a sanction depends upon how these magnitudes weigh against the cost to the target of acquiescing, and the benefit to the sender of achieving its objective. While some measures harm both parties, others, such as cutting off aid, might benefit the sender. In many cases, whether the measure costs or benefits the sender is unclear. Trade sanctions could reduce the gains from trade to both parties, or they could constitute a move toward the sender's optimal tariff. Even if there are no overall trade gains, powerful groups within the sender state might benefit.

2. HISTORICAL BACKGROUND. According to historians of sanctions, their first recorded use was an Athenian embargo of imports from Megara around 433 BC (see Carter 1988 or Malloy 1990), ostensibly in reprisal for the kidnapping of three courtesans. Here sanctions were imposed by the leader of a government (Pericles). Elagab (1988) cites episodes in the 1600s of individuals seeking redress for losses suffered at the hands of a foreign government with their own sovereign, who would issue a 'letter of marque' authorizing seizure of the offender's property commensurate with the initial loss.

An early appearance of sanctions in US history was the boycott of British goods by American colonists leading to the repeal of the 1765 Stamp Act a year later. An early use of sanctions to punish sovereign default was the commercial reprisal that Andrew Jackson threatened to take when the French Chamber of Deputies failed to appropriate funds to repay debts to the United States. British intermediation resolved the dispute, so the measures were never taken (see Elagab 1988). Sanctions began to serve US trade objectives in 1886 when Congress authorized the President to exclude vessels from countries that discriminate against US commerce from US ports (see Malloy 1990).

The League of Nations Charter established the first centralized system for administering sanctions (see Kuyper 1978). The League oversaw a commercial boycott of Greece that succeeded in coaxing a withdrawal from Bulgaria, as well as the less successful sanctions against Italy (see Doxey 1980 or Hufbauer et al. 1990).

3. ASPECTS OF THE CURRENT LEGAL FRAMEWORK. A web of international agreements and national laws govern the use of sanctions in the current world order. Chayes and Chayes (1995) distinguish among 'treaty-based sanctions'

undertaken to enforce an international agreement, 'membership sanctions', expelling or suspending a member of an international organization for noncompliance, and 'unilateral' sanctions, those initiated by national legislation. The distinction is often blurry, however. Treaties typically leave enforcement up to individual members, offering wide latitude for interpretation.

Sanctions and the United Nations. The United Nations Charter contains provisions for sanctions in response to 'any threat to peace, breach of peace, or act of aggression'. While the UN assembly can authorize sanctions, their enforcement is the exclusive domain of the governments of member states (see Stremlau 1996).

Before the end of the Cold War UN sanctions were implemented only twice, against Rhodesia during 1966–1979 and against South Africa during 1979–1994. Since then, however, they have been invoked against Iraq (1990–present), Yugoslavia (1991–95), Libya (1992–present), Haiti (1993–94), Liberia (1992–present), Somalia (1992–present), UNITA/Angola (1993–present), and Rwanda (1994–95). In at least half of these cases, sanctions were aimed at influencing the behaviour of governments toward their own citizens rather than toward other states (see Stremlau 1996).

WTO/GATT. While the enforcement of UN sanctions is delegated to individual members, the General Agreement of Trade and Tariffs (GATT) left both the initiation and imposition of reprisals up to members harmed by the noncompliance of another member. Article XXIII of the agreement established provisions for dispute settlement. If a member had 'nullified or impaired' the benefit of a GATT 'concession' to another member, the injured party could be authorized to retaliate by suspending its own GATT 'concessions' to the offender. In practice, such authorization was never given, so the system relied on unilaterally determined sanctions outside the formal ambit of Article XXIII.

Article XIX of GATT provides an 'escape clause', permitting members to suspend a GATT obligation in the face of an increase in imports that imposes a 'serious injury' to a domestic industry. Absent any agreement about compensation, affected exporting members are authorized to suspend 'equivalent concessions or other obligations' (see Sykes 1991).

The Uruguay Round establishing the World Trade Organization (WTO) took steps to reform the GATT dispute resolution mechanism. In particular, the WTO authorizes retaliation in response to a finding of noncompliance by a WTO panel, eliminating the need for unilateral determination of sanctions (see Chayes and Chayes 1995).

The Montreal Protocol. The Montreal Protocol, which went into force in 1988, imposes controls phasing out ozone-threatening chlorofluorocarbons (CFCs). According to Parson (1993), a major factor in getting a large number of countries to sign on was a provision banning imports of CFC-producing substances from countries not in compliance. South Korea and Taiwan, which were nonparties, nevertheless unilaterally decided to adhere to the Protocol's standards in order to avoid the ban.

This Protocol appears to be unusual among international treaties in specifying quite precisely what measures members should take against countries not in compliance. It has also been successful in meeting its targets for reducing production, although doubt remains as to whether CFC emissions have been cut in time to reverse the damage to the ozone layer in the near future.

Sanctions in US law. A wide range of US laws govern the use of sanctions. Malloy (1990) distinguishes between sanctions serving 'foreign policy, military or strategic objectives', from sanctions that constitute 'trade regulation'. The first target either specific countries (e.g., South Africa) or countries identified through some external mechanism (e.g., declaration of a national emergency, declaration of war, UN resolution). The second 'involve penalties imposed on *any* exporting nation that violates basic rubrics of trade with the United States' (see Malloy 1990).

Among the first type, the Export Administration Act, the Trading with the Enemies Act, and the International Emergency Economic Powers Act give the executive the authority to impose sanctions against countries for various national security purposes. The United Nations Participation Act authorizes US participation in UN sanctions. Finally, the Comprehensive Anti-Apartheid Act of 1986 imposed sanctions against South Africa in response to its apartheid policies. Unlike the other statutes, this law targeted a specific country, and was passed over a presidential veto. Measures were lifted in the mid 1990s in response to the dismantling of apartheid (see Malloy 1990, 1996).

Among US statutes constituting 'trade regulation', most important is the Tariff Act of 1930, along with the Trade Act of 1974 and other recent statutes. Section 301 of the 1974 Act authorizes retaliation against a wide range of 'unfair' practices. Some break treaty obligations (301(a)) while others are simply 'unreasonable or discriminatory' (301(b)) (see Sykes 1992).

The United States Trade Representative (USTR) administers the law. She first identifies, either by petition from a private group or by her own initiative, any foreign government practice that 'infringes upon US rights under a trade agreement or is otherwise "unjustifiable", "unreasonable", or "discriminatory"'. She then negotiates with the relevant government to try to get it to stop the practice. If negotiations fail, she is authorized to impose measures against the country in question which are 'equivalent in value to the burden being imposed by that country on US commerce' (see Sykes 1992). In the case of 301(a), retaliation by the USTR is 'mandatory', although the President can reverse any action (see Sykes 1990). (Partan 1990 compares the US law with its European counterpart.)

While the act is primarily aimed at promoting US exports, it has also taken aim at alleged impediments to US investment abroad and to practices restricting US access to raw materials abroad. The 'Special 301' provision aims at foreign infringement of US intellectual property.

Section 301 threatens sanctions in order to promote trade. When it fails, however, it triggers measures in the form of import barriers, having the opposite effect. US law also calls for measures in response to foreign practices that expand trade: antidumping duties target alleged 'dumping' in US markets by foreign firms, while countervailing duties offset export subsidies by foreign governments. Finally, Section 337 authorizes the 'exclusion' of foreign products in response to 'unfair methods of competition and unfair acts in . . . importation', often interpreted as infringement of US intellectual property (see Jackson 1991). Whether antidumping law, countervailing duties, or the Section 337 constitute 'sanctions' is unclear. One interpretation is that they punish practices that the US government would like to discourage. Another is that they simply offset their effect on US firms.

Numerous other US laws, some of which are discussed below, authorize or mandate retaliation in various circumstances.

4. THEORY. What does economic theory have to say about the effectiveness of sanctions as a tool of statecraft? The absence of a supra-national enforcement agency means that relations among nations must be self-enforcing. Developments in economic theory over the last two decades have provided a better, but still very sketchy, picture of how self-enforcing relationships work.

Sykes (1990) depicts sanctions as a simultaneous-moves game between a target and sender: The target chooses to acquiesce (A) to the sender's demand, or to balk (B) at it, while the sender decides to impose a threatened measure (P) or to condone (C) the target's behaviour. The two choices determine the four possible outcomes ST, $S = P$, C, and $T = B$, A. Denoting the sender's payoff in outcome ST as ST^S and the target's as ST^T, the following payoff matrix results:

sender \ target	B	A
P	PB^S, PB^T	PA^S, PA^T
C	CB^S, CB^T	CA^S, CA^T

The problem at hand implies some natural restrictions on payoffs. Since the sender wants the target to do something it wouldn't do on its own, $CB^S < CA^S$ while $CB^T > CA^T$. For the measure to be harmful enough to get the target to comply requires that $CA^T > PB^T$ (so that $CB^T > PB^T$). Finally, the restriction $PB^S < CA^S$ precludes the sender preferring the measure to the objective.

For simplicity assume for now that each party's preference for each choice is independent of the other choice. Hence $CB^T > CA^T$ implies $PB^T > PA^T$ (the target also prefers balking when the measure is in place); $CB^S < CA^S$ implies $PB^S < PA^S$ (the sender prefers the target to comply when the measure is in place); and $CB^T > PB^T$ implies $CA^T > PA^T$ (the measure harms the target even when it acquiesces). These additional inequalities arise, for example, if the two decisions affect payoffs independently.

The major remaining issue is the relationship between CB^S and PB^S and, hence, between CA^S and PA^S. Is punishing costly to the sender?

Sanctions as a solution to the Prisoner's Dilemma. As discussed above, some measures could benefit the sender, meaning that $CB^S < PB^S$ (and $CA^S < PA^S$). In this case the interaction between the sender and target becomes a prisoner's dilemma, with punishment and balking the two 'cheating' strategies and condoning and acquiescing the two 'cooperative' strategies. While both parties prefer the outcome CA to PB, P is a dominant strategy for the sender while B is the dominant strategy for the target. Hence the one-play Nash equilibrium outcome is PB.

A great deal of game theory has focused on overcoming the prisoner's dilemma. With repeated, simultaneous interaction, players might adopt decision rules that lead to the mutually preferred outcome, but these strategies require that the parties respond to past actions in deciding what to do currently, and value future as well as current payoffs (see, e.g., Fudenberg and Tirole 1991). If the two parties are sufficiently forward-looking, a simple (subgame perfect) equilibrium that supports cooperation has each party cooperating as long as neither had unilaterally cheated for some time, but not cooperating otherwise. An episode of unilateral cheating thus triggers a period of noncooperation in which everyone suffers. Sanctions, then, can be seen as the period of noncooperation to punish cheating.

A criticism of this equilibrium is that it is not 'renegotiation proof'. If either party unilaterally cheats then the two jointly do better by agreeing to ignore the infraction and to cooperate henceforth. But the anticipation of this renegotiation eliminates any incentive to cooperate in the first place. There are, however, 'renegotiation proof' equilibria that can support cooperation, but they are more complicated (see Fudenberg and Tirole 1991).

Note that, since the relationship between the two parties is symmetric, the sender can cheat by imposing the measure just as the target can cheat by balking. A danger is that sender might opportunistically claim a violation as an excuse to impose the measure (see Sykes 1990).

Costly sanctions: the Punisher's Dilemma. If the measure is costly to the sender as well as target then $CB^S > PC^S$ and $CA^S > PA^S$. Imposing the measure is then a dominated strategy for the sender. The only Nash equilibrium outcome of a single interaction is unpunished noncompliance. Is there any way, then, for a sender credibly to threaten a costly measure?

Once again, if the parties interact indefinitely and value the future then sanctions can work. Consider, for example, the following pair of decision rules: (1) The sender imposes the measure if: (i) the target has balked within the last N periods and (ii) the sender has always imposed the measure for N periods after any previous balking. Otherwise it condones the target's behaviour. (2) The target acquiesces unless the sender failed to impose the measure in any of N periods after any episode of balking, in which case it balks.

With sufficient value placed on future payoffs and appropriate N, this behaviour can sustain a subgame-perfect outcome in which the threat succeeds. The sender's desire to maintain its reputation for toughness renders the threat credible. If it fails to deliver on its threat then it can never use it again.

Again, this equilibrium unravels if the parties can renegotiate. Both would benefit by forgetting any balking in order to avoid the costly punishment. But anticipation of renegotiation removes any incentive for the target to acquiesce. Here the only renegotiation-proof outcome is unpunished balking.

The result that the potential for renegotiation unravels any possible effectiveness of a costly measure does not extend to situations in which compliance is a matter of degree. But costly sanctions cannot sustain compliance at the maximum feasible level. For sanctions to work, the target must compensate the sender for the cost of imposing the penalty by complying at a supernormal level (by paying reparations, for example). The more the measure costs the sender, the lower the highest normal level of compliance (see Eaton and Engers 1992). Hence a costly measure can still be effective in achieving an objective, but its effectiveness is limited by the cost of imposing it (even though, in equilibrium, it is not actually used).

Rules vs. discretion: the role of commitment. The examples so far make some highly simplistic assumptions about such things as timing, the number of parties, and information to make basic points. Some departures from these assumptions yield additional insights about how sanctions work.

Possibly more plausible than treating the two choices as simultaneous is to assume that the target first decides whether to acquiesce or to balk at a demand of the sender. The sender then decides whether to punish or condone the target's decision.

In order for the sender to achieve any clout, it has to convince the target that the measure depends on the target's behaviour. The problem is the time-inconsistency of the sender's optimal policy, which here is the punishment contingent on balking (see Kydland and Prescott 1977). In the examples above, repeated interaction created a motive for the sender to follow through in order to maintain a reputation for making good on its threats and promises.

The theory of agency suggests how delegation might provide another way to achieve commitment (see Fershtman and Judd 1987). The sender might delegate enforcement to an agent whose contract provides contingent payoffs $PB^S > CB^S$ and $CA^S > PA^S$. Seeing that sanctions are in the hands of an agent with these incentives, the target would comply. By analogy, the police are both rewarded for punishing criminals and penalized for punishing the innocent.

Such delegation arises quite naturally if sanctions are governed by statutes created by a legislature but enforced by an executive. While laws can be changed, doing so takes time. In the meantime the executive must impose measures according to existing law. Indeed, legislative sluggishness can enhance a government's ability to commit to a course of action. In the United States, this division of authority occasionally generates squabbles between a Congress wanting to set 'rules' mandating measures in particular circumstances and a President wanting the 'discretion' to waive them.

Whaling provides an example. The International Whaling Commission (IWC) was established in 1946 to limit whaling. As with many international arrangements, enforcement was left to member states who, for a long time, did little to carry out its provisions (see Borga 1996). The 'Pelly amendment' to the US Fisherman's Protective Act required the Secretary of Commerce to monitor foreign whaling to determine if it diminished 'the effectiveness of an international fishery conservation program'. In the event of a positive finding it authorizes, but does not require, the President to prohibit imports of fish products from the offending state. In 1974 the Commerce Secretary cited both Japan and the Soviet Union for their objections to an IWC quota. President Ford refused to impose the measure, however, on the grounds that it would be too costly to the United States, and that he expected these countries to abide by IWC quotas in the future anyway (see Lyster 1985).

Congressional frustration led to the 1976 Magnuson Fishery and Conservation Act, which specified a different measure and removed Presidential discretion: Any country cited would lose access to US fishing waters. The measure hit hard at Japan, but did not impose any cost on the United States. When Japan objected to an IWC decision to end commercial whaling in 1986, the US reduced Japan's fishing quota by 50 percent (see Lyster 1985). The eventual response was a halt to Japanese whaling except for 'scientific' purposes.

Three factors contributed to the eventual success of sanctions in reducing commercial whaling: (1) Sanctions were enforcing an international treaty, so US retaliation was legal. (2) Success was achieved by switching to a measure that was less costly to the United States. (3) Legislation restricted the executive's discretion.

While both the Pelly and Packwood–Magnuson amendments remain on the books, the major whaling countries no longer have access to US fishing waters anyway, so the measure imposed by the second no longer has any bite. President Clinton has chosen not to invoke the Pelly amendment in response to Norway's recent resumption of whaling (see Borga 1996).

The extent of Presidential discretion has also played a role in US trade legislation. While under Section 301 the President reserves the right to avoid retaliation, doing so after 1988 amendments may require a public 'veto' of a USTR recommendation (see Sykes 1990).

To what extent can laws that mandate costly measures in response to offending actions achieve a sender's objective? Eaton and Engers (1992) model a sender who periodically specifies a level of compliance that the target must achieve to avoid a costly measure. How much compliance the sender can elicit increases with the harm that the measure imposes on the target and decreases with its cost to the sender, even though, in equilibrium, the measure is not actually imposed.

Imperfect information: a role for discretion. In the examples so far all parties are perfectly informed about their own and each other's payoffs. The sender can then achieve its objective more effectively by binding its behaviour to a set of rules. But unforeseen contingencies may arise that call for deviation from statutory requirements.

If the cost to the target of compliance outweighs the benefit to the sender, both parties do better if the target balks, but compensates the sender accordingly. Discretion facilitates the negotiated settlement of such mutually beneficial opportunities. If imposing the measure itself compensates the sender for the target's balking, then noncompliance is an 'efficient breach' (see Sykes 1992).

The 1962 Hickenlooper Amendment to the US Foreign Assistance Act provides an example in which the scope for Presidential discretion was widened to avoid measures deemed too costly relative to what they would achieve. Initially the law required that the executive suspend foreign aid to countries that took US property or violated contracts with US citizens without full compensation. In 1972 the law was substantially weakened by allowing the President to waive the requirement if he 'determines and certifies that such a waiver is important to the national interests of the United States'.

Eaton and Engers (1994) model sanctions and compensation as alternative means of influencing a target with an unknown cost of compliance. Using carrots creates the possibility of a 'hold up'. Even though the cost of compliance is low, the target might refuse an initial offer that exceeds its cost of complying to try to get a higher offer in the future. Efficient compliance is delayed and, when it is achieved, the sender spends more than the target's cost of compliance. In contrast, a sender can achieve compliance cheaply and efficiently if it can credibly threaten a measure that imposes more harm on the target than the maximum possible cost of compliance. But if the measure is less harmful another inefficiency can arise: The target might balk at the initial threat, triggering retaliation, to try to signal that its cost of compliance is so high that the threat won't work in the future. Since the measure is costly to both parties, the sender doesn't threaten it again. The sender not only fails to achieve its objective, it also suffers the cost of imposing the sanction before giving up.

Multiple senders. Interaction is more complex still in the presence of multiple parties. Martin (1992) analyses the interaction of two potential senders who share an objective. There are three types of outcome: (1) Both countries individually find sanctions worth pursuing, so both impose them unilaterally. (2) One country free rides on the other's sanctions, which are less effective than joint sanctions. (3) Neither country finds unilateral sanctions effective enough to be worth pursuing on its own, even though their joint pursuit would achieve their objective. The outcome is a prisoner's dilemma between the two potential senders in which sanctions are not pursued.

5. EVIDENCE. A fundamental difficulty arises in trying to assess empirically the role of sanctions in international relations. On one hand, when sanctions are obviously futile the sender may not bother threatening them in the first place (their symbolic use aside). On the other, if they are bound to succeed then no explicit threat may be needed to achieve compliance (see Shavell 1987). Hence we might expect to see measures actually invoked only when there was initial doubt about the outcome. (An exception is when both the measure and the objective are lumpy: see Fernandez and Glazer 1991 and Eaton and Engers 1992.) The threat of sanctions might very effectively keep most countries in line even if, when measures are actually taken, they rarely persuade their particular target to capitulate. The target may have balked in the first place because it had an unusually high cost of compliance or low vulnerability to the measure. Senders might invoke them anyway simply to maintain their reputation for toughness.

Even so, several quantitative studies examining the explicit use of sanctions find that they often succeed. Most comprehensive is Hufbauer et al. (1990), which considers 116 episodes in which measures were actually imposed since the beginning of World War I. They judge sanctions to have been a success in slightly over a third of these cases.

They relate the sender's success to a host of objective and subjective measures. Broadly consistent with theory they find success is more likely when: (1) the goal was a modest policy change or destabilization (as opposed to disrupting the target's 'minor military adventure', weakening it militarily, or seeking a major policy change); (2) the measure is more costly to the target, (3) it is less costly to the sender; (4) the sender occupies a large share of the target's trade; and (5) the target does not receive support from third countries. Other factors leading to success are: (1) a closer prior relationship between the sender and target; (2) an unstable target; (3) a world war. Export controls (embargoes) are less successful as measures than those involving import controls (boycotts) and financial controls. Somewhat surprisingly, they do not find international cooperation in the imposition of the measure significant in success.

Martin (1992) provides a quantitative analysis of senders' success in achieving cooperation from third parties. Her major findings are that a sender country is more likely to enlist help if international institutions are involved, and if imposing sanctions is very costly to the individual sender country. She also finds evidence of a 'bandwagon' effect in the imposition of measures in that the variance in the number of countries participating is greater than would be the case if countries decide to participate independently of each other.

Three studies focus specifically on cases brought under Section 301 of the US Trade Act. Sykes (1992) analyses 83 cases to open markets for US exports (including attacks on barriers to US investment and on infringement of US intellectual property). Forty-eight were brought under Section 301(a), alleging violations of existing agreements. He finds that in 31 of these cases the target responded, either by changing the practice in question or by providing compensatory concessions. Thirteen cases remained unresolved. Of the remaining four one was dropped, one was resolved by the Tokyo Round, one was resolved by a change in US policy, and one resulted in cancellation of the agreement. Retaliation occurred in seven cases, and remained in place in six at the time of the study. The general picture is that actions brought under the statute have been quite successful, and the use of measures quite modest. The picture for actions brought under 301(b) is similar. Of the 35, 27 were successful. One failed. (The remaining seven were dismissed, withdrawn, settled in the Uruguay Round, or remained open.) Retaliation occurred twice.

Bayard and Elliott (1994) evaluate 72 Section 301 cases, finding that they typically succeeded in eliminating the targeted practices without disrupting trade, but found the effect on US exports at most modest. Elliott and Richardson (1997) expand the data set to include an additional 15 cases, and conduct a multinomial probit analysis to identify the determinants of success. Their principal findings are that success is more likely the more the target sells to the United States, and the larger its trade surplus with the United States. They also find weak evidence that actions initiated by the USTR are more likely to work than those brought by a private petitioner.

Episodes in which measures are actually imposed provide only a very narrow window on the role of sanctions in maintaining the world order. Instances of potential senders not bothering to use sanctions because they know they would fail are not a matter of record. Nor can we usually measure how much potential targets change their ways to avoid sanctions. On occasion a new international treaty or unilateral legislation has provided indirect evidence on the second, however. For example, according to Milner (1990), the 'Super 301' provision of the 1988 United States Omnibus Trade and Competitiveness Act 'seemed to "scare" some countries into opening their markets' (Milner 1990: 178).

6. CONCLUSION. Within the borders of a sovereign country, government authority enhances economic efficiency by enforcing contracts, protecting property rights, and correcting externalities. International sanctions lengthen the arm of this power beyond the national borders, bringing these benefits to the global economy. Sanctions achieve these objectives only very imperfectly, however. Problems of free riding and collective action abound; measures are often inadequate to the task; and countries differ significantly both in their power as potential senders and in their vulnerability as potential targets. While international agreements have made progress toward addressing these deficiencies, much remains to be done.

By their very nature, measures used to punish countries for their behaviour introduce an inefficiency in the world economy. In an ideal world, they would never be taken. But the threat of such measures can nevertheless play a useful role in discouraging behaviour that harms others.

JONATHAN EATON AND ALAN SYKES

See also ANTIDUMPING; COMMITMENT; COUNTERVAILING DUTIES; DISCLOSURE AND UNRAVELLING; PRISONERS' DILEMMA.

Subject classification: 1d(ii); 2g; 5a(v).

STATUTES

United Nations Charter

UN Charter Article 1(1).

International Treaties

The General Agreement on Tariffs and Trade, *opened for signature* Oct. 30, 1947, art. XXIII, 61 Stat. A5, A7, TIAS No. 1700, 55 UNTS 187, arts. XIX, XXVIII; Agreement on Interpretation and Application of Articles VI, XVI, and XXIII of the General Agreement on Tariffs and Trade, *done* Apr. 12, 1979, 31 UST 513, TIAS No. 9619.

International Convention for the Regulation of Whaling, with Schedule of Whaling Regulations, Dec. 2, 1946, 62 Stat. 1716, 161 UNTS 72. The Convention was implemented in United States law by the Whaling Convention Act of 1949, 16 USC §916 (1988).

Montreal Protocol on Substances that Deplete the Ozone Layer, Sept. 16, 1987, S. Treaty Doc. No. 10, 100th Cong., 1st Sess., 26 ILM. 1550 (entered into force Jan. 1, 1989).

Federal Statutes

Comprehensive Anti-Apartheid Act. Pub. L. No. 99–440, 100 Stat. 1086 (1986), *as amended*, H.J. Res. 756, Pub. L. No. 99–631, 100 Stat. 3515, 22 USC §§5001–5116.

Export Administration Act. Pub. L. No. 91–184, Dec. 30, 1969, 83 Stat. 841, 50 USC app. §2401 et seq.

Fishermen's Protective Act of 1967. Aug 27, 1954, ch. 1018, 22 USC §1971 et seq.

International Emergency Economic Powers Act (IEEPA). Pub. L. No. 95–223, Dec. 28, 1977, 91 Stat. 1626, 50 USC §1701 et seq.

Jackson–Vanik amendment to the Trade Act of 1974. Pub. L. No. 93–618, Jan. 3, 1975, 88 Stat. 2004 (conditioning trade to emigration rights and relevant waiver codified at 19 USC §§2432 (a)–(e); § 2439(b)).

Magnuson Fishery Conservation and Management Act. Pub. L. No. 94–265, Apr. 13, 1976, 90 Stat. 331, 16 USC §1801 et seq.

Pelly Amendment to the Fisherman's Protective Act. Pub. L. No. 92–219, 85 Stat. 786, codified as amended at 22 USC §1978 (monitoring of foreign whaling for effect on fishery conservation codified at 22 USC §1978 (a)–(h)).

Tariff Act of 1930, ch. 497, 46 Stat. 590.

Trade Act of 1974. Pub. L. No. 93–618, §§ 301–09, 88 Stat. 1978, 2041 (1975), *as amended by* Omnibus Trade and Competitiveness Act of 1988, Pub. L. No. 100–418, 102 Stat. 1107, 1164, 19 USC §§ 2411–2419 (1988).

Trading with the Enemies Acts. Oct. 6, 1917, ch. 106, 40 Stat. 411, 50 USC app. § 1et seq.

United Nations Participation Act of 1945. Dec. 20, 1945, ch. 583, 59 Stat. 619, 22 USC §287.

1962 Hickenlooper Amendment to the US Foreign Assistance Act. Pub. L. No. 88–633, pt III, §301 (d)(4), Oct. 7, 1964, 78 Stat. 1013 (presidential waiver codified at 22 USC §2370 (e)(1), (2)).

BIBLIOGRAPHY

Bartlett, B. 1985. Sanctions almost never work. *Wall Street Journal*, 19 August.

Bayard, T.O. and Elliott, K.A. 1994. *Reciprocity and Retaliation in U.S. Trade Policy*. Washington, DC: Institute for International Economics.

Bhagwati, J.N. and Patrick, H.T. 1990. (eds.) *Aggressive Unilateralism: America's 301 Trade Policy and the World Trading System*. Ann Arbor: University of Michigan Press.

Borga, M. 1996. Managing international open access resources: empirical evidence from the International Whaling Commission. PhD dissertation, Department of Economics, Boston University.

Carter, B.E. 1988. *International Economic Sanctions*. Cambridge: Cambridge University Press.

Chayes, A. and Chayes, A.H. 1995. *The New Sovereignty: Compliance with International Regulatory Agreements*. Cambridge, MA: Harvard University Press.

Doxey, M.P. 1980. *Economic Sanctions and International Enforcement*. New York: Oxford University Press.

Eaton, J. and Engers, M. 1992. Sanctions. *Journal of Political Economy* 100: 899–928.

Eaton, J. and Engers, M. 1994. Threats and promises. NBER Working Paper No. 4849.

Elagab, O.Y. 1988. *The Legality of Non-Forcible Counter-Measures in International Law*. Oxford: Clarendon Press.

Elliott, K.A. and Richardson, J.D. 1997. Determinants and effectiveness of 'aggressively unilateral' U.S. trade actions. In *The Effects of U.S. Trade Protection and Promotion Policies*, ed. R.C. Feenstra, Chicago: University of Chicago Press.

Fernandez, R. and Glazer, J. 1991. Striking for a bargain between two completely informed agents. *American Economic Review* 81: 240–52.

Fershtman, C. and Judd, K.L. 1987. Equilibrium incentives in oligopoly. *American Economic Review* 77: 927–40.

Fudenberg, D. and Tirole, J. 1991. *Game Theory*. Cambridge, MA: MIT Press.

Hufbauer, G.C., Schott, J.J. and Elliott, K.A. 1990. *Economic Sanctions Reconsidered: History and Current Policy, Second Edition*. Washington, DC: Institute for International Economics.

Jackson, J.H. 1991. *The World Trading System: Law and Policy of International Economic Relations*. 2nd edn, Cambridge, MA: MIT Press, 1997.

Kuyper, P.J. 1978. *The Implementation of International Sanctions: The Netherlands and Rhodesia*. Alphen aan den Rijn: Sijthoff and Noordhoff.

Kydland, F.E. and Prescott, E.C. 1977. Rules rather than discretion: the inconsistency of optimal plans. *Journal of Political Economy* 85: 473–91.

Lyster, S. 1985. *International Wildlife Law*. Cambridge: Grotius Publications Ltd.

Malloy, M.P. 1990. *Economic Sanctions and U.S. Trade*. Boston: Little, Brown.

Malloy, M.P. 1996. *Economic Sanctions and U.S. Trade: 1996 Supplement*. Boston: Little, Brown.

Martin, L.L. 1992. *Coercive Cooperation: Explaining Multilateral Economic Sanctions*. Princeton: Princeton University Press.

Milner, H. 1990. The political economy of U.S. trade policy: a study of the Super 301 provision. In *Aggressive Unilateralism: America's 301 Trade Policy and the World Trading System*, ed. J.N. Bhagwati and H.T. Patrick, Ann Arbor: University of Michigan Press.

Parson, E.A. 1993. Protecting the ozone layer. In *Institutions for the Earth: Sources of Effective International Environmental Protection*, ed. P.M. Haas, R.O. Keohane and M.A. Levy, Cambridge, MA: MIT Press.

Partan, D.G. 1990. Retaliation in United States and European Community trade law. *Boston University International Law Journal* 8: 333–49.

Schelling, T.C. 1960. *The Strategy of Conflict*. Cambridge, MA: Harvard University Press.

Schelling, T.C. 1966. *Arms and Influence*. New Haven: Yale University Press.

Shavell, S. 1987. The optimal use of nonmonetary sanctions as a deterrent. *American Economic Review* 77: 584–592.

Stremlau, J. 1996. *Sharpening International Sanctions*. New York: Carnegie Commission on Preventing Deadly Conflict.

Sykes, A.O. 1990. 'Mandatory' retaliation for breach of trade agreement: some thoughts on the strategic design of Section 301. *Boston University International Law Journal* 8: 301–24.

Sykes, A.O. 1991. Protectionism as a 'safeguard': a positive analysis of the GATT Escape Clause with normative speculations. *University of Chicago Law Review* 58: 255–305.

Sykes, A.O. 1992. Constructive unilateral threats in international commercial relations: the limited case for Section 301. *Law and Policy in International Business* 23: 263–330.

Internet. *See* COMPUTER LAW.

investment incentives and property rights. As long as economists have discussed property rights at all, they have been concerned with how such rights affect economic decisions of key importance, such as investment. This essay considers what theoretical links have been proffered to explain the link between investment behaviour and property rights and what empirical evidence we have on such links. Our primary focus will be on the considerable body of work that has used modern econometric techniques to investigate these issues using data from a number of countries.

Any study that seeks to investigate the impact of property rights on behaviour requires, at a minimum, two things: (i) a measure of investment and (ii) a source of variation (preferably exogenous) in rights. Economists have considerable experience in modelling and measuring investment in a variety of contexts. Even so, for developing economy agriculture, from which most of the evidence below is drawn, there are considerable difficulties in defining and measuring investments since much of this involves unpurchased inputs. Indeed investment may simply mean a changed intensity of effort put into land improvements, rather than conventional purchases of fixed inputs. Finding reliable measures of property rights that vary appropriately is less straightforward still and constitutes a major challenge. Moreover, these measures of rights need to vary across investing units and/or over time for estimation of their effect on investment to be possible.

Fully developed economies are in many ways the least promising candidates for studying the relationship between investment and property rights. In almost every country, systems of property rights are well codified and do not vary much cross-sectionally or over time. This reflects the fact that property laws have typically evolved over long periods. Wars and other infrequent events such as coups may disrupt property rights and generate time series data. However, because so much else that affects investment varies during such events they do not provide very promising episodes for the study of investment and property rights.

Empirical work on growth in a cross-section of countries has tried to proxy for cross-sectional differences in property rights using measures such as revolutions and coups (see, for example, Barro 1997). However, these can proxy for so much else that differs across countries that an interpretation in terms of attenuated property rights is often strained. Moreover, the evidence that we have does not suggest that there is a strong and statistically reliable link between investment and such episodes. History teaches a great deal about the relationship between investment and property rights. However, statistical estimation of the relationship is typically not feasible from the evidence of developed countries, even though much important qualitative evidence exists. Nonetheless, De Long and Shleifer (1993) suggested a creative use of historical data to look at these issues. They used growth of cities as a proxy for investment and the nature of the controlling political regime as a proxy for property rights. They found evidence that more despotic regimes in medieval and early modern Europe were associated with more limited city growth.

Most of the formal evidence that we have on investment

and property rights comes from less developed countries where both times series and cross-sectional variation in property rights can be found. Our discussion of evidence presented below focuses on this case. In such countries, formal legal systems are often less important than social custom and traditional agencies in determining rights to operate and transfer property. Nonetheless, most countries have made some transition towards formalization in recent times. Indeed, large scale efforts at titling land are common (as, for example, in Thailand and Kenya). Such programmes result in gradual change and the cross-sectional variation in rights that we see in such countries represents a patchwork of formal and traditional systems. With sufficient time, one might also be able to study the effect of such changes over time. However, change can often be quite gradual and might require much longer periods of data than are likely to be available.

In practice the kind of variation needed to study investment comes from the agricultural sector. The key property rights are those that determine how individuals own and operate land. With large agriculturally based populations, one has a natural laboratory for studying the effect of rights. However, the kind of data that one would typically require for acceptable estimation is still rather demanding.

It is important to be mindful of the heterogeneity in the rights that individuals could enjoy. In this context, it would be a mistake to think of a right as a discrete variable that conveys full rights to dispose of an asset in any way that one chooses. It is quite possible that some systems make it possible to sell land only to certain individuals because social customs (such as those embodied in the caste system in India) do not permit such transactions. Traditional land rights might recognize the right to bequeath land, but not to sell it. Many of the studies that we discuss below look carefully at rights and how to codify them. It is not surprising therefore that this area has been a fruitful one for collaboration between economists and anthropologists.

1. THEORY. We discuss the three main channels by which we would expect to find a link between property rights and investment decisions. We also discuss the difference between common property and individual property rights and reasons why land rights might evolve as the result of investment decision so that the rights are jointly determined with the decision to invest.

1.1 *Risk of expropriation.* The risk of expropriation is perhaps the first case that comes to mind when thinking about property right insecurity and investment decisions. Formally, property right insecurity is equivalent to a random tax on the returns to investment where the 'tax' is the share of the investment that is captured by the expropriator plus anything destroyed in the conflict over the land. Such risks create two effects on investment. There is a *level* effect that would (absent income effects) lead us to expect less investment. This is because the overall return to investment has fallen. The *composition* effect follows from the change in relative prices of different investments. This results in investment being diverted towards assets where the risk of expropriation is lower. For example, the person who is currently cultivating the land might switch his/her investment to more portable assets such as livestock, rather than fixed assets such as trees and irrigation.

1.2 *Gains from trade.* Incomplete property rights typically impair trade in land. This is particularly true of rights to rent and sell land. Part of the gain to investing may be realized in situations where the land is disposed of to someone who has a better use for it. Improving the possibilities for trade in land can therefore also improve investment incentives when the gains from trade raise he marginal return to land. Besley (1995) has produced a formal version of this argument where an investor faces stochastic trading opportunities for land and improvements in rights are modelled as reductions in transactions costs, so that there is more land trading after rights are improved. He derives conditions under which the gains from trade argument go through. Note that this argument, if appropriate, suggests that rights to sell and rent land would be the most important rights to explain investment.

1.3 *Collateral and credit markets.* The third argument emphasizes indirect benefits to secure property rights. Consider a world in which improvements in land rights encourage lenders to recognize land as collateral. Suppose also that lenders who invest are dependent on access to credit for their investment in the land. Then there are at least two ways in which land rights can be linked to investments through the credit market. In a competitive credit market without information problems, improved access to collateral reduces the risk premium on lending and hence reduces the interest rate faced by a borrower. This can encourage investment. With credit market imperfections (such as those due to asymmetric information) collateral can reduce agency problems in a number of ways. Again this can enhance access to credit – for example by reducing credit rationing, and thereby enhance investment incentives.

1.4 *Community versus individual rights.* A key difference between property rights systems is the extent to which they emphasize the claims of the community to the output of land versus the claims of the individual. It is well known (see, for example, Sen 1966) that in situations where the rights to the output from land accrue to the community rather than the individual who owns the land, and investment is decentralized, then a free-rider problem can arise with investment and input levels being too low. Hence in community oriented systems of land-holding, we would expect mechanisms to be in place to mitigate such problems. For example, investment decisions that are made collectively should not suffer from this problem. This would make it possible to internalize the externality associated with the investment.

In some societies, China being a notable recent case, there has a been shift away from community rights to land and a shift to more individualized notions of property rights. To the extent that the former system was unable to find ways around the free-rider problem, we would expect this to encourage investment in land.

1.5 *Endogenous property rights.* There are good reasons to suppose that rights are not exogenous and may be the product of individuals' actions. Indeed, in economies with poorly developed systems of land rights, individuals typically take defensive measures to protect their land. DeMeza and Gould (1992) develop a theoretical analysis along these lines. The following examples illustrate two possibilities and why this could impart bias into the study of how land rights affect investment.

- Example 1. Land-titling: In countries with land titling programmes, the decision to seek title is often in the hands of the land operator and there is typically incomplete registration of land. Hence, the decision to title (and hence the measured land right) is endogenous. An observed positive effect of land rights on investment could be picking up unobserved characteristics that are correlated with the decision to seek title.
- Example 2. Investment Protects Land Rights: If property rights are insecure then certain kinds of investments can help to enhance claims. In Ghana, for example, planting trees is often seen as a way of increasing claims to land as, while title to land may be in dispute, the title to the trees is not. Again this will tend to bias the analysis in favour of finding an effect of land rights on investment.

This kind of issue can represent serious difficulties in identifying the impact of land rights on investment. A large number of the studies that we discuss below have this as a potential caveat to their findings. In econometric studies, it may be possible to deal with this problem by finding an instrumental variable for rights (i.e. something which can reasonably be thought of as affecting rights but not the investment decision). However, it is very difficult to identify such variables in practice and few studies have proceeded down this route.

2. EVIDENCE. There are now many studies that have looked at links between property rights and investment incentives in a number of contexts. Tables 1 to 3 summarize the findings and the underlying studies are in the bibliography. We divide the evidence geographically.

2.1 *Africa.* Africa appears to have spawned the largest number of economic studies. This probably reflects the relevant recent transitions in property rights systems from those that have emphasized community control of land to more individualized notions. Pre-modern systems of property rights typically required community cooperation for individuals to be able to transfer land by selling, renting or bequeathing. Over time more standard 'western' formalizations of property rights have been superimposed on this traditional structure. This creates the kind of variation in rights that can be exploited to study the effect of investment. Hence some studies look to see whether land titling programmes have resulted in a change in farming practices and measures of farm investment. Others look at a snap shot in the transition process where farmers can have varying property rights on the land that they operate to see if there is any apparent effect on their investment portfolio.

A broad summary of the evidence is collected in Table 1. Most use data that were collected especially for the purpose of investigating property rights. As the table reveals quite clearly, there is very mixed evidence on the effects of rights. While this can always be attributed to measurement and specification problems, it is still striking to see that the evidence does not strongly confirm what the theory suggests we should find.

2.2 *Asia.* A summary of studies for Asia is given in Table 2. As well as studies of security the Chinese experience makes it possible to test for the effects of the introduction of the household responsibility system in agriculture to replace the commune system. The work of Lin (1988, 1992) suggests that this change enhanced investment incentives. This is consistent with the commune system failing to internalize the externality associated with investment.

On the issue of security, Feder et al. (1992) investigated whether land insecurity appears to have reduced investment in China. Using a subjective measure of insecurity, they find no evidence of this. For Thailand, Feder et al. (1988) argued for a credit based link between investment and rights. They find that farmers who have titled their land appear to use more credit and engage in more improvements.

2.3 *Latin-America.* Table 3 contains a summary of evidence for Latin America where a number of countries have made efforts to encourage land titling by farmers. The broad ranging study of Stanfield (1990) puts together evidence from a number of countries with a focus on the impact of these formal titling programmes. Consonant with the findings from Africa, there appears to be little systematic evidence to support a positive association between land rights and investment. This could reflect the fact that formal titles may be a poor guide to actual feelings of security.

However, in contradiction to this finding, Alston, Libecap and Schneider (1996) investigate the response of farmers in two Brazilian states to land titling programmes. In addition to testing for the effect of investment (which is positive), they show that titling has a positive impact on land values, which is a further indirect measure of investment effects. Mindful of possible endogeneity problems, they also estimate the determinants of titling. Here they find, among other things, that years spent on the farm and proximity to titling centres make it more likely that a farmer claims title.

2.4 *Assessment.* This brief tour of available evidence shows that most currently available econometric studies fail to find strong evidence of significant effects of property rights on investment. While endogeneity of land rights may be important, it is not an obvious explanation to support these findings since most endogeneity arguments would suggest reasons why we would find a spurious positive association between land rights and investment. Hence, it is more likely to cast doubt on those studies that have found effects and have not sought to guard against potential endogeneity. Nonetheless, there is an argument based on endogeneity of titling which suggests a bias towards finding no effect. This would be the case of individuals without titles who may choose to remain in that state because they do not fear problems of expropriation, while those with more insecure rights make efforts to

Table 1
Africa

Author	Year	Country	Objective of Study	Index of Tenure Status	Methodology	Results
Matlon	1984–85	Burkina Faso	Impact of indigenous tenure system on investment	Categorisation based on mode of acquisition and origins of the land	Regression analysis – Tobit model	Positive but marginal impact of tenure security on investment
Besley	1995	Ghana	Link between property rights and investment incentives, with a view to endogeneity of land rights	Index of the number of rights held over a plot of land	Regression analysis – linear probability model for investment	Mixed results, on the whole positive impact of land rights on investment. Endogeneity remains a concern
Migot-Adholla, Benneth, Place, Atsu	1987	Ghana	Impact of tenure security on credit, land improvements, input use and productivity	Bundle of rights over land	Regression analysis – logit model	Weak impact of land rights on credit and productivity, mixed impact on investment, no impact on input use
Place and Hazell	1987–88	Ghana, Kenya and Uganda	Impact of land rights on credit use, land improvements, input use and parcel yields	Index of land tenure security based on a bundle of rights	Formal econometrics – fixed effects and error component techniques	Results on the whole show a neglectable impact of land rights on the aforementioned variables
Migot-Adholla, Hazell, Blarel, Place	1987–88	Ghana, Kenya, Rwanda	Whether land rights evolve towards individualisation and whether they constrain productivity	Bundle of rights over land	Regression analysis – fixed effects and error component models	Low incidence of credit; mixed impact of land rights on investment, no impact on productivity
Carter, Wiebe, Blarel	1989	Kenya	Impact of land titling on land productivity; distinction between demand and supply-side effects	Possession of a legal title to land	Regression analysis and comparison of descriptive statistics	Title does not significantly affect productivity; demand-side effects cannot be identified
Migot-Adholla, Place, Oluoch-Kosura	1988	Kenya	Impact of land title on investment and productivity	Bundle of rights over land, with attention to possession of title	Regression analysis – logit model for investment	No impact of land rights/title on investment; very weak impact on crop yields
Pickney and Kimuyu	1991–92	Kenya, Tanzania	Evolution of land rights in the two countries and their impact on credit, investment and productivity	Possession of legal title to land (Kenya) vs. no title (Tanzania)	Case study – cross country comparison	No systematic differences between the two countries due to land titling – traditional systems prevail
Blarel	1988	Rwanda	Impact of tenure security on credit, investment and land yields	1) Bundle of rights over land; 2) Number of disputes.	Regression analysis – multinomial logit model	No impact of land rights on credit and yields; positive correlation between land rights and investment
Golan	1987	Senegal	Impact of tenure security on investment and land transactions.	Bundle of rights over land	Case study, cross village comparison	No impact of tenure status on investment and land transactions
Roth, Unruh, Barrows	1987–89	Somalia	Relationship between land registration, tenure security, credit use and investment	Possession of legal title	Tabular comparison and formal econometric analysis	Possession of title increases land value but has no significant effect oncredit and investment
Roth, Cochrane and Kisamba-Mugerwa	1987	Uganda	Impact of Pilot Land Registration Scheme on tenure security, credit use and agricultural investment	Possession of legal title and purposeful vs. compulsory registration	Tabular comparison and formal econometrics – logit model for investment	Marginal impact of title on credit use, positive impact on investment (potential endogeneity problem)

Table 2
Asia

Author	Year	Country	Objective of Study	Index of Tenure Status	Methodology	Results
Choe	1996	China	Understand the determinants of dynamics of private and public investment in post-reform China	N/A: the author compares the HRS with the commune system pre-'78	Theoretical model of peasants' choice with positive externality	Private investment decreased after 1978 because of the inability of farmers to internalise the externality involved in infrastructure investment
Feder, Lau, Lin and Luo	1992	China	Clarify the importance of factors related to tenure .security, farm size and credit on agricultural investm.	Farmers' perceived probability of reallocation of land	Formal econometric analysis – OLS and Tobit models	Productive investment is not affected by land size, availability of credit and perception of tenure insecurity
Lin	1988	China	Analysis of the commune system and the impact of the HRS on labour incentives and growth	N/A: the author compares the HRS with the commune system pre-'78	Theoretical model and formal econometric analysis	The HRS increased labour supply and had a major impact on the rates of growth of agricultural and sideline production
Lin	1992	China	Untangle the determinants of agricultural output growth in China in 1978–1984	N/A: the author compares the HRS with the commune system pre-'78	Formal econometric analysis and growth accounting	The shift to the HRS accounts for 48.69% of total output growth for the period considered
Feder, Onchan, Chalamwong and Hongladarom	1988	Thailand	Assess impact of land titling land value and farm productivity in 4 regions of Thailand	Possession of legal title to on land (various typologies of title are identified)	Formal econometric analysis	Title has a strong positive impact on credit use, land values, land improvements and farm productivity

Table 3
Latin Ameica

Author	Year	Country	Objective of Study	Index of Tenure Status	Methodology	Results
Alston, Libecap and Schneider	1996	Brazil	Determinants and impact of land titling in Brazil, with particular attention to frontier settlements	Possession of a legal title to land	Formal econometric analysis – log-linear specifications	Land title has a positive impact on land value and investment both at the individual and the county level
Alston, Fuller, Libecap and Mueller	1996	Brazil	Uncovering the determinants and the effects of the violent land conflicts in Brazil in the 1980s–1990s	N/A: the authors look at farms being illegally occupied by squatters	Game-theoretic model tested through formal econometric analysis	Violent conflicts more likely the higher land concentration and increase in land value; conflicts reduce land values and investments
Seligson	1982	Costa Rica	Assess the impact of the land titling programmes carried out in the country since 1971	Possession of legal title to land	Case study, comparison of titled vs. untitled farmers	Title improves access to credit and technical assistance but re-enforces inequality of land distribution
Stanfield	1990	Latin America & Caribbean	Impact of property rights in a few Latin American countries – focus on social justice considerations	Possession of legal title to land	Survey of existing works on the subject (references quoted)	Evidence on land concentration and tenure security is mixed. Title does not appear to increase productivity and investment

secure their titles. Hence titling would be associated with less secure property rights in some cases.

There are other explanations of the findings beyond the obvious one that the theory is not supported. Perhaps the chief among these is the difficulty of getting accurate and reliable measures of the de facto rights that individuals enjoy. Whether one owns a title to land may ultimately have very little bearing on how secure one's right is to that land. That depends upon one's trust in the legal system and the assumption that a legal title is unassailable may not be accurate in many contexts. There are also a host of standard problems in controlling properly for a whole range of other influences on investment. Hence, it may be too soon to pronounce that we can be sure that no effect is found. Moreover, there are sufficient studies that do find an effect to keep alive a possibility that the theory can be supported.

In appraising the generally negative results in the literature, one should not underestimate the difficulties in accurately measuring investment decisions in the context where the theory has been tested. Investment could involve hard-to-measure aspects of land cultivation such as intensity of effort and quality of investments. Since much investment comes from non-purchased inputs, it is inevitably difficult to be sure that one is picking up those aspects of investment that are most important in one's data. If one were not accurately measuring that part of investment that responds to property rights then one would not find an effect of rights on investment. In light of this, it is not surprising that relatively easy-to-measure events such as tree planting appear to have provided some of the more supportive findings to date.

Less progress has been made in distinguishing between different theoretical models. Feder et al. (1988) found evidence that access to credit is improved by titling. This agrees with Seligson's (1982) study of Costa Rica. However, Besley (1995) finds no evidence for a credit based link in Ghana. For the most part, however, authors have not tried to investigate which theoretical explanation is to be favoured. There is certainly scope for further work that tries to test between theories more systematically.

3. CONCLUDING COMMENTS. Secure land rights are frequently mentioned as an important prerequisite to investment and growth. There has been a good deal of work that has tried to examine this question, with agricultural activity in developing countries being a key context. Here, we have discussed the methodological issues that arise in assessing whether there is an empirical link. The literature has found it surprisingly difficult to establish such a link empirically. Hence, in spite of its theoretical importance, empirical support based on quantitative analysis for the importance of secure property rights to investment is limited.

TIMOTHY BESLEY

See also COMMON PROPERTY; EVOLUTION OF PROPERTY RIGHTS; FIRST POSSESSION; LAND TITLE SYSTEMS; LOCAL COMMON PROPERTY RIGHTS; PROPERTY RIGHTS; SELF-GOVERNANCE OF COMMON-POOL RESOURCES.

Subject classification: 2b(i).

BIBLIOGRAPHY

Alston, L.J., Fuller, J.R., Libecap, G.D. and Mueller, B. 1996. Competing claims to land: the sources of violent conflict in the Brazilian Amazon. Manuscript.

Alston, L.J., Libecap, G.D. and Schneider, R. 1996. The determinants and impact of property rights: land titles on the Brazilian frontier. *Journal of Law, Economics and Organization* 12: 25–61.

Barro, R. 1997. *Determinants of Economic Growth: A Cross-Country Empirical Study*. Cambridge, MA: MIT Press.

Barrows, R. and Roth, M. 1990. Land tenure and investment in African agriculture: theory and evidence. *Journal of Modern African Studies* 28: 265–97.

Besley, T. 1995. Property rights and investment incentives: theory and evidence from Ghana. *Journal of Political Economy* 103: 903–37.

Blarel, B. 1994. Tenure security and agricultural production on under land scarcity. In *Searching for Land Tenure Security in Africa*, ed. J.W. Bruce and S.E. Migot-Adholla, Dubuque, IA: Kendall/Hunt.

Brada, J.C. and King, A.E. 1993. Is private farming more efficient than socialised agriculture? *Economica* 60: 41–56.

Carter, M.R., Wiebe, K.D. and Blarel, B. 1994. Tenure security for whom? Differential effects of land policy in Kenya. In *Searching for Land Tenure Security in Africa*, ed. J.W. Bruce and S.E. Migot-Adholla, Dubuque, IA: Kendall/Hunt.

Choe, C. 1996. Incentive to work and disincentive to invest: the case of China's rural reform, 1979–1984. *Journal of Comparative Economics* 22: 242–66.

De Long, J., Bradford and Shleifer, A. 1993. Princes and merchants: European city growth before the industrial revolution. *Journal of Law and Economics* 36: 671–702.

De Meza, D. and Gould, J.R. 1992. The social efficiency of private decisions to enforce property rights. *Journal of Political Economy* 100: 561–80.

Feder, G. and Feeny, D. 1991. Land tenure and property rights: theory and implications for development policy. *The World Bank Economic Review* 5: 135–53.

Feder, G., Lau, L.J., Lin, J.Y. and Luo, X. 1992. The determinants of farm investment and residential construction in post-reform China. *Economic Development and Cultural Change* 41: 1–26.

Feder, G. and Onchan, T. 1987. Land ownership security and farm investment in Thailand. *American Journal of Agricultural Economics* 69: 311–20.

Feder, G. and Onchan, T. 1989. Land ownership and farm investment: reply. *American Journal of Agricultural Economics* 71: 215–16.

Feder, G., Onchan, T., Chalamwong, Y. and Hongladrom, C. 1988. *Land Policies and Farm Productivity in Thailand*. Baltimore: Johns Hopkins University Press for The World Bank.

Golan, E.H. 1994. Land tenure reform in the peanut basin of Senegal. In *Searching for Land Tenure Security in Africa*, ed. J.W. Bruce and S.E. Migot-Adholla, Dubuque, IA: Kendall/Hunt.

Johnson, D.G. 1988. Economic reforms in the People's Republic of China. *Economic Development and Cultural Change* 36 (supplement): S 225–45.

Lin, J.Y. 1988. The household responsibility system in China's agricultural reform: a theoretical and empirical study. *Economic Development and Cultural Change* 36 (supplement): S 199–224.

Lin, J.Y. 1992. Rural reforms and agricultural growth in China. *American Economic Review* 82: 34–51.

Matlon, P. 1994. Indigenous land use systems and investment in soil fertility in Burkina Faso. In *Searching for Land Tenure Security in Africa*, ed. J.W. Bruce and S.E. Migot-Adholla, Dubuque, IA Kendall/Hunt.

Migot-Adholla, S.E., Benneth, G., Place, F. and Atsu, S. 1994. Land, security of tenure and productivity in Ghana. In *Searching for*

Land Tenure Security in Africa, ed. J.W. Bruce and S.E. Migot-Adholla, Dubuque, IA: Kendall/Hunt.

Migot-Adholla, S.E., Hazell, P., Blarel, B. and Place, F. 1991. Indigenous land rights systems in sub-Saharan Africa: a constraint on productivity? *The World Bank Economic Review* 5: 155–75.

Migot-Adholla, S.E., Place, F. and Oluoch-Kosura, W. 1994. Security of tenure and land productivity in Kenya. In *Searching for Land Tenure Security in Africa*, ed. J.W. Bruce and S.E. Migot-Adholla, Dubuque, IA: Kendall/Hunt.

Pickney, T.C. and Kimuyu, P.K. 1994. Land tenure reform in East Africa: good, bad or unimportant? *Journal of African Economies* 3: 1–28.

Place, F., Roth, M. and Hazell, P. 1993. Productivity effects of indigenous land tenure systems in sub-Saharan Africa. *American Journal of Agricultural Economics* 75: 10–19.

Place, F., Roth, M. and Hazell, P. 1994. Land tenure security and agricultural performance in Africa: overview of research methodology. In *Searching for Land Tenure Security in Africa*, ed. J.W. Bruce and S.E. Migot-Adholla, Dubuque, IA: Kendall/Hunt.

Platteau, J.-P. 1996. The evolutionary theory of land rights as applied to sub-Saharan Africa: a critical assessment. *Development and Change* 27: 29–86.

Roth, M., Barrows, R., Carter, M. and Kanel, D. 1989. Land ownership security and farm investment: comment. *American Journal of Agricultural Economics* 71: 211–14.

Roth, M., Cochrane, J. and Kisamba-Mugerva, W. 1994. Tenure security, credit use, and farm investment in the Rujumbura Plot Land Registration Scheme, Uganda. In *Searching for Land Tenure Security in Africa*, ed. J.W. Bruce and S.E. Migot-Adholla, Dubuque, IA: Kendall/Hunt.

Roth, M., Unruh, J. and Barrows, R. 1994. Land registration, tenure security, credit use, and investment in the Shebelle region of Somalia. In *Searching for Land Tenure Security in Africa*, ed. J.W. Bruce and S.E. Migot-Adholla, Dubuque, IA: Kendall/Hunt.

Seligson, M.A. 1982. Agrarian reform in Costa Rica: the impact of the Title Security Program. *Interamerican Economic Affairs* 35: 31–56.

Sen, A.K. 1966. Labour allocation in a co-operative enterprises. *Review of Economic Studies* 33: 361–71.

Stanfield, D. 1990. *Rural Land Titling in Latin America and the Caribbean: Implications for Rural Development Programs*. Land Tenure Center, University of Wisconsin, Madison.

invisible hand explanations. Invisible hand explanations explain how social institutions may come about not as a product of anyone's intentions. The notion of the invisible hand is commonly attributed to the great eighteenth-century Scottish Enlightenment figures of David Hume, Adam Smith and Adam Ferguson. Putting the idea in context, we may observe that phenomena were traditionally classified as either 'natural' or 'artificial'. 'Natural' phenomena are characterized as those that are wholly independent of the human sphere, and 'artificial' phenomena as those that involve human agency. If it is said, however, that the realm of the 'natural' consists of everything that is the result neither of human action nor of human design, while the realm of the 'artificial' consists of everything that is the result of both, what is seen to be missing is the realm of everything that is the result of human action but not of human design.

It is to the Scottish thinkers that we owe the idea that this realm is real rather than merely hypothetical: Adam Smith is credited with coining the expression 'invisible hand' (Smith [1776] 1976: I, 456), Adam Ferguson formulated the splendid phrase about nations that 'stumble upon establishments, which are indeed the result of human action, but not the execution of any human design' (Ferguson [1767] 1995: 119); and David Hume is generally acknowledged to have laid the philosophical foundations for these ideas. Moreover, their insights justify us in seeing this third realm as the realm of the *social*. This terminology should not be taken to imply, however, that all social institutions belong here. Some are, of course, the product of human execution of a human plan, and as such belong to the 'artificial' category (see Hayek [1960] 1972: ch. 2; 1967: 96–105).

In tracing the historical roots of the notion of the invisible hand, it is possible to go still further back. In Bernard Mandeville's famous *Fable of the Bees*, subtitled *Private Vices Publick Benefits*, the idea is articulated that complex social order forms itself without design. Orderly social structures and institutions – law, morals and language, the market and money and many more – spontaneously grow up without men having deliberately planned them or even anticipated them, and it is these institutions which bring it about that men's divergent interests are reconciled. In discussing the growth of law, Mandeville says that

> we often ascribe to the excellency of man's genius, and the depth of his penetration, what is in reality owing to length of time, and the experience of many generations . . . (Mandeville [1729] 1924: II, 142).

However, even though the idea *that* order may form itself without design was expounded by Mandeville, the question *how* remained unaddressed. The initial breakthroughs in suggesting some sort of mechanisms for the workings of the invisible hand were made by the Scottish social and moral thinkers. Their work made it possible to delineate a mechanism that can show in specific detail how the actions of numerous individuals who pursue their own divergent interests may actually aggregate so as to bring about a well-structured yet undesigned social institution. Only when an invisible hand mechanism can be pointed to can the spell of an explanation which postulates a creator, a designer, or a conspiracy, be effectively broken.

F.A. Hayek talks about the 'shock caused by the discovery that [not only the *kosmos* of nature but] the moral and political *kosmos* was also the result of a process of evolution and not of design' (Hayek 1978: 190). What he alludes to here is the natural human response to the phenomenon of order. Upon encountering orderliness and patterned structures, people tend naturally to interpret these as the products of someone's intentional design. If complex order is exhibited by an artifact – say, a clock – the postulated designer would be a human agent, an artisan or an engineer. If complex order is exhibited by the physical world – say, the lunar period – the postulated designer would be a superhuman agent, God. The 'argument from design' (or the cosmological argument, as it is sometimes called) is a most powerful argument, psychologically, for the existence of God. At the very core of religious sensibility is the conviction that the world is not just the product of divine will, but that it is the manifestation of divine, cosmic design.

Against this background, the idea that the *kosmos* can be seen as the result of a process of evolution rather than design can indeed come as a shock. To this shock, moreover, Hayek goes on to attribute a significant contribution in the production of 'what we call the modern mind' (Hayek 1978: 190). And as the nineteenth-century notion of evolution, or spontaneous order, is itself rooted in the eighteenth-century notion of the invisible hand, there is a sense in which the notion of the invisible hand expresses a major anti-religious intuition. This notion was meant to replace that of the 'Finger of God', or 'Divine Providence'. It was to play a central role in forging modern, secular, sensibility.

In this context we may allude to Wittgenstein's notion of being 'in the grip of a picture': the picture is the theological picture, and its grip owes to the force of the 'argument from design'. The liberating role from the grip of this picture is assumed by an invisible hand explanation which succeeds in showing, through spelling out the workings of an appropriate mechanism (or process), how the social institution in question could have come about 'as a result of human action but not of human design'. This liberating role firmly establishes the notion of the invisible hand as a cornerstone in the secular, rationalist world view which we associate with the Enlightenment.

INVISIBLE HAND EXPLANATIONS: THE AGGREGATE MODEL. Here are three paradigmatic examples which go beyond Smith's classical account of the equilibrial pricing system that develops within the perfectly competitive market.

(1) *The creation of money within the banking system.* The early goldsmiths used to be paid a small fee for the safekeeping of people's gold and valuables. With time they came to realize, first, that they did not necessarily have to give back to the customers the exact same pieces of gold that they had deposited, and secondly, that not all deposits were withdrawn together. Inasmuch as new deposits tended to balance withdrawals, they eventually came to realize that only a small percentage of the cash entrusted to them is needed in the form of vault cash at any given time. From here the goldsmiths-turned-bankers are just a step away from investing most of the money deposited with them in securities and loans. And when we consider the impact of this embryonic banking system as a whole, rather than that of each small establishment taken in isolation, we get a neat account of the continuous creation of money within this system (Samuelson 1958: ch. 15).

(2) *The development of media of exchange.* The direct barter system is obviously inconvenient, and the metal gold – which is not only beautiful, but is also scarce, divisible, non-perishable, portable and immutable – is obviously valuable. As Ludwig von Mises famously pointed out, following Carl Menger, when these two considerations are put together an invisible hand account of the emergence of gold as a medium of exchange is forthcoming (Mises [1912] 1953: 30–4). Neither an enlightened ruler nor an explicit agreement need be posited.

(3) *The rise of the ultra-minimal state.* Nozick's account of this is consciously styled as an invisible hand explanation. 'Out of anarchy, pressed by spontaneous groupings, mutual-protection associations, divisions of labor, market pressures, economies of scale, and rational self-interest there arises something very much resembling a minimal state' (Nozick 1974: 16–17). Spelled out, the account begins with a Locke-like state of nature and lists the problems concerning the enforcement of individuals' rights therein. The successive stages that follow are: the formation of naive and inefficient mutual-protection associations, where each member is liable at any time to be called upon to assist any of the other members in defending or enforcing their rights; then the formation of the more professional private protection agencies, where there is division of labour and exchange in that some people are hired to perform protective functions; and finally, the emergence of a single protective agency which dominates a geographical area. All that remains is to supply arguments as to why this dominant protective agency already has the essential attributes of an ('ultra-minimal') state.

In all three examples the phenomenon explained is shown to be the product neither of centralized planning nor of explicit decisions or agreements to bring it about. But in order to better focus on the distinctive features of these explanations, here are a few negative examples, i.e. cases which should not be considered invisible hand explanations even though they may look like one. (1) Consider a crater so regular, and so well suited to its function as a water reservoir, that it is assumed to have been dug specially for that purpose. Suppose, however, that newly obtained stratigraphical data enable the geologists to explain the crater as a product of ancient volcanic activity, rather than as a result of human design. (2) Consider the loud noise produced in a large and crowded hall, which results from everyone's being engaged in conversation in their normal tone of voice. (3) Suppose several drivers receive flat tyres because of some broken glass strewn in a particular street. A 'hidden-hand' explanation may be offered, in terms of someone having spread the broken glass there intentionally. This may even be blown up to a 'conspiracy' explanation, when the existence of a service station down that street is taken into consideration. Suppose, however, that it is established that the broken glass was there completely 'by accident', and that the whole incident is satisfactorily explained in terms of the innocent tripping of a delivery boy carrying a crateful of bottles earlier that morning.

We note that the crater of the first example, while being explained not as the result of human design, is at the same time shown not to be the result of human action at all; the loud noise of the second example, while unintended, is a mere amplification of the separate individual actions being combined; and the series of punctured tyres of the third example merely shows how an explanation in terms of human intentions may be replaced by an explanation in terms of the accidental consequences of human action. None of these should qualify as invisible hand explanations.

In light of both the paradigmatic and the negative examples, here is a working characterization: An invisible hand explanation explains a well-structured social pattern (institution, norm, practice). It typically replaces an easily forthcoming and initially plausible explanation according to which the *explanandum* phenomenon is the product of intentional design. It purports to show the pattern in question as the 'output' of a process which aggregates, as its 'input', the separate, self-interested actions of numerous individuals who need neither foresee it nor intend to bring it about.

Because of the central role that the mechanism aggregating the individual actions plays in these explanations, they will be referred to as invisible hand explanations of the aggregate model. This is to distinguish them from the second model of invisible hand explanations, to be introduced shortly. I shall now proceed to comment on three aspects of the working characterization: (1) the availability and plausibility of the alternative explanation, (2) the invisible hand process, (3) the explicatory import of invisible hand explanations.

(1) Our ordinary explanations of human actions and their results are in terms of the beliefs and intentions of the agents. All the more so when what we are called upon to explain exhibits structure, order, design. As was pointed out earlier, our tendency to postulate a designer whenever we encounter orderliness and patterned structure accounts for the peculiar force, within the realm of the physical universe, of the so-called argument from design. In addition, when the cases we encounter look like ones involving complex coordinated activity, the association we tend to make, which comes from the realm of the biological universe, is to a central nervous system. Hence the rather natural 'inference' to the existence of a central planning agency that governs and coordinates the dispersed individual activity and directs it in accordance with its intended scheme. This inference is further enhanced when the *explanandum* phenomenon is considered to perform a valuable social *function*. (More on functions below.)

These considerations show that the more structured the pattern to be explained is, the more it exhibits orderliness, coordination, and in certain cases function as well, the more likely it is that an explanation in terms of intentional design will naturally suggest itself and will look considerably plausible. At the same time, the more structured and complex the pattern, the greater the challenge it poses to a proposed invisible hand explanation thereof, and the more potentially satisfying will such an explanation be.

(2) By 'the invisible hand process' is meant the aggregate mechanism which takes as 'input' the dispersed actions of the participating individuals and produces as 'output' the overall social pattern. It is this process which bears the explanatory brunt of invisible hand explanations. As emerges from the paradigmatic examples presented above, the invisible hand process is typically conveyed by means of a 'story'. The story consists of successive stages, the last of which being the pattern whose explanation is sought. As such, the full-fledged description of the invisible hand process falls under Hempel's category of *genetic explanations* which, as he says, 'present the phenomenon under study as a final stage of a developmental sequence, and accordingly account for the phenomenon by describing the successive stages of that sequence' (Hempel 1965: 447).

In order for the stories to form the backbone of good invisible hand explanations, they should be constrained by the following considerations. First, the description of the first stage in the sequence, as well as of every subsequent one, is to consist of nothing but the private interests, beliefs, intentions and actions of the participating individuals. Moreover, since these individuals need neither foresee the resulting pattern nor intend to bring it about, the pattern need not be referred to at all in the narrative. Second, the process has to be natural. That is, the stages of the process have to be described as the ordinary and normal course of events. The more extraordinary, freakish or science fiction-like the story, the less explanatory import will the resulting invisible hand explanation afford. Nevertheless, invisible hand explanations do involve an element of surprise. The surprise, however, ought not to come from within the explanation, as it were. It comes, instead, from the very existence of the explanation. The surprise consists in that what looks like the product of intentional design is shown to be explainable otherwise. And the bigger the surprise, the more satisfying the explanation.

(3) An invisible hand explanation may be judged a felicitous explanation on internal standards, independently of its truth. It will be judged a more felicitous explanation the higher the degree of structure exhibited by the social pattern explained, the higher the degree of complexity and sophistication of the invisible hand process, the higher the degree of naturalness of the narrative stages involved, and in general the further removed in type the social pattern explained is from the individual actions that bring it about. True as well as felicitous explanations are always valuable. However, an idiosyncratic aspect of felicitous invisible hand explanations is that they are valuable independently of their truth.

Consider a social pattern or institution for the emergence of which an invisible hand explanation is offered. Suppose, further, that the available historical evidence is inconclusive as to whether or not the explanation is indeed the correct account of how this institution actually came about. Had it been known to be true, this explanation would be said to have explanatory import. The point is that even when the question of truth is unsettled, the explanation can be said to have explicatory value. An account of how something could have emerged is generally viewed as a rational reconstruction of it, and as such it is taken to perform an explicatory task (see Carnap [1950] 1962: 576–7). The value of the explication in the case of felicitous invisible hand explanations is enhanced, moreover, since the sense of 'could' in the expression 'how something could have emerged' is restricted in them from mere logical possibility to something like 'could have emerged in the normal course of events'. An additional consideration which enhances this explicatory import has to do with reduction. The social pattern in question is shown by the invisible hand explanation to arise through a process which aggregates the actions of individuals who need not have this pattern in mind. Hence there should in principle be no reference to the *explanandum* phenomenon in the *explanans*; it is neither mentioned nor used in the course of the explanation. These considerations, which establish the explicatory worth of felicitous invisible hand explanations, may be taken to justify the intuitive feeling that these explanations yield considerable insight into the nature of the social institutions explained. There is even a sense in which the fact that such an explanation proves false may be felt to be peculiarly irrelevant. The fact that someone happened to have been smart and quick enough to bring about an institution which would otherwise have emerged invisible-handedly may be felt to shed no special light on its nature.

INVISIBLE HAND EXPLANATIONS: THE EVOLUTIONARY MODEL. It is one thing to say that the eighteenth-century idea of the invisible hand paved the way for the nineteenth-century idea of evolution, and it is quite another to conflate the two ideas. Evolutionary explanations, whether in the biological or in the social domain, have an obvious invisible hand aspect. It consists in the fact that when an item, be it a social institution or a biological organism, is claimed to be the product of an evolutionary process, its existence is thereby explained without any reference to a designing agent. Evolutionary explanations are candidates for qualifying as invisible hand explanations, then, insofar as they are liberated from the grip of the formative – yet in a way primitive – picture according to which to account for the existence of something is to point to its creator.

The expression 'to account for something's existence', however, can be taken in more than one way. The two different ways in which this expression is construed distinguish evolutionary explanations from invisible hand explanations as so far presented. One way to account for something's existence is as an answer to the question of origin: how did it come into being, how did it begin to exist? The other is as an answer to the question of endurance: why does it persist (regardless of how it came about in the first place), why does it continue to exist? The distinction, then, is between an explanation of emergence and an explanation of endurance. While invisible hand explanations of the aggregate model clearly address the first question, evolutionary explanations address the second. We are now in a position to turn our attention to invisible hand explanations of the evolutionary model, whose central conceptual tool of 'natural selection', along with its concomitant notion of 'survival of the fittest', account for continued existence, not for origins.

However, an important difference between evolutionary explanations within biology, and evolutionary explanations in the domain of society and culture, has to be noted. In the biological case some sort of an account (or a placeholder for an account) of origins is part and parcel of the explanatory apparatus. It is, namely, spontaneous and random mutations which are supposed to account for the emergence of the items (organisms, organs) whose continued existence is evolutionarily explained. No analogue to the notion of mutation exists in the socio-cultural case: an evolutionary explanation of a social institution involves no commitment, and tells no causal story, as to its historical origins. There is yet another difference within evolutionary explanations, between the biological and the social ones, which bears on the comparison between aggregate and evolutionary invisible hand explanations. It involves the notion of function. In the biological case, where the item to be explained (say an organ, like a kidney) is known to have withstood the generations-long evolutionary test, it may safely be assumed – or, at least, rebuttably presumed – that the item in question has some survival value to the organism containing it, that it fulfils a positive function contributing to its overall fitness. Matters are notably different in the social domain. When a social item is to be explained (a practice, a norm, an institution), it cannot in general be assumed that it has withstood the generations-long evolutionary test – for one thing, it may be too recent for that. Nor can it in general be assumed that it fulfils a positive function which contributes to the survival and wellbeing of the society incorporating it – it may, for example, promote sectarian interests, or it may lack a function (in the relevant sense) altogether. The attributes of lastingness and of overall positive functionality, in the case of an item from the social domain, have to be *ascertained*, case by case, rather than presupposed.

So, what an evolutionary explanation in the social domain does is the following: first of all, it ascertains that the institution in question fulfil a useful social function and identifies it (say, the continuous creation of money within the banking system); that is, it establishes its contribution to the equilibrial well-being and survival of the society incorporating it. Once this is ascertained, the explanatory schema can flow on. It assumes that by performing its useful function, even the faint beginnings of the social institution in question – whatever their origins – are with time reinforced and selected for. Consequently, this institution is seen as contributing to the evolutionary 'success' of the society incorporating it, and this success, in turn, accounts for the perpetuated existence of the institution in that society. What we have here, then, is a non-man-made process of selection: a large scale evolutionary mechanism scans, as it were, the inventory of societies and of their social structures at any given period of time, and screens through to the next phase those societies whose structures and institutions serve them best. But for all that this explanation tells us, the social institution thus explained could have come about in any one of a number of ways. It could have originated, somehow, through people's 'stumbling' upon an arrangement which proves beneficial. However, it could also, for that matter, have come about as a result of intentional design and careful execution by some enlightened ruler or clever committee – and yet the explanation of its continued existence would still count as an invisible hand explanation of the evolutionary kind.

In order for an evolutionary explanation in the social domain to take off, the social institution to be explained has, as we saw, to fulfil some useful function, whether manifest or latent. Only institutions that perform a beneficial function for the society incorporating them can be candidates for an evolutionary explanation. Put somewhat differently, only institutions that promote the well-being and the survival of their society better than any alternative arrangements which happened to have been historically tried can have their continued existence explained through the evolutionary explanatory apparatus. Note, in contrast, that for an invisible hand explanation of the aggregate variety to go through, nothing in particular need be assumed about the social pattern which is a candidate for this sort of explanation – except that it be *structured* in some interesting sense. When the existence of a social institution is accounted for by means of an aggregate invisible hand explanation, there is no assumption, explicit or implicit, that it is a good institution, a valuable one, one which ought to be preserved or revered. This is why invisible hand explanations of the aggregate type are value free, while those of the evolutionary type can be value laden.

It is through this door that conservative ideology is sometimes brought to bear on invisible hand explanations. Ideology enters the stage when the delicate distinction is blurred between *requiring* that the institution which is the *explanadum* phenomenon have a socially beneficial function, and *presupposing* that it has such a function. It is by not distinguishing between the two models of invisible hand explanations that the notion of the invisible hand is sometimes being put to ideological use nowadays by conservative circles, to promote reverence toward tradition and to serve as a weapon against liberals and social planners. This is ironic in view of the fact that, when first introduced by the Scottish thinkers, the notion of the invisible hand was thought to promote ideals of secular, enlightened progress.

There is an interesting sense in which the two types of invisible hand explanations may be superimposed upon each other. It is entirely possible that an institution whose emergence is accounted for through an invisible hand explanation of the aggregate model turns out, as a matter of empirical fact, to fulfil a function which contributes to the survival or well-being of the society incorporating it. If it does, then its endurance may be subjected to the other, i.e. to the evolutionary, model of invisible hand explanations. Indeed, it may even be the case that many, or most, of the social institutions whose emergence can be explained by the aggregate invisible hand explanation are relevantly 'functional' and hence also amenable to an evolutionary invisible hand explanation. But such a connection, if it exists, is an empirical, not an analytical, one. And as a matter of ideological hygiene, it is important to keep these two models conceptually apart.

RELATED NOTIONS

(1) *The cunning of reason.* Hegel's idea of the cunning of reason is historically related to the idea of the invisible hand, and commentators on Hegel often point to an affinity between the two notions. The affinity, however, is superficial, and the doctrines served by these notions are profoundly different.

Hegel transformed Kant's comments on 'the hidden plan of nature' into his doctrine: 'This is to be called the cunning of reason, that it lets the passions do its work' (Hegel [1917] 1930: I, 83). The higher purposes of reason are realized, obliquely, through the exercise of the passions, self-interests and motives of individuals. The historical agent, by acting out his own will, inadvertently acts as an instrument of reason; his 'passions, ambition, jealousy, greed and the like are thus viewed as the handmaids of reason working in history' (Avineri 1972: 232).

The point of contact is what is sometimes referred to as the 'dialectical tension' between intent and outcome. Both the doctrine of the invisible hand and the doctrine of the cunning of reason focus on the fact that the result of human action need not be the outcome of any human design. Moreover, both doctrines spring from the recognition that some unintended and unexpected consequences of human action may fulfil a purpose, may serve a valuable function, may lead to progress or to perfection. This, indeed, is why these unintended consequences appear (misleadingly) to be the result of some superb – if not superhuman – planning. And it is precisely this which the two doctrines attempt to address in terms other than superhuman planning.

This point of contact, while striking, does not go very far. For one thing, the notion of the cunning of reason is meant to apply to the actions of a few great men only – to the actions of the historical heroes, or the 'world-historical individuals', as Hegel calls them. This feature of his doctrine stands in marked contrast to its parallel feature in the doctrine of the invisible hand. Namely, for an invisible hand explanation to go through, a multitude of (non-heroic) individuals have to be postulated as privately pursuing their own particular purposes.

All told, the doctrines which the notions of the cunning of reason and the invisible hand were devised to serve differ on several fundamental counts. They differ as to the domain within which the explanation applies, as to what it is that is being explained, and as to the nature of the explanatory mechanism. In the case of Smith and Ferguson the domain is the social order, the phenomena to be explained are social structures, practices and institutions, and the explanation consists in showing how they come about as the result of the actions of numerous ordinary humans and of no design whatever. In the case of Hegel the domain is spiritual history, the phenomenon to be explained is humanity's ever growing self-understanding, and the explanation consists in showing how history uses as its vehicles the results of the actions of a few heroic humans so as to unfold the execution of Reason's design.

Interestingly, both notions are currently being put to political uses. While the invisible hand serves as a conservative weapon against social reform, the cunning of reason is taken to account for the spectacle of leaders who carry out a policy which is antithetical to their true desires and declared intentions. An impressive number of big political decisions in recent times can be described as having been made by leaders who betrayed their constituencies as well as their own past. Thus: de Gaulle who quitted Algiers, Nixon who went to China, de Klerk who terminated apartheid, Begin who withdrew from the Sinai, and more. In Hegelian terms these leaders were being used by Reason as an instrument for carrying out their counter-policy. A desire/ability dialectics is at work here, whereby the leader who wants to bring about a certain dramatic state of affairs is often politically unable to do so, while the opposing leader who intends to – and is elected in order to – prevent it, will end up bringing it about, if forced to by reality. And the irony is that the leader who strongly and credibly opposes a certain move often has the larger manoeuvrability for making it, once reality brings him or her around to recognizing its imperativeness: the support of those who are anyway in favour of this move is guaranteed, while the trust of this leader's own followers will bring many of them around as well. Indeed, in political argumentation today it is this understanding of the notion of the cunning of reason which is sometimes cynically cited by people as a justification for supporting a political candidate who in their judgment will be *capable* of carrying out the policy they favour, rather than the candidate who *intends* to carry it out.

2. *Hidden-hand explanations.* Robert Nozick proposes to see a hidden-hand explanation as the *opposite* of an invisible hand explanation. The latter explains what looks to be the product of someone's intentional design. A hidden-hand explanation, conversely, 'explains what looks to be merely a disconnected set of facts that (certainly) is not the product of intentional design, as the product of an individual's or group's intentional design(s)' (Nozick 1974: 19). (Recall the case of the series of flat tyres discussed above.) He suggests, further, that not only are invisible hand explanations satisfying, but that some people also find hidden-hand explanations satisfying, 'as is evidenced by the popularity of conspiracy theories' (ibid).

3. *The hiding-hand principle.* In discussing development projects in the third world, Albert O. Hirschman offers the principle of the hiding hand as a general principle of action that beneficially hides difficulties from us and thus helps explain or reinterpret certain aspects of human economic activity:

> Since we necessarily underestimate our creativity, it is desirable that we underestimate to a roughly similar extent the difficulties of the tasks we face so as to be tricked by these two offsetting underestimates into undertaking tasks that we can, but otherwise would not dare, tackle (Hirschman 1967: 13).

EDNA ULLMANN-MARGALIT

See also ADAM SMITH AND THE LAW; FERGUSON, ADAM; HAYEK, FRIEDRICH VON; MENGER, CARL; SCOTTISH ENLIGHTENMENT AND THE LAW; SPONTANEOUS ORDER.

Subject classification: 1b(i).

BIBLIOGRAPHY

Avineri S. 1972. *Hegel's Theory of the Modern State.* Cambridge: Cambridge University Press.

Carnap, R. 1950. *Logical Foundations of Probability*. London: Routledge & Kegan Paul; 2nd edn, 1962.

Ferguson, A. 1767. *An Essay on the History of Civil Society*. Ed. F. Oz-Salzberger, Cambridge: Cambridge University Press, 1995.

Hayek, F.A. 1960. *The Constitution of Liberty*. Chicago: Gateway Edition, 1972.

Hayek, F.A. 1967. *Studies in Philosophy, Politics and Economics.* London: Routledge & Kegan Paul.

Hayek, F.A. 1978. Dr. Bernard Mandeville. In *The Essence of Hayek*, ed. C. Nishiyama and K.R. Leube, Stanford: Hoover Institution Press, 1984.

Hegel, G.W.F. 1917. *Philosophie der Weltgeschichte*. Ed. G. Lasson, Leipzig: Felix Meiner, 1930.

Hempel, C.G. 1965. *Aspects of Scientific Explanation*. New York: The Free Press.

Hirschman, A.O. 1967. *Development Projects Observed.* Washington, DC: The Brookings Institution.

Mandeville, B. 1729. The *Fable of the Bees*, Part II, ed. F.B. Kaye, Oxford: Clarendon Press, 1924.

Mises, Ludwig von. 1912. *Theorie des Geldes und der Umlaufsmittel.* Munich and Leipzig: Duncker and Humblot. New edition, in English, published in 1953 as *Theory of Money and Credit*, New Haven, CT: Yale University Press.

Nozick, R. 1974. *Anarchy, State, and Utopia*. New York: Basic Books.

Rothschild, E. 1994. Adam Smith and the invisible hand. *American Economic Review, Papers and Proceedings* 84: 319–22.

Samuelson, P.A. 1958. *Economics.* 4th edn, New York: McGraw-Hill.

Smith, A. 1776. *An Inquiry Into the Nature and Causes of the Wealth of Nations.* Ed. R.H. Campbell, A.S. Skinner and W.B. Todd, Oxford: Clarendon Press, 1976.

Ullmann-Margalit, E. 1978. Invisible hand explanations. *Synthese* 39: 263–91.

Ullmann-Margalit, E. 1997. The invisible hand and the cunning of reason. *Social Research* 64: 181–98.

issue entrepreneurs. *See* REGULATORY CAPTURE.

J

joint and several liability. The law and economics analysis of the comparison of joint and several liability with non-joint (several only) liability focuses on the relative incentives for deterrence and for settlement generated by the two rules. Part I provides a brief background of the legal regimes. Parts II and III compare, respectively, the deterrence and settlement effects of the two rules.

I. LEGAL REGIMES. The choice between joint and several liability and non-joint liability arises in situations in which the plaintiff's injury results from the actions of multiple parties. Under joint and several liability, if the plaintiff litigates against many defendants and prevails against only one, it can recover its full damages from that defendant; if the plaintiff prevails against all defendants but some are insolvent, it can recover its full damages from the solvent defendants; and if the plaintiff prevails against all defendants and all are solvent, it can nonetheless choose to recover its full judgment from any defendant or to recover a portion from each. In contrast, under non-joint liability, the plaintiff can recover from a losing defendant only the share of the damages attributable to that defendant.

For joint and several liability, the legal regime needs to be specified further. As shown in Kornhauser and Revesz (1993), the various choices presented below can affect the economic analysis of the consequences of joint and several liability.

First, a right of contribution permits a defendant that has paid a disproportionately large share of the plaintiff's damages as a result of the application of joint and several liability to obtain compensation from a defendant that has paid a disproportionately small share of these damages. Absent a right of contribution, such reallocation is not possible. Second, contribution shares are usually determined either *pro rata* (equal division among the defendants) or by reference to comparative fault.

Third, the question of an appropriate set-off rule arises when the plaintiff settles with one defendant and litigates against the other. Under the *pro tanto* set-off rule, the plaintiff's claim against the non-settling defendant is reduced by the amount of the settlement. In contrast, under the apportioned share set-off rule (sometimes referred to as a proportional set-off rule), the plaintiff's claim against the non-settling defendant is reduced by the share of the liability attributable to the settling defendant.

Fourth, under the *pro tanto* set-off rule, when one defendant settles and the other litigates and ultimately loses, the question arises whether the settling defendant is protected from contribution actions. Fifth, the legal regime must also specify whether settling defendants are entitled to bring contribution actions against defendants who settled for less than their share of the liability.

Sixth, under the *pro tanto* set-off, if the plaintiff enters into an inadequately low settlement with one defendant, the other defendant is responsible for the shortfall if it litigates and loses. To protect the interests of non-settling defendants, courts sometimes require 'good faith' hearings on the adequacy of settlements.

Seventh, if the plaintiff joins all the joint tortfeasors in a single suit, its claims against all of them will be adjudicated in the same proceeding. If the plaintiff chooses not to join all the tortfeasors as defendants, the question arises whether a named defendant can join another tortfeasor as a third-party defendant. Otherwise, the named defendant would have to file a separate action for contribution after the adjudication of its liability to the plaintiff.

II. DETERRENCE. We compare here the deterrence effects of joint and several liability and non-joint liability, when coupled with both rules of negligence and strict liability. We perform the comparison first for cases in which the defendants are fully solvent (Kornhauser and Revesz 1989) and then consider the effects of limited solvency (Kornhauser and Revesz 1990).

We develop our argument by reference to a model in which two firms, Row and Column, dump hazardous wastes at a single landfill. The actors benefit from this dumping because the wastes are the byproduct of profitable economic activity. At some time in the future, these wastes may leak into the environment and cause serious damage; we think of this damage as the cost of cleaning up the landfill and the surrounding area affected by the release. We take the damage function to be convex (the additional damage caused by one unit of waste increases with increasing amounts of waste in the landfill).

The expected damage of a release is a 'social' loss because it does not fall directly on the dumpers absent a legal provision shifting the liability to them. Instead, it falls on the victim that would have legal responsibility for the cleanup, or, alternatively, that would suffer the consequences if the problem were left unattended. Under our model, each dumper chooses the amount of waste that it will dump.

The socially desirable amount of waste is that which maximizes the social objective function: the sum of the benefits derived by the actors minus the social loss. An economically rational firm, however, does not make its decision based on the social objective function. Instead, it seeks to maximize its private objective function: the benefit that it derives from the activity that leads to the production of the waste minus whatever share of the social loss the legal regime allocates to it.

We model a joint and several liability regime with

contribution shares determined by reference to the amount of waste dumped. (Other rules are considered in Landes and Posner 1980; Kornhauser and Revesz 1989; Tietenberg 1989; and Wright 1988: 1169–79.) We assume that a plaintiff, say for example the government, sues both defendants in the same proceeding, and we exclude the possibility of settlement (the deterrence effects of joint and several liability when settlement is possible are analysed in Kahan 1996 and Spier 1994).

A. FULL SOLVENCY. (1) *Negligence.* We assume in the case of negligence that the standard of care will be chosen at the level that maximizes social welfare; departures from the social optimum in setting the standard of care are considered in Kornhauser and Revesz (1989: 862–70). For expositional convenience, we assume that negligent actors are liable only for the losses that would have been prevented through due care (in this example, for the additional losses that result if a firm dumps more than the socially optimal amount, rather than the socially optimal amount). We show in Kornhauser and Revesz (1989) that essentially the same results hold if negligent actors are responsible for the full losses (even ones that would have occurred with due care).

Under these circumstances, joint and several liability will produce the socially optimal result. If one of the actors, say Row, is non-negligent, it would not be rational for Column to be negligent. If this actor were contemplating dumping more than the standard of care, she would face liability for the full increase in the resulting damage. If the standard of care is set at the social optimum, the increased benefits that this actor would obtain through negligent conduct would be less than the increase in the damage for which she would be liable. Thus, assuming that one of the actors is non-negligent, the remaining actor will be non-negligent as well. This argument shows that it is a Nash equilibrium for each actor to meet its standard of care.

We now show that this efficient Nash equilibrium is unique. Consider whether it would be rational for both actors to be negligent. These actors will, jointly, face liability equal to the full increase in the resulting damage. If negligent action on the part of these actors were preferable to non-negligent action for each of them, then the total social welfare would exceed that attainable when all actors meet the standard of care, which, once again is not possible if the standard of care is set at the social optimum. Thus, regardless of how the increased damage were allocated between the defendants, at least one of them would have to pay more than the increased benefit that it obtained by acting negligently. An equilibrium in which both actors are negligent is therefore not possible.

The analysis is different for a non-joint liability rule, under which a negligent defendant would not be liable for the share of the damage attributable to the non-negligent defendant. Instead, the negligent defendant would be liable for an amount proportional to waste that it had dumped. Assume that Row is non-negligent and that Column is contemplating dumping more than the standard of care. Column would then pay only a fraction of the increase in damage. Under this apportionment rule, the remainder of the increase would be attributable to Row and would be unrecoverable by the plaintiff as a result of Row's lack of negligence. Thus, in this situation, non-joint liability leads to under-deterrence.

(2) *Strict liability.* The analysis is different for strict liability. Under strict liability, as long as both actors are fully solvent, there is no difference between joint and several liability and non-joint liability. Strict liability ensures that the victim is compensated for the full damage, and thus the question whether the victim will have to bear the share of the damage caused by the actions of non-negligent defendants does not arise.

Assume that Row is dumping the optimal amount of waste (the amount that would have met the standard of care if a rule of negligence had been in effect) and that Column is contemplating whether to dump more than this amount. Such a decision on the part of Column would, of course, increase the damage to the victim. Column would, in turn, be liable for a larger share of the damage, as it would pay in proportion to the amount of waste that it dumped. As long as the damage function is convex, however, the increase in Column's liability is less than the increase in the social loss. Thus, Column's decision to dump more than the socially optimal amount has the effect of increasing Row's liability as well. As a result of this externality, strict liability leads to under-deterrence, regardless of whether it is coupled with joint and several liability or non-joint liability.

Miceli and Segerson (1991) consider a modification of the strict liability rule that does in fact lead to efficiency both in terms of the level of care adopted and of entry into the activity. Under their formulation, each actor is responsible for the marginal damage that it causes. This rule, coupled with the assumption of convex costs, implies that the total payments from the two defendants would exceed the plaintiff's actual damages.

B. LIMITED SOLVENCY. Here, each defendant is defined not only by its benefit function (the rate at which its generation of waste is transformed into net benefits) but also by a fixed solvency, which represents the actor's available amount of assets to offset its share of the social loss. Under this formulation of the problem, the actors cannot shed their solvencies over time. We present here the analysis for strict liability, which makes it possible to present the basic intuitions. The comparison of joint and several liability and non-joint liability under negligence when the actors have limited solvency is presented in Kornhauser and Revesz (1990).

Consider a situation under which Row's solvency is zero and Column's solvency is infinite, and that both firms are otherwise identical. The liability rule thus transmits no deterrence incentive to Row. Row will therefore dump up to the point at which any additional benefit (in terms of reduced costs of production) from additional dumping becomes zero. This amount, which we call x^H, is greater than $x(\infty)$, the amount that Row would have dumped if both defendants had been infinitely solvent. Note that, as a result of the under-deterrence caused by strict liability, discussed above, $x(\infty)$ is in turn larger than x^*, the socially optimal amount of dumping by Row.

Under joint and several liability, because Row has no solvency, Column will be responsible for the whole liability and will dump an amount a (smaller than x^*), which is the optimal amount of dumping by Column conditional on Row being insolvent. The equilibrium is thus (x^H, a). If Column is not infinitely solvent, there are two possible equilibria: (x^H, a), if Column's solvency is greater than a critical solvency which we call s_j, or (x^H, x^H), if Column's solvency is lower.

In contrast, under non-joint liability, Column is not responsible for the whole liability, but only for its proportional share. If Column has infinite solvency, it will dump b, an amount larger than a, though smaller than x^*. Here, too, there are two possible equilibria if Column is not infinitely solvent: (x^H, b), if Column's solvency is greater than a critical solvency which we call s_{nj}, or (x^H, x^H), if Column's solvency is lower. Because for any level that it dumps Column faces less liability under a rule of non-joint liability, over a larger range of solvencies it chooses to act as if it were infinitely solvent rather than wholly insolvent. Thus, s_{nj} is smaller than s_j. Table I summarizes the relevant equilibria.

Table I

Equilibria Under Joint and Several Liability and Non-Joint Liability

Region	Column's Solvency	Equilibria Joint and Several Liability	Non-Joint Liability
A	$0 - s_{nj}$	(x^H, x^H)	(x^H, x^H)
B	$s_{nj} - s_j$	(x^H, x^H)	(x^H, b)
C	$s_j - \infty$	(x^H, a)	(x^H, b)

In region C in Table I, joint and several liability is therefore preferable to non-joint liability. From a social welfare perspective, an equilibrium at (x^H, a) is preferable to an equilibrium at (x^H, b). When one actor is generating x^H, joint and several liability makes the other actor see the full social cost of its actions, whereas non-joint liability does not. Thus, a is the optimal response by Column to Row's choice of x^H.

In region B, however, the reverse is true. Joint and several liability induces Column to act in the same manner that it would if it were wholly insolvent, dumping x^H, whereas non-joint liability induces Column to act in the same manner that it would if it were infinitely solvent, dumping b. Thus, in this region, non-joint liability has better social welfare properties. (Of course, in region A, both rules have the same properties.)

This discussion illustrates that, when solvency is limited, neither rule dominates the other. (The same is true under negligence: Kornhauser and Revesz 1990.) The intuition behind this result is that Row's insolvency creates a 'domino' effect, leading Column, under certain circumstances, to act as if it were insolvent as well. Because under joint and several liability Column is responsible for a greater proportion of the total harm, the range under which this 'domino' effect occurs is greater. In a model in which an actor's probability of insolvency is independent of the other actor's solvency (or probability of insolvency), a 'domino' effect is not possible and the results are different (Watts, forthcoming).

III. SETTLEMENTS. The basic framework for the analysis of the impact of joint and several liability on settlements is set forth in Kornhauser and Revesz (1994a), which deals with fully solvent defendants, and Kornhauser and Revesz (1994b), which deals with potentially insolvent defendants. The discussion here proceeds by reference to a numerical example, as in Kornhauser and Revesz (1993 and 1995), which serves to illustrate in a straightforward manner the game-theoretic interactions generated by the competing rules.

We model the following rule of joint and several liability. First, there is a right of contribution among defendants found jointly and severally liable. Second, in contribution actions, the relevant shares are determined by reference to the amount of waste dumped. Third, following a settlement, the plaintiff's claim against the nonsettling defendants is reduced by the amount of the settlement (a *pro tanto* set-off rule); the effects of different formulations of the apportioned share set-off rule are analysed in Kornhauser and Revesz (1993: 465–9) and Klerman (1996). Fourth, a settling defendant is protected from any contribution actions. Fifth, a settling defendant can bring contribution actions against non-settling defendants. Sixth, there is no detailed judicial supervision of the substantive adequacy of settlements. Seventh, the claims involving the joint tortfeasors are litigated together in a single proceeding. Kornhauser and Revesz (1993) shows that the results derived here are robust to many changes in the legal regime governing joint and several liability.

To perform the comparison between joint and several liability on the one hand, and non-joint liability on the other, we consider a situation in which the plaintiff has a claim of $100 against two defendants, Row and Column, each equally at fault. All the parties are risk neutral. We assume initially that the defendants are sufficiently solvent that they can satisfy the plaintiff's judgment. Later, we consider the effects of limited solvency.

The probability that the plaintiff will prevail against each defendant is 50%. All the parties have accurate information about this value and the costs of litigation are zero. As shown in Kornhauser and Revesz (1994a), the results derived here hold even if the two defendants were not equally at fault, if the plaintiff's probability of success were not 50%, and if litigation costs are not zero.

With respect to the relationship between the plaintiff's probabilities of success against the two defendants, we consider two polar situations. In the first, these probabilities are independent. Thus, the plaintiff's probability of success against one defendant is 50% regardless whether the plaintiff has prevailed against, lost to, or settled with the other defendant.

In the second case, the probabilities are perfectly correlated. Thus, if the plaintiff litigates against both defendants, it either prevails against both (with a probability of 50%) or loses to both (also with a probability of 50%).

The parties may either litigate or settle the claim. Settlement negotiations have the following structure. The plaintiff makes settlement offers to the two defendants. Row and Column decide simultaneously whether to accept these offers. (The effects of different offer structures are examined in Donohue 1994; the effects of 'Mary Carter' agreements between the plaintiff and a subgroup of defendants are analysed in Bernstein and Klerman 1995.) We assume that defendants' costs of coordinating their actions are sufficiently high that they act non-cooperatively. The plaintiff then litigates against the non-settling defendants, if any. We adopt the convention that, if a party is indifferent between settlement and litigation, it settles.

The central conclusion of our analysis is that the comparison of the settlement inducing properties of joint and several liability and non-joint liability depends critically on the correlation of the plaintiff's probabilities of success. When these probabilities of success are independent, joint and several liability unambiguously discourages settlements, relative to non-joint liability. When, in contrast, these probabilities are perfectly correlated, joint and several liability has a more complex effect: it encourages settlement when the litigation costs are low, but may discourage settlements when these costs are high (Kornhauser and Revesz 1994a). Earlier analyses had focused, implicitly, only on perfectly correlated probabilities (Easterbrook, Landes and Posner 1980; Polinsky and Shavell 1981).

A recent experimental study of auditors' liability considers a more complicated correlation structure under which the probabilities are perfectly correlated if the manager is not liable (because under the securities' laws the auditor then cannot be liable) but independent if the manager is liable (Dopuch, Ingberman and King 1997).

A. NON-JOINT LIABILITY. The analysis of the choice between settlement and litigation under non-joint liability is straightforward. The plaintiff's expected recovery from litigation is \$50: it has a 50% probability of obtaining \$50 from each defendant; each defendant's expected loss is therefore \$25. Absent litigation costs, the plaintiff and the defendants are indifferent between litigation and settlement. For any level of litigation costs, settlement becomes preferable. For example, if each party's litigation costs were \$5, the plaintiff's expected recovery from litigation would be only \$20 and each defendant's expected loss would be \$30. The plaintiff and each defendant would prefer any settlement between \$20 and \$30 to litigation.

The result that under non-joint liability the parties are indifferent between settlement and litigation in the absence of litigation costs and prefer to settle for any level of litigation costs does not change if the defendants have limited solvency. Say, for example, that Row's solvency is only \$20. Then, in the absence of litigation costs, the plaintiff and Row are indifferent between litigation and a settlement for the plaintiff's expected recovery of \$10 (a 50% probability of recovering Row's solvency of \$20). For any level of litigation costs, the parties prefer to settle. Thus, while limited solvency affects the expected value of the plaintiff's claim as well as the amount at which the case would settle, it does not affect the choice between settlement and litigation.

B. JOINT AND SEVERAL LIABILITY. (1) *Independent probabilities.* As a consequence of joint and several liability, the plaintiff recovers its full damages not only if it prevails against both defendants but also if it prevails against one and loses to the other. When the plaintiff's probabilities of success against the two defendants are independent, each of four different scenarios carries a probability of 25%: that the plaintiff prevails against both defendants, that the plaintiff prevails against Row and loses to Column, that the plaintiff prevails against Column and loses to Row, and that the plaintiff loses to both defendants. In the first three cases, carrying an aggregate probability of 75%, the plaintiff recovers its full damages of \$100. Thus, its expected recovery from litigating with both defendants is \$75. In turn, each defendant's expected loss is \$37.50. We proceed by analysing a situation in which litigation costs are zero.

A risk-neutral plaintiff will not accept a settlement with both defendants that yields less than \$75, but would find acceptable an aggregate settlement for \$75 or more. What would happen if the plaintiff made settlement offers to the two defendants for \$37.50 each, so that its aggregate recovery was equal to the expected recovery of litigating against both defendants? If one defendant, say Row, accepted the offer, would the other defendant accept it as well? Column would accept the settlement only if its expected loss from litigation is at least \$37.50. Under the *pro tanto* set-off rule, Column's exposure in the event of litigation is reduced to \$62.50: the plaintiff's damages of \$100 minus Row's settlement of \$37.50. But Column faces only a 50% probability of losing the litigation. Thus, in light of Row's settlement, its expected loss from litigation is only \$31.25.

It therefore follows that if the plaintiff were to make offers of \$37.50 to each defendant, at least one of them would reject the offer. The plaintiff's expected recovery would then be \$68.75 (Row's settlement of \$37.50 plus an expected recovery of \$31.25 from litigating against Column). This amount is lower than the plaintiff's expected recovery from litigating against both defendants. Thus, the plaintiff would never make offers of \$37.50 to each defendant. Similar logic establishes that no other pair of offers would give the plaintiff an expected recovery of at least \$75 and yet be acceptable to the two defendants. Also, there is no scenario under which the plaintiff would receive an expected recovery of at least \$75 by settling with one defendant and litigating against the other.

This phenomenon has two sources: (1) the surplus that the plaintiff obtains from litigation as a result of joint and several liability when its probabilities of success against the defendants are independent, and (2) the benefit that a non-settling defendant receives from the set-off created by the plaintiff's settlement with the other defendant.

If the plaintiff were litigating against only one defendant rather than two, its expected recovery from litigation would be \$50 rather than \$75: it would have a 50% probability of recovering from that defendant its full damages of \$100. Similarly, as we have indicated, if the plaintiff were litigating against two defendants under non-joint liability, its expected recovery would also be \$50: it has a 50% probability of recovering \$50 from each of the defendants. Finally, if the plaintiff were litigating against two defendants under joint and several liability but its probabilities of success against the defendants were perfectly correlated, it would also have an expected recovery of only \$50 (a 50% probability of recovering its full damages if it prevails against both defendants).

As a result of the surplus that the plaintiff obtains from litigating under joint and several liability when the probabilities of prevailing are independent, the plaintiff will not accept from one defendant a settlement that is too low even if it intends to litigate against the other. Say, for example, that the plaintiff accepted a settlement of $0 from Row and litigated against Column. Its expected recovery would then be only $50 (a 50% probability of recovering $100); the settlement with Row would have reduced its expected recovery by $25. If the plaintiff accepted a settlement of $10 from Row, its expected recovery from litigating with Column would be $45 (a 50% probability of recovering $90), for a total expected recovery of $55; the loss from the low settlement with Row would be $20.

So as not to lose its surplus, the plaintiff would thus have to demand a sufficiently high settlement from Row. But a settlement that is sufficiently desirable for the plaintiff to accept confers a benefit upon Column. If, for example, the plaintiff were to settle with Row for $25, Column's expected loss from litigation would be $37.50 – the same expected loss as if Row litigated. Any higher settlement with Row reduces Column's expected loss. We have already shown that a settlement with Row for $37.50 reduces Column's expected loss from $37.50 to $31.25, giving it a benefit of $6.25. In order to recover $75, the plaintiff would have to obtain from Row a settlement of $50 (which would leave an expected recovery from Column of $25 and confer upon Column a benefit of $12.50). Row, however, would not agree to such a settlement because, given that Column litigates, it is better off litigating as well and facing an expected loss of only $37.50.

We have thus illustrated why the plaintiff cannot capture the full benefit of Row's settlement if its probabilities of success are independent. Part of this settlement confers an external benefit upon Column. It is this externality that stands in the way of settlement. Indeed, the only way that the plaintiff can obtain the full benefit of a defendant's payment is by litigating, because if it settles part of the benefit accrues to the other defendant, reducing the plaintiff's expected recovery from litigation.

The role of joint and several liability in discouraging settlements is not limited to the case in which litigation costs are zero. The externality described above also impairs the possibility of settlement when litigation costs are positive but lower than a particular threshold.

(2) *Perfectly correlated probabilities.* The problem changes considerably when the plaintiff's probabilities of success against both defendants are perfectly correlated. If the plaintiff litigates against both defendants, it either prevails against both (with a probability of 50%) or loses against both (also with a probability of 50%). Its expected recovery from litigation is $50 rather than $75; each defendant's expected loss is then $25.

In the case of perfectly correlated probabilities, the plaintiff will settle with both defendants. It is easy to see that the plaintiff will settle with at least one of the defendants. Say that the plaintiff settles with Row for $10. It faces a 50% probability of recovering $90 from Column, and its total expected recovery is $55 – $5 higher than its recovery from litigating against both defendants. The effect of this settlement is to give the plaintiff $10 with certainty, but to reduce its expected recovery from litigation by $5. As a result, settlement with one defendant and litigation against the other is always more attractive to the plaintiff than litigation against both defendants. Unlike the case of non-joint liability, where the parties are indifferent between settlement and litigation when litigation costs are zero, here there is a positive surplus that the plaintiff and a defendant can divide if a settlement takes place.

It is also easy to show that, for the example that we are analysing, the plaintiff in fact settles with both defendants, for $25 and $37.50, respectively. Given that Row settles for $25, Column's expected loss through litigation is $37.50 (a 50% probability of paying the plaintiff's damages of $100 minus Row's settlement of $25), and would therefore accept a settlement for that amount. Moreover, given that Column settles for $37.50, Row's expected loss through litigation is $31.25 (a 50% probability of paying the plaintiff's damages of $100 minus Column's settlement of $37.50), and would therefore prefer to settle for $25 (a settlement offer of no more than $25 to one of the defendants is necessary to rule out an equilibrium in which both defendants litigate). The same argument establishes that the plaintiff would be no better off settling with one defendant and litigating against the other.

We show elsewhere that, for perfectly correlated probabilities, the plaintiff settles with both defendants if their shares of the liability are sufficiently similar, and settles with one defendant – the one with the larger share of the liability – and litigates against the other if the defendants' shares of the liability are sufficiently different (Kornhauser and Revesz 1994a).

(3) *The effects of limited solvency.* As indicated above, under non-joint liability, the limited solvency of the defendants does not affect the choice between settlement and litigation. The situation is different under joint and several liability. We consider first how limited solvency would affect the choice between settlement and litigation if the plaintiff's probabilities of success are independent. If one of the defendants, say Row, has limited solvency, the plaintiff nonetheless litigates against both defendants if this solvency is above a threshold. For example, if Row's solvency is $80 and the plaintiff litigates against both defendants, its expected recovery is $37.50 from Column but only $32.50 from Row (with a probability of 25%, the plaintiff prevails against both defendants and recovers $50 from Row, and, also with a probability of 25%, the plaintiff prevails only against Row and recovers Row's solvency of $80 rather than its full damages of $100). In contrast, if the plaintiff settles with Column for $37.50, Row's expected loss from litigation, and consequently the maximum settlement that it would offer, would be only $31.25 (a 50% probability of paying the plaintiff's damages of $100 minus Column's settlement of $37.50).

When Row's solvency is sufficiently low, however, the plaintiff settles with both defendants. Consider the case in which Row's solvency is $40. If the plaintiff litigates against both defendants its expected recovery is $60 (with a probability of 25%, it prevails only against Column and recovers $100; with a probability of 25%, it prevails against both and recovers \$40 from Row and \$60 from Column; and with a probability of 25%, it prevails only against Row and recovers \$40). In turn, Row's expected loss is \$20 and Column's expected loss is \$40.

If the plaintiff offered Row a settlement of \$20, its expected recovery from Column is \$40 (a 50% probability of recovering its damages of \$100 minus Row's settlement of \$20), and Column would be willing to settle for this amount. In turn, if the plaintiff offered Column a settlement of \$40, its expected recovery from Row is \$20 (a 50% probability of recovering its solvency of \$40), and Row would be willing to settle for this amount. Thus, as in the case of non-joint liability, when the solvency of one of the defendants is sufficiently low and litigation costs are zero, the parties are indifferent between settling and litigating.

In summary, the result that joint and several liability discourages settlements when the plaintiff's probabilities of success are independent holds over a range of solvencies. A similar analysis (Kornhauser and Revesz 1994b) establishes that, when the plaintiff's probabilities of success are perfectly correlated, joint and several liability promotes settlements over a range of solvencies. For solvencies below a given threshold, however, joint and several liability has the same settling-inducing properties as non-joint liability. The relevant results are summarized in Table II.

Table II
Effects of Joint and Several Liability on Settlements, Under Different Levels of Solvency, Relative to Non-Joint Liability

	High Solvency	Low solvency
Independent probabilities	Discourages settlement	Neutral effect
Perfectly correlated probabilities	Encourages settlement	Neutral effect

In sum, from the perspectives of both inducing deterrence and inducing settlements, there is no dominant relationship between joint and several liability and non-joint liability. From a deterrence perspective, the comparison between the two rules turns on the levels of solvency of the defendants. In contrast, from a settlement perspective, the comparison turns on the correlation of the plaintiff's probabilities of success against the defendants.

LEWIS A. KORNHAUSER AND RICHARD L. REVESZ

See also CAUSATION AND TORT LIABILITY; DUE CARE; LEGAL STANDARDS OF CARE; REGULATION OF HAZARDOUS WASTES; SETTLEMENT OF LITIGATION.

Subject classification: 1d(ii); 5d(ii).

BIBLIOGRAPHY

Bernstein, L. and Klerman, D. 1995. An economic analysis of Mary Carter settlement agreements. *Georgetown Law Journal* 83: 2215–70.

Donohue, J. 1994. The effect of joint and several liability on the settlement rate – mathematical symmetries and metaissues about rational litigant behavior: comment on Kornhauser and Revesz. *Journal of Legal Studies* 23: 543–58.

Dopuch, N., Ingberman, D. and King, R. 1997. An experimental investigation of multi-defendant bargaining in joint and several and proportional liability regimes. *Journal of Accounting and Economics* 23: 189–221.

Easterbrook, F., Landes, W. and Posner, R. 1980. Contribution among antitrust defendants: a legal and economic analysis. *Journal of Law and Economics* 23: 331–70.

Kahan, M. 1996. The incentive effects of settlements under joint and several liability. *International Review of Law and Economics* 16: 389–95.

Klerman, D. 1996. Settling multidefendant lawsuits: the advantage of conditional setoff rules. *Journal of Legal Studies* 25: 445–62.

Kornhauser, L. and Revesz, R. 1989. Sharing damages among multiple tortfeasors. *Yale Law Journal* 98: 831–84.

Kornhauser, L. and Revesz, R. 1990. Apportioning damages among potentially insolvent actors. *Journal of Legal Studies* 19: 617–51

Kornhauser, L. and Revesz, R. 1993. Settlements under joint and several liability. *New York University Law Review* 68: 427–93.

Kornhauser, L. and Revesz, R. 1994a. Multidefendant settlements: the impact of joint and several liability. *Journal of Legal Studies* 23: 41–76.

Kornhauser, L. and Revesz, R. 1994b. Multidefendant settlements under joint and several liability: the problem of insolvency. *Journal of Legal Studies* 23: 517–42.

Kornhauser, L. and Revesz, R. 1995. Evaluating the effects of alternative superfund liability rules. In *Analyzing Superfund: Economics, Science, and Law*, ed. R. Revesz and R. Stewart, Washington, DC: Resources for the Future.

Landes, W. and Posner, R. 1980. Joint and multiple tortfeasors: an economic analysis. *Journal of Legal Studies* 9: 517–55.

Miceli, T. and Segerson, K. 1991. Joint liability in torts: marginal and infra-marginal efficiency. *International Review of Law and Economics* 11: 235–49.

Polinsky, A.M. and Shavell, S. 1981. Contribution and claim reduction among antitrust defendants: an economic analysis. *Stanford Law Review* 33: 447–71.

Spier, K. 1994. A note on joint and several liability: insolvency, settlement, and incentives. *Journal of Legal Studies* 23: 559–68.

Stanley, T. 1994. An analysis of the rules of contribution and no contribution for joint and several liability in conspiracy cases. *Santa Clara Law Review* 35: 1–122.

Tietenberg, T. 1989. Indivisible toxic torts: the economics of joint and several liability. *Land Economics* 65: 305–19.

Watts, A. forthcoming. Insolvency and division of cleanup costs. *International Review of Law and Economics*.

Wright, R. 1988. Allocating liability among multiple responsible causes: a principled defense of joint and several liability for actual harm and joint exposure. *University of California at Davis Law Review* 21: 1141–1211.

joint ventures. A joint venture is a type of firm that is owned and actively co-managed by independent firms that pool resources for a specific objective. Firms enter into joint ventures for some of the same reasons they combine in other ways (Brodley 1982; Jorde and Teece 1990; Carlton and Salop 1996). These reasons include increasing economies of scale or scope; eliminating wasteful duplication; exploiting firms' technological or other complementarities; and preventing appropriation of research and development. A joint venture among many firms in an industry can achieve efficient standardization or can reduce 'network externalities' that otherwise would keep separate competing networks from achieving efficient size (Farrell and Saloner 1988).

Joint ventures are hybrids between firms and long-term contracts such as cross-licensing agreements. A joint venture differs from a conventional contract and resembles a firm in that it substitutes a governance mechanism allocating control, ownership and profits for spot market dealings or *ex ante* contractual determination of prices and quantities (Coase 1937; Williamson 1979). On the other hand, a joint venture differs from complete integration through merger or similar mechanisms in that each venturer normally retains significant control over its contribution through a veto power. The venturers compete or deal at arms' length outside the limited sphere of their venture. Joint ventures therefore may be closer to relational contracts in which the firms make long-term commitments and save many decisions for later negotiation (MacNeil 1978; Williamson 1975, 1985). The hybrid nature of joint ventures affects both the internal rules governing the venture, which are designed to encourage cooperation despite the venturers' differing private incentives, and the application of the antitrust laws, which are supposed to prevent competitors from inefficiently restricting competition.

DEFAULT RULES. The joint venture agreement normally governs dealings between the venturers and between the venture and third parties. Default rules of the applicable business association statute fill gaps in the agreement. A contract that the parties designate as a joint venture or that has the characteristics of a joint venture and is not incorporated or formed as any particular type of business association generally is treated as a partnership in most countries (Heenen 1975). Partnership is a basic type of business in which owners directly participate in management, are both agents of the other partners and principals, and are personally liable for the firm's debts. The following discussion focuses on United States partnership law, which is similar to the partnership law of many other countries (see PARTNERSHIP).

Partnership is defined under US law as any 'association of two or more persons to carry on as co-owners a business for profit' (UPA §6(1); RUPA §202). This definition fits joint ventures. Like other co-owners (Grossman and Hart 1986), joint venturers share the residual claim to earnings and rights to control and manage the joint venture property (UPA §7 and 18, RUPA §202 and 401). Unlike an agent–principal relationship, a joint venture has no single dominant party that exercises ultimate control and has a right to the entire residual.

Partnership default rules may be inappropriate for many joint ventures because of the hybrid nature of such firms. As discussed above, the venturers may be more like independent parties to a conventional long-term contract than co-owners of a firm. As a result, venturers may not want to have partnership-type liability for the firm's debts or fiduciary duties to the firm. They may therefore contract for other terms or explicitly adopt a non-partnership standard form of business association. In particular, they may incorporate in order to limit their liability. However, corporate default rules may be even less appropriate for joint ventures than partnership rules because they are designed for larger firms with passive owners. Even incorporated joint ventures may take on many of the attributes and rules of partnership other than personal liability. Alternatively, joint venturers may organize as a limited liability company or comparable firm that combines partnership-type governance rules with limited liability.

MANAGEMENT AND VOTING. Governance rules for joint venturers are provided in the absence of contrary agreement by the business association standard form the parties select. Partner-venturers or their agents by default each have an equal vote regardless of capital contribution (UPA §18(e) and RUPA §401(f)). A majority of the partners by default must approve 'ordinary' decisions while all must approve extraordinary decisions, including amendment of the agreement and admission of new partners (UPA §18(h)–(i) and RUPA §401(i)–(j)). These rules are designed for a very closely held firm such as a joint venture in which the members make credit and service as well as capital contributions.

Under US corporate law, an incorporated joint venture is managed by default by directors elected by a majority of the share ownership, subject to majority shareholder vote on important decisions such as amendment of the agreement or charter. These rules are designed for firms that are owned mostly by passive investors who make only financial contributions and who do not want to participate in management. By contrast, joint venturers are active owners who normally would not agree to let a venturer who contributes slightly more than half the assets elect the entire board and control all major decisions of the firm. Accordingly, venturers normally vary the corporate rules in their agreement. Even if they do not, a court may apply partnership default rules or hold that a joint venture agreement that antedated incorporation continues to apply even after incorporation (Bromberg and Ribstein 1988–97, §7.21(b)(3)).

The act or consent of one joint venturer may or may not bind the firm in transactions with third parties. Under partnership rules, venturers or their agents are co-managers who can bind the firm in ordinary business transactions with third parties (UPA §9–13, RUPA §301–305). Similarly, the chief executive officer of an incorporated joint venture can bind the firm to ordinary transactions, while a director or shareholder vote may be necessary to bind the firm to extraordinary transactions. The limited scope of the venture may restrict the 'ordinary' transactions in which a venture's agents have apparent authority to bind the venture.

Neither partnership nor corporate default rules may be appropriate for joint ventures. Since a joint venture may resemble a long-term contract in which the parties retain ultimate decision-making power, each party may expect to hold a veto power that permits it effectively to maintain control over its contribution to the venture. As in other long-term agreements, the venturers often must rely more on renegotiation and reputational incentives than on their contractual governance mechanism (Brodley 1982; Halonen 1997). This carries over to dealings with third parties. Thus, a court may hold that a single venturer cannot bind the firm even in ordinary transactions, at least with third parties who have notice that they are dealing with a joint venture (Brelsford 1980).

VICARIOUS LIABILITY. If the venture is not a statutory limited liability firm the venturers may have to pay the firm's debts out of their personal assets. As profit-sharers and co-managers, joint venturers are, in effect, co-monitors (Alchian and Demsetz 1972). As such, they have both the opportunity and the incentive to see that the firm does not injure third parties. Thus, if the firm contracted with creditors in advance concerning owner liability, the owners arguably often would contract with third party creditors to assume this monitoring burden. Vicarious owner liability for the firm's debts bonds the venturers' promise to monitor (Sykes 1984; Carr and Mathewson 1990). Vicarious liability may not, however, be appropriate for joint venturers because they are more like independent actors than co-owners and therefore may not monitor the venture's operations as do partners in standard-form partnerships. That is one reason why venturers may opt out of personal liability by forming a corporation or other limited liability firm.

FINANCIAL PROVISIONS. Venturers often attempt to allocate the venture's surplus to reflect the value of their contributions. These values may be difficult to determine, particularly for contributions of intellectual property. Sharing rules in research joint ventures also must provide optimal *ex ante* incentives for effort and disclosure of know-how (Gandal and Scotchmer 1993; Morash 1995; Perez-Castrillo and Sandonis 1997). The venturers may decide on an equal split to reflect their substantial contributions and the difficulty of making a more precise allocation (Darrough and Stoughton 1989). This is the statutory default rule for ventures organized as partnerships (UPA §18(a), RUPA §401, Ribstein 1997).

An incorporated venture's profits are generally allocated according to the parties' financial contributions alone, in the absence of contrary agreement. The parties may contract around this rule if, as in the usual case, they have made non-financial contributions or in order to achieve optimal incentive design. Alternatively, a court may apply partnership default rules on the assumption that this is what the parties intended even if they incorporated for liability purposes.

FIDUCIARY DUTIES. In order to minimize agency costs, the law provides for default fiduciary duties that require the venture's managers to exercise their power in the venture's interests. However, joint venture managers are also agents of their venturer-employers, who compete or deal at arms' length with each other outside the limited scope of the venture. The managers' conflicting duties may be relevant where, for example, a manager decides whether to expand into a venturer's territory, buys the venture's inputs from or sells its output to his employer, or takes business opportunities that the venture could have exploited (Shishido 1987; Jorde and Teece 1990). The joint venture agreement may explicitly permit some conflicts (Ribstein 1997). However, it may be costly for the venturers to anticipate, at the time of writing the joint venture agreement, such everyday matters as sourcing and distribution. Although the parties can authorize specific questionable conduct on a case-by-case basis, a venturer's consent may not be viable if it is obtained without disclosure of material facts. Disclosure may be impracticable because it would reveal venturers' confidential information. A court therefore may have to reconcile the venture managers' duties to the venture and to their venturer-employers. It may conclude that the venturers expected to be able to act selfishly, so that their agents have no fiduciary duties to the venture. In contrast to other fiduciary duty contexts, such as parent-subsidiary relationships, the ventures can protect their interests by exercising their governance rights and dissolution power. Moreover, broad fiduciary duties may be quite costly, as where they require disclosure of proprietary information to a co-venturer who can use the information for competitive advantage outside the venture. The parties therefore may rely on reputational incentives and negotiation rather than legal duties (Compton 1993: 868; Kattan 1993: 945).

DISSOLUTION AND BUYOUT. Rules for dissolution of joint ventures should balance the costs and benefits of providing venturers with easy exit. The venturers' power to withdraw or dissolve affects their *ex ante* incentives to contribute to the venture. Contributions may be devalued by dissolution or opportunistically appropriated by withdrawing venturers (Ribstein 1987). On the other hand, exit rights operate in effect as property rules that allow venturers to exercise control and reduce agency costs by removing their investments from joint management and control (Levmore 1995). Moreover, the venturers can select the type of venture and other aspects of their relationship in order to enhance cooperation and long-term stability (Kogut 1989).

The default rules that apply in the absence of contrary agreement depend on choice of business form. Each party by default can dissolve and compel the liquidation of a partnership venture, or can at least obtain the value of its investment less any damages for exiting before the agreed time (UPA §§31, 38, RUPA §§701, 801). The parties to an incorporated venture have no comparable default buyout right and can dissolve only by majority shareholder vote, which may effectively be a unanimity requirement in a 50–50 joint venture. The parties may incorporate for liability purposes but include partnership-type exit or dissolution rules in their agreement. Alternatively, a court may imply such an agreement even in an incorporated venture.

ANTITRUST LAW. The laws regulating competition significantly influence the use and structure of joint ventures. The hybrid nature of joint ventures is again important. Unlike an ordinary contract, a joint venture partially integrates the ventures by placing control of some of their resources in a separate entity. By expanding the constituent firms' capabilities, integration creates greater efficiencies, and therefore may increase competition, as compared with simple cartel-like coordination which simply raises prices by restricting output (Berg and Friedman 1977). This suggests that joint ventures should be less regulated than cartels. At the same time, joint ventures may produce less efficiency than complete integration of two firms by merger or other combination, though they may reduce competition less than eliminating the separate entities (Reynolds and Snapp 1986).

Determining the appropriate level of antitrust regulation requires balancing the long-run costs of joint ventures against their efficiency benefits (Brodley 1982; Ordover and Willig 1985; Grossman and Shapiro 1986; Jorde and Teece 1990; Carlton and Salop 1996). The application of antitrust or competition law to research joint ventures generally depends on the tradeoff between the static effects of reducing competition between the venturers and the dynamic welfare gains from permitting such agreements (Bowman 1973; Ordover and Baumol 1988).

Joint ventures typically restrict non-members' access to resources or facilities created by the joint venture (Brodley 1982; Carlton and Salop 1996). As with many vertical restraints, such restrictions place non-members at a competitive disadvantage. The restrictions nevertheless may be necessary to achieve the venture's efficiency-promoting activities. For example, by protecting against free-riding and appropriation inherent in the creation of intellectual property, forming a research and development joint venture and limiting access to members encourages the creation of this property and thereby increases competition (Ordover and Willig 1985; Grossman and Shapiro 1986). Thus, blocking non-member access and competition between members should not be condemned on antitrust grounds solely because of its effect on static competition. This is a specific example of the role of interfirm contractual arrangements in creating the appropriate conditions for industrial development (Schumpeter 1942: 88). In this respect, access restrictions resemble a single firm's use of a trade secret, serving as an alternative to patent protection, which is not available for all intellectual property (Kitch 1980; Yu 1981; Kaplow 1984; Bittlingmayer 1988; Kobayashi and Yu 1993).

Appropriate antitrust regulation of joint ventures depends on the respective roles of rules and standards (Ehrlich and Posner 1974; Kobayashi 1997). Courts and agencies may err in applying a relatively vague rule of reason to the difficult problem of balancing static and dynamic efficiency. Even if the courts draw the line in the right place, efficient joint ventures may be deterred because the parties cannot easily anticipate at the time of forming the venture where courts ultimately will draw the line (Carlton and Salop 1996). The courts also have significant flexibility in applying even a nominally per se rule of legality (Easterbrook 1984). A statutory per se rule may be clearer, and therefore may deter fewer efficient joint ventures, than the comparable judicial rule. Accordingly, it may be appropriate to establish statutory safe harbours for joint ventures that are likely to have net benefits (Brodley 1990; Jorde and Teece 1990; Shapiro and Willig 1990). For example, Congress has relaxed antitrust standards for research and development and production joint ventures (National Cooperative Research Act of 1984; National Cooperative Production Amendments of 1993). The US antitrust agencies also have promulgated antitrust guidelines for research joint ventures (1980) and for intellectual property issues (1995). However, these efforts to clarify antitrust enforcement are incomplete, and have led to continuing efforts by the antitrust agencies to reduce the significant uncertainty regarding enforcement policies (Federal Trade Commission, Comment and Hearings on Joint Venture Project 1997).

LARRY E. RIBSTEIN AND BRUCE H. KOBAYASHI

See also FIDUCIARY DUTIES; INCENTIVES TO INNOVATE; PARTNERSHIP; RESIDUAL RIGHTS OF CONTROL; VICARIOUS LIABILITY.

Subject classification: 5g(v).

STATUTES AND REGULATIONS

National Cooperative Research Act of 1984, 15 USC §§4301–4305 (1988).

National Cooperative Production Amendments of 1993, amending 15 USCA §§4301–4305 (West Supp. 1994).

Uniform Partnership Act of 1914.

Revised Uniform Partnership Act (1996).

US Department of Justice. 1980. Antitrust guide concerning research joint venture. Washington, DC: US Government Printing Office.

US Department of Justice and the Federal Trade Commission. 1995. Antitrust guidelines for the licensing of intellectual property, reprinted in *4 Trade Regulation Reporter* (CCH) para. 13, 132.

US Federal Trade Commission. 1997. Notice: comment and hearings on joint venture project. 62 *Federal Register* 22945–8.

BIBLIOGRAPHY

Alchian, A.A. and Demsetz, H. 1972. Production, information costs, and economic organization. *American Economic Review* 62: 777–95.

Berg, S.V. and Friedman, P. 1977. Joint ventures, competition, and technological complementarities: the evidence from chemicals. *Southern Economic Journal* 43: 1330–37.

Bittlingmayer, G. 1988. Property rights, progress, and the aircraft patent agreement. *Journal of Law and Economics* 31: 227–48.

Bowman, W.S. 1973. *Patent and Antitrust Law*. Chicago: University of Chicago Press.

Brelsford, J.F. 1980. Apparent authority and the joint venture: narrowing the scope of agency between business associations. *University of California Davis Law Review* 13: 831–67.

Brodley, J.F. 1982. Joint ventures and antitrust policy. *Harvard Law Review* 95: 1523–90.

Brodley, J.F. 1990. Antitrust law and innovation cooperation. *Journal of Economic Perspectives* 4(3): 97–112.

Bromberg, A. and Ribstein, L.E. 1988–1997. *Bromberg & Ribstein on Partnership*. New York: Aspen Publishing Co.

Carlton, D. and Salop, S. 1996. You keep on knocking but you can't come in: evaluating restrictions on access to input joint ventures. *Harvard Journal of Law and Technology* 9: 319–51.

Carr, J.L. and Mathewson, G.F. 1990. The economics of law firms: a study in the legal organization of the firm. *Journal of Law and Economics* 33: 307–30.

Coase, R.H. 1937. The nature of the firm. *Economica* 4: 386–405.

Compton, C.T.C. 1993. Cooperation, collaboration, and coalition: a perspective on the types and purposes of technology joint ventures. *Antitrust Law Journal* 61: 861–95.

Darrough, M. and Stoughton, N. 1989. A bargaining approach to profit sharing in joint ventures. *Journal of Business* 62: 237–70.

Easterbrook, F.H. 1984. Vertical arrangements and the rule of reason. *Antitrust Law Journal* 53: 135–73.

Ehrlich, I. and Posner, R.A. 1974. An economic analysis of legal rulemaking. *Journal of Legal Studies* 3: 257–86.

Farrell, J. and Saloner, G. 1988. Coordination through committees and markets. *RAND Journal of Economics* 19: 235–52.

Gandal, N. and Scotchmer, S. 1993. Coordinating research through research joint ventures. *Journal of Public Economics* 51: 173–93.

Grossman, G.M. and Shapiro, C. 1986. Research joint ventures: an antitrust analysis. *Journal of Law, Economics, and Organization* 2: 315–37.

Grossman, S. and Hart, O.D. 1986. The costs and benefits of ownership: a theory of vertical and lateral integration. *Journal of Political Economy* 94: 691–719.

Halonen, M. 1997. A theory of joint ownership. University of Bristol Department of Economics Discussion Paper No. 97/437.

Heenen, J. 1975. Partnerships and other personal associations for profit. In *International Encyclopedia of Comparative Law* Vol. XIII (The Hague: J.C.B. Mohr): 187–8.

Jorde, T.M. and Teece, D.J. 1990. Innovation and cooperation: implications for competition and antitrust. *Journal of Economic Perspectives* 4(3): 75–96.

Kaplow, L. 1984. The patent-antitrust intersection: a reappraisal. *Harvard Law Review* 97: 1813–92.

Kattan, J. 1993. Antitrust analysis of technology joint ventures: allocative efficiency and the rewards of innovation. *Antitrust Law Journal* 61: 937–73.

Kitch, E.W. 1980. The law and economics of rights in valuable information. *Journal of Legal Studies* 9: 683–723.

Kobayashi, B.H. 1997. Game theory and antitrust: a post-mortem. *George Mason Law Review* 5: 411–21.

Kobayashi, B.H. and Yu, B.T. 1993. Indexing inventors: the 'Sources of Invention' revisited. *Journal of Economic Behavior and Organization* 21: 205–22.

Kogut, B. 1989. The stability of joint ventures: reciprocity and competitive rivalry. *Journal of Industrial Economics* 38: 183–98.

Levmore, S. 1995. Love it or leave it: property rules, liability rules, and exclusivity of remedies in partnership and marriage. *Law and Contemporary Problems* 58: 221–49.

MacNeil, I.R. 1978. Contracts: adjustment of long-term economic relations under classical, neoclassical, and relational contract law. *Northwestern Law Review* 72: 854–905.

Morasch, K. 1995. Moral hazard and optimal contract form for R&D cooperation. *Journal of Economic Behavior and Organization* 28: 63–78.

Ordover, J.A. and Baumol, W.J. 1988. Antitrust policy and high-technology industries. *Oxford Review of Economic Policy* 4: 13–34.

Ordover, J.A. and Willig, R.D. 1985. Antitrust for high-technology industries: assessing research joint ventures and mergers. *Journal of Law and Economics* 28: 311–33.

Perez-Castrillo, J.D. and Sandonis, J. 1997. Disclosure of know-how in research joint ventures. *International Journal of Industrial Organization* 15: 51–75.

Reynolds, R.J. and Snapp, B.R. 1986. The competitive effects of partial equity interests and joint ventures. *International Journal of Industrial Organization* 4: 141–53.

Ribstein, L.E. 1987. A statutory approach to partner dissociation. *Washington University Law Quarterly* 65: 357–426.

Ribstein, L.E. 1995. Linking statutory forms. *Law and Contemporary Problems* 58: 187–220.

Ribstein, L.E. 1997. Fiduciary duty contracts in unincorporated firms. *Washington and Lee Law Review* 54: 537–94.

Schumpeter, J.A. 1942. *Capitalism, Socialism and Democracy*. New York: Harper & Bros.

Shapiro, C. and Willig, R.D. 1990. On the antitrust treatment of production joint ventures. *Journal of Economic Perspectives* 4(3): 113–30.

Shishido, Z. 1987. Conflicts of interest and fiduciary duties in the operation of a joint venture. *Hastings Law Journal* 39: 63–123.

Sykes, A. 1984. The economics of vicarious liability. *Yale Law Journal* 93: 1231–80.

Williamson, O.E. 1975. *Markets and Hierarchies: Analysis and Antitrust Implications*. New York: Free Press.

Williamson, O.E. 1979. Transaction-cost economics: the governance of contractual relations. *Journal of Law and Economics* 22: 233–61.

Williamson, O.E. 1985. *Economic Institutions of Capitalism: Firms, Markets, Relational Contracting*. New York: Free Press.

Yu, B.T. 1981. Potential competition and contracting in innovation. *Journal of Law and Economics* 24: 215–38.

judgment-proofness. A party is said to be judgment-proof if she avoids the full degree of liability she should rightly face. There are several ways an individual can do this. Before the case comes to court, and after the accident has been caused, she can expend resources either to deter or to escape court action. After the case goes to court, the injurer can find loopholes in the law, or engineer a reduction in the extent of liability. These methods are not sufficient for judgment-proofness. If the courts can assess the probability of such manipulation, then they may be able to levy punitive damages, so that individuals face the appropriate level of expected liability. Thus, a more accurate definition of judgment-proof is that the party not have sufficient court-accessible funds to cover the sum of actual and punitive damages.

Examples of judgment-proofness are ubiquitous. One which is frequently cited is the asset-poor reckless driver, who risks others' lives and property. Similarly, the harm caused to someone injured on another person's property could plausibly exceed the value of that property, and any additional assets held by the owner. While being relevant for liability of individuals, judgment-proofness is also a significant potential problem with firms. Well-known examples of this are the series of cases associated with a company called Life Sciences Products (LSP). Two individuals set up LSP and produced a dangerous pesticide called Kepone. The owners borrowed $75,000 from a local bank and each contributed equity of $1000. The company ran into difficulties when it generated pollution that posed serious environmental risks. However, LSP's assets could not cover the damage: the bank's loan had priority over the environmental claims – only the $2000 in equity could be used to pay for environmental damage. Pitchford (1995) examines, among other things, the incentive of firms to change their capital structure from equity towards secured debt as a strategy to avoid liability. The most famous recent example of judgment-proofness involved the vessel *Exxon Valdez*. Although Exxon is a large oil company, and probably had sufficient resources to cover the cost of most conceivable damages, the captain of the ship, and other employees who may have been in the best position to avoid the accident, were clearly judgment-proof.

Socially insufficient care is the basic policy problem that courts and governments face as a result of judgment-proofness. Consider a situation where a single injurer influences the chance of an accident, as a result of which a victim suffers harm h. The injurer takes care c costing $\$c$ that determines the (decreasing and convex) probability $p(c)$ of an accident. The efficient level of care, which I shall call c^*, minimizes the expected cost $p(c) \cdot h + c$ of the accident. Now suppose the injurer has limited wealth w, and faces a strict liability regime. Due to limited wealth, the injurer effectively faces liability $l = \min\{h, w\}$, and chooses care to minimize her expected cost $p(c) \cdot \min\{h, w\} + c$. Consequently, injurers who are judgment-proof, and so have wealth that falls below h, choose care below c^*. They have no economic reason to take account of the additional social loss $h - w$ that they may cause.

Although insufficient care is a predicted outcome of judgment-proofness, this depends on the kind of liability regime, or regulations that are in place, and how costly it is to monitor the actions that lead to an accident. In the case of strict liability above, if care is observable at low cost (relative to expected benefits) by an outsider, and the accident process could be halted to prevent the consequences of insufficient care, it would make more sense to regulate. The regulation would stipulate that care no less than c^* be taken, or otherwise the party not be allowed to engage in the potentially harmful activity. For example, it would make no sense to allow people to juggle grenades in public – this activity is curtailed by banning grenades – so this and similar activities are not subject to strict liability in practice, but are instead subject to regulation. Regulation is possible whenever some device can be installed at sufficiently low expense to ensure that care less than c^* is impossible.

If care is observable by an outsider at high cost (relative to potential harm) then it makes less sense to incur the costs of regulation. *Ex post* mechanisms like liability rules and fines are cheaper to implement because costs are only incurred in the event of damage, unlike direct regulatory costs, which are usually incurred independently of whether damage is caused or not. Since care is observable, despite such observation being costly, a negligence rule may also be feasible. Shavell (1986) and Summers (1983) examine the effectiveness of a negligence rule when injurers are judgment-proof. When it is feasible, the negligence rule dominates strict liability because it induces some injurers with wealth below h to take optimal care. Specifically, under negligence there exists a lower limit $\underline{w} < h$ below which injurers will take insufficient care, and above which injurers will choose optimal care. To see why, note that under negligence, the injurer need only demonstrate that care c^* was chosen to avoid liability. This costs the injurer $\$c^*$. Clearly, an injurer with zero wealth has nothing to lose, and will choose $c = 0$. As injurer wealth increases, however, the injurer's expected costs, $p\ (c\ (w)) \cdot w + c\ (w)$ (where $c\ (w)$ is the privately optimal care given that w will be lost in the event of an accident), increase from zero. An injurer with wealth $\underline{w}$ such that $c^* = p\ (c\ (\underline{w})) \cdot \underline{w} + c\ (\underline{w})$ is indifferent between choosing care c^*, and care $c\ (\underline{w})$. To see why, note that the negligence rule does not levy a penalty if c^* is observed, but levies penalty $\underline{w}$ with probability $p\ (c\ (\underline{w}))$ if care $c\ (\underline{w}) < c^*$ is observed. An injurer with slightly higher wealth than $\underline{w}$ who chooses $c\ (w)$ incurs a higher expected cost than c^*. Therefore, it will be optimal for such an injurer to choose c^* instead, and avoid any liability. Moreover, the wealth threshold $\underline{w}$ is less than h since $p\ (c^*) \cdot h + c^* > c^* = p\ (c\ (\underline{w})) \cdot \underline{w} + c\ (\underline{w})$. Injurers with wealth between $\underline{w}$ and h are induced to take optimal care under negligence, whereas strict liability induces care $c\ (w) < c^*$. Put less technically, injurers with wealth in-between $\underline{w}$ and h are induced to take the optimal care because this saves them the expected penalty they would otherwise pay. Note however that the negligence rule does not eliminate the problem of inadequate care when wealth falls below $\underline{w}$.

Judgment-proofness has effects other than simply reduced care. It also leads to excessive engagement in activities that cause harm, relative to the optimum (Shavell 1986). For example, suppose the activity choice is driving a car or not, and care relates to how safely the car is driven. Since some of the cost of an accident is externalized, more individuals at a given level of wealth will be induced to buy a car than otherwise, let alone drive their car with less care. Two other effects of judgment-proofness stem from the fact that an injurer's payoff is decreasing in her court-accessible wealth (as the examples above demonstrated). First, the activity could become dominated by low wealth injurers through self-selection, which leads to further reductions in care. Second, injurers have an incentive to engage in wealth-hiding strategies to increase their payoffs. The last two possibilities have been examined by Ringleb and Wiggins (1990) in the context of the hypothesis that large firms have been replaced by smaller firms for productive activities carrying the risk of sizeable lawsuits. This hypothesis is consistent with either a deliberate spin-off strategy by larger (asset-rich) firms, or entry by small (asset-poor) firms. This is one explanation for the events involving Life Sciences Products. The two individuals who set up LSP were former employees of Allied Chemicals. Allied purchased the chemicals that LSP manufactured, and probably had sufficient assets to cover the liabilities associated with the damages caused by the pesticide Kepone.

These considerations point to an important aspect of judgment-proofness, namely that accidents often involve parties other than injurers and victims. In many cases of relevance a third party is present who might share some of the risk of liability with the injurer. For example, an injurer could have a contract with an insurance company that offers some cover in the event of an accident: the asset-poor reckless driver or the hapless home owner could purchase third party insurance cover. If the injurer is a worker, her employer may be held vicariously liable for accidents she causes. If the injurer is a firm, then the downstream firms that buy its products, and that may have divested their risky divisions in the first place, may be held liable. Similarly a firm's creditors may be held liable. Creditor liability has had substantial attention in the law and economics literature, and is potentially very significant, particularly for environmental liabilities:

> The risk for lenders is not only that their borrowers' environmental liabilities will lead to the loss of loans because of diminution of collateral's value or inability of borrowers to repay their loans, but they also face the risk of possible liability under the Comprehensive Environmental Response, Compensation, and Liability Act. While the law in this area is in its infancy, under certain circumstances lenders could be liable for cleanup costs that could exceed the value of the loan involved (Chadd et al. 1991: A-83).

Given their empirical significance, economic analysis of judgment-proofness should take account of the relationships, contractual or otherwise, with a third party. Shavell (1986) considers the case where an injurer can have a contract with an insurance company. Several interesting issues emerge. If insurance is voluntary, a potentially judgment-proof injurer's incentive to purchase coverage is reduced. The injurer clearly has a low incentive to pay for coverage that exceeds her assets, as such excess does not benefit her, beyond altruism. This factor is present whether or not insurers can observe care, whether or not injurers are subject to strict liability or negligence, and even if injurers are risk averse. Under-insurance is more important, in the case of strict liability, the lower the wealth of the injurer. The theme that judgment-proofness leads to insufficient care remains intact with voluntary insurance, at least when injurers have sufficiently low wealth. If full insurance coverage is mandatory, there are starkly different outcomes depending on whether or not the insurer can observe the injurer's care. With observability, the injurer will be compelled by the insurer, who bears the accident cost, to take optimal care. However, when care is not observable, the injurer will choose the minimum feasible care. The combination of unobservable care and compulsory full insurance gives the injurer no incentive to be careful, since there is no penalty associated with an accident.

The technical analysis in some of the preceding paragraphs is more specifically suited to injurers who are individuals rather than injurers that are firms. Several different issues emerge when the focus is on firms. One is that employees, such as the captain and crew of the *Exxon Valdez*, or the engineers at Bhopal in India, are often the principal parties in control of the risk of an accident. The other is that firm owners with limited wealth typically must borrow in order to produce. When firms are involved with accidents, the structure of the firm might be altered in the face of different liability rules. The contract between the party who controls the risk of an accident – the agent – and the party who provides finances, or bears liability for the agent's actions – the principal – will change depending on the nature of the liability rule which is imposed.

Pitchford (1995) develops a model of a potentially judgment-proof agent, a principal who contracts with the agent, and a potential victim. All agents are assumed risk neutral. The effects on social welfare and the probability of an accident under different kinds of government intervention are examined. Consider the case where the principal is a creditor, and the agent is an owner (or small group of owners) of an enterprise which can cause an accident. Several questions arise naturally in this framework. What is the effect of bankruptcy law, which typically places secured debt ahead of the claims of accident victims? Is it better to make an exception to the absolute priority rule and make the lender liable for any harm caused by an accident that is not covered by the firm's assets?

Consider the first of these questions. If secured debt is immune from the claims of accident victims, then firm owners will lower the amount of equity they choose. In fact, in the simple model described in Pitchford (1995), firm owners and creditors will agree on an all-debt firm, much as Life Sciences Products appeared to be. Provided that firm owners can hide their wealth, the strategy of choosing an all-debt firm reduces the funds available to an accident victim simply to current profits.

A wealth-hiding capital structure affects the care taken by the owners. Suppose that current profits are v, and consider the framework introduced earlier where there is an accident state that occurs with probability $p(c)$, and a no-accident state that occurs with the complementary probability. The owner of the firm loses profit v if an accident occurs, provided harm h exceeds v. The owner therefore minimizes $p(c) \cdot v + c$, which leads to care $c(v) < c(h) \equiv c^*$. If the firm is not very profitable, then a rule which allows debt priority over accident victim's claims might lead to significantly low care and a high accident probability.

Suppose that instead of zero liability, the lender is liable for an amount $l \leq h$ of the damage caused by an accident. In what way will the capital structure of the firm change in response to this regime? Will this result in care above $c(v)$? Subtle issues arise in analysing this case. If an accident occurs, the creditor must pay for the difference between l and any penalty which it levies on the owners of the firm as a result of the accident which they caused. It turns out that in an optimal debt contract between creditor and owner, the owner must put all its wealth as equity into the firm. This is optimal, because if the owner was very wealthy, it would be best for it to have no debt and face the full cost of its actions. Thus, when the lender is liable, equity is at a maximum of w, and when the lender is not liable, equity is at a minimum of 0, and debt is at a maximum. Despite this, making the lender liable does not necessarily lead to a rise in care!

To see why, one must carefully consider the incentives that the owners of the firm face when the creditor is liable for l. As a first step, consider how the lender–owner contract changes as l increases. A creditor in a competitive capital market (who therefore makes zero expected profit) must subsidize the loss $l-(v+w)$ it makes in the accident state, by charging a premium $x(l)$ to the owners when there is no accident. This premium is increasing in l because creditors must cover greater liability in the accident state. The owner's care decision is affected as follows. Owners receive $v+w-x$ if there is no accident, and nothing if there is an accident, and consequently choose care $c(v+w-x)$. A rise in l means that owners are rewarded less in the no-accident state as x rises. However, there is no change in their payoff when an accident occurs. Consequently, care *declines* with an increase in lender liability.

To answer the question, how does care differ when the creditor is immune from liability compared with the situation where the creditor is fully liable with $l = h$, one compares $c(v)$ with $c(v+w-x)$. If wealth is low, and harm is high, the premium can be sufficiently high so that full lender liability results in care below that which obtains if the lender faces no liability!

It is clear from examining $c(v+w-x)$ that the best policy to pursue is one which minimizes the premium x. This occurs where the creditor's liability is limited to $l = v+w$. Any increase in liability above $v+w$ leads to an increase in the no-accident state premium x. Since the owners always become bankrupt in the accident state, such a policy can only have the effect of decreasing the level of care. Limiting the liability of creditors is optimal precisely because it limits the perverse effect that higher premiums have. Limited liability may, however, be at odds with victim compensation. Although creditor liability above gross firm wealth results in decreased care, the victim does receive greater compensation. Compensation policy may have to account for a tradeoff between higher victim compensation and an increased accident probability.

There are several other important caveats to the conclusion that care declines when liability increases when $l > v+w$. First, such liability may lead to investments in monitoring technology that improve the situation relative to the case where creditors are not liable. This is possible, as discussed above, if monitoring is not too costly. There is a second offsetting effect. Consider a situation where there is a set of firms with different costs of care prevention. While increased creditor liability leads to a decrease in the level of care of viable firms, it also reduces their profits. Firms on the margin of entering the risky business may be deterred from entering the business by the increased premia that higher creditor liability implies. There is a trade-off between lower care by incumbents, and a reduction in the number of dangerous firms. Empirical analysis is needed to determine whether these offsetting effects outweigh the perverse effect of higher premia.

The model described can be applied to a situation of vicarious liability of an employer (rather than a creditor) who hires an employee (rather than an owner) whose actions might cause an accident. However, due to specialization, an employer may have a greater ability to monitor the efforts of an employee than a creditor does of a firm, although it may have less ability to discern the worker's wealth. Employers may also be able to take actions themselves that reduce the chance of an accident.

ROHAN PITCHFORD

See also BANKRUPTCY AND ITS REFORM; CORPORATE BANKRUPTCY; CRIMINAL SANCTIONS FOR PRODUCT SAFETY; DUE CARE; PUNITIVE DAMAGES; REGULATION OF HAZARDOUS WASTES; REGULATION OF TOXIC SUBSTANCES; VICARIOUS LIABILITY.

Subject classification: 5d(iv).

CASES

Life Sciences Products (LSP) series of cases as follows:

Case No. 1, *Life Sciences Products Company v. Occupational Safety and Health Review Commission*, OSHRC Docket No. 1490 (1977).

Case No. 2, *William P. Moore v. Allied Chemical Corporation, The Travelers Indemnity Company, and Hooker Chemicals & Plastic Corp.*, 480 F Supp. 377 (Va 1979).

Case No. 3, *Pruitt, Lorie Q., et al. v. Allied Chemical Corporation* (Va 1980).

Case No. 4, *Lorie Q. Pruitt, et al. v. Allied Chemical Corporation*, 523 F Supp. 975 (Va 1981).

BIBLIOGRAPHY

Chadd, C.M., Satinoven, T., Bergeson, L.I., Neuman, R.W. and Bryant, C.R. 1991. *Avoiding Liability for Hazardous Waste: RCRA, CERCLA and Related Corporate Law Issues*. Washington, DC: Corporate Practice Series 57, The Bureau of National Affairs.

Pitchford, R. 1995. How liable should a lender be? The case of judgment-proof firms and environmental risk. *American Economic Review* 85(5): 1171–86.

Ringleb, A.H. and Wiggins, S.N. 1990. Liability and large-scale, long-term hazards. *Journal of Political Economy* 98(3): 574–95.

Shavell, S. 1986. The judgment proof problem. *International Review of Law and Economics* 6: 45–58.

Summers, J.S. 1983. The case of the disappearing defendant. *University of Pennsylvania Law Review* 132: 145–85.

Sykes, A.O. 1981. An efficiency analysis of vicarious liability under the law of agency. *Yale Law Journal* 91(1): 168–206.

judicial independence. Although judicial independence is a concept that scholars routinely tout, they find it hard to define, and it is harder still to explain its persistence. The hardest questions about 'judicial independence' are what it is, and why it is sometimes observed (whatever it might be).

Independence from the parties. The definitional puzzle begins with the question 'independent from what?'. Independence from the parties to the dispute, observers sometimes reply – a judge is independent if he or she does not expect his or her welfare (financial or otherwise) to be correlated with a decision in favour of one or the other party. Obviously, one would not expect complete independence by this measure. If nothing else, the intellectual integrity of a judge's decision will usually – and, most would say, properly – affect his or her professional standing. When observers criticize judges who take bribes from the Mob or applaud those who risk their lives to convict drug lords, they usually have this answer in mind.

Indeed, independence from the parties to the dispute is surely an important part of what most people want from their judges. Judges who decide disputes in favour of the most violent or the best-paying party do not give the public much of a service. Those who succumb to threats simply serve as lackies to the Mob; those who take bribes simply serve as another set of rent-extracting bureaucrats.

Accordingly, it is easy to understand why politicians in modern democracies try to keep judges independent from the parties: putting Mob lackies or rent-extracting bureaucrats on the public payroll does not win votes. So long as politicians face competitive electoral markets and the costs of enforcing this version of judicial independence are relatively modest, most politicians will try to keep their judges independent.

Independence from the government. A more problematic definition of 'judicial independence' refers to a judge's independence from elected politicians. The definition raises a host of questions, for it is far from clear why (or when) rational politicians would find it advantageous to insulate judges from themselves. After all, voters elect politicians in part to implement policies and programmes. Independent judges can stop politicians from delivering those policies and programmes. The puzzle, therefore, is why (or when) politicians will find it advantageous to provide judges who can and may cheaply stop politicians from giving voters what they want.

The rest of this essay explores this puzzle. It does so by considering three issues: when politicians would most likely appoint judges on a non-partisan basis (Section I); when they would most likely ensure that the judges they appointed do not face politically skewed career incentives (Section II); and when – independent of any career incentives – sitting judges would be most likely to issue decisions that track the political preferences of elected politicians (Section III).

I. It is a staple of political science that US legislators and presidents politicize judicial appointments. A host of empirical studies seems to confirm that point. More recently, de Figueiredo and Tiller (1996) argue that this concern for politically acceptable appointments is a primary cause of politicians' expanding the courts only when the same party controls the House, the Senate and the Presidency.

Yet the evidence is mixed. In a sophisticated recent study, Ashenfelter, Eisenberg and Schwab (1995) find little relation between an appointing President's ideology and the way a judge decides a case. They take all federal civil rights and prisoner cases (cases one might have thought politically charged) in three federal districts, and look for correlations between case outcomes and the identity of the appointing President. Surprisingly, they find no significant relationship.

Logically, the politicization of appointments and the politicization of careers should be complementary: *ex ante* screening and *ex post* monitoring should substitute for each other. An elementary testable implication follows from this: *all else equal, politicians will politicize judicial appointments most strongly in those systems where they exercise the least control over a judge's later career.* In other words, if voters consider it crucial for their representatives not just to enact policies but to implement them as well, then politicians will politicize either appointments or judicial career incentives. If they give their sitting judges only weak political incentives *ex post*, they will screen them politically *ex ante*. If they monitor them more carefully *ex post*, they will screen them less scrupulously *ex ante*. Turn, therefore, from screening to monitoring.

II. *The logic*. Both judges and bureaucrats are government employees. Yet politicians in modern democracies do not usually keep their bureaucrats independent from themselves. Because politicians seldom intervene overtly in bureaucracies, most scholars assumed for decades that bureaucrats ran their own lives. It was a mistake, however, and stemmed from the fact that 'the process of policy administration by autonomous [ministries] is observationally equivalent to that under strict [legislative] control' (Calvert, Moran and Weingast 1987: 501). Ultimately, overt intervention is out-of-equilibrium behaviour. In equilibrium, politicians will not openly intervene. But they will not intervene only because bureaucrats know they *can* intervene, and therefore do what the politicians want from the start.

To test bureaucratic independence, modern scholars instead study times of change. Suppose rival politicians take control, or suppose that the incumbents change their policy preferences. Do bureaucrats track these changes? According to recent studies of the US, they do. Some scholars find that the US Congress (and particularly Congressional committees) controls bureaucrats (Coate, Higgins and McChesney 1990). Others find that Presidents exercise considerable control as well (Moe 1987). Scholars debate the relative power of Presidents and legislators, but few now claim that bureaucrats act autonomously.

Well paid and prestigious to be sure, judges are government bureaucrats all the same. The puzzle is why (or when) rational politicians will treat them differently from their other bureaucrats. Consider three distinct approaches. First, Landes and Posner (1975) suggested that independent courts solved a credible-commitments problem (for which see Williamson 1985). Since politicians sell legislation to interest groups for cash, if rational they will try to maximize their returns from the sales. In the absence of independent courts, they face a credibility problem. They can sell a programme in time one, but in time two they will have an incentive to threaten to kill it unless the interest group pays again. Since interest groups know politicians have that incentive, they will pay less in advance. The inability of politicians to tie their hands *ex post* thus limits the amounts they can extort *ex ante*.

Politicians are not likely to repeal a statute formally. In most legislatures, doing so would require the renegotiation of so many deals that it would not pay to bother. Nevertheless, politicians can often cheaply tell their bureaucrats to ignore a statute. There, to Landes and Posner, is precisely where independent judges matter. By giving constituents the right to enforce legislation in court, politicians can use independent courts to prevent themselves from using bureaucrats to renege on their promises.

As Landes and Posner acknowledged, independent judges will not necessarily enforce a statute according to the terms of the original deal between the politicians and the rent-seeking constituents. Precisely because of their independence, they need not follow 'any canon of statutory construction or . . . any particular approach to legislation . . . Quite the contrary, [they can] develop whatever theories of statutory construction [capture] their fancy' (Epstein 1990: 851). So long as judges only rarely nullify statutes, however, even random nullification will extend the length of a rent-seeking deal. If so, then even completely capricious courts will increase the price that politicians can extract for their statutes.

Politicians also have other ways of making their promises credible. Most obviously, they can select long-term and well-paid party leaders. Suppose that a majority party has high odds of staying in power, that experienced politicians from safe electoral districts control it, and that these leaders earn very large legal or illegal returns from their posts. Effectively, these leaders play a repeated game that earns them efficiency wages. If so, then they will be more likely than other politicians to find independent judges redundant. Hence the testable implication of this theory: *all else equal, judges should be least independent in political jurisdictions where well-paid party leaders from safe seats have stable control over the government.*

Second, McCubbins and Schwartz (1984) argue that independent courts help politicians to monitor their bureaucrats. Politicians, they observed, have the jobs they do because they deliver policies and programmes, rather than just enact them. To do that effectively they need bureaucrats they can trust. Yet most politicians lack a comparative advantage in roaming their agencies to root out agents who are rude, lazy or stupid. They are not, as McCubbins and Schwartz put it, much good at 'police-patrol monitoring'.

Instead, most rational politicians will adopt what McCubbins and Schwartz called 'fire-alarm' monitoring schemes. Rather than monitor their bureaus themselves, they will give constituents the right and the incentive to complain – to sound a 'fire alarm' – if bureaucrats perform inappropriately. One such fire alarm is litigation. In this scheme, politicians can ensure that a bureaucrat does as he is told by giving disaffected constituents the right to sue the government if he does anything else. The suit will notify the politicians that all is not well, and the politicians can then intervene if necessary. To ensure that constituents have the incentive to sue, politicians will keep their judges reasonably independent of the executive branch.

Politicians can also devise 'fire-alarms' other than courts. In some countries, they cultivate the 'personal vote' (Cain, Ferejohn and Fiorina 1987) by maintaining large staffs who regularly help constituents with governmental problems. If so, they will be more likely than other politicians to find independent courts redundant. Hence, again, the testable implication of the theory: *all else equal, judges should be least independent in political jurisdictions where majority politicians offer extensive bureaucratic interventionist services.*

Third, some scholars have tied judicial independence to political turnover in electoral markets (e.g. Ramseyer 1994). Suppose politicians largely solve the credible-commitments and monitoring problems through strong party leaders and large local offices. When in power, they will find that independent judges hamper their ability to do what they want. As a result, they will be more likely to consider independent courts appealing when they are out of power. They will then find independent judges attractive because they reduce their rivals' ability to do as they please.

Accordingly, majority politicians will have stronger incentives to keep courts independent if they expect to lose power soon; they will have weaker incentives if they expect to stay in power long. Posit two countries, A and B. In country A, parties 1 and 2 regularly alternate in power. Party 1 is in power now, but sees only a thirty percent chance that it will stay in power for the next ten years. By contrast, in country B party 1 has been in power for thirty years. Although its leaders cannot be sure they will stay in power, they calculate their odds of remaining in power for the next ten years at ninety percent.

If we hold the credible-commitments and monitoring problems constant, then party 1 has a stronger incentive to keep the courts independent in A than in B. In country B, the odds that party 1 will lose power are low enough for it to have little to gain by keeping courts independent. In country A, party 1 may well lose power soon. Party 2 will then take power, but it too may lose office quickly. Given that both parties in country A anticipate alternating in power, and given that both may want to lower the costs of being out of office, judicial independence can (but need not) emerge as the cooperative equilibrium to this repeated game. Again, the testable implication follows: *all else equal, judges should be least independent in political jurisdictions where one party faces high odds of staying in office.*

Empirics. Testable as these theories may be in form, measurement problems continue to plague scholars in practice. Higgins and Rubin (1980), for instance, explored whether the prospect of promotions limited judicial independence in the US. More specifically, they asked whether federal district judges wrote their opinions with an eye toward a job on the Court of Appeals. Tentatively, they answered 'no'. Although high reversal rates lowered a judge's chance for promotion, the effects were trivial. Had reversals mattered, Higgins and Rubin would have expected older judges to be reversed more often since they would care less about promotion. Consistent with the basic irrelevance of reversals, however, they found that older judges are reversed no more often than younger ones.

In a more recent series of studies, Cohen (1989, 1991, 1992) concluded otherwise. First, he examined sentencing decisions in antitrust cases (1989, 1992). He found that Democratic (though not Republican) judges were more likely to impose higher fines when there was an appellate vacancy in their district (suggesting better odds of promotion). Also, younger judges were more likely to impose harsher sentences than older. Harsher sentences increase promotion odds, Cohen explained, but increase it more among the younger judges since politicians already have substantial information about older judges.

Second, Cohen (1991) studied judicial opinions on the constitutionality of the (officially promulgated) federal sentencing guidelines. He found two effects relevant here. First, judges with crowded dockets were more likely to find the guidelines unconstitutional. Many judges thought the guidelines would increase trials by reducing prosecutorial discretion, and the most over-worked judges were most likely to find them unconstitutional. Second, the judges with the best chance of a promotion to the Court of Appeals were most likely to find the guidelines constitutional. The administration wanted the guidelines, Cohen suggests, and holding them constitutional helped a judge earn a promotion.

Ramseyer and Rasmusen (1997) similarly looked to the effect of potential promotions on judicial output, but used data from Japan. Under the Japanese judicial system, judges from lower courts are appointed to the national judiciary – but not to specific courts in specific cities. As a result, they move from court to court at the whim of the judicial personnel office. That office answers to the Supreme Court, and the Supreme Court is appointed directly by the cabinet. Potentially, therefore, the rotation of lower-court judges could reflect political considerations transmitted to the personnel office through the politically appointed Supreme Court. Ramseyer and Rasmusen asked whether the rotations reflected political factors, and on several dimensions found that they did.

First, during the three-decade long rule of the conservative Liberal Democratic Party (LDP), those judges who joined a leftist bar group were more likely to receive worse assignments. Confessed political unreliability, it seems, translated into a career penalty. Second, if the government was a party to a case, those judges who decided the case against it were more likely to receive worse assignments. Like everyone else, the government litigates cases because it wants to win, and judges who get in the way can suffer. Last, in at least one series of constitutional law cases, judges who decided the law against the ruling party were more likely to receive worse assignments. Some cases raise legal issues dear to the heart of politicians. When judges decide such issues contrary to the way politicians want, they too can suffer.

Crucially but unfortunately, the data from Japan do not let one distinguish among the various theories. During the period at stake, the ruling Japanese party enjoyed strong and stable electoral support; its leaders collected large amounts of legal and illegal cash; and politicians from the ruling party offered their constituents elaborate bureaucratic interventionist services. Whether under the credible-commitments, monitoring or political-variance hypotheses, one would have expected Japanese politicians to have little interest in keeping their judges institutionally independent. According to the evidence, they did not.

Few things are more basic to law and economics than money, and several scholars have asked whether judges face financial incentives in deciding cases. Unfortunately, they reach inconclusive results. Toma (1991) looked at the relation between the US Supreme Court's budget and several measures of the difference between the political complexion of Congress and the political complexion of the Court's decisions. She found both that the more closely the Court follows Congressional preferences, the higher the budget it receives, and that the higher the budget the Court receives, the more it tracks Congressional preferences.

By contrast, Anderson, Shughart and Tollison (1989) took the opposite tack. If by Landes and Posner's logic independent courts are more likely to enforce legislative wealth transfers, then politicians will value independent courts more highly than other courts. If they value them more highly, all else equal they will pay them more money. To prove this proposition, Anderson, Shughart and Tollison studied the salaries of state supreme court chief justices. They found that the salary was positively correlated with how often a court overturns statutes or regulations, and negatively correlated with whether the judges are elected. The more independent the judges (if they overturn legislation often, or if they need not run for the job), the more money they made.

III. Finally, ask when – given constant career incentives – judges will be most likely to decide cases according to the preferences of politicians. To explore the question, Gely and Spiller (1990, 1992) turned to the McCubbins, Noll and Weingast (1987, 1989) model of the way politicians influence bureaucrats (sometimes called 'positive political theory'). To understand the intuition behind the model, take three political principals: the President, the Senate and the House. Collectively, the three can overturn bureaucratic activity by statute, yet each of the three can veto any statute. Because of that veto, each can block any legislation that does not move bureaucratic policy closer to its own preferences.

As a result, these three principals can overturn some – but only some – agency policy. On some agency decisions, there will be other potential policy outcomes that all of the three principals prefer. If so, the politicians will reverse the decision by statute. On other agency decisions, there will be no unanimously favoured alternative. By choosing the latter and avoiding the former, an agency can ensure that its decisions stand. The larger the disagreement among the three principals, the greater the range of non-overturnable policies from which it can pick.

Gely and Spiller argued that this logic explains the game courts play: judges calculate the odds of legislative repeal, and decide cases at the point that is closest to their preferred point but within the set of policies for which there is no unanimously favoured alternative. If judges do this, moreover, Congress will never legislatively repeal court decisions. It will not repeal them, however, only because judges correctly calculate the scope of their discretion and assiduously stay within it. More precisely, as Cooter and Drexl put it:

> The court's discretionary power of interpretation over a given stock of laws corresponds to the set of possible laws that are Pareto efficient relative to the preferences of the decision-makers who must propose and enact fresh legislation (1994: 315).

This theory too yields testable implications, as Ferejohn (1995: 203–11) and Cooter and Ginsburg (1996) made clear. First, the range of discretion which judges have will depend on the extent of the disagreement among the parties holding vetoes over legislation. Judges will appear to act most independently and 'imaginatively' when the disagreement is large. They will seem to decide cases most 'mechanically' when the disagreement is minor.

Second (and importantly for international comparisons) judges will act most independently in presidential systems and least independently in parliamentary systems. In the former, disagreements among the several players with vetoes can give judges wide discretion. In the latter, parliament's nearly exclusive control over legislation will let it easily nullify the effect of a court decision that flouts majority party preferences.

Cooter and Drexl applied this logic to the European Community (EC). They asked how the EC might foster a court that will act independently. Importantly, they concluded that the court's apparent independence will depend on the structure that the EC chooses for its other branches of government. Should it choose unicameral majoritarian rules, the court will seem relatively less independent; should it choose unanimity rules or a bicameral form, the court will appear to act more independently.

There has been some testing of this theory. Using ideological ratings, Spiller and Gely (1992) studied how ideological change in Congress or the Presidency affects the way the US Supreme Court decides labour cases. '[E]ven though Congress may not be actively legislating,' they noted, 'it does not follow that it has actually relinquished legislative responsibility to the Court' (1992: 465). Instead, in labour cases Congressional preferences affect how the Court decides cases, and affect it in ways that account for the institutional structure of the legislative process. As Spiller and Gely put it, 'the Court seems to make its decisions so as to maximize its (ideologically based) preferences, taking into account the relevant political constraints' (1992: 489).

Cooter and Ginsburg (1996) applied the Gely–Spiller framework internationally. They first asked whether the willingness of judges to innovate depends on the number of veto gates in government. After all, the more players who can veto a statute, the harder legislative reversal will be. Second, they asked whether the judicial willingness to innovate is a function of political stability. Again, the more unstable the government, the harder legislative reversal will be. Using a panel of many countries, they predicted (1996: 299) – and found – that:

judicial discretion is lowest in those countries with a low number of vetoes and a high average coalition duration ... Judicial discretion [is] highest in countries with either a large number of vetoes, such as the United States, or low average cabinet duration, such as Italy and Israel.

Three points seem relevant. First, most politicians in modern democracies usually provide judges with substantial (even if incomplete) independence from the parties to the dispute. Second, in many (but not all) modern democracies they also provide judges with substantial independence from themselves. Why (and when) they would do the latter remains largely unanswered. Third, so long as judges incur a non-trivial cost when reversed by statute, they will sometimes follow election returns even when their careers seem insulated from electoral politics. Yet how readily politicians can pass a statute depends on the organizational structure of government. Accordingly, a court's apparent independence will in turn depend on that structure.

J. MARK RAMSEYER

See also AGENCY COST AND ADMINISTRATIVE LAW; BUREAUCRACY; CONSTITUTIONAL ECONOMICS; DIVISION OF POWERS IN THE EUROPEAN CONSTITUTION; JUDICIAL REVIEW; LEGISLATIVE INTENT; POLITICAL CONTROL OF THE BUREAUCRACY; PUBLIC CHOICE AND THE LAW; REGULATORY AGENCIES AND THE COURTS; STATUTORY INTERPRETATION AND RATIONAL CHOICE THEORIES.

Subject classification: 3d; 3e; 5a(ii).

BIBLIOGRAPHY

Anderson, G.M., Shughart, W.F. II and Tollison, R.D. 1989. On the incentives of judges to enforce legislative wealth transfers. *Journal of Law and Economics* 32: 215–28.

Ashenfelter, O., Eisenberg, T. and Schwab, S. 1995. Politics and the judiciary: the influence of judicial background on case outcomes. *Journal of Legal Studies* 24: 257–81.

Cain, B., Ferejohn, J. and Fiorina, M. 1987. *The Personal Vote: Constituency Service and Electoral Independence*. Cambridge, MA: Harvard University Press.

Calvert, R., Moran, M. and Weingast, B. 1987. Congressional influence over policy making: the case of the FTC. In *Congress: Structure and Policy*, ed. M. McCubbins and T. Sullivan (New York: Cambridge University Press) 493.

Coate, M.B., Higgins, R.S. and McChesney, F.S. 1990. Bureaucracy and politics in FTC merger challenges. *Journal of Law and Economics* 33: 463–82.

Cohen, M.A. 1989. The role of criminal sanctions in antitrust enforcement. *Contemporary Policy Issues* 7: 36–46.

Cohen, M.A. 1991. Explaining judicial behavior or what's 'unconstitutional' about the Sentencing Commission? *Journal of Law, Economics, and Organization* 7: 183–99.

Cohen, M.A. 1992. The motives of judges: empirical evidence from antitrust sentencing. *International Review of Law and Economics* 12: 13–30.

Cooter, R. and Drexl, J. 1994. The logic of power in the emerging European constitution: game theory and the division of powers. *International Review of Law and Economics* 14: 307–26.

Cooter, R. and Ginsburg, T. 1996. Comparative judicial discretion: An empirical test of economic models. *International Review of Law and Economics* 16: 295–313.

de Figueiredo, J.M. and Tiller, E.H. 1996. Congressional control of the courts: a theoretical and empirical analysis of expansion of the federal judiciary. *Journal of Law and Economics* 39: 435–62.

Epstein, R.A. 1990. The independence of judges: the uses and limitations of public choice theory. *Brigham Young University Law Review* 1990: 827–55.

Ferejohn, J. 1995. Law, legislation, and positive political theory. In *Modern Political Economy: Old Topics, New Directions*, ed. J. Banks and E. Hanushek (New York: Cambridge University Press): 191–215.

Gely, R. and Spiller, P.T. 1990. A rational choice theory of Supreme Court statutory decisions with applications to the *State Farm* and *Grove City* cases. *Journal of Law, Economics, and Organization* 6: 263–300.

Gely, R. and Spiller, P.T. 1992. The political economy of Supreme Court constitutional decisions: the case of Roosevelt's court-packing plan. *International Review of Law and Economics* 12: 45–67.

Higgins, R.S. and Rubin, P.H. 1980. Judicial discretion. *Journal of Legal Studies* 9: 129–38.

Landes, W.M. and Posner, R.A. 1975. The independent judiciary in an interest-group perspective. *Journal of Law and Economics* 18: 875–901.

McCubbins, M., Noll, R. and Weingast, B.R. 1987. Administrative procedures as instruments of political control. *Journal of Law, Economics, and Organization* 3: 243–77.

McCubbins, M., Noll, R. and Weingast, B.R. 1989. Structure and process, politics and policy: administrative arrangements and the political control of agencies. *Virginia Law Review* 75: 431–82.

McCubbins, M. and Schwartz, T. 1984. Congressional oversight overlooked: police patrols versus fire alarms. *American Journal of Political Science* 28: 165–79.

Moe, T.M. 1987. An assessment of the positive theory of 'Congressional dominance'. *Legislative Studies Quarterly* 12: 475–520.

Ramseyer, J.M. 1994. The puzzling (in)dependence of courts: a comparative approach. *Journal of Legal Studies* 23: 721–47.

Ramseyer, J.M. and Rasmusen, E.B. 1997. Judicial independence in civil law regimes: the evidence from Japan. *Journal of Law, Economics, and Organization* 13: 259–86.

Spiller, P.T. and Gely, R. 1992. Congressional control or judicial independence: the determinants of U.S. Supreme Court labor-relations decisions, 1949–1988. *RAND Journal of Economics* 23: 463–92.

Toma, E.F. 1991. Congressional influence and the Supreme Court: the budget as a signaling device. *Journal of Legal Studies* 20: 131–46.

Weingast, B.R. 1984. The Congressional-bureaucratic system: a principal – agent perspective (with applications to the SEC). *Public Choice* 44: 147–91.

Weingast, B.R. and Moran, M.J. 1983. Bureaucratic discretion or Congressional control? Regulatory policymaking by the Federal Trade Commission. *Journal of Political Economy* 91: 765–800.

Williamson, O.E. 1985. *The Economic Institutions of Capitalism*. New York: The Free Press.

judicial review. A court exercises judicial review when it agrees to hear, and then decide, a case or controversy arising directly or indirectly from an action (or inaction) of a legislative, executive, administrative, or putatively subordinate judicial body. The plaintiff seeking relief from the action ordinarily appeals to a higher law than the one he challenges. The plaintiff may sue to overturn a legislative act by appealing to a constitutional provision, for example, or to a higher, controlling common law precedent.

Occasionally, however, the court itself invokes such a higher law, even though neither party had raised the issue in that form (*Mapp v. Ohio*, *Erie R.R. v. Tompkins*, *Teague v. Lane*, and *Marbury v. Madison*; see also Elhauge 1991: n. 173).

Judicial review finds its fullest development under the United States Constitution ratified in 1789 and various congressional acts defining the jurisdiction of federal courts. But the practice enjoys precedents under the common law of England (*Dr. Bonham's Case*; but see Scalia, 1997: 129–30), and on the same or similar grounds it has clear antecedents in the pre-Revolutionary American colonies (Quincy 1865: 469–88, as quoted in Chase and Ducat 1978: 221). The meaning and significance of judicial review depends crucially on particular constitutional arrangements. Where there is no written constitution or separate provision for a judiciary to review legislation, one does not expect to find the practice flourishing. (But see Salzberger 1993 on the Israeli judiciary.) Accordingly, this discussion concentrates entirely on judicial review in the United States.

While courts may review acts of administrative and regulatory agencies, of chief executive officers (governors and presidents), and decisions of lower courts (both state and federal), today the term 'judicial review' applies most commonly to the judicial scrutiny of legislation.

Legal scholarship on judicial review, not to mention various judges' opinions, attends largely to the problem of an 'unelected' judiciary trumping the decisions of elected representatives (Bickel [1970] 1978; Ely 1980). A mixture of positive science and normative argument, by contrast, marks the treatment of judicial review in the law and economics literature. Since the mid-1960s economists and political scientists, explicitly interpreting the legislative process in game-theoretic terms (see, e.g., Shepsle 1970, 1979; McKelvey 1979), have identified a theoretical instability in the political process arising from the absence of pure-strategy equilibria (Condorcet winner or core) in legislative voting. As well, there has been concern over public policies that share no patent welfare-regarding justifications. Scholars have also developed positive theories of the political process that partly explain the political attractiveness of these policies as a form of welfare-degrading rent-seeking by interest groups and rent-provision by politicians. Those who have investigated either problem sometimes regard the judiciary as a palliative. And, the limitations on governmental action found in the US Constitution, enforced through judicial review, they believe, offer some support for their argument (Aranson 1987). Those scholars who remain more sanguine about the desirability of the challenged public policies, by comparison, have questioned the applicability of rent-seeking and disequilibrium models (Farber and Frickey 1991); they have also asked whether courts might be susceptible to the same problems (Eskridge 1988; Stout 1992; Stearns 1994).

This essay first describes certain aspects of judicial review and then explores these two contributions that economic theory makes to an understanding of it: disequilibrium (from social choice theory and positive political theory), and rent-seeking (from public choice theory). But economic analysis also helps to explain a variety of judicial doctrines and characteristics, and particularly those with special significance for judicial review. These include standing (Jensen, Meckling, and Holderness 1986; Stearns 1995a, 1995b), *stare decisis* (Kornhauser 1989; Macey 1989; O'Hara 1993; Schwartz 1992), and the persistence of an independent judiciary (Landes and Posner 1975; Salzberger 1993).

Hamilton's Federalist Paper No. 78 provides a clear and early gloss of judicial review:

> The interpretation of the laws is the proper and peculiar province of the courts. A constitution is in fact, and must be regarded by the judges as, a fundamental law. It therefore belongs to them to ascertain its meaning as well as the meaning of any particular act proceeding from the legislative body, and, in case of irreconcilable difference between the two, to prefer the will of the people declared in the constitution to that of the legislature as expressed in the statute.

This passage enunciates two principles. First, courts are empowered to interpret both statutory law and the law of the Constitution. When courts interpret statutes and constitutions, which logically precedes judgment, they are engaged in 'statutory construction'. This interpretive activity is crucial, because it can profoundly affect the court's eventual judgment and the future scope of both the Constitution and the law subject to challenge. (See generally Ferejohn and Weingast 1992, Rodriguez 1992, and Shepsle 1992.)

Second, the Constitution is superior to other laws, and all parties must follow its terms. The Supremacy clause of the United States Constitution explicitly provides for this superiority:

> This Constitution, and the laws of the United States which shall be made in pursuance thereof, and all treaties made, or which shall be made, under the authority of the United States, shall be the supreme law of the land; and the judges in every State shall be bound thereby, anything in the Constitution or laws of any State to the contrary notwithstanding. (US Constitution, article VI, clause 2)

This provision does not mean that all federal laws control state actions, for the states enjoy a residuum of sovereignty in matters that the Constitution itself explicitly or by implication delineates as beyond federal powers. (See, e.g., *Printz v. US*, *New York v. US*, and *Gregory v. Ashcroft*.) But where the Constitution allows, and where the federal legislature has enacted appropriate statutes that the Supreme Court finds to preempt the state's action, contradictory state laws or administrative or judicial actions must give way.

ASPECTS OF JUDICIAL REVIEW. A brief discussion of judicial review requires oversimplification and the initial treatment of institutions as independent entities, without endogeneity or strategic responsiveness in their relationships to other institutions. Consider a court, such as the US Supreme Court, engaged in judicial review, and an individual justice on that Court casting one of nine votes. As a matter of positive science, how will the justice vote in a particular case? The matter has received little study in the law and economics literature (but see Posner 1994), although political scientists have attended to it more closely (see, e.g., Rohde and Spaeth 1976).

The justice might vote for the plaintiff-appellant if the opinion writer bases the decision on one argument but for the defendant-appellee if the opinion writer bases it on another (the Chief Justice chooses himself or another Justice to write the opinion if the Chief Justice is in the majority; the senior justice in the majority chooses the opinion writer if the Chief Justice is in the minority). Or, the justice might agree with the majority opinion on the merits but write a concurring opinion; or, he might join the minority (dissenting) opinion or write his own dissenting opinion concurring partly or completely with the other dissenters. It is also not uncommon to find justices concurring with a decision in part while dissenting in part.

One gains an appreciation for the various bases of the justice's votes by considering three cases. In the first, *Griswold v. Connecticut*, plaintiffs challenged a Connecticut statute prohibiting the use of birth control pills and devices (defendants below were convicted as accessories, for giving advice about the use of such methods). There was a plurality opinion, three opinions concurring in the judgment of the Court, and two dissenting opinions. In Justice Stewart's dissent, joined by Justice Black, one finds these words:

> I think this is an uncommonly silly law. [But] we are not asked in this case to say whether we think this law is unwise or even asinine. We are asked to hold that it violates the United States Constitution. And that I cannot do . . .
>
> What provision of the Constitution . . . does make this state law invalid? The Court says it is the right of privacy 'created by several fundamental constitutional guarantees.' With all deference, I can find no such general right of privacy in the Bill of Rights, in any other part of the Constitution, or in any case ever before decided by this Court . . ..

If Justice Stewart had been a legislator, he would have voted against the act, or for its repeal. But as judges, neither he nor Justice Black could find a basis in the Constitution for declaring the Connecticut statute without effect.

In *CTS Corp. v. Dynamics Corp. of America*, the Supreme Court upheld an Indiana statute that makes it difficult to use a hostile takeover to assume control of a corporation chartered there. CTS Corporation had challenged the statute, on the grounds that a federal statute (the Williams Act) preempted the state's ability to regulate corporate takeovers in the manner the statute sought to accomplish. Justice Scalia's concurring opinion wholly rejects any public policy grounds for overturning Indiana's statute:

> Nothing in the Constitution says that the protection of entrenched management is any less important a 'putative local benefit' than the protection of entrenched shareholders, and I do not know what qualifies us to make that judgment (95).

Justice Scalia does advert to the public policy question at issue. But he dismisses it as a basis for judgment in the same manner as does Justice Stewart in *Griswold*. 'I do not share the Court's apparent high estimation of the beneficence of the state statute at issue here. But a law can . . . be both economic folly and constitutional. The Indiana . . . [law] is at least the latter' (96–7).

Finally, in *Planned Parenthood of Southeastern Pennsylvania v. Casey*, the Court heard a challenge to the Pennsylvania Abortion Control Act of 1982. The Act required, *inter alia*, that a woman's husband be notified in most cases before such a procedure could occur. Commentators widely interpreted *Planned Parenthood* to be an attack on the Court's first major abortion decision, *Roe v. Wade*. In her plurality opinion Justice O'Connor acknowledges the controversy surrounding *Roe* and *Planned Parenthood* (850–851) and the possibility that the Court's ruling in *Roe* was mistaken (857). But in reaffirming *Roe* she grounds her analysis partly on *stare decisis*, and particularly on the reliance people have come to place on a woman's right to have an abortion unfettered by state statutes that would impermissibly limit that right.

> [F]or two decades of economic and social developments, people have organized intimate relationships and made choices that define their views of themselves and their places in society, in reliance on the availability of abortion in the event that contraception should fail. The ability of women to participate equally in the economic and social life of the Nation has been facilitated by their ability to control their reproductive lives. . . . The Constitution serves human values, and while the effect of reliance on *Roe* cannot be exactly measured, neither can the certain cost of overruling *Roe* for people who have ordered their thinking and living around that case be dismissed (856).

These three cases identify aspects of judicial review that distinguish it from an ordinary legislative process. In *Griswold*, Justice Stewart's dissent and vote on the merits grow out of a concern for institutional legitimacy, quite apart from the public policy grounds on which he might have voted to overturn the Connecticut law. In *CTS Corp.* Justice Scalia's vote on the merits upholds a statute that he plainly finds less than desirable. And in *Planned Parenthood* Justice O'Connor's plurality opinion upholds a public policy and a prior decision of the Court (*Roe*) that, some speculate, she finds less than agreeable. In all three examples the respective justice takes a position that does not relate to, indeed may go against, his or her own public policy preferences. That is, the grounds for these opinions and votes on the merits remain orthogonal to the public policy dimensions involved. Hence, it may not be possible to place an appellate judge's position on an issue dimension common to legislators faced with the same or similar questions (Schwartz 1992). This problem alone makes the placement of the judiciary within the lawmaking process a difficult matter.

JUDICIAL REVIEW AND LEGISLATIVE DISEQUILIBRIUM. The Arrow problem finds limited though increasing attention in the literature on judicial review. But there are really two separate questions that the literature often conflates. The first concerns Arrow's theorem itself, a topic within the normative literature of social choice theory (Arrow [1951] 1963; Mueller 1989: 96–111; 384–407). Arrow, and those whose work explores the problem he identifies, first posits a set of normative criteria that a mechanism aggregating individual preferences into a social choice should meet. Arrow then asks if any mechanism, or institution, simultaneously can meet those conditions in the presence of ordinal preferences. He proves that no such institution exists.

The second issue concerns the positive question: within a particular institution does a pure-strategy equilibrium exist? And if it does exist, what is its location? The positive science aspect of disequilibrium holds implications for judicial review. First, in interpreting the meaning of a constitutional provision, judges may find some difficulty in understanding what that provision means. To resolve doubt they sometimes advert to historical records, including those reporting on the constitutional convention itself (Farrand et al. [1911] 1986). This method is subject to the attack of those who prefer to interpret the Constitution according to its plain meaning, and not the intent of those who wrote it (Scalia 1997). But the problem that economic analysis identifies with this method is that the constitutional convention itself was a political institution, subject to the same disequilibrium possibilities that afflict any other aggregative procedure. Indeed, Riker (1984) identifies a case of strategic manipulation during the constitutional convention, which led to the provisions for an electoral college to choose the president. The underlying induced preference configuration likely had no equilibrium.

Second, when judges seek to interpret state and federal statutes, the disequilibrium problem grows more severe. Even when a pure-strategy equilibrium prevails in a voting body, leading to the passage of legislation, there may not be a single maximand that all legislators share. And even if such a maximand prevails, although with different solutions (spending levels, for example) for different legislators, there may be only one legislator at the equilibrium (median) position, and legislators' expectations for the law's execution and effects may differ. If no pure-strategy equilibrium exists, of course, then the legislative result may reflect accident or agenda control or even artifice through the process of proposing and voting on amendments (Riker 1958). Hence, interpreting legislative actions in pursuit of statutory construction may remain difficult, perhaps impossible, leading Shepsle (1992) to refer to legislative intent itself as an 'oxymoron'. (But see Posner 1986, compared with Posner 1982, 1985.)

Third, there is the problem that Ely (1980: 4–5) identifies as 'the central problem . . . of judicial review: a body that is not elected or otherwise politically responsible in any significant way is telling the people's elected representatives that they cannot govern as they'd like'. One finds appellate judges often expressing this sentiment, as the opinions in *Griswold, CTS Corp.*, and *Planned Parenthood* suggest. But if the legislative process itself is palpably incoherent, if legislative majorities happen by accident, by agenda control, or by strategic dithering with the amendment process, then the connection of voters to their representatives may be happenstance, and of representatives to the laws they pass may be chimerical. Accordingly, because of the conclusions of positive political theory concerning disequilibrium, the oft repeated normative deference that judges give to legislation may find its basis substantially weakened.

The disequilibrium problem extends well beyond questions about the desirability of judicial review. More generally, it holds implications for all democratic institutions and representative government itself. And, it sets limits on the ability of those institutions to form welfare-regarding, coherent public policies (Riker 1982). In its most extreme form, disequilibrium implies that democratic institutions remain wholly incoherent, making any outcome possible (Schofield 1978; McKelvey 1979). Not surprisingly, the literature in positive political theory contains important attempts to limit the domain of incoherence (Tullock 1979; Miller 1980, 1983a), to identify conditions (usually uncertainty) that avoid it (Shepsle 1970; Coughlin and Nitzan 1981; Ledyard 1984), and to find institutional arrangements that have the effect, whether intended or not, of circumventing the problem (Shepsle 1979; Shepsle and Weingast 1981).

Concerning the position that in the light of legislative disequilibrium judges should apply judicial review more aggressively, the most insightful set of criticisms relies on the notion that collegial appellate courts are themselves voting bodies. Hence, their decisions too remain subject to disequilibrium. While the literature on disequilibrium in judicial processes is not extensive, it is growing. Murphy (1964: 85–87) makes an early passing mention of the problem and raises the issue of the power of the chief justice to order the agenda. He also briefly explores the order of voting (justices vote in reverse order of seniority). But he appears not to believe that the problem is serious.

Easterbrook (1982, 1983) develops a careful analysis to show that, over time, the possibility of disequilibrium could lead the Supreme Court to contradictory, incoherent results. He offers as examples the Court's decision in *United States v. DiFrancesco*, which ruled that a prosecutor may seek an increase in a defendant's penalty, which the Court followed one year later with *Bullington v. Missouri*, holding that a prosecutor may not seek an increase in a defendant's penalty at a separate trial, which will be held anyway in the light of other events (Easterbrook 1982: 811 n. 25). Easterbrook offers other real and theoretical examples, to show that disequilibrium may be widespread in Supreme Court opinions, compared one to another. As Epstein (1990: 841) summarizes the matter, '[t]he problem of cyclical voting . . . can independently undermine the output of judges just as it undermines the output of any political body.'

Eskridge (1988) and Farber and Frickey (1988) have raised serious questions about the likelihood that the legislative process is incoherent, and about the judiciary's role as a corrective to legislative incoherence. But the most extended criticism of the disequilibrium literature appears in the work of Stearns (1994; see relatedly Stearns 1995a; 1995b; 1997). He is far less concerned than are Easterbrook and Epstein, for example, with unalloyed expectations of disequilibrium arising from legislative and judicial processes. Stearns, like Farber and Frickey, as well as

Eskridge, observes that all voting bodies are subject to disequilibrium and its related decisional incoherence. Accordingly, he identifies a proposed reliance on judicial review to correct political failures as an instance of the 'Nirvana Fallacy', the comparison of a real institution (the legislature) with a theoretical ideal (a process with pure-strategy equilibria) (Demsetz 1969). The proper allocation of decisional authority, therefore, requires the comparison of real institutions, warts and all, and the interrelationships between and among them.

Stearns constructs a variety of examples, and adverts to some actual examples, to show that decisions taken by collegial, appellate courts can and do cycle. But he also goes through an extended exercise to explore the manner in which each institution – Court and Congress – violates one or more of Arrow's conditions. Congress gains coherence, for example, because it can remain with the status quo. But the Supreme Court must respond when an appellant properly places a case before it. In this comparative respect congressional decisions may appear more coherent than those of the Court. But the Court's decisional range is limited, whereas that of Congress is far less so. Hence, in this respect the Court's decisions may appear more coherent. The Court also can adopt background rules that, in Stearns's view, help to stabilize the legislative process, especially when the Court confronts statutes that have vague or contradictory provisions.

As a theoretical matter, the possibilities for disequilibrium remain a function of rules, procedures, and naturally occurring phenomena such as the nature of preferences arising from the questions that the members of an institution must answer. These possibilities seem far more general than a close attention to Arrow's social choice conditions would warrant. (Hence, the importance of keeping separate the otherwise closely related analyses of social choice and positive political theory.) So, for example, the Supreme Court may hear appeals whose possible range of answers is extremely limited, compared with the far more expansive issues that Congress faces. Without more extensive theoretical and empirical studies, however, it is not possible to say in which institution there persists a greater likelihood of disequilibrium.

Is it likely that disequilibrium characterizes legislative, and more particularly, judicial decision making? The empirical evidence remains inconclusive. Riker (1958, 1986) spent a lifetime collecting examples of cyclical majorities. But his complete list seems vanishingly small as a proportion of total congressional enactments. It is a simple matter to find instances where the Supreme Court has produced contradictory, incoherent decisions (Easterbrook 1983; Epstein 1990; Stearns 1994). But one (perhaps unsatisfactorily) can explain those instances by a change of mind, by the departure of one justice and the elevation to the Court of another, and by a distinguishing of cases that a simple vote on the merits fails to disclose.

Surely, there is evidence of strategic voting on the Supreme Court. Caldeira et al. (1996), for example, show that this activity is pervasive. The justices, when choosing which cases to hear, consistently take into account the likely decisions of their colleagues. Hence, they act more like price searchers, oligopolists, than like price takers in competitive markets. Rohde and Spaeth (1976) find similar activities with respect to opinion assignment and reactions to threats to the Court itself. And Schwartz (1992) explains individual justices' choices by incorporating a trade-off between the decision on the merits and the formation of a precedent. As Caldeira et al. note, these theoretical works and empirical findings tend to confirm the substance of judicial biography and popular writing (see, e.g., Woodward and Armstrong 1979: ch. 20), concerning the presence of strategic actions in Supreme Court deliberations.

While strategic action is neither necessary nor sufficient to establish that an underlying disequilibrium in preferences exists, it is empirically suggestive. But there is also suggestive empirical evidence to the contrary. Rohde and Spaeth's (1976) study finds a substantial amount of regularity in a variety of Supreme Court decisions. They construct a three-dimensional model, including the justices' individual attitudes toward 'freedom' (civil liberties), 'equality', and 'New Dealism' (government *versus* business), as reflected by their votes on the merits. Their scaling technique succeeds in capturing nearly all of the variations in the votes of individual justices, and in predicting the Court's overall decisions.

More important, their analysis demonstrates a substantial amount of consistency in the justices' ideologies, compared two issues at a time. These findings tend to support Dahl's (1957) early claim, that the Supreme Court does indeed 'follow the election results'. But national elections tend to collapse issues along single dimensions, over which each voter's preference remains single-peaked. Hence, the electorate at large will tend to display stability, not disequilibrium. If Supreme Court justices do recapitulate voters' conceptualization about issues, doctrinal concerns about institutional legitimacy to the contrary, then the Court itself should render far more stable decisions than much of the preceding discussion would suggest.

JUDICIAL REVIEW AND LEGISLATIVE RENT-PROVISION. The second positive approach to judicial review, though one with patent normative implications, focuses on rent-seeking and rent-provision. The classical example is governmental cartelization of producers/sellers in a market, to restrict output, raise price, and capture rents–returns to factors greater than necessary to bring goods and services to market. But the term 'rent-seeking' now covers a wider set of phenomena, the public provision of private benefits at collective cost, including most legislative actions that enjoy less than obvious welfare justifications.

Rent-seeking and disequilibrium are two closely related phenomena (Aranson 1989). Suppose, for example, that voters' preferences form a cyclical majority. If so, a candidate who takes forthright positions on the issues will lose to an opponent who delays announcing his own public policy intentions; for, under such circumstances there is no Condorcet winner, a strategy that defeats or ties all other strategies. In response to this problem, an election candidate might adopt a 'strategy of ambiguity', removing from the electorate information about his intentions (Shepsle 1970, 1972). But this strategy will make voters' acquisition of information more costly, leading to a deeper form of rational ignorance (Aranson 1989/1990), which in turn will deprive voters of information about special interest bargains. Hence, rent-seeking and rent-provision will grow less costly.

Rent-seeking, legislative rent-provision, and the degradation of welfare that accompanies them are widely disparaged. Not surprisingly, several proposals seek to restrict their ambit through judicial review. One set of proposals offers general rules that would have courts restrict or give no effect to the associated legislation. Easterbrook (1984), for example, asks judges to apply the old maxim that 'statutes contrary to the common law should be strictly construed'. Sunstein (1984) proposes a similar strategy. As well, Easterbrook would have judges faithfully and narrowly apply the terms of rent-providing legislation, as expressed within the four corners of the original law. Rents would then erode merely by the subsequent entry of competition from substitute goods or services. But courts would not extend protection against these new competitors, whom the original legislation did not contemplate. Macey (1986), in a similar vein, urges judges to read statutes as if they were welfare-regarding, thereby resolving any ambiguities against interpretations that would perpetuate welfare losses. And Siegan (1980) argues for a renaissance of Lochner-era substantive due process review of economic legislation.

Aranson, Gellhorn and Robinson (1982) propose an attack on rent-providing regulation by a renewal of the delegation doctrine (*A.L.A. Schechter Poultry Corp. v. United States*). They build on a theory of Fiorina (1982, 1986), which identifies the conditions under which legislators prefer the execution of the laws through regulation (the administrative process) to their execution through the judicial process. Regulation, Aranson et al. argue, becomes the preferred technology of rent-provision when some costs of delivering the rents fall on cohesive groups or firms. Congress then enacts a general statute empowering an agency to regulate in 'the public interest, safety, and convenience', but without further instructions apart from background administrative law. Aranson et al. would have the courts give such legislation no effect, on the theory that Congress would find it too costly to enact statutes that effectively settle the question of winners and losers. Mashaw (1985) attacks this proposal on every imaginable ground.

A second, more specific set of proposals finds a close correspondence between constitutional limits on government, on the one hand, and economic liberties unrestrained by rent-providing (or other forms of welfare-degrading) legislation, on the other. Epstein's writing dominates this genre. He (1987) proposes that the commerce clause (US Constitution, article I, sec. 8, clause 3) be read narrowly, to limit most federal regulation of the production of goods and services. So, for example, 'commerce', as in *United States v. E.C. Knight*, would be distinguished from 'manufacture', which would remain largely beyond the boundaries of congressional action. He (1984) argues for the judicial invalidation of much state regulation through the strict enforcement of the contracts clause (US Constitution, article I, sec. 10, clause 1). And, he (1985) would have courts give sweeping scope to the 'takings clause' of the fifth amendment, to invalidate an entire landscape of legislation where losers from legislation go uncompensated.

Considering the persistence of such proposals, one would expect them to be a constant part of future legal and economic writing. But what are the chances that any one of them will gain acceptance sufficient to trigger more intensive judicial review? One contribution, that of Landes and Posner (1975), suggests that such an occurrence remains unlikely. Their theory of judicial action relies on the (specifically unstated) assumption that the legislative process takes place along rent-seeking margins. The theory explains why courts ordinarily acquiesce in legislative decisions and simultaneously remain 'independent' from legislative attempts to control them. The essential idea is that those interest groups that demand publicly provided benefits from the legislature, as well as those legislators who supply such benefits, must choose how long each government programme will be in existence. *Ceteris paribus*, each prefers a programme that runs in perpetuity to one that lasts for only a period or two. Both prefer permanence, *inter alia*, because it economizes on transaction costs. And legislators also prefer it because they can capitalize their *pro rata* share of payments flowing from the perpetual grant (of rents) they have made, even if they will not long remain in the legislature.

Two forces threaten the persistence of these bargains. The first occurs within the legislature itself. Future lawmakers who did not participate in the original bargain always find it in their interest to rescind old programmes, to pay for new ones. But several legislative institutions and rules make it difficult to do so. These include the committee system, which gives high demanders a veto over rescinding legislation, and the filibuster in the Senate, which only a supermajority can end. These processes make the passage of new legislation difficult, but they make rescinding of old legislation commensurately more costly. Landes and Posner suppose that while these rules and practices make it more difficult to enact new programmes, the permanence they convey to existing bargains more than overcomes this potential disadvantage.

The existence of a court that can review legislation provides a second threat to legislation whose benefits flow over long periods. An individual legislator, a group of legislators, or even a majority of the legislature, finding itself stymied in its attempt to abrogate old bargains, may turn to the courts to do their work for them. Statutory construction is sufficiently elastic to allow such a process, but the courts ordinarily will not engage in second guessing the original legislation. In that sense the courts maintain their independence from the political process, but the cost of this independence is a limitation on their ability to act as censors of undesirable legislation. The Supreme Court's decision in *CTS Corp.*, reviewed earlier, is of this character.

This understanding of judicial review appears pessimistic from the perspective of the proposals just reviewed. The judiciary, according to the Landes–Posner theory, has become a permanent fixture in making interest-group legislation permanent. Indeed, the 'Court goes beyond not tampering with prior enactments to finding ways to enhance their survival. . . . [E]ven when the Court confronts an otherwise unconstitutional statute, it usually tries to narrow . . . [its] scope . . . or otherwise interpret its terms so that it will pass constitutional muster. . .'. The aim of such readings is 'to preserve as much of the original bargain's intent as possible' (Aranson and Ordeshook 1985: 147–8). (See e.g. *Kent v. Dulles*; *National Cable Television Association v. United States.*)

The final question concerning judicial review as a palliative for legislative rent-provision is its desirability. There are strong arguments against the practice. Some of these arguments focus on the appropriateness of rent-provision to offer equality to minorities (Miller 1983b). The notion is that rent-provision can form a workable technology for redistribution, thereby enhancing political stability. But this kind of policy calculation may underlie a theory of Pareto-improving redistribution (Hochman and Rogers 1969). And, the calculation would require an accounting for the costs of rent-seeking, including the opportunity costs of not redistributing using superior technologies.

There remain stronger arguments against the use of judicial review as a tool to suppress legislative rent-provision. Elhauge (1991), who appears not to be an apologist for rent-seeking, does not find the arguments for palliative judicial review to be wholly persuasive. First, he predicts that a distaste for particular public policies, if imported into the legal process, would simultaneously import those value judgments that inform the negative assessment itself. In Elhauge's view, one reminiscent of Justice Holmes's dissent in *Lochner v. New York* ('The Fourteenth Amendment does not enact Mr. Herbert Spencer's Social Statics'), this concentration on substance, not process, is inappropriate to the judicial function.

Second, the legal process itself is susceptible to interest-group politics, and that susceptibility would intensify were judicial review to become a tool for suppressing rent-provision. Confirmation hearings would be even more controverted than they have already become, and the rent-seeking process would begin before the stage of nomination itself. Considerations of judicial pay scales and perquisites of office would rise to the level of national policy debates. And legislative attempts to control appellate jurisdiction would flourish.

Third, one cannot predict the direction that legal change would take were courts to use judicial review in the manner proposed. Because this kind of review would move rent-seeking explicitly into the judicial process, it could harness that review itself to embed the resulting policies more firmly while making desirable legal change more difficult. Elhauge here adds a version of Miller's argument, that rent-seeking may remain the only way for minorities to counter majoritarian excesses.

JUDICIAL REVIEW IN A DEMOCRATIC POLITY. Elhauge's final argument brings the discussion full circle. Apparently ignoring the role of rational ignorance in instantiating welfare-degrading public policies, he speculates that legislators may provide rents because citizens of a democracy want it that way. This argument returns us to core normative questions about judicial review in a democracy, including speculations about institutional competence and legitimacy.

These questions remain difficult to address because they are fraught with ideology on both (or all) sides of the issue of judicial review in a democracy. That is, one seldom finds a discussion of judicial review as an abstract proposition. Instead, one finds commentators adverting to the desirability of judicial review in a specific policy context. Consider again, for example, the arguments over the Supreme Court's first major abortion decision, *Roe v. Wade*. The popular press, and nearly all commentary today, cite *Roe* for the proposition that a woman has a privacy right that incorporates her derivative right to terminate a pregnancy. And that is a reasonable gloss of the Court's holding.

What often goes unrecognized, however, is the federalism issue, coupled with the issue of democratic governance to which Ely adverts. *Roe* challenged a Texas statute that outlawed abortions except those performed to save a woman's life. That is, *Roe* also stands for the proposition that the fourteenth amendment provides the Supreme Court with grounds for overturning the decisions of a democratically elected legislature. Some find arguments about legislative incoherence to be inadequate for withdrawing judicial deference, and they oppose judicial review as a means for restricting the ambit of rent-providing legislation. (See, e.g., Elhauge 1991; Farber and Frickey 1991.)

Accordingly, these authors reject appeals to ideology as the basis for judicial review, while they argue that preferences for stable political processes and against welfare-degrading legislation are themselves ideological. Their problem in justifying *all* forms of judicial review of which they *do* approve, perhaps including the decision in *Roe*, thus grows immeasurably more difficult. And, one could construct a similar example to attack the argument that courts should review legislation aggressively to achieve virtually any public policy goals.

PETER H. ARANSON

See also AGENCY COST AND ADMINISTRATIVE LAW; COMPARATIVE ADMINISTRATIVE LAW; JUDICIAL INDEPENDENCE; LEGISLATIVE INTENT; POLITICAL CONTROL OF THE BUREAUCRACY; STATE POWER; STATUTORY INTERPRETATION AND RATIONAL CHOICE THEORIES.

Subject classification: 3c; 3e; 5a(ii).

CASES

A.L.A. Schechter Poultry Corp. v. US, 295 US 495 (1935).
Bullington v. Missouri, 451 US 430 (1981).
CTS Corp. v. Dynamics Corp. of America, 481 US 69 (1987).
Dr. Bonham's Case (1610) 8 Co. Rep. 1136.
Erie R.R. v. Tompkins, 304 US 64 (1938).
Gregory v. Ashcroft, 501 US 452 (1991).
Griswold v. Connecticut, 381 US 479 (1965).
Kent v. Dulles, 357 US 116 (1958).
Lochner v. New York, 198 US 45 (1905).
Mapp v. Ohio, 367 US 643 (1961).
Marbury v. Madison, 5 US 137 (1803).
National Cable Television Assoc. v. US, 415 US 336 (1974).
New York v. US, 488 US 1041 (1992).
Planned Parenthood of Southeastern Pennsylvania v. Casey, 505 US 833 (1992).

Printz v. US, No. 95–1478, decided June 27, 1997.
Roe v. Wade, 410 US 113 (1973).
Teague v. Lane, 489 US 288 (1989).
US v. DiFrancesco, 449 US 117 (1980).
US v. E.C. Knight, 156 US 1 (1895).

BIBLIOGRAPHY

Aranson, P.H. 1987. Procedural and substantive constitutional protection of economic liberties. *Cato Journal* 7: 345–75.

Aranson, P.H. 1989. The democratic order and public choice. In *Politics and Process: New Essays in Democratic Thought*, ed. G. Brennan and L.E. Lomasky, New York: Cambridge University Press.

Aranson, P.H. 1989/1990. Rational ignorance in politics, economics, and law. *Journal des Economistes et des Etudes Humaines* 1: 25–42.

Aranson, P.H. 1990. Models of judicial choice as allocation and distribution in constitutional law. *Brigham Young University Law Review* 1990: 729–825.

Aranson, P.H., Gellhorn, E. and Robinson, G.O. 1982. A theory of legislative delegation. *Cornell Law Review* 68: 1–67.

Aranson, P.H. and Ordeshook, P.C. 1985. Public interest, private interest, and the democratic polity. In *The Democratic State*, ed. R.Benjamin and S. Elkin, Lawrence, KS: University Press of Kansas.

Arrow, K.J. 1951. *Social Choice and Individual Values.* 2nd edn, 1963, New York: John Wiley and Sons.

Bickel, A.M. [1970] 1978. *The Supreme Court and the Idea of Progress.* New Haven: Yale University Press.

Caldeira, G.A., Wright, J.R. and Zorn, C.J.W. 1996. Strategic voting and gatekeeping in the Supreme Court. Paper prepared for presentation at the Annual Meeting of the American Political Science Association, August 29-September 1, San Francisco.

Chase, H.W. and Ducat, C.R. 1978. *Edward S. Corwin's The Constitution and What it Means Today.* 14th edn, Princeton: Princeton University Press.

Coughlin, P.J. and Nitzan, S. 1981. Electoral outcomes with probabilistic voting and Nash social welfare maxima. *Journal of Public Economics* 15: 113–21.

Dahl, R.A. 1957. Decision-making in a democracy: the Supreme Court as a national policy-maker. *Journal of Public Law* 6: 279–95.

Demsetz, H. 1969. Information and efficiency: another viewpoint. *Journal of Law and Economics* 12: 1–22.

Easterbrook, F.H. 1982. Ways of criticizing the court. *Harvard Law Review* 95: 802–32.

Easterbrook, F.H. 1983. Statutes' domains. *University of Chicago Law Review* 50: 533–52.

Easterbrook, F.H. 1984. The Supreme Court, 1983 term. Forward: the Court and the economic system. *Harvard Law Review* 98: 4–60.

Elhauge, E.R. 1991. Does interest group theory justify more intrusive judicial review? *Yale Law Journal* 100: 31–110.

Ely, J.H. 1980. *Democracy and Distrust: A Theory of Judicial Review.* Cambridge, MA: Harvard University Press.

Epstein, R.A. 1984. Toward a revitalization of the contracts clause. *University of Chicago Law Review* 51: 703–51.

Epstein, R.S. 1985. *Takings: Private Property and the Power of Eminent Domain.* Cambridge, MA: Harvard University Press.

Epstein, R.A. 1987. The proper scope of the commerce power. *Virginia Law Review* 73: 1387–1455.

Epstein, R.A. 1990. Independence of judges: the uses and limitations of public choice theory. *Brigham Young University Law Review* 1990: 827–55.

Eskridge, W.N., Jr. 1988. Politics without romance: implications of public choice theory for statutory interpretation. *Virginia Law Review* 74: 275–338.

Farber, D.A. and Frickey, P.P. 1988. Legislative intent and public choice. *Virginia Law Review* 74: 423–69.

Farber, D.A. and Frickey, P.B. 1991. *Law and Public Choice: A Critical Introduction.* Chicago, IL: University of Chicago Press.

Farrand, M., Hutson, J.H. and Rapport, L. 1911. *The Records of the Federal Convention of 1787.* Revised edn, New Haven: Yale University Press, 1986.

Ferejohn, J.A. and Weingast, B.R. 1992. A positive theory of statutory interpretation. *International Review of Law and Economics* 12: 263–79.

Fiorina, M.P. 1982. Legislative choice of regulatory forms: legal process or administrative process? *Public Choice* 39: 33–66.

Fiorina, M.P. 1986. Legislator uncertainty, legislative control, and the delegation of legislative power. *Journal of Law, Economics, and Organization* 2: 33–51.

Hochman, H.D. and Rogers, J.D. 1969. Pareto optimal redistribution. *American Economic Review* 59: 542–57.

Jensen, M.C., Meckling, W.H. and Holderness, C.G. 1986. Analysis of alternative standing doctrines. *International Review of Law and Economics* 6: 205–16.

Kornhauser, L. 1989. An economic perspective on stare decisis. *Chicago-Kent Law Review* 65: 63–92.

Landes, W.M. and Posner, R.A. 1975. The independent judiciary in an interest-group perspective. *Journal of Law and Economics* 18: 875–901.

Landes, W.M. and Posner, R.A. 1976. Legal precedent: a theoretical and empirical analysis. *Journal of Law and Economics* 19: 249–307.

Ledyard, J.O. 1984. The pure theory of large two-candidate elections. *Public Choice* 44: 7–41.

Macey, J.R. 1986. Promoting public-regarding legislation through statutory interpretation: an interest group model. *Columbia Law Review* 86: 223–68.

Macey, J.R. 1989. The internal and external costs and benefits of stare decisis. *Chicago-Kent Law Review* 65: 93–112.

Mashaw, J. 1985. Prodelegation: why administrators should make political decisions. *Journal of Law, Economics, and Organization* 1: 81–100.

McKelvey, R.D. 1979. General conditions for global intransitivities in formal voting models. *Econometrica* 47: 1085–1112.

Miller, N.R. 1980. A new solution set for tournaments and majority voting: further graph-theoretical approaches to the theory of voting. *American Journal of Political Science* 24: 68–96.

Miller, N.R. 1983a. The covering relation in tournaments: two corrections. *American Journal of Political Science* 27: 382–5.

Miller, N.R. 1983b. Pluralism and social choice. *American Political Science Review* 77: 734–47.

Mueller, D.C. 1989. *Public Choice II.* New York: Cambridge University Press.

Murphy, W.F. 1964. *Elements of Judicial Strategy.* Chicago: University of Chicago Press.

O'Hara, E. 1993. Social constraint or implicit collusion? toward a game theoretic analysis of stare decisis. *Seton Hall Law Review* 24: 763–78.

Quincy, J. 1865. *Reports of Cases.* Boston: Little, Brown & Co.

Posner, R.A. 1982. Economics, politics, and the reading of statutes and the Constitution. *University of Chicago Law Review* 49: 263–5.

Posner, R.A. 1985. *The Federal Courts: Crisis and Reform.* Cambridge, MA: Harvard University Press.

Posner, R.A. 1986. Legal formalism, legal realism, and the interpretation of statutes. *Case Western Reserve Law Review* 37: 179–217.

Posner, R.A. 1994. What do judges and justices maximize? (the same thing everybody else does). *Supreme Court Economic Review* 3: 1–41.

Riker, W.H. 1958. The paradox of voting and congressional rules for voting on amendments. *American Political Science Review* 52: 349–66.

Riker, W.H. 1982. *Liberalism Against Populism: A Confrontation between the Theory of Democracy and the Theory of Social Choice.* San Francisco: W.H. Freeman & Co.

Riker, W.H. 1984. The heresthetics of constitution making: the presidency in 1787, with comments on determinism and rational choice. *American Political Science Review* 78: 1–16.

Riker, W.H. 1986. *The Art of Political Manipulation*. New Haven: Yale University Press.

Rodriguez, D.B. 1992. Statutory interpretation and political advantage. *International Review of Law and Economics* 12: 217–31.

Rohde, D.W. and Spaeth, H.J. 1976. *Supreme Court Decision Making*. San Francisco: W.H. Freeman & Co.

Salzberger, E.M. 1993. A positive analysis of the doctrine of separation of powers, or: why do we have an independent judiciary? *International Review of Law and Economics* 13: 349–79.

Scalia, A. 1997. *A Matter of Interpretation: Federal Courts and the Law*. Edited by A. Gutmann with commentaries by G.S. Wood, L.H. Tribe, M.A. Glendon, and R. Dworkin. Princeton: Princeton University Press.

Schofield, N. 1978. Instability of simple dynamic games. *Review of Economic Studies* 45: 575–94.

Schwartz, E.P. 1992. Policy, precedent, and power: a positive theory of Supreme Court decision-making. *Journal of Law, Economics, and Organization* 8: 219–52.

Shepsle, K.A. 1970. A Note on Zeckhauser's 'Majority Rule with Lotteries on Alternatives': a case of the paradox of voting. *Quarterly Journal of Economics* 84: 705–9.

Shepsle, K.A. 1972. The strategy of ambiguity: uncertainty and electoral competition. *American Political Science Review* 66: 555–68.

Shepsle, K.A. 1979. Institutional arrangements and equilibrium in multidimensional voting models. *American Journal of Political Science* 23: 27–59.

Shepsle, K.A. 1992. Congress is a 'they,' not an 'it': legislative intent as oxymoron. *International Review of Law and Economics* 12: 239–56.

Shepsle, K.A. and Weingast, B.R. 1981. Structure-induced equilibrium and legislative choice. *Public Choice* 37: 503–19.

Siegan, B. 1980. *Economic Liberties and the Constitution*. Chicago, IL: University of Chicago Press.

Stearns, M.L. 1994. The misguided renaissance of social choice. *Yale Law Journal* 103: 1219–93.

Stearns, M.L. 1995a. Standing and social choice: historical evidence. *University of Pennsylvania Law Review* 144: 309–462.

Stearns, M.L. 1995b. Standing back from the forest: justiciability and social choice. *California Law Review* 83: 1309–1413.

Stearns, M.L. 1997. *Public Choice and Public Law: Readings and Commentary*. Cincinnati: Anderson Publishing Company.

Stout, L.A. 1992. Strict scrutiny and social choice: an economic inquiry into fundamental rights and suspect classifications. *Georgetown Law Journal* 80: 1787–1834.

Sunstein, C.R. 1984. Naked preferences and the Constitution. *Columbia Law Review* 84: 1689–1732.

Tullock, G. 1979. The general irrelevance of the general impossibility theorem. *Quarterly Journal of Economics* 81: 256–70.

Woodward, B. and Armstrong, S. 1979. *The Brethren: Inside the Supreme Court*. New York: Simon & Schuster.

juries. The jury is a very old institution, but it is not the normal human way of dealing with crimes or disputes. If we look at the world as a whole it has not been used a great deal. The more normal ways are a professional judge or judges or, in many cases, simply an executive officer who has judicial decisions as one of his duties. The district commissioner of the old British Empire, the magistrate in the old Chinese Empire, and the Roman Emperor are all examples.

As an introduction to the study of the jury, let us begin by inquiring why anyone might want a jury to make decisions as opposed to the other two methods that I have just mentioned. Let us begin with a little investigation of relatively pure theory.

ATHENIAN JURIES. Consider, for example, Athens. I should here emphasize that the origin of the American or English jury was not the Athenian jury. Indeed the Norman jury from which our system started was quite radically different. It seems unlikely, granted the fact that this was before the full revival of classical learning, that any of the people involved actually even knew about the Athenian jury. Nevertheless, our present jury oddly enough resembles the Athenian jury more closely than it does its actual historical antecedents.

The Athenian jury is not only to some extent similar to ours but also permits a more sensible theoretical investigation than do the early juries which were in fact the ancestors of ours. The voting population, which was a large part of the total population, assembled on the Pynx to vote on various governmental matters.

We can divide the things that they dealt with into two rough classes, depending on the importance of the issue. Clearly, deciding individual legal cases would tend to be less important than: 'Shall we go to war?' Going to the Pynx and voting was a tedious activity, so tedious that many of the citizens only went there occasionally. A way of factoring out the less important cases would seem sensible, and hence the delegating of law cases to a smaller group.

One way of doing this would be to draw a random sample of the potential voters and let them hear the evidence and make up their mind on the less important decisions. This was the method chosen by Athens. There could be two possible justifications for this. The most important one is simply that it would produce, with some random variance, the same solution as would the meeting of the entire citizen body on the Pynx dealing with the same case.

Obviously this random variance could be easily calculated by modern statistical methods to which the Athenians had no access. Nevertheless, they were presumably aware of the fact that on occasion juries would bring in a different result than would the entire people if it had been presented to them. In a way it was a low cost method of approximating a meeting of the entire body politic.

In so far as juries are drawn randomly this is still true, although our present juries are small enough that the random variance would presumably be quite high. Note that the random variance here would depend on what one might call the strength of the evidence on both sides. In conclusive cases, the citizen body voting as a whole would presumably be close to unanimous and hence random samples drawn from it would tend to come close to unanimity too. In more difficult cases the citizen body might split, so one would expect that the juries would have a good deal of variance in their outcome. This would account for the failure to use juries for such things as declarations of war.

RATIONALE FOR JURIES, I. There are two possible explanations for this desire to get a decision similar to what the populace as a whole have produced. One of these is simply a democratic feeling that what everybody wants is what should be done. The majority, in other words, is its own justification.

Even if one doesn't feel that the majority should control such things as criminal cases one might still feel that domestic peace would be best maintained if decisions were always those which the majority would probably approve. Thus, the jury would produce a result which could be depended on not to set off riots or other difficulties.

This argument would apply not just to democracies but to despotisms. Napoleon was a great proponent of the use of jury. Probably he was less interested in whether John Smith did indeed murder Jane Smith than in preventing popular discontent over the outcome of the case. If the case is decided by a random sample of the population, disturbances are on the whole unlikely because the population will probably approve of the decision and will, in any event, not blame the despot. Whether this is important or not, I do not know.

RATIONALE FOR JURIES, II. We return later to the question of getting the same decision by the jury method as the populace as a whole would reach. Let us turn now to the second possible reason for regarding the jury as desirable: that it is a good way of getting at the truth. Mr Simpson either did or did not murder his wife. Is the jury or, in this case, two juries, a good way of reaching this decision?

I have difficulty in believing that anyone would think that it is a good way to reach the truth. In so far as I know there is no place in our entire governmental or private decision making processes where we call in a group of twelve people who know nothing about the subject, have advocates on both sides present arguments, require unanimity in most cases, and then accept their decision. The US Constitution, Article seven, says 'No fact tried by a jury shall be otherwise re-examined in any court of the United States than according to the rules of common Law'.

In any event, bias is by no means absent from the jury. Today, in 1997, we are in the process of recovering from the two jury trials of Mr Simpson for murder. In the first trial a jury which consisted of ten African-Americans, one Mexican-American and one white woman, found him innocent.

The civil suit was decided by a non-African-American jury. This jury found him guilty. Thus, as can be seen, there was a complete racial break on the decision in this matter. These were exceptional cases, however. Normally the juries do not have this degree of ethnic purity. Racially mixed juries do not show such apparent extreme racial determinism.

In practice, the higher courts sometimes find ways of avoiding the decision of a jury once made, but it is certainly true that this group of citizens, who know very little about the case when they come in, and frequently know very little about it at the end of trial (a matter which we will discuss below), usually makes the final decision. This is true even if the subject matter is the execution of an individual or a civil suit in which perhaps hundreds of millions of dollars are involved. The famous *Texaco v. Pennzoil* case involved more than half a billion dollars.

It should perhaps be mentioned that although the jury is probably a pretty good measure of what the average citizen would do, in the United States most non-federal judges are subject in one way or another to an election process and hence are probably apt to respond to the average person's preferences also. The judicial selection process tends to be complicated and perhaps heavily biased, but is still subject to popular control.

Judges in most state courts are probably not as close to the average citizen as would be a randomly selected jury, but they are not wildly different. In the 1980s a man who believed in the Law of Moses, i.e. the Bible as the ultimate law code, was *elected* to the Texas Supreme Court. This was apparently because he had the same name as a recently deceased, highly popular Senator.

ACCURACY OF JURY. Consider the jury procedure as a way of determining the truth. The author of this essay has published several books containing measurements of the likely error in jury cases. I also used it as a theme in my presidential address to the Western Economic Association Annual Meeting in 1995. I have also dealt with it in a number of unpublished lectures. None of these computations has aroused comment. This is quite notable, because the empirical data that I used to calculate these error measures have always been collected by others, who have themselves never used them to calculate the probable accuracy of the courts.

I rather suspect that jury accuracy or inaccuracy is a taboo subject. After all, any person is subject to the prospect of being falsely accused of a crime and finding that he has to convince a group of twelve people that he is innocent. Thinking about the likelihood that the twelve people will go wrong is painful and apparently most scholars refrain from doing so.

POSSIBILITY OF CORRUPTION. Another possibility is the feeling that the majority is more likely to be factually right than is the decision of some specialist or a high-ranking executive official. When I talk to people about this they normally present bias and bribery as arguments for the jury. I see no reason to believe that the specialist is more likely to be biased than the people as a whole. Aristides was, after all, exiled, Socrates put to death, and Aristotle found it necessary to flee Athens. Jury bias, of course, would be in the direction of current public opinion.

The bribery argument is to some extent true since directly bribing a large number of people would be difficult. Still, historically popular assemblies have been strongly influenced by combining the decision on one proposal with another, the second proposal being to give everybody or some powerful block some advantage. American Justices of the Peace were for a long time compensated by keeping half of any fine they levied. It is frequently alleged that this led them to be particularly likely to convict. Juries would probably respond to a similar fee system much like the Justices of the Peace. Fortunately, this is not our practice. It should be pointed out that popular assemblies and for that matter elected assemblies do behave that way. The farm programme of practically any democratic government may be used as an example.

There is a better example in Athens itself. The Athenian government developed the habit, voted on by the citizens, of paying a fee to every citizen who turned up to vote. This had much to do with the decline of Athenian power since it led to fiscal stringency and a decline in appropriations for the navy.

Nevertheless, preventing bribery of judges should be fairly easy if the government in fact wants to do it. In order for the judge to be bribed he must let the litigants know that he is in the market. In other words, he must discreetly advertise. A police that really wanted to prevent corruption on the part of judges (or juries) could presumably look out for such advertisements and make the arrest.

ANGLO-SAXON ORIGINS. So much for a basically theoretical discussion of juries. We will return to factual measures of how they perform in a moment, but let us first consider actual historic origins of the jury in England and Normandy about the time of the Conquest. As we will see the early juries were almost the exact opposite of present juries. Instead of selecting a group of people who did not know the case and presenting evidence to them, the jury was expected to make the decision on its own without evidence because the people selected were thought to know the truth.

It should be realized that in a small isolated village such as most of the English population lived in around 1100, that its leading citizens would know who had committed crimes recently is not a terribly unlikely hypothesis. In any event there was to some extent in the previous Anglo-Saxon government and in the Norman government in France a system of obtaining information for government use by conscripting a small collection of normally prominent and trustworthy local citizens, and asking them to make statements under oath. The Domesday Book, for example, seems to have been compiled largely by this method.

This procedure was carried out with respect to crimes and civil suits, in so far as there were civil suits in those days, as well as for collecting data for taxes and the like. In the beginning a person that was found guilty of a crime by some of his more prominent neighbours, who had heard no evidence, could ask for a trial by ordeal or abjure the realm. If he were a noble he could, of course, choose trial by battle.

HISTORICAL DEVELOPMENT. The gradual shift of the jury from a collection of people who were expected to know whether the defendant was guilty or innocent to a system where they were expected to make their decision on the evidence is not well documented.

In 1219 the Lateran Council prohibited priests from participating in trials by ordeal, and since the priest's presence was necessary in such trials, England suddenly found itself without any real trial procedure at all. Although the history here is rather vague, the English courts seem then to have fallen back on the jury.

The original jury clearly was assumed to know the truth, with the consequence that it was not necessary to present evidence; but, with time, evidence began to be presented. Even though defendants were legally prohibited from having a lawyer, producing evidence which might be helpful was something which the defendants could still do, and of course the crown would produce evidence on the other side.

There is once again some difficulty here, but it would appear that with time the jury which decided that somebody should be tried and the jury which actually conducted the trial (if the defendant was not simply 'known' to be guilty by public knowledge) became separate. The juries, however, still depended very strongly on their own local knowledge. Indeed as late as the reign of Edward VI it was formally decided that the evidence could not overbalance the prior knowledge of the jury.

It should be emphasized that the juries, even when they began to be primarily people who listened to evidence and made a decision on that, were not random selections from the population. They tended to be substantial upper-class citizens.

To the present day a member of the peerage has the right to be tried by the House of Lords, although it has been quite a while since any of them has availed him or herself of the right. It seems likely that if one did, the right would rapidly disappear.

In the United States, on the other hand, from the beginning we had a much wider part of the population eligible for juries. In recent years England has followed in the same path. Of course the introduction of the arrangement under which lawyers can play a considerable role in selecting who actually sits on the jury is also a relatively recent innovation.

CONTINENTAL PROCEDURE. If we leave the English-speaking countries, there are still various remnants of Napoleon's desire to impose the jury all over Europe. Indeed it is even being expanded: Spain has just adopted the jury as its basic trial method, and the jury has been adopted in some parts of Russia since the reform. Considering the nature of the Russian judiciary, that was probably an improvement. In most places where the Napoleonic juries have left behind some remnants, only very special cases are tried by jury.

There is a good deal of difference in jury procedures. Some of the Swiss cantons until recently used a jury of fifteen, which convicted on two-thirds majority and acquitted on a simple majority. In the American and English jury, unanimity is generally required, so hung juries are quite possible. In recent years a number of states in the United States have adopted ten out of twelve for at least civil juries and in some cases juries may be set at numbers other than the sacred twelve. The author of this essay was called as an expert witness in a case where there were only six jurors.

Recently in a number of European countries there has been another effort to get laymen into court proceedings. The bench in a trial will consist of one professional judge and two laymen. The way the laymen are selected varies from country to country, but they normally hold office for only very short periods of time. The actual trial is largely conducted by the professional judge, although the laymen are of course free to ask questions, and the three of them then retire and make their decision.

The argument for this, and it is also sometimes offered as an argument for the jury, is that they do not want the procedure to be too legalistic. To be frank I have never understood this. If you don't like the laws, the sensible thing to do is to change or repeal them, not keep them on the statute books but then deliberately fail to enforce them.

EMPIRICAL STUDIES. But to return to the issue of jury accuracy and the facts, we find scattered through judicial opinions and legal commentaries remarks about 'the great practical knowledge' of the jury and nearly no research to indicate that this is indeed 'great'. There is, however, some research which makes it possible to make calculations on the accuracy of our courts.

Kalven and Zeisel at the University of Chicago sent letters to judges in about three thousand cases in which they asked them various questions about individual cases. These were all jury cases although somewhat more than half of American trials are conducted by the judge alone.

One of the questions was whether they agreed with the jury. In one-quarter of the cases they did not. Kalven and Zeisel (1966) say you cannot tell how accurate the jury is because you do not know what the actual truth is, but if the judge and jury disagree, at least one of them must be wrong. When they agree it is possible that they are both wrong. This is an elementary problem in high school algebra. The minimum number of errors which will generate the numbers reported by Kalven and Zeisel is about one case in eight.

Baldwin and McConville (1979) repeated more or less the same experiment in Britain, with considerably more methodological sophistication. Their sample was somewhat smaller, but the numbers permit calculating the accuracy of the courts with about the same results as Kalven and Zeisel. Note that they, like Kalven and Zeisel, did not calculate the accuracy themselves.

There is another obvious way of measuring the accuracy of juries, which is to let a number of juries watch the same trial. There is only one case in which this was even experimented with. It was in Chicago and was given up before any significant results had been developed.

EXPERIMENTS. It is possible, however, to produce a film strip of a case and then show that to a number of juries. Presumably the juries would not be quite so conscientious in making their decisions as if something really turned on them, but it is still a good research design. Hastie, Penrod and Pennington (1983) used this method. They took a perfectly genuine murder case and with the assistance of a trial judge impanelled, one after another, sixty-nine juries.

These were ordinary juries conscripted in the usual way and then asked if they wished to participate in an experiment, or go back into the regular pool. About 75% chose to participate, so these juries were relatively normal, except that they had passed only an abnormally brief *voir dire* procedure, which is a part of a normal trial that permits the attorneys to do some things to make the jurymen more likely to be biased on their side.

The experimental case was presided over by the judge who presided over the original case and the prosecuting and defence attorneys were those who participated in the original case. In general, the original case was duplicated as closely as was practicable.

There were four possible outcomes here. The defendant made a rather feeble effort to convince people that he acted in self defence. This was largely ignored. This left the choice of one of three outcomes, first degree murder, second degree murder, or manslaughter, for the jury to decide. The jury verdicts were split: 6 first degree murder, 39 second and 20 for manslaughter. Four juries were hung. The judge and the two attorneys thought that second degree murder was the correct decision, and the jury in the actual trial had reached the same conclusion.

This performance is better than random, but far from distinguished. It is likely that juries have more difficulty with essentially legal questions than with matters of fact. Since the distinctions between the various types of illegal killing are less than perfectly clear, the variance here may have been greater than in cases where only factual matters must be decided. Advocates of the jury, however, never suggest that they should not decide cases where they must judge legal problems as well as factual.

Hastie et al. made no effort to compute the accuracy of the juries. Their experiment had been designed to test which of various jury voting rules was best. The results cast no light on this question. Their failure to calculate accuracy from their data, however, does suggest the existence of some sort of taboo on that subject.

After the trial was over a test was administered to the juries to test their recall of the evidence and the judge's instructions on the law. The jurymen answered the questions right 60% of the time for facts and 30% in matters of law.

LEGAL COMMENTS ON THE JURY. It is not only the more or less scientific studies I have been discussing thus far that show inaccuracy of the jury. The courts themselves seem to distrust them. There are a large number of rules requiring the exclusion of various types of evidence. The Nutshell series is a set of reference books for law students. Paul F. Rothstein in the Evidence volume (1970) summarizes the standard view:

> Many (if not most) of the exclusionary rules of evidence exclude evidence because judges have felt that juries would be inclined to give the evidence more effect than they ought. That is, juries could not be trusted to give the evidence its logical, rational weight, or to perceive that it had none, but instead would, perhaps because of the emotional impact of the evidence, allow it to be more persuasive or influential than they should. This can happen where the evidence has some warranted weight as well as where it has none, so long as there is the danger that the jury will not evaluate it properly, but will over-inflate its role to an extent that renders the trial better off without the evidence, but clearly the courts do not have much confidence in juries.

FURTHER ON THE RATIONALE OF THE JURY. So far I have talked about the reasons for believing that the jury is not a wonderful technique, if what one is trying to do is to find out the truth. If what one is trying to do is to produce the democratic outcome, i.e., the outcome which the people as a whole would vote for if they were given a chance, the jury is an excellent technique. If that is our purpose, however, we could make large economies by throwing away most of the existing law libraries and shortening legal training.

If the jury is as bad as I think it is, why do we continue to use it? It could be that I am mistaken, but it is also possible that there are good reasons why even an inept scheme will be continued. For several centuries doctors regularly bled people for whatever ailed them, although bleeding (with a dirty knife) is bad for almost every disease.

The most obvious explanation is simply inertia. That was no doubt one of the reasons that bleeding was continued for such a long time, and in political matters inertia is certainly a very strong factor.

Although inertia is an obvious explanation, it is usual for Public Choice scholars like myself to try to seek out some special group or power which has either the ability to create some institution or to retain it. In this case the obvious group is the trial lawyers. Historically, lawyers have earned a good deal of money by arguing before jurors and there is no doubt that the length of time and skill needed to present a case to jurors is a good deal higher than that needed to present a case to three judges, as in the continental procedure.

This doesn't seem a terribly strong argument over the long period of history, but American legislatures have been dominated by lawyers throughout most of our history.

Today in the United States there is a very obvious set of very powerful interests that want to retain the jury. These are the tort lawyers, who are very organized, very wealthy, and who give very large gifts to the candidates for various government offices. There are also experts who testify before the jury for high fees. Their major expertise is looking sincere, and that would probably not impress judges. The strength of this combination is illustrated by the long series of lawsuits which forced Dow-Corning into bankruptcy in spite of the weak, indeed almost nonexistent, scientific evidence.

Further, the tort lawyers are experts at convincing the average citizen. They have beaten a number of referendums aimed at weakening their power by the use of basically the same persuasive strategy as in influencing a jury.

Once again, it seems that the pressure that the organized lawyers can exert would have been less in the past. In England, where the barrister and solicitor appear to have less power, the jury seems to be in a process of gradual abandonment. It's pretty much gone in civil litigation and there are signs that it will be sharply restricted in criminal matters also.

The present discussion of the reasons for retaining the jury are not very conclusive. Indeed, some of my colleagues believe that inertia is the obvious and total explanation and I am far from certain that they are wrong. It may be that inertia is simply reinforced by the pressure groups I have listed above.

JURY SELECTION. Rules differ a good deal from place to place, but in much of the United States, particularly in state courts, attorneys are permitted to question the potential jurors and throw some of them out either because they can convince the judge that the candidate would be biased, or arbitrarily since they usually have a certain number of arbitrary challenges.

In recent years the Supreme Court has been taking an interest in this matter and ruling that the use of arbitrary challenges to get rid of blacks or women may be improper. In the first Simpson trial the defence seems to have used its powers to get rid of as many whites as possible, but the courts have not held that improper.

The federal courts have a great deal of freedom in choosing their jurors. My own recent experience was in a case of considerable importance where they had called 114 jurors to be sure that they would have enough for the case after the attorneys had objected to some.

The Chief Judge of the federal court in Tucson went around the 114 candidates and asked each one of them three or four questions. Then we were removed and the lawyers who had been sitting quietly while this was going on flocked to the bench. We were then called back and 14 (12 members and two alternates) were announced as the jury by the judge, and the rest of us dismissed.

This is a federal court where the judges have a good deal of discretion, and apparently the Chief Judge thought that this was a suitable system. In the state court, in general, the matter would have taken a great deal more time and the attorneys would have questioned the candidates in the hope of selecting people who, if not biased in favour of their side, at least were not biased against it.

I should perhaps say that if you are called for jury and don't want to serve, simply exhibiting bias or incoherence during this question period will get you out; say: 'I am completely impartial, I just want to know if he was drunk at the time.'

FURTHER RESEARCH. It used to be that juries were instructed not to speak to anyone about the deliberations after they were over, and it was contempt of court to question them. This is no longer so and the jurymen are routinely questioned after the trial by the attorneys who want to find out what they did right or wrong and reporters who hope for a story. In so far as I know, academics have not devoted serious research time to this kind of questioning of jurors.

Here in Tucson we are about to have a new experiment. Several trials are going to be carried out with television cameras not only in the court room but actually in the jury room. The results are to be broadcast over cable. The number of cases is very small and I doubt that the jurors will behave under these circumstances as they would in a closeted jury. I am not sure that the information will be valuable, but students probably should look at it.

SUMMING UP. The jury is not a good technique and personally I would prefer to be tried by a professional judge if I were falsely accused. Nevertheless, it is not true that juries do not take the matter seriously. The evidence we have indicates that they think the matter over and discuss it. The problem is they may not fully understand the case or they may be seriously biased. Further, as a general rule they do not know the law, and the judges' instructions are normally confusing. If they did know the law they would still be likely to follow their own ethical principles even if they conflicted with the law.

The statement that the United States is a country ruled by law and not by men is false when juries make the final decision.

GORDON TULLOCK

See also ACCURACY IN ADJUDICATION; CIVIL PROCEDURE IN THE USA AND CIVIL LAW COUNTRIES; CONTRIBUTORY AND COMPARATIVE NEGLIGENCE: EMPIRICAL COMPARISONS; ENGLISH COMMON LAW; EXPERIMENTAL LAW AND ECONOMICS; INALIENABILITY; PLEA BARGAINING; A COMPARATIVE APPROACH; PRODUCTS LIABILITY; RULES OF EVIDENCE AND STATISTICAL REASONING IN COURT; TULLOCK, GORDON.

Subject classification: 5a(iv); 5e.

CASES

Texaco, Inc. v. Pennzoil, 729 SW2d 768 (Tex. 1987).

BIBLIOGRAPHY

Baldwin, J. and McConville, M. 1979. *Jury Trials*. Oxford: Clarendon Press.

Hastie, R., Penrod, S. and Pennington, N. 1983. *Inside the Jury*. Cambridge, MA: Harvard University Press.

Kalven, H. and Zeisel, H. 1966. *The American Jury*. Boston: Little-Brown.

Rothstein, P.F. 1970. *Evidence in a Nutshell*. St. Paul, MN: West Publishing Company; 5th edn, 1974.

Tullock, G. 1971. *The Logic of the Law*. New York: Basic Books.

Tullock, G. 1980. *Trials on Trial*. New York: Columbia University Press.

Tullock, G. 1996. Legal heresy. *Economic Inquiry* 34(1): 1–9.

just compensation. *See* COMPENSATION FOR REGULATORY TAKINGS; EMINENT DOMAIN AND JUST COMPENSATION; TAKINGS.

justice. The concept of justice informs our sense of justice, rather than being formed by it. The concept escapes circularity, resting as it does on foundations that are independent of notions of justice.

I. FINDINGS AND JUDGMENTS. Answers to questions about what justice demands are commonly, and misleadingly, called judgments. Misleadingly, because the same word is used to denote two radically different types of statement, and much hinges on the difference.

One type deals with points of fact. They are true or false, for facts are ultimately ascertainable, and once ascertained, exclude *bona fide* disagreement. They are *intersubjectively* valid. Points of fact in a strict sense include 'points of law', for what a text states, what the custom of a place is, or what conduct a social norm dictates, are also ascertainable. The world being what it is, texts may be poorly drafted, evidence may be blurred or missing, custom and convention may be falling into disuse. Findings in the face of such imperfect information may not be reached without a degree of help from judgments, which then appear as the product of personal intuition about what the facts would show if only they were fully accessible. For example, at one time interpersonal comparisons of utility were represented as 'objective', more like findings to support advocacy of income redistribution. (Later, these efforts came to be seen as misdirected because the problem was no longer conceived as one of facts but of value judgments.) In their role as substitutes for information, judgments function as surrogate findings.

Judgments properly speaking are expressions of moral intuitions, sharply distinct from surrogate findings which seek to express empirical conjectures. Judgments reflecting moral intuitions answer questions of justice that are deemed not to be matters of fact. Such judgments may seem right or wrong to another, perhaps rival moral intuition, but they are neither true nor false. Nothing in the rules of logic or epistemology compels two *bona fide* persons to agree on the same judgment; there can be no question of intersubjective validity. A shared religion, shared value judgments, shared interests may bring different persons' moral intuitions closer to each other, and the contrary may occur when these influences affect different persons differently. Genuine judgments are intrinsically personal, enjoying a latitude that has no very obvious limits.

Latitude in judgment means discretionary justice. The task of a firm, well-defined concept of justice is to reduce discretion in which my say-so can oppose your say-so. It accomplishes this, in a seeming paradox, by constricting the scope of judgment in justice.

It will be argued in this essay that the world of justice is neatly divided into two adjacent realms, with no overlap between them. The two realms are ruled by two regulating maxims, '*suum cuique*' (to each, his own) and 'to each, according to . . .' (i.e. one reference variable). In the realm of '*suum cuique*', the concept of justice leaves little space for judgments. Findings do nearly all the work. Where, on the other hand, 'to each, according to . . .' is the master rule, there is an irreducible role left to judgment. This is perhaps no very bad thing as long as discretion is kept in its irreducible place.

If the thesis presently to be unfolded is anywhere near right, the concept of justice requires that where findings furnish complete answers, they should be left to do so. The persistent invasion of one realm of justice by the regulating maxim of the other brings incoherence, confusion and discredit to justice.

Disorderly minds, discretionary justice. Conceptual analysis often has recourse to two sources, the behavioural and the linguistic. They furnish evidence of how people understand a concept as witnessed by their reactions and by their use of the corresponding words in ordinary speech.

By the first source, then, a just state of affairs is one that people agree to. However, outside actual contracts, agreement may not be signified by any positive act. It may be tacit acceptance, which in turn may reveal nothing more definite than acquiescence born of indifference or impotence. An enormous latitude in states of affairs is compatible with tacit acceptance. Moreover, one and the same mind can manifest tacit acceptance of mutually incompatible states of affairs. Many theories of justice 'finesse' the problem of tacit acceptance by postulating hypothetical agreements that would be reached under specified conditions, e.g. under ignorance of one's particular identity, endowments and interests, under uncertainty, under a desire to agree to anything reasonable, under mutual insight into each other's intentions, and so on. However, what hypothetical persons would agree to in hypothetical circumstances, while perhaps an interesting subject of speculation, cannot reliably predict what actual people will agree to in actual circumstances, and reveals only one of many possible versions of what they understand by 'just'.

Is usage of words like 'just' or 'fair' in ordinary speech a better witness to the common understanding of the concept? People will unhesitatingly say 'Due process of law should be observed (but) the wife-slayer should not get off by hiring high-priced lawyers'; 'People are free to spend their own money as they choose (but) should not get better medical care by paying more for it'; or 'The given word must be kept and contracts honoured (but) great inequalities of income and wealth are unjust'. The near-impossibility of reconciling the two members of these and similar pairs does not prevent them from being uttered in the same breath.

It is well known from social choice theory that it is not, in general, possible to obtain a coherent hierarchical ordering of states of affairs by aggregating, according to a plausible rule of aggregation, disparate individual orderings of such states. We may find X ranked above Y, Y above Z but Z above X. If collective entities, such as a society, were supposed to have a collective mind, we should have to say that it was a disorderly one, unable or unwilling to sort out its own incoherences. When one and the same individual is found to hold incoherent preferences, opinions, judgments, unconsciously and without embarrassment disagreeing with himself, the disorderly mind is not a symptom of the impossibility of adding up orderly ones, but a fairly predictable feature of human imperfection.

Disorderly minds can harbour mutually incompatible judgments, and discretionary justice. This is not to suggest that people should wake up and tidy up their minds. It is to suggest that the concept of justice needs more coherent foundations than most people's understanding of what is just.

Before justice: some foundations. Manifestly, justice is not a self-evident concept that reveals itself to the intuition of everyman. To what extent can one derive it from elements more basic, more self evident than itself, and that are independent of, and prior to, any notion of justice? If it is a composite, what are its components; if an edifice, what are its foundations?

Five foundation stones seem to bear most of its weight, doing so unobtrusively, beneath the surface. They are *verifiability* and *falsifiability*; *feasibility; harm*; and *trust*. Only briefly identified here, their role in carrying the edifice will emerge in detail in subsequent sections.

'There is a hippopotamus in the room' is an affirmation we can both verify and falsify with the same ease. 'There is a needle in the haystack' is a statement that the person affirming it can verify, but that we can only falsify with great difficulty and, in the limiting case of the infinitely great haystack, not at all. All data statements, i.e. statements with empirical content that, if confirmed, can pass for findings, are either verifiable, or falsifiable, or both. Which they are (and if they are both, which confirmatory operation is less onerous) appears, in an obvious but little noticed manner, to govern the placing of the burden of proof on one of a pair of contradictory answers to a question of justice. The allocation of the burden of proof, in turn, gives rise to such crucial principles as the presumptions of liberty, of innocence, of title and of equal treatment.

Feasibility sets limits to the requirements of justice in the same truistic way as 'ought implies can' does to the commands of morals. A person's feasible set of acts – what his environment and his possessions and claims on others permit him to choose – will generally contain some acts that sufficient reasons show to be inadmissible. These acts are unjust because they are inadmissible on independent grounds, and not inadmissible because they are unjust. No circularity is involved, as there would be if ruling an act admissible depended on prior knowledge of what justice required. All residual acts that have, for the time being, no sufficient reason speaking against them, are by implication, and for the time being, admissible. They are 'liberties'. Infringing them is unjust because they are liberties in the absence of reasons to the contrary, rather than being liberties because it would be unjust to infringe them. More concisely, liberty is the baseline; it is the restrictions upon it that need to be justified.

Sufficient reasons for ruling feasible acts inadmissible cannot be exhaustively classified, but some can be catalogued with some certainty. One class of such reasons has to do with harm, another with trust, both of which are foundation stones in their own right of the concept of justice.

Whoever cripples me, slanders me or takes away what is mine and what I value harms me in a non-trivial way. This is not a trite proposition, and some may even consider it far from self-evident, if only because neither 'non-trivial' nor 'mine' are non-controversial. As to the former, it is perhaps fair to say that when a harm is really on the borderline, the question whether it just passes muster as non-trivial is itself relatively trivial. As to the latter, what is duly 'mine' is clearly a central preoccupation of any analysis of justice. It cannot be resolved right at the outset, and must for a little while be held in abeyance. Notwithstanding any reservations on this score, harm is a robust enough idea to serve in the argument from feasibility to admissibility and hence to justice.

Trust enters into justice in a fundamental, constituent way through what one might call the belief-soliciting nature of statements. When making a statement, a speaker conveys words to a listener with the general objective of inducing in the latter a degree of belief – and the higher the better – that the statement is true or that he, the speaker, holds it to be true. The intrinsic purpose of saying *these* words must be to induce such a belief, for otherwise it would not matter whether it was these words or some others that were conveyed. The intrinsic purpose of a promise, a particularly important type of statement, is to induce a belief in the promisee that the promise will be fulfilled, or failing that, that the promisor intends to fulfil it. The promise is essentially a trust-soliciting statement. Breach of the promise betrays the trust that the promise was intended to induce. Contract is reciprocal promise. Whatever other reasons may be marshalled in support of the institution of contract, a self-evident one is that default betrays the trust the defaulting party has solicited. As such, it is an unjust act. It is perfectly possible to accept this conclusion, derived from the responsibility assumed by the promisor when he solicits the trust of the promisee, even if the proper remedy for the breach of promise is in dispute. An influential view in modern jurisprudence holds that when the breach of a contract causes no assessable damage, no remedy is applicable. In this view, when a contract is partly executed, remedy is restitution of the defaulter's gain or the damage caused by the default, while if the contract is unexecuted, remedy need only be brought for damage caused by the reliance of the plaintiff on its expected execution. This view appears to excuse the breach if it causes no damage to the promisee's interest. It reflects 'rights-based' theories of justice that derive rights from interests and obligations from rights. Such theories commingle issues of justice with those of welfare, and are not conducive to a clear concept of justice.

II. CONSTITUENT PRINCIPLES. Principles can be identified that rest on the foundations described in the preceding section and, perhaps together with other and compatible ones that are not specifically identified, constitute justice. Three such principles seem necessary, though we should not expect them to be sufficient, to constitute the essential concept: *responsibility*, *presumption* and *convention*.

Responsibility. The principle of responsibility results from the relation between a state of affairs and its putative cause – a relation that is normally a matter of empirical findings. A state of affairs in which we find disabled orphans, destitute old people, young people vainly looking for something useful and gainful to do, a region devastated by flood, an industry dying on its feet is readily described as an unjust world. Calling it unjust as distinct from sad or infuriating or crying out for some help, however, is implicitly to impute it to an unjust act committed by someone at some stage. Failing such imputation, one would in effect be saying that injustices can be self-generating – loose talk at best, nonsense at worst.

In the occasionally helpful language of game theory, Nature is a player whose moves have no discernible motive. Nature does not, as far as we can tell, seek to maximize anything. Nor does it deliberately help or hinder the human players who do. To say that an unjust state of affairs has come about without anyone committing an unjust act that could have caused it is saying that Nature has committed an unjust act. People sometimes do say this of Nature or of God in ordinary speech. They may even call Nature, God, history, chance, 'the system' or some similarly elusive entity 'responsible'. But they do not mean the responsibility that is a ground for being called to account, and if they did, they would sound as strange as the primitive tribe that burns the effigy of the river demon for causing the flood, or the medieval villagers who punished the cattle guilty of straying into the standing crop. Such doings would be thought laughable by the very thinkers who hold that what justice demands first and above all is the undoing of the effects of chance, the accidents of heredity and history and the acts of Nature on human lives.

It is not within our scope to speculate what the Herculean task of ceaselessly undoing what Nature keeps doing would require in terms of social and economic organization. On the other hand, it is pertinent to the concept of justice that the task of evening out the work of chance would entail arranging redress, not for injustices in the sense of acts that call for restitution and retribution, but for every human act that was either helped or hindered by chance. People would have to bear residual responsibility for the consequences of their own choices. Which consequence was imputable to choice and which to chance would have to be judged, offering almost infinite scope to judgmental justice and making it conceptually so vague as to be virtually indeterminate. This may not be the chief objection to it, but for the present purpose it seems telling enough.

It may be worth making it explicit that if an act of Nature, say a calamitous flood, is held to be an injustice to the flood victims, then the actor committing the injustice cannot be made responsible for repairing it. If the injustice is to be repaired just the same, the repair must be exacted from those who had the prudence or blind luck not to build their homes on the flood-plain; but making them repair the injustice they have not committed is an injustice, suggesting that a concept of justice that demands this is incoherent, a product of disorderly minds. If the non-victims are to be made to help the victims of the flood, some other ground than justice, e.g. some notion of an interpersonal sum of welfare, must be invoked to defend the injustice involved.

Presumption. A hypothesis and its negation form a pair such that it suffices to verify one member of the pair to falsify the other, or vice versa. A feasible act is either sufficiently harmless, unobjectionable, hence free, or it is not sufficiently harmless, objectionable, liable to sanction, unfree. A person is either innocent, or guilty. A holder either has title to an asset in his possession, or he has not. A case (raising a question of justice) is either relevantly like another case, or it is not. It is obviously redundant to prove one member in such pairs *and* disprove the other. The burden of proof need only be placed on one of the two, but it must be placed on one of them for a conclusion to be reached at all. Whichever side the burden of proof is placed, the opposite side is treated as the privileged hypothesis; a presumption is established in its favour. Unless the contrary hypothesis is successfully proved, the privileged hypothesis is presumed to be true and for the time being treated as such. Just as the presumption of innocence means that a man is treated as innocent until he is proved guilty, so the presumption of guilt means that he is treated as guilty until he is proved innocent. The two alternatives look symmetrical, though of course they are not. It is tempting to suppose that in our age and civilization we put the burden of proof where we do, because opting for the presumption of innocence, of freedom, of possession, of equal treatment of like cases, is intuitively just and ranges us on the side of the angels. Supposing this, however, is to suppose that we already know what is just and which side is that of the angels. There is, instead, an independent reason that makes these presumptions prevail, due to their being asymmetrical to their opposites in a way that makes them dominant quite regardless of ages, civilizations and intuitions about justice.

Consider feasible acts. An actor proposes to perform an act. There could be an objector, an authorized representative of society or just another party speaking for himself, who might affirm that the act would cause sufficient harm to a public or a private interest to justify its being stopped, prohibited, sanctioned. The presumption of liberty implies that the act will remain free and will not be stopped until the affirmation of its objectionable nature is not only made, but also verified. The opposite presumption would stop the actor doing the act in question until he could show it to be proof against possible objection. There is an indefinitely large number of potential objectors having a potentially infinite number of objections, some of which may be sufficiently strong. To falsify the hypothesis that the act is objectionable, and therefore not one of the actor's liberties, is a needle-in-the-haystack type of task, very difficult and costly if the set of potential objections is large, and logically impossible if the set is not finite (which, in a strict sense, it never is). Taking the haystack apart blade by blade to falsify the supposition of its harbouring a needle would take long enough to mean an indefinite suspension of the act whose free performance depended on there being no needle. Taken literally, the presumption that every act may be harmful and hurt some interest would freeze everything into total immobility; this could only be attenuated by society granting advance clearance to a specific list of demonstrably innocuous acts, like visiting one's ailing aunt, whose safety and lack of threat to any conceivable aspiration, wish, interest or value would not have to be established before they could be undertaken. However, opting for the presumption of liberty is hardly a matter of ethics, of a liberal temperament, or even of efficient social and economic organization. It is a matter of epistemology, of how knowledge works and how verification differs from falsification.

The way knowledge works directs, perhaps imperatively so, the burden of proof to be placed on interdictions, on the assumption of guilt, on the supposition that possession is illicit or title has some vice, and on the claim that some case is relevantly different from some precedent, some other case. The presumptions of liberty, of innocence, of title to possession and of like treatment of like cases, do not stand on their particular merits, genuine as those may be, but are the automatic consequences of where the burden of proof falls – a matter about which sensible thought leaves little choice.

Equal treatment, with the burden of proving that two cases are relevantly unlike, has a pivotal place among the presumptions that enter into the concept of justice. If equal treatment is to be presumed, and if one person benefits from the presumption of liberty, of innocence, of good title or other favourable presumptions if there are any, then all other persons must also benefit from the same presumptions unless it can be shown that their case differs in a relevant respect from that of the first person. It is intuitively appealing that the principle of presumption is general because it is just that it should be so. However, as was argued above, its generality has an independent source in knowledge that can be recognized before any knowledge of justice. Circularity is avoided; we have a constituent principle of justice, rather than one that is derived from the requirements of a justice that already exists in our intuitive understanding.

Convention. If there existed a truly pre-social state of affairs, or one where everyone was suddenly struck by amnesia, there would be no precedents to follow and no patterns of behaviour to fall in with. Could questions of justice be resolved with any degree of predictability, or for that matter at all? Take two cases. In the first, two persons board a (pre-social) bus with only one empty seat. Which of them should sit and which stand? In the second, a man's honour is mortally offended. May he kill the offender, perhaps by giving him a chance in a duel? 'Before justice', there is no predictable answer to either question; letting only their moral intuition speak, some people will give one answer, others another. Yet in a firm concept of justice, there must be guidelines that will narrow down the just resolution of such cases to a fairly predictable range. Once we all know what is just, the guidelines will be laid down in just laws. But if a concept of justice must precede just law, what will precede justice itself?

It is such considerations that suggest that there is a place for at least one more principle, in addition to the principles of responsibility and presumption, to enable the concept to be constituted from elements not dependent on prior ideas of justice. This principle is simply that where social conventions guide behaviour, questions of justice should be resolved according to such guidance.

Conventions are most intriguing phenomena both as regards their origin and their enforcement. Lack of space forces us to take their emergence, their functionality and their limited but nonetheless real self-enforcing features for granted here. For our purpose, they fall into two classes: conventions that foster civility, and those that discourage torts.

With two passengers aspiring to one vacant seat, they are both worst off when they fight each other over it. The next-worse solution is that they both remain standing, each fearing to look boorish if he sat down. If one sits and the other stands, at least one of them is better off and the other is no worse off. This is the Nash equilibrium solution, where neither can improve his own situation without the other accepting to worsen his. However, there are two equilibria, depending on who sits and who agrees to stand. This inequality of outcome is a source of conflict. Consequently, it is not self-evident that one or the other of the two equilibria will in fact be reached. Many if not most conventions of civility guide the parties in such conflicts round the issue and achieve an equilibrium. With the convention of first come, first served, both passengers know that he who boarded first is supposed to get the seat. We incorporate this into justice and have little hesitation saying that it is just that the first-comer should have first pick. For certain contingencies, a different and stronger convention may supersede the basic standard: for example, the aged and the infirm may get priority over the first-comer. Lest this story should give too Panglossian a view of social coexistence, it should be noted that conventions of civility tend to have a rather weak self-enforcing capability. The brutish driver, the lout spoiling the party, the queue-jumper face only mild sanctions, perhaps nothing more severe than contemptuous looks. It is also relevant to note that breaches of those conventions that are weakly sanctioned tend not to be called unjust acts in ordinary speech, and vice versa. Which way the causation runs should provide food for deep and probably fruitless thought.

Conventions against torts discourage serious harms to person and property and, more generally, non-trivial violations of the liberties of others except where this is done as a sanction employed to enforce the convention itself.

These conventions are largely self-explanatory. They are ancient, as old as society itself in the truistic sense that a society is formed by its members starting to adhere to such conventions in favour of each other. They are also cross-culturally stable, most societies treating much the same acts as torts. Doing one's bit to enforce the conventions, outlawing murderers, helping to catch the fugitive thief, watching the neighbours' property, putting peer pressure on defaulters and lending a hand in getting contracts duly executed, used to be norms of behaviour in conformity, as it were, to a convention to enforce the conventions. Though the enforcing function has to a great extent been taken over by state authorities, vestigial traces of it still subsist in many social groups.

The substance of the conventions against torts, including the mandatory character of the enforcement usually combining restitution and retribution, forms a stable and readily grasped part of the concept of justice.

III. THE TWO REALMS OF JUSTICE. Standard usage talks of two kinds of justice, commutative and distributive. The first sees to the full commutation of deserts into rewards and punishments. The second ensures that rewards and punishments are distributed as they ought to be. Assuming that 'deserts' means, broadly, all good grounds for rewarding and punishing, so that people in a just state of affairs get *all* they deserve, *and* deserve all they get, the supposed duality of justice is baffling. If commutative justice has been satisfied, it must have duly discharged the distributive function by the just allocation of rewards and punishments, benefits and burdens. Likewise, it is hard to see how distributive justice can be satisfied if it is not by the execution of commutative justice. The confusion has irked many logical minds, provoking them to deny that there could be any such thing as distributive justice. While this seems to be a mistaken view for reasons to be put forward in Section V, the commutative–distributive distinction is not very helpful, and obscures another kind of duality in the concept of justice. This concerns the two types of situation in which justice is a pertinent consideration.

The two kinds of situations are regulated by two complementary maxims. First enunciated by Cicero, the maxim '*suum cuique*' ('Render unto each his own') has survived as the common nucleus of two golden rules put forward by the third-century Imperial Roman legal thinker Ulpian in his *Digesta*.

The other maxim of 'to each, according to' is the generalized schema of 'to each, according to his needs, from each, according to his abilities', proposed by the revolutionary writer Louis Blanc in 1839 and made famous by Marx in the *Critique of the Gotha Programme*. Despite appearances, the two maxims are not rivals. They regulate two separate realms, and where one applies, the other does not.

Under '*suum cuique*', justice operates with an initial datum telling it what is a person's own. It is an ascertainable fact, or failing that, a presumption, that he has certain liberties, good title to his possessions and valid claims to what is owing to him under outstanding contracts. He has his own, and gets his own, as long as he and others do no more than exercise their liberties and fulfil their obligations, with their interactions being confined to voluntary exchanges and the rendering of unilateral benefits. '*Suum cuique*' is breached when a person's liberties are violated, his possessions are taken from him or trespassed upon, when his obligor defaults or when he is forced to render involuntary benefits to others. Under '*to each, according to*' each person in some defined class must get some benefit, or carry some burden, according to some defined criterion. For Marx, the criterion for benefits was need, and for burdens ability, while he left open and undefined the class of persons who shall benefit or carry burdens. But the maxim in its general form leaves undefined both the class of persons and the reference criterion, to be decided on the merits of the case. All it lays down unambiguously is that all who benefit should do so according to the same reference criterion, as should all who are made to suffer or carry burdens. In 'let all guilty persons be punished according to their crime', both the class of persons and the criterion according to which a punishment is to be meted out to them suggest themselves and appear to make the choice obvious enough. Yet even in this case, the choice remains a judgmental one, while in many other cases it is much less obvious and leaves great latitude to judgment.

Manifestly, both '*suum cuique*' and 'to each, according to' cut right across the somewhat questionable distinction between commutative and distributive justice. Each has to do with just distributions and the rectification of unjust ones, where 'distribution' must of course be understood in a general, all-inclusive sense.

The distinction between the two realms of justice ruled by the two maxims is a different, and very much sharper, one. Under '*suum cuique*', the exercise by everyone of their liberties and the fulfilment of their obligations distributes benefits and burdens. A just state of affairs prevails *unless* an unjust act violates it.

Under 'to each, according to', certain benefits or burdens must be distributed to chosen persons according to a common criterion. The class of persons and the distributive criterion must be chosen justly. Unlike in the realm of '*suum cuique*', the distribution here is the product of a deliberate act. Failing that act, there is no distribution; failing it being just, the distribution cannot be just. An unjust state of affairs ensues *unless* a certain just act is performed.

IV. 'SUUM CUIQUE'. What is a person's own is fundamentally a question of what, within his set of feasible acts, he is at liberty to perform. By the same token, knowledge of what '*suum cuique*' implies can be reached by knowing what particular persons' liberties are. Most, if not all, of this knowledge derives from the foundations and constituting principles of justice which dictate the division of any feasible set into admissible and inadmissible acts.

Admissible acts. Before Friday arrived, any act Robinson Crusoe was capable of performing he was at liberty to perform. There was no potential objector, raising questions of freedom, no one to tell him what to do, raising questions of obligation and duty, and no one his acts would inconvenience or harm, raising questions of civility, nuisance and tort. Feasibility and admissibility coincide for the solitary person. This need not mean that all his feasible acts are morally irreproachable, that he cannot do any wrong that is not wrong on consequentialist grounds. What it does mean is that the solitary person may be restrained by ethics but need not restrain himself on grounds of justice; he cannot be unjust without being unjust to others. Nothing in the concept of justice suggests that doing oneself an injustice is anything but a figure of speech.

Admissible acts are either *liberties* we are free to perform unless sufficient cause is shown why we should not, or *obligations* we are not free not to perform if called upon to do so by the holder of the right that was created when the obligation was assumed, or *duties* that we have moral reasons to perform but are not obliged, and normally cannot be forced by others, to perform.

The simplest liberties are acts that are matters of indifference to others and create no externalities. My reading in my study is undoubtedly indifferent to everyone else. My walking in the wood could be a negative externality to some people who like to take solitary walks. My driving to work is almost certainly a negative externality to other road-users, as is their driving to me. However, society in its wisdom has not evolved conventions about not entering the wood when someone has gone for a walk there, nor about desisting from driving into dense traffic. In the absence of a broadly recognized convention, such acts, for all the negative externalities they generate, remain liberties. Smoking in public is an interesting borderline case; in some societies, a convention seems to be evolving against it, though the spontaneity of its emergence is questionable in view of the influence exerted by the public health authorities and by tort litigation. 'Imposing a convention', an oxymoronic idea on a par with inventing a tradition or decreeing a custom, apart from other and probably more fatal flaws, confuses the issue of how we know what is just. For an 'imposed convention', unlike ones that emerge unaided by what Edmund Burke called 'artificial government', presupposes a concept of justice and is not an independent source of knowledge contributing to it.

A different and more serious problem is posed by imposed obligations. Making a promise or entering into a contract is to assume an obligation and to solicit the trust of the promisee that his right to the performance thus promised will in fact be honoured. Not to fulfil the obligation is therefore *prima facie* unjust. However, certain schools of thought assert that rights can arise not only by promise or contract, but by the recognition that the right in question would serve a very important interest. Along these lines, a right to the satisfaction of basic needs, a right to work, a right to education are said to exist and may be decreed by government. For the rights to be exercised, others must be placed under the obligation to provide the wherewithal. Unless it can be successfully argued that the involuntary, coerced obligors are in fact responsible for the basic needs of others being unmet, employment opportunities or educational facilities lacking, it is an injustice to coerce them to provide redress and serve these putative rights, however important they are. If the coercion in question is to be justified, it must be on grounds other than justice, and more powerful than justice.

In addition to exercising one's liberties and fulfilling one's obligations, doing one's duty completes the typology of admissible acts. It suits the structure of our argument to treat it presently in its negative form, i.e. as the breach of one's duty.

Inadmissible acts. Acts are inadmissible on general and on specific grounds. The general ground for inadmissibility is the prevention, frustration or obstruction (without sufficient reason) of another's admissible act – what is sometimes called interference with his liberty. Questions of deliberate intent, negligence or strict liability may enter here, affecting in particular the problem of redress and sanction. They cannot adequately be treated here. Deliberately raising the opportunity cost of an admissible act may or may not be inadmissible; this is part of the problem of coercion, and will be treated in that context. It is clear on the whole that to the extent that the reasons that make admissible acts admissible come to be integrated into the concept of justice, inadmissible acts that override these reasons are unjust.

The general ground for inadmissibility is that the act in question interferes with a liberty without sufficient reason. This means that, at least if sufficiency is so defined as to be empirically meaningful and verifiable, a reason may be furnished and may on occasion be found sufficient. Although the presumption of liberty prevails and therefore acts interfering with liberties are presumed to be inadmissible on general grounds, some such acts may nevertheless come to be admitted on examination of their merits. Inadmissibility on specific grounds forms part of the general case with, however, a particular reinforcing feature: the act in question is inadmissible *both* because it interferes with a liberty, *and* because it is in breach of a recognized rule, namely the social convention whose function is to protect that and other liberties. Thus, my stealing your money is inadmissible both because it deprives you of the chance to do certain things you would have otherwise been at liberty to do, and because it breaks the convention that forbids stealing. Roughly speaking, the first ground is consequential, the second deontological. Specific grounds for inadmissibility are, as it were, fully catalogued in the set of conventions in defence of civility and against torts. Anyone living in the society in question has ready access to the catalogue. If there can be sufficient reasons for interfering with a liberty, it seems immaterial whether they rest on general or on specific grounds. All one can say to reaffirm the difference between them, then, is that specific norms of conduct including specific interdictions, are not meant to be examined case by case on their merits.

Coercion calls for particular attention among inadmissible acts. Suppose racketeers offer protection against burglary to all shops in a street. Some agree to pay protection money. Those who do not become more attractive targets for the freelance burglars, and suffer increased losses. This raises for them the opportunity cost of not paying protection money, but contrary to how this predicament will be loosely described, does not 'force' or 'coerce' them to pay it. Coercion begins when the racketeers threaten the recalcitrant shopkeepers with burglary or worse unless they start paying. Short of threatening to commit a tort, the racketeers have not exercised coercion.

Property as a liberty. It seems self-evident enough that an act a person can perform and which is not inadmissible is one of 'his' liberties. '*Suum cuique*' applies unambiguously. It is equally easy to grasp how and why a person's life and limbs, his good name, his personal belongings are 'his' and what justice requires with respect to them. 'Property' in a wider sense, going beyond personal chattels, and including the freedom of disposition over valuable assets, the freedom to exclude all others from access to them and to the income they produce, while perhaps no harder to grasp, is notoriously controversial, if only because many people feel less compunction about coveting, and wanting to redistribute to themselves or to others, the 'impersonal' assets of some owner than about taking his personal belongings or the money in his wallet. What 'to each, his own' dictates becomes apparently less obvious and unequivocal as the property becomes larger, more abstract and more distant from the putative owner's daily life. Yet there is nothing intrinsic in property that would make it more or less legitimate according to its kind or size. The concept of justice speaks with equal clarity to its various manifestations, private or public, large or small, tangible or intangible, earned or inherited.

Owners acquire title to assets by two main means. One is by not consuming current income – what an earlier generation of economists approvingly called 'abstinence' – the other by voluntary exchange or the acceptance of bequests and gifts. We must leave the third means, the finding of unowned resources, discoveries, inventions on one side for a moment.

Not consuming current income is *prima facie* not unjust, but is it perhaps unjust to have the income in the first place? Many would say that it is unjust if large enough to permit so much saving. However, since current income is the produce of voluntary exchanges including the exchange of one's personal exertions, and of income-producing assets, if these can be justified, then income need not separately be justified. Assets acquired from a previous owner in voluntary exchange, giving value for value received, is an exercise of their liberties by both and as such fully respect the command of '*suum cuique*'. What, however, of the previous owner? And what of the owner before him? There is an old and familiar argument that at the end of a long chain of voluntary exchanges, each of which is as legitimate and just as the one preceding it, we ultimately arrive, at the end of the chain, to an acquisition that was not an exchange with a previous owner. It is then argued, though this does not follow at all from the chain having an end, that unless the first acquisition at the far end of the chain was justified, the whole chain unravels and property loses its justification. It will be borne in mind through what follows that this reasoning rests on the presumption that possession, far from permitting suppositions about title, places the burden of proof of title on the possessor. In the chain argument, title is presumed to have a vice until the contrary is proven. This remains a requirement through the length of the chain.

Along these lines the Western, and especially the Anglo-American, doctrine of property is wedded to the Lockean tradition, in which first acquisition is by taking first possession of a resource, say land, and where this is justified only on condition that the well-known Lockean proviso, namely that 'enough and as good' is left to others, is satisfied. Locke himself had no doubt that his proviso would in fact always be satisfied, both by virtue of the open frontier whose closing he did not foresee, and by virtue of enclosed land, as he put it, producing ten times or more of the produce of common waste. Perhaps comforted by his belief that what is valuable is not necessarily scarce, he did not seem to appreciate the logical quandaries his proviso creates.

In the first place, if resources are finite, any discovery, any finding and appropriation of a resource by the first individual reduces the probability of an equally valuable finding by each subsequent seeker. This can be seen either in terms of a declining marginal value of finds, or an increasing marginal finding cost of finds of equal value. With finite resources, the Lockean proviso cannot possibly be satisfied. The plain man, who finds that there is not 'enough and as good left' for him as some others possess, need not be able to appreciate the fine logical point to be convinced.

In the second place, however, one must ask the more fundamental question: why ever should one accept the Lockean proviso as a condition of the justice of property? Speaking in terms of land, if an individual must safeguard the interests of others before taking first possession of a tract of land, this *means* that the others had some interest in that tract, i.e. that is was not unowned, but had already been appropriated by them in some way. In equity, he must compensate the others; yet the others cannot object to his appropriating the tract if, in equity, they are compensated. The situation is manifestly one of a joint tenancy. The first individual is one of the joint tenants, and the tract he takes out of the joint tenancy must be small enough to leave the remaining joint tenants as well off on their remaining land as they were before. It is only this situation that makes the Lockean proviso just.

However, imputing some kind of prior ownership to a

joint tenancy just shunts the conundrum a little way off, to be faced again. For how does the joint tenancy justify *its* appropriation of the land? Only two ways can be tried. One is by showing that it has satisfied the Lockean proviso and taken the land out of an antecedent, and more encompassing, joint tenancy by leaving to the latter 'enough and as good' as it took. This, in turn, begs the question of how that more encompassing joint tenancy came to own the land, and leaves the Lockean proviso dangling from the end of an infinite regress. The other way to try is to assert that while the individual, taking first possession, owes a liability to a joint tenancy, the joint tenancy owes no liability to anyone because the land it had taken possession of was unowned, unclaimed, unencumbered by anybody's prior interest. Accepting this purely hypothetical assertion is to give the benefit of presumption of title to the joint tenancy while refusing it to the individual who had taken first possession. The joint tenancy is *presumed* to have good title, while the individual is expected to *prove* his good title by showing that he has satisfied the Lockean proviso. If this is its last line of defence, the doctrine of property had better not be based on the Lockean proviso.

Intellectual property merits a minor digression at this juncture. If one creative act, e.g. an invention, does not reduce the probability of an equally valuable one by someone else in the future, the Lockean proviso with respect to intellectual property is meaningless, for how can you fail to leave 'enough and as good' of infinity?

For property of all kinds to find its place in the scheme of justice, it needs a doctrine that is neither impossible to observe when resources are finite, nor nonsensical when they are infinite, nor unjust in distributing the burden of proof.

'Finders, keepers' is a starting point that, perhaps alone among starting points, is a question of ascertainable facts and does not beg questions of justice in order to draw conclusions about justice. To find something valuable is an admissible act as long as no one can show a valid prior claim to the find; it benefits from the presumption of liberty. It also benefits from chance, over which justice neither can nor must pretend to rule, and it is protected against arbitrary challenges by the convention of 'first come, first served'. Where valid prior claims exist, acquisition is justified by the voluntariness of exchange. Incremental acquisition of property *means* saving from income and is justified as an admissible act, a liberty, if the income itself is justified and if income is understood at large, to include windfalls. Bequests raise problems when they are mandatory, but if both the leaving and the accepting of them are free, they can be assimilated to voluntary exchanges, as can gifts for the same reason. If finding and appropriating what is unowned is a liberty, abstaining from consumption is a liberty, and voluntary exchange is a liberty, then property is a liberty. Under '*suum cuique*' a person's property is *his* if and because the acts that led to his possessing it were *his* liberties.

If this is established, the problem of property without possession is easy to fit into the concept of justice. Property is a liberty, or more precisely a set of liberties that the owner can choose to exercise. He is also at liberty to surrender such liberties, by voluntarily exchanging them for value received. He may, for example, let the use of his house to another in exchange for rent. By entering into such contracts, others acquire certain property rights and assume certain obligations, and so does he. His former liberties become pairs of obligations-and-rights, which are the reciprocals of the rights-and-obligations of his contract parties. Speaking of 'property rights', instead of simply of property, draws attention to the presence of as yet unexecuted or partly executory contracts of this kind, signifying undischarged obligations.

Duty and its breach. An obligation is a relation between two persons, the obligor and the obligee or right-holder, on the one hand, and an (onerous) act on the other that the obligor must perform at the right-holder's option. The relation is a consequence of a special kind of reciprocal promise, the contract whose existence and terms are normally verifiable. Breach of contract is inadmissible and an injustice. The conventions against torts provide for remedies against breaches of contract at least within the bounds of unconscionability. What, however, is a duty and how does it arise? One of our less errant and more uniform moral intuitions leads us to say that parents owe certain duties to their dependent children, employers to their employees, officers to their men, judges to the accused, kings to their subjects, and that these duties are matters of justice in a different way from obligations. Duty appears to be a complex consequence of a relation between a person in authority and others depending from it, with the authority exercised in the distribution of certain benefits or burdens, rewards or punishments among the dependents in a just manner. What inserts duties into the concept of justice is that only some distributions pass for just.

There is good reason, in the presumption of like cases requiring like treatment, why we hold that it is unjust for a parent to overfeed one child and starve another, for the teacher to give teacher's pet better marks than his course work deserves, or for the officer to assign the dangerous or unpleasant mission always to the same men. The parent, the teacher, the officer are in breach of their duty, yet the victims of the unjust use of their authority, unlike parties to a contract who have, so to speak, bought rights to the performance of certain obligations, have little recourse beyond grumbling, sullen resistance and the hope of one day getting their own back.

At best, the dependent recipients of a distribution by authority have a legitimate expectation that the authority will be exercised in a just manner. But if it is not, since they are not being deprived of anything that was theirs to begin with, '*suum cuique*' does not take care of their case.

In an attempt to repair this gap, it is sometimes said that relations of authority and dependence, command and obedience must really be understood as tacit contracts between the parties concerned, one agreeing to respect authority in exchange for the other exercising it in a non-arbitrary manner, though what the latter condition is meant to entail may call for further definition. A classic version of this attractive metaphor is the social contract between ruler and ruled. Evidently, if such relations were as good as explicit contracts, the requirements of justice could be derived from them; all distribution would fall into the realm of '*suum cuique*' and ensuring its justice would be reduced to contract-enforcement. With voluntary cooperation and command-obedience brought under the same rule, the concept of justice would be a simpler one than it proves to be when it is stripped of such pleasing fictions.

Where '*suum cuique*' stops, ceasing to offer reliable or indeed any guidance, 'to each, according to' takes over to fill the void, though its manner of doing so is neither above *bona fide* contestation nor always predictable.

V. 'TO EACH, ACCORDING TO . . .'. When the parent has pocket money to give his children, the teacher papers to mark, the officer duties to assign and the judge sentences to hand down and the government taxes to levy, the salient common feature is that without certain persons in authority performing certain acts within their competence, the children would get no pocket money, the papers would not get marked, the fatherland would not be defended, criminals would not be sentenced, and the tax burden would not be allocated. Under the rule of '*suum cuique*', at the end of a day of liberties exercised and obligations discharged, everybody has got his own and nothing is left to distribute. Under 'to each, according to' things fail to get distributed unless someone sees to their distribution. He can see to this in infinitely many different ways, for the rule he must follow, namely 'to each member of some class of persons, distribute the benefit or the burden according to something they have in common', is so general as to be virtually useless as a constraint. Can one be any more definite about which distributions will be more just than others?

Is there a presumption of equality? The same questions of justice must have the same answers; it is self-evident that like cases must be treated alike. However, every case is like every other case (for otherwise they would not all be *cases*), yet every case is also unlike every other (for otherwise they would not be *other* cases but one and the same case). Likeness in some respect is coupled with unlikeness in some other respect. Which respect is relevant?

The general proposition that the case of one person differs from the case of another in some respect that is relevant to what share each should get in some distribution is a needle-in-the-haystack hypothesis, unfalsifiable if the number of respects that could be relevant in a distribution is undenumerable. Therefore the burden of proof cannot be borne by the negation and must be placed on the assertion of a relevant difference between cases. This appears to establish the presumption of equality, interpreted to mean that until some difference between the cases of two persons is proved relevant, they should get the same share. Such a presumption, in turn, may partly explain why the idea of equality carries a connotation of justice, albeit in a somewhat vague and diffuse way.

However, there is some misfit between this presumption and justice. 'To each (child), the same (pocket money)', 'to each (student), the same (marks)', 'to each (athlete), the same (laurels)', 'to each (criminal), the same (sentence)', 'to each (patient), the same (medical attention)', 'to each (poor family), the same (allowance)', 'from each (taxpayer), the same (tax)' makes for an implausible and incongruous series of recommendations that radical egalitarians might be the first to protest against.

Equiproportionality. Clearly, if the presumption of equality means 'to each, the same', its general application would yield bizarre results. We would all want athletes to get laurels according to their prowess, and at least some of us would want good students to get better marks than bad ones. We would usually think it just that sentences should be the heavier the graver the crime, and wish that serious illness should get more medical attention than a head cold. What appears to have gone wrong with 'to each, the same' is that it is a special case of 'to each, according to' where the relevant reference criterion, that triggers off the distribution of a reward or a penalty, is not a quality, condition or circumstance of each person's case, but the person himself. It is the athlete and not his prowess, it is the patient and not his illness, the family and not its need, the criminal and not his crime. In this special case, the chosen reference criterion is the person, and since the reference criterion is a constant as between the cases to be treated, the result is also a constant: 'to each, the same'.

Were the reference criterion a variable, such as prowess, scholastic achievement, illness, need, crime, exertion at work, capacity to pay taxes, or any other among the variety that may be thought suitable as the 'according to' of a distribution rule, the result would of course also be a variable. For the general form of the rule, to which the presumption of equality guides us, is that in each distribution there shall be an equal proportion between the reference variable and the distributive share it triggers off. The generalized form of the rule produces equiproportionality ('Aristotlean equality'), of which absolute equality is a special case that will obtain when the reference variable is held invariant between persons.

Nothing in 'to each according to' determines how the blanks shall be filled, who shall be included in the distribution and what reference variable shall be taken as relevant. The rule leaves the filling of the blanks ultimately to moral intuition.

To find that intuition enters dominantly into deciding what is just, is to see the flashing of warning lights. Self-evident propositions, findings of ascertainable facts, the logic of the burden of proof, agreements and conventions go to shape a concept of justice that is largely unequivocal in resolving questions arising from '*suum cuique*'. Given the facts of the case, there is a vast area of determinacy about who owns what and what others owe to him. Just acts lead to just states of affairs without seeking to do so. Manifestly, however, this ceases to be true when distributions, instead of emerging as the by-products of the sum of just acts serving other purposes, must be consciously chosen by a distributor. The choice is left indeterminate in two of its variables, leaving it to moral intuitions, value judgments and perhaps also to partisanship, ideological fashion or sheer opportunism to decide what shall be deemed the just distribution.

When a distributor distributes something, all the concept of justice tells him is that he must treat like cases alike, different cases differently, i.e. follow the presumption of equality. However, for each set of possible recipients of a distribution of a benefit, positive or negative, there are indefinitely many ways of following the presumption of equality. Should everybody do military service, or only the young, or only able-bodied young males? Should family allowances be means-tested? Should all students get scholarships, and should they all get the same? – and if not, should grants vary according to parental income, some measure of honest plodding, or innate ability and the prospect of glory to the school? Formally, equality is satisfied by each and every one of these alternatives, and by none more than any other. And how else can one satisfy equality, if following the rule satisfies it only formally and doing it formally fails to warm the heart?

The latitude left to decisions about who shall share in a distribution, and according to what his share should be fixed, leads to a predictable consequence. The value judgments, and related uses of moral and emotional discretion that enter into the rival answers different people finally give to these questions, are mistaken for parts of the concept of justice itself.

All is there to be distributed. The vast bulk of the world's goods, tangible and intangible, is produced and distributed as a matter of course as and when liberties are exercised and mutually agreed obligations are discharged. In this, the realm of '*suum cuique*', no distributive decisions as such need, or indeed can, be taken. The question of the justice of distributive acts can properly speaking only arise in the realm of 'to each, according to', where judgment and discretion are dominant and where theories of justice may play a role in educating, and perhaps explaining if that is indeed possible, our moral intuitions that inspire them.

Contemporary theories of justice, however, tend to maximize their scope by obliterating '*suum cuique*'. The space thus vacated becomes one where everything worth having or escaping, and that is transferable among persons, is necessarily the subject of a deliberate distributive decision that is either just or unjust. Where '*suum cuique*' is tacitly or overtly laid aside and distributions are not *prejudged* by it, they can and must be *judged*. All things function like cakes waiting to be sliced and shared out by respecting the presumption of equality. One theory may favour one reference variable as the basis of distribution, the other another, but all have in common the starting point of the cake that is just there. Nobody had to provide the wherewithal for it, nobody had to bake it, no prior claims attach to it, and its distribution would be unjust or fail to take place altogether unless it was effected according to a just act.

The move to take an unowned cake, baked without anybody having been responsible for baking it, as the natural starting point may be overt or veiled. An example of the overt move is to propose to deduce justice from the solution of the problem of an agreed sharing out of manna from heaven. Covert moves are less blunt. Perhaps the best-known one is to take it that fair-minded people will accept, as a matter of fairness, principles of justice they would agree on if they ignored all the advantages with which nature or luck had endowed them. Given such a veil of ignorance, it is not known who contributed how much to producing the cake, and it is equally unknown who must contribute how much to reproduce it once it is eaten. Finally, '*suum cuique*' was set aside by some theories by claiming that the past and present exercise of liberties and rights does not establish title to property. For one thing, it is contended that it is society, by a collective effort, that provides for individuals the legal framework they need for exercising liberties and rights. No one could own property if society did not protect it from predators, and no one could earn income if society did not enforce contracts. Any distribution is really willed by society, and it is incumbent upon society to bring about a just distribution by a just act. For another, *pace* the marginal productivity theory of income distribution and Euler's theorem, it is argued that what people get in current income is no indication of what they really contribute to the social product, nor is the pattern of wealth ownership evidence of past contributions to the stock of wealth. Everybody's share is owed to everybody else's contributions in effort, saving, invention and the transmission of experience from Day One to the present. The stock of material and moral wealth is one vast positive externality, as is the current product. It is said to be meaningless to pretend that anybody has contributed any particular quantity of it and as a result owns any part of it: there is no '*suum cuique*'. Instead, there is a social obligation to distribute goods and bads according to proper criteria conforming to the presumption of equality what would otherwise be distributed randomly and unjustly.

It is in these various ways that all that is valuable and transferable is assimilated to the basic fiction of the cake that nobody baked and that needs cutting into just slices. 'To each, according to' is extended over all aspects of life where justice can have any relevance. Being judgmental and indeterminate in specific content, it is invested with criteria that would indeed have plausibility in a fictitious situation, or to which fictitious persons might indeed agree in such situations. The interest and significance of the theories that set aside '*suum cuique*' and make 'to each, according to' the universal rule is the greater, the less importance is attached to real facts and notably to real, as distinct from hypothetical, agreements. However, the importance we do attach to such things is not altogether a matter we decide at our pleasure. Its short anchors in logic and epistemology, conventions and agreements allow justice but little leeway.

ANTHONY DE JASAY

See also CONVENTIONS; CONVENTIONS AT THE FOUNDATION OF LAW; DISTRIBUTIVE JUSTICE; FIRST POSSESSION; HUME, DAVID; LOCKE, JOHN; MODERN UTILITARIANISM; SOCIAL JUSTICE; STATE OF NATURE AND CIVIL SOCIETY.

Subject classification: 3b.

just price. In medieval and early modern times, jurists, philosophers and moral theologians agreed that the parties to an exchange ought to trade at a just price. A person who charged too much or paid too little acted unjustly. As jurists interpreted the Roman law that was in force in much of continental Europe, if the discrepancy from the just price was sufficiently great, the victim could demand that the contract be rescinded or that the just price be paid. Philosophers and theologians explained this remedy by a theory of equality in exchange built on ideas taken from Aristotle.

Since the nineteenth century, few jurists or economists have believed that prices can be just or unjust. Yet still European and American courts give relief when contracts seem seriously one-sided. We seem to be clinging in practice to rules we can no longer explain in theory. Medieval and early modern ideas about the just price may be worth reconsidering.

THE ROMAN LEGAL TRADITION. About the year 1100, a man named Irnerius began lecturing in Bologna on the *Corpus iuris civilis*, a compilation of Roman legal texts made in the sixth century by the Emperor Justinian. Bologna rapidly became a centre of legal studies attracting thousands of students. The authority of Roman law was soon accepted throughout Italy and southern France. It eventually became accepted throughout most of continental Europe.

The texts in the *Corpus iuris* that dealt with the fairness of prices seemed inconsistent. According to one text, when people contract, the seller will ask for a higher price and the buyer for a lower one until eventually they reach agreement. Thus, the text concludes, 'each party is allowed to overreach (*circumscribere*) the other' (*Digest* 19.2.23.3). Another text, ascribed to the Emperor Diocletian but possibly interpolated by Justinian, gave a remedy to a person who sells land for less than half its just price. The buyer must, at his option, either rescind the contract or make up what is lacking in the just price (*Code* 4.44.2). Modern historians do not try to reconcile these texts. They explain that conditions had changed by the time the second was written: the economy was under tighter control, landowners were in greater need of protection, and Christian ideas were having an influence (Zimmermann 1990: 259–61).

The medieval jurists tried to reconcile them. At an early date, they interpreted the second text broadly so that it gave a remedy to buyers as well as sellers and to parties to analogous contracts (*Brachylogus* III.xii.8; Hugolinus §253). Thus they created a generalized remedy for what they called 'severe injury' or *laesio enormis*. They read the first text narrowly: it merely meant that one party could outreach the other when the deviation from the just price was less than half (*Glossa ordinaria* to C.4.44.2 to *humanum est*).

It is not at all clear why the medieval jurists generalized the second text rather than the first. Some historians think that they believed in a just price because they lived in a world without developed markets in which prices would not fluctuate (Atiyah 1979: 61–3). It is true that in some pre-commercial societies, people are supposed to trade goods at the same price all the time (Pospisil 1963: 305; Firth [1939] 1965: 347–8; Gluckman 1965: 189; Cashdan 1990: 259–78). The reason, however, is that prices fluctuate the most wildly when markets are thin and poorly organized. So people protect themselves by trading with a regular partner at a price that reflects long-run, but not short-run, supply and demand (Plattner 1989: 214–16; Cashdan 1990: 264–7; Gordley 1997: §8). Some of the price legislation of Charlemagne may reflect the conditions of such a pre-commercial society. It condemns those who buy low at harvest hoping to sell high in a time of scarcity. (Nymwegen Capitulary c.17). It urges lords to provide for their families and retainers from the produce of their own lands. They should sell only if they had a surplus, and then only at fixed prices (Nymwegen Capitulary c.18).

By the twelfth century, however, when Roman law was rediscovered, Italy was undergoing an urban and commercial revolution. Cities were growing. Merchants were buying low and selling high, and Church authorities had concluded that they could legitimately do so (Baldwin 1959: 37–41). The jurists themselves explained that prices fluctuate. They said that the just price was a market price that could differ from day to day and from region to region (*Glossa ordinaria* to D.13.4.3 [vulg. 13.4.4] to *varia*). As the great medieval jurist Accursius pointed out, one who bought something and later sold it for less than half the purchase price might not receive a remedy, for 'it could be . . . that when the sale of the object to him occurred, it was worth more than when he now sells' (*Glossa ordinaria* to C.4.44.4 to *auctoritate iudicis*).

The jurists do not explain why they thought the market price was fair. Most likely, they had no theory. They merely knew that if they declared the market price to be unjust, they would upset thousands of seemingly normal transactions. Their closest approach to a theory was to describe the remedy for an unjust price as a kind of fraud, 'fraud that appears from the transaction itself' (*dolus ex re ipsa*). They classified fraud as either 'causal' or 'incidental'. 'Causal fraud' leads a person to contract who would not have done so otherwise. For example, the seller of a horse might tell some lie to make the buyer think he would soon lose his own horse. The victim of causal fraud could escape from the contract. 'Incidental fraud' leads a person to contract on more disadvantageous terms. For example, the seller might lie about the age of the horse to get a better price. The victim of incidental fraud could demand the price he would otherwise have obtained as long as he was the victim of fraud in the normal sense, that is, as long as the other party had deceived him deliberately (*ex proposito*). If the terms were more disadvantageous than they should have been and yet the advantaged party had not used deliberate deceit, then, the jurists said, the 'fraud' appeared from the transaction itself (*ex re ipsa*). The victim then had the remedy for *laesio enormis* if the contract price deviated by half from the just price (Vacarius iv. 51 to D. 19.2.23.3; Rogerius to C.4.44; Azo to C.2.20 no. 9; see Fransen 1946: 49–55). The jurists who developed this classification were not trying to explain why, in principle, relief should be given absent deliberate deceit. They were merely noting, for purposes of classification, that the effect of *laesio enormis* was like that of incidental fraud perpetrated by deliberate deceit: the terms were unduly disadvantageous.

THE ARISTOTELIAN PHILOSPHICAL TRADITION. A theory of why relief should be given was eventually developed by using ideas taken from Aristotle. Aristotle's works on ethics, politics, metaphysics and physics became accessible to medieval thinkers in the late twelfth and early thirteenth centuries. In the *Nicomachean Ethics*, Aristotle distinguished distributive justice 'which is manifested in distributions of honor or money or other things that fall to be divided among those who have a share in the constitution', from commutative or corrective justice which 'plays a rectifying part in transactions between man and man' (*Nicomachean Ethics* V.ii 1130^a–31^a). Commutative justice preserved each person's share of resources. It was either involuntary or voluntary. In the case of involuntary commutative justice, one person deprived another of resources against his will, and had to restore equality by repaying an amount equal in value to the resources he had taken or destroyed. In the case of voluntary commutative justice, the parties agreed to exchange resources. Equality was preserved if each party gave resources equal in value to those he received (V. ii 1131^a).

The thirteenth century theologian Thomas Aquinas accepted this account. In principle, the parties should always exchange resources of equal value. Because of practical difficulties, he said, Roman law only gave a remedy when the disparity in the value of the resources exchanged was great (*Summa theologiae* II–II, q.77, a.1, obj. 1 & ad 1).

Like the medieval jurists, Thomas identified the just price with the market price. He put the case of a merchant who arrived with ship filled with grain at a famine-stricken city knowing that enough other grain ships were on the way to relieve the famine. Thomas took it for granted that the just price was the famine-level price. He asked whether the merchant could sell at that price without revealing that the other grain ships would soon arrive. He answered that the merchant could remain silent and sell (*Summa theologiae* II–II, q.77, a.3 ad 4).

For centuries thereafter, jurists and philosophers continued to explain *laesio enormis* by the Aristotelian principle of commutative justice. They identified the just price, which maintained equality, with the market price. Moreover, they recognized that market prices rose and fell to reflect three factors which they called cost, scarcity and need. These three factors had been mentioned, albeit cryptically, by Thomas (*In x libros ethicorum expositio* lib. 5, lec. 9; *Summa theologiae* II–II, q.77, a.3 ad 4). They were discussed by medieval commentators on Aristotle (Langholm 1979: 61–143); by the members of a sixteenth century school of philosopher-jurists known to historians as the late scholastics (Soto 1556: lib.6, q.2, a.3; Molina 1613: disp. 348; Lessius [1605] 1628: lib.2, cap.21, dub.4); and by the seventeenth century founders of the northern natural law school, Hugo Grotius and Samuel Pufendorf (Grotius [1625] 1939: II.xii.14; Pufendorf [1672] 1688: V.i.6).

These factors resemble the ones modern economists have in mind when they speak of supply and demand. To these earlier writers, cost meant the labour, expenses, and risk entailed in producing goods. Scarcity meant the quantity available. Need meant the amount people would pay for goods, an amount that might be quite different from their intrinsic worth or usefulness (Gordley 1991: 94–102). In a non-economic sense, these writers believed, a man was intrinsically worth more than an animal, and an animal was worth more than a stone. Bread, which sustains life, was more useful than luxuries such as diamonds. But, they pointed out, if prices were based on intrinsic worth or usefulness, then a mouse or a loaf of bread would sell for more than a diamond (Soto 1556: lib.6, q.2, a.3; Molina 1613: disp. 348).

A modern economist, however, conceives of supply and demand as separate schedules intersecting to determine an equilibrium price at which the market clears. These earlier writers did not. As Odd Langholm notes, this 'basic failure to separate demand and supply as separate arguments in the value formula' was 'a defect in the market model that was never quite straightened out in the scholastic tradition' (Langholm 1979: 116). Their explanation of how the market responds to cost, scarcity and need was a simpler one. Buyers and sellers make a judgment of the price that adequately reflects these factors. The market price is set by the common judgment (*communis aestimatio*). In their view, the common judgment could be wrong. If government authorities thought it was wrong, they might fix a different price at which everyone must trade. But unless they did so, the just price was the market price which reflected the judgment of buyers and sellers generally (Soto 1556: lib.6, q.2, a.3; Molina 1613: disp. 348; Lessius [1605] 1628: lib.2, cap.21, dub.2; Grotius [1625] 1939: II.xii.14 & 23; Pufendorf [1672] 1688: V.i.8).

The puzzle is why these writers thought that this fluctuating market price preserved equality in the resources of the parties. Some historians once claimed that they must have equated the just price of goods with their cost of production (Kaulla 1906: 53; Schreiber 1913: 120; Hagenauer 1931). That interpretation seemed to explain how the just price would preserve equality. If seller recovered neither more nor less than his own expenses and labour, the sale would make him neither richer nor poorer. The buyer would become neither richer nor poorer since he could always resell the goods for the price he had paid less any amount he had consumed. This interpretation also seemed to explain a famous passage in which Aristotle said that in an exchange between a house builder and a shoemaker, the house must be to the shoes as the builder is to the shoemaker (*Nicomachean Ethics* V 1133^a–1133^b). Thomas Aquinas and his teacher Albertus Magnus thought that Aristotle meant that the price of houses must be to the price of shoes as the expenses of producing the one are to the expenses of producing the other. If the price of houses were lower, Albertus said, then houses would not be built. (Thomas Aquinas, *In x libros ethicorum expositio* lib.5, lec.9; Albertus Magnus, *Ethica* V.ii. 9–10).

Nevertheless, as historians now recognize, none of these writers could have meant that the just price of goods is always equal to their cost of production. (Noonan 1957: 82–8; de Roover 1958: 418; Ambrosetti 1973: 28). They thought that the just price also depends on need and scarcity, and they identified it with a fluctuating market price. They were familiar with the passage from Aristotle about the builder and the shoemaker, but they must have taken it to mean that the builder and the shoemaker should recover their cost of production (although they will not do so in every transaction), and that if they do not do so (normally or eventually) they will cease to produce.

It does not seem to have troubled them that the seller will sometimes recover more or less than his costs. Perhaps they were not troubled because they knew that prices must fluctuate to take account of need and scarcity. If these fluctuations were necessary lest worse evils ensue, then the inequalities they produced in individual transactions had to be tolerated. If they were not necessary, then public authority could intervene and establish a regulated price. Thus, absent regulation, the market price was just in the sense that it preserved equality to the extent feasible. There was no need to tolerate the further inequalities that arose when, as the late scholastic Leonard Lessius put it, one party took advantage of the other's 'ignorance' or 'necessity' to sell to him for more than the market price or to buy for less (Lessius [1605] 1628: lib. 2, cap. 21, dub. 4). Similarly, there was no need to tolerate the artificially high prices set by monopolists which did not reflect need and scarcity but the desire of a small group to enrich themselves.

Moreover, these writers may have thought that as long as the seller would recover his costs normally or eventually, it did not matter that he sometimes recovered more or less. Over enough contracts, the end result would be equal. Moreover, in any particular transaction, the seller who received less than his costs might equally well have received more. Thus, the transaction would be equal in the sense that a bet is fair when each party has an equal risk of gain and loss. The late scholastic Domingo Soto made such an argument. He said that a merchant must bear his losses if 'bad fortune buffets him, for example, because an unexpected abundance of goods mounts up', and he may sell for more if 'fortune smiles on him and later there is an unexpected scarcity of goods':

> For as the business of buying and selling is subject to fortuitous events of many kinds, merchants ought to bear risks at their own expense, and, on the other hand, they may wait for good fortune (Soto 1556: lib. 6, q. 2, a. 3).

REPUDIATION. In the eighteenth century, the German jurist Thomasius claimed that those who believed that a price could be just must be imagining value to be an intrinsic property of things. But value depends on the 'mere judgment of men', and, in a contract, it should depend on the judgment of the contracting parties (Thomasius [1706] 1777: cap. 2, §14). In the nineteenth century, mainstream French and German jurists rejected the doctrine of the just price for similar reasons. Things did not have a just price but were worth different amounts to different people. Moreover, for a court to interfere with the price the parties had set would be a paternalistic interference with freedom of contract (Demolombe 1854–82: 24, §194; Laurent 1869–78: 15, §485; Endemann 1882: 2, §261).

French jurists therefore denied that relief should be given for *lésion* (the French version of *laesio enormis)* because the price was unfair. Some claimed that relief was really given because of some sort of fraud or duress or mistake (Duranton [1820] 1834–7: 10, §§200–01; Demante and Colmet de Santerre [1849] 1883: 5, §28 bis; Marcadé [1854] 1859: 357–8). Others claimed that relief for *lésion* should be abolished (Demolombe 1854–82: 24, §194; Laurent 1869–78: 15, §485). German jurists usually said relief was given for reasons of humanity. They claimed that such relief was an exception to the normal principles of contract law (Vangerow [1839] 1848: 3, §611 n.1; Windscheid [1862–9] 1891: 2, § 396 n.2).

Nevertheless, relief was not abolished. In France, article 1674 of the Civil Code of 1804 had preserved a remedy for *lésion* for the sale of land at a low price. That was the only case in which French customary law had traditionally permitted relief. In the nineteenth and twentieth century, special statutes were enacted which gave a remedy to those who pay an excessive amount for fertilizer, seeds, and fodder (Law of 8 July 1907) or for a rescue at sea (Law of 29 April 1916, art. 7) or after an aviation accident (Law of 31 May 1925, art. 57). Another statute gave a remedy to those who receive too little when selling artistic or literary property (Law of 11 March 1957). In other cases, courts have sometimes given relief by declaring the contract was procured by fraud, duress or mistake even though the victim had neither been told a lie nor threatened, and his only mistake concerned the value of what he bought or sold (e.g. Cass. req., 27 April 1887; Cass. req., 27 Jan. 1919; Cass. civ., 29 Nov. 1968; Douai, 2 June 1930; Paris, 22 Jan. 1953).

In Germany, although some local statutes limited relief, judges refused to limit the traditional remedy for *laesio enormis* despite the urging of some scholars. At the end of the century, the first draft of the German Civil Code of 1900 abolished relief. But an amendment (now article 138 par. 2) reinstated a remedy whenever one party obtained a 'disproportionate advantage' by exploiting the difficulties, indiscretion or inexperience of the other party. Since 1936, German courts have been willing to give relief for a violation of 'good morals' (German Civil Code, art. 138 par. 1) if the contract is sufficiently one-sided even if such a weakness were not exploited (RG, 13 March 1936).

In England and the United States, Roman law was never adopted and, consequently, neither was the remedy for *laesio enormis*. Nevertheless, relief from unfair bargains was traditionally available from certain courts called courts of equity, though not from other courts called courts of common law.

The courts of common law adopted the rule that while a promise must have 'consideration' to be enforceable, anything the other party gave up of whatever value would count as consideration. As Simpson has noted, this rule often had nothing to do with the enforcement of hard bargains (Simpson 1975: 445–9). It was used in sympathetic cases to enforce a promise that seemed to have no consideration at all by finding consideration in some trivial act to be performed by the promisee. Before the nineteenth century, English and American lawyers had simply accepted the rule without trying to explain it. In the nineteenth century, they began to say that the true explanation was that courts should not give relief when a bargain seemed one-sided. They made the same two arguments as their continental contemporaries. Things did not have a just price, and interference with the parties' bargain would be paternalistic (Chitty 1826: 7; J. Story [1836] 1918: 1, 339; W.W. Story [1844] 1851: 435; Pollock [1876] 1885: 172).

They therefore found it difficult to explain why courts of equity gave relief when a bargain was so harsh as to be 'unconscionable'. The reason, according to most Anglo-American lawyers, was not that the price was unfair but that the advantaged party might have committed fraud (J. Story [1836] 1918: 1, 399; W.W. Story [1844] 1851: 437–8; see Simpson 1977: 569). That was an odd explanation since relief was frequently given to people who never claimed they had been told a lie.

As on the continent, courts continued to give relief. In the United States, the courts of equity did so at least as generously in the nineteenth and early twentieth centuries as in the eighteenth (Gordley 1991: 154–8). Moreover, in the last thirty years, in the United States, the doctrine of unconscionability has seen a renaissance. Article 2–203 of the Uniform Commercial Code allows a court to give relief in law or in equity when a contract to sell goods is severely unfair. Section 208 of the American Law Institute's authoritative *Second Restatement of Contracts* provides for similar relief in other types of contracts. American courts have held the price to be unconscionable when home appliances were sold for over three times their usual retail price (*Jones v. Star Credit Corp.*; *Frostifresh v. Reynoso*) and homeowners were charged extravagant amounts for windows and sidewalls (*American Home Improvement Co. v. MacIver*).

REAPPRAISAL. Although the doctrine of the just price was repudiated in the nineteenth century, courts have not only continued to give relief but they have done so in the same types of cases as before. They have not given relief to those who received the market price but to those who paid significantly more or received significantly less than that amount. Today, most European and American jurists approve of the relief courts are giving. But few of them try to explain how a price can be unfair and why the market price should be considered a just price.

Some adherents of the law and economics movement explain the relief courts give in terms of efficiency rather than fairness. Landes and Posner argue that when courts give relief to the captain of a ship in distress who promised a huge amount to his only possible rescuer, they are preventing shipowners from investing too much in safety equipment that would enable the ship to rescue itself (Landes and Posner 1978). This economic approach does not explain why judges and other non-economists sympathize with the plight of the captain. Certainly, it is not because they want to optimize investment in safety equipment. Moreover, this approach does not explain all of the instances in which courts give relief. They do so when no feasible precaution would have prevented the ship from needing a rescue. They do so when the advantaged party exploited the inexperience or weak character of the victim. Presumably, they are not trying to prevent overinvestment in overcoming one's personal weaknesses.

Some jurists admit that relief is given because the contract is unfair, but they sidestep the problem of explaining how a price can be unfair. They claim that relief is not given merely because the price is too high or low. Nearly always, some weakness of the other party was exploited. He was ignorant of the market price, and remained ignorant because of his weak will or lack of experience, or, as in the rescue at sea case, because he was not offered the array of choices that a competitive market provides. American writers have referred to the exploitation of such weaknesses as 'procedural unconscionability' as distinguished from the 'substantive unconscionability' of the unfair price itself.

It is surely true that no one will pay more or charge less than the market price unless some such weakness is exploited. Either he must be ignorant of the market price, or, as in the case of rescue at sea, he must be cut off from the market. These are the circumstances Lessius called 'ignorance' and 'necessity'. But one cares about these circumstances only because they prevent a person from obtaining the market price. If he contracted at the market price, he will not be given relief however ignorant or necessitous he may have been. Procedural unconscionability matters, then, only because it leads to substantive unconscionability. So the question again arises, why the market price is fair.

At least the earlier writers faced that question and tried to answer it. Moreover, their answer was a coherent one. One might paraphrase it in this way. A society committed to promoting a fair distribution of purchasing power should also be committed to preserving the distribution it has achieved. If this distribution is imperfect, it should be changed through some common plan, and not by random events. Very often, admittedly, we must allow random events to redistribute purchasing power because otherwise worse evils will ensue. Changes in the market price redistribute purchasing power but, as modern economists point out, if we freeze prices, goods will pile up unsold or there will be waiting lines of buyers. That is a reason for enforcing contracts at the market price but not a reason for enforcing contracts that deviate from it. To tolerate the deviations is to allow a party to redistribute purchasing power in his own favour simply because he has met someone whose ignorance or necessity allow him to get by with it.

JAMES GORDLEY

See also EQUITY; ROMAN LAW; UNCONSCIONABILITY; UNJUST ENRICHMENT; WESTERN LEGAL TRADITION.

Subject classification: 3b; 4a(ii); 4b(ii).

PRIMARY SOURCES

Legislation (France):

Law of 8 July 1907, *Dalloz, Recueil périodique* 1908. IV. 173, as amended by Law of 8 July 1937, *Dalloz, Recueil périodique* 1938.IV.168.

Law of 29 April 1916, art. 7, *Dalloz, Recueil périodique* 1919.IV. 285, current version Law of 7 July 1967, art. 15, *Recueil Dalloz et Sirey* 1967.258.

Law of 31 May 1925, art. 57, 1925 *Dalloz, Recueil périodique* IV.41, 45, current version in Civil Aviation Code (Code de l'aviation civile) art. L. 142–1.

Law of 11 March 1957, art. 33, *Recueil Dalloz* 1957.102, 104.

Cases (France):

Cour de cassation. Chambre civile, decision of 29 Nov. 1968, *Gazette du Palais* 1969.J.63.

Cour de cassation, Chambre des requêtes, decision of 27 Jan. 1919, *Recueil Sirey* 1920.I.198.

Cour de cassation, Chambre des requêtes, decision of 27 April 1887, *Dalloz, Recueil périodique* 1988.I.263.

Cour d'appel, Paris, decision of 22 Jan. 1953, *Semaine juridique et Juris-Classeur périodique* 1953.II.7435.

Cour d'appel, Douai, decision of 2 June 1930, *Jurisprudence de la Cour d'appel de Douai* 1930.183.

Cases (Germany):

Reichsgericht, decision of 13 Mar. 1936, *Entscheidungen des Reichsgerichts in Zivilsachen* 150, 1.

Cases (United States):

American Home Improvement Co. v. MacIver, 201 A2d 886 (NH 1964).

Frostifresh Corp. v. Reynoso, 274 NYS2d 757 (NY 1966), *rev'd as to damages*, 281 NYS2d 964 (App. 1967).

Jones v. Star Credit Corp., 298 NYS2d 264 (NY 1969).

Roman law:

Codex Iustinianus (cited as *Code*). Ed. P. Krueger, Berlin: Weidmann, 1877.

Digesta Iustiniani Augusti (cited as *Digest*). Ed. P. Krueger and T. Mommsen, Berlin: Weidmann, 1870.

Carolingian law:

Capitulare missorum Niumagae datum (cited as Nymwegen Capitularies). In 1883. *Capitularia Regum Francorum* 1: 130–32, ed. A. Boretius. In *Monumenta Germaniae Historica legum sectio II* Hannover: Bibl. Hahniani.

Medieval jurists:

Accursius. *Glossa ordinaria*. Lyon: H. a Porta and A. Vincentius, 1551.

Anonymous. *Brachylogus iuris civilis*. Ed. E. Boeking, Berlin: F. Dummler, 1929.

Azo Portius. *Summa codicis*. Lyons: P. Fradin, 1557. Photographic reproduction, Frankfurt am Main: Minerva, 1968.

Hugolinus de Presbyteriis, *Diversitates sive dissensiones dominorum*. Ed. G. Haenel, Leipzig: I.C. Hinrichs, 1834.

Rogerius. *Summa codicis*. In *Bibliotheca iudiica medii aevi* 1. Ed. A. Gaudentius, Soc. Azzoguidiana: Bologna, 1913.

Vacarius. *Liber pauperum*. Ed. F. Zulueta, London: Quaritch, 1927.

Ancient and medieval philosophers and theologians:

Aristotle. *Nicomachean Ethics*. Quotations are from *The Basic Works of Aristotle*. Ed. R. McKeon, New York: Random House, 1941.

Albertus Magnus. *Ethica*. In *Opera omnia* 15. Ed. A. Borgnet, Paris: Vives, 1890.

Thomas Aquinas. *In decem libros ethicorum Aristotelis ad Nicomachum expositio* (cited *In x libros ethicorum expositio*). Ed. A.M. Pirotta, Taurini: Marietti; 2nd edn, 1934.

Thomas Aquinas. *Summa theologiae*. Leonine Text. Madrid: Matriti; 3rd edn, 1963.

Late scholastics:

Lessius, L. 1605. *De iustitia et iure, ceterique virtutibus cardinalis libri quatuor*. Paris: I. Fovet; 1628.

Molina, L. 1613. *De iustitia et iure tractatus*. Venice: Sessas.

Soto, D. 1556. *De iustitia et iure libri decem*. Salamanca: Andreas a Portonariis.

17th- and 18th-century jurists:

Grotius, H. 1625. *De iure belli ac pacis libri tres*. Ed. B.J.A. de Kanter-van Ketting Tromp, Leiden: E.J. Brill, 1939.

Pufendorf, S. 1672. *De iure naturae et gentium libri octo*. Amsterdam: A. van Hoogenhuysen; 1688.

C. Thomasius, 1706. De aequitate cerebrina legis II. Code de rescind. vend. et eius usu practio. In C. Thomasius, *Dissertationum academicarum varii inprimis iuridici argumenti*. Halle a. d. Saale: Vid. Gebaveri et filii, 1777.

19th-century jurists (France):

Demante, A.M. and Colmet de Santerre, E. 1849. *Cours analytique de Code civil*. Paris: G. Thorel; 2nd edn, 1883.

Demolombe, C. 1854–82. *Cours de Code Napoléon*. Paris: Imprimerie générale.

Duranton, A. 1820. *Cours de droit français suivant le Code civil*. Paris: Alex-Gobelet; 3rd edn, 1834–7.

Laurent, F. 1869–78. *Principes de droit civil français*. Paris: A. Durand and P. Lauriel.

Marcadé, V. 1854. *Explication théorique et pratique du Code Napoléon*. Paris; 5th edn, 1859.

19th-century jurists (Germany):

Endemann, W. 1882. *Handbuch des deutschen Handels-, See-, und Wechselrechts*. Leipzig: Fues's Verlag.

von Vangerow, K. 1839. *Leitfaden für Pandekten-Vorlesungen*. Marburg: Elwert; 3rd edn, 1848.

Windscheid, B. 1862–9. *Lehrbuch des Pandektenrechts*. Frankfort-am-Main: Rutten and Loening; 7th edn, 1891.

19th-century jurists (England and the United States):

Chitty, J. 1826. *A Practical Treatise on the Law of Contracts Not Under Seal and Upon the Usual Defences to Actions Thereon*. London: Sweet.

Pollock, F. 1876. *Principles of Contract: Being a Treatise on the General Principles concerning the Validity of Agreements in the Law of England*. London: Stevens & Sons; 4th edn, 1885.

Story, J. 1836. *Commentaries on Equity Jurisprudence as Administered in England and America*. Ed. W.H. Lyon, Jr., Boston: Little, Brown & Co.; 14th edn, 1918.

Story, W.W. 1844. *A Treatise on the Law of Contracts Not Under Seal*. Boston: Little and Brown; 3rd edn, 1851.

SECONDARY SOURCES

Ambrosetti, 1973. Diritto privato ed economia nella seconda scolastica. In *La seconda scolastica nella formazione del diritto privato moderno*, ed. P. Grossi, Milano: Giuffre.

Atiyah, P.S. 1979. *The Rise and Fall of Freedom of Contract*. Oxford: Clarendon Press.

Baldwin, J. 1959. *Medieval Theories of the Just Price Romanists, Canonists, and Theologians in the Twelfth and Thirteenth Centuries*. Philadephia: The American Philosophical Society.

Cashdan, E. 1990. Information costs and customary prices. In *Risk and Uncertainty in Tribal and Peasant Economies*, ed. E. Cashdan, Boulder, CO: Westview Press.

Firth, R. 1939. *Primitive Polynesian Economy* London: Routledge & K. Paul; 2nd edn, 1965.

Fransen, G. 1946. *Le Doi dans la conclusion des actes juridiques*. Gembloux: J. Duculot.

Gluckman, M. 1965. *Ideas in Barotse Jurisprudence*. New Haven: Yale University Press.

Gordley, J. 1981. Equality in exchange. *California Law Review* 69: 1587–1656.

Gordley, J. 1991. *The Philosophical Origins of Modern Contract Doctrine*. Oxford: Clarendon Press.

Gordley, J. 1997. Contract law in historical perspective. In *The Law of Contract*, ed. A. von Mehren. In *The International Encyclopedia of Comparative Law 7*, ed. U. Drobnig, Tubingen: Mohr.

Hagenauer, S. 1931. *Das 'justum pretium' bei Thomas von Aquino*. Stuttgart: W. Kohlhammer.

Kaulla, R. 1906. *Die geschichtliche Entwicklung der modernen Werttheorien*. Tubingen.

Landes, W. and Posner, R. 1978. Salvors, finders, Good Samaritans and other rescuers: an economic study of law and altruism. *Journal of Legal Studies* 7: 83–128.

Langholm, O. 1979. *Price and Value in the Aristotelian Tradition*. Bergen: Universitetsforlaget.

Noonan, J. 1957. *The Scholastic Analysis of Usury*. Cambridge, MA: Harvard University Press.

Plattner, S. 1989. Economic Behavior in Markets. In *Economic Anthropology*, ed. S. Plattner, Stanford: Stanford University Press.

Pospisil, L. 1963. *Kapauku Papuan Economy*. New Haven: Dept of Anthropology, Yale University Press.

de Roover, R. 1958. The concept of the just price and economic policy. *Journal of Economic History* 18: 418–34.

Schreiber, E. 1913. *Die volkswirtschaftlichen Anschauungen der Scholastic seit Thomas von Aquin*. Jena: G. Fischer.

Simpson, A.W.B. 1975. *A History of the Common Law of Contract*. Oxford: Clarendon Press.

Simpson, A.W.B. 1977. The Horwitz thesis and the history of contracts. *University of Chicago Law Review* 46: 533–601.

Zimmermann, R. 1990. *The Law of Obligations. Roman Foundations of the Civilian Tradition*. Cape Town: Juta & Co.

K

Kaldor–Hicks compensation. The need to judge one situation better than another motivates much of economics, and almost all of welfare economics. There are questions on the level of the individual: When is y is better than x for one particular person? And if y is better, by how much? How much does the person gain by going from x to y? There are similar-looking questions on the level of society: When is y better than x for society? And if it is better, by how much? Economists have had a fair amount of success in analysing and answering the individual-level questions. They have had less success with the societal-level questions.

In the view of nineteenth-century utilitarian philosophers and economists, a person's degree of happiness, or satisfaction, or *utility*, could in theory be measured much like a physical attribute such as weight. Measured utility would have the obvious characteristic of reflecting preferences – so $u(y) > u(x)$ if the individual prefers y to x, and $u(y) = u(x)$ if he likes them equally well. But it would also reflect strength of preference, so, for example, $u(y) - u(x) > u(w) - u(z)$ if the individual finds the utility advantage of y over x exceeds the utility advantage of w over z, and, for example, $u(y) = 5u(x)$ if the individual finds y five times as good as x. Moreover, according to classical utilitarians, utility, like weight, is comparable between individuals. This last means that, if u_a = Adam's utility and u_e = Eve's utility, it makes sense to add $u_a(x)$ and $u_e(x)$ together, and it makes sense to say $u_a(y) + u_e(y) > u_a(x) + u_e(x)$ when, and only when, situation y is better for society than situation x.

In short, for nineteenth-century utilitarians, *utility is an interpersonally comparable, cardinal metric*. It can be applied to both individual-level questions and societal-level questions, and it can be relied upon to answer questions about when y is better than x, and by how much. However, although there are still some utilitarians among us, most twentieth-century economists have turned away from this approach, mainly because of the impossibility of measurement. No one has derived a generally accepted way to measure one person's utility function. No one knows how to test the statement that $u(y) = 5u(x)$. No one is sure about how to scale Adam's and Eve's utilities so that the sum $u_a(x) + u_e(x)$ makes sense.

Modern economic analysis leans on two axioms, the first being that utility is ordinal. That is, writing $u(y) > u(x)$ when the individual prefers y to x (and $u(y) = u(x)$ when he is indifferent) makes sense, but a utility function has no meaning beyond this. It shows only *preference*. It does not show *strength of preference*, and it is not *comparable* between Adam and Eve (see, e.g., Morey 1984). The second axiom is that money is observable, measurable and comparable. That is, for example, \$2 is more than \$1 (ordinality); but, moreover, \$2 is twice as much as \$1 (cardinality); if Adam has \$1 under x and \$3 under y, he gains \$2 in the switch from x to y (cardinality); and if Eve has \$2 under x and \$1 under y, then society has a net gain of \$1 in the switch from x to y (cardinality plus interpersonal comparability). In short, *money is an interpersonally comparable, cardinal metric*. Unfortunately, as we shall see, these two axioms of economics do not mesh well.

HICKS, KALDOR, SCITOVSKY AND SAMUELSON. If utility is ordinal, and no utility comparisons between individuals are permitted, it seems almost impossible to make judgments about whether situation y is better for society than situation x. This is because, in most real policy choices, the switch from x to y produces some gainers (those for whom $u(y) > u(x)$), *and* some losers (those for whom $u(y) < u(x)$), as well as some who are indifferent. If interpersonal utility comparisons are prohibited, how can one judge the gains of the gainers against the losses of the losers?

To facilitate such judgments, Kaldor (1939) and Hicks (1939) developed the *compensation criterion* that bears their names. Consider a move from policy x to policy y. (In Kaldor the switch is the repeal of the English Corn Laws in 1846, which harmed landowners but helped consumers of bread.) If those who gain from the switch could *in theory* compensate those who have been harmed, and remain better off, then the move is desirable, and y is better for society than x. Note that the compensation is *not necessarily paid*; it is a theoretical possibility, not a fact.

For the economist to make his case for a reform, according to Kaldor:

> . . . it is quite sufficient for him to show that even if all those who suffer as a result [of the reform] are fully compensated for their loss, the rest of the community will still be better off than before. Whether the landlords, in the free-trade case, should in fact be given compensation or not, is a political question on which the economist, *qua* economist, could hardly pronounce an opinion (1939: 550).

Hicks proposes the same criterion: '. . . the reforms we have studied are marked out by the characteristic that they will allow of compensation to balance that loss, and they will still show a net advantage' (1939: 711). Hicks does not recommend that compensation of the losers always be made, although he does urge economists/reformers to be more explicit about what compensation policies (e.g. adjustments of taxes) would be appropriate.

So the *Kaldor–Hicks compensation criterion* involves the

theoretical possibility of compensation payments. The payments, if made, would leave everyone as well off after the reform as they were before, and leave some better off. A reform which in fact (not in theory) makes everyone as well off and some people better off (and which would therefore get unanimous support) is called a *Pareto improvement*, and consequently the Kaldor–Hicks criterion is sometimes called the *potential Pareto improvement* test. Also, note that those theoretical compensation payments are clearly not transfers of utility. They are potential transfers of goods, or of money. And so there are two types of analysis that can be done here, analysis in terms of goods transfers, or of money transfers.

Shortly after Hicks and Kaldor proposed compensation tests, Scitovsky (1941) used a careful goods-transfer model to reveal a troubling problem with the Kaldor–Hicks test. Scitovsky's model has two individuals, say Adam and Eve, and two goods, say A and B. There are two alternatives, say x and y, between which society must choose. Each alternative is an allocation of the two goods between the two people, and each allocation involves certain totals of the two goods. In a move from x to y, the total quantity of one good rises, and the total quantity of the other good falls. Given y (or x), society could in theory redistribute the totals of goods A and B between Adam and Eve, so as to achieve any redistribution with the same respective totals. In Scitovsky's example, the distributions x and y are both *Pareto optimal* or *efficient* given the respective totals. (That is, it is impossible to redistribute those totals so as to make one individual better off, without hurting the other.) Now Scitovsky shows (with his graphical example) that the move from x to y is a Kaldor–Hicks move. In other words, the gainer, say Adam, could potentially transfer some of one or both goods to the loser, say Eve, so as to fully compensate her, and remain better off than he was at x. However, at the same time, the reverse move from y to x is also a Kaldor–Hicks move. That is, in a move from y to x the gainer, Eve, could potentially transfer some of both goods to the loser, Adam, so as to fully compensate him, and remain better off than she was at y.

In other words, when the total quantity of one good is increasing but the total quantity of another good is decreasing, and when the theoretical compensation payments are mapped out in terms of goods transfers, the attractive Kaldor–Hicks criterion may be logically inconsistent. It may say y is better than x, and, at the same time, x is better than y, which Scitovsky rightly calls an 'absurd result'. His remedy is a two-edged test: 'We must first see whether it is possible in the new situation so to redistribute income as to make everybody better off than he was in the initial situation; secondly, we must see whether starting from the initial situation it is not possible by a mere redistribution of income to reach a position superior to the new situation, again from everybody's point of view. If the first is possible and the second impossible, we shall say that the new situation is better than the old was' (1941: 86–7). In other words, the move from x to y satisfies the *Scitovsky compensation criterion* if it is a Kaldor–Hicks move, but the move from y to x is not.

Samuelson (1950) uses a utility frontier diagram to analyse the Scitovsky criterion, similar to Figure 1 below. For the purpose of this diagram, any ordinal utility representation of Adam's preferences may be used, as well as any ordinal utility representation of Eve's preferences. (So this is *not* an exercise in (cardinal) utilitarian analysis, no meaning being attached to terms like $u_a(x) + u_e(x)$; all that matters are inequalities like $u_a(y) > u_a(x)$.)

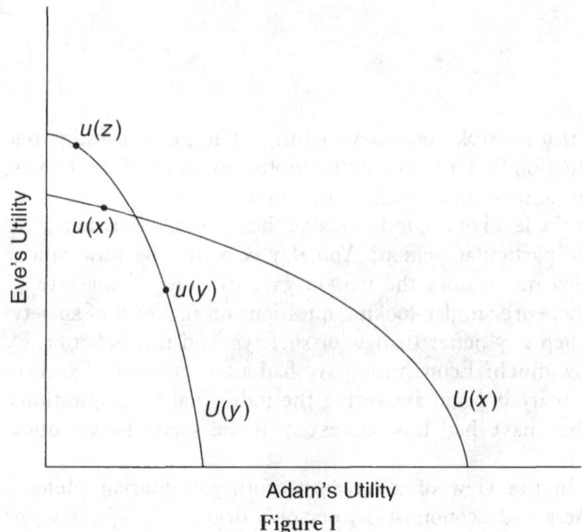

Figure 1

In Figure 1, Adam's utility is shown on the horizontal axis and Eve's on the vertical. Each point shows both a utility level for Adam and for Eve; for instance, $u(x) = (u_a(x), u_e(x))$ shows their utility levels given the initial situation x. Now, if situation x is chosen, there are many possible compensation transfers that could in theory be made, and they give rise to a large set of resulting utility combinations for Adam and Eve; the outer boundary of this set is the *utility frontier* $U(x)$. The fact that $u(x)$ is on the frontier $U(x)$ means that, given the goods totals or whatever other fundamental constraints are produced by the choice of situation x, the distribution of goods between Adam and Eve is Pareto optimal or efficient. Figure 1 illustrates a pair of alternatives, x and y, with Scitovsky reversal. The move from x to y is a Kaldor–Hicks move because the point $u(x)$ lies well inside the frontier $U(y)$. But for a completely analogous reason ($u(y)$ is inside the frontier $U(x)$), the move from y to x is also a Kaldor–Hicks move. On the other hand, situation z (which is one of the possibilities that could be reached from y) is better than situation x according to the two-edged Scitovsky test. That is, the move from x to z is a Kaldor–Hicks move, but the move from z to x is not. Not only does Figure 1 illustrate the kind of reversal that makes the Kaldor–Hicks compensation criterion unsatisfactory; it also reveals the potential weakness of the Scitovsky compensation criterion: the Scitovsky test finds z is better than y. But Figure 1 shows the set of utility possibilities based on z, which is the same as the set based on y, i.e. $U(y)$, is not at all more attractive than the set based on x, i.e. $U(x)$.

Samuelson writes that what Scitovsky should have done is make 'the comparison depend on the totality of all *possible* positions in each situation' (1950: 11). That is, for y to be declared better than x, the utility frontier $U(y)$ should lie entirely outside the utility frontier $U(x)$. Call this the *Samuelson compensation criterion*.

The main purpose of Samuelson's paper was to discover what is the connection, if any, between an increase in real national income – roughly speaking, the money value of the goods and services consumed by society – on the one hand, and an increase in the welfare of society on the other. (This connection had been explored earlier by many economists, including Hicks (1940).) Suppose, for example, that in situation x the list of prices of goods and services is $p_x = (p_{x1}, p_{x2}, \ldots)$, and that in situation y the list of prices is $p_y = (p_{y1}, p_{y2}, \ldots)$. Suppose, further, that there is a shift in relative prices as society goes from x to y; that is, the p_y vector is not proportional to the p_x vector. Finally, let x_a be the bundle of goods and services consumed by Adam under situation x, with similar definitions for x_c, y_a and y_c.

Now, everyone knows that it would be wrong to infer anything about Adam's welfare from a comparison of the money he spends under x with the money he spends under y, or $p_x \cdot x_a = p_{x1}\, x_{a1} + p_{x2}\, x_{a2} + \ldots$ with $p_y \cdot y_a$. There might, for example, be general price inflation or deflation between x and y, which would render such a comparison meaningless. So the alternative bundles x_a and y_a must be evaluated at one set of prices only.

If the evaluation is done at the prices corresponding to y, the test for Adam would be to see if $p_y \cdot y_a > p_y \cdot x_a$. If this inequality holds when society moves from x to y (and relative prices as well as consumption bundles change), then Adam is buying a new bundle of goods y_a when he could more than afford his old bundle x_a, and he must therefore be better off. This raises two questions: (1) Is $p_y \cdot y_a - p_y \cdot x_a$ a correct dollar measure of Adam's increase in welfare? (2) If $p_y \cdot y_a + p_y \cdot y_c > p_y \cdot x_a + p_y \cdot x_c$, can we conclude that society is better off because of the move from x to y? Samuelson's answer to the latter question is negative: the price–quantity inequality says nothing at all about whether the utility frontier $U(y)$ lies outside the utility frontier $U(x)$. The former question is related to a concept called consumer's surplus.

CONSUMER'S SURPLUS. Starting with the work of Dupuit (1844) and Marshall (1890), economists and others have attempted to measure the money gains from desirable public projects like roads or bridges, or from the existence of markets for given goods, and the money losses from undesirable things like monopolies, or taxes, or tariffs. This kind of measurement is essential for intelligent judgment about alternative microeconomic policies. The Kaldor–Hicks compensation criterion judges y better than x if the gainers in the move from x to y could in theory compensate the losers. To measure those gains and losses, according to Hicks (1941), the apparatus to use is consumer's surplus.

Marshall's definition of consumer's surplus seems straightforward. Suppose a consumer is purchasing something. He pays some price for the quantity he buys, but if he were given a choice between paying a higher price for that quantity, or going entirely without, there is some maximum amount he would be willing to pay. The difference between the maximum he would he willing to pay, and what he actually does pay, is his consumer's surplus. This is a money measure of the value of his opportunity to buy the commodity at the given price.

Hicks formalized the Marshallian notion of consumer's surplus in two ways (see especially Hicks 1942). Suppose a change from x to y is proposed. As before, p_x and p_y represent the pre- and post-change lists of prices, and x_a and y_a represent the pre- and post-change bundles of goods and services consumed by Adam. The *compensating variation* measure of Adam's gain from the x to y move is the answer to the following question: Starting at y_a and based on the p_y prices, what is the maximum amount of money Adam could give up, and remain as well off as he was at his original position x_a? This measure is illustrated in Figure 2.

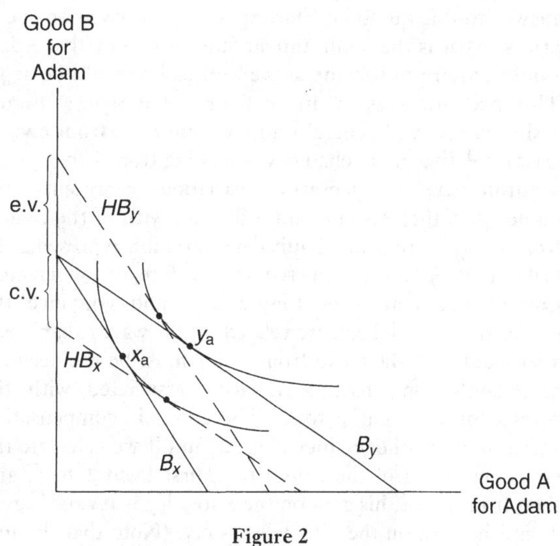

Figure 2

Figure 2 shows two budget lines for Adam, a pre-change budget B_x and a post-change budget B_y, and, as well, Adam's chosen bundles, x_a pre-change and y_a post-change. Note that the change from x to y makes Adam better off – in fact, the figure represents a change that simply involves a drop in the price of good A, with Adam's income and the price of good B remaining constant. Assume without loss of generality that the price of good B is normalized at 1 – so \$1 of income is equivalent to one unit of good B. In the figure, HB_x and HB_y are hypothetical budget lines; HB_x has a slope determined by the p_y prices but is located so that it would make Adam exactly as well off as he is at x_a; HB_y has a slope determined by the p_x prices but is located so that it would make Adam exactly as well off as he is at y_a. Under the assumption that the good B price equals 1, the vertical intercept of any budget line gives the income level corresponding to that budget.

With all this apparatus in place, we can now note that the compensating variation measure of Adam's gain must be equal to the difference, on the vertical axis, between the intercept of the B_y budget – that is, his expenditure level, contingent on prices p_y, when he is at the post-change point – and the intercept of the HB_x budget – that is, his expenditure level, also contingent on prices p_y, if his income is reduced so much that he is exactly as well off as he is at x_a. This difference is labelled c.v. in the figure.

Note that c.v. is close to, but not exactly equal to, the measure $p_y \cdot y_a - p_y \cdot x_a$ mentioned in the last section. It was asked there whether $p_y \cdot y_a - p_y \cdot x_a$ is a correct dollar measure of Adam's increase in welfare, and we can now see that the answer is 'not exactly'. (To find $p_y \cdot y_a - p_y \cdot x_a$, draw another line, through x_a and with the same slope as B_y, find its intercept on the vertical axis, and take the difference between that intercept and the B_y intercept.)

Note that the compensating variation measure meshes perfectly with what is required for the Kaldor–Hicks test; one can imagine taking away a sum of money (or good 2) from Adam, up to the amount c.v., and transferring that money to the loser Eve so as to compensate her for her loss.

The second formalization of consumer's surplus that Hicks provides is the *equivalent variation* measure. It is the answer to this question: Starting at x_a and based on the p_x prices, what is the minimum amount of money that Adam would require to become as well off as he would be at y_a? This is identified as e.v. in the figure. Note that, as Figure 2 shows, c.v. will generally differ somewhat from e.v., at least if relative prices change when going from x to y.

Intuitively, compensating variation represents the money gain that Adam could bribe Eve with, if the change from x to y were made; equivalent variation represents the bribe that Adam would require to forego the change. Careful examination of Figure 2 should convince the reader that c.v. and e.v. are related in this way: Adam's e.v. associated with the move from x to y must be the negative of Adam's compensating variation associated with the reverse move, from y to x. Therefore, if compensating variation is the money metric used, and if we calculate the effect on Adam of the round trip, first from x to y, and then from y to x, his gain on the x to y leg is c.v. of Figure 2, and his loss on the y to x leg is e.v. (Note that the loss from the y to x leg seems greater than the gain from the x to y leg; this should puzzle and disturb the reader.)

At this point we have an embarrassment of riches for measuring Adam's gain when society moves from x to y, a collection of more or less intelligently devised money metrics. These include $p_y \cdot (y_a - x_a)$, already introduced, which is close to what is wanted but not exact; compensating variation; equivalent variation; and various related demand-curve-based measures connected to c.v. and e.v. It turns out that both c.v. and e.v. are in fact exact representations of Adam's preferences, in the limited sense that they must be positive when Adam prefers y to x, zero when he is indifferent, and negative when he prefers x to y.

A great deal has been written about how the c.v. and e.v. money metrics are close to each other and close to observable areas under Marshallian demand curves (Willig 1976); about how the classical Marshallian 'deadweight loss' triangles are approximately equal to the properly calculated c.v. or e.v. welfare change measures; about how classical formulae for welfare change, such as $1/2\ (p_x + p_y) \cdot (y_a - x_a)$, are appropriate or close to appropriate (Weitzman 1988; Diewert 1992). We can safely say at this stage that, from the standpoint of theory and empirical work, there are good money measures for Adam's gain from a move from x to y.

CONSUMERS' SURPLUS. Note well the position of the apostrophe in this section's heading. Can we now combine, in a logically consistent way, consumer's surplus for Adam and for Eve, so as to determine with a *consumers'* surplus money metric whether or not *society* gains in the move from x to y?

Under some circumstances we can. If there is only one good, there is no logical problem with aggregating gains and losses. This is the underlying assumption of much law and economics theorizing, wherein a legal rule is chosen to maximize aggregate wealth. The money metric for Adam or Eve becomes the quantity of the one good he or she possesses. Society's gain in going from x to y becomes $(y_a + y_e) - (x_a + x_e)$, which may be easily measurable, and, although perhaps morally unattractive to some, this approach creates no internal contradictions.

Or, if there are two or more goods but relative prices do not change when society moves from one alternative to another, there is no logical problem with aggregating the money metric gains and losses. This case is essentially equivalent to the one-good case. This invariance of relative prices is the standard underlying assumption of economic cost–benefit studies.

Or, if relative prices do change when society moves from one alternative to another, but Adam's and Eve's preferences are such that they do not substitute one good for another as the first becomes relatively cheaper, there is again no logical problem with aggregating the money metrics. Or, if Adam's and Eve's preferences are (i) homothetic – meaning that as income changes, if relative prices are held constant, the proportions of various goods in their consumption bundles will not change – and (ii) identical – at least close to the alternative points – then there is no logical problem with aggregating the money metrics. Many of these results and the negative results below are surveyed in Blackorby and Donaldson (1990).

However, in the general case, where relative prices do change, where Adam and Eve do substitute cheaper for dearer goods, where their preferences do differ, the consumer's surplus money metric is logically inconsistent, just as the Kaldor–Hicks compensation test is logically inconsistent.

The fatal problem was discovered by Boadway (1974). In the spirit of Scitovsky (1941), Boadway constructs an example in which society (that is, Adam and Eve) move from x to y, where both x and y are Pareto optimal or efficient allocations. In Boadway's example, unlike Scitovsky's, x and y are efficient points in the same Edgeworth–Pareto box diagram. (Because both are efficient and the goods totals are constant, neither can be superior to the other in terms of the Kaldor–Hicks test.) However, x and y do differ in the sense that (i) the move from x to y makes Adam better off and Eve worse off, and (ii) relative prices are different at x and y. Boadway shows that, in the move from x to y, the sum of Adam's and Eve's compensating variations must be positive. But if society moves back, from y to x, the sum of the compensating variations is *again* positive. Since the move out is a social improvement, and the move back is also, the c.v. money metric is inconsistent, a Scitovsky-style 'absurd result'.

Nor is Boadway's example unique. Blackorby and Donaldson (1990) demonstrate that, in general, for an exchange economy model or an exchange and production model, when society moves from an efficient x to an efficient y, the sum of compensating variations will always be non-negative and will generally be positive (the latter if there are relative price changes, and substitution). Hence, by the criterion of positive summed compensation variations, the move from x to y will almost always seem to make society better off, as will the move from y to x, and Boadway inconsistency is the rule, not the exception. In fact, the compensating variation money metric is a worse (i.e. more logically inconsistent) test than the Kaldor–Hicks compensation test discussed above: whenever the Kaldor–Hicks test is inconsistent, the compensating variation money metric test will also be inconsistent, and, as the Boadway example shows, the compensating variation test will sometimes be inconsistent even when the Kaldor–Hicks criterion is not.

In conclusion, from the perspective of the economic theorist who seeks a consistent method which allows judgments about when the move from x to y is a social improvement, a method that does not require constant relative prices or very similar consumers with very special preferences, all of the compensation criteria discussed in this essay are fundamentally disappointing.

However, for the applied economist, the policy-maker, or the law-maker interested in economic efficiency, it is necessary to hope that relative price changes are not too large, to make a leap of faith, and to weigh together Eve's losses and Adam's gains. The applied economist uses cost–benefit analysis, consumers' surplus measures and the Kaldor–Hicks test to boldly go where the theorist fears to tread.

ALLAN M. FELDMAN

See also COMPENSATION FOR REGULATORY TAKINGS; CONTINGENT VALUATION; EMINENT DOMAIN AND JUST COMPENSATION; LAW-AND-ECONOMICS FROM THE PERSPECTIVE OF CRITICAL LEGAL STUDIES; PARETO OPTIMALITY; TAKINGS; VALUE MAXIMIZATION; WEALTH MAXIMIZATION.

Subject classification: 2a(ii); 4c(ii); 6c(iv).

BIBLIOGRAPHY

Blackorby, C. and Donaldson, D. 1990. A review article: the case against the use of the sum of compensating variations in cost-benefit analysis. *Canadian Journal of Economics* 23(3): 471–94.

Boadway, R. 1974. The welfare foundations of cost-benefit analysis. *Economic Journal* 84: 926–39.

Diewert, W. 1992. Exact and superlative welfare change indicators. *Economic Inquiry* 30(4): 565–82.

Dupuit, J. 1844. De la mesure de l'utilité des travaux publics. *Annales des Ponts et Chaussées*. Trans. by R.H. Barback in 1952 as 'On the measurement of the utility of public works', *International Economic Papers* 2: 83–110.

Hicks, J.R. 1939. The foundations of welfare economics. *Economic Journal* 49: 696–712.

Hicks, J.R. 1940. The valuation of social income. *Economica* N.S. 7: 105–24.

Hicks, J.R. 1941. The rehabilitation of consumers' surplus. *Review of Economic Studies* 8(2): 108–16.

Hicks, J.R. 1942. Consumers' surplus and index-numbers. *Review of Economic Studies* 9(2): 126–37.

Kaldor, N. 1939. Welfare propositions of economics and interpersonal comparisons of utility. *Economic Journal* 49: 549–52.

Marshall, A. 1890. *Principles of Economics*. London: Macmillan.

Morey, E. 1984. Confuser surplus. *American Economic Review* 74(1): 163–73.

Samuelson, P.A. 1950. Evaluation of real national income. *Oxford Economic Papers* N.S. 2: 1–29.

Scitovsky, T. 1941. A note on welfare propositions in economics. *Review of Economic Studies* 9(1): 77–88.

Weitzman, M. 1988. Consumer's surplus as an exact approximation when prices are appropriately deflated. *Quarterly Journal of Economics* 103(414): 543–53.

Willig, R. 1976. Consumer's surplus without apology. *American Economic Review* 66(4): 589–97.

Karl Llewellyn and the early law and economics of contract. Karl Llewellyn (1893–1962) taught law at the Yale, Columbia and Chicago Law Schools from the early 1920s to the 1950s (the standard biography is Twining 1973). Llewellyn is best known to lawyers for three major contributions: he wrote the first casebook on the law of sales (Llewellyn 1930); he was the leading drafter of the Uniform Commercial Code, America's most important commercial statute; and he was perhaps the most important scholar in the legal realist movement. Llewellyn is also known to the wider world for his original contributions to legal anthropology.

It is less well known that Llewellyn developed a normative theory of contracts to help decisionmakers regulate commercial transactions. Llewellyn's theory drew heavily on economics, and was an important precursor of the modern law and economics approach to contracts and commercial law. This essay sketches Llewellyn's theoretical contribution and argues that while his general approach remains relevant to moderns, his solutions to particular commercial problems are not. This is because Llewellyn lacked the economic tools, such as game theory and finance, that the contract theorists of today employ to resolve these problems. The essay that follows is drawn from the thirteen Llewellyn works cited in the bibliography below.

The decisionmakers that Llewellyn's theory was meant to help were courts and private law reform organizations. Legislatures played a minor role. The substantive part of the theory told decisionmakers what to do. The institutional part matched decisionmakers to the problems they could best solve and also specified the appropriate level of abstraction that particular rules should assume.

Regarding substance, Llewellyn explicitly rejected distributional norms because he thought they could not be effectively pursued in contracting contexts. The commercial parties in the theory were commonly both buyers and sellers. As a consequence, a rule that sought to shift wealth to sellers would hurt actual commercial sellers, because they were also buyers, and similarly for pro-buyer rules. The regnant norm in Llewellyn's contract theory was thus efficiency, as an intelligent law professor then would understand it.

Llewellyn's particular applications of the efficiency norm followed from three premises:

(1) Courts should interpret contracts in light of the parties' commercial objectives given the context in which they dealt;
(2) Decisionmakers should complete contracts either with rules that reflect the deal which typical parties would make in the circumstances or with rules that reduce transaction costs;
(3) A court should not enforce a contract without an independent inquiry into its substantive fairness if one party's consent to the contract was unconscionably procured.

Scholars today commonly pursue efficiency in the contract area by identifying the cost-minimizing solution to a contracting problem. For example, an analyst will develop a model to show what contract term respecting damages would be efficient for a particular transaction type. The scholar will then recommend that the law adopt this term as the default solution when the parties' contract is silent concerning damages. Llewellyn seldom worked in this way because the economics of his time was too primitive. Continuing with the example, optimal contract terms respecting damages are derived today as the equilibria of asymmetric information contracting games. Game theory had not been developed when Llewellyn wrote, so he could not identify game-theoretic solutions to the contracting problems his theory had to solve.

Llewellyn thus used commercial practice as the best evidence of the efficient transaction. Parties, he believed, pursued their self interest when contracting. Hence, the parties' consent to a deal was good evidence that the deal was efficient.

Llewellyn was sensitive to freedom of contract issues because when one party dictated the contract terms, the analyst could infer only that those terms maximized the utility of the powerful party, not that the deal maximized social welfare. Dictation would occur, in Llewellyn's view, if one party had structural market power or was more knowledgeable or sophisticated than the other. Contracts imposed by power or obtained through exploitation lacked the epistemological relevance of bargained contracts. To use practice as evidence of efficiency thus required Llewellyn to develop a theory that would permit courts to distinguish actual contracting processes that commonly would produce welfare maximizing solutions from actual contracting processes that commonly would not. His efforts in this respect are explored below.

The parties' consent, obtained in ideal conditions, was strong evidence of efficiency, and so also, scholars of the time then thought, was evidence of common commercial practices. Llewellyn was appropriately cautious about inferring the efficient solution from such evidence. Thus, he believed that while trade custom could be good evidence of the efficient arrangement, the existence of a custom was often irrelevant to adjudication. Custom is commonly challenged in law suits: one party claims that the custom provides the court with a rule for decision while the other claims that the custom, even if it exists, does not apply to the case at bar. Llewellyn was sympathetic to these challenges. Customs, he thought, reflect the solutions to normal business problems, but the disputes that come to court are often caused by exogenous economic shocks. A custom meant to govern in normal times could shed no light on the efficient resolution of unusual – 'trouble' – cases. Rather, the decisionmaker must solve directly for the best solution. (Modern contributions respecting the normative relevance of custom to Commercial Law are summarized and extended in Kraus 1997.)

Llewellyn also questioned the epistemological relevance of trade association rules. If all parties whom a rule affects are represented in the trade association, the rule is like a contract between parties of equal bargaining power: the rule is good evidence of the efficient arrangement. Trade associations, however, often imposed rules on outsiders such as unorganized consumers, and these rules were like contracts between parties of unequal bargaining power; one could not conclude that such a rule was efficient because sophisticated business persons chose it.

In addition to inferring the efficient solution from what parties did or from evidence of practice, Llewellyn also sometimes sought to derive the transaction cost minimizing solution directly. For example, he argued that sellers should be permitted to sue for the price when buyers rejected in distant markets. A successful price action would make the buyer the owner of the goods, and thus bear the burden of reselling them. This would be efficient because distant rejecting buyers have a comparative advantage at minimizing resale losses: the goods are in the buyer's market and he commonly knows that market well.

Contrary to Llewellyn's reputation among some modern scholars, Llewellyn did not believe that decisionmakers could infer values from facts, nor did he think that the state should delegate lawmaking power to private groups. Rather, Llewellyn believed that decisionmakers should enforce, facilitate and enact efficient commercial arrangements.

Respecting the institutional part of the theory, Llewellyn believed that the parties' commercial goals were seldom obvious to courts. On the other hand, a judge could become sophisticated by repeated acquaintance with the facts. In his view, then, courts that saw many commercial cases or courts with unusually capable judges could make good commercial rules. The ordinary judge needed help, however. He could find it from three sources: arbitrators; custom; and trade association rules. Arbitrators were useful because Llewellyn's goal was to enforce the deal the parties actually made: an arbitrator could often best tell whether the seller rendered a conforming performance – whether, for example, she tendered contract grade goods.

Llewellyn also considered other nonjudicial decisionmakers. Contract law rules performed two major functions in Llewellyn's theory: to complete incomplete contracts; and to place appropriate constraints on the parties' freedom to contract. Creating rules to perform these functions requires expertise, and the rules themselves must be clear. The need for expertise underlay Llewellyn's view that commercial law rules are best created by administrative agencies and specialized law reform organizations.

Whichever institution acted, the resulting legal rules should ask courts to find facts – which party had possession of the goods when the fire struck? – rather than require conceptual analysis – which party had title when the fire struck? Llewellyn, however, rejected conceptual analysis only at the level of rule application. Otherwise, he admired this form of analysis and sometimes engaged in it.

Llewellyn's views about commercial codes were a major exception to his view that legal rules should call for narrow factual inquiries. Codes are difficult to amend, and so must be applied in quite varied commercial circumstances. He concluded from this fact that code rules should not reflect solutions to specific contracting problems, but rather should constitute normative premises for reasoning or help courts decide which facts are relevant to decision. Llewellyn's position concerning the appropriate level of abstraction on which Uniform Commercial Code rules should be written thus does not reflect his thought on rules generally.

Llewellyn's general substantive and institutional approaches to Sales and Contract Law rules remain relevant to us. Modern law and economics scholars believe that the state should pursue efficiency in the contract area because efficiency is the only implementable goal. And efficiency should be pursued in some of the ways that Llewellyn advocated: courts should enforce the deals that parties make, which requires courts to understand the economics of commercial transactions; and doctrine or statute should attempt to reduce the costs to parties of making deals by choosing the efficient contract term as the default solution. Llewellyn's major achievement was to develop this general approach to the legal analysis of contract.

Many of Llewellyn's specific analyses are mistaken, however, and one therefore should not rely on his recommendations to resolve concrete cases. Without the concepts and tools of modern economic analysis, Llewellyn could not understand how market power is acquired and exercised, and so his unconscionability theories are too primitive. He also had perceptive insights respecting when rules should be mandatory or defaults and which transaction costs the state could likely reduce. But Llewellyn could not understand these concepts as moderns do, and so his work is often unhelpful. This essay next proceeds to give examples of Llewellyn's method.

Llewellyn sometimes pursued transaction cost reduction explicitly. In his view, sales law rules should facilitate prompt renegotiation. This theme led Llewellyn to advocate a cover remedy. When Llewellyn wrote, a disappointed promisee could recover market damages – the difference between the contract and market prices measured at the time of breach. Llewellyn argued that the promisee in the alternative should be permitted to seek cover damages – the difference between the contract price and the price of a substitute transaction. The availability of cover damages would permit parties to avoid expensive actions to prove a market price. Cover would also facilitate renegotiation, which reduces the costs of resolving disputes. When only market damages were available, Llewellyn argued, a breached-against buyer would make a substitute purchase at once; for if the buyer waited and the market rose, market damages would not make the buyer whole: the buyer would have 'covered' at the high price but will have his damages measured by the lower price prevailing at breach time. The market damage rule thus discouraged a buyer from attempting to salvage the deal privately. The buyer, however, would negotiate with his seller for a reasonable time after breach if he could have his damages measured by the cost of a substitute purchase should the negotiations break down.

As with many of Llewellyn's specific substantive claims, the economics of the argument are not exactly correct. Legal disputes that are triggered by the difference between the contract price and the price at performance time most commonly arise in markets that exhibit considerable short term price volatility, such as commodity markets. The modern view holds that today's price in such markets incorporates all publicly available information. Therefore, new price affecting information arrives unexpectedly. Market participants thus regard the next period price for goods as partly random: it is today's price plus interest plus an error term with mean zero. Applying this theory, a buyer who could get only market damages faces conflicting incentives. Contrary to Llewellyn's argument, the buyer also has an incentive not to purchase at once. If the market fell after breach, the buyer would prefer to have waited; for then he could have covered at the low price but will have his damages measured by the high price that existed on the date of breach. Thus under market damages, the possibility of a price rise after breach creates an incentive for the buyer to repurchase at once while the possibility of a decline creates an incentive for the buyer to wait. Since both possibilities are equally likely, the buyer would ignore them, negotiating with the breaching seller if that seemed profitable and otherwise buying on the market when convenient. The market damage rule thus did not discourage renegotiation.

In addition, adding cover damages to the remedies a disappointed buyer can assert would produce overcompensation. To see why, recall that when cover becomes available, the buyer is permitted to measure damages at the more favourable of two dates – breach or cover time. The buyer is thus given a free option to speculate after breach. Because options are valuable, adding a free option to the buyer's damage remedies produces overcompensation.

Llewellyn's advocacy of a cover remedy was troublesome because making cover available will not increase the likelihood of renegotiation. Also, Llewellyn never analysed the decisionmaker's real choice, which is whether to facilitate deals by reducing the promisee's costs of proving damages or to impede deals by adding a supra compensatory remedy. The primitive state of financial economics in Llewellyn's time would likely have caused any analyst to make these errors.

Llewellyn's views on the perfect tender rule illustrate the strengths and weaknesses of his substantive analyses. The perfect tender rule permits the buyer to reject for *any* defect, however trivial. Llewellyn's analysis of this rule evidences his careful attention to context. He recognized that perfect tender is appropriate for consumers and for buyers of machines for use. In the former case, the rule 'fits the case of the wallpaper which is just enough off-color, or the radio which is just enough off true, to edge the nerves'. In the latter case, perfect tender is appropriate because even slightly defective machines can disrupt manufacturing processes. Perfect tender is never appropriate for mercantile buyers.

Llewellyn objected to a perfect tender rule in mercantile transactions because the rule would encourage strategic behaviour: in particular, buyers would exploit trivial defects to reject when the market fell after purchase. Such rejections are breaches of the real contract that the parties thought they had made (which allocated the risk of price increases to the seller and of declines to the buyer). To enforce the real contract is thus to preclude rejection, but the real contract also did not require the buyer to pay the full price for defective goods. When the goods could be graded, the custom, Llewellyn believed, was to have price allowances. A decisionmaker would enforce the true deal – premise (1) of Llewellyn's theory – by following this custom.

Llewellyn's reform proposal was to generalize the custom by having the legal default permit courts to bar rejection but order price allowances in all mercantile transactions. He urged an amendment to a proposed Federal Sales Act that would have banned rejection in sales between merchants if

> the delivery offered in no material manner increases the risk resting on the buyer, and is of such character as to reasonably meet the buyer's operating requirements, so that an appropriate reduction of the price can serve as adequate compensation for failure of exact performance (Llewellyn 1940: 566).

This reform is unsatisfactory because it assumes that courts will have information that ordinarily is unverifiable. To apply the proposed rule, a court must find 'the risk resting on the buyer' in order to decide whether the defective tender increased that risk in a 'material manner'; know the buyer's production function in order to decide whether the defective tender 'reasonably meets the buyer's operating requirements'; and evaluate the consequences to the buyer of a 'failure of exact performance'. Information respecting these issues is seldom cost justified to produce in lawsuits.

A seller may attempt to exploit the court's ignorance by forcing the buyer to take a defective tender: the seller may plausibly think that the buyer could not rebut the seller's claim that the tender 'reasonably met the buyer's operating requirements'. In addition, there is seldom a market price for every quality level of a product. Thus, establishing an 'appropriate reduction of the price' for a defective tender would be hard for a court to do. Unsurprisingly, actual merchants respond to the strategic rejection concern with contract terms that are more precise than this proposed rule (e.g., Bernstein 1996).

Llewellyn paid considerable attention to freedom of contract issues – see premise (3) – because of the epistemological role that actual contracting played in his theory. When parties contract under ideal conditions, both can rationally expect to do better in the deal they make than in any other possible transaction. In Llewellyn's view, however, conditions were often less than ideal. This view led to his unconscionability thesis: contracts that were substantively objectionable ('lop-sided') should not be enforced when the bargaining process that produced them was procedurally defective. This thesis not only justified a court in refusing to enforce a particular term, but also supported mandatory statutory rules. When the factors that would support a finding of unconscionability in a particular case obtain generally in an economy, the state should prohibit bad terms and require good ones. Default rules are only appropriate when bargaining power is roughly equal. Otherwise, to permit contracting out would benefit the strong at the expense of the weak.

These perceptive views helped to organize the modern unconscionability debate. They did not help to provide solutions to concrete problems. A workable theory of unconscionability should provide criteria specifying when a contract is too lop-sided to enforce and when a contracting process is importantly defective. Llewellyn was unable to develop these criteria. Respecting the substantive aspect, Llewellyn could not say when a set of contractual risk allocations was too unbalanced to be allowed. Rather, he resorted to unsatisfactory methodological fixes. For example, he urged courts to read contracts as containing the terms that a consumer would reasonably expect. But he also thought it was reasonable of consumers to expect balanced contracts. Thus, Llewellyn's reasonable expectations standard for substantive unconscionability only restated the question, when is a contract sufficiently balanced to enforce?

As regards the contracting process, the current view holds that a mass contract is procedurally defective when it was the product of a market flawed by information imperfections or monopoly power. Thus, a term would be procedurally defective if firms imposed it in consequence of consumers' lack of search rather than because the term was the equilibrium outcome of a competitive process. Llewellyn understandably had no information economics and thus could not approach procedural unconscionability issues in this way.

Rather, he again used questionable arguments to justify his view that certain terms, such as warranty disclaimers, should be unenforceable because the terms were routinely used in unconscionable ways. As one example, he thought that the presence of a substantial price for an article implied the existence of a warranty against defects in manufacture. Hence, when the price was high, courts should strike the disclaimer.

This view is incorrect because a 'high' price can coexist with a disclaimer of warranties, in the sense that the consumer would not infer the absence of a disclaimer from the size of the price. To see why, consider a simple example. A firm sells a stereo that is produce at a constant marginal cost of c. The probability of a defect is π, and a defect makes the stereo worthless. The firm makes a replacement warranty. The firm must thus produce more units than it makes sales in order to be able to replace nonconforming units; the replacement units also could be defective. Thus, a firm that warrants would have to produce $1/(1-\pi)$ units to support each sale. If the firm sells x stereos in a period, its total variable cost is $cx/(1-\pi)$ and its marginal cost is $c/(1-\pi)$. When the firm prices at the minimum of its average cost curve, the fixed cost that each sale recovers is f. The stereo's competitive price with a warranty is thus $P = f + c/(1-\pi)$. The stereo's price without a warranty would be $P_{nw} = f + c$. Suppose that $f = \$100$, $c = \$1{,}000$ and $\pi = 0.01$. The transaction price when the firm warrants would be $1,110.10 and the price when it disclaims would be approximately one percent lower, $1,100. This example shows that rational buyers would pay almost as much for products with disclaimers as for products with warranties. It is thus incorrect to claim that whenever the price is nontrivial, buyers expect their sellers to have made warranties.

Llewellyn's mistake here may seem obvious to moderns. Moderns should recognize, however, that current explanations of the functions that warranties serve are derived from the hidden information/hidden action paradigm (see Emons 1989). This paradigm was unavailable when Llewellyn wrote. Therefore, Llewellyn lacked a direct intellectual counter-weight to the general ethos of the 1930s, which encouraged analysts to develop exploitation explanations for common commercial phenomena.

Karl Llewellyn's contract theory can be analysed on two levels of abstraction. On the high level, Llewellyn's approach to the legal regulation of contracting behaviour remains current. Llewellyn believed that the law should enforce the parties' actual deal, create default rules to complete incomplete contracts and set the limits of freedom of contract. Llewellyn justified the law's performance of the first task on efficiency grounds and used the efficiency norm to help the law perform the second task. Llewellyn's commitment to efficiency also generated his analysis of freedom of contract, for he thought that efficiency was unlikely when the bargaining process was conducted under much less than ideal conditions; the results of such flawed processes were not entitled to the law's deference. On the lower level of application of the approach, Llewellyn is seldom relevant today. He could only work with the tools he had, and those tools were too primitive for the task he set himself. No analyst could make much progress on the creation of good default rules or on developing criteria for efficient interventions in markets without a knowledge of game theory, transaction cost economics and the economics of information. Because these bodies of knowledge were created after Llewellyn worked, many of his particular applications were mistaken. Nevertheless, Llewellyn's general approach accommodated itself to the use of new tools and indeed facilitated their introduction. In this significant sense, he began what we now do.

ALAN SCHWARTZ

See also AMERICAN LEGAL REALISM; BREACH REMEDIES; CONTRACT FORMATION AND INTERPRETATION; CONTRACTS; DEFAULT RULES FOR INCOMPLETE CONTRACTS; PRIVATE COMMERCIAL LAW; UNCONSCIONABILITY; UNJUST ENRICHMENT.

Subject classification: 4c(i); 5c(i).

BIBLIOGRAPHY

Bernstein, L. 1996. Merchant law in a merchant court: rethinking the code's search for immanent business norms. *University of Pennsylvania Law Review* 144: 1765–1821.

Casebeer, K. 1977. Escape from liberalism: fact and value in Karl Llewellyn. *Duke Law Journal* 1977: 671–703.

Danzig, R. 1975. A comment on the jurisprudence of the Uniform Commercial Code. *Stanford Law Review* 27: 621–35.

Emons, W. 1989. The theory of warranty contracts. *Journal of Economic Surveys* 3: 43–57.

Fischer, W., Horowitz, M. and Reed T. (eds). 1993. *American Legal Realism.* New York: Oxford University Press.

Heffernan, W. 1983. Two stages of Karl Llewellyn's thought. *International Journal of the Sociology of Law* 11: 134–65.

Hillinger, I. 1985. The Article 2 Merchant rules: Karl Llewellyn's attempt to achieve the Good, the True, the Beautiful in commercial law. *Georgetown Law Journal* 73: 1141–84.

Kalman, L. 1986. *Legal Realism at Yale, 1927–1960.* Chapel Hill, NC: University of North Carolina Press.

Kamp, A. 1995. Between-the-wars social thought: Karl Llewellyn, legal realism, and the Uniform Commercial Code in context. *Albany Law Review* 59: 325–97.

Kraus, J.S. 1997. Legal design and the evolution of commercial norms. *Journal of Legal Studies* 26: 377–411.

Kronman, A. 1993. *The Lost Lawyer.* Cambridge, MA: Harvard University Press: 196–201.

Leiter, B. 1996. Rethinking legal realism: toward a naturalized jurisprudence. Manuscript.

Llewellyn, K. 1925. The effect of legal institutions upon economics. *American Economic Review* 15: 665–683.

Llewellyn, K. 1930. *Cases and Materials on the Law of Sales.* Introduction. Chicago: Collaghan and Company.

Llewellyn, K. 1931. What price contract? An essay in perspective. *Yale Law Journal* 40: 704–751.

Llewellyn, K. 1936. On warranty of quality and society I. *Columbia Law Review* 36: 699–744.

Llewellyn, K. 1937. On warranty of quality and society II. *Columbia Law Review* 37: 341–409.

Llewellyn, K. 1938a. On our case-law of offer and acceptance I. *Yale Law Journal* 48: 1–36.

Llewellyn, K. 1938b. The rule of law in our case-law of contract. *Yale Law Journal* 47: 1243–71.

Llewellyn, K. 1938c. Through title to contract and a bit beyond. *New York University Law Review* 15: 159–209.

Llewellyn, K. 1939a. Across sales on horseback. *Harvard Law Review* 52: 725–46.

Llewellyn, K. 1939b. Book review. *Harvard Law Review* 52: 700–12.

Llewellyn, K. 1939c. On our case-law of offer and acceptance II. *Yale Law Journal* 48: 779–818.

Llewellyn, K. 1939. The first struggle to unhorse sales. *Harvard Law Review* 52: 873–904.

Llewellyn, K. 1940. The needed Federal Sales Act. *Virginia Law Review* 26: 558–66.

Patterson, D. 1989. Good faith, lender liability, and discretionary acceleration: of Llewellyn, Wittgenstein, and the Uniform Commercial Code. *Texas Law Review* 68: 169–211.

Rumble, W., Jr. 1968. *American Legal Realism.* Ithaca, NY: Cornell University Press.

Schwartz, A. 1997. Karl Llewellyn and the origins of contract theory. Forthcoming in *The Jurisprudence of Corporations and Commercial Law*, ed. J. Krause and S. Walt, 1998.

Twining, W. 1973. *Karl Llewellyn and the Realist Movement.* London: Weidenfeld & Nicolson.

Twining, W. 1993. The ideal of juristic method: a tribute to Karl Llewellyn. *Miami Law Review* 48: 119–58.

Williamson, O. 1996. Revisiting legal realism: the law, economics and organization perspective. Working Paper No. 95–12, Program in Law and Economics, School of Law, Berkeley.

Wiseman, Z. 1987. The limits of vision: Karl Llewellyn and the merchant rules. *Harvard Law Review* 100: 465–542.

Kelsen, Hans (1881–1973). The most famous legal positivist of this century was born in Prague. From 1883 until 1930 Kelsen lived in Vienna. He played a major role in the drafting of the Austrian Federal Constitution of 1920, particularly in the provisions creating a central constitutional court. From 1919 until 1930 he was a professor of Public and Administrative Law at the University of Vienna, as well as a member of the Austrian Constitutional Court. In 1930 the Constitutional Court justices were removed from office after a political conflict and Kelsen subsequently accepted a professorship in Public International Law in Cologne. In 1933 he was ousted by the Nazi regime on account of his Jewish ancestry. He accepted an offer to work at the Graduate Institute of International Studies in Geneva, where he stayed until his emigration to the United States in 1940. First he taught on a temporary basis at Harvard Law School, Wellesley College and the University of California. From 1945 until his retirement in 1952 he was a professor in political science at the University of California in Berkeley. He lived in Berkeley until his death.

Kelsen is the founder of the Vienna School of the Pure Theory of Law. The sister school was the Brno School, founded by Kelsen's lifetime friend Franz Weyr (1879–1951). The Pure Theory of Law is a general theory of positive law and not of any special system of law. It is pure because it aims to free legal science of all foreign elements (Kelsen [1934] 1992: 7). This means a separation of law and facts on the one hand and of law and morality on the other. Important characteristics of the theory are its acceptance of the neo-Kantian duality of 'is' and 'ought', its rejection of natural law doctrines, and its analysis of the concept of a legal system as a hierarchical structure grounded in a basic norm (Kubeš and Weinberger 1980: 10–15).

In 1934, the year in which the first edition of *Pure Theory of Law* (*Reine Rechtslehre*) was published, Roscoe Pound called Hans Kelsen 'unquestionably the leading jurist of the time' (Pound 1934: 526). In 1962, nearly thirty years later and two years after publication of the second, completely revised and expanded edition of *Pure Theory of Law*, Herbert Hart described Kelsen as 'the most stimulating writer on analytic jurisprudence of our day' (Hart 1963: 728; Tur and Twining 1986: 2; Paulson 1992: xviii). At that time Kelsen was still to begin the work that would result in his *General Theory of Norms*, published posthumously in 1979.

Although Anglo-Saxon analytic jurisprudence appears to prefer realistic and utilitarian approaches to Kelsen's neo-Kantian line of thinking, he has had an indirect influence. The concept of the *ultimate rule of recognition* is clearly the result of Herbert Hart's struggle with that peculiar mixture of fascination and resistance that Kelsen's elusive concept of the basic norm (*Grundnorm*) tends to arouse in the minds of 'ordinary language' philosophers (Hart [1961] 1994: 292).

Kelsen's publications start in 1905 with a study of the political philosophy in Dante's *De Monarchia* and end with the posthumous *General Theory of Norms* in 1979. Besides legal theory, his publications range from constitutional law, administrative law and public international law to the theory of justice, sociology and political philosophy. The final bibliography of Kelsen's works includes 387 titles (Walter 1985).

Despite 'an impassioned resistance rarely seen in the history of legal science', as Kelsen himself put it in 1934 (Kelsen [1934] 1992, 1), at that time the Pure Theory of Law was already widely recognized on the European continent as one of the leading schools in legal theory, and it has kept its leading position there ever since. The theory's reception in the UK had to wait until after publication of H.L.A. Hart's *The Concept of Law* in 1961. Although *The Concept of Law* pays relatively little close attention to Kelsen, much of the work was plainly profoundly influenced by his theory (Paulson in Kelsen [1934] 1992: 146). The interest that British analytic jurisprudence takes in the Pure Theory of Law is mainly a consequence of Hart's indirect disputes with Kelsen. By contrast, positivist legal theory in the US tends to ignore Kelsen's work. Although Kelsen lived in the US for over thirty years, his 'formalistic' and 'constructivist' theory failed to capture much sympathy from American legal realists and pragmaticists (Paulson 1988).

Outlines of the Pure Theory of Law can best be sketched by quoting Kelsen himself on its characteristics: (i) the neo-Kantian dualism of 'is' and 'ought'; (ii) the positivist separation of morality and law; and (iii) the conception of the legal system as a hierarchical structure founded on a basic norm.

The Pure Theory of Law was from the outset grounded on the Kantian antithesis between 'is' (*Sein*) and 'ought' (*Sollen*). This is shown by a passage from the Preface to the second edition (1923) of Kelsen's first major work, *Die Hauptprobleme der Staatsrechtslehre* (Main Problems in the Theory of Public Law) of 1911:

> *Main Problems* takes as its point of departure the fundamental dichotomy between *Sollen* and *Sein*, between *ought* and *is*, first discovered, so to speak, by Kant in his effort to establish the independence of theoretical reason as against practical reason, value as against reality, morality as against nature (Kelsen [1911] 1923: VI).

In the 1960 edition of *Pure Theory of Law*, Kelsen writes about this antithesis:

> The difference between *is* and *ought* cannot be explained further. We are immediately aware of the difference. Nobody can deny that the statement: 'something is'–that is, the statement by which an existent fact is described–is fundamentally different from the statement: 'something ought to be'–which is the statement by which the norm is described. Nobody can assert that from the statement that something is, follows a statement that something ought to be, or vice versa (Kelsen [1960] 1967: 5–6).

Legal science must restrict itself to the 'ought': 'If legal science is not to merge into the natural sciences, the law must be contrasted with nature as sharply as possible' (Kelsen [1934] 1992: 8).

Being a legal positivist *pur sang*, Kelsen is a fierce defender of the separability thesis, the thesis claiming the separability of law and morals (Paulson 1992: xxiv):

> Here, above all, the task is to unfetter the law, to break

the connection that is always made between the law and morality. What is rejected thereby is not, of course, the dictate that the law ought to be moral and good; that goes without saying, though what it really means is another question. Rather, what is rejected is simply the view that the law as such is part of morality, and that therefore every law, as law, is in some sense and to some degree moral (Kelsen [1934] 1992: 15).

The Pure Theory of Law is

> . . . radically anti-ideological; and on precisely this point, traditional legal theory launches the fiercest resistance, finding it intolerable that the system of the Soviet Union is to be conceived of as a legal system in exactly the same way as is that of Fascist Italy or democratic, capitalistic France (ibid.: 25).

This passage was published in 1934, after Kelsen had already been driven away from Cologne by the Nazi regime.

According to Kelsen, the legal system is a hierarchical structure of issued legal norms that derive their legal validity from an appeal made to a higher-level norm. Higher-level norms are in turn valid owing to a similar appeal to a norm at a still higher level and so on. The sequence continues until the constitutional level is reached. Here Kelsen is left with the problem of legitimizing the constitution.

> If one goes on to ask about the basis of the validity of the constitution, on which rest all statutes and the legal acts stemming from those statutes, one may come across an earlier constitution, and finally the first constitution, historically speaking, established by a single usurper or a council, however assembled. What is to be valid as norm is whatever the framers of the first constitution have expressed as their will – this is the basic presupposition of all cognition of the legal system resting on this constitution ([1934] 1992: 57).

This presupposition is the 'basic norm'. Since the basic norm can no longer be conceived of as having been established by appeal to a higher-level norm, it is hypothetically valid.

> This final norm's validity cannot be derived from a higher norm, the reason for its validity cannot be questioned, such a presupposed highest norm is referred to in this book as basic norm ([1960] 1967: 195).

In *General Theory of Norms* Kelsen goes even further. Here he informs us that the basic norm is not a hypothesis at all but a mere fiction. And then there follows one of those typical sentences leaving the reader amazed at the lightness with which Kelsen could deliver the most ominous messages:

> A fiction differs from a hypothesis in that it is accompanied – or ought to be accompanied – by the awareness that reality does not agree with it ([1979] 1991: 256).

DICK W.P. RUITER

See also HART, H.L.A.; LEGAL POSITIVISM.

Subject classification: 4a(i); 7c.

SELECTED WORKS

1911. *Die Hauptprobleme der Staatsrechtslehre entwickelt aus der Lehre vom Rechssatze.* Tübingen: J.C.B. Mohr; 2nd edn, 1923.

1934. *Reine Rechtslehre.* Vienna: Deuticke; repr. Aalen: Scientia, 1985. Trans. by B. Litschewski Paulson and S.L. Paulson as *Introduction to the Problems of Legal Theory: A Translation of the First Edition of the* Reine Rechtslehre. Oxford: Oxford University Press, 1992.

1945. *General Theory of Law and State.* Cambridge, MA: Harvard University Press.

1957. *What is Justice?* Berkeley: University of California Press.

1960. *Reine Rechtslehre. Zweite, vollständig neu bearbeitete und erweiterte Auflage.* Vienna: Deuticke. Trans. by M. Knight as *Pure Theory of Law.* Berkeley: University of California Press, 1967.

1974. *Essays in Legal and Moral Philosophy*, ed. O. Weinberger. Dordrecht: Reidel.

1979. *Allgemeine Theorie der Normen.* Vienna: Manzsche Verlag. Trans. by M. Hartney as *General Theory of Norms.* Oxford: Oxford University Press, 1991.

BIBLIOGRAPHY

Hart, H.L.A. 1961. *The Concept of Law.* 2nd edn with a postscript (ed. P.A. Bulloch and J. Raz), Oxford: Oxford University Press, 1994.

Hart, H.L.A. 1963. 'Kelsen Visited'. *UCLA LAW Review* 10: 709–28. Repr. in H.L.A. Hart, *Essays in Jurisprudence and Philosophy* (Oxford: Clarendon) 1983: 286–308.

Hartney, M. 1991. Introduction: the final form of The Pure Theory of Law. In H. Kelsen, *General Theory of Norms.* Oxford: Oxford University Press.

Kubeš, V. and Weinberger, O. (eds). 1980. *Die Brünner rechts theoretische Schule (Normative Theorie).* Schriftenreihe des Hans Kelsen-Instituts, Band 5. Vienna: Manzsche Verlag.

Métall, R.A. 1969. *Hans Kelsen. Leben und Werk.* Vienna: Deuticke.

Paulson, S.L. 1988. Die Rezeption Kelsens in Amerika. In *Reine Rechtslehre im Spiegel ihrer Fortsetzer und Kritiker*, ed. O. Weinberger and W. Krawietz (Vienna: Springer): 179–202.

Paulson, S.L. 1992. Introduction, xvii-xlii; Biographical Outline, 139–143; Appendix III: Short Annotated Bibliography of Secondary Literature in English, 145–53. In H. Kelsen, *Introduction to the Problems of Legal Theory: A Translation of the First Edition of the* Reine Rechtslehre, Oxford: Clarendon Press.

Paulson, S.L. (ed). 1998. *Normativity and Norms: Critical Perspectives on Kelsenian Themes.* Oxford: Clarendon Press.

Pound, R. 1934. Law and the science of law in recent theories. *Yale Law Journal* 43: 525–36.

Tur, R. and Twining, W. 1986. *Essays on Kelsen.* Oxford: Clarendon Press.

Walter. R. 1985. *Hans Kelsen: Ein Leben im Dienste der Wissenschaft.* Vienna: Manzsche Verlag.

L

land development controls. Both economists and lawyers have written extensively on land development issues. However, this essay is concerned not with the separate contributions of the two disciplines but with the particular perspective on land development control associated with the law-and-economics movement. Controls on land use are exercised by regulatory bodies throughout the developed world. The traditional economic case for land development controls based on externality reasoning is developed and the alternative of private solutions examined in the first part. Next, land use control systems are analysed. Although there are three broad systems – development control, zoning and master planning (Cheshire and Sheppard 1997) – this essay is concerned with the first two. It will argue that the systems of development control as applied in the United Kingdom and zoning as operated in the United States are, in practice, similar systems. The two systems are briefly described, emphasizing the treatment of landowners' property rights and the role which courts play in supervizing the application of the regulatory framework. Thereafter, a general model of the land use control process is presented using the analytic framework of property rule/liability rule developed by Calabresi and Melamed (1972) and applied to land use regulation by Fischel (1985) and Stephen (1987).

AN ECONOMIC CASE FOR LAND DEVELOPMENT CONTROLS. Like many forms of regulation, the regulation of land use has been justified by economists on the basis of *market failure* (Willis 1980; Corkindale 1996). Here the market failure arises from the external effects which the users of a parcel of land might impose on the users of contiguous or adjacent parcels of land. Such *externalities* may arise from noise or air pollution, obstruction of a desirable view etc. In other words, uses of property are in conflict. Ronald Coase (1960), of course, pointed out that such conflicts of use are bilateral. Each party is imposing a cost on the other. Positive externalities may be generated by locating similar activities together. Such joint location may reduce the quantity of an ancillary service consumed by the activity or the resources needed to produce that service, i.e. there are agglomeration economies from the collocation of the activities.

Strictly speaking, talking of an externality implies that an uncompensated effect of the activities of one party on another has not been resolved through direct negotiation between the parties, i.e. the spillover remains uncompensated. Fischel (1985: 119–20) argues that many situations classified as externalities are not so since what is observed is the outcome *after* negotiation has exhausted the gains from trade.

Alternative to development controls. Alternatives to regulation via land use controls include direct regulation of particular externality generating activities to control the level of externality (e.g. emission controls on factories, restrictions on night-time activity at airports etc.), taxation of externality generating activities in order that the polluter 'internalize' the externality, private law remedies available under the *law of nuisance* and private negotiation between the parties involved resulting in restrictive covenants or easements (Willis 1980; Knetsch 1983).

It is sometimes argued that private solutions to externality problems such as the use of the law of nuisance or the negotiation of easements or restrictive covenants are flawed because they are reactive and thus only come into play after the externality has occurred. It might be more efficient, being less wasteful of resources, to use regulation via zoning and development control to lay out in advance what types of development will be permitted in a particular area and what types will not, or at least to have a public body deliberate on the acceptability of a particular development in a particular location before the development takes place. In one sense this criticism of private remedies is misplaced. It ignores the deterrent effect of nuisance law and the proactive use of restrictive covenants and easements.

The use to which a plot of land will be put will be conditioned by whether or not it will give rise to a nuisance claim. Consequently, a use which is incompatible with existing adjacent uses (in terms of existing nuisance law) is unlikely to take place unless the rights of adjacent users are bought out in some way (an easement is acquired). Indeed, the rights of *future* owners of adjacent land could be bought out by purchasing an easement from a current owner which, because it 'runs with the land', had the effect of removing the future landowner's right to take out a nuisance action against its neighbour (Knetsch 1983: 146; Fischel 1985: 164). Conversely, a landowner or prospective purchaser of a plot of land wishing to ensure that no incompatible use was made of adjacent land could purchase a restrictive covenant from its owner precluding the use of the land for such incompatible purposes (Ellickson 1973; Fischel 1985: 27, 164).

Clearly such restrictive covenants and easements could only be obtained at a price. Their price would have to be no less than the fall in the value of the adjacent land brought about by the loss of the property right restricted by the covenant or easement in order for the exchange to be attractive to the owner of the adjacent land. It would also have to be less than the value to the acquirer of the benefits from the covenant or easement. Thus the benefit to the acquirer would have to exceed the loss to the donor, thus satisfying the Kaldor–Hicks criterion. Not only that but since compensation would actually be paid it would be a Pareto improvement. Viewed in this way only value enhancing restrictions on the use of land would come into being. In contrast, land-use regulation might result in restrictions on development being imposed which were not value enhancing because such mutual benefit mechanisms are absent or because political considerations, rent-seeking, etc. may be present (Corkindale 1996).

Prior to the introduction of zoning and development control private remedies were widely used by property owners and even developers to control the future uses to which a property which they were selling could be put, e.g. restricting occupancy of residential dwellings built on the land to single family occupancy or restricting the use of the property to residential occupancy. Such mechanisms are still used by landowners and developers today even though regulation through zoning and development control is widespread. Houston, Texas, has not adopted a zoning ordinance yet some observers claim that single-use districts have evolved suggesting that regulatory zoning is not necessary (Siegan 1972). It is not clear that the Houston experience can be used to reject zoning. What would the situation have been if there had been zoning? Clearly, Houston works but would welfare levels be higher with zoning? Fischel (1985: 233) argues that the evidence from Houston does not demonstrate the case against zoning.

The picture of what can be achieved by private solutions as described above is quite appealing. They appear to avoid the bureaucracy and potential rent seeking which could be involved under regulation. However, our description of the operation of such a private law system may suffer from what Demsetz has called *nirvana economics*. We have been comparing the imperfect world of zoning and development control with an idealized world of nuisance law, covenants and easements. More particularly, we have been assuming that the Coase Theorem holds. In other words there are no impediments to property owners contracting with each other to achieve the distribution of property rights over land which will result in all land being allocated to its highest valued use. However, a comparison of systems for regulating land use requires that all systems are viewed as they will operate in reality. An evaluation of the private solutions requires that we consider whether the assumptions underlying the Coase Theorem are met in this context. Of importance here is the assumption of zero transaction costs. Transaction costs in the real world are patently not zero. In this context transaction costs arise from the need to find the relevant parties with whom to bargain, and the potential for strategic behaviour.

Finding the relevant parties with whom to bargain may not seem much of an impediment to bargaining. Where there is no public regulation of land use a developer wishing to develop a parcel of land by installing a noxious use might easily identify adjacent landowners with whom to negotiate an easement. However, those adversely affected may be more than the immediate neighbours. How far should the net be cast? The law governing easements considers proximity of the dominant and servient tenements as a pertinent issue in whether or not to enforce such agreements. This may introduce some uncertainty where the net is cast widely. Perhaps more importantly, the larger the number of affected land owners the more likely it is that there will be a holdout problem, i.e., a landowner will behave strategically to extract a major share of the benefits to the developer of the easements from surrounding land owners. Clearly, the use of easements to avoid a nuisance action will break down if one party (of the many) who might succeed in a nuisance action refuses to grant an easement. Furthermore, each potential grantor will have an incentive to behave strategically in this way. Thus where a number of easements are required the potential for holdout is great. A similar set of problems arises when a landowner wishes to obtain restrictive covenants from adjacent landowners to forestall any future noxious uses. Land use regulation may be seen as a way of reducing the transaction costs associated with such private agreements and increasing certainty (Knetsch 1983: 145–6). Of course, there will be administrative costs associated with land use regulation. Whether or not such costs are less than those associated with the alternatives is an empirical question which is not dealt with here.

ZONING AND DEVELOPMENT CONTROL SYSTEMS. Any system of land-use controls can be seen as withdrawing from the bundle of property rights, which constitute the ownership of land, the stick which represents the 'right to develop'. However, under different constitutional frameworks the withdrawal of such a right has different implications. How this issue has been resolved in the United States and the United Kingdom is discussed below. In both systems the exercise of the right by a public body to control land use is, however, subject to judicial scrutiny. We argue below that for most analytical purposes development control and zoning may be viewed as the same system.

United Kingdom. Development control has operated in the United Kingdom since the passing of the Town and Country Planning Act 1947 and the Town and Country Planning (Scotland) Act 1947 (hereafter, the Town and Country Planning Acts) together with subsequent amendments. Cullingworth and Nadin (1994) argue that prior to the passage of these Acts the system of land use control was one of zoning (see below). The powers of development control are exercised by organs of local government authorized by the Acts to do so. These organs are supervized in the exercise of these powers by departments of central government.

In the United Kingdom the doctrine of parliamentary supremacy gives Parliament very wide discretion in the framing of statutes. Inhibitions on the exercise of power by Parliament derive from the political process rather than from the legal system. Nevertheless, the Town and Country Planning Acts of 1947 provided compensation for those landowners who lost 'development value' due to the passage of those Acts (Stephen 1987).

Decisions of the authorities (both local and central government) exercising powers of development control in the UK are subject to the doctrines of administrative law as evolved by the courts. Where courts believe an administrative decision (including a development control decision) involves an abuse of the statutory powers conferred by Parliament or goes beyond the powers conferred by Parliament it will use the *ultra vires* doctrine to declare the decision unlawful. It should be noted that in the UK local government bodies are the creation of Parliament and are only entitled to exercise those powers granted to them by Parliament.

Commentators have argued that the UK statutes governing development control are sufficiently vague in the delineation of powers that considerable scope is given to the judiciary in interpreting the Acts and constraining the regulatory bodies (Underwood 1981). In particular, in the area of development control the courts in applying the *ultra vires* doctrine have used the concept of 'unreasonableness' to quash decisions of the relevant regulatory bodies (*Newbury District Council v. Secretary of State for the Environment* [1981] AC 578). Indeed, it is arguable that the statues are sufficiently vague in defining the powers of the regulatory bodies that the law of development control has been made as much by the courts as by Parliament (Stephen 1987).

The Acts allow the regulatory body to refuse to grant permission for a development. The courts have subjected the exercise of this power to a particular test of unreasonableness: that the regulatory body consider, *but only consider*, material considerations in reaching their decision. The Acts also allow the regulatory bodies to permit a development '*subject to such conditions as they think fit*'. However, conditions attached to a permission are subject to three tests which the House of Lords in *Newbury District Council* laid down as: (i) they must be for a planning purpose; (ii) they must fairly and reasonably be related to the permitted development; (iii) they must not be unreasonable.

United States. Zoning ordinances have been widely adopted by local governments in the United States since the passing of the Standard State Zoning Enabling Act 1926. The Federal Government plays no role in the zoning process. However, in some states bodies have been created at regional level (by state legislatures) which have the power to override zoning decisions of local government (see Fischel 1985: 26). Zoning ordinances lay down the type of development which will be permitted in specified locations within a local government's jurisdiction. In principle any conforming development may take place within a given use zone. This would appear to provide a stable, predictable and non-bureaucratic system. However, Ellickson and Tarlock (1981) argue that when combined with zoning variance procedures and subdivision controls this system becomes discretionary. It then bears many similarities to a system of development control.

In the United States the protection of private property afforded by the Fifth Amendment to the US Constitution requires that any regulation beyond the exercise of police powers be subject to just compensation. In its early years the use of zoning (under which no compensation is paid) was subject to challenges as to its constitutionality. However, the US Supreme Court in *Village of Euclid v. Ambler Realty Co.* (272 US 365 (1926)) upheld the constitutionality of zoning. Although, the plaintiff in *Euclid* alleged a taking, no compensation was sought and the case was decided on due process grounds rather than as a takings issue (Fischel 1985: 47). Zoning figures prominently in the US literature on regulatory takings, i.e. where it is claimed that a regulatory body has exceeded its 'police powers' to regulate an activity and has effectively taken an asset without compensation.

In the United States courts provide safeguards against procedural irregularities in the application of zoning powers by local governments. However, a wider role exists for the courts than in the UK because of constitutional issues. Fischel (1985: 43–55) identifies three types of clause in state and federal constitutions which have given rise to litigation in the field of zoning: those governing due process, equal protection and takings.

(i) Due process cases are concerned with whether the procedures laid down in the statutes have been applied (procedural due process) or whether the procedures laid down are themselves reasonable (substantive due process).

(ii) The equal protection clauses require that the law be applied impersonally and in a non-discriminatory manner. It has been used to challenge 'exclusionary zoning' ordinances which it has been argued deny certain categories of persons (e.g. low income families) access to a community by restricting the types of residential property that may be constructed in it.

(iii) The takings clause protects owners of property against the expropriation of their property by a public body without just compensation. This is a complex area of US law. It is sufficient for present purposes to note that restricting the use of land through a zoning ordinance does not necessarily constitute a taking, but a zoning ordinance which required undeveloped land previously zoned for residential use to be left as vacant land would.

Although devised under different constitutional frameworks and having superficially different administrative arrangements, development control and zoning as practised in the UK and US are very similar land use control systems. They grant to directly or indirectly elected regulatory bodies the right to control the development of land within their jurisdiction subject to scrutiny by the courts. In what follows we treat zoning and development control as a single system of land use regulation.

THE LAW-AND-ECONOMICS OF LAND DEVELOPMENT CONTROL SYSTEMS. Fischel (1985) has argued that the distinction between the Coasean (or the property rights approach as he calls it) analysis of land use control issues and the externality analysis is largely one of approach rather than objective. Because it focuses on the institution of property rights and the impediments to exchange of these rights, he argues that it is more likely to point the analyst in the direction of the most effective solution to land use problems. Similarly, the Coasean approach and the concepts which have subsequently been developed in the law-and-economics literature allow us to obtain greater clarity on some of the issues that have bedevilled discussion of land use regulation and development control.

In what follows we analyse a generalized land use control system which captures the main features of the US zoning system and the UK development control systems discussed above. We characterize such a system as consisting of a 'planning authority' vested with powers granted by a higher legislative authority to regulate land use within a specified geographical area. The planning authority is assumed to be directly or indirectly elected such that it may be assumed to be interested in maintaining the support of the median voter in the political arena corresponding to its area of jurisdiction. However, the planning authority is constrained in the use of its authority by the right of an aggrieved applicant to appeal to an appropriate court. The court has the role of ensuring that the planning authority has not exceeded its constitutional or statutory rights in exercising its role.

Following Fischel (1985) and Stephen (1987), the generalized planning system is analysed below using what Fischel has called an entitlements diagram. The analysis is aided by using the property rule and liability rule terminology developed by Calabresi and Melamed (1972). Unlike the externality literature which considers only technological externalities (i.e. effects on production functions or utility functions), the present analysis also encompasses the pecuniary externalities of a development (i.e. financial or distributional effects). It is clear that the actions of the actors involved in the planning process will be motivated by the financial effects of the decisions on them or their constituents (Stephen 1987: 89).

Consider a proposal to develop a plot of land as an apartment block in an area otherwise occupied by single family residential properties. The application may be thought of as one for a zoning variance in an area currently zoned for single family housing or as an application for substantial development under a development control regime. Assume that the development as envisaged by its promoter would impose a negative externality on residents of adjacent land through increased traffic congestion and parking in the streets surrounding the commercial development. Also assume that it is possible to reduce these external effects by modifying the development in such a way as to provide on-site parking spaces and enhancement of the local road system. The development as envisaged by its promoter maximizes the profit to be derived from developing the site: any of the modifications to the development which reduce the externality also reduce the benefit to be derived from the site by the developer. In other words, developing the site with an apartment block can be achieved by a range of specifications but the 'higher' the specification the lower the profitability of the development for its promoter.

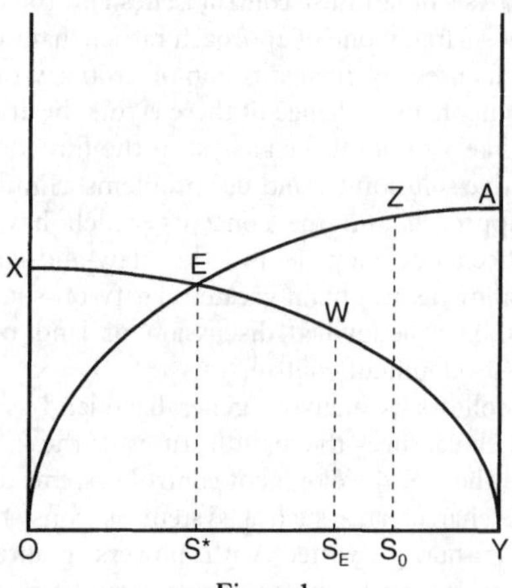

Figure 1

Figure 1 is drawn showing specification on the horizontal axis as a continuum increasing to the right from the developer's profit maximizing specification (O). With each increase in specification the development cost rises as shown by the curve OA, which is the developer's *marginal cost of compliance curve*. When the specification level is S_O the developer makes zero profit. This implies that the developer would make profits equal to the area OZS_O at the profit maximizing specification (O). As the specification rises the external effect on local residents is reduced as shown by XY, the *marginal benefit of compliance curve*. At specification S_E the external effects on the residents of the adjacent land arising from the development are zero. Thus the total externality imposed by the development at specification O is the area $OXWS_E$. Specifications above S_E generate net benefits for the occupants of adjacent land.

The marginal benefit and marginal cost curves intersect at E. At this point the marginal cost of compliance equals the marginal benefit of compliance, thus maximizing the welfare of the parties concerned. Specification S* is that which achieves this optimum. It maximizes the net benefit of the development to the developer and the local residents. At specifications below S* the marginal benefit to residents of increasing specification exceeds the marginal cost to the developer, indicating that an increased specification will increase the net benefit to society. Conversely, at specifications above S* the marginal cost of compliance exceeds the marginal benefit of compliance, indicating that a reduction in specification would increase the net benefit to society.

The Coase Theorem tells us that if transaction costs are zero the developer and local residents would negotiate towards specification S* regardless of the initial specification. It should be noted that at the optimum specification (S*) the development generates externalities equal to the area S^*EWS_E and costs of complying with specification S* equal to the area OES*. However, who bears the burden of the costs of compliance and the externality depends on the initial specification, i.e. the specification from which the bargaining begins. Which specification that is will depend on the entitlements of the parties.

It has been argued above that transaction costs are reduced under a land use regulation system by the planning authority representing the interests of the local community. Thus in analysing a development decision such as that represented in Figure 1 the entitlements of concern are those of the developer and the planning authority. The earlier discussion of the land use systems in the UK and US suggest that entitlements will lie with the planning authority. This is the position taken by Stephen (1987) and Fischel (1985). The former argues that UK courts are unlikely to settle the entitlement beyond S_E whilst the latter argues that US courts have given zoning boards entitlements which go beyond S_E.

If, as is argued by Fischel (1985) and Stephen (1987), the local planning authority's entitlement is at S_E in Figure 1 or to the right of it, the resulting specification will be inefficient in terms of the Kaldor–Hicks criterion. Efficiency would require a movement to S*. The entitlements are seen to be defended by a property rule which leaves the local planning authority in the driving seat. Furthermore, bargaining only involves a 'leasing' of the right to develop: the property right on making planning decisions remains with the local planning authority.

Were we dealing with individuals and transaction costs were low we would expect private bargaining to result in a reallocation of property rights which would move the parties to S*. However, here we are dealing with an agent of local government which has the right to regulate. Should regulation be subject to bargaining? Both Fischel (1985) and Stephen (1988) argue that such bargaining takes place and is necessary. In the case of the UK this was done via 'planning agreements', renamed 'planning obligations' in a recent Act of Parliament. The payment in kind by developers is termed 'planning gain' in the UK. Fischel (1985) argues that such bargains are of a restricted nature because they are restricted to bartering a reduced level of specification for some (usually physical) facility or benefit to the community. Such 'bargaining' is seen to promote efficiency. However, the courts ensure that the local planning authority cannot exploit its position merely to raise revenue or reduce taxation (Fischel 1985; Stephen 1987). Planners and planning lawyers are highly critical of such a bargaining process but economists sensitive to a world of 'trade offs' cannot but see their benefit.

FRANK H. STEPHEN

See also COMPENSATION FOR REGULATORY TAKINGS; EMINENT DOMAIN AND JUST COMPENSATION; LAND TITLE SYSTEMS; LAND-USE DOCTRINES; RESTITUTION FOR BENEFIT OR LIABILITY FOR HARM; TAKINGS; UNITIZATION.

Subject classification: 6c(iv).

STATUTES

Town and Country Planning Act 1947, 10 & 11 Geo. VI, c.51.

Town and Country Planning (Scotland) Act 1947, 10 & 11 Geo. VI, c.57.

CASES

Newbury District Council v. Secretary of State for the Environment [1981] AC 578.

Village of Euclid v. Ambler Realty Co., 272 US 365 (1926).

BIBLIOGRAPHY

Calabresi, G. and Melamed, D. 1972. Property rules, liability rules and inalienability: one view of the cathedral. *Harvard Law Review* 85: 1089–1128.

Cheshire, P. and Sheppard, S. 1997. The welfare economics of land use regulation. Paper presented at UK Law and Economics Study Group, 1996.

Coase, R. 1960. The problem of social cost. *Journal of Law and Economics* 3: 1–44.

Corkindale, J. 1996. *Economics of Land Use Planning*. Department of the Environment, London, March.

Cullingworth, J.B. and Nadin, V. 1994. *Town and Country Planning in Britain*. 11th edn, London: Routledge.

Ellickson, R.C. 1973. Alternatives to zoning: covenants, nuisance rules and fines as land use controls. *University of Chicago Law Review* 40: 681–782.

Ellickson, R.C. and Tarlock, A.D. 1981. *Land-Use Controls: Cases and Materials*. Boston: Little, Brown & Co.

Fischel, W.A. 1985. *The Economics of Zoning Laws*. Baltimore: The Johns Hopkins University Press.

Knetsch, J.A. 1983. *Property Rights and Compensation*. Toronto: Butterworths.

Siegan, B.H. 1972. *Land Use without Zoning*. Lexington, MA: Lexington Books.

Stephen, F.H. 1987. Property rules and liability rules in the regulation of land development: an analysis of development control in Great Britain and Ontario. *International Review of Law and Economics* 7: 33–49.

Stephen, F.H. 1988. *The Economics of the Law*. London: Harvester Wheatsheaf.

Underwood, J. 1981. *Development Control: A Review of Research and Current Issues*, Progress in Planning, v. 16 pt.3. Oxford and New York: Pergamon Press.

Willis, K.G. 1980. *The Economics of Town and Country Planning*. London: Granada Publishing.

land title systems. Legal protection of property rights in land is essential if owners are to maximize the value of land by transferring it to higher valuing users and investing in improvements to the point where marginal social benefits and costs are equal. Providing such protection is an important function of a land title system. In a world of certainty about previous transfers of land, such a system could simply enforce the rights of current owner-possessors in the knowledge that all previous transfers were consensual (that is, no competing claims exist). But when there is uncertainty about whether previous transfers were consensual, a prospective buyer of land cannot be sure that he will have good title to the land as against a previously defrauded owner. In that case, the basic problem facing a land title system is to resolve such claims in a way that promotes the maximal exchange of land and optimal investment in improvements.

Baird and Jackson (1984: 300) state this problem succinctly as follows: 'In a world where information is not perfect, [the land title system] can protect a later owner's interests fully, or [it] can protect the earlier owner's interests fully. But [it] cannot do both.' Epstein (1986: 674) portrayed this choice in terms of the tension between *first possession* as the determinant of title in an ideal world and *current possession* as the most practical determinant: 'As a matter of high principle, what comes first is best; as a matter of proof, however, what comes last is more reliable and more certain.' John Stuart Mill ([1848] 1987: 220) suggested the following resolution of this tradeoff:

> Possession which has not been legally questioned within a moderate number of years, ought to be . . . a complete title. Even when the acquisition was wrongful, the dispossession . . . by revival of a claim which has been long dormant, would be . . . almost always a greater private and public mischief, than leaving the original wrong without atonement.

(The logic of this proposal is embodied in the doctrine of adverse possession, which I discuss below.)

Actual title systems. Historically, common law countries have developed two systems for protecting title. Under the registration system, a landowner registers his land with the government, at which time a legal proceeding is undertaken to determine the status of title. In the absence of a legitimate claim, the government issues a certificate that gives the owner good title against any future claims. Subsequent purchasers need only inspect the certificate to verify ownership, and if a claimant should appear, he is only entitled to monetary compensation from a public fund financed by registration fees (Cribbet 1975: 298–9; Bostick 1987). The idea of land registration was borrowed from the practice of registering ownership interests in ships by Sir Robert Torrens (son of the classical economist) while he was serving as Registrar General of the Province of South Australia in 1858. Since then, the Torrens system of land registration has spread to many countries and a few jurisdictions in the US (Cribbet 1975: 298; Shick and Plotkin 1978: 17–20). In 1925, England enacted land reform that, among other things, instituted land registration as the principal form of title assurance, replacing the 'cumbersome examination of title deeds' that had arisen out of the feudal system (Cribbet 1975: 309).

In contrast, the United States has, since colonial days, relied for the most part on the recording system. This system, which originated with the recording acts, requires the maintenance of a public record of land transfer that can be inspected by prospective buyers to establish evidence of good title, thereby easing land transfer (Rose 1994: 205). In contrast to land registration, however, examination of the record does not *guarantee* title; depending on the thoroughness of the search and differences in lawyers' opinions about the title history, the risk of a claim to title remains. As a result, the history is searched anew with each land transfer (or at least is updated), and owners typically purchase private title insurance to provide monetary compensation in the event of a future claim (Cribbet 1975: 309–10; Rose 1994: 207).

From an economic perspective, the fundamental difference between these two systems is who receives the land, and who receives monetary compensation in the event of a claim. Under land registration, the owner-possessor retains the land and the claimant receives monetary compensation, whereas under the recording system with title insurance, the reverse is true.

ECONOMIC INCENTIVES OF LAND TITLE SYSTEMS. An economic approach to land title systems views them as creating incentives to maximize the value of land in the presence of the above uncertainties. This involves both *exchange efficiency*, or insuring that land ends up in the hands of the highest valuing user, and *productive efficiency*, or providing incentives for owners to improve the land to the point where the marginal benefit of the investment equals the marginal cost.

Exchange efficiency. The analysis of exchange efficiency focuses on two parties: the possessor of a parcel of land and a claimant. Assume that the possessor believes he holds legal title to the land (this is not always the case; see the discussion of adverse possession below), but that the possibility of a title defect leaves the chance that another individual will assert a claim of ownership. The purpose of the title system is to assign ownership in such a case. (Many claims are not for full ownership but instead arise over easements or boundary disputes. The basic argument is the same in these cases.)

Let the possessor's initial utility be $U(W_0, L_0)$, where W_0 is his wealth and L_0 is his holding of land. Assume that this is the utility maximizing portfolio of assets, so that the possessor's indifference curve, labelled U_1, is tangent to the budget line at point A in Figure 1, where the slope of the budget line is the negative of the price per unit of land, p. Note that the convexity of the indifference curve implies that the possessor does not view land and wealth as perfect substitutes. For example, the maximum amount of money that he would accept in return for his entire parcel is given by the distance DW_0, whereas the market value of the parcel is given by the smaller distance BW_0 (that is, $BW_0 = pL_0$). The difference between these amounts reflects the possessor's subjective value of the land, an amount that presumably grows over time as the possessor (or his progeny) continues to occupy the land (Holmes 1897: 477; Radin 1986: 741; Stake 1995). An important function of land title systems (and market systems based on voluntary exchange in general) is to protect subjective valuations of this sort by preventing non-consensual transfers of title.

The preceding model implies that the possessor would strictly prefer a title system that awards him title to the land rather than its market value in the event of a legitimate claim, where the distance BD is the dollar amount by which market value would under-compensate him. Presumably, however, the possessor would be indifferent between this system and a system that awards the land to the claimant and pays the possessor full compensation (i.e., the amount DW_0). The problem is that this quantity is unobservable, so compensation is ordinarily set at market value. (Knetsch and Borcherding (1979) address this issue in the context of eminent domain acquisitions.) In contrast, since claimants are not occupiers of the land and may never have occupied it, it is reasonable to suppose that they have little or no subjective value of the land beyond its financial (market) value. Thus, their valuation of the land will be roughly equal to its market value, or the distance BW_0 in Figure 1.

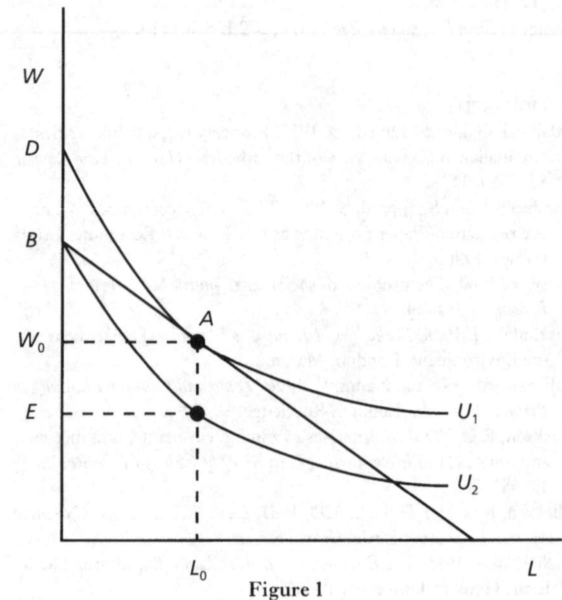

Figure 1

This analysis suggests that a system that awards the land to the possessor and market value compensation to the claimant both maximizes the value of the land (i.e., awards the land to the party that values it the most), and avoids undercompensating the loser.This conclusion is only partly correct, however, since under a system that awards the land to the claimant, it is possible that the possessor will re-acquire the land from the claimant in a consensual transfer. To see why, note that, beginning from point B, the maximum amount the dispossessed individual will pay to re-acquire the land is given by the distance BE. In contrast, the claimant, who merely has a financial interest in the land, will accept any amount greater than the land's market value BW_0. Since the dispossessed individual's willingness to pay exceeds the claimant's reservation price (i.e., since $BE > BW_0$), a mutually beneficial bargain is possible. Thus, as long as transaction costs are low enough, the disposed individual will re-acquire the land from the claimant, thereby achieving the value-maximizing outcome (Miceli and Sirmans 1995a).

The foregoing analysis is an example of the Coase Theorem, which states that if transaction costs are low enough then the efficient allocation of resources will be achieved regardless of the initial assignment of legal rights (Coase 1960). In the current setting this implies that, regardless of how the title system assigns title to the land in the event of a claim, the land will end up with the highest valuing user. In this case, the only impact of the title system is distributive. That is, the system that awards the land to the possessor leaves him at his original utility level, U_1, while the claimant receives the market value of the land as compensation. In contrast, when the claimant receives the land, the possessor, after re-purchasing the land, has utility somewhere between U_1 and U_2 (depending on how much above the market value he paid the claimant for the land), while the claimant receives an amount of money between the market value and the possessor's subjective value (i.e., between BW_0 and BE). Thus, although the value of the land is maximized under both title systems, on distributive grounds, both parties prefer the system that awards them the land.

The comparison between the two title systems differs when transaction costs are high since in that case there is no guarantee that the parties will be able to correct an inefficient assignment of title through voluntary exchange. When this is true, the title system matters for efficiency as well as for distribution. An efficient title system should therefore minimize impediments to transfers of land, for example by economizing on the costs to prospective buyers of locating and bargaining with the true possessor (Johnson 1972; Rose 1994: 205).

Janczyk (1977) explicity examined this criterion by comparing the operating costs of the Torrens system and the recording system in Cook County, Illinois, where the two systems coexist. He considered two costs: the average cost of transferring title under the two systems, and the cost of switching a parcel from one system to the other. His results indicated that title transfer is cheaper under the Torrens system, and that, despite a one-time switching cost, a substantial savings could be realized by converting all parcels to the Torrens system. Shick and Plotkin (1978) offer a less favourable assessment of the cost advantages of the Torrens system compared to the recording system, while also questioning its ability to provide equal benefits in terms of title protection. Their assessment, however, may primarily reflect the marginal status of the Torrens system in the US rather than its true merits in an ideal setting.

In some cases, transaction costs will be so high as to prevent bargaining. When this is true, efficiency can only be achieved if the title system assigns the land up front to the party that values it the most (Cooter and Ulen 1996: 89–90). The above analysis suggests that this objective will generally be accomplished by awarding the land to the possessor, given that the latter will ordinarily value the land more highly than the claimant. Although it is conceivable that claimants might occasionally value the land more than the possessor, this would not seem to be the norm. (An exception might be a case in which the claimant has squatted on the land for a long time, a situation that I will discuss below in the context of adverse possession.) Thus, on average, the value of land will be maximized, and the transaction costs of re-sale will be minimized, by assigning title to occupiers. By these criteria, the registration system appears superior to the recording system.

Productive efficiency. In addition to exchange, the value of land can be enhanced by improvements. From a social perspective, efficiency requires that improvements in land be made to the point where the marginal return on the investment equals the marginal cost (ignoring externalities). In the presence of uncertainties about title, however, possessors of land may underinvest for fear of not realizing the full return (Johnson 1972; Besley 1995; Alston, Libecap and Schneider 1996). Thus, the title system plays an important role in providing incentives for efficient investment in land, both by providing information up front about the security of title and possibly by promising compensation to possessors in the event of a claim. (A related problem is when a person mistakenly improves land owned by another (Dickinson 1985); in that case, however, the only issue is the appropriate compensation for the improver, not the assignment of title since the latter is not in dispute.)

To illustrate the impact of title security on land investment, let $V(x)$ be the value of land to the possessor as a function of the dollar investment in improvements, x, where $V' > 0$ and $V'' < 0$. Further, suppose that x, once spent, is non-salvageable. The efficient level of improvements, x^*, equates the marginal return on the investment to the last dollar invested, or

$$V'(x) = 1. \quad (1)$$

Now suppose that at the time of the investment, the possessor knows that a claim will arise in the future with probability q. In that case, his level of investment will depend on the title system in place. If the system awards title to the land and improvements to the possessor, then he will make the efficient level of investment because he faces no risk of loss (i.e., he is fully insured). In contrast, if the system awards title to the claimant without indemnifying the possessor, he will invest to the point where:

$$(1-q)\,V'(x) = 1, \qquad (2)$$

resulting in too little investment as long as $q > 0$.

Suppose, however, that under the latter system, the possessor can purchase title insurance which provides full compensation in the event of a claim. In that case, he will choose x to maximize $V(x) - x - \pi$, where π is the insurance premium. If the possessor prepays the premium (and therefore views it as sunk), he will invest efficiently since he is fully insured against loss. In equilibrium, the insurance premium will therefore be $\pi = qV(x^*)$.

The preceding shows that the registration system and the recording system with title insurance can both yield efficient investment incentives. Two potential differences, however, are worthy of note. First, market insurance may not be able to insure against the loss of subjective value (because of its unobservability). This could result in underinvestment under the recording system if a component of the marginal return ($V'(x)$) is subjective value. Second, although possessors pay for public insurance under the registration system in the form of a registration fee which, if the insurance is actuarially fair, would also equal π, one might expect that private title insurers with a profit motive will do a better job of identifying title flaws up front as compared to public insurance. Thus, depending on the structure of incentives for public insurers, fewer claims might be expected under private insurance (i.e., q would be lower), resulting in lower costs of dispute resolution and lower insurance premiums. This is not a fundamental difference between the systems, however, since private insurance for claimants (or at least efficiently structured incentives for public insurers) could be used under the registration system (Miceli and Sirmans 1995a: 86).

Failure of land registration in the US. The foregoing comparison of the two title systems has generally pointed to the superiority of land registration over the recording system from an economic perspective. This result is seemingly at odds with the failure of the registration system to replace (or even to offer a viable alternative to) the recording system in the US (Cribbet 1975: 309). As Shick and Plotkin note (1978: 2), 'use of Torrens in the US has been limited almost entirely to urban areas and for purposes associated with the elimination of historical title defects'. For example, its adoption in Cook County, Illinois, was a response to the Great Chicago Fire of 1871 which destroyed the public land records. The most likely explanation for the failure of Torrens in the US is historical. The recording system was instituted at an early date, and when land registration was introduced later in a few jurisdictions, it was optional and switching was costly. In addition, private title insurers have resisted competition from government (public) insurance (Cribbet 1975: 316–17; Friedman 1985: 434; Rose, 1994: 208), and mortgage lenders often require that borrowers purchase title insurance even for registered land (Shick and Plotkin 1978: 69). Thus, while many commentators have concluded that land registration is the better choice if one were establishing a new system 'in virgin land' (Cribbet 1975: 318; Bostick 1987), it is likely to remain a marginal system in the US as a result of the nature of existing property institutions.

LEGAL LIMITS ON THE TRANSFER OF TITLE. The discussion to this point has emphasized the economic benefits associated with an owner's right to transfer title freely (including the right to refuse a transfer). The law, however, places several limits on the alienability of title. For example, the government can physically acquire title to land, or transfer it from one party to another, without the owner's consent (Stake 1995). This section offers economic explanations for two such involuntary transfers: eminent domain, and adverse possession.

Eminent domain. Acquisition of property by eminent domain represents an involuntary transfer of title in that the government (or a private party endowed by the government with eminent domain power) need not negotiate with an owner before acquiring his property; it can simply seize the property provided that it puts it to 'public use' and pays the owner 'just compensation' (interpreted by the courts to mean market value). A common justification for this power is that it prevents individuals from refusing to sell their property to the government at a 'reasonable' price. This explanation is incorrect, however, because it assumes that an owner's subjective value (i.e., his value above the market price) is not worthy of protection in economic exchange. The correct economic argument for eminent domain is based instead on the transaction costs that arise when the government needs to assemble a large amount of land to build a public project like a highway. When the plans for such a project become known, private owners whose land is necessary for the project acquire monopoly power in their dealing with the government, thereby raising the cost of the land above its opportunity cost (including subjective value) and endangering the success of the project. The power of eminent domain allows the government to avoid this 'hold-out' problem and the associated transaction costs by eliminating the owner's right to refuse the transaction (Posner [1973] 1992: 56–7).

The logic of this argument suggests two further points. First, the government should not have the right to coerce exchange when it is acquiring *individual* parcels since in this case the hold-out problem is not present. Although the takings clause suggests no such limit, Fischel (1995: 74) argues that the transaction costs of acquiring property by eminent domain are sufficiently high compared to market acquisition (in the absence of the hold-out problem) that the power is 'self-limiting'. Second, private developers often face the hold-out problem and, based on the logic of the above argument, they should also have the power of eminent domain to overcome it. The public use requirement apparently prevents this, but Fischel (1995: 72–7) notes that courts have nevertheless routinely granted the power to private enterprises (like railroads) who face significant hold-out problems.

Adverse possession. Adverse possession is a doctrine under which a trespasser (or 'squatter') can acquire title to a piece of land by occupying it in a manner consistent with ownership for a statutory period of time, provided that the true owner does not protest. In effect, adverse possession is a time limit to an owner's right to exclude trespassers or wrongful possessors. The traditional economic explanations for this doctrine relate to both exchange and productive efficiency. Regarding the former, adverse possession clears uncertain title to land so as to facilitate exchange. Regarding the latter, it prevents productive land from being left idle for long periods of time (Epstein 1986; Netter, Hersch and Manson 1986; Cooter and Ulen 1996: 131–2). Neither of these explanations, however, is entirely satisfactory. First, modern land records make the cost of identifying owners relatively cheap, and second, land left idle is not necessarily being used inefficiently given the option value of waiting for the optimal time to develop.

Stake (1995) offers an alternative explanation for adverse possession based on the notion of 'loss aversion'. Psychological experiments reveal that people generally demand more compensation for losing an object than they are willing to pay to acquire it. This is consistent with the above notion that the longer a possessor of land occupies it, the larger will be his loss if he is dispossessed of it. Further, an owner's failure to expel a wrongful possessor during the statutory period is evidence that he does not have a strong attachment to land apart from its financial value. Based on this argument, awarding the land to the possessor by adverse possession minimizes the loss suffered by the party who must give up possession.

A related explanation is based on the objective of minimizing the cost associated with boundary errors, which are the primary sources of adverse possession claims. Specifically, suppose that a landowner, when improving his land, inadvertently encroaches on a neighbour's property. According to the loss aversion argument, the encroacher's valuation of this land will grow over time as he occupies it. Thus, the shorter is the period during which the owner can expel a wrongful possessor, the smaller will be the potential costs that the latter might have to endure. Offsetting this is the fact that a shorter statutory period would create an incentive for landowners to seek opportunities to encroach in an effort to acquire land outside of the market (a form of rent seeking behaviour). The optimal statutory period balances these two effects (Ellickson 1986; Miceli and Sirmans 1995b).

THOMAS J. MICELI

See also ADVERSE POSSESSION; COASE, RONALD; COASE THEOREM; EMINENT DOMAIN AND JUST COMPENSATION; FIRST POSSESSION; HOLDOUTS; POSSESSION; TRESPASS AND NUISANCE.

Subject classification: 5b(ii); 6c(iv).

BIBLIOGRAPHY

Alston, L., Libecap, G. and Schneider, R. 1996. The determinants and impact of property rights: land titles on the Brazilian frontier. *Journal of Law, Economics, and Organization* 12: 25–61.

Baird, D. and Jackson, T. 1984. Information, uncertainty, and the transfer of property. *Journal of Legal Studies* 13: 299–320.

Besley, T. 1995. Property rights and investment incentives: theory and evidence from Ghana. *Journal of Political Economy* 103: 903–37.

Bostick, C. 1987. Land title registration: an English solution to an American problem. *Indiana Law Journal* 63: 55–111.

Coase, R. 1960. The problem of social cost. *Journal of Law and Economics* 3: 1–44.

Cooter, R. and Ulen, T. 1996. *Law and Economics*. 2nd edn, Reading, MA: Addison-Wesley.

Cribbet, J. 1975. *Principles of the Law of Property*. 2nd edn, Mineola, NY: The Foundation Press.

Dickinson, K. 1985. Mistaken improvers of real estate. *North Carolina Law Review* 64: 37–75.

Ellickson, R. 1986. Adverse possession and perpetuities law: two dents in the libertarian model of property rights. *Washington University Law Quarterly* 64: 723–37.

Epstein, R. 1986. Past and future: the temporal dimension in the law of property. *Washington University Law Quarterly* 64: 667–722.

Fischel, W. 1995. *Regulatory Takings: Law, Economics, and Politics*. Cambridge, MA: Harvard University Press.

Friedman, L. 1985. *A History of American Law*. 2nd edn, New York: Touchstone.

Holmes, O.W. 1897. The path of the law. *Harvard Law Review* 10: 457–78.

Janczyk, J. 1977. An economic analysis of the land title systems for transferring real property. *Journal of Legal Studies* 6: 213–33.

Johnson, O. 1972. Economic analysis, the legal framework and land tenure systems. *Journal of Law and Economics* 15: 259–76.

Knetsch, J. and Borcherding, T. 1979. Expropriation of private property and the basis for compensation. *University of Toronto Law Journal* 29: 237–52.

Miceli, T. and Sirmans, C.F. 1995a. The economics of land transfer and title insurance. *Journal of Real Estate Finance and Economics* 10: 81–8.

Miceli, T. and Sirmans, C.F. 1995b. An economic theory of adverse possession. *International Review of Law and Economics* 15: 161–73.

Mill, J.S. 1848. *Principles of Political Economy*. Ed. W. Ashley; repr. Fairfield, NJ: Augustus M. Kelley, 1987.

Netter, J., Hersch, P. and Manson, W. 1986. An economic analysis of adverse possession statutes. *International Review of Law and Economics* 6: 217–27.

Posner, R. 1973. *Economic Analysis of Law*. 4th edn, Boston: Little, Brown & Co, 1992.

Radin, M. 1986. Time, possession, and alienation. *Washington University Law Quarterly* 64: 739–58.

Rose, C. 1994. *Property and Persuasion: Essays on the Theory and Rhetoric of Ownership*. Boulder, CO: Westview Press.

Shick, B. and Plotkin, I. 1978. *Torrens in the United States: A Legal and Economic History and Analysis of American Land-Registration Systems*. Lexington, MA: Lexington Books.

Stake, J. 1995. Loss aversion and involuntary transfers of title. In *Law and Economics: New and Critical Perspectives*, ed. R. Malloy and C. Braun, New York: Peter Lang.

land-use doctrines. This essay discusses the common law land-use doctrines of real covenants, equitable servitudes, easements, profits, and licences. Unfortunately, there is no appropriate single term to describe this collection of interests. Some authorities use 'servitudes', but that term could cause confusion by leading the reader to think only of equitable servitudes. 'Encumbrances' includes all of these interests, but is too broad in that it also refers to liens, mortgages and other interests not in the family of interests relating to the private control of land uses. 'Land-use doctrines' is descriptive, but could be read to include the rules relating to zoning and other public controls on use of land. As this essay is limited to the private arrangements regarding the use of land, perhaps 'land promises' would be most descriptive.

Private land-use controls remain a viable means of controlling externalities, even in this era of public zoning. Zoning has the advantages of economies of scale and obsolete restrictions can be removed by a simple majority. However, land promises can be more carefully tailored to particular situations and are supported by more meaningful 'consent' of the governed. They are relatively free from bureaucratic misdiagnosis of landowner concerns and self-serving implementation and enforcement. And they may be more reliable.

A person having the right to possess land holds an 'estate in land'. A covenant, servitude, easement or profit is not an estate in land, but is an interest in land, a right held by someone other than the estate holder. A common real covenant requires owners in a residential subdivision to keep their lawns mowed. A typical equitable servitude prevents them from using their homes for businesses. Countless easements allow utilities to bury their service lines under private lawns. A profit might allow one person to harvest timber from the land of another. And a licence (or 'license' in the US), which unlike the others is not an interest in land, could give a neighbour the right to drive across a corner of the pasture. Land-use doctrines govern the separation of such non-possessory rights from the rights of possession ordinarily thought of as ownership.

This essay addresses the enforceability, outside the landlord–tenant context, of covenants, servitudes, easements, profits and licences. The discussion of the categories should not, however, give the reader the idea that the categories do not overlap. These various land promises have much in common, both in substance and in doctrine. A promise by an owner to keep his driveway cleared might be found by a court to be a covenant, a servitude or an easement. The form of and label on the promise do not control. A promise to refrain from renting to college student tenants described as a 'real covenant' in a deed might be enforced as an equitable servitude. Even the elements of the doctrines overlap. For example, both the servitude and covenant doctrines require that the promise 'touch and concern' land in order for it to be enforceable.

THE AGE AND COMPLEXITY OF LAND-USE DOCTRINE. The complex rules of land promises have confused, frightened, bored and wearied many generations of students. Indeed, frustration with the level of detail in this law seems to be a major force behind the efforts in the United States to reform the law of land promises through the upcoming Restatement of the Law Third Property (Servitudes), drafts of which have proposed radical simplification.

Why did the rules become so elaborate and why have the intricacies resisted simplification? One reason that land law is so complex is that it is so old. Time allows simple organisms to mutate and evolve into complex ones. With more time for cases to arise, there is more opportunity for judges and legislatures to see that a small exception would improve the law. Property law is very old and, therefore, might be expected to be more complex than relatively recent areas of the law. Indeed, its complexity might signal the degree to which it has been adapted to the needs of society.

But the age of the law is not the whole answer. Another key to understanding the complexity of land-use doctrine is the age of land, its indestructibility. Because land lasts, human relationships regarding land, i.e. interests in land, may last too. Indeed, one of the functions of land-use doctrine is to allow parties to create relationships that span generations. Lasting legal relationships create inertia within the legal institutions governing those relationships. Neither immediate nor prospective reform works well.

With many connections ongoing, it is difficult to start afresh, shifting completely from old to new rules, without affecting thousands upon thousands of existing legal relationships. Parties to those relationships rely on their legal viability and would be upset by change. Meanwhile, parties contemplating new relationships involving land need to be able to count on continuing viability. It is hard to change the law without shaking confidence in nascent arrangements. At each point in time, therefore, the costs of reform might well outweigh the benefits of a simpler (or otherwise improved) set of rules.

It is possible, of course, to make changes prospectively, to apply reforms only to relationships begun in the future. But that too has its costs. Reform that is only prospective increases administrative costs during the period of transition. During the interim, lawyers and parties must learn and understand two sets of rules. Lawyers must know the old rules as long as there exist old relationships upon which people rely. Because promises relating to land can last forever, so can reliance on them. Not only does a long transition generate substantial transitional costs, but it also greatly reduces the value of the benefits ultimately achieved. A prospective-only transition in land law takes so long to complete that the advantages of the improved state amount to little when discounted back over the transition period.

It is easier for a court to create an exception than to reverse a previous ruling. This is especially so in the land law because established rules are so hard to change. For that reason, this area of the law is more dependent than many on the path it has followed in the past. Once rulings are made and repeated, future rulings must, in the usual property case, take that branch of the law for granted and graft an exception onto it, rather than pruning it back to start anew. In addition, another whole layer of complexity is added by the large number of US and English jurisdictions, the property law in each developing along its own path. The English and various American systems are sufficiently different that a rule that makes sense in one system might not in another.

Because many of the rules of land-use law are old, we cannot expect judges and legislatures to have justified their rulings with sophisticated economic rationales, at least not in current terminology, or to have adopted explicitly economic formulae for decision-making (such as Learned Hand's formula for negligence). Much of the doctrine and legal theory predates modern economic discourse. Moreover, because the law was quite formalistic and jurisprudence was less instrumental, judges supported their decisions with legal doctrine, rather than economics. For those reasons, we can rarely say with any confidence that a rule was intended to serve an economic purpose. Often, the best we can do is to try to determine whether the rule served or serves some economic end, regardless of the reasoning offered to support its adoption.

Some paths of the law, being now no more than historical accident, may resist economic explanation. The difference between the English and American rule regarding which side of the road to drive on might not yield to economic analysis. Furthermore, because the law is old and by now carefully tailored to serve our purposes, the surviving rules do a good job, leaving no obvious improvements to be made, and so the land-use doctrine has invited little economic attention. Perhaps in part for these reasons, not enough economic analysis has been done to date to make sense of the whole of land-use doctrine. Indeed, very little of the law of land promises has received proper economic treatment. Nevertheless, economic rationales for some of the requirements, distinctions and differences in the law will be suggested here.

THE ECONOMIC NEED FOR SUBDIVIDED RIGHTS. The basic economic rationale for allowing the set of all rights to use a piece of land to be carved up into smaller packages of rights would appear to be the same as the rationale for allowing the ownership of England to be broken geographically into smaller parcels and allowing the ownership of one lot to be sliced temporally into the rights of landlord and tenant; the sum of the parts is often worth more than the whole.

Assume that it is worth no more than $100 to Ben to remain legally able to operate a retail business on his land, Whiteacre. Assume also that his neighbour Sara, the owner and resident of Blackacre, is willing to pay $200 to prevent Ben from any retail business usage. As with any contract, Ben and Sara could improve their positions by an exchange, in this case Sara's $150 for Ben's promise not to operate a business. The land-use situation differs from the ordinary contractual situation, however, in that Sara's real interest is not in what Ben does, but in what any person does on Whiteacre, which Ben happens to own at the moment. Sara does not want anyone to operate a business on the land, whether it be Ben, or a tenant to whom Ben rents, or a buyer to whom Ben sells. Sara's goal cannot be achieved by contract because Ben cannot bind others to perform his contract.

The problem can be solved by separating out the right to determine whether Whiteacre is used for retail business from Ben's other rights in Whiteacre. The right to control business use of Whiteacre is worth more to Sara than to Ben, although the right to control everything else about Whiteacre is worth more to Ben than Sara. Put another way, agreements as to future land uses can minimize negative externalities from land use. Over the centuries, the tremendous gains to be had from exchanging rights to control the use of land have driven owners to seek legal mechanisms to accomplish those exchanges. And courts have obliged.

The interesting economic issues relate not to why rights in Whiteacre can be subdivided according to usage, but rather why the law fetters the subdivision of rights, as it does, and whether there is any current utility to having multiple doctrines with differing rules by which rights are subdivided. One concern, supporting constraints, is that subdivision of rights will lead to situations in which later purchasers think they are buying complete packages of rights when, in fact, they are not. During the initial development of the common law, England had no recording system to give purchasers notice of promises attached to land. Without such a system, mistakes and fraud become more likely, reducing the liquidity of land markets and undermining the basis for assuming that a voluntary exchange of rights is a genuine Pareto improvement (meaning the state *ex-post* exchange is Pareto-superior to the state *ex-ante*).

Curtailing the number of promises affixed to land with restrictive doctrine reduces the occasions for incomplete or false information. In addition, peculiar restrictions and obligations impressed on land by a capricious or imprudent owner may continue to burden land in perpetuity. Indeed, if severe enough, such private restrictions could deprive the land of its productive power forever.

In part for those reasons, judges and scholars have been quite reluctant to allow burdens to run to successors and have imposed the many limitations found in land-use doctrine. English courts have long held that burdens of covenants cannot run at law (although this rule was occasionally overcome by the 'pure principle of benefit and burden'). Even when they allowed burdens to run in equity, they restricted the doctrine by holding that there must be a benefited (dominant) parcel nearby before the burden could run. English courts also gave narrow compass to negative easements, restricting them to a few well-defined types.

American authorities have been somewhat more willing to let burdens run with land. An economic explanation of this variation might start by noting that the population density is lower in the United States, and this difference was greater in the past than it is at present. With lower density, externalities are generally less of a problem. If externalities were not as important, the American public and courts may have developed a stronger attitude that landowners should be able to do what they want, including making restrictive covenants. (The people settling each new state, and forming its early laws, might also have been more distrustful of the State than those remaining behind in England.) Another consequence of lower density is that land has a lower value. When the value is lower, wasted land does less harm. If wasted land is less offensive, then unduly restrictive land promises, which have the potential to nullify value, are not as dangerous.

COVENANTS RUNNING WITH LAND AT LAW. Covenants running with land at law have been called 'real covenants', 'real covenants at law', 'covenants running with the land', 'running covenants', 'running covenants at law', and 'deed covenants'. For simplicity, 'covenants running with the land at law' will be referred to here as 'real covenants'. Real covenants started with medieval warranties of title, but were expanded in *Pakenham's Case* (1368) to include other covenants affecting land.

A real covenant is a promise. A real covenant is distinguished from a contractual promise in that the promise in a real covenant is stuck to, 'appurtenant' to, some interest in land and passes automatically to each owner of that interest rather than staying with the original parties to the promise. The law of real covenants sets forth a number of 'elements' that must be met for a promise to 'run' with land: as covenants, they must be in writing; they must be intended to run; they must 'touch and concern the land' rather than being irrelevant to the ownership of interests in land; there must be 'horizontal' and 'vertical' 'privity of estate', abstruse requirements explained below; and, under modern recording acts, grantees of the affected interests in land must have notice of the covenants.

These requirements apply separately to the burden (duty to perform) and the benefit (right to performance) of the covenant. The parcel to which the burden is appurtenant is known as the 'servient' tenement. The benefit is appurtenant to the 'dominant' tenement. Whether the burden runs to future holders of the servient parcel and whether the benefit runs to holders of the dominant parcel are, for the most part, independent issues. The covenanting parties must intend, for example, that the burden of the promise run to the successors of the burdened party for the burden to run and must intend that the benefit run in order that the benefit run. An examination of the doctrinal elements follows next.

Intent. We can be reasonably confident that the parties to a real covenant will reap gains from their exchange only if the law enforces what the parties intended. If the law expands the rights exchanged, the chances that the outcome will not be a Pareto improvement increase dramatically. Furthermore, if covenanting parties thought the law might increase the duration of the rights exchanged beyond what was intended, they might pass up a beneficial exchange. Therefore, it is essential that courts find that the parties intended that the real covenant run before holding that it will do so.

For most real covenants, there is at least one dominant parcel and one servient parcel. For some covenants, one of the two parcels is missing. If there is no dominant parcel, the benefit of the covenant is 'in gross' rather than appurtenant, and is tied to a person (or persons) rather than being tied to an interest in land. If there is no servient parcel, the burden is in gross. A real covenant might be found to be in gross because one end of the promise was not intended to be appurtenant to any parcel or because one end does not touch and concern any parcel.

Although the running of the benefit and burden are usually independent, English (see *London County Council v. Allen*) and a few American authorities have linked the two. These authorities hold that the burden of a real covenant will not run with land if the benefit is in gross.

The cost of this rule is that it prevents many beneficial divisions of rights in land. Suppose, for example, a talented gardener has worked hard to make his house a showcase for his horticultural abilities. Suppose also that his family has outgrown this house, and he would like to sell if he could be assured that his successors would maintain his garden. He cares what happens to his garden no matter where he moves; he wants to hold the benefit in gross. If the running of the burden is tied to the running of the benefit, he cannot hold the benefit in gross, and he must forego the sale or give up control of his garden.

The advantage of this intent-frustrating rule is that it makes a real covenant easier to terminate by private negotiation, in that it will usually be possible to find the holder of the benefit, since it is tied to land. A successor willing to pay more than the gardener's price to convert the garden to another use might have a hard time finding the gardener. Thus transaction costs could prevent the successor from buying his way free of the promise. The requirement that the benefit run helps keep down the costs of terminating promises. This justification seems to have failed to convince most American commentators, perhaps because the problem of locating benefit holders could be solved less confiningly by legislation requiring holders of benefits in gross to place their mailing address on record if they wish to keep the promise from lapsing.

Touch and concern. Courts require that the benefit of the real covenant touch and concern (or 'touch or concern') Blackacre for the benefit to run to the owner of Blackacre and the burden touch and concern Whiteacre for the burden to run. A promise to keep a party wall in good repair touches and concerns, but promises to pay money, promises enforcing ideologies and promises for personal services usually do not. The touch and concern element has been defended on the grounds that tying to land the sorts of promises that do not touch and concern to land could reduce efficiency, democracy or personal freedom (see Reichman 1978).

Some promises have proved hard for courts to categorize, and this touch and concern element has long been criticized as being 'indeterminate'. Rarely, however, do the critics identify an actual case that has been decided badly because the court failed to find that the promise touched and concerned. Rather, the harm from indeterminacy is that it generates litigation, increases the costs of exchanges, or dissuades parties from using covenants (see Epstein 1982).

The amount of litigation generated by the touch and concern requirement remains uncertain. The reported appellate cases in the United States in the twentieth-century in which that element has played an important part number in the hundreds. A Lexis search on 10 August 1996 for '"touch and concern" and (covenant or servitude)' in the 'mega' file containing all US federal and state cases yielded 264 cases. Although the reported appellate cases are only the tip of the iceberg, this tip is so small that the whole might not be of huge concern. It is unknown to what degree the touch and concern element deflects parties from desirable transactions or raises the drafting costs of completed transactions.

The element may be less indeterminate than the critics suggest. According to one extensive examination of American cases, the element can be understood as a mechanism for efficiently allocating the burden or benefit of the promise (see Stake 1988). If the benefit of the promise is likely to be enjoyed more by the successor than the original promisee, the court will find that the benefit touches and concerns. In other words, the benefits will be allocated to the person who would enjoy them most.

On the burden side, courts act as if they intend to allocate the burden efficiently. If placing the burden of performance on the successor to the promisor would be more efficient than leaving the burden with the original promisor, the court will find that the covenant touches and concerns. In some cases it is a simple matter of allocating the burden to the party that can perform the obligation more easily. For example, the new owner of a barn is better able to perform a promise to keep the barn painted because he can monitor its condition and has the necessary physical access when it is time to paint. In other cases the court improves the allocation of resources by avoiding situations fraught with potential inefficiencies, such as when the court passes burdens to pay homeowners' association dues on to those who will be spending those dues. If the court were to find that the covenant did not touch and concern, the homeowners in charge of the association would in theory have the power to make improvements and charge them to former homeowners, a group not represented in the decisions to purchase.

There are other economic tests for determining whether a covenant touches and concerns land. Under one (see Nelson, Stoebuck and Whitman 1996), a covenant touches and concerns if it was set up to regulate externalities generated by the use of one parcel. Another intuitive approach is to ask whether ownership of some particular land makes the burden easier to perform or the benefit more enjoyable. Neither of these latter two approaches will, however, predict the court's decisions in homeowners' association dues cases as accurately as the efficiency approach first stated. In many, but not all, cases challenging the running of homeowners' association dues, the courts have upheld the promises to pay dues, finding them to touch and concern the land despite the usual rule that the burdens of promises to pay money do not touch and concern. The externalities approach does not explain this result because homeowners' association dues are often not imposed in order to regulate externalities created by the use of land. The intuitive approach does not predict the judicial results, because it is not significantly easier for the successor to pay the dues than the original promisor.

Successful positive explanation of touch and concern does not justify the element's interference with the parties' intent that the covenant run. One justification for interfering with intent is that people make mistakes. The effect of the touch and concern element is to keep promises from running to successors. When the original parties erred in predicting the preferences of their successors, that limitation will be beneficial. When the original parties correctly predicted the preferences of their successors, the touch and concern requirement deprives the successors of the benefits of the exchange. The key to the beneficial operation of the touch and concern element is that the costs of privately rectifying errors of the parties and errors of the law are asymmetrical.

Assume that a group of neighbours agreed that they and, after them, their successors would play poker together once a week. Assume that one of them sells to a new owner who refuses to play poker. If the group tries to enforce the covenant, the court will not enforce it because the burden fails to touch and concern his land.

Assuming that this covenant as applied to the new owner has become inefficient, generating less wealth than it costs to perform, the judicial refusal to enforce it against the new owner enhances efficiency. This non-enforcement is valuable because it might not be accomplished easily by the parties. Because all the parties must agree to let one player out of the group, all are in a position to hold out. Thus, the touch and concern element beneficially prevents some inefficient promises from running to parties that might find it hard to buy their way free of the obligation.

Assuming, on the other hand, that the old covenant generates more good than harm for the new parties, the element causes the court to keep an efficient agreement from running. This error is relatively easy for the parties to remedy. When a covenant for the new group of neighbours to play poker would be efficient, transaction costs will rarely prevent the negotiation of that new covenant. No owner has the power to hold out or free ride, because no owner is necessary to the agreement; the group can simply get someone else to play. Therefore, private extension of the erroneously limited covenant is comparatively unproblematic. The very fact that the covenant does not touch and concern helps to assure us that the judicial error will not be difficult to reverse.

The touch and concern element might also be criticized for depriving some promisees of the benefit of their bargain. This assumes the promisee incorrectly predicted the operation of the law. However, if the covenant is unenforceable against the successor because it does not touch and concern, it does not run, and it is presumably enforceable against the original promisor. The mistaken promisee loses a remedy against the successor, but gains a remedy against the original promisor. Thus, the distributional effects of the touch and concern element are mitigated.

The American Law Institute (1991) has proposed 'superseding' the touch and concern element with a judicial inquiry into whether the promise in question violates public policy. It is not clear how this approach will make the law more determinate. Nor is there any assurance that this new test will interfere less with private intent, since the traditional touch-and-concern approach has prevented few covenants from running. It is also not apparent how the new test could take advantage, as the common law does, of the asymmetrical costs of repairing judicial and private error. Finally, the touch and concern element in no way impedes enforcement of the promise between the original parties, as the reformed test could, judging by the language of Section 3.1 of the Third Restatement. Recommending the supersedure of touch and concern with a general inquiry into public policy fails to recognize that it could be useful to have a rule that upholds a promise between the original parties but declares the promise not binding on successors.

Notice. For the burden of a covenant to run, usually the successor to the promisor must have actual or constructive notice of the covenant before purchasing the servient tenement. The notice element requires that the successor to the promisor have some opportunity to find out about the burden of the covenant before purchasing the land.

Notice was not a requirement under the common law rules governing real covenants. However, American recording acts generally prevent interest holders from asserting their rights against subsequent holders of conflicting interests who are *bona fide* purchasers without notice (see Cunningham, Stoebuck and Whitman 1984). In the context of covenants, these acts prevent promisees from asserting claims against successors (to the promisor) that paid valuable consideration and took without notice. This statutory notice requirement does not protect a promisor's successor who did not pay for her deed or, in some states, did not record her deed.

Requiring notice is often justified on the grounds that it would be unfair to hold successors to promises they did not know about. Holding unknowing successors liable would also create an incentive and opportunity for promisors to free themselves of the promise by selling land to an unaware buyer, who might place a lower value on the burdened land than did the seller.

A writing. Real covenants are widely held to be interests in land for purposes of the Statute of Frauds. Therefore, the parties must commit their agreement to writing for the burden to be enforceable.

Horizontal privity. According to many authorities, the original parties must have a special connection, called 'horizontal privity', for their covenant to run to either of their successors. There are three different views regarding what relationship is required to establish horizontal privity. Under the narrowest definition, supported by English precedent, the parties must be in a relationship of tenure, as are a landlord and tenant, to establish horizontal privity.

An intermediate approach requires that the covenanting parties have simultaneous interests in the land involved in the covenant, such as when a dominant tenant owns an easement in the servient parcel. This approach has been justified on the ground that there is a big difference between an encumbered parcel and an unencumbered parcel and that once land is encumbered (here, by the easement) it does little marginal harm to encumber it further with the burden of a covenant.

Under the most relaxed definition, the parties are in horizontal privity if they have simultaneous interests or successive interests, i.e. at the time of the covenant one party conveys to the other an interest in the dominant or servient parcel. Even in this relaxed view, the horizontal privity requirement prevents neighbours from creating a real covenant to keep their lawns mowed without their exchanging some interest in their lands at the same time. Thus, this element imposes substantial costs on parties attempting to create a real covenant.

A fourth approach, which also has some support, is not to require horizontal privity at all. Only under this fourth approach can two neighbours simply exchange promises that will run. The legal world is still waiting for a convincing policy analysis explaining why courts should, by requiring horizontal privity, continue to impose costs on neighbours wishing to exchange running promises.

Vertical privity. A promisor and his successor are in 'vertical privity' if the promisor transfers his entire estate in land to the successor. Only in such cases is the successor bound by a real covenant. Therefore, if Ben merely leases the servient parcel, Whiteacre, to Jake, Jake is not liable on the real covenant not to operate a business on the land, and Ben remains liable.

The traditional doctrinal rule is the same on the benefit side; the promisee's successor can enforce a real covenant only if she has acquired the entire estate of the promisee. Because strict vertical privity is lacking, a tenant of Sara's cannot enforce the promise against Ben. The American Restatement of Property (1944) (section 547) (see Nelson, Stoebuck and Whitman 1996) and the English Law of Property Act 1925 (section 78) (see Megarry and Wade [1957] 1984) have relaxed this requirement on the benefit side, allowing any transferee of the promisee to enforce the real covenant. A possible rationale for the traditional requirement of vertical privity will be suggested in the section on equitable servitudes.

Termination. Real covenants terminate if all dominant and servient tenements come under the same ownership and also may terminate automatically by their own terms. Alternatively, judges will sometimes refuse to enforce a covenant on the ground that the holders of the dominant tenement have abandoned the covenant or acquiesced in its violation. In England there is a statutory procedure for discharging obsolete or destructive covenants. Additionally, real covenants can be terminated privately if the holders of the benefit waive their rights or release the burdened parties from their obligations. When real covenants involve a number of owners, holdouts will often prevent such private termination. For that reason, many modern covenants include a provision that the covenants can be terminated by the vote of a majority or super majority of the parties.

Real covenants are also terminated if the government condemns the servient parcel and uses it in violation of the covenant. The cases are divided as to whether the holder of the dominant parcel should obtain a portion of the condemnation award and, if so, how much that award should be. Cases limiting the total compensation awarded to the value of an unrestricted fee simple would seem to ignore that the value of the sum of the divided interests is probably higher than the value of the unencumbered fee. Such cases also undercut the allocative-efficiency rationale for requiring compensation, which is to make sure that the rights taken by the government are worth at least as much to the government as to the private landowners.

EQUITABLE SERVITUDES. Courts of equity, which have now merged with courts of law, have enforced promises stuck to land at least since *Tulk v. Moxhay* (1848). When a court sitting in equity enforces a promise attached to land, the promise is called an 'equitable servitude', 'equitable restriction', 'servitude', or even 'restrictive covenant'. Sitting in equity, the court applies the requirements of intent, touch and concern, and notice in much the same manner as when it sits at law and enforces the promise as a real covenant. One theoretical difference is in the source of the notice requirement. The Lord Chancellor Cottenham's opinion in *Tulk v. Moxhay* made it clear that a court of equity requires notice before enforcing a servitude against a successor, whereas the notice requirement for real covenants stems from modern recording acts. Since 1925, English statutes have required that servitudes be registered to be enforceable (see Megarry and Wade [1957] 1984). Another difference is that courts of equity sometimes overlook the writing requirement, which allows equitable servitudes to be implied, often from a common plan for a neighbourhood. A final difference, in England, is that the burden will not run unless there is a dominant parcel.

Changed conditions. Judges have refused to enforce equitable servitudes under the 'changed-conditions', 'change of conditions', 'changed-circumstances', or 'changed-neighbourhood' doctrine. This doctrine says that enforcement will be denied if conditions in the area affected by the covenant have so changed that the covenant can no longer achieve its purpose.

The doctrine creates bad incentives. By destabilizing servitude law, it invites litigation and deters parties from beneficial exchanges of rights or shunts them to more reliable but less appropriate legal mechanisms such as defeasible estates. If Sara thinks Ben's promise not to use Whiteacre for a business might be terminated because of changed conditions, she can instead purchase Whiteacre and sell Ben an interest (a fee simple determinable) that will terminate if he ever starts a business use. Or she could place Whiteacre in a trust for the benefit of Ben, with instructions to the trustee not to use the land for a business. Thus the changed-conditions doctrine creates an incentive to use some other, clumsier restriction rather than a servitude.

On the other hand, there are allocative efficiency benefits from the changed-conditions doctrine if judges correctly reallocate land-use rights in situations where strategic bargaining, especially by holdouts, would prevent the parties from privately terminating the servitude. Surely, use of restricted land is improved by the changed-conditions doctrine so long as the doctrine is applied only if the challenged restriction generates no conceivable benefit to neighbours and is being asserted only to capture some of the gains from changing the use of the servient parcel. It is not clear whether judges will also apply this doctrine to real covenants. Efficiency benefits can be achieved without great distributional unfairness (but perhaps at considerable administrative cost; see Reichman 1978) if judges adhere to the distinction between law and equity, allowing the holders of dominant tenements to assert rights only to damages (see Stake 1991).

Privity. The primary difference in requirements for real covenants and equitable servitudes is that courts of equity require neither horizontal nor vertical privity. Because the equitable servitude doctrine does not include privity elements, it is easier for a promisee's successor to assert the benefits of a promise in equity than at law. Any real covenant may also be enforced in equity as an equitable servitude, but some equitable servitudes cannot be enforced at law as real covenants. At first blush, this seems anomalous, because the usual rule is that a court will grant equitable relief (an injunction) only if there is a legal right but the legal remedy (damages) is inadequate.

The practical consequence of enforcement of a servitude in equity is that the court will issue an injunction against the covenantor's successor, requiring him to do, or not to do, an act. The court will order Jake not to operate a business on Whiteacre. By contrast, the remedy (at law) for violation of a real covenant is money damages. Sara can seek money damages from the landlord, Ben, rather than from the tenant, Jake. Making Ben liable for any monetary damages caused by the business use of Whiteacre seems appropriate, especially if Ben failed to tell Jake about the covenant. But Sara can enforce the equitable servitude directly against Jake, who is in possession, rather than having to find Ben and get him to control Jake's use of Whiteacre. Thus, it is possible that this arrangement of burdens approximates what parties would choose for themselves if they thought about it. Moreover, when the vertical privity requirement does not yield results that fit the parties' needs, the parties can often privately mitigate the requirement. For example, if Ben wants Jake to be liable at law for damages for breach of the promise, Ben can put that term in his lease.

If the burdened owner passes his entire interest to a successor, the successor is bound by the promise in both law (in America) and equity. Assuming that the original covenanting parties were not landlord and tenant (and assuming in England that the transferor is not the original covenantor), the transferor is released from any burden of the promise. It would unduly burden commerce in land if owners were to remain forever liable for breach of covenants attached to lands they once owned. But where the servient owner has not stepped out of the picture entirely by a complete transfer of his interest, it may be desirable to create an incentive for him to inform his tenant or other successor about the covenant. Making him liable for damages at law on a breach maintains that incentive for the transferor.

Affirmative and negative promises. The law of equitable servitudes in the United States differs importantly from English equity. In the US, both affirmative (or positive) promises, i.e. promises to do something, and restrictive (or negative) promises, i.e. promises to refrain from an act, can be enforced as servitudes. In England, equity will enforce a promise that is negative in nature, but will not enforce a positive promise. If Ben had promised Sara that he would keep Blackacre in good repair and then sold to Jake, English courts following the traditional rule would not order Jake to perform that promise, though they would enjoin him to honour Ben's promise not to operate a business. The English courts will not require a successor to put his hand into his pocket. This rule is under substantial attack (see Megarry and Wade [1957] 1984).

PROFITS À PRENDRE. Profits and easements are interests held by one person in land possessed by another. Where real covenants and equitable servitudes usually involve promises by the servient owner that he will do or not do something, easements and profits usually involve rights of the dominant owner to do something without interference from the servient owner, such as walk across land, lay a drainage pipe, use a lavatory, or otherwise enjoy the servient tenement. The two groups of interests overlap somewhat in the narrow area of negative easements.

A *profit à prendre* (or more simply, profit) is a right to sever and remove some substance, like minerals, gravel or timber, from land possessed by another. Rules governing creation and termination of profits are quite similar to those governing easements and some American authorities have abandoned the term 'profits'. In England, the rules for profits and easements differ in that profits, unlike easements, can be held in gross. Profits are often accompanied by an easement allowing access over the servient tenement to get to its resources.

Easements and profits may terminate by their own terms, by express release, by adverse use or by abandonment, though the last is hard to prove. Easements and profits terminate by the ancient doctrine of merger if the servient tenement and the easement come into the same hands. In such cases the easement is not created anew when the once-dominant or once-servient parcel is sold. This rule creates problems for future holders of the dominant parcel that wrongly assume the old easement still exists. However, the merger rule might be justified on the ground that it reduces the costs of selling the unencumbered fee in the future; each seller of the once-servient parcel need not specify that he is transferring both interests, the previously encumbered fee and the right to be free of the encumbrance. On the reasonable assumption that sellers wish to transfer all their rights more often than they wish to transfer a previously divided subset of their rights, the rule reduces transaction costs.

LICENCES. A licence differs from an easement or profit in that the licence is ordinarily revocable or terminable at the will of the grantor, whereas the easement or profit is not. Unlike profits and easements, licences are not interests in land and may be created without complying with the statute of frauds, i.e. without a writing.

EASEMENTS. Easements can be either appurtenant to a dominant parcel or in gross. Ben might grant to neighbour Sara an easement to walk across Whiteacre to get to town from Blackacre. If that easement is appurtenant to Blackacre, it runs to successive owners of Blackacre. In the United States, the easement in the servient tenement, Whiteacre, could also be held in gross by Janet, who owns no nearby land benefited by the easement. As was true under Roman law, English courts do not recognize easements in gross; there must be a dominant parcel, and it must be near the servient parcel.

Questions over the scope and location of easements generate substantial litigation. It is not clear how the law might be changed so that there would be less room for litigation, or at what cost such changes would come. One rule that has come under attack is the rule that the location of the easement, once established, cannot be changed without mutual agreement. Alternative rules allowing unilateral relocation could avoid the bilateral monopoly problems that may prevent parties from making best use of the dominant or servient parcels, but might generate even more litigation.

Use of land beyond the scope of an easement is ordinarily a *per se* misuse of the easement, often resulting in a trespass. An easement appurtenant can be used for the benefit of only the dominant parcel. Suppose Ben, Sara and Janet own lots 1, 2 and 3, in a row, and Ben grants to Sara an easement so that she can get from her house to the road passing Ben's lot. Sara then buys Janet's lot and decides to move her house to that lot. Sara now uses her easement for the benefit of lot 3, which is a *per se* imposition of a surcharge on the servient tenement even though there is no more harm to Ben than he anticipated at the time of the grant.

This rule obviously puts Ben and Sara in a bilateral monopoly situation, with the possible result that a Pareto-improving exchange of rights will not take place because of strategic bargaining. One justification for the *per se* rule is that, unlike the example above, most extensions of easements to benefit parcels other than the dominant tenement will indeed generate greater costs to the servient land, and it is administratively easier to lump all extensions together than to sort out the harmless extensions from all others. The *per se* rule also creates an incentive for the holder of the easement to negotiate with the servient owner before extending or modifying her use of the easement in any way.

Subdivisions of the dominant tenement and divisions of easements in gross are handled with a different rule. A holder may subdivide an easement when she subdivides the dominant parcel, and all new owners become easement holders, unless the burden on the servient parcel exceeds the burden the parties contemplated in the original grant. Similarly, in many states today, a utility company holding an easement in gross can transfer a portion of that easement to another utility for its lines, unless the burden exceeds what was originally contemplated. This modern approach has to some extent displaced the 400-year-old 'one-stock' rule. That rule said that the holder of an easement in gross could transfer a portion of the easement to another only if the two used the easement together, as 'one stock'.

Express easements. Easements can be created by express or implied grant or reservation and, unlike real covenants and equitable servitudes, can be created by prescription (long-standing use). Like real covenants and equitable servitudes, easements can be divided into negative (or restrictive) easements and positive (or affirmative) easements. Early English decisions recognized four types of negative easement: easements of light, air, building support, and flow of water in artificial streams.

For a number of reasons, courts cabined the development of negative easements with the rule that only those four types could be created; no new forms were allowed. One economic rationale is that negative easements are harder for prospective purchasers of the servient parcel to discover than affirmative easements, such as shortcut footpaths, and the common law of easements did not require notice for the purchaser to be burdened. Similarly, English courts usually refused to enforce, as easements, obligations that would require the expenditure of money, and that reluctance may have carried over to servitudes in the rule that equitable servitudes cannot compel owners to spend money.

Both English and American law allow negative easements of light and air to be created by express grant or reservation. Such easements allow the dominant tenement owner to restrain the servient tenement holder from erecting buildings that interfere with the light and air reaching the dominant land. A seventeenth-century English case rejected the possibility of easements of view or prospect: '[P]rospect . . . is a matter only of delight, and not of necessity, . . . But the law does not give an action for such things of delight' (*William Aldred's Case*, 58b, 821). By contrast, a number of states in the US allow easements of view or prospect, perhaps because delight was more easily acknowledged in cases arising in less Puritanical times. In addition, American statutes authorize conservation easements, which allow the easement owner, who may hold in gross, to prevent the fee-holder from building on the land except as specified in the grant.

There is still some authority in the United States for the old proposition that an easement cannot be reserved for the benefit of a 'stranger to the deed', a person other than the grantor or grantee of the possessory estate (see *Estate of Thompson v. Wade*). The rule has been eliminated in some states, has been rejected by the Restatement Third and, where it still exists, has been riddled with exceptions. The rule is not very confining, as it can be avoided by granting an easement before conveying the servient parcel. Nevertheless, why the law should prevent a grantor from transferring by a single deed an easement to one person and the servient parcel to another has yet to be justified by careful economic analysis.

Implied easements. Easements can be implied from prior (or pre-existing) use, from necessity, and from a plat. Suppose Ben owned both Blueacre and Greenacre and sold Greenacre to Sara. If it is apparent that Ben used Blueacre to get to and from Greenacre, courts will imply into his conveyance of Greenacre to Sara an additional grant of an easement to cross Blueacre based on prior use. Some courts purport to require that the pre-existing use be 'apparent', 'continuous' and 'necessary', but the enforcement of these requirements has been far from rigid.

Even if Blueacre had never been used for access to Greenacre, a court may imply the grant of an easement based on necessity if there is no other way, or perhaps no other reasonable way, for Sara to get to Greenacre immediately after her purchase from the common owner, Ben. While an easement implied from prior use is permanent, an easement implied from necessity lasts only as long as necessary.

If Ben had sold Blueacre instead of Greenacre, he might later urge a court to find that he implicitly reserved an easement over Blueacre. Courts are much more reluctant to imply the reservation of an easement on the grounds that such a reservation is in derogation of the grantor's deed. Necessity might be enough to imply the reservation of an easement, but prior use is not. If Ben wanted an easement, he could have expressly reserved it. Requiring Ben to do so decreases the possibility that the buyer thought she was getting more than she did and increases our confidence that Ben's sale of Blueacre was a Pareto improvement.

Prescriptive easements. A person who uses land of another in a particular way for a long time may gain an easement by prescription, which allows that person (and possibly her successors) to continue using the land in that way. There are two basic theories supporting easements by prescription. One is that once a wrongful act continues long enough, the aggrieved (servient) owner cannot enforce his rights, just as the doctrine of adverse possession and statutes of limitation bar many other stale claims. The other, and older, theory is that longstanding use of land indicates that an easement was once granted but the grant has been lost. In jurisdictions lacking a prescription statute, the lost-grant approach would appear to have stronger historical support.

Unfortunately, which theory a court adopts can make a big difference. Suppose the owner of the servient parcel acquiesced while the owner of the dominant parcel made use of the servient land. That fact supports the conclusions that there had once been a grant creating the claimed easement and that the use by the person claiming the easement was not wrongful. A court could, applying the 'acquiescence' requirement of the lost-grant theory, hold that an easement had been created. On the other hand, a court could, on the basis of the same acquiescence, find that no wrong had occurred, no cause of action had arisen, no statutory limitation period had run and, therefore, no easement had been created by prescription.

Judicial freedom to choose between theories is freedom to determine the outcome of the case. Thus, the law of prescription encourages litigation and makes it difficult for people to plan. The economic consequences of one theory, or the other, have yet to be sorted out. Given the confusion and uncertainty in the courts, a good examination of the economic consequences of requiring or prohibiting or ignoring acquiescence could influence the doctrine's development. Here, at least, there seems to be a need for proper economic analysis.

Not only is it unclear which version of prescription would be better, and on what criteria, but it is also unclear whether the law ought to allow prescription at all. In 1966, the Law Reform Committee debated total abolition of prescription in England. US Constitutional 'takings' doctrine and adverse possession have been defended on the grounds that depriving persons of longstanding uses carries high costs, higher than would be recognized if valuations of the loss were calculated by reference to the amount the owners would be willing to pay for the property (see Stake 1995). Perhaps prescription might be justified on a similar rationale.

Aside from the debatable 'acquiescence' element, the law of prescriptive easements resembles the law of adverse possession. One other difference from adverse possession is that most courts do not require the easement claimant's use to be as 'exclusive'. The claimant need not exclude the servient tenement owner, or others, to gain an easement by prescription. If, however, the claimant has not excluded and has shared use with members of the public, the prescriptive easement might be a public easement rather than a private easement.

Under the English doctrine of ancient lights, which has been rejected in the US, easements of light can be created by longstanding use of light passing across the servient parcel. It is clear that the doctrine of ancient lights can interfere with development of land uses that block the sun and that it can encourage development of land uses that rely on sunlight. It is not clear whether England and the United States have adopted rules appropriate to their varying economic conditions.

The rules of prescription provide a good example of how much the development of land-use doctrine depends on earlier paths taken. The possibility in England that negative easements can be created by prescription explains the English judicial reluctance to allow new types of negative easements. If new negative easements could be created by longstanding non-use, any new use of land could be met with a neighbour's objection that she had a prescriptive negative easement preventing such use. The law cannot allow new negative easements to be created by prescription without creating great uncertainty regarding to what new uses land may be put. In the United States, where most courts have held that negative easements cannot be created by prescription, allowing new sorts of negative easements is not so problematic and need not be proscribed.

J.E. Stake

See also EQUITY; INHERITANCE LAW; LAND DEVELOPMENT CONTROLS; PROPERTY RIGHTS; STATUTE OF FRAUDS.

Subject classification: 5b(ii); 6c(iv).

STATUTES

Law of Property Act 1925 (15 & 16 Geo. 5, c.20) s. 78.

CASES

Estate of Thomson v. Wade, 509 NE2d 309 (1987).

London County Council v. Allen [1914] 3 KB 642.

The Prior's Case (also known as *Pakenham's Case*) (1368) YB 42 Edw III, pl 14; Co. Litt. 385a.

Tulk v. Moxhay (1848) 2 Ph. 774, 41 Eng. Rep. 1143.

William Aldred's Case (1610) 9 Co. Rep. 57b, 77 Eng. Rep. 816.

BIBLIOGRAPHY

American Law Institute. 1944. *Restatement of The Law of Property, Vol. V: Servitudes*. St Paul, MN: American Law Institute Publishers.

American Law Institute. 1991. *Restatement of the Law Third: Property (Servitudes)*, Tentative Draft No. 2. Philadelphia, PA: American Law Institute.

Bruce, J.W. and Ely, J.W. Jr. 1984. *Cases and Materials on Modern Property Law*. St Paul, MN: West Publishing Company; 3rd edn, 1994. (A casebook by the authors of a treatise on easements.)

Clark, C.E. 1928. *Real Covenants and Other Interests which 'Run with Land'*. Chicago, IL: Callaghan and Company; 2nd edn, 1947. (The most exhaustive discussion of American land-use doctrines before 1950.)

Cunningham, R.A., Stoebuck, W.B. and Whitman, D.A. 1984. *The Law of Property*. St. Paul, MN: West Publishing Company.

Dukeminier, J. and Krier, J.E. 1981. *Property*. Boston, MA: Little, Brown and Company; 3rd edn, 1993. (Probably the most economically orientated casebook on property.)

Dunham, A. 1965. Promises respecting the use of land. *Journal of Law and Economics* 8: 133–65.

Epstein, R.A. 1982. Notice and freedom of contract in the law of servitudes. *Southern California Law Review* 55: 1353–68.

Hughes, W.T., Jr. and Turnbull, G.K. 1996. Restrictive land covenants. *Journal of Real Estate Finance and Economics* 12: 9–21.

Kurtz, S.F. and Hovenkamp, H. 1987. *Cases and Materials on American Property Law*. St Paul, MN: West Publishing Company; 2nd edn, 1993.

Law Reform Committee. (1966). 14th Report, Cmnd. 3100.

Megarry, R. and Wade, H.W.R. 1957. *The Law of Real Property*. London: Stevens & Sons Limited; 5th edn, 1984. (A detailed treatment of English property law.)

Nelson, G.S., Stoebuck, W.B. and Whitman, D.A. 1996. *Contemporary Property*. St Paul, MN: West Publishing Company. (A property casebook with substantial notes and text, and occasional commentary, on servitudes.)

Posner, R.A. 1973. *Economic Analysis of Law*. Boston, MA: Little, Brown & Co.; 4th edn, 1992; 5th edn, 1997.

Reichman, U. 1978. Judicial supervision of servitudes. *Journal of Legal Studies* 7: 139–64.

Robinson, G.O. 1991. Explaining contingent rights: the puzzle of 'obsolete' covenants. *Columbia Law Review* 91: 546–80.

Simpson, A.W.B. 1961. *An Introduction to the History of the Land Law*. London: Oxford University Press. The second edition was renamed *A History of the Land Law* (Oxford: Clarendon Press); 2nd edn, 1986. (A concise and authoritative summary of the development of many English land-use doctrines.)

Stake, J.E. 1988. Toward an economic understanding of touch and concern. *Duke Law Journal* 1988: 925–75.

Stake, J.E. 1991. Status and incentive aspects of judicial decisions. *Georgetown Law Journal* 79: 1447–97.

Stake, J.E. 1995. Loss aversion and involuntary transfers of title. In *Law and Economics: New and Critical Perspectives*, ed. R.P. Malloy and C.K. Braun (New York: Peter Lang Publishing, Inc.): 331–60.

last clear chance. Should a person be liable for not rescuing someone if the cost of rescue is trivial? If a motorcycle is parked illegally in the middle of the road and a truck smashes into it, who should be liable for the damage to the motorcycle? When a factory emits sulphur fumes that kill a neighbouring crop, what should be the extent of the factory owner's liability?

In all of the above examples, each person controls a different input into the production of the output; but unlike many problems in the law, these inputs are characterized by a clearly defined sequence: the motorcycle is parked in the middle of the road and then a truck comes; the sulphur fumes are in the air and then the crop is planted.

When these inputs occur simultaneously, a variety of liability rules create the proper incentives for an efficient outcome. For example, under a rule of negligence with contributory negligence, the owner would be liable for all of the damage to her motorcycle. This would discourage owners of motorcycles from inefficiently parking their motorcycles in the middle of the road in the future.

However, when the inputs occur sequentially, none of the damage-based liability rules create the optimal incentives both for long-run efficiency and for second-best outcomes when the long-run efficient choice is not made. For example, a comparative negligence rule cannot discourage truck drivers from smashing into motorcycles and simultaneously discourage motorcyclists from leaving their motorcycles in the middle of the road. If comparative negligence provides the correct incentives for truck drivers to swerve and avoid hitting parked motorcycles, then motorcyclists will have insufficient incentive to park their motorcycles in appropriate areas in the first place; if comparative negligence provides insufficient incentives for truck drivers to optimally avoid damage to motorcycles, then there will be fewer motorcycles parked in the middle of the road, but those that are will be needlessly damaged. In a nutshell, none of the standard liability rules can provide the right incentives for both equilibrium and out-of-equilibrium behaviour. Making the motorcyclist liable for the damage will discourage most motorcyclists from parking their motorcycles on the road most of the time, but when they do park their motorcycles on the road, these damage-based liability rules will not provide sufficient incentives for other drivers to avoid smashing into them.

The way out of this dilemma is to have a marginal *cost* liability rule. In this particular example, the motorcyclist would pay for the additional cost (swerving) that she imposes on others even in the absence of any damage from an accident. The truck driver is then liable for any costs that he imposes on the motorcyclist beyond those that would occur if he had acted optimally in response to the dangerous situation. This logic will now be elucidated within a more formal presentation. Those who are less interested in a detailed mathematical analysis may skip the formal presentation and proceed directly to the next section on applications.

A. MARGINAL COST LIABILITY – A FORMAL PRESENTATION

Let X be the injurer and Y be the injured party (for simplicity, we will assume that all damages fall on Y). Damage, D, is a decreasing function of x and of y, the amount spent on damage prevention by X and Y, respectively. In the example at hand, y might be the cost to Y of parking her motorcycle on the side of road while x might be the cost of keeping the truck's brakes in good order and the cost in wear and tear on the tyres from sudden swerving and braking.

$D(x, y) =$ damage. $D_x < 0$; $D_y < 0$; $D_{xx} > 0$; $D_{yy} > 0$; $D_{xy} > 0$; and $D_{xx}D_{yy} > D_{xy}D_{xy}$. A subscript stands for a partial derivative. The second order conditions are standard. $D_{xy} > 0$ implies that the inputs are substitutes – more x reduces the marginal productivity of y.

Economic efficiency dictates that society minimize the sum of damage and prevention costs. The optimal amount of damage prevention by X and Y is achieved when the last dollar spent on damage prevention by X (Y) reduces damage by one dollar. Beyond this optimal amount of expenditure (denoted by x^{Ω}, y^{Ω}), a dollar's worth of prevention reduces damage by less than one dollar. Until then, an extra dollar of prevention reduces damage by more than a dollar. More formally:

$$\text{Society minimizes } C^S(x, y) = D(x, y) + x + y.$$

First-order conditions are:

$$C^S_x = D_x(x, y) + 1 = 0$$
$$C^S_y = D_y(x, y) + 1 = 0.$$

The solution to the first order conditions is denoted by x^{Ω}, y^{Ω}. x^{Ω}, y^{Ω} are the efficient levels of x and y, respectively; in legal terms, X is negligent if x is below x^{Ω} and Y is negligent if y is below y^{Ω}.

We now turn our attention to the family of marginal cost liability rules. If Y is first, then Y is liable to X for any additional cost-effective preventive activity that *should* be undertaken by X given Y's decision; and X is liable to Y for any damage to Y beyond that which would have occurred had X undertaken the best response to Y's inefficient behaviour. These concepts will now be developed more formally.

Let $x^{\wedge} = B^x(y)$ be the optimal amount of x for a *given* y. B stands for best response. This is the explicit solution of x in the first order condition for minimizing social cost, $C^S_x = D_x(x, y) + 1 = 0$, for a given y. Clearly, if $y = y^{\Omega}$, then $x^{\wedge} = x^{\Omega}$; if $y < y^{\Omega}$, then $x^{\wedge} > x^{\Omega}$ (by our assumption that $D_{xy} > 0$); we will ignore the situation where $y > y^{\Omega}$.

For $y \leq y^{\Omega}$, the cost to each party under the marginal cost rule when Y goes first (yf) and X goes second (xs) is:

$$C^{\text{yf:mc}} = y + D(B^x(y), y) + B^x(y) - x^{\Omega} \text{ for Y, and}$$
$$C^{\text{xs:mc}} = x + D(x,y) - D(B^x(y), y) - B^x(y) + x^{\Omega} \text{ for X.}$$

In words, Y is responsible for her prevention costs, y, and the prevention costs that X should take beyond the prevention costs that would ordinarily be optimal, $B^x(y) - x^{\Omega}$, and for any resulting damage, $D(B^x(y), y)$, that would occur if X best responds to Y's behaviour.

This rule is always efficient. Suppose that Y has chosen y^{Ω}, then $B^x(y) = x^{\Omega}$ and

$$C^{\text{yf:mc}} = y^{\Omega} + D(x^{\Omega}, y^{\Omega}) + x^{\Omega} - x^{\Omega} \text{ for Y, and}$$
$$C^{\text{xs:mc}} = x + D(x, y^{\Omega}) - D(x^{\Omega}, y^{\Omega}) - x^{\Omega} + x^{\Omega} \text{ for X.}$$

Given $y = y^{\Omega}$, X will want to choose x^{Ω} since it is at that point where X minimizes his costs. As a consequence, $C^{\text{xs:mc}} = x^{\Omega}$.

Y is liable for the marginal costs which she imposes on others. Therefore, the externality is fully internalized, and Y will act so that social cost is minimized (i.e., y^{Ω} will be chosen).

Suppose, however, that Y has chosen $y < y^{\Omega}$, then

$$C^{\text{xs:mc}} = x + D(x, y) - D(B^x(y), y) - B^x(y) + x^{\Omega}.$$

Since all the costs now fall on X, he will minimize his cost by choosing $x = B^x(y)$. As a result,

$$\begin{aligned} C^{\text{xs:mc}} &= x + D(x, y) - D(B^x(y), y) - B^x(y) + x^{\Omega} \\ &= B^x(y) + D(B^x(y), y) - D(B^x(y), y) \\ &\quad - B^x(y) + x^{\Omega} = x^{\Omega}. \end{aligned}$$

So if X best responds to Y, his cost will be x^{Ω} regardless of what Y chooses.

All of this can be seen by looking at the first order conditions. For Y, the first-order conditions for cost minimization are:

$$C^{\text{yf:mc}}_y = [1 + D_y(B^x(y), y)] + [1 + D_x(B^x(y), y)]\, \frac{dB^x(y)}{dy} = 0.$$

From the first order conditions for social cost minimization, at x^{Ω}, y^{Ω} the terms in brackets will equal zero and therefore the first-order conditions for Y's cost minimization will also be satisfied.

For X the first order conditions for cost minimization are:

$$C_x^{\text{xs:mc}} = 1 + D_x(x, y) = 0.$$

These conditions, too, are identical to society's first order conditions for cost minimization.

Hence under the marginal cost liability rule, Y will always have the incentive to act optimally; but if she does not, X will have the appropriate incentive to best respond to Y's suboptimal behaviour.

There are other variations of this rule with similar incentive effects. Suppose that $B^x(y) - x^\Omega$ went to the government instead of to X; for example, $B^x(y) - x^\Omega$ might be a fine for parking in the middle of the road. From Y's point of view, the incentive effects are the same. Turning to X, he is no longer receiving $B^x(y) - x^\Omega$, but this is a fixed amount independent of his care level. Hence, not receiving compensation from Y will not affect X's level of care (but, possibly, will affect his decision whether to drive in the first place).

The same logic holds when X is the first and Y is the second mover (as would be the case if the truck were parked in the middle of the road and the motorcycle slammed into it). Then the implied liability rules and the resulting cost functions are as follows:

$$C^{\text{xf:mc}} = x + D(x, B^y(x)) - D(x^\Omega, y^\Omega) + B^y(x) - y^\Omega \quad \text{for X (when } x \leq x^\Omega)$$

$$C^{\text{ys:mc}} = y + D(x, y) + D(x^\Omega, y^\Omega) - D(x, B^y(x)) + y^\Omega - B^y(x) \text{ for Y.}$$

Looking at X's cost function, X is liable for his own prevention costs plus any additional cost and additional damage imposed on Y. The additional cost is the difference between Y's best response given x and Y's best response given x^Ω $(B^y(x) - y^\Omega)$; the additional damage is the difference in damage that occurs when Y best responds to x and the damage that occurs when x^Ω, y^Ω are chosen $(D(x, B^y(x)) - D(x^\Omega, y^\Omega))$. Clearly, X's cost minimizing strategy is to choose x^Ω with a resulting cost to X of x^Ω.

For Y, the only terms under her control are the first two. She will therefore minimize cost for a given x; that is, she will best respond to x. If X has chosen x^Ω, Y will choose y^Ω and the total cost to Y will be $y^\Omega + D(x^\Omega, y^\Omega)$; if X has chosen $x < x^\Omega$, then Y will choose $B^y(x)$ and Y's cost will again be $y^\Omega + D(x^\Omega, y^\Omega)$.

Once again there are variants on the basic liability rule with similar incentives for due care. For example, the comparison point might be zero damage rather than optimal damage so that the cost functions would be the following:

$$C^{\text{xf:mc}'} = x + D(x, B^y(x)) + B^y(x) - y^\Omega \quad \text{for X (when } x < x^\Omega)$$

$$C^{\text{ys:mc}'} = y + D(x, y) - D(x, B^y(x)) + y^\Omega - B^y(x) \text{ for Y.}$$

Since the only difference between these cost functions and the previous pair is $D(x^\Omega, y^\Omega)$, care levels are unaffected.

Insight into the power of the marginal cost liability rule is gained if we consider two alternative situations: (A) a different price is chosen, and (B) the actual prevention cost of the first mover differs from the average.

No other price will generate the optimal result. Suppose, for example, that Y is the first mover and Y's liability to X is set higher than $B^x(y) - x^\Omega$. Then Y will be overly cautious and may not shift the prevention cost onto X even if it is optimal to do so from a social cost–benefit calculation. That is, there will be a lower than optimal supply of people needing rescue. On the other hand, if Y's liability to X is set below $B^x(y) - x^\Omega$, then either there will be too many people needing rescue and being rescued (if the low price does not affect the supply of potential rescuers) or there will be too few rescuers and as a consequence too few people putting themselves at risk (if the low price reduces the supply of rescuers below the optimal).

Standards of due care work on averages (the reasonable man); in general, the courts are not able to determine whether the particular person's prevention cost is above or below average. If Y is the first mover and Y actually has higher than average cost in preventing damage, then cost minimization would suggest that Y shift the costs onto X on average (we use the word average since the cost function of X also varies around the mean). The marginal cost liability rule encourages this outcome. Under the marginal cost liability rule, if and only if the actual prevention cost to Y is greater than the additional expected cost to X, will Y actually shift the cost of prevention onto X.

B. APPLICATIONS

1. *Mitigation of damages in contract law.* In contract law, marginal cost liability is known as the doctrine of mitigation of damages. The plaintiff in a breach-of-contract case cannot collect for losses (damages) that he could have avoided by reasonable effort without risk of substantial loss or injury. In economic terms, 'reasonable effort' means best response. The plaintiff can collect, however, for the avoidance costs that he should undertake. His recovery against the defendant will be exactly the same regardless of whether he makes the effort to mitigate his loss.

For example, in *Daley v. Irwin* (1922), the plaintiff purchased defective seed and he found out the seed was defective before he planted it. The court ruled that a buyer who plants defective seed, knowing of its defects and having an opportunity to avoid loss of crop, cannot recover damages for the losses on the doomed-to-fail crop. The buyer's recovery is limited to the difference in market value between the seed as warranted and the defective seed delivered.

As another example we take an illustration from the *Restatements of the Law of Contracts* (1932). A sells to B a quantity of pork packed in barrels of brine with a warranty that the barrels will not leak. B finds that some of the barrels are leaky but does not repack the pork in good barrels. B can get judgment for only the cost of repacking in good barrels and not the value of the pork spoiled after his discovery of the defects.

In situations where a breach of contract does not give the plaintiff a last clear chance to avoid damages (i.e., the inputs do not take place sequentially but are simultaneous), the plaintiff can collect for the full amount of damages. In *Parkersburg Rig & Reel Co. v. Freed Oil & Gas Co.* (1922), the court held that the plaintiff need not build dams in anticipation of breaks in oil tanks built by the defendant (a breach of contract), and therefore could recover for all damages. Another situation where the plaintiff does not have the last clear chance is when the defendant assures the plaintiff that the contract is not repudiated. In these cases, too, the defendant is liable for all damages.

Contract law involves relatively low transaction costs. The marginal cost liability rule reduces transaction costs still further since it is a reasonable starting point for any negotiations. That is, the rule provides a good estimate of the likely agreement if the breach were anticipated beforehand.

2. *Last clear chance in accident law.* The doctrine of last clear chance makes the last person who could have reasonably avoided an accident liable. This doctrine originated in 1842 in the case of *Davies v. Mann.* The plaintiff negligently left his donkey tied up along the highway, and the defendant, driving at an excessive speed, hit the donkey. The donkey subsequently died. Had the defendant swerved in time, the donkey would not have been killed. The court found the driver liable as he had the last clear chance to avoid the accident.

To illustrate the role of marginal cost liability we consider *McKee v. Malenfant* (1954), a modern version of *Davies v. Mann.* This case involved a collision between a moving truck and one that had been negligently left standing on the highway. The person (Y) who left her truck on the road was the least-cost avoider; but *given* that the truck was already on the road, the driver of the other truck (X) should be encouraged not to smash into parked vehicles. Making Y fully liable will, in the future, discourage people from parking their trucks on the highway, but not *sufficiently* discourage others from smashing into parked vehicles. Making X fully liable will create the proper incentives for X to avoid smashing into Y but will not sufficiently discourage people from parking on the highway. As demonstrated earlier, the appropriate rule is to make Y liable for the marginal costs that she imposes on X (braking, swerving, etc.), whether there is an accident or not, and to make X liable for the marginal costs that he imposes on Y if he fails to respond properly to the dangerous situation.

In *McKee v. Malenfant* the court held that the driver of the moving vehicle was solely liable because he had ample opportunity to avoid the accident (he had the last clear chance), notwithstanding the negligence of the other party in leaving the vehicle in an improper place. The person (Y) who left her truck standing on the road should pay (to the extent feasible) for the marginal costs she imposes on others. In this way Y will make efficient choices. Clearly, a system of liability to all drivers who swerve or drive on another road in *order* to avoid hitting the truck is totally impractical. Liability to individual drivers is minimal, but the sum total to all the drivers may be quite significant; therefore, we want the driver of the parked vehicle to pay for the cost she shifts onto others. The appropriate solution is to charge Y a fine equal to the total marginal cost imposed on others (a Pigovian tax on the input). This fine will create the same incentives for Y as marginal cost civil liability. Whether Y pays to the state or to an individual, the effect on Y is basically the same. If Y is not always caught parking illegally on the highway, the fine can be increased to compensate for the reduction in probability. For example, if Y is caught only half the time, the fine would be twice as large as it would be if she were caught all the time.

We now investigate the effect of this solution on the other drivers. Under a marginal cost *liability* scheme, the other drivers are compensated for the cost of preventive behaviour, whether or not they do in fact take preventive measures. Compensation does not affect their behaviour since it is not based on any decision they make, but rather on the decision Y makes. Consequently, if Y pays a fine to the state instead of being liable to other drivers, her payment (assuming no wealth effects) will have no effect on the care level of other drivers. In other words, compensation for marginal costs that should be incurred is not necessary for the system to work properly.

We want the 'other drivers' to take into account the marginal costs that they impose. The doctrine of last clear chance, by making the other drivers liable for the damage when they are truly the second in the sequence, encourages them to make efficient decisions. Thus, a tax on the owner of the parked vehicle and liability for the damage on the driver of the moving truck because he had the last clear chance is a marginal cost liability rule applied in sequence.

Herein lies an important reason for fining people for inputs such as drunken or reckless driving instead of only for the resulting damage. Other drivers may swerve out of the way to avoid an accident (and the legal system should encourage them to do so). To the extent that these other drivers are successful, reckless drivers will not pay for their behaviour if liability depends only on actual damage. Reckless drivers are not *sufficiently* deterred if the costs of protection are shifted onto other drivers. In other words, if liability were only based on damages, reckless drivers would not pay for *some* of the negative externalities that they create. Therefore, we have fines to make these reckless drivers liable for the cost of damage prevention they shift onto others.

As demonstrated earlier, when there is a sequence of events, marginal cost liability should be applied regardless of whether there is damage or who is actually damaged. The law, in fact, reflects the symmetry of this analysis. A person is fined for illegal parking regardless of whether an accident occurred. Depending on which party had the last clear chance, the doctrine can be used against the defendant in favour of the plaintiff or against the plaintiff in favour of the defendant.

In accident law, marginal cost *civil* liability is rare, but in contract law it is the rule. These two areas of law have different methods of determining liability for several reasons. First, the party who has the last clear chance (i.e., the second party in the sequence who can mitigate damages) in contract law always knows who created the initial wrong – the breacher of the contract. But if a car swerved suddenly to avoid hitting someone walking negligently across the street, it could be very difficult to discover afterwards who this pedestrian was. Second, when a breach of contract occurs, cost-effective preventive action by the person who has the last clear chance may be very costly in comparison to the costs of preventive actions such as braking and swerving – the typical use of the doctrine of last clear chance in accident law. Therefore, it pays for the plaintiffs in breach-of-contract cases to sue even when there is 'no damage' because sufficient marginal costs are involved in preventive action to make it worthwhile for the plaintiff to collect for these costs (which are also known as damages in the legal literature). In contrast, the amount of liability that any one driver could collect for swerving (and thereby avoiding an accident) would not be enough to compensate for the cost of litigation. Finally, because it is much easier to determine sequence (who was first and who was last) in breach-of-contract cases than in accidents, we would expect the sequence of events to be much more important for breach of contract – where mitigation of damages is the rule – than for accidents where last clear chance is rarely applied. The differences in the two areas of civil law are thus due to the different costs of information and the benefits of litigation.

3. *Avoidable consequences and coming to the nuisance.* In nuisance law when 'damages' are awarded, they are typically for the costs of reasonable preventive behaviour by the plaintiff and any damage occurring (or that would have occurred) after preventive action had been taken. In other words, there is marginal cost liability. For example, in *United Verde Extension Mining Co. v. Ralston* (1931: 262), the court held that the plaintiff need not plant a hopeless crop that would be swept by sulphur fumes and should not recover for the damage to the crop if he did. In this case, the plaintiff had the last clear chance and could have mitigated damages and prevented wasted seed and crop damage by not planting. However, the plaintiff recovered for profits foregone in not planting the crop. Thus, we have marginal-cost liability or, in legal terminology, the doctrine of avoidable consequence:

> This doctrine states that a party cannot recover damages flowing from consequences which the party could reasonably have avoided . . . . The doctrine has a necessary corollary – the person who reasonably attempts to minimize his damages can recover expenses incurred.

Marginal-cost liability was also employed in *Spur Industries v. Del E. Webb Development Co.* (1972). In this case, action was brought by a real estate developer to enjoin a cattle-feeding operation that the defendant had set up in an agricultural area well outside the boundaries of any city before the developer had established an extensive retirement community on land nearby. The court held that the developer was entitled to enjoin the cattle-feeding operation as a nuisance, but it was required to indemnify the cattle feeder for the reasonable cost of moving or shutting down. This novel solution by the court reflects the fact that there are three stages to this sequential game: the feedlot was there first; the developer should have built elsewhere and thus had the last clear chance (the plaintiff had 'come to the nuisance'); but given that the plaintiff had built next to it, the feedlot had the last 'last clear chance' to mitigate the damage. The location of the feedlot far away from any city imposes little marginal cost on potential developers as they could readily avoid the nuisance by building elsewhere. However, given that the developer had located near the feedlot, it was best to have the feedlot move. Since the developer imposed the marginal costs, he should pay for them.

4. *The Good Samaritan rule.* A person is lying unconscious across a railroad track. Should a passerby be compensated for saving the unconscious person's life and/or be found liable for not saving? Clearly this is analogous to the situation involving a motorcycle parked on the road, and the solution is analogous also. Thus, the Continental (but not the Anglo-American) rule, which imposes Good Samaritan duties on mere bystanders when the cost of rescue is *trivial* but entitles the successful rescuer to a reward, makes perfect economic sense. The rescued person imposes costs on the bystander if the bystander rescues her and therefore the bystander should be compensated for rescue. If a person needs rescuing, it is most efficient that she be helped since by assumption her rescue has a low cost. If the bystander fails to rescue, he is now liable for failure to act just as the driver of the truck was liable when he smashed into the parked vehicle. The rescued person compensates the 'Good Samaritan' for marginal costs of the rescue. This amount is less than the liability of the passerby if he does not rescue – the marginal cost that the potential rescuer imposes by not rescuing. Since the amount of compensation is based on the marginal cost faced by the average rescuer, the rescued person will on average pay the marginal cost she imposes. But if a particular rescuer would incur higher than average costs in rescuing, we want him to rescue if his costs are less than the damage from not doing so. Therefore, we make the non-rescuer liable for damage, just as we make the truck driver who has the last clear chance liable when he smashes into the parked vehicle.

C. CONCLUSION

Economic theory has been used to unravel some of the difficult philosophical problems intrinsic to the concept of last clear chance and other cases involving sequential inputs.

Marginal-cost liability has been shown to be an optimal method of pricing sequential inputs. When the second person is forced to increase protection because of the negligence of the first, the first person should compensate the second for the cost of this protection. When it is not feasible to pay those who protect, the first person should pay the equivalent amount to the state. If the alternative protection were perfect, there would never be any *ex post* damage. Thus, the system cannot just charge the first person for *ex post* damage and must instead regulate the input.

DONALD WITTMAN

See also CAUSATION AND TORT LIABILITY; COMING TO THE NUISANCE; COMPARATIVE NEGLIGENCE; DUE CARE; ECONOMIC THEORY OF LIABILITY RULES; GOOD SAMARITAN RULE; LEGAL STANDARDS OF CARE; RESCUE.

Subject classification: 5d(ii).

CASES

Daley v. Irwin, 205 P 76 (Cal. 1922).

Davies v. Mann (1842) 10 M&W 546, 152 Eng. Rep. 588.

Island Express, Inc. v. Frederick, 171 A 181 (Del. 1934).

McKee v. Malenfant (1954) 4 DLR (2d) 785.

Parkersburg Rig & Reel Co. v. Freed Oil & Gas Co., 205 P 1020 (Cal. 1922).

Spur Industries Inc. v. Del E. Webb Development Co., 494 P2d 700 (Ariz. 1972).

United Verde Extension Mining Co. v. Ralston, 296 P 262 (Ariz. 1931).

BIBLIOGRAPHY

Restatement of Contracts (1932) § 336 at 538.

Shavell, S. 1983. Torts in which victim and injurer act sequentially. *Journal of Law and Economics* 26: 589–612.

Wittman, D.A. 1977. Prior regulation versus post liability: the choice between input and output monitoring. *Journal of Legal Studies* 6: 193–211.

Wittman, D.A. 1984. Liability for harm or restitution for benefit? *Journal of Legal Studies* 13: 57–80.

law and biology. The study of law and biology combines six theories: it is, at once, a theory of individual behaviour, of ethology, of history, of communications, of games, and of philosophy and morals.

1. INDIVIDUAL BEHAVIOUR. Law and Biology comes closest to classical economics in its fundamental assumption that natural selection favours the individual that leaves the most surviving offspring. The theory thus rests on the idea that individual members of a species, humans included, will organize their lives to produce as many surviving offspring as they can. Natural selection is the principal mechanism of evolutionary change. It works to select the behaviours best adapted to reproductive success. Adaptation is a behaviour or trait that has been shaped by natural selection to perform a specific role. The capacity to learn is an evolved trait.

Evolution, natural selection, and adaptation are theories. But they have made predictions confirmed by observations from diverse fields such as comparative anatomy, embryology, ethology, geology, paleontology, botany, genetics, biochemistry and zoology. Evolutionary theory is strongly functionalist. It is thought to underlie what seem to be beautifully designed and specialized behavioural features seen everywhere in nature. Thus, members of the cat family have razor-edged teeth that enable them to cut meat with greater efficiency. Members of the horse family have broad teeth with low ridges well suited to the task of grinding up harsh grasses. Plants in the rain forest have developed waxy leaves and 'drip points' that enable them to shed the excess rainwater that comes their way.

Evolutionary theory offers accounts of 'spite', which is behaviour that inflicts costs on actor and recipient alike, and of 'altruism', which is defined as behaviour that brings advantages to others at a cost to the giver. Both of these behaviours are difficult to explain since they are superficially opposed to natural selection's action on each party.

One extension of social theory is based on the idea of kin-selection, which holds that the reproductive 'best' must be measured not strictly from the individual's perspective but from the entire group of related individuals. The idea is called inclusive fitness. It says that reproductive success in the individual can be achieved by helping collateral relatives and by producing and helping descendant relatives. Inclusive fitness theory has been confirmed by observations of heroic and sacrificial acts among the social insects and of 'auntie' behaviour among Florida jays who forego their own reproductive opportunities to lend a hand in the rearing of relatives.

Given a quantitative cast, inclusive fitness would predict that an individual would sacrifice itself to save three siblings. In this way, it could pass along 150% of its genes. Others have said that a person should be willing to lay down his life for two brothers or eight cousins. In law, inclusive fitness theory raises nice questions about the duty to rescue. It obviously points to differences in behaviour anticipated from strangers or from relatives.

Another variation on 'altruism' that has been elaborated by evolutionary biologists draws on the theory of reciprocal altruism. This is the trading of altruistic acts over time so that each party can enjoy a net gain. This behaviour can get started and thrive among individuals with long memories, frequent interactions, and stable social networks. It has been observed in a number of unusual nonhuman contexts – the trading of blood among vampire bats, the medical-service/food interactions between so-called host fish and their cleaners who remove parasites, joint hunting parties of coyote and badger where both benefit from a speed/digging combine.

Reciprocal altruism has considerable power in the explanation of human behaviour. Writers have linked it to the development of behaviours such as aggressive moralism that is aimed at cheaters; gratitude and sympathy that enhance the probability of receiving an altruistic act; and guilt because it motivates the cheater to compensate for a misdeed. It figures importantly in many analyses of effective law. To mention but one example, studies of successful management of resource commons worldwide identify the sorts of factors that allow reciprocity to get established among nonhuman species. These include frequent interactions, close oversight, and the capacity to help or hurt would-be cooperators.

The cooperative circles of reciprocal altruism have been extended outwards by other theories. Under the theory of indirect reciprocity, A's kindness to B is expected to be returned not by B but by any observers C, D, and E. This implicates reputation and status, which is constantly assessed under biological theory.

Another version of reciprocity theory is known as the commitment model, where 'altruistic' acts are the product not of self-interested calculation but of an emotional disposition to 'do the right thing'. The idea is that, over time, it might pay to conduct social acts without prior conscious calculation, even if mistakes can result. This theory has been invoked to explain any number of 'altruistic' deeds, including the passing up of 'golden opportunities' such as the returning of a lost wallet.

To illustrate the differences between the theories, a life-risking 'altruistic' act to rescue a drowning victim might be explained as assistance to a relation, a payback for a friend, a daring deed that would win recognition and reward, or the intuitive reaction of a man who makes friends first and asks questions later.

At the level of the individual, evolutionary theory is rich with insights on the origins of human conflict. It has developed ideas of parental investment, which is the investment made in the rearing of the young. The greater investment of the female is thought to lie behind differences in male–female mating strategies, attitudes toward casual sex, and strategies of child-rearing. Male–male competitions for females are thought to explain male attitudes toward risk-taking, competition and violence. Evolutionary biologists believe they can explain why the prisons worldwide are filled with males.

Evolutionary biology has developed accounts of weaning conflicts, which pit mother against child; sibling rivalry, which pits sibling against sibling; and birth order, which accounts for the different strategies and behaviours of first-borns and later-borns.

In recent years, writers in Law and Biology have applied ideas from evolutionary biology to seek to explain the motivations of the founders of the US Constitution, enforceability of the environmental laws, child abuse, self-deception in legal argumentation, the rule against perpetuities in property, the doctrine of undue influence in wills and estates, and discrimination against women in the workplace. These writers have sought to account for behaviours such as racism, the search for scapegoats, optimism in the face of uncertainty, the pursuit of critics and whistleblowers.

2. ETHOLOGY. Ethology is the biological study of animal behaviour. It is taken seriously in Law and Biology because of the assumption that all organisms on earth are descended from a few, early ancestors. Behaviours common to animals and humans are thought to have common evolutionary origins. This suggests shared explanatory accounts.

Ethology's major contributions to Law and Biology have been methodological. Ethology emphasizes direct observations of animals in their natural habitats and its Nobel Prize-winners have included Karl von Frisch, Konrad Lorenz and Niko Tinbergen. Lorenz is best known for his imprinting studies, which showed that a newborn greylag goose will follow any large object that supplies certain key stimuli. This line of work figured importantly in the 'Baby M' case in the US that raised a legal question of the enforceability of a surrogacy contract under which a woman agreed to artificial insemination, to carry the child to term, to bear it, and to deliver it to the contracting parties. The contract was held not enforceable for the reasons of attachment that had arisen between mother and child.

Researchers in ethology have contributed to the understanding of concepts such as gene-environment interactions, critical moments of development, and learning theory. One behaviour widely observed in nature is the practice of infanticide among males that have successfully entered a population of females from which they were otherwise excluded. Among African lions, for example, these males will systematically destroy (and cannibalize) all the young sired by their predecessors, behaviour that is thought to be in their reproductive interest because females without cubs are more readily available to bear their cubs.

Among humans, the rate of child abuse by stepfathers grossly exceeds that of natural fathers. This outcome would be predicted by evolutionary biology. Note, however, that no obvious policy is recommended. Kindly stepfathers exceed abusive ones by a wide margin. The data suggests though that the law might not be totally indifferent about the biological relationship between the 'legal' father and child. There is at least a potential conflict between the privacy interests of a stepfather and the best interests of the child.

3. HISTORY. One of the enduring lessons of evolutionary biology is that change is constrained by the past. Future options are a product of past directions. This historical bias is confirmed by what appear to be 'maladaptations' in biological evolution. The panda's thumb is a famous evolutionary sign of history that shows the get-by opportunism, borrowings and fusion that make the best of what has come before.

Frequently, changing environments will render 'maladaptive' behaviours that were efficient and adaptive in an earlier environment. Cats' tails were a wonderful signalling device in an earlier time. They are a liability in a world of closing doors. Chattering in squirrels evolved to discourage predation by the great horned owl. It is a 'maladaptive' behaviour in a new environment where the principal predator is a human armed with a rifle.

Preadaptation is a term used by biologists to describe behaviours and traits that can be modified by natural selection to perform functions quite unlike those served by the original design. The wings of the bat are an example where an ordinary flap for gliding or fly-catching or body-heating became the mechanism for flight. It is a nice example of an efficient accident. This widespread 'maladaptation' in nature is a frequent target of law. The human brain that evolved in an historic environment is frequently making 'mistakes' in the modern world. There are perfectly believable evolutionary accounts of why humans are prone to sweets and tobacco, suspicious of strangers, vengeful in small matters, careless at well-travelled intersections, and tending to error in risk assessment. But the law need not accept any of these behaviours. Indeed, the more interesting questions in law are not those where the prohibition (e.g., the incest taboo) coincides overwhelmingly with human predilections. The interesting questions are the strategies of legal design that can work to defeat individual behaviours that are widely engaged in though they are socially destructive.

Thus it is not a convincing objection to say that law is opposed to the strong predilections of human beings. Much if not most law fights a resistance action against stubborn human behaviours. But an empirical knowledge that compliance does not come easily might encourage other approaches more compatible with predictable behaviours.

Any historical evolutionary system may display ambiguous features of gradualism and episodic response. Rates of evolutionary change will be a subject of debate. Evolutionary systems show also chaotic, nonlinear, and unpredictable characteristics. Both rates of change and directional shifts are of interest to law. Frequently, the law will seek to change social evolutionary trajectories by 'resetting' the starting points through court decision or legislation. The good news is that these interventions might make a difference. The bad news is that the unpredictable consequences of the intervention are frequently undisclosed.

Students of Law and Biology will use models of Darwinian evolution in a metaphorical sense. The only necessary ingredients for a functioning evolutionary model are a population of 'things' (e.g., artifacts, ideas, rules), a means for introducing variation into the population, and a method of differential selection from the population. In this sense, it is serviceable to think about the 'evolution' of laws or business behaviour or any other identifiable social phenomenon.

In the field of environmental law, one model of statutory evolution depicts the legislative process as a prisoners' dilemma played over time between competing lawmakers (see Rodgers 1989). This displays cooperation but with distinct, end-of-the-game, last-play features of defection. It predicts a package of 'consensus' and 'betrayal' features. Among the latter are legislative 'sleepers', which are measures hidden and sprung in surprise upon legislative adversaries. The prediction of 'sleepers' has been confirmed repeatedly in the legislative process.

Another model of statutory evolution in environmental law used the prisoners' dilemma approach to explain how a credit-claiming competition among Presidential aspirants (in this case, Richard Nixon and Edmund Muskie) produced a Clean Air Act that was tougher than either one would have preferred (see Elliot et al. 1985). This model borrows, and gives content to, several concepts from the field of evolutionary biology. These include historical constraint, selection, coevolution, adaptation (e.g., the pursuit of federal preemption strategies as second-best alternatives to no regulation), and even predation (e.g., political cost-externalization, defined as achieving a benefit for constituents at somebody else's expense).

4. COMMUNICATIONS. Deception is behaviour that is well developed throughout the animal world. Some species regularly use false warning signals, in the form of bluffs, bluster and feints. There are distraction displays, typified by the mother bird that feigns a broken wing to lead predators away from the nest. There is luring behaviour where predators dress themselves up as prey to attract the unsuspecting. Some species of angler fish have lures that look like a dangling worm built into their anatomy. There is camouflage behaviour. There are startle displays. There are 'playing dead' methods.

Two reasons are invoked to explain acts of deception among nonhumans. Both of them have provocative implications for the practice of truth-telling among members of the human species. The first is that the biological costs of deceit are customarily low. It is easy to tell a lie; it can be done with a word, an expression, a mere change in body language. A feint can become an act of second nature, a fib can rush forth without rehearsal. This lie-telling business requires no long journeys, heavy caloric intake, or years of careful study. Among strangers at least, lies can flow as easily as a smile.

The systematic lie, to be sure, as distinguished from the occasional lie, the helpful lie, or the white lie, can exact a price in social relations. Truth-telling is an important commodity in ongoing relations. It shades into reputation. In these contexts, small lies can work large damage, which can be attested to by many a fibbing spouse, deceitful colleague, and lie-mongering public official.

Most theories of animal communication presume that the purpose of the exercise is not to transmit accurate information but to bring about a change in the behaviour of the recipient of the message. This theoretical view has profound implications for law. If truth is a coincidental option, it puts a large number of legal tell-the-truth obligations in a different light. If advocacy is more about persuasion than truth, it puts the legal profession in a different light.

For our purposes, self-deception can be defined as a misrepresentation of reality to oneself. Immediately, one accustomed to evolutionary thinking is hard put to explain self-deception. The key theme in Darwinism is a powerful functionalism where every feature, trait, tendency, or habit is presumed to be serviceable to advance the overall goals of successful life and reproduction. But where in this theory is there room for self-deception? Do the more gullible thrive and survive? Will the biggest fools inherit the earth? Is there some extraordinary payoff hidden within the disposition to readily believe what isn't so?

Self-deception is a powerful force in the service of deception. Put another way, the best liars are true believers, which means they are not deceivers as normally defined by law because there is no intent to transmit inaccurate information to the audience. They tell the truth as they misperceive it. The emergence of self-deception as a powerful force in human affairs can be viewed also as an example of maladaptation where the traits that are highly functional in environment A (brashness, confidence, an ability to act quickly and decisively) emerge in environment B as the dangerous seeds of self-deception.

The lens of self-deception also has powerful explanatory potential in law. To mention but one example, the entire system of precedent rests upon a pillar of consistency in law. But the theory of self-deception would suggest that what is maintained is an illusion of consistency where past experiences are rewritten to make them consistent with present realities. Research in self-deception, which is now pursued in a variety of experimental contexts, thus has wide implications for law.

5. GAMES. An important change in theoretical perspectives in Law and Biology is introduced by game theory. Generally, in game theory the theoretical best strategy for a player depends upon the strategy adopted by the other players. This is to be distinguished from various optimality theories applied to decisionmaking. The approach in evolutionary biology that seeks to explain behaviours or strategies as fitness-maximizing is an optimality theory.

Evolutionary thinking is highly receptive to game-theory approaches. Axelrod's work on the *Evolution of Cooperation* shows how various strategies, played over time, yield interesting results in games described as iterative prisoners' dilemmas. Axelrod shows how a tit-for-tat strategy is remarkably robust in a number of different contexts. Interestingly, legal conflicts offer many contexts for exploring the ideas raised in this work. Legal topics as diverse as pleas in criminal cases, environmental law enforcement, custody negotiations, and long trials have features of iterative games that can be examined through these theoretical lenses.

Shubik's famous dollar auction is another well-known game-theoretical approach with implications for Law and Biology (Poundstone 1992). This is a bidding game where each bidder is held to the price of the bid even if she does not win the bid. Shubik actually auctions off one dollar in his classes. He finds that he can secure bids that average \$2.40. This game is a useful vehicle for exploring ideas such as sunk costs and historical constraints. The law is filled with many of these good-money-after-bad conundrums where rational choice is compromised by prior commitments.

Coalition theory is another example of gaming applications useful in Law and Biology. Ethologists have shown, for example, that the status and power structure in a chimpanzee colony is sustained by a delicate coalition of the No. 2 and No. 3 ranking males who combine against No. 1 who is physically superior to each. Political scientists and others are interested in these strategically constructed social configurations.

6. PHILOSOPHY AND MORALS. Law and Biology is a theory of philosophy because it opens up inquiries into topics such as the sense of justice, the evolution of morality, and the development of human ideas of right and wrong.

In all likelihood, the human emotion that we call a sense of justice arose in the context of reciprocal dealings among members of our own species. It takes the form of moralistic aggression against nonreciprocators. The targets of these emotions can be indiscriminately chosen. It is certainly possible for this sense of justice to be aimed at those who may have offended the elite or violated other inconsequential norms. With a victim 'erroneously' chosen, we might call this sense of justice an example of seeking the proper scapegoat.

Researchers in the field of Law and Biology would deny that morality is exclusively the domain of philosophy. They have specified conditions for the evolution of morality that include value of the group (e.g., for defence or finding food), cooperation and reciprocal exchange within the group, and individual members with disparate interests (see de Waal 1996). With these conditions, intragroup conflict must be resolved through a balancing of individual and collective interests. This can be done by one-on-one interactions. It also can be achieved through community mechanisms, including mediated reconciliation, peaceful arbitration, appreciation of altruistic behaviour, encouragement, and contributions to the quality of the social environment. This would give us the rudiments of a system of morality and, with necessary trappings, a system of justice.

WILLIAM H. RODGERS, JR.

See also EVOLUTIONARY GAME THEORY; NEOINSTITUTIONAL ECONOMICS; PRISONERS' DILEMMA; RESCUE.

Subject classification: 4c(i).

CASES

In the Matter of Baby M, 537 A2d 1227 (NJ 1988).

BIBLIOGRAPHY

Alexander, R.D. 1987. *The Biology of Moral Systems*. Hawthorne, NY: A. de Gruyter.

Axelrod, R. 1984. *The Evolution of Cooperation*. New York: Basic Books.

Beckstrom, J.H. 1985. *Sociobiology and the Law: The Biology of Altruism in the Courtroom of the Future*. Urbana: University of Illinois Press.

Beckstrom, J.H. 1985. The potential dangers and benefits of introducing sociobiology to lawyers. *Northwestern University Law Review* 79: 1279–92.

Browne, K.R. 1995. Sex and temperament in modern society: a Darwinian view of the glass ceiling and the gender gap. *Arizona Law Review* 37: 971–1106.

Cooter, R.D. 1996. Decentralized law for a complex economy: the structural approach to adjudicating the new Law Merchant. *University of Pennsylvania Law Review* 144: 1643–96.

Dawkins, R. 1995. *River Out of Eden: A Darwinian View of Life*. New York: Basic Books, Harper Collins.

de Waal, F. 1989. *Peacemaking Among Primates*. Cambridge, MA: Harvard University Press.

de Waal, F. 1996. *The Origins of Right and Wrong in Humans and Other Animals*. Cambridge, MA: Harvard University Press.

Diamond, J. 1997. *Guns, Germs, and Steel: The Fates of Human Societies*. New York: W.W. Norton & Co.

Elliott, E.D. 1997. Law and biology: the new synthesis. *St. Louis University Law Journal* 41: 595–615.

Elliott, E.D., Ackerman, B.A. and Millian, J.C. 1985. Toward a theory of statutory evolution: the federalization of environmental law. *Journal of Law, Economics & Organization* 1: 313–40.

Elliott, E.D. 1985. The evolutionary tradition in jurisprudence. *Columbia Law Review* 85: 38–94.

Fikentscher, W. and McGuire, M.T. 1994. A four-function theory of biology for law. *Rechtstheorie* 25: 291–309.

Frank, R.H. 1988. *Passions Within Reason: The Strategic Role of the Emotions*. New York: W.W. Norton & Co.

Frolik, L.A. 1996. The biological roots of the undue influence doctrine: what's love got to do with it? *University of Pittsburgh Law Review* 57: 841–92.

Grady, M.F. and McGuire, M.T. 1997. A theory of the origin of natural law. *Journal of Contemporary Legal Issues* 8: 1–43.

Gruter, M. 1991. *Law and the Mind: Biological Origins of Human Behavior*. Newbury Park, CA: Sage Publications.

Gruter, M. and Masters, R.D. (eds) 1986. *Ostracism: A Social and Biological Phenomenon*. New York: Elsevier.

Gruter, M. and Masters, R.D. (eds) 1992. *The Sense of Justice: Biological Foundations of Law*. Newbury Park, CA: Sage Publications.

Gruter, M. 1977. Law in sociobiological perspective. *Florida State University Law Review* 5: 181–218.

Hovenkamp, H. 1985. Evolutionary models in jurisprudence. *Texas Law Review* 64: 645–85.

Jones, O.D. 1996. Genes, behavior, and law. *Politics & Life Sciences* 15: 101–35.

Jones, O.D. 1997. Evolutionary analysis in law: an introduction and application to child abuse. *North Carolina Law Review* 75: 1118–1242. (The most complete bibliography of sources on law and biology.)

Keller, E.F. and Lloyd, E.A. (eds). 1992. *Keywords in Evolutionary Biology*. Cambridge, MA: Harvard University Press.
Konner, M. 1990. *Why the Reckless Survive and Other Secrets of Human Nature*. New York: Viking.
Masters, R.D. 1996. *Machiavelli, Leonardo, and the Science of Power*. Notre Dame, IN: Notre Dame Press.
McGinnis, J.O. 1996. The once and future property-based vision of the First Amendment. *University of Chicago Law Review* 63: 49–76.
McGinnis, J.O. 1996. The original constitution and our origins. *Harvard Journal of Law and Public Policy* 19: 251–92.
Norman, D.A. 1988. *The Psychology of Everyday Things*. New York: Basic Books.
Posner, R.A. 1992. *Sex and Reason*. Cambridge, MA: Harvard University Press.
Poundstone, W. 1992. *Prisoner's Dilemma*. New York: Doubleday.
Ridley, M. 1994. *The Red Queen: Sex and the Evolution of Human Nature*. New York: Macmillan, Inc.
Rodgers, W.H., Jr. 1982. Bringing people back: toward a comprehensive theory of taking in natural resources law. *Ecology Law Quarterly* 10: 205–52.
Rodgers, W.H., Jr. 1989. The lesson of the owl and the crows: the role of deception in the evolution of the environmental statutes. *Journal of Land Use and Environmental Law* 4: 377–95.
Rodgers, W.H., Jr. 1993. Where environmental law and evolutionary biology meet: of pandas' thumbs, statutory sleepers, and effective law. *University of Colorado Law Review* 65: 25–75.
Rodgers, W.H., Jr. 1995. Deception, self-deception, and myth: evaluating long-term environmental settlements. *University of Richmond Law Review* 29: 567–79.
Rodgers, W.H., Jr. 1996. The sense of justice and the justice of sense: native Hawaiian sovereignty and the second 'trial of the century.' *Washington Law Review* 71: 379–401.
Ruhl, J.B. 1996. Complexity theory as a paradigm for the dynamical law-and-society system: A wake-up call for legal reductionism and the modern administrative state. *Duke Law Journal* 45: 849–928.
Ruhl, J.B. 1996. The fitness of law: using complexity theory to describe the evolution of law and society and its practical meaning for democracy. *Vanderbilt Law Review* 49: 1407–90.
Schermer, M. 1997. *Why People Believe Weird Things: Pseudoscience, Superstition, and Other Confusions of Our Time*. New York: W.H. Freeman & Co.
Stake, J.E. 1990. Darwin, donations, and the illusion of dead hand control. *Tulane Law Review* 64: 705–81.
Sulloway, F.J. 1996. *Born to Rebel: Birth Order, Family Dynamics, and Creative Lives*. New York: Pantheon Books.
Tiger, L. 1992. *The Pursuit of Pleasure*. Boston: Little, Brown & Co.
Trivers, R. 1985. *Social Evolution*. Menlo Park, CA: Benjamin/Cummings Pub. Co.
Wax, A. 1996. Against nature – on Robert Wright's *The Moral Animal*. *University of Chicago Law Review* 63: 307–18.
Wright, R. 1994. *The Moral Animal – Evolutionary Psychology and Everyday Life* New York: Pantheon Books.

law-and-economics from a feminist perpective. For many, 'feminist law-and-economics' will seem an oxymoron: feminism and law-and-economics are conventionally graphed as opposite poles on the interdisciplinary terrain of modern legal scholarship. Seeing only opposition in these forms of legal analysis, however, concedes too much to a particular, if dominant, approach to economic analysis in law, an approach associated with politically conservative strains in legal thought. Whereas feminism and law-and-economics have typically stood in critical relation only, feminist law-and-economics moves beyond mere criticism to an effort to take what is useful in an economic analysis and apply it to feminist problems. Finding what is for feminism a useful kernel in economic analysis of law requires going to first principles in the discipline and sorting from that kernel the chaff of particular anti-feminist presumptions.

Describing feminist law-and-economics is, at the current state of the art, largely an exercise of vision and optimism. For reasons that may derive from the predominantly male make-up of the economics profession and the emphasis on abstract and mathematical reasoning, feminism has been slow to infiltrate economic thought. Women have indeed been involved in economics for a very long time, but their work has until recently been largely on the margins in distinctly 'female' areas: home economics in the earlier years of this century, for example, and, more recently, empirical work on female labour supply. Critiques of economic analysis by feminists have been predominantly totalistic, rejecting the elements of the paradigm that distinguish modern neoclassical work; feminists in economics, to the extent they could be identified at all, tended to work outside of the mainstream, drawing more on radical or Marxist strands of economic thinking than conventional theory. Not only are there small numbers of women working in the dominant fields in modern economics, but until recently the idea that these women might bring to the subject distinctively feminist insights has been practically inconceivable, so committed has the profession been to the concept that economic analysis, particularly mathematical economics, is ethically and politically neutral.

Nevertheless, it is increasingly the case that feminists working in economics, (see, e.g., Ferber and Nelson 1993) are beginning to bring feminist insights to bear on the core issues in these fields. Indeed, perhaps because of legal theory's greater exposure to multiple interdisciplinary perspectives, feminist perspectives on law-and-economics appear in the mainstream much more clearly than they do in mainstream economic analysis *per se*. This essay explores several of the different ways in which this emerging feminist perspective on law-and-economics manifests itself.

FEMINIST QUESTIONS. The most straightforward integration of feminism and law-and-economics occurs when conventional law-and-economic analysis is used to analyse a question or issue of particular importance to women. This is minimalist feminism, but nonetheless an important part of doing feminist work. As has been recognized by feminist and other critical approaches to scientific disciplines claiming objectivity, one of the most direct ways in which the values of a researcher influence the shape of the subject is in the determination of the phenomena that are investigated and the answers that are considered adequate (Harding 1995). Richard Posner's law-and-economics analysis of sex (Posner 1992), for example, was distorted by the subset of questions he asked about the nature of sexuality and its regulation (see Hadfield 1992). Failing to ask how women's decisions about sexuality and work are affected by economics and sexual regulation, he proposed a causal relationship running from economic variables to sexual conduct and regulation which overlooked the important (and, from an economist's point of view, conventional) causal relationships running in the opposite direction, that is, from sexual conduct and regulation to economic behaviour, in particular women's economic behaviour. Informed by a feminist attention to the agency of women and feminist scepticism about the naturalness or inescapability of women's economic inequality, the critique of Posner is an example of how feminist questions influence law and economics scholarship. Hadfield (1993) similarly critiques the law-and-economic analysis of the gender gap in wages for its failure to investigate the question why the household is structured on gender lines, despite the fact that the gendered structure of the household is the central explanation offered by economists for the wage gap.

Some of the best examples of 'asking the woman question' in law-and-economics are found in the area of family law. The investigation of questions of family law using law-and-economics techniques is not feminist *per se*; indeed, law-and-economic analysis of the family is in many instances the antithesis of feminism. What makes some of the work in this area feminist is its normative concern with the impact of family law on women and thus its selection of questions of importance to feminism. Brinig and Crafton (1994), for example, use economic analysis to theorize that the transition to no-fault divorce, which can be seen as a failure to enforce the marriage contract, leads to an increase in a particular form of opportunism, namely domestic violence; they then employ conventional econometric techniques (with conventional limitations, specifically the impossibility of ruling out mere correlation) to demonstrate that such a relationship is borne out in the data. While large numbers of feminists would challenge this finding and its normative implications (should we reintroduce fault into divorce law?), the use of law-and-economics techniques to investigate an issue of importance to feminists is one of the ways in which feminism has had an impact on the dimensions of law-and-economics scholarship. Other examples of such work include Carbone (1990), Carbone and Brinig (1991), Singer (1994) and Brinig (1995).

What unifies this area of work is the employment of largely conventional economic analysis – positive and normative – to investigate issues of particular salience to women. This is an area of work that, despite being the most straightforward integration of feminist politics and law-and-economic analysis, has been largely underdeveloped. Yet it holds out substantial promise for feminism if for no other reason than that it permits feminists to respond to the use of economic analysis to support law and policy that detract from rather than promote women's wellbeing. The use of law-and-economics by feminists is a particularly potent response, for it does not require that the audience to whom it is addressed be itself feminist. Feminists who use law-and-economics to investigate the tradeoffs between economic growth and redistribution goals in tax policy, the implications of efficiency analysis for welfare reform, or the impact of market reforms in transitional economics on the economic incentives facing women, participate, and participate powerfully, in these debates.

FEMINIST MODELS. As the first stage of feminist analysis, asking feminist questions is minimalist in the sense that it does not require any shift in the methodology of law-and-economics analysis. This is, as suggested above, part of the virtue of law-and-economics for feminists engaged in policy debates with political conservatives who rely on law and economics. Interestingly, however, it is difficult to ask feminist questions without subtle shifts in method. The initial such shift is evident in what we could call 'feminist models'. These models are not only addressed to questions of importance to women, they incorporate assumptions and specifications that reflect feminist perspectives. In doing so they do not depart from conventional economic analysis in the sense that they employ the model of rational utility maximization and, to the extent they are normative, the efficiency criterion. They do, however, conceptualize differently by dividing the world up into categories different from those of conventional economic analysis.

Hadfield (1996a), for example, reexamines the question of the sexual division of labour, an important determinant of the economic inequality between men and women, using conventional game theoretic and microeconomic techniques but beginning with the unconventional (as compared to Becker 1981) assumption that men and women do not differ in inherent productivity. Doing so results in a model of how apparently inherent and long-standing male-female differences in economic activity can be derived from incentives rooted in the economics of organization rather than biology. Such a model generates very different implications for law and policy than does a model based on biological differences.

The most significant way in which asking feminist questions leads feminists to shift ground from conventional economic assumptions, however, is with respect to the basic concepts of 'value', 'cost', 'benefit' and so on. When feminists using economic theory examine welfare and tax policy, for example, they are led to wonder whether children are 'public goods' or 'private goods'. Is welfare policy or the deductibility of child care expenses 'subsidization' which leads to an 'externality' on taxpayers? Or is it a mechanism of capturing contributions from individual taxpayers for the 'private benefits' they receive from the 'public good' of well-cared-for children? Feminists using economics to analyse family law (Carbone 1990; Singer 1994; Brinig 1996) ask, what are the 'benefits' associated with marriage: higher consumption through specialized division of labour? the relational goods of love and intimacy? How does marriage contribute to the acquisition of human capital by the spouses and access to the non-market goods of the affection of children and the satisfactions of parenting? They also ask, is marriage best analysed as a contract or a status relation? Which model best captures what seems important about marriage from a feminist perspective? And they wonder about the appropriate measure – market or non-market – for household contributions (Staudt 1996). Feminists studying the organization of institutions and firms will ask, are the costs associated with the integration of work and family or the promotion of relationships in the workplace 'transaction costs' or 'production costs'? And feminists studying sexuality and sexual regulation will wonder what is the appropriate way to model the choices men and women make in this area? How do economic conditions constrain the choices made? What are the 'benefits' and 'costs' of sexuality? What information asymmetries attend choices, such as the choice to enter into a surrogacy contract? (Trebilcock 1993; Brinig 1995).

What is most important about these shifts in the assumptions made by feminists using economic analysis in law is the way in which they highlight a principle tenet of feminist critique in a wide range of disciplines, namely the view that the structure of models and theories is normative (Harding 1995). Not only does the determination of what question to ask reflect the values and perspectives of the researcher; so too does the very way in which the world is divided into the categories necessary for analysis. There is nothing necessary about the determination, for example, to treat the household as if it possessed a joint utility function defined over a set of public and private goods and as if this utility function were maximized by a benevolent head of household (Becker 1981). Seeking to understand not only the ways in which marriage benefits women but also the ways in which it disadvantages them or contributes to their diminished wellbeing relative to men, feminists begin with a different model, one that examines bargaining and strategic behaviour in this relationship, one that replaces Becker's assumption of perfect coordination of interests or altruism with an assumption of self-interest (see, e.g., Lundberg and Pollak 1994). Guided by research interests rooted in feminist concerns, scholars are led to choose different starting points for their analysis and so make plain the fact that theorists of all stripes (including those who claim to be stripe-less) make choices in modelling and framing an analysis that is reflective of their interests.

FEMINIST CRITERIA. So far we have been considering the relatively minimalist ways in which feminists modify conventional law-and-economics to investigate issues of importance to women; what is 'feminist' about this law-and-economics is the orientation of the question and the premises on which the analysis is built. Feminist concerns, however, often prompt feminist scholars using economics to make a more dramatic departure from conventional law-and-economics; that departure is the abandonment of efficiency as a normative criterion. The departure is dramatic because, unlike economics *per se* where there are large literatures devoted to purely positive analysis and empirical investigation only marginally dependent on the concept of efficiency, economic analysis in law has been overwhelmingly dominated by a normative focus on efficiency. Indeed, many will assume that the very feature that makes analysis 'law-and-economics' is the fact that it asks at least one of two questions: What is the efficient legal rule in this setting? Are the existing legal rules efficient? Feminist law-and-economics appears, from this perspective, to be not law-and-economics at all if it asks questions that have nothing to do with efficiency. But this is to mistake the domain of the field with the preoccupations of its current practitioners.

What, then, is law-and-economics without efficiency? The easy answer is that it is analysis marked by the agnosticism of positive theory, the type of analysis that uses economic theory to predict and explain the behaviour of individuals and institutions but does not go further to offer judgment about whether that behaviour is desirable or not. But this answer does not capture the distinctively normative concerns that animate feminist theory, nor indeed the normative concerns that are the focus of the bulk of legal scholarship. Answering the question, is this a justifiable legal rule, institution or practice, is central to the project of law. And so there must be more to a feminist law-and-economics that does not adopt efficiency than agnosticism.

The 'more' is the marriage of criteria drawn from normative theories other than economics – distributive justice, anti-discrimination, care – with appropriate elements from economics as a conceptualization and theory of behaviour. Hadfield (1995a), for example, draws on economics to consider the normative question of what the test for sexual harassment should be under employment equity legislation. The analysis takes as its normative criterion the idea as a first principle that non-job-related discrimination on the basis of gender is unjustifiable and that the economic inequality that results from such discrimination is unjust. (By way of contrast, there is a literature in conventional law-and-economics examining the question whether employment equity legislation is efficient: Donohue 1986; Posner 1987; Epstein 1992.) It then uses the concepts and organizing structures from economics to consider how a test for sexual harassment intended to eliminate discrimination might be constructed; in particular, the analysis begins with the concept that men and women make maximizing choices among job alternatives based on wage and non-wage costs and benefits and argues that sexual harassment is discriminatory when it distorts these choices for women but not men. In addition, the analysis draws on economics to demonstrate the ways in which sexual harassment contributes to economic inequality.

When the positive and normative components of conventional law-and-economics are disaggregated, we discover that economics' organizing concepts and behavioural theory are valuable resources for feminist analysis. The virtue of economic analysis is that the way in which it organizes an analysis – the identification of a decision-maker, the goals of that decision-maker, the values associated with different decisions, the ways in which decisions made by disparate individuals interact (intentionally, strategically or not) – permits the analysis to reach far and often surprisingly beyond its premises. This is what is meant by the power of economic reasoning: the employment of simple concepts to organize and gain a deeper understanding of complex phenomena. The normative efficiency criterion is not necessary to this power. Certainly, for those for whom the premise is congenial, the efficiency criterion expands the power of economic analysis by providing a simple and sharp (indeed mathematical) test for the desirability of legal rules, institutions and practices. But by another token the idea that economic analysis is tied exclusively to efficiency as a normative criterion is limiting: efficiency analysis may be powerful but it is only powerful in its domain; it is inert in those normative domains that ask more of law than that it not make anyone worse off relative to the status quo. By the same token, feminist analysis is made more powerful, not less, by the possibility of drawing on the concept of human capital to understand the equities of marriage and its bargains (Singer 1994), information asymmetries to think about the pain of surrogacy (Brinig 1995), or the labour/leisure tradeoff to reconsider whether household work should be taxed to accomplish redistributive and other feminist goals related to the valuation of women's work (Staudt 1996; see also McCaffery 1993 and Alstott 1996). Disaggregating law-and-economics from efficiency puts economics in the service of the normative project of feminism, rather than the other way around.

FEMINIST PRAGMATICS. Many feminists will be uneasy with the idea of using positive economic analysis to analyse feminist questions. This unease stems from a tenet of feminist theory that we have already considered, namely the recognition that the tools and categories of analysis are inevitably normative themselves. That is, feminism generally rejects the very distinction between positive and normative analysis that is the workhorse of law-and-economics and the basis for the idea that economics has powerful tools to offer even those who adopt alternative, feminist, normative criteria. This distrust of the easy distinction between positive and normative analysis is itself a useful resource for feminism to the extent that it leads to care and scepticism in the employment of particular economic concepts as opposed to outright rejection. Economics becomes a truly feminist tool when it is employed as part of what we might call feminist pragmatics.

Pragmatism is, of course, part of the orientation of many conventional law-and-economics scholars, notably Richard Posner (1990, 1995). What makes pragmatism pragmatism, however, is that it is not defined by a particular normative view but rather by an attitude towards the best means of understanding what one's normative scheme makes important.

> Pragmatism is willing to take anything, to follow either logic or the senses and to count the humblest and most personal experiences . . . Her only test of probable truth is what works best in the way of leading us, what fits every part of life best and combines with the collectivity of experience's demands, nothing being omitted (James [1907] 1976: 38).

Whereas for Posner the force of pragmatism is importantly empirical in the economist's statistical sense, for feminist law-and-economics pragmatism is a route to admission of the wider 'ways of knowing' (Belenky et al. 1986) characteristic of feminism.

As an element of feminist pragmatics, economic concepts are employed to the extent that they pass the pragmatic test that they 'work best' and accord with 'the collectivity of experience's demands'. Analysing sexual harassment using the economic conception of a choice-making agent in the labour market or divorce using the concepts of human capital, self-interest and opportunism, fits with a feminist pragmatics to the extent that what is lost by these analyses (those elements of employment, choice, sexuality, marriage, love and so on that are omitted from the economic abstraction) is repaid by what is gained in terms of the development of powerful, if partial, argument and understanding. Feminists engaged in a pragmatic exercise are choosy consumers of economics: what does not fit with (a particular) feminist understanding of the world is discarded, what does not further the project of understanding what feminism makes normatively important is set aside. (For examples in family law, see Estin 1995a, 1995b; for a discussion relative to contract law, see Hadfield 1995b.)

A pragmatic approach to the use of economics in feminist analysis of law also seeks to integrate economics with other theories, methodologies and sources of knowledge. Feminist narrative might help us understand what problems are in need of investigation or what the limits of an abstract concept might be. Feminist ethics can remind us that autonomy and individual welfare are not the only goals at stake; feminist political theory can question the very conceptualization of what it means to be 'autonomous'. Sociology can provide us with facts about how household work is accomplished and perceived; psychology with an understanding of motivation that sheds light on what is captured and what is not by the economist's behavioural model; biology with a basis for accepting or rejecting premises about productivity or sexuality. And so on. The essential point is that economic concepts are viewed as tools to be used when and where it is pragmatic to do so, in light of a broad array of positive and normative perspectives on the subject at hand. In this way, economics becomes integrated with multiple perspectives in legal analysis.

FEMINIST THEORY. As we move from 'minimalist' feminist law-and-economics (the use of law-and-economics techniques to analyse feminist questions) to a more thoroughgoing feminist pragmatics which picks and chooses among economic concepts, criteria and perspectives, economic theory is progressively displaced from centre stage; when it does appear, however, it retains its recognizable neoclassical shape. This then leaves us with a further possible progression in the integration of feminism and law-and-economics and that is a reformulation of economic analysis itself in response to feminism. Here the waters are indeed difficult to navigate and any effort to describe what a truly feminist theory of law-and-economics would look like must be aspirational. But it is nonetheless useful to imagine where the integration of feminism and economics in law might lead.

One way in which we might imagine how feminism could change economic theory is by reconsidering the feminist pragmatist. We conceived of this type of work as involving the adoption or rejection of conventional economic analysis as the feminist scholar saw fit in light of her positive and normative tenets. Earlier, however, we emphasized the value of economics in the power that came from the adoption of a small set of sharply defined concepts to analyse complex phenomena. This suggests that our feminist pragmatist might at times feel reluctant to abandon economic theory in the places in which it did not fit because the alternative tools are so much less powerful. At such a juncture, the feminist pragmatist might consider as an alternative to rejection of economic theory a reconfiguration of pieces of the theory. By returning to first principles – what is 'value'? what motivates 'choice'? how do individuals deal with 'uncertainty'? – the feminist pragmatist could modify economic analysis itself.

Anderson (1993) is an example, from philosophy, of how attention to feminist concerns can lead to a reformulation of first principles. Motivated originally by a feminist concern with the legal treatment of surrogacy contracts, Anderson was led to examine the concept of value underlying rational choice theory in general and economic analysis in particular. Her inquiry led her to a reformulation of rational choice theory on the basis of the idea that, in contrast to the economist's presumption that all goods can be compared on a single value metric, value is pluralistic: goods are valued not only in different amounts, but in different, incommensurate, ways. Moreover, valuation is not a purely private, subjective matter, as the economist sees it, but rather a partly public, socially-mediated process. Hadfield (1996b) then considers how Anderson's theory of rational choice might lead to conclusions about contract enforcement and damages different from conventional law-and-economics, and specifically reexamines three contract settings of importance to feminists: surrogacy contracts, marital separation agreements and spousal loan guarantees.

Whether such work is ultimately 'economic' depends on how we define the domain of 'economics'. Is economics a methodology, equivalent to a set of assumptions about individual utility, maximizing behaviour, and so on? Or is it defined by its subject – the systematic analysis of choice-making? On the former, using Anderson's theory of rational choice to analyse contract law is a departure from law-and-economics; on the latter, it is a new form of law-and-economics. Similarly, whether such work is ultimately 'feminist' depends on the domain of 'feminism'. Is feminism a methodology and a set of normative presuppositions? Or is it an approach to existing and conventional theory that demands attention to feminist problems, suppositions and normative tenets but that, when it produces theory, produces theory that is intended to modify conventional theory for non-feminists also? Anderson's theory, though growing out of a feminist perspective on why existing analyses of choice are inadequate to capture what is at stake in choice, is nonetheless ultimately not distinctively feminist: it is offered as any progression on conventional theory is offered, that is, as a better theory, period (see Harding 1995). Similarly, if feminism modifies law-and-economics at the level of first principles, it may be that the theory that emerges is also not distinctively feminist; to the extent that Hadfield (1996b) suggests a modification, it too is motivated by but not ultimately defined by feminism.

This view of what a 'feminist' theory of law-and-economics could look like and how it might emerge is distinct from what others have suggested for a feminist law-and-economics. Dennis (1993), for example, examines the comparable worth debate between conventional neoclassical economists and feminist economists and proposes 'a feminist vision of law-and-economics' that takes institutions such as job categories, rather than the individual, as the primary economic unit, measures national economic 'health' not only by gross national product but also the distribution of wealth, and promotes stability and long-term employment rather than economic growth. While features of Dennis's 'vision' may indeed emerge from the interplay of feminism and law-and-economics in the multiple ways outlined above, it is unlikely that a thoroughgoing 'feminist' paradigm can be designed by feminists to replace the conventional law-and-economics paradigm; that is simply a project of insufficient intellectual respect for the complexity of law, economics and feminism. Such grand theorizing is, indeed, counter to both the feminist appreciation for complexity and particularity and the economist's incremental approach to theory-building.

Feminist law-and-economics is, in the end, an unknown quantity for precisely the reason that we cannot yet know what will emerge from the marriage of these conventionally opposed movements in legal scholarship. Feminism's critical relationship with conventional law-and-economics is a foil against which any merged analysis will be tested also. Feminism's pragmatism, however, should lead to increasing efforts to cull from conventional law-and-economics those insights, concepts and analytical techniques that are of value to feminist scholarship. What emerges theoretically will be of value to both feminism and law-and-economics.

GILLIAN K. HADFIELD

See also DIVORCE; MARRIAGE AS CONTRACT; NO-FAULT DIVORCE; SEXUAL HARASSMENT.

Subject classification: 4c(i); 6d(v).

BIBLIOGRAPHY

Alstott, A.L. 1996. Tax policy and feminism: competing goals and institutional choices. *Columbia Law Review* 96: 2001–81.

Anderson, E. 1993. *Value in Ethics and Economics*. Cambridge, MA: Harvard University Press.

Becker, G.S. 1981. *A Treatise on the Family*. Cambridge, MA: Harvard University Press; 2nd edn 1991.

Belenky, M.F., Clinchy, B.M., Goldberger, N.R. and Tarvle, J.M. 1986. *Women's Ways of Knowing*. New York: Basic Books.

Brinig, M.F. 1995. A maternalistic approach to surrogacy. *Virginia Law Review* 81: 2377–99.

Brinig, M.F. 1996. Men, women and children: the law and economics of the family. *Feminism and Legal Theory Workshop: Feminism Confronts Economic Theory*, Columbia Law School, New York.

Brinig, M.F. and Crafton, S.M. 1994. Marriage and opportunism. *Journal of Legal Studies* 23: 869–94.

Carbone, J. 1990. Economics, feminism, and the reinvention of alimony: a reply to Ira Ellman. *Vanderbilt Law Review* 43: 1463–1501.

Carbone, J. and Brinig, M.F. 1991. Rethinking marriage: feminist ideology, economic change, and divorce reform. *Tulane Law Review* 65: 953–1010.

Dennis, J.M. 1993. The lessons of comparable worth: a feminist vision of law and economic theory. *UCLA Women's Law Journal* 4: 1–35.

Donohue, J.J. 1986. Is Title VII efficient? *University of Pennsylvania Law Review* 134: 1411–31.

Epstein, R.A. 1992. *Forbidden Grounds: The Case Against Employment Discrimination Laws*. Cambridge, MA: Harvard University Press.

Estin, A.L. 1995a. Love and obligation: family law and the romance of economics. *William and Mary Law Review* 36: 989–1087.

Estin, A.L. 1995b. Economics and the problem of divorce. *University of Chicago Law School Roundtable* 2: 517–97.

Ferber, M.A. and Nelson, J.A. (eds). 1993. *Beyond Economic Man: Feminist Theory and Economics*. Chicago: University of Chicago Press.

Hadfield, G.K. 1992. Flirting with science: Richard Posner on the bioeconomics of sexual man. *Harvard Law Review* 106: 479–503.

Hadfield, G.K. 1993. Households at work: beyond labor market policies to remedy the gender gap. *Georgetown Law Journal* 82: 89–107.

Hadfield, G.K. 1995a. Rational women: a test for sex-based harassment. *California Law Review* 83: 1151–89.

Hadfield, G.K. 1995b. The dilemma of choice: a feminist perspective on *The Limits of Freedom of Contract*. *Osgoode Hall Law Journal* 33: 337–51.

Hadfield, G.K. 1996a. A coordination model of the sexual division of labour. Manuscript, Faculty of Law, University of Toronto.

Hadfield, G.K. 1996b. A feminist perspective on rational choice in the law. *Feminism and Legal Theory Workshop Papers: Feminism Confronts Economic Theory*, Columbia Law School, New York.

Harding, S. 1995. Can feminist thought make economics more objective? *Feminist Economics* 1: 7–32.

James, W. 1907. *Pragmatism*. Cambridge, MA: Harvard University Press, 1976.

Lundberg, S. and Pollak, R. 1994. Noncooperative bargaining models of marriage. *American Economic Review Papers and Proceedings*, 84: 132–7.

McCaffery, E.J. 1993. Slouching towards equality: gender discrimination, market efficiency, and social change. *Yale Law Journal* 103: 595–675.

Posner, R.A. 1987. The efficiency and efficacy of Title VII. *University of Pennsylvania Law Review* 136: 513–21.

Posner, R.A. 1990. *The Problems of Jurisprudence*. Cambridge, MA: Harvard University Press.

Posner, R.A. 1992. *Sex and Reason*. Cambridge, MA: Harvard University Press.

Posner, R.A. 1995. *Overcoming Law*. Cambridge, MA: Harvard University Press.

Singer, J.B. 1994. Alimony and efficiency: the gendered costs and benefits of the economic justification for alimony. *Georgetown Law Journal* 82: 2423–60.

Staudt, N.C. 1996. Taxing housework. *Georgetown Law Journal* 84: 1571–1647.

Trebilcock, M.J. 1993. *The Limits of Freedom of Contract*. Cambridge, MA: Harvard University Press.

law-and-economics from a philosophical perspective. The phrase 'law-and-economics' has come in recent years to refer to a research programme that analyses the law from the perspective of economic theory. One can distinguish between normative and descriptive (positive) approaches to such a study. The normative approach is concerned with showing that legal rules should conform to certain economic principles or standards. The descriptive approach is concerned with showing that certain past and present legal rules do in fact conform to the same. In the following, the discussion is confined for the most part to philosophical issues that arise regarding normative versions of law and economics, although it must be acknowledged that positive accounts of the economic analysis of law pose interesting philosophical issues as well.

The leading normative thesis of the economic analysis of law, reduced to its simplest form, is that legal rules should satisfy principles of economic efficiency. The criterion of efficiency most often employed in economic theory is that associated with Pareto, which is based on comparing how two social arrangements, x and y, impact on the welfare of the individuals involved. If the welfare of each person in x is at least as great as that in y, and at least one person's welfare is greater in x than in y, then x is Pareto superior (or efficient relative) to y. Correspondingly, if it is impossible to modify an arrangement x such that everyone is at least as well off and some even better off (alternatively, if any change from x to some other arrangement would leave some individual worse off), then x is Pareto optimal.

Economists have characteristically interpreted individual welfare as a matter of preference satisfaction. They have also customarily assumed a number of other things about the content, structure, and identification of such preferences. First, the preferences of any given agent are typically not sensitive to the preferences of other agents. Second, for any given individual, all options are taken to be preferentially comparable, i.e., the preference ordering is connected. Third, individual preferences are often assumed to be monetizable, that is, the individual can put a dollar value on how much he or she prefers one alternative to another. Fourth, in more formal treatments, it is customary to 'operationalize' the concept of individual preference by supposing that for a person to prefer x to y is consistently to choose x over y in a variety of settings in which both options are available. If it becomes important to identify preferences in contexts in which such choice behaviour cannot be observed, so that one has to resort to verbal reports of preferences, the reporting setting is presumed to be one that persons do not approach strategically, i.e., they can be expected to report their true preferences.

The Pareto principles have usually been regarded (but not invariably – see, for example, Sen 1970, Ch. 6) as relatively uncontroversial criteria for the evaluation of social arrangements. They are informationally much less demanding than many other criteria, since they do not presuppose any interpersonal comparisons of preferences or utilities. The Pareto criteria are most clearly suited to the domain which is the preoccupation of the microeconomist, namely, competitive market systems. In that setting, choices can be observed, and there is no call for strategic behaviour. The celebrated formal theorems of welfare economics, to the proof of which much ingenious energy has been expended, establish, among other things, that when production and consumption decisions are disciplined by the workings of a perfectly competitive market system, the outcome is a state which is Pareto optimal (Debreu 1959; Arrow and Hahn 1971).

Finally, it must be noted that the Pareto criteria can function in either of two ways, as very weak, or as relatively strong, conditions on changes in arrangements. On the weak formulation, the claim is simply that a change that can be shown to be both Pareto superior to the existing arrangement, and Pareto optimal, is, *ceteris paribus*, defensible. On the strong formulation, the Pareto superiority and optimality of a proposed change is a necessary condition for the justification of that change. The weak formulation has the disadvantage that typically any number of different and conflicting changes will satisfy the Pareto conditions, so that it becomes necessary to invoke other criteria in order to defend one change over another. On the strong formulation the problem is simply that, in many contexts, arguably justifiable changes will fail to satisfy the Pareto conditions.

It is ironic that the seminal result in the area of law and economics details the conditions under which the allocation of legal rights and liabilities is irrelevant to the production of Pareto optimality. Coase (1960) had famously argued that when there are no transaction costs and the parties involved are perfectly rational, the way in which rights and liabilities are assigned makes no difference from the point of view of the Pareto criteria. If their assignment did not satisfy the optimality criterion, the individuals involved would trade with one another until an arrangement is reached that is Pareto superior to that original assignment, and Pareto optimal. This is not to say that the law itself is irrelevant to efficient market transactions. On virtually any account, certain basic legal institutions, including a system of property rights, contract law, and procedures for their enforcement, are preconditions for markets themselves.

As Coase noted, a result about a world with no transaction costs is important, for the most part, because it directs attention to the problems that arise when there are transaction costs. Now the manner in which rights are assigned makes an economic difference. If they are not assigned to the party who would be disposed to purchase them, post assignment exchanges will have to take place, and transaction costs will then be incurred. These transaction costs may even be sufficiently high to block any transition to a superior and optimal arrangement, in which case the original assignment will have precluded the realization of an optimal outcome.

Coase's original article did not propose any general solution to the problems caused by transaction costs. Nevertheless, a natural suggestion is that, in these cases, the law should be used to mimic what the market would have done if there were no transaction costs (Posner 1977). That is, legal rights should be assigned to the parties who would have secured them in market exchange, if they did not already possess them. The objective is to try to ensure that the legal decision yields an outcome having the virtues of the one that would have resulted from competitive market exchanges.

If these virtues are explicated in terms of the Pareto criterion, however, there are a number of problems. In this framework, one must appeal to hypothetical (counterfactual) markets, within which choice cannot be observed. This means that judgments of which arrangements are Pareto superior to others cannot be based on an operationalized account of individual preferences. Moreover, strategic behaviour now becomes a problem. Individuals may well have a motive to misrepresent their preferences, and this, in turn, may lead to an outcome that is not Pareto optimal.

What is most important, if the combination of Pareto superiority and optimality is taken as a necessary condition for legal changes, is that there may be no legitimate way for the law to mimic the market. The market process is supposed to yield an outcome that is Pareto superior to the one that would result if no exchange takes place. But there is no assurance that legal intervention in the form of a rights assignment will have this effect (Coleman 1984: 669–70). The movement, for example, from a negligence regime to one of strict liability in the area of products liability has, arguably, made consumers richer and manufacturers poorer (see Kornhauser 1980: 607–8). If there is an economic defence of this change, then, it will have to be by reference to something other than the principle that requires Pareto superiority as a condition of any change.

Yet, if the Pareto criteria are downgraded from strong necessary conditions to weak sufficient conditions, additional principles will have to be invoked in order to rule out certain allocations that diverge from the market solution. In legally unregulated areas, for example, it can be argued that any rights assignment will be Pareto optimal. Losers – the persons who are not awarded the legal right – cannot complain of being made worse off by the new legal regime, because they do not lose a right that they already had. Any legal rule of assignment, therefore, is likely to make some better off without making anyone worse off. And any such assignment is likely to be optimal. This is because it is likely that no uncompensated change to another legal rule will be Pareto superior because any such change will make the original winner worse off. This is true even if the winner would have sold his or her right in a perfectly competitive marketplace.

In order to deal with such cases, law-and-economics advocates have tended to appeal to some other principle than those of Pareto superiority and optimality, some principle that is weak enough to allow individual welfare to be aggregated in a way that permits rights-assignments which benefit some at the expense of others, yet strong enough to rule out certain distributions which would never arise under conditions of perfect competition. One obvious candidate for such a guiding principle, of course, is the utilitarian principle, which calls for maximizing the sum (or, alternatively, the average) of individual welfare, and which thus allows for rights-assignments that decrease the welfare of some, so long as these 'losses' are sufficiently offset by increases to the welfare of others. Similarly, the utilitarian principle would forbid any allocation of entitlements if mutual trades could make each party even better off.

But an appeal at this point to some utilitarian principle throws one right back into a setting in which, methodologically, one must deal with the problem of interpersonal comparisons of welfare. Moreover, since one must still draw inferences about counterfactual situations, the problem of operationalizing the concept of individual preference or welfare remains. And finally, the appeal to a utilitarian principle raises a variety of substantive normative issues that are nicely avoided so long as one appeals only to the Pareto criteria. In particular, one now must contend with all the moral objections that have been raised against utilitarianism.

A distinct approach, which Posner (1977, 1979, 1980) takes, involves an appeal to the principle of wealth maximization. Wealth, according to Posner,

> is the value in dollars or dollar equivalents of everything in society. It is measured by what people are willing to pay for something, or, if they already own it, what they demand in money to give it up. The only kind of preference that counts in a system of wealth maximization is thus one that is backed up by money – in other words, that is registered in a market (1979: 119).

Treating welfare in terms of wealth solves the problem of interpersonal comparisons, since wealth is naturally subject to comparison, regardless of who possesses it. It is also plausible to suppose that persons have a connected preference ordering over increasing amounts of wealth. More generally, there is now a substantial body of literature dealing with how wealth can be measured, and the various logical properties of such a measure of social welfare (see WEALTH MAXIMIZATION). Wealth maximization, however, is no methodological panacea, and is subject to a wide range of objections (see Coleman 1980a, 1980b and 1984; Dworkin 1980a and 1980b; Kornhauser 1980). First, Posner is clear that he intends his notion of value to apply in cases where markets are only implicit, or 'counterfactual'. But prices will have to be specified for such contexts, if one is to show that one assignment generates greater wealth than another. How, in the absence of actual markets, are claims about prices to be verified? Second, a troublesome problem about intrapersonal preference comparability arises in connection with wealth maximization. While some (although it should be noted, not all – see here Levi 1986) are prepared to think that an individual must preferentially rank all possible alternatives, the thesis that an individual must always attach a monetary equivalent to each option seems very doubtful. On a familiar way of thinking, some things – love, friendship, trust, life itself – simply do not have a price. Third, the wealth maximization principle suffers from the kind of problem that was shown to beset the Kaldor–Hicks 'potential' compensation principle (Scitovsky 1941). Under certain circumstances there could be two alternative legal arrangements, such that a move from either one to the other would be superior from a wealth maximizing perspective. In such cases, the wealth maximization principle will not yield a coherent social ordering (see, again, WEALTH MAXIMIZATION).

The wealth maximization principle is also open to virtually all the substantive moral objections to which the utilitarian principle is subject, and then some. Notably, the wealth maximization criterion has perverse distributional tendencies. While classical utilitarianism is officially insensitive to distributional considerations, it does tend to favour roughly egalitarian distributions, assuming, as most utilitarians do, the diminishing marginal utility of income. On the other hand, wealth maximization appears to favour those with greater wealth, insofar as they are the ones who are willing to pay more for a certain good than those less fortunate (Baker 1975; but see the rejoinder to this in Coleman 1984: 661–4). Moreover, wealth maximization avoids the methodological problems of utilitarianism only by attenuating its connection to what is typically thought to be one of the main concerns of morality, i.e., human happiness. On an intuitive level, willingness to pay does not seem to be directly correlated with levels of happiness. A given person might be willing to pay more for x than another would, but this might simply indicate that the first is wealthier than the second, and thus can afford to pay a higher price for x. While utilitarianism may be deficient because it sacrifices individual happiness to the happiness of the group, at least it is about human happiness.

Suppose, however, that these various methodological and moral problems can be resolved. There is still the question of how to justify the wealth maximization principle itself. The great advantage of taking Pareto superiority and optimality as part of a sufficient condition for a change in legal rules is that, as weak as such a standard is, it is well grounded in the notion of pragmatic rationality, in the notion that it is rational to be disposed to support arrangements that work to everyone's, and hence one's own, advantage. Moreover, when formulated as a necessary condition on change, the Pareto conditions capture what many have taken to be an essential feature of an individualistic, contractarian approach to social, political, and legal, no less than economic, arrangements. There does not appear to be anything like a comparable argument for taking wealth maximization as either a sufficient or a necessary condition for change.

The problem is compounded by the consideration that some possible defences of wealth maximization, or any aggregation principle for that matter, are clearly not open to those who seek, as most advocates of the economic analysis of law have, to remain within an individualistic framework. One could, of course, appeal to some 'organic' conception of the state (see Kornhauser 1980), or to some communitarian or group conception of the good, but neither approach is likely to appeal very much to those who have worked in the law and economics tradition. Within that tradition, the central justificatory question has to be whether there is some liberal, individualistic standpoint from which wealth maximization can be defended.

Posner's (1980) own approach is to appeal to what he characterizes as the idea of consent, or *ex ante* compensation. The basic idea is to explore the implications of supposing that persons are sufficiently uncertain about the future, and in particular, about how they will be affected by any particular assignment of rights. Under such conditions, he claims, one might agree to the application of some aggregation principle such as wealth maximization (or, alternatively, the Kaldor–Hicks potential compensation principle) for the evaluation of certain kinds of legal arrangements. Recognizing that the operation of such a rule will mean that on certain occasions one's own interests will be sacrificed for the interests of others, still one may expect that over the long-run one will be a net gainer – that more often than not one will be advantaged rather than disadvantaged, given the operation of some such principle. This might very well be the case, for example, if the operation of a wealth maximization rule for assigning rights and liabilities resulted in substantial savings, over the long haul, in transaction costs.

Such a line of reasoning would seem to involve appealing, in effect, to Pareto superiority and optimality as a *sufficient* condition for change, adjusted to the level of what each *expects* to gain, to show why, at least in certain classes of cases, it would not be rational to insist upon a case-by-case application of the Pareto-criterion as a *necessary* condition for change. As Posner notes, a parallel approach to the Kaldor–Hicks potential compensation principle is to be found in the work of Polinsky (1972) and Michelman (1980). There is also a parallel argument, in Buchanan and Tullock (1962), adjusted to welfare rather than wealth, according to which rational persons would agree to allow certain classes of decisions to be settled by appeal to a majoritarian voting rule.

In each of these cases, the justificatory issue concerning how various rules or policies are to be evaluated is interestingly relocated within the more general setting of a theory of rational decision-making under conditions of risk and uncertainty. Posner notes, however, that his appeal to choice under conditions of uncertainty should be distinguished from the 'original position' arguments employed by Harsanyi (1955, 1978) and Rawls (1971), both of whom appeal to a model of deep or radical uncertainty. What Posner proposes instead is a model in which one imagines

> ... actual people, deploying actual endowments of skill and energy and character, making choices under uncertainty ... that is, ... choice under conditions of natural ignorance ... [rather than] choice under the artificial ignorance of the original position (1980: 499).

Posner's desire to distance himself from such models of radical uncertainty is understandable, for those arguments are subject to two very worrisome objections. The first is that there is no consensus regarding what a rational person would choose under conditions of complete uncertainty. Despite the elaborate constructions of Bayesian subjectivists (see, for example, Savage 1954), it remains the case that radical uncertainty calls into play alternative axiomatic constructions that, taken together, generate nothing but impossibility theorems (see Luce and Raiffa 1957: ch. 13). Second, no one has offered a very convincing argument as to why, here and now in the real world, one should be guided by those evaluative principles one would adopt under the counterfactual conditions of radical uncertainty.

Does Posner's own approach, involving an appeal to 'natural' rather than 'artificial' uncertainty, avoid these problems? The suggestion appears to be that 'uncertainty' can be explicated in terms of the less controversial notion of probabilistically defined risk, so that losses in specific cases can be balanced off by a 'sufficient probability that an individual will benefit in the long run' (Posner 1980: 492, fn. 13). And, of course, the appeal to 'natural' uncertainty is designed to avoid the problem of having to provide a bridge back from a counterfactual world to the real world.

Despite these advantages, changing the initial choice situation in this way complicates the task of justifying the wealth maximization principle. The 'original position' arguments of Rawls and Harsanyi have one very distinctive feature, namely, that they are designed to yield a solution that is maximal from the perspective of *each* individual participant. The choice behind the thick veil of ignorance places each participant in the position of being a representative of each other person, and the choice that the rational person is alleged to make maximizes the return to each (from the perspective of whatever is taken to be the appropriate rule, maximin payoff for Rawls, average payoff for Harsanyi). The rule agreed upon, therefore, is not a 'compromise' solution: each is satisfied that, given the special nature of the situation, each has done the best possible. Posner, however, cannot claim that, under conditions of 'natural' uncertainty, the wealth maximization principle is such a maximal solution. All he can claim is that, in certain contexts, the adoption of the wealth maximization principle is rational for many, but not for everyone. Thus, for example, the poor might prefer to reject the wealth maximization principle, for they might be better off under an alternative arrangement that discriminates on the basis of initial endowments. At the very least, it would seem, one must now move to some sort of bargaining model to develop a theory of how a consensus could be possible. But this, in turn, poses a serious problem, since there is no consensus on what is to count as an adequate bargaining model, nor about what is to be taken as the base-line against which mutual gains are to be explored, and compromises reached (see McClennen 1990).

In response, it might be argued that courts should not fashion legal rules which are sensitive to the parties' initial endowments, given that this amounts to a redistribution of wealth, and courts are ill-suited to this task. Shavell (1981) and Kaplow and Shavell (1994), for example, show that an inefficient common law rule can impose a 'tax' that introduces more distortion than would, say, a direct income tax. They argue that certain distributional goals are better promoted by a system of taxation than through common law. Wealth maximization is justified on this account by demonstrating that everyone would be better off with an efficient common law rule and a redistributive income tax.

One clear problem with this argument is that its recommendation that courts promote wealth maximization presupposes that other state agencies will engage in a rather aggressive form of wealth redistribution. Absent some radical restructuring of current political systems, however, this proposal must reside within what is sometimes called 'ideal' political theory. Moreover, even if courts are bad at redistributing wealth, it does not follow that they would be good at maximizing it. Even if we assume that judges are sufficiently competent to fashion economically efficient rules, the amount of information necessary for such a task is staggering (Hanson and Hart 1996).

Not only would the legitimacy of wealth maximization presuppose radical political restructuring, but its pursuit would result in a radical restructuring of current legal systems. No longer would the plaintiff-class be restricted to those who have been harmed and the defendant-class to those who have caused the harm. If gains in efficiency could be had by letting third parties sue, then they should be given incentives to bring suit. Similarly, if third parties are more effective cost-minimizers than those who actually caused the harm, then they should be proper objects of legal actions. In a legal system that took wealth maximization seriously, private law would be completely gobbled up by public law. Courts would no longer fulfil one of their traditional tasks, which is the meting out of justice between private parties (Coleman 1988). Whether such a system would ultimately be desirable is an open question and one usually not faced by those who advocate the wealth maximization principle.

For all this, the preoccupation of Posner and others with wealth maximization deserves not to be dismissed out of hand. In the rush to criticize the law and economics approach, and especially Posner's work, few have paused to reflect that for Rawls, as well as for many other 'liberal' theorists, wealth is a primary good, that is, the sort of good that agents should be concerned to secure, whatever their specific objectives or interests. It can be argued, then, that wealth maximization is a neutral principle with respect to rival views of the good life, and that it thus is well suited to a liberal conception of society. And despite the caveats expressed above to the line of argument pursued by Kaplow and Shavell, one might still want to insist that a strong case can be made for wealth maximizing in the area of commercial law as distinct from personal rights.

Nevertheless, the fate of the law-and-economics movement does not rest on the viability of the wealth maximization principle. It should be recalled that Coase himself, who provided the inspiration for the law and economics movement, calls at the end of his landmark article on social cost (1960: 43) for an evaluative approach that takes into account more than just wealth:

> In this article, the analysis has been confined, as is usual in this part of economics, to comparisons of the value of production, as measured by the market. But it is, of course, desirable that the choice among different social arrangements for the solution of economic problems should be carried out in broader terms than this and that the total effect of these arrangements in all spheres of life should be taken into account.

Whether the principles are based on wealth maximization, or some more expansive welfarist criterion, however, the law-and-economics movement has found itself faced, at this level, with a set of foundational problems that have, in the more general setting of normative political economy, proved to be quite intractable. It is perhaps not surprising, then, that recent work has tended to concentrate instead on much more applied and positive questions. The unfortunate effect of this has been that important foundational matters have not so much been settled as allowed to fall into desuetude.

Given the movement's general lack of interest in scrutinizing, let alone discussing, the normative foundations of their field, it is understandable why many critics have seen the almost exclusive emphasis on positive and applied questions as unmotivated, even intellectually dishonest. Such charges are not totally fair, however. In many ways, the desire to detail the effects that legal rules have on rational behaviour falls squarely within the mainstream tradition of jurisprudence which seeks to understand the law from a 'practical' perspective. That is, the law is regarded as an normative institution which is capable of guiding conduct by affecting the practical reasoning of those subject to its authority.

We might say that the distinctive contribution made to this jurisprudential tradition is the movement's commitment to study and evaluate the law from a 'rational choice' perspective. Researchers routinely employ the techniques of cost-benefit analysis, decision and game theory, and statistics to determine whether the goals sought by the law – whatever they might be – are best served by the legal rules in place. To be sure, the goals most often studied are those relating to economic efficiency. Yet, as the quote from Coase indicated, researchers allow that other goals may, and should, be pursued by the law and are committed to the idea that the pursuit of these goals should be scrutinized using many of the same analytical techniques. It is the emphasis on 'maximization,' not on the economic maxim and of wealth, which, perhaps, can claim to be the core commitment of this tradition. It is unsurprising, therefore, that one of the greatest proponents of the rational critique of the law, Oliver Wendell Holmes, should also have prophesied the rise of the law-and-economics movement:

> For the rational study of the law the black-letter man may be the man of the present, but the man of the future is the man of statistics and the master of economics (Holmes 1897).

While this rational choice approach has produced a sizeable body of empirical results documenting the significant effects that legal rules have on behaviour and normative arguments recommending certain modifications in those rules, it has also started to reveal the limit of the law's ability to effect change. Noting that legal rules are often costly to learn and enforce, researchers have argued that, in situations of repeated play, it is efficient for parties to develop dispute-resolution mechanisms which bypass the formal legal machinery. As Robert Ellickson has shown in his now-famous study of Shasta County ranchers and farmers, the resort to the law is often seen as a defection from an informal scheme of social cooperation, rather than as a method for enforcing the terms of that cooperation (Ellickson 1991). It is somewhat ironic that current research in law and economics is confirming the Coasean prediction, if for completely opposite reasons. Changes in legal entitlements are often irrelevant to the production of economic efficiency not because rational actors will end up trading those entitlements, but rather because they will ignore the changes, just as they ignored the initial allocation. Both when transactions costs are very low and very high, rational actors will tend to bypass the law. Nevertheless, for a broad range of cases which lie in between these extremes, legal rules can guide conduct and it is here where normative recommendations are in order.

While the increasing emphasis on the behavioural consequences of the law is philosophically sound, it is nonetheless worrisome that the law-and-economics tradition has been committed to the Holmesian view that legal actors, no less than market-place actors, are motivated to follow legal rules only because they wish to avoid the sanctions associated with their violation. That is, sanctions are viewed as operating as prices that legal actors will factor into their decision whether to comply with a law or not. The problem with this 'bad man' view of the law is simply that if all rule-following is motivated by the desire on the part of the agent to avoid sanctions, it is unclear why legal officials apply legal rules that they find go against their own interests. The standard economic reply is that legal officials will try to avoid the negative reputational impact that would result from censure by officials with higher authority or by the public. But why would members of the public criticize persons for acting as they themselves would act in those situations, and why would legal officials care about their reputation for acting against their own interest? More generally, this view seems to deny what many people take to be an incontrovertible fact about human experience, namely, that people act out of a sense of moral or social obligation, and not just to avoid sanctions. The economic approach to law, that is, seems to take a purely 'external' approach to rule-guided behaviour, to borrow H.L.A. Hart's terminology (see RULE-GUIDED BEHAVIOUR). What is needed is an 'internal' approach, which factors into the equation the fact that people are capable of following rules out of a sense of obligation, and not solely to avoid sanctions.

SCOTT SHAPIRO AND EDWARD F. MCCLENNEN

See also KALDOR-HICKS COMPENSATION; LAW-AND-ECONOMICS FROM THE PERSPECTIVE OF CRITICAL LEGAL STUDIES; PARETO OPTIMALITY; POSNER, RICHARD A.; RULE-GUIDED BEHAVIOUR; VALUE MAXIMIZATION; WEALTH MAXIMIZATION.

Subject classification: 4c(i).

BIBLIOGRAPHY

Arrow, K.J. and Hahn, F.H. 1971. *General Competitive Analysis*. San Francisco: Holden-Day.

Baker, C.E. 1975. The ideology of the economic analysis of law. *Philosophy and Public Affairs* 5: 3–48.

Buchanan, J.M. and Tullock, G. 1962. *The Calculus of Consent*. Ann Arbor: University of Michigan Press.

Coase, R. 1960. The problem of social cost. *Journal of Law and Economics* 3: 1–44.

Coleman, J.L. 1980a. Efficiency, auction and exchange. *California Law Review* 68: 221–49. Reprinted in Coleman, J.L., *Markets, Morals and the Law*, Cambridge: Cambridge University Press, 1988.

Coleman, J.L. 1980b. Efficiency, utility and wealth maximization. *Hofstra Law Review* 8: 509–551. Reprinted in Coleman, J.L., *Markets, Morals and the Law*, Cambridge: Cambridge University Press, 1988.

Coleman, J.L. 1984. Economics and the law: a critical review of the foundations of the economic approach to law. *Ethics* 94: 649–79.

Coleman, J.L. 1988. The structure of tort law. *Yale Law Journal* 97: 1233–53.

Debreu, G. 1959. *Theory of Value*. New York: John Wiley & Sons, Inc.

Dworkin, R.M. 1980a. Is wealth a value? *Journal of Legal Studies* 9: 191–226.

Dworkin, R.M. 1980b. Why efficiency? *Hofstra Law Review* 8: 563–90.

Ellickson, R.C. 1991. *Order Without Law: How Neighbors Settle Disputes*. Cambridge, MA: Harvard University Press.

Hanson, J.D. and Hart, M.R. 1996. Law and economics. In *A Companion to the Philosophy of Law and Legal Theory*, ed. D. Patterson, Oxford: Blackwell.

Harsanyi, J.C. 1955. Cardinal welfare, individualistic ethics, and interpersonal comparisons of utility. *Journal of Political Economy* 63: 309–21.

Harsanyi, J.C. 1978. Bayesian decision theory and utilitarian ethics. *American Economic Review Papers and Proceedings* 68: 223–8.

Holmes, O.W. 1897. The path of the law. *Harvard Law Review* 10: 457–78

Kaplow, L. and Shavell, S. 1994. Why the legal system is less efficient than the income tax in redistributing income. *Journal of Legal Studies* 23: 667–81

Kornhauser, L.A. 1980. A guide to the perplexed claims of efficiency in the law. *Hofstra Law Review* 8: 591–639.

Levi, I. 1986. *Hard Choices*. Cambridge: Cambridge University Press.

Luce, R.D. and Raiffa, H. 1957. *Games and Decisions: Introduction and Critical Survey*. New York: John Wiley & Sons, Inc.

McClennen, E.F. 1990. Foundational explorations for a normative theory of political economy. *Constitutional Political Economy* 1: 67–99.

Michelman, F. 1980. Constitutions, statutes, and the theory of efficient adjudication. *Journal of Legal Studies* 9: 431–61.

Polinsky, A.M. 1972. Probabilistic compensation criteria. *Quarterly Journal of Economics* 86: 407–25.

Posner, R. 1977. *Economic Analysis of Law*. 2nd edition, Boston: Little, Brown & Co.

Posner, R. 1979. Utilitarianism, economics, and legal theory. *Journal of Legal Studies* 8: 103–40.

Posner, R. 1980. The ethical and political basis of the efficiency norm in common law adjudication. *Hofstra Law Review* 8: 487–507.

Rawls, J. 1971. *A Theory of Justice*. Cambridge, MA: Harvard University Press.

Savage, L.J. 1954. The Foundations of Statistics. New York: John Wiley & Sons, Inc.; 2nd revised edn, New York: Dover Press, 1972.

Scitovsky, T. 1941. A note on welfare propositions in economics. *Review of Economic Studies* 9: 77–88.

Sen, A.K. 1970. *Collective Choice and Social Welfare*. San Francisco: Holden-Day.

Shavell, S. 1981. A note on efficiency vs. distributional equity in legal rulemaking: should distributional equity matter given optimal income taxation? *American Economic Review (Papers and Proceedings)* 71: 414–18.

law-and-economics from the perspective of critical legal studies. Critical legal studies was a left-wing political/academic movement that now exists only as a school of thought in legal academia. Between the late 1970s and the late 1980s, a few of us produced a critique of mainstream economic analysis of law. It had little effect on its targets, though quite a few of its propositions have been vindicated by later work by others unaware of our earlier low-tech effort. This is a selective synthesis of elements from the critique, inevitably informed by hindsight.

I begin by putting the emergence of mainstream law and economics in the historical context of developments in economics and developments in legal theory. From the side of economics, the theory of the efficiency of perfectly competitive equilibrium required a response to the problem of externalities. The private law rules that define the functioning of the institution of the 'free market' permit far more externalities than economists before Coase had recognized. These same private law rules posed a problem for legal theorists because courts make and unmake them according to criteria that seem patently open to ideological (liberal vs. conservative) manipulation, with significant distributional consequences. The solution of mainstream law and economics to these two problems was that courts should make market-defining private law rules according to the Kaldor–Hicks definition of efficiency, leaving distributional questions to legislatively enacted tax and transfer programmes.

In the second part of this essay, I outline a version of the critical legal studies critique of this solution.

(1) The mainstream proposal that courts adopt Kaldor–Hicks as the criterion of decision between different possible legal rules is a bad idea, practically unworkable, incoherent on its own terms, and just as open to alternating liberal and conservative ideological manipulation as the open-ended policy analysis it was supposed to replace.

(2) When we interpret mainstream law and economic analysis as an attempt to develop an efficient code of private law rules defining a free market, leaving distributive questions to tax and transfer, we come up against the problem that the outcome of a series of partial equilibrium analyses is radically path dependent while a general equilibrium solution setting all the rules at once will produce multiple solutions.

(3) A more sophisticated understanding of the relevance of neo-classical micro theory to legal rule-making undermines the policy bias, shared by liberal and conservative economists, that we should avoid trying to redistribute wealth, income and social power by reconfiguring the ground rules of property and contract that define a 'free market', and stick instead to tax and transfer (supposing that we don't want to socialize the economy).

THE EFFICIENCY OF THE FREE MARKET DEPENDS ON A SOLUTION TO THE PROBLEM OF EXTERNALITIES. The abstract model of an efficient, perfectly competitive equilibrium in a system of commodity production obviously has the idea of a commodity built into it, and this is commonly specified as meaning that everything of value is private property and there is freedom of contract. These institutions are understood to be imposed by the state, or by some other agent external to the competing owners. This much state intervention is part of the definition of the market, and when the intervention goes no further, then we have 'the free market'.

The efficiency of perfectly competitive free market equilibria is important in the construction of economists' policy discourse (a) because it gives rise to the contrast between free market and regulatory solutions to policy questions, and (b) because it underpins the idea that the valid bases for regulation of the free market are (i) to achieve potentially Pareto-superior results by responding to market failures, and (ii) to achieve distributive objectives, but only when the efficiency costs of regulation are not too great, and are less than those of some other mode of redistributive intervention (e.g., tax and transfer or government ownership of some activity).

In the economists' model of competitive equilibrium, we imagine that factor owners own something like factor chips, discrete physical objects, that are combined with other chips to make final good chips, which are also discrete physical objects that their owners consume. In this context, private property means that the state (a) prevents players from taking each other's chips without consent, and (b) doesn't dictate private parties' allocation of their chips to different uses. Free contract means (a) the state forces people to honour their voluntary agreements about chips, and (b) players are free to make any agreements they want about the use and transfer of chips. By contrast with a free market solution, 'regulation' means promulgating state restrictions either on how owners use or dispose of property or on what contracts they can make.

In order for there to be a presumption on efficiency grounds in favour of a free market, and therefore an efficiency equity tradeoff if the free market produces inequality, it was necessary to deal with the problem of externalities. The Pigovian solution of fines and bounties was 'regulatory' because it just assumed that the only way to deal with the externality was for the government to identify it and then deal directly with the causer, either by fining or by bountying, thereby interfering with the free market solution, under which the property-owner was free to use his property as he wished.

From a lawyer's point of view, what was odd about this approach was that it ignored the fact that externalities were externalities only because there was no private law rule requiring the cost imposer to desist or to pay the victim, or requiring the beneficiary of an externality to pay the person who generated it. Private law specifies when the state will intervene to support a private actor's demand for some kind of remedy (injunction or damages) for injury by another private actor. Private law rules say when I can get redress for breach of contract, compensation for injuries to my person and property, and restitution of things taken from me.

In the English-speaking world, most private law rules are made by judges rather than by legislators. Legislatures (within constitutional limits) have the power to change the rules the judges have made, and to deal with new situations by making new rules. It is the private law rules, governing a vast array of behaviour that is neither required nor forbidden by criminal law, that establish the property and contract regime that we think of as a 'free market'.

Modern law and economics was born with Coase's realization (1960) that the judge-made private law rules that had been taken by economists to provide a specification of their notion of property and contract, also involved deciding what to do about externalities, indeed amounted to resolving to internalize or not some particular cost to some particular actor. Moreover, the actual legal regimes permitted owners of property, including owners of property in their own labour or other kinds of activity, to cause injuries to others, including other owners of things, in many, many situations, far more than had ever been included in the limited Pigovian category of externalities combined with the standard analysis of public goods.

THE PROBLEM OF EXTERNALITIES IS BIGGER THAN ECONOMISTS SEEM TO REALIZE. To see how big the problem of externalities becomes when we focus on the actual content of private law rules, we need to add another way in which the legal/economic real world differs from the chip trading model.

With respect to things:

A. Some things (not public goods) you can't have property in at all.

B. For the domain of things in which you can have property, it turns out that the concept is relative, so that you can have more or less protection depending on the kind of thing. The three main axes of variation are the number of people against whom you have protection, the 'mental element' required before we say that someone who has interfered with your thing has to compensate you for injury, and the kind of redress you can get for interference.

C. Even with respect to things in which you can have 'full' ownership, full ownership turns out to include rights to use the thing in ways that impose costs on others, so that what lawyers mean by a full property right over a thing has two 'sides' – rights not to be interfered with and Hohfeldian privileges to use in a way that interferes with others. The combination of these rights to hurt with rights not to be hurt differs for different kinds of property. This is what is meant when lawyers say that 'property governs relations between persons with respect to things, rather than relations of persons to things,' and that 'property is just a bundle of rights' (see Hohfeld 1917; Vandevelde 1980; Singer 1982).

The sources of utility include not just objects but actions of people. If everything that can be a source of utility has to be property in order for competitive equilibrium to be efficient, then there obviously has to be property in labour, one of the main factors of production, and in human performances that are final goods for consumers. And since the states of our bodies and minds, quite apart from the ownership of objects, are important sources of utility, we need some rules about what one person can do to another by way of injury. So we have in the model that people in some sense own themselves (there are personal rights as well as property rights), and the imagined legal regime of a free market has to include rules defining what it means to own oneself and to have the right to alienate oneself.

With respect not to things but to utility generating actions of others, there are many things that people can do to you that reduce your utility but which give rise to no right of legal redress. There are interests (sources of utility) that receive no legal protection at all, as for example the interest in the aesthetic enjoyment generated by the environment. But even if the legal system regards your interest as one that is worthy of protection, the degree of protection varies widely. So the interest in bodily security receives different levels of protection depending on the nature of the invasion, the interest in emotional security another, and the interest in business goodwill yet a third. Just as with things, 'the human commodity' turns out to be multiform, providing rights sometimes against only a few injurers, sometimes against many, sometimes against injury no matter why or how inflicted (strict liability), sometimes only against people whose interference is not just intentional but positively malicious.

To make matters even worse, the Coase theorem leads to the conclusion that we can't limit our concern to situations in which the legal system permits one party to cause injury to another without compensation. Coase was highly conscious that the problem of externalities had been understated in the Pigovian tradition, for the reason that the notion of causation falsely simplified appearances. For Coase the issue was joint costs, rather than costs 'imposed' on one activity by another. If we are worried about how to allocate joint costs, with a view to efficiency, there is no reason to presume that the party we would intuitively identify as 'active' should have to pay, and that the intuitively 'passive' party should not. We may be able to say with confidence that A polluted the river to the injury of B's fishing rights, and it would be absurd to say that B's fish injured themselves by gobbling up the pollutants. But it does not follow that dead fish are a cost of the polluting activity, rather than that restricting the polluting activity is a cost of having a fishing industry (see Epstein 1973).

In practical terms, this means that in myriad situations in which the legal system forces the active party to internalize a given joint cost, thereby 'subsidizing' the activity of the passive party, we need to do an economist's quick review to see if efficiency is being served or impeded. Maybe in the particular case it would have been optimal to cut back on fishing rather than on the polluting activity.

So far we have been dealing with the problem of externalities in the regime of private property. Things are no simpler with respect to freedom of contract. The actual legal systems of developed capitalist societies may: (a) refuse to enforce many contracts by (i) categorically excluding some, (ii) excluding others on grounds of defects in formation, and (iii) excusing performance for one reason or another based on subsequent events; (b) provide very different levels of support for people trying to enforce contracts, with consequences for how meaningful or valuable the promise will turn out to be; (c) require contracts in many situations; and (d) impose terms in many kinds of contracts regardless of the agreement of the parties.

Looking at this multitude of rules from the point of view of the economist committed to the idea that perfectly competitive equilibrium in a free market is efficient (with consequent policy consequences), one might get rid of this problem in a number of ways. The most obvious would be to show that all the particular rules are just instantiations of the two general ideas that private property gives owners absolute control of whatever is of value, and, second, that free contract enforces voluntary agreements. To see why this is not the solution of modern law and economics, we now turn to the legal side of the historical context.

THERE ARE POLITICAL STAKES IN THE PROBLEM OF EXTERNALITIES. The modern mainstream law and economics movement is a confluence of economists' and lawyers' concerns, all in a particular political context. From the law side, there is a single salient fact: in the late nineteenth century, legal theorists believed that they could decide what the legally valid rules of property and contract were by deriving them from the same very abstract definitions that the economists were then (and are still) using. Property rights protected anything of value and contract enforced the will of the parties. Legal theorists and economists had a common project: to show that the judge-made rules of private law already were or could easily be changed so that they would be just workings-out of these two ideas (see Kennedy 1985).

At about the same time that economists abandoned the idea that there was something called 'value' that underlay or caused 'price', American legal theorists began to question the idea that real world legal practice reflected core concepts of property and contract. The ideas of absolute owner control and of enforcement of voluntary agreements were either too vague, or, when specified, insufficiently coherent to provide clear answers, and when they did provide clear answers it appeared that many long established or recently established rules must have been based on something else because they contradicted the intuitively obvious notions of what it meant to have property and contract.

By World War II, American legal theorists had lost their faith in the possibility of deriving the multitude of rules in this way, and had decided that the only rational course was for judges to decide on specific rule definitions through 'policy analysis', by which they meant a situationally specific consideration of the conflicting rights, conflicting moral principles and conflicting utilitarian considerations that were at stake in choosing a rule, all in the light of the institutional and administrative considerations relevant in the circumstances (see Singer 1988; Kennedy 1993: 83–125).

This shift in perspective undermined the crucial legal distinction between legislation and adjudication. Adjudication – what judges do – is supposedly different from legislation – what legislatures do – because adjudication is, if not just 'law application', then at least law-making according to established procedures that get the politics out of it. Legislation is for questions that can't be resolved by these non-political reasoning techniques. The erosion of the distinction was an important development because during the whole twentieth century in the US, judges doing adjudication have continually made decisions that have had massive political consequences.

Looked at strictly from the political point of view, American courts made private law rules that roughly corresponded to a conservative policy agenda up to the Depression, and then shifted dramatically to a liberal perspective after that. Areas affected include antitrust, labour law, industrial accident law, racial and sexual discrimination, sexual harassment, consumer protection and especially products liability, landlord/tenant, and environmental law. Legal theorists came to see these decisions as posing a problem of legitimacy: if judges decided according to policy analysis, and policy analysis seemed obviously open to *sub rosa* ideological influence, then it was arguable that they were usurping the role of the legislature (see Hackney 1995; Kennedy 1997: 97–130).

Conservative legal theorists had a much more concrete reason for alarm. After World War II, the courts became a major arm of political liberalism, pursuing all kinds of objectives that could no longer be achieved through the legislatures except during brief periods of liberal legislative dominance (for example, the Great Society period). Conservatives saw three problems here: first, it was undemocratic for liberals to use the courts to impose their value judgments when they couldn't get the people to agree to them through the electoral process; second, because the courts could only modify the private law rules, and couldn't tax or transfer, they were distorting the allocative efficiency of the free market far more than the liberals would have needed to do if the latter had been able to act legislatively; third, pursuing liberal redistributive objectives by modifying private law rules was often blatantly counterproductive, according to the conservative understanding of the working of the market, so that liberal judicial activism was futile as well as being undemocratic and costly in efficiency terms.

These liberal results were legitimated by appeal to the requirements of correct legal reasoning in the mode of policy analysis. Therefore, the search was on, from World War II onwards, for a new method to replace the deductive approach of the late nineteenth century with some criterion for judicial lawmaking other than open-ended, contextualized policy analysis, one that would be plausibly non-political. For conservatives, the goal was a new method that would produce results more in tune with their views of economic rationality, thereby preventing the liberals from making an end run around the political process. For liberals, the goal was a method that would legitimate the gigantic liberal law reform project they had carried out in the courts after World War I. Modern law and economics is as much a response to this challenge as it is a development internal to economics (see Horwitz 1981; Kennedy 1981).

THE MAINSTREAM SOLUTION: KALDOR–HICKS FOR JUDGES. After a number of interesting false starts (e.g. Calabresi 1970), liberals and conservatives hit on a solution that has stuck, in the sense of still guiding applied mainstream law and economics. It involved a complex adaptation of the Coase theorem to the needs of lawyers. Coase had been concerned to show that Pigovian externalities analysis was mistaken in ways that gave far too much support to various kinds of statism. There were two branches to his critique. Where transaction costs were low or nonexistent, there was no reason to worry about externalities because bargaining would lead to efficient outcomes no matter how the rules initially set liability or non-liability for joint costs. Where transaction costs were present, the situational calculus of the effects of various kind of state intervention (by which he meant Pigovian fines and bounties) would be so complex and uncertain as not to be worth the candle. Coase didn't address the question of how judges should make the property and contract rules in the first place, probably because as an economist allied with conservative lawyers he wasn't clued in to the post-realist crisis in the theory of adjudication.

The mainstream solution shared by liberal and conservatives had two parts. First, they made a sharp distinction between efficiency oriented and distributively oriented decision-making, a distinction that had been ignored or finessed by the previous generation of liberal policy analysts responsible for the judicial-activist remaking of private law. Second, they argued that there was a nonpolitical, objective, determinate method for judicial efficiency analysis in the presence of transaction costs, but no way to make distributive decisions except according to arbitrary, subjective, inherently political biases. Third, they argued that if judges made private law rules to promote efficiency, then the free market could do its work of maximizing the pie, and we could leave distributive questions to the legislature, which was (a) institutionally appropriate because these decisions were political and should be decided by majority vote, and (b) economically appropriate because it was only the legislature that had the power to do the kind of tax and transfer programmes that were the best way to do redistribution at minimal efficiency cost or with maximum targeted effectiveness (e.g. Posner [1973] 1992; Cooter and Ulen [1988] 1996).

The methodology they adopted was conceptually

simple. Take a rule, assuming all other rules constant and existing budget constraints. Ask how the allocation of resources that the rule affects would be different if there were no transaction costs. Devise a change in the rule to get as close as possible to that outcome. Recommend the change no matter what the distributive consequences.

In the absence of the legal theorists' commitment to get the courts out of the business of making distributive judgments, it might have made sense for the analyst to ask some such question as this: supposing that we have a distributive objective that cuts against going to the Kaldor–Hicks efficient rule, would it be cheaper to achieve it through tax and spend (which can be done only by the legislature) or by a legislative or judge-made regulatory regime? In practice, the mainstream solution was, and in the vast majority of cases still is, to assume, usually implicitly, that tax and transfer is always superior to any kind of regulation, so that there is no efficiency cost to keeping courts out of the distribution business.

This form of cost–benefit analysis may at first seem open to the critique that it deals with dollar values rather than with utilities. But it is arguably a good idea nonetheless. Measuring efficiency in terms of dollar asking or offer prices produces a conclusion about how to maximize efficiency given the budget constraints of all economic actors. These reflect the actual distribution of wealth and income. Bids based on budgets are (hypothetical) 'facts' rather than 'values', and courts can approach their job as essentially empirical. True, the utility outcomes that are generated by establishing a legal regime that is efficient in this sense may be normatively undesirable, because, for example, there is too much income or wealth inequality, or because the utility associated with a given income differs so much among persons that we feel we need to take the differences into account. In such cases, the legislature is the appropriate institution to adjust budget constraints through tax and transfer, or to devise regulations that will redistribute more cheaply than tax and transfer.

CRITIQUE OF KALDOR–HICKS FOR JUDGES. Would it be a good idea for courts to make private law rules (the rules that define the free market) by choosing the rule that appears to them to be the most efficient, in the sense of producing an allocation of resources that maximizes the dollar value of output, regardless of the distributive consequences? Here again some institutional details are necessary to assess the proposal.

Courts make private law rules case by case, in the sense that they take up rules as they are presented by litigants in disputes, with some but limited control over the sequence in which they are considered. Courts have power to overrule their own decisions, although there are rules about overruling, of which the most important is that it should be an exceptional procedure responding to a clear sense that an established rule is wrong. If courts set out to apply Kaldor–Hicks, they could in principle, over time, change every rule of private law to make it correspond to the new criterion, and decide the vast number of new questions of rule definition in accord with it.

Courts have no power to tax, or to set up government transfer programmes, though they can and constantly do order parties to pay damages for violation of legal norms. Legislatures can enact codes, meaning statutes that set out the whole body of rules governing some subject matter area (contrast judicial case-by-case rule-making), though they rarely do so, sticking mainly to occasional modification of what judges have done. Legislatures never, ever pass statutes that adjust tax and transfer programmes to make up for the impact of modifications of private law rules (though of course they could if they wanted to). Note that all these apparently stark distinctions are relative, and there are cases in which courts do things that look very legislative and vice versa.

If the courts were to adopt Kaldor–Hicks, the mainstream literature proposes somewhat different procedures for the different kinds of rules that constitute a 'free market' structure. There are rules that govern interactions between parties who have a buyer–seller relationship and rules governing relationships without a price bond. The second case is simpler than the first, and is illustrated by the law of nuisance.

Suppose that lots of cement plants typically emit lots of pollutants that affect neighbouring residential housing. Suppose that the residents would pay 10 to the factories to stop emitting and that the factories would ask 20. Suppose transaction costs make it impossible for the residents to get together, but that a resident goes to court for an injunction against emissions, and the court has jurisdiction to decide on a rule.

Now suppose that there is a rule in effect that the emissions are illegal, and that any resident injured by them can get them enjoined. Under Kaldor–Hicks, the court reasons that if there were no transaction costs, the outcome of bargaining would be that the factory would continue to emit, regardless of whether the rule favoured the factory or the residents. If the court enjoined the emissions, in the no-transaction-cost case, the factory would bribe the residents to accept the pollution; if no injunction, the factory could pollute at will. But there are transaction costs, so that if the court enjoins, the factories will stop emitting because they can't practically buy permission from all the residents.

If the only two possible rules are an injunction or no liability, then the court chooses the Kaldor–Hicks preferable rule of no liability, ignoring the fact that the residents are radically impoverished compared to their position under the old rule. The new solution is more efficient than the alternative, and it is up to the legislature to take care of any adverse distributive consequences by tax and transfer programmes.

But what about the solution of a rule requiring the plants to pay damages? This possibility is always present, but it doesn't solve the obvious problems with Kaldor–Hicks. First, it may be that because of transaction costs and the expenses of litigation, very few of the residents will ever avail themselves of a damage remedy. In this case, damages have only a somewhat lesser distributive effect than a rule of no liability.

Second, supposing that we could make the industry pay everyone damages, Kaldor–Hicks does not tell us whether to go for damages or for no liability, supposing that in either case the factory will continue to emit. The test seems to yield two efficient rules with opposite distributive consequences. This problem of the indeterminacy of the test arose here because it was possible to award the losing party damages without interfering with the efficiency of the outcome. Following a famous article by Calabresi and Melamed (1972), legal economists have shown that in many situations such a choice of rules exists. But this is only one of a number of sources of this kind of indeterminacy.

Another is that wealth effects or a Tverskian cognitive bias may operate in such a way that if we presume a right to pollute in the cement industry, pollution will be efficient, because the homeowners wouldn't offer enough to get the industry to stop, whereas if we start with a right in the homeowners, pollution will be inefficient, because the industry's offer will be less than the homeowners' asking price for permission. And remember that if transaction costs are small relative to the surplus that would be disposed in the bargain, there will be an efficient outcome however the entitlements are set, with attendant wealth effects, and no basis in Kaldor–Hicks for choosing between liability and no liability. (See Kelman 1979b; Kelman 1980; Bebchuk 1980; Kennedy 1981; Kelman 1987.)

There is a third point: what if we have not an on/off choice about emissions and a fixed number of residents locked in place, but variability on both sides, both in terms of activity levels and of what precautions are taken (the factory can vary output and install different degrees of scrubbing equipment; homeowners can move away or use air conditioners). In this case, if there are transaction costs, it is likely that the optimal solution is levels of activity and precautions for both parties that are different from the ones they would adopt in the absence of the joint cost. Since no lump-sum payment will induce this solution, the court will have to proceed by enjoining the parties to adopt it, and then order the payment of damages (which could go in either direction according to the distributive judgment) to fit its distributive view. Now imagine that cost and benefit conditions vary from area to area, and that they change continuously, with consequent changes in the efficient injunction (see Shavell 1980; Kennedy 1981).

Wherever there are joint costs and the parties can't be expected to bargain, problems like each of these three are likely to arise: the distributive effects are likely to be great but there is no likelihood that the legislature will respond by tax and transfer; there are likely to be several legal rules with different distributive consequences that are equally good from a Kaldor–Hicks point of view; and taking the Kaldor–Hicks programme seriously would seem to put the courts in the position of micro managing the economy.

In real life, courts don't do anything like this because they use not cost benefit analysis by itself but an analysis that appeals to precedent, rights, morality, the 'public interest' or 'general welfare', and administrative and institutional considerations as well. These discourses suggest decision making on grounds that are not, at least on their face, about efficiency. Richard Posner tried but failed to show that they nonetheless lead courts to efficient results by a kind of institutional invisible hand (see Kelman 1987: 115–16). It seems more likely that these criteria lead to decisions in many cases that are different from those that are at least apparently the obviously efficient ones. And the grounds are 'distributive', though not in the sense of 'income redistribution' or 'wealth redistribution'. They are about distribution of losses and surpluses between individuals based on norms and sequences of events, rather than between groups defined in terms of income or wealth. The defendant who is violating a well established rule, or acting immorally, or violating a right, should lose and pay damages no matter what the comparative bids of plaintiff and defendant would be for the right to injure or the right to protection.

Moreover, the courts are constantly guided *sub rosa* by either a liberal or a conservative ideology, both of which incorporate an implicit social welfare function. Liberals want to redistribute in the direction of the less well off, or avoid redistribution in the opposite direction, but their ideology also prohibits anything like confiscation or 'class warfare' through the courts. Liberals are 'moderates'. And so are conservatives, who believe the courts should redistribute in favour of those they view as the productive or wealth generating parts of society, but don't believe the courts should go 'too far' in that direction, whether out of libertarian respect for rights, because it would be institutionally inappropriate, or because they believe that big redistributions in favour of the rich would be politically dangerous (see Kennedy 1997: 39–70).

The combination of the discourses of the public interest, morality, rights, precedent and institutional competence, along with *sub rosa* ideological projects, is hardly a determinate method for making these distributive judgments. But remember that the Kaldor–Hicks solution will be radically indeterminate in the vast number of cases where there are two available efficient rules with different distributive consequences. In these cases, the courts can't use efficiency and ignore distribution. Where the solution is determinate it may amount to bringing about a big redistribution that is final in fact, even if in theory the legislature could somehow counteract it, and random from the point of view of the available discourses of fairness (rights, morality, etc.).

In light of these difficulties, it is hard to take seriously the proposal that the courts should just apply Kaldor–Hicks and stay out of distributive questions. But the most common liberal alternative, which is that courts should in some obscure sense balance efficiency considerations against the other values reflected in precedent, rights, morality and institutional competence (see Calabresi and Melamud 1972; Calabresi and Hirschoff 1972), turns out to be incoherent. As Ronald Dworkin (1980) pointed out, wealth is not a 'value' that can be set against, say, adherence to precedent or observance of a right, unless we go through the operation of assessing utilities through a social welfare function. We would want to take into account massive 'waste' generated by a legal rule – say the whole range of utility consequences of shutting down the cement industry in our nuisance example – and that might persuade us to disregard the homeowners rights, or the precedent that protected those rights. But we could do this only on the basis of our substantive views of justice in the circumstances, the very consideration that the mainstream wants the courts to leave to the legislature.

Criticism of this kind suggests that legal economists who

want to be helpful to courts and to other policy makers would do well to produce elaborate analyses of the distributive consequences of different private law rules. On the basis of these, courts can make the complex judgment about what outcome best fits the heterogeneous set of criteria of justice under the circumstances. But the critique has had no effect at all on the practice of mainstream economic analysis of law. Indeed, after a brief moment of debate in the early 1980s, legal economists stopped discussing the kinds of questions just canvassed, and adopted the project of extending the basic methodology – Kaldor–Hicks, assuming all other rules constant, leading to a policy recommendation that leaves all non-efficiency questions to tax and transfer legislation – to dozens and dozens of particular judge-made rules.

Of course, even if the critique is right, it *might* be the case that the particular question at hand yielded just one determinate solution, and that none of the various kinds of non-efficiency considerations just mentioned seem to point clearly in one direction or another, or that these considerations wash out or balance out over time as a sequence of decisions randomly helps and hurts different parties. And, as in any normal scientific enterprise, the thrill of the chase for a technically impressive solution to the problem at hand is far more engaging than an interminable and indeterminate methodological discussion that involves all kinds of non-technical or even anti-technical rhetoric.

A second reason for ignoring the critique is that both liberal and conservative legal economists prefer to pursue their political projects with respect to the economy by manipulating the apparently value neutral, technocratic discourse of efficiency to support their preferred outcomes, rather than by arguing on more overtly distributive or justice oriented grounds, that is, on the ideological grounds that half-consciously motivate them. This strategy of ideological conflict via manipulation of the efficiency norm is particularly evident in the area of problems that arise when there is a price nexus between plaintiff and defendant.

The initial free market paradigm seems to suggest a relatively simple procedure: freedom of contract is efficient unless there is either market failure in the sense of imperfect competition, or market failure because transaction costs prevent the parties from making the contracts that would be in their mutual best interests, or because the contract affects the interests of third parties who are prevented by transaction costs from buying relief. However, efficiency is no more apolitical as a guide for contract law than it is for property and tort law.

For reasons of space, I will merely summarize this point here. The law of contract actually in force makes enforceability depend on the absence of fraud and duress, and is loaded with compulsory terms, governing, in particular, just about all consumer transactions. The interpretation of the formation rules and the choice of compulsory terms are patently motivated by judicial and legislative concern with the distribution of transaction surplus (both between buyer and seller and among buyers), and with situations in which the transaction is arguably utility-reducing rather than utility-enhancing for the buyer (see Kelman 1979a; Kennedy and Michelman 1980; Kennedy 1982; Kelman 1987; Eastman 1996). Liberals favour many regimes of compulsory terms and conservatives oppose them. In mainstream law and economics, the issue is extensively debated, but in the context of Kaldor–Hicks. Liberal and conservative analysts pursue paternalist and distributive objectives through such devices as the manipulation of the assumption of perfect information, hypothesizing different kinds of insurance market failure, and accommodating the administrative needs of the court system (compare Schwartz 1983 with Bratton and McCahery 1997, Croley and Hanson 1990, and Schill 1991).

The point of the critical legal studies critique is that Kaldor–Hicks provides a rhetoric within which liberals debate conservatives, rather than an analytic sufficiently determinate to solve the legitimacy problem created by the erosion of the legislation/adjudication distinction.

THE IDEA OF AN EFFICIENT CODE. What about the argument that the normal science of mainstream law and economics, that is, the cost benefit analysis of particular legal rules, has value for the long run even if courts don't and even shouldn't adopt efficient rules case by case regardless of other considerations? Mainstream legal economists might be trying to establish through case by case analysis a collection of efficient rules for a capitalist economy. Eventually, we will arrive at an efficient code, which may not be a complete set of rules, but will nonetheless represent 'best practices' where it is possible to determine them. At that point, it might make sense to adopt it all at one time, assess the distributive consequences, and take care of all of them (perhaps most would cancel each other out) through tax and transfer (see Kaplow and Shavell 1994).

The objection to this understanding of the enterprise is that a sequence of partial equilibrium solutions, even if each was convincingly determinate, would produce a code whose provisions were radically path dependent. By this I mean that taking up the rules one by one, deciding each keeping all other rules constant, would produce wealth effects for each decision that would modify all the following decisions. If we took up a different rule first, we would get different wealth effects that would produce different efficient rules in the next round. Remember that for all the cases in which the rules operate with low transaction costs and in which there are multiple efficient solutions, we will have to decide on the basis of non-efficiency criteria. These decisions generate a further set of massive wealth effects (see Kennedy 1981).

Wouldn't it be possible to overcome these objections by imagining that the legislature delegated to legal economists the job of working out a general equilibrium solution to the problem of the efficient code, and then enacted the whole thing at the same time, taking into account all the undesirable distributive consequences through tax and transfer?

This won't work because the general equilibrium solution for all the legal rules is going to be hopelessly indeterminate, in the sense that there will be a different set of efficient rules for each of the multiple efficient solutions to the general equilibrium problem (see Kennedy 1981).

The basis of the general equilibrium solution would have to be imagining the outcome of costless bargaining between all economic actors, on the basis of endowments but without the institution of competition to stabilize the division of transaction surplus (without transaction costs there is no competition – just negotiations between coalitions of buyers and sellers).

Endowment (factor, entitlement) defining rules are the rules of the bargaining game that will produce the no transaction cost solution. In order to define endowments, we have to specify the legal attributes of the commodity – that is, deal with the problem of externalities – because the value of a given endowment to a player in the bargaining game is radically dependent on what can and can't be done with it.

The question of how to set these rules can't be resolved by resort to Kaldor–Hicks because by hypothesis there are no transaction costs and all settings lead to efficient outcomes. Instead we have to rely on rights, morality, the public interest, in short on politics, philosophy, ideology (see Baker 1975, 1980). There are obviously an indefinitely large number of rules that we might select, each with vast consequences for the wealth of the parties to the hypothetical bargaining game. Once we have chosen the rules, the game itself has many possible outcomes, depending on the black box of bargaining power and skill. Each of the many possible outcomes includes a distribution (no longer uniquely determined by the initial factor endowments because we no longer have competition) and an associated allocation of resources.

We then modify our initial set of legal rules for costless bargaining so that, when we play the game of competition in the real world of transaction costs, we come as close as possible to the allocation that emerged under our choice of rules for the no transaction cost game. The set of efficient rules under transaction costs should be different for every initial set of endowment (factor, entitlement) definitions. We then modify the distributive outcome by tax and transfer to produce the distribution that occurred in the no transaction cost game.

Because there are multiple equilibria, each leading to a different set of real world efficient legal rules and a different tax and transfer programme, there is no efficient code. Even the efficient code that corresponds to one of the indefinite number of possible no transaction cost outcomes will be valid only so long as the 'real world' continues to correspond to the world we assumed when we translated the no transaction cost settlement into a particular set of rules. Every significant change in the actual pattern of costs changes the optimal solution.

In light of all this, it seems to me that the mainstream enterprise of trying to build an efficient code is best described as quixotic.

REDISTRIBUTION THROUGH THE BACKGROUND RULES. We come now to the third critique of mainstream law and economics, which is that its practitioners have underestimated the economic plausibility of redistribution of wealth and income through the modification of private law rules, the rules that constitute a free market. As I've been arguing, it is an elemental premise of the mainstream that the free market is efficient so long as there is perfect competition, that the correct response to market failure is government regulation designed to get us to more efficient outcomes, and that distributive objectives are best pursued via tax and transfer. I will call these 'the maxims'.

An important implication of the analysis above is the tenuousness or even the incoherence of the distinction between a free market solution and a regulatory solution. There is no way to set the private law rules through the abstract definitions of private property and freedom of contract. Setting the rules in their details by applying Kaldor–Hicks is neither practically nor theoretically feasible. As a matter of fact, courts and legislatures patently take a whole range of non-efficiency goals into account in deciding issues like the scope of the law of nuisance and whether or not to impose compulsory terms in consumer and labour contracts.

In this context, the setting of the private law ground rules that define a free market seems inherently 'regulatory', in the sense of involving case by case or sector by sector, *ad hoc* governmental decision-making designed to encourage the baking of a large pie and a fair distribution thereof. We can still distinguish market solutions from state ownership, and within the private law regime we can distinguish rule systems according to how much paternalism they pursue and according to how much attention they pay to egalitarian distributive objectives. But an antipaternalist regime that makes no effort to use private law for distributive purposes nonetheless regulates, in the sense that it is among the causes of the outcome of bargaining within its frame. The decision maker who ignores this is making policy just as surely as is the decision maker who decides to use it for his or her purposes (see Kennedy and Michelman 1980).

If the free market collapses into regulation, so does tax and transfer, once we recognize that the economists' position relegates not just the division of social product among groups but also rights, morality, paternalism, the public interest and institutional concerns to the domain of distribution. Assume that the state is going to try to achieve all of these, as well as income–class distributive objectives, through the tax and transfer apparatus. Then the tax code will have to say things like: anyone who commits the tort of sexual harassment in this particular way will pay a tax of x, and the social security programme is amended so that anyone who has been the victim of sexual harassment of this particular type shall receive a one-time payment of x. The 'distorting' effect of this kind of tax and transfer would be exactly the same as that of a private law rule or a regulation providing for the same set of payments (see Croley and Hanson 1990).

The disintegration of the distinctions between free market, regulatory and tax and transfer solutions is a parallel development to the loss of faith in the ability to define the details of the ground rules through working out the definitions of free contract and private property. What happens when you lose faith in the distinctions?

You begin to see that the arguments against radical redistributions are much weaker than economists assume they are. The reason for this is not that efficiency becomes irrelevant, given the critique, far from it. It is still the case that we need and earnestly desire sophisticated economic analysis of the likely consequences, in terms of markets, prices and other economic variables, of the choice of a private law rule structure. But in deciding on policy, it is no longer plausible that there should be a presumption against the design of property and contract rules with the explicit idea of furthering non-efficiency goals, such as greater equality and some degree of paternalistic control of choices that do not appear to maximize utility. Of course, the same argument supports the overt pursuit of the ideologically opposite goals of eliminating or at least minimizing egalitarian and paternalist designs (see Singer 1988; Kennedy 1993).

As I argued above, the rhetoric of Kaldor–Hicks is so thoroughly manipulable that liberals and conservatives can pursue agendas of these kinds within its strictures, even acknowledging, as I do, that the rhetoric will sometimes point unambiguously in one direction or another. Conceding for the sake of argument that I have shown convincingly that the maxims are all useless, because the distinctions between free market, regulation, and tax and transfer collapse when we try to deploy them in practice, there remains a question. What are the political effects of the general belief in their validity?

I would say that the effect of the analytic mistakes embedded in the maxims is centrist – supportive of liberalism and conservatism together, seen as a bloc in opposition to more left and right wing positions. What the liberal and conservative members of the centrist bloc have in common is moderation, statism, and rationalism.

The belief that private law rules can and should be set according to a non-political logic of the free market restricts the alternatives available for those who want to achieve redistribution and suggests (happily for conservatives, tragically for liberals) a trade-off between equity and efficiency (moderation). It suggests that the appropriate locus of reformist zeal is the central government, which alone can regulate the whole economy to counteract market failures, and which alone can devise tax and transfer (statism). And it suggests that the domain of politics can and should be sharply restricted – to central legislative deliberation – while the economic technocrats take care of the thousands of decisions that define the ground rules of everyday interaction in civil society (rationalism).

Looked at from outside its left boundary, the moderate statist bias means that it is difficult or impossible to get economists to focus on the following kind of question (typical of recent critical legal studies work in law and economics): is it possible for a neighbourhood legal services organization to use the compulsory warranty of habitability in residential leases selectively to improve the housing situation of poor tenants over what it would be without intervention? In recent work, we've tried to show that economic analysis of distributive consequences – while no more determinate in the abstract than Kaldor–Hicks – strongly suggests that this strategy could work in two typical market situations: when the neighbourhood is unravelling downward through disinvestment and abandonment, and when it is unravelling upward through gentrification (see Kennedy 1987; Kolodney 1991; Alexander and Skapsa 1994).

Of course, the analysis won't tell you whether you ought to do it, supposing that it would work. That depends on the local decision-makers' institutional constraints and on their view of the comparative claims of poor tenants, landlords, and rich in-movers. But the discussion about whether or not to do it gains enormously, first, from the clarification of the issues the economic analysis provides, and, second, from the opening up of the non-efficiency dimensions once Kaldor–Hicks is rejected as the criterion for action.

There are other motives than a vaguely anarchist leftism (such as my own) for pursuing the critique of the legal economists' claims to objectivity and their characteristic policy maxims. These have to do with the general cultural conflict between advocates of hard methods and soft methods. The crits have seen hard methods, in technical legal analysis as well as in economic analysis of law, not as bad in themselves, but as a vehicle for technocratic imperialism, at the expense of participatory modes of decision making. It is not that hard methods fall to a global critique that simply invalidates them. It is rather that case by case internal critique can often show that their pretensions and their prestige are unwarranted. That seemed clearly to be the case for the economic analysis of law.

DUNCAN KENNEDY

See also AMERICAN LEGAL REALISM; COASE, RONALD; COASE THEOREM; KALDOR–HICKS COMPENSATION.

Subject classification: 4c(i).

BIBLIOGRAPHY

Alexander, G. and Skapsa, G. 1994. *A Fourth Way? Privatization, Property, and the Emergence of New Market Economies*. New York: Routledge.

Baker, E. 1975. The ideology of the economic analysis of law. *Philosophy and Public Affairs* 5: 3–41.

Baker, E. 1980. Starting points in the economic analysis of law. *Hofstra Law Review* 8: 939–72.

Bebchuk, L. 1980. The pursuit of a bigger pie: can everyone expect a bigger slice? *Hofstra Law Review* 8: 671–709.

Bratton, W. and McCahery, J. 1997. An inquiry into the efficiency of the limited liability company, of the theory of the firm and regulatory competition. *Washington and Lee Law Review* 54: 629–86.

Calabresi, G. 1970. *The Costs of Accidents*. New Haven: Yale University Press.

Calabresi, G. and Hirschoff, J. 1972. Toward a test for strict liability in tort. *Yale Law Journal* 81: 1055–92.

Calabresi, G. and Melamed, D. 1972. Property rules, liability rules and inalienability: one view of the cathedral. *Harvard Law Review* 85: 1089–1128.

Coase, R.H. 1960. The problem of social cost. *Journal of Law and Economics* 3: 1–44.

Cooter, R. and Ulen, T. 1988. *Law and Economics*. Glenview, IL: Scott, Foresman; 2nd edn, Addison Wesley, Reading, MA.: 1996.

Croley, S. and Hanson, J. 1990. What liability crisis? An alternative explanation for recent events in products liability. *Yale Journal on Regulation* 8: 1–111.

Dworkin, R. 1980. Is wealth a value? *Journal of Legal Studies* 9: 323–56.

Eastman, W. 1996. Everything's up for grabs: the Coasean story in game theoretic terms. *New England Law Review* 31: 1–37.

Epstein, R. 1973. A theory of strict liability. *Journal of Legal Studies* 2: 151–204.

Hackney, J. 1995. The intellectual origins of American strict products liability: a case study in American pragmatic instrumentalism. *The American Journal of Legal History* 39: 443–509.

Heller, T. 1976. The importance of normative decisionmaking: the limitations of legal economics as a basis for a liberal jurisprudence – as illustrated by the regulation of vacation home development. *Wisconsin Law Review* 1976: 385–502.

Hohfeld, W.N. 1917. Fundamental legal conceptions as applied in judicial reasoning. *Yale Law Journal* 26: 710–58.

Horwitz, M. 1981. Law and economics: science or politics? *Hofstra Law Review* 8: 905–12.

Kaplow, L. and Shavell, S. 1994. Why the legal system is less efficient than the income tax in redistributing income. *Journal of Legal Studies* 23: 667–81.

Kelman, M. 1979a. Choice and utility. *Wisconsin Law Review* 1979: 769–97.

Kelman, M. 1979b. Consumption theory, production theory and ideology in the Coase theorem. *Southern California Law Review* 52: 669–98.

Kelman, M. 1980. Spitzer and Hoffman on Coase: a brief rejoinder. *Southern California Law Review* 53: 1215–32.

Kelman, M. 1983. Misunderstanding social life: a critique of the core premises of law and economics. *Journal of Legal Education* 33: 274–312.

Kelman, M. 1984. Trashing. *Stanford Law Review* 36: 293–354.

Kelman, M. 1987. *A Guide to Critical Legal Studies*. Cambridge, MA: Harvard University Press.

Kennedy, D. 1981. Cost–benefit analysis of entitlement problems: a critique. *Stanford Law Review* 33: 387–447.

Kennedy, D. 1982. Distributive and paternalist motives in contract and tort law with special reference to compulsory terms and unequal bargaining power. *Maryland Law Review* 41: 563–658.

Kennedy, D. 1985. The role of law in economic thought: essays on the fetishism of commodities. *American University Law Review* 34: 939–1001.

Kennedy, D. 1987. The effect of the warranty of habitability on low income housing: 'milking' and class violence. *Florida State Law Review* 15: 485–519.

Kennedy, D. 1993. The stakes of law, or Hale and Foucault! In *Sexy Dressing, Etc.*, Cambridge, MA: Harvard University Press.

Kennedy, D. 1997. *A Critique of Adjudication: fin de siècle*. Cambridge, MA: Harvard University Press.

Kennedy, D. and Michelman, F. 1980. Are property and contract efficient? *Hofstra Law Review* 8: 711–70.

Kolodney, L. 1991. Eviction free zones: the economics of legal bricolage in the fight against displacement. *Fordham Urban Law Journal* 18: 507–43.

Posner, R. 1973. *Economic Analysis of Law*. Boston: Little Brown; 4th edn, 1992.

Shavell, S. 1980. Strict liability vs. negligence. *Journal of Legal Studies* 9: 1–25.

Schill, M. 1991. An economic analysis of mortgagor protection laws. *Virginia Law Review* 77: 489–538.

Schwartz, A. 1983. The enforceability of security interests in consumer goods. *Journal of Law and Economics* 26: 117–53.

Singer, J. 1982. The legal rights debate in analytical jurisprudence from Bentham to Hohfeld. *Wisconsin Law Review* 1982: 975–1059.

Singer, J. 1988. Legal realism now. *California Law Review* 76: 465–544.

Vandevelde, K. 1980. The new property of the nineteenth century: the development of the modern concept of property. *Buffalo Law Review* 29: 325–67.

law-and-economics from the perspective of economics. Modern scholars of law and economics identify the genesis of the discipline in the year 1960 when Ronald Coase published his famous article, 'The Problem of Social Cost'. From the purely modern perspective, no doubt they are correct. However, this perspective is myopic, since the great political philosophers and economists of the Scottish Enlightenment had made the link between law and economics some two centuries prior to Coase. From a quite different perspective, Jeremy Bentham's *Fragment on Government* (1776) followed by his *Introduction to the Principles of Morals and Legislation* (1789) also paved the way for a methodological approach to modern law and economics sharply at odds with that of the Scottish Enlightenment.

Since these two perspectives have both played important roles in the development of modern law and economics, it is helpful to review the principal contributions at the outset of this essay.

1. SCHOLARS OF THE SCOTTISH ENLIGHTENMENT. It is instructive briefly to review the writings of David Hume (1739), Adam Ferguson (1767) and Adam Smith (1776) on the central relationship between economics and the law within the broader then-emerging discipline of political economy.

David Hume. In his masterpiece *A Treatise of Human Nature* (1739), David Hume, perhaps the supreme realist of the Scottish Enlightenment, begins his study of what we now call law and economics with the statement: *'that 'tis only from the selfishness and confin'd generosity of men, along with the scanty provision nature has made for his wants, that justice derives its origin'* (Hume [1739] 1978: 495). Justice must be blind, available to all individuals in society, irrespective of their personal merits or needs:

> Whether a man be generous, or a miser, he is equally well receiv'd by her, and obtains with the same facility a decision in his favours, even for what is entirely useless to him (502).

On this basis, Hume builds up a legal framework which, in many respects, mirrors that favoured by such a leading exponent of modern law and economics as Richard Epstein (1986). The general rule that possession is to be stable must not be applied by particular judgments, but by other general rules, which must extend to the whole of society, and which must be inflexible. His justification for rules for property – occupation, prescription, accession and succession – conform precisely to Richard Epstein's utilitarian arguments, explicated more than two centuries later, in favour of first possession, adverse possession and inheritance (Epstein 1986).

Useful as the stability of possession may be, Hume recognizes the importance of the principle of voluntary alienation. For the initial endowment of rights may not suit future productivity: 'As these depend very much on chance, they must frequently prove contradictory both to men's wants and desires; and persons and possessions must often be very ill adjusted' (1739 [1978]: 514). All of this 'requires a mutual exchange and commerce; for which reason the translation of property by consent is founded on a law of nature, as well as its stability without such a consent' (ibid.).

Hume was also acutely aware of the importance of a law of contract for the enforcement of promises, arguing that '*a promise wou'd not be intelligible, before human conventions had establish'd it*; [and] *that even if it were intelligible, it wou'd not be attended with any moral obligation*' (516). He was also aware of the problem for an exchange economy posed by a lack of simultaneity of exchange in the absence of a law of contract:

> Your corn is ripe today; mine will be so to-morrow. 'Tis profitable for us both that I shou'd labour with you to-day, and that you shou'd aid me tomorrow. I have no kindness for you, and know you have as little for me . . . Here then I leave you to labour alone: You treat me in the same manner. The seasons change; and both of us lose our harvests for want of mutual confidence and security (520–21).

Hume thus sets out the three fundamental laws of nature upon which the peace and security of human society entirely depend, namely that of stability of possession, that of transference by consent and that of the performance of promises. The modern economic analysis of the common law of property (with the important exception of Epstein 1986) and contract (with the important exceptions of Epstein 1995 and Trebilcock 1993) has done no better; indeed, as I shall suggest, in certain ways it has performed markedly worse.

Adam Ferguson. In his classic book, *An Essay on the History of Civil Society* (1767), Adam Ferguson focuses attention on the law as a fundamental element in the securing and maintenance of civil liberty.

> Where men enjoy peace, they owe it either to their mutual regards and affections, or to the restraints of law. Those are the happiest states which procure peace to their members by the first of these methods: But it is sufficiently uncommon to procure it even by the second (Ferguson 1767: 155).

In Ferguson's judgment, law is a treaty to which members of the same community have agreed, and under which the magistrate and the subject continue to enjoy their rights, and to maintain the peace of society. Since 'The desire of lucre is the great motive to injuries' (156), law has a principal reference to property, determining the different methods by which property may be acquired, as by prescription, conveyance and succession. The law also makes the necessary provisions for rendering the possession of property secure.

The rights of an individual to property are fundamental to the freedom that nature requires: 'Where the citizen is supposed to have rights of property and of station, and is protected in the exercise of them, he is said to be free; and the very restraints by which he is hindered from the commission of crimes, are a part of his liberty' *(idem.)*. The rule of law, thus described, owes a great debt to Rome and to England:

> The first has left the foundation, and great part of the superstructure of its civil code, to the continent of Europe: the other, in its island, has carried the authority and government of law to a point of perfection, which they never before attained in the history of mankind (166).

Ferguson comments on the remarkable similarity between the rule of law prescribed by the civil code of the Roman Empire, and the rule of law that emerged through the common law of England:

> Under such favourable establishments, known customs, the practice and decisions of courts, as well as positive statutes, acquire the authority of laws; and every proceeding is conducted by some fixed and determinate rule (*idem.*).

Law and economics scholarship has far from consistently adhered to this fundamental principle of the rule of law. In their zeal for economic efficiency, too often its practitioners have shown themselves willing to rationalize the casting aside of well established precedents on which individuals had long based their daily lives (Brenner and Spaeth 1995; Scalia 1997; Tullock 1997).

Adam Smith. In his *magnum opus, The Wealth of Nations* (1776), Adam Smith recognizes the importance of property in determining an appropriate system of justice:

> Among nations of hunters, as there is scarce any property, or at least none that exceeds the value of two or three days labour; so there is seldom any established magistrate or any regular administration of justice. Men who have no property can injure one another only in their persons or reputations. But when one man kills, wounds, beats, or defames another, though he to whom the injury is done suffers, he who does it receives no benefit (Smith [1776] 1961, Bk. V, ch. 1 pt. II: 231).

Such is not the case where injuries to property are concerned: 'The benefit of the person who does the injury is often equal to the loss of him who suffers it' (ibid.). In such circumstances, individuals cannot live together with tolerable security in the absence of a civil magistrate: 'It is only under the shelter of the civil magistrate that the owner of that valuable property, which is acquired by the labour of many years, or perhaps of many successive generations, can sleep a single night in security' (232). For this reason, Smith suggests that

> Civil government, so far as it is instituted for the security of property, is in reality instituted for the defence of the rich against the poor, or of those who have some property against those who have none at all (236).

The notion that a system of justice may be a profit-maximizing venture is also evident in *The Wealth of Nations.* Smith notes that

> The judicial authority of such a sovereign, however, far from being a cause of expence, was for a long time a source of revenue to him. The persons who applied to the sovereign for justice were always willing to pay for it (*idem.*).

Those who were found guilty were always forced to pay an amercement to the sovereign to recompense him for disturbing the king's peace:

> In those days, the administration of justice, not only afforded a certain revenue to the sovereign, but to procure this revenue seems to have been one of the principal advantages which he proposed to obtain by the administration of justice (237).

Such a scheme of making the administration of justice subservient to the purposes of revenue was open to obvious abuses. Those who offered large presents would obtain something more than justice, while those who offered small presents would obtain less than justice. The amercement of the guilty was also an incentive to find the defendant in the wrong regardless of the merits of the case.

When the sovereign thus abused his powers, he could not be called to make redress, because he was above the law: 'In all barbarous governments, accordingly, in all those ancient governments of Europe in particular, which were founded upon the ruins of the Roman empire, the administration of justice appears for a long time to have been extremely corrupt' (238).

The turning point for the administration of justice occurred once the sovereign could no longer rely upon his private estate for defraying the expense of the sovereignty. As it became necessary for the people to contribute towards this expense through taxes, they insisted in return that there should be no private remuneration for any person involved in the administration of justice, including the sovereign. Fixed salaries were provided to the judges to recompense them for the loss of their share in the private emoluments. Justice was then said to be administered gratis.

As Smith wryly notes:

> Justice, however, never was in reality administered gratis in any country. Lawyers and attornies, at least, must always be paid by the parties; and if they were not, they would perform their duty still worse than they actually perform it (239).

Court fees, in Smith's judgement, were an effective method of defraying the costs of the judge and the courthouse, and would not add materially to the expense of litigation, given the relatively low incomes of the judges. Such fees were the principal source of support of the various courts of justice in England, with keen competition between the courts for business: 'it came in many cases, to depend altogether upon the parties before what court they would chuse to have their cause tried; and each court endeavoured, by superior dispatch and impartiality, to draw to itself as many causes as it could' (241–2).

Smith was, in certain respects, in advance of the law and economics movement in his comprehension of the factors that might lead to efficiency in the administration of justice. For example, normative law and economics still tends to focus on the comparative statics approach of Paretian welfare economics to the relative exclusion of issues of process efficiency central to *The Wealth of Nations* (1776) and more recently emphasized both by public choice scholars and by modern Austrian economists.

2. THE APPROACH OF JEREMY BENTHAM. In his own copy of *A Fragment on Government* (1776), Bentham made the handwritten note that 'this was the very first publication by which men at large were invited to break loose from the trammels of authority and ancestor-wisdom on the field of the law' (Harrison 1988: vi). Bentham was a dedicated disciple of Descartes, arguing on the first page of the *Fragment* that 'The age we live in is a busy age; in which knowledge is rapidly advancing towards perfection' (Bentham 1776:3). The secrets have been discovered and now only await application. Central to this discovery is Bentham's fundamental axiom: '*it is the greatest happiness of the greatest number that is the measure of right and wrong*' (ibid.). This principle, variously called by him 'the greatest happiness principle' or 'the principle of utility', was not claimed by Bentham as his original discovery. His original contribution was to pursue the axiom through the medium of legislation (Harrison 1988).

Thus, Bentham argued that the theory and practice both of politics and of law could be reconstructed from first principles. The objective, as he put it at the start of his *Introduction to the Principles of Morals and Legislation* (1789), was to rear the fabric of felicity by the hands of reason and of law. Creating correct law would lead to happiness; and the creation of correct law meant reasoning from first principles rather than adopting the piled up rubbish of ancient authority.

The central idea of all of Bentham's scholarship, therefore, was to create laws so that individuals would behave and act so as to bring about the greatest happiness. Bentham did not believe in the invisible hand. Self-interest would only lead to the greatest happiness if the law was correctly devised. Therefore, the legislator should plan rewards and punishments to persuade self-interested individuals to do as they ought. Bentham set out to advise the legislator about the effects of various laws so that he might choose accordingly in pursuit of utilitarian goals.

Bentham's theoretical innovations were not striking (Welch 1987: 770). Much in line with earlier utilitarians, he argued that men were pleasure seeking and that the promotion of happiness should be the criterion of moral goodness. What was unique about his contribution was the notion that utilitarianism was both scientific and systematic. Thus, he stated unequivocally that pleasure was homogeneous and quantifiable. All his images were designed to promote this vision: 'felicific calculus', 'axioms of mental pathology', 'table of the springs of action' (ibid.: 771).

It was to take 150 years for economics to disengage itself from Bentham's erroneous suggestion that utility was measurable on a cardinal scale and was comparable between individuals (Robbins 1938). It has been the singular achievement of certain modern law and economics scholars (notably Richard A. Posner) to rehabilitate Bentham's axiom albeit in a somewhat modified form and to impose it as a working normative principle in the economic analysis of law.

3. IMMEDIATE ANTECEDENTS TO THE LAW-AND-ECONOMICS MOVEMENT. The law-and-economics movement originated in the United States and was transmitted subsequently to other countries. Almost inevitably,

therefore, the immediate antecedents to the movement came from within the United States, even though the founding article (by Ronald Coase) was penned by a quintessential Englishman who had emigrated to the United States only nine years earlier in 1951, when already in mid-career at the age of 41.

American jurisprudence since 1870 is characterized by complex patterns of ideas, and not, as is argued commonly (see e.g., Mercuro and Medema 1997), by a pendulum swing between formalism and realism (Duxbury 1995: 2). In reality, there was never any complete revolt against formalism and there was no realist movement, only two transient realist intellectual moods, one in the 1930s and the other in the 1970s and 1980s.

Formalism was prevalent in many areas of knowledge during the late nineteenth century as scholars sought to treat particular fields as if they were governed by 'interrelated, fundamental and logically demonstrable principles of science' (Duxbury 1995: 10). This trend was discernible in legal thought during the post-Civil War period of American legal history, arguably taking two conceptions. In the universities, there emerged the Langdellian science of law; in the courts, there became somewhat entrenched the philosophy of *laissez-faire.*

By the mid-nineteenth century, American law was developing its own identity, somewhat distinct from that of the English common law. As American law developed its own momentum, the American Bar was forced to raise its professional standards, extending beyond its original admissions requirement of a grasp of the basic principles of English common law.

In 1870, Harvard University appointed Christopher Columbus Langdell to the newly created post of Dean of the Harvard Law School. Langdell determined to respond to the perceived crisis in American legal education by promoting the case method of legal instruction. 'It is the idea that law is a science, and the promotion of this idea by the use of the case method, which constitutes his sole yet fundamental contribution to American legal education' (Duxbury 1995: 14).

Langdellian legal science consisted of four elements. First, there was a great respect for *stare decisis.* This indeed is the key to the science of law. Second, most reported cases are simply repetitious of extant principles and precedents. Third, since only a small number of cases are truly relevant to the science of law, the number of fundamental legal doctrines is similarly limited. Fourth, the task of the legal scientist is to classify these fundamental doctrines and to demonstrate their logical interconnection. This revolution in legal instruction swept through the American academy and provided the basis for a legal formalism that dominated American legal education for at least a half century.

The second aspect of legal formalism – the tradition of *laissez-faire* – was a product of the courts. *Laissez-faire* was conceived of by the courts as the freedom of the individual to strike or not to strike a bargain. This was viewed as a cornerstone of a genuine legal science (Duxbury 1995: 26). In particular, the United States courts were strongly influenced by the writings of Herbert Spencer whose books, *Social Statics* (1851) and *Man versus The State* (1884), ushered in the notion of Social Darwinism, or the survival of the fittest.

This conception involved the courts in ensuring that the burden of regulation was focused on the private realm of the market and not on the public realm of government. The appropriate framework for settling economic disputes was private rather than public law. 'Private relations between economic actors were to be governed not by statutes, but by the contractual rights and duties accepted by those actors' (Duxbury 1995: 30).

From the United States Supreme Court downwards in the federal court system, and throughout the large majority of state court systems, the courts opposed government regulation of private economic relations and put in place a Social Darwinist legal system that was to survive more or less intact until the mid-1930s. Inevitably, the judgments recorded by these courts became part of the science of law as discovered through the case method in the formalist United States legal academies.

As early as the late nineteenth century Social Darwinism was challenged both in the academies and in the courts by forerunners of the legal realist intellectual mood. For the most part, these early challengers retained respect for legal formalism in its more general form. Their attack was directed more at Social Darwinism than at the prevailing doctrine of legal science, though of course, in matters of economic regulation, they could not attack the one without the other. Best known among such challengers are Oliver Wendell Holmes, Jr., Benjamin Nathan Cardozo and Roscoe Pound.

Perhaps the best example of this challenge to Social Darwinism occurred in the dissenting judgment of Justice Holmes in the Supreme Court decision in the case of *Lochner v. New York* (1905). In this case, the Court declared that a New York statute setting a ten-hour maximum work-day for bakers violated the stipulation in the Fourteenth Amendment that 'No State shall . . . deprive any person of life, liberty, or property, without due process of law'. Dissenting, Justice Holmes observed that 'The Fourteenth Amendment does not enact Mr. Herbert Spencer's *Social Statics*' (75–6). This sentence became something of a rallying cry for the legal realist intellectual mood that was to follow some fifteen years later.

By the end of the First World War, formalism had become stale, leaving a void in American legal scholarship. The mood of legal realism evolved out of this void which threatened to stifle the creativity of legal scholars. For the most part, this mood did not manifest itself in an outright hostility to scientific method. Rather, it shifted attention away from the increasingly deductive logic of the natural sciences to the perceived inductive logic of the social sciences (though strictly this was already a misperception in the case of economics).

It is important not to exaggerate the scepticism of the legal realists. For the most part, they did not view the law simply as what judges do when settling disputes on the basis of the whim and fancy of the moment. Rather, the mood of the realist was one of dissatisfaction with the notion that twentieth-century legal thought should be dominated by a nineteenth-century legal world view. The key contributors to the mood, Karl Llewellyn, Jerome Frank, Underhill Moore, William O. Douglas and Robert Hale, did not always agree with each other on the meaning of realism itself, though they coalesced in a dislike of Langdellian formalism. The Universities of Yale and Columbia became centres for this dissident approach, though they also suffered from internal dissent.

The real significance of legal realism is to be found not in any concrete linkage between law and social sciences, for this simply did not occur in practice, but rather in the avenue that it opened up for a future marriage between law and certain social sciences, notably economics. The early intersections between law and economics under the influence of legal realism provide an illustration of this limited linkage.

Late nineteenth-century developments in economics in the United States had challenged the validity of classical economics, most especially its support for the idea of free exchange. An influential group of institutional economists, including Thorstein Veblen, John Bates Clark, Henry Carter Adams, Richard T. Ely and E.R.A. Seligman, many of whom were influenced by the perceived success of the German Bismarckian welfare state, attacked the more extreme version of *laissez-faire* on the ground that it had failed to resolve problems of unemployment and poverty. They argued in favour of social justice without socialism, or for a qualified form of interventionism.

As progressive lawyers became drawn to the methods of the social sciences, it is not surprising that institutional economics of this form proved to be an attractive proposition. Thus it was that legal realism, following the intellectual lead provided by the institutional economists, came to challenge legal formalism in the courts. Most especially, during the 1930s, legal realism in this form contributed to the demise of the private law emphasis of the United States Supreme Court, following the decision in *West Coast Hotel Co. v. Parrish* in 1937, which overturned a long line of judgments conforming to the precedent set in *Lochner v. New York* in 1905.

Ultimately, legal realism was to lose its dynamic, largely because it failed to lead to any well-defined methodology or subject of inquiry. '[By] the late 1930s, it had faded from the scene' (Kitch 1983: 165) as American lawyers became preoccupied with the emergence of totalitarianism across large parts of continental Europe and retreated into formalism as a means of protecting political values and moral principles founded on genuine social consensus (Duxbury 1995: 159). The demise of legal realism, however, did not imply the end of experimentation in legal education. The environment remained highly receptive to the introduction of economics into United States law schools (Kitch 1983: 165).

4. THE EARLY LAW-AND-ECONOMICS MOVEMENT AT CHICAGO. The path towards law-and-economics was undoubtedly smoothed by the legal realist challenge to formalism which opened up American legal education to the study of the social sciences. Yet the relationship should not be exaggerated.

The law-and-economics movement developed within an economics tradition more favourable to the free exchange model of classical political economy than was mainstream neoclassical economics at that time. It was, moreover, an economics tradition markedly hostile to the earlier interventionist, institutional approach which had so attracted the legal realists.

In a sense it also turned out to be a movement which incorporated some of the formalism of the Langdellian era, albeit a formalism which was based on the notion that laws should be economically efficient, rather than that they should rest on *stare decisis* and precedent. Crucial to this emphasis was the fact that the law-and-economics movement emerged at the University of Chicago, home to the world's leading free market economics programme at that time.

The scene was unwittingly set for the Chicago Law School to exercise an influential role in establishing law-and-economics when it appointed its first professor of economics to the law faculty in 1939. Henry Simons was not viewed at that time as an inspired appointment. He had pursued an unsuccessful non-tenured academic career in the Chicago department of economics since 1927, publishing relatively little and building a reputation as an ineffective teacher (Kitch 1983: 176–8). By the time that he joined the law school his scholarship was more that of an anthropologist or psychologist than that of an economist (Duxbury 1995: 331).

The law school appointment was designed as a compromise in a tenure battle over Simons waged between his mentor Frank Knight and his principal antagonist, Paul Douglas. By tenuring Simons in the law school, the Chicago economics department relieved itself of an ongoing embarrassment. In return, Henry Simons, a fine price theorist trained by Jacob Viner, was to rise to the occasion and to introduce economics to Chicago law school students on a more systematic basis than was available elsewhere.

Simons, at least when he was writing in the trough of the Great Depression, was not an unwavering advocate of *laissez-faire*. In his 1934 pamphlet, *A Positive Program for Laissez Faire*, Simons claimed that: 'Competition and laissez faire have not brought us to heaven' (Simons 1934: 6) and that 'there is now imperative need for a sound, positive program of economic legislation' (2). He supported an aggressive policy of antitrust and a thorough-going progressive income tax system.

Nevertheless, by the left-leaning standards of the United States academy in the 1930s, Simons was viewed as a conservative, both inside and outside Chicago. Following his law school appointment, and with the easing of the Great Depression, Simons was to become more closely aligned to the emerging Chicago free market economic philosophy (Kitch 1983: 178–9). He was also to become a markedly more effective teacher, educating Law School students in basic microeconomic theory via his course entitled 'Economic Analysis of Public Policy'.

By the time of his early death in 1946, Simons was establishing himself as more of a classical liberal than as an economic interventionist. From this perspective he established within the Law School a free market, substantially non-interventionist economic programme that came to dominate the early law-and-economics movement. This programme would be reinforced by the teaching of his successor in the Chicago law school, Aaron Director, a former student of Frank Knight.

In 1945, Henry Simons had sent to Friedrich von Hayek, then at the London School of Economics, a proposal that an Institute of Political Economy should be established at Chicago with Director as its head. This proposal was quickly superseded by the idea of a Free Market Study, which Hayek enthusiastically endorsed. Hayek negotiated funding for this project with the Volker Fund and helped to persuade the Chicago law school to appoint Director as research associate, with the rank of professor, to direct this project. Before the programme could be instituted, Simons died and the Volker Fund was persuaded to allow Director to assume his teaching responsibilities.

Director was not a prolific writer and the research project soon foundered. However, he was a creative thinker and an exceptional teacher, influenced significantly by the price theory course that he had received from Jacob Viner. He was especially effective in steering the law school away from an interventionist approach to antitrust policy and more generally in reinforcing the powerful anti-government message initiated by Henry Simons.

Through Volker Fund grants, Director brought John McGee, Ward Bowman, Robert Bork and William Letwin and others to the law school, each of whom would go on to make significant contributions to scholarship. He established excellent relationships with certain economists at Chicago, most notably Milton Friedman and George Stigler. He was largely responsible in 1950 for bringing Hayek to The Committee on Social Thought at Chicago after the economics department had rejected his candidature (Kitch 1983: 187). Director also became the editor in 1958 of the *Journal of Law and Economics*, newly established by Edward Levi, the Dean of the Chicago Law School (Coase 1993: 251). Throughout the duration of his editorship, from 1958 until he retired in 1964, Director emphasized the importance of free markets in the solution to economic problems.

Director could not have exerted the influence that he did upon law and economics at Chicago in the absence of powerful support from the Department of Economics. Frank Knight and Jacob Viner had set the scene for the pro-market stance of Chicago during the Great Depression when so many in the economics profession flirted with socialism. George Stigler and Milton Friedman reinforced this view in the post-World War II environment, while simultaneously shifting the emphasis of Chicago economics towards the positivist, empirical methodology that was to become its hallmark.

5. THE CONTRIBUTION OF RONALD H. COASE. The anvil on which the law-and-economics movement was forged was not located at the University of Chicago. As so often happens, law-and-economics was an unexpected consequence of a seemingly unrelated research initiative launched at the London School of Economics in 1937 by Ronald Coase.

In his famous essay, 'The Nature of The Firm' (1937), Coase explores why a firm emerges at all in a specialized exchange economy and why such firms as do emerge vary in size. His struggle for an answer to this previously unexplored question leads him to confront the issue of transaction costs – an issue that has preoccupied him throughout his subsequent career.

If a command structure such as that of the firm successfully supersedes the price system as a means of resource allocation, this must occur, he argues, because the cost of using the price mechanism exceeds the cost of using a command system. In his 1937 essay, Coase analyses in a perfunctory manner the nature of such costs, their implications for the changing sizes of firms, and the relevance of such costs in defining the marginal product of the entrepreneur.

Institutionally perceptive, Coase noted that firms of all sizes and shapes coalesced in free market economies. He therefore inferred that high transaction costs were prevalent in market economies. This recognition he carried forward through the following two decades, ultimately to use as a fulcrum on which he would launch the law-and-economics research programme (Coase 1988). In 1960, he launched the programme with another famous essay, entitled 'The Problem of Social Cost', written at the University of Virginia in response to criticisms by Chicago economists levelled at his essay entitled 'The Federal Communications Commission', which had been published in 1959 by Aaron Director in the second volume of the *Journal of Law and Economics*.

'The Problem of Social Cost' was concerned with 'those actions of business firms which have harmful effects on others' (Coase 1960: 1). In essence it was an attack on Pigou's solution to this problem as outlined in *The Economics of Welfare* (1920):

> The traditional approach has tended to obscure the nature of the choice that has been made. The question is commonly thought of as one in which A inflicts harm on B and what has to be decided is: how should we restrain A? But this is wrong. We are dealing with a problem of a reciprocal nature. To avoid the harm to B would inflict harm on A. The real question that has to be decided is: should A be allowed to harm B or should B be allowed to harm A? The problem is to avoid the more serious harm (Coase 1960: 2).

On the initial assumption that the pricing system works smoothly and without cost, Coase deploys the example where straying cattle destroy crops on neighbouring land to demonstrate that the value of production will be maximized whether liability falls upon the cattle owner or upon the farmer. Coase recognizes that it is necessary to know which party is liable 'since without the establishment of this initial delimitation of rights there can be no market transactions to transfer and recombine them' (Coase 1960: 8). He proceeds to illustrate his argument further by reference to a number of important common law cases, both English and American, which are now part of the litany of law-and-economics courses (Barnes and Stout 1992).

From the viewpoint of maximizing the value of production, assuming zero transaction costs, the decision confronting the courts concerning the assignment of liability is not a decision that will affect the final outcome:

> It is always possible to modify by transactions on the market the initial legal delimitation of rights. And, of course, if such market transactions are costless, such a rearrangement of rights will always take place if it would lead to an increase in the value of production (Coase 1960: 15).

It is important to note that this was only the end of the beginning of Coase's 1960 essay. In section VI of the essay, he explicitly rejects as unrealistic the assumption that there are no costs involved in carrying out market transactions: 'These operations are often extremely costly, sufficiently costly at any rate to prevent many transactions that would be carried out in a world in which the pricing system worked without cost' (ibid.).

In such circumstances, Coase is clear that the decision of a court, for example in granting an injunction or in imposing liability to pay damages, may result in outcomes that do not maximize the value of production. Internalization of the externality through merger of the two parties potentially might raise the value of production by comparison with the market outcome, although such will not always be the case. Even government regulation might be warranted on efficiency grounds, though Coase is not favourable to this solution, arguing that the alternative of doing nothing might often be value maximizing in situations of market failure:

> The kind of situation which economists are prone to consider as requiring corrective Government action is, in fact, often the result of Government action. Such action is not necessarily unwise. But there is a real danger that extensive Government intervention in the economic system may lead to the protection of those responsible for harmful effects being carried too far (Coase 1960: 28).

Three things are clear from a close reading of 'The Problem of Social Cost'. First, Ronald Coase is interested in the law exclusively from the perspective of its impact on economics and not *vice versa*. His essay does not address the issue of how legal rules might be formulated to maximize the value of production, although he does point out that judges 'seemed to show a better understanding of the economic problem than did many economists' (Coase 1993: 251). Rather, Coase accepts the legal rules as exogenous and reviews the economic implications of those rules under differing transaction cost scenarios: 'My interest is primarily in the economic system'.

Second, Coase's argument about reciprocity not only undermines Pigovian economic analysis, but also casts doubt on the common law notion of causality as a basis for assigning responsibility (Duxbury 1995: 387). In the hands of scholars who *are* concerned about the legal system and its rules, this doubt becomes important in the scenario of high transaction costs, since the notion of placing the burden of adjustment on the *least cost avoider* may conflict with the causality based notion of determining liability.

Third, the world inhabited by Coase is a world of positive and not of zero transaction costs. It is ironic that Coase became famous, to those unacquainted with his 1960 essay, as the originator of a theory of a zero transaction cost world which he always rejected as unrealistic. George Stigler formalized this misconception as *The Coase Theorem:* 'under perfect competition private and social costs will be equal' (Stigler 1966: 113). This unfortunate emphasis has led unwary scholars of law-and-economics into an excessively benign view of the impact of legal rules on economic performance (Williamson 1993).

When Ronald Coase joined the Chicago Law School in 1964 (initially in a joint appointment with the Business School) to fill Aaron Director's place on his retirement, two factors influenced his positive decision. The stick was impending trouble at the University of Virginia, where a left-leaning administration had placed the economics department under critical review. The carrot was the opportunity to assume the editorship of the *Journal of Law and Economics*:

> Indeed, it is probable that without the *Journal* I would not have come to Chicago. What I wanted to do was to encourage the type of research which I had advocated in 'The Problem of Social Cost,' and I used my editorship of the *Journal* as a means of bringing this about (Coase 1993: 252).

Coase achieved that and a great deal more. From 1964 until 1974 as sole editor, and from 1974 until his retirement in 1982 as joint editor with William M. Landes, Coase opened up the new academic discipline of law-and-economics to a new generation of scholars who would otherwise have found it treacherous to research in a field unknown to the leading journals of economics and of law. Coase used the *Journal* to support faculty research, to grant fellowships and to make available financial assistance as well as to offer the opportunity for publication (Coase 1993: 253). In 1991, the award of the Nobel Prize in Economic Science not only honoured Ronald Coase for his personal contributions to knowledge, but also placed the seal of recognition on a new discipline which by then had made its distinctive mark within the broader discipline of economics.

6. THE NEW BENTHAMITES. The law-and-economics programme has assumed both a normative and a positive dimension. In this section, I shall focus attention on the normative scholarship of a few key contributors who have tended to follow the utilitarian path first outlined by Jeremy Bentham.

Bentham's brand of utilitarianism comprises a combination of three conditions (Sen 1987: 69), namely:

(1) *Welfarism*, which requires that the goodness of a state of affairs be a function only of utility information regarding that state of affairs;

(2) *Sum-ranking*, which requires that utility information regarding any state of affairs be assessed in terms of the sum of all individuals' utilities concerning that state of affairs; and

(3) *Consequentialism*, which requires that every choice in society be determined by the goodness of the consequent state of affairs.

Modern utilitarians are more circumspect than was Bentham in adhering to these conditions. The ordinalist revolution, combined with a recognition that utility is not comparable across individuals, has resulted in a much weaker form of utilitarianism, based on the Pareto principle (Pareto 1897), in some cases extended by the principle of Kaldor–Hicks potential compensation (Kaldor 1939, Hicks 1939). The scholars whose work is reviewed in this section adhere to one or other of these two principles, and are prepared to deploy such a principle in an instrumentalist manner, to reform the legal system according to its precepts.

Henry Simons. It is not surprising that law-and-economics assumed an instrumentalist, utilitarian direction, given the early leadership of Henry Simons. The essay for which Simons is best known, 'A Positive Program for Laissez Faire', published in 1934, is a propagandist tract, more an essay in political philosophy than economics (Coase 1993: 240).

It was also an interventionist tract, arguing for example that

> *the state should face the necessity of actually taking over, owning, and managing directly, both the railroads and the utilities, and all other industries in which it is impossible to maintain effectively competitive conditions* (Simons 1934: 11–12, italics in original).

For other industries, he argued that 'there still remains a real alternative to socialization, namely the establishment and preservation of competition as the regulative agency' (ibid: 12). To achieve this end, the US antitrust laws should be deployed: 'The Federal Trade Commission must become perhaps the most powerful of our governmental agencies' (19).

In formulating such proposals, Simons provided no empirical support; nor was he disposed seriously to investigate the likely impact of his reforms on economic efficiency; nor was he much concerned about whether or not the Federal Trade Commission would perform as he suggested it should. Of course Simons was writing well in advance of the public choice revolution, and it was not then unknown, even at Chicago, for economists to place their faith in government agencies. Nevertheless, as Coase concludes: 'Stigler's description of Simons is eminently just: Simons was a utopian' (Coase 1993: 242).

Gordon Tullock. The only formal training in economics received by Gordon Tullock was the course provided in the Chicago Law School by Henry Simons. It is not surprising, therefore, that his first contribution to law-and-economics, *The Logic of the Law* (1971), has a distinctly Benthamite tone. In this, the first book ever published in law-and-economics, Tullock explicitly refers to Bentham's failed reforms of the English legal system, claiming that: 'Since we now have a vast collection of tools that was not available to Bentham, it is possible for us to improve on his work' and 'Hopefully this discussion, together with empirical research, will lead to significant reforms' (Tullock 1971: xiv).

The tools on which Tullock draws come from the new welfare economics, essentially the Pareto principle buttressed by Kaldor–Hicks potential compensation. By focusing on potential reforms from a long-term *ex ante* perspective similar to that adopted by Buchanan and Tullock in *The Calculus of Consent* (1962), Tullock seeks to show that some reforms that would be rejected *ex post* by those who benefit from the *status quo* might nevertheless satisfy the Pareto criterion from the perspective of a veil of uncertainty.

On this basis, Tullock launches a review of the foundational principles of the law, and shows what happens when, abandoning the traditional view of civil and criminal law as an extension of broad moral philosophy, we apply some of the concepts and procedures of Paretian welfare economics to the US legal system. In a wide-ranging discussion that covers all the major areas of law and law enforcement – from contracts and negligence law to robbery and murder, from the treatment of children and incompetents to the punishment of habitual offenders – Tullock derives optimal rules and procedures markedly different from those that prevailed in 1971.

Because it represented a foundational challenge to the legal system rather than a textbook for lawyers, and because it brought into question the relevance of legal formalism in a somewhat arcane manner, Tullock's book failed to make the impression on law-and-economics that Richard Posner's 1973 book would achieve. In a fundamental sense, however, Tullock was the precursor to Posner in the normative economic analysis of law.

Richard A. Posner. Unequivocally, Richard A. Posner has remained the most important scholar in law-and-economics since his textbook *Economic Analysis of Law* was first published in 1973. More than any other single scholar he has been responsible for the shape that post-Coaseian law-and-economics has taken, both in its normative and in its positive dimensions. This achievement is all the more remarkable because Posner has no formal training in economics and, since 1983, has combined a prodigious output of scholarship as Senior Lecturer in the University of Chicago Law School with a full time appointment as a highly productive Judge in the US Court of Appeals, Seventh Circuit.

It is interesting to note that Posner's interest in normative economics runs counter to the positivist emphasis of the University of Chicago economics department, exposing him no doubt to his mentor George Stigler's pejorative remarks about economic preaching (Stigler 1982). Posner's contributions have refocused the direction of post-1973 law-and-economics away from Coase's earlier interest in the implications of legal rules for economic efficiency towards the use that can be made of economic theory to explain the common law. Once again, this shift of emphasis runs somewhat counter to the general lack of interest in institutions displayed by some leading figures of the post-Friedman, Chicago Economics Department (Rowley 1997). Finally, it is noteworthy that Posner overcame an initial handicap imposed by his legal training at Harvard University to embrace free market economics, joining the University of Chicago law faculty in 1969 and eventually becoming a leading member of the Chicago School.

Posner was never a thorough-going Benthamite in his normative predisposition, claiming that 'Bentham's major weaknesses as a thinker were the sponginess of the utility principle as a guide to policy, his lack of interest in positive or empirical analysis, and his excessive, if characteristically modern, belief in the plasticity of human nature and social institutions' (Posner 1981: 42). For these reasons, Posner sought out an alternative principle 'that supports Blackstonian rights and other stabilizing features of social structure' (47). Indeed, Posner clearly recognized the current philosophical hostility to utilitarianism and sought out at an early stage in his research programme 'a firmer base for ethical theory than utilitarianism' (48).

In his 1973 textbook, Posner defines efficiency to mean 'exploiting economic resources in such a way that human satisfaction as measured by aggregate consumer willingness to pay for goods and services is maximized' (Posner 1973: 4). The term that he designates for this concept is wealth maximization. Whether his work is to be read as embracing a narrow definition of wealth or a broader definition inclusive of any utility that is increased through exchange (Duxbury 1995: 398) is debatable, depending on which contribution by Posner is under scrutiny (compare for example Posner 1973, 1981, 1990 and 1995 for significant variations on a theme).

The purpose of this summary is best served by focusing on Posner's most careful and thorough review of the wealth maximization principle (Posner 1985). In this essay, Posner attempts to define a concept of wealth maximization that 'serves as a common denominator for both utilitarian and individualist perspectives' (Posner and Parisi 1997: xi). To this end, Posner identifies the economists' concept of *expected utility* as being equivalent to his concept of wealth. He notes that the economists' concept of expected utility is distinct from the utilitarian concept of utility as happiness, 'though wealth and happiness are positively correlated' (Posner 1985: 88).

Because Posner must apply his concept of wealth maximization to potential transactions as well as to actual transactions, he is forced to fall back upon a Kaldor–Hicks potential compensation principle grounded on expected utility. Inevitably, this leaves him open to the charge that his concept is arbitrary, and that wealth maximization exposes individuals to the discretionary judgment of third parties as well as to potential coercion. Still, he might claim with some justice that in these regards his concept fares no worse than the Kaldor–Hicks principle as deployed deterministically in economics.

More difficult for him, however, is his claim that wealth maximization has affinities with property rights concepts such as those espoused by John Locke (1690). If Posner is correct, for example, in asserting that liability rules in defence of property are economically more efficient than property rules in situations of high transaction costs, then wealth maximization runs directly counter to the imprescriptible right of an individual to the exclusive use of his own property. If Posner is correct that in some circumstances the rule of negligence with contributory negligence in the law of tort is economically more efficient than the rule of strict liability, once again the right of an individual to 'life, liberty and property' is eroded by the application of Posner's principle.

In his 1985 essay, Posner recognizes that wealth maximization comes up short in its limited defence of property rights. He does not regard this as a serious deficiency, however, in its narrower role as a guide to the courts in areas where the Constitution or legislation does not deprive them of initiative or discretion (Posner 1985: 103). He justifies this claim by asserting that: 'Wealth maximization combines elements of utilitarianism and individualism, and in so doing comes closer to being a consensus political philosophy in our contentiously pluralistic society than any other overarching political principle' (Posner 1985: 104).

As a good Chicagoan, Richard Posner recognizes an unsubstantiated assertion when he sees one. He knows what would have happened to him had he made such a statement in a Chicago industrial organization seminar chaired by George Stigler!

Steven Shavell. Almost inevitably, as neoclassical economists have turned their research programmes towards law-and-economics, mathematical rigour has tended to substitute for the linguistic skills of those trained exclusively in the law. Indeed, there is an oral tradition at Chicago in which Aaron Director is held to have said in the early 1960s that by the year 2000 there would be no point in anyone submitting a learned article written in the English language to an economics journal, because the editor would not be able to understand it! Fortunately, perhaps, this has not turned out to be a correct prophecy.

Nevertheless, there is a discernible trend in law-and-economics towards the deployment of rigorous modelling techniques and in this respect Steven Shavell, Professor of Economics and Law at Harvard University, is perhaps the most distinguished contributor. In his 1987 book, which draws together much of his earlier scholarship on the economic analysis of accident law, Shavell defends his technical approach to the problem, asserting that: 'The advantage of studying models is that they allow predictive and normative questions to be answered in an unambiguous way' (Shavell 1987: 3).

Shavell is quite explicit in his instrumental approach to the analysis of accident law: 'Citations refer mainly to literature with an economic orientation, or at least to works that view the liability system in a frankly instrumental way' (ibid.). The first eight chapters of his book develop rigorous mathematical models of the behaviour of all actors in the accident situation, including tortfeasors and victims, insurance companies and the courts. In Chapter 9, Shavell introduces the social welfare function on which his reform conclusions will be predicated. The social welfare function that he endorses is that in which social welfare is assumed equal to the sum of parties' expected utilities. This is identical to wealth maximization as defined by Richard Posner. As Shavell explicitly recognizes, the interests of tortfeasors are treated equally in this model with those of the victims: 'protection of risk-averse injurers against risk is just as important a determinant of social welfare as is protection of risk-averse victims, other things being equal' (207).

The danger of this approach becomes evident in Chapter 13, when Shavell confronts potential criticisms of his approach. In responding to the question: *What is the normative value of the analysis?* Shavell argues that:

> The analysis should be of aid in assessing the desirability of legal rules, presuming as I do that the criterion of social welfare in which the reader is interested will reflect the value of parties engaging in their activities, the costs of taking precautions, the losses due to accidents, compensation of risk-averse parties, and administrative costs (293).

Surely the reader will be interested in such matters, and Shavell's positive analysis will have helped some of them to come to terms with the implications of alternative legal rules. However, strong value judgments have been slipped in through the social welfare function without explicit recognition. The unwary reader will miss these value judgments and come to think that Steven Shavell has unambiguously established the superiority of a strict liability over a negligence rule in the law of accidents.

Now it may be true that the principle of *caveat emptor* should apply just as much with respect to academic scholarship as with respect to product liability. But note that *caveat emptor* is not a principle on which Steven Shavell (1987) has relied in arguing in favour of a strict liability rule in the case of product liability.

7. THE LAW-AND-ECONOMICS OF DR. PANGLOSS. From the outset, Ronald Coase (1960) had set law-and-economics on a primarily positive compass point. Initially, Richard Posner (1973) was ambivalent to this lead, steering his vessel simultaneously in a normative and in a positive direction. Given his stated commitment to the continued stability of the common law (Posner 1985), it is singularly fortunate that Posner encountered an essential consistency between the two directions; otherwise he would surely have wrecked his ship.

For his adventure into the positive analysis of law and economics Richard Posner was singularly fortunate to join forces with a brilliant Chicago economist, William M. Landes, whose mentor was Ronald Coase, and who was joint editor of the *Journal of Law and Economics* from 1974 until 1991. Together these two scholars embarked on a research programme in law-and-economics, commencing in the mid-1970s and continuing through the present time, which has fundamentally changed mainstream American common law jurisprudence.

Thus it came to pass that Chicago methodology (Friedman 1953) dominated the early programme of research in positive law-and-economics. Theories concerning the wealth maximizing characteristics of the common law – property, contract and tort – as well as the criminal law were formulated using rational choice theory complemented by sound microeconomic theory. Econometric models reflecting the specifications imposed by such theory were then evaluated against carefully screened data, exposing theory to the predictive test recommended by Milton Friedman. The results appear by and large not to falsify an important premise of Chicago law-and-economics, namely that judge-made law is the result of an effort to induce efficiency outcomes (see for example, Landes and Posner 1978, 1980, 1981a, 1981b, 1983, 1984 and 1985).

Law-and-economics scholars have been less successful in explaining the process through which wealth-maximizing characteristics of the common law occur than in inferring such efficient outcomes from their regression models. It has been argued, for example, that the central tenets of the common law emerged during the nineteenth century during a period when the professional classes (which included judges) were influenced by utilitarian ideals. Even if this were true, it would not explain how the common law, especially the law of tort, has evolved in an efficient manner during the second half of the twentieth century, when a more socialist ethic has predominated.

It has been argued that an evolutionary process of selection generates efficient legal rules. This occurs either because parties litigate inefficient rules more frequently than they litigate efficient rules (Rubin 1977) or because litigation is driven by the cost of inefficient rules (Priest 1977). This argument depends at least in part on far-sighted litigators, presumably insurance companies, corporations or labour unions, who expect to be in court repeatedly through time. It also depends on litigators having *some* faith in *stare decisis* and precedent, something that the New Benthamites would not necessarily endorse. Furthermore, as Posner recognizes, 'The intervals over which the common law has evolved are too short for a random process to have generated efficient rules' (Posner 1990: 372).

It has also been suggested that the conditions of judicial appointment are intended to make the judge indifferent, from the standpoint of his pecuniary interest, to how he decides. This argument is full of holes. Approximately fifty per cent of state judges in the United States are elected and presumably behave like politicians. Tenure and income are not as secure for the remainder as is the case for US federal judges, who only occasionally become involved in common law adjudication, either through diversity suits, or on appeal from the states.

Moreover, tenure and income security do not always produce policy eunuchs, as Posner would be quick to allow (Posner 1995). Furthermore, there is no obvious reason why policy eunuchs would pursue wealth maximization in a society in which redistributive goals tend to dominate wealth creation. The theory of judicial motivation remains an important empty law-and-economics box which must be filled before outsiders will evidence great confidence in regression results, however skilfully achieved.

In this short section, it is impossible to do justice to the many advances that are currently under way in positive law-and-economics or to offer an overview of the many counter-results to the Chicago hypothesis that have been published. It is worth stating, however, that this area of law-and-economics is by no means a closed book. Recent applications of game theory, both strategic and evolutionary, offer real promise of extending the economic analysis of law not least to the processes of adjudication (Baird, Gertner and Picker 1994). Extensions of law-and-economics to areas of the law well outside what is conventionally known as common law also offer a major testing ground for the efficiency hypothesis in predictably less favourable terrain.

Finally, there is a vast amount of research awaiting scholars of customary law systems and civil code systems to determine whether either or both of these are more or less efficient than the common law system as it has evolved in the late twentieth century (Tullock 1997).

8. SOME NOTES OF DISSENT. It should not be thought that the law-and-economics research programme outlined above is devoid of criticism. In this section, two important areas of dissent are identified.

(a) Critical insights from Austrian economics. Economists broadly identified as members of the Austrian School have focused their criticisms on the tendency of law-and-economics scholars to attach objective meaning to such concepts as economic efficiency and transaction costs and to model the behaviour of courts as if information costs typically are low. These are powerful criticisms with significant implications both for New Benthamite thinking and for positive economic analysis.

In *The Counter-Revolution of Science* (1952) Friedrich von Hayek identifies the abuse of reason which characterized much of the hostility to methodological individualism during the late nineteenth and early twentieth centuries. Central to this abuse, in his view, was the attempt to replicate the methods of natural science within the social sciences. Most especially, Hayek is alarmed by the tendency of social scientists to introduce notions of objective specificity and precision widely used in the natural sciences into disciplines which involve human action. Such attempts he labels with the pejorative term *scientism* (Hayek 1952: 25).

Hayek suggests that the social sciences 'are concerned with man's actions, and their aim is to explain the unintended or undesigned results of the actions of many men' (ibid.). In a fundamental sense the facts deployed in social science 'are merely opinions, views held by the people whose actions we study' (28). Since the social scientist cannot directly observe the minds of those who act in response to external stimuli, his approach is essentially subjective. Unlike the natural scientist, the data deployed by the social scientist 'never exists as a consistent and coherent body. It only exists in the dispersed, incomplete, and inconsistent form in which it appears in many individual minds' (29–30).

In Hayek's judgment, recognizing the subjectivity of data is nowhere more important than in economics: 'it is probably no exaggeration to say that every important advance in economic theory during the last hundred years was a further step in the consistent application of subjectivism' (31). Whether or not Hayek is fully justified in this assertion no doubt is a matter for continuing debate. Nevertheless, this insight has profound consequences for Austrian economists in their contributions to law-and-economics.

The insight plays a key role, for example, in Mario Rizzo's 1980 article entitled 'The Mirage of Efficiency'. The focus of this article is 'on elucidating the tremendous information requirements that make pursuit of the efficiency norm impractical' (Rizzo 1980: 642). As he correctly notes, both the normative and the positive analysis of law must define what ought to be included in wealth and what are the appropriate shadow prices for each of those components. This is an impossible task in a science of human action.

Suppose, for example, that *ex post* compensation of victims, regardless of whether the defendant was negligent, is a public good. Then its exclusion from consideration in the determination of wealth maximizing liability arrangements might lead to an inefficient outcome. How do outside researchers know whether or not to include this in the wealth concept? The problems of information in law-and-economics need not be laboured further in this section.

Suppose now that we recognize the subjectivity of cost. This has profound implications for law-and-economics. Buchanan (1969), writing in a London School of Economics cost tradition heavily influenced by Hayek, noted that opportunity cost is subjective in any theory of choice and must be evaluated in a utility dimension. In such circumstances, outside observers simply cannot know the choice-influencing costs that determine decisions. Only the decision-makers themselves confront opportunity costs *ex ante* at the moment of decision. The consequences of such cost are not opportunity costs in the choice-influencing sense, and even they must be measured in subjective utility space.

It does not take a genius like Hayek to understand the implications of this insight for court judgments in which the judges, or (worse still) the jurors, are called upon to determine whether transaction costs are high or low in order to establish an appropriate legal rule from an efficiency perspective. Nor does it take a genius to understand the grave problems that subjectivity of cost pose for scholars who set out to test whether or not particular legal rules are wealth maximizing for society.

(b) Critical insights from public choice. There is a sense in which law-and-economics scholarship in the late 1990s resembles neoclassical economics immediately prior to the emergence of public choice in the late 1950s. For the most part, law-and-economics scholars view the common law as invulnerable to political market pressures. This is a dangerously naive viewpoint.

As Gordon Tullock has shown in his 1997 monograph *The Case Against the Common Law*, the common law is far from immune from public choice pressures. Federal judges are appointed through a political process in the United States – a process which is far distant from the peer review mechanism utilized for example in England and Wales. State judges are either appointed through a political process or directly elected. Inevitably such processes of selection impact upon judicial decision-making.

Public prosecutors' offices are financed from the public purse and their budgets are not immune from success or failure in pursuing politically unpopular crimes. Trial locations are selected increasingly in response to political pressures with an eye to influencing jury selection. Jury selection is no longer a random process, at least in high profile cases where psychological tests are now the norm and ethnic, racial and cultural characteristics are closely monitored. Even the penalties imposed both in civil and in criminal cases undergo detailed public scrutiny, opening up opportunities for special interests to bias expected penalties and for judges to hunt for deep pockets rather than to abide by criteria of proximate cause in the judgments that they pass down.

David Friedman (1987) correctly recognized the bias that political markets impose on judicial decision-making:

> The most obvious implication of this line of analysis is that laws will tend to favour concentrated interests at the expense of dispersed interests, since the former will be better able to raise money from their members to lobby for the laws they prefer (Friedman 1987: 147).

Even Posner is not unaware of the relevance of public choice for the economic analysis of the common law, though he has not commented explicitly on its efficiency implications:

> In a way, the systematic incorporation of public choice theory into the economic approach to law may serve to bridge the conflicting, normative perspectives in law and economics, at least by bringing the debate on to the more solid ground of collective choice theory (Posner and Parisi 1997: xii).

To this author, at least, collective choice theory is more of a quicksand than solid ground (Rowley 1993). Furthermore, public choice has more to say at the positive than at the normative level of analysis and what it has to say is very unfavourable to efficiency (Rowley 1989). Law-and-economics scholars, like ostriches, still have their heads firmly in the sand on this important aspect of their discipline.

9. THE IMPORTANCE OF ECONOMICS IN LAW-AND-ECONOMICS. Economics has played an important role in the development of law-and-economics. It has provided the new research programme with its normative framework and its positive methodology (Rowley 1981). It has provided it with its principal analytical tools – mathematical modelling, game theory and econometric techniques. It has provided, in short, the glue that holds the new research programme together and that gives it its distinctive flavour.

In my view, law-and-economics is a distinctive *research programme* in its own right. To pursue the programme effectively is increasingly open only to scholars who have a first-class grounding in economics and in the law. For much the same reasons, it is also now a sub-discipline in economics, and, more rarely, in the law. It is unlikely, however, that law-and-economics will ever achieve the status of an entirely separate *discipline*. The law is too diverse to be grounded effectively only in the normative and positive framework provided by economics. It is an insufficiently general area of study to warrant economists devoting all their studies to its institutions.

The future of law-and-economics is extremely bright and although Chicago cannot expect to dominate the future of the discipline as effectively as it has dominated the past thirty years, it has surely earned an eternal reputation as the founding father of what is perhaps, with public choice, one of the two most successful research programmes in the social sciences of the second half of the twentieth century.

CHARLES K. ROWLEY

See also ADAM SMITH AND THE LAW; AMERICAN LEGAL REALISM; BENTHAM, JEREMY; CALABRESI, GUIDO; COASE, RONALD; DIRECTOR, AARON; FERGUSON, ADAM; HAYEK, FRIEDRICH VON; HUME, DAVID; OPPORTUNITY COSTS AND LEGAL INSTITUTIONS; POSNER, RICHARD A.; PUBLIC CHOICE AND THE LAW; SCOTTISH ENLIGHTENMENT AND THE LAW; SIMONS, HENRY C.; TULLOCK, GORDON; WEALTH MAXIMIZATION.

Subject classification: 4c(i).

CASES

Lochner v. New York 198 US 45 (1905).
West Coast Hotel Co. v. Parrish 300 US 379 (1937).

BIBLIOGRAPHY

Baird, D.W., Gertner, R.H. and Picker, R.C. 1994. *Game Theory and the Law*. Cambridge, MA: Harvard University Press.

Barnes, D.W. and Stout, L.A. 1992. *Cases and Materials on Law and Economics*. St. Paul, MN: West Publishing Co.

Bentham, J. 1776. *A Fragment on Government*. Edited by J.H. Burns and H.L.A. Hart, Cambridge: Cambridge University Press, 1988.

Bentham, J. 1789. *An Introduction to the Principles of Morals and Legislation*. Edited by J.H. Burns and H.L.A. Hart, London: Athlone Press, 1970.

Blackstone, W. 1765–69. *Commentaries on the Laws of England*. Chicago: University of Chicago Press, 1979.

Brenner, S. and Spaeth, H.J. 1995. *Stare Indecisis: The Alteration of Precedent on the Supreme Court, 1945–1992*. Cambridge and New York: Cambridge University Press.

Buchanan, J.M. 1969. *Cost and Choice: An Inquiry in Economic Theory*. Chicago: Markham Publishing Company.

Buchanan, J.M. and Tullock, G. 1962. *The Calculus of Consent*. Ann Arbor: University of Michigan Press.

Calabresi, G. 1961. Some thoughts on risk distribution and the law of torts. *Yale Law Journal* 70: 499–553.

Coase, R.H. 1937. The nature of the firm. *Economica*, N.S. 4: 386–405.

Coase, R.H. 1959. The Federal Communications Commission. *Journal of Law and Economics* 2: 1–40.

Coase, R.H. 1960. The problem of social cost. *Journal of Law and Economics* 3: 1–45.

Coase, R.H. 1988. *The Firm, the Market and the Law*. Chicago: University of Chicago Press.

Coase, R.H. 1993. Law and economics at Chicago. *Journal of Law and Economics* 36: 239–54.

Duxbury, N. 1995. *Patterns of American Jurisprudence*. Oxford: Clarendon Press.

Epstein, R.A. 1986. Past and future: the temporal dimension in the law of property. *Washington Law Quarterly* 64(3): 667–722.

Epstein, R.A. 1995. *Simple Rules for a Complex World*. Cambridge, MA: Harvard University Press.

Ferguson, A. 1767. *An Essay on the History of Civil Society*. Edited by L. Schneider, New Brunswick, NJ: Transaction Publishers, 1980.

Friedman, D. 1987. Law and economics. In *The New Palgrave: A Dictionary of Economics*, ed. J. Eatwell, M. Milgate and P. Newman (London: Macmillan): vol. 3, 144–8.

Friedman, M. 1953. The methodology of positive economics. In M. Friedman, *Essays in Positive Economics*, Chicago and London: University of Chicago Press.

Harrison, R. 1988. Introduction to J. Bentham, *A Fragment on Government*. Cambridge: Cambridge University Press: vi-xxiii.

Hayek, F.A. von. 1952. *The Counter-Revolution of Science: Studies on the Abuse Of Reason*. 2nd edn, Indianapolis: Liberty Press, 1979.

Hicks, J. 1939. *Value and Capital*. Oxford: Clarendon Press.

Hume, D. 1739. *A Treatise of Human Nature*. Edited by P.H. Nidditch, Oxford: Oxford University Press, 1978.

Kaldor, N. 1939. Welfare propositions of economics and interpersonal comparisons of utility. *Economic Journal* 49: 549–52.

Kitch, E.W. 1983. The fire of truth: a remembrance of law and economics at Chicago, 1932–1970. *Journal of Law and Economics* 26: 163–234.

Landes, W.M. and Posner, R.A. 1978. Salvors, finders and Good Samaritans and other rescuers: an economic study of law and altruism. *Journal of Legal Studies* 7: 83.

Landes, W.M. and Posner, R.A. 1980. Joint and multiple tortfeasors: an economic analysis. *Journal of Legal Studies* 9: 517–55.

Landes, W.M. and Posner, R.A. 1981a. An economic theory of intentional torts. *International Review of Law and Economics* 1: 127–54.

Landes, W.M. and Posner, R.A. 1981b. The positive theory of tort law. *Georgia Law Review* 15: 851–924.

Landes, W.M. and Posner, R.A. 1983. Causation in tort law: an economic approach. *Journal of Legal Studies* 12: 109–34.

Landes, W.M. and Posner, R.A. 1984. Tort law as a regulatory regime for catastrophic personal injuries. *Journal of Legal Studies* 13: 417–34.

Landes, W.M. and Posner, R.A. 1985. A positive economic analysis of products liability. *Journal of Legal Studies* 14: 535–67.

Landes, W.M. and Posner, R.A. 1987. *The Economic Structure of Tort Law*. Cambridge, MA.: Harvard University Press.

Locke, J. 1690. *Two Treatises of Government*. Edited by Peter Laslett, Cambridge: Cambridge University Press, 1960.

Mercuro, N. and Medema, S.G. 1997. *Economics and the Law: From Posner to Post-Modernism*. Princeton: Princeton University Press.

Pareto, V. 1897. The new theories of economics. *Journal of Political Economy* 5: 485–502.

Pigou, A.C. 1920. *The Economics of Welfare*. London: Macmillan.

Posner, R.A. 1973. *Economic Analysis of Law*. Boston: Little, Brown & Co.

Posner, R.A. 1981. *The Economics of Justice*. Cambridge, MA: Harvard University Press.

Posner, R.A. 1985. Wealth maximization revisited. *Notre Dame Journal of Law, Ethics and Public Policy* 2(1): 85–106.

Posner, R.A. 1987. The law and economics movement. *American Economic Review, Papers and Proceeding* 77: 1–13.

Posner, R.A. 1990. *The Problems of Jurisprudence*. Cambridge, MA: Harvard University Press.

Posner, R.A. 1995. *Overcoming Law*. Cambridge, MA: Harvard University Press.

Posner, R.A. and Parisi, F. 1997. Law and economics: an introduction. In *Law and Economics*, ed. R.A. Posner and F. Parisi, Volume 1, Cheltenham, UK and Lyme, NH: Edward Elgar.

Priest, G.L. 1977. The common law process and the selection of efficient rules. *Journal of Legal Studies* 6: 65–82.

Rizzo, M. 1980. The mirage of efficiency. *Hofstra Law Review* 8(3): 641–58.

Robbins, L. 1938. Interpersonal comparisons of utility: a comment. *Economic Journal* 48: 635–41.

Rowley, C.K. 1981. Social sciences and law: the relevance of economic theories. *Oxford Journal of Legal Studies* 1(1): 391–406.

Rowley, C.K. 1989. The common law in public choice perspective: a theoretical and institutional critique. *Hamline Law Review* 12(2): 355–83.

Rowley, C.K. 1993. Introduction. In *Social Choice Theory, Vol. 1: The Aggregation of Preferences*, ed. C.K. Rowley, Aldershot: Edward Elgar: xi–xlviii.

Rowley, C.K. 1997. Donald Wittman's *The Myth of Democratic Failure*. *Public Choice* 92 (1–2): 15–26.

Rubin, P.H. 1977. Why is the common law efficient? *Journal of Legal Studies* 6: 51–63.

Scalia, A. 1997. *A Matter of Interpretation: Federal Courts and the Law*. Princeton: Princeton University Press.

Sen, A. 1987. Rational behaviour. In *The New Palgrave: A Dictionary of Economics*, ed. J. Eatwell, M. Milgate and P. Newman (London: Macmillan), vol. 4: 68–76.

Shavell, S. 1987. *Economic Analysis of Accident Law*. Cambridge, MA: Harvard University Press.

Simons, H. 1934. *A Positive Program for Laissez-faire: some proposals for liberal economic policy*. Ed. H.D. Gideonse, Chicago: Chicago University Press, 1948.

Smith, A. 1776. *The Wealth of Nations*, Volume 2. Ed. E. Cannan, London: Methuen & Co, 1904; repr. 1961.

Spencer, H. 1851. *Social Statics: or, the Conditions Essential to Human Happiness Specified, and the First of Them Developed*. London: Chapman.

Spencer, H. 1884. *Man Versus The State*. Caldwell, ID: The Caxton Printers, 1940.

Stigler, G.J. 1966. *The Theory of Price*. 3rd edn, New York: Macmillan.

Stigler, G.J. 1982. *The Economist as Preacher and Other Essays*. Chicago: University of Chicago Press.

Trebilcock, M.J. 1993. *The Limits of Freedom of Contract*. Cambridge, MA: Harvard University Press.

Tullock, G. 1971. *The Logic of the Law*. New York: Basic Books.

Tullock, G. 1997. *The Case Against the Common Law*. The Blackstone Commentaries, No. 1, Durham, NC: Carolina Academic Press.

Welch, C. 1987. Utilitarianism. In *The New Palgrave: A Dictionary of Economics*, ed. J. Eatwell, M. Milgate and P. Newman (London: Macmillan), vol. 4: 770–76.

Williamson, O.E. 1993. Transaction cost economics meets Posnerian law and economics. *Journal of Institutional and Theoretical Economics* 149(1): 99–118.

law-and-economics from the perspective of law. To appreciate the significance of law-and-economics from the perspective of law requires an overview of the impact that the interdisciplinary approach has had on legal thought. For this purpose, it is helpful to classify developments in the literature.

The so-called 'old law-and-economics' (Posner 1975: 758–9), which involved traditional micro-economic analysis of the law governing explicit economic systems, for example competition and public finance, had initially only a marginal impact on lawyers working within these areas and was little noticed by others. The beginning of 'new law-and-economics' is usually identified with Coase's seminal paper on social costs (Coase 1960), but this became widely known in legal circles only when its implications had been taken up by lawyer-economists active in the law schools, notably Posner at Chicago (Posner 1973). Posner's rigid insistence on a narrow set of behavioural assumptions and obsession with the alleged wealth-maximizing function of the common law contrasted with the broader approach taken by Calabresi in his pioneering study of accident law (Calabresi 1970). The latter was rapidly assimilated by tort scholars and significantly reorientated legal debate.

For the next decade, the Chicago approach dominated the literature and quickly established itself in North America as a major input to legal scholarship, capable of addressing a wide range of normative issues (Duxbury 1995: ch. 5). European legal scholars were slower to respond and the movement took root there only in the 1980s (Van den Bergh 1992). The training in economics undertaken by many American judges (and their influential law clerks) and the appointment of some leading lawyer–economists (including Posner) to the Federal Bench gave rise to expectations that law-and-economics would significantly influence judicial decision-making. Its impact on antitrust doctrine is clear (Kovacic 1992), but there is an unresolved debate as to how far the influence has spread into other areas of law (Culp 1987).

The influence of law-and-economics on legal thought has been perceived by one commentator as having lost its upward trajectory at some time in the 1980s (Ellickson 1989). This may be true in relation to private law, the literature on which has become dominated by economists, working with increasingly technical and sophisticated models. But it does not apply to public law for, as will be seen, legal scholarship here has benefited much from economic analysis, both by applying public-choice theory and by reacting against it. More generally, lawyers have responded positively to what has been described as 'post-Chicago law-and-economics', an approach taken by a new generation of lawyer–economists, concerned to reduce the dogma associated with the earlier work and to relate their analysis to other social science disciplines (Barnett and Coleman 1989; Rubin 1996).

If, taken as a whole, law-and-economics has had a very marked influence on legal thought, it would be simplistic to attribute this to an enthusiastic acceptance of its normative claims. Very few lawyers consider allocative efficiency to be the sole or conclusive goal of the legal order. As regards positive analysis, it is important to distinguish between two varieties. One important stream of law-and-economics addresses the hypothesis that the legal system and its participants are strongly influenced by a concern to promote allocative efficiency (Posner 1975, 1992). Although this form of analysis has fascinated lawyers seeking a universal explanation of how law evolves, it has nevertheless been received with scepticism. The problem lies in the testing of the hypothesis: judicial decisions constitute qualitative, rather than quantitative, data and their interpretation is necessarily a subjective exercise (Veljanovski 1986). 'Positive analysis' can, however, be given its more usual meaning with models, incorporating legal rules and legal institutions as exogenous variables, being deployed to predict the impact on behaviour of variation in such rules and institutions. Whether or not the predictions are tested by empirical studies – and there is still an insufficient amount of this work being undertaken – they generate major insights for lawyers and enrich legal discourse (Ackerman 1984).

To substantiate this last proposition, it is necessary to identify the environments in which legal discourse takes place and to explore the differences between law-and-economics and traditional legal reasoning.

PRIVATE LAW. The first wave of law-and-economics literature was mainly concerned with, and had its greatest impact on, the general principles of private law, that area of law that is much dependent on judicial decision-making. No doubt law-and-economics was able to establish its own identity as a distinct branch of economic analysis in this field because judicial doctrine was a novel terrain for investigation and because some degree of legal know-how was necessary to complement economic skills (Hansmann 1983). But there were more important reasons for the receptiveness of private law scholarship to law-and-economics.

Fundamentally, judicial decision-making involves the application of a relatively stable body of established doctrine to individual cases. At the same time, it has an open texture that allows for refinement at the margins, whether by extension or retraction. The major challenge for judges (and for jurists interpreting their decisions) is to articulate the reasons for making the adjustments at the margin. To accomplish this task successfully requires both an appreciation of the goals implicit in the basic doctrine and a coherent rationalization of how the specific rules derived from the doctrine, including the marginal adjustments, implement those goals. In practice, judges are generally reluctant to specify explicitly the goals of the basic doctrine; rather, they reason by analogy, concentrating on the similarities and differences in various applications of it (Levi 1948).

In comparison with law-and-economics, this method is unhelpful in predicting the consequences of legal rulings. On the other hand, it may provide a broader input into normative analysis, since it is not constrained to evaluate all types of assets according to the same metric, that of willingness to pay (Sunstein 1993: 787–8). Of course, if, and to the extent that, the basic legal doctrine seeks to achieve allocative efficiency, then law-and-economics can facilitate the judicial task. Where, as is typically the case, decision-makers must resolve a tension between that economic goal and other goals, notably procedural justice, corrective justice and distributional justice, law-and-economics is no less important. Its introduction into legal discourse should induce decision-makers to address the goals in a more systematic way and can indicate what economic sacrifices (opportunity costs) are involved in the pursuit of non-economic goals (Calabresi 1982).

Further, because lawyers exposed to law-and-economics have to confront a different analytical framework and structure of argument, that should sharpen their awareness of characteristics of the problem that are often masked in traditional legal reasoning (Easterbrook 1984; Veljanovski 1986).

Legal doctrine is shaped by judges resolving disputes in a selection of cases, in relation normally to events that have already occurred. The *ex post* appraisal will often lead them to search for 'just' outcomes to the individual dispute, subordinating to that any concern for the *ex ante* impact of the ruling on future behaviour. In Anglo-Saxon legal systems this tendency is enhanced by the adversarial culture inherent in the judicial process. In contrast, law-and-economics adopts a predominantly *ex ante* perspective, predicting the impact of a ruling, or of some alternative to it, on aggregate social behaviour. Moreover, because the data are not limited to those that relate to the legal claim brought in the individual case, the analysis can potentially take account of a broader range of economic variables.

One of the important insights provided by the Coase Theorem (Coase 1960) was that the opportunity (or lack of it) for contracting should vitally affect how legal rights are formulated; another was that legal notions of causation may over-simplify the interaction between resource uses, thus unduly narrowing perceived policy options (Ackerman 1984). Law-and-economics thus suggests that legal disputes often arise from a multiplicity of factors, sometimes operating within a long timescale, rather than from the limited events that are highlighted in a specific legal claim.

'The forms of action we have buried, but they still rule us from their graves' (Maitland [1909] 1963: 2). Judges reach decisions, and develop rules, within an elaborate network of generally discrete legal concepts. A claim brought under the tort of negligence will evoke a different mode of reasoning than one asserting a property right or alleging a breach of contract. Law-and-economics traverses traditional legal boundaries (for example, tort being viewed as a proxy contract where there are high transaction costs), thereby rationalizing the relationships between the concepts, imparting coherence to the structure and facilitating its orderly development (Cooter 1985).

At the end of the last century, Mr Justice Holmes had already recognized the power of economics to predict the effects of law on individual behaviour (Holmes 1897: 469). The strength of much modern analysis is its focus on marginal effects. Agents acting rationally will respond to minor changes by reference to the costs and benefits to which such changes give rise, irrespective of the incidence of past costs and benefits. Since judges invariably make decisions *ex post*, they tend to have regard to the gross (and thus average) effects of their rulings and are less sensitive to marginal effects (Easterbrook 1984). A disregard of marginal effects may generate outcomes unintended by the decision-makers. If, for example, a legal doctrine is interpreted as rendering unenforceable an exemption clause in a contract, thereby increasing the potential liability costs of a supplier, the marginal effect may be for the supplier to shift the additional burden to the purchaser by other means, such as skimping on product quality.

Emphasizing these differences between economic and legal reasoning, law-and-economics scholars have applied basic behavioural models widely to most areas of private law. If the early literature was characterized by a simplification of how law operates in the real world, this paradoxically enhanced its value to many lawyers: 'the simplicity of the law and economics paradigm was one of its chief virtues; simplicity makes ideas more accessible, applications more obvious' (Ellickson 1989: 24). Some of the contributions of law-and-economics to legal discourse have, therefore, been received with little or no resistance. This has typically occurred where the analysis has provided lawyers with a systematic means of ordering legal doctrine in a way that is consistent with their intuitions: defining property rights by reference to what allocation will enable resources to be put to their most productive use, having regard in particular to the incidence of transaction costs (Demsetz 1967); and selecting appropriate legal forms of organization (discrete short-term contracts, longer-term 'relational' contracts, partnerships, corporations) according to which form can, at lowest cost, constrain opportunistic behaviour (Williamson 1985).

In some areas, the restrictive assumptions of the economic models have proved more troublesome and have led lawyers to question the reliability of the analysis. For example, the prediction that certain liability rules, or a combination of them, will generate optimal care by both injurers and victims is based on the assumption of each party's awareness not only of the precautions (and their costs) that he can take, but also of those of the other party (Schwartz 1978: 709). As a partial retort, law-and-economics authors could show that much of what passed for functional analysis in traditional legal critical writing involved assumptions about economic behaviour (e.g. monopolistic power) that were not rendered explicit and reasoning that was simply 'bad economics' (Hansmann 1983: 227).

Undoubtedly, greatest controversy has attended that branch of law-and-economics literature that displays an obsession with allocative efficiency and an insistence on reaching strong normative conclusions. And critical responses have been strengthened by the fact that the conclusions have evoked scepticism even within the ranks of mainstream welfare economics: they have been held to be sustainable only if the limitations of general equilibrium theory are ignored and the difficulties of 'second best' theory avoided (Markovits 1975).

There is perhaps discernible a new wave of law-and-economic scholarship that attempts to analyse private law principles by comparing the impact of efficiency and non-efficiency values (Hadfield 1996, reviewing Trebilcock 1993). Whether or not this approach takes root, it has to be recognized that even the more controversial dimensions of law-and-economics have their value: 'The role of law and economics as an intellectual *agent provocateur* should not be underestimated and should be seen as a strength to be nurtured' (Trebilcock 1983: 290). When lawyers are confronted with what is, for many of them, a new and unsettling perspective, it forces them to reflect on the values and assumptions of legal doctrine. This can be illustrated by a few general examples. Traditionally, the law of tort has been viewed as a body of principles to determine in what circumstances it is 'fair' for the inflicter of harm to compensate the injured party. By focusing instead on how the principles operate as incentives on risk-takers to exercise care, economic analysis sharpens awareness of how selection of an appropriate liability rule may facilitate the minimization of accident costs, precaution costs and administrative costs (Shavell 1987). Conventionally, contractual remedies have been treated as devices to secure the performance of promises or, failing that, to provide adequate compensation to promisees. The law-and-economics literature alerts decision-makers to the possibility that breach of the contract may generate welfare gains and thus counsels them to ensure that a given remedy does not deter this outcome (Ulen 1984). Historically, the development of company law has been much influenced by a concern that, with the increasing separation of management and ownership, shareholders' legal powers over the firm need to be strengthened. Exponents of law-and-economics direct attention instead to the way in which financial markets, through their evaluation of corporate performance, already exert a powerful constraint on productive inefficiency (Manne 1967).

CRIMINAL LAW AND FAMILY LAW. These areas of law (the first, largely public law; the second, a combination of private and public law) differ from others in two important respects. They have attracted economists not otherwise known for their work in law-and-economics, notably Becker, who has made pioneering theoretical contributions in both areas (Becker 1968, 1981); and economic analysis has provoked considerable hostility from mainstream legal scholars and other social scientists.

The economics of crime assumes potential offenders to be rational utility maximisers who weigh the cost of penal sanctions, as discounted by the probability of apprehension, prosecution and conviction, against the benefit to be derived from an unlawful act. The analysis of the principles of criminal liability, the type, and severity, of sanctions and the level of law enforcement ignores notions of moral responsibility and non-deterrence functions of the criminal law, both of which are regarded by lawyers as fundamental to criminal justice systems (Gibbons 1982).

The argument used by lawyers, that economic analysis is artificial because it strips the subject-matter of more fundamental values, may miss the point. There clearly is an important economic dimension to criminal behaviour. The isolation of that dimension, and its subjection to rigorous analysis, can generate insights that, provided they are not treated as conclusive determinants, are valuable for policy-making purposes. This has been recognized by those dealing with white-collar crime and regulatory offences and, to a lesser extent, those involved in the management of law-enforcement.

Likewise with family law. Viewing marriage as a long-term contract, with a high degree of transaction-specific investment and subject (unfortunately) to seriously imperfect information (Cohen 1987), or investigating the market for adopting children (Landes and Posner 1978), may appear to trivialize the emotional and societal content of human relationships (Bennett 1991). But attention to the economic parameters highlights how legal structures may seriously affect behavioural incentives, which might otherwise be neglected.

PUBLIC LAW. Economic analysis of public law was slower to emerge as an identifiable and coherent branch of law-and-economics scholarship. There might appear to be a simple explanation for this: because public law is so diverse and the range of economic theory which can be brought to bear on it so broad, it is not clear what should properly be defined as 'law-and-economics' in this area. But more important reasons can be located in the intellectual agendas of the two disciplines.

From Adam Smith to Hayek and beyond, economists have written profusely on systems of government. But the (typically) abstract level of their analysis could not easily be transplanted into the framework of discourse traditionally adopted by public lawyers. Public law scholarship was dominated by legal process theory, which assumed that government institutions acted rationally to achieve public interest goals (Duxbury 1995: ch. 4). Take, for example, the central issues of constitutional law: how powers, particularly law-making powers, are to be allocated; and what rights, particularly individual rights, are to be protected against the ordinary exercise of those powers. A paper published in 1983 suggested that, at that time, constitutional lawyers had shown 'little consideration of the efforts of economic . . . theorists to understand the driving forces behind the problems, great and small, that present themselves for constitutional adjudication' (Gellhorn and Robinson 1983: 261). This observation may seem to have done less than justice to a branch of the law-and-economics literature dealing with issues of individual rights (Posner 1981: chs 12–14). But that literature did not purport to address the central normative issues. Rather, by employing conventional models of the impact of law on market behaviour, it sought to demonstrate that the adoption of rights-based laws may be counter-productive. The tendency of fair employment laws to increase the demand for workers from disadvantaged sections of the community can, for example, be blunted if the same laws require equal pay (Landes 1968).

Economists had also always been involved in analysis of those areas of public law that deal explicitly with economic markets, notably competition law and public finance (the 'old law-and-economics'). Such work did eventually influence legal thought, although in the case of taxation it had to overcome a doctrinal obsession with concepts of fairness and a seeming indifference to questions of behavioural impact (Hansmann 1983: 221–2). As regards antitrust, lawyers had traditionally focused on the distributive goals of the legislation. A significant change occurred in the 1970s and 1980s: Chicagoan efficiency analysis began to pervade both legal scholarship and judicial reasoning – the latter development no doubt being aided by the appointment of several prominent law-and-economics scholars to the bench (Duxbury 1995: 348–64).

The 'old law-and-economics' may have made a necessary technical input into areas of public law that inherently required economic expertise. But it had little impact on the main intellectual task undertaken by public lawyers more generally: a critical evaluation of how well institutional arrangements and administrative principles and instruments serve the public interest. In the 1980s and 1990s the scene was transformed by a fresh wave of law-and-economics scholarship.

Its origins lay in the incomplete analysis of institutions in the early literature of the 'new law-and-economics'. As we have seen, that literature was largely driven by the hypothesis that legal institutions generated efficient outcomes. For this purpose a sharp distinction was drawn between legislatures and the judiciary. Pluralist, democratic decision-making was seen as incompatible with efficiency, since any prospect of economic rationality would necessarily be distorted by the self-seeking of politicians and the impact of interest-group influence. Judicial decisions, in contrast, were considered free from such pressures. What was needed was a more comprehensive and rigorous theory for explaining the behaviour of legislatures and other public agencies and working through its implications for institutional arrangements.

That need was supplied by the rapid expansion of public choice theory and its assimilation by a growing number of law-and-economics exponents. The energy and rigour with which those theorists applied their models, both positively, to explain how 'trade' between self-interested politicians, public officials and private groups produced laws generally adverse to the public interest, and normatively, to prescribe constitutional arrangements best available to control the processes, persuaded many that the economic analysis of public law could lead to major insights. And the political environment, in which governments were actively seeking to redefine the relationship between state and markets, helped to foster that conviction.

The first wave of public choice-inspired economic analysis of public law was treated with scepticism by some legal scholars (Farber and Frickey 1991), but this was not to prove decisive. Many public lawyers now found the central tenets of legal process theory to be simplistic and were searching for a broader understanding of the functioning of public institutions. The public law principles requiring officials and agencies to apply standards of transparency and administrative rationality to their decision-making had, within the traditional framework, been deemed necessary to ensure that the activity was consistent with public interest goals. The new perspective provoked both positive and negative reactions to the traditional principles. On the one hand, the vulnerability of public institutions to capture by private interests as well as to the self-interest of the decision-makers themselves, would seem to imply an enhanced need for the principles. On the other hand, the notion that legislatures function primarily to confer benefits on private interest groups has suggested to some the futility of the conventional principle of statutory interpretation, requiring courts to ascertain the public interest goal of legislators (Easterbrook 1984).

At a more general level, exposure to the economic models forced lawyers to re-examine the fundamental features of constitutional arrangements. 'We need to know who wins and who loses and by how much, when thinking about public policy. Not only is this a necessary part of strategic public management, it is crucial to a normative consideration of whether the legislation is in the public interest' (Mashaw 1989: 145). And if the predictions of public choice theory are well founded, that can lead to arguments that the power to make distributive decisions on the basis of majoritarian democratic processes should be constrained (Macey 1988).

However, the rich insights generated by the economic analysis of public law have not arisen simply from applications of public choice theory. They have also resulted from reactions to, and criticisms of, that theory. One approach starts with the public choice conception of legislation as the distribution of costs and benefits among different groups but seeks to explain it by reference to a broader set of motivations than simply the desire of politicians to maximize their prospects of reelection, or of bureaucrats to maximize their budgets or their chances of an easy life (Levine and Forrence 1990). Another recognizes that any and every resource allocation problem is, in principle if also imperfectly, capable of resolution by alternative institutional mechanisms, notably the market, private law and government action, and that the main task is to analyse comparatively the strengths and weaknesses (benefits and costs) of each such mechanism in relation to a given problem, or set of problems (Ackerman 1984; Komesar 1994).

If the latter two approaches have, to some extent at least, fed on the basic menu derived from public choice theory, a third mode of analysis, no less important, has proceeded in another direction. Even in an era of deregulation, public law continues to play a vital role in dealing with market failure and pursuing other public interest goals, including redistribution. 'Progressive law and economics', as it has been called (Rose-Ackerman 1988), employs the tools of traditional welfare economics to analyse externalities, information asymmetry and imperfect competition and to fashion appropriate public policy solutions. Its protagonists 'are similar to Chicagoans in recognizing the value of markets in promoting efficiency and the importance of economic incentives in both the private and public sectors. They are trying to get the economic incentives right, not eliminate them' (Rose-Ackerman 1988: 344). In similar vein, principal–agent theory has been used to address issues of central concern to public lawyers: the location of law-making powers; the breadth of discretion in decision-making; the accountability of public institutions; and the role of process values (Bishop 1990).

The juxtaposition of the rival models emerging from the public interest and public choice literature respectively undoubtedly renders the study of public law concepts more complex, but both types of economic analysis are vital for a proper understanding of the key normative issues (Ogus 1994). Thus, in considering the relative merits of centralized and decentralized decision-making, scholars have drawn on the 'economics of federalism' literature, which analyses how the meeting of local citizen preferences is affected by population mobility, information costs and externalities (Tiebout 1956). However, what this analysis prescribes as optimal may be distorted by models of interest group activity, which has differential impacts according to the location of decision-making (Noam 1982). Similarly, principal–agent theory may suggest an efficient breadth of administrative discretion, and cost-reducing mechanisms of accountability (Bishop 1990), but consideration has also to be given to bureaucrats' own motivations, as well as their vulnerability to capture (Aranson et al. 1983).

So too with the study of regulatory forms and institutions. Lawyers, trained within a framework of legal process ideals, had to come to terms with the 'economic theory of regulation'. The latter is an offshoot of public choice theory, postulating that much regulation, apparently designed to further public interest goals, in fact conferred rents on the regulatees, and resulted from 'trade' in the political market-place (Peltzman 1976). Indeed, the elaboration of the theory and the empirical testing of the hypotheses became a major industry, with its products filling many pages in the law-and-economics journals. Some brave efforts by legal scholars to challenge this literature (Kelman 1988) could not stem the tide, and it is reasonable to infer that it exerted not a little influence on the deregulatory policies of the 1980s and 1990s.

In its turn, the deregulation movement prompted an investigation of how regulation could be rendered more efficient, a task to which 'progressive law-and-economics' was able to make a major contribution. The key input has been an enhanced understanding of the incentive effects of different legal forms (Dewees 1983). The analysis essentially involves studying the varying incidence of information costs (to regulators and regulatees) and monitoring costs (to regulators). The general outcome has been a normative orientation towards less prescriptive regulation and harnessing interventionist measures to the incentives operating in ordinary competitive markets. This suggests, for example, a preference for financial devices (notably taxes) over 'command-and-control' standards, enforced by the criminal law (Baumol 1972); for public franchises awarded on the basis of competitive tender over the price regulation of natural monopolies (Demsetz 1968); and for mandatory information disclosure over behavioural control instruments (Colantoni et al. 1976).

LEGAL HISTORY AND COMPARATIVE LAW. Since law-and-economics purports to provide scientific explanations for the existence and character of legal rules, one would expect it also to contribute to an understanding of changes in the rules. Legal historians have increasingly looked to political, social and (macro-) economic factors, external to the law, to explain developments in the law. They have, nevertheless, largely ignored that branch of law-and-economics scholarship which explores the impact on legal evolution of specific micro-economic variables. This literature seeks to establish a systematic relationship between the demand of economic agents for cost-reduction and the supply of legal rules, or amended legal rules, to meet that demand (Clark 1981).

Analysis of the supply side has tended to focus on judge-made law, reflecting the obsession of the earlier law-and-economics studies with the judicial process and the 'efficiency of the common law' hypothesis. The engine for inducing change is assumed to be predominantly litigant behaviour: in aggregate, it is argued, disputants will tend to settle claims based on legal rules which are efficient, but challenge rules which are inefficient. Over time, therefore, efficient rules will survive and prevail over inefficient rules (Rubin 1983).

Lawyers may be justified in treating this analysis with suspicion. It over-simplifies the motives for litigation; and the criterion of 'efficiency' is problematic, since it seems to take no account of externalities or the fact that many affected by legal rules will not have the resources to challenge them (Kornhauser 1980). Nor does it deal with legislation, which remains the major instrument for legal change. As to this, it is, of course, a primary implication of public choice theory that, in contrast to common law, legislation does not evolve towards efficiency. However, its predictions are not always easy to sustain. How, for example, is the phenomenon of deregulation to be explained? It has been suggested that dwindling profits from existing regulatory forms force the industrial interest groups to push for reform (Jarrell 1984). But this does not easily stand with the fact that many of the reforms have been opposed by the industrial interests which benefited from the status quo.

Legal change can also be considered from a comparative perspective. The 'transplant' of legal doctrine from one system to another is a phenomenon much studied by comparative lawyers, but without any clear theoretical explanation of why such borrowing should occur. Law-and-economics is capable of filling this gap. Although, for reasons given in the preceding paragraphs, one should be wary of overarching theories of evolution towards efficiency, there are important reasons why legal systems should be sensitive to economic pressures. With the increasing mobility of capital and labour between different jurisdictions, there must emerge a degree of competition between legal systems to meet the preferences of firms and individuals. There is already a sizeable law-and-economics literature on whether competition between national regulatory regimes generates efficiency, or rather results in a 'race to the bottom' (Bratton et al. 1996). The analysis can clearly be extended to private law concepts. Since, presumptively, settlors can achieve their aims at lower cost with the Anglo-American legal device of a trust than with alternative property concepts available under civilian legal systems, this provides a powerful explanation of why the latter have been forced to recognize, and in some instances, adopt, the device: the '[t]rust has obtained an easy and well-deserved victory in the competition in the market of legal doctrines' (Mattei 1994: 10).

ANTHONY I. OGUS

See also CALABRESI, GUIDO; CHICAGO SCHOOL OF LAW AND ECONOMICS; COASE, RONALD; ECONOMIC APPROACH TO CRIME AND PUNISHMENT; POSNER, RICHARD A.; PROPERTY RIGHTS; PUBLIC CHOICE AND THE LAW; REGULATORY COMPETITION; STATUTORY INTERPRETATION AND RATIONAL CHOICE THEORIES; WEALTH MAXIMIZATION.

Subject classification: 4c(i).

BIBLIOGRAPHY

Ackerman, B.A. 1984. *Reconstructing American Law*. Cambridge, MA: Harvard University Press.

Aranson, P., Gellhorn, E. and Robinson, G. 1983. A theory of legislative delegation. *Cornell Law Review* 68: 1–67.

Barnett, R.E. and Coleman, J.L. (eds). 1989. Symposium on post-Chicago law and economics. *Chicago–Kent Law Review* 65: 3–194.

Baumol, W. 1972. On taxation and the control of externalities. *American Economic Review* 62: 307–22.

Becker, G.S. 1968. Crime and punishment: an economic approach. *Journal of Political Economy* 76: 169–217.

Becker, G.S. 1981. *A Treatise on the Family*. Cambridge, MA: Harvard University Press.

Bennett, B. 1991. The economics of wiving services: law and economics on the family. *Journal of Law and Society* 18: 206–18.

Bishop, W. 1990. A theory of administrative law. *Journal of Legal Studies* 19: 489–530.

Bratton, W., McCahery, J., Picciotto, S. and Scott, C. 1996. *International Regulatory Competition and Coordination: Perspectives on Economic Regulation in Europe and the United States*. Oxford: Clarendon Press.

Calabresi, G. 1970. *The Cost of Accidents: A Legal and Economic Analysis*. New Haven, CT: Yale University Press.

Calabresi, G. 1982. The new economic analysis of law: scholarship, or self-indulgence? *Proceedings of the British Academy* 68: 85–108.

Clark, R.C. 1981. The interdisciplinary study of 'legal evolution'. *Yale Law Journal* 90: 1238–74.

Coase, R.H. 1960. The problem of social cost. *Journal of Law and Economics* 3: 1–44.

Cohen, L. 1987. Marriage, divorce, and quasi-rents; or 'I gave him the best years of my life'. *Journal of Legal Studies* 16: 267–303.

Colantoni, C.S., Davis, O.A. and Swaminuthan, M. 1976. Imperfect consumers and welfare comparisons of policies concerning information and regulation. *Bell Journal of Economics* 7: 602–15.

Cooter, R. 1985. Unity in tort, contract, and property: the model of precaution. *California Law Review* 73: 1–51.
Culp, J.M. (ed.) 1987. Economists on the bench. *Law and Contemporary Problems* 50(4): 1–286.
Demsetz, H. 1967. Toward a theory of property rights. *American Economic Review Papers & Proceedings* 57: 347–59.
Demsetz, H. 1968. Why regulate utilities? *Journal of Law and Economics* 11: 55–65.
Dewees, D.N. (ed.) 1983. *The Regulation of Quality: Products, Services, Workplaces and the Environment*. Toronto: Butterworths.
Duxbury, N. 1995. *Patterns of American Jurisprudence*. Oxford: Clarendon Press.
Easterbrook, F.H. 1984. Foreword: the court and the economic system. *Harvard Law Review* 98: 4–60.
Ellickson, R.C. 1989. Bringing culture and human frailty to rational actors: a critique of classical law-and-economics. *Chicago–Kent Law Review* 65: 23–55.
Farber, D.A. and Frickey, P.P. 1991. *Law and Public Choice: A Critical Introduction*. Chicago: University of Chicago Press.
Gellhorn, E. and Robinson, G.O. 1983. The role of economic analysis in legal education. *Journal of Legal Education* 33: 247–73.
Gibbons, T. 1982. The utility of economic analysis of crime. *International Review of Law and Economics* 2: 173–91.
Hadfield, G.K. 1996. The second wave of law and economics. *University of Toronto Law Journal* 46: 181–200.
Hansmann, H. 1983. The current state of law-and-economics scholarship. *Journal of Legal Education* 33: 217–36.
Holmes, O.W. 1897. The path of the law. *Harvard Law Review* 10: 457–78.
Jarrell, G.A. 1984. Change at the exchange: causes and effects of deregulation. *Journal of Law and Economics* 27: 273–312.
Kelman, M. 1988. On democracy-bashing: a sceptical look at the theoretical and 'empirical' practice of the public choice movement. *Virginia Law Review*. 74: 199–273.
Komesar, N.K. 1994. *Imperfect Alternatives: Choosing Institutions in Law, Economics, and Public Policy*. Chicago: University of Chicago Press.
Kornhauser, L.A. 1980. A guide to the perplexed claims of efficiency in the law. *Hofstra Law Review* 8: 591–639.
Kovacic, W.E. 1992. The influence of economics on antitrust law. *Economic Inquiry* 30: 294–306.
Landes, E.M. and Posner, R.A. 1978. The economics of baby shortage. *Journal of Legal Studies* 7: 323–48.
Landes, W.M. 1968. The economics of fair employment laws. *Journal of Political Economy* 76: 507–52.
Levi, E.H. 1948. *An Introduction to Legal Reasoning*. Chicago: University of Chicago Press.
Levine, M. and Forrence, J. 1990. Regulatory capture, public interest, and the public agenda: toward a synthesis. *Journal of Law, Economics and Organization* 6 (special issue): 167–98.
Macey, J.R. 1988. Transaction costs and the normative elements of the public choice model: an application to constitutional theory. *Virginia Law Review* 74: 471–518.
Maitland, F.W. 1909. *The Forms of Action at Common Law*. Ed. A.H. Chaytor and W.J. Whittaker. Cambridge: Cambridge University Press 1963.
Manne, H.G. 1967. Our two corporate systems: law and economics. *Virginia Law Review* 53: 259–84.
Markovits, R. 1975. A basic structure for microeconomic policy analysis in our worse-than-second-best world: a proposal and related critique of the Chicago approach to the study of law and economics. *Wisconsin Law Review* 1975: 1950–2080.
Mashaw, J.L. 1989. The economics of politics and the understanding of public law. *Chicago–Kent Law Review* 65: 123–60.
Mattei, U. 1994. Efficiency in legal transplants: an essay in comparative law and economics. *International Review of Law and Economics* 14: 3–19.
Noam, E. 1982. The choice of governmental level in regulation. *Kyklos* 35: 278–91.
Ogus, A. 1994. *Regulation: Legal Form and Economic Theory*. Oxford: Clarendon Press.
Peltzman, S. 1976. Towards a more general theory of regulation. *Journal of Law and Economics* 19: 211–40.
Posner, R.A. 1973. *Economic Analysis of Law*. Boston: Little, Brown; 4th edn, 1992.
Posner, R.A. 1975. The economic approach to law. *Texas Law Review* 53: 757–82.
Posner, R.A. 1981. *The Economics of Justice*. Cambridge, MA: Harvard University Press.
Rose-Ackerman, S. 1988. Progressive law and economics – and the new administrative law. *Yale Law Journal* 98: 341–68.
Rubin, E.L. 1996. The new legal process, the synthesis of discourse, and the microanalysis of institutions. *Harvard Law Review* 109: 1393–1439.
Rubin, P.K. 1983. *Business Firms and the Common Law: The Evolution of Efficient Rules*. New York: Praeger.
Schwartz, G.T. 1978. Contributory and comparative negligence: a reappraisal. *Yale Law Journal* 87: 697–727.
Shavell, S. 1987. *Economic Analysis of Accident Law*. Cambridge, MA: Harvard University Press.
Sunstein, C. 1993. On analogical reasoning. *Harvard Law Review* 106: 741–91.
Tiebout, C.M. 1956. A pure theory of local government expenditure. *Journal of Political Economy* 64: 416–24.
Trebilcock, M.J. 1983. The prospects of 'law and economics': a Canadian perspective. *Journal of Legal Education* 33: 288–93.
Trebilcock, M.J. 1993. *The Limits of Freedom of Contract*. Cambridge, MA: Harvard University Press.
Ulen, T.S. 1984. The efficiency of specific performance: toward a unified theory of contract remedies. *Michigan Law Review* 83: 341–403.
Van den Bergh, R. 1992. Law and economics in Europe: present state and future prospects. In *Bibliography of Law and Economics*, ed. B. Bouckaert and G. de Geest, Dordrecht: Kluwer.
Veljanovski, C. 1986. Legal theory, economic analysis and the law of torts. *In Legal Theory and Common Law*, ed. W. Twining, Oxford: Blackwell.
Williamson, O.E. 1985. *The Economic Institutions of Capitalism: Firms, Markets, Relational Contracting*. New York: Free Press.

law-and-economics in action. Law-and-economics is based on legal and economic concepts which have a long history in the writings of lawyers, judges, economists and politicians. Nonetheless, the birth of law-and-economics and its most notable practical accomplishments can be reasonably traced back to the University of Chicago Law School in the period from approximately 1940 to 1960. From a quite early stage, law-and-economics has been nourished by the coincidental rapid development of financial economics, with its strong emphasis on efficient capital markets, in schools of business and traditional economics departments. In the US, law-and-economics' outlook on some key subjects, such as the market for corporate control, generally has been indistinguishable from mainstream financial economics.

Law-and-economics has been highly influential in two quite separate ways. In its prosaic non-doctrinal form – more economics in law and more law in economics – it is a resounding practical success around the world. There is much more economics in law schools, more lawyers and judges are familiar with economics and more economists are concentrating on law-related work.

Since 1960, most large law schools in the US have adopted economics programmes. Many traditional law school courses such as contracts, torts, agency, and corporations are taught from an economics point of view. The same is true with variations in many other parts of the world. As a result, law school graduates are much more familiar with basic economic concepts, particularly price theory and financial economics, than they were in the past. Trial lawyers in the US expertly comb the literature of economics for ideas to buttress theories of liability and defense. It is a common practice in US litigation for lawyers to make extensive, quite sophisticated uses of economists as advisors and expert witnesses. On the other hand, law-and-economics has had little effect on the day-to-day practice techniques of office lawyers. Here the big influences have been a sharp increase in competition among lawyers and innovations in office equipment, such as machines for word processing, copying and computer research.

Academic economists are increasingly studying and publishing articles and books on legal issues. The *Journal of Law and Economics*, published at the University of Chicago since 1958, and the *Journal of Law, Economics, and Organization*, published at Yale University since 1985, are but two of the numerous journals devoted to the relationship between law and economics. And most traditional law reviews and economics journals now regularly publish articles on law-and-economics subjects. The US judiciary and administrative and enforcement agencies also show the influence of law-and-economics. For example, three of law-and-economics' most prolific and ingenious exponents, Richard Posner, Frank Easterbrook and Guido Calabresi, are federal courts of appeal judges. And on the US Supreme Court, Justices Stephen Breyer and Antonin Scalia have more than a passing familiarity with economics and law-and-economics doctrine.

In its doctrinal form, law-and-economics espouses a free-market economic analysis of the law which is highly flavoured by an efficient capital markets viewpoint. Here, there have been practical successes and failures as well as mixed outcomes. Recent changes in US antitrust enforcement policy and the auctioning of radio spectrum are examples of successes of law-and-economics. Law-and-economics has made many contributions in the debate over takeover defence although it failed in its opposition to the auctioning of takeover targets. The outstanding example of the failure of a key law-and-economics doctrine to influence change is the worldwide endorsement of legal prohibitions on insider trading despite strong criticism from some central law-and-economics figures.

With a big push from law-and-economics, US antitrust enforcement has adopted some free-market principles after a twisty legalistic passage through most of the twentieth century. Law-and-economics writers such as Robert Bork (1967, 1978), a 1953 graduate of the University of Chicago Law School, have urged that the main purpose of antitrust law should be to maximize consumer welfare. Large-scale business or combinations of businesses, Bork argued, should not in itself be viewed as bad. It is results that should matter. US antitrust enforcement agencies and courts now place much more emphasis on the likely effects of antitrust enforcement on consumers rather than on strict adherence to complex legalistic rules. The most important practical result has been an easing of restrictions on business combinations. Mergers of huge companies in the same industry, which would have been inconceivable twenty-five years ago, are common now without disabling interference by antitrust enforcement agencies. At the same time, in a political tit-for-tat, there is much more and much tougher enforcement against price fixing and other producer conspiracies because they are considered to be harmful to consumers and are otherwise without redeeming merit. The acceptance of this approach to antitrust enforcement has important causes unrelated to law-and-economics, such as product innovation, increases in competition and the expansion of international markets. Nonetheless, these changes in antitrust enforcement policies must be regarded as a major practical achievement of law-and-economics.

Auctioning of radio spectrum by the US government is another important practical although incomplete success of law-and-economics. The idea of using market pricing principles to allocate radio spectrum was explained and advocated by Leo Herzel in 1951 while a student at the University of Chicago Law School, and in 1959 by Ronald Coase, an economist educated at the London School of Economics who subsequently joined the University of Chicago Law School faculty and became the editor of its *Journal of Law and Economics*. Coase was awarded the Nobel prize in economics in 1991 in part for his article on the radio spectrum.

Before 1927, radio spectrum was allocated in the US on a first-come, first-served basis. In 1927, Congress changed the law and until 1981 rights to radio spectrum were allocated by the Federal Communications Commission (FCC) in administrative proceedings using a public interest standard. In 1981, Congress adopted a lottery procedure for the allocation of a part of radio spectrum. This had the salutary effect of depoliticizing the allocation of this part of radio spectrum, but lotteries conferred windfall gains on the lucky winners. Much more important politically, lotteries lost the United States revenue – $46 to $80 billion from cellular licences according to a 1990 Department of Commerce estimate.

In 1993, Congress authorized the FCC to allocate some radio spectrum rights through an auction procedure which has garnered billions of dollars of revenue for the US government. Auctions of radio spectrum cannot, however, be viewed as a complete success for law-and-economics. Herzel and Coase had suggested auctions as a means to an end: a free market in radio spectrum. This has not been fully achieved. The property rights that are being auctioned are incomplete because the same old restrictions on technology and use remain (DeVany 1997). Moreover, auctions have not been extended to television or radio broadcasting in the US for which FCC licences are still allocated by the FCC according to a public interest standard. Several other countries have begun to use auctions in allocating radio spectrum, some of them more extensively than the US (Crandall 1997).

Law-and-economics has strongly supported the takeover market and opposed takeover defences and auctions of takeover targets. While there have been a few dissident law-and-economics voices who have defended auctions of takeover targets. (Herzel, Schmidt and Davis 1979; Bebchuk 1982), it is fair to say that these views are not mainstream law-and-economics.

The pioneer law-and-economics theorist and proponent of the market for corporate control is Henry Manne, a 1952 graduate of the University of Chicago Law School. In 1965, Manne argued in a classic article that there is a close association between a company's managerial efficiency and the market price of its shares and that this correlation provides the economic incentives on which the market for corporate control is based. Managements which exploit or neglect their shareholders, Manne said, depress their stock prices, which leads to takeovers by managers who are more responsive to shareholders. In the same vein, Manne argued that the market for corporate control provides a solution to the corporate governance conundrum posed by Berle and Means (1933) in their important book on the separation of share ownership and management control. Like Bork, Manne argued that antitrust concerns over market control are usually misguided.

Manne's 1965 article set the groundwork for Frank Easterbrook and Dan Fischel, also graduates in 1973 and 1977 respectively (and teachers) at the University of Chicago Law School. They wrote several influential articles in the early 1980s extolling the takeover market and sharply criticizing takeover defence and takeover auctions. They included in their criticism of takeover defence anything which interfered with the takeover process, as, for example, the delays in the closing of tender offers, and the disclosures, mandated by the federal securities laws, which facilitate auctions. Easterbrook and Fischel, like Bork, had a talent for advocacy and sharp, unacademic ears for the telling phrase, which helped their articles to be widely read and cited.

Following Manne, Easterbrook and Fischel based their arguments on efficient capital markets theories and the corollary belief that a company's stock price is the best estimate of its value. Tender offer premiums, they urged, are accurate indicators that target assets can be utilized more effectively to provide higher returns to bidders. To support their arguments, Easterbrook and Fischel relied heavily on the rapidly growing literature of financial economics. It was not until several years later that the disinterested accuracy of bidders' judgments in these matters began to be questioned in the literature of financial economics (Jensen 1989).

Easterbrook and Fischel, again following Manne, urged that in order to encourage changes in the control of companies, controlling shareholders should be entitled to keep any special control premiums they receive, so long as other shareholders are not made worse off than they were before the transaction. In practice in the US today, there are occasions when controlling shareholders are paid a premium while other shareholders are excluded from the transaction. Such transactions are generally viewed as legal unless there are special facts. On the other hand, it is generally considered legally risky and unfair for controlling shareholders to be paid higher prices than other shareholders are paid in the same or related transactions. The law and practice on this subject have not really changed much since Manne and Easterbrook and Fischel wrote.

Most remarkably, Easterbrook and Fischel entirely rejected the promotion of takeover auctions by boards of directors of target companies, and urged instead a requirement of complete passivity for target boards of directors who are faced with tender offers. Even in the UK, where there is a takeover market and a strong policy against takeover defence, target director passivity has never been required and auctions are common.

Easterbrook and Fischel offered two main arguments in support of target director passivity: boards of directors of targets have insurmountable conflicts of interest; and shareholder wealth in the aggregate would be maximized by director passivity, not by auctions. Higher takeover prices, they said, create a chilling effect on the takeover market and are bad for shareholders generally. They disposed of the argument that target boards have a legal obligation to their shareholders to bargain for the highest possible price by asserting that auctions, like pollution, have detrimental side-effects and harm shareholders generally.

Although the Easterbrook and Fischel articles are cited widely, and usually approvingly, neither Congress nor state legislatures adopted their policy recommendations against takeovers. However, their arguments against takeover defence did influence courts in the US to be more sceptical of arguments justifying such defences.

Federal legislation in the US has not been affected much by law-and-economics' opposition to auctions of takeover targets. The key federal statute which governs tender offer procedure in the US, the 1968 Williams Act amendments to the Securities Exchange Act of 1934, remains safely intact. The main economic effect of the Williams Act is that it greatly increases the likelihood of well-informed auctions. It encourages competing bids by mandating delays and disclosures during the tender offer process and by imposing detailed disclosure requirements on anyone who accumulates more than five percent of a public company's shares. Securities Exchange Commission (SEC) rules under the Williams Act require tender offers to remain open for at least 20 business days and if there is a material change in the tender offer terms, the tender offer must be kept open for ten business days after the change is announced. In practice, these delays and disclosures usually provide enough time and information for potential competing bidders and their advisers to carefully evaluate bids and to prepare their own competing bids. There appears to be no politically significant investor, business or public-interest constituency in the US in favour of making fundamental changes in the Williams Act.

In state legislatures, law-and-economics' opposition to both takeover defence and auctions fared badly. During the 1980s, the states raced one another to enact more extreme anti-takeover legislation. Even the most moderate of these statutes, such as Delaware's, are designed to increase the bargaining power of target boards and shareholders to exact higher prices from bidders.

For a while, the courts did appear to be paying close attention to law-and-economics' opposition to state anti-takeover statutes. For example, in *Edgar* 1982, the US Supreme Court held an early Illinois anti-takeover statute unconstitutional with some kind words for Easterbrook's and Fischel's 1981 *Harvard Law Review* article. However, subsequently in *CTS* 1987, the Court held a complicated

Indiana anti-takeover statute constitutional. Since then, lawyers have had little difficulty in drafting a large variety of tough state anti-takeover statutes that are constitutional. In theory some of these statutes could stop takeovers completely; in fact they have not. Target boards bend to market pressures.

In the 1980s, state and federal courts also began permitting many quite extraordinary non-statutory takeover defences. Shareholder approval is not required for some of these defences, such as poison pills. Takeover bidders relied heavily on law-and-economics' insights, and the testimony of its experts, in fighting these takeover defences in the courts. Generally, the courts listened to the arguments of law-and-economics that target boards should not have the right to 'just say no' to high premium tender offers, although there are occasional exceptions (*Moore* 1995) which provide material for law-and-economics handwringing. On the other hand, courts, disregarding law-and-economics, usually allow target boards of directors plenty of time to hold auctions under the protection of statutory and non-statutory takeover defences; and courts are not reluctant to push unwilling target boards into auctions (*Paramount* 1994).

Law-and-economics has had little direct influence on corporate governance. Since Henry Manne, law-and-economics generally has concentrated on the market for corporate control as the primary solution to corporate governance problems. In the late 1980s and early 1990s, it became apparent that the takeover market does not solve all corporate governance problems. Bidders were overpaying for acquisitions probably due to the same kinds of blunders and conflicts of interest for which target managements had been blamed (Jensen 1989). Leveraged buyout (LBO) transactions, which had been highly admired in the law-and-economics literature because of their emphasis on combining equity ownership and management control, also began to show fissures. There were the same problems in different forms: overpayment for acquisitions and conflicts of interest (Jensen 1991). Moreover, the German and Japanese economic systems appeared to be performing very well with no takeover bids. As a result, prominent law-and-economics scholars began studying the corporate governance systems in Japan and Germany (Roe 1993; Kaplan 1994). They also began to re-examine corporate governance in the American past (Jensen 1991, 1993; Roe 1994). Some of them looked longingly at the superior economic performance of the US early in this century, when merchant bankers with large equity interests served on boards of directors of corporations, and they saw cause and effect (Jensen 1991, 1993). Most recently, law-and-economics scholars have been using evolutionary theory to explain the development of corporate governance institutions in the US and elsewhere (Gilson 1996; Roe 1996). This new research is interesting, often ingenious, but unlike Henry Manne's model of the market for corporate control, it does not lead readily to simple, convincing policy recommendations.

As a result, institutional investors and conventional lawyers and economists using orthodox legal and corporate governance concepts have been dominating the revision of corporate governance in the US. Organizations such as the National Association of Corporate Directors and the Investor Responsibility Research Center are successfully putting pressure on public companies for more independent directors, independent board chairmen, and committees of independent directors to control crucial board functions such as the nomination and evaluation of directors, audit and compensation. Independent directors are also taking control of target responses to takeover bids and other kinds of corporate crises. Similar moves to increase the importance of independent directors are taking place in other parts of the world, although more slowly.

Surprisingly, these conventional approaches to corporate governance appear to be helping to resolve some of the main takeover defence problems that have concerned law-and-economics, although not always in accordance with its prescriptions. For example, special committees of independent directors, advised by independent investment bankers and independent lawyers, usually have little taste for hard-line 'just say no' defences to high-premium takeover bids. On the other hand, independent directors generally have no interest in selling out quickly and cheaply to the first bidder. As a result of these conventional corporate governance reforms, takeover auctions are being institutionalized in the US and hard-line takeover defence generally is becoming little more than skilful bargaining for higher prices. It is fair to say this is only a change in degree from past practice.

Manne (1966) established the framework for the law-and-economics arguments justifying insider trading. He argued that insider trading causes no important harm; the only losers are traders who would have traded anyway. On the other hand, he said, investors in general benefit from insider trading by more accurate stock prices; insider trading opportunities give managers incentives to perform better; insider trading rules are easily avoided; and policing insider trading is costly. Carlton and Fischel (1983) refined the incentives argument by urging that insider trading could be used as an efficient form of management compensation. They argued that before there were legal rules against insider trading, corporations never prohibited insider trading in their own securities because they recognized that insider trading serves a useful purpose. Haddock and Macey (1987), using 'a private interest model of government behavior', attempted to provide a new negative explanation of insider trading regulation. They identified stock-market professionals as the private interest group that is responsible for the regulations prohibiting insider trading because, they said, stock market professionals want to eliminate competition from corporate insiders who have better information.

Whether or not it was willed by market professionals, insider trading by corporate insiders has almost disappeared in the US. Enforcement of insider trading laws against them is easy due to SEC reporting rules, and there are very strong financial and political incentives which encourage civil and criminal enforcement of insider trading laws. On the other hand, insider trading appears to be flourishing among market professionals where violations are very difficult to detect although the incentives for enforcement are at least equally as strong. There appears to be some evidence that market professionals are using insider trading rules as a weapon against competitors, such as Drexel Burnham, who are too aggressive (Fischel 1995).

This would not be the first time ethical codes have been used to restrict competition.

Insider trading laws and enforcement are becoming more stringent in the US and are spreading rapidly to other jurisdictions which have important financial markets, such as EU countries and Japan. Probably the most important reason for the failure of the opposition of law-and-economics to insider trading regulation is that investors who use financial markets value openness. In particular, they fear special privileges for corporate insiders and market professionals. The rapid growth of international financial markets has accentuated this concern because foreigners are afraid that they are at a special disadvantage to local insiders and market professionals when they invest abroad. As a result, international competition for financial business encourages the spread of insider trading restrictions and other legal rules which require openness. A 1988 US House Report is an example of this viewpoint, stating that efforts to curb insider trading are crucial to the capital formation process which 'depends on investor confidence in the fairness and integrity of our financial markets'.

Another reason for the failure of law-and-economics to discourage insider trading regulation is that some of its main arguments are not convincing. For example, it is difficult to take seriously the use of insider information as a form of compensation for corporate executives. The problem of assuring a reasonable correspondence between access to insider information and the proper amount of compensation appears to be insoluble; and there are so many simpler, better ways to accomplish the same result.

Law-and-economics achieved failure through success when the US Supreme Court adopted a fraud-on-the-market theory of causation of injury (*Basic* 1988). The Court cited law-and-economics proponents in support of its assertion that the market price of shares traded on well-developed markets reflects all publicly available information and held that a plaintiff claiming securities fraud need not show reliance on the defendant's false statement or omission. Rather, the Court said, the plaintiff need only show that the market relied on the false information, and that this could be proved through an unnatural drop or an unnatural rise in the stock's price. If the plaintiff traded the stock during the period in which the stock price was affected, there was no need to show causation separately and a court could infer damages. The fraud-on-the-market theory opened the way for more class action litigation. Anybody who traded a company's stock during the affected period could be a plaintiff. Damages in theory could be enormous. The Private Securities Litigation Reform Act of 1995 attempts to limit some of the more egregious claims.

Law-and-economics has had surprisingly little bearing on the major controversies over accounting policies as, for example, whether pooling of interests accounting should be replaced entirely by purchase accounting and how executive stock options should be accounted for. The main influences here have been the accounting profession itself, the SEC, and business and public interest pressure groups. Maybe this is because there is nothing useful for law-and-economics to say about accounting policies; maybe law-and-economics just has an uneasy relationship to disclosure. In any event, when there is adequate disclosure of the facts, differences about accounting policies may involve mainly arithmetical transformations and pressure group rhetoric.

A discussion of the influence of law-and-economics would be incomplete without mentioning Blum's and Kalven's *Uneasy Case for Progressive Taxation* (1953). Blum and Kalven were key members of the University of Chicago Law School faculty for many years. They were close to but not quite part of law-and-economics – probably too independent to join any party. Their scholarly, sceptical analysis of the shaky theoretical foundations of progressive income taxation may have contributed intellectual self-confidence to the bold move by the Reagan Administration in 1986 to sharply reduce income tax progression. But since then progression has bounced back to some extent in the US and the practical prospect for dislodging it entirely appears negligible in the US and Europe.

Why, circa 1940–1960, did ideas from around the world – Edinburgh, London, Cambridge, Vienna, among many other places – combine in the sombre city on Lake Michigan to become law-and-economics? Probably, World War II has an important relationship to the explanation, but it is better not to be drawn into speculation here on this fascinating subject. It would be highly useful to have some day the results of an old-fashioned sociology-of-knowledge inquiry into the psychological and social origins of this remarkable development.

LEO HERZEL AND ADDISON D. BRAENDEL

See also AGENCY COSTS AND CORPORATE GOVERNANCE; ANTITRUST POLICY; AUCTIONS AND TAKEOVERS; BOARDS OF DIRECTORS; CHICAGO SCHOOL OF LAW AND ECONOMICS; COASE, RONALD; COMPARATIVE CORPORATE GOVERNANCE; INSIDER TRADING; LAWYERS AS TRANSACTION COST ENGINEERS; MARKET FOR CORPORATE CONTROL; PROPERTY RIGHTS IN THE ELECTROMAGNETIC SPECTRUM; TENDER OFFERS.

Subject classification: 4c(i); 5a(iii); 5g(iii).

STATUTES

Private Securities Litigation Reform Act of 1995. USC 15: §78u–4.

Williams Act. USC 15: §§78g, 78l – 78n, 78s.

CASES

Basic Inc. v. Levinson, 485 US 224 (1988).

CTS Corporation v. Dynamics Corporation of America, 481 US 69 (1987).

Edgar v. MITE Corporation, 457 US 624 (1982).

Moore Corp. Ltd v. Wallace Computer Services, Inc., 907 F Supp 1545 (Del. 1995).

Paramount Communications Inc. v. QVC Network, Inc., 637 A2d 34 (1994).

BIBLIOGRAPHY

Bebchuk, L.A. 1982. The case for facilitating competing tender offers. *Harvard Law Review* 95: 1028–56.

Berle, A. and Means, G. 1933. *The Modern Corporation and Private Property*. New York: Macmillan.

Blum, W.J. and Kalven, Jr., H. 1953. *The Uneasy Case for Progressive Taxation*. Chicago: University of Chicago Press.

Bork, R.H. 1967. Antitrust and monopoly: the goals of antitrust policy. *American Economic Review Papers and Proceedings* 57: 242–53.

Bork, R.H. 1978. *The Antitrust Paradox: A Policy at War with Itself*. New York: Basic Books.

Carlton, D.W. and Fischel, D.R. 1983. The regulation of insider trading. *Stanford Law Review* 35: 857–95.

Coase, R.H. 1959. The Federal Communications Commission. *Journal of Law and Economics* II: 1–40.

Crandall, R. 1997. New Zealand spectrum policy: a model for the United States? *Journal of Law and Economics*, forthcoming.

DeVany, A. 1997. Implementing a market-based spectrum policy. *Journal of Law and Economics*, forthcoming.

Easterbrook, F.H. and Fischel, D.R. 1981. The proper role of a target's management in responding to a tender offer. *Harvard Law Review* 94: 1161–1204.

Easterbrook, F.H. and Fischel, D.R. 1982a. Corporate control transactions. *Yale Law Journal* 91: 698–737.

Easterbrook, F.H. and Fischel, D.R. 1982b. Auctions and sunk costs in tender offers. *Stanford Law Review* 35: 1–50.

Fischel, D.R. 1995. *Payback: The Conspiracy to Destroy Michael Milken and His Financial Revolution*. New York: Harper Business.

Gilson, R.J. 1996. Corporate governance and economic efficiency: when do institutions matter? *Washington University Law Quarterly* 74: 327–45.

Haddock, D.H. and Macey, J.R. 1987. Regulation on demand: a private interest model with an application to insider trading regulation. *Journal of Law and Economics* 30: 311–52.

Herzel, L. 1951. Public interest and the market in color television regulation. *University of Chicago Law Review* 18: 802–16.

Herzel, L., Schmidt, J. and Davis, S. 1979. Why corporate directors have a right to resist tender offers. *Chicago Bar Record* 61: 152–62.

Jensen, M.C. 1989. Eclipse of the public corporation. *Harvard Business Review* 5: 61–74.

Jensen, M.C. 1991. Corporate control and the politics of finance. *Journal of Applied Corporate Finance* 4: 13–33.

Jensen, M.C. 1993. The modern industrial revolution, exit, and the failure of internal control systems. *Journal of Finance* 48: 831–80.

Kaplan, S.N. 1994. Top executives, turnover, and firm performance in Germany. *Journal of Law, Economics, and Organization* 10: 142–59.

Manne, H. 1965. Mergers and the market for corporate control. *Journal of Political Economy* 73: 110–20.

Manne, H. 1966. *Insider Trading and the Stock Market*. New York: Free Press.

Roe, M. 1993. Some differences in corporate structure in Germany, Japan, and the United States. *Yale Law Journal* 102: 1927–2003.

Roe, M. 1994. *Strong Managers, Weak Owners: The Political Roots of American Corporate Finance*. Princeton: Princeton University Press.

Roe, M. 1996. Chaos and evolution in law and economics. *Harvard Law Review* 109: 641–68.

United States House Report Number 100–910 (House Energy and Commerce Committee). 1988.

law firms. The organization of law firms is part of a more general theory of the efficiency of the organization of firms. In the market for more complex services such as law, medicine and accounting, there are a number of critical issues surrounding ownership rules. Are sole proprietorships or partnerships more efficient in the delivery of these services to clients? How do small and large demanders organize their efforts to obtain the best deals in the marketplace? How does competition discipline suppliers to serve these uninformed consumers? In our view, agency considerations are central to these issues: specifically, the creation of brand-name capital is key to addressing these questions. Monitoring is also critical.

The North American legal service industry provides an interesting institutional framework in which to examine the above questions. In particular, consider four sets of facts concerning the organization of law firms which need to be explained.

(1) Lawyers practise law both as solo practitioners and as members of partnerships of varying sizes. For example, in the US, as a percentage of all lawyers in private practice, the number of lawyers practising solo is substantial but has been declining. In 1960, the percentage solo was 64; the corresponding figure for 1970 was 52 and for 1980 was 49 (see Curran 1985). Internal Revenue Service data also corroborates the decline in solo practice in the US. Between 1950 and 1987, the number of solo practitioners filling returns increased 86 percent from 122,000 to 227,000, whereas the number of partnership returns increased by 145 percent from 58,000 to 142,000 (see Rosen 1992).

(2) Some law firms use a sharing rule known as a lock-step system, whereby a lawyer's share is determined according to the lawyer's vintage in the partnership, independent of measures of individual lawyer productivity. (For a discussion of these systems see Ronald Gilson and Robert Mnookin 1985 and Mark Stevens 1987.) Some observers (see Marc Galanter and Thomas Palay 1991) claim that if the lock-step system was ever the norm, it was not the prevailing practice in the US by the 1960s. Other rules reward lawyers according to their billings, amended by some judgement of the lawyer's contributions to the firm through *pro bono* work such as lecturing at law faculties or promotion of the firm's reputation by committee duty for the local law society or the general promotion of business for the partnership.

(3) There is a claim that in-house counsel are becoming increasingly important for many large corporations. In-house lawyers have increased in numbers and a growing proportion of a firm's legal business is now handled internally – vertical integration for much of the business formerly contracted to outside law firms. The one exception has been litigation, where outside counsel still predominate. Corporate clients have shown an increased willingness to shop for outside legal advice in contrast to the historical rule of using a single outside firm for all legal matters. Corporate clients may break up their work across several law firms, using one for their corporate business and another for antitrust matters for example. Not surprisingly with changes in information storage and retrieval through computers, large clients demand detail on the invoices submitted by law firms, and reveal an increased willingness to bargain over these details and to monitor more assiduously the specific actions taken by outside counsel in litigation and other matters (see Freund 1985). In short, as the cost of information has fallen, clients demand better and more frequent control over case matters, hoping to avoid costly litigation and to settle matters outside the court room.

(4) Recently, there has been the emergence of 'boutique' or specialized law firms, many of which specialize in litigation. There are other features of the modern market for legal services such as the growth in demand that we will not discuss here. Sherwin Rosen (1992) reports that in the US legal market, legal services accounted for 0.6% of GDP in 1960 and increased to 1.39% in 1987. Rosen discusses this growth and other related issues.

One feature common to the markets for complex services is an inherent asymmetry of knowledge about the product: professionals supplying the good are knowledgeable; consumers demanding the good are uninformed. Consumers, however, are aware of their disadvantage. They seek assurance from the market in the form of commitments for honest delivery of services. A competitive market brings the required discipline to guarantee the efficient provision of these services to consumers.

A simple model offers an explanation of the above organizational features. (A more formal elaboration of this model is set out in Carr and Mathewson 1990.) Consider the following. Absent shirking by the lawyer, a client's case yields a known payoff (Y). If, however, the lawyer shirks and is not detected, this payoff is reduced by some known amount (L). The probability that shirking by the lawyer remains undetected by the client is given by $0 \leq \Theta \leq 1$. In the extreme, detected shirking is non-contentious so that a law suit for damages would be invariably successful; punitive damages beyond L, however, are ruled out in our model. This means that if the lawyer shirks, the expected pay-off to the client is given by $Y - \Theta L$.

Legal cases can vary according to both Θ and L. For example, complex cases involving esoteric legal precedents can be represented by high values of Θ: uninformed consumers who know little of the law may face a low likelihood of detecting shirking by the legal specialist. A straightforward case such as a minor traffic offence, a notarization or a standard agreement to purchase can hold little potential damage for a client (i.e., it has a small L). Frequently, in such cases, legal matters are sufficiently simple that the client either does not retain counsel or seeks the services of only a paralegal. These cases are defined by a loss $L^0 = 0$ and labelled as 'simple' cases. In other cases, the damage from shirking by the lawyer is strictly positive. For our purposes, it is useful to define two other higher degrees of damage, L^2 ('high' potential damage) $> L^1$ ('moderate' potential damage) > 0, where the role for this damage potential will become clear subsequently.

Moral hazard plays a role only for cases with strictly positive potential damage. In such cases, when legal specialists know that their clients have incomplete information, lawyers may reduce their inputs without being detected by the client. In particular, imagine that a lawyer faces a simple discrete choice. If the lawyer does not shirk, his input is fixed (at 1 by assumption); if the lawyer does shirk, his input is reduced to $1 - K$, where K is sold on an exterior market (has an alternative value). Suppose further that the conserved resource input of the lawyer is proportional to the loss facing the client so that $K \equiv kL$. Then, L is a scale variable defining the magnitude of both the potential loss to the client and the potential gain to the lawyer if legal inputs are reduced.

For illustrative purposes, assume a one-shot transaction between the lawyer and the client. Reputational effects are present when lawyers signal their expertise through investment in legal training and law firms signal their commitment not to shirk through their investment in brand-name capital. This brand-name capital is a sunk investment. (This is identical to the role of brand-name capital as a sunk investment associated with product quality in the model of Klein and Leffler 1981.) Examples of an investment in brand-name capital include advertising, both formal and word-of-mouth, the expenses associated with the solicitation of new clients, the accumulation of satisfied clients, the firm's fulfilment of its commitments including the punishment of shirkers, *pro bono* work, 'in-house' non-billable work done by lawyers to position the firm to solicit legal business in specific areas of law, underbilling on precedent-setting cases and the difference between the stipends paid to members of the firm for teaching in law schools relative to their billing rate.

The *ex ante* sale of cases by clients to lawyers will not cure the problem. If permitted, such a sale would resolve the moral hazard dilemma for clients by making lawyers residual income recipients. Lawyers, however, would be exposed to a potential client hold-up. A client paid Y for the case prior to trial could refuse to cooperate with the lawyer. For example, by failing to testify after the receipt of Y, the client could lower the expected value of the case. This means that there is a double moral hazard problem which prevents a resolution by assigning the residual return to the agent with the superior information.

SOLO PRACTITIONER. For sole proprietorship, holding constant the level of potential gain to a lawyer from shirking, our simple framework yields the following interpretation. A competitive case assignment is that with low probabilities of successful shirking, brand-name capital is unimportant and a non-specialized lawyer, or even a paralegal, gets the case as the lower-cost provider of the basic service. As the probability of successful shirking rises, the case is assigned to a specialized lawyer with sunk brand-name capital. As the likelihood of successful shirking rises even further, enforcing due care by the lawyer through a premium payment could become uneconomic.

PARTNERSHIP. How are these results altered by the possibility of partnership agreements? A partnership facilitates the assembly of wealth for investment in brand-name capital if required. Professional lawyers in a partnership monitor their fellow legal specialists even though their specialties are not perfect substitutes. The lower the degree of substitutability across legal specializations, the higher is the cost of internal monitoring. Monitoring takes place because members of a team know that any fraudulent behaviour by their partners places both joint and specific capital investment at risk. A partner who monitors may even know before the payout is received by the client whether the lawyer on the case is shirking. A monitor that detects *ex ante* shirking by the partner could find it profitable to take remedial action. In general, lower costs from both monitoring and remedial action push partnerships towards organizations of similar legal specialists. Team production where clients require diversified groups of legal talent, however, pushes in the opposite direction. Which force dominates is uncertain.

Partnerships dominate solo practices when partnerships signal to clients that the ability of partners to monitor each other works to the client's advantage: uninformed clients will get their 'money's worth' because lawyers in a partnership can impose punishment on shirkers. The added cost to the client of a partnership is the cost of the monitor. In the partnership agreement, the incentives for the lawyer not to shirk must be maintained. It is well known that lawyers in a partnership have an incentive to reduce effort if they must now share their revenues with others. Any tendency in this direction must be more than offset by the enhanced expected sanctions that monitors can levy on lawyers detected of shirking. Furthermore, the expected sanctions must be credible in the sense that the monitor must have an incentive to execute the sanctions should monitoring reveal that the lawyer shirked. In general, a partnership creates a liability externality among the partners of the firm that under some conditions can compensate the client for any informational disadvantage. In other words, the clients are on balance better off if the partnership delivers honest behaviour at a lower price.

This framework permits insight into the decline in the incidence of solo practitioners. Wealthier societies are characterized by legal matters which are more complex (higher L's) and because of this increased complexity the likelihood of detecting shirking is lower (larger Θ's). Galanter and Palay (1991, ch. 4) discuss the transformation in the demand for legal services. They note that 'the amount of law has increased . . . (and) the amount of regulation has multiplied.' They also remark on the view that 'the business world of today is more complex than the business world of a generation ago: there are more players, more products, more intense competition, . . . and more uncertainty about the rewards of risk.' With these forces at work, a competitive legal market would thus yield an increase in the talent marketed though monitored partnerships at the expense of solo lawyers or even paralegals.

What happens if the signal to the client and internal partner/monitor are not simultaneous but the internal monitor sees shirking before the client, perhaps before a case goes to trial or a legal matter is settled? Remedial action becomes a possibility when the monitor detects ongoing shirking on the part of the legal specialist. Partnerships take remedial action selectively to preserve sufficiently high quasi-rent streams.

BOUTIQUE LAW FIRMS. Partnerships alone facilitate remedial action; the feasibility of remedial action is increased if the monitor and legal specialist share common specialties. This consideration may move partnerships towards organizations of similar specialists ('boutique' law firms) as opposed to the more traditional coalition of diverse legal talents. The emergence of 'boutique' or specialized firms can be explained as a rational response to the increased gains from monitoring and early detection. With boutique firms, remedial action on the part of the monitor facilitated by the high degree of substitutability between the skills of the monitor and the lawyer reduce the premia and brand-name investment for the firm. Specialized firms with highly substitutable legal talents and smaller brand-name investments together with external direct monitoring by the client have become more efficient organizational structures.

LOCK-STEP COMPENSATION. These results also allow us to interpret an anomaly concerning remuneration in many large law firms. As noted above, many large law firms remunerate lawyers according to their vintage, a lock-step rule. Relative productivity is reflected in the assignment of returns between practising lawyers and monitors. If competitive partnership contracts require additional brand-name investment, then the relative shares are altered with monitors taking proportionately more than lawyers. But the owners of the larger share of brand-name capital who perform the monitoring role together are typically the senior members of the partnership.

Furthermore, their brand-name shares and monitoring functions may be more or less equal according to their vintage, making the application of a lock-step procedure an efficient rule. As a result, the traditional rule follows from competitive pressures to seek organizational arrangements that guarantee the delivery of legal services at the lowest cost to the relevant set of consumers.

IN-HOUSE COUNSEL. Consider high damage cases (as defined by L^2). For each corporate client, high damage suits may be sufficiently rare that it does not pay a client to hire a litigation expert as a permanent member of their corporate legal staff. If so, the client retains outside legal talent. If the issues are sufficiently complex and the potential awards sufficiently large, it will pay the client to seek expert legal advice from a monitored partnership. The cost of this advice itself can amount to a significant expense for the client. In the presence of these features, clients may employ direct monitors, for example lawyers who lack the skills to provide the special legal service but who can monitor any outside legal specialists. There is a minimum scale of damage that warrants such investment.

Enhanced monitoring by corporate counsel increases the knowledge of clients about the services of outside counsel, reduces the need for brand-name capital as a sunk commitment to assuring the delivery of quality and reduces the corresponding quasi-rent stream. This reduces the value of a traditional full-line service firm used by clients for all of their outside legal needs and promotes the emergence of specialty areas even within the larger law firms. Another argument for the growth of in-house counsel is that the explosion of regulatory law in the 1960s and 1970s has resulted in an increase in the number of routine legal tasks that could be handled internally within the firm (see Kronman 1993).

As an illustration of the role of direct monitoring by an agent of the client, consider the nature of such monitoring in medicine and law. In medical cases requiring a specialist and in criminal law, the cost from shirking can be very high. For example, a patient with operable cancer suffers greatly if the diagnostician spends too little time in the examination and misses the telltale signs. In criminal law, an innocent defendant may suffer large penalties if his lawyer provides an inferior defence because of inadequate preparation. In these cases with large potential damages, generalists should aid their clients in both selecting and monitoring specialists. Specialist doctors are more typically organized as owner-managed firms rather than monitored partnerships. In medicine, the family doctor refers patients to the specialist and acts as a monitor on the specialist's performance. While North American litigation specialists may be in monitored partnerships, this is not the case in the UK where clients first consult a solicitor on litigation matters. Only when the case proceeds to court does the solicitor hire a barrister as an expert on behalf of his client. Barristers in the UK are typically solo specialists. They receive much of their work through referral and the solicitor monitors the barrister on behalf of his current and future clients. In the UK, organization in litigation resembles organization in the medical market.

CONCLUSION. Analysing the nature of bonding and monitoring in the supply of legal services under competition provides insight into organizational arrangements in law firms. Moral hazard issues arise when suppliers of the service are more knowledgeable than their clients. Monitoring coupled with an appropriate distribution of ownerships rights on the firm's reputational capital creates lower price services to clients and guarantees protection of clients' interests. By creating joint brand-name capital that is at risk, lawyers in a partnership bond themselves to deliver honestly their professional services. What is critical is that the monitor's self-interests coincide with the client's. This may require the monitor to own a substantial portion of the firm's brand-name capital. In this case, senior law partners who hold a proportionately greater interest in the firm should also serve as the principal managers of client accounts, the case for most large law firms. Legal partnerships dominate solo lawyers when cases are large and the detection of shirking is low. For large corporate clients, it may pay to hire lawyers directly using them to monitor outside legal counsel. The larger the client's assets, the larger the premium required to cover the sunk brand-name capital investment, and the less expensive the in-house legal service, the more likely are clients to have legal experts on staff to monitor their outside counsel. With a sequential equilibrium in the market for legal services, however, lawyers, aware of their clients' monitoring activities, incorporate these activities into their own decisions on revenue sharing, monitoring within the partnership, and investment in brand-name capital. More monitoring by clients reduces the need for law firms to post brand-name capital.

Direct client monitoring and the reduction in brand-name capital yield a demand for specialized outside counsel, for example for litigation purposes alone. In-house counsel handle the more routine legal matters and monitor the external litigation experts. Outside firms that specialize in narrow legal matters may emerge as more efficient coalitions of legal talent – 'boutique' law firms. Such firms have the added advantage that monitoring within these partnerships itself is reduced as it is less costly for lawyers who are experts in the same field to monitor each other and to take remedial action should shirking be detected.

JACK CARR AND FRANK MATHEWSON

See also EMPLOYEE OWNERSHIP OF FIRMS; HOLD-UP PROBLEM; LAWYERS AS TRANSACTION COST ENGINEERS; PARTNERSHIP; PROFESSIONAL CORPORATIONS AND LIMITED LIABILITY; REGULATION OF THE PROFESSIONS.

Subject classification: 5a(iii); 5g(v).

BIBLIOGRAPHY

Carr, J.L. and Mathewson, G.F. 1988. Unlimited liability as a barrier to entry. *Journal of Political Economy* 96(4): 766–84.

Carr, J. and Mathewson, G.F. 1990. The economics of law firms: a study in the legal organization of the firm. *Journal of Law and Economics* 33(2): 307–30.

Curran, B. 1985. *The Lawyer Statistical Report*. New York: M. Beider.

Freund, J. 1985. Comment on Chayes and Chayes. *Stanford Law Review* 37: 301–12.

Galanter, M. and Palay, T. 1991. *Tournament of Lawyers*. Chicago: University of Chicago Press.

Gilson, R.J. and Mnookin, R.H. 1985. Sharing among the human capitalists: an economic inquiry into the corporate law firm and how partners split profits. *Stanford Law Review* 37: 313–92.

Klein, B. and Leffler, K. 1981. The role of market forces in assuring contractual performance. *Journal of Political Economy* 89: 615–41.

Kronman, A. 1993. *The Lost Lawyer*. Cambridge, MA: The Belknap Press of Harvard University Press.

Rosen, S. 1992. The market for lawyers. *Journal of Law and Economics* 35: 215–46.

Stevens, M. 1987. *Power of Attorney*. New York: McGraw-Hill Book Company.

Weil, R., Bower, W.W. and Roy, P. 1987. Paying partners and stockholders. *Legal Economics* 13: 26–36.

Law Merchant. *Lex mercatoria*, the Law Merchant, generally refers to the customary law governing European commercial interactions during the medieval period. Despite its customary nature, however, the medieval Law Merchant constituted a true system of law in the sense defined by Hart (1961), as there were well known 'primary rules of obligation' along with obvious and effective 'secondary rules' or institutions to induce recognition of, resolve disputes under, and facilitate change in primary rules. Indeed, in contrast to Hart's (1961: 89–96) contention that custom tends to be static and inefficient, the Law Merchant was a dynamic system of evolving law that significantly enhanced the potential for efficient exchange (Berman 1983; Benson 1989). Virtually every aspect of commercial transactions in Europe was governed for several centuries by this privately produced, privately adjudicated and privately enforced body of law (Bewes 1923: 1; Trakman 1983: 13; Benson 1989).

The Law Merchant was gradually absorbed and altered by royal law, particularly in England. Thus, the Law Merchant became less recognizable as royal courts supplanted merchant courts, and as statutes, precedents and treaties supplanted or supplemented business tradition and practice. Nonetheless, it has survived in varying degrees within national legal systems (Benson 1989, 1990, 1995; Chen 1992), and particularly in international trade (Trakman 1983; Berman and Dasser 1990; Benson 1989, 1990, 1992). Indeed, custom as an important source of international commercial law has been increasingly recognized by some legal scholars, and beginning in the mid-1950s, *lex mercatoria* has been increasingly applied to characterize certain aspects of modern international commercial law (De Ly 1992: 1). Depending upon which period is being discussed, Law Merchant is now typically prefaced with either 'medieval' or 'modern' (or 'new').

There is actually considerable debate about the existence, or at least the legal character, of both the medieval and the modern Law Merchant (for instance, see Ebke 1987, Goldman and Mann 1990, De Ly 1992). This debate is not reviewed here, but the presentation is structured in reflection of it, the objective being to illustrate that the Law Merchant was and is a true system of law as defined by Hart (1961). The primary and secondary rules and institutions of the medieval Law Merchant are described in Section I, the process of royal absorption is discussed in Section II and the modern institutions of the international Law Merchant are examined in Section III.

I. THE MEDIEVAL LAW MERCHANT. From the sixth to the tenth centuries commercial trade was almost nonexistent in Europe relative to what had occurred before in the Roman Empire and what would come after. However, rapid expansion in agricultural productivity during the eleventh and twelfth centuries meant that less labour was needed to produce sufficient food and clothing to sustain the population. Agricultural commodities were produced at levels which stimulated greater trade and population began to move into towns, many of which rapidly became cities. One consequence of and, simultaneously, one impetus for the increased productivity in agriculture and the urbanization which followed was the emergence of a class of professional merchants to trade in agricultural commodities and in the products of the new urban centres (Berman 1983: 335).

Customary law in the form of accepted business practices and contracts had been a significant source of the rules of commerce throughout history (Bewes 1923: 1–11; Trakman 1983: 7–8). This law, however, was highly localized in Europe during the early eleventh century. Furthermore, merchants spoke different languages and had different cultural backgrounds, geographic distances often prevented direct communication let alone the building of strong interpersonal bonds to facilitate trust, and numerous middlemen were frequently required to bring about an exchange, including, buyer, seller and shipping agents. All of this generated mistrust between merchants (Trakman 1983: 11). Law, essentially to facilitate or substitute for trust, was required (Benson 1989). It was during this period that

> the basic concepts and institutions of modern Western mercantile law – *lex mercatoria* ('the law merchant') – were formed, and, even more important, it was then that mercantile law in the West first came to be viewed as an integrated, developing system, a *body* of law (Berman 1983: 333).

In fact, the commercial revolution could not have occurred without the rapid development of this system of law (Berman 1983: 336). This legal system was the product of the decentralized merchant community, however, rather than of centralized state government.

Recognition. How could merchants from such far-ranging backgrounds (both culturally and geographically) produce law that all were willing to recognize? Fuller (1964: 23) proposes three conditions for 'optimal efficacy of the notion of duty': (1) the reciprocity out of which duty arises must be a reflection of voluntary agreement; (2) the reciprocal commitments of the parties must be, by some measure, equal despite being different; and (3) frequent interaction is necessary so that the duty can be reversible (i.e., the interaction must take place in what we would now call a repeated-game setting). Fuller (1964: 24) also notes that the kind of society in which these conditions are most likely to be met

> is a surprising one: in a society of economic traders. By definition the members of such a society enter direct and voluntary relationships of exchange. As for equality it is only with the aid of something like a free market that it is possible to develop anything like an exact measure for the value of disparate goods. Without such a measure, the notion of equality loses substance and descends to the level of a kind of metaphor. Finally economic traders frequently change roles, now selling, now buying. The duties that arise out of their exchanges are therefore reversible, not only in theory but in practice.

Markets were expanding rapidly during the eleventh and twelfth centuries, and given Fuller's argument, it should not be too surprising that the reciprocity necessary for the recognition of rules of obligation arose, in part, from the mutual gains generated by developing repeated exchange relationships within the international merchant 'community' (Benson 1989). As Milgrom et al. (1990: 1) explain, a valuable ongoing relationship with a trading partner can serve as a bond, because a trader will sacrifice the relationship only if the expected benefits of dishonest behaviour are large relative to the value of the relationship.

Long-term (repeated-game) effects were not the only source of legal recognition. In particular, each merchant had dealings (entered into many games) with different merchants. Thus, the spread of information, primarily through word of mouth, about fraud, or other breaches of widely held rules of conduct within one exchange could affect a merchant's reputation and limit his ability to enter into other exchanges (Benson 1989; Milgrom et al. 1990). In order to maintain a reputation for dealing under recognized rules of behaviour, most merchants' dominant strategy was to behave as expected in all interactions, whether it was a repeated or a one-shot game.

The importance of reputations and repeated dealings meant that the merchant community could impose a significant threat or sanction if someone did not behave as expected. In a very real sense, each trader's valuable reputation and repeated-dealing arrangements were held hostage by the rest of the community. Thus, the Law Merchant was ultimately backed by the threat of ostracism by the merchant community at large, a threat that was probably even more effective than threats of physical coercion since the result was that the guilty party would no longer be a merchant (Wooldridge 1970: 95–6). Nevertheless, this boycott sanction, while a real threat, was not often required (Trakman 1983: 10):

> Good faith was the essence of the mercantile agreement. Reciprocity and the threat of business sanctions compelled performance. The ordinary undertakings of merchants were binding because they were 'intended'

to be binding, not because any law compelled such performance.

As the size of the merchant community grew, the costs to merchants of obtaining information about the reputation of others increased; word of mouth was no longer a sufficient information mechanism (Milgrom et al. 1990: 6). Therefore, some individuals began to specialize in the gathering of information, and/or the application of commercial law. Itinerant consuls travelled with groups of traders of a particular nationality, for instance, watching over their interests at each market or fair and judging disputes that arose within the group (Bewes 1923: 85). In some fairs, permanent consuls took on the duty of attending travelling merchants, representing them in matters connected with the fair. They were also a source of information about reputations. Before finalizing a contract, each merchant was free to check with a consul to see if the other party in the exchange had any unpaid judgments against him (Milgrom et al. 1990: 10–14). In that way, merchants learned who to boycott and who to trade with. The consuls also were part of the evolving system of merchant courts, as they served as arbitrators for disputes between merchants.

Adjudication. Merchants established their own courts for several reasons. For instance, royal courts typically would not consider disputes arising from contracts made in another nation, and they would not honour any contractual agreement which involved the payment of interest. Any interest was usurious. Common-law courts in England would not consider books of account as evidence despite the fact that merchants held such records in high regard. Thus, merchants needed their own courts so they could be sure that their own rules would be enforced (Trakman 1983: 15).

Commercial disputes also often had to be achieved after consideration of highly technical issues. Merchant court judges were merchants chosen from the relevant merchant community (fair or market), and when technical issues were involved, merchant experts in the relevant area of commerce could be chosen as judges. Lawyers and royal judges often had no knowledge of such issues, so the risk of judicial error was lower in a merchant court.

As trade became more complex and widespread, merchant organizations and their courts also became more formal. For example, the Italian merchants trading in Champagne were organized into a corporation in the thirteenth century, with a captain or rector chosen to settle disputes within the group (Bewes 1923: 83). Within the corporation, merchants from each of the different Italian cities were represented by a consul. Merchant guilds also arose, both to provide protection for foreign merchants away from their homes, and to protect against unknown foreign merchants who might take advantage of a local merchant and then never be seen again (Milgrom et al. 1990: 4). The consuls that developed to distribute reputation information in the major trading towns that were frequent stops for travelling merchants also evolved into permanent courts, ultimately becoming the basis for the municipal courts that would arise in these urban centres (Bewes 1923: 81–3; Berman 1983: 356–403).

Perhaps the most widely cited characteristics of the merchant courts were their speed and informality (Berman 1983: 347). This characteristic was in response to the needs of merchants, and a third reason for participatory merchant courts (Mitchell 1904: 13; Bewes 1923: 19). Merchants of the time had to complete their transactions in one market or fair and quickly move to the next, so a dispute had to be settled quickly to minimize disruption of business affairs. This speed and informality could not have been equitably achieved without the use of judges knowledgeable of commercial issues, whose judgments would be respected by the merchant community at large.

In this same light, appeals were forbidden in order to avoid undue delay and disruption of commerce (Trakman 1983: 16). Similarly, rules of evidence and procedures were kept simple and informal: lengthy testimony under oath was avoided; notarial attestation was usually not required as evidence of an agreement; debts were recognized as freely transferable through informal 'written obligatory', a process developed by merchants to simplify the transfer of debt; actions by agents in transactions were considered valid without formal authority, and ownership transfers were recognized without physical delivery (ibid.: 14). All these legal innovations were validated in merchant courts despite their frequent illegality in royal courts. All were desirable as business practices because they promoted speed and informality in commerce and reduced transactions costs. Indeed, this brings up a fourth reason for participatory merchant courts. The fact is that royal judges simply would not or could not adapt and change as fast as the rapidly changing commercial system required (Bewes 1923: 19; Trakman 1983).

Change. Naturally, the Law Merchant did not spring from a void. Parts of it trace to Roman commercial law (Berman 1983: 339). Parts also trace to Lex Rhodia, the customary commercial law of the Mediterranean identified in the third century (Trakman 1983: 8), and to the Middle East where commercial interactions arose earlier and persisted longer than in much of Europe. Indeed, Bewes (1923: 11) suggests that 'Europe may be indebted to the East for the earliest form of shipping documents, as well as for the law merchant generally.' From these foundations, however, the continued evolution of legal institutions in European commercial society was spontaneous and undesigned. The Law Merchant evolved just as markets evolve, from the bottom up through individual interaction (relevant evolutionary processes are discussed in EVOLUTION OF COMMERCIAL LAW). Indeed,

> [the] customary nature of the Law Merchant was by far the most decisive factor in its development: it made the law eminently a practical law adapted to the requirements of commerce; and as trade expanded and new forms of commercial activity arose – negotiable paper, insurance, etc. – custom everywhere fashioned and framed the broad general principles of the new law (Mitchell 1904: 12).

Observation and imitation were very important in the evolution of the Law Merchant, particularly as Europe began to emerge from a highly localized agrarian economy dominated by localized custom. As an example, Jewish merchants in the Mediterranean who wanted to develop international marketing arrangements initially relied upon traditional sources of trust: family and ethnic/religious affiliation. A Jewish merchant wishing to establish a position in a distant market would send a member of his family to take up a permanent position in that market, learn local customs, and establish relationships with other Jewish merchants (Greif 1989). As such merchants began to transact business across political, cultural and geographic boundaries they learned about foreign trade practices. Since similar circumstances create similar legal problems, they are likely to be resolved similarly, so many trade practices in different localities were found to have much in common (Bewes 1923: 9). But where conflicts arose or where innovative trade practices were developed, those practices which proved to be the most efficient at facilitating commercial interaction tended to supplant those which were less efficient (Trakman 1983: 11). After all, merchants had incentives to adopt those rules which minimized their expected transactions costs. By the twelfth century all important principles of commercial law were international in character (Mitchell 1904: 7–9; Bewes 1923: 138).

Another mechanism for instituting change was merchant-court dispute resolution. Some of the merchant judges in the participatory merchant courts went into considerable detail in justifying rulings (Gross 1974), thus providing clear reasons for adopting a new rule. Indeed, as the Law Merchant developed merchant court records were increasingly maintained (Gross 1974; Berman 1983). The speed and informality that characterized these courts suggests, however, that detailed rulings may not have been the norm. Of course, in general, even if the reasons for a decision are not explicitly stated, potentially affected parties should perceive some reason and adjust their conduct accordingly (Fuller 1981: 90), and this presumably applied for medieval merchants. A ruling actually only applied to the parties directly involved, of course, but if others considered the dispute resolution (or contract form, as suggested below) to be useful, they adopted the same practice in their future interactions, so the rule spread through a process of voluntary acceptance. Indeed, it was only after a business practice came into common usage that the 'practice and usage' became a rule of the Law Merchant which merchants in general were expected to recognize.

Many innovative changes in the Law Merchant were also initiated through contract as individuals agreed to new practices in the face of new circumstances. For example, by the twelfth century barter trade had been virtually replaced by commercial middlemen who bought and sold using commercial contracts involving credit. Indeed, the commercial revolution which followed was not fuelled by cash, but by collaboration through the use of credit (Berman 1983: 351). The main forms of credit extended by sellers to buyers were promissory notes and bills of exchange. When such commercial instruments developed in Europe during the late eleventh and twelfth centuries, they served as a substitute for money because, like money they acquired the character of independent negotiable obligations (Berman 1983: 350). The negotiability of credit instruments, which did not exist prior to this period, was 'invented' by merchants seeking an improved means of exchange. Many other kinds of credit instruments were developed. For instance, buyers extended credit to sellers through the use of various contracts for future delivery of goods. Third parties (e.g. bankers) extended credit to buyers, and in order to protect these creditors, devices such as mortgages of movables were developed. Hayek (1973: 38) notes that while spontaneous orders are not necessarily complex, when circumstances demand it they are able to achieve a considerable degree of complexity relative to deliberately designed orders. The Law Merchant illustrates this. In fact, many other aspects of the Law Merchant could be examined to emphasize the evolution and integration of a wide variety of principles, concepts, rules and procedures into a system of law (Berman 1983: 349). The evolutionary story is, in each instance, similar to the development of commercial credit devices. The point is that the Law Merchant was an evolving system, and given the time and place, this evolution was quite rapid (Berman 1983: 354–5).

Dramatic change in the Law Merchant occurred in a relatively short time. In fact, Berman (1983: 350) concludes that 'a great many if not most of the structural elements of the modern system of commercial law were formed in this period [from 1000 to 1200, but particularly between 1050 and 1150].' By the twelfth century, commercial law in Europe provided alien merchants with substantial protection against potential discrimination under local laws, including local customs (Berman 1983: 342), and by the early thirteenth century the Law Merchant clearly was a universal, integrated system of principles, concepts, rules and procedures. The rapid evolution of the Law Merchant continued through the thirteenth, fourteenth, and fifteenth centuries so that as commercial opportunities expanded, commercial law became even more objective, precise, uniform and integrated, and its dispute resolution procedures became more regularized (Berman 1983: 350).

Rules of obligation. The medieval Law Merchant might be characterized as the law of commercial contract for the medieval period. Draetta et al. (1992: xiii) describe the modern Law Merchant as the 'customary principles and detailed rules which are generally applied in international business contracts', for instance, but this is too narrow a description for the medieval Law. Certainly, the rules that came to dominate the medieval Law Merchant 'commanded merchants to do that which they themselves had promised to do' (Trakman 1983: 18). The agreement was the overriding force in regulating business conduct (ibid.: 10). Thus, many rules developed about and through contracting, and much of the merchant courts' business was focused on contract issues. Berman (1983: 349–55) discusses significant Law Merchant developments relating to negotiable instruments, bankruptcy, business associations such as joint ventures, and insurance, for instance (also see Mitchell 1904). However, Mitchell (1904: 16), Berman (1983: 343), and Trakman (1983: 12) also stress the Law Merchant requirements of 'equity', further suggesting that issues treated today as 'criminal' such as fraud, duress or other abuses of the will or knowledge of either party in an exchange meant that the transaction would be invalidated in a merchant court.

Similarly, as indicated above, procedural and evidentiary rules were also part of the Law Merchant. Therefore, while many of the modern classifications of legal issues (e.g., criminal versus civil, equity, contract versus property versus tort) were obviously not explicitly recognized under the Law Merchant (nor, for that matter, under Royal law, at least during the early years of the Law Merchant), and its most significant lasting developments were in regard to contract law, this legal system ruled over virtually every aspect of commercial interaction in the fairs, markets and seaports (Berman 1983: 341), and the merchant courts would consider any matter that might arise between merchants.

Commercial law can be conceived of as coordinating the self-interested actions of individuals, but perhaps an equivalently valuable insight is gained by viewing it as coordinating the actions of people with limited knowledge and trust (Benson 1989). Markets coordinate the diffused knowledge, but diffused knowledge necessarily implies that some people are ignorant of what others know and commercial law evolved to facilitate or coordinate exchange in the light of such complexity. The Law Merchant therefore evolved as international commerce developed in the middle ages, in order to keep commercial transactions as simple as possible. Furthermore, complexities that might hinder communication and thereby inhibit trade were avoided. Thus, over the period from 1000 to 1200 the 'rights and obligations' of merchants in their dealings with each other 'became substantially more objective and less arbitrary, more precise and less loose' (Berman 1983: 341).

When it is recognized that individuals had to *voluntarily* adopt a certain practice before it could become common usage it becomes clear why commercial law had to be objective and impartial. Reciprocity, in the sense of mutual benefits and costs, is the very essence of trade. However, the legal principle of reciprocity of rights, as it was developed in the late eleventh and early twelfth centuries and still is understood today, involves more than mutual exchange. It involves an element of fairness in exchange (Mitchell 1904: 16; Trakman 1983: 12). Beyond such procedural issues, however,

> Substantively, even an exchange which is entered into willingly and knowingly must not impose on either side costs that are excessively disproportionate to the benefits to be obtained; nor may such exchange be unduly disadvantageous to third parties or to society generally (Berman 1983: 344).

Fairness was a required feature of the Law Merchant, of course, precisely because its recognition arose voluntarily in order to achieve mutual benefits (Benson 1989). No one would *voluntarily* recognize such a legal system that was not expected to treat him fairly. This emphasis on fairness also encouraged merchants to recognize the Law Merchant and, therefore, increased the likelihood of efficiency gains through trade.

II. ROYAL LAW VERSUS THE LAW MERCHANT. Around the twelfth century, European kings began systematically collecting and codifying the customary rules of the Law Merchant (Berman 1983: 341). Kings were asserting claims to legal authority in competition with other claimants such as the Roman Church (canon law), and the powerful aristocracy (manor law), and they clearly wanted to claim authority over commercial matters as well (*see* EVOLUTION OF COMMERCIAL LAW for discussion of the interplay between custom and authority in commercial law). Early codifications, however, did not substantially alter the customary underpinnings of commercial law (Mitchell 1904: 11). After all, royal authority was far from complete. In fact, competition for authority meant that merchants in particular actually had several legal systems to choose from beyond their own. Merchants could and did take disputes to ecclesiastical courts, for example. The Church was a major trader (Bewes 1923: 9), and in addition, many of the major fairs were held at important priories and abbeys, so it was clearly in the interests of the Church's leaders to remain on good terms with the merchant community by offering them a source of dispute resolution that would recognize their customs and practices, at least when they did not conflict with canon law. Similarly, merchants naturally used the developing urban courts which evolved from the earlier market courts, and which merchants continued to dominate.

The availability of numerous alternative dispute resolution forums, including the courts of the fairs and markets, meant that the universal Law Merchant remained a source of protection against the growing centralized power of kings (Berman 1983: 343). As Hayek (1973: 81–2) explains,

> The growth of the purpose-independent rules of conduct which can produce a spontaneous order will ... often have taken place in conflict with the aims of the rulers who tended to try to turn their domain into an organization proper. It is in the *ius gentium*, the law merchant, and the practices of the ports and fairs that we must chiefly seek the steps in the evolution of law which ultimately made an open society possible.

Even as the Law Merchant began to be absorbed into royal law, royal courts had to grant merchants similar safeguards and privileges to those provided in merchant, urban, and ecclesiastical courts in order to attract commercial disputes away from their competitors. Thus, early codifications and interjurisdictional competition meant that the customary laws of the Law Merchant provided the foundation upon which government-enforced commercial law would evolve (Bewes 1923: 19). It was only after alternative courts were displaced that the Law Merchant could be more fully absorbed and altered. This would take some time. Nonetheless, the power and attraction of the Law Merchant as an independent legal system began to be undermined as claims of royal authority in commercial matters were established. In addition, codification in geographically defined kingdoms undermined the uniformity, consistency and continuity of the Law Merchant in Europe, raising doubts as to whether there was a unique system of commercial law (Trakman 1983: 21).

The development of royal influences in commercial law was not just motivated by those wishing to supply authoritarian law. Some members of the merchant 'community' also saw advantages in having royal authority established over commercial matters (Ogilvie 1984: 115; Benson 1989).

Indeed, much of authoritarian law is initiated by powerful interest groups seeking special advantages from a legal authority, and parts of the business community have, for centuries, been very effective in the political arena. In this context, one early development in the gradual process of absorption of the Law Merchant into royal law was cooperation by royal authorities in applying sanctions to back the Law Merchant (Berman 1983: 343). This does not imply that the merchants could not enforce their own laws through boycott sanctions (see Benson 1989, 1995), but some merchants clearly found it beneficial to shift the burden of enforcement. Another result of the growing political power of some domestic merchants was a more significant factor leading towards more royal influence over commercial matters, however. A merchant who wants to become wealthy in an unregulated competitive market must be concerned primarily with maintaining a reputation for fair dealing, because other merchants and consumers can always choose to buy from someone else. Similarly, a universally recognized legal system is vital in order to create the incentives to cooperate in trade for everyone's mutual benefit. But the increasing authoritarian power of some kings offered an alternative. In England, for instance, developing economic regulation involved domestic merchants trading support and money to kings in exchange for special privileges such as royal grants of monopoly rights, the power to form exclusive guilds and entry restrictions (Ekelund and Tollison 1980). The full development of monopolization through economic regulation and the associated incentives that tended to undermine recognition of the Law Merchant did not occur overnight, of course. Indeed, it could not, in part because kings often faced competition for authority from sources within their kingdoms. In England, for example, at various times, competition was intense between barons and the kings, between Parliament and the king *and* between different royal courts, and each tried, at various times, to attract support from wealthy domestic merchants by offering them special favours and privileges.

There were three powerful common law courts in England by the fourteenth century – the Court of Common Pleas, the Court of the King's Bench and the Court of the Exchequer – when specialty courts also began evolving from the King's Council. These 'conciliar courts' or 'prerogative courts' included the Court of the Admiralty, which attracted considerable commercial dispute resolution business (Mitchell 1904), as well as the Court of Chivalry, the Court of the Chancery (or equity), the Star Chamber and the Court of Requests. Furthermore, the functional separation of the organs of government towards the end of that century intensified the competition between the powers represented in Parliament, the king with his prerogative courts, and the common law courts. Some judges felt that the common law courts should be the supreme source of law rather than either the king or the Parliament, but they clearly did not have the power to achieve this goal. Most common law judges recognized that they had to pick sides, and over time their interests tended to become more aligned with Parliament (Ekelund and Tollison 1980: 584), in part because many common law lawyers and judges were members of Parliament (Holdsworth [1903] 1924: 210–11). Therefore, many common law judges characterized Parliament as simply a common law court, supreme in that it could overturn other common law court decisions, legislate jurisdictional boundaries, and dictate other characteristics of the courts, but also dependent on the other common law courts to facilitate the implementation of the law.

Competition continued. In order to promote royal ends, for instance, Henry VIII supported the prerogative courts' in aggression against common law jurisdictions and encouraged application of Continental civil law rather than common law. However, the common law courts had gained superiority over the 'weaker' competitors (e.g., ecclesiastical, manor and hundred courts) by the later part of Elizabeth's reign, and at that time they attacked the jurisdiction of the prerogative courts (Holdsworth [1903] 1924: 414). To achieve significant reductions in royal authority, common law judges asserted that the law emanating from Parliament and other common law courts was the supreme source of law, in part by attacking any remaining non-royal sources of law as well. For instance, the great common law jurist and parliamentarian, Sir Edward Coke, who was intimately involved in the struggle between parliamentary and royal authority, ruled that decisions of merchant courts could be reversed by common law judges, claiming that the merchant courts' purpose was to find a suitable compromise while judges ruled on the legal merits of the case (*Vynior's Case*, 4). In essence, Coke asserted that the Law Merchant was not a separate identifiable system of law, but rather that it was 'part of the law of this realm' (Trakman 1983: 26). Furthermore and significantly, contracts to submit to arbitration were declared to be revocable. The use of merchant courts in England declined dramatically after this, and they continued to function only in a few places (Gross 1974: xix). The doctrine of revocability was justified and reinforced in England (*Kill v. Hollister*, 1) when contracts to arbitrate were declared revocable because they 'oust courts of their jurisdiction'. Thus, the earliest judicial defenders of the revocability doctrine spoke of the courts' interests, suggesting that the common law judges of England saw arbitration as an undesirable threat to their control of dispute resolution.

The increasing concentration of legal authority in Europe meant that some nation states were in a position to regulate both domestic and international commerce, and distinct national systems of commercial/regulatory law developed, reflecting domestic political considerations (Trakman 1983: 24). Civil law countries were more receptive to the Law Merchant than was English common law, however (Trakman 1983: 24). Some fragmentation in the Law Merchant occurred across Europe, but there was little difference in substance, because trade between these geographically contiguous countries continued to be relatively important. In contrast, the English Parliament passed acts of trade and navigation throughout the seventeenth century in an effort to make its empire self sufficient by having the colonies supply raw materials exclusively to England and purchase only British goods, all on British ships. In this environment, Trakman (1983: 27) argues that the Law Merchant suffered in England:

> By restricting the dynamic use of trade custom in various ways, the English common law courts precluded resort to the pliable framework of the Law Merchant. Either they refused to admit custom into the legal system in any form whatever, or custom was required to satisfy onerous tests of admissibility before it was received into English law . . . custom had to comply with the rules of positive law. It had to be truly 'ancient' in its origins in order to be admitted in law, and it had to be consistently practiced, notwithstanding the changing environment of business itself . . . In this way, the Law Merchant became rigid as post-medieval English judges sought to integrate the Law Merchant into the established confines of a centralized common law.

Even so, Bewes (1923: 14) contends that despite the refusal of common law judges to recognize the Law Merchant as a distinct branch of law (in contrast to other European countries) and their rejection of some of its important principles, sufficient similarity remained between England's common law of commerce and the law applied in France's commercial courts to imply that the Law Merchant was still an underlying source of much of England's commercial law. Furthermore, the Law Merchant continued to evolve in international commerce, moving the form and content of international contracts away from domestic contracts in both common law and civil law countries (Draetta et al. 1992: 3).

Deliberate efforts to thwart the spontaneous evolution of customary law often sets off spontaneous reactions, so the path of subsequent evolution may be altered in unanticipated and unintended ways. The evolution of commercial custom and practice was clearly altered in England from what it might have been as the common law began to influence and often change the basic character of the Law Merchant (Trakman 1983: 30). Thus, numerous conflicts between English common law and the international Law Merchant developed. But this could not continue. The rigidity of the common law, including economic regulations passed by Parliament, began to raise transactions costs for English businessmen. After all, England was faced with increasing resistance to its trade and navigation acts in parts of its colonial empire, and ultimately began to lose its hold on the colonies. Thus, facing the loss of captured markets and an increasingly international competitive environment, the business community demanded recognition of their evolving business practices as a source of law. In the late seventeenth century, particularly with Sir John Holt, and then in the eighteenth century with Lord Mansfield, common law decisions once again began to recognize customs and usages of English merchants as a source of changes in English common law (Mitchell 1904: 77–8). Mansfield used merchant juries to consider commercial disputes, for instance (Draetta et al. 1992: 11). While Mansfield's role in the revival of customary sources of legal change in common law was particularly important [there also were political motivations behind Mansfield's efforts (Ogilvie 1984: 116)], a significant impetus for once again recognizing merchants' evolving custom, appears to be that as international trade became relatively more significant, common law courts were forced to compete with foreign courts and legal systems to regulate international commerce (Trakman 1983: 28). Still, substantial differences between civil law and common law in commercial matters remain, in part perhaps because of the influence that the common law had over evolving business practices during the period when the civil law was more receptive to the Law Merchant. For instance, common law turns to money damages first when a breach of contract occurs, while the civil law relies much more heavily on specific performance (Ebke 1987: 612). Even civil law jurisdictions' contract law can differ from the law of international contracting under the modern Law Merchant, however (Draetta et al. 1992).

III. THE MODERN LAW MERCHANT. Customary commercial law is still a primary source of order in international trade (Berman and Dasser 1990; Benson 1992, 1995; Draetta et al. 1992). This source of order is becoming increasingly important during the twentieth century, for at least two reasons. First, as Cooter (1994: 216) explains, increasingly complex economies require more decentralized lawmaking for efficiency rather than less, and second, as Lew (1978: 589) emphasizes, the development of international economic and political 'blocks' made up of several nations makes international businessmen increasingly uncertain about national courts' impartiality and abilities to resolve business disputes appropriately. Thus, the Law Merchant continues to govern for both efficiency and equity reasons. Indeed, while the focus here is on the international Law Merchant, the same characterization of commercial law applies, at least to some extent, within many countries, including the United States (Benson 1995, 1997).

Recognition. The agreements that arise in international trade and disputes resolved through private sources of dispute resolution (e.g., negotiation, mediation, arbitration), as discussed below, are still backed by the desires of businessmen to maintain their reputations and repeated-dealing arrangements, and therefore, ultimately, by the threat of boycott. Trade associations in particular are in a position to take measures against non-performance. In some cases a threat to inform the membership when some member refuses to comply with accepted rules is more than sufficient to support compliance. In addition, non-performance can be punishment by temporary suspension or complete expulsion from the trade association (David 1985: 358). Today, for instance, almost all international trade contracts expressly exclude adjudication by the national courts of the trading parties and refer any dispute that cannot be resolved through negotiation (perhaps with the aid of a mediator) to arbitration (Berman and Dasser 1990: 33). Some nations provide sanctions if an arbitration settlement is not complied with, while others do not, but in fact other considerations are much more important. In particular, as David (1985: 357) stresses, the most powerful incentives come from a desire to maintain a reputation for fair dealing and/or from fear that non-performance will be interpreted to imply that the firm is in financial distress and therefore may be unable to fulfill other obligations, along with the threat of business community sanctions. Another sanction in some trade associations, and also with some arbitration tribunals such as the International Chamber of Commerce (ICC), is that the defaulting party will no longer be allowed to use the arbitration tribunal, significantly curtailing the potential for trade since most trading partners will insist on arbitration clauses.

Adjudication. Most business disputes are resolved through negotiation or mediation, but when a third party with the power to impose a solution is required, international traders almost always turn to arbitration (Berman and Dasser 1990). There are many potential sources of arbitration for international business disputes. A large number of international trade associations have their own conflict resolution procedures, using arbitrators with special expertise in trade matters of concern to association members. Other traders rely on the ICC's arbitration institution. ICC arbitrators are experts in international commerce, and are typically chosen from a different national origin than those of the parties in the dispute.

International arbitration procedures are speedy and flexible, in reflection of commercial interest. These private commercial dispute resolution processes are modern versions of the medieval fair and market courts. Arbitration is not preferred just because it is fast and flexible, however. It is also chosen because international traders generally assume that national courts will not enforce obligations derived solely from the Law Merchant (Chen 1992: 100). After all, in contrast to some national courts, international arbitrators readily turn to commercial custom to determine awards (Berman and Dasser 1990: 33). Indeed, international arbitration tribunals are not simply alternatives to courts: 'Owing no allegiance to any sovereign State, international commercial arbitration has a special responsibility to develop and apply the law of international trade' (Lew 1978: 589).

Change. International commercial law continues to evolve through contractual innovations and arbitration rulings. Indeed, as Draetta et al. (1992: 3) explain, international contracts have evolved to such a degree that they now clearly differ in many distinct ways from domestic contracts under both civil law and common law jurisdictions. Similarly, an international arbitrator applies customary commercial rules (Lew 1978: 581–5; Berman and Dasser 1990), as explained below, but when no clear rule applies they must determine the appropriate new rule. To do so, they 'denationalize' their awards and attempt to make them acceptable by showing their consistency with several accepted rules (Lew 1978: 584–5). Thus, international arbitration has characteristics often attributed to the common law, as arbitrators, in extending the modern Law Merchant to new issues, look to past arbitration rulings, as well as to customary rules developed through practices and usage. Such rulings do not apply universally, however, until and unless they are widely adopted in future contracts.

Rules of obligation. Statutes and government court precedent, as well as treaties and trade agreements between nations, may influence international commercial law, of course, so the role of custom can be masked. In fact, many government proclamations are simply codifications of custom (Berman and Dasser 1990: 24–5). For instance, article 9 of the 1980 United Nations Convention on International Sales of Goods, which has been adopted in statutes by many nations, states that the parties are bound by any usage and practices which they have established between themselves, as well as usage that they knew or ought to have known and which is widely known in international trade and regularly observed in contracts of the type that the parties in trade are employing. Of course, other statutes and treaties may attempt to impose rules on commerce that depart from or conflict with business custom.

An indication of the relative role of such statutes and treaties, and of international customary law can be seen by examining arbitration settlements. Lew's (1978) detailed analysis of available records reveals that the source of law applied in international arbitration is business practice and custom (also see Trakman 1983 and Draetta et al. 1992). In fact, in principle, 'The answer to every dispute is to be found *prima facie* in the contract itself. What did the parties intend, what did they agree and what did they expect?' (Lew 1978: 581). When arbitrators cannot discover the parties' intent explicitly stated in the contract, which is likely to be the case, they must decide what the parties expected or should have expected and, in this regard, Lew (1978: 582–3) finds that arbitrators generally do not refer to any nationalized system of law unless the parties have specified or expected that a particular system should apply. Instead, they generally apply the customary rules which are commonly recognized within the 'private international law systems from which the parties come' (Lew 1978: 585). Arbitrators avoid the limitations of nationalized legal systems, in part because these legal systems are frequently less concerned with fairness and justice than with issues of political power (Gardner 1958: 17–18). In fact, even though many national governments may be unable to agree on common rules for trade between their citizens, relative uniformity in international commercial law is established as businessmen use arbitrators rather than state courts, thereby replacing conflicting state laws with accepted business custom (David 1985: 138). Thus, in international trade at least, the Law Merchant continues to govern.

BRUCE L. BENSON

See also ARBITRATION IN THE SHADOW OF THE LAW; CUSTOMARY LAW; EMERGENCE OF LEGAL RULES; ENGLISH COMMON LAW; EVOLUTION OF COMMERCIAL LAW; FULLER, LON L.; INFORMAL CONTRACT ENFORCEMENT: LESSONS FROM MEDIEVAL TRADE; PRIVATE COMMERCIAL LAW; ROMAN LAW.

Subject classification: 4a(iii); 4b(iii); 5a(v); 5c(ii).

CASES

Kill v. Hollister (1746) 1 Wils. KB 129.
Vynior's Case (1609) 8 Co. Rep. 80a, 80b.

BIBLIOGRAPHY

Benson, B.L. 1989. The spontaneous evolution of commercial law. *Southern Economic Journal* 55: 644–61.

Benson, B.L. 1990. *The Enterprise of Law: Justice Without the State*. San Francisco: Pacific Research Institute for Public Policy.

Benson, B.L. 1992. Customary law as a social contract: international commercial law. *Constitutional Political Economy* 3(1): 1–27.

Benson, B.L. 1995. An exploration of the impact of modern arbitration statutes on the development of arbitration in the United States. *Journal of Law, Economics, & Organization* 11: 479–501.

Benson, B.L. 1997. Arbitration. In *The Encyclopedia of Law and Economics*, ed. B. Bouckaert and G. De Geest, Aldershot: Edward Elgar (forthcoming).

Berman, H.J. 1983. *Law and Revolution: The Formation of Western Legal Tradition*. Cambridge, MA: Harvard University Press.

Berman, H.J. and Dasser, F.J. 1990. The 'new' Law Merchant and the 'old': sources, content, and legitimacy. In *Lex Mercatoria and Arbitration: A Discussion of the New Law Merchant*, ed. Thomas E. Carbonneau, Dobbs Ferry, NY: Transnational Juris Publications.

Bewes, W.A. 1923. *The Romance of the Law Merchant: Being an Introduction to the Study of International and Commercial Law With Some Account of the Commerce and Fairs of the Middle Ages*. London: Sweet & Maxwell.

Chen, J.C. 1992. Code, custom, and contract: the Uniform Commercial Code as Law Merchant. *Texas International Law Journal* 27: 91–135.

Cooter, R.D. 1994. Structural adjudication and the new Law Merchant: a model of decentralized law. *International Review of Law and Economics* 14: 215–31.

David, R. 1985. *Arbitration in International Trade*. Deventer, The Netherlands: Kluwer Law and Taxation Publishers.

De Ly, F. 1992. *International Business Law and Lex Mercatoria*. Amsterdam: North Holland.

Draetta, U., Lake, R.B. and Nanda, V.P. 1992. *Breach and Adaptation of International Contracts: An Introduction to Lex Mercatoria*. Salem, NH: Butterworth Legal Publishers.

Ebke, W.F. 1987. Review of *The Law Merchant: the Evolution of Commercial Law*, by Leon E. Trakman. *The International Lawyer* 21: 606–16.

Ekelund, R.B. and Tollison, R.D. 1980. Economic regulation in mercantile England: Heckscher revisited. *Economic Inquiry* 18: 565–72.

Fuller, L. 1964. *The Morality of Law*. New Haven: Yale University Press.

Fuller, L. 1981. *The Principles of Social Order*. Durham, NC: Duke University Press.

Gardner, R.N. 1958. Economic and political implications of international commercial arbitration. In *International Trade Arbitration: A Road to World-Wide Cooperation*, ed. Martin Domke, New York: American Arbitration Association.

Goldman, B. and Mann, F.A. 1990. Introduction. In *Lex Mercatoria and Arbitration: A Discussion of the New Law Merchant*, ed. Thomas E. Carbonneau, Dobbs Ferry, NY: Transnational Juris Publications.

Greif, A. 1989. Reputation and coalitions in medieval trade. *Journal of Economic History* 49: 857–82.

Gross, C. (ed.) 1974. *Selected Cases Concerning the Law Merchant, A.D. 1270–1638*. London: Professional Books Limited.

Hart, H.L.A. 1961. *The Concept of Law*. Oxford: Clarendon Press.

Hayek, F.A. 1973. *Law, Legislation, and Liberty*, Vol. 1. Chicago: University of Chicago Press.

Holdsworth, Sir W. [1903] 1924. *A History of English Law*, Vol. I. London: Methuen & Co.

Lew, J.D.M. 1978. *Applicable Law in International Commercial Arbitration: A Study in Commercial Arbitration Awards*. Dobbs Ferry, NY: Oceana Publications.

Milgrom, P.R., North, D.C. and Weingast, B.R. 1990. The role of institutions in the revival of trade: the Law Merchant, private judges, and the Champagne Fairs. *Economics and Politics* 2: 1–23.

Mitchell, W. 1904. *An Essay on the Early History of the Law Merchant*. Cambridge: Cambridge University Press.

Ogilvie, M.H. 1984. Review of Leon Trakman's *The Law Merchant: The Evolution of Commercial Law*. *Canadian Bar Review* 62: 113–16.

Trakman, L.E. 1983. *The Law Merchant: The Evolution of Commercial Law*. Littleton, CO: Fred B. Rotham & Company.

Wooldridge, W.C. 1970. *Uncle Sam, The Monopoly Man*. New Rochelle, NY: Arlington House.

lawyers as transaction cost engineers. In 1937, Ronald Coase first focused attention on transaction costs as a central determinant of how economic activity is organized (Coase 1937). The choice between organizing productive activity within a firm or across a market and, in turn, the internal structure of the firm, itself a nexus of contracts among participants in the venture (Jensen and Meckling 1976), and the choice among types of contractual arrangements, are driven by economizing on transaction costs. Recognition that organizational and transactional structure can be understood as mechanisms that economize on information, bargaining, and agency costs has given rise to a large and important literature that explains the existence and efficiency of particular institutional arrangements by reference to the transaction-cost properties of the activity involved. For example, arrangements as diverse as vertical integration (Klein, Crawford and Alchian 1978), franchising (Rubin 1978), corporate governance (Williamson 1984), and movie contracts (Goldberg 1997), have been usefully explicated by reference to transaction cost considerations.

The question, then, is what mechanisms drive the transaction-cost economizing process itself. One might simply dismiss the inquiry by reference to the neoclassical assumption that, in the end, competition drives economic activity into the most cost-efficient forms. But it would be strange if an economic orientation that focused on market imperfections to explain observed patterns of organizing economic activity fell back on the invisible hand (and the institutionless features) of market-driven selection to explain the mechanisms of transaction cost economizing. The New Institutional Economics (Williamson 1985) should also be concerned with the institutional characteristics of the economizing process (Gilson and Kraakman 1984).

Observation of imperfect markets discloses a common institutional mechanism that facilitates transaction-cost economizing. Across different kinds of markets, we observe intermediaries – specialists operating to ameliorate contracting and organization costs by positioning themselves between potential participants in exchange, whether within a firm or across a market, to reduce the transaction cost wedge that otherwise separates them. The role of intermediaries is well recognized in the study of financial markets. For example, information intermediaries offer economies of specialization, scale and scope that are not available to individual acquirers of information (Leland and Pyle 1977). Similarly, reputational intermediaries, like investment banks in connection with initial public offerings (Gilson and Kraakman 1984; Booth and Smith 1986), minimize the barriers that a new seller, without its own reputation, faces in participating in the IPO market.

Now consider the difficulty of crafting transaction cost efficient contracts and internal organizational structures. Each market participant could try to internalize the transaction design effort. Alternatively, we might observe organizational intermediaries whose function is to design transaction cost efficient structures through which to carry out productive activities, a role I have called that of a *transaction cost engineer* (Gilson 1984). Across a wide range of transactions, business lawyers – that is, lawyers providing non-litigation services to clients engaged in business activities – serve as transaction cost engineers. Understanding that role illuminates both the economic function of lawyers and the institutional framework in which transaction cost economizing occurs.

THE CONCEPTUAL FRAMEWORK. Most transactions involve, in one guise or another, the pricing of a capital asset. This is most apparent in an explicit asset sale; however, the phenomenon is the same in the creation of a new enterprise, such as a joint venture or partnership: the object of the creation and often the parties' contribution, are capital assets which must be valued. Under the Capital Asset Pricing Model (CAPM), modern finance theory's paradigm of how assets should be valued under uncertainty, an asset's value is dependent on its expected return and systematic risk. As long as the capital market is relatively efficient in informational terms, the activity of arbitrageurs who identify an asset whose market price is different from what would be expected based on the asset's systematic risk would push prices toward the predicted level.

Although there have been important criticisms of this formulation of asset pricing theory (Gilson and Black 1995), they do not blunt its central insight for our purposes: *In a world in which assets are priced according to any version of capital asset pricing theory, there is little role for business lawyers.* Because capital assets will be priced correctly as a result of simple market arbitrage, the activities of business lawyers cannot increase the value of a transaction by reducing transaction costs. Indeed, absent a regulatory-based explanation for a business lawyer's participation, the fees charged by business lawyers would *decrease* the value of the transaction. In that circumstance, business lawyers would hardly be instruments of transaction cost economizing. And that, after all, is what Coase (1960) said.

Consistent with the centrality of market imperfections to transaction cost economics, the role for a transaction cost intermediary appears with closer attention to the simplifying assumptions necessary to derive CAPM. Four are of particular importance:

(1) All investors have common time horizons – i.e., they measure the return to be earned from an asset over the same period.
(2) All investors have the same expectations about the future risk and return associated with an asset.
(3) There are no transaction costs.
(4) All information is costlessly available.

These basic asset pricing theory assumptions can be reduced to the simple statement that there are no costs of transacting; neither transaction costs nor informational disparities separate the parties valuing a capital asset. In this Coasean world, private outcomes are always optimal (Calabresi 1968, 1991; Dahlman 1979). Of course, these assumptions do not describe the real world; all are descriptively false. It is the very failure of these perfect market assumptions that provides the opportunity for transaction cost intermediaries, and business lawyers in particular, to create value. When markets fall short of perfection, incentives exist for private innovation.

Thus, the potential for a link between legal skills and transaction value is the business lawyer's ability to create a transactional structure that constrains the extent to which conditions in the real world deviate from the theoretical assumptions of asset pricing theory. As transaction cost engineers, business lawyers devise efficient structures which bridge the gap between asset pricing theory's hypothetical perfect markets and the less than perfect reality of transacting in this world.

AN EXAMPLE OF TRANSACTION COST ENGINEERING BY BUSINESS LAWYERS: THE CORPORATE ACQUISITION AGREEMENT. A typical corporate acquisition agreement usefully demonstrates the transaction cost engineering role played by business lawyers. The agreement is composed of essentially four parts (Freund 1975). The initial (and usually most straightforward) part describes the transaction's overall framework: the parties are identified, and the overall structure of the transaction – a merger, sale of assets or triangular variation – is described.

The second part of the agreement focuses on the price to be paid and the medium and timing of payment. When the transaction contemplates the immediate payment of cash, the text is quite straightforward. Where the payment is made over time, or the amount paid depends on the occurrence of subsequent events, or when the medium of payment is the buyer's stock or debt, the document's complexity expands significantly.

The third part of the agreement consists of representations and warranties made by the seller and, typically to a lesser extent, the buyer. These provisions consist of a series of detailed statements of fact concerning the business being sold. The seller commonly warrants, among other things, the accuracy of its financial statements; the absence of any liabilities for taxes or other matters not appearing on its financial statements; the ownership and condition of assets important to the operation of the business; and the extent to which employees of the business are unionized.

The fourth part of the agreement – covenants and conditions – results from the fact that there is often a significant gap between the date the agreement is executed and the date the agreement is closed, during which time the buyer undertakes a close investigation of the business being sold and any regulatory barriers or consents are eliminated or obtained. Covenants govern the operation of the business during the period before closing, and conditions specify those requirements which, if not satisfied, relieve the buyer of its obligation to complete the transaction.

The business lawyer's role as a transaction cost engineer appears from the manner in which different elements of the acquisition agreement – the primary artifact of the business lawyer's participation in the transaction – respond to the problem of constraining the real world's deviation from asset pricing theory's world of perfect markets. Important parts of the agreement, and hence an important part of the business lawyer's efforts, are best understood as responding to deviations from the assumptions on which asset pricing theory is built: that all investors have homogeneous expectations; that they share a common time horizon; that information is costlessly available; and that there are no other transaction costs.

THE FAILURE OF THE HOMOGENOUS-EXPECTATIONS ASSUMPTION: CONTINGENT PRICING. As long as the buyer and seller agree about the size and risk of the future income stream associated with the business, they have no cause to disagree about its price. However, buyers and sellers typically do not share common expectations about the future of the business.

Suppose the parties agree on the proper metric for valuing the business, say $1 in purchase price for $1 in sales. The problem is that the buyer and seller still may disagree about the future performance of the business. A substantial disagreement could 'kill' the deal, because of the failure of the homogenous expectations assumption. This failure creates the opportunity for the lawyer to create value by acting as a transaction cost engineer: to 'bridge the negotiating gap between a seller who thinks his business is worth more than its historical earnings justify' and a purchaser who needs to be shown rather than merely told the truth (Freund 1975: 205).

Economists call the solution that business lawyers resort to for this problem state-contingent contracting, and lawyers call it an 'earnout'. Because differences in expectations will ultimately disappear as time transforms a prediction of next year's sales into historical fact, lawyers respond by delaying the determination of the purchase price until next year's sales are known. Payment of the difference in value resulting from the parties' differing expectations is put off until after the uncertainty has been resolved, thereby allowing each party to act *as if* his expectations were shared by the other. In effect, each party bets on the accuracy of his expectation, with a settling up only after the uncertainty has been eliminated and the parties really do have homogeneous expectations.

THE FAILURE OF THE COMMON-TIME HORIZON ASSUMPTION: CONDUCT OF THE BUSINESS DURING THE EARNOUT PERIOD. The failure of a second assumption – this time that investors measure risk and return over the same period – provides an additional opportunity for business lawyers to create value. This can be seen by reference to the earnout concept just considered. Efforts to operationalize this response to the failure of the homogeneous expectations highlights the absence of a common time horizon and the resulting potential for opportunistic behaviour. Where the parties have different time horizons, each has an incentive to maximize value over the period relevant to it, even at the expense of a decrease in value in the period relevant to the other party. The potential for such strategic behaviour reduces the value of the transaction regardless whether the seller or the buyer retains management control during the earnout period. For example, if the earnout period is one year after the closing of the transaction, the seller will try to maximize performance over that period – by increasing advertising expenditures if the earnout formula is keyed to sales; or by deferring maintenance and reducing research and development if the earnout formula is keyed to profits. If the buyer is in control, its incentives are reversed but no more balanced.

Efforts to respond to the failure of the common time horizon assumption results in the earnout formula taking the form of a complicated state-contingent contract. By carefully specifying in advance the impact on the purchase price of all events that might occur during the relevant period, the formula substantially reduces the room for opportunistic behaviour. However, no formula can completely specify the production function for the business, let alone identify all possible exogenous events that might occur during the earnout period and their impact on the formula. Moreover, the cost of such detailed contracting – not just in lawyer's fees, but in the time and especially the goodwill of the parties – will be substantial, and in many cases prohibitive. But the possibility that the costs of ameliorating the failure of the homogenous expectations and common time horizon assumptions will be too great merely constrains, but does not eliminate, the potential for business lawyers to create value by designing structures that economize on transaction costs. It is value creation of the sort that reflects what clients mean by the comment that a particular layer has good 'judgment', to know when the game is not worth the candle.

THE FAILURE OF THE COSTLESS-INFORMATION ASSUMPTION: REPRESENTATIONS, WARRANTIES, INDEMNIFICATIONS AND OPINIONS. In transactional terms, the most important assumption of all is that information is costlessly available to all parties. The portion of the acquisition agreement dealing with representations and warranties is commonly the lengthiest part of an acquisition agreement and the portion that requires the most lawyer's time to negotiate (Freund 1975). Its primary purpose is to remedy the information asymmetry between the seller and the buyer that arises from the fact that information is typically not only costly, but differentially so for the buyer and seller. To see how representations and warranties serve to economize on information costs, it is helpful to distinguish between the costs of acquiring new information and the costs of verifying previously acquired information.

Costs of acquiring information. During the negotiation, the buyer and seller will face different costs of information acquisition for two reasons. First, simply because of its prior operation of the business, the seller will already have large amounts of information concerning the business that the buyer does not have, but would like to acquire. Second, there will usually be information that neither party has, but that one or both would like and which one or the other can acquire more cheaply. The question is then how the acquisition agreement reduces these informational gaps at the lowest cost. The effort to locate the least-cost producer will be in both parties' interests because the buyer's total purchase price is the sum of the amount paid to the seller and the transaction costs, including the costs of information acquisition, incurred by the buyer in effecting the transaction.

The acquisition agreement confronts the task of minimizing information costs in three general ways: (1) by facilitating the transfer to the buyer of information the seller already has; (2) by allocating the responsibility of producing new information to the party who can acquire it most cheaply; and (3) by controlling overspending on information acquisition by identifying not only the type of information that should be acquired, but also how much should be spent in the process.

(1) The transfer of existing information from seller to buyer accounts for the quite detailed picture of the seller's business that the standard set of representations and warranties presents. Among other facts, the identity, location and condition of the assets of the business are described, the nature and extent of liabilities are specified, and the character of employment relationships – from senior management to production employees – is described (California Continuing Education of the Bar 1997). This is information that the buyer wants and the seller already has; provision by the seller minimizes acquisition costs to the benefit of both parties.

(2) A similar analysis applies when the buyer needs information that the seller has not already produced. For example, the buyer may desire information about aspects of the seller's business that bear on the opportunity for synergy between its own business and that of the seller but that, prior to the transaction, the seller had no reason to create. While the analysis here is similar to that with respect to existing information, the result of the analysis is somewhat different. Not only will the seller not always be the least-cost information producer, but there also will be a substantial role for third-party information producers.

Consider information concerning the impact of the acquisition on, for example, the seller's existing contracts. Among other things, it will be important to know whether existing contracts are assignable or assumable: The continued validity of the seller's leasehold interests will depend on whether a change in control of the seller operates – as a matter of law or because of the specific terms of a lease – as an assignment of the leasehold (Friedman 1974). Similarly, the status of the seller's existing liabilities, such as its outstanding debt, will depend on whether the transaction can be undertaken without creditor consent (American Bar Foundation 1971).

In both cases, the seller's lawyer is likely the lowest-cost information producer. An acquisition agreement's common requirement of an 'Opinion of Counsel for the Seller' is best understood from this perspective. Any significant acquisition agreement requires, as a condition to the buyer's obligation to complete the transaction, that the buyer receive an opinion of seller's counsel with respect to items such as the assignability of contracts and the impact of the transaction on existing debt (Jacobs 1980).

(3) Emphasis on selecting the lowest cost producer of information raises a related question. The demand for information, as for any good, is more or less price elastic. Information production is costly even for the most efficient producer, and the higher the cost, the less parties will choose to produce. Thus, some fine tuning of the assignment of information-production roles will be necessary. We would expect some limits on the kind of information to be produced and on how much should be spent even for information the production of which is desired.

The provisions of a standard acquisition agreement impose precisely these kinds of controls. While the buyer will want information about the seller's existing contracts, it may not want the seller to go to the expense of detailing every small contract, and to the extent that these contracts are simply a normal part of the seller's business, the information may have no impact on the pricing of the transaction.

From this perspective, the function of certain common qualifications of the seller's representations and warranties becomes apparent. First, representations concerning a seller's existing contracts are typically limited to only *material* contracts. If particular contracts are not in themselves important, then there is no reason to incur the costs of producing information about them. Variations on the theme include qualifications that limit a warranty to contracts involving more than a specified dollar amount, or on the relationship of the contracts to 'the ordinary course of business' (Freund 1975; California Continuing Education of the Bar 1997).

A second common limit on the information costs to be incurred operate as instructions concerning how hard to look for information whose subject matter cannot be excluded as unimportant ahead of time. Here the idea is to qualify not the object of the inquiry, but the diligence of the search. For example, consider the common representation concerning the absence of defaults under disclosed contracts. While it might involve little cost to determine whether the seller, as lessee, has defaulted under a lease, it may well be quite expensive to determine whether the lessor is in default. In that situation, the buyer might consider it sufficient to be told everything that the seller had thought appropriate to find out for its own purposes, without regard to the acquisition, but to require no further investigation.

This type of qualification, limiting the representation to information the seller already has and requiring no further search, is the domain of the familiar 'knowledge' qualification. In form, the seller's representation concerning the existence of breaches is qualified by the phrase 'to the seller's knowledge'. In function, the qualification serves to limit the scope of the seller's search to information already within its possession; no new information need be sought.

The same analysis also explains the variation in form that a knowledge qualification often takes. Within the same acquisition agreement one may see all of the following variations: 'to the seller's knowledge'; 'to the best of seller's knowledge'; 'to the best of seller's knowledge and after diligent investigation'.

What seems to be at work, at least implicitly (and think how much more effective explicit treatment would be (Gilson 1984)), is a hierarchy of search effort that must be undertaken with respect to information of different levels of importance.

Costs of verifying information. Problems of information cost do not end when the information is acquired. Even after cooperation in reducing the cost of producing information, another information-cost problem remains: How can the buyer determine whether the information it has received is accurate when the buyer, who has provided it, has a clear incentive to mislead the buyer into overvaluing the business?

Just as the seller has an interest in reducing the total costs of information production, so too does it have an interest in verifying the accuracy of the information it provides the buyer to avoid a lemons market (Akerlof 1970; Grossman 1981; Klein and Leffler 1981) at the lowest possible cost. And like efforts to reduce information production costs, verification techniques can be implemented both by the parties themselves and through the efforts of third parties.

With respect to verification techniques by the parties, the most familiar approach reflects what Oliver Williamson calls a 'hostage' strategy (Williamson 1983): an artificial second period in which misrepresentations in the first period – the acquisition transaction – are penalized. If any of the seller's information turns out to be inaccurate, the seller will be required to make the buyer whole; in effect, the seller posts a bond that it has provided accurate information. Consistent with the 'hostage' metaphor, the buyer's warranty of the accuracy of the information it has provided through its representations is often secured by the buyer's or a third party's retention of a portion of the consideration as a fund to assure the seller's performance of its indemnification obligation (Freund 1975).

Verification by the parties, even through holding back a portion of the consideration, will not be completely effective. For example, the indemnification obligation may be limited to the amount of the consideration held back, and typically is limited in time: A contractual statute of limitations restricts the period in which claims for indemnification may be asserted (Freund 1975). Ultimately, all verification techniques relying on the parties are imperfect because they do not entirely eliminate the potential for opportunism inherent in the one-time character of an acquisition transaction. Party-based techniques all operate to reduce final-period problems by adding an artificial second round. For this reason, all share a common limit on their effectiveness: As long as gains from cheating in the first round can exceed the penalties if caught in the second – because the probability of being caught is less than 1.0 – the buyer still lacks complete assurance that the information provided by the seller can be entirely trusted.

A critical role is thus left for third parties to close the verification gap left by the seller's residual final period problems. This gap can be filled by reputational intermediaries – someone paid to verify another party's information. For example, it is a common occurrence for companies about to make an initial public offering to switch to a Big Six auditor who, presumably, would not risk its reputation by taking on an unreliable client (Carpenter and Strawser 1971; DeAngelo 1981). From this perspective, lawyers and accountants commonly play the role of reputational intermediaries in acquisition transactions. Acquisition agreements commonly require that an opinion of *seller's* counsel be delivered to the buyer as a condition to the buyer's obligation to close the transaction. Typically, counsel's opinion will cover some of the same information separately covered by the seller's own representations and warranties. It is also common to further condition the buyer's obligation on receipt of an opinion of seller's independent accountant – the 'cold comfort' letter (Freund 1975).

A particular opinion commonly requested from the seller's lawyer that 'we are not aware of any factual information that would lead us to believe that the agreement contains an untrue statement of a material fact or omits a fact necessary to make the statements made therein not misleading' (Bermant 1974), and the accountant's cold comfort letter to the effect that there have been no changes in specified financial statements since the last audited financial statements, share a common underpinning that is reputationally based. The central characteristic of both opinions is that neither alters the total *quantity* of information that had been produced for the buyer. Rephrased, the lawyer's statement is simply that a third party who has been intimately involved in the *seller's* production of information for the buyer does not believe the seller has misled the buyer. It is quite clearly the *lawyer's* reputation – for diligence and honesty – that is intended to be placed at risk. Similarly, the cold comfort letter adds no new facts to those that have already been produced by means of the seller's representations and warranties; the accountant's letter adds only the imprimatur of a respectable third party verifying the accuracy of the information produced by the seller.

WHY LAWYERS? The analysis of a typical acquisition agreement provides empirical verification for the proposition that business lawyers serve as transaction cost engineers, whose role is to design a transactional structure that allows the parties to act, with respect to their transaction, *as if* they were acting in a Coasean world. But the question remains: Why lawyers? There is nothing traditionally *legal* about the role of transaction cost engineer. One need not be able to recite Latin incantations to bless the union of the parties' interests through exchange. Why do lawyers dominate the structuring of transactions in which capital assets are transferred or created? Answering the question requires introducing the existence of regulation.

In the United States, the transfer of significant capital assets is surrounded by substantial regulatory structures. In a corporate acquisition, tax law, antitrust law, labour law, products liability law, ERISA, securities law, and corporate law, hardly exhaust the spectrum of regulatory oversight that may influence the format of a particular transaction (Gilson and Black 1995). Most such regulatory systems express the boundaries of their application and the detail of their requirements in formal terms: Transactions that take a particular outward form are covered. So, for example, different types of acquisitions – sales of assets, mergers and tender offers – are treated differently under many regulatory regimes. This approach to regulation serves as an invitation to targets of regulation to engineer the structure of their transaction so that its form falls outside the jurisdictional boundaries of the regulation without altering its substance. The regulatory eternal triangle is completed by the courts which, in the end, must determine whether to credit the form in which the transaction is cast, or look beyond the formal terms of the regulatory structure to its 'purpose' and through the formal structure of the transaction to its financial substance.

The critical importance of transactional structure for purposes of regulation provides the core of an explanation for the success of lawyers as transaction cost engineers. Because the lawyer must play an important role in designing the structure of the transaction in order to assure the desired regulatory treatment, economies of scope should give them an advantage in performing the nonregulatory aspects of transaction structuring as well. Note, however, that this argument explains the importance of lawyers as transaction cost engineers; it does not necessarily dictate whether these lawyers will provide them from within a traditional law firm, or from within organizations composed of different kinds of professionals, such as the multi-disciplinary accounting firms in Europe, or investment banks in the United States. The efficiency considerations bearing on the internal structure of the organization through which transaction cost engineering services are provided raise interesting issues (Gilson and Mnookin 1985; Galanter and Palay 1991), but are beyond the scope of this essay.

EXTENSIONS. The discussion so far focuses on business lawyers and the example of corporate acquisitions. The concept of lawyers as transaction cost engineers can be usefully extended into other business settings and, indeed, even into litigation.

Focusing on a corporate acquisition agreement, the quintessential one-shot business transaction, ignores the fact that much transactional activity occurs between parties with longstanding business relationships. This alters significantly the character of the transaction costs confronting the parties, the role of structure as opposed to repeat dealings in offsetting opportunism, and the tools brought to bear by the transaction cost engineer. Thompson (1995), L. Bernstein (1995), Suchman (1995), E. Bernstein (1995), Okamoto (1995), Lambert (1995) and Utset (1995) consider the lawyer's transaction cost engineering function in different legal and transaction cost settings.

Understanding the transaction cost engineering skills of business lawyers leads to one of the most interesting extensions of the concept: into dispute resolution and litigation. Once one recognizes that dispute resolution involves trades between the parties – assets are transferred, liabilities extinguished, old relationships are sometimes adjusted, and new relationships created – then the potential for value creation by lawyers through engineering the structure of dispute resolution appears (Mnookin 1993; Gilson and Mnookin 1994; Arrow et al. 1995). For example, Gilson and Mnookin (1994) demonstrate how lawyers can serve as reputational intermediaries to overcome the incentives toward conflict inherent in the prisoner's dilemma characteristics of litigation between one-shot litigants.

RONALD J. GILSON

See also BARGAINING WITH REGULATORS; COASE, RONALD; HORIZONTAL MERGERS; LAW-AND-ECONOMICS IN ACTION; LAW FIRMS; LEGAL ADVICE; MARKET FOR CORPORATE CONTROL; NEOINSTITUTIONAL ECONOMICS.

Subject classification: 2e; 5a(iii).

BIBLIOGRAPHY

Akerlof, G.A. 1970. The market for 'lemons': quality uncertainty and the market mechanism. *Quarterly Journal of Economics* 84: 488–500.

American Bar Foundation. 1971. *Commentaries on Indentures*. Chicago: American Bar Foundation.

Arrow, K., Mnookin, R.H., Ross, L., Tversky, A. and Wilson, R. 1995. *Barriers to Conflict Resolution*. New York: W.W. Norton.

Bermant, G. 1974. The role of opinion of counsel – a tentative reevaluation. *California State Bar Journal* 49: 132–8, 186–91.

Bernstein, E.A. 1995. Law and economics and the structure of value adding contracts: a contract lawyer's view of the law and economics literature. *Oregon Law Review* 74: 189–237.

Bernstein, L. 1995. The silicon valley lawyer as transaction cost engineer? *Oregon Law Review* 74: 239–55.

Booth, J.R. and Smith, R.L. 1986. Capital raising, underwriting and the certification hypothesis. *Journal of Financial Economics* 15: 261–81.

Calabresi, G. 1968. Transaction costs, resource allocation and liability rules – a comment. *Journal of Law and Economics* 11: 67–73.

Calabresi, G. 1991. The pointlessness of Pareto. *Yale Law Journal* 100: 1211–36.

California Continuing Education of the Bar. 1997. *Drafting Agreements for the Sale of Businesses*. Berkeley, CA: Continuing Education of the Bar.

Carpenter, C.G. and Strawser, R.H. 1971. Displacement of auditors when clients go public. *Journal of Accounting* 131: 55–8.

Coase, R.H. 1937. The nature of the firm. *Economica* 4: 386–405.

Coase, R.H. 1960. The problem of social cost. *Journal of Law and Economics* 3: 1–44.

Dahlman, C.J. 1979. The problem of externality. *Journal of Law and Economics* 22: 141–62.

DeAngelo, L.E. 1981. Auditor size and quality. *Journal of Accounting and Economics* 3: 183–99.

Friedman, M. 1974. *Friedman on Leases*. New York: Practicing Law Institute.

Freund, J. 1975. *Anatomy of a Merger*. New York: New York Law Journal Press.

Galanter, M. and Palay, T. 1991. *Tournament of Lawyers*. Chicago: University of Chicago Press.

Gilson, R.J. 1984. Value creation by business lawyers: legal skills and asset pricing. *Yale Law Journal* 94: 239–313.

Gilson, R.J. and Black, B.S. 1995. *The Law and Finance of Corporate Acquisitions*. Mineola, NY: Foundation Press.

Gilson, R.J. and Kraakman, R. 1984. The mechanisms of market efficiency. *Virginia Law Review* 70: 549–644.

Gilson, R.J. and Mnookin, R.H. 1985. Sharing among the human capitalists: an economic inquiry into the corporate law firm and how partners split profits. *Stanford Law Review* 37: 313–92.

Gilson, R.J. and Mnookin, R.H. 1989. Coming of age in a corporate law firm: the economics of associate career patterns. *Stanford Law Review* 41: 567–95.

Gilson, R.J. and Mnookin, R.H. 1994. Disputing through agents: cooperation and conflict between lawyers in litigation. *Columbia Law Review* 94: 509–66.

Goldberg, V.P. 1997. The net profits puzzle. *Columbia Law Review* 97: 524–50.

Grossman, S.J. 1981. The informational role of warranties and private disclosure about product quality. *Journal of Law and Economics* 24: 461–83.

Jacobs, A. 1980. *Opinion Letters in Securities Matters: Text-Clauses-Law*. New York: Clark Boardman.

Jensen, M. and Meckling, W. 1976. Theory of the firm: managerial behavior, agency costs, and ownership structure. *Journal of Financial Economics* 3: 305–60.

Klein, B., Crawford, C.A. and Alchian, A.A. 1978. Vertical integration, appropriable rents, and the competitive contracting process. *Journal of Law and Economics* 21: 297–326.

Klein, B. and Leffler, K. 1981. The role of market forces in assuring contractual performance. *Journal of Political Economy* 89: 615–41.

Lambert, F.W. 1995. A preliminary inquiry into the transcendence of value creation. *Oregon Law Review* 74: 121–45.

Leland, H.E. and Pyle, D.H. 1977. Information asymmetries, financial structure and financial intermediation. *Journal of Finance* 32: 371–87.

Mnookin, R.H. 1993. Why negotiations fail: an exploration of barriers to the resolution of conflict. *Ohio State Journal on Dispute Resolution* 8: 235–49.

Okamoto, K.S. 1995. Reputation and the value of lawyers. *Oregon Law Review* 74: 15–55.

Rubin, P.H. 1978. The theory of the firm and the structure of the franchise contract. *Journal of Law and Economics* 21: 223–33.

Suchman, M.C. 1995. Transaction costs: a comment on sociology and economics. *Oregon Law Review* 74: 257–73.

Thompson, R.B. 1995. Value creation by lawyers within relational contracts and in noisy environments. *Oregon Law Review* 74: 315–26.

Utset, M.A. 1995. Producing information: initial public offerings, production costs, and the producing lawyer. *Oregon Law Review* 74: 275–314.

Williamson, O.E. 1983. Credible commitments: using hostages to support exchange. *American Economic Review* 73: 519–40.

Williamson, O.E. 1984. Corporate governance. *Yale Law Journal* 93: 1197–1230.

Williamson, O.E. 1985. *The Economic Institutions of Capitalism*. New York: Free Press.

Learned Hand rule. The Learned Hand rule is a way of identifying negligence based on comparing the cost of a potential precaution with its probabilistic expected benefits. The rule is named after Judge Learned Hand, one of the great twentieth-century American appellate judges, who identified the criterion in a 1947 decision in a case about a runaway barge in New York harbour.

In *United States v. Carroll Towing Co.*, Judge Hand analysed the liability for damages resulting from the breaking away of a barge moored in New York harbour. The barge went on to hit a tanker, whose propeller tore a hole below the barge's water line, whereupon the barge and its cargo sank. The barge owner employed a bargee whose task was to be on the barge. However, at the time of the accident, a January afternoon in the full tide of wartime shipping activity in a very busy harbour, the bargee was off the barge, and had not been there for almost twenty-four hours. Furthermore, the bargee had apparently fabricated a story as to why he had not been on the barge at the time of the accident. Judge Hand held that it was a fair requirement for the owner to have a bargee on board during the working hours of daylight. Judge Hand, apparently for rhetorical reasons, chose to use algebraic terms to state his view on the duty to take precautions in the case at hand. He said that:

> the owner's duty, as in other similar situations, to provide against resulting injuries is a function of three variables: (1) The probability that she will break away; (2) the gravity of the resulting injury, if she does; (3) the burden of adequate precautions. Possibly it serves to bring this notion into relief to state it in algebraic terms: if the probability be called P; the injury, L; and the burden, B; liability depends upon whether B is less than L multiplied by P: i.e., whether B is less than PL (*Carroll Towing*, 173).

Carroll Towing, though an ordinary case on its facts, is one of the most widely cited opinions in the literature on law and economics. Its appeal arises because it has been used in the literature as a bridge between the logic of common law judges deciding tort cases and the theorizing by economists and lawyers about those decisions. For some authors, 'The Learned Hand rule' has become a shorthand for the economic analysis of torts. For others, it is a shorthand for the logic judges use to decide tort cases. It is attractive to those using it because it invokes the name of one of the great judges of the century on behalf of the view of economic analysis of law and because it states the decision to be made in algebra, suggesting the general nature of the analysis in a form congenial to traditional economic analysis. A statement in algebraic terms did indeed bring the notion into relief, and the Learned Hand rule has been widely cited in the literature in law and economics.

THE LINKAGE BETWEEN THE LEARNED HAND RULE AND THE DECISION-MAKING OF COMMON LAW JUDGES. It is worthwhile here to review the two linkages of the Learned Hand rule: the linkage to the decision-making of common law judges, and the linkage to the economic analysis of law.

Evidence from the Carroll Towing case itself. Judge Hand did not hold that the presence of a bargee on the barge was required under all circumstances:

> It becomes apparent why there can be no such general rule, when we consider the grounds for such a liability. Since there are occasions when every vessel will break from her moorings, and since, if she does, she becomes a menace to those about her; the owner's duty as in similar situations, to provide against resulting injuries is a function of three variables (*Carroll Towing*, 173).

Instead, Judge Hand wanted to characterize the circumstances under which the owner would be held liable for not posting a bargee to the barge. Those circumstances would properly vary with the likelihood of accident, the potential harm if an accident were to take place, and the cost of the precaution. To provide that characterization, he stated the inequality which was to become the Learned Hand rule.

There are some interesting aspects of the case to note. First, Judge Hand was considering the issue of contributory negligence, not negligence. He had already determined that Carroll Towing Company, the owner of the tugboat, was negligent. He then turned to whether or not the owner of the barge was contributorily negligent, as well. Judge Hand determined that the owner was indeed contributorily negligent.

Second, the failure discussed was that the bargee was missing at the time of the accident. Though this was the fault of the errant bargee, its consequences were attributed in the first instance to Connors Marine Co., the owner of the barge.

Third, the judge states the inequality, in a manner that is a rhetorical aside: ('Possibly it serves to bring this notion into relief to state it in algebraic terms'). Having done so, however, he then does not find it necessary to evaluate quantitatively the elements of the inequality in the case at hand. He does not explicitly weigh the cost of precautions, the probability of the accident, nor the gravity of the accident, though he does do so indirectly and qualitatively.

For the cost of the precautions, he determines that there was no excuse for the absence of the bargee, that is, there was no significant cost for the precaution untaken.

The effect on probability of the accident of not taking the precaution of stationing a bargee was handled as follows:

> At the locus in quo – especially during the short January days and in the full tide of war activity – barges were being constantly 'drilled' in and out. Certainly it was not beyond reasonable expectation that, with the inevitable haste and bustle, the work might not be done with adequate care.

That is, barges were constantly being drilled in and out, and it was not unlikely that the moorings would not have been done properly. In that case, the judge found that there was not the slightest ground to believe that the bargee could have successfully protested to the deckhand and harbourmaster before it broke away from its moorings. He did find, however, that he could have called for help after determining the scope of the damage to the barge and called for help from the tugs, which could have kept the barge afloat and beached her, and saved her cargo. The change in probability in the barge breaking away is nil, but the impact on the probability of saving the cargo is one.

The costs of the accident were manifest and large. Judge Hand divided the cost into collision damages and sinking damages, because the barge owner was partially responsible for only the sinking damages, not the collision damages.

> In such circumstances we hold – and it is all that we do hold – that it was a fair requirement that the Connors company should have a bargee aboard (unless he had some excuse for his absence), during the working hours of daylight.

The judge thereby identified a part of the duty of care, enough to decide the case. He did not feel it necessary to fully determine the appropriate level of due care in all its dimensions. So much for the need for direct computation.

Evidence from earlier cases. Landes and Posner (1987) found similar language in *Mackintosh v. Mackintosh*, a Scottish case from 1864: 'The amount of care [taken by a prudent man] will be proportionate to the degree of risk run and to the magnitude of the mischief that may be occasioned' (at 681). They also cite *Chicago B. & Q. R. Co. v. Krayenbuhl*, a Nebraska railroad case from 1902, where the judge discussed at some length the tradeoff between dangers and costly precautions, whether with rail turntables or with covering wells on vacant land frequented by children.

Finally, the Learned Hand rule has withstood twenty years of review by scholars. As a result, it seems appropriate to think of the Learned Hand rule as simply a restatement of traditional legal analysis, not a novel test.

THE LINKAGE BETWEEN THE LEARNED HAND RULE AND THE ECONOMIC ANALYSIS OF LAW. Learned Hand decided Carroll Towing more than twenty years before there was a formal economic analysis of negligence law, so he was clearly not explicitly attempting to provide linkage with the body of economic analysis of law that has grown up in the meantime.

The early history of the economic analysis of law is represented by the work of Calabresi (1970), Posner (1972), Brown (1973), Diamond (1974), Landes and Posner (1983) and Shavell (1980). Another, earlier strand of the literature begins with Coase's classic work, 'The Problem of Social Cost' (1960).

The standard economic analysis. The now standard economic analysis of tort law shows simplified circumstances under which common law negligence rules provide incentives to take efficient levels of precautions. Efficient levels of precautions are those levels of precautions by both injurer and victim which would be taken if both the injurer and the victim were under common control and the level of precautions were taken to minimize overall costs of accidents and precautions taken together. It is a mathematical property of minimization that the marginal benefit of taking a precaution equals the marginal cost of taking the precaution. In this context the marginal benefit of taking a precaution is probabilistic; it is the probability of an accident multiplied by the cost of the accident avoided. To say that the marginal benefit of precautions equals the marginal cost of precautions is equivalent to saying that efficient levels of precaution are being taken. The economic theory of liability focuses on the similarity between the rules of negligence and the properties of efficient choices of precaution. (See ECONOMIC THEORY OF LIABILITY RULES.)

The marginal rereading of the rule. The Learned Hand Rule, as stated, needs minor amendment to conform to the standard economic theory. One must convert it to a *marginal* rule. To achieve cost minimization, the *marginal* benefit should be compared to the *marginal* expected cost. When that is done, the Learned Hand rule is identical to the marginal conditions of the economic theory of liability. At the combination of precautions that minimizes the social cost of accidents, including the cost of precautions, the marginal cost of each precaution will be equal to the marginal expected benefit. But the marginal interpretation of the Learned Hand rule also makes sense in interpreting how courts work. Here, plaintiffs look for precautions that the defendant could have taken, should have taken, and did not take. 'Should have taken' can be interpreted as a precaution where the incremental expected benefit is greater than the incremental cost of the precaution. Indeed, when one is talking about marginal precautions, such as keeping a bargee on board a barge during daylight working hours, then the Learned Hand rule, as Judge Hand stated it, is a marginal rule. There is little doubt that judges understand this marginal concept, and there is equally little doubt that Judge Hand would have found the marginal rereading of his rule to be consistent with his intent – a friendly amendment.

Discrete v. continuous precautions. It is a standard tactic of economic research to simplify the relevant technology, in this case the technology of precautions, to be a continuous function, so that the output (accident reduction) is a continuous function of the inputs (precautions). This makes the analysis simpler by availing one of calculus and the standard marginal conditions. This tactic has been taken in the economic analysis of liability since the 1973 article by Brown.

In the continuous economic model it is sensible to talk about equalities: adjust precautions until their marginal cost just equals the marginal benefit they obtain. In a discontinuous world, one will seldom find equalities, but will normally have to deal with inequalities: the precautions taken were less than appropriate, or there has been a breach of duty. To meet a duty is to meet or exceed a standard. In this sense, an economic theory stated in continuous terms is necessarily a simplification and approximation to the underlying reality of cases before judges.

Cases before judges are not continuous. They are replete with complex and sometimes unclear facts which are typically discrete and lumpy, not continuous. To decide a case, it is not necessary to identify the standard of care; it is sufficient to determine whether or not the standard was met. Of course, one way for a plaintiff to meet his responsibility and show that a duty was breached is to find a precaution untaken, which, if taken, would have had a greater marginal benefit than its marginal cost.

This point was made in 1973 by Brown. There he said that the Learned Hand rule, read marginally, is

> a good approximation, I think, of the way that courts actually proceed. The attorney for the plaintiff will try to find some act which, if the defendant had taken it, would have significantly reduced the probability of the accident at low cost. But that is precisely the statement that the increment in the expected loss was greater than the cost of avoidance, which is the definition of the Incremental Standards of negligence. The defendant will try to respond that the expected benefits of the proposed act were, in fact, less than the costs of undertaking it. When the court is asked to decide between the two points of view it is being asked to compare the incremental expected benefits with the incremental costs (Brown 1973: 334–5).

The same point was made by Landes and Posner:

> We find that the courts do consider marginal rather than total values in applying the standard. The court asks, 'What additional care inputs should the defendant have used to avoid this accident, given his existing level of care?' The focus on the particular accident and on the particular inputs that could have prevented it invites a marginal analysis (Landes and Posner 1987:87).

CONCLUSION. A rhetorical aside by Learned Hand in his decision in *Carroll Towing* has been used by the literature in law-and-economics as a shorthand for the equivalency of the simple economic theory of liability and the way that judges decide negligence cases. The shorthand is a reasonable, simple first approximation of the way that judges decide negligence cases. Appropriately understood, the Learned Hand rule is also a proper shorthand for the simple central characteristics of the economic theory of liability.

JOHN PRATHER BROWN

See also DUE CARE; ECONOMIC THEORY OF LIABILITY RULES; LEGAL STANDARDS OF CARE.

Subject classification: 5d(ii).

CASES

Chicago B. & Q. R. Co. v. Krayenbuhl, 91 NW 880 (Neb. 1902).

Mackintosh of Holme v. Mackintosh of Farr (1864), 2 Macpherson 1357.

United States v. Carroll Towing Co., 159 F2d 169 (2d Cir. 1947).

BIBLIOGRAPHY

Brown, J.P. 1973. Toward an economic theory of liability. *Journal of Legal Studies* 2: 323–49.

Calabresi, G. 1970. *The Cost of Accidents: a Legal and Economic Analysis*. New Haven: Yale University Press.

Coase, R.H. 1960. The problem of social cost. *Journal of Law and Economics* 3: 1–44.

Diamond, P.A. 1974. Accident law and resource allocation. *Bell Journal of Economics and Management Science* 5: 366–405.

Landes, W.M. and Posner, R.A. 1983. Causation in tort law: an economic approach. *Journal of Legal Studies* 12: 109–134.

Landes, W.M. and Posner, R.A. 1987. *The Economic Structure of Tort Law*. Cambridge, MA: Harvard University Press.

Posner, R.A. 1972. A theory of negligence. *Journal of Legal Studies* 1: 29–96.

Shavell, S. 1980. An analysis of causation and the scope of liability in the law of torts. *Journal of Legal Studies* 9: 463–516.

legal advice. Legal advice is the information that lawyers (or other experts on law) provide to clients about the nature of legal rules, about the probability and magnitude of sanctions for their violation, and about litigation and legal procedure. Thus, for example, advice might concern the current understanding of the definition of negligence in the design of a product, the likelihood of tax audit, the desirability of bringing a suit for losses suffered in an automobile accident, or the best way of presenting evidence in litigation about such an accident. The provision of legal advice is not taken to be coextensive with the provision of legal services in general, however. Some legal services (such as, often, the making of argument in court) are better regarded as the performance of specialized tasks than as the provision of information.

A client may obtain legal advice *ex ante* – when he is contemplating an action – or he may secure it *ex post* – after he has acted or someone has been harmed, which is to say, at the stage of possible or actual litigation. Advice of these two types will be considered separately because of their distinctive aspects. A notable difference between the types of advice is that *ex ante* advice can channel behaviour directly in conformity with law, whereas *ex post* advice comes too late to accomplish that (although it has indirect effects on behaviour). *Ex ante* legal advice was first studied from an economic theoretical perspective in Shavell (1988) and Kaplow and Shavell (1992); *ex post* legal advice was initially investigated from this standpoint in Kaplow and Shavell (1989, 1990); what is reviewed here is in many respects a synthesis of those articles. Legal advice was further studied in Bundy and Elhauge (1991, 1993).

Several assumptions will be maintained in most of the discussion in this essay: that advice is not purposely subversive of the law (for instance, that advice is not intended to enable a person to perpetrate a financial fraud); that lawyer–client communications and legal work product are confidential; and that lawyers are truthful to clients and endeavour to provide them with good advice. However, each of these assumptions will be examined in later sections. Additionally, the term 'social welfare' and its cognates will have the usual economic interpretation – referring to an individualistic social welfare function (which in some models will reduce to a simple aggregate, such as the amount of production, less production costs, precautionary costs, harm done, and litigation-related costs).

ADVICE ABOUT CONTEMPLATED ACTS. Advice will have private value to a party who is considering taking some action with a possible legal consequence if the advice might lead him to alter his decision. Suppose, for example, that a firm is deciding whether to release a chemical waste from a holding tank into a river rather than to spend on transport of the chemical to a dump site – but the firm does not know whether a discharge of the chemical would violate an antipollution statute. One possibility is that, without advice, the firm would elect to discharge the chemical into the river (suppose the firm thinks this probably does not violate the statute). In such situations, advice would have private value if it might lead the firm instead to transport the chemical to the dump site (the advice might be that a discharge would in fact violate the statute), because advice would then enable the firm to avoid sanctions for violating the antipollution statute. The converse possibility is that, in the absence of advice, the firm would decide to transport the chemical to the dump site (suppose the firm believes that a discharge would violate the statute). Here advice would have value to the firm if it might lead the firm instead to discharge the chemical into the river (the advice might be that a discharge would not violate the statute), because advice would then save the firm transport costs.

In general, the private value of legal advice is the expected value of the private gain from possible changes in a party's decision. This notion of the private value of legal advice is, it may be noted, just an application of the conventional definition of the expected value of information to a decisionmaker, as presented for instance in Raiffa (1968).

The social, as opposed to the private, value of *ex ante* legal advice inheres in the social desirability, or lack thereof, of advice-induced changes in parties' behaviour. Suppose that it is socially desirable that the chemical not be discharged (because the harm from a discharge would exceed the cost of transport to the dump site). Then if advice would result in the firm deciding against discharging the chemical, the advice would be socially desirable. But if advice would lead the firm to discharge the chemical (say, because the firm would learn that the probability of sanctions is low), the advice would not be socially desirable. The social value of advice is the expected value of the potential social gains and losses produced by the advice.

Comparison of the social and the private values of *ex ante* legal advice is of interest for, among other reasons, it informs us whether the amount of such legal advice that is purchased does or does not tend toward the socially correct level. In particular, when the private value of advice exceeds the social, the amount of advice demanded will tend to be socially excessive, and in the reverse situation the demand for advice will tend to be socially inadequate.

The comparison between the social and the private values of legal advice depends on the form of liability: whether it is strict (under which a party pays for any harm caused) or based on the negligence rule (under which a party pays for harm only if he was negligent). In the consideration of these rules, it will be assumed that law enforcement is perfect in the sense that a sanction equal to harm is imposed whenever parties are supposed to be liable for harm. Then the situations when there is underenforcement or misapplication of legal rules will be addressed.

When parties are strictly liable, the private value of legal advice is the same as its social value. This basic and important conclusion follows essentially because a party's liability burden will equal the harm he causes. If a party learns through advice that taking some precaution will reduce his liability from $15,000 to $5,000, this also means that the precaution will lower harm by $10,000. Hence, it should not be surprising that the private and social values of advice are equivalent.

The conclusion is different when liability is based on negligence; under this rule, the private value of legal advice tends to exceed its social value. The explanation is suggested by two points. First, if a party avoids negligence because of advice, the party's liability saving will generally be larger than the reduction in expected harm he accomplishes. Suppose that, without advice, the party just mentioned would not take the precaution and would be found negligent and liable for the harm of $15,000. And suppose that, with advice, the party would take the precaution and thereby avoid liability for negligence. Thus the advice would lead to a reduction in liability for the party of $15,000 – an amount exceeding the $10,000 reduction in harm. The reason that the private liability saving from advice is larger than the reduction in harm is that, under the negligence rule, a party escapes having to pay for any harm caused when he acts nonnegligently (the party escapes having to pay for the $5,000 of harm he still generates if he takes the precaution). The second point is similar. If a party would learn from advice that he can relax somewhat his level of precautions and will continue not to be found negligent, his saving will be the full amount of the reduction in precautionary costs. However, society will not save as much as the party, for when precautions fall, expected harm rises.

Consider now the situation when legal rules (whether based on strict liability or on negligence) are underenforced, that is, when the probability of having to pay for harm is less than 100 percent or when the level of damages is less than harm. When this is so and expected sanctions thus fall short of expected harm, it might seem that the private incentive to obtain legal advice is less than socially appropriate. Nevertheless, that is not clear. The explanation involves the observation that when a party obtains legal advice, he will not necessarily be induced to act in a socially desirable way: advice may lead him to act undesirably precisely because he may learn that the law is underenforced. In consequence, it is ambiguous whether the private value of legal advice is socially excessive or inadequate when the law is poorly enforced.

Finally, consider the case where legal rules are sometimes incorrectly formulated or applied. For example, an environmental authority might mistakenly omit a truly harmful chemical from its list of substances for which discharge will result in a penalty, or it might mistakenly include on its list a chemical that is truly harmless. When rules are erroneously applied and legal advice gives a party foreknowledge of error, the only possible effects of the advice are undesirable (either to discharge the substance when it should not be, or not to discharge it when it should be). Thus, the social value of advice is negative – it would be best for parties not to obtain advice – even though its private value is positive.

ADVICE ABOUT ACTS ALREADY COMMITTED. The private value of *ex post* legal advice, advice provided after acts have been committed, is analogous to the private value of *ex ante* legal advice. It resides in the possibility that the advice will lead a party to change his decisions, but now about whether to sue or how to conduct litigation (including settlement negotiation) rather than about the party's earlier, substantive behaviour. *Ex post* legal advice can affect not only what legal arguments to pursue, but also how to develop evidence, what evidence to present and not to present, and how to challenge false arguments. It is virtually inevitable that *ex post* legal advice will have substantial private value because of the complicated nature of legal procedure and the unlikelihood that potential litigants will know the law in real detail.

In considering the social value of *ex post* advice and comparing it to the private value of *ex post* advice, let us begin with advice about whether a harmed party should bring suit. The social value of this advice derives principally from the effect of suit on the prior behaviour of parties who might be sued, that is, on their precautions and participation in potentially harm-producing activity. This incentive effect of suit could be small or large, and either be exceeded by or surpass the expected private gain from suit; see Shavell (1982). To illustrate, if there is little that injurers can do to prevent harm, suit will not have much social benefit, but the private motive of injured parties to bring legal actions may be high (especially under strict liability) because they can collect damages for harm sustained. In such a situation, legal advice about whether to bring suit would be likely to have greater private value than social value (assuming that the advice would tend to promote suit). If, on the other hand, injurers can take inexpensive steps to prevent harm and would do so if sued, suit may have substantial social value, but relatively small private value if the magnitude of harm is not significant. In this situation, legal advice about whether to bring suit would be likely to have greater social value than private value (again assuming that the advice would foster suit).

Now consider legal advice that parties obtain during litigation. As noted in the introduction, because such advice is, by its nature, imparted to parties only after they have acted, it cannot have aided them in conforming with the law, in choosing how to act if they were uncertain about the law. (The firm that does not know whether discharging a chemical waste into a river will violate an antipollution statute cannot be led to behave appropriately by learning what the law is after it decides about discharging the chemical.) This simple but fundamental observation means that *ex post* advice does not raise social welfare in the direct way that *ex ante* advice does. Nonetheless, *ex post* advice certainly may influence behaviour and social welfare.

One way that *ex post* advice may affect social welfare is by lowering sanctions for those who knowingly violate the law, that is, *ex post* advice may dilute deterrence of undesirable conduct. Lawyers may lower expected sanctions by advantageous use of legal strategy, and importantly by counselling defendants on the selection of evidence to present and to suppress. Given that individuals anticipate that their expected sanctions for causing harm will be reduced due to the subsequent availability of legal advice, fewer individuals will be deterred from engaging in undesirable behaviour. Thus, legal advice may have negative social value, a point that was early emphasized by Bentham (1827). (In principle, a partial remedy for this problem, though, would be for the state to raise sanctions overall to offset the dilution of deterrence due to advice.)

However, *ex post* advice may also enhance social welfare by raising otherwise inadequate sanctions that would be imposed on those who knowingly commit sanctionable acts. Advice may raise expected sanctions because lawyers may help *plaintiffs* to obtain higher judgments, better reflecting the harms they have sustained, than they would receive if they did not have legal advice.

Additionally, *ex post* advice may raise social welfare by lowering sanctions for defendants who did not violate the law, or who face higher sanctions than they should. If parties anticipate that, if they ever incorrectly face a legal sanction, advice will help them to avoid that sanction, they will not be undesirably discouraged from engaging in many useful activities or be led to take expensive and inordinate precautions.

There is no way on the basis of logic alone to conclude whether or not *ex post* advice provided during litigation is on balance socially desirable – whether or not its socially undesirable effect, due to dilution of deterrence, is less important than its desirable effect, due to increased accuracy of legal outcomes for the guilty and for the innocent. Either effect could outweigh the other, depending on context.

Let us next restrict attention to *ex post* legal advice that does increase the accuracy of legal outcomes and ask how the generally positive social value of this advice compares to its private value. The general answer to this question is that either the private value of the advice or its social value could be larger, so that the private incentive to spend on the advice could be socially excessive or it could be inadequate. The reason, as discussed in Shavell (1997), is essentially that explained above with respect to the bringing of suit: the social value of legal advice that increases accuracy inheres in its incentive effect on prior behaviour of parties; and this has little connection to the private incentive to spend on advice, for that derives from the amount at stake in litigation.

In some contexts, however, the private value of accuracy enhancing advice will tend to exceed the social value, so that too much of the advice will be purchased. Notably, consider advice that will enable a party to establish accurately the degree of harm suffered in an adverse event. If the presently estimated harm deviates from the truth by $100, a party will be willing to spend up to $100 on legal advice to prove the correct amount (if the estimate exceeds the correct level, the defendant will spend on legal help; and if the estimate is below the correct level, the plaintiff will spend on legal help). It can be shown that the social value of the more accurate estimate tends, however, generally to be lower than $100, essentially because the social value of accuracy is based on its effects on incentives. Indeed, there would be little or no beneficial incentive benefit from accurate assessment of harm if all that potential injurers know when choosing their precautions (for instance, how carefully to drive on the road) is the probability distribution of possible harm (the range of possible damage that could occur in an automobile accident). For development of this point, see Kaplow and Shavell (1996).

In sum, the social value of *ex post* legal advice is complicated to determine, possibly negative and possibly positive, and not closely related to its private value. In certain domains, a plausible conjecture is that, in an appropriate average sense, the private value of *ex post* advice exceeds the social.

SUBVERSION OF THE LAW. It has been assumed for the most part above that legal advice is purely informational in character, conveying knowledge about the law and legal sanctions but not altering expected sanctions. Yet lawyers are sometimes able to subvert the law by effectively lowering sanctions or their probability. As mentioned above, lawyers may inappropriately reduce expected sanctions by selecting only favourable evidence to present. Also, lawyers may diminish the real magnitude of sanctions by helping clients to hide assets; and lawyers can also decrease the likelihood of sanctions if they have knowledge of enforcement strategies (such as how the tax authorities choose whom to audit). Such legal assistance is to be distinguished from advice that lowers expected sanctions for bona fide reasons, for example, by demonstrating that an asserted harm was not a true harm. Of course, lawyers are not supposed to thwart law enforcement, but they have an economic incentive to do so and can fairly easily avoid punishment for it (lawyers give advice in private and can phrase their advice in hypothetical but readily understood terms). From the social perspective, legal advice that frustrates law enforcement is obviously undesirable.

CONFIDENTIALITY OF ADVICE. The legal system protects the confidentiality of communications between lawyers and their clients under wide circumstances, and this protection has been implicity assumed in the above discussion. Confidentiality of legal advice will benefit clients when there is positive probability that disclosure of advice would lower its value. This would usually be true of advice about the selection of evidence to present in litigation: such advice generally would be robbed of effectiveness if it were disclosed to the opposing side and the court. Confidentiality is also of obvious importance to those obtaining advice subversive of the law. By contrast, confidentiality often should not matter to parties obtaining advice about the legality of an act or about magnitude or likelihood of sanctions, because disclosure of such advice will usually not disadvantage them. For example, disclosure of the *ex ante* advice that a party obtains about what is considered negligent behaviour ordinarily should not matter to the party.

Still, whatever is the character of legal advice, maintaining the confidentiality of much information *about clients* that is revealed to lawyers in the course of their dealings with clients will frequently be of importance to the clients. For instance, a firm would usually not want information pertaining to its business plans revealed to others, and an individual would ordinarily not want information of a personal nature disclosed to outsiders.

Because protection of confidentiality can benefit clients (and is never a disadvantage to them), it encourages clients to consult with and reveal information to their lawyers. This in itself is sometimes thought to imply that confidentiality is socially desirable. That reasoning, however, is mistaken: confidentiality is socially desirable only if the legal advice that confidentiality encourages is socially desirable, and as has been explained above, that may not be the case.

PROTECTION OF LEGAL WORK PRODUCT. The legal system also protects the confidentiality of legal work product – documents and other records of lawyers' effort – that they generate on behalf of clients in expectation of litigation. The protection of work product is accomplished principally by denying opposing litigants the legal right to discover work product (that is, the right to order the party with work product to produce it). The effect of work product protection is similar to that of protection of confidentiality, so it can be very briefly considered. As Easterbrook (1981) stressed, protection of work product encourages lawyers to engage in research on and development of their clients' cases, for much of the value of such research and development would be lost if it became immediately known to the other side. (Thus, the protection functions analogously to copyright.) Because protection of work product raises the value and quality of legal advice, it inures to clients' benefit. But whether protection of work product is socially desirable is not evident *a priori*; for it depends on whether or not the advice that the work product supports is socially desirable. A further complication is that, even when the advice is socially desirable, the private value of advice, and thus the amount of work product, may be socially excessive.

QUALITY AND TRUTHFULNESS OF ADVICE. The issue of lawyers' incentives to supply good advice and to be truthful to clients has not been addressed above. To the degree that poor or dishonest advice would be discovered and that lawyers would suffer penalties for having provided such advice, they will have reason not to do so. There are two basic types of penalty lawyers face for furnishing unsound legal advice: loss of business because of damage to reputation; and legal sanction, in the form of a damage judgment arising from a malpractice action, a fine assessed by a court, or a punishment imposed by a professional association. For a general treatment of these ways of regulating lawyer conduct, see Wilkins (1992).

Several observations are worth making about penalties for unsound advice. First, the ability of clients to discover that they were given subpar advice varies according to context. Poor advice about well-defined legal questions is more likely to be detected than poor advice about areas of law that are unsettled or than poor advice about the probability of a legal outcome (probabilities are hard to verify objectively, and lawyers may be able to ascribe adverse legal results suffered by their clients to bad luck). In some domains, lawyers' motivations to provide good advice are particularly perverse. For example, lawyers have reason to exaggerate the probability of winning cases when they give advice about bringing suit, for this will generate business for themselves. To some extent, this problem of dishonest reporting of the chance of prevailing may be mitigated through contingency fee arrangements, whereby lawyers bear most legal expenses and receive a fraction of any settlement or court award.

Second, the existence of law firms serves to foster provision of advice of good quality. Firms have a greater reputational stake than individuals, and a continuing one. Additionally, firm members are often able to (and have reason to) check on the advice that one another are providing to clients.

CONCLUSION. Perhaps the most important lessons of the foregoing review of the subject of legal advice are two. First, *ex ante* advice, given when parties are contemplating actions with possible legal consequences, is quite different from *ex post* advice, provided at the stage of possible or actual litigation. Second, for a variety of reasons, the private incentive to obtain legal advice may deviate from (and often exceed) the social reason to do so.

STEVEN SHAVELL

See also DISCOVERY; LAW-AND-ECONOMICS IN ACTION; LAWYERS AS TRANSACTION COST ENGINEERS; LEGAL AID; PRIVACY; PRIVATE INFORMATION AND LEGAL BARGAINING; SELECTION OF CASES FOR TRIAL.

Subject classification: 4c(ii); 5a(iii).

BIBLIOGRAPHY

Bentham, J. 1827. *Rationale of Judicial Evidence*, Vol. V. London: Hunt and Clarke.

Bundy, S. McG. and Elhauge, E.R. 1991. Do lawyers improve the adversary system? A general theory of litigation advice and its regulation. *California Law Review* 79: 313–420.

Bundy, S. McG. and Elhauge, E.R. 1993. Knowledge about legal sanctions. *Michigan Law Review* 92: 261–335.

Easterbrook, F. 1981. Insider trading, secret agents, evidentiary privileges, and the production of information. *Supreme Court Review* 1981: 309–65.

Kaplow, L. and Shavell, S. 1989. Legal advice about information to present in litigation: its effects and social desirability. *Harvard Law Review* 102: 565–615.

Kaplow, L. and Shavell, S. 1990. Legal advice about acts already committed. *International Review of Law and Economics* 10: 149–59.

Kaplow, L. and Shavell, S. 1992. Private versus socially optimal provision of ex ante legal advice. *Journal of Law, Economics, and Organization* 8: 306–20.

Kaplow, L. and Shavell, S. 1996. Accuracy in the assessment of damages. *Journal of Law and Economics* 39: 191–210.

Raiffa, H. 1968. *Decision Analysis*. Reading, MA: Addison-Wesley.

Shavell, S. 1982. The social versus the private incentive to bring suit in a costly legal system. *Journal of Legal Studies* 11: 333–9.

Shavell, S. 1988. Legal advice about contemplated acts: the decision to obtain advice, its social desirability, and protection of confidentiality. *Journal of Legal Studies* 17: 123–50.

Shavell, S. 1997. The fundamental divergence between the private and the social motive to use the legal system *Journal of Legal Studies* 26: 575–612.

Wilkins, D.B. 1992. Who should regulate lawyers? *Harvard Law Review* 105: 799–887.

legal aid. The legal system is sometimes represented as a mechanism which gives agents incentives to anticipate externalities associated with their actions, while simultaneously giving other parties a means of redressing externalities which do occur. As an efficient outcome would occur when the marginal social cost of actions to reduce externalities equals the marginal social benefit of avoiding further externalities, there is an efficiency justification for ensuring that individuals can bear the costs of using the law (Posner [1973] 1986). There may also be equity-based justifications: if justice is seen as a fundamental right distinguishable from most other services or goods, excluding individuals from the legal system on grounds of income will be an infringement of this right, particularly where defendants have to participate in criminal or personal injury proceedings which may have severe personal consequences.

From an efficiency perspective, the fundamental policy dilemma is to find a mechanism enabling individuals of limited personal means to obtain legal redress, while avoiding further efficiency losses by creating new incentives for providers and users. From an equity perspective, the key question is whether all legal services are an equally fundamental right, and if not how they can be differentiated. Trade-offs between these efficiency and equity objectives are likely to be inevitable, making any policy choice a second-best for any single objective.

Ensuring access to law could be done via a number of mechanisms: an insurance market which allowed individuals to shift their risks of injury, loss or legal costs; or a contingency fee system, in which the plaintiff shifted risk onto a lawyer whose remuneration was contingent on the outcome of the case; or, finally, a redistribution of income such as a means-tested subsidy to individuals with insufficient personal means to ensure access to the legal system.

The policy emphasis inevitably varies substantially across jurisdictions. In the US, access to civil legal services for people of limited means is promoted by the widespread use of contingency fees for personal injury litigation, coupled to small volumes of *pro bono* work, in which lawyers agree voluntarily to perform for a low or zero fee cases which the client would otherwise be unable to afford. Federal and private funding for criminal and civil legal aid work also exists, but at a relatively low level: in the fiscal year 1994 the Legal Services Corporation – the main source of public funding for legal aid in America – received a budget of $400 million.

In other countries, the policy emphasis has been focused more exclusively on legal aid schemes as a way of promoting access to people of limited means, particularly during the post-war period of expanding welfare systems. The precise scope and administrative arrangements for these schemes vary enormously between jurisdictions, but the essential feature of most is that they offer conditional financial support, funded from taxation, to individuals whose financial circumstances would prevent them from taking or defending proceedings without assistance with their legal costs.

Legal aid, like many other professional services, is characterized by a high degree of uncertainty and ignorance on the part of the consumer, who is likely to be an infrequent user with limited knowledge of the range of appropriate and available services and their likely costs and outcomes, and with limited ability to assess the competence of legal practitioners. This clearly locates legal aid within a larger class of principal–agent relationships, which invariably contain potential conflicts between each party's own interests and those of the other party (Rees 1987). The legal aid system can be seen as a variant of the principal–agent relationship. The basic principal–agent relationship is between the assisted person and the lawyer but this is invariably mediated by a third party, such as the Legal Aid Board in England and Wales, which acts as the assisted person's agent by providing information, negotiating remuneration and monitoring quality, but which also has a principal–agent relationship with the lawyer. This is analogous to an insurer acting on behalf of the insured by transacting with the insured's agent. Thus three sets of contract are of interest in this particular context: between the assisted person and the lawyer, the third party and the lawyer, and the third party and the assisted person. Each of these contracts generates incentives and potential incentive problems.

One incentive problem likely to arise is *adverse selection*, where the insurer has insufficient information to discriminate fully between risks and tends therefore to equalize premiums, which increases the likelihood that high-risk individuals will seek insurance cover, and that low-risk individuals will opt out: this is adverse selection. Although the legal aid system can be seen as an insurance system where the state subsidises premiums, the risks of adverse selection are reduced because payment is generally compelled via taxation. Hence the legal aid system can be seen as a response to insurance market failure.

A second incentive problem likely to arise is *moral hazard*, in the form of producer's moral hazard (or supplier-induced demand) where the incentives facing producers lead them to provide their clients or agents with more (or fewer) services than the client would choose in the absence of information asymmetry, or in the form of consumer's moral hazard, where the existence of some form of insulation (such as insurance) against the financial consequences of an action encourages the insured to increase consumption of services.

Moral hazard in legal aid can arise between the assisted person/potential assisted person and the third party, and between the third party and the lawyer. The potential assisted person, aware of the existence of legal aid, may act in a way which increases the likelihood of requiring legal services. And once an action has commenced, the assisted person may have less incentive to reach pre-trial settlement, and more incentive to pursue a larger settlement.

Moral hazard between the lawyer and the third party depends on the nature of the remuneration contract and its effect on strategic decisions made within a complex web of principal–agent relationships. In Australia, legal aid is provided in part by fee for service arrangements with private practitioners, but increasingly in recent years via salaried in-house lawyers, who are also the principal delivery mechanism of the US Legal Services Corporation. In the UK, the standard pattern of remuneration until recently has been fee per item of service. The moral hazard issues raised by fee per item of service remuneration are well rehearsed, and in recent years there has been a move towards prospectively defined standard fees to replace fees per item of service, but there remain great difficulties in measuring and monitoring the quantity and quality of a lawyer's inputs to a legally aided case. And other aspects of procedure and case financing may also influence outcomes through their influence on principal–agent relationships. For example, in the UK legal aid reduces the legally aided parties' exposure to their opponents' legal costs, which is likely to influence the party's decision to settle or continue a case.

LEGAL AID EXPENDITURE. Despite intense interest in recent years in the costs of legal aid, very few countries have been able to produce detailed information that might facilitate economic analysis. There are few reliable comparative international data on legal aid systems: one estimate of legal aid expenditure in 1989 in eight European countries had the UK devoting 0.05% of Gross Domestic Product to legal aid, compared to 0.04% in The Netherlands, 0.025% in Sweden, 0.02% in Germany, 0.01% in Spain, 0.005% in France and Ireland, and 0.002% in Belgium (Cousins 1994). An alternative estimate of legal aid spending per head of population in 1989 was 4.1 European Currency Units (ECUs) in Germany, 6.7 ECUs in The Netherlands and 15.5 ECUs in England and Wales (Blankenburg 1992).

Despite these international variations in levels of legal aid expenditure, total spending on legal aid grew fairly rapidly in most countries during the 1980s and early 1990s:

for example, over the period 1970 to 1989 legal aid expenditure rose in real terms by 366% in Germany and by approximately 220% in England and Wales. In some jurisdictions the problem was perceived to be a failure of real expenditure on legal aid to accommodate rising pressures: for example in Australia judicial decisions widening the scope of legal aid combined with relatively low expenditure growth during the 1980s and early 1990s to engender a debate on whether national funding of legal aid was adequate.

The difficulties experienced in many jurisdictions of providing satisfactory legal aid systems at sustainable levels of expenditure have led to the efficiency and equity of legal aid systems themselves being subjected to close scrutiny and to policy reforms, notably but not exclusively in the UK. In the UK, legal aid experienced a volume growth of approximately 4% per annum over the period from 1980 to 1993 in the number of civil matrimonial and criminal cases, and of almost 12% per annum for civil non-matrimonial cases. In addition, real expenditure per case grew by approximately 3–5% per annum over that period. There was clear evidence that volume inputs of legal practitioner services to the average criminal case rose sharply over this period: between 1980 and 1992 the average number of hours spent in attendance, preparation, advocacy, travelling and waiting in court rose by 76%, the average number of letters and telephone calls rose by 126% and 95% respectively, and the average number of dates spent in advocacy rose by 48%. The average length of each case also rose substantially, by 52% over the period 1988–1992 alone (Gray 1994).

Hence the legal aid system in England experienced both a rising volume of cases and a rising real cost per case. Both phenomena would be consistent with the presence of moral hazard influences on producers (practitioners) and consumers (clients),

The remuneration system over this period was primarily a fee per item of service system which placed the onus of calculating the items of service required to perform a case firmly on the lawyer; this could systematically engender moral hazard manifested in growing volumes of inputs per case and hence rising unit costs. The incentives to behave in this way would be mediated by the opportunity cost of performing legal aid work compared to other legal work: for example, a slump in alternative work such as property transactions – as occurred in the UK following the housing slump in 1989 and the deregulation of the property transaction market – would reduce the opportunity cost of performing legal aid work and reinforce incentives to put more into each case.

Moral hazard amongst consumers might also have an impact on the volume of cases insofar as legal aid increased the likelihood of assisted individuals becoming involved in legal action, or on the unit cost of cases insofar as it discouraged assisted persons from reaching a pre-trial settlement. For example, there is some English evidence that individuals who are eligible for free civil legal aid are approximately six times more likely to be involved in legally aided non-matrimonial litigation than are individuals who are eligible for legal aid but have been assessed as liable for some contribution towards the costs of the litigation (Lord Chancellor's Department 1991). Unfortunately there is less evidence on the propensity to litigate of those not eligible for legal aid, or how this has changed over time.

It is worth noting that a number of explanations other than (or in addition to) moral hazard would be consistent with a rising volume or unit cost of legally aided cases. First, an increasing demand arising from higher crime rates and/or an increasing propensity to use the law to resolve civil or matrimonial disputes could result in a greater volume of legally aided cases. Evidence illustrating both these trends is available from many countries, and both have been linked with many factors other than the availability of subsidised legal assistance. Second, a decrease in the efficiency of the legal aid system or the administration of justice system within which it operates, such as the courts, could result in longer waiting times, more frequent cancellations, lengthened case times and higher unit costs for all legal cases including those which were legally aided. Third, changes in the quality of legal services, such as higher standards of representation or tighter requirements concerning evidence, would also tend to increase costs per case.

In summary, the little evidence available indicates that growing legal aid expenditure in England and Wales during the 1980s and early 1990s resulted from both volume growth and rising unit costs, phenomena which were compatible with the existence of moral hazard on the part of producers and consumers, but were also consistent with many other possible factors. However, the moral hazard arguments were emphasised by a number of commentators arguing for reform to the system (Bevan, Holland and Partington 1994), and exerted a strong influence on a range of far-reaching reforms introduced in 1996 (Lord Chancellor's Department 1996).

REFORMING LEGAL AID. Ideally, optimal levels of legal aid provision could be estimated using the kind of efficiency and equity arguments outlined above, and from this perspective rising legal aid expenditure is not in itself an indication of a problem. However, a rising share of national income devoted to legal aid cannot be sustained indefinitely, and this has underlain the reforms proposed in many jurisdictions. These fall into three categories: those directed at the legal aid system directly; potential alternatives to legal aid; and reforms aimed at the wider legal services industry.

Insofar as moral hazard is a contributory factor in rising expenditure, the orthodox responses to producers would be to introduce more rigorous procedures for monitoring and assessing the work lawyers do, and/or to devise an alternative system of payment more related to output rather than input, such as standard fees per case: these should reduce moral hazard and thus restrain unit cost increases. In England and Wales there has been a significant move towards prospective standard fees for legally aided cases, and in the reforms introduced in 1996 this move will be accentuated. Prospectively set standard fee systems, however, may simply alter rather than remove moral hazard amongst producers. Such systems almost invariably require cases to be differentiated by size or complexity, with triggers or thresholds at which higher standard fees are paid or fee per item is used. This creates incentives to reach trigger points or to redefine cases, problems which have been well documented in the diagnosis-related group (DRG) prospective payment system which is now widely used in the public part of the American health care system (Hodgkin and McGuire 1994), but which has failed to prevent rapid cost inflation continuing in that sector.

To address these issues, the English reforms propose a system whereby regional purchasers of legal aid are given annual global budgets and central guidance on legal aid priority areas; they then enter into contracts with providers which may take the form of block contracts covering all work for a specified period or a set price per case to a maximum volume; finally, the contracts are monitored and efficiency incentives are operated through a franchising system which ensures minimum standards and gives preferential treatment to providers meeting pre-specified performance targets. It seems clear that the major challenge facing this contracting mechanism – which forms the core of the English reforms – will be the monitoring of quality standards amongst providers, given the information asymmetries discussed earlier.

A standard response to potential moral hazard amongst consumers or potential consumers of legal aid is the use of charges or insurance co-payments. In effect the means test in the English system provides this mechanism by determining eligibility and liability to contribute towards the cost of the proceedings. The impact of this can be gauged by the fact that a substantial proportion of all those who initiate legal proceedings and then are offered legal aid conditional on a contribution then decline to continue the proceedings. As with prospective payment systems, co-payment systems have been used extensively in the health sector, and have been shown to induce substantial changes in health care use (Newhouse 1993); however, their role in containing health expenditure growth over time has been limited.

Turning to potential alternatives to legal aid, contingent funding may provide lawyers with incentives to accept certain cases by offering them a stake in a successful outcome to the action. This can take a number of forms: a straight percentage of any award (the American system); the costs awarded against a losing side (in Scotland); or an increment or 'uplift' to normal fees if the outcome is successful (the English 'conditional fee' variant). There is no experience to date of any variant of contingency funding acting as a complete substitute for some form of legal aid. However, between 1995 and 1997 around 30,000 cases in England involving money or damages claims were fought on a conditional fee basis, and in October 1997 the Lord Chancellor announced that the UK Government intended to remove from the scope of civil legal aid most cases involving claims for money or damages which it believed could be funded through conditional fee agreements, with the possible exception of medical negligence litigation in which high investigative costs may be required to establish a case. This represents a major policy experiment.

Another potential alternative to legal aid is some form of insurance cover for legal expenses; this could be on a voluntary or compulsory basis, possibly with some state subsidization of premiums to ensure affordability to all sections of the population. In some countries the percentage of the population covered by such insurance is quite high: 50% in Germany and 80% in Sweden; the comparable figure in the UK is around 7%. However, even where coverage is high such policies tend to exclude areas covered by legal aid schemes, and surveys tend to reveal dissatisfaction amongst policy holders over areas such as refusal to renew policies following claims; confusing documentation which fails to state exclusions clearly; imposed time restrictions on the reporting of claims which were likely to exclude many cases; and failure to provide adequate means of arbitration in the event of disputes. Again, experience from the health insurance sector has reflected some of these problems, providing neither physicians nor patients with incentives for cost control. In addition, voluntary legal expenses insurance might produce widespread adverse selection, and hence it is not evident that legal expense insurance could be an alternative to legal aid, at least without a number of other changes to the legal system more generally (for example, the climate for legal expenses insurance is more favourable in Germany in part because the costs of particular cases are more predictable than in other jurisdictions such as Australia). The more widespread introduction of conditional fees in the UK in place of legal aid will depend on the development of new 'before the event' and 'after the event' insurance products, with the hope that this will be aided by greater predictability in costs as a result of wider civil justice reforms.

Another potential alternative to legal aid would be a legal loans market, in which lenders held the impending action as an asset and funded the costs of pursuing the case. A limited scheme of this kind operates in certain states of Australia, but difficulties in assessing merits and promptly establishing the financial status of the litigant have severely restricted the scheme's adoption.

A contingency legal aid fund, in which litigants apply for support from a fund and agree to pay back a surcharge on their costs if successful, has been used in Hong Kong, but raises problems of moral hazard and adverse selection: successful applicants have no incentives to settle, while litigants with particularly strong cases are unlikely to make use of the scheme.

An alternative way of potentially improving access to legal services is by making broader reforms to the legal system, such as removing restrictions on legal services advertising or on the use of paraprofessionals, changing the nature of the legal firm, or altering the institutional context within which the legal market is set (Evans and Wolfson 1982). Thus it might be anticipated that more competition between providers would increase efficiency, reduce prices and enhance access to those of limited means. However, these policy options have frequently been debated and even introduced with little theoretical or empirical support. For example, it is not clear that competition in legal services will necessarily be manifested in lower prices; evidence from the health sector suggests that competition may engender an expansion in facilities and rising costs.

In conclusion, it seems clear that there has been considerable confusion over the policy objectives of legal aid systems, with an unwillingness to consider the weights to attach to efficiency and equity objectives and the likely trade-offs. It also seems clear that a priority in law and economics is to attain a broader theoretical and empirical understanding of legal aid systems set within their broader legal service industries.

ALASTAIR M. GRAY

See also ALTERNATIVE DISPUTE RESOLUTION; CONDITIONAL FEES IN BRITAIN; CONTINGENT FEES; COST OF JUDICIAL SERVICES; DISPUTE RESOLUTION IN JAPAN AND THE UNITED STATES; EQUITY; LAW FIRMS; LEGAL ADVICE; LIABILITY RIGHTS AS CONTINGENT CLAIMS.

Subject classification: 3b; 5a(iii).

BIBLIOGRAPHY

Bevan, G., Holland, T. and Partington, M. 1994. *Organising Cost-Effective Access to Justice*. London: Social Justice Foundation, Memorandum No. 9.

Blankenburg, E. 1992. Comparing legal aid schemes in Europe. *Civil Justice Quarterly* 11: 106–14.

Cousins, M. 1994. The politics of legal aid. *Civil Justice Quarterly* 13: 111–32.

Evans, R.G. and Wolfson, A.D. 1982. Cui bono – who benefits from improved access to legal services? In *Lawyers and the Consumer Interest: Regulating the Market for Legal Services*, ed. R.G. Evans and M.J. Trebilcock, Toronto: Butterworths.

Gray, A. 1994. The reform of legal aid. *Oxford Review of Economic Policy* 10(1): 51–67.

Hodgkin, D. and McGuire, T.G. 1994. Payment levels and hospital response to prospective payment. *Journal of Health Economics* 13: 1–29.

Lord Chancellor's Department. 1991. *Review of financial conditions for legal aid: eligibility for civil legal aid: a consultation paper*. London: Lord Chancellor's Department.

Lord Chancellor's Department. 1996. *Striking the Balance: The Future of Legal Aid in England and Wales*. London: HMSO.

Newhouse, J.P. and the Insurance Experiment Group. 1993. *Free for All? Lessons from the RAND Health Insurance Experiment*. Cambridge, MA: Harvard University Press.

Posner, R.A. 1973. *Economic Analysis of the Law*, 3rd edn. Boston: Little, Brown & Co., 1986.

Rees, R. 1987. The theory of principal and agent. In *Surveys in the Economics of Uncertainty*, ed. D. Hey and P.J. Lambert, Oxford: Basil Blackwell.

legal bargaining. *See* PRIVATE INFORMATION AND LEGAL BARGAINING.

legal error. *See* LEGAL STANDARDS OF CARE.

legal formalities. Suppose that two actors such as A and B in Figure 1 wish to establish between them the legal relationship $R(x)$ with respect to some vector of property entitlements x. For instance, x might be a tract of land which A wishes to convey to B, so that R would be the relationship of vendor–vendee of land. Similarly, x might be a good or service that A wishes to sell to B, and R would be the contractual relationship of buyer–seller. The same basic structure describes even superficially dissimilar legal relations. It may be that R is the relationship of marriage, and x the vector of entitlements to property of various sorts that are affected by the creation of the marriage relationship. Or x may be thought of as property owned by A, in which B takes a security interest, denoted by the relationship R, or which has been passed to B via a testamentary relationship R.

For the purposes of this essay, a *legal formality* will be defined as that set of *ex ante observable* and *ex post verifiable* actions which must be taken by A and/or B to make the relationship R legally enforceable and valid (or superior to) as against claims by third parties, represented by C in Figure 1. These actions may in general be taken either at the time the relationship is created, or a short time afterward. This definition limits the scope of this essay to what might be called transactional or exchange formalities. It excludes procedural formalities – those actions which must be taken at the time a party seeks to invoke the legal process to enforce his rights. *Ex ante* observability and *ex post* verifiability (see Schwartz 1992; Hart 1995) are economic characteristics. Their significance for legal formalities is discussed in Section 3 below.

$$\begin{array}{c} R(x) \\ A \text{———} B \\ \\ C \end{array}$$

Figure 1

1. SOME EXAMPLES OF LEGAL FORMALITIES

(1) *Written instruments, the seal and other contractual formalities.* The English Statute of Frauds of 1677 provided that certain types of promises must be evidenced by a signed writing in order to be enforceable at law. As discussed in more detail elsewhere (see STATUTE OF FRAUDS), although the Statute of Frauds for contracts was repealed in England in 1954, similar versions of the statute were enacted by every state legislature in the United States, where such laws continue in effect and where for the sale of goods, the Statute of Frauds as found in Article 2–201 of the Uniform Commercial Code governs.

Related to the general legal formality of a writing is the set of formalities required for the legal effectiveness of a will. The original 1677 English Statute of Frauds also covered wills, requiring that a will devising or bequeathing land or tenements be in writing and attested by three or four credible witnesses to be legally effective. The 1837 Wills Act applied more generally to any will and required for legal validity that the will be (1) in writing, (2) executed by being signed by the testator, and (3) witnessed in its execution by at least two witnesses. In the United States, the Uniform Probate Code provisions adopted by many states relax the formal requirements somewhat (for example, by allowing non-contemporaneous witnessing, and following French authorities in recognizing holographic or handwritten wills that would otherwise fail to meet the formal requirements). The formality of a signed, properly witnessed written will remains the standard in the

United States as well as in England (see Scoles and Halbach 1993: 129–45).

When gifts are to be made legally effective before death, the common law of both England and America is rather more severe in restricting the relationships *R* that will be deemed legally enforceable. For a gift from *A* to *B* of some entitlement *x* to be legally valid (even as between *A* and *B*), the Anglo-American common law requires delivery. This formality, apparently as old as the common law itself (Mechem 1926), views delivery as ordinarily meaning the actual transfer of possession of the object of property *x*. Until delivery, the gift is not valid and enforceable. In particular, promises to make gifts are generally unenforceable in Anglo-American common law.

The doctrine of consideration is the primary means by which the common law limits the legal enforceability of promises to make gifts ('gratuitous promises'). This doctrine requires that for a promissory relationship *R* to be legally enforceable, *A* and *B* must each have both given and received – exchanged – a promise or performance. Most importantly, this disqualifies any relationship in which only one of the parties has made a promise to the other. Such promises fail the formal requirements of consideration and therefore are unenforceable even as to the parties.

Legal scholars often hold consideration to be a paradigmatic instance of a legal formality. Insofar as it makes a certain type of mutual action – an exchange – prerequisite to legal enforceability, consideration meets the definition of a formality which I have set out above. However, comparison with any of the other formalities discussed thus far reveals that consideration is rather more, and less, than a legal formality. Unlike the formalities of a writing, or attestation with witnesses, or even registration, consideration requires more than that a relationship *R* be accompanied by certain acts. Rather, it requires that the relationship *R* itself *consist* of a certain set of actions. In this sense it has a substantive component that the other formalities lack. On the other hand, consideration is not sufficiently abstract or general (see Fuller 1941). The formality of a writing is abstract and general in that it may apply to any contractual relationship *R*. A writing, or attestation by signature and witnesses, is something which private actors may use to make legally enforceable any arbitrary promissory relationship *R*. Since consideration limits the set of relationships *R* which are to be deemed legally enforceable, it lacks this quality.

Indeed, consideration arose as a requirement for enforceability only when the common law (via the action of *assumpsit*) began to enforce informal, oral promises (see the discussion in Simpson 1987: chs. 4–7). Until this time (roughly the sixteenth century), only sealed covenants and penal bonds were enforced. The covenant was a sealed obligation to pay a definite sum; likewise, penal bonds were promises under seal to forfeit the bond *unless* the bond had been discharged by performance (Plucknett 1956: 633–6; Simpson 1986a: 2–3). The seal began as a wax bearing the imprint of an individualized signet ring, but gradually neither wax nor an impression was required (see American Law Institute 1981: 263; Holmes 1996: 350). The seal functioned to authenticate an instrument without an illiterate promisor's signature (Holmes 1996: 348). In England today, promises made under seal are enforceable even if they lack consideration (Treitel 1983: 120). A similar rule once existed in the United States. However, American courts and/or legislatures gradually expanded the set of acts viewed as constituting a 'seal', to include a printed device, word, scrawl, the printed initials 'L.S.' ('*locus sigilli*' – place of the seal) or a printed recital of a sealing (see Eisenberg 1982). This expansion in what counted as a 'seal' culminated in the deterioration of the legal significance of the seal: currently, about one-half of the states give no legal effect to the seal, while in the others, the effect of the seal is at most to give to a (rebuttable) presumption that the contract was supported by consideration (American Law Institute 1981: 255–9). In contracts involving the sale of goods, the seal is ineffective in all states (save Louisiana; see UCC Section 2–203). At the same time, since contracts involving the sale of goods between merchants are presumptively exchange transactions, under the Uniform Commercial Code, a signed, written offer to sell is irrevocable for the time stated regardless of whether there is any consideration for the (call) option thereby created (see UCC 2–205).

(2) *Recording formalities for land and credit transactions:* Land recording statutes illustrate yet another sort of formality. Under the typical land recording statute, a written instrument creating or transferring an interest in land is fully effective as between the parties (*A* and *B* in Figure 1) but is not effective in establishing the purchaser *B*'s rights as against a subsequent purchaser *C* unless and until the essential terms of the transfer have been recorded and made part of the public record by filing the documents creating or transferring the interest. Recording Acts are universal in the United States (see, for instance, Burke 1978). Under all of the American recording acts, copies of the filed land transfer documents are retained in a central, public location, such as the office of the county recorder of deeds. About half of the states have so-called notice recording statutes, under which a purchaser such as *C* would take priority over *B*'s prior unrecorded interest if and only if *C* had no notice of *B*'s interest. The remaining states have so-called 'race-notice' statutes, under which *C* must not only have no notice of *B*'s prior unrecorded interest but also record his interest before *B*. Such statutes set up a race to record first (Axelrod, Berger and Johnstone 1986). Recording statutes were a very early Colonial adaptation, taking their present form and function as early as 1640 (see Aigler 1924; Haskins 1941). While the early American statutes may have been influenced by English legislation, such as the Statute of Enrollments and registry acts for the countries of Middlesex and Yorkshire, and although English legislation in this century has provided for the enrollment of deeds, there has never been a general formal requirement of land transfer registration in England (Haskins 1941).

The formality of registration is not limited to land transfers. In the United States, registration is required not only to establish priority over another purchaser of an interest in land, but also to establish the priority of a creditor's security interest in personal property. Suppose that the relationship between *A* and *B* is that of debtor and creditor, respectively. As collateral for his loan to *A*, the lender

B requires the pledge of some item of personal property *x*. This gives *B* an entitlement to *x* which arises if and only if *A* is in default on his obligation to repay what he has borrowed from *B*. Under the 'notice' filing systems which were universal in the United States by the mid-twentieth century, *B*'s claim entitlement to the property *x* would only have priority to the claim of some other creditor *C* in the same property if *B* was first-to-file and neither knew nor reasonably should have known of an existing claim (see Baird and Jackson 1984: 313). Unlike land, however, such formal requirements apply only if *B* is not in actual possession of the property *x*, and the filing system does not require a description of either the property or the credit relationship (ibid.: 308). Article 9 of the American Uniform Commercial Code has adopted a race system for security interests in personal property, which, like the land registration race systems, gives priority to the first party to file, regardless of knowledge of other competing claims to the property.

(3) *Negotiability and facial formalities.* Records of interests in land or personal property are kept in centralized locations, and recording formalities require that certain actions be taken at these locations to give priority to a legal relationship created at another time and place. Contractual obligations accepted as payment in lieu of currency – such as cheques, bills of exchange and promissory notes – are also a kind of recording, but they are also, of course, a kind of contract. Such 'negotiable instruments' are promises by *A* to pay *B* which may be legally enforced against *A* by any holder of the instrument, such as *C*. Like record of title to land or property, such a negotiable instrument records the legal relationship between *A* and *B*, but unlike a land record, the negotiable instrument is intended to transfer a right to *C* rather than extinguish *C*'s conflicting claim. As a medium of exchange, such an instrument is unlike an ordinary contract, in that only the holder *C* may enforce the promise. And to serve this function, it must be that *C* may determine quickly and with a high degree of certainty whether a particular note is or is not legally negotiable. For this reason, under both the common law and contemporary commercial statutes, the negotiability of a written instrument is 'purely a matter of form' and the determination is made solely from the face of the instrument (Hart and Willier 1997: vol. 2, 1B–12). Negotiability hinges on the presence of three formalities: (1) the sum payable must be certain and unconditional and payable to the bearer or to order at the time it is first issued or comes into the possession of a holder; (2) the instrument must be payable on demand, or at a fixed and determinate future time; and (3) the instrument must not contain an order or promise to do anything in addition to the payment of money. (Hart and Willier 1997: vol. 2, 1B–13; on the common law requirements, see Chafee 1919: 754).

2. THE ORIGINS AND FUNCTIONS OF LEGAL FORMALITIES

Some legal formalities mirror social practice or economic practice. For example, in the law of gifts, delivery is almost surely the typical or normal way that a gift is made. As one early legal commentator observed, were *A* to say to *B*, 'I hereby give my watch to you,' but then return the watch to his own pocket, both parties would feel that the transaction was not quite what it seemed to be: *A* would wonder what he was doing putting the watch into his own pocket, and *B* would suppose that *A* was just joking (Mechem 1926: 346). In a similar way, courts derived the formal requirements for a negotiable instrument by asking what qualities were required by businesspeople in order to treat a note as negotiable. The business purpose or function – free circulation as a substitute for cash – defined negotiability. Courts inferred the formal requisites of negotiability as a concise statement of what businesspeople needed an instrument to possess in order to be certain enough to serve as a medium of exchange (See Chafee 1919: 751–2). Finally, the formalities or solemnities now requisite to legal marriage under Anglo-American law emerged from religious tradition, and while a separate legal ceremony of marriage may now substitute for a religious ceremony, the religious ceremony itself still usually suffices as the required legal solemnity (Clark 1987: 90–92). Formalities of this type, which originate in social or economic conventions, may be termed *conventional formalities*.

Other formalities, such as those surrounding the making of a contract, originated in early legal or quasi-legal customs. The earliest contractual formality in Roman law was the verbal *stipulato*, a highly formulaic and yet precise question and answer dialogue between the parties (Zimmermann 1996: 68–9). As with other very early formalities, such as possession, compliance with the formal acts required by the stipulation was not viewed as something additional necessary to make the promises legally binding, but as the actual legal effect itself (Zimmermann 1996: 82). Gradually, under the influence of commercial practice in the Hellenistic provinces, the classical stipulation weakened in importance as the practice of recording transactions in writing came to be seen as essential to legal validity (Zimmerman 1996: 78–9).

The early common law contractual formalities of the sealed bond or covenant functioned to gave the promisee a direct and unconditional right to payment (or, to the thing, in the case of covenant). That is, with such instruments, the promisor effectively gave the promisee security against non-performance. Such instruments originated in old Teutonic and merchant practices whereby items of personal property and even living hostages were given as security (Hazeltine 1910: 608–9). Of course, security of any sort is valuable only insofar as the party holding it has a quite clear right to the security if performance does not occur. In other words, security must also serve as conclusive (or virtually conclusive) evidence that a promise was made. The evolution of contractual formalities is marked by the gradually increasing importance of this evidentiary function. In merchant practice, pledges of goods came to replace living hostages, and pledges of goods became less substantial, functioning less as security for the promise than as symbol and evidence of it (Pollock 1893: 392–4). At the medieval commercial fairs, for instance, it was

> very good mercantile custom . . . to 'wet a bargain' by having a drink in a tavern near the site of the commercial fair where the deal was struck. Moreover,

immediately after agreement was reached, the parties would exchange a coin or ring as earnest money and/or shake hands in a very public ritual signalling the fact of agreement (Bewes 1923: 28–9, 31).

Italian merchants brought notaries who documented transactions upon which a debt remained due (Rabel 1947: 177). These formalities arose despite the fact that, under the Law Merchant, mere verbal promises were binding. Even after the law too recognized and enforced such promises, merchants continued to formalize and record their transactions in official registers, records of brokers, and other notarial instruments (Rabel 1947: 177).

Whether by seal, public exchange of personal tokens or written record, all of these early contractual formalities had the effect of creating reliable *ex post* evidence of the agreement. They exemplify what may be called *evidentiary formalities.* The formalities required by the recording statutes similarly originated in common law customs which served to publicize the creation of the legal relationship. However awkwardly, the common law custom was that a security interest in real property was created only when the debtor actually transferred possession of the property to the creditor (Baird and Jackson 1984: 307). The early common law method of conveying land was by an enfeoffment ceremony. This was a public ceremony in which the landowner and the grantee actually went upon the land (or in sight of it) and made a symbolic transfer of seisin or possession. In the presence of virtually the entire local community, the owner delivered a twig, clod of earth or other token of possession to the grantee, and spoke formal words of seisin (Powell 1997: vol. 14, section 82.01). At a time when land was not often transferred and ownership was well-known locally, and when most of the population was illiterate, such a ceremony was a very effective means of recording ownership. In 1535 the English Statute of Uses made it impossible to convey title to real property without a public enfeoffment ceremony (see Simpson 1986b: 173–207). Possession or the public symbolic transfer of possession would of course operate as solid proof of an ownership interest in *ex post* legal proceedings. But whereas many early contractual formalities – such as recording, or the seal – would generally not be open and available to the public prior to a legal dispute, possessory formalities necessarily broadcast the creation of the legal relationship to as many people as possible as soon as possible after its creation. In this regard, possessory formalities exemplify what I shall call *publicizing formalities.*

3. THE ECONOMIC SIGNIFICANCE OF LEGAL FORMALITIES

(1) *Observability, verifiability and the strategic role of legal formalities.* The distinction between conventional, evidentiary and publicizing formalities has been drawn on the basis of somewhat idealized versions of legal formalities. In American law especially, virtually all of the formalities described above have become riddled with exceptions. Judges have created such exceptions when confronted by cases in which the relationship was evidenced or publicized despite the failure to comply with the formality (Langbein 1979; Rose 1988; see also STATUTE OF FRAUDS); or in which, conversely, formal compliance may have been used by a more sophisticated party to trick the naive into legal liability. Still, the functional significance of legal formalities explains how modern formalities have evolved from their common law (or pre-legal) origins. Interests in land and property are now formalized by recording rather than by possession or ceremonies of possession, for possession does not effectively publicize the existence of an interest in land when many interests in land do not necessarily imply possession; likewise, ceremonies of possession do not suffice when interests in land are routinely purchased and sold by strangers to a local community. If a debtor would need to surrender possession of personal property for the creditor to obtain priority for his security interest in the property, the practice of extending personal property as collateral for loans could never have become an effective method for businesses to use their assets as collateral (see Baird and Jackson 1984: 308). As the use of personal property as security for loans became conventional, possession no longer effectively publicized the existence of a security interest.

As the formality of possession demonstrates, social or economic conventions often both evidence and publicize the existence of a legal relationship. On the other hand, evidentiary formalities need not publicize the relationship, and publicizing formalities need not provide reliable *ex post* evidence of the relationship. A written contract or will may provide low cost and reliable *ex post* evidence of the relationship R. However, merely requiring that a contract be in writing for it to be enforceable by its makers does nothing to raise the likelihood that third parties will easily and quickly gain knowledge of the contractual relationship. And when it comes to wills, the literary staple of the surprises in store for the heirs upon the formal reading of the written will suggests that a written will may do more to keep private the set of relationships created by the testator than to publicize them. Conversely, merely recording the fact of the relationship in a public repository of records may effectively publicize its existence, but, as is true of security interests in personal property, need not provide much in the way of *ex post* evidence describing the relationship (Baird and Jackson 1984: 308–9).

Recent work in the economic theory of contracts sharpens these distinctions. The creation of the relationship R is done by virtue of acts which both A and B can observe. These acts are not necessarily, however, the sort which can be proven *ex post* to a legal decisionmaker. To be effective in evidencing the relationship *ex post*, a formality must consist of acts which are not only *observable ex ante* by the parties, but which are also *verifiable ex post* by a third party, the legal decisionmaker (see Schwartz 1992; Hart 1995). To be effective in publicizing the relationship so as to establish rights prior to those of another market participant, such as C, the acts specified by the formality must in addition be verifiable by such market participants. On the other hand, the publicizing function of a formality does not depend upon the observability of the actions it requires: registration by B establishes a verifiable record of his interest superior to C's, but there is no need for A to observe the act. Finally, it would seem that most conventional formalities satisfy both observability and verifiability: the face of a commercial note is readily observable by both parties *ex ante* and verifiable to third party market participants and legal decisionmakers.

These differences suggest immediately that evidentiary, publicizing and conventional formalities each may be viewed as solving a distinct sort of economic problem involving strategic behaviour in contracting. As the strategic significance of evidentiary formalities are discussed elsewhere (see STATUTE OF FRAUDS), the focus here is on publicizing and conventional formalities.

(2) *Law and the evolution of conventional formalities.* Following Lewis (1969) and Young (1996), I define a convention as a behavioural regularity which is self-enforcing in the sense that everyone conforms, everyone expects others to conform and it is in fact best for everyone to conform when everyone else is expected to do so. Under this definition, conventions solve social coordination problems, and they do so by virtue of the fact that the convention is common knowledge. The problem of choosing which side of the road to drive on is a classic illustration of a social coordination problem (see Young 1996). Common knowledge of a practice, say, of driving on the right hand side, requires that every driver know the practice, and know also that every other driver knows the practice, and that everyone knows that every other driver knows that this driver knows . . . and so on. (On common knowledge, see, for example, Geanakoplos 1994.)

One can easily think of legal rules that have mapped social or economic conventions which meet this formal definition, such as the above-mentioned rules regarding which side of the road to drive upon (see Young 1996: 112–16). More importantly, many of the social or economic conventions from which legal formalities have arisen also meet this definition of a convention. Consider, for instance, a trade creditor deciding whether to accept a note in payment of an obligation. The note will be acceptable if and only if the creditor expects that his creditors will accept the note who in turn will accept the note provided that everyone in the relevant community is expected to accept the note – i.e., the note is a conventional means of payment. Insofar as the formal legal requirements for negotiability simply map the requirements that are present if and only if a note is conventionally accepted as payment, the legal formality of negotiability rests upon a convention in the rather strict sense defined above. Even more strongly, some conventions, such as that a gift requires an actual transfer of possession of the thing given, would seem to be language conventions: that is, the meaning of 'gift' includes delivery of possession because everyone in the relevant community uses the word 'gift' in this sense and expects everyone else to do so, and it is best to use the word in this sense precisely because everyone in the relevant community does.

As the example of marriage formalities suggests, it is perhaps more likely that legal formalities arise in conventions than that actual substantive legal rules fixing liability should so arise. The problem of choosing *how* to become married is a coordination problem solved by conventions. If Mr X and Ms Y are trying to decide between two ways of solemnizing their marriage, they will conform to the conventional ceremony precisely because everyone is expected to conform and when everyone in fact conforms it is best for Mr X and Ms Y to do so. A radically different strategic dilemma is raised by the issue of *whether* Mr X and Ms Y should become married at all. The status of marriage not only establishes a set of potential legal claims to a vector of property rights x, but triggers a range of social expectations and social sanctions. Conventional means of formalizing the creation of the marriage and other relationships may arise to publicize and evidence its existence so that extralegal sanctions and economic sanctions may be applied in the event a violation of substantive social or economic norms is alleged. It is important to stress that substantive norms regarding behaviour within the relationship arise as solutions to games of conflict, not coordination. While there may be equilibria with credible social sanctions for the violations of such norms (see Kandori 1992; Ellison 1994), such substantive norms are not generally self-enforcing in the sense that coordination game conventions are.

An important, but as yet largely unaddressed research topic (see, however, Bernstein 1996), is the effect that adoption of such self-enforcing social and economic conventions as legal formalities will have on the structure of the social incentives to maintain such conventions. In the case of commercial paper, the instrument by which A promises to pay B is acceptable to B if and only if B expects C to accept it from him. That the law grants C a right to bring an action against A on this instrument does not *create* the conventions defining an acceptable instrument, for these almost surely have arisen on the expectation that payment will be made rather than refused. The law might stabilize conventions by clarifying and broadcasting them. If there is some uncertainty, then by stating the formal requirements simply enough, the law increases the certainty with which instruments may be taken as payment, lowering the cost of trade to everyone in the system. However, the law's adoption of these conventions may itself alter the conventions. This is especially likely if occasional errors are made by courts in discerning the conventions. Suppose, for instance, that it is common knowledge within the business community that a particular type of note is accepted as payment. If there is even a small chance, however, that a court might determine the note to be non-negotiable, and this is common knowledge, then there is no longer common knowledge of the negotiability of the note. There is *almost* common knowledge (or approximate common knowledge as it is known in the game-theoretic and computer science literature; see Morris and Shin 1996) which may be quite different from a strategic point of view.

(3) *Strategic behaviour and the publicizing function of formalities.* Publicizing formalities such as registration or filing for interests in land and security interests in personal property enable a third party like C to determine cheaply whether B has already established an interest in the property *before* C himself acquires such an interest. As noted above, evidentiary formalities such as a writing, the seal, or attestation, do not necessarily enable C to determine the existence of a prior interest, but rather facilitate proof of the contract or will in *ex post* litigation. This raises the question of why the law does not require the formality of registration for *all* legal relationships.

John Austin, one of the giants of English jurisprudence, gave a very legalistic answer to this question. According to Austin (1879: 939, 941), as a matter of contract law, *A* is free to promise to sell the same good or service to both *B* and *C*; neither *B* nor *C* may bring an action against the other, but whomever does not get the good or service may sue *A* for breach of contract. With respect to land and security interests in personal property, however, the disappointed promisee, *B* for example, not only gets to sue *A*, but also may sue *B* to have his right to the land or goods declared superior to *B*'s. There is, according to Austin, need for the formality of registration only when *B* may lose out to *C* – that is, when one of their claims will be declared subordinate to the other's – but no need when both *B* and *C* may with equal validity assert a right to performance of a contract.

From an economic point of view, Austin's answer is superficial, for it explains the formality of registration by reference to a system of rights which itself must be explained. While space does not permit a complete economic explanation of why registration is sometimes required and sometimes not, the following sketch indicates how such an explanation would proceed.

When *A* promises to provide a good or service to *B* as well as to *C*, there necessarily will be some time at which *B* and *C* know whether or not *A* has performed as promised. It may well be that social costs could be lowered were a disappointed contracting party to be informed earlier rather than later that performance would not be forthcoming, but the law assumes that the existence of a remedy against *A* for nonperformance will ordinarily suffice both to encourage *A* to perform or breach efficiently and to discourage *B* and *C* from overinvesting in reliance upon *A's* promise. (See, however, Craswell 1988 on the difficulty of optimizing both reliance and breach decisions.) With land or security interests in personal property, it may be very costly or even impossible, absent a registration system, for *B* and *C* to determine whether *A* has in fact performed, for since the interest conveyed often has nothing to do with possession of the good or land, performance means not only conveying the promised interest to *A* or *B*, but also not conveying any conflicting interest to anyone else. That is, unlike the contract situation, where *A*'s performance involves an observable act, *A*'s performance vis-à-vis promises to convey interests in land and personal property cannot generally be observed, at least in large, relatively anonymous communities, because performance is defined by the *failure to act inconsistently*, which generally cannot be observed directly. Hence even if there were an effective remedy against *A* – such as a damage award for failure to convey the promised interest – there would be no certain time at which *B* or *C* would know whether to invoke that remedy. In the meantime, any subsequent transaction by *B* or *C* attempting to convey all or part of the interest presumably obtained from *A* would be burdened by the uncertainty surrounding the existence of competing claims. The further down the chain of title (in the case of land), the greater would be the possible number of competing claims, and hence the greater the uncertainty and/or cost of resolving those claims and the lower (for risk averse individuals) the value of the interest conveyed.

Matters in fact will be much worse than this, for when the interest conveyed is a conditional right to land or personal property as security for a loan, the purpose of obtaining the interest in the first place will typically have been to secure some other promise by *A* against his breach. Such an interest is most valuable precisely when there will be no other effective remedy in the event of *A*'s breach. When the privately created interest itself is intended to serve as a remedy for the breach of some related promise (to pay interest and repay principal at a promised date), the law must provide some cheap and ready means by which the state of the interest may be observed, or else the value of such interests will be severely lessened.

Observe that not all acts will create common knowledge of *B*'s interest $R(x)$. An act done by *C* cannot become common knowledge at the time of the transaction between *A* and *B* because *C* follows *B*. This is the problem with notice as a formality: making *B*'s interest depend upon what *C* knew or should have known about *B*'s interest does not give *B* knowledge in time to effect *B*'s transaction with *A*. Land formalities originated in practices by *B* which were directly observed by *C*, thus meeting the ideal of immediate common knowledge and no uncertainty. In this light, registration may be viewed as the best means available of creating common knowledge, given that immediate observability by *C* is not generally possible.

Publicizing formalities affect efficiency by eliminating strategic behaviour due to private information and thereby increasing the certainty of the transactions in publicized interests. More concretely, publicizing formalities destroy the possibility of strategic behaviour (fraud, in lawyer's terms) which arises when *A* has private information that he has created and been paid for the interest $R(x)$ by *B*. When this information is private, it may be that the equilibrium involves all the bad *A*s (who have already sold or granted an interest) mimicking the good *A* types (who haven't) by selling the same interest to both *B* and *C*. With this risk, there is a very large downside risk to *C* types that they will pay something and get nothing. This may cause all purchasers such as *B* and *C* to take costly and socially wasteful self-protective action, which in the limit would mean completely eschewing dealings in the unobservable interest $R(x)$. In this light, publicizing formalities are a very efficient sort of self-protection for *B* and *C*, which if effective eliminate *A*'s private information and allow for the creation of an active market in various otherwise unobservable interests *R* in land and personal property. Efficiency is enhanced, because the elimination of uncertainty due to unobservability allows future *A*s to obtain a higher price for land or a lower interest rate against collateral than they could otherwise obtain. As mutually beneficial trades will occur which would not otherwise, the innovation of publicizing formalities marks a Pareto improvement.

4. COMPARISON WITH TRADITIONAL EXPLANATIONS

The explanation and typology of legal formalities set out above differs rather markedly from traditional jurisprudential thinking about formalities by failing to say anything about what is called the *cautionary* or *deterrent* function of form (see Fuller 1941: 800; Austin 1879: 940 (prevention of 'inconsiderate engagements'); Gulliver and Tilson 1941 (similar 'protective function' of wills); see also Posner 1996). As traditionally understood, this refers to the effect that legal formalities may have in deterring undeliberate (or even, with wills, coerced) promises and transactions. The absence of such a function from the discussion given here does not reflect a naive or simplistic economic conception that all actors are always rational and never make undeliberate promises. It instead reflects my view that there is no particular explanatory content in the cautionary function. To say that the need to perform a certain ceremony such as affixing a seal or speaking marriage vows encourages deliberation is to beg the question of *what* one means by deliberation and *why* some acts encourage deliberation and others do not. If by deliberation one means thinking carefully about the promised undertaking, then it may be that a silent prayer better encourages deliberation than any outward formality. Even if one understands deliberation in a narrower economic sense, as the careful calculation of the expected costs and benefits of the relationship in light of its legal enforceability, then there is no reason to think that an arbitrary act ought to trigger such calculation. Rather, it would seem that what causes an increased degree of care in calculating the costs and benefits of creating some legal relationship is the primary effect of formalities in evidencing and publicizing the relationship. Like the so-called channelling function (see Fuller 1941: 800) discussed earlier, the cautionary function of legal formalities is more usefully analysed as an indirect effect of legal formalities than as a defining function.

JASON SCOTT JOHNSTON

See also COMMON KNOWLEDGE; CONTRACT FORMATION AND INTERPRETATION; CONVENTIONS; EFFICIENT NORMS; ENGLISH COMMON LAW; GRATUITOUS PROMISES; LAND TITLE SYSTEMS; LAND-USE DOCTRINES; STATUTE OF FRAUDS.

Subject classification: 1b(i); 5a(i); 5b(i).

STATUTES

The Statute of Frauds, 29 Car. II, c. 3 (1677).

The Statute of Uses, 27 Hen. VIII, c. 10 (1535).

The Statute of Wills, 32 Hen. VIII, c. 1 (1540).

Uniform Commercial Code, Uniform Laws Annotated, vols. 1–2. St. Paul, MN: West Publishing Co. 1989.

Wills Act, 7 Wm. IV & Vict., c. 26, §IX (1837).

CASES

Pillans v. Van Mierop (1765) 3 Burr. 1664.

BIBLIOGRAPHY

Aigler, R.W. 1924. The operation of the recording acts. *Michigan Law Review* 22: 405–20.

American Law Institute. 1981. *Restatement (Second) of the Law of Contracts*. St. Paul, MN: West Publishing.

Austin, J. 1879. Fragments – on contracts. In J. Austin, *Lectures on Jurisprudence*, vol. II, ed. R. Campbell, 4th edn, London: John Murray.

Axelrod, A., Berger, C. and Johnstone, Q. 1986. *Land Transfer and Finance*. 3rd edn, Boston: Little, Brown & Co.

Baird, D. and Jackson, T. 1984. Information, uncertainty, and the transfer of property. *Journal of Legal Studies* 13: 299–320.

Baker, J.H. 1986. Origins of the 'doctrine' of consideration. In J.H. Baker, *The Legal Profession and the Common Law: Historical Essays*, London: The Hambledon Press.

Bewes, W.A. 1923. *The Romance of the Law Merchant*. London: Sweet & Maxwell.

Bernstein, L. 1996. Merchant law in a merchant court: rethinking the Code's search for immanent business norms. *University of Pennsylvania Law Review* 144: 1765–1821.

Burke, D. 1978. *American Conveyancing Patterns*. Lexington, MA: Lexington Books.

Chafee, Z. 1919. Acceleration provisions in time paper. *Harvard Law Review* 32: 747–88.

Clark, H.H. 1987. *The Law of Domestic Relations in the United States*. 2nd edn, St. Paul, MN: West Publishing.

Craswell, R. 1988. Contract remedies, renegotiation and the theory of efficient breach. *Southern California Law Review* 61: 629–70.

Eisenberg, M.A. 1982. The principles of consideration. *Cornell Law Review* 67: 640–65.

Ellison, G. 1993. Learning, local interaction and coordination. *Econometrica* 61: 1047–71.

Ellison, G. 1994. Cooperation in the prisoner's dilemma with anonymous random matching. *Review of Economic Studies* 61: 567–88.

Fuller, L.L. 1941. Consideration and form. *Columbia Law Review* 41: 799–824.

Furmston, M.P. 1986. *Cheshire, Fifoot and Furmston's Law of Contract*. 11th edn., London: Butterworths.

Geanakoplos, J. 1994. Common knowledge. In *Handbook of Game Theory with Economic Applications* vol. 2, ed. R.J. Aumann and S. Hart, Amsterdam: Elsevier Science.

Gibbons, R. 1992. *Game Theory for Applied Economists*. Princeton: Princeton University Press.

Gulliver, A. and Tilson, C. 1941. Classification of gratuitous transfers. *Yale Law Journal* 51: 1–39.

Hart, F.M and Willier, W.F. 1997. *Negotiable Instruments under the Uniform Commercial Code*. New York: Matthew Bender.

Hart, O. 1995. *Firms, Contracts and Financial Structure*. Oxford: Clarendon Press.

Haskins, G.L. 1941. The beginning of the recording system in Massachusetts. *Boston University Law Review* 21: 281–304.

Hazeltine, H.D. 1910. The formal contract of early English law. *Columbia Law Review* 10: 608–17.

Holmes, E.M. 1996. *Corbin on Contracts*. vol. 3. St. Paul, MN: West Publishing.

Kandori, M. 1992. Social norms and community enforcement. *Review of Economic Studies* 59: 63–80.

Langbein, J. 1979. The crumbling of the Wills Act: Australians point the way. *American Bar Association Journal* 65: 1192–5.

Lewis, D. 1969. *Convention: A Philosophical Study*. Cambridge, MA: Harvard University Press.

Mechem, P. 1926. The requirement of delivery in the law of gifts of chattels and choses in action evidenced by commercial instruments. *Illinois Law Review* 21: 341–74.

Morris, S. and Shin, H.S. 1996. Approximate common knowledge and co-ordination: recent lessons from game theory. CARESS Working Paper No. 96–07, University of Pennsylvania Center for Analytical Research in Economics and the Social Sciences, Philadelphia, PA.

Plucknett, T.F.T. 1956. *A Concise History of the Common Law*. 5th edn, Boston: Little, Brown & Co.

Pollock, F. 1893. Contracts in early English Law. *Harvard Law Review* 6: 389–404.

Posner, E.A. 1996. Norms, formalities, and the Statute of Frauds: a comment. *University of Pennsylvania Law Review* 144: 1971–86.

Powell, R. 1997. *Powell on Real Property*. New York: Matthew Bender.

Rabel, E. 1947. The Statute of Frauds and comparative legal history. *Law Quarterly Review* 63: 174–84.

Rose, C.M. 1988. Crystals and mud in property law. *Stanford Law Review* 40: 577–610.

Schwartz, A. 1992. Relational contracts in the courts: an analysis of incomplete agreements and judicial strategies. *Journal of Legal Studies* 21: 271–318.

Scoles, E.F. and Halbach, E.C. Jr. 1993. *Problems and Materials on Decedent's Estates and Trusts*. 5th edn, Boston: Little, Brown & Co.

Simpson, A.W.B. 1986a. Historical introduction. In M.P. Furmston, *Cheshire, Fifoot and Furmston's Law of Contract*, 11th edn, London: Butterworths.

Simpson, A.W.B. 1986b. *A History of the Land Law*. Oxford: Clarendon Press.

Simpson, A.W.B. 1987. *A History of the Common Law of Contract*. Oxford: Clarendon Press.

Summers, R.A. and Atiyah, P.J. 1987. *Form and Substance in Anglo-American Law*. Oxford: Clarendon Press.

Treitel, G. 1983. *The Law of Contract*. 6th edn, London: Stevens.

Young, H.P. 1993. The evolution of conventions. *Econometrica* 61: 57–84.

Young, H.P. 1996. The economics of convention. *Journal of Economic Perspectives* 10: 105–22.

Zimmermann, R. 1996. *The Law of Obligations: Roman Foundations of the Civilian Tradition*. Oxford: Clarendon Press; Cape Town: Juta & Co. Ltd, 1990.

legal formants. The notion of legal formants has been developed in recent work on comparative law. A recent study of 'legal formants' explains that

> [T]here often is not, in a given legal system, a single rule on a particular point, but rather a series of different (sometimes conflicting) formulations of the applicable rule, depending on the kind of source consulted. The code may say one thing, the courts another, scholars may state the rule differently; the rule actually followed may again be different from what anyone says it is (Schlesinger et al. 1994: 78)

The theory of legal formants, also known as the dynamic approach to comparative law, focuses on law as a social activity: a formant of the law may be a group, a type of personnel, or a community, institutionally involved in the activity of creating law. From this point of view we find in the western legal tradition an established legal profession, and three main types of personnel within it: the practising lawyer; the legal policymaker (a legislator, an appellate court judge, or upper level administrator); and the legal scholar (law professors and the like). Judges, legislators and legal theorists are all interacting and competing legal formants.

These professionals produce different kinds of texts: statutes, opinions, holdings, articles, treatises, briefs, summons, broad principles, narrow rules, and so on. They have an archive (previous writers, precedents, etc.) and a professional, tested style to transform old documents and produce new ones. These texts and documents, and the way they are produced, the way they are interlocked, the way they are re-used by others, and so on, become a key feature in the understanding of the working of the law. To cope with these documents, the formants approach adopts a new kind of form criticism, in the widest sense, as a method to uncover, separate, and explain the various materials used to produce the texts. This approach looks for differences of all kinds between and within the documents. This is a direct refutation of the principle of the unity of the law. The law is not an harmonious set of elements, but a composite of different models and clashing texts reconciled by ingenious lawyers.

In the standard legal approach, more or less characterized by so-called legal positivism, a constitution, for example, is a unitary document interpreted by lawyers and applied by judges, even if disputes may arise about its meaning. In the formant approach a constitution is also a document, derived from a number of sources, but a decision 'explaining its meaning' is simply another autonomous connected text. What we call the meaning of a legal text is just the link, established by lawyers, between the previous text and another document: a plea, a scholarly article, or a decision.

The law can then be reconstructed as a set of interlocked documents used by professionals according to their personal or institutional strategies. Thus the very idea of the legal tradition is to be seen as the result of an actual strategy of considering a variety of independent documents and texts competing for hegemony as interlocked in a pattern of continuity.

Since the theory is deeply rooted in comparative law, it is especially fit to uncover the different sources of law in terms of legal transplants: a Roman text, embodying a principle, becomes linked with another text, a provision of the German code, to be discussed by an American scholar, whose text is re-transplanted in Europe by comparativists, and becomes part of the opinion of an Italian judge. The theory offers a picture of laws as bundles of transplants of competing sources of law.

The formant approach is then a totally comparative approach based on a kind of 'external' study of the law as a form of sociological and economic appraisal of lawyers' activities, coupled with an 'internal' analysis of documents as a kind of form criticism. This approach has then two major implications. First, the legal process is seen as a competitive arena of different types of elite groups. Second there is a total refusal of the metaphysics of the unity of the law and of the 'meaning' of legal propositions. We shall discuss by means of examples the former implication in the next section and the latter in the last section.

FORMANTS AND THE LEGAL PROCESS. The main idea is to substitute the model of the law as a more or less consistent system of interrelated, hierarchically connected propositions, by a model of competing formants within the unique setting and constraints of one legal tradition. We offer an 'internal example' related to the actual competition of formants within a system, and some 'external examples' involving the comparison of different laws.

As an internal example we note the present growth of a new European law. A quite strong competition can be seen among a bureaucratic law tending towards uniformity by means of common administrative regulations and model acts (e.g. directives on products liability); a judge-made law developed by the European Court of Justice, trying to advance broad new doctrines of judicial activism (e.g., a new doctrine on State tortious liability for *non* enactment of European standards in national laws); and several scholarly efforts endeavouring to rediscover or rebuild a European 'Common Law' based on shared principles, ideas and categories (e.g. Mattei's project on the common core of European private laws, or Lando's Restatements on converging principles on contracts, or even Zimmerman's rediscovery of Roman law as a still working pillar for a newer legal education). All these institutional actors express themselves in texts competing for hegemony in framing modern European law. This competitive model captures the tremendous complexity of the law much better than the artificial idea of a coherent hierarchy.

Take the distinction between the Common and the Civil Law; the former being more centred on the role of courts, and the latter more grounded on that of legislation. Within the Civil Law a sharp distinction separates the French and the German model. The former is much more centred on a bureaucratic organization of courts in the interpretation of codes, whereas in the latter legal scholars played a central role in shaping legislation and in paving the way for court decisions. Also within the *Common Law* the role of legal education and legal scholars is much different in the UK and in the US, where important aspects of the legal process are influenced by the national law schools as distinctive American institutions.

In contrast, traditional Islamic law has been essentially based on the prestige of a caste of scholars in law and divinity, who were not professional lawyers, in an institutional setting where judges did not deliver opinions, and where little or no room was left to legislation.

From a historical perspective Roman law evolved without regular courts, but as a law managed by private arbitrators; only in later times did it become grounded upon imperial legislation, and imperial courts made by crown servants. When the Empire collapsed in the West, a common system of local courts (royal, mercantile, ecclesiastical, manorial, and so on) developed. Only in the twelfth century was legal education reorganized in the newly invented universities around Justinian Roman texts; but this innovation was refused in England, where the legal profession was already self-organized in strong professional elites around the royal courts. This early organization of the English Bar prevented a reception of the renewed Roman law. For centuries English law has been taught at the Inns of Court and not at the universities, whereas the Civil Law has been much more influenced by scholarly models and cultural revolutions. Indeed when rationalism became a dominant paradigm, it was received also within the continental legal culture, paving the way for codification in the nineteenth century, another novelty refused in England. The French Revolution also introduced a class of legal bureaucrats, which became an overwhelming factor affecting the legal process in several countries, to the detriment of legislation, courts, and scholarship.

As we may see by these sketches, the theory is designed to cope with the different fabrics of the law, conceived as a battleground of competing sources and elites of professionals.

FORMANTS AND CRITIQUE. The theory of competing legal formants has some consequences in the field of legal criticism, interpretation and hermeneutics. A precedent, a statute, and the like, have only the meaning attached to them by competing elite groups, placed under different institutional constraints, and with different incentive structures.

From this point of view the theory draws a distinction between the working rules, the practices of a legal system, and the symbolic set, the discourse used by lawyers to describe, justify and rationalize the rules. Take medical malpractice as an example. In America it is classified as a tort, whereas in France it is considered a breach of contract. French contractual liability is strict, so that the victim need not allege the doctor's fault, whereas tortious medical malpractice in America is based on negligence. The two systems are at opposites. But French lawyers introduced a distinction between two different kind of contractual obligations: *obligations de moyen* and *obligations de resultat*. In the former case a party is under a duty not to perform the obligation, but just to use his skill as best he can, so the victim of a breach *must* allege a fault. According to French courts in routine cases a doctor is under a duty *de resultat*, and so the victim has not to allege fault; but in non-routine cases she is under a duty *de moyen*, which means that she just promises to use her professional skill, and so the victim must allege a doctor's fault, to prove the breach.

American malpractice law is based on negligence, but American courts decided that in routine cases they can apply the doctrine of *res ipsa loquitur*, so that the victim's damage is evidence of the doctor's fault. *Res ipsa loquitur* is not applied in *non* routine cases, and so the victim must prove a specific breach of the duty by the doctor.

It is easy to see similarities and differences. The working rules and the practices are the same: routine cases lead to no-fault; non-routine cases imply fault. However, the symbolic set, the discourses used to state these rules, are totally different: in France: contract, strict liability, different kind of obligations, necessity of fault in non-routine cases; in America: tort, negligence standard, *res ipsa loquitur*, non-necessity of fault in routine cases.

A lot of similar examples have been detected by comparative lawyers, to show how practical similarities are often hidden by justifications and categories. Without indulging in such technical matters, the consequence of the theory is that in the law practices and discourses have independent lives. Rules do not follow from the premises, but the premises are selected, for many different symbolic reasons, and *then* arranged around the rules. Similar premises may lead to opposite rules, and identical rules can be explained by opposite premises.

The theory implies that it is always necessary to *deconstruct* the law to reach its working level, beyond the peculiar legal discourse of any one tradition. This deconstruction is necessary not only for the sake of comparison, but also for making meaningful economic analysis of the law. Deconstructive criticism is neither a luxury nor a philosophical intruder, but a necessity coming from within. From this standpoint the theory of formants is a *global internal critique* of the legal discourse. It is beyond the task of the theory to raise external critiques, but it certainly entails an anti-formalistic appraisal, and in the field of legal hermeneutics it disfavours the metaphysics of meaning.

Why are practices and discourses independent? It is less surprising, indeed, when we find similar practices beneath different discourses in quite similar modern societies. We can simply imagine that there are common economic, or the like, reasons inducing real uniformity beyond apparent variety. It is much harder to explain real divergences, when they occur in similar westernized systems. For instance the rules about transfer of property, or formation of contracts, diverge totally in France, Germany, England, Austria, Italy etc. Both subjects are classical legal topics on which generations of western scholars have written long books and thoughtful papers. For example, a property in goods is transferred at the moment of delivery in Germany even without a previous contract of sale; it is transferred at the moment of contract in France and delivery is unimportant; you need both a valid contract and a delivery in Austria; you can transfer the property at the moment of contract or at the moment of delivery in England. A similar variance also affects the rules about formation of contract.

A suggestion of the theory is that in these cases the 'rules' are essential only to the legal profession, but are socially irrelevant. This means that it is important for society to have a rule, but it is irrelevant which one is adopted. This seems to be true especially in many 'classical' topics of private law theory. So the formant approach accepts the view of a purely technical, maybe a-political, merely professional, evolution of many legal rules, just because the choice of the adopted rule is in these cases socially irrelevant. This is a first step toward a reconstruction of a theory of legal change, distinguishing in the law between what is socially important and what is not.

Finally, as we saw, the formants approach clashes with positivism as a pattern in jurisprudence. At least in the Kelsen approach the law is depicted as a pyramid of state norms consistently improved by state officials. The sketch we now derive by the formant approach is that of several sources of the law, and the 'state' looks more like a permanently unstable compromise among competing legal sources. The Harvard Legal Process School shared similar views but with a strong bias toward equilibrium, and a strong commitment to classic liberal values. In the new formant approach the effort is merely deconstructivist. Values and commitments are not metaphysically embodied in The Process, but they are more to be seen as complex strategies of the opposing legal actors. So in terms of jurisprudence the formant approach is similar to some radical form of American realism, with two main differences: first, the formant approach is grounded on comparison as 'the' tool of understanding law; and second, in the formant approach the essential of the law is not reduced to working rules and the role of judges; narratives and discourses are as important as the practices for the purpose of social communication and social stability, and judges are but one of the factors, more apparent but often less important than others.

P.G. Monateri and Rodolfo Sacco

See also AMERICAN LEGAL REALISM; COMPARATIVE LAW AND ECONOMICS; HARMONIZATION OF LAW IN THE EUROPEAN UNION; KELSEN, HANS; LEGAL PLURALISM; LEGAL POSITIVISM; MEDICAL MALPRACTICE; WESTERN LEGAL TRADITION.

Subject classification: 4b(iv).

BIBLIOGRAPHY

Mattei, U. 1997. *Comparative Law and Economics*. Ann Arbor: University of Michigan Press.

Monateri, P.G. 1984. Règles et technique de la dèfinition en France et en Allemagne. *Revue internationale de droit comparé* 36: 77f.

Sacco, R. 1991. Legal formants: a dynamic approach to comparative law. *American Journal of Comparative Law* 39: 1–34; 343–402.

Schlesinger, R.B. 1995. The past and future of comparative law. *American Journal of Comparative Law* 42: 477–81.

Schlesinger, R.B., Baade, H.W., Damaska, M.R., Herzog, P.E. and Wise, E.M. 1994. *Comparative Law*. Westbury, NY: Foundation Press.

Watson, A. 1983. Legal change: sources of law and legal culture. *University of Pennsylvania Law Review* 131: 1121–55.

Watson, A. 1995. From legal transplants to legal formants. *American Journal of Comparative Law* 43: 469–76.

legal obligation, non-compliance and soft budget constraint. One requirement for smooth operation of a market economy is financial discipline. This means enforcing four simple rules: (i) Let buyers abide by their sales agreements and pay for their purchases. (ii) Let debtors observe their credit agreements and pay their debts. (iii) Let taxpayers pay their taxes. (iv) Let firms cover costs out of revenues.

In a consolidated market economy, there is a legal obligation to comply with the first three rules. Compliance with the fourth is imposed by the nature of an economy based on private property. Persistent losses lead sooner or later to ruin and an exit from commercial life.

Non-compliance with the rules of financial discipline occurs in all real economies. The syndrome known as soft budget constraint (*SBC*) is a special case of such non-compliance. (This essay uses the abbreviations *BC* for budget constraint and *SBC* for soft budget constraint.)

CLARIFYING THE CONCEPTS. The concept of *SBC*, coined by the author (Kornai 1979, 1980 and 1986), was borrowed from the microeconomic theory of the household. Take the functioning of a firm, disregarding for a moment the possibility of credit. In a static model, the firm's total spending, like the household's in the standard microeconomic model, cannot exceed the *BC* – the stock of money at its disposal. Let us call this a pure case, where the *BC* on the firm is truly effective or *hard*.

In a real economy, processes occur over time, and there is credit. An intertemporal *BC* can be called hard if the firm's spending stream, including debt servicing, does not persistently exceed its income stream, including the credit it raises.

Consider a situation where the requirement of a hard *BC*, and thereby rule (iv) of financial discipline, fails to apply. The firm's spending stream exceeds its income stream over a protracted period; it makes steady losses. This means it cannot fulfil various financial obligations, which flouts rules (i), (ii) and (iii) of financial discipline. For instance, it may fail to pay for ordered, delivered goods, pay wages for hours worked, pay installments and interest on loans, pay taxes, or commit several such omissions. Each omission implies a forced loan. Those to whom payments are due are forced to give the firm credit, against their will.

Then two things may happen. The internal regularities of the market dictate that a persistently loss-making firm ceases to exist. The losses are borne by the firm's owners and forced creditors, in proportions depending on the circumstances of the liquidation, for instance the terms of the law.

However, there is another possibility. The firm may be *bailed out.* Some forced creditor may resign himself and waive the debt, or tolerate late repayment. This constitutes collaboration between the offender breaching financial discipline and the injured party. Alternatively, an institution (such as the state) may give active assistance (for instance a budget subsidy). The bailout, allowing the firm to survive its persistent losses and insolvency, *softens* the *BC*.

A few more comments are needed for clarification.

There is no sense in referring to an *SBC* on a single firm and its operation over a single period. If a loss-making firm was bailed out once, that does not justify saying its *BC* was soft. The *BC* is rightly called soft only when whole groups of firms are rescued frequently, bail-outs occur time and again over a long period, in a foreseeable fashion, and the collective experience of these rescues becomes imprinted in management expectations. The *SBC* syndrome is not a 'financial' phenomenon, but a *behavioural regularity* of firms, an attribute of expectations, a specific social relation between the firm and the rescuer.

Ultimately, there lies behind the *SBC* syndrome a dynamic dilemma of commitment and credibility, which will be dealt with in more detail later. The state (or other rescuing institution) would like to induce the firm to cover its expenditure with its income. So it makes statements committing itself not to bail the firm out. However, it fails to abide by these under certain conditions. The more frequently this happens, the less credible the commitment becomes.

BC stringency is not a dichotomous variable. Between the extremes of perfect hardness and perfect softness lies a continuum. The degree of hardness or softness expresses the certainty of the firm's expectations, the subjective probability that a breach of financial discipline will be tolerated and a bail-out ensue.

To understand the *SBC* syndrome more closely, let us look at the instruments available for softening the constraint, remaining with the firm and cases where the state or a state institution applies them.

The most obvious instrument, most often mentioned by writers, is a budget subsidy covering a firm's losses.

A second, equivalent instrument, but less conspicuous than this, is a tax concession. There are several variants. Rather than setting a uniform rate of taxation, the state may tailor it to each sector or industry's profitability. Alternatively, there may be a uniform rate, with room for exceptions. Or the state may tolerate firms breaching rule (iii) by not paying taxes on time. The last does not mean a situation where the firm taxed finds a legal loophole or commits an undetected act of illegal tax evasion. The situation within the scope of *SBC* is one where the tax authorities knowingly overlook a breach of the law, as the firm's tacit accomplice, lest it collapse under the weight of taxation.

A third category of instruments ties in with credit. Let us confine the discussion for now to cases where the bank is state-owned and controlled by the government's financial apparatus. The *BC* softens if the state bank fails to apply strict, prudential criteria to its lending, and allows credit applications even if it knows debtors will be unable to meet their obligations. This is a kind of lifeline the state often throws to a troubled firm. The softness may continue when instalments, interest and repayment of the loan fall due. This breach of rule (ii) of financial discipline, where non-compliance with the credit agreement is tolerated, eases the firm's payment problems temporarily. The instruments applied within the credit system are far less conspicuous than fiscal instruments, and survive more stubbornly, even in an environment resistant to softening the *BC*.

The fourth and final category of instruments can be applied where prices are regulated by an administrative authority. The difference between a soft and a hard administrative price can be sensed intuitively. One adapts passively to prevailing costs, according to a mechanical 'cost-plus' formula. This largely sanctions the actual costs, even if they result from inefficient management. The latter calls for effort by the firm, which can only make a profit at the administratively fixed price by producing economically and efficiently. It is easier to set a harder price, of course, if there is some available basis for doing so, such as the cost level of more efficient firms in the country, or the foreign price of a tradable good. The risk of softening is greater if the producer has a national monopoly, or the product or service is not tradable.

There has been a debate about the concept of *SBC* in economic literature. Several authors have suggested alterations, or tried to subdivide the syndrome (see, for instance, Gomulka 1986). However, a broad range of theoretical, empirical and economic-policy writing adopts the conceptual framework just outlined. This is the sense in which the concept is used in the rest of this essay.

THE SBC FRAMEWORK: A VERTICAL RELATION. Market transactions produce a horizontal linkage between two partners of equal rank, buyer and seller. There is no superiority or subordination. The information flows horizontally, as does the product or service provided and the payment made for it. The *SBC* syndrome can occur when a vertical relation of superiority and subordination replaces or imposes itself on the horizontal relation. This clearly occurs under the socialist system. (Here the socialist system denotes the actual, historical formation that existed for decades in many countries, including the Soviet Union and several countries in Eastern Europe. It is synonymous with what is often known elsewhere as the 'communist system' or 'Soviet-type economy'.) In this case the state stands 'above' the enterprise, as its owner and the main coordinator running the command economy.

The official doctrine of the socialist system endorses rule (iv) of financial discipline: a firm must cover costs from income. However, the principle does not actually apply because relations between the state and state-owned enterprises are permeated by the *SBC* syndrome.

This has been the area of main concern in literature dealing with the *SBC*. However, researchers recognized from the outset that it is much more widespread, and appears under other systems, if only sporadically. Let me list some other relations that display *SBC* phenomena and are not system-specific (having developed under either the capitalist or the socialist system). In each case the relation is vertical, and I have signified which party is 'above' and which 'below'. The superior party tolerates the non-performance or initiates the rescue. The subordinate party breaks the rules and benefits from the rescue:

* Above: the state.
  Below: production firms (for instance, in declining industries), either state-owned or privately owned.
* Above: the state.
  Below: investment projects implemented with a state subsidy.
* Above: the state.
  Below: banks, either state-owned or privately owned.
* Above: the state.
  Below: off-budget, non-profit institutions (for instance, the social insurance system).
* Above: central government.
  Below: local government (see Qian and Roland 1996).
* Above: a bank with a credit monopoly.
  Below: debtors.

The concept of an *SBC* can be broadened further. Phenomena related to it in many respects occur, for instance, in relations between the centre of a large conglomerate and its member-companies. Another example is the handling of a debt crisis affecting several countries. There the international financial community is above (the international financial institutions, major banks, and perhaps governments of creditor countries), while the countries requiring a bail-out are below.

The remarks that follow are largely confined to the spheres in which the conceptual and analytical apparatus originally developed: to relations between the state and subordinate organizations, primarily firms.

THE SYNDROME'S EFFECTS. *Weakening of market instincts, adverse selection.* One prominent aspect of standard microeconomic theory is the recognition that firms strive to maximize profits. The theory of the *SBC* adds a further dimension. A firm's behaviour is also influenced by how intensely it strives to act efficiently: feebly or strongly. The market mechanism and market competition perform a process of natural selection. If the *BC* is hard, profitability becomes a matter of life and death. If the *BC* is soft, so that the firm's survival is assured, its pursuit of profits growth will be feebler, because it needs to strive less hard to survive.

The theory of the *SBC* complements the literature that arose in the wake of Schumpeter's theory of business enterprise. Schumpeter (in 1911 and 1942) drew attention to the process of creative destruction. The literature deals extensively with the creative side of the process, with freedom of enterprise and competitive entry, with the forms and conditions of competition, and with innovation. Schumpeter's entrepreneur introduces new products, technologies and methods of organization, and wins new markets. The theory of the *SBC* focuses on the destructive side. Softening the *BC* impedes the destruction that market selection should be carrying out. Acting symmetrically with the phenomena emphasized by Schumpeter, the *SBC* sustains the old products, and old technologies, forms of organization and markets, in cases where they should have been replaced by new ones. This conservation continues to tie down resources that market selection would free for new, more efficient purposes. Indeed the way the *SBC* syndrome supported obsolete firms was among the main reasons for the socialist system's low efficiency.

The *SBC* syndrome does not simply weaken the *ex ante* selection produced by exit. It also creates adverse selection *ex post*, making an entrepreneur entering the market less concerned about risks and more willing to proceed even if costs are unfavourably high, because the firm can expect to be bailed out if there is trouble.

The effect of the *SBC* resembles what is known in the economic theory of insurance as 'moral hazard'. Indeed with an *SBC* in force, the state (superior organization) more or less assumes the role of an insurer, compensating for losses. That dulls the debtor's sense of responsibility, saps his eagerness to prevent losses, or if the losses have already been made, to minimize them.

All these developments strongly affect the mentality and behaviour of managers. It may be more important to have good connections with those who decide on budget subsidies, tax concessions, soft credits, and administrative prices that allow costs to run away, than to strive for more favourable procurement and marketing, or more efficient production. Here analysis of the *SBC* intersects with the theory of rent-seeking. The latter sets out to explain how the entrepreneur wants to optimize his or her relations with the political sphere and the bureaucracy. This includes the case where an already profitable enterprise succeeds in gaining a rent. The *SBC* theory examines the relation between firm and state (and other, analogous vertical relations) *from a specific angle*, directing attention to losses, insolvency, exit, the problems of demise and survival of the organization.

Weakening responsiveness to prices and costs. The customary demand functions describe the buyer's varying reactions to relative prices of different products. The tightness of the *BC* adds another dimension to the examination of price responsiveness. If the firm is sure it will be compensated for its losses and its survival not be jeopardized by insolvency, it becomes less responsive to prices and costs. It feels it is less important to react to cost and price changes by altering its technology or product mix.

Coordination problems, damaging monetary and fiscal effects. If the *SBC* syndrome is confined to a narrow field of the economy, it may not have cumulative, spillover effects. It is a different matter if it prevails over most of the economy, as it typically did under the socialist system. This can be felt strongly at certain stages of the post-socialist transition.

Predominance of the *SBC* syndrome can lead to inordinate expansion of the credit supply, for instance through forced lending. One obvious example is the phenomenon of 'chains of debt' that cause serious problems in several post-socialist countries. This places serious strains on the whole banking system and the state budget, and puts on pressure for excessive monetary expansion and for fiscal deficit. If the government reacts by using its usual softening instruments – successively bailing out those in worst trouble – it can prevent serious coordination problems in the short term. At the same time it spells out a message that it does not matter if a firm cannot pay its debts, because it will be rescued, and the long-term disciplinary effects of that are very damaging.

Bailing out the large banks that suffer a financial crisis is especially problematic. If they are not rescued, there could be catastrophic knock-on effects. On the other hand, the repeated state assistance they have received in most post-socialist countries sends out harmful signals to the financial sector. It reduces the severity with which the bank treats credit transactions that represent a bad risk (see Begg and Portes 1993).

Runaway demand. If buyers feel they can spend more than their *BC* allows without running a serious risk, their demand ceases to be constrained by present and future income. So the *SBC* syndrome causes runaway demand. There is no way of establishing accurately what degrees of softness in the *BC* will generate what amounts of additional demand. Due to the softening process, demand tends to depart from the buyer's ability to pay, as the expression 'runaway' implies. The effect of *SBC* on demand has been confirmed theoretically by Goldfeld and Quandt (1988, 1990 and 1993) and Kornai and Weibull (1983). Goldfeld and Quandt call this reaction the 'Kornai effect'.

There was debate about whether the effect plays a significant part in explaining the chronic shortage characteristic of the socialist system. Although the syndrome was certainly not a *sufficient* condition for a chronic shortage economy to develop, it was, along with other factors, among the *necessary* conditions for this (see Kornai 1992, chs 11 and 12; and Qian 1994).

The effect is most striking on investment decisions. It is noticeable also in a traditional market economy that actual costs far outstrip the original budget for a project if it is completed wholly or partly with state funds. That applies to many military installations. Two classic examples of such overruns involving Britain and France were the Concorde supersonic airliner and the Channel Tunnel. In all such cases, those initiating and implementing the project calculate that the state will not abandon the project once it has started.

The phenomenon applied to almost every investment carried out under the socialist system. The *SBC* suffices to explain a typical feature of the economic system: investment hunger. The heads of every enterprise and state institution want to invest, because they can do so without risk of financial failure (see Kornai 1980; Huang 1996). The investment hunger constantly reproduced under the socialist economic system is among the main components of the runaway of aggregate demand.

The connection between the *SBC* syndrome and demand has important theoretical implications. Standard equilibrium theory tacitly assumes the *BC* on every decision-maker is hard. The assumption that Say's Principle applies is equivalent to assuming that the *BC* exists and is hard. According to Clower, the *BC* is not an accounting identity, but a rational postulate about behaviour, for 'no transactor consciously plans to purchase units of any commodity without at the same time planning to finance the purchase either from profit receipts, or from the sale of units of some other commodity . . .' (see Clower 1965; Clower and Leijonhufvud 1975 and 1981.) Where the *SBC* syndrome applies, this postulate is breached on a mass scale on a micro level, and consciously so, as Clower puts it. To remain with the example of investment, the investor, though aware that the planned income stream will never cover the planned expenditure stream, embarks on the project nonetheless. This starts a process of inordinate additional demand that the additional-supply process cannot oppose at prevailing prices.

MEASUREMENT. Like other complex social and economic phenomena, the hardness or softness of the *BC* cannot be measured directly, only indirectly.

One possible way of quantifying it is to observe the extent to which the various softening instruments are applied and the frequency with which this occurs. For instance, how large are the budget subsidies and how are they distributed? How differentiated are the tax rates? To what extent do unpaid taxes accumulate? What is the composition of the banks' stock of outstanding credit, in terms of servicing and repayments? What is the proportion of non-performing loans? What is the distribution of profitable and loss-making firms among the debtors to banks, or in more general terms, what relationship pertains between the extending of credit and business profitability? According to the conservative principle of banking, the best borrower would be one who could continue to operate without credit. It is possible to observe whether the principle applies. There are numerous examples of this method of measurement found in literature on the subject (see, for instance, Kornai and Matits 1990; Raiser 1995; Perkins and Raiser 1995).

Another way of measuring is to try to examine the primary effects of the *SBC*. In line with the account given earlier, one can describe as secondary or ultimate effects occurrences such as declining efficiency, weakening responses to prices and costs, disturbances of coordination, and runaway demand. The question then remains what other factors contributed to these ultimate effects, besides the *SBC* syndrome. On the other hand, there is a fairly direct relation between *SBC* and the following three primary effects:

(A) The strength of the correlation between the profitability of a firm and its survival. The complementary issue to this is the closeness of the correlation between the exit and the losses of a firm, and the frequency of the various types of bail-out actions.

(B) One form the *SBC* syndrome takes is bureaucratic redistribution of business profits. Most of the profits of enterprises operating fairly profitably are siphoned off through various channels and transferred to those that are less profitable or make losses. This levelling of profits dulls the profit motive. The scale of the redistribution can be gauged numerically (see Kornai and Matits 1990; Schaffer 1990.)

(C) Under a hard *BC*, a persistently profitable enterprise

has a greater chance of self-financing its investment and of receiving long-term investment credit. It is a sign of softening if there is a loose correlation between the profitability of a firm and its development, expansion and investment activity. This can also be measured numerically (see Kornai and Matits 1990; Perkins and Raiser 1995).

There is a danger of comprehensive, manifold measurement being eschewed in favour of observing one or two randomly chosen indices, such as reduction of budget subsidies. This can lead to false conclusions. The post-socialist transition has slashed fiscal subsidies to the business sphere in many countries. Nonetheless, there are no grounds for complacency. The hardening of the *BC* has been much less radical. Into the foreground have come softening techniques such as extending soft loans, or tolerating firms' non-fulfilment of loan-servicing and taxpaying obligations. It is essential to track the course of the *SBC* syndrome through a collection of indices.

THE EXPLANATORY FACTORS. Since it is the state, in most cases, that softens the constraint, it may initially seem baffling to know why it should do something that harms the state interest.

Several explanations have been advanced (for a review of the theories, see Dewatripont, Maskin and Roland 1996; Maskin 1996). One criterion for grouping the theories is by whether they attribute this behaviour in an *endogenous* fashion to the internal interests of a softening institution 'above', or whether an *exogenous* explanation applies, for in the second group of explanations, a strong, even a key part is played by the relation of the actor performing the softening with the surrounding political and social environment and the external economic factors.

Endogenous explanations. The pioneering work is a study by Dewatripont and Maskin (1995), whose model shows how the *SBC* syndrome can be analysed with the apparatus of game theory. A superior organization, such as a bank, is deciding whether to finance investment projects. Projects come in two types: 'good' investments, which can be completed in a specified period, and 'bad' investments, whose completion will be delayed and cost more than 'good' projects. Although each project manager knows beforehand the likely completion period, this information is kept from the bank, and some projects accepted are bad. At the end of the initial period, the managers of bad, incomplete projects request refinancing. Since the initial investment is a sunk cost, it may be that the bank prefers to refinance a loan, because the marginal benefit of refinancing exceeds the marginal cost. This situation may occur even though the total sum invested will end up being higher than the returns it generates. So the bank is using softening instruments in its own commercial interest, not because of outside factors. However, its behaviour results later in adverse selection. Future project managers count on the bank's willingness to refinance and have no qualms about requesting money for bad projects. The only way the bank can avoid this is by committing itself in advance (and abiding by its commitment) not to give refinancing under any conditions – but in that case it would often have to act against its commercial interest. The study analyses the conditions in which the bank will choose repeated refinancing, along with its damaging side-effects, and those in which it commit itself to refusing refinancing. In particular, it shows that decentralization of credit can make refinancing more difficult to achieve, which can contribute to hardening budget constraints.

The credibility of a commitment by an institution 'above' lies at the centre of many other theoretical investigations (for instance, see Schaffer 1989; Qian and Xu 1991).

Bai and Wang (1996) emphasize the information side of the problem. Those personally responsible to their superiors for a previous bad decision are afraid it will shed a bad light on their screening activity to cancel the half-complete project. It will be less conspicuous to continue the project, even at a higher cost.

Exogenous explanations. The following are those that deserve the closest attention.

(1) The socialist system headed by the communist party was imbued with the concept and practice of state paternalism. This left its mark on the state's relationship with firms, as well as individuals. The state treated its enterprises like children, patronizing them and intervening in every detailed decision. On the other hand it did not abandon them when they were in trouble.

In effect, the party apparatus, the economic bureaucracy and the enterprise management group formed an inseparable whole, a uniform, cohesive stratum of leaders. Managers of firms could count on help from their colleagues (see Kornai 1980).

Explanation 1 is system-specific, deriving from the political and sociological nature and official ideology of the socialist system. Explanations 2–5 are not system-specific.

(2) Governments may make *SBC*-type interventions for reasons of employment policy. They want to avoid mass insolvency and liquidation among firms, so as to save jobs and reduce the insecurity of employees.

(3) Governments and parties may apply mainly fiscal instruments of state assistance that soften the *BC*, in order to gain political support. This lies behind the fiscal support won by farming lobbies, or the assistance to some declining, crisis-ridden industries or regions. This explanation for the *SBC* syndrome gains support from inferences of public-choice theory.

(4) The possibility of corruption cannot be excluded. A loss-making firm may bribe a politician or bureaucrat who can influence whether fiscal assistance or other softening instruments are applied.

(5) The state feels it has no option but to bail out a troubled firm if its demise would cause external damage greater than the cost of rescue. This effect may occur in the real economy. For instance, if a firm is in a monopoly position, elimination of its production may upset other firms as well, and precipitate a serious loss to society (see Newbery 1991; Segal 1993). On the other hand, it may appear in the monetary economy. Mention was made earlier of the reproduction of insolvency and the grave coordination problems that may arise. The desire to avert serious external damage explains why the state normally saves large banks in financial difficulties, not only in a

socialist or post-socialist economy, but in every developed country that operates traditionally as a market economy. A surge of withdrawals by depositors leads to panic, which spreads and can grow into a national catastrophe. As a rule, the state forestalls this with a bail-out.

The various endogenous and exogenous explanations often act together on the factors that induce softening, reinforcing each other.

Examining the explanatory factors makes clearer something already mentioned when the concepts were clarified: why the *SBC* syndrome is more widespread, prevalent and resilient under the socialist than under the capitalist system. In the former, all the explanatory factors listed are constantly present in all spheres of the economy. However, most of these factors can also appear in the latter, if more sporadically and over a narrower sphere. *SBC* phenomena tend to appear more extensively the greater the intertwining between politics and business, the bigger the state sector, and the wider the bureaucracy's sphere of action. Thus the *SBC* syndrome is quite common in developing countries, for instance.

CONCLUSIONS FOR ECONOMIC POLICY. Identifying the damage the *SBC* syndrome causes leads to a general conclusion: it is worth working to harden the *BC* on firms and other organizations.

While this applies to every economic formation, there is good reason to single out economic policy in the socialist countries, where the *SBC* syndrome causes most trouble. Historical experience seems to support the following statement. Partial reforms with cosmetic changes will not suffice to harden the *BC*. The socialist system has to give way to a capitalist market economy.

Most policy programmes and expert recommendations for the post-socialist transition treat hardening the *BC* as a key issue. The need for a radical change in property relations should be specially emphasized. It helps to harden the *BC* if the relative weight of the private sector is raised substantially and most enterprises hitherto owned by the state are privatized. There is also a fairly general consensus on the following statement: it is hopeless to expect the *BC* on firms to harden while state ownership remains dominant (see Boycko, Shleifer and Vishny 1992 and 1995). On the other hand, Bardhan (1993) expresses confidence about the compatibility of public ownership and a hard *BC*. The situation changes when private ownership becomes dominant and the state-enterprise sector narrows. It can be observed empirically that it then ceases to be impossible (although it remains far from easy) to give the remaining state-owned enterprises fuller autonomy and harden their *BC* (see Pinto, Belka and Krajewski 1993).

These are some other measures that help to eliminate or minimize the *SBC* syndrome:

* Introduction and consistent enforcement of an accounting law compatible with a market economy. This limits the concealment of losses, as does the spread of the joint-stock company form.
* Introduction and consistent enforcement of an up-to-date banking law. This makes it harder to conceal losses or irresponsible lending.
* Reduction of fiscal subsidies, introduction of uniform tax rates, and elimination or strict limitation of tax concessions. 'Fiscalization' of concealed subsidies, so that they appear plainly in the budget, which tends to reduce them.
* Introduction and consistent enforcement of a bankruptcy and liquidation law, and development of the judicial system required.
* Where possible, action against the appearance of monopolies.
* Where possible, price liberalization, to limit the scope for using administrative prices as a softening instrument.
* Decentralization, where practicable, of the state organization, including fiscal decision-making. If possible there should be overlap and multiplication among state bodies, to create competition among them that helps to overcome the *SBC* syndrome (see Raiser 1995; Qian and Roland 1996).

While most experts agree on the desirability of hardening the *BC*, this can never be accomplished rigidly or dogmatically, at a stroke. In some cases exceptions must be made, for instance if the external damage would be too great compared with the gain from hardening the constraint. Under some conditions, there have to be temporary concessions, to prevent insolvencies and liquidations caused by the hardening having serious knock-on effects that destabilize the economy or political democracy. Attention needs paying to regional differences within the country, and to social and employment problems caused by market selection. Adaptation takes time, so that the option of temporary subsidies should not be utterly rejected in a doctrinaire manner. If such subsidies are given, it is worth announcing beforehand a timetable for phasing them out. This allows preparations to be made for a hard *BC* regime. There has been debate about when such softening of the *BC* is permissible and what scale the concessions should assume.

Observation of the hardness or softness of the *BC* and assessment of the change have passed from the realm of theoretical studies into the practical language of economic policy. Reports on the post-socialist transformation frequently take the *BC* as a yardstick. Activity (or absence of activity) to harden the *BC* makes a good gauge of the responsibility, foresight and resolve behind government policy.

JÁNOS KORNAI

See also BUREAUCRACY IN EASTERN EUROPE AND THE FORMER SOVIET UNION; COMMITMENT; PRIVATIZATION; PRIVATIZATION IN CENTRAL AND EASTERN EUROPE; RENT SEEKING; TRANSITION IN EASTERN EUROPE.

Subject classification: 2d(i); 3f(ii).

BIBLIOGRAPHY

Bai, C. and Wang, Y. 1996. Agency in project screening and termination decisions: Why is good money thrown after bad? Mimeo, University of Minnesota.

Bardhan, P.K. 1993. On tackling the soft budget constraint in market socialism. In *Market Socialism: The Current Debate*, ed. P.K.

Bardhan and J.E. Roemer, New York, Oxford: Oxford University Press.

Begg, D. and Portes, R. 1993. Enterprise debt and economic transformation: Financial restructuring in Central and Eastern Europe. In *Capital Markets and Financial Intermediation*, ed. C. Mayer and X. Vives, Cambridge, New York: Cambridge University Press.

Boycko, M., Shleifer, A. and Vishny, R. 1992. Property rights, soft budget constraints and privatization. Mimeo, Harvard University.

Boycko, M., Shleifer, A. and Vishny, R. 1995. *Privatizing Russia*. Cambridge, MA: MIT Press.

Clower, R. 1965. The Keynesian counter-revolution: a theoretical appraisal. In *The Theory of Interest Rates*, ed. F.H. Hahn and F.P.R. Brechling, London: Macmillan.

Clower, R. and Leijonhufvud, A. 1975. The coordination of economic activities: a Keynesian perspective. *American Economic Review, Papers and Proceedings* 65: 182–8.

Clower, R. and Leijonhufvud, A. 1981. Say's principle: What it means and doesn't mean. Reprinted in A. Leijonhufvud, *Information and Coordination*, Oxford: Oxford University Press.

Dewatripont, M. and Maskin, E. 1995. Credit and efficiency in centralized and decentralized economies. *Review of Economic Studies* 62: 541–55.

Dewatripont, M., Maskin, E. and Roland, G. 1996. Soft budget constraints and transition. Manuscript.

Goldfeld, S.M. and Quandt, R.E. 1988. Budget constraints, bailouts and the firm under central planning. *Journal of Comparative Economics* 12: 502–20.

Goldfeld, S.M. and Quandt, R.E. 1990. Output targets, the soft budget constraint and the firm under central planning. *Journal of Economic Behavior and Organization* 14: 205–22.

Goldfeld, S.M. and Quandt, R.E. 1993. Uncertainty, bailouts, and the Kornai effect. *Economics Letters* 41: 113–19.

Gomulka, S. 1986. Kornai's soft budget constraint and the shortage phenomenon: A criticism and restatement. In *Growth, Innovation and Reform in Eastern Europe*, Economics of Technological Change series, Madison: University of Wisconsin Press.

Huang, Y. 1996. *Inflation and Investment Controls in China. The Political Economy of Central-Local Relations during the Reform Era*. Cambridge: Cambridge University Press.

Kornai, J. 1979. Resource-constrained versus demand-constrained systems. *Econometrica* 47: 801–19.

Kornai, J. 1980. *Economics of Shortage*. Amsterdam: North Holland.

Kornai, J. 1986. The soft budget constraint. *Kyklos* 39: 3–30.

Kornai, J. 1992. *The Socialist System: The Political Economy of Communism*. Princeton: Princeton University Press and Oxford: Oxford University Press.

Kornai, J. and Matits, Á. 1990. The bureaucratic redistribution of firms' profits. In J. Kornai, *Vision and Reality, Market and State: New Studies on the Socialist Economy and Society*, Budapest: Corvina; Hemel Hempstead: Harvester-Wheatsheaf; New York: Routledge.

Kornai, J. and Weibull, J.W. 1983. Paternalism, buyers' and sellers' market. *Mathematical Social Sciences* 7: 153–69.

Maskin, E.S. 1996. Theories of the soft budget-constraint. *Japan and the World Economy* 8: 125–33.

Newbery, D.M. 1991. Sequencing the transition. Discussion Paper 575, Centre for Economic Policy Research, London.

Perkins, F. and Raiser, M. 1995. State enterprise reform and macroeconomic stability in transition economies. Economics Division Working Papers 95/1, Research School of Pacific and Asian Studies, ANU.

Pinto, B., Belka, M. and Krajewski, S. 1993. Transforming state enterprises in Poland: microeconomic evidence on adjustment. Working Paper 1101, Transition and Macroadjustment, Washington, DC: The World Bank.

Qian, Y. 1994. A theory of shortage in socialist economies based on the 'soft budget-constraint'. *American Economic Review* 84: 145–56.

Qian, Y. and Roland, G. 1996. Federalism and the soft budget constraint. Manuscript.

Qian, Y. and Xu, C. 1991. Innovation and financial constraints in centralized and decentralized economies. Mimeo, London School of Economics.

Raiser, M. 1995. Decentralization, autonomy and efficiency: Inconsistent reforms and enterprise performance in China. Kiel Working Paper 689, Institut für Weltwirtschaft an der Universität Kiel.

Schaffer, M.E. 1989. The credible-commitment problem in the center-enterprise relationship. *Journal of Comparative Economics* 13: 359–82.

Schaffer, M.E. 1990. State-owned enterprises in Poland: taxation, subsidization, and competition policies. In *European Economy* (Brussels: Commission of the European Communities), No. 43: 183–202.

Schumpeter, J.A. 1911. *Theorie der Wirtschaftlichen Entwicklung. The Theory of Economic Development.* Leipzig: Duncket & Humblot, 1912. Trans. by R. Opie as *An Inquiry into Profits, Capital, Credit, Interest and the Business Cycle*, Cambridge, MA: Harvard University Press 1934; reprinted New York: Oxford University Press, 1961.

Schumpeter, J.A. 1942. *Capitalism, Socialism and Democracy*. New edn, New York: Harper & Row, London: Allen & Unwin, 1976.

Segal, I. 1993. Monopoly and soft budget-constraint. Manuscript.

legal paternalism and efficiency. Paternalistic laws are ones which deliberately restrict people's freedom of decision in order to bring benefits *to those people*. In other words, legal paternalism interferes with people's freedom of choice, such as the freedom to sell a right or the freedom to consent to an injury inflicted by another person. There are innumerable laws which are hard to justify on other grounds and which arguably have a paternalistic intent. Examples of such laws can be found in a wide range of traditional law categories, such as contract, tort, and regulatory statutes. In contract law among the many examples are the non-disclaimable duty of good faith in contract performance, the undue influence doctrine, and the non-waivable product seller's guarantee against injury due to product defect. Each of these examples is an interference with the freedom of contract, in effect through the imposition of compulsory terms. Tort law examples include landlords' duties to tenants which the tenants cannot waive, and the non-waivable duties of employers not to wrongfully discharge their employees. Paternalistic regulatory statutes range widely, from the safety cases (seat belts in cars, protective clothing in hazardous occupations, design requirements for toys, etc.) to the regulation of financial institutions and the legislative restrictions on insurance and employment contracts.

PRINCIPLES IN THE ANALYSIS OF LEGAL PATERNALISM. Economists and lawyers have not been keen to make explicit the paternalistic motivation of many laws. Consequently there have been very few attempts to formulate the principles upon which legal paternalism should be based. However, a few brave authors have insisted on pointing to the difficulty of rationalizing many laws solely on the basis of distributive arguments. In contract, for example, there are myriad restrictions on contract terms which do not redistribute the contract gains between the parties because the contracts are formed, and the price of the contract performance is determined, in the knowledge that the restrictions apply. As a result the contract price will reflect, for example, any non-waivable duty imposed on the contract performer (Kennedy 1982).

Paternalistic law is most easily explained as a means of improving the efficiency of the activities which it is designed to control. As we shall see, however, the pursuit of such efficiency gains must be balanced against the consequences which the legal interventions have for the freedom of all of the parties affected. Conventional economic theory is rather stymied in its ability to analyse paternalistic law by its adherence to the assumption that people have complete and fixed preferences. Legal paternalism, on the contrary, tends to derive from the incompleteness, the variability through time and other problematic aspects, of people's preferences.

Law-and-economics has taken a narrow view of human rationality, in line with most economic theory. The narrow interpretation, called *logical rationality* (Kahneman 1994), assumes that people's preferences are internally consistent, constant and evident to the people concerned. Logical rationality is not concerned with the *content* of people's preferences; and this kind of rationality is concerned only with the form of the preferences – it takes no interest in, and is not judged by, the *consequences* of rational behaviour. By contrast *substantive* rationality is concerned with the extent to which a person's behaviour is successful in pursuing his own good. It can only be judged in terms of the individual's experience of the consequences of his decisions. For an analysis of legal paternalism it proves to be important to go beyond the narrow conception of logical rationality to consider the consequences of people's decisions and of legal interference with those decisions.

The instrumentalist argument for free choice. A good starting point for an analysis of legal paternalism, which essentially is an interference with free choice, is the assumptions which underlie the most widely used argument for allowing free choice. This argument, called the instrumentalist argument, concerns both logical *and* substantive rationality.

The instrumentalist argument adopts two premises, (a) and (b), that together imply a conclusion, (c), in favour of freedom of choice (Burrows 1993):

(a) The outcomes of private choices should be valued only in terms of the chooser's manifest, *ex ante* preferences (that is those preferences that the chooser is aware of before a choice is made, and which are reflected in his choice);

(b) A person will make private choices which produce outcomes that better satisfy his *ex ante* manifest preferences than would any alternative decision process.

Therefore

(c) The freedom to make private choices necessarily is in the individual's best interests, in the instrumental sense of leading to outcomes that are at least as valuable to him as any alternative available outcomes.

This preference-choice-value (PCV) proposition underlies the liberal recommendation of free choice. Yet it is by no means certain that the premises (a) and (b) will be plausible for all kinds of decision. Consider the conditions under which the PCV proposition will be *most compelling*.

Condition 1: the individual's *ex ante* manifest preferences are considered, non-impulsive, consistent, and complete in the sense of covering all the potential alternatives.

There are a number of doubts about how well this condition is satisfied in practice. For example, numerous experimental studies have shown that people's preferences display a variety of inconsistencies which violate the requirements of logical rationality. Secondly, if people are impetuous then the content of the preferences which guide their decisions makes them an unreliable guide to their deeper values. If a person's preferences are ill-considered, impulsive or incomplete there is no guarantee that *ex post* he will retrospectively accept the basis on which he made his initial judgement.

Condition 2: the preferences that determine choices reflect fully any feedback from experience that would align those preferences most closely with the person's good.

This condition relates to the endogenous nature of people's preferences. If the preferences are dependent on experience then clearly discrepancies between *ex ante* and *ex post* preferences are likely, *even if* the *ex ante* preferences are consistent, considered and as complete as is feasible prior to the preference-altering experience. When such discrepancies arise it is an extremely strong assumption to insist (as does part (a) of the PCV proposition) that alternative choices should be judged solely in terms of a person's *ex ante* preferences. It is more convincing, perhaps, to suggest that if different choices lead to different later preferences then decisions ideally should consciously reflect a judgement on which of the possible later preferences would be the most closely aligned with the person's good. But this is a very demanding requirement of substantively rational individual choice, because it needs the chooser to *foresee* (at the point of making the choice) the changes in his preferences that would result from the alternative experiences which could follow from his various options. A number of obstacles to fully rational choice, in this sense, can easily be imagined.

For one thing, experimental evidence does not suggest that people are good at predicting changes in their preferences (Kahneman 1994). Consequently there is no guarantee that their choices will derive from a perception of the preference-creating potential of their decisions. For another, the learning feedback from experience to preferences and choices will be weak in those circumstances in which the choices are infrequent, so that the possibility of altering the decisions is small even when preferences are changing through experience. Finally, there are situations in which a person faces the risk of a catastrophic event (such as fatality or serious injury), but even a lengthy experience of taking that risk does little to alter his perception of the potential consequences. Thus, one may drive for years and luckily experience no events that could make one appreciate fully the consequences of being unrestrained in a collision, until it is too late.

Condition 3: the first two conditions are concerned with the nature of people's *ex ante* and *ex post* preferences. The third condition relates to people's skill in decision making: even if a person's preferences have all the desirable characteristics needed to align them with his wellbeing, successful choices still require an ability to identify the best route to satisfying those preferences. Yet some kinds of choices require both considerable imagination (to recognize the full range of options available) and a high degree of analytical ability (in order to be able to connect the alternative outcomes of choices with the person's preferences). There now exists an extensive literature, on the boundary between psychology and economics, which recounts a significant number of biases in the way people make decisions (Hogarth 1987, ch. 10), in particular in the way they collect and process information. These fallibilities in decision making include, for example, the selective collection of information to protect preconceived notions of the 'best' choice, and the refusal to contemplate some of the possible, painful outcomes.

The instrumentalist argument for free choice is therefore founded upon several assumptions which are much more plausible for some kinds of decisions (such as those where there are few options and where the outcomes are easily predictable without experience) than for others. Neither theory nor evidence therefore appears to dictate that we reject out of hand the case for paternalistic interventions for all choice contexts. A preferable approach seems to be to eschew a *general* stance in favour of or against such interventions in favour of an evaluation of each proposed intervention in its own specific context.

Paternalism, efficiency and freedom. If a paternalistic legal intervention is capable of creating benefits for people whose freedom of choice it restricts, then there is a *prima facie* case for the intervention on *efficiency* grounds. Naturally this *prima facie* case requires that the legal system be capable of identifying *ex ante* the contexts within which such benefits are attainable. And the appropriate *ex post* judgement on the value of the intervention should be based upon the benefits to the constrained individuals as they perceive them *ex post*. There are three routes by which legal interventions may generate such benefits: the enhancement of a person's physical wellbeing, the stimulation of the creative development of a person's preferences, and the moderation of impulsive, self-damaging decisions.

This interpretation of the possible consequences of legal paternalism sees the paternalistic and efficiency objectives as synonymous. The main objection to the pursuit of such an objective lies in the belief that interfering with free choices is an infringement of people's freedom. Thus there is an apparent confrontation between the efficiency objective and people's rights. An extreme liberal opinion would assert that people have a fundamental right to autonomy and self-determination (so long as these are compatible with the similar rights of other people). This fundamental right, the argument goes, is paramount and should not be infringed through restrictions on the freedom of choice, *however great* the potential efficiency benefits to people might be and *however small* their loss of freedom might be.

There are two important counter-objections to this extreme liberal stance: it seriously oversimplifies the consequences of legal paternalism for people's freedom, and it asserts a degree of dominance of freedom of choice that society does not generally try to implement. The oversimplification lies in the fact that it limits the freedom argument to the protection of negative freedom (the right to make free choices) to the exclusion of positive freedom (the right to have access to an enhanced set of options, the right to develop and fulfil one's potential). If a legal intervention assists an individual to follow a path that develops his preferences and thereby expands his set of fulfilling options, it could be seen as *enhancing* positive freedom. The intervention then has conflicting negative and positive freedom effects, and it is not necessarily the case that any efficiency advantage it generates must be balanced against a loss of freedom overall.

The second counter-objection is that even if the effect on positive freedom were disregarded it would be far from obvious that most people would subscribe to the extreme liberal position, which denies any possibility of a trade-off between efficiency gains and negative freedom. While not denying the importance of people's rights to negative freedom, society in general, and the law in particular, accepts many situations in which minor intrusions on rights are allowed in the pursuit of efficiency gains. For example, in principle I could claim that it infringes my autonomy if another person once lays, uninvited, the lightest of fingers on me in the street. In principle legal action could be brought by the police for assault, but in practice the efficiency gain from not using public resources to try to prevent such trivial intrusions is accepted by everyone.

A more reasonable attitude to legal paternalism than that implied by the extreme liberal opinion is that the balance of argument concerning the efficiency and positive freedom benefits, together with the adverse consequences for negative freedom, should be judged on a context-by-context basis. For some legal interventions the balance may lie in favour of paternalism, in others against. On this argument the courts and legislatures must make the judgments without the assistance of a great, over-riding principle in support of or hostile to legal paternalisms. The consideration of a number of specific examples of legal paternalism (Burrows 1993, section IV, and 1995, section III) reveals that in each of them the complexity of the paternalistic objectives, and of the various risks of harm to negative freedom, is such that fine judgment is required in the drawing of the line between justifiable and unjustifiable legal paternalisms.

CONCLUSION. A fruitful analysis of legal paternalism requires the recognition of the instrumentalist arguments both for freedom of choice and for legal restrictions on such freedom. The strength of these conflicting arguments will depend upon the degree to which the conditions required for successful free choices are satisfied, as well as upon the ability of the legal system to identify situations in which legal paternalism will generate benefits for the people who are restricted by it. In addition, a final judgment on the case for a particular legal paternalism needs to incorporate its implications for both positive and negative freedom. Only then could the courts or the legislature be confident that they have made a fully rational judgment on the merits and disadvantages of the legal paternalism.

PAUL BURROWS

See also BOUNDED RATIONALITY; COGNITION AND CONTRACT; CONSUMER PROTECTION; INHERITANCE LAW; MENGER, CARL; PRECOMMITMENT AND PROHIBITION; PREFERENCE SHAPING BY THE LAW; RULE-GUIDED BEHAVIOUR; VALUING LIFE AND RISKS TO LIFE.

Subject classification: 4c(ii).

BIBLIOGRAPHY

Burrows, P. 1993. Patronising paternalism. *Oxford Economic Papers* 45: 542–72.

Burrows, P. 1995. Analysing legal paternalism. *International Review of Law and Economics* 15: 489–508.

Hogarth, R.M. 1987. *Judgement and Choice*. 2nd edn, Chichester: Wiley.

Kahneman, D. 1994. New challenges to the rationality assumption. *Journal of Institutional and Theoretical Economics* 150(1): 18–36.

Kennedy, D. 1982. Distributive and paternalist motives in contract and tort law, with special reference to compulsory terms and unequal bargaining power. *Maryland Law Review* 41: 563–658.

legal pluralism. Legal pluralism describes a situation in which in a single country various legal systems coexist and each of them applies to different groups of individuals, so that the same social or economic relationship may be differently regulated if it involves different categories of persons. Seen from another perspective, legal pluralism is a situation in which an individual is subject to more than one legal system. Such is the case, for instance, when state law applies to everybody as the 'general law' of the country, while various customary and religious laws apply to different ethnic or religious groups as the 'personal law' of their own members.

The relationship between general and personal law varies in different countries and in different historical periods. During the Middle Ages, for instance, common law (*jus commune*), which mainly stemmed from Romanistic principles and was supported by the authority of the Catholic church, was loosely but fairly generally applied throughout most of continental Europe, while at the same time each individual was also subject to a personal law (*jus proprium*), based on local customs, feudal privileges or the bylaws of professional groups. Both common and personal laws were later gradually replaced by the unitary legal system created and codified by the nation states of the seventeenth and eighteenth centuries. In England, however, common law, developed by the royal courts' jurisdiction, soon prevailed over the customary laws administered by local courts, but had to face competition from equity jurisdiction until the two systems were unified at the end of the nineteenth century.

Due to the great variety of local situations and the different views of legal scholars and anthropologists on what should be regarded as 'law', there is still no general agreement on what is meant by 'legal pluralism' as a specific phenomenon. Indeed, historical, anthropological and comparative law studies show that practically all legal systems provided (or still provide) different rules for people of different status (such as nobles, priests, slaves, women, public officials, etc.) or capacity (e.g., minors or the mentally handicapped).

Although it will later be argued that legal pluralism is not as unusual as generally thought, it can be agreed at the outset that the mere presence of different rules for different peoples is not *per se* a situation of legal pluralism. The latter is characterized by the coexistence of bodies of rules so different as to constitute a plurality of potentially autonomous legal systems, each resting on its own jurisprudential principles, legal technicalities and enforcing machinery.

A typical situation of legal pluralism was created by colonization in Africa. Here, imported European law came to coexist (and potentially to conflict) with the pre-existing traditional (customary and religious) law of local societies. Let us take family law, for instance. Africans were encouraged by missionaries to enter into Christian marriage, and if a couple did so, colonial legislation often declared that both spouses and their children were thereafter subject to European law in matters related to family relations and succession. However, as marriage in Africa was (and to a great extent still is) an event of wide social relevance and implications, as far as the local community was concerned the couple remained subject to their own traditional law. If problems arose later, for instance on the monogamous character of the marriage, on divorce or maintenance, the two legal systems would be in conflict and neither would accept the solution provided by the other.

In the colonial context the two legal systems were generally kept separate. The imported law with its judicial machinery was mainly reserved for European subjects, while customary and religious laws (mainly Islamic *sharia*), with their own dispute-solving systems, were left for the local population, unless Western morality and colonial interests were directly involved.

Apart from practical reasons of colonial administration, this separation, recently termed 'deep legal pluralism', was also due to a reluctance to make the 'superior' European legal system available to people of a different civilization. For their part, Africans regarded European rule, with its unintelligible laws, as totally alien to their own political system and legal culture, which they continued to regard as the only legitimate and binding source of law.

Legal pluralism, however, requires some form of relationship between the coexisting legal systems. In the colonial context this relationship existed both in theory and in practice, and it has been termed a 'dominant–servient' relationship. Colonial enactments were officially regarded as the general law of the territory, while the imported European laws on the one hand and customary and religious laws on the other were regarded as the personal laws of the people living in the colony. From the practical point of view, apart from possibile shifts from customary to

European law as shown in the marriage example above, customary law was influenced by the European presence, for instance in gradually recognizing previously unknown individual land rights in response to the pressing demands put forward by colonial agriculture.

Independence came as a challenge to legal pluralism, but in general it actually changed more the form than the substance of the relationship between imported European laws and local legal traditions. Some African states actually retained the legal dualism of colonial origin, but many others officially abolished it and declared the unity of the national legal system. Imported European laws, however, far from being cancelled became the backbone of the new state legal system and were made binding for all citizens. Customary law, if not drastically abrogated or simply ignored, was officially incorporated into – but not really amalgamated with – the state legal system, sometimes through a process of restatement. In all cases, however, it continued to exist and govern the traditional life of the vast majority of the population, especially in rural areas. One can here recall the case of a Minister visiting a rural province of an African socialist state and, as a start to the new land reform, distributing nationalized land to local peasants, who never dared to use it because the traditional 'guardian of the land' (officially banned by the government) simply did not endorse what had been granted by the Minister.

The behaviour of those peasants was not illogical. They did not contradict the traditional authority because they did not wish to opt out of their customary legal system, which they felt still offered them more security than the state legal system. Without the people's consent the land reform was destined to remain on paper, unless the state resorted to the use of force in order to implement it. Later on the same country (no longer governed by a socialist regime) took a different approach. Not only did it recognize the customary land tenure system, but it also officially involved the traditional authorities in a grassroots programme aimed at modernizing the local agricultural system and transforming its subsistence economy into a market economy. The example shows how socio-economic development may be better served by accepting legal pluralism rather than ignoring it or imposing a powerless unitarian legal system modelled on foreign laws.

Unfortunately, accepting legal pluralism was not always easy in developing countries. One reason was that foreign laws enjoyed a misplaced prestige with the governing elites and international financing bodies, who had little confidence in customary law, which was relatively unknown and unjustly labelled 'backward'. Deeper anthropological studies have shown how sophisticated so-called 'primitive' law is in relation to social stability and how finely tuned it is with local environmental conditions. A better knowledge of traditional law and a new emphasis on participatory and sustainable development now seem to provide the conditions for accepting legal pluralism as a fertile situation in which the foreign-modelled legal system of the state and traditional systems can complement each other and gradually evolve into an integrated system according with local needs and conditions.

Although legal pluralism is particularly relevant in developing countries, it is also present in industrialized states, where too legal anthropology has greatly contributed to the study of both old and new minorities, such as Native American and immigrant communities in North America. Thanks to these studies and to a new interpretation of the principle of equality that includes the right to diversity, industrialized states are increasingly giving space to the legal systems of these minorities.

While from the social point of view accepting legal pluralism is thus becoming an important aspect of the protection of human rights, from the economic point of view deregulation and globalization can also be regarded as paving the way towards a particular type of legal pluralism. Indeed, nowadays many states allow business organizations to have their own rules and dispute-solving mechanisms, which are so independent from state law as to form a sort of separate legal system of a transnational nature similar to the merchant common law (*lex mercatoria*) of medieval Europe.

The widespread presence of legal pluralism is of course reflected in the way the idea of law is perceived in Western legal theory. Legal pluralism is thus both a field of operation for the lawmaker and an instrument of scientific research for the legal scholar. In the study of law the plural approach, like an optical lens, allows us to bring nearer faraway objects, such as the world legal systems that are more distant from the Western-centred idea of law and justice. Furthermore, it helps to magnify the most hidden components of the legal rule and therefore enhances our understanding (and use) of it.

A first scientific aspect of legal pluralism is a widening of the concepts of law and justice in order to accommodate the less state-oriented legal cultures of non-Western societies. Their traditional principles of mediation and arbitration, for instance, are changing the Western concept of the rule of law, as well as suggesting models for alternative dispute resolution which are sorely needed by most industrial countries, where the state machinery is increasingly unable to cope efficiently with both criminal and civil justice.

A second effect of accepting legal pluralism as a scientific concept relates to the way in which world legal systems are classified by comparative law scholars. Until recently such systems were grouped – different authors following different criteria – in a few major 'families', in which every national system was fixed in a central or lateral position. The family picture of common law, for instance, was dominated by England, with the USA to her side and surrounded by her former colonies. Similarly, the family picture of civil law had France and Germany at the top, most other countries of continental Europe one step down and below them their many former colonies ranging from South America to Southern Africa and Southeast Asia. However, the presence of former colonies in such pictures always appeared to be somehow artificial, as in early colonial photographs where local chiefs look strange when dressed in Western ceremonial clothes. Moreover, new states do not always like to be bound into their adoptive colonial family, and sometimes opt out of it by partly or totally changing their inherited legal system in favour of other foreign models. Sudan, for instance, opted out of common law by adopting (unsuccessfully) a French-modelled civil code in 1971 and later by shifting toward an integralist Islamic state. More recently, Mozambique, having inherited a civil law system from Portugal, joined the British Commonwealth after abandoning a previous option for socialist law.

A better framework for classifying world legal systems was therefore needed, and it has been suggested that legal pluralism could satisfactorily provide such a framework. At any given time, law in a society is the result of a process of stratification of different legal systems over various periods. In general, the new layer does not completely cover and cancel the previous ones, but interacts with them and/or leaves them operating in certain areas. The result of the process of stratification is thus a situation of legal pluralism, where different legal systems coexist and interact with one another. The process of stratification is obviously a dynamic one, with both sudden and continuous changes. Such changes are seldom the result of new laws locally produced. More often they are the outcome of spontaneous or forced borrowing from foreign models. The French Civil Code is a good example: created by Napoleon's legal experts after the Revolution it was thereafter imposed or received in a great number of civil law countries inside and outside Europe.

While in the past legal borrowing was fairly predictable along political lines (such as colonial or socialist links), it has become more eclectic in recent times. Many reforming states feel free (or even eager) to adopt solutions from a wide-ranging variety of sources, disregarding any 'family' membership. Thus Eritrea, one of the newest independent states (1991), is looking at both American and the Southeast Asian models for reforming the partly socialist and partly civil law legal system inherited from Italian and Ethiopian domination. In the past, the resulting combination of different foreign models and local solutions would have been negatively termed a 'hybrid' legal system, while now it can be seen as a fertile and dynamic situation of legal pluralism.

A new classification of the world legal systems can be built on such plural and dynamic foundations. If each national legal system is seen as a changing combination of various legal systems, the world legal panorama is no longer a static and hierarchical picture. It is, rather, an open field where each country can (and actually does) move freely according to its changing legal choices, with its position at any time being given by its proximity to or distance from any other world legal system.

Moving from the general world perspective to the specific, a plural approach to the scientific analysis of any particular legal system allows us to discover how its basic element, the legal rule, is not simple, as it usually appears, but rather a combination of different elements. The plural approach suggests that what is usually regarded as a single legal system is actually made up of a variety of separated but interacting bodies of rules, such as statutory legislation, judicial decisions, legal textbooks, legal practice, etc. Some of these bodies, labelled as 'sources of law', have an official lawmaking character. Others are not officially supposed to produce law, but rather to implement or explain it. However, the actual legal rule provided by the whole system to any given case is often not the one stated by the official sources of law, but is rather the combination of the various solutions provided for that case by the different bodies of rules.

Let us take an example from a country where legal rules are officially supposed to be set forth by statutes only, while judicial decisions are simply expected to apply them and textbooks to provide their scholarly explanations. In such a country the basic statutory rule of ancient origin provides that: '*Damages, whether from intentional or negligent wrongdoing, shall be compensated.*' While expounding to law students the general principles of the local legal system, classic university textbooks write that: '*As far as compensation of damages is concerned, intentional and negligent wrongdoing are in principle equally treated.*' However, a careful examination of modern judicial decisions shows that in practice on most occasions judges are allowed, by special legal provisions or by contractual arrangements, to award greater compensation for damages arising from intentional wrongdoing. Therefore, if we reframe the statutory rule and its judicial application in the wording of a general principle we should rather say that: '*Normally damages from intentional or negligent wrongdoing are differently compensated.*' Hence, a plural approach to a legal system of this type shows that the actual rule on the issue has become just the opposite of what may appear by simply reading the official legal source of that system, where the basic statutory rule mentioned above is actually no longer a principle of general application, but has become a provision of residuary and limited relevance.

MARCO GUADAGNI

See also ANTHROPOLOGICAL LAW-AND-ECONOMICS; CHOICE OF LAW; CONFLICT OF LAWS; CUSTOMARY LAW; LAW MERCHANT; LEGAL FORMANTS; RULE OF LAW; WESTERN LEGAL TRADITION.

Subject classification: 1c; 4b(iv); 5a(v).

BIBLIOGRAPHY

Abel, R. (ed.) 1982. *The Politics of Informal Justice*. New York: Academic Press.

Allott, A.N. 1980. *The Limits of Law*. London: Butterworth.

Burman, S. and Harrell-Bond, B. 1979. *The Imposition of Law*. New York: Academic Press

Chiba, M. 1989. *Legal Pluralism*. Tokyo: Tokyo University Press.

Falk Moore, S. 1978. *Law as Process*. London and Boston: Routledge and Kegan Paul.

Gilissen, J. (ed.) 1972. *Le pluralisme juridique*. Bruxelles: Éditions de l'Université Libre de Bruxelles.

Grande, E. (ed.) 1995. *Transplants, Innovation and Legal Tradition in the Horn of Africa*. Turin: L'Harmattan.

Griffiths, J. 1986. What is legal pluralism? *Journal of Legal Pluralism and Unofficial Law* 24: 1–55.

Hooker, M.B. 1975. *Legal Pluralism: an Introduction to Colonial and Neo-colonial Laws*. Oxford: Clarendon Press.

Llewellyn, K.N. and Hoebel, E.A. 1941. *The Cheyenne Way*. Norman: University of Oklahoma Press.

Mattei, U. 1997. Three patterns of law. Taxonomy and change in legal systems. *American Journal of Comparative Law* 48: 5–44.

Nader, L. 1997 (1969). *Law in Culture and Society*. Berkeley: University of California Press.

Pospisil, L.J. 1971. *Anthropology of Law: a Comparative Theory*. New York: Harper & Row.

Reyntjens, F. 1991. Note sur l'utilité d'introduire un système juridique 'pluraliste' dans la macro-comparaison des droiys. *Revue de Droit International et de Droit Comparé* 75: 41–50.

Rouland, N. 1991. *Aux confins du droit*. Paris: O. Jacob.

Sacco, R. 1991. Legal formants: a dynamic approach to comparative law. *American Journal of Comparative Law* 39: 1–34 and 343–400.

Tamanaha, B.Z. 1993. The folly of the 'social scientific' concept of legal pluralism. *Journal of Law and Society* 20: 192–217.

Woodman, G.R. 1996. Legal pluralism and the search for justice. *Journal of African Law* 40: 153–67.

legal positivism. 'Legal positivism', in English-speaking countries, refers to that style of jurisprudence initiated in the late eighteenth and early nineteenth centuries by Jeremy Bentham and John Austin. It purports to make a conceptual claim about the nature of law. Those who defend it, and especially those who condemn it, do so, however, by reference to a variety of political–philosophical arguments having to do with the proper role of legislators, judges and other lawyers. In that way debates which take the form of conceptual controversies highlight important issues of legal philosophy which are not, at bottom, conceptual at all.

Bentham and Austin asserted two propositions. (1) All municipal law is 'posited', that is, deliberately created by human beings; we may call this 'the deliberate creation thesis'. (2) What the law is as to any matter can be discovered by empirical investigation and does not require satisfaction of any substantive moral test so that, contingently, what the law is may always diverge from what the law ought to be; this is the 'separation thesis'. Many legal positivists qualify one or both of these theses. Anti-positivists mount a root-and-branch attack on either or both of them. There are as well self-proclaimed critics of legal positivism who maintain that, even if both theses are correct, it still is the case that legal systems necessarily promote moral values. The latter position is not one legal positivists need deny.

The 'positivism' in legal positivism is not to be confused with a battery of other theoretical claims styled 'positivist'. Legal positivism has no necessary connection with 'positivism' in the social sciences – aspirations to provide value-free descriptions of the evolution of human societies, first inspired by Auguste Comte; nor with 'value positivism' – the view popularized by Max Weber that all values are the result of human choices; nor with 'logical positivism' – the style of cognitive dogmatics of the 1920s and 1930s (associated especially with A.J. Ayer) which denied sense to all propositions other than the tautological and the empirically verifiable. In the early 1970s F.A. Hayek was advertised to be giving a lecture at the London School of Economics on 'The Destruction of Liberalism by Logical Positivism'. Philosophers turned up in droves, intrigued by a suggested connection between such disparate systems of thought, only to be told:

> There has been an error in the notice. Professor Hayek's lecture is entitled: 'The Destruction of Liberalism by Legal Positivism'.

Bentham, the reformer, advocated codification of the law based, 'scientifically', on the principle of utility. He was appalled by those parts of Blackstone's *Commentaries* in which the ramshackle common law of his day received the accolade of 'reason'. The cause of this mischief was, as he saw it, the tradition of natural-law thinking. In theory, it placed reason at the centre of our apprehension of law. In practice, it conceded 'legal' (and therefore 'moral') status to every accrued complex of doctrine. He was equally unimpressed by novel doctrines, such as those contained in the American Declaration of Independence, which invoked 'natural rights' as a revolutionary banner. Clear-eyed criticism and reform of our institutions must begin by recognizing the conceptual truths that the only law is positive law and the only rights those which positive law creates. The conceptual under-brush once cleared away, bad law could be exposed and replaced by codified good law. We may call this the 'critique and reform' argument for legal positivism.

Hayek's condemnation of legal positivism is directed exclusively against the deliberate creation thesis. He accuses legal positivists of confusing two kinds of orders of rules: 'grown' and 'made' orders. Law had evolved as a set of negative rules of just conduct, protecting the domain of each person's free control over his or her body and resources. Technical elaboration of these rules, in the hands of common law judges, was guided, not by some spurious master plan, but by consistency in maintaining a system of expectations. Along came the legal positivists. They hijacked the word 'law' for the inner order of deliberately constructed associations and applied this mistaken concept to the 'law' of the state. As a result, legislatures in advanced economies were endowed with a new role. Instead of acting as occasional helpmeets to the judges by ironing out inconsistencies or expunging anomalies within the rules of just conduct, they began the deliberate manufacture of whole swathes of 'law': to direct and control industry; to institute bureaucratic agencies of all kinds; and to re-allocate wealth in the name of welfare. Thus the morality of the market upon which the 'great society' of the enlightenment world depended was subverted and 'liberalism' – by which Hayek means libertarian individualism – was destroyed. We may call this the 'legislature, hands off!' argument against legal positivism.

If the only indictment against legal positivism were that it has focused attention on a conception of law which enables legislation to be used as a deliberate engine of reform, let it be acquitted. Few of us would wish to slough off all the planned legislative programmes of the last two centuries. Even those who favour reining in the interventionist state apparently see no mileage in attaching their aspirations to a conceptual claim about 'true law'. For example, the Chicago School dedicated to the economic analysis of law, championed by Richard Posner, proclaims the 'efficiency' of common law adjudication and decries 'inefficient' legislative initiatives in the work-place, the sale of consumables and the environment.

But they have not felt the need to hitch their critique to a denial of the deliberate creation thesis. Indeed, the Chicago School is Bentham's heir, but with a methodological agenda for measuring beneficient outcomes which his felicific calculus clearly lacked. There are free marketeers and anti-egalitarian libertarians a-plenty; but as to the idea that a refutation of the conceptual claims of legal positivism is a necessary step towards forwarding their aims, Hayek is a voice crying in the wilderness.

Modern legal positivists maintain variants of the critique and reform argument, and have added others. Most of them, however, would modify the classical version of the deliberate creation thesis.

Bentham and Austin took over the concept of political sovereignty they found in writers such as Bodin and Hobbes and devised from it a highly implausible elucidation of the empirical test for law. They claimed that all laws in a modern state were the commands of a sovereign individual or body, or of one of his (or their) subordinates; and that the sovereign could be readily identified by the factual test of habitual obedience. Taken literally, this would mean that, if you want to discover the law of a country, you only have to find out who is habitually obeyed there and then collate his commands. The late Herbert Hart attacked many features of this picture. A state's laws might include customs which had been deliberately made by no one. Much more importantly, the very rules by which we identify the sovereign legislature might not result from deliberate creation; and all the rules of a legal system rested, ultimately, on a master 'practice' rule, which Hart called 'the rule of recognition'.

Nevertheless, Hart insisted on the separation thesis, for Benthamite critique-and-reform reasons, and for two other reasons as well. The vital question of determining whether we are morally bound to obey the law is subverted if we build morality into the definition of law – the 'obedience' argument for legal positivism. Secondly, the social phenomenon which law represents must be empirically defined if explanatory theorizing is to have a clear focus – the 'social theory' argument for legal positivism. The rule of recognition, he said, is constituted by a complex practice of judges and other officials wherein they accord 'validity' to particular rules of the legal system. Its existence is an empirical question of social fact. Validity did not depend on a substantive moral test.

The major onslaught of our day on the separation thesis has come from those who shift the focus of inquiry from the legislature to the judge. Everyone agrees that judges 'develop' the law. They do not merely apply rules contained in legislative enactments or in the *rationes decidendi* of earlier cases. In developing the law, they invoke, among other things, considerations of moral responsibility, fairness and justice. On the face of it, they take the law to be that which, morally speaking, it ought to be. That facet of the judicial role cannot (it is said) be squared with the separation thesis – the 'judicial declaratory' argument against legal positivism.

Ronald Dworkin is a leading exponent of this argument. It is the business of the judge, he says, to declare as 'law' the best politics which will fit the extant legal materials. In doing that, he must conscientiously answer questions of moral truth about justice, fairness and procedural due process. He must do this, not just in special 'hard' cases, but every time – although many cases will be 'easy' precisely because the requirement of 'fit' with legal materials will rule out many moral options.

How did Hart deal with this feature of adjudication? He suggested that there were many instances in which judges were vested with a (often highly circumscribed) discretion to declare what the law ought to be. True, they usually would not announce that they were engaged in law-creation; but the observer was entitled to describe what they did as 'interstitial legislation'. Before the court ruled, a lawyer might report that valid law, as tested by the rule of recognition, gave no determinate solution to the point in issue, but that there were many considerations, including moral ones, which a judge might (and perhaps should) take into account in developing the law.

Yet how could the separation thesis be maintained in the face of specific provisions of positive law which, in terms, made some moral concept dispositive of a legal question? This is the 'overt moralizing' argument against legal positivism. Of course, if such a prescription were understood as pointing to the community's conventional morality, it would not threaten the separation thesis. Moral conventions, like conventions about interpreting statutes or reading precedents, are, in principle, discoverable empirically. But it might be understood as a direction to apply the critically correct moral answer, all things considered. In the view of some commentators on American constitutional law, provisions in the Bill of Rights, which import concepts such as 'cruel and unusual punishment', 'equal protection of the laws' or 'due process', have just this effect.

In the posthumously published postcript to *The Concept of Law*, Hart made the following concession. He announced that he now espoused 'soft positivism'. Laws might, contingently, make answers to legal questions turn on substantive issues of morality. Joseph Raz, in contrast, continues to affirm 'hard' or 'strict' positivism. According to Raz, not merely the existence, but also the content, of every law is discoverable empirically and without answering moral questions. Provisions of the sort just discussed should be understood as authorizations to courts to fill gaps in the law. Raz supports this position by the following conceptual reasoning. 'Law' is not just a set of power relations. It is a social institution which asserts 'authority'. That is, it claims to be the ultimate arbiter over all reasons for action. It could not fulfil this definitional function if it delegated right answers to morality; although it can, and frequently does, delegate to judges the power to add new law based on their own views of morality. This is the 'authority' argument for legal positivism.

Why should we relate different perceptions of the judicial role to the conceptual debate about the nature of law represented by affirmations or denials of the separation thesis? Dworkin claims that legal positivists must be committed to a particular justificatory theory which he calls 'conventionalism': state force is justified when applied in accordance with pre-announced conventions, but when conventions run out judges must choose what they think to be the best solution. The right justificatory theory is, however, 'law as integrity': the judge is to administer state force in such a way as to show that the community seeks to treat its citizens with equal concern and respect. Hart and Raz deny that positivism, as such, is committed to any particular justificatory theory. They claim, indeed, that

Dworkin's own prescriptions for judges in hard cases would be compatible with the separation thesis.

The disagreement then ascends to meta-theoretical controversy about the point of theory itself. Dworkin denounces 'semantic sting' theorizing, that is, claims about the nature of law based on how the word 'law' is used in ordinary language. (This is a straw-man critique since no positivist has ever founded his position solely on a supposed univocal usage of the word 'law'.) Semantics set aside, argues Dworkin, a theory of law must necessarily be politically committed. It must interpret the practices generally understood to be involved in law in their best light – the 'committed theory' argument against legal positivism. To the contrary, argues Hart, theory has a legitimate explanatory role in setting out the salient characteristics of legal institutions. Since the history of the world is rife with bad laws as well as good, theory achieves its explanatory objectives best if it starts with the separation thesis.

Anglo-American jurisprudential theory of our day tends to be court-centred. To a continental writer it may seem parochial to suggest that the truth or falsity of the separation thesis should turn on how we read the language of common law judges in troublesome cases. The most famous advocate of legal positivism in the twentieth century was Hans Kelsen. For him, the point of departure were the thousands of occasions in daily life in which people give information about the law. Such *rechtsetze* assert the existence (validity) of norms. They are verifiably true or false because they refer to norms within a positive legal order which is by and large effective. They constitute 'juristic science'. Kelsen (in his later writings) accepted the deliberate creation thesis without qualification: all norms of a positive legal order are created by acts of will. From first to last he accepted the separation thesis: the validity of a legal norm could never be challenged for failure to meet a moral test.

Kelsen embraced the social theory argument for legal positivism, and added to it his own 'purity' argument. We must separate genuine *rechtsetze* from the many instances, to be found in traditional juristic science, where an author smuggles his subjective moral or political opinions into purported descriptions of the law. Pure legal-information-giving must be isolated. To do that it was necessary to provide an amoral basis for the use made within *rechtsetze* of vocabulary also employed both when people convey information about positive morality and also when they voice opinions about supposed objective values. Thus Kelsen tackled, from a positivist perspective, a problem which Bentham and Austin had ignored – the inherent 'oughtness' of law, law's normativity.

The normativity of legal discourse is seen by some as a basis for undermining the separation thesis. M.J. Detmold contends that, if we acknowledge that the law prescribes what we ought to do, then it must be unified with all other features of practical discourse. We cannot say that morally speaking we ought to do X, whilst legally we ought to do the opposite of X, because the logic of 'ought' allows for no such contradiction. Hence law and morality cannot be separated. It follows, he says, that a Roman Catholic judge who issues a decree of divorce misunderstands his role as a judge; and a judge who believes capital punishment to be morally wrong cannot, as a judge, pass sentence of death, whatever the statute may say. (Presumably, by the same logic, a judge who thinks that, morally, a murderer ought to die must order him to be hanged even if the legislature has purported to abolish capital punishment.) This is the 'ought logic' argument against legal positivism.

Raz avoids these bizarre implications of law's supposed normativity in the following way. An expositor of the law employs fully moralized terminology by making 'detached statements' from the stance of a hypothetical 'legal man' (one who supposes that moral duties coincide with the prescriptions of positive law). Such detached statements are fully compatible with any private beliefs the expositor may have about the moral soundness of the law. Raz draws an analogy with a non-vegetarian telling a vegetarian friend whether he ought to eat some item of food; and with a well-informed non-believer giving advice to a subscriber to a particular religious faith about what the latter's religious duties are. Kelsen's solution is different. Law's normativity is comprised of evaluations which are relative only to the wills of those who laid down that particular constitution from which all the laws of a system derive their validity.

Kelsen saw legal phenomena as follows. Whenever a community has a legal system, we find that there are one set of people (legislators) issuing conditional directives to another set of people (officials) about the circumstances in which coercion should be applied to citizens. By and large, when citizens fulfil the conditions stipulated in these directives, officials apply the prescribed coercive measures to them. All of that could be interpreted sociologically, in terms of cause and effect. But that would leave out of account a third set, those who clothe the directives with 'oughts' and measure conduct by them. They are engaged in juristic science. Their statements employ the terminology of rights, duties, delicts and so forth; but they must be understood in an amoral sense since they might refer to valid norms which neither the speaker nor anyone else approves on moral grounds. The normativity so deployed is no more than what I have called 'Kelsen's pallid normativity'. Juristic statements are issued 'as if' those who promulgated a written constitution, or those whose behaviour created a customary constitution, had been vested with authority to lay down the fundamental terms for all legitimate coercion. The law's normativity is rooted in history, not in justice. To make the point more dramatically, Kelsen says that all legal-information-giving presupposes a fictive 'basic norm' authorizing the creation of the 'historically first constitution' in the case of any by and large effective system of positive law.

As support for his analysis, Kelsen points to changes in juristic presuppositions which follow a successful revolution. Legal information is conveyed in normative terms as if the revolutionaries were empowered to promulgate their constitution. That assessment of revolutions has opened Kelsen to the charge that his theory endorses might as right. That is a misreading since his theory 'endorses' nothing. It makes a historical claim about the practice of juristic science. Lawyers characteristically top-dress the coercion-relevant prescriptions effective within a territory with a normativity which does no more than presuppose that the constitution was authorized and hence ought to be obeyed. The pallid nature of law's normativity ensures that there is no question of 'right' in any substantive moral sense.

Bentham and Kelsen opposed their conceptions of positive law to theories of natural law. Opponents of legal positivism need not, however, be natural lawyers as our discussion of Hayek, Dworkin and Detmold demonstrates. In what sense is natural law theory itself inherently anti-positivist?

Two theses sometimes associated with natural law would directly confront, respectively, the deliberate creation and separation theses of legal positivism. The first claims that moral prescriptions become 'law' without the need for enactment by legislators or articulation by courts or juristic opinion. The second suggests that a blue pencil test may be applied to enacted law, crossing out those provisions which flout natural law. Some writers, like Deryck Beyleveld and Roger Brownsword, are prepared to give a central role to these claims. For the main tradition which derives from the medieval summation of natural law theory made by St Thomas Aquinas, however, they are side shows. The central concern of the tradition is the global relationship between those aspects of morality which are discoverable by reason and systems of positive law. That which is self-evidently obligatory on X, or self-evidently due to Y, ought to be enacted into positive law and, if it is, positive law binds in conscience. Positive law continues to be morally binding so long as it aims at what Aquinas called 'determinationes' of more abstract requirements; but if it flatly contradicts some fundamental moral prescription, it becomes a corruption of law. From this perspective the objection to legal positivism, if there is one, is not its espousal of either the deliberate creation or the separation theses, but rather its failure to identify the intrinsic moral worth of positive law.

One of the inherent goods claimed for law arises from rule-of-law values. Starting from that, Lon Fuller advanced his theory of the 'inner morality of law' or 'procedural natural law'. Law, he said, is the 'enterprise of subjecting human conduct to the governance of rules'. Legal positivism misunderstood this enterprise by characterizing law in the same terms as managerial direction, as a set of prescriptions issued from above. The enterprise should be seen as a cooperative endeavour, as is shown by the requirements of the rule of law that prescriptions must observe the constraints of universalizability and congruence between official behaviour and declared rule. Some have questioned whether these and other rule-of-law requirements necessarily confer moral value on a system of rules. Whether they do or not, it is difficult to see why a 'positivist' should disavow them.

The most influential modern exposition of natural law theory is that of John Finnis. He plays down the two strictly anti-positivistic theses. Seldom does practical reason yield concrete specifications of what ought not to be done, or of what ought to be rendered to others; and, even when it does, enactment is required before they become 'law' in an institutional sense. *'Lex injusta non est lex'* is not to be understood in a blue pencil sense. The main quarrel with legal positivists, as Finnis sees it, is their failure to articulate the 'focal meaning' of law. That relates to law's morally valuable function as coordinator of the common good. There are certainly legal systems which are administered for the selfish ends of ruling elites, or which derogate from other features of just human association; but then they deviate from the focal sense of 'law' in which positive law is the worthy promoter of those conditions under which all may participate, so far as possible, in the self-evidently valuable facets of human flourishing.

Finnis's categories of self-evidence are open to challenge and it may well be that most writers who have proclaimed themselves 'legal positivists', as well as many who have not, would reject them. Even if one accepts everything he advances under this head, however, it is clear that one could still affirm both the deliberate creation and the separation theses. Thus one could be both a legal positivist and a believer in natural law.

I suggest that many of the anti-positivist positions discussed here have 'positivism' in their sights because, for one reason or another (and the reasons diverge wildly), a writer conceives the very word 'positivist' as carrying undesirable connotations for legal roles. What is to be contested is, for Hayek, untrammelled legislative initiatives; for Dworkin, judges or theorists who will not acknowledge the essentially politicized nature of what they do; and for Finnis, any lawyer who denies a role-commitment to view law constantly in the light of the good purposes which good law should serve. It seems to me to be fruitless to package all the issues of legal philosophy which this heterogeneous collection of debates has cast up in terms of a single conceptual designation – legal positivism versus anti-positivism.

J.W. HARRIS

See also AUSTIN, JOHN; BENTHAM, JEREMY; BLACKSTONE, WILLIAM; CHICAGO SCHOOL OF LAW AND ECONOMICS; CONVENTIONS AT THE FOUNDATION OF LAW; EMERGENCE OF LEGAL RULES; FULLER, LON L.; HART, H.L.A.; HAYEK, FRIEDRICH VON; KELSEN, HANS; RULE OF RECOGNITION.

Subject classification: 4a(i).

BIBLIOGRAPHY

Aquinas, St Thomas. [n.d.]. *Selected Political Writings*. Ed. A.P. d'Entreves, Oxford: Basil Blackwell, 1959.

Austin, J. 1832. *The Province of Jurisprudence Determined and the Uses of the Study of Jurisprudence*. Ed. H.L.A. Hart, London: Weidenfeld and Nicolson, 1954.

Bentham, J. 1776, 1789. *A Fragment on Government and An Introduction to the Principles of Morals and Legislation*. Ed. W. Harrison, Oxford: Basil Blackwell, 1960.

Bentham, J. 1970. *Of Laws in General*. Ed. H.L.A. Hart, London: Athlone Press.

Beyleveld, D. and Brownsword, R. 1994. *Law as a Moral Judgment*. 2nd edn, Sheffield: Sheffield Academic Press.

Detmold, M.J. 1984. *The Unity of Law and Morality: a Refutation of Legal Positivism*. London: Routledge & Kegan Paul.

Dworkin, R. 1986. *Law's Empire*. London: Fontana.

Finnis, J. 1980. *Natural Law and Natural Rights*. Oxford: Clarendon Press.

Fuller, L.L. 1969. *The Morality of Law*. 2nd edn, New Haven and London: Yale University Press.

George, R.P. (ed.). 1996. *The Autonomy of Law: Essays on Legal Positivism*. Oxford: Clarendon Press.
Harris, J.W. 1979. *Law and Legal Science*. Oxford: Clarendon Press.
Harris, J.W. 1997. *Legal Philosophies*. 2nd edn, London: Butterworths.
Hart, H.L.A. 1982. *Essays on Bentham: Studies in Jurisprudence and Political Theory*. Oxford: Clarendon Press.
Hart, H.L.A. 1983. *Essays in Jurisprudence and Philosophy*. Oxford: Clarendon Press.
Hart, H.L.A. 1994. *The Concept of Law*. 2nd edn, Oxford: Clarendon Press.
Hayek, F.A. 1973. *Law, Legislation and Liberty*, Vol 1: *Rules and Order*. London: Routledge & Kegan Paul.
Kelsen, H. 1960. *The Pure Theory of Law*. Trans. M. Knight, Berkeley: University of California Press, 1967.
Kelsen, H. 1979. *General Theory of Norms*. Trans. M. Hartney, Oxford: Oxford University Press, 1991.
Posner, R.A. 1973. *Economic Analysis of Law*. 4th edn, Boston and Toronto: Little, Brown & Co., 1992.
Raz, J. 1979. *The Authority of Law*. Oxford: Clarendon Press.
Raz, J. 1990. *Practical Reason and Norms*. 2nd edn, Princeton: Princeton University Press.
Raz, J. 1994. *Ethics in the Public Domain*. Oxford: Clarendon Press.
Waluchow, W.J. 1994. *Inclusive Legal Positivism*. Oxford: Clarendon Press.

legal reform in Eastern Europe. While there has been substantial research on the legal transition in Eastern Europe, most of it has been by scholars in comparative systems, not law and economics. As a result, law and economics scholars are missing an important opportunity for interesting research. There are several reasons why they should find the transition worth studying. First, many economists (including the author) believed that merely removing government impediments to markets would lead to rapid economic growth in the former Communist economies. In fact, it has turned out that a legal infrastructure is a necessary component of a successful market economy. Since those of us specializing in law and economics study this infrastructure, the transition has provided evidence of the value of our work. Second, legal institutions in advanced economies have evolved over hundreds of years. We see them in an advanced state, and the study of their evolution is difficult because it occurred slowly and in small steps. In the transition economies, however, we can observe the beginning and rapid evolution of the fundamental legal institutions of a market economy. Third, the transition can provide useful examples in our teaching. Just as the effects of controlled prices can illustrate the power of demand and supply in markets, so the effects of the absence of property rights and contracts can illustrate the power of legal institutions in developed economies. Finally, agents in transition economies are currently attempting to design efficient institutions. Those of us schooled in law and economics may be in a position to assist in this design, and thus create real wealth in the world.

There are 27 countries in the former Soviet bloc in Eastern Europe (including Mongolia). It will be impossible to discuss all of these countries. This essay will concentrate on Poland, Hungary, the Czech Republic, and most specifically on Russia. There are several reasons for this emphasis on Russia. First, it is the largest and potentially richest of the relevant countries, so that any useful suggestions for reform would be more valuable than elsewhere. Second, because it is the largest, there is more information available. Third, while each legal system is unique, there are nonetheless useful parallels between the Russian system and others. Finally, because the legal system in Russia is in more disarray than many others, it is the most interesting to study.

To see the relevance of the Russian system, consider Table 1 (de Melo et al. 1996). It represents an estimate of the degree of 'liberalization' of the 27 countries undergoing the transition. While this is not a direct measure of legal reform, it is closely related and the values in Table 1 are closely related to perceptions of legal development. Moreover, de Melo et al. (1996: 8) indicate that 'there is a high degree of complementarity in designing and implementing different types of reform', so that once again we would expect the legal system to also be correlated with this index. Note that Russia is in about the middle of the table, so that its experience is relevant for understanding at least some additional countries. Fischer et al. (1996) show that this index is significantly and positively related to economic growth.

Table 1
Indices of Liberalization

Advanced Reformers	Slovenia; Poland; Hungary; Czech Republic; Slovakia
High Intermediate Reformers	Estonia; Bulgaria; Lithuania; Latvia; Albania; Romania; Mongolia
Low Intermediate Reformers	Russia; Kyrgyzstan; Moldova; Kazakhstan
Slow Reformers	Uzbekistan; Belarus; Ukraine; Turkmenistan
'War'	Croatia; Macedonia; Armenia; Georgia; Azerbaijan; Tajikistan

Source: de Melo et al., 1996: 7, 38–42.

Rankings are included for Vietnam ('Advanced') and China ('High Intermediate'). 'Liberalization' is based on liberalization of domestic prices, liberalization of the foreign trade regime, and privatization and banking reform, for the period 1989–1994.

This essay will concentrate on the governance of voluntary agreements. This includes contract law, although, as shown below, many agreements that one might expect to be governed by contract in a more developed economy will have other governance terms in Russia. It will also include a brief discussion of corporate governance issues. I do not discuss privatization. There are many excellent summary sources available on this topic (see Brada 1996; Rapaczynski 1996; and, for a book-length study, Blasi et al. 1997). Additionally, Rapaczynski makes the point that most 'property' in modern economies is actually in the form of a claim on certain streams of payments, so that contractual enforcement is an important part of privatization.

In Western countries, business and law developed simultaneously. As new business institutions were developed, the law facilitating the functioning of these institutions developed and evolved. In the former Communist countries, this was not so. Large amounts of investment in physical capital occurred under the previous regime, and laws were not developed to govern this capital. Thus, there are large industrial sectors but no legal governing framework. There are two major implications of this difference.

First, there are disputes involving substantial amounts, but insufficient trained judges to hear such disputes. The judicial system has been thrown into a market economy which generates disputes with large amounts at stake, because there are substantial capital investments at issue, but judges lack training or experience in operating in a market economy. As a result, all countries seem to suffer from inefficient judicial systems. However, one might expect that in time this problem will be resolved.

A second problem is more serious. Rent seeking takes a different form than that seen in western economies. It is generally argued that in the west, most common law rules are relatively free of rent seeking (with the possible exception of American tort law: see Rubin and Bailey 1994). In the east, however, property and contract law are subject to substantial rent seeking by those in control of the established enterprises. This rent seeking plays an important part in the analysis.

The point is this: in the west, an entrepreneur desiring finance for an enterprise would be forced to provide guarantees to lenders in order to induce them to invest in the firm ((Jensen and Meckling 1976). While such contracts are subject to some opportunistic post-contractual manipulation, the basic terms provide some limits to wealth appropriation. In the east, however, managers have acquired control of enterprises with no need for concessions to lenders. As a result, the developing laws of corporate governance and of enterprise bankruptcy have been heavily influenced by the interests of these entrenched managers. It may be more difficult to restructure law to eliminate such rent seeking because those in power may effectively resist any attempts to do so. Thus, it is not certain that the law will develop efficiently, and it is possible that different countries will reach different equilibria.

Law in eastern Europe is in a substantial disequilibrium, and so is changing rapidly. At any point in time, all that one can do is provide a snapshot of the situation at that time. Moreover, there is really no theory to predict where the final equilibrium will be. Thus, this essay will be relatively more fact intensive and more ephemeral than most. I see no way around this problem.

SOURCES OF LAW. There are equivalents in contract law to the 'big bang' proposals for rapid privatization of property. One is the suggestion made by several authorities (e.g. Leijonhufvud 1993) that the post-Communist economies adopt entirely the civil code of some capitalist economy such as Finland or the Netherlands. Such a code would be difficult to interpret for an economy with no tradition of markets. Indeed, even translating the terms from Finnish or Dutch into Russian or Polish would be difficult. The terms are defined only by their use in a market economy and in actual existing transactions and decisions. Leoni (1961) discusses the difficulty of translating legal terms from one language to another because words are rooted in institutions that may be lacking in the second culture. Leoni's discussion is in the context of translating between language used in relatively free economies; the problems would be exacerbated in trying to translate terms used in market economies to languages spoken in societies that have not had markets and the corresponding institutions for many years. Murrell (1992) makes a similar point by suggesting that a legal code has embedded in it large amounts of practical knowledge, so that a transfer would not be feasible.

Similarly, it would not be feasible for authorities to generate an entire body of contract law *de novo*. Difficulties are not a result of incorrect drafting by the legislature, and could not be corrected by better craftsmanship. A body of law such as contract law is in some sense organically grown over a long period of time. It has numerous components that must interact with each other and with other large complex bodies of law (securities law, corporate law, labour law, to name only a few). As Hayek says (1973: 65),

> The parts of a legal system are not so much adjusted to each other according to a comprehensive overall view, as gradually adapted to each other by the successive application of general principles to particular problems. . . .

Laws must also be adapted to existing institutions in an economy. For anyone or any group to be able to craft such a body of law is as unlikely as for a single decision-maker to be able to design a complex economy *de novo*. It was of course the impossibility of this latter task (the socialist calculation problem) that caused the current situation in the former Soviet empire.

All the countries here under consideration have some sort of pre-existing contract law. Therefore, the choice is not between starting *de novo* or adopting a body of law. Rather, the choice is between modifying an existing body of law or adopting some other body of law. However, even if some other country's law were to be adopted, it would require modification to tailor the law to local conditions, where these conditions include the long time absence of market institutions. Thus, in either case, the issue is the most efficient method of modifying some currently maladapted law. In fact, countries have not chosen to adopt outside law, although they have used some parts of such laws in drafting local laws (e.g. Blumenfeld 1996). Nonetheless, most legal codes in Eastern Europe have been relatively home grown.

Many have argued that it is desirable for private parties to develop rules for governing relationships that may later be adapted into a formal legal system (Rubin 1994; Cooter 1996; Hay et al. 1996). This was at least in part the basis for the development of the common law, and it is likely to be efficient in developing countries as well. Rubin argued that this process would be facilitated if courts committed themselves to enforce private arbitration agreements.

THE CZECH REPUBLIC, HUNGARY, POLAND. As indicated in Table 1, the Czech Republic, Hungary and Poland are much more similar to each other than any is to Russia, and are among the most advanced countries. It is interesting that these countries were apparently the most dissatisfied with Communism, as indicated by the various attempted revolutions each staged during the Communist era. The civil codes of the countries in the former Soviet Union are based on pre-Soviet European Civil Codes and 'many of the principles are not inconsistent with a market economy' (IMF 1991: 247). In many cases, these have been adopted from pre-Communist codes. This is also true of the Czech Republic, Poland and Hungary. At the beginning of the transition, these three countries had in place a set of basic contract laws.

Gray (1993: 16) provides a summary of the situation in the Central and Eastern European (CEE) countries (Bulgaria, the Czech Republic, Hungary, Poland, Romania, and Slovenia) soon after the transition:

> All the CEE countries are moving rapidly to create legal frameworks conducive to private sector development and the growth of a market economy. New or amended constitutions proclaim the new market orientation of these economies, provide a level playing field for all forms of property ownership, and establish a system of judicial oversight to limit government interference . . .
>
> Yet there are major challenges ahead to implement the new laws that are on the books. The interests of former owners of property are clashing with those of current tenants, leading to a surge in new disputes now entering the courts . . . The courts, suffering from understaffing as well as relatively low pay and prestige, are unlikely to be able to handle this surge . . . All in all, it is a time of great progress, great confusion, and great challenge.

The benefit of relatively efficient laws is continuing. Poland and the Czech Republic are greatly benefiting from the legal certainty, and Hungary is benefiting to a lesser extent (Hungary's main problem seems to be a reluctance to privatize, rather than direct contractual uncertainty). One piece of evidence is negative: the US business press, in writing about these countries, never mentions difficulties with the 'rule of law' or with the legal system. Even in describing cases where western investments have been unsuccessful in the Czech Republic, Hungary and Poland, the discussion is in terms of business reasons for the failures, rather than contractual or legal difficulties (see for example Branegan 1994). This is totally different from the case of Russia; there, virtually every article discusses legal uncertainty and difficulties with contract enforcement. Moreover, in comparing eastern Europe with Russia, the point is often made that legal systems are much more advanced in the former countries (e.g. Pennar, Galuszka and Miller 1994). Foreign companies are finding sufficient certainty in all three countries so that there are substantial business links between Eastern and Western Europe, in the form of acquisitions, partnerships and supplier networks.

Thus, the evidence from at least three of the former Communist countries indicates that if correct measures are taken, then it is possible to emerge successfully from the desolation created by Communism. One part of the required effort includes creation or recreation of a rule of law, and these three countries have undertaken the investments needed to do so. However, the starting point for these countries was perhaps more favourable to capitalism and development than in many other countries.

However, there are still weaknesses in law. Borish and Noel (1996) provide a summary of conditions in Poland, Hungary, the Czech Republic and Slovakia. (This is an excellent factual source for information regarding the state of these economies, including their legal systems, in 1996). They summarize the weaknesses in law in all the Visegrad countries:

> (i) restrictive Collateral Laws, inadequate property registries, and unclear title to property, which undermine the use of collateral for secured transactions; (ii) slow or cumbersome registration procedures, disincentives to companies to start-up and register with higher levels of founding capital, and problems associated with corporate governance; (iii) weak or unclear Commercial codes, insufficient judicial infrastructure, and underdeveloped market mechanisms for contract enforcement; and (iv) ineffective or limited use of bankruptcy and liquidation procedures to enhance market discipline and contract enforcement (Borish and Noel 1996: 3).

Thus, although these countries are farther down the road to a legal system and rule of law, there is still a distance to go. Many of these weaknesses are directly related to the ability of managers to protect their positions in newly privatized firms. To the extent that powerful interests benefit from these inefficiencies, it will be more difficult to correct them.

RUSSIA. Russia has a less well adapted body of law than the countries discussed so far. This may be because Russia was Communist for longer than the others, so that existing pre-Communist law is older than in the other countries and there are more generations of people who have had no actual exposure to markets. Moreover, at the time of the Revolution Russia was less economically advanced than were the other countries when they became Communist.

The formal legal system. The major legal weaknesses do not seem to be only in the area of contract law itself. There is a large body of Russian contract law that was used under the Soviet system to govern transactions between enterprises, which differs from contract law in market economies. However, it is not as different as we might expect. 'More surprising, perhaps, is the substantial convergence of contractual norms in Soviet and Anglo-American legal systems despite significant differences in the organization of capitalist and socialist economies' (Kroll 1987: 147). Attorneys and businessmen in Russia indicated in private conversations that difficulties in doing business are due more to uncertainty about government actions than contractual weaknesses.

One example of forces leading to legal uncertainty in Russia is what has been called the 'war of laws'. Various levels of government may pass conflicting laws, and there is no mechanism for resolving such conflicts. This makes business planning difficult. 'At the time of this writing, the problem of lack of clarity and uniformity exists at all levels of government and involves uncertainty concerning the location of authority to legislate and implement the laws, the nature and extent of the legislative and executive powers, and the appropriate means and methods for enforcement' (IMF 1991: 226). While the splitting of the Soviet Union into independent countries may have reduced these problems, it has not solved them all, and local laws are continually changing. There are inconsistencies in rules and interpretations by various ministries and departments of Russia. The multiplicity of fora for resolution of commercial disputes is more severe in economies that lack a well-developed body of commercial law because different courts may use different and inconsistent rules and laws.

There are over 800 ministries, and many of these can stop any given deal (Kvint 1993: 26). Obtaining approval from all relevant parties to undertake a deal in Russia has been called 'death by committee' (Poe 1993: 54). Building one property development in Moscow required permits from 130 different committees. This leads to possibilities of substantial corruption. Shleifer and Vishny (1993) indicate that the most dangerous form of corruption is that in which several authorities have the power to stop an activity, so that bribes must be paid to many potential enforcers and an actor cannot be certain that he has bribed all the relevant officials; they indicate that this is the case in Russia. Poe (1993) describes the same situation. Mauro (1995) provides evidence that societies with more corruption invest less and grow more slowly. Erlanger (1994) also indicates that official corruption is an ongoing problem in Russia, and may be more of a detriment to investment than organized crime. An important theme of Handelman (1995) is that there may be little difference between official corruption and organized crime, and that there are close links between criminals and government officials.

The law used in the formal legal system in Russia has been inadequate in many dimensions. The basic commercial law in use until recently was a 1964 law. This was modified by many subsequent decrees and laws, but was nonetheless seriously incomplete. Moreover, there are inconsistencies among the various laws passed or adopted since the fall of communism. Thus, the body of law governing commercial relationships is weak and difficult to use. For example, debt collection has been difficult. Banks have had difficulty in seizing certain collateral for loans in default. As a result, loans have tended to be for short time periods, such as 90 days. Banks have also made loans only to customers they know well (Blasi et al. 1997: 158). On the other hand, the 29 May 1992 Russian mortgage law does allow for the use of real property as collateral for bank loans. Moreover, this law is quite flexible in allowing parties to choose whatever terms are most congenial (Osakwe 1993: 354–5). However, although there are six private mortgage registers, as of 1995 there was no central register where a lender can establish the priority of his mortgage. More recently, it has been reported that banks' rights to foreclose are still not defined. As a result, mortgages tend to be for short terms (no more than ten years, and often six months to one year, with an option to renew). Down payments are high, typically 30–40%. As of September 1995, there had been only about 1000 mortgages reported.

An additional difficulty is that there are three separate court systems (Vlasihin 1993). There is a system of business courts, the Arbitration Courts (which is not an Arbitration Court in the Western sense), that hear disputes between businesses. However, if one party to a dispute is a private citizen, another court system is involved. There is yet another system, the Constitutional Court. It is not always clear which court will hear a particular dispute. Moreover, since there are three systems that might hear similar disputes, the rate of development of precedents and predictability of the law will be retarded. While there are potential benefits from competing court systems, this does not seem to be the case in Russia because the parties do not seem able to choose *ex ante* which system will govern their dispute.

Aslund (1995), although generally optimistic, also discusses difficulties in passing relevant laws. He suggests that the conflicts between the government and the Supreme Soviet, between the government and ministries remaining from the Communist era, and between the central government and regional governments created great difficulties. Moreover, even when laws are passed, problems remain. This is because of delays in passing relevant laws and inefficiencies that exist between the passage of laws. Even today, insufficient laws have been passed to enable the economy to function at a high level. This may be a pervasive feature of a legal system based on codes when legal change is difficult and there are lags. I will discuss three major laws.

The 1990 Law 'On Property in the RSFSR'. This law was seriously incomplete. The needed subordinate legislation was delayed because of political difficulties, and much is still lacking. Moreover, 'there was no clear distribution of state property between the Federation and its member republics, districts, and regions' (Topornin 1993: 17). These problems in allocation of property rights and conflict between governmental units still plague the country today; examples are provided below. It also appears that in Russia, more than in the other countries, there remain people in authority with some hostility towards the adoption of markets, and the number of such people may be increasing.

The 1992 Arbitration Procedural Code (APC) established a nationwide system of arbitration courts and provided rules for binding arbitration and enforcement. This law was a major improvement because it did provide more authority for arbitration. However, the APC was a procedural code, and it still depended on the existing body of substantive law. Some of the difficulties addressed by Greif and Kandel (1995) have been remedied by subsequent legislation (the 10% fee for arbitration has been reduced, and the legislature has recently passed a new substantive commercial law, as discussed below) but other problems, problems of competence of judges and lack of enforcement, remain. Moreover, the new Commercial Code does not mention arbitration at all.

The official arbitration courts suffer additional problems. For domestic disputes, the major court is the Supreme Arbitration Court. The Arbitration Court is the basic commercial court in Russia. The Chairman of the Supreme Arbitration Court, Veniamin Yakovlev, indicates that his court has difficulty in obtaining enforcement of its orders (Yakovlev 1994). He also indicates that the long delays in hearing disputes create severe problems. He blames the 'bloody squabbles' among entrepreneurs on the delays in using the court. Nineteen courts, including the Moscow Court, do not have independent physical facilities. The judges in this court are the same as in the Soviet era, and, because of low pay, many of the best have left (Black et al. 1996). Middle level judges earn only $160 per month and are largely dependent on the goodwill of others in the system for other benefits, such as housing (*Economist* 1995b, at 48).

Pistor (1995) indicates that court enforcement of private arbitration decrees is sometimes possible, particularly if assets are available in banks. However, there are risks, and she indicates that on occasion assets will be 'siphoned off by enforcers'. While the number of cases handled by the Arbitration Court has fallen by almost 30% from 1993 to 1994, the number of debt collection cases has fallen by only 8%, suggesting that users of courts are less unhappy with the courts as debt collectors than with other functions of the courts. She also indicates that the Arbitration Court has in general been willing to enforce awards from private arbitrators, and treats these orders as final and binding. Nonetheless, Pistor indicates that private arbitration courts are used very little. However, more optimistically, Langer and Buyevitch (1995) indicate that the number of cases heard by the International Arbitration Court of the Russian Federation Chamber of Commerce and Industry tripled from 1993 to 1994.

The Russian Arbitration Court attached to the Russian chamber of Commerce and Industry (discussed in Viechtbauer, 1993) handles international disputes. This court is descended from a Soviet court, the Foreign Trade Arbitration Court. However, there are numerous difficulties with this court as well. There are not enough qualified arbitrators. The Court will not allow the parties to specify the law to govern a dispute; only Court rules will be followed. Enforcement of awards is difficult and not automatic. As a result, relatively few disputes are brought to this court; western businesses are more likely to name third country (often Swedish) arbitrators. Nonetheless, this court has the most experience in Russia with capitalist economic dealings. It is also beginning to publish its most important decisions, so that disputants may be able to determine in advance the likely outcome of an arbitration. This may also be a step towards a more common law like process in Russia, as advocated above.

The 1995 Commercial Code. A newly adopted Commercial Code went into effect on 1 January 1995 (Russian Federation 1994; for a generally favourable view of this Code, see Blumenfeld 1996). This consolidated and updated many laws, so that the law actually in use will be greatly improved. The new code is a definite advance over previous law. One severe problem has been inflation. In the past, with very high inflation rates, the value of settlements decreased substantially as there were delays in collection. Parts of the new code may address this issue. Article 337 says that '. . . a pledge shall secure a demand in that amount which it has at the moment of satisfaction, in particular, interest, compensation of losses caused by delay of performance . . .', and this may be interpreted as allowing some inflation adjustment. Payments for 'Maintenance of Citizen' (apparently compensation for lost wages and earnings) will be indexed with the minimum wage ('amount of payment for labour established by law': Article 319). On the other hand, the section on Bankruptcy of an Entrepreneur (Article 25) makes no similar provisions. Since bankruptcy is often used as a method of debt collection, this lack may be costly.

Although a definite improvement, the new code is by no means a panacea. Many difficulties remain. First, the judges are the same and, as already noted, one serious problem with the legal system is the competence and ability of judges. Second, many problems stem from difficulties in enforcing decrees and rulings of the courts, and enforcement problems also remain. Third, while Article 11 indicates that there are three types of courts, it does nothing to clarify their relationship. Fourth, there is an insufficient number of lawyers in Russia. Most Soviet era lawyers were criminal lawyers, and there were relatively few of them. Now, there are too few lawyers for a large market economy and relatively few of these lawyers are skilled in commercial matters (Siltchenkov 1993). There are only 20,000 independent lawyers in Russia, and 28,000 public prosecutors. Although the US has too many lawyers, Russia has only one-eighth as many (*Economist* 1995b, at 43).

Finally, the entire code is only 127 pages long and deals with several areas of law, including all of contract law, property law, and the law of business associations. This means that there are of necessity large ambiguities in the law, and thus parties will remain uncertain about outcomes of litigation. It is planned that future parts of the Code will correct some of these ambiguities, but these parts have yet to be written or adopted. Unless Russian courts are willing to adopt some sort of common law type system to codify interpretations of the law, it will be difficult for litigants to predict the outcome of cases. To its credit, the law does indicate that in the event of interpretative uncertainty, the outcome of a dispute 'shall be determined by the customs of business turnover applicable to the relations of the parties' (Article 419).

There are some other likely difficulties with this law which are important. The law adopts many of the errors in contemporary American contract law. Article 333 limits contractual damages to an amount which is not 'clearly incommensurate to the consequences of the violation', equivalent to common law courts' (mistaken) unwillingness to enforce contractually specified damages viewed as 'punitive'. Article 426 allows dissolution of 'contracts of adhesion'. In addition, Article 10 states: 'The use by commercial organization of civil rights for the purpose of limiting competition, and also abuse by them of their dominant position in the market, shall not be permitted.' This is an extremely open-ended antitrust law, with great potential for abuse. Blumenfeld (1996), while generally favourable to the Code, nonetheless points out some additional weaknesses.

Thus, while the revision in the commercial code is useful and needed, nonetheless, even after this revision, difficulties will remain.

Opportunism. Both government units and private enterprises behave opportunistically. Efficient contract law would limit the possibility for private opportunism. However, if the government itself behaves opportunistically and fails to honour its own commitments, then it is unlikely that private parties will be able to rely on the government for efficient enforcement. Thus, although private contract is the subject of this essay, government behaviour is also relevant. (For additional examples and references, see Rubin 1997.)

Part of the problem is that there are several levels of government, and the central government may be lacking sufficient power to compel lower level governments to honour their agreements. A common pattern is for the government to offer terms to a foreign investor to induce specific investments in Russia and then opportunistically to change the terms so as to appropriate some or all of the quasi-rents associated with the investment. For example, the Raddison Corporation negotiated an agreement with the Kremlin to build a hotel in Moscow. Once the property was completed, however, the Moscow City Council demanded a partnership before allowing the hotel to open. Negotiations delayed the opening for about one year, and the city did get a partnership (Thomas and Sutherland 1992: 147).

Governments may also arbitrarily change tax rates after investments have been sunk, thus appropriating part of the value of the investment. For example, the Moscow city government initially allowed joint ventures to pay taxes at the same rate as Russians, about $3,500 per hectare. However, after some investments had been sunk, they changed the method of taxing such land. The rate was increased to up to $465,000 per hectare, the rate paid by foreigners. This decree was only one in a series of changes in tax and land-ownership laws making it difficult for foreign and Russian firms to lease property for office space and development in the capital. For example, the City Council has annulled leases signed by the mayor's office and passed legislation calling for lease agreements to be renegotiated. These new tax rates mean that some past investments may not be profitable, and many would not have been undertaken.

Government has no monopoly on opportunism. An important form of this behaviour is by corporations, mainly through expropriation of stockholder wealth. Corporate governance structures are exceedingly weak in Russia. Companies sometimes refuse to register or acknowledge investors. There are also instances of stock watering, where additional shares are issued to favoured investors. Though attempts are being made to control this behaviour, so far they have not been completely successful. (This issue is discussed at length in Blasi et al. 1997.)

A recent survey of investors has indicated the extent of the problems associated with an ineffective legal system (Craik 1995; Halligan and Teplukhin 1996). According to the survey, the 'most important restraints to investment' are 'fear for shareholder rights and weak contract law'. Craik begins: 'Russia's ever-shifting and poorly enforced legal system is by far the biggest single impediment to a much-needed investment boom that could provide the impetus for reform a survey of domestic and international business operating here shows.' The survey indicates that the main legal problem is the difficulty of enforcing stock market investments, because of problems with share registers. The second major concern was contract law, 'which was seen as complex and difficult to implement'. Respondents indicate that the Civil Code has made an improvement but 'businesses say that in practice, many courts lack the expertise to implement the system'. Broken promises by the government itself (discussed above) are counted as part of the difficulty with contract law. 'Political instability' rated as the third most serious concern.

Recently, Dmitri Vasiliev, the executive director of the Russian Securities Commission, has defended the investment climate in Russia (Vasiliev 1995). However, as of July 1995, the strongest arguments made are that 'Regulations *now being written* will govern all aspects of market activity . . .' and '*Soon*, the Securities Commission will also have formal enforcement mechanisms at its disposal . . .' (emphasis added). Vasiliev does claim that some companies have adequately protected shareholders' rights, but the example (the Red October chocolate factory) is a company needing additional capital. However, the *Economist* (1995a) does indicate that there are several reforms being planned or implemented to make the Russian stock market more reliable. Kranz (1995a) indicates that there are institutions that register shares, such as the Moscow Central Depository, and that Chase Manhattan Bank has a cooperative arrangement with this organization. She indicates that certainty and stability in the stock market are increasing (1995a, 1995b). Liesman (1995) indicates that as of October 1995, American investors were reluctant to invest in Russia, in part because new securities, tax-reform and corporate laws promised by the government had not yet been passed. Articles in the US business press sometimes advise against investing in Russia (e.g. Dunkin 1995).

One strategy for dealing with such legal inconsistency is to enter the market on a small scale and observe what happens. Many foreign firms, for example, have small investments in Russia, often involving only retailing of products. Poe (1993) recommends a similar strategy in determining the reliability of a potential Russian partner. To the extent that quicker or larger investments would occur if there were increased certainty, then the uncertainty is imposing real costs on the Russian economy.

In addition to issues relating to corporate governance, there are other forms of opportunism by managers. One is simple looting of assets. Oil and other natural resources sell for prices in Russia that are below world market levels. Many managers have gotten rich by acquiring such assets, for example by selling them at Russian prices to companies they own, and then reselling them on the world market. (This source of ill-gotten gains is discussed, for example, in Blasi et al. 1997: 24–25, 33–35, and elsewhere.) Another widespread form of opportunism is the apparent practice of many Russian firms to delay paying their workers for long periods of time (discussed, for example, in Schmetzer 1996).

Bases for legal uncertainty. Part of the difficulty with contract enforcement is caused by uncertainty and the associated high discount rates. Many of the mechanisms for contractual enforcement depend on reputations and on other long term investments (e.g., in self-enforcing agreements). If parties believe that legal or property institutions are likely to change in the near future, they will be willing to invest less in such agreements. Blanchard and Kremer (1997) argue that if firms expect customers and suppliers to go bankrupt, then investments in reputations will not occur and opportunism will make many exchanges impossible. Blasi et al. (1997) indicate that no more than one-quarter of Russian firms are very likely to remain in business. Thus, a short time horizon and the associated uncertainty are understandable. This may explain the widely noted tendency of Russian negotiators to drive excessively difficult bargains. Such bargaining may mean that the Russian participants receive lower long term returns from the agreement, but if parties have short time horizons, this will be less significant.

Short time horizons may also explain some otherwise puzzling behaviour by political authorities. If a political authority radically changes the tax rate faced by businesses, then this can be profitable in the short run because the jurisdiction can appropriate the quasi-rents from the completed investment. However, this policy has long term costs because other businesses will be less willing to invest in this jurisdiction. But a short time horizon means that the present value of the appropriated investments can outweigh the long term losses from lost future investments.

Again, the problem is uncertainty. If governments breach agreements, they can expect greatly reduced future investment as other potential investors refrain from investing. However, if the relevant officials do not expect the government to last, there is less cost from opportunism and such appropriation becomes more likely. Other potential transactors, observing that the state does not even honour its own agreements, would understandably place relatively little weight on the state as a neutral enforcer of other contracts. Shleifer and Vishny (1996) indicate that this uncertainty has caused the market to place low values on Russian assets. For example, a barrel of oil owned by a western company is valued at $4–$5.00; by a Russian company, at $.05. Boettke (1995) indicates that this uncertainty about the stability of government policies and commitment of the government to particular reforms is a continuation of similar uncertainty from the Soviet era. Since such uncertainty and unpredictability have a long history in Russia, it may be difficult to convince the people that any given policy or reform will be stable.

The Coase theorem (Coase 1960) shows that with well-defined property rights and sufficiently low transactions costs, the final use of resources is efficient and invariant with respect to initial rights assignments. Most criticisms of the theorem have focused on the second condition, the magnitude of transactions costs. However, the situation in Russia today is one in which the theorem may not hold because the first condition, the existence of well-defined property rights, is not satisfied. The problem is not anarchy. Rather, it is the existence of too many governments, with lines of power insufficiently well defined between them. Property rights are not well defined because it is not clear who has the power to define them. The result is that resources will not be used efficiently.

For private enforcement mechanisms to function requires investments of exactly the sort that may not be worthwhile, given the levels of uncertainty in Russia today. Required investments are of several sorts. The simplest is investment in reputation for honesty. By demonstrating a willingness to refrain from exploiting a situation to its fullest (as, for example, by not offering high quality and supplying low quality goods when detection of quality is impossible before purchase) a firm can establish a reputation for honesty. However, this investment will pay only with sufficiently low discount rates. Otherwise, the gains from exploiting the immediate situation will outweigh the gains from greater future profits. Similarly, self-enforcing agreements work only because the present value of future profits from the expected sequence of exchanges between two parties is greater than the immediate gains from cheating. This again is a form of investment and requires sufficiently low discount rates to make the agreement actually self enforcing.

It is important to separate multilateral mechanisms that are open to any member from those based on religious or ethnic solidarity (Landa 1981). The traditional pattern of trade in Russia has been based on such ethnic or cultural groups. Greif (1994) indicates that this pattern of trade is associated with 'collectivist' as opposed to 'individualist' culture, and that the latter is more common in developed economies. While groups based on ethnic solidarity are useful for some purposes, such groups enable trade to occur only between members. Valuable transactions with non-members become impossible, and therefore resources are unable to flow to their highest valued use. (Such ethnic solidarity is also often the basis for criminal gangs, in Russia and elsewhere, for the same reason: contract enforcement by courts is unavailable to criminals.)

The argument advanced here has both normative and positive implications for Russia. The normative implication is that agents should form groups based on characteristics other than ethnic solidarity. Businesses should actively seek to generate such organizations, and advisors to businesses should suggest the formation of such associations. Governments should facilitate the formation of groups engaging in multilateral enforcement. Such facilitation should be active, for example, by passing laws encouraging the formation of multilateral enforcement mechanisms. The most important such law would be to agree to enforce private arbitration decisions where the parties have agreed to voluntary arbitration. Government should provide passive support, for example, by not overzealously applying antitrust laws to such groups. The new Russian Commercial Code does indicate that 'The creation of associations of commercial and/or non-commercial organizations in the form of associations (or unions) shall be permitted' (Article 50). This means that there is a possibility for such multilateral enforcement organizations to form.

The positive implication is that we should expect to observe spontaneous formation of voluntary trade and other associations whose purpose is enforcement of agreements in exactly the ways discussed above. Some such mechanisms are being created (for more detailed discussion, see Rubin 1997). Regional trading associations of brokers have been established with the encouragement of the recently empowered Russian Federation Commission on Securities and Exchanges and with the assistance of US government financed resident advisors. These associations will be self regulating, with a director of enforcement and compliance rules based on US and international standards.

Several large industrial firms and investment funds signed an agreement with respect to shareholders' rights in 1994. These firms agreed to provide detailed audited financial information to shareholders and to have independent managers maintain possession and control of shareholder registers so that shareholders can be guaranteed that their holdings will indeed be registered. At least three associations (the Association of Broker-Dealers, the League of Investment Funds, and the Russian Association of Investment Funds) have been established and undertake some self-policing, although significant problems with shareholder rights still exist and investors view these as being highly troublesome, as discussed above.

Another agency that does perform the functions identified above is the 'commodity exchange'. These are trading centres, with many firms as members. They trade a wide variety of goods – not merely 'commodities' as defined in the US. There are at least 165 commodities exchanges in Russia, including twenty in Moscow (Wegren 1994). Participants understand that methods of dispute resolution between participants are necessary. Moreover, most exchanges require a recommendation from two members and an examination of financial and reputational capital before admitting a new member. However, there does not seem to be a strong system of enforcement of promises. Contracts are often not honoured and payments are often not made. In 1992, approximately 30% of the contracts were not fulfilled.

Greif and Kandel (1995) report on several related mechanisms. There are several private arbitration courts, including courts set up by commodities exchanges, banking associations, and the Bar Association. In 1993 over 100 companies (Russian and foreign) each paid a fee to establish the Moscow Commercial Court, a permanent arbitration committee. The Moscow Arbitration Court, the Moscow branch of the basic business court of Russia, will enforce its decisions. Additionally, 'business groups' are associations of businessmen that join together for one time deals. However, members will engage in several such deals over time. If anyone reneges, they will be prohibited from participating in future deals. These voluntary groups based on multiple interlocking transactions are not cultural or ethnic groups, but they do have common interests and a common code of behavior.

Moreover, a fear of organized crime may contribute to unwillingness of firms to provide public information. The head of one association, the Russian Business Round Table, was poisoned. His associates indicate that the motive may have been the unwillingness of the Association to allow criminal firms to join (Stanley 1995). More generally, any public information useful for establishing a reputation can be used by criminals to target profitable or successful firms for purposes of extortion. This is only one aspect of the danger to the Russian economy from criminal enterprises.

Criminals as enforcers? It may be that criminals will act as enforcers for contracts. Leitzel et al. (1995) claim that the 'main benefit' of the Russian Mafia (sometimes called the 'Mafiya' to distinguish it from its Sicilian namesake) is contract enforcement. Similarly, Erlanger (1994) says that '. . . the inability to get redress through the courts leads to more crime, as businesses hire muscle to enforce deals otherwise unenforceable'. Black et al. (1996) indicate that violence is a real option in enforcement of corporate law. Aslund (1995: 169) also suggests that 'banks take recourse to using gangsters, who force people to pay under threat of physical harm'. Kranz (1995b) indicates that 'with the judicial system in shambles . . . guns, bombs and grenades take the place of arbitration courts'.

On the other hand, Greif and Kandel (1995: 308) indicate that 'there is no evidence that gangs actively enforced contracts except in those cases that directly concerned their interests' (Leitzel et al. provide no evidence for their claim, nor do Black et al.) Grief and Kandel do indicate (1995: 316) that, with respect to security firms, 'contract enforcement on their part would be natural'. Handelman (1995) discusses the role of criminals as debt collectors at various places in his study of organized crime in Russia (e.g. 69, 168). However, whenever he mentions the debt collection function of thugs, he also indicates that they 'stave off unfriendly creditors' and 'intimidate creditors' so that there may be no net effect. Handelman indicates that gangsters have become associated with many firms, and that such associations are a normal and necessary part of doing business in Russia. Such associations would be consistent with the claim of Greif and Kandel, that criminals collect only their own debts. Kranz (1995b) indicates that 40,000 enterprises in Russia may have Mafia connections, and that the Mafia sometimes infiltrates big business by first extending loans and then demanding management control. But Blasi et al. (1997) argue that claims of major Mafia ownership of large corporations is probably exaggerated, although they agree that the Mafia is a serious problem in Russia and that many businesses probably pay protection.

Aslund (1995: 169–70) indicates that one-third of bank employees are security guards, suggesting that banks either use these guards to fight the Mafia or that banks are 'infested with the Mafia'. Kranz (1995b) indicates that criminals sometimes try to take over companies by taking control of the company's bank, and that 'as many as 10 of Russia's big banks may also have Mafia connections'.

However, while data are obviously lacking, there are reasons to doubt that the Mafia will actually provide anything like an efficient level of contract enforcement. In particular, the discount rate is again relevant. A criminal gang hired to collect a debt has two options: keep the entire debt or turn over the contractual share to the original creditor. Which strategy is optimal depends on the discount rate. If this is high enough, then the gang may forego the future gains from additional enforcement contracts and simply keep the money (or even extort additional money).

If discount rates are sufficiently high, then creditors, expecting criminals to keep the debt, will not hire them and there will not be contractual enforcement by criminals.

Intriligator (1994), who claims that criminalization is destroying the Russian economy, also argues that the Mafias have very short time horizons. Even Leitzel et al. (1995), who are more optimistic regarding the role of the Mafia than is Intriligator, believe that the Mafiosi have short time horizons because of uncertainty. Handelman's suggestion that criminals are equity owners in many firms and Kranz's (1995b) discussion of this issue are consistent with this argument. Aslund (1995), overall, is optimistic about the future of Russia, but even he admits (171) that 'if no serious action is taken [with respect to crime], the legitimacy of democratic rule will be undermined.'

RUSSIA: SUMMARY. The evidence cited here is largely anecdotal. Data are lacking for a more systematic examination of the issues. However, potential investors in Russia are confronted with the same problem, and the data used here may be similar to the data used by such investors. As indicated above, the problems identified are the same as the problems that investors consider in making decisions about future commitments (Craik 1995; Halligan and Teplukhin 1996). The US Embassy, in providing advice to Americans considering investing in Russia, makes similar points (US Embassy Moscow 1996: 26). In discussing Russian 'business customs' they indicate that:

- many Russians want to keep their wealth and their business dealings secret;
- while Americans prefer to base their business relationships on legally enforceable contracts, many Russians still doubt the value of their business laws and courts;
- most Russian business dealings are based on strong personal relationships, with the contract considered to be merely a formality;
- Americans think 'win-win'; most Russians think 'win-lose'.

These 'customs' are based on the issues discussed in this essay, and are rational responses to the sort of uncertainty discussed here.

There is insufficient ability to enforce contracts in Russia today. The law is weak, and even when decisions are obtained from courts, enforcement of decisions is often difficult. As a result, parties use private mechanisms for such enforcement. However, the power of such mechanisms is also weak. Firms have not yet established valuable reputations, so that they do not have valuable reputation capital to use to guarantee agreements. There are barriers to creation of such reputations, in the form of fear of expropriation by criminals or by tax collectors, or by corrupt officials. Some multilateral enforcement organizations have been formed, and they are aware of the problems associated with contract enforcement. However, many of them do not seem willing or able actually to take the steps needed to enforce agreements.

What does this mean? Things are bad, but perhaps improving. The question is, will they improve fast enough to enable Russia to become a fully developed economy, or will the economy remain trapped in a low level institutional equilibrium? We know from the examples of the Czech Republic, Hungary and Poland that it is possible for an economy to emerge successfully from the wasteland created by Communism. However, since the situation is unique in human history, I cannot at this time predict if Russia will succeed or not.

The true danger may be that if the legal system cannot function, then the criminal underground may become more and more powerful in both market and nonmarket activities (Erlanger 1994; Intriligator 1994; Handelman 1995; Kranz 1995b). Jeffrey Sachs (1995), a former adviser to the Russian government, indicates that 'Russia's corruption is singularly deep' and appears pessimistic about the future. George Soros, a well-known successful investor in Eastern Europe, indicates that although he is investing in Russia because of the potential return, he is 'cautiously pessimistic' about the country. He believes the country is dominated by 'robber capitalism', defined as a 'breakdown of legal and financial controls', and that the economy is characterized as a struggle between rival gangs, including the Communists as one such gang (Gordon 1995). A World Bank publication (*Transition*, 1996), quoting a publication at Gottingen University, ranks Russia 47 out of 54 rated countries in 'Corruption'. (The ranking 1 is least corrupt; the rates for other former communist countries are Poland: 24; Czech Republic: 25; Hungary: 31.)

On the other hand, Aslund (1995) believes that Russia is on the road to a successful transition. Galuszka et al. (1994) in a special *Business Week* report indicate optimism, and suggest that Russia has begun to develop and is no longer in danger of collapse. Layard and Parker (1996) and Poe (1993) believe that Russia will prosper, and both books (aimed at potential American investors in Russia) refer in their titles to the 'Coming Russian Boom'. But Tourevski and Morgan (1993) and Kvint (1993) in books aimed at the same audience are less optimistic. I have myself collected a large file of business press articles on events in Russia, and about as many report favourable as unfavourable outcomes.

As I have stressed throughout, the issue is predictability. If the system becomes sufficiently stable and predictable to make investment in creation of a rule of law and a set of contract enforcing institutions worthwhile, then the problems I have discussed will be solved. If this happens, then I believe that the other problems facing the Russian economy will also become manageable. If the system continues to be unpredictable and if agents continue to lack faith in the future, then the problems will persist. At this time, I cannot foretell which will happen; nor, I believe, can anyone.

PAUL H. RUBIN

See also ANTHROPOLOGICAL LAW-AND-ECONOMICS; ARBITRATION; CONFLICT OF LAWS; CORRUPTION IN TRANSITION ECONOMIES; ECONOMIC LEGALITY AND TRANSITION IN RUSSIA AND EASTERN EUROPE; GANGS AND THE STATE OF NATURE; ORGANIZED CRIME; PRIVATE COMMERCIAL LAW; PROPERTY RIGHTS; RULE OF LAW; TRANSFER OF PROPERTY RIGHTS IN EASTERN EUROPE; TRANSITION IN EASTERN EUROPE.

Subject classification: 1a(ii); 3f(ii).

BIBLIOGRAPHY

Aslund, A. 1995. *How Russia Became a Market Economy*. Washington, DC: Brookings Institution.

Black, B.S., Kraakman, R.H. and Hay, J. 1996. Corporate law from scratch. In *Corporate Governance in Central Europe and Russia*, ed. R. Frydman, C. Gray and A. Rapaczynski, Budapest: Central European Press.

Blanchard, O. and Kremer, M. 1997. Disorganization. Working Paper, Massachusetts Institute of Technology, Cambridge, MA.

Blasi, J.R., Kroumova, M. and Kruse, D. 1997. *Kremlin Capitalism*. Ithaca: ILR Press of Cornell University Press.

Blumenfeld, L.H. 1996. Russia's new Civil Code: the legal foundation for Russia's emerging economy. *The International Lawyer* 30: 477–515.

Boettke, P.J. 1995. Credibility, commitment, and Soviet economic reform. *Economic Transition in Eastern Europe and Russia: Realities of Reform*, ed. E. Lazear, Stanford: Hoover Institution Press.

Borish, M.S. and Noel, M. 1996. *Private Sector Development During Transition*. Washington, DC: The World Bank.

Brada, J.C. 1996. Privatization is transition – or is it? *Journal of Economic Perspectives* 10: 67–86.

Branegan, J. 1994. White Knights need not apply. *Time*, 31 October.

Coase, R.H. 1960. The problem of social cost. *Journal of Law and Economics* 3: 1–44.

Cooter, R.D. 1996. The theory of market modernization of law. *International Review of Law and Economics* 16: 141–72.

Craik, E. 1995. Investors rate legal mess as key obstacle. *Moscow Times*, 1 April: 1.

De Melo, M., Denizer, C. and Gelb, A. 1996. From plan to market: patterns of transition. Washington, DC: World Bank Policy Research Paper 1564.

Dunkin, A. 1995. After the fire in emerging markets. *Business Week*, 23 January.

Economist. 1995a. Boris the Broker evolves: Russia's primitive stockmarket is at last becoming more sophisticated. 8 July: 69–70.

Economist. 1995b. Russian law: groping ahead. 2 September: 42–8.

Erlanger, S. 1994. Russia's new dictatorship of crime. *New York Times*, 15 May.

Fischer, S., Sahay, R. and Vegh, C.A. 1996. Economies in transition: the beginnings of growth. *American Economic Review*, 86: 229–33.

Galuszka, P., Kranz, P. and Reed, S. 1994. Russia's new capitalism: it's still chaotic, but private companies are forging a vital economy. *Business Week*, 10 October.

Gordon, M.R. 1995. Cautiously pessimistic investor eyes Russia. *The New York Times*, 22 December.

Gray, C.W. and associates. 1993. *Evolving Legal Frameworks for Private Sector Development in Central and Eastern Europe*. Washington, DC: World Bank Discussion Paper 209, July.

Greif, A. 1994. Cultural beliefs and the organization of society: a historical and theoretical reflection on collectivist and individualist societies. *Journal of Political Economy* 102: 912–50.

Greif, A. and Kandel, E. 1995. Contract enforcement institutions: historical perspective and current status in Russia. *Economic Transition in Eastern Europe and Russia: Realities of Reform*, ed. E. Lazear, Stanford: Hoover Institution Press.

Halligan, L. and Teplukhin, P. 1996. Investment disincentives in Russia. *Communist Economics and Economic Transformation* 8: 29–51.

Handelman, S. 1995. *Comrade Criminal: Russia's New Mafiya*. New Haven: Yale University Press.

Hay, J.R., Shleifer, A. and Vishny, R.W. 1996. Toward a theory of legal reform. *European Economic Review* 40: 559–67.

Hayek, F.A. 1973. *Law, Legislation and Liberty; Volume 1: Rules and Order*. Chicago: University of Chicago Press.

International Monetary Fund (IMF), The World Bank, Organization for Economic Co-Operation and Development, and European Bank for Reconstruction and Development. 1991. *A Study of the Soviet Economy*. Washington, DC.

Intriligator, M.D. 1994. Privatization in Russia has led to criminalization. *Australian Economic Review* 6: 4–14.

Jensen, M. and Meckling, W. 1976. Theory of the firm: managerial behavior, agency costs, and ownership structure. *Journal of Financial Economics* 3: 305–60.

Kranz, P. 1995a. Russia isn't Siberia for investors anymore. *Business Week* (International Edition), 17 April.

Kranz, P. 1995b. Russia's really hostile takeovers. *Business Week*, 14 August.

Kroll, H. 1987. Breach of contract in the Soviet economy. *Journal of Legal Studies* 16: 119–48.

Kvint, V. 1993. *The Barefoot Shoemaker: Capitalizing on the New Russia*. New York: Arcade Publishing.

Landa, J.T. 1981. A theory of the ethnically homogeneous middleman group: an institutional alternative to contract law. *Journal of Legal Studies* 10: 349–62.

Langer, R. and Buyevitch, A. 1995. Russia's courts take courage. *Moscow Times*, 18 July: 17.

Layard, R. and Parker, J. 1996. *The Coming Russian Boom*. New York: Free Press.

Leijonhufvud, A. 1993. Problems of socialist transition: Kazakhstan 1991. In *The Political Economy of the Transition Process in Eastern Europe* ed. L. Samogyi, Aldershot: Edward Elgar: 289–311.

Leitzel, J., Gaddy C. and Alexeev, M. 1995. Mafiosi and Matrioshki: organized crime and Russian reform. *Brookings Review* 26–29 (Winter).

Leoni, B. 1961. *Freedom and the Law*. Indianapolis: Liberty Fund, 1991.

Liesman, S. 1995. For US investors, Russia rates caution: enthusiasm fades as Moscow's market fizzles. *Wall Street Journal*, 23 October.

Mauro, P. 1995. Corruption and growth. *Quarterly Journal of Economics* 110: 681–712.

Murrell, P. 1992. Conservative political philosophy and the strategy of economic transition. *East European Politics and Societies* 6: 3–16.

Osakwe, C. 1993. Modern Russian law of banking and security transactions: a biopsy of post-Soviet Russian commercial law. *Whittier Law Review* 14: 301–82.

Pennar, K., Galuszka, P. and Miller, K.L. 1994. Frontier economies: enter if you dare. *Business Week*, 18 November.

Pistor, K. 1995. Supply and demand for contract enforcement in Russia: courts, arbitration, and private enforcement. Prepared for presentation for the John M. Olin Seminar Series, The Rule of Law and Economic Reform in Russia, Harvard University.

Poe, R. 1993. *How to Profit from the Coming Russian Boom: The Insider's Guide to Business Opportunities and Survival on the Frontiers of Capitalism*. New York: McGraw-Hill.

Rapaczynski, A. 1996. The roles of the state and the market in establishing property rights. *Journal of Economic Perspectives* 10: 87–103.

Rubin, P.H. 1994. Growing a legal system in the post-communist economies. *Cornell International Law Journal* 27: 1–47.

Rubin, P.H. 1997. *Promises, Promises: Contracts in Russia and Other Post-Communist Economies*. Shaftesbury Papers, Edward Elgar and the Locke Institute, in press.

Rubin, P.H. and Bailey, M.J. 1994. The role of lawyers in changing the law. *Journal of Legal Studies* 23: 807–31.

Russian Federation. 1994. *Civil Code of the Russian Federation*. Studies on Russian Law, the Vinogradoff Institute, Faculty of Laws, University College, London.

Sachs, J.D. 1995. Why corruption rules Russia. *The New York Times*, 29 November: A19.

Schmetzer, U. 1996. Unpaid for months, Russians see no resolution to wage crisis. *Chicago Tribune*, 25 October.

Shleifer, A. and Vishny, R.W. 1996. A survey of corporate governance. NBER Working Paper No. 5554.

Shleifer, A. and Vishny, R.W. 1993. Corruption. *Quarterly Journal of Economics* 108: 599–617.

Siltchenkov, D. 1993. A stranger in a strange land: practicing law after the breakup of the USSR. *Whittier Law Review* 14: 503–14.

Stanley, A. 1995. To the business risks in Russia, add poisoning. *New York Times*, 9 August.

Thomas, B. and Sutherland, C. 1992. *Red Tape: Adventure Capitalism in the New Russia*. New York: Dutton.

Topornin, B.N. 1993. *The Legal Problems of Economic Reform in Russia*. Edinburgh: The David Hume Institute.

Tourevski, M. and Morgan, E. 1993. *Cutting the Red Tape: How Western Companies Can Profit in the New Russia*. New York: Free Press.

Transition, 1996. Corruption – an international comparison. July-August, 16–17 (World Bank).

US Embassy, Moscow. 1996. 1997 Russia Country Commercial Guide. Internet: http://www.itaiep.doc.gov/bisnis/country/ruccg.html.

Vasiliev, D. 1995. We Russians can mind our own markets. *Wall Street Journal*, 7 July: A10.

Viechtbauer, V. 1993. Arbitration in Russia. *Stanford Journal of International Law* 29: 355–457.

Vlasihin, V.A. 1993. Toward a rule of law and bill of rights for Russia. In *Law and Democracy in the New Russia*, ed. B.L.R. Smith and G.M. Danilenko, Washington, DC: Brookings Institution.

Wegren, S.K. 1994. Building market institutions. *Communist and Post-Communist Studies* 27: 195–224.

Yakovlev, V.F. 1994. Interview. *Moscow Rossiyskaya Gazeta*. Reprinted in *Federal Broadcast Information Service-USSR-077*, 19 July.

legal rules. *See* EMERGENCE OF LEGAL RULES.

legal standards of care. Two methods are employed to induce a potential injurer to take socially optimal care to reduce either the probability that a victim will be harmed or the magnitude of the harm to the victim should he be harmed, or both. One, termed strict or absolute liability, makes the injurer responsible for all harm that is caused. The injurer, in her own interest, takes socially optimal care because by doing so she minimizes the sum of precaution costs and the costs imposed on the victim. Since she bears both of these costs she will wish to make them as low as possible. Thus, under a strict liability regime, a potential injurer is induced to act in a socially desirable way not by being offered the possibility of escaping liability for harm caused but rather by the certainty that she will be liable for all harm which is caused.

THE LEGAL STANDARD. By contrast, an injurer can be induced to take socially optimal care by setting a legal standard for her conduct and holding her liable if she does not conform to it. Most commonly, that standard requires the injurer to 'take reasonable care' or, equivalently, refrain from acting 'negligently'.

If we assume that the legal standard in all instances is set at what constitutes socially optimal care for the injurer (and this is known by the injurer), it can be predicted that the injurer will endeavour to act in accordance with the legal standard of care. However, the reasoning underlying the injurer's decision to conform to the legal standard will depend on the applicable causality rule determining whether or not the injurer is liable for harm which would have occurred even if the injurer had conformed to the legal standard.

The difference between the two causality rules (which becomes important at several points in the discussion which follows) can be made clear by considering a case in which the issue is whether a sufficiently high fence has been built to protect spectators at a baseball game from being hit by a ball. Assume that a socially optimal fence is ten feet high and this is what is required under the legal standard. The issue that distinguishes the two causality standards is whether, if a fence of less than ten feet is built, liability will be imposed for harm resulting from a ball flying so high that it would have gone over the legally mandated ten-foot fence had it been built. Under one causality rule liability will be imposed and under the other it will not.

If it is assumed that liability will be imposed, the injurer reasons that she can escape all liability by building a ten-foot fence (she need build one no higher to avoid liability). By contrast, if she builds a fence less than ten feet high she is liable for all harm, including that harm which would not have been prevented by the ten-foot fence. As a result she has a powerful incentive to build the ten-foot fence.

If the other causality rule applies the reasoning of the injurer is different (see Grady 1983; Kahan 1989). If she fails to build the ten-foot fence she is liable only for that harm which the ten-foot fence would have prevented. Her choice whether to build the ten-foot fence, as a result, depends on a comparison between its cost and the costs associated with the harm that will be prevented if the fence is built. More precisely, she continually compares cost and benefit in harm avoided and chooses the fence which minimizes the sum of her precaution costs and expected liability. (Notably, this reasoning is identical to what would occur if the controlling legal rule were strict liability.) Since we are now assuming that the legal standard is set at what constitutes socially optimal care for the injurer, the injurer will conform to the legal standard.

What is crucial, however, is that under this causality rule the injurer will take socially optimal care. She will, consequently, conform to the legal standard only if it mandates socially optimal care. By contrast, under the other causality rule, the injurer will conform to the legal standard to avoid all liability. As we shall see, this incentive may be powerful enough to induce the injurer to take care which exceeds socially optimal care if the legal standard mandates such care.

THE REASONABLE MAN (PERSON) STANDARD. We have so far assumed that a legal standard is set for each injurer, requiring the injurer to take what is, for that injurer, socially optimal care to avoid causing harm to victims. In the great majority of instances, however, the legal standard requires the injurer not to take the care that is optimal for that injurer, but rather the care that would be taken, until very recently, by the 'reasonable man' and, currently, in our more enlightened times, the 'reasonable person'. If the legal standard is set at one level for all injurers the question arises of how those injurers whose optimal level of care is either above or below the required level will respond.

The answer with respect to those injurers whose optimal

level of care exceeds the required level is clear. Since they escape all liability by taking the prescribed level of care they have no reason to take more even if it is socially optimal for them to do so. In apparent recognition that this is so, the law generally requires injurers for whom it is optimal to take more care than the 'reasonable man', now 'reasonable person', to do so.

With rare exceptions, however, an injurer cannot escape conforming to the specified level of care by demonstrating that her optimal level of care is below the specified level (see Schwartz 1989). The question then arises how injurers whose optimal level of care is below the specified level adapt to a legal standard which requires that, in order to avoid liability, they take more care than is optimal for them.

The answer to this question depends on which causality rule is assumed to apply. If an injurer who fails to take the required level of care is liable for all harm caused, including that harm which would not have been prevented by taking the mandated care, it will often be privately worthwhile for the injurer to take the required care, even if it exceeds optimal care, because by doing so she escapes liability for all harm, not only the harm which is prevented by taking the mandated care. By contrast, if an injurer who fails to take the required level of care is liable only for the harm which would have been prevented by taking the requisite level of care, the injurer will take optimal care rather than the greater level of care required under the legal standard.

To see why this is so, consider the example of the fence discussed above. Suppose that a socially optimal fence for the injurer is ten feet high but the legal standard requires one that is eleven feet high. The injurer wants to know what is gained by increasing the size of the fence from the optimal ten feet to the legally required eleven feet. Since, under the causality rule now assumed to apply, the injurer will not be liable for any balls which would go over the eleven-foot fence, and the ten-foot fence will block all balls flying no higher than ten feet, increasing the size of the fence from ten to eleven feet will avoid liability only for those balls which would go over a ten-foot fence but not an eleven-foot fence. If, however, the cost of increasing the fence from ten to eleven feet was less than the associated reduction in liability it would be optimal for the higher fence to be built. Since it is our present assumption that the increase from ten to eleven feet is not optimal, it follows that the higher fence will not be built even if liability can only be avoided by building it.

The foregoing analysis suggests two related questions. (1) Why is a single standard which exceeds optimal care for some injurers employed despite the fact that, under one causality rule (which we shall see often applies), it induces some injurers to take excessive care and, under the other causality rule, it induces injurers to take the same care they would take if required to take the care that was optimal for them? (2) Under the causality rule which may induce injurers to take excessive care, how should this possibility be taken into account in deciding the single level of care which should be required?

Traditional legal theory has long supplied a partial answer to the first of these two questions. If a single standard is imposed, the costs of deciding what level of care is optimal for the particular injurer are avoided. This answer is, however, inadequate, essentially for two reasons: (1) there are also process costs associated with deciding what the single standard should be, and (2) (as discussed above) employing a single standard may induce some injurers to take excessive care.

The effort to determine the circumstances in which, in light of these factors, a single standard, or a legal standard, requiring each injurer to take the care that is optimal is relatively more efficient has revealed a second objective, which is achieved by employing a single standard (see Shavell 1987; Schwartz 1989). There are some actors who, because of their poor ability to take care to avoid injuring victims when engaging in an activity, should not engage in the activity. Determining how effective a particular actor will be in avoiding harm to others, when engaging in a particular activity, is a costly and error-prone process. If, instead, the single required level of care is set so that persons for whom it is optimal to take at least that much care should engage in the activity, injurers will be induced to self-select and only those who should engage in the activity will engage in it.

This insight provides the beginning for deciding what single level of care should be required. It is, however, not desirable to set the required level of care at the minimum that is optimal in order for it to be desirable for the injurer to engage in the activity. If this were done (assuming the causality rule imposing liability on an injurer for all harm caused), some injurers, for whom it would not be optimal to take the specified level of care, would nevertheless do so because (as discussed above) they could escape liability for all harm. To constrain the taking of excessive care by some injurers, and their engaging in the activity as a result when they should not do so, the required level of care must be set above the minimal level which must be optimal for an injurer if the injurer should engage in the activity. Doing this is, however, constrained by the fact that the level which is set will, necessarily, be excessive for some injurers who should engage in the activity. Consequently, they will be induced to take excessive care in order to meet the standard and avoid liability. The optimal single standard is derived by minimizing the sum of the misallocative costs resulting from (a) some injurers who should not engage in the activity taking excessive care and engaging in the activity, and (b) some injurers who should engage in the activity being obliged to take excessive care (Shavell 1987: 86–91).

It would appear that deriving the single standard is much less complicated, and the use of a single standard to deter entry into an activity by injurers who should not engage in it more effective, if the causality role limiting an injurer's liability to the harm which would have been prevented by the mandated care applies. For under this rule the complication of injurers taking excessive care to meet the legal standard simply does not arise. The analysis in the literature, however, assumes that the causality rule holding the injurer liable for all harm controls and, as a result, does not consider how an optimal single standard would be derived under the other causality rule (see Shavell 1987: 86–91; Schwartz 1989).

The analysis of the use of a single standard may be

further refined in a number of respects. The discussion of the process for determining the optimal single standard assumes that all injurers derive the same benefits from engaging in the activity (Shavell 1987). If injurers derive different benefits, an optimal single standard would have to be determined for each class of injurers deriving the same benefits (Schwartz 1989). The use of a single standard also has an impact on earlier decisions of an injurer which are relevant in determining what will be the optimal level of care for the injurer when engaging in the activity (Schwartz 1989). Essentially, the tendency to take excessive care to avoid all liability operates with respect to these decisions as well. While this incentive effect will not yield optimal decisions, it may, on balance, be better than having no liability imposed for sub-optimal behaviour in those acts which precede entry into the activity. While in principle these acts could be scrutinized and lead to liability if found to be unreasonable, doing so is a costly and error-prone process in which courts rarely engage.

UNCERTAIN LEGAL STANDARDS. We have so far analysed the behaviour of an injurer when the injurer is certain what legal standard will be applied and believes that it will be (uninterestingly) equal to what is optimal care for the injurer or either above or below the optimal level. What remains to be analysed is how the injurer will act when there is uncertainty as to the legal standard which will control. In those circumstances the injurer anticipates that there will be a distribution of outcomes, with the required level sometimes set at the optimal level for the injurer, and sometimes above or below it. Once again, the analysis depends on which causality rule is assumed to apply. It is much simpler if it is assumed that an injurer is liable only for the harm that would have been prevented by taking the mandated care. For, under this assumption, the possibility that the required level of care will exceed the optimal level of care for the injurer has no impact on the injurer's choice of care. As demonstrated above, even if the injurer believed that the required level of care would always exceed the optimal level of care, the injurer would, nevertheless, choose to take optimal care and accept liability for the harm which would have been prevented by taking the mandated care.

Under the causality rule which is now assumed to apply, the possibility that the required level of care will be less than what is optimal for the injurer will have an effect and induce the injurer to take less than optimal care. This is so because, in deciding how much care to take, the injurer compares the cost of care with the benefit of care in reducing expected liability. If the injurer were certain that liability would be imposed, the comparison would be between the costs of the precaution and the reduction in harm caused. If, however, there is only some probability that the injurer will be held liable, the private benefit of taking care is the harm prevented multiplied by the probability of being held liable. Thus, for example, if an expenditure of one hundred dollars will prevent one hundred and fifty dollars of harm it will, nevertheless, not be worthwhile for an injurer who anticipates being held liable only one half of the time. As a result, the possibility that an injurer will sometimes be exonerated even if less than optimal care is taken systematically induces injurers to take less than optimal care.

The incentive effect of the possibility that an injurer will be exonerated even if less than optimal care is taken is the same if it is assumed that the alternative causality rule, holding the injurer liable for all harm, including the harm which would have occurred even if the mandated care had been taken, applies. However, as discussed above, if this causality rule controls, the possibility that the required level of care will be set above the optimal level may lead the injurer to take excessive care.

The level of care chosen by the injurer is thus determined by the relative importance of the tendency to take less than optimal care induced by the possibility of being exonerated, even if less than optimal care is taken, and the tendency to take excessive care in order to meet the standard requiring that excessive care be taken and, thus, avoid all liability (Goetz 1984: 299; Craswell and Calfee 1986). In general, in the absence of great variance in the distribution of the levels of care that the injurer anticipates will be required, the tendency to take excessive care will dominate.

Since the discussion so far establishes that the incentive effects of having a single standard applicable to all injurers, or uncertainty as to what level of care will be required, depend on the causality rule that applies, it becomes important to know which rule is, in fact, applied. There is no simple answer to this question. The rule that limits liability to harm which would have been prevented by taking the mandated care seems theoretically sound. For, after all, the failure to build a ten-foot fence has not caused injury to a victim hit by a ball flying at a height of eleven feet. However, because application of this rule requires what will, in many circumstances, be a determination of the hard (perhaps impossible) question of what harm would have occurred even if the mandated care had been taken, courts often simply ignore the issue and assume that the harm to the victim who is suing would have been prevented had the mandated care been taken.

In the posited case involving the fence it is easy to understand and determine the question of whether a ball flying at a given height would have gone over a fence of a particular height. Consider, however, the example of a case in which the injurer is a driver who drives above the mandated speed. It is true, and explicitly assumed in standard analysis, that the driver might have injured someone even if driving at or below the mandated level. It is, however, very difficult to determine what the probability of harm would have been at the mandated level. It is, moreover, difficult, if not impossible, to know whether the particular victim who is suing is a member of the class of persons who would not have been hurt if the speed of the car had not been excessive or of the class of persons who would have been hurt even if the car had not been driven at excessive speed. If this cannot be determined, some probabilistic method of computing damages would have to be employed.

Unless it is easy to separate the harm that would have been prevented by taking the mandated care from the harm that would have occurred even if the mandated care had been taken, as in the posited case of the ball going over a fence, courts may simply ignore the issue and assume that the harm to the victim who is suing would have been prevented by taking the mandated care. As a result the possibility of injurers being induced to take excessive care if more than optimal care is required to avoid liability seems to be a real one.

There is a second body of scholarship which analyses legal uncertainty using a different conceptual framework (see P'ng 1986; Polinsky and Shavell 1989; Kaplow 1994). The analysis above essentially asks how a class of identically situated injurers will choose a level of care when it anticipates that in some instances the required level of care will exceed the optimal level and in others be less than the optimal level. The alternative theoretical approach posits a binary choice by a universe of heterogeneous injurers between complying with the controlling rule, or violating it, when sometimes an injurer will be exonerated, even though the rule has been violated, and sometimes held liable, even though the injurer has complied with the rule. Both of these possibilities make the alternative of violating the law more desirable for an injurer making the choice than would be the case if an injurer were always held liable if the controlling rule were violated and always exonerated if the injurer complied with the controlling result. Under this analysis, legal uncertainty induces 'under-deterrence' in the sense that some injurers are induced to violate the rule.

The essential difference between the two approaches derives from two interrelated consequences of positing the compliance choice as a binary one: (1) the person making a compliance choice cannot adapt her behaviour to the legal system by taking into account the variations in the probability of being held liable associated with doing more or less to avoid the harm which the legal rule is designed to prevent, and (2) under the binary approach error consists in imposing liability on the 'innocent' or convicting the 'guilty'. There is no place in the analysis for different magnitudes of error. Under the continuous approach, however, 'legal error' consists of arriving at a standard which departs from the social optimum. There are consequently more or less egregious errors, depending on how far the standard departs from the social optimum. Moreover, the magnitude and frequency of these errors matter because the person making a compliance choice takes them into account in choosing how much will be done to avoid causing the harm which the legal rule is designed to prevent. It is in this process of adaptation that the incentive to over-comply arises. By doing more than is socially optimal, the probability of being held liable can be reduced. This possibility is not taken into account when the compliance choice is posited as a binary one.

The most important conclusions of the above analysis may be summarized as follows. The most significant consequence resulting from the use of a legal standard, rather than a rule of strict or absolute liability, to induce injurers to take socially optimal care, is the discontinuity which is created because all liability can be avoided by taking the required level of care. This discontinuity exists, however, only if the theoretically incorrect, but practically unavoidable, causality rule applies, holding the injurer liable for all harm, including that which would have occurred even if the mandated care had been taken.

Our understanding of the relative efficacy of either employing a single legal standard applicable to all injurers, or requiring each injurer to take what is for that injurer optimal care, can fairly be described as being at a primitive stage. It is now clear that a meaningful comparison must include a consideration both of the process costs and incentive effects associated with the two regimes. The development of the theory required to do this has only recently begun. We have no idea what the empirical magnitudes implicated by the theory are.

The analysis of legal uncertainty is particularly useful in providing a means for understanding and evaluating various procedural features. Most fundamentally, under all of the analyses discussed above, legal uncertainty causes the behaviour of persons subject to a legal regime to depart from the social optimum. A change in the system which reduces uncertainty will, consequently, cause behaviour to conform better to the social optimum. It is thus possible to decide whether the change should be made by comparing its costs with the value of the associated improvement in behaviour.

Once again, however, we have virtually no empirical evidence as to the uncertainty which characterizes various legal regimes or the impairment of incentives resulting from that uncertainty which does exist. The analysis of legal uncertainty does provide good reason for caution in assessing the efficacy of actual or proposed legal regimes. Those regimes will not be implemented with complete accuracy and consistency. Persons subject to them will adapt to the resultant uncertainty as to what legal standard will be applied if they are charged with violating the law. We do not, however, now have the basis for estimating with any precision exactly what these adaptations are or would be under various actual or proposed legal regimes.

WARREN F. SCHWARTZ

See also ACCURACY IN ADJUDICATION; CAUSATION AND TORT LIABILITY; COMPARATIVE NEGLIGENCE; DUE CARE; LEARNED HAND RULE.

Subject classification: 5a(i); 5d(ii).

BIBLIOGRAPHY

Craswell, R. and Calfee, J. 1986. Deterrence and uncertain legal standards. *Journal of Law, Economics and Organization* 2: 279–303.

Goetz, C.J. 1984. *Cases and Materials on Law and Economics*. St Paul, MN: West Publishing Company.

Grady, M. 1983. A new positive economic theory of negligence. *Yale Law Journal* 92: 799–829.

Kahan, M. 1989. Causation and incentives to take care under the negligence rule. *Journal of Legal Studies* 18: 421–47.

Kaplow, L. 1994. The value of accuracy in adjudication: an economic analysis. *Journal of Legal Studies* 23: 307–401.

P'ng, I.P.L. 1986. Optimal subsidies and damages in the presence of legal error. *International Review of Law and Economics* 6: 101–5.

Polinsky, A.M. and Shavell, S. 1989. Legal error, litigation, and the incentive to obey the law. *Journal of Law, Economics and Organization* 5: 99–108.

Schwartz, W.F. 1989. Objective and subjective standards of negligence: defining the reasonable person to induce optimal care and optimal populations of injurers and victims. *Georgetown Law Journal* 78: 241–82.

Shavell, S. 1987. *Economic Analysis of Accident Law*. Cambridge, MA: Harvard University Press.

legal transplants. *See* COMPARATIVE LAW AND ECONOMICS.

legislative intent. A perennial issue in the debate over legislative interpretation concerns what authority, if any, to accord to the proferred intent of the legislature. A fundamental precept of most normative theories of statutory interpretation is that the essential enterprise of the interpreter, be it a judge, an administrative agency, or any citizen potentially subject to the legislation, is to discern what the legislature intended with its enactment of a particular statutory provision (Blackstone [1765] 1979: 59–62). Such approaches can be labelled 'intentionalist' in the sense that they are concerned with implementing the intentions of the framers of the legislation. In its weakest sense, this intentionalist interpreter looks at evidence of one or another legislative meaning in instances in which the text of the statute is ambiguous and, therefore, the interpretive issue cannot be resolved solely by reference to the 'plain meaning' of the statute (see Eskridge and Frickey [1988] 1995: 525–31). Stronger versions of intentionalism are characterized by reliance on expressions of legislative intent in all instances of interpretation. So, even where the text of the statute seems to point clearly in one direction, the interpreter is entitled to look past the statute's words and towards indicia of the legislature's intent (see e.g. *Church of the Holy Trinity v. United States*).

Many of the modern controversies about statutory interpretation concern the question whether and to what extent it is proper to look at legislative intent to discern statutory meaning in either the 'weak' or the 'strong' senses described above. Moreover, there is substantial disagreement concerning the appropriate methods of discerning legislative intent, supposing that such intent is relevant to legislative interpretation. The economic analysis of law has made important contributions to these spirited debates. In particular, the contributions of public choice theory and positive political theory continue to bring important insights to the literature on legislative interpretation and, on the relationship among legislatures, courts, executive officials, and regulatory agencies.

1. LEGISLATIVE INTENT AND STATUTORY PURPOSE: A CONCEPTUAL FRAMEWORK

1.1. *Legislative intent and its critics.* The key jurisprudential tradition of modern American law is legal positivism. The core insight of our positivistic tradition is, following H.L.A. Hart ([1961] 1994: 185–6), that 'it is in no sense a necessary truth that laws reproduce or satisfy certain demands of morality, though in fact they have often done so'. Instead, what accords legitimacy to law is that it reflects the command of the sovereign as developed through proper, socially acceptable procedures (see Fuller 1964: 106–18). The principal contribution of the legal positivists to the enterprise of legislative interpretation is the following idea: The aspiration of statutory construction must be to discern the will of the law-giver, that is, the legislature. It is only by recovering this will – this *intent* – that we can accord the deference due to that institution whose responsibility it is to create the statutory law which binds individuals and institutions. Many modern legal theorists, most notably Ronald Dworkin, have vigorously criticized this positivistic premise (Dworkin 1986: 33–43). To them, the ambition of legal interpretation is quite different than that supposed by defenders of the view that law is the command of the sovereign and thus interpretation entails understanding the intent of this sovereign. To critics of legal positivism, then, legislative intent is a conceptual irrelevancy. Even supposing that something like a legislature's intent could be discerned, we ought to reject it, say critics of positivism, for there are other, superior ambitions for the enterprise of statutory interpretation (Moore 1985; Dworkin 1986; Hurd 1990; Eskridge 1994).

There is a very different critique of this positivistic insight, however, which does not rest on a non-positivisic jurisprudence. Rather, it rests on an empirical foundation, and one which comes along with its own set of descriptive theories about legislative behaviour and conduct. Critics object that legislative intent is not discernible; it is, for them, a chimerical concept, one which rests on a seriously flawed, and even incoherent, description of legislative decision-making. When we consider, in Part II, the contributions of public choice theory to statutory interpretation, we will address this critique in more detail. For now, it is sufficient just to describe the basic elements of the critique:

- Legislative intent supposes that a collective body can have an 'intent'. This is false, critics argue, for it relies on an analogy between the psychological make-up of an individual, an individual who has some degree of (free) will and can have the capacity to form intentions, purposes, make choices, and the like (Moore 1985: 348). This is a flawed analogy, however, since the legislature is a collective institution made up of n individuals, each with their own matrix of intentions and purposes.
- The conventional expressions of legislative intent relied upon by courts and agencies in the process of interpreting statutes are fundamentally unreliable. To the critics, so-called 'legislative history' is a patchwork quilt of incomplete, manufactured and ambiguous statements of self-selected legislators, each with their own axes to grind (see Easterbrook 1988: 63; Scalia 1997: 32–7). Thus, even if there were something like a collective intent of the legislature, we would be unlikely to discern it through the traditional mechanisms of legislative history and its translation through judicial and administrative excavations and interpretations.
- There is a critical failure to distinguish between the meaning of statutory words and phrases as *understood* by legislators when they are considering proposed legislation which is before them and the avowed *hopes* of the legislators with respect to how the legislation will be interpreted in the future (Dworkin 1985: 321–4). The difficulty of distinguishing between the legislature's understanding of the meaning of legislation and the legislature's hopes and wishes with respect to future interpretations confounds efforts to get at the legislature's *intent*.

Each of these critiques, and others, has been made over a long period of time by scholars and by judges. As evidenced by judicial outcomes, these critiques have had a substantial influence on the use of legislative intent by modern courts (see, e.g., *Wisconsin Public Intervenor v. Mortier* (Scalia, J., concurring); *K Mart v. Cartier*; *Macarthys Ltd. v. Smith*). Moreover, the leading scholarly perspectives on statutory interpretation are, in their own different ways, powerfully influenced by these empirical critiques of the use of legislative history and legislative intent (Sunstein 1990; Eskridge 1994).

1.2. *From intent to purpose – and back to intent.* An important effort to reclaim intentionalist interpretation from the critics of legislative history and intent was that of the 'Legal Process' theorists of the 1950s and 60s (see Eskridge and Frickey [1988] 1995: 395–8). Legal process scholars emphasized that the better enterprise of legislative interpretation was the recovery of the *purpose* of the statute, rather than the 'true' intent of the founding legislature. To Legal Process theorists, a consideration of purpose would be informed by, but not beholden to, expressions of legislators' individual and collective intentions. Where there were found conflicts between evidence of legislative intentions and statutory purposes, the proper role of the interpreter would be to implement the latter (see, e.g., *Moragne v. States Marine Lines, Inc.*).

Critics of this well-known approach objected that the notion of legislative purpose was also incoherent. How can an interpreter discern the purpose of a statute without relying in the end on the words of the statute itself and, where the text fails, the expressions of legislative intent as described in the statute's history? And, moreover, modern regulatory statutes frequently have multiple purposes. It became a commonplace to highlight complicated, ambiguous statutes and to use them to illustrate the descriptive and normative flaws in the 'purposive' account. As Cass Sunstein puts it, 'in the face of multimember institutions . . . the task of describing legislative "purpose" becomes as much creation as discovery' (1990: 124).

Yet, still and all, there proved to be something relentlessly appealing about the 'purposive' approach. Prominent legal scholars have offered important insights into how contemporary regulatory statutes can be understood and implemented more effectively by close attention to the multifaceted, manifest purposes underlying the regulatory programme constructed by the legislature (see Calabresi 1982; Sunstein 1990: 106–92). In the end, most contemporary commentators on statutory interpretation, save for those who are concerned with critiquing the basic jurisprudential traditions of American law and in offering a different vision of legal interpretation, are wedded to at least some version of legislative intent (see, e.g., Maltz 1988: 9–13; Shapiro 1992: 941–50; Schachter 1995: 593–95). The *intent* at issue, to be sure, is not solely or perhaps even especially the intent of the collective legislature *qua* legislature; it may be, per these more 'purposive' approaches, the intent of the legislation and the regulatory programme constructed by pieces of legislation as they are enacted by different legislatures over a period of time. Nonetheless, the attention is drawn in these views toward legislative intent and toward the ambition of discerning this intent through sophisticated, theoretically informed processes of interpretation (see Farber 1989, 1991).

There are two key sets of questions which lie at the heart of the spirited scholarly and judicial debate over the role of legislative intent in the interpretation and implementation of legislation. The first set of questions is informed by many of the issues described above: How should we think about legislative intent and its use in light of the serious empirical critiques of the concept? If we are not prepared yet to abandon the use of legislative intent in statutory interpretation, are there more fruitful ways to frame the idea of legislative intent with respect to particular statutes or to the enterprise of statutory interpretation more generally? The second set of questions concerns what role legislative intent plays in shaping decision-making by those individuals and institutions responsible for implementing statutes. Whatever the strength of the critiques of legislative intent, those who carry out statutory mandates emphasize the profound pertinence of legislative intent as expressed through legislative history in their own day-to-day operations. Any plausible positive and normative theory of legislative intent must account for the relationship among political institutions – including legislative institutions, agencies, courts, executive officials, business firms, and the like – as structured by the phenomena of expressed legislative intent *beyond* the four corners of the statute's text (see Pierce 1989).

As we will see in the remainder of this essay, the economic analysis of law and legal institutions has contributed in important ways to answering both these sets of questions. Two separate strands of analysis have been especially pertinent to the economic analysis of legislative intent. The first is the application of modern public choice theory to the understanding of legislative decision-making and, correlatively, legislative intent. The second is the more recent use of positive political theory to examinate legislative intent both with respect to positive and normative theories of statutory interpretation and also with respect to the political control of agencies and courts.

2. ECONOMIC ANALYSIS AND LEGISLATIVE INTENT: PUBLIC CHOICE

Work in the political economy tradition has contributed to positive and normative theories of legislative intent. The contributions of public choice, in particular, have reshaped many public law scholars' approaches to considering how legislative intent can be and should be used in interpreting legislation. By 'public choice' we mean to include two distinct strands of thinking about the application of economic theory to the study of political institutions: interest-group theory and social choice theory (see generally Farber and Frickey 1991; Mueller 1989).

2.1. *Interest group theory.* The standard view among legal scholars of the 1950s and 60s of the legislative process was summarized by Professors Henry Hart and Albert Sacks in their classic work on the legal process (1958). They described the legislature as an institution made up of 'reasonable persons pursuing reasonable aims reasonably'.

While this description was intended to communicate an essentially normative point about modern legislatures and their behaviour, this rosy view of legislative motivations was taken by legal scholars as a description of how legislators actually behave (see Rodriguez 1989). This account of legislative behaviour was subject to frank critique, of course, and much of standard pluralist political science of that same era, as exemplified in the work of Truman (1951), Dahl (1956), Lindblom (1965) and others, raised serious objections to this picture of benign, public-regarding lawmakers. Very much opposite to this view was the emerging public choice account offered by economists working within the Chicago–Virginia School tradition. In the writings of leading economists such as Buchanan and Tullock (1962), Stigler (1971), Peltzman (1976) and Becker (1983), public choice theory painted a picture of legislators acting with an eye toward re-election and thus carrying out their legislative responsibilities in a private-regarding, calculating fashion (see Stigler 1988; Farber and Frickey 1991). The critical behavioural assumption underlying the public choice theory of legislatures is that legislators are driven relentlessly toward the aim of re-election (see Mueller 1989: 1). The mechanisms of legislator self-interest are the ordinary sum and substance of legislating, including passage and defeat of legislation, regulatory oversight, appropriations decision-making, and legislative-executive contests. Also critical in the public choice account is the pervasive role of interest groups outside the legislature, groups which each press their own agenda on legislators. These groups have ubiquituous weapons to use on legislators, including the granting and withholding of favours, campaign contributions, information, and other resources, without which legislators would be unable to pursue effectively their aim of re-election. The legislative process, in this public choice account, is essentially a transmission belt for the translation of interest group preferences into public law (see Tollison 1988: 347–66).

Law and economics scholars building upon these interest group theories have drawn from the account of rent-seeking legislators descriptions of legislative intent and its proper impact on the enterprise of legislative interpretation (see Farber and Frickey 1988; Eskridge 1989). In an early important paper, Landes and Posner described the legislative process as a mechanism for supplying goods to interest groups which demanded such goods more or less along the lines described by textbook supply-and-demand principles (Landes and Posner 1975). The key problem, though, is that the bargains struck among interest groups and legislators, as manifest in statutes and regulations, could be unravelled by subsequent judicial interpretations. In the face of this risk, the costs which interest groups are willing to pay in the form of economic rents to self-regarding legislators are less than what would be expected in a market in which bargains are efficiently and reliably enforced (877–85). The solution to this predicament, argued Landes and Posner, was the commitment of the judiciary to enforcing the legislative bargain (885–7). This commitment was not the product of a benevolent, respectful judiciary but, instead, a result of the continuing dependence of the judiciary on legislative rewards and sanctions. The role played by legislative intent in this account is roughly as follows: The manifestations of legislative intent communicate to the courts the terms of the interest-group/legislator bargains struck. The intent of the statute makers is exactly like the intent of parties to a contract (see Hadfield 1992). Moreover, just as contemporary contract law absorbs the principle that contracts ought to be construed to implement drafters' intent, statutory interpretation will be – and perhaps ought to be – concerned with recovering the intent of the framers of the statute. In this account, public choice offers a simple heuristic for viewing the relationship among courts, legislators, and interest groups in the construction and subsequent enforcement of legislative intent (see Eskridge 1991; Farber 1991).

Relying upon public choice theory, Jonathan Macey (1986) provides an interesting and novel account of the use of legislative history in statutory interpretation. Macey relies on public choice theory to describe the essentially private-regarding behaviour of legislators in the statutory enactment process. Rather than concluding, however, that the legislation which gets enacted through this pernicious process is transparently private-regarding, he points out that many modern regulatory statutes speak in public-regarding terms (252–3). The environmental and consumer safety statutes of the 1960s and 70s, for example, reveal to the reader a picture of the benevolent federal government working to ensure clean air and water, safety in the workplace and on the highways. And civil rights legislation of the past quarter century similarly speaks in terms of the larger public interest, and not in terms of the narrow, factionalist concerns of pressure groups which were critical in securing the passage of these landmark statutes. So what explains this? To Macey, the idea is this: Legislators act self-interestedly, but still persist in maintaining a public-regarding face. To reveal themselves otherwise, that is, to behave as steely-eyed rent-seekers, would be to relinquish their public commitment to deliberative decision-making and representative democracy. In economic terms, behaving this way would increase substantially the transaction costs of legislating, in that legislators would have to communicate their private-regarding agendas expressly through statutory provisions and indicia of legislative history (227–33). And this is precisely the aim of Macey's prescriptive analysis. He argues that, on the basis of this public choice account, courts ought to require legislators to put their agendas up front; otherwise, courts should be instructed to interpret legislation in order to further the *expressed* (although, as public choice theory indicates, not real) intent of the legislature, that is, to pursue public-regarding goals (261–6).

Although interest group theory has contributed conspicuously to the analysis of legislative intent, it has rather serious limitations as an analytical source of insight (see Pildes and Anderson 1990; Stearns 1994). To begin with, it is empirically problematic to describe the contemporary legislative process as *solely* or even *mostly* characterized by raw wealth-transfers from the public fisc to interest groups (see Kelman 1988: 205–23). To be sure, if we broaden our definition of interest groups to include clusters of factions and pressure groups who are motivated to overcome collective action problems and participate in influencing the legislative process, then the public choice account is more likely to be descriptively accurate, but trivially so. The analytic punch of public choice theory lies in its view of the legislative process as rife with rent-seeking behaviour and economic wealth transfers. The strong view, as exemplified by lawyers and economists working within the traditions set by the Chicago–Virginia School, have added substantial but, in the end, limited contributions to unravelling the conundrum of legislative intent.

2.2. *Social choice theory.* Social choice theory frames the issue of legislative intent in two opposite ways. First, the standard social choice picture, following Arrow (1951) and Black (1958) reveals the legislature as subject to cycling and thus prone to chaos. Legislative outcomes are, if not entirely random, then not necessarily indicative of the preferences of the collective as made up of *n* legislators at a given point in time (see McKelvey 1976; Austen-Smith and Riker 1987). No suitable equilibria are possible in a decision-making environment in which legislative decisions come up more or less randomly and in which legislators face multifaceted, interdependent choices among a range of alternatives. Thus, to speak of legislative intent is to chase a chimera; the revealed intent is no more nor less than what happens to emerge at the final stage of the process when legislators are asked to cast a vote for or against the proposal which is currently on the table (Easterbrook 1983; Shepsle 1992). To be sure, we can rely on the expression of intent as gleaned from the text of the legislation, but the utility of legislative history in communicating the true intent of the legislature when the statute's text is ambiguous disappears in the face of the Arrovian characterization of the legislative process as chaotic and unstable.

A very different framing of the issue of legislative intent is provided by the recent efforts of political economists to describe how chaos may be met by institutional structures and procedural rules. Arrow himself, of course, noted ways in which decision-making cycles could be corrected by procedural devices under a number of conditions (Arrow [1951] 1963: 22 et seq.). And much of the work in the vein of structure-induced equilibrium (SIE) theory explains theoretically and empirically how the otherwise chaotic legislative process is addressed deliberately by rational legislators (Shepsle 1979; Tullock 1981; Shepsle and Weingast 1987). Examples of these structures include the regulatory power of the US Congress's Rules Committee (Weingast 1992), the system of bicameralism (Levmore 1992), and the assorted rules of legislative committee jurisdiction and procedures (Shepsle and Weingast 1987).

The strand of social choice theory reflected in SIE theory and related work has a more ambivalent relationship to the notion of legislative intent than do other strands of public choice theory. On the one hand, the idea that legislators craft structures and procedures to enable themselves to pursue legislative strategies does undergird the idea that legislators have purposes and even intentions. While these intentions may be more malevolent than benign and are, at any rate, strategic rather than exclusively principled, we might still recover from an economic perspective on the legislative process a theory of the intent of the enacting legislature. What is more problematic, though, is creating from this positive theory of legislative intent any fruitful normative suggestions.

2.3. *Public choice theory as normative theory.* The public choice account, and especially Chicago–Virginia-style interest group theory, paints a rather bleak picture of legislative behaviour and statute-making processes. It is no coincidence, surely, that with the rise of public choice theory as an influential analytic framework for understanding legislation and public law, there has been a growing scepticism among legal scholars about the utility of legislative intent in statutory interpretation. As mentioned in Part 1 of this essay, there is hardly anyone among contemporary public law scholars who make use of public choice theory to any degree who defends vigorously the idea of legislative intent as a coherent concept which can be and should be used by agencies and courts in implementing and interpreting legislation.

If public choice theory is swallowed whole as a complete theoretical account of legislative processes, then it becomes difficult to prescribe the use of legislative intent; and it is correspondingly easier to criticize, as do judges such as Supreme Court Justice Antonin Scalia (1997) and circuit judges Frank Easterbrook (1983, 1988) and Alex Kozinski (*Wallace v. Christensen*), the still commonplace reliance on legislative history as indicia of legislative intent in statutory interpretation cases. Yet, the more sophisticated political economists have reconsidered in recent years the standard public choice critiques of legislative intent and interpretation and have generated fruitful economic accounts of legislative decision-making and court-legislative-agency relationships which, if connected to prescriptive theory in sensible ways, may frame the debate about legislative intent and its (mis)use in much more interesting terms. In the remaining section of this essay, we will consider some of the applications of *positive political theory* to the study of legislative intent.

3. ECONOMIC ANALYSIS AND LEGISLATIVE INTENT: POSITIVE POLITICAL THEORY

In recent years, a number of prominent political economists have been exploring, through the lens of game theory and principal-agent theory, the structure and behaviour of political institutions. Following Riker and Ordeshook (1973), these political economists have labelled this cluster of approaches *positive political theory* (PPT), meaning the application of rational choice theory to the study of political institutions (Farber and Frickey 1992: 462). These contributions differ fundamentally from the public choice enterprise in that they do not presuppose a re-election-maximizing, rent-seeking legislature, nor do they argue that legislation is primarily the product of external interest group influence. Instead, the enterprise of positive political theorists who study legislatures is to consider how rational legislators carry out legislative and regulatory functions within the structure of political and legal institutions, institutions with sets of *ex ante* rules, norms, and patterns of conduct. One of the key insights of PPT is that legislators must take account of the actions and reactions of other rational political actors each with their own set of incentives and political weapons (see Marks 1988; Eskridge and Ferejohn 1992). The elements of game theory, in both very simple and more complicated iterations, have yielded many original and arresting conclusions about the nature of legislative decision-making and of court–legislature–executive relationships (see Rodriguez 1994: 42–110).

One key idea expressed memorably by Kenneth Shepsle (1992) is that the legislature is a 'they' not an 'it'. In contrast, to standard median-voter models of legislative behaviour (models with homogenized collective legislative action which thereby undergird the view that the legislature can have, as an individual, an *intent*), Shepsle stresses the fact that the legislature is more accurately described as a nexus of institutions, institutions with cross-cutting responsibilities and functions. Building upon different strands of economic theory, including social choice theory and structure-induced equilibrium theory, Shepsle and his PPT cohort explain that legislative intent will always be difficult to express through the heuristic of individual, quasi-psychological concepts such as *intentions* and *purposes*. Instead, we would do well to understand the multifaceted quality of legislative behaviour by considering inter-institutional relationships organized around the strategies of legislators working within the structures of the law-making process, including all of its legislative, executive, and judicial features.

Each of these institutions is situated differently with respect to legislative intent. For example, legislators craft and oversee the progress of legislative proposals through the committee system. Much of the fundamental decision-making which goes into the shape of the legislative proposal that comes to the floor for the consideration of the body proceeds through strategizing by rational legislators at the committee and even the pre-committee (through self-selection onto committees) stage (Shepsle and Weingast 1987: 88–90; Weingast and Marshall 1988: 143–55). Yet much of what is conventionally labelled pertinent legislative history is constructed post-committee. These include legislator floor statements, conference committee reports, and presidential signing statements (Rodriguez 1992). It is difficult to draw from a PPT model of legislative bargaining, then, a justification for traditional uses of legislative history.

Another key insight of PPT is the dichotomy stressed between the *enacting* legislative coalition and the *current* coalition. Conventionally, reliance on legislative intent in statutory interpretation means reliance on the intent of the legislature which enacted the statute, even if this legislature is, after all, long gone. At the same time, the superintendence of regulatory policy-making, including the legislative reactions to certain implementations and interpretations of a statute, is carried out not by the framers of the original statute, but by the current legislature. While we might hope, as a normative matter, that the current legislative majority will pay suitable fidelity to the expectations of the enacting majority coalition, a rational, self-interested group of legislators may well have little incentive to so circumscribe their own conduct. Using game-theoretic models of legislature/court/agency action under conditions of perfect information and inconsequential transaction costs, PPT explains how this tension between the will of the enacting legislature and the will of current legislators plays out in single-dimensional and multiple-dimensional policy spaces (Ferejohn and Weingast 1992a).

Schwartz, Spiller and Urbitzondo (1994) have considered, by means of game theoretic analysis, the role of legislative intent in signalling to courts the preferences of legislators. The basic idea is that, to the extent that it is costly to legislators to enact specific laws, legislation that is itself ambiguous signals to the courts that it is less important to self-interested legislators. Moreover, one way to communicate these preferences is through use of supplementary materials to indicate the legislators' intent. 'To the extent that legislative history and other supplementary materials can provide as informative a signal as can more precise statutory language, these materials may be a preferable source of that signal, as they can be provided at lower cost' (ibid., 72).

PPT leaves us with a basic normative question, however, to wit: Ought we to pay complete fidelity to the will of the enacting legislature on the theory that it is only this will which should, given our democratic theories, govern us? Or should we, as a matter of *realpolitik*, work to accommodate processes of regulatory decision-making to the often competing wills of legislators across periods of time? Recent PPT work has addressed itself to this and related normative questions. McNollgast (1992, 1994) and others have described the legislative–judicial relationship as an essentially *communicative* activity. Rational, self-interested legislators are concerned not only with the enacting process, but also with the process of conveying their majority will into implementation through suitable interpretations. They wish to do so not only through careful statutory drafting (an ambition which is not always possible considering the cross-cutting incentives of legislative opponents), but also through the creation of self-serving legislative histories. Much of this constructed history is an elaborate project of spin control; legislators communicate their spin on the meaning of legislative phrases and sections. At the same time, the statute's opponents simultaneously insist upon a different, and frequently more narrow, explanation of ambiguous statutory language (Ferejohn and Weingast 1992b: 570–74; McNollgast 1994: 21–9).

An interesting feature of this communicative process noted by PPT scholars such as McNollgast is that the legislative coalitions are multiple; there are not only *supporters* and *opponents* of legislation but, rather, ardent supporters, ardent opponents, and pivotal legislators, the latter group consisting of legislators whose support is critical to the enactment of legislation and whose expressions of views concerning the meaning of statutory provisions are, and should be, often decisive in construing the intent and purpose of controversial legislation (McNollgast 1994: 16–21; but see Jorgensen and Shepsle 1994). In one study, the authors considered the the passage of the Civil Rights Act of 1964 and described the pivotal role of Republican moderates, and especially Senator Everett Dirksen of Illinois, who craftily steered the very liberal House-reported version of the civil rights legislation toward a more moderate course (Rodriguez and Weingast 1995). Despite the fact that throughout the entire deliberation process, and continuing on into the aftermath, ardent supporters such as Senator Hubert Humphrey trumpeted the Act as a far-reaching, ultra-liberal piece of legislation, the true process reveals a much more complex, ambiguous, and ultimately moderate legislative outcome.

From a normative perspective, this complexity is welcome. The process of communication within and among members of legislative coalitions enables ideological legislators, each pursuing their own interests however constituted, to get things done. McNollgast have suggested a series of *positive canons*, essentially guides to statutory construction which would, if employed, tie the process of statutory interpretation to a more sensible and sophisticated reading of legislative intent (1992). These canons include a closer look at the makeup of the three legislative coalitions described above. Since attention to legislative intent usually means attention to the views expressed by particular legislators at a given point in time, a concern with 'where these legislators are coming from' is a prudent mechanism for recollecting more accurate legislative intent (1992: 718–25). Another valuable positive canon is the attention to the structure and dynamics of intra-legislative institutions such as conference committees; these committees are often the most revealing of the nature and scope of legislative compromise, insofar as the final decisions about legislative content are shaped through communications among these select groups of legislators (1992: 725–7).

Among the avenues of future PPT contributions to our understanding of legislative intent, three stand out. First, more refinements of the notion of legislative communication are called for, especially with regard to empirical studies of specific legislative episodes and events. PPT scholars can gain greater purchase in understanding the interrelationships among legislative coalitions in the process of statute-making and, as well, the relationships among legislators, courts, and agencies in the implementation of legislative bargains, by developing more fully this idea of communicative action. Second, economic theory can be useful in exploring, through the idea of scarcity, the role of transaction costs in the consideration of legislative decision-making and the construction of legislative intent. Legislators face ubiquitous transaction costs in the course of statute-making. These costs include monitoring costs, opportunity costs, and error costs. Through the application of PPT, the role of costs ought to be considered more systematically and, in particular, by close attention to the way in which intra-legislative transaction costs can shape legislative and regulatory outcomes (see Schwartz et al. 1994; Rodriguez 1997). Finally, PPT can be a useful way to compare and contrast different legislative systems. While much of the focus of PPT work has been on the United States Congress, we can also consider how to evaluate the performance of other legislative institutions (state and local) within the United States, as well as legislative systems abroad.

4. CONCLUSION

The mystery of legislative intent has confounded the project of statutory interpretation since the time of Blackstone. Efforts to unravel the intentions and purposes of the heterogeneous legislature will always be problematic since collective institutions, by their nature, are filled with complex, inchoate motivations and clusters of preferences. Reducing the legislative 'they' to an 'it' has left us with a very unsatisfying account of the structure of modern legislation and its meaning. Nonetheless, our commitment to legal positivism requires us to continue to try to give a theoretically sophisticated account of legislative intent. Economic analysis, through the contributions of both public choice theory and positive political theory, has provided able assistance to that end.

DANIEL B. RODRIGUEZ

See also AGENCY COST AND ADMINISTRATIVE LAW; JUDICIAL INDEPENDENCE; JUDICIAL REVIEW; LEGAL POSITIVISM; POLITICAL CONTROL OF THE BUREAUCRACY; PUBLIC CHOICE AND THE LAW; STATE POWER; STATUTORY INTERPRETATION AND RATIONAL CHOICE THEORIES.

Subject classification: 3c; 3e.

CASES

Church of the Holy Trinity v. US, 143 US 457 (1892).
K Mart v. Cartier, Inc., 486 US 281 (1988).
Macarthys Ltd v. Smith [1979] 3 All ER 325.
Moragne v. States Marine Lines, Inc., 398 US 375 (1970).
Wallace v. Christensen, 802 F2d 1539 (9th Cir. 1986).
Wisconsin Public Intervenor v. Mortier, 501 US 597 (1991).

BIBLIOGRAPHY

Arrow, K. 1951. *Social Choice and Individual Values*. New York: John Wiley; 2nd edn, 1963.

Austen-Smith, D. and Riker, W. 1987. Asymmetric information and the coherence of legislation. *American Political Science Review* 81: 897–918.

Becker, G. 1983. A theory of competition among pressure groups for political influence. *Quarterly Journal of Economics* 98: 371–400.

Black, D. 1958. *The Theory of Committees and Elections*. Cambridge: Cambridge University Press.

Blackstone, W. 1765. *Commentaries on the Laws of England*, Volume I. Facsimile reprint, Chicago: University of Chicago Press, 1979.

Buchanan, J. and Tullock, G. 1962. *The Calculus of Consent*. Ann Arbor: University of Michigan Press.

Calabresi, G. 1982. *A Common Law for the Age of Statutes*. Cambridge, MA: Harvard University Press.

Dahl, R. 1956. *A Preface to Democratic Theory*. Chicago: University of Chicago Press.

Dworkin, R. 1985. *A Matter of Principle*. Cambridge, MA: Harvard University Press.

Dworkin, R. 1986. *Law's Empire*. Cambridge, MA: Harvard University Press.

Easterbrook, F. 1983. Statutes' domains. *University of Chicago Law Review* 50: 533–52.

Easterbrook, F. 1988. The role of original intent in statutory construction. *Harvard Journal of Law and Public Policy* 11: 59–66.

Eskridge, W., Jr. 1989. Politics without romance: implications of public choice theory for statutory interpretation. *Virginia Law Review* 74: 275–338.

Eskridge, W., Jr. 1991. Reneging on history? Playing the court/congress/president civil rights game. *California Law Review* 79: 613–84.

Eskridge, W., Jr. 1994. *Dynamic Statutory Interpretation*. Cambridge, MA: Harvard University Press.

Eskridge, W., Jr. and Ferejohn, J. 1992. The Article I, Section 7 game. *Georgetown Law Journal* 80: 523–64.

Eskridge, W., Jr. and Frickey, P. 1988. *Cases and Materials on Legislation: Statutes and the Creation of Public Policy*. St. Paul, MN: West Publishing Company; 2nd edn, 1995.

Eskridge, W., Jr. and Frickey, P. 1994. Foreword: law as equilibrium. *Harvard Law Review* 108: 26–104.

Farber, D. 1989. Statutory interpretation and legislative supremacy. *Georgetown Law Journal* 78: 281–318.

Farber, D. 1991. Legislative deals and statutory bequests. *Minnesota Law Review* 75: 667–89.

Farber, D. and Frickey, P. 1988. Legislative intent and public choice. *Virginia Law Review* 74: 423–69.

Farber, D. and Frickey, P. 1991. *Law and Public Choice: A Critical Introduction*. Chicago: University of Chicago Press.

Farber, D. and Frickey, P. 1992. Foreword: positive political theory in the nineties. *Georgetown Law Journal* 80: 457–76.

Ferejohn, J. and Weingast, B. 1992a. A positive theory of statutory interpretation. *International Review of Law and Economics* 12: 263–79.

Ferejohn, J. and Weingast, B. 1992b. Limitation of statutes: strategic statutory interpretation. *Georgetown Law Journal* 80: 565–82.

Fuller, L. 1964. *The Morality of Law*. New Haven: Yale University Press.

Hadfield, G. 1992. Commentary: incomplete contracts and statutes. *International Review of Law and Economics* 12: 257–59.

Hart, H.L.A. 1961. *The Concept of Law*. Oxford: Clarendon Press; 2nd edn, 1994.

Hart, H. and Sacks, A. 1958. *The Legal Process: Basic Problems in the Making and Application of Law*. Cambridge, MA: Harvard University Press; rev. edn, ed. W. Eskridge, Jr. and P. Frickey, Westbury, NY: Foundation Press, 1994.

Hurd, H. 1990. Sovereignty in silence. *Yale Law Journal* 95: 945–1028.

Jorgensen, M. and Shepsle, K. 1994. A comment on the positive canons project. *Law and Contemporary Problems* 57: 43–9.

Kelman, M. 1988. On democracy-bashing: a skeptical look at the theoretical and 'empirical' practice of the public choice movement. *Virginia Law Review* 74: 199–273.

Landes, W. and Posner, R. 1975. The independent judiciary in an interest-group perspective. *Journal of Law and Economics* 18: 875–901.

Levmore, S. 1992. Bicameralism: when are two decisions better than one? *International Review of Law and Economics* 12: 145–62.

Lindblom, C. 1965. *The Intelligence of Democracy: Decision Making through Mutual Adjustment*. New York: Free Press.

Macey, J. 1986. Promoting public-regarding legislation through statutory interpretation: an interest group model. *Columbia Law Review* 86: 223–68.

Maltz, E. 1988. Statutory interpretation and legislative power: the case for a modified intentionalist approach. *Tulane Law Review* 63: 1–28.

Marks, B. 1988. A model of judicial influence of Congressional policy making: *Grove City College v. Bell*. Hoover Institution Working Paper, Stanford University, Stanford, CA.

McKelvey, R. 1976. Intransitivities in multidimensional voting models and some implications for agenda control. *Journal of Economic Theory* 12: 472–82.

McNollgast [McCubbins, M., Noll, R. and Weingast, B.]. 1992. Positive canons: the role of legislative bargains in statutory interpretation. *Georgetown Law Journal* 80: 705–42.

McNollgast. 1994. Legislative intent: the use of positive political theory in statutory interpretation. *Law and Contemporary Problems* 57: 3–37.

Moore, M. 1985. A natural law theory of interpretation. *Southern California Law Review* 58: 279–398.

Mueller, D. 1989. *Public Choice II*. Cambridge: Cambridge University Press.

Peltzman, S. 1976. Toward a more general theory of regulation. *Journal of Law and Economics* 19: 211–40.

Pierce, R. Jr., 1989. The role of the judiciary in implementing an agency theory of government. *New York University Law Review* 64: 1239–85.

Pildes, R. and Anderson, E. 1990. Slinging arrows at democracy: social choice theory, value pluralism, and democratic politics. *Columbia Law Review* 90: 2121–2214.

Posner, R. 1989. Legislation and its interpretation: a primer. *Nebraska Law Review* 68: 431–53.

Posner, R. 1990. *The Problems of Jurisprudence*. Cambridge, MA: Harvard University Press.

Riker, W. and Ordeshook, P. 1973. *An Introduction to Positive Political Theory*. Prentice-Hall Contemporary Political Theory Series; Englewood Cliffs, NJ: Prentice Hall.

Rodriguez, D. 1989. The substance of the new legal process. *California Law Review* 77: 919–53.

Rodriguez, D. 1992. Statutory interpretation and political advantage. *International Review of Law and Economics* 12: 217–31.

Rodriguez, D. 1994. The positive political dimensions of regulatory reform. *Washington University Law Quarterly* 72: 1–150.

Rodriguez, D. 1997. The transaction costs of legislating. Mimeo, University of California, Berkeley, CA.

Rodriguez, D. and Weingast, B. 1995. Legislative history, statutory interpretation, and the Civil Rights Act of 1964. Mimeo, University of California, Berkeley.

Rubin, E. 1991. Beyond public choice: comprehensive rationality in the writing and reading of statutes. *New York University Law Review* 66: 1–64.

Scalia, A. 1989. The rule of law as a law of rules. *University of Chicago Law Review* 56: 1175–1188.

Scalia, A. 1997. *A Matter of Interpretation*. Princeton: Princeton University Press.

Schachter, J. 1995. Metademocracy: the changing structure of legitimacy in statutory interpretation. *Harvard Law Review* 108: 593–663.

Schwartz, E., Spiller, P. and Urbitzondo, S. 1994. A positive theory of legislative intent. *Law and Contemporary Problems* 57: 51–74.

Shapiro, D. 1992. Continuity and change in statutory interpretation. *New York University Law Review* 67: 921–59.

Shepsle, K. 1979. Institutional arrangements and equilibrium in multidimensional voting models. *American Journal of Political Science* 23: 27–59.

Shepsle, K. 1992. Congress is a 'they' not an 'it': legislative intent as oxymoron. *International Review of Law and Economics* 12: 239–56.

Shepsle, K. and Weingast, B. 1981. Structure-induced equilibrium and legislative choice. *Public Choice* 37: 503–19.

Shepsle, K. and Weingast, B. 1987. The institutional foundations of committee power. *American Political Science Review* 81: 85–104.

Stearns, M. 1994. The misguided renaissance of social choice. *Yale Law Journal* 103: 1219–93.

Stigler, G. 1971. The theory of economic regulation. *Bell Journal of Economics and Management* 2: 3–21.

Stigler, G. (ed.) 1988. *Chicago Studies in Political Economy*. Chicago: University of Chicago Press.

Sunstein, C. 1990. *After the Rights Revolution*. Cambridge, MA: Harvard University Press.

Tollison, R. 1988. Public choice and legislation. *Virginia Law Review* 74: 339–71.

Truman, D. 1951. *The Governmental Process*. New York: Alfred A. Knopf.

Tullock, G. 1981. Why so much stability? *Public Choice* 37: 189–202.

Weingast, B. 1992. Fighting fire with fire: amending activity and institutional change in the postreform Congress. In *The Postreform Congress*, ed. R. Davidson, New York: St. Martin's Press.

Weingast, B. and Marshall, W. 1988. The industrial organization of Congress; or why legislatures, like firms, are not organized as markets. *Journal of Political Economy* 96: 132–63.

Zeppos, N. 1990. Legislative history and the interpretation of statutes: toward a fact-finding model of statutory interpretation. *Virginia Law Review* 76: 1295–1374.

leveraged buyouts. A leveraged buyout, put simply, is a corporate control transaction in which new investors of a firm acquire a modest equity stake while the firm itself takes on significant new debt and uses this new debt to repurchase the equity held by the old shareholders. There is a *buyout*, because the equity of the firm has changed hands. The buyout is *leveraged* because the firm now carries a much higher debt burden. Hence, understanding leveraged buyouts requires us to understand the link between ownership of a firm and its capital structure. Doing this, however, requires us to solve the central mystery of finance (see Myers 1984). As long as this mystery persists, our ability to understand either the economic forces underlying leveraged buyouts or the legal rules that govern them will necessarily remain incomplete. At present, the best we can do is set out a few basic landmarks.

BACKGROUND. The bedrock of modern corporate finance is the Modigliani and Miller indifference proposition (see Modigliani and Miller 1958). It establishes that, in perfect capital markets, a firm's capital structure has no effect on its value. In increasing its debt, a firm makes its cost of equity cheaper, but at the same time raises its cost of debt by an equal and offsetting amount. By establishing the irrelevance of capital structure in perfect capital markets, the Modigliani and Miller indifference proposition tells us that we can talk coherently about capital structure only if we are able to identify the ways in which capital markets are imperfect. The Modigliani and Miller indifference proposition, for example, assumes away the different tax treatment accorded debt and equity. Similarly, it does not take account of the effects of a buyout on pre-existing investors (see Miller 1988). If leveraged buyouts take place only because investors enjoy tax benefits or only because new owners are benefited at the expense of old ones, there is no harm if the law discourages them.

At this point, however, we should not get ahead of ourselves. Before we approach the giant transactions, such as the $20 billion buyout of RJR-Nabisco, we should look at the situation in which the leveraged buyout most commonly arose before the 1980s and which, in absolute numbers if not total asset value, remains the most common.

Much economic activity takes place in small, closely held firms. We tend to underestimate its magnitude, because so much of it is invisible to the consumer. The first-aid kit we buy may bear the label of a Fortune 500 company, but the firm that made the metal box in which the medicine and bandages are stored is likely a closely held firm. The breakfast cereal we eat may bear the label of a giant corporation, but the firm that printed the label is likely privately held. Such firms may have hundreds of employees and annual revenues in the tens of millions of dollars. All told, they account for perhaps 40% of all economic activity in the United States. Many of these firms (almost a third) have no institutional debt. The only debt may be a mortgage on the real property and short-term trade debt, the amount of which is trivial in comparison to the asset value of a firm (see Petersen and Raghuram 1993).

These firms typically have a single owner-manager or a small group of owner-managers. Indeed, for such firms, there are substantial benefits from having ownership and control in the same hands. Hence, when the principal retires, not only will management change, but a transfer of ownership to the new manager is both likely and desirable. This issue is now one of crucial importance in the United States because so many closely held firms came into being shortly after World War II and their owners are now retiring. The United States will see a transfer of wealth from one generation to another over the next ten to fifteen years that is unprecedented in human history, and much of this wealth is tied up in closely held firms.

Let us imagine a manufacturing firm with sales of $10 million a year and profits each year of $1 million. The firm is worth $10 million. There are short-term trade creditors, but this debt turns over completely every sixty days and the total amount is never more than $200,000. The founder of the firm brought his son-in-law into the business some years before, and he has proved an able manager. Over time, the son-in-law has acquired an equity stake of 25%. When the founder of such a firm decides to retire, a leveraged buyout is often a most sensible course. The founder wants to keep a minority interest in the firm, but wants to sell 50% of the firm's equity to obtain a fixed income stream, not only for his own peace of mind, but because he needs to provide for his wife who will likely live longer than he.

The son-in-law does not have sufficient wealth to buy the founder's stake outright. The fixed assets of the business, however, are themselves worth several million, and the founder is willing to take a note to be paid out over a period of time in addition to some cash. The leveraged buyout begins with a secured bank loan of $2 million and an equity contribution of the son-in-law of $1 million. The founder then sells 50% of the equity for $3 million in cash and the firm's promissory note. The note is subordinated to the obligation to the bank. All the trade creditors are informed of the transaction. The firm goes from one that had assets of $10 million and perhaps $200,000 in debt to one that still has assets of $10 million, but liabilities in excess of $4 million.

This transaction seems unobjectionable. The firm is one in which the owner and manager of the firm should be one and the same, but the optimal owner-manager (the one with both the requisite skill and the firm-specific human capital) had insufficient liquidity for the firm to remain an all-equity firm. The bank's loan is fully secured, but, even if it were not, the bank entered the transaction with its eyes open. The trade creditors face a riskier debtor, but they are fully informed about the transaction and, because their debt is short-term, they can simply cease shipping goods to the firm on open account. More to the point, even after the leveraged buyout, the firm is not that highly leveraged relative to other firms in the same industry.

This mundane transaction helps us keep things in perspective. The advanced tools of corporate finance do much to help us understand a wide variety of complicated transactions. For the most common and basic leveraged buyouts, however, the transactions take place and are desirable for straightforward reasons. Much of our economy depends on firms in which ownership and management are one and the same. Some transfers of this dual role will be to a person or small group of people who face liquidity constraints that the initial owner-manager may not have had. It is only when the leveraged buyouts become more exotic that explanations for them become harder to find. It is to that subject that we turn next.

LEVERAGED BUYOUTS OF LARGE FIRMS. It is not easy to explain why the 1980s brought a sudden increase in the number of leveraged buyouts. Our inability to explain why a transaction takes place undercuts our ability to understand the legal rules that should govern it. Most of the obvious explanations for leveraged buyouts are wanting because they explain either the buyout or the leverage, but not why the two take place together.

Some, for example, have suggested that leveraged buyouts involve a wealth transfer from workers to the shareholders. It is possible that the buyout may bring in owners who are willing to change the norms that had previously governed relations between workers and management. New managers who lack any relationship with the workers and feel no obligation to them might be willing to alter the pension plan or alter compensation schemes to exploit the firm-specific human capital that long-time employees had sunk into the firm. The wealth effects of such changes, however, seem able to explain only a small part of the premium that the new owners pay in leveraged buyouts (see Lichtenberg and Siegal 1990). Nor is it obvious why old and new managers should have different sentiments about the workers. In any event, one has to ask not only why the new managers could take actions that the old managers did not, but also why these managers also wanted to increase the firm's debt at the same time.

New owners can exploit workers without borrowing more than the old owners did. Nothing in the nature of things suggests that owner-managers who are particularly hard-nosed with respect to labour relations should also want a lot of debt. In the typical leveraged buyout, the new shareholders and creditors are typically a small group of old managers, venture capitalists, banks and junk-bond financiers. They can create any capital structure they want and divide the returns from the enterprise any way they want. There are not liquidity, regulatory or other obvious constraints that would push them towards high leverage.

Another explanation begins with the idea that a sudden increase in the debt of a firm makes existing creditors worse off and equity holders correspondingly better off. The available empirical evidence, however, suggests that wealth transfers from creditors to shareholders rarely drive these transactions (see Asquith and Wizman 1990). For example, the premium offered to the stockholders of RJR-Nabisco was in the region of $10 billion. The total amount owed to pre-existing creditors was only half this amount. Even if the creditors lost everything (and they lost only a tenth as much), their losses still could not explain why the new investors were willing to buy the old shareholders out at an enormous premium.

More to the point, creditors face these losses in any case in which the firm enters into a transaction involving shareholders that has the same economic effect as a dividend. A leveraged buyout is only one way of engaging in this kind of transaction. By having the firm repurchase stock, existing equity holders could capture wealth from creditors without selling their stake. Astute creditors can sharply limit the ability of the shareholders to engage in all such transactions. Nothing compels the shareholders to enter into a leveraged buyout to capture these gains. Again, increasing the value of equity by shifting risk to creditors explains the leverage, but not the buyout.

Leveraged buyouts can bring tax benefits. Tax explanations for leveraged buyouts, however, founder on the same two objections lodged against the idea that buyouts came into being to transfer large sums of wealth from existing creditors to the new investors. (US corporate tax law, for example, allows a firm to deduct interest from its income, but not dividend payments. Higher leverage may therefore reduce a firm's overall tax bill.) The available empirical evidence does suggest that such tax benefits can be quite substantial. They may approach and, in some cases, even exceed the size of the premium the old shareholders receive. Nevertheless, in the aggregate, they explain less than half of the premium that is paid for the old shares (see Kaplan 1989). Even if tax benefits drive the transactions, they do not explain why the transaction includes a change in ownership.

A convincing explanation for leveraged buyouts must connect the change in control with the change in corporate structure (see Jensen 1989). One might begin by positing that the kind of agency costs a firm faces may change as it becomes more or less leveraged. As the nature of these costs shifts, the ownership structure that minimizes them might need to change as well. For example, assume that a change in tax law makes it advantageous for the firm to be highly leveraged. Because of this change, even a small change in the business climate will put the lenders' money at risk. Moreover, both the managers and the shareholders have incentives to take risks that they might not assume under other circumstances.

A change in governance structure that made monitoring more direct might be desirable (see Jensen 1986). In short, a shift to more debt may itself make a different form of ownership more attractive. The assets of a mature firm may be put to their best use in the hands of a new group of owners. Leverage makes it possible for those who provide equity, but do not manage the firm, to sit on the board. The smaller the equity in the firm, the easier it becomes for a few individuals to own the bulk of it. A small group of venture capitalists may be better able to navigate financial distress than dispersed public shareholders and, for this reason, this group can take advantage of the discipline that a high debt load imposes on managers. By tying up the cash flow of the firm, the managers of the firm will have to re-enter credit markets in order to start new ventures. The market subjects the managers to far greater scrutiny than they would receive if they could reinvest large internal cash flows into new projects. This outcome may be desirable in a mature industry (such as the food or petrochemical industry, for example) where billions should not be lightly invested in new plant and equipment.

The leveraged buyout allows managers, even of large firms, to hold large equity stakes. It therefore increases the extent to which losses from bad investments come out of the pockets of the managers. Managers are less likely to spend hundreds of millions on a state-of-the-art factory that makes a cookie that is a little less likely to break when packaged. Similarly, managers are less apt, after a buyout, to want to maintain corporate jets or sink a fortune into redecorating their offices if such expenses come out of their own pockets. Not only have they invested in the firm with their own assets, but they may have issued personal guarantees on the bank loans. A failure of the firm will lead to the loss of their homes. This prospect, like that of being hanged in a fortnight, concentrates the mind wonderfully.

LEVERAGED BUYOUTS AND THE LAW'S ROLE. A leveraged buyout, like any other kind of transaction, may bring with it losers as well as winners. It by no means follows, however, that legal intervention is necessary or even desirable. Indeed, the foundations of our modern understanding of corporate law send a note of caution. Corporate law is at bottom contractual (see Easterbrook and Fischel 1991). Creditors rely on their loan covenants (see Smith and Warner 1979). In the closely held firm, the institutional lender will usually include in the loan agreement the right to declare a default when there are 'reasonable grounds for insecurity', a clause broad enough to ensure that a default could be declared whenever there was a leveraged buyout. Loan agreements often also include covenants that sharply limit the ability of a firm to take on substantial additional debt or issue dividends (or their economic equivalent). Through any of these devices, large creditors can prevent leveraged buyouts from reducing the value of their rights.

One can take things a step further. Not only can creditors protect themselves from the bad effects of leveraged buyouts through contract, but the leveraged buyout itself is a device that plays an important role in ensuring that the market for corporate control curbs the agency costs associated with the separation of ownership and management. The most colourful part of the RJR-Nabisco buyout concerned the abuses of the existing managers, such as the use of a corporate jet to transport the CEO's German shepherd and extravagant outings to corporate-sponsored golf tournaments. The CEO was heard, when questioned about such things, to observe, 'A few million dollars are lost in the sands of time' (Burrough and Helyar 1990: 72). Whatever else, the buyout put a stop to all these excesses. Whenever the market itself may curtail mischief, one has to worry that a legal rule, by constraining market mechanisms, may do as much harm as good.

To be sure, the perceived abuses in RJR may not so much justify leveraged buyouts as suggest that stronger laws are needed to limit the ability of managers to profit at the expense of shareholders. Indeed, one might argue further that the ability of the managers to join with outsiders in leveraged buyouts and capture unknown gains is exactly one of the abuses that legal rules should prevent, because shareholders cannot easily contract for such protections.

Devising such legal rules, however, is easier said than done. As hard as it may be for shareholders to control managerial abuse, it may be even harder to craft general legal rules that do any better. In a second-best world, a legal system's refusal to limit leveraged buyouts, notwithstanding their potential costs, may be preferable to the legal rules we would have to add to keep managerial abuse at the same level. The ability of outsiders to use a leveraged buyout limits excessive perks and other abuses not only when a buyout takes place, but also in those cases where managers fear a buyout. The fear itself instils restraint.

THE REGULATION OF LEVERAGED BUYOUTS. The role the law should play in leveraged buyouts is perhaps only a small one, but there are several distinct problems that may be appropriately subject to legal rules. First, we can ask whether legal rules are needed to protect shareholders. After some leveraged buyouts, the firm's equity will cease to be publicly traded. The firm removes itself from much of the federal regulation of securities. Some special problems may arise. For example, those who had been public shareholders may have insufficient information to assess how well they were treated when the transaction itself insulates the firm from further public scrutiny. The more valuable the disclosure rules of our securities laws, the more important this problem becomes.

Shareholders who are bought out during a leveraged buyout may capture a large part of the efficiency gains that the buyout brings. A leveraged buyout, however, may involve cashing out of only some of the shares. The remaining shareholders enjoy none of the benefits of the buyout. They face the same risks as the new shareholders without having acquired their shares at a price that reflected these risks. These issues, however, may not require special rules. How minority shareholders are or should be protected when there is a takeover or sale of the firm is an issue that is both well explored and not peculiar to leveraged buyouts (see Easterbrook and Fischel 1991).

Creditors, much more than shareholders, face special problems from leveraged buyouts. In the wake of a leveraged buyout, each pre-existing creditor's loan becomes riskier. As noted, however, creditors have considerable power to protect themselves in the wake of buyouts and other transactions that put them at risk, but only a limited ability to call off legal rules that, while designed to protect them, do not advance their interests in a particular transaction. Given that it is easy for creditors to fashion new terms but hard to opt out of those that the law supplies, legal rules that protect creditors are easy to justify only if they make sense in virtually every transaction between debtor and creditor. We may, however, be able to justify fraudulent conveyance law, the law that governs leveraged buyouts, on exactly these grounds.

The law of fraudulent conveyances applies only in narrow situations. Its general principles are uncontroversial (see Clark 1977), and, for this reason, much of its application to leveraged buyouts is uncontroversial as well.

The debate is largely over its reach. How far we should extend it depends on our assessment of the ability of creditors to protect themselves through covenants, the ability of judges to apply its principles to transactions that take place long before the litigation, and our own ability to craft alternative legal regimes.

We begin with the most uncontroversial use of fraudulent conveyance law in leveraged buyouts, which is to allow creditors to prevent leveraged buyouts whose principal purpose is to defraud them. *Tabor Court Realty*, one of the leading cases on leveraged buyouts and fraudulent conveyances, was a case involving a number of shady figures, and the scent of corruption lay heavily in the air. Since the 1570s, fraudulent conveyance law has protected creditors when their debtor intentionally tries to delay, hinder or defraud them. Such laws are among the easiest to justify because it is hard to imagine arm's length bargains in which creditors grant their debtor the ability to defraud them.

Fraudulent conveyance law, however, goes beyond cases of outright fraud. Painting with broad strokes, fraudulent conveyance law typically allows creditors to set aside any leveraged buyout that leaves a corporation insolvent. The idea is simple: If a buyout leaves the firm insolvent, there is not, by definition, enough left to pay the creditors. Assets should go to shareholders only when the firm is left with enough to pay the creditors in full.

If courts could assess without error whether a firm was solvent, the logic of applying fraudulent conveyance law to leveraged buyouts would be unassailable. Courts, however, look at the firm with the benefit of hindsight. Litigation typically takes place only after the firm has gone through the buyout and then failed. Courts have to distinguish between firms that were left insolvent by a buyout and firms that failed because the firm made bad decisions or encountered unexpected economic changes after the buyout. Applying fraudulent conveyance law to buyouts therefore makes sense only if courts are adept at making these distinctions.

Once a court finds that a leveraged buyout left a firm insolvent, a second issue arises – identifying those against whom suit can be brought (see *Lippi v. City Bank*). Potential targets include the old shareholders who were cashed out as well as the new creditors who financed the buyout. There are few cases, however, in which a court will find that a fraudulent conveyance took place, but that the party in question is not subject to suit.

One might compare the way in which fraudulent conveyance law works with alternative ways in which legal rules might protect creditors. We might provide for legal scrutiny at the time of the transactions rather than after the fact when things have already gone badly. For example, one might have a rule that granted a safe harbour to those who engaged in leveraged buyouts if they gave all known creditors notice of the transaction. Anyone who received notice would have to object to the transaction at that time. The time for attacking a leveraged buyout would be moved forward to the time of the transaction. Requiring the creditors to act immediately prevents bad transactions from taking place in the first instance.

Confronting the issue immediately also removes a source of uncertainty from the transaction. Unlike a simple dividend, a leveraged buyout requires that some parties contribute new capital to the enterprise. A rule that focuses attention on the time of the transaction brings its own disadvantages. Such an approach must, by its nature, generate more litigation than a rule that comes into play only when the firm fails. A rule that requires litigation only after the ship sinks may be cheaper to implement than one that requires litigation before each voyage.

There are other ways to protect creditors from the harm that leveraged buyouts might cause them, that would come into play at the time of the transaction rather than after the fact. For example, the law might require notice to existing creditors on recapitalization and also allow all creditors to accelerate their loans unless they waived the right at the outset. Such an acceleration provision may make sense as an off-the-rack term in every debt contract. The term is found in many loan agreements that are elaborately dickered. This rule is analogous to the appraisal remedy in corporate law.

There are, however, several difficulties in implementing this approach. First, identifying a firm's creditors is not as easy as looking at a balance sheet. Creditors, in this sense, include buyers with claims on warranties, disputed or unknown tax obligations, and anyone with a lawsuit against the firm. Second, even if these claims are identified, paying them off may be costly. One may not want to settle all outstanding lawsuits or lose the benefit of a loan at a favourable interest rate.

In short, current law relies on judicial scrutiny after the fact to protect creditors from the ill effects of a leveraged buyout. We could provide no legal rule at all (except for cases of outright fraud) and force each creditor to rely on private contracting. Alternatively, we can create a legal regime that imposes earlier scrutiny. These choices between contract and mandatory rule and between *ex ante* and *ex post* rules pervade our legal system and are a common theme in law-and-economics. Our ultimate choice, here as elsewhere, must turn both on our intuitions and on the wisdom that comes from experience.

We should not, however, leave the subject of the legal rules governing leveraged buyouts without noting a feature of existing US law that cannot be easily defended. In bankruptcy, fraudulent conveyance law allows all creditors to object to the leveraged buyout, even those who lent after the buyout and with full knowledge of it (see *Moore v. Bay*). This rule seems to make little sense. Outside the narrow domain of situations in which creditors can pierce the corporate veil, a creditor has no grounds for complaint simply because it lent money to a firm that was too thinly capitalized. Hence, it seems odd that creditors of a firm that went through a leveraged buyout in the past should be able to enjoy the fruits of a fraudulent conveyance action even though they came on the scene after the buyout and had notice of it.

EMPIRICAL OBSERVATIONS AND NEW DIRECTIONS. Empirical work in law-and-economics has done much to illuminate the explanations of why leveraged buyouts have increased dramatically in recent years. In addition, we can use leveraged buyouts as a natural experiment to understand capital structures and the law of corporate reorganizations.

Law-and-economics scholarship has explored the virtues of Chapter 11 under United States law and alternatives to Chapter 11, such as mandatory sales of the firm (either as a going concern or piecemeal). The empirical issue commonly raised is one of assessing the costs of financial distress in worlds with and without Chapter 11. The costs of financial distress are, more generally, at the heart of some of the most important questions in corporate finance. The Modigliani and Miller irrelevance proposition assumes away the costs of financial distress. Hence, the cost of reorganizing the firm in the event that the firm could not meet its debt payments may be one of the explanations for equity in a world in which there are tax benefits to carrying debt.

Identifying the costs of financial distress, however, has always been hard. A firm is frequently in financial distress because it is in economic distress as well. The restaurant that cannot pay its debts is often the restaurant with surly waiters and terrible food. In order for the firm to regain its footing, the staff has to be trained (or fired) and the menu needs to be redesigned. These costs, however, have nothing to do with the firm's capital structure. A restaurant with no debt at all would have to incur the same costs to become a viable enterprise.

Leveraged buyouts provide cases in which financial distress can be seen in isolation (see Denis and Denis 1995). The leveraged buyouts and the other highly leveraged transactions of the 1980s involved firms much like others in their industry. Indeed, by virtue of the buyout, the firms may have been better run than most. The problems these firms faced in Chapter 11 were quite different from those of bad restaurants and give us an opportunity to measure the costs of acquiring a new capital structure and the costs, both direct and indirect, associated with it.

Andrade and Kaplan (1996) find that the costs of financial distress include unexpected cuts in capital expenditures, undesired asset sales and costly managerial delay. Most of these costs, however, occur before the firm enters Chapter 11. Moreover, the costs of Chapter 11 seem relatively modest. Their sample contains large, well-known firms and publicly traded securities. These are exactly those in which market-based alternatives to Chapter 11 appear most attractive. The low costs that these leveraged buyouts experienced may lead law-and-economics scholars away from market-based alternatives to Chapter 11 to studying its inner mechanics and how the agency costs it generates can be reduced.

There is a second, and perhaps more important lesson from these empirical studies. If the costs of financial distress are small, the benefits that the leveraged buyout may bring in the form of greater discipline and tighter management do not need to be large for us to conclude that legal rules should facilitate or at least not interfere with leveraged buyouts. In short, here as elsewhere, we must be sensitive to the possibility that changes in legal rules can do more harm than good.

DOUGLAS G. BAIRD

See also AGENCY COSTS AND CORPORATE GOVERNANCE; AUCTIONS AND TAKEOVERS; CHAPTER 11; CORPORATE LAW; CORPORATE REORGANIZATIONS; EMPLOYEE OWNERSHIP OF FIRMS; FRAUDULENT CONVEYANCE; MARKET FOR CORPORATE CONTROL; OWNERSHIP OF THE FIRM; TENDER OFFERS.

Subject classification: 5g(iii); 5g(iv).

CASES

Moore v. Bay, 284 US 4 (1931).
Lippi v. City Bank, 955 F2d 599 (9th Cir. 1992).
United States v. Tabor Court Realty Corp., 803 F2d 1288 (3d Cir. 1986), cert. denied, 483 US 1005 (1987).

BIBLIOGRAPHY

Andrade, G. and Kaplan, S. 1996. How costly is financial (not economic) distress? Evidence from highly leveraged transactions that became distressed. Manuscript, Graduate School of Business, University of Chicago, Chicago, IL.
Asquith, P. and Wizman, T.A. 1990. Event risk, covenants, and bondholder returns in leveraged buyouts. *Journal of Financial Economics* 27: 195–213.
Baird, D. 1991. Fraudulent conveyances, agency costs, and leveraged buyouts. *Journal of Legal Studies* 20: 1–24.
Burrough, B. and Helyar, J. 1990. *Barbarians at the Gate: The Fall of RJR Nabisco*. New York: Harper and Row.
Clark, R.C. 1977. The duties of the corporate debtor to its creditors. *Harvard Law Review* 90: 505–62.
Denis, D.J. and Denis, D.K. 1995. Causes of financial distress following leveraged recapitalizations. *Journal of Financial Economics* 37: 129–57.
Easterbrook, F. and Fischel, D. 1991. *The Economic Structure of Corporate Law*. Cambridge, MA: Harvard University Press.
Jensen, M.C. 1986. Agency costs of free cash flow, corporate finance and takeovers. *American Economic Review* Papers and Proceedings 76: 323–9.
Jensen, M.C. 1988. Takeovers: their causes and consequences. *Journal of Economic Perspectives* 2 (1): 21–48.
Jensen, M.C. 1989. Eclipse of the public corporation. *Harvard Business Review* 67: 61–74.
Kaplan, S. 1989. Management buyouts: evidence on taxes as a source of value. *Journal of Finance* 44: 611–32.
Kaplan, S. 1994a. Campeau's acquisition of Federated: post-bankruptcy results. *Journal of Financial Economics* 35: 123–36.
Kaplan, S. 1994b. Federated's acquisition and bankruptcy: lessons and implications. *Washington University Law Quarterly* 72: 1103–26.
Lichtenberg, F.R. and Siegal, D. 1990. The effect of ownership changes on the employment and wages of central office and other personnel. *Journal of Law and Economics* 33: 383–408.
Miller, M.H. 1988. The Modigliani–Miller propositions after thirty years. *Journal of Economic Perspectives* 2 (4): 99–120.
Modigliani, F. and Miller, M.H. 1958. The cost of capital, corporation finance, and the theory of investment. *American Economic Review* 48: 261–97.
Myers, S.C. 1984. The capital structure puzzle. *Journal of Finance* 39: 575–92.
Petersen, M.A. and Raghuram, R.G. 1993. The benefits of firm-creditor relationships: evidence from small business data. Manuscript, Graduate School of Business, University of Chicago, Chicago, IL.
Smith, C.W. and Warner, J.B. 1979. On financial contracting: an analysis of bond covenants. *Journal of Financial Economics* 7: 117–61.

liability insurance. *See* INSURANCE, DETERRENCE AND LIABILITY.

liability rights as contingent claims. A contingent claim is a right to receive money or goods should a possible event actually occur. Different people place different values on the risks represented by contingent claims. These differences create potential gains from trade that an efficient market exhausts. Beginning in the 1950s, general equilibrium theorists produced increasingly robust proofs that a complete set of competitive markets for contingent claims allocates risks efficiently (Arrow and Hahn 1971). These theorists apparently had in mind such contingent claims as stock options, insurance, and commodity futures. Their arguments, however, also apply in principle to legal liability for some kinds of harm.

A liability right is conventionally defined as a right of the victim to receive money compensation from the injurer in the event that possible harm actually occurs (Calabresi and Melamed 1972), and thus combines the victim's right and the injurer's liability. A liability right is contingent upon conditions stipulated in law, such as the injurer's negligence causing the victim's harm (Cooter 1991). When the contingencies occur, a liability right matures into a legal right of action with a claim to damages.

In principle, the victim could transfer his right to receive damages to someone else, and the injurer could pay someone else to assume his obligation to pay damages. The transfers could occur before or after the liability right matures. To illustrate transfer of an unmatured liability right, a person who purchases medical insurance typically assigns to the insurer any legal rights to compensation for medical costs arising from accidents ('subrogation clause'). Similarly, a company that purchases liability insurance pays the insurer to assume liability. To illustrate transfer of matured liability rights, an accident victim who sues the injurer in the US typically retains an attorney on a contingent fee, which assigns approximately one-third of any court judgment to the plaintiff's attorney.

Different people place different values on the risks that trigger liability, and these different valuations create potential gains from trade. To realize these gains, a potential victim should sell the right to receive damages to someone who values it more, and a potential injurer should pay someone else to bear liability who can do so at less cost. If perfectly competitive markets for liability rights existed, they would reach equilibrium when every right to receive damages is owned by the party who values it the most, and every duty to pay damages is held by the party who can bear it at least cost. Such an equilibrium is Pareto efficient with respect to the allocation of matured and unmatured liability rights.

Law often impedes or forbids the exchange of liability rights, especially liability arising from accidents. For example, consumers and manufacturers cannot usually contract to modify the rights of consumers to receive compensation for injuries caused by defective products. Courts disallow so many contracts to waive, disclaim, modify, or transfer liability for accidental harm that the mainstream in tort scholarship proclaims the decline or death of contracts for liability rights (Gilmore 1974; Calabresi 1976; Atiyah 1979). Lawyers or law firms in the US and elsewhere apparently cannot buy unmatured liability rights (prohibition of 'champerty'). Contingent fees allow lawyers in the US to buy a fraction, but not all, of a matured liability claim. Continental Europe typically prohibits contingent fees.

Inefficiencies in liability law impose high costs on society (Huber 1988; Viscusi 1996). Would removing the legal impediments to markets for liability rights solve these problems? No one can accurately predict how markets would develop. Presumably some markets would flourish and others would fail. Some legal theorists favour allowing disclaimers and waivers, or developing new contracts to exchange liability rights (Priest 1981; Havighurst 1986; Cooter 1989; Choharis 1995; Rubin 1997), and other scholars are more circumspect or hostile to contract remedies in torts (O'Connell and Joost 1986; Bell 1990; Sugarman 1992; Croley and Hanson 1993; Geistfeld 1994).

I believe that many of the historical abuses of contracts for liability rights resulted from the absence of competition. Competitive exchange holds promise as a remedy for inefficient tort laws. Instead of impeding exchange, law should facilitate competition in markets for liability rights. I will examine the main causes of potential gains from trade, describe the legal impediments, and speculate on how markets might emerge if the legal impediments were removed.

DETERRENCE VERSUS INSURANCE. Potential victims of accidents desire deterrence and insurance. I will explain how this desire creates a strong incentive to exchange liability rights. In simple tort models, optimal deterrence requires injurers to internalize the external benefit of avoiding accidents. In these simple models, injurers internalize the external benefits of precaution when they are liable for perfectly compensatory damages (Brown 1973). Damages are perfectly compensatory when they restore the victim to the same level of utility as he would have enjoyed without the injury. In other words, the victim is indifferent between no injury or an injury with perfectly compensatory damages.

Courts distinguish between economic and non-economic losses caused by accidents. The economic losses include property damage, lost wages, and medical costs. The non-economic losses include pain, suffering, emotional distress, and lost companionship. Optimal deterrence requires perfect compensation, and perfect compensation requires damages for economic and non-economic losses. To illustrate concretely, assume an accident causes losses of 20 for hospitalization, 50 for lost wages, and 30 for pain and suffering. Perfect compensation requires damages equal to 100. Assume the injurer can take precautions that reduce the probability of an accident. When the injurer decides how much precaution to take, liability of 100 causes the injurer to internalize the full gain that more precaution conveys upon the potential victim. Consequently, the injurer balances his own costs of precaution against its benefit to the victim.

The right to receive perfectly compensatory damages fully insures potential victims against the destruction of value in accidents where the injurer is liable. Full insurance, however, may not be optimal. People buy insurance in order to shift money from a state of the world in which money is needed less to a state of the world in which money is needed more. In other words, people buy insurance against accidents that increase the marginal utility of money. In the typical case, economic losses cause the marginal utility of money to rise, so people will buy insurance against economic losses. In the typical case, however, non-economic losses do not cause the marginal utility of money to rise, so people will not buy insurance against non-economic losses (Cook and Graham 1977). (Rare examples of people buying insurance against pain may be found in Croley and Hanson 1995.)

Law that pursues the ideal of perfect compensation or the goal of optimal deterrence awards damages for economic and non-economic losses, thus over-insuring. Law that pursues the goal of optimal insurance does not award damages for non-economic losses, thus under-deterring. To illustrate, a tort system similar to those of the United States, which provide large awards for pain and suffering, will set liability approximately at 100 in the preceding example and optimally deter the injurer. The victim, however, probably has no desire to insure against pain and suffering. A tort system similar to Germany's, which provides little compensation for pain and suffering, will set liability closer to 70, thus under-deterring the injurer and supplying the efficient amount of insurance to the victim.

Combining optimal deterrence and optimal insurance requires the potential injurer to pay relatively high damages and the potential victim to receive relatively low damages. In private law, the injurer's obligation to pay damages usually *equals* the victim's right to receive damages. This equality creates a tradeoff between the two goals, and different legal systems respond differently to this trade-off. To achieve both goals, law must decouple payments to the injurer and victim. Specifically, law can require the injurer to pay a relatively high fine to the state and relatively low damages to the victim (Polinsky and Che 1991).

Instead of decoupling by law, which has disadvantages, decoupling can occur through markets. When the liability system provides the potential accident victim with unwanted insurance, a market for liability rights permits him to sell it. If the buyer is anyone other than the potential injurer, the sale reduces insurance without reducing deterrence. To illustrate, a potential victim with liability rights equal to 100, who wants insurance equal to 70, can sell the right to recover damages equal to 30. The buyer might be a law firm specializing in accidents. After completing the sale, the victim of an injury recovers 70 in damages as required for optimal insurance, and the injurer pays a total of 100 (70 to the victim and 30 to the law firm), as required for optimal deterrence. Thus sales of unmatured tort claims by potential victims to third parties eliminates unwanted insurance without reducing the injurer's incentives for precaution.

FIRST PARTY OR THIRD PARTY INSURANCE? I explained that liability law provides unwanted insurance and creates an incentive to sell liability rights. The preceding discussion assumed that insurance is unwanted because the harm does not increase the marginal utility of money. Another reason why the victim may not want the injurer to provide insurance is that the victim can buy it cheaper.

To illustrate, consider a manufacturer who sells a product to a retailer, who resells the product to a consumer. If the manufacturer is strictly liable for consumer product injuries, then the manufacturer in effect sells a joint product consisting of a manufactured good plus an insurance policy. In contrast, a rule of no liability exposes the consumer to the risk of injury, thus providing an incentive for the consumer to purchase his own insurance. No-liability induces first-party insurance, and strict liability induces third-party insurance. If third-party insurance is cheaper than first-party insurance, then a rule of strict liability is more efficient than a rule of no liability in simple tort models. Conversely, if first-party insurance is cheaper than third-party insurance, then a rule of no liability is more efficient than a rule of strict liability in simple tort models.

Priest argues that the legal doctrine of enterprise liability replaced relatively cheap first-party insurance with relatively expensive third party insurance (Priest 1985; 1991). If Priest is right, lawmakers created the wrong rule, which imposes excessive insurance costs upon consumers. A market for liability rights can correct this mistake. By assumption, the consumer can insure at less cost than the manufacturer, so an exchange of liability rights creates a surplus. The manufacturer can profitably buy the consumer's liability right at a price exceeding the consumer's cost of insurance. A consumer who sells a liability right and buys insurance converts third-party insurance into first-party insurance.

TRANSACTION COSTS. Schwartz (1985) found that the plaintiffs' legal costs in the typical American tort suit equal between 29% and 44% of the damages awarded. Assuming defendant's legal costs are similar in magnitude, total legal costs exceed 60% of the damages awarded. Reducing the costs of resolving disputes motivates many proposals for tort reform, including proposals to replace fault-based liability with no-fault rules (O'Connell and Joost 1986).

Instead of restricting sales to third parties, suppose the potential victim can sell a liability right to the potential injurer. The potential injurer who buys an unmatured liability right extinguishes the potential plaintiff's claim before an accident occurs. In the event of an accident, no one will incur the high cost of litigation and the victim will bear his own accident costs. Thus the sale of liability rights can effectively convert liability from fault to no fault without actually changing the law. Saving the transaction costs of dispute resolution provides a motive for victims to sell liability rights to injurers.

What is the effect on deterrence? In simple tort models, a reduction in liability reduces the injurer's incentives for precaution. To illustrate by the preceding example, an injurer who buys the victim's right to receive damages of 30 reduces his liability from 100 to 70. After the transaction, the injurer internalizes only 70% of the benefit of avoiding an accident, so the injurer may reduce his precaution and the number of accidents may increase.

Competition, however, tends to prevent this erosion of incentives. The market price of liability rights responds to the frequency and magnitude of damages. To be more precise, in competitive equilibrium the price of an unmatured liability right roughly equals the expected judgment in the event of an accident, discounted by the probability of an accident (Cooter 1989). By reducing precaution and increasing the number of accidents, an injurer causes the price of liability rights to rise. The rise in price reduces the profitability of the injurer's strategy of buying liability rights in order to reduce precaution.

To illustrate, assume that an injurer planned to purchase liability rights from potential victims and then reduce his precaution. Competitors who understand the injurer's strategy will buy liability rights in anticipation of a rise in their price. The rise in the price of liability rights increases the cost to the injurer of pursuing his strategy. As an alternative strategy, the injurer could commit to taking efficient precaution, thus reducing the market price that the injurer must pay to buy liability rights from victims.

The transaction costs of markets for liability rights are large. Successful markets must aggregate unmatured rights and sell them in bulk. Insurers could play an important role as a broker in bulk sales. For example, automobile insurers could offer lower premiums to drivers in exchange for their liability rights arising from automobile accidents, including the right to damages for pain and suffering. In the event of an accident involving two drivers with such insurance, the drivers would make claims against their insurance companies and the insurance companies would resolve liability with each other. Insurance companies might contract to pre-settle such claims, thus eliminating court proceedings.

As another example, assume that you buy a used Volvo and the manufacturer is liable for accidental harm caused by a manufacturing defect. You might get a reduction in your vehicle insurance premium in exchange for transferring to the insurer your liability right against Volvo. Your insurer would then resell such liability rights in bulk to Volvo, thus extinguishing any possible suit. If Volvo gets too careless, a law firm specializing in liability rights might outbid Volvo and purchase a block of liability rights from the insurer.

The same exchange might occur for the right to recover damages from injuries caused by medical malpractice. Specifically, the patient could transfer his right to recover damages for medical malpractice to his insurance company in exchange for lower premiums, and the insurance company could resell the right to the patient's doctors or their insurers.

CONSENT. The best rationale for disallowing contracts for liability rights concerns asymmetrical information. A person who does not know the quality of a product cannot value it correctly. Similarly, a person who does not know the probability and magnitude of a loss cannot value it correctly. If competition drives the price of liability to their value, however, ignorant individuals can transact in these markets simply by knowing the market price.

To illustrate by analogy, consider a competitive market for fire insurance. Most homeowners know little about the probability of a fire. Competition among insurers, however, tends to equate the insurance premium with the expected value of claims plus administrative costs. Consequently, every consumer can be ignorant of probabilities and magnitudes of losses, and yet all consumers who pay the competitive price for insurance receive it at cost. A competitive market for liability rights would work the same way. Instead of trying to learn about probabilities, most rational individuals would focus on learning about the prices of liability rights. Thus an ignorant consumer, who knows nothing about the probability or magnitude of accidents, would receive full value for liability rights.

CONCLUSION. Regarding liability rights as contingent claims invites an extension of models of competitive exchange to liability law, which could change law in theory and practice. The extension could replace intuition in legal theory with rigour and bring a new perspective to regulating risks. Exchange in a complete set of perfectly competitive markets allocates liability rights efficiently, regardless of the initial allocation by law. Legal reforms could facilitate the development of competitive markets for liability rights, rather than impeding exchange. Competitive exchange could solve the problems of deterrence and insurance, lower the transaction cost of dispute resolution, and improve the quality of consent to waivers of liability.

Since law impedes or prohibits markets for liability rights, no one knows how they would work. The success of such markets would depend upon the ability of entrepreneurs to develop new contingent commodities by unbundling and repackaging liability rights. If large, unrealized surpluses from such exchanges exist, pressure will build to liberalize markets for liability rights.

ROBERT COOTER

See also CLASS ACTIONS; CONDITIONAL FEES IN BRITAIN; CONTINGENT FEES; INSURANCE, DETERRENCE AND LIABILITY; MEDICAL MALPRACTICE; PRODUCTS LIABILITY; PUBLIC CHOICE AND THE LAW.

Subject classification: 5d(ii).

BIBLIOGRAPHY

Arrow, K.J. and Hahn, F. 1971. *General Competitive Analysis*. Edinburgh: Oliver & Boyd; San Francisco: Holden-Day, Inc.

Atiyah, P.S. 1979. *The Rise and Fall of Freedom of Contract*. Oxford: Clarendon Press.

Bell, P.A. 1990. Analyzing tort law: the flawed promise of neocontract. *Minnesota Law Review* 74: 1177–1249.

Brown, J. 1973. Toward an economic theory of liability. *Journal of Legal Studies* 2: 323–49.

Calabresi, G. 1976. Torts – the law of the mixed society. In *American Law: The Third Century*, ed. B. Schwartz, South Hackensack, NJ: Rothman & Co., for New York University School of Law.

Calabresi, G. and Melamed, D. 1972. Property rules, liability rules and inalienability: one view of the cathedral. *Harvard Law Review*. 85: 1089–1128.

Choharis, P.C. 1995. A comprehensive market strategy for tort reform. *Yale Journal on Regulation* 12: 435–525.

Cook, D. and Graham, P.J. 1977. Demand for insurance and protection: the case of irreplaceable commodities. *Quarterly Journal of Economics* 91: 143–56.

Cooter, R.D. 1989. Towards a market in unmatured tort claims. *University of Virginia Law Review* 75: 383–411.

Cooter, R.D. 1991. Economic theories of legal liability. *Journal of Economic Perspectives* 5(3): 11–30.

Croley, S.P. and Hanson, J.D. 1993. Rescuing the revolution: the revived case for enterprise liability. *Michigan Law Review* 91: 683–797.

Croley, S.P. and Hanson, J.D. 1995. The nonpecuniary costs of accidents: pain-and-suffering damages in tort law. *Harvard Law Review* 108: 1785–1917.

Geistfeld, M. 1994. The political economy of neocontractual proposals for products liability reform. *Texas Law Review* 72: 803–47.

Gilmore, G. 1974. *The Death of Contract*. Columbus: Ohio State University Press.

Havighurst, C. 1986. Private reform of tort-law dogma: market opportunities and legal obstacles. *Law and Contemporary Problems* 49: 143–72.

Huber, P.W. 1988. *Liability: The Legal Revolution and its Consequences*. New York: Basic Books.

O'Connell, J. and Joost, R.H. 1986. Giving motorists a choice between fault and no-fault insurance. *Virginia Law Review* 72: 61–9.

Polinsky, A.M. and Che, Y.-K. 1991. Decoupling liability: optimal incentives for care and litigation. *RAND Journal of Economics* 22: 562–70.

Priest, G.L. 1981. A theory of consumer product warranty. *Yale Law Journal* 90: 1297–1352.

Priest, G.L. 1985. The invention of enterprise liability: a critical history of the intellectual foundations of modern tort law. *Journal of Legal Studies* 14: 461–527.

Priest, G.L. 1991. The modern expansion of tort liability: its source, its effect, and its reform. *Journal of Economic Perspectives* 5: 31–50.

Rubin, P.H. 1997. Juries and the tort-contract boundary. Paper read at George Mason Colloquium on Torts and the Revival of Contract Law, at the School of Law, George Mason University.

Schwartz, G. 1985. Directions in contemporary products liability scholarship. *Journal of Legal Studies* 14: 763–77.

Sugarman, S.D. 1992. American Law Institute Reporter's Study, enterprise responsibility for personal injury. *Stanford Law Review* 44: 1163–1208.

Viscusi, W.K. 1996. Regulating the regulators. *University of Chicago Law Review* 63: 1423–61.

liability rules. *See* CALABRESI, GUIDO; ECONOMIC THEORY OF LIABILITY RULES.

libel. *See* PRIVACY.

licensing and certification systems. When participants have incomplete or asymmetric information, market outcomes may be less than optimal. If buyers cannot distinguish between high and low quality goods, then all goods must sell for the same price. If supplying high quality costs more than supplying low quality, a reduction in price may reduce the fraction of high-quality goods that trade, reduce the average price that prevails in the market, and reduce the returns to bringing high-quality goods to market. In extreme cases, markets may cease to exist entirely, or only low-quality goods may trade (Akerlof 1970).

The existence of such 'lemons' markets in practice remains a matter of dispute. Studies of the market for used trucks, for example, have been unable to detect evidence for the theoretical implication that trucks that are traded should tend to need more repairs than those that are not (Bond 1982, 1984; Pratt and Hoffer 1984). In part, the lack of empirical support reflects the wide range of market institutions that seek to reveal information, thereby avoiding the lemons phenomenon.

Licensing and certification systems, whether voluntary, private systems or mandatory and governmental, are one form of response to the demand for better information about products and services. Certification essentially reveals information. The information may be continuous information (as with weight or purity), it may be categorical (as with bond ratings), or it may simply identify products above some minimum standard. Sellers may self-certify, or they may obtain certification from a third party or the government.

Any form of certification requires some underlying standard that provides the basis for the measurement or specifies the product characteristics that matter. Frequently, those standards are private consensus standards, developed under the auspices of the American National Standards Institute (ANSI), the American Society for the Testing of Materials (ASTM) or, in Europe, the International Organization for Standardization. The standards may seek to measure product performance characteristics, they may specify certain design requirements that products must meet or, especially in the case of services, they may examine inputs in the production process such as the amount and kinds of training that a provider has received. In each case, the standard can be thought of as identifying a particular bundle of information.

Conceptually, certification reveals information that parties may either use or not use. Thus transactions in uncertified products can occur. In many instances, however, certification is so important to buyers that few, if any, uncertified products could survive. Although this 'market power' of certifying organizations and the underlying standards developers has raised antitrust concerns (Federal Trade Commission 1978), its source is a market judgment about the value of certain information. Nonetheless, existing firms frequently dominate the standards development process, and may seek to use standards to exclude innovative new products.

If certification allows a market test of the value of certain information, licensing imposes a judgment that the information is crucial. Products (or providers) who fall short of some standard (that could equally well provide the basis for a certification) are prohibited. Sellers will only engage in voluntary certification if the information is valuable to buyers, but buyers have no choice in the face of licensing requirements.

CERTIFICATION. Perhaps the most obvious solution to the lack of information about the quality of goods or services is for sellers of high quality to identify themselves. Such seller-provided information can be thought of as self-certification. It is limited, however, by the obvious incentives of sellers to misrepresent quality. Rational buyers who cannot observe quality directly have an incentive to discount sellers' claims.

Nonetheless, self-certification can be credible in a wide variety of circumstances. First, sellers can create a warranty for their certification. As long as quality can be observed *ex post*, and sellers can make a binding (and enforceable) promise to pay if the characteristic is not as claimed, sellers will have incentives to reveal quality accurately. Moreover, because rational buyers will assume that sellers will disclose and warrant their claims if they are of high quality, buyers will assume the worst about a seller that does not disclose. Thus all but the worst sellers will have an incentive to reveal their true quality (Grossman 1981; Ippolito and Mathios 1990; Rubin 1991).

Thus sellers can credibly self-certify objective, readily measured product attributes such as weight, or the capacity of a memory chip or disk drive, because the truth can be readily observed after purchase. Moreover, self-certification is credible even if quality is not directly observable, so long as there is a set of problems that depend only on quality and can be observed *ex post*. In such circumstances, sellers can offer a warranty covering the observable problems (Grossman 1981). Claims of greater durability or fewer quality problems that are backed by a warranty are credible, because the seller will incur greater expenses if those claims are false.

When private standards exist for more complex product characteristics, such as safety standards for bicycle helmets or product specifications for plastic pipes for various uses, self-certification can also function effectively. Whether the product in fact conforms to the standard can be observed *ex post*. Sellers can thus warrant that the product conforms to the specifications of a particular standard. The existence of a standard allows sellers to summarize more complex product characteristics and convey that information to buyers who are aware of the standard.

Second, when buyers and sellers interact repeatedly, a quality-assuring premium can provide an incentive for honest self-certification. If high-quality goods sell for a sufficient premium (relative to marginal cost) over low-quality goods, and if buyers cease to make purchases from a seller who promises high quality but delivers low quality, then a profit-maximizing seller will truthfully certify quality. Although a seller who misrepresents quality gains from selling low-quality goods at a high-quality price for a single period, he will lose the premium for high-quality goods in all future periods (Klein and Leffler 1981). Consumers are willing to pay a premium price, above and beyond the higher costs of quality, because it gives the firm an incentive to maintain quality. Investments in intangible assets such as advertising and trademarks, which have little or no residual value if the firm cheats on quality, can serve a similar function by acting as a bond that is forfeit if quality is reduced (Ippolito 1990). Empirical evidence indicates that for consumer goods, a significant portion of higher than competitive returns is in fact a premium for brand-specific quality characteristics (Thomas 1989).

For self-certification to function effectively, the credibility of the seller's warranty of that certification is crucial. In some instances, however, the problem may be readily observable, but the warranty will have little or no value if the problem occurs. For example, a seller of a bond may promise to repay, but in the event of problems, a warranty would add nothing. Potential buyers must either conduct their own assessment of quality, or obtain certification from an independent third party.

The economic characteristics of information are an important determinant of the structure of such third party certification systems. Once information is produced, it is not used up (though it may depreciate as circumstances change). Thus, there is an obvious economy in having a third party conduct a single assessment of quality, rather than having each buyer evaluate quality independently (Barzel 1982). When certification is a matter of judgment, however, competing judgements may be desirable. In the United States bond market, there are two ratings services, for example, and buyers apparently value both. When issues have split ratings, yields more closely resemble the yield of other issues with the lower rating. When the rating services agree, however, yields are lower than on issues receiving the rating from only one agency (Thompson and Vaz 1990).

Once it is produced, the marginal cost of disseminating information is relatively low. Moreover, those who have obtained information from its producer can pass it on to others. Because some who benefit do not pay the producer of the information, markets would tend to produce too little information. Sellers, however, benefit from all users of the information. In effect, they can internalize the free-rider externality (Beales, Craswell and Salop 1981). Thus, certification systems are commonly paid for by sellers, and disseminated without additional charge to buyers. Bond issuers pay for evaluation by one or more ratings agencies, television stations and networks pay a major share of the cost of audience measurement services, and manufacturers pay for certification from institutions such as Underwriters Laboratory.

Certification may be valuable even when products or services are already known to meet some minimum quality standard because of the existence of licensing requirements. Physicians, for example, must be licensed to practice medicine. They have the option of seeking board certification in a speciality. Physicians who are eligible for board certification earn more than otherwise similar physicians who are not, and those who actually obtain board certification earn still more (Wilensky and Rossiter 1983; Ohsfeldt, Culler and Becker 1987).

Even if information already exists and is publicly available, there may be value in a third party's certification of that information. A.M. Best & Co., for example, rates the financial soundness of insurance companies. When ratings change, however, there is no significant impact on stock prices, suggesting that the ratings are summarizing information that is already available to the capital markets. The value of the certification is thus to policyholders, rather than to potential investors (Singh and Power 1992).

LICENSING. Although the underlying rationale for licensing and certification systems is quite similar, they utilize very different mechanisms. Certification systems seek to reveal information: to make the unobservable observable, or, more generally, to reduce the costs of obtaining information. Licensing systems, in contrast, seek to make information irrelevant by prohibiting trade in goods or services that do not meet the licensing standard.

Occupational licensing in the form of minimum training and educational requirements is widespread for many learned and not so learned professions, ranging from law and medicine to barbers and beauticians. Such requirements raise the cost of entry, and reduce the supply of professionals in occupations subject to licensure.

Licensing, whether explicit or implicit, is also common in product markets. Requirements for prior governmental approval of new prescription drugs or food additives are effectively licence requirements. Developing the necessary data to support approval raises the cost of entry, and the time necessary for review of requests to enter necessarily delays entry into the market. Similarly, requirements such as product safety standards can also be thought of as a form of licensing, even if no formal 'licence' is issued. Unlike prior approval requirements, however, such standards do not necessarily restrict new firms or new products, as long as the new entrant conforms to the existing standards.

The public interest defence of all licensing requirements is that they protect buyers from low quality products or services. If consumers cannot observe quality, a licensing requirement that eliminates low quality goods will increase the average quality of goods that are traded, and may enhance consumer welfare. If producers choose the standards, however, they will likely choose to enhance profitability by choosing standards that are too restrictive (Leland 1979). Similarly, licensing requirements for professionals based on years of education may enhance quality if the marginal cost of providing higher-quality services is lower for those with more training (Shapiro 1986). The limitations of occupational licensing are discussed in more detail in Beales (1980).

Whether licensing requirements actually do increase quality is an empirical question on which the evidence remains somewhat scanty. Product standards presumably lead to products that conform to the standard, but they may not accomplish their intended objectives. Where product features and consumer caution are substitutes in reducing risk, a mandated safer product may lead to less consumer caution, with little or no effect on overall accident rates. Consumers who must purchase medicines with child-resistant caps, for example, may use less care in keeping medicine out of the reach of children. Studies of the effect of the US Consumer Product Safety Commission have found no statistically significant effect on accident rates, either in general or for accident categories that have been the particular subject of regulatory attention (Linneman 1980; Viscusi 1985). The evidence is more mixed on the effects of automobile safety standards. Although some authors have found significant reductions in highway fatalities as a result of safety standards (Crandall and Graham 1984), others have found no significant effects (Peltzman 1975).

The evidence is even more scant on the impact of occupational licensing on quality of services actually consumed. Some studies have examined whether incidental restrictions such as those on advertising or commercial practice have an impact on quality, and found none (Kwoka 1984), but virtually no reliable studies have examined whether licensing itself actually has the predicted effect of raising quality.

The problem with the public interest argument for licensing is that an equivalent certification system that simply identifies providers who meet a certain standard seems to be a generally superior alternative. With certification, consumers who do not value higher quality as much as the added costs of producing it can choose a lower-quality, lower-price alternative. Similarly, consumers who prefer to reduce risk by exercising high levels of care can do so, without the need to purchase higher cost products with built-in safety features that may be less effective than simply being careful.

Licensing restrictions do impose costs. Studies of the drug approval process in the United States have found that the tighter licensing requirements adopted in the 1960s substantially reduced the flow of new products to market, and imposed significant net costs (Peltzman 1973). Drugs are available in other countries significantly earlier than they are in the US (Kaitin et al. 1989), with no evidence that the incidence of side effects or ineffective products differs significantly. To some extent, the costs of the US process may stem from the particular standards adopted, rather than from licensing itself. Although less restrictive standards would reduce costs, it is unlikely that the costs of licensing could be eliminated.

Occupational licensing also imposes costs. With entry restricted, the expected effect of licensing is an increase in the price of services. Indeed, in the public interest story of excluding low quality producers, it is the increase in price that creates incentives for provision of higher quality services. Incomes of physicians are higher than they would be in the absence of licensing (Leffler 1978), and lack of reciprocity agreements in dentistry raises the income of dentists (Shepard 1978). Broader studies across professions have found that restrictions on competitive behaviour (such as prohibitions on advertising or price competition) raise professional incomes, but have been unable to disentangle the direct effects of licensing itself (Muzondo and Pazderka 1983).

An interesting variant on the conventional public interest explanation for licensing relies on its anticompetitive effect. Because licensing restricts entry and creates a stream of rents for those who are licensed, it may create a quality assuring premium of the sort discussed above. Licensed professionals, fearing the loss of future rents that would result from detection and licence revocation, would be more likely to provide high-quality services (Svorny 1992). An implication of this argument is that, even though licensure increases prices, the quantity of services consumed should increase, if the net effect of licensing is to benefit consumers. At least for physicians, however, states with more restrictive licensure requirements also have lower levels of consumption of physicians' services (Svorny 1987). Thus, even if it does enhance quality, physician licensing appears to enhance physician incomes even more.

Of course, certification instead of licensing imposes on buyers the costs of identifying, processing, and using the relevant information. Consumers who want high quality must bear these costs, but consumers who are willing to accept low quality need not do so. Indeed, one theoretical effect of licensing requirements in the professions is that licensing may generate a cross subsidy from buyers who would choose low quality to those who prefer higher quality (Shapiro 1986). If all consumers have similar preferences, then simply mandating the alternative that informed consumers would choose avoids the costs of search that would otherwise be necessary. For example, virtually all consumers would presumably choose a non-carcinogenic colour additive over a carcinogenic one. Licensing requirements that ban carcinogenic additives when virtually perfect substitutes are available are likely superior to certification systems. On the other hand, consumers may differ substantially in their willingness to make other quality tradeoffs. Because consumers may differ in their willingness to trade off small cancer risks for reductions in calories, a certification (or disclosure) approach to regulating artificial sweeteners may be superior to licensing.

In general, certification appears to be a superior policy solution to problems of asymmetric information. Certification leaves choices to consumers and the market process, rather than imposing an *a priori* judgment that some products or services are not worth buying.

J. HOWARD BEALES III

See also CONSUMER PROTECTION; DISCLOSURE AND UNRAVELLING; PHARMACEUTICAL REGULATION; PRODUCTS LIABILITY; REGULATION OF THE PROFESSIONS; TRADEMARKS.

Subject classification: 6b.

BIBLIOGRAPHY

Akerlof, G. 1970. The market for 'lemons': quality uncertainty and the market mechanism. *Quarterly Journal of Economics* 84: 488–500.

Barzel, Y. 1982. Measurement cost and the organization of markets. *Journal of Law and Economics* 25: 27–48.

Beales, J.H. 1980. The economics of regulating the professions. In *Regulating the Professions: A Public Policy Symposium*, ed. R.D. Blair and D.L. Kaserman, Lexington, MA: Lexington Books.

Beales, H., Craswell, R. and Salop, S. 1981. The efficient regulation of consumer information. *Journal of Law and Economics* 24: 491–539.

Bond, E.W. 1982. A direct test of the 'lemons' model: the market for used pickup trucks. *American Economic Review* 72: 836–40.

Bond, E.W. 1984. Test of the 'lemons' model: reply. *American Economic Review* 74: 801–4.

Crandall, R.W. and Graham, J.D. 1984. Automobile safety regulation and offsetting behavior: some new empirical estimates. *American Economic Review* 74: 328–31.

Federal Trade Commission Staff Report. 1978. *Standards and Certification*. Washington, DC: Government Printing Office.

Grossman, S. 1981. The informational role of warranties and private disclosure about product quality. *Journal of Law and Economics* 24: 461–83.

Ippolito, P.M. 1990. Bonding and nonbonding signals of product quality. *Journal of Business* 63: 41–60.

Ippolito, P.M. and Mathios, A. 1990. The regulation of science based claims in advertising. *Journal of Consumer Policy* 13: 413–45.

Kaitin, K.I., Mattison, N., Northington, F.K. and Lasagna, L. 1989. The drug lag: an update of new drug introductions in the United States and in the United Kingdom, 1977 through 1987. *Clinical Pharmacology and Therapeutics* 86: 121–38.

Klein, B. and Leffler, K.B. 1981. The role of market forces in assuring contractual performance. *Journal of Political Economy* 89: 615–41.

Kwoka, J.E. 1984. Advertising and the price and quality of optometric services. *American Economic Review* 74: 211–16.

Leffler, K.B. 1978. Physician licensure: Competition and monopoly in American medicine. *Journal of Law and Economics* 21: 165–86.

Leland, H.E. 1979. Quacks, lemons, and licensing: a theory of minimum quality standards. *Journal of Political Economy* 87: 1328–46.

Linneman, P. 1980. The effects of consumer safety standards: the 1973 mattress flammability standard. *Journal of Law and Economics* 23: 461–79.

Muzondo, T.R. and Pazderka, B. 1983. Income-enhancing effects of professional licensing restrictions: a cross-section study of Canadian data. *Antitrust Bulletin* 28: 397–415.

Ohsfeldt, R.L., Culler, S.D. and Becker, E.R. 1987. Sex differences in the economic advantages of physician board certification. *Southern Economic Journal* 54: 343–50.

Pratt, M.S. and Hoffer, G.E. 1984. Test of the 'lemons' model: comment. *American Economic Review* 74: 798–800.

Peltzman, S. 1973. An evaluation of consumer protection legislation: the 1962 drug amendments. *Journal of Political Economy* 81: 1049–91.

Peltzman, S. 1975. The effects of automobile safety regulation. *Journal of Political Economy* 83: 677–725.

Rubin, P.H. 1991. The economics of regulating deception. *Cato Journal* 10: 667–90.

Shapiro, C. 1986. Investment, moral hazard, and occupational licensing. *Review of Economic Studies* 53: 843–62.

Shepard, L. 1978. Licensing restrictions and the cost of dental care. *Journal of Law and Economics* 21: 187–201.

Singh, A.K. and Power, M.L. 1992. The effects of Best's rating changes on insurance company stock prices. *Journal of Risk and Insurance* 59: 310–17.

Svorny, S.V. 1987. Physician licensure: a new approach to examining the role of professional interests. *Economic Inquiry* 25: 497–509.

Svorny, S.V. 1992. Should we reconsider licensing physicians? *Contemporary Policy Issues* 10: 31–8.

Thomas, L.G. 1989. Advertising in consumer goods industries: Durability, economies of scale, and heterogeneity. *Journal of Law and Economics* 32: 163–93.

Thompson, G.R. and Vaz, P. 1990. Dual bond ratings: a test of the certification function of rating agencies. *Financial Review* 25: 457–72.

Viscusi, W.K. 1985. Consumer behavior and the safety effects of product safety regulation. *Journal of Law and Economics* 28: 527–53.

Wilensky, G.R. and Rossiter, L.F. 1983. Economic advantages of board certification. *Journal of Health Economics* 2: 87–94.

limited and extended liability regimes.

> The economic historian of the future may assign to the nameless inventor of the principle of limited liability, as applied to trading corporations, a place of honour with Watt and Stephenson, and other pioneers of the Industrial Revolution. The genius of these men produced the means by which man's command of natural resources was multiplied many times over; the limited liability company [provided] the means by which huge aggregations of capital required to give effect to their discoveries were collected, organized and efficiently administered (*Economist*, 18 December 1926).

In 1855 English companies were permitted to operate under limited liability following the passage of the Limited Liability Act. Contrary to the quotation above, the virtues of limited liability were not accepted by all participants in the debate surrounding the introduction of limited liability. The defenders of the then prevailing unlimited liability rule argued that limited liability would result in uncompensated wealth transfers from shareholders to creditors and ultimately result in a reduction in the availability of credit and in corporate activity. The proponents of limited liability argued that investment would be facilitated both by wealthy investors who under joint and several unlimited liability faced significant potential loss, and by the poor and middle classes who would not worry about their personal wealth when they made an investment in equity. (See Halpern et al. 1980 for a discussion of the arguments presented in the debate and for citations to other work.) It has been noted that limited liability in England was slow to spread (see Smart 1996, who argues that companies were signalling high-risk activities when they selected limited liability). At that time, the arguments did not need to address the situation of large tort damages that potentially could bankrupt the firm. In the United States, the joint and several unlimited liability regime was the general American rule until the early nineteenth century. By 1850, most states had enacted statues providing for limited liability but, even after the change to limited liability, provisions for double liability were prevalent. In California, *pro rata* shareholder liability (defined below) survived until 1931.

While the virtues of limited liability and its positive effect on the growth of capital markets have remained unassailed for many years, in the early 1980s a number of articles were published that evaluated possible liability regimes and presented an efficiency argument for limited liability as the default regime in corporate law. Subsequent research has confirmed the efficiency of limited liability in this context. With the rise of large tort damages, there has been renewed interest in identifying a liability structure that will provide incentives to companies to take appropriate amounts of care if they operate in hazardous industries. While hinted at in earlier studies, two papers focus on this issue in recommending *pro rata* unlimited liability regimes for widely held companies. One of the papers has generated responses which suggest the unlimited liability in torts would be neither feasible nor viable.

INTRODUCTION. When, due to operating reasons or a judgment against the firm, the firm cannot meet its liabilities by liquidating its assets, the impact on shareholders will depend upon the liability rule in operation. If there is a limited liability rule, the company liquidates its assets and from this value covers some or all of the claims to creditors and claimants. If there is a deficiency of assets over claims, the creditor loses since the shareholders are not responsible for meeting any of this deficiency. In an unlimited liability regime, the equity holders are responsible for the deficiency. There is a range of liability rules that can and have been utilized. At one extreme is the pure limited liability rule, under which shareholders have no additional financial obligation. The limited liability rule can be extended to cover some of the deficiency based on a multiple of the book value of equity per share. Alternatively, if the shares have no book value, the excess can be stated as a fixed dollar amount per share. This form of liability is referred to as assessibility and is an example of extended or excess liability. An example is 'double liability' where the shareholders are responsible for unpaid claims up to the per share book value of equity (see Macey and Miller 1992 for the history and implications of this form of excess non-joint and several liability as applied to the banking system in the United States). While this rule is not joint and several liability, it is possible to construct such a rule. In this situation, the creditors could pursue each shareholder and shareholders could sue each other. Unlimited liability is also an excess liability regime but instead of pure unlimited liability in which each shareholder faces joint and several responsibility, there can be *pro rata* liability under which the shareholder is responsible for his or her proportionate share of the deficiency of assets over claims. A shareholder owning ten percent of the shares of the firm, will be responsible only for ten percent of the deficiency. Note that any excess liability regime is *de facto* limited at values less than the contracted amounts since it is always limited directly by the shareholder's personal wealth determined in accordance with bankruptcy laws.

The literature has considered the efficiency of various liability rules described above and whether or not there are inherent benefits to a particular liability rule. The analyses are usually undertaken with respect to different creditor classes and different ownership structures of the firm. Considering creditor class, the distinction is made between voluntary and involuntary creditors. Included in the latter category are individuals who purchase products or use services, tort creditors, and situations where damage is done to the environment. The relevant difference between the creditor classes is the ability of creditors to negotiate the terms of the credit and engage in monitoring behaviour to ensure that certain situations do not occur. For the tort creditor, negotiations are impossible and, unlike voluntary creditors, internalization by the corporation of costs imposed on these parties, *ex ante*, is not possible in the absence of a particular liability regime.

The ownership structure refers to close corporations, sole proprietorships, and widely held companies. For the widely held firm, management typically owns a small percentage of the equity and receives little direct benefit from shifting wealth from creditors to equity holders. It is observed that small sole proprietorships typically have to contract around pure limited liability to generate unlimited liability when dealing with voluntary creditors. This is observed through the use of personal guarantees by the owner managers. In the case of involuntary creditors there remains serious concern over the inadequate incentives to reducing risk provided by limited liability. The close corporation is truly distinct and the bulk of the analysis focuses on the widely held company.

EXAMPLE OF LIABILITY RULES AND WEALTH EFFECTS. A simple example is presented to capture the essence of the liability rule issues. The example considers contractual creditors only. Consider a firm which starts today with initial capital of $10,000 and has issued debt that has a promise to pay of $6000 at the end of the period. Assume the initial book value and the par value of the equity are synonymous. The funds are invested in a project which will last only one year. At the end of the year, the company is liquidated and the funds distributed first to the debtholders to cover principal and interest payments and any remaining funds to the equity holder. There are no corporate taxes and assume the equity is owned by one individual. In addition, there are no transactions or information costs incurred by either creditors or shareholders, both *ex ante* and subsequent to the liquidation of the assets. This is an unrealistic assumption which is relaxed in the subsequent analysis. In fact, it is the relationship of *ex ante* and *ex post* transactions costs to the liability structure that leads to recommendations concerning the appropriateness of particular liability regimes. The market value of the company at any point in time during the period is equal to the present value of the expected company cash flows at the end of the period. The market value of equity will equal the residual cash flows after the payment of debt obligations from the liquidation value of the firm's assets; the equity cash flows in turn depend upon the liability structure under which the company operates.

Table 1

Panel A: Unlimited Liability

		Payoffs ($)		
State	Probability	Asset	Debt	Equity
Good	0.6	15,000	6,000	9,000
Bad	0.4	5,000	6,000	–1,000
Market values		10,000	5,714	4,286

Panel B: Limited Liability

		Payoffs ($)		
State	Probability	Asset	Debt	Equity
Good	0.6	15,000	6,000	9,000
Bad	0.4	5,000	5,000	0
Market values		10,000	5,286	4,714

Consider first the situation of unlimited liability. With a single owner, the issue of joint and several liability is not relevant. Under unlimited liability, the equity investor is responsible for any excess of creditors' claims over and above the liquidation value of the firm. For the purpose of the example assume when the assets of the firm are liquidated, the equity holder will have sufficient personal assets to pay any deficiency value and will not declare personal bankruptcy. In Table 1, Panel A, there are two possible outcomes, a good state with a probability of 0.6 and a bad state with a 0.4 probability. If the good state occurs, the assets have a liquidation value of $15,000, whereas in the bad state the value of the assets is $5,000. In the good state there is no problem paying the debt holders the full value of $6,000 and there is $9,000 available to the equity holders. Under the bad state, the liquidation value of the assets is $5,000 and not sufficient to cover the creditors' claims. This results in an additional claim on the equity holder of $1,000. Thus the equity holder has a negative payoff – a contribution – of $1,000 to the creditors.

Under unlimited liability and the assumptions used, the debt is riskless since there is no question that the creditor will receive full value on the credit and the interest rate will equal a risk-free interest rate. The market value of the project cash flows is equal to $10,000, the value of the initial capital. Since the debt is riskless, assuming a 5% risk-free discount rate, the market value of debt is $5714, leaving a market value of equity of $4286.

Note that the market value of the corporation as of the start date is the same as it would be if no debt were introduced. The unlimited liability regime does not change the overall risk of the assets and the size of the potential debt payment does not affect the market value of the assets. Second, the market value of the equity falls but this reflects the issuance of risk-free debt and the repurchase of equity to alter the capital structure. The creditors before investing their funds would evaluate the expected cash flows they would receive at the end of the period and set the terms of the credit in order to protect themselves. Since they have a risk-free position, the equity holder has a very risky position. This is reflected in the spread of the payoffs to the equity holder. However, the actual per share value of the equity will not be affected by the debt–equity shift under unlimited liability (Modigliani and Miller 1958). The number of shares has been reduced and the increased risk to the equity is offset by the higher expected return.

Now consider the same firm, project and financing but under a limited liability regime – the equity holder is not responsible to cover any deficit of the creditors' claims over and above the cash flows available from the liquidation of the firm's assets. Thus the equity value is derived from the value of the underlying firm assets at the end of the period and the debt obligations that have first priority. In Table 1, panel B, the cash flows to all investors in the firm are presented along with the market values of the claims. Since we have assumed no transactions costs in the event of default, the market value of the assets, i.e. the market value of the firm, remains at $10,000. The creditors, while receiving the full value of their claim in the good state, receive only the liquidation value of the assets, which is less than their claim of $6,000, in the bad state. Thus creditors now face a risky cash flow stream and must adjust the terms of their credit including a higher interest rate on credit.

Note that the equity of the firm receives either a positive amount or zero at the end of the period; this is equivalent to a call option written on the underlying assets of the firm with a strike or exercise price equal to the promised debt payments at the end of the period. Options are called derivative securities since their value is derived from the cash flow characteristics of the underlying securities (Hull 1995). Using option theory, the value of the equity is calculated to be $4,714 and the market value of debt is equal to $5,286. Just as in the previous example, the movement from an unlevered to a levered firm has no effect on the market value of the assets, decreases the market value of equity, and has no impact on the share price of the equity. The equity holder now has a risky stream and the expected return on the equity is sufficient to just compensate for the added risk. These observations are consistent with the Miller and Modigliani propositions in a no-tax world. The independence of the share price from the form of liability regime depends upon the fact that the creditors can negotiate the terms of their credit and hence the market value of the credit based on the liability structure.

Comparing the limited and unlimited liability scenarios we observe that the market value of equity is higher by $428 in the limited liability regime. This increase is exactly equal to the lower market value of the creditors' claims. Suppose there were a unilateral change in liability regime from limited to unlimited liability. We know that this would result in a higher risk to equity holders and a lower risk to bondholders. Market prices of equity would be unchanged after the announcement as long as the terms of the credit are renegotiated so that the increase in market value of the debt is passed on to the equity holders, who now have a higher risk. If, however, there is no chance of recontracting, the shift to the unlimited liability regime will result in a windfall to the creditors.

Notice that in this example the overall risk and value of the enterprise along with the cost of capital are unaffected by the liability structure of the firm. The liability structure shifts risk and values among the various claimants to the cash flow. While we have chosen the two extreme or pure cases of liability regime, the intermediate positions, *pro rata* and assessibility, would have impacts on the equity value and the risk to the creditors (and thereby the yields charged for credit) between the two extremes. For example with *pro rata* liability, the risk to the creditor is greater and the risk to the equity holder is less than under a pure unlimited liability regime.

The above conclusions assume that the creditors are able to collect from the equity holders the full amount of the excess liability up to the legal amount. However, this assumption becomes the crux of the debate among the researchers as to the efficacy of extended liability. For any specific form of extended liability, the creditors will assess the probability of collecting in the event of a bankruptcy; this probability will depend upon the wealth of the investors and their ability to circumvent the excess liability structure. For the former, the creditors must incur search costs which are unrelated to the underlying profitability of the firm. Clearly if the liability rule has a joint and several element to it, the information costs are larger. The creditors then determine a yield on the credit based on their ability to collect. The less likely they are to collect, the higher their risk, the larger the yield and the less risk to the equity holders – given that overall risk remains constant. If the creditors believe that they will be unable to collect anything in the event of a default, even in a excess liability regime, the regime is effectively a limited liability. If it is observed that transactions costs are higher under unlimited liability, contractual provisions may be introduced to convert unlimited to limited liability.

Also of concern to researchers are the attempts by equity holders to frustrate an unlimited liability regime and generate uncompensated shifts in wealth. Suppose the firm operates in an unlimited liability regime and the creditors have evaluated the risk of default and their expected payoffs in the event of liquidation and have set the yields appropriately. While equity holders have a riskier stream there is the offsetting benefit of a lower cost of credit. However, it is in the equity holder's interests to institute various techniques ranging from hiding personal assets to selling (in the extreme giving) shares to low-wealth individuals. To the extent the current equity holders are successful in these operations and this behaviour is unexpected by creditors, they convert unlimited liability closer to limited liability. The equity holders now have claims worth more to them than before and their wealth has increased at the expense of the wealth of debt holders. The incentive to engage in this behaviour increases with the probability of default, the risk of the assets, and the amount of debt.

In the original arguments concerning the introduction of limited liability, the major concern was increased risk taking by owners of companies to the detriment of the corporation and its creditors. It is necessary to understand the situations in which this risk taking will arise. With an unchanged cost of capital, there should be no bias toward riskier projects. However, the concerns raised in the original arguments are correct and are quickly demonstrated in the following examples.

Table 2

Limited Liability

		Payoffs ($)		
State	Probability	Asset	Debt	Equity
Good	0.6	7,000	6,000	1,000
Bad	0.4	3,000	3,000	0
Market values		4,737	4,267	470

Panel A: Shift risk

		Payoffs ($)		
State	Probability	Asset	Debt	Equity
Good	0.05	50,000	6,000	44,000
Bad	0.95	100	100	0
Market values		1,996	324	1,672

Panel B: Double Liability

		Payoffs		
State	Probability	Asset	Debt	Equity
Good	0.05	50,000	6,000	44,000
Bad	0.95	100	4,100	–4,000
Market values		1,996	3,981	–1,985

Panel C: Unlimited Liability

		Payoffs		
State	Probability	Asset	Debt	Equity
Good	0.05	50,000	6,000	44,000
Bad	0.95	100	6,000	–5,900
Market values		1,996	5,714	–3,718

Limited liability introduces the prospect of opportunistic behaviour – moral hazard and adverse selection (Milgrom and Roberts 1992, chs 5 and 6) – which are attempts by equity holders under certain situations to shift wealth from creditors to themselves. An example of moral hazard is that bondholders evaluate the credit worthiness of a company and adjust the terms of credit accordingly. However, once the credit is in place, under certain circumstances the company may undertake behaviour which was not anticipated in order to increase the equity holders' wealth at the expense of the creditors. The bondholder class is most susceptible to this problem since it has a long-term contract. To demonstrate the situations under which this opportunistic behaviour will arise and how the liability regime will impact on the incentive to engage in this behaviour, consider the examples presented in Table 2. Our illustrative limited liability firm invests its $10,000 and immediately after the investment the economy goes into a recession and the outcomes in the good and bad state are reduced to $7000 and $3000 respectively. The value of the firm falls to $4737, the market value of debt is $4267 and equity, $470. (As a point of comparison the market values of debt and equity under unlimited liability are $5714 and –$977 respectively.) This firm faces a substantial risk of default and the equity holders have an incentive to undertake actions that will shift wealth from the creditors to themselves. To do this, the assets of the firm are liquidated and invested in a very risky project, one which has a low probability of a very high payoff and a high probability of effectively a zero payoff (see panel A, Table 2). In this situation, the total value of the assets fall to $1996, the value of debt falls to $324 but the value of equity *increases* to $1672. The creditors' loss in value, related to the increased risk they now face in the firm's operations, reflects the loss in value of the assets and the gain to the equity holders. The equity holders are clearly better off compared to the previous situation. (Smith and Warner (1979) identify other methods by which wealth can be shifted from bondholders to equity holders.) The incentive to engage in these actions increases with the amount of debt outstanding and the probability of default. Clearly if the firm is successful, the benefits provided by limited liability are not as valuable as the situation in which the firm is likely to be in default. The creditors are not powerless to prevent some of these actions since they can incur expenses and monitor more closely and introduce covenants in the trust indenture which will curtail certain types of behaviour and force provision of information to creditors before the firm undertakes certain actions.

Would the incentive be the same under different liability regimes? In panels B and C the payoffs and values of creditors' and equity holders' claims are presented under a form of excess (double) liability and unlimited liability. Under double liability with a risk increase, in the very likely event of default, the equity holder would have to make a payment to the creditors equal to the difference between the liquidation value of assets and the debt claim up to a maximum of the original book value of the equity, $4000. The value of the debt would thus be higher ($3981) and the value of the equity is now negative, –$1985. Since the likelihood of a default and a payment by the equity holder is so high, the equity holder by undertaking risk increasing decisions would lose value and hence would not do it. Under the pure unlimited liability regime, the payment by the equity holder conditional on the bad state occurring will cover the complete excess of the creditor claim above the value of the assets and this claim must be paid by the equity holder. In this case the debt is riskless and the shares of the firm have a value of –$3718. Again the incentive to engage in risk increasing behaviour is blunted significantly. Therefore, under any excess liability regime, the incentive to engage in wealth shifting behaviour is reduced since the value of the equity expected by this behaviour is reduced.

The example demonstrates one of the shortcomings of any excess liability regime: to the extent that the equity holder can reduce or eliminate payments to creditors in the event of default, the incentive to diminish risk-taking behaviour is frustrated and there are again uncompensated shifts in wealth. For example, in the double liability case, if investors can structure their affairs such that there is no collection in excess of the amount under limited liability, the equity holder has returned the situation to one of limited liability. The problem of avoiding the excess liability payoffs becomes increasingly severe with the amount of the excess liability and if it is joint and several liability. Thus the incentive to avoid payments is greatest under the joint and several rule, decreases under the *pro rata* unlimited liability and continues to decrease under excess limited liability as the deviation from pure limited liability is reduced. Of course, bondholders are not unaware of the possibility of frustration of the excess liability rule and will adjust the credit terms appropriately. In the extreme, the limited liability rule is found.

EFFICIENCY OF LIABILITY REGIME: CONTRACTUAL CREDITORS. In concluding which liability regime is efficient, all researchers identify two issues: the relationship between liability regime and the functioning and efficiency of the capital market and the transactions costs imposed on creditors and investors. Consider first the capital market issue. In order to have correct corporate investment decisions, there must be a separating between corporate investment and production decisions and owners' personal consumption decisions. The existence of a capital market in which shares can be freely traded facilitates this separation. Individuals who own shares need not be concerned about the dividend policy of the firm in respect of their consumption decisions but can sell sufficient number of shares to generate funds for consumption. A shareholder with a particular risk preference who finds that a firm in which he or she owns shares makes a good investment decision but of above-average risk need only sell some shares to return his or her portfolio to the desired risk exposure. In addition there should be no incentive for investors to accumulate shares and thereby reduce the liquidity of the market. Finally, the information costs of both equity investors and grantors of credit should be minimized. In all of these factors, the liability structure has an important impact.

In the pure unlimited liability world, the rate of return earned by any investor depends not only on the cash flows of the firm and the wealth of the individual investor but also the wealth of other investors. If a wealthy investor purchases one share and there is a default, creditors in a cost-minimizing strategy will aggressively pursue the wealthy shareholder. If this individual has sufficient wealth to cover the excess of claims over assets, the individual faces a very unusual probability distribution of possible returns: with no default there is a payoff related to the cash flows for one share, yet in the event of default the investor is exposed to the loss of the entire firm. This is not the probability distribution faced by an investor who has less or no personal wealth. Therefore, under the pure unlimited liability regime, investors have different probability distributions for the same share and hence pricing securities becomes very difficult for the market. In addition, as long as the wealthy investor maintains his or her private wealth available in event of default, this investor would prefer to alter the probability distribution by owning an increasing amount of the shares of the firm. Since the outcome in the event of a default is the same, the greater number of shares provides a greater payoff in the good states. This result is recognized in the literature and for this reason, a pure unlimited liability regime is mentioned as a possible rule but quickly dismissed. Note that in the pure limited liability rule, each individual investor faces the same probability distribution, there is no incentive to accumulate shares for risk modifying reasons, and securities markets can price securities. Under this rule, shares are transferable and markets can perform their function.

It is also true that any excess liability rule which does not have a joint and several element will permit markets to price securities. For each equity investor, the distribution of outcomes is the same provided payment is made. Thus, security holders need not worry about the wealth of other equity investors and each investor faces the same probability distribution. Note, however, that creditors are not indifferent between the liability regimes since with extended liability they incur transactions costs to assess the capacity of investors to pay in the event of a default. On the investor side, the sale of shares by a wealthy investor to a poorer one will have an impact on the amount of recovery and hence creditors will take this into consideration. One way to ensure the full benefit of unlimited liability through lower credit costs is to have majority holdings and limitations on transactions so that the creditor can have an easier time assessing the wealth and capacity to pay. Thus, extended liability rules may generate a problem of reduced trading. The stronger the excess liability, the more the reduced trading. While securities can be priced, transactions may not occur, thereby inhibiting the functioning of markets.

In considering the transactions costs of creditors, an extended liability regime will introduce significant costs both *ex ante* and *ex post*. All of the costs are related to the amount of the payments to the creditors in the event of default relative to the actual amount that should be paid and the probability that equity holders will engage in activities that reduce the payout in the event of default.

On an *ex ante* basis, creditors need to identify the terms under which they will grant credit and this requires identification of the wealth of all individual investors and assurances that the wealth will be available in the event of default. Thus search costs prior to the initiation of the credit and ongoing monitoring costs of the shareholders' identity and wealth as the firm approaches default are necessary. The ongoing monitoring will be costly and, in some situations, impossible. The costs are greatest in a joint and several regime but any excess liability regime will require ongoing monitoring of shareholder wealth and ownership structure.

After a default, the transactions costs incurred will depend upon the liability rule in operation. Under a joint and several rule, the creditors will pursue all shareholders but clearly will anticipate collections from the wealthiest shareholder(s). Collection costs can be very large, especially in a widely held company. As the excess liability rule becomes weaker, the creditors will still pursue the wealthiest shareholders since they have the greatest likelihood of making payments in the event of default in amounts equal to those imposed by the liability regime.

There is very little empirical work undertaken on the impact of liability structure. One interesting piece is the analysis of extended liability presented in Macey and Miller (1992) in the context of 'double' liability in the banking industry. Over the period roughly from the Civil War to the Great Depression, during which the extended liability regime was in force, most small banks were closely held and the larger banks were parts of holding companies. Macey and Miller observed that recoveries for depositors and other creditors were about 51% of the amount assessed, arguably a small proportion given the less developed capital market and the closely held status of the companies. Also they found that most banks were liquidated voluntarily before they went into insolvency, thereby keeping losses to creditors low. However, this observed behaviour is more likely due to management owning the bulk of the shares and thus liquidating while they can still obtain a payoff. They also note a number of administrative issues that had to be faced.

One that has direct relevance to our discussion is the determination of who is liable in the event of a default and judgment against shareholders. It was determined that liability followed ownership provided the shares had been sold in good faith at a time when the bank was solvent. In addition, there were opportunistic transfers to insolvent parties in an attempt by shareholders to evade liability in default. Rules were established in order to determine whether the transactions undertaken either in insolvency or prior to insolvency were undertaken with the sole purpose of avoiding assessment. Finally, enforcement of assessment in the event of a default presented problems. Suing a large number of shareholders was costly and cumbersome and enforcing assessments in remote jurisdictions was problematic. In the latter case receivers did not pursue shareholders.

Even though this liability structure was operational in its context, it may not provide much information as to the operation of extended liability regimes in the context of well-developed capital markets, widely held shares, and foreign investors. It is interesting to note that the excess liability was removed since it 'effectively bankrupt(s) many innocent stockholders who have taken no part in the active management and control of the bank' (Macey and Miller 1992: 37). The idea that innocent shareholders are being punished for actions of others is an important issue in applying extended liability in the context of tort creditors.

Carr and Mathewson present an agency cost argument

in which mandated unlimited liability results in a higher cost of capital, smaller firms and less growth. Intuitively the cost of capital is higher due to higher transactions and monitoring costs under unlimited liability. Unlimited liability must be mandated, otherwise firms would either shift to limited liability or would write contracts with creditors to introduce limits to their liability. The authors test their theory on two different data sets: Scottish banks over the period 1795 to 1882 and US law firms. The authors find evidence consistent with their position in both data sets. In the Scottish banking system there were three Edinburgh banks that had limited liability while entry was open to others, provided the entrants' shareholders accepted unlimited liability. While a public policy argument could be made that an unlimited (joint and several) liability regime would reduce risk taking behaviour, thereby lowering the probability of default and hence increasing the stability of the banking system (see Macey and Miller 1992 for a similar argument), Carr and Mathewson argue that there was a private interest explanation for mandated unlimited liability. They find limited liability banks were more profitable and larger than unlimited liability banks. Findings on average size of law firms and lawyers' incomes based on liability regime are also consistent with their hypothesis. A comment on the paper by Gilson (1991) concerning the law firm data set suggests that Carr and Mathewson have the causation of liability status and growth reversed. The reason for incorporation of legal professionals reflects a tax advantage, and those firms which have grown the most and have the most to lose will incorporate while those with low growth will not. Gilson is of the view that liability status has no influence *per se*. There continues to be disagreement over the interpretation of new empirical evidence.

Finally, there is some empirical evidence presented for German start up companies (Horvath and Woywode 1996) which suggests that holding constant size, age, and industry, the growth rates of companies differ according to the liability structure chosen. Those which choose limited liability have higher growth rates compared to those which choose unlimited liability, even after controlling for a number of variables. The paper also observes that companies with limits on the owners' liability display an increased likelihood of exiting via filing for bankruptcy.

CONCLUSION ON LIABILITY REGIME: CONTRACTUAL CREDITORS. For contractual creditors the research has recognized that there are problems with limited liability in terms of the incentive to engage in risk enhancing and other wealth diverting behaviour. However, all researchers have concluded that limited liability should be the default rule. This conclusion rests on the observation that creditors in a limited liability regime can protect themselves *ex ante* by choosing appropriate terms for the credit instruments they provide to the firm including restrictive covenants, monitoring, information provision requirements, and personal guarantees. In addition, transactions costs to creditors, both *ex ante* and *ex post*, are lower under limited liability than under any of the excess liability regimes. The transactions costs faced by shareholders are lowest under limited liability, although the excess liability rules without joint and several elements will permit transactions costs to approach but not equal those under limited liability. With limited liability as the default rule, companies are free to contract around it as they see fit.

TORT CREDITORS: LARGE COMPANIES WITH PUBLICLY TRADED EQUITY. The conclusion to maintain limited liability in the context of voluntary creditors is a result of the costs and benefits of limited liability and the observation that any risk increasing behaviour is partially internalized due to the behaviour of creditors. However, there are situations in which negotiations with a potential creditor are indirect or even non-existent. For example in a product liability situation, the consumer purchases the product and potentially could have included in the purchase decision, and hence in the price paid, the probability of a product liability claim. In other situations, the consumer may take the service provided but not be able to differentiate in price based on the probability of a problem. There are also environmental torts such as the Exxon Valdez oil spill which can have significant costs. These are examples of corporate torts and the issue of the impact of the liability regime on the incentive to undertake behaviour which can increase the likelihood of tort claims is an important one in the literature.

Consider a company with limited liability in an industry that is prone to high risk events. Note that high risk industries can be identified *ex ante* by market participants. In this industry, the firm would typically engage in costly risk reducing activity; however, in order to increase cash flows, the firm decides to reduce or eliminate the risk reducing investments. Analogously, the firm may decide not to undertake needed risk reducing investment activity. The probability of a harmful event occurring increases, and even though the probability is very small, given the size of some tort claims the potential expected costs to the firm can be substantial. Note that the gain in wealth by eliminating the risk reducing activity or not engaging in it is at the expense of the tort creditors who are unable to negotiate with the corporation and require the risk reducing activity. If potential tort victims could identify that the company altered its risk strategy and consequently could adjust the product prices appropriately and engage in monitoring to ensure that the company does not engage in opportunistic behaviour concerning the product liability risk, there would be no gain to equity holders of risk changing behaviour in high risk industries. Even though the relative infrequency of these types of risk increasing activities is accepted by Hansmann and Kraakman (1991), they still believe that the incentives provided by an excess liability scheme are important and should be introduced.

With proportionate liability the market will assess the expected value of the possible tort claims and the share price will fall to reflect the incorporation of this information. The reduced price will provide an incentive to the firm to increase the funds devoted to risk reducing activities and thereby result in an increase in share price. The risk reducing activities will continue up to the point where the marginal cost equals the marginal benefit. In this way the risk of tort claims is internalized in the decision making of the corporation. However, given the structure of the marginal costs and benefits, it may be rational for the company not to engage in any risk reducing activities.

Another way to internalize the costs of tort damages is through the purchase of insurance by the corporation. The premium paid for the insurance will reflect the expected damages and thus the incentive for risk reducing is manifest in a reduction in the insurance premium. However, there is a question whether the insurance company will write an unlimited payoff policy and the monitoring costs incurred by the insurance company may be substantial.

Leebron (1991) investigates proportionate liability for tort claims and concludes that the case for limited liability for corporate torts has been overestimated and other liability regimes should be investigated. In the absence of enforcement transactions costs, which Leebron considers may be significant, the optimal liability rule would be *pro rata* (proportional) unlimited liability, at least for severely injured tort victims. However, any decision as to the appropriate liability rule requires 'a context-specific analysis and an examination of diversification opportunities, risk bearing, and transactions costs' (Leebron 1991: 1568). In addition, he suggests that a final resolution of liability regime for widely held companies awaits more theoretical and empirical work.

Hansmann and Kraakman (1991) argue that a well-designed *pro rata* unlimited liability rule is feasible, can be introduced at the state level, and will neither impair the marketability of securities nor impose excessive collection costs. The authors recognize that the rule has to be designed very carefully, collection costs could be large, and there could be collection only against the large/wealthy shareholders. In an attempt to address the collection costs issue, they introduce a concept of portfolio insurance – insurance that covers the individual investor's portfolio in the event of a tort claim. This type of insurance does not currently exist and it is not obvious that this type of insurance will be written. What distinguishes this insurance from the traditional type of insurance is the open-ended nature of the possible loss. Equally important is the possibility of evasion of payments in the event of a tort liability. Evasion techniques have been described above (see Macey and Miller 1992), and Hansmann and Kraakman add to the list the issuance of debt and the repurchase of equity in order to reduce the amount of assets available to the tort creditor and the disaggregation of companies into less risky assets held by the company and higher risk assets that are sold to individuals who have few personal assets. Note that risk is in the context of potential tort liability and not underlying operating risk. These individuals who acquire the risky assets are described by the authors as 'high rollers'; they suggest that high rollers are limited in supply and hence not an important problem is the operation of the *pro rata* rule in the event of tort. With the size of environmental tort claims, high rollers exist even under a limited liability regime. These individuals stand ready to purchase the risky assets of companies and thus remove the tort risk exposure from the original company.

Independent of the theoretical arguments for and against the use of proportionate liability in corporate torts, two papers suggest that the use of extended liability will not achieve the results strongly supported by Hansmann and Kraakman. The reasons proposed are the existence of 'liquid equity traded in a world with innovative capital markets and minimal transactions costs' (Grundfest 1992: 390), and procedural problems of implementation, especially in the context of obtaining funds to cover the excess liabilities in the event of tort liability (Alexander 1992: 394). The papers are complementary; Grundfest considers the influence of capital markets on the efficacy of excess liability regimes and Alexander considers the administrative problems encountered in implementing proportionate liability for tort claims at the state level. Taken together the papers suggest that the expected reduction of share prices of risky firms will not arise. Without the reduction in share price, the incentive to reduce tort risk is diminished and corporate behaviour is no different than under limited liability.

The Alexander paper is a compelling argument concerning the difficulty of implementing (*pro rata*) unlimited liability, focusing on the problems of the choice of law and personal jurisdiction. She argues that without federal legislation, it would not be feasible to adopt unlimited liability in tort and thus individual states cannot proceed on their own. Hansmann and Kraakman (1992a) acknowledge the importance of procedural issues and agree that federal legislation is the preferred mechanism to implement unlimited liability in torts but disagree that it is the only route. Their comment on the Alexander paper addresses the issues of jurisdiction and conflicts of law which they conclude would still permit implementation of unlimited liability at the state level.

Grundfest presents an intriguing argument for the inability of any extended liability regime to influence share prices. His position is based on the reactions of sophisticated, well functioning capital markets to the introduction of unlimited liability, the response of corporations with high tort risk activities by issuing equity-like securities that do not have unlimited liability, and the reaction of financial intermediaries. Grundfest argues that the response expected if excess liability for torts is instituted is identical to the arbitrage of tax and regulatory barriers by imaginative wealth maximizing capital market participants. In fact regulatory constraints intended to stop the arbitrage lead to further arbitrage behaviour.

From the investor perspective, Grundfest argues that any reduction in share price for risky firms will result in the emergence of a clientele composed of attachment proof investors who will hold the risky securities and pay up to the same price as would exist under limited liability; shareholders with substantial assets will form another clientele that holds the securities of less risky companies in less risky industries. Grundfest refers to this behaviour as arbitrage and, if successful, there will be no price signal associated with the introduction of excess liability, no reduction in risky activities, and no increase in the pool of assets available to satisfy claims. The arbitrage result is restricted only by transactions costs. The attachment proof investors need sufficient wealth in aggregate to be effective in the arbitrage and must be without assets available to satisfy a claim at the individual level.

The clientele arises as a result of US constitutional issues at the state level and from the practical and jurisdictional problems arising from attempts to collect from domestic and foreign shareholders of firms that have insufficient assets to satisfy tort claims and the fact that jurisdiction cannot be established for foreign investors. In making these arguments Grundfest relies on the paper by Alexander (1992), who deals in depth with these issues. Alexander uses an example where the tort occurs in an excess liability state and the firm and some shareholders are found in different limited liability states. Alexander argues as summarized in Grundfest (1992: 395–6):

> . . . the simple passive ownership of stock in a corporation that commits a tort cannot satisfy the minimum contacts test for assertion of jurisdiction. This holds true even if the tort occurs in the forum state, the corporation is incorporated in the forum state, and the shareholders derive economic benefit from the corporation's activity in the forum state (Alexander, citing *World-Wide Volkswagen v. Woodson*, 444 US 286 (1977)). For jurisdiction to lie, the corporation's shareholders would probably have to be subject to personal service in the forum state, reside in the state, engage in continuous and substantial business dealings in the state, or have litigation-related contacts with the forum state. Because of these constitutional limitations, only a fraction of any corporation's shareholders would be subject to excess liability in any given state, and that fraction would depend on random factors, such as the locus of the specific tort at issue and the residences of each of the corporation's shareholders. Moreover, because it would be against a state's self interest to make its residents liable for torts while residents of other states could readily avoid jurisdiction, the prospect that proportionate liability would be adopted at the state level seems doubtful.

With respect to obtaining jurisdiction over foreign shareholders and attaching their assets, the problems here make the collection problems associated with smaller domestic shareholders seem trivial. First, courts may not assert jurisdiction over foreign shareholders. Further, any attempt to extend jurisdiction will face potential impacts on international relations. Even if the jurisdictional issue is solved, the problem of collection is challenging. Foreign courts may not enforce US court judgments in their country, may not recognize default judgments, and may only enforce judgments that are consistent with their corporate law. Further, it will be difficult to identify ownership of the shares, especially where shares are held in street or bearer name or where the shares are held in account in countries with bank secrecy laws. Finally, the cost of pursuing foreign shareholders will be very high and greater than the cost of pursuing domestic shareholders.

Grundfest also notes that the formation of clienteles can result in unbalanced portfolios compared to the set of portfolios each investor would have under limited liability. However, he notes that the same portfolio risk that obtained under limited liability can be obtained under *pro rata* liability through the use of derivative securities such as futures, options and swaps of index portfolios composed of risky and non-risky stocks. Thus, what could be done under limited liability can be attained under unlimited liability. Further, these derivative securities are attachment proof in the sense that they do not reflect direct ownership of any equity security.

In addition to the clientele effect, corporate issuers can react to the instigation of extended liability by restructuring balance sheets towards attachment proof security issues. Debt-equity exchanges will reduce the equity component and the use of convertible debt, high risk debt, warrants and complex securities, all of which have equity characteristics but are attachment proof, will arise. Hansmann and Kraakman (1992b) respond that these reactions will just focus the unlimited liability in the remaining equity. While this is true, it does not negate the argument that arbitrage will occur on this smaller remaining equity and in fact the arbitrage may be easier since there is less equity outstanding. Finally, Grundfest suggests that intermediaries such as investment banks, commercial banks and mutual funds will arise to provide investment vehicles that are attachment proof. For example, a foreign government or governmental agency can issue foreign debt that has a value that is contingent on the price of a security of a domestic company which is risky in respect to tort liability. This structure provides an attachment proof position to the domestic investor since the investor is not an equity holder in the domestic corporation directly and the tort claimants would have to assert jurisdiction over lenders in a foreign government. To similar effect, foreign companies in safe industries can issue debt that has value contingent on the price of a security of a domestic risky company. The most direct methods to avoid a payment in the event of a tort claim are the use by domestic investors of offshore mutual funds which hold the shares of risky domestic companies or the direct investment in the equity of risky companies by wealthy individuals through their foreign accounts. In these situations there will be significant difficulty in attaching the assets of the investors. The resolution of the Grundfest and Hansmann–Kraakman positions will be based on empirical evidence. The empirical evidence available on the reaction of capital markets to certain factors such as tax differences and differential regulatory requirements both domestically and internationally provides support to the Grundfest position.

TORT CREDITORS: CLOSELY HELD COMPANIES. In any discussion of liability rules, especially in the context of tort liability, the close corporation takes up a large amount of energy and passion. It is generally accepted that for most close corporations the entrepreneur or small ownership group has invested a substantial amount of its personal wealth in the venture. This results in an undiversified portfolio and generally a higher cost of capital than a comparable corporation in which the owners have been able to diversify their risk. In addition, the ability to bear loss in the close corporation is much restricted compared to a company with a large number of shareholders. These arguments suggest at first blush that a limited liability regime is appropriate for the close corporation.

The owner/manager of the close corporation obtains the full benefit of any opportunistic behaviour with respect to involuntary creditors. Thus there is the strong incentive for opportunistic behaviour. The paradigmatic example of the problem of limited liability in torts is *Walkovszky v. Carlton*, in which the owner of a fleet of taxicabs separately incorporated a company for each taxicab. The owner is thus able to limit his potential liability exposure to the assets within the individual company in the event of a tort claim. The result is an incentive to increase opportunistic behaviour.

Recognizing the problem, the research papers suggest resolutions ranging from the introduction of unlimited liability, to a more vigorous approach to piercing the corporate veil, to the retention of limited liability in conjunction with the introduction of other mechanisms intended to reduce the opportunistic behaviour.

Piercing the corporate veil permits creditors to reach the personal assets of the shareholder of the firm. Easterbrook and Fischel (1985: 109) argue that veil piercing can be understood as an attempt by the court to trade off the benefits of limited liability against its costs. They note that almost every veil-piercing case has involved a close corporation. However, Leebron (1991: 1628, fn. 19) notes that even in the close corporation, courts are more inclined to pierce the veil in order to hold a parent corporation liable for debts of a subsidiary than reaching the personal assets of the shareholders (*Walkovszky v. Carlton*).

Alternatives to veil piercing which retain limited liability have also been discussed by many of the authors. These alternatives include the identification of minimum capital requirements in order to reduce the impact of thin capitalization on incentives to undertake risky behaviour, changing the priority of tort claimants to a position prior to the secured creditors in the event of a tort claim, mandatory corporate insurance, introduction of managerial liability (which is often eliminated through the purchase of insurance) and finally the regulation of inputs in a risky industry (gatekeeper function). These approaches may be workable but introduce a number of administrative costs and questions and significant difficulties in identifying the correct levels of intervention. As an example Leebron concludes that in situations in which:

> limited liability is irrelevant because controlling shareholders and other investors taking an active role in the enterprise may be held directly liable . . . the shareholders ought to be granted limited liability subject to the three constraints put forth. First, controlling shareholders should not be able to limit their liability by artificially separating a unitary business. Or closely related enterprises, into separate corporations. Second, shareholders of close corporations should not be allowed to unilaterally determine the capital available to involuntary creditors by using personally guaranteed corporate debt instead of equity to finance the enterprise. Finally, shareholder/managers should have an obligation to provide adequate insurance to meet the claims of foreseeable tort victims (Leebron 1991: 1636).

Finally, the argument for unlimited liability is presented by Hansmann and Kraakman (1991) in which they conclude that some small firms may not be viable under unlimited liability due to the diversification and risk bearing arguments presented before, but there is no reason to believe that such small firms should exist. Further, they argue that the presence of liability insurance for businesses strengthens the argument for unlimited liability. However, as noted above, insurance is costly and limits on the liability covered due to difficulty of monitoring may make unlimited liability less feasible than the authors suggest. The ultimate resolution of the appropriate liability regime is again an empirical issue; the lack of empirical evidence on important issues is best demonstrated in Hansmann and Kraakman (1991: 1890) where they quote a telephone conversation that 'writers of liability insurance for businesses claim to be able to control moral hazard by inspecting their insured and employing experience ratings'. There is no doubt this is true, but it is coverage of well-known risks and limited, not unlimited, coverage.

PAUL HALPERN

See also BANKRUPTCY AND ITS REFORM; CORPORATE BANKRUPTCY; CORPORATE LAW; JOINT AND SEVERAL LIABILITY; PARTNERSHIP; PRODUCTS LIABILITY; PROFESSIONAL CORPORATIONS AND LIMITED LIABILITY; UNLIMITED SHAREHOLDER LIABILITY.

Subject classification: 5g(ii).

CASE

Walkovszky v. Carlton 223 NE 2d 6 (NY 1966).

BIBLIOGRAPHY

Alexander, J. 1992. Unlimited shareholder liability through a procedural lens. *Harvard Law Review* 106: 387–445.

Carr, J. and Mathewson, G.F. 1988. Unlimited liability as a barrier to entry. *Journal of Political Economy* 96: 766–84.

Carr, J. and Mathewson, G.F. 1991. Reply to Professor Gilson. *Journal of Political Economy* 99: 426–8.

Easterbrook, F. and Fischel, D. 1985. Limited liability and the corporation. *University of Chicago Law Review* 52: 89–117.

Gilson, R. 1991. Unlimited liability and law firm organization: tax factors and the direction of causation. *Journal of Political Economy* 99: 420–5.

Grundfest, J. 1992. The limited future of unlimited liability: a capital markets perspective. *Yale Law Journal* 102: 387–425.

Halpern, P., Trebilcock, M. and Turnbull, S. 1980. An economic analysis of limited liability in corporation law. *University of Toronto Law Journal* 30: 117–50.

Hansmann, H. and Kraakman, R. 1991. Towards unlimited shareholder liability for corporate torts. *Yale Law Journal* 100: 1879–1934.

Hansmann, H. and Kraakman, R. 1992a. A procedural focus on unlimited shareholder liability. *Harvard Law Review* 106: 446–59.

Hansmann, H. and Kraakman, R. 1992b. Do capital markets compel limited liability? a response to Professor Grundfest. *Yale Law Journal* 102: 427–36.

Horvath, M. and Woywode, M. 1996. Entrepreneurs and the choice of limited liability. John M. Olin Working Paper 129, Stanford Law School, Stanford, CA.

Hull, J. 1995. *Introduction to Futures and Options Markets*. Englewood Cliffs, NJ: Prentice Hall.

Leebron, D. 1991. Limited liability, tort victims, and creditor. *Columbia Law Review* 91: 1565–1650.

Macey, J. and Miller, G. 1992. Double liability of bank shareholders: history and implications. *Wake Forest Law Review* 27: 31–62.

Mayers, D. and Smith, C., Jr. 1982. On the corporate demand for insurance. *Journal of Business* 55: 281–96.

Milgrom, P. and Roberts, J. 1992. *Economics, Organization and Management*. Englewood Cliffs, NJ: Prentice Hall.

Modigliani, F. and Miller, M. 1958. The cost of capital, corporation finance and the theory of investment. *American Economic Review* 48: 261–97.

Smart, M. 1996. On limited liability and the development of capital markets: an historical analysis. Law and Economics Working Paper Series, Faculty of Law, University of Toronto.

Smith, C. and Warner, J. 1979. On financial contracting: an analysis of bond covenants. *Journal of Financial Economics* 7: 117–61.

Woodward, S. 1985. Limited liability in the theory of the firm. *Zeitschrift für die gesamte Staatswissenschaft* (*Journal of Institutional and Theoretical Economics*) 141: 601–11.

liquidated damages. *See* COGNITION AND CONTRACTS; PENALTY DOCTRINE IN CONTRACT LAW.

litigation. *See* SETTLEMENT OF LITIGATION.

litigation costs. *See* ALLOCATION OF LITIGATION COSTS: AMERICAN AND ENGLISH RULES; CONTINGENT FEES.

Llewellyn, Karl. *See* KARL LLEWELLYN AND THE EARLY LAW AND ECONOMICS OF CONTRACT.

Lloyd's of London. *See* OCCUPATIONAL DISEASE AND THE TORT SYSTEM: THE CASE OF ASBESTOS.

local common property rights. Local common property rights are property rights exercised in common by members of a group that is sufficiently small for these members to be able to observe and react to one another's behaviour, and consequently to have an interest in cooperating with each other in the right circumstances. Typical examples of assets managed under common property systems include many kinds of environmental resource such as village grazing lands, inshore fisheries, underground aquifers, canal systems, forests and watersheds – but also other kinds of institutions such as partnerships, joint-stock companies, collective farms, research joint ventures and cabinet government, the management of which raises intriguingly similar incentive issues. Understanding these issues requires a careful analysis of the differences between these and other kinds of property right.

First of all, what are property rights? Ownership of an asset typically involves at least three conceptually distinct rights: the right to enjoy the stream of benefits it yields, the right to manage the asset (or to decide who else will manage it), and the right to transfer ownership to someone else. Sometimes these rights may be vested in different parties, as when a trust is managed on behalf of beneficiaries (who have the right to enjoy the stream of benefits without the right of management). It is quite usual for common proprietors of environmental resources to have limited or non-existent rights of transfer, as when village grazing lands are the joint property of all and only village inhabitants, or when members of a housing collective can sell their property only with the approval of other members. In general this essay will assume that common property rights imply rights of both ownership and management, and will consider separately the issues raised by rights of transfer.

Common property rights in a resource are distinguished from other kinds of property along three distinct dimensions. First, it must be impossible (or prohibitively costly) for members of the group to exclude other members from consumption of the resource, though they will typically be able to exclude non-members. By contrast, private property implies complete excludability of others from consumption: my purchase of a restaurant meal means nobody else will consume that meal. At the other extreme, open access implies that consumption of the resource is available to anybody, so that any agreements between co-owners are vulnerable to being undermined by the entry of outsiders. In a sense, therefore, common property is to oligopoly what private property is to monopoly, and what open access is to competition with free entry.

The second feature of common property, and the one that makes its analysis most interesting, is the absence of a complete set of contractual relations governing which member of the group is entitled or required to do what. Timeshare systems, for example, are not really a form of common property since the rights of each owner are fairly precisely defined. With true common property rights the owners are obliged by circumstances to seek co-operative solutions to management problems without the benefit of complete contractual enforceability.

The third feature of common property, and one without which there would be no management problems to solve, is that there is rivalry in consumption between members of the group: an increase in the amount consumed by one individual reduces the amount remaining for others to consume. This means that, in the absence of agreements to cooperate, self-interested decisions by individuals will impose negative externalities on others, resulting in over-consumption of the resource and under-investment in its upkeep. By contrast, pure public goods (such as broadcasting, or national defence) do not involve rivalry in consumption since one person's consumption leaves unaffected the consumption possibilities of others. The same is true of uncongested toll goods such as motorways (where excludability is possible), though when these goods become congested individuals begin to impose negative externalities upon each other.

Local common property rights are distinguished from global commons in two main ways. First, the main members of the local community are few enough to be known to each other; some of their actions are observable; and consequently they have the ability and sometimes the incentive to build reputations for behaving in certain ways. By contrast, some global commons problems, such as global warming, involve billions of us. However, it is sometimes useful to analyse global commons as involving a limited set of known players, namely governments; what distinguishes these cases from classic local commons is a second feature, namely the absence of even the potential for intervention by a state that is more powerful than any of the individuals.

Figure 1 shows in matrix form the relation between local common property and other forms, along the three main dimensions just outlined.

The presence of externalities between members of a group enjoying common property rights has sometimes been taken to imply that common property resources will always be inefficiently managed – deforestation, overgrazing and excessive mineral depletion being the standard instances. In terms of the theory of games, common property rights lead to a Prisoners' Dilemma, where non-cooperative behaviour is a dominant strategy for all players. In a classic article, Garrett Hardin (1968) referred to this outcome as the 'tragedy of the commons'. Such arguments are sometimes taken to imply that public policy should seek to alter property rights to replace common property by private property wherever this is feasible.

However, the empirical literature on the management of local commons has shown that, while instances of inefficiency and excessive depletion abound, there are also many examples in which collective owners can work together to manage a resource in a remarkably efficient way (see Berkes 1986; Wade 1988; Chopra et al. 1989; Feeny et al. 1990; Ostrom 1990; Ostrom and Gardner 1993; Seabright 1993, 1997; White and Runge 1994). Economic theory – in particular the theory of repeated games – suggests a number of ways in which economic agents who interact repeatedly may have an incentive to cooperate in order to induce future cooperation on the part of others (see Seabright 1993 for a survey). For this inducement to be effective, three conditions must hold. First, the future must matter enough to outweigh the immediate benefits to any individual of failing to cooperate; that is, other players must have at their disposal retaliatory strategies that 'hurt' the defector from a cooperative agreement sufficiently in future periods, even when future payoffs are discounted. So, for instance, excluding those who breach their fishing quotas from the fishing grounds in the future must be a sufficiently damaging prospect to outweigh any immediate gains from over-fishing.

Secondly, these retaliatory strategies must be credible, which means that once an individual has defected, it must be in the others' interest to put the retaliation into effect. For example, excluding those who have breached their fishing quotas must not require an unreasonable level of effort on the part of others in policing the fishing grounds. Abandoning an agreement to restrict extraction rates of a mineral asset (as a punishment for free-riding by some parties to that agreement) must not reduce its stock so substantially as to damage the interests of the retaliators by more than the original free-riding did.

So when will retaliation be credible? It may be credible naturally (retaliation may be what they would do anyway in the circumstances, as when it involves playing a Nash equilibrium of the one-shot prisoners' dilemma game). Alternatively, it may be so because of a credible agreement between the affected parties to put the retaliation into effect. In the latter circumstance, retaliation is itself a form of collective action, which must therefore be credible if the original collective action is to be credible. It is in this respect that one can think of the setting up of police forces, inspectorates and similar institutions as a central form of common property resource management.

Thirdly, the benefits of cooperation in the future must themselves be sufficiently probable to act as an incentive to cooperation in the present. Sheer repetition of the game is not enough to ensure this. For example, if the game is to be played a fixed number of times, then both players will know before the last repetition of the game that defection in the last round cannot be punished and that therefore cooperation is unlikely in that round. But knowing that, they will each defect in the penultimate round. And knowing that, the argument by backward induction holds that they will defect even in the original round.

For future cooperation to be a sufficiently probable incentive, one of a number of conditions must hold. The game may be infinitely repeated, or there may be sufficient uncertainty about how many times it will be repeated. An alternative solution is 'reputation': even a very small probability that the player is of a type that intrinsically prefers to cooperate acts as an incentive to all types of players to behave cooperatively, so long as the game is sufficiently far from its final period for the loss of a reputation for cooperation to be costly. Another is bounded rationality, where a small probability that the player is of a type to cooperate 'irrationally' has much the same effect. Finally, the one-shot game may have multiple Nash equilibria over which

Excludability	Complete	Partial		None	
Contractual status	Complete	Complete	Incomplete	Complete	Incomplete
Rivalry in Consumption	Private Goods	Toll Goods (congested)	Local or National Commons	Open Access	Global Commons
No Rivalry	Free Goods	Toll Goods (uncongested)	Local Public Goods	Pure Public Goods	Pure Public Goods

Figure 1 Classification of Resource Types

all players have a strict preference ordering. In all cases, the possibility of cooperation depends upon players' not discounting future payoffs too heavily (or equivalently, on their interacting at sufficiently frequent intervals); if they don't place much value on the future, the gains from short-term self-interested behaviour may be too great for any future inducements to outweigh. They must also be able to observe one another's behaviour with sufficient reliability to observe whether agreements are being kept.

To this point, the considerations discussed in this section are all essentially forward-looking: people will cooperate if they expect to gain in the future from doing so. Much of the empirical literature on the management of common property resources, however, stresses that historical considerations also play an extremely important part in accounting for successful collective action. In particular, traditions and institutions of collective action can increase the likelihood of successful collective action in the future, and we often observe that cooperative institutions work more successfully when they are embedded in a context in which collective action has worked in the past. Alternatively put, cooperation can be habit-forming.

Two main kinds of explanation have been advanced to account for the persistence of traditions of successful collective action: those based on trust, and those based on reciprocity. Trust-based explanations suggest that individuals assess the likelihood that others will cooperate on the basis of their observed tendency to cooperate in the past. This will be particularly important in circumstances where the sustainability of cooperation is a marginal matter, either because of high discount rates (relative to the frequency with which opportunities occur for repeated interaction), or because of one-off benefits from defection that are high relative to the per period costs to the defector of retaliation. These circumstances imply that it makes a significant difference to individuals whether they cooperate anticipating similar behaviour on the part of others, or choose instead to defect without waiting for others to do so first. A good analogy is a cease-fire during a civil war: if each side expects the cease-fire to hold, it has less of an incentive to make a pre-emptive strike, and consequently the cease-fire is more likely to hold.

This presence or absence of trust may itself depend on past traditions and institutions. Trust is therefore understood as a kind of capital good, embodied either in individuals or in the organizations to which they belong, and which acts as a state variable whose value influences the probability of future co-operation independently of the direct payoffs associated with such co-operation. Attempts to apply such notions empirically include Fukuyama (1995), Putnam (1993), Sako (1992) and Seabright (1997).

In addition, informal institutions that enhance cooperative management of common property resources may also act in other ways to change the direct payoffs. They may act as monitoring mechanisms, for example: by helping members to observe the behaviour of others, they may make it easier to implement retaliation strategies. An alternative, more subtle possibility is that in circumstances where it is unclear what kind of behaviour is consistent with optimal resource management, institutions may help members to coordinate on relatively simple (and therefore more easily monitored) standards of acceptable behaviour (Kreps (1990) suggests this to be the main function of a corporate culture). A number of empirical studies have reported the successful evolution within relatively short periods of time of collective management institutions whose primary function is monitoring and the clarification of rules (Feeny et al. 1990: 10–11).

Explanations based on reciprocity appeal to the idea that cooperative behaviour towards others tends to elicit cooperative behaviour from them in return, regardless of whether the parties expect to meet again subsequently. Such a hypothesis is normally hard to test empirically, since in most circumstances where individuals interact enough to reciprocate they will also expect to continue interacting in the future. However, a set of ingenious laboratory experiments by Ernst Fehr and colleagues has shown that individuals receiving generous treatment from others they know they will not meet again nevertheless respond generously to them in return. For instance, in a labour market game (Fehr et al. 1993), firms that paid more to workers than their reservation wage received effort levels from the workers well above the minimum that the firm was able to monitor. Given the dependence of productivity on effort, the firms paying higher wages were the more profitable. Although there are important unresolved questions about the wider applicability of results obtained under laboratory conditions, these findings suggest not only that cultures of cooperation may persist through reciprocity, but also that groups in which cooperative habits have developed may be more economically successful than those in which more narrowly self-interested behaviour is the norm.

So both theoretical and empirical studies have clearly rejected the view that common property rights are necessarily less efficient than private property. Nevertheless there remain many well-documented instances in which common property has resulted in significant efficiency losses (see Stevenson (1991) for a careful econometric comparison of private and common property pasturing in Switzerland, and Lele (1981) for a survey of case studies of producer cooperatives in developing countries in the 1970s). In addition, many studies of public enterprises in which high wages coexist with low productivity indicate that reciprocity effects are far from reliable. There are therefore many circumstances in which the replacement of common property by private property rights has seemed an attractive solution.

The term 'privatization', however, is ambiguous. Sometimes it refers to the physical division of an asset, so that separate rights of ownership and control can be exercised over its component parts. This is most common in the case of areas of land, where physical barriers can be erected to exclude non-owners from access to the land. Provided exclusion is complete, privatization in this sense is indeed likely to improve incentives for efficiency, though it may result in severe inequities towards those who have depended upon access to common land in the past (Jodha (1986) provides evidence that diminished access to common property resources has significantly hurt the Indian rural poor). Nevertheless, the internalization of externalities may often be incomplete, so that privatization can have perverse results. For example, privatizing grazing land may not completely prevent encroachment, but may reduce the incentives of those without private rights to prevent erosion on the land belonging to those who do. Privatizing forest land, by making forest-dwellers unable to rely on traditional sources of food or fuelwood, may encourage more destructive practices (say of slash-and-burn) and discourage care of newly planted saplings. In addition, it is difficult to frame formal contractual rights so as to safeguard traditional entitlements (a clause requiring landowners to grant 'reasonable' access to 'responsible' grazers or forest dwellers would be very hard to enforce). In fact, it is quite possible that by diminishing incentives for informal cooperation, privatization may make both parties worse off – including the owner of the newly created property right (see Seabright 1993: 124–9).

A quite different sense of the term 'privatization' applies in circumstances where the asset itself cannot be physically divided, but where separate shares are created in the ownership of the asset and are sold to individual owners. In this case, although the shares become private property the asset itself remains common property. The classic instance is the creation of the joint-stock company, which is best described as a form of common property with privately owned and traded shares. There has been a substantial literature on the free-rider problems associated with joint-stock companies (see Grossman and Hart 1980), as well as on the possible adverse incentive consequences of creating freely tradeable markets in shares (Shleifer and Summers 1988). Privatization of state-owned enterprises in the formerly planned economies has also given rise to a large literature comparing the different incentives associated with what are in effect different forms of common property (Blanchard and Aghion 1996).

In large industrial enterprises the free-rider problems associated with common ownership are usually resolved in part by the delegation of day-to-day control of the enterprise to a group of managers. The many incentive issues that arise in the management of firms have a ready application to many other forms of common property, where common owners frequently delegate some or all of the ordinary tasks to agents working on their behalf. The richness and multiplicity of these applications demonstrate that common property resources are far from being unusual or atypical examples of property in complex modern societies, and they certainly do not represent outmoded traditional institutions. If anything it is private property in the strict sense that is unusual: most of the important and difficult economic decisions taken by citizens of advanced industrial societies involve attempts to cooperate in the management of resources in which they hold some form of common property rights.

PAUL SEABRIGHT

See also COMMON PROPERTY; CORPORATE GOVERNANCE; PROPERTY RIGHTS; SELF-GOVERNANCE OF COMMON-POOL RESOURCES; TRUST.

Subject classification: 2b(i).

BIBLIOGRAPHY

Berkes, F. 1986. Local-level management and the commons problem: a comparative study of Turkish coastal fisheries. *Marine Policy* 10: 215–29.

Blanchard, O. and Aghion, P. 1996. On insider privatisation. *European Economic Review* 40: 759–66.

Chopra, K., Kadekodi, G. and Murty, M. 1989. People's participation and common property resources. *Economic and Political Weekly* 24: A–189–95.

Feeny, D., Berkes, F., McCay, B. and Acheson, J. 1990. The tragedy of the commons: twenty-two years later. *Human Ecology* 18: 1–19.

Fehr, E., Kirchsteiger, G. and Riedl, A. 1993. Does fairness prevent market clearing? An experimental investigation. *Quarterly Journal of Economics* 108: 437–59.

Fukuyama, F. 1995. *Trust: the Social Virtues and the Creation of Prosperity*. New York: Free Press.

Grossman, S. and Hart, O. 1980. Takeover bids, the free-rider problem and the theory of the firm. *Bell Journal of Economics* 11: 42–64.

Hardin, G. 1968. The tragedy of the commons. *Science* 162: 1243–8.

Jodha, N. 1986. Common property resources. *Economic and Political Weekly* 21: 1169–81.

Kreps, D. 1990. Corporate culture and economic theory. In *Perspectives on Positive Political Economy*, ed. J. Alt and K. Shepsle, Cambridge: Cambridge University Press.

Lele, U. 1981. Cooperatives and the poor: a comparative perspective. *World Development* 9: 55–72.

Ostrom, E. 1990. *Governing the Commons*. Cambridge: Cambridge University Press.

Ostrom, E. and Gardner, R. 1993. Coping with asymmetries in the commons: self-governing irrigation systems can work. *Journal of Economic Perspectives* 7(4): 93–112.

Putnam, R. 1993. *Making Democracy Work: Civic Traditions in Modern Italy*. Princeton: Princeton University Press.

Sako, M. 1992. *Prices, Quality and Trust*. Cambridge: Cambridge University Press.

Seabright, P. 1993. Managing local commons: theoretical issues in incentive design. *Journal of Economic Perspectives* 7(4): 113–34.

Seabright, P. 1997. Is cooperation habit-forming? In *The Environment and Emerging Development Issues*, ed. P. Dasgupta and K.-G. Mäler, Oxford: Clarendon Press.

Shleifer, A. and Summers, L. 1988. Breaches of trust in hostile takeovers. In *Corporate Takeovers: Causes and Consequences*, ed. A. Auerbach, Chicago: University of Chicago Press.

Stevenson, G. 1991. *Common Property Economics – a General Theory and Land Use Applications*. Cambridge: Cambridge University Press.

Wade, R. 1988. *Village Republics: Economic Conditions for Collective Action in South India*. Cambridge: Cambridge University Press.

White, T.A. and Runge, F. 1994. Common property and collective action: lessons from cooperative watershed management in Haiti. *Economic Development and Cultural Change* 43(1): 1–41.

Locke, John (1632–1704). John Locke was born on 29 August 1632 in a small thatched cottage in Wrington, Somerset. One of his ancestors was Sir William Locke, mercer to Henry VIII, alderman and sheriff of London. John Locke, a direct descendant, derived his coat of arms from this relative. Locke's grandparents were of the Puritan trading class, his paternal grandfather a clothier and his maternal grandfather a tanner. Locke's father was a lawyer, clerk to the Justices of the Peace and a small landowner. Locke had two younger brothers; one died in infancy, the other died in 1663 in his mid-twenties.

The Civil War began within a week of Locke's tenth

birthday. His father was a captain in the Parliamentary Army under the Justice of the Peace, Colonel Popham. After the Parliamentary Army was routed at Devizes in July 1643, Locke's father withdrew from military service and became the county clerk for sewers. In 1647 Colonel Popham recommended that John Locke be admitted to Westminster School, where he was a pupil at the time of the execution of Charles I; although the headmaster, Richard Busby, was a royalist, he taught his pupils to think independently about politics. Locke learned Latin, Greek and Hebrew and was elected a King's Scholar in 1650. This qualified him to compete for a scholarship to Christ Church, Oxford, or Trinity College, Cambridge. He was placed last of the six candidates admitted to Oxford and was awarded a scholarship to Christ Church in 1652, at the age of nineteen.

The university had been purged by the Puritans when Cromwell took office as Lord Protector; they had appointed many new teachers and enforced attendance at sermons but had neglected to reform the curriculum. In later life, Locke was to berate the education offered him at Oxford: the unquestioning study and reverence for the Classics, and the formal disputation techniques. In February 1656 Locke received his BA and became a Master in Arts in June 1658.

In 1660 the monarchy was restored and in December of that year Locke was elected Lecturer in Greek at Christ Church and tutor to ten students. His father died in early 1661 and Locke became a small landholder. In 1663 he was appointed Lecturer in Rhetoric and Censor of Moral Philosophy, an appointment of twelve months, and gave a series of lectures on the Law of Nature, the product of previous discussions about the State of Nature with his friend Towerson, of Queen's College. Locke worked at the same time on a refutation of Richard Filmer's *Patriarcha*, a defence of the divine right of kings.

To secure a permanent position at Oxford, Locke needed an appointment to one of sixty senior studentships. Fifty-five were reserved for the clergy, two for law, two for medicine, and one for moral philosophy. Locke considered becoming a clergyman, but decided to study medicine instead. He became friendly with Robert Boyle, the father of modern chemistry, and participated in unorthodox experiments in Boyle's High Street rooms. He studied husbandry, metallurgy and pharmacology, and became an outstanding physician and advocate of empirical methods.

In 1666 Anthony Ashley Cooper, later to became the first Earl of Shaftesbury, came to Oxford to take medicinal waters and his doctor asked Locke to administer the draught. Ashley was impressed by Locke's conversation, and their lasting friendship began. Ashley's influence helped Locke secure a studentship at Oxford without taking holy orders; he was able to cease tutoring and began to study Descartes.

In spring 1667, Lord Ashley invited Locke to Exeter House in the Strand to become his personal physician, secretary, confidant and children's tutor. Ashley's primary interests were in promoting trade, stockholding and colonial expansion and his ideas undoubtedly affected the development of Locke's economic thought. It was in this year that Locke first drafted his *Essay on Toleration*. In May 1668 he performed a novel operation on Lord Ashley, draining an abscess on his liver that saved his life. When Locke was made a Fellow of the Royal Society for scientific pursuits in November 1668, he was sponsored not from Christ Church but from Exeter House by Sir Paul Neile, a founder of the Royal Society and one of Ashley's political associates.

In 1668 Locke wrote most of *Some Considerations of the Lowering of Interest and Raising the Value of Money*, although it was not published until 1692. He also wrote a memorandum entitled *Some of the Consequences That Are Like to Follow upon Lessening of Interest to 4 percent*. When Ashley became Chancellor of the Exchequer, Locke was appointed secretary to the Lords Proprietor of Carolina. In this role, he assisted in drafting a constitution, *The Fundamental Constitutions for the Government of Carolina*, designed to maintain the Lords Proprietor's powers over the colonists. Lord Ashley and Locke shared a dislike for religious and political absolutism, and the Carolina Constitutions provided for a remarkable liberality in religious affairs.

In 1671 Locke began to draft an *Essay Concerning Human Understanding*, which was not published until the 1680s. Locke advised Charles II on the legality of the Declaration of Toleration. In 1672 Ashley was appointed Lord Chancellor and became the First Earl of Shaftesbury. Locke took a minor post as Secretary of Presentations where he supervised the ecclesiastical matters which were under the Chancellor's control.

From 1673 onwards Shaftesbury began to intrigue against the king and Locke helped him with several anonymous pamphlets. *Some Modest Reflections of the Commitment of the Earl of Shaftesbury* appears to have been written by the earl with Locke's assistance, but Locke appears to be the primary author of *No Protestant Plot*. The need for secrecy is reflected in Locke's preserved papers, which are written in a modified shorthand, with ciphers, signatures and names cut out and even invisible ink. In 1676 Shaftesbury was sent to the Tower, where he remained for twelve months.

From 1679, Shaftesbury became involved with the plot to secure the succession of the Duke of Monmouth. Locke discreetly assisted the movement, possibly by drafting the *Two Treatises of Government*, a theoretical justification for resistance to a sovereign. In 1682, the Monmouth Rebellion failed and Shaftesbury went into hiding in Holland, where he died in 1683. In the same year Locke fled to Amsterdam, where he lived under an assumed name. In 1684, Locke was expelled from Christ Church at Charles II's express demand, ending fifteen years of association with Oxford, a traditionalist institution that had long rejected his radical views on philosophy and economics.

In Utrecht, in 1684–5, Locke wrote an *Essay Concerning Human Understanding*. The work reflects the influence of the *ad hoc* empiricism of Newton and Boyle and the systematic rationalism of Descartes. Additionally, Locke composed an *Essay on Toleration* and published a *Letter on Toleration* in Latin. In 1687–8 he wrote a number of reviews in *Bibliotheque Universelle* for LeClerc; these were the first publications to which Locke signed his name.

In 1687, Locke moved to Rotterdam where he lived as a

paying guest with a Quaker, Benjamin Furley. He became friendly with influential people such as Viscount Mordaunt at The Hague and William Penn. In 1688 Penn obtained a pardon for Locke from King James II, who that year abdicated the throne in favour of William of Orange.

In February 1689 Locke returned to England, where William and his wife Mary had both been offered the English throne. William attempted to persuade Locke to become an ambassador but he refused, possibly because of ill health, preferring to take the lowlier office of Commissioner of Appeals.

In 1689 Locke modified the *Two Treatises of Government* for anonymous publication. It constituted a response to Filmer's book, which had defended the divine right of kings, as well as providing a theoretical defence of the Whig Revolution. It is difficult to tell when the *Treatises* were first written. They were published by Churchill, a Whig supporter, who was originally to have printed *An Essay on Human Understanding*. Locke destroyed all correspondence concerning the *Treatises*, and was obsessive about concealing his authorship. 1689 saw the publication of the first of three letters concerning toleration, or *Epistola de Tolerantia*, the others released in 1690 and 1692. The *Essay on Human Understanding*, Locke's first major work that was not anonymous, was published in 1689.

In December 1695 Locke was appointed a Commissioner for Trade and Plantations by the King with parliamentary approval and a salary of £1000 per annum. Locke's decision to take this office is not surprising given his previous experience, his interest in economics and his financial interests in the raw silk trade, Bahama Adventurers and the Royal Africa Company, which was involved in the slave trade. The Board of Trade did not begin its work until 1696. Locke took a leading role and devoted an enormous number of hours to ensuring the acceptance of his views. In 1700, Locke resigned his commissions due to ill health and retired to the country. In 1697, he had commenced writing *The Conduct of Understanding*. This work was never completed.

Towards the end of his life, Locke became increasingly interested in his young cousin Peter King. King began his career as a grocer and ultimately became Lord Chancellor. In 1704, Locke sensed death coming and made preparations to dispose of his effects. He left his personal papers to King, and they remained the property of the Lord Chancellor's descendants, later the Earls of Lovelace, until 1948, when they were sold to the Bodleian Library, Oxford.

1. THE LOCKEIAN STATE OF NATURE. In all his major writings, but most especially in the *Two Treatises of Government*, Locke distinguishes clearly between the political relationship and other forms of personal and social relationship. In particular, he contrasts the consensual political relationship (civil or political society) with two kinds of nonconsensual relations among individuals that may precede or even reemerge from the political relationship (Simmons 1993:11), namely *the state of nature* and *the state of war*. Locke writes also of the nonconsensual relationship between parent and child, a relationship between individuals who are not moral equals, but this relationship is less relevant to an understanding of the political relationship, which can be forged only among mature adults.

The state of nature is the fulcrum from which Locke establishes the boundaries of the the political relationship. Indeed, it is the concept with which Locke introduces the *Second Treatise* (II, para. 4): 'To understand political power right, and derive it from its original, we must consider what state all men are naturally in.' Locke was not the first scholar to make use of the concept of the state of nature as a cornerstone of his political philosophy. Indeed, many scholars have argued that he resurrected the concept from the writings of his immediate predecessor, Thomas Hobbes, in *Leviathan* (1651). In this judgment, they are unequivocally wrong. Locke's concept of the state of nature differs significantly from that of Hobbes, both in moral and in positive characteristics (Rowley 1996: 6–12).

The social characterization of the state of nature by Hobbes is unambiguous. The state of nature is a situation characterized by the absence of effective government. Life in this state is 'solitary, poor, nasty, brutish and short', a condition of war 'of every man, against every man', a war in which there is no industry, no culture, and no real society (Hobbes [1651] 1946, ch. 13, paras. 8–9). According to Hobbes, individuals have no rights or duties in the state of nature – 'The notions of right and wrong, justice and injustice have there no place' (ch. 13, para. 13). Furthermore, according to Hobbes, only groups of individuals can be viewed as being in or out of the state of nature. The sovereign remains in the state of nature even with regard to the subjects who have placed themselves without it (ch. 28, para. 2).

Locke's depiction of the state of nature is somewhat different, as is evident from the opening statement of the *Second Treatise*: 'a *state of perfect freedom* to order their actions, and dispose of their possessions, and persons as they think fit, within the bounds of the law of nature, without asking leave, or depending upon the will of any other man' (para. 4). Yet, this state of perfect freedom is not a state of licence. It 'has a law of nature to govern it which obliges every one' (para. 6). Specifically, 'no one ought to harm another in his life, health, liberty or possessions' (ibid.). In order to restrain all men from invading others' rights, the law of nature provides that 'every one has a right to punish the transgressors of that law to such a degree, as may hinder its violation' (para. 7). Specifically, each individual possesses an executive right (and duty) in the state of nature to punish transgressors to the extent necessary to achieve reparation and to restrain or prevent subsequent transgressions of a similar nature. Every man in the state of nature thus has a power to kill a murderer, even though he is the judge in his own case.

It is important to note that Locke's state of nature is not the condition of men without effective government as a number of Locke scholars have claimed (Simmons 1993: 15). Indeed, men may be living under highly organized governments – such as the USSR – and still be in the state of nature if those governments are illegitimate with respect to them. '*Want of a common judge with authority, puts all men in a state of nature*' (Locke II, para. 19); and 'Men living together according to reason, without a common superior on earth, with authority to judge between them, is *properly the state of nature*' (ibid.). Wherever no one is entitled to settle controversies between two persons, these persons are in the state of nature.

The existence of a referee or umpire in itself does not end the state of nature, as Locke clearly intimates: 'For 'tis not every compact that puts an end to the state of nature between men, but only this one of agreeing together mutually to enter into one community, and make one body politick; other promises and compacts, men may make one with another, and yet still be in the state of nature' (Locke II, para. 14).

Evidently, individuals may enter into contracts with each other, transfer rights and undertake obligations without leaving the state of nature. In creating a civil society, individuals must give up not only their rights to interpret and execute natural law, but must also create for their government the right to make and to enforce civil laws, the content of which extends beyond that prescribed by the law of nature (paras. 128–30). Thus, the special agreement that creates a civil society involves the surrendering by individuals of far more rights than would any simple agreement to set up a common judge with authority.

Drawing upon this discussion, Simmons (1993: 21) infers a definition of Locke's state of nature as taking the following form: 'A is in the state of nature with respect to B if and only if A has not voluntarily agreed to join (or is no longer a member of) a legitimate political community of which B is a member'. As a special case of this definition, Simmons adds: 'A is in the state of nature (simpliciter) if and only if A has not voluntarily agreed to join (or is no longer a member of) any legitimate political community'. This definition accounts for Locke's claim that aliens, children and madmen are in the state of nature even within legitimate civil societies, as are those who have not consented to join such a society even though they are eligible so to do. It also accounts for Locke's claim that those individuals whose communities are destroyed by foreign conquest and those whose rights are abused by otherwise legitimate governments are returned to the state of nature.

What is the social characterization of the state of nature? Locke sets out two contrasting situations. At one extreme, he describes the state of nature as 'a state of peace, good will, mutual assistance and preservation' (Locke II, para. 19). At the other extreme, he describes the state of war as 'a state of enmity, malice, violence, and mutual destruction' (ibid. II, para. 19). '*Force without right, upon a man's person, makes a state of war*, both where there is, and is not, a common judge' (ibid.).

Locke has been chastised for inconsistency in posing these sharply conflicting scenarios. He is not guilty. Both descriptions are of *possible* states of nature, but neither is of *the* state of nature (Simmons 1993: 28). Where individuals typically abide by the laws of nature, the state of nature will be one of peace, goodwill and the like; where they typically disregard these laws, the state of nature will resemble the state of war. Reality typically falls between these extremes. Enjoyment of the freedom provided by the state of nature 'is very uncertain, and constantly exposed to the invasion of others' (Locke II, para. 123). It is, in essence, a state of significant but not desperate inconveniences, of limited safety and considerable uncertainty. 'Thus mankind, not withstanding all the privileges of the state of nature, being but in an ill condition, while they remain in it, are quickly driven into society' (para. 127).

2. NATURE AND NATURAL LAW. Locke's understanding of nature and natural law is encapsulated only to a limited extent in the *Two Treatises*. Much more detail is provided in his unpublished *Questions Concerning the Law of Nature* and in his *Essay Concerning Human Understanding*, although the crucial break with natural law tradition becomes most clear in Locke's treatment of it in the *Two Treatises*.

Locke has few illusions about the role of nature in the absence of natural law. In Question 4 of *Questions*, he discusses the likely behaviour of human beings who have no guide other than nature:

> How far removed are the morals of these men from virtue, how alien are they to any sense of humanity! Nowhere is there such fickle faith, so much perfidy, such monstrous cruelty; and by murdering men and shedding kindred blood, they sacrifice both to their gods and to their own 'genius.'

Those men who live exclusively under the guidance of nature 'spend their lives wretchedly in rapine, theft, debauchery and murder'. They do not achieve that happiness promised by the natural law endorsed by Locke (*Questions*, fol. 41). This notion of man as a fallen angel fits squarely within the classical liberal tradition of which Locke was a founding father.

In 1688, the English Whigs, for the most part, were adherents to the natural law expounded by Grotius in *De iure belli ac pacis* (On the law of war and peace) in 1625. By 1750, Locke had become firmly ensconced as the Whig theorist of natural law and his theories were to become the foundation stones of the American Revolution. The shift of emphasis was non-trivial. Locke essentially reformed natural law, refuting the immanentist version of Grotius in favour of a transcendent version (Zuckert 1994: 207). Specifically, whereas Grotius had argued that the law of nature would exist even in the absence of God, Locke insisted that God is indispensable to the law of nature, indeed defining the latter as 'the command of the divine will, knowable by the light of nature, indicating what is and what is not consonant with a rational nature, and by that very fact commanding or prohibiting' (*Questions*, fols. 11–12).

Furthermore, Locke explicitly challenged the view of Grotius, adopted by Thomas Hobbes (1651), which identified the law of nature as a dictate of right reason, insisting that 'less accurately some say it is a dictate of reason; for reason does not so much lay down and decree this law of nature as it discovers and investigates a law which is ordained by a higher power' (*Questions*, fol. 12). If God is the source of law, human reason cannot be that source even though, as Locke consistently emphasized, the law of nature is 'a law which each individual can discover by that light alone which is implanted in us by nature' (ibid.).

In Locke's judgment, God is required for the law of nature to have obligatory force. In the case of the law of nature, this duty or obligation is what 'is incumbent on each individual as something which must be performed by reason of one's own nature' (ibid.). However, nature itself cannot impose obligation: 'No one can oblige or constrain us to do anything unless he has a right and power over us' (fol. 83). In this respect, Locke undoubtedly was influenced by Pufendorf's *Elementa iuris universalis* (Elements of Universal Law), published in 1660. Pufendorf in turn had been influenced by Thomas Hobbes's notion of law as the will of a superior. However, Locke focused much more than Pufendorf on theological themes and rejected outright Pufendorf's emphasis on the Roman lawyers' notion of natural law (Zuckert 1994: 192–3).

Locke's natural law is transcendent because knowledge of that law and its obligations depends on rational knowledge of the existence and will of the transcendent God. Central to Locke's doctrine of natural law, indeed, was his rational proof for the existence of God. In this respect, Locke's understanding of natural law broke sharply with that of all his predecessors. Nevertheless, he ended up with a doctrine that overlapped with that of Grotius on the centrality of rights and the importance of compact (Zuckert 1994: 215), an overlap that would became especially evident in the *Second Treatise*.

3. NATURAL LAW AND NATURAL RIGHTS. In the *Two Treatises*, Locke significantly advanced his challenge to the natural law tradition of Grotius by drawing important inferences from his notion of human beings as the property of their maker, God. If human beings by nature are free and equal, yet they remain within the bounds of the law of nature (Locke, II, para. 4). The natural law prescriptions prescribed in the early chapters essentially have the character of limits on natural freedom (Zuckert 1994: 217). If human beings belong to God, they cannot belong to one another, or even to themselves.

Since God is the sole proprietor, no one else has the right to 'take away, or impair the life, or what tends to the preservation of the life, liberty, health, limb, or goods of another' (Locke II, para. 6). From this more general restriction, Locke infers limits on what human beings may appropriate from 'that which God gave to mankind in common . . . The same law of nature that does . . . give us property, does also bound that property too' (ibid., II, 25, 31). Likewise, 'a man [has] not . . . power over his own life' (para. 24).

Contrary to Grotius, Locke embraced without qualification the concept of inalienability. 'For a man, not having the power of his own life, *cannot*, by compact, or his own consent, *enslave himself* to any one, nor put himself under the absolute, arbitrary power of another, to take away his life, when he pleases' (para. 23). From this embrace, follows most of the characteristic strands of Lockeian classical liberalism, notably his categorical rejection of absolutism and his enunciation of a natural right to resistance against those who threaten a man's life, liberty or possessions. As I shall suggest in section 5, however, inalienability as espoused by Locke is of a somewhat idiosyncratic nature.

In the *Two Treatises*, in sharp contrast to *Questions*, the sanctions called forth to reinforce the law of nature, the so-called *executive power* discussed in section 1, take on a much more worldly form (Zuckert 1994: 221). The absence of rational knowledge of the soul's immortality does not here vitiate the natural law. To the set of natural law limits or obligations, Locke now adds a right to execute the law, 'the true original of political power'. In making this addition, Locke evidently retreats from his transcendent theory towards the immanent theories of Grotius, Pufendorf and Hobbes. He does so by rendering his original 'no harm' principle inoperative. The law of nature, via the natural executive power, seemingly validates an extensive right to harm others. 'Contrary to the initial impression, there will be much violence in the state of nature, much, perhaps most, of it morally allowable under the law of nature' (Zuckert 1994: 236).

4. OF PROPERTY. At one level, Locke developed a theory of property in the *Second Treatise* from the basis of transcendent natural law and in a manner that explicitly challenged the contractual basis promulgated by Grotius (and Pufendorf): 'I shall endeavour to shew, how men might come to have a *property* in several parts of that which God gave to mankind in common, and that without any express compact of all the commoners' (para. 25). At another level, however, Locke outlined an alternative, more immanent theory of property which grounds private property on much more earthly considerations: 'Though the earth, and all inferior creatures be common to all men, yet every man has a *property* in his own *person*. This no body has any right to but himself' (para. 27).

This tension between the transcendent and the immanent theory continues throughout Chapter V of the *Second Treatise*, though Zuckert (1994: 288) decisively concludes that the transcendent foundation 'never was the basis on which the building was actually constructed'. If Zuckert is correct, this may explain why Locke's theory of property has remained relevant to a late twentieth-century philosophic discourse in which theistic viewpoints tend to be much less dominant than was the case in late seventeenth-century England.

Locke defined property in very broad terms, embracing all the natural rights of an individual in the language of property: 'Lives, liberties and estates which I call by the general name, *property*' (Locke, II, para. 123). For this reason, Locke's discussion of property must be viewed as the central feature of the *Second Treatise* as Locke himself was acutely aware, commending his then anonymous work to Richard King, in a letter of 25 August 1703, in the following terms: 'Property, I have found nowhere more clearly explained than in a book entitled, *Two Treatises of Government*' (Laslett, Introduction, 15.) Certainly, no other aspect of his political philosophy has produced as much controversy in interpretation.

To understand Locke's theory of property correctly it is important to bear in mind the purpose of the *Second Treatise* as spelled out right at the outset of the book:

> To this purpose, I think it may not be amiss, to set down what I take to be political power. That the power of a *magistrate* over a subject, may be distinguished from that of a *father* over his children, a *master* over his servant, a *husband* over his wife, and a *lord* over his slave (para. 2).

Chapter V, entitled *Of Property*, essentially explains the master–servant relation even though there are only a few references in the entire chapter to these concepts (II, paras. 28, 29, 41). Once this connection is made, as I shall explain, most of the controversy over Locke's theory of property collapses.

Locke justified private property on utilitarian grounds, recognizing the tragedy of the commons long before the concept was formally enunciated:

> though all the fruits it naturally produces, and beasts it feeds, belong to mankind in common, as they are produced by the spontaneous hand of nature; and no body has originally a private dominion, exclusive of the rest of mankind, in any of them, as they are thus in their natural state: yet being given for the use of men, there must of necessity be a means *to appropriate* them some way or other before they can be of any use, or at all beneficial to any particular man (para. 26).

Locke developed his theory of property from the basis that 'every man has a *property* in his own *person*' (para. 27). From this, he argued that 'The *labour* of his body, and the *work* of his hands, we may say, are properly his' (ibid.). From this followed perhaps the most famous passage of the *Second Treatise* which justified the privatization of non-human capital:

> Whatsoever then he removes out of the state that nature hath provided, and left it in, he hath mixed his *labour* with, and joyned to it something that is his own, and thereby makes it his *property*. It being by him removed from the common state nature placed it in, hath by this *labour* something annexed to it, that excludes the common right of other men. For this *labour* being the unquestionable property of the labourer, no man but he can have a right to what that is once joyned to, at least where there is enough, and as good left in common for others.

The introduction of money implies 'that men have agreed to disproportionate and unequal possession of the earth, they having by a tacit and voluntary consent found out a way, how a man may fairly possess more land than he himself can use the product of, by receiving in exchange for the overplus, gold and silver, which may be hoarded up without injury to any one, these metalls not spoileing or decaying in the hands of the possessor' (para. 50).

Thus, a process takes place whereby certain individuals legitimately own nothing but their own bodies and must sell their labour to others in order to survive. Chapter 5 clearly explains, in this manner, the emergence of the master–servant relationship in the state of nature as a process of consent.

From this perspective, it is possible to make sense of the famous Lockean proviso 'at least where there is enough, and as good left in common for others' (para. 27). Locke is committed to the idea that lawful appropriation from the commons must be limited to what an individual can use and to what is no more than his fair share. This is the core idea with which Locke begins his discourse (Simmons 1992: 281). However, his arguments are complicated by a number of factors: the emergence of subsequent generations of would-be appropriators, the consequent increased demands on a relatively fixed pool of resources, and the invention of money. Bearing these complications in mind, how best can we interpret Locke's basic ideas concerning the privatization of the commons?

At first sight, there seems to be two distinct limits on natural property in the *Second Treatise* with quite different interpretations for an individual's share of the commons. The first limit is that set by the equal rights of others to appropriate (II, para. 27), and is usually referred to as the *Lockeian proviso*. Under conditions of general scarcity, this proviso is sometimes interpreted to imply that a fair share is, roughly, an equal share. This is the source of the socialist interpretation of Locke, an interpretation, I must say, that runs counter to the spirit of all of Locke's scholarship.

The second limit is that set by an individual's own use of the property in question and is usually referred to as the *spoliation limit*. Locke introduces this limit by noting that God has only given property to mankind to enjoy: 'As much as any one can make use of to any advantage of life before it spoils; so much he may by his labour fix a property in. Whatever is beyond this, is more than his share, and belongs to others' (para. 31). This limit defines an individual's share as whatever he can use. To take more than one can use is 'useless as well as dishonest' (para. 51), since it deprives others of opportunities and wastes one's own labour.

There is an apparent inconsistency between these two limits (Simmons 1992: 282). For the first limit seems to set an individual's share in terms of what is left for others, whereas the second limit sets an individual's share in terms of his capacity to make use of it. There is no reason to suppose that the two limits will always determine the same level of appropriation. This discrepancy has been used by scholars of differing persuasion to give licence to their particular agendas. In my view, however, the two limits are clearly reconcilable within Locke's general theory of property as defining the master–servant relationship.

The Lockean proviso is a factual statement by Locke about acquisition in the early ages of man when there was always enough and as good left for others after a taking of property by the mixing of a man's labour with the land. This fact changed with the conditions of scarcity of land that arose in later ages. In such latter circumstances, there is simply no way in which the Lockeian proviso could be made to hold. Fortunately, the invention of money freed humanity from the limit of the Lockeian proviso.

If the surplus product of a man's labour can be stored in the form of money, it is no longer a foolish thing to hoard up more than he can make use of. In such circumstances, great tracts of common land are unlikely to persist: 'Tho' this can scarce happen amongst that part of mankind, that have consented to the use of money' (para. 45).

From this perspective, the invention of money produced a situation of possession and dispossession in which some individuals own more than they can use and in which others own nothing but themselves. This situation makes possible the master–servant relationship under circumstances in which the entire commons has been privatized. From Locke's perspective, this dispossession occurs not through conflict, but by consent. For by consenting to the use of money 'men have agreed to disproportionate and unequal possession of the earth' (para. 50).

The dispossessed is not truly dispossessed. He lacks land but '(by being master of himself, and *proprietor of his own person*, and the actions or labour of it) had still in himself *the great foundation of property*' (para. 44). His right to property is recognized in his ability to sell his labour and to derive the fruits of that sale. In such circumstances, he is better off than would be the case if he lived off the commons, 'And a king of a large and fruitful territory [in the Americas] there feeds, lodges, and is clad worse than a day labourer in *England*' (para. 41).

As Zuckert correctly argues, Locke justifies the system of property that he describes both in terms of the natural rights of individuals and in terms of its consequences. The proper standard for judging the distribution of benefits is not the equal distribution of the existing stock of property, as many students of social justice suggest, but rather the original position before it was improved by human action.

Evidently, as Locke advances his theory of property he withdraws somewhat from the transcendent version of his theory of natural law. Increasingly, he identifies natural law as the law of reason. He talks about the triad of life, liberty and property within the generic term of property. Yet, the right to life clearly is the primary right with the other two derivative of that right. The right to property, in particular, takes its bearing from the general good of mankind, and not from the sovereign fact of divine ownership (Zuckert 1994: 273).

The claim to property in one's own person is central to this development, marking Locke's break with conventional natural law. If individuals are self-owners, then divine ownership at best takes on a much more metaphysical dimension. Furthermore, the claim to property in one's own person offers a right to exclusivity that distinguishes Locke's natural property from Hobbes's right of nature. One individual's claim, and the limits on others implicit in that claim, implies a system of rights and concomitant duties for all in the state of nature. If there is property in self and in the things appropriated by self, then there is injustice in interference with this property, even in the absence of civil or political society. There is no such injustice in the Hobbesian state of nature.

5. OF POLITICAL SOCIETY. According to Locke, the law of nature essentially reflects the moral claim of each individual to *negative freedom* and the corresponding duty of all other individuals to uphold the negative freedom of that individual. To this end, in the state of nature, each individual has an executive power to punish transgressors of the law of nature 'to such a degree, as may hinder its violation' (para. 7).

Indeed, those individuals who choose to transgress the law of nature may ultimately forfeit their own rights to life, liberty, and property. The constant danger of the state of nature degenerating into a state of war is a principal reason advanced by Locke to explain why a state of nature may be transformed into a political society: 'The great and *chief end* therefore, of means uniting into commonwealths, and putting themselves under government, *is the preservation of their property*. To which in the state of nature there are many things wanting' (para. 124).

This leads naturally to a discussion of the nature of the right to property in Locke's political philosophy. This right is clearly not inalienable, at least in the modern sense of that term. If we define an inalienable, right as a right that cannot be lost in any way, then such a right would incorporate both a disability and an immunity; the possessor of the right would not be able to dispose of it, voluntarily or involuntarily. Nor would any other person, group or institution be able to dispossess him of it. Property clearly does not fall into this category of a right since it can be given away or exchanged voluntarily (*alienated*) and it can be lost involuntarily through negligence or wrongdoing (*forfeited*).

The natural right to property does imply, however, that property cannot be taken away by some other party, including a government (*prescribed*). In this sense, we may denote the natural right to property as an *imprescriptible right*. What revolutionary writers such as Locke had in mind was that the right to property was a right that no government could take away legitimately without the owner's consent. This formed the basis for Locke's contractarian notion of political society.

In Locke's view, man is born free in the state of nature, and is not born into a political society. Individuals are not naturally citizens but must explicitly choose so to become. By agreeing to leave the state of nature and to enter into civil or political society, individuals necessarily sacrifice their right to judge and to punish breaches of their natural rights by others. This is no small sacrifice and will not rationally be countenanced by property holders unless political society is strictly limited with respect to the powers that it subsumes:

> The *supream power cannot take* from any man part of his *property* without his own consent. For the preservation of property being the end of government, and that for which men enter into society, it necessarily supposes and requires, that the people should *have property*, without which they must be suppos'd to lose that by entring into society, which was the end for which they entered into it, too gross an absurdity for any man to own (para. 138).

According to Locke, governments do not possess rights naturally; only individuals have that capacity. There is only one process through which political rights can be secured, and that is voluntary alienation of rights by the right-holder's consent, contract or trust: 'Men being, as has been said, by nature, all free, equal and independent, no one can be put out of this estate, and subjected to the political power of another, without his own *consent*' (para. 95).

Locke's recognition that individual consent could justify political society in no sense implies that he endorsed democratic politics in the modern sense of one man-one vote. The *Second Treatise* is deliberately vague with respect to the form that political society might take. It is highly unlikely, however, that Locke would have courted the hostility of the very landed classes on which he depended to oust the Stuart monarchy. It was to be the men of property, the industrious and the rational, who had substantial interests to protect, who would actively covenant to enter into political society. It was they also who subsequently would govern. The labouring classes could never be full political members of society, primarily because their hand-to-mouth existence prevented them from fully developing their rational faculties. Beggars and the idle poor were viewed as morally depraved (Macpherson 1962), existing only because of the relaxation of discipline and the corruption of manners (Laslett, Introduction, 1960).

In a number of places in the *Second Treatise* Locke declares that the legislative power is the supreme power in government: 'This *legislative* is not only the *supream power* of the commonwealth, but sacred and unalterable in the hands where the community have once placed it' (para. 134). Yet, he argues, there are limits to its powers. The legislative power is pre-eminent among the institutions of government, but its domain and range of authority is strictly limited: 'yet the legislative being only a fiduciary power to act for certain ends, there remains still *in the people a supream power* to remove or *alter the legislative*, when they find the *legislative* act contrary to the trust reposed in them' (para. 149).

With the special exception of, property, the specific limitations that Locke would impose on the legislative power are procedural in nature. The legislative power must not be exercised arbitrarily, or contrary to God's will. Laws must be duly promulgated: 'And therefore whatever form the common-wealth is under, the ruling power ought to govern by *declared* and *received laws*, and not by extemporary dictates and undetermined resolutions' (para. 137). Locke was concerned not with the problem of absolute power in itself, but with the problem of absolute arbitrary power (Bex 1996).

Of course, the limitation on government that has received the greatest attention is Locke's statement that: 'The *supream power cannot take* from any man any part of his *property* without his own consent' (II, para. 138). This statement should be interpreted as an absolute limit on the legislative power, even though Locke himself saw no need for a specific substantive protection of property. Since in seventeenth-century England those who elected the legislature were without question men of property, there was simply no need to provide the substantive constraint. Such would not be the case at all once the franchise was extended to include the property-less.

Locke's *Second Treatise* was written in justification of revolution in the face of arbitrary absolute power. Yet, the revolution envisaged by Locke in no sense takes the modern form of a broadly popular, egalitarian uprising. Even during a revolution, the social community will remain, and with it, the set of relationships that was entered into originally by covenant for the better protection of property. Even in the post-revolutionary environment, Locke envisages a community dominated by the propertied classes, through a powerful governmental authority exercised by an elite oligarchy.

Locke's political philosophy provides strong claims rights that allow the justified revolutionary a moral high ground to stand on in resisting illegitimate government (Simmons 1993: 152). When an aggrieved citizen defends his rights, those who oppose him wrong him by breaching their duty with respect to his rights. In so doing, they place themselves outside political society, and into a state of war against the people.

Locke employs two distinct lines of argument in justifying a 'popular' right of resistance to oppressive government. In the first line of argument, he justifies such resistance on the ground that a state of war exists between the people and their government. Here, Locke focuses on the case of tyrranical executive power (James II). However, he notes that the legislative may also expose itself to justifiable revolution by delivering the people into subjection by a foreign power: 'The delivery also of the people into the subjection of a foreign power, either by the prince, or by the legislative, is certainly *a change of the legislative*, and so a *dissolution of the government*' (II, para. 217).

Most important of all, as a justification of revolution, is the situation where legislators endeavour to take away or to destroy the property of the people:

> The reason why men enter into society, is the preservation of their property; and the end why they chuse and authorise a legislative, is, that there may be laws made, and rules set as guards and fences to the properties of all the members of the society, to limit the power, and moderate the dominion of every part and member of the society (para. 222).

Whenever the legislative behaves in such a fashion, it puts itself into a state of war with the people, who are then absolved from any further obedience, and who are returned to their former liberties. The people, then, are free to establish a new legislative. Those who have abused their authority forfeit all rights under the law of nature and may be killed or used at will by any other person.

When a government is dissolved, and society is deprived of its referee, the people are not necessarily returned to the state of nature: 'The usual, and almost only way whereby *this union is dissolved*, is the inroad of foreign force making a conquest upon them' (para. 211). Otherwise people are at liberty to provide for themselves, by erecting a new legislative, which will differ from its predecessor in ways dictated by circumstances, as free individuals seek out new avenues to preserve and to protect their rights.

CHARLES K. ROWLEY

See also CIVIL SOCIETY; EVOLUTION OF PROPERTY RIGHTS; HOBBES AND CONTRACTARIANISM; HUME, DAVID; PROPERTY RIGHTS; STATE OF NATURE AND CIVIL SOCIETY.

Subject classification: 2b(i); 3a; 7b.

SELECTED WORKS

1823. *The Fundamental Constitutions of the Government of Carolina*. In *The Works of John Locke*, vol. 10, London: Thomas Davison.

1876. *An Essay Concerning Toleration*. In H.R. Fox Bourne, *The Life of John Locke*, New York: Harper.

1960. *Two Treatises of Government*. Ed. P. Laslett. Cambridge: Cambridge University Press (cited as Locke II).

1975. *An Essay Concerning Human Understanding*, Ed. P.H. Nidditch, Oxford: Clarendon Press.

1990. *Questions Concerning the Law of Nature*, ed. R. Horwitz, J.S. Clay and D. Clay, Ithaca: Cornell University Press.

BIBLIOGRAPHY

Aaron, R.I. 1937. *John Locke*. London: Oxford University Press.

Ashcraft, R. 1987. *Locke's Two Treatises of Government*. London: Allen & Unwin.

Bex, B. 1996. *The Origins of Liberalism*. Hagerstown, MD: The Remnants Trust.

Blaug, M. 1986. *Great Economists Before Keynes*. Cambridge: Cambridge University Press.

Bobbio, N. 1993. *Thomas Hobbes and the Natural Law Tradition*. Chicago: University of Chicago Press.

Cranston, M. 1985. *John Locke: A Biography*. Oxford: Oxford University Press.

Dunn, J. 1969. *The Political Thought of John Locke*. Cambridge: Cambridge University Press.

Filmer, Sir Robert. 1949. *Patriarcha and Other Political Works*. Ed. P. Laslett, Oxford: Basil Blackwell.

Fox-Bourne, H.R. 1876. *The Life of John Locke*. New York: Harper.

Gray, J. 1989. *Liberalisms: Essays in Political Philosophy*. London: Routledge

Gray, J. 1993. *Post-Liberalism: Studies in Political Thought*. London: Routledge.

Hobbes, T. 1651. *Leviathan*. Ed. M. Oakeshott, Oxford: Basil Blackwell, 1946.

Macpherson, C.B. 1962. *The Political Theory of Possessive Individualism*. Oxford: Clarendon Press.

Rowley, C.K. 1996. *What is Living and What is Dead in Classical Liberalism?* In *The Political Economy of the Minimal State*, ed. C.K. Rowley, Cheltenham: Edward Elgar.

Simmons, A.J. 1992. *The Lockean Theory of Rights*. Princeton: Princeton University Press.

Simmons, A.J. 1993. *On the Edge of Anarchy: Locke, Consent, and the Limits of Society*. Princeton: Princeton University Press.

Tarcov, N. 1984. *Locke's Education for Liberty*. Chicago: University of Chicago Press.

Vaughn, K.I. 1980. *John Locke: Economist and Social Scientist*. Chicago: University of Chicago Press.

Vaughn, K.I. 1987. *Locke, John*. In *The New Palgrave: A Dictionary of Economics*, ed. J. Eatwell, M. Milgate and P. Newman, London: Macmillan, vol. 3. pp. 229–30.

Wood, N. 1984. *John Locke and Agrarian Capitalism*. Berkeley: University of California Press.

Zuckert, M. 1994 *Natural Rights and the New Republicanism*. Princeton: Princeton University Press.

M

mafia. *See* CIVIL LIABILITY UNDER RICO: UNINTENDED CONSEQUENCES OF LEGISLATION; GANGS AND THE STATE OF NATURE; LEGAL REFORM IN EASTERN EUROPE; ORGANIZED CRIME.

Maine, Sir Henry James Sumner (1822–1888). Maine's most influential work is *Ancient Law* (1861, henceforth *AL*), whose subtitle was 'Its connection with the early history of society and its relation to modern ideas'. He sought to demonstrate the gradual historical development of the legal notions current in the legal systems of his own time, such as property, contract, disposition by will and crime. He was not concerned with the majority of societies, which had remained 'stationary', but rather with the relatively rare 'progressive' societies. These may be compared with the 'nobler nations' that formed a model for Savigny's theory of legal evolution.

The distinction between stationary and progressive societies seems to have been derived from the *Traité de legislation* (4 volumes, 1827) of Charles Comte, which purported to identify 'the general laws according to which peoples progress, decline or remain stationary' and identified people of 'Caucasian race' as more progressive than others. For Maine, progressive societies were all Indo-European and he showed no interest in other societies. Like Savigny, he was interested in the parallels between the development of a people's language and the development of its legal institutions and he was influenced by current theories of the fundamental unity of Indo-European languages.

Maine saw his work as scientific; he saw no difference between the truth of the natural scientist and that of the historian. His methodological model was the uniformitarian geology of Sir Charles Lyell's *Principles of Geology* (1830), whose argument was that changes in the earth's surface were not caused by unpredictable sudden catastrophes but were the result of regular physical forces in constant, gradual and almost imperceptible change. So the earliest ideas of law 'are to the jurist what the primary crusts of the earth are to the geologist. They contain, potentially, all the forms in which law has subsequently exhibited itself' (*AL*: 3).

In Maine's view the typical progressive societies were those of ancient Rome and of England. Although he himself regarded his work as inductive and empirical, in most cases he generalized from the experience of ancient Roman law. This was the subject he had taught when he held the Regius Chair of Civil Law at Cambridge, to which he had been appointed at the age of twenty-five, and of lectures at the Inns of Court in London. The fact that the development of Roman law could be traced from written records over a thousand years required that it be taken as a model. For Roman law bore 'in its earliest portions the traces of the most remote antiquity' and in its developed form 'the staple of the civil institutions by which modern society is even now controlled' (*AL*: v), and Maine approached each topic through the categories established by Roman law.

Maine was opposed to Jeremy Bentham's idea that all law was legislation, the command of a sovereign. The farther we go back in time, 'the farther we find ourselves from a conception of law which at all resembles a compound of the elements which Bentham determined' (*AL*: 7–8). It is 'unfruitful' to say that societies modify their laws according to modifications of their views of general expediency, for that merely recognizes that change takes place. An inquiry into the nature of law must be scientific and Bentham's error was 'analogous to the error of one who, in investigating the laws of the material universe, should commence by contemplating the existing physical world as a whole, instead of beginning with the particles which are its simplest ingredients' (119).

The earliest forms of law recorded in writing, such as the Twelve Tables in Rome, the Laws of Solon in Athens and the Laws of Manu in India, which Maine called 'ancient codes', were not legislation in the modern sense but rather authoritative written records of what had previously been unwritten custom. Society was originally controlled by arbitrary and isolated decisions, which purported to be divinely inspired, handed down by a king or patriarch, which Maine called 'Themistes'. When small groups of aristocrats replaced the kings, they claimed to be the collective custodians of the traditional rules by which disputes were settled. Customary law therefore came to mean whatever this privileged caste decided. Their claim to a monopoly of legal knowledge was challenged by 'popular movements which began to be universal in the western world' (*AL*: 15). It was the agitation of such movements, such as that of the Roman plebeians in the early Republic, who doubted the impartiality of aristocratic interpretation of custom, which produced the 'ancient codes'.

In most societies there was no further legal development after this stage: '. . . much the greatest part of mankind has never shown a particle of desire that its civil institutions should be improved since the moment when external completeness was first given to them by their embodiment in some permanent record' (*AL*: 22). In progressive societies, on the other hand, there is a deliberate effort to adapt the law to changing social conditions.

First this was by fictions, which pretend that the legal

rule is unchanged, although a new class is admitted to its scope, so that the change is concealed. Adoption of a child into a new family is an early example of such a fiction. Although not biologically his child, the adopted child is legally the child of his adoptive father. Secondly, recourse is made to equity, 'a set of legal principles entitled by their intrinsic superiority to supersede the older law' (*AL*: 44). It is always introduced by a magistrate, the praetor in Rome and the chancellor in England, and is typically explained as the recovery of an ancient rule that had been lost. Only at a third stage is the law changed by open legislation in the modern sense.

Maine held that in early societies, the unit with which the law dealt was not the individual but the family group. Relations between the members of a family were controlled by their position within the family. The primitive family is dominated by the patriarch and its members are subject to his power. He represents the family to the outside world.

> [T]he persons theoretically amalgamated into a family by their common descent are practically held together by common obedience to their highest living ascendant, the father, grandfather or great-grandfather. The patriarchal authority of a chieftain is as necessary an ingredient in the notion of the family group as the fact (or assumed fact) of its having sprung from his loins' (*AL*: 133).

The patriarch's descendants through females are in the power of another patriarch and are not therefore 'included in the primitive notion of family relationship' (148).

At this point Maine generalizes the history of Roman law to the maximum, when he explained how the law gradually took account of the individual:

> The movement of progressive societies has been uniform in one respect. Through all its course it has been distinguished by the gradual dissolution of family dependency, and the growth of individual obligation in its place. The Individual is steadily substituted for the Family, as the unit of which civil laws take account. The advance has been accomplished at varying rates of celerity . . . But, whatever its pace, the change has not been subject to reaction or recoil, and apparent retardations will be found to have been occasioned by the absorption of archaic ideas and customs from some entirely foreign source. Nor is it difficult to see what is the tie between man and man which replaces by degrees those forms of reciprocity in rights and duties which have their origin in the Family. It is Contract. Starting . . . from a condition of society in which all the relations of Persons are summed up in the relations of Family, we seem to have steadily moved towards a phase of social order in which all these relations arise from the free agreement of Individuals (*AL*: 168–9).

Thus the status of the slave, that of the female under tutelage, and that of the son in his ancestor's power all disappeared. Maine's argument reached its climax with his most famous generalization. If we limit the word status to 'these personal conditions only, and avoid applying the term to such conditions as are the immediate or remote result of agreement, we may say that the movement of the progressive societies has hitherto been a movement *from Status to Contract*' (170).

Maine presented his theory in a way that made it easy for the reader to deduce that a situation in which the legal position of individuals resulted from negotiation with others was more progressive than one in which their position was determined in advance by their personal condition. Thus any legal rule which appeared to be based on status was ripe for reform.

Similarly in discussing the development of property, Maine showed that individual ownership only gradually replaced some form of co-ownership. In early Rome there was some evidence of the existence of family ownership before the recognition of the ownership of the family property by the family head. Maine gave particular attention to village communities in India, which in his view exemplified the expansion of the family into a larger group of co-owners. The Indian village community was 'at once an organised patriarchal society and an assemblage of co-proprietors. The personal relations to each other of the men who compose it are indistinguishably confounded with their proprietary rights' (*AL*: 260). Such communities were also found in early Slav societies, where they appeared to be almost exact repetitions of the Indian communities. After the publication of *Ancient Law*, Maine served from 1862 to 1869 as Legal Member of the Viceroy's Council in India, an experience which enabled him to deepen his interest in such communities and resulted in *Village Communities in the East and West*, published in 1871.

In dealing with succession on death, Maine argued that in most societies the power of the family head to dispose of family property by will is recognized relatively late. Where wills were accepted from the later Middle Ages, they were not allowed to interfere with the rights of the widow and of the children to fixed shares of the estate.

Maine's theories about the evolution of basic legal institutions, particularly his emphasis on the gradual unfolding of the idea of the self-determination of the free individual, although not themselves influenced by Darwinism, fitted into the fashion of thinking in terms of biological evolution. They were regarded as forming a natural history of law. Later, Maine himself accepted the parallel when, discussing the motives which impel man to the labour and pain which produce wealth in increasing quantities, he wrote that

> they are the springs of action called into activity by the strenuous and never-ending struggle for existence, the beneficent private war which makes one man strive to climb on the shoulders of another and remain there through the law of the survival of the fittest'. The setting for the struggle was 'the sacredness of contract and the stability of private property, the first the implement and the last the reward, of success in the universal competition (1885: 70–71).

Maine's theories were the object of sustained detailed criticism both from anthropologists and from historians of English law. The former tended to prefer matriarchy, rather than patriarchy, as the basis of early social organization and argued that Maine had seriously underestimated the influence of magic and of religion in shaping legal institutions. F.W. Maitland, the greatest English legal historian, observed (1897: 340–56) that to speak of land being owned by communities before it was owned by individuals, is not really to speak of ownership in the sense of rights to dispose of the land. Rather, such language was concerned with control over the way the land was used. Talk of ownership was an anachronism in that co-ownership presupposes prior individual ownership.

Maine wrote with a patrician air of authority and was a master of the memorable phrase. His views were received enthusiastically by conservative thinkers who were opposed to proposals for legal reform, since he was taken as having shown that the law somehow adapts itself to new social and economic conditions, without the need for legislation. Maine himself was opposed to democracy on the ground that it was unprogressive. The ordinary man's innate conservatism would, in his view, make him oppose changes which science and knowledge showed more enlightened members of society to be desirable.

Although Maine had cautiously stated that the movement of societies had hitherto been from status to contract, his readers took it to be a general law of legal progress. The ever increasing autonomy of the individual's will was expressed through contracts, through the fullest disposition of property and through unlimited testamentary freedom. He seemed thus to provide a scientific justification for laissez-faire individualism.

PETER STEIN

See also ADOPTION; BENTHAM, JEREMY; CUSTOMARY LAW; EMERGENCE OF LEGAL RULES; EQUITY; EVOLUTION OF COMMERCIAL LAW; INHERITANCE LAW; LEGAL PLURALISM; ROMAN LAW; SAVIGNY, FRIEDRICH VON; SOCIAL NORMS AND THE LAW; WESTERN LEGAL TRADITION.

Subject classification: 4a(ii); 7c.

SELECTED WORKS

1861. *Ancient Law: its Connection with the Early History of Society and its Relation to Modern Ideas.* London: Murray; (= *AL*).

1871. *Village Communities in the East and West: Six Lectures delivered at Oxford.* London: Murray.

1875. *Lectures on the Early History of Institutions.* London: Murray; New York: Holt.

1883. *Dissertations on Early Law and Custom: Chiefly Selected from Lectures delivered at Oxford.* London: Murray; New York: Holt.

1885. *Popular Government: Four Essays.* London: Murray.

BIBLIOGRAPHY

Maitland, F.W. 1897. *Domesday Book and Beyond: three essays in the early history of England.* Cambridge: Cambridge University Press.

mandatory disclosure. A wide range of transactions and interactions occurs between differentially informed parties. Customers are not always fully informed concerning the quality of the products and services they purchase. Corporate management has better information regarding the future profitability of their firm than do prospective investors. Traders in securities markets have access to different information regarding security values. Candidates for election, but not voters, know the identities of major political contributors. Parties to lawsuits do not share the same information regarding the merit of their cases. Job applicants are better informed about their skills and employers are better informed about working conditions. The list goes on. In some of these settings, governments have imposed mandatory disclosure rules requiring that certain parties disclose particular pieces of information.

There are numerous mandatory disclosure rules in the United States. The Food and Drug Administration requires that producers of food products disclose information concerning ingredients and nutritional information. Automobile manufacturers must disclose estimated fuel mileage as measured by the Environmental Protection Agency. Sellers and lessors of multifamily residences are required to disclose any information that they possess regarding the presence of lead-based paint hazards. This rule does not require abatement of a hazard, just disclosure. Firms with publicly traded securities must disclose financial information at the time the securities are issued and on a continuing basis thereafter. Certain individuals are required to disclose their stock market trades. The Federal Election Campaign Act requires political candidates to file periodic reports disclosing the money they raise and spend. The rules of evidence and discovery determine how information is used (or not used) in legal proceedings.

What is the effect of such mandatory disclosure rules? Who gains and who loses compared to a system of purely voluntary disclosure and thus who has the incentive to lobby for such rules? This essay addresses these questions with regard to disclosures that can be verified, that is, disclosures that can be supported with the necessary data to ensure that the disclosure is truthful. We do not consider the issues associated with fraudulent disclosures.

The analyses of Grossman and Hart (1980), Grossman (1981) and Milgrom (1981) imply that if disclosure is costless, then individuals involved in such transactions have the incentive to disclose all of their private information voluntarily. We will present their argument for the case of a seller who is better informed regarding product quality than his customers. The intuition, however, carries over to other applications. As an example, consider disclosure regarding the fat content of a particular food. Without disclosure, customers are unable to observe directly whether the food is high or low in fat (presume that, other things equal, customers prefer the latter). The producer, however, has this information and can disclose it on the label. What are customers to infer if the producer fails to disclose this information? A natural inference is that the food must be high in fat. For if it was low in fat, and if this is what customers prefer, then it would have been in the producer's interest to disclose this information. More generally, customers would infer that quality must be low if the seller withholds information regarding quality. Given this inference, a strategy of full disclosure is best for the seller. Informing customers of the true product quality must lead to higher profits than having customers believe product quality is low.

This intuition is formally modelled as follows. Suppose a seller privately observes his product's quality, $q \in Q$, where q measures the value of the product to customers and Q is the set of possible product quality levels. There are n risk-neutral customers. The seller can costlessly make a verifiable disclosure of q. Suppose there was an equilibrium in which the seller does not disclose if quality is such that $q \in \bar{Q}$ (where $\bar{Q}$ is a subset of Q). Then a seller who does not disclose sells his product for a price equal to the average quality in the subset $\bar{Q}$, i.e., $E[q \mid q \in \bar{Q}]$. However, a seller with $q \in \bar{Q}$ and with a quality that exceeds the average quality in $\bar{Q}$, $q > E[q \mid q \in \bar{Q}]$, has the incentive to deviate from the proposed equilibrium, disclose q and sell his product for q. Hence, equilibrium must entail disclosure by all $q \in Q$, except perhaps for the lowest value of q.

This argument implies that mandatory disclosure rules are redundant since voluntary disclosure would be forthcoming. Thus, this argument cannot explain the mandatory disclosure rules that we observe in practice. The argument, however, relies on some strong assumptions. It is assumed that disclosure is costless, that all customers understand the information that the seller might disclose, and that the exact extent of the seller's private information is publicly known. We will examine the implications for mandatory disclosure rules when these assumptions are relaxed. For concreteness, we will continue to discuss disclosure in terms of the problem facing a seller with private information on product quality.

In practice, disclosure is costly. There are direct costs associated with the production and dissemination of verifiable data. There may also be indirect costs such as those associated with revealing trade secrets to competitors. Once we acknowledge these disclosure costs, we no longer have the result that voluntary disclosure is always forthcoming (see Jovanovic 1982, Verrecchia 1983 and Dye 1986). With disclosure costs, the threat that customers will infer the worst if there is no disclosure cannot induce all sellers to disclose. Sellers with sufficiently low quality, even if not the lowest quality possible, will not find it profitable to incur the disclosure cost. Thus, disclosure costs induce an outcome in which sellers with relatively high-quality products disclose and sellers with relatively low-quality products do not disclose.

Formally, suppose the seller must pay c to disclose q. Then, in equilibrium, the seller discloses if q exceeds a threshold. To see this, consider an equilibrium in which the seller does not disclose if $q \in \bar{Q}$. A seller with quality q has a payoff of $nq - c$ if he discloses q and a payoff of $nE[q \mid q \in \bar{Q}]$ if he does not disclose q. The seller would disclose if $nq - c \geq nE[q \mid q \in \bar{Q}]$, or $q \geq E[q \mid q \in \bar{Q}] + c/n$. This implies that the equilibrium entails seller disclosure for $q \geq q^*$, where $q^* = E[q \mid q < q^*] + c/n$. Note that the size of the market, as measured by the number of customers, n, is important in determining the extent of disclosure (unlike the costless disclosure scenario).

What is the effect of mandatory disclosure in this case? Customers are indifferent. Since they pay the expected value of the product conditional on whatever information they have, they have an expected payoff of zero with mandatory or voluntary disclosure. The seller is worse off with mandatory disclosure. If quality is relatively high, $q \geq q^*$, the seller would voluntarily disclose anyway. But if quality is relatively low, $q < q^*$, the seller's gain from disclosure, $n(q - E[q \mid q < q^*])$ is outweighed by the cost. So no one is better off with mandatory disclosure. Thus, while accounting for disclosure costs can explain a lack of full voluntary disclosure, it still cannot identify any interest group that would benefit from, and thus lobby for, mandatory disclosure rules.

Fishman and Hagerty (1996) consider the implications of relaxing the assumption that all customers understand the meaning of a seller's disclosure. For instance, not everyone understands the health implications of the nutritional information that is provided on food packaging. Not all investors understand the implications for future profitability of the data contained in a firm's financial statements. The implication of limited understanding is that voluntary disclosure may not be forthcoming even if disclosure is costless. The reason is as follows. The benefit of disclosure for a seller with a high-quality product is that customers are willing to pay more. This benefit is limited, though, if not all potential customers will understand what the disclosure means. In this case, mandatory disclosure can be in the interest of customers, though counter to the interest of the seller.

Formally, suppose that if the seller discloses $q = q'$, only m of the n customers understand that $q = q'$. The other $n - m$ customers observe that a disclosure was made but they do not understand it; that is, the disclosure does not inform them of the particular value of q. Suppose there is a relatively low number of customers who could understand the disclosure, that is, m/n is low. In this case, even if disclosure is costless, there is an equilibrium in which the seller does not disclose q, sets a price equal to $E[q]$, and all n customers buy the product. Customers have an expected payoff of zero; price equals expected value. The seller's payoff is $nE[q]$. Unlike the Grossman–Hart–Milgrom model, a seller with $q > E[q]$ does not have the incentive to deviate from the proposed equilibrium by disclosing and setting a price equal to q. This is because $n - m$ of the customers will not understand the disclosure and these customers will not buy the product.

There is also an equilibrium in which the seller discloses q. In this equilibrium, there is a threshold quality level, $\hat{q}$, such that a seller with quality $q < \hat{q}$ sets a price equal to q and a seller with quality $q \geq \hat{q}$ sets a price equal to $\hat{q}$. In equilibrium, all n customers buy the product. For $q > \hat{q}$, the seller's price is below the product's value. This pricing credibly signals to the $n - m$ customers who do not understand the disclosure that the product is worth purchasing. A lower-quality seller will not choose this price since the gain from overcharging the $n - m$ customers who do not observe q is outweighed by the loss of business from the m customers who know that the product is overpriced. In this equilibrium, customers have an expected payoff of $E[q - \hat{q} \mid q \geq \hat{q}]\text{Prob}(q \geq \hat{q}) > 0$. The seller has an expected payoff of $nE[\min\{q, \hat{q}\}]$.

With voluntary disclosure, either of these equilibria may prevail. The customers prefer the equilibrium with disclosure because they pay a price below value for high-quality products; they pay $\hat{q}$ for quality levels $q > \hat{q}$. Because of this underpricing, the seller receives less, on average, in the equilibrium with disclosure; $nE[\min\{q, \hat{q}\}] < nE[q]$. Therefore, by ruling out the equilibrium with no disclosure, mandatory disclosure can result in a transfer from the seller to the customers and thus the customers are the constituency that would support such a rule. Fishman and Hagerty (1996) also consider an extended model in which (i) the customers who understand the seller's disclosure may value the product more because they are able to use it more efficiently; and (ii) m is endogenous. In the extended model, there are circumstances under which both the customers and the seller are better off with mandatory disclosure.

Now consider the assumption that the seller is known to have private information regarding the product for sale. In practice this may not be the case. For instance, a home may be subject to a health hazard, involving, say, lead-based paint, asbestos or radon. The homeowner may or may not be informed regarding the presence of a hazard. Moreover, an uninformed homeowner would likely be unable to verify that he is in fact uninformed. For how does one verify that they don't know something? Hence, failure to present evidence that the dwelling is free of such hazards should not be taken as evidence that a hazard is certainly present. In this case, a seller will disclose if he is informed and quality is relatively high. A seller will not disclose if either he is informed and quality is relatively low, or if he is uninformed. So while, on average, no disclosure means bad news, it does not mean sufficiently bad news so as to induce every informed seller to disclose. In such circumstances, requiring a seller who actually is informed to disclose the information, like the rule cited above regarding the presence of lead-based paint, is beneficial for the seller. Such a rule eliminates the negative inference that otherwise accompanies a lack of disclosure. Matthews and Postlewaite (1985), Farrell (1986), and Shavell (1994) all analyse this setting.

This intuition is formalized as follows. Following Shavell (1994) most closely, suppose it is costly for the seller to become informed of quality, q. The cost, c, is a random variable privately observed by the seller. If the seller pays to observe q, then it is costless to disclose q. In equilibrium, a seller acquires information if the cost is sufficiently low, i.e., $c < c^*$, and then discloses the information if quality is sufficiently high, i.e., $q \geq q^*$. The seller's payoff if he acquires and discloses the information about quality is $nq - c$. To determine the seller's payoff if he acquires but does not disclose product quality information, consider a customer's inference in response to a lack of disclosure. With some probability, the seller actually is informed but quality is low. Conditional on this possibility, a customer's valuation of the product is $E[q \mid q < q^*]$. With some probability, the seller actually is uninformed. Conditional on this possibility, a customer's valuation of the product is $E[q]$. Therefore, the seller's payoff if he acquires but does not disclose product quality information is $n\{E[q \mid q < q^*]\alpha + E[q](1-\alpha)\} - c$, where α is the equilibrium probability that the seller is informed given that he made no disclosure.

In equilibrium, the threshold q^* is the quality for which the seller is indifferent between disclosing and not disclosing; that is, $q^* = E[q \mid q < q^*]\alpha + E[q](1-\alpha)$. Also, in equilibrium, the threshold c^* is the cost for which the seller is indifferent between acquiring information and not acquiring information; that is, $c^* = n(E[q \mid q \geq q^*] - q^*)$ $\text{Prob}(q \geq q^*)$. The seller's expected payoff is $nE[q] - E[c \mid c < c^*]\text{Prob}(c < c^*)$, which is the expected revenue less the expected cost of acquiring information. Customers' expected payoffs are zero; the price they pay equals the expected value of the product conditional on their information.

Now, consider a rule that mandates disclosure if the seller is informed but does not mandate that the seller become informed. Customers are indifferent; they still have an expected payoff of zero. The seller, however, is better off. With mandatory disclosure, if the seller becomes informed, he must disclose his information and his expected payoff is $nE[q] - c$. If he remains uninformed his expected payoff is $nE[q]$. By eliminating the option to remain silent when informed, mandatory disclosure eliminates the incentive to become informed. This benefits the seller by eliminating the adverse selection problem that otherwise exists between seller and customers. Shavell (1994) also derives a similar result in an extended model in which there is social value to disclosure because customers who know q use the product more efficiently. In that case, with voluntary disclosure, the seller acquires information if $c < c^*$ and with mandatory disclosure, the seller acquires information if $c < c^{**}$, where c^{**} is the socially optimal cutoff and $c^{**} < c^*$. Again, the seller is better off with mandatory disclosure and customers are indifferent (either way, the price customers pay equals the expected value of the product conditional on their information).

It is interesting that a mandatory disclosure rule which actually reduces the likelihood of disclosure raises social welfare. Given the assumptions underlying the analysis, however, it is not clear how to enforce such a rule. If it is not observable whether the seller is informed, then how can an informed seller be compelled to disclose his information? Though some of the issues being considered differ, a number of other articles on disclosure also feature the idea that whether a party is informed is unobservable, e.g., Dye (1985), Dye and Sridhar (1995), and Dye (1996).

Various other assumptions in the basic disclosure model can also be relaxed. Milgrom (1981) analyses a setting in which it is not feasible for a seller to disclose all of his information. Specifically, a seller observes S signals but can only disclose $K < S$ of the signals. In equilibrium, the seller discloses the K most favourable signals. Consider the case of $K = 1$. An interpretation is that the seller is a firm issuing securities and each signal represents a different method of preparing the financial statements. Different methods can convey different information but for reasons of cost and brevity, only one set of financial statements is prepared. Fishman and Hagerty (1990) show that a rule limiting the seller's discretion as to which signals can be disclosed may be beneficial. Limiting discretion has the effect of controlling the information content of the disclosure. This is because how favourable a disclosure appears depends on how much discretion the seller has in making the disclosure. This type of disclosure rule resembles the restriction that financial statements be prepared in accordance with generally accepted accounting principles.

So far, we have discussed situations in which an informed party sells something to uninformed parties. The same results can be derived if the buyer is informed rather than the seller. Consider the original Grossman–Hart–Milgrom voluntary disclosure result in such a context. If an informed buyer withholds any information, an uninformed seller will infer that the withheld information must be favourable. Grossman and Hart (1980) apply this version of the argument to the problem facing an informed party who seeks to acquire control of a firm through a tender offer to uninformed shareholders.

Now consider a case in which the informed party might be a buyer or a seller. For example, consider a corporate insider who has private information regarding his firm and who can anonymously trade his firm's shares. Suppose disclosure is voluntary and the insider discloses nothing. Are other investors to infer that the insider has good news or bad news? If the former, then perhaps the insider will profit by selling shares and if the latter then perhaps the insider will profit by buying shares. Therefore, there is not necessarily any inference that induces voluntary disclosure. This implies that if disclosure is to be forthcoming it may need to be mandated. Fishman and Hagerty (1995) analyse this situation. There, the information to be disclosed pertains to an insider's trades. The circumstances under which there is an equilibrium with voluntary disclosure are characterized.

In all of the analyses discussed here, all disclosures were known to be truthful. Any cost of verifying a disclosure was paid up front. Suppose instead that it is feasible to disclose without immediately paying the cost to verify the disclosure. This raises the possibility of fraud and the interesting question of whether deterring fraud is best accomplished through private contracting or through the law. For a discussion of this issue, see Easterbrook and Fischel (1991).

Finally, the basic model discussed here has also been used to analyse mandatory disclosure in non-commercial settings, like trials. Shavell (1989) and Sobel (1989) examine the incentive for individuals to disclose information during pretrial bargaining. The results discussed above suggest that if a plaintiff with private information regarding his damages withholds his information, then the defendant may infer that the plaintiff's damages were low. Similarly, if a defendant withholds information, then the plaintiff may infer that the defendant's information suggests that he is liable. This could induce full voluntary disclosure during pretrial bargaining. As shown by Shavell (1989) and Sobel (1989), however, there are other possibilities. If litigation costs are high, then there may be no voluntary disclosure. This is because, to avoid a trial, one party may make a generous settlement offer irrespective of whether the other party discloses his private information. In this case, mandatory disclosure during the discovery phase of a trial can benefit one of the two parties.

MICHAEL J. FISHMAN AND KATHLEEN M. HAGERTY

See also CONSUMER PROTECTION; DISCLOSURE AND UNRAVELLING; DISCOVERY; FRAUD-ON-THE-MARKET; OWNERSHIP OF MARKET INFORMATION; PRIVATE INFORMATION AND LEGAL BARGAINING; PRODUCTS LIABILITY; SECURITIES REGULATION; SETTLEMENT OF LITIGATION; TENDER OFFERS.

Subject classification: 6c(i); 6c(iii).

BIBLIOGRAPHY

Dye, R.A. 1985. Disclosure of nonproprietary information. *Journal of Accounting Research* 23: 123–45.

Dye, R.A. 1986. Proprietary and nonproprietary disclosures. *Journal of Business* 59: 331– 66.

Dye, R.A. 1996. Investor sophistication and voluntary disclosures. Accounting Department working paper, Northwestern University.

Dye, R.A. and Sridhar, S.S. 1995. Industry-wide disclosure dynamics. *Journal of Accounting Research* 33: 157–74.

Easterbrook, F.H. and Fischel, D.R. 1991. *The Economic Structure of Corporate Law*. Cambridge, MA.: Harvard University Press.

Farrell, J. 1986. Voluntary disclosure: robustness of the unraveling result, and comments on its importance. In *Antitrust and Regulation*, ed. R. Grieson, Lexington, MA: Lexington Books.

Fishman, M.J. and Hagerty, K.M. 1990. The optimal amount of discretion to allow in disclosure. *Quarterly Journal of Economics* 105: 427–44.

Fishman, M.J. and Hagerty, K.M. 1995. The mandatory disclosure of trades and market liquidity. *Review of Financial Studies* 8: 637–76.

Fishman, M.J. and Hagerty, K.M. 1996. Mandatory vs. voluntary disclosure in markets with informed and uninformed customers. Finance Department working paper, Northwestern University.

Grossman, S.J. 1981. The informational role of warranties and private disclosure about product quality. *Journal of Law and Economics* 24: 461–83.

Grossman, S.J. and Hart, O.D. 1980. Disclosure laws and takeover bids. *Journal of Finance* 35: 323–34.

Jovanovic, B. 1982. Truthful disclosure of information. *Bell Journal of Economics* 13: 36–44.

Matthews, S. and Postlewaite, A. 1985. Quality testing and disclosure. *RAND Journal of Economics* 16: 328–40.

Milgrom, P.R. 1981. Good news and bad news: representation theorems and applications. *Bell Journal of Economics* 12: 380–91.

Shavell, S. 1989. Sharing of information prior to settlement or litigation. *RAND Journal of Economics* 20: 183–95.

Shavell, S. 1994. Acquisition and disclosure of information prior to sale. *RAND Journal of Economics* 25: 20–36.

Sobel, J. 1989. An analysis of discovery rules. *Law and Contemporary Problems* 52: 133–59.

Verrecchia, R.E. 1983. Discretionary disclosure. *Journal of Accounting and Economics* 5: 179–94.

Manne, Henry Girard (1928–). Henry Manne has made three distinct contributions to the field of law and economics which taken together constitute a unique and impressive legacy. The first contribution consists of Manne's foundational scholarship in the law and economics of corporate law and securities regulation. To this day his seminal work on takeovers, insider trading, corporate disclosure and the role of regulatory agencies provides a basic starting point for scholarship by lawyers and economists doing research in corporate finance and market micro-structure as well as corporate law and securities regulation.

The second stage of his career in law and economics began in 1974 when he founded the Law and Economics Center at the University of Miami Law School. The Law and Economics Center, which was moved briefly to Emory University en route to its current home at George Mason Law School, began innovative programmes supporting research and teaching in law and economics in a variety of forums.

The third contribution made by Manne to the field of law and economics is comprised of the decade between 1986 and 1996, when he served as the Dean of the George Mason Law School. During this period, he single-handedly transformed a sleepy backwater of American legal education into a major intellectual centre for the study of law and economics.

Manne received his training in law and economics at the University of Chicago Law School where he studied with Aaron Director. Soon Manne, followed by Judge Richard Posner and Judge Guido Calabresi, was one of the pioneers in the use of economic analysis to provide insights into legal problems. In his words, the application of economic analysis to the law is 'the only really high quality work systematically going on in law today' (Marx 1994: 1) After receiving his *juris doctor* (J.D.) at Chicago, Manne began teaching at a series of universities including St. Louis University, the George Washington University and the University of Rochester, where he was William R. Kenan Professor of Law and Political Science. Along the way, he also earned a doctorate in law (S.J.D.) from Yale.

SCHOLARLY CONTRIBUTION. For decades after its publication, the prevailing theory of American corporate governance was that of Adolf Berle and Gardiner Means (1932), who argued that the separation of ownership (shareholding) and control (management) in publicly traded corporations allows managers to run such corporations for their own benefit, to the exclusion of the interests of shareholders and society as a whole (Kaufman 1994: 52). Manne's scholarship on mergers and the market for corporate control constituted a powerful refutation of this approach. In part, the power of Manne's approach derives from the fact that he was the first person to use economic analysis in the corporate law area.

In his pathbreaking article, 'Mergers and the Market for Corporate Control' (1965), Manne recognized that corporate control is a commodity, or good, which, like any other commodity, has a market. He established that the 'agency cost' problems of separation of ownership and control in corporations with diffuse shareholders posited by Berle and Means were exaggerated since managers must keep share prices high in order to avoid being displaced in a hostile takeover. In other words, the best defence against a hostile takeover is to keep share prices sufficiently high that rival management teams cannot earn positive rates of return by purchasing control and ousting incumbent management. The market for corporate control thus provides incentives for managers to act in shareholders' interests. As Manne described it, the threat of a corporate takeover, 'afford[s] strong protection to the interests of vast numbers of small, non-controlling shareholders' (1965: 113). Observing that the takeover market constrained managers to work in the interests of shareholders, Manne pointed out that the market for corporate control gives 'power and protection' to shareholders by providing potential outside bidders with incentives to monitor incumbent management teams on behalf of shareholders.

Manne's article is generally considered the seminal work in law and economics on agency theory in corporate governance. It caused a paradigm shift in our understanding of the governance of the publicly held corporation. Its central premises – that there is an active market for corporate control in publicly held corporations which functions to safeguard the interests of shareholders and that this market is the superior guardian of shareholders' rights – are the foundation for much of the current work in corporate finance and securities regulation being carried out in law schools, economics departments and business schools. This early work was well received by many traditional scholars, although the Securities and Exchange Commission resisted the *laissez faire* policy implications of Manne's conclusions (Manne 1970: 547). Manne's work still provides the basic paradigm for current scholarly work on takeovers and mergers.

Manne's pathbreaking article made two other significant observations. First, in the context of developing a point made by economist Donald Dewey, he pointed out that mergers are often a low-cost substitute for bankruptcy. Manne observed that in market economies it is important that poorly performing firms fail so that the assets of these firms can be redeployed in more productive uses. Because bankruptcy is costly, mergers are often a superior mechanism for redeploying the assets of underperforming firms. He also observed that mergers can occur while a firm is on the path to insolvency, thereby redeploying underutilized assets more promptly.

Second, Manne observed that the protection which small shareholders receive in an economy with a robust market for corporate control is a substitute for other mechanisms for protecting shareholders, including litigation, proxy fights, and bureaucracies like the Securities and Exchange Commission (SEC) (Manne 1965: 113). Manne stressed that unsolicited tender offers are the most important instrument of corporate governance, noting that 'any move that lowers the return from *bona fide* takeovers diminishes the effectiveness of the market for corporate control and the protection of all shareholders' (1988: 29).

Manne's analysis of the market for corporate control led him to important insights about antitrust policy as well as securities regulation. These conclusions flowed from his fundamental insight that the threat of a takeover must be credible in order to encourage managerial efficiency in potential target firms. Manne was thus highly critical of the Celler–Kefauver Act of 1950 which tightened federal regulation of corporate mergers, noting that the best judge of merger activity was the market (which evaluates the economic efficiency of a transaction *ex ante*) rather than federal regulators (who evaluate transactions *ex ante*) (Kaufman 1994: 54). Manne was also highly critical of the Williams Act, which amended the Securities Exchange Act of 1934 and raised the costs of hostile takeovers by requiring disclosures in tender offers and by large block purchasers of stock. Manne correctly saw the Williams Act as a political gambit to protect well-connected incumbent management teams at the expense of small, diffuse, less politically powerful shareholders. By weakening the property rights of outside bidders, the Williams Act transferred wealth from shareholders to incumbent management teams, particularly those management groups that exploited management positions for private gain at the expense of shareholders.

The Williams Act, enacted in 1967, requires anyone purchasing five percent of the stock of a company to publicly disclose their takeover plans. These disclosure requirements enable the target company to take defensive measures aimed at making takeovers more costly. They also diminish bidders' incentives to engage in takeovers by limiting their potential profits. Manne presciently predicted that the Williams Act would '. . . seriously diminish realizable profits, and thus takeover incentives' (1966b: 91), allowing inefficient management to become entrenched.

Manne is perhaps best known for his foundational work on the law and economics of insider trading. He has vigorously opposed the regulation of insider trading, which he described as a victimless crime which, '. . . took a lot of teaching to get people to look on . . . as wrong' (1974: 25). According to Manne, the presence of insiders works to reduce the luck factor on both sides and gives outsiders something closer to a fair shake when they trade (1974: 84). Additionally, when insiders trade on their information, they make the pricing function of the market more efficient, reducing the volatility of stock prices. 'For all the rhetoric about the unfairness of insider trading,' Manne observes, 'its operational effect is to make the stock market a fairer game than it otherwise would be' (*idem.*). In a 1968 newspaper column following the landmark insider trading decision in *SEC vs. Texas Gulf Sulfur Co.*, Manne argued that even if insider trading actually harms investors, SEC rules against insider trading are futile since, 'it will in fact be impossible for the SEC to gain substantial compliance with rules against insider trading' (1968: 16).

Manne has also maintained that the practice of trading on non-public information plays an important role in corporate governance. Insider trading can, according to Manne, transform corporate managers from bureaucrats with little real interest in risk-taking into entrepreneurs whose outlook and time horizon are closely tied to that of the shareholders. He was among the first to recognize that the right to trade on material, non-public information about a corporation was a property right that a firm should be able to allocate in order to maximize the overall value of the enterprise. He predicted that, if legalized, insider trading would evolve into an important element in a fully incentive-compatible compensation contract for managers.

By the early 1980s, events conspired to unite Manne's scholarship on insider trading with his scholarship on the market for corporate control. As Manne himself pointed out, the Williams Act put the SEC's insider trading policy 'on a collision course with desirable takeover policy' (1986: 27). This conflict arose because potential corporate raiders, in order to circumvent the reporting requirements of the Williams Act, began enlisting the help of arbitrageurs who could acquire large blocks of a target company's stock without arousing a target company's suspicion. Raiders, contrary to the provisions of the Williams Act, shared their secret takeover intentions with these arbitrageurs who could perform the share-gathering task which the Williams Act prevented the raiders from doing themselves. In this way, trading on inside information became a key component of takeovers in the post-Williams Act era. To cope with the crisis, the SEC pressed for increasingly strict sanctions against those suspected of insider trading. Manne derided this as an SEC effort 'to impart its moral attitudes to the business community . . . without heed to the economic or business consequences of their move' (1968: 5).

Manne's work on insider trading strongly influenced an entire generation of scholars in law and economics. Well into the 1990s Manne's work on the SEC, on insider trading and on takeovers provided the starting point for virtually all of the serious analytical work at major universities in the United States.

MANNE AND THE CENTER FOR LAW AND ECONOMICS. Henry Manne founded the first Center for Law and Economics at the University of Miami in 1974. Today, every law school of note in the United States contains a centre devoted to the study of law and economics, and all these centres can be traced to Henry Manne's academic entrepreneurship in the early 1970s. A cornerstone of Manne's Law and Economics Center has been its programme of instruction in law and economics for federal judges and for professors, the Summer Institute for Law Professors in Rochester, New York, which began in 1971. By 1990 over 900 professors had received instruction in law (for economists) or in economics (for lawyers), and 350 judges (40% of the federal judiciary) had received instruction in law and economics from such outstanding academics as Armen Alchian, Orley Ashenfelter, George Benston, and Noble Laureates Milton Friedman and Paul Samuelson (Crovitz 1990: A25). As a result, Manne's influence in the development of the discipline of law and economics has been prodigious.

MANNE'S WORK AT GEORGE MASON UNIVERSITY. In 1980 Manne moved the Law and Economics Center from Miami to Emory Law School in Atlanta, Georgia. Then in 1986 he was named Dean of the George Mason University School of Law in northern Virginia, close to Washington, DC. Upon assuming the deanship at George Mason, Dean Manne was not given significant new resources. He was, however, authorized to add five new faculty positions, and he brought with him significant resources from charitable individuals and institutions that previously had supported law and economics in the United States. Manne radically altered the law school's curriculum and introduced a philosophy of legal education based on the idea that 'understanding economics is crucial for the understanding of anything fundamental about law' (Matthews 1993: F4). He reshaped the faculty into one with a firm economic grounding, encouraging professors who either lacked interest or aptitude in economics to leave the university. Dean Manne also provided funding for several professors to return to graduate school to earn PhDs in economics, and enriched the curriculum's law and economics offerings. Manne introduced requirements that law students at

George Mason enroll in a quantitative methods course where they learn basic economic principles, as well as statistics, accounting, finance, and econometric techniques. A fundamental part of the restructured curriculum was the development of specialized courses of study through which students could elect to acquire in-depth expertise in a particular legal sub-specialty (1991: 14). In just a few years under Manne's guidance, the number of applicants to George Mason had tripled. The law school was labelled as 'one of the up-and-coming law schools in the United States' (1991: 14), and it was recognized as one of the few law schools in the US interested in serious interdisciplinary scholarship.

In 1996 Manne resigned as dean of George Mason. In 1997 Mark Grady, a professor from UCLA whose legal scholarship had been in the field of torts, became Dean of George Mason Law School. Dean Manne's ties with the Law and Economics Center of George Mason have been severed. He remains a University Professor at George Mason University, but the future of the Law and Economics Center is unclear. It is noteworthy that the law and economics centres that Manne previously established at Emory University in Atlanta, Georgia, and the University of Miami (Florida) did not long survive after Manne ended his associations with those institutions, and neither of those institutions sponsors significant research in law and economics today.

JONATHAN R. MACEY

See also AUCTIONS AND TAKEOVERS; CHICAGO SCHOOL OF LAW AND ECONOMICS; INSIDER TRADING; LAW-AND-ECONOMICS IN ACTION; MARKET FOR CORPORATE CONTROL; SECURITIES REGULATION; TENDER OFFERS.

Subject classification: 4c(i); 7c.

STATUTES

Celler–Kefauver Act (1950), 29 December, ch. 1184, 64 Stat. 1125.
Securities and Exchange Act (1934), 6 June, ch. 404, 48 Stat. 881.
Williams Act (1968), 29 June, Pub. L. 90–439, 82 Stat. 454.

CASES

SEC v. Texas Gulf Sulfur Co., 401 F2d 833 (2d Cir. 1968).

SELECTED WORKS

1961. Current views on the 'modern corporation'. *University of Detroit Law Journal* 38: 559–88; reprinted in *Corporate Practice Commentator* (1962) 4: 1–40.
1964. Some theoretical aspects of vote sharing, *Columbia Law Review* 64: 1427–45.
1965. Mergers and the market for corporate control. *Journal of Political Economy* 73: 110–20.
1966a. *Insider Trading and the Stock Market*. New York: Free Press.
1966b. Tender offers and the free market. *Mergers and Acquisitions* 91: 90–115.
1967. Our two corporation systems: law and economics. *Virginia Law Review* 53: 259–84.
1968. Prohibition on Wall Street? *Barron's* 16 December: 5, 16–18.
1970. Insider trading and the law professors. *Vanderbilt Law Review* 23: 547–90.
1971. The parable of the parking lots. *The Public Interest* 23: 10–15.
1972 (with H.C. Wallich). *The Modern Corporation and Social Responsibility*. Washington, DC: American Enterprise Institute.
1974 (with E. Solomon). Economic aspects of required disclosure under federal securities law. In *Wall Street in Transition*, New York: New York University Press.
1986. The real Boesky-case issue. *New York Times*, 25 November: A27.
1988. The SEC v. the American shareholder: the Drexel Burnham case. *National Review*, 25 November: 26–9.
1991. In specialization, George Mason was first. *National Law Journal* 23: 14.
1993. An intellectual history of the School of Law, George Mason University. Monograph published by the Law and Economics Center of George Mason.

BIBLIOGRAPHY

Berle, A.A., Jr. and Means, G.C. 1932. *The Modern Corporation and Private Property*. New York: Macmillan.
Crovitz, G. 1990. George Mason's entrepreneurial Dean preaches economics. *Wall Street Journal*, 4 April: A25.
Kaufman, A. 1994. Kohlberg Kravis Roberts & Co. and the restructuring of American capitalism. *Business History Review*, 22 March, 67: 52–97.
Marx, C. 1994. *Investor's Business Daily*, 20 January: 1–3.
Matthews, J. (quoting Henry Manne). 1993. Business tries to shape legal system, report says. *The Washington Post*, 19 May: F4.
Seligman, D. 1983. An economic defense of insider trading. *Time*, 5 September: 27.

marginal deterrence. *See* CRIMINAL ATTEMPTS; PUBLIC ENFORCEMENT OF LAW.

market for corporate control. If managers of firms do not indulge in activities that maximize the wealth of shareholders, most economists today would say that those managers should be given the proper incentives, replaced, or punished by the market for corporate control. The market for corporate control values the rights of owners to set the compensation level of top managers, structure their compensation contracts, and to hire and fire these managers. Accordingly, the market for corporate control is an important part of the managerial labour market wherein alternative teams compete for the rights to manage corporate resources (Jensen and Ruback 1983). This market operates both within and outside the firm. Rather than list all mechanisms within the market for corporate control and do injustice to all of them, we have detailed a few important internal and external control mechanisms.

INTERNAL CONTROL MECHANISMS. There are a number of internal control mechanisms that help in aligning managerial and shareholder interests. Among the most important are (1) equity ownership of top managers, (2) performance-related chief executive officer (CEO) compensation, (3) mechanisms for matching jobs and human capital, and (4) boards of directors.

(1) *Equity ownership of top managers.* Research on managerial compensation has logically focused on two areas of examination: (i) the equity ownership of all top managers and/or members of the board, and (ii) the entire compensation contract of the chief executive officer. We

begin with the relationship of firm value and the equity ownership of the top managers.

Berle and Means (1933) were the first to posit that when principals such as shareholders do not have the necessary information or skills to manage the firm, they rely on agents or managers who may hold little equity in the firm. Such an arrangement may lead some agents to shirk or undertake suboptimal investment projects to maximize their own benefits, rather than maximizing principals' wealth. More recently, researchers have argued that managers deviate from shareholder wealth-maximization by consuming perquisites when they do not have an ownership stake in the firm (Jensen and Meckling 1976). Accordingly, more managerial ownership aligns managerial interests with shareholder interests. Alternatively, in another information setting, managers may use ownership stakes to signal to markets that they have projects of a high quality (Leland and Pyle 1977). Hence more managerial ownership can be associated with a higher market value of the firm.

There is no reason to believe that a relationship between managerial stakes and firm performance is linear. For example, Stulz (1988) models the takeover process as a game between managers and an outside bidder vying for the voting rights of a number of small, competitive and passive shareholders. Increases in managerial ownership stakes force the outside bidder to pay higher premiums to gain control of the firm. When the managerial ownership stake is so large that a takeover is not profitable to the bidder, however, high managerial ownership levels reduce *ex ante* market value. Accordingly, increases in managerial ownership increase the premium that the bidder must offer, but decrease the probability that the bidder makes a bid. These two opposing forces imply that the firm's market value first increases and then decreases with each increase in the managerial ownership stake.

In an empirical line of inquiry, Mørck, Shleifer and Vishny (1988) estimate a piecewise-linear relationship between board ownership stakes and average Tobin's Q (where Q is the sum of market value of equity, debt, and preferred stock divided by the replacement value of assets). They find that Tobin's Q increases and then decreases with increases in managerial ownership, and suggest that the firm's market value is adversely affected at managerial ownership levels between 5% and 25%. In this range of ownership stakes, managers are entrenched and can indulge in non-value-maximizing activities without being disciplined by their shareholders. The authors find that for managerial ownership levels greater than 25%, the relationship between board ownership and Q once again turns positive. Nonlinearity in the relationship between managerial ownership and firm performance has been corroborated in a number of settings. McConnell and Servaes (1990), using a larger data set, find a quadratic relationship between managerial ownership and Tobin's Q. Further, they find the relationship to turn slightly negative when managerial ownership reaches approximately 40% to 50% of the firm. Hubbard and Palia (1995a) examine mergers, and find that the bidder's excess returns increase until ownership levels of 5% are reached and turn negative thereafter.

To summarize, cross-sectional studies have generally concluded that the relationship between firm value and insider ownership (i.e., ownership of top managers, and in some cases, ownership of the total board of directors), is nonmonotonic though there are differences across studies about the point at which the relationship becomes positive or negative. This finding may be at odds with the more general notion that firms are governed by a network of relationships, and that once one controls for observed firm characteristics and unobserved heterogeneity (via firm fixed effects), there is no effect of changes in managerial ownership on firm performance. Accordingly, firms are in equilibrium with respect to unobserved contracting characteristics and focusing on one such endogenous relationship is inappropriate (Demsetz and Lehn 1985; Himmelberg, Hubbard and Palia 1996).

(2) *Performance-related CEO compensation.* In principle, pay-performance sensitivity, and not just the level of pay, is important for optimal compensation policy. In one investigation, Jensen and Murphy (1990) suggest that a large part of the pay-performance sensitivity is from the value of stock owned by the CEO and from the value of unexercised options. Examining the sensitivity of different components of CEO pay to shareholder wealth, they find that each $1,000 change in shareholder wealth corresponds to an average increase in this year's and next year's salary and bonus of only two cents. Dismissals do not appear to be an important part of managerial incentives, because the increases in dismissal probability due to poor performance and its associated penalties are extremely small. Jensen and Murphy estimate an upper bound for stock options and other compensation components of $0.75 per $1,000 change in shareholder wealth; the greatest sensitivity comes from the value of stock owned by the CEO, estimated to be $2.50 for each change in firm value of $1,000. Thus their combined estimate of the CEO pay-performance sensitivity is only $3.25 per $1,000 change in shareholder wealth. Such a small estimated sensitivity may be attributed to political forces that operate in the contracting process that implicitly or explicitly constrain the type of contracts that can be written between managers and shareholders. Jensen and Murphy suggest that forces operating in the political sector and within organizations appear to have a major impact on the CEO's compensation contract. The impact of these forces is both informal and indirect, and is therefore difficult to document. For example, they suggest that public disapproval of high rewards seems to have truncated the upper tail of the compensation contract for CEOs. This sentiment would indirectly be absorbed by the board of directors of the corporation and the compensation committee members that design the CEO's contract. Because, in addition, a CEO's wealth constraint would make very large penalties for poor performance impossible, one would expect to find a more compact distribution for the sensitivity of CEO compensation to performance.

In another view, variations in CEO compensation and pay-performance sensitivity reflect differences in investment opportunities and in the executive talent required to manage them. For example, Smith and Watts (1992) examine sixteen industries, of which three are regulated, and find that industries with lower investment opportunities (measured as the ratio of market value of equity plus book value of assets minus book value of equity to book value of assets) have lower CEO compensation and less frequent use of both option and bonus plans. Smith and Watts attribute these findings to a contracting hypothesis. Firms with less promising investment opportunities have managerial actions that are more readily observable and therefore do not need a strong pay-performance relationship to align managerial and shareholder interests. In this case, the larger are growth options relative to firm value, the higher the pay-performance sensitivity. In addition, they find that regulated firms have lower levels of CEO pay because higher levels of compensation in firms with higher growth options are necessary for managers to make decisions; the skills associated with the selection of investment projects commands a higher equilibrium wage than those associated with the supervision of existing assets in place. Regulated firms appear to have a lower level of pay and a lower pay-performance relationship than unregulated manufacturing firms (Joskow, Rose and Shepard 1993), and Palia (1996) finds that most of the differences in the pay-performance sensitivities between utilities and unregulated firms arise from differences in options and stock ownership.

(3) *Finding the appropriate human capital.* While many empirical studies have examined the differences in pay levels and the pay-performance sensitivities (i.e., the provision of incentives), such studies largely ignored one function of the managerial labour market: to select executives and assign or match their talents to different jobs (i.e., select the appropriate human capital). In addition to providing performance incentives, one of the functions of the executive labour market is to identify competent and talented managers (Rosen 1992). Does the quality of managerial talent and the executive labour market have an impact on company performance? Some researchers have even concluded that the allocation of talent has significant effects on the growth rate of a country (Murphy, Shleifer and Vishny 1991). Individuals with significant increasing returns to ability (or 'superstars') choose occupations where much of the rent on their talent can be retained. Murphy, Shleifer and Vishny find evidence that countries with a higher proportion of engineering college majors grow faster, and countries with a higher proportion of law concentration majors grow more slowly.

In a study that examines the privatization of Russian shops, Barberis, Boycko, Shleifer and Tsukanova (1996) conclude that the presence of new owners and managers increases the likelihood of restructuring, whereas giving equity incentives to old managers does not promote restructuring. This suggests that recent research in the analysis of executive pay may have stressed incentives to the point of ignoring the potential for 'slotting' people into jobs. As a related point, there may be quality sorting in the managerial labour market in the presence of regulation (Peltzman 1993; Hubbard and Palia 1995b; Palia 1996).

(4) *Boards of directors.* If the board of directors of a company is a perfect external monitor, shareholders would not need to use managerial compensation to align managerial and shareholder interests. Generally, the quality of the board has been proxied in two dimensions: size of the board, and the proportion of outsiders on the board (for a detailed list of studies, see Palia 1996). Some have suggested that small boards are more effective, because large boards are easier for the CEO to control, and have found evidence consistent with such a relationship. Research on the composition of the board of directors, as measured by the proportion of outside directors on the board, is ambiguous in its effect on firm-value. Some studies have found a positive impact of the proportion of directors from outside the firm on: firm-value, CEO turnover, takeovers, management buyouts, and poison-pill adoptions. By contrast, other studies have found either no significant relationship or a significant negative relationship of the composition of the board on firm-value.

EXTERNAL CONTROL MECHANISMS. There are a number of external control mechanisms that assist shareholders in taking care of their interests. They are (1) ownership by large shareholders, (2) takeovers, and (3) debt.

(1) *Ownership by large shareholders.* Recently, the proportion of total shares owned by pension funds and mutual funds has increased dramatically. It is possible that large shareholders gain a lot from monitoring (given the larger amount of shares they own), and the presence of a large shareholder is associated with a higher firm value (Shleifer and Vishny 1986). Such benefits of large shareholder control have been found to be valuable in a number of studies. Holderness and Sheehan (1988) estimate a positive stock price reaction to announcement of trades where a shareholder controls more than 50%, but less than 100%, of the firm. They also find that new directors and officers were appointed after such trades, suggesting active involvement of the large shareholder. Some studies have found that shares that are identical with respect to dividend receipts but with differential voting rights trade at different prices, with the higher voting share receiving a premium. For example, large blocks of equity appear to trade at a substantial premium to the post-trade price of smaller block of shares (Barclay and Holderness 1992).

(2) *Takeovers.* If other methods to control managerial discretion prove to be inadequate, mergers and acquisition markets can be used to alter corporate control. Jensen and Ruback (1983) and Jarrell, Brickley and Netter (1988) summarize papers that examine the gains to bidders and target firms. They find that target firms earn around 15% to 30% abnormal returns over the market, whereas the abnormal returns to the bidding firms have generally been found to be non-positive. These results suggest that takeovers increase the value of the combined firm.

Several theoretical studies have suggested that takeovers help in disciplining managers. Target firms are often poorly performing firms whose managers are removed after the takeover. Hubbard and Palia (1995b) examine a sample of banks and find an increasing CEO pay-performance sensitivity and a competitive corporate control market to be positively correlated. Jensen (1986) suggests that takeovers help some firms to distribute their excess free cash flow to their shareholders which otherwise would have been kept as a managerial buffer or used in negative present value projects.

Other researchers have suggested that recent takeovers and divestitures in the 1980s have reversed the managerial non-shareholder-wealth-maximizing behaviour that was implemented in the 1960s. Their studies have examined whether the benefits or costs of firm-level diversification vary according to whether acquisitions are in related or diversifying lines of business. Lang and Stulz (1994) examine Tobin's *Q* in the late 1970s and through the 1980s, and find that diversified firms have lower-than-average *Q* values, all else being equal, while single-industry firms have a high *Q*. This diversification discount is robust to controlling for size, industry, and access to capital markets. Further, they find that the value of the diversified firm is less than the value of its divisions standing alone. Some studies have found that diversified firms were also more active buyers and sellers in the market for corporate control in the 1980s. They also find that firms generally became more focused in the 1980s and that diversified firms were no more able to exploit economies of scope than focused firms. When examining divestitures, for a sample of acquisitions, no significant differences were found in the returns earned *ex ante* among acquirer-related acquisitions and diversifying acquisitions. This result suggests surprisingly weak support for arguments that diversifying acquisitions decreased value *ex ante*. In addition, acquirers were found more likely to divest unrelated than related acquisitions.

Recently, research has examined why diversifying acquisitions actually took place in the 1960s. Some have examined the stock market reactions to acquisition announcements and found evidence that the abnormal returns for diversifying acquisitions can be attributed to 'synergies' between the acquiring and target firms. Hubbard and Palia (1996) examine the entire conglomerate merger wave in the 1960s. They analyse whether there are any significant differences between conglomerate firms and focused firms, and look for differences in the abnormal returns earned by these two categories of firms in making diversifying or related acquisitions. They find that the conglomerate firm that makes a related acquisition actually earns the highest returns. In contrast to the findings of research examining the announcement effect of takeovers, some studies have found that conglomerate firms traded at a discount to single-segment firms during the 1960s (Servaes 1996).

(3) *Debt.* The role of debt in disciplining managers in the presence of agency costs has been suggested by a number of authors (see Shleifer and Vishny 1996 for a review). For example, debt can force the manager to precommit to paying out free cash flow and may even help the manager to distribute free cash flow. Some authors have suggested that, under some circumstances, the debt overhang is an effective deterrent to new investment. Others have suggested that debt is a contract that gives the creditor the right to collateral in case of default. Fear of such liquidation enables the creditors to receive their promised payment. Debt can also be valuable in the context of default, upon which creditors can restrict the firm from raising future funds in the capital markets. Managerial shirking can be avoided because of the negotiating ability of debt holders after default. In addition, stringent covenants are a credible threat that helps creditors ensure managerial obedience. To that extent, studies have found that debt restricts bad investments, especially for firms with poor prospects. While all these arguments suggest the benefits of debt, some recent papers have started to examine costs of high leverage in the presence of aggregate risk (Gertler and Hubbard 1993) and whether concentrated equity with voting rights can achieve Pareto improvement over a debt contract (Myers 1996). To summarize, research has generally shown that for a group of (generally poorly-performing) firms, debt is beneficial in its role of restricting managerial discretion and shirking.

NEW AVENUES OF RESEARCH. While most studies have focused attention on the benefits and costs of individual mechanisms for corporate control, one can think more broadly about competition among alternative means of supplying efficient corporate control (as in Stigler 1958). Toward that end, many researchers are examining the evolution of corporate control markets within countries and across countries (see the review in Shleifer and Vishny 1996). These international differences in the corporate control market and their evolution promise to be an important area for future empirical research.

R. GLENN HUBBARD AND DARIUS PALIA

See also AGENCY COSTS AND CORPORATE GOVERNANCE; AUCTIONS AND TAKEOVERS; BOARDS OF DIRECTORS; COMPETITION FOR STATE CORPORATE LAW; CORPORATE GOVERNANCE; CORPORATE LAW; MANNE, HENRY G.; INDEPENDENT DIRECTORS; LAW-AND-ECONOMICS IN ACTION; LEVERAGED BUYOUTS; OWNERSHIP AND CONTROL IN EUROPE; TENDER OFFERS.

Subject classification: 5g(iii).

BIBLIOGRAPHY

Barberis, N., Boycko, M., Shleifer, A. and Tsukanova, N. 1996. How does privatization work? Evidence from the Russian shops. *Journal of Political Economy* 104: 764–90.

Barclay, M. and Holderness, C. 1992. The law and large-block trades. *Journal of Law and Economics* 35: 265–94.

Berle, A. and Means, G. 1933. *The Modern Corporation and Private Property*. New York: Macmillan.

Demsetz, H. and Lehn, K. 1985. The structure of corporate ownership: causes and consequences. *Journal of Political Economy* 93: 1155–77.

Gertler, M. and Hubbard, R.G. 1993. Corporate financial policy, taxation, and macroeconomic risk. *RAND Journal of Economics* 24: 286–303.

Himmelberg, C., Hubbard, R.G. and Palia, D. 1996. Understanding determinants of managerial ownership and the link between ownership and performance. Working paper, Columbia University.

Holderness, C. and Sheehan, D. 1988. The role of majority shareholders in publicly held corporations: an exploratory analysis. *Journal of Financial Economics* 20: 317–46.

Hubbard, R.G. and Palia, D. 1995a. Benefits of control, managerial ownership, and the stock returns of acquiring firms. *RAND Journal of Economics* 26: 782–92.

Hubbard, R.G. and Palia, D. 1995b. Executive pay and performance: evidence from the U.S. banking industry. *Journal of Financial Economics* 39: 105–30.

Hubbard, R.G. and Palia, D. 1996. A re-examination of the conglomerate merger wave in the 1960s. Working paper, Columbia University.

Jarrell, G.A., Brickley, J.A. and Netter, J.M. 1988. The market for corporate control: the empirical evidence since 1980. *Journal of Economic Perspectives* 2: 49–68.

Jensen, M.C. 1986. Agency costs of free cash flow, corporate finance, and takeovers. *American Economic Review* Papers and Proceedings 76: 323–9.

Jensen, M.C. and Meckling, W. 1976. Theory of the firm: managerial behavior, agency costs and ownership structure. *Journal of Financial Economics* 3: 305–360.

Jensen, M.C. and Murphy, K.J. 1990. Performance pay and top-management incentives. *Journal of Political Economy* 98: 225–64.

Jensen, M.C. and Ruback, R. 1983. The market for corporate control: the scientific evidence. *Journal of Financial Economics* 11: 5–50.

Joskow, P.L., Rose, N.L. and Shepard, A. 1993. Regulatory constraints on CEO compensation. *Brookings Papers on Economic Activity (Microeconomics)*: 1–72.

Lang, L. and Stulz, R. 1994. Tobin's *Q*, corporate diversification and firm performance. *Journal of Political Economy* 102: 1248–80.

Leland, H.E. and Pyle, D.H. 1977. Informational asymmetries, financial structure, and financial intermediation. *Journal of Finance* 32: 371–87.

McConnell, J.J. and Servaes, H. 1990. Additional evidence on equity ownership and corporate value. *Journal of Financial Economics* 27: 595–612.

Mørck, R., Shleifer, A. and Vishny, R.W. 1988. Management ownership and market valuation. *Journal of Financial Economics* 20: 293–315.

Murphy, K.M., Shleifer, A. and Vishny, R.W. 1991. The allocation of talent: implications for growth. *Quarterly Journal of Economics* 5(106): 503–30.

Myers, S. 1996. Inside and outside equity financing. Working paper, Massachussets Institute of Technology.

Palia, D. 1996. The impact of regulation on CEO labour markets. Working paper, Columbia University.

Peltzman, S. 1993. Comment. *Brookings Papers on Economic Activity (Microeconomics)*: 63–6.

Rosen, S. 1992. Contracts and the market for executives. In *Contract Economics*, ed. L. Werin and H. Wijkander, Oxford: Blackwell.

Servaes, H. 1996. The value of diversification during the conglomerate merger wave. *Journal of Finance* 51: 1201–26.

Shleifer, A. and Vishny, R.W. 1986. Large shareholders and corporate control. *Journal of Political Economy* 94: 461–88.

Shleifer, A. and Vishny, R.W. 1996. A survey of corporate governance. NBER Working paper No 5554, April.

Smith, C.W. and Watts, R.L. 1992. The investment opportunity set and corporate financing, dividend and compensation policies. *Journal of Financial Economics* 32: 263–92.

Stigler, G.J. 1958. The economics of scale. *Journal of Law and Economics* 1: 54–71.

Stulz, R.M. 1988. Managerial control of voting rights: Financing policies and the market for corporate control. *Journal of Financial Economics* 20: 25–54.

markets and incommensurability. Questions about what constitute the appropriate limits of the market domain have inspired a significant amount of legal-economic inquiry (see Trebilcock 1993; Sunstein 1997). One particular question accorded considerable attention recently is whether certain goods and activities are ill-suited to commodification – either to the extent that they should be accorded special protection in the market domain or even to the extent that they should never be made the subject of commercial exchange. Arguments recommending that particular goods and activities be accorded special protection or deemed market-inalienable often proceed from the idea of incommensurability. This essay provides: (i) an account of the notion of incommensurability as used in legal–economic reasoning; (ii) an explanation of incommensurability-based objections to particular instances of commodification; and (iii) some critical observations on these objections.

INCOMMENSURABILITY. Incommensurability is the concept which philosophers tend to use when attempting to demonstrate that certain things are not comparable along the same metric. As applied to market reasoning, the incommensurability thesis is that since market valuations are monistic in nature – since they require that diverse goods and activities be valued in terms of a single metric – they can sometimes degrade that which is being valued. Radin's 'personhood' theory of private property is a specific illustration of the incommensurability argument (Radin 1993). Inspired principally by Hegel, Radin purports to identify a distinction between what she terms fungible and personal property. Whereas fungible property has a purely economic or instrumental value, personal property is that with which the owner becomes bound up to such a degree that its loss would cause him pain that could not be relieved simply by replacing the object with other goods of equal market value. A credit card is likely to be fungible. By contrast, many items of jewellery will (for their owners) have more personal significance. Not all property can be straightforwardly categorized as fungible or personal. One's word-processor, for example, might fall into either category, depending on what is stored on the hard disk. But Radin's point is that all private property will be more fungible than personal or *vice versa* – that there is, as it were, a continuum between personal and fungible property rights – and that its categorization in this way ought to have important implications for the manner in which it is regulated.

By and large, Radin claims, there should be a presumption that rights to personal property deserve greater legal protection than rights to fungible property. In endeavouring to support this claim, she considers the regulation of residential tenancies. Whereas landlords usually have only a commercial interest in their properties, tenants generally have a personal interest in them. Since preservation of one's home is intuitively more exigent than preservation of one's business, the law ought to put the interests of tenants before those of landlords (Radin 1993: 79). Critics of Radin's personhood perspective have observed that if residential tenancies are regulated in the manner which she prescribes, few people will be inclined to make their properties available on the residential leasehold property market (see Brennan 1988; Greenberg 1990). Her proposal, if implemented, might actually harm tenants (or certainly prospective tenants).

Whereas, generally, the notion of incommensurability is used to denote the impossibility of evaluating two or more things according to a common metric, in relation to market reasoning it is often employed to denote the inappropriate reduction of a single good or activity to a monetary valuation (see Anderson 1993: 118). Radin's argument about personhood illustrates the point: when the market is used to value property rights, she believes, there is always the risk that the peculiarly personal nature of certain rights will be underestimated or neglected, since, within the market domain, personal and fungible rights are valued alike – that is, in monetary terms. The incommensurability thesis can be expanded – and, as a critique of market reasoning, seems somewhat more interesting once it is expanded – to cover goods and activities which are not commonly subjected to explicit monetary valuation. Friendship offers a simple illustration: placing a price on friendship seems inconsistent with the manner in which one normally values friends. In advancing the incommensurability thesis, legal theorists have tended to present human body tissue, sexual activity and parental rights as principal examples of goods and activities which are somehow degraded if commodified (see Radin 1996).

INCOMMENSURABILITY-BASED OBJECTIONS TO MARKET REASONING. The essence of incommensurability-based objections to market reasoning is that the intrinsic dignity and value of humanity will be undermined if peculiarly personal goods and activities, such as human tissue, surrogacy and sex, are legitimately traded. To commodify our entire being, so the argument goes, can only be injurious to ourselves. This argument sometimes seems compelling because it is bound up with other, more convincing arguments against particular instances of commodification. Where a market in human tissues and organs is established, for example, there may be an increased risk of abuse and exploitation of the vulnerable and the poor, need may be displaced by ability and willingness to pay, altruism might well decline and the market may generate a supply of infected materials. While certain of these problems might be countered by appropriate regulation (such as the development of mechanisms for monitoring quality of material supplied), the potential costs of creating regulations to facilitate the operation of the market – not to mention the risks of regulatory failure – will themselves count against arguments for commercialization. Similarly, if sale of parental rights to children were permitted, there would be a risk of children being bought and sold for immoral purposes, pricing would likely be affected by factors such as skin colour and disability and the wealthy would buy the 'best' babies (see Prichard 1984). Whatever one makes of these various arguments, however, the fact of the matter is that they are distinct from the incommensurability-based argument against market reasoning. When that argument is considered on its own – rather than as one of a collection of general arguments against specific instances of commodification – it seems, for two reasons, to be remarkably weak.

CRITICAL OBSERVATIONS ON INCOMMENSURABILITY. There are two fundamental, interconnected problems with incommensurability-based objections to market reasoning. The first is that such objections are disputable because there exists no criterion which facilitates objective comparisons of value. The second is that such objections seem by themselves to be not especially persuasive when considered against the reasons for favouring commodification. Let us consider each of these problems in turn.

The objectivity problem is exemplified by Radin's argument concerning property and personhood. The viability of her argument depends entirely on what personhood is taken to mean (see Duxbury 1995: 663–74). Her claim is that property rights ought to be deemed inappropriate for commodification or accorded special protection within the market domain (rent control being but one example of such protection) when they are very clearly and importantly bound up with one's personhood. Yet, since people are likely to differ in their intuitions as to where particular property rights lie on the personal-fungible continuum, personhood-based arguments in support of limiting the scope of markets will always be vulnerable to the accusation that they are too idiosyncratic to be used as a basis for determining regulatory strategies.

This problem besets incommensurability-based objections to market reasoning more generally (see Duxbury 1996). Individual beliefs as to what is and is not appropriately commodifiable will differ; and even where there exists substantial consensus concerning how particular goods and activities ought to be treated, that consensus may shift over time. During the early part of the nineteenth century, for example, the notion of life insurance was considered sacrilegious. The sanctity of human life would be undermined, it was believed, if life itself were made the subject of commercial speculation. By the end of the century, however, with increasing industrialization and the flourishing of the market economy, economic valuations of death – and therefore life insurance – became more acceptable. Indeed, with the promotion of life insurance as a form of altruism – as a means, that is, of providing for one's dependants after death – such valuations became ever more desirable (see Zelizer 1979: 150–53). Intuitions about the degrading effects of markets tend to vary from one person, one place and one point in time to another. It is for this reason that incommensurability-based arguments in favour of restricting the scope of markets prove highly contestable.

Since there exists no objective criterion which enables us to compare values among persons, we ought to conclude that individuals should be permitted to value things in whatever ways they like. This does not mean that people should be allowed to do whatever they like. The proposition, rather, is that restrictions on human activity cannot be justified merely because there exists considerable feeling that the activity in question is being inappropriately valued. Of course, restrictions on activities may be imposed for other reasons – for example, because the relevant activity involves coercing or otherwise causing harm to others – but such reasons stand independent from the proposition that an activity ought to be restricted if it entails an inappropriate valuation.

Incommensurability-based arguments against particular instances of commercialization seem rather weak, furthermore, when compared with the reasons that tend to be offered in favour of commercialization. Consider, in this regard, proposals for the commodification of human body materials. The principal argument in support of the market system is simple: reliance on altruism condemns the sick. A donation-based system cannot generate a supply of human tissues and organs which matches demand; consequently, under any such system, those in need are more likely to suffer. A market system would not only alleviate scarcity, but would ensure significant gains for vendors and recipients alike. In the language of welfare economics, markets in human tissues and organs are likely to prove allocatively efficient (see Hansmann 1989). Likewise with adoption. If adoption agencies were permitted to use surplus income generated by their adoption fees to pay women contemplating abortion to have the baby instead and put it up for adoption, this may prove allocatively efficient at various levels: in cases of unwanted pregnancy, women would be provided with an extra option – that is, with an incentive neither to abort nor to raise the baby in burdensome circumstances; furthermore, since the existence of such an incentive should ensure an increase in the number of children available for adoption, the range of choice available to prospective adoptive parents would also be increased (Landes and Posner 1978).

This is not to suggest that permitting markets in human tissues and organs or commercial adoption would prove unproblematic. It is important to try to ascertain, where such markets are proposed, that the benefits of creating such a system will outweigh the costs. The point to be stressed, however, is not that there are powerful arguments on either side of the relevant debates but that – as compared with these various arguments – the incommensurability-based objection to commercialization seems unconvincing. In the debate over whether or not it ought to be permissible to commodify the parent–child relationship, for example, the argument that the relationship is degraded by the presence of the market seems trivial as compared with, say, the argument that commodification ought to be encouraged where it improves allocative efficiency or the argument that markets ought to be stringently regulated where they generate widespread opportunities for exploitation.

In law, as elsewhere, choices impose prices. No doubt there are occasions when the presence of the market can seem somehow inappropriate or undignified. Yet such a price may well be worth paying. For if the argument in favour of commodification is that it is likely to improve or even save lives, the counter-argument that commodification is wrong because it represents an affront to human dignity is unlikely to carry much weight.

There may, of course, be no guarantee that commodification will generate improvements. Indeed, there may exist certain activities which are considered by many people to be somehow degrading, but which also, when commodified, seem to generate few benefits. Imagine a situation in which a circus freak willingly exhibits his disfigurement for a price. The principal argument in favour of commercialized adoption and surrogacy and markets in human tissues and organs is that commodification in these contexts is intended to generate significant benefits beyond the gain in wealth which falls to the seller. By contrast, the benefit to be gained from commodifying the exhibition of disfigurement – employment for the circus freak and the entertainment or thrill that some people might derive from seeing him – might be regarded as somewhat superficial. Considering also that many people are likely to find the very idea of commercialising disfigurement to be degrading and offensive, might one not conclude here that the degradation which accompanies commodification, despite the presence of consent, comes at too high a cost? Is this not, in short, an instance where incommensurability represents a valid argument against market reasoning?

This question ought to be answered in the negative. The first point to note is that, in the case of the circus freak (as with trade in pornography and animal furs), commodification cannot be said to be the cause of degradation. Exhibition of disfigurement is likely to be considered by many people to be degrading and offensive even if it attracts no fee. That, however, is not the reason for the answer offered here. The problem with the claim that certain markets, such as markets in the exhibition of disfigurement, ought not to be permitted because they generate few benefits while encouraging degradation which causes considerable offence is that it is, in essence, arbitrary. Such a claim can be sustained only if it proves possible to demonstrate that a line can be drawn between those purportedly degrading market activities which are sufficiently beneficial and those which are not. The very fact that different people value goods and activities in different ways, however, ensures that any such line-drawing must always be a matter of personal intuition. Possibly there will be a good deal of agreement among people that a market in the exhibition of disfigurement cannot generate the same sorts of benefits as could a market in, say, human organs; but in relation to certain goods and activities – sexual activity, for example – the question of whether or not markets are more beneficial than costly is likely to prove contentious. No one can ever say for sure that, where markets are perceived to cause or to exacerbate the degradation of particular goods or activities, commodification is too costly.

It is on this last proposition that the argument advanced in this essay depends. The argument can only be sustainable so long as it is accepted that perceived degradation, for all that it may constitute a cost, can never be regarded as a sound reason for controlling market activity. If we accept that, in certain circumstances, markets ought to be prohibited because concerns about degradation weigh more heavily than the meagre benefits which commodification brings, we place ourselves in the position of having to decide where the benefits of permitting an activity which is considered to be degrading outweigh the costs of causing offence. The necessarily idiosyncratic nature of such decisions, we have seen, undermines arguments based on incommensurability. If the argument presented here allowed for such decisions, it would be equally untenable.

Neil Duxbury

See also ADOPTION; INALIENABILITY; LEGAL PATERNALISM AND EFFICIENCY; PROPERTY RIGHTS IN PRISONERS OF WAR; RENT CONTROL.

Subject classification: 2b(i); 4c(i).

BIBLIOGRAPHY

Anderson, E. 1993. *Value in Ethics and Economics*. Cambridge, MA: Harvard University Press.

Brennan, T.J. 1988. Rights, market failure and rent control: a comment on Radin. *Philosophy and Public Affairs* 17: 66–79.

Duxbury, N. 1995. Law, markets and valuation. *Brooklyn Law Review* 61: 657–701.

Duxbury, N. 1996. Do markets degrade? *Modern Law Review* 59: 331–48.

Greenberg, D. 1990. Radin on personhood and rent control. *The Monist* 73: 642–59.

Hansmann, H. 1989. The economics and ethics of markets for human organs. *Journal of Health Politics, Policy and Law* 14: 57–85.

Landes, E.M. and Posner, R.A. 1978. The economics of the baby shortage. *Journal of Legal Studies* 7: 323–48.

Prichard, J.R.S. 1984. A market for babies? *University of Toronto Law Journal* 34: 341–57.

Radin, M.J. 1993. *Reinterpreting Property*. Chicago: University of Chicago Press.

Radin, M.J. 1996. *Contested Commodities*. Cambridge, MA: Harvard University Press.

Sunstein, C.R. 1997. *Free Markets and Social Justice*. New York: Oxford University Press.

Trebilcock, M.J. 1993. *The Limits of Freedom of Contract*. Cambridge, MA: Harvard University Press.

Zelizer, V.A. 1979. *Morals and Markets: The Development of Life Insurance in the United States*. New York: Columbia University Press.

marriage as contract. Although far more than a contract from religious, cultural, biological, psychological and philosophical perspectives, marriage is also a contract, the essence of which is transparent in the marriage vows. The man promises that he will be a husband, the woman that she will be a wife, and each promises that they will perform their duties in a spirit of 'loving', 'honouring', and 'cherishing' their spouse. That spirit is a material requirement of the contract, because the value to the recipient of spousal services and their cost, or value, to the provider, is crucially dependent on the attitude with which they are delivered and received. In reliance on these assurances, each spouse invests in this particular marriage, thereby sacrificing current actual, and future potential, love interests, and other life choices.

The complexity, subtlety and exigent quality of the almost infinite set of duties that each party must perform make it inefficient, if not impossible, to specify them with any precision at the time of marriage. The meaning of husband and wife and the specific rights and duties that attach to each role are normally inferred from the subculture and social class in which the parties were raised, and from their prenuptial relationship.

But, some expectations are universal and expressly voiced. All marriages promise a lifetime commitment. Often, however, that promise is broken, and the parties seek to dissolve the agreement, i.e. to divorce. Because marriage is a species of contract, many of the problems inherent in fashioning an efficient and equitable law of divorce, alimony and property division are variations and special cases of the difficulties that surface in the enforcement of commercial contracts.

Before beginning the analysis of marriage as contract two qualifications are necessary. First, while the inherent qualities of men and women, and much of the nature of the conjugal relation, may be universal, cultures and peoples differ. Therefore the ethos, the legal and social constraints, and the specific matrix of costs and benefits that confront men and women likewise differ across societies and eras. Much of the analysis that follows addresses the institution of marriage in 1990s America. It will apply with considerably less force to societies that differ sharply from that time and place.

Second, in the discussion that follows no consideration is given to the effects on third parties that are generated by dissolving a marriage. The principal such externality is experienced by, and through, children. Children usually suffer massively from their parents' divorce, and the rest of society suffer negative externalities directly from the effect on the children's future behaviour and indirectly from the existence of the option of divorce on the institution of marriage. Marriage, divorce, child siring, child bearing and child rearing are all pieces of a jointly endogenous mosaic: for example, the more attractive and secure marriage, the less the demand for out-of-wedlock birth, and vice versa. Despite the significance of these external effects, they have not been systematically integrated into the literature of marriage as contract and for this reason the remainder of this essay will make no further mention of them.

Given the profound restriction on personal freedom demanded by marriage, and the obvious difficulty of predicting the continuation of one's ardour, the popularity of the long-term contract-like commitment of marriage requires an explanation. In most commercial contracts, the gains of contracting are purely instrumental. The only joy generated at the formation of the contract arises from the anticipation of its performance. In marriage, by contrast, there are two significant gains garnered from the mere formation of the contract. First, the entrance into a consecrated state spiritually joining two souls strikes a religious/psychological chord deep in the human soul. Second, the offer of a lifetime commitment indicates a deep and abiding love and is valued as evidence that one is worthy of such love.

That said, it is still the instrumental gains from marriage that are central. First, and most important, marriage allows for investment in assets of peculiar value to this relationship. Neither the man nor the woman would normally desire a long-term contract if no investment by either were to be undertaken that would be of peculiar value only within this relationship. Each would prefer to be free to take advantage of as yet unknown opportunities. If each knows that the other will make an approximately equal and reasonably modest specific investment in this relationship then each, while desiring the protection of a long-term contract, might be willing to proceed with the relationship without such protection, relying on the other's self-interest. If, however, either party expects to make a very large investment or a significantly larger investment than the other, that party would normally insist on a long-term contract to protect the value of their investment.

In the conjugal relationship by far the most significant investment in a specific asset centres on procreation. The existence and presence of children are, in general, valued particularly by their natural parents. And both the cost of, and return from, children span a lifetime. Therefore, when a conjugal relationship between a mother and father terminates each parent will still have significant costs to bear in a situation in which the associational value of the children will be diminished. Thus a fundamental reason to marry is to allow for optimal investment in assets peculiar to the relationship – primarily, but not exclusively, children.

The magnitude of a parent's investment in their children differs systematically between the sexes. Women as a group – perhaps as a result of evolutionary adaptation – have a greater concern for, and desire to raise, their children. Thus it is they who are most anxious to obtain the contractual guarantee of marriage before undertaking the investment of bearing the children of a particular man. Were it not for the prospect of procreation it is doubtful that the lifetime pledge of the traditional marriage would be anything other than an anomalous high-risk adventure entered into by a few foolhardy souls.

Although children are the principal reason for marriage they are not the only reason. The vow to fulfil one's duty 'for richer, for poorer, in sickness and in health' reflects that marriage is also a species of insurance contract. One gives up the opportunity to find a new companion in the event that one's own prospects have improved, in exchange for the other party making a symmetrical sacrifice.

Thus there are substantial reasons to marry. But, over a lifetime, preferences, information and opportunities of both marriage partners change, and frequently one or the other will have an incentive to breach the contract. When a marriage contract is breached and terminates in divorce the wronged party loses a lifetime stream of spousal services.

The market for spouses is monopolistically competitive. All men are potential husbands; all women, potential wives. Although some men are close substitutes for one another, most others are very imperfect substitutes. Nonetheless, there is substantial choice and competition in this market. Therefore, it is reasonable to view the typical husband or wife as having foregone an alternative spouse of nearly equivalent *ex ante* value to the one they actually married. As in commercial contracts then, the loss to the wronged party from breach and divorce is at least the cost of acquiring a new spouse of equivalent *ex ante* value, and if none is available it is the present value of the loss in quasi-rents that were expected under the breached contract.

We begin with transaction costs. The marriage market is highly developed. It offers a rich variety of competing paths to finding a spouse. While a highly developed market usually results in low transaction costs, in the case of marriage this is not so. The highly developed character of this market is itself the result of the high costs and extraordinary difficulty of finding a good match.

Why are the costs so high? Because this is a barter market. Not only must a man find a woman to whom he is willing to offer a lifetime commitment, that woman must be simultaneously willing to make the reciprocal promise to him as well. A careful search is vital for both parties because neither men nor women are fungible.

Even if dating and other such search activities were pure consumption for the divorced, and transaction costs were consequently zero, it is likely that one party, or both, will not be able to do as well the second time around. Why? First, one spouse may have suffered the stochastic change in value that the marriage vows expressly insured against (for example, the great athlete who has been crippled by disease). Second, predictable changes often result from an investment in assets specific to this marriage. Children, being the most significant investment in a specific marital asset, also represent the greatest consequent cost in the search for a replacement spouse. Women, because they generally gain custody of their children, suffer this cost most heavily. Third, and perhaps most importantly, wives and husbands are fundamentally different capital assets. They are not characterized by the same time profile of growth and depreciation, and consequently the costs and difficulties of finding a new spouse are not symmetrical for men and women. Women usually lose value in the marriage market relative to men, solely as a function of age.

Because marriage is a barter market, demonstrating women's loss of value analytically or empirically is extremely difficult. Men and women bear no price tags. The only measure of their value is the 'quality' of spouses they can acquire, who similarly bear no price tags. The prospective bride (or husband) is simultaneously the commodity purchased, the currency used to purchase a husband (or wife), and the purchaser of the husband (or wife). In addition, the lack of transitivity of tastes across purchasers further obscures the issue. We are faced with an intractable identification problem.

Despite these handicaps and qualifications, the statistical evidence that is available is suggestive that, with childbearing and the passage of time, women lose value on the marriage market relative to men. Two facts stand out: (1) divorced men remarry at a faster rate than do divorced women; and (2) for every age group except fourteen to twenty-four, women tend to marry men who are older than themselves and as they age the gap increases. This age gap has a benign explanation with respect to the first marriages of the young. Being a husband or wife requires certain skills and capacities that do not come to fruition at the same age for men and women: the ability of a man to support his wife and children financially takes more time to establish than the domestic skills traditionally required of a wife. But that disparity disappears rather quickly once both parties enter their twenties. Why then does the median excess of husbands' ages over wives' increase as the age of the groom increases?

Both empirical observations are fully consistent with the hypothesis that older men need not restrict their marital search to their own close contemporaries but may instead fish in the likely more attractive pool of younger women. Thus, older women have a yet smaller pool of their own contemporaries who are interested in them. Returning to our identification problem, however, from the data *per se* we cannot determine whether we are seeing men's preference for and success with younger women or women's preference as they age for (1) older men, (2) a more thorough search of the market, or (3) remaining unmarried.

Following divorce, mothers almost always obtain custody of their children. Caring for children imposes two significant costs on women in the marriage market: (1) it makes it more difficult for them to search and advertise; and (2) men usually prefer to marry childless women.

Here too the empirical evidence is consistent with the hypothesis that motherhood hurts women on the marriage market. Divorced women with children remarry at a significantly slower pace than those without children. Naturally, this observation can also be interpreted as evidence of mothers' taste for not remarrying rather than men's taste for childless women.

Although we have no prices for husbands and wives we can generate supply and demand data that support the hypothesis that women lose value on the marriage market with time. While slightly more live births are male than female, a higher mortality rate for males of all ages (even prenatally) creates an ever increasing abundance of women as the cohort ages. But this abundance radically understates the increasing difficulties women confront in finding a spouse as they age. The percentage of men who are married rises steadily as a function of age up to the age of sixty-five. Therefore, the ratio of unmarried women to unmarried men rises faster than the overall sex ratio. In the United States it is less than one for 20-year-olds and over two for 55-year-olds. Further, a subset of the unmarried are the unmarriageable. Because of physical handicaps, mental disabilities, imprisonment etc., they do not offer enough to attract a spouse. As the cohort ages the unmarriageable become an ever increasing proportion of the unmarried. Thus the ratio of unmarried but marriageable women to unmarried but marriageable men rises at a still faster rate.

Aside from differing mortality rates and child custody patterns, women lose value in the marriage market as they age quite simply because men prefer younger women, while women do not seem to have as strong or even a similar age preference with regard to men. Wives and husbands are reciprocal, not symmetrical, roles performed by spouses. Since what a man wants in a wife is different from what a woman wants in a husband, the ability to satisfy these requirements need not, and does not, vary with age at the same rate.

At the time of formation, the marriage contract promises gains to both the parties. Yet the period of time over which these gains are realized is not symmetrical. As a rule, and relatively speaking, men gain early in the relationship, and women late. The creation of this long-term imbalance provides the opportunity for strategic behaviour whereby one of the parties, generally the man, might find it in his interest to breach the contract unless otherwise constrained.

This problem is well understood in long-term commercial contracts as one of appropriable quasi-rents. Much of the law of contract is an effort to design rules and institutions that prevent this kind of strategic behaviour, the control of which is in the *ex ante* interest of both parties.

In commercial contracts the uncompensated breach by one party will usually not affect the *ex post* allocation of resources, but result only in a wealth transfer to the breacher of a large portion of the other's quasi-rents. Reasoning by analogy, and *wrongly* assuming negotiation between spouses to be a low transaction cost encounter, leads to the conclusion that if continuing breach and termination of the marriage were more costly to the wife (the wronged spouse) than its value to the husband (the breaching spouse), the parties would reach a Coasean bargain in which the wife offers the husband compensation intermediate between the value of breaching to him and the value of continuing the marriage to her.

On occasion something that bears a passing resemblance to a Coasean bargain is struck: for example, rather than terminate a marriage, a wife may accept a husband who is periodically unfaithful. On other occasions the wealth effect version of the Coase Theorem (Coase 1988: 170–4) seems to apply: i.e. if the husband must compensate the wife for breaching he will be unwilling to do so, and if she must compensate him for refraining from breaching she will be unwilling to do so. But, even if making post-contractual opportunistic adjustments, or declining to renegotiate the contract to forestall breach and recission, were *ex post* efficient, their anticipation would generate severe *ex ante* inefficiencies. Women who expect that much of the benefit of the bargain of marriage will not be forthcoming will adjust their behaviour *ex ante*. They will: marry less frequently; choose to marry a different sort of man; and invest less in their marriages.

More often than not, however, not even a pale imitation of a Coasean bargain can be reached, and not because breaching is worth more to the husband than it costs the wife. The value in receipt, and cost in provision, of spousal services is crucially dependent on the perceived attitude of the other party. And so breach and its threat do not merely transfer rents, they destroy them. Deterring breach by offering compensation would merely make it all too apparent that the proper marital spirit is absent. The transaction costs of renegotiating the contract are thus prohibitive, since the very act of renegotiation destroys the value of the services performed.

The possibility for substantial breaches of the marriage contract has always existed. Until recent times the religious consciousness of the people who participated in and sanctioned the institution placed substantial internal psychological and external social costs on the parties in the event of breach. Rather than the formal legal constraints that prove to be tenuous and imperfect, it was the informal social and psychological constraints that by and large protected marriages. As those institutions have declined, the inadequacies of the legal structures have come to the fore.

Before considering legal responses to the problems of marital breach let us briefly catalogue the private responses to the problem. In many commercial contexts post-contractual opportunism can be anticipated and averted by vertical integration. This solution is not feasible in the case of marriage. The crux of the problem is not the legal prohibition of a person selling themself to another, rather, it is that the man (or woman) cannot in any meaningful way purchase the person who can be a wife (or husband); he cannot purchase her in such a way that he acquires the same stake in her welfare that she has in herself.

Another contractual device to consider is hostage taking. This requires that the wife or her family hold something of value of the husband's until she is assured of his performance of the contract. An ancient form of hostage taking was the 'bride price' (Posner 1981: 163–8). Unfortunately, for a variety of reasons the bride-price regime is unsuitable for a modern western country. First, arranged marriages are the rare exception, and the parties themselves may be too young and immature to foresee the possibility of future breach. Second, bridegrooms are generally far more well endowed with human capital than with physical or money capital; as they cannot transfer their human capital to their wife, they have very little to offer as a hostage. Third, most couples would prefer to spend all their income in the early years of their marriage; the holding of a substantial amount of property by the wife as a hostage would constrain family consumption. Fourth, the need to guarantee performance is partially symmetric; a wife as well as a husband can breach. Finally, a bride-price regime grounded solely in efficiency concerns unconnected to cultural or religious roots would likely be offensive; the party asked to supply a bride price (or a dowry) might well feel that the relationship had been reduced to commerce.

A child is a more promising hostage than a bride price. Mothers usually receive custody of their children following a divorce. Knowing this, a husband who fears the loss of close contact with his children will refrain from breaching. Children, however, also have their limitations as hostages. They are useless to the childless wife and of only limited value to the wife whose children are adults. Moreover, in order to serve effectively as hostages, the husband must anticipate their absence as a severe deprivation. If he does not, or if his expected visitation rights following a divorce are liberal enough, he may not anticipate much cost. And, while it is in the wife's *ex ante* interest to threaten to deprive her husband of access to his children, it is frequently in her *ex post* interest that he maintain close contact with them.

Another strategy that women can adopt is to marry a man older than they otherwise would. If a man and a woman are of equal value on the marriage market at the age of twenty, and the woman's value, as the capital asset wife, declines fairly steadily, while the man's value, as the capital asset husband, rises initially before declining, then over a large span of their marriage the husband's value will exceed the wife's and he will have an incentive to terminate the marriage. A woman can protect herself from this threat by marrying an older man. She would in effect be sacrificing an investment in the future for current consumption. The greater consumption may, but need not exclusively, be in the form of higher money income. This strategy is a species of constrained maximization – her choice among men not only reflects her desires but includes their expected future opportunities for breach – and thus represents some net social loss.

Finally, there is the pre-emptive solution. If the quasi-rents expected from an investment in marital-specific assets can not be assured, then invest less in the marriage! The tendency of middle-class wives to have fewer children and for women to acquire more marketable skills are both consistent with the hypothesis that women are investing fewer resources in being wives and mothers out of fear of uncompensated breach.

If the informal social mechanisms are insufficient to protect marriage partners, then legal methods of protection increase in importance. The question is, which forms of legal arrangements best prevent the destruction and appropriation of marital rents? The legal tools include both voluntary prenuptial agreements and the standard-form marriage contract that is provided by the state, in large measure through its divorce laws.

The use of prenuptial marriage contracts has increased in recent years. These contracts take a variety of forms. The polar archetypes may be characterized as the traditional, the remarriage, the counter-culture and the feminist.

The traditional prenuptial marriage contract was motivated by a desire to protect assets accumulated prior to a marriage from appropriation by the spouse following a divorce. Most often it is the groom who seeks such a contract when he has accumulated a great deal of wealth or expects a high income. On occasion the family of one of the marriage partners seeks such a contract.

The remarriage contract, a variant of this traditional prenuptial agreement, normally is employed when one or both of the parties seeks to protect the future welfare of the children from a prior marriage. To forestall anxiety and uncertainty, the marriage partners will negotiate and specify how their property will be divided in the event of either divorce or death.

Counter-culture marriage contracts arise out of distaste for traditional marital roles. The panoply of traditional duties that the community implied but did not expressly state in sanctioning marriage is replaced by an express and sometimes detailed statement of alternative duties. The law, having been unwilling to enforce traditional duties, in the sense of requiring specific performance, has also been chary of enforcing the terms of these contracts.

The feminist marriage contract is, at least in part, motivated by the concerns voiced in this entry, namely, that women often do not receive a fair shake in a divorce. So it is one that recognizes that divorce deprives women of quasi-rents that represent a return to sacrificed opportunities. These contracts seek to shift the weight of post-marital rights, duties and property division in favour of the wife. Ironically, it is probably those women who are most likely to be victimized by the divorce laws – those who embrace the role of the traditional wife – who are least likely to negotiate a feminist marriage contract.

These formal prenuptial contracts offer some opportunity to the parties to protect themselves, and, especially with second marriages, they can do quite well in specifying the devolution of property to children after death. Nonetheless, they are of limited use in the ordinary marriage, largely because of the difficulties they face in specifying the appropriate level of damage payments, if any, to be paid in the event of breach. Any such marriage contract must specify a variety of damage amounts, each reflecting the stage in the marriage when the breach occurs, the circumstances of the parties at the time of marriage and the circumstances at the time of breach. Further, they must contend with the question of whether fault should be taken into account, and how it is to be determined.

What of the legislative approaches to the question of divorce? There are four distinct legal structures available:

(1) unilateral divorce with no property settlement; (2) mutual consent divorce with mutually agreed property settlement; (3) indissoluble marriage; and (4) judge-determined divorce and property settlements. These four structures represent the polar forms of which all actual divorce laws are combinations.

Unilateral divorce without property settlement is the marriage analogue to the contract at will; each party is completely free to walk away from the marriage. In commercial contexts the at-will contract tends not to be used when the parties must make differential investments in specific assets, or when either party must make a massive investment, for then the risks of opportunistic behaviour or a simple miscalculation of the other party's interest are simply too great. In marriage, usually both parties, but certainly the wife who bears children, must make a massive investment in specific assets. Unilateral divorce allows one spouse (typically the husband) freely to abandon the marriage after his spouse has made her disproportionate contributions to the relationship. This simple regime of divorce is therefore unsuitable for long-term marriage contracts; it is the problem, rather than the solution, that marriage contracts must overcome.

Mutual-consent divorce is the family-law analogue to the contractual remedy of specific performance: it requires performance of the contract unless a release is granted. At first, this solution appears robust: yielding divorce always, *and only*, when it is efficient. And perhaps it was so once, but much of its vigour has been sapped by modern life. The essential problem is that specific performance is not really available as an enforceable remedy. First, many of the acts that a spouse has implicitly contracted to perform cannot be specified nor their performance monitored. Second, the marital duties are to be performed in a certain spirit, and no court can succeed in forcing an unwilling spouse to perform marital duties in a spirit of love and devotion. Therefore, while the law may not permit the party who wishes to breach the marriage agreement to obtain a divorce without the permission of their spouse, neither can it make them perform the duties of the contract in any meaningful way. And so the parties are free to breach the contract while remaining nominally married.

If this strategy necessarily imposed substantial costs specifically on the breaching party, his incentive to obtain the consent to divorce from his spouse would persist. The reality, however, is that in our era of relaxed sexual mores and community values a married man can live separated from, or with, his wife for an indefinite period without either party being inordinately restricted in their sexual, social and business activities. Nor is there much reason to believe that what costs there are of not obtaining a divorce will bear more heavily on one spouse or the other – breacher or victim, husband or wife. Thus, rather than placing a cost and therefore a constraint on inefficient breachers, a requirement of mutual consent will instead result in fewer breaches terminating in divorce, rather that in fewer inefficient breaches.

While the prospect of breach without divorce suggests that the desire of the breacher to obtain the consent of his spouse to divorce is less than one would at first suppose, the destructibility of quasi-rents suggests that the benefits to the innocent spouse of not consenting to a divorce may be minimal. Marital breach destroys much of the value of the remainder of the contract to the wronged party. And so, when a marriage is breached, often neither party wants it to continue. It is then likely that a property settlement can be worked out that is *ex post* satisfactory. Such an agreement will be far different from what would have been specified *ex ante*.

Much of the expected quasi-rents of the innocent spouse from continuing the marriage will be destroyed regardless of the divorce regime. But the problem will be exacerbated in a mutual-consent regime. The requirement of mutual consent creates an incentive for the breaching party to act more egregiously and thereby destroy more of the rents of his spouse. As the quasi-rents are destroyed, the marriage falls in value to the innocent party, whose consent to a divorce can then be obtained at a lower price.

In light of the short-comings of unilateral and mutual consent standards of divorce, indissoluble marriage appears to have many virtues: it seems to eliminate the possibility of inefficient divorce; it provides powerful incentives for the exercise of greater care in choosing a spouse; the destruction of the value of the marriage to the innocent party generated by the very act of seeking a divorce is eliminated; and it provides no incentive for either party to destroy rents solely for the purpose of obtaining the consent of the other to a divorce.

What are the apparent costs of indissoluble marriage? Some marriages are better terminated. If the law requires the parties to carry out the marriage contract in spite of their desire to dissolve it, efficient dissolutions of marriage will be sacrificed, and some couples at the margin will refrain from marrying because of the unavailability of dissolution.

But both these costs and benefits are largely illusory. The law can prevent divorce, but it is unable to require and enforce performance of the marriage contract in all but a perfunctory sense. Therefore, as in the case of a mutual consent regime so too here, one can breach without obtaining a divorce. And indissoluble marriage provides no effective remedy for the wronged party.

The final legislative alternative is to allow the court to grant divorce at its discretion and determine the property settlement independent of the agreement of the parties. The court would be called on to ascertain the future stream of quasi-rents that the non-breaching party had a right to expect prior to the breach and award them the present value of that future stream. The result would be that only *ex ante* efficient divorces took place, and the demands of both justice and efficiency would be satisfied.

Interestingly, the relationship between this remedy – *if damages are properly measured* – and mutual-consent divorce represents a reversal of the usual liability rule/property rule dichotomy (Calabresi and Melamed 1972). In the typical commercial case a liability rule is a less generous vehicle for vindicating the rights of the wronged party than a property rule. The property rule normally permits the wronged party to take a portion of the gain that the breaching party would reap. But, in the case of marriage, because of the personal nature of the duties and the destructibility of quasi-rents, a property rule (i.e.

mutual-consent divorce) will often leave the wronged party worse off than a liability rule.

There is only one shortcoming to this treatment of divorce: it is much easier to say than to do. In order to implement this regime effectively, courts must determine who breached and the damages to the non-breaching party. The determination of breach is a substantial test but is dwarfed by the difficulties of specifying the loss in quasi-rents occasioned by marital breach. Furthermore, the damages will often be so great that the breacher is effectively judgment-proof.

CONCLUSION. The application of the general theory of long-term contracts to the contract of marriage does not yield any obvious or optimistic conclusions as to the proper way to structure the marriage arrangement. The nature of the underlying duties assumed by the marriage partners is not capable of precise definition, much less effective legal enforcement. Yet the success of the marriage often requires the two partners to invest heavily in the relationship even though they may be able to salvage little of their original investment should the marriage turn bad. To make matters more difficult, the roles of men and women are not symmetrical. It is typically the wife who has more to lose by divorce. What, if anything, can be done to insure the integrity of the long-term marriage arrangement, which redounds *ex ante* to the benefit of both marriage partners? Neither antenuptial marriage contracts nor the various legal regimes of divorce and property settlement offer much hope for the general population. There is much to be said for the older view that relies on informal and social sanctions and the good moral sense of the parties for the greatest protection of the marriage relationship.

LLOYD R. COHEN

See also COMMITMENT; CONTRACT FORMATION AND INTERPRETATION; CONTRACTS; CONTRACTS AND RELATIONSHIPS; DIVORCE; LAW-AND-ECONOMICS FROM A FEMINIST PERSPECTIVE; RELATIONAL CONTRACT; SOCIAL NORMS AND THE LAW.

Subject classification: 5c(iii); 5f.

BIBLIOGRAPHY

Allen, D. 1992. Marriage and divorce: comment. *American Economic Review* 82(3): 679–93.

Becker, G.S. 1981. *A Treatise on the Family*. Cambridge, MA: Harvard University Press.

Becker, G.S. 1985. Human capital, effort, and the sexual division of labor. *Journal of Labor Economics* 3(1), Part II: S33–58.

Becker, G.S., Landes, E.M. and Michael, R.T. 1977. An economic analysis of marital instability. *Journal of Political Economy* 85 (6): 1141–87.

Becker, G.S. and Murphy, K. 1988. The family and the State. *Journal of Law and Economics* 31(1): 1–18.

Brown, B. et al. 1977. *Women's Rights and the Law*. New York: Praeger.

Calabresi, G. and Melamed, D.A. 1972. Property rules, liability rules, and inalienability: one view of the cathedral. *Harvard Law Review* 85 (6): 1089–1128.

Carbone, J. and Brinig, M. 1991. Rethinking marriage: feminist ideology, economic change, and divorce reform. *Tulane Law Review* 65 (5): 953–1010.

Coase, R.H. 1988. *The Firm, The Market, and The Law*. Chicago: University of Chicago Press.

Cohen L. 1987. Marriage, divorce, and quasi rents or 'I gave him the best years of my life'. *Journal of Legal Studies* 16 (2): 267–303.

Cohen, L. 1995. Rhetoric, the unnatural family, and women's work. *Virginia Law Review* 81 (8): 2275–2303.

Ellman, I.M. 1989. The theory of alimony. *California Law Review* 77 (1): 1–81.

Epstein, R. 1984. In defense of the contract at will. *University of Chicago Law Review* 51 (4): 947–82.

Glendon, M.A. 1977. *State, Law and Family: Family Law in Transition in the United States and Western Europe*. New York: North Holland.

Klein, B., Crawford, R. and Alchian, A. 1978. Vertical integration, appropriable rents, and the competitive contracting processing. *Journal of Law and Economics* 21 (2): 297–326.

Koo, H. and Suchindran, C.M. 1978. Relationships among fertility, marital dissolution and remarriage. Final report, National Institute of Child Health and Human Development, Research Triangle Institute.

Lichtenstein, N. 1985. Marital misconduct and the allocation of financial resources at divorce: a farewell to fault. *University of Missouri at Kansas City Law Review* 54 (1): 1–18.

Mott, F. and Moore, S. 1983. The tempo of remarriage among young women. *Journal of Marriage and Family* 45 (5): 427–36.

Neely, R. 1979. Marriage contracts, for better or for worse marital and non-marital contracts. *Section of Family Law ABA* 6.

Parkman, A. 1992. *No-Fault Divorce: What Went Wrong*? Boulder, CO: Westview Press.

Parkman, A. 1996. Reform of the divorce provisions of the marriage contract. *Brigham Young University Journal of Public Law* 8 (1): 91–106.

Peters, E. 1983. The impact of state divorce laws on the marital contract. Discussion Paper No. 83–19 *Economic Research Center/Norc*.

Peters, E. 1986. Marriage and divorce: informational constraints and private contracting. *American Economic Review* 76 (3): 437–54.

Pollak, R. 1985. A transactions cost approach to families and households. *Journal of Economics Literature* 23(2): 581–608.

Posner, R.A. 1981. *The Economics of Justice*. Cambridge, MA: Harvard University Press.

Stake, J. 1992. Mandatory planning for divorce. *Vanderbilt Law Review* 45 (2): 397–454.

Trost, J. 1975. Married and unmarried cohabitation: the case of Sweden and some comparisons. *Journal of Marriage and the Family* 37 (3): 677–82.

US Bureau of Census, Current Population Reports 5, table E (Ser. P-20, No. 380, Marital Status and Family Status: March 1982).

US National Center for Health Statistics, Vital Statistics of the United States, Vol. 3, Marriage and Divorce, annual reports.

US National Center for Health Statistics, Monthly Vital Statistics Reports, Suppl., Advance Report. Final Divorce Statistics: 1976, tables 2, 4 and 5 (Vol. 27, No. 5).

Wallerstein, J. and Kelly, J. 1980. *Surviving The Breakup*. New York: Basic Books.

Weiss, Y. and Willis, R. 1985. Children as collective goods and divorce settlements. *Journal of Labor Economics* 3 (3): 268–92.

Weitzman, L. 1981. *The Marriage Contract*. New York: Free Press.

Weitzman, L. 1985. *The Divorce Revolution*. New York: Free Press.

Williamson, O. 1980. Mitigating contractual hazards using hostages to support exchange. Discussion Paper No. 126, Center for the Study of Organizational Innovation, University of Pennsylvania, April 1980.

Zelder, M. 1993. Inefficient dissolutions as a consequence of public goods: the case of no-fault divorce. *Journal of Legal Studies* 22 (2): 503–20.

medical malpractice. The traditional common law of medical malpractice holds health-care providers liable for medically caused (iatrogenic) injuries that are caused by negligence. Adverse outcomes that are consistent with the normal risks of customary medical care are the burden of the patient and first party insurance. The rationale for liability of medical providers, as for other professionals, is asymmetric information between consumers and producers. In competitive markets, if consumers misperceive risks, a rule of *caveat emptor* leads to nonoptimal levels of risky activities and nonoptimal care per unit of activity (Spence 1977; Shavell 1980). In the medical context, if patients misperceive the risks and benefits of alternative treatments and cannot readily monitor the quality of care delivered, then there may be too little care per procedure and too many risky procedures. In theory, a negligence rule of liability for failure to take due care can correct this distortion and create incentives for optimal care per treatment. The optimal level of risky treatments can be achieved by extending the definition of negligence to include liability for performing 'unnecessary' procedures.

Liability is only one of several mechanisms that may correct the distortions that result from asymmetric information in medical markets. Altruism, professional or ethical concerns may motivate physicians to act as better agents for patients than would be predicted from models that assume purely self-interested income maximization (Danzon 1994c). In most countries, other regulatory and institutional mechanisms, including professional licensure, peer review and hospital credentialling committees, provide coarse screens to identify and eliminate persistent incompetence or misconduct by medical providers. More recently, third-party payers in the US are demanding evidence of quality of care. Nevertheless, tort liability may in theory still enhance incentives for care on a case-by-case basis. Liability also serves as a source of compensation for victims of iatrogenic injury.

Under a perfectly functioning negligence rule there would be no negligence and no claims, since by definition it is cheaper to prevent injuries that would be deemed negligent than to pay for the resulting damages (Shavell 1982). In practice, much of the scholarly and policy literature on medical malpractice is concerned with the allegedly excessive costs, distortions and inequities of the traditional malpractice system and with evaluation of proposals for reform. In the 1970s, many states in the US modified traditional liability rules for medical malpractice, while Sweden and New Zealand replaced tort liability with quasi no-fault systems of compensation for medical injuries. In the 1980s and 1990s, proposals for no-fault and other radical alternatives have been discussed in several countries, including the US, the UK and Canada.

This essay reviews issues that distinguish medical malpractice from other areas of tort liability, including evidence on the operation of current malpractice systems and proposals for reform. Most of the empirical evidence relates to the US, where dissatisfaction with the status quo has led to more numerous and more extensive studies of iatrogenic injury rates, claims and claims disposition, in an attempt to distinguish fact from allegation. Experience in other countries is reported where available.

I. THE MALPRACTICE SYSTEM IN OPERATION

1. *Imperfect information.* The discrepancies between the negligence system in theory and its operation in practice arise primarily because the decision-makers – courts, doctors, patients, liability insurers – lack the information that is assumed by the models (Danzon 1991). Asymmetric information leads to systematic bias in standards of care, which undermines the potential efficiency gains from the liability system. The unpredictability of legal standards of care creates incentives for physicians to practice defensive medicine – excessive care designed to reduce the probability of suit – and incentives for plaintiffs and defence to invest heavily in litigation. These three factors – biased and unpredictable standards of care, defensive medicine and high costs of litigation – undermine the potential efficiency gains from the liability system.

Because of the technical complexity of medical care, courts defer to customary practice of the medical profession to define the standard of care. Only very rarely have courts attempted to define the appropriate standard of care by comparing the costs and expected benefits of additional precautions, as prescribed by the Learned Hand rule and as required to achieve efficient investments in injury prevention. By definition, a custom standard of care cannot correct any systematic deviations of customary care from optimal care that may result from imperfect information on the part of consumers and other market participants. Thus malpractice liability, using a custom standard of care, may at best prevent significant deviations from the norms that consumers have come to expect. But by deferring to custom, the courts forego any attempt to correct any systematic bias in customary care that results from risk misperceptions and asymmetric information in the market.

The prevalence of private and social insurance for medical care creates further systematic bias in customary care. The extent and nature of the biases depend on the structure of insurance contracts, in particular, systems of patient co-payments and provider reimbursement and the resulting financial incentives. In insurance systems where providers are paid fee-for-service and patients face low co-payments, patient moral hazard leads to overuse of costly procedures, relative to a first best optimum. Since provider moral hazard may lead to excessive fee levels, payers attempt to control costs by regulating fees per visit or per procedure. Strict fee regulation creates incentives for physicians to reduce real resources per unit of care, leading to increased frequency of very short visits, particularly in Germany and Japan. Thus fee-for-service reimbursement leads to a high volume of procedures and reimbursable visits; however, low fees per encounter create a risk of low care per encounter.

Capitation forms of payment are increasingly being adopted in managed care in the US and in other countries, particularly for primary care physicians, to correct these tendencies for overuse under fee-for-service reimbursement. Since the capitated physician faces a positive marginal cost but receives zero marginal revenue per unit of additional service or effort, capitation creates incentives for suboptimal quantity and quality of care. Thus with heavily insured patients and imperfectly informed patients and insurers, the safe conclusion is that customary care is likely to deviate systematically from optimal care, both in quantity and quality. The direction and extent of bias depends on the level and form of provider reimbursement, the money and time costs of patients and on the extent to which third party payers control or monitor outcomes. More on this below.

In addition to systematic bias in custom-based standards of care, imperfect information on the part of courts leads to unpredictable legal rulings, which creates uncertainty for providers. With a custom standard, some variability is inevitable because of significant differences in medical opinion and variations in medical practice patterns across areas within any country. Craswell and Calfee (1986) have shown that with uncertain legal standards, a negligence rule is likely to create nonoptimal deterrence incentives. With uncertainty, doctors cannot be sure that they will avoid liability simply by taking the required level of care. Unpredictability creates incentives for 'defensive medicine', that is, excessive levels of care and practice patterns designed to reduce the probability of successful suit, with little if any effect on the probability of injury. Moreover, the more variable are practice norms and legal rulings, the greater the incentive for plaintiff and defence to invest in legal expense in an attempt to influence the outcome in their favour. Uncertain legal standards also contribute to errors by patients in filing claims. The evidence from several studies in the US indicates that many valid claims are not filed and many invalid claims are filed (Danzon 1985; Weiler et al. 1993).

Unpredictability of claims and legal standards leads physicians to demand comprehensive liability insurance, including legal defence insurance. Liability insurance would not interfere with deterrence if it were perfectly experience-rated, with premiums adjusted to reflect the actuarial risk implied by the physician's actual level of care. The rating of malpractice liability insurance, however, is based primarily on broad correlates of claims experience, such as location and medical specialty. Within these broad rating categories, individual experience-rated adjustments are infrequent and rarely based simply on the number of claims filed or paid. Ellis, Gallup and McGuire (1990) have shown that experience-rating based on a simple count of claims filed or paid would expose providers to significant risk of inappropriate surcharges, because of the large number of false positive claims.

The lack of experience-rating of liability insurance does not necessarily imply that deterrence incentives are nonexistent or even suboptimal, as some have argued. Physicians with consistently bad claims experience, adjusted for specialty, are likely to face a surcharge on their premium, restrictions on their scope of covered practice (for example, no surgery) or be denied coverage. Moreover, the threat of significant out-of-pocket costs, time and embarrassment of being sued probably serves as a potent deterrent to most physicians. However, an important implication of pervasive liability insurance that has at best rough experience-rating is that deterrence probably derives more from the frequency of claims than the size of awards. This has important implications for reforms that propose limits on the size of awards.

2. *Evidence on rates of injury, claims and insurance costs.* The best empirical evidence on the incidence of iatrogenic injuries comes from two broad-based surveys of medical records of hospitalized patients, the first in California (Mills et al. 1977) and the second in New York in 1984 (Weiler et al. 1993, hereafter Harvard study). In both studies, a stratified random sample of hospital records was reviewed by experts in legal medicine, to determine the incidence of any injury due to medical care and the incidence of injury due to negligence. The California study concluded that 4.6 percent of hospitalized patients suffered an injury due to medical care; of these, 17 percent (or one in 126 patients) involved negligent injury. The results from the New York data were similar: 4.2 percent of patients suffered an injury due to medical care and of these, 28 percent (roughly one percent of all patients) involved negligence.

This apparently high rate of iatrogenic injury in part reflects the broad definition of injury used in both studies. The Harvard study defined an iatrogenic injury as 'any disability caused by medical management that prolonged the hospital stay by at least one day or persisted beyond the patient's release from hospital'. Thus the count of injuries reflects the standard of care implicitly assumed by study reviewers, their expectation of an appropriate length of stay and reasonable medical outcomes. The California study explicitly defined negligence in terms of the standards likely to be applied by a jury. Since neither study attempted to define negligence by weighing marginal costs and benefits of additional precautions, the resulting count of 'injuries' does not necessarily correspond to adverse outcomes that, on efficiency grounds, should be prevented.

Given the broad definition of injury, it is not surprising that the majority of the injuries were minor. Nevertheless, in the Harvard study 14 percent of injuries were fatal and over half of these were deemed attributable to negligence. This may be a downward biased estimate of the total number of negligent injuries because injuries in ambulatory settings were excluded, unless they resulted in a hospitalization, and because of underreporting in hospital records. While these studies are confined to US data, it seems unlikely that injury rates are significantly lower in other countries. Incentives for injury avoidance are probably higher in the US, because the higher frequency and cost of malpractice claims creates both direct deterrence incentives and has led hospitals to implement more extensive quality assurance and risk management protocols than exist in most other countries.

The difference among providers in claim rates may be consistent with some bad apples but also suggest significant error in filings. In the Harvard study, adverse event rates varied tenfold between individual hospitals, after controlling for patient age and diagnosis. Similarly, analysis of claims experience of individual physicians indicates that, after controlling for medical specialty, the distribution of claims is more concentrated than would be expected based on chance alone (Rolph 1981; Ellis, Gallup and McGuire 1990). These findings are consistent with the hypothesis that malpractice claims are disproportionately due to a minority of providers who are of below-average competence. However, since these simple claim counts do not adequately control for case-mix and volume of work, it is also possible that some providers have worse claims experience in part because they treat a more complex case mix or higher volume. Consistent with this interpretation, Sloan et al. (1989) find that board certified physicians and physicians who work longer hours have more claims. Surgical specialties have claim frequency rates several fold higher than non-surgical specialties. Assuming that surgeons are not consistently more careless than non-surgical specialists, a plausible explanation of these specialty differences is that the consequences of surgical errors or simple bad luck are more likely to be severe and obvious, hence lead to larger potential awards and greater incentives to file claims than for non-surgical specialties.

Both the California and the Harvard data indicate that the number of claims filed was less than one-tenth of the number of negligently caused injuries as defined by the study. Moreover, there appear to be both false negatives – failure to file valid claims – and false positives – claims filed in the absence of a negligent injury. The ratio of claims to negligent injuries was much higher for serious injuries: roughly one claim is filed for every three such injuries and one in six is paid (Weiler et al. 1993). Based on these and other data, White (1994) calculates that the probability of a claim is .026 per negligent injury, .01 per non-negligent injury and .001 per noninjury. This much higher probability of suit for negligent treatment than for non-negligent treatment should provide a significant deterrent effect, despite the high overall error rate in claiming.

Although the Harvard study concluded that many of the claims filed lacked evidence of a medically caused injury, this could reflect the limited information available to the reviewers and the very small number of claims. In a study of claims data with more complete information on injury causation as evaluated by independent reviewers, Farber and White (1991) concluded that negligence was present in 35 percent of claims, not present in 42 percent, with the remainder uncertain. For claims with negligence, the probability of receiving compensation was .66 and the mean payment was $205,000; for claims without negligence, the probability of payment was only .16 and the average payment was $41,800. Similar results are reported in two other studies of claims data.

These findings suggest that negligent care is more likely to result in a claim being filed, compensation being paid and a higher mean amount than when care is non-negligent. Thus extreme criticisms of the tort system as a random lottery are exaggerated. Moreover, the apparent mismatch between claim rates and negligent injury rates overall does not necessarily imply that deterrence incentives and compensation are too low or that the goal of reforms should be to stimulate more claims. Given the existence of professional norms and other forms of regulatory and market-driven quality assurance mechanisms, the optimal degree of sanction through the tort system is certainly less than in the absence of these alternative sanctions. Thus compensating small claims through the tort system may not be cost-effective, given the availability of other forms of social and private insurance that provide adequate compensation for minor injuries at lower overhead cost.

3. *Trends in malpractice claim frequency.* Although medical malpractice liability has existed for centuries, such actions were rare until the late 1960s. In the US from the early 1970s to the mid-1980s malpractice claim frequency (number of claims per 100 physicians) increased at more than 10 percent a year. Claim severity (the average payment per claim paid) increased at roughly twice the rate of general inflation. The number of claims filed per 100 physicians per year reached a peak of about 16 in 1986, and has since stabilized at roughly 13. The unexpected surge in claim costs precipitated 'crises' in liability insurance markets in the mid-1970s and mid-1980s, which in turn led many states to adopt tort reforms designed to reduce claim costs.

Several studies have attempted to understand the factors that have contributed to these trends in claims and to the persistent differences across states. The acceleration of claims in the 1960s can be attributed partly to changes in medical care, and in particular to the increased frequency of invasive surgery. Pro-plaintiff shifts in legal doctrine also contributed. For example, the abolition of the locality rule substituted a national standard for a local standard, which increased the number of actionable events and made it easier for plaintiffs to obtain expert testimony against the alleged 'conspiracy of silence' fostered by the locality rule; the abolition of charitable and government immunity exposed not-for-profit hospitals to suit; the doctrine of *respondeat superior* extended the liability of hospitals for actions of their employees; and informed consent was defined as requiring information that a reasonable patient would want, rather than what was customary for physicians to provide. These changes in traditional rules, that expand the grounds for malpractice claims or reduce plaintiff costs, have no doubt contributed to the higher rate of claims in the US than in other countries (see below). But these factors had run their course by the mid-1970s and cannot explain the continued growth in claims in the 1980s, which paralleled similar growth in product liability claims in the US.

The slowing of claim growth since the late 1980s also remains largely unexplained. Some of the tort reforms enacted in the 1970s and early 1980s had their intended effects. In particular, caps on awards and collateral source offset reduced the growth of awards and settlements; shorter statutes of limitations and collateral source offset slowed claim frequency (Danzon 1984a, 1986; Zuckerman et al. 1990). Others changes appear to have had no effect or negligible effect.

This acceleration of malpractice claims was not confined to the US. During the 1980s the rate of increase in the number of claims and size of payments was at least as rapid in the UK and Canada as in the US (Danzon 1990). But in 1987 physicians in the US were still five to six times more likely to be sued than physicians in Canada and the UK. The average award was somewhat higher in the US than in Canada. However, for several reasons the available data do not permit a cross-country comparison of net compensation for comparable injuries. Medical costs are deducted from the tort award and shifted to public health care systems in the UK and Canada. The attorney's contingent fee (typically one-third) is subtracted from the award to the plaintiff in the US, whereas the UK and most Canadian provinces apply the English rule, that the loser pays costs. Moreover, the mean observed award depends on the actual mix of cases, which may differ across countries. In particular, to the extent that the higher frequency of claims in the US includes disproportionately more minor injuries or cases of dubious merit which settle for a relatively low expected value, the mean observed payment in the US provides a downward biased estimate for the expected compensation for the case mix in Canada or the UK, where the absence of contingent fees is likely to deter more cases with low stakes or low probability of winning.

The UK and Canada experienced very sharp increases in malpractice premiums in the 1980s, which precipitated a perception of crisis parallel to the liability crisis in the US. The increase in malpractice premiums in the UK and Canada reflected not only the rising cost of claims but also an attempt to move from pay-as-you-go to partial funding of incurred liabilities and an attempt to differentiate rates for surgeons. The squeeze of sharply rising premiums but constrained reimbursement under public health systems generated intense pressure for reforms. In the UK, the National Health Service agreed to indemnify doctors for the costs of malpractice insurance. While this solved the income squeeze on physicians, it may undermine the deterrent function of liability, reducing it to a costly and inequitable social compensation scheme.

There is no evidence from other countries on the number of injuries and hence the relationship between claims and injuries. However, if the rate of injury is at least as high as in the US, then since the rate of claims is much lower in other countries, the shortfall between injuries and claims is likely to be even larger in other countries than it is in the US.

II. MEDICAL LIABILITY AS A COMPENSATION SYSTEM

The standard of compensation in malpractice claims, as in other tort claims, is to make the plaintiff whole, including both monetary and non-monetary damages. During the 1970s and 1980s, the average award for medical malpractice claims increased more rapidly than general inflation in the US, the UK and Canada, implying an increase in real compensation to malpractice claimants. An increase in payment levels could be appropriate, if prior levels were too low. For monetary loss, the available data from insurance claim files are unfortunately not sufficiently accurate to evaluate whether current payments are excessive or inadequate on average. In addition to missing and misreported data, assessment of the adequacy of compensation begs the fundamental question of defining compensable expense. While certain elements of wage loss and essential medical care may be clear cut, many medical and quasi-medical services – for example, home help, private duty nursing – enhance the quality of life but are not essential to sustain life. Thus even the definition of monetary loss is discretionary and hence may be subject to moral hazard and influence through litigation.

A valid concern is that awards for pain, suffering and other nonmonetary loss may exceed optimal levels of compensation for irreplaceable loss, at least in the US. Optimal compensation for such losses depends on the effect of injury on the marginal utility of income, which may differ with the type of injury, the preferences of the patient and the extent of compensation for monetary loss (Cook and Graham 1977). For example, a partially disabling injury may reduce the range of consumption activities that can be enjoyed but increase the utility derived from such services as attendant care and home help. If these quasi-medical services are paid for as a component of monetary loss, then the marginal utility from additional discretionary spending in the post-injury health state may be lower than in the pre-injury health state; however, if compensation for monetary loss does not cover these quasi-medical services, then the marginal utility of income could be higher in the post-injury state than in the pre-injury state.

Although theory does not permit broad generalization, the evidence suggests that payments for pain and suffering exceed optimal levels of compensation in the US (Danzon 1984b). Suggestive evidence on this point is that no other form of private or social insurance provides compensation for pain and suffering. Although this 'gap' in other insurance coverages may be a second best optimum, constrained by the unobservability of such losses and hence the exposure to moral hazard and claim exaggeration, similar potential for excessive claiming applies in the tort systems. Thus very large awards for pain and suffering are probably not consistent with optimal insurance. As argued earlier, deterrence effects of the tort system appear to derive less from the size of awards than from the frequency of claims, both because time costs are more closely related to frequency than size and because the crude forms of experience rating used by liability insurers are based primarily on frequency, because severity is considered highly random. These considerations have led several commentators to advocate replacing the current open-ended system of payments for noneconomic loss with a schedule of limits that vary with the severity of the injury (Danzon 1984b; Weiler 1991).

Tort awards are often criticized for providing unequal compensation for seemingly similar injuries. Although equal compensation for similar injuries might be appropriate if compensation were the sole goal of liability, deterrence may require unequal payment for similar injuries depending on the cause of the injury. A simple negligence rule requires that an injury be compensated if and only if it was caused by negligence. Theory and empirical evidence suggest that out-of-court settlements in practice adjust payments for the degree of negligence, even where comparative fault is not formally the rule. This is potentially consistent with efficient deterrence – and with some definitions of fairness. Several empirical studies confirm that the disposition of claims, including court awards and out-of-court settlements, provides higher payments in cases involving negligence and higher awards for cases involving severe injury (Danzon and Lillard 1983; Farber and White 1991). Nevertheless, significant unpredictability of awards remains, conditional on the degree of negligence; this undermines deterrence, creates incentives for defensive medicine and litigation, and contributes to volatility in liability insurance markets.

III. COSTS OF OPERATING THE MALPRACTICE SYSTEM

The medical malpractice system entails high overhead costs of litigation, administration and defensive medicine. These costs are the focus of many criticisms of the status quo. They must be offset against any deterrence benefits of the liability system to obtain an overall evaluation of its net benefit, positive or negative.

Overhead costs. Compared with either public or private first-party insurance, tort liability is grossly inefficient as a system of compensation and insurance since it involves high overhead costs, uncertainty and delays in payment. Roughly 40 cents of the malpractice insurance premium dollar reach the patient as compensation, compared to over 90 cents for large first-party private or public health insurance programmes. An additional 40 cents of the liability insurance dollar is spent on litigation, roughly equally divided between plaintiff and defence attorneys. Other real but hidden costs of tort liability litigation include the time and anxiety costs borne by the litigants and delay in claim disposition.

Defensive medicine. Defensive medicine should be defined as changes in medical practice that occur because of the threat of liability and that would not be desired by well-informed patients, given their insurance coverage. This definition distinguishes defensive medicine from efficient deterrence, defined as changes in practice that are cost-justified (positive expected net benefits) and hence that would be desired by well-informed patients. Defensive medicine should also be distinguished from care that is not cost-justified but that results from moral hazard under first party health insurance contracts. As discussed earlier, insurance with low co-payment and fee-for-service provider reimbursement creates incentives for overuse of services, regardless of the liability rule. Such insurance-induced overuse of care should not be included in measures of defensive medicine.

Incentives for defensive medicine arise because courts lack good information about the optimal standard of care. With imperfectly informed decision-makers, physicians may anticipate that they can reduce their expected liability – either probability of being held liable or award if liable – by taking additional, highly visible precautions, such as ordering unnecessary tests, beyond the level that is cost-justified or desired by patients given their insurance coverage. Note, however, that if patients are fully insured, they would want any test or procedure that offers any positive expected benefit. A physician who is a good agent would comply and, if reimbursement is fee-for-service, such compliance also serves the physician's own financial interest. Thus much of the excess care that is commonly called defensive medicine in the US would probably exist even in the absence of liability. Consistent with this, casual evidence suggests that concern over so-called defensive medicine has declined with the growth of managed care, which reduces the physician's financial gain from over-provision of care.

Several studies have attempted to estimate the extent of defensive medicine. Some are widely cited, but none is convincing, because of failure to distinguish excess care induced by liability as opposed to insurance. However, given the uncertainty with respect to the due care standard, theory suggests that defensive medicine may add substantially to the overhead costs of the malpractice system, even though convincing empirical evidence to support this prediction remains elusive.

Given the high administrative costs of operating the liability system and – plausibly – significant additional costs from defensive medicine, it is clear that if the sole function of liability is to provide compensation, this can be done more efficiently through other private and social insurance mechanisms. The high overhead costs of the tort system are only worth incurring if it also serves to deter negligence. In other words, the costs of investigation and determination of causation and responsibility for injuries are worth incurring *only* if there are offsetting benefits in deterrence of future injuries.

IV. EVIDENCE ON DETERRENCE

Measuring the deterrence benefits, if any, of the malpractice system has also proved elusive. Since rates of iatrogenic injury are not readily observable, any change in injury rates due to the deterrence effect of liability is also not readily observable. The only credible estimates are based on the New York data on medical injuries, as analysed in Weiler et al. (1993). These estimates exploit the variation in claim rates between different localities in New York state. The tentative conclusion of this analysis is that injury rates would be significantly higher, were it not for the threat of liability, and that the deterrence benefits of the malpractice system may well outweigh its costs, even ignoring such intangible benefits as retribution or fairness. This empirical evidence on deterrence benefits is consistent with rough calculations by Danzon (1985), that under reasonably conservative assumptions about the magnitude of deterrence, the malpractice system pays for itself. This perhaps surprising conclusion is possible, despite the high overhead rate on malpractice claims, because of the low ratio of claims to injuries. Because the high administrative loading is incurred on only a small percentage of injuries, a fairly small percentage reduction in injury rates is sufficient to offset reasonable estimates of overhead and defensive medicine costs. Even if the benefits of the current system do outweigh its costs, however, the high deadweight costs make the search for more cost-effective alternatives an important policy question.

V. TORT REFORMS

Most of the problems with traditional malpractice liability – imperfect deterrence, mismatch between claims and injuries, unpredictability of liability findings and awards, defensive medicine, uncertain compensation and high litigation costs – are at bottom attributable to imperfect information on the part of courts, plaintiffs, insurers and providers. With perfect information, courts could costlessly make accurate findings of negligence, liability insurance premiums could be perfectly experience-rated, hence providers would face incentives to take due care but not excessive care, with no incentive to practice defensive medicine. The rationale for a negligence rule of liability derives from imperfect information on the part of consumers. However, simply changing the liability rule does not, by itself, improve information. Similarly, several of the proposed reforms of the traditional tort system do little to improve information. In general, any reforms should be designed to reduce opportunities for exploitation of asymmetric information and to make better use of the information that is available. The practical choice is between imperfect alternatives.

In evaluating proposed reforms, this discussion assumes that the objective is to minimize the total cost of injuries, including the utility costs of injuries (after optimal compensation), prevention, litigation and other overhead. Providing optimal compensation to victims is implied by this criterion, as a necessary condition for minimizing the utility cost of injuries. Reducing the cost of liability insurance premiums, which has been the goal of most actual reform proposals, may simply shift costs with no net efficiency gain.

1. *Limits on awards for non-monetary loss.* A schedule of limited awards for non-economic loss has been proposed by several authors. Plausibly, it would be consistent with optimal insurance and would reduce litigation with minimal if any loss in deterrence. Sweden and some other European countries use such schedules. A schedule based on the severity of injury and the plaintiff's life expectancy provides more appropriate compensation and is more equitable than a single cap for all cases, as proposed in most reform proposals in the US. A single cap is likely to be unfair and suboptimal for young, severely injured plaintiffs. Scheduled payments or guidelines may also be useful for components of economic loss that are currently subject to much discretion, such as private nursing and education costs.

Scheduled awards are likely to reduce litigation expenditures by reducing the parties' expected payoff from investments to influence the outcome. Limits on non-economic damages are unlikely to undermine deterrence, because the very large losses are typically covered by insurance and are not used for rating individual (as opposed to class) premiums, since they are viewed as random bad luck, beyond the control of the insured.

Empirical evidence from states that have set limits on awards shows that such caps do significantly reduce liability claim costs. Although only a small minority of claims are affected at current limits – for example, $250,000 for non-economic damages – these few very large awards account for a significant fraction of total expense. In one study, five percent of claims accounted for roughly fifty percent of the total dollars paid (Danzon and Lillard 1983). Thus a reduction in these few very large payments can significantly affect total claim costs and hence lower malpractice insurance premiums. Plaintiffs' attorneys have strongly opposed award limits. Since the attorney's contingent fee is typically a percentage of the award, any reduction in the gross award reduces the attorney's fee by the same percentage. The attorney's net revenue, after subtracting costs, is reduced by an even larger percentage, assuming that there are significant fixed costs in filing a claim.

2. *Periodic payments.* Periodic payment of compensation for future damages enables the defendant to provide the patient's compensation through the purchase of an annuity or a similar financial instrument. This minimizes the cost to the defendant of providing the target level of compensation intended for the plaintiff. Note, however, that to preserve incentives for rehabilitation, the amounts of such future payments should be fixed at the time of claim disposition. Evidence from workers' compensation insurance confirms that periodic payments that are contingent on the actual reported loss tend to increase the duration and size of claims (Ruser 1985).

3. *Collateral source offset.* Collateral source offset reduces the tort award to the plaintiff by the amount of compensation available from specified private first party or public insurance. This occurs automatically in countries such as Sweden, the UK and Canada, where medical costs that are covered under national health systems are not compensable in tort. The rationale is to prevent double compensation to the plaintiff.

However, the goal of preventing double compensation to the plaintiff can be achieved either by collateral source offset or by subrogation. Subrogation preserves full internalization of costs to the tort feasor and hence preserves stronger incentives for deterrence than collateral source offset, which shifts costs from the tort feasor to other social insurance programmes and ultimately to taxpayers. This reduction in the potential tort award that results from collateral source offset could significantly reduce plaintiffs' incentives to bring claims and hence undermine deterrence. The empirical evidence tends to support this concern. Collateral source offset rules have not only reduced claim severity but also claim frequency, consistent with the predicted feedback effect from lower awards to fewer claims. Nevertheless, because subrogation may entail higher transactions costs than collateral source offset, the optimal mechanism for eliminating double compensation is an empirical question.

4. *Limits on contingent fees.* Several states have imposed limits on the attorney's contingent fee percentage, typically a sliding scale that decreases with the size of the award. The rationale for this approach is weak. Contingent fees provide a potentially efficient risk-sharing arrangement for bearing the costs of investment in litigation with uncertain payoff. An attorney with a portfolio of cases is a more efficient bearer of this risk than an individual plaintiff, for whom the legal expense may be a significant fraction of wealth. If the goal is to reduce large awards, this is better achieved directly by imposing scheduled limits. If the goal is to reduce litigation expense and payments to attorneys, this is better achieved directly by reducing uncertainty and the ability of litigants to influence the outcome, which would reduce the incentives to invest in litigation.

If the goal is to reduce frivolous litigation, the English rule for shifting costs to the losing party is a promising approach. However, in order to protect risk-averse plaintiffs and make the system even-handed in application, defence costs should be applied against the plaintiff's attorney, if paid on a contingent basis, rather than against the individual plaintiff. Such a rule would expose plaintiff attorneys to greater uncompensated expense in the event that they take a case and lose. This would make them more reluctant to bring cases that lack clear evidence of negligence, while making them more willing to take cases with strong evidence of negligence but small monetary value.

5. *Alternative dispute resolution (ADR).* Several states have adopted forms of alternative dispute resolution (ADR) that are intended to expedite claim disposition, eliminate frivolous claims and reduce litigation expense. These include screening, mediation panels and nonbinding arbitration, that are intended to expedite claim resolution within the context of the traditional jury system, and binding arbitration that replaces the judge and jury with a mutually agreed panel as ultimate arbiters of the case. The success of these procedures depends on their effect on the incentives and constraints of the parties to the litigation.

Theory and evidence indicate that mandatory screening, without significant penalties for appeal and without the panel's findings being admissible evidence in court, may simply add an additional tier of delay and costs. For ADR to reduce litigation delay and costs, it must create incentives for the parties to substitute the informal process for more costly trial in a large percentage of cases. This implies that formal arbitration proceedings should be binding. For less formal procedures, the parties should face significant penalties for proceeding to trial against the recommendation of the panel. One model is to apply the English rule of cost-shifting to post-ADR litigation. Thus a party who rejects an ADR finding and who receives the same or a lower award at court could be required to pay the other side's legal costs of going to trial, up to a limit. Because most plaintiffs would be risk averse and often could not pay the court costs of both sides, such cost shifting should be applied to the plaintiff's attorney, who should be permitted to increase the contingent percentage to reflect the added risk. President Clinton's Health Security Act proposed a system of mandatory non-binding arbitration, with results inadmissible as evidence at trial and with no penalties for proceeding to trial. Such an approach is likely to add rather than reduce the costs and delay of litigation.

An example of a promising form of ADR is the early neutral evaluation (ENE) programme (Rosenberg and Folberg 1994) that has been adopted in northern California. The ENE is designed to provide each side with additional information about the other's case, including a prompt and neutral evaluation. If combined with a system of early binding offers and a fee-shifting rule for frivolous rejection of an offer and consequent pursuit of litigation, the costs and delay of claim disposition could be significantly reduced. An early binding offer system, combined with the English rule, creates incentives for each party to act on their true information, whereas bluff and strategic manipulation are penalized. By contrast, screening and mediation, without significant penalties for strategic post-screening behaviour, simply increase delay and costs.

VI. 'NO-FAULT' ALTERNATIVES

In the 1970s, Sweden and New Zealand adopted radical alternatives to tort liability for accidents, including medical malpractice. These models are often cited as offering potential savings from replacing the negligence rule of liability with a no-fault (causation-only) criterion of compensability. In the US, proposals for strict enterprise liability (for example, Weiler 1991) would replace the negligence liability of the individual physician with a rule of strict liability on the hospital with which the physician is associated, by analogy with the workers' compensation system whereby employers are strictly liable for all work-related injuries and diseases. In fact, the Swedish and New Zealand systems are very different from the strict enterprise liability proposals in the US and hence provide little evidence relevant to how enterprise liability might function. In particular, the low reported overhead costs of these systems omit significant hidden costs and in any case are not due to the use of a causation-only criterion for compensation. Nevertheless the experience of these two systems is instructive. For more detail, see Danzon (1994a, 1994b).

1. *The Swedish Patient Compensation Insurance (PCI).* The Patient Compensation Insurance (PCI) was established in 1975 by voluntary contract between medical providers and a consortium of insurers. The aim was to preempt a proposal for statutory expansion of tort liability that was intended to reduce barriers to compensation of victims under traditional tort procedures. Although Swedish patients retain the right to sue in tort under traditional negligence rules, tort claims have been extremely rare until recently. A key feature of the Swedish model is its decoupling of compensation and deterrence. Patient compensation is provided by the PCI, while the discipline of medical providers is handled by the Medical Responsibility Board (MRB). No information is transmitted between these two institutions, in order to obtain the doctors' cooperation with the PCI. The PCI is administered by a consortium of insurers, with potential appeal to a special advisory panel and ultimately to arbitration.

The superficial appeal of the Swedish model is its apparently low budget cost and low overhead rate, and its widespread acceptance by medical providers. Claim frequency has stabilized at about 21 claims per 100 physicians per year, compared to 13–16 claims per 100 physicians in the US; in both countries roughly 40 percent of these claims receive compensation. But the PCI costs roughly 0.16 percent of health care costs in Sweden, whereas medical malpractice insurance premiums are about one percent of higher health expenditures in the US. Thus the per capita budget cost of the Swedish PCI appears to be roughly one-tenth of US malpractice premiums. Administrative overhead is 14–18 percent of total PCI premiums, compared to roughly 60 percent in the US. This low overhead rate is often cited as evidence of the potential savings from switching from a negligence rule to a no-fault (causation-only) rule of compensability for medical injuries (Weiler 1991), analogous to the strict liability of employers for workplace injuries under workers' compensation.

However these inferences are based on a misunderstanding of the PCI. The low budget cost of the PCI, despite the higher claim frequency, reflects primarily two factors. First, the collateral offset rule shifts most of the wage loss and medical expense of iatrogenic injuries to other social insurance programmes, thereby undermining cost internalization and general deterrence and leading to a severe understatement of the true cost of compensating iatrogenic injuries in Sweden. Second, awards for noneconomic loss are below those in most other European countries and significantly lower than in the US. The mean payment for noneconomic loss was $3,800 in 1987, with a maximum of $117,070. Nevertheless, payments for noneconomic loss account for roughly 74 percent of total PCI payments, because economic loss is largely covered through collateral insurance.

The low PCI payment levels are possible because Sweden's tort regime offers an even lower schedule of payments and higher costs for plaintiffs than the PCI. The PCI must offer plaintiffs an expected payoff that at least matches their expected tort recovery, net of costs, in order to deter tort claims, since patients select the PCI alternative voluntarily. Among other obstacles, Swedish tort plaintiffs allegedly have difficulty obtaining the expert testimony required to prove negligence under the custom standard of care.

Because a plaintiff's expected net tort recovery sets the floor that must be matched by any voluntary contractual alternative, countries with more pro-plaintiff tort systems, such as the US, could not adopt the Swedish model or any other voluntary contractual alternative and expect to realize costs as low as in Sweden, unless they were also to restrict patients' tort rights significantly. In fact, the out-of-court settlement process already offers a voluntary contractual alternative that operates in the shadow of the formal tort system. In the US, over 90 percent of malpractice claims are settled out of court, dropped or dismissed, and less than 10 percent are taken to verdict. This suggests that much of the potential savings from a voluntary contractual alternative may already be realized through the settlement process.

The PCI's low overhead percentage is not the result of using a causation-only test for compensability; hence any analogy to strict liability and workers' compensation is misplaced. Although the PCI is often called no-fault, this is misleading. From the patient's perspective, the criteria of compensability are quite similar to a custom-based negligence rule. An injury is compensable if (1) it occurred with 'substantial probability' as a direct consequence of medical intervention, and (2) either the treatment was not medically justified or the injury could have been avoided by performing the treatment differently. Thus although the terminology of fault and negligence have been eliminated, compensation requires some notion of 'error'. Adverse outcomes caused by medical care are explicitly excluded, if the treatment was medically justified.

But from the provider's perspective, the PCI is not only no-fault but also no liability. The PCI eliminates all reference or inquiry into fault or negligence, does not require the patient to identify a particular provider who failed in a duty of care, and entails neither financial nor reputational consequences for the provider. This 'no-fault' scheme bears no resemblance to strict liability, as applied in workers' compensation and product liability, or as proposed for strict enterprise liability of hospitals or health plans in the US. All of these systems would place responsibility for the payment of damages on the liable defendant, in order to preserve deterrence incentives, whereas the PCI foregoes any attempt at deterrence.

The low litigation expense of the PCI reflects primarily the fact that neither plaintiffs nor physicians have strong incentives to oppose or appeal the claim adjudication decisions of the insurer consortium. Physicians face no financial or reputational penalty if one of their patients is compensated; this is viewed as an essential condition for achieving physicians' cooperation rather than opposition to patient compensation. Although patients have the right to appeal to a review panel and ultimately to arbitration, their expected gain from appeal is small. The panel has ruled in favour of the insurers in 90 percent of cases and both forums have been closed to the press and public. Thus the key factors contributing to low litigation rates under the PCI are the elimination of all links between patient compensation and provider liability and deterrence, and the lack of more attractive alternatives for the patient. Although the PCI database on iatrogenic injuries might in theory be used for risk management purposes, in practice the information collected is insufficiently detailed. Although clinics and hospitals are informed about their claims experience, the responsible individuals and sometimes even the nature of the injury are not identified.

Patients can file a claim with the Medical Responsibility Board if they feel that their treatment was negligent or contrary to the statutory code of medical practice. They bear their own filing costs and receive no compensation. Providers may be sanctioned by a reprimand or warning, but this has no financial consequence and probably at most a minor reputation effect. There are roughly six MRB claims per 100 physicians per year, of which one in six receives some sanction. Thus the ratio of MRB sanctions to paid PCI claims is less than one in ten – a rough measure of the loss in potential deterrence that results from decoupling compensation from medical discipline.

The main lesson from the Swedish PCI experience is that a sufficient and possibly a necessary condition for low overhead costs is to forego all links between patient compensation and provider deterrence. Whether or not the savings in litigation costs from such separation are offset by an increase in injury costs because of weakening of deterrence incentives, remains an important but unanswered empirical question. The answer may differ across countries, depending on the costs and benefits of their tort systems and on the costs and effectiveness of other systems of quality control. Although in principle tort liability and other systems of quality control should be substitutes, casual evidence from several countries suggests a complementary relationship. For example, hospital investments in risk management and quality assurance have certainly been influenced by concern to reduce liability costs. However as institutional health care purchasers – health insurers in the US, fundholding GPs in the UK, sickness funds in Germany – become increasingly active as consumer surrogates in monitoring quality of care, the incremental benefit from tort liability may diminish.

2. *The New Zealand Accident Compensation Corporation (ACC).* The New Zealand Accident Compensation Corporation (ACC) was established in 1974 as a comprehensive no-fault compensation system for victims of 'personal injury by accident', including 'medical misadventures'. Unlike the Swedish PCI, the ACC preempts tort actions. Claims are administered by the ACC, with appeal to a special ACC Authority. Compensation was set at a relatively high percentage of wage loss for workers, plus scheduled lump sum payments for noneconomic loss. Non-workers received only the lump sum payments. Medical costs were borne by the national health service (NHS), except that the ACC paid directly for services in private hospitals, co-payments and services not covered by the public system. The system was financed by broad payroll and general taxes. Medical injuries were not distinguished from other injuries, hence financing was hidden in payroll and general taxation, with no separate assessment on medical providers.

This system is commonly cited for its low overhead costs, at less than 10 percent of total expenditures, and prompt compensation of claimants. However, far from indicating efficiency, the low overhead simply reflects the ACC's practice of accepting over 80 percent of claims as filed, relying largely on physicians as gatekeepers to certify that a claim is a 'personal injury by accident' and, in cases of permanent disability, that continued benefits are necessary. Physicians had no incentive to oppose claims; indeed until recently physicians could benefit from supporting an ACC claim, since the ACC paid higher fees than did the NHS and a patient who received ACC compensation is barred from filing a tort claim.

Between 1975 and 1989 total expenditures under the ACC grew by over twenty percent a year in nominal terms, or roughly six percent a year after adjusting for inflation. The emphasis on economizing on overhead costs, with minimal investigation of claims or investment in data collection and analysis, have doubtless contributed to the rapid cost escalation. Because the data collected on injury causation are so limited – for example there is, no attempt to identify iatrogenic injuries – the database cannot be used for injury prevention and loss control. Overall, the ACC experience suggests that economizing on overhead may be 'penny wise but pound foolish': skimping on the administrative expense necessary to control excessive claiming and injury rates can lead to higher real social costs of injuries.

Dissatisfaction with this explosion of costs, the inequity of the incidence of costs (low risks subsidizing high risks) and the neglect of injury prevention led to significant reforms of the ACC in 1992. The rules for compensation for medical injuries that were adopted were remarkably similar to traditional negligence rules, although there is no interest in restoring the tort system for claims adjudication. The problems with the original ACC and the proposed solutions are instructive.

'Personal injury by accident' was broadly defined by the original ACC statutes to include 'physical and mental damage caused by medical, surgical, dental and first aid misadventure'. The intent was to exclude illness and normal risks of medical care but to include medical injuries that fall outside the realm of normal risk, including but not limited to those caused by negligence. In practice, adverse outcomes that have either very low probability or unexpected severity have been considered compensable. This is similar to the criterion of 'unintended and unexpected' adverse consequences of medical care proposed by Weiler (1991), which was rejected by the founders of the PCI as an unworkable criterion for compensation (Oldertz 1988).

Defining compensability in terms of an outcome that is unexpected or of unexpected severity suppresses but does not eliminate the need to determine whether the care was appropriate. If 'expected' is defined in terms of statistical probability, the probability distribution depends on the level of care, which thus begs the question of the appropriateness of care, given the patient's medical condition. Moreover, even if an appropriate level of care is implicitly or explicitly assumed, this leaves open whether the 'expected' outcome is to be defined on objective or subjective grounds. Rulings and commentary in New Zealand have differed on this point, creating the potential for inconsistent and arbitrary outcomes.

Difficulties in implementing this definition led to numerous proposals for change, including defining injuries as categorized by the International Classification of Diseases (ICD-9). Others urged extending the system to all incapacity, reasoning logically that there is no equitable justification for compensating victims of medically-caused injuries, while denying compensation to others in similar condition, once the compensation system has eliminated defendant-specific liability and hence has abandoned the deterrence rationale for drawing a distinction based on causation. This objection applies to any system that provides tax-financed compensation to victims of medical injury, with no attempt at deterrence, while denying compensation to others in similar condition.

The 1992 ACC reforms adopted a far more restrictive definition of compensable injury that largely restores a negligence criterion for compensability, without the terminology of fault and without placing liability on the individual provider. 'Medical misadventure' is now defined as 'personal injury resulting from medical error or medical mishap'. 'Medical error' is 'the failure . . . to observe a standard of care and skill reasonably to be expected in the circumstances'. 'Medical mishap' is determined largely on the basis of 'rarity and severity' of the outcome, specifically, less than a 1% probability of occurring, provided that the injury severity exceeds a threshold. This category specifically excludes abnormal reactions and complications of procedures, and injuries related to lack of informed consent, misdiagnosis or treatment omissions, unless resulting from negligence.

The 1992 reforms require the ACC to pay for all medical costs incurred by beneficiaries, effectively restoring the traditional collateral source rule, in the interests of accountability and internalization of costs. By shifting most medical expenses incurred by ACC claimants to the public health system, the previous system undermined the ACC's incentives to control the cost and duration of claims. The 1992 reforms also proposed measures to increase deterrence of medical injuries. The ACC was authorized to establish a medical misadventure account, funded by premiums levied on registered health care professionals, with experience rating and no-claims bonuses. Potentially negligent medical misadventures may be reported to the appropriate disciplinary body. However these changes have remained discretionary.

The New Zealand experience under the original ACC structure illustrates pitfalls to be avoided rather than a useful prototype that other countries might copy. The original definition of a compensable event raised practical and ethical issues that led almost inevitably to proposals to expand the system to include all incapacity. However the huge budget costs of such a system and the difficulty of setting bounds on the definition of incapacity led to the restoration of a quasi-negligence criterion of patient compensation. But, as in the PCI, the terminology of fault has been eliminated and so far individual providers are not accountable for the injuries that they cause. As in the Swedish PCI, the low administrative cost is not an indicator of efficiency; rather, it reflects the elimination of all links between compensation and deterrence. As in Sweden, the elimination of all provider liability, explicit and implicit, was considered key to the non-adversarial adjudication of claims. However, economizing on overhead certainly contributed to the rapid increase in claim costs. The true overhead of an insurance or accident compensation scheme includes not only the measured overhead but also the deadweight loss from unnecessary injuries and inappropriately compensated claims (Danzon 1992). This is not observable, but in the ACC it is likely to be very high.

3. *Enterprise liability*. Proposals for enterprise liability call for the shifting of liability entirely from individual physicians to larger enterprises, either hospitals or health plans. More restrictive variants would simply add these institutions as additional defendants under theories of vicarious and agency liability. Weiler et al. (1993) and Abraham and Weiler (1994) argue for holding the hospital strictly liable for all injuries arising out of care by the physicians on their staff, including injuries that occur outside the hospital. They argue that this would improve efficiency of deterrence, because hospitals are best placed to coordinate the allocation of resources to reduce injuries; provide more accurate internalization of costs, because experience-rating of liability insurance is more accurate if applied to hospitals than to individual physicians; and reduce the costs of legal defence.

The evidence suggests that liability is already being shifted through voluntary contract in circumstances where such shifting offers potential efficiency gains, notably health maintenance organizations (HMOs) and hospitals that have an exclusive relationship with their physicians and pay them on a salary basis. The fact that liability is not shifted by voluntary contract in the majority of physician/hospital arrangements, integrated delivery systems and managed care plans, strongly suggests that to mandate such shifting would reduce efficiency. This is plausible, because the relationship between the plan or hospital and the individual physicians is often not an exclusive relationship; the plan or hospital is not in close physical proximity; and it lacks the information necessary to control efficiently the day-to-day practice of the physician.

The hospital is particularly inappropriate as a bearer of liability given current trends away from inpatient care towards greater use of outpatient or day surgery. Moreover, since care often involves several providers, there is no reason to single out one as the locus of liability unless that one has an informational advantage and is responsible for coordinating care. Neither condition is met in the typical physician-hospital relationship.

Of greater practical concern is the trend towards holding health plans liable for the negligence of their participating providers. If plans are held liable for the negligence of their participating providers, this is likely to lead to tighter integration, more strict control by plans over their providers and exclusive plan-provider arrangements, with each provider participating in only one plan. Such exclusive arrangements would limit patients' choice of providers and increase travel time for consumers. The current rapid growth of managed care plans that offer patients flexibility in choice of provider – independent practice associations (IPAs) and point-of-service plans – indicates that patients are willing to pay for greater choice of providers than is offered by more tightly integrated plans that require an exclusive arrangement between plan and providers. IPAs and, *a fortiori*, point-of-service plans, do not fit the enterprise liability model. Thus if enterprise liability is imposed by legislation or by the courts, the evolution of managed care organizations will be obstructed.

The argument that enterprise liability would reduce defence costs while at the same time improving efficiency of deterrence is not convincing. Standards of care can only meaningfully be defined for providers who ultimately make decisions about the delivery of care. Health plans, by contrast, as financial intermediaries and residual claimants that define and enforce coverage decisions, can only meaningfully be held liable in contract for performance of their contractual obligations and for care in credentialling providers.

If plans are held liable for the negligence of their participating providers, a reasonable standard of care must still be applied at the level of the provider. In that case, the provider will be called to defend the claim and savings in defence costs are likely to be minimal. If individual providers are not called as defendants, then the standard of care for plans is likely to evolve into strict liability for any adverse outcome, for lack of any reasonable basis that defines due care.

A rule of strict liability in theory eliminates the need for courts to make a finding of negligence. But determining whether an injury was caused by medical care, rather than by the underlying disease, would require a similar inquiry, as would the no-fault rules that exclude 'normal risks' of medical care. Thus, the likely evolution is towards a very broad social insurance scheme for all imperfect health outcomes. It is unclear what efficiency or equity goals would be served by such a scheme.

A simple causation-only strict liability system, if combined with experience-rated premiums, would create incentives for providers to avoid high risk patients and treatments, unless they could charge differential fees to reflect the higher expected liability costs. Retaining a fault principle for errors of omission might constrain the incentive to avoid high risk treatments but the incentive to avoid high risk patients would remain. Proponents of enterprise liability also claim potential overhead savings from the use of an administrative disposition process and scheduled damage payments, rather than traditional tort rules. These changes can be made without switching from fault to a strict liability rule. Moreover a strict liability rule is more vulnerable to court errors in setting damages and requires administration of many more cases.

CONCLUDING COMMENTS

The available data are – and are likely to remain – inadequate for a full evaluation of the benefits of a malpractice system relative to its costs. The available evidence suggests that both the extreme criticisms and the unquestioning defences of the current system are overstated. However, the current system in the US could probably be made more cost-effective by some simple reforms. Reforms should be designed to improve the accuracy of the decision-making process, with incentives to use the information available and sanctions for abuse and strategic behaviour, with benefits based on sound insurance principles. Reforms that merely shift costs in an attempt to reduce the more visible budget costs are likely to result in higher real social costs, including higher real injury costs.

In general, the trend in health care markets towards consumer choice between comprehensive networks of care offers new opportunities for experimentation with contractual alternatives for liability. The forum for dispute resolution, the criteria for compensation and the levels of compensation could be specified as terms of the health plan contract. Consumers could then express their willingness to pay for liability alternatives, just as they do for other dimensions of quality and quantity of services. Given the active role of employers and public purchasers in monitoring and selecting among plans, the concern that consumers might consistently be misled on quality is much diminished relative to the traditional, atomistic, fee-for-service medical market place. Moreover, as noted earlier, if plans are to compete by eliminating low-valued care, it is essential that this not be preempted by exposure to liability. Thus clarification of the terms of the health care coverage and the liability coverage could go hand in hand.

PATRICIA M. DANZON

See also ACCURACY IN ADJUDICATION; ALTERNATIVE DISPUTE RESOLUTION; ARBITRATION IN THE SHADOW OF THE LAW; CONTINGENT FEES; CUSTOMARY PRACTICES AND THE LAW OF TORTS; INSURANCE, DETERRENCE AND LIABILITY; LEARNED HAND RULE; LEGAL STANDARDS OF CARE; LIABILITY RIGHTS AS CONTINGENT CLAIMS; REGULATION OF THE PROFESSIONS.

Subject classification: 5d(v); 6d(iii).

BIBLIOGRAPHY

Abraham, K.S. and Weiler, P.C. 1994. Enterprise medical liability and the evolution of the American health system. *Harvard Law Review* 108: 381–438.

Cook, P.J. and Graham, D.A. 1977. The demand for insurance and protection: the case of irreplaceable commodities. *Quarterly Journal of Economics* 91: 143–56.

Craswell, R. and Calfee, J. 1986. Deterrence and uncertain legal standards. *Journal of Law, Economics and Organization* 2(2): 279–303.

Danzon, P.M. 1984a. The frequency and severity of medical malpractice claims. *Journal of Law and Economics* 27: 115–48.

Danzon, P.M. 1984b. Tort reform and the role of government in private insurance markets. *Journal of Legal Studies* 13(3): 517–49.

Danzon, P.M. 1985. *Medical Malpractice: Theory, Evidence and Public Policy*. Cambridge, MA: Harvard University Press.

Danzon, P.M. 1986. New evidence on the frequency and severity of medical malpractice claims. *Law and Contemporary Problems* 5(49): 57–84.

Danzon, P.M. 1990. The 'crisis' in medical malpractice: a comparison of trends in the United States, Canada, the United Kingdom and Australia. *Law, Medicine and Health Care* 18(1–2).

Danzon, P.M. 1991. Liability for medical malpractice. *Journal of Economic Perspectives* 5(3): 51–69.

Danzon, P.M. 1992. Hidden overhead costs: is Canada's system really less expensive? *Health Affairs*, Spring 11(1): 21–43.

Danzon, P.M. 1994a. The Swedish patient compensation system: myths and realities. *International Review of Law and Economics* 14: 453–66.

Danzon, P.M. 1994b. Tort reform: the case of medical malpractice. *Oxford Review of Economic Policy* 10(1): 84–98.

Danzon, P.M. 1994c. Alternative liability regimes for medical malpractice: results from simulation analysis. *Journal of Risk and Insurance* 61(2): 219–44.

Danzon, P.M. and Lillard, L. 1983. Settlement out of court: the disposition of medical malpractice claims. *Journal of Legal Studies* 12: 345–77.

Ellis, R.P., Gallup, C.L. and McGuire, T.G. 1990. Should medical professional liability insurance be experience rated? *Journal of Risk and Insurance* 57(1): 66–78.

Farber, H.S. and White, M. 1991. Medical malpractice: an empirical examination of the litigation process. *RAND Journal of Economics* 22: 199–217.

Mills, D.H., Boyden, J.S. and Rubsamen, D.S. 1977. *Report on the Medical Insurance Feasibility Study* (sponsored jointly by California Medical Association and California Hospital Association). San Francisco: Sutter Publications.

Oldertz, C. 1988. The patient, pharmaceutical and security insurances. In *Compensation for Personal Injury in Sweden and Other Countries*, ed. C. Oldertz and E. Tildefelt (Stockholm: Juristforlaget): 51–78.

Rolph, J.E. 1981. Some statistical evidence on merit rating in medical malpractice insurance. *Journal of Risk and Insurance* 48(2): 247–60.

Rosenberg, J.D. and Folberg, H.J. 1994. Alternative dispute resolution in a civil justice reform act demonstration district: findings, implications and recommendations. *Stanford Law Review* 46.

Ruser, J. 1985. Workers' compensation insurance, experience-rating, and occupational injuries. *RAND Journal of Economics* 16(4): 487–503.

Shavell, S. 1980. Strict liability versus negligence. *Journal of Legal Studies* 9: 1–25.

Shavell, S. 1982. On liability and insurance. *Bell Journal of Economics* 13: 120–32.

Sloan, F.A., Mergenhagen, P.M., Burfield, W.B., Bovbjerg, R.R. and Hassan, M. 1989. Medical malpractice experience of physicians: predictable or haphazard? *Journal of the American Medical Association* 262 (23): 3291–7.

Spence, M. 1977. Consumer misperceptions, product failure and product liability. *Review of Economic Studies* 44: 561–72.

Weiler, P.C. 1991. *Medical Malpractice on Trial.* Cambridge, MA: Harvard University Press

Weiler, P.C., Howard, H.H., Newhouse, J.P., William, G.J., Troyen, A.B. and Lucian, L. 1993. *A Measure of Malpractice: Medical Injury, Malpractice Litigation and Patient Compensation*. Cambridge, MA: Harvard University Press.

White, M.J. 1994. The value of liability in medical malpractice. *Health Affairs* 13(4): 75–87.

Zuckerman, S., Bovbjerg, R.R. and Sloan, F.A. 1990. Effects of tort reforms and other factors on medical malpractice insurance premiums. *Inquiry* 27: 167–82.

Menger, Carl (1840–1921). In the history of economic thought Carl Menger is remembered, in particular, for three reasons. For having, with his *Grundsätze der Nationalökonomie* (*Principles of Economics*), and alongside William Stanley Jevons and Léon Walras, laid the foundations for the marginalist revolution in economics. For his dispute with Gustav Schmoller in what has become known as the *Methodenstreit*, the 'dispute about method'. And, finally, but most importantly, for being the founder of the Austrian School of Economics.

Menger was born on 28 February 1840, in Neu-Sandec, Galicia (in today's Poland), the son of a lawyer. Like his two brothers, Anton (a legal philosopher and historian of socialist doctrine) and Max, he studied at the universities of Vienna (1859–60) and Prague (1860–63). After taking the degree of Doctor of Law at the University of Cracow in 1867 he worked as a journalist for papers in Lemberg and Vienna before he entered, in 1871, the Austrian civil service in the press department of the prime minister's office in Vienna. In the same year he published his first and main book, *Grundsätze der Nationalökonomie*, which he presented in 1872 to the faculty of law and political economy (Rechts- und Staatswissenschaften) at the University of Vienna, in order to obtain his 'Habilitation' as Privatdozent of political economy. When, one year later, in 1873, he was installed as extraordinary professor, he left his position in the Civil Service for a career in academia. In 1876 Menger was appointed one of the tutors of Crown Prince Rudolf of Austria, then eighteen years of age, whom he accompanied on extensive travels across Europe in 1877 and 1878. In the summer of 1878 he resumed teaching at the University of Vienna. In 1879 he was promoted to ordinary professor and appointed to the chair of political economy. Four years later Menger published his second major work, the *Untersuchungen über die Methode der Sozialwissenschaften und der politischen Ökonomie insbesondere* (*Investigations into the Method of the Social Sciences with Special Reference to Economics*), a publication which triggered the dispute with the leader of the younger German Historical School, Gustav Schmoller. In the 1890s Menger devoted himself to issues of Austrian monetary policy as well as to general questions in monetary theory. He became, in 1892, a member of the Austrian currency commission and published, during the same year, several contributions on monetary issues, including his handbook article, *Geld*, a work which F.A. Hayek (1992:88) said 'must be ranked as the third and last of Menger's main contributions to economic theory'. After 1892, during the remaining three decades of his life, Menger published only occasional shorter articles, even though he resigned in 1903 from his teaching position, eight years before the official retirement age, in order to be able to devote more time to his project of preparing a second edition of the *Grundsätze*, which had long been out of print, and of completing his comprehensive treatise on economics of which the *Grundsätze* had been meant to be only the first, introductory part. Both projects remained, however, uncompleted when Menger died on 26 February 1921. His son Karl published a revised edition of the *Grundsätze* in 1923, incorporating some of the material from the manuscripts which his father had left behind and which are today archived in the Special Collections Department of the Perkins Library of Duke University (Barnett 1990).

The simultaneous and independent discovery of the principle of marginal utility by Menger, Jevons and Walras is generally regarded as the beginning of the modern, neoclassical period in the development of economics, and historians of thought have traditionally focused on the commonalities that unite the theoretical approaches of these three authors. More recently, however, attention has increasingly shifted to significant differences that set Menger's approach apart from that of his fellow founders of the marginal utility doctrine, in particular the contrast between his focus on *market processes* and the *equilibrium-centred* perspective that has come to dominate the Walrasian, mainstream neoclassical tradition. As R. Wagner has put it,

> [Menger] was more concerned with price formation than price determination. He was concerned with the working of the market process, not with the particular characteristics that would be obtained once that process had worked itself out. . . . For Walras the market process . . . was subsumed in a black box. In contrast, Menger's analytical efforts were guided precisely by a desire to understand how this black box works. . . . The question that Walras begged through his fiction of tâtonnement was precisely the question that Menger chose to address (Wagner et al. 1978: 66).

Like Jevons and Walras, Menger sought to rectify what he recognized as fundamental inadequacies of the value theory of classical economics, by making the subjective value of goods to individuals the central explanatory variable of a 'price theory based upon reality and placing all price phenomena (including interest, wages, ground rent, etc.) together under one unified point of view' (Menger [1871] 1981: 49). Yet what distinguished him was his ambition to proceed from the notions of subjective value and marginal utility to a theoretical understanding of the market process as a process that is ultimately driven, in all its respects, by consumer choices. He aimed at an all-inclusive price theory that consistently integrates the theory of production into a general consumer valuation theory that explains the prices of all goods, services and productive inputs in utility terms, i.e. in terms of opportunity costs to consumers.

While the classical cost-of-production theory sought to explain the value of goods as a derivative of the costs of the inputs that went into making them, Menger recognized that the true relationship is exactly the reverse, in the sense that the value or price of inputs is a derivative of the value that the final products have to consumers. Goods that serve directly in the satisfaction of human wants he called first order goods, and goods that are used as inputs in the production of other goods he called second, third or higher order goods, depending on their remoteness from the final consumption goods. Menger's fundamental claim was that the price of goods of higher order can only be explained in terms of the prospective value of their products, ultimately the prospective value of the final consumption goods to the production of which they contribute.

As noted, and as indicated by its subtitle, '*Erster, allgemeiner Theil*' (First, general part), Menger had intended his *Grundsätze* to be the lead volume of a comprehensive treatise on economics. Yet, after publishing the first part, he redirected his efforts away from a further substantive exposition of his theory, toward a general methodological defence of *theoretical* research, resulting in the 1883 publication of his *Untersuchungen über die Methode der Sozialwissenschaften*. Apparently, this was caused by his frustration about the lack of attention that his *Grundsätze* had received among his German colleagues, who were 'influenced by the anti-theoretical attitude of the younger historical school' (Hayek 1992: 78, fn.). As one can conclude from Menger's dedication of the *Grundsätze* to Wilhelm Roscher, as well as from the words of praise for the achievements of German political economy that he voiced in the preface, the German economists clearly were the audience whose recognition Menger had hoped to obtain and his failure to do so must have been a great disappointment to him. Menger ([1883] 1985: 26f.) explicitly noted in the introduction to the *Untersuchungen* that he was 'far from overrating the significance of methodology' and considered detours into methodological investigations only justified in extraordinary situations when in a field of knowledge 'the progress of a science is blocked because erroneous methodological principles prevail'. This was, however, what he judged to be the case in 'the presently prevailing state of research in the field of political economy in Germany' (27), where 'historical understanding' was thought to be 'the exclusively justified and attainable goal of research' (25) and where the search for general laws, independent of spatial and temporal conditions, was regarded as an 'inadmissible and misconceived' effort involving 'an undue abstraction from the "full empirical reality" of phenomena' (24). In concluding the preface (31), Menger noted that the 'largely polemic character' of his methodological treatise should only be understood as reflecting the seriousness of his intention to make 'research in the field of political economy in Germany aware of its real task again', and to 'contribute to bringing it back to the right paths'.

However well meant Menger's critique of the historical school's methodological orientation might have been, it was by no means kindly received. Yet at least it drew attention. It provoked, in particular, what Hayek (1992: 80) describes as 'a magisterial rebuke' from Gustav Schmoller (1883), to which Menger again sharply responded with his 1884 pamphlet *Die Irrtümer des Historismus in der deutschen Nationalökonomie* (Menger 1970: 1–98). The review copy that had been sent to him Schmoller not only returned unopened with an insulting letter, he even published the letter in his journal. While this put an end to the direct quarrel between Menger and Schmoller, the *Methodenstreit*, the 'dispute about method', was to be carried on for a while by several disciples on each side. The passionate exchange caused, as Hayek (1992: 50) reports, 'such a rift between the two groups that the German universities came to be filled more and more exclusively by members of the historical school and the Austrian universities by members of Menger's school'.

From today's perspective much of the exchange between the contending parties in the *Methodenstreit* may seem strange, and, in fact, the true significance of this debate does not necessarily lie in what appears to have been its principal issue, i.e. the role assigned to historical-descriptive versus theoretical-analytical research in political economy. Beneath its surface the *Methodenstreit* was a *conflict of paradigms*, a conflict between fundamentally different theoretical outlooks at economic phenomena, and it was, even less explicitly stated, a conflict between fundamentally different views on the role of economic policy. On the one side of the paradigm-conflict there was Menger's claim that all social and economic phenomena are ultimately to be explained as aggregate outcomes, intended and unintended, of individual human actions that are directed at individual human purposes, a claim that was combined with an essentially classical liberal understanding of the working of market processes and the limits of government intervention. On the other side of the conflict there was Schmoller's advocacy of a collectivist perspective that looks at economies as historic organic wholes and interprets all economic phenomena as integral parts of such wholes, along with his preference for a more activist state and his rejection of what he labelled as Menger's *Manchester-individualism*.

Although they were not Menger's direct students, but had left the University of Vienna just before Menger started teaching there, Eugen von Böhm-Bawerk (1851–1914) and Friedrich von Wieser (1851–1926) were to become the principal builders of the Menger School or, as it was to be named, the Austrian School of Economics. They had been among the first to read Menger's *Grundsätze*, a reading that made them instant and enthusiastic followers, as they were convinced to have found in Menger's book the 'Archimedean point' from which to approach economic theory (Wieser 1923: 88). Both were to take their 'Habilitation' with Menger, Böhm-Bawerk in 1880 and Wieser in 1883. Because of his intention to prepare revised editions, Menger did not allow his *Grundsätze* nor his *Untersuchungen* to be reprinted during his lifetime. It was, therefore, Böhm-Bawerk's and Wieser's works that came to be widely read rather than Menger's, and it was mainly through them that his ideas were developed further and became more widely known. It was also their works that were soon translated into English, while 'Menger's book had to wait 80 years till it was made available in an English version' (Hayek 1992: 105). Probably the most influential period in the teaching of Mengerian-Austrian economics came when, after Menger's early retirement, Wieser assumed Menger's chair in 1903, and when one year later Böhm-Bawerk also took a chair at the University of Vienna that had been specifically established for him. In the decade before World War I the famous Böhm-Bawerk Seminar became the intellectual centre of the Austrian School out of which the third generation of Austrian economists was to emerge, including Ludwig von Mises who continued the tradition of Böhm-Bawerk, and Hans Mayer who worked in the Wieser tradition.

There has been some recent discussion on whether Carl Menger can truly be said to have originated a new theoretical approach in economics that could justly be regarded as constituting a distinct 'Austrian' perspective. In particular Erich Streissler (1989, 1990a, 1990b) has argued in a number of articles that, counter to commonly held opinion, Menger was by no means a revolutionary innovator of subjectivist value theory, but was simply carrying on arguments that were well developed in German economic teaching in the middle of the nineteenth century. As he puts it: 'It is easy to show that very few of the basic ideas of Menger's Principles cannot be found foreshadowed in the books of German economics that he knew well' (Streissler 1990b: 33). Yet, his strong rhetoric notwithstanding, Streissler's 'new' account does not, in the end, say much more in substance than what others, like Hayek (1992: 64, 98ff.) or even Menger himself, have said about the influence of German economics on the writing of the *Grundsätze*. Of his initial strong claim not too much seems to be left when Streissler (1990b: 61) arrives at the conclusion that what one may 'think of as peculiarly Austrian economics as distinct from and in contrast to *standard* neoclassical theory – the process-analytic approach, the 'time-error' paradigm, capital theory, the strict methodological individualism – has *no* recognisable forebears in German economics.'

Without ignoring the potential importance of contributions such as Streissler's for a more complete account of the place of Menger and the Austrian School in the history of economic thought, they unduly play down the fundamental significance and the paradigmatic nature of the research programme that Menger initiated. The principal, and interrelated, ingredients of the paradigm that Menger originated, and that can be regarded as the foundation upon which the Austrian School of Economics has been built, consist in his *methodological individualism* (to use the term that Schumpeter [1908] later coined), in his thoroughgoing *subjectivism* and in his *causal-genetic*, or *process-oriented* approach. Menger's methodological individualism must be distinguished from another central aspect of his approach, namely his emphasis on what may be called *invisible-hand explanations*, i.e. explanations of socio-economic phenomena as *unintended* outcomes of individual efforts. The two principles are not always sufficiently separated even though they are concerned with different issues. The first concerns the general methodological issue of whether aggregate or collective social phenomena can be explained in terms of individual human behaviour. The second concerns the more specific issue of whether particular social phenomena can be explained as *unintended outcomes* of separate individual actions, aimed at individual purposes. Invisible-hand explanations represent a particular kind of individualistic explanation, one that is appropriately applied to social phenomena that are, in Menger's terminology, of 'organic' origin, by contrast to social phenomena of 'pragmatic' origin, i.e. those that are the product of deliberate collective or concerted action directed at their creation, or, as Menger ([1883] 1985: 145) put it, that are 'products of the agreement of members of society, or of positive legislation, results of the purposeful common activity of society'. Quite obviously, invisible-hand-explanations are appropriate only for social phenomena of 'organic' origin, but there is no reason why Menger's methodological individualism should not be equally applicable to phenomena of 'pragmatic' origin, even if Menger's own explanatory focus has been on the former.

Menger's methodological individualism is reflected in the maxim that economic phenomena ought to be explained 'by reducing them to their elements, to the *individual* factors of their causation' (ibid.: 159). It is a methodological principle that aims at providing a unified theoretical account of all aggregate or collective phenomena – of market phenomena, such as prices of goods or interest rates, as well as of social structures and institutions – by explaining them as resultants of individual human efforts that are aimed at individual purposes, but interact with each other in more or less complex ways and may produce outcomes that none of the individual actors involved intended. Inherently associated with Menger's methodological individualism is a thorough-going subjectivist perspective on human behaviour that not only emphasizes the *subjectivity of utility*, or human valuations, but also the *subjectivity of human knowledge*, i.e. of individuals' perception of the world and of the conjectures and theories upon which their actions are based. Menger persistently stresses that the properties of goods and services are not simply a matter of their inherent attributes as such, but are a matter of relations between things and acting persons (Menger [1871] 1981: 74, 120f.). Far from ascribing to individuals perfect knowledge and foresight, Menger saw them as guided in their actions by limited knowledge and fallible expectations, and as subject to uncertainty and error. It is, in particular, this *knowledge-subjectivism* that separates the Mengerian vision of the market-process from neoclassical accounts. As Lachmann (in Wagner et al. 1978: 59) has put it: 'Menger's readiness to take the human mind with all its limitations as his starting point is what really distinguishes Menger from Jevons and Walras.'

Menger's thorough-going subjectivism leads, in turn, to his *causal-genetic* or *process-oriented* perspective. If social and economic phenomena are the product of human choices, if human actions are guided by subjective preferences as well as by subjective theories about the world, and if we can, ultimately, know about other persons' preferences and theories only from their choices, then studying the nature of these choices and the ways in which they interact to produce social outcomes must be the principal avenue of research through which we can hope to arrive at an understanding and explanation of social and economic phenomena. If persons are diverse, not only in their valuations of things but also in their knowledge and conjectures about the world, if their knowledge continuously changes as they learn from their own experience as well as from others, and if the imagination and creativity of the human mind can introduce novelty at any point, it can hardly be the task of economics to theorize about what specific outcomes may emerge from the innumerable choices and market-interactions of such individuals. Instead, the only task that, from a Mengerian perspective, economic theory can properly assume is the different, and more modest project to study the working properties of socio-economic processes, and to provide an understanding of the general *kinds* of outcomes that processes of a certain nature can be expected to generate. In its emphasis on the diversity of, and differences among individuals, Menger's paradigm can be said to share the principal characteristic of an evolutionary perspective that concentrates on the dynamics of adaptive change, over time, in the composition of populations of diverse individuals. In Menger's approach, just as in evolutionary approaches generally, it is the individual differences that matter, not the properties of the aggregate as such, and it is from changes in the diversity of individuals that changes at the aggregate level are explained.

Menger ([1871] 1981: 191) insisted that the force that drives all economic processes is that individuals 'strive to better their economic position as much as possible'. Accordingly, a causal-genetic or process explanation of aggregate phenomena, such as market prices or social structures and institutions, has to 'explicate the *sequence* of actions' (Kirzner 1987: 148) that bring them about. In other words, it has to provide a theoretical reconstruction of the processes through which social structures and institutions emerge from individuals striving to better their position. Such explication or theoretical reconstruction is not meant to provide a detailed recount of the singular sequence of actions or of the actual historical process from which market prices or social institutions have emerged in particular instances. It is, instead, meant to provide a general theoretical account of the typical features of such processes, what Hayek (1973: 24) has called 'explanations of the principle', i.e. a theoretical reconstruction of hypothetical processes that could *in principle* have produced the type of phenomena that are under investigation. The paradigmatic example in Menger's work of such *in-principle-explanations* is his account of the origin of money (Menger [1871] 1981: 260f.; 1984: 13ff.; [1883] 1985: 151ff.), an account that shows how the institution of money can be explained as the outcome of a process that is totally blind in regard to its eventual result, but is driven only by individual human actions, each of which is guided only by limited individual purposes and limited knowledge.

Menger's explanation of the evolution of money is a paradigmatic example also of the critical role that learning plays in Mengerian process explanations. What Hayek was to discuss later under the heading of *competition as a discovery procedure* is a notion that was clearly captured in Menger's emphasis on the fact that it is the experimenting of diverse individuals with diverse goods and diverse economic strategies that allows for discoveries of successful strategies to be made by pioneers that then provide the model from which others can learn. As Menger notes with regard to individuals' knowledge of the economic advantages that they can realize by accepting, in exchange for their commodities, goods that are more marketable, even if in themselves they may be useless to them:

> This knowledge will never be attained by all members of a people at the same time. On the contrary, only a small number of economising individuals will at first recognise the advantage accruing to them from the acceptance of other, more saleable commodities in exchange for their own whenever a direct exchange of their commodities for the goods they wish to consume is impossible or highly uncertain. . . . There is no better way in which men can become enlightened about their economic interests than by observation of the economic success of those who employ the correct means of achieving their ends ([1871] 1981: 261).

Menger's view of the market process as a process of discovery and learning that is ultimately governed by consumer preferences provides an important clue to the policy implications of his approach. It has often been observed that, in Menger's work, one does not find many explicit statements on issues of economic policy, and there has been some speculation on whether he – or his early followers, Wieser and Böhm-Bawerk – can justly be said to have taken the kind of liberal outlook at market competition that has become one of the principal attributes of the Austrian School of Economics. Streissler (1989: 133), for instance, has noted that, judging from Menger's only noteworthy statement on economic policy, an 1891 newspaper article on 'The Social Theories of Classical Economics and Modern Economic Policy', one might be inclined to conclude that Menger was a moderate interventionist or social liberal rather than a classical liberal. This conclusion, Streissler (1990a: 189f.) has recently suggested, may need to be corrected, though, in light of newly discovered notebooks of Crown Prince Rudolf, that had been written under Menger's tutorial guidance and that provide evidence, if only indirectly, of Menger's classical liberal stance.

Whatever significance one may want to attribute to the Crown Prince's notebooks, and however scarce the explicit discussion on matters of economic policy may be in Menger's work, there can be no doubt that Menger saw an important purpose of theoretical economics in the guidance that it may provide to economic policy. To him the study of economic policy was but the practical or applied side of theoretical economics, concerned with 'the general principles, the maxims by which national economy can be benefited' ([1883] 1985: 203). It is therefore appropriate to ask what kind of policy approach would appear to be most plausible from the point of view of Menger's theoretical paradigm or, in other words, would follow 'from the inner logic of the system' (Raico 1995: 23). Streissler (1990a: 186) rightly notes that Menger's methodological individualism, as well as his emphasis on the limits and fallibility of human knowledge, articulate fundamental arguments in support of a sceptical liberal view of the promises of government intervention. One can, however, be even more specific about Menger's policy perspective in the sense that a closer reading of his work must lead one to the conclusion that he not only conjectured that consumer choices *do*, de facto, govern economic processes, but that he also believed that consumer preferences *ought* to govern the economic processes. To be sure, since 'ought-statements' cannot be logically derived from 'is-statements' this normative principle does not follow as a direct logical conclusion from Menger's conjectures about the factual role of consumer preferences in economic processes. Yet, it is a principle that clearly makes good sense in the overall context of his work. And it is a normative principle that has definite implications for economic policy, whether or not they have been explicitly stated by Menger.

The notion that consumer preferences rather than producer interests should govern the economic process is, of course, a normative principle that has been central to the classical liberal tradition ever since Adam Smith's ([1776] 1981: 660) famous critique of the mercantile system as one that is governed by the interests of producers in protectionist privileges, at the expense of consumers. It is an ideal for which Hutt ([1936] 1990: 257) has coined the name *consumer sovereignty*. In Menger's work the notion of 'economic governance exercised by consumer preferences' (Kirzner 1990b: 99) is not meant to be equally descriptive of just any kind of economic process or any kind of 'market economy', nor is it meant as a description of the economy of Menger's contemporary Austria. It is, instead, meant as a normative standard against which actual economies can be measured. It is an ideal of a desirable economic order, an ideal that can be approached more or less by real economies, and towards which real economies may be moved by suitable institutional reforms.

To say that the principle of *consumer sovereignty* can be considered the natural *normative* complement to Menger's theory of the economic process as a consumer-driven process does not mean, though, that to the theoretical-explanatory part of the Mengerian paradigm a 'normative economics' was added that specializes in advancing normative claims. Instead, Menger's view of the relation between economic theory and the study of economic policy clearly implies that the task of the latter is to state testable conjectures about what are and what are not suitable means to promote consumer sovereignty, i.e. means that are suitable to make the economic system more responsive to consumer preferences. It is in this sense that Menger can be said to be part of the liberal tradition that advocates market-competition as a suitable arrangement for promoting consumer sovereignty. It should be mentioned, as an aside, that neither to Menger nor Adam Smith or other liberal advocates of consumer sovereignty was this normative principle a dogmatic postulate. It was, instead, based on the implicit conjecture that an economic system governed by consumer preferences is more capable to promote its constituents' welfare than one governed by producer interests, and that therefore the former is more desirable for them than the latter.

If the principle of consumer sovereignty is, indeed, the fundamental normative premise in Menger's approach, then certain conclusions for economic policy can be drawn, whether or not they have been explicitly discussed by Menger himself, and whether or not he has always been consistent in drawing them. One conclusion that immediately suggests itself concerns the already noted fact that, even if consumer preferences can be viewed as the ultimate driving force in all economic systems (Hutt [1936] 1990: 261), the effective controlling power that consumer choices are able to exert surely varies across different kinds of economic arrangements. As Smith had argued, and as Menger clearly knew, in the mercantile system there were obviously serious obstacles that reduced the controlling force of consumer choices, and the same is most definitely true for the socialist experiments in economic organization that Menger had little opportunity to observe. This means, however, that alternative economic systems or legal-institutional frameworks can be compared, against the measuring rod of *consumer sovereignty*, as to the governing role that they actually allow consumer choices to play. It also means that proposals for reforms in legal-institutional frameworks can be examined as to whether their predictable effect will be to strengthen or to weaken consumer sovereignty.

Just as Menger's theoretical paradigm has a procedural focus (i.e., it is concerned with the study of processes rather than with outcomes as such), the policy perspective that his approach suggests also has a procedural focus. It directs attention to the issue of how consumer choices can be made more effective controllers of the economic process, rather than to the issue of how particular outcomes may be achieved. And just as Menger's theoretical account of the market process is, in its procedural focus, paradigmatically different from standard neoclassical accounts, so a Mengerian policy approach can be said to be, in its procedural focus, categorically different from neoclassical welfare economics. There are essentially two ways in which the policy issue of 'what should be done' can be approached. One can either apply outcome criteria that allow for outcomes to be evaluated directly, independent of the ways in which they have come about. Or one can employ procedural criteria that allow for an evaluation of the processes or procedures through which outcomes are generated. In the second case outcomes are evaluated only indirectly, in the sense that outcomes are considered 'good' if they result from 'good' processes. Given the subjectivity of individuals' valuations and theories, there is no way for the economist-analyst to judge outcomes directly as to their contribution to the satisfaction of consumer preferences. The policy perspective must, instead, focus on the nature of the choice process through which consumer preferences are made effective, and on the issue of how, by way of institutional reforms, the 'economic governance exercised by consumer preferences' (Kirzner 1990b: 99) may be improved. By its very nature, the ideal of consumer sovereignty is a procedural norm that can only be implemented by procedural or institutional means, not by interventionist measures directly aiming at outcomes as such. The question that it poses to economic policy is not what substantive outcomes serve consumer preferences best, but rather, what kind of institutional frameworks offer the best prospects for consumer choices to play their governing role.

The procedural-institutional focus of the principle of consumer sovereignty can help to clarify the issue of the alleged social-interventionist leanings of Menger's liberalism. To the extent that the realization of the ideal of consumer sovereignty depends on the presence of suitable institutional framework-conditions, and to the extent that such conditions cannot be expected to be assured by the natural course of things, a liberal advocate of consumer sovereignty must argue for government policies that bring about and maintain such conditions. In this sense, it is certainly true, as Kirzner (1990b: 101) comments, that Menger's emphasis on the role of consumer valuations does not lead him to an 'unqualified endorsement of pure laissez faire'. Yet, that does not mean that Menger was an 'interventionist social liberal'. It would seem to be more appropriate to classify him under the rubric of *constitutional liberalism*, in the sense in which this label applies, for instance, to the Ordo-Liberals of the Freiburg School of Economics or to the Constitutional Economics pioneered by James Buchanan.

In light of the policy issue of how economic systems can be made to work more effectively in the service of consumer interests, an aspect of Menger's theoretical argument can be clarified that has puzzled even some of the most sympathetic readers of his work, namely Menger's notion of 'economic prices' as distinguished from observable, real-world prices (Menger [1871] 1981: 249). While the latter are the prices that form in the real world where human choices are subject to error, 'economic prices' are supposed to be prices that, as Kirzner puts it, would 'prevail in the absence of error' (Kirzner 1990b: 102). On first look the notion of 'economic prices', and its contrast to 'uneconomic prices' (Menger [1871] 1981: 218), may seem inconsistent with Menger's subjectivism, yet it makes good sense when his argument on the role of human error is interpreted in a strictly procedural sense, as the logic of his paradigm requires. If consumer choices are informed by subjective preferences as well as by subjective theories about the factual consequences of choice-alternatives, and if such theories may be mistaken, then the normative principle of consumer sovereignty must be interpreted as implicitly supposing that individuals' *informed choices* rather than their erroneous beliefs about the properties of alternative options should govern economic processes if these processes are to improve people's well-being effectively. Menger's use of the concept of 'economic prices' does not mean, as Kirzner (1990b: 102) seems to suppose, that the theoretical model of the consumer-driven economic process only applies to a world in which error is absent. Nor does it mean that the Mengerian approach leads to the conclusion that somebody other than the consumers themselves is better equipped to decide what is good for them. It leads, instead, to the policy issue of how economic processes may be framed by rules and institutions so as to enable consumers to make better informed choices, choices that allow them more effectively to realize their well-informed preferences.

What has to be carefully separated here is, on the one side, the theoretical claim that consumer choices ultimately – though in different economic systems more or less effectively – govern economic processes, and, on the other side, the normative principle that economic processes should be institutionally framed such that the controlling power of informed consumer choices is strengthened. In the broader context of the Mengerian paradigm, the notion of 'economic prices' has to be interpreted as a procedural 'ideal', the informational complement to the ideal of consumer sovereignty, against which real-world economic processes can be judged, and against which proposals for institutional reform may be measured. While it would be clearly inconsistent with the overall thrust of Menger's paradigm to have the problem of error in consumer choice cured by political paternalism, it is perfectly consistent with his vision to assign to political economy the task of investigating into how economic processes may be institutionally framed in order to help consumers to make better informed choices and to have their choices more effectively control the economic process. There is, in other words, clearly a constitutional or *Ordnungspolitik*-dimension implied in the logic of Menger's argument that points to the issue of how suitable institutional framing may help to improve the role that market competition may play as a process of learning and discovery by allowing economic actors to eliminate errors more speedily and at less cost.

In Menger's work the foundations have been laid for a research programme that integrates, in a coherent manner, an explanatory paradigm and a policy paradigm that, together, can be said to constitute the hard core of the Austrian School of Economics, and that can provide guidance for a progressive development of that school. Menger's explanatory paradigm is based on a *methodological individualism* in the sense that it seeks to explain all social and economic phenomena as the resultants of individual human choices and their more or less complex interaction. Though Menger himself has mainly focused on the explanation of what he called 'organic' phenomena – i.e. socio-economic phenomena that emerge spontaneously, and without deliberate coordination, from separate individual choices – it should be obvious that his individualist methodology can be, and should be, equally applied to phenomena of 'pragmatic' origin, i.e. to products of collective choices in their various forms. The latter has been done, to a considerable extent, by modern Public Choice theory as well as by other branches of the New Institutional Economics, and their findings can, in parts, be seen as contributions to a progressive development of the Mengerian explanatory paradigm. Menger's policy paradigm, on the other hand, can be said to be based on a *normative individualism* in the sense that it evaluates socio-economic processes and arrangements in terms of their suitability to promote the interests of the individual actors involved. Though Menger's own application of this policy paradigm has mainly concentrated on the study of market processes and the notion of consumer sovereignty, there is no reason why it could not be interpreted in a more general sense in which it could equally well be applied to the study of collective choice processes, in particular political processes. In such applications the notion of *citizens' sovereignty* could play, for the realm of politics, the same role the notion of consumer sovereignty plays with regard to markets. While the notion of consumer sovereignty points to the issue of how, i.e. by what institutional means, market processes can be made to be more effectively governed by consumer choices, the notion of citizens' sovereignty directs attention to the issue of how well the rules of politics enable citizens to have their preferences govern the political process. A progressive development of the Mengerian research programme should seek not only to develop further the study of the institutional foundations of consumer sovereignty, but also to extend the individualist policy paradigm to the realm of politics and to collective choice processes more generally. Some of the work that has been done in these areas of inquiry, for instance by the Freiburg School of Law and Economics and in constitutional economics, can be counted among the contributions to such development.

VIKTOR J. VANBERG

See also AUSTRIAN SCHOOL OF ECONOMICS AND THE EVOLUTION OF INSTITUTIONS; CONVENTIONS; CONVENTIONS AND TRANSACTION COSTS; HAYEK, FRIEDRICH VON; INVISIBLE HAND EXPLANATIONS; LEGAL PATERNALISM AND EFFICIENCY; SPONTANEOUS ORDER.

Subject classification: 1b(i); 2a(i); 7a.

SELECTED WORKS

1871. *Grundsätze der Volkswirtschaftslehre*. Translated as *Principles of Economics* by J. Dingwall and B.F. Hoselitz with an Introduction by F.A. Hayek, New York and London: New York University Press, 1981.

1883. *Untersuchungen über die Methode der Sozialwissenschaften und der politischen Ökonomie insbesondere*. Translated as *Investigations into the Method of the Social Sciences with Special Reference to Economics* by F.J. Nock, edited by L. Schneider, with a new Introduction by L.H. White, New York and London: New York University Press, 1985.

1884. *Die Irrtümer des Historismus in der deutschen Nationalökonomie*. Reprinted in Carl Menger, *Gesammelte Werke*, Vol. III, 1–98.

1887. *Zur Kritik der politischen Ökonomie*. Reprinted in Carl Menger, *Gesammelte Werke*, Vol. III, 99–131.

1888. *Zur Theorie des Kapitals*. Reprinted in Carl Menger, *Gesammelte Werke*, Vol. III, 133–183.

1889. *Grundzüge einer Klassifikation der Wirtschaftswissenschaften*. Reprinted in Carl Menger, *Gesammelte Werke*, Vol. III, 185–218.

1891. *Die Sozialtheorien der klassischen Nationalökonomie und die moderne Wirtschaftspolitik*. Reprinted in Carl Menger, *Gesammelte Werke*, Vol. III, 219–245.

1892a. *Geld*. Reprinted in Carl Menger, *Gesammelte Werke*, Vol. IV, 1–116.

1892b. On the origin of money. *Economic Journal* 2, 239–55. Reprinted as Monograph Number 40, April 1984 by Committee for Monetary Research and Education, Greenwich, CT.

1923. *Grundsätze der Volkswirtschaftslehre*. Zweite Auflage. (Mit einem Geleitwort von Richard Schüller. Aus dem Nachlass herausgegeben von Karl Menger), Leipzig: G. Freytag; Vienna: Hölder-Pichler-Tempsky.

1968–70. *Gesammelte Werke* (Collected Works), 2nd edition, edited by F.A. Hayek, Tübingen: J.C.B. Mohr (Paul Siebeck). Vol. I: *Grundsätze der Volkswirtschaftslehre*, 1968. Vol. II: *Untersuchung über die Methode der Sozialwissenschaften und der politischen Ökonomie insbesondere*, 1969. Vol. III: *Kleinere Schriften zur Methode und Geschichte der Volkswirtschaftslehre*, 1970. Vol. IV: *Schriften über Geldtheorie und Währungspolitik*, 1970.

BIBLIOGRAPHY

Barnett, M. 1990. The papers of Carl Menger in the Special Collections Department, William R. Perkins Library, Duke University. In Caldwell (ed.): 15–28.

Butos, W.N. 1985. Menger: a suggested interpretation. *Atlantic Economic Journal* 13: 21–30.

Caldwell, B.J. (ed.) 1990. *Carl Menger and his Legacy in Economics*. Annual supplement to volume 22, *History of Political Economy*, Durham and London: Duke University Press.

Hayek, F.A. 1973. *Law, Legislation and Liberty*, Vol. 1. London: Routledge & Kegan Paul.

Hayek, F.A. 1992. Carl Menger (1840–1921). In *The Fortunes of Liberalism, Essays on Austrian Economics and the Ideal of Freedom*, The Collected Works of F.A. Hayek, Vol. IV (Chicago: University of Chicago Press): 61–107.

Hutt, W.H. 1936. *Economists and the Public. A Study of Competition and Opinion*. London: Jonathan Cape. Reprinted New Brunswick, NJ, and London: Transaction Publishers, 1990.

Kirzner, I.M. 1987. Austrian School of Economics. In *The New Palgrave: A Dictionary of Economics*, ed. J. Eatwell, M. Milgate and P. Newman (London: Macmillan) Vol. 1: 145–51.

Kirzner, I.M. 1990a. Carl Menger und die subjektivistische Tradition in der Ökonomie. In *Vademecum zu einem Klassiker der subjektiven Wertlehre und des Marginalismus*, ed. H.C. Recktenwald (Düsseldorf: Verlag Wirtscharg und Finanzen): 61–82.

Kirzner, I.M. 1990b. Menger, classical liberalism, and the Austrian school of economics. In Caldwell (ed.): 93–106.

Kirzner, I.M. 1995. The subjectivism of Austrian economics. In *New Perspectives on Austrian Economics*, ed. G. Meijer (London and New York: Routledge): 11–22.

Raico, R. 1995. The Austrian School and classical liberalism. *Advances in Austrian Economics* 2: 3–38.

Schmoller, G. 1883. Zur Methodologie der Staats- und Sozialwissenschaften. Reprinted (as: Die Schriften von K. Menger und W. Dilthey zur Methodologie der Staats- und Sozial-Wissenschaften) in G. Schmoller, *Zur Literaturgeschichte der Staats- und Sozialwissenschaften*, Leipzig (1888): 275–304.

Schumpeter, J. 1908. Der methodologische Individualismus. In *Das Wesen und der Hauptinhalt der theoretischen Nationalökonomie*, Berlin: Duncker & Humblot, 88–98.

Smith, A. 1776. *An Inquiry into the Nature and Causes of the Wealth of Nations*. 2 vols, Indianapolis: Liberty Classics, 1981.

Streissler, E.W. 1989. Carl Menger (1840–1921). In *Klassiker des ökonomischen Denkens*, ed. J. Starbatty, Zweiter Band (München: C.H. Beck): 119–134.

Streissler, E.W. 1990a. Carl Menger, der deutsche Nationalökonom. In *Studien zur Entwicklung der ökonomischen Theorie X*, ed. B. Schefold, Berlin: Duncker & Humblot, 153–95.

Streissler, E.W. 1990b. The influence of German economics on the work of Menger and Marshall. In B.J. Caldwell (ed.): 31–68.

Streissler, E.W. and M. Streissler (eds.) 1994. *Carl Menger's Lectures to Crown Prince Rudolf of Austria*. Aldershot: Edward Elgar.

Vanberg, V.J. 1994. Carl Menger's evolutionary and John R. Common's collective action approach to institutions: a comparison. In V.J. Vanberg, *Rules and Choice in Economics* (London and New York: Routledge): 144–163.

Vaughn, K.I. 1987. Menger, Carl (1840–1921). In *The New Palgrave: A Dictionary of Economics*, ed. J. Eatwell, J. Eatwell, M. Milgate and P. Newman (London: Macmillan), Vol. 3: 438–44.

Wagner, R.E. et al. 1978. Carl Menger and Austrian economics. *Atlantic Economic Journal* 6 (3), September, Special Issue. Contributions by R.E. Wagner, S. Bostaph, L.S. Moss, I. Kirzner, H.N. Gram and V.C. Walsh, L.M. Lachmann and K.I. Vaughn.

Wieser, F. von. 1923. Karl Menger. In *Neue österreichische Biographie*. Abt. 1 (Wien: Amalthea Verlag): 84–92

Zuckerkandl, R. 1927. Carl Menger. In *Deutsches biographisches Jahrbuch*, Vol. 3 (Stuttgart: Deutsche verlags-anstalt Stuttgart): 192–200.

mergers. *See* HORIZONTAL MERGERS; VERTICAL MERGERS AND MONOPOLY LEVERAGE.

minimum wage regulation. When workers who devote most of their energies to the service of their employers are nevertheless found to be living in poverty, there is a strong legislative urge to do something about it. The obvious thing to do is to require employers to pay a 'living wage'. Such legislation has now been in force in various countries for over a hundred years, and economists have been discussing the issue much longer than that. While recognizing the alleviation of poverty as a primary goal of policy, economists have almost uniformly opposed minimum wage legislation, at least until very recently. To some extent, this opposition reflects the division of labour. John Stuart Mill (1848) remarked on the many minimum wage plans current in his time, and went on to describe, at some length, the adverse consequences of such plans. As Marshall (1897) put it, '. . . there is popularity in the doctrine of a living wage; so we had better leave politicians to praise it and set ourselves to criticize it.' More recently, the attempt by Card and Krueger (1995) to debunk the conventional economic wisdom on minimum wages has again generated much popular support, and much criticism by other economists.

EMPLOYMENT EFFECTS. The main economic objection to minimum wage laws is that some workers will lose their jobs. As a theoretical proposition, this is easily demonstrated, under general conditions. Consider a profit-maximizing employer paying n^* workers the minimum wage m, and making (maximal) profits π. Suppose the minimum wage rises to M (with no effect on other prices, or on the demand for the employer's product). If this increase is granted, and nothing else changes, profits fall by $n^*(M-m)$. Let N^* be the number of workers employed after all profit-maximizing adjustments have been made, and note that the new profit level must be at least $\pi-n^*(M-m)$. Now consider what would happen if the wage is restored to its old level: starting from $\pi-n^*(M-m)$, the employer's profit rises by $N^*(M-m)$. But if N^* is above n^*, the profit would then be higher than its original level, contradicting the assumption that profit was maximal to begin with. So N^* cannot be above n^*, and if the employer has any way to partially offset wage increases through adjustments in production methods, N^* must be strictly below n^*. This argument has nothing to do with the details of the firm's operations, nor with whether the firm has some monopoly power. The only assumption (beyond profit maximization) is that if N^* workers are available at the higher wage, then they are also available at the lower wage, so the result fails if the employer can only attract more workers by paying higher wages, that is, if the employer has some monopsony power.

The argument that a monopsony might find it profitable to increase employment in response to minimum wage regulation is exactly analogous to the argument that a monopoly might find it profitable to increase output in response to maximum price regulation. Let m now represent a wage freely chosen by a monopsony employer to maximize profit, where the profit-maximizing employment level n^* is the total number of workers available at the wage m. Suppose that a minimum wage level M is set slightly above m (so that the difference $\delta = M-m$ is small), with N^*-n^* extra workers available at the higher wage. Observe that before the minimum wage law, the employer did not find it profitable to increase the payroll by the amount MN^*-mn^*, in order to gain the extra revenue resulting from the addition of N^*-n^* workers. But this must have been a close call, because the employer did find it profitable to increase employment up to n^*, and since δ is small, the difference N^*-n^* must also be small, assuming that the number of workers available responds smoothly to increases in the wage offered. Now after the wage M is imposed, the employer is forced to increase the payroll by Mn^*-mn^*, with no offsetting increase in revenue, and must then consider whether a further payroll increase of MN^*-Mn^* is worth the gain in revenue generated by N^*-n^* extra workers. The answer to this must be yes, given that the employer was on the margin of hiring the extra workers anyway, when it would have been more expensive to do so. It follows that a minimum wage set slightly above the level that was freely chosen by the employer must necessarily increase employment. Further increases in the minimum must eventually cause employment to decline, however, since beyond some point the number of workers available is more than the employer wishes to hire, and the situation is then as it was in the first case discussed above, so the same analysis applies. Thus, as Stigler (1946) pointed out, even if monopsony is the relevant case, a national minimum wage cannot be imposed without fear of employment losses, because the appropriate wage level will vary from one employer to the next.

POVERTY. If the purpose of the minimum wage is to ensure that workers can achieve a decent standard of living, then, as Mill (1848) stressed, some provision has to be made for those who are laid off when the minimum constraint binds. There is then the familiar tension between alleviating poverty and providing incentives to work. If those who are laid off are covered by a welfare system that guarantees a minimum standard of living, then there is no incentive to work unless the minimum wage is substantially above this level. On the other hand, if the minimum is set high enough to provide an incentive to work, then some jobs that were initially viable will be eliminated for no good reason, which is clearly wasteful. This problem is endemic in all schemes designed to alleviate poverty, and the wasteful effects of minimum wage regulation should be judged in relation to the alternatives. In this context Stigler (1946) advocated a negative income tax as the best alternative.

There are several reasons to favour other means of reducing poverty. First, if the objective is to provide a decent living standard for each household, then it is unnecessary to intervene in a situation where the sub-standard earnings of one household member are offset by the high earnings of other members. Second, it is a mistake to think that all workers found to be earning less than a living wage at a point in time are trapped in poverty: most low-wage workers move on to higher-paying jobs.

LEGISLATION. By far the best-known example of minimum wage legislation is the US Fair Labor Standards Act of 1938. This was preceded in the US by more limited legislation at the state level (setting minimum wages for women and minors only), beginning in Massachusetts in

1912, and in eight other states in 1913 (see US Department of Labor 1915a). The early US legislation was partly stimulated by the living wage movement in New Zealand and in Australia, which led to the New Zealand Industrial Conciliation and Arbitration Act of 1894, and the Factories and Shops Act of 1896 in Victoria. While the stated purpose of the New Zealand legislation was the peaceful settlement (through arbitration) of wage disputes that might otherwise lead to strikes or lockouts, the Victoria measure established wage boards empowered to raise wages in a few 'sweated' trades. Within a few years, the wage board system spread throughout Australia and New Zealand, with more and more trades being covered, and a similar system was established in Great Britain by the Trade Boards Act of 1909.

Prior to the passage of the State minimum wage laws in the US in 1913, there were extensive feasibility studies by various *ad hoc* Commissions. These studies drew on a massive report by the US Bureau of Labor, authorized by an act of Congress in 1907, detailing (in 19 volumes covering about 1,200 pages) the conditions of employment of women and children (see US Department of Labor 1915b). The quality of the data on women's wages is remarkable: for example, the Massachusetts commission in 1911 collected individual wage schedules for 6,900 people, and supplemented this with wage data from the Bureau of Labor study for some 8,000 women.

One result of particular importance from these investigations was that wages were found to vary greatly from one establishment to another, for no apparent reason. For example, the Bureau of Labor study tabulated women's wages in 13 establishments in the glass industry, and found that for four distinct categories of relatively unskilled work, the wage paid by the establishment at the top of the distribution was twice the wage paid at the bottom. The conclusion drawn from this was that if one establishment can pay high wages and compete successfully with others paying low wages, there should be little reason to fear that minimum wage laws would cause workers to lose their jobs. Indeed, this kind of evidence seriously undermines the theoretical argument for employment losses given earlier, since it appears from the data that employers do not take the wage as given, as the theory supposes. There is no suggestion that monopsony is the source of these wage variations; the interpretation is rather that some employers are not managing their businesses efficiently, or that they are making excessive profits at the expense of their workers. Whatever the reason, the finding of large unexplained wage variations is characteristic of many field studies of labour markets, and it is echoed in studies of wage variation across industries, such as Krueger and Summers (1988).

The US Fair Labor Standards Act of 1938 largely resolved the long series of political and legal struggles over state minimum wage laws (see Grossman 1978 for an accessible summary of the legislative history of this Act). Amendments have subsequently expanded the coverage of the Act, and the minimum wage has been raised 19 times since it was originally set at 25 cents an hour in 1938; the most recent amendment, passed in August 1996, raised the minimum to $5.15 in September 1997. Yet the struggle continues: the amendments have been preceded by long series of Congressional hearings, sometimes extending over several Congresses, and often calling forth passionate testimony on both sides.

EVIDENCE ON EMPLOYMENT EFFECTS. The bulk of the evidence on the effects of minimum wages is concerned with the effects of the Fair Labor Standards Act, as amended. Figure 1 shows the monthly history of the real minimum wage (deflated by the Consumer Price Index), in relation to real average hourly earnings of production workers in manufacturing. The vertical lines show the months in which increases in the nominal minimum were implemented, and the downward drift between each pair of lines shows the declining value of a dollar. One might expect to find that each jump in the minimum would be accompanied by a reduction in employment, particularly for workers employed in low-wage jobs, such as teenagers, or workers in retail industries. Brown, Gilroy and Kohen (1982) surveyed many regression studies using time-series data to test this hypothesis, leading to the conclusion that 'In summary, our survey indicates a reduction of between one and three percent in teenage employment as a result of a 10 percent increase in the federal minimum wage.' But as Card and Krueger (1995) pointed out, these are fragile results that are unlikely to convince those who are sceptical about the practical relevance of economic theory.

One reason why it is difficult to find evidence on the employment effects of minimum wages is that there are many ways to circumvent the effect of an apparently binding minimum wage, even if we ignore the real problem of outright noncompliance. A simple example is the trade-off between wages and fringe benefits: if the minimum is increased, benefits can be cut. Employers also spend money to make the workplace more pleasant, or give discounts on goods and services, or adopt flexible rules on work scheduling, and so forth. These things are easily adjusted, especially in the long run, and from the worker's point of view, they just transfer money from one pocket to another. If a minimum wage regulation merely changes the composition of the worker's pay packet, it should not have any effect on the employment decision.

Another reason for the lack of strong empirical evidence on employment effects is that, as Figure 1 suggests, the minimum wage has never been high enough to affect more than a small minority of workers, and these are the very workers whose employment patterns are most volatile in any case, so the signal to noise ratio in any time-series study is not favourable. Moreover, although the minimum wage series depicted in Figure 1 has about 700 observations, the amount of relevant information in this series is effectively the number of times the minimum was increased by a substantial amount, and the increase was not quickly erased by inflation.

The most recent innovation in the empirical analysis of minimum wage effects is the work of Katz and Krueger (1992) and of Card and Krueger (1995), using original survey data to examine the effects of changes in state minimum wage laws on fast food restaurants in Texas and New Jersey. This research returns to the painstaking methods of the older Bureau of Labor Statistics studies (although the authors of the older studies had many more

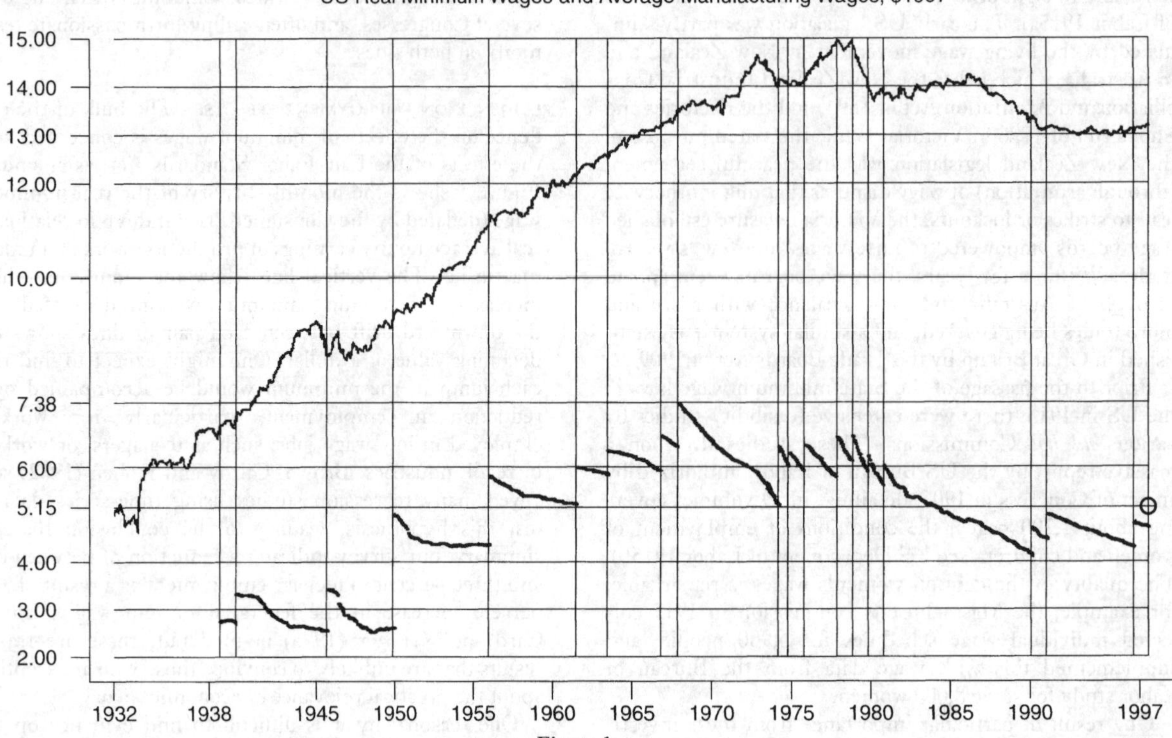

Figure 1

Source

The figure shows a real wage and a real minimum wage. In each case the deflator is the CPI, for which the source is as follows: Consumer Price Index – Urban Wage Earners and Clerical Workers; Series ID: CWUR0000SA0; US City average; not seasonally adjusted; Base Period: 1982–84 = 100; http://stats.bls.gov/top20.html#CPI

The wage series is: Average hourly earnings of production or nonsupervisory workers, seasonally adjusted; Manufacturing; Series ID: EES30000006; http://stats.bls.gov/cesbtabs.htm

The minimum wage can be found at: http://www.dol.gov/dol/esa/public/minwage/chart.htm

research workers at their disposal). The most controversial finding was that when New Jersey raised the minimum wage to $5.05 in 1992, while the minimum in neighbouring Pennsylvania remained at the Federal level of $4.25, employment appeared actually to *increase* in New Jersey relative to Pennsylvania, after the change took effect. As discussed in Kennan (1995), this result becomes less impressive when it is recognized that the relative increase in employment resulted not from an increase in New Jersey, where the minimum wage had increased, but rather from a decrease in Pennsylvania, where nothing had apparently changed. Without tracing the source of the decrease in Pennsylvania, it is difficult to have confidence that the same decrease would have occurred in New Jersey if the minimum wage law had not been put into effect.

As is illustrated by the remarkable reaction to the work of Card and Krueger (1995), the political economy of minimum wages is at least as vital now as it was in John Stuart Mill's time, even though the economic importance of this kind of regulation does not seem large, after a century of experience.

JOHN KENNAN

See also ARBITRATION; ASSET RESTRUCTURING AND UNION BARGAINING; DISCRIMINATION IN EMPLOYMENT; EMPLOYEE OWNERSHIP OF FIRMS; EMPLOYMENT CONTRACT LAW; JUST PRICE; REGULATION AND DEREGULATION; RENT CONTROL.

Subject classification: 6c(v).

BIBLIOGRAPHY

Brown, C., Gilroy, C. and Kohen, A. 1982. The effect of the minimum wage law on employment and unemployment. *Journal of Economic Literature* 20: 487–528.

Card, D. and Krueger, A. 1995. *Myth and Measurement: The New Economics of the Minimum Wage*. Princeton: Princeton University Press.

Grossman, J. 1978. Fair labour standards act of 1938: maximum struggle for a minimum wage. *Monthly Labour Review*, v. 101 no.6 June: 22–30. *http://www.dol.gov/dol/esa/public/minwage/history.htm.*

Katz, L. and Krueger, A. 1992. The effect of the minimum wage on the fast-food industry. *Industrial and Labour Relations Review* 46: 6–21.

Kennan, J. 1995. The elusive effects of minimum wages. *Journal of Economic Literature* 33: 1950–65.

Krueger, A.B. and Summers, L.H. 1988. Efficiency wages and the inter-industry wage structure. *Econometrica* 56: 259–93.

Marshall, A. 1897. The old generation of economists and the new. *Quarterly Journal of Economics* 11: 115–35.

Mill, J.S. 1848. *Principles of Political Economy*. New York: Co-operative Publication Society; revised edn, 1900.

Stigler, G. 1946. The economics of minimum wage legislation. *American Economic Review* 36: 358–65.

US Department of Labor. 1915a. *Minimum Wage Legislation in the United States and Foreign Countries*. Bureau of Labor Statistics, Bulletin 167. Washington, DC: Government Printing Office.

US Department of Labor. 1915b. *Summary of the Report on Condition of Woman and Child Wage Earners in the United States*. Bureau of Labor Statistics, Bulletin 175. Washington, DC: Government Printing Office.

mistakes in contracts. *See* BREACH REMEDIES; INCOMPLETE CONTRACTS.

mitigation of damages. *See* IMPOSSIBILITY DOCTRINE IN CONTRACT LAW; LAST CLEAR CHANCE; SPECIFIC PERFORMANCE.

modern contractarianism. Contractarianism is the political philosophy that government is or ought to be created or empowered in some sense by the consent of the citizens, who agree to cooperate in certain ways to enable the government. There are many variant visions of just what level of agreement is required. It can range from actual to tacit to hypothetical to, most recently, so-called reasonable agreement. David Hume (1748) famously ridiculed the doctrine of contractarianism by pointing out that no then-extant state had been created by agreement and that yet many of them seemed, in some plausible sense, morally acceptable.

No leading contractarian today holds that there must be actual agreement. The focus of contemporary contractarians is on what citizens, under certain, sometimes quite abstract, circumstances, would supposedly consent to or ought, either rationally or morally, to consent to. Interpretation of these abstract circumstances to bring them down to ground enough to allow criticism or judgment of actual states is commonly beyond the enterprise of contractarian philosophy. Thomas Hobbes (1651) argued that citizens ought rationally comply, in their own self interest, with an extant state, even a relatively harsh state. Succeeding generations of contractarians have generally abandoned this rational criterion and have grounded their arguments in moral claims or in metaphysical, as opposed to self-interest, claims of what is rational.

The urgency of the focus on consent seems, except in Hobbes, to depend on finding a ground for making citizens obligated to obey government within certain limits. For Hobbes it was sufficient to oblige citizens with the threat of coercion. However, he often used the word obligation when his modern sense was to be obliged by force. Indeed, he said there are 'two species of Natural obligation': being obligated to submit to laws of physics and to fear of the stronger (Hobbes [1642] 1983: ch. 15, ¶7). Such slippage in the meaning of obligation has been a frequent problem in political analysis, especially in contractarian theory. In particular, scholars often moralize Hobbes's contractarian arguments.

The move to grounding obedience in normative obligation that is derived from consent is the familiar moral move of grounding an obligation to fulfil a promise in the fact of one's having consensually promised. What is at issue in promise keeping is usually an exchange (see generally, Hardin 1988). I promise to do something for you in return for your first doing something for me. There is less agreement, and a ridiculously large philosophical literature, on the strength of the obligation, if any, to fulfil a gratuitous promise, such as the notorious deathbed promise, especially if the person who has been promised something has incurred no costs in anticipation of fulfillment. In the law of some nations, gratuitous promises are not legally enforceable. In political contractarianism, however, the structure of the consent or the promise is potentially confused. Do I promise my government to obey? Or do I promise my fellow citizens? If government is not a moral agent analogous to a person, then the bite of the promise must depend on its being a promise to my fellow citizens. What then do my fellow citizens exchange with me? Their own forbearance in obedience to our government.

For Hobbes, our coordination on our government gives it the power to maintain order in our interest. Hence, he has no need of consent. John Locke (1690) argued that anyone who accepts benefits from the state has tacitly agreed to its rule. This view seems grossly simplistic. For example, it seems to entail that the trapped slave who accepts the benefit of police protection therefore agrees to the regime that supports slavery. Many contemporary writers evidently hold that hypothetical consent, but not tacit consent, is morally compelling: If I would have agreed, I can be treated as though I actually did agree. However, the emphasis in contemporary political philosophy is not on the obligation of citizens to obey but rather on the justification of a political order. For such justification, the philosopher Thomas Scanlon (1982) argues that agreement need merely be reasonable, that one must accept a government that one could not reasonably reject. Unfortunately, this move seems merely to shift the burden of understanding from 'agreement' to 'reasonable' and plausibly to undercut the original point of contractarianism. Instead of grounding obligation to obey government in consent we ground it in what the philosopher asserts it would have been reasonable to agree to.

The normative doctrine of contractarianism apparently has a very strange pedigree. It came into vogue with the death of theological grounds for claiming citizens must behave in certain ways. One might call theological politics a matter of obligation to god or an obligation to follow god's will. But, given the power of god to demolish those who disobey, this sounds rather more like being obliged by force than like being obligated by the rightness of god's demands. Hence, the duty of obeisance to government under theological accounts was a matter of the citizen-believer's self interest. With god no longer in the theory of the state, the problem of invoking a duty of obeisance became acute. One solution to that problem was simply to suppose citizens actually have a moral duty that they themselves voluntarily take on through agreement, essentially through contracting. This was a very odd move. It translated the self-interest notion of political duty under theological theories to a purely normative notion of moral obligation.

This move left a major difficulty in political theory: How do we explain actual behaviour of citizens if their only incentive for obeisance is the normative incentive of having promised to do what, in the event, often turns out to be against their interests? Under god's indirect rule, at least in many theories, interest and obeisance were perfectly coordinated. Under normative consent theories, they often are contrary. This grievous difficulty has never been overcome in any contractarian theory. There are essentially three moves that have commonly been made to address the apparent difficulty. One of these is simply to assert that obeisance to the state is a normative matter, that it is simply right. This move runs against the grim fact that obeisance to many states cannot plausibly have been good and cannot plausibly therefore be right. Hence, we require specific argument for why this particular state merits obeisance.

The second move is the quasi-logical move of Kantians and others to assert that, among other things, failing to keep a promise is inconsistent and incoherent. This transcendental move simply makes no sense to many theorists but seems compelling to others.

Finally, it is supposed by John Rawls and others that humans in a just society will become just, so that such a society will actually be supported by moral motivations. There might be difficulties in making the transition to such a just society but, if Rawls's psychological argument is roughly right, there is no incoherence in supposing there could be one at least in principle.

THE BACKGROUND: HOBBES, LOCKE, ROUSSEAU, KANT. Although there were forerunners, the most important early contractarian was Hobbes. In *Leviathan* (1651) he proposed that there are two ways that government could be created to resolve the problem of social order in a particular community. That problem is acute because, in the so-called state of nature, Hobbes supposed life without government must be nasty, brutish, and short. Each person would independently attempt to defend against attacks from others by, often, attacking pre-emptively. This would be true even if most people were not vicious and were not inclined to steal from others. Hobbes supposed that most people are essentially self-seeking and centrally concerned with their own welfare. Hence, he posed solutions to the problem of disorder that depend on the rational, self-interested actions of people.

Order among such people could come about in two ways. First, members of an anarchic community could agree with each other to establish government as if by contract. Hobbes was writing before the heyday of contract law, but modern readers commonly interpret his argument as an analogue of the self-interested signing of a contract of exchange. And second, an extant government of some other power or a usurper could impose order. Hobbes called these two resolutions government by institution and by imposition, respectively. The actual problem that motivated him was the turmoil and disorder of the mid-seventeenth-century England in which he lived. For that problem his actual complaint was that deliberately attacking an extant government was self-destructive because it could lead to the collapse of that government and hence to disorder, under which virtually all would suffer great losses.

It is clear that the central problem for Hobbes was that order be established and maintained. He did not expect to achieve that with moral commitments but only with rational incentives for obedient behaviour. What was needed, he therefore thought, was merely coordination on a powerful sovereign or government that could be relied upon to suppress disorderly activities. In the absence of the threat of disorder and theft, individuals could then go on to prosper in their own ways. Oddly, although he is commonly regarded as a, or even the, major contract theorist, contract was at most only a device for reaching coordination on a sovereign and it was not the only device. Indeed, Hobbes himself thought it might never actually have been used. Yet he nevertheless thought that the extant, non-contractarian governments of the world, which at some point in their histories had been imposed rather than contractually established, were governments that should generally be obeyed.

Locke (1690) had a more sanguine vision of the state of nature as a time in which people could come together and agree on a government. Moreover, he was more inclined than Hobbes to argue as though there really had been such an agreement. (He was presumably the main object of Hume's [1748] criticism of contract theorists.) But he saw clearly that there is still a problem of the consent of later generations who were not parties to any supposed past contract. He resolved this problem with his doctrine of tacit consent from accepting advantages from a government. His vision seems clearly to be one of moral, and not only rationally self-interested, commitment to obey government. That moral vision has arguably dominated contract thinking since his time. That is a somewhat odd twist on later visions of contract in the law, which is often seen as rationally rather than morally grounded. Worse, it raises the problem that it does not likely motivate many people in actual states. It seems therefore to ground state policies to coerce those who do disobey. For a theory whose proponents often claim grounding in a vision of autonomous free agents, this is a disconcerting twist.

If Locke saw clearly the problem of the obligations of future generations to a contract they did not sign, as though you and I were obligated for the contractual debts of our distant forebears, Jean-Jacques Rousseau (1762) saw, with Hume, the implausibility that any real society of any complexity could have unanimously agreed to a government. Because he nevertheless wanted to motivate obedience to the state with the moral obligation to live up to one's consent, he invented the notion of the General Will. Even many of those who are ardent exponents of Rousseau's thought have difficulty putting this notion into simple, comprehensible words. It is about the abstract idea that we do want order. The order Rousseau wanted clearly goes beyond Hobbes's relatively minimal demand for order to include strong positive commitments to the community.

On such a notion, Rousseau supposed, we could unanimously agree. Thereafter, we could make specific decisions with less than unanimity. Locke similarly saw the need for unanimity in his moral vision. But he restricted the demand to the stage of agreeing to reach a decision on the form of government. That is, we have to agree to enter a room together in order then to design a government. But once in the room, we can vote by majority rule on actual elements of the design. Rousseau seems to have demanded much more than this, but it is very hard to say just what he wanted.

Immanuel Kant (1785) resolved this problem in Rousseau's vision with his so-called transcendental argument about what any rational agent could will. Kant supposed that the moral law could only be grounded in principles that any rational agent could will to be universal laws in the sense that they would apply to all rational agents equally. Hence, I could not will a law that would make an exception for me. He supposed further that all rational agents would reach the same conclusions about whether any proposed principle could be a moral law. If this were true, then we could plausibly come together and will at least the elements of the principles that would underlie a morally acceptable government. Hence, we could contract on the uniquely correct form of government. That government would be republican in the sense that it would represent us all. It would not, however, be democratic because a merely democratic government could allow a majority to legislate against a minority. It could therefore be a government of interests and not a government of right.

Both Rousseau's and Kant's contractarian arguments might seem to ignore a problem that becomes immediately clear in a strategic or game theoretic understanding of the problem of contracting for social order. We could all agree in the abstract that we do want order. But it does not follow that we could ever agree on the form that the order would take. Hobbes saw this grievous difficulty in his contractarian account but could ignore it as irrelevant in his account of why we should not rebel against any established government. We should not rebel for the simple reason that the costs to us of moving to a form of government more beneficial to us would outweigh the gains we would get from the change. This is, of course, a social scientific and not a merely logical or conceptual claim and it might well be false in many instances, as for example in Czechoslovakia in 1989. It seems also to have been arguably true in some instances, as for example in the US civil war. A Kantian account could perhaps escape this difficulty if it were true that there is only one rationally determinable best form of government. But this seems to be utterly implausible. Indeed, contingent considerations generally seem to argue against a purely rationalist resolution of the problem of social order.

CONSENT. The moral core of contractarian arguments is that we obligate ourselves by consent or that our order is justified by consent. Consider how this core fits with the various notions of consent in which contractarian theories have been grounded: actual, tacit, and hypothetical consent. Let us first address actual and tacit consent and then turn in the next section to hypothetical consent, especially in its contemporary variants. It is the failure or implausibility of arguments from actual and tacit consent that sets up the contemporary arguments.

A commonplace claim is that there have been some cases of very nearly genuine contractual agreement on social order when peoples have, through representatives, written and adopted constitutions. If this were true, then we could suppose that even actual-agreement contractarianism has a field of play. The outstanding early case of such a supposed social contract is the US constitution of 1787–88. The adoption of that constitution, however, lacked the essential features of a contractual agreement (Hardin, forthcoming). First, perhaps most obviously, it lacked an external enforcement agency so that it was binding, if at all, only morally or from endogenous constraints. Second, it also lacked the unanimous consent of an ordinary contract. Some state conventions voted only narrowly for it and two states at first voted against it. Prior to that, some states and some important interests were represented not at all or only briefly or poorly at the constitutional convention. Slaves and women were not represented at all; small farmers were represented if at all only indirectly, although they were the great bulk of the white male population; and the eventual anti-Federalists were poorly represented because many of them refused to attend or stay at a convention with an apparently illegal purpose. Both the Philadelphia constitutional and the subsequent state ratifying conventions were meetings of the elite. Hobbes (1651: 203) asserted, and most writers on promise-keeping would agree, that 'no man is obliged by a covenant of which he was not the author'. Third, it set up future changes in the relations between the citizens who were party to it, changes that would not require even the degree of consent that adoption of the constitution itself required. Moreover, it continues to constrain generations who never agreed to it.

The most critical difference between that constitutional experience and an ordinary contract is that the actual problem of the creation of a new government lacked the strategic structure of such a contract. An ordinary contract governs an exchange. I do something for you – I build you a house – in return for your doing something for me – you pay me. It would, of course, be in my interest to have you do your something for me while I do nothing for you so that I walk away with your payment without having the burden of building your house. In the constitution of 1787–88, however, the people of New York who favoured the constitution could not have said it was their interest to have the people of Virginia adopt the constitution while they did not. The constitutional order could be of value to either only if both coordinated on it. The value of the constitution came from enabling Virginians, New Yorkers, and others to trade more easily, to interdict beggar-thy-neighbour foreign trade policies, and to defend themselves against foreign attack. The constitution resolved a massive problem of coordination on order for such purposes. It enabled the future resolution of countless exchanges by setting up an enforcer – government – that was external to the exchanges. But it was not an act of exchange itself.

An implication of its being a coordination rather than a contract is that the enforcement of the constitutional order could readily be endogenous – it would not require an external enforcing agency. We follow the constitutional order because the costs of recoordinating on an alternative make it not our interest to recoordinate. This might follow even when the new coordination would be substantially superior to the one it replaced. This is a very grand and complex instance of the general nature of coordination. But it has the central features of simpler coordination problems. For example, the convention that we all drive on the right or that we all drive on the left coordinates us all to our mutual advantage. Olaf Palme decided that Sweden's convention of driving on the left was too costly because it meant accidents on the open road with, especially, German tourists who were accustomed to the opposite convention. At substantial cost, the Swedish government changed its driving convention in 1967 (Hardin 1988). There was a similar concern in the United Kingdom, but there the costs of a recoordination seemed plausibly to outweigh the benefits of making it. Within either convention, however, there is little need for an external enforcing agency. Drivers are compelled by the coordination itself to follow the convention in their own interest. Enforcement of acquiescence is endogenous to the system.

One response to these seemingly non-contractarian aspects of the US constitution is the claim that contract simply does not mean what it once did in the early contract tradition, and modern contracts are often like constitutions. Unfortunately, this response guts any claim that I am morally bound to the constitutional order because I consented to it or that the order is justified by my consent.

Alternatively, it can be argued, as Locke already did argue, that I have tacitly consented to that order by taking advantage of the benefits it offers me. This is an odd claim. It seems to imply that even the revolutionary who detests and wishes to destroy the constitutional order but who, on the way to doing that, must use weapons created under that order is morally bound to comply with the order. Hence, actual agreement and tacit agreement are implausible candidates for moralizing social order under a supposed social contract.

The crux of our problem is the moral nature of consent. We might suppose that consent is itself right-making, or we might suppose consent is merely an indicator of what it would be right or good to do. If we have the latter view, we might go further and suppose consent is morally binding: I morally must do what I have consented to do. Recent contractarians reject actual-agreement and tacit-agreement contractarianism. They want it to be true in some sense that what we would consent to under certain circumstances is right. The phrase 'under certain circumstances' suggests, rightly, that their concern is with hypothetical agreement. They also sometimes seem to want to hold that our consent binds us, although it is unclear why there is any further need for binding us morally in those theories in which we are already rationally bound. Turn then to the complex contemporary views.

CONTEMPORARY CONTRACTARIANS: RAWLS, BUCHANAN, SCANLON. A striking difference between the Hobbesian and Lockean views is the following. Hobbes supposed that moral obligations of many social kinds, such as the obligation to abide by ordinary contracts, is derivative from the prior existence of a powerful sovereign who can enforce such obligations. Locke implicitly supposed on the contrary that morality is prior to politics and that we can derive the moral status of a government from the prior morality of consent to it. For Locke, it would be wrong to break a promise even in the state of nature. For Hobbes, nothing is wrong in the state of nature if it conduces to survival. It is an odd quality of most contemporary contractarian thinking that it follows Locke in this respect. Much of it does so, however, not so clearly from Locke's influence as perhaps from Kant's (1785). (Contemporary contractarianism therefore has a metaphysical ring to it that irritates many of its critics, although the contractarians themselves are often irritated in turn by the accusation that they practise dreaded metaphysics.)

Buchanan (1975) argues that, in constitutional debate, we must reach unanimous agreement on principles for government. Hence, we start from here and now. That is to say, everything is not up for reconsideration *de novo*. The current distribution of property constrains what can be done hereafter to the extent that constitutionally determined expropriation would not receive unanimous consent. This makes Buchanan the theorist who is nearest to being an actual-agreement contractarian, although he writes of hypothetical agreement.

Rawls (1971) argues that we should seek principles of justice that a representative person could agree to from behind a veil of ignorance. That is to say, we should seek principles that we think are generally compelling independently of who we are, and not principles that would contingently happen to serve particular interests. Hence, Rawls can be said to be a hypothetical-agreement contractarian. However, there is an odd quality to his position that seems very uncontractarian. One person alone, a representative person, should be able to decide on the principles of justice for our society. If this is true, then presumably just any such person would reach the same conclusion on what those principles should be. And indeed, Rawls proposes what those principles are. But if this is possible, then the principles sound suspiciously rationalist. They are deducible from more or less pure reason, as Kant's moral principles are. Agreement with them is more nearly like agreement with laws of physics than like the kind of agreement we might make on some mutual accommodation. After being criticized on this point, Rawls (1985) came to defend his views with specific reference to Kant's rationalist theory, although he also has strongly defended his vision against dismissive claims that it is metaphysical.

Against Rawls's argument from behind the veil, or from what he calls the original position, which is partly defined by ignorance, note that John Harsanyi (1955) had argued nearly two decades before Rawls that we should establish social and moral principles from a supposition of individuals' ignorance of the advantages that would flow specifically to them from our chosen rules. His conclusion was that we would choose strictly utilitarian distributional principles because under these our expected individual benefits would be maximized. Rawls blocks this conclusion by stipulating an unusually strong principle of risk aversion that many scholars find objectionable and even perverse. Even with his principle of risk aversion, however, Rawls's derivation seems likely to permit a somewhat distorted utilitarian maximization, although this is a hotly contested claim. Rawls's defence of his principle of fairness, on which his theory is based, depends heavily on his assumption of risk aversion. It seems likely that any effort to obtain principles of social justice from rationalist deduction must start from strong constraining assumptions, for example, either of Rawls's risk aversion or of Harsanyi's risk neutrality. Otherwise, we cannot adequately narrow the range of principles from which we wish to choose. They must seemingly be narrowed to a set that includes only one, unique, principle. But this means that our initial assumptions, which are themselves in no sense contractarian, heavily determine our contractarian conclusions.

Scanlon (1982) in essence addresses this problem of a purely rationalist deduction. He allows what might be a substantial multiplicity of principles or of distributions. Rather than stipulate what our principle must be, he stipulates that it must be one which we could not reasonably reject. This definition packs, of course, a lot of its concern into the notion of reasonable. Presumably, a fairly wide array of principles could be reasonable. If we actually have a social order that meets Scanlon's criterion of reasonableness, then it follows that we should not attempt to change it to meet another order that also meets the criterion. Hence, Scanlon's reasonableness is a more restrictive variant of Hobbes's conclusion that we should support any government that successfully maintains order. If our social order does not meet Scanlon's criterion, the criterion yields some constraint on what reforms we could seek, but it might not restrict our choices enough to make consensus possible. Hobbes thought that three quite different forms of government could be rationally supportable: monarchy, oligarchy, and democracy. But he also thought monarchy best, so that, if we were without government, we should plump for monarchy. His preference for monarchy turned, of course, on social scientific claims, not on analytical or normative claims, although he stated is as though it were a conceptual matter. Scanlon's reasonableness might yield no definitive conclusion without also invoking social scientific claims to narrow our range of choice.

MOTIVATING MORAL PRINCIPLES. Most of the contractarians, classical and contemporary, have been driven by one of two main motivating moral principles: mutual advantage and fairness. The theories of Hobbes and Locke seem straightforwardly to be driven by a concern with mutual advantage. Hobbes openly stated this concern, although he granted that some individuals, such as religious fanatics and glory seeking aristocrats, might not see any advantage for themselves in an orderly society. Locke's concern with consent captures his concern with mutual advantage. One might read Rousseau as also concerned with mutual advantage. But it would be difficult to read Kant's contractarianism as essentially responsive to mutual advantage even though it might suggest an order that would be mutually advantageous. One might claim that his concern is some version of fairness, although it is not easy to articulate such a principle in his terms. Among contemporary contractarians, Buchanan is most emphatically concerned with mutual advantage. In his view, we start from here and we improve things for everyone – or at least we do not harm anyone.

Rawls greatly complicates the notion of distributive justice by grounding it in an odd combination of mutual advantage and fairness. Pure fairness might seem to require equality of distribution. What we distribute is, of course, what we have first produced plus whatever might be available to us without effort. But suppose we could produce so much more by distributing unequally that we could then make everyone, including those who would be worst off, better off than anyone would be under the perfectly equal distribution. As a rule, most modern economists suppose this to be the nature of our problem of production and Rawls grants that they might be right. He supposes that a rational person behind the veil would choose to be better off at the cost of some inequality rather than to be worse off in a state of equality. He therefore allows inequalities that make the worst off class of citizens best off. This is his difference principle. One might conclude, with typical economists, that distributive justice (taken as equality) trades off with productive efficiency. Rawls supposes, however, that distributive justice includes both concerns, equality and efficiency, and that the trade off between them is internal to the conception of distributive justice.

It is a distinguishing central insight of Rawls that fairness cannot stand alone as a theory of the good or the right because it is fully consistent with egalitarian misery. Hence, inequality that produces greater overall welfare can trump pure equality. Those who dislike this assertion sometimes argue against it with an implicit dismissal of the possibility that inequality could have this effect or with claims that all we need is to correct aberrant psychologies to get people to produce for the general good rather than merely for selfish benefit.

In his theory, Rawls is concerned with fairness of an odd kind. Fairness in the allocation of the joint social product is at issue just because that product is joint. I might claim to 'deserve' a fair part of it because I contributed to its production. If market wages and profits really mirrored contributions, allocation according to desert would reduce to little more than what markets do. Rawls clearly thinks market wages and profits do not mirror contributions. We cannot causally relate your effort strictly to your share of the social product. Your wages are related to the supply and demand functions for your talents, rather than directly to your output. What you produce may stay constant while your wage changes, or vice versa. Rawls's theory of justice may therefore entail a distribution other than what the market would produce.

Yet, his theory does not simply correct for any supposed distortions that supply and demand might impose on your wage. Nor does Rawls want a simple desert model in which you get what you deserve as a result of your effort or whatever. Rawls does not tie your desert to *what* you produce. He ties it merely to the fact *that* you produce. The fact that you produce gives you a claim on a share of the joint product. The capitalist or well paid professional may think she deserves what she gets from market relations. A Rawlsian and virtually any contemporary economist would reject such desert claims and would say that the capitalist or professional is merely in part very lucky to be in the right place at the right time. Bill Gates is not in any plausibly meaningful sense worth the four billion dollars a year that he has recently been making, but that is what our somewhat distorted market yields him. Still, Rawls's theory retains an odd tie to desert or entitlement. Since your entitlement depends on your producing something, your entitlement is nothing if you cannot contribute anything to the joint product. Hence, the severely disabled and plausibly the citizens of other nations are not entitled to a share of our nation's product, although we might altruistically choose to give them something. Brian Barry (1995) breaks this minimal tie to desert with his theory of impartiality. Those who like desert talk might say he wants to base desert in simple humanity, not in any specific capacity or accomplishment.

CONCLUDING REMARKS. Contractarians are commonly concerned to *justify* government, especially its coercive power. We would not need a normative theory to *explain* the success of government. The modern equivalent of the theological theory would suffice: When we typically obey government we can see that it is in our interest to do so. In large part because this is in fact true, moral justification may play little or no role in explanation. Indeed, given that the contractarian moral justifications are the relatively arcane and hotly argued theories of, mostly, philosophers, it would be surprising if they were the reasons actual people do obey governments.

It is one of the sometimes implicit claims of self-interest theories that they can explain even what the actors apparently do not understand. So for example, many people readily assert that it is in individuals' interest to contribute to public provisions of various kinds. Yet, rational choice theory suggests that it is not in their interest individually to do so and they commonly do not. Hence, people seem to be motivated by interests that they do not understand and that they often even deny. Perhaps one could suppose that a hypothetical agreement is in some sense similarly binding even on those who do not understand the issue. However, the facts in the rational choice case are that behaviour often fits the theory rather than the understanding.

Do the facts of behaviour fit the contractarian programme? This is not generally a question that has been addressed. For a social order to work seems to require more that people acquiesce in the order than that they consent to it. This is a fundamentally Hobbesian conclusion that runs against the tradition of the social contract theory of which he is often thought to be the father. Hobbes supposed that acquiescence follows, of course, from interests rather than from moral commitment. Therefore he was happy with government by imposition, as when a usurper seizes power or when a foreign power invades and conquers, and he did not require contractual agreement either for the establishment or the maintenance of order.

This still leaves the questions whether government would work better if it is consensual and whether it would be more consensual if it is fair. Surely the answer to the first question is typically that it would, although consensual support of government can depend on many things other than its fairness. For example, nationalist hysteria can produce consensual support. The answer to the second question might seem self evident to some, but there is remarkably little evidence, although there are some very modest results that show that fairness in the system of justice leads to greater acceptance of its decisions (Tyler 1990). In any case, consensus *per se* is not requisite for fairness nor fairness for consensus. Perhaps it should therefore not be surprising that, even theoretically, contractarianism, which originally began as a consent theory, has become rationalist in its modern guises. Talk of consent in such theory today is little more than metaphorical.

Given the virtually total unworkability of contractual creation or justification of actual governments, one might suppose that moral theorists concerned with government would focus on how to make governments good in various ways. At its best, social contract theory might be seen as an ideal theory that commends standards to which we should aspire. It might also commend reforms to which we should be committed. But it is not easy to make a convincing argument that what we should first focus on is reforms that enhance consent rather than reforms that enhance governmental performance. (The move to broader consent by a minority dictatorial government in Burundi led recently to a bloodbath.) This is especially true if the consent that is to be enhanced is hypothetical consent. Moreover, one might suppose that enhancing political equality requires enhancing educational and economic opportunities, which might well be prior to making consent workable.

RUSSELL HARDIN

See also BUCHANAN, JAMES M.; HOBBES AND CONTRACTARIANISM; HUME, DAVID; JUSTICE; LOCKE, JOHN; MODERN UTILITARIANISM; STATE OF NATURE AND CIVIL SOCIETY.

Subject classification: 3a.

BIBLIOGRAPHY

Barry, B.M. 1995. *Justice As Impartiality*. Oxford: Oxford University Press.

Buchanan, J.M. 1975. *The Limits of Liberty*. Chicago: University of Chicago Press.

Hardin, R. 1988. *Morality within the Limits of Reason*. Chicago: University of Chicago Press.

Hardin, R. (forthcoming.) *Liberalism, Constitutionalism, and Democracy*. Oxford: Oxford University Press.

Harsanyi, J.C. 1955. Cardinal welfare, individualistic ethics, and interpersonal comparisons of utility. *Journal of Political Economy* 63: 309–21.

Hobbes, T. 1642. *De Cive*. First published in Latin, English trans. 1651. Ed. Howard Warrender, Oxford: Clarendon Press, 1983.

Hobbes, T. 1651. *Leviathan*. London: Andrew Cooke.

Hume, D. 1748. Of the original contract. In David Hume, *Essays Moral, Political, and Literary*, ed. E. Miller, Indianapolis: Liberty Press, 1985.

Kant, I. 1785. *Grounding for the Metaphysics of Morals*. Indianapolis: Hackett, 1981.

Locke, J. 1690. *Two Treatises of Government*. London: Awnsham and John Churchill. Ed. Peter Laslett, Cambridge: Cambridge University Press, 1960.
Rawls, J. 1971. *A Theory of Justice*. Cambridge, MA: Harvard University Press.
Rawls, J. 1985. Justice as fairness: political not metaphysical. *Philosophy and Public Affairs* 14: 223–51.
Rousseau, J.-J. 1762. *On the Social Contract*. Trans. Maurice Cranston, London: Penguin.
Scanlon, T.M. 1982. Contractualism and utilitarianism. In *Utilitarianism and Beyond*, ed. A. Sen and B. Williams (Cambridge: Cambridge University Press): 103–28.
Tyler, T.R. 1990. *Why People Obey the Law*. New Haven: Yale University Press.

modern utilitarianism. Utilitarianism is the view that one should do whatever will bring about the greatest amount of good. It was first clearly propounded in the eighteenth century by the philosopher Jeremy Bentham (1789). Leading figures in its subsequent development were John Stuart Mill (1863) and Henry Sidgwick (1874), both philosophers with a strong interest in economics. Throughout its history, economists have had a strong influence on the development of utilitarian thinking. Recently, work by the economist John Harsanyi (1953, 1955, 1977a) has been particularly influential. Important recent writings include Griffin (1986), the debate contained in Smart and Williams (1973) and the collection in Sen and Williams (1982).

The broad and imprecise statement that one should do whatever will bring about the greatest amount of good leaves plenty of scope for differing opinions among utilitarians, and there is no more precise formulation of their doctrine that all utilitarians would accept. Indeed, some would not accept even this broad statement. But it will be helpful to have a more detailed formulation as a benchmark for comparing alternative versions of utilitarianism. One formulation is the conjunction of the following principles.

Consequentialism. Of the acts that are available, one should do the one that will have the best consequences – that is to say, the one that will bring about the best state of affairs.
Personal good. The goodness of a state of affairs is its goodness for people.
Additivity. The goodness of a state of affairs for people is the total wellbeing of individual people.
Hedonism. A person's wellbeing is the preponderance of pleasure over pain in her life.

This is now an old-fashioned sort of utilitarianism, and few modern authors would accept all these principles without reservation. But they provide a convenient scheme for classifying the points that are at issue in modern utilitarian thinking. This essay will take the principles of consequentialism, personal good, additivity and hedonism in turn, and discuss some of the questions raised by each. Many of the new ideas that have entered utilitarianism recently are responses to objections that were made against earlier versions of the doctrine. So this tour of the issues will also provide a picture of the present standing of utilitarianism, and its unsolved problems.

CONSEQUENTIALISM: DIRECT AND INDIRECT UTILITARIANISM. 'Indirect' utilitarianism has become popular in recent decades. The most familiar version of it is rule utilitarianism (see Harsanyi 1977b; Hooker 1996), but other versions are possible. For instance, there is character utilitarianism and virtue utilitarianism. All versions accept the principles of ordinary, direct utilitarianism, except that they deny consequentialism: they deny you should do the act that will bring about the best consequences. Instead, they first of all make a claim about which rules you should live by, or what sort of character you should have, or what virtues you should espouse: you should live by the rules that will have the best consequences – that will most promote total wellbeing – or have the character that will have the best consequences, or espouse the virtues that will have the best consequences. Then these theories say you should do whatever act is prescribed by the rules you should live by, or issues from the character you should have, or from the virtues you should espouse.

The attraction of indirect utilitarianism is that it seems to offer a way of overcoming some of the objections that are commonly levelled against the direct version. Here are four of these objections and the indirect utilitarian's replies.

The first objection is that some implications of utilitarianism are intuitively simply wrong. For example, suppose the police are holding a person whom they know to be innocent, but whom the public believes to be guilty of a terrible crime. Suppose there will be riots if this person is not punished, leading to many deaths and great destruction. Direct utilitarianism will dictate that the innocent person should be punished, to avert the greater harm that will be caused by the riots. But intuition suggests it is wrong to punish an innocent person, even if there will be beneficial consequences, because it is unjust. On the other hand, a rule utilitarian can argue that on balance it best promotes total wellbeing to adopt rules of justice rather than rules of expediency, even if this occasionally leads to destructive riots. A just society is happier than an unjust one. So rule utilitarianism can support rules of justice, and agree with the intuition that it is wrong to punish the innocent person on this occasion.

A second objection is that even by a utilitarian's own criterion, people must live by some rules. Otherwise society would collapse, and that would be bad for total wellbeing. For instance, people must normally keep promises. If they did not, no one would be able to trust anyone else, and most social interaction would become impossible. Direct utilitarianism says one should keep a promise only if keeping it will contribute more to total wellbeing than breaking it will. But if you break a promise whenever it turns out better for the total wellbeing to do so, your promises cannot be relied on. If people commonly followed the prescription of direct utilitarianism, the whole institution of promising would fail, and this would be very bad for total wellbeing. On the other hand, adopting the rule of keeping your promises (except perhaps when the consequences will be extremely bad) may well have better consequences than adopting some other rule about promises. If so, rule utilitarianism will tell you to adopt this rule, and keep your promises, and that will be good for total wellbeing.

A third objection is that direct utilitarianism requires people to adopt a cold impartiality towards others, because it requires them to give equal weight to each person's wellbeing. But in a happy human society, people are inevitably partial. They care more for their loved ones and their neighbours than for other people. To require impartiality would make the world a much less happy place. It would damage the total of wellbeing, so direct utilitarianism would once more fail by its own criterion. On the other hand, indirect utilitarianism in the form of character utilitarianism would say that people ought to cultivate warm and loving characters, which make them partial towards people close to them, because having this sort of character best promotes total wellbeing.

A fourth objection is known as the 'demandingness' objection (see Kagan 1989). It says that, in asking us always to do what will bring about the most good, utilitarianism is implausibly demanding. For example, those of us who live in rich countries could do more good by sending most of our wealth to feed the world's poor than by keeping most of it for ourselves. So direct utilitarianism says this is what we should do. But the objectors find it implausible that morality really demands so big a sacrifice from us. One response to their objection is to adopt a version of rule utilitarianism. This version says we should act according to the rules that would have the best consequences if they were generally adopted. If people who live in rich countries generally adopted the rule of sending, say, 30% of their wealth to the poor, perhaps that would have better consequences than other rules, such as the rule of sending 70%. So according to this version, 30% is the proportion each of us should send. The fraction that would be most beneficial were it adopted as a general rule is no doubt not actually 30%, but whatever it is, it will definitely be less than the fraction of a person's wealth that would do the most good when considered on its own. So this version of rule utilitarianism is definitely less demanding than direct utilitarianism.

Some of these objections arise from a misunderstanding of direct utilitarianism. Few direct utilitarians would apply their theory only to overt acts such as keeping or breaking a promise. They will apply it to all acts, including the act of adopting a rule or undertaking some character-forming activity. For instance, a direct utilitarian would think you should adopt the rule of keeping your promises, if adopting this rule will contribute more to total wellbeing than failing to adopt it would. Indeed many direct utilitarians would apply utilitarianism to character traits and other dispositions, as well as to acts. So a direct utilitarian might think you should have the disposition of partiality towards your loved ones, if having this disposition better contributes to total wellbeing than other dispositions you might have, such as cool impartiality.

Indeed, direct and indirect utilitarians generally agree about the rules you should adopt and the dispositions you should have. They differ in what they think about the rightness of the acts that issue from these rules or dispositions. Suppose you ought to adopt the rule of keeping promises, and you have indeed adopted it. Now suppose that, following this rule, you keep a promise on some particular occasion. Rule utilitarians think you are automatically right to do so, because you are following a rule you ought to have adopted. Direct utilitarians think you are right only if keeping this particular promise better promotes total wellbeing than breaking it would have done. They believe that following a rule you ought to have adopted may sometimes lead you to do things you ought not to do. Similarly, a disposition you ought to have may lead you to do something you ought not to do. Intuitively, this seems to happen often. Surely, people ought to care more for their loved ones than for the general good, but sometimes this partiality, which they ought to have, leads them to do things they ought not to do. For instance, they may promote a relative in her job when she does not deserve it.

The issue between direct and indirect utilitarianism is over the truth of intuitions like this. Intuition is not always on the side of direct utilitarianism. In the example of punishing an innocent person, which I mentioned above, intuition suggests that, not only ought we to adopt rules of justice, but on each particular occasion we ought to follow them, even if the result is to reduce total wellbeing. This conflicts with direct utilitarianism. So the debate between direct and indirect utilitarianism continues.

CONSEQUENTIALISM: MORAL SUBJECTS. Utilitarianism is addressed to all of us. It tells each of us to pursue the total wellbeing of everyone. On the other hand, many economists assume that actually each of us will pursue only our own wellbeing – a view known as 'psychological egoism'. If psychological egoism is true, utilitarianism tells us to do something that actually we will not do, and this seems to make it a pointless doctrine, at best. But in fact many authors have found utilitarianism compatible with psychological egoism. Indeed, the founding figure Jeremy Bentham himself seems to have been a psychological egoist. He was not very interested in personal morality, but in the institutions and activities of government, and particularly in the law. He treated utilitarianism as a theory of public rather than private morality; he thought the law should be designed to bring about the greatest total of wellbeing. Similarly, utilitarianism has been used by some economists as a theory of public morality. For example, some modern economists have adopted it as a principle for designing the tax system (see, for instance, Mirrlees 1971, 1982). This public role is its typical application in law and economics. It restricts the scope of consequentialism: it says only that the government or social institutions should do what will have the best consequences, not people in general. This is one way of dealing with the demandingness objection too. As a personal morality, utilitarianism may be implausibly demanding, but it may nevertheless be a credible public morality.

The view of utilitarianism as a public morality does raise a question about the behaviour of legislators and public officials. These people are supposed to execute the public morality. But they are only people, so according to psychological egoism they will pursue only their own wellbeing. How can they be influenced in their public acts by the total wellbeing of everyone, as public utilitarianism requires them to be? It seems that public utilitarianism may require public officials to be utilitarian in their individual acts, so it may indeed conflict with psychological egoism.

PERSONAL GOOD: POPULATION. The principle of personal good claims that the goodness of a state of affairs is its goodness for people. Nearly all modern utilitarians would add in the good of animals as well. That is not now controversial, and when in this essay I speak of people's good, I implicitly include the good of animals with it.

However, there is a great deal of controversy over issues that involve the creation and destruction of people (or animals). The principle of personal good is intended to express a concern for people's wellbeing, which is one of the hallmarks of utilitarianism. Utilitarians are concerned to make people better off: to improve their wellbeing. But this concern can easily find itself misdirected when we come to evaluate acts that cause births or deaths, and it turns out that the principle of personal good does not express it accurately.

To see why, think of some putative act of policy that will cause the population to be bigger than it would otherwise have been (a change in the tax laws for families, for instance). To keep things simple, suppose the policy will add some new people to the population but make no difference to the wellbeing of existing people. To decide whether the policy is a good one according to the principle of personal good, we have to compare how good the world will be for people if the policy is implemented with how good it will be if the policy is not implemented. This depends on how the good of different people is aggregated together.

Additivity is one principle of aggregation, and let us first try out that one. Then the goodness of the world for people is the total of people's wellbeing. This total will be increased by adding new people, provided the wellbeing of the new people is positive. So our principles including additivity imply that the policy is a good one if this proviso is satisfied. But no one is made better off by this policy; the existing people are simply left as well off as they were anyway. So this conclusion does not properly reflect the utilitarian concern for making people better off. Adding people to the world does not meet this concern. It increases total wellbeing, but not by making anyone better off.

At first it may seem the problem is in the additive principle of aggregation. This thought seems to have been the stimulus for a new version of utilitarianism that has been dominant among utilitarian economists for the last fifty years. It is known as 'average utilitarianism', and it has a different aggregation principle. It takes the goodness of the world to be the average, rather than the total, of people's wellbeing. The idea is that the number of people who exist does not matter, what matters is the quality of life of those who do exist. Average utilitarianism is intended to express the utilitarian concern for making people better off. But actually it fails in this intention. Think about some policy that leaves all existing people exactly as well off as before, but adds some new people who are better off than the average. Adding these people will increase average wellbeing, so it is favoured by average utilitarianism. Nevertheless, it benefits no one; it does not satisfy the concern for making people better off. Indeed, one version of average utilitarianism has an opposite implication. It implies it is a good thing to kill people whose wellbeing is below the average, because this increases average wellbeing. Of course, this conclusion is absurd, and better versions of average utilitarianism are not committed to it. (They value the average of people's lifetime wellbeing: their wellbeing aggregated over their lives as a whole. Since killing a person reduces her lifetime wellbeing, it inevitably reduces the average.)

The real source of the problem is not in the aggregation principle at all. However we choose to aggregate wellbeing across people, there will always be some way of increasing the aggregate by adding people to the population, without benefiting existing people at all. Consequently, no aggregation principle can properly capture the concern to make people better off. The principle of personal good tries to express this concern, but whatever aggregation principle it is coupled with, it fails to do it properly. In recent years there has been a flood of literature that tries to accommodate changes of population within utilitarianism in a way that truly reflects the concern for people's wellbeing, or that at least reaches an acceptable compromise. (As a small sample, see Bayles 1976, Blackorby, Bossert and Donaldson 1997, Dasgupta 1994, Narveson 1967 and Parfit 1984, Part IV.) It has proved extraordinarily difficult to find principles that do not lead to paradoxes or implausible conclusions. This is one of the most hotly disputed areas of utilitarian thinking.

ADDITIVITY: THE VALUE OF EQUALITY. According to the principle of additivity, all that matters is the total of people's wellbeing. How that wellbeing is distributed amongst people does not matter at all. So utilitarianism gives no value to equality, at least not directly.

Surprisingly perhaps, in its early days utilitarianism had a reputation as an egalitarian doctrine. This was not entirely undeserved. One of Bentham's slogans was 'Each to count for one and none for more than one'. That is to say, utilitarians value the wellbeing of everyone in the society equally, whether they are lords or peasants. This is certainly a sort of egalitarianism. But valuing everyone's wellbeing equally is not the same as valuing equality in everyone's wellbeing. If it turns out that the way to maximize the total wellbeing is for a few people to be very well off indeed, and others very miserable, then this unequal arrangement is what utilitarianism recommends.

This inegalitarian potential within utilitarianism was recognized long ago. For one, the utilitarian economist Francis Edgeworth (1881) pointed it out, and embraced the inegalitarian conclusion. But for a long time other utilitarian economists – notably Alfred Marshall ([1890] 1920) and A.C. Pigou (1920) – insisted their doctrine did in fact favour equality, despite initial appearances. They relied on the assumption of diminishing marginal benefit. It is plausible to assume that the richer you are the greater is your wellbeing. But it is also plausible to assume that as you get richer, each addition to your wealth increases your wellbeing by less and less: additions have diminishing marginal benefit. If this is so, these economists argued, then any addition to a nation's wealth will add more to total wellbeing if it goes to poorer people rather than to richer ones. So the utilitarian aim of maximizing total wellbeing is best promoted by diverting wealth from the rich towards the poor.

This is a bad argument. It relies on a further hidden

assumption. Diminishing marginal benefit is an assumption about the benefits wealth brings to a single person; it says nothing about comparative benefits to different people. On its own, therefore, it cannot imply anything about the merits of redistributing wealth between people. The argument's hidden assumption is that the relation between a person's wealth and her wellbeing is the same for everyone. This is plainly false. No doubt some people are more 'susceptible' than others to the benefits of wealth, as Edgeworth put it: they derive more benefit than other people do from any given amount of wealth. The utilitarian aim is then best promoted by concentrating wealth disproportionately on to more susceptible people, rather than by distributing it equally. The egalitarian attitude of Marshall and Pigou results from a false assumption.

The inegalitarian implications of utilitarianism are by now well recognized. John Rawls expressed this complaint against it when he said that utilitarianism 'adopt[s] for society as a whole the principle of rational choice for one man' (Rawls 1971: 26–7). His point is that a single person might reasonably adopt the additive principle over her life, but not society as a whole over its members. A single person might reasonably sacrifice some wellbeing at one time in her life for the sake of a greater gain in wellbeing at another time; the greater gain more than compensates her for the lesser loss. Utilitarianism treats relations between people similarly: one person may be asked to make a sacrifice of wellbeing for the sake of a greater gain to someone else. Rawls thinks this is unjustified, because one person cannot be compensated for a loss by a gain to someone else.

ADDITIVITY: MODIFIED UTILITARIANISM. Rawls's own response was to reject utilitarianism wholesale in favour of a radically different theory of justice. A less radical response is to modify utilitarianism by adopting an aggregation principle that differs from the additive one in a way that gives some value to equality. This idea has been popular among many welfare economists (e.g. see Atkinson and Stiglitz 1980: 340). The idea is that we should value the wellbeing of badly off people more than the wellbeing of well-off people. Indeed, wellbeing itself has diminishing marginal value; the better off a person is, the less valuable it is to bring her more wellbeing. The value of wellbeing is not a linear function of wellbeing, but a strictly concave function. We do not assess the goodness of a state of affairs just by adding up people's wellbeing. Instead, we first transform each person's wellbeing by a strictly concave function that represents the value of her wellbeing. Then we add up the resulting transforms across people. The additive principle is:

$$G = g_1 + g_2 + g_3 + \ldots \quad (1)$$

where G is the goodness of a state of affairs for people, and g_1, g_2, g_3 and so on are the people's wellbeings. The new modified principle is:

$$G = f(g_1) + f(g_2) + f(g_3) + \ldots \quad (2)$$

where f is the strictly concave transformation that represents the value of a person's wellbeing.

In the philosophical literature, this idea is often called 'the priority view' or 'giving priority to the worse off' (e.g. Scanlon 1978; Temkin 1993). The additively separable form of (2) shows it is not strictly egalitarian, because it values each person's wellbeing independently of everyone else's. It does not compare one person's wellbeing with another person's, as an egalitarian would. Nevertheless, it does have the egalitarian consequence that, given some total of wellbeing, the more equally this wellbeing is distributed the better. The priority view is not strictly egalitarianism, but it has this egalitarian consequence whilst preserving many of the features of utilitarianism.

ADDITIVITY: HARSANYI'S DEFENCE. On the other hand, recent years have also seen a forceful new defence of the additive principle as a component of utilitarianism, particularly by John Harsanyi. In the 1950s Harsanyi developed no less than two new arguments for additivity. Both are founded on a theory of rationality that is not itself a moral theory: the standard theory of rational decision in the face of uncertainty, known as 'expected-utility theory'. Expected-utility theory says that a rational person, faced with a choice, chooses the option that has the greatest expectation of a quantity called 'utility'. Controversially, Harsanyi takes utility to be a measure of how well off a person is: utility measures wellbeing, that is to say.

Harsanyi's first argument (Harsanyi 1953) is of a type that was later taken up by Rawls to reach a different conclusion. It uses the idea of an 'original position'. Harsanyi imagines a person who is free to choose among a range of different societies to live in, each having the same population. She can choose any society, but she must do so behind a 'veil of ignorance': she does not know which position in the society she will occupy. She will have a chance of being the best-off person, and the same chance of being the worst-off person, or anywhere in between. This is a choice under uncertainty, because the subject has to choose a society whilst uncertain what the result will be for herself. So expected-utility theory can be applied. Under Harsanyi's interpretation of the theory, the person will, if rational, choose the society where her expectation of wellbeing is greatest. This is the society with the greatest average wellbeing. Since the populations are all the same, it will also have the greatest total wellbeing. Because this is the society a rational person would choose from behind a veil of ignorance, Harsanyi claims it is the best society. So he derives the additive principle: the best society is the one with the greatest total wellbeing.

Harsanyi's second argument for additivity (Harsanyi 1955) also sets out from expected-utility theory. It works by means of a remarkable piece of mathematics that is too complicated to reproduce here. It is not transparent. Nevertheless, it is a genuine and significant argument and not merely sleight-of-hand. Harsanyi's arguments together give significant new strength to the additive principle of utilitarianism. But of course they are not conclusive, and leave plenty of room for debate. One important bone of contention is Harsanyi's interpretation of utility as a measure of wellbeing (see Sen 1977, Broome 1991, Weymark 1991).

HEDONISM: THE PREFERENCIST ALTERNATIVE. Bentham took the view – hedonism – that a person's wellbeing consists in having pleasure and avoiding pain. He seems to have assumed that pleasure and pain were quantities that could be added and subtracted, and were comparable between people. To most modern authors these assumptions seem implausible. They believe there are more good and bad things in life than pleasure and pain. For example, there are achievement and failure, being loved and being hated, and so on. These things seem valuable in themselves, apart from the pleasure and pain they may lead to. Moreover, it seems implausible that pleasure and pain are simple, interpersonally comparable quantities.

If there are other good and bad things besides pleasure and pain, the question arises of how they are to be weighed against each other in determining a person's overall wellbeing. Many modern authors are subjectivist about this: they believe that what is good for a person is what the person herself values. And they often take her preferences to indicate what she values. So we arrive at:

Preferencism. One state of affairs is better for a person than another if and only if the person prefers it to the other.

Actually, preferencism in this form has few defenders. Most authors recognize that a person's preferences may be a poor indication of what she values, because they may be badly formed, perhaps hastily or imprudently, or on the basis of inaccurate information. So most authors rely on preferences that are idealized in some way, rather than on people's actual preferences (e.g., Brandt 1979). For instance, they may claim that one state of affairs is better for a person than another if and only if the person would prefer it if she were rational and well informed. Idealized preferencism is a modern alternative to hedonism. These two are by no means the only accounts of wellbeing that are available to utilitarians (see, e.g., Sen 1979; Griffin 1986), but they represent two broad schools amongst utilitarians: those who value the having of good experiences and those who value the satisfaction of desires.

Although preferencism is a radically different view from hedonism, economists sometimes fail to distinguish the two properly. The word 'satisfaction' can cause confusion. According to preferencism, what is good for a person is to have her preferences satisfied. It is easy to suppose that having her preferences satisfied will give a person a feeling of satisfaction. This feeling is a sort of pleasure. So it is easy to suppose that preferencism identifies a person's wellbeing with this sort of pleasure. But that is a bad mistake. The satisfaction of preferences is a quite different matter from feelings of satisfaction. Satisfying your preferences does not necessarily give you a feeling of satisfaction. For example, you may prefer that your children should prosper after you are dead, rather than endure a miserable life. If this preference is satisfied, you will feel no satisfaction, since you will be dead.

Historically, preferencism seems to have entered utilitarian thinking through the work of economists. Like utilitarianism, economic theory had Benthamite sources. W.S. Jevons (1871) was particularly responsible for importing Bentham's ideas into economics, and he expressed his economic theory in terms of pleasure and pain. But in the first decades of the twentieth century economists learnt to express themselves in terms of preferences. This led to a neater economic theory. Moreover, it was held to be sounder on epistemic grounds, because preferences were claimed to be observable, whereas pleasure and pain were not (see Robbins 1932). When economists turned to utilitarian moral theory it was natural for them to speak in terms of preferences there too.

HEDONISM: PROBLEMS OF PREFERENCISM. However, preferencism (idealized or not) is not enough for utilitarian purposes. Preferences can only determine whether one state of affairs is better or worse for a person than another. They do not determine how much better or worse. But utilitarianism needs to add up wellbeing across people, so it needs a quantitative – 'cardinal' – scale of wellbeing, and moreover one that is comparable between people. Something must be added to preferencism to achieve this, and the obvious thing to add is a notion of intensity of preference.

Expected-utility theory can supply a notion of intensity. Utility as defined within expected-utility theory is cardinal, and can plausibly be taken as a cardinal measure of intensity of preference. If intensity of preference is in turn taken to determine a quantitative scale of wellbeing, utility will be a cardinal measure of wellbeing. This measure is particularly agreeable to the spirit of preferencism, because expected-utility theory derives a person's utility entirely from her preferences. So utility inherits the epistemic privilege that is claimed for preferences: it is observable. Nevertheless, it remains controversial whether utility does truly measure a person's wellbeing (see Sen 1977; Broome 1991; Weymark 1991), and its epistemic advantage seems irrelevant to that question.

It is controversial whether utility measures wellbeing for a single person, but a bigger stumbling-block is comparisons between people. If preferencism is to be successfully adopted into utilitarianism, intensities of preferences must be comparable between people. And if the spirit of preferencism is to survive, the comparisons must themselves be based on preferences. But people's preferences seem to give us no basis for comparing intensities between people. This single point has led, and still leads, a great many economists to abandon utilitarianism. They take preferencism for granted, and they believe a measure of wellbeing must be based on preferences. Preferences supply no basis for interpersonal comparisons of wellbeing. Yet utilitarianism requires these interpersonal comparisons. Therefore utilitarianism has to go. During the last half-century, much of utilitarianism has been squeezed out of large areas of welfare economics, leaving only this one small residue:

Pareto principle. One state of affairs is better than another if one person prefers the one to the other and no one prefers the other to the one.

The Pareto principle assumes preferencism but requires no comparisons of wellbeing between people. Since it offers only a sufficient condition for one state of affairs to be better than another, and since the condition is rarely satisfied, it gives us only a very weak and fairly useless moral theory. Still, it does seem to be the natural end of preferencism.

There have been some attempts to construct interpersonal comparisons of wellbeing on a preferencist basis. The most detailed is John Harsanyi's (1977a: ch 4). Harsanyi uses the notion of an 'extended preference'. Suppose you would prefer to be Antony rather than Cleopatra; that is an example of an extended preference. An extended preference is a preference between possessing all the personal features of one person, and living that person's life, and possessing all the personal features of someone else, and living that person's life. Harsanyi hopes to construct interpersonal comparisons of wellbeing on the basis of extended preferences. His attempt remains controversial (see Broome 1998), and has so far made little impression on the body of utilitarian thinking.

CONCLUSION. Until the 1970s, utilitarianism held a dominating position in the practical moral philosophy of the English-speaking world. Since that time, it has had a serious rival in contractualism, an ethical theory that was relaunched into modern thinking in 1971 by John Rawls's *A Theory of Justice*. There were even reports of utilitarianism's imminent death. But utilitarianism is now in a vigorous and healthy state. It is responding to familiar objections. It is facing up to new problems such as the ethics of population. It has revitalized its foundations with new arguments. It has radically changed its conception of human wellbeing. It remains a credible moral theory.

JOHN BROOME

See also BENTHAM, JEREMY; DISTRIBUTIVE JUSTICE; HUME, DAVID; JUSTICE; MODERN CONTRACTARIANISM; PARETO OPTIMALITY; RULE-GUIDED BEHAVIOUR; SOCIAL JUSTICE.

Subject classification: 3a; 3b.

BIBLIOGRAPHY

Atkinson, A.B. and Stiglitz, J.E. 1980. *Lectures on Public Economics*. New York: McGraw-Hill.

Bayles, M.D. (ed.) 1976. *Ethics and Population*. Cambridge, MA: Schenkman Publishing Co.

Bentham, J. 1789. *An Introduction to the Principles of Morals and Legislation*. Oxford: Clarendon Press, 1996.

Blackorby, C., Bossert, W. and Donaldson, D. 1997. Critical level utilitarianism and the population-ethics dilemma. *Economics and Philosophy* 13: 197–230.

Brandt, R. 1979. *A Theory of the Good and the Right*. Oxford: Clarendon Press; New York: Oxford Press University Press.

Broome, J. 1991. *Weighing Goods: Equality, Uncertainty and Time*. Oxford: Blackwell.

Broome, J. 1998. Extended preferences. In *Preferences*, ed. C. Fehige, G. Meggle and U. Wessels, New York: W. de Gruyter.

Dasgupta, P. 1994. Savings and fertility: ethical issues. *Philosophy and Public Affairs* 23: 99–127.

Edgeworth, F.Y. 1881. *Mathematical Psychics*. London: Kegan Paul.

Griffin, J. 1986. *Well-Being: Its Meaning, Measurement and Moral Importance*. Oxford: Clarendon Press.

Harsanyi, J.C. 1953. Cardinal utility in welfare economics and in the theory of risk-taking. *Journal of Political Economy* 61: 434–5.

Harsanyi, J.C. 1955. Cardinal welfare, individualistic ethics, and interpersonal comparisons of utility. *Journal of Political Economy* 63: 309–21.

Harsanyi, J.C. 1977a. *Rational Behavior and Bargaining Equilibrium in Games and Social Situations*. Cambridge: Cambridge University Press.

Harsanyi, J.C. 1977b. Rule utilitarianism and decision theory. *Erkenntnis* 11: 25–53.

Hooker, B. 1996. Ross-style pluralism versus rule-consequentialism. *Mind* 105: 531–52.

Jevons, W.S. 1871. *The Theory of Political Economy*. London: Macmillan.

Kagan, S. 1989. *The Limits of Morality*. Oxford: Clarendon Press; New York: Oxford University Press.

Marshall, A. 1890. *Principles of Economics*. London: Macmillan, 8th edn, 1920.

Mill, J.S. 1863. *Utilitarianism*. In his *Collected Works*, Volume 10, Toronto: University of Toronto Press, 1969.

Mirrlees, J.A. 1971. An exploration in the theory of optimum income taxation. *Review of Economic Studies* 38: 175–208.

Mirrlees, J.A. 1982. The economic uses of utilitarianism. In *Utilitarianism and Beyond*, ed. A.K. Sen and B. Williams, Cambridge: Cambridge University Press.

Narveson, J. 1967. Utilitarianism and new generations. *Mind* 76: 62–72.

Parfit, D. 1984. *Reasons and Persons*. Oxford: Oxford University Press.

Pigou, A.C. 1920. *The Economics of Welfare*. London: Macmillan.

Rawls, J. 1971. *A Theory of Justice*. Cambridge, MA: Harvard University Press.

Robbins, L. 1932. *An Essay on the Nature and Significance of Economic Science*. London: Macmillan.

Scanlon, T.M. 1978. Rights, goals and fairness. In *Public and Private Morality*, ed. S. Hampshire, Cambridge: Cambridge University Press.

Sen, A.K. 1977. Non-linear social welfare functions: a reply to Professor Harsanyi. In *Foundational Problems in the Special Sciences*, ed. R. Buts and J. Hintikka, Dordrecht: Reidel.

Sen, A.K. 1979. Utilitarianism and welfarism. *Journal of Philosophy* 76: 463–89.

Sen, A.K. and Williams, B.A.O. (eds). 1982. *Utilitarianism and Beyond*. Cambridge: Cambridge University Press.

Sidgwick, H. 1874. *The Methods of Ethics*. London: Macmillan, 7th edn, 1907.

Smart, J.J.C. and Williams, B.A.O. 1973. *Utilitarianism: For and Against*. Cambridge: Cambridge University Press.

Temkin, L. 1993. *Inequality*. New York: Oxford University Press.

Weymark, J.A. 1991. A reconsideration of the Harsanyi–Sen debate on utilitarianism. In *Interpersonal Comparisons of Well-Being*, ed. J. Roemer and J. Elster, Cambridge: Cambridge University Press.

moral hazard. *See* INSURANCE LAW.

moral rights. *See* COPYRIGHT; DROIT DE SUITE.

most-favoured-customer clauses. Most-favoured-customer clauses (MFCCs) are contractual terms that guarantee buyers the right to purchase on terms as favourable as those offered to any other buyer; similar arrangements can also be crafted to provide such protection for sellers. They have attracted considerable attention among economists in recent years for their ability to help firms create credible commitments. Three types of commitment have been studied fairly extensively. First, MFCCs may help firms commit to eschew price discounting to particular customers, thereby facilitating tacit collusion. For example, if a manufacturer of gasoline additives commits to sell to all buyers at the same price, then he no longer has much incentive to compete aggressively for the business of particularly price-sensitive customers, and market prices may rise. Second, MFCCs can help Coasian durable-goods monopolists avoid the temptation to cut future prices and undermine monopoly profits. For instance, if a manufacturer of turbines for the generation of electricity promises current customers that they will receive retroactively any discounts offered to future customers, he becomes less likely to cut price to increase future sales. While both these forms of commitment present concerns about anticompetitive behaviour, there is also a third, efficiency-enhancing rationale for the use of MFCCs: they may aid the parties to a long-term contract in achieving efficient price adjustment while avoiding opportunistic renegotiation. For example, a small natural gas producer may be hesitant to lock himself into a long-term sales contract with a large pipeline, for fear that the buyer will refuse to adjust future prices fairly as market conditions evolve. This concern may be ameliorated, however, if contractual prices are indexed to the prices obtained by other sellers in the producer's locality.

MFCCs vary both in how many parties are involved and which time periods are covered. *Two-party MFCCs* link the price in a given buyer-seller transaction to the price in another transaction in which one of the two parties is involved; they thus commit a party to eschew price discrimination. *Three-party MFCCs* (or *meeting competition* clauses) link the price in a given transaction to the prices charged by one or more third parties in separate transactions; they may have more subtle and far-reaching effects than the two-party variety. *Contemporaneous MFCCs* link various prices charged at a single point in time, while *retroactive MFCCs* link current prices to past prices charged during some prespecified period.

Perhaps the best-known instance of the use of MFCCs was in the sale of turbine generators by General Electric and Westinghouse during the 1960s, both of whom employed retroactive two-party MFCCs. Another much-discussed case was the use of contemporaneous two-party MFCCs in the 1970s by the Ethyl Corporation and other firms manufacturing lead-based anti-knock additives for gasoline. These two cases attracted intense antitrust scrutiny, and motivated economists to study whether MFCCs may serve as 'facilitating practices' that foster tacit collusion among a group of firms. Salop (1986) initiated this line of inquiry with a thought-provoking discussion of these two cases along with a description of a third example, the use of MFCCs in natural gas contracts. (As is discussed below, gas contracts have used both two-party and three-party MFCCs, generally of the contemporaneous variety.) These three examples have served as a remarkably large share of the motivation for the growing formal game-theoretic literature that examines the economic effects of the use of MFCCs. The most important additional example is probably the familiar use of three-party contemporaneous MFCCs by retailers who promise to 'meet or beat' the prices offered by competitors.

The bulk of the literature on MFCCs to date is game-theoretic, and studies multistage games to examine how commitment to an MFCC in the initial stage of the game affects pricing behaviour in later stages. There are also a few papers that examine the empirical effects of MFCCs; both the theoretical and the empirical work are discussed below.

THE ECONOMIC ROLE OF MFCC. As mentioned earlier, MFCCs can serve several economic functions. One of these is reducing the level of price competition within an industry. While explicit price-fixing arrangements are illegal *per se* in the United States, such formal agreements may not be needed in order to sustain cooperative pricing among oligopolists who recognize their mutual interdependence. An industry with only a handful of rivals may be able to sustain prices above the competitive level simply out of the fear that even price cuts to carefully targeted customers might trigger a retaliatory price war. This sort of mutual forbearance from price competition is often referred to as 'tacit' collusion or 'conscious parallelism'. As the number of firms in an industry grows, however, or market conditions become more turbulent, coordination becomes more difficult to achieve, and it may be aided through the adoption of practices such as uniform delivered pricing, advance notice of price changes, or MFCCs. Current antitrust practice holds that conscious parallelism in the setting of prices is not enough to establish a conspiracy to fix prices, and that the use of some number of 'plus factors' or 'facilitating practices' such as those just mentioned must also be present as well.

From an antitrust perspective, contemporaneous two-party MFCCs can be viewed as commitment devices that allow a buyer or seller to avoid the temptation to engage in third-degree price discrimination. A monopolist, of course, always profits from such price discrimination in any given period, though it is well known that the welfare effects of such discrimination are ambiguous in general. Oligopolists, however, may be better off if they can commit not to discriminate. Consider, for example, a differentiated-product oligopoly in which each seller has a group of price-inelastic 'loyal' customers but also competes for sales to price-elastic customers who are willing to 'shop around'. A firm can link the prices it charges in the two segments using a contemporaneous two-party MFCC, thereby making itself a 'softer' competitor in the price-elastic market. The key to this softening effect is that price reductions are now more costly for the firm, since they must be applied across the board rather than only to the most elastic customers. Besanko and Lyon (1993) show that, under the right conditions, this relaxation of price competition can more than compensate for the reduction in rents collected from the inelastic segment of the market. They also find that adoption of MFCCs is less profitable the larger the number of firms in the industry, and that a 'bandwagon effect' emerges, so that in symmetric equilibrium either all firms adopt MFCCs or none do.

Retroactive two-party MFCCs can also facilitate tacit collusion among firms, as Cooper (1986) shows. In Cooper's model, the two customer groups are differentiated by time of purchase, rather than elasticity of demand, but the logic is much the same as in the contemporaneous case. A firm that adopts a retroactive MFCC in the first period reduces its incentives to compete vigorously on price in the second period, and thereby softens price competition between firms. Retroactive MFCCs appear to be more powerful facilitating devices than the contemporaneous sort, for Cooper finds that in duopolistic equilibrium at least one firm always adopts a retroactive MFCC. In fact, the power of this result also suggests that the model is missing some key aspects of the real world, since MFCCs are not ubiquitous in practice. For example, in Cooper's model the non-adopter reaps greater benefits than the adopting firm, so that in a dynamic setting a waiting game might be expected to emerge.

Three-party MFCCs, also known as 'meeting competition clauses' (MCCs), are even more powerful anticompetitive devices than their two-party cousins. Imagine a homogeneous-product oligopoly in which all firms but one have adopted MCCs, thereby committing themselves to match the price set by the remaining firm. As Belton (1987) points out, the dominant strategy for this 'price leader' is then to set the monopoly price! Again, however, the generality and power of the result raises questions about its empirical relevance.

A second function MFCCs may play is to provide intertemporal pricing commitment for sellers of durable goods. Coase (1972) argued that a monopolistic seller of a durable good would maximize profits by selling a restricted quantity of output, but is unable to precommit not to exploit residual demand by lowering prices in the future. Butz (1990) pointed out, however, that a retroactive MFCC (with an infinite horizon) can solve this problem. Thus, MFCCs can be anticompetitive even in a monopolistic setting by preventing the monopolist from competing with his future self.

Additional complexities arise when the buyers of the monopolist's product use it as an intermediate factor input and compete among themselves in a downstream market. Then each buyer fears loss of competitive position if his rivals renegotiate their contracts with the monopolist. Furthermore, the monopolist has incentives to cut a special deal with the last buyer, offering him a lower marginal cost in exchange for a higher fixed fee. McAfee and Schwartz (1994) argue that two-party MFCCs cannot prevent this sort of opportunistic price-cutting if the MFCC applies jointly to all terms of a contract, since other buyers may find it unprofitable to renegotiate to the contract with higher fixed fee. DeGraba (1996), however, shows that MFCCs can provide commitment against opportunistic price cutting when they allow buyers to choose a mix of desired terms from any of the contracts provided to rivals. Whether MFCCs stimulate competition or simply strengthen monopoly power thus appears to turn on a number of factors including the number of competing sellers and the exact nature of the contractual terms.

A third function for MFCCs is in facilitating price adjustment in long-term contracts. A primary difficulty for parties signing long-term contracts is adjusting prices over time to reflect changes in market conditions while avoiding opportunistic renegotiation. Unlike the multilateral contracting problems discussed in the preceding paragraph, the price adjustment problem arises even in bilateral monopoly situations. As pointed out initially by Goldberg (1991) and elaborated by Crocker and Lyon (1994), an MFCC – by linking the price in a bilateral contract to external events – may facilitate the efficient adjustment of prices over time. For example, long-term contracts for wellhead supply of natural gas have often included three-party MFCCs that link the purchase price to the prices paid in neighbouring fields. This practice allows the contract price to adjust to the changing opportunity cost of sellers over the life of the contract. Of course, as mentioned above, three-party MFCCs could in theory facilitate tacit collusion between buyers, so their impact is ultimately an empirical question.

Finally, it is worth noting that Levy (1996) offers an alternative efficiency rationale for the use of MFCCs in the case of new products whose quality is initially unknown to buyers. He shows that a firm offering a retroactive MFCC can signal that its quality is high, and that it will not have to cut its price sharply after consumers find out about the product's quality.

EMPIRICAL EVIDENCE. Given the theoretical ambiguity regarding the competitive effects of MFCCs, and the interest they have raised in antitrust circles, it is obviously important to know what effect these clauses play in practice. Unfortunately, as in much of the industrial organization literature, the available empirical evidence is scarce. What is known, however, suggests that concerns about the role of MFCCs in tacit collusion may have been overstated, at least for MFCCs used in long-term contracts. Consider in turn the three key examples from Salop's original paper (1986).

Begin with the GE/Westinghouse case, probably the most widely cited in the MFCC literature. In the first formal model of MFCCs, Cooper (1986) showed that in a duopoly at least one firm adopts a retroactive two-party MFCC. Work by Neilson and Winter (1993), however, shows that joint adoption of MFCCs is an equilibrium only if one is willing to make the assumption that an individual firm's demand is more responsive to changes in its rival's price than to changes in its own price. The turbine generator market of the 1960s was one in which products were substantially differentiated, and in which each firm had its share of loyal repeat customers. With this structure, it is highly likely that own-price elasticity was higher than cross-price elasticity. Thus, squaring the model with the facts of the case (in which both firms adopted MFCCs) is difficult. Furthermore, the purchase of a turbine generator is probably best conceived of as a long-term contract rather than a spot purchase, since the lag between placing an order for a turbine generator and its actual delivery could easily reach three years or more. As a result, efficiency arguments for the use of MFCCs as a price adjustment tool within a long-term contract have force in the GE/Westinghouse context. Overall, the GE/Westinghouse case is a shaky foundation for a theory of MFCCs as facilitating practices.

The *Ethyl* case is even less convincing as an example of the anticompetitive use of MFCCs. It is known that MFCCs were in use even during the period when there was only one firm in the lead-based antiknock additive industry, and since additives are not durable goods the presumption must be that MFCCs were initially used to commit the seller against opportunism. Even after the entry of rivals, questions remain about whether MFCCs facilitated tacit collusion. The experimental work of Grether and Plott (1984) suggests that under the conditions of the *Ethyl* case, the adoption of MFCCs alone (apart from the other practices that were also used, such as advance notice of price changes and uniform delivered pricing) would have lowered industry-average prices. Thus, the anticompetitive effects of MFCCs, if any, can only be understood in the context of the entire set of sales practices used in the industry, as argued by Holt and Scheffman (1987).

Turn finally to the natural gas market. This is the area in which the role of MFCCs has been analysed in the most rigorous empirical fashion. Here the anticompetitive concern is with tacit collusion by pipeline buyers rather than by members of the structurally competitive wellhead supply industry. Crocker and Lyon (1994) study a set of 239 contracts from the 1970s, 74% of which contained three-party MFCCs. They highlight three main characteristics of the use of MFCCs in these contracts. First, the use of MFCCs is strongly and positively associated with the number of buyers in the relevant wellhead market. This is entirely consistent with the efficiency argument that an MFCC can help track changes in the seller's outside options, since more buyers mean a greater chance that the seller's outside option will diverge significantly from the contractual price over the life of the contract. The positive association is inconsistent with a tacit collusion interpretation, however. The benefits of attempting collusion fall with the number of buyers, since collusive success becomes unlikely, yet the costs of verifying MFCC price quotes increase. On balance, the use of MFCCs to facilitate collusion should, at least beyond some threshold number of buyers, decline with further increases in the number of buyers. (Fraas and Greer's (1977) empirical investigation finds exactly this type of inverse-U shaped relationship between the number of firms in a market and the use of formal devices to facilitate collusion. They argue that formal facilitating practices are unnecessary for small numbers of firms and ineffective for large numbers, but may be profitable for groups of intermediate size.) Second, the pattern of use of MFCCs is very similar to the pattern of use of fuel price indices, which few would argue are tools to facilitate collusion. Third, and perhaps most strikingly, the areas on which the MFCCs are defined are surely suboptimal from the perspective of collusion. Most MFCC regions in gas contracts are quite small, often just a handful of counties in a particular state. This reflects the apparent intention to use MFCCs to track the seller's relevant outside options. The competition-softening effect of MFCCs, however, would be maximized by having them cover the largest possible number of buyers, i.e. the entire production region. On all three counts, MFCCs in gas contracts appear to be used to facilitate efficient price adjustment rather than tacit collusion.

Complementary results are obtained by Hubbard and Weiner (1991), who study gas contracts from the 1950s, during which time two-party MFCCs were used in a majority of contracts. They argue that in this period of rapid demand growth, MFCCs were used to help pipelines commit to eschew opportunism while retaining some price flexibility in contracts, and were not an exercise of market power. Why the gas market shifted from two-party MFCCs during the 1950s to three-party MFCCs in the 1970s is an interesting but unresolved question. A possible explanation is that as demand growth slowed in the 1970s, each pipeline was signing fewer new contracts and could not commit to efficient price adjustment by indexing solely to its own contracts, so instead had to reference the contracts of others as well.

The empirical results on the pro-competitive use of MFCCs in contracts should not be too surprising. Long-term contracts are typically used when large transaction-specific investments necessitate a move from spot market transactions to specifically-crafted contracts. This very process tends to isolate the contractual transaction from other transactions, making coordination across firms less valuable. As mentioned earlier, procurement of turbine generators during the 1960s and 1970s took place under long-term contracts that reflected delivery lags. Since generators were typically customized for particular buyers, each transaction also possessed idiosyncratic elements. Under these circumstances, it is possible that the MFCCs in these purchase agreements were facilitating price adjustment rather than tacit collusion. It is important to note that GE and Westinghouse adopted a collection of marketing practices simultaneously, of which MFCCs were only one. Thus, as in the *Ethyl* case, it may be misleading to attempt to isolate the effect of MFCCs apart from the other contractual measures employed.

It is possible that MFCCs are more likely to be anticompetitive in spot markets as opposed to long-term contracts. Unfortunately, there has been no empirical study of the effects of 'meeting competition clauses' in the retail markets where they are common. However, Morton (1995) has studied the adoption by Medicaid of a MFCC requirement in its procurement of pharmaceuticals, under which sellers were legally obligated to give Medicaid the lowest price charged to any other buyer. She finds that the effect was to increase the average price of branded products, and to increase the price of generic products in markets where there was a single branded competitor. Although government buyers were able to reduce their expenditures on pharmaceuticals, the overall welfare effect of the MFCC appears to have been negative.

CONCLUSIONS. Most-favoured-customer clauses are powerful devices for shaping relationships between buyers and sellers. They may be tailored to specific situations in a variety of different ways, and thus may be expected to have a variety of different economic effects. They clearly present the potential for both pro- and anti-competitive uses. On balance, the evidence from natural gas markets suggests that MFCCs used as part of long-term contracts are likely to be facilitating efficient price adjustment rather than collusion. Detailed 'revisionist' case analysis of *United States v. General Electric* and *In re. Ethyl Corporation*, using recent theory as a guide to separate anticompetitive from efficiency explanations, would be valuable. The use of meeting-competition clauses for retail purchases on a spot basis is perhaps more likely to facilitate tacit collusion. There should be no strong presumption to this effect, though, since existing models neglect the consumer search costs that might be saved by the use of such clauses in the retail setting, and since there has been no rigorous empirical testing of the question. These issues remain as important topics for future research.

THOMAS P. LYON

See also ANTITRUST POLICY; ASSET SPECIFICITY AND VERTICAL INTEGRATION; CARTELS AND TACIT COLLUSION; CHEAP TALK AND COORDINATION.

Subject classification: 1d(ii); 6c(ii).

CASES

In re Ethyl Corp., No. 9128 (FTC Initial Decision 5 Aug. 1981) 729 F2d 128 (2d Cir. 1984).

United States v. General Electric Co., Competitive Impact Statement, 42 Fed. Reg. 17003 (30 March 1977) (consent decree).

BIBLIOGRAPHY

Belton, T.M. 1987. A model of duopoly and meeting or beating competition. *International Journal of Industrial Organization* 5: 399–417.

Besanko, D. and Lyon, T.P. 1993. Equilibrium incentives for most-favoured customer clauses in an oligopolistic industry. *International Journal of Industrial Organization* 11: 347–67.

Butz, D.A. 1990. Durable-good monopoly and best-price provisions. *American Economic Review* 80: 1062–76.

Coase, R.H. 1972. Durability and monopoly. *Journal of Law and Economics* 15: 143–9.

Cooper, T.E. 1986. Most-favoured-customer pricing and tacit collusion. *RAND Journal of Economics* 19: 377–88.

Crocker, K.J. and Lyon, T.P. 1994. What do 'facilitating practices' facilitate? An empirical investigation of most-favoured-nation clauses in natural gas contracts. *Journal of Law and Economics* 37: 297–322.

DeGraba, P.J. 1996. Most-favoured-customer clauses and multilateral contracting: when nondiscrimination implies uniformity. *Journal of Economics and Management Strategy* 5: 565–79.

DeGraba, P.J. and Postlewaite, A. 1992. Exclusivity clauses and best-price policies in input markets. *Journal of Economics and Management Strategy* 1: 423–54.

Fraas, A.R. and Greer, D.F. 1977. Market structure and price collusion: an empirical analysis. *Journal of Industrial Economics* 26: 21–44.

Goldberg, V.P. 1991. The *International Salt* puzzle. *Research in Law and Economics* 14: 31–49.

Grether, D.M. and Plott, C.R. 1984. The effects of market practices in oligopolistic markets: an experimental examination of the *Ethyl* case. *Economic Inquiry* 22: 479–507.

Holt, C.A. and Scheffman, D.T. 1987. Facilitating practices: the effects of advance notice and best-price policies. *RAND Journal of Economics* 18: 187–97.

Hubbard, R.G. and Weiner, R. 1991. Efficient contracting and market power: evidence from the U.S. natural gas industry. *Journal of Law and Economics* 34: 25–67.

Levy, S. 1996. Most-favoured customer clauses as signals of quality. Working Paper, Indiana University School of Business, Bloomington, IN.

McAfee, R.P. and Schwartz, M. 1994. Opportunism in multilateral vertical contracting: nondiscrimination, exclusivity, and uniformity. *American Economic Review* 84: 210–30.

Morton, F. Scott. 1995. The strategic response by pharmaceutical firms to the MFN clause in the Medicaid rebate rules of 1990. Mimeo, Stanford University Department of Economics, Stanford, CA.

Neilson, W.S. and Winter, H. 1993. Bilateral most-favoured-customer pricing and collusion. *RAND Journal of Economics* 24: 147–55.

Salop, S.C. 1986. Practices that (credibly) facilitate oligopoly co-ordination. In *New Developments in the Analysis of Market Structure*, ed. J. Stiglitz and G.F. Mathewson, Cambridge, MA: MIT Press.

most-favoured-nation obligations in international trade. A country may, either unilaterally or by agreement with other countries, grant 'most favoured nation' (MFN) status to certain of its trading partners. A nation entitled to MFN treatment is assured that it will be treated no less favourably than the most favoured trading partner – that is, it will not be subject to discrimination that disfavours its commercial interests. For example, an MFN commitment respecting tariff rates assures trading partners that imported goods from their country will not be subject to a higher tariff than imported goods from other countries.

Prior to the formation of the General Agreement on Tariffs and Trade (GATT) in 1947, the United States and other countries often followed a policy of non-discrimination in their tariff policies voluntarily, without any international obligation to do so. Article I of the GATT, now incorporated into the treaty creating the World Trade Organization (WTO), made the MFN obligation binding. It contains a commitment by all WTO members to afford to each other MFN treatment with respect to tariffs and other customs charges affecting trade in goods. Article XIII of the GATT contains a similar obligation with respect to quotas and other quantitative restrictions. The General Agreement on Trade in Services (GATS) has begun to extend MFN obligations to various service sector matters, although the applicability of MFN obligations in the services arena remains much more limited.

A number of important exceptions to the MFN obligation are contained within the WTO/GATT system. Probably the most important of these exceptions permits the members of free trade areas or customs unions to eliminate tariffs on trade among the members without the need to extend such treatment to non-members. Other exceptions include the ability of nations to offer trade preferences to their former colonies, and to developing countries. Nations may also discriminate under certain conditions when protecting their declining industries from increased import competition under the 'safeguards' provisions of GATT Article XIX.

From an economic standpoint, MFN obligations (and their exceptions) have important consequences both *ex post* and *ex ante*. *Ex post*, they operate as constraints on the trade policies that nations may pursue, shaping the extent to which they may adopt discriminatory trade policies for various political or economic reasons. *Ex ante*, they affect the bargaining game among nations engaged in trade negotiations over the opening of their markets. Reciprocal trade agreements such as those of the WTO/GATT system involve commitments by nations to lower their trade barriers in exchange for commitments by other countries to do the same. Because of the MFN obligation of Article I, any tariff concession made to one member of the

WTO/GATT during the course of a trade negotiation must be extended to all members, and thus the potential for 'free riding' exists. Likewise, unless an exception to the MFN obligation applies, members are foreclosed during bargaining from entering certain preferential agreements that they might otherwise like to enter.

Economic analysis of MFN obligations and their exceptions is of two kinds. Normative analysis inquires whether MFN policies enhance economic welfare, conventionally defined, from either the global or national perspective. Such analysis is of the 'second best' in an important sense because it presupposes that some (probably inefficient) trade restrictions will exist, and the second-best question is whether they ought be discriminatory or non-discriminatory. Since the seminal work of Viner (1950) and Lipsey (1960), it has been clear that non-discriminatory trade restrictions are less detrimental to welfare (at least from the global perspective), *other things being equal*, than discriminatory trade restrictions. The reason is that discriminatory restrictions cause 'trade diversion' – the substitution of high cost suppliers for low cost suppliers – whenever the cost disadvantage of the higher cost suppliers is smaller than the magnitude of any trade preference that extends to them. Non-discriminatory restrictions avoid this substitution of high cost for low cost suppliers and its attendant deadweight losses. Other things may not be equal, however, and discriminatory trade restrictions may also result in 'trade creation' – the expansion of trade with efficient suppliers – if the opportunity to discriminate results in more market opening initiatives. Thus, from a normative standpoint, it is usually considered an empirical question whether an MFN regime will enhance global welfare: MFN policy sacrifices some trade creation to avoid some trade diversion, with the net effect being ambiguous. Kemp and Wan (1976) show, however, that discriminatory customs unions can always be designed to enhance global welfare if an appropriate adjustment is made in the external tariffs applicable to non-members.

Positive economic analysis seeks to determine why the MFN policies and exceptions that are in place have been adopted. Drawing on the lessons of public choice, it begins with a recognition that governments do not seek to maximize global or even national economic welfare as conventionally defined. In the trade policy field in particular, well-organized producer groups will typically be much more influential than consumer groups, and the influence of different producer groups will vary as well to some extent. Accordingly, standard welfare analysis is not likely to offer an adequate positive theory of trade policies in practice, and indeed the most cursory inspection of the international trading system reveals far more protectionism, whether on an MFN basis or otherwise, than can possibly be explained by conventional welfare models. The harder task, of course, is to construct a satisfactory alternative theory.

Because the normative analysis of discrimination in trade policy has been fairly well developed for decades, we will emphasize the more recently studied and far less settled positive issues. The discussion has three parts. First, we consider the unilateral choice between a discriminatory and a non-discriminatory policy by a country wishing to afford protection to a local industry. The next section addresses the virtues of an MFN policy for a cooperative trading agreement on the assumption that the transaction costs of bargaining among nations are zero. The final section considers the effects of MFN rules in a costly bargaining process between parties to a trade agreement, and in particular on the possible free rider difficulties that MFN obligations may create and that exceptions to them may ameliorate. All three sections draw heavily on the analysis in Schwartz and Sykes (1996).

1. THE UNILATERAL CHOICE BETWEEN DISCRIMINATION AND NON-DISCRIMINATION. Assume for the moment that nations perceive themselves as Nash actors, taking the trade policies of other nations as fixed. Even when nations anticipate no retaliation for trade discrimination, however, their incentive to do so is limited by a number of factors.

(a) Discrimination to increase tariff revenues. The opportunity to increase tariff revenues by imposing different tariffs on goods originating from different countries exists only for a country with a degree of monopsony power with respect to the good in question. If a country without monopsony power (facing a perfectly elastic import supply curve) attempts to impose a higher tariff on goods originating from certain supplier countries, producers in those countries will simply sell their goods in other markets.

Nations that face an upward-sloping import supply curve, however, do have the opportunity to exploit their monopsony power. Indeed, they can do so without discriminating – the theory of the 'optimal tariff' imagines that such countries maximize national welfare as a single-price (non-discriminating) import monopsonist (Bhagwati and Srinivasan 1983: 175–9). Such a country can in principle do even better, however, by practising a species of price discrimination. In the limiting case of perfect price discrimination, a distinct tariff could be placed on each unit of each imported good equal to the difference between its supply price (given by its location on the import supply curve) and the market price to consumers in the importing nation. Such a policy would maximize tariff revenue conditional on the market price, the latter chosen to achieve whatever level of protection for home market producers of the good that the government desires to achieve.

Perfect price discrimination of this sort will rarely be possible, of course, and an alternative form of imperfect price discrimination might charge a different tariff on goods from different exporting nations. Familiar principles of optimal taxation suggest how this discriminatory tariff ought to be structured – the tariff should be higher on the exporting nations with less elastic export supply curves.

Any effort to implement such a policy in practice, however, faces severe difficulties. Most obviously, it is necessary to know the costs of suppliers in different countries at the time the tariffs are set, and to update that information and the commensurate tariffs over time as cost conditions change. It is not at all clear how an importing government is to obtain such information. Further, the enforcement of a discriminatory policy also requires the importing nation to identify accurately the country of origin of imported goods. This task is not easy as exporters in countries subject to high tariffs will have an incentive to use various concealment devices, including fraudulent indications of origin, transshipment, and so on, so that their goods receive more favourable treatment.

Even if these informational and enforcement problems can be overcome, a discriminatory policy designed to increase tariff revenues is largely self-defeating in the long run. It induces entry by high-cost producers in countries subject to low tariffs and exit by low-cost producers in countries subject to high tariffs. Thus, in the long term, a country practising discrimination will be served primarily by high-cost producers subject to low tariffs, whose exports yield little revenue. Although a country could take entry and exit into account and design an optimal discriminatory policy to vary over time, such a policy requires so much information that it is doubtful that any country could implement it. Even for nations with considerable monopsony power, therefore, the successful implementation of a discriminatory tariff policy designed to increase tariff revenues seems unlikely to occur very often.

(b) Discrimination to subsidize particular trading partners. A government may have preferences as to which foreign suppliers should capture the producer surplus from sales in its protected market. If so, it may be possible to give favoured suppliers more producer surplus by imposing relatively lower tariffs on their goods. The effectiveness of such a policy is limited by the entry of additional producers into the industry of the favoured country, which will cause rents to be competed away over time. Nonetheless, as long as long-run supply in the favoured country is not perfectly elastic, some long-run surplus will be realized. From the international perspective, of course, such a policy is welfare-decreasing because it leads to trade diversion.

The frequency with which discriminatory trade policy will be employed for these purposes depends, in large measure, on its effectiveness and political acceptability, as compared to alternative means, such as direct subsidies, for conferring benefits on favoured countries. Tariff preferences are off budget, and may thus at times seem more palatable than other means of subsidizing favoured nations. Indeed, the use of discrimination to benefit favoured countries seemingly occurs with some frequency. Tariff preferences for developing countries or former colonies constitute the most important example. The US–Israel Free Trade Agreement is perhaps another. We thus suspect that this motive for discrimination is more important than the price discrimination motive discussed previously, and would result in some measure of discrimination by nations behaving as Nash actors. Likewise, we view some of the exceptions to the MFN requirement in the WTO/GATT system, including the waiver for the Generalized System of Preferences for developing countries and the Article I preferences for former colonies, as resulting from this motivation for discrimination.

II. DISCRIMINATION IN COOPERATIVE AGREEMENTS – THE CASE OF COSTLESS BARGAINING. Suppose that a group of self-interested political officials assembles for the purpose of negotiating a trade agreement among their nations. Each official has an objective function that gives heavy weight to the welfare of domestic producer groups (who will reward the official for increasing their surplus), gives more modest weight to consumer interests (and thus leads to a preference for protectionism in some industries), and finally gives significant weight to government revenue (which the officials can distribute to favoured interest groups in exchange for their political support). In this section, we also assume that the transaction costs of bargaining among these officials are zero. Will an optimal agreement among them permit tariff discrimination in favour of imports from certain countries, or embody an MFN requirement?

(a) The virtue of MFN. As elaborated in Schwartz and Sykes (1996), a trade agreement that achieves the Pareto frontier for the political officials who enter the agreement will not in general prohibit discrimination. Some producer groups are better organized than others, and we would not expect the producers in a given industry to be equally well-organized everywhere. A politically savvy agreement might then tend to disadvantage exporters who were poorly organized and favour exporters of competing goods from other countries who were well organized, resulting in a discriminatory tariff structure.

Yet, an MFN requirement has an interesting property that may make it politically attractive as a baseline rule. In particular, non-discriminatory trade restrictions have the property that they maximize the global sum of producer surplus and government revenue *conditional* on the level of protection in any given market in any importing country. The intuitive partial equilibrium proof is quite simple. Consider an importing nation facing some set of supply curves for a particular good from its trading partners. For simplicity, let transport costs be zero. The market price in the importing nation will be a function of the quantity of imports permitted to enter; greater levels of protection for home market producers of the good can be achieved by reducing that quantity. Consider an arbitrary level of protection for home market producers achieved by permitting a quantity of imports equal to q^*, and assume initially that a non-discriminatory tariff is used to achieve exactly this quantity. Domestic producer and consumer surplus are determined by the price that results with imports of q^*. Now imagine that the importing nation begins to charge discriminatory tariffs, but holds constant the quantity of imports at q^*. Exporters from favoured countries move up their supply curves to regions of higher marginal cost, and exporters from disfavoured countries move down their supply curves to regions of lower marginal cost. A deadweight loss arises because marginal imports from each country are no longer produced at the same marginal cost. Domestic producer and consumer surplus remain the same, however, because q^* remains the same. Thus, the existence of the deadweight loss implies that the move to a discriminatory tariff policy must have reduced government tariff revenue, foreign producer surplus, or both, since these are the only other components of global surplus in partial equilibrium. It follows that for any level of protection in an importing nation (i.e., any quantity of imports allowed to enter), the sum of global producer surplus and tariff revenue will be at a maximum under an MFN tariff structure.

This observation suggests a possible reason why political officials might want to adopt an MFN obligation as a baseline rule, as it seems plausible that any policy which increases the sum of producer surplus and government revenue will prove beneficial to political officials on average. Yet, we would also expect a savvy agreement to permit deviation from an MFN policy in cases where clear political gains could be realized. It is noteworthy that the WTO/GATT system has exactly this sort of structure – a baseline MFN requirement, subject to exceptions. In the remaining sections we consider some of those exceptions and their possible rationale.

(b) Declining vs. prosperous industries. In general, declining industries will value protection from competition to a greater extent than prosperous industries, and thus work harder in the political process to obtain it. The reason is that declining industries, more or less by definition, are earning less than a competitive rate of return on sunk investments. If they can secure protection and raise their prices toward the long run break-even level (but not above), no entry by new firms will be induced, and the increased profits will be retained as long as protection remains in place. Prosperous industries, by contrast, benefit less from protection if its effect is simply to attract further entry that causes returns to be competed down to the competitive level in reasonably short order (see Friedman 1990: 549–50).

For the same reasons, exporters will typically be more upset about restrictions on their exports – and thus press their political representatives more to avert those restrictions – if restrictions cause returns to fall below the competitive level. Where restrictions on exports simply reduce supracompetitive returns that would have been competed away by entry anyway, the exporters will be less motivated to resist them.

Much the same points can be made about unions and other worker organizations. Workers in declining industries with specific human capital investments will work hard to protect their quasi-rents from further erosion or to restore them. Potential workers in expanding industries, who have not yet incurred sunk investments and who expect no better than a competitive return on them once they are incurred, are not likely to organize to create or protect those investment opportunities.

These observations suggest why declining industries tend to receive more protection than prosperous industries in general. They also suggest why an international trade agreement might permit member nations to protect declining domestic industries against surges in import competition from prosperous exporting industries. This is the explanation offered in Sykes (1991) for 'safeguards measures' under the GATT, which permit signatories to revoke tariff concessions when a domestic industry is 'seriously injured' by increased import competition.

Parallel reasoning supports the use of discriminatory trade restrictions when implementing such protection. Consider an importing nation with a declining industry that suffers from increased import competition. Some imports come from exporters that are themselves high cost, declining firms, while recent increases in imports come from exporters elsewhere that are low cost producers by global standards and who are prospering and expanding. If the declining industry in the importing nation is to be protected, the political logic above suggests that new trade restrictions should not be imposed on an MFN basis. Rather, political officials will jointly prefer that the prosperous exporters bear the brunt of new restrictions, and that exports by declining firms be spared. This structure of discrimination is precisely the departure from the MFN obligation that is authorized by Article 5 of the WTO Agreement on Safeguards. Such a structure, of course, is quite at odds with the teachings of conventional welfare economics, because it restrains the growth of efficient producers while inhibiting the contraction of inefficient producers.

III. THE MFN OBLIGATION AND THE MULTILATERAL BARGAINING PROCESS. Attention to the transaction costs of multilateral trade negotiations suggests two other considerations that affect the wisdom of an MFN obligation, one a virtue of MFN and one a vice. The additional benefit of MFN further reinforces our argument as to why an MFN obligation is a politically valuable baseline rule to include in a multilateral trade agreement, if accompanied by appropriate exceptions. The additional disadvantage may afford an explanation for the most important exception to the MFN obligation in the WTO/GATT system, which permits the formation of customs unions and free trade areas.

The WTO system now has over 120 members. Multilateral trade negotiations in a system with so many players will be complicated and costly, owing in substantial part to the fact that trade concessions affect the interests of many parties, with or without an MFN obligation in place. To see why, consider first the situation that would prevail without an MFN obligation. Country A might secure a concession from country B in return for some concession by country A, only to discover shortly afterward that country C had obtained an even better concession on the same goods from country B. As a result, the expectations of country A under its original bargain with country B would be frustrated. For this reason, negotiations in the absence of an MFN obligation would have to take one of two forms: either all of the parties with interests in trade in a particular good as importers or exporters would have to sit down and negotiate simultaneously with no final deals possible until everyone had reached agreement, or the parties to any smaller numbers negotiation would have to promise each other not to frustrate each others' expectations by offering unexpected future deals to others. The first option would be exceedingly cumbersome, with holdouts and other forms of strategic behaviour making it difficult to reach closure. The second option would also prove quite cumbersome if the promises made to protect expectations had to be negotiated good-by-good and country-by-country with respect to every country not a party to the negotiation that might be a potential exporter of the goods at issue.

An alternative is for nations engaged in smaller numbers negotiations to make a generic promise to protect each others' expectations rather than negotiating specific promises on each good. The most favoured nation obligation is precisely that – 'I will not give anyone else a better deal than I have just given you. If I do, you will also be entitled to the benefits of it.' The simplicity of such a generic promise perhaps makes it an attractive focal point. Indeed, we see it in other contexts, as in negotiations between the United Auto Workers and individual US auto manufacturers. Further, as noted in the last section, it has the nice property in the trade area of ensuring that the global sum of producer surplus and government revenue will be at a maximum conditional on the level of protection ultimately negotiated for each market.

But the introduction of the MFN obligation creates another problem – free riders. Just as it protects the parties to smaller numbers negotiations from the frustration of their expectations due to unexpected, more favourable concessions granted to others, it also extends the benefits of any concessions negotiated among smaller numbers of countries to additional countries that have not participated in the negotiation. Nations may then be tempted to offer few concessions themselves and hope to take advantage of the concessions secured by others. As a result of this strategic behaviour, mutual concessions that may be politically valuable may never be made.

Schwartz and Sykes (1996) suggest that the WTO/GATT provisions which permit the formation of customs unions and free trade areas may facilitate jointly valuable trade liberalization that might otherwise be thwarted by free rider problems. These provisions permit preferential trade concessions to be made between two or more members of the WTO system, as long as those concessions entail the *elimination* of trade impediments on 'substantially all' trade between them. As a result of these provisos, customs unions and free trade areas usually take many years to negotiate and are widely anticipated by the trading community at large. Their creation is thus less likely to frustrate expectations, and thus less likely to undermine one of the most important functions of the MFN obligation in the first instance.

Furthermore, the restrictions on customs unions and free trade areas may tend to discourage the formation of such agreements if they create a great deal of trade diversion, and thus if they might destroy a great deal more producer surplus for non-members than they create for members. The argument here, though tentative, runs as follows: When trade preferences result in considerable trade diversion, governments are sacrificing revenue without transferring comparable surplus to producer groups, who by hypothesis have high costs and thereby dissipate many of the rents that they might otherwise capture from having preferential access to a foreign market. Nevertheless, absent a baseline MFN requirement, nations might be tempted to enter trade diverting discriminatory arrangements to bestow modest benefits on a handful of politically powerful industries, creating a loss of global surplus that would be difficult to prevent because of the transaction costs of organizing the affected producer groups elsewhere to oppose these arrangements with appropriate counter offers.

But when the existing MFN requirement is coupled with the exceptions for free trade areas and customs unions, such targeted and unproductive arrangements are prohibited. Instead, nations can only discriminate if they wipe out trade restrictions between them across the board. These across the board arrangements, if trade diverting to a large extent, will be doubly costly to the treasuries of the member nations because of their scope, while again conferring only modest surplus on their producers. And here, the modest benefits that are conferred on producer groups in the member states will not be limited to the politically powerful industries that could secure trade diverting preferences in the absence of an MFN requirement, but will be spread throughout the economy to all producer groups, whether or not they are well-organized and influential. In short, the existing legal structure prohibits trade diverting arrangements to favour individual industries with lots of political power, and requires nations that wish to discriminate to do so in a way that favours all producer groups in the preferred trading partners. Were trade diversion the predominant consequence of such an arrangement, the large loss of government revenue that attends the preferences would buy relatively modest producer surplus by comparison, and thus it seems unlikely that across-the-board preferences that create a great deal of trade diversion will prove attractive politically.

CONCLUSION. Although the normative economics of discrimination in international trade and its antithesis – the MFN obligation – are reasonably well understood, the positive economics of existing institutional structures that promote or inhibit discrimination is comparatively undeveloped. Although we have advanced some tentative thoughts on the matter, much remains to be done to understand the detailed legal obligations of the international trading system. The reader will note, for example, that we have said nothing in this essay about non-discrimination obligations in the services area, which presents a more complicated and mixed picture than trade in goods. Likewise, we have said little about the factors that may lead some nations to invoke certain exceptions to the general MFN obligation for trade in goods, such as the right to form a customs union or free trade area. The development of useful theories to explain who joins these entities, and when, remains on the agenda for further research.

WARREN F. SCHWARTZ AND ALAN O. SYKES

See also ANTIDUMPING; COUNTERVAILING DUTIES; HOLDOUTS.

Subject classification: 2g.

BIBLIOGRAPHY

Bhagwati, J. and Srinivasan, T.N. 1983. *Lectures on International Trade*. Cambridge, MA: MIT Press.

Friedman, D. 1990. *Price Theory*. Cincinnati: South-Western.

Kemp, M. and Wan, H. 1976. An elementary proposition concerning the formation of customs unions. In M. Kemp and H. Wan, *Three Topics in the Theory of International Trade: Distribution, Welfare and Uncertainty*, Amsterdam: North-Holland.

Lipsey, R. 1960. The theory of customs unions: a general survey. *Economic Journal* 70: 496–513.

Schwartz, W. and Sykes, A. 1996. Toward a positive theory of the most favoured nation obligation and its exceptions in the WTO/GATT system. *International Review of Law and Economics* 16: 27–51.

Sykes, A. 1991. Protectionism as a safeguard: a positive analysis of the GATT 'escape clause' with normative speculations. *University of Chicago Law Review* 58: 255–305.

Viner, J. 1950. *The Customs Union Issue*. New York: Carnegie Endowment for International Peace.

N

National Conference of Commissioners of Uniform State Laws (NCCUSL). *See* PRIVATE LAW-MAKING AND THE UNIFORM COMMERCIAL CODE.

natural law. *See* BLACKSTONE, WILLIAM; LEGAL POSITIVISM; LOCKE, JOHN; SCOTTISH ENLIGHTENMENT AND THE LAW.

negligence. *See* COMPARATIVE NEGLIGENCE; DUE CARE; LEGAL STANDARDS OF CARE; PUNITIVE DAMAGES.

neoinstitutional economics. There has been much debate and confusion over a name for the field here referred to as neoinstitutional economics. Some years ago I made a distinction between neoinstitutional economics and the new institutional economics (Eggertsson 1990: 6). I labelled a revival of the old American institutionalism as the new institutional economics, and applications of basic methods of modern economics as neoinstitutional economics. In assigning the label neoinstitutional economics, I considered whether a particular study or a research programme assumed rational choice. After applying this test, I concluded, prematurely, that studies which assume bounded rationality differ qualitatively from studies based on rational choice.

My classification has not stood the test of time. The term new institutional economics has come to represent in the literature all shades of institutionalism, including new–old, holistic, evolutionary, biological, and neoclassical approaches. At the same time neoinstitutional economics, for most people, still brings to mind a subdiscipline of neoclassical economics which leads off, but not far off, the beaten track of mainstream economic analysis. In this essay I will consider the terms neoinstitutional economics and economics of institutions as perfect substitutes.

To make life even more complicated, however, in recent years the methods of neoinstitutional economics have increasingly differed from those of neoclassical economics, although only on select margins. While neoinstitutional economics treats choices and transactions as fundamental units of analysis, it has come to recognize that standard rational choice methods are sometimes inappropriate – for instance, when analysing long-term evolution of social systems and fundamental uncertainty (see Denzau and North 1994). In the view of neoinstitutional economics, many questions require a richer, more sophisticated model of choice, along with theories for explaining how people form preferences and model their social environment. The field has also departed from mainstream economics by considering alternative ways of aggregating behaviour. Because neoinstitutional economics proposes that individual decisions are made in a social context, it demands a model of aggregation or selection to explain social outcomes. For some purposes, evolutionary social theories provide appropriate tools at this level of analysis (see Witt 1993), but they do not exclude other approaches, such as models of political processes based on individual choices (see Alt and Shepsle 1990). Finally, neoinstitutional economics has modified the role it assigns to individual human actors and has given more weight to organizations, which it views as social systems that collect, process, and use information, and that act in a manner which transcends and survives individual members of the organization (see Hutchins 1995). It must be added that some neoinstitutional economists feel that approaches which modify the rational choice model, rely on evolutionary theories, or treat organizations as actors lack a solid theoretical base.

Until recently, the institutional literature could not agree on a common definition of its key theoretical term, institution, but now most scholars are converging on a definition. Institutions are social constraints that emerge when rules, ranging from constitutions to social norms, are enforced (see North 1990). Social constraints join the familiar constraints of income and technology in standard economic theory, and influence people's incentives and shape their choices.

Together, sets of institutions make up systems for allocating scarce resources, systems of property rights. We have a little problem here, however, because common usage gives the terms property rights and institutions different meanings than they have in economics. An institution for many people is an organization, such as a firm, hospital, or a school, rather than a set of rules; I write these words at the Hoover Institution. In law, the term property rights refers to a narrow category of legal rules, but not to social constraints in general. Some readers see property rights as a code word for exclusive private ownership and a policy of *laissez-faire*. For example, a reviewer once recommended to me that I avoid the phrase property rights because of recent electoral victories by the Right. In addition, the word 'rights' in property rights suggests moral rights both to opponents and defenders of private ownership. A distinguished scholar (see Scott 1983) has written an essay about 'property rights and property wrongs'. Although I recognize that economics has a long history of borrowing words from common usage and reinventing their meaning, it is important to avoid unnecessary misunderstanding. Therefore, I often alternate the term system of control with the terms institutional environment or system of property rights, so the reader may understand that I am talking about social constraints in general.

WHY ECONOMICS NEEDS NEOINSTITUTIONAL ECONOMICS. Modern mainstream economics needs a complementary research programme to analyse variations in the structure of economic systems and their transformation over time. We need a theory where the social system itself is a variable, a theory that uses modern social science to revive the research programme of the classical economists from Smith to Marx and to continue the work of Schumpeter and Hayek.

Neoinstitutional economics is an interdisciplinary approach which explores how the economic system relates to other parts of the social system. It integrates learning from a wide range of fields, such as sociology, anthropology and political science, law, public choice, history, demography and, lately, from psychology and cognitive science. Although it borrows from a number of scholarly disciplines, neoinstitutional economics derives its identity from a specific research agenda: an investigation into the link between institutions and wealth. The explorations into sociology, politics and psychology are motivated by a search for better understanding of the performance and dynamics of economic systems.

Neoinstitutional economics, therefore, has the role of both defining research questions appropriate for research into the structure of economics systems, and of exploring the extent to which traditional methods of economics must be modified to deal with these questions. Coase's (1937) essay on the nature of the firm is a classic manifestation of this approach. Coase asks why some transactions are made in markets but others within firms, and what factors determine the allocation of transactions between the two spheres. He then introduces the idea of costly transactions which eventually evolved into the concept of transaction costs, now an essential ingredient of the economics of institutions.

Neoinstitutional economics, then, differs from fields such as sociology, political science and psychology because it is a branch of economics. We should not be so eager to emphasize the difference between regular economics and the economics of institutions that we forget the link between the two. Research into the institutional structure of economic systems must build on findings in macroeconomics and microeconomics, and, similarly, economics cannot avoid recognizing differences in institutional environments.

CONTROL AND INFORMATION. The study of economic systems revolves around two related issues: methods for rationing scarce resources, or the control problem, and implications of scarce information for social organization, the information problem.

The human condition is shaped by information scarcity which limits not only our technical knowledge but also our capacity to coordinate and verify transactions, measure complex attributes, interpret data, and understand social systems. Although social scientists have struggled long to better understand how the interplay of control, information, and incentives shapes economic performance, the results are relatively meager. In the early twentieth century, F.A. Hayek initiated an information revolution in social science, and made major contributions that still lack the general recognition they deserve. Neoinstitutional economics took off in the 1970s with a surge of studies on information-control issues (see Eggertsson 1990). Important ideas came from many quarters and not always from people who saw themselves as institutionalists. I became familiar with the economics of property rights and transaction costs through scholars whose work may be referred to as the Los Angeles–Seattle–Chicago approach: A. Alchian (Los Angeles), H. Demsetz (Chicago and Los Angeles), R.H. Coase, and G.J. Stigler (Chicago), Y. Barzel, S.N.S. Cheung and D.C. North (Seattle). Others have entered the field differently, for instance on the public choice path. These early approaches to neoinstitutional economics were summarized by Furubotn and Pejovich (1972) who themselves made important contributions. The information-control perspective was also used to analyse political organizations and processes. For me, the approaches that originated at the University of Rochester and at CalTech (W.H. Riker, K.A. Shepsle, B.R. Weingast, R.H. Bates) have been particularly important, while many others, such as J.M. Buchanan, G. Tullock, A. Downs and M. Olson, have played a central role. O.E. Williamson (1985) has had great impact on neoinstitutional economics with a theory of economic organization under capitalism. Finally, an economic historian, D.C. North (1993), put the pieces together and argued convincingly that the control–information perspective could serve as the theoretical base for a modern theory of economic systems and their evolution through time.

Transaction costs, a somewhat elusive concept (see Allen 1991), is the unifying theoretical tool of neoinstitutional analysis. The best way to grasp their meaning is to see transaction costs as reflecting uncertain control of resources. The control problem arises because competition for scarce resources must be resolved in one way or another, for instance, through private control and exchange in markets, through direct allocation by the state or communal ownership, or through races and physical struggles. Within these broad categories, we find elaborate mosaics of rights, duties, enforcement mechanisms and procedures for dispute resolution. Transaction costs arise because control systems are contested, and because measurement and enforcement are costly: control is costly.

People lose their hold on resources in two ways: either because someone outright appropriates the resources or because partners in voluntary transactions are opportunistic and cheat. The distinction between losses in voluntary and involuntary transactions is obviously murky. The theft of your car on a dark night and the withholding of information about hidden flaws when you buy a car have similar implications – involuntary loss of resources. Expected transaction costs, the costs of enforcing control, profoundly influence behaviour, both the way in which people organize their business and also what investment projects they choose.

People's expectations about the costs of maintaining reasonable control over their resources depend on the support they expect to receive from the state and their fellow citizens. The control that individuals have over resources has two sources: an internal and an external source. Protection provided by the state (laws, police, the courts) and by other members of society (law abidance, commercial morality) determines the degree of external control, and efforts by owners themselves (locks, guards, monitoring) determine the level of internal control. Individuals expect low transaction costs, when, in the absence of substantial private investment in protection and enforcement, the chances of someone expropriating their resources are thought to be low.

The institutional environment of a community does more than influence the general cost of doing business; it also promotes certain activities and forms of organization (see North 1990). The institutions may penalize private firms, encourage ballet, create an unfavourable environment in agriculture, promote heavy industry, and discourage technological innovation. By channeling effort into favoured areas, the institutional environment affects the amount and character of intellectual capital and the long-term direction of the social system.

Economists usually frown on policies that explicitly favour particular activities, because such policies tend to misallocate resources. In the long run, however, and from the viewpoint of dynamic rather than static efficiency, institutions that favour specific activities can be either enormously productive or destructive. Destructive arrangements are adopted both to satisfy demands of politically powerful special interest groups and because governments in a world of scarce information misread the future.

The issue of control of resources points directly to the information problem. Many scholars have tried to visualize the implications of scarce information by attempting to theorize about a world of full information. Such exercises have led to unproductive disputes, for instance, over the validity of the Coase theorem, which concerns the allocation of property rights when there are no transaction costs (see Cooter 1982). The controversies usually arise because the disputants, implicitly or explicitly, make different assumptions about the information environment of the actors. I find it useful to think of information scarcity as involving three issues: the supply of data to actors, their capacity to process information, and their stock of knowledge.

The first phase of neoinstitutional economics, and the information revolution in economics (see Stiglitz 1994), primarily explored the implications of scarce data, and what happens when access to data varies from one type of an actor to another (asymmetric information, moral hazard, adverse selection). In contractual relations, the parties with relatively cheap access to information have, other things equal, relative advantage in manipulation and cheating, which gives an incentive to actors with limited information to find ways to protect themselves. However, those who are in a position to cheat easily are not trusted, and they sometimes find it advantageous to make a binding commitment to honest behaviour, for instance by supplying various explicit or implicit collaterals. Organizational forms reflect such concerns (see Williamson 1985; Barzel 1989).

Many scholars now use the term bounded rationality in a general sense to represent all aspects of the information problem, but the version of bounded rationality that I was introduced to dealt with limits to human computing – hardware problems in the language of computers. A rational response to limits on one's capacity to compute is to proceed in measured steps toward increasingly better outcomes, with each step aiming at basic satisfaction rather than optimality (see Simon 1957). The process was labelled satisficing.

People's efforts to understand their environments involve more than collection and processing of data. The data are filtered through theories and models that interpret the data. These mental models belong to each individual's stock of knowledge and reflect his or her experience (see Clark 1997). Many social scientists find it difficult to recognize that variations in behaviour may depend on different models, rather than on different interests, basic preferences, or constraints. Yet everybody recognizes that macroeconomists often read different interpretations into the same set of data because of their theoretical orientation – as do also economic and political actors in their daily business.

That a theorist allows for limited supply of data does not require significant departure from standard methods in economics; and for many neoinstitutional economists the information revolution stopped here. The early literature on regulation, search in labour markets, and rent seeking was concerned with supply of (and demand for) data. Similarly, microeconomists with an interest in institutions and organization, such as Barzel and Cheung, did not break with traditional economic methods when they embraced transaction costs. Barzel and Cheung linked transaction costs closely to the cost of measurement, and used traditional economic tools to think about the measurement of complex commodities and about efforts to enforce control. However, the early neoinstitutionalists made a big leap forward by asking new questions, questions concerning behaviour and outcomes under incomplete control, and about the use of contracts, market practices, and organizations to enforce control and lower transaction costs (see Milgrom and Roberts 1992). These questions were asked about both economic and political transactions (see Banks and Hanushek 1995).

The idea that actors have limited ability to process data has, in my opinion, not led to particularly interesting insights, beyond those produced by the assumption of positive transaction costs: applications usually present the idea in terms of constrained maximization. Yet it must be admitted that concern with limits on data processing (unlike concern with costly measurement) raises questions about cognition and how the mind works.

Inquiry into the relationship between cognition and mental models, institutions, and social outcomes reaches beyond standard methods of economics. In searching for a sophisticated model of choice, some neoinstitutionalists have turned to evolutionary psychology, cognitive science and related fields. Findings in these disciplines indicate that the human brain does not use a single overarching decision model, as traditional rational choice methods suggest (see Cosmides and Tooby 1994). Instead, the brain economizes by employing specialized decision models and frequently relies on simple rules of behaviour, rules of thumb. Further, past learning influences how people interpret new data and makes thinking path dependent.

Neoinstitutional economics and cognitive psychology represent different levels of analysis – one field studies the economic system, the other the cognitive system – which complicates transfer of findings between the two fields. Yet neoinstitutional economics struggles with several questions that cognitive science could possibly help to solve. There is the perennial question of the origins of cooperation and law abidance. Does cooperative behaviour always reflect strategic considerations or does cooperation sometimes reflect the influence of path dependent norms and models of social behaviour that vary between human groups? A related issue concerns the long-term survival of dysfunctional social systems, which is usually attributed to factors such as calculating elites who associate reforms with an uncertain future for themselves; silent critics who hide their views to avoid retaliation (Kuran's (1995) preference falsification); and ineffective leaders who are unable to build support for reforms because their promises are not credible (Weingast's (1994) political risk). Many neoinstitutionalists are satisfied with explanations along these lines, explanations that are essentially framed in terms of traditional economic methods. Other argue that the story is more complex than the traditional view suggests, that phenomena such as the rise and fall of the Soviet Union involve complex cognitive issues, knowledge, and modelling, in addition to individual calculations of net gain (Eggertsson 1997). And, on a light note, does disagreement among social scientists over the interpretation of social change reflect different theoretical models or strategic posturing?

NEOINSTITUTIONAL ECONOMICS AND PROFESSOR PANGLOSS. Probably the most common misconception that many social scientists have of the field is that neoinstitutional economics is a modern extension of the teachings of Professor Pangloss – his lesson that all is for the best in this best of all possible worlds. I have puzzled over this misunderstanding because many neoinstitutionalists, including myself, entered the field looking for explanations of why economic systems fail, and why people tolerate institutional arrangements that perform poorly. I can think of two explanations why reasonable people could argue that neoinstitutional economics sees all institutions and organizations as efficient in the neoclassical sense.

First, neoinstitutionalists usually represent choice as optimization under constraints, which leads some people to believe that the field paints a rosy picture of the world: if everyone makes an optimal decision, the outcome must be pretty good. In truth, the approach suggests no such general optimality. The optimal choice for a person with a wounded leg sometimes is to have the leg amputated, and the optimal choice for many consumers in the old Soviet Union was to get up at five in the morning to wait in line for their local grocery store to open. Obviously, it is not optimal in some general sense to lose a leg, and the Soviet consumer was not in a state of Nirvana. The approach only claims that people tend to pick the best available alternative.

The second possible explanation of the misunderstanding is more complex. Several prominent neo-institutionalists, often with deep roots in neoclassical economics, have studied the economic logic of contracts and economic organization in competitive markets (see Demsetz 1988). These studies frequently conclude that specific institutional arrangements and forms of organization are optimal in some general sense – they minimize costs in a world with transaction costs. These studies rely, implicitly or explicitly, on Alchian's (1950) filter of competition – relatively costly forms of organization do not survive the market test. We should be clear about what these scholars are attempting. They are trying to build a theory of organizations and market practices in an ideal-type competitive market with transaction costs. These studies have shown that some forms of organization which standard economics sees either as irrational or as attempts to monopolize markets have a useful economizing function. The findings also serve as a benchmark, but they represent only a subset of the neoinstitutional research programme. The main conclusion of the current body of research is that in terms of technical possibilities, wasteful economic organization is more the rule than the exception (Olson 1996).

NEOINSTITUTIONAL ECONOMICS AND POWER. The criticism that neoinstitutional economics is an exercise in Panglossian philosophy is often reinforced with a claim that the approach ignores the distribution of power and the use of power to extort wealth, but instead puts the emphasis on voluntary exchange. According to this criticism, the neoinstitutional approach sees institutions and organizations as joint efforts by equal partners to solve certain transaction problems.

It is true that neoinstitutional economists seldom use the word power; indeed, economists, as a group, seldom do, but they do not ignore it either. The choice sets and constraints of various categories of actors measure their relative power. An analysis of how actors with unequal choice sets play their cards is a study in power, even when the word is not mentioned. And neoinstitutional economics investigates not only behaviour in the economic arena, but also in the political arena where actors, again with unequal choice sets, exercise power and set rules for economic activity.

The reader must also be careful not to identify voluntary exchange with equal status – equal social standing or equal power – among the traders. For exchange to be voluntary requires only that the traders control the resources which they trade – otherwise the stronger party would simply appropriate the commodity or the service that he desires. Theoretically it is possible for individuals to control no resources at all, which means that they cannot engage in voluntary exchange. But, even extreme disempowerment usually does not entirely deprive actors of control of scarce resources. A powerful employer, a monopsonist, may offer a worker a bonus for working more intensively because high costs of measurement and enforcement (transaction costs) provide the worker with some measure of control over her level of effort. Both sides can benefit from the exchange, given their circumstances, but obviously the power relationship between the two is unequal; voluntary exchange does not imply equality. Additionally, if we want to study why the two parties came to be in a given relative position of power, we step back and examine previous choices, and transactions at other levels of analysis, for instance, in the political sphere.

THE DETERMINACY DILEMMA. Now we come to a problem or a dilemma which for me is of more substance than the critique that I discussed above: is it true that neoinstitutional economics makes social processes and institutional change determinate by attempting to explain too much? In other words, does the attempt to explain economic and political processes, and even sociological variables, in terms of rational individual choices, make social change determinate? Are only unexpected exogenous events, such as change in climate, capable of shifting the social system to a new equilibrium path? The new notion of path dependence further reinforces a sense of determinacy in institutional change by suggesting that early choices by social actors lock them in a particular scenario and put them on a path that they cannot leave, except perhaps in the very long run.

Initially, the theory of path dependence attempted to show how increasing returns to scale could make the choice of a particular technology rule out future choices of alternative superior technologies (see Arthur 1994). Scholars subsequently argued that social constraints and investment in knowledge also involve lock-ins and path dependence, with the accumulated stock of knowledge and prior choice of social constraints determining future social organization (see North 1990; David 1994).

So far, the question of social determinacy has received little attention in the neoinstitutional literature, presumably because research has aimed primarily at explaining the logic of various social structures. But the considerable success of the field, and an urgent need for systematic institutional policy, for instance to guide the transition of the former soviet economies, has put pressure on neoinstitutional economists to give advice on institutional change. Request for advice on policy raises questions of determinancy, path dependence, and degrees of freedoms in institutional reforms. I turn finally to a discussion of the contribution of neoinstitutional economics to institutional policy.

LESSONS FROM THE OLD THEORY OF ECONOMIC POLICY. Neoinstitutional economists need to think more systematically about their role in institutional reforms. I have found it useful to consult the old theory of economic policy which Ragnar Frisch, Jan Tinbergen, and other developed in the years around World War II (see Eggertsson 1997b). The theory of economic policy was a response to developments in contemporary economic theory, especially the theories of Maynard Keynes. Economists believed that they knew how to control and direct economic systems, even in detail. The purpose of the new policy science was to provide a systematic framework for thinking about policy.

The Tinbergen (1956) approach emphasizes that systematic public policy requires a (formal or informal) model of the economy that identifies the relationship between a set of instruments and targets. The instruments are variables controlled by the policymakers, and the targets are variables that represent policy goals. The policy process involves policymakers (administrators, politicians) and experts (economists). Policy makers describe their preferences and provide support for measures taken. Experts specify the policy model, relate instruments to targets, and recommend measures (values for instruments) that maximize the (weighted average of) target variables.

The old theory of economic policy saw experts as having relative advantage in technical knowledge of the relationship between instruments and targets. They were engineers who knew how to repair the economic machine, while the general public and politicians lacked such knowledge. And, reflecting contemporary views, the old policy perspective did not allow for strategic responses to policy measures by the public. Although the Tinbergen policy approach reflects theoretical perspectives that have lost their lustre, it still carries an important message for institutional policy: successful reforms require that we identify available instruments and specify how they relate to policy goals. Until now, neoinstitutional economics has paid little attention to the choice set of economic experts.

LESSONS FROM RECENT DEVELOPMENTS IN ECONOMICS. The theory of institutional policy can also learn from recent developments in political macroeconomics, rational expectations macroeconomics, and bounded rationality macroeconomics.

Political macroeconomics explicitly recognizes that personal goals of policymakers influence their behaviour, and that political pressures limit what they are capable of doing (see Alesina 1995). The old theory of economic policy vaguely assumes that the authorities maximize a social welfare function that is often seen as balancing justice and aggregate wealth.

Rational expectations macroeconomics introduces strategic interactions between policymakers and the people to whom the measures are directed. In its chaste early formulation, rational expectations macroeconomics assumes that the two parties, the authorities and the public, are endowed with accurate policy models (see Lucas 1990). The public, for instance, is assumed to know how the government changes its policy in response to exogenous shocks, and also take advantage of that knowledge. The notion of strategic public reactions to policy is an important insight, which a theory of institutional policy cannot ignore.

Finally, bounded rationality macroeconomics recognizes strategic interactions but introduces the idea that both the authorities and the public rely on imperfect policy models; the parties do not fully understand the structure of the social system. Bounded rationality macroeconomics emphasizes the development of policy models through learning and updating (see Sargent 1993). The theory recognizes that the actors can either arrive at policy models that bring satisfactory outcomes or develop models and strategies that lead to poor social outcomes.

THOUGHTS ABOUT INSTITUTIONAL POLICY. Advisors on institutional reform can learn a few things about their limits and opportunities from the theory of macroeconomics policy. The first lesson concerns the need to establish the true preferences of the policy elite, identify the set of available instruments, and establish whether available instruments can reach the desired goals. The experts must also ask: How does the political process limit choices? How reliable are the best available policy models? Does it make better sense to aim for explicit targets or to initiate a guided process of learning-by-doing that will bring some range of outcomes? And how much should we sacrifice to maintain flexible institutions and have the option of reversing, at low cost, institutional reforms that prove unsatisfactory?

Experts must reckon with policy determinacy and anticipate situations where their efforts are wasted. Their degrees of freedom will vary with circumstances. When experts step into a power vacuum, their role is likely to be relatively great, as it will be when their advice comes backed by threats, such as threats of withdrawal of credit from international lenders. When policy models are contested, experts can influence the course of events by promoting their particular solutions – *laissez faire*, central planning, free trade, industrial policy, specific methods of privatization or regulation. Somewhat paradoxically, here the policy models themselves have become intermediate targets of policy. Finally, the role of experts is relatively large when social systems crash and discredit policy models with which they have been associated (see Eggertsson 1997a). Events such as the Great Depression, the demise of the soviet system, or failure of a regulatory regime in an industry increase the demand for experts who offer alternative models.

Periodic crashes of social systems, both at the macro and micro levels, and the resulting fundamental uncertainty, is a fascinating and important topic of which modern social science knows little. We can view the dynamics of social systems over time as being associated with revisions of the policy models by private and public actors who interact in institutional environments such as regulated industries, labour markets, national health programmes, or centrally managed economies. Interactions of policy models lead to changes in behaviour and to adjustments in institutions that either gradually improve performance or lead the system down a path of decline (Lindbeck 1995). The dynamics of institutional change over time is the greatest unsolved riddle of social science, in spite of valiant efforts by Smith, Malthus, Ricardo, Marx, Schumpeter, and many others.

Finally, if we temporarily forget about the problem of policy determinacy and assume that all concerned are waiting eagerly for our recommendation, what should be our advice? I have four suggestions:

(1) Many formal institutional arrangements were designed without regard for information scarcity and transaction costs. Such arrangements should be reevaluated.

(2) When appropriate, which is often, a central authority should set only the general rules of the game; select the main categories of players (with an eye to their incentives and access to information); and make arrangements to increase the supply of information, for instance, lower the cost of obtaining information from abroad by facilitating international cooperation. Details of institutional arrangements should emerge in trial-and-error experiments among people closely involved in the relevant activity (see Ostrom 1990).

(3) Political risks often block implementation of highly productive institutional reforms (Weingast 1994). When political risks are high, reforms are not credible to those whose support is needed for the measures. Support is lacking because people doubt the government's capacity to properly implement the measures or they expect that all future benefits will go to the political leaders and their cronies. Experts can have a large impact on institutional reforms by inventing new ways to make proposed reforms credible. Credibility is established, for instance, by measures that prevent a corrupt bureaucracy from undermining reforms or make it very costly for governments to default on their promises.

(4) Experts need to recognize the power of informal institutions – norms and social values. They must strive to identify important informal social constraints, and, when possible, try to align formal rules and enforcement with prevailing social norms. When norms are consistent with policy goals, they should be enforced by introducing comparable formal rules. Decentralized procedures of rule making tend to have a relative advantage over centralized ones in recognizing the opportunities and constraints associated with informal institutions (see Cooter 1996).

THRÁINN EGGERTSSON

See also BOUNDED RATIONALITY; COASE, RONALD; COASE THEOREM; PATH DEPENDENCE; STATE POWER.

Subject classification: 1c; 2e.

BIBLIOGRAPHY

Alchian, A.A. 1950. Uncertainty, evolution and economic theory. *Journal of Political Economy* 58: 211–21.

Alesina, A. 1995. Elections, party structure, and the economy. In *Modern Political Economy: Old Topics, New Directions*, ed. J.S. Banks and E.A. Hanushek, Cambridge and New York: Cambridge University Press.

Allen, D.W. 1991. What are transaction costs? *Research in Law and Economics* 14: 1–18.

Alt, J.E. and Shepsle, K.A. (eds.) 1990. *Perspectives on Positive Political Economy*. Cambridge: Cambridge University Press.

Arthur, W.B. 1994. *Increasing Returns and Path Dependence in the Economy*. Ann Arbor: University of Michigan Press.

Banks, J.S. and Hanushek, E.A. 1995. *Modern Political Economy. Old Topics, New Directions*. Cambridge and New York: Cambridge University Press.

Barzel, Y. 1989. *Economic Analysis of Property Rights*. Cambridge: Cambridge University Press.

Clark, A. 1997. Economic reason: the interplay of individual learning and external structure. In *The Frontiers of the New Institutional Economics*, ed. J.N. Drobak and J.V.C. Nye, San Diego, CA: Academic Press.

Coase, R.H. 1937. The nature of the firm. *Economica* 4: 386–405.

Cooter, R. 1982. The cost of Coase. *Journal of Legal Studies* 11: 1–33.

Cooter, R. 1996. Decentralized law for a complex economy: the structural approach to adjucating the new Law Merchant. *University of Pennsylvania Law Review* 144: 1643–96.

Cosmides, L. and Tooby, J. 1994. Better than rational: evolutionary psychology and the invisible hand. *American Economic Review, Papers Proceedings* 84(2): 327–32.

David, P.A. 1994. Why are institutions the 'carriers of history'? Path dependence and the evolution of conventions, organizations, and institutions. *Structural Change and Economic Dynamics* 5: 205–20.

Demsetz, H. 1988. *The Organization of Economic Activity*, 2 vols. Oxford: Basil Blackwell.

Denzau, A.T. and North, D.C. 1994. Shared mental models: ideologies and institutions. *Kyklos* 47: 3–31.

Eggertsson, T. 1990. *Economic Behavior and Institutions*. Cambridge and New York: Cambridge University Press.

Eggertsson, T. 1997a. When the state changes its mind: the puzzle of discontinuity in government control of economic activity. In *Privatization at the turn of the Century*, ed. H. Giersch, Berlin: Springer.

Eggertsson, T. 1997b. The old theory of economic policy and the new institutionalism. *World Development* 25: 1187–1203.

Furubotn, E.G. and Pejovich, S. 1972. Property rights and economic theory: a survey of recent literature. *Journal of Economic Literature* 10: 1137–62.

Hutchins, E. 1995. *Cognition in the Wild*. Cambridge, MA: MIT Press.

Kuran, T. 1995. *Private Truths, Public Lies: The Social Consequences of Preference Falsification*. Cambridge, MA: Harvard University Press.

Lindbeck, A. 1995. Welfare state disincentives with endogenous habits and norms. *Scandinavian Journal of Economics* 97: 477–94.

Lucas, R.E. Jr. 1990. Supply-side economics: an analytical review. *Oxford Economic Papers* 42: 293–316.

Milgrom, P. and Roberts, J. 1992. *Economics, Organization, and Management*. Englewood Cliffs, NJ: Prentice Hall.

North, D.C. 1990. *Institutions, Institutional Change, and Economic Performance*. Cambridge: Cambridge University Press.

North, D.C. 1993. Economic performance through time. Nobel Memorial Prize Lecture, reprinted in *Empirical Studies in Institutional Change*, ed. L.J. Alston, T. Eggertsson and D.C. North, Cambridge: Cambridge University Press, 1996.

Olson, M., Jr. 1996. Big bills left on the sidewalk: why some nations are rich, and others poor. *Journal of Economic Perspectives* 10: 3–24.

Ostrom, E. 1990. *Governing the Commons: The Evolution of Institutions for Collective Action*. Cambridge: Cambridge University Press.

Sargent, T.J. 1993. *Bounded Rationality in Macroeconomics*. Oxford: Oxford University Press.

Scott, A. 1983. Property rights and property wrongs. *Canadian Journal of Economics* 16: 555–73.

Simon, H.A. 1957. *Models of Man*. New York: Wiley.

Stiglitz, J.E. 1994. *Whither Socialism?* Cambridge, MA: MIT Press.

Tinbergen, J. 1956. *Economic Policy: Principles and Design*. Amsterdam: North-Holland.

Weingast, B.R. 1994. The political impediment to economic reform: political risk and enduring gridlock. Working Paper, Hoover Institution, Stanford University, CA.

Williamson, O.E. 1985. *The Economic Institutions of Capitalism: Firms, Markets, Relational Contracting*. New York: The Free Press.

Witt, U. (ed.) 1993. *Evolutionary Economics*. Aldershot: Edward Elgar.

network effects and externalities. Network externality has been defined as a change in the benefit, or surplus, that an agent derives from a good when the number of other agents consuming the same kind of good changes (Katz and Shapiro 1985). As fax machines increase in popularity, for example, your fax machine becomes increasingly valuable since you will have greater use for it. This allows, in principle, the value received by consumers to be separated into two distinct parts. One component, which elsewhere we have labelled the autarky value, is the value generated by the product even if there are no other users. The second component, which we have called synchronization value, is the additional value derived from being able to interact with other users of the product, and it is this latter value that is the essence of network effects.

An illustration: As this essay is being written, commentators are speculating whether Apple computer will survive, since some analysts think that its network (base of users) is shrinking below a minimum acceptable level. Because the actual quantity of Apple computers being sold is still amongst the very largest of all personal computer manufacturers, allowing Apple to take advantage of any economies of scale in production, and its computers are not thought to be deficient in terms of quality, any lack of viability must be due to the fact that the network of Apple computer users is too small. In other words, the synchronization value of Apple computers is thought to be too low.

First a definitional concern: Network effects should not properly be called network externalities unless the participants in the market fail to internalize these effects. After all, it would not be useful to have the term 'externality' mean something different in this literature than it does in the rest of economics. Unfortunately, however, the term externality has indeed been used somewhat carelessly. Although the individual consumers of a product are not likely to internalize the effect of their joining a network on the network's other members, the owner of the network may very well internalize such effects. When the owner of a network (or technology) is able to internalize such network effects, they are no longer externalities. This distinction, first discussed in Liebowitz and Margolis (1994), now seems to be adopted by some authors (e.g. Katz and Shapiro 1994) but has not been universally adopted.

Putting aside definitional concerns, the import of network effects comes largely from the belief that they are endemic to new, high-tech industries, and that accordingly such industries experience problems that are different in character from the problems that have, for more ordinary commodities, been solved by markets (Katz and Shapiro 1985; Farrell and Saloner 1985; Arthur 1996). The purported problems due to network effects are several, but the most arresting is a claim that markets may adopt an inferior product or network in the place of some superior alternative. Thus if network effects are a typical characteristic of modern technologies, the theory suggests that markets may be inadequate for managing the fruits of such technologies.

The concept of network externality has been applied in the economics of standards, where a primary concern is the choice of a correct standard (Farrell and Saloner 1985; Katz and Shapiro 1985; Besen and Farrell 1994; Liebowitz and Margolis 1996). The concept has also played a role in discussions of path dependence (David 1985; Arthur 1989, 1990; Liebowitz and Margolis 1990, 1995a).

Two types of network effects have been identified. *Direct* network effects have been defined as those generated through a direct physical effect of the number of purchasers on the value of a product (e.g. fax machines). *Indirect* network effects are 'market mediated effects' such as cases where complementary goods (e.g. toner cartridges) are more readily available or lower in price as the number of users of a good (laser printers) increases. In early contributions, however, this distinction was not carried into models of network effects. Once network effects were embodied in payoff functions, any distinction between direct and indirect effects was ignored in developing models and drawing conclusions. However, our 1994 paper demonstrates that the two types of effects will typically have different economic implications. It is now generally agreed (Katz and Shapiro 1994) that the consequences of internalizing direct and indirect network effects are quite different. Generally, indirect network effects are pecuniary in nature and therefore should not be internalized. Pecuniary externalities do not impose deadweight losses if left uninternalized, whereas they do impose (monopoly or monopsony) losses if internalized. An interesting aspect of the literature on network externalities is that it has seemed to ignore, and thus repeat, earlier mistakes regarding pecuniary externalities (for the resolution of pecuniary externalities see Young 1913; Knight 1924; Ellis and Fellner 1943).

Concern about marginal adjustment of the level of network activity has not been the primary focus of network externality modelling; it has focused, instead, primarily on selection among competing networks. The discussion below follows this relative emphasis. It briefly considers the issue of levels of network activities in the next section, and then turns to the choice of networks.

1. LEVELS OF NETWORK-RELATED ACTIVITIES. Harvey Leibenstein's work on bandwagon and snob effects (1950) anticipated much of the current discussion of network effects. His main result was that demand curves are more elastic when consumers derive positive value from increases in the size of the market.

One branch of the more recent network literature would fit easily into the Leibenstein framework. Such research has reexamined various economic models with network effects introduced. For example, an analysis of the impacts of unauthorized software copying will change when network effects are introduced. Since unauthorized users increase the size of a network just as do authorized users, and larger network sizes increase the value derived by authorized (paying) users, any harm from unauthorized copying might be mitigated, or perhaps reversed.

The difference between a network effect and a network externality lies in whether the impact of an additional user on other users is somehow internalized. Since the synchronization effect is almost always assumed to be positive in this literature, the social value from another network user will always be greater than the private value. If network effects are not internalized, the equilibrium network size may be smaller than is efficient. For example, if the network of telephone users were not owned, it would likely be smaller than optimal since no agent would capture the benefits that an additional member of the network would confer on other members. (Alternatively, if the network effects were negative a congestion externality might imply that networks tend to be larger than optimal.) Where networks are owned, this effect is internalized and under certain conditions the profit maximizing network size will also be socially optimal (see Liebowitz and Margolis 1995b).

Perhaps surprisingly, the problem of internalizing the network externality is largely unrelated to the problem of choice between competing networks that is taken up in the next section. In the case of positive network externalities, all networks are too small. Therefore, it is not the *relative* market shares of two competing formats but rather the overall level of network activity that will be affected by this difference between private and social values. This is completely compatible with standard results on conventional externalities. For reasons that we will expand on below, this is a far more likely consequence of uninternalized network effects than the more exotic cases of incorrect choices of networks, standards or technologies.

Network size is a real and significant issue that is raised by network effects. Nevertheless, this issue has received fairly little attention in contemporary discussions of network externality, perhaps because it is well handled by more conventional economic models.

2. CHOICE AMONG COMPETING NETWORKS UNDER INCREASING RETURNS. Recent work on network externalities challenges economists' traditional use of decreasing returns and grants primacy to economies of scale. Positive network effects, which raise the values received by consumers as markets get larger, have impacts that are very similar to conventional firm-level economies of scale. If we start an analysis with the assumption that firms produce similar but incompatible products (networks), and that the network effects operate only within classes of compatible products, then competitors (networks) with larger market shares will have an advantage over smaller competitors, *ceteris paribus*. If larger networks have a forever widening advantage over smaller networks, we have entered the realm of natural monopoly, which is exactly where most models that address network and standards choices find themselves.

It is critical to note, however, that network effects are not in general *sufficient* for natural-monopoly-type results. In cases where average production costs are falling, constant, or nonexistent, network effects would be sufficient for a result of natural monopoly. Many, if not most, models in this area ignore production costs and thus with any assumption of positive network effects are unavoidably constructed as instances of natural monopoly. But notice that if production costs exhibit decreasing returns, and if these decreasing returns overwhelm the network effects, then natural monopoly is not implied, and competing incompatible networks (standards) will be possible.

Though economists have long accepted the possibility of increasing returns, they have generally judged that, except in fairly rare instances, the economy operates in a range of decreasing returns. Some proponents of network externalities models predict that as newer technologies take over a larger share of the economy, the share of the economy described by increasing returns will increase. Brian Arthur has emphasized these points to a general audience:

> [R]oughly speaking, diminishing returns hold sway in the traditional part of the economy – the processing industries. Increasing returns reign in the newer part – the knowledge-based industries . . . They call for different management techniques, strategies, and codes of government regulation. They call for different understandings (Arthur 1996: 101).

If the choice of a standard or network is dominated by natural monopoly elements, then only one standard will survive in the market. It is thus of great importance that the standard that comes to dominate the market also be the best of the alternative standards available. Traditionally it has been assumed that the natural monopolist who comes to dominate a market will be at least as efficient as any other producer. This assumption is challenged in the network literature although specifics differ across the many models populating it. The issue that recurs time and again, however, is that we lose the usual assurances that the products that prevail in markets are those that yield the greatest surpluses.

The mere existence of network effects and increasing returns is not sufficient to lead to the choice of an inferior technology. For that, some additional assumptions are needed. One common assumption that can generate a prediction of inefficient network choice is that the network effect differs across the alternative networks. In particular, it is sometimes assumed that the network offering the greatest surplus when network participation is large also offers the smallest surplus when participation is small. This condition, however, is not likely to be satisfied, since synchronization effects are likely to be uniform. For example, if there is value in a cellular telephone network becoming larger, this should be equally true whether the network is digital or analog. Similarly, the network value of an additional user of a particular videorecorder format is purported to be the benefits accrued by having more opportunities to exchange video tapes. But this extra value does not depend on the particular format of videorecorder chosen. If network effects are the same for all versions of a given product, it is very unlikely that the wrong format would be chosen if both are available at the same time (see PATH DEPENDENCE).

3. COMMON RESTRICTIONS IN NETWORK EFFECTS MODELS. As we have noted, network externality models often feature particular outcomes: Survival of only one network or standard, unreliability of market selection, and the entrenchment of incumbents. In formal models, these results follow inevitably from assumptions that are common simplifications in economic theory and that appear to be relatively unrestrictive. As applied in these network models, however, these assumptions are both critically responsible for the results and unappealingly restrictive.

Two important limitations of many network externalities models are the assumptions of constant marginal production cost and network value functions that rise without limit (see, for example, Katz and Shapiro 1986: 829; Chou and Shy 1990: 260; Farrell and Saloner 1992: 16 and Church and Gandal 1993: 246). Matutes and Regibeau (1992) consider issues of duopoly and compatibility under a similar structure. Such assumptions impose an inexhaustible economy of large-scale operation. If network size could reach a point where additional participation did not provide additional value to participants, then increases in scale would no longer be advantageous and it would be possible for multiple networks to compete at an efficient output.

Without investigation, it seems unreasonable that in all or most new-technology industries the law of diminishing marginal product is somehow suspended. While the scale properties of a technology pertain to the simultaneous expansion of all inputs, it seems evident that resource limitations do ultimately constrain firm size. Economists have long supposed that limitations of management play a role in this, a relationship formalized in Radner (1992). The resource constraints faced by America Online in early 1997 is an example of this type of effect, even if it was only a short-run phenomenon at that time.

Another limitation is the common assumption that consumers are identical in their valuations of competing networks. Once heterogeneous tastes are allowed it becomes feasible for competing networks to coexist with one another even though each exhibits natural monopoly characteristics (e.g., if some computer owners much prefer Macintoshes and others much prefer the PC, they could both coexist).

A further restriction in the modelling is the undifferentiated value received by consumers when another consumer joins a network, regardless of who the new consumer is. If economists, for example, much prefer to have other economists join their network as opposed to, say, sociologists, then a sociologist has a smaller network effect than another economist. Such differential network impacts make it possible for economists to form a coalition that switches to a new standard even if the new standard fails to attract many sociologists. This latter point will prove to be of great importance when examining empirical examples of choosing the wrong standard, where large entities such as multinational firms and governments play an important role.

4. THE EMPIRICAL RELEVANCE OF NETWORK EFFECTS AND INCREASING RETURNS. Although many technologies have tended to evolve into single formats (e.g. home-use VCRs are almost all of the VHS variety) some portion of these may actually have evolved for reasons having little to do with either network effects *or* increasing returns. We should not be surprised to find that where there are differences in the performance of various standards, one may prevail over the others simply because it is better suited to the market.

First of all, the extent (and homogeneity) of network effects may be much more limited than is commonly assumed. For example, in the case of word-processors, it may be quite important for a small group of collaborators to use identical software so as to be perfectly compatible with each other. Similarly, compatibility may be important for employees within a firm. But compatibility with the rest of the world may be relatively unimportant, unimportant enough to be overwhelmed by differences in preferences, so that multiple networks could survive. Networks that serve niche markets well (such as word-processors specializing in mathematical notation), might not be significantly disadvantaged by network effects.

As an illustration, consider the empirical examples of tax software and financial software. By far the dominant firm in North America is Intuit, with its Turbo-Tax products and Quicken financial software. This market seems to have tilted strongly toward a single producer. Yet network effects should be virtually nonexistent for these products. Consumers do *not* exchange this type of information with one another. A superior explanation that is consistent with the product reviews in computer magazines is that these products are simply *better* than the alternatives.

Similarly, for large firms, compatibility within the firm should be of great importance, but compatibility outside the firm might be of little consequence. For many products where the majority of customers are large firms, producers will not encounter natural monopoly elements since there may be little or no network advantage in selling to multiple firms. Firms using spreadsheets, for example, will likely benefit from compatibility within the firm and there will be strong network effects *within* a firm. Across firms, however, network effects might be nonexistent. If the only natural monopoly element in spreadsheet production were the network effect (e.g. constant or increasing spreadsheet-production costs), we might find multiple producers of spreadsheets, each with a natural monopoly over the firms that had adopted that particular spreadsheet, but with no producer being a natural monopolist for the market as a whole.

Regarding increasing returns in production leading to a single product or standard (independent of network effects), it is true that the past decades have evidenced a number of technologies that have experienced enormous declines in prices and tremendous growth in sales. Nevertheless, it is not clear that this is the result of increasing returns to (network) scale *per se*. Since bigger has been cheaper, it has often been assumed that bigger causes cheaper. But an available alternative explanation is that as technologies have advanced with time, the average cost curves (derived under *ceteris paribus* assumptions) have themselves been shifting down over time. If that is the case, the implied causality may be reversed: Cheaper causes bigger. Consider for example the history of old technologies, such as refrigerators and automobiles, or of a modern product such as the personal computer. These industries, currently thought to exhibit conventional decreasing returns in production beyond a minimum efficient scale, experienced tremendous cost decreases, along with tremendous increases in utilization, early in their histories. Changes in technology may have been more important than changes in scale. (For a related discussion of increasing returns and monopolization, see Stigler 1941: 68–76.)

5. POLICY IMPLICATIONS. The theory of network externality is currently playing a role in several antitrust actions, the most prominent of which are the investigations of Microsoft by the Justice Department over various aspects of Microsoft's behaviour, including its attempted purchase of Intuit, the inclusion of the Microsoft Network as an icon in Windows 95, Microsoft's attempt to wrest control of the web browser market from Netscape, and so forth. The claim seems to be that since markets cannot be relied upon to choose the best standards or bring about the right networks, governments might wish to investigate and control firms' efforts to make standards or establish networks. These theories played a central role in the *amicus curiae* brief against the Microsoft consent decree presented by four anonymous parties (*United States v. Microsoft Corp.*).

Clearly the potential to misuse such as yet unsubstantiated theories in antitrust actions by competitors unable to win in the marketplace is very great, not unlike that of various theories of predation. With so little empirical support for these theories, it appears at best premature and at worst simply wrong to use them as the basis for antitrust decisions.

It is also possible that network effects may cast in a new light the role of copyright and patent laws. First, networks are likely to be too small if network effects are not internalized. Intellectual property laws are one means by which such network effects can be internalized, since ownership is an ideal method of internalization.

The possibility that networks can compete with each other suggests a further consideration regarding intellectual property law. Where one standard is owned and another is not, we can have less confidence that an unowned but superior standard will be able to prevail against an owned standard, since the owner of a standard can appropriate the benefits of internalizing any network effects. Although we do not have any evidence that inferior standards have prevailed against superior standards (in free markets), this may be in large part because most standards are supported by companies that have some form of ownership such as patent, copyright, or business positioning. The greatest chance for some form of third-degree path dependence (see PATH DEPENDENCE) to arise would be if an unowned standard with dispersed adherents were to engage in competition with a standard that had well defined ownership. Further research in this area is needed before any firm conclusions can be drawn, however.

6. CONCLUSIONS. Network effects are undoubtedly real and important phenomena. The popular and very compelling example is the telephone network. Who would deny that the value of phone service depends heavily on the number of other people who have phone service? Contemporary technologies expand that example enormously.

The enthusiasm for recognizing and understanding these phenomena should not, however, lead us to inappropriate or premature conclusions. As we have noted above, there are distinctions and reservations that ought to be maintained. The first and broadest is that between network effects and network externalities. A further distinction is between pecuniary externalities and real ones. Even for the set of real externalities, it is important to note the distinction between the problem of network size and that of network choice, the boundedness of the network effect, the likely symmetry of network effects for alternative products, the ability of large consumers to self-internalize network effects, and the influence of differences in tastes.

Finally, we would urge some reservation about the empirical validity of economies of production scale for many high-tech products. If these products have diseconomies of scale at some production level, these production costs may overturn other natural monopoly elements. Improvements in production costs, as with many other economic results, may have more to do with being smarter than with being bigger.

S.J. LIEBOWITZ AND STEPHEN E. MARGOLIS

See also ANTITRUST POLICY; CHEAP TALK AND COORDINATION; INFORMATIONAL CASCADES AND SOCIAL CONVENTIONS; NETWORK EXTERNALITY AND CONVENTION; PATH DEPENDENCE.

Subject classification: 1b(ii).

CASES

United States v. Microsoft Corp., 159 FRD 318, 333–38 (1995) (Sporkin, J.), rev'd and remanded, 56 F3d 1448 (DC Cir. 1995).

BIBLIOGRAPHY

Arthur, W.B. 1989. Competing technologies, increasing returns, and lock-in by historical events. *Economic Journal* 99: 116–31.

Arthur, W.B. 1990. Positive feedbacks in the economy. *Scientific American* 262: 92–9.

Arthur, W.B. 1996. Increasing returns and the new world of business. *Harvard Business Review* 72: 100–109.

Besen, S.M. and Farrell, J. 1994. Choosing how to compete: strategies and tactics in standardization. *Journal of Economic Perspectives* 8: 117–31.

Chou, C. and Shy, O. 1990. Network effects without network externalities. *International Journal of Industrial Organization* 8: 259–70.

Church, J and Gandal, N. 1993. Complementary network externalities and technological adoption. *International Journal of Industrial Organization* 11: 239–60.

David, P.A. 1985. Clio and the economics of QWERTY. *American Economic Review, Papers and Proceedings* 75: 332–7.

Ellis, H.S. and Fellner, W. 1943. External economies and diseconomies. *American Economic Review* 33: 493–511.

Farrell, J. and Saloner, G. 1985. Standardization, compatibility, and innovation. *RAND Journal of Economic* 16: 70–83.

Farrell, J. and Saloner, G. 1992. Converters, compatibility, and control of interfaces. *Journal of Industrial Economics* 40: 9–35.

Katz, M.L. and Shapiro, C. 1985. Network externalities, competition, and compatibility. *American Economic Review* 75: 424–40.

Katz, M.L. and Shapiro, C. 1986. Technology adoption in the presence of network externalities. *Journal of Political Economy* 94: 822–41.

Katz, M.L. and Shapiro, C. 1994. Systems competition and network effects. *Journal of Economic Perspectives* 8: 93–115.

Knight, F.H. 1924. Some fallacies in the interpretation of social cost. *Quarterly Journal of Economics* 38: 582–606.

Leibenstein, H. 1950. Bandwagon, snob, and Veblen effects in the theory of consumer's demand. *Quarterly Journal of Economics* 64: 183–207.

Liebowitz, S.J. and Margolis, S.E. 1990. The fable of the keys. *Journal of Law and Economics* 33: 1–25.

Liebowitz, S.J. and Margolis, S.E. 1994. Network externality: an uncommon tragedy. *Journal of Economic Perspectives* 8: 133–50.

Liebowitz, S.J. and Margolis, S.E. 1995a. Path dependence, lock-in and history. *Journal of Law, Economics and Organization* 11: 205–26.

Liebowitz, S.J. and Margolis, S.E. 1995b. Are network externalities a new source of market failure? *Research In Law and Economics* 17: 1–22.

Liebowitz, S.J. and Margolis, S.E. 1996. Market processes and the selection of standards. *Harvard Journal of Law and Technology* 9: 283–318.

Matutes, C. and Regibeau, P. 1992. Compatibility and bundling of complementary goods in a duopoly. *Journal of Industrial Economics* 40: 37–54.

Radner, R. 1992. Hierarchy: the economics of managing. *Journal of Economic Literature* 30: 1382–1415.

Stigler, G.J. 1941. *Production and Distribution Theories*. New York: Macmillan.

Young, A.A. 1913. Pigou's *Wealth and Welfare*. *Quarterly Journal of Economics* 27: 672–86.

network externality and convention. Your decision to get an electronic mail account may increase the value of an Internet connection to other current and potential users. This effect is an example of a positive network externality. Other examples include decisions as to which computer to buy, which language to learn, and which currency to hold.

The essence of network externality is that the value of an activity to the individual depends on how many other individuals engage in the same activity. Problems with this feature are discussed in the literature also using terms such as *adoption externalities* or *critical mass* phenomena (see e.g. Schelling 1978; Dybvig and Spatt 1983). In the case of a positive relationship between the number of adopters and the expected utility of adoption, which is the case we will be concerned with here, there is a close connection between the idea of network externality and that of convention. A convention, following Lewis (1969), is a commonly known and observed regularity of behaviour that solves some recurrent coordination problem. Consider the problem of deciding which currency to accept in exchange. It is not of primary importance to you what shape or colour the associated pieces of paper have – the fundamental question is how many other people will later in turn accept them as payment for goods or services. The more widespread the use of the currency you accept, the greater the probability of your being able to use it later, and the greater the value of that currency to you. Equivalently, the common use of a particular currency is a convention that solves the coordination problem of indirect exchange.

The power of the network effect embodied in a convention is often underestimated or forgotten. In the 1964 movie *Goldfinger*, secret agent James Bond stops a diabolical scheme by the eponymous villain to destroy the gold reserves in Fort Knox. The idea is that destroying the gold will cause the world economy to collapse by making the American dollar worthless, allowing Goldfinger to take control. Something is wrong with this logic, plausible though it may seem at first glance. Clearly the value of the American dollar does not depend on whether there is gold in Fort Knox or not. Few people could directly verify whether this is the case or not, and yet they willingly accept dollars in payment for goods or services. They do so because they expect other people to do likewise. A public announcement to the effect that there is no gold in Fort Knox would cause the value of the dollar to drop to zero only insofar as it instantly makes everyone believe that no one will accept dollars in exchange – and, perhaps, only so long as there is some viable alternative for coordinating expectations.

Because of network effects, existing conventions are not necessarily efficient, in the sense that no other feasible convention exists that would be preferred by everyone. Even though Esperanto may be a superior language in some absolute sense, you have no use for it if nobody you meet speaks Esperanto. Yet, although the term network externality is firmly established, care should be taken in using it. Liebowitz and Margolis (1994) point out that there are network effects that are not externalities in the usual sense of non-contractible side-effects inducing deviations from Pareto optimality. This is clear, for example, insofar as the effect works through the price mechanism. If the market price for computer software written for a particular operating system is indirectly affected by the number of consumers who buy the operating system, this is part of the normal workings of a market, which may involve transfers of wealth, and not a Pareto-relevant external effect. When we speak of inefficiency in the following text, this is not meant to suggest that government intervention is called for or even possible. In the typically global contexts we are concerned with here, involving conventions of language or media of exchange, the activities of particular local governments are usually irrelevant, at least in the long run. Furthermore, in order to discuss the role of government in these matters, it is clearly necessary to have a theory of the political process and government regulatory activities. As pointed out by authors such as Tullock (1967) and Stigler (1971), the parties who have the most clearly focused interests in regulation, and thus the incentive to try to affect it, are typically the regulated firms themselves. Thus, for example, the setting of product standards through regulation may serve to induce inefficiences rather than alleviate them.

The basic problem of coordination inherent in any situation with network effects is captured by the simple two-player game of Table 1, where two players independently have to choose one of two actions, a_1 and a_2. The left-hand number of a cell of this matrix is the utility accruing to the row player, the right-hand number that of the column player. A Nash equilibrium is a combination of action choices such that no player wishes to change his choice given that he expects the other player to stick to his. The example game therefore has three equilibria – one where both players choose a_1, another where both players choose a_2, and a third where the players randomize their choices in such a fashion that they undertake action a_1 with probability 1/3.

Table 1
A coordination game

	a_1	a_2
a_1	2, 2	0, 0
a_2	0, 0	1, 1

In this example, both players would prefer the situation where both play a_1 and both get a payoff of 2 – that is, the (a_1, a_1) equilibrium is efficient. Yet there is no guarantee of this happening. An equilibrium is simply a pair of strategies such that when both players' expectations are coordinated on it, neither one has an incentive to deviate. In particular, both (a_1, a_1) and (a_2, a_2) fulfil this requirement.

The industrial organization literature on network effects (see e.g. Farrell and Saloner 1985; Katz and Shapiro 1985, 1986) is concerned mainly with issues of standardization and the introduction of new technologies. Our simple example game illustrates the logic of technology choice and network effects in what Katz and Shapiro (1994) call systems markets. Consider the following problem. A firm is considering whether to adopt a new, superior product standard. The good marketed by the firm is such that a consumer's utility is increasing in the number of other users of a good adhering to the same standard. Then there may be multiple equilibria just as in our example game. If each consumer expects all other consumers to switch, it is rational for the individual consumer to switch, and those expectations are indeed fulfilled. Conversely, if each consumer expects all other consumers to stay with the status quo, it is rational not to switch, so this is another fulfilled expectations equilibrium.

We have an intuition that the possibility of communication solves coordination problems. Yet this intuition is not easily captured in formal game-theoretical terms. This is because it seems most sensible to model verbal utterances as practically costless. Adding the possibility of such actions to a game then only nominally affects the set of equilibria. Assume the agents in our example game verbally agree to both play a_1. If they thereupon both play a_2, that is still a Nash equilibrium. In fact, since the messages do not affect the ultimate payoffs, any combination of messages followed by an equilibrium of the original game is an equilibrium of the game extended with communication. From the standpoint of orthodox game theory, any attempt to label the inefficient equilibria implausible will have to be based on intuition. The formal logic of equilibrium does not exclude them. Talk is cheap and only actions that directly affect payoffs matter. We have no theory of why it should be rational to act in accordance with the conventional meanings of talk – but we do have theories of why the only stable assignments of meaning are those that result in coordination (see Wärneryd 1991).

If decisions in a coordination game do not have to be simultaneous, and the player who goes second can observe the decision of the first player before making his own choice, the set of plausible solutions is narrowed dramatically. For consider now the choice of the second player. If he has observed that the first player has played a_1, his only rational option is to choose a_1 also. If the first player has played a_2, the second player's only rational option is a_2. Given that the player who goes first knows that the second player will behave rationally, his best choice is a_1. Thus this process of backwards induction suggests that common knowledge of rationality implies that the efficient outcome will always occur in a game of this type when moves are sequential. (In game-theoretic terminology, (a_1, a_1) is the unique subgame perfect outcome of the sequential game.) A similar conclusion holds for analogous games with many players. Consider, for example, a game with two alternatives, where an individual gets a positive payoff only if everyone has chosen the same alternative. As long as the population is finite and decisions are made sequentially with perfect observability, the logic of backwards induction shows that each player must rationally choose the alternative that is preferred by all. Farrell and Saloner (1985) use this type of logic to argue that firms who have the option of switching to a standard that would be preferred by all firms if all adopted it will in fact switch if they make their decisions sequentially.

On the other hand, this solution depends critically on the choice made by the first decision-maker. If the player who goes first deviates and makes the wrong choice, it is rational for all who come later to follow him, which in turn leads to an inefficient outcome. This illustrates that there may be a bias toward the *status quo* in situations where there is a past history of decisions. Such *lock-in*, *inertia*, or *path dependence* effects are studied by, for example, Arthur (1994). A much-cited historical example is the continued use of the QWERTY standard for the layout of typewriter and computer keyboards, even though supposedly there exist superior alternatives (e.g. the Dvorak keyboard). The QWERTY standard is argued to be a historical accident that has become locked in because of the strong bias, given an installed base of typists trained on the QWERTY keyboard, for later keyboard manufacturers to conform to the precedent set by the original developers (see David 1985).

A more subtle network effect arises from the possibility of what is now known as *informational cascades* (see Bikhchandani, Hirshleifer and Welch 1992). Suppose you face a decision problem where the utility you derive from the various alternatives does not depend fundamentally on the decisions of other people, but you are uncertain about the relative merits of the alternatives. Then if other decision-makers have private information about the desirability of different choices, observing their choices reveals information and may make you wish to conform. Lewis (1969) uses the following example. A person who observes other people wearing raincoats on the street may conclude that they have heard weather forecasts warning of rain to come, and may thus rationally decide to wear a raincoat himself. This in turn makes it rational for later decision-makers to don their raincoats. As the evidence of past decisions accumulates, it may become inevitable that all agents ignore their own information and put on their raincoats based on the information revealed by previous decisions. Lewis argues that such behaviour does not constitute a convention in his sense, precisely because there is no fundamental need for coordination. However, there is clearly a higher-level coordination problem in these situations, arising from informational asymmetries, that has much the same structure as any other coordination game, so similar mechanisms are at work.

The discussion so far has centred on examples with a small number of players, and we have noted a number of ways in which coordination might plausibly occur in these cases. The term convention is of course typically reserved for regularities of behaviour that solve coordination problems involving *large* numbers of individuals. For example, the convention of shaking hands solves the problem of greeting strangers in at least the entire Western world. In problems involving such large numbers, it does not seem reasonable to assume that the stringent assumptions, such as rationality being common knowledge, that guarantee an equilibrium outcome in small-number cases hold.

Consider again the two-player game of Table 1, but now assume it is played by two players who have been drawn randomly from a large population of identical players. Think of strategy a_1 as offering your right hand in greeting to a stranger, and a_2 as using your left hand. Suppose that n_1 is the share of the population who use their right hand, and $n_2 = 1 - n_1$ is the share of the population who use their left. These are then also the approximate probabilities of encountering the respective strategies under random matching.

The expected utility of using a particular strategy is now an increasing function of the number of other people who use the same strategy. The expected utility of using strategy a_1 is equal to

$$u_1(n_1) := n_1 \cdot 2 + n_2 \cdot 0 = 2n_1,$$

and the expected utility of using strategy a_2 is equal to

$$u_2(n_1) := n_1 \cdot 0 + n_2 \cdot 1 = 1 - n_1.$$

These functions are graphed in Figure 1.

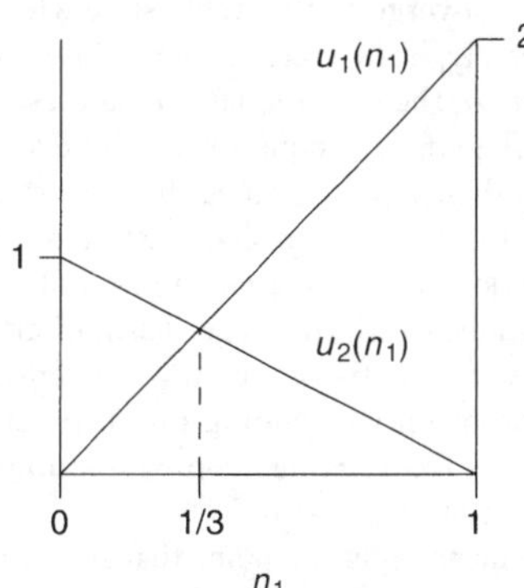

Figure 1 The critical mass

If we have $n_1 < 1/3$, it is better to use strategy a_2. If we have $n_1 > 1/3$, it is better to use strategy a_1. Thus $n_1^* = 1/3$ is a threshold population share for strategy a_1, or *critical mass*, such that if it is exceeded, all individuals would prefer to play strategy a_1.

Suppose the population is initially at the inefficient equilibrium, i.e. everybody plays a_2. With a large number of individuals involved in a coordination problem, it seems unreasonable to assume that they could all coordinate to switch simultaneously. It is therefore natural instead to take an evolutionary approach. What if new generations of players enter the population, possibly experimenting with new ways of behaving? Which conventions are stable under such a process?

A simple approach to this stability question is provided by the concept of an *evolutionarily stable strategy* (ESS) originally introduced by Maynard Smith (see, e.g., Maynard Smith 1982) in evolutionary biology. The ESS notion captures the idea that an equilibrium strategy should be stable against small invasions of 'mutants' playing some other strategy. Consider a general symmetric two-player game with strategy set $S := \{s_1, s_2, \ldots, s_m\}$ and payoff function u: $S \times S \to \mathbb{R}$. A strategy $s \in S$ is said to be evolutionarily stable if for all $s' \neq s$ we have that

$$u(s, s) > u(s', s), \text{ or}$$

$$u(s, s) = u(s', s) \text{ and } u(s, s') > u(s', s').$$

That is, a strategy s is an ESS if either it is a strict best reply against itself (in which case (s, s) is a strict Nash equilibrium), or there is a potential mutant strategy that does equally well against s, but strictly worse against itself than does s against the mutant.

Since both pure-strategy equilibria of our example game are strict equilibria, both are ESSs. The ESS concept, although static, is closely related to that of stable stationary states of payoff-monotonic dynamical systems based on games (see, e.g., Weibull 1995). An evolutionary selection process is payoff-monotonic if the relative growth rate of a strategy's population share is proportional to its current average payoff. Thus under any payoff-monotonic evolutionary dynamics, starting from some point to the left of $n_1^* = 1/3$ in our example, where the average payoff from playing a_2 is higher than from playing a_1, the population will eventually converge to the stable state where all agents play a_2. Conversely, if the starting-point has a greater share than n_1^* playing a_1, the evolutionary dynamics will take the population to the efficient equilibrium. The set of population shares less than n_1^* is said to be the *basin of attraction* of a_2, while the set of population shares greater than n_1^* is the basin of attraction of a_1. If a starting-point is chosen at random, the strategy with the larger basin of attraction will be more likely to be the long-run convention. In our example, the probability of ending up in the efficient convention is thus 2/3, starting from a randomly selected initial configuration.

This argument neglects the point that realistic evolutionary processes based on, e.g., individual experiment- ation, must typically be subject to *constant* mutation. Kandori, Mailath and Rob (1993) study a model of such a process in 2 × 2 games. Suppose, by way of an example, that the population only consists of ten individuals. The agents occasionally reconsider their strategy choices, and when they do, they normally pick a best reply against the current population distribution. But with some small probability ε an individual will pick the wrong strategy when he updates. Call this phenomenon a mutation. Suppose the population is initially at the inefficient equilibrium, i.e., all individuals play a_2. Then, clearly, we need four simultaneous mutations in order for a_1 to become a best reply. That is, four people constitute the critical mass necessary for a switch from the inefficient situation. Conversely, if we start at the efficient situation where all players play a_1, seven simultaneous mutations are necessary for a switch to a_2. Thus a switch to the efficient equilibrium is more likely than the other way around. Kandori et al. go on to show that in the long run, as time approaches infinity, and as ε approaches zero, the relative proportion of time spent at the efficient equilibrium in this system approaches one. Although both switch probabil-ities become smaller as ε falls, the probability of a switch to the inefficient equilibrium becomes smaller at a faster rate.

In general, Kandori et al. show that this process of constant mutation leads to the evolutionary selection of the *risk dominant* strategy in 2 × 2 games (also see Young 1993). A strategy is risk dominant if it is a best reply when both strategies are equally likely (see Harsanyi and Selten 1988). The simple reason for the result is that a risk dominant strategy has the larger basin of attraction.

Table 2
The medium-of-exchange game

	M	B
M	u_M	0
B	r	$u_B + r$

In the pure coordination games we have studied so far, the risk dominance and efficiency criteria coincide. We conclude by considering a slightly more specific example, involving a model of medium-of-exchange choice (see also Wärneryd 1989).

Wallace (1983) argues that the only reason individuals hold government-issued paper money is that legal tender laws force them to. Government money has the disadvantage as a capital good that it does not yield any interest. If people were free to use whatever they wished as money, a switch would occur to bonds or other interest-bearing instruments.

This argument ignores the coordination problem inherent in medium-of-exchange choice. Even if using bonds as money were to be an efficient convention, individuals would not recoordinate their expectations on this basis alone if legal tender laws were to be abolished. Instead, as long as agents expected a sufficient number of others to continue to hold government money, the original convention would still be in force. Nevertheless, we shall now argue that a switch may occur with certainty in the *very long* run discussed by Kandori et al.

We may investigate the conditions for a switch to occur by modelling this problem as a simple coordination game. Suppose we have a large population of agents who meet randomly in pairs for exchange interaction. Exchange can only take place if both players in a match use the same medium of exchange. Suppose medium M is such that it yields its user a utility of u_M if a successful transaction takes place, and zero otherwise. Suppose there is also another potential medium, B, which in addition to the utility u_B from a successful transaction also always yields an interest payment r. Thus B-users always get at least utility r, even if no exchange takes place. We summarize this payoff structure in Table 2.

Suppose the share of the population using M is n_M, and the share using B is $n_B = 1 - n_M$. These are also the probabilities of encountering the respective strategies under random matching. Then the expected utility of an M-user is $n_M u_M + n_B \cdot 0 = n_M u_M$, and the expected utility of a B-user is $n_M r + n_B(u_B + r) = (1 - n_M) u_B + r$. We note that the expected utilities of both activities are increasing in the share of their respective adherents. Suppose we have $r < u_M$, i.e. it is better to conclude a successful exchange transaction in medium M than to just have the interest payment from B. Then there is some population share n^*_M of M-users such that an agent is indifferent between the two instruments, i.e. such that $n^*_M u_M = (1 - n^*_M)u_B + r$. We have $n^*_M = (u_B + r)/(u_M + u_B)$.

If we have $n_M > n^*_M$, all individuals would prefer holding M. Conversely, if we have $n_M < n^*_M$, all individuals would prefer to hold B. Thus $n^*_B = 1 - n^*_M = (u_M - r)/(u_M + u_B)$

is the critical mass necessary for a switch from the M convention, if it is in force.

We now note that

$$n^*_B < 1/2 \Leftrightarrow u_B + 2r > u_M, \text{ and}$$

$$0.5r + 0.5(u_B + r) > 0.5u_M \Leftrightarrow u_B + 2r > u_M.$$

Thus the critical mass for a switch to the B-convention, starting at the M-convention, is less than 1/2 exactly when the B-convention is risk dominant. It is not sufficient for the M-convention to be efficient for it to have the greater critical mass, since we could have $u_M > u_B + r$ but $u_M < u_B + 2r$. That is, even if the B-convention is inefficient, it could have a small critical mass, and thus a larger basin of attraction under evolutionary dynamics. In the latter case, the analysis of Kandori et al. suggests that, in the long run, the B-convention would in fact win out in a statistical sense.

KARL WÄRNERYD

See also ANTITRUST POLICY; CHEAP TALK AND COORDINATION; CONVENTIONS AND TRANSACTION COSTS; COORDINATION GAMES; EVOLUTIONARY GAME THEORY; INFORMATIONAL CASCADES AND SOCIAL CONVENTIONS; NETWORK EFFECTS AND EXTERNALITIES; PATH DEPENDENCE.

Subject classification: 1b(ii); 1d(ii).

BIBLIOGRAPHY

Arthur, W.B. 1994. *Increasing Returns and Path Dependence in the Economy*. Ann Arbor: University of Michigan Press.

Bikhchandani, S., Hirshleifer, D. and Welch, I. 1992. A theory of fads, fashion, custom, and cultural change as informational cascades. *Journal of Political Economy* 100: 992–1026.

David, P. 1985. Clio and the economics of QWERTY. *American Economic Review* Papers and Proceedings, 75: 332–7.

Dybvig, P.H. and Spatt, C.S. 1983. Adoption externalities as public goods. *Journal of Public Economics* 20: 231–47.

Farrell, J. and Saloner, G. 1985. Standardization, compatibility, and innovation. *RAND Journal of Economics* 16: 70–83.

Harsanyi, J.C. and Selten, R. 1988. *A General Theory of Equilibrium Selection in Games*. Cambridge, MA: MIT Press.

Kandori, M., Mailath, G.J. and Rob, R. 1993. Learning, mutation, and long run equilibria in games. *Econometrica* 61: 29–56.

Katz, M.L. and Shapiro, C. 1985. Network externalities, competition, and compatibility. *American Economic Review* 75: 424–40.

Katz, M.L. and Shapiro, C. 1986. Technology adoption in the presence of network externalities. *Journal of Political Economy* 94: 822–41.

Katz, M.L. and Shapiro, C. 1994. Systems competition and network effects. *Journal of Economic Perspectives* 8(2): 93–115.

Lewis, D.K. 1969. *Convention. A Philosophical Study*. Cambridge, MA: Harvard University Press.

Liebowitz, S.J. and Margolis, S.E. 1994. Network externality: an uncommon tragedy. *Journal of Economic Perspectives* 8(2): 133–50.

Maynard Smith, J. 1982. *Evolution and the Theory of Games*. Cambridge: Cambridge University Press.

Schelling, T.C. 1978. *Micromotives and Macrobehavior*. New York: Norton.

Stigler, G.J. 1971. The theory of economic regulation. *Bell Journal of Economics and Management Science* 2: 3–21.

Tullock, G. 1967. The welfare costs of tariffs, monopolies, and theft. *Western Economic Journal* 5: 224–32.

Wallace, N. 1983. A legal restrictions theory of the demand for 'money' and the role of monetary policy. *Federal Reserve Bank of Minneapolis Quarterly Review* 7: 1–7.

Wärneryd, K. 1989. Legal restrictions and the evolution of media of exchange. *Journal of Institutional and Theoretical Economics* 145: 613–26.

Wärneryd, K. 1991. Evolutionary stability in unanimity games with cheap talk. *Economics Letters* 36: 375–8.

Weibull, J.W. 1995. *Evolutionary Game Theory*. Cambridge, MA: MIT Press.

Young, H.P. 1993. The evolution of conventions. *Econometrica* 61: 57–84.

NEV suits. *See* SUITS WITH NEGATIVE EXPECTED VALUE.

Newcomb's paradox. *See* PRISONERS' DILEMMA AND THE THEORY OF THE STATE.

no-fault automobile insurance. *See* AUTOMOBILE ACCIDENTS, INSURANCE AND TORT LIABILITY.

no-fault divorce. Although most of the law and economics literature is concerned with the American version of no-fault divorce, most industrial nations have many of the same laws. Finland remains the only European nation to have unilateral no-fault grounds for divorce, although Sweden (since 1973) and Great Britain (under 1996 legislation which takes effect in 1999) have no-fault bilateral and unilateral divorce. The other European nations, like the majority of United States jurisdictions, have added no-fault to the traditional fault grounds (*International Law Digest* 1996), with Ireland finally permitting divorce in November of 1996.

England's former law of divorce, enacted in 1973, allowed for bilateral and 'irretrievable breakdown' divorce specifying various fault grounds. In the early 1990s, faced with the highest divorce rates in recorded history (Freeman 1996: 199), the British Government proposed a 'back to basics' philosophy that would lengthen the waiting period for divorce to twelve months (eighteen months where there were minor children), during which mediation and reflection would take place. This no-fault law was finally enacted by Parliament in July 1996. Although the grounds for divorce under the new bill made fault completely irrelevant, the change was welcomed by conservatives because it makes divorce less hasty than the fault divorces most people obtained under the old statute. Since the mediation and counselling provisions add substantial transaction costs and encourage reconciliation, the idea is that the divorce rate should first increase over the next several years, then decrease (*New Statesman and Society* 1996). However, two British economists recently decried the system because the 'legal reforms have reduced the incentive for commitment in marriage' (Ormerod and Rowthorn 1996). Likening marriage to the formation of a joint business venture, these writers note that the availability of specific performance or damages in case of contractual breach provide potential partners with the security required to invest wealth and energies in the venture. The empirical work necessary to substantiate such claims for and against no-fault systems comes almost entirely from the United States.

'No fault' divorce was first introduced in the US in 1969 in California, which until then had adultery as its only ground for divorce. After the advent of no-fault, California divorces could be granted upon 'irretrievable breakdown of the marriage', eliminating not only the necessity for showing fault but also the need for both spouses to agree to divorce. Its proponents heralded the statute as a release from moribund marriages. Some feminists argued that with greater financial opportunities available to women and no barriers to exit from marriage, women ought to be free to reach their true potential. In addition, the threat of fault divorce, with its disastrous economic consequences, would no longer be there to penalize women if they left a bad marriage (Regan 1992: 1464–5). As discussed in more detail below, Parkman (1992: 61–3) notes public choice reasons for the change to no-fault, such as pressure upon male-dominated legislatures by easily organized divorced men's groups.

Freedom from the restrictions of fault divorces (i.e., a non-fault liability rule) proved troublesome for alimony. Since fault (breach), which had previously been the trigger for alimony (damages), was no longer necessary for divorce, alimony was to provide for the needy spouse who could not support him- or herself because of lack of job training or education or the competing burdens of child care. Economic equality was to be secured through property distribution, which could be made without regard to fault and with a recognition that each spouse contributed to the marriage as a partner.

However, the changes in the financial attributes of divorce have not been complete solutions. Since many women do not earn as much as their husbands (Fuchs 1988: 44–5), they have lower opportunity costs, and frequently remain primary caretakers for their children despite gender-neutral custody laws. In those marriages that do not last long enough to accumulate significant tangible property, many divorcing women have found themselves with less wealth than before no-fault divorce. This presumably unintended consequence of no-fault divorce has been noted by many writers; the citations appear in Brinig and Crafton (1994: 878–9).

There is yet another repercussion of no-fault divorce that is less prominent in the literature, and that is its effect upon the marriage contract itself. The marriage obligations have been rendered unenforceable because no penalties can be exacted for breach of any marital promises (Ormerod and Rowthorn 1996). There are therefore few incentives other than moral obligations or feelings of affection to prevent either party from behaving opportunistically. Some legislatures have tried to meet this problem by compensating spouses who make sacrifices during marriages in addition to splitting marital property. Courts struggling with this difficulty have modified existing legal doctrines to recognize additional assets as 'property' (*O'Brien v. O'Brien*, 1985). Privately, more and more couples have written marital contracts that can be the basis for actions for breach (Trebilcock and Keshvani 1991: 565–7). There has, however, been relatively little recognition of the changing economic incentives.

In a reaction against no-fault divorce, Louisiana amended its Civil Code (art. 102 and 103) to provide for covenant marriages. This legislation went into effect on 15 August 1997. At the time of marriage, Louisiana couples may now elect whether to be governed by a mixed fault and no-fault regime (with a six-month separation for unilateral no-fault divorces) or, after counselling about the nature of its lifetime commitment, a covenant marriage. Covenant marriages may only be dissolved upon serious fault grounds (adultery, commission of a felony with a sentence of death or imprisonment at hard labour, desertion, or physical or sexual abuse of spouse or child). The new provisions have sparked considerable debate in the academic and popular press (Gallagher 1997; Pollit 1997; Ryan 1997; Scott and Scott 1997; Shipley 1997).

There has been no apparent decrease in opportunistic behaviour in marriage. For one thing, more and more cases of abuse are reported (Brinig and Crafton 1994: 888). Of course, this may be due either to better reporting facilities or to the increasing consciousness of women, who may newly believe that something may be done if they complain about abuse. If this were all, however, we would expect the increase in reporting to occur across all states. Second, more and more couples litigate around sacrifices made to advance one spouse's career. This behaviour lags, in the sense that the investments in human capital characteristic of the reported 'degree division' cases occur prior to the time when the spouse realizes that such investments might never be recouped. Predictably, there will eventually be fewer such marriage-specific investments. Thus, women will be less likely to specialize in household production or in their husbands' careers and more likely to continue working to advance their own careers. The consequent increase in the labour force participation of women may undermine marriage (Stake 1992: 405–6; Parkman 1992: 78), but others argue that it has decreased divorce rates (Brinig and Buckley 1997; Parkman 1997).

These observations are consistent with the change from a regime that recognized that marriage provides occasions for opportunism. In the older system, the rule of fault limited such behaviour through its delineation of marital covenants, violation of which led to breach, with its concomitant damage remedy, alimony (Brinig and Crafton 1994: 880).

The wife may have even less power in those states where fault is irrelevant than she did in the divorceless form of marriage, because the only threat she can make is that it may take the husband some time to replace her 'household services' after their divorce. It is more difficult for the woman to remarry, and she usually earns far less than the husband in the job market, for a variety of reasons (Regan 1992: 1465–6). Upon leaving, therefore, she loses more than he does, giving him more bargaining power within the marriage. The cost of deviant behaviour has decreased, so that isolating no-fault divorce from other factors, there should be more divorces and more opportunistic behaviour by spouses (Cohen 1987: 288–9; Brinig and Crafton 1994: 872–94).

This strategic behaviour should occur primarily in marriages entered into under the old rules. Spouse abuse is one way to measure the effect of the change in regimes upon those marriages entered into before no-fault divorce was introduced, or at least upon those marriages begun without sufficient understanding of what the new system might mean in terms of divorce compensation. Where marital fault imposes no costs, there is significantly more abuse, other things held equal (Brinig and Crafton 1994: 887). With marriages begun in the no-fault era, we would expect other effects: decreases in the number of marriages contracted and in the number of children. No-fault states in fact show fewer marriages and fewer births over the last twenty years than in the states retaining fault (Brinig and Crafton 1994: 884–7).

Peters (1986) maintained and claimed to demonstrate empirically that whatever the legal regime, couples will bargain for efficient divorces, and reject inefficient ones. Divorce levels would thus be independent of the legal regime. This divorce irrelevance proposition has been criticized for failing to account for transaction costs (Marvell 1989; Allen 1992). In a bilateral divorce regime, transaction costs (including legal fees, court costs and other bargaining costs) might prevent the husband who seeks a divorce from securing his wife's consent, and thus decrease divorce rates. In a unilateral regime, where divorce may be obtained at the instigation of either spouse, impediments to bargaining such as the inability to enforce agreements not to divorce, or the indivisibility of many marital assets (including the marital home or children), might prevent the wife who seeks to preserve her marriage from persuading her husband to abandon divorce, and so result in higher divorce rates. Because of the emotionalism and spite that bargaining over whether or not to stay married may engender, the parties may fail to exploit all options that might actually be preferable, including preserving the marriage and refraining from disturbing behaviour.

There are other reasons to question the divorce law irrelevance proposition. Endowment effects underlie Martin Zelder's public goods explanation of what he calls 'inefficient' divorces (Zelder 1993a, 1993b). Zelder assumes that children are public goods, in the sense that their value to the parents is higher in marriage than in divorce, since both parties can share time with them during the marriage. Since both have complete access to the children when the family lives together, even if a bargain not to divorce were enforceable, time with the children could not be used as a side payment to prevent divorce. For example, a child might be worth 100 to his mother when she is married, but only 60 after divorce, since she will then see less of him. Having less utility after divorce, she will have less to transfer to her husband as a side payment to preserve the marriage. Zelder's model does not explain why couples might stay together 'for the sake of the kids', though it notes that the change in legal regime affects bargaining position. The no-divorce result under the bilateral regime and the divorce result under the unilateral regime are both 'efficient', in the sense that the parties cannot continue bargaining and be jointly better off.

There are additional reasons why divorce rules should matter. Suppose that, in the above example, the husband would gain only $5000 from divorce. Since the wife would be prepared to pay $10,000 to preserve the marriage, we might expect them to bargain accordingly. But divorce rights cannot be waived, so that the husband's promise not to divorce would be unenforceable. He might pocket the $10,000 and sue for divorce the next day (*Capps v. Capps*, 1975). This explains both why such contracts are not made, and why the shift to unilateral divorce can be expected to increase divorce levels.

Finally, the divorce law irrelevance proposition might not hold as a consequence of moral hazard. In a unilateral regime, the party who initiates divorce proceedings need not pay the spouse to waive veto rights. Divorce will therefore be cheaper, and the matrimonial faults which might have occasioned it will become less costly. Because adultery or abuse costs less, there will be more of it (Posner 1992: 249; Brinig and Crafton 1994), and more straying or outraged spouses seeking divorce. With a greater probability of divorce, the parties will also invest less in marriage-specific assets such as children, further increasing divorce levels.

It is unsurprising that divorce rates doubled in the United States when states moved from fault to no-fault laws (see Figure 1). Since 1985, an at-fault party can obtain a divorce in every state on no-fault grounds, such as irreconcilable differences, an irretrievable breakdown of the marriage, or a short term separation. Therefore, the levelling-off of divorce rates in the 1980s was also predictable.

Since 1980, most of the legal change had already occurred, though while an innocent party has everywhere lost the right to veto the divorce, some 32 states still permit him or her to raise the spouse's fault as grounds for altering the split of matrimonial assets (American Law Institute 1996). The innocent party might commence divorce proceedings on fault grounds or counterclaim on fault grounds when the guilty party has sought a no-fault divorce. Bargaining in the shadow of fault in these mixed-regime states, the parties may decide not to divorce at all, or they may agree to seek a divorce on no-fault grounds, but with a more one-sided division of assets than they would have agreed to in the absence of fault.

A number of empirical studies consider whether no-fault divorce or some other factor, such as increased women's labour force participation, is responsible for the United States' divorce rates, which are twice as high as those in other industrialized nations (see Table 1). The question is obviously relevant for the many jurisdictions considering reform of divorce statutes (Clark 1996), and apparently played a role in the adoption of a no-fault regime in the UK in the summer of 1996 (*New Statesman* 1996). Clearly there was at least a short-term boost in state divorce rates as the laws took hold. Although the empirical issue remains in doubt after ten years of studies of United States divorces, the greater number, at least, seem to find more divorces in the long-run in states with no-fault regimes.

In the most widely cited study, Peters (1986) looked at panel data for a three-year period in the late 1970s and reported that they were uncorrelated with no-fault divorce laws. From this she concluded that no one seeking divorce will be kept in a marriage, and where fault is required the parties will produce it. In an econometric battle using Peters' data set, Allen (1992) contested her findings in the

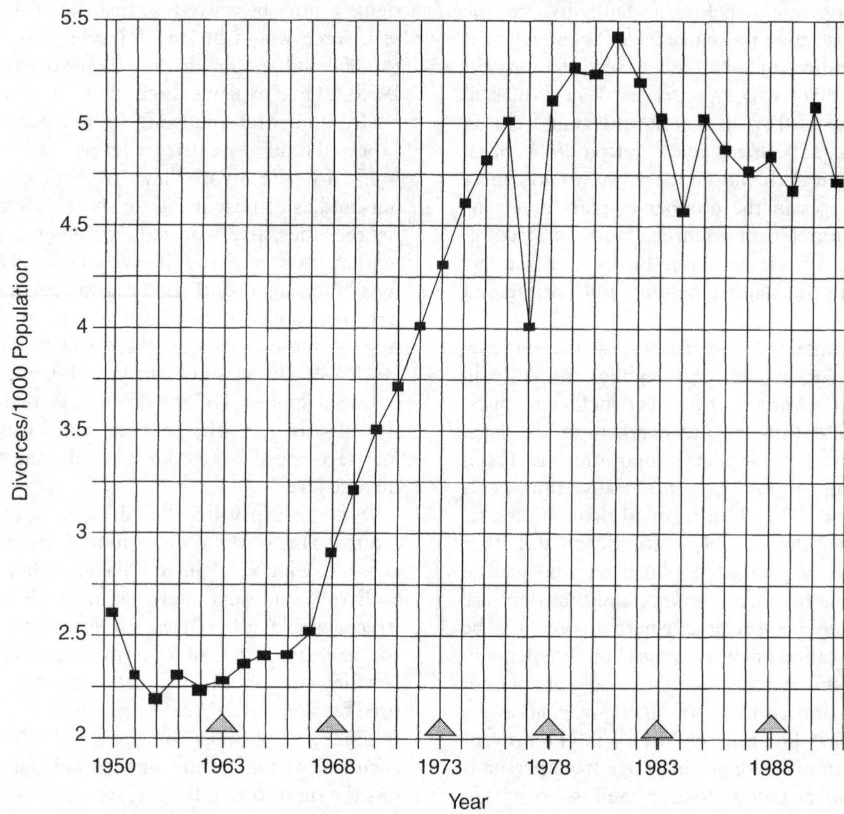

Figure 1 US Divorce Rates

American Economic Review and was in turn criticized by her (Peters 1992).

Marvell (1989) reported an increase in divorce rates using a different panel data set and regional variables. Another panel study by Martin Zelder of pre-1982 divorces reported that a no-fault dummy variable, taken alone, was not correlated with increased divorce levels (Zelder 1993b). Where the dummy variable was multiplied by a measure of expenditures on children (Zelder's (1993a) 'public goods'), however, he found a significant relationship with increased divorce. Zelder concluded that transaction cost barriers do not prevent the parties from bargaining around the divorce regime, but that divorce law irrelevance does not hold when the parties have children.

More recently, Nakonezny, Shull and Rodgers (1995) reported that states enacting no-fault laws saw a significant increase in divorce rates over the following three years. However, the authors did not attempt to demonstrate a long-term effect. The short-term effect is easy to imagine: some couples who sought a divorce around the time of the legal change delayed proceedings until the new law was enacted in order to reduce divorce costs.

Table 1
Divorce Systems and Divorce Rates

Country	Type of Law	Date of Enactment	Divorce Rate per 1,000 Married Women (1980)	Divorce Rate per 1,000 Married Women (1992)
United States	mixed fault and no-fault or no-fault	1969 to 1985	23	21
Canada	mixed fault and no-fault		10	11
France	mixed fault and no-fault		6	N/A
Germany	mixed fault and no-fault		6* (West Germany)	7
Italy	mixed fault and no-fault		1	2
Japan	bilateral or fault		5	N/A
Sweden	bilateral and unilateral	1973	11	12
United Kingdom	mixed fault and no-fault (becomes no-fault only in 1999)	1973	12	12

Brinig and Buckley (1997) found that the change to a no-fault legal regime is significantly correlated with increased divorce levels over a relatively lengthy time period, employing social as well as legal and economic variables, and using a variety of techniques of analysis. Since the immediate effect of enactment of the statutes had largely worn off, the longer time period may have permitted a sharper picture of the determinants of divorce than the Peters study. Their definition of no-fault was different from Peters', because they counted a state as retaining fault if fault was relevant at the financial settlement stage. This meant that they characterized as fault states several states Peters had considered no-fault. They made greater use of religious and regional differences, reasoning that if the change to no-fault resulted in an increased social acceptance of divorce, such effects were more likely to be detected with a model including social predictors.

A closely related matter concerns the division of property on divorce. In a fault regime, the at-fault party is penalized for his fault through equitable distribution. However, there is little evidence that the move to no-fault affected the bargaining over the matrimonial assets. An early article used panel data to show that alimony awards were indeed lower in states that had adopted no-fault divorce laws (Landes 1978). Similarly, Weitzman's study of property settlements before and after passage of a no-fault divorce law in California concluded that women's standards of living diminished dramatically following divorce, while men's improved (Weitzman 1981). More recently, however, several writers have reported that property settlements did not change much with no-fault. An empirical study of New York divorces found that no-fault settlements differed little from those of the earlier fault-based divorce era (Garrison 1991). A national study of panel data found little difference in divorce settlements between fault and no-fault states (Weiss and Willis 1993). Brinig and Alexeev (1993) compared 1987 divorce settlements in Virginia (a fault state) and Wisconsin (a no-fault state), and found nearly identical payouts.

A final puzzle is that most divorce petitions are brought by women, even after the move to no-fault (Friedman and Percival 1976: 69; Gunter and Johnson 1978; Brinig 1993: 466). However, there is an easy explanation for this, even assuming that husbands are more likely to have committed matrimonial fault. A husband who wishes to terminate a marriage will often leave his wife and children without initiating divorce, since he can usually take his investments in human capital with him (Landes 1978). The abandoned wife must then begin divorce proceedings to enforce his support duties and formalize custody arrangements (Brinig and Carbone 1988: 863–4).

No-fault's origin, as well as its consequences, have been the subject of discussion by law and economics scholars. Allen Parkman speculated that no-fault divorce reform first occurred in male-dominated legislatures (Parkman 1992: 61–3), 'in a process of benign neglect' reinforced by the lobbying efforts of male interest groups. He points out that it was not merely the change in divorce, property and alimony laws that has changed the atmosphere in the United States, but also the push which the no-fault movement made toward negotiated settlements.

At first, the organized American Bar considered divorced mediation (third-party structured settlement) inconsistent with professional ethics. First, non-attorney mediators would violate 'unauthorized practice of law' rules. Second, attorneys would be unable to represent both (necessarily adversary) spouses, and would therefore be involved in conflicts of interest. Because of their extensive training in legal rules as opposed to counselling, lawyer-mediators would be unable to resist giving legal advice. From a public choice perspective, it appears that the protests of the organized bar were little more than a smokescreen to protect entry into what had been lawyers' sole province (Kressel and Hochberg 1987), since in most cases divorce does not raise difficult legal issues.

In fact, American lawyers ultimately capitulated to the inevitable, and most states now allow mediation by both attorney and non-lawyer mediators. But the states have raised the stakes considerably for the non-lawyers. Since the advent of no-fault divorce, and contemporaneously with the rise of mediation, the practice of family law has shifted from being a rather disreputable one (only slightly above criminal defence work, and perhaps below ambulance-chasing and loan collection in terms of public perception) to a practice that looks very much like a general business law practice. The modern tendency to model the divorcing family on corporate dissolutions (Starnes 1993) is particularly attractive to economists (Ormerod and Rowthorn 1996). The effective modern family law practitioner is not only counsellor and strategist. He or she must also know a good bit about taxation, finance, and human capital theory. In fact, the work in some American states has spawned a valuation industry in which the experts testify in divorces as well as business dissolutions.

M.F. Brinig

See also ALIMONY; CHILD CUSTODY; DIVORCE; MARRIAGE AS CONTRACT.

Subject classification: 5f.

CASES

Capps v. Capps, 219 SE2d 901 (Va. 1975).

O'Brien v. O'Brien, 489 NE2d 712 (NY 1985).

BIBLIOGRAPHY

Allen, D.W. 1992. Marriage and divorce: a comment. *American Economic Review* 82: 679–85.

American Law Institute. 1996. *Principles of the Law of Family Dissolution* (Tentative Draft). Philadelphia: American Law Institute.

Becker, G.S. 1991. *A Treatise on the Family*. 2nd edn, Cambridge, MA: Harvard University Press.

Brinig, M.F. 1993. The law and economics of no-fault divorce. *Family Law Quarterly* 26: 453–70.

Brinig, M.F. and Alexeev, M.V. 1993. Trading at divorce. *Ohio State Journal on Dispute Resolution* 8: 279–97.

Brinig, M.F. and Buckley, F.H. 1997. No-fault laws and at-fault people. *International Review of Law and Economics* (forthcoming).

Brinig, M.F. and Carbone, J.R. 1988. The reliance interest in marriage and divorce. *Tulane Law Review* 62: 870–82.

Brinig, M.F. and Crafton, S.M. 1994. Marriage and opportunism. *Journal of Legal Studies* 23: 869–94.

Carbone, J.R. and Brinig, M.F. 1991. Rethinking marriage: feminist ideology, economic change and divorce reform. *Tulane Law Review* 65: 953–1010.

Clark, C.S. 1996. Marriage and divorce. *CQ Researcher* (May 10) 6: 411–12.

Cohen, L. 1987. Divorce and quasi-rents or 'I gave him the best years of my life'. *Journal of Legal Studies* 16: 267–303.

CQ Researcher. 1996. Is it time to crack down on easy divorces? (May 10) 6: 409–32.

Duncan, G.J. and Hoffman, S. 1985. A reconsideration of the economic consequences of marital dissolution. *Demography* 22: 485–99.

Freeman, M.D.A. 1996. England in the international year of the family. In *The International Survey of Family Law 1994*, ed. A. Bainham, The Hague: Kluwer Law International, 199–225.

Friedman, L. and Percival, R. 1976. Who sues for divorce? *Journal of Legal Studies* 5: 61–82.

Fuchs, V. 1988. *Women's Quest for Economic Equality*. Cambridge, MA: Harvard University Press.

Gallagher, M. 1997. Covenants inspire marriages with new commitment. *Sacramento Bee*, 21 July 1997 at B7.

Garrison, M. 1991. Good intentions gone awry: the impact of New York's equitable distribution law on divorce outcomes. *Brooklyn Law Review* 57: 679–754.

Glendon, M.A. 1989. *The Transformation of Family Law: State Law and Family in the United States and Western Europe*. Chicago: University of Chicago Press.

Gunter, B.G. and Johnson, D.P. 1978. Divorce filing as role behavior: effect of no-fault on divorce filing patterns. *Journal of Marriage and the Family* 40: 571–87.

International Law Digest 1996. Summit, NJ: Martindell-Hubbell.

Kressel, S. and Hochberg, D. 1987. Divorce attorneys: assessment of a topology and attitudes towards legal reform. *Journal of Divorce* 10: 1–13.

Landes, E. 1978. The economics of alimony. *Journal of Legal Studies* 7: 35–63.

Leitzel, J. 1989. Reliance and contract breach. *Law and Contemporary Problems* 52: 87–105.

Marvell, T. 1989. Divorce rates and the fault requirement. *Law and Society Review* 23: 543–67.

Muris, T.J. 1981. Opportunistic behavior and the law of contracts. *Minnesota Law Review* 65: 521–90.

Nakonezny, P.A., Shull, R.D. and Rodgers, J.L. 1995. The effect of no-fault divorce law on the divorce rate across the 50 states and its relation to income, education, and religiosity. *Journal of Marriage and the Family* 57: 477–88.

New Statesman and Society. 1996. Don't kill the divorce bill. 9(405): 15.

Ormerod, P. and Rowthorn, B. 1996. It's the family, stupid! *Daily Mail*, 20 November, p.8.

Parkman, Allen W. 1992. *No-Fault Divorce: What Went Wrong?* Boulder, CO: Westview Press.

Parkman, A.W. 1997. Why are married women working so hard? *International Review of Law and Economics* (forthcoming).

Peters, H.E. 1986. Marriage and divorce: informational constraints and private contracting. *American Economic Review* 76: 437–54.

Peters, H.E. 1992. Marriage and divorce: reply. *American Economic Review* 82: 686–93.

Peterson, R. 1996. Reevaluation of the economic consequences of divorce. *American Sociological Review* 61: 528–36.

Pollitt, K. 1997. Why 'covenant marriages' could be harmful to kids. *Sacramento Bee*, 12 July 1997 at B7.

Posner, R.A. 1992. *Sex and Reason*. Cambridge, MA: Harvard University Press.

Regan, M.C. 1992. Divorce reform and the legacy of gender. *Michigan Law Review* 90: 1453–94.

Rheinstein, M. 1956. The law of divorce and the problem of marriage stability. *Vanderbilt Law Review* 9: 663–89.

Ryan, K. 1997. Super vows' aim to put marriages to the test: Louisiana covenant measure may boost other efforts to curb divorce. *Dallas Morning News*, 29 June 1997 at 1A.

Scott, E.S. 1990. Rational decisionmaking about marriage and divorce. *Virginia Law Review* 76: 9–94.

Scott, E.S. and Scott, R.E. 1997. Marriage as relational contract. Donner Series on Freedom of Contract, Law and Economics Center, George Mason University.

Shavell, S. 1984. Design of contract and remedies for breach. *Quarterly Journal of Economics* 99: 121–48.

Shipley, S. 1997. Making vows last longer in Louisiana. *Christian Science Monitor*, 1 July 1997, p. 1.

Stake, J.E. 1992. Mandatory planning for divorce and marriage. *Vanderbilt Law Review* 45: 397–454.

Starnes, C. 1993. Playing with paper dolls, partnership buyouts and the law of the displaced homemaker. *University of Chicago Law Review* 60: 67–139.

Teitelbaum, L.E. 1989. Placing the family in context. *University of California-Davis Law Review* 22: 801–27.

Trebilcock, M. and Keshvani, R. 1991. The role of private ordering in family law: a law and economics perspective. *University of Toronto Law Journal* 41: 533–90.

Weiss, Y. and Willis, R. 1993. Transfers among divorced couples. *Journal of Labor Economics* 11: 629–79.

Weitzman, L. 1981. The economics of divorce: social and economic consequences of property, alimony and child support awards. *U.C.L.A. Law Review* 28: 1181.

Zelder, M. 1993a. Inefficient dissolutions as a consequence of public goods: the case of no-fault divorce. *Journal of Legal Studies* 22: 503–20.

Zelder, M. 1993b. The economic analysis of the effect of no-fault divorce law on the divorce rate. *Harvard Journal of Public Policy* 16: 241–67.

non-cooperative games. Non-cooperative game theory is concerned with the analysis of strategic situations. A *strategic situation* involves a group of people, each of whom has discretion over his behaviour, in which what a person does has a non-trivial impact on the wellbeing of each of the others. This interdependence between what others do and how ones fares creates the essential feature of a strategic situation: an individual's appropriate course of action is contingent on how the others are expected to behave. Such situations abound in society and include debt renegotiations under Chapter 11 of the Federal bankruptcy laws, the battle between a plaintiff and a defendant in a tort case, and the process by which politicians and special interests determine our laws. In analysing such situations – whether it is with the objective of understanding individual behaviour or developing a recommended course of action – game theory contributes in two ways. First, it provides a framework for describing a strategic situation concisely. Second, it offers an array of tools for solving a game and deriving implications about behaviour.

The distinction between non-cooperative and cooperative game theory is one of both emphasis and structure. In non-cooperative game theory, the individual agent is the fundamental unit of analysis and the focus is individual behaviour. In contrast, the coalition – a group of players – is the fundamental unit in cooperative game theory and the foci are coalition formation and the allocation of resources.

Whether any particular allocation can actually be realized (that is, agents would willingly go along with such an allocation) is a non-issue in a cooperative game in that it is presumed that binding contracts are available (due to the presence of a legal institution with enforcement powers) to implement any allocation. Non-cooperative game theory either makes no presumption of the availability of binding contracts or, if it does, there is an explicit modelling of how those contracts are used by agents.

I. CONSTRUCTING A GAME. Given a social setting about which we want to describe or prescribe individual behaviour, the initial task is to develop a representation of this situation that is rich enough to capture the primary forces at play but simple enough to be tractable so that insight can be derived. While there is no recipe for efficacious modelling, game theory provides a scaffolding – referred to as a *game form* – upon which a model can be constructed. Non-cooperative game forms include the extensive form and the strategic (or normal) form; for brevity, attention here will be devoted to the latter, though the extensive form is of comparable importance.

The *strategic form* of a game is defined by three elements. First, the *set of players*. This set consists of all individuals who have choices to make and who are the agents whose behaviour we are trying to understand. Second, a *strategy set* for each player. In game theory, a *strategy* is a complete description of a player's behaviour over the course of the game. It is an array of contingency plans which assign an action to any state in which the player might find himself. A player's strategy set is composed of all feasible strategies. Under this conceptualization, all decision-making is compressed into the choice of a strategy. Once selected, the behaviour of an agent is nothing more than the execution of that strategy. For example, in a bargaining context in which individuals have to divide $100 and one individual makes a take-it-or-leave it offer, a strategy for that individual – the proposer – is a proposed allocation of $100. His strategy set then includes all the ways in which to allocate $100. There are 101 of these if he is constrained to no finer a denomination than a dollar. In response to a proposed allocation, the other player – the responder – can either 'accept' or 'reject' the offer. However, her strategy set is not described by the two elements 'accept' and 'reject'. Rather, it is an array of contingency plans each of which assigns either 'accept' or 'reject' to any offer that might be put forth. A strategy for the responder might be: 'accept' if offered at least $40 and 'reject' if offered less than $40. With 101 feasible allocations, there are then 2^{101} strategies in the responder's strategy set! Clearly, the notions of a strategy and strategy set are idealizations, but useful idealizations.

The third and final element of the strategic form is a *payoff function* for each player. A payoff function captures a player's evaluation, in terms of his own wellbeing, of the feasible strategy profiles where a *strategy profile* is a list of strategies, one for each player. Typically, a payoff function assigns a number to each strategy profile where this number measures a player's utility when that strategy profile is used. While players are not presumed to care intrinsically about strategies (one cannot consume a decision rule), a given strategy profile induces a particular outcome to the game (that is, some sequence of actions) and a payoff function measures how a player evaluates that outcome. Returning to the bargaining context, a player's payoff function depends on the strategies of the proposer and responder. Any such strategy profile induces a sequence of actions. For example, consider the proposer using the strategy of proposing that he get $55 and the responder using a strategy which says to accept the allocation if and only if he gets at least $40. For this strategy profile, the induced sequence of actions has the proposer suggesting that he get $55 and the responder accepting the offer. If one presumes that each player only cares about his own wealth, the payoff the proposer assigns to this strategy profile is the incremental utility he gets from $55 and the responder's payoff is the incremental utility from $45.

A standard assumption in non-cooperative game theory is that the game – whether it is described by the strategic form or the extensive form – is *common knowledge* to all players. In the context of a strategic form game, this not only requires that players' strategy sets and payoff functions be known by all players but also that each player knows that all other players have this information and that each player knows that each other player knows that all other players have this information *ad infinitum*.

One of the primary uses of a formal model is to understand how a change in the environment affects behaviour. An attractive feature of the strategic form is that it is sufficiently rich in its structure as to be capable of encompassing most of the relevant changes in the agents' environment that one is interested in analysing. For example, laws which mandate that a firm give advance notice of a plant closing to workers can be reflected in a shrinking of a firm's strategy set in that the action of non-disclosure is eliminated. Alternatively, if compliance is an issue, advance notice laws might be better modelled through the payoff functions by allowing firms to maintain the option of not providing advance notice and having their payoff functions reflect the legal penalty associated with failure to provide advance notice.

II. SOLVING A GAME. Having modelled a strategic situation as a non-cooperative game, the next task is to solve it. Solving a game means applying a set of criteria for discriminating among strategy profiles. These criteria should be based upon some fundamental principles regarding how agents do behave or should behave (depending on the objective of the exercise). A *solution concept* embodies such a set of criteria and is a device for selecting among strategy profiles. With a solution concept, one plugs in a game and out pops a strategy profile or some set of strategy profiles which are the solution(s). Ideally, a solution is a unique strategy profile. However, this ideal is often not attained, in that commonly used solution concepts may yield many solutions or may yield nothing, in which case the theory is vacuous.

While there are various approaches to solving a game, the standard and most widely used approach for solving non-cooperative games is predicated upon players being rational. In the context of a non-cooperative game, a player is *rational* if his behaviour can be represented as the maximization of his expected payoff *given* his beliefs as to how other players will behave (as well as his beliefs over any other source of uncertainty such as Nature). Within the rationality approach, methods differ according to the specification of a player's beliefs over other players' strategies. One class of methods – equilibrium analysis – requires that beliefs be consistent with what actually transpires. This approach does not deal with the issue of how players come to have such accurate beliefs. The second class of methods focuses on this issue by modelling the process of belief formation. Of primary interest is to understand the set of beliefs (and associated behaviour) to which this process converges.

A. Equilibrium and the specification of consistent beliefs. The canonical equilibrium approach imposes the restriction that each player's beliefs over other players' strategies be consistent with the actual strategies employed; that is, beliefs over strategies are accurate. This approach is embodied in the notion of a Nash equilibrium. A strategy profile is a *Nash equilibrium* if each player's strategy maximizes his payoff given the strategies used by the other players. In other words, each player has an accurate conjecture of the other players' strategies and uses a strategy which maximizes his payoff for those beliefs. A strategy can be part of a Nash equilibrium even if there are other strategies which give just as high a payoff, as long as there is no other strategy which yields a strictly higher payoff.

By way of example, let us return to the bargaining context though with an alternative formulation. Players have still to allocate $100 but we now suppose they move simultaneously rather than sequentially in that *both* players propose an allocation. What is meant by 'simultaneous' here is that each player proposes an allocation without knowing what the other has submitted. Specifically, each player proposes how much he is to get and we will let x_i denote the amount (in dollars) proposed by player i, $i = 1, 2$. Each player's strategy set is $\{0,1, \ldots,100\}$. The rules of bargaining in this example are that both players get their demands met if $x_1 + x_2 \leq 100$; that is, if both demands are feasible. If instead $x_1 + x_2 > 100$ then both players get nothing as a result of their failure to agree on a feasible allocation. Player i's payoff from a strategy profile is specified to equal the amount of money he receives, which is x_i when $x_1 + x_2 \leq 100$ and 0 when $x_1 + x_2 > 100$. This is known as the Nash demand game (Nash 1953).

What are the Nash equilibria for this game? To begin, any strategy profile which leaves money on the table is not a Nash equilibrium, as a player could always have increased his payoff by demanding more. Consider the strategy profile $(\bar{x}_1, \bar{x}_2)$ and suppose $\bar{x}_1 + \bar{x}_2 < 100$. Player 1's payoff is $\bar{x}_1$ from using strategy $\bar{x}_1$ but he could receive a higher payoff of $\bar{x}_1 + 1$ by raising his demand by one dollar (that is, by using strategy $\bar{x}_1 + 1$). In that player 1's strategy of $\bar{x}_1$ does not maximize his payoff, $(\bar{x}_1, \bar{x}_2)$ is not a Nash equilibrium. Therefore, if a strategy profile is a Nash equilibrium, it must have $x_1 + x_2 \geq 100$. In fact, any strategy pair for which $x_1 + x_2 = 100$ is a Nash equilibrium as no player can increase his payoff by changing his strategy. If a player raises his demand, his payoff will be zero (as then the demands will exceed 100), which cannot be higher than that received from playing his original strategy. If he reduces his demand, he can only lower his payoff. It can be shown that the only other Nash equilibrium is for each to propose 100.

A central attraction of Nash equilibrium is that it is a profile of strategies and beliefs which, once achieved, would seem likely to persist over time were the encounter to occur repeatedly. For if players are using the strategies associated with a Nash equilibrium and have accurate beliefs, then no player has an incentive to change his actions or his beliefs. What is problematic is how players might come to settle on a Nash equilibrium. This equilibration process is of central importance in game theory and a topic to which we will return.

Properties of Nash equilibria. Various properties are known about Nash equilibria for general classes of games. Ideally, we would like a solution always to exist and, furthermore, for it to be unique. Multiplicity makes it difficult to draw definitive and precise conclusions while non-existence makes for a vacuous theory. Unfortunately, neither existence nor uniqueness is generally true. It is easy to construct games for which Nash equilibria do not exist (consider the childhood game of Rock, Paper, Scissors) and games for which there exist many Nash equilibria (such as the Nash demand game). However, the issue of existence can be assured for finite games – that is, those with a finite number of strategies and a finite number of players – if we allow players to randomize in their selection of a strategy. A *mixed strategy* is a randomization over a player's strategy set (the elements of which we now refer to as a *pure strategy*). Every finite game has at least one Nash equilibrium in mixed strategies (Nash 1950). Though there is considerable controversy regarding the relevance and plausibility of mixed strategies, it does have the virtue of assuring the existence of a solution for a large class of games.

A significant property of Nash equilibria concerns collective rationality. A strategy profile is defined to be *Pareto-inefficient* if there exists another strategy profile which gives every player a strictly higher payoff. A strategy profile is Pareto-efficient when such a strategy profile does not exist. For a wide class of games, Nash equilibria are typically Pareto-inefficient (Dubey 1986). That is, there is another strategy profile which gives every player a strictly higher payoff than that achieved at a Nash equilibrium. This property highlights the fact that while each player is maximizing his own payoff at a Nash equilibrium, this does not imply that the players, as a group, are doing as well as they can.

As an example of the Pareto-inefficiency of Nash equilibria, consider the game in Figure 1 which involves a lender and a debtor in a situation where debt contracts are unenforceable. The associated payoffs to any strategy profile are shown in the matrix where the first number in a cell is the payoff of the player who is selecting a row (in this case, the debtor) and the second number is the payoff of the player selecting a column (in this case, the lender). The lender chooses between L(end) and D(o Not Lend) while the debtor, in the event he receives a loan, chooses P(ay back) or R(enege). If the loan is not made – the lender chooses D – then both players receive a payoff of zero. If the loan is made and the debtor repays – the strategy profile (P, L) – both players earn a payoff of 2. Since they both do better than if the loan were not made, the implicit assumption is that the loan is a worthy one, the profit it would generate for the debtor being more than sufficient to provide adequate interest and return of principal to the lender. If the loan is made but the debt is not paid back – the strategy profile (R, L) – then the debtor does very well with his payoff of 4 but the lender loses out with her payoff of –2. The unique Nash equilibrium is (R, D) so that the loan is not made. But this outcome is Pareto-inefficient since (P, L) gives each player a higher payoff.

		Lender	
		Lend	Do Not Lend
Debtor	Pay Back	2, 2	0, 0
	Renege	4, −2	0, 0

Figure 1

One possible way out of the problem of Pareto-inefficiency is through repetition. When players repeat the game indefinitely, they can achieve a Pareto-efficient outcome – even if it is not a Nash equilibrium when the game is played just once – as long as players attach sufficient importance to future payoffs (Fudenberg and Maskin 1986). In that a strategy for the repeated game which induces a Pareto-efficient outcome may not maximize the payoff received from the current period's encounter, there is a short-run incentive to act differently from that prescribed by this strategy. When the game is played just once, it is this incentive that causes the Pareto-efficient arrangement to unravel. However, with the prospect of future encounters and players caring about their future payoffs, behaviour that diverges from the Pareto-efficient outcome can be deterred by the threat of punishing the one who defaults in his future encounters with the group and thereby lowering his future payoff. If players sufficiently value future payoffs, this threatened punishment can be sufficient to sustain behaviour which supports a Pareto-efficient outcome. Of central importance, however, is that the punishment be credible in the sense that the other players would want to go along with it. Returning to the debt game, if the debtor and lender interact repeatedly – the debtor seeks to get a new loan each period from the lender – they may be able to sustain the preferred outcome of (P, L) by the threat that the lender will never make another loan if the debtor ever defaults. As long as the debtor sufficiently values future payoffs, he will want to continue to repay his loans so as to maintain creditworthiness.

Alternative equilibrium approaches. While Nash equilibrium represents the canonical equilibrium approach to solving a game, there are other methods of equilibrium analysis. Refining the Nash equilibrium concept – which involves placing additional restrictions on beliefs – was a major avenue of research in the 1970s and 1980s. This work was partly motivated by the multiplicity of Nash equilibria – hoping that additional restrictions will narrow down the solution set – and partly by the unfortunate fact that some Nash equilibria for some games are unreasonable – hoping to eliminate such strategy profiles. A modification of Nash equilibrium that instead imposes weaker conditions is that of *self-confirming equilibrium* (Fudenberg and Kreps 1988; Fudenberg and Levine 1993). It requires that beliefs be consistent with observed play; that is, actual (equilibrium) play never runs counter to a player's expectation about others' behaviour. Such a restriction can be milder than requiring that a player accurately conjectures other players' strategies. In particular, it is sufficient to conjecture accurately those contingency plans embodied in other players' strategies which are actually called into play. Thus, a player's beliefs about what the other players would do for unrealized contingencies could be wrong.

B. Formation of beliefs. Rather than require that beliefs be consistent, an alternative methodology for deriving beliefs and solving a game is to model the process by which beliefs are formed. There are two approaches to be covered: eduction and adaptive play (for an early discussion along these lines, see Binmore 1990).

Eduction. One approach to modelling the formation of beliefs is to model the process by which a player might reason from basic principles as to what others will do. In modelling eduction, players are presumed not only to be aware of their own thought processes – and thus can consciously assess what they should do and decide whether a line of reasoning makes sense – but also to possess a theory of mind. A construct used in psychology, a *theory of mind* refers to the attribution of self-awareness and reasoning to others. A theory of mind is what allows someone to put himself in the place of another so as to try and figure out what the other will do.

What are the logical bases from which a player might determine what others will do? One candidate is the extent to which other players are believed to be rational and what they believe about other players' beliefs. By way of example, consider the following foundation: each player believes all players are rational. Our analysis will be constructed upon this assumption about beliefs along with the standard assumption that the game is common knowledge to the players. An eductive approach derives those beliefs over players' strategies which are implied by these assumptions. One is then deriving beliefs over strategies by specifying beliefs over the more primitive object of how players reason. To see how this works, consider the game in Figure 2. Player 1 chooses either T(op) or B(ottom) while player 2 chooses either L(eft) or R(ight). In deciding how to behave, player 1 does not need to formulate any beliefs over what player 2 will do since his optimal strategy is independent of those beliefs. Strategy B yields a higher payoff for player 1 whether two is expected to use L or R. Now consider player 2. Strategy L is optimal if player 2 believes one will use T (as it yields a payoff of four while strategy R yields a payoff of one) but R is optimal if he thinks one will use B. Thus, player 2's payoff-maximizing behaviour hinges on her beliefs regarding player 1's strategy. What should player 2 believe player 1 will do? Well, she believes that player 1 is rational and, as reasoned above, rationality implies that player 1 uses B. Thus, player 2 should expect player 1 to use B. Given that belief, the optimal strategy for player 2 is R. Based on the specified beliefs regarding rationality, eduction implies that the solution is (B, R). While this is not generally the case, note that (B, R) happens to be the unique Nash equilibrium.

		Player 2	
		Left	Right
Player 1	Top	2, 4	0, 1
	Bottom	3, 2	2, 3

Figure 2

In the above example, one level of beliefs was specified. More structure could be imposed through the specification of additional levels. For example, here are three levels of beliefs for a two-player game:

Level 1: 1 believes 2 is rational
2 believes 1 is rational

Level 2: 1 believes 2 believes 1 is rational
2 believes 1 believes 2 is rational

Level 3: 1 believes 2 believes 1 believes 2 is rational
2 believes 1 believes 2 believes 1 is rational.

And one need not stop there. Indeed, we say that *rationality is common knowledge* if players' beliefs conform to an infinite number of levels of knowledge regarding the rationality of players. Furthermore, a strategy is *rationalizable* if it is optimal for beliefs which are consistent with rationality being common knowledge (Bernheim 1984; Pearce 1984). There is even an algorithm for deriving the set of rationalizable strategies (which is a generalization of what we did with the game in Figure 2). One should first eliminate all of a player's strategies which are not optimal for any beliefs over other players' strategies. This is done for each player. If at least one strategy has been eliminated in this fashion, the process is repeated on the reduced game (that is, the original game less those strategies which are never optimal). This process is iterated until no more strategies are eliminated. The surviving set of strategies, which must be non-empty, are the rationalizable ones.

While such an eductive process may be aesthetically pleasing in its logical structure, it does presume that players are quite sophisticated and, even with all that sophistication, it may still fail to deliver precise predictions about behaviour. Any strategy which is part of a Nash equilibrium is rationalizable, so that if there are many Nash equilibria then there are many rationalizable strategies (Pearce 1984). In some if not many games, most if not all strategies are rationalizable.

Adaptive play. Rather than engage in careful reasoning, players might instead seek to learn about other players' strategies by observing past play and then adjusting their play to that information. This is referred to as *adaptive play*. This approach requires that the game under consideration be embedded in a 'larger' structure. Suppose we want to consider adaptive play for the game in Figure 3 (which, for reasons we need not go into, is called the Battle of the Sexes). Rather than assume that players play it just once, suppose that players repeatedly play this game but each player is myopic in that she always tries to choose an action to maximize her payoff in the current encounter. We are then imposing a certain simplicity to strategies in that a strategy only concerns what to do in today's encounter and ignores the indefinite future. Alternatively, we could rationalize the myopia by imagining two large populations of players. In each period, someone is randomly selected from population I to play the role of player 1, and from population II to play the role of player 2. Since the chances of being matched again are very slim (given random matching and a large population), myopia makes sense for each of the individuals selected.

		Player 2	
		Left	Right
Player 1	Top	2, 1	0, 0
	Bottom	0, 0	1, 3

Figure 3

Most methods of adaptive play go to the other extreme from that of eduction in that they assume players simplistically extrapolate from history and make no effort to try to 'outthink' other players. One such method of experiential learning is *fictitious play* (Brown 1951; though see Binmore 1992 for a more recent treatment). Fictitious play has a player assign a probability to another player using a particular strategy which equals the relative frequency with which that strategy was played in the past. Suppose the game in Figure 3 has been played fifty times and player 2 used strategy L fourteen times and R thirty-six times. According to fictitious play, player 1 assigns probability .28 (= 14/50) to player 2 using L and .72 (= 36/50) to her using R. Given these beliefs, we then apply the assumption of rationality in specifying that player 1 use the strategy which maximizes his expected payoff. In the above game, his expected payoff from using T is .28(2) + .72(0) = .56 and from using B is .28(0) + .72(1) = .72. According to fictitious play and this particular history, player 1 uses B.

Though fictitious play imagines simple-minded players who do not strategize at all but instead engage in a rudimentary extrapolation of past play, when fictitious play converges – players settle down to using the same strategy over time – it converges to a Nash equilibrium. Thus, the plausibility of Nash equilibrium as a description of behaviour is not contingent upon players being sophisticated and, indeed, may do better as a description of simpletons (for recall that there can be many rationalizable strategies). There are games, however, for which fictitious play does not converge. Furthermore, if play is initially at a Nash equilibrium (in pure strategies) then fictitious play results in that strategy profile persisting. But then it is the initial play which drives behaviour and that is an issue on which fictitious play is mute.

Another version of adaptive play modifies fictitious play

in several important ways. Here we describe the work of Young (1993a, 1993b) but see also the related work of Kandori, Mailath and Rob (1993). First, suppose that players can draw only from the recent past in that play from more than T periods ago is not available. Second, a player obtains information about K out of the last T plays, where those K plays are drawn randomly without replacement. These K observations make up the history that is used to form beliefs where, like fictitious play, a player's probability is set equal to the relative frequency (for those K observations) with which a strategy was played. Third, there is a small exogenous probability that a player randomly selects a strategy. The introduction of this 'noise' into the process is quite important as it prevents initial play from necessarily driving all that happens.

To see what this learning process generates, let us return to the Nash demand game (Young 1993b). Given that there is noise, play never literally settles down though what can happen is that particular strategies occur most of the time. If $K/T \leq 1/2$ (that is, agents sample at most half of the records that are available) then, as the amount of noise goes to zero, there is one allocation (or at most two) that occurs almost all the time. Furthermore, if we let the feasible set of allocations become increasingly fine (that is, we go from units being in dollars to dimes to cents to 1/10ths of a cent and so forth), then agents settle upon an even split. Through experiential learning and the associated adaptation of play, agents come to settle on a particular way of splitting the pie. In the presence of many Nash equilibria, a convention develops for resolving this indeterminacy. While further advances in modelling are required, adaptive play may ultimately come to explain various conventions in society including the US convention that attorneys for the plaintiff in tort cases receive compensation equal to one third of awarded damages.

C. Evolutionary game theory. Thus far solutions to a game have been predicated upon players choosing strategies which maximize their expected payoff given their beliefs over other players' strategies. An alternative approach which skirts the entire issue of strategy selection by individual players is to model the dynamics of a population of agents using notions of natural selection. This branch of the discipline is known as *evolutionary game theory* (Maynard Smith 1982; Weibull 1995). Initially developed by biologists, evolutionary game theory is the product of importing (and then modifying) game theory into biology.

The idea is to specify a population of agents who interact to play a game. Each player has a series of encounters with the other players, where each encounter involves the game under consideration. The performance of a particular strategy is measured by the average payoff it generates for a player who uses that strategy in his interaction with the population. The static evolutionary approach is comprised of modifications of Nash equilibrium which identify stable populations (in terms of the strategies that players use). Here, a central concept is an *evolutionarily stable strategy* or ESS (Maynard Smith and Price 1973). Suppose all players are using strategy X and then a few new players come along playing strategy Y. For strategy X to be an ESS, the average payoff that it generates when interacted with the population (most of whom use X but a small number of whom use Y) must exceed the average payoff that strategy Y generates. An ESS is thought to be stable – and thus of interest since it will tend to persist over time – because an ESS outperforms any new strategy and, using the idea of natural selection, its representation in the population would be expected to grow until all players are once again using that strategy. In other words, an ESS is viewed as being immune to 'mutations' in which a small proportion of the population use a different strategy.

An alternative approach is to specify the dynamic which drives the population rather than use a static concept motivated by dynamic stories. One such dynamic is the *replicator dynamic* which specifies that the growth rate of the population share of a strategy is proportional to the average payoff of a player using that strategy (when matched with all other players in the population) *less* the average payoff of all players in the population. Thus, those strategies that do better than average find their relative presence in the population growing while those that do worse than average shrink. An ESS is known to be asymptotically stable in the replicator dynamic which means that if the mix of strategies in the population is near an ESS and if the change in that mix is governed by the replicator dynamic then the mix will eventually converge to that ESS.

While this evolutionary line of reasoning is a fresh and promising perspective to behaviour in strategic situations, proper exploitation of its potential requires, in the opinion of this writer, the explicit embodiment of those features that make social evolution distinct from biological evolution. Equating a strategy's payoff with a strategy's (evolutionary) fitness is a *non sequitur*. Of particular concern is that dynamics encompass the mechanism by which strategies are transferred. In the social context, it is not reproduction and genetics but rather social learning such as imitation. While the payoff that a strategy generates is certainly relevant to its imitation, it is not the only force likely to be influential. The ease with which a strategy can be inferred from a player's past play is also of importance and the dynamics we specify should reflect that. Recent work suggests that the future of non-cooperative game theory may be closely tied to concepts of social learning.

RECOMMENDED READING. This essay has covered some of the main issues and methods within non-cooperative game theory. To learn more directly of its usefulness in law and economics, the reader is referred to Baird, Gertner and Picker (1994). They examine the impact of legal institutions on individual behaviour. A second use of game theory within law and economics is to understand why we have the laws that we do. Such work includes the modelling of legislative processes, interaction within and between primitive societies, and the evolution of common law. For a comprehensive treatment of non-cooperative game theory, Binmore (1992), Gibbons (1992), Colman (1995) and Gardner (1995) provide well-written introductions for the first-timer to the subject. A lighter and less systematic treatment is provided in Dixit and Nalebuff (1991) as they show the power of game-theoretic reasoning through a series of entertaining anecdotes.

JOSEPH E. HARRINGTON, JR.

See also COMMON KNOWLEDGE; COORDINATION GAMES; EVOLUTIONARY GAME THEORY; GAME THEORY AND STATES OF THE WORLD; GAME THEORY AND THE LAW; PRISONERS' DILEMMA.

Subject classification: 1d(i).

BIBLIOGRAPHY

Baird, D.G., Gertner, R.H. and Picker, R.C. 1994. *Game Theory and the Law*. Cambridge, MA: Harvard University Press.

Bernheim, B.D. 1984. Rationalizable strategic behaviour. *Econometrica* 52: 1007–28.

Binmore, K. 1990. *Essays on the Foundations of Game Theory*. Oxford, UK; New York: Basil Blackwell.

Binmore, K. 1992. *Fun and Games*. Lexington, MA.: D.C. Heath & Co.

Brown, G.W. 1951. Iterative solutions of games by fictitious play. In *Activity Analysis of Production and Allocation*, ed. T.J. Koopmans, New York: John Wiley & Sons.

Colman, A.M. 1995. *Game Theory and Its Applications in the Social and Biological Sciences*. Oxford: Butterworth–Heinemann.

Dixit, A. and Nalebuff, B. 1991. *Thinking Strategically*. New York: W.W. Norton & Co.

Dubey, P. 1986. Inefficiency of Nash equilibria. *Mathematics of Operations Research* 11: 1–8.

Fudenberg, D. and Kreps, D.M. 1988. A theory of learning, experimentation and equilibrium in games. Mimeo, Stanford University, Stanford, CA.

Fudenberg, D. and Levine, D.K. 1993. Self-confirming equilibrium. *Econometrica* 61: 523–45.

Fudenberg, D. and Maskin, E.S. 1986. The folk theorem in repeated games with discounting or with incomplete information. *Econometrica* 54: 533–54.

Gardner, R. 1995. *Games for Business and Economics*. New York: John Wiley & Sons.

Gibbons, R. 1992. *Game Theory for Applied Economists*. Princeton: Princeton University Press.

Kandori, M., Mailath, G.J. and Rob, R. 1993. Learning, mutation, and long run equilibria in games. *Econometrica* 61: 29–56.

Maynard Smith, J. 1982. *Evolution and the Theory of Games*. Cambridge: Cambridge University Press.

Maynard Smith, J. and Price, G.R. 1973. The logic of animal conflict. *Nature* 246: 15–8.

Nash, J.F., Jr. 1950. Equilibrium points in n-person games. *Proceedings of the National Academy of Sciences of the United States* 36: 48–9.

Nash, J.F., Jr. 1953. Two-person cooperative games. *Econometrica* 21: 128–40.

Pearce, D.G. 1984. Rationalizable strategic behavior and the problem of perfection. *Econometrica* 52: 1029–50.

Robinson, J. 1951. An iterative method of solving a game. *Annals of Mathematics* 54: 296–301.

Weibull, J. 1995. *Evolutionary Game Theory*. Cambridge, MA: MIT Press.

Young, H.P. 1993a. The evolution of conventions. *Econometrica* 61: 57–84.

Young, H.P. 1993b. An evolutionary model of bargaining. *Journal of Economic Theory* 59: 145–68.

nonprofit firms. *See* OWNERSHIP OF THE FIRM.

norm cascades. *See* INFORMATIONAL CASCADES AND SOCIAL CONVENTIONS.

nuisance, law of. *See* TRESPASS AND NUISANCE.

nuisance suits. One of the chief problems of court reform in recent years has been the nuisance suit or frivolous suit. I will define this as *a lawsuit with a low probability of success at trial, brought even though the plaintiff knows that his probability of prevailing would not justify his costs if the judicial process were to be completed instantly*. This is one of many possible definitions, and, as we shall see, trying to define the term helps to illuminate a variety of problems that arise in the courts. Note, too, that I have chosen a definition which depends on existing law and procedure; a filing that is a nuisance suit in one jurisdiction might win in another.

Let us begin with a model of a civil suit in tort. The plaintiff pays amount F to file suit against the defendant, an amount meant to include all initial expenses. The suit has probability α of prevailing and winning damages of D, facts known to both sides and the court. The plaintiff then makes a take-it-or-leave-it offer to settle for amount S. If the defendant rejects, the plaintiff decides whether to go to trial at additional cost c_p or to drop the suit. If he goes to trial, the defendant must pay c_d to defend himself. What makes this a nuisance suit is that $-F - c_p + \alpha D < 0$. In the extreme, the suit has no chance of winning, and $\alpha = 0$. This is essentially the model of Shavell (1982). (Note that all results below will carry through with more elaborate settlement bargaining and when the parties are uncertain of the parameter values.)

SETTLEMENT EXTORTION. One misconception can be dispelled immediately: the idea that the plaintiff can extract a settlement from the defendant simply because the defendant has greater costs of going to trial.

Suppose that c_d is large, much larger than c_p and $c_p > \alpha D$. What will the settlement amount be?

The value to the defendant of not going to trial is $\alpha D + c_d$. The value to the plaintiff of going to trial is $\alpha D - c_p$. One might think that the settlement would be between these values – at the upper extreme, $\alpha D + c_d$, with take-it-or-leave-it offers; or $\alpha D + (c_d - c_p)/2$, with equal bargaining power. That is false. The catch is that the plaintiff's threat to go to trial must be credible, but if his settlement offer is turned down, he will give up rather than pay c_p for a probability α of D. Hence, the size of c_d is irrelevant.

There are, however, twists to the situation that can make the plaintiff's threat to go to trial credible, so suit-for-settlement becomes plausible.

Sunk costs. Suppose the plaintiff has sunk most of his costs up front. Even though this is a nuisance suit, so $c_p + F > \alpha D$, it can also be true that $c_p < \alpha D$. Then the threat to go to trial is credible; once the plaintiff has paid F, and if c_d is large, a big settlement can be extorted.

Both F and c_p may be small in terms of opportunity cost, if not accounting cost, because the plaintiff has prepaid most of his legal costs. This could occur, for example, when the plaintiff pays a flat salary to his in-house counsel, though only if he has no other use for the counsel's time. Prepayment could, however, be a strategic move, reversing the typical advice to delay payments and hasten receipts. Making the cost F irrecoverable, the plaintiff's threat to go to trial becomes credible and his bargaining position improves.

The first model in which the timing of costs was crucial, Rosenberg and Shavell (1985), has a slightly different twist. After the plaintiff pays F, the defendant must pay c_d before the plaintiff pays c_p, because the defendant must prepare some defence to the initial filing or lose by summary judgment, whereas the plaintiff can rest on the merits until the actual trial. This means that the plaintiff can offer to settle for c_d immediately after filing, and the defendant will accept, even though both know that the plaintiff would never go to trial.

US federal independent prosecutors illustrate the importance of prepaid costs. They have liberal budgets – indeed, no fixed budgets at all – so it is not surprising that their results have been poor by comparison with regular prosecutors. Since the client has authorized the expenditure in advance, before the quality of the case is determined by the prosecutor, the prosecutor has little incentive to drop cases that are unlikely to win at trial.

It is worth noting as an empirical matter that even if a case is frivolous, the defendant is often well advised to make heavy expenditures in defending himself. An apt case is *Bonsignore v. City of New York*, 521 F Supp 394 (NY 1981). The wife of a policeman successfully sued the city after he shot her, claiming the city was negligent in not requiring all policemen to take tests for mental disorders. Judge Sofaer upheld the jury verdict, noting with disapproval that the city had brought no witnesses, whereas Mrs Bonsignore had brought fifteen.

Divisible costs. Bebchuk (1996) carries the idea of sunk costs further. Suppose that the plaintiff cannot pay his legal expenses first, but both sides incur costs in T stages, and at $T - 1$, once most costs are sunk, the plaintiff finds it worthwhile to incur the costs of the last stage so as to have a chance at the trial judgment. He can then extract a settlement. Going back to $T - 2$, however, the plaintiff would be willing to pay expenses of that stage, as the price of admission to the profitable settlement of $T - 1$. The reasoning continues back to Stage 1. The result is like the loser-pays 'dollar auction' of Shubik (1971), with settlement as an agreement by both players to exit a costly rivalry that is profitable at each stage but ruinous overall.

Defendant ignorance. Bebchuk (1988) points out that if the plaintiff knows $\alpha = 0$ but the defendant does not, the plaintiff can bring suit and extort a profitable settlement. What is relevant to the defendant's acceptance of a settlement offer is the defendant's subjective probability of winning, not the plaintiff's, nor the true probability. Even if the defendant is uncertain of the probability, and assigns positive probability to the plaintiff dropping the case if no agreement is reached, the partially credible threat is still credible, if not quite as frightening.

The defendant's disadvantage can arise from two sources. He might literally have worse information, especially before the discovery process begins. Before discovery, the tort defendant usually has little evidence available with which to dispute the plaintiff's claims. Or, he might not know the law, especially before he hires a lawyer. Many stories exist of government regulatory claims of this kind. The agency claims a violation where it knows none exists, threatening prosecution unless the defendant's behaviour is changed. Note that such suits are never actually filed in court (though the plaintiff still incurs costs), and hence court reforms cannot help.

Incomplete information about the plaintiff. With positive probability, the plaintiff might be irrational or motivated by one of the reasons not involving settlement listed below. All types of plaintiff will pretend to be of this litigious type. Suppose there is a probability β that the plaintiff will go to trial even though $c_p > \alpha D$. The defendant's expected cost from turning down the settlement offer is then $(1 - \beta) * (0) + \beta(\alpha D + c_d)$. Thus, the plaintiff can make a settlement demand of $\beta(\alpha D + c_d)$, which might well exceed F, even if it is much smaller than c_d.

Plaintiff reputation. The plaintiff might want to maintain a reputation for carrying out threats. If there is even a very small probability that the plaintiff is irrational – much smaller than necessary as a basis for the reason discussed in the previous paragraph – the plaintiff can use it for leverage to support a reputation equilibrium in the style of the Kreps–Milgrom–Roberts–Wilson (1982) 'Gang of Four' model. For explanation of this subtle model, see Rasmusen (1994: ch. 5 and 6). The essential requirement is that the plaintiff expects to be in future litigation and is willing to take a loss on the present case to preserve his reputation.

REASONS NOT INVOLVING SETTLEMENT. Other nuisance suits seem to exist which are not brought solely in the hopes of extorting a settlement (though a generous settlement is always welcome).

Plaintiff mistake. The plaintiff may not know α is low. Mistakes can always occur. In a sense, either $\alpha = 0$ or $\alpha = 1$, and any suit that loses is a nuisance suit, *ex post*. I will mention only two of the many reasons for mistakes. (1) A man is not just a poor judge in his own case, but often a sincerely poor judge, unable to see what is obvious to others: that his suit is hopeless. This is the origin of the 'empty-head, pure-heart' suit. (2) The plaintiff faces an agency problem, because he relies on an attorney's advice. If the attorney is paid an hourly wage, he has incentive to convince the plaintiff to sue – which is, of course, a major reason for contingency fees, though their dampening effect on the number of nuisance suits is little noted (and even reversed, somehow, in the *Restatement of Torts* §675h). One-third of zero, plus a reputation for losing cases, is not attractive to ambulance chasers.

Benefits from litigation. It may happen that there is a benefit just from bringing the case – the litigation cost C is negative. The *Restatement of Torts*, §676 (Propriety of Purpose) has a good discussion of this. The plaintiff may derive utility from the disutility of the defendant – a grudge suit. The plaintiff may value the publicity, as is commonly suspected of public prosecutors who bring sensational but legally dubious civil or criminal suits. (This is distinct from wanting a reputation for toughness for use in other court proceedings, discussed above.) The plaintiff may value the delay that litigation brings. If the suit includes a preliminary injunction, or if the plaintiff can win with a biased lower court even if he knows he will lose on appeal, he is able to delay something costly, e.g. suffering the death penalty. In civil cases, defendants may be able to delay yielding up property or complying with rules. Also, especially in land-use disputes, delay may enable a litigant to lobby to change the relevant law to his advantage.

Indirect benefits from winning. An apparent nuisance suit may turn out not to be one when indirect benefits to success are included. These include the utility of official vindication of one's cause, and advantages in later legal proceedings. Failure to prosecute patent and copyright infringement can waive the protection, and similar losses of rights occur in other areas of the law. An appellate victory can establish a precedent that a plaintiff can use in future litigation, or which changes the law in a way that he finds personally satisfying.

Court error and unjust law. A somewhat different explanation for meritless suits is court error (distinct from defendant error, one of the earlier reasons). Even if it is true that α *should* be zero, it may be that α is positive because of court error. Many suits that appear ridiculous do win, but while one is tempted to call these nuisance suits, they do not fall under the definition of this essay. A suit may be a long shot and still have positive net expected value. In *Bigbee v. Pacific Telephone and Telegraph Co.* (1983), for example, a man in a telephone booth sued the telephone company for improper design and maintenance because it was hard to escape as a drunk driver careered towards him out of the street, over a kerb and across a parking lot. The California Supreme Court unanimously upheld his right to a jury trial. Defending this suit against summary judgment was clearly not frivolous; it won by a large margin, and hence is not a nuisance suit. The problem is not procedure, but substance, and the proper derogatory term is 'court error' or 'unjust law', depending on whether other courts would replicate the same bad result. Such suits, however, may make up the bulk of what the public complains of as nuisance suits, as I explain in Rasmusen (1995), and are hard to remedy by procedural reform, as Bebchuk and Chang (1996) explain.

Any of this second set of reasons to go to trial can be leveraged up by the possibility of settlement. Once the threat to go to trial is credible, the plaintiff can demand a bigger settlement, the prospect of which makes filing suit in the first place more attractive.

Note also that the second set of reasons need not arise only under the adversarial system of civil litigation. They apply to government-sponsored criminal and civil suits as well as to suits brought for profit. The problem of nuisance suits extends beyond common-law countries and beyond a profit-seeking plaintiff's bar.

SOLUTIONS. The goal of reducing the number of nuisance suits is often confused with the entirely separate, and dubious, goal of reducing litigation. A reform such as the English Rule, which leads to lower costs for meritorious plaintiffs, could actually increase the total amount of litigation. For efficiency and justice, this is good; for minimizing court caseloads, it is bad.

Fee-shifting rules. The American rule is that each litigant pays his own legal fees, except in unusual cases such as those covered by the Civil Rights Attorney's Fee Award Act of 1976, where plaintiffs can recover their costs, and in the state of Alaska (see Wade 1986: 487). The English Rule is that the loser pays. There is a large literature in economics on this, surveyed in Cooter and Rubinfeld (1989). By reducing the payoff at trial, the English Rule reduces the credibility of threats to go to trial with meritless suits.

Procedural rules. These rules delegate the deterrence of nuisance suits to the judge in the original proceedings, subject to review by higher courts.

First, the rules on how suit is brought can make nuisance suits difficult. These include rules on standing, limiting who can bring suit; on forum shopping, preventing plaintiffs from going to sympathetic or corrupt judges; on removal, allowing defendants to avoid such judges; on pleadings, requiring a specific-enough filing that its lack of merit is apparent; on evidence, barring hearsay and limiting expert testimony; and on discovery, limiting the demands each litigant can impose on the other. See Olson (1991) (for America), and the Woolf Report (1996) (for England and Wales) for discussion of these rules – highly legalistic and largely ignored by economists. Given these rules, the judge has the ability to dismiss suits by summary judgment.

Second, the judge can punish as well as dismiss. Courts have inherent powers to control bad-faith conduct, and the US Supreme Court has on this basis upheld sanctions even for acts outside the courtroom: *Chambers v. Nasco*, 501 US 32 (1991). In addition, judges are often granted statutory powers: The Federal statute 28 USC §1927 allows fee-shifting under certain circumstances, Federal tax rule 26 USCS §6673 assesses penalties for frivolous or dilatory proceedings, and many states have similar statutes. The best-known sanction in the United States is Rule 11 of the Federal Rules of Civil Procedure, as amended in 1983. It says, in the concise 1983 version (expanded less elegantly in the 1993 amendments), that an attorney may file suit only if

> . . . to the best of his knowledge, information, and belief formed after reasonable inquiry it is well grounded in fact and is warranted by existing law or a good faith argument for the extension, modification, or reversal of existing law, and that it is not interposed for any improper purpose, such as to harass or to cause unnecessary delay or needless increase in the cost of litigation.

Imposition of Rule 11 sanctions is common, but although the 1993 amendments, the Supreme Court, and many economists have emphasized that its purpose is deterrence, lower courts seem to pay little attention. They tend to use the sanctions for compensation to the aggrieved party, and only after a motion by that party. See *Cooter & Gell v. Hartmarx* (1990), Polinsky and Rubinfeld (1993) and, for further analysis of the 1993 amendments, Kobayashi and Parker (1993).

It is frequently observed that a good rule can be bad policy when applied by uncooperative judges. Judges often condone, or even praise, aggressive litigation. See *Golden Eagle v. Burroughs* (1986) and *Zaldivar v. City of Los Angeles* (1986), which admire Rule 11 in the abstract while overruling it in particular cases, or *Eastway v. City of New York* (1986), in which an unhappy trial judge required by an appellate court to impose Rule 11 sanctions decided to include only attorneys' fees, and to reduce them from $58,550 to $1,000 because of mitigating factors. Perhaps as a surrender to this kind of judge nullification, Rule 11 was amended in 1993 to say that the trial judge *may* rather than *shall* impose sanctions. More study needs to be done of judges' motives, both personal and political; Macey (1994) is one step in this direction.

Tort rules. If legislatures and judges are unwilling to stop nuisance suits, the public might be able to rely on the plaintiff's bar, resorting to judo tort reform which uses the opponent's strength and momentum against him. A nuisance suit is an injury, often intentional, and reckless by definition. Can the victim sue?

Economists have not addressed this topic, but Wade (1986) has an excellent survey of state law. Judges have been uniformly hostile to suits brought on general tort grounds of negligent harm, but this is perhaps because of the existence of special causes of action for malicious prosecution, both criminal and civil. What their effect has been is unclear, but suits for civil malicious prosecution lose much of their force in the absence of the English Rule on costs, unless they can obtain punitive damages as in *Bertero v. National General Corp.* (1975).

CONCLUSION. Law-and-economics research in the area of nuisance suits has been active since the early 1980s, but though it has illuminated extortionary settlement and the effects of fee-shifting, it has neglected many other aspects of the problem. Perhaps the biggest blanks are in the areas of public choice theory and theory-driven empirical study. Reforming a system against the inclinations of those who staff it is no easy problem, but scholarship has concentrated on the effect of successful proposals rather than implementation. The incentives of litigants are studied in great detail; the incentives of judges, not at all. Empirical work would also be helpful, particularly to delineate the extent of the problem and which of the many plausible explanations for nuisance suits are most common in practice.

ERIC B. RASMUSEN

See also ACCURACY IN ADJUDICATION; ALLOCATION OF LITIGATION COSTS: AMERICAN AND ENGLISH RULES; CIVIL PROCEDURE IN THE USA AND CIVIL LAW COUNTRIES; COMPARATIVE COMMON LAW: THE CONSEQUENCES OF DIFFERING INCENTIVES TO LITIGATE; DISCOVERY; PRIVATE INFORMATION AND LEGAL BARGAINING; SETTLEMENT OF LITIGATION; SUITS WITH NEGATIVE EXPECTED VALUE.

Subject classification: 5a(iv).

STATUTES

28 USC §1927 (fee-shifting under unusual circumstances).

USCS, Federal Rules of Civil Procedure §11 (sanctions for frivolous suits).

26 USCS §6673 (1996) (tax court sanctions for frivolous suits).

42 USC 1988, Civil Rights Attorney's Fee Award Act of 1976 (plaintiffs can recover their costs).

CASES

Bertero v. National General Corp., 13 Cal 3d 43 (Cal. 1975) (punitive damages can be assessed for malicious civil prosecution).

Bigbee v. Pacific Telephone and Telegraph Co., 34 Cal 3d 49 (Cal. 1983) (suing the telephone-booth maker).

Bonsignore v. City of New York, 521 F Supp 394 (NY 1981) (wife shot by policeman sued city).

Chambers v. Nasco, Inc., 501 US 32 (1991) (inherent court powers).

Cooter & Gell v. Hartmarx Corp., 496 US 384 (1990) (Rule 11 is meant to deter).

Eastway Construction Corp. v. City of New York, 637 F Supp 558 (NY 1986).

Golden Eagle Distribution Corp. v. Burroughs Corp., 801 F2d 1531 (9th Cir. 1986) (false statements *per se* cannot be sanctioned by Rule 11).

Zaldivar v. City of Los Angeles, 780 F2d 823 (9th Cir. 1986) (extent of frivolity that requires Rule 11 sanctions).

BIBLIOGRAPHY

American Law Institute. 1977. *Restatement of the Law, Second: Torts 2d.* St Paul, MN: American Law Institute.

Bebchuk, L. 1988. Suing solely to extract a settlement offer. *Journal of Legal Studies* 17: 437–50.

Bebchuk, L. 1996. A new theory concerning the credibility and success of threats to sue. *Journal of Legal Studies* 25: 1–26.

Bebchuk, L. and Chang, H. 1996. An analysis of fee shifting based on the margin of victory: on frivolous suits, meritorious suits, and the role of Rule 11. *Journal of Legal Studies* 25: 371–403.

Cooter, R. and Rubinfeld, D. 1989. Economic analysis of legal disputes and their resolution. *Journal of Economic Literature* 27: 1067–97.

Kobayashi, B. and Parker, J. 1993. No armistice at 11: a commentary on the Supreme Court's 1993 amendment to Rule 11 of the Federal Rules of Civil Procedure. *Supreme Court Economic Review* 3: 93–152.

Kreps, D., Milgrom, P., Roberts, J. and Wilson, R. 1982. Rational cooperation in the finitely repeated prisoners' dilemma. *Journal of Economic Theory* 27: 245–52.

Macey, J. 1994. Judicial preferences, public choice, and the rules of procedure. *Journal of Legal Studies* 23: 627–46.

Olson, W. 1991. *The Litigation Explosion.* New York: Dutton.

Polinsky, A.M. and Rubinfeld, D. 1993. Sanctioning frivolous suits: an economic analysis. *Georgetown Law Journal* 82: 397–435.

Rasmusen, E. 1994. *Games and Information.* 2nd edn, Oxford: Basil Blackwell.

Rasmusen, E. 1995. Predictable and unpredictable error in tort awards: the effect of plaintiff self selection and signalling. *International Review of Law and Economics* 15: 323–45.

Rosenberg. D. and Shavell, S. 1985. A model in which lawsuits are brought for their nuisance value. *International Review of Law and Economics* 5: 3–13.

Shavell, S. 1982. Suit, settlement, and trial: a theoretical analysis under alternative methods for the allocation of legal costs. *Journal of Legal Studies* 11: 55–81.

Shubik, M. 1971. The dollar auction game: a paradox in noncooperative behaviour and escalation. *Journal of Conflict Resolution* 15: 109–11.

Wade, J. 1986. On frivolous litigation: a study of tort liability and procedural sanctions. *Hofstra Law Review* 14: 433.

Woolf. 1996. *Access to Justice: Final Report to the Lord Chancellor on the Civil Justice System in England and Wales.* London: Her Majesty's Stationery Office.

O

occupational disease and the tort system: the case of asbestos. From the 1930s through the 1960s, the use of asbestos grew rapidly, as did the exposure of workers to high concentrations of airborne asbestos fibres. Throughout this period, asbestos manufacturers quietly settled small numbers of claims by workers for illness or death caused by asbestos exposure and suppressed information that would link asbestos to disease. But by the time that Clarence Borel won a product-liability suit in 1971 and its appeal two years later, thousands of asbestos workers were dying every year from past exposures. *Borel v. Fibreboard* started an avalanche of tort litigation that generated 10,000 claims by 1980 and perhaps 200,000 claims by 1990, bankrupting more than a dozen major manufacturing firms and overwhelming the US civil courts. This essay examines the role that tort litigation played in deterring these worker exposures and in compensating the victims.

1. THE ROLE OF THE TORT SYSTEM FOR OCCUPATIONAL DISEASE. Early this century, workers in North America abandoned their common law right to sue the employer in negligence for injuries arising out of the workplace in exchange for no-fault administrative compensation through workers' compensation (WC) systems. In the United Kingdom, workers' compensation was not an exclusive remedy, leaving workers with a choice of accepting the administrative compensation or suing in tort. Workers' compensation first dealt with accidental injuries but grew to cover work-related illness including respiratory disease, and asbestos was generally covered in the US and the UK by the late 1930s. Since then (and in the UK since 1948 through Social Security), workers have been compensated for workplace injuries and illness throughout the United States, Canada and the UK at levels specified by state or provincial statutes, regulations or policies.

Because employers' workers-compensation premiums are generally set in relation to the claims history of the employer or industry, and because workers-compensation insurers often operate loss-management programmes, worker compensation provides some incentive for the employer to avoid worker injuries (Moore and Viscusi 1990). Workers who are aware of workplace hazards and have some bargaining power may bargain for higher wages for hazardous work or for reductions in those hazards. Thus the market may provide a powerful incentive for workplace safety. In addition, state and federal occupational safety and health regulations provide worker protection. We cannot evaluate the effectiveness of the tort system in isolation from these other forces.

While workers' compensation provides the principal means of compensating victims of industrial disease, tort lingers in the background. In some cases, the worker who is dissatisfied with a compensation award may challenge that award in court, generally seeking judicial review of the award process but in some jurisdictions asking for a trial *de novo* of his claim. More importantly, *Borel* established in 1971 that while the worker must usually rely on workers' compensation as against his employer, he may still bring a product liability action against the supplier of a product to the employer. Many product liability actions in the United States arise out of workplace injuries and illness (Dewees, Duff and Trebilcock 1996: ch 4). The flood of asbestos cases that overwhelmed the US asbestos manufacturers and the civil courts in the 1970s and 1980s were work-related product liability actions.

2. THE ROLE OF PRODUCT LIABILITY ACTIONS IN THEORY. Looking first at compensation, if the workers-compensation system is well designed, it is hard to justify the addition of tort to satisfy the goal of distributive justice. However, in cases where the employer's or supplier's behaviour caused the illness and that behaviour was wanton, reckless or intentional, corrective justice might justify compensation from the wrongdoer not only for pecuniary loss but also for pain and suffering. This could justify allowing tort lawsuits against the wrongdoer in these situations.

The deterrent effect of workers' compensation on the employer is blunt in part because the insurance aspect does not impose on most employers the full cost of claims paid on that employer's policy. More aggressive risk-rating of workers-compensation premiums improves the incentives but weakens the insurance. Adding tort liability may not help because employers would simply purchase tort liability insurance, again blunting the deterrent. Tort liability might be justified on deterrence grounds only in situations involving wanton, reckless or intentional conduct. This would ensure that the individual firm would face the full costs of its actions when by definition the costs of avoidance would be less than the harm caused. Thus theory could justify creating an exception to the exclusive remedy of workers' compensation to rectify the weakening of incentives caused by insurance.

The supplier of a defective product to an employer would be deterred by the employer facing higher workers-compensation premiums arising from higher worker claims caused by the product. Here again the incentive on the supplier will be blunted by the insurance aspect of compensation. As with employers, one might justify allowing tort lawsuits in cases where the supplier of the product behaved in a wanton, reckless or intentional manner.

These theoretical conclusions must be tempered by

several special features of asbestos disease. First, there is usually a latency period of ten to thirty years between the worker's exposure and the manifestation of asbestosis or cancer. If the potential liability for tort damages will only arise several decades in the future, a rational firm that discounts such liability at its internal rate of return will virtually ignore the liability even though society might discount the future harm at a lower rate (Dewees 1986). Second, causation is only probabilistic and the risk of contracting lung cancer is not zero in the absence of asbestos exposure. This risk increases with the extent and duration of exposure and it may depend on the type of asbestos. Thus even if an asbestos-exposed worker dies of lung cancer one can never be certain that the exposure caused the lung cancer, and in most cases one can only say that the asbestos exposure increased the risk of lung cancer fatality. Workers-compensation administrators have agonized over the drafting of rules that will tend to compensate those whose disease was caused by the exposure without compensating other victims of that disease.

A third practical problem arising from the first two bedevils any attempt to use tort to compensate for asbestos disease: product identification and exposure. How do we determine the extent of exposure of an asbestos worker in a workplace many years ago when airborne fibre measurements were rare? If a worker has been exposed to asbestos while working for several employers, which should pay for his disease? This is not a problem in Ontario, where a single agency handles workers' compensation for the entire province, but it is a problem in those US jurisdictions where different employers may be served by competing insurers. If the worker sues the asbestos supplier, how does he establish the *product* that caused his injury? The records of asbestos suppliers may not survive the long latency periods between exposure and manifestation of the disease. Accounts of the early asbestos litigation reveal the difficulty faced by plaintiffs who clearly suffered from asbestos disease but could not prove which suppliers should be held responsible (Brodeur 1985).

The result of these problems is that product liability suits by asbestos-exposed workers are very costly and complicated to litigate, with less than 40 percent of defendants' costs being paid to plaintiffs (Kakalik et al. 1984).

3. THE HISTORY OF ASBESTOS USE AND DISEASE. Asbestos is a family of naturally occurring fibrous hydrated silicates, of which three have been commercially important: chrysotile, amosite and crocidolite. Asbestos has high tensile strength, flexibility and durability, and is resistant to heat, wear and corrosion (ORCA 1984: 75–92). Over one thousand years ago, asbestos fibres were woven into fireproof cloth and mixed with clay to add strength to pottery. In the twentieth century, asbestos has been used as a fire retardant in textiles, as fireproofing and thermal insulation, as a component in friction products such as brake pads, as reinforcement in asbestos-cement pipes and other products, to provide wear resistance in vinyl floor coverings, for acid resistance in packings and gaskets, for filtering in gas masks and as a filler in resins, plastics, caulking and sealants. Chrysotile asbestos has accounted for the vast majority of the commercial asbestos consumed. During the 1930s builders began to spray asbestos insulation in commercial buildings for thermal insulation, decorative purposes and noise control and in ships for fireproofing. The 1950s saw rapid growth in the use of sprayed asbestos in buildings to protect structural steel from excessive heat in case of fire. In addition, asbestos was commonly used to insulate boilers and steam pipes in buildings and ships beginning in the 1920s. These uses grew through the 1960s and then collapsed in the 1970s as fear of asbestos exposure grew and as regulations limited and then banned the installation of friable asbestos. These uses in buildings and ships also gave rise to enormous worker exposures and much later to a tragic toll of disease among those workers.

High levels of asbestos exposure give rise to three major disease risks. Asbestosis is a chronic, restrictive, progressive and irreversible lung disease which produces scarring in the lung and reduced lung function that gradually reduces the worker's strength and activity level and life expectancy. It is common among heavily exposed asbestos workers. Mesothelioma is a rare and usually fatal cancer of the lining of the lung and abdomen that is usually caused by asbestos exposure. Lung cancer is not specifically associated with asbestos exposure, but high exposure levels appear to increase the risk of lung cancer, especially in smokers.

Before 1920, doctors had reported deaths and lung disease arising from asbestos exposure in France, Great Britain Canada and in the United States (ORCA 1984: 104). In 1927, Dr Cooke coined the name 'asbestosis' for the pulmonary fibrosis suffered by asbestos textile workers. A 1930 report to the UK Parliament recognized that prolonged asbestos exposure could lead to serious fibrosis, and recommended dust suppression that was adopted in a 1931 asbestos regulation. Studies in the 1930s in the US and Canada confirmed the risk of lung disease arising from heavy asbestos exposure. In 1947 a high incidence of cancer was noted among asbestos workers, and in 1955 Sir Richard Doll documented a tenfold increase in lung cancer rates among textile workers, although a later study of Quebec miners showed no excess cancer risk. Mesothelioma was proven to arise from exposures to crocidolite in South Africa by 1960. Then, in 1964, Dr Irving Selikoff reported very high mortality and disease rates among highly exposed US insulation workers (ORCA 1984: 109). By this time, two decades had elapsed since the heavy shipyard exposures of World War II and those workers were developing high disease and mortality rates that would attract public attention for the next decade and more. By the 1980s, the US mortality rate from workplace asbestos exposure was thought to be up to 10,000 per year.

4. ASBESTOS REGULATION. Early in the twentieth century, workplace safety legislation required that harmful dust, gases and vapours in the workplace air be controlled, but airborne asbestos dust was not regulated until 1931 when the UK passed the Asbestos Industry Regulations requiring extensive provisions for dust control (ORCA 1984: 128). In 1946, the American Conference of Governmental Industrial Hygienists (ACGIH) adopted a Threshold Limit Value (TLV) for asbestos of five million particles per cubic foot and governments in the US and Canada used

the TLV as an indication of satisfactory dust control in the workplace. Then in 1968 the British Occupational Hygiene Society recommended that occupational exposures to chrysotile asbestos be limited to two fibres per cubic centimetre (f/cc) and that crocidolite be limited to 0.2 f/cc in order to reduce the risk of workers contracting asbestosis to one percent. In 1970, the ACGIH proposed lowering the TLV to five f/cc for all asbestos types, and formally adopted this TLV in 1973. The US Occupational Safety and Health Administration (OSHA) adopted five f/cc as an emergency temporary standard in 1971, recommended a two f/cc standard in 1972 and adopted two f/cc in 1976. Ontario adopted a guideline of two f/cc for all types of asbestos in 1973 and then limited exposures to amosite and crocidolite to 0.2 f/cc in 1975. In 1979 the UK Advisory Committee on Asbestos recommended limits of 1.0 f/cc for chrysotile, 0.5 f/cc for amosite and 0.2 f/cc for crocidolite, limits which were embodied in regulations in Ontario in 1982 (ORCA 1984; 130). In 1980 the ACGIH reduced its TLV to 2, 0.5, and 0.2 f/cc for the three types of asbestos. In 1983 OSHA adopted an emergency temporary standard of 0.5 f/cc and then adopted a 0.2 f/cc regulation for all types of asbestos in 1986.

In 1973, the US Environmental Protection Agency banned the spraying of asbestos-containing materials in buildings and began to require precautions in working with friable asbestos. By the late 1970s, governments in the US and Canada had banned the installation of all friable asbestos-containing insulation in buildings, so that asbestos use was confined to hard products in which the asbestos fibres were firmly encapsulated and unlikely to escape. Governments also began to regulate the inspection, maintenance, precautions and removal of asbestos in buildings. In 1986 the EPA proposed a ban and phaseout of all asbestos products which was adopted in 1989 and overturned by the 5th Circuit Court of Appeal in 1991 on the grounds that EPA had not supported the rule by substantial evidence (*Corrosion Proof Fittings v. EPA*).

By the 1980s, workplace asbestos exposures in North America and the UK were a small fraction of those in the 1930s to 1960s, but the long latency of asbestos disease meant that the number of workers dying of asbestos disease climbed during the 1980s and would not decline significantly until early in the twenty-first century.

As asbestos consumption declined in the 1970s, building maintenance workers remained at risk from exposure to the large stock of friable asbestos in buildings and regulations were adopted to limit their exposure. Fear spread to building occupants as parents worried about the safety of their children when they observed maintenance workers wearing 'moon suits' as they worked on or around asbestos in schools. Enormous sums were spent to remove asbestos from schools and other buildings during the 1970s and 1980s before the general public finally accepted that the exposures of building occupants were a tiny fraction of the exposures of the workers who had installed the insulation and that the risks to building occupants of asbestos in good condition that was not being disturbed were insignificant. One study noted that risks to occupants were less than the risk of a fatal traffic accident while commuting to and from the building (ORCA 1984: 579–85). Massive lawsuits were filed by building owners against asbestos manufacturers and installers to recover both the past and projected expenditures for asbestos control.

5. TORT LITIGATION. In 1930, asbestosis was not a compensable occupational disease under US workers' compensation laws. But by 1933, Johns-Manville Corporation was being sued for negligence by 11 workers suffering from asbestosis. These suits and others were generally settled out of court. The volume of negligence suits grew during the mid-1930s and the industry finally supported the listing of asbestosis as a compensable disease in order to eliminate the tort litigation (Motley and Nial 1992: 1924). Once asbestos disease became compensable, litigation in the US dwindled as workers' compensation is the exclusive remedy of an injured worker. This changed when Clarence Borel's attorney successfully argued that his asbestos disease was caused by his exposure to asbestos products that were unreasonably dangerous, that the manufacturers failed to warn users of the risks, and that the manufacturers were therefore strictly liable for the resulting harm under the 1965 revision to the *Restatement of Torts*. This case unleashed a flood of product-liability suits against asbestos manufacturers by workers employed by users of those products.

The plaintiff in *Borel* argued that the health risks posed by asbestos were foreseeable at the time of Borel's exposure so that the manufacturer had a duty to warn its customers and their employees. In fact, no warning labels appeared on asbestos products until the mid-1960s. The asbestos manufacturers argued that the health risks were not well known, given the medical 'state of the art' until the Selikoff studies in 1964, but the plaintiff introduced evidence of earlier medical literature and claims settlements by the manufacturers. Still, the manufacturers enjoyed some success with a 'state of the art' defence until documents were discovered in the late 1970s showing that some high officials of the companies had known about worker disease since the early 1930s and had decided to settle negligence claims and workers compensation claims quietly and to avoid informing workers and the public about these risks.

The asbestos litigation has created enormous problems for the US civil courts because of its volume and complexity. The introduction of 10,000 new claims per year is by itself a major burden on the system. But each claim presents important factual problems: when was the worker exposed; what were the exposure levels; what types of asbestos were used; who produced the asbestos; what health damage has the worker suffered? Because exposures may have varied within a single plant and over time, each claimant may require careful fact finding. Furthermore many claimants may have only pleural plaques which may be a precursor to asbestosis but do not in themselves impair the worker's lung function. If the worker cannot recover for plaques, the statute of limitations may have run by the time that asbestosis or cancer can be diagnosed, yet only a fraction of workers with plaques will later develop disabling disease. And if a class action is brought on behalf of injured workers from a particular workplace, what is the legal status of workers whose injury is manifest after the class is certified? The courts have been overwhelmed by the task of finding these facts in mass trials where the common law of several states must be applied.

The asbestos litigation also gave rise to complex questions regarding insurance coverage. Most defendants purchased comprehensive general liability insurance policies from various insurers over the years. These policies cover liability for bodily injury occurring during the policy period. But with a long latency disease when does the injury 'occur'? The courts have found injury at the time of exposure, at the time when a fibre damages a cell in the lung, and at the time when the disease becomes manifest (Khan 1992). Some courts have followed *Keene v. INA* in adopting the 'triple trigger', holding that insurers at any of these times are liable. Furthermore where more than one insurer is found to be 'on the risk' the court must apportion the liability among the insurers. These issues have been the subject of extensive litigation between defendants and their insurers, rivalling in cost and complexity the litigation between workers and manufacturers.

The asbestos litigation was part of the product liability litigation that grew in the US following the adoption in 1965 of strict liability for unreasonably dangerous products. Asbestos losses hit insurance companies at about the same time as other pollution losses such as the cost of cleaning up toxic waste sites. These unanticipated losses devastated the balance sheets of US insurance companies and of their international reinsurance companies. Nowhere were these losses more painful than at Lloyds of London, where insurance coverage is provided by syndicates of individuals (Names) who have pledged their assets without limit to cover losses that exceed premium revenues. Some Lloyds syndicates wrote extensive reinsurance during the 1970s and early 1980s that covered asbestos liability in the US. Lloyds' Asbestos Working Group warned insiders in 1980 of the high risks posed by US asbestos litigation, saying that reserves of $75,000 should be set aside for each anticipated claim. These warnings, however, were allegedly not communicated to the Names who were recruited to syndicates with large asbestos exposure. By the early 1990s, Lloyds' losses were estimated to be in the billions of US dollars. Since all Names face unlimited liability, those who invested in these syndicates suffered great personal and financial tragedies including many bankruptcies and some suicides. Lawsuits have been launched by groups of Lloyds Names alleging negligence and fraud by Lloyds syndicates, adding to the overall litigation burden of asbestos. While insurance usually spreads losses incurred by a few victims over many who have paid premiums, in this case the losses of hundreds of thousands of US asbestos claimants are being borne, in part, by a smaller number of Lloyds Names.

6. THE CONTRIBUTION OF TORT. Did tort litigation or the fear of tort litigation help to control worker exposure to airborne asbestos fibres? One study found that if an employer expected to be liable for the full cost of workers' compensation, or for typical compensatory tort damages, for all workers injured or killed by asbestos exposure in the plant this would not have created a significant incentive to reduce worker exposures. A profit-maximizing employer would not have reduced worker exposures on this account (Dewees 1986: 312). The principal reason is that tort awards for premature fatality compensate for discounted lost earnings which are approximately one-tenth as great as the value of life revealed by studies of the compensating wage necessary to induce workers to accept increased risks of fatality on the job. A simulation assuming that the firm would be liable for amounts based on the compensating wage differential showed the firm adopting maximum controls in most cases. A second reason is that the value of that future liability discounted over the several decades from the exposure to the fatality is quite small. Proof of causation for asbestos disease is difficult today even in the case of highly exposed workers, leading to great uncertainty about the magnitude of liability that might arise. And when workers were highly exposed, knowledge about the dose-response function for asbestos disease was quite primitive, so that firms could not generally have predicted their potential liability with any accuracy. This is a shaky foundation on which to build effective deterrence.

The actual performance of the tort system seems consistent with this theoretical analysis. Some workers brought negligence claims against US asbestos firms in the 1930s but settlement of the claims did not change the firms' worker-protection practices. When the avalanche of product liability claims hit the manufacturers in the US following *Borel*, the use of asbestos and the exposure of workers to asbestos both declined rapidly. But these declines coincided with US regulatory activity as the ACGIH adopted the five f/cc TLV in 1973, OSHA proposed a two f/cc standard in 1972 and adopted it in 1976, and the EPA banned the installation of sprayed asbestos in buildings in 1973. The regulatory system began to provide serious worker protection at about the time that the tort system began to impose substantial liability on the industry. By the time that it was clear that liability for asbestos disease would be enormous, when Johns–Manville declared bankruptcy in 1982, government regulation was highly protective.

Canadian uses of asbestos were similar to those in the US. Many of the same firms operated in both countries and their regulatory history is similar, yet Canada experienced no flood of tort litigation by asbestos victims because its workers' compensation laws generally prevent workers from suing *any* employer, not just the worker's employer. The time profile of asbestos use in both countries is very similar, peaking in 1973 and declining rapidly thereafter. Limited comparisons of actual worker exposures appear similar in both countries in the late 1970s when US litigation was growing rapidly. It is not apparent that tort litigation brought greater protection to US workers than arose for Canadian workers who could not sue.

Tort litigation might serve to generate and disseminate information about asbestos risks in the workplace and thereby help to control worker exposure. However, the negligence claims of the 1930s were settled quietly by the manufacturers and appear to have been forgotten for decades, as were claims in the 1950s. The successful *Borel* case and its successors brought greater notoriety to the injured asbestos workers than would have otherwise arisen, but the increasing death toll among the large cohort of World War II shipyard insulation workers was quickly generating publicity on its own.

It seems quite unlikely that the evidence of industry knowledge of and concealment of asbestos health risks during the 1930s, 1940s and 1950s would have come to light in the absence of the tort litigation. But discovery of this evidence in the late 1970s only served to increase the magnitude and number of the tort awards by limiting the state of the art defence. It does not appear to have contributed significantly to reductions in worker exposure.

The contribution of the tort system to the compensation of asbestos victims is uncertain. Asbestos workers could generally claim workers' compensation benefits if they could demonstrate that workplace asbestos exposure had caused their disease. There were serious restrictions on the compensation for long-latency diseases offered by workers-compensation systems in many states and many asbestos workers failed to file claims. Successful claimants often received compensation that fell far short of the full financial losses caused by the disease. Indeed, the plight of asbestos workers was one factor that led to reform of workers' compensation for industrial disease during the 1970s. The tort recoveries that began with *Borel*, however, were highly uneven, with some plaintiffs settling for a fraction of their lost wages and others receiving full compensation plus punitive damages. Similarly situated plaintiffs in one state might expect $15,000 and those in an adjoining state $1.5 million. The tort system looks less like an efficient compensation mechanism in the case of asbestos disease and more like an expensive lottery.

As the defendants have declared bankruptcy (15 major asbestos manufacturers by 1992) and insurers have exhausted their coverage, efforts have been made to secure a body of assets that can cover existing and future claims in a fair way. But the steady flow of new claims has included workers with less proven exposure to asbestos, with less evidence of current disease, and in some cases with fraudulent claims filed by over-anxious plaintiffs' lawyers. Plaintiffs have waited years for compensation. Legal costs have devoured available assets. The tort system has proven to be a very expensive means of compensating asbestos victims.

Has tort achieved corrective justice in holding the wrongdoer responsible for the harm that has been caused? It has certainly imposed enormous costs on the corporations that were responsible for exposing workers to dangerous airborne asbestos fibre levels over many decades and on their insurers. The shareholders who suffered in the 1980s, however, were not necessarily the same shareholders who profited between 1930 and 1970. The executives who concealed information, often long ago, were generally not punished individually in these suits. The millions of insurance policy holders of all types whose increased premiums helped to cover the asbestos claims are not wrongdoers, nor are the thousands of Lloyds Names. These factors seriously limit the achievement of corrective justice.

The exposure of millions of workers to harmful concentrations of airborne asbestos fibres was tragic and their undercompensation through workers' compensation in the US compounded the tragedy. The tort system, however, has contributed little to worker protection and has contributed slowly, unevenly and at great expense to the compensation of those injured asbestos workers.

DONALD N. DEWEES

See also CAUSATION AND TORT LIABILITY; CLASS ACTIONS; INSURANCE FOR WORKPLACE INJURIES; LIABILITY RIGHTS AS CONTINGENT CLAIMS; OCCUPATIONAL HEALTH AND SAFETY REGULATION; PRODUCTS LIABILITY; PUNITIVE DAMAGES; REGULATION OF HAZARDOUS WASTES; REMOTE RISKS AND THE TORT SYSTEM; RISK ASSESSMENT; RISK REGULATION.

Subject classification: 5d(v); 6d(iii).

CASES

Borel v. Fibreboard Paper Products Corp., 493 F2d 1076 (5th Cir. 1973), *cert. den.*, 419 US 869 (1974).

Corrosion Proof Fittings et al. v. The Environmental Protection Agency 947 F2d 1201 (5th Cir. 1991), *clarified* No. 89–9596, 1991 US App. LEXIS 26,930 at *2 (5th Cir. Nov. 15, 1991).

Keene Corp. v. Insurance Company of North America, 667 F2d 1034 (DC Cir. 1981), *cert. den.* 456 US 951 (1982).

BIBLIOGRAPHY

Brodeur, P. 1985. *Outrageous Misconduct*. New York: Pantheon.

Dewees, D.N. 1986. Economic incentives for controlling industrial disease: the asbestos case: *Journal of Legal Studies* 15: 289–319.

Dewees, D.N., Duff, D. and Trebilcock, M.J. 1996. *Exploring the Domain of Accident Law: Taking the Facts Seriously*. New York: Oxford University Press.

Kakalik, J. et al. 1984. *Variation in Litigation Compensation and Expenses*. Santa Monica: Institute for Civil Justice, Rand Corporation.

Khan, L.J. 1992. Untangling the insurance fibers in asbestos litigation: toward a national solution to the asbestos injury crisis. *Tulane Law Review* 68: 195–240.

Moore, M.J. and Viscusi, W.K. 1990. *Compensation Mechanisms for Job Risks: Wages, Workers' Compensation and Product Liability*. Princeton: Princeton University Press.

Motley, R.L. and Nial, S. 1992. A critical analysis of the Brickman administrative proposal: who declared war on asbestos victims' rights? *Cardozo Law Review* 13: 1919–48.

Ontario Royal Commission on Asbestos [ORCA]. 1984. *Report of the Royal Commission on Matters of Health and Safety Arising from the Use of Asbestos in Ontario*. Toronto: Queen's Printer.

Wikeley, N.J. 1993. *Compensation for Industrial Disease*. Aldershot: Dartmouth Publishing.

occupational health and safety regulation. Accidents and illnesses in the workplace result in significant numbers of employees each year experiencing pain and suffering, interruption to their work activities, and consequent loss in production for their employers. Estimates from the Labour Force Survey in England and Wales put the numbers of workplace injuries which involved consultation with a doctor or absence from work at almost 1.5 million each year, representing about one in sixteen of the workforce (Stevens 1992).

Given the substantial nature of these costs, it is natural to ask whether this burden is simply the inevitable by-product of a set of complex and uncertain technologies. However Shavell (1987) has defined accidents as 'harmful outcomes that neither injurers nor victims wished to occur – although either might have affected the likelihood or severity of the outcomes'. In other words many, if not most, accidents are to some extent avoidable by someone taking care. It is this combination of chance and deterministic behaviour which makes the study of health and safety regulation such a fruitful area for economists. Recent advances in the economics of risk and incentives have helped address some of the normative issues concerning the form and structure of the regulations, while insights into the agency relationships between regulator and regulated have shed some light on the practice and effectiveness of regulatory enforcement.

WHO BEARS THE COST? There are two stages to determining who bears the financial cost of any given occupational accident or illness. First, who is obliged by law to meet those costs; and second, has there been a subsequent contractual agreement to transfer that obligation to someone else? The tort liability system offers one way of deciding the first of these questions: under a negligence system such as in the UK, if a court decides that an employee's accident was caused by the negligence of the employer, then he or she has to pay for the losses; if not, the losses are borne by the employee. Under a strict liability system such as in most US states, losses from work-related accidents are borne by employers, irrespective of negligence. Whatever the liability system, if the resulting *ex ante* allocation of risk is not acceptable to employees or employers, they can then contract with each other (through mutually agreed wage premiums) or with insurers (who are pooling many independent risks) in order to improve that allocation. Ultimately, therefore, the cost of any one accident can be spread widely throughout the community, and indeed, given the sophisticated use of reinsurance, throughout the world. If the employee takes out insurance to spread his risk, we refer to this as first party insurance; if the employer takes out insurance to spread his risk, we refer to this as third party or liability insurance. In a sense, these are all substitutes: the cost of a given accident which is not internalized within the firm can be spread through first party insurance or liability insurance, or a combination of both depending on who is responsible in tort. In the US, employers take out insurance against their compulsory Workers' Compensation liabilities, whereas in the UK, employers liability insurance is compulsory against the costs of negligently caused accidents only. The cost of some non-negligent losses are then borne by government through welfare payments, or by first party disability insurers. On the face of it, if the cost of an accident is shared widely in this way rather than resting wholly on the individual(s) best placed to avoid or minimize the losses, then no one has an interest in taking such action – there is a trade-off between risk shifting and incentives.

WHY REGULATE? Of course, there are conditions under which the allocation of risk and incentives described above is Pareto optimal. If employees, employers and insurers are aware of the precise risks faced in the workplace and the actions taken to influence these risks, and if there are no obstacles to bargaining, then they will achieve this first best allocation through contracting with each other: liability rules have no relevance for efficiency in these circumstances (Coase 1960). However, if some or all of the parties have incomplete information and misperceive the risk of injury, or if other obstacles to bargaining exist, then the form of *ex post* liability rules may be relevant in the search for a second best outcome (Spence 1977). Similarly, direct *ex ante* regulation of employer behaviour may also be justified on second best grounds if litigation is costly, as might the monitoring of employer behaviour by insurers or the use of incomplete incentive contracts by employers. In other words, occupational health and safety regulation is one mechanism amongst several which might be used, separately or together, in order to obtain the best feasible allocation of risk and care incentives in the workplace, taking into account the relative costs of administration (Shavell 1984). Because these mechanisms are to an extent substitutable, a debate has emerged in relation to the appropriate boundaries to be drawn between them (Diamond 1977; Rea 1981). Moreover, one further element in this debate has been been the argument that the coercive power of the state in enacting regulations governing one sector of the community is potentially open to manipulation by interest groups, such that the regulations will be framed or enforced in their favour (Peltzman 1976; Keenan and Rubin 1988). In essence, this argument, as with the public interest position, can only be resolved by reference to empirical evidence: that is, by a comparison of the level and distribution of both impact benefits and compliance costs associated with regulation. We return to this issue below after first considering some historical background to the issues.

HISTORY. This debate over the role of the state in governing employer behaviour with respect to employee safety has its roots in the parallel developments of industrial injury compensation and workplace regulation in most developed economies. In the UK, nineteenth-century legislation governing conditions of employment was introduced initially in response to concerns over the employment of children and women, but subsequently was extended to cover matters such as the fencing of machinery and the reporting of workplace accidents, as well as the whitewashing and ventilation of factories. These Factory Acts were introduced against a background of severe obstacles to the use of civil litigation by injured employees, and *inter alia* established the first paid inspectorate to enforce the regulations. A complex combination of interest groups – reformers, bureaucrats, industrialists – were responsible for determining the scope and stringency of the controls imposed on employers (Bartrip and Hartwell 1997). Moreover, the inspectorate, under pressure of limited resources and low penalties, soon evolved towards an approach to enforcement which relied on negotiation rather than formal prosecution. Towards the end of the nineteenth century, the reform process moved towards the removal of some of the common law barriers which effectively prevented employees from bringing claims against their employers, culminating in the *Employers' Liability Act* 1880, and as a consequence employers began to insure themselves against the potential cost of liability to negligently harmed employees. From that point onwards, occupational health and safety inspections in the UK have been performed to varying degrees by both regulators and liability insurers. Moreover, the financial consequences to the employer of a poor safety record could in principle consist of a combination of regulatory fines and premium loadings, although in practice neither of these were particularly significant as a cost of doing business.

As in the UK, the early concerns over workplace safety in the US were driven by the recognition of the difficulties faced by injured employees seeking compensation through the courts, which in turn were seen to dilute incentives for employers to prevent accidents. By contrast with the UK experience, however, in the US the early responses originated in the form of workers' compensation laws. These required the employer to pay damages to injured employees irrespective of who was at fault. Given that most employers sought insurance against these potential liabilities, the insurance companies were, in a competitive market, concerned to relate premiums to risk as well as encouraging employers directly to adopt loss-prevention programmes in the workplace. However, dissatisfaction with the impact of these market incentives on employers grew, and after the patchy implementation of state regulation, the Occupational Safety and Health Act 1970 finally introduced a federal regulatory agency (OSHA) with responsibilities for workplace safety. Again, while the origins of this legislation were embedded in the concerns of reformers over occupational health and safety, it was fairly soon exposed to critical review from the public choice perspective (Nichols and Zeckhauser 1977), arguing that serious consideration had not been given by the legislators to approaches other than direct regulation. Ironically, while OSHA's emphasis on formal prosecutions of cited violations led to suggestions that they were imposing unjustifiable costs on industry, the movement in the early 1980s towards flexibility and informality through on-site consultations could lead to suggestions that it is ineffective.

STANDARD SETTING. The establishment by government of an agency responsible for occupational health and safety regulation implies the delegation of certain powers. The extent of this delegation, and the degree of discretion consequently possessed by the agency, can vary across different agencies and across different areas of intervention. In some cases, the legislative basis for enabling agency powers is couched in very general terms, so that the agency has considerable discretion in setting standards with respect to matters such as conditions of work, the fencing of machinery etc. In other cases, standards may be very tightly defined in the relevant legislation, so that the agency is simply invited to secure compliance with, say, a mandated maximum level of airborne exposure to a given toxic substance. In principle, whoever sets them, these standards could be established by reference to health benefits and compliance costs at the margin for the average employee and average employer. In practice, in the absence of information on the value of health benefits accruing from additional safety measures, standards are often the outcome of a political as much as an economic process. Moreover, the same standard normally applies to all regulated workplaces, irrespective of the variations in risks and compliance costs between employers. It is this perceived constraint on the regulator's discretion which underpins the orthodox textbook arguments against direct *ex ante* regulation by contrast with *ex post* financial incentives, where the latter facilitate efficient solutions for each employer.

ENFORCEMENT. Both the British Health and Safety Executive and OSHA in the US are faced with broadly similar enforcement problems: they have a given budget and responsibility for a very large number of workplaces so that they can visit only a small proportion of employers in a given year. Moreover, fines are typically low relative to the costs of violations. Consequently the general deterrence effect of enforcement activity in relation to occupational health and safety would appear to be minimal. Implicit in this view of the world is the assumption that the regulated employer's compliance decision is determined by a comparison of the expected cost of non-compliance (the product of the probability of prosecution and the likely penalty) with the expected cost of compliance (installation of new technology, monitoring costs, etc.). This effectively treats the regulatory enforcement decision as identical to the orthodox economic approach to crime and punishment (Becker 1968; Stigler 1970). The enforcement mechanism here relies on information about fines and detection measures becoming available to potential offenders who then base decisions under uncertainty on an expected value criterion. The relationship between the regulator and any one potential offender is irrelevant to the latter's decision whether to comply.

While this assumption may be plausible for modelling some areas of the criminal justice system, there is a large body of observational evidence from social scientists which suggests that regulatory enforcement agents tend to negotiate with individual offenders, with formal prosecution only rarely used (Hawkins 1984; Scholz 1984). This suggests that a more fruitful direction for the modelling of health and safety enforcement recognizes the information asymmetry which exists between the regulator and regulated firms: because of the infrequency with which premises can be inspected by a budget-constrained regulator, it will usually be the case that the employer knows far more than the regulator in relation to breaches of the law (Ricketts and Peacock 1986). One possibility in such circumstances is that the regulator could use readily observable data on outcomes – accidents, industrial diseases, etc. – and attach penalties to these outcomes. Then the regulated firm could negotiate more lenient outcome-related penalties in exchange for revealing some of its private information on compliance. Ricketts and Peacock view the appointment by firms of 'safety officers' with a duty to provide information to the regulator as a manifestation of this implied principal-agent contract. Moreover, this approach is consistent with more general models of optimal law enforcement with self-reporting of behaviour. As Kaplow and Shavell (1994) point out, self-reporting offers two advantages over schemes without self-reporting: enforcement resources are saved by the regulator, and uncertainty over penalties is reduced for the regulated firm.

Even in the absence of self-reporting, it may be possible for the regulator to (partially) observe non-compliance with standards. Inspectors typically monitor compliance during the course of a visit to an employer's premises. Hence data on compliance which are available continuously to the employer are also available at discrete intervals to the regulator. While the frequency of these intervals is necessarily low, as pointed out previously, they do suggest the possibility of a strategic element entering into the principal-agent relationship (Ayres and Braithwaite 1992). So-called 'negotiated compliance' involves strategic behaviour on the part of both regulator and firm, as threats of prosecution are made contingent on the promise of future compliance after an offence has been detected (Scholz 1984). Clearly, the more credible a promise of compliance is, the more likely it is that negotiated compliance will be the equilibrium solution to the enforcement game. Fenn and Veljanovski (1988) suggest that credible promises can result either through the technology of compliance (for example, irreversible engineering modifications) or through the evolution of a cooperative relationship with the regulator. Using data on enforcement practices of the British Factory Inspectorate, they find significant variations in the use of informal rather than formal enforcement measures depending on the perceived compliance costs of the offender and previous history of cooperative behaviour by the firm's management. Of course, it is difficult to use this evidence to distinguish between models of regulatory behaviour which stress the regulator's concern for the public interest and those which emphasize regulatory capture. What is needed is additional evidence in relation to the impact which enforcement has on actual behaviour.

EFFECTIVENESS. Establishing the effectiveness of a given regulation can sometimes be a simple question of comparing time series data on an indicator of success, such as injury rates, before and after the regulation becomes law. However, there are two significant difficulties with this approach. First, there are many factors which change over time and which may also cause a gradual improvement in workplace health and safety. Second, introducing a specific regulation at a given time does not by itself imply a change in workplace behaviour without some means of enforcement. The first of these problems indicates the need to consider cross-sectional data on measures of regulatory effectiveness, either at industry, firm, or, preferably, plant level. The second problem suggests that these data requirements should reflect an understanding of the enforcement process, and the inputs used in that process.

Arguably the effectiveness of regulation should ultimately be measured in terms of employee welfare: that is, within a cost–benefit framework. However, willingness to pay measures of intangible health and safety benefits are notoriously difficult to obtain. Measures such as improvements in injury rates, illness rates or lost workdays are alternative measures of final output enabling a cost-effectiveness approach to be adopted. However, there may be a large amount of stochastic variation in these variables which masks the impact of regulation. Consequently, an alternative approach emphasizes the link between regulatory enforcement and *compliance* with the regulation in question – an intermediate output. While this approach improves the chances of finding an impact of regulation where one exists, it does require a leap of faith (or a practical demonstration) that regulatory compliance does confer real health benefits on the workforce.

Measuring enforcement inputs is not simply a question of counting the number of inspectors, inspections, and prosecutions. As outlined above, the *absence* of prosecution may, on some assumptions, be a means to the end of negotiated compliance. Informal measures such as threats, warnings, and notices to improve matters may play an important role in this process, as might follow-up visits to monitor compliance. Targeting of enforcement activity on firms believed to be at greatest risk of non-compliance is often observed, and this can lead to serious simultaneity issues in estimating the impact of inspection frequency: a positive correlation between visits and injury rates can result from *either* specific deterrence *or* targeting behaviour by inspectors.

Most of the modern research on regulatory impact in this area has arisen from the concern of US economists to evaluate the impact of OSHA: its establishment coincided with a period of scepticism by economists over the benefits of regulation in general. The early years of OSHA witnessed a number of studies using aggregate industry data and found no effect on either injury rates or safety investment (Smith 1976; Viscusi 1979; Bartel and Thomas 1985). Later, the increasing availability of plant-level data permitted a more disaggregated approach, in which the injury rates and lost workdays could be subsequently monitored for those establishments which were inspected in a given year (Smith 1979; Cooke and Gautschi 1981; McCaffrey 1983). Smith's results implied a 16% reduction in injuries for small hazardous plants inspected in 1973, although Viscusi (1986) points out that this result could be due to a combination of targeted inspections and regression to the mean; that is, plants inspected in 1973 are typically those with unusually high injury rates, which are more likely to fall in the following year. A series of studies followed which attempted *inter alia* to address the statistical problems caused by targeted inspections (Viscusi 1986; Ruser and Smith 1988, 1991; Scholz and Gray 1990; Gray and Jones 1991). The consensus from these studies would appear to support a small but significant effect on workplace safety as measured by firm-specific accident rates. Finally, there have been a few studies emerging which focus on the impact of enforcement measures on compliance with specific standards, rather than injury rates. Viscusi (1985) investigated the effect of cotton dust regulations on worker exposure, and inferred from the results that some 6,000 cases of byssinosis were prevented per year. Weil (1996) analysed the determinants of establishment level compliance with a set of standards governing machine-guarding in the custom woodworking industry. The levels of compliance observed, particularly for second and subsequent inspections, was far higher than predicted from the underlying expected penalties in relation to compliance costs. Weil suggests a number of explanations: employers may misperceive the penalties which are likely; there may be informational benefits from OSHA inspections; organizational factors such as unionization may play a role; and non-compliance may have consequences for litigation and/or insurance premiums.

CONCLUSION. Occupational health and safety regulation is perhaps best viewed as a complementary mechanism to employee litigation and insurer monitoring of workplace safety, and its evolution over time in both the US and UK can be seen in this context. Regulatory agencies have both standard setting and enforcement roles, and the most interesting contributions by economists have involved the analysis of agency discretion in both of these roles. In their 1989 survey article, Gruenspecht and Lave argue in favour of more research on the interaction mechanisms between firms and regulators. It is only by obtaining a full understanding of this interaction that a convincing evaluation can be made of the economic benefits from health and safety regulation.

PAUL FENN

See also BARGAINING WITH REGULATORS; DUE CARE; INSURANCE, DETERRENCE AND LIABILITY; INSURANCE FOR WORKPLACE INJURIES; OCCUPATIONAL DISEASE AND THE TORT SYSTEM: THE CASE OF ASBESTOS; PUBLIC CHOICE AND THE LAW; REGULATORY CAPTURE; REGULATORY IMPACT ANALYSIS: A CROSS-COUNTRY COMPARISON; RISK REGULATION; VALUING LIFE AND RISKS TO LIFE.

Subject classification: 6d(iii).

BIBLIOGRAPHY

Ayres, I. and Braithwaite, J. 1992. *Responsive Regulation: Transcending the Deregulation Debate*. New York: Oxford University Press.

Bartel, A. and Thomas, L. 1985. Direct and indirect effects of regulation: a new look at OSHA's impact. *Journal of Law and Economics* 28: 1–25.

Bartrip, P. and Hartwell, M. 1997. Profit and virtue: economic theory and the regulation of occupational health in nineteenth and early twentieth century Britain. In *The Human Face of Law*, ed. K. Hawkins, Oxford: Oxford University Press.

Becker, G. 1968. Crime and punishment: an economic approach. *Journal of Political Economy* 76: 169–217.

Coase, R. 1960. The problem of social cost. *Journal of Law and Economics* 3: 1–44.

Cooke, W. and Gautschi, F. 1981. OSHA, plant safety programs, and injury reduction. *Industrial Relations* 20: 245–57.

Diamond, P. 1977. Insurance theoretic aspects of workers' compensation. In *Natural Resources, Uncertainty and General Equilibrium Systems: Essays in memory of Rafael Lusky*, A. Blinder and P. Friedman, New York: Academic Press.

Fenn, P. and Veljanovski, C. 1988. A positive theory of regulatory enforcement. *Economic Journal* 98: 1055–70.

Gray, W. and Jones, C. 1991. Longitudinal patterns of compliance with OSHA regulations in the manufacturing sector. *Journal of Human Resources* 26: 623–53.

Gruenspecht, H. and Lave, L. 1989. The economics of health, safety and environmental regulation. In *Handbook of Industrial Organization, Vol. II*, ed. R. Schmalensee and R. Willig, Amsterdam: North Holland.

Hawkins, K. 1984. *Environment and Enforcement*. Oxford: Clarendon Press.

Kaplow, L. and Shavell, S. 1994. Optimal law enforcement with self-reporting of behaviour. *Journal of Political Economy* 102: 583–606.

Keenan, D. and Rubin, P. 1988. Shadow interest groups and safety regulation. *International Review of Law and Economics* 8: 21–36.

McCaffrey D. 1983. An assessment of OSHA's recent effect on injury rates. *Journal of Human Resources* 18: 131–46.

Nichols, A. and Zeckhauser, R. 1977. Government comes to the workplace: an assessment of OSHA. *Public Interest* 49: 40–41.

Peltzman, S. 1976. Toward a more general theory of regulation. *Journal of Law and Economics* 19: 211–40.

Rea, S. 1981. Workmen's compensation and occupational safety under imperfect information. *American Economic Review* 71: 80–93.

Ricketts, M. and Peacock, A. 1986. Bargaining and the regulatory system. *International Review of Law and Economics* 6: 3–16.

Ruser, J. and Smith, R. 1988. The effect of OSHA records-check inspections on reported occupational injuries in manufacturing establishments. *Journal of Risk and Uncertainty* 1: 415–35.

Ruser, J. and Smith, R. 1991. Reestimating OSHA's effects; have the data changed? *Journal of Human Resources* 26: 212–23.

Scholz, J. 1984. Cooperation, deterrence, and the ecology of regulatory enforcement. *Law and Society Review* 18: 179–224.

Scholz, J. and Gray, W. 1990. OSHA enforcement and workplace injuries: a behavioural approach to risk assessment. *Journal of Risk and Uncertainty* 3: 283–305.

Shavell, S. 1984. A model of the optimal use of liability and safety regulation. *RAND Journal of Economics* 15: 271–80.

Shavell, S. 1987. *Economic Analysis of Accident Law*. Cambridge, MA: Harvard University Press.

Smith, R. 1976. *The Occupational Safety and Health Act: its goals and achievements*. Washington, DC: American Enterprise Institute.

Smith, R. 1979. The impact of OSHA inspections on manufacturing injury rates. *Journal of Human Resources* 14: 147–70.

Spence, M. 1977. Consumer misperceptions, product failure, and producer liability. *Review of Economic Studies* 44: 561–72.

Stevens, G. 1992. Workplace injury: a view from HSE's trailer to the 1990 Labour Force Survey. *Employment Gazette*: 621–40.

Stigler, G. 1970. The optimum enforcement of laws. *Journal of Political Economy* 78: 526–36.

Viscusi, W.K. 1979. The impact of occupational health and safety regulation. *Bell Journal of Economics* 10: 117–140.

Viscusi, W.K. 1985. Cotton dust regulation: an OSHA success story? *Journal of Policy Analysis and Management* 4: 325–43.

Viscusi, W.K. 1986. The impact of occupational health and safety regulation 1973–83. *RAND Journal of Economics* 17: 567–80.

Weil, D. 1996. If OSHA is so bad, why is compliance so good? *RAND Journal of Economics* 27: 618–40.

offset rule. *See* TOTAL OFFSET RULE IN DAMAGE AWARDS.

opportunistic behaviour in contracts. Opportunistic behaviour in contracts is of interest in its own right: Does such behaviour exist? What forms does it take? Is it consequential? Mainly, however, opportunistic behaviour in contracts is interesting because a farsighted awareness of the hazards that accrue to opportunism elicits contractual and organizational responses that have the purpose and effect of mitigating those hazards. That is where the chief economic and legal importance of opportunism resides.

Opportunism is a type of self-interest seeking and may be contrasted both with stewardship (unself-interest seeking) and with simple self-interest seeking (look to your interests but keep all of your promises). Opportunism contemplates self-interest seeking with guile – to include the incomplete or distorted disclosure of information, especially calculated efforts to mislead, distort, disguise, obfuscate or otherwise confuse. Courts of law attempt to annihilate opportunism by asking witnesses to take an oath to 'tell the truth, the whole truth, and nothing but the truth', to which strong penalties for perjury are applied.

The world of contract in the absence of opportunism is uninteresting: all contracts become self-enforcing by asking the parties to promise to behave responsibly throughout (Williamson 1985: 48). Yet opportunism does not, by itself, pose a serious contracting problem. For that it is further necessary that contracts be incomplete (by reason of bounded rationality) and that the transaction possess attributes for which classical market contracting is poorly suited. Put differently, opportunism in contracts is not a free-standing concept but requires, additionally, that bounded rationality and transaction attributes be introduced.

I therefore examine opportunism in this larger context. As set out in Section 1, orthodox economics and law were poorly suited to interpret non-standard and unfamiliar business practices. The transaction-cost economics approach to economic organization is sketched in Section 2. Hazards and their mitigation are examined in Section 3. Concluding remarks follow.

1. ORTHODOXY

Many lenses have and continue to be used to interpret contractual and organizational variety. Sociologists have an abiding interest in such issues and have usefully called our attention to intertemporal process transformations and their consequences (Williamson 1996: 225–32). These are beyond the scope of this essay. I focus here principally on orthodoxy of economic and contract law kinds.

Orthodox economics. Different theories of the firm and of contract inform different issues. Orthodox economics was long preoccupied with the study of price and output (Arrow 1971: 180). To describe firms as production functions to which a profit maximization purpose was ascribed was sufficient for this purpose. Relatedly, contracts were predominantly of a simple spot contracting kind: 'sharp in by clear agreement; sharp out by clear performance' (Macneil 1974: 738). Conflicts were mainly ignored because, should they arise, these were costlessly resolved by the courts.

Albeit useful for many purposes, such a conception of firms and contracts left a large amount of commercial activity unexplained. Puzzles for which explanations were needed and public policy issues for which economists were expected to have recommendations included the following:

(1) What explains non-standard and unfamiliar forms of contracting in intermediate product markets?
(2) What explains extending the boundaries of the firm beyond those for which a technological rationale suffices?
(3) What explains the limits to firm size?
(4) What purposes are served by labour unions?
(5) What should be done to control natural monopoly?
(6) What economic purposes are served and what public policy issues are posed by product differentiation?

Note that issues of *both* firm and market are posed by this list of questions. That is important and will be developed further below. What is pertinent here is that orthodoxy interpreted all contractual practices and organizational structures that could not easily be attributed to technology (economies of scale or scope) as suspect. Monopoly was the lurking hazard.

Monopoly explanations took various forms. One explanation is that non-standard practices were devised to effect price discrimination, as with block-booking and tie-ins. Another explanation is that they had the purpose and effect of creating barriers to entry, as in vertical integration for which no physical or technical rationale could be supplied. Or possibly they were intended to realize monopsony, as with labour unions. And product differentiation took advantage of information asymmetries to the detriment of consumers (Williamson 1985: 183–6).

Working, as it did, out of a simple technological setup in which little or no provision was made for affirmative but non-technological purposes, the 'inhospitality tradition' in antitrust took hold. A presumption of antisocial purpose and effect was routinely ascribed to contractual and organizational variety. As Ronald Coase put it, 'if an economist finds something – a business practice of one sort or other – that he does not understand, he looks for a monopoly explanation. And as we are very ignorant in this field, the number of ununderstandable practices tends to be rather large, and the reliance on a monopoly explanation is frequent' (Coase 1972: 67).

Orthodox law. The orthodox legal approach to contract is that of 'legal centralism', according to which 'disputes require "access" to a forum external to the original social setting of the dispute [and that] remedies will be provided as prescribed in some body of authoritative learning and dispensed by experts who operate under the auspices of the state' (Galanter 1981: 1). The courts were the obvious candidate for that role.

In effect, both law and economics took the easy way out – in that antitrust lawyers in the law schools and in the antitrust enforcement agencies readily subscribed to the firm as a production function construction, while economists were content to work out of the fiction of costless court ordering. Indeed, some of the latter continues today. As Gordon Tullock puts it, the standard law and economics approach 'assumes that the courts will get it right' (Tullock 1996: 5).

2. TRANSACTION-COST ECONOMICS: A SKETCH

Private ordering. James Buchanan has argued that as 'economics comes closer to being a "science of contract" than a "science of choice", . . . [t]he maximizer must be replaced by the arbitrator, the outsider who tries to work out compromises among conflicting claims' (1975: 229). Transaction-cost economics subscribes to this science of contract conception but moves it back a stage to include not merely an arbitrator but an institutional design specialist. The study of governance is implicated.

Note in this connection that the science of contract works from but goes beyond the economics of property rights, which has played a crucial role in the law and economics movement. Kenneth Scott's remarks about contract in primitive and modern societies apply:

> In primitive societies, . . . there would be a role for the principles of tort law, but not much of a role for contract principles. Cooperation and exchange would be very immediate and short-term. In legal terms, such dealings as occurred would be close to spot contracts. . . .
>
> With the Industrial Revolution, production becomes, by orders of magnitude, more complex and interdependent. . . . Long range planning and coordination require the ability to rely on long term promises (Scott 1996: 57).

The move from primitive society to complex organization is thus attended by a move from property to contract. Thus although the definition and enforcement of property rights by the state (Michelman 1967) remain important, the study of contract, given property rights, is predominantly concerned with private ordering, with the courts being reserved for ultimate appeal.

Karl Llewellyn's concept of contract as framework, as against legal rules, is pertinent (1931: 736–7):

> . . . the major importance of legal contract is to provide a framework for well-nigh every type of group organization and for well-nigh every type of passing or permanent relation between individuals and groups . . . – a framework highly adjustable, a framework which almost never accurately indicates real working relations, but which affords a rough indication around which such relations vary, an occasional guide in cases of doubt, and a norm of ultimate appeal when the relations cease in fact to work.

This last is important, in that ultimate appeal delimits threat positions, but the main contractual action takes place in the context of private ordering. This is what transaction-cost economics is principally concerned with.

This rival concept of contract – which places primary reliance on private ordering, with backup reliance on the courts – better comports with the facts. Most disputes, including many that under current rules could be brought to a court, are resolved by avoidance, self-help, and the like (Galanter 1981: 2). That is because in 'many instances the participants can devise more satisfactory solutions to their disputes than can professionals constrained to apply general rules on the basis of limited knowledge of the dispute' (ibid.: 4). The assumption that 'the courts will get it right' is a convenient but overweening simplification.

Respect for private ordering invites the idea that organization is important. More generally, the need is to study the governance of contractual relations. The comparative institutional analysis of markets, hybrids, hierarchies, bureaus is implicated.

Lon Fuller's definition of eunomics as 'the science, theory or study of good order and workable arrangements' (1954: 477) is very much in the spirit of governance. So, too, is John R. Commons's insistence that 'the ultimate unit of activity . . . must contain in itself the three principles of conflict, mutuality, and order. This unit is a transaction' (1932: 4). The efficient alignment of transactions with alternative modes of governance is what comparative contracting is all about. Governance is the means by which order is accomplished in a relation in which potential conflict threatens to undo or upset opportunities to realize mutual gains.

A farsighted, as against a myopic, approach to contracting is vital to this exercise. George Schultz's reflections on the importance of his training in economics are pertinent (1995: 1):

> . . . my training in economics has had a major influence on the way I think about public policy tasks, even when they have no particular relationship to economics. Our discipline makes one think ahead, ask about indirect consequences, take note of variables that may not be directly under consideration.

Note that this is very different from the more familiar view that 'What economics has to export . . . is . . . a very particular and special form of [rationality] – [that] of the utility maximizer' (Simon 1978: 2) – which is the science of choice, rather than the science of contract, conception of economics.

Behavioural assumptions. Herbert Simon has argued that 'Nothing is more fundamental in setting our research agenda and informing our research methods than our view of the nature of the human beings whose behavior we are studying' (1985: 303). He thereafter describes human actors in terms of their cognitive ability and their self-interestedness. Bounded rationality – behaviour that is *intendedly* rational but only *limitedly* so – is the cognitive condition to which Simon refers. 'Frailties of motive' describes the condition of self-interestedness (Simon 1985: 303).

Transaction-cost economics interprets limits on rationality to mean that all complex contracts are unavoidably incomplete. But transaction-cost economics also makes provision for intended rationality, where this is taken to mean that economic actors are farsighted. Specifically, parties to a long-term contract will look ahead, perceive problems, and fold these back into the contractual agreement. The resulting contracting process is thus described as 'incomplete contracting in its entirety'.

Some of the potential problems to which contracts are subject may be relieved by making more complete provision for contingencies. There are limits to that, however, especially if parties have incentives to behave strategically. Whereas Simon minifies the latter by describing self-interestedness in relatively benign terms – frailty of motive – transaction-cost economics makes express provision for opportunism, which contemplates self-interest seeking of a strategic kind.

It is useful in this connection to distinguish between day-to-day routines and occasional disturbances of less familiar or non-standard kinds. As between frailty of motive and opportunism, which applies where?

I submit that frailty of motive adequately describes day-to-day activity most of the time. People usually will do what they say (and some will do more) without self-consciously asking whether the effort is justified by expected discounted net gains. If they slip, it is a normal friction and often a matter of bemusement.

Suppose, however, we should ask another question:

Which assumption better takes us into the deep structure of economic organization? Specifically, if our concern is not with day-to-day affairs but with long-term contractual relations, how should we proceed?

Long-term (but incomplete) contracts are reserved for transactions for which the continuity of a trading relation is the source of added value. The stakes are raised for transactions of this kind, in that maladaptation costs will accrue if the parties decline to behave cooperatively. Considerations of opportunism arise when disturbances push the parties off the contract curve.

Opportunism is a disconcerting behavioural assumption and economists have been loathe to employ it. Bad enough that they were engaged in the 'dismal science'. As it has become clear, however, that the concept of opportunism is vital to an understanding of contract and organization, acceptance of the concept has been growing.

Interestingly, economists are Johnnies-come-lately to the opportunism scene. Organization theorists were alert to the conditions much earlier. Michael Crozier, for example, referred to the 'active tendency of the human agent to take advantage, in any circumstances, of all available means to further his own privileges' (1964: 194) – which is a stronger statement than I think is needed. And guile is clearly contemplated by Irving Goffmann's reference to 'false or empty, that is, self-disbelieved, threats and promises' as the means by which to realize advantage (1969: 105). Moreover, the concepts of informal rewards, managerial discretion, information distortion and non-disclosure, and subgoal pursuit were well established among organization theorists at a time when economists were still insistent on single-minded profit maximization (supported by stewardship behaviour).

Faced with a long-term contract, an important part of the exercise now is to look ahead, perceive hazards and fold these back into the organizational design – in all significant contractual contexts whatsoever (intermediate product market, labour market, capital market etc.). If candid reference to opportunism alerts us to avoidable dangers, which the more benign reference to frailties of motive would not, then there are real hazards in the more benevolent construction.

The parallel between the concept of opportunism, as it applies to contract, and that of oligarchy, in relation to democracy, is striking. Robert Michels concluded his famous book *Political Parties* with the observation that 'nothing but a serene and frank examination of the oligarchical dangers of democracy will enable us to minimize these dangers' (1966: 370). The corresponding proposition on opportunism is this: nothing but a serene and frank examination of the hazards of opportunism will enable us to mitigate these hazards.

Credible contracting. Were it that mere promise, unsupported by credible commitments, were self-enforcing, then the economics of organization would reduce to a mere technical problem – even, as Avinash Dixit puts it, 'a design engineering problem' (1996: 2). The cartel problem would vanish, because no firms would defect. The difficulties of externalities and public goods would vanish, because individuals would self-disclose true values. Adverse selection and moral hazard would be absent from insurance and more generally. Firms would reliably maximize profits, there being no agency problem on separating ownership from control. Interfirm contracts would also operate smoothly, as disturbances would elicit cooperative responses, thereby to restore the parties to the contract curve (the resulting gains to be divided according to the prespecified sharing rule). Regulation for natural monopoly would be unneeded (Arrow 1969).

In fact, the world of contract and organization does not conform to this description. What to do?

The idea of credible contracting effected through governance is a crucial and unifying concept. If, on looking ahead, contractual hazards are in prospect, then the attempt will be made to craft cost-effective safeguards in advance. If firm and market are usefully thought of as alternative modes for organizing the very same transactions, and if the credible contracting attributes of each mode vary systematically with the transactions, then work out the logic that determines which goes where. Commons's (1934) three principles of mutuality (benefit), order (governance) and conflict (hazard) are all implicated. Contrary to the myopic advice of Machiavelli – get them before they get us – the wise prince is one who seeks both to give and receive credible commitments. A huge number of otherwise puzzling or even troubling contractual and organizational practices are explained by this farsighted approach to incomplete contract.

3. HAZARDS AND THEIR MITIGATION

Suppose that contracts are incomplete and that economic agents are given to opportunism. What are the ramifications? Which contracts pose hazards of what kind and in what degree? Which transactions go where?

Discriminating alignment. Transaction-cost economics maintains that the action resides in the details of transactions and governance. If transactions differ in their attributes in ways that give rise to differential hazards, then these features need to be explicated. If governance structures – spot markets, various forms of long-term contract, firms, bureaus – are each defined by distinct syndromes of attributes that are differentially responsive to the needs of transactions, then that needs to be worked out. Upon dimensionalizing transactions and governance structures (Williamson: 1979, 1991, 1996), the logic of discriminating alignment applies: align transactions, which differ in their attributes, with governance structures, which differ in their costs and competencies, so as to effect a transaction-cost economizing result.

Contractual hazards and their mitigation are central to the exercise. The argument is developed here in two parts. What I consider to be the 'main hazards' are described first. Added hazards are described thereafter.

The main hazards. The principal dimensions out of which transaction cost economics originally worked are the frequency with which transactions recur, the disturbances to which they are subject and the extent to which they are supported by transaction-specific assets. This last gives rise to the hazards of bilateral dependence, which turns out to be a widespread condition. The hazards that accrue to weak property rights are also pertinent.

(a) *Bilateral dependence.* Asset specificity is the big locomotive out of which transaction-cost economics works. Investments in durable assets that cannot be redeployed to alternative uses and users without loss of productive value give rise to a condition of bilateral dependency. What may have been a large-numbers supply condition at the outset is, by reason of asset specificity, transformed into a small-numbers exchange relation during contract execution and at the contract renewal interval. The resulting bilateral dependency is the source of contractual hazard. All complex contracts being incomplete, much of the burden for effecting hazard mitigation is borne by the mechanisms of *ex post* governance. A huge amount of contractual and organizational variety has these origins.

Without purporting to be exhaustive, asset-specificity distinctions of six kinds have been made: (1) site specificity, as where successive stations are located in a cheek-by-jowl relation to each other so as to economize on inventory and transportation expenses; (2) physical asset specificity, such as specialized dies that are required to produce a component; (3) human asset specificity that arises in a learning-by-doing fashion; (4) dedicated assets, which are discrete investments in general purpose plant that are made at the behest of a particular customer; to which (5) brand-name capital and (6) temporal specificity have been added.

Although the contractual/organizational ramifications of asset specificity vary among the six kinds, all are similar in the following respect: the faceless contracting, out of which orthodox economics works, gives way to contracting in which the pairwise identity of the parties matters. Added hazards thereby arise, principally in conjunction with disturbances which push the parties off the contract curve. Restoring the parties to the contract curve will thus yield gains, provided that this can be done in a cost-effective way.

Small or routine disturbances rarely pose problems. In consideration of the dependency condition and expectations of reciprocity, each party will not only do what it said it would do but will attempt to be cooperative in responding to small disturbances. Major disturbances, however, imply major departures from the contract curve. Big stakes are posed; the presumption of accommodation begins to wobble; the hazards of opportunism intrude.

Farsighted agents will, of course, recognize such hazards. One response would be to price the hazard out, by charging a risk premium. A second would be to avoid the hazard by substituting a generic technology for the specific technology, but this would sacrifice the benefits of the specialized assets. A third would be to mitigate the hazards by introducing *ex post* governance. Examples include provision for added information disclosure, auditing of data claims, bilateral negotiations to restore efficiency and divide the resulting gains, and arbitration in the event that bilateral efforts fail. Also, penalties for premature termination (liquidated damages) may be agreed to at the outset.

More generally, hostages may be created to deter unwanted breach and support exchange across a wider range of disturbances. Indeed, simple contracts (A supplies B) may be supplanted by reciprocal trading (A and B supply each other), thereby to equilibrate hazards. Not only will A and B supply different products to each other on conditional terms, but A and B may be observed to exchange identical amounts of *identical* product in reciprocal trade, albeit in different geographic areas (petroleum exchanges are a common illustration). Take-or-pay contractual provisions may also appear (Masten and Crocker 1985).

As described above, such non-standard and unfamiliar contracting practices were regarded with deep suspicion when interpreted under the lens of applied price theory. On making the transaction the basic unit of analysis and adopting a comparative contractual approach to economic organization, many of these practices are perceived to have the purpose and effect of safeguarding the transactions in question against the hazards of opportunism. Simple spot contracts thus give way to a variety of more complex agreements (of a relational or hybrid contracting kind). In the limit, as asset specificity and/or disturbances build up and the problems with interfirm contracting between autonomous agents become more severe, transactions may be taken out of the market and organized internally. As against technological and monopolizing explanations for vertical integration, therefore, transaction-cost economics advances an efficiency rationale.

But this also poses a puzzle. What prevents a firm, taking a transaction out of the market and organizing it internally, from replicating the market in all state realizations where the market works well and intervening only but always where expected net gains accrue to the exercise of authority? What is responsible for limits to firm size?

Whereas economic orthodoxy – the firm-as-production function – was perplexed by this query, transaction-cost economics addresses it directly. The puzzle of selective intervention is answered by working through the mechanisms of selective intervention. Because firms and markets differ in discrete structural ways, selective intervention turns out to be impossible. Thus, although a firm can make or buy (sometimes does both) to its own needs, these two work differently because each is defined by a distinctive syndrome of attributes (Williamson 1991).

The argument has a connection, moreover, with contract law. As Clyde Summers has argued, the idea of a single, all-purpose law of contract needs to give way to that of contract laws (plural). His distinction between black-letter law on the one hand and a more circumstantial approach to contract law on the other is pertinent: 'The epitome of abstraction is the *Restatement*, which illustrates its black letter rules by transactions suspended in mid-air, creating the illusion that contract rules can be stated without reference to surrounding circumstances and are therefore generally applicable to all contractual transactions' (Summers 1969: 566). Such a conception does not and cannot provide a 'framework for integrating rules and principles applicable to all contractual transactions' (*ibid.*). A broader conception of contract, with emphasis on the affirmative purposes of the law and effective governance relations, is needed if that is to be realized.

The successive development of contract law from classical transactions, of a simple *quid pro quo* kind (the ideal transaction in both law and economics), to neoclassical contracts that are longer term and more adjustable, to relational contracts of a still more elastic kind (Macneil 1974, 1978) is a reflection of these concerns. The proposition that each generic mode of governance is supported by a distinctive form of contract law (Williamson 1991) is an extension to such reasoning. Specifically, the implicit form of contract law that distinguishes internal organization is that of forbearance. Thus, whereas courts routinely grant standing to firms should there be disputes over prices, the damages to be ascribed to delays, failures of quality and the like, courts will refuse to hear disputes between one internal division and another over identical technical issues. Access to the courts being denied, the parties must resolve their differences internally: in effect, hierarchy is its own court of ultimate appeal.

To be sure, there is more to the market and hierarchy comparison than these contract law differences. Such differences are nevertheless important and contribute to the incentive and bureaucratic differences that distinguish market and hierarchy. More generally, identifying and explicating the syndromes of attributes that define alternative modes of governance is vital to an understanding of economic organization. Such an exercise is alien to the firm-as-production function tradition.

(b) *Weak property rights.* Consider two private-sector regimes, one in which property rights are well defined and easy to protect under the law and the other in which property rights are poorly defined and costly to protect. Parties that organize economic activities in the first regime examine the adaptive properties and associated costs of each feasible mode and choose the least-cost form (Williamson 1991). Components that can be produced more cheaply by outside suppliers thus are bought rather than made.

Matters become more complicated when private-sector property rights are poorly defined and costly to enforce. Firms in these circumstances may decide to make rather than buy because outside procurement runs the risk that valued know-how will leak out (Teece 1986). Also, manufacturers' agents sometimes incur added expenses, over and above those needed to develop the market, because these added expenses strengthen customer bonds in a cost-effective way, thereby deterring manufacturers from entering into the distribution stage and expropriating market development investments (Heide and John 1988). Similarly, franchisors sometimes impose costly bonding on franchisees in order to deter franchisees from violating quality norms (Klein and Leffler 1981).

The common thread that runs through all these examples is that insecure but legitimate property rights are supported by added governance apparatus in the degree to which these are perceived to be a cost-effective way to protect against the loss of value. What has been referred to as 'inefficiency by design' (Williamson 1996: 198–202) arises in this way. Specifically, organizational forms that are judged to be inefficient in relation to a zero transaction-cost ideal but for which no feasible superior alternative can be described and implemented with expected net gains should be regarded as presumptively efficient instead. As developed elsewhere, this 'remediableness criterion' has ramifications not only for economics but also (perhaps especially) for politics (Dixit 1996).

Other hazards. Bilateral dependency and the losses through leakage that accrue to weaknesses of property rights are the main hazards with which transaction-cost economics has been concerned. However, hazards can take many forms. Non-convergent expectations are one type (Malmgren 1961). Interdependencies that link spillovers are another (Williamson 1996: 270–71 My focus here is on quality hazards (especially in final product markets) and the hazards of common agency. As with the main hazards described above, these hazards would vanish were it not for opportunism. Also, as a consequence of these hazards, additional non-standard forms of organization take shape.

(a) *Quality.* The branch of transaction-cost economics that is concerned with 'measurement costs' has been especially concerned with problems of quality. A familiar example is the problem of judging the quality of oranges from visual inspection (Barzel 1982; North 1990: 29–30). Because information asymmetries are more pronounced in final goods markets than in intermediate goods markets, the measurement problem is more serious in the former.

Note in this connection that one of the little-remarked purposes served by organization is that it is a means by which to relieve information asymmetries. This is especially evident when two firms are dealing with each other. Thus, it will often be cost effective for each firm to hire specialists. Lawyers can craft precautions into the contract. Engineers and other technical specialists can assess the competence of would-be suppliers and can perform inspection and testing of work-in-process and delivered product. Repeat-purchase reputation-effects introduce added incentives for contractual integrity. Information sharing through trade associations can buttress these incentives.

By contrast, individual consumers can rarely support the costs of hiring specialists. Moreover, experience rating is more haphazard. There are, however, things that can be done to infuse added integrity into transactions in the final product market. Many of these are of a private ordering kind.

Note in this connection that suppliers that are alert to the hazards of opportunism that quality shading poses for consumers have incentives to work through the contractual logic set out earlier. Thus, firms could sell 'plain vanilla' rather than differentiated products, albeit at a sacrifice if differentiation has value. Also, firms that merely purport to offer 'valued features' should expect consumers to discount these claims, which would show up as a lower price. More responsively and proactively, firms could take actions that would provide added security. Branding, dating, warranties, standardization, demonstrations, trial usage and the like can all be interpreted as credible contracting instruments.

To be sure, mixed motives – for credible contracting *and* monopoly – are sometimes operative. The latter, however, requires the support of monopoly power. Also, other public-policy issues can arise. Those that take the form of health hazards with long latency periods are especially troubling. Government regulation (through the FDA, for example) is sometimes warranted on this account.

(b) *Common agency*. Bengt Holmstrom and Paul Milgrom (1991) have addressed the problem of common agency, whereby an agent has several tasks to perform, some of which are competing. The core argument has been summarized by Avinash Dixit as follows (1996: 96):

> The agent's priorities over these tasks do not coincide with those of the principal, perhaps because they require different qualities of effort, or because new tasks have less values to the agency in terms of its original mission. In any case, the principal must devise an incentive scheme to alter the effort allocation of the agent. The choice will depend on the degree of observability of different inputs and outputs, as well as on the differences in values between the two parties.
>
> Holmstrom and Milgrom find two important results. First, if the result of one task is very poorly observable, then the incentive scheme for a competing task must have lower power in order to avoid excessive diversion of effort away from this task to more observable ones. Second, if some tasks are primarily of value to the agent, and can be controlled in an all-or-nothing fashion, then it may be desirable for the principal to simply prohibit these, rather than try to give extra incentives for others. This point is especially important if the incentives for other tasks must be low-powered in conformity with the first result.

The theme of earlier sections thus repeats: farsighted agents will look ahead: if hazards are posed, then the ramifications will be worked through; incentive alignment and *ex post* governance changes will be made in response.

4. CONCLUDING REMARKS

It is beyond the scope of this essay to do anything but sketch the applications of the foregoing contractual logic. I trust, however, that it is evident that transaction-cost economics offers different and, I think, more veridical responses to the list of six questions that were posed at the outset than does orthodox law and economics. Indeed, in addition to the firm- and market-organization issues posed there, the same contractual themes repeat, with variation, to the study of capital markets (Williamson 1988), to regulation (Goldberg 1976; Williamson 1976; Priest 1993), to economic development (Weingast 1993; Levy and Spiller 1994), and to politics (Stigler 1992; Williamson 1996: ch. 8; Dixit 1996).

This is not to suggest that transaction-cost economics is an all-purpose theory that informs all of the phenomena that are 'out there'. Neither is it equally informative of all the issues to which it has been applied. Any issue, however, that arises as or can be construed as a contracting problem is usefully examined in transaction-cost-economizing terms. A huge number of issues plainly qualify.

OLIVER E. WILLIAMSON

See also ASSET SPECIFICITY AND VERTICAL INTEGRATION; BOUNDED RATIONALITY; COMMONS, JOHN R.; CONTRACTS AND RELATIONSHIPS; HOLD-UP PROBLEM; INCOMPLETE CONTRACTS; RELATIONAL CONTRACT.

Subject classification: 2e; 5c(i).

BIBLIOGRAPHY

Arrow, K.J. 1969. The organization of economic activity: issues pertinent to the choice of market versus nonmarket allocation. In *The Analysis and Evaluation of Public Expenditure: The PPB System*. Vol. 1. US Joint Economic Committee, 91st Congress, 1st Session, Washington, DC: US Government Printing Office: 59–73.

Arrow, K.J. 1971. *Essays in the Theory of Risk-Bearing*. Chicago: Markham.

Barzel, Y. 1982. Measurement cost and the organization of markets. *Journal of Law and Economics* 25: 27–48.

Buchanan, J. 1975. Microeconomic theory: conflict and contract. *American Economic Review, Papers and Proceedings* 65: 225–36.

Coase, R.H. 1972. Industrial organization: a proposal for research. In *Policy Issues and Research Opportunities in Industrial Organization*, ed. V.R. Fuchs, New York: National Bureau of Economic Research: 59–73.

Commons, J.R. 1925. Law and economics. *Yale Law Journal* 34: 371–82.

Commons, J.R. 1932. The problem of correlating law, economics, and ethics. *Wisconsin Law Review* 8: 3–26.

Crozier, M. 1964. *The Bureaucratic Phenomenon*. Chicago: University of Chicago Press.

Dixit, A. 1996. *The Making of Economic Policy: A Transaction-Cost Politics Perspective*. Cambridge, MA: MIT Press.

Fuller, L.L. 1954. American legal philosophy at mid-century. *Journal of Legal Education* 6(4): 457–85.

Galanter, M. 1981. Justice in many rooms: courts, private ordering, and indigenous law. *Journal of Legal Pluralism* 19: 1–47.

Goffmann, E. 1969. *Strategic Interaction*. Philadelphia, PA: University of Pennsylvania Press.

Goldberg, V. 1976. Regulation and administered contracts. *Bell Journal of Economics* 7: 426–48.

Heide, J. and John, G. 1988. The role of dependence balancing in safeguarding transaction-specific assets in conventional channels. *Journal of Marketing* 52: 20–35.

Holmstrom, B. and Milgrom, P. 1991. Multi-task principal–agent analyses. *Journal of Law, Economics, and Organization* 7 (Special Issue): 24–52.

Klein, B., Crawford, R.A. and Alchian, A.A. 1978. Vertical integration, appropriable rents, and the competitive contracting process. *Journal of Law and Economics* 21: 297–326.

Klein, B. and Leffler, K.B. 1981. The role of market forces in assuring contractual performance. *Journal of Political Economy* 89: 615–41.

Levy, B. and Spiller, P. 1994. The institutional foundations of regulatory commitment: a comparative analysis of telecommunications regulation. *Journal of Law, Economics, and Organization* 10(2): 201–46.

Llewellyn, K.N. 1931. What price contract? An essay in perspective. *Yale Law Journal* 40: 704–51.

Macneil, I.R. 1974. The many futures of contracts. *Southern California Law Review* 47: 691–816.

Macneil, I.R. 1978. Contracts: adjustments of long-term economic relations under classical, neoclassical, and relational contract law. *Northwestern University Law Review* 72: 854–906.

Malmgren, H. 1961. Information, expectations and the theory of the firm. *Quarterly Journal of Economics* 75: 399–421.

Masten, S. and Crocker, K. 1985. Efficient adaptation in long-term contracts: take-or-pay provisions for natural gas. *American Economic Review* 75: 1083–93.

Michelman, F. 1967. Property, utility and fairness: comments on the ethical foundations of 'just compensation' law. *Harvard Law Review* 80: 1165–1257.

Michels, R. 1966. *Political Parties*. New York: The Free Press.

Nelson, R.R. and Winter, S.G. 1982. *An Evolutionary Theory of Economic Change*. Cambridge, MA: Harvard University Press.

North, D. 1990. *Institutions, Institutional Change, and Economic Performance*. New York: Cambridge University Press.

Priest, G. 1993. The origins of utility regulation and the 'theories of regulation' debate. *Journal of Law and Economics* 36: 289–323.

Schultz, G. 1995. Economics in action: ideas, institutions, policies. *American Economic Review, Papers and Proceedings* 85: 1–8.

Scott, K. 1996. The evolving roles of contract law. *Journal of Institutional and Theoretical Economics* 152: 55–8.

Simon, H. 1957. *Administrative Behavior*. New York: Macmillan, 2nd edn.

Simon, H. 1978. Rationality as process and as product of thought. *American Economic Review, Papers and Proceedings* 68: 1–16.

Simon, H. 1985. Human nature in politics: the dialogue of psychology with political science. *American Political Science Review* 79: 293–304.

Stigler, G. 1969. In President's Task Force Report on Productivity and Competition. Reprinted in Commerce Clearing House, *Trade Regulation Reporter* 419.

Stigler, G. 1992. Law or economics? *Journal of Law and Economics* 35: 455–68.

Summers, C. 1969. Collective agreements and the law of contracts. *Yale Law Journal* 78: 537–75.

Teece, D.J. 1986. Profiting from technological innovation. *Research Policy* 15: 285–305.

Tullock, G. 1996. Legal heresy: Presidential address to the Western Economic Association Annual Meeting. *Economic Inquiry* 34(1): 1–9.

Weingast, B. 1993. Constitutions as governance structures. *Journal of Institutional and Theoretical Economics* 149: 286–311.

Williamson, O.E. 1976. Franchise bidding for natural monopolies – in general and with respect to CATV. *Bell Journal of Economics* 7: 73–104.

Williamson, O.E. 1979. Transaction-cost economics: the governance of contractual relations. *Journal of Law and Economics* 22: 233–61.

Williamson, O.E. 1985. *The Economic Institutions of Capitalism*. New York: Free Press.

Williamson, O.E. 1988. Corporate finance and corporate governance. *Journal of Finance* 43: 567–91.

Williamson, O.E. 1991. Comparative economic organization: the analysis of discrete structural alternatives. *Administrative Science Quarterly* 36: 269–96.

Williamson, O.E. 1996. *The Mechanisms of Governance*. New York: Oxford University Press.

opportunity costs and legal institutions. The word *cost* may be used to convey several meanings. When *opportunity* is put in place as an antecedent modifier, the set of possible meanings is restricted. Opportunity suggests the presence of something of value that may or may not be chosen; the word *opportunity* connects cost to human choice. And *opportunity cost* suggests that something, a course of action, is rejected in order to achieve something else. That which might have been can, of course, never be. Hence, any realization of a foregone opportunity is a logical contradiction.

How, then, is opportunity cost measured at all? The value of that alternative that might have been chosen but that can never be becomes quantifiable only in the internal or subjective calculus of the person who makes the relevant choice, and this value exists temporally only at the moment of choice itself. Opportunity cost is, therefore, necessarily reckoned in a utility dimension that cannot be observed externally. At best, tolerably acceptable proxies for opportunity cost can be introduced under carefully specified institutional settings (Buchanan 1969).

Because the value of a foregone opportunity is reckoned in a utility rather than a commodity or monetary dimension, non-physical attributes of choice alternatives can readily be entered into the evaluation. The anticipated value of the course of action not chosen may include any attribute that either enhances or retards the intrinsic worth of the 'thing in itself'. The opportunity cost of the road chosen by Robert Frost's traveller may depend on whether or not the road not chosen does or does not imply trespass on private property.

Legal institutions affect human action largely through their impact on the relative opportunity costs of alternatives faced by persons in their varying capacities or roles as choosers – whether as prospective purchasers of end-items in consumer-goods markets; as prospective sellers of resource services (including labour) in markets for inputs; as prospective investors of accumulated funds in financial markets; as prospective entrepreneurs in organizing the production of value; politically, as prospective voters-choosers, including all of the participating roles in the politics of democracy (electoral, bureaucratic, executive, legislative, judicial); and, finally, as prospective members of the continuing constitutional evaluation of the alternative sets of constraints that define the integrated legal-political-economic-social regime of interaction.

Inclusively interpreted, this essay's title is such as to allow almost anything within the umbrella rubric of comparative social structures to be discussed. If we accept the presupposition that human beings, everywhere and at any time, are described, at least in part, by general proclivities that can be operationally defined, and, further, if we eschew situationalistic explanations for everything, we are left with potential variability in political-social-legal institutions as the primary means through which betterment of the human condition may be furthered. In a persuasive paper, Mancur Olson (1996) argued that differences in observed levels of personal well-being among separate nations are to be explained by differences in the set of political-legal-social institutions that act to constrain behaviour. Dispute may well arise over whether or not 'the law', as it exists, has been, or should be, designed, explicitly or implicitly, to achieve economic purpose. But there is no disputing the obvious point that 'the law', whether actual or potential, does indeed exert significant effects on behaviour and that these ultimately influence measured levels of economic well-being.

Human beings achieve their potential for satisfaction only in a social order that both describes and proscribes the rules within which they act, one with another, whether in one-to-one, market-like exchange transactions or in more complex, many-person interaction processes. In an inclusive definitional sense, the whole set of such rules may be summarized under the rubric of 'the law', independently of any consideration of origins or means of enforcement. And, at this level of abstraction, the rules that constrain persons in their behaviour towards one another are not different, in kind, from the constraints of the natural world. It is folly to swim against the raging torrent; it is also folly to steal gold from the well-guarded treasury. In both cases, the opportunity costs of such choices are prohibitively high.

At yet another level of analysis, however, a distinction

between natural and non-natural constraints emerges from the recognition that the set of rules, 'the law', is, itself, artifactual, even if much of it may have evolved without conscious or explicit design aimed at the accomplishment of specific purpose. What is important here is the acknowledgement that, in prospect, law can be *made*, or reformed, at some margins of adjustment, even if evolutionary processes may successfully explain how many of the existing rules came into being. Some such acknowledgement becomes a necessary prerequisite to improvement in the human condition. When reform or change enters the discussion, the subject is almost always centred on changes in law, in rules, in legal institutions – changes that are directly translated into shifts in the relative opportunity costs of alternative behavioural options that persons confront.

REFORM BY RULES CHANGE: A CLASSIC EXAMPLE. The discussion may be facilitated through usage of a familiar example, the now classic Prisoners' Dilemma, used here as a two-person metaphor for a large-number social interaction. Consider the simple two-by-two payoff matrix in Figure 1, where person *A* chooses between Rows and person *B* chooses between Columns. Ordinal payoffs in each cell are as shown, with the left number for *A*, the right for *B*. Rational choice dictates that *A* choose Row 2 and that *B* choose Column 2, generating a solution or outcome in Cell IV. Each person faces a dominant choice; no matter what action the other is predicted to take, the payoff structure dictates a singular pattern of behaviour. Note that the solution or outcome in Cell IV *emerges* from the separately made choices of *A* and *B*; this solution, as such, is not explicitly chosen by either person. And, of course, it is not the most preferred position for either person, or even by the collectivity of both players. Hence, the familiar label, the dilemma, or, in a large-number setting, the 'tragedy of the commons'.

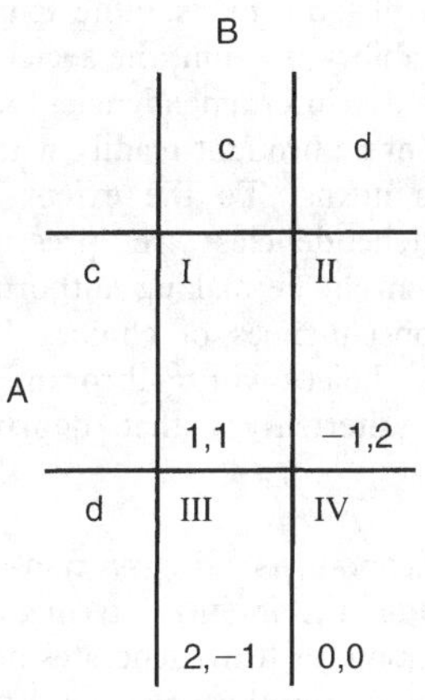

Figure 1

This interaction may be discussed specifically in opportunity-cost terminology. For person *A*, the foregone opportunity of choosing Row 2 is the expected value of the payoff that would emerge from a choice of Row 1 – a payoff that is less than that which would emerge from a choice of Row 2. And vice versa for person *B*. There is no behavioural incentive for either person to initiate independent action that will allow escape from the dilemma.

Suppose, however, that both persons fully recognize the situation that they each separately confront in this interaction. Clearly there is a potential for both persons to be made better off if some agreement can be reached on arrangements that will modify the payoffs faced. Institutional reform might be of several types. Agreement might be reached on a set of penalties for behaviour deemed to be harmful and/or rewards for behaviour deemed to be beneficial. For illustration, suppose *A* and *B* agree to impose penalties on *d*-like behaviour (Figure 1). This change will reduce the opportunity cost for *A* in taking the Row 1 action and that for *B* in taking the Column 1 action. Sufficiently high penalties on *d*-like behaviour (or sufficiently high rewards for *c*-like behaviour) will generate an emergent solution in Cell I, where both (all) persons secure higher payoffs than in the initial Cell IV equilibrium. Indeed, in its simplest sense, the situation in Cell IV, if understood, should prompt the classic call 'there ought to be a law'.

Implementation of any effective set of penalties (or rewards) aimed at generating the mutually preferred (Pareto-superior) result requires agreement, or, more specifically, collectivization or politicization of the interaction. The institutional regime that allows persons separately to make independent choices among alternatives must be modified, either through some change in incentives that will cause persons to choose differently or through more explicit political selection of the behavioural combination that will produce preferred results. Instead of a system of rewards and penalties on good and bad behaviour, agreement may be reached that will, simply, declare bad behaviour 'against the law'. In the simple matrix of Figure 1, person *A* can no longer choose a Row 2 action; person *B* cannot choose a Column 2 action, but must choose the *c* alternative, generating the preferred Cell I solution. The off-diagonal attractors in Cells II and III no longer exist.

PRIVATIZATION. Another institutional means of escaping from the dilemma – and a means that may prove more efficacious in many settings than in others – involves a change in rules that operates to remove or to reduce the payoff (utility) interdependence among persons that creates the difficulty in the first place. This approach requires that we ask the question: Why are the payoffs of one person dependent on behaviour of the other? Does the observed interdependence stem from some necessary feature of an interaction or is it amenable to elimination or reduction by a change in law?

Here the familiar 'tragedy of the commons' illustration is expositionally helpful. Consider the setting in which each of several (or many) ranchers grazes steers on an open range – the commons that is freely available to all users. Overgrazing results and the valuable pasture is used up in the sense that no recognition of its value enters into the calculus of the separate users. A collective-political solution might involve some set of penalties (prices) on usage of the pasture, as in our earlier example. Instead of this scheme, however, more effective rules-change here might take the form of 'privatization'. Individuals – either one, several or many – might be assigned ownership rights in the valued resource that carry with them the legally enforceable authority to exclude others from usage.

Reform that establishes or reassigns property rights in valued resources may be preferred to direct political manipulation for several reasons. Efficient usage of a valued resource emerges from the rational choices of separate owners rather than from a politically determined set of prices (penalties) on usage. In any situation, choice-makers face opportunity costs that reflect anticipated value of alternatives that are not chosen. But these rejected alternatives may vary in their incidence as between the chooser and others who are in the relevant interdependence relationship.

The rancher who adds a steer to the commons foregoes only a small share of the anticipated value of the grass that the steer will eat. By comparison, under private ownership of the grazing range, the rancher who adds a steer foregoes the full amount of the anticipated value of the grass to be eaten – value that would be available if the steer is not added. Some numbers will make the illustration concrete. Suppose, in the first setting, there are 1000 steers on the commons, only 10 of which belong to the single rancher who, correctly, anticipates that an additional steer will eat $1000-worth of grass, thereby reducing the value of all other grazing animals. To the individual rancher, however, only 1/100 of this value, or $10, will be reflected in the loss in value to his own steers. Again by comparison, think of the rancher who owns a separately bounded parcel of the range land. The anticipated value of grass that might be eaten by a steer is again $1000, but this anticipated shortfall in value will all show up as reduction in value of the rancher's own herd.

The example demonstrates precisely how law and legal institutions affect allocative results indirectly through their influence on incentives that confront individual choosers. In a strict resource-using sense, adding the steer has identical effects in the two settings. A value of $1000 is somehow sacrificed or given up. But, when translated into the opportunity cost of choices faced by those persons who confront the alternatives, the two settings seem quite different. Predictably, differing allocative results will emerge.

In effect, what privatization of a valued resource accomplishes is a matching between decision or choice authority with those consequences of choice that should be reckoned in any efficiency calculus. Note, however, that efficiency emerges from, and indeed is defined by, the separate decisions of owner-users who confront opportunity costs that reflect the full value of sacrificed alternatives. In this indirect sense, the law of property does, indeed, serve the purpose of promoting economic efficiency – a principle that has been recognized at least since Aristotle.

The commons example is also helpful in introducing the critical distinction that must be made between the establishment of ownership (exclusion) rights as a means of internalizing the consequences of choices in resource usage and the particularized assignment of such rights as among persons in the relevant political community. The efficiency-enhancing purpose of the law of property is achieved under *any* assignment, subject only to the proviso that competitive conditions generally prevail. That is to say, no matter which set of persons in the community succeeds in securing rights of ownership in the valued resource, their own decision calculus, separately exercised, will ensure that efficient usage occurs. It matters not at all whether the previously open commons be assigned to ranchers *a, b, c* through *m* or to ranchers *n, o, p* through *z*. The law of property will have met its purpose upon the assignment itself; the distribution is irrelevant.

Economists will be familiar with this neutrality result; versions of it are widely discussed under the rubric of 'the Coase Theorem'. The important principle to be stressed is that while the particular assignment of ownership rights among persons is of little or no economic consequence, the assignment of ownership rights, as such, is the *sine qua non* for efficiency in allocation. It matters not *who* owns the valued pasture; it matters much that it be owned by *someone*, anyone.

The implementation of reform that establishes and assigns separate ownership-exclusion rights can be interpreted as a response to the plaint that 'there ought to be a law', noted earlier. In this perspective, the law of property finds its *raison d'être* in the efforts of persons to improve their economic well-being. But what are the limits? If someone, anyone, owns everything that is valued, and if the law of property and contract operates with reasonable efficacy, is there more that 'the law' need do?

Unfortunately, perhaps, not all that is valued can be separately and privately owned. Persons live, one with another, in many non-privatized dimensions; each person (family) does not exist in a protected bubble all her own from which she departs only to engage in reciprocal exchange (market) transactions. There are 'natural' commons, so to speak, that cannot be privatized, at least in the ordinary sense. Further, there may be economies of scale in the usage of some goods, quite apart from the technology of excludability. In sum, the social order cannot be wholly privatized; interdependencies among persons remain that cannot be brought readily within the inclusive market-exchange nexus. To the extent that such non-exchange interdependencies are present, there is a mismatch between choice-making authority and the incidence of the consequences of choice. The opportunity costs that inform choices will tend to undervalue the estimated foregone alternatives that deprive all but the choosers.

EXTERNALITY. Economists discuss non-exchange interdependencies under the inclusive term *externality*. If the activity of one person (or firm) generates non-compensated benefits or harms on another, the opportunity costs that inform choices may not fully incorporate the spillover or external components since these do not impact directly on the utility (wealth) of the chooser. The interdependence is not internalized as it would be in an ordinary market exchange transaction. The slight increase in the city's smog is a consequence of a freeway trip, but individuals other than the prospective driver bear the major incidence. The impact of the driver's choice on others may not be appropriately weighted in the decision calculus.

The early neoclassical welfare economics, derived from the analysis of Pigou (1932), suggested that, once an externality is identified, the generating action should be subjected to political correction, either through some collectively imposed structure of penalties (or rewards) or through direct political management. The object of the politicization, in either case, is that of bringing 'private' cost into line with 'social' cost. Institutional reform embodies directed changes in the opportunity costs faced by relevant choosers.

Two flaws in this seemingly straightforward Pigovian logic were exposed in the last half of this century. First, the normative structure was based on the romanticized notion that those who hold authority to make political-bureaucratic choices are themselves basically benevolent as well as omniscient. Public choice theory, sometimes called 'politics without romance' (Buchanan 1979), carries the implication that persons who make choices, no matter under what authority, confront the opportunity costs peculiar to the choice setting; there is no basis for any presumption that a political decision maker will either be able or be motivated to choose among options in such fashion as to reflect 'social' costs, if, indeed, the whole notion has any meaning in this context. Explicitly politicized corrections for externalities may or may not result in improvements over the uncorrected market interaction, externalities and all. Pragmatic, case-by-case comparison is indicated.

A second major flaw in the Pigovian construction lies in its failure to relate the postulated economic interdependence with the legal structure – a failure that was exposed in Coase's now classic paper (1960), which stimulated a major part of the whole law-and-economics research programme. When a person or firm inflicts damage or harm to another (or others) the obvious question is whether or not that action that is observed is within or without the law, whether the person who carries out the action does so within her legal rights or goes beyond these rights to invade the rights of another (or others). If the action is not within the law, that is, if the actor invades the rights of another (or others), the primary means of corrective adjustment is effective enforcement of either criminal or tort law, or both – enforcement that will effectively prohibit the damage-causing action from taking place.

If the action that is taken is within the law, that is, if the actor imposes damages on some third party or parties while staying within her defined legal rights, the economist should ask: Why does the market fail to work here? The removal of a non-compensated harm is equivalent to the addition of an ordinary good. And, in any exchange equilibrium, goods are traded until all mutual gains are eliminated. Hence, at a genuine trading equilibrium, the observed presence of a non-compensated harm must suggest either that the externality is infra-marginal or that it is Pareto irrelevant; that is, the harm to the person or persons externally affected is not valued as highly as the benefit to the acting person or firm (Buchanan and Stubblebine 1962). In either case, the observation of non-compensated harm does not imply distortion in the allocation of resources and a need for correction. Relevant opportunity costs are internalized to those charged with choice authority.

A neutrality theorem was introduced in the third section, with reference to the assignment of ownership rights. The logical equivalent of this theorem emerges in the externality setting, but its validity is less apparent due to institutional differences in the two cases. Consider a particular course of action that a person (or firm) might take that will impose damages on another. Does it matter whether the actor is assigned a legal right to undertake the action? Or whether the person potentially damaged is assigned a legal right to prevent the action? Economists will recognize this setting as that in which the Coase Theorem embodying the neutrality result initially emerged.

On first consideration, the opportunity costs of taking the action in question would seem to be quite different in the two legal settings. The actor, if assigned the right to take the action, would more heavily weight the impact of the no-action alternative on her own anticipated well-being, thereby possibly neglecting the impact on the utilities of others. By contrast, the acted-on would reverse the weighting. But what this initial consideration neglects is the market or exchange process as a means through which the relative values of goods and bads among separate potential traders are adjusted towards equality. The actor who fails to take into account adequately the value of the avoidance of potential spillover damage to the acted-on may be underestimating the opportunity costs of taking the action in question. That which the acted-on would pay to avoid the damage is a part of the opportunity cost for the actor, even in the setting where there is a clearly assigned legal right to take the action in question.

Conversely, in the setting where the potentially acted-on holds the legal right to prevent the action, the opportunity cost of exercising such a right must include the payment that the actor would be willing to make for permission. When these across-exchange payments are taken into account, the neutrality theorem again applies. No matter what the assignment of rights, efficiency tends to emerge. It is the assignment of rights, as such, that matters, not the specific distribution.

As noted, however, the neutrality result is less apparent in the externality setting because the institutional structure differs from that discussed earlier. Here there is a more explicit recognition that rational behaviour on the part of participants in the nexus requires exploitation of mutually profitable exchange opportunities when these are available. Further, there is the evident presumption that the legal structure that facilitates exchange remains invariant under differing rights assignments.

Most importantly, neutrality in the externality setting requires small numbers on both sides of the interaction, precisely because the result emerges from exchanges, which can only be effectively consummated at relatively low transactions costs. Properly interpreted, Coase's neutrality theorem requires that transactions costs be low or non-existent. If either or both sides of the externality account involve large numbers of persons, transactions costs may be such as to make exchange difficult and indirectly to rehabilitate elements of the Pigovian construction. Consider a setting where one person, the actor, may impose external or spillover damage simultaneously on a large number of other people. If the actor holds a legal right to take the action at issue, she may underestimate the value of the foregone alternative to others, and she may not be in error when she fails to incorporate a value for a payment that might be secured from refraining from taking the action (or for taking action in the external economics setting). The large group of affected parties may find it difficult to organize any joint payment.

On the other hand, should the large group, collectively, hold a legal right to prevent the action, the potential actor, who might be willing to make some payment for permission, might find the required payment prohibitively high, since the members of the affected group might not readily agree on the distribution, among themselves, of shares in smaller payments.

In situations where potential trades must, in either case, be worked out by many persons, acting as a group, on one or both sides of the interaction, it seems evident that the actual allocation of resources may be quite different in separate assignments of legal authority. (For extended discussion of the effects of numbers in externality relationships, see Buchanan 1973).

The neutrality result does not apply because there remains an externality or publicness relationship among members of any large group on either one or both sides of the potential 'externality exchange'. There remains a commons problem among parties, and incentives are such as to prevent low-cost organization of efficiency-generating transactions with acting persons or firms. We are left with the prospect of comparing possibly inefficient market outcomes, left uncorrected, and possibly inefficient politicized outcomes, under collectivized corrective institutions. In such cases, reassignment of rights may not suffice to ensure that opportunity costs are effectively internalized.

UNCERTAINTY AND AMBIGUITY IN THE LAW. To this point, the discussion has been based on an implicit presumption that the legal rights to undertake particular actions are assigned with certainty and are, therefore, readily enforceable. Under this presumption, in the relevant small-number settings, the neutrality theorem applies, and the economic interdependencies between parties is effectively internalized regardless of how rights are assigned. Persons face opportunity costs that reflect the full consequences of the choices to be made.

Consider what the introduction of uncertainty and/or ambiguity in the assignment of rights does in this setting. Suppose that a person who might potentially take an action that would exert harm on another does not know whether or not she will be held liable for damages. Nor does the person who might be damaged know whether or not claims for liability can be enforced, after the action is taken. In this situation, it may seem more profitable for the potentially damaged person to plan to seek legal recourse through claims for damage than to seek to prevent the damage being imposed through some exchange-like agreement with the acting party. This pattern of action seems likely to take place when the potentially damaged party overestimates the prospects of recovering damages relative to the estimates made by the actor.

It seems clear that the extended market or exchange-like internalization that might validate the neutrality theorem loses credibility in settings of legal uncertainty. The opportunity costs that inform choices in a regime of legal uncertainty need not reflect the value of the alternatives among which choices must be made. Allocative distortions may emerge even in an imaginary regime in which the uncertainties in the law are resolved costlessly by some random device. The distortions loom much larger in any regime of legal uncertainty where disputed claims are settled through litigation that requires resource usage, as represented by the activities of lawyers, judges and courts. These outlays are deadweight losses, over and beyond the allocative or excess burden losses.

Who suffers the ultimate costs measured by the resource wastage of lawyers? And how can changes in constraints be implemented that will prove mutually beneficial? The standard externality solutions do not seem to apply.

In one interpretation, lawyers become spoilers in that they act to destroy economic value. Consider an extension of the commons example used earlier. Onto the stylized post-commons, privatized, pastorally efficient setting, let us now introduce a predator who removes the borderline fences and blurs the boundaries beyond recognition. The valued resource is neither owned–used in common, nor is it owned–used privately–separately. The range wars and territorial disputes that describe the fictionalized American West find their modern equivalents in the burgeoning litigation that saps the economy's productive potential. The tragedy of the distributional conflict reflected by the modern litigation explosion is not amenable to reform in a way comparable to the straightforward privatization of the commons. Reform must go beyond assignment of ownership rights; reform must extend to insurance of predictability of claims. Resource owners must be protected against claims for liability invented by the legal entrepreneurs, whose value product can only be negative.

CONCLUSIONS. As noted earlier, this essay might have allowed discussion of many subjects in the intersections of law, politics and political economy. Somewhat arbitrarily, perhaps, attention has been centred on the role of legal institutions, and notably those of property and contract, in creating the conditions within which choices are made by individuals, and, in particular, on the behavioural differences that might be predicted to emerge in differing legal settings.

Legal institutions determine the incidence of the consequences of choice, and an objective for legal–political–constitutional reform must be that of achieving a closer correspondence between consequences of choice and the authority to make choices. To the extent that consequences can be effectively internalized to the chooser, there need arise none of the familiar problems summarized as dilemmas, tragedies or externalities.

Internalization means that both the anticipated benefits and the opportunity costs of a prospective course of action, as faced by whomever is in a position of authority to choose, impact largely if not exclusively on the utility of the chooser, rather than on others. Individuals can be left 'free to choose' because they suffer the full consequences. Legal institutions offer the structural means through which adjustments may be made so as to secure the relevant matching as far as is practically possible.

JAMES M. BUCHANAN

See also COASE, RONALD; COASE THEOREM; COMMON PROPERTY; PRISONERS' DILEMMA; PROPERTY RIGHTS.

Subject classification: 1d(ii); 2b(i); 4c(i).

BIBLIOGRAPHY

Buchanan, J.M. 1969. *Cost and Choice: An Inquiry in Economic Theory*. Chicago: University of Chicago Press.

Buchanan, J.M. 1973. The institutional structure of externality. *Public Choice* 14: 69–82.

Buchanan, J.M. 1979. Politics without romance: a sketch of positive public choice theory and its normative implications. *IHS Journal, Zeitschrift des Instituts für Höhere Studien* 3: B1–11.

Buchanan, J.M. and W.C. Stubblebine. 1962. Externality. *Economica* N.S. 29: 371–84.

Coase, R.H. 1960. The problem of social cost. *Journal of Law and Economics* 3: 1–44.

Olson, M. 1996. Big bills left on the sidewalk: why some nations are rich, and others poor. *Journal of Economic Perspectives* 10(2): 3–24.

Pigou, A.C. 1920. *The Economics of Welfare*. London: Macmillan; 4th edn, 1932.

options contracts. *See* CONTRACT RENEGOTIATION AND OPTION CONTRACTS; DERIVATIVE SECURITIES REGULATION.

options pricing and contract remedies. The theory of options valuation has found many uses outside the realm of finance. One of these is to illuminate the common law's preference for money damages over specific performance as the usual remedy for breach of contract, as shown by Mahoney (1995).

Justice Holmes (1897: 462) famously noted that a contractual undertaking is a promise either to perform or to pay damages. Under the common law, specific performance is an 'extraordinary' remedy, granted only when money damages would be inadequate to compensate the promisee for the lost value of the performance. We can therefore think of the promise as constituting the sale of the performance coupled with the purchase of an option to buy back the performance for a price equal to the damages awarded for breach. The option is valuable, and its value should be reflected as a decrease in the price that the promisee pays for the performance compared to an otherwise identical contract in which the remedy would be specific performance. Consideration of the option value embedded in a contract for which the remedy will be money damages shows why specific performance is not the preferred remedy.

For the sake of simplicity, consider a bilateral executory contract in which Seller agrees to sell a marketable good to Buyer for a fixed price on a defined date in the future. At the time of contracting, Seller's cost of performance (that is, the cost of making or acquiring the good and of foregoing a spot sale at the time of performance) is unknown, but we will assume that the parties agree as to its probability distribution. The same is true of the value of that performance to Buyer, but for expositional clarity we can consider that value as fixed and focus only on the variability in Seller's cost. When the time for performance arrives, depending on the realized cost of performance, performance may be inefficient – i.e., it may cost more than the value of the good to Buyer.

A specific-performance remedy and a money-damages remedy are two different ways of allocating the value that can be created by rescinding the contract if the cost of performance exceeds its value to Buyer. If Seller may breach and pay money damages, the amount of those damages under the standard expectationary measure will be the value of the good to Buyer less the unpaid portion of the contract price. Seller will therefore capture the full gain from termination, which is the cost of performance to Seller less the (smaller) value of that performance to Buyer. On the other hand, if Buyer is entitled to specific performance, Buyer has the right to demand performance regardless of its cost to Seller. When termination is efficient, by definition Seller would be willing to pay more to be released from that obligation than Buyer would be willing to pay for the good. Excluding transaction costs, therefore, Seller will offer, and Buyer will accept, a sum greater than expectationary damages but less than Seller's full cost of performance to be released from the contract. Thus Buyer will obtain some or all of the value of termination.

Consider a simple example. In period 1, Buyer agrees to pay \$100 for a good that Seller will manufacture and deliver in period 2. There are two possible states in period 2, and each is equally likely. In the first state, Seller's cost of performance is \$60 and in the second it is \$120. The value of the good to Buyer is \$110 in both states. In the high-cost state, performance is inefficient in the sense defined above, and a money-damages remedy permits Seller to escape performance by paying Buyer \$10 (the difference between the value of the performance to Buyer and the contract price). A specific-performance remedy entitles Buyer to insist on performance in either state. In the high-cost state, Buyer's insistence on performance will provide it with a \$10 net benefit at a net cost to Seller of \$20. Both parties will be better off if Seller pays Buyer some amount greater than \$10 but less than \$20 to terminate the contract. This suggests that Seller will again escape performance, but at a higher price than was true under a money-damages regime.

So long as the rule is clear, the parties are identically informed and risk-neutral, and transaction costs low, the parties should be indifferent between the two remedies. In either case, as the Coase theorem (see Coase 1960) suggests, Seller will perform when it is efficient to do so and won't when it is not. As in the above example, the rule will affect the distribution of the gain from termination when termination is efficient, but this also will not matter, because the parties can agree to a contract price that reflects the additional value of the contract to Buyer when the remedy is specific performance.

This is where the theory of option valuation steps in. Option pricing techniques can be used to calculate the difference in value between a contractual obligation coupled with a money-damages remedy and the identical obligation coupled with a specific-performance remedy. The difference is the value of a call option on the performance, with the damages award as the strike price. More importantly, the option approach helps to show why the choice of remedy *does* matter in many situations.

In effect, the money-damages 'option' enables Seller to hedge his exposure from the contract. Seller is, in financial parlance, 'short' the performance – that is to say, Seller is obligated to deliver the performance at a future date. By holding an option to purchase the performance, Seller caps the potential loss from his short position. A risk-averse Seller would be better off holding the short position coupled with a fairly priced option than holding the short position alone. In financial markets, we see traders take short positions without hedging, because those traders are engaged in speculation; they are attempting to profit from what they perceive to be their insight into the future returns on a financial asset. In markets for products and services, we would imagine that most people in Seller's position hope to profit from their ability to provide the product or service efficiently, rather than their ability to forecast the returns on that product or service. We therefore frequently observe hedging in such markets, and indeed we would expect most people in Seller's position to desire the hedge that money damages provides.

The analysis is similar from Buyer's perspective. Buyer's likely objective is to acquire the good or service for use in Buyer's business or for consumption. If Buyer holds a 'long' position in the performance without writing (that is, selling) an option to Seller, Buyer is speculating on Seller's cost of performance, and in doing so is giving up cash-in-hand in the amount of the option value. Buyer would presumably rarely wish to do this, so long as money damages are an adequate substitute for performance (see Craswell 1988; Schwartz 1990).

The option analysis supplements the conventional way of thinking about the choice between money damages and specific performance, which focuses on the transaction costs associated with each (see Kronman 1978; Schwartz 1979). Money-damages awards are thought to be systematically undercompensatory. Indeed, standard doctine regarding the calculation of money damages fails to provide compensation for some of the costs incurred by a promisee in the event of breach. Courts award damages only to the extent that they are reasonably certain, and no compensation is given for some of the incidental costs that accompany a contract breach (such as legal fees). Money damages are therefore an imperfect substitute for performance. Specific performance may solve that problem, but it introduces another imperfection. When performance would be inefficient, specific performance requires negotiation of an appropriate payment from Seller to Buyer in lieu of performance. Bargaining is costly, and there is always the possibility that Seller and Buyer will fail to reach agreement even though it is clearly the efficient thing to do. As described in detail by Bishop (1985), the relative magnitudes of these imperfections vary with the context, and so too will the preferred remedy.

The transaction-costs argument, while correct, provides only limited help in making sense of what courts do. In all but the most extreme cases, the relative magnitudes of the transaction costs associated with money damages and specific performance are not obvious. In most circumstances, it is difficult to argue persuasively that the imperfections noted above are very significant, and harder still to argue that one or the other clearly dominates.

The options approach, by contrast, explains in a reasonably straightforward way both the strong general preference for money damages and the most important exceptions. The most prominent exception to the money-damages rule involves contracts to sell a 'unique' good. In such cases, courts award specific performance on the grounds that money damages would be insufficient, and commentators have generally explained the result by noting that money damages would not adequately protect the subjective value that Buyer sees in the good. Note that the reference to 'subjective value' suggests that Buyer's purpose in entering into the contract is more analogous to that of the unhedged speculator in financial markets than to the hedged producer or user of a commodity in markets for goods. This becomes even more plausible when we look at the sorts of goods at stake in the classic specific-performance cases. Specific performance is routinely granted in cases involving 'unique' goods. The paradigmatic unique good, and the one most often at issue, is real estate (see *Kann v. Wausau Abrasives Co.*). Other cases have involved works of art (see *Falcke v. Gray*), race horses (see *Elliott v. Jones*) and shares of stock with a limited public market (see *Mutual Oil Co. v. Hills*). Each of these cases shares important characteristics with financial markets. It is likely that the motivation for the contract is Seller's and Buyer's differing beliefs about the future value of the good. The good in question is pre-existing; that is, Seller is not manufacturing the good for Buyer. Thus opportunity costs are the most relevant component of Seller's cost of performance, and Seller's estimate of those costs may rise prior to performance if Seller concludes that it has underestimated the future returns on the asset. Should Seller then breach, Buyer may be unable to take advantage of his insights into the future value of the good unless those returns have already materialized at the time of suit. In short, Buyer and Seller are in a position very closely analogous to the speculative buyer and seller of a financial asset (except that the efficiency of financial markets makes it much more likely that information about future returns will be promptly reflected in market prices), and a specific performance remedy is merely a means of permitting them to hold unhedged positions.

The drafters of the Uniform Commercial Code identified another class of cases as warranting specific performance. These are cases involving long-term supply contracts. Interestingly, courts have not routinely awarded specific performance for breach of such contracts. There is an important subset of cases, however, in which courts have often concluded that money damages are insufficient and awarded specific performance. The typical case is one in which a regulated entity, such as a public utility, enters into a long-term contract for the purchase of one of its inputs; for example, an electric company buying oil or coal. The cost of the input rises substantially, and the seller insists on contract renegotiation or simply breaches.

The options perspective outlined above explains the courts' tendency to grant specific performance in such cases by focusing on the parties' respective desires to bear risk. For a public utility subject to rate regulation, predictability in the prices of its major inputs is critical. The utility is typically permitted to charge rates that represent some fixed margin over its costs, and thus it must pass on variability in input costs to its customers. Its customers, particularly if households, will wish to avoid the risk of wildly fluctuating utility costs, and accordingly the public utility will enter into long-term, fixed-price supply contracts and seek a high degree of certainty that it will retain the benefit of the fixed price. Contrast this with the position of the seller, which is often a publicly held natural resource company. The seller can spread the risk of price fluctuations over a large portfolio of contracts for the sale and/or purchase of the resource; moreover, its shareholders would consider commodity price variability to be a diversifiable risk. Thus, there is likely to be a substantial asymmetry between the attitudes of the buyer and seller to the risk of price fluctuations, and a specific-performance remedy better accommodates both parties than a money-damages remedy.

There will, of course, be cases in which the parties have idiosyncratic reasons for preferring an overcompensatory remedy. For example, both parties may recognize that Seller is much better informed about the distribution of the cost of performance than Buyer. Seller could agree to an overcompensatory remedy as a means of signalling credibly to Buyer that Seller believes that the cost of performance has a low variance. Expressed in option terms, Seller may be unwilling to pay the cost of the money-damages option because Seller believes that the variance of the underlying asset is low, and accordingly the value of the option is low. When this occurs, and the situation is not one in which specific performance is otherwise likely, we would expect to see the parties agree to liquidated damages, which can mimic the risk-shifting effects of specific performance (see Polinsky 1983). The same is true if the parties have some reason to believe that a court is particularly likely to award insufficient damages in their situation. The options perspective therefore supplements the arguments that have been made in favour of the presumptive enforceability of liquidated damages clauses.

This analysis of the choice between money damages and specific performance from an options perspective demonstrates how even very elementary insights from options theory can be usefully deployed in analysing legal rules. There is a recent and rapidly growing body of literature that supplements the traditional analysis of investment decisions by firms, in which investments are made if, and only if, they have positive net present value, with a perspective drawn from options theory. That literature has already had an impact on legal theory.

The option perspective on investment decisions shows that there are some investments that should not be made today even if they have a positive net present value. Imagine, for example, that a project will cost $1000, and once spent, the $1000 cannot be recovered. Imagine further that one period from now, the project will pay off (in present value terms) either $500 or $1600, each with probability 1/2. Because the expected present value is $1050, which exceeds the cost, standard theory would conclude that the investment should be made. It may be, however, that a decision to undertake the project can be delayed for one period, at which time it will be known whether the project will be worth $500 or $1600. At that later date, the project could be undertaken if profitable and abandoned if unprofitable.

In this latter case, the firm can be thought *ex ante* to have an option to undertake the project. The value of the option resides in the possibility of making an investment decision only after it is known whether the project will be profitable. Once the decision to invest is made, the option is exercised and its value lost. Consequently, in many instances it would not make sense to undertake the investment in period 1, despite its positive net present value. The investment is worth making in period 1 only if the expected profits foregone by delaying the investment for one period exceed the value of the option.

A similar analysis shows that, in some circumstances, it would make sense to invest in a project that has a negative net present value if that project brings with it a valuable option. Consider an opportunity to purchase a patent for $1000. It will cost an additional $5000 to develop the patented product, and one period hence the product will provide a profit stream worth either $8000 or $3000 in present value, each with probability 1/2. It would not make sense to spend a total of $6000 for an expected payoff of $5500.

However, once again it may be possible to delay development of the product until it is known whether the payoff will be $8000 or $3000. In that event, the patent should be considered an option to develop the product. The firm should purchase the patent if the value of the option to develop exceeds $1000.

As noted by Dixit and Pindyck (1994), from whom the above discussion is drawn, wherever it is possible to delay a decision to invest, and the investment once made cannot be recovered, the investment decision can be described in option terms. Many legal issues can be so described, and legal scholars are increasingly turning to options theory. Recent uses include modelling an anticipatory breach decision as the extinguishment of an option to perform (see Triantis and Triantis 1998), and modelling the decision to bring suit as the purchase of a sequence of options to proceed through preliminary motions, to discovery, and ultimately to trial (see Grundfest and Huang 1996). The use of options methodology to address legal questions will undoubtedly increase.

PAUL G. MAHONEY

See also CONTRACT RENEGOTIATION AND OPTION CONTRACTS; CONTRACTS; SPECIFIC PERFORMANCE.

Subject classification: 5c(ii).

CASES
Elliott v. Jones, 101 A 874 (Del. 1917).
Falcke v. Gray (1859) 4 Drew. 651.
Kann v. Wausau Abrasives Co., 129 A 374 (NH 1925).
Mutual Oil Co. v. Hills, 248 F 257 (9th Cir. 1918).

BIBLIOGRAPHY
Bishop, W. 1985. The choice of remedy for breach of contract. *Journal of Legal Studies* 14: 299–320.
Coase, R.H. 1960. The problem of social cost. *Journal of Law and Economics* 3: 1–44.
Craswell, R. 1988. Contract remedies, renegotiation, and the theory of efficient breach. *University of Southern California Law Review* 61: 629–70.
Dixit, A.K. and Pindyck, R.S. 1994. *Investment Under Uncertainty*. Princeton, NJ: Princeton University Press.
Grundfest, J.A. and Huang, P.H. 1996. Real options and the economic analysis of litigation: a preliminary inquiry. John M. Olin Working Paper 131, Stanford Law School, Stanford, CA.
Holmes, O.W. 1897. The path of the law. *Harvard Law Review* 10: 457–78.
Kronman, A.T. 1978. Specific performance. *University of Chicago Law Review* 45: 351–82.
Mahoney, P.G. 1995. Contract remedies and options pricing. *Journal of Legal Studies* 24: 139–63.
Polinsky, A.M. 1983. Risk sharing through breach of contract remedies. *Journal of Legal Studies* 12: 427–44.
Schwartz, A. 1979. The case for specific performance. *Yale Law Journal* 89: 271–306.
Schwartz, A. 1990. The myth that promisees prefer supracompensatory remedies: an analysis of contracting for damage measures. *Yale Law Journal* 100: 369–407.
Triantis, A.J. and Triantis, G.G. 1998. Timing problems in contract breach decisions. *Journal of Law and Economics* 51 (forthcoming).

organized crime. With origins dating back to classical economists such as Jeremy Bentham, rational choice theories of crime were formalized in seminal papers by Gary Becker (1968) and by Becker and George Stigler (1974). This literature models participation in criminal activity as the outcome of a rational deliberation by a perpetrator who weighs the monetary and psychic benefits from crime against his costs of participation, including prospective penalties and foregone legitimate employment or consumption alternatives. By treating perpetrators' decisions as the deliberate response to changes in this set of benefits and costs, models of rational criminal behaviour seek to understand what circumstances prompt crime. Relatively little attention has been paid, however, to understanding what factors explain the organizational structure of criminal markets.

Crime, like any economic activity, may be supplied under a variety of market structures. For example, a loan shark may supply his own capital and self-protect from police scrutiny (i.e., vertically integrate), or he may contract in the market for these inputs to his primary line of business (i.e., vertically specialize). If the loan shark chooses to contract in the market, he transacts with what Thomas Schelling (1967, 1971) has defined as the 'organized criminal firm'. An organized criminal firm specializes in providing goods and services to other criminals and, to a much lesser degree, carrying out illegal activities with the public as final consumers or victims. Schelling's organized criminal firm is characterized by (a) a primary line of business that is illegal, (b) ongoing, illegal market transactions with other specialized firms, and (c) a formal governance system to enforce these market transactions. Included in Schelling's definition is the traditional view of organized crime as La Cosa Nostra or the Mafia. Excluded are firms that occasionally engage in illegal activity (such as fraud) that is ancillary to their regular line of legitimate business, and criminals who sometimes organize themselves into groups (such as burglary rings) but who are not highly specialized vertically and who lack elaborate governance systems.

WHY DOES ORGANIZED CRIME EXIST? To explain organized crime's existence, economists were drawn initially to the theory of monopoly. Schelling (1971:75) argued that 'we find "organized crime" in the lines of business that lend themselves to monopoly', and Rubin (1973: 155) deemed 'a crime to be "organized" if criminals in that line have some market power'. Coincident with this approach, economists also focused on extortion as the primary line of business among organized criminal firms. Thus Abadinsky (1981: 21) described organized crime as an enterprise that 'strives for monopoly power . . . to appropriate downstream profits through extortion or monopoly pricing of its services'.

Equating organized crime with monopoly power and limiting attention to extortion, however, are at variance with a careful examination of the facts. While some lines of business in which organized crime participates – such as racketeering, protection and extortion – are usually monopolized so as to define and enforce property rights, many others – including prostitution, smuggling, fencing and narcotics importation – involve substantial competition among downstream suppliers. Thus while some organized crimes may involve monopolization, monopoly theory is unlikely to provide a general explanation for the existence of organized criminal firms. Further, there is evidence of regular turnover in the ethnic composition of particular criminal markets, which arguably is more consistent with fluid competition than with persistent monopoly. Finally, while many economists have interpreted organized crime's use of violent business tactics as evidence of monopoly power, a competing explanation is that violent firms may have a comparative advantage in illegal markets where victims of violence have no legal recourse (Becker 1968). Alternatively, the direction of causality may be the opposite: violence may best exclude competition, so that organized crime leads to monopoly rather than *vice versa*.

Because organized crime did not fit neatly within the monopoly framework, economists later shifted their attention to consider alternative paradigms. Gambetta (1993) modelled the Mafia as a loose association of independent firms (or 'families') whose business is the production and sale of private protection. In Gambetta's analysis, the Mafia provides a substitute for mutual trust or reputational guarantees between private parties, and for the enforcement of contracts by the state.

Another viewpoint was developed by Skaperdas and Syropoulos (1995), who interpreted organized criminal firms as active competitors to the state for control over economic activity. In their analysis, organized crime acted as an alternative civil authority for taxing individuals and businesses through extortion. Grossman (1995) similarly viewed organized crime as a competitor to the state, but focused on the firm's primary role as being an alternative enforcer of property rights. A third approach, associated with Anderson (1995) and Dick (1995), has treated the Mafia as a profit-maximizing firm which may facilitate markets' efficient operation – or, in a stronger sense, ensure that some markets exist at all. Their analysis was grounded in the transaction-cost literature (Coase 1937; Williamson 1979), which posits that firms arrange their supply decisions to minimize their combined production and organization costs.

Like its legal counterpart, the organized criminal firm only will create a market when it can organize and undertake production at a cost that is lower than the expenditure a downstream firm would incur to supply in-house the same goods or services. Consider again the loan shark who seeks protection from the police. The loan shark may self-protect by bribing police directly to shield his business from unwanted scrutiny, or he may contract in the market with an organized criminal firm that specializes in supplying protection from police. The loan shark's choice between self-protecting and contracting for protection depends on the relative cost of transacting under the two supply modes.

An additional dimension that both the loan shark and the organized criminal firm must consider is the enforcement of illegal market transactions, because they cannot be enforced by the state. The organized criminal firm may assist contract enforcement by developing a Mafia honour code that specifies expected behaviour on the part of the organized criminal firm and downstream transactors. This code can also be used to facilitate trade between several organized criminal firms. The cost of developing and implementing these substitute means of enforcement introduces an additional determinant of criminal market structure. A further complication is introduced by the existence of uncertainty, which can raise enforcement costs and may require introduction of direct monitoring among transactors.

The transaction-cost approach offers two analytical strengths. First, because the framework remains relevant under both perfect and imperfect competition, it is capable of explaining a broad range of empirical phenomena. Second, the framework unifies seemingly disparate objectives among organized criminal firms. While monopoly theory had treated organized criminal extortion as distinct from the firm's specialized supply of inputs to downstream criminals, both activities are explainable by transaction-cost principles. Extortion can be interpreted as selling the avoidance of property damage or personal injury to the victim. The victim jointly minimizes his production plus organization costs to choose between a market transaction – paying extortion – and an internal transaction – self-protecting or self-insuring against the threatened violence.

WHEN DOES ORGANIZED CRIME PAY? The transaction cost framework highlights four primary determinants of organized crime's scale and scope: production costs, organization costs, enforcement costs and uncertainty. Each determinant contributes towards explaining empirical regularities documented by criminologists.

Production costs. Consider first the influence of production costs, and recall the loan shark who seeks protection from police scrutiny. An organized criminal firm generally will be able to produce this protection at lower cost than the loan shark could himself because the criminal firm can more fully exploit economies of scale and scope. Unlike an individual loanshark, the organized criminal firm can spread fixed bribery expenditures across multiple markets to lower its average cost of supplying protection. The organized criminal firm can also better exploit external economies when cultivating relations with the police, and can better establish property rights over the return from its bribery investments (Schelling 1967). Organized crime's production advantage tends to decline, however, as the good or service being supplied grows more specific to the downstream purchaser. For example, if rotating police patrols are replaced by having one officer assigned to monitor each loan shark, then protection becomes a specific input to the loan shark's business. As input specificity rises, economies of scale, scope and externalities decline in importance, and this reduces the organized criminal firm's cost advantage relative to self-production.

Production-cost considerations may explain why organized crime supplies protection from police more frequently to 'victimless' criminal trades. The prostitute, loan shark and bookmaker require public visibility to practice their trades. If these businesses self-protected from police scrutiny by reducing their visibility, they would lower their accessibility to potential customers. The organized criminal firm, by contrast, which bribes police to reduce law-enforcement scrutiny of downstream criminals, does not sacrifice its clientele's public visibility. Organized crime's opportunity to exploit scale and scope economies when cultivating relations with the police magnifies this production-cost advantage. The same calculus does not apply to 'victimizing' criminal trades. A victimizing criminal who self-protects against police scrutiny by lowering his visibility receives the *positive* byproduct of reducing visibility among his potential victims. Theory therefore predicts that the organized criminal firm's production cost advantage should be greater for victimless than for victimizing criminals. In fact, criminologists have found that organized crime's incidence is greater in the victimless criminal trades of prostitution, pornography, narcotics, bookmaking and loan sharking than it is in the victimizing trades of burglary, theft and embezzlement.

Production-cost considerations also may explain why organized criminal firms tend to transact more frequently with illegal trades, both for extortion and input supply. An illicit business has little legal recourse against extortion by the organized criminal firm, in contrast to the legitimate business-owner, who may rely partially upon the police and courts for protection. Stated in another way, the state partially defrays the production cost of self-protecting for the legitimate business firm but not for the illicit business owner. Gambetta (1993) also draws this conclusion, arguing that the Mafia's private enforcement services are especially valuable when the state is unwilling to enforce contracts. By similar reasoning, it will be relatively less costly for the loan shark than for the legitimate money-lender to hire the organized criminal firm to forcefully collect outstanding debts. The state partially subsidizes the legitimate money-lender's production costs for collecting debts by making these obligations enforceable in court. By contrast, debts incurred from gambling are not enforceable in court and therefore the loan shark must bear the full production cost for debt collection. The organized criminal firm therefore will tend to be a more attractive alternative to self-collection of debts for the loan shark than for the legitimate lender. Criminologists have in fact found that organized criminal firms both extort and supply inputs more frequently to illegal than legal trades. The same theory also explains why organized crime often withdraws from illicit activities when they are legalized. For example, organized criminal protection of liquor wholesalers fell precipitously after the repeal of Prohibition, organized crime's involvement with bookmakers declined following legalization of off-track betting, and organized crime withdrew from Nevada's prostitution market after its legalization.

Organization costs. While organized criminal firms generally enjoy a production-cost advantage, this may be partially or completely offset by organization-cost disadvantages. Organization costs arise from the need to arrange and order separate tasks, to coordinate those tasks, and to adapt to contingencies. Organized crime will tend to face higher organization costs when supplying inputs that are specific to downstream purchasers. First, the organized criminal firm will often be less flexible and slower to adapt to unexpected events when inputs are specific. For example, if new police patrols are unexpectedly added, a loan shark may be able to respond faster by self-protecting than by relying on the organized criminal firm to intercede on his behalf. (To some extent, this may be offset by organized crime's heightened incentive to invest in intelligence gathering by dint of its greater scale and scope.) Second, as inputs grow more specific, trading partners become mutually dependent and this raises the risk of opportunism in market transactions. The organized criminal firm could opportunistically undersupply protection or demand additional payment to continue shielding the loan shark from police. The more that the loan shark fears being a victim of opportunism, the more he will prefer self protection. The possibility that the loan shark himself may behave opportunistically, for example by understating his receipts to evade payment, also discourages market supplied protection because the organized criminal firm must raise its supply price to offset its higher expected collection costs.

It follows that organized crime should more frequently supply non-specific inputs and should shy away from settings that are prone to opportunism. The criminology literature identifies financing, bribery to secure protection, and extortion as inputs that are supplied frequently by organized criminal firms. These inputs tend to be non-specific to downstream purchasers as evidenced by significant opportunities for exploiting economies of scale from spanning indivisibilities, internalizing external costs, and pooling risk. Indivisibilities from overlapping jurisdictions and enforcement authority create scale economies in bribery (Anderson 1973). A large firm's ability to internalize external costs from violence creates scale economies in extortion (Schelling 1967). Finally, risk pooling provides the major source of scale economies in financing downstream illegal activities (Rubin 1973). Input specificity may also explain why, in contrast, criminologists have found that organized crime rarely supplies customers to brothels and rarely directly controls outstanding debt accounts for loan sharks and book makers.

Enforcement costs. In markets where contracts cannot be court enforced, private mechanisms including reputation and Mafia codes of honour can provide substitute means for contract enforcement. As an example, organized crime has developed a 'corporate culture' to inject honour among thieves. Organized criminal firms provide their own policing and adjudication and administer a range of penalties for infractions. The effectiveness of a Mafia honour code is bolstered by organized crime's reliance on intermarriage, screening of members, and ethnic bonding which create kinship and facilitate policing efforts (Ianni 1972; Abadinsky 1981).

Downstream, organized criminal firms can economize on their enforcement costs by transacting with parties who have longer horizons. Firms with longer horizons risk suffering a larger penalty, in the form of foreclosed access to lower-cost market transactions, if they commit opportunism. Empirically, criminologists have found that organized crime does tend to transact with longer lived entities. For example, organized criminal firms transact more frequently with downstream businesses that have lower turnover rates. Lower turnover and arrest rates among prostitutes employed by brothels and escort services, as compared with street prostitutes, are consistent with organized crime's tendency to protect only the former. Organized crime finances and protects narcotics importing and wholesaling, where turnover rates and risks of detection generally are lower, yet tends to shy away from retail drug distribution. Finally, organized crime more often provides protection and fencing services to large, established cargo theft rings than it does to individual thieves whose continuity is subject to greater uncertainty.

Uncertainty. Contract enforcement costs will tend to be higher in markets with substantial uncertainty. Uncertainty hinders verification of transactors' actions. Transaction complexity, lags in communication of past performance, and delays in punishment further complicate private enforcement efforts in uncertain environments (Williamson 1991). In general, therefore, organized criminal firms will need to directly monitor transactors to assure contract compliance. As the transaction environment becomes less certain, we may expect the criminal firm to adopt contract terms to assist with monitoring downstream firms' behaviour.

This final consideration provides a complementary explanation for organized crime's tendency to transact in victimless criminal markets. Suppliers of illicit goods and services require visibility among their potential clientele, and this visibility lowers the organized criminal firm's monitoring costs. For similar reasons, organized crime transacts more often with downstream producers of relatively simple and standardized goods and services where specialized knowledge of the business is not required for monitoring – prostitution and loan sharking, but not embezzlement or securities fraud; restaurants and laundromats, but not banks or insurance companies.

Organized crime may tailor its contract terms to assist monitoring. Criminologists have found that legal businesses such as restaurants and bars with highly variable income streams generally pay extortion through input purchase requirements for liquor, linen services, and vending machines. This form of payment facilitates the organized criminal firm's task of metering downstream victims' revenues more accurately. Other examples are found in the fact that loan sharks tend to borrow capital directly from organized criminal firms, pornography distributors typically are required to rent film projectors and use organized crime-controlled labs to process film, and early book makers generally leased wire services from organized crime. By contrast, criminologists have found that organized criminal firms typically receive lump-sum or direct money-skimming payments in racketeering and casino gambling. One explanation for this difference may be that non-salvageable investments tend to be larger in these industries. The organized criminal firm thus would be better able to rely on threats of asset seizure to assure payment.

PUBLIC POLICY. Decriminalizing victimless crimes has occasionally been proposed as a reform to curb organized crime's influence. Transaction-cost theory predicts, and empirical observation tends to indicate, that organized crime predominantly supplies victimless criminal trades. Theory also predicts, and again historical experience generally confirms, that legalization of previously illicit activities tends to discourage organized crime's participation. Transaction-cost theory therefore predicts that decriminalization of victimless crimes such as prostitution and bookmaking should reduce the demand for organized criminal-supplied inputs and lead to increased self-supply among individual criminal enterprises. Fighting organized crime, therefore, may not be synonymous with fighting crime, and may instead lead the market to substitute towards 'disorganized crime'. That is, the criminals and their opportunities might remain largely undisturbed, with merely a lesser degree of organization than before.

Arguing that if a monopoly in the supply of 'goods' is socially undesirable, then a monopoly in the supply of 'bads' should be socially desirable, Schelling (1967) and Buchanan (1973) have contended thac an appropriate public policy might actually favour organized crime. They note that disorganized criminals will have a smaller incentive to internalize external costs associated with crime such as violence and will tend to over supply 'social nuisances' (such as prostitution and gambling). Schelling raises the example of an individual criminal who might be tempted to kill a witness to his activities. The Mafia firm might be more reluctant, Schelling argues, because it will take into account the likelihood that its actions would raise its future costs of doing business by prompting general public outrage and heightened police scrutiny. While an individual criminal's actions could prompt the same outrage and scrutiny, these effects would be spread over the entire criminal population and therefore would not be internalized to the same degree by the actual perpetrator. Because of these differing incentives to internalize violence, therefore, decriminalization of victimless trades might inadvertently increase the total supply of violence and social bads by substituting supply away from organized and towards disorganized crime. On the other hand, because disorganized criminals will usually be less well situated to exploit economies of scale and scope in undertaking crimes, the pervasiveness and breadth of victimless crimes might fall when organized crime's involvement is reduced. The loss of organized criminal firms' superior enforcement services, compared to disorganized criminals, could also tend to reduce the aggregate level of crime. Whether on balance decriminalization would increase or decrease criminal activity, therefore, is an empirical question. More generally, transaction cost theory highlights how policies designed to raise the cost of business among organized criminal firms may simply alter the organizational structure that crime assumes, while having an ambiguous impact on its net supply.

ANDREW DICK

See also CIVIL LIABILITY UNDER RICO: UNINTENDED CONSEQUENCES OF LEGISLATION; CONSPIRACY; CORRUPTION IN TRANSITION ECONOMIES; DRUG PROHIBITION; ECONOMIC APPROACH TO CRIME AND PUNISHMENT; GANGS AND THE STATE OF NATURE; GUN CONTROL; LEGAL REFORM IN EASTERN EUROPE; TRUST.

Subject classification: 1a(ii); 5e.

BIBLIOGRAPHY

Abadinsky, H. 1981. *Organized Crime*. Boston: Allyn & Bacon.

Anderson, A.G. 1973. Comment. In *The Economics of Crime and Punishment*, ed. S. Rottenberg, Washington, DC: American Enterprise Institute.

Anderson, A.G. 1995. Organized crime, Mafia and governments. In *The Economics of Organised Crime*, ed. G. Fiorentini and S. Peltzman, London: Cambridge University Press.

Becker, G.S. 1968. Crime and punishment: an economic approach. *Journal of Political Economy* 76: 169–217.

Becker, G.S. and Stigler, G.J. 1974. Law enforcement, malfeasance, and compensation of enforcers. *Journal of Legal Studies* 3: 1–18.

Buchanan, J.M. 1973. A defense of organized crime? In *The Economics of Crime and Punishment*, ed. S. Rottenberg, Washington, DC: American Enterprise Institute.

Coase, R.H. 1937. The nature of the firm. *Economica* 4: 386–405.

Dick, A.R. 1995. When does organized crime pay? A transaction cost analysis. *International Review of Law and Economics* 15: 25–45.

Gambetta, D. 1993. *The Sicilian Mafia: The Business of Private Protection*. Cambridge, MA: Harvard University Press.

Grossman, H.I. 1995. Rival kleptocrats: the Mafia versus the State. In *The Economics of Organised Crime*, ed. G. Fiorentini and S. Peltzman, London: Cambridge University Press.

Ianni, F.A.J. 1972. *A Family Business: Kinship and Social Control in Organized Crime*. New York: Russell Sage Foundation.

Rubin, P.H. 1973. The economic theory of the criminal firm. In *The Economics of Crime and Punishment*, ed. S. Rottenberg, Washington, DC: American Enterprise Institute.

Schelling, T.C. 1967. Economics and the criminal enterprise. *Public Interest* 7: 61–78.
Schelling, T.C. 1971. What is the business of organized crime? *Journal of Public Law* 20: 71–84.
Skaperdas, S. and Syropoulos, C. 1995. Gangs as primitive states. In *The Economics of Organised Crime*, ed. G. Fiorentini and S. Peltzman, London: Cambridge University Press.
Williamson, O.E. 1979. Transaction cost economics: the governance of contractual relations. *Journal of Law and Economics* 22: 233–61.
Williamson, O.E. 1991. Economic institutions: spontaneous and intentional governance. *Journal of Law, Economics, and Organization* 7: 159–87.

organized markets. *See* SELF-REGULATION OF PRIVATE ORGANIZED MARKETS.

ownership. *See* OWNERSHIP OF THE FIRM; POSSESSION; PROPERTY RIGHTS; RESIDUAL RIGHTS OF CONTROL.

ownership and control in Europe. Berle and Means (1932) described how dispersed ownership has given rise to a separation of ownership and control. While some European countries, most notably the UK, correspond to the Berle and Means description, others do not: in many Continental European countries there are very high levels of concentration of ownership. As discussed by Demsetz and Lehn (1985), ownership patterns should reflect a tradeoff between the risk of concentrated ownership capturing private benefits and its potential for exercising control. What is puzzling is that the resolution of this tradeoff should have taken such different forms in different countries. In the UK there is an active market in corporate control with more than forty hostile bids annually, whereas in Germany there have been only a handful of hostile takeovers since 1945. This essay compares the different patterns of ownership in the stock markets of France, Germany and the UK and shows how this has shaped the markets for corporate control.

I. PATTERNS OF OWNERSHIP IN FRANCE, GERMANY AND THE UNITED KINGDOM

The stereotypic description of the structure of corporate sectors is that there are small companies privately owned by individuals, families and partners, whereas large companies are traded on the stock market with ownership held by a large number of individual shareholders, usually through financial intermediaries, in particular, pension funds, life assurance firms and mutual funds.

Support for this description comes from looking at ownership patterns of UK firms. Of the top 700 companies in the UK, nearly 80% are quoted on the stock market. In total, there are about two thousand companies traded on the stock market in comparison with an extant population of around half a million firms. The value of companies quoted on the stock market is around 81% of GDP and approximately two-thirds of equity of quoted companies is held by financial institutions.

However, this pattern is by no means universally observed. On the contrary, it is the exception rather than the rule. While the US has more quoted companies than the UK, the value of these as a proportion of GDP is somewhat less than it is in the UK. But in most Continental European countries, the number of quoted companies is far fewer than in the UK. In Germany, there are fewer than 700 quoted companies and in France there are fewer than 500. In both countries, the value of quoted companies amounts to one quarter of GDP. Moreover, in the past six years in Germany there have been only 77 new stock market listings compared with 3,000 in the US.

In the UK and the US, ownership is dispersed across a large number of institutions or individuals. In the UK, most equity is held by institutions but rarely does one institution own a large stake in any one company. In the US, most equity is held directly by a large number of individuals. In other countries ownership is concentrated. Graph 1 shows the ownership patterns of approximately the largest 170 quoted companies in France, Germany and the UK. It records the percentage of companies in which

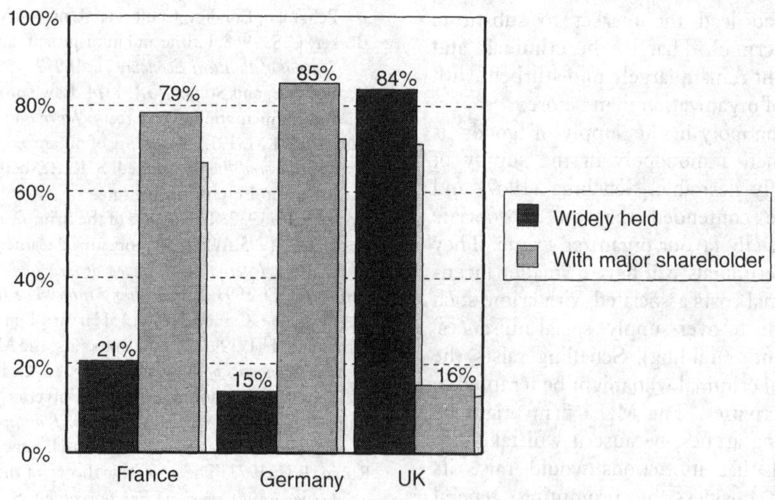

Graph 1 Ownership of a sample of French, German and UK quoted companies

there was at least one shareholder who owned more than 25% of the equity of a firm. There is a striking difference. In the UK, in only 16% of companies was there a single shareholder owning more than 25% of shares in any one company. In contrast, in Germany in nearly 85% of companies there was at least one shareholder owning more than 25% of the shares in any one company. In France, in nearly 80% of companies there was at least one shareholder holding more than 25% of shares. Concentration of ownership is therefore much greater outside the UK and the US. Prowse (1992) makes a similar observation in a comparison of ownership in Japan and the US. In the case of Japan, the largest group of shareholders consists of financial institutions.

In Germany by far the single largest group of shareholders is the corporate sector itself. Graph 2 breaks down large share stakes in Germany by different groups of investors: banks, investment institutions, companies, government, etc. It reveals that a majority of the large share stakes are held by companies. The next largest group is families, followed by trusts, institutional investors and foreign companies. Banks come far down the list of large shareholders in Germany. However, the significance of banks is greater than their direct equity holdings would suggest: as holders of bearer shares they are able to exercise proxy votes on behalf of shareholders. Where companies are widely held, shareholders will often give their proxies to banks, so that they are able to exercise the voting rights on their behalf.

While the share stakes held by trusts, institutional investors and banks are rarely majority holdings, in one-third of cases, families are majority shareholders. Contrary to the stylized description that was presented at the beginning, large-scale family ownership is a particular feature of the largest enterprises in Germany. This raises an interesting question of how and why German families hold onto equity so much longer than their UK counterparts. The other group that emerges as having majority shareholdings is other companies.

A remarkably similar pattern emerges for France. Firstly, as described above, the proportion of large stakeholdings in total is about the same as in Germany. Graph 3 records that a majority of these are associated with other companies. Foreign companies, families and banks are other large shareholders. There are some large stakes held by insurance companies but these are rarely majority holdings. Banks have some large minority shareholdings, often in excess of 25%. However, as in Germany, it is families and other companies that have the largest proportion of majority shareholdings.

The ownership patterns of individual firms reveal a number of characteristics that aggregate data hide. Graphs 4, 5 and 6 show the pattern of ownership of three prominent German companies – Renk AG, Kromschroder AG and Metallgesellschaft AG. Graph 7 describes ownership of the French water company, Degremont. Together, they show the equity holdings of corporates in each other. These investments are frequently in quoted companies and are often by firms in a related or the same industry. The first graph shows a large holding by MAN AG, a large German engineering company producing buses, lorries and machines, in Renk AG, another mechanical engineering company. Ruhrgas is a gas company which owns Elster, another gas company.

An important feature of these ownership patterns is that the other corporates are frequently not trading partners. The gas company Elster holds Kromschröder, a precision mechanics and optics company. A second feature is that banks and insurance companies often emerge higher up in the ownership tree. For example, Allianz, an insurance company, and Deutsche Bank between them have a

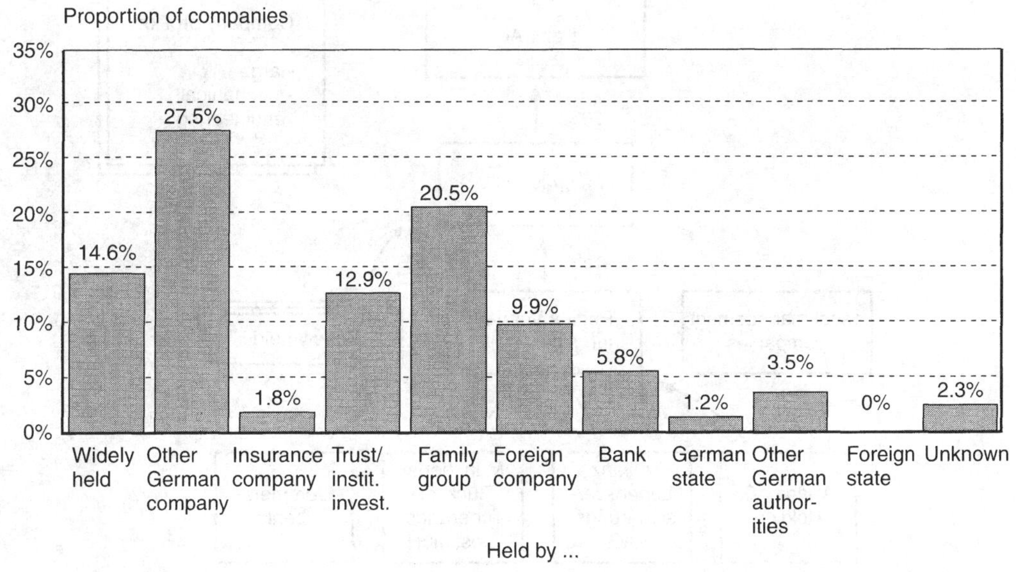

Graph 2 Share stakes in excess of 25% in 171 German industrial and commercial quoted companies in 1990

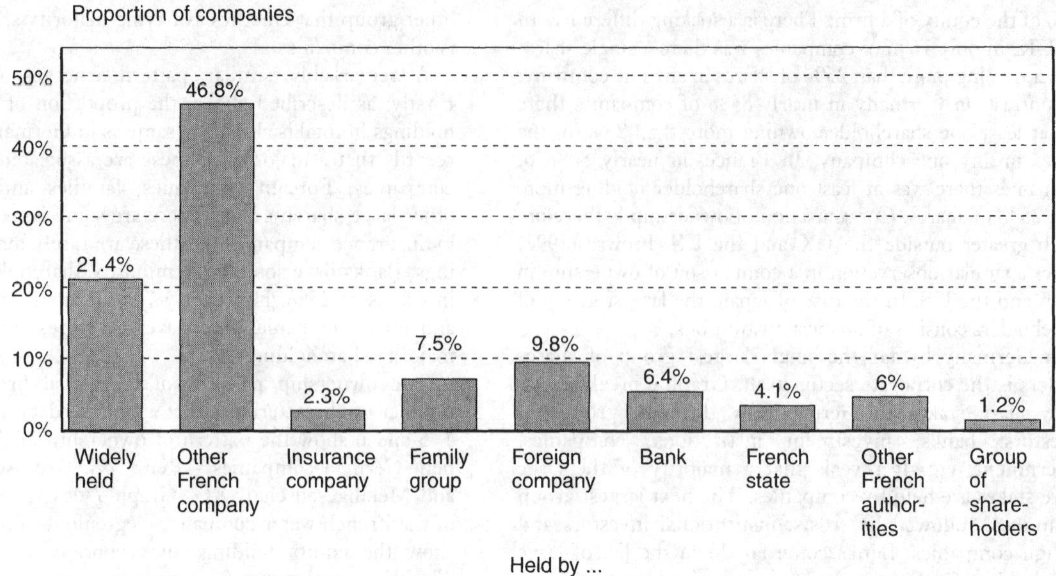

Graph 3 Share stakes in excess of 25% in 155 French industrial and commercial quoted companies in 1990

controlling interest in the holding company of Metallgesellschaft. Allianz and Commerzbank have a controlling interest in a holding company in MAN. UAP, Compagnie Financière de Suez and Crédit Lyonnaise have significant holdings in Societé Lyonnaise des Eaux-Dumex, which owns Degremont. The presence of institutional owners is common to all countries. However, in the UK institutional ownership is diversified, while in France and Germany it is far more concentrated.

One implication of this ownership pattern is that dispersed outside shareholders are even less important than the small number of quoted companies in France and Germany would suggest. Even where companies are quoted on the stock market, in many cases controlling shareholdings reside with other companies. These systems are therefore appropriately described as *insider systems* (Graph 8). Insider systems are ones in which the corporate sector has controlling interests in itself, and outside investors, while able to participate in equity returns through the stock market, are not able to exert much control. In contrast, the UK and US are *outsider systems* of corporate control in which there are few large, controlling

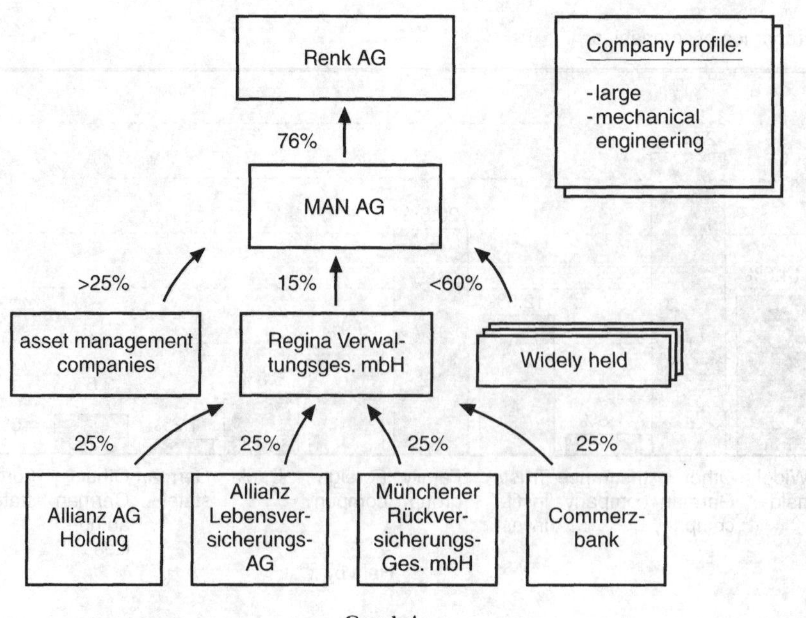

Graph 4

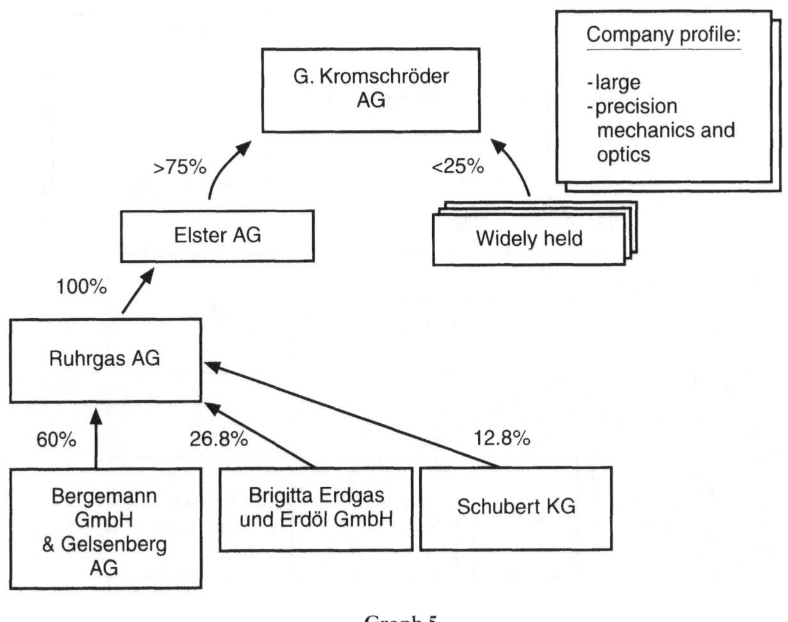

Graph 5

shareholdings and these are rarely associated with the corporate sector itself.

These differences in ownership give rise to very different forms of corporate control across countries.

2. THE MARKET FOR CORPORATE CONTROL IN THE UK AND GERMANY

UK. The takeover market is active in the UK. Franks and Mayer (1990) report that during the merger waves at the beginning of the 1970s and the end of the 1980s up to 4% of the total UK capital stock was acquired by takeover (or merger) in one year. Furthermore, Jenkinson and Mayer (1994) record that, through much of the 1980s, around 25% of takeovers were hostile in the sense of being rejected initially by the incumbent management. Of those bids that were hostile in nature, approximately one-half were successfully completed.

Most empirical studies of takeovers do not distinguish takeovers that are associated with the correction of managerial failure from those that are not; see, for example, Jensen and Ruback (1983), Meeks (1977) and Ravenscraft and Scherer (1987). Two exceptions are Martin and

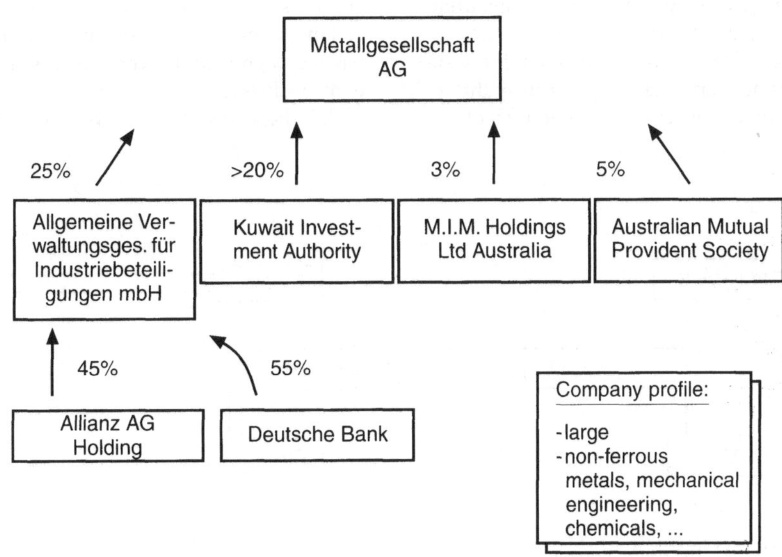

Graph 6

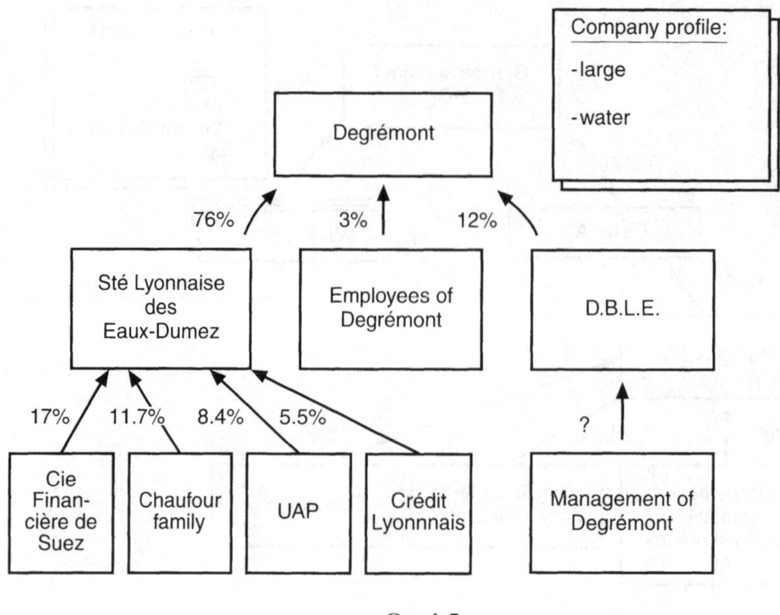

Graph 7

McConnell (1991) and Franks and Mayer (1996). Martin and McConnell (1991) investigate the disciplinary role of corporate takeovers in the US over the period 1958 to 1984, using a sample of 253 successful tender offers. They classify a takeover as disciplinary where there is turnover of the top manager of the target firm. They report no difference in bid premiums associated with disciplinary and non-disciplinary takeovers and only weak evidence of differences in the share price performance of targets of disciplinary and non-disciplinary bids prior to takeover.

Franks and Mayer (1996) report similar results for a sample of 80 contested bids in the UK in 1985 and 1986. They find that for a range of financial variables (including share price returns, dividends and cash flow rates of return) the performance of targets of hostile bids in the six years prior to a bid was not statistically significantly different from that of samples of either accepted bids or non-merging firms. In contrast, the dividend performance of targets of both friendly and hostile bids was quite different from that of firms in the lowest deciles of share performance. Targets of hostile and friendly bids rarely reduced their dividends in the two years prior to a bid; however, poorly performing firms frequently reduced their dividends.

Martin and McConnell classify correction of managerial failure by changes in managerial control rather than opposition by management. Franks and Mayer repeat their analysis of UK takeovers using a similar criterion. Again they find little evidence that control changes in takeovers are a response to poor managerial performance: the financial performance of bids that prompted control changes was not significantly worse than bids where there were no control changes.

All these results question the common association of

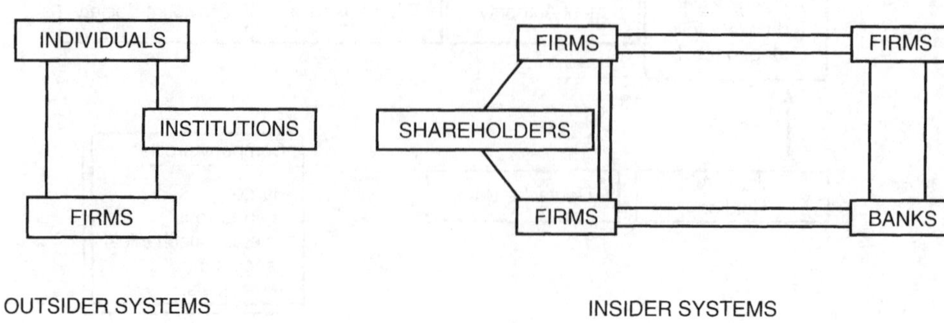

Graph 8

markets for corporate control with the correction of managerial failure. However, Franks and Mayer do report considerable post merger restructuring even where there is no evidence of poor pre-bid performance. Levels of asset disposals and restructurings were significantly higher in Franks and Mayer's study where bids were either hostile or prompted managerial control changes. Furthermore, their study reported a close association between the two classifications: managerial dismissals and therefore control changes were much higher in hostile than in friendly bids. In hostile bids, nearly 80% of executive directors could expect to resign or be dismissed within two years of a successfully completed hostile bid.

While the market for corporate control does not therefore appear to be associated with the correction of managerial failure as measured by past corporate performance, it does give rise to substantial corporate restructurings with high asset disposals and executive dismissals. Franks and Mayer (1990) use the terms *ex ante* and *ex post* failure to distinguish between the two types of acquisition. One interpretation of their results is that hostile bids can occur in the absence of any evidence of poor performance in the past (*ex post* failure) in the expectation that the acquiring firm will implement a superior policy in the future (*ex ante* failure). In addition, Franks and Mayer (1996) report much larger bid premiums for the targets of hostile than friendly bids. Larger bid premiums are consistent with higher expected benefits from hostile bids.

In a detailed analysis of 42 cases of hostile bids in the UK, Jenkinson and Mayer (1994) provide some support for this distinction. They make similar observations to Franks and Mayer (1996), *viz*: that there is only a weak relation between both pre-bid share price and accounting performance of firms and the risk of being a target of a bid or the probability of being able to resist a bid – poor financial performance does not appear to be associated with a greater propensity to be a takeover target or the victim of a successful rather than an unsuccessful bid. In Franks and Mayer's terms there is, therefore, little evidence of *ex post* failure.

They also report that hostile bids are as often motivated by the corporate strategy of the acquiring firm as the failure of the target firm. Executive dismissals are a reflection of disputes over corporate strategy (the *ex ante* failures of Franks and Mayer) and these are mirrored in high levels of restructuring after acquisition.

Germany. Franks and Mayer (1990) report that the total number of takeovers in Germany was around one-half of that in the UK during the 1980s. More significantly, in contrast to the active market in corporate control in the UK, there have been just four recorded cases of hostile takeovers in Germany since World War II and three have occurred within the last six years.

Several explanations have been suggested for the low level of hostile takeovers in Germany. The first explanation comes from the dominant position of banks in owning corporate equity and sitting on the supervisory boards of many quoted German companies. As recorded above, German banks' holdings of equity are a quite modest proportion of the total. Instead, the system of proxy votes is thought to be an important source of bank influence.

The second explanation is that restrictions on voting rights prevent predators from acquiring controlling interests in firms. German companies frequently pass resolutions at shareholders meetings limiting the voting right of any one shareholder to a maximum of 5%, 10% or 15% of total votes, irrespective of the size of the shareholding. The justification for this is that, in the absence of a UK style takeover code, such restrictions protect minority shareholders from predators acquiring controlling shareholding interests and diluting the value of the minority's investments.

The third explanation for the low level of activity is that it is difficult to remove members of the supervisory board and thereby gain control of a company, even when a majority of the shares are tendered. The supervisory board comprises representatives of both shareholders and employees. For an AG (public limited company), 50% of the board is composed of employee representatives who by tradition vote with the incumbent management.

Case studies of hostile takeovers in Germany reported in Franks and Mayer (1997) provide evidence of the effectiveness of these institutional features as barriers to takeover. The unwelcome bid by Pirelli for Continental, Germany's largest tyre manufacturer, was launched in September 1990. During the course of the bid substantial share stakes were acquired by allies of the two parties: Italmobiliare, Mediobanca and Sopaf in the Pirelli camp; BMW, Daimler-Benz and Volkswagen in the Continental camp. These share stakes were in large part acquired from individual investors and investment institutions.

At the time of the Pirelli bid, there was a 5% limitation on the voting rights that could be exercised by any one shareholder. Prior to launching the bid, Pirelli attempted to have the 5% limitation removed so as not to dilute the voting rights of its own (and its partners') holdings. The motion for removal of the restriction was brought to a shareholders' meeting in March 1991 which supported its removal and thereby paved the way for Pirelli to launch a tender bid for Continental. However, the removal was delayed (and never implemented) due to a court action by objecting shareholders.

The Continental case illustrates that voting right restrictions can introduce a two-stage procedure into German takeovers. In the first stage, predators solicit the support of small shareholders to have voting right limitations removed. In the second stage, a normal tender can be launched. The Continental case suggests that the first stage can represent a significant though not necessarily insurmountable barrier to takeover.

The case suggests that neither proxy votes nor voting right restrictions are absolute defences against hostile takeovers, though the latter certainly slows down the process. Furthermore, if it sees fit, the supervisory board can remove members of the management board. Instead, the main impediment to an Anglo-American market for corporate control is the ownership structure of German companies. It is significant that in the Continental case there was no major shareholder who owned a stake of 25% or more, thus allowing Pirelli and its partners to build large holdings. Two other hostile takeovers, that for Feldmühle Nobel and the bid by Krupp for Hoesch, were also for firms in the small set of companies with dispersed shareholdings. In the latter case, Krupp was able to amass a stake of 24.9% without the knowledge of Hoesch or the investment banking community. The purchase of this stake took more than five months to complete, involved purchases on the German, London and Swiss stock exchanges, and was a crucial tactic in gaining control. Without such a stake, a merger would have proved unlikely or impossible, since all previous attempts at friendly mergers in the industry had failed.

From the evidence described above, it appears that there is an active market for corporate control in the UK and a virtual absence of one in Germany. However, Franks and Mayer (1997) document that in Germany there is an active market in share stakes, with owners of large share blocks selling to other parties. During the two-year period 1990–1991, they found that 7.2% per annum of the disclosed share stakes turned over, and this level is substantially in excess of takeover activity in the UK. They suggest that such a market in share stakes may perform a similar role to markets for corporate control in the UK and US.

3. AN EVALUATION

The above suggests eight empirical generalizations on ownership and control which warrant explanation:

(1) There are marked differences in the ownership patterns of similar companies in different countries.
(2) Intercorporate holdings of companies are very significant in some countries but not others.
(3) Large shareholdings by families are of much greater importance in some countries than others.
(4) Markets for corporate control are little in evidence in countries with concentrated ownership. However, there is an active market in share stakes which may perform some of the functions of a market for corporate control.
(5) Even where companies are widely held, markets for corporate control are seriously impeded in some countries.
(6) Bank control is primarily associated with widely held companies where the market for corporate control is impeded.
(7) There is little association of the market for corporate control with *ex ante* managerial failure (in the sense of Franks and Mayer (1990)).
(8) Markets for corporate control give rise to substantial *ex post* correction even in the absence of *ex ante* failure.

These observations raise several puzzles. How can similar forms of technology give rise to such different patterns of ownership? If intercorporate holdings are justified by complementarities between firms, why are there such marked differences in complementarities giving rise to much larger intercorporate holdings in some countries than others? Do families really possess much greater managerial skills or have much greater private benefits in some countries than in others? If markets for corporate control improve corporate efficiency, why are they largely absent in some countries? In particular, why are markets for corporate control impeded in widely held companies in some countries and bank intermediation used instead? If the market for corporate control is associated with the correction of managerial failure, why is there little evidence of poor pre-bid performance? Why is there substantial *ex post* correction in the absence of poor pre-bid performance?

It is very difficult for theories of either ownership or control to provide adequate explanations for the organization and operation of both UK and Continental European capital markets. There is clearly more to the determination of ownership than complementarity in production and the market for corporate control does not appear to be associated with the traditional form of the correction of managerial failure. The financing of investment or the liquidity of securities markets cannot provide explanations for these observations. External equity can be raised while retaining control through the use of dual class shares and the pyramiding to which reference was made above. Active secondary markets can be organized in shares other than the controlling block in companies with concentrated share ownership. Holmstrom and Tirole (1993) argue that this may be an important source of information for structuring incentives for management.

According to Demsetz and Lehn (1985) concentrated ownership will occur where there is control potential and there are private benefits of control. Concentrated ownership allows investors to exert direct control as against the indirect control of takeover markets. However, unless direct and indirect control are close substitutes or families attach very different values to private benefits in different countries, the diverse forms of ownership are not readily explained.

The hypothesis that will be advanced here is that the patterns of ownership are associated with different forms of corporate control that allow for different types of correction. Correction of managerial failure in an *ex post* sense is more closely associated with concentrated ownership and large share stakes. Dispersed ownership allows *ex ante* correction to take place in the absence of *ex post* failure.

At first sight, this would appear to permit systems with dispersed ownership to achieve more efficient resource allocation than those with concentrated ownership. The problem that dispersed ownership presents is that it is not possible for a large number of small shareholders to commit to a single shareholder. A simple example illustrates the point. Suppose that there are 100,000 investors all owning one share in a firm. Suppose assurance that current investment policies are to be retained requires the continuing presence of at least half of these shareholders. A prospect then emerges that offers some investors a higher return elsewhere. Since each shareholder has a negligible effect on policy decisions of the firm and since, on their own, their decision to retain or sell shares will have no effect on any one else, they will evaluate the alternative prospect purely on its financial merits. However, if more than 50,000 investors act similarly then collectively their decision to sell will cause a change in the policy of the firm. Even though investors may wish to make a commitment to maintain policies unchanged, they are unable to provide this. Other stakeholders (suppliers, purchasers and employees) who require long-term commitment from investors will be discouraged from making long-term investment commitments themselves.

Shareholders want to be able to take advantage of profitable alternative investment opportunities but they do not wish to suffer the consequences of the changes in control. In that respect the Continental system is a very effective system of ownership. It allows a large number of small investors to trade in investment opportunities without having any effect on control. There are large investors that know that if they trade then there will be a change in control. If encouraging investment by other stakeholders is important then the large investors will have no incentive to trade while the small investors may.

The advantage of dispersed shareholding is that owners are not tied down to prior commitments and can seek the highest value control group at any point in time. Dispersed shareownership achieves value maximization but at the expense of being unable to sustain relations that are required to encourage investment by other stakeholders, such as suppliers, purchasers and employees. It is in this sense that the UK and US financial markets may be short term. It does not result from mispricing of securities or excessive trading of shares but from the structure of ownership. Dispersed shareholders cannot commit in the way in which concentrated owners can and cannot therefore sustain the same set of prior relations. This provides the basis for the Shleifer and Summers (1988) assertion that shareholders are unable to make commitments to other stakeholders and employ managers to do this on their behalf. The observation here is that through concentrated ownership some financial systems permit investors to make commitments. Not being committed has its merits as well as its deficiencies. Where little investment is required of other stakeholders, or can be sustained through explicit contracting, then dispersed share ownership can achieve more efficient allocation of resources than owners who are burdened by prior commitments.

While it is possible to provide a rationale for high levels of concentration of ownership, majority or large minority inter-corporate ownership remains a puzzle. One interpretation of the insider system is that there are complex webs of intercorporate holdings that retain control within the corporate sector itself and prevent control from being exerted by either individuals or families. The corporate sector owns and controls itself through intercorporate holdings and corporate representatives on supervisory boards.

This would run contrary to the conventional principal–agent description of the corporate sector as an agent of investors. The difficulty it poses is that where control is retained within the corporate sector through large corporate shareholdings, management is likely to enjoy a high degree of protection from external influences: managerial failure will not be corrected either directly by large outside shareholders such as families or indirectly by takeovers, as in economies with dispersed shareownership.

4. CONCLUSIONS

This paper has recorded marked differences in the ownership patterns of corporate sectors across countries. It has been noted that the UK and US have large quoted sectors with share ownership dispersed across a large number of investors. In the case of the UK, the dominant shareholding group is institutional investors; in the US, it is individual investors.

In contrast, France and Germany have small quoted sectors. More significantly, even the largest quoted companies in general have at least one shareholder owning more than 25% of the equity and frequently a majority shareholding. These large shareholdings are in particular associated with family and other corporate investors. A contrast was therefore drawn between insider systems of corporate ownership as observed in France and Germany with the outsider system of the UK and US.

The different ownership systems are associated with very different forms of corporate control. There is an active market for corporate control in the UK and the US and there is very little in the way of a market for corporate control in France and Germany. In the case of Germany, even in the comparatively small widely held component of the quoted sector, the market for corporate control is impeded by proxy votes and voting right restrictions that confer more power on banks than in the concentrated ownership segment.

Theories of corporate ownership are mainly concerned with the complementarities in production that exist in vertical relations and which require joint ownership on account of transaction costs or incomplete contracts. However, the patterns of ownership that are observed in France and Germany do not appear to be particularly closely associated with trading relations. More significantly, similar companies have quite different ownership structures in the UK on the one hand and France and Germany on the other.

In theory, the market for corporate control should be closely associated with the correction of managerial failure. In practice, there is very little evidence of a relation between the incidence of hostile takeovers and poor corporate performance. The performance of targets of hostile takeovers in the UK is close to that of the average quoted company. Despite this, the hostile takeovers result in considerable restructuring and managerial turnover. There is therefore *ex ante* correction even in the absence of evidence of *ex post* failure.

In the last section the thesis was advanced that the distinct patterns of ownership create different incentives and forms of correction. Concentrated ownership allows relations involving commitment on the part of investors to be sustained. Dispersed ownership permits correction to occur even in the absence of past failure largely because owners are unable to commit. It would therefore be expected that the different forms of ownership would be suited to promoting different types of activity. Concentrated ownership is required where investment by other stakeholders is important and cannot be promoted contractually. Dispersed ownership will be advantageous where little investment is required by other parties or adequate contracts can be written. What, however, is difficult to explain is the high level of intercorporate holdings which are likely to create insider systems largely immune to sanction by outside investors.

JULIAN FRANKS AND COLIN MAYER

See also AGENCY COSTS AND CORPORATE GOVERNANCE; AUCTIONS AND TAKEOVERS; COMPARATIVE CORPORATE GOVERNANCE; CORPORATE GOVERNANCE; LEVERAGED BUYOUTS; MARKET FOR CORPORATE CONTROL; REGULATION OF CAPITAL MARKETS IN THE EUROPEAN UNION; TENDER OFFERS.

Subject classification: 3f(i); 5g(iii); 6c(ii).

BIBLIOGRAPHY

Berle, A. and Means, G. 1932. *The Modern Corporation and Private Property*. New York: Macmillan.

Demsetz, H. and Lehn, K. 1985. The structure of corporate ownership: causes and consequences. *Journal of Political Economy* 93: 1155–77.

Franks, J. and Mayer, C. 1990. Takeovers: capital markets and corporate control: a study of France, Germany and the UK. *Economic Policy* 10: 189–231.

Franks, J. and Mayer, C. 1995. Ownership and control. In *Trends in Business Organization: Do Participation and Co-operation Increase Competitiveness*?, ed. H. Siebert, Tubingen: J.C.B. Mohr.

Franks, J. and Mayer, C. 1996. Hostile takeovers and the correction of managerial failure. *Journal of Financial Economics* 40: 163–81.

Franks, J. and Mayer, C. 1997. The ownership and control of German corporations, London Business School, mimeo.

Holmstrom, B. and Tirole, J. 1993. Market liquidity and performance monitoring. *Journal of Political Economy* 101: 678–709.

Jenkinson, T. and Mayer, C. 1994. *Hostile Takeovers*. London: Macmillan; New York: McGraw Hill.

Jensen, M. and Ruback, R. 1983. The market for corporate control: the scientific evidence. *Journal of Financial Economics* 11: 5–50.

Martin, K.J. and McConnell, J. 1991. Corporate performance, corporate takeovers, and management turnover. *Journal of Finance* 46: 671–87.

Meeks, G. 1977. *Disappointing Marriage: A Study of the Gains from Merger*. Cambridge: Cambridge University Press.

Prowse, S. 1992. The structure of corporate ownership in Japan. *Journal of Finance* 47: 1121–40.

Ravenscraft, D. and Scherer, F. 1987. *Mergers, Sell-Offs and Economic Efficiency*. Washington, DC: Brookings Institution.

Shleifer, A. and Summers, L. 1988. Breaches of trust in hostile takeovers. In *Corporate Takeovers: Causes and Consequences*, ed. A. Auerbach, Chicago: University of Chicago Press for National Bureau of Economic Research.

ownership of market information. Not only is the idea of ownership generally not simple, it is even more opaque than normal when applied to the price and quote data emanating from a market or an exchange (Lee 1995 and 1998, ch. 7). Ownership may be viewed as the bundle of rights and obligations associated with the purchase and sale, or more generally the use and distribution, of a particular item (Honoré 1961). Many factors make this concept extremely perplexing in the context of price and quote data.

In any one jurisdiction, there are several bodies of law and regulation that impinge on the dissemination of this type of information. These frequently conflict, and it is not always clear which takes priority. Furthermore, there are many such areas that are either in the process of being reformed or the subject of great controversy. The ease with which data are transmitted globally also makes cross-border concerns important and adds additional difficulties. National law and regulation governing the same topics can differ substantially, conflict between different jurisdictions' laws is common, and only infrequently is there any international law or treaty governing how such conflicts should be resolved.

There is also great contractual complexity and uncertainty regarding the use and distribution of price and quote data. Advances in computer and data-transmission technology have made it relatively cheap to receive information electronically, to manipulate it, and then to redistribute it. The traditional industry model of how price and quote data were distributed around a market assumed a simple three-stage path: an exchange disseminated them to vendors, and vendors in turn re-disseminated them to end-users. Now, however, the flow of data typically follows a much more labyrinthine path. Furthermore, the commercial strategies of market participants have become blurred as the number of participants and the range of services offered have grown, and the rapidity with which it is possible to enter new markets has increased. Market participants are therefore using a variety of untested legal approaches in an attempt to protect what they perceive as their rights.

There are four key ownership questions of critical interest to all users and suppliers of price and quote data: What precise types of data are published? To whom and how quickly are they disseminated? What prices are charged for them? And what constraints, if any, are placed on their use – most importantly regarding their manipulation and redistribution, and their employment in establishing proprietary trading systems? Answers to these questions determine not only the distribution of profits between all the different types of market participants – for example between suppliers, transmitters, manipulators and users of data; between financial intermediaries and end-users; between different types of financial intermediaries; and between different exchanges. They also affect the structure of markets, by changing the relative costs and benefits of different types of order-routing and execution facilities.

Consider an exchange's viewpoint. The dissemination by an exchange of its price and quote data affects three critical concerns of the exchange: the extent to which, and the manner in which, deals are executed both on and off the exchange's trading system; the pursuit of the interests of the exchange's owners; and the amount of revenue that the exchange receives from the dissemination of the information. An exchange must disseminate some information in order to attract trading – market participants will not normally send their orders to a trading arena without some knowledge of the quotes and prices obtaining there. The very dissemination of price and quote information, however, makes off-exchange trading easier. Trading systems that do not bear the costs incurred by the exchange may use the exchange's quotes as the basis for the execution of trades off the exchange.

Such trading is undertaken both to avoid the charges associated with dealing on the exchange and to escape any exchange rules that might hinder the execution of trades. It harms the exchange directly by reducing the fees the exchange receives for its trading services. Indirectly, it reduces liquidity on the exchange and therefore the exchange's desirability as a location to which other orders may be sent, and also allows market participants other than the members of the exchange to profit at the members' expense. If sufficient order flow were diverted, such off-exchange trading could in addition reduce the value of the exchange's price and quote data. If an exchange cannot forbid re-dissemination of its data, then the revenues that the exchange receives from the sale or licensing of such data will also be under threat. Once the exchange has passed the data to a single company, that company can compete with the exchange in selling the data to other market participants.

Five branches of law and regulation relevant for the ownership of price and quote data in a range of jurisdictions are outlined here. They govern, respectively, intellectual property rights, confidentiality, competition, a new *sui generis* property right in databases, and the securities markets. Other pertinent areas of law and regulation are ignored. In the US, for example, these include the law and regulation governing contracts (National Conference of Commissioners on Uniform State Laws 3/5/1996), trade secrets (*Board of Trade of the City of Chicago v. Christie Grain and Stock Company*), and commercial misappropriation (*International News Service v. Associated Press* and *National Basketball Association v. Sports Team Analysis and Tracking Systems, Inc.*). The ownership of other types of market information, such as price indices and research reports, are also ignored.

COPYRIGHT. The owner of a copyright in a work has the right to prevent unrestricted copying or use of the work for an extended period. Most exchanges therefore claim copyright in the price and quote data they disseminate, in order to restrict copying of such data other than on a historical basis. It is universally held that copyright does not subsist in facts. Compilations of facts or databases may, however, attract copyright, and the criteria for assessing whether they do, differ across jurisdictions.

In the UK, the primary statutory criterion for assessing whether copyright subsists in a compilation is whether it exhibits sufficient originality (Section 1(1), Copyright, Designs and Patents Act 1988). The central judicial criterion that has been developed to assess whether a work should be deemed original is whether enough labour, skill and capital have been expended by the author in creating it (*University of London Press Ltd. v. University Tutorial Press Ltd.*). Since 1896, it has been assumed that a list of stock exchange prices exhibits sufficient originality to warrant copyright protection (*Exchange Telegraph Co. v. Gregory and Co.*). The value of an exchange's copyright in a compilation of its price and quote data may, however, be limited, as it may not take much embellishment to obtain copyright in a slightly modified work. Most other market participants who disseminate data derived from an exchange's data may themselves also be able to claim copyright in these compilations.

Although the primary statutory criterion for the assignment of copyright is also that of originality in the US (Section 102(a), Copyright Act 1976), judicial interpretation of the term there has been quite different than in the UK. In particular, it is the 'creative selection approach' that has been confirmed as the key test of originality in the US (*Feist Publications, Inc. v. Rural Telephone Service Co., Inc.*). This holds that copyright subsists in a compilation only if it exhibits a minimal amount of creativity in its selection and arrangement of facts. The expenditure of labour, capital or other assets in the production of the compilation is therefore irrelevant for assessing whether it is protected by copyright or not. As such it is arguable that a list of exchange prices and quotes does not exhibit sufficient originality to warrant copyright, given that the selection and arrangement criteria used to create this type of list could not be more obvious. Furthermore, even if such a compilation were to attract copyright, it would only subsist in the compilation's selection and arrangement. Other market participants would therefore be allowed to employ the data of which the compilation was composed, and re-package and redistribute them as they saw fit.

CONFIDENTIALITY. An obligation of confidentiality arises when one party imparts to another party secret information, on the understanding that the information is to be used only for a restricted purpose. Many exchanges therefore attempt to impose a contractual obligation of confidentiality upon all parties receiving their information not to divulge it in a proscribed manner.

In order for a breach of confidence to be actionable in the UK, three criteria must be fulfilled (*Coco. v. Clark (A.N.) (Engineers) Ltd.*, and more generally Gurry 1981). First, the information in question must have the necessary quality of confidence about it, meaning that it must not be public knowledge. The courts have tended to evaluate the confidentiality of commercial information by assessing whether any special economic effort would be necessary to reproduce it. They have also been concerned about how much revelation of the information is required before it is deemed to be in the public domain. Although the legal response to the question of when any 'relative secrecy' disappears has been stated as being dependent on the technology currently available (*Franchi v. Franchi*), 'widespread use' of information has been viewed as 'driv[ing] a hole into the blanket of confidence' (*Dunford & Elliott Ltd. v. Johnston and Firth Brown Ltd.*).

The second criterion that must be met for a breach of confidence to be actionable stipulates that the person receiving the information should have done so in circumstances importing an obligation of confidence on him. A confidant will thus be subject to an obligation of confidentiality if he is aware of the obligation, or if he ought to be aware of the obligation. An obligation of confidentiality is also imposed on third parties, namely people who obtain confidential information indirectly as a result of a breach of confidentiality on the part of a direct confidant, as soon as such third parties become aware that they received the information as a result of an initial breach of confidentiality. The third criterion requires that the confidant must make an unauthorized use of the information, possibly to the detriment of the party initially confiding the information.

When an exchange disseminates its price and quote data, it has the express aim of disseminating them as widely as possible, for the appropriate fees. For an exchange to attempt to classify these data as confidential, when its aim in releasing them is to publicize them as much as practicable, may be considered perverse. The very act by an exchange of offering to sell its prices and quotes to whomever is willing to buy them may thus dispel any notion of confidentiality imposed on the purchasers of the information. Establishing a duty of confidentiality regarding the distribution of price and quote data in other more restricted contexts, for example when brokers submit their bids and offers to an inter-dealer broker, may, however, be easier.

COMPETITION. If an exchange captures a large percentage of the trading in a commodity, or if it is granted any property rights in the information it disseminates, it may become the dominant or even the sole source of information about trading in the commodity. Such an exclusive position may bring the exchange within the remit of anti-trust legislation and regulation. Two important instances of potentially anti-competitive conduct by an exchange concerning the dissemination of its information are when it charges too much for its information, and when it discriminates between different clients (*Pont Data Australia v. Australian Stock Exchange and Australian Stock Exchange Operations*).

The determination of what is a fair price for an exchange's price and quote data when the exchange is the sole source of the data has been contentious. Two opposite approaches may be taken in deciding how the costs of running an exchange should be apportioned to the production of its price and quote information. On the one hand, an exchange may be viewed primarily as the operator of a trading system. The production of price and quote information is then seen as a by-product of this function, and the cost of producing the information is thus seen as marginal. On the other hand, an exchange may be perceived primarily as an organization for making prices. The cost of producing this information is then seen as being the total cost of running the exchange. Lee (1995: 185–92) argues that neither of these approaches is valid. The attempt to apportion costs either to the production of trading services, or to the production of information, cannot be made on anything other than an arbitrary basis, given that information and trading services are joint products.

Competition law, the general aim of which is to dismantle exclusive arrangements, by its very nature conflicts with the assignment of an intellectual or economic property right that grants exclusivity over the right to sell or reproduce a particular good or service. This conflict has proved particularly acute in the European Union (EU) for two reasons. First there is little harmonization of EU copyright law, and thus for the most part it is national legislation which determines copyright. The diversity of such national legislation has been thought to obstruct trade between Member States, and thus to act as an impediment to the development of an integrated market. Both the freedom of movement and competition provisions in the Treaty of Rome (Articles 30–36, 59–66, and 85–86) have therefore been employed to attenuate the perceived adverse effects of such diversity.

The second reason why the conflict between competition and intellectual property rights has been so intense is that there is a tension between different elements of the Treaty itself. The right to move goods freely throughout the EU is subject to the exemption that it not be allowed to prevent restrictions on the protection of industrial and commercial property. Intellectual property has been taken to be included in such industrial and commercial property. The Treaty also requires, however, that such restrictions not constitute a means of arbitrary discrimination or a disguised restriction on trade between Member States. In addition, these prohibitions often conflict with the Treaty's competition provisions. The question of which part of the Treaty is pre-eminent, and of whether the protection of industrial and commercial property on the one hand, or the pursuit of competition or free trade on the other, should dictate policy, has therefore had to be resolved in the courts.

The European Court recently repeated its traditional view that mere ownership of an intellectual property right was not sufficient to confer a dominant position in a market (*RTE and ITP Ltd. v. EC Commission*). It confirmed, however, that when an organization enjoyed a *de facto* monopoly over some information, this *de facto* monopoly might allow the organization to prevent competition, and therefore to occupy a dominant position. In the case in question, the Court found three instances of anti-competitive activity. These were: first, when a company's refusal to provide certain information prevented the appearance of a new product that the company did not offer, and for which there was a potential consumer demand; second, when there was no justification for this refusal, either in the activity the company undertook or in that of a derivative activity; and finally, when by denying others access to the information that was indispensable to their activities, the company reserved to itself a secondary market thereby excluding all competition. Given these anti-competitive abuses, the Court maintained it was unnecessary to examine the conflict between national intellectual property rights and the freedom to trade between Member States.

Given that most exchanges operate a *de facto* monopoly as the sole source of the price and quote data emanating from their trading systems, they are likely to be seen as having a dominant position in the market for the provision of these data. Any refusal by an exchange to license the use of its data, notwithstanding any copyright claimed in them, would therefore probably also be viewed as abusive in the EU.

SUI GENERIS RIGHTS. A *sui generis* right has recently been developed in the EU to protect databases (Directive 96/9/EC), and a similar right is currently under legislative scrutiny in the US (US Congress: House of Representatives 1996). The goal of the EU's *sui generis* right is to ensure that the creator of a database can protect his investment against any harm, misappropriation or copying, that does not infringe whatever copyright that might exist in the arrangement of the database. The maker of a database was given the right to prevent the extraction and re-utilization of the whole, or a substantial part, of the contents of the database. The term of the right was set at fifteen years. The term could also be extended if the database was changed in an appropriate manner.

The extra protection granted to database owners was believed necessary for several reasons. The diversity of national copyright legislation in the EU governing the protection of databases, together with the fact that in some Member States databases were not clearly protected, were seen as major impediments to the achievement of the Single Market. It was also recognized that the development of electronic databases required considerable investment, that they could often be cheaply copied and accessed, and that in the absence of a harmonized system of unfair-competition legislation or of case-law, other measures in addition to copyright were required to protect them.

Exchanges are likely to be able to protect their price and quote data under this *sui generis* right (Bull 1997). As with any copyright held, however, if an exchange has a monopolistic position regarding the database of its price and quote information, competition law would probably require it to license the use of the database on fair and non-discriminatory terms.

SECURITIES MARKETS. The most detailed legislation and regulation supervising the dissemination of price and quote information in securities markets has been developed in the USA. The Securities Exchange Act 1934 (SEA) lays out a complex hierarchy of objectives which the Securities and Exchange Commission (SEC) is obliged to pursue. At the most general level, it is required to further the public interest, to protect investors, and to maintain fair and orderly markets. Five subsidiary objectives have been set out as part of the National Market System, the most important of which in this context is that information with respect to quotations for, and transactions in, securities be made available to brokers, dealers, and investors. In order to deliver this objective the SEC has mandated that the prices, sizes and locations of all trades and all quotes in the largest exchange-listed and NASDAQ-listed equities be published via the Consolidated Tape Association and the Consolidated Quotation System (Code of Federal Regulations, Sections 240.11Aa3–1, 240.11Ac1–1 and 240.11Ac1–2).

The SEA imposes a range of constraints on exchanges that are relevant for the dissemination of price and quote data, and also on so-called 'exclusive securities information processors'. These are organizations that act on an exclusive basis on behalf of exchanges in collecting, processing, and preparing for distribution the exchanges' information about trades and quotes. Exclusive securities information processors are viewed as both monopolists and public utilities, and as such are required to be absolutely neutral with respect to all market centres, market makers, and private firms, to make their services available on reasonable and nondiscriminatory terms, and not to set unreasonable charges.

The SEC has made a series of key decisions concerning the dissemination of price and quote information. It has ruled that an exclusive securities information processor may set a fixed access charge for the price and quote information which it sells (SEC 1978). It has also determined, however, and been backed judicially, that if an exclusive securities information processor also retails its information, it should only recover those costs it would incur if it operated a pure pass-through system, when setting its charges (*NASD Inc. v. SEC and Instinet*). In certain very restricted circumstances, and particularly in an attempt to repatriate order flow to the USA, the SEC has relaxed the amount of price and quote information that an exchange is required to release (SEC 1990a and 1990b). The SEC's most recent ruling with regard to transparency was in its order execution rules (SEC 29 August 1996).

Regulatory examination of transparency in other jurisdictions has also been undertaken. The Office of Fair Trading (OFT) in the UK, for example, has examined the rules of the London Stock Exchange several times (OFT 1990 and 1994), and has concluded that a delay in the publication of the details of large trades by the exchange was likely to restrict and distort competition significantly. It argued that delaying trade publication would increase the information risk associated with taking on a trade, with the attendant consequences of increasing spreads, increasing transactions costs, reducing market liquidity and possibly declining trading volume.

To date the only supranational law that determines how markets should be regulated across jurisdictions is the Investment Services Directive (ISD) of the EU (Council directive 93/22/EEC). The Directive provides the legal basis under which a 'regulated' market from one Member State may operate in other Member States. In order to be classified a 'regulated' market, an institution must satisfy the so-called transparency provisions of the Directive. These stipulate the minimum data, with respect to prices, quotes, and volumes on the market, that the market must disseminate publicly. Given the controversial nature of the negotiations that culminated in the ISD, particularly with regard to transparency, it is unsurprising that in order to reach a compromise the actual text agreed in the Directive is essentially so ambiguous as to be meaningless (Lee 1996: 198). The international controversy over transparency has also been reflected in other relevant global discussions (International Organization of Securities Commissions 1992).

An assessment of the influence of transparency on markets is difficult for many reasons: the multiplicity of criteria by which the policy may be judged, the possibility of disagreement about the appropriateness of the criteria, the difficulty of obtaining an objective assessment of many of them, and the problem of evaluating how much of what occurred in a marketplace happened on the one hand as a result of the presence of transparency or on the other hand despite its presence. It is in the US that a policy requiring the full publication of trades and quotes in the securities markets has been employed for the longest period, namely since 1975, and it is there too that the strongest supporters of this approach are found. The SEC, for example, has claimed many times that transparency has played a major role in effecting the success of the American markets (SEC 1994: IV-1).

Notwithstanding the strength with which this view is held, however, the opposing position has also been argued as being as, if not more, convincing (Mulherin, Netter and Overdahl 1991a,1991b; Lee 1995: 224–6). Unless competition is impaired, mandated transparency in the securities markets is an inappropriate regulatory policy for a range of reasons. Our current state of knowledge about the economic effects of transparency can best be characterized as one of ignorance, confusion and uncertainty. What theoretical intuitions and empirical evidence we do have appear relevant for only very specific environments and in many instances contradict each other. The risk of creating regulation that does not deliver the intended consequences is therefore not insignificant. All attempts to impose a regulatory structure for transparency have also been subject to such a level of inconsistency as to lead to significant regulatory difficulties and inequalities. Finally, as long as competition is not impaired, market participants themselves face the appropriate incentive to disseminate enough information. In order both to attract order flow to their trading systems, and to ensure the perceived fairness and integrity of their markets, exchanges have sufficient motive to publish speedily details of their prices and quotes.

CONCLUSION. A specification of the rights and obligations that are associated with the ownership of price and quote information is difficult. Many bodies of law and regulation are relevant; many of them conflict, and most of them are in the process of being reformed. An assessment of what should be an appropriate allocation of these ownership rights and obligations is even harder. Ignorance, uncertainty and differences of opinion are widespread. These difficulties will not be easily resolved.

RUBEN LEE

See also COPYRIGHT; DISCLOSURE AND UNRAVELLING; INSIDER TRADING; INTELLECTUAL PROPERTY; MANDATORY DISCLOSURE; REGULATION OF AUTOMATED TRADING SYSTEMS; SECURITIES REGULATION; SELF-REGULATION OF PRIVATE ORGANIZED MARKETS; TRADE SECRET.

Subject classification: 5b(iii); 6c(iii).

STATUTES

Code of Federal Regulations 1975, Section 240: 11A.

Copyright Act of 1976, 17 United States Code.

Copyright, Designs and Patents Act 1988 (c. 48).

Council directive 93/22/EEC, 1993 OJ L 141/27, of 10 May 1993 on investment services in the securities field.

Directive 96/9/EC, 1996 OJ L 77/20, of the European Parliament and of the Council on the legal protection of databases.

Securities Exchange Act of 1934, 15 United States Code.

Treaty Establishing the European Economic Community, as amended (Treaty of Rome), 1957.

CASES

Board of Trade of the City of Chicago v. Christie Grain and Stock Company, 198 US 236 (1905).

Coco v. Clark (A.N.) (Engineers) Ltd [1969] RPC 41.

Dunford & Elliott Ltd v. Johnston and Firth Brown Ltd [1978] FSR 143.

Exchange Telegraph Co. Ltd v. Gregory and Co. [1896] 1 QB 147.

Feist Publications, Inc. v. Rural Telephone Service Company, Inc., 499 US 340 (1991).

Franchi v. Franchi [1967] RPC 149.

International News Service v. Associated Press, 248 US 215 (1918).

NASD, Inc. v. SEC, 801 F2d 1415 (DC Cir. 1986).

National Basketball Association v. Sports Team Analysis and Tracking Systems, Inc. WL 444278, 1 (1996 NY).

Pont Data Australia Pty Ltd v. Australian Stock Exchange and Australian Stock Exchange Operations Pty Ltd (1991) 100 ALR 125.

RTE and ITP Ltd v. EC Commission [1995] ECR I-808 Joined Cases C-241/91 P and C-242/91 P.

University of London Press Ltd v. University Tutorial Press Ltd [1916] 2 Ch. 601.

BIBLIOGRAPHY

Bull, G. 1997. Data law: market data rights bingo. *Computer Law and Security Report* 13: 75–86.

Gurry, F. 1981. *Confidential Information.* Oxford: Oxford University Press.

Honoré, A.M. 1961. Ownership. In *Oxford Essays in Jurisprudence*, ed. A.G. Guest, Oxford: Clarendon Press.

International Organization of Securities Commissions, Technical Committee, Working Party on the Regulation of Secondary Markets. 1992. *Transparency on Secondary Markets: A Synthesis of the IOSCO debate.*

Lee, R. 1995. *The Ownership of Price and Quote Information: Law, Regulation, Economics and Business.* Oxford: Oxford Finance Group.

Lee, R. 1996. Supervising EC capital markets: do we need a European SEC? In *European Economic Business Law: Legal and Economic Analyses on Integration and Harmonization*, ed. R. Buxbaum, G. Hertig, A. Hirsch, and K. Hopt, Berlin and New York: Walter de Gruyter.

Lee, R. 1998. *What is an Exchange? Automation and the Regulation of Trading Markets.* Oxford: Oxford University Press, forthcoming.

Mulherin, J.H., Netter, J.M. and Overdahl, J. 1991a. Prices are property: the organization of financial exchanges from a transaction cost perspective. *Journal of Law and Economics* 34: 591–644.

Mulherin, J.H., Netter, J.M. and Overdahl, J. 1991b. Who owns the quotes? A case study into the definition and enforcement of property rights at the Chicago Board of Trade. *Review of Futures Markets* 10: 108–129.

National Conference of Commissioners on Uniform State Laws. 3/5/1996. *Uniform Commercial Code (Private), Article 2B, Licenses.* Draft.

Office of Fair Trading. 1990. *Financial Services Act 1986: Trade Publication and Price Transparency on the International Stock Exchange.*

Office of Fair Trading. 1994. *Trade Publication Rules of the London Stock Exchange.*

Securities and Exchange Commission. 1978. *In the Matter of Bunker Ramo Corporation, GTE Information Systems Incorporated, Options Price Reporting Authority.* Release No. 15372, File No. 4–280.

Securities and Exchange Commission. 1990a. *SROs; Notice of Filing of Proposed Rule Change by the NYSE relating to the NYSE's Closing-Price Session of its Off-Hours Trading Facility.* Release No. 34-28639; File No. SR-NYSE-90-52.

Securities and Exchange Commission. 1990b. *SROs; Notice of Filing of Proposed Rule Change by the NYSE relating to the NYSE's Aggregate-Price Session of its Off-Hours Trading Facility.* Release No. 34-28640; File No. SR-NYSE-90-53.

Securities and Exchange Commission, Division of Market Regulation. 1994. *Market 2000: An Examination of Current Equity Market Developments.*

Securities and Exchange Commission. 1996. *Order Execution Obligations.* Release No. 34–37619; File No. 57–30–95. 29 August 1996.

US Congress: House of Representatives. 1996. *A Bill to amend title 15, United States Code, to promote investment and prevent intellectual property piracy with respect to databases.* HR 3531, 104th Congress 2d Session.

ownership of the firm. In modern economies, large-scale enterprise exhibits a variety of ownership forms. Most common and familiar is ownership by those persons – individuals or organizations – that supply the firm with financial capital. Other forms of ownership are important as well, however,

Employee ownership, for example, has long been prominent in the service professions – such as law, accounting and investment banking – and has recently expanded noticeably in the industrial sector. Farmer-owned producer cooperatives dominate the markets for most basic agricultural commodities, and in a number of cases have integrated downstream into processing and marketing. Consumer-owned utilities play a prominent role in generating and distributing electricity and in providing telephone service. Mutual companies account for a substantial fraction of all insurance sold – both in life insurance and in property and casualty insurance – and are important in the banking industry as well. Business-owned wholesale, supply, and service cooperatives are key firms in a variety of businesses, from credit cards to hardware to news reporting, with brand names that are frequently well known to consumers. Condominiums and cooperatives have been rapidly displacing investor-owned rental housing in recent decades. And nonprofit firms, which have no owners at all, account for a conspicuous share of all non-governmentally provided health, education, child care, and old age care. Moreover, it appears that the share of economic activity represented by non-investor-owned enterprise has been growing among the leading economies in recent decades, and is largest in the most developed economies.

This diverse pattern of ownership raises several questions for students of law and economics. First, to what extent do underlying economic factors account for variation in ownership forms across industries, across societies, and across time? Second, what is the influence of law upon these patterns? Third, to what extent has law, and particularly organizational law, adapted to facilitate the formation and management of the forms of ownership that have evolved?

I. A THEORY OF OWNERSHIP. Ownership of a firm, as the term is conventionally understood, comprises two rights: the right to control the firm, and the right to appropriate the firm's net earnings. While these two rights could in theory be separated and assigned to different persons, in practice they are typically joined. There are obvious incentive reasons for this: where control is in the hands of persons who do not participate in earnings, the incentive to maximize – or even to pay – those earnings is diminished.

In large firms, and especially in firms where (as is common) ownership is shared among a large class of persons, the two rights that constitute ownership are often substantially attenuated. Control is commonly limited to the right to vote in periodic elections for the firm's board of directors and for the approval of fundamental transactions, such as merger or dissolution. Participation in earnings is commonly limited to the right to receive distributions at intervals when and as declared by the firm's elected directors. Regardless of how attenuated these rights may be, however, there is typically an easily distinguished class of persons to whom they are assigned in any given firm, and there is a set of basic economic factors that tend to govern membership in that class – factors that show substantial regularity across industries and across national economies.

Nonprofit firms are the conspicuous exception to the joinder of the two basic rights of ownership. The defining characteristic of a nonprofit firm is, in fact, that the individuals who control the firm have no right to appropriate the firm's net earnings. Consequently, nonprofit firms have no owners. The same economic factors that determine to whom ownership of a firm is assigned, however, also determine when it is efficient for a firm to have no owners at all.

Ownership is nearly always held by one or another class of the firm's patrons, where by 'patrons' we mean persons who have some transactional relationship with the firm aside from ownership, either as suppliers of a factor of production (capital, labour, or some other input) or as purchasers of one or more of the goods or services that the firm produces. The reason for assigning ownership of a firm to its patrons is evidently to reduce the costs of contracting. Simple market contracting – that is, contracting between otherwise unrelated parties – is often subject to imperfections that can impose substantial costs on the transactions involved. Those costs can be reduced by giving ownership of the firm to the parties with whom the firm is transacting.

In general, high costs of contracting between a firm and its patrons result from the simultaneous presence of (1) some strategic advantage that the firm has over those patrons, such as market power or private information, and (2) the firm's willingness to exploit that advantage to its benefit – that is, to behave opportunistically. Assigning ownership of the firm to the patrons involved can reduce the costs of contracting in two ways. First, it may diminish the firm's strategic advantage *vis-à-vis* those patrons – for example, by giving the patrons access to information held by the firm. Second, and more important, when the patrons own the firm, the firm largely loses its incentive to behave opportunistically toward them.

It follows that, as a first approximation, ownership of a firm is most efficiently assigned to that class of the firm's patrons for whom the costs of contracting, in the absence of ownership, would be highest. But two other important considerations also enter in. First, some patrons are more effective owners than others. For example, some patrons are in a better position to control the firm's managers, or to bear the risks associated with the firm's fluctuating stream of net earnings. Second, the character of the firm's owners may affect the costs of contracting with patrons who are *not* owners. For example, some classes of patrons may have greater opportunity or incentive than others to exploit opportunistically the strategic advantages that the firm enjoys over other classes of patrons.

An efficient assignment of ownership is therefore one that minimizes the sum of (a) the costs of contracting – that is, the total costs of transactions between the firm and its various classes of patrons – and (b) the costs of ownership – that is, the costs of controlling (or failing to control) the firm's managers and of bearing the risks associated with the firm's earnings (see Hansmann 1988, 1996). If market forces tend to promote the survival of firms that have efficient ownership structures, then the patterns of ownership we observe should reflect these various costs.

Clearly there are obstacles that frustrate efficient assignment of ownership. We shall survey some of these obstacles below. But there are also strong forces that promote the selection of efficient ownership forms. It is common for firms to be organized initially by entreprenuers who then sell the firm to one or another class of its patrons. For example, condominium and cooperative housing is generally first constructed or acquired by developers who then secure occupants for the building and organize the transaction through which the building is sold collectively to those occupants. Likewise, many of the worker cooperatives that have populated the American plywood industry since the 1920s were initially organized by brokers. These entrepreneurs and brokers have an incentive to sell the firm to the patrons who will be the most efficient owners, since that will generally maximize the entrepreneur's returns. Transactions that convert ownership from one class of patrons to another – for example, from employees to investors, or from investors to customers – are also relatively common and apparently can often be organized without excessive transaction costs. The sale of a majority of the stock of United Air Lines – a publicly traded company – to the firm's employees in 1994 is a conspicuous example. Consequently, there are good reasons to expect that observed patterns of ownership reflect at least rough efficiency.

II. COSTS OF CONTRACTING. The potential inefficiencies in contracting that most strongly influence patterns of ownership can be organized conveniently into a small number of categories.

A. Market power. As a consequence of economies of scale, cartelization, or regulation, firms frequently have a degree of market power toward some of their customers or suppliers. Where this is the case, there is an obvious incentive for the affected patrons to own the firm, for they can thereby avoid both the social inefficiencies of monopoly pricing and the even larger private costs that monopoly pricing imposes on them.

The roughly 1,000 electric utilities in the United States that are organized as consumer cooperatives are a conspicuous example. Since consumer ownership largely removes the threat of monopoly pricing in these firms, they are generally exempted from the awkward system of price regulation that is imposed on investor-owned utilities. Another obvious example is the extensive system of consumer retail cooperatives in Sweden. The large market share of the Swedish retail cooperatives, which contrasts markedly with the relatively small market share that retail cooperatives have in most other countries, evidently developed as a direct response to the extensive cartelization of Swedish consumer goods industries.

Indeed, the generally high level of competition that – absent legal cartelization, as in Sweden – generally prevails in retail markets is evidently important in explaining the modest role of retail consumer cooperatives in most economies. The situation is quite different at the wholesale level, and among suppliers of goods and services to retail business, where economies of scale are often large and competition is consequently attenuated. For example, while retail cooperatives account for less than half of one percent of the market for groceries in the US, retailer-owned wholesale cooperatives account for nearly 15% of groceries at the wholesale level, and nearly one-third if vertically integrated chain stores are excluded.

Market power has also played a strong role in the formation of producer cooperatives. For example, the farmer-owned marketing cooperatives that today dominate the markets for staple grains in the United States received their initial impetus from a combination of natural monopoly and cartelization that largely eliminated competition among grain elevators – the farmers' principal customers – in the late nineteenth century.

B. Asymmetric information. Contracting can also be costly when a firm possesses better information than its patrons concerning important aspects of their transactions, and where the ordinary tools of contracting are insufficient to prevent the firm from exploiting that advantage. As with market power, patron ownership can reduce these costs by removing the firm's incentive to exploit its strategic advantage.

A simple example can be found in agricultural fertilizers and livestock feed. When those products first began to be commercially marketed to US farmers in the early twentieth century, the farmers had difficulty determining the quality of what they were buying. The consequence was a classic 'lemons' problem, and the quality of the commercial products tended to be low. Farmers responded by forming their own supply cooperatives to manufacture and distribute fertilizer and feed whose quality they could trust.

Life insurance offers an even more conspicuous example. When life insurance began to be marketed in the first half of the nineteenth century, the only companies that survived were mutual companies owned by their policyholders; none of the investor-owned companies that sought to enter the business succeeded. The reason for this was evidently that purchasers of insurance would not trust an investor-owned company to perform on a contract under which the purchasers would have to pay currently for the right to a return payment from the company to be made many years in the future; such a company simply had too much uncontrollable discretion to speculate with, or simply divert, the purchaser's funds before the time came to perform. Although mutual life insurance companies had the same informational advantage over their customers as did investor-owned companies, the mutuals had little incentive to exploit that advantage, and thus purchasers were willing to trust them. Investor-owned life insurance companies began to compete successfully with the mutuals only with the advent, in the second half of the nineteenth century, of governmental regulation of the quantity and quality of the financial reserves maintained by life insurance companies – regulation that effectively enabled the investor-owned companies to guarantee to their policyholders that they would not behave in a way that might render them incapable of paying off on their policies.

C. Lock-in. The potential costs of contracting in the presence of asymmetric information can be substantially aggravated when for some reason patrons tend to become locked into their transactional relationship with a firm in the sense that, once they begin patronizing a firm, they cannot shift their patronage to one of the firm's competitors without incurring substantial costs.

(1) *Contractual lock-in.* Sometimes lock-in is contractual. Life insurance again offers an example. The typical life insurance contract is front-end loaded, in the sense that the premiums paid by the policyholder in the early years of the contract substantially exceed the cost to the company of insuring the policyholder during those years. An important reason for this is to avoid the problem of adverse selection, in which policyholders have an incentive to drop their insurance in favour of a cheaper policy if they subsequently discover that they are unusually healthy, leaving the company to continue insuring only the worst risks. When policyholders are thus locked in, however, the insurance company is in an even stronger position than it would otherwise be to exploit the policyholders by maintaining inadequate reserves. Foreseeing this vulnerability, purchasers of insurance have an even stronger reason to patronize a mutual company.

Investor-owned firms offer another example. The alternative to investor ownership is for the firm to borrow all of the financial capital it needs – that is, to have only a contractual relationship with its suppliers of capital. But when a firm borrows all of the financial capital it needs, familiar problems of asymmetric information arise that are much like those presented by life insurance: the firm has both the incentive and the ability to speculate inefficiently with the funds it has borrowed, or simply to siphon them off to the firm's owners, since the lenders will bear a disproportionate share of the losses in the event of insolvency. This problem might be manageable if borrowing could always be made short-term, so that the lenders could withdraw their loans at the first suspicion that the firm is behaving opportunistically. This approach is unworkable, however, where firms must – as is common – invest the money they borrow in assets that are to a degree firm-specific and hence illiquid. For one thing, short-term borrowing would bring the costs of repeatedly renegotiating terms of credit. For another, short-term borrowing would bring the potential for inefficient runs on the firm's assets by its creditors. When some of the firm's creditors came to suspect that the firm might be unable to repay its debts – or even to believe that other creditors might suspect this – they would have an incentive to race to withdraw their loans, creating a multi-person prisoners' dilemma among the lenders. Borrowing long term mitigates these problems, but at the price of locking in the lenders and exposing them to greater opportunism by the firm. Giving ownership to some or all of the long-term lenders – that is, making the firm investor-owned – is a response to that problem of opportunism.

(2) *Transaction-specific investments.* Sometimes lock-in is the result of patrons' transaction-specific investments – that is, investments whose value will be substantially diminished if the patrons stop dealing with the firm.

Franchising provides an example. Franchisees must often make substantial investments whose value is dependent on retaining the franchise. These investments might include construction of a facility specialized to the franchise, local advertising and other goodwill development tied to the franchisor's brand name, or acquisition of knowledge and skill specialized to the franchisor's products. The result is to give the franchisor the power to act opportunistically toward the franchisee – for example, by altering the terms of the franchise contract to the franchisee's disadvantage, or by seeking to reacquire the franchise at a bargain price. One common response to this problem of potential franchisor opportunism is to make the franchisees, collectively, the owners of the franchisor. This is the pattern found, for example, in the US consumer hardware business, which is dominated by a number of large franchises – the largest four of which each have between 3,000 and 8,000 local hardware stores as franchisees – that are owned collectively by their franchisees. Another prominent example is the credit card industry. Both MasterCard and Visa are franchises in which the franchisees are local banks that individually market cards – for which the local bank provides the credit – bearing the Visa or MasterCard name. And both MasterCard and Visa are cooperatives that are collectively owned by the local banks that are their franchisees.

Labour contracting arguably provides another example. Workers must often make investments that are specific to their employer. Such investments may include the expense of acquiring skills and information that are specialized to the employer, as well as the opportunity costs incurred from the atrophy of skills that would be useful in employment elsewhere. Other firm-specific investments may include – at least if alternative employment would mean leaving town – personal investments such as renovation of a house to suit one's personal tastes, friendships with individuals in the local community, and a spouse's employment ties. Protection of these investments may be one incentive for the formation of worker-owned firms, though in fact employee ownership is most common in firms in which the employees' firm-specific investments seem unusually small. (For further analysis and evidence concerning these and other aspects of employee-owned firms, which will not be treated here in detail, see EMPLOYEE OWNERSHIP.)

Following a theme well developed in the literature on vertical integration (see Williamson 1985), the theoretical literature on ownership of the firm has often emphasized the efficiency of giving ownership to the patrons who must make the most important transaction-specific investments in their dealings with the firm (see, prominently, Hart and Moore 1990). It is important to appreciate, however, that the need to protect transaction-specific investments is just one – and by no means always the most important – of the various costs of contracting that ownership can serve to mitigate.

D. Risks from long-term contracts. We have noted above several situations in which contracts between a firm and its patrons must generally be written with long terms. One is life insurance, in which long-term contracts mitigate problems of adverse selection. Another is borrowing financial capital, in which long-term contracting avoids runs on a firm's credit and other liquidity problems. Long-term contracts such as these commonly constitute substantial gambles between the firm and the patrons involved, creating private risk where there is no social risk. For example, if (as has historically been common) the contracts are written in terms of nominal currency values, they create a gamble on future rates of inflation and future interest rates. If the patrons own the firm, this gamble is eliminated, offering another important efficiency advantage for policyholder ownership of life insurance companies and investor ownership of capital-intensive industrial firms.

E. Who owns whom? The costs of contracting we have surveyed here could be mitigated, not just by having the patrons collectively own the firm, but also by having the firm own its patrons. The latter solution is in fact common. Producers of brand-name goods, for example, sometimes integrate downstream to obtain ownership of their retail outlets rather than deal with franchisees or entirely independent stores.

Where the patrons in question constitute a numerous class, however, having the firm own its patrons is not the same as having the patrons own the firm, and sometimes the latter is the only practical alternative. For example, where the patrons in question are retail outlets, having their common supplier own them dulls their incentives (or those of their managers) to minimize costs and maximize income, and the efficiency losses from these dulled incentives may more than offset any gains from removing the supplier's incentive to act opportunistically toward the retailers. And, where the patrons in question are not firms but individuals such as workers, ownership of the patrons by the firm is obviously infeasible, not just because of practical incentive problems but also owing to prohibitions on personal servitude.

F. Controlling patron opportunism. When discussing asymmetric information, we focused on situations in which the firm possesses information that its patrons lack. In some cases, however, the problem of asymmetric information is the reverse: contracting is costly because the patrons have information that the firm lacks. For example, employees may engage in various forms of shirking that are difficult for their employer to monitor, and franchisees may free-ride on the franchisor's brand name by skimping on service or quality. Where, for the reasons discussed immediately above, such problems cannot be solved by having the firm own its patrons, there arises the question whether patron ownership of the firm is an alternative solution.

The obvious difficulty here is the '1/N problem': when N patrons share ownership of a firm, each individual patron receives, by virtue of its ownership share, only 1/N of the returns to the firm from any extra effort it makes, which is a trivial incentive where N is at all sizeable. Patron ownership may, however, bring indirect productivity incentives that are more powerful than these direct financial incentives. One is simply a salience effect: if patrons own some or all of the firm, then they are likely to keep much better informed about, and focused on, the firm's overall financial performance. Another is mutual monitoring: shared ownership gives patrons an incentive to apply pressure to each other to be productive, with cumulative effects that could be substantial where shirking by fellow patrons is fairly obvious and sanctioning of fellow patrons – for example, by simple social shaming – is relatively costless.

With respect to employee ownership, the available evidence is ambiguous. Empirical studies of the relationship between employee ownership and employee productivity have yet to confirm a strong positive correlation. Moreover, employee ownership is most common in industries, such as legal and accounting services, in which monitoring of employees by the firm seems unusually easy. The pattern of patron ownership in franchises also suggests that patron ownership can have important weaknesses in mitigating opportunistic conduct by patrons. Franchisee ownership of franchisors seems most commonly found in businesses – such as hardware and credit cards – in which the value of the franchisor's brand name is not particularly vulnerable to free-riding by the franchisees. In contrast, franchisee ownership seems largely absent in businesses – such as fast foods – in which careful policing of franchisee quality seems important.

Nevertheless, there are situations in which mutual patron monitoring seems to be an important reason for adoption of patron ownership. The rotating credit associations that are common in developing economies – and whose character was shared by the early mutual savings and loan associations in the United States – are an example. Apparently some of the smaller mutual casualty and liability insurance companies also involve substantial mutual monitoring; the numerous local farmers' mutual fire insurance companies that arose in the United States in the late nineteenth century are one clear historical example.

III. COSTS OF OWNERSHIP. While assigning ownership to any given class of a firm's patrons is likely to reduce their cost of contracting with the firm, it also necessitates that those patrons bear the costs associated with ownership. Those costs will be higher, or harder to bear, for some types of patrons than for others.

A. Risk bearing. We noted above that, for some patrons, ownership can actually reduce risk by eliminating inefficient gambles between those patrons and the firm. The risk that remains, however – the variability in the firm's earnings – must be borne in large part by the firm's owners.

Clearly some patrons are in a better position to bear this risk than are others. Suppliers of financial capital are, of course, generally good risk bearers, since they can often diversify their investments by taking a small ownership stake in each of a number of firms. Employees, in contrast, are often poor risk bearers, since generally they can supply labour only to a single firm.

While risk-bearing capacity is surely significant, and

helps explain why investor ownership is dominant in capital-intensive industries, it does not appear overwhelmingly important in explaining observed patterns of ownership. Employee ownership, for example, does not correlate well with the risk level of the firms involved. The extensive development of farm marketing and supply cooperatives also suggests that risk-bearing is not of primary importance in explaining ownership. Since farmers are typically employee-owners of their own farms, and since farming is a highly capital intensive and highly volatile industry, farmers necessarily bear a great deal of risk simply from their basic farm operations. Nevertheless, farmers add further to this risk by participating extensively in ownership of both their suppliers and their customers through cooperatives whose residual returns are strongly correlated with those of the farms they serve.

B. Controlling managers. The owners of a firm must also bear the costs – commonly labelled 'agency costs' – of controlling the firm's managers. There are two principal components to these costs. The first, which we can label 'monitoring costs', consists of the costs of exercising effective authority over the firm's managers. The second consists of the costs of the managerial opportunism that results from the owners' failure to monitor the managers with perfect effectiveness. (The classic exposition is Jensen and Meckling 1976.)

Monitoring costs include the costs to the owners of (1) informing themselves about the operations of the firm, (2) making decisions, and (3) assuring that the firm's managers adhere to the decisions that the owners make. These costs are clearly lower for some classes of a firm's patrons than they are for others.

For customers of retail stores, for example, these costs are generally quite high. Retail customers are commonly both numerous and transient, making them difficult to organize, and the value of an individual customer's purchases from any one firm is often too modest to justify devoting significant effort to participation in the firm's governance. This is presumably another reason why retail cooperatives are relatively uncommon today in most developed countries. The situation is different if we move back a step in the chain of distribution and examine retail stores that purchase their supplies from a common supplier. Often a retailer's relationship with its supplier is stable over time and accounts for a large share of the retailer's expenditures. It is not surprising, therefore, that retailer-owed wholesale and supply cooperatives are quite common. Likewise, the extensive development of farmer-owned marketing and supply cooperatives presumably reflects, in part, the ease of organizing farmers for effective oversight of those firms. And the frequency with which multi-unit residences are organized as cooperatives or condominiums surely owes much to the ease of organizing and informing a building's occupants, and the large stake each occupant has in the efficient management of the building.

Sometimes, however, one finds ownership shared by a class of patrons for whom monitoring costs are conspicuously high. This is true, for example, of mutual life insurance companies in the United States, in which policyholders have never – since the initial founding of such firms in the 1840s – exercised any meaningful degree of direct control over the firms' managers. The same is famously true of the dispersed shareholders in many of the investor-owned firms in the United States whose stock is publicly traded; while the threat of hostile takeover helps to discipline managers of such firms, historically that threat has often been remote for many firms, and in any event takeover involves a change in ownership. In firms such as these, the principal cost of control that the owners must bear is the cost of *failing* to control the firm's managers, including in particular the losses suffered as a consequence of managerial slack and self-dealing.

The fact that firms with weak owners are so common suggests two things. First, the costs of managerial opportunism – the managerial slack and self-dealing that result when owners are unable to monitor managers perfectly – often remain within acceptable bounds even when managers are largely autonomous. Evidently factors other than the direct exercise of authority by the firm's owners – factors such as personal reputation, morality, and legally enforceable fiduciary duties – can also place substantial limits on managerial opportunism.

Second, it can be worthwhile to assign ownership to a given class of a firm's patrons even when those patrons are capable of exercising little or no direct control over the firm's managers. This is particularly so in the case where the patrons in question face unusually high costs of contracting because they are highly vulnerable to opportunistic behaviour by the firm. Even though the patrons, as owners, may be capable of exercising no direct authority, they can still benefit from the fiduciary duties and other forms of indirect influence that ownership gives them over managers. Moreover, and perhaps more important, ownership gives highly vulnerable patrons the advantage that no *other* class of persons has ownership, and hence there is nobody else who has both the authority and the incentive to induce the firm's managers to exploit the vulnerable patrons in question. Although transacting with managers who are only nominally responsible to your authority may be disadvantageous, it is far preferable to transacting with managers who are actively seeking to exploit you for the advantage of someone else.

Thus, even mere beneficial ownership of a firm – that is, the right to have the firm operated for one's benefit, but without the effective capacity to control the firm's managers directly – can be important. Moreover, as between two different classes of a firm's patrons – one for which monitoring costs are high, but for which the costs of contracting are also quite high, and the other for which both monitoring costs and the costs of contracting are low – the former patrons, with the high monitoring costs, may well be the more efficient owners. Minimizing the agency costs of delegated management evidently figures less importantly in the assignment of ownership than reducing the incentive for the firm to exploit opportunistically its advantages in contracting.

This is evidently why life insurance companies were owned by their policyholders rather than by investors in the middle of the nineteenth century. It is also evidently among the reasons why most large firms today are owned by their investors rather than by their employees. While employees are generally in a much better position than are the firm's shareholders to monitor management and to act collectively to make their voice felt, they are also generally less vulnerable to opportunistic behaviour on the part of the firm (which is not to say, of course, that they are not vulnerable at all).

C. Collective decision-making. When ownership of a firm is shared by many persons, there are likely to be differences of opinion among the individual owners concerning the management of the firm. While these differences of opinion may arise because of differences in the owners' personal preferences or circumstances, the most important are likely to derive from differences in the individual owners' relationships with the firm. When a worker-owned firm has two plants, for example, and must close one of them for lack of business, the workers at the two plants are unlikely to be of the same mind as to which should be closed.

Firms with multiple owners must employ some form of collective choice mechanism to resolve these differences of opinion. Voting is the method most commonly used, and the one that is embodied as the standard method in organizational law, such as the law of business corporations, cooperatives, and partnerships. But, as the public choice literature emphasizes, voting, like all other collective choice mechanisms, has necessary weaknesses as a means of aggregating preferences.

First, voting is a costly process: its informational requirements are high and its procedures are cumbersome. Second, even when the individuals voting are well informed and representative of the preferences of the group as a whole, voting can produce substantive decisions that are inefficient. At best, voting is likely to favour the preferences of the median rather than the mean voter. More seriously, voting can result in substantial exploitation of the minority by the majority, or even exploitation of the majority by a minority that captures control of the agenda.

To some extent, the pathologies of voting can be mitigated by checking mechanisms, such as fiduciary duties, that effectively remove some of the most inefficient or exploitative outcomes from the available decision set. But fiduciary duties are themselves a crude form of control that work poorly when there is no simple yardstick by which to judge clearly if, and to what degree, one group is exploiting another. When all of a firm's owners are identically situated, a simple rule of equal treatment is easy to prescribe and enforce. But when owners differ significantly in the kinds of transactions they have with the firm, enforceable rules of fairness are elusive.

It follows that ownership is likely to bring special costs of collective decision-making when the owners have substantially heterogeneous interests. These costs are conceptually distinct from the agency costs of controlling managers discussed above. They can be high even in firms, such as modest-sized partnerships, in which there are no hired managers and hence no important agency costs. And they can be low in large corporations in which ownership is widely dispersed and hence agency costs are high, but in which all the owners have essentially identical interests.

These costs of collective decision-making appear to be extremely important in determining assignments of ownership. It is uncommon to find a firm in which ownership is shared among a class of persons who display substantial heterogeneity of interest. To begin with, in any given firm ownership is generally assigned only to a single class of patrons – investors of capital, employees, customers, or suppliers of a particular factor of production. In theory, shared ownership among several or even all classes of a firm's patrons would serve to reduce the costs of contracting for each of them. But evidently the high costs of collective decision-making among patrons with conflicting interests makes shared ownership of this sort infeasible.

Furthermore, the class of patrons that has ownership of any given firm is nearly always highly homogeneous. The common shareholders in an investor-owned firm are an obvious example. All have lent money to the firm on essentially identical terms. While the firm may have other classes of securityholders, such as preferred stockholders, who have invested on different terms, those other securityholders rarely vote together with the common shareholders. Likewise, the agricultural marketing cooperatives are generally owned by farmers who sell to the cooperative a single highly homogeneous crop. In the unusual cases in which a single cooperative handles more than one crop, residual returns are computed separately for each crop and shared only among the farmers who supply that crop – thus foregoing opportunities for risk-sharing across crops in favour of avoiding conflicts of interest among the cooperative's farmer-owners. Worker ownership provides further examples. In successful worker-owned firms, ownership is typically shared only among a class of employees who have highly homogeneous interests in the firm.

The strong advantages of homogeneity of interest among a firm's owners evidently constitute an important reason why ownership of large-scale enterprise is commonly in the hands of investors of financial capital. In most firms those investors are the only substantial class of patrons whose interests are, or can be structured to be, highly homogeneous. In the less common situation in which some other class of patrons with which the firm transacts exhibits substantial homogeneity of interest, that other class – rather than investors of capital – often has ownership. This latter fact suggests that it is not some other consideration, such as risk-sharing, that is primarily responsible for the predominance of investor ownership. Thus, it appears that modern societies are predominantly capitalist in substantial part because of the deficiencies of collective choice mechanisms.

IV. NONPROFIT FIRMS. Where both the costs of contracting and the costs of ownership are extremely high for a given class of patrons, a nonprofit firm – that is, a firm with no owners at all – is frequently the solution chosen.

Simple donative charities provide a clear example. Individuals who make donations to an organization that provides aid to the needy are, in effect, purchasing services from that organization that are to be delivered to third parties – the organization's beneficiaries. In theory, a proprietary firm could sell the same services. But the customers of a proprietary firm would face very high costs of contracting, since it would be difficult for them to write and enforce an agreement obligating the firm to perform services of a given quality and quantity in return for the sum contributed. The fact that the services are being provided to third parties who are strangers to the contributor, and that the services are often provided in a bulk form that makes the individual contributor's marginal purchase difficult to differentiate, renders monitoring of the organization by the purchaser extremely difficult. Consequently, few contributors would choose to patronize a proprietary firm. Thus, if the organization is to be owned by anyone, it must be owned by its contributors.

Yet giving ownership of the organization to the contributors may yield little benefit. The individual contributions may well be so small, and the contributors so numerous, transient, and dispersed, that it is not worthwhile to seek to make the contributors an effective governing group. The solution chosen, therefore, is to have an unowned organization that is not just *de facto* but formally under the control of autonomous self-appointing managers. The agency costs that result from this extreme managerial autonomy are evidently acceptable, and much smaller than would be the costs of contracting between the contributors and a proprietary firm in which managers are in the close service of the firm's owners.

In some nonprofit firms, ultimate control – the right to elect the organization's directors – is put in the hands of the firm's patrons (i.e., its contributors). Yet in such cases the contributors are not given the second defining right of ownership – the right to have the organization's net earnings distributed to themselves – and thus they are not true owners. Why is this right not retained by the patrons as well – making the organization a cooperative rather than a nonprofit – given that the patrons are effectively the firm's beneficial owners in any case? Presumably because the right to distributions of net earnings would be of little use to the patrons, while it might provide an opportunity for abuse if control of the organization were to be captured by a self-interested minority.

In any event, there may often be only modest differences between, on the one hand, a proprietary organization whose owners are ineffective at monitoring its managers and, on the other, a nonprofit organization; both can play a similar patron protection role. Savings banks are a case in point. In the early nineteenth century, when savings banks first arose in substantial numbers in the United States and Europe, investor-owned banks – like investor-owned life insurance companies – were too unreliable to be trusted to hold an individual's funds for any length of time. Consequently, for most of the nineteenth century savings banks were organized either as nonprofit institutions or as mutual institutions. Although the mutuals were initially small institutions under the effective control of their depositors, they soon grew sufficiently large that their managers became effectively autonomous and self-appointing, with the result that the nonprofit savings banks and the mutual savings banks became – and remain – largely indistinguishable in functional terms.

Because nonprofit institutions have no owners from whom the firm can be purchased, transactions converting nonprofit firms to other forms of ownership can be accomplished only with the consent of the firms' managers, who are likely to have a personal stake in resisting such a conversion. Consequently, in contrast to other forms of ownership, the nonprofit form is one on which the forces of market selection work slowly, with the result that there are some industries – such as banking and hospital care – in which nonprofit firms have retained a large market share long after changes in the nature of those industries deprived the nonprofit form of its principal efficiency advantages.

V. REGULATION VERSUS OWNERSHIP. Governmental regulation that reduces the costs of contracting for a particular kind of transaction can have a substantial impact on patterns of ownership. A conspicuous example we have already noted is provided by the life insurance industry, where investor-owned firms competed successfully with mutuals only after governments began regulating financial reserves. Regulation of the reserves of savings banks – also a late-nineteenth-century innovation – had the same effect, allowing commercial banks to move into an industry previously dominated by nonprofit and mutual firms. State statutes mandating accurate disclosure of the contents of agricultural fertilizers, adopted early in the twentieth century, allowed investor-owned firms to compete with farmer-owned supply cooperatives in that business. And, as we also noted earlier, the absence of effective antitrust enforcement in Sweden evidently goes far in explaining the extensive role of consumer cooperatives there. In short, governmental regulation has helped make the world safe for capitalism.

Conversely, alternative assignments of ownership can serve as a substitute for regulation – as in the case of electric utilities, where consumer cooperatives obviate the need for the rate regulation that is applied to investor-owned utilities.

VI. LEGAL FORMS. Not surprisingly, the standard forms for enterprise organization provided for by law are adapted to prevailing forms of ownership. In the United States, for example, most states have long had statutes providing for three general types of incorporated (limited liability) enterprise: the business corporation, the cooperative corporation, and the nonprofit corporation. The first two of these – the basic forms for large-scale proprietary enterprise – clearly contemplate ownership of the firm by its patrons. This is patent in the cooperative statutes, which by their terms provide that earnings and votes are to be distributed according to members' 'patronage', which can involve purchasing the firm's products or services or supplying the firm with any factor of production – including labour – with the exception of capital. The business corporation statutes make up for the latter exception, in effect providing for a specific type of producers' cooperative – the capital or lenders' cooperative – in which votes and earnings are apportioned according to contributions of capital. In principal there is no need for the separate business corporation statutes; the cooperative statutes, which are the more general form, could be employed for forming capital cooperatives as well. Presumably the business corporation statutes exist simply because it is convenient to have a more finely-tuned form specialized for the most common type of cooperative.

A still more general corporation statute would not presume that votes and earnings are distributed according to acts of patronage of any sort. Rather, it would simply provide for juridical personality and limited liability, and permit voting control and earnings to be apportioned in any fashion desired – much as is typically done in general partnership statutes. While more general corporation statutes of this sort exist in some jurisdictions – for example, in the form of business trust statutes – their general absence is testimony to the fact that ownership in large firms is nearly always used to mitigate the costs of contracting between the firm and one or another class of its patrons.

HENRY HANSMANN

See also AGENCY COSTS AND CORPORATE GOVERNANCE; COMPARATIVE CORPORATE GOVERNANCE; CORPORATE GOVERNANCE; CORPORATE LAW; EMPLOYEE OWNERSHIP OF FIRMS; FIDUCIARY DUTIES; FRANCHISE CONTRACTS; PUBLIC CHOICE AND THE LAW; RESIDUAL RIGHTS OF CONTROL.

Subject classification: 5g(i); 5g(iii).

BIBLIOGRAPHY

Hansmann, H.B. 1988. Ownership of the firm. *Journal of Law, Economics, and Organization* 4: 267–304.

Hansmann, H.B. 1996. *The Ownership of Enterprise*. Cambridge, MA: Harvard University Press.

Hart, O. and Moore, J. 1990. Property rights and the nature of the firm. *Journal of Political Economy* 98: 1119–58.

Jensen, M. and Meckling, W. 1976. Theory of the firm: managerial behavior, agency costs and ownership structure. *Journal of Financial Economics* 3: 305–60.

Williamson, O.E. 1985. *The Economic Institutions of Capitalism*. New York: Free Press.